D0930773

BUSINESS STATISTICS
OF THE
UNITED STATES

PATTERNS OF ECONOMIC CHANGE

14TH EDITION
2009

BUSINESS STATISTICS OF THE UNITED STATES

PATTERNS OF ECONOMIC CHANGE

14TH EDITION
2009

Edited by Cornelia J. Strawser

Associate Editor
Mary Meghan Ryan

3 2210 00328 5282

Bernan Press

Lanham, Maryland

NORTH BABYLON PUBLIC LIBRARY

Published in the United States of America
by Bernan Press, a wholly owned subsidiary of
The Rowman & Littlefield Publishing Group, Inc.
4501 Forbes Boulevard, Suite 200
Lanham, Maryland 20706

Bernan Press
800-865-3457
info@bernan.com
www.bernan.com

Copyright © 2009 by Bernan Press

All rights reserved. No part of this publication may be reproduced,
stored in a retrieval system, or transmitted in any form or by any
means, electronic, mechanical, photocopying, recording, or otherwise,
without the prior permission of the publisher. Bernan Press does not claim
copyright in U.S. government information

ISBN-13: 978-1-59888-305-3
eISBN: 978-1-59888-334-3
ISSN: 1086-8488

∞™ The paper used in this publication meets the minimum requirements of
American National Standard for Information Sciences—Permanence of
Paper for Printed Library Materials, ANSI/NISO Z39.48-1992.
Manufactured in the United States of America.

CONTENTS

PREFACE

Business Statistics of the United States: Patterns of Economic Change, 14th Edition, 2009 is a basic desk reference for anyone requiring statistics on the U.S. economy. It contains about 3,500 economic time series in all, portraying the period since World War II in comprehensive detail, and, in the case of about 200 key series, the period from 1929 through 1948 as well. The data are predominantly from federal government sources. Of equal importance are the extensive background notes for each chapter, which help users to understand the data, use them appropriately, and, if desired, seek additional information from the source agencies.

THE 2009 EDITION

Compiled in the midst of a dramatic downturn in the United States economy, the 14th edition of *Business Statistics* provides an abundance of data enabling the user to understand the background of recent developments and compare today's economy with past history, going all the way back to 1929. Two more years' worth of current data have been added, bringing most series up to date through the end of 2008, while incorporating all data revisions made as of spring 2009 and maintaining a complete historical record back to the 1940s or before for the most important series. New features in this edition include:

- An expanded series of graphs, Figures 18-1 through 18-5, depicting the U.S. economy from 1929 through 1948. Currently there is much public discourse about the policies pursued during the "Great Depression" and World War II and their effects, but surprisingly little understanding of the actual course of the economy. The term "Great Depression" does not even have a specific economic definition. These graphs of employment, unemployment, output, price change, interest rates, money, and credit should provide new insight into the history of the period and its similarities to, and differences from, the U.S. economy today.
- A new series in Table 12-3 showing total Federal Reserve asset holdings, the "Fed's balance sheet," which expanded to a startling degree in 2008 as the monetary authority used new tools to maintain and expand the flow of credit.
- Three broader measures of labor underutilization calculated by the Bureau of Labor Statistics, which have been added to Table 10-5, Unemployment Rates and Related Data. One of the new measures adds discouraged workers to the unemployment count, a second adds other "marginally attached" workers to unemployment, and a third includes the "underemployed" who want to work full-time but can only find part-time work. These measures are available back to 1994.

Finally, there has been considerable interest recently in the importance to GDP of various components of demand, especially consumption spending. Many journalists and analysts repeatedly quote a statistic derived from a table published by the Bureau of Economic Analysis in the National Income and Product Accounts (NIPAs) entitled "Percentage Shares of Gross Domestic Product." In that table, the value of personal consumption expenditures (PCE) is shown to be approximately 70 percent of the value of gross domestic product (GDP). Typically, in press accounts this becomes "consumption comprises" or "consumption accounts for" 70 percent of the U.S. economy. But those statements cannot be true, because PCE includes the value of imported goods and services—including the value of the imported materials incorporated in domestically-produced goods and services—while GDP includes only domestic production and specifically excludes the entire value of imported goods and services.

In fact, in this NIPA table, the positive sources of demand—PCE, investment, government spending, and exports—add up to 117 percent of GDP; imports—which are not a source of demand for U.S. output—amount to 17 percent of GDP and must be *subtracted* to make this table balance to 100 percent. This table, while arithmetically "correct," does not give a convincing answer to the question about how much GDP is accounted for by each source of demand.

Ideally, we would want to be able to allocate the value of imports to each of the positive demand categories, and then subtract them, to arrive at the net demand for domestic production that would truly "account for" total GDP. Data are not available to do this. But we can get a start on approximating it by moving imports from the "demand" category, where they appear as a negative, to the "supply" side of the equation. If we do this we see that the sum of the four positive demands—C + I + G + X, or aggregate demand—is equal to the sum of the two sources of supply—GDP + M, or aggregate supply. If the proportionate import content of each component of demand is roughly equal to the average import content of total aggregate demand, then the shares of aggregate demand provide a rough first approximation of the shares of GDP.

In this edition of *Business Statistics,* new Table 1-8, Shares of Aggregate Supply, shows that imports have risen from 4 percent of aggregate supply in the 1950s to 15 percent recently. New Table 1-9, Shares of Aggregate Final Demand, indicates that PCE has been around 60 percent of aggregate final demand ever since 1951, suggesting that it may "account for" closer to 60 percent than to 70 percent of GDP.

THE PLAN OF THE BOOK

The history of the U.S. economy is told in major U.S. government sets of statistical data: the national income and product accounts compiled by the Bureau of Economic Analysis (BEA); the data on labor force, employment, hours, earnings, and productivity compiled by the Bureau of Labor Statistics (BLS); the price indexes collected by BLS; and the financial market data compiled primarily by the Board of Governors of the Federal Reserve System (FRB). All of these sets exist in annual and either monthly or quarterly form beginning in 1946, 1947, or 1948, and many are available, at least annually, as far back as 1929.

In Part A, *Business Statistics* presents annual values for major indicators and their significant components back as far as space and availability permit, along with recent quarterly or monthly data. This enables easy calculation of growth rates and more flexible comparisons of recent values with historical data.

However, historical data with a higher frequency than annual are required for many purposes, including comparisons of activity before and after business cycle turning points. For the main series presented in Part A, historical quarterly or monthly data are presented in Part C that go all the way back to the beginning of the postwar period, where available. Part C also includes, for the same series, the annual values back to the end of World War II that had to be dropped from the tables in Part A for space reasons.

In both Part A and Part C, the presentations begin with the national income and product accounts, or NIPAs. The NIPAs comprise a comprehensive, thorough, and internally consistent data set. They measure the value of the total output of the U.S. economy (the gross domestic product, or GDP) and they allocate that value between its quantity, or "real," and price components. They show how the value of aggregate demand is distributed among consumers, business investors, government, and foreign customers; how much of aggregate demand is supplied by imports and how much by domestic production; and how the income generated in domestic production is distributed between labor and capital.

Production estimates covering only the "industrial" sectors of the economy—manufacturing, mining, and utilities—follow the presentation of the overall accounts.

Then, more detail is presented for the components of economic activity. GDP by definition consists of the sum of consumption expenditures, business investment, government purchases of goods and services, and exports minus imports—the elementary economics blackboard equation "GDP = C + I + G + X – M." Chapters on each of these components—consumption, investment, government, and foreign trade—are presented in Part A.

Following these chapters, there are a chapter on prices, two chapters on the compensation of labor and capital inputs and the amount and productivity of labor input, one chapter on energy inputs into production and consumption, and one chapter on money and financial markets.

While GDP is initially defined and measured by adding up its demand categories and subtracting imports, this output is produced in industries—some in the old-line heavy industries such as manufacturing, mining, and utilities, but an increasing share in the huge and heterogeneous group known as "service-providing" industries. Part A gives a number of summary measures of activity classified by industry or industrial sector: industrial production, profits, and employment-related data. Further industry information is provided in the next section of the book.

In Part B, *Business Statistics* first presents a general description of the current system of industrial classification, the North American Industry Classification System (NAICS), and its differences from its predecessor the Standard Industrial Classification system (SIC). This is followed by a table summarizing the structure of the U.S. economy as specified in NAICS. This table indicates how the NAICS statistical system is organized and shows—very roughly, in some cases—how each NAICS industry relates to the earlier SIC industries. The chapters that follow show GDP, income, employment, hours, and earnings by industry, followed by statistics for key sectors such as petroleum, housing, manufacturing, retail trade, and services.

Part C, Historical Data, contains in Chapter 18 graphs and tables summarizing annual values for important economic aggregates for the years 1929 through 1948, giving information about the enormous changes the economy went through as it experienced the Great Depression and the New Deal, mobilized for and fought World War II, and then demobilized.

In Chapters 19 and 20, postwar annual and quarterly or monthly values for the most important NIPA series and other major indicators complete the record shown in Part A for the period since the end of World War II.

Part D, State and Regional Data, contains annual data by state and region on personal income and employment back to 1958, and annual values and quantity indexes for GDP by state and region back to 1977.

Notes and definitions. Productive use of economic data requires accurate knowledge about the sources and meaning of the data. The notes and definitions for each chapter, shown immediately after that chapter's tables, contain definitions, descriptions of recent data revisions, and references to sources of additional technical information. They also include information about data availability and revision and release schedules, which allows users to readily access the latest current values if they need to keep up with the data month by month or quarter by quarter.

THE HISTORY OF *BUSINESS STATISTICS*

The history of *Business Statistics* began with the publication, many years ago, of the first edition of a volume with the same name and general purpose by the U.S. Department of Commerce's Bureau of Economic Analysis (BEA). After 27 periodic editions, the last of which appeared in 1992, BEA found it necessary, for budgetary and other reasons, to discontinue both the publication and the maintenance of the database from which the publication was derived.

The individual statistical series gathered together here are publicly available. However, the task of gathering them from the numerous different sources within the government and assembling them into one coherent database is impractical for most data users. Even when current data are readily available, obtaining the full historical time series is often time-consuming and difficult. Definitions and other documentation can also be inconvenient to find. Believing that a *Business Statistics* compilation was too valuable to be lost to the public, Bernan Press published the first edition of the present publication, edited by Dr. Courtenay M. Slater, in 1995. The first edition received a warm welcome from users of economic data. Dr. Slater, formerly chief economist of the Department of Commerce, continued to develop *Business Statistics* through four subsequent annual editions. The current editor worked with Dr. Slater on the fourth and fifth editions. In subsequent editions, she has continued in the tradition established by Dr. Slater of ensuring high-quality data while revising and expanding the book's scope to include significant new aspects of the U.S. economy and longer historical background.

Nearly all of the statistical data in this book are from federal government sources and are available in the public domain. Sources are given in the applicable notes and definitions.

The data in this volume meet the publication standards of the federal statistical agencies from which they were obtained. Every effort has been made to select data that are accurate, meaningful, and useful. All statistical data are subject to error arising from sampling variability, reporting errors, incomplete coverage, imputation, and other causes. The responsibility of the editor and publisher of this volume is limited to reasonable care in the reproduction and presentation of data obtained from established sources.

The 2009 edition has been edited by Cornelia J. Strawser, in association with Mary Meghan Ryan, who prepared all the tables and graphs and whose ability and experience have been essential in producing a timely and accurate reference work.

Dr. Strawser is the senior economic consultant to Bernan Press. She edited the seventh through thirteenth editions and was the co-editor of two previous editions of *Business Statistics*. She was co-editor of *Foreign Trade of the United States, 2001,* and also worked on the *Handbook of U.S. Labor Statistics*. She was formerly a senior economist for the U.S. House of Representatives Budget Committee and has also served at the Senate Budget Committee, at the Congressional Budget Office, and on the Federal Reserve Board staff.

The editor assumes full responsibility for the interpretations presented in this volume.

BUSINESS STATISTICS IN TURBULENT TIMES

This 14th edition of *Business Statistics of the United States* presents data on U.S. economic performance through December 2008—the 12th month of the 11th recession of the postwar period, according to the chronology maintained by the National Bureau of Economic Research. This recession has already been longer than the postwar average of just over 10 months. As we assemble these data in the first half of 2009, there are indications that this recession will turn out to be longer than the two longest previous postwar recessions—each of which lasted 16 months—and some observers have predicted that it will be the worst since the Great Depression.

This article begins with a general discussion of business cycles in the United States economy, including a chronology of the cycles occurring in the years covered by this volume, and a discussion of the meaning of the term "The Great Depression."

- Following this is an example of the use of monthly data, such as those provided in this book, to track recession and recovery.
- Then, other examples are provided of important analytical techniques for extracting key information from a statistical record and elucidating growth issues.
- Following that section, and illustrating the use of the techniques described, is a comparison of the latest completed cycle of recession, recovery, and growth—between 2000 and 2007—with the previous cycle that ran from 1990 through 2000.
- Subsequent sections deal with measuring the standard of living and with the relationships between inflation and unemployment.
- A section from earlier editions on the effects of hurricanes and other disasters is reprinted.
- An upcoming comprehensive revision in the national income and product accounts, scheduled for release in July 2009, is briefly described and discussed.

BUSINESS CYCLES IN THE U.S. ECONOMY

The study of economic fluctuations in the United States was pioneered by Wesley C. Mitchell and Arthur F. Burns early in the twentieth century; it was carried on subsequently by other researchers affiliated with the National Bureau of Economic Research (NBER), an independent, nonpartisan research organization. These analysts observed that indicators of the general state of business activity tended to move up and down over periods that were longer than a year and were therefore not accounted for by seasonal variation. Although these periods of expansion and contraction have not been uniform in length, and thus not "cycles" in any strict mathematical sense, their recurrent nature caused them to be called

"business cycles." NBER has identified 32 business cycles over the period beginning with December 1854.

The first NBER-established business cycle dates were published in 1929. Currently, the dates are established by the NBER Business Cycle Dating Committee, first formed in 1978. It consists of eight economists who are university professors, associated with research organizations, or both.

Business cycle dates are based on monthly data, and have been identified for periods long before the availability of quarterly data on real gross national product (GDP). Even in the recent period when such data are available, the identification of a recession does not always coincide with the frequently cited definition of recession as two consecutive quarters of decline in real GDP.

The monthly and quarterly dates of the cycles from before the Great Depression to the latest announced turning point—the December 2007 peak ending the expansion that began in November 2001—are shown in Table A-1 below. Quarterly turning points are identified by Roman numerals. NBER considers that the trough month is both the end of the decline and the beginning of the recovery, based on the concept that the actual turning point was some particular day within that month. Thus, the latest expansion ended in December 2007, and the recession also began in December 2007.

For additional information on NBER and its business cycle studies, see the NBER Web site at <http://www.nber.org/cycles>.

What was the Great Depression?

Note that most of the 1930s, after the March 1933 trough, is identified as a period of expansion by NBER, in apparent conflict with the fact that the entire decade is often considered to be in the "Great Depression." The NBER does not identify "depressions;" the popular usage denotes a prolonged period of idle resources.

People interested in the economics and politics of the 1930s may wish to distinguish, as NBER does, between that part of the period when output and employment declined precipitously—the 43-month collapse from August 1929 through March 1933—and the subsequent period when output and employment, though still far below a likely trend line, were rising most of the time, before accepting at face value statements like "the New Deal failed to end the Depression."

In this edition of *Business Statistics*, Chapter 18 has been expanded; it now includes five graphs depicting the eco-

Table A-1. BUSINESS CYCLE REFERENCE DATES 1927–2007

TROUGH	PEAK
NOVEMBER 1927 (IV)	AUGUST 1929 (III)
MARCH 1933 (I)	MAY 1937 (II)
JUNE 1938 (II)	FEBRUARY 1945 (I)
OCTOBER 1945 (IV)	NOVEMBER 1948 (IV)
OCTOBER 1949 (IV)	JULY 1953 (II)
MAY 1954 (II)	AUGUST 1957 (III)
APRIL 1958 (II)	APRIL 1960 (II)
FEBRUARY 1961 (I)	DECEMBER 1969 (IV)
NOVEMBER 1970 (IV)	NOVEMBER 1973 (IV)
MARCH 1975 (I)	JANUARY 1980 (I)
JULY 1980 (III)	JULY 1981 (III)
NOVEMBER 1982 (IV)	JULY 1990 (III)
MARCH 1991 (I)	MARCH 2001 (I)
NOVEMBER 2001 (IV)	DECEMBER 2007 (IV)

SOURCE: NATIONAL BUREAU OF ECONOMIC RESEARCH, HTTP://WWW.NBER.ORG/CYCLES.

nomic course of the Depression and World War II periods, accompanied by some explanatory narration. New emphasis is placed on Federal Reserve data on money and credit. The Notes and Definitions to this chapter discuss the business cycle dates for this period and the important issue of the statistical treatment of work relief employment during the Depression.

Tracking recessions: total payroll employment

Figure A-1 shows how current data can be tracked month by month in comparison with earlier business cycles. The figure depicts proportional movements in total payroll employment (see Tables 10-7 and 20-4 and the associated Notes and Definitions), beginning with the cycle peak and continuing over the following 23 months.

Many economists would prefer to track cycles monthly using a comprehensive measure of aggregate output, not employment. However, we do not have a satisfactory monthly measure of gross domestic product [GDP]; attempts to estimate it have proved to be volatile, "noisy," and subject to excessive revision.

There is a reliable and long-established monthly index of industrial production—manufacturing, mining, and utilities—presented in Chapter 2 of this volume. Mining and utilities are of little significance in the business cycle process—in fact, short-term variation in the utility sector is mostly influenced by unusual weather conditions. As a result, the cyclical movements of the industrial production index are dominated by the manufacturing sector. Because manufacturing now accounts for only about 10 percent of total nonfarm employment, the industrial production index is limited as a general business cycle gauge, but it is still one of the major indicators monitored by the Business Cycle Dating Committee.

The employment count—covering the entire nonfarm economy, based on a large and long-established sample of large and small businesses, and available shortly after the end of each month—is a widely accepted indicator, more reliable and less subject to revision and excessive random variation than any available broad production measure. It is viewed as "the most reliable comprehensive estimate of employment" by the Business Cycle Dating Committee.

For ease of comparison in this graph, the employment totals for each recession period are converted to indexes with the peak month set at 100. To illustrate, the line labeled "From July 1981" represents employment in each successive month, July 1981 through June 1983, divided by the July 1981 value and multiplied by 100. The line labeled "From December 2007" represents employment in each successive month, December 2007 through a preliminary value for March 2009, divided by the December 2007 value and multiplied by 100.

Looked at in this way, the similarities among the four recessions in the first 10 months of decline are striking: nearly a year after the peak, employment was down about 1½ percent in each case. Two months later, the four declines no longer look similar: employment had leveled off in 1991 and 2002, but lurched sharply downward in winter 2007–2008 as it did in mid-1982. Thus, it appears that this recession will be comparable in length and severity to, at least, the 1981–82 recession, rather than to the mild recessions of more recent decades.

Figure A-1 shows that the slide in employment from the July 1981 peak continued for a year and a half and then began a brisk recovery. Can we hope for that by the end of 2009? Both periods saw fiscal stimulus enacted, but the monetary conditions are strikingly different.

A look at Table 20-6 shows that the federal funds rate (the rate banks charge on overnight loans, set by Federal Reserve open market operations) was 19 percent in July 1981, fell to 13 percent in July 1982, and was 9 percent by July 1983. The Fed had maintained a very tight policy in early 1981 to break the back of inflation, then had plenty of room to reduce rates once the recession was under way.

In contrast, the federal funds rate was already close to zero in December 2007, and the obstacles to renewed credit flows were not high interest rates but deflation and deteriorating financial balance sheets. These are the conditions that have led some to fear a slide like the one that started in August 1929 and lasted 3½ years, similarly fed by deflation and financial institution failures.

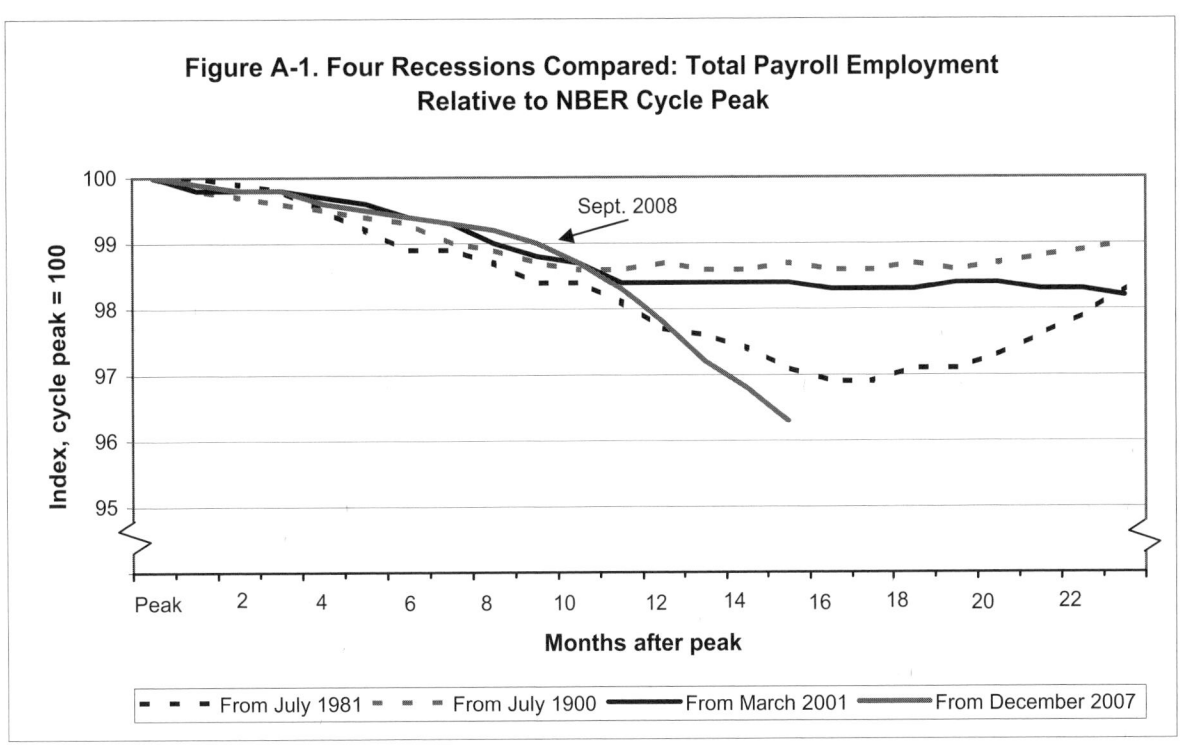

Figure A-1. Four Recessions Compared: Total Payroll Employment Relative to NBER Cycle Peak

As mentioned above, Chapter 18 of this edition of *Business Statistics* includes a statistical picture of the Depression years, as an indication of what today's policymakers are struggling to prevent. Two of today's highest economic officials—Chairman Ben Bernanke of the Federal Reserve Board, and Chairman Christina Romer of the President's Council of Economic Advisers—are respected academic scholars of the Great Depression. The policies they pursue today, including efforts to get credit flowing again that might produce results comparable to the interest rate declines of 1982–83, are undertaken in the light of their knowledge of the failures of the policies of 1929–33. That said, the guidance of history is limited when so many circumstances are different, and much uncertainty remains.

ANALYTICAL TECHNIQUES FOR GROWTH ISSUES

In assessing the performance of an economy over longer periods of time, it is important to use analytical techniques that highlight the most important aspects of the series. In this article and in the graphs and text that accompany nearly every *Business Statistics* data chapter, the editor will frequently make use of three powerful tools: the ratio-scale graph, the calculation of compound annual growth rates, and the use of cyclically comparable years to estimate trends and to separate trend from cyclical behavior. Econometricians use more elaborate methods of statistical analysis to estimate relationships and construct models, but much can be discerned just by using these relatively simple techniques.

Ratio-scale graphs. At the beginning of Chapter 1 (Figure 1-1) is a time series graph of output per capita from 1946

through 2008, drawn on a ratio scale. Output per capita is the constant-dollar value of each year's U.S. gross domestic product (GDP), divided by the size of that year's U.S. population.

The reader will quickly see that equal distances on the vertical scale of this graph do not represent equal differences in 2000-dollar values. However, equal vertical distances do represent equal <u>percent changes</u>. Any upward-sloping straight line plotted on this scale represents a constant percentage rate of growth over the period, and any downward-sloping straight line represents a constant percentage rate of decline.

This ratio-scale graph was produced by the following three steps: (1) The values to be graphed were converted into natural (base e) logarithms. (2) The natural logarithms were graphed. (3) For ease of interpretation, the vertical scale on this graph of the logarithms was re-labeled, replacing the numerical value of the logarithm that was plotted with the numerical value of its antilog—that is, the original value of per capita output.

This technique is only valid for data series that do not include zeroes or negative numbers, for which logarithms do not exist. Because percentage values such as the unemployment rate and percent changes such as the inflation rate are already in percentage terms, and because percent changes may include zero and/or negative values, they are not graphed in this fashion.

Compound annual growth rates. In the text of this article and in the highlights pages that precede and accompany most of the chapters, the editor often uses compound annual growth rates to summarize the history of important economic processes such as economic and demographic growth and inflation.

The compound annual growth rate is the percentage rate which, when compounded annually, would cause a quantity or price "X(t)" observed in a period "t" to grow (or decline) to a quantity or price "X(t+i)" over a period of "i" years. Using this procedure, growth percentages for different periods spanning different numbers of years can be reduced to a common scale—the annual rate—for comparison. The formula for calculating such a growth rate, "r," is as follows:

$$r = \left(\sqrt[i]{X(t+i)\Big/ X(t)} - 1 \right) x100.$$

When growth rates are functionally related to each other, such as the growth rates for output, hours worked, and output per hour worked (productivity), those rates will be arithmetically consistent as in the following formula, where "o" is the percentage growth rate for output, "h" the rate for hours worked, and "p" the growth rate for output per hour worked:

$$p = \left[\big[(100 + o)/(100 + h) \big] - 1 \right] x100$$

When the percentage growth rates are not very far from zero, relationships of this kind can be approximated or verified by simple addition or subtraction of the relevant percentage rates. For example, the productivity growth rate of 2.2 percent in output per hour at nonfarm business from 1948 to 2000 is approximately the difference between the output growth rate of 3.7 percent and the hours growth rate of 1.5 percent in that period.

Using cyclically comparable end points. For economic processes that have significant business-cycle components, such as output and employment, it is important to use comparable points in the business cycle for estimating underlying growth rates. One commonly used method is to calculate growth rates between years with similar, high rates of resource utilization. The broadest readily available measure of resource utilization is the unemployment rate, which was 3.8 percent in 1948, 4.0 percent in 2000, and 4.6 percent in 2007. (See Table 10-4.) A narrower measure that focuses on capital rather than labor, namely capacity utilization in manufacturing, was 82.5 percent in 1948, 80.1 percent in 2000, and 79.4 percent in 2007. (See Table 2-3.) For calculation of trends for the postwar period as a whole, either of the latter years could be considered as a possible end point.

For comparisons using monthly or quarterly data, calculations can be made by using the actual monthly or quarterly dates of business cycle peaks. In the analysis that follows, however, the editor will use annual averages, because they are less volatile, and also because it is thereby possible to include on a consistent basis data that are only available annually from the Census Bureau's Current Population Survey of household income and earnings.

With the designation of December 2007 as the peak ending the latest expansion, it is possible to compare the two most recent cycles using peak-to-peak growth rates. In the table that follows, the editor will compare growth rates from 1990 to 2000 (representing the July 1990–March 2001 cycle) with rates from 2000 to 2007 (representing the March 2001–December 2007 cycle).

It should be noted that the peak-to-peak definition used here includes the recessions themselves as part of the cycle, as well as the subsequent recoveries. The strength and speed of early cyclical recovery tends to be inversely related to the depth and speed of the preceding recession. Hence, a comparison of recoveries that began with the cyclical troughs would overestimate the underlying strength of the economy and the sustainable increases in incomes in periods preceded by deep recessions.

Comparison of the last two completed business cycles

Table A-2 presents a number of comparisons of the last two completed business cycles, including peak-to-peak calculations. All of these comparisons use data published in *Business Statistics*, and the annual rates of change are calculated using the formula shown earlier in this article.

To begin with we show measures of the length in months of the two cycles—the length of the full cycle and of its expansion phases. Although the recessions at the beginnings of the two periods here compared were of equal length (8 months) and mildness, the full 2000–2007 cycle was markedly shorter than the 1990–2000 cycle. Also, the actual expansion in employment took longer to get started in the later period, as can be seen by comparing the length of the NBER-designated expansion phase with the length of the expansion in employment.

A further dimension is the "what happened next" question, since performance after a cycle is over can reflect imbalances that grew up during that cycle. For example, some look at the Great Depression as affected by the imbalances in income distribution and the speculative excesses of the 1920s. The relative severity of the recessions of 1973–1975 and the early 1980s was a response to the inflationary buildup of the 1960s and 1970s. The recession following December 2007 is, as has been pointed out above, already more severe than the one that followed March 2001, and appears to reflect a more pervasive buildup of debt problems.

Turning to the measurements of economic performance in Table A-2, the rates of growth in real GDP per capita, real disposable income per capita, and employment were all slower in the 2000–2007 cycle than in 1990–2000. Growth in

Table A-2. Two Business Cycles Compared

(Number, percent.)

Description	July 1990 to March 2001	March 2001 to December 2007
GENERAL DESCRIPTION OF CYCLE		
Length of full cycle, months	128	81
Length of expansion phase, months	120	73
Length of employment expansion	118	52
Length of following recession, months	8	15+
Percent change in real GDP	-0.4	-3.2 -
ECONOMIC MEASUREMENTS OF CYCLE, BASED ON ANNUAL AVERAGES FOR 1990, 2000, AND 2007		
Real per capita product and income growth (percent changes, annual rate, Table 1-7):		
Real gross domestic product per capita	2.03	1.35
Real disposable (after-tax) personal income per capita	1.81	1.69
Total civilian employment (CPS, Table 10-2):		
Change in jobs, millions	18.1	9.2
Percent change, annual rate	1.43	0.93
Nonfarm payroll employment (CES, Table 10-7):		
Change in jobs, millions	22.3	5.8
Percent change, annual rate	1.87	0.62
Capital stock growth (percent change, annual rate, in quantity index for the net stock of fixed assets, Table 5-6):		
Private nonresidential	2.90	1.88
Private residential	2.46	2.80
Federal government	0.09	0.27
State and local government	2.47	2.55
Productivity growth (percent change, annual rate, output per hour, nonfarm business, Table 9-3)	2.04	2.45
Growth in real pre-tax compensation and incomes (percent change, annual rate, deflated using CPI-U-RS):		
Employment cost index, all private industry (nonfarm) workers (Tables 9-1, 9-2, and 8-2):		
Total compensation	1.00	0.79
Wages and salaries	0.86	0.36
Median earnings, full-time year-round workers (Table 3-1):		
Men	0.52	0.08
Women	0.82	0.86
Median household income (Table 3-1)	0.94	-0.09
Gap between productivity growth and compensation growth rates:		
Total	1.04	1.66
Caused by deflator difference	0.69	0.49
Unexplained	0.35	1.17
Ratio to GDP of credit market debt owed (Tables 12-5 and 1-1):		
Federal and related:		
Beginning of period	0.67	0.78
End	0.78	0.91
Nonfederal:		
Beginning of period	1.70	1.98
End	1.98	2.71

Sources: National Bureau of Economic Research chronology, National Income and Product Accounts, Bureau of Labor Statistics data, Census Bureau data, Federal Reserve Flow-of-Funds Accounts.

Note: Credit market debt includes that owed by both financial and nonfinancial entities. "Federal and related" credit market debt includes Treasury securities held by the public (including by the Federal Reserve), budget agency securities and mortgages, debt of government-sponsored enterprises (GSEs), and debt of agency- and GSE-backed mortgage pools.

the private nonresidential capital stock—generally considered the part of the capital stock most relevant to growth in economic productivity—was a full percentage point slower. Growth in the private residential capital stock was more rapid in the later period, reflecting the housing bubble, and growth in government-owned capital was also somewhat more rapid—reflecting the defense buildup in the case of the Federal government stock. Indeed, constant-dollar defense investment, which declined 33 percent from 1990 to 2000, rose 60 percent in the following seven years, as can be seen in Table 6-6.

Despite the slower growth in nonresidential capital in the 2000–2007 period, private nonfarm productivity grew faster, perhaps as a delayed result of earlier investment. The faster productivity growth was associated with slower employment growth, as fewer workers were required to produce a given level of output.

Productivity growth is generally welcomed, and even sought as a policy goal, because it has theoretically and historically been associated with growth in real wages. In 2000–2007, however, growth in real wages and in real median worker earnings fell well behind productivity growth.

There are some valid reasons that growth in hourly worker pay can differ from productivity growth, and these factors are displayed in Table A-2. One is that employers must pay the costs of total compensation, not just wages and salaries. Total compensation includes not only wages and salaries but also employer social insurance taxes and the cost of health, retirement, and other benefits. In recent years, growth in health benefit costs has outpaced hourly wage and salary rates. This can be seen by comparing real growth in the two categories that are shown for the employment cost index, total compensation and wages and salaries. But growth in the index for total compensation still falls far short of productivity growth, and it slows down in the 2000–2007 period even when productivity growth is speeding up.

A second reason for differences between productivity and compensation growth is that the price index used to calculate real compensation—a specially-constructed index of consumer prices, the CPI-U-RS (see Chapter 8)—has a somewhat different trend from the productivity price index. The prices of what U.S. workers produce have gone up less than the prices of what they buy, mainly because business sector output includes a greater share of high-tech products—whose prices have decreased dramatically—than the average consumer market basket. So even if workers get a constant share of the current-dollar value of output, their earnings lose ground in relative purchasing power. (Economists call this a deterioration in the "terms of trade.") But this deflator difference actually shrank in 2000–2007 compared with the previous cycle period, and the unexplained difference between productivity growth and compensation growth grew, weakening the case for a link between productivity and worker well-being.

Finally, using data from the Federal Reserve Flow of Funds accounts in Chapter 12, we can look at the ratio of credit market debt to GDP over the course of the cycle. These are comprehensive measures of debt, including that owed by both financial and nonfinancial entities. Both Federal and nonfederal debt grew relative to GDP in both periods, but the growth in the later cycle was greater, particularly for nonfederal debt, which started the cycle at twice the annual value of GDP and ended at a ratio of 2.7. This gives some indication of the debt levels now overhanging current levels of spending and activity, measures of which are shown in more detail in Chapter 12.

Whose standard of living?

Some of the measures discussed in the preceding section are averages, such as GDP and personal income per capita and output per hour worked. It is important to note that the average, known technically to statisticians as a "mean," is only one way of describing the central tendency of any set of statistical data, and is not necessarily the method that produces the most representative number.

Most researchers who are interested in the economic well-being of a typical American family or household judge that the best single number to characterize that well-being is the standard of living of the family or household situated at the middle of the income distribution. Half of all families or households have higher incomes and half have lower incomes. This is the measure known as the "median." Medians are not the same as averages or means, and in the case of income distributions, they are invariably lower.

This reason behind this difference is sometimes illustrated by calling up the image of a billionaire walking into a working-class bar. The "average income" (mean income) of each person in the bar would jump, as a billion dollars was added to the numerator of the average and just one unit was added to the denominator. However, the median would be little if at all changed—at most, the addition of one person to the group might mean that the median income moved up from one worker to the next best-paid worker—and this would accord with an accurate perception that the typical person in that bar had not experienced any significant increase in his income. Thus, when a few individuals or households have very high incomes, means are higher than medians and not representative of the typical individual or household.

Furthermore, if over time the incomes of people at the upper end of the distribution increase faster than the incomes of those at the middle and bottom of the distribution (which is what happens when the income distribution becomes more unequal), then the means will also increase more than the medians.

Once a year, as a supplement to the Current Population Survey, the Census Bureau collects data on the incomes of its sample of households. These data are used to produce a report on median incomes, the distribution of incomes, and the poverty rate, providing extensive data on the economic well-being of households and individuals throughout the income distribution. This survey is the source for all of the data in Chapter 3 of *Business Statistics,* including the median earnings and median household income data that are also used to calculate the growth rates shown in Table A-2.

Inflation and unemployment

A number of important price indicators are presented in *Business Statistics,* both in Chapter 8: Prices and in Table 1-5, which shows chain-type price indexes for GDP and various subsectors. Users should note that price indexes measure the average level of prices, relative to some base year that is set to equal 100, while "inflation" is the annual percent rate of change in a price index.

Accurate measurement of prices is challenging in a dynamic economy. Various biases have been identified over the years in the most widely used price indicators, the official Consumer Price Index for All Urban Consumers (CPI-U) and its close relative, the Consumer Price Index for Urban Wage Earners and Clerical Workers (CPI-W). Improved methods to remove these biases are frequently introduced into the calculation of the indexes going forward, but the official Consumer Price Indexes are not retroactively corrected. However, there are some alternative versions of the CPI that carry the current improved methodologies back for a number of years to create a consistent historical record. These are presented in *Business Statistics;* see Tables 8-2 and 8-3 and their associated notes and definitions. One of these alternatives, the CPI-U-RS, is used by the Bureau of Labor Statistics to calculate historical values of real compensation (Chapter 9), by the Census Bureau to calculate historical values of real median income (Chapter 3), and by the editor of *Business Statistics* to calculate the real compensation and wage and salary growth shown in Table A-2.

Because of this and other perceived shortcomings of the official CPIs, economists at the Federal Reserve, among others, pay particular attention to the chain-type price indexes for personal consumption expenditures in the NIPAs. The NIPA indexes use many of the same basic price observations that are collected for the CPIs. However, the NIPA indexes are defined to cover a somewhat broader universe of prices. In compiling the NIPA indexes, the Bureau of Economic Analysis processes the data in a more consistent fashion and regularly revises past data to correct biases. (See Table 1-5 and the notes and definitions to Chapter 1.) The chain-weighting procedure means that the weights are continually and consistently updated.

Still, all of these indexes tell a similar story about the behavior of inflation over the postwar period. As Figure 8-1 in Chapter 8 shows, inflation was high in 1946 and 1947, as World War II price controls were dismantled and pent-up purchasing power from the war period was released. Prices declined in the 1949 recession but rose sharply in 1950 and 1951 with recovery and the outbreak of the Korean War. Inflation was negative again in 1955 in the aftermath of that war's end and the 1954 recession. Inflation rose during two recoveries in 1956–1957 and 1960, but fell back to about 1 percent—generally judged to represent price stability because of remaining and irremediable biases in the price indexes—in the slack years of 1961 and 1962.

However, as the 1960s progressed, the federal government embarked on a stimulative fiscal policy with the intent of attaining unemployment rates lower than those observed in the 1950s and early 1960s. (Tables 10-4 and 10-5) As the buildup in military spending for the Vietnam War accelerated, fiscal policy became even more stimulative, without any attempt to raise taxes or cut back on other spending until late in the decade. (Chapter 6) Monetary policy tended to accommodate the fiscal policy, that is, to hold down interest rates in the face of increased federal borrowing. To offset these causes of inflation, an attempt was made to hold wages and prices down using voluntary "guidelines" in the early 1960s. The guidelines collapsed in 1966, however, and inflation continued to accelerate during the sustained period of very low unemployment through 1969.

The 1970 recession failed to bring inflation down, and the 1971 recovery was weak. Moves to accelerate the recovery, including monetary stimulus and depreciation of the dollar, were undertaken. New price controls and guidelines were introduced, with some initial effect on inflation. But the 1972 decline in inflation was short-lived, followed by new highs as the price controls collapsed and commodity prices soared. The severe 1975–1976 recession provided only a temporary and incomplete respite from inflation, which soared to double digits in 1979 through 1981 with recovery and new commodity price shocks.

Finally, under the impact of a tough monetary policy that led to the 1981–1982 recession—the most severe recession of the postwar period up to that time—inflation ratcheted down to a core rate of about 4 percent, which prevailed during the 1982–1990 expansion. A recession in 1990 ushered in even lower inflation rates throughout the rest of the 1990s, despite the achievement in the late 1990s of the lowest unemployment rates since 1969.

As the above narrative indicates, the 1950s and 1960s were characterized by an apparent inverse relationship, often interpreted as a "trade-off," between inflation and high employment, with inflation falling as an apparent consequence of unemployment rising. By the 1970s, inflation became more stubborn and failed to respond proportionately and negatively to increases in unemployment. Indeed, at times inflation and unemployment rose together, a phenomenon known as "stagflation." This has often been ascribed to "supply shocks"—for example, bad harvests, oil embargoes, and OPEC price increases—which, unlike decreases in aggregate demand, tend to increase inflation even while depressing output. However, not all supply shocks are really independent of demand forces. In retrospect, some "supply" shocks should perhaps be considered as delayed reactions to demand shocks. To give an important example, oil prices tend to increase when the dollar has declined, and they tend to fall during worldwide recessions—as they did in 1986 and at the end of 2008. (See the general price data in Chapter 8, the oil price data in Chapter 17, and the data on the international value of the dollar in Table 13-8.) Since a decline in the dollar is an expected consequence of expansionary monetary policy, the resulting increase in the price of oil could be considered part of the inflationary effect of such a policy. And OPEC's power to set prices is clearly dependent on the general state of the world economy in both booms and recessions.

In attempting to explain stagflation, economists now attempt to take account of the role of expectations about future inflation in maintaining the momentum of a given inflation rate even in the presence of rising unemployment. Employers and workers may continue to expect high inflation, perhaps based on an expectation of expansionary government policy, despite current decreases in the demand for labor, and therefore agree to continue high rates of wage and price increase. This mechanism is believed by many to explain the worsening of the tradeoff in the 1970s.

But many economists were again surprised by the combination of low unemployment and low inflation in the late 1990s. The surprise was greater among those economists who looked to the unemployment rate as the sole measure of resource utilization. In fact, the level of capacity utilization also plays a role in determining to what extent changes in aggregate demand affect prices and to what extent they lead to expanded volume of production instead. Capacity utilization measures are not available for all sectors of the economy, but the Federal Reserve Board does maintain utilization series for the industrial sector. (Table 2-3) Figure 2-1 shows a clear downtrend in peak capacity utilization ever since the 1960s from one cycle high to the next, indicating progressively less upward pressure on prices.

The issues involved in the relationships between inflation, economic growth, and unemployment are far from settled. Debate continues about the relative roles of monetary policy, tax rates and other aspects of fiscal policy, global competition, other supply considerations, labor market institutions, and expectations.

With respect to monetary policy, *Business Statistics* provides data on the monetary and reserve aggregates in Tables 12-1 through 12-3. Rates of change in money and reserves have provided increasingly inaccurate forecasts of inflation and are not widely considered to be valid indicators of the state of monetary policy any more. In fact, the Federal Reserve has discontinued publication of M3, the broadest monetary aggregate. The data on interest rates provided in Table 12-9—especially the federal funds rate, which is directly controlled by the Federal Reserve—are currently the subject of more attention in assessing the monetary policy stance. Table 12-9 now includes an estimate by the editor of *Business Statistics* of the "real" (inflation-adjusted) federal funds rate. A real rate near or below zero suggests that Federal Reserve policy is stimulative and potentially inflationary, while high positive rates such as those observed in the early 1980s suggest contraction and disinflation. A market-based, longer-term real rate is included as well.

In 2008, the usual measures of monetary easing—both the interest rates and the money and reserve aggregates—show an extremely easy policy, yet the economy showed little response. For that reason the Federal Reserve undertook new methods of "quantitative easing" and direct intervention in credit markets to encourage borrowing, which are measured in the dramatic expansion of the Federal Reserve balance sheet, newly added to Table 12-3.

Effects of hurricanes and other disasters

This section explains how the national income and product accounts (NIPAs) reflected the effects of Hurricane Katrina in the third quarter of 2005. The same principles of measurement apply to the NIPA treatment of other hurricanes, earthquakes, and the terrorist attacks of September 11, 2001.

As the Bureau of Economic Analysis (BEA) explains, "Gross domestic product (GDP) is not directly affected by the destruction of previously produced property." ("The Impact of the Third-Quarter Hurricanes on the NIPAs," *Survey of Current Business*, December 2005, p. 4). Some commentators like to point out that GDP can even be, perversely, increased by an episode of destruction, once people start buying and producing to replace the lost assets.

What these observers may not realize is that the NIPAs also include series that do recognize destruction of capital, namely several income measures and the net national product (NNP). BEA statisticians estimate the amount of loss in such disasters that is over and above normal depreciation and include it in "consumption of fixed capital" (CFC), which is deducted from GDP to yield NNP. See Table 1-10 in Chapter 1 and the associated notes and definitions for the relationship of gross and net product and income.

Since personal income and net factor incomes are also measured net of CFC, the dip in NNP caused by the destruction of assets also causes a dip in income.

In Tables 19-6 and 19-8, it will be seen that total "rental income of persons," which includes the imputed rent on owner-occupied homes, was actually negative in the third quarter of 2005, as the value of hurricane destruction of property exceeded the entire national value of rentals paid or imputed on the equity value of the remaining residential stock. Smaller declines in that quarter can also be seen in corporate profits and proprietors' income.

Insurance payments ameliorate some of the economic losses to individuals. The insurance payments do not of themselves restore the assets, either in reality or as the accounts measure them; that happens only when new construction and other investment start to take place. The insurance payments appear in non-production income components of the NIPAs as transfer payments of various kinds, and they appear when the insured losses occur, not when the actual monetary payments are made. In the third quarter of 2005, there were large business transfers to persons, increasing personal income and decreasing net business transfer receipts (receipts minus payments). As a result, personal income in total declined not by the amount of the total property loss as recorded in the rental payment component but by the value of the uninsured loss—the property loss minus the estimated insurance receipts. Also included in the accounting are net receipts of insurance payments by business from government and a minus entry in payments to the rest of the world, indicating net receipts from overseas reinsurance companies. (See the notes and definitions for Tables 7-9 through 7-16 for a discussion of the treatment of international insurance service flows.)

BEA has made disaster adjustments of this nature for Hurricanes Andrew and Iniki in 1992; the Midwest floods and the East Coast storms in 1993; the California Northridge earthquake in 1994; Hurricane Opal in 1995; Hurricane Floyd in 1999; Tropical Storm Allison in 2001; the terrorist attacks of September 11, 2001; Hurricanes Charley, Frances, Ivan, and Jeanne in 2004; and Hurricanes Katrina, Rita, and Wilma in 2005. These adjustments apply not only to the national figures, but also to state and local estimates, such as those shown in Chapter 21 of this book.

REFERENCES (all available on the BEA Web site)

Further information can be found in the following resources: "The Impact of the Third-Quarter Hurricanes on the NIPAs," *Survey of Current Business,* December 2005, p. 4; "Final Estimates for the Third Quarter of 2005," *Survey of Current Business,* January 2006, p. 1–3; "Disaster Adjustments," in "XI.Technical Notes," April 2006, <http://www.bea.gov/bea/regional/articles/lapi2004/technote.pdf> (Accessed Jan. 4, 2007); and "Frequently Asked Questions," *How Are Disasters (Such as Hurricanes and Earthquakes) Treated in the National Accounts?*, <http://www.bea.gov/bea/faq/national/0805PIKtnaffects.htm> (Accessed Jan. 4, 2007).

Upcoming NIPA revision

In July 2009 the Bureau of Economic Analysis will release a comprehensive, or benchmark, revision of the NIPAs.

Current-dollar estimates will be revised—especially for the most recent four years—because of data updating and classification and statistical changes. Users of the constant-dollar estimates and the quantity and price indexes will also, and immediately, notice a change in the reference year for the chain-type quantity and price indexes and the chained-dollar estimates, from 2000 (as used in the data in this volume) to 2005.

The change in the reference year will cause conspicuous differences in the <u>levels</u> of the constant-dollar measures and the price and quantity indexes, but this does not of itself affect the <u>rates of change</u>—the growth and inflation rates calculated from these data—which are based on chain-weighted indexes whatever the reference base year is. After the revision, historical growth and inflation trends are likely to be similar to those that can be derived from the data in this volume, except for revisions occasioned by new data for the most recent several years.

BEA also plans changes in the treatment of disasters and a new classification system for personal consumption expenditures.

These and all of the other planned changes are described in "Preview of the 2009 Comprehensive Revision of the NIPAs: Changes in Definitions and Presentations," *Survey of Current Business,* March 2009, available at <http://www.bea.gov>.

GENERAL NOTES

These notes provide general information about the data in Tables 1-1 through 21-2. Specific notes with information about data sources, definitions, methodology, revisions, and sources of additional information follow the tables in each chapter.

Main divisions of the book

The tables are divided into four main parts:

Part A (Tables 1-1 through 13-8) pertains to the U.S. economy as a whole. Generally, each table presents annual averages as far back as data availability and space permit, and quarterly or monthly values for the most recent year or years. (For the most important series, full quarterly or monthly histories and annual averages back to the beginning of the postWorld-War-II period are shown in Part C.) Some chapters present data for the United States only in aggregate, while others—such as the chapters concerning industrial production and capacity utilization (chapter 2), capital expenditures (chapter 5), profits (chapter 9), and employment, hours, and earnings (chapter 10)—also have detail for major industry groups.

Data by industry on industrial production and capacity utilization (Tables 2-2 and 2-3), capital expenditures (Table 5-11), profits (Tables 9-4 through 9-6), and payroll employment, hours, and earnings (Tables 10-7 through 10-12) are classified using the new North American Industry Classification System (NAICS), as far back as such data are made available by the source agencies.

Part B focuses on the individual industries that together produce the gross domestic product (GDP).

Chapter 14 provides an overview of NAICS, presenting the overall structure of the classification system, the definition of each major industry group, and the approximate relationships of each group to the industries in SIC (Standard Industrial Classification), the previous system.

Chapter 15 contains data on GDP, quantity production trends, and factor income by NAICS industry group.

Chapter 16 provides further detail on payroll employment, hours, and earnings classified according to NAICS.

Chapter 17 presents various data sets for key economic sectors. Some of the tables are based on definitions of products, rather than of producing establishments, and are valid for either classification system. This is the case for Tables 17-1, Petroleum and Petroleum Products; 17-2, New Construction; 17-3, Housing Starts and Building Permits, New House Sales, and Prices; and 17-8, Motor Vehicle

Sales and Inventories. Tables 17-4 through 17-7 and 17-9, 17-11, and 17-12, which cover manufacturing and retail and wholesale trade, show data classified according to NAICS. Tables 17-13 and 17-14 present data for services industries classified according to NAICS.

NAICS is fully described in U.S. Office of Management and Budget's, *North American Industry Classification System: United States, 2002* which was published by Bernan Press in 2003. Additional information is available on the Census Bureau Web site <http://www.census.gov>.

Part C presents further historical detail.

Chapter 18 shows selected data for the years 1929 through 1948. Generally, these are shown on an annual basis only, as many of the series are not available in quarterly or monthly detail. At the beginning of the chapter, graphs with brief narration highlight some of the most important characteristics of the Depression and World War II eras. Chapters 19 and 20 present quarterly or monthly data back to the earliest postwar year available for major series, along with available annual data back to 1946 that are not shown in Part A.

Part D presents data by state and region, calculated by the Bureau of Economic Analysis; data are available on an annual basis only. Table 21-1 contains data on GDP and Table 21-2 shows data on personal income, population, and employment.

Characteristics of the tables and the data

The subtitles or column headings for the data tables normally indicate whether the data are *seasonally adjusted*, *not seasonally adjusted*, or *at a seasonally adjusted annual rate*. These descriptions refer to the monthly or quarterly data, rather than the annual data. Annual data by definition require no seasonal adjustment. Annual values are normally calculated as totals or averages (as appropriate) of unadjusted data. Such annual values are shown in either or both adjusted or unadjusted data columns.

Seasonal adjustment removes from the time series the average impact of variations that normally occur at about the same time each year, due to occurrences such as weather, holidays, and tax payment dates.

A simplified example of the process of seasonal adjustment, or deseasonalizing, can indicate its importance in the interpretation of economic time series. Statisticians compare actual monthly data for a number of years with "moving average" trends of the monthly data for the 12 months centered on each month's data. For example, they may find that in November, sales values are usually about 95 percent of the moving average, while in December, usual sales values are 110 percent of the average. Suppose that actual November sales in the current year are $100 and December sales are $105. The seasonally adjusted value for November will be $105 ($100/0.95) while the value for December will be $95 ($105/1.10). Thus, an apparent increase in the unadjusted data turns out to be a decrease when adjusted for the usual seasonal pattern.

The statistical method used to achieve the seasonal adjustment may vary from one data set to another. Many of the data are adjusted by a computer method known as X-12-ARIMA, developed by the Census Bureau. A description of the method is found in "New Capabilities and Methods of the X-12-ARIMA Seasonal Adjustment Program," by David F. Findley, Brian C. Monsell, William R. Bell, Mark C. Otto and Bor-Chung Chen (*Journal of Business and Economic Statistics*, April 1998). This article can be downloaded from the Bureau of the Census Web site at <http://www.census.gov>.

Production and sales data presented at *annual rates*—such as NIPA data in dollars, or motor vehicle data in number of units—show values at their annual equivalents: the values that would be registered if the seasonally adjusted rate of activity measured during a particular month or quarter were maintained for a full year. Specifically, seasonally adjusted monthly values are multiplied by 12 and quarterly values by 4 to yield seasonally adjusted annual rates.

Percent changes at seasonally adjusted annual rates for quarterly time periods are calculated using a compound interest formula, by raising the quarter-to-quarter change in a seasonally adjusted series to the fourth power. See the preceding article for an explanation of compound annual growth rates.

Indexes. In many of the most important data sets presented in this volume, aggregate measures of prices and quantities are expressed in the form of indexes. The most basic and familiar form of index, the original Consumer Price Index, begins with a "market basket" of goods and services purchased in a base period. The value weight ascribed to each component of the market basket is moved forward by the observed change in the price of the item selected to represent that component. These weighted component prices—the quantities in the base period repriced in the prices of subsequent periods—are aggregated, divided by the base period aggregate, and multiplied by 100 to provide an index number. An index calculated in this way is known as a *Laspeyres index*. In general, economists believe that Laspeyres price indexes have an upward bias, showing more price increase than if account were taken of consumers' ability to change spending patterns and maintain the same level of satisfaction in response to changing relative prices.

A *Paasche index* is one that uses the weights of the current period. Since the weights in the Paasche index change in each period, Paasche indexes only provide acceptable indications of change relative to the base period. Paasche indexes for two periods neither of which is the base period cannot be correctly compared: for example, a Paasche price index might increase even if no prices changed because of a change in the composition of output toward prices that had previously increased more from the base period. When the national income and product account (NIPA) measures of real output were Laspeyres measures, using the weights of a single base year, the implicit deflators (current-dollar values divided by constant-dollar values) were Paasche indexes. Just as Laspeyres price indexes are upward-biased, Paasche price indexes are downward-biased because they overestimate consumers' ability to maintain the same level of satisfaction by changing spending patterns.

In recent years, government statisticians (with the aid of elaborate computer programs) have developed measures of real output and prices that minimize bias by using the weights of both periods and updating the weights for each period-to-period comparison. Such measures are described as chained indexes and are used in the NIPAs, the index of industrial production, and an experimental consumer price index. Chained measures are discussed more fully in the notes and definitions for Chapter 1, Chapter 2, and Chapter 8. The "Fisher Ideal" index, the "superlative" index, and the "Tornqvist formula" are all types of chained indexes that use weights for both periods under comparison.

Detail may not sum to totals due to rounding. Since annual data are typically calculated by source agencies as the annual totals or averages of not-seasonally-adjusted data, they therefore will not be precisely equal to the annual totals or averages of monthly seasonally-adjusted data. Seasonal adjustment procedures are typically multiplicative rather than additive, and as a result, seasonally-adjusted data may not add or average to the annual figure. Percent changes and growth rates may have been calculated using unrounded data and therefore differ from those using the published figures.

The data in this volume are from federal government sources and may be reproduced freely. A list of data sources is shown below.

The tables in this volume incorporate data revisions and corrections released by the source agencies through April 2009.

Data sources

The source agencies for the data in this volume are listed below. The specific source or sources for each particular data set are identified at the beginning of the notes and definitions for the relevant data pages.

Board of Governors of the Federal Reserve System
20th Street & Constitution Avenue NW
Washington, DC 20551

Data Inquiries and Publication Sales:
    Publications Services
    Mail Stop 127
    Board of Governors of the Federal Reserve System
    Washington, DC 20551
    Phone: (202) 452-3245

Quarterly Publication:
    As of 2006, the *Federal Reserve Bulletin* is available
    free of charge and only on the Federal Reserve Web
    site.

URL:
    http://www.federalreserve.gov

Census Bureau
U.S. Department of Commerce
4700 Silver Hill Road
Washington, DC 20233

URL:
    http://www.census.gov

Ordering Data Products:
    Call Center: (301) 763-INFO (4636)

E-mail Questions:
    webmaster@census.gov

E-sales:
    http://www.census.gov/mp/www/censtore.html

Bureau of Economic Analysis
U.S. Department of Commerce
    Washington, DC 20230

Data Inquiries:
    Public Information Office
    Phone: (202) 606-9900

Monthly Publication:
    Survey of Current Business
    Available online and by subscription; call (202) 512-1800
    or visit **http://bookstore.gpo.gov.**

URL:
    http://www.bea.gov

Bureau of Labor Statistics
U.S. Department of Labor
2 Massachusetts Avenue NE
Washington, DC 20212-0001
(202) 691-5200

URL:
    http://www.bls.gov

Data Inquiries:
    Blsdata_staff@bls.gov

Monthly Publications available online:
    Monthly Labor Review
    Employment and Earnings
    Compensation and Working Conditions
    Producer Price Indexes
    CPI Detailed Report

Employment and Training Administration
U.S. Department of Labor
200 Constitution Avenue NW
Washington, DC 20210
(877) US2-JOBS

URL:
    http://www.doleta.gov
    http://www.itsc.state.md.us

Energy Information Administration
U.S. Department of Energy
1000 Independence Avenue SW
Washington, DC 20585

Data Inquiries and Publications:
    National Energy Information Center
    Phone: (202) 586-8800
    E-mail: infoctr@eia.doe.gov

Monthly Publication:
    Monthly Energy Review, as of 2007 available only on
    the EIA Web site, free of charge.

URL:
    http://www.eia.doe.gov

Federal Housing Finance Agency
FHFAinfo@FHFA.gov
(202) 414-6921,6922
(202) 414-6376

URL:
    http://www.ofheo.gov/hpi

U.S. Department of the Treasury
Office of International Affairs
Treasury International Capital System

URL:
    http://www.treas.gov/tic

To order government publications
    Superintendent of Documents
    Government Printing Office
    Washington, DC 20402
    (202) 512-1800

URL:
    http://bookstore.gpo.gov

PART A

THE U.S. ECONOMY

CHAPTER 1: NATIONAL INCOME AND PRODUCT

Section 1a: Gross Domestic Product: Values, Quantities, and Prices

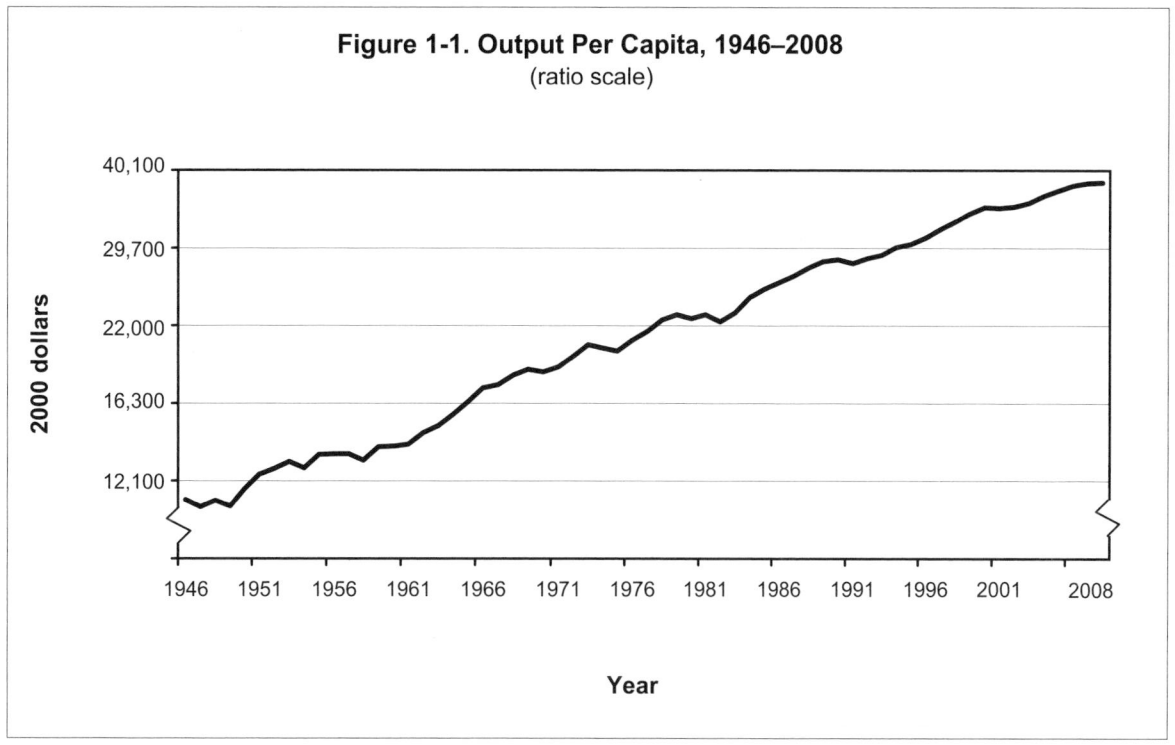

Figure 1-1. Output Per Capita, 1946–2008
(ratio scale)

- Total output of goods and services in the United States (real gross domestic product, or GDP), expressed in constant 2000-value dollars to remove the effect of inflation, rose from $1.64 trillion in 1948 to $11.65 trillion in 2008. (Tables 1-2 and 19-2) This was a seven-fold increase in real value over the 60-year period, with an annual average growth rate of 3.3 percent per year.

- Real GDP per capita—the constant-dollar average value of production for each man, woman, and child in the population—rose from $11,206 (2000 dollars) in 1948 to $38,262 in 2008, a growth rate of 2.1 percent per year. (Tables 1-7 and 19-7) This value is charted in Figure 1-1. It is graphed on a "ratio scale," with equal vertical distances signifying equal percent changes.

- The figure indicates that growth is not always smooth or uninterrupted. There are times when output levels off or declines, marking the periods identified as recessions in economic activity. According to the National Bureau of Economic Research, the 11th recession of the post-World-War-II period began in December 2007; it is not clearly apparent in the annual average data shown above, but on a quarterly basis, real GDP peaked in the second quarter of 2008 and declined 3.3 percent over the next three quarters. (See article at the front of this book, "Business Statistics in Turbulent Times.")

- Measured in current dollars, the value of GDP has increased even faster, reflecting increases in the average price level. Current-dollar GDP rose from $269 billion in 1948 to over $14 trillion in 2008. (Tables 1-1 and 19-1) The price level in 2008 was more than 7 times that in 1948, reflecting an average inflation rate of 3.4 percent per year. (Tables 1-5 and 19-4) Annual rates of increase in the chain-type price index for GDP ranged from 9 percent or more in 1947, 1974–1975, and 1980–1981 to changes of no more than 1.2 percent in 1949–1950, 1954, 1959, 1961, 1963, and 1998. Over the last 10 years, inflation averaged 2.4 percent per year. (Table 1-5)

Table 1-1. Gross Domestic Product

(Billions of dollars, quarterly data are at seasonally adjusted annual rates.)   **NIPA Tables 1.1.5, 5.6.5A, 5.6.5B**

Year and quarter	Gross domestic product	Personal consumption expenditures	Gross private domestic investment						Exports and imports of goods and services			Government consumption expenditures and gross investment		
			Total	Fixed investment		Change in private inventories			Net exports	Exports	Imports	Total	Federal	State and local
				Nonresidential	Residential	Farm	Nonfarm							
1950	293.8	192.2	54.1	27.8	20.5	-0.1	5.9		0.7	12.4	11.6	46.8	26.0	20.7
1951	339.3	208.5	60.2	31.8	18.4	1.0	8.9		2.5	17.1	14.6	68.1	45.1	23.0
1952	358.3	219.5	54.0	31.9	18.6	1.4	2.1		1.2	16.5	15.3	83.6	59.2	24.4
1953	379.4	233.1	56.4	35.1	19.4	0.7	1.2		-0.7	15.3	16.0	90.6	64.4	26.1
1954	380.4	240.0	53.8	34.7	21.1	0.2	-2.1		0.4	15.8	15.4	86.2	57.3	28.9
1955	414.8	258.8	69.0	39.0	25.0	-0.6	5.6		0.5	17.7	17.2	86.5	54.9	31.6
1956	437.5	271.7	72.0	44.5	23.6	-1.0	4.9		2.4	21.3	18.9	91.4	56.7	34.7
1957	461.1	286.9	70.5	47.5	22.2	0.1	0.7		4.1	24.0	19.9	99.7	61.3	38.3
1958	467.2	296.2	64.5	42.5	22.3	2.0	-2.3		0.5	20.6	20.0	106.0	63.8	42.2
1959	506.6	317.6	78.5	46.5	28.1	-1.6	5.5		0.4	22.7	22.3	110.0	65.4	44.7
1960	526.4	331.7	78.9	49.4	26.3	0.6	2.7		4.2	27.0	22.8	111.6	64.1	47.5
1961	544.7	342.1	78.2	48.8	26.4	0.9	2.1		4.9	27.6	22.7	119.5	67.9	51.6
1962	585.6	363.3	88.1	53.1	29.0	0.6	5.5		4.1	29.1	25.0	130.1	75.3	54.9
1963	617.7	382.7	93.8	56.0	32.1	0.5	5.1		4.9	31.1	26.1	136.4	76.9	59.5
1964	663.6	411.4	102.1	63.0	34.3	-1.2	6.0		6.9	35.0	28.1	143.2	78.5	64.8
1965	719.1	443.8	118.2	74.8	34.2	0.8	8.4		5.6	37.1	31.5	151.5	80.4	71.0
1966	787.8	480.9	131.3	85.4	32.3	-0.5	14.1		3.9	40.9	37.1	171.8	92.5	79.2
1967	832.6	507.8	128.6	86.4	32.4	0.9	9.0		3.6	43.5	39.9	192.7	104.8	87.9
1968	910.0	558.0	141.2	93.4	38.7	1.4	7.7		1.4	47.9	46.6	209.4	111.4	98.0
1969	984.6	605.2	156.4	104.7	42.6	0.0	9.2		1.4	51.9	50.5	221.5	113.4	108.2
1970	1 038.5	648.5	152.4	109.0	41.4	-0.8	2.8		4.0	59.7	55.8	233.8	113.5	120.3
1971	1 127.1	701.9	178.2	114.1	55.8	1.7	6.6		0.6	63.0	62.3	246.5	113.7	132.8
1972	1 238.3	770.6	207.6	128.8	69.7	0.3	8.8		-3.4	70.8	74.2	263.5	119.7	143.8
1973	1 382.7	852.4	244.5	153.3	75.3	1.5	14.4		4.1	95.3	91.2	281.7	122.5	159.2
1974	1 500.0	933.4	249.4	169.5	66.0	-2.8	16.8		-0.8	126.7	127.5	317.9	134.6	183.4
1975	1 638.3	1 034.4	230.2	173.7	62.7	3.4	-9.6		16.0	138.7	122.7	357.7	149.1	208.7
1976	1 825.3	1 151.9	292.0	194.4	82.5	-0.8	18.0		-1.6	149.5	151.1	383.0	159.7	223.3
1977	2 030.9	1 278.6	361.3	228.7	110.3	4.5	17.8		-23.1	159.4	182.4	414.1	175.4	238.7
1978	2 294.7	1 428.5	438.0	280.6	131.6	1.4	24.4		-25.4	186.9	212.3	453.6	190.9	262.6
1979	2 563.3	1 592.2	492.9	333.9	141.0	3.6	14.4		-22.5	230.1	252.7	500.8	210.6	290.2
1980	2 789.5	1 757.1	479.3	362.4	123.2	-6.1	-0.2		-13.1	280.8	293.8	566.2	243.8	322.4
1981	3 128.4	1 941.1	572.4	420.0	122.6	8.8	21.0		-12.5	305.2	317.8	627.5	280.2	347.3
1982	3 255.0	2 077.3	517.2	426.5	105.7	5.8	-20.7		-20.0	283.2	303.2	680.5	310.8	369.7
1983	3 536.7	2 290.6	564.3	417.2	152.9	-15.4	9.6		-51.7	277.0	328.6	733.5	342.9	390.5
1984	3 933.2	2 503.3	735.6	489.6	180.6	5.7	59.7		-102.7	302.4	405.1	797.0	374.4	422.6
1985	4 220.3	2 720.3	736.2	526.2	188.2	5.8	16.1		-115.2	302.0	417.2	879.0	412.8	466.2
1986	4 462.8	2 899.7	746.5	519.8	220.1	-1.5	8.0		-132.7	320.5	453.3	949.3	438.6	510.7
1987	4 739.5	3 100.2	785.0	524.1	233.7	-6.4	33.6		-145.2	363.9	509.1	999.5	460.1	539.4
1988	5 103.8	3 353.6	821.6	563.8	239.3	-11.9	30.4		-110.4	444.1	554.5	1 039.0	462.3	576.7
1989	5 484.4	3 598.5	874.9	607.7	239.5	0.0	27.7		-88.2	503.3	591.5	1 099.1	482.2	616.9
1990	5 803.1	3 839.9	861.0	622.4	224.0	2.4	12.2		-78.0	552.4	630.3	1 180.2	508.3	671.9
1991	5 995.9	3 986.1	802.9	598.2	205.1	-1.3	0.9		-27.5	596.8	624.3	1 234.4	527.7	706.7
1992	6 337.7	4 235.3	864.8	612.1	236.3	6.2	10.1		-33.2	635.3	668.6	1 271.0	533.9	737.0
1993	6 657.4	4 477.9	953.4	666.6	266.0	-6.2	27.0		-65.0	655.8	720.9	1 291.2	525.2	766.0
1994	7 072.2	4 743.3	1 097.1	731.4	301.9	12.1	51.8		-93.6	720.9	814.5	1 325.5	519.1	806.3
1995	7 397.7	4 975.8	1 144.0	810.0	302.8	-11.1	42.2		-91.4	812.2	903.6	1 369.2	519.2	850.0
1996	7 816.9	5 256.8	1 240.3	875.4	334.1	8.6	22.1		-96.2	868.6	964.8	1 416.0	527.4	888.6
1997	8 304.3	5 547.4	1 389.8	968.7	349.1	3.2	68.8		-101.6	955.3	1 056.9	1 468.7	530.9	937.8
1998	8 747.0	5 879.5	1 509.1	1 052.6	385.8	1.4	69.4		-159.9	955.9	1 115.9	1 518.3	530.4	987.9
1999	9 268.4	6 282.5	1 625.7	1 133.9	424.9	-2.7	69.6		-260.5	991.2	1 251.7	1 620.8	555.8	1 065.0
2000	9 817.0	6 739.4	1 735.5	1 232.1	446.9	-1.3	57.8		-379.5	1 096.3	1 475.8	1 721.6	578.8	1 142.8
2001	10 128.0	7 055.0	1 614.3	1 176.8	469.3	0.0	-31.7		-367.0	1 032.8	1 399.8	1 825.6	612.9	1 212.8
2002	10 469.6	7 350.7	1 582.1	1 066.3	503.9	-2.5	14.4		-424.4	1 005.9	1 430.3	1 961.1	679.7	1 281.5
2003	10 960.8	7 703.6	1 664.1	1 077.4	572.4	0.4	13.9		-499.4	1 040.8	1 540.2	2 092.5	756.4	1 336.0
2004	11 685.9	8 195.9	1 888.6	1 154.5	675.5	8.0	50.5		-615.4	1 182.4	1 797.8	2 216.8	825.6	1 391.2
2005	12 421.9	8 694.1	2 086.1	1 273.1	769.6	0.3	43.0		-713.6	1 311.5	2 025.1	2 355.3	875.5	1 479.8
2006	13 178.4	9 207.2	2 220.4	1 414.1	757.0	-3.9	53.3		-757.3	1 480.8	2 238.1	2 508.1	932.2	1 575.9
2007	13 807.5	9 710.2	2 130.4	1 503.8	630.2	1.6	-5.2		-707.8	1 662.4	2 370.2	2 674.8	979.3	1 695.5
2008	14 264.6	10 057.9	1 993.5	1 552.8	487.7	-2.4	-44.6		-669.2	1 859.4	2 528.6	2 882.4	1 071.9	1 810.4
2006														
1st quarter	12 959.6	9 026.3	2 236.7	1 375.5	808.1	1.0	52.1		-761.7	1 423.2	2 184.9	2 458.4	922.8	1 535.5
2nd quarter	13 134.1	9 161.9	2 253.7	1 408.3	779.6	-6.9	72.8		-777.2	1 462.8	2 240.0	2 495.7	928.5	1 567.2
3rd quarter	13 249.6	9 283.7	2 231.7	1 433.0	736.2	-6.7	69.3		-792.7	1 492.5	2 285.2	2 526.9	935.5	1 591.4
4th quarter	13 370.1	9 357.0	2 159.5	1 439.6	704.0	-3.0	18.8		-697.7	1 544.5	2 242.2	2 551.4	941.7	1 609.7
2007														
1st quarter	13 510.9	9 524.9	2 117.8	1 456.4	677.0	-2.1	-13.5		-728.8	1 560.5	2 289.4	2 597.0	950.3	1 646.8
2nd quarter	13 737.5	9 657.5	2 147.2	1 493.7	654.4	2.9	-3.8		-723.1	1 614.4	2 337.5	2 655.9	974.6	1 681.3
3rd quarter	13 950.6	9 765.6	2 164.0	1 522.9	618.1	-0.2	23.2		-682.6	1 714.9	2 397.5	2 703.5	994.0	1 709.5
4th quarter	14 031.2	9 892.7	2 092.3	1 542.1	571.3	5.7	-26.7		-696.7	1 759.7	2 456.5	2 742.9	998.3	1 744.6
2008														
1st quarter	14 150.8	10 002.3	2 056.1	1 553.6	528.1	0.2	-25.8		-705.7	1 820.8	2 526.5	2 798.1	1 026.5	1 771.6
2nd quarter	14 294.5	10 138.0	2 000.9	1 571.9	505.0	-4.1	-71.9		-718.2	1 923.2	2 641.4	2 873.7	1 056.1	1 817.6
3rd quarter	14 412.8	10 163.5	2 010.9	1 581.2	479.4	-4.2	-45.5		-707.7	1 968.9	2 676.6	2 946.1	1 098.0	1 848.1
4th quarter	14 200.3	9 927.9	1 906.1	1 504.3	438.4	-1.5	-35.0		-545.1	1 724.7	2 269.7	2 911.4	1 107.0	1 804.4

Table 1-2. Real Gross Domestic Product

(Billions of chained [2000] dollars, quarterly data are at seasonally adjusted annual rates.)   NIPA Tables 1.1.6, 5.6.6A, 5.6.6B

Year and quarter	Gross domestic product	Personal consumption expenditures	Gross private domestic investment Total	Fixed investment Nonresidential	Residential	Change in private inventories Farm	Nonfarm	Net exports	Exports	Imports	Government Total	Federal	State and local	Residual
1950	1 777.3	1 152.8	227.7	...	...	-0.3	20.8	...	50.3	59.3	405.3	...	...	0.5
1951	1 915.0	1 171.2	228.3	...	...	1.7	25.8	...	61.7	61.7	553.5	...	...	-38.0
1952	1 988.3	1 208.2	206.5	...	...	2.5	6.7	...	59.0	67.1	666.3	...	...	-84.6
1953	2 079.5	1 265.7	216.2	...	...	1.6	4.1	...	55.1	73.4	713.9	...	...	-98.0
1954	2 065.4	1 291.4	206.1	...	...	0.4	-6.8	...	57.7	69.8	665.1	...	...	-85.1
1955	2 212.8	1 385.5	256.2	...	...	-1.5	17.0	...	63.9	78.2	640.7	...	...	-55.3
1956	2 255.8	1 425.4	252.7	...	...	-2.6	14.2	...	74.4	84.5	641.0	...	...	-53.2
1957	2 301.1	1 460.7	241.7	...	...	0.4	2.2	...	80.9	88.1	669.5	...	...	-63.6
1958	2 279.2	1 472.3	221.7	...	...	4.7	-7.0	...	70.0	92.3	690.9	...	...	-83.4
1959	2 441.3	1 554.6	266.7	...	...	-3.8	17.9	...	77.2	101.9	714.3	...	...	-69.6
1960	2 501.8	1 597.4	266.6	...	...	1.4	8.8	...	90.6	103.3	715.4	...	...	-64.9
1961	2 560.0	1 630.3	264.9	...	...	2.1	7.0	...	91.1	102.6	751.3	...	...	-75.0
1962	2 715.2	1 711.1	298.4	...	...	1.4	18.3	...	95.7	114.3	797.6	...	...	-73.3
1963	2 834.0	1 781.6	318.5	...	...	1.2	17.0	...	102.5	117.3	818.1	...	...	-69.4
1964	2 998.6	1 888.4	344.7	...	...	-3.1	19.7	...	114.6	123.6	836.1	...	...	-61.6
1965	3 191.1	2 007.7	393.1	...	...	2.0	27.4	...	117.8	136.7	861.3	...	...	-52.1
1966	3 399.1	2 121.8	427.7	...	...	-1.1	45.2	...	126.0	157.1	937.1	...	...	-56.4
1967	3 484.6	2 185.0	408.1	...	...	2.1	28.4	...	128.9	168.5	1 008.9	...	...	-77.8
1968	3 652.7	2 310.5	431.9	...	...	3.3	23.7	...	139.0	193.6	1 040.5	...	...	-75.6
1969	3 765.4	2 396.4	457.1	...	...	0.0	27.8	...	145.7	204.6	1 038.0	...	...	-67.2
1970	3 771.9	2 451.9	427.1	...	...	-1.9	7.8	...	161.4	213.4	1 012.9	...	...	-68.0
1971	3 898.6	2 545.5	475.7	...	...	3.3	18.5	...	164.1	224.7	990.8	...	...	-52.8
1972	4 105.0	2 701.3	532.1	...	...	0.3	24.2	...	176.5	250.0	983.5	...	...	-38.4
1973	4 341.5	2 833.8	594.4	...	...	1.5	36.6	...	209.7	261.6	980.0	...	...	-14.8
1974	4 319.6	2 812.3	550.6	...	...	-3.6	35.1	...	226.3	255.7	1 004.7	...	...	-18.6
1975	4 311.2	2 876.9	453.1	...	...	4.7	-19.2	...	224.9	227.3	1 027.4	...	...	-43.8
1976	4 540.9	3 035.5	544.7	...	...	-1.3	34.0	...	234.7	271.7	1 031.9	...	...	-34.2
1977	4 750.5	3 164.1	627.0	...	...	5.9	32.1	...	240.3	301.4	1 043.3	...	...	-22.8
1978	5 015.0	3 303.1	702.6	...	...	1.7	40.9	...	265.7	327.6	1 074.0	...	...	-2.8
1979	5 173.4	3 383.4	725.0	...	...	3.5	21.5	...	292.0	333.0	1 094.1	...	...	11.9
1980	5 161.7	3 374.1	645.3	...	...	-5.8	0.0	...	323.5	310.9	1 115.4	...	...	14.3
1981	5 291.7	3 422.2	704.9	...	...	8.2	25.5	...	327.4	319.1	1 125.6	...	...	30.7
1982	5 189.3	3 470.3	606.0	...	...	6.1	-24.6	...	302.4	315.0	1 145.4	...	...	-19.8
1983	5 423.8	3 668.6	662.5	...	...	-14.2	10.2	...	294.6	354.8	1 187.3	...	...	-34.4
1984	5 813.6	3 863.3	857.7	...	...	5.1	66.5	...	318.7	441.1	1 227.0	...	...	-12.0
1985	6 053.7	4 064.0	849.7	...	...	5.7	17.5	...	328.3	469.8	1 312.5	...	...	-31.0
1986	6 263.6	4 228.9	843.9	...	...	-1.8	10.1	...	353.7	510.0	1 392.5	...	...	-45.4
1987	6 475.1	4 369.8	870.0	...	...	-7.4	37.7	...	391.8	540.2	1 426.7	...	...	-43.0
1988	6 742.7	4 546.9	890.5	...	...	-10.7	32.7	...	454.6	561.4	1 445.1	...	...	-33.0
1989	6 981.4	4 675.0	926.2	...	...	0.0	28.8	...	506.8	586.0	1 482.5	...	...	-23.1
1990	7 112.5	4 770.3	895.1	595.1	298.9	2.1	13.2	-54.7	552.5	607.1	1 530.0	659.1	868.4	-91.1
1991	7 100.5	4 778.4	822.2	563.2	270.2	-1.5	1.0	-14.6	589.1	603.7	1 547.2	658.0	886.8	-96.0
1992	7 336.6	4 934.8	889.0	581.3	307.6	5.8	10.3	-15.9	629.7	645.6	1 555.3	646.6	906.5	-89.1
1993	7 532.7	5 099.8	968.3	631.9	332.7	-6.1	27.7	-52.1	650.0	702.1	1 541.1	619.6	919.5	-78.6
1994	7 835.5	5 290.7	1 099.6	689.9	364.8	11.2	52.0	-79.4	706.5	785.9	1 541.3	596.4	943.3	-63.7
1995	8 031.7	5 433.5	1 134.0	762.5	353.1	-10.6	41.3	-71.0	778.2	849.1	1 549.7	580.3	968.3	-51.1
1996	8 328.9	5 619.4	1 234.3	833.6	381.3	6.8	21.7	-79.6	843.4	923.0	1 564.9	573.5	990.5	-38.5
1997	8 703.5	5 831.8	1 387.7	934.2	388.6	2.9	68.5	-104.6	943.7	1 048.3	1 594.0	567.6	1 025.9	-23.8
1998	9 066.9	6 125.8	1 524.1	1 037.8	418.3	1.4	71.2	-203.7	966.5	1 170.3	1 624.4	561.2	1 063.0	-14.6
1999	9 470.3	6 438.6	1 642.6	1 133.3	443.6	-3.0	71.5	-296.2	1 008.2	1 304.4	1 686.9	573.7	1 113.2	-5.8
2000	9 817.0	6 739.4	1 735.5	1 232.1	446.9	-1.3	57.8	-379.5	1 096.3	1 475.8	1 721.6	578.8	1 142.8	0.2
2001	9 890.7	6 910.4	1 598.4	1 180.5	448.5	0.0	-31.8	-399.1	1 036.7	1 435.8	1 780.3	601.4	1 179.0	1.6
2002	10 048.8	7 099.3	1 557.1	1 071.5	469.9	-2.5	15.2	-471.3	1 013.3	1 484.6	1 858.8	643.4	1 215.4	3.0
2003	10 301.0	7 295.3	1 613.1	1 081.8	509.4	0.4	14.0	-518.9	1 026.1	1 545.0	1 904.8	687.1	1 217.8	3.4
2004	10 675.8	7 561.4	1 770.2	1 144.3	560.2	5.9	48.2	-593.8	1 126.1	1 719.9	1 931.8	715.9	1 215.8	-0.3
2005	10 989.5	7 791.7	1 873.5	1 226.2	595.4	0.2	39.1	-616.6	1 205.3	1 821.9	1 939.0	724.5	1 214.3	-11.8
2006	11 294.8	8 029.0	1 912.5	1 318.2	552.9	-3.2	46.3	-615.7	1 314.8	1 930.5	1 971.2	741.0	1 230.2	-35.3
2007	11 523.9	8 252.8	1 809.7	1 382.9	453.8	1.0	-3.7	-546.5	1 425.9	1 972.4	2 012.1	752.9	1 259.0	-55.1
2008	11 652.0	8 272.1	1 689.1	1 405.4	359.5	3.6	-34.3	-390.2	1 514.1	1 904.3	2 070.2	798.2	1 273.0	-24.7
2006														
1st quarter	11 217.3	7 947.4	1 946.3	1 295.2	596.5	1.0	45.4	-636.0	1 284.3	1 920.2	1 960.5	740.6	1 219.9	-29.2
2nd quarter	11 291.7	8 002.1	1 944.3	1 315.4	570.1	-5.6	63.3	-619.4	1 301.4	1 920.9	1 966.6	737.7	1 228.8	-32.2
3rd quarter	11 314.1	8 046.3	1 917.8	1 332.7	536.7	-5.6	59.9	-623.0	1 312.6	1 935.7	1 974.9	741.1	1 233.7	-37.0
4th quarter	11 356.4	8 119.9	1 841.6	1 329.3	508.4	-2.7	16.4	-584.3	1 361.1	1 945.3	1 982.7	744.4	1 238.2	-42.4
2007														
1st quarter	11 357.8	8 197.2	1 795.9	1 340.4	486.4	-3.9	-10.7	-618.6	1 363.2	1 981.8	1 987.1	737.5	1 249.3	-49.8
2nd quarter	11 491.4	8 237.3	1 822.9	1 373.8	471.7	-0.1	-2.6	-571.2	1 392.2	1 963.4	2 006.4	749.6	1 256.6	-53.5
3rd quarter	11 625.7	8 278.5	1 838.7	1 402.9	445.3	-2.5	19.2	-511.8	1 466.2	1 978.0	2 025.3	762.7	1 262.6	-55.3
4th quarter	11 620.7	8 298.2	1 781.3	1 414.7	411.6	10.5	-20.6	-484.5	1 482.1	1 966.5	2 029.4	761.7	1 267.5	-62.1
2008														
1st quarter	11 646.0	8 316.1	1 754.7	1 423.1	383.0	6.0	-17.9	-462.0	1 500.6	1 962.6	2 039.1	772.6	1 266.7	-56.3
2nd quarter	11 727.4	8 341.3	1 702.0	1 431.8	369.6	2.4	-55.1	-381.3	1 544.7	1 926.0	2 058.9	785.0	1 274.4	-44.3
3rd quarter	11 712.4	8 260.6	1 703.7	1 425.7	353.7	2.2	-33.3	-353.1	1 556.1	1 909.1	2 088.1	810.8	1 278.7	-16.4
4th quarter	11 522.1	8 170.5	1 596.0	1 341.1	331.6	3.7	-31.1	-364.5	1 454.9	1 819.4	2 094.7	824.5	1 272.3	19.3

Note: Chained (2000) dollar series are calculated as the product of the chain-type quantity index and the 2000 current-dollar value of the corresponding series, divided by 100. Because the formula for the chain-type quantity indexes uses weights from more than one period, the corresponding chained-dollar estimates are usually not additive. The residual column is the difference between the total and the sum of the most detailed components shown in the Bureau of Economic Analysis (BEA) published data.

. . . = Not available.

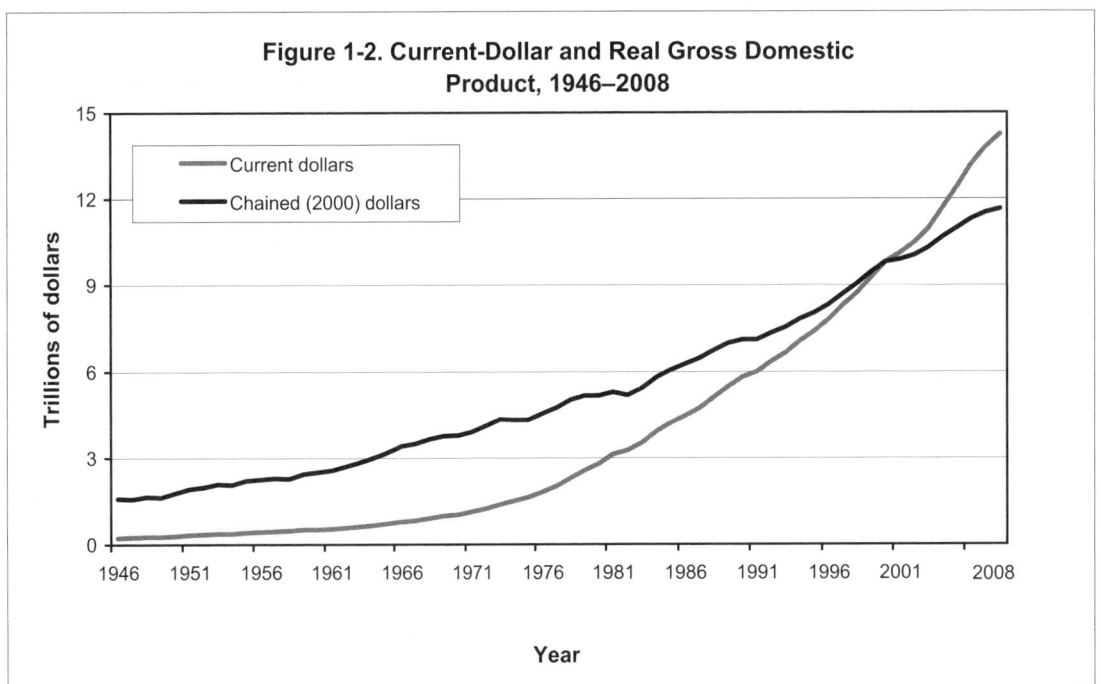

Figure 1-2. Current-Dollar and Real Gross Domestic Product, 1946–2008

- Figure 1-2 shows the value of GDP in both current dollars and real terms (chained 2000 dollars). Since real GDP is expressed in dollar values from the year 2000, the two are the same in that year. As prices increase in nearly every year, the current-dollar measure grows faster than the measure of real, or constant-dollar, GDP. (Tables 1-1, 19-1, 1-2, and 19-2)

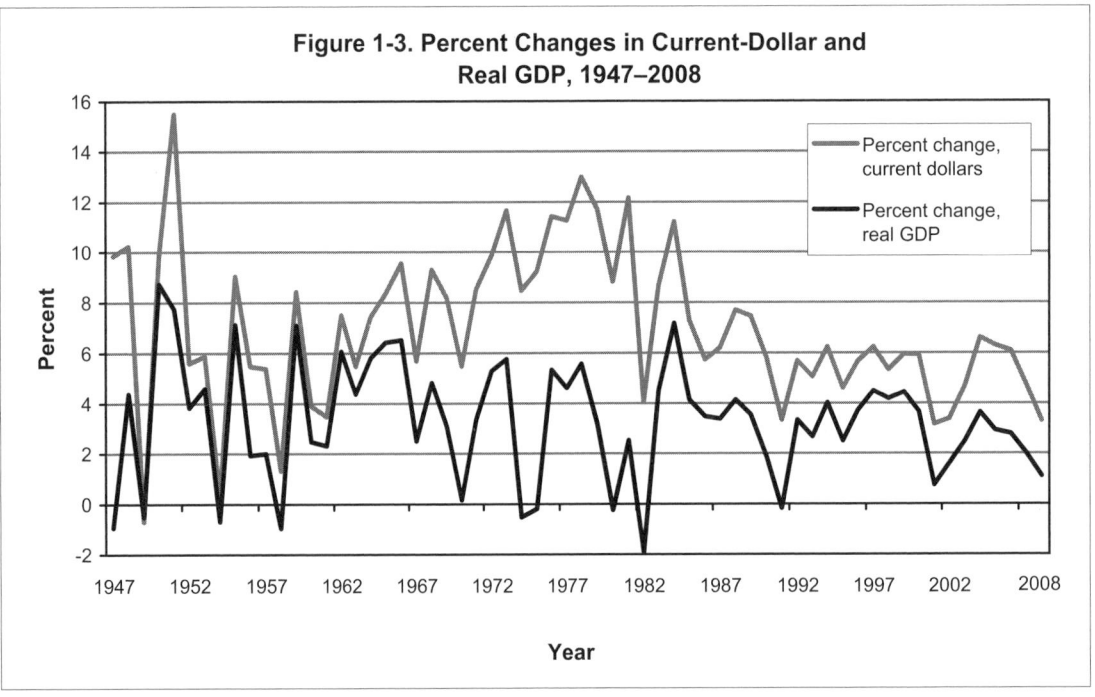

Figure 1-3. Percent Changes in Current-Dollar and Real GDP, 1947–2008

- The arithmetic scale used in Figure 1-2 seems to suggest ever-accelerating growth in GDP, but users should not interpret it in this way. (See "Business Statistics in Turbulent Times" in the introductory material to this book.) Figure 1-3 depicts the same data in the form of year-to-year percent changes. The annual changes in real GDP, though quite variable, fluctuate around their average value of 3.3 percent. The changes in nominal GDP, which are roughly the sum of the real change and the inflation rate, are more volatile. During years of low inflation, they are quite similar to (though somewhat higher than) the changes in real GDP. In years of high inflation, they are far above the changes in real GDP. Some years of high nominal change, notably 1947, 1974, and 1975, have seen the real GDP actually decline. (Tables 1-1, 19-1, 13, and 19-3)

Table 1-3. Contributions to Percent Change in Real Gross Domestic Product

(Percent, percentage points.)   NIPA Table 1.1.2

Year and quarter	Percent change at seasonally adjusted annual rate, real GDP	Personal consumption expenditures	Gross private domestic investment				Exports and imports of goods and services			Government consumption expenditures and gross investment		
			Total	Fixed investment		Change in private inventories	Net exports	Exports	Imports	Total	Federal	State and local
				Nonresidential	Residential							
1950	8.7	4.28	5.74	0.86	2.03	2.84	-1.31	-0.66	-0.65	0.02	-0.56	0.58
1951	7.7	1.05	0.05	0.44	-1.14	0.75	0.81	0.98	-0.17	5.84	5.78	0.06
1952	3.8	1.95	-1.65	-0.18	-0.10	-1.37	-0.59	-0.22	-0.37	4.11	4.00	0.11
1953	4.6	2.91	0.70	0.80	0.18	-0.28	-0.70	-0.31	-0.39	1.67	1.33	0.34
1954	-0.7	1.25	-0.69	-0.20	0.42	-0.91	0.40	0.19	0.21	-1.64	-2.25	0.60
1955	7.1	4.57	3.45	1.01	0.90	1.54	-0.04	0.44	-0.48	-0.84	-1.39	0.55
1956	1.9	1.79	-0.23	0.55	-0.49	-0.29	0.37	0.70	-0.33	0.01	-0.24	0.25
1957	2.0	1.53	-0.71	0.16	-0.32	-0.54	0.25	0.43	-0.18	0.93	0.46	0.47
1958	-1.0	0.50	-1.25	-1.12	0.05	-0.18	-0.89	-0.69	-0.20	0.69	-0.01	0.70
1959	7.1	3.55	2.80	0.73	1.21	0.86	0.00	0.45	-0.45	0.76	0.42	0.34
1960	2.5	1.73	0.00	0.52	-0.39	-0.13	0.72	0.78	-0.06	0.03	-0.35	0.39
1961	2.3	1.30	-0.10	-0.06	0.01	-0.05	0.06	0.03	0.03	1.07	0.51	0.56
1962	6.1	3.11	1.81	0.78	0.46	0.57	-0.21	0.25	-0.47	1.36	1.07	0.29
1963	4.4	2.56	1.00	0.50	0.58	-0.08	0.24	0.35	-0.12	0.58	0.01	0.57
1964	5.8	3.71	1.25	1.07	0.30	-0.13	0.36	0.59	-0.23	0.49	-0.17	0.65
1965	6.4	3.91	2.16	1.65	-0.15	0.66	-0.30	0.15	-0.45	0.65	0.00	0.66
1966	6.5	3.50	1.44	1.29	-0.43	0.58	-0.29	0.36	-0.65	1.87	1.24	0.63
1967	2.5	1.81	-0.76	-0.15	-0.13	-0.49	-0.22	0.12	-0.34	1.68	1.17	0.51
1968	4.8	3.50	0.90	0.46	0.53	-0.10	-0.30	0.41	-0.70	0.73	0.10	0.63
1969	3.1	2.27	0.90	0.78	0.13	0.00	-0.04	0.25	-0.29	-0.06	-0.42	0.37
1970	0.2	1.42	-1.04	-0.06	-0.26	-0.73	0.34	0.56	-0.22	-0.55	-0.86	0.31
1971	3.4	2.38	1.67	0.00	1.10	0.58	-0.19	0.10	-0.29	-0.50	-0.85	0.36
1972	5.3	3.80	1.87	0.92	0.89	0.06	-0.21	0.42	-0.63	-0.16	-0.42	0.26
1973	5.8	3.05	1.96	1.50	-0.04	0.50	0.82	1.12	-0.29	-0.08	-0.41	0.33
1974	-0.5	-0.47	-1.30	0.09	-1.13	-0.27	0.75	0.58	0.18	0.52	0.08	0.44
1975	-0.2	1.42	-2.98	-1.14	-0.57	-1.27	0.89	-0.05	0.94	0.48	0.03	0.45
1976	5.3	3.48	2.84	0.52	0.90	1.41	-1.08	0.37	-1.45	0.10	0.00	0.09
1977	4.6	2.68	2.43	1.19	0.99	0.25	-0.72	0.20	-0.92	0.23	0.19	0.04
1978	5.6	2.76	2.16	1.69	0.35	0.12	0.05	0.82	-0.78	0.60	0.22	0.38
1979	3.2	1.52	0.61	1.23	-0.21	-0.41	0.66	0.82	-0.16	0.37	0.20	0.17
1980	-0.2	-0.17	-2.12	-0.04	-1.17	-0.91	1.68	0.97	0.71	0.38	0.39	-0.01
1981	2.5	0.90	1.59	0.74	-0.35	1.20	-0.15	0.12	-0.27	0.19	0.42	-0.23
1982	-1.9	0.87	-2.55	-0.51	-0.71	-1.34	-0.60	-0.73	0.12	0.35	0.35	0.01
1983	4.5	3.65	1.45	-0.16	1.33	0.29	-1.35	-0.22	-1.13	0.77	0.63	0.13
1984	7.2	3.44	4.63	2.05	0.64	1.95	-1.58	0.63	-2.21	0.70	0.30	0.40
1985	4.1	3.31	-0.17	0.82	0.07	-1.06	-0.42	0.23	-0.65	1.41	0.74	0.67
1986	3.5	2.62	-0.12	-0.36	0.55	-0.32	-0.30	0.54	-0.84	1.27	0.55	0.71
1987	3.4	2.17	0.51	-0.01	0.10	0.42	0.17	0.78	-0.61	0.52	0.36	0.17
1988	4.1	2.66	0.39	0.57	-0.05	-0.14	0.82	1.24	-0.42	0.27	-0.15	0.42
1989	3.5	1.86	0.64	0.61	-0.14	0.17	0.52	0.99	-0.47	0.52	0.14	0.39
1990	1.9	1.34	-0.53	0.05	-0.37	-0.21	0.43	0.81	-0.39	0.64	0.18	0.46
1991	-0.2	0.11	-1.20	-0.57	-0.37	-0.26	0.69	0.63	0.06	0.23	-0.02	0.24
1992	3.3	2.18	1.07	0.32	0.47	0.29	-0.04	0.68	-0.72	0.11	-0.15	0.26
1993	2.7	2.23	1.21	0.83	0.31	0.07	-0.59	0.32	-0.91	-0.18	-0.35	0.17
1994	4.0	2.52	1.93	0.91	0.39	0.63	-0.43	0.85	-1.29	0.00	-0.30	0.30
1995	2.5	1.81	0.48	1.08	-0.14	-0.46	0.11	1.04	-0.93	0.10	-0.20	0.30
1996	3.7	2.31	1.35	1.01	0.33	0.02	-0.14	0.91	-1.05	0.18	-0.08	0.26
1997	4.5	2.54	1.95	1.33	0.08	0.54	-0.34	1.30	-1.64	0.34	-0.07	0.41
1998	4.2	3.36	1.63	1.28	0.32	0.03	-1.16	0.27	-1.43	0.34	-0.07	0.41
1999	4.5	3.44	1.33	1.09	0.27	-0.03	-0.99	0.47	-1.46	0.67	0.14	0.54
2000	3.7	3.17	0.99	1.06	0.03	-0.10	-0.86	0.93	-1.79	0.36	0.05	0.31
2001	0.8	1.74	-1.39	-0.52	0.02	-0.88	-0.20	-0.60	0.40	0.60	0.23	0.37
2002	1.6	1.90	-0.41	-1.06	0.22	0.43	-0.69	-0.23	-0.46	0.80	0.43	0.37
2003	2.5	1.94	0.54	0.10	0.41	0.04	-0.44	0.12	-0.56	0.47	0.44	0.02
2004	3.6	2.56	1.48	0.56	0.53	0.39	-0.68	0.93	-1.61	0.27	0.29	-0.02
2005	2.9	2.13	0.95	0.71	0.37	-0.13	-0.21	0.71	-0.93	0.07	0.09	-0.01
2006	2.8	2.13	0.35	0.77	-0.45	0.03	-0.02	0.96	-0.98	0.32	0.16	0.16
2007	2.0	1.95	-0.90	0.52	-1.02	-0.40	0.58	0.95	-0.37	0.40	0.11	0.28
2008	1.1	0.16	-1.02	0.17	-0.93	-0.26	1.40	0.76	0.64	0.57	0.43	0.14
2006												
1st quarter	4.8	2.86	1.15	1.62	-0.23	-0.24	0.09	1.70	-1.61	0.72	0.66	0.06
2nd quarter	2.7	1.88	-0.02	0.71	-1.11	0.38	0.59	0.58	0.01	0.23	-0.11	0.34
3rd quarter	0.8	1.52	-0.92	0.59	-1.40	-0.11	-0.12	0.39	-0.51	0.32	0.13	0.19
4th quarter	1.5	2.55	-2.68	-0.09	-1.18	-1.41	1.33	1.66	-0.33	0.30	0.12	0.18
2007												
1st quarter	0.1	2.71	-1.63	0.33	-0.91	-1.06	-1.20	0.06	-1.25	0.17	-0.26	0.43
2nd quarter	4.8	1.42	0.94	1.07	-0.60	0.47	1.66	1.01	0.65	0.77	0.47	0.30
3rd quarter	4.8	1.44	0.54	0.91	-1.06	0.69	2.03	2.54	-0.51	0.75	0.51	0.24
4th quarter	-0.2	0.67	-1.93	0.36	-1.33	-0.96	0.94	0.53	0.40	0.16	-0.04	0.19
2008												
1st quarter	0.9	0.61	-0.89	0.26	-1.12	-0.02	0.77	0.63	0.14	0.38	0.41	-0.03
2nd quarter	2.8	0.87	-1.74	0.27	-0.52	-1.50	2.93	1.54	1.39	0.78	0.47	0.31
3rd quarter	-0.5	-2.75	0.06	-0.19	-0.60	0.84	1.05	0.40	0.65	1.14	0.97	0.17
4th quarter	-6.3	-2.99	-3.47	-2.56	-0.80	-0.11	-0.15	-3.44	3.29	0.26	0.52	-0.25

Table 1-4. Chain-Type Quantity Indexes for Gross Domestic Product and Domestic Purchases

(Index numbers, 2000 = 100.)   **NIPA Tables 1.1.3, 1.4.3, 2.3.3**

Year and quarter	Gross domestic product, total	Personal consumption expenditures Total	Excluding food and energy	Private fixed investment Total	Nonresidential	Residential	Exports	Imports	Total	Federal	State and local	Gross domestic purchases
1950	18.1	17.1	13.7	13.0	8.6	32.3	4.6	4.0	23.5	35.6	17.5	17.7
1951	19.5	17.4	13.8	12.4	9.0	27.0	5.6	4.2	32.2	59.0	17.6	18.9
1952	20.3	17.9	14.2	12.2	8.8	26.6	5.4	4.5	38.7	76.8	17.9	19.7
1953	21.2	18.8	14.9	13.0	9.6	27.5	5.0	5.0	41.5	82.9	18.8	20.8
1954	21.0	19.2	15.2	13.3	9.4	29.8	5.3	4.7	38.6	72.0	20.5	20.6
1955	22.5	20.6	16.5	15.0	10.4	34.6	5.8	5.3	37.2	65.5	21.9	22.0
1956	23.0	21.2	16.9	15.0	11.0	31.8	6.8	5.7	37.2	64.3	22.6	22.4
1957	23.4	21.7	17.3	14.9	11.2	29.8	7.4	6.0	38.9	66.6	24.0	22.8
1958	23.2	21.8	17.4	13.8	10.0	30.2	6.4	6.3	40.1	66.6	26.0	22.8
1959	24.9	23.1	18.6	15.7	10.8	37.8	7.0	6.9	41.5	68.7	27.0	24.4
1960	25.5	23.7	19.2	15.9	11.4	35.1	8.3	7.0	41.6	66.8	28.2	24.8
1961	26.1	24.2	19.7	15.8	11.3	35.2	8.3	7.0	43.6	69.6	29.9	25.4
1962	27.7	25.4	20.9	17.2	12.3	38.6	8.7	7.7	46.3	75.5	30.8	27.0
1963	28.9	26.4	22.0	18.6	13.0	43.2	9.4	8.0	47.5	75.5	32.7	28.1
1964	30.5	28.0	23.5	20.4	14.5	45.7	10.5	8.4	48.6	74.5	34.9	29.7
1965	32.5	29.8	25.1	22.5	17.0	44.3	10.7	9.3	50.0	74.5	37.3	31.7
1966	34.6	31.5	26.6	23.7	19.2	40.4	11.5	10.6	54.4	82.7	39.6	33.8
1967	35.5	32.4	27.6	23.3	18.9	39.1	11.8	11.4	58.6	91.0	41.6	34.8
1968	37.2	34.3	29.2	24.9	19.7	44.4	12.7	13.1	60.4	91.7	44.0	36.6
1969	38.4	35.6	30.4	26.5	21.2	45.7	13.3	13.9	60.3	88.5	45.5	37.7
1970	38.4	36.4	31.0	25.9	21.1	43.0	14.7	14.5	58.8	82.0	46.8	37.6
1971	39.7	37.8	32.5	27.9	21.1	54.8	15.0	15.2	57.6	75.7	48.2	39.0
1972	41.8	40.1	34.7	31.2	23.1	64.5	16.1	16.9	57.1	72.6	49.3	41.1
1973	44.2	42.0	36.9	34.1	26.4	64.1	19.1	17.7	56.9	69.5	50.7	43.1
1974	44.0	41.7	36.9	32.0	26.7	50.9	20.6	17.3	58.4	70.1	52.6	42.6
1975	43.9	42.7	37.7	28.5	24.0	44.3	20.5	15.4	59.7	70.4	54.5	42.1
1976	46.3	45.0	39.8	31.4	25.2	54.7	21.4	18.4	59.9	70.4	54.9	44.9
1977	48.4	47.0	41.8	35.9	28.0	66.4	21.9	20.4	60.6	71.9	55.1	47.3
1978	51.1	49.0	44.1	40.2	32.2	70.6	24.2	22.2	62.4	73.7	56.9	49.8
1979	52.7	50.2	45.5	42.5	35.5	68.0	26.6	22.6	63.5	75.5	57.8	51.1
1980	52.6	50.1	45.4	39.7	35.4	53.6	29.5	21.1	64.8	79.0	57.7	50.1
1981	53.9	50.8	46.4	40.6	37.4	49.3	29.9	21.6	65.4	82.8	56.6	51.4
1982	52.9	51.5	47.1	37.7	36.0	40.4	27.6	21.3	66.5	86.0	56.6	50.8
1983	55.2	54.4	50.3	40.5	35.5	57.1	26.9	24.0	69.0	91.7	57.3	53.7
1984	59.2	57.3	53.6	47.3	41.8	65.6	29.1	29.9	71.3	94.6	59.3	58.4
1985	61.7	60.3	56.9	49.8	44.6	66.6	30.0	31.8	76.2	102.0	63.0	61.0
1986	63.8	62.7	59.6	50.4	43.3	74.8	32.3	34.6	80.9	107.8	67.1	63.2
1987	66.0	64.8	61.8	50.7	43.3	76.3	35.7	36.6	82.9	111.7	68.0	65.2
1988	68.7	67.5	64.4	52.4	45.5	75.5	41.5	38.0	83.9	109.9	70.6	67.3
1989	71.1	69.4	66.4	53.9	48.1	73.2	46.2	39.7	86.1	111.6	73.0	69.2
1990	72.5	70.8	67.8	52.8	48.3	66.9	50.4	41.1	88.9	113.9	76.0	70.2
1991	72.3	70.9	67.9	49.4	45.7	60.5	53.7	40.9	89.9	113.7	77.6	69.6
1992	74.7	73.2	70.6	52.3	47.2	68.8	57.4	43.7	90.3	111.7	79.3	72.0
1993	76.7	75.7	73.2	56.8	51.3	74.4	59.3	47.6	89.5	107.1	80.5	74.3
1994	79.8	78.5	76.2	62.1	56.0	81.6	64.4	53.3	89.5	103.1	82.5	77.6
1995	81.8	80.6	78.6	66.1	61.9	79.0	71.0	57.5	90.0	100.3	84.7	79.4
1996	84.8	83.4	81.7	72.0	67.7	85.3	76.9	62.5	90.9	99.1	86.7	82.4
1997	88.7	86.5	85.3	78.7	75.8	86.9	86.1	71.0	92.6	98.1	89.8	86.4
1998	92.4	90.9	90.1	86.7	84.2	93.6	88.2	79.3	94.4	97.0	93.0	90.9
1999	96.5	95.5	95.2	93.9	92.0	99.3	92.0	88.4	98.0	99.1	97.4	95.8
2000	100.0	100.0	100.0	100.0	100.0	100.0	100.0	100.0	100.0	100.0	100.0	100.0
2001	100.8	102.5	102.9	97.0	95.8	100.4	94.6	97.3	103.4	103.9	103.2	100.9
2002	102.4	105.3	105.9	92.0	87.0	105.1	92.4	100.6	108.0	111.2	106.4	103.2
2003	104.9	108.2	109.0	95.1	87.8	114.0	93.6	104.7	110.6	118.7	106.6	106.1
2004	108.7	112.2	113.2	102.0	92.9	125.3	102.7	116.5	112.2	123.7	106.4	110.4
2005	111.9	115.6	116.7	109.0	99.5	133.2	109.9	123.5	112.6	125.2	106.3	113.7
2006	115.1	119.1	120.5	111.1	107.0	123.7	119.9	130.8	114.5	128.0	107.6	116.7
2007	117.4	122.5	124.2	107.7	112.2	101.5	130.1	133.7	116.9	130.1	110.2	118.3
2008	118.7	122.7	125.0	102.4	114.1	80.4	138.1	129.0	120.3	137.9	111.4	118.0
2006												
1st quarter	114.3	117.9	119.3	112.9	105.1	133.5	117.1	130.1	113.9	128.0	106.7	116.2
2nd quarter	115.0	118.7	120.0	112.2	106.8	127.6	118.7	130.2	114.2	127.5	107.5	116.8
3rd quarter	115.3	119.4	120.7	110.8	108.2	120.1	119.7	131.2	114.7	128.0	108.0	117.0
4th quarter	115.7	120.5	122.0	108.6	107.9	113.8	124.2	131.8	115.2	128.6	108.3	117.1
2007												
1st quarter	115.7	121.6	123.3	107.7	108.8	108.8	124.3	134.3	115.4	127.4	109.3	117.4
2nd quarter	117.1	122.2	123.9	108.5	111.5	105.6	127.0	133.0	116.5	129.5	110.0	118.3
3rd quarter	118.4	122.8	124.7	108.2	113.9	99.6	133.7	134.0	117.6	131.8	110.5	119.0
4th quarter	118.4	123.1	124.9	106.5	114.8	92.1	135.2	133.3	117.9	131.6	110.9	118.7
2008												
1st quarter	118.6	123.4	125.2	105.0	115.5	85.7	136.9	133.0	118.4	133.5	110.8	118.7
2nd quarter	119.5	123.8	125.7	104.5	116.2	82.7	140.9	130.5	119.6	135.6	111.5	118.7
3rd quarter	119.3	122.6	125.0	103.1	115.7	79.2	141.9	129.4	121.3	140.1	111.9	118.3
4th quarter	117.4	121.2	123.9	96.9	108.8	74.2	132.7	123.3	121.7	142.5	111.3	116.5

Table 1-5. Chain-Type Price Indexes for Gross Domestic Product and Domestic Purchases

(Index numbers, 2000 = 100.) NIPA Tables 1.1.4, 1.6.4, 2.3.4

Year and quarter	Gross domestic product												Gross domestic purchases
	Gross domestic product, total	Personal consumption expenditures		Private fixed investment			Exports and imports of goods and services		Government consumption expenditures and gross investment			
		Total	Excluding food and energy	Total	Nonresidential	Residential	Exports	Imports	Total	Federal	State and local	
1950	16.5	16.7	16.8	22.2	26.3	14.2	24.5	19.6	11.5	12.6	10.4	16.2
1951	17.6	17.8	17.8	24.1	28.8	15.2	27.7	23.7	12.3	13.2	11.4	17.4
1952	18.0	18.2	18.2	24.7	29.5	15.7	27.9	22.8	12.6	13.3	11.9	17.7
1953	18.2	18.4	18.6	24.9	29.7	15.8	27.8	21.8	12.7	13.4	12.2	17.9
1954	18.4	18.6	18.9	25.1	30.0	15.8	27.4	22.1	13.0	13.7	12.4	18.1
1955	18.7	18.7	19.1	25.5	30.4	16.2	27.7	22.0	13.5	14.5	12.6	18.4
1956	19.4	19.1	19.6	27.0	32.8	16.6	28.6	22.4	14.3	15.2	13.4	19.0
1957	20.0	19.6	20.2	27.9	34.5	16.6	29.7	22.6	14.9	15.9	14.0	19.7
1958	20.5	20.1	20.6	28.0	34.7	16.6	29.4	21.7	15.3	16.6	14.2	20.1
1959	20.8	20.4	21.0	28.3	35.1	16.6	29.4	21.9	15.4	16.5	14.5	20.4
1960	21.0	20.8	21.4	28.4	35.3	16.7	29.8	22.1	15.6	16.6	14.7	20.6
1961	21.3	21.0	21.6	28.3	35.1	16.8	30.3	22.1	15.9	16.9	15.1	20.9
1962	21.6	21.2	21.9	28.3	35.1	16.8	30.4	21.8	16.3	17.2	15.6	21.1
1963	21.8	21.5	22.2	28.3	35.1	16.7	30.3	22.3	16.7	17.6	15.9	21.4
1964	22.1	21.8	22.5	28.4	35.3	16.8	30.6	22.7	17.1	18.2	16.2	21.7
1965	22.5	22.1	22.8	28.9	35.7	17.3	31.5	23.1	17.6	18.7	16.7	22.1
1966	23.2	22.7	23.2	29.5	36.2	17.9	32.5	23.6	18.3	19.3	17.5	22.7
1967	23.9	23.2	23.9	30.4	37.1	18.5	33.7	23.7	19.1	19.9	18.5	23.4
1968	24.9	24.2	24.9	31.6	38.4	19.5	34.5	24.0	20.1	21.0	19.5	24.4
1969	26.2	25.3	26.1	33.1	40.0	20.9	35.6	24.7	21.3	22.1	20.8	25.6
1970	27.5	26.4	27.3	34.6	41.9	21.5	37.0	26.1	23.1	23.9	22.5	27.0
1971	28.9	27.6	28.5	36.3	43.9	22.8	38.4	27.7	24.9	26.0	24.1	28.4
1972	30.2	28.5	29.5	37.9	45.4	24.2	40.1	29.7	26.8	28.5	25.5	29.6
1973	31.9	30.1	30.5	40.0	47.1	26.3	45.4	34.8	28.7	30.4	27.5	31.3
1974	34.7	33.2	32.8	43.9	51.7	29.0	56.0	49.8	31.6	33.2	30.5	34.5
1975	38.0	36.0	35.5	49.4	58.8	31.7	61.7	54.0	34.8	36.6	33.5	37.8
1976	40.2	37.9	37.7	52.2	62.0	33.7	63.7	55.6	37.1	39.2	35.6	39.9
1977	42.8	40.4	40.1	56.3	66.3	37.1	66.3	60.5	39.7	42.2	37.9	42.6
1978	45.8	43.2	42.8	61.1	70.7	41.7	70.3	64.8	42.2	44.8	40.4	45.7
1979	49.6	47.1	45.7	66.6	76.4	46.4	78.8	75.9	45.8	48.2	43.9	49.7
1980	54.1	52.1	49.9	72.9	83.2	51.4	86.8	94.5	50.8	53.3	48.9	54.9
1981	59.1	56.7	54.2	79.7	91.2	55.6	93.2	99.6	55.8	58.5	53.7	59.9
1982	62.7	59.9	57.8	84.0	96.3	58.6	93.6	96.2	59.4	62.4	57.1	63.3
1983	65.2	62.4	60.8	83.9	95.4	59.9	94.0	92.6	61.8	64.6	59.7	65.5
1984	67.7	64.8	63.4	84.4	95.2	61.6	94.9	91.8	65.0	68.4	62.3	67.8
1985	69.7	66.9	65.8	85.5	95.9	63.2	92.0	88.8	67.0	70.0	64.7	69.8
1986	71.3	68.6	68.2	87.5	97.6	65.9	90.6	88.9	68.2	70.4	66.6	71.3
1987	73.2	70.9	70.8	89.1	98.4	68.6	92.9	94.3	70.1	71.2	69.4	73.5
1988	75.7	73.8	73.8	91.4	100.6	70.9	97.7	98.8	71.9	72.7	71.5	76.0
1989	78.6	77.0	76.9	93.6	102.7	73.2	99.3	100.9	74.1	74.7	73.9	78.9
1990	81.6	80.5	80.2	95.5	104.7	74.9	100.0	103.8	77.1	77.1	77.4	82.1
1991	84.5	83.4	83.3	97.0	106.3	75.9	101.3	103.4	79.8	80.2	79.7	84.8
1992	86.4	85.8	86.1	96.7	105.4	76.8	100.9	103.6	81.7	82.6	81.3	86.8
1993	88.4	87.8	88.3	97.8	105.5	79.9	100.9	102.7	83.8	84.8	83.3	88.7
1994	90.3	89.7	90.4	99.1	106.0	82.8	102.0	103.6	86.0	87.1	85.5	90.6
1995	92.1	91.6	92.4	100.3	106.2	85.8	104.4	106.4	88.4	89.5	87.8	92.5
1996	93.9	93.5	94.1	100.0	105.0	87.6	103.0	104.5	90.5	92.0	89.7	94.1
1997	95.4	95.1	95.6	99.8	103.7	89.8	101.2	100.8	92.1	93.5	91.4	95.4
1998	96.5	96.0	96.9	98.9	101.4	92.2	98.9	95.4	93.5	94.5	92.9	96.1
1999	97.9	97.6	98.3	98.9	100.1	95.8	98.3	96.0	96.1	96.9	95.7	97.6
2000	100.0	100.0	100.0	100.0	100.0	100.0	100.0	100.0	100.0	100.0	100.0	100.0
2001	102.4	102.1	101.9	101.0	99.7	104.6	99.6	97.5	102.5	101.9	102.9	102.0
2002	104.2	103.5	103.7	101.7	99.5	107.2	99.3	96.3	105.5	105.6	105.4	103.6
2003	106.4	105.6	105.2	103.3	99.6	112.4	101.4	99.7	109.8	110.1	109.7	106.0
2004	109.5	108.4	107.3	106.8	100.9	120.6	105.0	104.5	114.8	115.3	114.4	109.2
2005	113.0	111.6	109.6	111.6	103.8	129.3	108.8	111.2	121.5	120.8	121.9	113.3
2006	116.7	114.7	112.1	116.4	107.3	136.9	112.6	115.9	127.2	125.8	128.1	117.1
2007	119.8	117.7	114.5	118.0	108.7	138.9	116.6	120.2	132.9	130.1	134.7	120.3
2008	122.5	121.6	117.0	118.7	110.5	135.6	122.8	132.7	139.2	134.3	142.2	124.2
2006												
1st quarter	115.5	113.6	111.1	115.2	106.2	135.4	110.8	113.8	125.4	124.6	125.9	115.8
2nd quarter	116.3	114.5	111.9	116.2	107.1	136.7	112.4	116.6	126.9	125.9	127.5	116.9
3rd quarter	117.1	115.4	112.5	116.6	107.5	137.1	113.7	118.1	128.0	126.2	129.0	117.7
4th quarter	117.7	115.2	113.0	117.5	108.3	138.4	113.5	115.3	128.7	126.5	130.0	117.9
2007												
1st quarter	118.9	116.2	113.7	118.0	108.7	139.2	114.5	115.5	130.7	128.9	131.8	118.9
2nd quarter	119.5	117.2	114.2	117.9	108.7	138.7	116.0	119.1	132.4	130.0	133.8	119.9
3rd quarter	120.0	118.0	114.8	117.8	108.6	138.8	117.0	121.2	133.5	130.3	135.4	120.6
4th quarter	120.8	119.2	115.5	118.2	109.0	138.8	118.8	124.9	135.2	131.1	137.6	121.8
2008												
1st quarter	121.6	120.3	116.2	118.1	109.2	137.9	121.4	128.7	137.2	132.9	139.9	122.8
2nd quarter	122.0	121.5	116.8	118.4	109.8	136.7	124.6	137.1	139.6	134.6	142.6	124.1
3rd quarter	123.1	123.0	117.5	119.0	110.9	135.5	126.6	140.2	141.1	135.4	144.5	125.5
4th quarter	123.3	121.5	117.7	119.4	112.2	132.2	118.6	124.7	139.0	134.3	141.8	124.2

Table 1-6. Final Sales

(Quarterly dollar data are at seasonally adjusted annual rates.)   **NIPA Tables 1.4.4, 1.4.5, 1.4.6**

Year and quarter	Final sales of domestic product			Final sales to domestic purchasers		
	Billions of dollars	Billions of chained (2000) dollars	Chain-type price index, 2000 = 100	Billions of dollars	Billions of chained (2000) dollars	Chain-type price index, 2000 = 100
1950	288.0	1 763.8	16.3	287.3	1 787.4	16.1
1951	329.4	1 889.4	17.4	326.9	1 900.0	17.2
1952	354.8	1 990.0	17.8	353.7	2 013.6	17.6
1953	377.4	2 087.7	18.1	378.1	2 127.1	17.8
1954	382.3	2 092.5	18.3	381.9	2 123.4	18.0
1955	409.8	2 209.2	18.6	409.3	2 242.8	18.3
1956	433.5	2 259.0	19.2	431.2	2 285.0	18.9
1957	460.3	2 316.9	19.9	456.2	2 338.3	19.5
1958	467.6	2 299.0	20.3	467.0	2 341.1	20.0
1959	502.7	2 442.7	20.6	502.3	2 487.4	20.2
1960	523.2	2 506.8	20.9	519.0	2 534.8	20.5
1961	541.7	2 566.8	21.1	536.8	2 594.6	20.7
1962	579.5	2 708.5	21.4	575.4	2 744.8	21.0
1963	612.1	2 830.3	21.6	607.2	2 862.4	21.2
1964	658.8	2 999.9	22.0	651.9	3 024.5	21.6
1965	709.9	3 173.8	22.4	704.3	3 211.2	21.9
1966	774.2	3 364.8	23.0	770.3	3 415.5	22.6
1967	822.7	3 467.6	23.7	819.2	3 528.1	23.2
1968	900.9	3 640.3	24.8	899.6	3 715.3	24.2
1969	975.4	3 753.7	26.0	974.0	3 832.6	25.4
1970	1 036.5	3 787.7	27.4	1 032.6	3 854.0	26.8
1971	1 118.9	3 893.4	28.7	1 118.2	3 969.3	28.2
1972	1 229.2	4 098.6	30.0	1 232.6	4 186.9	29.4
1973	1 366.8	4 315.9	31.7	1 362.7	4 373.4	31.2
1974	1 486.0	4 305.5	34.5	1 486.8	4 329.7	34.3
1975	1 644.6	4 352.5	37.8	1 628.6	4 338.2	37.5
1976	1 808.2	4 522.3	40.0	1 809.8	4 556.2	39.7
1977	2 008.6	4 721.6	42.5	2 031.7	4 789.5	42.4
1978	2 268.9	4 981.6	45.6	2 294.3	5 047.9	45.5
1979	2 545.3	5 161.2	49.3	2 567.9	5 194.2	49.4
1980	2 795.8	5 196.7	53.8	2 808.9	5 142.8	54.6
1981	3 098.6	5 265.1	58.9	3 111.2	5 217.9	59.6
1982	3 269.9	5 233.4	62.5	3 289.9	5 218.2	63.1
1983	3 542.4	5 454.0	65.0	3 594.1	5 507.3	65.3
1984	3 867.8	5 739.2	67.4	3 970.5	5 877.3	67.6
1985	4 198.4	6 042.1	69.5	4 313.6	6 204.2	69.5
1986	4 456.3	6 271.8	71.1	4 589.0	6 452.0	71.1
1987	4 712.3	6 457.2	73.0	4 857.5	6 626.5	73.3
1988	5 085.3	6 734.5	75.5	5 195.7	6 849.7	75.9
1989	5 456.7	6 962.2	78.4	5 544.8	7 041.6	78.8
1990	5 788.5	7 108.5	81.4	5 866.5	7 157.4	82.0
1991	5 996.3	7 115.0	84.3	6 023.8	7 115.2	84.7
1992	6 321.4	7 331.1	86.2	6 354.7	7 333.0	86.7
1993	6 636.6	7 522.3	88.2	6 701.6	7 566.4	88.6
1994	7 008.4	7 777.8	90.1	7 102.0	7 853.6	90.4
1995	7 366.5	8 010.2	92.0	7 457.9	8 076.8	92.3
1996	7 786.1	8 306.5	93.7	7 882.3	8 383.1	94.0
1997	8 232.3	8 636.6	95.3	8 333.9	8 740.4	95.3
1998	8 676.2	8 997.6	96.4	8 836.2	9 203.2	96.0
1999	9 201.5	9 404.0	97.8	9 462.0	9 701.3	97.5
2000	9 760.5	9 760.5	100.0	10 140.0	10 140.0	100.0
2001	10 159.7	9 920.9	102.4	10 526.7	10 320.5	102.0
2002	10 457.7	10 036.5	104.2	10 882.1	10 505.3	103.6
2003	10 946.5	10 285.1	106.4	11 445.9	10 799.5	106.0
2004	11 627.3	10 619.8	109.5	12 242.7	11 205.2	109.3
2005	12 378.6	10 947.3	113.1	13 092.1	11 555.4	113.3
2006	13 129.0	11 249.3	116.7	13 886.4	11 858.5	117.1
2007	13 811.2	11 523.4	119.9	14 519.0	12 066.0	120.3
2008	14 311.6	11 681.0	122.5	14 980.7	12 063.6	124.2
2006						
1st quarter	12 906.5	11 167.6	115.6	13 668.3	11 796.5	115.9
2nd quarter	13 068.3	11 232.1	116.4	13 845.5	11 844.6	116.9
3rd quarter	13 187.1	11 257.8	117.1	13 979.7	11 874.1	117.7
4th quarter	13 354.3	11 339.7	117.8	14 052.0	11 918.6	117.9
2007						
1st quarter	13 526.5	11 370.5	119.0	14 255.3	11 983.2	119.0
2nd quarter	13 738.4	11 490.5	119.6	14 461.5	12 057.0	119.9
3rd quarter	13 927.6	11 605.0	120.0	14 610.1	12 114.1	120.6
4th quarter	14 052.3	11 628.0	120.9	14 749.0	12 109.8	121.8
2008						
1st quarter	14 176.4	11 653.7	121.7	14 882.2	12 113.3	122.9
2nd quarter	14 370.5	11 778.8	122.0	15 088.7	12 153.0	124.2
3rd quarter	14 462.5	11 739.2	123.2	15 170.2	12 084.1	125.5
4th quarter	14 236.9	11 552.2	123.2	14 782.0	11 904.0	124.2

Table 1-7. Per Capita Product and Income and U.S. Population

(Dollars, except as noted; quarterly data are at seasonally adjusted annual rates.)   **NIPA Table 7.1**

Year and quarter	Current dollars							Chained (2000) dollars						Population (mid-period, thousands)
	Gross domestic product	Personal income	Disposable personal income	Personal consumption expenditures				Gross domestic product	Disposable personal income	Personal consumption expenditures				
				Total	Durable goods	Nondurable goods	Services			Total	Durable goods	Nondurable goods	Services	
1950	1 937	1 510	1 385	1 267	203	648	417	11 717	8 306	7 600	509	3 324	3 607	151 684
1951	2 199	1 672	1 497	1 352	194	708	450	12 412	8 408	7 591	456	3 354	3 728	154 287
1952	2 283	1 754	1 550	1 399	187	731	481	12 668	8 534	7 698	436	3 427	3 826	156 954
1953	2 378	1 829	1 621	1 461	205	738	517	13 032	8 802	7 932	482	3 477	3 923	159 565
1954	2 342	1 813	1 627	1 478	196	737	545	12 719	8 757	7 952	472	3 460	4 011	162 391
1955	2 509	1 913	1 714	1 566	235	755	576	13 389	9 177	8 383	566	3 564	4 148	165 275
1956	2 601	2 019	1 801	1 615	227	777	611	13 410	9 450	8 474	534	3 621	4 279	168 221
1957	2 692	2 094	1 867	1 675	233	800	641	13 435	9 508	8 528	529	3 622	4 365	171 274
1958	2 683	2 119	1 898	1 701	215	814	672	13 088	9 433	8 455	479	3 597	4 456	174 141
1959	2 860	2 218	1 979	1 793	241	838	714	13 782	9 685	8 776	527	3 682	4 612	177 130
1960	2 912	2 277	2 022	1 835	240	846	750	13 840	9 735	8 837	527	3 662	4 721	180 760
1961	2 965	2 335	2 078	1 862	227	852	782	13 932	9 901	8 873	499	3 669	4 838	183 742
1962	3 139	2 448	2 171	1 947	251	872	823	14 552	10 227	9 170	549	3 727	5 000	186 590
1963	3 263	2 534	2 246	2 022	273	888	861	14 971	10 455	9 412	594	3 751	5 153	189 300
1964	3 458	2 681	2 410	2 144	295	931	918	15 624	11 061	9 839	640	3 880	5 393	191 927
1965	3 700	2 860	2 563	2 283	325	986	972	16 420	11 594	10 331	712	4 035	5 610	194 347
1966	4 007	3 072	2 734	2 446	347	1 062	1 037	17 290	12 065	10 793	763	4 208	5 821	196 599
1967	4 189	3 262	2 895	2 555	354	1 092	1 108	17 533	12 457	10 994	767	4 228	6 039	198 752
1968	4 533	3 547	3 114	2 780	402	1 174	1 203	18 196	12 892	11 510	843	4 377	6 292	200 745
1969	4 857	3 840	3 324	2 985	424	1 249	1 313	18 573	13 163	11 820	864	4 449	6 529	202 736
1970	5 064	4 090	3 587	3 162	414	1 326	1 421	18 391	13 563	11 955	826	4 504	6 712	205 089
1971	5 427	4 350	3 860	3 379	467	1 375	1 538	18 771	14 001	12 256	898	4 528	6 886	207 692
1972	5 899	4 729	4 140	3 671	526	1 467	1 678	19 555	14 512	12 868	1 001	4 677	7 200	209 924
1973	6 524	5 241	4 616	4 022	583	1 619	1 820	20 484	15 345	13 371	1 094	4 784	7 466	211 939
1974	7 013	5 716	5 010	4 364	572	1 798	1 994	20 195	15 094	13 148	1 009	4 645	7 570	213 898
1975	7 586	6 181	5 498	4 789	618	1 948	2 223	19 961	15 291	13 320	999	4 668	7 775	215 981
1976	8 369	6 762	5 972	5 282	728	2 102	2 452	20 822	15 738	13 919	1 116	4 848	8 012	218 086
1977	9 219	7 414	6 517	5 804	823	2 257	2 725	21 565	16 128	14 364	1 207	4 915	8 274	220 289
1978	10 307	8 255	7 224	6 417	906	2 472	3 039	22 526	16 704	14 837	1 258	5 046	8 569	222 629
1979	11 387	9 161	7 967	7 073	952	2 774	3 347	22 982	16 931	15 030	1 240	5 123	8 734	225 106
1980	12 249	10 134	8 822	7 716	940	3 057	3 719	22 666	16 940	14 816	1 129	5 057	8 785	227 726
1981	13 601	11 266	9 765	8 439	1 006	3 299	4 134	23 007	17 217	14 879	1 132	5 066	8 844	230 008
1982	14 017	11 951	10 426	8 945	1 034	3 392	4 519	22 346	17 418	14 944	1 120	5 065	8 944	232 218
1983	15 092	12 635	11 131	9 775	1 198	3 547	5 030	23 146	17 828	15 656	1 272	5 187	9 349	234 333
1984	16 638	13 915	12 319	10 589	1 381	3 742	5 466	24 593	19 011	16 343	1 445	5 346	9 644	236 394
1985	17 695	14 787	13 037	11 406	1 524	3 894	5 988	25 382	19 476	17 040	1 577	5 443	10 098	238 506
1986	18 542	15 466	13 649	12 048	1 674	3 982	6 391	26 024	19 906	17 570	1 714	5 587	10 302	240 683
1987	19 517	16 255	14 241	12 766	1 736	4 181	6 849	26 664	20 072	17 994	1 728	5 670	10 652	242 843
1988	20 827	17 358	15 297	13 685	1 851	4 421	7 413	27 514	20 740	18 554	1 816	5 802	10 983	245 061
1989	22 169	18 545	16 257	14 546	1 907	4 716	7 923	28 221	21 120	18 898	1 839	5 907	11 205	247 387
1990	23 195	19 500	17 131	15 349	1 895	4 996	8 457	28 429	21 281	19 067	1 813	5 932	11 398	250 181
1991	23 650	19 923	17 609	15 722	1 790	5 068	8 864	28 007	21 109	18 848	1 688	5 840	11 438	253 530
1992	24 668	20 870	18 494	16 485	1 882	5 179	9 424	28 556	21 548	19 208	1 763	5 878	11 680	256 922
1993	25 578	21 356	18 872	17 204	2 024	5 300	9 881	28 940	21 493	19 593	1 877	5 956	11 855	260 282
1994	26 844	22 176	19 555	18 004	2 210	5 455	10 339	29 741	21 812	20 082	2 009	6 088	12 058	263 455
1995	27 749	23 078	20 287	18 665	2 294	5 571	10 800	30 128	22 153	20 382	2 073	6 147	12 228	266 588
1996	28 982	24 176	21 091	19 490	2 419	5 767	11 304	30 881	22 546	20 835	2 209	6 230	12 443	269 714
1997	30 424	25 334	21 940	20 323	2 538	5 931	11 854	31 886	23 065	21 365	2 370	6 321	12 705	272 958
1998	31 674	26 880	23 161	21 291	2 717	6 096	12 478	32 833	24 131	22 183	2 608	6 498	13 090	276 154
1999	33 181	27 933	23 968	22 491	2 927	6 461	13 103	33 904	24 564	23 050	2 880	6 718	13 454	279 328
2000	34 761	29 849	25 473	23 864	3 057	6 895	13 912	34 761	25 473	23 864	3 057	6 895	13 912	282 413
2001	35 500	30 579	26 243	24 729	3 097	7 070	14 561	34 668	25 704	24 222	3 157	6 964	14 102	285 294
2002	36 346	30 834	27 183	25 518	3 208	7 220	15 091	34 885	26 253	24 646	3 349	7 072	14 235	288 055
2003	37 701	31 519	28 076	26 498	3 242	7 533	15 722	35 432	26 588	25 093	3 510	7 234	14 374	290 729
2004	39 836	33 159	29 592	27 939	3 354	7 989	16 596	36 393	27 302	25 776	3 698	7 423	14 696	293 348
2005	41 961	34 691	30 611	29 368	3 448	8 493	17 428	37 122	27 434	26 320	3 832	7 609	14 934	296 036
2006	44 101	36 791	32 263	30 812	3 521	8 986	18 305	37 798	28 134	26 869	3 966	7 815	15 159	298 820
2007	45 760	38 654	33 706	32 181	3 589	9 389	19 203	38 192	28 648	27 351	4 117	7 929	15 398	301 737
2008	46 842	39 742	34 946	33 028	3 360	9 737	19 931	38 262	28 741	27 164	3 903	7 810	15 481	304 529
2006														
1st quarter	43 526	36 211	31 791	30 316	3 515	8 831	17 970	37 674	27 991	26 692	3 940	7 761	15 062	297 743
2nd quarter	44 015	36 572	32 078	30 704	3 516	8 986	18 202	37 841	28 018	26 817	3 949	7 804	15 133	298 399
3rd quarter	44 287	36 955	32 422	31 031	3 525	9 113	18 393	37 818	28 101	26 895	3 972	7 828	15 167	299 175
4th quarter	44 572	37 420	32 754	31 194	3 528	9 014	18 652	37 859	28 424	27 070	4 003	7 867	15 273	299 965
2007														
1st quarter	44 940	38 162	33 307	31 681	3 581	9 185	18 915	37 778	28 664	27 265	4 082	7 917	15 354	300 644
2nd quarter	45 589	38 421	33 478	32 049	3 602	9 351	19 096	38 135	28 555	27 336	4 123	7 936	15 374	301 332
3rd quarter	46 177	38 828	33 858	32 325	3 596	9 422	19 307	38 482	28 702	27 403	4 136	7 940	15 424	302 108
4th quarter	46 328	39 199	34 179	32 664	3 576	9 596	19 492	38 369	28 670	27 399	4 129	7 925	15 440	302 865
2008														
1st quarter	46 626	39 409	34 351	32 957	3 529	9 722	19 705	38 372	28 560	27 401	4 076	7 901	15 500	303 498
2nd quarter	47 001	39 957	35 531	33 335	3 483	9 951	19 901	38 561	29 234	27 427	4 039	7 960	15 494	304 128
3rd quarter	47 275	39 920	35 096	33 337	3 333	9 986	20 017	38 418	28 525	27 095	3 871	7 794	15 453	304 872
4th quarter	46 464	39 682	34 805	32 484	3 096	9 289	20 099	37 701	28 644	26 734	3 627	7 586	15 475	305 619

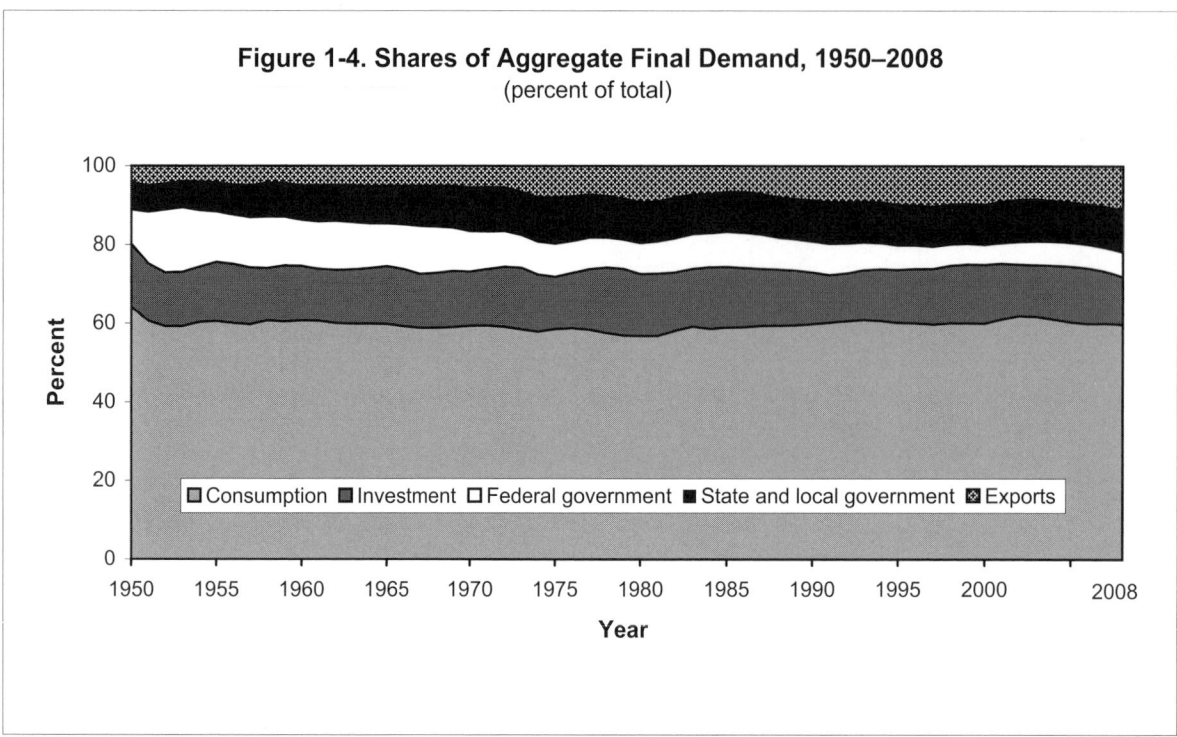

Figure 1-4. Shares of Aggregate Final Demand, 1950–2008
(percent of total)

- People want to know how various sources of demand, especially consumption spending, affect GDP. It is often stated, for example, that consumption "accounts for" about 70 percent of GDP. Such statements are based on a NIPA table showing the components of GDP as a percent of total GDP. It can readily be seen in Table 1-1 that in 2008, personal consumption expenditures (PCE) amounted to 70.5 percent of total GDP, and that this is up from a range of 60 to 65 percent earlier in the postwar period. (All such calculations must be made in current dollars, since for reasons stated in the notes and definitions, the 2000-dollar values do not sum to the total GDP.)

- Can this be interpreted as "accounting for" 70.5 percent of GDP? No, because the value of PCE includes imported goods and services—coffee, cocoa, and bananas; crude oil from the Middle East, transformed into gasoline; clothing, cars, and toys manufactured overseas—even the money that U.S. consumers spend when they travel. The import content of PCE doesn't contribute to demand for U.S. GDP, which excludes imports; it contributes to demand for GDP in China and other countries that export to us.

- It is not possible with NIPA data to estimate and subtract out the import content of PCE, and so there is no way to estimate PCE's contribution to GDP. What we can do is calculate PCE and the other sources of aggregate final demand for U.S. output as shares of total final demand; this is shown in Table 1-9 and Figure 1-4. These shares would measure contributions to GDP if each demand source had the same percentage "import content" as total GDP.

- Consumption spending has been around 60 percent of final demand ever since 1951. (It was greater in 1946 through 1950, as consumers made up for wartime deprivations.) The shares of exports and state and local government spending have increased to about 11 percent each, while the federal government direct spending share has declined from Korean War highs to about 6 percent currently. (This measure of government spending does not include government financing of medical care and other consumption spending through transfer payment programs such as Social Security and Medicare.) Investment is the most variable share. (Table 1-9)

- Imports now supply about 15 percent of the total supply of goods and services in the U.S. market, with the remaining 85 percent coming from domestic production (GDP). In the 1950s, domestic production supplied 96 percent and imports just 4 percent. (Table 1-8)

Table 1-8. Shares of Aggregate Supply

(Billions of dollars, quarterly dollar data are at seasonally adjusted rates, percents.)   **NIPA Table 1.1.5**

Year and quarter	Aggregate supply (billions of dollars)			Shares of aggregate supply (percent)	
	Total	GDP	Imports	Domestic production (GDP)	Imports
1950	305.4	293.8	11.6	96.2	3.8
1951	353.9	339.3	14.6	95.9	4.1
1952	373.6	358.3	15.3	95.9	4.1
1953	395.4	379.4	16.0	96.0	4.0
1954	395.8	380.4	15.4	96.1	3.9
1955	432.0	414.8	17.2	96.0	4.0
1956	456.4	437.5	18.9	95.9	4.1
1957	481.0	461.1	19.9	95.9	4.1
1958	487.2	467.2	20.0	95.9	4.1
1959	528.9	506.6	22.3	95.8	4.2
1960	549.2	526.4	22.8	95.8	4.2
1961	567.4	544.7	22.7	96.0	4.0
1962	610.6	585.6	25.0	95.9	4.1
1963	643.8	617.7	26.1	95.9	4.1
1964	691.7	663.6	28.1	95.9	4.1
1965	750.6	719.1	31.5	95.8	4.2
1966	824.9	787.8	37.1	95.5	4.5
1967	872.5	832.6	39.9	95.4	4.6
1968	956.6	910.0	46.6	95.1	4.9
1969	1 035.1	984.6	50.5	95.1	4.9
1970	1 094.3	1 038.5	55.8	94.9	5.1
1971	1 189.4	1 127.1	62.3	94.8	5.2
1972	1 312.5	1 238.3	74.2	94.3	5.7
1973	1 473.9	1 382.7	91.2	93.8	6.2
1974	1 627.5	1 500.0	127.5	92.2	7.8
1975	1 761.0	1 638.3	122.7	93.0	7.0
1976	1 976.4	1 825.3	151.1	92.4	7.6
1977	2 213.3	2 030.9	182.4	91.8	8.2
1978	2 507.0	2 294.7	212.3	91.5	8.5
1979	2 816.0	2 563.3	252.7	91.0	9.0
1980	3 083.3	2 789.5	293.8	90.5	9.5
1981	3 446.2	3 128.4	317.8	90.8	9.2
1982	3 558.2	3 255.0	303.2	91.5	8.5
1983	3 865.3	3 536.7	328.6	91.5	8.5
1984	4 338.3	3 933.2	405.1	90.7	9.3
1985	4 637.5	4 220.3	417.2	91.0	9.0
1986	4 916.1	4 462.8	453.3	90.8	9.2
1987	5 248.6	4 739.5	509.1	90.3	9.7
1988	5 658.3	5 103.8	554.5	90.2	9.8
1989	6 075.9	5 484.4	591.5	90.3	9.7
1990	6 433.4	5 803.1	630.3	90.2	9.8
1991	6 620.2	5 995.9	624.3	90.6	9.4
1992	7 006.3	6 337.7	668.6	90.5	9.5
1993	7 378.3	6 657.4	720.9	90.2	9.8
1994	7 886.7	7 072.2	814.5	89.7	10.3
1995	8 301.3	7 397.7	903.6	89.1	10.9
1996	8 781.7	7 816.9	964.8	89.0	11.0
1997	9 361.2	8 304.3	1 056.9	88.7	11.3
1998	9 862.9	8 747.0	1 115.9	88.7	11.3
1999	10 520.1	9 268.4	1 251.7	88.1	11.9
2000	11 292.8	9 817.0	1 475.8	86.9	13.1
2001	11 527.8	10 128.0	1 399.8	87.9	12.1
2002	11 899.9	10 469.6	1 430.3	88.0	12.0
2003	12 501.0	10 960.8	1 540.2	87.7	12.3
2004	13 483.7	11 685.9	1 797.8	86.7	13.3
2005	14 447.0	12 421.9	2 025.1	86.0	14.0
2006	15 416.5	13 178.4	2 238.1	85.5	14.5
2007	16 177.7	13 807.5	2 370.2	85.3	14.7
2008	16 793.2	14 264.6	2 528.6	84.9	15.1
2006					
1st quarter	15 144.5	12 959.6	2 184.9	85.6	14.4
2nd quarter	15 374.1	13 134.1	2 240.0	85.4	14.6
3rd quarter	15 534.8	13 249.6	2 285.2	85.3	14.7
4th quarter	15 612.3	13 370.1	2 242.2	85.6	14.4
2007					
1st quarter	15 800.3	13 510.9	2 289.4	85.5	14.5
2nd quarter	16 075.0	13 737.5	2 337.5	85.5	14.5
3rd quarter	16 348.1	13 950.6	2 397.5	85.3	14.7
4th quarter	16 487.7	14 031.2	2 456.5	85.1	14.9
2008					
1st quarter	16 677.3	14 150.8	2 526.5	84.9	15.1
2nd quarter	16 935.9	14 294.5	2 641.4	84.4	15.6
3rd quarter	17 089.4	14 412.8	2 676.6	84.3	15.7
4th quarter	16 470.0	14 200.3	2 269.7	86.2	13.8

Table 1-9. Shares of Aggregate Final Demand

(Billions of dollars, quarterly dollar data are at seasonally adjusted rates, percents.)   NIPA Table 1.1.5

| Year and quarter | Aggregate final demand (billions of dollars) | | | | | | | Shares of aggregate final demand (percent) | | | | | |
| | Total | Consumption (PCE) | Nonresidential fixed investment | Residential investment | Exports | Government consumption and gross investment | | PCE | Nonresidential investment | Residential investment | Exports | Federal government | State and local government |
						Federal	State and local						
1950	299.6	192.2	27.8	20.5	12.4	26.0	20.7	64.2	9.3	6.8	4.1	8.7	6.9
1951	343.9	208.5	31.8	18.4	17.1	45.1	23.0	60.6	9.2	5.4	5.0	13.1	6.7
1952	370.1	219.5	31.9	18.6	16.5	59.2	24.4	59.3	8.6	5.0	4.5	16.0	6.6
1953	393.4	233.1	35.1	19.4	15.3	64.4	26.1	59.3	8.9	4.9	3.9	16.4	6.6
1954	397.8	240.0	34.7	21.1	15.8	57.3	28.9	60.3	8.7	5.3	4.0	14.4	7.3
1955	427.0	258.8	39.0	25.0	17.7	54.9	31.6	60.6	9.1	5.9	4.1	12.9	7.4
1956	452.5	271.7	44.5	23.6	21.3	56.7	34.7	60.0	9.8	5.2	4.7	12.5	7.7
1957	480.2	286.9	47.5	22.2	24.0	61.3	38.3	59.7	9.9	4.6	5.0	12.8	8.0
1958	487.6	296.2	42.5	22.3	20.6	63.8	42.2	60.7	8.7	4.6	4.2	13.1	8.7
1959	525.0	317.6	46.5	28.1	22.7	65.4	44.7	60.5	8.9	5.4	4.3	12.5	8.5
1960	546.0	331.7	49.4	26.3	27.0	64.1	47.5	60.8	9.0	4.8	4.9	11.7	8.7
1961	564.4	342.1	48.8	26.4	27.6	67.9	51.6	60.6	8.6	4.7	4.9	12.0	9.1
1962	604.7	363.3	53.1	29.0	29.1	75.3	54.9	60.1	8.8	4.8	4.8	12.5	9.1
1963	638.3	382.7	56.0	32.1	31.1	76.9	59.5	60.0	8.8	5.0	4.9	12.0	9.3
1964	687.0	411.4	63.0	34.3	35.0	78.5	64.8	59.9	9.2	5.0	5.1	11.4	9.4
1965	741.3	443.8	74.8	34.2	37.1	80.4	71.0	59.9	10.1	4.6	5.0	10.8	9.6
1966	811.2	480.9	85.4	32.3	40.9	92.5	79.2	59.3	10.5	4.0	5.0	11.4	9.8
1967	862.8	507.8	86.4	32.4	43.5	104.8	87.9	58.9	10.0	3.8	5.0	12.1	10.2
1968	947.4	558.0	93.4	38.7	47.9	111.4	98.0	58.9	9.9	4.1	5.1	11.8	10.3
1969	1 026.0	605.2	104.7	42.6	51.9	113.4	108.2	59.0	10.2	4.2	5.1	11.1	10.5
1970	1 092.4	648.5	109.0	41.4	59.7	113.5	120.3	59.4	10.0	3.8	5.5	10.4	11.0
1971	1 181.3	701.9	114.1	55.8	63.0	113.7	132.8	59.4	9.7	4.7	5.3	9.6	11.2
1972	1 303.4	770.6	128.8	69.7	70.8	119.7	143.8	59.1	9.9	5.3	5.4	9.2	11.0
1973	1 458.0	852.4	153.3	75.3	95.3	122.5	159.2	58.5	10.5	5.2	6.5	8.4	10.9
1974	1 613.6	933.4	169.5	66.0	126.7	134.6	183.4	57.8	10.5	4.1	7.9	8.3	11.4
1975	1 767.3	1 034.4	173.7	62.7	138.7	149.1	208.7	58.5	9.8	3.5	7.8	8.4	11.8
1976	1 959.3	1 151.9	192.4	82.5	149.5	159.7	223.3	58.8	9.8	4.2	7.6	8.2	11.4
1977	2 191.1	1 278.6	228.7	110.3	159.4	175.4	238.7	58.4	10.4	5.0	7.3	8.0	10.9
1978	2 481.1	1 428.5	280.6	131.6	186.9	190.9	262.6	57.6	11.3	5.3	7.5	7.7	10.6
1979	2 798.0	1 592.2	333.9	141.0	230.1	210.6	290.2	56.9	11.9	5.0	8.2	7.5	10.4
1980	3 089.7	1 757.1	362.4	123.2	280.8	243.8	322.4	56.9	11.7	4.0	9.1	7.9	10.4
1981	3 416.4	1 941.1	420.0	122.6	305.2	280.2	347.3	56.8	12.3	3.6	8.9	8.2	10.2
1982	3 573.2	2 077.3	426.5	105.7	283.2	310.8	369.7	58.1	11.9	3.0	7.9	8.7	10.3
1983	3 871.1	2 290.6	417.2	152.9	277.0	342.9	390.5	59.2	10.8	3.9	7.2	8.9	10.1
1984	4 272.9	2 503.3	489.6	180.6	302.4	374.4	422.6	58.6	11.5	4.2	7.1	8.8	9.9
1985	4 615.7	2 720.3	526.2	188.2	302.0	412.8	466.2	58.9	11.4	4.1	6.5	8.9	10.1
1986	4 909.4	2 899.7	519.8	220.1	320.5	438.6	510.7	59.1	10.6	4.5	6.5	8.9	10.4
1987	5 221.4	3 100.2	524.1	233.7	363.9	460.1	539.4	59.4	10.0	4.5	7.0	8.8	10.3
1988	5 639.8	3 353.6	563.8	239.3	444.1	462.3	576.7	59.5	10.0	4.2	7.9	8.2	10.2
1989	6 048.1	3 598.5	607.7	239.5	503.3	482.2	616.9	59.5	10.0	4.0	8.3	8.0	10.2
1990	6 418.9	3 839.9	622.4	224.0	552.4	508.3	671.9	59.8	9.7	3.5	8.6	7.9	10.5
1991	6 620.6	3 986.1	598.2	205.1	596.8	527.7	706.7	60.2	9.0	3.1	9.0	8.0	10.7
1992	6 989.9	4 235.3	612.1	236.3	635.3	533.9	737.0	60.6	8.8	3.4	9.1	7.6	10.5
1993	7 357.5	4 477.9	666.6	266.0	655.8	525.2	766.0	60.9	9.1	3.6	8.9	7.1	10.4
1994	7 822.9	4 743.3	731.4	301.9	720.9	519.1	806.3	60.6	9.3	3.9	9.2	6.6	10.3
1995	8 270.0	4 975.8	810.0	302.8	812.2	519.2	850.0	60.2	9.8	3.7	9.8	6.3	10.3
1996	8 750.9	5 256.8	875.4	334.1	868.6	527.4	888.6	60.1	10.0	3.8	9.9	6.0	10.2
1997	9 289.2	5 547.4	968.7	349.1	955.3	530.9	937.8	59.7	10.4	3.8	10.3	5.7	10.1
1998	9 792.1	5 879.5	1 052.6	385.8	955.9	530.4	987.9	60.0	10.7	3.9	9.8	5.4	10.1
1999	10 453.3	6 282.5	1 133.9	424.9	991.2	555.8	1 065.0	60.1	10.8	4.1	9.5	5.3	10.2
2000	11 236.3	6 739.4	1 232.1	446.9	1 096.3	578.8	1 142.8	60.0	11.0	4.0	9.8	5.2	10.2
2001	11 559.6	7 055.0	1 176.8	469.3	1 032.8	612.9	1 212.8	61.0	10.2	4.1	8.9	5.3	10.5
2002	11 888.0	7 350.7	1 066.3	503.9	1 005.9	679.7	1 281.5	61.8	9.0	4.2	8.5	5.7	10.8
2003	12 486.6	7 703.6	1 077.4	572.4	1 040.8	756.4	1 336.0	61.7	8.6	4.6	8.3	6.1	10.7
2004	13 425.1	8 195.9	1 154.5	675.5	1 182.4	825.6	1 391.2	61.0	8.6	5.0	8.8	6.1	10.4
2005	14 403.6	8 694.1	1 273.1	769.6	1 311.5	875.5	1 479.8	60.4	8.8	5.3	9.1	6.1	10.3
2006	15 367.2	9 207.2	1 414.1	757.0	1 480.8	932.2	1 575.9	59.9	9.2	4.9	9.6	6.1	10.3
2007	16 181.4	9 710.2	1 503.8	630.2	1 662.4	979.3	1 695.5	60.0	9.3	3.9	10.3	6.1	10.5
2008	16 840.1	10 057.9	1 552.8	487.7	1 859.4	1 071.9	1 810.4	59.7	9.2	2.9	11.0	6.4	10.8
2006													
1st quarter	15 091.4	9 026.3	1 375.5	808.1	1 423.2	922.8	1 535.5	59.8	9.1	5.4	9.4	6.1	10.2
2nd quarter	15 308.3	9 161.9	1 408.3	779.6	1 462.8	928.5	1 567.2	59.8	9.2	5.1	9.6	6.1	10.2
3rd quarter	15 472.3	9 283.7	1 433.0	736.2	1 492.5	935.5	1 591.4	60.0	9.3	4.8	9.6	6.0	10.3
4th quarter	15 596.5	9 357.0	1 439.6	704.0	1 544.5	941.7	1 609.7	60.0	9.2	4.5	9.9	6.0	10.3
2007													
1st quarter	15 815.9	9 524.9	1 456.4	677.0	1 560.5	950.3	1 646.8	60.2	9.2	4.3	9.9	6.0	10.4
2nd quarter	16 075.9	9 657.5	1 493.7	654.4	1 614.4	974.6	1 681.3	60.1	9.3	4.1	10.0	6.1	10.5
3rd quarter	16 325.0	9 765.6	1 522.9	618.1	1 714.9	994.0	1 709.5	59.8	9.3	3.8	10.5	6.1	10.5
4th quarter	16 508.7	9 892.7	1 542.1	571.3	1 759.7	998.3	1 744.6	59.9	9.3	3.5	10.7	6.0	10.6
2008													
1st quarter	16 702.9	10 002.3	1 553.6	528.1	1 820.8	1 026.5	1 771.6	59.9	9.3	3.2	10.9	6.1	10.6
2nd quarter	17 011.8	10 138.0	1 571.9	505.0	1 923.2	1 056.1	1 817.6	59.6	9.2	3.0	11.3	6.2	10.7
3rd quarter	17 139.1	10 163.5	1 581.2	479.4	1 968.9	1 098.0	1 848.1	59.3	9.2	2.8	11.5	6.4	10.8
4th quarter	16 506.7	9 927.9	1 504.3	438.4	1 724.7	1 107.0	1 804.4	60.1	9.1	2.7	10.4	6.7	10.9

Section 1b: Income and Value Added

Figure 1-5. Factor Income by Type, 1948 and 2008

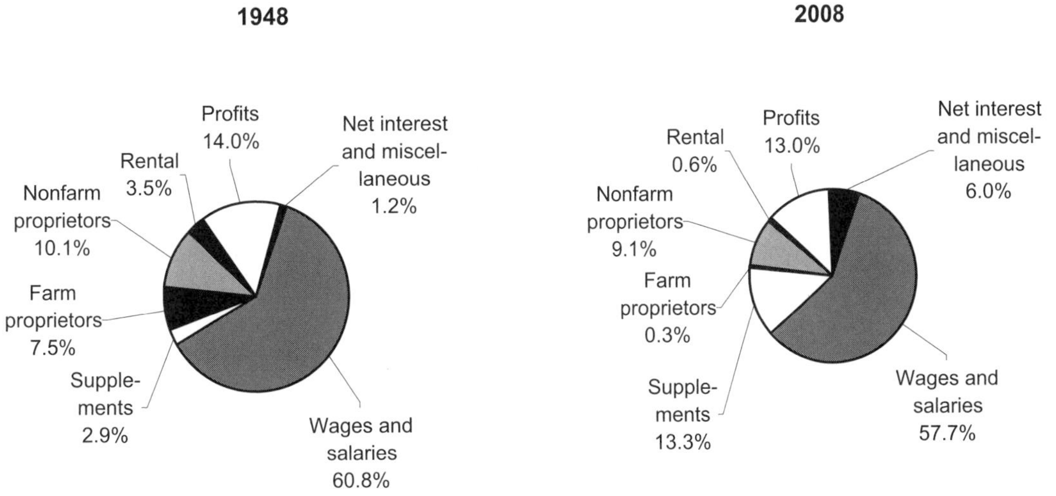

1948

- Profits 14.0%
- Rental 3.5%
- Nonfarm proprietors 10.1%
- Farm proprietors 7.5%
- Supplements 2.9%
- Net interest and miscellaneous 1.2%
- Wages and salaries 60.8%

2008

- Profits 13.0%
- Rental 0.6%
- Nonfarm proprietors 9.1%
- Farm proprietors 0.3%
- Supplements 13.3%
- Net interest and miscellaneous 6.0%
- Wages and salaries 57.7%

- The changing distribution of the national income over the postwar period is shown in the figure above, based on data in Tables 1-12 and 19-8. The total income concept whose distribution is shown in this graph is called "net national factor income," formerly known as simply "national income," and is the sum of the income components identified in the graph.

- Labor compensation rose from 63.7 percent of the total in 1948 to 71.0 percent of the total in 2008. However, the wage and salary share declined from 60.8 percent to 57.7 percent over this period. The increase in the total labor share is entirely accounted for by supplements to wages and salaries, which are the costs of fringe benefits—including health insurance—and taxes ("employer contributions") to pay for Social Security and Medicare.

- The farm proprietors' share dropped from 7.5 percent in 1948 to less than 1 percent in 2008. Shares going to nonfarm proprietors declined slightly. Proprietors' income includes the return to their labor input as well as to their land and other capital, so it cannot be unequivocally attributed to either capital or labor.

- The share of rental income of persons declined from 3.5 percent in 1948 to less than 1 percent in 2008. This may seem surprising, as the share includes the imputed rental income of homeowners, and homeownership increased over the period. However, the rental income imputed to homeowners is net of all the costs of owning a home, including interest, depreciation, taxes, and purchased inputs. Table 12-7 shows that home mortgage debt has been increasing relative to real estate value. Accordingly, interest costs in recent years have absorbed a much greater share of the gross rental value of homeownership than in 1948, leaving a smaller return to the homeowner's equity.

- The share of capital incomes other than rental income rose from 15.2 percent to 19.0 percent, with the interest portion rising while corporate profits edged down. Corporations, like homeowners, have increased their debt relative to their equity.

Table 1-10. Relation of Gross Domestic Product, Gross and Net National Product, National Income, and Personal Income

(Billions of dollars, quarterly data are at seasonally adjusted annual rates.)   NIPA Table 1.7.5

Year and quarter	Gross domestic product	Plus: Income receipts from the rest of the world	Less: Income payments to the rest of the world	Equals: Gross national product	Less: Consumption of fixed capital									Equals: Net national product
					Total	Private					Government			
						Total	Domestic business			House-holds and institutions	Total	General government	Government enterprises	
							Total	Capital consumption allowances	Less: Capital consumption adjustment					
1950	293.8	2.2	0.7	295.2	29.4	21.5	18.1	14.9	-3.2	3.3	8.0	7.5	0.5	265.8
1951	339.3	2.8	0.9	341.2	33.2	24.6	20.7	17.1	-3.6	3.8	8.7	8.1	0.6	308.0
1952	358.3	2.9	0.9	360.3	35.7	26.1	21.9	18.8	-3.1	4.2	9.6	8.9	0.6	324.6
1953	379.4	2.8	0.9	381.3	37.8	27.3	22.9	21.0	-1.9	4.4	10.5	9.8	0.7	343.5
1954	380.4	3.0	0.9	382.5	39.9	28.7	24.1	23.0	-1.1	4.7	11.2	10.4	0.7	342.6
1955	414.8	3.5	1.1	417.2	42.1	30.3	25.3	25.7	0.4	5.0	11.8	11.0	0.8	375.1
1956	437.5	3.9	1.1	440.3	46.4	33.6	28.1	27.9	-0.2	5.5	12.8	11.9	0.9	393.9
1957	461.1	4.3	1.2	464.1	49.9	36.3	30.4	30.3	-0.1	5.8	13.6	12.7	0.9	414.3
1958	467.2	3.9	1.2	469.8	52.0	38.1	32.1	31.6	-0.4	6.1	13.9	12.9	1.0	417.8
1959	506.6	4.3	1.5	509.3	53.0	38.6	32.2	33.5	1.4	6.4	14.5	13.5	1.0	456.3
1960	526.4	4.9	1.8	529.5	55.6	40.5	33.9	35.3	1.4	6.7	15.0	13.9	1.1	473.9
1961	544.7	5.3	1.8	548.2	57.2	41.6	34.7	36.7	2.0	6.9	15.6	14.4	1.2	491.0
1962	585.6	5.9	1.8	589.7	59.3	42.8	35.6	41.0	5.4	7.2	16.5	15.3	1.2	530.5
1963	617.7	6.5	2.1	622.2	62.4	44.9	37.5	43.5	6.0	7.5	17.5	16.2	1.3	559.8
1964	663.6	7.2	2.3	668.5	65.0	46.9	39.0	46.2	7.2	7.9	18.1	16.7	1.4	603.5
1965	719.1	7.9	2.6	724.4	69.4	50.5	41.9	49.5	7.6	8.5	18.9	17.4	1.5	655.0
1966	787.8	8.1	3.0	792.9	75.6	55.5	46.3	53.5	7.2	9.2	20.1	18.5	1.6	717.3
1967	832.6	8.7	3.3	838.0	81.5	59.9	50.0	57.9	7.8	9.9	21.6	19.8	1.8	756.5
1968	910.0	10.1	4.0	916.1	88.4	65.2	54.4	62.6	8.2	10.8	23.1	21.1	2.0	827.7
1969	984.6	11.8	5.7	990.7	97.9	73.1	61.2	68.9	7.7	12.0	24.8	22.6	2.2	892.8
1970	1 038.5	12.8	6.4	1 044.9	106.7	80.0	67.2	73.9	6.7	12.9	26.7	24.2	2.5	938.2
1971	1 127.1	14.0	6.4	1 134.7	115.0	86.7	72.5	79.5	6.9	14.2	28.3	25.5	2.8	1 019.7
1972	1 238.3	16.3	7.7	1 246.8	126.5	97.1	80.9	88.9	8.1	16.2	29.5	26.4	3.1	1 120.3
1973	1 382.7	23.5	10.9	1 395.3	139.3	107.9	89.9	97.0	7.1	18.0	31.4	27.8	3.5	1 256.0
1974	1 500.0	29.8	14.3	1 515.5	162.5	126.6	105.9	107.6	1.7	20.7	35.9	31.6	4.3	1 353.0
1975	1 638.3	28.0	15.0	1 651.3	187.7	147.8	124.4	118.5	-5.9	23.4	40.0	34.9	5.1	1 463.6
1976	1 825.3	32.4	15.5	1 842.1	205.2	162.5	136.9	128.6	-8.3	25.6	42.6	37.1	5.5	1 637.0
1977	2 030.9	37.2	16.9	2 051.2	230.0	184.3	155.3	146.2	-9.1	29.0	45.7	39.7	6.0	1 821.2
1978	2 294.7	46.3	24.7	2 316.3	262.3	212.8	179.3	165.5	-13.7	33.6	49.5	42.8	6.7	2 054.0
1979	2 563.3	68.3	36.4	2 595.3	300.1	245.7	206.9	190.0	-16.9	38.8	54.5	46.9	7.6	2 295.1
1980	2 789.5	79.1	44.9	2 823.7	343.0	281.1	236.8	217.1	-19.8	44.3	61.8	53.1	8.8	2 480.7
1981	3 128.4	92.0	59.1	3 161.4	388.1	317.9	268.9	269.3	0.4	49.0	70.1	60.2	10.0	2 773.3
1982	3 255.0	101.0	64.5	3 291.5	426.9	349.8	297.3	309.4	12.1	52.5	77.1	66.3	10.9	2 864.6
1983	3 536.7	101.9	64.8	3 573.8	443.8	362.1	307.4	347.8	40.4	54.7	81.7	70.2	11.5	3 130.0
1984	3 933.2	121.9	85.6	3 969.5	472.6	385.6	328.0	393.4	65.4	57.6	87.0	74.8	12.2	3 496.9
1985	4 220.3	112.4	85.9	4 246.8	506.7	414.0	353.0	445.4	92.4	61.0	92.7	79.8	12.9	3 740.1
1986	4 462.8	111.4	93.6	4 480.6	531.3	431.8	366.9	458.4	91.5	64.9	99.5	85.7	13.8	3 949.3
1987	4 739.5	123.2	105.3	4 757.4	561.9	455.3	385.7	475.1	89.4	69.5	106.7	92.1	14.6	4 195.4
1988	5 103.8	152.1	128.5	5 127.4	597.6	483.5	408.9	501.0	92.1	74.6	114.1	98.4	15.6	4 529.8
1989	5 484.4	177.7	151.5	5 510.6	644.3	522.1	440.6	523.1	82.5	81.5	122.2	105.3	16.9	4 866.3
1990	5 803.1	189.1	154.3	5 837.9	682.5	551.6	466.4	521.1	54.7	85.1	130.9	113.1	17.9	5 155.4
1991	5 995.9	168.9	138.5	6 026.3	725.9	586.9	497.4	530.1	32.7	89.5	139.1	120.2	18.8	5 300.4
1992	6 337.7	152.7	123.0	6 367.4	751.9	607.3	510.5	544.9	34.4	96.8	144.6	124.8	19.8	5 615.5
1993	6 657.4	156.2	124.3	6 689.3	776.4	624.7	524.6	569.3	44.7	100.1	151.8	130.6	21.1	5 912.9
1994	7 072.2	186.4	160.2	7 098.4	833.7	675.1	568.0	615.1	47.1	107.1	158.6	135.9	22.7	6 264.7
1995	7 397.7	233.9	198.1	7 433.4	878.4	713.4	600.2	651.8	51.6	113.2	165.0	141.4	23.6	6 555.1
1996	7 816.9	248.7	213.7	7 851.9	918.1	748.8	630.7	696.7	66.1	118.2	169.3	144.6	24.6	6 933.8
1997	8 304.3	286.7	253.7	8 337.3	974.4	800.3	675.2	756.5	81.3	125.1	174.1	148.2	25.9	7 362.8
1998	8 747.0	287.1	265.8	8 768.3	1 030.2	851.2	718.3	809.6	91.4	132.9	179.0	151.9	27.1	7 738.2
1999	9 268.4	320.8	287.0	9 302.2	1 101.3	914.3	769.8	883.6	113.7	144.5	187.0	158.4	28.6	8 200.9
2000	9 817.0	382.7	343.7	9 855.9	1 187.8	990.8	836.1	943.9	107.8	154.8	197.0	166.4	30.6	8 668.1
2001	10 128.0	322.4	278.8	10 171.6	1 281.5	1 075.5	903.7	1 028.7	124.9	171.7	206.0	172.7	33.3	8 890.2
2002	10 469.6	305.7	275.0	10 500.2	1 292.0	1 080.3	893.6	1 109.3	215.7	186.8	211.6	178.3	33.4	9 208.3
2003	10 960.8	336.8	280.0	11 017.6	1 335.5	1 118.3	916.6	1 123.6	207.0	201.7	218.2	183.2	35.0	9 681.1
2004	11 685.9	437.5	361.3	11 762.1	1 436.1	1 206.0	970.2	1 148.2	178.0	235.8	230.2	192.4	37.7	10 326.0
2005	12 421.9	573.5	480.5	12 514.9	1 612.0	1 359.7	1 062.3	987.8	-74.5	297.4	252.3	207.5	44.9	10 902.9
2006	13 178.4	725.4	647.1	13 256.6	1 623.9	1 356.0	1 085.5	1 006.1	-79.4	270.5	268.0	223.7	44.3	11 632.7
2007	13 807.5	861.7	759.3	13 910.0	1 720.5	1 431.1	1 147.0	1 055.5	-91.5	284.1	289.4	241.4	48.0	12 189.5
2008	14 264.6	798.3	665.1	14 397.8	1 832.3	1 523.1	1 225.0	1 305.6	80.5	298.1	309.2	258.1	51.1	12 565.5
2006														
1st quarter	12 959.6	661.9	582.4	13 039.2	1 582.7	1 323.1	1 059.8	997.9	-61.9	263.3	259.5	216.8	42.8	11 456.5
2nd quarter	13 134.1	720.0	634.8	13 219.4	1 612.5	1 346.8	1 077.8	1 002.7	-75.1	268.9	265.8	221.8	43.9	11 606.8
3rd quarter	13 249.6	745.9	679.4	13 316.1	1 638.3	1 367.8	1 094.5	1 008.5	-86.0	273.3	270.5	225.8	44.7	11 677.7
4th quarter	13 370.1	773.7	691.8	13 452.0	1 662.2	1 386.2	1 109.7	1 015.2	-94.5	276.5	275.9	230.2	45.7	11 789.8
2007														
1st quarter	13 510.9	788.2	715.8	13 583.3	1 684.3	1 402.1	1 123.6	1 043.8	-79.8	278.4	282.2	235.5	46.7	11 899.0
2nd quarter	13 737.6	852.8	793.2	13 797.2	1 707.0	1 420.0	1 138.5	1 051.6	-86.9	281.5	287.0	239.5	47.6	12 090.1
3rd quarter	13 950.6	898.5	786.3	14 062.8	1 731.9	1 440.1	1 154.4	1 059.4	-95.1	285.7	291.8	243.4	48.4	12 330.8
4th quarter	14 031.2	907.4	742.0	14 196.6	1 758.6	1 462.3	1 171.4	1 067.2	-104.2	290.9	296.3	247.1	49.2	12 438.0
2008														
1st quarter	14 150.8	843.2	705.1	14 289.0	1 778.0	1 477.5	1 186.1	1 286.0	100.0	291.4	300.5	250.8	49.7	12 511.1
2nd quarter	14 294.5	822.8	708.9	14 408.3	1 803.1	1 497.4	1 205.6	1 295.2	89.6	291.8	305.7	255.2	50.5	12 605.2
3rd quarter	14 412.8	815.6	688.7	14 539.6	1 898.1	1 585.9	1 266.0	1 323.6	57.6	320.0	312.1	260.6	51.5	12 641.6
4th quarter	14 200.3	711.6	557.7	14 354.3	1 850.1	1 531.7	1 242.5	1 317.5	75.0	289.2	318.4	265.8	52.6	12 504.2

Table 1-10. Relation of Gross Domestic Product, Gross and Net National Product, National Income, and Personal Income—*Continued*

(Billions of dollars, quarterly data are at seasonally adjusted annual rates.)   **NIPA Table 1.7.5**

Year and quarter	Net national product	Less: Statistical discrepancy	Equals: National income	Corporate profits with IVA and CCAdj	Taxes on production and imports less subsidies	Contributions for government social insurance	Net interest and miscellaneous payments on assets	Business current transfer payments, net	Current surplus of government enterprises	Wage accruals less disbursements	Personal income receipts on assets	Personal current transfer receipts	Equals: Personal income	Addendum: Gross national income
1950	265.8	1.4	264.4	36.0	22.4	5.5	3.2	0.9	. . .	0.0	18.6	14.0	229.0	293.8
1951	308.0	3.6	304.3	41.2	24.0	6.6	3.7	1.2	. . .	0.1	19.1	11.4	258.0	337.6
1952	324.6	2.8	321.8	39.3	26.7	6.9	4.1	1.3	. . .	0.0	19.9	11.9	275.4	357.5
1953	343.5	4.0	339.5	39.7	29.0	7.1	4.7	1.2	. . .	-0.1	21.6	12.5	291.9	377.2
1954	342.6	3.2	339.4	38.8	29.0	8.1	5.6	1.0	. . .	0.0	23.2	14.3	294.5	379.3
1955	375.1	2.5	372.7	49.5	31.7	9.1	6.2	1.4	. . .	0.0	25.7	15.7	316.1	414.8
1956	393.9	-1.7	395.6	48.5	33.9	10.0	6.9	1.7	. . .	0.0	28.2	16.8	339.6	441.9
1957	414.3	0.0	414.3	48.4	36.0	11.4	8.0	1.9	. . .	0.0	30.6	19.5	358.7	464.1
1958	417.8	1.0	416.8	43.5	36.8	11.4	9.5	1.8	. . .	0.0	31.9	23.5	369.0	468.8
1959	456.3	0.5	455.8	55.7	40.0	13.8	9.6	1.8	1.0	0.0	34.6	24.2	392.8	508.9
1960	473.9	-0.9	474.9	53.8	43.4	16.4	10.6	1.9	0.9	0.0	37.9	25.7	411.5	530.4
1961	491.0	-0.6	491.6	54.9	45.0	17.0	12.5	2.0	0.8	0.0	40.1	29.5	429.0	548.8
1962	530.5	0.4	530.1	63.3	48.2	19.1	14.2	2.2	0.9	0.0	44.1	30.4	456.7	589.4
1963	559.8	-0.8	560.6	69.0	51.2	21.7	15.2	2.7	1.4	0.0	47.9	32.2	479.6	623.0
1964	603.5	0.8	602.7	76.5	54.6	22.4	17.4	3.1	1.3	0.0	53.8	33.5	514.6	667.7
1965	655.0	1.6	653.4	87.5	57.8	23.4	19.6	3.6	1.3	0.0	59.4	36.2	555.7	722.8
1966	717.3	6.3	711.0	93.2	59.3	31.3	22.4	3.5	1.0	0.0	64.1	39.6	603.9	786.6
1967	756.5	4.6	751.9	91.3	64.2	34.9	25.5	3.8	0.9	0.0	69.0	48.0	648.3	833.4
1968	827.7	4.6	823.2	98.8	72.3	38.7	27.1	4.3	1.2	0.0	75.2	56.1	712.0	911.5
1969	892.8	3.2	889.7	95.4	79.4	44.1	32.7	4.9	1.0	0.0	84.1	62.3	778.5	987.6
1970	938.2	7.3	930.9	83.6	86.7	46.4	39.1	4.5	0.0	0.0	93.5	74.7	838.8	1 037.6
1971	1 019.7	11.6	1 008.1	98.0	95.9	51.2	43.9	4.3	-0.2	0.6	101.0	88.1	903.5	1 123.1
1972	1 120.3	9.1	1 111.2	112.1	101.4	59.2	47.9	4.9	0.5	0.0	109.6	97.9	992.7	1 237.7
1973	1 256.0	8.6	1 247.4	125.5	112.1	75.5	55.2	6.0	-0.4	-0.1	124.7	112.6	1 110.7	1 386.7
1974	1 353.0	10.9	1 342.1	115.8	121.7	85.2	70.8	7.1	-0.9	-0.5	146.4	133.3	1 222.6	1 504.6
1975	1 463.6	17.7	1 445.9	134.8	131.0	89.3	81.6	9.4	-3.2	0.1	162.2	170.0	1 335.0	1 633.6
1976	1 637.0	25.1	1 611.8	163.3	141.5	101.3	85.5	9.5	-1.8	0.1	178.4	184.0	1 474.8	1 817.0
1977	1 821.2	22.3	1 798.9	192.4	152.8	113.1	101.1	8.4	-2.6	0.1	205.3	194.2	1 633.2	2 028.9
1978	2 054.0	26.6	2 027.4	216.6	162.2	131.3	115.0	10.6	-1.9	0.3	234.8	209.6	1 837.7	2 289.7
1979	2 295.1	46.0	2 249.1	223.2	171.9	152.7	138.9	13.0	-2.6	-0.2	274.7	235.3	2 062.2	2 549.2
1980	2 480.7	41.4	2 439.3	201.1	190.9	166.2	181.8	14.4	-4.8	0.0	338.7	279.5	2 307.9	2 782.3
1981	2 773.3	30.9	2 742.4	226.1	224.5	195.7	232.3	17.6	-4.9	0.1	421.9	318.4	2 591.3	3 130.4
1982	2 864.6	0.3	2 864.3	209.7	226.4	208.9	271.1	20.1	-4.0	0.0	488.4	354.8	2 775.3	3 291.2
1983	3 130.0	45.7	3 084.2	264.2	242.5	226.0	285.3	22.5	-3.1	-0.4	529.6	383.7	2 960.7	3 528.0
1984	3 496.9	14.6	3 482.3	318.6	269.3	257.5	327.1	30.1	-1.9	0.2	607.9	400.1	3 289.5	3 954.9
1985	3 740.1	16.7	3 723.4	330.3	287.3	281.4	341.3	34.8	0.8	-0.2	654.0	424.9	3 526.7	4 230.1
1986	3 949.3	47.0	3 902.3	319.5	298.9	303.4	366.8	36.6	1.3	0.0	695.5	451.0	3 722.4	4 433.6
1987	4 195.4	21.7	4 173.7	368.8	317.7	323.1	366.4	33.8	1.2	0.0	717.0	467.6	3 947.4	4 735.7
1988	4 529.8	-19.5	4 549.4	432.6	345.5	361.5	385.3	34.0	2.5	0.0	769.3	496.6	4 253.7	5 147.0
1989	4 866.3	39.7	4 826.6	426.6	372.1	385.2	432.1	39.2	4.9	0.0	878.0	543.4	4 587.8	5 470.9
1990	5 155.4	66.2	5 089.1	437.8	398.7	410.1	442.2	39.4	1.6	0.1	924.0	595.2	4 878.6	5 771.6
1991	5 300.4	72.5	5 227.9	451.2	430.2	430.2	418.2	39.9	5.7	-0.1	932.0	666.4	5 051.0	5 953.8
1992	5 615.5	102.7	5 512.8	479.3	453.9	455.0	388.5	42.4	7.6	-15.8	910.9	749.4	5 362.0	6 264.7
1993	5 912.9	139.5	5 773.4	541.9	467.0	477.7	365.7	40.7	7.2	6.4	901.8	790.1	5 558.5	6 549.8
1994	6 264.7	142.5	6 122.3	600.3	513.5	508.2	366.4	43.3	8.6	17.6	950.8	827.3	5 842.5	6 955.9
1995	6 555.1	101.2	6 453.9	696.7	524.2	532.8	367.1	46.9	11.4	16.4	1 016.4	877.4	6 152.3	7 332.3
1996	6 933.8	93.7	6 840.1	786.2	546.8	555.2	376.2	53.1	12.7	3.6	1 089.2	925.0	6 520.6	7 758.2
1997	7 362.8	70.7	7 292.2	868.5	579.1	587.2	415.6	49.9	12.6	-2.9	1 181.7	951.2	6 915.1	8 266.6
1998	7 738.2	-14.6	7 752.8	801.6	604.4	624.2	487.1	64.7	10.3	-0.7	1 283.2	978.6	7 423.0	8 783.0
1999	8 200.9	-35.7	8 236.7	851.3	629.8	661.4	495.4	67.4	10.1	5.2	1 264.2	1 022.1	7 802.4	9 337.9
2000	8 668.1	-127.2	8 795.2	817.9	664.6	702.7	559.0	87.1	5.3	0.0	1 387.0	1 084.0	8 429.7	9 983.1
2001	8 890.2	-89.6	8 979.8	767.3	673.3	731.1	566.3	92.8	-1.4	0.0	1 380.0	1 193.9	8 724.1	10 261.3
2002	9 208.3	-21.0	9 229.3	886.3	724.4	750.0	520.9	84.3	0.9	0.0	1 333.2	1 286.2	8 881.9	10 521.2
2003	9 681.1	48.8	9 632.3	993.1	759.3	778.6	524.7	83.8	1.7	15.0	1 336.6	1 351.0	9 163.6	10 968.8
2004	10 326.0	19.1	10 306.8	1 231.2	819.2	828.8	491.2	83.0	-4.2	-15.0	1 432.1	1 422.5	9 727.2	11 742.9
2005	10 902.9	-71.2	10 974.0	1 447.9	868.9	874.3	569.1	70.0	-13.4	5.0	1 596.9	1 520.7	10 269.8	12 586.0
2006	11 632.7	-163.0	11 795.7	1 668.5	926.4	925.5	631.2	85.4	-8.6	1.3	1 824.8	1 603.0	10 993.9	13 419.7
2007	12 189.5	-81.4	12 270.9	1 642.4	963.2	965.1	664.4	100.2	-7.9	-6.3	2 000.1	1 713.3	11 663.2	13 991.4
2008	12 565.5	135.8	12 429.7	1 476.5	983.1	996.0	682.7	103.6	-8.1	0.0	2 037.7	1 869.1	12 102.6	14 262.0
2006														
1st quarter	11 456.5	-154.6	11 611.1	1 634.2	908.5	917.1	615.5	85.1	-7.8	-20.0	1 735.4	1 567.6	10 781.6	13 193.8
2nd quarter	11 606.8	-131.7	11 738.5	1 681.6	923.8	918.9	629.7	83.5	-8.3	0.0	1 809.5	1 594.5	10 913.2	13 351.0
3rd quarter	11 677.7	-170.8	11 848.6	1 713.8	932.0	925.5	630.1	86.0	-9.1	0.0	1 865.8	1 620.1	11 056.1	13 486.9
4th quarter	11 789.8	-194.9	11 984.7	1 644.5	941.5	940.4	649.3	86.8	-9.2	25.0	1 888.6	1 629.8	11 224.7	13 646.9
2007														
1st quarter	11 899.0	-188.4	12 087.4	1 617.8	955.2	959.8	645.8	98.3	-10.8	-25.0	1 930.9	1 695.7	11 473.0	13 771.7
2nd quarter	12 090.1	-143.4	12 233.6	1 672.5	956.4	959.1	660.8	97.4	-8.5	0.0	1 982.5	1 699.2	11 577.5	13 940.6
3rd quarter	12 330.8	-7.8	12 338.6	1 668.3	965.7	966.0	663.0	102.2	-5.5	0.0	2 030.9	1 720.6	11 730.4	14 070.6
4th quarter	12 438.0	13.9	12 424.1	1 611.1	975.3	975.3	688.1	103.1	-6.7	0.0	2 056.2	1 737.8	11 872.1	14 182.7
2008														
1st quarter	12 511.1	63.4	12 447.6	1 593.5	975.1	992.2	662.3	103.2	-7.1	0.0	2 054.1	1 778.1	11 960.5	14 225.6
2nd quarter	12 605.2	136.6	12 468.6	1 533.3	988.5	995.4	683.4	102.1	-7.7	0.0	2 052.3	1 926.3	12 152.2	14 271.7
3rd quarter	12 641.6	150.2	12 491.4	1 514.8	993.8	1 000.0	656.6	92.1	-8.0	0.0	2 055.7	1 872.7	12 170.4	14 389.4
4th quarter	12 504.2	193.0	12 311.2	1 264.5	974.9	996.4	728.6	116.8	-9.6	0.0	1 988.5	1 899.3	12 127.5	14 161.3

. . . = Not available.

Table 1-11. Gross Domestic Income by Type of Income

(Billions of dollars, quarterly data are at seasonally adjusted annual rates.)   **NIPA Tables 1.1.5, 1.10**

Year and quarter	Gross domestic income	Compensation of employees, paid			Taxes on production and imports	Less: Subsidies	Net operating surplus	Private enterprises				
		Total	Wage and salary accruals	Supplements to wages and salaries			Total	Total	Net interest and miscellaneous payments, domestic industries	Business current transfer payments, net	Proprietors' income with IVA and CCAdj	Rental income of persons with CCAdj
1950	292.4	155.2	147.2	8.0	23.0	0.6	. . .	85.4	3.1	0.9	37.6	9.2
1951	335.7	181.4	171.6	9.8	24.8	0.7	. . .	97.0	3.5	1.2	42.7	10.1
1952	355.6	196.2	185.6	10.5	27.1	0.4	. . .	97.0	4.0	1.3	43.1	11.2
1953	375.3	210.2	199.0	11.2	29.1	0.1	. . .	98.4	4.6	1.2	42.1	12.5
1954	377.2	209.2	197.3	11.9	28.9	-0.1	. . .	99.1	5.4	1.0	42.3	13.5
1955	412.3	225.8	212.2	13.5	31.5	-0.2	. . .	112.8	6.1	1.4	44.3	13.9
1956	439.2	244.6	229.1	15.5	34.3	0.4	. . .	114.3	6.8	1.7	45.8	14.2
1957	461.1	257.6	240.0	17.6	36.6	0.7	. . .	117.6	8.0	1.9	47.9	14.6
1958	466.2	259.6	241.4	18.2	37.7	0.9	. . .	117.7	9.4	1.8	50.1	15.4
1959	506.1	281.1	259.9	21.1	41.1	1.1	132.0	131.0	9.5	1.8	50.7	16.2
1960	527.3	296.6	273.0	23.6	44.6	1.1	131.8	130.8	10.4	1.9	50.8	17.1
1961	545.3	305.4	280.7	24.8	47.0	2.0	137.6	136.8	12.1	2.0	53.2	17.9
1962	585.3	327.2	299.5	27.8	50.4	2.3	150.6	149.7	13.8	2.2	55.4	18.8
1963	618.5	345.3	314.9	30.4	53.4	2.2	159.6	158.3	14.7	2.7	56.5	19.5
1964	662.8	370.7	337.8	32.9	57.3	2.7	172.4	171.1	16.9	3.1	59.4	19.6
1965	717.5	399.5	363.8	35.7	60.8	3.0	190.9	189.6	19.1	3.6	63.9	20.2
1966	781.5	442.6	400.3	42.3	63.3	3.9	204.0	203.0	21.9	3.5	68.2	20.8
1967	828.0	475.1	429.0	46.1	68.0	3.8	207.2	206.2	24.9	3.8	69.8	21.2
1968	905.4	524.3	472.0	52.3	76.5	4.2	220.5	219.3	26.7	4.3	74.3	20.9
1969	981.4	577.6	518.3	59.3	84.0	4.5	226.5	225.5	33.2	4.9	77.4	21.2
1970	1 031.2	617.2	551.5	65.7	91.5	4.8	220.6	220.6	39.9	4.5	78.4	21.4
1971	1 115.5	658.9	584.5	74.4	100.6	4.7	245.7	245.9	44.2	4.3	84.8	22.4
1972	1 229.2	725.1	638.8	86.4	108.1	6.6	276.1	275.6	48.9	4.9	95.9	23.4
1973	1 374.1	811.2	708.8	102.5	117.3	5.2	311.4	311.8	57.5	6.0	113.5	24.3
1974	1 489.1	890.3	772.3	118.0	125.0	3.3	314.6	315.6	72.7	7.1	113.1	24.3
1975	1 620.6	949.2	814.9	134.3	135.5	4.5	352.7	356.0	83.2	9.4	119.5	23.7
1976	1 800.1	1 059.4	899.8	159.6	146.6	5.1	394.1	396.0	85.2	9.5	132.2	22.3
1977	2 008.7	1 180.6	994.2	186.4	159.9	7.1	445.3	447.9	99.8	8.4	145.7	20.7
1978	2 268.1	1 336.2	1 121.3	214.9	171.2	8.9	507.4	509.3	116.2	10.6	166.6	22.1
1979	2 517.3	1 500.8	1 255.9	245.0	180.4	8.5	544.4	547.0	141.5	13.0	180.1	23.8
1980	2 748.1	1 651.9	1 377.7	274.2	200.7	9.8	562.3	567.2	183.0	14.4	174.1	30.0
1981	3 097.5	1 826.0	1 517.7	308.3	236.0	11.5	658.9	663.9	228.9	17.6	183.0	38.0
1982	3 254.7	1 926.0	1 593.9	332.1	241.3	15.0	675.4	679.4	267.0	20.1	176.3	38.8
1983	3 490.9	2 042.8	1 684.8	358.0	263.7	21.2	761.9	765.0	283.1	22.5	192.5	37.8
1984	3 918.6	2 255.8	1 855.3	400.5	290.2	21.0	920.9	922.8	327.1	30.1	243.3	40.2
1985	4 203.6	2 424.9	1 995.7	429.2	308.5	21.3	984.7	983.9	352.6	34.8	262.3	41.9
1986	4 415.8	2 571.9	2 116.6	455.3	323.7	24.8	1 013.7	1 012.4	386.6	36.6	275.7	33.5
1987	4 717.8	2 751.6	2 272.1	479.5	347.9	30.2	1 086.6	1 085.4	395.1	33.8	302.2	33.5
1988	5 123.3	2 968.1	2 453.8	514.2	374.9	29.4	1 212.1	1 209.6	417.8	34.0	341.6	40.6
1989	5 444.7	3 146.5	2 597.6	548.9	399.3	27.2	1 281.8	1 276.9	471.7	39.2	363.3	43.1
1990	5 736.8	3 340.5	2 756.3	584.2	425.5	26.8	1 315.1	1 313.5	481.1	39.4	380.6	50.7
1991	5 923.4	3 448.0	2 825.7	622.3	457.5	27.3	1 319.3	1 313.6	461.6	39.9	377.1	60.3
1992	6 235.0	3 638.4	2 967.5	670.9	483.8	29.9	1 390.8	1 383.2	428.9	42.4	427.6	78.0
1993	6 517.9	3 804.7	3 092.5	712.2	503.4	36.4	1 469.7	1 462.4	407.4	40.7	453.8	95.6
1994	6 929.7	4 001.2	3 253.8	747.5	545.6	32.2	1 581.3	1 572.8	413.3	43.3	473.3	119.7
1995	7 296.5	4 197.4	3 439.8	757.7	558.2	34.0	1 696.4	1 685.0	420.0	46.9	492.1	122.1
1996	7 723.2	4 394.7	3 627.3	767.3	581.1	34.3	1 863.6	1 850.9	438.9	53.1	543.2	131.5
1997	8 233.7	4 666.1	3 879.1	787.0	612.0	32.9	2 014.1	2 001.5	489.2	49.9	576.0	128.8
1998	8 761.6	5 023.9	4 187.3	836.7	639.8	35.4	2 103.1	2 092.8	564.1	64.7	627.8	137.5
1999	9 304.1	5 362.3	4 476.6	885.7	674.0	44.2	2 210.7	2 200.6	577.9	67.4	678.3	147.3
2000	9 944.1	5 787.3	4 833.8	953.4	708.9	44.3	2 304.5	2 299.1	661.2	87.1	728.4	150.3
2001	10 217.6	5 947.2	4 947.9	999.3	728.6	55.3	2 315.6	2 317.0	687.2	92.8	771.9	167.4
2002	10 490.6	6 096.6	4 986.3	1 110.3	762.8	38.4	2 377.6	2 376.8	640.7	84.3	768.4	152.9
2003	10 912.0	6 331.1	5 133.4	1 197.7	807.2	47.9	2 485.1	2 483.4	627.6	83.8	811.3	133.0
2004	11 666.8	6 662.5	5 385.7	1 276.9	863.8	44.6	2 748.9	2 753.1	602.3	83.0	911.6	118.4
2005	12 493.0	7 037.2	5 683.1	1 354.1	928.2	59.3	2 974.9	2 988.3	709.1	70.0	959.8	40.9
2006	13 341.4	7 440.4	6 035.1	1 405.3	976.2	49.7	3 350.6	3 359.2	813.8	85.4	1 014.7	44.3
2007	13 889.0	7 819.4	6 362.8	1 456.6	1 015.6	52.3	3 386.0	3 393.9	899.6	100.2	1 056.2	40.0
2008	14 128.8	8 062.3	6 557.4	1 504.9	1 033.8	50.7	3 251.1	3 259.2	928.8	103.6	1 072.4	64.4
2006												
1st quarter	13 114.3	7 324.6	5 933.0	1 391.6	962.7	54.2	3 298.5	3 306.4	780.0	85.1	1 004.7	52.8
2nd quarter	13 265.8	7 370.7	5 972.7	1 398.0	973.6	49.8	3 358.8	3 367.1	807.7	83.5	1 018.3	45.6
3rd quarter	13 420.4	7 448.5	6 040.7	1 407.8	980.1	48.2	3 401.6	3 410.8	817.6	86.0	1 013.4	40.4
4th quarter	13 565.0	7 618.0	6 194.1	1 423.9	988.3	46.8	3 343.4	3 352.6	850.0	86.8	1 022.4	38.2
2007												
1st quarter	13 699.3	7 715.6	6 275.6	1 440.0	1 002.7	47.5	3 344.2	3 355.1	864.8	98.3	1 037.2	35.1
2nd quarter	13 881.0	7 767.2	6 317.7	1 449.4	1 012.3	55.9	3 450.3	3 458.8	897.0	97.4	1 050.2	44.6
3rd quarter	13 958.4	7 846.4	6 384.8	1 461.6	1 019.2	53.5	3 414.4	3 419.9	900.1	102.2	1 063.8	41.8
4th quarter	14 017.4	7 948.3	6 472.8	1 475.5	1 027.7	52.3	3 335.2	3 341.9	936.7	103.1	1 073.8	38.6
2008												
1st quarter	14 087.4	8 017.0	6 525.2	1 491.7	1 025.8	50.6	3 317.4	3 324.5	915.4	103.2	1 071.7	39.1
2nd quarter	14 157.8	8 040.7	6 538.5	1 502.2	1 039.4	50.8	3 325.5	3 333.3	935.8	102.1	1 076.9	58.6
3rd quarter	14 262.6	8 100.2	6 589.1	1 511.1	1 044.1	50.3	3 270.6	3 278.6	901.0	92.1	1 080.5	68.5
4th quarter	14 007.3	8 091.6	6 576.9	1 514.7	1 026.1	51.2	3 090.8	3 100.4	963.1	116.8	1 060.6	91.4

. . . = Not available.

Table 1-11. Gross Domestic Income by Type of Income—*Continued*

(Billions of dollars, quarterly data are at seasonally adjusted annual rates.)

NIPA Tables 1.1.5, 1.10

Year and quarter	Net operating surplus—*Continued*						Consumption of fixed capital			Statistical discrepancy	Gross domestic product
	Private enterprises—*Continued*					Current surplus of government enterprises	Total	Private	Government		
	Corporate profits with IVA and CCAdj, domestic industries										
	Total	Taxes on corporate income	Profits after tax								
			Total	Net dividends	Undistributed corporate profits						
1950	34.7	17.9	16.8	7.9	9.0	. . .	29.4	21.5	8.0	1.4	293.8
1951	39.5	22.6	16.9	7.4	9.5	. . .	33.2	24.6	8.7	3.6	339.3
1952	37.4	19.4	18.0	7.5	10.5	. . .	35.7	26.1	9.6	2.8	358.3
1953	37.9	20.3	17.6	7.8	9.9	. . .	37.8	27.3	10.5	4.0	379.4
1954	36.9	17.6	19.3	7.9	11.4	. . .	39.9	28.7	11.2	3.2	380.4
1955	47.2	22.0	25.1	8.9	16.2	. . .	42.1	30.3	11.8	2.5	414.8
1956	45.7	22.0	23.7	9.5	14.2	. . .	46.4	33.6	12.8	-1.7	437.5
1957	45.3	21.4	23.8	9.9	14.0	. . .	49.9	36.3	13.6	0.0	461.1
1958	41.0	19.0	22.0	9.8	12.2	. . .	52.0	38.1	13.9	1.0	467.2
1959	53.0	23.7	29.2	10.7	18.5	1.0	53.0	38.6	14.5	0.5	506.6
1960	50.6	22.8	27.9	11.4	16.4	0.9	55.6	40.5	15.0	-0.9	526.4
1961	51.5	22.9	28.6	11.5	17.1	0.8	57.2	41.6	15.6	-0.6	544.7
1962	59.5	24.1	35.4	12.4	23.0	0.9	59.3	42.8	16.5	0.4	585.6
1963	64.9	26.4	38.5	13.6	25.0	1.4	62.4	44.9	17.5	-0.8	617.7
1964	72.0	28.2	43.8	15.0	28.9	1.3	65.0	46.9	18.1	0.8	663.6
1965	82.8	31.1	51.7	16.9	34.8	1.3	69.4	50.5	18.9	1.6	719.1
1966	88.7	33.9	54.8	17.8	37.0	1.0	75.6	55.5	20.1	6.3	787.8
1967	86.6	32.9	53.7	18.3	35.3	0.9	81.5	59.9	21.6	4.6	832.6
1968	93.2	39.6	53.5	20.2	33.4	1.2	88.4	65.2	23.1	4.6	910.0
1969	88.8	40.0	48.8	20.4	28.4	1.0	97.9	73.1	24.8	3.2	984.6
1970	76.5	34.8	41.8	20.4	21.4	0.0	106.7	80.0	26.7	7.3	1 038.5
1971	90.2	38.2	52.0	20.3	31.7	-0.2	115.0	86.7	28.3	11.6	1 127.1
1972	102.6	42.3	60.2	21.9	38.3	0.5	126.5	97.1	29.5	9.1	1 238.3
1973	110.6	50.0	60.6	23.1	37.5	-0.4	139.3	107.9	31.4	8.6	1 382.7
1974	98.3	52.8	45.5	23.5	22.1	-0.9	162.5	126.6	35.9	10.9	1 500.0
1975	120.2	51.6	68.6	26.4	42.2	-3.2	187.7	147.8	40.0	17.7	1 638.3
1976	146.8	65.3	81.5	30.1	51.4	-1.8	205.2	162.5	42.6	25.1	1 825.3
1977	173.3	74.4	98.9	33.7	65.2	-2.6	230.0	184.3	45.7	22.3	2 030.9
1978	193.8	84.9	108.9	39.6	69.3	-1.9	262.3	212.8	49.5	26.6	2 294.7
1979	188.6	90.0	98.6	41.5	57.1	-2.6	300.1	245.7	54.5	46.0	2 563.3
1980	165.7	87.2	78.5	47.3	31.1	-4.8	343.0	281.1	61.8	41.4	2 789.5
1981	196.4	84.3	112.1	58.3	53.8	-4.9	388.1	317.9	70.1	30.9	3 128.4
1982	177.1	66.5	110.6	61.3	49.2	-4.0	426.9	349.8	77.1	0.3	3 255.0
1983	229.2	80.6	148.5	71.3	77.2	-3.1	443.8	362.1	81.7	45.7	3 536.7
1984	282.0	97.5	184.5	78.5	106.0	-1.9	472.6	385.6	87.0	14.6	3 933.2
1985	292.2	99.4	192.8	85.7	107.1	0.8	506.7	414.0	92.7	16.7	4 220.3
1986	280.0	109.7	170.4	88.3	82.1	1.3	531.3	431.8	99.5	47.0	4 462.8
1987	320.8	130.4	190.4	95.6	94.8	1.2	561.9	455.3	106.7	21.7	4 739.5
1988	375.7	141.6	234.0	98.0	136.0	2.5	597.6	483.5	114.1	-19.5	5 103.8
1989	359.5	146.1	213.4	126.4	87.0	4.9	644.3	522.1	122.2	39.7	5 484.4
1990	361.7	145.4	216.3	144.1	72.2	1.6	682.5	551.6	130.9	66.2	5 803.1
1991	374.7	138.6	236.1	156.4	79.8	5.7	725.9	586.9	139.1	72.5	5 995.9
1992	406.2	148.7	257.5	159.9	97.7	7.6	751.9	607.3	144.6	102.7	6 337.7
1993	465.0	171.0	294.0	182.2	111.7	7.2	776.4	624.7	151.8	139.5	6 657.4
1994	523.2	193.7	329.5	197.4	132.0	8.6	833.7	675.1	158.6	142.5	7 072.2
1995	603.9	218.7	385.2	221.6	163.7	11.4	878.4	713.4	165.0	101.2	7 397.7
1996	684.3	231.7	452.6	257.3	195.3	12.7	918.1	748.8	169.3	93.7	7 816.9
1997	757.5	246.1	511.5	283.9	227.6	12.6	974.4	800.3	174.1	70.7	8 304.3
1998	698.7	248.3	450.4	309.2	141.2	10.3	1 030.2	851.2	179.0	-14.6	8 747.0
1999	729.8	258.6	471.1	295.7	175.5	10.1	1 101.3	914.3	187.0	-35.7	9 268.4
2000	672.2	265.2	407.0	348.4	58.6	5.3	1 187.8	990.8	197.0	-127.2	9 817.0
2001	597.6	204.1	393.5	330.1	63.4	-1.4	1 281.5	1 075.5	206.0	-89.6	10 128.0
2002	730.5	192.6	537.9	351.3	186.5	0.9	1 292.0	1 080.3	211.6	-21.0	10 469.6
2003	827.7	243.3	584.4	392.8	191.6	1.7	1 336.5	1 118.3	218.2	48.8	10 960.8
2004	1 037.8	307.4	730.5	491.7	238.8	-4.2	1 436.1	1 206.0	230.2	19.1	11 685.9
2005	1 208.5	413.7	794.8	316.5	478.3	-13.4	1 612.0	1 359.7	252.3	-71.2	12 421.9
2006	1 401.0	468.9	932.1	628.8	303.3	-8.6	1 623.9	1 356.0	268.0	-163.0	13 178.4
2007	1 297.8	450.4	847.4	671.1	176.3	-7.9	1 720.5	1 431.1	289.4	-81.4	13 807.5
2008	1 090.0	366.6	723.3	663.9	59.4	-8.1	1 832.3	1 523.1	309.2	135.8	14 264.6
2006											
1st quarter	1 383.7	453.8	929.9	548.2	381.6	-7.8	1 582.7	1 323.1	259.5	-154.6	12 959.6
2nd quarter	1 412.0	474.8	937.1	583.1	354.0	-8.3	1 612.5	1 346.8	265.8	-131.7	13 134.1
3rd quarter	1 453.3	487.2	966.0	642.9	323.1	-9.1	1 638.3	1 367.8	270.5	-170.8	13 249.6
4th quarter	1 355.1	459.8	895.4	740.9	154.5	-9.2	1 662.2	1 386.2	275.9	-194.9	13 370.1
2007											
1st quarter	1 319.7	448.5	871.2	653.8	217.5	-10.8	1 684.3	1 402.1	282.2	-188.4	13 510.9
2nd quarter	1 369.7	468.5	901.1	661.7	239.4	-8.5	1 707.0	1 420.0	287.0	-143.4	13 737.5
3rd quarter	1 311.9	451.1	860.8	662.2	198.6	-5.5	1 731.9	1 440.1	291.8	-7.8	13 950.6
4th quarter	1 189.7	433.5	756.3	706.6	49.7	-6.7	1 758.6	1 462.3	296.3	13.9	14 031.2
2008											
1st quarter	1 195.1	402.9	792.1	654.9	137.2	-7.1	1 778.0	1 477.5	300.5	63.4	14 150.8
2nd quarter	1 159.8	406.8	753.0	681.6	71.4	-7.7	1 803.1	1 497.4	305.7	136.6	14 294.5
3rd quarter	1 136.4	393.5	742.9	647.3	95.6	-8.0	1 898.1	1 585.9	312.1	150.2	14 412.8
4th quarter	868.6	263.2	605.3	671.8	-66.5	-9.6	1 850.1	1 531.7	318.4	193.0	14 200.3

. . . = Not available.

Table 1-12. National Income by Type of Income

(Billions of dollars, quarterly data are at seasonally adjusted annual rates.)   **NIPA Tables 1.7.5, 1.12**

Year and quarter	National income, total	Compensation of employees								Proprietors' income with IVA and CCAdj			Rental income of persons with CCAdj
		Total	Wage and salary accruals			Supplements to wages and salaries				Total	Farm	Nonfarm	
			Total	Government	Other	Total	Employer contributions for:						
							Employee pension and insurance funds	Government social insurance					
1950	264.4	155.3	147.3	22.6	124.6	8.0	4.7	3.4		37.6	12.9	24.7	9.2
1951	304.3	181.4	171.6	29.2	142.4	9.8	5.7	4.1		42.7	15.3	27.4	10.1
1952	321.8	196.2	185.6	33.4	152.3	10.5	6.4	4.1		43.1	14.3	28.8	11.2
1953	339.5	210.2	199.0	34.3	164.7	11.2	7.0	4.2		42.1	12.1	30.0	12.5
1954	339.4	209.2	197.3	34.9	162.4	11.9	7.3	4.6		42.3	11.7	30.6	13.5
1955	372.7	225.7	212.2	36.6	175.6	13.5	8.4	5.2		44.3	10.6	33.7	13.9
1956	395.6	244.5	229.0	38.8	190.2	15.5	9.8	5.7		45.8	10.5	35.4	14.2
1957	414.3	257.5	240.0	41.0	198.9	17.6	11.2	6.4		47.9	10.4	37.4	14.6
1958	416.8	259.5	241.3	44.1	197.2	18.2	11.9	6.3		50.1	12.3	37.8	15.4
1959	455.8	281.0	259.8	46.1	213.8	21.1	13.3	7.9		50.7	10.0	40.6	16.2
1960	474.9	296.4	272.9	49.2	223.7	23.6	14.3	9.3		50.8	10.5	40.3	17.1
1961	491.6	305.3	280.5	52.5	228.0	24.8	15.2	9.6		53.2	11.0	42.2	17.9
1962	530.1	327.1	299.4	56.3	243.0	27.8	16.6	11.2		55.4	11.0	44.4	18.8
1963	560.6	345.2	314.9	60.0	254.8	30.4	18.0	12.4		56.5	10.8	45.7	19.5
1964	602.7	370.7	337.8	64.9	272.9	32.9	20.3	12.6		59.4	9.6	49.8	19.6
1965	653.4	399.5	363.8	69.9	293.8	35.7	22.7	13.1		63.9	11.8	52.1	20.2
1966	711.0	442.7	400.3	78.4	321.9	42.3	25.5	16.8		68.2	12.8	55.4	20.8
1967	751.9	475.1	429.0	86.5	342.5	46.1	28.1	18.0		69.8	11.5	58.4	21.2
1968	823.2	524.3	472.0	96.7	375.3	52.3	32.4	20.0		74.3	11.5	62.8	20.9
1969	889.7	577.6	518.3	105.6	412.7	59.3	36.5	22.8		77.4	12.6	64.7	21.2
1970	930.9	617.2	551.6	117.2	434.3	65.7	41.8	23.8		78.4	12.7	65.7	21.4
1971	1 008.1	658.9	584.5	126.8	457.8	74.4	47.9	26.4		84.8	13.2	71.6	22.4
1972	1 111.2	725.1	638.8	137.9	500.9	86.4	55.2	31.2		95.9	16.8	79.1	23.4
1973	1 247.4	811.2	708.8	148.8	560.0	102.5	62.7	39.8		113.5	28.9	84.6	24.3
1974	1 342.1	890.2	772.3	160.5	611.8	118.0	73.3	44.7		113.1	23.2	89.9	24.3
1975	1 445.9	949.1	814.8	176.2	638.6	134.3	87.6	46.7		119.5	21.7	97.8	23.7
1976	1 611.8	1 059.3	899.7	188.9	710.8	159.6	105.2	54.4		132.2	17.0	115.2	22.3
1977	1 798.9	1 180.5	994.2	202.6	791.6	186.4	125.3	61.1		145.7	15.7	130.0	20.7
1978	2 027.4	1 336.1	1 121.2	220.0	901.2	214.9	143.4	71.5		166.6	19.6	147.1	22.1
1979	2 249.1	1 500.8	1 255.8	237.1	1 018.7	245.0	162.4	82.6		180.1	21.8	158.3	23.8
1980	2 439.3	1 651.8	1 377.6	261.5	1 116.2	274.2	185.2	88.9		174.1	11.3	162.8	30.0
1981	2 742.4	1 825.8	1 517.5	285.8	1 231.7	308.3	204.7	103.6		183.0	18.7	164.3	38.0
1982	2 864.3	1 925.8	1 593.7	307.5	1 286.2	332.1	222.4	109.8		176.3	13.1	163.3	38.8
1983	3 084.2	2 042.6	1 684.6	324.8	1 359.8	358.0	238.1	119.9		192.5	6.0	186.5	37.8
1984	3 482.3	2 255.6	1 855.1	348.1	1 507.0	400.5	261.5	139.0		243.3	20.6	222.7	40.2
1985	3 723.4	2 424.7	1 995.5	373.9	1 621.6	429.2	281.5	147.7		262.3	20.8	241.5	41.9
1986	3 902.3	2 570.1	2 114.8	397.0	1 717.9	455.3	297.5	157.9		275.7	22.6	253.1	33.5
1987	4 173.7	2 750.2	2 270.7	422.6	1 848.1	479.5	313.2	166.3		302.2	28.7	273.5	33.5
1988	4 549.4	2 967.2	2 452.9	451.3	2 001.6	514.2	329.6	184.6		341.6	26.8	314.7	40.6
1989	4 826.6	3 145.2	2 596.3	480.2	2 116.2	548.9	355.2	193.7		363.3	33.0	330.3	43.1
1990	5 089.1	3 338.2	2 754.0	517.7	2 236.3	584.2	377.8	206.5		380.6	31.9	348.7	50.7
1991	5 227.9	3 445.2	2 823.0	546.8	2 276.2	622.3	407.1	215.1		377.1	26.7	350.4	60.3
1992	5 512.8	3 635.4	2 964.5	569.2	2 395.3	670.9	442.5	228.4		427.6	34.5	393.0	78.0
1993	5 773.4	3 801.4	3 089.2	586.8	2 502.4	712.2	472.4	239.8		453.8	31.2	422.6	95.6
1994	6 122.3	3 997.2	3 249.8	606.2	2 643.5	747.5	493.3	254.1		473.3	33.9	439.4	119.7
1995	6 453.9	4 193.3	3 435.7	625.5	2 810.2	757.7	493.6	264.0		492.1	22.7	469.5	122.1
1996	6 840.1	4 390.5	3 623.2	644.4	2 978.8	767.3	492.5	274.9		543.2	37.3	505.9	131.5
1997	7 292.2	4 661.7	3 874.7	668.1	3 206.6	787.0	497.5	289.5		576.0	34.2	541.8	128.8
1998	7 752.8	5 019.4	4 182.7	697.3	3 485.5	836.7	529.7	307.0		627.8	29.4	598.4	137.5
1999	8 236.7	5 357.1	4 471.4	729.3	3 742.1	885.7	562.4	323.3		678.3	28.6	649.7	147.3
2000	8 795.2	5 782.7	4 829.2	774.7	4 054.5	953.4	609.9	343.5		728.4	22.7	705.7	150.3
2001	8 979.8	5 942.1	4 942.8	815.9	4 126.9	999.3	642.7	356.6		771.9	19.7	752.2	167.4
2002	9 229.3	6 091.2	4 980.9	865.9	4 115.0	1 110.3	745.1	365.2		768.4	10.6	757.8	152.9
2003	9 632.3	6 325.4	5 127.7	904.4	4 223.3	1 197.7	815.6	382.1		811.3	29.2	782.1	133.0
2004	10 306.8	6 656.4	5 379.5	943.1	4 436.4	1 276.9	868.5	408.3		911.6	37.3	874.3	118.4
2005	10 974.0	7 030.8	5 676.7	980.7	4 695.9	1 354.1	926.0	428.1		959.8	34.1	925.7	40.9
2006	11 795.7	7 433.8	6 028.5	1 023.0	5 005.5	1 405.3	956.8	448.5		1 014.7	16.2	998.6	44.3
2007	12 270.9	7 812.3	6 355.7	1 075.2	5 280.5	1 456.6	991.9	464.7		1 056.2	44.0	1 012.2	40.0
2008	12 429.7	8 055.1	6 550.1	1 129.5	5 420.6	1 504.9	1 026.9	478.0		1 072.4	34.6	1 037.9	64.4
2006													
1st quarter	11 611.1	7 318.0	5 926.4	1 007.7	4 918.7	1 391.6	946.6	445.0		1 004.7	17.3	987.5	52.8
2nd quarter	11 738.5	7 364.2	5 966.2	1 013.2	4 953.0	1 398.0	952.9	445.1		1 018.3	9.8	1 008.4	45.6
3rd quarter	11 848.6	7 441.9	6 034.2	1 029.4	5 004.8	1 407.8	959.5	448.2		1 013.4	13.8	999.6	40.4
4th quarter	11 984.7	7 611.1	6 187.2	1 041.9	5 145.3	1 423.9	968.1	455.8		1 022.4	23.7	998.7	38.2
2007													
1st quarter	12 087.4	7 709.0	6 269.0	1 059.9	5 209.0	1 440.0	977.6	462.3		1 037.2	39.3	997.9	35.1
2nd quarter	12 233.6	7 760.1	6 310.7	1 068.1	5 242.5	1 449.4	987.7	461.7		1 050.2	42.3	1 007.9	44.6
3rd quarter	12 338.6	7 839.3	6 377.7	1 080.8	5 297.0	1 461.6	996.5	465.1		1 063.8	47.4	1 016.4	41.8
4th quarter	12 424.1	7 941.0	6 465.5	1 092.1	5 373.4	1 475.5	1 005.9	469.6		1 073.8	47.1	1 026.7	38.6
2008													
1st quarter	12 447.6	8 009.7	6 518.0	1 109.7	5 408.3	1 491.7	1 015.3	476.4		1 071.7	41.6	1 030.1	39.1
2nd quarter	12 468.6	8 033.5	6 531.3	1 123.4	5 407.9	1 502.2	1 024.4	477.8		1 076.9	38.0	1 039.0	58.6
3rd quarter	12 491.4	8 092.9	6 581.8	1 138.3	5 443.5	1 511.1	1 031.2	479.9		1 080.5	32.4	1 048.2	68.5
4th quarter	12 311.2	8 084.1	6 569.4	1 146.7	5 422.8	1 514.7	1 036.7	478.0		1 060.6	26.3	1 034.2	91.4

Table 1-12. National Income by Type of Income—*Continued*

(Billions of dollars, quarterly data are at seasonally adjusted annual rates.)   **NIPA Tables 1.7.5, 1.12**

| Year and quarter | Corporate profits with IVA and CCAdj | | | | | Net interest and miscellaneous payments | Taxes on production and imports | Less: Subsidies | Business current transfer payments, net | | | Current surplus of government enterprises | Addendum: Net national factor income |
| | Total | Taxes on corporate income | Profits after tax | | | | | | Total [1] | To persons | To government | | |
			Total	Net dividends	Undistributed corporate profits								
1950	36.0	17.9	18.1	8.8	9.3	3.2	23.0	0.6	0.9	0.6	0.3	. . .	241.2
1951	41.2	22.6	18.6	8.6	10.1	3.7	24.8	0.7	1.2	0.9	0.3	. . .	279.1
1952	39.3	19.4	19.9	8.6	11.3	4.1	27.1	0.4	1.3	0.9	0.4	. . .	293.9
1953	39.7	20.3	19.4	8.9	10.6	4.7	29.1	0.1	1.2	0.8	0.4	. . .	309.3
1954	38.8	17.6	21.2	9.3	11.9	5.6	28.9	-0.1	1.0	0.6	0.4	. . .	309.4
1955	49.5	22.0	27.5	10.5	17.0	6.2	31.5	-0.2	1.4	0.9	0.4	. . .	339.6
1956	48.5	22.0	26.5	11.3	15.3	6.9	34.3	0.4	1.7	1.2	0.5	. . .	359.9
1957	48.4	21.4	26.9	11.7	15.2	8.0	36.6	0.7	1.9	1.4	0.5	. . .	376.4
1958	43.5	19.0	24.5	11.6	13.0	9.5	37.7	0.9	1.8	1.2	0.6	. . .	378.1
1959	55.7	23.7	32.0	12.6	19.4	9.6	41.1	1.1	1.8	1.3	0.4	1.0	413.1
1960	53.8	22.8	31.0	13.4	17.6	10.6	44.6	1.1	1.9	1.3	0.5	0.9	428.7
1961	54.9	22.9	32.0	13.9	18.1	12.5	47.0	2.0	2.0	1.4	0.7	0.8	443.7
1962	63.3	24.1	39.2	15.0	24.1	14.2	50.4	2.3	2.2	1.5	0.7	0.9	478.8
1963	69.0	26.4	42.6	16.2	26.4	15.2	53.4	2.2	2.7	1.9	0.8	1.4	505.3
1964	76.5	28.2	48.3	18.2	30.1	17.4	57.3	2.7	3.1	2.2	0.9	1.3	543.6
1965	87.5	31.1	56.4	20.2	36.2	19.6	60.8	3.0	3.6	2.3	1.4	1.3	590.7
1966	93.2	33.9	59.3	20.7	38.7	22.4	63.3	3.9	3.5	2.1	1.4	1.0	647.2
1967	91.3	32.9	58.4	21.5	36.9	25.5	68.0	3.8	3.8	2.3	1.5	0.9	683.0
1968	98.8	39.6	59.2	23.5	35.6	27.1	76.5	4.2	4.3	2.8	1.5	1.2	745.4
1969	95.4	40.0	55.4	24.2	31.2	32.7	84.0	4.5	4.9	3.3	1.6	1.0	804.3
1970	83.6	34.8	48.9	24.3	24.6	39.1	91.5	4.8	4.5	2.9	1.6	0.0	839.7
1971	98.0	38.2	59.9	25.0	34.8	43.9	100.6	4.7	4.3	2.7	1.6	-0.2	908.1
1972	112.1	42.3	69.7	26.8	42.9	47.9	108.1	6.6	4.9	3.1	1.8	0.5	1 004.4
1973	125.5	50.0	75.5	29.9	45.6	55.2	117.3	5.2	6.0	3.9	2.0	-0.4	1 129.7
1974	115.8	52.8	63.0	33.2	29.8	70.8	125.0	3.3	7.1	4.7	2.4	-0.9	1 214.2
1975	134.8	51.6	83.2	33.0	50.2	81.6	135.5	4.5	9.4	6.8	2.6	-3.2	1 308.8
1976	163.3	65.3	98.1	39.0	59.0	85.5	146.6	5.1	9.5	6.7	2.8	-1.8	1 462.7
1977	192.4	74.4	118.0	44.8	73.2	101.1	159.9	7.1	8.4	5.1	3.3	-2.6	1 640.4
1978	216.6	84.9	131.8	50.8	81.0	115.0	171.2	8.9	10.6	6.5	4.1	-1.9	1 856.5
1979	223.2	90.0	133.2	57.5	75.7	138.9	180.4	8.5	13.0	8.2	4.8	-2.6	2 066.8
1980	201.1	87.2	113.9	64.1	49.9	181.8	200.7	9.8	14.4	8.6	5.7	-4.8	2 238.9
1981	226.1	84.3	141.8	73.8	68.0	232.3	236.0	11.5	17.6	11.2	6.4	-4.9	2 505.2
1982	209.7	66.5	143.2	77.7	65.4	271.1	241.3	15.0	20.1	12.4	7.8	-4.0	2 621.8
1983	264.2	80.6	183.6	83.5	100.1	285.3	263.7	21.2	22.5	13.8	8.7	-3.1	2 822.4
1984	318.6	97.5	221.1	90.8	130.3	327.1	290.2	21.0	30.1	19.7	10.4	-1.9	3 184.8
1985	330.3	99.4	230.9	97.6	133.4	341.3	308.5	21.3	34.8	22.3	12.6	0.8	3 400.5
1986	319.5	109.7	209.8	106.2	103.7	366.8	323.7	24.8	36.6	22.9	13.6	1.3	3 565.6
1987	368.8	130.4	238.4	112.3	126.1	366.4	347.9	30.2	33.8	20.2	13.6	1.2	3 821.1
1988	432.6	141.6	291.0	129.9	161.1	385.3	374.9	29.4	34.0	20.6	13.4	2.5	4 167.3
1989	426.6	146.1	280.5	158.0	122.6	432.1	399.3	27.2	39.2	23.5	15.7	4.9	4 410.3
1990	437.8	145.4	292.4	169.1	123.3	442.2	425.5	26.8	39.4	22.2	17.2	1.6	4 649.4
1991	451.2	138.6	312.6	180.7	131.9	418.2	457.5	27.3	39.9	17.9	22.0	5.7	4 752.1
1992	479.3	148.7	330.6	187.9	142.7	388.5	483.8	29.9	42.4	19.6	24.5	7.6	5 008.8
1993	541.9	171.0	370.9	202.8	168.1	365.7	503.4	36.4	40.7	14.4	26.6	7.2	5 258.4
1994	600.3	193.7	406.5	234.7	171.8	366.4	545.6	32.2	43.3	15.1	28.6	8.6	5 556.9
1995	696.7	218.7	478.0	254.2	223.8	367.1	558.2	34.0	46.9	19.0	26.5	11.4	5 871.4
1996	786.2	231.7	554.5	297.6	256.9	376.2	581.1	34.3	53.1	22.9	31.1	12.7	6 227.6
1997	868.5	246.1	622.4	334.5	287.9	415.6	612.0	32.9	49.9	19.4	29.7	12.6	6 650.6
1998	801.6	248.3	553.3	351.6	201.7	487.1	639.8	35.4	64.7	26.0	35.0	10.3	7 073.3
1999	851.3	258.6	592.6	337.4	255.3	495.4	674.0	44.2	67.4	34.1	35.9	10.1	7 529.4
2000	817.9	265.2	552.7	377.9	174.8	559.0	708.9	44.3	87.1	42.4	43.7	5.3	8 038.3
2001	767.3	204.1	563.2	370.9	192.3	566.3	728.6	55.3	92.8	50.0	47.5	-1.4	8 215.0
2002	886.3	192.6	693.7	399.2	294.5	520.9	762.8	38.4	84.3	37.3	46.6	0.9	8 419.8
2003	993.1	243.3	749.9	424.7	325.1	524.7	807.2	47.9	83.8	34.3	47.9	1.7	8 787.4
2004	1 231.2	307.4	923.9	539.5	384.4	491.2	863.8	44.6	83.0	26.4	48.1	-4.2	9 408.9
2005	1 447.9	413.7	1 034.2	577.4	456.9	569.1	928.2	59.3	70.0	38.8	31.8	-13.4	10 048.5
2006	1 668.5	468.9	1 199.6	702.1	497.5	631.2	976.2	49.7	85.4	24.9	57.9	-8.6	10 792.5
2007	1 642.4	450.4	1 192.0	788.7	403.4	664.4	1 015.5	52.3	100.2	31.9	61.4	-7.9	11 215.5
2008	1 476.5	366.6	1 109.9	832.1	277.8	682.7	1 033.8	50.7	103.6	34.7	63.3	-8.1	11 351.1
2006													
1st quarter	1 634.2	453.8	1 180.3	652.8	527.5	615.5	962.7	54.2	85.1	24.6	55.6	-7.8	10 625.3
2nd quarter	1 681.6	474.8	1 206.8	688.8	518.0	629.7	973.6	49.8	83.5	23.8	57.5	-8.3	10 739.4
3rd quarter	1 713.8	487.2	1 226.6	720.9	505.6	630.1	980.1	48.2	86.0	24.7	58.8	-9.1	10 839.7
4th quarter	1 644.5	459.8	1 184.8	745.8	439.0	649.3	988.3	46.8	86.8	26.7	59.8	-9.2	10 965.6
2007													
1st quarter	1 617.8	448.5	1 169.3	761.5	407.8	645.8	1 002.7	47.5	98.3	30.4	60.8	-10.8	11 044.8
2nd quarter	1 672.5	468.5	1 204.0	779.2	424.8	660.8	1 012.3	55.9	97.4	31.7	61.1	-8.5	11 188.3
3rd quarter	1 668.0	451.1	1 217.3	797.6	419.7	663.0	1 019.2	53.5	102.2	32.5	61.5	-5.5	11 276.3
4th quarter	1 611.1	433.5	1 177.6	816.4	361.2	688.1	1 027.7	52.3	103.1	33.1	62.1	-6.7	11 352.5
2008													
1st quarter	1 593.5	402.9	1 190.6	832.5	358.1	662.3	1 025.8	50.6	103.2	32.2	63.0	-7.1	11 376.4
2nd quarter	1 533.3	406.8	1 126.5	846.4	280.0	683.4	1 039.4	50.8	102.1	32.4	63.6	-7.7	11 385.6
3rd quarter	1 514.8	393.5	1 121.3	841.1	280.3	656.6	1 044.1	50.3	92.1	41.5	46.4	-8.0	11 413.4
4th quarter	1 264.5	263.2	1 001.2	808.3	192.9	728.6	1 026.1	51.2	116.8	32.8	80.2	-9.6	11 229.1

[1] Includes net transfer payments to the rest of the world, not shown separately.
. . . = Not available.

Table 1-13. Gross and Net Value Added of Domestic Corporate Business

(Billions of dollars, quarterly data are at seasonally adjusted annual rates.)   **NIPA Table 1.14**

Year and quarter	Gross value added of corporate business, total	Consumption of fixed capital	Net value added											Gross value added of financial corporate business
						Net operating surplus								
									Corporate profits with IVA and CCAdj					
											Profits after tax			
			Total	Compensation of employees	Taxes on production and imports less subsidies	Total	Net interest and miscellaneous payments	Business current transfer payments	Total	Taxes on corporate income	Total	Net dividends	Undistributed	
1950	160.4	11.6	148.8	98.7	14.8	35.3	-0.1	0.7	34.7	17.9	16.8	7.9	9.0	7.3
1951	183.9	13.2	170.7	114.6	15.9	40.3	-0.2	1.1	39.5	22.6	16.9	7.4	9.5	8.2
1952	192.6	14.0	178.6	123.0	17.3	38.2	-0.2	1.1	37.4	19.4	18.0	7.5	10.5	9.2
1953	206.2	14.8	191.4	134.0	18.5	38.9	0.0	1.0	37.9	20.3	17.6	7.8	9.9	10.2
1954	203.6	15.7	188.0	132.2	17.9	37.8	0.2	0.8	36.9	17.6	19.3	7.9	11.4	10.8
1955	229.5	16.6	212.9	144.6	19.8	48.5	0.2	1.2	47.2	22.0	25.1	8.9	16.2	11.8
1956	245.6	18.7	226.9	158.2	21.5	47.2	0.0	1.5	45.7	22.0	23.7	9.5	14.2	12.9
1957	256.9	20.5	236.4	166.5	22.8	47.1	0.2	1.7	45.3	21.4	23.8	9.9	14.0	13.8
1958	251.8	21.6	230.2	164.0	23.1	43.0	0.6	1.5	41.0	19.0	22.0	9.8	12.2	14.7
1959	281.9	21.8	260.1	180.3	25.6	54.2	-0.2	1.5	53.0	23.7	29.2	10.7	18.5	15.9
1960	293.9	23.3	270.6	190.7	27.8	52.0	-0.2	1.6	50.6	22.8	27.9	11.4	16.4	17.5
1961	302.1	23.9	278.2	195.6	28.9	53.7	0.4	1.8	51.5	22.9	28.6	11.5	17.1	18.4
1962	329.0	24.6	304.4	211.0	31.2	62.2	0.7	2.0	59.5	24.1	35.4	12.4	23.0	19.3
1963	349.5	26.0	323.5	222.7	33.2	67.7	0.4	2.4	64.9	26.4	38.5	13.6	25.0	19.7
1964	377.7	27.2	350.4	239.2	35.6	75.7	0.8	2.9	72.0	28.2	43.8	15.0	28.9	21.6
1965	414.4	29.4	385.0	259.9	37.8	87.3	1.2	3.3	82.8	31.1	51.7	16.9	34.8	23.2
1966	454.1	32.7	421.4	288.5	38.9	94.0	2.3	3.0	88.7	33.9	54.8	17.8	37.0	25.1
1967	479.3	35.6	443.6	308.4	41.4	93.8	4.0	3.3	86.6	32.9	53.7	18.3	35.3	28.1
1968	529.1	39.1	490.1	341.3	47.8	100.9	3.9	3.8	93.2	39.6	53.5	20.2	33.4	31.3
1969	576.7	44.2	532.5	378.6	52.9	101.0	7.8	4.4	88.8	40.0	48.8	20.4	28.4	36.2
1970	597.8	48.9	548.9	400.2	57.0	91.7	11.3	3.9	76.5	34.8	41.8	20.4	21.4	39.4
1971	646.1	52.9	593.2	425.3	62.8	105.2	11.5	3.5	90.2	38.2	52.0	20.3	31.7	43.1
1972	716.8	59.1	657.7	472.5	67.3	117.9	11.3	4.0	102.6	42.3	60.2	21.9	38.3	47.3
1973	802.6	65.9	736.6	533.9	74.1	128.6	13.0	5.0	110.6	50.0	60.6	23.1	37.5	51.8
1974	869.9	78.2	791.7	587.4	78.6	125.6	20.7	6.6	98.3	52.8	45.5	23.5	22.1	60.0
1975	944.4	92.9	851.6	614.9	84.5	152.2	23.4	8.6	120.2	51.6	68.6	26.4	42.2	67.8
1976	1 062.9	102.8	960.1	695.2	91.4	173.5	18.8	7.9	146.8	65.3	81.5	30.1	51.4	73.2
1977	1 205.2	117.4	1 087.8	784.8	100.0	203.0	23.3	6.4	173.3	74.4	98.9	33.7	65.2	85.8
1978	1 376.4	136.0	1 240.4	901.9	108.7	229.8	27.5	8.5	193.8	84.9	108.9	39.6	69.3	103.6
1979	1 530.7	157.2	1 373.4	1 023.4	115.0	235.0	34.9	11.5	188.6	90.0	98.6	41.5	57.1	114.7
1980	1 666.0	180.1	1 485.8	1 122.6	128.6	234.6	55.9	13.0	165.7	87.2	78.5	47.3	31.1	128.8
1981	1 893.3	205.3	1 688.0	1 243.9	154.4	289.7	77.7	15.6	196.4	84.3	112.1	58.3	53.8	147.3
1982	1 971.4	227.5	1 743.9	1 297.5	161.3	285.2	90.0	18.1	177.1	66.5	110.6	61.3	49.2	165.2
1983	2 121.0	236.0	1 885.0	1 371.2	177.4	336.3	86.6	20.6	229.2	80.6	148.5	71.3	77.2	188.0
1984	2 378.0	252.9	2 125.1	1 520.3	195.6	409.2	98.8	28.3	282.0	97.5	184.5	78.5	106.0	210.5
1985	2 535.3	274.0	2 261.3	1 630.9	209.0	421.4	96.9	32.3	292.2	99.4	192.8	85.7	107.1	233.3
1986	2 649.8	284.4	2 365.4	1 728.6	219.6	417.2	107.0	30.1	280.0	109.7	170.4	88.3	82.1	262.3
1987	2 837.9	300.0	2 537.9	1 849.6	233.4	454.8	108.3	25.6	320.8	130.4	190.4	95.6	94.8	280.8
1988	3 071.3	318.9	2 752.3	1 988.9	252.0	511.4	108.7	27.1	375.7	141.6	234.0	98.0	136.0	299.7
1989	3 235.0	344.6	2 890.4	2 097.6	267.5	525.3	129.4	36.5	359.5	146.1	213.4	126.4	87.0	322.7
1990	3 382.0	367.5	3 014.5	2 208.1	284.5	521.9	125.3	34.9	361.7	145.4	216.3	144.1	72.2	340.5
1991	3 468.9	395.7	3 073.2	2 253.0	307.9	512.3	101.7	35.8	374.7	138.6	236.1	156.4	79.8	369.2
1992	3 643.1	408.7	3 234.4	2 377.0	325.9	531.5	79.3	46.0	406.2	148.7	257.5	159.9	97.7	407.1
1993	3 824.8	421.3	3 403.5	2 489.2	343.5	570.8	72.1	33.7	465.0	171.0	294.0	182.2	111.7	427.0
1994	4 103.4	456.6	3 646.9	2 633.0	375.6	638.3	74.9	40.2	523.2	193.7	329.5	197.4	132.0	433.9
1995	4 354.5	486.9	3 867.6	2 774.1	384.1	709.3	66.4	39.1	603.9	218.7	385.2	221.6	163.7	475.0
1996	4 626.5	513.6	4 112.9	2 916.1	397.4	799.4	70.0	45.1	684.3	231.7	452.6	257.3	195.3	517.0
1997	4 983.6	553.6	4 430.0	3 125.0	415.7	889.3	95.4	36.3	757.5	246.1	511.5	283.9	227.6	581.8
1998	5 313.6	589.0	4 724.6	3 397.6	429.8	897.2	143.3	55.2	698.7	248.3	450.4	309.2	141.2	658.6
1999	5 655.0	632.0	5 023.0	3 645.2	449.4	928.4	142.3	56.3	729.8	258.6	471.1	295.7	175.5	704.1
2000	6 051.8	690.0	5 361.8	3 957.7	477.1	926.9	178.1	76.6	672.2	265.2	407.0	348.4	58.6	779.6
2001	6 099.4	752.5	5 346.9	4 016.7	473.6	856.6	171.3	87.7	597.6	204.1	393.5	330.1	63.4	805.9
2002	6 225.8	742.1	5 483.7	4 044.5	502.7	936.5	135.9	70.1	730.5	192.6	537.9	351.3	186.5	854.1
2003	6 456.9	759.8	5 697.1	4 156.9	528.8	1 011.4	120.8	63.0	827.7	243.3	584.4	392.8	191.6	898.5
2004	6 895.0	797.1	6 097.9	4 352.7	568.3	1 176.9	70.4	68.7	1 037.8	307.4	730.5	491.7	238.8	938.6
2005	7 431.1	858.9	6 572.2	4 601.3	611.0	1 359.9	83.0	68.4	1 208.5	413.7	794.8	316.5	478.3	1 034.9
2006	7 962.5	892.8	7 069.7	4 876.2	640.8	1 552.7	95.2	56.5	1 401.0	468.9	932.1	628.8	303.3	1 099.1
2007	8 195.3	945.3	7 249.9	5 110.1	663.9	1 476.0	100.5	77.8	1 297.8	450.4	847.4	671.1	176.3	1 120.2
2008	8 182.0	1 011.1	7 170.9	5 227.3	675.4	1 268.2	104.4	73.9	1 090.0	366.6	723.3	663.9	59.4	1 011.6
2006														
1st quarter	7 830.4	871.6	6 958.8	4 800.2	631.7	1 526.9	91.5	51.7	1 383.7	453.8	929.9	548.2	381.6	1 059.2
2nd quarter	7 915.6	886.2	7 029.3	4 829.8	639.1	1 560.4	94.9	53.5	1 412.0	474.8	937.1	583.1	354.0	1 098.0
3rd quarter	8 028.0	900.1	7 127.9	4 876.3	643.5	1 608.1	95.9	58.9	1 453.3	487.2	966.0	642.9	323.1	1 096.3
4th quarter	8 076.0	913.2	7 162.8	4 998.4	649.0	1 515.4	98.3	61.9	1 355.1	459.8	895.4	740.9	154.5	1 142.7
2007														
1st quarter	8 118.2	925.5	7 192.6	5 045.1	655.4	1 492.2	98.1	74.4	1 319.7	448.5	871.2	653.8	217.5	1 118.5
2nd quarter	8 219.9	938.4	7 281.6	5 075.5	661.7	1 544.4	100.0	74.7	1 369.7	468.5	901.1	661.7	239.4	1 153.2
3rd quarter	8 235.9	951.8	7 284.2	5 125.4	666.4	1 492.4	100.1	80.4	1 311.9	451.1	860.8	662.2	198.6	1 137.3
4th quarter	8 207.1	965.7	7 241.4	5 194.4	672.1	1 374.9	103.6	81.6	1 189.7	433.5	756.3	706.6	49.7	1 071.6
2008														
1st quarter	8 233.3	978.8	7 254.5	5 222.3	670.4	1 361.8	100.6	66.1	1 195.1	402.9	792.1	654.9	137.2	1 114.0
2nd quarter	8 224.4	996.5	7 227.9	5 219.5	678.8	1 329.6	105.2	64.7	1 159.8	406.8	753.0	681.6	71.4	1 071.4
3rd quarter	8 304.1	1 039.4	7 264.7	5 246.3	682.0	1 336.5	102.5	97.6	1 136.4	393.5	742.9	647.3	95.6	1 043.4
4th quarter	7 966.1	1 029.7	6 936.4	5 221.1	670.4	1 044.9	109.2	67.1	868.6	263.2	605.3	671.8	-66.5	817.5

Table 1-14. Gross Value Added of Nonfinancial Domestic Corporate Business in Current and Chained Dollars

(Billions of dollars, quarterly data are at seasonally adjusted annual rates.)   **NIPA Table 1.14**

Year and quarter	Current-dollar gross value added													Gross value added in billions of chained (2000) dollars
	Total	Consumption of fixed capital	Net value added											
			Total	Compensation of employees	Taxes on production and imports less subsidies	Net operating surplus								
						Total	Net interest and miscellaneous payments	Business current transfer payments	Corporate profits with IVA and CCAdj					
									Total	Taxes on corporate income	Profits after tax			
											Total	Net dividends	Undistributed	
1950	153.1	11.3	141.8	94.4	14.4	33.1	0.9	0.6	31.6	16.8	14.8	7.4	7.4	675.3
1951	175.7	12.9	162.9	109.8	15.4	37.7	1.0	0.8	35.9	21.1	14.8	7.0	7.7	714.0
1952	183.4	13.6	169.7	117.8	16.8	35.2	1.2	0.9	33.1	17.7	15.5	7.1	8.4	738.8
1953	195.9	14.4	181.6	128.2	17.9	35.5	1.3	1.0	33.2	18.4	14.9	7.2	7.6	792.6
1954	192.9	15.2	177.7	125.9	17.3	34.4	1.6	0.9	31.9	15.5	16.4	7.4	9.0	783.0
1955	217.7	16.1	201.7	137.9	19.2	44.6	1.6	1.0	41.9	20.1	21.8	8.4	13.4	878.0
1956	232.7	18.1	214.6	150.8	20.8	43.0	1.8	1.1	40.2	19.9	20.2	9.0	11.2	907.2
1957	243.1	19.9	223.2	158.4	22.0	42.7	2.2	1.2	39.4	19.0	20.4	9.2	11.2	919.1
1958	237.1	21.0	216.2	155.2	22.3	38.6	2.8	1.2	34.6	16.1	18.6	9.1	9.5	882.5
1959	266.0	21.1	244.9	170.8	24.4	49.7	2.9	1.3	45.5	20.7	24.8	9.8	15.0	980.4
1960	276.4	22.6	253.8	180.4	26.6	46.8	3.2	1.4	42.2	19.1	23.1	10.5	12.6	1 012.0
1961	283.7	23.2	260.5	184.5	27.6	48.4	3.7	1.5	43.2	19.4	23.8	10.6	13.2	1 033.6
1962	309.8	23.9	285.9	199.3	29.9	56.8	4.3	1.7	50.8	20.6	30.2	11.6	18.6	1 120.7
1963	329.9	25.2	304.7	210.1	31.7	62.9	4.7	1.7	56.5	22.8	33.8	12.4	21.3	1 186.7
1964	356.1	26.4	329.7	225.7	33.9	70.2	5.2	2.0	63.0	23.9	39.2	14.0	25.2	1 270.3
1965	391.2	28.4	362.8	245.4	36.0	81.4	5.8	2.2	73.3	27.1	46.2	16.2	30.0	1 375.1
1966	429.0	31.5	397.4	272.9	37.0	87.6	7.0	2.7	77.9	29.5	48.4	16.8	31.6	1 472.6
1967	451.2	34.3	416.8	291.1	39.3	86.4	8.4	2.8	75.2	27.8	47.3	17.3	30.1	1 508.9
1968	497.8	37.6	460.2	321.9	45.5	92.8	9.7	3.1	80.0	33.5	46.5	19.0	27.5	1 604.8
1969	540.5	42.4	498.1	357.1	50.2	90.8	12.7	3.2	74.9	33.3	41.6	19.0	22.5	1 667.6
1970	558.3	46.8	511.5	376.5	54.2	80.7	16.6	3.3	60.9	27.3	33.6	18.3	15.3	1 649.9
1971	603.0	50.7	552.4	399.4	59.5	93.4	17.6	3.7	72.1	30.0	42.1	18.1	24.0	1 716.6
1972	669.5	56.4	613.2	443.9	63.7	105.6	18.6	4.0	83.0	33.8	49.2	19.7	29.5	1 846.4
1973	750.8	62.7	688.1	502.2	70.1	115.8	21.8	4.7	89.4	40.4	49.0	20.8	28.2	1 957.7
1974	809.8	74.1	735.7	552.2	74.4	109.1	27.5	4.1	77.5	42.8	34.7	21.5	13.1	1 925.4
1975	876.7	87.9	788.7	575.5	80.2	133.1	28.4	5.0	99.6	41.9	57.7	24.6	33.2	1 898.8
1976	989.7	97.0	892.7	651.4	86.7	154.7	26.0	7.0	121.7	53.5	68.2	27.8	40.5	2 050.0
1977	1 119.4	110.5	1 008.8	735.3	94.6	178.9	28.5	9.0	141.4	60.6	80.9	30.9	50.0	2 200.0
1978	1 272.9	127.8	1 145.1	845.3	102.7	197.0	33.4	9.5	154.1	67.6	86.6	35.9	50.6	2 344.1
1979	1 415.9	147.3	1 268.6	959.9	108.8	200.0	41.8	9.5	148.8	70.6	78.1	37.6	40.5	2 418.7
1980	1 537.1	168.2	1 368.9	1 049.8	121.5	197.6	54.2	10.2	133.2	68.2	65.0	44.7	20.4	2 394.6
1981	1 746.0	191.5	1 554.5	1 161.5	146.7	246.4	67.2	11.4	167.7	66.0	101.7	52.5	49.2	2 491.5
1982	1 806.2	211.2	1 594.9	1 203.9	152.9	238.1	77.4	8.8	151.9	48.8	103.1	54.1	49.0	2 430.6
1983	1 933.0	217.6	1 715.4	1 266.9	168.0	280.5	77.0	10.5	192.9	61.7	131.2	63.2	68.0	2 545.1
1984	2 167.5	230.7	1 936.8	1 406.1	185.0	345.7	86.0	11.7	248.0	75.9	172.0	67.2	104.8	2 772.8
1985	2 302.0	247.4	2 054.6	1 504.2	196.6	353.8	91.5	16.1	246.3	71.1	175.2	72.0	103.2	2 896.3
1986	2 387.5	255.3	2 132.2	1 583.1	204.6	344.5	95.1	27.3	222.1	76.2	145.9	72.9	73.0	2 963.3
1987	2 557.1	266.5	2 290.6	1 687.8	216.8	386.0	96.4	29.9	259.7	94.2	165.5	76.3	89.2	3 119.6
1988	2 771.6	281.6	2 490.0	1 812.8	233.8	443.4	109.8	27.4	306.2	104.0	202.3	82.2	120.1	3 300.7
1989	2 912.3	301.6	2 610.7	1 914.7	248.2	447.9	142.0	23.0	282.9	101.2	181.7	105.4	76.4	3 361.8
1990	3 041.5	319.2	2 722.3	2 012.9	263.5	445.8	146.2	25.4	274.3	98.5	175.8	118.3	57.5	3 404.0
1991	3 099.7	341.4	2 758.3	2 048.4	285.7	424.2	135.9	26.7	261.5	88.6	172.9	125.5	47.4	3 376.2
1992	3 236.0	353.6	2 882.3	2 154.1	302.5	425.7	111.3	25.2	289.2	94.4	194.8	134.1	60.7	3 479.5
1993	3 397.8	363.4	3 034.4	2 244.8	318.8	470.8	102.0	29.6	339.2	108.0	231.2	149.1	82.1	3 575.5
1994	3 669.5	391.5	3 278.0	2 381.5	349.6	546.9	101.0	30.0	415.9	132.9	283.1	157.9	125.2	3 797.9
1995	3 879.5	415.0	3 464.5	2 509.8	356.9	597.8	115.2	30.2	452.5	141.0	311.4	178.0	133.5	3 977.4
1996	4 109.5	436.5	3 673.0	2 630.8	369.1	673.1	111.9	38.0	523.2	153.1	370.1	197.5	172.6	4 196.4
1997	4 401.8	467.1	3 934.7	2 812.9	385.5	736.3	124.0	39.0	573.4	161.9	411.5	215.9	195.6	4 469.3
1998	4 655.0	493.3	4 161.7	3 045.6	398.7	717.4	143.8	35.2	538.3	158.6	379.7	241.0	138.7	4 725.4
1999	4 950.8	523.8	4 427.0	3 267.7	416.6	742.7	160.2	45.0	537.6	171.2	366.3	224.6	141.7	5 011.0
2000	5 272.2	567.8	4 704.3	3 544.4	443.4	716.5	191.7	48.4	476.4	170.2	306.2	251.3	54.8	5 272.2
2001	5 293.5	646.8	4 646.7	3 595.9	439.1	611.8	204.0	50.6	357.2	111.7	245.5	245.4	0.1	5 224.5
2002	5 371.7	643.6	4 728.2	3 611.9	465.5	650.8	167.4	54.0	429.4	97.0	332.3	254.8	77.5	5 269.7
2003	5 558.4	657.5	4 900.9	3 703.2	488.5	709.2	152.6	64.4	492.1	135.7	356.4	292.7	63.8	5 387.5
2004	5 956.4	687.4	5 269.0	3 865.2	523.9	879.9	138.9	59.3	681.6	191.0	490.7	367.0	123.7	5 662.1
2005	6 396.1	743.9	5 652.2	4 075.6	563.2	1 013.5	153.6	58.5	801.4	274.5	526.9	184.2	342.7	5 916.1
2006	6 863.4	775.2	6 088.3	4 316.8	591.1	1 180.3	169.6	71.8	939.0	309.3	629.7	474.4	155.3	6 156.4
2007	7 075.1	822.3	6 252.8	4 525.3	611.9	1 115.5	179.4	68.1	868.1	321.1	547.0	503.4	43.5	6 243.1
2008	7 170.4	882.4	6 288.0	4 634.6	622.5	1 031.0	185.4	57.6	788.0	270.7	517.3	508.6	8.7	6 326.0
2006														
1st quarter	6 771.2	755.7	6 015.5	4 264.7	582.7	1 168.1	165.1	73.0	930.0	302.6	627.4	404.7	222.7	6 126.1
2nd quarter	6 817.5	769.3	6 048.3	4 282.3	589.5	1 176.4	169.4	72.0	935.0	312.3	622.7	431.7	191.0	6 132.4
3rd quarter	6 931.7	781.9	6 149.7	4 318.3	593.6	1 237.8	169.8	71.3	996.7	323.3	673.4	484.3	189.1	6 198.2
4th quarter	6 933.3	793.7	6 139.6	4 401.9	598.7	1 139.0	174.1	70.7	894.2	299.1	595.1	576.9	18.2	6 169.0
2007														
1st quarter	6 999.6	804.6	6 195.0	4 464.1	604.1	1 126.9	174.6	68.8	883.6	319.8	563.8	491.9	71.9	6 166.5
2nd quarter	7 066.7	816.0	6 250.7	4 497.4	609.9	1 143.5	178.9	68.0	896.6	330.9	565.7	496.1	69.5	6 230.2
3rd quarter	7 098.6	828.1	6 270.6	4 537.2	614.2	1 119.1	178.8	67.7	872.6	318.9	553.7	492.7	61.0	6 271.2
4th quarter	7 135.5	840.7	6 294.8	4 602.7	619.5	1 072.6	185.4	67.7	819.5	314.7	504.7	533.0	-28.3	6 304.4
2008														
1st quarter	7 119.3	852.6	6 266.7	4 623.0	617.9	1 025.8	180.5	57.9	787.4	279.8	507.6	494.0	13.6	6 283.0
2nd quarter	7 153.1	868.5	6 284.6	4 630.8	625.6	1 028.2	186.7	58.2	783.2	294.0	489.2	514.2	-25.0	6 375.1
3rd quarter	7 260.7	909.8	6 350.9	4 653.6	628.6	1 068.8	180.9	52.6	835.3	303.7	531.6	498.4	33.2	6 410.9
4th quarter	7 148.6	898.7	6 249.9	4 630.9	617.9	1 001.2	193.5	61.5	746.2	205.3	540.9	527.7	13.2	6 235.0

Table 1-15. Rates of Return and Related Data for Domestic Nonfinancial Corporations

| Year | Rates of return (percent) | | | | | Shares of net value added (percent) | | | | | Value of produced assets (billions of dollars) | Tax liability as a percent of produced assets | Q3 ratio |
| | Net operating surplus | | Corporate profits | | Net interest | Net operating surplus | | Corporate profits | | Net interest | | | |
	Before tax	After tax	Before tax	After tax		Before tax	After tax	Before tax	After tax				
1960	9.6	5.7	8.7	4.7	0.7	18.4	10.9	16.6	9.1	1.3	487.5	3.9	0.50
1961	9.7	5.8	8.7	4.8	0.7	18.6	11.1	16.6	9.1	1.4	498.3	3.9	0.64
1962	11.1	7.1	9.9	5.9	0.9	19.9	12.7	17.8	10.6	1.5	512.9	4.0	0.61
1963	11.9	7.6	10.6	6.4	0.9	20.7	13.2	18.6	11.1	1.5	530.9	4.3	0.68
1964	12.7	8.3	11.4	7.1	0.9	21.3	14.0	19.1	11.9	1.6	554.8	4.3	0.80
1965	13.8	9.2	12.4	7.8	1.0	22.4	15.0	20.2	12.7	1.6	590.3	4.6	0.88
1966	13.7	9.1	12.2	7.6	1.1	22.0	14.6	19.6	12.2	1.8	640.6	4.6	0.70
1967	12.4	8.4	10.8	6.8	1.2	20.7	14.1	18.0	11.4	2.0	697.6	4.0	0.88
1968	12.2	7.8	10.6	6.1	1.3	20.2	12.9	17.4	10.1	2.1	758.6	4.4	0.99
1969	10.9	6.9	9.0	5.0	1.5	18.2	11.5	15.0	8.4	2.6	831.7	4.0	0.73
1970	8.9	5.9	6.7	3.7	1.8	15.8	10.5	11.9	6.6	3.2	910.1	3.0	0.64
1971	9.4	6.4	7.3	4.3	1.8	16.9	11.5	13.1	7.6	3.2	991.1	3.0	0.70
1972	9.8	6.7	7.7	4.6	1.7	17.2	11.7	13.5	8.0	3.0	1 076.5	3.1	0.81
1973	9.7	6.3	7.5	4.1	1.8	16.8	11.0	13.0	7.1	3.2	1 198.5	3.4	0.52
1974	7.7	4.7	5.4	2.4	1.9	14.8	9.0	10.5	4.7	3.7	1 426.6	3.0	0.19
1975	8.1	5.5	6.1	3.5	1.7	16.9	11.6	12.6	7.3	3.6	1 645.7	2.6	0.35
1976	8.6	5.6	6.8	3.8	1.4	17.3	11.3	13.6	7.6	2.9	1 801.0	3.0	0.41
1977	9.0	5.9	7.1	4.1	1.4	17.7	11.7	14.0	8.0	2.8	1 991.8	3.0	0.31
1978	8.8	5.8	6.9	3.9	1.5	17.2	11.3	13.5	7.6	2.9	2 243.8	3.0	0.29
1979	7.8	5.0	5.8	3.0	1.6	15.8	10.2	11.7	6.2	3.3	2 577.1	2.7	0.30
1980	6.7	4.4	4.5	2.2	1.8	14.4	9.5	9.7	4.8	4.0	2 961.1	2.3	0.36
1981	7.4	5.4	5.0	3.0	2.0	15.9	11.6	10.8	6.5	4.3	3 350.5	2.0	0.28
1982	6.6	5.2	4.2	2.9	2.1	14.9	11.9	9.5	6.5	4.9	3 619.9	1.4	0.30
1983	7.5	5.8	5.2	3.5	2.1	16.4	12.8	11.3	7.7	4.5	3 744.6	1.7	0.34
1984	8.8	6.9	6.3	4.4	2.2	17.9	13.9	12.8	8.9	4.4	3 911.5	1.9	0.30
1985	8.6	6.9	6.0	4.3	2.2	17.2	13.8	12.0	8.5	4.5	4 119.3	1.7	0.39
1986	8.1	6.3	5.2	3.4	2.2	16.2	12.6	10.4	6.8	4.5	4 267.9	1.8	0.47
1987	8.7	6.6	5.9	3.7	2.2	16.9	12.7	11.3	7.2	4.2	4 440.9	2.1	0.45
1988	9.4	7.2	6.5	4.3	2.3	17.8	13.6	12.3	8.1	4.4	4 695.5	2.2	0.48
1989	9.0	7.0	5.7	3.7	2.9	17.2	13.3	10.8	7.0	5.4	4 967.2	2.0	0.59
1990	8.5	6.7	5.3	3.4	2.8	16.4	12.8	10.1	6.5	5.4	5 225.4	1.9	0.56
1991	7.9	6.2	4.9	3.2	2.5	15.4	12.2	9.5	6.3	4.9	5 391.8	1.6	0.79
1992	7.7	6.0	5.3	3.5	2.0	14.8	11.5	10.0	6.8	3.9	5 508.9	1.7	0.93
1993	8.2	6.4	5.9	4.0	1.8	15.5	12.0	11.2	7.6	3.4	5 716.9	1.9	1.00
1994	9.1	6.9	6.9	4.7	1.7	16.7	12.6	12.7	8.6	3.1	6 015.6	2.2	0.92
1995	9.4	7.2	7.1	4.9	1.8	17.3	13.2	13.1	9.0	3.3	6 371.1	2.2	1.12
1996	10.0	7.8	7.8	5.5	1.7	18.3	14.2	14.2	10.1	3.1	6 712.3	2.3	1.21
1997	10.4	8.1	8.1	5.8	1.8	18.7	14.6	14.6	10.5	3.2	7 056.0	2.3	1.41
1998	9.7	7.6	7.3	5.1	2.0	17.2	13.4	12.9	9.1	3.5	7 419.0	2.2	1.53
1999	9.5	7.4	7.0	4.7	2.1	16.8	12.9	12.1	8.3	3.6	7 809.2	2.2	1.84
2000	8.6	6.7	5.8	3.8	2.4	15.2	11.6	10.1	6.5	4.1	8 295.2	2.1	1.35
2001	7.0	5.8	4.1	2.8	2.4	13.2	10.8	7.7	5.3	4.4	8 705.2	1.3	1.11
2002	7.3	6.2	4.8	3.7	1.9	13.8	11.7	9.1	7.0	3.5	8 950.8	1.1	0.74
2003	7.7	6.8	5.7	4.3	1.8	14.5	12.7	10.6	8.1	3.4	9 185.0	1.4	0.93
2004	9.1	7.4	6.8	5.1	1.7	16.7	13.4	12.3	9.2	3.1	9 682.7	1.7	0.91
2005	9.0	7.5	7.9	5.4	1.7	16.9	13.2	13.9	9.5	3.0	10 474.0	2.5	0.79
2006	9.0	...	...	...	...	17.2	...	...	...	...	11 261.6	...	0.70
2007	8.2	...	...	...	...	16.0	...	...	...	...	11 906.4	...	0.58

Note: See notes and definition for explanation.
. . . = Not available.

NOTES AND DEFINITIONS

TABLES 1-1 THROUGH 1-15 AND 19-1 THROUGH 19-11 NATIONAL INCOME AND PRODUCT

Source: U.S. Department of Commerce, Bureau of Economic Analysis (BEA)

All data in these tables are from the national income and product accounts (NIPAs). The data are as published in the 2003 comprehensive NIPA revisions, updated and revised in each annual revision through August 2008, and continued through the fourth quarter of 2008 in the estimates released on March 26, 2009.

Upcoming NIPA Revision

In July 2009 the Bureau of Economic Analysis will release a comprehensive, or benchmark, revision of the NIPAs.

Current-dollar estimates will be revised—especially for the most recent four years—because of data updating and classification and statistical changes. Users of the constant-dollar estimates and the quantity and price indexes will also, and immediately, notice a change in the reference year for the chain-type quantity and price indexes and the chained-dollar estimates, from 2000 (as used in the data in this volume) to 2005.

The change in the reference year will cause conspicuous differences in the *levels* of the constant-dollar measures and the price and quantity indexes, but this does not of itself affect the *rates of change*—the growth and inflation rates calculated from these data—which are based on chain-weighted indexes whatever the reference base year is. Significant changes are not expected in historical growth and inflation trends from those that can be derived from the data in this volume, other than the revisions occasioned by new data for the most recent several years.

BEA also plans changes in the treatment of disasters and a new classification system for personal consumption expenditures.

These and all of the other planned changes are described in "Preview of the 2009 Comprehensive Revision of the NIPAs: Changes in Definitions and Presentations," *Survey of Current Business,* March 2009, available at <http://www.bea.gov>.

Definitions and notes on the data:
Basic concepts of total output and income (Tables 1-10 through 1-12)

The NIPAs depict the U.S. economy in several different dimensions. The basic concept, and the measure that is now most frequently cited, is gross domestic product (GDP), which is the market value of all goods and services produced by labor and property located in the United States.

In principle, GDP can be measured by summing the values created by each industry in the economy. However, it can more readily be measured by summing all the final demands for the economy's output. This final-demand approach also has the advantage of depicting the origins of demand for economic production, whether from consumers, businesses, or government.

Since production for the market necessarily generates incomes equal to its value, there is also an income total that corresponds to the production value total. This income can be measured and its distribution among labor, capital, and other income recipients can be depicted.

The structure and relationships of several of these major concepts are illustrated in Table 1-10. The definitions of these concepts are as follows:

Gross domestic product (GDP), the featured measure of the value of U.S. output, is the market value of the goods and services produced by labor and property located in the United States. Market values represent output valued at the prices paid by the final customer, and therefore include taxes on production and imports, such as sales taxes, customs duties, and taxes on property.

The term "gross" in gross domestic product is used to indicate that capital consumption allowances (economic depreciation) have not been deducted.

GDP is primarily measured by summing the values of all of the final demands in the economy: personal consumption expenditures (PCE), gross private domestic investment (including change in private inventories and before deduction of charges for consumption of fixed capital), net exports of goods and services, and government consumption expenditures and gross investment. GDP measured in this way excludes duplication involving "intermediate" purchases of goods and services (goods and services purchased by industries and used in production), the value of which is already included in the value of the final products. Production of any intermediate goods unused in production in the current period is captured in the measurement of inventory change.

In concept, GDP is equal to the sum of the economic value added by (formerly referred to as "gross product originating in") all industries in the United States. This, in turn, also makes it the conceptual equivalent of *gross domestic income (GDI),* a new concept introduced in the 2003 revision. GDI is the sum of the incomes earned in each domestic industry, plus the taxes on production and imports and less the subsidies that account for the difference between output value and factor input value. This derivation is shown in Table 1-11. Since the incomes and taxes can be measured directly, they can be summed to a total that is equivalent to GDP in concept but differs due to imperfections in measurement. The difference between the two is known as the *statistical discrepancy*. It is defined as GDP minus GDI, and is shown in Table 1-11.

Gross national product (GNP) refers to all goods and services produced by labor and property supplied by U.S. residents—whether located in the United States or abroad—expressed at market prices. It is equal to GDP, plus *income receipts from the rest of the world,* less *income payments to the rest of the world. Domestic* production and income refer to the *location* of the factors of production, with only factors located in the United States included; *national* production and income refer to the *ownership* of the factors of production, with only factors owned by United States residents included.

Before the comprehensive NIPA revisions that were made in 1991, GNP was the commonly used measure of U.S. production. (The terminology survived in popular cultural references, including the name of a musical group and the "Gross National Parade.") However, GDP is clearly preferable to GNP when used in conjunction with indicators such as employment, hours worked, and capital utilized—for example, in the calculation of labor and capital productivity—because it is confined to production taking place within the borders of the United States. It is also the measure used by almost all other countries, thus facilitating international comparisons such as those shown in Chapter 13.

The income-side aggregate corresponding to GNP is *gross national income (GNI),* shown as an addendum to Table 1-10. It consists of gross domestic income plus income receipts from the rest of the world, less income payments to the rest of the world. It is used as the denominator for a national saving-income ratio, presented in Chapter 5. National income is the preferred measure for calculating and comparing saving, since it is the income aggregate from which that saving arises. As with GDP and gross domestic income, the statistical discrepancy indicates the difference between the product-side and income-side measurement of the same concept.

Net national product is the market value, net of depreciation, of goods and services attributable to the labor and property supplied by U.S. residents. It is equal to GNP minus the *consumption of fixed capital (CFC)*. CFC relates only to fixed capital located in the United States. (Investment in that capital is measured by private fixed investment and government gross investment.) In periods in which extraordinary property destruction occurs, such as a severe hurricane or a terror attack, normal capital consumption is augmented by the estimated value of the lost assets.

National income has been redefined and now includes all net incomes (net of the consumption of fixed capital) earned in production. It now includes not only "factor incomes"—net incomes received by labor and capital as a result of their participation in the production process, but also "nonfactor charges"—taxes on production and imports, business transfer payments, and the current surplus of government enterprises, less subsidies. This change has been made to conform with the international guidelines for national accounts, *System of National Accounts (SNA) 1993*. According to *SNA 1993,* these charges cannot be eliminated from the input and output prices.

Since national income now includes the nonfactor charges, it is conceptually equivalent to *net national product* and differs only by the amount of the statistical discrepancy.

The concept formerly known as "national income," which excludes the nonfactor charges, is still included in the accounts as an addendum item called "net national factor income." It is shown in Table 1-12 and used as the denominator in Figure 1-5. *Net national factor income* consists of compensation of employees, proprietors' income with inventory valuation and capital consumption adjustments (IVA and CCadj, respectively), rental income of persons with capital consumption adjustment, corporate profits with inventory valuation and capital consumption adjustments, and net interest.

By definition, national income and its components exclude all income from capital gains (increases in the value of owned assets). Such increases have no counterpart on the production side of the accounts. This exclusion is partly accomplished by means of the inventory valuation and capital consumption adjustments, which will be described in the definitions of the components of product and income.

Definitions and notes on the data: Imputation

The term *imputation* will appear from time to time in the following definitions of product and income components. Imputed values are values estimated by BEA statisticians for certain important product and income components that are not explicitly valued in the source data, usually because a market transaction in money terms is not involved. Imputed values appear on both the product and income side of the accounts; they add equal amounts to income and spending, so that no imputed saving is created.

One important example is the imputed rent on owner-occupied housing. The building of such housing is counted as investment, yet in the monetary accounts of the household sector, there is no income from that investment nor any rental paid for it. In the NIPAs, the rent that each such dwelling would earn if rented is estimated and added to both national and personal income (as part of rental income receipts) and to personal consumption expenditures (as part of expenditures on housing services).

Another important example is imputed interest. For example, an individual keeps a monetary balance in a bank or other financial institution. He or she receives either no interest or below-market interest, but receives the institution's services, such as clearing checks and otherwise facilitating payments, with little or no charge. Where is the product generated by the institution's workers and capital? In the NIPAs, the depositor is imputed a market-rate-based interest return on his or her balance, which is then imputed as a service charge received by the institution, and therefore included in the value of the institution's output.

Definitions and notes on the data:
Components of product (Tables 1-1 through 1-5)

Personal consumption expenditures (PCE) is goods and services purchased by persons residing in the United States. PCE consists mainly of purchases of new goods and services by individuals from businesses. It includes purchases that are financed by insurance, such as government-provided and private medical insurance. In addition, PCE includes purchases of new goods and services by nonprofit institutions, net purchases of used goods ("net" here indicates purchases of used goods from business less sales of used goods to business) by individuals and nonprofit institutions, and purchases abroad of goods and services by U.S. residents traveling or working in foreign countries. PCE also includes purchases for certain goods and services provided by government agencies. (See the notes and definitions for Chapter 4 for additional information.) New annual accounts separate household and nonprofit institution expenditures and incomes, providing the data presented in Table 4-6.

Gross private domestic investment consists of gross private fixed investment and change in private inventories.

Private fixed investment consists of both nonresidential and residential fixed investment. The term "residential" refers to the construction and equipping of living quarters for permanent occupancy. Hotels and motels are included in *nonresidential fixed investment*, as described in this section.

Private fixed investment consists of purchases of fixed assets, which are commodities that will be used in a production process for more than one year, including replacements and additions to the capital stock. It is measured "gross," before a deduction for consumption of existing fixed capital. It covers all investment by private businesses and nonprofit institutions in the United States, regardless of whether the investment is owned by U.S. residents. The residential component includes investment in owner-occupied housing; the homeowner is treated equivalently to a business in these investment accounts. (However, when GDP by sector is calculated, owner-occupied housing is no longer included in the business sector. It is allocated to the households and institutions sector.) Private fixed investment does not include purchases of the same types of equipment and structures by government agencies, which are included in government gross investment, nor does it include investment by U.S. residents in other countries.

Nonresidential fixed investment is the total of nonresidential structures and nonresidential equipment and software.

Nonresidential structures consists of new construction, brokers' commissions on sales of structures, and net purchases of used structures by private business and by nonprofit institutions from government agencies (that is, purchases of used structures from government minus sales of used structures to government). New construction also includes hotels and motels and mining exploration, shafts, and wells.

Nonresidential equipment and software consists of private business purchases on capital account of new machinery, equipment, and vehicles; purchases and in-house production of software; dealers' margins on sales of used equipment; and net purchases of used equipment from government agencies, persons, and the rest of the world (that is, purchases of such equipment minus sales of such equipment). It does not include the estimated personal-use portion of equipment purchased for both business and personal use, which is allocated to PCE.

Residential private fixed investment consists of both residential structures and residential producers' durable equipment (including such equipment as appliances owned by landlords and rented to tenants). Investment in structures consists of new units, improvements to existing units, purchases of manufactured homes, brokers' commissions on the sale of residential property, and net purchases of used residential structures from government agencies (that is, purchases of such structures from government minus sales of such structures to government). As noted above, it includes investment in owner-occupied housing.

Change in private inventories is the change in the physical volume of inventories held by businesses, with that change being valued at the average price of the period. It differs from the change in the book value of inventories reported by most businesses; an *inventory valuation adjustment (IVA)* converts book value change using historical cost valuations to the change in physical volume, valued at average replacement cost.

Net exports of goods and services is *exports of goods and services* less *imports of goods and services*. It does not include income payments or receipts or transfer payments to and from the rest of the world.

Government consumption expenditures is the estimated value of the services produced by governments (federal, state, and local) for current consumption. Since these are generally not sold, there is no market valuation and they are priced at the cost of inputs. The input costs consist of the compensation of general government employees; the estimated consumption of general government fixed capital, including software (CFC, or economic depreciation); and the cost of goods and services purchased by government less the value of sales to other sectors. The value of investment in equipment and structures produced by government workers and capital is also subtracted, and is instead included in government investment. Government sales to other sectors consist primarily of receipts of tuition payments for higher education and receipts of charges for medical care.

This definition of government consumption expenditures differs in concept—but not in the amount contributed to GDP—from the treatment in existence before the 2003 revision of the NIPAs. In the new definition, goods and services purchased by government are considered to be intermediate output. In the previous definition, they were considered to be final sales. Since their value is added to the other components to yield total government consumption expenditures, the dollar total contributed to GDP is the same. The only practical difference is that the goods purchased disappear from the goods account and appear in the services account instead. In the industry sector accounts, the value added by government is also unchanged. It continues to be measured as the sum of compensation and CFC, or equivalently as gross government output less the value of goods and services purchased. The new definition increases U.S. conformity with *SNA 1993*.

Gross government investment consists of general government and government enterprise expenditures for fixed assets (structures and equipment and software). Government inventory investment is included in government consumption expenditures.

Definitions and notes on the data:
Real values, quantity and price indexes (Tables 1-2 through 1-7)

Real, or chained (2000) dollar, estimates are estimates from which the effect of price change has been removed. Prior to the 1996 comprehensive revision, constant-dollar measures were obtained by combining real output measures for different goods and services using the relative prices of a single year as weights for the entire time span of the series. In the recent environment of rapid technological change, which has caused the prices of computers and electronic components to decline dramatically relative to other prices, this method distorts the measurement of economic growth and causes excessive revisions of growth rates at each benchmark revision. The current, chained-dollar measure changes the relative price weights each year, as relative prices shift over time. As a result, historical growth rates do not get revised as a result of recent changes in relative prices.

Chained-dollar estimates, although expressed for continuity's sake as if they had occurred according to the prices of a single year (currently 2000), are usually not additive. This means that because of the changes in price weights each

year, the chained (2000) dollar components in any given table for any year other than 2000 usually do not add to the chained (2000) dollar total. The amount of the difference for the major components of GDP is called the *residual* and is shown in Table 1-2. In time periods close to the base year, the residual is usually quite small; over longer periods, the differences become much larger. For this reason, BEA no longer publishes chained-dollar estimates prior to 1990, except for selected aggregate series. For the more detailed components of GDP, historical trends and fluctuations in real volumes are represented by *chain-type quantity indexes*, which are presented in Tables 1-4, 4-4, 5-4, 5-6, 6-6, 6-7, 6-11, 6-16, 7-2, 7-3, 15-2, 19-4, and 21-1.

Chain-weighting leads to complexity in estimating the contribution of economic sectors to an overall change in output; it becomes difficult for someone without access to the complicated statistical methods that BEA uses to find the correct answers to questions such as "How much is the rise in defense spending contributing to GDP growth?" Because of this, BEA is now calculating and publishing estimates of the contribution of each major component to the total change in real GDP. *Business Statistics* reproduces these calculations in Tables 1-3 and 19-3. For further information, see J. Steven Landefeld, Brent R. Moulton, and Cindy M. Vojtech, "Chained-Dollar Indexes: Issues, Tips on Their Use, and Upcoming Changes," *Survey of Current Business* (November 2003); and J. Steven Landefeld and Robert P. Parker, "BEA's Chain Indexes, Time Series, and Measures of Long-Term Economic Growth," *Survey of Current Business* (May 1997).

GDP price indexes measure price changes between any two adjacent years (or quarters) for a fixed "market basket" of goods and services consisting of the average quantities purchased in those two years (or quarters). The annual measures are chained together to form an index with prices in 2000 set to equal 100. Using average quantities as weights and changing weights each period eliminates the substitution bias that arises in more conventional indexes, in which weights are taken from a single base period that usually takes place early in the period under measurement. Generally, using a single, early base period leads to an overstatement of price increase. (The CPI-U and the CPI-W are examples of such conventional indexes, technically known as "Laspeyres" indexes. See the "General Notes" at the beginning of this volume and the notes and definitions for Chapter 8 for further explanation.)

The chain-type formula guarantees that a GDP price index change will differ only trivially from the change in the implicit deflator (ratio of current-dollar to real value, expressed as a percent). Therefore, *Business Statistics* is no longer publishing a separate table of implicit deflators.

Definitions and notes on the data:
Aggregates of sales and purchases (Tables 1-4 through 1-6)

Final sales of domestic product is GDP minus change in private inventories. It is the sum of personal consumption expenditures, gross private domestic fixed investment, government consumption expenditures and gross investment, and net exports of goods and services.

Gross domestic purchases is the market value of goods and services purchased by U.S. residents, regardless of where those goods and services were produced. It is GDP minus net exports (that is, minus exports plus imports) of goods and services; equivalently, it is the sum of personal consumption expenditures, gross private domestic investment, and government consumption expenditures and gross investment. The price index for gross domestic purchases is therefore a measure of price change for goods and services purchased by (rather than produced by) U.S. residents.

Final sales to domestic purchasers is gross domestic purchases minus change in private inventories.

Definitions and notes on the data:
Per capita product and income estimates (Table 1-7)

In Table 1-7, annual and quarterly measures of product, income, and consumption spending are expressed in per capita terms—the aggregate dollar amount divided by the U.S. population. Population data from 1991 forward reflect the results of Census 2000.

National per capita totals, as shown in Table 1-7, are based on definitions of income and population that differ slightly from the sum of the states shown in Table 21-2. See the notes and definitions for Chapter 21 for further explanation.

Definitions and notes on the data:
Shares of aggregate supply and demand (Tables 1-8 and 1-9)

These tables, new in this edition of *Business Statistics*, are not official NIPA tables. They are components of current-dollar GDP rearranged by the editor in order to highlight relationships that are not always apparent in the official presentation of the NIPAs.

Aggregate supply combines the two sources that, between them, supply the goods and services demanded by consumers, businesses, and governments in the U.S. economy—domestic production (GDP) and imports. In this table the user can observe the growing share of imports that satisfy demands in the U.S. marketplace.

Aggregate final demand is the sum of all final demands for goods and services in the U.S. market—consumption spending, fixed investment, exports, and government consumption and investment. It is different from *final sales* (Table 1-6) because imports are not subtracted; in this table, imports are considered a source of supply, not a negative element of demand. It is different from *domestic purchases* (Tables 1-4 through 1-6) because it includes exports, since they are a source of demand for U.S. output.

Table 1-9 provides alternative data on the question of the relative importance of consumption spending and other final demands to the U.S. economy. NIPA statistics on PCE as a percent of GDP are frequently cited, but there is a problem with this, since PCE includes the value of imports while GDP does not.

Definitions and notes on the data:
Components of income (Tables 1-11 and 1-12)

There are now two different presentations of aggregate income for the United States: *gross domestic income* (Table 1-11) and *national income* (Table 1-12). As noted above, domestic income refers to income generated from production within the United States, while national income refers to income received by residents of the United States. This means that some of the income components differ between the two tables. Domestic income payments include payments to the rest of the world from domestic industries. National income payments exclude payments to the rest of the world but include payments received by U.S. residents from the rest of the world. These differences are seen in employee compensation, interest, and corporate profits. Taxes on production and imports, taxes on corporate income, business transfer payments, subsidies, proprietors' income, rental income, and the current surplus of government enterprises are the same in both accounts.

A third income aggregate is *personal income*. The derivation of this well-known statistic from national income is shown in Table 1-10. See Chapter 4 and its notes and definitions for more information.

Compensation of employees is the income accruing to employees as remuneration for their work. It is the sum of wage and salary accruals and supplements to wages and salaries. In the domestic income account, it is called "compensation of employees, paid." It refers to all payments generated by domestic production, including those to workers residing in the "rest of the world." In the national and personal income accounts, it is a different amount labeled "compensation of employees, received"—that is, received by U.S. residents—including from the rest of the world.

Wage and salary accruals consists of the monetary remuneration of employees, including the compensation of corporate officers; corporate directors' fees paid to directors who are also employees of the corporation; commissions, tips, and bonuses; voluntary employee contributions to certain deferred compensation plans, such as 401(k) plans; and receipts-in-kind that represent income. As of the 2003 revision, it also includes judicial fees to jurors and witnesses, compensation of prison inmates, and marriage fees to justices of the peace, all of which were formerly included in "other labor income."

In concept, wage and salary accruals include the value of the exercise by employees of "nonqualified stock options," in which an employee is allowed to buy stock for less than its current market price. (Actual measurement of these values involves a number of problems, particularly in the short run. Such stock options are not included in the monthly wage data from the Bureau of Labor Statistics, which are the main source for current extrapolations of wages and salaries, and are not consistently reported in corporate financial statements. They are, however, generally included in the unemployment insurance wage data that are used to correct the preliminary wage and salary estimates.) Another form of stock option, the "incentive stock option," leads to a capital gain only and is thus not included in the definition of wages and salaries.

Wage and salary accruals include retroactive wage payments for the period in which they were earned, not for the period in which they were paid. In the NIPAs, wages *accrued* is the appropriate measure for both domestic and national income, since the intent is to measure income associated with production. Wages *disbursed* is the appropriate measure for personal income, since the latter concept focuses on what individuals receive. The difference, *wage accruals less disbursements,* is shown in Table 1-10. Substantial entries appear for this item in 2003 and 2004 because there were 53 Fridays instead of 52 Fridays in the latter year. As a result, some of the wages disbursed in 2004 were actually accrued in 2003. In 2005, 2006, and 2007, this item reflects unusually large exercises of stock options and financial industry bonuses, paid in the year after they were earned.

Supplements to wages and salaries consists of *employer contributions for employee pension and insurance funds* and *employer contributions for government social insurance.*

Employer contributions for employee pension and insurance funds consists of employer payments (including payments-in-kind) to private pension and profit-sharing plans, private group health and life insurance plans, privately administered workers' compensation plans, government employee retirement plans, and supplemental unemployment benefit plans. This includes the major part of the former category "other labor income." The remainder of "other labor income" has been reclassified as wages and salaries (as noted above).

Employer contributions for government social insurance consists of employer payments under the following federal, state, and local government programs: old-age, survivors, and disability insurance (Social Security); hospital insurance (Medicare); unemployment insurance; railroad retirement; pension benefit guaranty; veterans' life insurance; publicly administered workers' compensation; military medical insurance; and temporary disability insurance.

Taxes on production and imports is included in the gross domestic income account to make it comparable in concept to gross domestic product. It consists of federal excise taxes and customs duties and of state and local sales taxes, property taxes (including residential real estate taxes), motor vehicle license taxes, severance taxes, special assessments, and other taxes. It is equal to the former "indirect business taxes and nontax liabilities" less most of the nontax liabilities, which have now been reclassified as "business transfer payments."

Subsidies (payments by government to business other than purchases of goods and services) are now presented separately from the current surplus of government enterprises, which is presented as a component of net operating surplus. However, for years before 1959, subsidies continue to be presented as net of the current surplus of government enterprises, since detailed data to separate the series for this period are not available.

Net operating surplus is a new aggregate introduced in the 2003 NIPA revision—a grouping of the business income components of the gross domestic income account. It represents the net income accruing to business capital. It is equal to gross domestic income minus compensation of employees, taxes on production and imports less subsidies (that is, the taxes are taken out of income and the subsidies are put in), and consumption of fixed capital (CFC). Net operating surplus consists of the surplus for private enterprises and the current surplus of government enterprises. The net operating surplus of private enterprises comprises net interest and miscellaneous payments, business current transfer payments, proprietors' income, rental income of persons, and corporate profits.

Net interest and miscellaneous payments, domestic industries consists of interest paid by domestic private enterprises and of rents and royalties paid by private enterprises to government, less interest received by domestic private enterprises. Interest received does not include interest received by noninsured pension plans, which are recorded as being directly received by persons in personal income. Both interest categories include monetary and imputed interest. In the *national* account, interest paid to the rest of the world is subtracted from the interest paid by domestic industries and interest received from the rest of the world is added. Interest payments on mortgage and home improvement loans and on home equity loans are included as net interest in the private enterprises account.

It should be noted that net interest does not include interest paid by federal, state, or local governments. In fact, government interest does not enter into the national and domestic income accounts, though it does appear as a component of personal income. The NIPAs draw a distinction between interest paid by government and that paid by business.

The reasoning behind this distinction is that interest paid by *business* is one of the income counterparts of the production side of the account. The value of business production (as measured by its output of goods and services) includes the value added by business capital, and interest paid by business to its lenders is part of the total return to business capital.

However, there is no product flow in the accounts that is a counterpart to the payment of interest by *government.* The output of government does not have a market value. For purposes of GDP measurement, BEA estimates the government contribution to GDP as the sum of government's compensation of employees, purchases of goods and services, and consumption of government fixed capital. (See above, and also the notes and definitions to Chapter 6.) This implies an estimate (described as "conservative" by BEA) that the net return to government capital is zero—that is, that the gross return is just sufficient to pay down the depreciation. Consequently, this assumption generates no income that might correspond to the government's interest payment.

Supporting the distinction between business and government interest payments, it may be noted that most federal government debt was not incurred to finance investment, but rather to finance wars, avoid tax increases and spending cuts during recessions, or stimulate the economy. Some of the largest and most productive government investments—investments for highways—are typically financed by taxes on a pay-as-you-go basis and not by borrowing.

Business current transfer payments, net consists of payments to persons, government, and the rest of the world by private business for which no current services are performed. Net insurance settlements—actual insured losses (or claims payable) less a normal level of losses—are treated as transfer payments. Payments to government consist of federal deposit insurance premiums, fines, regulatory and inspection fees, tobacco settlements, and other miscellaneous payments previously classified as "nontaxes." Taxes paid by domestic corporations to foreign governments, formerly classified as transfer payments, are now counted as taxes on corporate income.

In the NIPAs, capital income other than interest—corporate profits, proprietors' income, and rental income—is converted from the basis usually shown in the books of business and reported to the Internal Revenue Service to a basis that more closely represents income from current production. In the business accounts that provide the source data, depreciation of structures and equipment typically reflects a historical cost basis and a possibly arbitrary service life allowed by law to be used for tax purposes. BEA adjusts these values to reflect the average actual life of the capital goods and the cost of replacing them in the current period's prices. This conversion is done for all three forms of capital income. In addition, corporate and proprietors' incomes also require an adjustment for inventory valuation to exclude any profits or losses that might appear in the books, should the cost of inventory acquisition not be valued in the current period's prices. These two adjustments are called the *capital consumption adjustment (CCAdj)* and the *inventory valuation adjustment (IVA)*. They are described in more detail below.

Proprietors' income with inventory valuation and capital consumption adjustments is the current-production income (including income-in-kind) of sole proprietorships and partnerships and of tax-exempt cooperatives. The imputed net rental income of owner-occupants of farm dwellings is included, but the imputed net rental income of owner-occupants of nonfarm dwellings is included in rental income of persons. Fees paid to outside directors of corporations are included. Proprietors' income excludes dividends and monetary interest received by nonfinancial business and rental incomes received by persons not primarily engaged in the real estate business; these incomes are included in dividends, net interest, and rental income of persons, respectively.

Rental income of persons with capital consumption adjustment is the net current-production income of persons from the rental of real property (except for the income of persons primarily engaged in the real estate business), the imputed net rental income of owner-occupants of nonfarm dwellings, and the royalties received by persons from patents, copyrights, and rights to natural resources. Consistent with the classification of investment in owner-occupied housing as business investment, the homeowner is considered to be paying himself or herself the rental value of the house (classified as PCE for services) and receiving as net income the amount of the rental that remains after paying interest and other costs.

Corporate profits with inventory valuation and capital consumption adjustments (often referred to as "economic profits") is the current-production income, net of economic depreciation, of organizations treated as corporations in the NIPAs. These organizations consist of all entities required to file federal corporate tax returns, including mutual financial institutions and cooperatives subject to federal income tax; private noninsured pension funds; nonprofit institutions that primarily serve business; Federal Reserve Banks, which accrue income stemming from the conduct of monetary policy; and federally sponsored credit agencies. This income is measured as receipts less expenses as defined in federal tax law, except for the following differences: receipts exclude capital gains and dividends received, expenses exclude depletion and capital losses and losses resulting from bad debts, inventory withdrawals are valued at replacement cost, and depreciation is on a consistent accounting basis and is valued at replacement cost.

Since *national* income is defined as the income of U.S. residents, its profits component includes income earned abroad by U.S. corporations and excludes income earned by the rest of the world within the United States.

Taxes on corporate income consists of taxes on corporate income paid to government and to the rest of the world.

Taxes on corporate income paid to government (formerly "profits tax liability") is the sum of federal, state, and local income taxes on all income subject to taxes. This income includes capital gains and other income excluded from profits before tax. These taxes are measured on an accrual basis, net of applicable tax credits.

Taxes on corporate income paid to the rest of the world consists of nonresident taxes, which are those paid by domestic corporations to foreign governments. These taxes were formerly classified as "business transfer payments to the rest of the world."

Profits after tax is total corporate profits with IVA and CCAdj less taxes on corporate income. It consists of dividends and undistributed corporate profits.

Dividends is payments in cash or other assets, excluding those made using corporations' own stock, that are made by corporations to stockholders. In the domestic account, these are payments by domestic industries to stockholders in the United States and abroad; in the national account, these are dividends received by U.S. residents from domestic and foreign industries. The payments are measured net of dividends received by U.S. corporations. Dividends paid to state and local government social insurance funds and general government are included.

Undistributed profits is corporate profits after tax with IVA and CCAdj less dividends.

The *inventory valuation adjustment (IVA)* is the difference between the cost of inventory withdrawals valued at replacement cost and the cost as valued in the source data used to determine profits before tax, which in many cases charge inventories at acquisition cost. It is calculated separately for corporate profits and for nonfarm proprietors' income. Its behavior is determined by price changes, especially for materials. When prices are rising, which has been typical of much of the postwar period, the business-reported value of inventory change will include a capital gains component, which needs to be removed from reported inventory change on the product side in order to correctly measure the change in the volume of inventories, and from reported profits on the income side of the accounts in order to remove the capital gains element. At such times, the IVA will be a negative figure, which is added to reported profits to yield economic profits. Occasionally, falling prices—especially for petroleum and products—will result in a positive IVA. No adjustment is needed for farm proprietors' income, as farm inventories are measured on a current-market-cost basis.

Consumption of fixed capital (CFC) is a charge for the using-up of private and government fixed capital located in the United States. It is not based on the depreciation schedules allowed in tax law, but instead on studies of prices of used equipment and structures in resale markets. In periods in which extraordinary property destruction occurs, such as during a severe hurricane or a terror attack, normal capital consumption is augmented by the estimated value of the lost assets.

For general government and for nonprofit institutions that primarily serve individuals, CFC on their capital assets is recorded in government consumption expenditures and in personal consumption expenditures, respectively. It is considered to be the value of the current services of the fixed capital assets owned and used by these entities.

Private capital consumption allowances consists of tax-return-based depreciation charges for corporations and nonfarm proprietorships and of historical cost depreciation (calculated by BEA using a geometric pattern of price declines) for farm proprietorships, rental income of persons, and nonprofit institutions.

The *private capital consumption adjustment (CCAdj)* is the difference between private capital consumption allowances and private consumption of fixed capital. The CCAdj has two parts:

The first component of CCAdj converts tax-return-based depreciation to consistent historical cost accounting based on actual service lives of capital. In the postwar period, this has usually been a large positive number, that is, a net addition to profits and subtraction from reported depreciation. This is the case because U.S. tax law typically allows depreciation periods shorter than actual service lives. Tax depreciation was accelerated even further for 2001 through 2004. This component is a reallocation of gross business saving from depreciation to profits; gross saving is unchanged, with exactly offsetting changes in capital consumption and net saving.

The second component is analogous to the IVA: it converts reported business capital consumption allowances from the historical cost basis to a replacement cost basis. It is determined by the price behavior of capital goods. These prices have had an upward drift in the postwar period, which has been much more stable than the changes in materials prices. Hence, this component is consistently negative (serving to reduce economic profits relative to the reported data) but less volatile than the IVA.

In 1981 through 2004, positive values for the first component outweighed negative values for the second, resulting in a net positive CCAdj, an addition to profits. However, when the accelerated depreciation expired in 2005, there was a sharp decline in the consistent-accounting adjustment and it was outweighed by the price adjustment. This led to negative CCAdjs in 2005 and 2006, reducing profits from the reported numbers.

Definitions and notes on the data:
Gross value added of domestic corporate business (Tables 1-13 and 1-14)

Gross value added is the term now used for what was formerly called "gross domestic product originating." It represents the share of the GDP that is produced in the specified sector or industry. Tables 1-13 and 1-14 show the current-dollar value of gross value added for all domestic corporate business and its financial and nonfinancial components. For the total and for nonfinancial corporations, consumption of fixed capital and net value added are shown, as is the allocation of net value added among employee compensation, taxes and transfer payments, and capital income. Constant-dollar values are also shown for nonfinancial corporations.

The data for nonfinancial corporations are often considered to be somewhat sturdier than data for the other sectors of the economy, since they exclude sectors whose outputs are difficult to evaluate—households, institutions, general government, and financial business—as well as excluding all noncorporate business, in which the separate contributions of labor and capital are not readily measured.

Definitions and notes on the data:
Rates of return and related data for domestic nonfinancial corporations (Table 1-15)

Table 1-15 shows various measures of the return to capital in nonfinancial corporate business. The measure of capital is the *value of produced assets,* which is the current-cost value of the net stock of equipment and software and structures and the replacement-cost value of inventories. The basic measure of the total return to capital is the *net operating surplus,* which is the sum of corporate profits, net interest paid, and net business transfer payments; this is shown in Table 1-14. As in that table, corporate profits are adjusted to an economic profits basis by including the inventory valuation and capital consumption adjustments.

Rates of return are total net operating surplus and its major components, before and after corporate taxes, as a percent of the value of produced assets. *Tax liability* is also shown as a percent of produced assets.

Shares of net value added are total net operating surplus and its major components, before and after corporate taxes, as a percent of net value added in nonfinancial domestic corporate business. Net value added, shown in Table 1-14, is the value of the industry's output after deducting the consumption of fixed capital, and is the sum of compensation of employees, the net operating surplus, and taxes on production and imports less subsidies.

A *Q ratio* (often known as "Tobin's Q" for the economist James Tobin, who originally proposed it) is the ratio of the valuation of assets in financial markets to the current-cost value of produced assets. A value of Q above 1 indicates that newly produced physical assets may be purchased more cheaply than the ownership claims to existing assets. Table 1-15 shows the BEA calculation of a ratio termed *Q3*. The numerator is the sum of the market value of outstanding equity and an estimate of the market value of outstanding corporate bonds, minus net liquid assets and land. The denominator is the value of the net stock of produced assets.

The rate of return data do not follow the general NIPA publication and revision schedule. They were presented and described in "Note on the Returns for Domestic Nonfinancial Corporations in 1960–2005," *Survey of Current Business* (May 2006), pp. 6-10. The rate of return for the net operating surplus before tax, the share of net value added, the value of produced assets, and the Q3 ratio were revised and updated in "Returns for Domestic Nonfinancial Business," *Survey of Current Business* (May 2008), pp. 19-23.

Revisions

NIPA data normally undergo revision at the end of every July. In July 2009, there will be a comprehensive revision incorporating the results of the 2002 benchmark input-out-

put accounts. The reference year for the chain-type indexes and the chained-dollar estimates will be updated to 2005, and the entire time series will be revised back to 1929.

In mid-2002, BEA inaugurated a new revision schedule for wages and salaries and related income-side components of the NIPAs. When "final" estimates of a quarter's GDP are released, wages and salaries and related data will be revised for that quarter and the preceding quarter. Since these revisions only affect income-side components, GDP itself will not be revised for that previous quarter (and the statistical discrepancy will therefore change). The purpose of this schedule change is to achieve a more timely incorporation of the Bureau of Labor Statistics's quarterly tabulations of employees covered by state unemployment insurance. Previously, revisions based on these data were not incorporated until July of the following year. The same revision schedule will also be used in the monthly estimates of personal income.

Data availability

Annual data are available beginning with 1929. Quarterly data begin with 1946 for current-dollar values and 1947 for quantity and price measures such as real GDP and the GDP price index. Not all data are available for all time periods.

New data are normally released toward the end of each month. The first estimates for each calendar quarter are released in the month after the quarter's end. Revisions for the most recent quarter are released in the second and third months after the quarter's end. As described above, wage and salary and related income-side components may be revised for previous quarters as well.

The most recent data are published each month in the *Survey of Current Business.* Current and historical data may be obtained from the BEA Web site at <http://www.bea.gov> and the STAT-USA subscription Web site at <http://www.stat-usa.gov>.

References

The latest revision is described in "Annual Revision of the National Income and Product Accounts: Annual Estimates for 2005–2007, Quarterly Estimates for 2005:I–2008:I", *Survey of Current Business* (August 2008), vol. 88 number 8. Previous annual revisions are discussed in articles in earlier August issues.

"Measuring the Economy: A Primer on GDP and the National Income and Product Accounts" (September 2007), prepared by the Bureau of Economic Analysis (BEA), is available on the BEA Web site at <http://www.bea.gov>. It contains further references to NIPA concepts, framework, history, estimating methods and source data, and reliability.

The treatment of employee stock options is discussed in Carol Moylan, "Treatment of Employee Stock Options in the U.S. National Economic Accounts," available on the BEA Web site at <http://www.bea.gov>.

CHAPTER 2: INDUSTRIAL PRODUCTION AND CAPACITY UTILIZATION

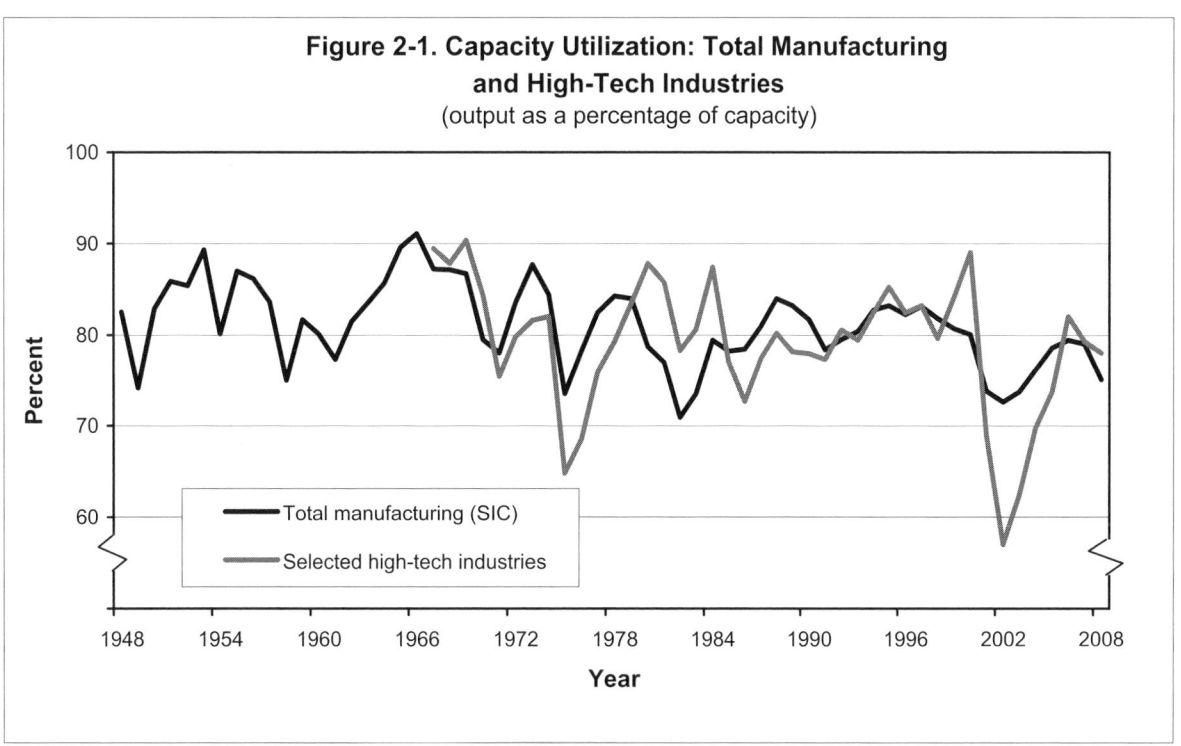

Figure 2-1. Capacity Utilization: Total Manufacturing and High-Tech Industries
(output as a percentage of capacity)

- Manufacturing capacity utilization is a key statistic for the U.S. economy, despite being limited to a sector that by some measures is diminishing in importance. (The Federal Reserve also provides measures of capacity utilization for "total industry"—manufacturing, mining, and utilities. However, mining and utilities are less significant in the context of business cycle analysis, and much of the variation in capacity use by utilities is a result of transitory weather variations, not economic factors.) Manufacturing utilization is an important indicator of inflationary pressure and also measures an important element in the demand for new capital goods. (Tables 2-3 and 20-1)

- By December 2008, manufacturing capacity utilization had fallen to 69 percent; three months later, according to preliminary data, only 66 percent of manufacturing capacity was in use—lower than utilization in any previous month in the entire postwar period. (Tables 2-3 and 20-1)

- Capacity utilization in the high-tech industries (computers and office equipment, communications equipment, and semiconductors and related electronic components) has been more volatile than in the rest of industry, as seen in Figure 2-1. High-tech cycles were also not precisely synchronized with the overall cycle. At the height of the dot-com boom in 2000, high-tech utilization soared to 89.0 percent, while capacity use declined elsewhere. In 2002, high-tech industries used only 57.0 percent of capacity. For most of 2006 through 2008, however, high-tech utilization exceeded the overall manufacturing average. (Table 2-3)

- Industrial production increased 184 percent from 1967 to 2007, which translates into an annual average growth rate of 2.6 percent. High-tech industries grew at an annual rate of 17.8 percent, while the aggregate of the rest of the manufacturing, mining, and utilities industries grew at a rate of 1.7 percent. (Table 2-2)

Table 2-1. Industrial Production Indexes by Market Groups

(Seasonally adjusted, 2002 = 100.)

Year and month	Total industrial production	Final products and nonindustrial supplies							
		Total	Consumer goods						
			Total	Durable consumer goods					Nondurable consumer goods
				Total	Automotive products	Home electronics	Appliances, furniture, and carpeting	Miscellaneous durable goods	Total
1967	39.2	38.5	45.1	31.0	29.8	1.5	44.2	47.3	52.1
1968	41.4	40.4	47.7	34.6	35.5	1.6	47.5	50.4	54.1
1969	43.3	41.9	49.5	36.1	35.8	1.6	50.1	54.5	55.9
1970	41.9	40.6	49.0	33.3	30.1	1.5	49.6	52.7	56.9
1971	42.5	41.2	51.8	37.7	38.4	1.6	52.4	55.5	58.5
1972	46.6	45.0	56.0	42.2	41.4	1.9	61.5	62.3	62.2
1973	50.4	48.4	58.5	45.4	45.0	2.2	66.4	65.1	64.1
1974	50.2	48.2	56.8	41.3	38.9	2.0	60.4	62.9	64.2
1975	45.8	44.9	54.5	37.5	37.5	1.7	51.7	55.8	63.1
1976	49.4	48.1	59.0	42.4	42.7	2.0	58.4	62.1	67.0
1977	53.1	52.0	62.7	47.6	48.3	2.4	65.6	68.8	69.4
1978	56.0	55.1	64.6	48.8	48.0	2.7	69.1	71.0	71.9
1979	57.7	56.9	63.7	47.0	43.2	2.7	69.3	71.6	71.5
1980	56.3	56.2	61.3	40.8	33.3	2.8	64.5	65.6	71.6
1981	57.0	57.3	61.7	41.4	34.3	2.9	63.7	66.6	71.9
1982	54.1	55.9	61.5	39.0	33.3	2.6	57.5	63.0	73.1
1983	55.6	57.4	63.8	43.4	38.7	3.7	63.5	64.8	73.9
1984	60.5	62.2	66.7	48.5	43.2	4.5	70.8	71.7	75.4
1985	61.3	63.8	67.3	48.5	43.2	4.7	70.2	71.7	76.4
1986	61.9	65.1	69.7	51.7	46.4	6.1	73.7	74.1	78.2
1987	65.1	68.3	72.6	54.7	49.5	6.0	77.7	78.7	81.0
1988	68.4	71.7	75.4	57.6	52.1	8.0	78.9	82.2	83.6
1989	69.1	72.4	75.7	59.0	54.2	8.4	79.7	82.7	83.4
1990	69.7	73.3	76.0	57.3	50.8	9.7	77.7	81.9	84.8
1991	68.7	72.2	75.9	54.8	47.4	11.6	72.4	79.0	86.0
1992	70.6	74.0	78.2	60.1	55.5	12.6	76.5	81.6	86.6
1993	72.9	76.3	80.7	65.2	61.3	16.0	80.9	85.2	87.8
1994	76.8	79.7	84.3	71.7	68.7	20.7	86.6	89.9	90.0
1995	80.4	82.9	86.9	75.1	70.8	30.9	86.2	92.5	92.2
1996	84.0	86.1	88.6	78.0	73.0	37.6	87.2	95.6	93.4
1997	90.1	91.8	91.8	83.4	78.5	51.8	91.0	97.8	95.6
1998	95.4	97.1	95.2	89.6	83.7	70.4	97.1	101.2	97.6
1999	99.5	100.0	97.1	96.0	91.7	87.8	100.4	103.5	97.6
2000	103.7	103.5	99.1	99.0	93.7	100.1	103.2	106.3	99.2
2001	100.1	100.8	98.1	94.7	90.8	100.1	98.6	98.6	99.4
2002	100.0	100.0	100.0	100.0	100.0	100.0	100.0	100.0	100.0
2003	101.3	101.2	101.4	103.4	105.6	109.8	99.9	100.1	100.6
2004	103.8	103.4	102.7	104.9	105.2	121.9	103.1	102.2	101.8
2005	107.2	107.4	105.4	105.4	103.0	131.8	105.2	105.1	105.3
2006	109.7	109.8	105.8	104.3	99.5	151.1	101.8	106.7	106.2
2007	111.3	111.1	106.8	104.7	101.5	161.1	96.7	106.5	107.4
2008	108.8	108.2	104.0	94.4	87.6	182.4	84.1	99.9	106.9
2007									
January	109.9	110.2	106.1	102.3	96.5	153.5	98.2	106.6	107.3
February	110.8	111.2	107.7	103.9	100.0	159.9	97.9	105.8	108.8
March	110.6	110.7	106.7	104.0	100.2	156.2	97.3	106.4	107.4
April	111.1	111.0	107.1	105.7	102.8	159.2	98.6	106.8	107.4
May	111.1	110.9	106.9	105.4	102.3	154.8	98.3	107.0	107.3
June	111.2	111.1	106.9	106.3	104.3	155.2	97.6	107.3	107.0
July	111.5	111.4	107.1	106.8	105.2	154.4	96.7	108.0	107.1
August	111.6	111.3	107.0	105.5	103.0	155.8	96.9	107.0	107.4
September	112.0	111.7	107.2	104.5	100.8	162.2	96.1	107.0	108.0
October	111.4	110.8	106.1	104.0	100.7	166.0	95.2	105.7	106.7
November	112.1	111.1	106.3	104.2	100.7	176.0	94.8	105.5	106.9
December	112.4	111.4	106.6	104.2	101.4	180.4	92.9	104.9	107.3
2008									
January	112.3	111.7	106.9	102.7	99.4	179.5	91.1	104.5	108.2
February	112.0	111.3	106.7	101.6	98.6	181.9	89.4	103.0	108.2
March	111.6	110.7	105.6	98.7	92.8	184.2	89.1	102.8	107.6
April	111.0	109.9	105.0	96.0	87.6	187.5	88.7	102.3	107.7
May	110.7	109.6	104.7	96.0	87.9	188.8	87.7	102.1	107.3
June	110.4	109.5	104.8	97.1	90.9	185.0	86.9	101.8	107.1
July	110.4	109.2	104.5	97.8	92.4	186.6	86.4	101.6	106.6
August	109.2	107.8	102.7	92.2	83.1	184.2	83.1	100.4	105.9
September	104.8	105.3	101.4	91.5	84.2	182.2	80.1	98.5	104.3
October	106.3	105.7	103.0	89.5	81.5	180.9	78.7	97.1	107.0
November	104.9	104.9	102.1	86.6	79.0	178.0	74.8	94.2	106.7
December	102.4	103.3	100.4	82.6	74.2	170.1	73.1	90.5	105.7

Table 2-1. Industrial Production Indexes by Market Groups—*Continued*

(Seasonally adjusted, 2002 = 100.)

Year and month	Nondurable non-energy consumer goods Total	Foods and tobacco	Clothing	Chemical products	Paper products	Consumer energy products	Business equipment Total	Transit	Information processing	Industrial and other	Defense and space equipment	Construction supplies	Business supplies
1967	53.7	57.8	163.8	23.9	53.7	43.2	20.4	77.2	1.5	53.9	88.4	49.5	33.8
1968	55.6	59.3	169.8	26.1	53.2	46.2	21.3	86.1	1.6	53.8	88.6	52.1	35.9
1969	57.2	60.9	172.5	27.4	55.0	49.4	22.7	84.9	1.8	57.3	84.3	54.3	38.2
1970	57.7	61.7	167.3	29.8	53.1	52.3	21.9	74.5	1.9	55.3	71.4	52.4	38.4
1971	59.2	63.6	166.5	31.5	54.2	54.8	20.8	72.0	1.8	52.9	64.2	54.1	39.5
1972	63.1	67.1	181.8	34.4	54.6	57.8	23.6	78.5	2.1	60.2	62.4	61.4	43.5
1973	65.2	68.9	185.6	37.0	56.5	58.9	27.4	93.8	2.4	68.5	68.4	66.6	46.2
1974	64.9	69.3	173.4	39.0	55.6	60.4	29.0	91.6	3.0	71.4	70.6	65.0	46.1
1975	63.2	68.1	168.2	37.6	52.4	61.8	25.9	80.5	2.8	62.5	71.2	55.1	42.5
1976	67.3	72.5	177.6	40.9	54.5	65.0	27.6	83.1	3.4	65.1	69.1	59.3	45.3
1977	69.7	73.9	186.7	42.5	59.6	67.5	31.9	98.7	4.4	70.9	61.9	64.6	49.1
1978	72.4	76.7	191.4	45.1	62.6	68.8	36.0	114.6	5.6	75.9	63.0	68.3	51.7
1979	71.5	76.2	180.4	45.2	63.3	70.5	40.5	125.7	7.0	80.6	67.5	70.0	53.5
1980	72.3	77.4	183.7	45.1	64.0	68.0	41.5	118.1	8.8	78.0	80.2	64.8	52.3
1981	72.8	77.7	183.5	45.7	65.7	67.5	42.8	110.1	10.5	77.8	86.9	63.7	53.5
1982	74.2	80.2	183.0	45.8	67.3	68.0	39.1	90.6	11.9	67.3	103.9	57.8	52.9
1983	75.2	80.4	188.2	46.3	70.2	68.5	39.3	89.1	13.7	62.3	96.2	61.9	55.4
1984	76.5	81.4	180.5	47.4	73.8	70.6	45.2	91.7	16.9	71.1	111.4	67.3	60.2
1985	77.7	83.8	180.3	47.8	77.6	70.6	46.9	94.7	18.2	72.0	125.7	69.0	61.8
1986	79.6	85.2	188.4	51.5	78.6	72.0	46.1	86.7	18.3	71.6	142.4	71.3	63.8
1987	82.4	87.1	189.9	55.5	83.2	74.6	49.3	88.4	21.0	74.2	145.4	75.9	67.6
1988	84.7	89.6	186.9	58.8	85.4	78.5	54.4	97.7	23.6	80.6	146.9	77.7	70.1
1989	84.3	89.0	178.2	60.0	85.7	79.0	56.3	102.0	24.4	83.2	147.1	77.4	71.1
1990	86.2	91.5	174.5	62.2	87.3	78.5	58.4	110.3	26.4	82.7	142.0	76.8	72.8
1991	87.1	91.9	173.9	64.4	87.8	80.9	57.4	115.5	26.4	78.3	131.5	72.6	71.8
1992	88.1	93.2	177.5	64.2	88.9	79.8	59.6	111.1	29.8	79.7	122.0	75.7	73.5
1993	88.8	92.4	180.8	65.9	91.0	83.3	62.3	102.5	32.4	85.0	115.3	79.0	75.8
1994	91.2	96.2	184.0	67.3	90.0	84.4	66.0	95.2	36.3	90.8	108.3	84.7	78.8
1995	93.4	98.7	183.1	70.1	90.6	86.6	71.7	91.7	43.3	96.5	105.2	86.7	82.1
1996	94.0	98.3	178.1	73.5	90.2	90.4	78.5	95.2	52.7	99.8	102.0	90.5	85.2
1997	96.8	99.8	177.3	77.7	98.2	89.8	90.3	114.0	66.5	105.9	100.7	95.0	91.3
1998	99.3	102.3	166.8	81.6	102.8	89.8	100.5	136.6	78.8	109.2	105.1	100.1	96.5
1999	98.7	100.4	160.8	82.9	104.9	92.9	106.4	135.7	95.3	106.7	102.2	102.7	100.6
2000	100.1	101.9	153.7	86.0	105.6	95.1	114.7	117.7	116.5	112.9	91.3	105.0	105.2
2001	100.1	101.8	132.4	90.8	103.0	96.2	108.0	112.1	114.9	102.1	100.0	100.1	101.0
2002	100.0	100.0	100.0	100.0	100.0	100.0	100.0	100.0	100.0	100.0	100.0	100.0	100.0
2003	100.6	101.3	94.4	101.9	96.2	100.5	100.0	91.9	105.0	99.6	106.7	99.7	101.7
2004	101.5	102.9	78.5	104.4	96.7	102.9	105.3	97.5	114.9	102.2	104.7	102.0	103.8
2005	104.8	106.3	74.1	109.8	95.8	107.1	112.6	107.4	123.8	107.8	115.8	106.6	107.3
2006	106.4	106.7	68.6	115.6	95.6	105.8	123.2	124.7	141.3	112.6	113.4	109.0	108.5
2007	107.2	109.0	68.8	113.7	95.3	108.4	126.4	121.7	149.4	115.5	117.6	106.9	109.9
2008	106.0	108.7	66.1	111.3	93.0	109.5	125.0	108.1	162.5	111.7	120.6	100.2	106.7
2007													
January	107.6	108.2	69.4	116.6	95.6	106.8	124.4	123.0	145.5	113.3	116.6	106.1	109.2
February	107.7	108.7	69.8	115.8	96.4	112.4	124.4	122.5	145.3	113.6	115.8	106.2	110.1
March	107.3	108.3	69.1	115.1	96.4	108.2	124.9	120.3	145.4	115.0	112.8	107.5	109.8
April	107.4	108.6	69.9	114.7	96.2	107.7	124.8	118.2	145.6	115.5	114.4	107.6	110.1
May	107.1	108.9	69.9	113.6	95.3	108.2	124.9	117.6	145.6	115.9	115.9	107.7	109.8
June	107.3	109.4	69.4	113.1	95.6	106.5	125.7	119.3	147.2	116.0	117.4	108.1	109.7
July	107.6	109.8	69.1	113.5	95.7	106.1	127.3	121.8	149.0	117.1	118.1	108.0	109.5
August	106.9	109.2	67.0	113.0	94.7	109.1	126.8	122.2	150.8	115.3	118.5	107.1	109.9
September	107.4	110.4	67.9	112.1	94.6	110.1	128.5	123.3	152.5	117.2	120.1	107.0	110.3
October	106.7	109.1	67.9	112.6	94.1	107.1	128.1	122.8	153.5	116.2	119.4	106.0	109.8
November	106.2	108.7	67.1	111.8	94.0	109.1	128.3	123.9	154.9	115.6	121.1	105.7	110.1
December	106.8	109.2	69.0	112.2	94.6	108.8	129.4	125.4	157.4	115.9	121.4	105.6	110.1
2008													
January	106.9	108.8	68.7	113.3	94.7	111.9	130.2	125.2	159.8	116.3	122.3	105.0	110.2
February	106.7	108.9	67.8	112.6	94.7	112.2	129.8	123.3	162.2	115.2	120.5	104.0	109.9
March	107.0	109.9	67.2	111.5	95.2	109.6	130.8	122.4	165.2	116.0	120.7	103.3	109.4
April	106.4	109.3	66.7	111.3	93.8	111.4	128.4	118.1	167.2	112.3	120.8	102.1	109.1
May	106.6	109.6	65.2	111.4	93.9	109.4	128.4	117.9	167.5	112.3	120.2	102.2	108.3
June	106.3	108.9	66.3	111.4	94.4	109.5	128.2	119.9	166.5	111.7	121.9	101.7	107.6
July	105.8	108.1	66.6	111.8	92.9	108.8	127.4	119.8	163.7	111.5	120.2	102.4	107.3
August	105.9	108.2	67.7	111.3	93.1	106.3	126.2	113.0	161.7	112.4	120.8	101.2	106.6
September	105.8	108.4	66.7	111.5	91.9	101.0	117.7	74.9	160.1	110.7	118.9	99.1	104.3
October	106.1	109.3	65.4	111.3	90.5	110.2	114.9	65.1	160.0	109.0	120.4	97.8	104.4
November	105.3	108.6	62.9	110.2	90.6	111.0	117.9	87.1	158.5	107.7	120.0	93.7	102.8
December	103.3	106.1	62.1	108.2	90.5	112.9	120.2	111.0	156.9	104.9	120.0	89.7	100.0

Table 2-1. Industrial Production Indexes by Market Groups—*Continued*

(Seasonally adjusted, 2002 = 100.)

Year and month	Materials Total	Non-energy materials Total	Durable Total	Durable Consumer parts	Durable Equipment parts	Durable Other	Nondurable Total	Nondurable Textile	Nondurable Paper	Nondurable Chemical	Energy materials
1967	39.1	32.2	25.7	47.6	7.7	58.5	48.2	79.5	49.8	33.7	68.8
1968	41.7	34.6	27.3	53.6	7.8	61.5	53.0	87.8	52.1	39.2	72.0
1969	44.1	36.7	28.7	54.0	8.4	65.5	57.3	90.1	56.5	43.6	75.6
1970	42.6	34.6	26.1	45.3	7.7	61.2	57.7	86.8	56.1	44.6	79.4
1971	43.2	35.2	26.1	50.1	7.7	58.8	60.1	91.0	58.5	47.2	80.1
1972	47.6	39.5	29.6	55.8	8.8	66.6	66.3	95.8	62.5	55.0	83.1
1973	51.9	43.8	33.8	64.8	10.4	73.8	69.6	93.1	67.4	60.6	85.2
1974	51.8	43.7	33.4	57.3	11.0	73.8	70.5	87.0	70.8	62.3	84.8
1975	46.1	37.5	28.0	46.2	9.5	61.7	63.2	85.2	61.5	52.2	84.0
1976	50.1	41.8	31.2	59.1	10.2	66.3	70.0	95.0	67.6	59.8	85.9
1977	53.6	45.2	34.0	64.7	11.5	70.2	75.1	101.3	70.7	66.5	88.6
1978	56.3	48.2	36.7	68.4	12.9	74.8	77.9	91.8	74.2	70.6	89.7
1979	57.8	49.5	37.9	64.6	14.2	76.7	79.4	99.3	77.2	73.5	92.1
1980	55.7	46.6	35.1	49.9	14.6	71.0	76.8	88.6	77.8	68.0	92.8
1981	56.0	46.7	35.2	47.4	15.0	71.1	77.4	94.8	79.3	68.5	93.7
1982	51.7	42.1	30.7	40.3	13.7	60.0	73.3	86.6	79.9	61.4	89.7
1983	53.0	45.0	32.7	49.0	14.0	62.7	78.5	97.2	85.0	67.9	86.9
1984	58.1	50.1	38.0	58.3	16.9	69.5	82.0	88.6	90.3	72.2	92.4
1985	58.0	50.2	38.2	60.6	16.9	69.0	81.3	91.7	89.8	70.9	91.9
1986	57.9	51.1	38.7	60.1	17.2	70.2	83.9	95.5	93.6	74.4	88.2
1987	61.0	54.5	41.4	61.7	18.8	75.2	88.9	107.2	98.2	80.8	90.3
1988	64.4	58.0	44.8	66.8	20.5	80.5	92.2	106.2	101.5	85.7	93.4
1989	64.9	58.4	45.0	63.3	21.2	80.8	93.0	108.5	101.4	86.9	94.3
1990	65.3	58.5	45.1	59.0	22.0	81.2	93.2	103.1	101.8	87.7	96.2
1991	64.3	57.2	43.7	55.8	21.9	77.7	92.2	103.0	99.6	86.5	96.3
1992	66.4	60.0	46.6	62.7	23.1	81.8	94.5	109.0	102.0	88.7	95.4
1993	68.6	62.7	49.7	70.9	24.6	85.0	95.6	113.5	102.0	89.1	95.7
1994	73.1	67.7	55.3	81.9	27.9	91.3	98.4	120.5	105.9	91.9	97.2
1995	77.2	72.4	61.1	85.2	34.1	94.7	99.4	118.4	108.6	92.6	98.7
1996	81.2	76.9	67.5	87.5	41.9	97.6	98.4	115.2	105.1	93.1	100.2
1997	87.8	85.0	76.9	94.2	53.1	102.5	103.1	120.3	106.3	99.8	100.0
1998	93.1	91.4	85.4	97.6	65.4	105.3	104.4	119.3	107.3	100.0	100.4
1999	98.7	98.5	95.0	107.4	80.1	107.0	105.7	116.3	109.2	102.9	99.9
2000	104.0	104.8	104.5	107.7	100.0	108.0	105.5	111.5	108.1	103.6	101.5
2001	99.1	98.7	98.9	95.7	99.4	100.1	98.4	98.6	101.6	95.8	100.3
2002	100.0	100.0	100.0	100.0	100.0	100.0	100.0	100.0	100.0	100.0	100.0
2003	101.3	101.8	103.5	98.7	111.5	99.4	99.0	94.8	96.3	100.6	100.0
2004	104.5	106.4	109.5	98.6	123.6	104.0	101.4	90.5	97.4	107.1	99.6
2005	107.0	110.7	115.4	99.3	138.2	106.6	103.3	93.3	98.0	109.2	98.4
2006	109.5	113.7	119.9	96.9	151.2	109.1	104.1	84.9	98.4	110.9	100.0
2007	111.7	116.0	122.8	93.9	163.7	109.3	105.8	78.8	97.7	115.4	101.8
2008	109.6	111.9	119.7	82.9	170.9	104.8	100.4	70.6	93.3	107.4	103.6
2007											
January	109.6	113.6	119.5	93.6	155.6	107.3	104.5	80.7	97.9	112.9	100.5
February	110.4	114.1	119.9	93.8	156.7	107.4	105.1	81.3	99.0	113.8	101.8
March	110.6	115.0	120.9	94.5	157.9	108.4	105.9	80.9	98.4	115.9	100.5
April	111.2	115.8	122.0	95.3	159.6	109.2	106.3	81.3	98.4	115.9	100.8
May	111.5	115.9	122.4	95.3	160.6	109.6	106.0	81.2	97.7	115.6	101.5
June	111.3	116.1	123.0	95.0	162.9	109.7	105.7	81.2	96.2	115.5	100.6
July	111.7	116.8	123.9	94.6	166.1	110.0	106.1	78.5	97.5	115.0	100.5
August	112.1	116.4	123.6	94.9	165.9	109.4	105.5	76.2	97.1	114.7	102.5
September	112.4	116.8	123.7	93.2	167.0	109.7	106.4	76.2	96.2	116.8	102.4
October	112.2	116.4	123.8	92.3	169.1	109.3	105.3	76.2	96.2	115.2	102.7
November	113.3	117.7	125.3	92.8	171.0	110.9	106.4	76.2	97.8	116.3	103.4
December	113.7	117.9	125.0	91.0	171.7	110.8	107.2	76.0	100.0	116.8	104.0
2008											
January	113.2	117.1	124.6	90.1	173.3	109.7	106.0	73.8	97.2	115.7	104.2
February	113.1	116.5	124.4	89.5	173.6	109.4	104.8	74.2	95.8	114.5	104.9
March	112.9	116.3	124.0	87.5	175.5	108.8	104.9	73.1	96.4	114.2	104.6
April	112.4	115.6	123.3	85.8	175.0	108.4	104.2	72.3	95.7	113.4	104.6
May	112.1	115.1	122.5	85.3	174.2	107.5	104.1	72.6	97.4	112.7	104.6
June	111.7	114.8	122.9	86.0	174.8	107.6	103.1	70.9	94.7	111.9	104.0
July	111.9	114.4	122.8	86.6	173.8	107.6	102.1	70.6	94.2	110.6	105.2
August	110.9	113.5	121.5	81.2	175.0	107.0	101.8	72.8	94.1	109.1	104.0
September	104.3	107.8	118.9	80.6	172.7	103.7	92.6	70.2	92.1	91.5	96.2
October	107.1	108.6	115.8	77.8	168.5	101.1	97.8	69.4	91.5	103.7	102.3
November	105.1	104.2	110.6	74.8	160.8	96.4	94.4	66.1	87.6	98.6	104.4
December	101.2	98.6	104.6	69.3	153.7	90.9	89.5	61.7	83.2	92.5	103.7

Table 2-1. Industrial Production Indexes by Market Groups—*Continued*

(Seasonally adjusted, 2002 = 100.)

Year and month	Energy						Non-energy					Total non-energy, excluding high-tech
								Selected high-tech				
	Total	Consumer energy products	Commercial energy products	Oil and gas well drilling	Converted fuels	Primary energy	Total	Total	Computers and office equipment	Communications equipment	Semiconductors and related components	
1967	57.8	43.2	30.8	. . .	57.0	79.7	35.8	0.3	. . .	. . .	. . .	52.9
1968	61.0	46.2	33.4	. . .	61.1	82.0	37.9	0.3	. . .	. . .	. . .	55.8
1969	64.2	49.4	35.1	. . .	65.3	84.8	39.6	0.3	. . .	. . .	. . .	58.1
1970	67.3	52.3	37.8	. . .	68.8	88.9	37.8	0.3	. . .	. . .	. . .	55.4
1971	68.5	54.8	39.7	. . .	70.6	88.2	38.3	0.3	. . .	. . .	. . .	56.4
1972	71.7	57.8	41.9	97.2	75.0	89.6	42.3	0.3	0.1	4.5	0.2	62.0
1973	73.6	58.9	44.2	83.1	77.9	90.7	46.2	0.4	0.1	5.0	0.3	67.4
1974	73.9	60.4	44.2	106.3	76.8	91.1	46.0	0.5	0.2	5.4	0.3	66.6
1975	74.2	61.8	45.9	111.6	74.1	91.9	41.1	0.5	0.2	5.2	0.3	59.4
1976	76.6	65.0	48.2	126.7	78.2	91.9	44.8	0.6	0.3	5.5	0.4	64.4
1977	79.5	67.5	49.9	163.2	81.1	94.6	48.6	0.8	0.4	6.7	0.5	69.3
1978	80.9	68.8	51.4	182.7	80.4	96.8	51.7	1.0	0.6	7.3	0.6	73.1
1979	83.3	70.5	53.7	187.0	83.4	99.0	53.2	1.3	0.8	8.7	0.7	74.4
1980	83.6	68.0	52.9	224.3	81.8	92.7	51.4	1.6	1.2	10.4	0.8	70.9
1981	84.9	67.5	54.2	272.8	80.6	94.7	52.1	1.9	1.6	11.2	0.9	71.1
1982	81.8	68.0	54.9	229.6	74.2	91.8	49.1	2.2	1.9	11.8	1.0	66.2
1983	79.4	68.5	56.0	180.4	74.0	95.8	51.5	2.6	2.7	12.6	1.2	68.7
1984	84.1	70.6	59.1	197.9	78.7	93.5	56.6	3.4	3.9	13.4	1.6	74.6
1985	83.8	70.6	61.2	180.0	78.3	92.9	57.6	3.6	4.6	13.0	1.6	75.7
1986	80.9	72.0	63.0	95.4	75.5	97.0	58.9	3.7	4.9	12.3	1.7	77.4
1987	83.2	74.6	66.3	91.8	79.4	97.7	62.2	4.5	6.3	13.7	2.1	81.0
1988	86.5	78.5	68.5	111.1	83.0	100.4	65.7	5.4	7.7	16.5	2.4	84.6
1989	87.4	79.0	71.1	96.4	86.1	99.7	66.2	5.7	8.1	17.4	2.6	85.0
1990	88.8	78.5	73.1	102.5	86.8	102.4	66.8	6.4	8.7	20.6	3.0	85.1
1991	89.3	80.9	74.1	80.1	86.9	102.5	65.4	6.9	9.0	20.9	3.3	82.8
1992	88.1	79.8	73.7	55.6	88.5	100.0	67.9	8.2	11.3	23.9	4.0	85.0
1993	89.7	83.3	75.9	77.3	90.2	99.1	70.3	9.6	14.0	27.0	4.6	87.3
1994	91.5	84.4	78.9	92.0	91.6	100.8	74.5	12.1	17.4	32.0	6.1	91.1
1995	93.4	86.6	81.7	89.6	92.9	102.3	78.4	16.9	24.3	38.9	9.1	93.4
1996	95.7	90.4	84.2	96.1	94.6	103.8	82.2	24.1	34.4	47.9	13.9	94.9
1997	96.1	89.8	87.7	110.1	96.1	102.6	89.3	35.3	48.8	65.1	21.6	99.6
1998	96.5	89.8	89.2	103.2	97.2	102.5	95.3	49.1	67.2	77.6	32.4	103.2
1999	97.1	92.9	92.7	80.7	98.9	100.5	100.0	70.0	88.2	97.2	51.8	104.5
2000	99.6	95.1	96.5	114.3	101.3	101.7	104.5	98.3	102.8	132.8	79.8	105.3
2001	99.7	96.2	98.1	138.7	97.8	101.6	100.2	101.3	103.8	127.4	86.5	100.1
2002	100.0	100.0	100.0	100.0	100.0	100.0	100.0	100.0	100.0	100.0	100.0	100.0
2003	101.0	100.5	104.8	116.2	100.3	99.8	101.3	120.5	108.2	107.1	134.5	100.0
2004	101.9	102.9	108.6	126.9	102.3	98.3	104.3	137.9	109.4	122.1	162.4	102.1
2005	102.6	107.1	111.4	142.5	103.1	96.3	108.4	158.8	130.2	121.6	197.2	105.4
2006	103.8	105.8	111.8	164.4	102.9	98.6	111.3	189.1	162.0	145.1	230.0	107.0
2007	105.9	108.4	113.9	170.3	107.0	99.5	112.7	213.7	197.4	149.1	264.4	107.6
2008	107.6	109.5	115.6	177.7	106.3	102.2	108.8	238.7	216.9	169.7	294.2	102.9
2007												
January	104.7	106.8	113.0	172.7	103.4	99.1	111.3	196.9	178.3	146.2	237.2	106.7
February	107.2	112.4	115.8	173.3	108.2	99.0	111.7	197.4	180.3	146.0	237.3	107.1
March	105.0	108.2	113.1	172.7	104.0	98.9	112.1	199.8	183.0	145.1	242.3	107.4
April	105.2	107.7	114.4	170.4	106.0	98.5	112.6	202.9	186.3	143.7	249.4	107.8
May	105.6	108.2	113.8	169.0	106.3	99.4	112.6	204.7	189.7	142.7	252.5	107.7
June	104.6	106.5	112.9	171.2	105.1	98.5	113.0	209.5	193.3	144.5	260.7	108.0
July	104.3	106.1	111.6	170.3	103.9	98.9	113.6	216.5	197.1	147.9	272.8	108.3
August	106.5	109.1	114.6	168.6	110.0	99.3	112.9	219.2	201.5	151.1	273.6	107.6
September	106.7	110.1	113.8	168.4	109.0	99.6	113.4	222.6	206.5	153.7	276.1	108.0
October	106.0	107.1	114.3	162.2	109.8	99.7	112.8	228.0	212.1	154.8	285.4	107.2
November	107.2	109.1	115.4	170.1	109.0	100.9	113.3	232.2	217.7	155.7	291.6	107.6
December	107.5	108.8	114.2	174.9	109.4	101.7	113.6	235.3	223.1	157.4	294.3	107.9
2008												
January	108.6	111.9	116.9	169.6	110.1	101.7	113.2	237.5	228.1	159.2	294.7	107.3
February	109.2	112.2	118.6	167.6	109.9	102.6	112.6	242.2	232.5	161.9	301.2	106.6
March	108.1	109.6	114.8	171.2	108.9	102.7	112.4	248.1	236.1	167.7	308.3	106.3
April	108.8	111.4	117.1	174.0	108.9	102.7	111.3	251.2	237.5	173.4	309.1	105.0
May	108.2	109.4	115.7	176.8	108.7	102.8	111.1	250.3	234.8	174.4	307.7	104.9
June	108.0	109.5	116.5	179.1	106.2	102.9	110.8	248.4	227.5	173.0	309.6	104.7
July	108.7	108.8	116.9	180.2	104.9	104.8	110.5	246.6	217.9	171.0	314.2	104.4
August	107.0	106.3	114.0	182.7	102.6	104.0	109.4	243.6	209.7	168.9	314.4	103.4
September	100.8	101.0	112.8	189.0	100.7	94.1	105.9	240.0	205.0	169.0	307.8	99.9
October	107.0	110.2	114.7	186.4	104.1	101.2	105.6	232.0	201.0	171.2	285.8	99.8
November	108.5	111.0	115.0	183.2	105.8	103.5	103.2	217.7	193.4	172.6	249.9	97.8
December	108.3	112.9	114.4	172.7	104.2	103.1	99.9	206.5	179.7	174.0	227.3	94.8

. . . = Not available.

Table 2-2. Industrial Production Indexes by NAICS Industry Groups

(Seasonally adjusted, 2002 = 100.)

Year and month	Total industrial production	Manu-facturing (SIC)	Manufacturing (NAICS) Total	Durable goods manufacturing Total	Wood products	Nonmetallic mineral products	Primary metals	Fabricated metal products	Machinery	Computer and electronic products	Electrical equipment, appliances, and components	Motor vehicles and parts	Aerospace and miscellaneous transport equipment
1967	39.2	36.1	. . .	. . .	. . .	. . .	. . .	. . .	. . .	. . .	. . .	. . .	. . .
1968	41.4	38.1	. . .	. . .	. . .	. . .	. . .	. . .	. . .	. . .	. . .	. . .	. . .
1969	43.3	39.8	. . .	. . .	. . .	. . .	. . .	. . .	. . .	. . .	. . .	. . .	. . .
1970	41.9	38.0	. . .	. . .	. . .	. . .	. . .	. . .	. . .	. . .	. . .	. . .	. . .
1971	42.5	38.6	. . .	. . .	. . .	. . .	. . .	. . .	. . .	. . .	. . .	. . .	. . .
1972	46.6	42.6	41.5	31.4	73.7	74.1	113.7	69.1	68.0	1.4	72.4	44.3	72.4
1973	50.4	46.4	45.3	35.3	71.3	79.5	133.7	76.3	78.5	1.7	81.5	50.7	82.4
1974	50.2	46.3	45.2	35.1	64.8	78.5	137.2	75.0	82.4	1.9	79.6	43.5	83.8
1975	45.8	41.5	40.4	30.5	60.1	70.3	104.7	64.8	71.8	1.7	63.9	38.0	79.6
1976	49.4	45.2	44.2	33.4	67.6	74.3	111.7	69.4	74.9	2.0	72.1	48.5	74.5
1977	53.1	49.1	47.9	36.6	73.0	79.1	112.9	75.3	81.8	2.6	79.5	55.1	75.1
1978	56.0	52.1	50.9	39.5	73.9	84.2	120.7	79.0	88.1	3.1	84.4	57.4	82.8
1979	57.7	53.7	52.5	41.5	71.5	84.1	123.8	82.5	93.0	3.9	87.9	52.6	96.4
1980	56.3	51.8	50.5	39.7	66.2	75.9	107.8	77.8	88.5	4.7	82.6	38.8	95.5
1981	57.0	52.4	51.0	40.1	64.7	72.7	107.9	77.3	87.6	5.4	81.5	37.8	90.4
1982	54.1	49.5	48.1	36.7	58.0	64.3	82.2	69.2	73.3	6.1	73.4	34.1	92.5
1983	55.6	51.9	50.4	38.5	67.3	69.2	84.2	69.8	66.1	7.1	75.9	43.5	88.3
1984	60.5	57.0	55.5	44.0	72.0	74.7	92.3	75.9	77.2	8.7	85.5	52.2	94.2
1985	61.3	57.9	56.3	44.9	72.9	76.1	85.2	77.0	77.4	9.3	84.2	54.2	100.7
1986	61.9	59.2	57.6	45.7	79.2	79.2	83.2	76.5	76.2	9.6	85.7	54.1	105.9
1987	65.1	62.5	60.8	48.4	86.4	83.6	89.7	77.9	77.8	11.0	86.9	56.1	109.8
1988	68.4	65.9	64.3	52.0	86.3	85.3	100.2	81.9	85.7	12.3	91.1	59.9	115.6
1989	69.1	66.4	64.9	52.6	85.0	84.6	97.9	81.3	88.8	12.7	89.7	59.3	122.5
1990	69.7	67.0	65.5	52.8	84.1	83.3	96.7	80.3	86.7	13.8	87.5	55.8	123.0
1991	68.7	65.6	64.3	51.2	78.6	76.7	90.8	76.6	81.4	14.3	82.9	53.3	118.7
1992	70.6	68.0	66.8	53.8	82.9	80.1	93.0	79.0	81.1	16.1	87.9	60.7	109.8
1993	72.9	70.4	69.2	56.8	83.9	81.8	97.5	82.0	87.2	17.7	93.4	67.0	102.3
1994	76.8	74.5	73.6	61.6	88.9	86.4	104.9	89.1	95.5	20.7	100.2	77.0	91.9
1995	80.4	78.5	77.6	66.9	91.0	88.9	106.0	94.6	102.2	26.7	102.5	79.3	87.3
1996	84.0	82.2	81.6	72.8	93.9	94.7	108.6	98.0	105.8	34.5	105.7	79.9	90.7
1997	90.1	89.2	88.5	81.6	96.7	97.8	113.3	102.5	111.6	46.1	109.6	86.1	101.2
1998	95.4	95.1	94.4	90.2	101.1	102.8	115.3	105.8	114.5	59.2	113.6	90.6	117.3
1999	99.5	99.9	99.3	97.8	105.3	103.6	115.1	106.4	112.0	77.2	115.5	100.5	113.1
2000	103.7	104.4	103.9	105.2	103.7	103.6	111.4	110.7	117.7	101.4	121.3	99.9	99.3
2001	100.1	100.1	99.8	100.4	97.1	99.7	99.5	102.6	104.2	103.3	109.3	91.4	105.9
2002	100.0	100.0	100.0	100.0	100.0	100.0	100.0	100.0	100.0	100.0	100.0	100.0	100.0
2003	101.3	101.3	101.6	102.7	100.7	100.5	99.1	98.7	99.7	114.3	97.3	103.5	95.8
2004	103.8	104.3	104.7	107.0	104.4	103.6	110.0	98.9	103.7	129.9	99.0	103.7	94.3
2005	107.2	108.5	109.1	112.8	110.4	108.1	108.0	103.4	110.2	144.5	100.7	103.9	105.0
2006	109.7	111.2	112.1	117.8	110.0	109.9	112.6	109.0	115.5	163.8	101.4	100.2	110.9
2007	111.3	112.7	113.8	120.2	99.2	106.9	110.0	112.1	116.4	176.7	104.8	97.4	121.7
2008	108.8	109.2	110.4	116.3	84.8	100.7	102.6	110.1	109.3	193.2	104.5	83.4	119.2
2007													
January	109.9	111.4	112.3	117.6	100.6	107.8	107.8	109.9	115.3	168.4	102.7	95.1	117.1
February	110.8	111.7	112.6	118.1	101.1	105.6	108.5	110.5	115.3	168.4	104.8	97.5	117.4
March	110.6	112.2	113.1	118.8	102.3	107.1	109.6	111.6	116.6	169.3	104.5	97.2	116.6
April	111.1	112.5	113.5	119.5	101.3	106.7	110.3	111.9	117.1	171.0	105.8	98.5	117.5
May	111.1	112.5	113.5	119.6	101.4	106.8	110.2	111.6	117.9	171.2	104.5	98.1	119.0
June	111.2	112.9	113.9	120.5	101.9	107.6	108.9	112.4	117.0	174.1	104.8	99.4	121.1
July	111.5	113.5	114.6	121.4	100.8	107.9	110.9	112.5	117.6	177.6	105.1	100.2	122.3
August	111.6	113.0	114.1	120.9	99.4	107.5	109.8	112.5	115.1	178.9	104.7	99.2	123.5
September	112.0	113.4	114.5	121.2	97.5	107.4	107.4	112.9	117.6	180.9	105.6	96.2	125.8
October	111.4	112.9	114.1	121.1	95.7	107.1	109.7	112.7	116.5	183.8	103.8	95.6	125.9
November	112.1	113.3	114.5	121.8	94.4	107.1	112.3	113.5	115.4	186.8	104.9	95.7	127.2
December	112.4	113.7	114.8	122.0	94.3	103.9	114.7	113.1	114.8	189.4	105.6	96.0	126.9
2008													
January	112.3	113.4	114.6	121.9	91.5	104.7	113.2	113.6	114.9	191.0	105.7	94.6	127.8
February	112.0	112.8	114.0	121.2	90.5	103.4	111.9	113.5	113.6	194.0	104.6	94.2	125.1
March	111.6	112.7	113.9	121.0	89.9	104.5	110.6	113.6	114.8	197.5	105.8	88.7	125.1
April	111.0	111.7	112.9	119.3	89.0	102.7	109.7	112.6	111.2	199.2	105.7	83.9	124.3
May	110.7	111.5	112.7	118.9	88.2	102.6	107.8	112.1	110.9	199.4	106.1	83.9	123.3
June	110.4	111.0	112.3	119.0	87.3	101.7	107.9	110.5	110.6	199.0	106.3	86.4	125.1
July	110.4	110.8	112.0	119.0	86.7	102.7	110.1	109.8	109.2	198.0	106.2	88.7	123.0
August	109.2	109.7	111.0	117.2	86.1	101.6	108.6	110.2	110.2	196.6	105.4	79.2	122.6
September	104.8	105.7	106.7	113.7	82.8	99.1	102.0	109.2	107.3	194.2	103.4	79.9	103.2
October	106.3	106.2	107.4	111.1	79.0	99.4	94.1	107.3	106.0	190.2	103.5	77.0	99.9
November	104.9	103.9	105.0	108.5	76.8	94.3	82.6	106.1	103.7	182.4	102.6	74.6	109.5
December	102.4	100.9	101.8	105.4	69.7	91.7	72.3	102.5	99.8	177.1	99.1	69.6	121.7

. . . = Not available.

Table 2-2. Industrial Production Indexes by NAICS Industry Groups—Continued

(Seasonally adjusted, 2002 = 100.)

Year and month	Durable goods manufacturing—Continued		Manufacturing (NAICS)—Continued — Nondurable goods manufacturing									Other manufacturing (non-NAICS)
	Furniture and related products	Miscellaneous manufacturing	Total	Food, beverage, and tobacco products	Textile and product mills	Apparel and leather	Paper	Printing and support	Petroleum and coal products	Chemical	Plastics and rubber products	
1967	. . .	. . .	. . .	. . .	. . .	. . .	. . .	. . .	. . .	. . .	. . .	. . .
1968	. . .	. . .	. . .	. . .	. . .	. . .	. . .	. . .	. . .	. . .	. . .	. . .
1969	. . .	. . .	. . .	. . .	. . .	. . .	. . .	. . .	. . .	. . .	. . .	. . .
1970	. . .	. . .	. . .	. . .	. . .	. . .	. . .	. . .	. . .	. . .	. . .	. . .
1971	. . .	. . .	. . .	. . .	. . .	. . .	. . .	. . .	. . .	. . .	. . .	. . .
1972	55.8	42.4	60.9	66.0	86.1	182.9	66.3	51.6	73.9	47.8	34.9	68.3
1973	58.4	43.7	63.8	66.7	85.2	186.1	71.6	54.2	72.6	52.3	39.2	70.5
1974	53.6	42.8	64.1	67.7	78.4	174.5	74.7	52.6	78.3	54.4	38.2	71.0
1975	45.7	39.9	59.4	66.5	75.8	169.8	64.6	49.1	77.2	47.8	32.7	67.5
1976	51.1	43.4	64.9	71.0	84.4	179.0	71.4	52.7	85.5	53.5	36.2	69.6
1977	58.6	47.2	69.3	72.6	92.3	188.1	74.5	57.1	91.6	58.2	42.6	76.3
1978	63.2	48.2	71.8	75.2	92.0	192.5	77.9	60.4	92.5	61.1	44.1	78.9
1979	62.7	48.4	72.2	74.8	91.8	180.3	79.0	62.2	98.8	62.5	43.4	80.6
1980	60.5	45.8	70.0	76.0	88.1	183.9	78.8	62.7	87.5	59.1	38.6	83.4
1981	60.0	47.5	70.6	76.8	86.2	183.7	79.9	64.3	83.5	60.1	40.9	85.4
1982	56.4	48.0	69.6	79.0	79.9	182.5	78.6	69.1	79.8	56.2	40.2	86.4
1983	61.9	48.0	72.8	79.2	90.1	187.7	83.7	74.3	81.1	60.1	43.7	88.8
1984	69.4	52.0	76.2	80.3	92.4	179.2	87.9	80.9	82.9	63.6	50.5	92.8
1985	69.9	52.7	76.6	82.9	89.2	178.8	86.2	84.2	81.7	63.1	52.5	96.5
1986	73.0	53.9	78.8	84.0	92.9	186.3	89.8	88.4	81.2	65.9	54.7	98.4
1987	78.2	58.0	83.0	85.6	102.5	188.2	92.7	94.9	85.1	71.0	60.6	104.1
1988	77.2	63.4	85.8	88.0	101.6	184.7	96.4	98.0	87.7	75.1	63.2	103.6
1989	76.9	64.2	86.3	87.5	103.4	176.5	97.4	98.4	86.8	76.5	65.4	102.1
1990	75.2	67.3	87.7	90.0	99.2	172.4	97.4	102.1	86.9	78.3	67.2	100.9
1991	69.5	68.6	87.4	90.6	97.8	171.2	97.6	98.9	85.7	78.0	66.5	96.8
1992	75.0	71.5	89.6	91.8	103.2	175.7	100.0	104.3	85.3	79.2	71.6	94.8
1993	78.3	75.5	90.9	91.5	107.2	179.2	101.1	104.6	85.8	80.1	76.7	95.5
1994	81.0	76.1	94.0	94.7	113.1	181.3	105.5	105.7	88.2	82.2	83.0	94.7
1995	82.4	79.0	95.7	97.4	112.0	179.9	107.0	107.3	89.8	83.5	85.1	94.7
1996	83.0	82.8	96.0	96.6	109.4	175.6	103.7	108.0	91.9	85.3	87.9	93.8
1997	91.9	84.9	99.5	98.6	115.4	175.1	105.9	110.2	95.0	90.3	93.4	101.7
1998	98.4	89.9	101.0	101.5	114.4	165.1	106.7	111.5	93.2	91.8	96.7	107.8
1999	101.8	91.7	101.7	99.7	114.1	158.0	107.6	112.4	97.1	93.6	101.9	110.9
2000	103.3	96.7	102.2	101.2	111.9	150.8	105.3	113.1	96.9	95.0	102.9	112.6
2001	96.7	95.5	98.9	100.9	100.3	128.2	99.3	106.3	96.4	93.4	96.9	105.7
2002	100.0	100.0	100.0	100.0	100.0	100.0	100.0	100.0	100.0	100.0	100.0	100.0
2003	98.2	103.0	100.1	102.0	96.0	93.3	96.8	96.2	97.9	101.3	100.3	97.1
2004	100.9	103.2	102.0	102.5	94.6	82.0	97.6	96.9	106.0	105.6	101.5	97.9
2005	104.6	109.9	104.8	106.2	96.7	80.4	97.5	99.2	110.1	109.3	102.3	97.6
2006	104.2	113.3	105.7	106.7	88.0	79.1	97.6	99.8	109.7	112.7	102.9	96.6
2007	101.0	118.3	106.7	109.6	81.2	79.3	95.9	100.6	109.1	114.1	104.7	95.3
2008	90.4	117.7	103.7	109.4	72.8	75.9	92.1	94.0	110.0	108.8	99.1	89.9
2007												
January	101.8	115.7	106.3	108.2	83.4	80.7	95.9	102.3	110.1	113.7	103.1	96.1
February	101.2	115.3	106.4	108.8	83.3	80.0	96.9	102.9	108.5	114.0	102.1	96.2
March	101.4	117.0	106.8	108.5	83.1	79.6	96.1	102.6	110.3	114.6	103.4	96.0
April	101.0	118.3	106.7	109.1	83.6	80.1	96.6	101.7	107.7	114.5	104.4	96.2
May	100.9	118.6	106.7	109.4	83.3	80.2	95.9	100.5	109.3	114.0	104.8	95.5
June	101.1	119.5	106.6	110.0	83.3	79.9	94.8	99.8	108.4	113.8	105.1	95.5
July	101.9	119.4	107.0	110.7	81.4	79.4	96.2	99.5	108.6	114.0	105.9	95.4
August	102.1	118.5	106.5	110.0	79.4	77.6	95.4	99.8	109.0	113.7	104.6	94.7
September	100.8	120.2	107.2	111.0	78.7	78.4	95.0	100.0	109.4	114.5	105.9	95.1
October	100.6	118.5	106.4	109.8	78.3	77.8	94.3	99.3	109.1	113.6	105.7	94.3
November	100.8	118.4	106.6	109.6	78.2	78.0	96.1	99.8	109.2	113.9	105.9	93.9
December	98.8	119.6	107.0	110.1	78.2	80.2	98.0	99.5	109.6	114.4	105.0	94.6
2008												
January	97.5	119.7	106.6	109.8	76.0	79.1	95.5	98.6	111.2	114.0	103.5	93.9
February	95.9	117.2	106.2	109.7	76.1	78.3	94.0	97.1	111.7	113.2	102.9	93.5
March	95.3	118.8	106.1	110.8	75.4	77.2	94.8	98.0	111.0	112.6	101.9	93.6
April	93.7	117.7	105.8	110.3	74.4	76.5	94.1	96.9	112.4	112.2	100.9	91.8
May	93.4	117.7	105.9	110.3	74.4	75.1	96.2	96.4	112.2	112.1	100.8	90.8
June	92.8	117.4	104.9	109.4	73.3	76.3	94.3	93.4	111.4	111.0	101.2	90.8
July	92.1	117.6	104.5	108.7	73.0	77.0	94.0	91.9	111.5	110.6	101.5	89.3
August	89.1	119.7	104.1	108.9	73.8	77.7	94.2	93.0	110.1	109.7	99.4	88.9
September	87.9	118.2	99.3	108.8	71.9	76.7	91.3	92.3	98.7	101.0	97.7	88.1
October	85.2	117.5	102.8	109.8	71.2	74.6	89.7	91.9	112.0	106.7	96.0	86.9
November	81.6	116.4	100.5	109.2	68.8	71.6	85.9	90.6	109.2	103.4	93.7	86.5
December	79.9	114.5	97.4	106.5	65.3	70.4	81.3	87.4	108.4	99.5	89.4	84.9

. . . = Not available.

Table 2-2. Industrial Production Indexes by NAICS Industry Groups—*Continued*

(Seasonally adjusted, 2002 = 100.)

Year and month	Mining	Utilities			Selected high-tech industries	Excluding selected high-tech industries	Stage-of-process groups		
		Total	Electric	Natural gas			Crude	Primary and semi-finished	Finished
1967	. . .	. . .	. . .	. . .	0.3	54.1	. . .	. . .	. . .
1968	. . .	. . .	. . .	. . .	0.3	57.1	. . .	. . .	. . .
1969	. . .	. . .	. . .	. . .	0.3	59.5	. . .	. . .	. . .
1970	. . .	. . .	. . .	. . .	0.3	57.5	. . .	. . .	. . .
1971	. . .	. . .	. . .	. . .	0.3	58.5	. . .	. . .	. . .
1972	99.4	50.3	40.9	101.9	0.3	63.9	88.3	46.0	40.1
1973	100.0	53.2	44.6	97.5	0.4	68.8	93.0	50.2	43.0
1974	98.5	53.0	44.8	93.9	0.5	68.2	94.2	49.6	42.5
1975	95.9	54.0	46.8	95.6	0.5	62.2	85.5	43.9	40.1
1976	96.7	56.4	49.7	94.6	0.6	66.8	90.4	47.9	44.0
1977	99.1	58.7	52.9	91.4	0.8	71.3	95.3	51.7	47.8
1978	110.8	60.2	54.6	92.2	1.0	74.7	97.1	54.2	50.8
1979	105.8	61.6	55.8	94.6	1.3	76.3	99.7	55.4	51.7
1980	107.8	62.0	56.7	92.6	1.6	73.6	90.6	51.8	50.8
1981	110.9	62.9	58.2	90.5	1.9	74.0	91.9	51.8	51.9
1982	105.0	60.9	56.8	85.0	2.2	69.6	93.4	47.6	51.0
1983	99.0	61.4	58.5	79.6	2.6	70.8	93.6	49.9	53.3
1984	105.9	65.0	61.8	84.5	3.4	76.4	99.8	54.8	58.1
1985	103.7	66.4	64.1	81.0	3.6	77.2	97.2	55.3	59.6
1986	103.9	67.0	65.4	77.0	3.7	77.9	99.6	56.2	61.7
1987	104.8	70.1	68.5	80.6	4.5	81.2	102.8	59.5	64.8
1988	107.5	74.1	72.4	85.5	5.4	84.8	106.2	62.6	68.5
1989	106.2	76.4	74.6	88.6	5.7	85.3	106.3	63.1	69.5
1990	107.8	77.9	76.7	85.6	6.4	85.6	107.9	63.1	70.8
1991	105.4	79.8	78.5	87.9	6.9	83.9	105.1	62.1	70.0
1992	103.1	79.7	78.1	90.4	8.2	85.5	104.2	64.6	71.8
1993	103.0	82.6	80.9	93.8	9.6	87.6	103.0	67.6	73.8
1994	105.4	84.2	82.7	94.4	12.1	91.1	105.2	72.3	76.8
1995	105.3	87.2	85.7	96.9	16.9	93.3	105.6	76.3	80.6
1996	107.1	89.7	87.9	101.5	24.1	94.9	105.3	80.7	83.8
1997	108.9	89.7	88.2	99.5	35.3	98.9	108.1	86.8	90.5
1998	107.2	92.0	91.8	93.1	49.1	101.9	106.2	92.5	96.8
1999	101.6	94.7	94.5	95.7	70.0	103.1	104.2	98.6	99.5
2000	104.2	97.4	97.2	98.6	98.3	104.3	104.6	103.7	103.3
2001	104.8	97.0	96.9	97.2	101.3	100.1	101.7	98.9	101.2
2002	100.0	100.0	100.0	100.0	100.0	100.0	100.0	100.0	100.0
2003	100.2	101.9	102.1	100.9	120.5	100.2	100.2	101.1	101.8
2004	99.6	103.3	104.2	98.8	137.9	102.0	101.5	103.9	104.4
2005	98.3	105.4	107.2	97.1	158.8	104.7	100.8	107.2	109.4
2006	101.5	104.8	107.8	91.3	189.1	106.2	103.6	108.5	113.2
2007	102.1	108.3	110.5	98.1	213.7	107.2	104.6	109.5	116.0
2008	104.2	108.4	110.2	100.2	238.7	104.2	104.5	106.0	113.8
2007									
January	101.1	106.4	109.2	93.8	196.9	106.3	103.5	108.2	114.5
February	101.4	112.6	113.1	109.9	197.4	107.2	104.1	109.5	115.0
March	101.5	106.7	109.3	94.9	199.8	106.9	104.3	109.0	114.9
April	101.4	108.4	110.1	100.9	202.9	107.2	104.2	109.5	115.6
May	102.2	108.3	110.9	96.2	204.7	107.3	104.7	109.5	115.5
June	101.9	106.4	108.8	95.5	209.5	107.2	104.3	109.3	116.1
July	101.9	105.0	107.0	96.0	216.5	107.4	104.3	109.4	117.0
August	101.7	109.9	111.7	101.6	219.2	107.4	104.1	110.0	116.4
September	102.4	109.5	111.8	98.9	222.6	107.7	105.0	110.1	117.0
October	101.8	108.2	112.3	89.6	228.0	107.0	104.1	109.5	116.5
November	103.4	109.4	111.6	99.1	232.2	107.5	106.1	110.1	116.5
December	104.5	108.9	110.6	101.1	235.3	107.8	107.1	109.9	117.3
2008									
January	104.2	110.9	112.4	103.8	237.5	107.7	106.6	110.0	117.3
February	105.0	111.4	112.7	104.9	242.2	107.3	106.9	109.8	116.6
March	104.7	108.8	110.5	100.5	248.1	106.8	106.9	109.0	116.6
April	104.9	109.7	111.5	101.3	251.2	106.1	106.7	108.7	115.1
May	104.9	108.2	109.7	100.9	250.3	105.8	106.9	108.0	115.0
June	104.8	109.4	111.8	98.5	248.4	105.6	105.8	107.9	115.1
July	106.9	107.9	110.1	97.6	246.6	105.6	107.3	107.4	114.7
August	106.4	104.3	106.0	95.9	243.6	104.4	106.8	105.9	113.5
September	96.4	105.7	108.0	95.2	240.0	100.2	95.3	102.9	111.4
October	103.5	106.8	108.4	99.1	232.0	101.8	102.7	103.7	110.6
November	105.2	108.9	110.6	101.0	217.7	100.7	102.6	101.2	110.2
December	103.2	109.4	110.5	103.7	206.5	98.3	99.8	97.9	108.8

. . . = Not available.

Table 2-3. Capacity Utilization by NAICS Industry Groups

(Output as a percentage of capacity, seasonally adjusted.)

Year and month	Total industry	Total manufac- turing (SIC)	Manufacturing (NAICS) Total	Durable goods manufacturing Total	Wood products	Nonmetallic mineral products	Primary metals	Fabricated metal products	Machinery	Computer and electronic products	Electrical equipment, appliances, and compo- nents	Motor vehicles and parts	Aircraft and miscel- laneous transpor- tation equipment
1967	87.0	87.2	. . .	87.5	. . .	75.7	85.0	86.4	90.4	. . .	. . .	78.9	94.1
1968	87.4	87.1	. . .	87.3	. . .	78.5	84.8	87.3	85.1	. . .	. . .	90.1	89.6
1969	87.4	86.7	. . .	87.1	. . .	79.8	88.2	86.2	86.7	. . .	. . .	86.6	84.8
1970	81.3	79.5	. . .	77.7	. . .	74.0	79.2	78.5	79.8	. . .	. . .	66.2	73.2
1971	79.7	78.0	. . .	75.5	. . .	75.7	72.8	78.5	73.9	. . .	. . .	78.9	64.3
1972	84.7	83.4	83.4	82.1	92.3	79.8	82.7	85.1	83.0	81.5	89.9	84.2	65.1
1973	88.3	87.6	87.8	88.5	87.6	84.3	94.5	90.9	92.3	85.1	97.7	91.9	73.2
1974	85.1	84.4	84.4	84.6	78.0	81.7	96.5	86.0	91.8	83.1	91.5	76.7	73.9
1975	75.7	73.5	73.4	71.6	70.2	73.0	75.0	72.0	77.6	68.5	70.5	65.6	70.7
1976	79.7	78.2	78.3	76.3	79.4	77.6	78.4	75.5	79.9	71.7	78.8	81.8	66.4
1977	83.4	82.4	82.4	81.2	86.1	82.6	79.1	79.9	85.5	77.7	85.9	89.9	66.8
1978	85.0	84.3	84.2	83.8	84.9	86.3	83.9	80.9	88.5	80.6	88.3	90.7	72.0
1979	85.0	84.0	83.9	84.1	80.2	84.2	85.9	81.7	90.2	83.8	89.5	81.3	81.5
1980	80.7	78.7	78.4	77.6	72.8	75.0	76.2	75.5	83.8	86.7	82.1	59.4	84.6
1981	79.6	77.0	76.6	75.2	70.8	72.2	77.4	73.5	80.8	84.4	79.0	57.3	76.7
1982	73.7	70.9	70.4	66.6	63.3	64.5	55.6	65.4	66.9	80.9	69.7	51.4	69.7
1983	74.9	73.5	73.0	68.7	74.4	70.9	59.2	66.4	60.7	81.9	72.8	67.5	66.1
1984	80.5	79.4	79.0	76.8	79.2	76.3	69.1	73.1	71.1	87.4	82.3	81.6	69.5
1985	79.3	78.2	77.7	75.7	78.8	75.9	66.9	73.8	70.7	80.2	78.9	83.2	72.3
1986	78.6	78.4	78.0	75.3	83.4	78.4	69.6	73.5	70.2	77.4	79.9	78.6	74.0
1987	81.2	81.0	80.5	77.6	86.5	80.9	78.2	75.2	72.0	79.8	82.1	77.4	75.6
1988	84.3	84.0	83.7	82.0	84.8	82.0	88.7	80.0	80.4	81.5	86.9	82.1	79.9
1989	83.7	83.2	83.1	81.6	83.1	81.2	86.7	79.7	84.0	78.8	86.0	79.8	85.2
1990	82.5	81.7	81.5	79.4	81.4	79.6	85.0	77.7	81.6	78.9	83.7	71.2	85.4
1991	79.8	78.4	78.3	75.1	76.4	73.5	79.0	74.1	76.3	77.6	78.9	63.3	83.1
1992	80.4	79.5	79.4	76.9	80.7	77.3	81.2	76.4	75.4	78.9	82.0	71.7	76.9
1993	81.5	80.4	80.3	78.6	81.3	78.9	85.8	77.4	79.5	77.3	86.5	78.5	72.6
1994	83.5	82.7	82.8	81.7	83.8	81.4	91.1	81.9	83.9	79.6	92.0	87.1	66.3
1995	84.0	83.2	83.3	82.5	82.2	81.7	89.9	83.9	85.8	83.2	91.7	84.7	63.8
1996	83.4	82.2	82.3	81.8	81.7	85.4	89.2	83.5	84.9	81.0	90.6	82.1	66.5
1997	84.2	83.2	83.1	82.7	81.1	84.6	89.8	82.6	84.4	81.5	89.3	83.6	73.3
1998	83.0	81.8	81.6	81.2	82.1	84.0	87.4	80.7	81.5	78.3	87.1	80.4	82.4
1999	81.9	80.7	80.4	80.4	82.1	81.0	85.1	78.3	76.8	80.7	84.6	84.2	77.3
2000	81.7	80.1	79.6	80.0	78.2	77.7	82.6	79.3	78.3	84.6	87.1	82.0	66.9
2001	76.1	73.8	73.3	71.4	71.9	72.2	73.7	73.0	68.8	69.3	77.6	72.7	70.7
2002	74.6	72.7	72.2	69.3	74.3	72.3	75.6	71.0	66.8	59.3	73.4	78.3	66.5
2003	75.8	73.7	73.3	70.6	76.9	73.0	74.0	71.5	68.3	63.3	74.6	78.4	63.8
2004	77.9	76.2	75.7	73.5	80.3	74.3	82.9	72.9	72.6	70.2	78.1	76.8	63.4
2005	80.1	78.6	78.3	76.3	84.2	76.3	80.5	75.8	77.5	73.1	81.6	77.0	71.0
2006	80.9	79.4	79.2	77.9	81.8	75.4	83.8	79.5	81.0	78.0	82.5	72.5	75.2
2007	80.6	79.0	78.9	77.2	72.1	71.4	82.4	80.4	80.8	75.3	83.7	71.0	81.6
2008	77.6	75.1	75.1	72.6	61.5	66.8	76.7	77.6	74.7	74.9	81.2	60.9	78.1
2007													
January	80.3	78.8	78.7	76.8	73.5	72.5	80.6	79.5	80.6	77.0	83.0	68.6	79.3
February	80.8	78.9	78.7	76.9	73.8	70.9	81.2	79.9	80.6	76.1	84.6	70.5	79.3
March	80.6	79.1	79.0	77.2	74.6	71.8	82.0	80.5	81.4	75.6	84.2	70.5	78.7
April	80.7	79.2	79.0	77.4	73.7	71.4	82.6	80.6	81.6	75.3	85.0	71.5	79.2
May	80.7	79.1	78.9	77.2	73.7	71.4	82.5	80.2	82.1	74.4	83.9	71.4	80.1
June	80.6	79.1	79.0	77.5	74.0	71.9	81.5	80.7	81.3	74.7	83.9	72.5	81.3
July	80.7	79.4	79.3	77.9	73.1	72.0	83.1	80.7	81.6	75.1	84.0	73.2	82.0
August	80.6	78.9	78.8	77.3	72.1	71.7	82.2	80.5	79.8	74.7	83.4	72.6	82.6
September	80.7	79.1	79.0	77.2	70.7	71.5	80.5	80.6	81.4	74.6	83.9	70.5	84.0
October	80.2	78.6	78.5	76.9	69.3	71.3	82.2	80.3	80.6	75.0	82.3	70.1	83.9
November	80.5	78.7	78.7	77.1	68.3	71.3	84.1	80.8	79.7	75.4	82.9	70.2	84.6
December	80.6	78.8	78.7	77.0	68.2	69.1	85.9	80.3	79.1	75.8	83.3	70.4	84.2
2008													
January	80.5	78.5	78.4	76.8	66.2	69.6	84.8	80.5	79.0	75.8	83.1	69.3	84.6
February	80.2	78.0	77.9	76.1	65.5	68.7	83.8	80.4	78.0	76.5	82.0	69.0	82.6
March	79.8	77.8	77.7	75.8	65.0	69.4	82.8	80.3	78.7	77.4	82.7	64.9	82.5
April	79.2	77.0	76.9	74.6	64.4	68.1	82.1	79.5	76.1	77.8	82.4	61.3	81.7
May	78.9	76.7	76.7	74.3	63.8	68.1	80.7	79.0	75.8	77.5	82.5	61.3	80.9
June	78.7	76.3	76.3	74.2	63.2	67.4	80.7	77.8	75.5	77.1	82.5	63.0	82.0
July	78.6	76.1	76.1	74.1	62.8	68.1	82.3	77.3	74.4	76.5	82.3	64.6	80.4
August	77.6	75.3	75.3	73.0	62.5	67.3	81.2	77.6	75.1	75.8	81.5	57.7	80.1
September	74.5	72.5	72.4	70.7	60.2	65.7	76.2	76.9	73.0	74.6	79.8	58.2	67.3
October	75.5	72.8	72.8	69.0	57.4	65.9	70.3	75.5	72.1	72.8	79.8	56.1	65.1
November	74.6	71.3	71.2	67.4	56.0	62.5	61.7	74.7	70.5	69.6	79.1	54.4	71.3
December	72.7	69.2	69.1	65.5	50.9	60.8	54.0	72.2	67.9	67.4	76.3	50.8	79.2

. . . = Not available.

Table 2-3. Capacity Utilization by NAICS Industry Groups—*Continued*

(Output as a percentage of capacity, seasonally adjusted.)

Year and month	Durable goods manufacturing—*Continued*		Manufacturing (NAICS)—*Continued* Nondurable goods manufacturing									Other manufacturing (non-NAICS)
	Furniture and related products	Miscellaneous manufacturing	Total	Food, beverage, and tobacco products	Textile and product mills	Apparel and leather	Paper	Printing and support	Petroleum and coal products	Chemical	Plastics and rubber products	
1967	91.9	. . .	86.3	85.0	. . .	. . .	89.7	. . .	94.9	78.9	88.3	. . .
1968	91.5	. . .	86.5	84.8	. . .	. . .	89.3	. . .	95.8	80.1	91.2	. . .
1969	93.1	. . .	86.2	85.1	. . .	. . .	91.0	. . .	96.4	79.1	90.4	. . .
1970	84.6	. . .	82.2	84.0	. . .	. . .	86.1	. . .	96.7	76.1	79.5	. . .
1971	85.7	. . .	81.9	84.0	. . .	. . .	86.7	. . .	95.6	75.4	80.1	. . .
1972	94.3	80.5	85.3	85.1	89.3	81.8	91.3	92.4	93.6	80.2	88.7	85.8
1973	95.4	79.4	86.6	84.8	86.2	82.0	94.8	94.0	90.4	83.9	92.4	84.7
1974	82.3	74.5	84.2	83.8	76.1	76.2	95.0	88.0	92.8	84.3	84.2	82.8
1975	67.8	67.9	76.0	80.1	72.1	74.6	80.6	79.6	83.6	71.8	70.0	77.2
1976	75.6	72.4	81.0	83.3	80.6	78.0	87.8	82.2	86.0	77.6	77.2	77.5
1977	84.4	77.6	84.2	82.6	88.1	81.8	90.4	86.0	87.6	80.9	88.5	83.3
1978	85.6	79.0	84.9	83.3	87.4	84.1	92.5	87.4	86.5	81.9	88.3	85.0
1979	79.9	78.6	83.6	81.2	87.0	79.0	91.1	86.0	88.8	82.1	83.8	85.7
1980	74.1	73.4	79.5	81.0	82.9	80.2	88.6	83.7	76.1	76.1	73.8	87.1
1981	71.8	75.9	78.8	80.5	80.3	79.0	87.2	81.2	72.8	75.8	76.9	87.5
1982	67.1	73.9	76.3	81.4	74.2	78.2	84.2	82.2	71.3	69.1	73.8	87.4
1983	73.5	70.8	79.5	80.9	83.8	82.1	89.1	86.3	74.4	72.8	80.7	88.1
1984	80.5	76.2	82.4	81.4	85.3	83.4	91.6	89.6	78.6	76.0	90.4	89.5
1985	78.2	74.5	80.8	82.7	80.9	80.2	88.3	85.3	80.1	73.8	86.3	90.3
1986	80.0	74.3	81.9	82.8	83.2	80.9	90.5	85.6	81.8	76.1	84.8	88.9
1987	83.4	77.4	84.8	83.8	90.8	82.6	90.4	89.3	82.5	81.2	89.0	90.7
1988	80.3	81.8	86.1	85.4	88.2	82.9	91.4	89.9	83.2	84.3	88.6	88.6
1989	78.3	79.7	85.0	83.6	88.0	81.0	90.6	88.7	84.2	83.5	86.7	85.3
1990	75.2	79.6	84.4	84.4	83.3	79.7	89.5	88.2	84.7	83.2	83.7	83.8
1991	70.2	78.2	82.4	83.4	81.5	81.1	88.0	83.3	82.8	81.1	78.6	81.0
1992	77.0	76.8	82.7	82.5	85.5	83.4	88.7	85.9	84.9	79.7	81.8	80.0
1993	79.9	77.8	82.6	80.8	87.8	84.6	89.1	85.7	88.0	78.8	86.1	81.2
1994	81.6	77.9	84.3	82.9	90.1	86.0	90.8	85.7	88.7	79.7	90.5	81.1
1995	81.2	80.1	84.3	84.0	87.0	85.5	89.4	85.1	89.5	79.9	88.7	82.0
1996	80.3	81.5	82.9	82.2	83.8	83.0	85.2	83.8	92.1	79.8	87.4	80.7
1997	84.6	79.5	83.6	82.1	85.8	82.2	87.3	82.1	94.1	81.3	88.2	84.9
1998	84.4	79.0	82.2	82.1	82.9	78.0	87.3	80.6	92.0	79.0	86.9	85.6
1999	81.5	77.0	80.3	78.5	81.2	78.0	86.8	78.9	91.1	77.3	86.6	86.1
2000	77.0	77.4	79.1	78.2	78.9	80.1	84.7	78.8	89.3	75.4	82.7	87.9
2001	70.1	72.9	75.8	77.4	71.2	74.7	80.4	76.5	88.2	71.1	76.2	83.4
2002	71.9	74.2	76.3	76.4	73.0	67.3	82.5	73.9	88.5	74.2	78.3	80.8
2003	71.3	75.9	76.9	77.8	72.6	71.6	81.9	72.2	89.2	74.0	79.3	82.0
2004	75.4	74.8	78.6	77.9	74.6	72.4	83.3	74.9	92.3	76.3	82.5	84.5
2005	79.5	77.0	80.6	79.6	78.7	75.8	83.8	78.5	91.5	77.5	84.0	84.4
2006	79.9	76.1	80.7	78.9	74.6	75.7	84.0	78.9	90.1	78.8	83.8	83.0
2007	78.1	75.6	80.8	80.0	72.6	78.0	82.2	79.2	87.7	79.0	84.1	81.3
2008	70.8	71.4	77.7	78.5	68.4	75.4	79.6	74.9	86.4	74.3	77.8	76.0
2007												
January	78.4	75.8	80.9	79.5	72.8	78.6	82.1	80.5	89.4	79.2	83.5	82.2
February	78.0	75.2	80.9	79.9	73.1	78.1	82.9	81.0	87.9	79.3	82.6	82.2
March	78.2	76.0	81.1	79.6	73.2	77.9	82.2	80.8	89.3	79.7	83.6	82.0
April	77.9	76.5	81.0	79.9	74.0	78.5	82.7	80.0	87.0	79.6	84.2	82.2
May	77.9	76.4	80.9	80.1	74.0	78.7	82.1	79.0	88.1	79.1	84.5	81.5
June	78.1	76.6	80.8	80.4	74.4	78.5	81.2	78.5	87.3	78.9	84.6	81.5
July	78.8	76.2	81.0	80.8	72.9	78.2	82.4	78.2	87.3	79.0	85.1	81.4
August	79.0	75.2	80.6	80.2	71.5	76.5	81.8	78.5	87.4	78.7	83.9	80.8
September	78.0	76.0	81.0	80.8	71.1	77.4	81.5	78.7	87.6	79.1	84.7	81.1
October	78.0	74.5	80.3	79.8	71.1	76.9	81.0	78.2	87.1	78.4	84.4	80.3
November	78.2	74.1	80.4	79.6	71.3	77.1	82.6	78.5	87.0	78.5	84.4	79.9
December	76.7	74.5	80.6	79.7	71.5	79.3	84.3	78.4	87.2	78.7	83.4	80.4
2008												
January	75.8	74.2	80.2	79.5	69.7	78.3	82.2	77.7	88.2	78.3	82.0	79.8
February	74.6	72.3	79.8	79.2	70.2	77.6	81.0	76.7	88.4	77.7	81.4	79.3
March	74.2	72.9	79.7	79.8	69.8	76.4	81.7	77.5	87.7	77.1	80.4	79.4
April	73.1	72.0	79.4	79.4	69.1	75.8	81.2	76.7	88.6	76.7	79.4	77.8
May	72.9	71.7	79.4	79.2	69.4	74.5	83.0	76.4	88.2	76.6	79.2	76.8
June	72.6	71.2	78.6	78.5	68.7	75.7	81.5	74.3	87.4	75.8	79.3	76.7
July	72.1	71.1	78.3	77.9	68.6	76.5	81.3	73.3	87.4	75.4	79.4	75.4
August	70.0	72.1	77.9	77.9	69.7	77.3	81.6	74.4	86.2	74.8	77.7	75.0
September	69.2	70.9	74.3	77.8	68.3	76.4	79.1	74.0	77.1	68.8	76.4	74.3
October	67.2	70.4	76.9	78.4	67.9	74.5	77.8	74.0	87.5	72.7	75.0	73.3
November	64.6	69.6	75.2	77.9	65.9	71.7	74.6	73.2	85.2	70.4	73.2	72.9
December	63.5	68.3	72.9	75.9	62.9	70.6	70.7	71.0	84.5	67.8	69.9	71.6

. . . = Not available.

Table 2-3. Capacity Utilization by NAICS Industry Groups—*Continued*

(Output as a percentage of capacity, seasonally adjusted.)

Year and month	Mining	Utilities	Selected high-tech industries				Measures excluding selected high-tech industries		Stage-of-process groups		
			Total	Computers and office equipment	Communications equipment	Semiconductors and related electronic components	Total industry	Manufacturing	Crude	Primary and semi-finished	Finished
1967	81.2	94.5	89.4	...	...	...	86.9	86.8	81.1	85.0	88.2
1968	83.6	95.1	87.8	...	...	...	87.2	87.0	83.4	86.8	87.1
1969	86.7	96.8	90.4	...	...	...	87.1	86.4	85.6	88.1	85.6
1970	89.1	96.3	84.3	...	...	...	81.0	79.3	85.1	81.5	78.2
1971	87.8	94.7	75.4	...	...	...	80.0	78.3	84.3	81.7	75.7
1972	90.7	95.3	79.8	84.6	73.9	84.9	84.9	83.6	88.5	88.2	79.7
1973	91.6	93.3	81.6	81.8	75.1	91.4	88.5	87.9	90.4	92.1	83.1
1974	90.9	86.9	82.0	88.4	73.4	87.4	85.2	84.5	91.1	87.4	80.1
1975	89.0	85.1	64.9	68.8	62.2	64.4	76.1	73.9	83.9	75.1	73.5
1976	89.4	85.5	68.5	76.2	61.9	69.5	80.1	78.7	86.9	80.0	76.7
1977	89.5	86.6	75.9	77.6	72.5	78.2	83.7	82.8	88.9	84.5	79.9
1978	89.6	86.9	79.3	78.6	77.4	82.1	85.2	84.5	88.4	86.2	82.1
1979	91.1	87.0	83.5	78.6	85.6	87.5	85.0	84.0	89.3	86.0	81.8
1980	91.1	85.5	87.8	86.8	91.8	85.3	80.5	78.2	88.9	78.8	79.5
1981	90.8	84.4	85.7	85.4	89.1	83.2	79.4	76.5	89.1	77.3	77.6
1982	84.2	80.2	78.3	70.4	87.0	81.5	73.4	70.5	82.2	70.5	73.3
1983	79.8	79.6	80.6	76.0	85.7	81.7	74.7	73.1	79.8	74.5	73.3
1984	85.7	82.1	87.4	85.4	85.0	91.2	80.1	78.9	85.6	81.1	77.4
1985	84.3	81.8	77.1	76.3	78.0	77.1	79.4	78.3	83.9	79.7	76.8
1986	77.6	81.0	72.7	72.7	74.7	71.3	79.0	78.8	79.3	79.7	77.1
1987	80.3	83.6	77.4	73.7	78.2	79.9	81.4	81.3	83.1	82.8	78.7
1988	84.3	86.6	80.2	76.2	83.8	81.6	84.5	84.3	86.8	85.8	81.6
1989	85.3	86.8	78.2	74.9	79.6	80.0	84.0	83.6	87.3	84.7	81.4
1990	86.9	86.5	77.9	71.4	82.5	80.9	82.8	81.9	88.2	82.7	80.6
1991	85.1	87.8	77.3	74.1	77.9	79.2	79.9	78.5	85.6	79.8	78.0
1992	84.6	86.3	80.5	78.9	79.8	81.4	80.4	79.4	85.6	81.5	77.9
1993	85.9	88.3	79.4	79.8	80.8	78.2	81.6	80.5	85.9	83.5	78.0
1994	87.7	88.4	82.4	76.7	81.7	85.5	83.6	82.7	88.2	86.5	79.0
1995	88.1	89.3	85.3	82.1	78.8	90.0	83.9	83.0	89.0	86.6	79.7
1996	90.4	90.8	82.4	85.8	76.9	84.0	83.5	82.2	88.8	85.8	79.2
1997	91.4	90.3	83.2	82.6	78.0	86.4	84.3	83.1	90.7	86.2	80.2
1998	89.2	92.7	79.6	80.5	83.6	77.0	83.3	82.1	87.7	84.3	80.4
1999	86.1	94.1	84.2	81.4	88.6	82.9	81.7	80.3	86.6	84.2	78.3
2000	90.7	93.8	89.0	77.0	90.5	93.7	81.1	79.1	88.5	84.4	77.1
2001	90.4	89.6	69.0	70.4	67.3	69.9	76.7	74.3	85.3	77.4	72.5
2002	86.1	87.7	57.0	69.7	44.6	61.1	76.1	74.2	82.7	76.6	70.7
2003	88.0	86.0	62.4	75.0	44.4	71.7	76.7	74.7	84.4	77.7	71.6
2004	88.3	84.8	69.7	79.0	52.7	78.1	78.4	76.7	86.1	79.8	73.3
2005	88.6	85.2	73.8	76.3	60.1	81.0	80.5	78.9	86.5	81.7	76.0
2006	90.4	83.4	82.0	76.4	80.3	85.8	80.8	79.2	88.3	81.7	77.1
2007	89.2	85.4	79.3	79.0	78.3	79.9	80.6	79.0	87.8	81.0	77.5
2008	90.0	83.7	78.2	81.9	76.7	77.5	77.5	74.9	86.6	77.3	74.1
2007											
January	88.8	84.3	80.9	78.7	81.6	81.6	80.3	78.7	87.5	80.8	77.3
February	89.0	89.2	79.8	78.2	80.9	79.9	80.9	78.8	87.8	81.6	77.4
March	89.0	84.5	79.3	78.0	79.8	79.6	80.6	79.1	87.9	81.2	77.3
April	88.8	85.8	79.0	77.9	78.2	80.0	80.8	79.2	87.7	81.3	77.6
May	89.4	85.6	78.1	77.8	76.8	78.9	80.8	79.1	88.0	81.2	77.4
June	89.0	84.0	78.4	77.8	76.8	79.5	80.7	79.2	87.5	80.9	77.6
July	88.9	82.8	79.4	77.8	77.6	81.2	80.7	79.4	87.5	80.8	78.0
August	88.7	86.5	78.9	78.3	78.2	79.6	80.7	78.9	87.2	81.2	77.5
September	89.3	86.1	78.8	79.1	78.4	78.7	80.8	79.1	87.8	81.1	77.7
October	88.7	84.9	79.4	80.2	77.8	79.8	80.2	78.5	87.1	80.5	77.2
November	90.0	85.7	79.7	81.5	77.1	80.2	80.6	78.7	88.5	80.9	77.0
December	90.9	85.1	79.8	83.0	76.9	79.9	80.7	78.8	89.4	80.6	77.3
2008											
January	90.6	86.5	79.7	84.5	76.7	79.1	80.5	78.4	88.8	80.6	77.1
February	91.2	86.7	80.7	86.0	77.0	80.2	80.2	77.8	88.9	80.3	76.6
March	90.8	84.5	82.1	87.4	78.7	81.6	79.7	77.5	88.8	79.6	76.3
April	90.9	85.1	82.7	88.3	80.3	81.5	79.1	76.6	88.5	79.4	75.2
May	90.8	83.7	82.2	87.7	79.9	80.9	78.8	76.4	88.6	78.8	75.0
June	90.7	84.4	81.3	85.5	78.3	81.4	78.6	76.1	87.6	78.7	74.9
July	92.3	83.1	80.6	82.5	76.6	82.5	78.5	75.8	88.7	78.3	74.6
August	91.8	80.2	79.4	79.9	74.9	82.6	77.6	75.1	88.3	77.1	73.7
September	83.1	81.2	78.0	78.6	74.2	80.8	74.4	72.2	78.7	74.9	72.2
October	89.1	81.9	75.2	77.5	74.5	74.9	75.5	72.7	84.8	75.5	71.6
November	90.5	83.4	70.4	74.8	74.5	65.3	74.7	71.3	84.7	73.7	71.3
December	88.8	83.6	66.5	69.7	74.5	59.2	73.0	69.3	82.3	71.3	70.4

. . . = Not available.

NOTES AND DEFINITIONS

TABLES 2-1 THROUGH 2-3 AND 20-1
INDUSTRIAL PRODUCTION AND CAPACITY UTILIZATION

SOURCE: BOARD OF GOVERNORS OF THE FEDERAL RESERVE SYSTEM

The *industrial production index* measures changes in the physical volume or quantity of output of manufacturing, mining, and electric and gas utilities. *Capacity utilization* is calculated by dividing a seasonally adjusted industrial production index for an industry or group of industries by a related index of productive capacity.

Around the 15th day of each month, the Federal Reserve issues estimates of industrial production and capacity utilization for the previous month. The production estimates are in the form of index numbers (currently 2002 = 100) that reflect the monthly levels of total output of the nation's factories, mines, and gas and electric utilities expressed as a percent of the monthly average in the 2002 base year. Capacity estimates are expressed as index numbers, 2002 *output* = 100 (not 2002 *capacity*), and capacity utilization is measured by the production index as a percent of the capacity index. Since the bases of those two indexes are the same for each industry, this procedure yields production as a percent of capacity. Monthly estimates are subject to revision in each of the three subsequent months, as well as to annual and comprehensive revisions in subsequent years. Monthly series are seasonally adjusted using the Census X-12-ARIMA program.

Definitions and notes on the data

The index of industrial production measures a large portion of the goods output of the national economy on a monthly basis. That portion, together with construction, has also accounted for the bulk of the variation in output over the course of many historical business cycles. The substantial industrial detail included in the index illuminates structural developments in the economy.

The total industrial production index and the indexes for its major components are constructed from individual industry series (300 series for data from 1997 forward) based on the 2002 North American Industry Classification System (NAICS). See Chapter 14 of this publication for a description of NAICS and a table that outlines its structure.

The Federal Reserve has been able to provide a longer continuous historical series on the NAICS basis than some other government agencies. In a major research effort, the Fed and the Census Bureau's Center for Economic Studies re-coded data from seven Censuses of Manufactures, beginning in 1963, to establish benchmark NAICS data for output, value added, and capacity utilization. The resulting indexes are shown annually for the last 37 years (42 years for aggregate levels) in Tables 2-1 through 2-3.

The Fed's featured indexes for total industry and total manufacturing on the Standard Industrial Classification (SIC) basis do *not* observe the reclassifications under NAICS of the logging industry to the Agriculture sector and the publishing industry to the Information sector. (The reason cited by the Fed was to avoid "changing the scope or historical continuity of these statistics.") One advantage of the SIC index for capacity utilization is that it is a continuous series back to 1947 (shown in Table 20-1). On the new NAICS basis, production and capacity utilization are shown back to 1972 in Tables 2-2 and 2-3.

The individual series components of the indexes are grouped in two ways: market groups and industry groups.

Market groups. For analyzing market trends and product flows, the individual series are grouped into two major divisions: *final products and nonindustrial supplies* and *materials*. *Final products* consists of products purchased by consumers, businesses, or government for final use. *Nonindustrial supplies* are expected to become inputs in nonindustrial sectors: the two major subgroups are *construction supplies* and *business supplies*. *Materials* comprises industrial output that requires further processing within the industrial sector. This twofold division distinguishes between products that are ready to ship outside the industrial sector and those that will stay within the sector for further processing.

Final products are divided into *consumer goods* and *equipment*, and *equipment* is divided into *business equipment* and *defense and space equipment*. Further subdivisions of each market group are based on type of product and the market destination for the product.

Industry groups are typically groupings by 3-digit NAICS industries and major aggregates of these industries—for example, *durable goods* and *nondurable goods manufacturing*, *mining*, and *utilities*. Indexes are also calculated for *stage-of-process* industry groups—*crude*, *primary and semifinished*, and *finished* processing. The stage-of-process grouping was a new feature in the 2002 revision, replacing the two narrower and less well-defined "primary processing manufacturing" and "advanced processing manufacturing" groups that were previously published. *Crude processing* consists of logging, much of mining, and certain basic manufacturing activities in the chemical, paper, and metals industries. *Primary and semifinished processing* represents industries that produce materials and parts used as inputs by other industries. *Finished processing* includes industries that produce goods in their finished form for use by consumers, business investment, or government.

The indexes of industrial production are constructed with data from a variety of sources. Current monthly estimates of production are based on measures of physical output where possible and appropriate. For a few high-tech industries, the estimated value of nominal output is deflated by a corresponding price index. For industries in which such direct measurement is not possible on a monthly basis, output is inferred from production-worker hours, adjusted for trends in worker productivity derived from annual and benchmark revisions. (Between the 1960s and 1997, electric power consumption was used as a monthly output indicator for some industries instead of hours. However, the coverage of the electric power consumption survey deteriorated, and in the 2005 revision, the decision was made to resume the use of hours in those industries, beginning with the data for 1997.)

In annual and benchmark revisions, the individual indexes are revised using data from the quinquennial Censuses of Manufactures and Mineral Industries and the Annual Survey of Manufactures and Survey of Plant Capacity, prepared by the Census Bureau; deflators from the Producer Price Indexes and other sources; the *Minerals Yearbook*, prepared by the Department of the Interior; publications from the Department of Energy; and other sources.

The weights used in computing the indexes are based on Census value added—the difference between the value of production and the cost of materials and supplies consumed. (Census value added differs in some respects from the economic concept of industry value added used in the national income and product accounts [NIPAs]. Industry value added as defined in the NIPAs is not available in sufficient detail for the industrial production indexes. See Chapter 15 for data and a description of NIPA value added by major industry group.) Before 1972, a linked-Laspeyres formula is used. Beginning with 1972, the index uses a version of the Fisher-ideal index formula—a chain-weighting system similar to that in the NIPAs. See the "General Notes" article at the front of this book and the notes and definitions for Chapter 1 for more information. Chain-weighting keeps the index from being distorted by the use of obsolete relative prices.

For the purpose of these value-added weights, value added per unit of output is based on data from the Censuses of Manufacturing and Mineral Industries, the Census Bureau's Annual Survey of Manufactures, and revenue and expense data reported by the Department of Energy and the American Gas Association, which are projected into recent years by using changes in relevant Producer Price Indexes.

To separate seasonal movements from cyclical patterns and underlying trends, each component of the index is seasonally adjusted by the Census X-12-ARIMA method.

The index does not cover production on farms, in the construction industry, in transportation, or in various trade and service industries. A number of groups and subgroups include data for individual series not published separately.

Capacity utilization is calculated for the manufacturing, mining, and electric and gas utilities industries. Output is

measured by seasonally adjusted indexes of industrial production. The capacity indexes attempt to capture the concept of sustainable maximum output, which is defined as the greatest level of output that a plant can maintain within the framework of a realistic work schedule, taking account of normal downtime and assuming sufficient availability of inputs to operate the machinery and equipment in place. The 87 individual industry capacity indexes are based on a variety of data, including capacity data measured in physical units compiled by government agencies and trade associations, Census Bureau surveys of utilization rates and investment, and estimates of growth of the capital stock.

Revisions

Revisions normally occur annually. The latest was released on March 27, 2009, and its results are incorporated in this volume.

In the November 2005 revision, the indexes were all rebased from 1997 = 100 to 2002 = 100. A previous comprehensive revision in 1997 moved the reference year from 1987 to 1992 = 100 and introduced annual (instead of quinquennial) updating of the value-added weights for each industry. In the January 2001 revision, recalculation of the value-added weights each month was introduced.

Data availability

Data are available monthly in Federal Reserve release G.17. Current and historical data and background information are available on the Federal Reserve Web site at <http://www.federalreserve.gov>. The total Industrial Production index extends back to 1919.

Chain-weighting makes it difficult for the user to analyze in detail the sources of aggregate output change. An "Explanatory Note," included in each month's index release, provides some assistance for the user, including a reference to a an Internet location with the exact contribution of a monthly change in a component index to the monthly change in the total index.

References

The G.17 release each month contains extensive explanatory material, as well as references for further detail. The 2005 revision is described in "Industrial Production and Capacity Utilization: The 2005 Annual Revision," issued November 7, 2005.

An earlier detailed description of the industrial production index, together with a history of the index, a glossary of terms, and a bibliography is presented in *Industrial Production—1986 Edition*, available from Publication Services, Mail Stop 127, Board of Governors of the Federal Reserve System, Washington, DC 20551.

CHAPTER 3: INCOME DISTRIBUTION AND POVERTY

Section 3a: Household and Family Income

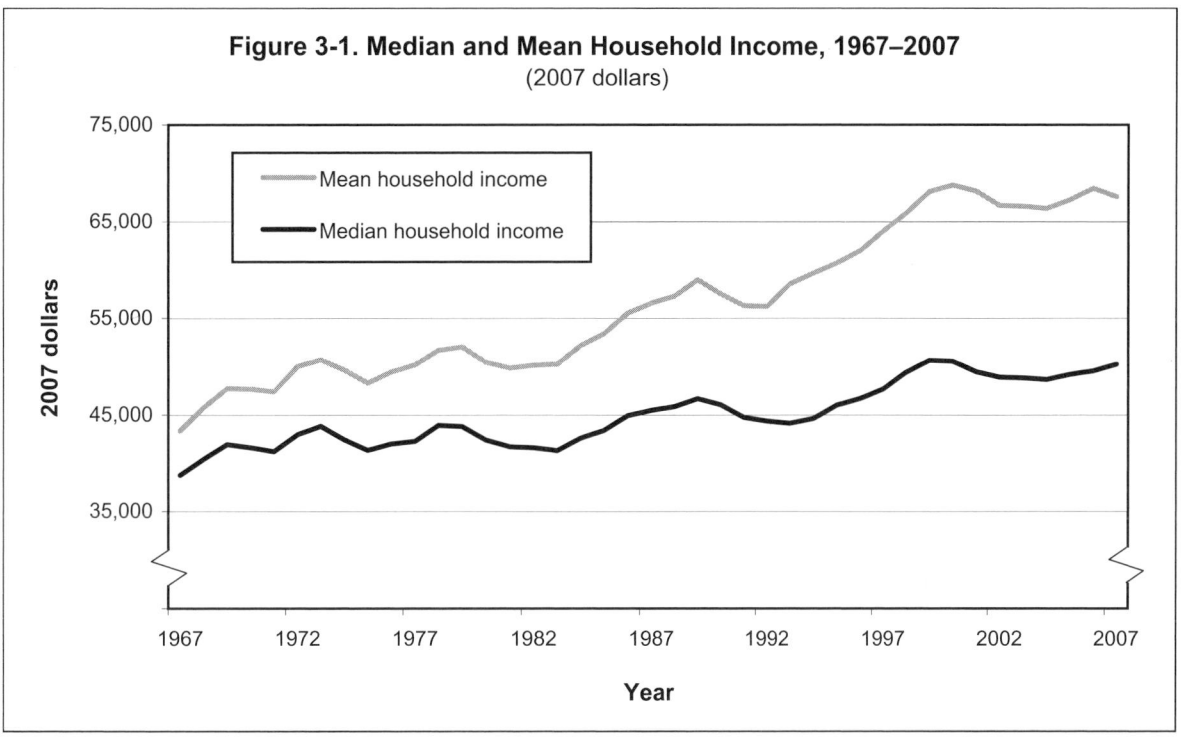

Figure 3-1. Median and Mean Household Income, 1967–2007
(2007 dollars)

- Measured as cash income before taxes, median household income in 2007 was $50,233, continuing its rise since 2004 and 2005 but down 0.8 percent in constant (2007) dollars from the 1999 all-time high of $50,641. Between the 1969 business cycle peak and 1999, real median household income rose an average 0.6 percent per year. (Table 3-1)

- The Census Bureau also tabulates "mean income," which is the sum of all the reported household incomes divided by the number of households. Mean income is higher than median income when the distribution of income is skewed upward, with very large incomes at the top of the distribution. It rises faster than median income when the income distribution becomes more unequal. (See "Whose Standard of Living?" in the article "Using the Data: The U.S. Economy in the New Century" at the beginning of this book.) Mean household income peaked one year later in 2000, rose at a 1.2 percent annual rate from 1969 to 2000, and in 2007 was 1.7 percent below its 2000 high. (Table 3-1)

- Measures of household income distribution confirm a trend increase in income inequality. The "Gini coefficient" rose from 0.386 in 1968 to 0.470 in 2006. It declined slightly in 2007, however, as incomes fell at the top part of the income distribution. (Table 3-4)

- The ratio of women's to men's earnings for year-round, full-time workers increased from 0.607 in 1960 to 0.778 in 2007. Men's earnings have been stagnant, or worse, since 1973, in real terms. In 2007, at $45,113, they were down 1.6 percent from a recent high in 2003, and 3.3 percent below 1973. Women's real earnings reached a new record of $35,102 in 2007 and were up 32.8 percent since 1973. (Table 3-1)

Table 3-1. Median and Mean Household Income and Median Earnings

(2007 dollars.)

Year	Median household income — All races	White Total	White Not Hispanic	Black	Asian [1]	Hispanic (any race)	Mean household income, all races	Median earnings — Male workers	Female workers	Ratio, female to male
1960	. . .	. . .	. . .	. . .	. . .	. . .	. . .	32 888	19 955	0.607
1961	. . .	. . .	. . .	. . .	. . .	. . .	. . .	33 938	20 108	0.592
1962	. . .	. . .	. . .	. . .	. . .	. . .	. . .	34 558	20 492	0.593
1963	. . .	. . .	. . .	. . .	. . .	. . .	. . .	35 426	20 883	0.589
1964	. . .	. . .	. . .	. . .	. . .	. . .	. . .	36 254	21 444	0.591
1965	. . .	. . .	. . .	. . .	. . .	. . .	. . .	36 770	22 035	0.599
1966	. . .	. . .	. . .	. . .	. . .	. . .	. . .	38 376	22 087	0.576
1967	38 771	40 432	. . .	23 475	. . .	. . .	43 363	38 983	22 525	0.578
1968	40 442	42 108	. . .	24 830	. . .	. . .	45 753	40 029	23 279	0.582
1969	41 945	43 775	. . .	26 460	. . .	. . .	47 720	42 275	24 885	0.589
1970	41 620	43 350	. . .	26 385	. . .	. . .	47 657	42 725	25 365	0.594
1971	41 215	43 109	. . .	25 465	. . .	. . .	47 401	42 908	25 533	0.595
1972	42 980	45 090	45 733	26 319	. . .	34 027	50 023	45 218	26 164	0.579
1973	43 848	45 954	46 359	27 050	. . .	33 971	50 710	46 659	26 425	0.566
1974	42 459	44 405	44 784	26 408	. . .	33 772	49 653	44 985	26 430	0.588
1975	41 348	43 240	43 566	25 958	. . .	31 063	48 282	44 704	26 294	0.588
1976	42 034	44 032	44 929	26 182	. . .	31 706	49 442	44 582	26 835	0.602
1977	42 300	44 481	45 363	26 249	. . .	33 183	50 179	45 585	26 860	0.589
1978	43 937	45 675	46 535	27 449	. . .	34 425	51 713	45 879	27 271	0.594
1979	43 814	45 939	46 585	26 971	. . .	34 714	52 047	45 286	27 019	0.597
1980	42 429	44 762	45 555	25 788	. . .	32 704	50 462	44 590	26 825	0.602
1981	41 724	44 085	44 721	24 738	. . .	33 469	49 847	44 319	26 252	0.592
1982	41 613	43 565	44 295	24 690	. . .	31 312	50 150	43 482	26 848	0.617
1983	41 322	43 334	. . .	24 591	. . .	31 471	50 257	43 293	27 532	0.636
1984	42 605	44 947	45 880	25 605	. . .	32 298	52 202	44 132	28 093	0.637
1985	43 402	45 772	46 801	27 232	. . .	32 095	53 413	44 462	28 712	0.646
1986	44 939	47 245	48 319	27 219	. . .	33 125	55 519	45 587	29 298	0.643
1987	45 502	47 941	49 260	27 363	56 266	33 760	56 587	45 301	29 526	0.652
1988	45 852	48 472	49 808	27 632	54 343	34 288	57 291	44 894	29 652	0.660
1989	46 670	49 091	50 147	29 196	58 288	35 392	58 963	44 127	30 303	0.687
1990	46 049	48 029	49 128	28 721	59 131	34 341	57 521	42 565	30 484	0.716
1991	44 726	46 869	47 988	27 922	54 114	33 688	56 301	43 680	30 514	0.699
1992	44 359	46 636	48 202	27 156	54 733	32 719	56 238	43 723	30 950	0.708
1993	44 143	46 572	48 286	27 600	54 184	32 338	58 537	42 965	30 728	0.715
1994	44 636	47 076	48 595	29 090	56 005	32 402	59 673	42 685	30 720	0.720
1995	46 034	48 317	50 225	30 251	54 867	30 882	60 708	42 549	30 392	0.714
1996	46 704	48 900	51 040	30 900	56 947	32 774	62 009	42 298	31 200	0.738
1997	47 665	50 199	52 266	32 266	58 284	34 299	64 007	43 375	32 167	0.742
1998	49 397	51 972	53 912	32 204	59 245	35 989	65 873	44 900	32 853	0.732
1999	50 641	52 668	54 948	34 731	63 414	38 260	68 114	45 284	32 747	0.723
2000	50 557	52 876	54 932	35 720	67 133	39 935	68 792	44 853	33 065	0.737
2001	49 455	52 136	54 230	34 514	62 815	39 310	68 171	44 826	34 215	0.763
2002	48 878	. . .	. . .	. . .	. . .	38 152	66 677	45 443	34 810	0.766
2003	48 835	. . .	. . .	. . .	. . .	37 200	66 590	45 847	34 637	0.755
2004	48 665	. . .	. . .	. . .	. . .	37 619	66 373	44 781	34 292	0.766
2005	49 202	. . .	. . .	. . .	. . .	38 200	67 277	43 955	33 836	0.770
2006	49 568	. . .	. . .	. . .	. . .	38 853	68 459	43 460	33 437	0.769
2007	50 233	. . .	. . .	. . .	. . .	38 679	67 609	45 113	35 102	0.778
By race										
Race alone										
2002	. . .	51 963	54 054	33 454	60 653	. . .	. . .	. . .	. . .	. . .
2003	. . .	51 443	53 862	33 421	62 793	. . .	. . .	. . .	. . .	. . .
2004	. . .	51 216	53 688	33 035	63 122	. . .	. . .	. . .	. . .	. . .
2005	. . .	51 569	53 937	32 774	64 887	. . .	. . .	. . .	. . .	. . .
2006	. . .	52 111	53 910	32 876	66 060	. . .	. . .	. . .	. . .	. . .
2007	. . .	52 115	54 920	33 916	66 103	. . .	. . .	. . .	. . .	. . .
Race alone or in combination										
2002	. . .	. . .	. . .	33 628	60 260	. . .	. . .	. . .	. . .	. . .
2003	. . .	. . .	. . .	33 470	62 300	. . .	. . .	. . .	. . .	. . .
2004	. . .	. . .	. . .	33 189	63 061	. . .	. . .	. . .	. . .	. . .
2005	. . .	. . .	. . .	32 876	64 838	. . .	. . .	. . .	. . .	. . .
2006	. . .	. . .	. . .	33 044	65 713	. . .	. . .	. . .	. . .	. . .
2007	. . .	. . .	. . .	34 091	65 876	. . .	. . .	. . .	. . .	. . .

[1] For 1987 through 2001, Asian and Pacific Islander.
. . . = Not available.

Table 3-2. Median Income and Poverty Rates by Race and Hispanic Origin Using 3–Year Moving Averages

(Income in 2007 dollars; percent of population)

Race and Hispanic origin	Median household income, 2007 dollars					
	2000–2002	2001–2003	2002–2004	2003–2005	2004–2006	2005–2007
All Races	49 630	49 056	48 793	48 901	49 145	49 668
White alone or in combination	52 278	51 778	51 445	51 321	51 546	51 846
White alone	52 325	51 847	51 541	51 409	51 632	51 932
Not Hispanic	54 405	54 049	53 868	53 829	53 845	54 256
Black alone or in combination	34 621	33 871	33 429	33 178	33 036	33 337
Black alone	34 563	33 796	33 303	33 077	32 895	33 189
American Indian and Alaskan Native alone or in combination	38 170	39 154	39 783	39 532	38 427	38 029
American Indian and Alaskan Native alone	37 671	37 219	36 286	35 719	34 650	34 941
Asian alone or in combination	63 403	61 792	61 874	63 400	64 537	65 476
Asian alone	63 534	62 087	62 189	63 601	64 690	65 683
Native Hawaiian and Other Pacific Islander alone or in combination	. . .	. . .	57 235	56 940	56 430	57 598
Native Hawaiian and Other Pacific Islander alone	. . .	. . .	56 689	57 697	56 551	56 278
Hispanic (any race)	39 132	38 221	37 657	37 673	38 224	38 577

Race and Hispanic origin	Poverty rates					
	2000–2002	2001–2003	2002–2004	2003–2005	2004–2006	2005–2007
All Races	11.7	12.1	12.4	12.6	12.5	12.5
White alone or in combination	9.9	10.3	10.6	10.7	10.7	10.5
White alone	9.9	10.2	10.5	10.6	10.6	10.4
Not Hispanic	7.7	8.0	8.3	8.4	8.4	8.2
Black alone or in combination	23.0	23.6	24.3	24.6	24.5	24.4
Black alone	23.1	23.7	24.4	24.7	24.6	24.6
American Indian and Alaskan Native alone or in combination	21.6	20.0	19.2	19.7	20.9	21.2
American Indian and Alaskan Native alone	23.1	23.3	24.3	25.3	27.2	26.6
Asian alone or in combination	10.0	10.7	10.5	10.8	10.3	10.4
Asian alone	10.1	10.7	10.6	10.9	10.4	10.5
Native Hawaiian and Other Pacific Islander alone or in combination	. . .	. . .	. . .	. . .	. . .	. . .
Native Hawaiian and Other Pacific Islander alone	. . .	. . .	. . .	. . .	. . .	. . .
Hispanic (any race)	21.6	21.9	22.1	22.0	21.4	21.3

. . . = Not available.

Table 3-3. Median Family Income by Type of Family

(2007 dollars.)

Year	All families	Married couples			Male householder [1]	Female householder [1]	4-person families
		Total	Wife in paid labor force	Wife not in paid labor force			
1947	24 612	25 245	. . .	. . .	23 840	17 637	26 731
1948	23 962	24 601	. . .	. . .	24 774	15 518	26 074
1949	23 652	24 322	29 361	23 279	21 475	16 009	25 715
1950	24 954	25 909	30 097	24 924	23 420	14 451	27 631
1951	25 844	26 736	32 269	25 322	24 053	15 469	28 722
1952	26 618	27 788	33 529	26 084	24 736	15 293	29 923
1953	28 832	29 709	36 737	27 983	27 956	16 686	. . .
1954	28 072	29 190	35 947	27 290	27 041	15 454	. . .
1955	29 895	31 120	38 042	29 273	28 352	16 720	33 285
1956	31 849	33 135	39 692	30 950	27 765	18 350	35 441
1957	32 037	33 269	39 617	31 179	29 553	17 825	35 405
1958	31 938	33 369	39 014	31 285	26 746	17 209	35 692
1959	33 732	35 257	41 752	33 109	28 725	17 211	37 798
1960	34 432	35 982	42 275	33 820	29 776	18 184	38 568
1961	34 787	36 619	43 601	33 920	30 747	18 155	39 045
1962	35 771	37 615	44 810	34 618	34 300	18 805	40 576
1963	37 020	39 058	46 143	35 776	33 827	19 022	42 286
1964	38 393	40 514	47 750	37 043	33 852	20 210	43 764
1965	40 045	41 818	49 486	37 944	35 389	20 331	44 898
1966	42 160	43 873	51 754	39 898	36 003	22 446	46 688
1967	43 059	45 816	54 039	41 311	36 985	23 307	48 818
1968	45 085	47 759	55 813	42 907	38 237	23 383	51 363
1969	47 165	50 005	58 145	44 395	41 700	24 110	53 115
1970	47 019	50 111	58 498	44 336	42 945	24 269	53 214
1971	46 953	50 172	58 677	44 483	39 818	23 347	53 075
1972	49 270	52 758	61 596	46 788	45 675	23 677	56 769
1973	50 268	54 343	63 557	47 627	44 807	24 181	57 188
1974	48 925	52 796	61 511	46 380	44 207	24 603	56 763
1975	48 072	52 094	60 399	44 683	45 535	23 982	55 532
1976	49 562	53 687	62 063	46 159	42 610	23 893	57 371
1977	49 895	54 904	63 169	46 947	45 248	24 201	58 354
1978	51 450	56 408	64 485	47 122	46 568	24 900	59 582
1979	52 135	57 038	66 173	47 128	44 738	26 298	59 920
1980	50 366	55 440	64 395	45 452	41 971	24 935	58 293
1981	48 974	54 830	63 978	44 461	43 507	23 975	57 474
1982	48 342	53 677	62 596	43 940	41 549	23 692	56 978
1983	48 633	53 987	63 526	43 311	43 222	23 325	57 742
1984	50 243	56 285	65 895	44 823	44 335	24 335	59 108
1985	50 967	57 151	66 948	45 126	41 572	25 102	60 233
1986	53 171	59 212	69 214	46 574	45 056	24 633	62 662
1987	54 073	60 898	71 151	46 513	44 013	25 636	64 752
1988	54 215	61 286	71 930	45 843	45 182	25 845	65 769
1989	55 238	62 235	73 083	46 413	44 960	26 546	65 813
1990	54 369	61 354	71 937	46 544	44 669	26 039	63 747
1991	53 357	60 863	71 514	44 651	42 091	24 782	63 923
1992	52 955	60 654	72 071	43 690	39 928	24 651	64 072
1993	52 223	60 766	72 351	42 698	37 398	24 647	63 812
1994	53 653	62 199	73 751	43 131	38 392	25 229	65 039
1995	54 863	63 578	75 413	43 736	41 012	26 601	67 124
1996	55 663	65 410	76 824	44 409	41 583	26 201	67 793
1997	57 407	66 453	78 146	46 405	42 455	27 079	68 719
1998	59 372	68 827	80 985	47 207	45 327	28 154	71 216
1999	60 764	70 309	82 724	47 884	46 464	29 569	74 358
2000	61 083	71 157	83 361	48 140	45 425	30 963	75 457
2001	60 206	70 662	82 958	47 762	42 853	30 151	74 108
2002	59 563	70 455	83 912	46 219	43 496	30 453	72 301
2003	59 389	70 213	84 744	46 359	42 876	29 931	73 383
2004	59 342	69 842	84 362	46 339	44 304	29 604	72 473
2005	59 683	69 998	83 645	47 217	43 663	28 935	74 677
2006	60 064	71 373	85 137	47 055	43 031	29 647	75 498
2007	61 355	72 589	86 435	47 329	44 358	30 296	75 675

[1]No spouse present.
. . . = Not available.

Table 3-4. Shares of Aggregate Income Received by Each Fifth and Top 5 Percent of Households

Year	Number (thousands)	Share of aggregate income (percent)						Mean household income (2007 dollars)						Gini coefficient
		Lowest fifth	Second fifth	Third fifth	Fourth fifth	Highest fifth	Top 5 percent	Lowest fifth	Second fifth	Third fifth	Fourth fifth	Highest fifth	Top 5 percent	
1967	60 813	4.0	10.8	17.3	24.2	43.6	17.2	8 684	24 061	38 413	53 746	96 724	152 576	0.397
1968	62 214	4.2	11.1	17.6	24.5	42.6	16.3	9 433	25 290	40 113	55 954	97 231	148 651	0.386
1969	63 401	4.1	10.9	17.5	24.5	43.0	16.6	9 660	26 080	41 675	58 375	102 600	157 925	0.391
1970	64 778	4.1	10.8	17.4	24.5	43.3	16.6	9 492	25 713	41 405	58 365	103 325	158 593	0.394
1971	66 676	4.1	10.6	17.3	24.5	43.5	16.7	9 550	25 241	40 927	58 184	103 096	158 130	0.396
1972	68 251	4.1	10.4	17.0	24.5	43.9	17.0	10 119	26 137	42 657	61 241	109 944	170 409	0.401
1973	69 859	4.2	10.4	17.0	24.5	43.9	16.9	10 591	26 629	43 677	62 835	112 427	173 173	0.400
1974	71 163	4.3	10.6	17.0	24.6	43.5	16.5	10 553	26 229	42 270	61 048	108 160	164 403	0.395
1975	72 867	4.3	10.4	17.0	24.7	43.6	16.5	10 193	25 040	41 081	59 695	105 394	159 938	0.397
1976	74 142	4.3	10.3	17.0	24.7	43.7	16.6	10 444	25 569	42 050	61 066	108 079	164 675	0.398
1977	76 030	4.2	10.2	16.9	24.7	44.0	16.8	10 394	25 585	42 321	62 010	110 580	169 164	0.402
1978	77 330	4.2	10.2	16.8	24.7	44.1	16.8	10 748	26 396	43 584	63 846	113 986	173 501	0.402
1979	80 776	4.1	10.2	16.8	24.6	44.2	16.9	10 663	26 521	43 727	64 169	115 159	175 630	0.404
1980	82 368	4.2	10.2	16.8	24.7	44.1	16.5	10 326	25 699	42 407	62 476	111 395	166 466	0.403
1981	83 527	4.1	10.1	16.7	24.8	44.3	16.5	10 067	25 078	41 543	61 926	110 618	164 378	0.406
1982	83 918	4.0	10.0	16.5	24.5	45.0	17.0	9 882	25 006	41 392	61 560	112 906	170 605	0.412
1983	85 407	4.0	9.9	16.4	24.6	45.1	17.0	9 998	25 114	41 522	62 309	114 398	172 845	0.414
1984	86 789	4.0	9.9	16.3	24.6	45.2	17.1	10 332	25 736	42 649	64 215	118 076	178 241	0.415
1985	88 458	3.9	9.8	16.2	24.4	45.6	17.6	10 317	26 144	43 396	65 277	121 934	188 092	0.419
1986	89 479	3.8	9.7	16.2	24.3	46.1	18.0	10 422	26 809	44 863	67 584	127 921	200 396	0.425
1987	91 124	3.8	9.6	16.1	24.3	46.2	18.2	10 706	27 209	45 492	68 762	130 769	206 026	0.426
1988	92 830	3.8	9.6	16.0	24.2	46.3	18.3	10 888	27 481	45 963	69 479	132 644	209 201	0.426
1989	93 347	3.8	9.5	15.8	24.0	46.8	18.9	11 292	28 094	46 700	70 640	138 089	223 104	0.431
1990	94 312	3.8	9.6	15.9	24.0	46.6	18.5	11 020	27 728	45 800	69 052	134 006	213 390	0.428
1991	95 669	3.8	9.6	15.9	24.2	46.5	18.1	10 728	26 946	44 759	68 230	130 837	204 183	0.428
1992	96 426	3.8	9.4	15.8	24.2	46.9	18.6	10 506	26 325	44 352	68 083	131 921	209 382	0.433
1993	97 107	3.6	9.0	15.1	23.5	48.9	21.0	10 398	26 361	44 187	68 670	143 070	245 556	0.454
1994	98 990	3.6	8.9	15.0	23.4	49.1	21.2	10 672	26 596	44 803	69 720	146 571	253 234	0.456
1995	99 627	3.7	9.1	15.2	23.3	48.7	21.0	11 274	27 555	46 075	70 828	147 807	255 094	0.450
1996	101 018	3.6	9.0	15.1	23.3	49.0	21.4	11 310	27 762	46 696	72 272	152 005	264 786	0.455
1997	102 528	3.6	8.9	15.0	23.2	49.4	21.7	11 385	28 464	47 887	74 170	158 129	277 497	0.459
1998	103 874	3.6	9.0	15.0	23.2	49.2	21.4	11 716	29 584	49 501	76 558	162 005	282 375	0.456
1999	106 434	3.6	8.9	14.9	23.2	49.4	21.5	12 338	30 294	50 709	78 922	168 303	292 525	0.458
2000	108 209	3.6	8.9	14.8	23.0	49.8	22.1	12 229	30 535	50 850	79 048	171 297	303 898	0.462
2001	109 297	3.5	8.7	14.6	23.0	50.1	22.4	11 871	29 827	49 925	78 279	170 953	305 043	0.466
2002	111 278	3.5	8.8	14.8	23.3	49.7	21.7	11 514	29 274	49 331	77 596	165 669	289 298	0.462
2003	112 000	3.4	8.7	14.8	23.4	49.8	21.4	11 269	28 948	49 139	77 781	165 810	285 492	0.464
2004	113 343	3.4	8.7	14.7	23.2	50.1	21.8	11 245	28 773	48 750	76 867	166 232	289 677	0.466
2005	114 384	3.4	8.6	14.6	23.0	50.4	22.2	11 317	29 055	49 176	77 346	169 491	298 611	0.469
2006	116 011	3.4	8.6	14.5	22.9	50.5	22.3	11 674	29 593	49 591	78 494	172 941	305 842	0.470
2007	116 783	3.4	8.7	14.8	23.4	49.7	21.2	11 551	29 442	49 968	79 111	167 971	287 191	0.463

Table 3-5. Shares of Aggregate Income Received by Each Fifth and Top 5 Percent of Families

Year	Number of families (thousands)	Share of aggregate income (percent)						Mean family income (2007 dollars)						Gini coefficient
		Lowest fifth	Second fifth	Third fifth	Fourth fifth	Highest fifth	Top 5 percent	Lowest fifth	Second fifth	Third fifth	Fourth fifth	Highest fifth	Top 5 percent	
1947	37 237	5.0	11.9	17.0	23.1	43.0	17.5	. . .	. . .	. . .	. . .	. . .	. . .	0.376
1948	38 624	4.9	12.1	17.3	23.2	42.4	17.1	. . .	. . .	. . .	. . .	. . .	. . .	0.371
1949	39 303	4.5	11.9	17.3	23.5	42.7	16.9	. . .	. . .	. . .	. . .	. . .	. . .	0.378
1950	39 929	4.5	12.0	17.4	23.4	42.7	17.3	. . .	. . .	. . .	. . .	. . .	. . .	0.379
1951	40 578	5.0	12.4	17.6	23.4	41.6	16.8	. . .	. . .	. . .	. . .	. . .	. . .	0.363
1952	40 832	4.9	12.3	17.4	23.4	41.9	17.4	. . .	. . .	. . .	. . .	. . .	. . .	0.368
1953	41 202	4.7	12.5	18.0	23.9	40.9	15.7	. . .	. . .	. . .	. . .	. . .	. . .	0.359
1954	41 951	4.5	12.1	17.7	23.9	41.8	16.3	. . .	. . .	. . .	. . .	. . .	. . .	0.371
1955	42 889	4.8	12.3	17.8	23.7	41.3	16.4	. . .	. . .	. . .	. . .	. . .	. . .	0.363
1956	43 497	5.0	12.5	17.9	23.7	41.0	16.1	. . .	. . .	. . .	. . .	. . .	. . .	0.358
1957	43 696	5.1	12.7	18.1	23.8	40.4	15.6	. . .	. . .	. . .	. . .	. . .	. . .	0.351
1958	44 232	5.0	12.5	18.0	23.9	40.6	15.4	. . .	. . .	. . .	. . .	. . .	. . .	0.354
1959	45 111	4.9	12.3	17.9	23.8	41.1	15.9	. . .	. . .	. . .	. . .	. . .	. . .	0.361
1960	45 539	4.8	12.2	17.8	24.0	41.3	15.9	. . .	. . .	. . .	. . .	. . .	. . .	0.364
1961	46 418	4.7	11.9	17.5	23.8	42.2	16.6	. . .	. . .	. . .	. . .	. . .	. . .	0.374
1962	47 059	5.0	12.1	17.6	24.0	41.3	15.7	. . .	. . .	. . .	. . .	. . .	. . .	0.362
1963	47 540	5.0	12.1	17.7	24.0	41.2	15.8	. . .	. . .	. . .	. . .	. . .	. . .	0.362
1964	47 956	5.1	12.0	17.7	24.0	41.2	15.9	. . .	. . .	. . .	. . .	. . .	. . .	0.361
1965	48 509	5.2	12.2	17.8	23.9	40.9	15.5	. . .	. . .	. . .	. . .	. . .	. . .	0.356
1966	49 214	5.6	12.4	17.8	23.8	40.5	15.6	13 126	29 140	41 695	55 818	95 263	146 278	0.349
1967	50 111	5.4	12.2	17.5	23.5	41.4	16.4	13 331	29 810	42 847	57 464	101 467	160 538	0.358
1968	50 823	5.6	12.4	17.7	23.7	40.5	15.6	14 368	31 338	44 771	59 876	102 313	157 718	0.348
1969	51 586	5.6	12.4	17.7	23.7	40.6	15.6	14 825	32 740	46 850	62 760	107 485	165 090	0.349
1970	52 227	5.4	12.2	17.6	23.8	40.9	15.6	14 601	32 285	46 680	62 968	108 281	164 883	0.353
1971	53 296	5.5	12.0	17.6	23.8	41.1	15.7	14 613	31 810	46 542	63 032	108 565	165 535	0.355
1972	54 373	5.5	11.9	17.5	23.9	41.4	15.9	15 252	33 278	48 880	66 751	115 768	177 479	0.359
1973	55 053	5.5	11.9	17.5	24.0	41.1	15.5	15 650	33 900	49 809	68 070	116 790	176 255	0.356
1974	55 698	5.7	12.0	17.6	24.1	40.6	14.8	15 927	33 620	49 084	67 248	113 313	165 279	0.355
1975	56 245	5.6	11.9	17.7	24.2	40.7	14.9	15 302	32 349	48 100	65 858	110 983	162 804	0.357
1976	56 710	5.6	11.9	17.7	24.2	40.7	14.9	15 672	33 167	49 475	67 600	113 775	166 521	0.358
1977	57 215	5.5	11.7	17.6	24.3	40.9	14.9	15 605	33 358	50 169	69 206	116 589	169 968	0.363
1978	57 804	5.4	11.7	17.6	24.2	41.1	15.1	15 826	34 320	51 535	71 003	120 485	176 558	0.363
1979	59 550	5.4	11.6	17.5	24.1	41.4	15.3	15 965	34 517	52 055	71 667	122 923	181 955	0.365
1980	60 309	5.3	11.6	17.6	24.4	41.1	14.6	15 359	33 435	50 510	70 076	117 986	167 727	0.365
1981	61 019	5.3	11.4	17.5	24.6	41.2	14.4	14 882	32 362	49 497	69 493	116 600	162 929	0.369
1982	61 393	5.0	11.3	17.2	24.4	42.2	15.3	14 039	31 853	48 637	68 997	119 223	170 578	0.380
1983	62 015	4.9	11.2	17.2	24.5	42.4	15.3	13 824	31 807	48 938	69 746	120 933	174 362	0.382
1984	62 706	4.8	11.1	17.1	24.5	42.5	15.4	14 296	32 731	50 499	72 213	125 505	181 457	0.383
1985	63 558	4.8	11.0	16.9	24.3	43.1	16.1	14 461	33 183	51 232	73 437	130 509	195 033	0.389
1986	64 491	4.7	10.9	16.9	24.1	43.4	16.5	14 869	34 333	53 189	75 999	136 886	207 870	0.392
1987	65 204	4.6	10.7	16.8	24.0	43.8	17.2	14 853	34 764	53 982	77 260	141 194	221 031	0.393
1988	65 837	4.6	10.7	16.7	24.0	44.0	17.2	14 981	34 886	54 288	77 966	143 054	223 518	0.395
1989	66 090	4.6	10.6	16.5	23.7	44.6	17.9	15 280	35 549	55 227	79 456	149 607	239 657	0.401
1990	66 322	4.6	10.8	16.6	23.8	44.3	17.4	15 122	35 271	54 321	78 120	145 182	227 797	0.396
1991	67 173	4.5	10.7	16.6	24.1	44.2	17.1	14 452	34 303	53 226	77 197	141 828	219 455	0.397
1992	68 216	4.3	10.5	16.5	24.0	44.7	17.6	13 880	33 478	52 889	76 876	143 059	225 236	0.404
1993	68 506	4.1	9.9	15.7	23.3	47.0	20.3	13 761	33 050	52 374	77 638	156 866	270 746	0.429
1994	69 313	4.2	10.0	15.7	23.3	46.9	20.1	14 370	33 999	53 689	79 364	159 939	274 390	0.426
1995	69 597	4.4	10.1	15.8	23.2	46.5	20.0	15 218	35 063	54 898	80 322	161 373	276 756	0.421
1996	70 241	4.2	10.0	15.8	23.1	46.8	20.3	14 986	35 328	55 882	81 654	165 313	286 018	0.425
1997	70 884	4.2	9.9	15.7	23.0	47.2	20.7	15 530	36 391	57 416	84 192	172 969	302 724	0.429
1998	71 551	4.2	9.9	15.7	23.0	47.3	20.7	15 912	37 452	59 277	86 929	178 922	313 164	0.430
1999	73 206	4.3	9.9	15.6	23.0	47.2	20.3	16 560	38 494	60 759	89 679	183 798	316 900	0.429
2000	73 778	4.3	9.8	15.4	22.7	47.7	21.1	17 003	38 877	61 101	90 051	188 936	334 797	0.433
2001	74 340	4.2	9.7	15.4	22.9	47.7	21.0	16 421	38 023	60 359	89 764	186 968	328 288	0.435
2002	75 616	4.2	9.7	15.5	23.0	47.6	20.8	16 155	37 482	59 781	88 912	183 597	321 315	0.434
2003	76 232	4.1	9.6	15.5	23.2	47.6	20.5	15 638	37 086	59 768	89 865	184 123	317 315	0.436
2004	76 866	4.0	9.6	15.4	23.0	47.9	20.9	15 586	37 099	59 542	88 958	185 140	322 543	0.438
2005	77 418	4.0	9.6	15.3	22.9	48.1	21.1	15 684	37 319	59 718	89 316	187 237	327 798	0.440
2006	78 454	4.0	9.5	15.1	22.9	48.5	21.5	15 980	37 812	60 144	90 902	192 705	341 112	0.444
2007	77 908	4.1	9.7	15.6	23.3	47.3	20.1	16 068	38 304	61 444	91 881	186 529	316 618	0.432

. . . = Not available.

Table 3-6. Median Household Income by State

(2007 dollars.)

State	1990	1995	1996	1997	1998	1999	2000	2001	2002	2003	2004	2005	2006	2007
United States	46 049	46 034	46 704	47 665	49 397	50 641	50 557	49 455	48 878	48 835	48 665	49 202	49 568	50 233
Alabama	35 920	35 112	39 874	41 140	46 070	45 110	42 652	41 178	43 339	42 000	40 207	39 456	39 029	42 212
Alaska	60 436	64 783	69 452	61 820	64 396	63 956	63 630	67 181	60 824	58 439	60 442	59 361	58 019	62 993
Arizona	44 943	41 694	41 631	42 171	47 117	46 036	47 900	50 013	45 795	46 409	48 129	48 054	47 981	47 215
Arkansas	35 042	34 873	35 691	33 699	35 144	36 936	35 756	39 045	37 327	36 078	38 402	38 934	38 108	40 795
California	51 196	49 997	51 073	51 129	52 000	54 291	56 368	55 351	54 673	55 579	54 031	54 968	56 888	55 734
Colorado	47 264	54 991	53 886	55 687	59 196	59 951	58 083	57 851	55 661	56 300	55 857	53 581	57 277	61 141
Connecticut	59 777	54 366	55 425	56 656	59 081	62 957	60 409	62 478	61 530	61 965	60 483	60 364	64 174	64 141
Delaware	47 373	47 185	51 727	55 430	52 666	58 023	60 641	58 092	57 223	55 262	52 743	54 416	53 926	54 589
District of Columbia	42 126	41 538	42 064	41 038	42 471	48 120	49 633	48 215	45 030	50 781	47 696	47 786	49 852	50 783
Florida	41 038	40 183	40 321	41 804	44 346	44 587	46 784	42 655	43 824	43 935	44 495	45 659	46 972	45 794
Georgia	42 385	46 065	42 762	47 225	49 118	49 060	50 450	49 863	49 489	47 843	44 988	48 777	50 744	48 641
Hawaii	59 856	57 889	54 968	52 726	51 864	55 380	62 063	55 558	54 518	58 436	61 736	63 285	62 185	64 022
Idaho	38 916	44 143	45 674	43 027	46 596	44 549	45 285	44 786	43 468	47 769	48 691	46 919	47 524	49 184
Illinois	50 046	51 431	52 049	53 175	54 851	57 652	55 463	54 073	49 225	50 904	50 578	51 403	50 052	52 506
Indiana	41 412	45 101	46 250	50 092	50 472	50 818	49 203	47 290	47 308	47 828	46 464	45 072	46 695	47 453
Iowa	41 966	47 984	43 700	43 515	47 027	51 142	49 355	47 989	47 310	46 655	47 630	49 387	49 491	48 908
Kansas	46 009	40 989	42 879	46 977	46 635	46 475	49 436	48 503	49 120	49 865	45 078	44 636	46 844	48 497
Kentucky	38 109	40 271	42 652	43 089	46 052	41 983	43 664	45 016	42 370	41 640	39 089	38 977	40 605	39 452
Louisiana	34 456	37 757	39 822	42 841	40 314	40 634	36 985	39 025	39 195	37 774	39 988	39 548	37 523	41 313
Maine	42 236	45 740	45 657	42 213	45 275	48 359	44 870	42 878	42 474	41 840	45 367	46 650	46 937	47 894
Maryland	59 757	55 444	57 891	60 134	63 537	64 963	65 662	62 692	65 011	58 977	62 682	64 269	65 474	65 630
Massachusetts	55 743	52 111	51 970	54 129	53 792	54 759	56 292	61 196	57 460	57 445	57 101	59 495	56 900	58 463
Michigan	46 039	49 209	51 616	49 902	53 127	57 352	54 798	52 757	49 231	50 756	46 384	48 785	50 027	49 370
Minnesota	48 389	51 245	53 940	54 825	60 882	58 533	65 320	61 698	62 954	59 551	61 585	57 581	57 806	58 058
Mississippi	31 031	35 851	35 104	36 709	36 992	40 415	41 297	35 323	35 593	36 896	38 150	34 916	35 718	37 279
Missouri	42 033	47 046	45 089	47 083	51 069	51 496	51 496	54 298	48 414	49 301	49 336	46 253	45 655	45 844	46 005
Montana	35 948	37 498	37 745	37 627	40 113	38 623	39 465	37 624	40 149	38 452	37 273	39 630	42 271	43 655
Nebraska	42 264	44 485	44 759	44 686	46 257	48 065	50 268	51 075	49 324	49 575	48 064	50 898	49 511	49 174
Nevada	49 247	48 747	50 715	50 047	50 504	51 593	55 094	53 174	51 816	50 939	51 815	51 202	53 765	54 058
New Hampshire	62 753	52 917	51 856	52 808	57 112	57 310	61 317	60 116	63 759	62 644	62 365	60 522	63 728	67 576
New Jersey	59 568	59 338	62 463	61 854	63 296	61 888	60 689	60 632	62 892	63 183	60 675	67 302	69 990	60 508
New Mexico	38 507	35 112	33 011	38 753	40 070	40 534	42 253	38 793	40 865	39 576	43 427	41 365	41 164	44 356
New York	48 583	44 619	46 596	46 110	47 503	49 762	49 057	49 322	48 367	48 237	49 011	50 105	49 590	48 944
North Carolina	40 491	43 201	46 847	46 164	45 526	46 358	46 135	44 694	42 085	42 027	44 169	44 667	40 926	43 513
North Dakota	38 853	39 297	41 411	40 782	38 496	40 645	43 340	41 919	41 722	45 557	43 052	44 812	42 211	47 205
Ohio	46 156	47 203	44 833	46 543	49 448	49 139	51 728	48 937	49 195	49 063	47 261	46 947	47 202	49 099
Oklahoma	37 500	35 544	36 104	40 382	42 845	40 670	39 049	41 704	42 019	40 474	43 484	39 982	39 940	43 216
Oregon	45 031	49 139	46 704	47 977	49 628	50 546	51 170	48 337	48 178	46 941	44 999	46 901	48 427	50 236
Pennsylvania	44 606	46 640	45 924	48 325	49 562	46 985	50 781	50 944	48 980	48 401	48 415	49 175	49 852	48 437
Rhode Island	49 163	47 768	48 670	44 821	51 685	53 159	50 807	53 549	48 887	50 405	52 618	52 556	55 260	54 210
South Carolina	44 191	39 273	45 616	44 132	42 260	45 373	45 236	44 195	43 580	43 380	42 471	42 728	40 741	44 213
South Dakota	37 787	39 958	38 853	38 248	41 649	44 584	43 917	46 461	43 650	44 556	45 123	45 830	46 716	46 418
Tennessee	34 744	39 197	40 517	39 461	43 307	45 447	41 053	41 907	42 678	42 302	41 791	41 853	41 847	41 195
Texas	43 411	43 283	43 520	45 179	45 457	48 143	46 487	47 853	46 273	44 273	45 441	43 994	44 536	46 053
Utah	46 355	49 282	48 738	55 097	56 275	57 304	57 252	55 445	55 162	55 551	55 841	58 216	56 178	53 529
Vermont	47 825	45 694	42 580	45 151	50 016	51 746	47 672	47 776	49 558	48 771	51 953	53 852	53 456	47 390
Virginia	53 938	48 933	51 598	55 332	55 074	56 859	56 786	58 840	57 202	61 760	56 137	55 137	58 739	59 161
Washington	49 384	48 050	48 262	57 399	60 241	58 586	51 202	49 762	52 075	53 559	54 799	53 790	56 275	58 080
West Virginia	34 044	33 611	33 223	35 406	33 923	36 457	35 412	34 752	33 837	36 936	36 633	38 708	39 509	42 091
Wisconsin	47 230	55 327	52 637	51 001	52 499	56 827	54 287	53 107	52 905	52 162	50 200	47 422	53 158	51 277
Wyoming	45 306	42 594	40 731	43 051	44 779	46 351	47 715	46 517	45 828	47 975	49 832	47 494	48 375	48 744

Section 3b: Poverty

Figure 3-2. Poverty Rates: Total, Children, and Seniors, 1959–2007
(percent of population in age group; age groups not available for 1960–1965)

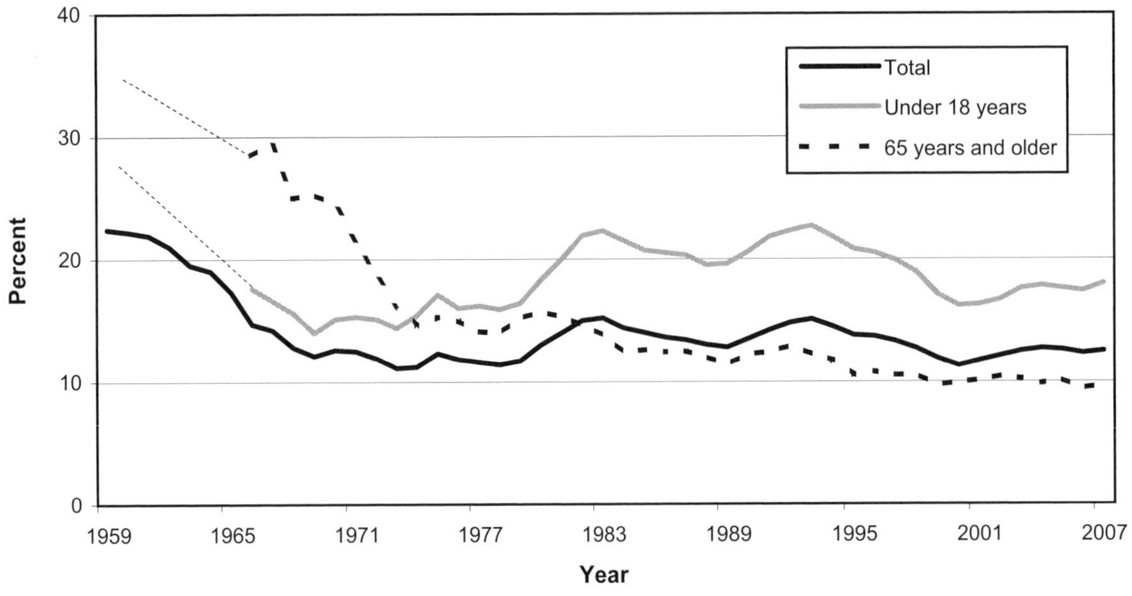

- The number of Americans with family incomes below the poverty line was 12.5 percent of the population in 2007, little changed since 2003. The most recent low for the poverty rate was 11.3 percent in 2000, essentially the same as at its all-time low in 1974. (Table 3-8)

- The poverty rate for senior citizens (age 65 years and older) was 9.7 percent in 2007, lower than the rate for people age 18 to 64 years. This has not always been the case. In 1959, the first poverty rate calculations showed more than one-third of all seniors as living in poverty, compared with 17 percent of working-age adults. (Table 3-10) Between 1959 and 1974, ad hoc legislative changes raised Social Security benefits by a cumulative 104 percent—exceeding the 69 percent increase in consumer prices—and since then, each year's benefits have been indexed to the rate of change in the Consumer Price Index, Urban Wage Earners and Clerical Workers (CPI-W). (See Chapter 8.) However, it should be noted that when medical expenses are taken into account, one set of recent Census Bureau estimates indicates that redefining both income and the poverty line would raise the poverty rate of the elderly above the poverty rate of working-age adults. (Table 3-18)

- The poverty rate for children, on the other hand, has always been higher than the average and remains so even when the rate is redefined as in Table 3-18. The gap between the official poverty rates for children and for working-age adults has been as high as 10 percentage points (in 1959 and the early 1990s, for example) and as low as 5.3 percentage points (in 1969). (Table 3-10)

- Poverty among Hispanics (who may be of any race) was 21.5 percent in 2007, compared with 8.2 percent for non-Hispanic Whites. Poverty among Blacks was 24.5 percent and poverty among Asians was 10.2 percent. (Table 3-8)

Table 3-7. Weighted Average Poverty Thresholds by Family Size

(Dollars.)

Year	Unrelated individuals			Families of 2 people			Families, all ages								CPI-U, all items (1982–1984 = 100)
	All ages	Under 65 years	65 years and older	All ages	House-holder under 65 years	House-holder 65 years and older	3 people	4 people	5 people	6 people	7 people or more (before 1980)	7 people	8 people	9 people or more	
1959	1 467	1 503	1 397	1 894	1 952	1 761	2 324	2 973	3 506	3 944	4 849	. . .	. . .	. . .	29.2
1960	1 490	1 526	1 418	1 924	1 982	1 788	2 359	3 022	3 560	4 002	4 921	. . .	. . .	. . .	29.6
1961	1 506	1 545	1 433	1 942	2 005	1 808	2 383	3 054	3 597	4 041	4 967	. . .	. . .	. . .	29.9
1962	1 519	1 562	1 451	1 962	2 027	1 828	2 412	3 089	3 639	4 088	5 032	. . .	. . .	. . .	30.3
1963	1 539	1 581	1 470	1 988	2 052	1 850	2 442	3 128	3 685	4 135	5 092	. . .	. . .	. . .	30.6
1964	1 558	1 601	1 488	2 015	2 079	1 875	2 473	3 169	3 732	4 193	5 156	. . .	. . .	. . .	31.0
1965	1 582	1 626	1 512	2 048	2 114	1 906	2 514	3 223	3 797	4 264	5 248	. . .	. . .	. . .	31.5
1966	1 628	1 674	1 556	2 107	2 175	1 961	2 588	3 317	3 908	4 388	5 395	. . .	. . .	. . .	32.5
1967	1 675	1 722	1 600	2 168	2 238	2 017	2 661	3 410	4 019	4 516	5 550	. . .	. . .	. . .	33.4
1968	1 748	1 797	1 667	2 262	2 333	2 102	2 774	3 553	4 188	4 706	5 789	. . .	. . .	. . .	34.8
1969	1 840	1 893	1 757	2 383	2 458	2 215	2 924	3 743	4 415	4 958	6 101	. . .	. . .	. . .	36.7
1970	1 954	2 010	1 861	2 525	2 604	2 348	3 099	3 968	4 680	5 260	6 468	. . .	. . .	. . .	38.8
1971	2 040	2 098	1 940	2 633	2 716	2 448	3 229	4 137	4 880	5 489	6 751	. . .	. . .	. . .	40.5
1972	2 109	2 168	2 005	2 724	2 808	2 530	3 339	4 275	5 044	5 673	6 983	. . .	. . .	. . .	41.8
1973	2 247	2 307	2 130	2 895	2 984	2 688	3 548	4 540	5 358	6 028	7 435	. . .	. . .	. . .	44.4
1974	2 495	2 562	2 364	3 211	3 312	2 982	3 936	5 038	5 950	6 699	8 253	. . .	. . .	. . .	49.3
1975	2 724	2 797	2 581	3 506	3 617	3 257	4 293	5 500	6 499	7 316	9 022	. . .	. . .	. . .	53.8
1976	2 884	2 959	2 730	3 711	3 826	3 445	4 540	5 815	6 876	7 760	9 588	. . .	. . .	. . .	56.9
1977	3 075	3 152	2 906	3 951	4 072	3 666	4 833	6 191	7 320	8 261	10 216	. . .	. . .	. . .	60.6
1978	3 311	3 392	3 127	4 249	4 383	3 944	5 201	6 662	7 880	8 891	11 002	. . .	. . .	. . .	65.2
1979	3 689	3 778	3 479	4 725	4 878	4 390	5 784	7 412	8 775	9 914	12 280	. . .	. . .	. . .	72.6
1980	4 190	4 290	3 949	5 363	5 537	4 983	6 565	8 414	9 966	11 269	13 955	12 761	14 199	16 896	82.4
1981	4 620	4 729	4 359	5 917	6 111	5 498	7 250	9 287	11 007	12 449	. . .	14 110	15 655	18 572	90.9
1982	4 901	5 019	4 626	6 281	6 487	5 836	7 693	9 862	11 684	13 207	. . .	15 036	16 719	19 698	96.5
1983	5 061	5 180	4 775	6 483	6 697	6 023	7 938	10 178	12 049	13 630	. . .	15 500	17 170	20 310	99.6
1984	5 278	5 400	4 979	6 762	6 983	6 282	8 277	10 609	12 566	14 207	. . .	16 096	17 961	21 247	103.9
1985	5 469	5 593	5 156	6 998	7 231	6 503	8 573	10 989	13 007	14 696	. . .	16 656	18 512	22 083	107.6
1986	5 572	5 701	5 255	7 138	7 372	6 630	8 737	11 203	13 259	14 986	. . .	17 049	18 791	22 497	109.6
1987	5 778	5 909	5 447	7 397	7 641	6 872	9 056	11 611	13 737	15 509	. . .	17 649	19 515	23 105	113.6
1988	6 022	6 155	5 674	7 704	7 958	7 157	9 435	12 092	14 304	16 146	. . .	18 232	20 253	24 129	118.3
1989	6 310	6 451	5 947	8 076	8 343	7 501	9 885	12 674	14 990	16 921	. . .	19 162	21 328	25 480	124.0
1990	6 652	6 800	6 268	8 509	8 794	7 905	10 419	13 359	15 792	17 839	. . .	20 241	22 582	26 848	130.7
1991	6 932	7 086	6 532	8 865	9 165	8 241	10 860	13 924	16 456	18 587	. . .	21 058	23 582	27 942	136.2
1992	7 143	7 299	6 729	9 137	9 443	8 487	11 186	14 335	16 952	19 137	. . .	21 594	24 053	28 745	140.3
1993	7 363	7 518	6 930	9 414	9 728	8 740	11 522	14 763	17 449	19 718	. . .	22 383	24 838	29 529	144.5
1994	7 547	7 710	7 108	9 661	9 976	8 967	11 821	15 141	17 900	20 235	. . .	22 923	25 427	30 300	148.2
1995	7 763	7 929	7 309	9 933	10 259	9 219	12 158	15 569	18 408	20 804	. . .	23 552	26 237	31 280	152.4
1996	7 995	8 163	7 525	10 233	10 564	9 491	12 516	16 036	18 952	21 389	. . .	24 268	27 091	31 971	156.9
1997	8 183	8 350	7 698	10 473	10 805	9 712	12 802	16 400	19 380	21 886	. . .	24 802	27 593	32 566	160.5
1998	8 316	8 480	7 818	10 634	10 972	9 862	13 003	16 660	19 680	22 228	. . .	25 257	28 166	33 339	163.0
1999	8 499	8 667	7 990	10 864	11 213	10 075	13 289	17 030	20 128	22 730	. . .	25 918	28 970	34 436	166.6
2000	8 791	8 959	8 259	11 235	11 589	10 418	13 740	17 604	20 815	23 533	. . .	26 750	29 701	35 150	172.2
2001	9 039	9 214	8 494	11 569	11 920	10 715	14 128	18 104	21 405	24 195	. . .	27 517	30 627	36 286	177.1
2002	9 183	9 359	8 628	11 756	12 110	10 885	14 348	18 392	21 744	24 576	. . .	28 001	30 907	37 062	179.9
2003	9 393	9 573	8 825	12 015	12 384	11 133	14 680	18 810	22 245	25 122	. . .	28 544	31 589	37 656	184.0
2004	9 646	9 827	9 060	12 335	12 714	11 430	15 066	19 307	22 830	25 787	. . .	29 233	32 641	39 062	188.9
2005	9 973	10 160	9 367	12 755	13 145	11 815	15 577	19 971	23 613	26 683	. . .	30 249	33 610	40 288	195.3
2006	10 294	10 488	9 669	13 167	13 569	12 201	16 079	20 614	24 382	27 560	. . .	31 205	34 774	41 499	201.6
2007	10 590	10 787	9 944	13 540	13 954	12 550	16 530	21 203	25 080	28 323	. . .	32 233	35 816	42 739	207.3

. . . = Not available.

Table 3-8. Poverty Status of People by Race and Hispanic Origin

(Thousands of people, percent of population.)

Year	Number of people, all races	All races		White		White, not Hispanic		Black		Asian [1]		Hispanic (any race)	
		Number	Poverty rate (percent)	Number	Poverty rate (percent)	Number	Poverty rate (percent)	Number	Poverty rate (percent)	Number	Poverty rate (percent)	Number	Poverty rate (percent)
1959	176 557	39 490	22.4	28 484	18.1	...	...	9 927	55.1	...	...	...	...
1960	179 503	39 851	22.2	28 309	17.8	...	...	...	...	...	...	...	...
1961	181 277	39 628	21.9	27 890	17.4	...	...	...	...	...	...	...	...
1962	184 276	38 625	21.0	26 672	16.4	...	...	...	...	...	...	...	...
1963	187 258	36 436	19.5	25 238	15.3	...	...	...	...	...	...	...	...
1964	189 710	36 055	19.0	24 957	14.9	...	...	...	...	...	...	...	...
1965	191 413	33 185	17.3	22 496	13.3	...	...	...	...	...	...	...	...
1966	193 388	28 510	14.7	19 290	11.3	...	...	8 867	41.8	...	...	...	...
1967	195 672	27 769	14.2	18 983	11.0	...	...	8 486	39.3	...	...	...	...
1968	197 628	25 389	12.8	17 395	10.0	...	...	7 616	34.7	...	...	...	...
1969	199 517	24 147	12.1	16 659	9.5	...	...	7 095	32.2	...	...	...	...
1970	202 183	25 420	12.6	17 484	9.9	...	...	7 548	33.5	...	...	...	...
1971	204 554	25 559	12.5	17 780	9.9	...	...	7 396	32.5	...	...	...	...
1972	206 004	24 460	11.9	16 203	9.0	...	...	7 710	33.3	...	...	2 414	22.8
1973	207 621	22 973	11.1	15 142	8.4	12 864	7.5	7 388	31.4	...	...	2 366	21.9
1974	209 362	23 370	11.2	15 736	8.6	13 217	7.7	7 182	30.3	...	...	2 575	23.0
1975	210 864	25 877	12.3	17 770	9.7	14 883	8.6	7 545	31.3	...	...	2 991	26.9
1976	212 303	24 975	11.8	16 713	9.1	14 025	8.1	7 595	31.1	...	...	2 783	24.7
1977	213 867	24 720	11.6	16 416	8.9	13 802	8.0	7 726	31.3	...	...	2 700	22.4
1978	215 656	24 497	11.4	16 259	8.7	13 755	7.9	7 625	30.6	...	...	2 607	21.6
1979	222 903	26 072	11.7	17 214	9.0	14 419	8.1	8 050	31.0	...	...	2 921	21.8
1980	225 027	29 272	13.0	19 699	10.2	16 365	9.1	8 579	32.5	...	...	3 491	25.7
1981	227 157	31 822	14.0	21 553	11.1	17 987	9.9	9 173	34.2	...	...	3 713	26.5
1982	229 412	34 398	15.0	23 517	12.0	19 362	10.6	9 697	35.6	...	...	4 301	29.9
1983	231 700	35 303	15.2	23 984	12.1	19 538	10.8	9 882	35.7	...	...	4 633	28.0
1984	233 816	33 700	14.4	22 955	11.5	18 300	10.0	9 490	33.8	...	...	4 806	28.4
1985	236 594	33 064	14.0	22 860	11.4	17 839	9.7	8 926	31.3	...	...	5 236	29.0
1986	238 554	32 370	13.6	22 183	11.0	17 244	9.4	8 983	31.1	...	...	5 117	27.3
1987	240 982	32 221	13.4	21 195	10.4	16 029	8.7	9 520	32.4	1 021	16.1	5 422	28.0
1988	243 530	31 745	13.0	20 715	10.1	15 565	8.4	9 356	31.3	1 117	17.3	5 357	26.7
1989	245 992	31 528	12.8	20 785	10.0	15 599	8.3	9 302	30.7	939	14.1	5 430	26.2
1990	248 644	33 585	13.5	22 326	10.7	16 622	8.8	9 837	31.9	858	12.2	6 006	28.1
1991	251 192	35 708	14.2	23 747	11.3	17 741	9.4	10 242	32.7	996	13.8	6 339	28.7
1992	256 549	38 014	14.8	25 259	11.9	18 202	9.6	10 827	33.4	985	12.7	7 592	29.6
1993	259 278	39 265	15.1	26 226	12.2	18 882	9.9	10 877	33.1	1 134	15.3	8 126	30.6
1994	261 616	38 059	14.5	25 379	11.7	18 110	9.4	10 196	30.6	974	14.6	8 416	30.7
1995	263 733	36 425	13.8	24 423	11.2	16 267	8.5	9 872	29.3	1 411	14.6	8 574	30.3
1996	266 218	36 529	13.7	24 650	11.2	16 462	8.6	9 694	28.4	1 454	14.5	8 697	29.4
1997	268 480	35 574	13.3	24 396	11.0	16 491	8.6	9 116	26.5	1 468	14.0	8 308	27.1
1998	271 059	34 476	12.7	23 454	10.5	15 799	8.2	9 091	26.1	1 360	12.5	8 070	25.6
1999	276 208	32 791	11.9	22 169	9.8	14 735	7.7	8 441	23.6	1 285	10.7	7 876	22.7
2000	278 944	31 581	11.3	21 645	9.5	14 366	7.4	7 982	22.5	1 258	9.9	7 747	21.5
2001	281 475	32 907	11.7	22 739	9.9	15 271	7.8	8 136	22.7	1 275	10.2	7 997	21.4
2002	285 317	34 570	12.1	...	...	...	...	...	...	...	...	8 555	21.8
2003	287 699	35 861	12.5	...	...	...	...	...	...	...	...	9 051	22.5
2004	290 617	37 040	12.7	...	...	...	...	...	...	...	...	9 122	21.9
2005	293 135	36 950	12.6	...	...	...	...	...	...	...	...	9 368	21.8
2006	296 450	36 460	12.3	...	...	...	...	...	...	...	...	9 243	20.6
2007	298 699	37 276	12.5	...	...	...	...	...	...	...	...	9 890	21.5
By race													
Race alone													
2002	...	...	...	23 466	10.2	15 567	8.0	8 602	24.1	1 161	10.1	...	...
2003	...	...	...	24 272	10.5	15 902	8.2	8 781	24.4	1 401	11.8	...	...
2004	...	...	...	25 327	10.8	16 908	8.7	9 014	24.7	1 201	9.8	...	...
2005	...	...	...	24 872	10.6	16 227	8.3	9 168	24.9	1 402	11.1	...	...
2006	...	...	...	24 416	10.3	16 013	8.2	9 048	24.3	1 353	10.3	...	...
2007	...	...	...	25 120	10.5	16 032	8.2	9 237	24.5	1 349	10.2	...	...
Race alone or in combination													
2002	...	...	...	...	...	...	...	8 884	23.9	1 243	10.0	...	...
2003	...	...	...	...	...	...	...	9 108	24.3	1 527	11.8	...	...
2004	...	...	...	...	...	...	...	9 411	24.7	1 295	9.7	...	...
2005	...	...	...	...	...	...	...	9 517	24.7	1 501	10.9	...	...
2006	...	...	...	...	...	...	...	9 447	24.2	1 447	10.1	...	...
2007	...	...	...	...	...	...	...	9 668	24.4	1 467	10.2	...	...

[1] For 1987 through 2001, Asian and Pacific Islander.
. . . = Not available.

Table 3-9. Poverty Status of Families by Type of Family

(Thousands of families, percent)

Year	Married couple families				Families with no spouse present						Unrelated individuals	
	Number of families		Poverty rate (percent)		Male householder			Female householder			Below poverty level	Poverty rate
	Total	Total below poverty level	Total	With children under 18 years	Familes below poverty level	Poverty rate (percent) Total	With children under 18 years	Familes below poverty level	Poverty rate (percent) Total	With children under 18 years		
1959	39 335	...	...	...	...	...	...	1 916	42.6	59.9	4 928	46.1
1960	39 624	...	...	...	...	...	...	1 955	42.4	56.3	4 926	45.2
1961	40 405	...	...	...	...	...	...	1 954	42.1	56.0	5 119	45.9
1962	40 923	...	...	...	...	...	...	2 034	42.9	59.7	5 002	45.4
1963	41 311	...	...	...	...	...	...	1 972	40.4	55.7	4 938	44.2
1964	41 648	...	...	...	...	...	...	1 822	36.4	49.7	5 143	42.7
1965	42 107	...	...	...	...	...	...	1 916	38.4	52.2	4 827	39.8
1966	42 553	...	...	...	...	...	...	1 721	33.1	47.1	4 701	38.3
1967	43 292	...	...	...	...	...	...	1 774	33.3	44.5	4 998	38.1
1968	43 842	...	...	...	...	...	...	1 755	32.3	44.6	4 694	34.0
1969	44 436	...	...	...	...	...	...	1 827	32.7	44.9	4 972	34.0
1970	44 739	...	...	...	...	...	...	1 952	32.5	43.8	5 090	32.9
1971	45 752	...	...	...	...	...	...	2 100	33.9	44.9	5 154	31.6
1972	46 314	...	...	...	...	...	...	2 158	32.7	44.5	4 883	29.0
1973	46 812	2 482	5.3	...	154	10.7	...	2 193	32.2	43.2	4 674	25.6
1974	47 069	2 474	5.3	6.0	125	8.9	15.4	2 324	32.1	43.7	4 553	24.1
1975	47 318	2 904	6.1	7.2	116	8.0	11.7	2 430	32.5	44.0	5 088	25.1
1976	47 497	2 606	5.5	6.4	162	10.8	15.4	2 543	33.0	44.1	5 344	24.9
1977	47 385	2 524	5.3	6.3	177	11.1	14.8	2 610	31.7	41.8	5 216	22.6
1978	47 692	2 474	5.2	5.9	152	9.2	14.7	2 654	31.4	42.2	5 435	22.1
1979	49 112	2 640	5.4	6.1	176	10.2	15.5	2 645	30.4	39.6	5 743	21.9
1980	49 294	3 032	6.2	7.7	213	11.0	18.0	2 972	32.7	42.9	6 227	22.9
1981	49 630	3 394	6.8	8.7	205	10.3	14.0	3 252	34.6	44.3	6 490	23.4
1982	49 908	3 789	7.6	9.8	290	14.4	20.6	3 434	36.3	47.8	6 458	23.1
1983	50 081	3 815	7.6	10.1	268	13.2	20.2	3 564	36.0	47.1	6 740	23.1
1984	50 350	3 488	6.9	9.4	292	13.1	18.1	3 498	34.5	45.7	6 609	21.8
1985	50 933	3 438	6.7	8.9	311	12.9	17.1	3 474	34.0	45.4	6 725	21.5
1986	51 537	3 123	6.1	8.0	287	11.4	17.8	3 613	34.6	46.0	6 846	21.6
1987	51 675	3 011	5.8	7.7	340	12.0	16.8	3 654	34.2	45.5	6 857	20.8
1988	52 100	2 897	5.6	7.2	336	11.8	18.0	3 642	33.4	44.7	7 070	20.6
1989	52 317	2 931	5.6	7.3	348	12.1	18.1	3 504	32.2	42.8	6 760	19.2
1990	52 147	2 981	5.7	7.8	349	12.0	18.8	3 768	33.4	44.5	7 446	20.7
1991	52 457	3 158	6.0	8.3	392	13.0	19.6	4 161	35.6	47.1	7 773	21.1
1992	53 090	3 385	6.4	8.6	484	15.8	22.5	4 275	35.4	46.2	8 075	21.9
1993	53 181	3 481	6.5	9.0	488	16.8	22.5	4 424	35.6	46.1	8 388	22.1
1994	53 865	3 272	6.1	8.3	549	17.0	22.6	4 232	34.6	44.0	8 287	21.5
1995	53 570	2 982	5.6	7.5	493	14.0	19.7	4 057	32.4	41.5	8 247	20.9
1996	53 604	3 010	5.6	7.5	531	13.8	20.0	4 167	32.6	41.9	8 452	20.8
1997	54 321	2 821	5.2	7.1	507	13.0	18.7	3 995	31.6	41.0	8 687	20.8
1998	54 778	2 879	5.3	6.9	476	12.0	16.6	3 831	29.9	38.7	8 478	19.9
1999	56 290	2 748	4.9	6.4	485	11.8	16.3	3 559	27.8	35.7	8 400	19.1
2000	56 598	2 637	4.7	6.0	485	11.3	15.3	3 278	25.4	33.0	8 653	19.0
2001	56 755	2 760	4.9	6.1	583	13.1	17.7	3 470	26.4	33.6	9 226	19.9
2002	57 327	3 052	5.3	6.8	564	12.1	16.6	3 613	26.5	33.7	9 618	20.4
2003	57 725	3 115	5.4	7.0	636	13.5	19.1	3 856	28.0	35.5	9 713	20.4
2004	57 983	3 216	5.5	7.0	657	13.4	17.1	3 962	28.3	35.9	9 926	20.4
2005	58 189	2 944	5.1	6.5	669	13.0	17.6	4 044	28.7	36.2	10 425	21.1
2006	58 964	2 910	4.9	6.4	671	13.2	17.9	4 087	28.3	36.5	9 977	20.0
2007	58 395	2 849	4.9	6.7	696	13.6	17.5	4 078	28.3	37.0	10 189	19.7

. . . = Not available.

Table 3-10. Poverty Status of People by Sex and Age

(Thousands of people, percent of population.)

Year	Poverty status of people by sex				Poverty status of people by age					
	Males below poverty level		Females below poverty level		Children under 18 years below poverty level		People 18 to 64 years below poverty level		People 65 years and older below poverty level	
	Number (thousands)	Poverty rate (percent)	Number (thousands)	Poverty rate (percent)	Number (thousands)	Poverty rate (percent)	Number (thousands)	Poverty rate (percent)	Number (thousands)	Poverty rate (percent)
1959	. . .	. . .	. . .	. . .	17 552	27.3	16 457	17.0	5 481	35.2
1966	12 225	13.0	16 265	16.3	12 389	17.6	11 007	10.5	5 114	28.5
1967	11 813	12.5	15 951	15.8	11 656	16.6	10 725	10.0	5 388	29.5
1968	10 793	11.3	14 578	14.3	10 954	15.6	9 803	9.0	4 632	25.0
1969	10 292	10.6	13 978	13.6	9 691	14.0	9 669	8.7	4 787	25.3
1970	10 879	11.1	14 632	14.0	10 440	15.1	10 187	9.0	4 793	24.6
1971	10 708	10.8	14 841	14.1	10 551	15.3	10 735	9.3	4 273	21.6
1972	10 190	10.2	14 258	13.4	10 284	15.1	10 438	8.8	3 738	18.6
1973	9 642	9.6	13 316	12.5	9 642	14.4	9 977	8.3	3 354	16.3
1974	10 313	10.2	13 881	12.9	10 156	15.4	10 132	8.3	3 085	14.6
1975	10 908	10.7	14 970	13.8	11 104	17.1	11 456	9.2	3 317	15.3
1976	10 373	10.1	14 603	13.4	10 273	16.0	11 389	9.0	3 313	15.0
1977	10 340	10.0	14 381	13.0	10 288	16.2	11 316	8.8	3 177	14.1
1978	10 017	9.6	14 480	13.0	9 931	15.9	11 332	8.7	3 233	14.0
1979	10 535	10.0	14 810	13.2	10 377	16.4	12 014	8.9	3 682	15.2
1980	12 207	11.2	17 065	14.7	11 543	18.3	13 858	10.1	3 871	15.7
1981	13 360	12.1	18 462	15.8	12 505	20.0	15 464	11.1	3 853	15.3
1982	14 842	13.4	19 556	16.5	13 647	21.9	17 000	12.0	3 751	14.6
1983	15 182	13.5	20 084	16.8	13 911	22.3	17 767	12.4	3 625	13.8
1984	14 537	12.8	19 163	15.9	13 420	21.5	16 952	11.7	3 330	12.4
1985	14 140	12.3	18 923	15.6	13 010	20.7	16 598	11.3	3 456	12.6
1986	13 721	11.8	18 649	15.2	12 876	20.5	16 017	10.8	3 477	12.4
1987	14 029	12.0	18 518	15.0	12 843	20.3	15 815	10.6	3 563	12.5
1988	13 599	11.5	18 146	14.5	12 455	19.5	15 809	10.5	3 481	12.0
1989	13 366	11.2	18 162	14.4	12 590	19.6	15 575	10.2	3 363	11.4
1990	14 211	11.7	19 373	15.2	13 431	20.6	16 496	10.7	3 658	12.2
1991	15 082	12.3	20 626	16.0	14 341	21.8	17 586	11.4	3 781	12.4
1992	16 222	12.9	21 792	16.6	15 294	22.3	18 793	11.9	3 928	12.9
1993	16 900	13.3	22 365	16.9	15 727	22.7	19 781	12.4	3 755	12.2
1994	16 316	12.8	21 744	16.3	15 289	21.8	19 107	11.9	3 663	11.7
1995	15 683	12.2	20 742	15.4	14 665	20.8	18 442	11.4	3 318	10.5
1996	15 611	12.0	20 918	15.4	14 463	20.5	18 638	11.4	3 428	10.8
1997	15 187	11.6	20 387	14.9	14 113	19.9	18 085	10.9	3 376	10.5
1998	14 712	11.1	19 764	14.3	13 467	18.9	17 623	10.5	3 386	10.5
1999	14 079	10.4	18 712	13.2	12 280	17.1	17 289	10.1	3 222	9.7
2000	13 536	9.9	18 045	12.6	11 587	16.2	16 671	9.6	3 323	9.9
2001	14 327	10.4	18 580	12.9	11 733	16.3	17 760	10.1	3 414	10.1
2002	15 162	10.9	19 408	13.3	12 133	16.7	18 861	10.6	3 576	10.4
2003	15 783	11.2	20 078	13.7	12 866	17.6	19 443	10.8	3 552	10.2
2004	16 399	11.5	20 641	13.9	13 041	17.8	20 545	11.3	3 453	9.8
2005	15 950	11.1	21 000	14.1	12 896	17.6	20 450	11.1	3 603	10.1
2006	16 000	11.0	20 460	13.6	12 827	17.4	20 239	10.8	3 394	9.4
2007	16 302	11.1	20 973	13.8	13 324	18.0	20 396	10.9	3 556	9.7

. . . = Not available.

Table 3-11. Poverty Status of People Inside and Outside Metropolitan Areas, and People In and Near Poverty

(Thousands of people, percent of population.)

Year	Inside metropolitan areas [1]		Central city [1]		Outside central city [1]		Outside metropolitan areas [1]		Total in and near poverty (income below 1.25 times the poverty level)		Near poor (income between 1 and 1.25 times poverty level)	
	Number (thousands)	Poverty rate (percent)	Number (thousands)	Poverty rate (percent)	Number (thousands)	Poverty rate (percent)	Number (thousands)	Poverty rate (percent)	Number (thousands)	Percent	Number (thousands)	Percent
1959	17 019	15.3	10 437	18.3	6 582	12.2	21 747	33.2	54 942	31.1	15 452	8.7
1960	. . .	. . .	. . .	. . .	. . .	. . .	. . .	. . .	54 560	30.4	14 709	8.2
1961	. . .	. . .	. . .	. . .	. . .	. . .	. . .	. . .	54 280	30.0	14 652	8.1
1962	. . .	. . .	. . .	. . .	. . .	. . .	. . .	. . .	53 119	28.8	14 494	7.9
1963	. . .	. . .	. . .	. . .	. . .	. . .	. . .	. . .	50 778	27.1	14 342	7.7
1964	. . .	. . .	. . .	. . .	. . .	. . .	. . .	. . .	49 819	26.3	13 764	7.3
1965	. . .	. . .	. . .	. . .	. . .	. . .	. . .	. . .	46 163	24.1	12 978	6.8
1966	. . .	. . .	. . .	. . .	. . .	. . .	. . .	. . .	41 267	21.3	12 757	6.6
1967	13 832	10.9	8 649	15.0	5 183	7.5	13 936	20.2	39 206	20.0	11 437	5.8
1968	12 871	10.0	7 754	13.4	5 117	7.3	12 518	18.0	35 905	18.2	10 516	5.3
1969	13 084	9.5	7 993	12.7	5 091	6.8	11 063	17.9	34 665	17.4	10 518	5.3
1970	13 317	10.2	8 118	14.2	5 199	7.1	12 103	16.9	35 624	17.6	10 204	5.0
1971	14 561	10.4	8 912	14.2	5 649	7.2	10 999	17.2	36 501	17.8	10 942	5.3
1972	14 508	10.3	9 179	14.7	5 329	6.8	9 952	15.3	34 653	16.8	10 193	4.9
1973	13 759	9.7	8 594	14.0	5 165	6.4	9 214	14.0	32 828	15.8	9 855	4.7
1974	13 851	9.7	8 373	13.7	5 477	6.7	9 519	14.2	33 666	16.1	10 296	4.9
1975	15 348	10.8	9 090	15.0	6 259	7.6	10 529	15.4	37 182	17.6	11 305	5.4
1976	15 229	10.7	9 482	15.8	5 747	6.9	9 746	14.0	35 509	16.7	10 534	5.0
1977	14 859	10.4	9 203	15.4	5 657	6.8	9 861	13.9	35 659	16.7	10 939	5.1
1978	15 090	10.4	9 285	15.4	5 805	6.8	9 407	13.5	34 155	15.8	9 658	4.5
1979	16 135	10.7	9 720	15.7	6 415	7.2	9 937	13.8	36 616	16.4	10 544	4.7
1980	18 021	11.9	10 644	17.2	7 377	8.2	11 251	15.4	40 658	18.1	11 386	5.1
1981	19 347	12.6	11 231	18.0	8 116	8.9	12 475	17.0	43 748	19.3	11 926	5.3
1982	21 247	13.7	12 696	19.9	8 551	9.3	13 152	17.8	46 520	20.3	12 122	5.3
1983	21 750	13.8	12 872	19.8	8 878	9.6	13 516	18.3	47 150	20.3	11 847	5.1
1984	. . .	. . .	. . .	. . .	. . .	. . .	. . .	. . .	45 288	19.4	11 588	5.0
1985	23 275	12.7	14 177	19.0	9 097	8.4	9 789	18.3	44 166	18.7	11 102	4.7
1986	22 657	12.3	13 295	18.0	9 362	8.4	9 712	18.1	43 486	18.2	11 116	4.7
1987	23 054	12.3	13 697	18.3	9 357	8.3	9 167	17.0	43 032	17.9	10 811	4.5
1988	23 059	12.2	13 615	18.1	9 444	8.3	8 686	16.0	42 551	17.5	10 806	4.4
1989	22 917	12.0	13 592	18.1	9 326	8.0	8 611	15.7	42 653	17.3	11 125	4.5
1990	24 510	12.7	14 254	19.0	10 255	8.7	9 075	16.3	44 837	18.0	11 252	4.5
1991	26 827	13.7	15 314	20.2	11 513	9.6	8 881	16.1	47 527	18.9	11 819	4.7
1992	28 380	14.2	16 346	20.9	12 034	9.9	9 634	16.9	50 592	19.7	12 578	4.9
1993	29 615	14.6	16 805	21.5	12 810	10.3	9 650	17.2	51 801	20.0	12 536	4.8
1994	29 610	14.2	16 098	20.9	13 511	10.3	8 449	16.0	50 401	19.3	12 342	4.7
1995	28 342	13.4	16 269	20.6	12 072	9.1	8 083	15.6	48 761	18.5	12 336	4.7
1996	28 211	13.2	15 645	19.6	12 566	9.4	8 318	15.9	49 310	18.5	12 781	4.8
1997	27 273	12.6	15 018	18.8	12 255	9.0	8 301	15.9	47 853	17.8	12 280	4.6
1998	26 997	12.3	14 921	18.5	12 076	8.7	7 479	14.4	46 036	17.0	11 560	4.3
1999	25 278	11.3	13 404	16.5	11 874	8.3	7 513	14.3	45 030	16.3	12 239	4.4
2000	24 603	10.8	13 257	16.3	11 346	7.8	6 978	13.4	43 612	15.6	12 030	4.3
2001	25 446	11.1	13 394	16.5	12 052	8.2	7 460	14.2	45 320	16.1	12 413	4.4
2002	27 096	11.6	13 784	16.7	13 311	8.9	7 474	14.2	47 084	16.5	12 514	4.4
2003	28 367	12.1	14 551	17.5	13 816	9.1	7 495	14.2	48 687	16.9	12 826	4.5
2004	. . .	. . .	. . .	. . .	. . .	. . .	. . .	. . .	49 693	17.1	12 653	4.4
2005 [1]	30 098	12.2	15 966	17.0	14 132	9.3	6 852	14.5	49 327	16.8	12 377	4.2
2006 [1]	29 283	11.8	15 336	16.1	13 947	9.1	7 177	15.2	49 688	16.8	13 229	4.5
2007 [1]	29 921	11.9	15 983	16.5	13 938	9.0	7 355	15.4	50 876	17.0	13 601	4.6

[1] Data by residence beginning in 2005 are based on new definitions of metropolitan and micropolitan statistical areas announced in 2003. The major categories are now entitled "inside metropolitan statistical areas" and "outside metropolitan statistical areas." The sub-categories within metropolitan statistical areas are now entitled "inside principal cities" and "outside principal cities." See "About Metropolitan and Micropolitan Statistical Areas" at <http://www.census.gov/population/www/estimates/aboutmetro.html>.
. . . = Not available.

Table 3-12. Poor People Age 16 Years and Older by Work Experience

(Thousands of people, percent of population [poverty rate], percent of total poor people.)

Year	Total number of poor people, 16 years and older	Worked		Worked year-round, full-time			Worked less than year-round or full-time			Did not work		
		Number	Percent of total poor	Number	Poverty rate (percent)	Percent of total poor	Number	Poverty rate (percent)	Percent of total poor	Number	Poverty rate (percent)	Percent of total poor
1978	16 914	6 599	39.0	1 309	. . .	7.7	5 290	. . .	31.3	10 315	. . .	61.0
1979	16 803	6 601	39.3	1 394	. . .	8.3	5 207	. . .	31.0	10 202	. . .	60.7
1980	18 892	7 674	40.6	1 644	. . .	8.7	6 030	. . .	31.9	11 218	. . .	59.4
1981	20 571	8 524	41.4	1 881	. . .	9.1	6 643	. . .	32.3	12 047	. . .	58.6
1982	22 100	9 013	40.8	1 999	. . .	9.0	7 014	. . .	31.7	13 087	. . .	59.2
1983	22 741	9 329	41.0	2 064	. . .	9.1	7 265	. . .	31.9	13 412	. . .	59.0
1984	21 541	8 999	41.8	2 076	. . .	9.6	6 923	. . .	32.1	12 542	. . .	58.2
1985	21 243	9 008	42.4	1 972	. . .	9.3	7 036	. . .	33.1	12 235	. . .	57.6
1986	20 688	8 743	42.3	2 007	. . .	9.7	6 736	. . .	32.6	11 945	. . .	57.7
1987	20 546	8 258	40.2	1 821	2.4	8.9	6 436	12.5	31.3	12 288	21.6	59.8
1988	20 323	8 363	41.2	1 929	2.4	9.5	6 434	12.7	31.7	11 959	21.2	58.8
1989	19 952	8 376	42.0	1 908	2.4	9.6	6 468	12.5	32.4	11 576	20.8	58.0
1990	21 242	8 716	41.0	2 076	2.6	9.8	6 639	12.6	31.3	12 526	22.1	59.0
1991	22 530	9 208	40.9	2 103	2.6	9.3	7 105	13.4	31.5	13 323	22.8	59.1
1992	23 951	9 739	40.6	2 211	2.7	9.2	7 529	14.1	31.4	14 212	23.7	59.3
1993	24 832	10 144	40.8	2 408	2.9	9.7	7 737	14.6	31.2	14 688	24.2	59.1
1994	24 108	9 829	40.8	2 520	2.9	10.5	7 309	13.9	30.3	14 279	23.6	59.2
1995	23 077	9 484	41.1	2 418	2.7	10.5	7 066	13.7	30.6	13 593	22.3	58.9
1996	23 472	9 586	40.8	2 263	2.5	9.6	7 322	14.1	31.2	13 886	22.7	59.2
1997	22 753	9 444	41.5	2 345	2.5	10.3	7 098	13.8	31.2	13 310	21.7	58.5
1998	22 256	9 133	41.0	2 804	2.9	12.6	6 330	12.7	28.4	13 122	21.1	59.0
1999	21 762	9 251	42.5	2 559	2.6	11.8	6 692	13.2	30.8	12 511	19.9	57.5
2000	21 080	8 511	40.4	2 439	2.4	11.6	6 072	12.1	28.8	12 569	19.8	59.6
2001	22 245	8 530	38.3	2 567	2.6	11.5	5 964	11.8	26.8	13 715	20.6	61.7
2002	23 601	8 954	37.9	2 635	2.6	11.2	6 318	12.4	26.8	14 647	21.0	62.1
2003	24 266	8 820	36.3	2 636	2.6	10.9	6 183	12.2	25.5	15 446	21.5	63.7
2004	25 256	9 384	37.2	2 891	2.8	11.4	6 493	12.8	25.7	15 871	21.7	62.8
2005	25 381	9 340	36.8	2 894	2.8	11.4	6 446	12.8	25.4	16 041	21.8	63.2
2006	24 896	9 181	36.9	2 906	2.7	11.7	6 275	12.6	25.2	15 715	21.1	63.1
2007	25 297	9 089	35.9	2 768	2.5	10.9	6 320	12.7	25.0	16 208	21.5	64.1

. . . = Not available.

Table 3-13. Poverty Rates by State

(Percent of population.)

State	1990	1995	1996	1997	1998	1999	2000	2001	2002	2003	2004	2005	2006	2007
United States	13.5	13.8	13.7	13.3	12.7	11.9	11.3	11.7	12.1	12.5	12.7	12.6	12.3	12.5
Alabama	19.2	20.1	14.0	15.7	14.5	15.2	13.3	15.9	14.5	15.0	16.9	16.7	14.3	14.5
Alaska	11.4	7.1	8.2	8.8	9.4	7.6	7.6	8.5	8.8	9.6	9.1	10.0	8.9	7.6
Arizona	13.7	16.1	20.5	17.2	16.6	12.2	11.7	14.6	13.5	13.5	14.4	15.2	14.4	14.3
Arkansas	19.6	14.9	17.2	19.7	14.7	14.7	16.5	17.8	19.8	17.8	15.1	13.8	17.7	13.8
California	13.9	16.7	16.9	16.6	15.4	14.0	12.7	12.6	13.1	13.1	13.2	13.2	12.2	12.7
Colorado	13.7	8.8	10.6	8.2	9.2	8.5	9.8	8.7	9.8	9.7	10.0	11.4	9.7	9.8
Connecticut	6.0	9.7	11.7	8.6	9.5	7.2	7.7	7.3	8.3	8.1	10.1	9.3	8.0	8.9
Delaware	6.9	10.3	8.6	9.6	10.3	10.4	8.4	6.7	9.1	7.3	9.0	9.2	9.3	9.3
District of Columbia	21.1	22.2	24.1	21.8	22.3	14.7	15.2	18.2	17.0	16.8	17.0	21.3	18.3	18.0
Florida	14.4	16.2	14.2	14.3	13.1	12.4	11.0	12.7	12.6	12.7	11.6	11.1	11.5	12.5
Georgia	15.8	12.1	14.8	14.5	13.5	12.8	12.1	12.9	11.2	11.9	13.0	14.4	12.6	13.6
Hawaii	11.0	10.3	12.1	13.9	10.9	10.8	8.9	11.4	11.3	9.3	8.6	8.6	9.2	7.5
Idaho	14.9	14.5	11.9	14.7	13.0	14.1	12.5	11.5	11.3	10.2	9.9	9.9	9.5	9.9
Illinois	13.7	12.4	12.1	11.2	10.1	9.9	10.7	10.1	12.8	12.6	12.3	11.5	10.6	10.0
Indiana	13.0	9.6	7.5	8.8	9.4	6.7	8.5	8.5	9.1	9.9	11.6	12.6	10.6	11.8
Iowa	10.4	12.2	9.6	9.6	9.1	7.4	8.3	7.4	9.2	8.9	10.9	11.3	10.3	8.9
Kansas	10.3	10.8	11.2	9.7	9.6	12.3	8.0	10.1	10.1	10.8	11.4	12.5	12.8	11.7
Kentucky	17.3	14.7	17.0	15.9	13.5	12.1	12.6	12.6	14.2	14.4	17.8	14.8	16.8	15.5
Louisiana	23.6	19.7	20.5	16.3	19.1	19.2	17.2	16.2	17.5	17.0	16.8	18.3	17.0	16.1
Maine	13.1	11.2	11.2	10.1	10.4	10.6	10.1	10.3	13.4	11.6	11.6	12.6	10.2	10.9
Maryland	9.9	10.1	10.3	8.4	7.2	7.3	7.4	7.2	7.4	8.6	9.9	9.7	8.4	8.8
Massachusetts	10.7	11.0	10.1	12.2	8.7	11.8	9.8	8.9	10.0	10.3	9.3	10.1	12.0	11.2
Michigan	14.3	12.2	11.2	10.3	11.0	9.7	9.9	9.4	11.6	11.4	13.3	12.0	13.3	10.8
Minnesota	12.0	9.2	9.8	9.6	10.3	7.3	5.7	7.4	6.5	7.4	7.0	8.1	8.2	9.3
Mississippi	25.7	23.5	20.6	16.7	17.6	16.2	14.9	19.3	18.4	16.0	18.7	20.1	20.6	22.6
Missouri	13.4	9.4	9.5	11.8	9.8	11.7	9.2	9.7	9.9	10.7	12.2	11.6	11.4	12.8
Montana	16.3	15.3	17.0	15.6	16.6	15.8	14.1	13.3	13.5	15.1	14.2	13.8	13.5	13.0
Nebraska	10.3	9.6	10.2	9.8	12.3	11.0	8.6	9.4	10.6	9.8	9.5	9.5	10.2	9.9
Nevada	9.8	11.1	8.1	11.0	10.6	11.3	8.8	7.1	8.9	10.9	10.9	10.6	9.5	9.7
New Hampshire	6.3	5.3	6.4	9.1	9.8	7.6	4.5	6.5	5.8	5.8	5.5	5.6	5.4	5.8
New Jersey	9.2	7.8	9.2	9.3	8.6	7.8	7.3	8.1	7.9	8.6	8.0	6.8	8.8	8.7
New Mexico	20.9	25.3	25.5	21.2	20.4	20.9	17.5	18.0	17.9	18.1	16.5	17.9	16.9	14.0
New York	14.3	16.5	16.7	16.5	16.7	14.2	13.9	14.2	14.0	14.3	15.0	14.5	14.0	14.5
North Carolina	13.0	12.6	12.2	11.4	14.0	13.8	12.5	12.5	14.3	15.7	14.6	13.1	13.8	15.5
North Dakota	13.7	12.0	11.0	13.6	15.1	13.1	10.4	13.8	11.6	9.7	9.7	11.2	11.4	9.3
Ohio	11.5	11.5	12.7	11.0	11.2	12.0	10.0	10.5	9.8	10.9	11.6	12.3	12.1	12.8
Oklahoma	15.6	17.1	16.6	13.7	14.1	12.8	14.9	15.1	14.1	12.8	10.8	15.6	15.2	13.4
Oregon	9.2	11.2	11.8	11.6	15.0	12.6	10.9	11.8	10.9	12.5	11.8	12.0	11.8	12.8
Pennsylvania	11.0	12.2	11.6	11.2	11.3	9.3	8.6	9.6	9.5	10.5	11.4	11.2	11.3	10.4
Rhode Island	7.5	10.6	11.0	12.7	11.6	10.0	10.2	9.6	11.0	11.5	11.5	12.1	10.5	9.5
South Carolina	16.2	19.9	13.0	13.1	13.7	11.7	11.1	15.1	14.3	12.7	14.9	15.0	11.2	14.1
South Dakota	13.3	14.5	11.8	16.5	10.8	7.7	10.7	8.4	11.5	12.7	13.5	11.8	10.7	9.4
Tennessee	16.9	15.5	15.9	14.3	13.4	11.9	13.5	14.1	14.8	14.0	15.9	14.9	14.9	14.8
Texas	15.9	17.4	16.6	16.7	15.1	15.2	15.5	14.9	15.6	17.0	16.5	16.2	16.4	16.5
Utah	8.2	8.4	7.7	8.9	9.0	5.7	7.6	10.5	9.9	9.1	10.1	9.2	9.3	9.6
Vermont	10.9	10.3	12.6	9.3	9.9	9.6	10.0	9.7	9.9	8.5	7.8	7.6	7.8	9.9
Virginia	11.1	10.2	12.3	12.7	8.8	7.9	8.3	8.0	9.9	10.0	9.4	9.2	8.6	8.6
Washington	8.9	12.5	11.9	9.2	8.9	9.6	10.8	10.7	11.0	12.6	11.4	10.2	8.0	10.2
West Virginia	18.1	16.7	18.5	16.4	17.8	15.7	14.7	16.4	16.8	17.4	14.2	15.4	15.3	14.8
Wisconsin	9.3	8.5	8.8	8.2	8.8	8.6	9.3	7.9	8.6	9.8	12.4	10.2	10.1	11.0
Wyoming	11.0	12.2	11.9	13.5	10.6	11.6	10.8	8.7	9.0	9.8	10.0	10.6	10.0	10.9

Section 3c: Alternative Measures of Income and Poverty

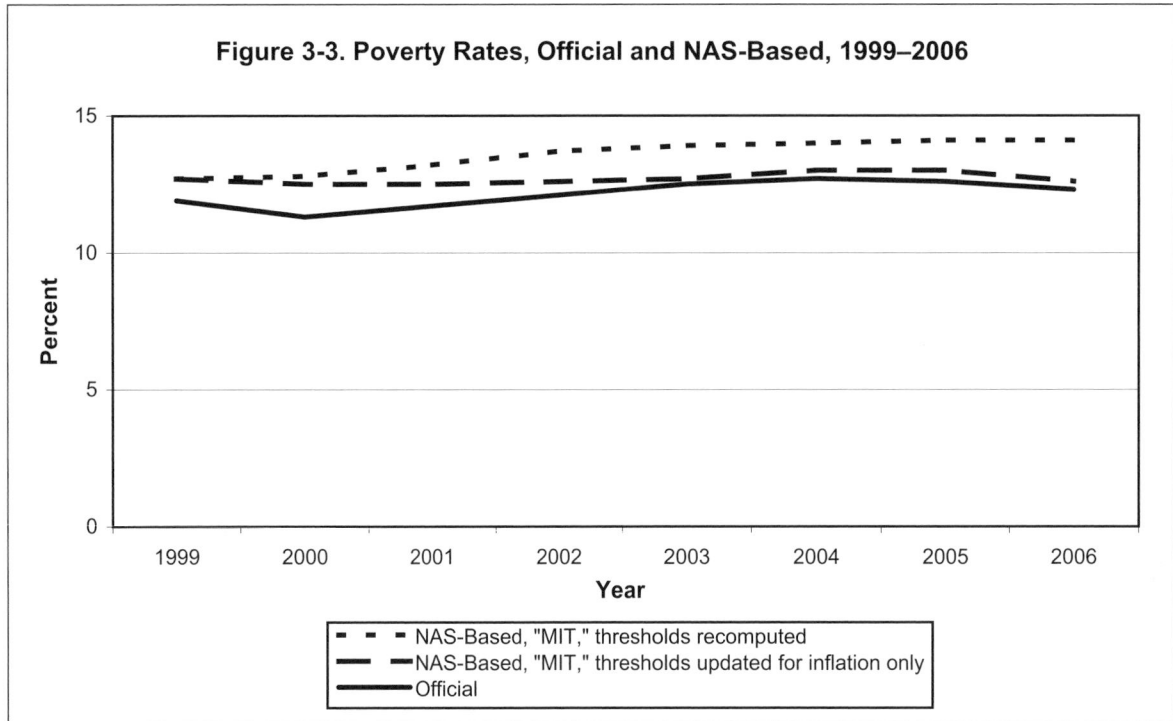

Figure 3-3. Poverty Rates, Official and NAS-Based, 1999–2006

- A special panel of the National Academy of Sciences (NAS) has recommended a complete overhaul of the poverty rate, redefining both needs and resources. For the years 1999 forward, the Census Bureau has calculated experimental poverty measures according to several versions of the NAS recommendations. In Figure 3-3, two of these experimental measures are compared with the official rate. The experimental measures use different approaches to the treatment of medical expenses; the two shown here both use the "MIT" approach, in which medical out-of-pocket expenses are included in the thresholds. (Table 3-17)

- The NAS-based thresholds are initially based on needs estimated for the year 1999; in that year, the two experimental measures shown indicated a poverty rate of 12.7 percent, compared with 11.9 percent in the official rate. (Table 3-17)

- One of the NAS-based measures shown above updates the thresholds for inflation only, using the CPI-U, just as is the case with the official series. This measure, while consistently higher than the official rate, shows a slight decline in poverty between 1999 and 2006, compared with the increase in the official series. (Table 3-17)

- The other NAS-based measure recomputes the thresholds each year using the increase in median expenditures on necessities instead of the CPI; thus, the thresholds represent a rising standard of living when such spending rises faster than inflation, but would represent a falling standard of living if the median spending were to fall in real terms. In the period in question, median spending has been increasing, and as a result the indicated poverty rate rises even in a year of economic expansion such as 2000, when the rates based on CPI-updated thresholds fall. (Table 3-17)

- In Table 3-15, by comparing poverty rates using "market income," "post-social-insurance income," and "disposable income" in a given year, the separate effects on poverty of social insurance programs (mainly Social Security) and taxes and means-tested transfers can be observed. The percentage point reduction in the poverty rate resulting from social insurance (from 18.5 percent to 12.5 percent in 2006) is more than 2½ times the reduction resulting from the net effect of taxes and means-tested transfers (12.5 to 10.2 percent). (Table 3-15)

Table 3-14. Median Household Income and Poverty Rates for People, Based on Alternative Definitions of Income

Year	Definition 1, MI: Money income excluding capital gains (current official measure)				Definition 4: Money income before taxes and cash transfers, plus realized capital gains (losses) and health insurance supplements			
	Median income (2003 dollars)	Poverty rate (percent)		Gini coefficient	Median income (2003 dollars) [2]	Poverty rate (percent)		Gini coefficient
		Official threshold	CPI-U-RS threshold [1]			Official threshold	CPI-U-RS threshold [1]	
1979	38 649	11.7	10.6	0.403	38 259	18.8	17.8	0.460
1980	37 447	13.0	11.5	0.401	36 346	20.1	19.0	0.462
1981	36 868	14.0	12.2	0.404	35 544	21.1	19.8	0.466
1982	36 811	15.0	13.2	0.409	35 118	22.0	20.6	0.475
1983	36 826	15.2	13.7	0.412	35 570	21.8	20.6	0.478
1984	37 767	14.4	12.8	0.413	36 739	20.8	19.5	0.477
1985	38 510	14.0	12.5	0.418	37 418	20.4	19.1	0.486
1986	39 868	13.6	12.2	0.423	38 937	19.9	18.7	0.505
1987	40 357	13.4	12.1	0.424	39 188	19.7	18.7	0.488
1988	40 678	13.0	11.7	0.425	39 727	19.7	18.5	0.489
1989	41 411	12.8	11.3	0.429	40 466	19.4	18.1	0.492
1990	40 865	13.5	11.9	0.426	39 348	19.9	18.7	0.487
1991	39 679	14.2	12.4	0.425	38 086	21.1	19.7	0.490
1992	39 364	14.8	13.1	0.430	37 679	22.1	20.6	0.497
1993	39 165	15.1	13.4	0.448	37 554	22.6	21.1	0.514
1994	39 613	14.5	12.6	0.450	38 438	22.0	20.3	0.515
1995	40 845	13.8	11.7	0.444	39 509	21.1	19.5	0.509
1996	41 431	13.7	11.6	0.447	40 300	20.8	19.1	0.511
1997	42 294	13.3	11.3	0.448	41 294	20.3	18.7	0.513
1998	43 825	12.7	10.6	0.446	42 643	19.3	17.4	0.509
1999	44 922	11.9	9.9	0.445	44 112	18.7	16.9	0.508
2000	44 853	11.3	9.7	0.447	44 197	18.0	16.5	0.506
2001	43 882	11.7	9.9	0.450	43 151	18.5	16.9	0.510
2002	43 381	12.1	10.1	0.448	42 422	19.0	17.4	. . .
2003	43 318	12.5	10.5	0.450	42 295	19.5	17.8	. . .
2004	. . .	12.7	10.8	0.450	. . .	20.0	18.3	0.503
2005	. . .	12.6	10.8	0.450	. . .	19.7	18.1	0.501
2006	. . .	12.3	10.5	0.447	. . .	18.9	17.3	0.495

Year	Definition 14, MI - Tx + NC: Income after all taxes and transfers				Definition 15, MI - Tx + NC + HE: Income after all taxes and transfers, plus net imputed return on equity in own home			
	Median income (2003 dollars)	Poverty rate (percent)		Gini coefficient [3]	Median income (2003 dollars)	Poverty rate (percent)		Gini coefficient [3]
		Official threshold	CPI-U-RS threshold [1]			Official threshold	CPI-U-RS threshold [1]	
1979	35 435	8.9	7.9	0.359	37 776	7.5	6.7	0.352
1980	34 290	10.1	8.6	0.354	37 804	8.2	7.0	0.347
1981	33 505	11.5	9.8	0.358	39 199	8.7	7.3	0.350
1982	33 831	12.3	10.6	0.366	38 398	9.9	8.5	0.359
1983	34 359	12.7	11.0	0.374	38 203	10.4	9.0	0.368
1984	35 049	12.0	10.4	0.378	39 262	9.9	8.6	0.372
1985	35 709	11.7	10.1	0.385	39 410	9.9	8.6	0.381
1986	37 197	11.3	9.8	0.409	40 026	10.1	8.6	0.404
1987	37 696	11.0	9.5	0.382	41 065	9.7	8.2	0.380
1988	37 796	10.8	9.4	0.385	41 195	9.4	8.2	0.384
1989	38 556	10.4	8.8	0.389	41 662	9.1	7.6	0.387
1990	37 960	10.9	9.3	0.382	40 526	9.8	8.3	0.381
1991	37 443	11.4	9.7	0.380	40 127	10.3	8.6	0.379
1992	37 741	11.9	10.2	0.385	40 026	10.7	9.1	0.381
1993	38 104	12.1	10.3	0.398	40 230	11.2	9.4	0.395
1994	38 740	11.1	9.2	0.400	41 113	10.0	8.3	0.395
1995	39 922	10.3	8.5	0.394	42 263	9.4	7.6	0.388
1996	40 295	10.2	8.4	0.398	42 444	9.3	7.6	0.392
1997	40 985	10.0	8.2	0.403	43 000	9.2	7.5	0.397
1998	42 459	9.5	7.7	0.405	44 302	8.8	7.1	0.399
1999	43 328	8.9	7.2	0.408	45 354	8.2	6.5	0.402
2000	43 285	8.8	7.2	0.410	45 634	8.0	6.5	0.402
2001	43 369	9.0	7.3	0.412	45 126	8.3	6.7	0.407
2002	43 155	9.3	7.7	0.394	44 884	8.6	7.1	0.388
2003	43 629	9.7	7.9	0.394	45 154	9.0	7.4	0.390
2004	. . .	9.6	7.9	0.404	. . .	8.8	7.2	0.398
2005	. . .	9.6	8.1	0.402	. . .	8.9	7.4	0.398
2006	. . .	9.3	7.9	0.405	. . .	8.7	7.4	0.400

Note: See notes and definitions for explanation of alternative definitions and thresholds and of the Gini coefficient.

[1] Before 1987, threshold based on CPI-U-X1.
[2] Years before 2002 linked by editor to Census 2002 figure based on changes in earlier Census Bureau estimates.
[3] Earlier years not comparable with 2002 and subsequent years because of a change in tax estimating model.
. . . = Not available.

Table 3-15. Median Household Income and Poverty Rates with Three-Parameter Poverty Thresholds, Excluding and Including Effects of Government Programs, 2003–2006

Year	Based on money income				Based on market income			
	Median income	Poverty rate (percent)		Gini coefficient	Median income	Poverty rate (percent)		Gini coefficient
		CPI-U threshold	CPI-U-RS threshold			CPI-U threshold	CPI-U-RS threshold	
2003 (2004 dollars)	44 483	12.5	10.4	0.450	41 983	19.3	17.3	0.492
2004 (2004 dollars)	44 389	12.6	10.6	0.450	41 648	19.4	17.6	0.496
2004 (revised, 2005 dollars)	45 817	12.7	. . .	. . .	43 589	18.8	. . .	. . .
2005 (2005 dollars)	46 326	12.6	. . .	0.450	43 701	18.9	. . .	0.493
2005 (revised, 2006 dollars)	47 845	. . .	. . .	. . .	45 134	. . .	. . .	. . .
2006 (2006 dollars)	48 201	12.2	10.4	0.447	45 700	18.5	16.6	0.492

Year	Based on post-social-insurance income				Based on disposable income			
	Median income	Poverty rate (percent)		Gini coefficient	Median income	Poverty rate (percent)		Gini coefficient
		CPI-U threshold	CPI-U-RS threshold			CPI-U threshold	CPI-U-RS threshold	
2003 (2004 dollars)	46 196	12.8	11.0	0.446	39 993	10.2	8.1	0.405
2004 (2004 dollars)	45 968	12.9	11.2	0.449	39 754	10.4	8.3	0.400
2004 (revised, 2005 dollars)	48 089	12.6	. . .	. . .	41 446	10.1	. . .	. . .
2005 (2005 dollars)	47 975	12.7	. . .	0.447	40 843	10.3	. . .	0.418
2005 (revised, 2006 dollars)	49 548	. . .	. . .	. . .	42 072	. . .	. . .	. . .
2006 (2006 dollars)	49 863	12.5	10.8	0.447	42 288	10.2	8.3	0.423

Note: See notes and definitions for explanation of the income definitions and poverty thresholds.

. . . = Not available.

Table 3-16. Official Poverty Thresholds and Three-Parameter Scaled Thresholds Used in Alternative Poverty Estimates: 2005

(Dollars.)

Size of family unit	Number of related children under 18 years								
	None	One	Two	Three	Four	Five	Six	Seven	Eight or more
Official Thresholds									
One personUnder 65 years	10 160	. . .	. . .	. . .	. . .	. . .	. . .	. . .	. . .
65 years or older	9 367	. . .	. . .	. . .	. . .	. . .	. . .	. . .	. . .
Two people									
Householder under 65 years	13 078	13 461	. . .	. . .	. . .	. . .	. . .	. . .	. . .
Householder 65 years or older	11 805	13 410	. . .	. . .	. . .	. . .	. . .	. . .	. . .
Three people	15 277	15 720	15 735	. . .	. . .	. . .	. . .	. . .	. . .
Four people	20 144	20 474	19 806	19 874	. . .	. . .	. . .	. . .	. . .
Five people	24 293	24 646	23 891	23 307	22 951	. . .	. . .	. . .	. . .
Six people	27 941	28 052	27 474	26 920	26 096	25 608	. . .	. . .	. . .
Seven people	32 150	32 350	31 658	31 176	30 277	29 229	28 079	. . .	. . .
Eight people	35 957	36 274	35 621	35 049	34 237	33 207	32 135	31 862	. . .
Nine people or more	43 254	43 463	42 885	42 400	41 603	40 507	39 515	39 270	37 757
Four-Person Threshold With Three-Parameter Equivalence Scale Thresholds									
One person	9 179	. . .	. . .	. . .	. . .	. . .	. . .	. . .	. . .
Two people	12 943	13 852	. . .	. . .	. . .	. . .	. . .	. . .	. . .
Three people	19 806	17 433	16 445	. . .	. . .	. . .	. . .	. . .	. . .
Four people	24 224	22 063	19 806	18 872	. . .	. . .	. . .	. . .	. . .
Five people	28 320	26 306	24 224	22 063	21 172	. . .	. . .	. . .	. . .
Six people	32 175	30 274	28 320	26 306	24 224	23 370	. . .	. . .	. . .
Seven people	35 841	34 029	32 175	30 274	28 320	26 306	25 482	. . .	. . .
Eight people	39 353	37 614	35 841	34 029	32 175	30 274	28 320	27 522	. . .
Nine people or more	42 735	41 059	39 353	37 614	35 841	34 029	32 175	30 274	29 499

. . . = Not available.

Table 3-17. Official and National Academy of Sciences (NAS)–Based Poverty Rates, 1999–2006

(Percent of population.)

Measurement method	1999	2000	2001	2002 (new tax model)	2003	2004 (revised)	2005	2006
Official measure	11.9	11.3	11.7	12.1	12.5	12.7	12.6	12.3
MSI-GA-CPI	12.1	12.0	12.2	12.1	12.3	12.5	12.5	12.2
MIT-GA-CPI	12.7	12.5	12.5	12.6	12.7	13.0	13.0	12.6
CMB-GA-CPI	12.8	12.6	12.8	12.7	12.9	13.2	13.1	12.9
MSI-NGA-CPI	12.2	12.1	12.3	12.3	12.4	12.7	12.6	12.4
MIT-NGA-CPI	12.8	12.7	12.7	12.8	12.7	13.1	13.0	12.8
CMB-NGA-CPI	12.9	12.8	12.9	12.9	13.0	13.3	13.3	13.0
MSI-GA-CE	12.1	12.3	12.9	13.2	13.4	13.4	13.3	13.6
MIT-GA-CE	12.7	12.8	13.2	13.7	13.9	14.0	14.1	14.1
CMB-GA-CE	12.8	12.8	13.1	13.4	13.7	13.9	13.9	14.0
MSI-NGA-CE	12.2	12.5	13.0	13.4	13.5	13.4	13.5	13.7
MIT-NGA-CE	12.8	13.0	13.4	13.9	14.1	14.1	14.2	14.2
CMB-NGA-CE	12.9	13.0	13.2	13.7	13.9	13.9	14.0	14.1

Note: The Census Bureau changed the way it modeled taxes, effective with the revised 2002 estimates. Consequently, comparisons of 2002 and later data with earlier years may be affected.

MSI means "Medical out-of-pocket expenses subtracted from income."
MIT means "Medical out-of-pocket expenses in the thresholds."
CMB means "Combined methods."
GA means "Geographic adjustment (of poverty thresholds)."
NGA means "No geographic adjustment (of poverty thresholds)."
CPI means "Thresholds were adjusted since 1999 using the Consumer Price Index for All Urban Consumers."
CE means "Thresholds were recomputed since 1999 using data from the Consumer Expenditure Survey."

See notes and definitions for further explanation.

Table 3-18. Comparison of NAS-Based and Official Poverty Rates by Selected Characteristics, 2006

(Percent of population.)

Characteristic	Official poverty rate (no geographic adjustment)	NAS-based rate, MIT, CPI adjustment of 1999 thresholds	
		Without geographic adjustment	With geographic adjustment
All People	12.3	12.8	12.6
People in families	10.6	10.9	10.8
Married-couple families	5.7	6.4	6.4
Families with female householder, no husband present	30.5	28.7	28.0
Families with male householder, no wife present	13.8	16.4	15.8
By age			
Under 18 years	17.4	15.2	15.0
18 to 64 years	10.8	11.8	11.7
65 years and older	9.4	12.9	12.5
Race and Hispanic origin			
White alone	10.3	11.2	11.1
Non-Hispanic White alone	8.2	9.1	8.4
Black alone	24.3	22.5	21.4
Asian alone	10.3	11.1	13.7
Hispanic (any race)	20.6	21.0	23.7
Region			
Northeast	11.5	11.0	13.1
Midwest	11.2	11.6	9.8
South	13.8	14.8	12.7
West	11.6	12.1	14.9

Note: MIT means "Medical out-of-pocket expenses in the thresholds."

NOTES AND DEFINITIONS

TABLES 3-1 THROUGH 3-18
INCOME DISTRIBUTION AND POVERTY

SOURCE: U.S. DEPARTMENT OF COMMERCE, BUREAU OF THE CENSUS

All data in this chapter are derived from the Current Population Survey (CPS), which is also the source of the data on labor force, employment, and unemployment used in Chapter 10. (See the notes and definitions for Tables 10-1 through 10-5.) Early each year, the 60,000 households in this monthly survey are asked additional questions concerning earnings and other income in the previous year. This survey, informally known as the "March Supplement," is now formally known as the Current Population Survey Annual Social and Economic Supplement (CPS-ASEC). It was previously called the Annual Demographic Supplement.

The population represented by the survey is the civilian noninstitutional population of the United States and members of the armed forces in the United States living off post or with their families on post, but excluding all other members of the armed forces. As it is a survey of households, homeless persons are not included.

Racial classification and Hispanic origin

In 2002 and all earlier years, the CPS required respondents to report identification with only one race group. Since 2003, the CPS has allowed respondents to choose more than one race group. Income data for 2002 were collected in early 2003; thus, in the data for 2002 and all subsequent years, an individual could report identification with more than one race group. In the 2000 census, about 2.6 percent of people reported identification with more than one race.

Therefore, data from 2002 onward that are classified by race are not strictly comparable with race-classified data for 2001 and earlier years. As alternative approaches to dealing with this problem, the Census Bureau has tabulated two different race concepts for each racial category in a number of cases. In the case of Blacks, for example, this means there is one income measure for "Black alone," consisting of persons who report Black and no other race, and one for "Black alone or in combination," which includes all the "Black alone" reporters *plus* those who report Black in combination with any other race. The tables in this volume show both the "alone" and the "alone or in combination" values where available.

The race classifications now used in the CPS are *White, Black, Asian, American Indian and Alaska Native,* and

---

THE ACS: NEW ESTIMATES OF INCOME AND POVERTY FOR STATES AND SMALLER AREAS

When the Census Bureau released the CPS income and poverty data for 2007 on August 26, 2008, it also released data on income and poverty for states and smaller areas based on a newer, separate survey—the American Community Survey (ACS). According to the Census Bureau, "The ACS offers broad, comprehensive information on social, economic, and housing data and is designed to provide this information at many levels of geography, particularly for local communities." The ACS is designed to replace the decennial census "long form" questionnaire which has been the source of decennial census data for small areas; the ACS will have the additional advantage of providing much more up-to-date information between censuses. The ACS is a much larger survey than the CPS, reaching 250,000 addresses each month, but is not designed to provide the same degree of continuity over time as the CPS. In many media outlets, ACS results are featured more prominently than the CPS findings, reflecting the ACS's abundance of local data.

ACS data are presented by Bernan Press in volumes entitled *County and City Extra.* These data, with their relatively short historical comparisons and their focus on small-area data, are outside the scope of *Business Statistics.* The Census Bureau recommends that the CPS data be used for national estimates, and *Business Statistics* will continue to present CPS data exclusively.

This volume also includes two tables of historical state data on household income and poverty *based on CPS data* (Tables 3-6 and 3-13). While the CPS data are not as well designed for yielding accurate state-level estimates as the ACS data, they provide perspective on the behavior of these variables at the state level over longer periods of time. These tables should be used with caution. Typically, the Census Bureau presents CPS state data accompanied by estimates of their often-large standard errors and encourages users to reduce excessive random sampling variation by using two- or three-year moving averages.

The August 26, 2008 press release mentioned above is available on the Census Bureau Web site; it provides information about both surveys and additional references for users who require data from the ACS. It can be found at <http://www.census.gov/Press-Release/www/releases/archives/income_wealth/012528.html>.

Native Hawaiian and Other Pacific Islander. (Native Hawaiians and other Pacific Islanders were included in the "Asian" category in the data for 1987 through 2001.) The last two of these five racial groups are too small to provide reliable data for a single year, but in new Census Bureau tables available on the website, household income and poverty data for all five groups are presented in 2- and 3-year averages. Table 3-2 displays some of these data.

Hispanic origin is a separate question in the survey—not a racial classification—and Hispanics may be of any race. A subgroup of *White non-Hispanic* is shown in some tables. According to the Census Bureau, "Being Hispanic was reported by 13.0 percent of White householders who reported only one race, 3.0 percent of Black householders who reported only one race, and 1.9 percent of Asian householders who reported only one race. Data users should exercise caution when interpreting aggregate results for the Hispanic population or for race groups because these populations consist of many distinct groups that differ in socioeconomic characteristics, culture, and recency of immigration." ("Income, Poverty, and Health Insurance Coverage in the United States: 2007," footnote 2, p. 2)

Definitions

Households consists of all persons who occupy a housing unit. A household includes the related family members and all the unrelated persons, if any (such as lodgers, foster children, wards, or employees), who share the housing unit. A person living alone in a housing unit or a group of unrelated persons sharing a housing unit as partners is also counted as a household. The count of households excludes group quarters.

Earnings includes all income from work, including wages, salaries, armed forces pay, commissions, tips, piece-rate payments, and cash bonuses, before deductions such as taxes, bonds, pensions, and union dues. This category also includes net income from nonfarm self-employment and farm self-employment. Wage and salary supplements that are paid directly by the employer, such as the employer share of Social Security taxes and the cost of employer-provided health insurance, are not included.

Income, in the official definition used in the survey, is money income, including *earnings* from work as defined above; unemployment compensation; workers' compensation; Social Security; Supplemental Security Income; cash public assistance (welfare payments); veterans' payments; survivor benefits; disability benefits; pension or retirement income; interest income; dividends (but not capital gains); rents, royalties, and payments from estates or trusts; educational assistance, such as scholarships or grants; child support; alimony; financial assistance from outside of the household; and other cash income regularly received, such as foster child payments, military family allotments, and foreign government pensions. Receipts not counted as income include capital gains or losses, withdrawals of bank deposits,

money borrowed, tax refunds, gifts, and lump-sum inheritances or insurance payments.

A *year-round, full-time worker* is a person who worked 35 or more hours per week and 50 or more weeks during the previous calendar year.

A *family* is a group of two or more persons related by birth, marriage, or adoption who reside together.

Unrelated individuals are persons 15 years old and over who are not living with any relatives. The poverty status of unrelated individuals is determined independently of and is not affected by the incomes of other persons with whom they may share a household.

Median income is the amount of income that divides the ranked income distribution into two equal groups, with half having incomes above the median, and half having incomes below the median. The median income for persons is based on persons 15 years old and over with income.

Mean income is the amount obtained by dividing the total aggregate income of a group by the number of units in that group. In this survey, means are higher than medians because of the skewed nature of the income distribution; see the section "Whose standard of living?" in the article "Using the Data: The U.S. Economy in the New Century," which can be found at the beginning of this book.

Where available, historical income figures are shown in constant *2007 dollars*. Some data are shown in dollars for an earlier year if that year is the latest year for which the Census Bureau provided that particular data set. All constant-dollar figures are converted from current-dollar values using the *CPI-U-RS* (the Consumer Price Index, All Urban, Research Series), which measures changes in prices for past periods using the methodologies of the current CPI, and is similar in concept and behavior to the deflators used in the NIPAs for consumer income and spending. See Chapter 8 for CPI-U-RS data and the corresponding notes and definitions.

Income distribution

Income distribution is portrayed by dividing the total ranked distribution of families or households into *fifths*, also known as *quintiles*, and also by separately tabulating the top 5 percent (which is included in the highest fifth). The households or families are arrayed from those with the lowest income to those with the highest income, then divided into five groups, with each group containing one-fifth of the total number of households. Within each quintile, incomes are summed and calculated as a share of total income for all quintiles, and are averaged to show the average or mean income within that quintile.

A statistical measure that summarizes the dispersion of income across the entire income distribution is the *Gini coefficient* (also known as Gini ratio, Gini index, or index of income concentration), which can take values ranging from 0 to 1. A Gini value of 1 indicates "perfect" inequality; that is, one household has all the income and the rest have none. A value of 0 indicates "perfect" equality, a situation in which all households have equal income.

There are small differences between the Gini coefficients presented in the report's main tables and those presented in the tables comparing alternative definitions of income. In the latter, the coefficients were recalculated, using a slightly different method, for comparability with the other income definitions.

The *number of people below poverty level,* or the number of poor people, is the number of people with family or individual incomes below a specified level that is intended to measure the cost of a minimum standard of living. These minimum levels vary by size and composition of family and are known as *poverty thresholds.*

The official poverty thresholds are based on a definition developed in 1964 by Mollie Orshansky of the Social Security Administration. She calculated food budgets for families of various sizes and compositions, using an "economy food plan" developed by the U.S. Department of Agriculture (the cheapest of four plans developed). Reflecting a 1955 Department of Agriculture survey that found that families of three or more persons spent about one-third of their after-tax incomes on food, Orshansky multiplied the costs of the food plan by 3 to arrive at a set of thresholds for poverty income for families of three or larger. For 2-person families, the multiplier was 3.7; for 1-person families, the threshold was 80 percent of the two-person threshold.

These poverty thresholds have been adjusted each year for price increases, using the percent change in the Consumer Price Index for All Urban Consumers (CPI-U).

For more information on the Orshansky thresholds (the description of which has been simplified here), see Gordon Fisher, "The Development of the Orshansky Thresholds and Their Subsequent History as the Official U.S. Poverty Measure" (May 1992), available on the Census Bureau Web site at <http://www.census.gov/hhes/poverty/povmeas/papers/orshansky.html>.

The *poverty rate* for a demographic group is the number of poor people or poor families in that group expressed as a percentage of the total number of people or families in the group.

Average poverty thresholds. The thresholds used to calculate poverty rates vary not only with the size of the family but with the number of children in the family. For example, the threshold for a three-person family in 2007 was $16,218 if there were no children in the family but $16,705 if the family consisted of 1 adult and 2 children. There are 48 different threshold values depending on size of household,

number of children, and whether the householder is 65 years old or over (with lower thresholds for the older householders). The full matrix of thresholds is shown in the report referenced below. To give a general sense of the "poverty line," the Census Bureau also publishes the *average* threshold for each size family, based on the actual mix of family types in that year. These are the values shown in Table 3-7 to represent the history of poverty thresholds. The *average* value for 3-person families in 2007, as shown in Table 3-7, was $16,530, a weighted average of the values actually used for the 3 different possible family compositions.

Metropolitan area status. Poverty status by residence for people *inside metropolitan areas* and *outside metropolitan areas,* and with the metropolitan area group subdivided into *central city* and *outside central city,* is shown in Table 3-11 for the years 1959 and 1967–2003. Data for 2004 are not available because the sample for that year was a mixture of 1990 census–based sample design and 2000 Census–based sample design, with different definitions for metropolitan areas. The data for 2005 and subsequent years shown in Table 3-11 reflect the new, somewhat different definitions, as explained in a footnote. The major categories are now entitled *inside metropolitan statistical areas* and *outside metropolitan statistical areas.* The sub-categories within the metropolitan statistical area group are now entitled *inside principal cities* and *outside principal cities.*

A person with *work experience* (Table 3-12) is one who, during the preceding calendar year and on a part-time or full-time basis, did any work for pay or profit or worked without pay on a family-operated farm or business at any time during the year. A *year-round* worker is one who worked for 50 weeks or more during the preceding calendar year. A person is classified as having worked *full time* if he or she worked 35 hours or more per week during a majority of the weeks worked. A *year-round, full-time worker* is a person who worked 35 or more hours per week and 50 or more weeks during the previous calendar year.

Toward better measures of income and poverty

The definition of the official poverty rate is established by the Office of Management of Budget in the Executive Office of the President and has not been substantially changed since 1969. Criticisms of the current definition are legion. In response to these criticisms, the Census Bureau has published extensive research work illustrating the effects of various ways of modifying income definitions and poverty thresholds. Some of the results of this work are published here in Tables 3-14 through 3-18 and explained in the notes and definitions below.

Improving the income concept

One type of criticism accepts the general concept of the Orshansky threshold but recommends making the income definition more realistic by including some or all of the following: capital gains; taxes and tax credits; noncash food, housing, and health benefits provided by government and employers; and the value of homeownership. There is debate about whether it is appropriate to use income data augmented in this way in conjunction with the official thresholds. The original 1964 thresholds made no allowance for health insurance or other health expenses—in effect, they assumed that the poor would get free medical care, or at least that the poverty calculation was not required to allow for medical needs—and because of the imprecision of Orshansky's multiplier it is not clear to what extent they include housing expenses in a way that is comparable with the inclusion of a homeownership component in income. Nevertheless, the Census Bureau has calculated and published income and poverty figures based on broadened income definitions and either the official thresholds or thresholds that are closely related to the official ones. Some of these calculations are presented in Tables 3-14, 3-15 and 3-16 and described below.

Still accepting the validity of the basic Orshansky threshold concept, some critics have also argued that use of the CPI-U in the official measure to update the thresholds each year has overstated the price increase, and that an inflator such as the CPI-U-RS should be used instead. (See the notes and definitions for Chapter 8.) Use of the CPI-U-RS leads to lower poverty thresholds beginning in the late 1970s, when the CPI began to be distorted by housing and other biases subsequently corrected by new methods. Tables 3-14 and 3-15 also show poverty rates using the lower CPI-U-RS thresholds. Use of the CPI-U-RS eliminates a presumed upward bias in the poverty rate *relative to the poverty rates estimated before the bias emerged*. This is a bias in the behavior of the time series *given the concept of the Orshansky threshold*, not necessarily a bias in the current *level* of poverty, since all the other criticisms of the Orshansky thresholds need to be considered when assessing the general adequacy of today's poverty measurements.

Alternative definitions of income with Orshansky-type poverty thresholds

The Census Bureau has calculated "alternative" income and poverty measures based on a number of different definitions of income. In many cases, these measures require simulation—use of data from sources other than the CPS to estimate elements of family and individual income and expenses. One system of income definition alternatives, shown in Table 3-14, was used for data through 2003, and selectively updated to 2006. The updated data for each year are shown on the website under the category "Detailed poverty tables." Another system for income definition was introduced in 2004 and has been used to compare adjacent years data through 2006; this system is shown in Table 3-15. Although these two systems differ from each other in a few details, both provide poverty rates including and excluding the effects of various government programs, demonstrating the effects of these programs in alleviating poverty.

Table 3-14

Table 3-14 shows household income and poverty data according to a system of alternative income definitions that was last used in published reports for 2003 data, issued in June 2005, and has been selectively updated to 2006 on the Website. The income data are expressed in 2003 dollars. This table provides the longest time span for comparisons of Gini coefficients and poverty rates using different income definitions.

Definition 1, also known as "MI," is the official Census Bureau definition of money income described above.

Definition 4 is Definition 1 income *minus* government cash transfers (Social Security, unemployment compensation, workers' compensation, veterans' payments, railroad retirement, Black Lung payments, government education assistance, Supplemental Security Income, and welfare payments), *plus* realized capital gains and employers' payments for health insurance coverage. Capital gains and health insurance are not collected in the CPS but are simulated using statistical data from the Internal Revenue Service and the National Medical Care Expenditure Survey. Definition 4 is the closest approach in this set of calculations to a measure of the income generated by the workings of the economy before government interventions in the form of taxes and transfer payments. In its last published report using this framework, the Census Bureau only showed income according to this definition for 2002 and 2003. The editor has extended this series back to 1979 on an estimated 2003-dollar basis, using estimates for the same concept of income published in earlier Census Bureau reports.

Definition 14, also known as "MI – Tx + NC," is income after all government income and earnings tax and transfer interventions. It consists of Definition 4 income minus payroll taxes and federal and state income taxes, plus the Earned Income Credit; plus all of the cash transfers listed above as being subtracted from money income to yield Definition 4; plus the "fungible" value of Medicare and Medicaid (see below for definition); plus the value of regular-price school lunches provided by government; and plus the value of noncash transfers, including food stamps, rent subsidies, and free and reduced-price school lunches. The tax information is not collected in the CPS but is simulated using statistical data from the Internal Revenue Service, Social Security payroll tax formulas, and a model of each state's income tax regulations.

The "fungible" value approach to medical benefits counts such benefits as income only to the extent that they free up resources that would have been spent on medical care. Therefore, if family income is not sufficient to cover the family's basic food and housing requirements, Medicare and Medicaid are treated as having no income value. Data on average Medicare and Medicaid outlays per enrollee are used in the valuation process.

Food stamp values are reported in the March CPS. Estimates of other government subsidy payments use data from the Department of Agriculture (for school lunches) and the 1985 American Housing Survey.

Definition 15 ("MI – Tx + NC + HE") is Definition 14 income plus the net imputed return on equity in owner-occupied housing—the calculated annual benefit of converting one's home equity into an annuity, net of property taxes. This concept can be thought of as measuring the extent to which equity in the home relieves the owner of the need for rental or mortgage payments. Information from the 1987 American Housing Survey is used to assign values of home equity and amounts of property taxes. Since disposable personal income in the national income and product accounts (NIPAs) includes the imputed rent on owner-occupied housing plus most of the cash and in-kind transfers included in Definitions 14 and 15, Definition 15 is the Census Bureau income definition closest to the NIPA concept.

Tables 3-15 and 3-16

In a separate data system entitled "The Effects of Taxes and Transfers on Income and Poverty (New Alternative Measures of Income and Poverty)", the Census Bureau calculated redefined alternative income measures and modified the set of Orshansky poverty thresholds, still maintaining the basic Orshansky concept. This system is described in "The Effect of Taxes and Transfers on Income and Poverty: 2005" and has been updated through 2006; the report and updated data are available on the Census Bureau Web site at <http://www.census.gov>. The updated data for recent years appear on the website under "Detailed poverty tables." Selected statistics from this report are shown in Tables 3-15 and 3-16.

In this system, the Orshansky poverty thresholds were modified using a more systematic formula to adjust the basic official 4-person, 2-child threshold for different family sizes and compositions. The distinction between families with householders over and under the age of 65 years was also dropped. Otherwise, these thresholds—called "three-parameter" thresholds—still derive from the basic Orshansky calculation of the cost of a food budget, augmented by multipliers derived from budgets observed in 1955. Table 3-16 shows the three-parameter thresholds for 2005 compared with the official thresholds. The thresholds are the same—$19,806—for the four-person family that includes two children, but the three-parameter thresholds are different for other family sizes and compositions, reflecting differing assumptions about how the addition of children affects spending, such as greater economies of scale in larger households.

Money income is the concept used in the official income and poverty measures, and consists of cash income received by household members 15 and older before deductions for taxes and other expenses. It does not include lump-sum payments, capital gains, or noncash benefits such as food stamps.

Market income includes money income except government cash transfers; includes imputed net realized capital gains; includes the imputed rate of return on home equity; and subtracts imputed work expenses *other than child care*. As an approach to an estimate of income generated by the economy before any government interventions, it is somewhat similar to "Definition 4" in the earlier measures, but differs in that it excludes health insurance, includes home equity return, and deducts certain work expenses.

Post-social-insurance income is market income plus government non-means-tested cash transfers, of which Social Security is the dominant example. Other non-means-tested transfers which are included in money income and which are added back to market income to yield post-social-insurance income include unemployment compensation and workers' compensation. This concept differs from the official money income measure in that it includes capital gains and losses and the return on home equity, is adjusted to exclude certain work expenses, and excludes means-tested cash transfers (family assistance, Supplemental Security Income, and means-tested veterans' payments).

Disposable income is post-social-insurance income plus means-tested cash transfers, plus the value of nonmedical means-tested noncash transfers (food stamps, public or subsidized housing, and free or reduced-price school lunches), minus federal payroll taxes, federal and state income taxes, and property taxes on owner-occupied homes. It also includes the Earned Income Tax Credit. Disposable income is roughly similar to Definition 15 in the earlier calculations defined above, except that neither health insurance nor government medical programs are included and imputed work expenses are deducted.

Improving the concepts of income and poverty together

Another type of criticism argues that the official thresholds are no longer relevant to today's needs, and that the concepts of income (or "resources") and of the threshold level that depicts a minimum adequate standard of living need to be rethought together. These critics cite the availability of more up-to-date and detailed information about consumer spending at various income levels. The Consumer Expenditure Survey (CEX), originally designed to provide the weights for the Consumer Price Index, is now conducted annually and provides extensive data on consumer spending patterns. To give just one example of the information available now that was not available to Mollie Orshansky, the CEX indicates that food now accounts for one-sixth, not one-third, of total family expenditures, even among low-income families. (For data and notes on the Consumer Expenditure Survey, see Bernan Press, *Handbook of U.S. Labor Statistics.*)

A special panel of the National Academy of Sciences (NAS) undertook a study that reconsidered both resources and thresholds. The Census Bureau now calculates and publishes poverty rates that have been developed following

NAS recommendations, which are presented in Tables 3-17 and 3-18.

Measures based on NAS recommendations—Tables 3-17 and 3-18

The most recent calculations of experimental poverty measures that redefine both income and need are presented in "Alternative Poverty Estimates in the United States: 2003" (see below for complete reference) and updated through 2006 on the Census Bureau Web site at <http://www.census.gov>.

To derive these estimates, a baseline set of poverty thresholds for the year 1999, based on data from the CEX for the years 1997–1999, was developed as follows:

A reference family type was selected: a 2-adult, 2-child family.

The definition of necessities for the purpose of the poverty threshold was expenditures on food, clothing, shelter, and utilities (FCSU), augmented by a multiplier of between 1.15 and 1.25 to include other needs such as household and personal supplies. The definition of food includes food away from home. Expenses on shelter include interest (but not principal repayment) for homeowners and rent for renters.

The numerical estimates were derived as follows: FCSU expenditures for reference families falling between the 30th and 35th percentile of the distribution of expenditures in the CEX, based on 1997–1999 data but expressed in 1999 dollars, were calculated and expanded by the multiplier percentages. The midpoint of these estimates was then selected as the poverty threshold; it turned out to be 96.725 percent of median FCSU expenditures.

For health care, three different treatments were developed; these treatments are described below.

Three-parameter equivalence scale adjustments were used to convert the threshold for the reference family to thresholds for other family sizes and compositions, accounting for the differing needs of adults and children and the economies of scale of living in larger families.

For some of the experimental measures, thresholds were adjusted geographically to reflect differences in the cost of living (in practice, difference in housing costs) in different areas.

The family incomes to be compared with these poverty thresholds were defined and measured to include the effects of all taxes, tax credits, and in-kind benefits such as food stamps, but not the value of homeownership, and to allow for expenses such as child care that are necessary to hold a job.

The 12 measures shown in Table 3-17 are as originally presented in Table B-3 in "Alternative Poverty Estimates in the United States: 2003," and updated in the table "Official and

National Academy of Sciences (NAS) Based Poverty Rates: 1999 to 2006," available on the Census Bureau Web site. The following abbreviations are used to define the alternative definitions of poverty that are presented in this table.

MSI indicates that in calculating the poverty rate, medical out-of-pocket expenses are subtracted from family income before comparing that income to the family's threshold.

MIT indicates that poverty thresholds were increased to take the family's potential medical out-of-pocket expenses into account, using the CEX and the 1996 Medical Expenditures Panel Survey, with the amounts depending on family size, age, and health insurance coverage.

CMB indicates that expected medical out-of-pocket expenses were included in the thresholds, and the difference between each family's spending and the expected spending was subtracted from family income—and if the difference was negative, the amount was added to income. This way, families that were "unexpectedly healthy" were classified as better off.

GA indicates that the thresholds were adjusted for geographic differences in the cost of living. Measures labeled *NGA* were not.

CPI indicates that the thresholds established for 1999 were updated to succeeding years using the percent change in the CPI-U. This means that the threshold for measures with this indication has been held constant in real (inflation-adjusted) terms since 1999, just as the official threshold has been held constant in real terms—except for bias in the price indexes since 1964.

CE indicates that the thresholds were updated using the percent change in <u>median</u> FCSU expenditures from the latest available 12 quarters of CEX data. This means that if the actual real FCSU spending of middle-income families rises (or falls), the real standard of living represented by the poverty thresholds will rise (or fall) commensurately.

In Table 3-18, poverty rates for 2006 using one of the NAS-based concepts—adjustment with the CPI, with medical out-of-pocket expenses in the threshold—are shown with and without the geographic adjustment to demonstrate the impact of the new methods and the geographic adjustment.

Notes on the data

The following are the principal changes that may affect year-to-year comparability of all income and poverty data from the CPS.

Beginning in 1952, the estimates are based on 1950 census population controls. Earlier figures were based on 1940 census population controls.

Beginning in 1962, 1960 census–based sample design and population controls are fully implemented.

With 1971 and 1972 data, 1970 census–based sample design and population controls were introduced.

With 1983–1985 data, 1980 census–based sample design was introduced; 1980 population controls were introduced; and these were extended back to 1979 data.

With 1993 data, there was a major redesign of the CPS, including the introduction of computer-assisted interviewing. The limits used to "code" reported income amounts were changed, resulting in reporting of higher income values for the highest-income families and, consequently, an exaggerated year-to-year increase in income inequality. (It is possible that this jump actually reflects in one year an increase that had emerged more gradually, so that the distribution measures for 1993 and later years may be properly comparable with data for decades earlier even if they should not be directly compared with 1992.) In addition, 1990 census–based population controls were introduced, and these were extended back to the 1992 data.

With 1995 data, the 1990 census–based sample design was implemented and the sample was reduced by 7,000 households.

Data for 2001 implemented population controls based on the 2000 census, which were carried back to 1999. Data from 2000 forward also incorporate results from a 28,000-household sample expansion.

For more information on these and other changes that could affect comparability, see "Current Population Survey Technical Paper 63RV: Design and Methodology" (March 2002) and footnotes to CPS historical income tables, both available on the Census Bureau Web site at <http://www.census.gov/hhes/income>.

Data availability

Data embodying the official definitions of income and poverty are published annually in late summer or early fall by the Census Bureau, as part of a series with the general title *Current Population Reports: Consumer Income, P60*. Most of the data in this chapter were derived from report P60-235, "Income, Poverty, and Health Insurance Coverage in the United States: 2007" (August 2008), and from the "Historical Income Tables" and "Historical Poverty Tables" on the Census Web site (see below).

The data in Table 3-14 were first published in two reports, both issued in June 2005: P60-228, "Alternative Income Estimates in the United States: 2003," and P60-227, "Alternative Poverty Estimates in the United States: 2003." Updates available on the website are cited in the table description above.

The most recent data in Table 3-15 became available in December 2007. The source reports are cited above in the table description.

The NAS-based data used in Tables 3-17 and 3-18 are posted on the Census Bureau Web site under the titles "Official and National Academy of Sciences (NAS) Based Poverty Rates: 1999 to 2006" and "Alternative Poverty Estimates Based on National Academy of Sciences Recommendations, by Selected Demographic Characteristics and by Region: 2006."

All these reports and related data, including historical tabulations, used in *Business Statistics* are available on the Census Bureau Web site at <http://www.census.gov>, under the general headings of "Income" and "Poverty."

References

Definitions and descriptions of the concepts and data of the official and alternative series are provided in the source documents listed above and in the references contained therein.

Additional descriptive material on the NAS-based experimental poverty measures is found in the Census report P60-216, "Experimental Poverty Measures: 1999" issued October 2001, available at <http://www.census.gov/prod/2001pubs/p60-216.pdf>; and in Kathleen S. Short and Thesia I. Garner, "A Decade of Experimental Poverty Thresholds 1990 to 2000," (June 27, 2002), available at <http://www.census.gov/hhes/www/povmeas/papers/decade.pdf>.

CHAPTER 4: CONSUMER INCOME AND SPENDING

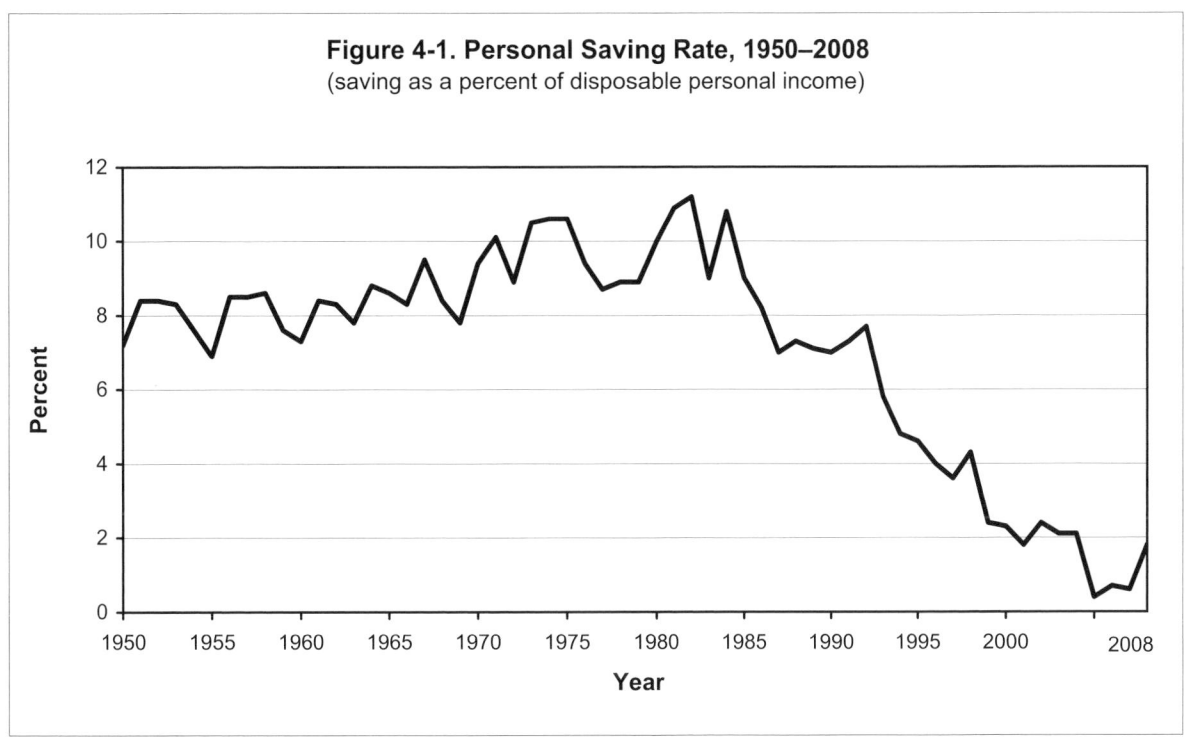

Figure 4-1. Personal Saving Rate, 1950–2008
(saving as a percent of disposable personal income)

- The personal saving rate—saving as a percent of disposable income—averaged 8 to 10 percent for much of the postwar period, but started to trend down around the mid-1980s. From 1999 through 2004, the saving rate averaged 2.2 percent. In 2005–2007, personal saving, which includes the saving of non-profits, averaged only 0.6 percent of income; in 2005, *household* saving was actually negative—only nonprofits had positive saving, while households borrowed and spent down their assets. In 2008, as assets began to lose value and borrowing slowed, the personal saving rate was 1.8 percent. (Tables 4-1 and 4-6, 12-5 through 12-8, and 12-10)

- It should be noted that personal income does not, by definition, include any capital gains. Despite that, taxes on realized capital gains are deducted from personal income to get after-tax income (along with all other income taxes). Capital gains are a source of spending power in addition to current disposable income; they can be, and in recent years have been, converted into cash by asset sales, refinancing, and home equity loans, which contributed to recent low saving rates. (Table 12-10)

- Labor compensation, excluding social insurance contributions, made up 58.3 percent of total personal income in 2008. This was down from 60.3 percent in 2000 and 65.4 percent in 1948. ("Contributions for social insurance," mainly Social Security taxes, are excluded from both the numerator and the denominator of this percentage.) Transfer receipts rose from 4.9 percent in 1948 to 12.9 percent in 2000 and 15.4 percent in 2008. It should be noted that "consumption expenditures" in the national income and product accounts includes all spending financed by government health insurance programs such as Medicare and Medicaid and personal income includes the amount of that spending, in the transfer receipts component. (Tables 4-1 and 19-6)

- The share of proprietors' income was little changed between 2000 and 2008 and only half of what it had been in 1948. The share of rental income declined to less than 1 percent, while the shares of dividend and interest income saw offsetting changes between 2000 and 2008 but were far above what they had been in 1948. (Tables 4-1 and 19-6)

Table 4-1. Personal Income and Its Disposition

(Billions of current dollars, except as noted; quarterly data are at seasonally adjusted annual rates.)   **NIPA Table 2.1**

Year and quarter	Personal income													
					Personal income receipts on assets			Personal current transfer receipts						
									Government social benefits to persons					
	Total	Compensation of employees, received	Propri-etors' income with IVA and CCAdj	Rental income of persons with CCAdj	Total	Personal interest income	Personal dividend income	Total	Total	Social Security and Medicare	Govern-ment unem-ployment insurance	Veterans	Family assistance	Other
1950	229.0	155.3	37.6	9.2	18.6	9.7	8.8	14.0	13.4	1.0	1.5	7.7	0.6	2.7
1951	258.0	181.4	42.7	10.1	19.1	10.5	8.6	11.4	10.5	1.9	0.9	4.6	0.6	2.6
1952	275.4	196.2	43.1	11.2	19.9	11.3	8.6	11.9	11.0	2.2	1.1	4.3	0.5	2.9
1953	291.9	210.3	42.1	12.5	21.6	12.7	8.9	12.5	11.7	3.0	1.0	4.1	0.5	3.0
1954	294.5	209.2	42.3	13.5	23.2	14.0	9.3	14.3	13.7	3.6	2.2	4.2	0.6	3.2
1955	316.1	225.7	44.3	13.9	25.7	15.2	10.5	15.7	14.8	4.9	1.5	4.4	0.6	3.3
1956	339.6	244.5	45.8	14.2	28.2	16.9	11.3	16.8	15.6	5.7	1.5	4.4	0.6	3.4
1957	358.7	257.5	47.9	14.6	30.6	18.9	11.7	19.5	18.1	7.3	1.9	4.5	0.7	3.7
1958	369.0	259.5	50.1	15.4	31.9	20.3	11.6	23.5	22.2	8.5	4.1	4.7	0.8	4.1
1959	392.8	281.0	50.7	16.2	34.6	22.0	12.6	24.2	22.9	10.2	2.8	4.6	0.9	4.5
1960	411.5	296.4	50.8	17.1	37.9	24.5	13.4	25.7	24.4	11.1	3.0	4.6	1.0	4.7
1961	429.0	305.3	53.2	17.9	40.1	26.2	13.9	29.5	28.1	12.6	4.3	5.0	1.1	5.1
1962	456.7	327.1	55.4	18.8	44.1	29.1	15.0	30.4	28.8	14.3	3.1	4.7	1.3	5.5
1963	479.6	345.2	56.5	19.5	47.9	31.7	16.2	32.2	30.3	15.2	3.0	4.8	1.4	5.9
1964	514.6	370.7	59.4	19.6	53.8	35.6	18.2	33.5	31.3	16.0	2.7	4.7	1.5	6.4
1965	555.7	399.5	63.9	20.2	59.4	39.2	20.2	36.2	33.9	18.1	2.3	4.9	1.7	7.0
1966	603.9	442.7	68.2	20.8	64.1	43.4	20.7	39.6	37.5	20.8	1.9	4.9	1.9	8.1
1967	648.3	475.1	69.8	21.2	69.0	47.5	21.5	48.0	45.8	25.8	2.2	5.6	2.3	9.9
1968	712.0	524.3	74.3	20.9	75.2	51.6	23.5	56.1	53.3	30.5	2.1	5.9	2.8	11.9
1969	778.5	577.6	77.4	21.2	84.1	59.9	24.2	62.3	59.0	33.1	2.2	6.7	3.5	13.4
1970	838.8	617.2	78.4	21.4	93.5	69.2	24.3	74.7	71.7	38.6	4.0	7.7	4.8	16.6
1971	903.5	658.3	84.8	22.4	101.0	75.9	25.0	88.1	85.4	44.7	5.8	8.8	6.2	20.0
1972	992.7	725.1	95.9	23.4	109.6	82.8	26.8	97.9	94.8	49.8	5.7	9.7	6.9	22.7
1973	1 110.7	811.3	113.5	24.3	124.7	94.8	29.9	112.6	108.6	60.9	4.4	10.4	7.2	25.7
1974	1 222.6	890.7	113.1	24.3	146.4	113.2	33.2	133.3	128.6	70.3	6.8	11.8	8.0	31.7
1975	1 335.0	949.0	119.5	23.7	162.2	129.3	32.9	170.0	163.1	81.5	17.6	14.5	9.3	40.2
1976	1 474.8	1 059.2	132.2	22.3	178.4	139.5	39.0	184.0	177.3	93.3	15.8	14.4	10.1	43.7
1977	1 633.2	1 180.4	145.7	20.7	205.3	160.6	44.7	194.2	189.1	105.3	12.7	13.8	10.6	46.7
1978	1 837.7	1 335.8	166.6	22.1	234.8	184.0	50.7	209.6	203.2	116.9	9.1	13.9	10.8	52.5
1979	2 062.2	1 501.0	180.1	23.8	274.7	217.3	57.4	235.3	227.1	132.5	9.4	14.4	11.1	59.6
1980	2 307.9	1 651.8	174.1	30.0	338.7	274.7	64.0	279.5	270.8	154.8	15.7	15.0	12.5	72.8
1981	2 591.3	1 825.7	183.0	38.0	421.9	348.3	73.6	318.4	307.2	182.1	15.6	16.1	13.1	80.2
1982	2 775.3	1 925.9	176.3	38.8	488.4	410.8	77.6	354.8	342.4	204.6	25.1	16.4	12.9	83.4
1983	2 960.7	2 043.0	192.5	37.8	529.6	446.3	83.3	383.7	369.9	222.2	26.2	16.6	13.8	91.0
1984	3 289.5	2 255.4	243.3	40.2	607.9	517.2	90.6	400.1	380.4	237.8	15.9	16.4	14.5	95.9
1985	3 526.7	2 424.9	262.3	41.9	654.0	556.6	97.4	424.9	402.6	253.0	15.7	16.7	15.2	102.0
1986	3 722.4	2 570.1	275.7	33.5	695.5	589.5	106.0	451.0	428.0	268.9	16.3	16.7	16.1	109.9
1987	3 947.4	2 750.2	302.2	33.5	717.0	604.9	112.2	467.6	447.4	282.6	14.5	16.6	16.4	117.3
1988	4 253.7	2 967.2	341.6	40.6	769.3	639.5	129.7	496.6	476.0	300.2	13.2	16.9	16.9	128.8
1989	4 587.8	3 145.2	363.3	43.1	878.0	720.2	157.8	543.4	519.9	325.6	14.3	17.3	17.5	145.3
1990	4 878.6	3 338.2	380.6	50.7	924.0	755.2	168.8	595.2	573.1	351.8	18.0	17.8	19.2	166.2
1991	5 051.0	3 445.3	377.1	60.3	932.0	751.7	180.3	666.4	648.5	381.7	26.6	18.3	21.1	200.8
1992	5 362.0	3 651.2	427.6	78.0	910.9	723.4	187.4	749.4	729.8	414.4	38.9	19.3	22.2	234.9
1993	5 558.5	3 794.9	453.8	95.6	901.8	699.6	202.2	790.1	775.7	443.4	34.1	20.1	22.8	255.3
1994	5 842.5	3 979.6	473.3	119.7	950.8	716.8	234.0	827.3	812.2	475.4	23.5	20.1	23.2	270.0
1995	6 152.3	4 177.0	492.1	122.1	1 016.4	763.2	253.2	877.4	858.4	506.8	21.4	20.9	22.6	286.7
1996	6 520.6	4 386.9	543.2	131.5	1 089.2	793.0	296.2	925.0	902.1	537.7	22.0	21.7	20.3	300.4
1997	6 915.1	4 664.6	576.0	128.8	1 181.7	848.7	333.0	951.2	931.8	563.2	19.9	22.5	17.9	308.3
1998	7 423.0	5 020.1	627.8	137.5	1 283.2	933.2	349.9	978.6	952.6	575.1	19.5	23.4	17.4	317.3
1999	7 802.4	5 352.0	678.3	147.3	1 264.2	928.6	335.6	1 022.1	988.0	588.9	20.3	24.3	17.9	336.7
2000	8 429.7	5 782.7	728.4	150.3	1 387.0	1 011.0	376.1	1 084.0	1 041.6	620.8	20.3	25.1	18.4	357.0
2001	8 724.1	5 942.1	771.9	167.4	1 380.0	1 011.0	369.0	1 193.9	1 143.9	668.5	31.7	26.7	18.1	398.9
2002	8 881.9	6 091.2	768.4	152.9	1 333.2	936.1	397.2	1 286.2	1 248.9	707.5	53.2	29.6	17.7	440.9
2003	9 163.6	6 310.4	811.3	133.0	1 336.6	914.1	422.6	1 351.0	1 316.7	741.3	52.8	32.0	18.4	472.2
2004	9 727.2	6 671.4	911.6	118.4	1 432.1	895.1	537.0	1 422.5	1 396.1	788.0	36.0	34.5	18.4	519.2
2005	10 269.8	7 025.8	959.8	40.9	1 596.9	1 022.0	574.9	1 520.7	1 481.9	844.5	31.3	36.8	18.2	551.1
2006	10 993.9	7 432.6	1 014.7	44.3	1 824.8	1 125.4	699.4	1 603.0	1 578.1	938.9	29.9	39.2	18.3	551.7
2007	11 663.2	7 818.6	1 056.2	40.0	2 000.1	1 214.3	785.8	1 713.3	1 681.4	999.4	32.3	41.9	18.8	588.9
2008	12 102.6	8 055.1	1 072.4	64.4	2 037.7	1 208.5	829.1	1 869.1	1 834.4	1 058.3	52.3	45.4	19.3	659.0
2006														
1st quarter	10 781.6	7 338.0	1 004.7	52.8	1 735.4	1 085.3	650.2	1 567.6	1 543.0	914.0	29.7	38.8	18.2	542.3
2nd quarter	10 913.2	7 364.2	1 018.3	45.6	1 809.5	1 123.4	686.1	1 594.5	1 570.7	934.9	29.6	39.2	18.2	548.8
3rd quarter	11 056.1	7 441.9	1 013.4	40.4	1 865.8	1 147.6	718.2	1 620.1	1 595.4	947.4	30.1	39.3	18.3	560.2
4th quarter	11 224.7	7 586.1	1 022.4	38.2	1 888.6	1 145.6	743.0	1 629.8	1 603.1	959.2	30.4	39.6	18.4	555.6
2007														
1st quarter	11 473.0	7 734.0	1 037.2	35.1	1 930.9	1 172.2	758.7	1 695.7	1 665.3	981.9	31.3	41.0	18.6	592.6
2nd quarter	11 577.5	7 760.1	1 050.2	44.6	1 982.5	1 206.1	776.5	1 699.2	1 667.5	997.5	31.2	41.9	18.7	578.2
3rd quarter	11 730.4	7 839.3	1 063.8	41.8	2 030.9	1 236.2	794.7	1 720.6	1 688.0	1 008.8	32.5	42.1	18.9	585.7
4th quarter	11 872.1	7 941.0	1 073.8	38.6	2 056.2	1 242.7	813.5	1 737.8	1 704.7	1 009.6	34.3	42.7	19.0	599.2
2008														
1st quarter	11 960.5	8 009.7	1 071.7	39.1	2 054.1	1 224.6	829.5	1 778.1	1 745.8	1 032.4	38.2	44.6	19.2	611.5
2nd quarter	12 152.2	8 033.5	1 076.9	58.6	2 052.3	1 208.7	843.6	1 926.3	1 893.9	1 050.0	41.4	44.9	19.3	738.4
3rd quarter	12 170.4	8 092.9	1 080.5	68.5	2 055.7	1 217.4	838.3	1 872.7	1 831.2	1 068.9	59.2	45.7	19.4	637.9
4th quarter	12 127.5	8 084.1	1 060.6	91.4	1 988.5	1 183.4	805.1	1 899.3	1 866.6	1 081.9	70.4	46.5	19.5	648.3

Table 4-1. Personal Income and Its Disposition—*Continued*

(Billions of current dollars, except as noted; quarterly data are at seasonally adjusted annual rates.)   **NIPA Table 2.1**

Year and quarter	Personal income—Continued		Less: Personal current taxes	Equals: Disposable personal income	Less: Personal outlays							Equals: Personal saving		Disposable personal income, billions of chained (2000) dollars
	Personal current transfer receipts—Continued, From business, net	Less: Contributions for government social insurance			Total	Personal consumption expenditures	Personal interest payments	Personal current transfer payments				Billions of dollars	Percent of disposable personal income	
								Total	To government	To the rest of the world, net				
1950	0.6	5.5	18.9	210.1	195.0	192.2	2.0	0.8	0.3	0.4		15.1	7.2	1 260.0
1951	0.9	6.6	27.1	231.0	211.5	208.5	2.2	0.7	0.3	0.4		19.5	8.4	1 297.3
1952	0.9	6.9	32.0	243.4	222.9	219.5	2.6	0.8	0.4	0.4		20.5	8.4	1 339.4
1953	0.8	7.1	33.2	258.6	237.1	233.1	3.2	0.9	0.4	0.5		21.5	8.3	1 404.5
1954	0.6	8.1	30.2	264.3	244.3	240.0	3.4	0.9	0.4	0.5		20.0	7.6	1 422.1
1955	0.9	9.1	32.9	283.3	263.6	258.8	4.0	0.8	0.4	0.4		19.7	6.9	1 516.7
1956	1.2	10.0	36.6	303.0	277.2	271.7	4.6	1.0	0.5	0.5		25.8	8.5	1 589.7
1957	1.4	11.4	38.9	319.8	292.8	286.9	4.9	1.1	0.6	0.5		27.0	8.5	1 628.5
1958	1.2	11.4	38.5	330.5	302.2	296.2	5.0	1.0	0.6	0.4		28.3	8.6	1 642.6
1959	1.3	13.8	42.3	350.5	323.9	317.6	5.5	0.8	0.3	0.5		26.7	7.6	1 715.5
1960	1.3	16.4	46.1	365.4	338.8	331.7	6.2	0.8	0.3	0.5		26.7	7.3	1 759.7
1961	1.4	17.0	47.3	381.8	349.6	342.1	6.5	1.0	0.5	0.5		32.2	8.4	1 819.2
1962	1.5	19.1	51.6	405.1	371.3	363.3	7.0	1.1	0.5	0.5		33.8	8.3	1 908.2
1963	1.9	21.7	54.6	425.1	391.8	382.7	7.9	1.2	0.5	0.7		33.3	7.8	1 979.1
1964	2.2	22.4	52.1	462.5	421.7	411.4	8.9	1.3	0.6	0.7		40.8	8.8	2 122.8
1965	2.3	23.4	57.7	498.1	455.1	443.8	9.9	1.4	0.6	0.8		43.0	8.6	2 253.3
1966	2.1	31.3	66.4	537.5	493.1	480.9	10.7	1.6	0.8	0.8		44.4	8.3	2 371.9
1967	2.3	34.9	73.0	575.3	520.9	507.8	11.1	2.0	1.0	1.0		54.4	9.5	2 475.9
1968	2.8	38.7	87.0	625.0	572.2	558.0	12.2	2.0	1.0	1.0		52.8	8.4	2 588.0
1969	3.3	44.1	104.5	674.0	621.4	605.2	14.0	2.2	1.1	1.1		52.5	7.8	2 668.7
1970	2.9	46.4	103.1	735.7	666.2	648.5	15.2	2.6	1.3	1.3		69.5	9.4	2 781.7
1971	2.7	51.2	101.7	801.8	721.2	701.9	16.6	2.8	1.5	1.3		80.6	10.1	2 907.9
1972	3.1	59.2	123.6	869.1	791.9	770.6	18.1	3.1	1.8	1.4		77.2	8.9	3 046.5
1973	3.9	75.5	132.4	978.3	875.6	852.4	19.8	3.4	1.8	1.5		102.7	10.5	3 252.3
1974	4.7	85.2	151.0	1 071.6	958.0	933.4	21.2	3.4	2.1	1.3		113.6	10.6	3 228.5
1975	6.8	89.3	147.6	1 187.4	1 061.9	1 034.4	23.7	3.8	2.5	1.3		125.6	10.6	3 302.6
1976	6.7	101.3	172.3	1 302.5	1 180.2	1 151.9	23.9	4.4	3.0	1.3		122.3	9.4	3 432.2
1977	5.1	113.1	197.5	1 435.7	1 310.4	1 278.6	27.0	4.8	3.5	1.3		125.3	8.7	3 552.9
1978	6.5	131.3	229.4	1 608.3	1 465.8	1 428.5	31.9	5.4	3.9	1.5		142.5	8.9	3 718.8
1979	8.2	152.7	268.7	1 793.5	1 634.4	1 592.2	36.2	5.9	4.3	1.6		159.1	8.9	3 811.2
1980	8.6	166.2	298.9	2 009.0	1 807.5	1 757.1	43.6	6.8	5.0	1.8		201.4	10.0	3 857.7
1981	11.2	195.7	345.2	2 246.1	2 001.8	1 941.1	49.3	11.4	6.0	5.5		244.3	10.9	3 960.0
1982	12.4	208.9	354.1	2 421.2	2 150.4	2 077.3	59.5	13.6	7.1	6.6		270.8	11.2	4 044.9
1983	13.8	226.0	352.3	2 608.4	2 374.8	2 290.6	69.2	15.0	8.1	6.9		233.6	9.0	4 177.7
1984	19.7	257.5	377.4	2 912.0	2 597.3	2 503.3	77.0	16.9	9.2	7.8		314.8	10.8	4 494.1
1985	22.3	281.4	417.4	3 109.3	2 829.3	2 720.3	90.4	18.6	10.4	8.2		280.0	9.0	4 645.2
1986	22.9	303.4	437.3	3 285.1	3 016.7	2 899.7	96.1	20.9	12.0	9.0		268.4	8.2	4 791.0
1987	20.2	323.1	489.1	3 458.3	3 216.9	3 100.2	93.6	23.1	13.2	9.9		241.4	7.0	4 874.5
1988	20.6	361.5	505.0	3 748.7	3 475.8	3 353.6	96.8	25.4	14.8	10.6		272.9	7.3	5 082.6
1989	23.5	385.2	566.1	4 021.7	3 734.6	3 598.5	108.2	27.8	16.5	11.4		287.1	7.1	5 224.8
1990	22.2	410.1	592.8	4 285.8	3 986.4	3 839.9	116.1	30.4	18.4	12.0		299.4	7.0	5 324.2
1991	17.9	430.2	586.7	4 464.3	4 140.1	3 986.1	118.5	35.6	22.6	13.0		324.2	7.3	5 351.7
1992	19.6	455.0	610.6	4 751.4	4 385.4	4 235.3	111.8	38.3	26.0	12.3		366.0	7.7	5 536.3
1993	14.4	477.7	646.6	4 911.9	4 627.9	4 477.9	107.3	42.7	28.5	14.2		284.0	5.8	5 594.2
1994	15.1	508.2	690.7	5 151.8	4 902.4	4 743.3	112.8	46.3	30.9	15.4		249.5	4.8	5 746.4
1995	19.0	532.8	744.1	5 408.2	5 157.3	4 975.8	132.7	48.9	32.6	16.2		250.9	4.6	5 905.7
1996	22.9	555.2	832.1	5 688.5	5 460.0	5 256.8	150.3	52.9	34.9	18.0		228.4	4.0	6 080.9
1997	19.4	587.2	926.3	5 988.8	5 770.5	5 547.4	163.9	59.2	38.2	21.0		218.3	3.6	6 295.8
1998	26.0	624.2	1 027.0	6 395.9	6 119.1	5 879.5	174.5	65.2	40.6	24.6		276.8	4.3	6 663.9
1999	34.1	661.4	1 107.5	6 695.0	6 536.4	6 282.5	181.0	73.0	44.7	28.3		158.6	2.4	6 861.3
2000	42.4	702.7	1 235.7	7 194.0	7 025.6	6 739.4	204.7	81.5	50.0	31.5		168.5	2.3	7 194.0
2001	50.0	731.1	1 237.3	7 486.8	7 354.5	7 055.0	212.2	87.2	54.2	33.0		132.3	1.8	7 333.3
2002	37.3	750.0	1 051.8	7 830.1	7 645.3	7 350.7	196.4	98.2	58.2	40.0		184.7	2.4	7 562.2
2003	34.3	778.6	1 001.1	8 162.5	7 987.7	7 703.6	182.5	101.5	61.3	40.2		174.9	2.1	7 729.9
2004	26.4	828.8	1 046.3	8 680.9	8 499.2	8 195.9	191.3	112.1	68.9	43.1		181.7	2.1	8 008.9
2005	38.8	874.3	1 207.8	9 062.0	9 029.5	8 694.1	215.0	120.4	72.5	47.9		32.5	0.4	8 121.4
2006	24.9	925.5	1 353.2	9 640.7	9 570.0	9 207.2	235.4	127.4	76.2	51.1		70.7	0.7	8 407.0
2007	31.9	965.1	1 492.8	10 170.5	10 113.1	9 710.2	265.4	137.5	81.2	56.3		57.4	0.6	8 644.0
2008	34.7	996.0	1 460.6	10 642.1	10 450.7	10 057.9	248.2	144.5	84.4	60.1		191.4	1.8	8 752.6
2006														
1st quarter	24.6	917.1	1 316.0	9 465.6	9 371.2	9 026.3	223.8	121.1	74.4	46.7		94.4	1.0	8 334.2
2nd quarter	23.8	918.9	1 341.1	9 572.1	9 518.0	9 161.9	228.5	127.6	75.6	52.0		54.2	0.6	8 360.4
3rd quarter	24.7	925.5	1 356.2	9 699.9	9 651.8	9 283.7	239.1	129.0	76.8	52.2		48.1	0.5	8 407.1
4th quarter	26.7	940.4	1 399.6	9 825.1	9 739.0	9 357.0	250.1	131.9	78.2	53.8		86.1	0.9	8 526.2
2007														
1st quarter	30.4	959.8	1 459.5	10 013.5	9 904.2	9 524.9	244.0	135.3	79.6	55.7		109.3	1.1	8 617.7
2nd quarter	31.7	959.1	1 489.4	10 088.0	10 056.9	9 657.5	262.6	136.9	80.8	56.0		31.1	0.3	8 604.5
3rd quarter	32.5	966.0	1 501.6	10 228.8	10 182.0	9 765.6	278.2	138.1	81.8	56.3		46.8	0.5	8 671.1
4th quarter	33.1	975.3	1 520.5	10 351.5	10 309.2	9 892.7	276.7	139.8	82.5	57.3		42.4	0.4	8 683.1
2008														
1st quarter	32.2	992.2	1 535.0	10 425.5	10 404.9	10 002.3	261.7	140.8	82.9	57.9		20.6	0.2	8 667.9
2nd quarter	32.4	995.4	1 346.1	10 806.0	10 538.2	10 138.0	253.8	146.4	83.7	62.7		267.9	2.5	8 891.0
3rd quarter	41.5	1 000.0	1 470.7	10 699.7	10 559.9	10 163.5	248.9	147.5	84.8	62.7		139.8	1.3	8 696.4
4th quarter	32.8	996.4	1 490.4	10 637.1	10 299.7	9 927.9	228.4	143.4	86.3	57.1		337.4	3.2	8 754.2

Table 4-2. Personal Consumption Expenditures: Current Dollars, Constant Dollars, and Price Indexes

(Billions of dollars, except as noted; quarterly data are at seasonally adjusted annual rates.)   NIPA Tables 1.1.6, 2.3.4, 2.3.5

Year and quarter	Personal consumption expenditures											
	Current dollars				Chained (2000) dollars				Chain-type price indexes (2000 = 100)			
	Total	Durable goods	Nondurable goods	Services	Total	Durable goods	Nondurable goods	Services	Total	Durable goods	Nondurable goods	Services
1950	192.2	30.7	98.2	63.3	1 152.8	. . .	. . .	. . .	16.7	39.8	19.5	11.6
1951	208.5	29.9	109.2	69.5	1 171.2	. . .	. . .	. . .	17.8	42.5	21.1	12.1
1952	219.5	29.3	114.7	75.4	1 208.2	. . .	. . .	. . .	18.2	42.9	21.3	12.6
1953	233.1	32.7	117.8	82.5	1 265.7	. . .	. . .	. . .	18.4	42.5	21.2	13.2
1954	240.0	31.9	119.7	88.4	1 291.4	. . .	. . .	. . .	18.6	41.6	21.3	13.6
1955	258.8	38.8	124.7	95.2	1 385.5	. . .	. . .	. . .	18.7	41.4	21.2	13.9
1956	271.7	38.1	130.8	102.8	1 425.4	. . .	. . .	. . .	19.1	42.5	21.5	14.3
1957	286.9	40.0	137.1	109.8	1 460.7	. . .	. . .	. . .	19.6	44.1	22.1	14.7
1958	296.2	37.4	141.7	117.0	1 472.3	. . .	. . .	. . .	20.1	44.9	22.6	15.1
1959	317.6	42.7	148.5	126.5	1 554.6	. . .	. . .	. . .	20.4	45.7	22.8	15.5
1960	331.7	43.3	152.8	135.6	1 597.4	. . .	. . .	. . .	20.8	45.4	23.1	15.9
1961	342.1	41.8	156.6	143.8	1 630.3	. . .	. . .	. . .	21.0	45.6	23.2	16.2
1962	363.3	46.9	162.8	153.6	1 711.1	. . .	. . .	. . .	21.2	45.8	23.4	16.5
1963	382.7	51.6	168.2	162.9	1 781.6	. . .	. . .	. . .	21.5	45.9	23.7	16.7
1964	411.4	56.7	178.6	176.1	1 888.4	. . .	. . .	. . .	21.8	46.1	24.0	17.0
1965	443.8	63.3	191.5	189.0	2 007.7	. . .	. . .	. . .	22.1	45.7	24.4	17.3
1966	480.9	68.3	208.7	203.8	2 121.8	. . .	. . .	. . .	22.7	45.5	25.2	17.8
1967	507.8	70.4	217.1	220.3	2 185.0	. . .	. . .	. . .	23.2	46.2	25.8	18.3
1968	558.0	80.8	235.7	241.6	2 310.5	. . .	. . .	. . .	24.2	47.7	26.8	19.1
1969	605.2	85.9	253.1	266.1	2 396.4	. . .	. . .	. . .	25.3	49.1	28.1	20.1
1970	648.5	85.0	272.0	291.5	2 451.9	. . .	. . .	. . .	26.4	50.1	29.4	21.2
1971	701.9	96.9	285.5	319.5	2 545.5	. . .	. . .	. . .	27.6	52.0	30.4	22.3
1972	770.6	110.4	308.0	352.2	2 701.3	. . .	. . .	. . .	28.5	52.5	31.4	23.3
1973	852.4	123.5	343.1	385.8	2 833.8	. . .	. . .	. . .	30.1	53.3	33.8	24.4
1974	933.4	122.3	384.5	426.6	2 812.3	. . .	. . .	. . .	33.2	56.7	38.7	26.3
1975	1 034.4	133.5	420.7	480.2	2 876.9	. . .	. . .	. . .	36.0	61.8	41.7	28.6
1976	1 151.9	158.9	458.3	534.7	3 035.5	. . .	. . .	. . .	37.9	65.3	43.3	30.6
1977	1 278.6	181.2	497.1	600.2	3 164.1	. . .	. . .	. . .	40.4	68.1	45.9	32.9
1978	1 428.5	201.7	550.2	676.6	3 303.1	. . .	. . .	. . .	43.2	72.0	49.0	35.5
1979	1 592.2	214.4	624.5	753.3	3 383.4	. . .	. . .	. . .	47.1	76.8	54.1	38.3
1980	1 757.1	214.2	696.1	846.9	3 374.1	. . .	. . .	. . .	52.1	83.3	60.4	42.3
1981	1 941.1	231.3	758.9	950.8	3 422.2	. . .	. . .	. . .	56.7	88.9	65.1	46.7
1982	2 077.3	240.2	787.6	1 049.4	3 470.3	. . .	. . .	. . .	59.9	92.4	67.0	50.5
1983	2 290.6	280.8	831.2	1 178.6	3 668.6	. . .	. . .	. . .	62.4	94.2	68.4	53.8
1984	2 503.3	326.5	884.6	1 292.2	3 863.3	. . .	. . .	. . .	64.8	95.6	70.0	56.7
1985	2 720.3	363.5	928.7	1 428.1	4 064.0	. . .	. . .	. . .	66.9	96.6	71.5	59.3
1986	2 899.7	403.0	958.4	1 538.3	4 228.9	. . .	. . .	. . .	68.6	97.7	71.3	62.0
1987	3 100.2	421.7	1 015.3	1 663.3	4 369.8	. . .	. . .	. . .	70.9	100.5	73.7	64.3
1988	3 353.6	453.6	1 083.5	1 816.5	4 546.9	. . .	. . .	. . .	73.8	101.9	76.2	67.5
1989	3 598.5	471.8	1 166.7	1 960.0	4 675.0	. . .	. . .	. . .	77.0	103.7	79.8	70.7
1990	3 839.9	474.2	1 249.9	2 115.9	4 770.3	453.5	1 484.0	2 851.7	80.5	104.6	84.2	74.2
1991	3 986.1	453.9	1 284.8	2 247.4	4 778.4	427.9	1 480.5	2 900.0	83.4	106.1	86.8	77.5
1992	4 235.3	483.6	1 330.5	2 421.2	4 934.8	453.0	1 510.1	3 000.8	85.8	106.8	88.1	80.7
1993	4 477.9	526.7	1 379.4	2 571.8	5 099.8	488.4	1 550.4	3 085.7	87.8	107.8	89.0	83.3
1994	4 743.3	582.2	1 437.2	2 723.9	5 290.7	529.4	1 603.9	3 176.6	89.7	110.0	89.6	85.7
1995	4 975.8	611.6	1 485.1	2 879.1	5 433.5	552.6	1 638.6	3 259.9	91.6	110.7	90.6	88.3
1996	5 256.8	652.6	1 555.5	3 048.7	5 619.4	595.9	1 680.4	3 356.0	93.5	109.5	92.6	90.8
1997	5 547.4	692.7	1 619.0	3 235.8	5 831.8	646.9	1 725.3	3 468.0	95.1	107.1	93.8	93.3
1998	5 879.5	750.2	1 683.6	3 445.7	6 125.8	720.3	1 794.4	3 615.0	96.0	104.2	93.8	95.3
1999	6 282.5	817.6	1 804.8	3 660.0	6 438.6	804.6	1 876.6	3 758.0	97.6	101.6	96.2	97.4
2000	6 739.4	863.3	1 947.2	3 928.8	6 739.4	863.3	1 947.2	3 928.8	100.0	100.0	100.0	100.0
2001	7 055.0	883.7	2 017.1	4 154.3	6 910.4	900.7	1 986.7	4 023.2	102.1	98.1	101.5	103.3
2002	7 350.7	923.9	2 079.6	4 347.2	7 099.3	964.8	2 037.1	4 100.4	103.5	95.8	102.1	106.0
2003	7 703.6	942.7	2 190.2	4 570.8	7 295.3	1 020.6	2 103.0	4 178.8	105.6	92.4	104.1	109.4
2004	8 195.9	983.9	2 343.7	4 868.3	7 561.4	1 084.8	2 177.6	4 311.0	108.4	90.7	107.6	112.9
2005	8 694.1	1 020.8	2 514.1	5 159.2	7 791.7	1 134.4	2 252.7	4 420.9	111.6	90.0	111.6	116.7
2006	9 207.2	1 052.1	2 685.2	5 469.9	8 029.0	1 185.1	2 335.3	4 529.9	114.7	88.8	115.0	120.8
2007	9 710.2	1 082.8	2 833.0	5 794.4	8 252.8	1 242.4	2 392.6	4 646.2	117.7	87.2	118.4	124.7
2008	10 057.9	1 023.2	2 965.1	6 069.6	8 272.1	1 188.5	2 378.4	4 714.3	121.6	86.1	124.7	128.8
2006												
1st quarter	9 026.3	1 046.5	2 629.3	5 350.5	7 947.4	1 173.1	2 310.8	4 484.7	113.6	89.2	113.8	119.3
2nd quarter	9 161.9	1 049.1	2 681.5	5 431.3	8 002.1	1 178.3	2 328.7	4 515.7	114.5	89.0	115.2	120.3
3rd quarter	9 283.7	1 054.4	2 726.3	5 502.9	8 046.3	1 188.4	2 342.0	4 537.6	115.4	88.7	116.4	121.3
4th quarter	9 357.0	1 058.2	2 703.8	5 595.0	8 119.9	1 200.7	2 359.8	4 581.5	115.2	88.1	114.6	122.1
2007												
1st quarter	9 524.9	1 076.6	2 761.5	5 686.8	8 197.2	1 227.3	2 380.1	4 616.1	116.2	87.7	116.0	123.2
2nd quarter	9 657.5	1 085.3	2 817.7	5 754.4	8 237.3	1 242.3	2 391.5	4 632.7	117.2	87.4	117.8	124.2
3rd quarter	9 765.6	1 086.2	2 846.6	5 832.8	8 278.5	1 249.4	2 398.6	4 659.8	118.0	86.9	118.7	125.2
4th quarter	9 892.7	1 083.0	2 906.2	5 903.5	8 298.2	1 250.6	2 400.2	4 676.1	119.2	86.6	121.1	126.3
2008												
1st quarter	10 002.3	1 071.0	2 950.7	5 980.6	8 316.1	1 237.0	2 397.9	4 704.3	120.3	86.6	123.1	127.1
2nd quarter	10 138.0	1 059.3	3 026.2	6 052.5	8 341.3	1 228.3	2 420.7	4 712.1	121.5	86.2	125.0	128.5
3rd quarter	10 163.5	1 016.2	3 044.6	6 102.7	8 260.6	1 180.1	2 376.3	4 711.3	123.0	86.1	128.1	129.5
4th quarter	9 927.9	946.3	2 839.0	6 142.5	8 170.5	1 108.6	2 318.6	4 729.4	121.5	85.4	122.5	129.9

. . . = Not available.

Table 4-3. Personal Consumption Expenditures by Major Type of Product

(Billions of dollars, quarterly data are at seasonally adjusted annual rates.)   **NIPA Table 2.3.5**

Year and quarter	Personal consumption expenditures, total	Durable goods				Nondurable goods					
		Total	Motor vehicles and parts	Furniture and household equipment	Other durable goods	Total	Food	Clothing and shoes	Gasoline and oil	Fuel oil and coal	Other nondurable goods
1950	192.2	30.7	13.7	13.7	3.3	98.2	53.9	19.6	5.5	3.4	15.8
1951	208.5	29.9	12.2	14.1	3.6	109.2	60.7	21.3	6.1	3.5	17.6
1952	219.5	29.3	11.4	14.0	3.9	114.7	64.1	22.0	6.8	3.5	18.4
1953	233.1	32.7	13.9	14.7	4.1	117.8	65.4	22.2	7.4	3.4	19.4
1954	240.0	31.9	12.8	14.8	4.3	119.7	66.8	22.3	7.8	3.5	19.3
1955	258.8	38.8	17.7	16.4	4.6	124.7	68.6	23.3	8.6	3.8	20.4
1956	271.7	38.1	15.8	17.3	5.0	130.8	71.4	24.4	9.4	3.9	21.7
1957	286.9	40.0	17.6	17.2	5.2	137.1	75.1	24.5	10.2	4.1	23.2
1958	296.2	37.4	15.1	16.9	5.4	141.7	77.9	24.9	10.6	4.2	24.2
1959	317.6	42.7	18.9	18.1	5.7	148.5	80.6	26.4	11.3	4.0	26.1
1960	331.7	43.3	19.7	18.0	5.7	152.8	82.3	27.0	12.0	3.8	27.7
1961	342.1	41.8	17.8	18.3	5.7	156.6	84.0	27.6	12.0	3.8	29.2
1962	363.3	46.9	21.5	19.3	6.1	162.8	86.1	29.0	12.6	3.8	31.4
1963	382.7	51.6	24.4	20.7	6.6	168.2	88.2	29.8	13.0	4.0	33.1
1964	411.4	56.7	26.0	23.2	7.5	178.6	93.5	32.4	13.6	4.1	35.0
1965	443.8	63.3	29.9	25.1	8.2	191.5	100.7	34.1	14.8	4.4	37.6
1966	480.9	68.3	30.3	28.2	9.8	208.7	109.3	37.4	16.0	4.7	41.4
1967	507.8	70.4	30.0	30.0	10.4	217.1	112.4	39.2	17.1	4.8	43.5
1968	558.0	80.8	36.1	32.9	11.8	235.7	122.2	43.2	18.6	4.7	47.0
1969	605.2	85.9	38.4	34.7	12.9	253.1	131.5	46.5	20.5	4.6	50.2
1970	648.5	85.0	35.5	35.7	13.7	272.0	143.8	47.8	21.9	4.4	54.1
1971	701.9	96.9	44.5	37.8	14.6	285.5	149.7	51.7	23.2	4.6	56.4
1972	770.6	110.4	51.1	42.4	16.9	308.0	161.4	56.4	24.4	5.1	60.8
1973	852.4	123.5	56.1	47.9	19.5	343.1	179.6	62.5	28.1	6.3	66.6
1974	933.4	122.3	49.5	51.5	21.3	384.5	201.8	66.0	36.1	7.8	72.7
1975	1 034.4	133.5	54.8	54.5	24.2	420.7	223.2	70.8	39.7	8.4	78.5
1976	1 151.9	158.9	71.3	60.2	27.4	458.3	242.5	76.6	43.0	10.1	86.0
1977	1 278.6	181.2	83.5	67.2	30.5	497.1	262.6	84.1	46.9	11.1	92.4
1978	1 428.5	201.7	93.1	74.3	34.3	550.2	289.6	94.3	50.1	11.5	104.7
1979	1 592.2	214.4	93.5	82.7	38.2	624.5	324.7	101.2	66.2	14.4	118.0
1980	1 757.1	214.2	87.0	86.7	40.5	696.1	356.0	107.3	86.7	15.4	130.6
1981	1 941.1	231.3	95.8	92.1	43.4	758.9	383.5	117.2	97.9	15.8	144.5
1982	2 077.3	240.2	102.9	93.4	43.9	787.6	403.4	120.5	94.1	14.5	155.2
1983	2 290.6	280.8	126.5	106.6	47.7	831.2	423.8	130.9	93.1	13.6	169.8
1984	2 503.3	326.5	152.1	119.0	55.4	884.6	447.4	142.5	94.6	13.9	186.3
1985	2 720.3	363.5	175.9	128.5	59.0	928.7	467.6	152.1	97.2	13.6	198.2
1986	2 899.7	403.0	194.1	143.0	66.0	958.4	492.0	163.1	80.1	11.3	211.9
1987	3 100.2	421.7	195.0	153.4	73.2	1 015.3	515.2	174.4	85.4	11.2	229.1
1988	3 353.6	453.6	209.4	163.7	80.5	1 083.5	553.5	185.5	88.3	11.7	244.5
1989	3 598.5	471.8	215.3	171.6	84.9	1 166.7	591.6	198.9	98.6	11.9	265.7
1990	3 839.9	474.2	212.8	171.6	89.8	1 249.9	636.8	204.1	111.2	12.9	285.0
1991	3 986.1	453.9	193.5	171.7	88.7	1 284.8	657.5	208.7	108.5	12.4	297.8
1992	4 235.3	483.6	213.0	178.7	91.9	1 330.5	669.3	221.9	112.4	12.2	314.7
1993	4 477.9	526.7	234.0	193.4	99.3	1 379.4	691.9	229.9	114.1	12.4	331.1
1994	4 743.3	582.2	260.5	213.4	108.3	1 437.2	720.6	238.1	116.2	12.8	349.5
1995	4 975.8	611.6	266.7	228.6	116.3	1 485.1	740.9	241.7	120.2	13.1	369.2
1996	5 256.8	652.6	284.9	242.9	124.8	1 555.5	768.7	250.2	130.4	14.3	391.9
1997	5 547.4	692.7	305.1	256.2	131.4	1 619.0	796.2	258.1	134.4	13.3	416.9
1998	5 879.5	750.2	336.1	273.1	141.0	1 683.6	829.8	270.9	122.4	11.5	449.0
1999	6 282.5	817.6	370.8	293.9	153.0	1 804.8	873.1	286.3	137.9	11.9	495.6
2000	6 739.4	863.3	386.5	312.9	163.9	1 947.2	925.2	297.7	175.7	15.8	532.9
2001	7 055.0	883.7	407.9	312.1	163.7	2 017.1	967.9	297.7	171.6	15.4	564.4
2002	7 350.7	923.9	429.3	323.1	171.6	2 079.6	1 001.9	303.5	164.5	14.2	595.5
2003	7 703.6	942.7	431.7	331.5	179.4	2 190.2	1 046.0	310.9	192.7	16.9	623.7
2004	8 195.9	983.9	436.8	355.7	191.3	2 343.7	1 113.1	325.0	231.4	18.3	655.9
2005	8 694.1	1 020.8	443.1	377.3	200.3	2 514.1	1 181.2	341.5	283.6	21.0	686.8
2006	9 207.2	1 052.1	434.0	403.5	214.6	2 685.2	1 257.4	360.2	313.8	22.4	731.4
2007	9 710.2	1 082.8	440.4	415.3	227.0	2 833.0	1 329.1	374.0	340.6	26.3	762.9
2008	10 057.9	1 023.2	379.9	411.7	231.6	2 965.1	1 399.2	373.6	381.8	30.0	780.5
2006											
1st quarter	9 026.3	1 046.5	431.5	401.4	213.6	2 629.3	1 233.2	354.4	305.3	20.1	716.3
2nd quarter	9 161.9	1 049.1	433.9	402.0	213.2	2 681.5	1 252.2	357.9	320.2	23.1	728.2
3rd quarter	9 283.7	1 054.4	436.6	403.7	214.2	2 726.3	1 265.4	362.5	338.4	23.8	736.2
4th quarter	9 357.0	1 058.2	434.0	406.7	217.4	2 703.8	1 278.8	366.1	291.2	22.8	744.9
2007											
1st quarter	9 524.9	1 076.6	442.0	413.7	220.9	2 761.5	1 297.7	374.6	307.1	25.4	756.7
2nd quarter	9 657.5	1 085.3	444.0	415.2	226.2	2 817.7	1 321.2	372.9	336.9	25.8	761.0
3rd quarter	9 765.6	1 086.2	437.9	417.2	231.1	2 846.6	1 337.9	375.4	341.6	25.5	766.1
4th quarter	9 892.7	1 083.0	437.8	415.3	229.9	2 906.2	1 359.8	373.2	376.7	28.6	767.9
2008											
1st quarter	10 002.3	1 071.0	424.7	415.1	231.3	2 950.7	1 380.5	375.5	393.4	30.2	771.1
2nd quarter	10 138.0	1 059.3	400.6	423.0	235.7	3 026.2	1 416.3	382.4	409.5	32.3	785.7
3rd quarter	10 163.5	1 016.2	370.7	411.2	234.3	3 044.6	1 418.4	374.4	432.7	30.9	788.2
4th quarter	9 927.9	946.3	323.8	397.4	225.2	2 839.0	1 381.7	362.1	291.4	26.7	777.1

Table 4-3. Personal Consumption Expenditures by Major Type of Product—*Continued*

(Billions of dollars, quarterly data are at seasonally adjusted annual rates.)   **NIPA Table 2.3.5**

Year and quarter	Services								
	Total	Housing	Household operation			Transportation	Medical care services	Recreation	Other services
			Total	Electricity and gas	Other household operation				
1950	63.3	21.7	9.5	3.3	6.2	6.0	7.2	3.9	15.0
1951	69.5	24.3	10.4	3.7	6.7	7.0	7.7	4.0	16.0
1952	75.4	27.0	11.2	4.1	7.1	7.4	8.5	4.3	17.1
1953	82.5	29.9	12.1	4.5	7.6	8.0	9.5	4.5	18.5
1954	88.4	32.3	12.7	5.0	7.7	8.2	10.5	4.8	20.0
1955	95.2	34.4	14.2	5.5	8.7	8.6	11.2	5.2	21.7
1956	102.8	36.7	15.4	6.1	9.3	9.2	12.1	5.6	23.8
1957	109.8	39.3	16.4	6.5	9.9	9.7	13.4	5.6	25.4
1958	117.0	42.0	17.5	7.1	10.4	9.9	14.8	5.8	27.0
1959	126.5	45.0	18.7	7.6	11.1	10.6	16.4	6.4	29.4
1960	135.6	48.2	20.3	8.3	12.0	11.2	17.7	6.9	31.3
1961	143.8	51.2	21.2	8.8	12.4	11.6	19.0	7.4	33.3
1962	153.6	54.7	22.4	9.4	13.0	12.3	21.2	8.0	35.0
1963	162.9	58.0	23.6	9.9	13.8	12.9	23.0	8.5	36.9
1964	176.1	61.4	25.0	10.4	14.6	13.8	26.4	9.1	40.4
1965	189.0	65.4	26.5	10.9	15.6	14.7	28.6	9.6	44.2
1966	203.8	69.5	28.1	11.5	16.6	15.9	31.5	10.4	48.4
1967	220.3	74.1	30.0	12.2	17.8	17.4	34.7	11.1	53.0
1968	241.6	79.8	32.3	13.0	19.2	19.3	40.1	12.5	57.7
1969	266.1	86.9	35.0	14.1	21.0	21.6	45.8	13.8	62.9
1970	291.5	94.1	37.8	15.3	22.4	24.0	51.7	15.1	68.8
1971	319.5	102.8	41.1	16.9	24.2	26.8	58.4	16.3	74.0
1972	352.2	112.6	45.4	18.8	26.7	29.6	65.6	17.6	81.4
1973	385.8	123.3	49.9	20.4	29.5	31.6	73.3	19.7	88.0
1974	426.6	134.8	55.8	24.0	31.8	34.1	82.3	22.5	97.1
1975	480.2	147.7	64.0	29.2	34.8	37.9	95.6	25.4	109.7
1976	534.7	162.2	72.5	33.2	39.3	42.5	109.1	28.4	120.1
1977	600.2	180.2	81.8	38.5	43.3	48.7	125.3	31.4	132.8
1978	676.6	202.4	91.2	43.0	48.2	53.4	143.1	34.7	151.8
1979	753.3	227.3	100.3	47.8	52.5	59.9	161.0	38.8	166.2
1980	846.9	256.2	113.7	57.5	56.2	65.2	184.4	43.6	183.8
1981	950.8	289.7	126.8	64.8	62.0	70.3	216.7	50.6	196.7
1982	1 049.4	315.2	142.5	74.2	68.3	72.9	243.3	56.8	218.8
1983	1 178.6	341.0	157.0	82.4	74.6	81.1	274.3	63.6	261.6
1984	1 292.2	374.5	169.4	86.5	82.9	93.2	303.2	69.7	282.1
1985	1 428.1	412.7	181.8	90.8	91.1	104.5	331.5	77.7	319.8
1986	1 538.3	448.4	187.7	89.2	98.5	111.1	357.5	83.7	349.9
1987	1 663.3	483.7	195.4	90.9	104.5	120.9	392.2	90.0	381.2
1988	1 816.5	521.5	207.3	96.3	111.0	133.4	442.8	102.1	409.4
1989	1 960.0	557.4	221.1	101.0	120.0	142.0	492.5	114.3	432.8
1990	2 115.9	597.9	227.3	101.0	126.2	147.7	556.0	125.9	461.0
1991	2 247.4	631.1	238.6	107.4	131.2	145.3	608.9	132.9	490.6
1992	2 421.2	658.5	250.7	108.9	141.9	157.7	672.2	146.6	535.5
1993	2 571.8	683.9	269.9	118.2	151.7	172.7	715.1	160.4	569.8
1994	2 723.9	726.1	286.2	120.7	165.5	190.6	752.9	171.4	596.7
1995	2 879.1	764.4	298.7	122.2	176.5	207.7	797.9	187.9	622.5
1996	3 048.7	800.1	318.5	129.4	189.1	226.5	833.5	202.5	667.6
1997	3 235.8	842.6	337.0	131.3	205.6	245.7	873.0	215.1	722.4
1998	3 445.7	894.6	350.5	129.8	220.7	259.5	921.4	229.3	790.5
1999	3 660.0	948.4	364.8	130.6	234.1	276.4	961.1	248.6	860.7
2000	3 928.8	1 006.5	390.1	143.3	246.8	291.3	1 026.8	268.3	945.9
2001	4 154.3	1 073.7	409.0	156.7	252.3	292.8	1 113.8	284.1	980.7
2002	4 347.2	1 123.1	407.7	152.5	255.2	288.4	1 206.2	299.1	1 022.7
2003	4 570.8	1 161.8	429.4	167.3	262.1	297.3	1 300.5	317.7	1 064.0
2004	4 868.3	1 226.8	449.0	175.4	273.5	308.2	1 395.5	341.8	1 147.1
2005	5 159.2	1 298.7	479.7	198.3	281.3	324.3	1 491.3	357.8	1 207.4
2006	5 469.9	1 388.7	502.4	209.6	292.9	341.2	1 575.8	380.1	1 281.6
2007	5 794.4	1 460.9	525.7	218.8	306.9	357.0	1 681.1	403.4	1 366.3
2008	6 069.6	1 513.7	553.0	232.3	320.6	373.0	1 781.2	412.6	1 436.1
2006									
1st quarter	5 350.5	1 351.8	495.5	208.0	287.5	334.8	1 548.5	369.2	1 250.6
2nd quarter	5 431.3	1 377.9	499.7	209.0	290.7	340.2	1 566.4	374.2	1 272.9
3rd quarter	5 502.9	1 401.8	506.1	211.6	294.5	343.0	1 583.0	383.4	1 285.6
4th quarter	5 595.0	1 423.5	508.4	209.7	298.8	347.0	1 605.1	393.7	1 317.3
2007									
1st quarter	5 686.8	1 440.1	517.5	216.8	300.7	350.6	1 649.1	396.0	1 333.5
2nd quarter	5 754.4	1 453.8	524.0	219.0	305.0	354.2	1 663.0	402.0	1 357.4
3rd quarter	5 832.8	1 466.9	526.9	218.3	308.6	360.4	1 690.2	405.9	1 382.5
4th quarter	5 903.5	1 482.7	534.3	221.1	313.2	362.9	1 721.9	409.7	1 392.0
2008									
1st quarter	5 980.6	1 495.1	541.7	228.1	313.6	368.8	1 746.6	408.2	1 420.2
2nd quarter	6 052.5	1 508.8	554.5	236.3	318.1	372.9	1 769.3	412.3	1 434.6
3rd quarter	6 102.7	1 520.9	555.8	231.9	323.9	376.8	1 792.9	415.8	1 440.4
4th quarter	6 142.5	1 529.7	559.9	233.0	326.9	373.6	1 816.1	413.9	1 449.3

Table 4-4. Chain-Type Quantity Indexes for Personal Consumption Expenditures by Major Type of Product

(Index numbers, 2000 = 100, seasonally adjusted.)   NIPA Table 2.3.3

Year and quarter	Personal consumption expenditures, total	Durable goods				Nondurable goods					
		Total	Motor vehicles and parts	Furniture and household equipment	Other durable goods	Total	Food	Clothing and shoes	Gasoline and oil	Fuel oil and coal	Other nondurable goods
1950	17.1	8.9	14.4	5.6	6.8	25.9	34.3	15.0	20.5	231.8	17.0
1951	17.4	8.1	12.2	5.3	6.9	26.6	35.2	14.9	22.3	231.2	17.7
1952	17.9	7.9	11.0	5.4	7.4	27.6	36.4	15.7	24.1	224.7	18.5
1953	18.8	8.9	13.6	5.6	7.7	28.5	37.7	15.9	25.4	217.2	19.2
1954	19.2	8.9	13.0	5.8	8.1	28.9	38.5	15.9	26.2	221.4	19.1
1955	20.6	10.8	17.8	6.5	8.9	30.3	40.1	16.7	28.5	235.3	20.1
1956	21.2	10.4	15.1	6.8	9.6	31.3	41.4	17.1	30.2	235.8	21.0
1957	21.7	10.5	15.8	6.6	9.7	31.9	42.2	17.0	31.4	233.8	21.7
1958	21.8	9.7	13.1	6.5	9.9	32.2	42.2	17.1	32.9	242.7	22.2
1959	23.1	10.8	15.6	7.0	10.5	33.5	43.7	18.0	34.6	231.8	23.5
1960	23.7	11.0	16.6	6.9	10.4	34.0	44.0	18.2	35.8	222.0	24.6
1961	24.2	10.6	14.9	7.0	10.3	34.6	44.5	18.5	36.1	211.4	25.9
1962	25.4	11.9	17.7	7.5	11.0	35.7	45.1	19.4	37.7	210.9	27.7
1963	26.4	13.0	20.0	8.0	11.7	36.5	45.6	19.7	38.8	221.3	29.0
1964	28.0	14.2	21.1	9.0	13.1	38.2	47.4	21.3	40.9	230.0	30.3
1965	29.8	16.0	24.5	9.9	14.5	40.3	50.0	22.1	42.9	240.8	32.1
1966	31.5	17.4	25.0	11.2	17.2	42.5	52.1	23.6	45.5	247.8	34.7
1967	32.4	17.6	24.4	11.7	18.0	43.2	52.8	23.8	47.0	247.9	35.6
1968	34.3	19.6	28.4	12.4	19.6	45.1	55.4	24.8	50.3	234.7	37.1
1969	35.6	20.3	29.6	12.8	20.5	46.3	56.8	25.2	53.7	222.4	38.2
1970	36.4	19.6	26.6	12.9	21.5	47.4	58.5	24.9	57.0	206.9	39.5
1971	37.8	21.6	31.7	13.4	21.8	48.3	59.1	26.1	59.8	199.9	39.7
1972	40.1	24.3	36.3	14.9	24.6	50.4	61.0	27.9	62.2	219.7	41.8
1973	42.0	26.8	39.6	16.5	27.7	52.1	61.2	29.8	65.4	238.6	44.6
1974	41.7	25.0	32.8	16.7	28.5	51.0	60.2	29.4	62.2	188.3	44.5
1975	42.7	25.0	33.0	16.3	29.6	51.8	61.7	30.4	64.1	184.8	43.0
1976	45.0	28.2	40.0	17.4	31.9	54.3	64.9	31.8	66.6	207.5	44.6
1977	47.0	30.8	44.2	18.9	34.2	55.6	66.1	33.6	68.7	200.9	45.3
1978	49.0	32.4	46.1	20.0	36.5	57.7	66.8	36.9	70.3	199.3	48.6
1979	50.2	32.3	43.1	21.1	37.9	59.2	68.1	38.8	69.3	185.2	51.4
1980	50.1	29.8	37.3	20.7	35.1	59.1	68.7	39.7	65.4	143.2	52.2
1981	50.8	30.1	38.1	20.7	35.6	59.8	68.8	42.2	66.3	120.1	53.3
1982	51.5	30.1	39.1	20.3	35.0	60.4	69.9	42.8	67.2	111.5	53.0
1983	54.4	34.5	46.7	23.1	37.0	62.4	71.9	46.0	68.7	111.6	54.3
1984	57.3	39.6	54.5	25.8	42.4	64.9	73.5	49.9	70.8	111.2	57.4
1985	60.3	43.6	61.6	28.1	44.4	66.7	75.2	52.2	72.2	112.5	58.8
1986	62.7	47.8	66.2	31.6	48.9	69.1	77.0	56.4	75.7	116.7	60.5
1987	64.8	48.6	63.8	33.9	52.0	70.7	78.0	58.4	77.8	115.1	62.9
1988	67.5	51.5	67.4	36.2	54.8	73.0	81.1	60.2	79.8	119.4	64.3
1989	69.4	52.7	67.3	38.1	56.0	75.0	82.5	63.6	81.5	116.5	66.4
1990	70.8	52.5	66.3	38.3	56.6	76.2	84.8	63.2	80.8	105.8	67.7
1991	70.9	49.6	58.6	38.7	54.1	76.0	84.7	63.4	79.9	104.8	67.4
1992	73.2	52.5	63.4	40.8	55.0	77.6	85.2	66.9	83.1	107.3	68.7
1993	75.7	56.6	67.1	45.1	59.2	79.6	86.7	69.7	85.2	109.6	71.1
1994	78.5	61.3	71.5	50.1	63.6	82.4	88.8	73.4	86.3	114.9	74.6
1995	80.6	64.0	70.4	55.4	67.8	84.2	89.4	76.4	87.9	118.2	77.7
1996	83.4	69.0	73.8	61.8	73.0	86.3	90.2	80.2	89.9	116.5	81.3
1997	86.5	74.9	78.8	69.1	77.7	88.6	91.4	82.6	92.7	107.0	85.7
1998	90.9	83.4	87.7	78.2	83.9	92.2	93.6	88.4	96.9	101.3	90.3
1999	95.5	93.2	96.4	89.7	92.6	96.4	96.6	95.0	100.4	103.7	95.4
2000	100.0	100.0	100.0	100.0	100.0	100.0	100.0	100.0	100.0	100.0	100.0
2001	102.5	104.3	105.0	106.0	99.6	102.0	101.6	102.0	101.5	95.8	103.1
2002	105.3	111.8	111.0	116.4	105.2	104.6	103.2	106.9	103.6	98.1	106.4
2003	108.2	118.2	114.4	127.1	111.8	108.0	105.7	112.3	104.3	97.4	111.3
2004	112.2	125.7	116.6	142.2	119.0	111.8	109.1	117.8	106.3	92.0	116.0
2005	115.6	131.4	116.4	156.9	125.1	115.7	113.2	125.1	106.7	83.2	119.6
2006	119.1	137.3	113.3	175.8	133.0	119.9	117.8	132.5	104.9	78.6	125.0
2007	122.5	143.9	115.6	189.8	139.3	122.9	120.0	138.7	105.0	86.5	129.0
2008	122.7	137.7	100.2	196.3	138.2	122.1	119.9	139.2	101.1	75.2	129.4
2006											
1st quarter	117.9	135.9	112.7	171.9	133.4	118.7	116.5	131.1	106.0	72.9	123.0
2nd quarter	118.7	136.5	113.1	174.0	132.1	119.6	117.9	131.3	104.3	79.4	124.5
3rd quarter	119.4	137.7	113.7	177.0	132.2	120.3	118.2	133.0	104.5	80.1	125.6
4th quarter	120.5	139.1	113.7	180.4	134.1	121.2	118.8	134.5	104.7	82.1	127.0
2007											
1st quarter	121.6	142.2	116.3	185.4	135.5	122.2	119.2	137.5	105.4	90.4	128.3
2nd quarter	122.2	143.9	116.8	188.0	138.9	122.8	120.0	138.4	104.9	87.3	129.0
3rd quarter	122.8	144.7	114.7	192.0	142.1	123.2	120.1	139.9	105.1	83.7	129.6
4th quarter	123.1	144.9	114.5	193.9	140.8	123.3	120.9	138.8	104.6	84.4	129.1
2008											
1st quarter	123.4	143.3	111.3	194.7	140.0	123.1	121.3	139.8	103.2	80.8	128.5
2nd quarter	123.8	142.3	105.4	201.2	140.8	124.3	122.5	143.5	102.0	75.5	130.4
3rd quarter	122.6	136.7	97.5	196.9	139.2	122.0	120.2	138.5	98.6	70.0	130.5
4th quarter	121.2	128.4	86.6	192.4	132.8	119.1	115.5	135.1	100.4	74.5	127.9

Table 4-4. Chain-Type Quantity Indexes for Personal Consumption Expenditures by Major Type of Product
—Continued

(Index numbers, 2000 = 100, seasonally adjusted.)

NIPA Table 2.3.3

Year and quarter	Services								
	Total	Housing	Household operation			Transportation	Medical care services	Recreation	Other services
			Total	Electricity and gas	Other household operation				
1950	13.9	15.0	14.2	14.1	13.6	18.7	10.0	10.0	15.4
1951	14.6	16.0	15.1	15.8	14.1	20.3	10.5	10.1	15.5
1952	15.3	17.1	15.6	17.2	14.0	20.6	11.0	10.3	16.1
1953	15.9	18.0	16.3	18.5	14.5	21.2	11.5	10.4	16.7
1954	16.6	18.9	17.0	20.3	14.5	20.9	12.3	10.6	17.4
1955	17.4	19.8	18.6	21.9	16.1	21.7	12.8	11.1	18.1
1956	18.3	20.8	19.9	23.8	17.1	22.6	13.6	11.7	18.8
1957	19.0	21.8	20.7	25.3	17.5	23.0	14.4	11.3	19.4
1958	19.8	22.9	21.4	26.7	17.9	22.6	15.3	11.3	20.2
1959	20.8	24.1	22.3	28.3	18.4	23.5	16.5	12.0	21.2
1960	21.7	25.4	23.4	29.9	19.2	24.3	17.1	12.7	21.9
1961	22.6	26.6	24.2	31.4	19.7	24.6	17.9	13.3	22.8
1962	23.7	28.1	25.4	33.6	20.4	25.5	19.4	14.0	23.3
1963	24.8	29.4	26.5	35.2	21.1	26.6	20.7	14.6	24.2
1964	26.3	30.8	27.8	37.1	22.1	28.0	23.0	15.2	25.8
1965	27.7	32.5	29.2	38.8	23.2	29.2	24.1	15.6	27.5
1966	29.1	34.0	30.6	41.0	24.3	30.8	25.4	16.3	28.9
1967	30.6	35.6	32.2	43.3	25.5	32.5	26.4	16.8	30.7
1968	32.1	37.4	33.6	45.8	26.3	34.5	28.4	17.8	31.8
1969	33.7	39.4	35.3	48.5	27.5	36.3	30.4	18.8	32.4
1970	35.0	40.8	36.6	50.8	28.3	37.3	32.1	19.6	33.7
1971	36.4	42.6	37.2	52.4	28.5	38.7	34.1	20.3	34.6
1972	38.5	45.1	39.2	55.5	29.9	41.1	36.5	21.3	36.2
1973	40.3	47.4	41.1	57.1	31.8	42.2	39.1	23.1	37.0
1974	41.2	49.8	41.6	57.8	32.1	42.5	40.5	24.7	36.1
1975	42.7	51.3	43.5	61.0	33.4	42.9	42.5	26.1	37.4
1976	44.5	52.8	45.3	63.2	34.9	44.2	44.5	27.9	39.1
1977	46.4	54.2	47.7	66.3	36.9	47.4	46.7	29.7	40.8
1978	48.6	56.8	50.2	69.2	39.1	49.0	48.9	31.1	42.6
1979	50.0	59.1	51.7	69.7	41.2	50.4	50.9	32.5	42.8
1980	50.9	60.9	53.1	71.6	42.2	47.9	52.7	34.1	42.5
1981	51.8	62.5	52.6	70.4	42.1	46.5	55.4	37.1	41.9
1982	52.9	62.8	53.0	71.3	42.3	45.9	56.2	39.7	44.5
1983	55.8	64.1	54.7	73.4	43.7	48.9	58.5	42.7	50.1
1984	58.0	66.8	56.1	73.9	45.8	53.6	60.2	44.8	52.0
1985	61.3	69.5	58.4	75.8	48.3	58.4	62.7	48.1	56.7
1986	63.1	71.3	59.4	75.0	50.5	60.7	65.2	49.9	58.1
1987	65.8	73.5	62.1	77.7	53.2	63.1	68.6	51.9	61.0
1988	68.5	75.8	65.0	81.6	55.4	66.3	72.0	56.7	62.5
1989	70.6	77.8	67.6	83.3	58.7	67.2	74.0	60.7	64.3
1990	72.6	79.7	68.3	81.9	60.5	67.2	77.7	63.6	65.7
1991	73.8	81.5	69.2	84.5	60.4	64.0	80.3	64.0	66.7
1992	76.4	82.7	71.1	84.0	63.8	66.7	84.1	68.6	69.1
1993	78.5	83.6	74.6	88.5	66.8	69.5	85.4	72.8	72.0
1994	80.9	86.4	77.8	89.9	70.9	75.0	86.4	76.3	73.6
1995	83.0	88.2	80.2	90.8	74.2	79.6	88.3	81.7	74.5
1996	85.4	89.5	83.9	94.0	78.2	85.0	89.8	85.2	77.2
1997	88.3	91.7	87.2	93.3	83.9	90.4	91.8	87.8	80.8
1998	92.0	94.3	91.5	95.4	89.4	93.4	94.5	91.3	86.9
1999	95.7	97.2	95.3	96.4	94.7	97.3	96.3	96.1	92.8
2000	100.0	100.0	100.0	100.0	100.0	100.0	100.0	100.0	100.0
2001	102.4	102.7	100.2	98.3	101.4	98.9	104.7	102.5	101.5
2002	104.4	103.5	100.8	101.1	100.6	96.2	110.7	104.8	102.2
2003	106.4	104.5	102.2	102.9	101.8	96.3	115.0	108.4	103.1
2004	109.7	107.7	104.7	104.1	105.1	97.7	118.5	113.7	106.9
2005	112.5	111.1	106.4	106.6	106.3	98.8	122.4	115.9	108.9
2006	115.3	114.7	106.0	103.5	107.8	100.9	125.6	119.5	111.6
2007	118.3	116.4	108.0	105.4	109.8	102.7	129.3	124.9	115.2
2008	120.0	117.5	107.7	103.3	111.0	102.1	133.9	123.8	116.9
2006									
1st quarter	114.1	113.6	104.2	100.6	106.9	99.8	125.0	117.3	110.4
2nd quarter	114.9	114.4	106.0	103.9	107.6	100.7	125.4	117.8	111.2
3rd quarter	115.5	115.1	106.8	104.8	108.2	101.0	125.6	119.7	111.6
4th quarter	116.6	115.7	107.0	104.5	108.7	102.0	126.5	123.4	113.2
2007									
1st quarter	117.5	116.1	107.5	105.7	108.7	102.2	128.2	124.0	114.3
2nd quarter	117.9	116.3	107.6	105.1	109.4	102.6	128.5	124.7	115.1
3rd quarter	118.6	116.5	108.0	105.4	109.9	103.2	129.7	125.5	115.9
4th quarter	119.0	116.8	108.7	105.5	111.0	103.0	130.9	125.4	115.6
2008									
1st quarter	119.7	117.0	109.2	107.5	110.4	103.4	132.5	123.9	116.8
2nd quarter	119.9	117.5	108.0	104.4	110.7	102.6	133.5	124.3	116.7
3rd quarter	119.9	117.7	105.7	98.5	111.3	102.0	134.3	123.8	116.8
4th quarter	120.4	117.8	107.8	102.9	111.5	100.3	135.3	123.5	117.2

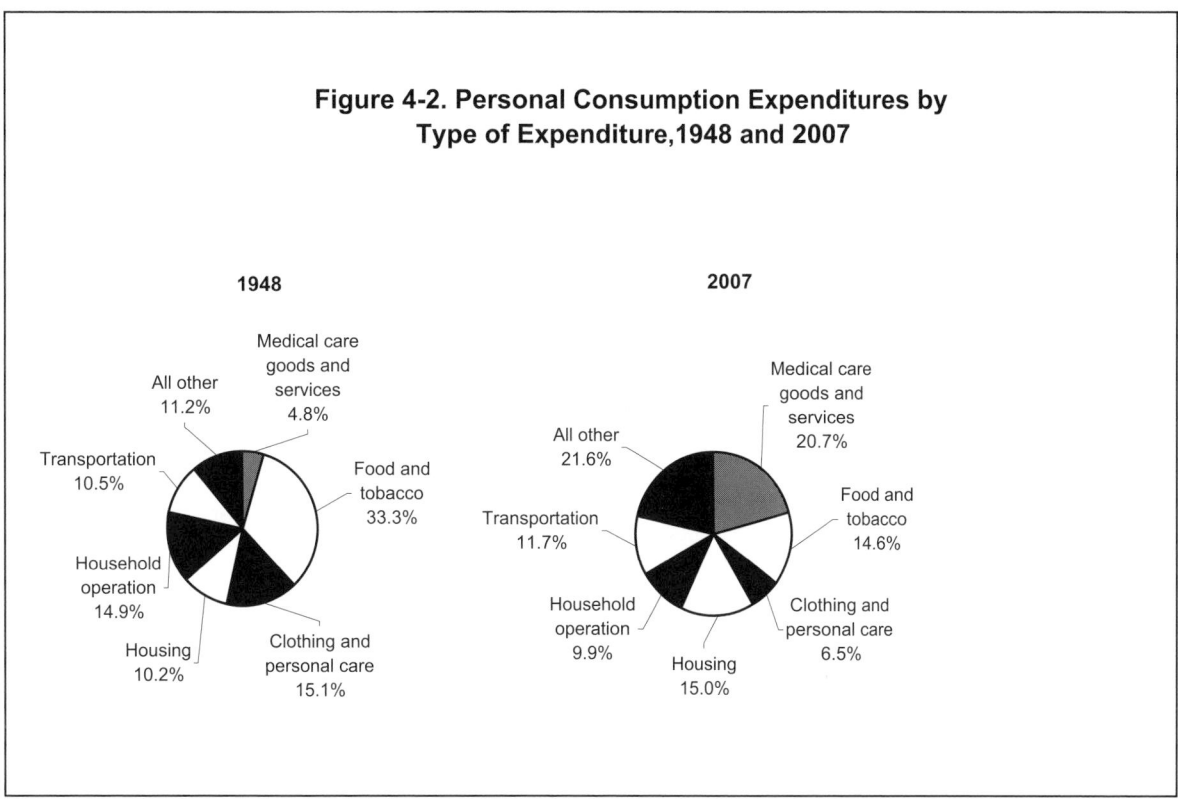

Figure 4-2. Personal Consumption Expenditures by
Type of Expenditure, 1948 and 2007

- Spending for medical care goods and services in 2007 made up 20.7 percent of personal consumption spending—more than four times the percentage in 1948. This includes medical care payments made by government and private insurance on behalf of individuals as well as out-of-pocket consumer payments. (Table 4-5)

- In 2007, much smaller shares were required for food and tobacco and for clothing and personal care than in 1948, as seen in the figure. Household operation claimed a smaller share of the total, but housing itself took a larger share. Transportation rose somewhat, and the "all other" share nearly doubled. It should be noted that the nonprofit sector is included in this tabulation, and its spending on education, research, religious, and welfare activities is included in the "all other" category. (Table 4-5)

Table 4-5. Personal Consumption Expenditures by Type of Expenditure

(Billions of dollars.) NIPA Table 2.5.5

Year	Personal consumption expenditures	Food and tobacco	Clothing, accessories, and jewelry	Personal care	Housing	Household operation	Medical care	Personal business	Transportation	Recreation	Education and research	Religious and welfare activities	Foreign travel and other, net
1939	67.2	20.9	8.4	1.0	9.4	9.6	3.1	3.0	6.5	3.5	0.7	1.0	0.2
1940	71.3	22.0	8.9	1.0	9.7	10.4	3.3	3.1	7.3	3.8	0.8	1.0	0.1
1941	81.1	25.4	10.5	1.2	10.4	11.8	3.6	3.2	8.6	4.3	0.8	1.1	0.1
1942	89.0	30.7	13.1	1.4	11.2	12.7	4.1	3.3	5.6	4.7	0.9	1.2	0.2
1943	99.9	35.8	16.0	1.6	11.8	13.1	4.5	3.7	5.6	5.0	1.1	1.5	0.3
1944	108.7	39.3	17.5	1.8	12.3	14.0	5.1	3.9	5.9	5.4	1.1	1.7	0.6
1945	120.0	43.5	19.6	2.0	12.8	15.5	5.4	4.1	6.8	6.2	1.1	1.8	1.2
1946	144.3	50.7	22.0	2.1	14.2	19.9	6.6	4.7	12.4	8.6	1.2	2.0	-0.1
1947	162.0	56.1	22.8	2.2	16.0	23.7	7.4	5.2	15.8	9.3	1.5	2.1	0.0
1948	175.0	58.2	24.2	2.3	17.9	26.1	8.4	5.6	18.4	9.7	1.7	2.3	0.3
1949	178.5	56.6	23.3	2.3	19.6	25.7	8.7	5.8	21.7	10.0	1.8	2.3	0.6
1950	192.2	58.1	23.7	2.4	21.7	29.1	9.4	6.4	25.2	11.2	1.9	2.4	0.7
1951	208.5	65.2	25.6	2.7	24.3	31.1	10.2	6.9	25.3	11.7	2.1	2.6	0.9
1952	219.5	69.0	26.6	2.9	27.0	31.5	11.2	7.2	25.6	12.3	2.2	3.0	1.1
1953	233.1	70.5	27.0	3.1	29.9	33.0	12.2	8.0	29.4	13.1	2.3	3.1	1.5
1954	240.0	71.7	27.2	3.4	32.3	33.7	13.3	8.8	28.8	13.6	2.5	3.3	1.5
1955	258.8	73.6	28.4	3.7	34.4	37.3	14.2	9.8	35.0	14.6	2.7	3.5	1.6
1956	271.7	76.7	29.7	4.1	36.7	39.8	15.5	10.7	34.4	15.5	3.0	3.9	1.7
1957	286.9	80.7	30.0	4.6	39.3	41.2	17.1	11.4	37.4	15.9	3.4	4.1	1.7
1958	296.2	83.9	30.3	4.9	42.0	42.4	18.7	12.2	35.5	16.3	3.7	4.4	1.9
1959	317.6	87.2	32.0	5.2	45.0	45.0	20.6	13.1	40.7	17.7	4.0	5.1	2.0
1960	331.7	89.2	32.7	5.6	48.2	46.7	22.2	14.1	42.8	18.5	4.4	5.2	2.1
1961	342.1	91.1	33.5	6.1	51.2	48.2	23.9	15.3	41.5	19.3	4.7	5.3	2.0
1962	363.3	93.3	35.0	6.7	54.7	51.0	26.5	15.9	46.4	20.8	5.1	5.5	2.3
1963	382.7	95.7	36.0	7.0	58.0	54.0	28.7	16.7	50.2	22.4	5.6	5.7	2.5
1964	411.4	101.1	39.1	7.5	61.4	58.4	32.3	18.4	53.3	24.6	6.2	6.6	2.6
1965	443.8	108.8	41.4	8.1	65.4	62.1	34.7	20.1	59.4	26.9	7.0	7.1	2.9
1966	480.9	117.8	45.5	9.0	69.5	67.2	38.0	22.0	62.2	30.9	8.0	7.7	3.1
1967	507.8	121.4	47.8	9.8	74.1	70.8	41.4	23.7	64.5	33.1	8.9	8.5	3.8
1968	558.0	131.6	52.5	10.5	79.8	76.3	47.7	26.0	73.9	36.7	10.1	9.3	3.7
1969	605.2	141.3	56.2	10.9	86.9	81.1	54.2	28.9	80.4	40.0	11.3	10.0	4.0
1970	648.5	154.6	57.6	11.5	94.1	84.8	61.3	31.8	81.5	43.1	12.7	11.0	4.5
1971	701.9	161.0	61.8	11.7	102.8	90.1	68.5	34.3	94.5	46.0	13.9	12.5	4.8
1972	770.6	173.6	67.1	12.3	112.6	99.5	76.7	37.7	105.1	51.5	15.3	14.0	5.2
1973	852.4	192.9	74.7	13.6	123.3	111.4	85.3	41.3	115.8	57.6	16.9	15.0	4.7
1974	933.4	215.9	79.3	14.8	134.8	123.6	95.5	46.6	119.7	63.4	18.5	16.7	4.7
1975	1 034.4	238.3	85.6	16.1	147.7	135.7	109.9	54.9	132.4	70.5	20.6	18.3	4.4
1976	1 151.9	259.3	93.7	17.5	162.2	152.0	124.7	60.5	156.8	78.2	22.5	20.8	3.8
1977	1 278.6	279.6	102.8	19.9	180.2	170.5	142.1	67.2	179.1	85.5	24.2	23.2	4.3
1978	1 428.5	307.8	115.1	21.9	202.4	189.6	162.3	78.9	196.7	96.1	26.8	26.6	4.3
1979	1 592.2	343.9	123.4	23.8	227.3	212.0	183.3	85.9	219.6	108.9	29.8	30.3	4.1
1980	1 757.1	376.8	132.3	25.5	256.2	233.3	209.6	95.2	238.9	117.5	33.5	34.8	3.5
1981	1 941.1	406.3	143.8	27.1	289.7	254.5	245.2	102.3	264.0	130.8	37.6	39.2	0.4
1982	2 077.3	427.7	147.0	28.0	315.2	271.9	274.8	115.1	270.0	140.9	41.3	43.0	2.5
1983	2 290.6	451.3	161.1	32.2	341.0	296.7	310.0	143.6	300.7	156.9	45.4	46.1	5.4
1984	2 503.3	476.6	175.8	35.5	374.5	322.8	343.7	151.8	339.9	174.8	49.4	51.8	6.6
1985	2 720.3	498.4	188.3	38.8	412.7	343.6	376.4	177.5	377.7	189.7	53.9	55.7	7.7
1986	2 899.7	524.2	204.1	42.3	448.4	359.6	407.4	198.3	385.2	206.9	58.1	61.9	3.3
1987	3 100.2	549.8	218.9	46.5	483.7	376.3	447.6	213.6	401.3	226.8	63.2	66.7	6.1
1988	3 353.6	588.2	235.7	50.1	521.5	398.6	505.0	224.2	431.1	251.7	70.2	74.4	2.8
1989	3 598.5	630.3	252.5	53.8	557.4	423.2	561.9	236.3	455.9	272.4	77.7	81.0	-3.7
1990	3 839.9	677.8	261.5	56.9	597.9	433.3	635.1	250.9	471.7	290.2	83.7	88.7	-7.7
1991	3 986.1	699.9	263.5	58.5	631.1	444.3	692.9	279.7	447.3	302.0	89.3	92.9	-15.2
1992	4 235.3	717.3	280.9	62.0	658.5	466.0	761.1	306.7	483.2	321.3	96.0	102.3	-20.0
1993	4 477.9	740.6	293.4	64.4	683.9	497.5	809.0	330.0	520.8	351.0	101.5	106.5	-20.6
1994	4 743.3	767.9	306.3	68.1	726.1	529.6	853.3	336.1	567.3	383.4	107.3	115.3	-17.4
1995	4 975.8	790.1	314.5	72.8	764.4	553.5	905.0	349.6	594.6	418.1	114.3	120.4	-21.4
1996	5 256.8	820.1	327.2	77.0	800.1	586.6	950.7	376.0	641.8	448.4	122.6	130.5	-24.2
1997	5 547.4	850.0	337.4	82.9	842.6	616.2	1 002.8	412.9	685.2	474.5	129.7	134.2	-21.1
1998	5 879.5	888.7	356.3	86.2	894.6	641.8	1 069.4	446.1	718.0	505.8	140.0	146.0	-13.3
1999	6 282.5	944.8	379.6	89.5	948.4	675.2	1 130.8	491.6	785.0	546.1	150.5	154.5	-13.5
2000	6 739.4	1 003.7	397.0	93.4	1 006.5	719.3	1 218.3	539.1	853.4	585.7	163.8	172.3	-13.0
2001	7 055.0	1 052.0	397.1	94.5	1 073.7	740.3	1 327.3	536.5	872.4	604.0	178.1	186.5	-7.4
2002	7 350.7	1 091.0	407.0	96.7	1 123.1	747.4	1 441.2	547.0	882.2	629.9	190.2	200.1	-5.1
2003	7 703.6	1 134.0	418.8	100.4	1 161.8	781.1	1 556.5	559.7	921.7	659.9	203.1	207.1	-0.5
2004	8 195.9	1 200.6	441.5	106.7	1 226.8	822.4	1 670.2	610.9	976.5	707.8	212.8	219.0	0.8
2005	8 694.1	1 269.5	464.5	111.9	1 298.7	875.3	1 781.0	646.0	1 051.0	745.3	226.3	224.5	0.1
2006	9 207.2	1 347.2	492.6	115.9	1 388.7	922.2	1 888.4	680.9	1 089.0	796.7	240.9	240.6	3.9
2007	9 710.2	1 422.5	511.9	120.4	1 460.9	959.5	2 008.0	741.0	1 138.0	841.0	257.3	252.7	-2.9

Table 4-6. Personal Saving: Households and Nonprofit Institutions Serving Household (NPISHs)

NIPA Table 2.9

Year	Personal saving (billions of dollars)			NPISH saving as a percent of total personal saving	Saving as a percent of disposable income		NPISH saving as a percent of income and receipts from sales
	Total personal	Household	NPISH		Total personal	Household	
1992	366.0	352.6	13.5	3.7	7.7	7.5	3.0
1993	284.0	271.4	12.6	4.4	5.8	5.6	2.7
1994	249.5	238.8	10.6	4.2	4.8	4.7	2.2
1995	250.9	235.7	15.2	6.1	4.6	4.4	3.0
1996	228.4	206.9	21.6	9.5	4.0	3.7	3.9
1997	218.3	176.5	41.8	19.1	3.6	3.0	7.0
1998	276.8	240.3	36.5	13.2	4.3	3.8	5.8
1999	158.6	114.0	44.6	28.1	2.4	1.7	6.7
2000	168.5	116.6	51.9	30.8	2.3	1.6	7.2
2001	132.3	107.8	24.5	18.5	1.8	1.4	3.3
2002	184.7	168.6	16.2	8.8	2.4	2.2	2.0
2003	174.9	166.4	8.5	4.9	2.1	2.0	1.0
2004	181.7	159.6	22.1	12.2	2.1	1.8	2.5
2005	32.5	-10.2	42.6	131.1	0.4	-0.1	4.4
2006	70.7	38.6	32.1	45.4	0.7	0.4	3.2
2007	57.4	39.3	18.1	31.5	0.6	0.4	1.7

NOTES AND DEFINITIONS

Source: U.S. Department of Commerce, Bureau of Economic Analysis (BEA)

All personal income and personal consumption expenditure series are from the national income and product accounts (NIPAs). All quarterly series are shown at seasonally adjusted annual rates. Current and constant dollar values are in billions of dollars. Indexes of price and quantity are based on the average for the year 2000, which equals 100.

Upcoming NIPA Revision

In July 2009 the Bureau of Economic Analysis will release a comprehensive, or benchmark, revision of the NIPAs.

Current-dollar estimates will be revised—especially for the most recent four years—because of data updating and classification and statistical changes. Users of the constant-dollar estimates and the quantity and price indexes will also, and immediately, notice a change in the reference year for the chain-type quantity and price indexes and the chained-dollar estimates, from 2000 (as used in the data in this volume) to 2005.

The change in the reference year will cause conspicuous differences in the *levels* of the constant-dollar measures and the price and quantity indexes, but this does not of itself affect the *rates of change*—the growth and inflation rates calculated from these data—which are based on chain-weighted indexes whatever the reference base year is. Significant changes are not expected in historical growth and inflation trends from those that can be derived from the data in this volume, other than the revisions occasioned by new data for the most recent several years.

BEA also plans changes in the treatment of disasters and a new classification system for personal consumption expenditures.

These and all of the other planned changes are described in "Preview of the 2009 Comprehensive Revision of the NIPAs: Changes in Definitions and Presentations," *Survey of Current Business,* March 2009, available at <http://www.bea.gov>.

Tables 4-1 through 4-5 cover all income and spending by the personal sector, which includes nonprofit institutions serving households. On an annual basis only, Table 4-6 shows income, spending, and saving estimated separately for households and for such nonprofit institutions.

In several cases, the notes and definitions below will refer to *imputations* or *imputed values.* See the notes and definitions to Chapter 1 for an explanation of imputation and the role it plays in national and personal income measurement.

See the article at the beginning of this book for an explanation of how Hurricane Katrina and other disasters are reflected in personal income.

TABLES 4-1 THROUGH 4-4 AND 19-6
SOURCES AND DISPOSITION OF PERSONAL INCOME; PERSONAL CONSUMPTION EXPENDITURES BY MAJOR TYPE OF PRODUCT

Definitions

Personal income is the income received by persons residing in the United States from participation in production, from government and business transfer payments, and from government interest, which is treated similarly to a transfer payment rather than as income from participation in production. *Persons* denotes the total for individuals, *nonprofit institutions that primarily serve households (NPISHs),* private non-insured welfare funds, and private trust funds. (Income, outlays, and saving excluding NPISHs are referred to as *household* income, outlays, and saving.) All proprietors' income is treated as received by individuals. Life insurance carriers and private noninsured pension funds are not counted as persons, but their saving is credited to persons.

Income from the sale of illegal goods and services is excluded by definition from national and personal income, and the value of purchases of illegal goods and services is not included in personal consumption expenditures.

Personal income is the sum of compensation received by employees, proprietors' income with inventory valuation and capital consumption adjustments (IVA and CCAdj), rental income of persons with capital consumption adjustment, personal receipts on assets, and personal current transfer receipts, less contributions for social insurance.

Personal income differs from national income in that it includes current transfer payments and interest received by persons, regardless of source, while it excludes the following income components: employee and employer contributions for social insurance; business transfer payments, interest payments, and other payments on assets other than to persons; taxes on production and imports less subsidies; the current surplus of government enterprises; and undistributed corporate profits with IVA and CCAdj. The relationships of GDP, gross and net national product, national income, and personal income are displayed in Table 1-10.

Compensation of employees, received is the sum of wage and salary accruals and supplements to wages and salaries, as defined in the *national* income account (see Table 1-12 and the notes and definitions to Chapter 1), minus an adjustment item *wage accruals less disbursements*. By subtracting this adjustment, BEA puts retroactive wage payments back into the quarter *in which* the wages were received by workers rather than the quarter *for which* they were paid. This adjustment item is zero in most quarters but appears more frequently in recent years. There are substantial entries in 2003 and 2004 because 53 Friday paydays fell in 2004 instead of the usual 52. In 2005, 2006, and 2007 there are entries for this item reflecting stock options and financial industry bonuses paid in the year after the activity with which they are associated. See the notes and definitions to Chapter 1. *Wage accruals less disbursements* is shown in Table 1-10, but is not shown separately in Tables 4-1 or 19-6.

As in *national* income, the *compensation of employees* component of personal income refers to compensation received by residents of the United States, including compensation from the rest of the world, but excludes compensation from domestic industries to workers residing in the rest of the world.

Wage and salary disbursements consists of the monetary remuneration of employees, including the compensation of corporate officers; corporate directors' fees paid to directors who are also employees of the corporation; the value of employee exercise of "nonqualified stock options"; commissions, tips, and bonuses; voluntary employee contributions to certain deferred-compensation plans, such as 401(k) plans; receipts in kind that represent income; and judicial fees to jurors and witnesses, compensation of prison inmates, and marriage fees to justices of the peace, all of which were formerly included in "other labor income."

Supplements to wages and salaries consists of employer contributions to employee pension and insurance funds and to government social insurance funds.

The following two categories, *proprietors' income* and *rental income,* are both measured net of depreciation of the capital (structures and equipment) involved. BEA calculates normal depreciation, based on the estimated life of the capital, and subtracts it from the estimated value of receipts to yield net income. In the case of a major disaster, such as a severe hurricane or the terrorist attacks, the extraordinary loss of capital is also estimated and subtracted from receipts in the quarter in which it occurs.

Proprietors' income with inventory valuation and capital consumption adjustments is the current-production income (including income-in-kind) of sole proprietors and partnerships and of tax-exempt cooperatives. The imputed net rental income of owner-occupants of farm dwellings is included. Dividends and monetary interest received by proprietors of nonfinancial business and rental incomes received by persons not primarily engaged in the real estate business are excluded. These incomes are included in personal income receipts on assets and rental income of persons, respectively. Fees paid to outside directors of corporations are included. The two valuation adjustments are designed to obtain income measures that exclude any element of capital gains: inventory withdrawals are valued at replacement cost, rather than historical cost, and charges for depreciation are on an economically consistent accounting basis and are valued at replacement cost.

Rental income of persons with capital consumption adjustment consists of the net current-production income of persons from the rental of real property (other than the incomes of persons primarily engaged in the real estate business), the imputed net rental income of owner-occupants of nonfarm dwellings, and the royalties received by persons from patents, copyrights, and rights to natural resources. The capital consumption adjustment converts charges for depreciation to an economically consistent accounting basis valued at replacement cost.

The recent behavior of rental income merits explanation. This component of personal income in 2007 was less than one-quarter of its level in 2001. A negative value is shown in the third quarter of 2005, reflecting the destruction of property caused by Hurricane Katrina; but even ignoring that, the downtrend in rental income was striking. Because rental income is net of interest and other expenses, it reflected increasing indebtedness and interest payments on owner-occupied and other housing, relative to its estimated rental value. Rental income began to rise during 2008, however, apparently reflecting falling interest rates. See Tables 12-5, 12-6, and 12-7.

Personal income receipts on assets consists of personal interest income and personal dividend income.

Personal interest income is the interest income (monetary and imputed) of persons from all sources, including interest paid by government to government employee retirement plans as well as government interest paid directly to persons.

Personal dividend income is the dividend income of persons from all sources, excluding capital gains distributions. It equals net dividends paid by corporations (dividends paid by corporations minus dividends received by corporations) less a small amount of corporate dividends received by general government. Dividends received by government employee retirement systems are included in personal dividend income.

Personal current transfer receipts is income payments to persons for which no current services are performed. It consists of government social benefits to persons and net receipts from business.

Government social benefits to persons (formerly called "government transfer payments to persons") consists of benefits from the following categories of programs:

Social Security and Medicare, consisting of federal old-age, survivors, disability, and health insurance;

Unemployment insurance;

Veterans' benefits;

Family assistance, which consists of aid to families with dependent children and (beginning in 1996) assistance programs operating under the Personal Responsibility and Work Opportunity Reconciliation Act of 1996;

Other, which includes pension benefit guaranty, workers' compensation, military medical insurance, temporary disability insurance, food stamps, Black Lung benefits, supplemental security income, public assistance (including Medicaid), educational assistance, and the earned income credit. Government payments to nonprofit institutions, other than for work under research and development contracts, also are included. Payments from government employee retirement plans are not included.

Contributions for government social insurance, which is subtracted to arrive at personal income, includes payments by employers, employees, self-employed, and other individuals who participate in the following programs: old-age, survivors, and disability insurance (Social Security); hospital insurance and supplementary medical insurance (Medicare); unemployment insurance; railroad retirement; veterans' life insurance; and temporary disability insurance. Contributions to government employee retirement plans are not included in this item.

In the 2003 revision, there was a change in the tabular presentation of contributions for government social insurance, though not in the concept of personal income. Before the revision, the components of personal income as presented in the tables entitled "Personal Income and its Disposition" included only wages and salaries and "other labor income." *Personal* contributions for social insurance were subtracted from that total. Since the revision, the total compensation concept presented in the table contains wages and salaries and *all* supplements, including the *employer* social insurance payments. Both the *employer* and *employee* contributions are then subtracted to arrive at personal income. In either case, the effect is to end up with a personal income figure that is net of all social insurance taxes but not net of personal income taxes.

Personal current taxes is tax payments (net of refunds) by persons residing in the United States that are not chargeable to business expenses, including taxes on income, on realized net capital gains, and on personal property. As of the 1999 revisions, estate and gift taxes are classified as capital transfers and are not included in personal current taxes.

Disposable personal income is personal income minus personal current taxes. It is the income from current production that is available to persons for spending or saving.

However, it is not the cash flow available, since it excludes realized capital gains. Disposable personal income in chained (2000) dollars represents the inflation-adjusted value of disposable personal income, using the implicit price deflator for personal consumption expenditures.

Personal outlays is the sum of *personal consumption expenditures* (defined below), *personal interest payments*, and *personal current transfer payments*.

Personal interest payments is nonmortgage interest paid by households. As noted above in the definition of rental income, mortgage interest is subtracted from gross rental or imputed rental receipts of persons to yield a net rental income estimate; hence, it is not included as an interest outlay in this category.

Personal current transfer payments to government includes donations, fees, and fines paid to federal, state, and local governments. These were formerly classified as "personal nontax payments" and included in the old "personal tax and nontax payments" total.

Personal current transfer payments to the rest of the world (net) is personal remittances in cash and in kind to the rest of the world less such remittances from the rest of the world.

Personal saving is derived by subtracting personal outlays from disposable personal income. It is the current net saving of individuals (including proprietors), nonprofit institutions that primarily serve individuals, life insurance carriers, retirement funds (including those of government employees), private noninsured welfare funds, and private trust funds. Conceptually, personal saving may also be viewed as the sum of the net acquisition of financial assets and the change in physical assets less the sum of net borrowing and consumption of fixed capital. In either case, it is defined to exclude both realized and unrealized capital gains.

Note that in the context of national income accounting, the term just defined is *saving,* not "savings." *Saving* refers to a *flow* of income during a particular time span (such as a year or a quarter) that is not consumed. It is therefore available to finance a commensurate *flow* of investment during that time span. Strictly defined, "savings" denotes an accumulated *stock* of monetary funds—possibly the cumulative effects of successive periods of *saving*—available to the owner in asset form, such as in a bank savings account.

See the reference below for an article on alternative measures of personal saving.

Personal consumption expenditures (PCE) is goods and services purchased by persons residing in the United States. Persons are defined as individuals and nonprofit institutions that primarily serve individuals. PCE mostly consists of purchases of new goods and services by individuals from business, including purchases financed by insurance (such as medical insurance). In addition, PCE includes purchases of new goods and services by nonprofit institutions, net purchases of used goods by individuals and nonprofit institutions, and purchases abroad of goods and services by U.S. residents traveling or working in foreign countries. PCE also includes purchases for certain goods and services provided by the government, primarily tuition payments for higher education, charges for medical care, and charges for water and sanitary services. Finally, PCE includes imputed purchases that keep PCE invariant to changes in the way that certain activities are carried out. For example, to take account of the value of the services provided by owner-occupied housing, PCE includes an imputation equal to what (estimated) rent homeowners would pay if they rented their houses from themselves. (See the discussion of imputation in the notes and definitions to Chapter 1.) Actual purchases of residential structures by individuals are classified as gross private domestic investment.

Tables 4-3 and 4-4 present personal consumption expenditures classified by major type of product: *durable goods, nondurable goods,* and *services.* Each of these three major categories is then subdivided according to type of expenditure.

In general, *durable goods* are commodities that can be stored or inventoried and that have an average life of at least three years. *Nondurable goods* are all other commodities that can be stored or inventoried.

This classification system is not particularly helpful with respect to the objective of spending. For example, the *medical care* component of services does not include drugs and medicines, which are included instead in nondurable goods. For a more precise classification of consumption spending by objective, see Table 4-5, Personal Consumption Expenditures by Type of Expenditure, and its description below. This classification by type of expenditure is only available on an annual basis.

Revisions

Data in this book reflect the 2003 comprehensive revisions to the NIPAs and all further revisions available through March 2009.

See the notes and definitions to Chapter 1 for an explanation of a new revision schedule for wages and salaries and related components of the income side of the NIPAs. This means quarterly revisions for as much as seven months of previous data, which affect income and saving while leaving PCE and other components of GDP untouched.

An important conceptual change was made in the 1999 comprehensive revision of the NIPAs, when it was decided to treat the retirement plans of federal, state, and local employees like private pensions. Previously, these employee retirement plans were treated as government social insurance programs. Both the employer contributions to and the dividends and interest received by these retirement funds are now treated as components of personal income, while benefits paid by the plans to retirees are treated as transactions within the personal sector rather than as transfer payments. This conceptual revision raised employer contributions for employee pension and insurance funds and dividends and interest, and reduced transfer payments received and personal contributions for social insurance. The effect was to move the accumulation of assets in these pension funds from the government surplus to personal saving.

Data availability

Monthly data are made available in a BEA press release, usually distributed the first business day following the monthly release of the latest quarterly national income and product account (NIPA) estimates. Monthly and quarterly data are subsequently published each month in the BEA's *Survey of Current Business.* Current and historical data are available on the BEA Web site at <http://www.bea.gov>, and may also be obtained from the STAT-USA subscription Web site at <http://www.stat-usa.gov>.

References

The latest revision incorporated in this volume is presented and described in an article on the national income and product accounts in the August 2008 *Survey of Current Business.* Other references can be found in the notes and definitions to Chapter 1. A discussion of monthly estimates of personal income and its disposition appears in the November 1979 edition of the *Survey of Current Business.* A more detailed description of concepts, sources, and methods used in estimating personal consumption expenditures appears in *Personal Consumption Expenditures* (NIPA Methodology Paper No. 6, 1990), available on the BEA Web site from the National Technical Information Service (NTIS Accession No. PB 90-254244) available online at <http://www.bea.gov/bea/ARTICLES/NATIONAL/NIPA/Methpap/methpap6.pdf>.

Additional and more recent information can be found in the articles listed in the notes and definitions for Chapter 1.

An article on "Alternative Measures of Personal Saving" by Marshall B. Reinsdorf appears in the February 2007 issue of the *Survey of Current Business,* pp. 7-13.

TABLE 4-5
PERSONAL CONSUMPTION EXPENDITURES BY TYPE OF EXPENDITURE

SOURCE: BUREAU OF ECONOMIC ANALYSIS (BEA)

In this table, also derived from the NIPAs, annual estimates of the current-dollar value of PCE are presented by "type of expenditure" instead of by "type of product." The latter is the classification scheme used in Tables 4-3 and 4-4. The "type of expenditure" tabulations provide a more precise delineation of consumer spending by its ultimate objective. These tabulations cut across the categories of durable goods, nondurable goods, and services that are used in the quarterly estimates. The definitions of the expenditure types given below explain the relationship of each to the categories used in the "type of product" tables.

Definitions

Food and tobacco includes food, beverages (including alcoholic beverages), and tobacco products, whether purchased for home consumption or on the premises of eating and drinking places. All of these components are included in nondurable goods in the "major type of product" classification system.

Clothing, accessories, and jewelry includes clothing and shoes from the nondurable goods category, jewelry and watches from the durable goods category, and cleaning, storage, and repair of clothing and shoes from the services category.

Personal care includes toilet articles and preparations from nondurable goods and barbershops, beauty parlors, and health clubs from services.

Housing includes rents paid for rental housing, imputed rent of owner-occupied dwellings, and rent of hotels, motels, clubs, schools, and other group housing. All components are from the services group.

Household operation includes furniture, appliances, and other durable household goods from durable goods; "semi-durable" furnishings (such as textile goods), household supplies, and stationery from nondurable goods; and utilities, communications, domestic service, maintenance, insurance, and miscellaneous services from services.

Medical care includes drug preparations and sundries from nondurable goods, ophthalmic and orthopedic products from durable goods, and the services of medical professionals, hospitals, nursing homes, and health insurance.

Personal business includes financial, legal, funeral, and miscellaneous services.

Transportation includes the purchase of motor vehicles and parts from the durable goods category, gasoline and oil from nondurable goods, and tolls, insurance, transit, taxi, rail, bus, airline, and other transportation services.

Recreation includes books, "wheel goods" (other than those classified in transportation), photo equipment, boats, pleasure aircraft, video, audio, musical instruments, computers, and software, all from durable goods; toys, sports supplies, flowers, seeds, and potted plants from nondurable goods; and a long list of recreational and cultural services, including legal gambling. (As noted earlier, purchases of goods and services that are illegal and the incomes from such purchases are outside the scope of the national income and product accounts.)

Education and research includes all education and research expenditures in the service category, including the research of nonprofit institutions.

Religious and welfare activities are all classified as services in the "major type of product" system. For nonprofits, this category equals current expenditures (including consumption of fixed capital) of religious, social welfare, foreign relief, and political organizations, and those of museums, libraries, and foundations. The expenditures are net of receipts—such as those from sales of meals, rooms, and entertainments—accounted for separately in consumer expenditures. They exclude relief payments within the United States and expenditures by foundations for education and research. For proprietary and government institutions, the value for this category equals receipts from users.

Foreign travel and other, net consists of foreign travel spending (services) and other expenditures abroad (nondurable goods) by U.S. residents *minus* expenditures in the United States by nonresidents (services) and personal remittances in kind to nonresidents (nondurable goods). Negative figures indicate that the sum of the first two terms is less than the sum of the second two terms. Beginning with 1981, foreign travel spending by U.S. residents includes U.S. students' expenditures abroad, and expenditures in the United States by nonresidents includes nonresidents' student and medical care expenditures in the United States.

Positive values for this foreign travel category, indicating that U.S. residents spent more abroad than foreigners spent here, appear in the 1980s when the dollar was strong against other major currencies. (The international value of the dollar is shown in Table 13-8.) Negative values in subsequent years resulted from the weakening of the dollar, which discouraged U.S. residents' travel abroad and encouraged tourism by foreigners in the United States. The negative sign does not indicate a drain on GDP—these effects of a weaker dollar are in fact positive for GDP—but rather reflects the fact that the goods and services purchased by foreigners in the United States must be subtracted from total consumer purchases in order to be added to other exports and classified in the category of exports rather than in the consumption spending of U.S. residents.

Data availability and revisions

Data are published once a year in supplemental NIPA tables in the *Survey of Current Business,* most recently in August 2008, reflecting the most recent NIPA revisions. They are also available on the BEA Web site at <http://www.bea.gov>.

TABLE 4-6
PERSONAL SAVING: HOUSEHOLDS AND NONPROFIT INSTITUTIONS SERVING HOUSEHOLDS

SOURCE: BUREAU OF ECONOMIC ANALYSIS (BEA)

As noted above, the "personal" sector includes not only households but also "nonprofit institutions serving households" (NPISHs). This category comprises all nonprofit institutions except those that are considered to be serving government and business, such as chambers of commerce and trade associations. Those institutions are included in the business sector instead.

For annual (not quarterly) data beginning with 1992, BEA now compiles and makes available tables showing personal income and its disposition for households and NPISHs separately. Each major type of income and expenditure is estimated separately for the two groups. Household receipts from NPISHs, purchases from NPISHs, and contributions to NPISHs are identified separately instead of being netted out as they are in the current quarterly accounts. These data provide answers to questions about how much of "per-

sonal" saving is in fact accounted for by NPISHs, and whether these institutions are a factor in the observed changes in personal saving behavior. This is one of the questions analyzed in the article "Alternative Measures of Personal Saving" cited above.

These results indicate that NPISHs accounted for a surprisingly large proportion of "personal" saving in the stock-market boom years of 1999 and 2000, and for more than all of it in 2005. In that year aggregate household saving was negative, as households borrowed and spent down assets to finance current consumption.

Data availability and references

These data and the data on income and outlays for the household and nonprofit sectors on which they are based become available about two months after the release of the midyear revision of the NIPAs. They are published in Table 2.9 in the NIPA tables on the BEA Web site at <http://www.bea.gov>. An article from the April 2003 *Survey,* "Income and Outlays of Households and of Nonprofit Institutions Serving Households," can also be found on the BEA Web site.

CHAPTER 5: SAVING AND INVESTMENT; BUSINESS SALES AND INVENTORIES

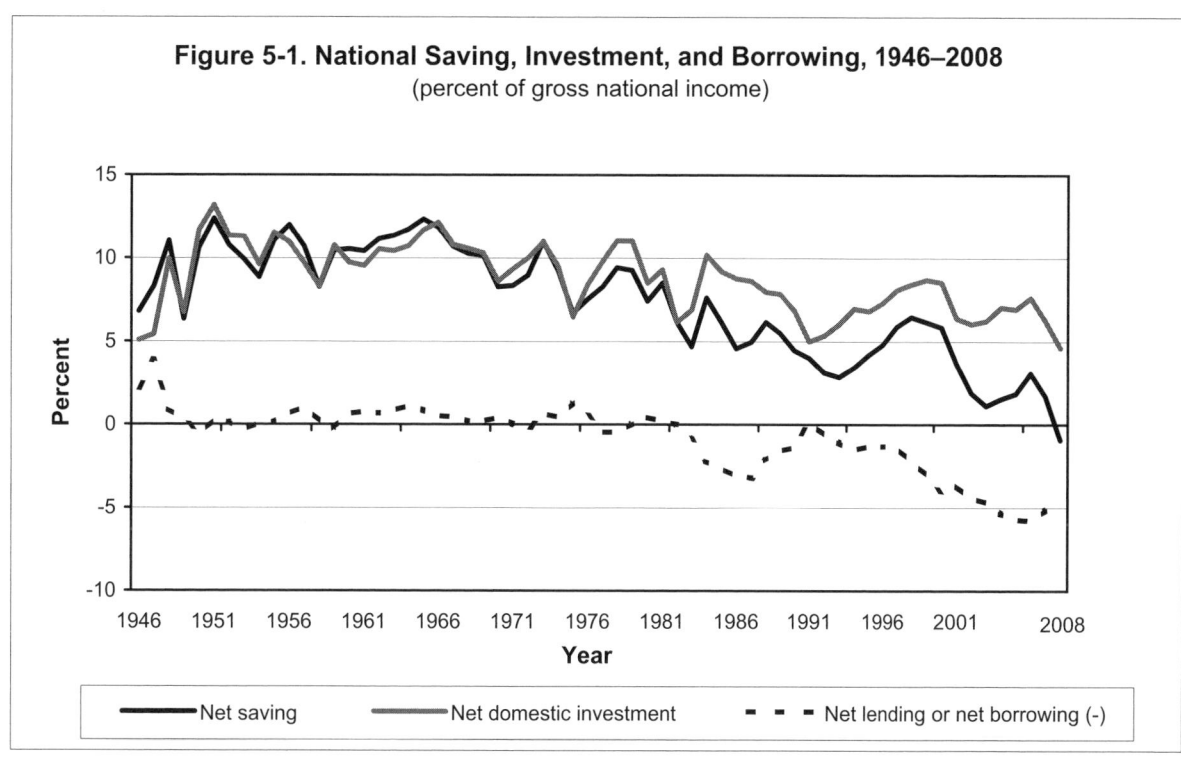

Figure 5-1. National Saving, Investment, and Borrowing, 1946–2008
(percent of gross national income)

- Net national saving—the middle line in Figure 5-1—averaged about 5 percent of gross national income (GNI) in the years 1984 through 2000, which was already lower than the rates seen in the 1950s and 1960s. Net saving is saving by U.S. persons, businesses, and governments, excluding the consumption of fixed capital—that is, saving available for investment over and above the replacement of the existing stock. The national saving rate was still lower in the years 2001–2007, averaging about 2 percent, and with the recession that began at the end of 2007, it fell into negative territory for the first time since the depression years of 1931 through 1934. (Tables 5-1, 18-1, and 19-9)

- What accounted for the decline in the saving rate in the 2000s? Comparing 2007 with 2000, retained profits were greater in 2007 relative to GNI, but personal and state and local saving were lower, and the federal government swung from a surplus of 1.9 percent of GNI to a deficit of 1.6 percent. (Table 5-1)

- Net domestic investment (gross investment minus consumption of fixed capital) reached rates over 8 percent of GNI in the late 1990s. After the 2001 recession, it recovered to a peak of 7.6 percent in 2006, before declining to 4.6 percent in 2008. This was the lowest investment rate in the entire postwar period—the lowest since net investment was negative in the early 1930s. (Tables 5-1, 18-1, and 19-9)

- The excess of investment over saving in the 2000s was financed by a further increase in borrowing overseas (a larger negative entry on the graph above), which reached a record 5.8 percent of GNI in 2006. (Table 5-1)

- In terms of physical quantities, residential investment rose 33.2 percent from 2000 to 2005—an annual rate of 5.9 percent—but then suffered a 40 percent collapse from 2005 to 2008. Nonresidential investment declined through 2002 but between 2002 and 2008 rose 31 percent, an annual rate of 4.6 percent. (Table 5-4)

Table 5-1. Saving and Investment

(Billions of dollars, except as noted; quarterly data are at seasonally adjusted annual rates.)   **NIPA Tables 1.7.5, 5.1**

Year and quarter	Gross saving Total	Net saving Total	Private Total	Personal saving	Undistributed corporate profits with IVA and CCAdj	Federal	State and local	Consumption of fixed capital Total	Private Total	Domestic business	Households and institutions	Federal	State and local
1950	60.6	31.2	24.4	15.1	9.3	5.5	1.3	29.4	21.5	18.1	3.3	5.8	2.1
1951	75.0	41.8	29.6	19.5	10.1	9.6	2.6	33.2	24.6	20.7	3.8	6.1	2.6
1952	74.2	38.5	31.8	20.5	11.3	3.7	3.0	35.7	26.1	21.9	4.2	6.8	2.7
1953	75.1	37.4	32.1	21.5	10.6	1.8	3.5	37.8	27.3	22.9	4.4	7.6	2.8
1954	73.4	33.5	31.9	20.0	11.9	-1.6	3.2	39.9	28.7	24.1	4.7	8.3	2.9
1955	88.0	45.9	36.7	19.7	17.0	5.7	3.5	42.1	30.3	25.3	5.0	8.7	3.1
1956	99.4	53.0	41.0	25.8	15.3	7.6	4.4	46.4	33.6	28.1	5.5	9.3	3.5
1957	99.6	49.7	42.2	27.0	15.2	3.3	4.2	49.9	36.3	30.4	5.8	9.8	3.9
1958	90.8	38.8	41.3	28.3	13.0	-5.4	2.9	52.0	38.1	32.1	6.1	9.9	4.0
1959	106.2	53.2	46.0	26.7	19.4	3.3	3.8	53.0	38.6	32.2	6.4	10.2	4.2
1960	111.3	55.8	44.3	26.7	17.6	7.2	4.3	55.6	40.5	33.9	6.7	10.6	4.4
1961	114.3	57.1	50.2	32.2	18.1	2.6	4.3	57.2	41.6	34.7	6.9	10.9	4.7
1962	124.9	65.7	57.9	33.8	24.1	2.5	5.2	59.3	42.8	35.6	7.2	11.5	5.0
1963	133.2	70.8	59.7	33.3	26.4	5.4	5.7	62.4	44.9	37.5	7.5	12.1	5.4
1964	143.4	78.4	71.0	40.8	30.1	1.0	6.4	65.0	46.9	39.0	7.9	12.3	5.7
1965	158.5	89.1	79.2	43.0	36.2	3.3	6.5	69.4	50.5	41.9	8.5	12.7	6.2
1966	168.7	93.1	83.1	44.4	38.7	2.3	7.8	75.6	55.5	46.3	9.2	13.2	6.9
1967	170.5	89.0	91.4	54.4	36.9	-9.4	7.0	81.5	59.9	50.0	9.9	14.0	7.5
1968	182.0	93.6	88.4	52.8	35.6	-2.3	7.5	88.4	65.2	54.4	10.8	14.8	8.3
1969	198.3	100.4	83.7	52.5	31.2	8.7	8.0	97.9	73.1	61.2	12.0	15.5	9.3
1970	192.7	86.0	94.0	69.5	24.6	-15.2	7.1	106.7	80.0	67.2	12.9	16.1	10.6
1971	208.9	93.9	115.8	80.6	34.8	-28.4	6.5	115.0	86.7	72.5	14.2	16.5	11.8
1972	237.5	111.0	119.8	77.2	42.9	-24.4	15.6	126.5	97.1	80.9	16.2	16.6	12.8
1973	292.0	152.7	148.3	102.7	45.6	-11.3	15.7	139.3	107.9	89.9	18.0	17.1	14.3
1974	301.5	139.0	143.4	113.6	29.8	-13.8	9.3	162.5	126.6	105.9	20.7	18.2	17.7
1975	297.0	109.2	175.8	125.6	50.2	-69.0	2.5	187.7	147.8	124.4	23.4	19.7	20.2
1976	342.1	137.0	181.3	122.3	59.0	-51.7	7.4	205.2	162.5	136.9	25.6	21.4	21.3
1977	397.5	167.5	198.5	125.3	73.2	-44.1	13.1	230.0	184.3	155.3	29.0	23.1	22.6
1978	478.0	215.7	223.5	142.5	81.0	-26.5	18.7	262.3	212.8	179.3	33.6	25.0	24.5
1979	536.7	236.6	234.9	159.1	75.7	-11.3	13.0	300.1	245.7	206.9	38.8	27.0	27.5
1980	549.4	206.5	251.3	201.4	49.9	-53.6	8.8	343.0	281.1	236.8	44.3	30.1	31.8
1981	654.7	266.6	312.3	244.3	68.0	-53.3	7.6	388.1	317.9	268.9	49.0	33.8	36.3
1982	629.1	202.2	336.2	270.8	65.4	-131.9	-2.2	426.9	349.8	297.3	52.5	37.6	39.5
1983	609.4	165.6	333.7	233.6	100.1	-173.0	4.9	443.8	362.1	307.4	54.7	40.8	40.9
1984	773.4	300.9	445.0	314.8	130.3	-168.1	23.9	472.6	385.6	328.0	57.6	44.6	42.3
1985	767.5	260.7	413.4	280.0	133.4	-175.0	22.3	506.7	414.0	353.0	61.0	48.1	44.6
1986	733.5	202.2	372.0	268.4	103.7	-190.8	21.0	531.3	431.8	366.9	64.9	51.6	47.9
1987	796.8	234.9	367.4	241.4	126.1	-145.0	12.4	561.9	455.3	385.7	69.5	55.2	51.4
1988	915.0	317.4	434.0	272.9	161.1	-134.5	17.9	597.6	483.5	408.9	74.6	59.3	54.8
1989	944.7	300.4	409.7	287.1	122.6	-130.1	20.8	644.3	522.1	440.6	81.5	63.5	58.7
1990	940.4	258.0	422.7	299.4	123.3	-172.0	7.2	682.5	551.6	466.4	85.1	67.9	63.0
1991	964.1	238.2	456.1	324.2	131.9	-213.7	-4.2	725.9	586.9	497.4	89.5	72.2	66.9
1992	948.2	196.3	493.0	366.0	142.7	-297.4	0.7	751.9	607.3	510.5	96.8	74.7	69.9
1993	962.4	186.0	458.6	284.0	168.1	-273.5	0.9	776.4	624.7	524.6	100.1	77.9	73.8
1994	1 070.7	237.1	438.9	249.5	171.8	-212.3	10.5	833.7	675.1	568.0	107.1	80.2	78.5
1995	1 184.5	306.2	491.1	250.9	223.8	-197.0	12.0	878.4	713.4	600.2	113.2	81.9	83.1
1996	1 291.1	373.0	489.0	228.4	256.9	-141.8	25.8	918.1	748.8	630.7	118.2	82.0	87.2
1997	1 461.1	486.6	503.3	218.3	287.9	-55.8	39.1	974.4	800.3	675.2	125.1	82.5	91.6
1998	1 598.7	568.6	477.8	276.8	201.7	38.8	52.0	1 030.2	851.2	718.3	132.9	82.8	96.2
1999	1 674.3	573.0	419.0	158.6	255.3	103.6	50.4	1 101.3	914.3	769.8	144.5	84.8	102.1
2000	1 770.5	582.7	343.3	168.5	174.8	189.5	50.0	1 187.8	990.8	836.1	154.8	87.2	109.8
2001	1 657.6	376.1	324.6	132.3	192.3	46.7	4.8	1 281.5	1 075.5	903.7	171.7	88.2	117.8
2002	1 489.1	197.1	479.2	184.7	294.5	-247.9	-34.2	1 292.0	1 080.3	893.6	186.8	88.9	122.7
2003	1 459.0	122.5	515.0	174.9	325.1	-372.1	-20.4	1 336.5	1 118.3	916.6	201.7	90.4	127.8
2004	1 618.1	182.0	551.1	181.7	384.4	-370.6	1.5	1 436.1	1 206.0	970.2	235.8	94.0	136.1
2005	1 844.2	232.2	494.4	32.5	456.9	-291.7	29.5	1 612.0	1 359.7	1 062.3	297.4	99.1	153.2
2006	2 038.5	414.5	569.5	70.7	497.5	-201.1	46.2	1 623.9	1 356.0	1 085.5	270.5	105.6	162.3
2007	1 956.0	235.6	454.5	57.4	403.4	-229.3	10.4	1 720.5	1 431.1	1 147.0	284.1	111.8	177.6
2008	1 700.0	-132.3	469.3	191.4	277.8	-521.5	-80.1	1 832.3	1 523.1	1 225.0	298.1	117.9	191.3
2006													
1st quarter	2 034.2	451.6	601.9	94.4	527.5	-207.9	57.5	1 582.7	1 323.1	1 059.8	263.3	103.0	156.5
2nd quarter	2 022.8	410.3	572.1	54.2	518.0	-225.0	63.1	1 612.5	1 346.8	1 077.8	268.9	105.0	160.8
3rd quarter	2 005.9	367.6	553.8	48.1	505.6	-218.4	32.2	1 638.3	1 367.8	1 094.5	273.3	106.7	163.9
4th quarter	2 090.9	428.7	550.1	86.1	439.0	-153.2	31.8	1 662.2	1 386.2	1 109.7	276.5	107.8	168.1
2007													
1st quarter	1 974.4	290.2	492.1	109.3	407.8	-225.2	23.2	1 684.3	1 402.1	1 123.6	278.4	109.8	172.5
2nd quarter	1 987.3	280.3	455.9	31.1	424.8	-211.4	35.8	1 707.0	1 420.0	1 138.5	281.5	111.0	176.0
3rd quarter	1 958.9	226.9	466.5	46.8	419.7	-244.3	4.7	1 731.9	1 440.1	1 154.4	285.7	112.5	179.3
4th quarter	1 903.6	145.0	403.6	42.4	361.2	-236.3	-22.3	1 758.6	1 462.3	1 171.4	290.9	113.9	182.4
2008													
1st quarter	1 773.6	-4.4	378.7	20.6	358.1	-330.7	-52.4	1 778.0	1 477.5	1 186.1	291.4	115.0	185.5
2nd quarter	1 634.6	-168.5	547.9	267.9	280.0	-649.6	-66.9	1 803.1	1 497.4	1 205.6	291.8	116.9	188.8
3rd quarter	1 670.5	-227.5	420.1	139.8	280.3	-544.0	-103.6	1 898.1	1 585.9	1 266.0	320.0	119.2	192.9
4th quarter	1 721.5	-128.6	530.3	337.4	192.9	-561.5	-97.4	1 850.1	1 531.7	1 242.5	289.2	120.5	197.9

Table 5-1. Saving and Investment—*Continued*

(Billions of dollars, except as noted; quarterly data are at seasonally adjusted annual rates.)   **NIPA Tables 1.7.5, 5.1**

| Year and quarter | Total | Gross domestic investment, capital account transactions, and net lending, NIPAs | | | Capital account transactions, net | Net lending or net borrowing (-), NIPAs | Statistical discrepancy | Net domestic investment | Gross national income | Gross saving as a percent of gross national income | Net saving as a percent of gross national income |
| | | Gross domestic investment | | | | | | | | | |
		Total	Private	Government							
1950	62.0	63.9	54.1	9.8	. . .	-1.8	1.4	34.4	293.8	20.6	10.6
1951	78.7	77.8	60.2	17.6	. . .	0.9	3.6	44.5	337.6	22.2	12.4
1952	77.0	76.3	54.0	22.3	. . .	0.6	2.8	40.6	357.5	20.7	10.8
1953	79.2	80.4	56.4	24.0	. . .	-1.3	4.0	42.7	377.2	19.9	9.9
1954	76.6	76.3	53.8	22.5	. . .	0.2	3.2	36.4	379.3	19.3	8.8
1955	90.5	90.0	69.0	21.0	. . .	0.4	2.5	47.9	414.8	21.2	11.1
1956	97.7	94.9	72.0	22.9	. . .	2.8	-1.7	48.5	441.9	22.5	12.0
1957	99.6	94.8	70.5	24.4	. . .	4.8	0.0	45.0	464.1	21.5	10.7
1958	91.9	91.0	64.5	26.5	. . .	0.9	1.0	38.9	468.8	19.4	8.3
1959	106.7	107.8	78.5	29.3	. . .	-1.2	0.5	54.8	508.9	20.9	10.4
1960	110.4	107.2	78.9	28.3	. . .	3.2	-0.9	51.6	530.4	21.0	10.5
1961	113.8	109.5	78.2	31.3	. . .	4.3	-0.6	52.3	548.8	20.8	10.4
1962	125.3	121.4	88.1	33.3	. . .	3.9	0.4	62.2	589.4	21.2	11.1
1963	132.4	127.4	93.8	33.6	. . .	5.0	-0.8	65.0	623.0	21.4	11.4
1964	144.2	136.7	102.1	34.6	. . .	7.5	0.8	71.7	667.7	21.5	11.7
1965	160.0	153.8	118.2	35.6	. . .	6.2	1.6	84.4	722.8	21.9	12.3
1966	175.0	171.1	131.3	39.8	. . .	3.9	6.3	95.5	786.6	21.4	11.8
1967	175.1	171.6	128.6	43.0	. . .	3.6	4.6	90.1	833.4	20.5	10.7
1968	186.6	184.8	141.2	43.6	. . .	1.7	4.6	96.5	911.5	20.0	10.3
1969	201.5	199.7	156.4	43.3	. . .	1.8	3.2	101.8	987.6	20.1	10.2
1970	200.0	196.0	152.4	43.6	. . .	4.0	7.3	89.3	1 037.6	18.6	8.3
1971	220.5	219.9	178.2	41.8	. . .	0.6	11.6	104.9	1 123.1	18.6	8.4
1972	246.6	250.2	207.6	42.6	. . .	-3.6	9.1	123.7	1 237.7	19.2	9.0
1973	300.7	291.3	244.5	46.8	. . .	9.3	8.6	152.1	1 386.7	21.1	11.0
1974	312.3	305.7	249.4	56.3	. . .	6.6	10.9	143.2	1 504.6	20.0	9.2
1975	314.7	293.3	230.2	63.1	. . .	21.4	17.7	105.6	1 633.6	18.2	6.7
1976	367.2	358.4	292.0	66.4	. . .	8.9	25.1	153.2	1 817.0	18.8	7.5
1977	419.8	428.8	361.3	67.5	. . .	-9.0	22.3	198.8	2 028.9	19.6	8.3
1978	504.6	515.0	438.0	77.1	. . .	-10.4	26.6	252.7	2 289.7	20.9	9.4
1979	582.8	581.4	492.9	88.5	. . .	1.4	46.0	281.2	2 549.2	21.1	9.3
1980	590.9	579.5	479.3	100.3	. . .	11.4	41.4	236.6	2 782.3	19.7	7.4
1981	685.6	679.3	572.4	106.9	. . .	6.3	30.9	291.2	3 130.4	20.9	8.5
1982	629.4	629.5	517.2	112.3	-0.2	0.0	0.3	202.6	3 291.2	19.1	6.1
1983	655.1	687.2	564.3	122.9	-0.2	-31.8	45.7	243.4	3 528.0	17.3	4.7
1984	788.0	875.0	735.6	139.4	-0.2	-86.7	14.6	402.4	3 954.9	19.6	7.6
1985	784.1	895.0	736.2	158.8	-0.3	-110.5	16.7	388.3	4 230.1	18.1	6.2
1986	780.5	919.7	746.5	173.2	-0.3	-138.9	47.0	388.4	4 433.6	16.5	4.6
1987	818.5	969.2	785.0	184.3	-0.4	-150.4	21.7	407.3	4 735.7	16.8	5.0
1988	895.5	1 007.7	821.6	186.1	-0.5	-111.7	-19.5	410.1	5 147.0	17.8	6.2
1989	984.3	1 072.6	874.9	197.7	-0.3	-88.0	39.7	428.4	5 470.9	17.3	5.5
1990	1 006.7	1 076.7	861.0	215.7	6.6	-76.6	66.2	394.2	5 771.6	16.3	4.5
1991	1 036.6	1 023.2	802.9	220.3	4.5	9.0	72.5	297.3	5 953.8	16.2	4.0
1992	1 051.0	1 087.9	864.8	223.1	0.6	-37.5	102.7	336.0	6 264.7	15.1	3.1
1993	1 102.0	1 172.4	953.4	219.0	1.3	-71.7	139.5	395.9	6 549.8	14.7	2.8
1994	1 213.2	1 318.4	1 097.1	221.4	1.7	-106.9	142.5	484.7	6 955.9	15.4	3.4
1995	1 285.7	1 376.7	1 144.0	232.7	0.9	-91.9	101.2	498.4	7 332.3	16.2	4.2
1996	1 384.8	1 485.2	1 240.3	244.9	0.7	-101.0	93.7	567.1	7 758.2	16.6	4.8
1997	1 531.7	1 641.9	1 389.8	252.2	1.0	-111.3	70.7	667.5	8 266.6	17.7	5.9
1998	1 584.1	1 771.5	1 509.1	262.4	0.7	-188.1	-14.6	741.3	8 783.0	18.2	6.5
1999	1 638.5	1 912.4	1 625.7	286.8	4.8	-278.7	-35.7	811.2	9 337.9	17.9	6.1
2000	1 643.3	2 040.0	1 735.5	304.5	0.8	-397.4	-127.2	852.1	9 983.1	17.7	5.8
2001	1 567.9	1 938.3	1 614.3	324.0	1.1	-371.5	-89.6	656.9	10 261.3	16.2	3.7
2002	1 468.1	1 926.4	1 582.1	344.3	1.4	-459.7	-21.0	634.4	10 521.2	14.2	1.9
2003	1 507.8	2 020.0	1 664.1	356.0	3.2	-515.5	48.8	683.5	10 968.8	13.3	1.1
2004	1 637.3	2 261.4	1 888.6	372.8	2.4	-626.5	19.1	825.3	11 742.9	13.8	1.5
2005	1 773.0	2 483.9	2 086.1	397.8	4.0	-714.9	-71.2	871.9	12 586.0	14.7	1.8
2006	1 875.5	2 647.0	2 220.4	426.7	3.9	-775.5	-163.0	1 023.1	13 419.7	15.2	3.1
2007	1 874.6	2 593.2	2 130.4	462.8	1.8	-720.4	-81.4	872.7	13 991.4	14.0	1.7
2008	1 835.9	2 489.5	1 993.5	496.0	2.4	-656.1	135.8	657.2	14 262.0	11.9	-0.9
2006											
1st quarter	1 879.6	2 648.4	2 236.7	411.7	6.9	-775.6	-154.6	1 065.7	13 193.8	15.4	3.4
2nd quarter	1 891.2	2 680.1	2 253.7	426.3	4.0	-793.0	-131.7	1 067.5	13 351.0	15.2	3.1
3rd quarter	1 835.1	2 660.6	2 231.7	428.9	2.1	-827.7	-170.8	1 022.3	13 486.9	14.9	2.7
4th quarter	1 896.0	2 599.1	2 159.5	439.6	2.5	-705.6	-194.9	936.9	13 646.9	15.3	3.1
2007											
1st quarter	1 786.0	2 563.6	2 117.8	445.8	2.2	-779.8	-188.4	879.3	13 771.7	14.3	2.1
2nd quarter	1 843.9	2 607.6	2 147.2	460.4	0.4	-764.2	-143.4	900.6	13 940.6	14.3	2.0
3rd quarter	1 951.1	2 633.1	2 164.0	469.1	2.5	-684.5	-7.8	901.2	14 070.6	13.9	1.6
4th quarter	1 917.4	2 568.4	2 092.3	476.1	2.3	-653.3	13.9	809.8	14 182.7	13.4	1.0
2008											
1st quarter	1 837.0	2 530.0	2 056.1	473.9	2.4	-695.4	63.4	752.0	14 225.6	12.5	0.0
2nd quarter	1 771.2	2 493.8	2 000.9	492.8	2.6	-725.2	136.6	690.7	14 271.7	11.5	-1.2
3rd quarter	1 820.7	2 517.2	2 010.9	506.3	2.6	-699.1	150.2	619.2	14 389.4	11.6	-1.6
4th quarter	1 914.5	2 417.0	1 906.1	510.9	2.2	-504.8	193.0	566.9	14 161.3	12.2	-0.9

. . . = Not available.

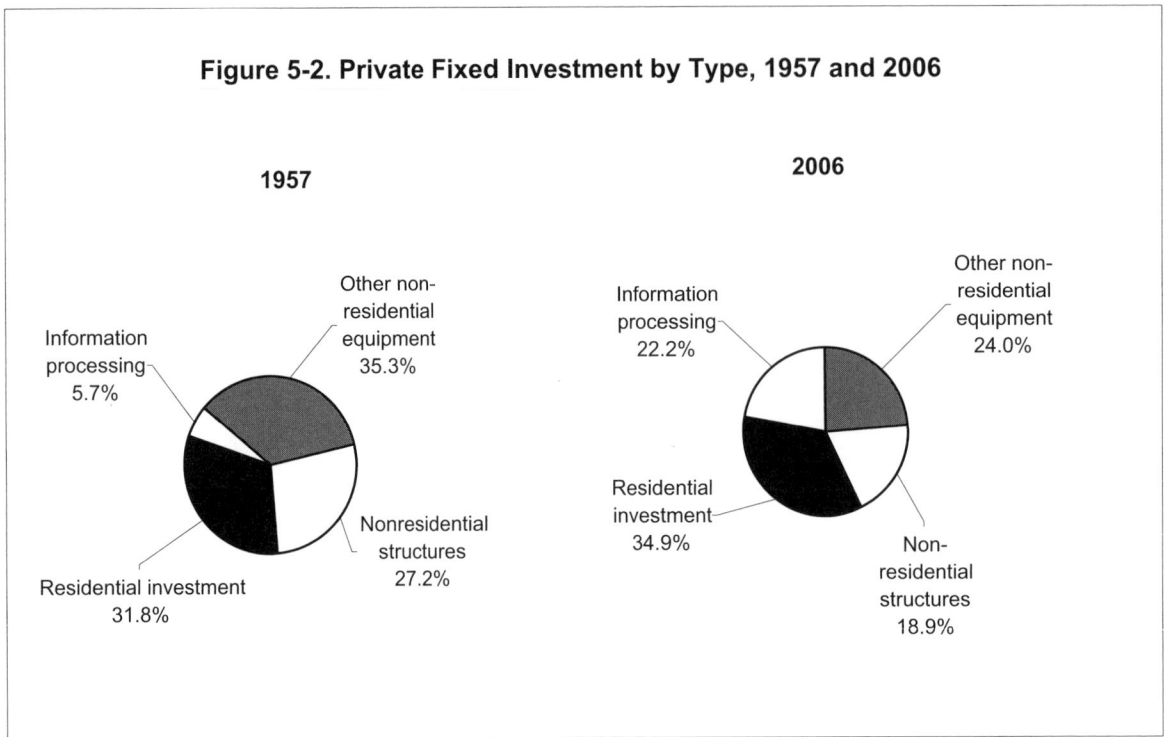

Figure 5-2. Private Fixed Investment by Type, 1957 and 2006

1957

2006

- Between 1957—a high year in an early postwar business cycle—and 2006, the recent high point for real investment, the quantity of aggregate gross private fixed investment increased more than seven-fold, with an average annual growth rate of 4.2 percent. Every major type of investment, except for structures for manufacturing (i.e., building new factories), grew in real terms between those two years. (Table 5-4)

- However, the composition of this investment changed markedly. Information processing software and equipment rose from 5.7 percent to 22.2 percent of current-dollar value during this period, while other equipment became relatively less important, going from 35.2 percent to 24.0 percent of current-dollar value. Nonresidential structures also lost relative importance, falling from 27.3 percent to 18.9 percent of current-dollar value, while residential investment grew from 31.8 percent to 34.9 percent of current-dollar value. (Table 5-2)

Table 5-2. Gross Private Fixed Investment by Type

(Billions of dollars, quarterly data are at seasonally adjusted annual rates.)   **NIPA Table 5.3.5**

Year and quarter	Total gross private fixed investment	Nonresidential									
		Total	Structures						Equipment and software		
			Total	Commercial and health care	Manufac-turing	Power and communi-cation	Mining exploration, shafts, and wells	Other non-residential structures	Total	Information processing equipment and software	
										Total	Computers and peripheral equipment
1950	48.3	27.8	10.0	1.8	1.1	2.8	1.4	2.9	17.8	1.8	...
1951	50.3	31.8	12.0	1.9	2.1	3.0	1.7	3.2	19.9	2.1	...
1952	50.5	31.9	12.2	1.6	2.3	3.1	2.0	3.3	19.7	2.4	...
1953	54.5	35.1	13.6	2.1	2.2	3.6	2.1	3.5	21.5	2.7	...
1954	55.8	34.7	13.9	2.6	2.0	3.3	2.3	3.6	20.8	2.4	...
1955	64.0	39.0	15.2	3.4	2.3	3.3	2.5	3.7	23.9	2.8	...
1956	68.1	44.5	18.2	4.2	3.2	4.1	2.7	4.0	26.3	3.4	...
1957	69.7	47.5	19.0	4.1	3.6	4.5	2.6	4.1	28.6	4.0	...
1958	64.9	42.5	17.6	4.2	2.4	4.4	2.4	4.2	24.9	3.6	...
1959	74.6	46.5	18.1	4.6	2.1	4.3	2.5	4.7	28.4	4.0	0.0
1960	75.7	49.4	19.6	4.8	2.9	4.4	2.3	5.2	29.8	4.9	0.2
1961	75.2	48.8	19.7	5.5	2.8	4.1	2.3	5.0	29.1	5.3	0.3
1962	82.0	53.1	20.8	6.2	2.8	4.1	2.5	5.2	32.3	5.7	0.3
1963	88.1	56.0	21.2	6.1	2.9	4.4	2.3	5.6	34.8	6.5	0.7
1964	97.2	63.0	23.7	6.8	3.6	4.8	2.4	6.2	39.2	7.4	0.9
1965	109.0	74.8	28.3	8.2	5.1	5.4	2.4	7.2	46.5	8.5	1.2
1966	117.7	85.4	31.3	8.3	6.6	6.3	2.5	7.8	54.0	10.7	1.7
1967	118.7	86.4	31.5	8.2	6.0	7.1	2.4	7.8	54.9	11.3	1.9
1968	132.1	93.4	33.6	9.4	6.0	8.3	2.6	7.3	59.9	11.9	1.9
1969	147.3	104.7	37.7	11.7	6.8	8.7	2.8	7.8	67.0	14.6	2.4
1970	150.4	109.0	40.3	12.5	7.0	10.2	2.8	7.8	68.7	16.6	2.7
1971	169.9	114.1	42.7	14.9	6.3	11.0	2.7	7.9	71.5	17.3	2.8
1972	198.5	128.8	47.2	17.6	5.9	12.1	3.1	8.6	81.7	19.5	3.5
1973	228.6	153.3	55.0	19.8	7.9	13.8	3.5	9.9	98.3	23.1	3.5
1974	235.4	169.5	61.2	20.6	10.0	15.1	5.2	10.3	108.2	27.0	3.9
1975	236.5	173.7	61.4	17.7	10.6	15.7	7.4	10.1	112.4	28.5	3.6
1976	274.8	192.4	65.9	18.1	10.1	18.2	8.6	11.0	126.4	32.7	4.4
1977	339.0	228.7	74.6	20.3	11.1	19.3	11.5	12.5	154.1	39.2	5.7
1978	412.2	280.6	93.6	25.3	16.2	21.4	15.4	15.2	187.0	48.7	7.6
1979	474.9	333.9	117.7	33.5	22.0	24.6	19.0	18.5	216.2	58.5	10.2
1980	485.6	362.4	136.2	41.0	20.5	27.3	27.4	20.0	226.2	68.8	12.5
1981	542.6	420.0	167.3	48.3	25.4	30.0	42.5	21.2	252.7	81.5	17.1
1982	532.1	426.5	177.6	55.8	26.1	29.6	44.8	21.3	248.9	88.3	18.9
1983	570.1	417.2	154.3	55.8	19.5	25.8	30.0	23.3	262.9	100.1	23.9
1984	670.2	489.6	177.4	70.6	20.9	26.5	31.3	28.1	312.2	121.5	31.6
1985	714.4	526.2	194.5	84.1	24.1	26.5	27.9	31.8	331.7	130.3	33.7
1986	739.9	519.8	176.5	80.9	21.0	28.3	15.7	30.7	343.3	136.8	33.4
1987	757.8	524.1	174.2	80.8	21.2	25.4	13.1	33.7	349.9	141.2	35.8
1988	803.1	563.8	182.8	86.3	23.2	25.0	15.7	32.5	381.0	154.9	38.0
1989	847.3	607.7	193.7	88.3	28.8	27.5	14.9	34.3	414.0	172.6	43.1
1990	846.4	622.4	202.9	87.5	33.6	26.3	17.9	37.6	419.5	177.2	38.6
1991	803.3	598.2	183.6	68.9	31.4	31.6	18.5	33.2	414.6	182.9	37.7
1992	848.5	612.1	172.6	64.5	29.0	33.9	14.2	31.0	439.6	199.9	44.0
1993	932.5	666.6	177.2	69.4	23.6	33.2	16.6	34.5	489.4	217.6	47.9
1994	1 033.3	731.4	186.8	75.4	28.9	31.2	16.4	34.9	544.6	235.2	52.4
1995	1 112.9	810.0	207.3	83.1	35.5	33.1	15.0	40.6	602.8	263.0	66.1
1996	1 209.5	875.4	224.6	91.5	38.2	29.2	16.8	49.0	650.8	290.1	72.8
1997	1 317.8	968.7	250.3	104.3	37.6	28.8	22.4	57.3	718.3	330.3	81.4
1998	1 438.4	1 052.6	275.2	115.4	40.5	33.6	23.4	62.3	777.3	363.4	87.2
1999	1 558.8	1 133.9	282.2	124.3	32.6	39.5	20.6	65.2	851.7	411.0	96.0
2000	1 679.0	1 232.1	313.2	137.6	31.8	46.8	27.2	69.9	918.9	467.6	101.4
2001	1 646.1	1 176.8	322.6	134.9	29.5	49.6	39.2	69.4	854.2	437.0	85.4
2002	1 570.2	1 066.3	279.2	116.8	17.8	49.5	35.6	59.5	787.1	399.4	77.2
2003	1 649.8	1 077.4	277.2	112.2	16.7	44.2	45.7	58.4	800.2	406.7	77.8
2004	1 830.0	1 154.5	298.2	122.1	18.5	39.1	55.7	62.9	856.3	429.6	80.3
2005	2 042.8	1 273.1	337.6	132.6	23.3	40.9	76.6	64.2	935.5	451.4	81.7
2006	2 171.1	1 414.1	410.4	152.8	27.4	48.4	107.9	74.1	1 003.7	482.3	88.8
2007	2 134.0	1 503.8	480.3	174.4	33.0	62.3	118.1	92.6	1 023.5	517.7	93.7
2008	2 040.5	1 552.8	553.4	179.3	48.4	76.0	142.7	106.9	999.4	535.8	89.8
2006											
1st quarter	2 183.6	1 375.5	377.4	143.1	25.2	47.0	94.0	68.1	998.1	476.6	86.9
2nd quarter	2 187.9	1 408.3	406.0	150.4	27.5	46.4	108.1	73.7	1 002.3	478.7	89.1
3rd quarter	2 169.2	1 433.0	424.4	157.4	29.1	49.0	113.6	75.4	1 008.6	487.5	90.3
4th quarter	2 143.6	1 439.6	433.9	160.1	27.8	51.1	115.9	79.0	1 005.6	486.5	88.8
2007											
1st quarter	2 133.4	1 456.4	449.6	168.0	29.6	54.6	115.4	82.1	1 006.8	503.1	92.5
2nd quarter	2 148.1	1 493.7	469.8	169.8	31.6	61.3	116.2	90.9	1 023.9	514.1	92.8
3rd quarter	2 141.0	1 522.9	492.9	177.1	33.4	65.0	120.7	96.7	1 030.0	521.1	93.7
4th quarter	2 113.4	1 542.1	508.7	182.6	37.3	68.2	120.0	100.6	1 033.4	532.5	95.7
2008											
1st quarter	2 081.7	1 553.6	522.7	182.2	38.9	72.6	125.0	104.0	1 030.9	539.6	95.8
2nd quarter	2 077.0	1 571.9	549.8	182.7	48.4	74.2	136.1	108.5	1 022.1	550.9	96.8
3rd quarter	2 060.6	1 581.2	572.4	179.9	51.5	77.9	153.5	109.7	1 008.8	544.5	89.2
4th quarter	1 942.7	1 504.3	568.4	172.5	55.1	79.2	156.4	105.3	935.8	508.2	77.4

. . . = Not available.

Table 5-2. Gross Private Fixed Investment by Type—*Continued*

(Billions of dollars, quarterly data are at seasonally adjusted annual rates.)   **NIPA Table 5.3.5**

Year and quarter	Information processing equipment and software—*Continued*		Industrial equipment	Transportation equipment	Other non-residential equipment	Residential Total	Residential structures Total	Permanent site Total	Single family	Multifamily	Other residential structures	Residential equipment
	Software [1]	Other information processing										
1950	...	1.8	4.5	6.4	5.1	20.5	20.2	16.1	...	...	4.0	0.4
1951	...	2.1	5.7	6.6	5.5	18.4	18.1	13.8	...	...	4.3	0.4
1952	...	2.4	5.9	5.7	5.6	18.6	18.2	13.4	...	...	4.9	0.4
1953	...	2.7	6.7	6.6	5.6	19.4	19.0	13.9	...	...	5.1	0.4
1954	...	2.4	7.1	6.0	5.3	21.1	20.7	15.4	...	...	5.3	0.4
1955	...	2.8	7.3	7.5	6.3	25.0	24.6	18.6	...	...	6.0	0.4
1956	...	3.4	8.8	7.4	6.7	23.6	23.1	16.5	...	...	6.6	0.5
1957	...	4.0	9.6	8.3	6.7	22.2	21.7	15.1	...	...	6.6	0.5
1958	...	3.6	8.2	6.1	6.9	22.3	21.9	15.4	13.1	2.3	6.4	0.5
1959	0.0	4.0	8.5	8.3	7.6	28.1	27.5	19.7	16.7	3.0	7.9	0.6
1960	0.1	4.6	9.4	8.5	7.1	26.3	25.8	17.5	14.9	2.6	8.3	0.5
1961	0.2	4.8	8.8	8.0	7.0	26.4	25.9	17.4	14.1	3.3	8.5	0.5
1962	0.2	5.1	9.3	9.8	7.5	29.0	28.4	19.9	15.1	4.8	8.5	0.5
1963	0.4	5.4	10.0	9.4	8.8	32.1	31.5	22.4	16.0	6.4	9.1	0.6
1964	0.5	5.9	11.4	10.6	9.9	34.3	33.6	24.1	17.6	6.4	9.5	0.6
1965	0.7	6.7	13.7	13.2	11.0	34.2	33.5	23.8	17.8	6.0	9.7	0.7
1966	1.0	8.0	16.2	14.5	12.7	32.3	31.6	21.8	16.6	5.2	9.8	0.7
1967	1.2	8.2	16.9	14.3	12.4	32.4	31.6	21.5	16.8	4.7	10.1	0.7
1968	1.3	8.7	17.3	17.6	13.0	38.7	37.9	26.7	19.5	7.2	11.1	0.9
1969	1.8	10.4	19.1	18.9	14.4	42.6	41.6	29.2	19.7	9.5	12.4	1.0
1970	2.3	11.6	20.3	16.2	15.6	41.4	40.2	27.1	17.5	9.5	13.2	1.1
1971	2.4	12.2	19.5	18.4	16.3	55.8	54.5	38.7	25.8	12.9	15.8	1.3
1972	2.8	13.2	21.4	21.8	19.0	69.7	68.1	50.1	32.8	17.2	18.0	1.5
1973	3.2	16.3	26.0	26.6	22.6	75.3	73.6	54.6	35.2	19.4	19.0	1.7
1974	3.9	19.2	30.7	26.3	24.3	66.0	64.1	43.4	29.7	13.7	20.7	1.9
1975	4.8	20.2	31.3	25.2	27.4	62.7	60.8	36.3	29.6	6.7	24.5	1.9
1976	5.2	23.1	34.1	30.0	29.6	82.5	80.4	50.8	43.9	6.9	29.6	2.1
1977	5.5	28.0	39.4	39.3	36.3	110.3	107.9	72.2	62.2	10.0	35.7	2.4
1978	6.3	34.8	47.7	47.3	43.2	131.6	128.9	85.6	72.8	12.8	43.3	2.7
1979	8.1	40.2	56.2	53.6	47.9	141.0	137.8	89.3	72.3	17.0	48.6	3.2
1980	9.8	46.4	60.7	48.4	48.3	123.2	119.8	69.6	52.9	16.7	50.2	3.4
1981	11.8	52.5	65.5	50.6	55.2	122.6	118.9	69.4	52.0	17.5	49.5	3.6
1982	14.0	55.3	62.7	46.8	51.2	105.7	102.0	57.0	41.5	15.5	45.0	3.7
1983	16.4	59.8	58.9	53.5	50.4	152.9	148.6	95.0	72.5	22.4	53.7	4.2
1984	20.4	69.6	68.1	64.4	58.1	180.6	175.9	114.6	86.4	28.2	61.3	4.7
1985	23.8	72.9	72.5	69.0	59.9	188.2	183.1	115.9	87.4	28.5	67.2	5.1
1986	25.6	77.7	75.4	70.5	60.7	220.1	214.6	135.2	104.1	31.0	79.4	5.5
1987	29.0	76.4	76.7	68.1	63.9	233.7	227.9	142.7	117.2	25.5	85.2	5.8
1988	34.2	82.8	84.2	72.9	69.0	239.3	233.2	142.4	120.1	22.3	90.9	6.1
1989	41.9	87.6	93.3	67.9	80.2	239.5	233.4	143.2	120.9	22.3	90.1	6.1
1990	47.6	90.9	92.1	70.0	80.2	224.0	218.0	132.1	112.9	19.3	85.8	6.0
1991	53.7	91.5	89.3	71.5	70.8	205.1	199.4	114.6	99.4	15.1	84.8	5.7
1992	57.9	98.1	93.0	74.7	72.0	236.3	230.4	135.1	122.0	13.1	95.3	5.9
1993	64.3	105.4	102.2	89.4	80.2	266.0	259.9	150.9	140.1	10.8	109.0	6.1
1994	68.3	114.6	113.6	107.7	88.1	301.9	295.6	176.4	162.3	14.1	119.2	6.2
1995	74.6	122.3	129.0	116.1	94.7	302.8	296.5	171.4	153.5	17.9	125.1	6.3
1996	85.5	131.9	136.5	123.2	101.0	334.1	327.8	191.1	170.8	20.3	136.7	6.3
1997	107.5	141.4	140.4	135.5	112.1	349.1	342.8	198.1	175.2	22.9	144.8	6.3
1998	124.0	152.2	146.4	144.0	123.5	385.8	379.3	224.0	199.4	24.6	155.3	6.6
1999	152.6	162.4	147.0	167.6	126.0	424.9	417.8	251.3	223.8	27.4	166.6	7.0
2000	176.2	190.0	159.2	160.8	131.2	446.9	439.5	265.0	236.8	28.3	174.5	7.4
2001	174.7	177.0	146.7	141.7	128.8	469.3	461.9	279.4	249.1	30.3	182.5	7.4
2002	167.6	154.5	135.7	126.3	125.7	503.9	496.3	298.8	265.9	33.0	197.5	7.6
2003	171.4	157.5	140.7	118.3	134.5	572.4	564.5	345.7	310.6	35.1	218.8	7.9
2004	183.0	166.4	139.7	142.9	144.0	675.5	667.0	417.5	377.6	39.9	249.5	8.4
2005	195.1	174.6	157.1	164.4	162.6	769.6	760.6	480.8	433.5	47.3	279.8	9.0
2006	205.7	187.8	171.2	177.0	173.1	757.0	747.4	468.8	416.0	52.8	278.7	9.5
2007	227.3	196.8	180.6	157.2	168.0	630.2	620.7	353.4	305.2	48.2	267.3	9.5
2008	240.5	205.5	180.6	112.2	170.8	487.7	478.5	230.3	186.1	44.2	248.2	9.2
2006												
1st quarter	201.3	188.4	164.7	183.3	173.5	808.1	798.5	517.4	465.5	51.9	281.2	9.5
2nd quarter	203.6	186.0	174.2	174.8	174.6	779.6	770.0	487.8	435.2	52.6	282.3	9.5
3rd quarter	206.8	190.4	172.6	176.3	172.2	736.2	726.7	450.9	398.8	52.2	275.7	9.5
4th quarter	211.3	186.5	173.4	173.4	172.3	704.0	694.6	419.2	364.6	54.6	275.4	9.5
2007												
1st quarter	218.2	192.5	172.1	168.1	163.4	677.0	667.4	390.9	338.1	52.8	276.5	9.6
2nd quarter	225.8	195.5	185.1	157.8	166.9	654.4	644.8	372.8	323.7	49.1	272.1	9.6
3rd quarter	229.5	197.9	185.2	154.6	169.2	618.1	608.6	345.8	299.2	46.6	262.8	9.5
4th quarter	235.6	201.2	179.9	148.4	172.6	571.3	561.8	304.2	259.8	44.4	257.6	9.5
2008												
1st quarter	241.8	202.0	182.0	142.1	167.3	528.1	518.7	263.4	219.7	43.7	255.3	9.3
2nd quarter	244.6	209.5	183.2	121.4	166.5	505.0	495.6	242.5	197.1	45.4	253.1	9.5
3rd quarter	242.5	212.9	182.2	105.5	176.6	479.4	470.2	222.6	177.1	45.5	247.6	9.2
4th quarter	233.0	197.8	175.1	79.8	172.7	438.4	429.6	192.8	150.7	42.1	236.8	8.8

[1] Excludes software "embedded," or bundled, in computers and other equipment.
. . . = Not available.

Table 5-3. Real Gross Private Fixed Investment by Type

(Billions of chained [2000] dollars, quarterly data are at seasonally adjusted annual rates.)   **NIPA Table 5.3.6**

Year and quarter	Total gross private fixed investment	Nonresidential Total	Structures Total	Commercial and health care	Manufac- turing	Power and communi- cation	Mining exploration, shafts, and wells	Other non- residential structures	Equipment and software Total	Information processing equipment and software Total	Computers and peripheral equipment [1]
1990	886.6	595.1	275.2	119.6	45.4	33.4	26.6	50.4	355.0	100.7	. . .
1991	829.1	563.2	244.6	92.9	41.8	39.6	26.0	43.8	345.9	105.9	. . .
1992	878.3	581.3	229.9	86.4	38.4	42.0	21.5	40.6	371.1	122.2	. . .
1993	953.5	631.9	228.3	89.9	30.2	39.3	24.8	43.8	417.4	138.2	. . .
1994	1 042.3	689.9	232.3	94.1	35.7	35.6	23.9	42.8	467.2	155.7	. . .
1995	1 109.6	762.5	247.1	99.7	42.1	36.3	20.3	47.9	523.1	182.7	. . .
1996	1 209.2	833.6	261.1	107.4	44.2	31.3	21.5	56.4	578.7	218.9	. . .
1997	1 320.6	934.2	280.1	118.6	42.3	30.1	25.3	63.9	658.3	269.9	. . .
1998	1 455.0	1 037.8	294.5	125.4	43.7	34.7	23.3	67.4	745.6	328.9	. . .
1999	1 576.3	1 133.3	293.2	129.4	33.9	40.8	21.3	67.9	840.2	398.5	. . .
2000	1 679.0	1 232.1	313.2	137.6	31.8	46.8	27.2	69.9	918.9	467.6	. . .
2001	1 629.4	1 180.5	306.1	130.3	28.5	48.2	32.0	66.6	874.2	459.0	. . .
2002	1 544.6	1 071.5	253.8	109.8	16.7	47.1	24.5	55.9	820.2	437.4	. . .
2003	1 596.9	1 081.8	243.5	102.6	15.4	41.0	29.0	53.4	843.1	462.7	. . .
2004	1 712.8	1 144.3	246.7	105.1	16.2	33.7	33.3	54.6	905.1	505.7	. . .
2005	1 829.8	1 226.2	249.8	104.3	19.0	32.7	36.5	51.9	989.6	546.7	. . .
2006	1 865.5	1 318.2	270.3	110.6	20.9	35.3	40.7	55.9	1 061.0	596.6	. . .
2007	1 808.5	1 382.9	304.6	119.7	23.9	43.5	44.5	66.7	1 078.9	653.9	. . .
2008	1 718.9	1 405.4	338.8	119.4	33.3	49.9	52.1	75.4	1 047.0	685.0	. . .
1998											
1st quarter	1 402.4	1 001.6	286.7	120.8	44.8	34.0	23.6	63.5	717.2	309.9	. . .
2nd quarter	1 444.5	1 032.5	298.0	126.7	44.6	34.9	24.0	67.9	737.3	322.7	. . .
3rd quarter	1 465.1	1 042.4	295.5	124.7	43.2	35.1	23.9	68.6	749.1	332.2	. . .
4th quarter	1 507.7	1 074.7	297.6	129.5	42.1	35.0	21.8	69.5	778.6	350.7	. . .
1999											
1st quarter	1 531.0	1 094.0	292.0	128.4	38.1	36.7	20.0	68.9	802.7	369.5	. . .
2nd quarter	1 568.6	1 127.3	294.1	129.5	34.3	39.2	21.7	69.6	833.5	395.8	. . .
3rd quarter	1 598.6	1 154.4	291.8	129.9	32.6	42.6	20.5	66.2	862.4	412.8	. . .
4th quarter	1 606.9	1 157.3	294.8	129.9	30.5	44.8	22.8	66.9	862.3	415.8	. . .
2000											
1st quarter	1 651.1	1 196.7	299.9	130.8	31.0	44.7	24.2	69.2	896.7	442.9	. . .
2nd quarter	1 689.1	1 238.6	312.5	136.7	33.0	45.7	26.9	70.2	926.0	465.7	. . .
3rd quarter	1 686.4	1 245.2	319.7	140.8	31.6	47.8	28.2	71.3	925.5	473.8	. . .
4th quarter	1 689.4	1 247.9	320.6	141.9	31.6	49.0	29.4	68.8	927.3	488.1	. . .
2001											
1st quarter	1 678.2	1 234.4	313.8	140.8	32.4	44.1	31.7	64.6	920.8	485.7	. . .
2nd quarter	1 640.5	1 190.2	310.6	135.4	30.2	47.6	32.6	64.4	879.2	461.4	. . .
3rd quarter	1 621.9	1 169.3	315.1	126.1	28.9	49.1	34.1	76.1	852.9	447.3	. . .
4th quarter	1 577.0	1 128.2	284.9	118.9	22.6	52.2	29.7	61.1	843.8	441.7	. . .
2002											
1st quarter	1 551.5	1 090.3	270.3	116.5	19.3	53.5	24.0	57.9	820.9	435.0	. . .
2nd quarter	1 545.9	1 073.3	256.4	111.2	17.3	47.9	23.4	57.4	819.0	437.1	. . .
3rd quarter	1 543.2	1 068.0	245.8	107.3	15.2	43.2	25.4	54.5	825.7	444.2	. . .
4th quarter	1 537.8	1 054.5	242.5	104.2	14.9	43.8	25.4	53.8	815.4	433.3	. . .
2003											
1st quarter	1 536.3	1 047.5	238.2	100.2	14.4	44.4	26.5	51.7	813.3	442.1	. . .
2nd quarter	1 575.6	1 074.5	246.5	101.4	15.7	42.3	30.0	54.8	831.7	446.0	. . .
3rd quarter	1 626.7	1 098.8	246.0	103.9	15.9	39.5	30.3	53.9	857.8	470.4	. . .
4th quarter	1 648.9	1 106.5	243.1	104.7	15.7	37.9	29.2	53.2	869.5	492.4	. . .
2004											
1st quarter	1 647.9	1 099.1	242.9	102.9	15.4	36.9	31.6	52.8	861.9	494.2	. . .
2nd quarter	1 698.7	1 127.5	246.5	107.1	15.1	31.4	33.7	55.1	887.4	499.3	. . .
3rd quarter	1 736.7	1 160.7	248.7	106.9	15.9	32.4	33.9	55.5	920.0	507.5	. . .
4th quarter	1 767.7	1 189.7	248.6	103.2	18.5	34.2	33.8	54.9	951.2	521.7	. . .
2005											
1st quarter	1 790.5	1 200.4	253.1	105.1	19.2	33.6	36.4	53.5	956.6	529.5	. . .
2nd quarter	1 823.5	1 219.0	252.3	104.6	18.6	32.6	38.5	51.3	977.9	540.3	. . .
3rd quarter	1 847.2	1 237.1	246.2	103.1	18.9	31.9	35.9	51.1	1 006.5	552.7	. . .
4th quarter	1 858.0	1 248.2	247.4	104.2	19.3	32.5	35.2	51.6	1 017.4	564.3	. . .
2006											
1st quarter	1 895.2	1 295.2	256.5	106.4	19.6	35.4	37.2	52.6	1 056.6	586.2	. . .
2nd quarter	1 883.1	1 315.4	268.3	109.8	21.1	34.2	40.4	56.0	1 061.2	590.9	. . .
3rd quarter	1 860.0	1 332.7	277.4	113.3	22.1	35.4	42.4	56.7	1 066.4	603.9	. . .
4th quarter	1 823.7	1 329.3	279.1	113.0	20.8	36.3	42.9	58.4	1 059.9	605.3	. . .
2007											
1st quarter	1 807.8	1 340.4	286.6	116.9	21.8	38.7	42.7	59.9	1 060.0	629.9	. . .
2nd quarter	1 821.3	1 373.8	298.9	117.3	23.0	43.1	43.6	65.9	1 077.9	647.3	. . .
3rd quarter	1 817.0	1 402.9	313.2	121.1	24.1	45.2	46.4	69.4	1 087.5	660.9	. . .
4th quarter	1 788.2	1 414.7	319.7	123.7	26.6	46.9	45.4	71.6	1 090.1	677.6	. . .
2008											
1st quarter	1 762.4	1 423.1	326.4	122.5	27.5	49.5	47.1	73.8	1 088.6	689.6	. . .
2nd quarter	1 754.9	1 431.8	340.5	122.6	34.0	49.5	50.4	76.8	1 074.7	702.9	. . .
3rd quarter	1 731.1	1 425.7	348.4	119.8	35.4	50.3	55.4	77.2	1 054.0	695.5	. . .
4th quarter	1 627.0	1 341.1	339.9	112.6	36.3	50.1	55.7	73.7	970.5	651.8	. . .

[1]See notes and definitions.
. . . = Not available.

Table 5-3. Real Gross Private Fixed Investment by Type—*Continued*

(Billions of chained [2000] dollars, quarterly data are at seasonally adjusted annual rates.)　　　　　**NIPA Table 5.3.6**

Year and quarter	Nonresidential—*Continued* Equipment and software—*Continued* Information processing equipment and software—*Continued* Software [2]	Other information processing	Industrial equipment	Transportation equipment	Other nonresidential equipment	Residential Total	Residential structures Total	Permanent site Total	Single family	Multifamily	Other residential structures	Residential equipment
1990	39.9	80.1	109.2	81.0	96.0	298.9	292.6	181.3	154.2	26.7	111.6	6.0
1991	45.1	79.6	102.2	78.8	82.0	270.2	264.0	156.1	135.1	20.6	107.8	5.8
1992	53.0	84.4	104.0	80.2	81.6	307.6	301.4	182.0	164.1	17.5	119.5	6.0
1993	59.3	90.9	112.9	95.1	89.3	332.7	326.4	194.3	179.7	14.1	132.1	6.1
1994	65.1	99.4	122.9	111.4	96.5	364.8	358.6	217.6	198.9	18.2	141.2	6.1
1995	71.6	107.0	134.9	120.6	101.7	353.1	346.8	203.2	180.6	22.6	143.4	6.2
1996	84.1	117.2	139.9	125.4	105.6	381.3	375.1	222.3	197.3	25.0	152.8	6.2
1997	108.8	127.3	143.0	135.9	115.8	388.6	382.4	223.5	196.6	26.9	158.8	6.1
1998	129.4	143.2	148.1	145.4	125.7	418.3	411.9	244.7	218.1	26.6	167.1	6.4
1999	157.2	158.0	147.9	167.7	126.7	443.6	436.6	262.9	234.2	28.7	173.6	7.0
2000	176.2	190.0	159.2	160.8	131.2	446.9	439.5	265.0	236.8	28.3	174.5	7.4
2001	173.8	181.7	145.7	142.8	126.9	448.5	441.1	266.6	237.1	29.5	174.5	7.4
2002	169.7	161.1	134.5	126.0	122.9	469.9	462.2	277.3	246.3	31.0	184.9	7.7
2003	177.3	167.1	138.4	113.8	130.4	509.4	501.2	304.5	272.6	31.9	196.7	8.1
2004	193.6	181.1	134.0	130.6	138.3	560.2	551.2	339.7	305.3	34.3	211.3	9.0
2005	207.0	191.6	145.3	149.5	150.4	595.4	586.0	363.7	325.9	37.8	222.0	9.3
2006	215.5	206.7	153.5	159.5	156.5	552.9	543.5	332.9	294.9	38.0	210.6	9.6
2007	237.0	218.0	155.7	139.4	148.4	453.8	444.9	247.1	214.1	33.1	199.4	9.5
2008	248.4	226.1	149.2	99.6	146.3	359.5	351.3	167.7	136.0	31.5	186.2	9.1
1998												
1st quarter	122.1	139.5	151.1	134.7	125.0	401.8	395.5	232.9	205.0	27.9	162.6	6.3
2nd quarter	126.2	142.2	149.4	140.3	127.8	412.9	406.5	239.5	213.5	26.1	166.9	6.4
3rd quarter	131.5	143.1	145.9	146.8	126.5	424.1	417.7	249.3	223.3	26.0	168.4	6.5
4th quarter	137.8	148.1	146.2	159.8	123.8	434.3	427.7	257.2	230.6	26.6	170.6	6.6
1999												
1st quarter	144.9	149.8	145.6	161.4	127.5	438.1	431.3	261.1	232.5	28.6	170.3	6.7
2nd quarter	154.5	157.0	147.4	165.7	125.1	441.8	434.9	260.3	231.8	28.4	174.6	7.0
3rd quarter	162.2	162.8	149.2	174.6	126.1	444.5	437.3	262.0	232.8	29.2	175.3	7.2
4th quarter	167.2	162.4	149.3	169.1	128.2	449.9	442.7	268.4	239.6	28.8	174.4	7.2
2000												
1st quarter	171.4	179.9	156.3	166.1	131.3	454.5	447.1	272.6	243.5	29.0	174.6	7.3
2nd quarter	175.8	187.7	159.7	167.0	133.6	450.4	443.1	268.8	239.7	29.1	174.3	7.3
3rd quarter	176.2	192.3	161.9	159.5	130.4	441.2	433.8	259.3	232.4	26.8	174.5	7.4
4th quarter	181.2	200.2	159.0	150.7	129.6	441.6	434.2	259.5	231.5	28.0	174.6	7.4
2001												
1st quarter	181.4	193.7	159.3	145.3	130.9	444.0	436.6	263.7	234.6	29.1	172.8	7.4
2nd quarter	174.1	182.9	147.3	144.5	126.3	450.1	442.7	268.4	239.1	29.3	174.3	7.4
3rd quarter	172.3	177.8	140.6	137.6	127.6	452.1	444.8	269.7	240.3	29.4	175.1	7.3
4th quarter	167.4	172.2	135.4	144.0	122.8	447.8	440.4	264.6	234.5	30.1	175.8	7.5
2002												
1st quarter	166.3	162.9	135.8	130.4	120.3	459.0	451.4	268.7	238.0	30.8	182.7	7.6
2nd quarter	170.2	162.6	132.7	126.1	123.8	469.5	461.8	277.3	245.9	31.4	184.5	7.7
3rd quarter	173.4	161.7	134.7	124.1	123.6	471.8	464.2	280.1	248.9	31.2	184.1	7.6
4th quarter	168.7	157.1	134.9	123.5	124.1	479.3	471.6	283.3	252.4	30.8	188.3	7.7
2003												
1st quarter	170.4	160.2	139.1	108.3	125.1	484.1	476.4	289.0	257.4	31.6	187.4	7.7
2nd quarter	171.8	162.4	142.7	116.6	127.1	496.3	488.3	293.8	262.4	31.4	194.6	8.0
3rd quarter	180.6	168.7	138.9	116.8	133.8	521.8	513.5	309.4	276.9	32.5	204.1	8.3
4th quarter	186.3	177.0	132.8	113.5	135.5	535.2	526.7	325.8	293.6	32.0	200.7	8.5
2004												
1st quarter	190.5	179.2	129.1	112.0	132.7	540.5	531.8	328.0	295.4	32.5	203.6	8.7
2nd quarter	190.5	183.0	131.5	125.5	135.3	561.7	552.8	339.5	305.6	33.8	213.2	8.8
3rd quarter	193.9	181.2	136.9	137.0	140.8	567.5	558.5	345.5	310.1	35.4	212.7	9.1
4th quarter	199.3	181.0	138.7	147.9	144.5	570.9	561.7	345.8	310.1	35.7	215.6	9.2
2005												
1st quarter	201.5	187.9	142.0	142.1	145.6	582.1	572.9	355.5	318.8	36.6	217.2	9.1
2nd quarter	206.8	188.4	140.9	148.5	150.5	595.8	586.4	361.3	323.5	37.8	225.0	9.3
3rd quarter	208.2	195.3	146.3	157.2	151.7	601.7	592.3	366.0	327.6	38.4	226.1	9.2
4th quarter	211.4	194.9	152.0	150.3	153.7	602.0	592.4	372.0	333.7	38.3	219.8	9.5
2006												
1st quarter	212.5	207.6	149.9	165.3	158.2	596.5	586.8	371.6	333.1	38.5	214.5	9.7
2nd quarter	213.2	205.1	157.2	157.9	158.7	570.1	560.6	346.8	308.7	38.2	213.6	9.7
3rd quarter	215.8	209.4	153.8	159.7	155.2	536.7	527.4	319.9	282.7	37.3	207.6	9.6
4th quarter	220.5	204.8	153.2	155.2	153.8	508.4	499.3	293.2	255.2	38.1	206.9	9.4
2007												
1st quarter	227.9	212.5	150.3	149.0	145.3	486.4	477.3	271.9	235.6	36.4	206.7	9.5
2nd quarter	235.7	216.2	160.3	139.4	147.5	471.7	462.8	261.0	227.3	33.8	203.2	9.5
3rd quarter	239.4	219.6	159.1	137.4	149.2	445.3	436.5	242.2	210.3	32.0	195.9	9.5
4th quarter	245.1	223.5	153.1	131.9	151.5	411.6	403.0	213.4	182.9	30.4	191.7	9.4
2008												
1st quarter	251.0	223.6	153.4	127.0	146.5	383.0	374.6	187.1	156.7	30.4	190.0	9.3
2nd quarter	252.3	230.6	152.0	108.6	145.3	369.6	361.1	175.2	142.9	32.1	188.5	9.5
3rd quarter	249.5	233.6	148.6	93.6	151.5	353.7	345.6	163.5	130.5	32.7	184.8	9.0
4th quarter	240.8	216.6	142.8	69.3	141.9	331.6	323.9	145.1	113.8	31.0	181.5	8.6

[2]Excludes software "embedded," or bundled, in computers and other equipment.

Table 5-4. Chain-Type Quantity Indexes for Private Fixed Investment by Type

(Index numbers, 2000 = 100, quarterly data are seasonally adjusted.)　　　　　　　　　　　　　　　　**NIPA Table 5.3.3**

Year and quarter	Total gross private fixed investment	Nonresidential									
		Total	Structures						Equipment and software		
			Total	Commercial and health care	Manufac- turing	Power and communi- cation	Mining exploration, shafts, and wells	Other non- residential structures	Total	Information processing equipment and software	
										Total	Computers and peripheral equipment
1950	13.0	8.6	26.4	10.8	27.8	42.9	45.6	34.9	5.1	0.2	. . .
1951	12.4	9.0	28.4	10.4	48.8	43.1	47.9	34.1	5.3	0.2	. . .
1952	12.2	8.8	28.3	8.1	52.2	43.5	53.3	34.3	5.1	0.2	. . .
1953	13.0	9.6	30.8	11.1	49.9	47.8	58.2	35.6	5.6	0.3	. . .
1954	13.3	9.4	31.9	13.8	46.7	43.7	64.4	37.5	5.3	0.2	. . .
1955	15.0	10.4	34.2	17.9	51.1	41.6	69.3	37.6	6.0	0.3	. . .
1956	15.0	11.0	37.8	20.3	67.1	48.6	67.0	37.2	6.2	0.3	. . .
1957	14.9	11.2	37.7	19.3	71.2	50.5	63.3	37.2	6.3	0.3	. . .
1958	13.8	10.0	35.7	20.3	49.1	48.5	59.2	38.9	5.4	0.3	. . .
1959	15.7	10.8	36.5	22.0	43.8	46.5	60.7	42.9	6.1	0.3	0.0
1960	15.9	11.4	39.4	23.4	59.3	47.0	57.0	47.7	6.3	0.4	0.0
1961	15.8	11.3	40.0	26.7	58.0	44.0	58.1	46.6	6.2	0.4	0.0
1962	17.2	12.3	41.8	29.7	58.6	44.3	60.9	47.6	6.9	0.5	0.0
1963	18.6	13.0	42.2	28.7	58.8	47.2	57.2	50.3	7.5	0.6	0.0
1964	20.4	14.5	46.6	31.2	70.7	51.4	61.2	55.2	8.5	0.7	0.0
1965	22.5	17.0	54.1	36.6	97.8	56.9	60.5	62.0	10.0	0.8	0.0
1966	23.7	19.2	57.8	35.7	121.5	64.9	57.3	64.4	11.6	1.1	0.0
1967	23.3	18.9	56.3	34.3	106.9	71.0	54.8	63.0	11.5	1.1	0.0
1968	24.9	19.7	57.1	37.5	102.9	78.9	55.1	55.8	12.3	1.2	0.0
1969	26.5	21.2	60.2	43.3	108.2	78.9	57.5	55.4	13.3	1.5	0.0
1970	25.9	21.1	60.4	43.9	104.5	86.3	54.1	52.1	13.2	1.7	0.0
1971	27.9	21.1	59.4	47.9	86.3	87.0	50.0	48.8	13.3	1.8	0.0
1972	31.2	23.1	61.2	52.3	75.4	90.7	53.7	49.3	15.1	2.0	0.0
1973	34.1	26.4	66.2	54.7	93.4	96.5	57.3	53.1	17.8	2.4	0.0
1974	32.0	26.7	64.8	51.3	106.4	90.4	68.1	48.7	18.3	2.7	0.0
1975	28.5	24.0	58.0	39.9	102.0	83.1	79.5	43.0	16.5	2.7	0.0
1976	31.4	25.2	59.4	39.4	94.2	90.6	85.8	45.2	17.6	3.1	0.1
1977	35.9	28.0	61.8	41.5	96.8	89.2	96.9	47.7	20.2	3.8	0.1
1978	40.2	32.2	70.8	47.3	129.1	93.5	110.5	54.1	23.3	4.9	0.2
1979	42.5	35.5	79.7	56.4	158.6	97.0	117.7	59.5	25.3	5.9	0.3
1980	39.7	35.4	84.4	61.9	132.7	97.9	165.4	57.7	24.4	6.9	0.5
1981	40.6	37.4	91.1	66.9	150.6	100.4	192.3	55.8	25.4	8.0	0.7
1982	37.7	36.0	89.5	72.8	145.4	94.8	177.7	52.7	24.1	8.5	0.9
1983	40.5	35.5	79.9	70.7	105.2	81.6	147.2	55.6	25.4	10.0	1.3
1984	47.3	41.8	91.0	86.0	108.8	83.3	167.3	65.1	30.5	12.6	2.2
1985	49.8	44.6	97.5	99.3	121.7	82.4	149.1	71.7	32.4	14.1	2.7
1986	50.4	43.3	86.8	92.3	102.3	87.9	87.3	67.4	33.0	15.2	3.1
1987	50.7	43.3	84.3	89.0	99.7	78.2	85.4	71.4	33.5	16.1	3.9
1988	52.4	45.5	84.9	91.6	105.2	73.8	93.7	66.5	36.0	18.0	4.5
1989	53.9	48.1	86.6	90.5	126.0	76.6	84.7	67.9	38.6	20.5	5.5
1990	52.8	48.3	87.9	86.9	142.8	71.3	97.9	72.1	38.6	21.5	5.4
1991	49.4	45.7	78.1	67.5	131.5	84.7	95.7	62.6	37.6	22.6	5.9
1992	52.3	47.2	73.4	62.8	120.7	89.8	79.2	58.1	40.4	26.1	8.0
1993	56.8	51.3	72.9	65.3	94.8	83.9	91.3	62.7	45.4	29.6	10.3
1994	62.1	56.0	74.2	68.4	112.2	76.0	88.1	61.3	50.8	33.3	12.8
1995	66.1	61.9	78.9	72.5	132.3	77.6	74.7	68.6	56.9	39.1	19.3
1996	72.0	67.7	83.4	78.1	139.1	66.8	79.3	80.7	63.0	46.8	27.8
1997	78.7	75.8	89.4	86.2	132.9	64.4	93.0	91.5	71.6	57.7	40.3
1998	86.7	84.2	94.0	91.2	137.4	74.2	85.8	96.4	81.1	70.3	58.2
1999	93.9	92.0	93.6	94.1	106.5	87.2	78.3	97.2	91.4	85.2	82.5
2000	100.0	100.0	100.0	100.0	100.0	100.0	100.0	100.0	100.0	100.0	100.0
2001	97.0	95.8	97.7	94.7	89.7	103.0	117.8	95.3	95.1	98.2	102.4
2002	92.0	87.0	81.0	79.8	52.4	100.6	90.3	80.0	89.3	93.5	107.3
2003	95.1	87.8	77.7	74.6	48.5	87.7	106.7	76.5	91.7	99.0	121.3
2004	102.0	92.9	78.8	76.4	50.9	72.1	122.4	78.1	98.5	108.1	135.1
2005	109.0	99.5	79.7	75.8	59.7	69.8	134.3	74.3	107.7	116.9	156.7
2006	111.1	107.0	86.3	80.4	65.8	75.5	149.9	80.0	115.5	127.6	195.4
2007	107.7	112.2	97.3	87.0	75.1	92.9	163.9	95.5	117.4	139.8	230.5
2008	102.4	114.1	108.2	86.8	104.7	106.5	191.9	107.9	113.9	146.5	245.5
2006											
1st quarter	112.9	105.1	81.9	77.3	61.7	75.7	137.0	75.3	115.0	125.4	181.8
2nd quarter	112.2	106.8	85.7	79.8	66.5	73.0	148.8	80.2	115.5	126.4	193.2
3rd quarter	110.8	108.2	88.6	82.4	69.6	75.7	156.0	81.1	116.0	129.1	202.6
4th quarter	108.6	107.9	89.1	82.1	65.4	77.5	158.0	83.5	115.3	129.4	204.2
2007											
1st quarter	107.7	108.8	91.5	85.0	68.4	82.6	157.1	85.8	115.4	134.7	217.3
2nd quarter	108.5	111.5	95.4	85.3	72.4	92.0	160.4	94.3	117.3	138.4	224.5
3rd quarter	108.2	113.9	100.0	88.0	75.8	96.6	170.9	99.4	118.3	141.3	234.7
4th quarter	106.5	114.8	102.1	89.9	83.8	100.3	167.2	102.5	118.6	144.9	245.3
2008											
1st quarter	105.0	115.5	104.2	89.1	86.4	105.7	173.3	105.7	118.5	147.5	254.7
2nd quarter	104.5	116.2	108.7	89.1	107.1	105.8	185.6	110.0	117.0	150.3	262.6
3rd quarter	103.1	115.7	111.3	87.1	111.2	107.6	203.8	110.5	114.7	148.7	246.5
4th quarter	96.9	108.8	108.5	81.9	114.0	107.0	205.0	105.4	105.6	139.4	218.1

. . . = Not available.

Table 5-4. Chain-Type Quantity Indexes for Private Fixed Investment by Type—*Continued*

(Index numbers, 2000 = 100, quarterly data are seasonally adjusted.)   **NIPA Table 5.3.3**

Year and quarter	Nonresidential—*Continued* Equipment and software—*Continued* Information processing equipment and software—*Continued* Software [1]	Other information processing	Industrial equipment	Transportation equipment	Other nonresidential equipment	Residential Total	Residential structures Total	Permanent site Total	Single family	Multifamily	Other residential structures	Residential equipment
1950	. . .	2.3	22.1	18.5	24.6	32.3	33.3	45.3	. . .	. . .	15.9	9.0
1951	. . .	2.5	24.8	17.8	24.8	27.0	27.8	36.2	. . .	. . .	15.7	8.3
1952	. . .	2.9	25.7	14.7	25.0	26.6	27.3	34.1	. . .	. . .	17.4	8.3
1953	. . .	3.2	28.3	17.4	24.4	27.5	28.2	35.2	. . .	. . .	18.1	8.7
1954	. . .	2.9	29.2	15.3	23.0	29.8	30.6	38.7	. . .	. . .	18.9	8.9
1955	. . .	3.3	29.0	19.4	27.0	34.6	35.6	45.7	. . .	. . .	20.9	10.2
1956	. . .	3.8	32.0	17.5	27.9	31.8	32.6	39.6	. . .	. . .	22.3	11.3
1957	. . .	4.3	32.4	18.7	26.3	29.8	30.5	36.0	. . .	. . .	22.5	11.3
1958	. . .	3.9	27.0	13.6	26.7	30.2	30.8	36.9	34.6	51.8	21.9	12.0
1959	0.0	4.2	27.4	18.0	28.7	37.8	38.7	47.0	44.0	66.6	26.6	13.8
1960	0.1	4.9	29.6	18.6	26.3	35.1	36.0	41.5	38.9	58.6	27.7	13.0
1961	0.1	5.2	28.0	17.6	26.0	35.2	36.1	41.3	36.8	73.9	28.3	13.0
1962	0.1	5.5	29.4	21.7	27.8	38.6	39.5	47.1	39.3	107.4	28.5	13.8
1963	0.2	5.7	31.8	21.0	32.3	43.2	44.2	53.4	41.9	144.2	30.7	15.4
1964	0.2	6.2	35.9	23.7	35.8	45.7	46.8	57.0	46.0	143.2	31.8	16.5
1965	0.3	7.1	42.4	29.7	39.7	44.3	45.3	54.5	45.0	128.7	31.7	18.4
1966	0.5	8.3	48.7	32.7	44.7	40.4	41.1	47.8	40.0	107.9	31.3	18.8
1967	0.6	8.3	48.9	31.6	42.2	39.1	39.8	45.6	39.2	93.7	31.2	19.3
1968	0.6	8.6	47.9	38.0	42.7	44.4	45.2	53.6	43.1	135.4	32.8	23.0
1969	0.8	9.9	51.1	39.5	45.6	45.7	46.4	55.1	41.0	168.5	33.5	26.2
1970	1.1	10.7	51.9	32.4	47.6	43.0	43.4	49.9	35.6	164.9	33.9	28.6
1971	1.1	10.8	47.6	35.0	47.5	54.8	55.5	67.2	49.4	209.9	38.5	32.0
1972	1.3	11.5	51.3	40.7	53.8	64.5	65.4	81.3	58.7	262.8	42.2	38.4
1973	1.5	13.9	60.7	48.9	62.8	64.1	64.8	80.9	57.4	270.2	41.3	43.2
1974	1.8	15.4	65.4	44.3	62.0	50.9	51.1	58.6	44.1	174.0	40.2	44.0
1975	2.1	14.8	55.4	38.2	57.4	44.3	44.3	44.8	40.2	77.6	43.6	41.0
1976	2.3	16.2	55.7	42.4	57.9	54.7	55.0	58.9	56.0	75.2	49.3	43.1
1977	2.4	19.5	59.0	51.6	65.2	66.4	67.0	76.0	72.0	99.6	53.9	47.2
1978	2.8	23.2	65.7	57.0	71.8	70.6	71.2	79.5	74.4	112.2	59.1	51.3
1979	3.5	26.0	70.4	59.5	73.2	68.0	68.4	74.4	65.9	137.1	59.7	56.2
1980	4.1	28.0	67.4	48.6	65.8	53.6	53.6	52.3	43.3	122.7	55.7	56.3
1981	4.8	29.6	66.3	47.2	67.6	49.3	49.2	48.2	39.4	118.0	50.8	56.2
1982	5.5	29.8	60.5	41.8	58.5	40.4	40.0	37.6	30.2	96.2	43.8	54.0
1983	6.5	31.3	55.7	47.1	56.3	57.1	57.0	61.4	52.5	131.8	50.8	60.3
1984	8.3	35.7	63.8	56.1	63.8	65.6	65.6	72.1	60.9	161.0	56.1	66.8
1985	9.8	36.8	66.7	58.3	64.4	66.6	66.5	71.2	60.4	156.9	59.8	72.1
1986	11.0	38.3	66.4	56.1	63.2	74.8	74.7	79.5	69.1	161.5	67.9	78.0
1987	12.5	36.8	64.8	53.3	65.0	76.3	76.2	80.6	74.7	127.4	69.9	81.2
1988	14.9	39.3	68.0	56.2	68.1	75.5	75.3	77.7	73.8	108.7	72.0	83.9
1989	19.2	41.1	72.8	50.6	76.1	73.2	73.0	75.7	71.7	108.5	69.1	84.4
1990	22.6	42.1	68.6	50.4	73.2	66.9	66.6	68.4	65.1	94.6	64.0	81.9
1991	25.6	41.9	64.2	49.0	62.5	60.5	60.1	58.9	57.1	72.9	61.8	78.7
1992	30.1	44.4	65.3	49.9	62.2	68.8	68.6	68.7	69.3	62.0	68.5	81.1
1993	33.7	47.9	70.9	59.1	68.1	74.4	74.3	73.3	75.9	50.0	75.7	82.7
1994	37.0	52.3	77.2	69.3	73.6	81.6	81.6	82.1	84.0	64.5	80.9	83.2
1995	40.7	56.3	84.7	75.0	77.5	79.0	78.9	76.7	76.3	80.0	82.2	84.3
1996	47.7	61.7	87.9	78.0	80.5	85.3	85.3	83.9	83.3	88.5	87.6	83.9
1997	61.8	67.0	89.8	84.5	88.3	86.9	87.0	84.3	83.0	95.3	91.0	83.2
1998	73.5	75.4	93.0	90.4	95.8	93.6	93.7	92.3	92.1	94.2	95.8	87.6
1999	89.2	83.1	92.9	104.3	96.6	99.3	99.3	99.2	98.9	101.7	99.5	95.3
2000	100.0	100.0	100.0	100.0	100.0	100.0	100.0	100.0	100.0	100.0	100.0	100.0
2001	98.7	95.6	91.5	88.8	96.7	100.4	100.4	100.6	100.1	104.3	100.0	100.4
2002	96.3	84.8	84.5	78.3	93.7	105.1	105.2	104.6	104.0	109.8	106.0	104.1
2003	100.6	87.9	86.9	70.7	99.4	114.0	114.0	114.9	115.1	112.7	112.7	110.3
2004	109.9	95.3	84.2	81.2	105.4	125.3	125.4	128.2	128.9	121.5	121.1	121.7
2005	117.5	100.8	91.3	93.0	114.6	133.2	133.3	137.2	137.6	133.6	127.2	126.3
2006	122.3	108.8	96.4	99.2	119.3	123.7	123.7	125.6	124.6	134.6	120.7	130.4
2007	134.5	114.7	97.8	86.7	113.1	101.5	101.2	93.2	90.4	117.3	114.3	128.6
2008	141.0	119.0	93.7	61.9	111.5	80.4	79.9	63.3	57.4	111.6	106.7	123.7
2006												
1st quarter	120.6	109.2	94.2	102.8	120.6	133.5	133.5	140.2	140.7	136.2	122.9	131.7
2nd quarter	121.0	107.9	98.7	98.2	121.0	127.6	127.5	130.8	130.4	135.0	122.4	131.3
3rd quarter	122.5	110.2	96.6	99.3	118.3	120.1	120.0	120.7	119.4	132.1	119.0	130.4
4th quarter	125.2	107.8	96.2	96.5	117.2	113.8	113.6	110.6	107.8	134.9	118.6	128.1
2007												
1st quarter	129.4	111.8	94.4	92.6	110.8	108.8	108.6	102.6	99.5	128.8	118.4	129.6
2nd quarter	133.8	113.8	100.7	86.7	112.4	105.6	105.3	98.5	96.0	119.6	116.4	128.5
3rd quarter	135.9	115.6	100.0	85.4	113.7	99.6	99.3	91.4	88.8	113.1	112.2	128.5
4th quarter	139.1	117.6	96.2	82.0	115.5	92.1	91.7	80.5	77.3	107.7	109.9	127.7
2008												
1st quarter	142.5	117.7	96.4	78.9	111.7	85.7	85.2	70.6	66.2	107.4	108.9	126.1
2nd quarter	143.2	121.3	95.5	67.5	110.8	82.7	82.1	66.1	60.4	113.5	108.0	128.6
3rd quarter	141.6	122.9	93.3	58.2	115.5	79.2	78.6	61.7	55.1	115.7	105.9	122.6
4th quarter	136.7	114.0	89.7	43.1	108.2	74.2	73.7	54.7	48.1	109.6	104.0	117.4

[1] Excludes software "embedded," or bundled, in computers and other equipment.
. . . = Not available.

Table 5-5. Current-Cost Net Stock of Fixed Assets

(Billions of dollars, year-end estimates.)

Year	Total	Private Total	Private Nonresidential Total	Private Nonresidential Equipment and software	Private Nonresidential Structures	Private Residential	Government Total	Government Nonresidential Equipment and software	Government Nonresidential Structures	Government Residential	Private and government Nonresidential Equipment and software	Private and government Nonresidential Structures	Private and government Residential	Government Federal	Government State and local
1947	729.8	515.4	248.0	68.0	180.0	267.4	214.4	62.0	146.8	5.6	130.1	326.8	273.0	121.1	93.3
1948	774.6	560.0	272.0	82.2	189.8	288.0	214.6	52.2	157.4	5.0	134.4	347.3	293.0	113.0	101.6
1949	779.1	579.4	276.9	86.0	190.9	302.5	199.8	44.3	150.3	5.2	130.3	341.2	307.7	102.8	96.9
1950	864.7	653.2	313.6	99.4	214.1	339.6	211.5	40.5	164.6	6.4	140.0	378.8	346.0	102.3	109.3
1951	947.2	710.5	341.8	109.3	232.4	368.7	236.7	44.3	184.5	7.9	153.6	417.0	376.6	113.9	122.9
1952	1 001.7	747.6	360.2	114.8	245.3	387.4	254.1	50.7	195.9	7.4	165.6	441.3	394.8	123.9	130.2
1953	1 037.0	777.7	375.9	124.2	251.7	401.9	259.3	57.5	193.9	7.9	181.7	445.6	409.7	130.5	128.8
1954	1 084.4	809.2	385.8	127.7	258.0	423.4	275.2	64.1	200.6	10.6	191.8	458.6	434.0	140.7	134.5
1955	1 178.3	881.4	425.2	140.3	284.9	456.2	296.9	69.5	219.7	7.6	209.9	504.7	463.8	147.5	149.4
1956	1 277.6	948.4	470.2	157.3	312.9	478.2	329.1	74.1	246.1	8.9	231.4	559.0	487.2	159.8	169.3
1957	1 339.6	996.5	502.2	171.3	331.0	494.2	343.2	76.2	257.5	9.4	247.5	588.5	503.6	165.7	177.4
1958	1 381.9	1 020.6	511.5	176.7	334.8	509.2	361.3	77.9	273.2	10.2	254.6	607.9	519.4	171.7	189.5
1959	1 436.4	1 064.8	533.5	185.7	347.7	531.3	371.6	82.4	278.1	11.1	268.1	625.8	542.4	175.9	195.7
1960	1 481.9	1 096.8	544.6	191.6	353.0	552.2	385.1	85.2	288.1	11.8	276.9	641.1	564.0	180.0	205.1
1961	1 536.4	1 132.0	559.7	194.8	364.8	572.3	404.4	89.2	302.7	12.6	284.0	667.5	584.9	187.0	217.4
1962	1 604.0	1 173.3	579.9	202.2	377.7	593.4	430.7	96.5	320.8	13.5	298.7	698.4	606.9	197.9	232.8
1963	1 660.6	1 209.0	601.0	210.7	390.3	608.0	451.6	99.2	338.7	13.7	309.9	729.0	621.8	203.5	248.1
1964	1 767.2	1 293.6	636.6	223.4	413.3	657.0	473.7	102.0	357.1	14.6	325.4	770.3	671.6	209.0	264.7
1965	1 883.5	1 379.4	681.9	240.7	441.1	697.6	504.0	104.6	384.1	15.3	345.4	825.2	712.9	216.0	288.0
1966	2 041.8	1 496.9	742.5	268.2	474.4	754.4	544.9	109.8	418.7	16.4	378.0	893.0	770.8	226.7	318.2
1967	2 197.0	1 608.5	802.8	293.8	509.0	805.7	588.6	116.4	454.9	17.3	410.2	963.9	823.0	240.9	347.7
1968	2 411.6	1 772.7	882.5	323.9	558.7	890.2	638.9	120.9	498.6	19.4	444.8	1 057.3	909.6	253.0	385.9
1969	2 627.6	1 924.5	972.1	357.4	614.7	952.3	703.2	125.1	556.5	21.6	482.5	1 171.2	973.9	267.4	435.8
1970	2 860.8	2 078.4	1 070.3	392.2	678.0	1 008.2	782.4	131.1	628.2	23.1	523.4	1 306.3	1 031.2	285.3	497.1
1971	3 159.1	2 311.6	1 178.4	419.8	758.6	1 133.2	847.5	132.2	689.5	25.9	552.0	1 448.0	1 159.1	299.5	548.0
1972	3 474.0	2 550.6	1 283.2	452.8	830.4	1 267.4	923.4	134.0	760.4	29.0	586.8	1 590.8	1 296.4	322.5	600.9
1973	3 938.4	2 899.6	1 447.3	505.4	941.9	1 452.3	1 038.8	136.2	869.9	32.8	641.5	1 811.8	1 485.0	349.5	689.3
1974	4 692.4	3 415.8	1 763.0	623.4	1 139.6	1 652.7	1 276.6	149.7	1 090.3	36.6	773.1	2 229.9	1 689.4	403.3	873.3
1975	5 075.8	3 734.7	1 942.9	713.9	1 228.9	1 791.8	1 341.1	164.4	1 136.6	40.1	878.3	2 365.5	1 832.0	426.6	914.5
1976	5 533.8	4 115.7	2 126.9	790.4	1 336.5	1 988.9	1 418.1	178.7	1 194.6	44.8	969.1	2 531.1	2 033.6	462.8	955.3
1977	6 194.0	4 686.9	2 365.7	887.7	1 477.9	2 321.2	1 507.1	195.0	1 260.6	51.5	1 082.7	2 738.6	2 372.7	485.7	1 021.4
1978	7 012.2	5 364.2	2 687.2	1 014.2	1 673.0	2 677.0	1 648.0	207.8	1 380.7	59.6	1 222.0	3 053.6	2 736.5	524.0	1 124.0
1979	8 087.7	6 210.7	3 102.4	1 178.5	1 924.0	3 108.2	1 877.0	225.2	1 581.0	70.9	1 403.7	3 504.9	3 179.1	583.9	1 293.1
1980	9 216.7	7 067.8	3 563.2	1 367.4	2 195.8	3 504.6	2 148.9	251.5	1 819.7	77.8	1 618.9	4 015.5	3 582.3	648.0	1 501.0
1981	10 163.3	7 802.6	4 032.9	1 525.1	2 507.8	3 769.7	2 360.7	282.9	1 992.6	85.2	1 808.0	4 500.5	3 854.9	697.1	1 663.6
1982	10 720.3	8 229.0	4 288.4	1 615.8	2 672.6	3 940.6	2 491.3	307.5	2 093.4	90.3	1 923.4	4 766.0	4 030.9	735.5	1 755.8
1983	11 067.2	8 516.4	4 416.7	1 669.4	2 747.3	4 099.7	2 550.9	337.9	2 112.2	100.8	2 007.3	4 859.4	4 200.5	772.4	1 778.5
1984	11 661.4	9 011.2	4 680.1	1 760.7	2 919.4	4 331.1	2 650.3	360.9	2 184.7	104.6	2 121.6	5 104.2	4 435.7	810.6	1 839.7
1985	12 275.5	9 509.0	4 944.3	1 865.6	3 078.6	4 564.7	2 766.5	383.7	2 277.0	105.8	2 249.3	5 355.6	4 670.6	842.4	1 924.1
1986	13 046.3	10 110.1	5 180.2	1 970.1	3 210.1	4 929.9	2 936.2	411.5	2 414.9	109.7	2 381.6	5 625.0	5 039.6	885.2	2 051.0
1987	13 803.5	10 710.8	5 462.3	2 071.2	3 391.1	5 248.5	3 092.6	437.2	2 535.8	119.6	2 508.4	5 926.9	5 368.2	921.5	2 171.1
1988	14 642.9	11 391.6	5 817.2	2 198.7	3 618.5	5 574.3	3 251.3	471.1	2 645.0	135.2	2 669.9	6 263.5	5 709.5	977.3	2 274.0
1989	15 480.2	12 051.7	6 168.1	2 335.2	3 832.9	5 883.6	3 428.5	508.3	2 775.8	144.4	2 843.4	6 608.7	6 028.0	1 031.2	2 397.4
1990	16 211.5	12 610.9	6 499.9	2 469.1	4 030.8	6 111.0	3 600.7	551.1	2 900.4	149.2	3 020.2	6 931.1	6 260.2	1 078.9	2 521.8
1991	16 602.8	12 880.7	6 632.4	2 541.1	4 091.4	6 248.3	3 722.1	583.9	2 988.0	150.2	3 125.0	7 079.4	6 398.5	1 122.5	2 599.6
1992	17 323.9	13 438.8	6 838.8	2 613.9	4 224.9	6 599.9	3 885.1	613.3	3 112.8	159.0	3 227.2	7 337.8	6 758.9	1 169.4	2 715.7
1993	18 231.0	14 166.8	7 161.9	2 728.2	4 433.7	7 004.9	4 064.3	637.0	3 257.0	170.3	3 365.2	7 690.7	7 175.1	1 209.0	2 855.2
1994	19 352.0	15 056.7	7 551.3	2 880.6	4 670.7	7 505.4	4 295.2	665.8	3 447.7	181.7	3 546.4	8 118.4	7 687.1	1 260.7	3 034.5
1995	20 298.9	15 794.3	7 954.4	3 067.4	4 887.1	7 839.8	4 504.7	674.8	3 641.7	188.2	3 742.1	8 528.8	8 028.0	1 291.3	3 213.4
1996	21 299.9	16 618.1	8 347.4	3 233.1	5 114.3	8 270.6	4 681.8	674.8	3 810.5	196.5	3 907.9	8 924.9	8 467.1	1 315.5	3 366.3
1997	22 450.5	17 549.3	8 818.7	3 394.6	5 424.1	8 730.6	4 901.2	671.4	4 032.9	196.8	4 066.1	9 457.0	8 927.5	1 334.7	3 566.5
1998	23 721.6	18 620.5	9 320.4	3 583.8	5 736.6	9 300.1	5 101.1	677.1	4 217.1	206.9	4 260.9	9 953.7	9 507.0	1 355.8	3 745.3
1999	25 246.1	19 847.2	9 860.4	3 822.1	6 038.4	9 986.7	5 398.9	698.2	4 480.7	219.9	4 520.3	10 519.1	10 206.7	1 398.9	4 000.0
2000	26 902.2	21 189.5	10 513.8	4 077.3	6 436.5	10 675.7	5 712.7	703.0	4 778.0	231.7	4 780.3	11 214.5	10 907.4	1 424.6	4 288.1
2001	28 464.7	22 484.8	11 020.0	4 203.2	6 816.8	11 464.8	5 979.9	711.3	5 021.9	246.7	4 914.5	11 838.7	11 711.5	1 446.8	4 533.1
2002	29 788.3	23 522.7	11 329.6	4 270.8	7 058.8	12 193.1	6 265.6	723.2	5 278.8	263.6	4 994.0	12 337.6	12 456.7	1 469.9	4 795.7
2003	31 424.4	24 916.9	11 692.0	4 380.8	7 311.3	13 224.7	6 507.5	738.2	5 489.8	279.5	5 119.0	12 801.1	13 504.3	1 498.9	5 008.6
2004	34 637.0	27 422.8	12 620.3	4 549.2	8 071.2	14 802.5	7 214.2	784.1	6 134.4	295.7	5 333.2	14 205.5	15 098.2	1 591.4	5 622.7
2005	38 167.7	30 223.7	13 726.0	4 760.4	8 965.5	16 497.7	7 944.1	817.7	6 791.7	334.7	5 578.1	15 757.2	16 832.4	1 722.6	6 221.4
2006	41 175.2	32 429.3	14 788.3	5 043.9	9 744.4	17 641.0	8 746.0	864.3	7 535.4	346.3	5 908.2	17 279.7	17 987.3	1 830.8	6 915.2
2007	42 592.0	33 381.2	15 512.1	5 286.1	10 226.0	17 869.0	9 210.9	897.0	7 990.2	323.7	6 183.1	18 216.2	18 192.7	1 700.6	7 510.2

Table 5-6. Chain-Type Quantity Indexes for Net Stock of Fixed Assets

(Index numbers, 2000 = 100.)

Year	Total	Private					Government				Private and government fixed assets			Government, by level	
		Total	Nonresidential			Residential	Total	Nonresidential		Residential	Nonresidential		Residential	Federal	State and local
			Total	Equipment and software	Structures			Equipment and software	Structures		Equipment and software	Structures			
1947	20.83	18.35	17.12	9.13	24.33	19.73	30.29	50.32	26.13	16.37	14.98	25.14	19.67	67.93	17.25
1948	21.14	19.16	17.89	10.04	24.90	20.60	28.63	39.61	26.39	16.67	14.26	25.57	20.52	60.29	17.59
1949	21.55	19.81	18.43	10.56	25.42	21.36	28.08	34.03	26.91	17.68	13.94	26.09	21.29	56.40	18.16
1950	22.17	20.68	19.07	11.17	26.03	22.49	27.64	28.55	27.59	18.57	13.71	26.73	22.41	52.62	18.86
1951	23.01	21.45	19.75	11.79	26.72	23.37	28.73	30.50	28.44	19.96	14.52	27.49	23.31	54.76	19.57
1952	23.89	22.17	20.35	12.30	27.39	24.21	30.23	34.07	29.46	21.53	15.46	28.31	24.16	58.56	20.29
1953	24.84	22.95	21.06	12.90	28.15	25.07	31.83	37.84	30.55	22.94	16.51	29.21	25.04	62.46	21.10
1954	25.73	23.72	21.66	13.29	28.93	26.02	33.20	39.81	31.80	23.59	17.12	30.19	25.99	64.78	22.13
1955	26.70	24.65	22.40	13.86	29.79	27.17	34.34	40.62	33.05	24.09	17.73	31.21	27.11	65.96	23.26
1956	27.67	25.56	23.24	14.47	30.81	28.16	35.47	41.38	34.30	24.74	18.36	32.33	28.10	67.04	24.40
1957	28.58	26.41	24.05	15.07	31.79	29.06	36.61	41.87	35.59	25.92	18.95	33.44	29.00	67.90	25.63
1958	29.40	27.10	24.58	15.28	32.62	29.94	37.94	42.57	37.04	28.01	19.23	34.53	29.92	69.14	27.01
1959	30.44	28.00	25.22	15.66	33.48	31.15	39.50	44.37	38.49	30.35	19.81	35.63	31.15	71.20	28.40
1960	31.43	28.88	25.94	16.10	34.45	32.22	40.91	45.53	39.93	32.09	20.36	36.80	32.23	72.70	29.78
1961	32.44	29.72	26.60	16.44	35.42	33.27	42.57	47.40	41.50	34.20	20.91	38.02	33.30	74.84	31.28
1962	33.58	30.71	27.43	16.99	36.47	34.44	44.31	49.62	43.08	36.56	21.70	39.29	34.51	77.17	32.82
1963	34.79	31.81	28.30	17.66	37.49	35.80	45.96	50.99	44.82	37.78	22.47	40.62	35.86	78.72	34.52
1964	36.14	33.07	29.41	18.57	38.70	37.24	47.64	52.14	46.64	39.10	23.42	42.09	37.30	79.99	36.36
1965	37.63	34.50	30.90	19.90	40.23	38.60	49.30	52.66	48.58	40.50	24.64	43.79	38.66	80.79	38.33
1966	39.19	35.98	32.63	21.59	41.85	39.75	51.15	53.72	50.64	42.02	26.25	45.60	39.82	81.95	40.43
1967	40.64	37.31	34.16	23.00	43.37	40.84	53.08	55.12	52.71	43.73	27.67	47.35	40.92	83.16	42.67
1968	42.14	38.74	35.71	24.47	44.89	42.12	54.82	55.31	54.81	45.40	28.97	49.12	42.21	83.16	44.99
1969	43.66	40.27	37.41	26.10	46.52	43.44	56.30	54.96	56.68	47.52	30.32	50.85	43.54	82.79	47.12
1970	45.00	41.63	38.91	27.43	48.11	44.62	57.53	54.36	58.28	49.69	31.38	52.44	44.75	82.16	49.00
1971	46.37	43.13	40.27	28.57	49.61	46.28	58.43	52.17	59.81	51.79	32.03	53.95	46.41	80.59	50.74
1972	47.94	44.89	41.82	30.09	51.11	48.29	59.29	50.41	61.20	53.55	33.07	55.41	48.42	79.33	52.35
1973	49.68	46.87	43.79	32.30	52.80	50.26	60.22	49.08	62.55	55.21	34.74	56.95	50.38	78.41	53.92
1974	51.16	48.47	45.59	34.33	54.35	51.63	61.27	48.78	63.84	56.79	36.43	58.38	51.76	78.03	55.46
1975	52.28	49.62	46.78	35.47	55.57	52.70	62.33	48.77	65.07	58.68	37.41	59.59	52.85	77.87	56.92
1976	53.57	50.98	48.03	36.74	56.76	54.20	63.38	49.11	66.25	60.15	38.54	60.78	54.34	77.95	58.32
1977	55.15	52.74	49.61	38.58	58.03	56.17	64.30	49.38	67.27	61.55	40.16	61.94	56.31	78.06	59.53
1978	57.04	54.84	51.68	41.05	59.68	58.28	65.37	49.70	68.50	62.72	42.32	63.41	58.40	78.26	60.93
1979	59.02	57.01	54.03	43.75	61.67	60.26	66.59	50.72	69.76	63.84	44.78	65.10	60.36	78.70	62.43
1980	60.65	58.74	56.11	45.66	63.84	61.59	67.83	51.93	70.99	65.27	46.60	66.87	61.69	79.31	63.90
1981	62.22	60.44	58.32	47.52	66.30	62.70	68.93	53.33	72.01	66.96	48.39	68.72	62.82	80.21	65.06
1982	63.41	61.68	60.00	48.47	68.58	63.43	69.92	55.11	72.82	68.53	49.46	70.38	63.57	81.28	66.03
1983	64.78	63.11	61.43	49.52	70.29	64.86	71.05	57.86	73.59	70.41	50.76	71.69	65.01	82.89	66.99
1984	66.67	65.12	63.65	51.63	72.56	66.64	72.48	61.47	74.56	72.01	53.09	73.41	66.78	84.91	68.21
1985	68.71	67.24	66.04	53.69	75.18	68.43	74.24	66.21	75.73	73.97	55.54	75.42	68.58	87.54	69.67
1986	70.70	69.24	67.94	55.37	77.22	70.56	76.17	71.37	77.03	76.07	57.72	77.14	70.70	90.42	71.26
1987	72.64	71.18	69.66	56.77	79.20	72.72	78.13	76.59	78.40	78.25	59.64	78.85	72.87	93.45	72.87
1988	74.56	73.13	71.49	58.50	81.07	74.81	79.91	80.59	79.77	80.19	61.68	80.52	74.95	95.43	74.57
1989	76.44	75.04	73.36	60.40	82.87	76.75	81.70	84.95	81.12	81.89	63.92	82.12	76.89	97.24	76.36
1990	78.22	76.77	75.14	61.91	84.85	78.41	83.67	89.40	82.66	83.79	65.84	83.92	78.55	99.10	78.37
1991	79.61	78.03	76.33	62.87	86.21	79.76	85.52	92.68	84.27	85.42	67.11	85.38	79.91	100.45	80.38
1992	81.05	79.39	77.42	64.08	87.16	81.41	87.28	95.38	85.86	87.21	68.53	86.61	81.57	101.57	82.36
1993	82.72	81.12	78.99	66.23	88.23	83.32	88.74	96.57	87.36	88.73	70.55	87.86	83.46	101.92	84.21
1994	84.54	83.08	80.79	69.09	89.15	85.44	90.03	96.91	88.83	89.98	73.06	89.01	85.57	101.71	86.04
1995	86.57	85.27	83.12	72.66	90.48	87.47	91.45	97.11	90.46	91.49	76.16	90.47	87.59	101.56	88.01
1996	88.88	87.76	85.81	76.72	92.08	89.75	93.11	97.41	92.35	93.04	79.70	92.19	89.85	102.02	90.08
1997	91.35	90.47	88.93	81.60	93.89	92.04	94.63	97.23	94.17	95.82	83.86	94.01	92.12	101.35	92.36
1998	94.08	93.50	92.42	87.20	95.88	94.58	96.24	97.75	95.95	97.32	88.74	95.91	94.64	100.85	94.68
1999	96.99	96.69	96.10	93.47	97.80	97.29	98.09	98.94	97.92	98.81	94.27	97.85	97.32	100.54	97.26
2000	100.00	100.00	100.00	100.00	100.00	100.00	100.00	100.00	100.00	100.00	100.00	100.00	100.00	100.00	100.00
2001	102.54	102.67	102.67	103.88	101.91	102.68	102.03	101.17	102.18	101.43	103.48	102.03	102.66	99.46	102.88
2002	104.76	104.89	104.23	106.00	103.14	105.53	104.27	102.92	104.52	102.99	105.55	103.73	105.48	99.36	105.89
2003	107.06	107.20	105.63	107.92	104.23	108.71	106.52	104.71	106.88	104.45	107.45	105.35	108.62	99.45	108.85
2004	109.54	109.75	107.17	110.40	105.24	112.16	108.77	107.25	109.13	105.99	109.95	106.88	112.03	99.94	111.66
2005	112.01	112.35	108.96	113.82	106.17	115.50	110.74	110.36	111.00	107.06	113.32	108.21	115.32	100.43	114.10
2006	114.77	115.28	111.38	118.15	107.65	118.89	112.85	114.16	112.99	107.60	117.57	109.91	118.64	101.21	116.63
2007	117.18	117.75	113.92	121.82	109.65	121.30	115.03	117.54	115.10	108.43	121.20	111.95	121.02	101.89	119.25

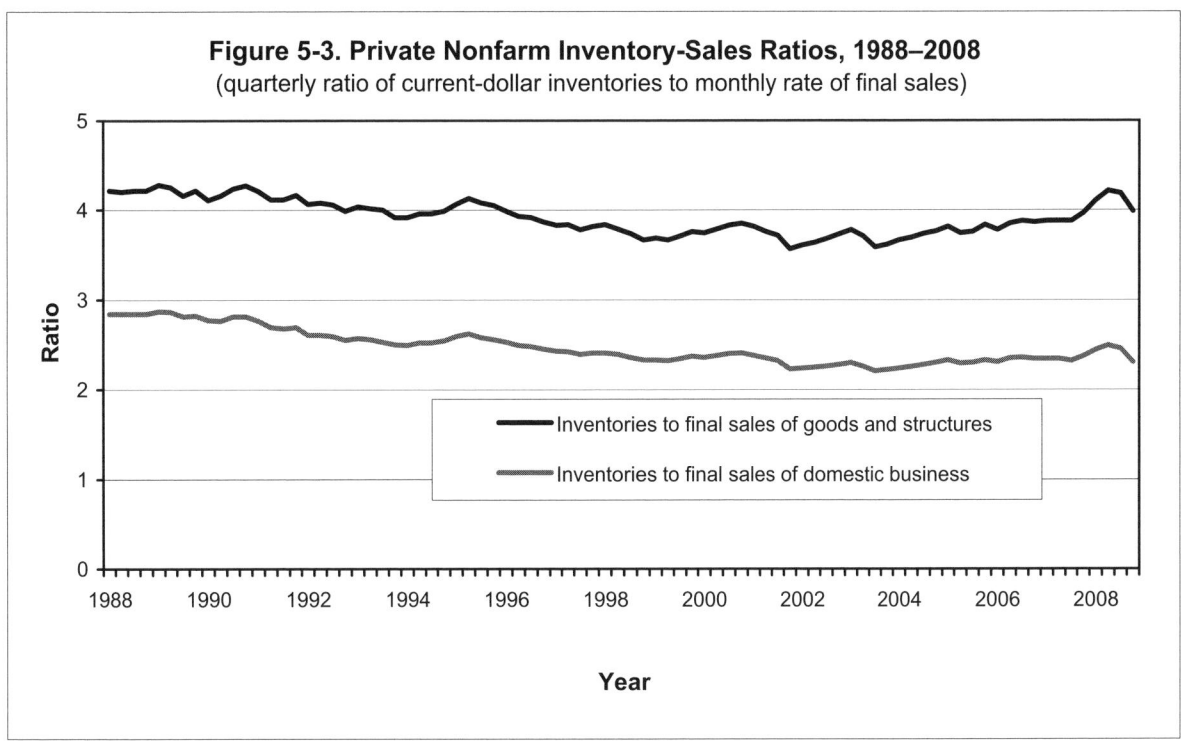

Figure 5-3. Private Nonfarm Inventory-Sales Ratios, 1988–2008
(quarterly ratio of current-dollar inventories to monthly rate of final sales)

- Inventories play a key role in the business cycle, and ratios of inventories to sales (I/S ratios) are important cyclical indicators. If production gets ahead of sales, or if sales take an unexpected dip, there can be "involuntary" inventory accumulation. In that case, I/S ratios rise and production has to be cut back. Sharply increasing ratios were associated with the 1974–1975 and 1981–1982 recessions. (Tables 5-7 and 19-7)

- Inventory liquidation contributed importantly to the 2001 recession and has already been observed in the recession that began at the end of 2007. Nonfarm stocks were cut $32 billion, in constant 2000 dollars, in 2001. Recently, inventory liquidation began in the fourth quarter of 2007, reached a $55 billion annual rate in the second quarter of 2008, and was still running at a $31 billion rate in the fourth quarter of 2008. Reports that General Motors factories will be closed for up to 9 weeks in summer 2009, in order to work off dealers' auto inventories, suggest that the period of inventory reduction did not end with 2008. (Table 1-2)

- The monthly inventory indicators in Tables 5-7 and 5-8 also suggest that there was still pressure to cut stocks at the end of 2008, despite the inventory reductions that had already taken place during that year. Ratios were up sharply for manufacturers and retail and wholesale trade.

- When inventories are liquidated—recorded in the NIPAs as negative inventory change—that means that production and imports are being held below the rate of current sales. In a normal growing economy, there is a modest positive rate of inventory investment, with production and/or imports running a little ahead of the current rate of final sales in order to grow stocks in line with growing sales.

- When a recession has involved inventory reductions, it means production is cut more than sales. Conversely, when sales level off and start to increase, firms stop cutting stocks; production will increase more than the sales increase, in order to maintain or build inventory levels, giving a temporary extra impetus to GDP growth. In other words, the existence of inventories makes production of storable goods more volatile than the sales of those goods.

Table 5-7. Inventories to Sales Ratios

(Seasonally adjusted, ratio of inventories at end of quarter to monthly rate of sales during the quarter, annual data are for fourth quarter.)

NIPA Tables 5.7.5A, 5.7.5B, 5.7.6A, 5.7.6B

Year and quarter	Ratio, total private inventories to final sales of domestic business		Ratio, nonfarm inventories to final sales of domestic business		Ratio, nonfarm inventories to final sales of goods and structures	
	Current dollars	Chained (2000) dollars	Current dollars	Chained (2000) dollars	Current dollars	Chained (2000) dollars
1950	5.70	3.53	3.00	2.24	3.68	3.39
1951	5.76	3.62	3.11	2.40	3.78	3.61
1952	5.16	3.61	3.02	2.39	3.69	3.59
1953	4.96	3.61	3.04	2.39	3.75	3.59
1954	4.67	3.40	2.85	2.23	3.54	3.35
1955	4.36	3.33	2.91	2.24	3.61	3.36
1956	4.41	3.33	2.99	2.30	3.74	3.48
1957	4.39	3.36	2.98	2.32	3.74	3.52
1958	4.44	3.33	2.87	2.25	3.62	3.42
1959	4.20	3.26	2.87	2.27	3.67	3.48
1960	4.17	3.27	2.86	2.29	3.67	3.51
1961	4.07	3.20	2.78	2.24	3.58	3.45
1962	4.09	3.21	2.79	2.29	3.60	3.51
1963	3.91	3.15	2.75	2.27	3.56	3.49
1964	3.75	3.07	2.73	2.26	3.54	3.49
1965	3.73	2.99	2.70	2.24	3.47	3.42
1966	3.88	3.16	2.89	2.44	3.74	3.75
1967	3.87	3.25	2.96	2.54	3.86	3.92
1968	3.76	3.23	2.87	2.53	3.76	3.91
1969	3.85	3.30	2.95	2.62	3.89	4.08
1970	3.78	3.29	2.94	2.63	3.92	4.13
1971	3.73	3.24	2.86	2.59	3.83	4.07
1972	3.72	3.09	2.75	2.50	3.66	3.90
1973	4.18	3.13	2.96	2.57	3.91	4.01
1974	4.49	3.37	3.52	2.82	4.73	4.50
1975	4.02	3.17	3.14	2.62	4.24	4.17
1976	3.93	3.14	3.17	2.63	4.32	4.21
1977	3.86	3.13	3.14	2.62	4.29	4.18
1978	3.95	3.06	3.12	2.58	4.20	4.06
1979	4.17	3.08	3.33	2.60	4.47	4.08
1980	4.23	3.05	3.42	2.60	4.69	4.13
1981	4.15	3.20	3.47	2.71	4.80	4.31
1982	3.95	3.15	3.28	2.64	4.67	4.26
1983	3.68	2.91	3.07	2.49	4.39	3.98
1984	3.70	2.98	3.14	2.56	4.50	4.07
1985	3.49	2.92	2.99	2.50	4.36	4.03
1986	3.23	2.84	2.80	2.44	4.12	3.92
1987	3.31	2.84	2.88	2.47	4.25	3.99
1988	3.27	2.75	2.84	2.43	4.22	3.92
1989	3.22	2.75	2.82	2.44	4.22	3.94
1990	3.21	2.77	2.81	2.46	4.27	4.02
1991	3.04	2.77	2.69	2.46	4.17	4.07
1992	2.90	2.67	2.55	2.36	3.99	3.90
1993	2.83	2.63	2.50	2.35	3.92	3.86
1994	2.87	2.67	2.54	2.38	3.99	3.88
1995	2.86	2.63	2.56	2.38	4.05	3.88
1996	2.74	2.56	2.45	2.30	3.87	3.74
1997	2.68	2.60	2.41	2.34	3.82	3.78
1998	2.56	2.59	2.33	2.35	3.67	3.75
1999	2.59	2.60	2.37	2.37	3.76	3.79
2000	2.63	2.62	2.41	2.40	3.85	3.86
2001	2.44	2.55	2.23	2.33	3.57	3.74
2002	2.51	2.58	2.28	2.37	3.73	3.85
2003	2.45	2.49	2.22	2.28	3.62	3.67
2004	2.53	2.49	2.30	2.28	3.77	3.68
2005	2.56	2.47	2.33	2.27	3.84	3.64
2006	2.56	2.45	2.34	2.26	3.87	3.65
2007	2.61	2.38	2.37	2.20	3.97	3.55
2008	2.56	2.39	2.31	2.19	3.99	3.64
2006						
1st quarter	2.52	2.45	2.31	2.25	3.78	3.60
2nd quarter	2.56	2.45	2.35	2.26	3.85	3.61
3rd quarter	2.58	2.47	2.36	2.28	3.88	3.66
4th quarter	2.56	2.45	2.34	2.26	3.87	3.65
2007						
1st quarter	2.57	2.44	2.34	2.26	3.88	3.65
2nd quarter	2.56	2.41	2.34	2.23	3.88	3.59
3rd quarter	2.55	2.39	2.32	2.21	3.88	3.56
4th quarter	2.61	2.38	2.37	2.20	3.97	3.55
2008						
1st quarter	2.71	2.37	2.44	2.19	4.11	3.56
2nd quarter	2.78	2.32	2.49	2.14	4.22	3.45
3rd quarter	2.74	2.34	2.46	2.15	4.19	3.48
4th quarter	2.56	2.39	2.31	2.19	3.99	3.64

Table 5-8. Manufacturing and Trade Sales and Inventories

| Year and month | Sales, billions of dollars | | | | | Inventories, billions of dollars, end of period, seasonally adjusted | | | | Ratios, inventories to sales, seasonally adjusted [1] | | | |
| | Not seasonally adjusted, total | Seasonally adjusted | | | | Total | Manufacturing | Retail trade | Merchant wholesalers | Total | Manufacturing | Retail trade | Merchant wholesalers |
		Total	Manufacturing	Retail trade	Merchant wholesalers								
1992	6 486.9	6 486.9	2 904.0	1 815.7	1 767.1	837.0	378.7	261.4	196.9	1.52	1.57	1.67	1.31
1993	6 811.0	6 811.0	3 020.5	1 942.2	1 848.2	864.0	379.7	279.5	204.8	1.50	1.51	1.69	1.31
1994	7 323.0	7 323.0	3 238.1	2 110.0	1 974.9	927.3	399.9	305.4	222.0	1.47	1.45	1.67	1.29
1995	7 861.2	7 861.2	3 479.7	2 222.5	2 159.0	986.1	424.8	322.9	238.4	1.48	1.44	1.73	1.30
1996	8 248.2	8 248.2	3 597.2	2 366.7	2 284.3	1 005.5	430.4	334.0	241.1	1.46	1.43	1.68	1.27
1997	8 686.5	8 686.5	3 834.7	2 474.0	2 377.8	1 046.8	443.6	344.6	258.6	1.42	1.37	1.65	1.26
1998	8 914.0	8 914.0	3 899.8	2 587.1	2 427.1	1 078.7	449.1	357.3	272.4	1.44	1.39	1.64	1.32
1999	9 439.6	9 439.6	4 031.9	2 808.6	2 599.2	1 139.0	463.6	385.0	290.3	1.41	1.35	1.60	1.30
2000	10 011.9	10 011.9	4 208.6	2 988.8	2 814.6	1 198.0	481.7	406.9	309.5	1.41	1.36	1.60	1.29
2001	9 823.4	9 823.4	3 970.5	3 067.7	2 785.2	1 120.8	428.1	394.7	297.9	1.43	1.38	1.59	1.32
2002	9 884.6	9 884.6	3 914.7	3 134.3	2 835.5	1 141.2	423.1	416.2	301.9	1.36	1.29	1.56	1.26
2003	10 243.1	10 243.1	4 015.4	3 265.5	2 962.3	1 148.3	408.3	432.4	307.6	1.34	1.25	1.57	1.23
2004	11 079.8	11 079.8	4 309.0	3 474.3	3 296.5	1 240.1	440.7	461.4	338.0	1.30	1.18	1.56	1.18
2005	12 005.1	12 005.1	4 742.1	3 688.1	3 575.0	1 307.3	472.9	472.0	362.5	1.28	1.17	1.52	1.18
2006	12 788.1	12 788.1	5 020.0	3 887.4	3 880.8	1 392.4	511.5	488.6	392.3	1.28	1.19	1.50	1.18
2007	13 271.9	13 271.9	5 081.1	4 040.4	4 150.5	1 450.1	530.7	502.8	416.6	1.28	1.23	1.48	1.16
2008	13 699.3	13 699.3	5 183.1	4 015.4	4 500.7	1 458.1	542.0	486.5	429.6	1.31	1.28	1.50	1.17
2004													
January	805.5	875.8	339.6	279.3	256.9	1 149.3	408.2	433.1	307.9	1.31	1.20	1.55	1.20
February	827.7	883.1	339.3	281.3	262.5	1 159.3	411.1	436.4	311.9	1.31	1.21	1.55	1.19
March	958.8	911.7	354.4	286.5	270.9	1 168.3	413.2	441.2	313.9	1.28	1.17	1.54	1.16
April	910.4	906.2	352.4	283.1	270.6	1 175.0	415.0	446.0	314.0	1.30	1.18	1.58	1.16
May	919.9	913.2	352.4	288.8	272.1	1 183.1	418.5	447.2	317.4	1.30	1.19	1.55	1.17
June	954.3	912.7	356.6	284.2	271.9	1 193.9	422.6	451.4	319.9	1.31	1.18	1.59	1.18
July	897.4	917.9	357.1	287.6	273.1	1 206.6	426.2	455.2	325.2	1.31	1.19	1.58	1.19
August	948.4	926.2	362.3	287.9	276.0	1 216.2	429.7	458.4	328.1	1.31	1.19	1.59	1.19
September	946.9	932.4	363.2	292.8	276.4	1 216.4	430.5	457.9	328.0	1.30	1.19	1.56	1.19
October	948.3	944.0	369.0	295.0	280.0	1 224.5	434.6	456.8	333.0	1.30	1.18	1.55	1.19
November	944.6	953.6	373.1	296.1	284.4	1 237.6	440.0	460.5	337.0	1.30	1.18	1.56	1.18
December	1 017.7	962.1	375.5	299.1	287.4	1 240.1	440.7	461.4	338.0	1.29	1.17	1.54	1.18
2005													
January	872.8	968.8	380.8	298.0	290.0	1 251.6	447.4	461.6	342.6	1.29	1.17	1.55	1.18
February	888.3	970.7	380.0	300.4	290.4	1 259.7	451.9	463.7	344.1	1.30	1.19	1.54	1.19
March	1 025.1	976.8	387.2	300.3	289.3	1 266.8	455.7	465.0	346.1	1.30	1.18	1.55	1.20
April	979.1	986.1	387.6	304.9	293.5	1 270.9	456.9	465.1	348.9	1.29	1.18	1.53	1.19
May	1 003.0	982.3	388.1	302.6	291.6	1 271.9	456.7	466.1	349.2	1.29	1.18	1.54	1.20
June	1 040.3	993.1	391.2	309.5	292.5	1 270.4	457.8	462.0	350.5	1.28	1.17	1.49	1.20
July	963.3	1 000.3	391.1	313.9	295.3	1 266.6	461.6	453.7	351.3	1.27	1.18	1.45	1.19
August	1 053.5	1 007.0	398.9	309.0	299.1	1 270.0	461.4	456.5	352.0	1.26	1.16	1.48	1.18
September	1 038.2	1 019.2	404.8	309.2	305.3	1 277.3	462.3	461.6	353.3	1.25	1.14	1.49	1.16
October	1 032.3	1 029.7	406.9	311.0	311.8	1 286.3	466.8	463.3	356.1	1.25	1.15	1.49	1.14
November	1 020.6	1 031.3	409.7	312.9	308.7	1 294.8	469.3	467.7	357.8	1.26	1.15	1.49	1.16
December	1 088.7	1 043.2	416.7	313.2	313.3	1 307.3	472.9	472.0	362.5	1.25	1.13	1.51	1.16
2006													
January	963.9	1 057.9	418.5	323.2	316.2	1 316.2	478.6	474.2	363.4	1.24	1.14	1.47	1.15
February	959.5	1 053.4	415.1	320.9	317.3	1 318.5	478.6	473.2	366.8	1.25	1.15	1.47	1.16
March	1 114.5	1 059.7	419.5	322.1	318.0	1 330.5	482.9	478.9	368.7	1.26	1.15	1.49	1.16
April	1 031.4	1 061.4	417.3	324.7	319.4	1 337.4	487.6	477.0	372.8	1.26	1.17	1.47	1.17
May	1 118.5	1 073.0	426.1	323.7	323.2	1 351.1	491.3	484.1	375.8	1.26	1.15	1.50	1.16
June	1 129.7	1 074.8	426.3	323.5	325.0	1 361.7	496.3	487.4	378.0	1.27	1.16	1.51	1.16
July	1 036.8	1 075.6	422.7	326.4	326.5	1 369.8	501.0	487.8	380.9	1.27	1.19	1.49	1.17
August	1 134.9	1 081.4	426.2	326.7	328.4	1 377.7	504.1	489.4	384.2	1.27	1.18	1.50	1.17
September	1 064.3	1 059.2	410.8	323.8	324.6	1 382.1	507.6	488.2	386.2	1.30	1.24	1.51	1.19
October	1 073.2	1 057.4	408.6	324.2	324.6	1 387.1	510.0	488.2	388.8	1.31	1.25	1.51	1.20
November	1 052.5	1 063.2	410.8	324.8	327.5	1 392.1	511.6	486.8	393.6	1.31	1.25	1.50	1.20
December	1 108.9	1 083.3	419.7	328.9	334.8	1 392.4	511.5	488.6	392.3	1.29	1.22	1.49	1.17
2007													
January	993.0	1 069.2	408.6	329.5	331.1	1 394.7	512.2	489.0	393.5	1.30	1.25	1.48	1.19
February	979.0	1 078.7	411.6	332.3	334.9	1 398.4	512.7	490.5	395.2	1.30	1.25	1.48	1.18
March	1 130.3	1 090.9	417.6	334.9	338.4	1 398.2	513.0	488.1	397.1	1.28	1.23	1.46	1.17
April	1 078.6	1 097.9	422.7	334.2	341.0	1 401.7	514.7	489.5	397.5	1.28	1.22	1.46	1.17
May	1 158.1	1 108.3	426.3	339.6	342.4	1 408.0	517.0	492.6	398.5	1.27	1.21	1.45	1.16
June	1 143.1	1 100.8	422.9	335.7	342.2	1 412.1	518.0	495.0	399.1	1.28	1.22	1.47	1.17
July	1 081.7	1 109.3	431.8	337.1	340.5	1 417.1	518.6	498.7	399.8	1.28	1.20	1.48	1.17
August	1 162.7	1 103.7	423.4	337.2	343.1	1 420.4	518.1	501.7	400.6	1.29	1.22	1.49	1.17
September	1 092.1	1 112.2	422.2	341.1	348.8	1 427.9	522.0	501.5	404.4	1.28	1.24	1.47	1.16
October	1 159.4	1 124.9	427.6	342.2	355.1	1 432.0	522.8	503.0	406.2	1.27	1.22	1.47	1.14
November	1 135.4	1 148.3	435.6	346.8	365.9	1 439.8	526.4	502.5	410.9	1.25	1.21	1.45	1.12
December	1 158.4	1 141.3	433.1	343.1	365.2	1 450.1	530.7	502.8	416.6	1.27	1.23	1.47	1.14
2008													
January	1 076.2	1 158.5	437.6	343.7	377.1	1 464.5	537.5	504.6	422.4	1.26	1.23	1.47	1.12
February	1 078.3	1 143.2	429.5	340.7	373.0	1 472.7	540.7	505.4	426.6	1.29	1.26	1.48	1.14
March	1 165.3	1 155.1	434.4	342.4	378.2	1 471.6	545.8	500.0	425.9	1.27	1.26	1.46	1.13
April	1 175.2	1 171.3	446.0	342.7	382.5	1 477.7	545.6	501.1	431.1	1.26	1.22	1.46	1.13
May	1 222.8	1 180.2	447.4	345.4	387.4	1 481.9	548.8	499.7	433.4	1.26	1.23	1.45	1.12
June	1 234.6	1 197.7	455.9	345.6	396.2	1 492.4	555.6	500.1	436.6	1.25	1.22	1.45	1.10
July	1 207.0	1 198.4	462.4	343.1	392.9	1 507.1	559.1	506.9	441.1	1.26	1.21	1.48	1.12
August	1 197.8	1 172.3	445.5	340.4	386.4	1 510.0	562.8	503.3	443.9	1.29	1.26	1.48	1.15
September	1 160.4	1 144.5	431.5	334.4	378.6	1 504.9	558.3	504.1	442.5	1.31	1.29	1.51	1.17
October	1 138.0	1 100.4	415.9	322.0	362.5	1 496.2	555.0	503.0	438.2	1.36	1.33	1.56	1.21
November	993.2	1 039.7	388.9	313.2	337.6	1 481.0	552.3	493.8	435.0	1.42	1.42	1.58	1.29
December	1 050.5	1 004.5	376.0	302.9	325.7	1 458.1	542.0	486.5	429.6	1.45	1.44	1.61	1.32

[1] Annual data are averages of monthly ratios.

Table 5-9. Real Manufacturing and Trade Sales and Inventories

(Billions of chained [2000] dollars, ratios; seasonally adjusted; annual sales figures are averages of seasonally adjusted monthly data.)

Year and month	Sales, monthly average				Inventories, end of period				Ratios, end-of-period inventories to monthly average sales			
	Total	Manufac-turing	Retail trade	Merchant wholesalers	Total	Manufac-turing	Retail trade	Merchant wholesalers	Total	Manufac-turing	Retail trade	Merchant wholesalers
1997	737.1	324.1	219.8	190.2	1 025.1	430.7	340.6	254.1	1.39	1.33	1.55	1.34
1998	774.7	335.6	234.2	203.2	1 081.4	449.3	357.9	274.4	1.40	1.34	1.53	1.35
1999	819.4	346.2	253.6	218.9	1 143.8	466.3	385.5	292.0	1.40	1.35	1.52	1.33
2000	844.8	350.2	265.9	228.7	1 188.3	474.2	407.1	307.0	1.41	1.35	1.53	1.34
2001	834.8	331.2	274.0	228.7	1 147.9	452.8	396.3	298.6	1.38	1.37	1.45	1.31
2002	845.0	327.7	284.5	232.9	1 168.4	447.0	420.6	300.5	1.38	1.36	1.48	1.29
2003	855.7	323.2	297.3	235.7	1 176.0	437.5	436.4	301.8	1.37	1.35	1.47	1.28
2004	888.8	330.0	312.8	247.8	1 217.3	440.1	458.6	318.9	1.37	1.33	1.47	1.29
2005	927.0	344.7	326.6	258.5	1 250.1	455.3	462.2	332.3	1.35	1.32	1.42	1.29
2006	956.4	348.9	342.2	269.6	1 284.8	467.1	472.1	345.2	1.34	1.34	1.38	1.28
2007	967.7	340.5	354.6	278.0	1 281.1	463.6	466.4	350.4	1.32	1.36	1.32	1.26
2008	940.5	321.1	347.4	276.7	1 264.5	453.9	451.6	357.8	1.34	1.41	1.30	1.29
2004												
January	867.3	322.9	306.9	238.5	1 174.8	436.5	437.3	300.7	1.35	1.35	1.43	1.26
February	868.6	320.5	307.3	242.2	1 179.9	437.2	439.2	303.3	1.36	1.36	1.43	1.25
March	891.2	332.4	312.3	248.5	1 183.7	437.4	442.6	303.6	1.33	1.32	1.42	1.22
April	882.6	328.7	308.5	247.0	1 186.2	436.9	447.1	302.1	1.34	1.33	1.45	1.22
May	882.4	325.4	312.3	246.8	1 190.1	437.5	448.5	304.1	1.35	1.35	1.44	1.23
June	882.4	329.1	306.6	248.2	1 194.7	438.9	449.8	306.0	1.35	1.33	1.47	1.23
July	887.7	329.9	312.2	247.7	1 201.8	440.1	451.1	310.6	1.35	1.33	1.45	1.25
August	893.2	332.9	312.5	249.9	1 208.0	440.8	454.2	313.0	1.35	1.32	1.45	1.25
September	897.3	332.4	317.8	249.2	1 205.0	438.6	454.0	312.6	1.34	1.32	1.43	1.25
October	896.9	333.6	317.0	248.5	1 211.1	439.0	456.4	315.9	1.35	1.32	1.44	1.27
November	903.0	335.2	318.3	251.8	1 217.1	441.1	457.8	318.3	1.35	1.32	1.44	1.26
December	912.8	337.5	322.5	255.4	1 217.3	440.1	458.6	318.9	1.33	1.30	1.42	1.25
2005												
January	915.0	340.6	320.4	256.3	1 226.5	445.0	459.4	322.1	1.34	1.31	1.43	1.26
February	913.0	337.8	322.0	255.6	1 231.9	447.6	461.5	322.8	1.35	1.33	1.43	1.26
March	912.6	341.5	321.5	251.9	1 233.4	449.4	460.9	323.0	1.35	1.32	1.43	1.28
April	920.4	341.9	325.3	255.9	1 234.1	449.5	459.2	325.3	1.34	1.32	1.41	1.27
May	922.1	344.3	324.3	256.2	1 233.3	449.3	458.7	325.1	1.34	1.31	1.41	1.27
June	929.9	345.2	331.6	256.4	1 234.7	450.4	457.6	326.4	1.33	1.31	1.38	1.27
July	930.1	342.6	334.5	256.8	1 232.0	453.5	450.7	326.9	1.33	1.32	1.35	1.27
August	930.4	346.7	327.5	259.0	1 233.9	452.6	453.3	327.3	1.33	1.31	1.38	1.26
September	927.9	346.5	323.1	260.6	1 237.0	451.7	457.2	327.6	1.33	1.30	1.42	1.26
October	933.1	345.3	325.6	264.8	1 241.9	453.3	459.6	328.6	1.33	1.31	1.41	1.24
November	942.5	350.9	331.1	263.9	1 243.8	453.6	460.6	329.2	1.32	1.29	1.39	1.25
December	947.0	353.5	332.1	264.8	1 250.1	455.3	462.2	332.3	1.32	1.29	1.39	1.26
2006												
January	956.2	353.7	341.3	266.0	1 254.3	458.3	463.6	331.8	1.31	1.30	1.36	1.25
February	955.1	352.0	339.5	267.6	1 253.3	456.7	462.0	334.2	1.31	1.30	1.36	1.25
March	958.7	354.4	340.9	267.9	1 260.3	458.9	466.9	334.2	1.32	1.30	1.37	1.25
April	953.4	349.9	341.6	266.3	1 262.8	460.9	463.8	337.4	1.32	1.32	1.36	1.27
May	958.3	355.1	339.8	267.3	1 268.0	461.5	467.6	338.5	1.32	1.30	1.38	1.27
June	954.4	351.2	339.6	267.5	1 272.3	463.0	469.5	339.4	1.33	1.32	1.38	1.27
July	954.9	348.6	341.3	269.1	1 274.9	464.2	469.2	341.0	1.34	1.33	1.38	1.27
August	957.8	349.2	341.0	271.5	1 279.5	464.7	470.9	343.4	1.34	1.33	1.38	1.27
September	951.0	341.6	341.0	272.7	1 283.2	466.2	471.5	345.0	1.35	1.37	1.38	1.27
October	959.1	344.2	344.8	274.0	1 283.0	467.3	468.6	346.3	1.34	1.36	1.36	1.26
November	954.6	341.6	346.2	271.2	1 285.7	467.8	468.6	348.6	1.35	1.37	1.35	1.29
December	963.4	345.3	348.8	273.8	1 284.8	467.1	472.1	345.2	1.33	1.35	1.35	1.26
2007												
January	955.7	338.7	349.7	272.1	1 282.2	467.2	469.8	344.4	1.34	1.38	1.34	1.27
February	957.4	338.8	352.1	271.5	1 283.3	466.7	471.2	344.8	1.34	1.38	1.34	1.27
March	962.1	340.9	353.3	273.3	1 279.6	465.3	469.0	344.7	1.33	1.37	1.33	1.26
April	965.4	342.8	352.2	275.7	1 280.0	464.7	470.1	344.7	1.33	1.36	1.34	1.25
May	971.9	343.9	357.2	276.7	1 279.1	464.6	469.1	344.8	1.32	1.35	1.31	1.25
June	965.0	339.2	353.1	277.9	1 278.8	463.4	469.1	345.8	1.33	1.37	1.33	1.24
July	971.3	345.0	353.8	277.5	1 281.5	462.4	472.7	346.4	1.32	1.34	1.34	1.25
August	973.7	340.5	355.5	283.3	1 281.6	460.9	473.1	347.6	1.32	1.35	1.33	1.23
September	973.0	337.6	357.6	283.8	1 284.4	462.8	471.5	349.9	1.32	1.37	1.32	1.23
October	979.5	343.6	356.8	284.6	1 283.6	461.9	472.8	348.8	1.31	1.34	1.33	1.23
November	973.8	338.7	359.1	281.9	1 281.7	462.6	469.5	349.2	1.32	1.37	1.31	1.24
December	963.2	335.9	354.6	277.9	1 281.1	463.6	466.4	350.4	1.33	1.38	1.32	1.26
2008												
January	968.4	337.9	355.4	280.5	1 286.6	466.6	467.1	351.8	1.33	1.38	1.31	1.25
February	954.4	328.9	354.5	276.6	1 286.2	466.5	465.7	352.9	1.35	1.42	1.31	1.28
March	954.9	328.8	355.6	276.1	1 280.7	467.0	461.8	350.2	1.34	1.42	1.30	1.27
April	965.0	336.2	356.0	278.4	1 276.9	463.2	460.1	352.0	1.32	1.38	1.29	1.27
May	962.7	331.3	357.5	279.9	1 272.9	461.1	458.3	352.1	1.32	1.39	1.28	1.26
June	960.6	329.9	354.6	281.3	1 272.3	460.5	457.8	352.6	1.32	1.40	1.29	1.25
July	951.5	329.5	349.8	276.9	1 275.9	458.3	462.1	355.0	1.34	1.39	1.32	1.28
August	939.0	318.5	347.9	277.2	1 273.8	457.9	458.1	356.7	1.36	1.44	1.32	1.29
September	918.1	307.8	342.2	272.6	1 269.9	454.1	458.7	356.7	1.38	1.48	1.34	1.31
October	919.9	310.5	333.8	278.5	1 268.6	453.8	458.5	355.9	1.38	1.46	1.37	1.28
November	898.9	298.2	333.4	270.7	1 269.9	455.9	455.6	357.4	1.41	1.53	1.37	1.32
December	892.3	295.8	328.1	271.9	1 264.5	453.9	451.6	357.8	1.42	1.54	1.38	1.32

Table 5-10. Capital Expenditures

(Millions of dollars.)

Capital expenditures	All companies									
	1998	1999	2000	2001	2002	2003	2004	2005	2006	2007
TOTAL	970 897	1 046 952	1 161 029	1 109 004	997 894	975 015	1 042 060	1 144 783	1 309 939	1 361 633
Structures	329 111	320 078	364 407	363 748	358 484	344 641	368 707	401 653	488 701	529 306
New	284 491	296 496	329 525	335 538	321 191	305 291	324 680	365 938	448 861	484 083
Used	44 620	23 583	34 882	28 210	37 293	39 350	44 028	35 715	39 840	45 224
Equipment	641 786	726 874	796 622	745 256	639 410	630 373	673 353	743 130	821 238	832 326
New	606 210	689 553	750 626	706 617	598 668	579 414	628 591	701 247	777 059	792 399
Used	35 577	37 321	45 996	38 639	40 741	50 960	44 762	41 884	44 179	39 928
Not distributed as structures or equipment	0	0	0	0	0	0	0	0	0	0
CAPITALIZED COMPUTER SOFTWARE [1]	. . .	. . .	. . .	. . .	. . .	. . .	. . .	. . .	. . .	. . .
Prepackaged	. . .	. . .	. . .	. . .	. . .	. . .	. . .	. . .	. . .	. . .
Vendor-customized	. . .	. . .	. . .	. . .	. . .	. . .	. . .	. . .	. . .	. . .
Internally-developed	. . .	. . .	. . .	. . .	. . .	. . .	. . .	. . .	. . .	. . .
CAPITAL LEASE AND CAPITALIZED INTEREST EXPENSES [1]										
Capital leases	16 533	17 140	19 545	15 529	15 334	15 641	17 996	18 103	24 442	20 210
Capitalized interest	. . .	. . .	. . .	. . .	. . .	. . .	. . .	. . .	. . .	. . .

Capital expenditures	Companies with employees									
	1998	1999	2000	2001	2002	2003	2004	2005	2006	2007
TOTAL	896 452	974 631	1 089 862	1 052 344	917 490	886 846	953 171	1 062 536	1 217 107	1 277 428
Structures	300 283	293 787	338 120	346 221	325 168	314 021	335 405	368 791	453 893	494 812
New	260 008	276 094	309 541	323 871	299 941	281 892	300 371	341 223	420 090	460 477
Used	40 275	17 693	28 579	22 349	25 227	32 128	35 034	27 568	33 802	34 335
Equipment	596 169	680 843	751 742	706 123	592 321	572 825	617 766	693 745	763 215	782 615
New	570 397	656 344	718 227	679 090	564 218	540 611	588 110	664 648	734 160	752 345
Used	25 773	24 499	33 515	27 033	28 103	32 214	29 656	29 096	29 055	30 271
Not distributed as structures or equipment	0	0	0	0	0	0	0	0	0	0
CAPITALIZED COMPUTER SOFTWARE [1]	. . .	. . .	. . .	. . .	. . .	49 869	49 868	49 149	58 522	62 893
Prepackaged	. . .	. . .	. . .	. . .	. . .	17 307	17 306	17 630	21 181	21 776
Vendor-customized	. . .	. . .	. . .	. . .	. . .	15 554	15 553	13 876	16 912	17 939
Internally-developed	. . .	. . .	. . .	. . .	. . .	17 008	17 008	17 643	20 433	23 177
CAPITAL LEASE AND CAPITALIZED INTEREST EXPENSES [1]										
Capital leases	15 631	16 594	19 184	15 500	15 092	15 137	17 526	17 640	23 923	19 432
Capitalized interest	9 799	9 591	11 423	11 969	. . .	. . .	. . .	. . .	. . .	. . .

Capital expenditures	Companies without employees									
	1998	1999	2000	2001	2002	2003	2004	2005	2006	2007
TOTAL	74 445	72 322	71 168	56 660	80 404	88 169	88 889	82 247	92 832	84 205
Structures	28 828	26 291	26 287	17 527	33 316	30 621	33 302	32 862	34 809	34 494
New	24 483	20 402	19 984	11 667	21 250	23 399	24 309	24 715	28 771	23 606
Used	4 345	5 889	6 303	5 860	12 066	7 222	8 993	8 146	6 038	10 888
Equipment	45 617	46 030	44 880	39 133	47 088	57 549	55 587	49 386	58 023	49 711
New	35 813	33 209	32 399	27 528	34 450	38 803	40 481	36 598	42 899	40 054
Used	9 804	12 821	12 481	11 605	12 638	18 746	15 106	12 787	15 124	9 657
Not distributed as structures or equipment	0	0	0	0	0	0	0	0	0	0
CAPITALIZED COMPUTER SOFTWARE [1]	. . .	. . .	. . .	. . .	. . .	. . .	. . .	. . .	. . .	. . .
Prepackaged	. . .	. . .	. . .	. . .	. . .	. . .	. . .	. . .	. . .	. . .
Vendor-customized	. . .	. . .	. . .	. . .	. . .	. . .	. . .	. . .	. . .	. . .
Internally-developed	. . .	. . .	. . .	. . .	. . .	. . .	. . .	. . .	. . .	. . .
CAPITAL LEASE AND CAPITALIZED INTEREST EXPENSES [1]										
Capital leases	902	546	361	29	242	504	469	463	519	778
Capitalized interest	. . .	. . .	. . .	. . .	. . .	. . .	. . .	. . .	. . .	. . .

[1]Included in structures and equipment data shown above.
. . . = Not available.

Table 5-11. Capital Expenditures for Structures and Equipment for Companies with Employees by Major NAICS Industry Sector

(Millions of dollars.)

Year and type of expenditure	Total	Forestry, fishing, and agricultural services (113–115)	Mining (21)	Utilities (22)	Construction (23)	Manufacturing (31–33)			Wholesale trade (42)	Retail trade (44–45)	Transportation and warehousing (48–49)	Information (51)
						Total	Durable goods industries (321, 327, 33)	Nondurable goods industries (31, 322–326)				
1998												
Total expenditures	896 452	854	40 424	36 010	26 867	203 587	117 901	85 685	29 169	57 276	51 287	96 487
Structures, total	300 283	206	26 503	18 574	7 062	39 028	19 406	19 622	7 480	25 105	13 036	24 721
New	260 008	158	24 714	17 771	4 749	37 122	18 449	18 673	6 738	23 104	12 365	24 218
Used	40 275	49	1 789	804	2 313	1 906	957	949	742	2 001	671	503
Equipment, total	596 169	648	13 921	17 436	19 805	164 559	98 496	66 063	21 690	32 171	38 251	71 766
New	570 397	603	12 625	17 266	15 346	159 363	95 571	63 792	20 470	30 359	33 409	70 827
Used	25 773	46	1 296	170	4 458	5 196	2 925	2 271	1 220	1 812	4 842	939
1999												
Total expenditures	974 631	1 716	30 586	42 802	23 110	196 399	117 005	79 394	32 442	64 063	57 299	122 827
Structures, total	293 787	344	17 626	21 241	1 753	33 985	17 320	16 665	7 264	29 494	14 122	34 924
New	276 094	331	17 039	20 784	1 505	32 814	16 581	16 233	6 508	28 670	13 859	33 733
Used	17 693	13	587	457	248	1 171	739	432	756	824	263	1 191
Equipment, total	680 843	1 371	12 960	21 561	21 356	162 414	99 685	62 729	25 179	34 569	43 178	87 903
New	656 344	1 190	12 167	20 545	18 600	157 715	96 434	61 281	23 714	33 567	40 425	85 310
Used	24 499	182	793	1 016	2 756	4 699	3 251	1 448	1 465	1 002	2 752	2 593
2000												
Total expenditures	1 089 862	1 488	42 522	61 302	25 049	214 827	133 786	81 041	33 579	69 791	59 851	160 177
Structures, total	338 120	139	28 620	29 472	2 803	39 434	21 228	18 207	8 923	32 037	13 457	41 502
New	309 541	134	25 500	29 258	2 583	36 643	19 748	16 895	8 364	30 413	13 190	40 062
Used	28 579	5	3 120	214	220	2 791	1 480	1 312	559	1 624	267	1 440
Equipment, total	751 742	1 350	13 902	31 830	22 245	175 393	112 558	62 835	24 656	37 754	46 394	118 675
New	718 227	1 086	12 854	27 937	17 788	169 454	108 703	60 751	23 610	36 428	43 455	117 835
Used	33 515	264	1 048	3 893	4 458	5 939	3 856	2 083	1 046	1 326	2 938	841
2001												
Total expenditures	1 052 344	1 532	51 278	82 823	24 802	192 835	118 875	73 959	29 981	66 917	57 756	144 793
Structures, total	346 221	226	32 678	38 093	3 859	39 815	22 032	17 784	6 932	30 010	16 594	41 742
New	323 871	149	31 825	36 504	3 389	38 001	20 701	17 301	5 357	29 118	14 479	41 384
Used	22 349	77	853	1 588	470	1 814	1 331	483	1 575	892	2 116	358
Equipment, total	706 123	1 306	18 600	44 731	20 943	153 019	96 844	56 176	23 049	36 906	41 161	103 051
New	679 090	1 091	17 567	42 939	17 432	148 397	94 251	54 145	20 757	35 074	38 521	102 410
Used	27 033	215	1 033	1 792	3 511	4 623	2 592	2 030	2 292	1 833	2 640	641
2002												
Total expenditures	917 490	1 910	42 467	65 502	24 773	157 243	84 062	73 181	26 789	59 316	47 124	88 156
Structures, total	325 168	184	30 685	29 893	1 890	32 643	15 133	17 510	5 885	26 286	14 498	33 607
New	299 941	118	29 775	29 008	1 254	31 022	14 396	16 626	5 447	25 051	13 870	33 472
Used	25 227	66	910	886	456	1 622	737	885	438	1 234	628	135
Equipment, total	592 321	1 726	11 783	35 609	23 063	124 600	68 929	55 671	20 904	33 030	32 626	54 550
New	564 218	1 319	10 262	34 816	19 257	118 621	66 112	52 510	18 562	31 157	29 178	54 247
Used	28 103	407	1 520	793	3 806	5 978	2 817	3 161	2 342	1 873	3 447	303
2003												
Total expenditures	886 846	1 894	50 548	54 569	23 159	149 065	80 226	68 839	26 014	65 868	44 460	80 524
Structures, total	314 021	202	36 617	24 841	1 676	31 108	13 330	17 778	5 615	29 675	13 005	30 765
New	281 892	177	35 897	24 580	1 424	29 315	12 631	16 685	4 921	27 393	11 779	30 406
Used	32 128	25	720	261	251	1 793	700	1 093	694	2 282	1 226	358
Equipment, total	572 825	1 692	13 931	29 729	21 484	117 956	66 895	51 061	20 399	36 193	31 454	49 759
New	540 611	1 267	12 135	29 044	16 170	112 102	62 810	49 292	19 457	32 162	26 786	47 857
Used	32 214	425	1 796	685	5 313	5 855	4 086	1 769	942	4 031	4 668	1 902
2004												
Total expenditures	953 171	2 081	51 253	50 409	28 627	156 651	85 119	71 532	32 314	72 170	46 054	83 488
Structures, total	335 405	324	34 564	24 398	4 511	31 823	13 606	18 217	7 133	33 308	13 992	28 636
New	300 371	309	33 583	23 626	4 167	30 016	12 818	17 198	6 555	31 486	13 018	26 253
Used	35 034	15	982	772	345	1 807	788	1 019	578	1 822	975	2 384
Equipment, total	617 766	1 757	16 689	26 011	24 115	124 828	71 513	53 315	25 181	38 862	32 062	54 852
New	588 110	1 507	15 415	25 724	18 939	120 481	68 904	51 576	21 888	36 965	28 472	53 120
Used	29 656	250	1 274	286	5 176	4 347	2 609	1 738	3 293	1 897	3 590	1 732
2005												
Total expenditures	1 062 536	2 702	66 746	58 032	30 072	165 634	92 180	73 455	40 578	73 531	56 926	91 373
Structures, total	368 791	344	46 433	24 186	2 544	34 132	14 735	19 397	9 184	34 119	17 855	31 977
New	341 223	283	45 655	23 485	2 247	32 564	14 033	18 531	8 830	33 360	16 954	31 716
Used	27 568	61	777	701	297	1 569	703	866	355	759	901	262
Equipment, total	693 745	2 358	20 313	33 847	27 528	131 502	77 444	54 058	31 394	39 412	39 072	59 396
New	664 648	2 016	18 495	33 083	22 082	126 387	73 889	52 498	28 224	38 301	34 953	59 071
Used	29 096	341	1 818	764	5 446	5 115	3 555	1 560	3 169	1 111	4 119	325
2006												
Total expenditures	1 217 107	2 672	99 309	69 757	30 257	192 364	106 843	85 521	36 600	86 735	68 021	104 373
Structures, total	453 893	391	68 662	30 587	2 556	41 617	17 515	24 103	10 375	43 188	20 852	31 947
New	420 090	316	67 322	29 294	2 217	39 419	16 243	23 176	9 956	41 985	19 765	31 621
Used	33 802	75	1 340	1 293	338	2 198	1 272	926	419	1 203	1 087	326
Equipment, total	763 215	2 281	30 647	39 170	27 701	150 747	89 328	61 419	26 226	43 547	47 168	72 425
New	734 160	1 846	28 813	37 617	23 276	146 551	86 637	59 914	24 366	41 943	41 258	71 830
Used	29 055	435	1 833	1 553	4 425	4 196	2 692	1 504	1 860	1 604	5 911	595
2007												
Total expenditures	1 277 428	2 149	121 733	83 621	36 725	196 953	107 989	88 964	31 756	84 235	68 536	105 336
Structures, total	494 812	469	86 231	38 507	3 542	42 725	18 306	24 419	7 798	41 830	24 799	28 597
New	460 477	286	84 455	35 976	2 718	41 486	17 859	23 627	7 339	40 568	23 894	27 824
Used	34 335	183	1 776	2 531	824	1 239	447	792	459	1 262	905	773
Equipment, total	782 615	1 681	35 502	45 114	33 183	154 228	89 683	64 545	23 958	42 405	43 737	76 739
New	752 345	1 368	33 157	44 045	27 342	149 681	86 892	62 788	21 979	40 812	39 336	76 094
Used	30 271	313	2 344	1 069	5 841	4 547	2 791	1 757	1 980	1 593	4 400	645

Note: Detail may not sum to total because of rounding.

Table 5-11. Capital Expenditures for Structures and Equipment for Companies with Employees by Major NAICS Industry Sector—*Continued*

(Millions of dollars.)

Year and type of expenditure	Finance and insurance (52)	Real estate and rental and leasing (53)	Professional, scientific, and technical services (54)	Management of companies and enterprises (55)	Administrative and support and waste management (56)	Educational services (61)	Health care and social assistance (62)	Arts, entertainment, and recreation (71)	Accommodation and food services (72)	Other services, except public administration (81)	Structure and equipment expenditures serving multiple industries
1998											
Total expenditures	118 173	85 184	22 277	1 821	13 110	12 983	47 109	8 994	20 822	20 627	3 392
Structures, total	27 221	36 775	4 886	753	4 288	9 109	23 971	5 045	12 045	13 737	738
New	16 858	24 109	4 572	502	3 745	8 734	21 328	4 838	10 402	13 280	699
Used	10 362	12 666	314	251	543	374	2 643	206	1 643	457	39
Equipment, total	90 952	48 409	17 390	1 068	8 822	3 874	23 138	3 949	8 777	6 890	2 654
New	90 058	46 877	16 868	1 030	8 346	3 825	22 465	3 752	8 005	6 296	2 609
Used	894	1 532	522	38	476	49	672	197	772	594	46
1999											
Total expenditures	130 101	100 629	29 546	6 065	16 227	13 532	51 342	13 355	23 328	16 902	2 359
Structures, total	20 080	33 903	6 780	1 668	2 875	9 767	25 922	8 119	13 431	9 975	516
New	17 918	30 295	6 168	1 509	2 773	9 140	24 159	7 971	11 391	9 033	495
Used	2 162	3 608	613	159	102	627	1 763	148	2 040	941	21
Equipment, total	110 021	66 726	22 766	4 397	13 353	3 766	25 420	5 236	9 897	6 928	1 843
New	109 577	63 555	22 153	4 319	12 323	3 668	24 945	5 125	9 324	6 370	1 752
Used	444	3 171	613	78	1 029	97	475	111	573	558	91
2000											
Total expenditures	133 684	92 456	34 055	5 054	17 506	18 223	52 166	19 125	26 307	21 125	1 572
Structures, total	23 010	24 815	8 141	1 570	4 032	13 699	26 868	12 245	13 873	13 274	206
New	20 298	17 793	7 470	955	3 504	12 965	23 999	11 627	12 879	11 705	200
Used	2 712	7 022	671	615	528	735	2 869	618	993	1 569	6
Equipment, total	110 675	67 641	25 914	3 484	13 475	4 523	25 299	6 880	12 434	7 852	1 366
New	109 678	62 175	24 847	3 403	12 723	4 338	24 407	6 161	11 501	7 192	1 357
Used	997	5 466	1 067	81	752	186	892	719	933	659	10
2001											
Total expenditures	131 105	82 674	30 464	3 035	15 785	17 377	52 932	14 974	21 365	29 006	911
Structures, total	22 744	20 489	7 258	933	3 527	12 852	27 030	8 998	12 248	20 031	163
New	19 571	17 325	6 793	869	3 367	11 860	25 241	8 157	11 402	18 918	162
Used	3 173	3 164	465	64	160	991	1 789	841	846	1 112	0
Equipment, total	108 361	62 185	23 206	2 102	12 258	4 525	25 902	5 976	9 117	8 976	749
New	107 268	60 295	22 330	2 019	11 644	4 238	24 573	5 590	7 921	8 300	725
Used	1 093	1 891	876	83	613	287	1 329	386	1 196	676	24
2002											
Total expenditures	128 444	94 529	25 864	3 430	14 719	19 532	59 311	13 169	22 409	21 269	1 532
Structures, total	24 308	35 579	7 129	933	3 276	14 655	30 291	7 758	12 157	13 261	250
New	19 748	30 227	6 424	913	2 948	13 601	27 273	7 332	10 848	11 363	248
Used	4 739	5 352	706	21	328	1 055	3 018	425	1 309	1 899	2
Equipment, total	103 956	58 949	18 735	2 497	11 443	4 876	29 021	5 412	10 252	8 007	1 282
New	103 421	56 847	18 021	2 481	10 585	4 690	28 196	5 132	9 290	6 858	1 276
Used	535	2 102	714	16	857	186	825	280	962	1 149	6
2003											
Total expenditures	120 787	87 952	24 703	3 298	16 612	16 667	61 151	11 029	21 036	26 035	1 476
Structures, total	26 200	25 028	5 314	925	3 976	11 984	30 996	6 800	10 568	18 518	209
New	17 908	16 446	4 671	869	3 213	11 569	28 885	6 532	9 417	16 288	202
Used	8 292	8 583	643	56	763	415	2 111	268	1 151	2 230	7
Equipment, total	94 587	62 923	19 389	2 373	12 636	4 683	30 155	4 229	10 468	7 517	1 267
New	94 205	61 253	18 675	2 368	11 374	4 569	29 497	4 038	9 684	6 706	1 263
Used	383	1 671	714	5	1 262	114	658	192	783	811	4
2004											
Total expenditures	153 629	91 606	26 688	2 825	17 455	18 919	64 561	12 165	20 641	19 701	1 572
Structures, total	43 919	27 277	6 007	860	2 567	13 728	32 608	7 360	9 860	12 278	321
New	30 216	21 610	5 714	798	2 309	12 781	30 668	7 196	9 126	10 867	307
Used	13 703	5 667	293	62	259	947	1 939	164	734	1 411	13
Equipment, total	109 710	64 329	20 681	1 965	14 888	5 190	31 953	4 804	10 781	7 423	1 252
New	109 244	61 947	20 081	1 931	12 692	4 965	31 280	4 677	10 373	6 788	1 248
Used	466	2 382	600	34	2 196	225	673	128	408	635	3
2005											
Total expenditures	161 389	103 022	33 066	2 809	18 194	17 484	73 825	14 165	30 718	20 105	2 163
Structures, total	39 383	24 791	8 717	857	3 051	12 711	39 089	9 242	17 679	12 036	460
New	31 023	17 341	7 633	795	2 759	11 913	37 493	8 805	16 567	11 350	452
Used	8 360	7 450	1 084	62	292	798	1 597	436	1 112	686	8
Equipment, total	122 005	78 231	24 350	1 951	15 143	4 773	34 736	4 924	13 039	8 069	1 703
New	121 511	76 894	23 887	1 917	13 523	4 597	34 110	4 757	11 950	7 209	1 681
Used	494	1 337	463	34	1 620	176	626	166	1 089	861	22
2006											
Total expenditures	163 069	132 073	30 284	3 306	19 231	22 615	75 296	17 156	36 217	25 959	1 813
Structures, total	41 326	40 794	6 971	875	3 613	17 537	41 197	11 733	22 585	16 621	467
New	34 028	30 240	6 375	799	3 485	16 203	37 765	11 326	21 774	15 754	446
Used	7 298	10 554	596	76	128	1 334	3 433	406	811	866	21
Equipment, total	121 743	91 280	23 313	2 432	15 618	5 078	34 099	5 424	13 632	9 339	1 346
New	121 157	88 957	22 867	2 188	14 932	4 983	33 508	5 121	13 161	8 463	1 322
Used	586	2 323	446	244	686	95	591	303	472	875	24
2007											
Total expenditures	172 481	123 043	31 814	4 426	18 805	23 232	83 763	18 769	38 427	29 541	2 080
Structures, total	45 102	44 516	7 440	1 368	4 271	17 863	45 084	12 589	22 311	19 165	603
New	36 340	36 820	6 930	1 295	4 089	17 238	43 244	11 894	21 220	16 263	597
Used	8 762	7 696	510	73	182	625	1 840	695	1 091	2 902	6
Equipment, total	127 379	78 528	24 374	3 058	14 534	5 369	38 678	6 180	16 116	10 376	1 476
New	126 384	76 368	23 955	2 931	13 825	5 230	38 138	5 916	14 855	9 454	1 475
Used	995	2 160	420	127	709	139	541	264	1 261	922	1

Note: Detail may not sum to total because of rounding.

NOTES AND DEFINITIONS

TABLES 5-1 THROUGH 5-4 AND 5-7
GROSS SAVING AND INVESTMENT ACCOUNTS; INVENTORIES TO SALES RATIOS

SOURCE: U.S. DEPARTMENT OF COMMERCE, BUREAU OF ECONOMIC ANALYSIS (BEA)

All of the data in these tables are from the National Income and Product Accounts, which are described in the Notes and Definitions to Chapter 1. All quarterly series are shown at seasonally adjusted annual rates. Current and constant dollar values are in billions of dollars. Indexes of quantity are based on the average for the year 2000, set to equal 100.

Definitions: Table 5-1

Gross saving is saving before the deduction of allowances for the consumption of fixed capital. It represents the amount of saving available to finance gross investment. *Net saving* is gross saving less allowances for fixed capital consumption. It represents the amount of saving available for financing expansion of the capital stock, and comprises private saving (the sum of personal saving and undistributed corporate profits) and the saving of federal, state, and local governments.

Personal saving is derived by subtracting personal outlays from disposable personal income. (See Chapter 4 for more information.) It is the current net saving of individuals (including proprietors of unincorporated businesses), nonprofit institutions that primarily serve individuals, life insurance carriers, retirement funds, private noninsured welfare funds, and private trust funds. Conceptually, personal saving may also be viewed as the sum for all persons (including institutions as previously defined) of the net acquisition of financial assets and the change in physical assets, less the sum of net borrowing and consumption of fixed capital. In either case, it is defined to exclude capital gains. That is, it excludes profits on the increase in the value of homes, securities, and other property—whether realized or unrealized—and includes the noncorporate inventory valuation adjustment and the capital consumption adjustment (IVA and CCAdj, respectively). (See notes and definitions to Tables 1-1 through 1-15.)

Undistributed profits are corporate profits after tax less dividends, with the corporate IVA and corporate CCAdj. (See notes and definitions for Tables 1-1 through 1-15.)

Government net saving was formerly called "current surplus or deficit (-) of general government." (See Chapter 6 for further detail from the government accounts.) Where current receipts of government exceed current expenditures, government has a current surplus (indicated by a positive value) and saving is made available to finance investment by government or other sectors—for example, by the repayment of debt, which can free up funds for private investment. Where current expenditures exceed current receipts, there is a government deficit (indicated by a negative value) and government must borrow, drawing on funds that would otherwise be available for private investment. In these accounts, current expenditures are defined to include a charge for the consumption of fixed capital.

Consumption of fixed capital is an accounting charge for the using-up of private and government fixed capital, including software, located in the United States. It is based on studies of prices of used equipment and structures in resale markets. For general government and nonprofit institutions that primarily serve individuals, consumption of fixed capital is recorded in government consumption expenditures and in personal consumption expenditures (PCE), respectively, as the value of the current services of the fixed capital assets owned and used by these entities. *Private consumption of fixed capital* consists of tax-return-based depreciation charges for corporations and nonfarm proprietorships and historical-cost depreciation (calculated by the Bureau of Economic Analysis [BEA] using a geometric pattern of price declines) for farm proprietorships, rental income of persons, and nonprofit institutions, *minus* the capital consumption adjustments. (In other words, in the NIPA treatment of saving, the amount of the CCAdj is taken out of book depreciation and added to income and profits—a reallocation from one form of gross saving to another.)

Gross private domestic investment consists of gross private fixed investment and change in private inventories. (See the notes and definitions for Chapter 1.)

Gross government investment consists of federal, state, and local general government and government enterprise expenditures for fixed assets (structures, equipment, and software). Government inventory investment is included in government consumption expenditures. For further detail, see Chapter 6.

Capital account transactions, net are the net cash or in-kind transfers between the United States and the rest of the world that are linked to the acquisition or disposition of assets rather than the purchase or sale of currently-produced goods and services. When positive, it represents a net transfer from the United States to the rest of the world; when negative, it represents a net transfer to the United States from the rest of the world. This is a definitional category that was introduced in the 1999 revision of the NIPAs. Estimates are available only from 1982 forward.

Net lending or net borrowing (-), NIPAs is equal to the international balance on current account as measured in the NIPAs (see Chapter 7) less capital account transactions, net. When positive, this represents net investment by the United States in the rest of the world; when negative, it represents net borrowing by the United States from the rest of the world. For data before 1982, net lending or net borrowing equals the NIPA balance on current account, because estimates of capital account transactions are not available.

By definition, gross national saving must equal the sum of gross domestic investment, capital account transactions, and net international lending (where net international borrowing appears as negative lending). In practice, due to differences in measurement, these two aggregates differ by the same *statistical discrepancy* calculated in the product and income accounts. (See Chapter 1.) Gross saving is therefore equal to the sum of gross domestic investment, capital account transactions, and net international lending minus the statistical discrepancy. Where the statistical discrepancy is negative, it means that the sum of measured investment, capital transactions, and net international lending has fallen short of measured saving.

Net domestic investment is gross domestic investment minus consumption of fixed capital.

Gross national income is national income plus the consumption of fixed capital. (See Chapter 1 for further information.) This is a new concept introduced in the 2003 revision. It is conceptually equal to gross national product, but differs by the statistical discrepancy. Gross national income is an appropriate denominator for the national saving ratios. Saving was previously shown as a percentage of gross national product; in the revision, it is instead shown as a percentage of the income-side equivalent of gross national product. Since saving is measured as a residual from income, it is appropriate to involve consistent measurements—and consistent imperfections in those measurements— in both the numerator and the denominator of the fraction.

Definitions: Tables 5-2 through 5-4

Gross private fixed investment comprises both nonresidential and residential fixed investment. It consists of purchases of fixed assets, which are commodities that will be used in a production process for more than one year, including replacements and additions to the capital stock. It is "gross" in the sense that it is measured before a deduction for consumption of fixed capital. It covers all investment by private businesses and nonprofit institutions in the United States, regardless of whether the investment is owned by U.S. residents. It does not include purchases of the same types of equipment and structures by government agencies, which are included in government gross investment, or investment by U.S. residents in other countries.

Gross nonresidential fixed investment consists of structures, equipment, and software that are not related to personal residences.

Nonresidential structures consists of new construction, brokers' commissions on sales of structures, and net purchases (purchases less sales) of used structures by private business

and by nonprofit institutions from government agencies. New construction includes hotels, motels, and mining exploration, shafts, and wells.

Other nonresidential structures consists primarily of religious, educational, vocational, lodging, railroads, farm, and amusement and recreational structures, net purchases of used structures, and brokers' commissions on the sale of structures.

Nonresidential equipment and software consists of private business purchases—on capital account—of new machinery, equipment, and vehicles; purchases and in-house production of software; dealers' margins on sales of used equipment; and net purchases (purchases less sales) of used equipment from government agencies, persons, and the rest of the world. (However, it does not include the personal-use portion of equipment purchased for both business and personal use. This is included in PCE.)

Software excludes the value of software "embedded," or bundled, in computers and other equipment, which is instead included in the value of that equipment.

Other information processing includes communication equipment, nonmedical instruments, medical equipment and instruments, photocopy and related equipment, and office and accounting equipment.

Other nonresidential equipment consists primarily of furniture and fixtures, agricultural machinery, construction machinery, mining and oilfield machinery, service industry machinery, and electrical equipment not elsewhere classified.

Residential private fixed investment consists of both *structures* and residential producers' durable *equipment*—that is, equipment owned by landlords and rented to tenants. Investment in *structures* consists of new units, improvements to existing units, manufactured homes, brokers' commissions on the sale of residential property, and net purchases (purchases less sales) of used structures from government agencies.

Other residential structures consists primarily of manufactured homes, improvements, dormitories, net purchases of used structures, and brokers' commissions on the sale of residential structures.

Real gross private investment (Table 5-3) and *chain-type quantity indexes for private fixed investment* (Table 5-4) are defined and explained in the notes and definitions to Chapter 1. The chained-dollar (2000) estimates in Table 5-3 are constructed by applying the changes in the chain-type quantity indexes, as shown in Table 5-4, to the 2000 current-dollar values. Thus, they do not contain any information about time trends that is not already present in the quantity indexes.

As the quantity indexes are chain-weighted at the basic level of aggregation, chained constant-dollar components generally do not add to the chained constant-dollar totals. For this reason, BEA only makes available year-2000-dollar estimates back to 1990 (except for the very highest levels of aggregation of gross domestic product [GDP]), since the addition problem is less severe for years close to the base year. However, the addition problem is so severe for computers that BEA does not even publish recent year-2000-dollar values for this component. BEA notes that "The quantity index for computers can be used to accurately measure the real growth rate of this component. However, because computers exhibit rapid changes in prices relative to other prices in the economy, the chained-dollar estimates should not be used to measure the component's relative importance or its contribution to the growth rate of more aggregate series." (Footnote to BEA Table 5.3.6, *Survey of Current Business*, available on the BEA Web site at <http://www.bea.gov>.) Accurate estimates of these contributions are shown in BEA Table 5.3.2, which is published in the *Survey of Current Business* and can be found on the BEA Web site.

Definitions: Table 5-7

Inventories to sales ratios. The ratios shown in Table 5-7 are based on the inventory estimates underlying the measurement of inventory change in the NIPAs. They include data and estimates for not only the inventories held in manufacturing and trade (see the following Tables 5-8 and 5-9), but also stocks held by all other businesses in the U.S. economy.

For the current-dollar ratios, inventories at the end of each quarter are valued in the prices that prevailed at the end of that quarter. For the constant-dollar ratios, they are valued in chained (2000) dollars. In both cases, the inventory-sales ratio is the value of the inventories at the end of the quarter divided by quarterly total sales at *monthly* rates (quarterly totals divided by 3). In other words, they represent how many months' supply businesses had on hand at the end of the period. This makes them comparable in concept and order of magnitude to the ratios shown in Tables 5-8 and 5-9. Annual data are those for the fourth quarter.

Data availability, revisions, and references

See the information on the NIPAs at the end of the notes and definitions to Chapter 1. All current and historical data are available on the BEA Web site at <http://www.bea.gov> or the STAT-USA subscription Web site at <http://www.stat-usa.gov>.

TABLES 5-5 AND 5-6
CURRENT-COST NET STOCK OF FIXED ASSETS; CHAIN-TYPE QUANTITY INDEXES FOR NET STOCK OF FIXED ASSETS

Source: U.S. Department of Commerce, Bureau of Economic Analysis (BEA)

The Bureau of Economic Analysis (BEA) calculates measurements, integrated with the national income and product accounts (NIPAs), of the level of the *stock* of fixed assets in the U.S. economy, or what is commonly called the "capital stock." (The fixed investment component of the GDP is a *flow*, or the increment of new capital goods into the capital stock.) Data on consumer stocks of durable goods are also included in the accounts, but are not shown here. Historical data are available back to 1901, with detailed annual estimates of net stocks, depreciation, and investment by type and by NAICS (North American Industry Classification System) industry. This volume of *Business Statistics* presents time series data on the net stock of fixed assets valued in current dollars and constant-dollar quantity indexes. Data for 1947 through 2007 are presented in Tables 5-5 and 5-6, and data for 1929 through 1948 are presented in Table 18-3.

Definitions and methods

The definitions of capital stock categories are the same as used in GDP investment categories. (See the notes and definitions to Tables 5-2 through 5-4 for more information.)

The values of fixed capital and depreciation typically reported by businesses are inadequate for economic analysis and are not typically used in these measures. In business reports, capital is generally valued at historical costs—each year's capital acquisition in the prices of the year acquired—and the totals thus represent a mixture of pricing bases. Reported depreciation is generally based on historical cost and on depreciation rates allowable by federal income tax law, rather than on a realistic rate of economic depreciation.

In these data, the *net stock of fixed assets* is measured by a perpetual inventory method. In other words, net stock at any given time is the cumulative value of past gross investment less the cumulative value of past depreciation, including damages from disasters and war losses that exceed normal depreciation (such as the terrorist attacks of September 11, 2001).

Gross investment is the gross fixed investment component of GDP. Depreciation for privately owned assets is the value of "consumption of fixed capital" in the NIPAs, which is subtracted from GDP in order to yield net domestic product. For government assets, the published NIPA value of consumption of fixed capital does *not* include disaster and war loss damage. The value of these damages is calculated by BEA and subtracted from capital stock assets for the purpose of fixed asset measurement.

The initial calculations using this perpetual inventory method are performed in real terms for each type of asset. They are then aggregated to higher levels using an annual-weighted Fisher-type index. (See the definition of *real or chained-dollar estimates* in the notes and definitions for Chapter 1.) This provides the *chain-type quantity indexes* shown in Table 5-6. Growth rates in these indexes measure real growth in the capital stock.

The real values are then converted to a *current-cost* basis to yield the values shown in Table 5-5. They are converted by multiplying the real values by the appropriate price index for the period under consideration. A major use of the current-cost net stock figures is comparison with the value of output in that year; for example, the current-cost net stock of fixed assets for the total economy divided by the current-dollar value of GDP yields a capital-output ratio for the entire economy. Growth rates in current-cost values will reflect both the real growth measured by the quantity indexes and the increase in the value at current prices of the existing stock.

Data availability

These data are updated each year following the mid-year revision of the NIPAs. The data in this volume were posted on the BEA Web site on August 21, 2008.

References

The latest comprehensive revision was presented and described in "Fixed Assets and Consumer Durable Goods for 1994–2004," *Survey of Current Business* (September 2005). Data for earlier years were presented and described in "Fixed Assets and Consumer Durable Goods: Preliminary Estimates for 2002 and Revised Estimates for 1925–2001," *Survey of Current Business* (May 2004). The fixed asset measures are described in *Fixed Assets and Consumer Durable Goods in the United States, 1925–97* (September 2003), available on the BEA Web site at <http://www.bea.gov>.

TABLES 5-8 AND 5-9
MANUFACTURING AND TRADE SALES AND INVENTORIES

SOURCES: U.S. DEPARTMENT OF COMMERCE, CENSUS BUREAU (CURRENT-DOLLAR SERIES) AND U.S. DEPARTMENT OF COMMERCE, BUREAU OF ECONOMIC ANALYSIS (BEA; CONSTANT-DOLLAR SERIES)

The current-dollar data on which these tables are based bring together summary data from the separate series on manufacturers' shipments, inventories, and orders; merchant wholesalers' sales and inventories; and retail sales and inventories, all of which are included in Part B of this book. Generally, current-dollar inventories are collected on a current cost (or pre-LIFO [last in, first out]) basis. See the notes and definitions for Tables 17-4, 17-5, 17-9, 17-11, and 17-12 for further information about these data.

Based on these current-dollar values and relevant price data, BEA makes estimates of real sales, inventories, and inventory-sales ratios. Note, however, that annual figures for sales are shown as annual *totals* in Table 5-8 but as *averages* of the monthly data in Table 5-9. Also note that constant-dollar detail may not add to constant-dollar totals because of the chain-weighting formula; see the discussion of chain-weighted measures in the notes and definitions for Chapter 1.

Inventory values are as of the end of the month or year. In Table 5-8, annual values for monthly current-dollar inventory-sales ratios are averages of seasonally adjusted monthly ratios. However, for the real ratios in Table 5-9, annual figures for inventory-sales ratios are calculated by BEA as year-end (December) inventories divided by the monthly average of sales for the entire year. In all cases, the ratios in these two tables (like those in Table 5-7) represent the number of months' sales on hand as inventory at the end of the reporting period.

Data availability

Sales, inventories, and inventory-sales ratios for manufacturers, merchant wholesalers, and retailers are published monthly by the Census Bureau in a press release entitled "Manufacturing and Trade Inventories and Sales." Recent and historical data are available on the Census Bureau Web site at <http://www.census.gov/mtis/www/mtis.html>. They can also be found by going to the general Census website, <http://www.census.gov>, going to the alphabetical index, finding "Economic Indicators" under "E" and then finding "Manufacturing and trade."

Sales and inventories in constant dollars are available on the BEA Web site at <http://www.bea.gov>. To locate these data on that site, click on "National Economic Accounts." Scroll down to "Supplemental Estimates," click "Underlying Detail Tables," and then click on "List of Underlying Detail Tables." For the most recent data, if there is more than one table with the same title, select the last table listed.

References

For information about the 1996 historical revisions to sales and inventories in constant dollars, see "Real Inventories, Sales, and Inventory-Sales Ratios for Manufacturing and Trade, 1977–95," *Survey of Current Business* (May 1996).

TABLES 5-10 AND 5-11
ANNUAL CAPITAL EXPENDITURES

SOURCE: U.S. DEPARTMENT OF COMMERCE, CENSUS BUREAU

These data are from the Census Bureau's Annual Capital Expenditures Survey (ACES). The survey provides detailed information on capital investment in new and used structures and equipment by nonfarm businesses.

The survey is based on a sample of approximately 46,000 companies with employees and 15,000 non-employer businesses (businesses with an owner but no employees). For companies with employees, the Census Bureau reports data for 132 separate industry categories from the North American Industry Classification System (NAICS); Table 5-11 shows these data for the major NAICS sectors. Total capital expenditures, with no industry detail, are reported for the nonemployer businesses and are shown in Table 5-10, where they can be compared with the totals for companies with employees. The 1999 ACES was the first to use NAICS, providing data for the years 1998 forward on that basis.

Definitions

Capital expenditures include all capitalized costs during the year for both new and used structures and equipment, including software, that were chargeable to fixed asset accounts for which depreciation or amortization accounts are ordinarily maintained. For projects lasting longer than one year, this definition includes gross additions to construction-in-progress accounts, even if the asset was not in use and not yet depreciated. For *capital leases*, the company using the asset (lessee) is asked to include the cost or present value of the leased assets in the year in which the lease was entered. Also included in capital expenditures are capitalized leasehold improvements and capitalized interest charges on loans used to finance capital projects.

Structures consist of the capitalized costs of buildings and other structures and all necessary expenditures to acquire, construct, and prepare the structures. The costs of any machinery and equipment that is integral to or built-in features of the structures are classified as structures. Also included are major additions and alterations to existing structures and capitalized repairs and improvements to buildings.

New structures include new buildings and other structures not previously owned, as well as buildings and other structures that have been previously owned but not used or occupied.

Used structures are buildings and other structures that have been previously owned and occupied.

Equipment includes machinery, furniture and fixtures, computers, and vehicles used in the production and distribution of goods and services. Expenditures for machinery and equipment that is housed in structures and can be removed or replaced without significantly altering the structure are classified as equipment.

New equipment consists of machinery and equipment purchased new, as well as equipment produced in the company for the company's own use.

Used equipment is secondhand machinery and equipment.

Capital leases consist of new assets acquired under capital lease arrangements entered into during the year. Capital leases are defined by the criteria in the Financial Accounting Standards (FASB) Number 13.

Capitalized computer software consists of costs of materials and services directly related to the development or acquisition of software; payroll and payroll-related costs for employees directly associated with software development; and interest cost incurred while developing the software. Capitalized computer software is defined by the criteria in Statement of Position 98-1, Accounting for the Costs of Computer Software Developed or Obtained for Internal Use.

Prepackaged software is purchased off-the-shelf through retailers or other mass-market outlets for internal use by the company and includes the cost of licensing fees and service/maintenance agreements.

Vendor-customized software is externally developed by vendors and customized for the company's use.

Internally-developed software is developed by the company's employees for internal use and includes loaded payroll (salaries, wages, benefits, and bonuses related to all software development activities).

Data availability

The *Annual Capital Expenditure Survey: 2007* was published by the Census Bureau on January 22, 2009, and—in addition to new data for 2007—contains revised data for 2006. A similar schedule was followed in earlier years. The "2008 Capital Spending Report: U.S. Capital Spending Patterns, 1999-2006" was released October 7, 2008. Current and past surveys are available on the Census Bureau Web site at <http://www.census.gov/csd/ace>.

CHAPTER 6: GOVERNMENT

Section 6a: Federal Government in the National Income and Product Accounts

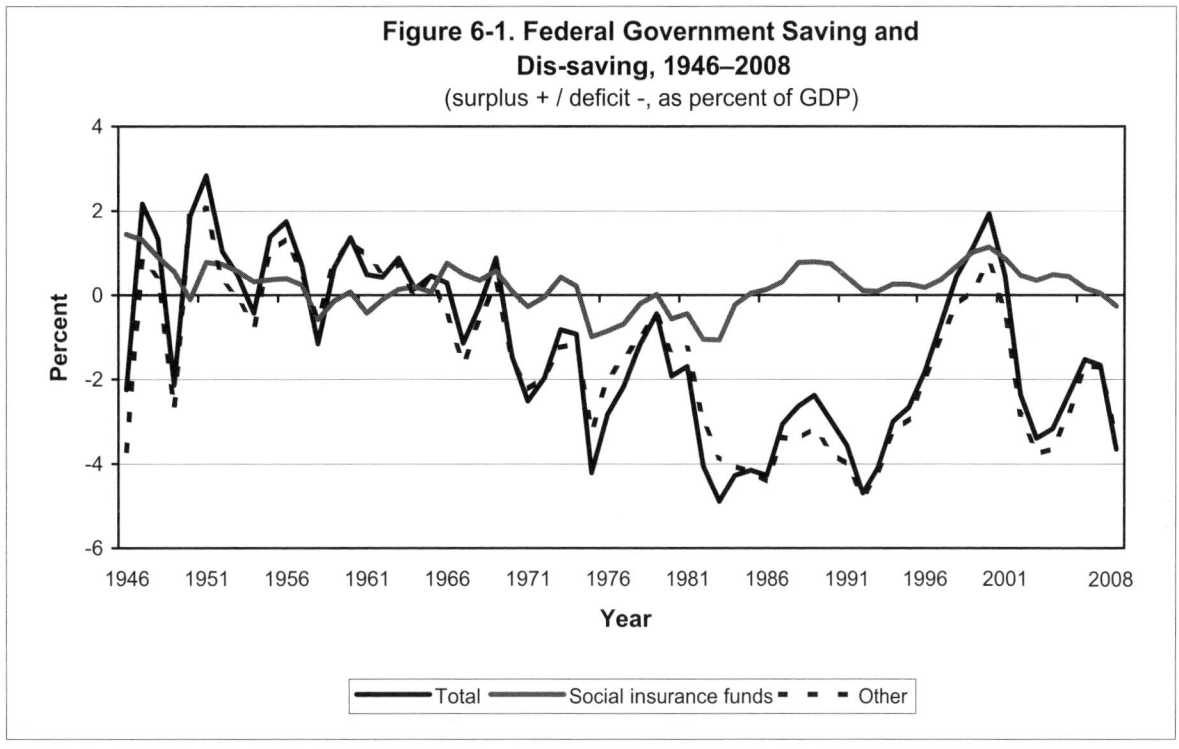

Figure 6-1. Federal Government Saving and Dis-saving, 1946–2008
(surplus + / deficit -, as percent of GDP)

- In the recovery and economic expansion of the 2000s, the federal budget never got back to a surplus such as those achieved in 1999 and 2000. With the onset of recession beginning in December 2007, the calendar 2008 NIPA budget deficit was 3.7 percent of GDP—4 percent by the fourth quarter—as receipts fell while expenditures continued to rise. (Tables 6-1, 1-1, 19-10 and 19-1)

- Total federal government current expenditures increased from 17.6 percent of gross domestic product (GDP) in 1953—the peak for Korean War spending—to 21.7 percent of GDP in 2008. The composition of expenditures changed significantly over that period. "Consumption" spending on defense and nondefense programs fell from 72 percent of total spending to 30 percent, while social benefits such as Social Security and Medicare rose from 13 percent to 45 percent. Grants to state and local governments increased from 3 percent to 13 percent, and interest outlays rose from 7 to 10 percent. (Tables 6-1 and 1-1)

- Federal government nondefense consumption spending, in real terms (as measured by the quantity index), increased at an annual rate of 2.5 percent from 1953 to 2008. Real federal nondefense gross investment spending rose 3.9 percent per year. (Table 6-6)

- Real defense consumption spending jumped 41 percent in the eight years since 2000, but in 2008 was still only 27 percent (an annual rate of 0.4 percent) above spending in 1953. Real defense investment spending was up 82 percent from 2000, but was only up 42 percent (an annual rate of 0.6 percent) from 1953. (Table 6-6)

Table 6-1. Federal Government Current Receipts and Expenditures

(National income and product accounts, calendar years, billions of dollars, quarterly data are at seasonally adjusted annual rates.)

NIPA Table 3.2

Year and quarter	Current receipts Total	Tax receipts Total¹	Personal current taxes	Taxes on production and imports Total¹	Excise taxes	Taxes on corporate income Total	Federal Reserve banks	Other	Contributions for government social insurance	Income receipts on assets Total	Interest receipts	Rents and royalties	Current transfer receipts	Current surplus of government enterprises
1950	48.8	43.3	17.4	8.7	8.2	17.2	0.2	17.0	5.3	...	...	...	0.2	...
1951	62.9	56.3	25.4	9.2	8.6	21.7	0.3	21.4	6.4	...	...	...	0.3	...
1952	65.8	58.9	30.2	10.1	9.6	18.6	0.3	18.3	6.6	...	...	...	0.3	...
1953	68.6	61.5	31.3	10.7	10.2	19.5	0.3	19.1	6.8	...	...	...	0.3	...
1954	62.5	54.4	28.1	9.5	9.0	16.9	0.3	16.6	7.8	...	...	...	0.3	...
1955	71.1	62.0	30.5	10.4	9.8	21.1	0.3	20.8	8.8	...	...	...	0.3	...
1956	75.8	65.9	33.9	11.0	10.3	20.9	0.4	20.5	9.6	...	...	...	0.4	...
1957	79.3	67.9	36.0	11.5	10.8	20.4	0.5	19.9	11.0	...	...	...	0.4	...
1958	76.0	64.7	35.5	11.2	10.4	18.0	0.5	17.4	11.0	...	...	...	0.4	...
1959	87.0	73.3	38.5	12.2	11.2	22.5	0.9	21.6	13.4	0.0	...	0.0	0.4	-0.1
1960	93.9	76.5	41.8	13.1	12.0	21.4	0.9	20.6	16.0	1.4	1.3	0.0	0.4	-0.3
1961	95.5	77.5	42.7	13.2	12.2	21.5	0.7	20.8	16.5	1.5	1.4	0.1	0.5	-0.5
1962	103.6	83.3	46.5	14.2	13.0	22.5	0.8	21.7	18.6	1.7	1.6	0.1	0.5	-0.5
1963	111.8	88.6	49.1	14.7	13.5	24.6	0.9	23.7	21.0	1.8	1.7	0.1	0.6	-0.3
1964	111.8	87.8	46.0	15.5	14.2	26.1	1.6	24.6	21.7	1.8	1.7	0.1	0.7	-0.3
1965	120.9	95.7	51.1	15.5	13.9	28.9	1.3	27.6	22.7	1.9	1.8	0.1	1.1	-0.3
1966	137.9	104.8	58.6	14.5	12.6	31.4	1.6	29.8	30.5	2.1	2.0	0.1	1.2	-0.6
1967	146.9	109.9	64.4	15.2	13.3	30.0	1.9	28.1	34.0	2.5	2.3	0.2	1.1	-0.6
1968	171.2	129.8	76.4	17.0	14.7	36.1	2.5	33.6	37.8	2.9	2.7	0.2	1.1	-0.3
1969	192.5	146.1	91.7	17.9	15.5	36.1	3.0	33.0	43.1	2.7	2.5	0.2	1.1	-0.5
1970	186.0	138.0	88.9	18.2	15.7	30.6	3.5	27.1	45.3	3.1	2.8	0.2	1.1	-1.5
1971	191.7	138.7	85.8	19.1	16.0	33.5	3.4	30.1	50.0	3.5	3.1	0.3	1.1	-1.6
1972	220.1	158.4	102.8	18.6	15.6	36.6	3.2	33.4	57.9	3.6	3.3	0.4	1.3	-1.1
1973	250.4	173.1	109.6	19.9	16.7	43.3	4.3	38.9	74.0	3.8	3.4	0.4	1.3	-1.8
1974	279.5	192.2	126.5	20.2	16.5	45.1	5.6	39.6	83.5	4.2	3.6	0.5	1.4	-1.8
1975	277.2	187.0	120.7	22.2	16.4	43.6	5.4	38.2	87.5	4.9	4.3	0.6	1.5	-3.6
1976	322.5	218.1	141.2	21.6	17.0	54.6	5.9	48.7	99.1	5.9	5.2	0.7	1.6	-2.2
1977	363.4	247.4	162.2	22.9	17.5	61.6	5.9	55.7	110.3	6.7	5.8	0.9	1.9	-2.9
1978	423.5	286.9	188.9	25.6	18.5	71.4	7.0	64.4	127.9	8.5	7.4	1.1	2.4	-2.1
1979	486.2	326.2	224.6	26.0	18.5	74.4	9.3	65.1	148.9	10.7	9.2	1.5	2.8	-2.3
1980	532.1	355.9	250.0	34.0	26.9	70.3	11.7	58.6	162.6	13.7	11.3	2.3	3.5	-3.6
1981	619.4	408.1	290.6	50.3	41.7	65.7	14.0	51.7	191.8	18.3	14.8	3.5	3.8	-2.5
1982	616.6	386.8	295.0	41.4	32.8	49.0	15.2	33.8	204.9	22.2	18.3	3.8	5.2	-2.4
1983	642.3	393.6	286.2	44.8	35.7	61.3	14.2	47.1	221.8	23.8	20.4	3.5	6.0	-2.9
1984	709.0	425.7	301.4	47.8	35.9	75.2	16.1	59.2	252.8	26.6	22.8	3.9	7.3	-3.4
1985	773.3	460.6	336.0	46.4	34.3	76.3	17.8	58.5	276.5	29.1	25.7	3.5	9.4	-2.4
1986	815.2	479.6	350.1	44.0	30.3	83.8	17.8	66.0	297.5	31.4	29.0	2.4	8.2	-1.5
1987	896.6	544.0	392.5	46.3	30.7	103.2	17.7	85.4	315.9	27.9	25.6	2.3	10.7	-2.0
1988	958.2	566.7	402.9	50.3	33.9	111.1	17.4	93.8	353.1	30.0	28.0	2.0	10.8	-2.3
1989	1 037.4	621.7	451.5	50.2	32.7	117.2	21.6	95.6	376.3	28.6	26.5	2.1	12.4	-1.6
1990	1 081.5	642.8	470.2	51.4	33.9	118.1	23.6	94.5	400.1	30.2	27.6	2.6	13.5	-5.1
1991	1 101.3	636.1	461.3	62.2	45.3	109.9	20.8	89.2	418.6	30.1	27.4	2.8	17.9	-1.4
1992	1 147.2	660.4	475.3	63.7	45.4	118.8	16.8	102.0	441.8	.25.7	23.1	2.6	19.4	-0.1
1993	1 222.5	713.4	505.5	66.7	46.9	138.5	16.0	122.5	463.6	26.2	23.5	2.7	21.1	-1.8
1994	1 320.8	781.9	542.7	79.4	57.9	156.7	20.5	136.3	493.7	23.4	20.6	2.7	22.3	-0.4
1995	1 406.5	845.1	586.0	75.9	56.1	179.3	23.4	155.9	519.2	23.7	21.2	2.5	19.1	-0.6
1996	1 524.0	932.4	663.4	73.2	54.0	190.6	20.1	170.5	542.8	26.9	23.0	4.0	23.1	-1.2
1997	1 653.1	1 030.6	744.3	78.2	58.6	203.0	20.7	182.3	576.4	25.9	21.4	4.5	19.9	0.3
1998	1 773.8	1 116.8	825.8	81.1	61.5	204.2	26.6	177.7	613.8	21.5	17.7	3.8	21.5	0.1
1999	1 891.2	1 195.7	893.0	83.9	64.7	213.0	25.4	187.6	651.6	21.5	18.0	3.5	22.7	-0.3
2000	2 053.8	1 313.6	999.1	87.8	66.7	219.4	25.3	194.1	691.7	25.2	20.1	5.1	25.7	-2.3
2001	2 016.2	1 252.2	994.5	85.8	65.2	164.7	27.1	137.6	717.5	24.9	18.4	6.5	27.1	-5.5
2002	1 853.2	1 075.5	830.5	87.3	67.4	150.5	24.5	126.0	734.3	20.2	15.4	4.9	24.8	-1.6
2003	1 879.9	1 070.8	774.5	89.7	68.2	197.8	22.0	175.8	758.9	22.9	16.4	6.5	25.0	2.3
2004	2 008.9	1 152.3	797.4	94.6	71.4	250.3	18.1	232.2	805.2	23.8	17.2	6.6	28.8	-1.2
2005	2 266.9	1 383.0	930.7	99.2	73.9	341.0	21.5	319.5	850.0	24.0	16.9	7.1	15.0	-5.0
2006	2 510.4	1 550.2	1 049.9	98.0	71.3	388.9	29.1	359.9	902.4	25.7	18.0	7.7	35.7	-3.6
2007	2 651.2	1 644.5	1 167.3	97.7	68.9	365.4	34.6	330.8	942.3	29.2	21.9	7.2	37.5	-2.2
2008	2 572.9	1 530.0	1 127.2	96.2	67.2	291.1	32.7	258.5	972.2	31.8	22.2	9.6	39.3	-0.5
2006														
1st quarter	2 453.6	1 504.7	1 018.8	97.8	72.1	377.3	26.6	350.7	893.6	23.7	16.4	7.3	34.7	-3.1
2nd quarter	2 487.6	1 535.1	1 031.6	98.2	71.2	394.4	28.9	365.5	895.7	24.9	17.1	7.8	35.5	-3.5
3rd quarter	2 531.9	1 570.9	1 056.0	98.6	71.1	404.6	30.7	373.9	902.6	26.0	18.1	7.9	36.0	-3.6
4th quarter	2 568.6	1 590.2	1 093.2	97.4	71.0	379.5	30.0	349.5	917.7	28.2	20.5	7.7	36.5	-4.0
2007														
1st quarter	2 612.8	1 615.2	1 139.5	97.7	69.4	365.6	35.1	330.5	937.1	28.4	21.4	7.1	37.0	-5.1
2nd quarter	2 648.1	1 648.2	1 157.1	96.9	68.8	381.5	35.4	346.1	936.4	29.0	22.3	6.8	37.2	-2.8
3rd quarter	2 664.9	1 654.4	1 178.1	98.2	69.4	365.1	34.4	330.7	943.3	29.8	22.5	7.3	37.6	-0.2
4th quarter	2 679.2	1 660.0	1 194.7	98.0	68.1	349.5	33.5	316.0	952.3	29.5	21.6	7.9	38.2	-0.8
2008														
1st quarter	2 672.5	1 634.9	1 201.2	95.8	66.8	322.5	32.9	289.6	968.9	29.9	21.7	8.2	39.4	-0.5
2nd quarter	2 478.8	1 436.0	999.8	96.9	67.5	324.4	28.5	296.0	971.8	31.7	21.9	9.8	40.0	-0.6
3rd quarter	2 595.7	1 565.0	1 141.7	94.7	66.1	313.4	31.6	281.7	976.0	32.4	22.4	10.1	22.4	-0.1
4th quarter	2 544.4	1 484.3	1 166.1	97.3	68.3	204.3	37.6	166.6	972.2	33.1	22.8	10.3	55.6	-0.7

¹Includes components not shown separately.
. . . = Not available.

Table 6-1. Federal Government Current Receipts and Expenditures—*Continued*

(National income and product accounts, calendar years, billions of dollars, quarterly data are at seasonally adjusted annual rates.)

NIPA Table 3.2

| Year and quarter | Current expenditures [1] | | | | | | | | | | Net federal government saving, NIPA (surplus + / deficit -) | | |
| | Total | Consumption expenditures | Government social benefits | | Other current transfer payments | | Interest payments | | | Subsidies | Total | Social insurance funds | Other |
			Total [1]	To persons	Total [1]	Grants-in-aid to state and local governments	Total	To persons and business	To the rest of the world				
1950	43.3	22.1	10.2	10.2	5.5	1.9	4.5	. . .	0.0	1.0	5.5	-0.3	5.8
1951	53.3	34.4	7.9	7.9	5.2	2.0	4.6	. . .	0.0	1.2	9.6	2.6	7.0
1952	62.1	44.2	8.1	8.1	4.3	2.2	4.6	. . .	0.1	0.9	3.7	2.6	1.1
1953	66.8	48.3	8.7	8.7	4.3	2.3	4.7	. . .	0.1	0.7	1.8	2.1	-0.3
1954	64.2	43.9	10.7	10.7	4.1	2.3	4.8	. . .	0.1	0.6	-1.6	1.2	-2.8
1955	65.3	43.9	11.5	11.5	4.5	2.4	4.8	. . .	0.1	0.6	5.7	1.5	4.2
1956	68.3	45.1	12.3	12.3	4.4	2.5	5.2	. . .	0.2	1.2	7.6	1.7	5.9
1957	76.0	49.5	14.5	14.5	4.7	2.9	5.7	. . .	0.2	1.6	3.3	1.1	2.2
1958	81.4	50.9	18.2	18.2	5.2	3.3	5.4	. . .	0.1	1.8	-5.4	-2.7	-2.7
1959	83.6	50.0	18.6	18.6	7.6	3.8	6.3	. . .	0.3	1.1	3.3	-0.7	4.0
1960	86.7	49.8	20.1	19.9	7.4	4.0	8.4	8.0	0.3	1.1	7.2	0.4	6.8
1961	92.8	51.6	23.3	23.1	8.0	4.5	7.9	7.6	0.3	2.0	2.6	-2.3	5.0
1962	101.1	57.8	23.7	23.5	8.6	5.0	8.6	8.3	0.3	2.3	2.5	-0.6	3.1
1963	106.4	60.8	24.9	24.6	9.2	5.6	9.3	8.9	0.4	2.2	5.4	0.8	4.5
1964	110.8	62.8	25.4	25.2	9.8	6.5	10.0	9.6	0.5	2.7	1.0	1.3	-0.2
1965	117.6	65.7	27.6	27.3	10.7	7.2	10.6	10.1	0.5	3.0	3.3	0.5	2.9
1966	135.7	75.9	30.2	29.9	14.0	10.1	11.6	11.1	0.5	3.9	2.3	6.0	-3.7
1967	156.2	87.1	36.9	36.5	15.7	11.7	12.7	12.1	0.6	3.8	-9.4	4.1	-13.5
1968	173.5	95.4	42.2	41.9	17.1	12.7	14.6	13.9	0.7	4.1	-2.3	3.2	-5.5
1969	183.8	98.4	46.1	45.8	19.0	14.6	15.8	15.0	0.8	4.5	8.7	5.7	3.0
1970	201.1	98.6	56.1	55.6	23.9	19.3	17.7	16.7	1.0	4.8	-15.2	1.0	-16.2
1971	220.0	102.0	66.6	66.1	29.0	23.2	17.9	16.1	1.8	4.6	-28.4	-3.0	-25.3
1972	244.4	107.7	73.3	72.9	38.6	31.7	18.8	16.1	2.7	6.6	-24.4	-0.6	-23.8
1973	261.7	108.9	85.2	84.5	39.7	34.8	22.8	19.0	3.8	5.1	-11.3	5.8	-17.1
1974	293.3	118.0	103.9	103.3	41.8	36.3	26.0	21.7	4.3	3.2	-13.8	3.2	-17.0
1975	346.2	129.6	133.0	132.3	50.5	45.1	28.9	24.4	4.5	4.3	-69.0	-16.2	-52.9
1976	374.3	137.2	143.9	143.1	54.6	50.7	33.8	29.3	4.5	4.9	-51.7	-15.6	-36.1
1977	407.5	150.7	152.9	152.1	60.0	56.6	37.1	31.6	5.5	6.9	-44.1	-13.8	-30.2
1978	450.0	163.3	163.3	162.4	69.4	65.5	45.3	36.7	8.7	8.7	-26.5	-4.6	-21.9
1979	497.5	179.0	183.7	182.8	70.8	66.3	55.7	44.6	11.1	8.2	-11.3	0.2	-11.4
1980	585.7	207.5	220.7	219.6	78.4	72.3	69.7	57.0	12.7	9.4	-53.6	-15.5	-38.1
1981	672.7	238.3	251.4	250.1	78.2	72.5	93.9	76.6	17.3	11.1	-53.3	-13.8	-39.5
1982	748.5	263.3	282.4	281.2	76.4	69.5	111.8	92.5	19.3	14.5	-131.9	-33.8	-98.1
1983	815.4	286.5	304.3	303.0	78.7	71.6	124.6	105.6	19.0	20.8	-173.0	-37.3	-135.7
1984	877.1	310.0	310.5	309.2	86.0	76.7	150.3	129.1	21.2	20.6	-168.1	-8.7	-159.4
1985	948.2	338.4	326.6	325.4	92.7	80.9	169.4	146.3	23.1	20.9	-175.0	1.7	-176.7
1986	1 006.0	358.2	345.3	343.7	99.9	87.6	178.2	153.5	24.6	24.5	-190.8	6.4	-197.2
1987	1 041.6	374.3	358.2	356.7	94.7	83.9	184.6	158.4	26.2	29.9	-145.0	15.2	-160.2
1988	1 092.7	382.5	379.1	377.5	102.8	91.6	199.3	167.6	31.7	29.0	-134.5	39.7	-174.1
1989	1 167.5	399.2	412.2	410.6	109.8	98.3	219.3	181.0	38.4	26.8	-130.1	43.1	-173.2
1990	1 253.5	419.8	447.2	445.4	122.7	111.4	237.5	196.7	40.8	26.4	-172.0	43.0	-215.0
1991	1 315.0	439.5	494.2	492.0	103.5	131.6	250.9	210.1	40.9	26.9	-213.7	25.7	-239.4
1992	1 444.6	445.2	551.7	549.8	167.0	149.1	251.3	212.2	39.1	29.5	-297.4	6.5	-303.9
1993	1 496.0	441.9	582.4	580.5	182.3	163.7	253.4	214.0	39.4	36.0	-273.5	5.6	-279.1
1994	1 533.1	440.8	607.6	605.5	191.6	174.7	261.3	217.1	44.2	31.8	-212.3	17.9	-230.3
1995	1 603.5	440.5	642.7	640.8	196.3	184.1	290.4	236.6	53.8	33.7	-197.0	19.0	-216.0
1996	1 665.8	446.3	680.0	677.9	208.2	191.2	297.3	232.0	65.3	34.0	-141.8	13.9	-155.7
1997	1 708.9	457.7	706.3	704.2	212.5	198.6	300.0	221.3	78.6	32.4	-55.8	30.6	-86.4
1998	1 734.9	454.6	719.2	716.9	227.4	212.8	298.8	219.6	79.3	35.0	38.8	59.0	-20.2
1999	1 787.6	475.1	738.0	735.7	248.0	232.9	282.7	208.1	74.5	43.8	103.6	94.1	9.6
2000	1 864.4	499.3	772.5	770.0	265.6	247.3	283.3	200.3	83.0	43.8	189.5	112.3	77.1
2001	1 969.5	531.9	841.4	838.7	290.0	276.1	258.6	176.2	82.4	47.6	46.7	87.0	-40.3
2002	2 101.1	591.5	919.6	916.9	323.4	304.6	229.1	152.4	76.6	37.5	-247.9	48.9	-296.8
2003	2 252.1	662.7	966.5	963.7	362.2	338.5	212.9	139.0	73.9	47.8	-372.1	39.0	-411.1
2004	2 379.5	723.7	1 015.3	1 012.3	375.2	349.1	221.0	138.4	82.5	44.2	-370.6	56.8	-427.4
2005	2 558.6	766.3	1 081.6	1 078.5	396.5	360.9	255.4	151.5	103.9	58.9	-291.7	54.1	-345.7
2006	2 711.6	811.8	1 180.4	1 177.1	387.7	358.0	282.3	147.3	135.0	49.4	-201.1	22.9	-224.1
2007	2 880.5	856.1	1 254.2	1 250.6	412.5	376.3	312.6	147.5	165.1	45.2	-229.3	6.4	-235.7
2008	3 094.3	931.9	1 382.3	1 378.6	424.2	388.3	308.2	141.2	167.0	47.7	-521.5	-37.6	-483.8
2006													
1st quarter	2 661.5	805.9	1 156.0	1 152.7	379.4	354.2	266.4	144.5	121.9	53.8	-207.9	35.5	-243.4
2nd quarter	2 712.5	809.2	1 176.4	1 173.0	390.1	358.7	287.4	155.8	131.7	49.4	-225.0	19.6	-244.5
3rd quarter	2 750.4	816.2	1 188.1	1 184.8	396.5	363.0	301.9	163.3	138.5	47.8	-218.4	15.9	-234.3
4th quarter	2 721.8	816.0	1 201.3	1 197.9	384.7	356.2	273.3	125.6	147.8	46.5	-153.2	20.7	-173.9
2007													
1st quarter	2 837.9	832.5	1 232.0	1 228.5	418.2	372.9	309.6	153.3	156.2	45.6	-225.2	17.6	-242.8
2nd quarter	2 859.5	851.1	1 250.4	1 246.8	402.3	376.8	310.5	144.9	165.6	45.2	-211.4	2.9	-214.3
3rd quarter	2 909.2	869.1	1 264.1	1 260.5	407.3	375.9	323.9	156.3	167.6	44.8	-244.3	-1.4	-242.9
4th quarter	2 915.6	871.6	1 270.1	1 266.5	422.4	379.6	306.4	135.5	170.9	45.1	-236.3	6.4	-242.7
2008													
1st quarter	3 003.2	898.0	1 305.3	1 301.7	423.9	379.9	329.4	158.3	171.1	46.6	-330.7	-3.2	-327.5
2nd quarter	3 128.4	918.2	1 443.1	1 439.4	417.0	384.4	302.3	130.3	172.0	47.8	-649.6	-19.8	-629.8
3rd quarter	3 139.8	954.2	1 376.5	1 372.7	418.4	386.6	342.6	176.4	166.2	48.2	-544.0	-50.5	-493.5
4th quarter	3 105.9	957.5	1 404.2	1 400.4	437.3	402.3	258.5	99.9	158.7	48.3	-561.5	-77.0	-484.5

[1]Includes components not shown separately.
. . . = Not available.

Table 6-2. Federal Government Consumption Expenditures and Gross Investment

(National income and product accounts, calendar years, billions of dollars, quarterly data are at seasonally adjusted annual rates.)

NIPA Tables 3.9.5, 3.10.5

| Year and quarter | Total | Consumption expenditures | | | | | Gross investment | | | | | | |
| | | Total | Compensation of general government employees | Consumption of general government fixed capital | Intermediate goods and services purchased [1] | Less: Own-account investment and sales to other sectors | Total | National defense | | | Nondefense | | |
								Total	Structures	Equipment and software	Total	Structures	Equipment and software
1950	26.0	22.1	11.1	5.8	5.7	0.4	3.9	2.4	0.5	1.9	1.6	1.2	0.4
1951	45.1	34.4	16.6	6.1	12.6	0.9	10.7	9.1	2.0	7.1	1.5	1.1	0.4
1952	59.2	44.2	19.3	6.8	18.7	0.6	15.0	13.4	3.3	10.1	1.6	1.1	0.5
1953	64.4	48.3	19.1	7.6	22.3	0.6	16.1	14.7	3.3	11.4	1.4	1.1	0.3
1954	57.3	43.9	18.3	8.2	18.1	0.7	13.3	12.1	2.7	9.4	1.2	0.9	0.3
1955	54.9	43.9	19.0	8.6	17.7	1.3	10.9	10.1	2.1	8.0	0.9	0.6	0.2
1956	56.7	45.1	19.6	9.2	17.1	0.8	11.6	10.5	2.1	8.4	1.2	0.9	0.3
1957	61.3	49.5	20.2	9.7	20.8	1.3	11.9	10.5	2.3	8.2	1.4	1.1	0.2
1958	63.8	50.9	21.3	9.8	21.1	1.3	12.9	11.3	2.6	8.7	1.6	1.4	0.2
1959	65.4	50.0	21.7	10.1	19.3	1.2	15.4	13.7	2.5	11.2	1.7	1.5	0.2
1960	64.1	49.8	22.6	10.5	17.8	1.1	14.3	12.3	2.2	10.1	2.0	1.7	0.3
1961	67.9	51.6	23.7	10.7	18.2	1.0	16.3	13.9	2.4	11.5	2.4	1.9	0.6
1962	75.3	57.8	25.2	11.3	22.4	1.1	17.4	14.5	2.0	12.5	2.9	2.1	0.8
1963	76.9	60.8	26.5	11.9	23.5	1.2	16.1	12.6	1.6	11.0	3.5	2.3	1.2
1964	78.5	62.8	28.5	12.2	23.3	1.2	15.6	11.5	1.3	10.2	4.2	2.5	1.6
1965	80.4	65.7	30.0	12.5	24.6	1.3	14.7	10.0	1.1	8.9	4.7	2.8	1.9
1966	92.5	75.9	34.3	13.0	30.3	1.7	16.7	11.8	1.3	10.5	4.9	2.8	2.1
1967	104.8	87.1	37.9	13.8	36.8	1.3	17.7	13.5	1.2	12.3	4.2	2.2	1.9
1968	111.4	95.4	41.9	14.5	40.3	1.3	16.0	12.2	1.2	10.9	3.8	2.1	1.7
1969	113.4	98.4	44.9	15.2	39.8	1.4	15.0	11.3	1.5	9.9	3.6	1.9	1.7
1970	113.5	98.6	48.3	15.8	35.9	1.4	14.8	11.1	1.3	9.8	3.8	2.1	1.7
1971	113.7	102.0	51.7	16.1	35.7	1.5	11.7	7.5	1.8	5.7	4.2	2.5	1.7
1972	119.7	107.7	55.4	16.2	38.4	2.3	12.0	7.5	1.8	5.7	4.5	2.7	1.8
1973	122.5	108.9	57.4	16.5	37.7	2.8	13.6	8.7	2.1	6.6	4.9	3.1	1.8
1974	134.6	118.0	62.0	17.6	41.7	3.4	16.6	11.1	2.2	8.9	5.6	3.4	2.2
1975	149.1	129.6	68.4	19.0	45.2	3.0	19.5	13.0	2.3	10.7	6.5	4.1	2.4
1976	159.7	137.2	73.3	20.5	46.2	2.8	22.6	15.3	2.1	13.2	7.3	4.6	2.7
1977	175.4	150.7	79.9	22.1	52.4	3.8	24.7	16.7	2.4	14.4	8.0	5.0	3.0
1978	190.9	163.3	85.8	24.0	58.2	4.5	27.6	17.8	2.5	15.3	9.8	6.1	3.7
1979	210.6	179.0	91.8	25.8	66.9	5.6	31.6	21.4	2.5	18.9	10.2	6.3	4.0
1980	243.8	207.5	102.5	28.7	82.3	6.2	36.3	24.3	3.2	21.1	12.0	7.1	4.9
1981	280.2	238.3	115.1	32.3	97.0	6.2	41.9	28.9	3.2	25.7	13.0	7.7	5.3
1982	310.8	263.3	125.3	36.0	108.2	6.1	47.5	34.7	4.0	30.8	12.7	6.8	6.0
1983	342.9	286.5	132.3	39.0	121.3	6.1	56.4	41.9	4.8	37.1	14.5	6.7	7.8
1984	374.4	310.0	149.4	42.8	124.5	6.7	64.4	48.7	4.9	43.8	15.7	7.0	8.7
1985	412.8	338.4	159.0	46.1	140.2	6.9	74.4	57.5	6.2	51.3	16.9	7.3	9.6
1986	438.6	358.2	163.1	49.6	152.4	6.9	80.4	62.9	6.8	56.1	17.5	8.0	9.5
1987	460.1	374.3	170.3	53.1	158.7	7.9	85.8	66.4	7.7	58.8	19.4	9.0	10.4
1988	462.3	382.5	178.0	56.9	156.4	8.7	79.8	61.3	7.4	53.9	18.6	6.8	11.7
1989	482.2	399.2	185.7	60.9	162.1	9.4	83.0	62.7	6.4	56.3	20.3	6.9	13.4
1990	508.3	419.8	193.9	65.1	171.2	10.3	88.5	65.9	6.1	59.8	22.6	8.0	14.6
1991	527.7	439.5	205.9	69.1	175.9	11.3	88.2	63.4	4.6	58.8	24.8	9.2	15.7
1992	533.9	445.2	210.7	71.4	174.3	11.3	88.8	61.6	5.2	56.3	27.2	10.3	16.9
1993	525.2	441.9	211.9	74.4	166.6	11.0	83.3	55.2	5.1	50.1	28.1	11.2	16.9
1994	519.1	440.8	209.8	76.4	167.6	13.0	78.3	52.9	5.7	47.2	25.4	10.5	14.9
1995	519.2	440.5	206.8	77.9	166.4	10.6	78.8	51.4	6.3	45.1	27.3	10.8	16.5
1996	527.4	446.3	210.7	78.0	168.8	11.1	81.1	52.1	6.7	45.4	29.1	11.2	17.9
1997	530.9	457.7	212.9	78.0	175.9	9.1	73.2	44.9	5.7	39.2	28.3	9.8	18.5
1998	530.4	454.6	215.1	78.0	171.5	9.9	75.8	45.0	5.1	39.9	30.8	10.6	20.2
1999	555.8	475.1	221.3	79.6	182.7	8.5	80.7	47.7	5.0	42.8	33.0	10.6	22.4
2000	578.8	499.3	233.8	81.6	193.8	9.8	79.5	48.8	5.0	43.8	30.7	8.3	22.3
2001	612.9	531.9	242.9	82.8	215.3	9.1	81.0	50.2	4.6	45.6	30.8	8.3	22.5
2002	679.7	591.5	269.4	83.5	248.0	9.4	88.1	55.4	4.4	51.0	32.7	9.9	22.8
2003	756.4	662.7	298.9	85.1	288.7	9.9	93.7	60.4	5.3	55.2	33.3	10.1	23.1
2004	825.6	723.7	324.1	88.5	321.7	10.5	101.9	67.8	5.6	62.2	34.1	9.4	24.6
2005	875.5	766.3	345.0	93.2	341.5	13.5	109.2	72.9	6.0	66.9	36.3	8.3	28.0
2006	932.2	811.8	360.6	99.5	364.4	12.7	120.3	79.5	6.3	73.2	40.8	9.9	30.9
2007	979.3	856.1	378.8	105.5	384.7	12.9	123.2	82.1	7.5	74.6	41.1	10.9	30.3
2008	1 071.9	931.9	404.6	111.4	428.2	12.2	140.0	95.2	9.8	85.4	44.8	12.6	32.2
2006													
1st quarter	922.8	805.9	358.3	97.1	363.2	12.6	116.9	75.2	5.4	69.8	41.7	9.6	32.1
2nd quarter	928.5	809.2	359.9	98.9	364.1	13.7	119.3	79.6	5.3	74.3	39.8	9.5	30.3
3rd quarter	935.5	816.2	361.1	100.6	367.9	13.4	119.4	78.7	6.7	72.0	40.7	9.6	31.1
4th quarter	941.7	816.0	363.2	101.6	362.5	11.3	125.7	84.7	7.9	76.8	41.0	10.9	30.1
2007													
1st quarter	950.3	832.5	375.5	103.5	366.3	12.8	117.7	77.9	6.5	71.5	39.8	10.3	29.5
2nd quarter	974.6	851.1	378.1	104.7	381.1	12.7	123.5	82.1	6.6	75.4	41.4	10.6	30.8
3rd quarter	994.0	869.1	380.1	106.2	396.8	14.0	124.9	83.7	7.7	76.0	41.2	11.0	30.2
4th quarter	998.3	871.6	381.4	107.5	394.8	12.1	126.7	84.6	9.2	75.4	42.1	11.5	30.6
2008													
1st quarter	1 026.5	898.0	393.9	108.5	407.4	11.8	128.5	86.1	7.9	78.2	42.4	12.1	30.3
2nd quarter	1 056.1	918.2	400.7	110.4	419.1	12.0	138.0	94.3	8.9	85.4	43.7	12.0	31.7
3rd quarter	1 098.0	954.2	408.1	112.7	446.3	12.9	143.9	99.9	10.7	89.2	44.0	12.7	31.3
4th quarter	1 107.0	957.5	415.6	113.9	440.2	12.1	149.5	100.4	11.5	88.9	49.1	13.8	35.3

[1] Includes general government intermediate inputs for goods and services sold to other sectors and for own-account investment.

Table 6-3. Federal Government Defense and Nondefense Consumption Expenditures by Type

(National income and product accounts, calendar years, billions of dollars, quarterly data are at seasonally adjusted annual rates.)

NIPA Table 3.10.5

Year and quarter	Defense consumption expenditures [1]						Nondefense consumption expenditures [1]					
	Total	Compensation of general government employees	Consumption of general government fixed capital	Intermediate goods and services purchased [2]			Total	Compensation of general government employees	Consumption of general government fixed capital	Intermediate goods and services purchased [2]		
				Durable goods	Nondurable goods	Services				Durable goods	Nondurable goods	Services
1950	17.2	8.0	5.2	1.7	0.9	1.5	4.9	3.1	0.6	0.1	0.5	0.9
1951	30.1	13.5	5.4	4.4	2.3	5.0	4.3	3.1	0.6	0.1	0.1	0.7
1952	38.9	16.1	6.2	8.0	2.8	6.1	5.3	3.2	0.6	0.1	0.5	1.3
1953	41.2	16.0	6.9	9.1	4.2	5.1	7.1	3.1	0.6	0.1	2.4	1.3
1954	37.1	15.4	7.6	6.8	3.2	4.2	6.9	2.9	0.6	0.1	2.2	1.4
1955	36.9	15.8	8.0	6.0	1.7	5.9	7.1	3.2	0.6	0.1	2.5	1.6
1956	38.8	16.1	8.5	6.1	1.7	6.7	6.3	3.5	0.6	0.1	0.8	1.7
1957	43.2	16.5	9.0	6.7	2.2	9.3	6.3	3.7	0.6	0.1	0.8	1.8
1958	44.1	17.0	9.1	7.1	2.1	9.5	6.8	4.3	0.7	0.0	0.7	1.7
1959	40.1	17.3	9.5	5.1	1.8	6.9	9.8	4.4	0.7	0.0	3.3	2.1
1960	41.0	17.7	9.8	4.4	1.9	7.7	8.7	5.0	0.7	0.1	1.1	2.5
1961	42.7	18.3	10.0	3.6	2.3	8.8	9.0	5.4	0.7	0.1	0.4	3.0
1962	46.6	19.4	10.6	4.6	2.9	9.6	11.3	5.8	0.8	0.2	1.5	3.6
1963	48.3	20.1	11.1	4.7	2.7	10.2	12.4	6.4	0.9	0.3	1.2	4.5
1964	48.8	21.6	11.2	4.0	2.9	9.7	14.0	7.0	1.0	0.4	1.1	5.3
1965	50.6	22.6	11.3	4.2	3.2	9.9	15.1	7.4	1.2	0.5	1.1	5.7
1966	60.0	26.3	11.6	6.2	4.7	12.2	15.9	8.0	1.5	0.5	0.4	6.4
1967	70.0	29.3	12.1	6.2	7.3	15.5	17.1	8.6	1.7	0.4	1.2	6.2
1968	77.2	32.4	12.7	7.5	8.4	16.4	18.3	9.5	1.8	0.4	1.9	5.7
1969	78.2	34.7	13.2	6.5	7.6	16.5	20.2	10.1	2.0	0.3	3.0	5.9
1970	76.6	36.6	13.6	6.1	5.4	15.2	22.1	11.7	2.1	0.3	2.0	7.1
1971	77.1	38.2	13.8	4.6	4.4	16.3	24.9	13.4	2.3	0.3	2.1	8.1
1972	79.5	40.5	13.8	5.7	4.7	15.5	28.2	14.8	2.4	0.3	2.4	9.9
1973	79.4	41.4	14.0	5.5	4.3	15.3	29.4	16.0	2.5	0.2	1.9	10.4
1974	84.5	44.1	14.7	5.2	5.2	16.9	33.4	18.0	2.8	0.2	2.6	11.7
1975	90.9	47.9	15.7	6.0	5.1	17.4	38.7	20.5	3.2	0.2	2.8	13.7
1976	95.8	50.3	17.1	5.8	4.5	18.8	41.4	23.1	3.4	0.3	3.5	13.3
1977	104.2	53.6	18.4	8.0	4.5	20.4	46.5	26.3	3.7	0.3	4.4	14.7
1978	112.7	57.5	20.0	9.6	4.9	21.7	50.6	28.3	4.0	0.4	4.9	16.7
1979	123.8	61.7	21.3	11.3	6.2	24.2	55.1	30.1	4.5	0.5	5.2	19.4
1980	143.7	68.6	23.5	12.8	10.0	30.2	63.8	34.0	5.2	0.7	7.4	21.3
1981	167.3	78.8	26.3	16.2	11.8	35.8	71.0	36.3	6.0	0.6	11.2	21.4
1982	191.2	87.4	29.2	19.6	11.5	45.4	72.1	37.9	6.7	0.6	9.1	22.1
1983	208.8	92.4	31.7	25.1	11.3	49.5	77.7	39.9	7.3	0.9	10.6	23.9
1984	232.9	107.5	34.8	27.1	10.4	54.7	77.1	41.8	7.9	0.9	6.4	24.9
1985	253.7	115.3	37.5	29.3	10.0	63.4	84.7	43.6	8.7	1.0	9.5	27.1
1986	268.0	118.8	40.2	31.9	10.2	68.7	90.3	44.3	9.3	1.0	12.4	28.2
1987	283.6	123.5	43.0	33.8	10.3	75.1	90.6	46.8	10.1	1.1	6.9	31.6
1988	293.6	126.9	46.0	33.5	10.6	79.0	88.9	51.1	10.9	1.2	-0.1	32.2
1989	299.5	131.7	49.1	32.0	10.8	78.3	99.7	54.0	11.8	1.3	5.7	33.9
1990	308.1	134.5	52.4	31.6	11.0	81.8	111.7	59.3	12.7	1.5	5.7	39.6
1991	319.8	141.8	55.5	31.0	10.7	84.3	119.7	64.0	13.6	1.6	6.3	42.1
1992	315.3	143.0	57.3	28.4	9.4	81.3	129.8	67.7	14.2	1.7	6.9	46.7
1993	307.6	138.7	59.5	26.4	8.5	78.8	134.2	73.3	14.8	1.6	7.4	43.9
1994	300.7	134.7	61.0	22.9	7.6	80.5	140.1	75.1	15.3	1.6	7.0	48.1
1995	297.3	130.8	61.8	20.9	6.3	81.1	143.2	76.0	16.1	1.7	7.3	49.1
1996	302.5	133.3	61.2	20.8	7.6	83.6	143.8	77.3	16.7	1.8	7.2	47.8
1997	304.7	132.8	60.4	20.9	7.6	86.5	153.0	80.1	17.6	1.8	8.2	51.0
1998	300.7	131.6	59.6	21.0	7.0	84.7	153.9	83.5	18.4	1.7	8.2	49.0
1999	312.9	133.5	59.8	22.3	8.2	92.2	162.2	87.8	19.8	1.7	6.7	51.6
2000	321.5	138.9	60.2	22.3	10.4	92.7	177.8	94.8	21.4	1.8	8.5	58.1
2001	342.4	145.7	60.4	22.5	10.3	107.2	189.5	97.2	22.4	1.9	9.9	63.6
2002	381.7	163.1	60.5	23.4	11.5	127.4	209.9	106.3	22.9	2.2	11.3	72.2
2003	436.8	183.3	61.6	25.9	13.4	157.0	226.0	115.5	23.4	2.1	12.6	77.6
2004	482.9	200.4	64.4	28.9	17.1	176.7	240.8	123.6	24.1	2.4	14.3	82.3
2005	515.2	216.2	67.8	29.9	21.0	185.7	251.1	128.9	25.4	2.7	16.8	85.5
2006	544.6	226.5	72.3	33.1	22.0	196.4	267.2	134.1	27.3	3.0	17.5	92.3
2007	580.1	237.9	76.6	36.0	23.7	212.1	276.0	140.9	28.9	2.9	17.8	92.2
2008	639.7	254.8	81.2	41.8	28.3	238.7	292.2	149.7	30.2	3.1	20.1	96.3
2006												
1st quarter	538.3	225.2	70.5	31.3	21.1	195.8	267.6	133.1	26.5	3.1	18.0	94.0
2nd quarter	543.6	225.3	71.8	31.9	21.4	199.7	265.6	134.5	27.1	2.9	17.4	90.8
3rd quarter	545.3	226.4	73.1	33.7	24.9	193.2	270.8	134.7	27.5	3.1	17.7	95.3
4th quarter	551.2	228.9	73.6	35.7	20.7	196.9	264.9	134.2	28.0	3.0	17.0	89.2
2007												
1st quarter	559.0	235.0	75.1	33.2	22.0	200.3	273.6	140.5	28.4	2.9	17.0	91.0
2nd quarter	574.8	237.1	76.0	35.0	23.2	209.1	276.4	141.0	28.7	2.9	17.6	93.1
3rd quarter	591.9	239.1	77.2	37.6	25.7	219.4	277.2	141.0	29.0	3.0	18.0	93.2
4th quarter	594.7	240.3	78.1	38.0	23.9	219.7	276.9	141.1	29.4	3.0	18.6	91.6
2008												
1st quarter	613.8	247.4	79.0	39.1	25.7	227.6	284.2	146.4	29.6	3.0	19.5	92.5
2nd quarter	629.0	251.8	80.5	40.9	30.5	230.4	289.2	148.9	29.9	3.0	19.9	94.4
3rd quarter	659.6	257.8	82.3	43.1	32.8	248.7	294.5	150.3	30.4	3.1	20.8	97.8
4th quarter	656.6	262.4	83.0	44.3	24.1	247.9	300.9	153.2	30.8	3.2	20.3	100.4

[1]Excludes government sales to other sectors and government own-account investment (construction and software).
[2]Includes general government intermediate inputs for goods and services sold to other sectors and for own-account investment.

Table 6-4. National Defense Consumption Expenditures and Gross Investment: Selected Detail

(National income and product accounts, calendar years, billions of dollars, quarterly data are at seasonally adjusted annual rates.)

NIPA Table 3.11.5

Year and quarter	Compensation of general government employees		Intermediate goods and services purchased [1]							Gross investment			
			Durable goods	Nondurable goods		Services				Equipment and software			
	Military	Civilian	Aircraft	Petroleum products	Ammunition	Research and development	Installation support	Weapons support	Personnel support	Aircraft	Missiles	Ships	Electronics and software
1972	27.0	13.5	2.7	1.8	2.0	5.1	4.4	1.6	1.7	2.6	1.5	1.8	0.8
1973	27.6	13.8	2.4	1.7	1.7	5.3	4.3	1.6	1.5	2.3	1.5	1.6	0.9
1974	29.1	15.0	2.0	2.8	1.4	5.7	4.7	1.8	1.8	2.3	1.7	2.2	1.0
1975	31.1	16.8	2.1	2.9	1.1	5.9	4.9	1.7	2.1	3.6	1.3	2.2	1.2
1976	32.4	17.8	2.0	2.5	0.6	6.4	5.4	1.9	2.3	3.4	1.4	2.4	1.3
1977	34.0	19.7	3.3	2.4	0.8	6.8	6.2	2.1	2.2	3.7	1.2	3.1	1.5
1978	36.2	21.3	3.5	2.5	1.0	7.1	6.3	2.4	2.6	3.7	1.1	3.9	1.8
1979	38.7	22.9	4.8	3.6	1.2	7.7	7.3	2.9	2.7	4.8	1.8	4.3	2.1
1980	43.5	25.1	5.6	6.8	1.4	10.2	8.5	4.4	3.0	6.1	2.3	4.1	2.6
1981	50.5	28.3	7.8	7.7	1.6	12.4	9.3	5.2	4.0	7.5	2.8	5.1	3.2
1982	56.6	30.8	10.2	6.8	2.1	14.1	13.7	6.0	5.8	8.4	3.4	6.2	3.8
1983	59.8	32.7	13.6	6.4	2.5	14.5	15.5	7.3	6.4	10.1	4.6	7.1	4.6
1984	72.8	34.8	14.0	5.9	2.2	16.2	17.0	8.6	6.7	10.9	5.7	8.0	5.6
1985	78.2	37.2	15.4	5.8	1.3	21.7	17.2	9.8	8.4	13.4	6.6	9.0	7.0
1986	80.6	38.1	17.2	3.6	3.6	23.8	18.5	10.4	9.4	17.9	7.9	8.9	7.8
1987	83.7	39.8	18.2	3.9	2.8	27.0	19.1	11.0	10.9	17.6	8.7	8.8	8.7
1988	85.2	41.7	17.9	3.5	3.5	31.5	19.0	9.8	11.4	13.5	7.8	8.6	9.2
1989	87.4	44.3	16.4	4.2	3.1	28.6	19.0	10.3	12.4	12.2	8.8	10.0	9.6
1990	89.1	45.4	14.8	5.3	2.8	26.1	22.1	11.7	13.0	12.0	11.2	10.8	9.9
1991	93.8	48.0	13.6	4.7	2.7	21.9	23.8	10.2	12.7	9.2	10.8	10.2	9.7
1992	93.2	49.8	12.2	3.5	2.6	23.7	23.2	8.5	14.4	8.3	10.6	10.1	9.8
1993	88.0	50.7	10.7	3.2	2.5	22.9	25.4	7.5	13.7	9.3	7.9	8.7	9.9
1994	84.3	50.4	9.2	3.0	1.8	22.5	26.3	8.6	14.7	10.5	5.7	8.1	9.3
1995	81.3	49.5	8.9	2.8	1.2	21.7	25.8	9.1	16.1	9.0	4.7	8.0	8.8
1996	84.0	49.4	8.8	3.4	1.4	24.8	26.0	7.2	17.0	9.2	4.1	6.8	9.0
1997	83.8	49.0	9.4	2.9	1.7	26.3	25.3	8.4	18.5	5.8	2.9	6.1	9.0
1998	83.4	48.2	9.9	2.1	1.9	23.6	24.7	8.7	19.3	5.8	3.3	6.4	9.1
1999	85.2	48.3	10.5	2.6	1.9	26.6	25.0	9.3	22.4	7.0	2.8	6.8	9.8
2000	89.4	49.5	9.8	4.1	1.8	26.3	24.9	9.6	22.9	7.8	2.7	6.6	10.1
2001	95.4	50.3	9.8	4.2	2.1	30.6	27.3	12.0	27.5	8.5	3.3	7.2	9.8
2002	108.6	54.4	9.8	4.6	2.5	38.4	30.7	13.8	34.0	9.4	3.1	8.7	9.9
2003	125.7	57.7	11.2	5.3	2.6	47.1	35.9	16.6	41.2	9.2	3.3	9.5	10.6
2004	136.1	64.3	11.9	7.0	3.6	48.9	36.5	22.5	52.1	11.1	3.9	10.0	11.5
2005	147.4	68.7	10.7	10.1	4.0	52.3	35.8	25.1	56.6	13.5	3.9	9.8	12.8
2006	154.8	71.6	11.0	11.2	4.1	59.0	36.1	24.6	61.7	13.6	4.5	10.7	14.3
2007	162.7	75.2	11.3	12.2	4.1	58.8	37.3	28.1	68.1	12.8	4.3	10.5	16.6
2008	175.9	79.0	12.8	15.9	4.5	63.6	41.8	32.7	79.4	13.9	4.3	11.3	20.2
2002													
1st quarter	106.0	54.2	9.2	3.6	2.4	33.8	29.4	12.5	31.0	7.3	3.4	8.1	9.9
2nd quarter	107.5	54.6	9.9	4.5	2.6	36.5	29.6	12.3	32.3	9.4	3.1	8.5	10.0
3rd quarter	108.0	54.5	10.2	4.3	2.7	35.7	31.2	14.1	35.2	10.2	2.9	8.9	10.2
4th quarter	113.0	54.4	9.9	5.9	2.4	47.5	32.6	16.1	37.7	10.5	3.1	9.0	9.6
2003													
1st quarter	122.6	57.5	9.7	8.0	2.1	37.3	32.9	13.5	36.1	9.4	2.7	8.5	10.4
2nd quarter	126.7	56.8	11.8	5.7	2.7	54.1	36.0	17.8	41.6	9.1	2.8	10.1	10.3
3rd quarter	126.7	57.7	11.4	3.0	2.8	45.1	37.1	17.7	42.9	8.5	3.3	10.1	11.1
4th quarter	126.6	58.5	11.8	4.5	2.9	52.0	37.5	17.5	44.2	9.9	4.3	9.4	10.6
2004													
1st quarter	135.3	62.3	11.3	6.5	3.4	48.1	36.7	22.1	49.8	8.6	3.7	10.0	10.7
2nd quarter	135.5	63.8	11.7	6.8	3.6	50.3	35.8	21.0	50.7	10.0	3.5	9.1	12.0
3rd quarter	136.3	65.7	12.5	9.2	3.8	48.5	38.3	24.8	55.6	11.8	4.3	11.5	11.5
4th quarter	137.5	65.4	12.1	5.7	3.8	48.9	35.2	22.1	52.3	13.8	4.2	9.5	11.8
2005													
1st quarter	148.8	67.9	10.7	6.9	3.7	50.7	34.2	23.7	54.2	12.6	3.1	9.9	11.7
2nd quarter	147.1	68.3	10.7	10.4	4.0	52.1	35.2	24.8	54.7	13.5	4.4	9.5	12.5
3rd quarter	146.9	69.6	10.6	12.2	4.2	53.0	38.4	29.7	61.7	14.0	3.4	10.6	13.5
4th quarter	147.0	69.1	10.9	10.8	4.2	53.4	35.2	22.3	56.1	14.1	4.8	9.2	13.7
2006													
1st quarter	154.3	70.9	10.6	9.9	4.1	58.9	36.3	24.5	59.7	13.0	4.7	9.8	13.4
2nd quarter	153.9	71.5	10.3	11.2	3.7	59.1	37.7	27.3	65.1	15.2	4.7	11.3	13.4
3rd quarter	154.8	71.6	10.8	14.1	4.2	56.6	35.0	22.5	60.8	11.9	3.4	10.9	14.9
4th quarter	156.4	72.6	12.5	9.7	4.4	61.6	35.5	24.2	61.2	14.3	5.3	10.9	15.7
2007													
1st quarter	160.2	74.8	10.1	10.2	4.2	60.4	35.6	24.6	62.5	12.1	5.3	10.0	15.1
2nd quarter	161.9	75.2	10.9	12.0	3.7	59.3	36.9	27.7	66.4	14.1	4.2	10.4	16.4
3rd quarter	164.1	75.0	11.8	13.7	4.4	56.5	38.8	30.7	71.4	13.2	3.9	10.4	17.2
4th quarter	164.6	75.7	12.5	13.0	3.9	59.1	37.9	29.5	72.2	11.7	3.7	11.3	17.6
2008													
1st quarter	170.3	77.2	11.4	13.6	4.5	58.9	40.7	31.4	75.9	10.5	3.7	10.0	18.9
2nd quarter	173.2	78.6	12.5	18.6	4.1	62.2	40.5	30.6	76.6	15.1	4.5	11.2	20.0
3rd quarter	177.9	79.9	13.4	20.3	4.6	62.6	44.1	36.3	84.2	14.9	4.8	11.9	21.1
4th quarter	182.2	80.2	14.1	11.1	4.7	70.6	42.1	32.4	81.0	15.1	4.1	12.0	20.9

[1] Includes general government intermediate inputs for goods and services sold to other sectors and for own-account investment.

Table 6-5. Federal Government Output, Lending and Borrowing, and Net Investment

(National income and product accounts, calendar years, billions of dollars, quarterly data are at seasonally adjusted annual rates.)

NIPA Tables 3.2, 3.10.5

Year and quarter	Output						Net lending (net borrowing -)							Net investment
	Gross		Value added		Intermediate goods and services purchased [1]		Net saving, current (surplus +, deficit -)	Plus: capital transfer receipts	Minus			Plus: Consumption of fixed capital	Equals: Net lending (borrowing -)	
	Defense	Non-defense	Defense	Non-defense	Defense	Non-defense			Gross investment	Capital transfer payments	Net purchases of non-produced assets			
1950	17.3	5.3	13.2	3.7	4.1	1.6	5.5	0.6	3.9	0.4	. . .	5.8	. . .	-1.9
1951	30.6	4.6	18.9	3.7	11.7	0.9	9.6	0.7	10.7	0.4	. . .	6.1	. . .	4.6
1952	39.1	5.7	22.3	3.8	16.9	1.9	3.7	0.8	15.0	0.5	. . .	6.8	. . .	8.2
1953	41.5	7.5	23.0	3.7	18.5	3.8	1.8	0.9	16.1	0.6	. . .	7.6	. . .	8.5
1954	37.3	7.3	23.0	3.5	14.3	3.8	-1.6	0.9	13.3	0.6	. . .	8.3	. . .	5.0
1955	37.3	7.9	23.7	3.8	13.6	4.1	5.7	1.0	10.9	0.7	. . .	8.7	. . .	2.2
1956	39.1	6.7	24.7	4.1	14.5	2.6	7.6	1.3	11.6	0.8	. . .	9.3	. . .	2.3
1957	43.7	7.1	25.5	4.4	18.1	2.7	3.3	1.4	11.9	1.3	. . .	9.8	. . .	2.1
1958	44.7	7.4	26.1	5.0	18.6	2.4	-5.4	1.3	12.9	2.3	. . .	9.9	. . .	3.0
1959	40.5	10.6	26.7	5.1	13.8	5.5	3.3	1.4	15.4	3.1	. . .	10.2	. . .	5.2
1960	41.5	9.4	27.4	5.6	14.0	3.7	7.2	1.8	14.3	2.6	0.5	10.6	2.1	3.7
1961	43.1	9.6	28.3	6.1	14.7	3.5	2.6	2.0	16.3	2.9	0.5	10.9	-4.2	5.4
1962	47.0	11.9	30.0	6.6	17.0	5.3	2.5	2.1	17.4	3.1	0.6	11.5	-5.0	5.9
1963	48.7	13.2	31.1	7.3	17.6	5.9	5.4	2.2	16.1	3.6	0.5	12.1	-0.5	4.0
1964	49.3	14.8	32.7	8.0	16.5	6.8	1.0	2.6	15.6	4.1	0.6	12.3	-4.4	3.3
1965	51.2	15.9	33.9	8.6	17.3	7.3	3.3	2.8	14.7	4.0	0.5	12.7	-0.4	2.0
1966	60.9	16.7	37.9	9.5	23.0	7.2	2.3	3.0	16.7	4.4	0.6	13.2	-3.2	3.5
1967	70.4	18.0	41.4	10.2	29.0	7.8	-9.4	3.1	17.7	4.3	-0.2	14.0	-14.0	3.7
1968	77.4	19.3	45.1	11.3	32.3	8.0	-2.3	3.1	16.0	6.0	-0.9	14.8	-5.4	1.2
1969	78.4	21.3	47.9	12.1	30.5	9.2	8.7	3.6	15.0	5.9	0.1	15.5	6.8	-0.5
1970	76.8	23.2	50.3	13.8	26.6	9.3	-15.2	3.7	14.8	5.3	-0.3	16.1	-15.2	-1.3
1971	77.3	26.1	52.0	15.7	25.3	10.4	-28.4	4.6	11.7	5.9	-0.4	16.5	-24.5	-4.8
1972	80.2	29.8	54.3	17.2	25.8	12.6	-24.4	5.4	12.0	6.0	-0.7	16.6	-19.7	-4.6
1973	80.5	31.2	55.4	18.6	25.1	12.6	-11.3	5.1	13.6	6.0	-3.2	17.1	-5.5	-3.5
1974	86.1	35.2	58.8	20.8	27.3	14.4	-13.8	4.8	16.6	7.9	-5.7	18.2	-9.6	-1.6
1975	92.1	40.4	63.7	23.7	28.5	16.8	-69.0	4.9	19.5	9.7	-0.4	19.7	-73.1	-0.2
1976	96.4	43.6	67.3	26.5	29.1	17.1	-51.7	5.6	22.6	10.6	-2.4	21.4	-55.5	1.2
1977	105.0	49.5	72.1	30.0	32.9	19.5	-44.1	7.2	24.7	11.1	-1.4	23.1	-48.3	1.6
1978	113.6	54.3	77.5	32.3	36.2	22.0	-26.5	5.2	27.6	11.9	-0.6	25.0	-35.1	2.6
1979	124.8	59.7	83.0	34.7	41.8	25.1	-11.3	5.5	31.6	14.4	-2.8	27.0	-22.0	4.6
1980	145.0	68.6	92.1	39.2	52.9	29.4	-53.6	6.5	36.3	16.6	-4.0	30.1	-65.9	6.2
1981	168.9	75.5	105.1	42.3	63.8	33.2	-53.3	6.9	41.9	15.6	-5.5	33.8	-64.6	8.1
1982	193.1	76.4	116.7	44.6	76.4	31.8	-131.9	7.5	47.5	14.6	-3.6	37.6	-145.1	9.9
1983	210.1	82.5	124.2	47.1	85.9	35.4	-173.0	5.8	56.4	15.5	-4.9	40.8	-193.5	15.6
1984	234.6	82.0	142.4	49.8	92.2	32.2	-168.1	6.0	64.4	17.7	-3.9	44.6	-195.6	19.8
1985	255.5	89.8	152.8	52.3	102.7	37.5	-175.0	6.4	74.4	19.4	-1.1	48.1	-213.2	26.3
1986	269.8	95.3	159.0	53.7	110.8	41.6	-190.8	7.0	80.4	20.0	-3.0	51.6	-229.6	28.8
1987	285.8	96.4	166.6	56.8	119.2	39.6	-145.0	7.2	85.8	19.0	-0.4	55.2	-186.9	30.6
1988	296.0	95.3	172.9	62.0	123.1	33.3	-134.5	7.6	79.8	19.6	-0.1	59.3	-166.9	20.5
1989	302.0	106.7	180.8	65.8	121.1	40.9	-130.1	8.9	83.0	20.1	-0.7	63.5	-160.1	19.5
1990	311.4	118.7	186.9	72.0	124.5	46.7	-172.0	11.6	88.5	28.1	-0.7	67.9	-208.3	20.6
1991	323.2	127.7	197.3	77.7	125.9	50.0	-213.7	11.0	88.2	26.3	0.2	72.2	-245.3	16.0
1992	319.4	137.1	200.3	81.8	119.1	55.3	-297.4	11.3	88.8	22.4	0.2	74.7	-322.9	14.1
1993	311.9	141.0	198.2	88.1	113.7	52.9	-273.5	12.9	83.3	24.5	0.2	77.9	-290.7	5.4
1994	306.7	147.1	195.7	90.5	111.0	56.7	-212.3	15.1	78.3	25.9	0.2	80.2	-221.4	-1.9
1995	301.0	150.2	192.6	92.1	108.3	58.1	-197.0	14.9	78.8	27.7	-7.4	81.9	-199.2	-3.1
1996	306.6	150.9	194.6	94.1	112.0	56.8	-141.8	17.5	81.1	28.2	-3.8	82.0	-147.8	-0.9
1997	308.1	158.6	193.2	97.7	115.0	60.9	-55.8	20.6	73.2	29.1	-7.6	82.5	-47.4	-9.3
1998	303.9	160.7	191.3	101.8	112.6	58.9	38.8	25.2	75.8	28.8	-5.6	82.8	47.8	-7.0
1999	315.9	167.6	193.3	107.6	122.7	60.0	103.6	28.8	80.7	36.1	-0.9	84.8	101.3	-4.1
2000	324.6	184.6	199.2	116.2	125.4	68.4	189.5	28.1	79.5	36.2	-0.3	87.2	189.4	-7.7
2001	345.9	195.1	206.0	119.6	139.9	75.4	46.7	28.0	81.0	40.8	-0.7	88.2	41.8	-7.2
2002	386.0	214.9	223.6	129.3	162.4	85.6	-247.9	25.3	88.1	48.4	0.3	88.9	-270.6	-0.8
2003	441.3	231.3	244.9	139.0	196.4	92.3	-372.1	22.0	93.7	62.4	-0.2	90.4	-415.6	3.3
2004	487.5	246.7	264.8	147.8	222.7	99.0	-370.6	24.6	101.9	63.1	0.0	94.0	-416.9	7.9
2005	520.5	259.3	284.0	154.2	236.5	105.0	-291.7	25.0	109.2	67.2	-0.5	99.1	-343.5	10.1
2006	550.3	274.2	298.8	161.4	251.6	112.9	-201.1	27.8	120.3	70.2	-13.3	105.6	-244.9	14.7
2007	586.3	282.7	314.5	169.7	271.8	113.0	-229.3	26.5	123.2	82.4	-1.3	111.8	-295.4	11.4
2008	644.8	299.4	336.0	179.9	308.8	119.5	-521.5	28.2	140.0	157.8	-27.0	117.9	-646.2	22.1
2006														
1st quarter	543.9	274.7	295.7	159.6	248.2	115.1	-207.9	29.0	116.9	72.9	0.2	103.0	-266.0	13.9
2nd quarter	550.2	272.7	297.2	161.6	253.0	111.1	-225.0	27.8	119.3	69.5	-2.3	105.0	-278.7	14.3
3rd quarter	551.4	278.2	299.5	162.2	251.9	116.0	-218.4	27.1	119.4	71.3	0.8	106.7	-276.1	12.7
4th quarter	555.9	271.4	302.6	162.2	253.3	109.2	-153.2	27.4	125.7	67.3	-52.1	107.8	-158.8	17.9
2007														
1st quarter	565.6	279.7	310.1	168.9	255.5	110.9	-225.2	25.0	117.7	74.1	-1.3	109.8	-280.9	7.9
2nd quarter	580.4	283.4	313.1	169.7	267.3	113.7	-211.4	26.7	123.5	80.1	-4.3	111.0	-273.0	12.5
3rd quarter	598.9	284.1	316.3	169.9	282.6	114.2	-244.3	26.9	124.9	86.0	2.2	112.5	-318.0	12.4
4th quarter	600.0	283.7	318.4	170.5	281.6	113.2	-236.3	27.4	126.7	89.6	-1.7	113.9	-309.6	12.8
2008														
1st quarter	618.8	291.0	326.4	176.0	292.4	115.0	-330.7	29.2	128.5	86.4	-7.7	115.0	-393.8	13.5
2nd quarter	634.1	296.1	332.3	178.8	301.8	117.3	-649.6	29.8	138.0	87.5	-92.6	116.9	-635.8	21.1
3rd quarter	664.7	302.4	340.0	180.7	324.6	121.7	-544.0	27.8	143.9	93.2	-6.6	119.2	-627.4	24.7
4th quarter	661.7	307.9	345.4	184.0	316.3	123.9	-561.5	25.9	149.5	364.1	-0.9	120.5	-927.8	29.0

[1] Includes general government intermediate inputs for goods and services sold to other sectors and for own-account investment.
. . . = Not available.

Table 6-6. Chain-Type Quantity Indexes for Federal Government Defense and Nondefense Consumption Expenditures and Gross Investment

(Seasonally adjusted, 2000 = 100.)   NIPA Tables 3.9.3, 3.10.3

| Year and quarter | Defense consumption expenditures [1] | | | Intermediate goods and services purchased [2] | | | Defense gross investment | Nondefense consumption expenditures [1] | | | Intermediate goods and services purchased [2] | | | Non-defense gross investment |
	Total	Compensation of general government employees	Consumption of general government fixed capital	Durable goods	Non-durable goods	Services		Total	Compensation of general government employees	Consumption of general government fixed capital	Durable goods	Non-durable goods excluding CCC inventory change	Services	
1950	48.3	94.4	45.7	39.0	58.3	8.6	22.2	25.3	61.3	12.2	12.4	17.8	10.5	22.6
1951	82.1	163.5	44.7	93.4	153.0	24.7	78.8	21.1	56.3	12.4	12.3	31.3	7.7	20.3
1952	106.1	188.2	49.7	165.6	200.0	33.3	114.0	24.8	55.0	12.4	11.3	19.5	13.1	19.7
1953	110.8	184.3	55.5	185.4	321.2	26.8	127.7	32.3	50.4	12.4	10.4	19.5	13.1	17.3
1954	96.5	172.8	59.4	134.9	211.2	22.5	104.1	31.1	47.8	12.4	11.7	18.9	14.2	15.6
1955	90.2	164.0	60.6	114.4	97.0	29.4	84.1	30.5	48.4	12.3	9.7	21.8	14.7	11.1
1956	90.4	159.7	60.9	108.2	95.7	33.0	80.5	26.8	49.5	12.1	9.9	33.9	16.1	14.2
1957	96.5	157.5	61.2	113.3	115.7	44.3	76.3	25.9	50.9	12.0	9.1	46.9	15.8	15.9
1958	94.3	148.3	61.2	117.4	117.8	43.6	81.3	25.9	52.5	12.1	7.1	20.9	14.6	18.8
1959	87.2	144.3	62.5	83.9	98.5	39.2	97.0	37.5	52.6	12.0	5.4	57.5	19.1	18.9
1960	88.2	144.2	64.2	71.3	105.6	44.5	87.4	32.9	56.9	11.9	6.5	45.5	22.4	22.2
1961	90.4	147.1	65.4	58.5	130.3	48.7	96.9	32.5	58.3	12.1	11.7	53.1	26.5	26.9
1962	96.6	153.4	67.4	72.4	165.1	51.0	100.3	39.6	61.4	12.8	19.0	52.8	30.8	31.4
1963	97.6	150.7	69.1	73.0	153.6	54.8	86.6	43.2	65.0	14.1	26.4	58.8	38.7	36.9
1964	95.1	150.6	69.9	61.7	169.6	50.1	78.6	46.2	66.5	15.7	34.2	63.2	44.4	42.4
1965	95.4	150.8	69.8	63.9	183.2	49.7	68.6	48.3	67.7	18.0	43.7	63.5	45.8	48.4
1966	108.9	166.1	70.0	93.1	261.3	59.2	79.3	48.6	70.4	20.5	45.4	74.4	49.8	49.8
1967	123.1	180.7	71.3	91.9	401.9	70.4	89.5	50.8	73.9	22.5	39.8	80.4	45.9	40.4
1968	128.4	183.1	72.4	106.4	460.2	71.6	78.5	50.9	75.6	23.8	31.8	64.5	40.6	35.4
1969	123.3	183.3	72.1	88.8	408.4	67.7	69.5	53.5	76.3	24.7	27.7	81.1	39.6	32.1
1970	112.1	170.0	71.0	79.5	284.3	61.8	63.3	53.3	77.3	25.3	22.1	83.1	45.0	30.4
1971	103.4	157.1	68.0	57.2	232.4	61.8	40.3	55.8	79.9	25.5	21.2	79.1	49.1	31.9
1972	97.1	145.1	64.3	73.1	236.8	54.9	30.1	60.1	82.2	25.6	22.8	88.9	58.1	33.0
1973	90.0	137.6	61.3	67.6	176.0	51.4	33.9	59.4	82.4	25.9	18.0	76.8	58.3	34.0
1974	87.1	135.5	59.3	58.4	152.1	52.1	41.4	62.7	86.5	26.3	15.6	84.5	59.0	35.0
1975	85.0	133.6	58.5	60.7	126.0	48.9	46.0	64.8	88.0	26.8	16.7	63.9	62.1	36.3
1976	83.5	130.9	58.5	54.5	102.8	49.7	50.1	64.7	92.4	27.5	18.0	80.9	55.7	39.0
1977	84.4	129.8	58.8	69.0	96.0	50.4	51.2	67.4	94.5	28.3	20.7	92.5	59.0	41.0
1978	85.3	130.6	59.1	77.1	96.8	49.7	50.9	70.2	96.9	29.6	26.1	108.1	63.4	48.5
1979	86.4	129.5	59.7	83.3	99.7	51.5	58.1	71.4	96.8	31.2	31.5	108.2	67.9	47.3
1980	89.7	130.3	60.8	87.3	109.0	58.0	62.2	75.1	99.4	33.1	36.8	106.8	67.5	51.0
1981	94.8	134.3	62.3	101.8	115.3	63.8	68.6	76.3	96.5	35.2	32.7	177.1	61.4	50.8
1982	101.2	137.4	64.4	111.7	114.8	76.5	77.1	73.0	94.7	37.2	28.1	126.2	59.1	47.2
1983	106.6	139.5	67.5	132.0	120.2	81.0	90.5	75.7	96.0	39.8	42.8	132.1	62.0	53.6
1984	109.8	141.5	71.8	133.4	113.8	87.2	103.3	73.0	96.1	43.2	46.4	138.1	62.6	57.6
1985	116.4	144.1	77.5	143.2	111.8	99.1	124.4	77.1	96.3	46.6	47.4	121.1	65.5	61.5
1986	121.8	144.8	84.1	153.0	141.1	104.7	142.5	80.0	94.9	50.0	47.8	107.0	65.5	63.0
1987	126.3	146.1	90.6	162.5	138.2	111.1	155.6	78.8	96.6	53.2	53.5	121.9	72.2	69.1
1988	127.7	144.3	95.9	167.1	133.2	114.0	144.0	75.0	99.0	56.5	55.9	120.0	71.8	64.7
1989	126.8	144.3	100.1	160.4	129.0	110.3	144.9	81.4	99.6	59.8	61.5	106.5	72.8	69.0
1990	125.9	143.4	104.0	154.6	115.2	110.3	149.3	88.0	104.5	63.3	70.0	113.6	82.4	75.3
1991	125.8	142.9	107.0	147.6	117.3	110.0	140.7	89.1	104.2	66.9	72.1	96.8	84.8	81.5
1992	119.3	134.5	108.8	132.8	108.5	103.7	135.3	94.6	106.1	69.7	78.1	118.8	92.7	90.0
1993	114.2	128.7	109.2	120.8	99.5	98.4	118.3	93.4	106.0	72.2	76.0	118.5	85.6	92.1
1994	109.0	122.1	108.3	103.7	90.6	98.2	110.2	94.1	103.0	74.1	76.2	115.0	92.0	82.2
1995	105.2	115.4	106.7	94.2	74.3	96.6	104.3	92.6	98.9	76.3	78.4	112.7	92.0	87.1
1996	103.3	110.5	105.1	93.5	82.1	97.9	105.1	90.6	96.3	79.7	87.3	108.4	88.6	93.3
1997	102.1	106.5	103.5	93.9	82.7	99.2	92.4	93.7	95.7	83.6	92.4	116.8	92.3	92.0
1998	99.5	103.2	101.8	94.9	85.6	95.3	93.4	92.7	96.8	88.1	92.5	114.9	87.8	101.8
1999	101.0	100.7	100.8	100.8	95.3	102.2	97.6	94.5	97.0	94.3	92.3	91.8	91.0	108.9
2000	100.0	100.0	100.0	100.0	100.0	100.0	100.0	100.0	100.0	100.0	100.0	100.0	100.0	100.0
2001	103.9	100.7	99.8	100.9	104.7	112.2	104.1	104.5	99.9	103.9	112.5	118.6	107.3	100.3
2002	110.9	103.4	99.7	104.8	125.6	130.1	116.1	111.0	101.9	107.1	130.3	144.6	119.0	107.3
2003	120.5	107.1	100.5	115.3	129.1	154.9	126.3	115.0	104.4	109.2	129.6	158.6	125.3	109.4
2004	126.8	109.1	102.3	127.2	147.0	168.4	139.3	116.2	103.4	111.3	148.6	185.0	128.3	110.8
2005	128.0	109.4	104.9	129.3	146.6	170.8	146.9	116.3	103.2	114.6	169.9	196.8	127.8	115.7
2006	129.1	107.6	108.0	140.1	141.3	174.9	157.2	119.3	103.0	120.3	189.8	195.2	133.5	128.1
2007	132.5	107.2	111.3	151.9	145.3	183.4	159.8	119.0	103.6	125.9	191.4	191.7	129.4	128.4
2008	140.8	111.4	114.9	175.5	141.8	199.4	181.5	122.5	107.5	130.5	206.8	197.3	130.3	138.9
2006														
1st quarter	128.9	107.4	106.8	134.3	141.9	176.6	150.2	120.4	102.7	118.1	191.9	204.9	137.7	131.6
2nd quarter	128.8	106.9	107.6	135.0	133.4	178.2	157.6	118.5	102.9	119.6	183.5	192.6	131.8	124.9
3rd quarter	128.8	108.1	108.4	141.6	153.4	170.9	154.5	120.7	103.5	121.1	192.9	195.7	136.9	127.6
4th quarter	129.9	108.1	109.2	149.3	136.6	173.9	166.5	117.6	102.9	122.5	190.9	187.5	127.8	128.2
2007														
1st quarter	129.3	107.0	110.1	139.5	147.1	175.4	152.6	118.6	103.4	124.0	184.8	187.3	129.0	124.3
2nd quarter	131.4	106.5	111.0	147.9	145.3	181.5	160.3	118.9	103.1	125.4	190.1	192.7	130.7	129.3
3rd quarter	134.8	107.7	111.8	159.3	156.5	188.9	162.4	119.4	103.8	126.5	192.9	192.0	130.3	128.6
4th quarter	134.3	107.9	112.5	161.1	132.2	188.0	163.6	119.2	104.1	127.6	197.9	195.0	127.7	131.2
2008														
1st quarter	136.8	108.7	113.3	165.5	136.1	193.2	166.0	120.1	105.5	128.5	198.8	197.4	127.2	132.1
2nd quarter	137.9	109.9	114.2	172.0	139.4	193.1	180.2	121.2	106.9	129.6	201.3	200.5	128.1	135.8
3rd quarter	143.5	112.5	115.4	180.4	147.8	205.4	189.6	122.9	107.8	131.1	208.7	194.2	131.1	136.3
4th quarter	144.8	114.5	116.7	184.2	143.9	205.7	190.3	126.0	109.8	132.7	218.5	197.1	134.9	151.5

[1]Excludes government sales to other sectors and government own-account investment (construction and software).
[2]Includes general government intermediate inputs for goods and services sold to other sectors and for own-account investment.

Table 6-7. Chain-Type Quantity Indexes for National Defense Consumption Expenditures and Gross Investment: Selected Detail

(Seasonally adjusted, 2000 = 100.)

NIPA Table 3.11.3

Year and quarter	Consumption expenditures									Gross investment			
	Compensation of general government employees		Intermediate goods and services purchased [1]							Equipment and software			
			Durable goods	Nondurable goods		Services							
	Military	Civilian	Aircraft	Petroleum products	Ammunition	Research and development	Installation support	Weapons support	Personnel support	Aircraft	Missiles	Ships	Electronics and software
1972	147.9	139.5	82.6	414.8	336.9	45.7	60.6	61.7	43.1	50.4	51.5	99.5	7.6
1973	139.5	133.7	69.0	262.5	262.8	45.7	55.2	58.0	34.8	44.3	53.8	84.0	8.3
1974	134.5	137.2	53.6	238.6	179.7	45.4	55.5	62.1	39.5	44.4	59.6	103.6	8.3
1975	131.6	137.2	49.4	200.8	125.1	43.5	52.9	54.1	39.4	67.2	43.5	92.7	9.6
1976	128.4	135.5	41.4	166.4	62.8	45.1	54.3	57.0	38.8	62.9	37.0	95.0	10.1
1977	127.3	134.2	63.2	141.5	85.8	46.6	57.1	56.7	34.2	65.7	29.0	110.9	11.2
1978	126.1	139.0	64.6	140.8	99.2	46.0	53.3	61.7	35.8	62.0	23.9	124.8	13.8
1979	124.1	139.6	80.4	143.2	110.2	47.6	56.9	67.8	34.2	77.7	48.1	128.4	15.1
1980	125.4	139.4	87.3	158.5	110.5	58.7	60.5	91.3	33.7	93.0	69.4	112.9	18.5
1981	129.4	143.4	112.5	155.7	124.8	68.0	62.1	97.6	41.3	107.6	80.5	128.7	22.0
1982	131.7	148.0	131.6	146.5	153.8	73.2	85.0	106.0	56.7	108.2	103.9	150.0	25.4
1983	134.0	149.8	160.2	156.9	180.4	72.3	93.1	123.2	60.6	122.9	131.5	166.7	31.0
1984	135.6	152.3	151.4	156.5	152.7	78.1	99.1	140.5	62.0	132.1	158.1	176.6	39.0
1985	137.6	156.4	162.7	159.2	91.1	103.1	97.3	155.5	75.7	180.4	180.3	194.1	49.9
1986	138.9	155.6	179.9	159.1	245.1	110.7	100.1	162.9	80.3	275.1	228.6	187.4	57.0
1987	140.6	156.0	192.7	163.4	186.0	124.6	99.9	168.4	87.5	315.6	260.0	182.3	65.2
1988	139.6	152.6	199.5	137.6	214.7	146.7	95.6	146.9	81.8	259.3	236.7	172.7	68.9
1989	138.9	154.1	188.1	151.1	179.6	130.9	94.8	148.4	83.6	237.2	271.1	191.7	72.1
1990	139.2	150.5	165.3	149.8	162.0	117.1	104.5	162.7	81.3	218.8	352.0	202.3	74.8
1991	140.7	145.8	147.9	148.0	152.8	96.6	110.6	135.6	74.6	157.4	354.0	181.5	73.6
1992	128.7	145.0	129.0	123.8	145.1	101.8	106.5	108.3	80.3	137.7	350.1	175.4	77.7
1993	122.1	141.0	111.8	119.0	144.0	96.8	114.9	91.4	74.4	148.8	254.0	147.9	78.3
1994	116.2	132.9	94.9	122.5	99.2	93.6	116.1	102.3	76.8	148.6	186.9	133.1	74.8
1995	110.2	125.0	90.4	111.2	63.5	90.0	109.8	106.1	81.0	120.1	158.1	125.3	71.6
1996	106.1	118.6	89.7	112.3	74.3	102.4	109.0	81.6	83.0	117.3	140.9	105.8	77.0
1997	103.3	112.4	95.8	100.9	91.3	105.9	105.2	92.9	88.5	81.6	104.2	93.8	80.9
1998	100.9	107.2	101.7	99.2	103.4	93.3	101.6	94.7	89.9	82.1	117.7	99.1	86.5
1999	99.1	103.4	107.4	108.5	105.2	103.4	101.9	99.3	101.5	85.4	105.7	105.0	95.7
2000	100.0	100.0	100.0	100.0	100.0	100.0	100.0	100.0	100.0	100.0	100.0	100.0	100.0
2001	102.0	98.3	98.6	122.0	114.3	114.5	106.4	122.2	115.3	116.8	126.9	109.6	99.0
2002	105.8	99.0	99.0	157.5	140.9	141.1	117.2	136.9	137.9	134.2	119.2	131.0	103.5
2003	111.5	98.8	111.2	135.2	143.7	168.1	131.9	160.9	161.8	133.0	122.8	142.0	113.2
2004	112.8	102.1	116.7	142.8	188.6	168.1	127.5	212.2	199.6	163.8	144.7	136.5	125.5
2005	112.2	104.5	104.2	135.0	199.3	171.7	119.7	231.0	211.7	205.6	141.3	125.9	142.3
2006	109.5	104.4	104.2	131.5	189.7	186.5	116.7	221.4	224.2	208.8	161.8	126.5	160.0
2007	108.7	105.0	108.8	134.5	182.8	180.9	116.5	247.6	238.8	196.6	150.9	118.7	187.8
2008	113.5	107.8	123.9	124.5	187.9	188.5	125.9	281.3	272.8	206.7	148.2	118.0	234.1
2002													
1st quarter	105.3	97.6	93.0	148.9	133.8	125.2	114.3	125.5	126.9	105.8	129.1	124.2	102.0
2nd quarter	105.9	99.2	99.7	187.7	145.7	134.7	113.6	122.6	131.2	136.2	118.9	129.5	104.0
3rd quarter	106.2	100.0	103.0	127.1	148.9	131.0	118.0	140.4	142.2	145.5	110.8	134.5	107.2
4th quarter	105.8	99.4	100.3	166.4	135.1	173.4	122.8	159.3	151.4	149.5	117.8	135.9	100.8
2003													
1st quarter	109.6	99.1	97.0	184.8	116.4	134.7	122.4	132.0	143.1	135.7	103.8	127.3	110.2
2nd quarter	112.7	97.3	117.6	155.7	149.9	193.6	132.6	173.2	164.2	131.3	104.7	150.5	109.5
3rd quarter	112.3	98.8	112.9	81.6	153.5	160.2	136.4	171.2	167.8	122.2	122.4	150.5	118.8
4th quarter	111.6	100.0	117.2	118.7	155.1	184.0	136.4	167.3	172.1	143.0	160.4	139.7	114.5
2004													
1st quarter	113.4	100.1	111.5	172.2	180.1	167.7	130.6	210.3	192.1	126.2	138.0	142.4	116.6
2nd quarter	112.3	100.8	114.7	145.4	185.7	173.9	126.1	198.8	194.8	147.3	128.8	125.0	130.3
3rd quarter	112.2	103.9	122.7	166.4	194.6	165.4	132.9	232.8	212.4	177.3	158.4	153.5	125.8
4th quarter	113.3	103.5	117.9	87.0	193.9	165.4	120.3	207.0	198.9	204.4	153.6	125.2	129.2
2005													
1st quarter	113.3	103.5	104.1	113.4	185.6	168.6	115.0	220.2	203.7	186.8	113.7	127.1	128.5
2nd quarter	112.0	104.4	103.7	149.6	195.6	171.7	118.7	228.2	204.9	204.9	158.7	123.0	137.9
3rd quarter	111.5	105.2	102.8	148.6	208.7	173.3	128.5	271.9	230.0	214.9	121.3	137.7	149.9
4th quarter	111.8	104.7	106.2	128.4	207.1	173.2	116.7	203.8	208.3	216.1	171.7	115.7	152.8
2006													
1st quarter	109.4	103.8	101.6	126.1	198.8	188.6	118.4	221.8	219.5	200.3	168.3	119.9	149.8
2nd quarter	108.8	103.8	97.0	123.6	173.7	187.0	122.3	245.9	237.7	232.9	169.6	134.7	149.1
3rd quarter	110.1	104.5	101.4	154.1	189.1	177.8	112.5	202.0	219.6	179.9	120.8	125.6	165.9
4th quarter	109.7	105.6	116.9	122.3	197.4	192.6	113.6	215.9	219.9	222.0	188.4	125.9	175.2
2007													
1st quarter	108.4	104.6	95.7	132.2	191.6	187.8	113.0	217.9	221.5	189.0	187.2	115.1	169.2
2nd quarter	107.8	104.4	104.6	136.7	168.3	182.9	115.8	245.2	233.3	220.4	149.5	116.6	184.3
3rd quarter	109.3	104.9	113.9	149.7	199.3	173.2	120.3	269.4	249.5	201.5	138.0	116.4	196.0
4th quarter	109.1	106.1	121.1	119.4	172.1	179.8	117.0	258.0	250.7	175.4	128.9	126.8	201.8
2008													
1st quarter	110.6	105.6	110.7	116.7	196.1	177.1	124.6	273.0	263.2	156.4	127.7	109.2	217.9
2nd quarter	111.4	107.3	121.4	124.3	171.6	185.5	122.0	264.2	264.2	224.8	156.9	117.0	231.9
3rd quarter	114.6	108.9	128.7	133.8	188.5	184.0	131.6	311.1	287.8	222.0	166.6	120.2	243.6
4th quarter	117.3	109.2	135.0	123.3	195.3	207.4	125.5	277.0	276.1	223.4	141.4	125.7	243.1

[1]Includes general government intermediate inputs for goods and services sold to other sectors and for own-account investment.

Section 6b: State and Local Government in the National Income and Product Accounts

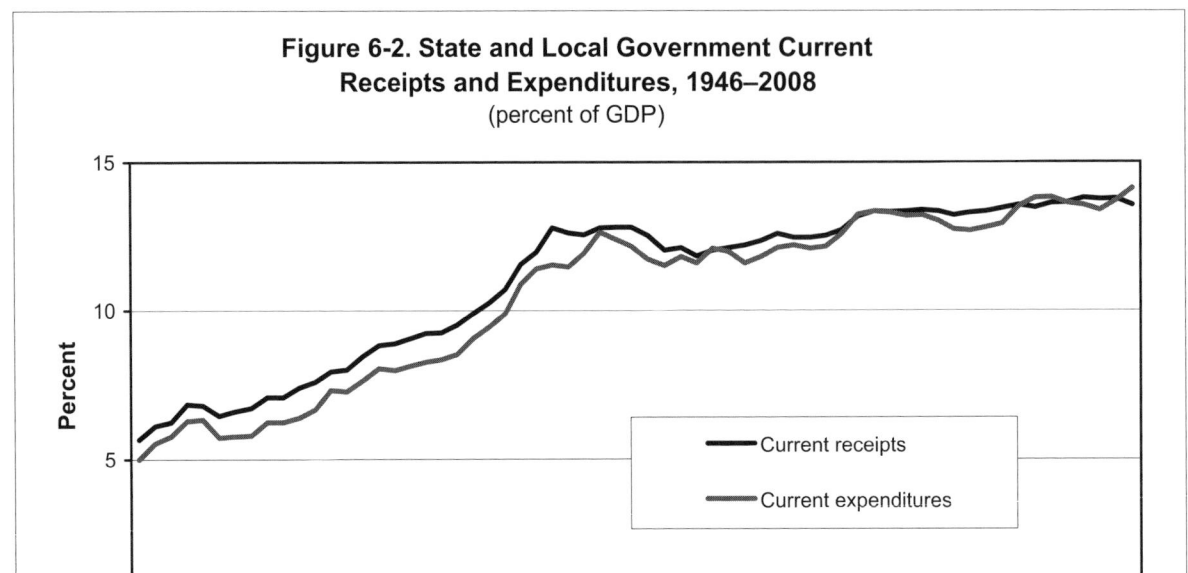

Figure 6-2. State and Local Government Current Receipts and Expenditures, 1946–2008
(percent of GDP)

- Current receipts of state and local governments began to decline in the third quarter of 2008, and their usual small surpluses turned to deficits beginning with the fourth quarter of 2007. (Table 6-8)

- Both current receipts and current spending of state and local governments have increased as a share of gross domestic product (GDP) over the postwar period. State and local governments, unlike the federal government, are bound by constraints on deficit spending, and have generally run modest surpluses ("net saving") in their current accounts. These governments were, however, collectively in current account deficit in 2002 and 2003. Surpluses returned in the following four years, but the deficit in 2008 was larger than the combined deficits of the early 2000s. (Tables 6-8, 1-1, 19-11 and 19-1)

- Despite the net saving usually registered in their current receipts and expenditures accounts, state and local governments on balance have not been suppliers of funds to the capital markets. Though they are constrained against deficits in their annual budgets, these governments can and do borrow—for investment, or just to cover shortfalls in current accounts—by issuing bonds. (Usually, the permission of voters in the state or local jurisdiction is required.) They have usually been net borrowers from the rest of the economy, even before the deficits of the 2000s. This has allowed their net investment usually to exceed the sum of their current surpluses, estimated capital depreciation allowances, and capital transfers (which are mainly federal highway grants). (Table 6-10)

- State and local gross investment rose at an annual rate of 3.2 percent in real terms from 1953 to 2008, compared with 3.9 percent for federal nondefense investment. (Tables 6-6 and 6-11)

Table 6-8. State and Local Government Current Receipts and Expenditures

(National income and product accounts, calendar years, billions of dollars, quarterly data are at seasonally adjusted annual rates.)

NIPA Table 3.3

Year and quarter	Total	Current receipts												
		Current tax receipts							Taxes on corporate income	Contributions for government social insurance	Income receipts on assets		
		Total	Personal current taxes		Taxes on production and imports						Total¹	Interest receipts	Rents and royalties
			Total¹	Income taxes	Total	Sales taxes	Property taxes	Other					
1950	20.0	16.5	1.5	0.8	14.2	4.8	7.1	2.3	0.8	0.2	0.5	0.3	0.2
1951	21.9	18.1	1.7	0.9	15.6	5.4	7.7	2.5	0.9	0.2	0.6	0.4	0.2
1952	23.7	19.7	1.8	1.0	17.0	5.8	8.4	2.8	0.8	0.3	0.7	0.4	0.2
1953	25.5	21.1	1.9	1.0	18.4	6.3	9.1	3.0	0.8	0.3	0.7	0.5	0.3
1954	26.9	22.2	2.1	1.1	19.4	6.5	9.7	3.2	0.8	0.3	0.8	0.5	0.3
1955	29.4	24.4	2.4	1.3	21.0	7.1	10.4	3.5	1.0	0.3	0.9	0.6	0.3
1956	32.4	27.0	2.7	1.6	23.3	8.0	11.5	3.8	1.0	0.4	1.0	0.7	0.3
1957	35.0	29.0	2.9	1.7	25.1	8.6	12.6	3.9	1.0	0.4	1.1	0.7	0.3
1958	37.1	30.6	3.1	1.8	26.5	10.0	13.8	2.8	1.0	0.4	1.1	0.8	0.4
1959	40.6	33.8	3.8	2.2	28.8	11.1	14.8	2.9	1.2	0.4	1.1	0.9	0.3
1960	44.5	37.0	4.2	2.5	31.5	12.2	16.2	3.1	1.2	0.5	1.3	1.0	0.3
1961	48.1	39.7	4.6	2.8	33.8	13.0	17.6	3.2	1.3	0.5	1.4	1.1	0.4
1962	52.0	42.8	5.0	3.2	36.3	14.0	19.0	3.3	1.5	0.5	1.5	1.1	0.4
1963	56.0	45.8	5.4	3.4	38.7	15.0	20.2	3.5	1.7	0.6	1.6	1.2	0.4
1964	61.3	49.8	6.1	4.0	41.8	16.5	21.7	3.7	1.8	0.7	1.9	1.5	0.4
1965	66.5	53.9	6.6	4.4	45.3	18.2	23.2	3.9	2.0	0.8	2.2	1.8	0.4
1966	74.9	58.8	7.8	5.4	48.8	20.0	24.5	4.3	2.2	0.8	2.6	2.1	0.5
1967	82.5	64.0	8.6	6.1	52.8	21.4	27.0	4.4	2.6	0.9	3.0	2.4	0.6
1968	93.5	73.4	10.6	7.8	59.5	25.1	29.9	4.6	3.3	0.9	3.5	2.8	0.7
1969	105.5	82.5	12.8	9.8	66.0	28.6	32.8	4.7	3.6	1.0	4.3	3.6	0.8
1970	120.1	91.3	14.2	10.9	73.3	31.6	36.7	5.0	3.7	1.1	5.2	4.3	0.8
1971	134.9	101.7	15.9	12.4	81.5	35.4	40.4	5.7	4.3	1.2	5.5	4.6	0.9
1972	158.4	115.6	20.9	17.2	89.4	39.8	43.2	6.4	5.3	1.3	5.9	4.9	1.0
1973	174.3	126.3	22.8	18.9	97.4	44.1	46.4	7.0	6.0	1.5	7.8	6.6	1.1
1974	188.1	136.0	24.5	20.4	104.8	48.2	49.0	7.7	6.7	1.7	10.2	8.9	1.3
1975	209.6	147.4	26.9	22.5	113.2	51.7	53.4	8.1	7.3	1.8	11.2	9.8	1.3
1976	233.7	165.7	31.1	26.3	125.0	57.8	58.2	9.0	9.6	2.2	10.4	9.0	1.3
1977	259.9	183.7	35.4	30.4	136.9	64.0	63.2	9.7	11.4	2.8	11.7	10.4	1.3
1978	287.6	198.2	40.5	35.0	145.6	71.0	63.7	10.9	12.1	3.4	14.7	13.3	1.3
1979	308.4	212.0	44.0	38.2	154.4	77.3	64.4	12.7	13.6	3.9	20.1	18.1	1.9
1980	338.2	230.0	48.9	42.6	166.7	82.9	68.8	15.0	14.5	3.6	26.3	23.1	3.1
1981	370.2	255.8	54.6	47.9	185.7	90.7	77.1	17.9	15.4	3.9	32.0	28.5	3.3
1982	391.4	273.2	59.1	51.9	200.0	96.2	85.3	18.5	14.0	4.0	36.7	33.1	3.5
1983	428.6	300.9	66.1	58.3	218.9	107.7	91.9	19.4	15.9	4.1	41.4	37.0	4.3
1984	480.2	337.3	76.0	67.5	242.5	121.0	99.7	21.8	18.8	4.7	47.7	42.6	4.9
1985	521.1	363.7	81.4	72.1	262.1	131.1	107.5	23.5	20.2	4.9	54.9	49.4	5.4
1986	561.6	389.5	87.2	77.4	279.7	139.9	116.2	23.7	22.7	6.0	58.4	52.0	6.2
1987	590.6	422.1	96.6	86.0	301.6	150.3	126.4	24.9	23.9	7.2	58.1	52.6	5.3
1988	635.5	452.8	102.1	90.6	324.6	162.4	136.5	25.7	26.0	8.4	60.5	55.9	4.4
1989	687.3	488.0	114.6	102.3	349.1	172.3	149.9	26.9	24.2	9.0	65.7	61.4	4.1
1990	737.8	519.1	122.6	109.6	374.1	184.3	161.5	28.3	22.5	10.0	68.4	64.1	4.2
1991	789.2	544.3	125.3	111.7	395.3	190.7	176.1	28.6	23.6	11.6	68.0	63.1	4.5
1992	845.7	579.8	135.3	120.4	420.1	204.3	184.7	31.1	24.4	13.1	64.8	59.6	4.8
1993	886.9	604.7	141.1	126.2	436.8	216.4	187.3	33.1	26.9	14.1	61.4	56.2	4.5
1994	942.9	644.2	148.0	132.2	466.3	231.4	199.4	35.5	30.0	14.5	63.2	57.9	4.5
1995	990.2	672.1	158.1	141.7	482.4	242.7	202.6	37.0	31.7	13.6	68.4	62.9	4.5
1996	1 043.3	709.6	168.7	152.3	507.9	256.2	212.4	39.4	33.0	12.5	73.3	67.3	4.6
1997	1 097.4	749.9	182.0	164.7	533.8	268.7	223.5	41.6	34.1	10.8	77.8	71.5	4.8
1998	1 163.2	794.9	201.2	183.0	558.8	283.9	231.0	43.9	34.9	10.4	80.9	74.6	4.6
1999	1 236.7	840.4	214.5	195.5	590.2	301.6	242.8	45.8	35.8	9.8	85.3	78.4	5.1
2000	1 319.5	893.2	236.6	217.3	621.1	316.6	254.6	49.9	35.5	11.0	92.2	84.0	6.3
2001	1 373.0	915.8	242.7	223.1	642.8	321.1	269.3	52.4	30.2	13.6	88.8	80.3	6.5
2002	1 410.1	929.0	221.3	200.8	675.5	330.2	290.1	55.2	32.2	15.8	78.2	69.6	6.6
2003	1 494.2	979.4	226.6	204.5	717.5	347.7	307.9	61.9	35.3	19.8	72.9	62.9	7.9
2004	1 594.3	1 061.2	249.0	225.0	769.2	370.0	327.5	71.7	43.0	23.6	75.4	64.3	8.7
2005	1 714.4	1 162.3	277.1	252.1	829.0	399.1	347.5	82.4	56.3	24.2	85.9	73.4	10.0
2006	1 811.4	1 242.2	303.3	277.0	878.2	421.5	369.6	87.1	60.7	23.1	94.7	80.6	11.4
2007	1 902.8	1 304.1	325.4	298.3	917.8	436.5	390.9	90.3	60.9	22.8	100.3	84.6	12.8
2008	1 935.1	1 318.6	333.4	305.9	937.6	436.3	404.6	96.7	47.6	23.7	103.7	87.7	13.1
2006													
1st quarter	1 781.7	1 221.2	297.2	271.2	864.9	416.5	361.2	87.2	59.2	23.5	92.2	78.7	10.8
2nd quarter	1 815.3	1 246.6	309.5	283.2	875.5	420.5	366.8	88.2	61.7	23.2	94.0	80.1	11.1
3rd quarter	1 820.4	1 244.8	300.2	273.8	881.5	423.0	372.4	86.1	63.1	22.9	95.5	81.3	11.5
4th quarter	1 828.4	1 256.2	306.4	279.8	890.9	426.1	377.9	86.9	59.0	22.8	96.9	82.2	12.0
2007													
1st quarter	1 877.5	1 285.9	320.0	293.2	905.0	432.2	383.3	89.5	60.8	22.7	98.5	83.2	12.5
2nd quarter	1 909.8	1 311.5	332.3	305.4	915.4	435.7	388.6	91.2	63.7	22.7	99.8	84.3	12.8
3rd quarter	1 905.5	1 305.3	323.5	296.3	921.0	438.4	393.6	89.1	60.9	22.8	101.1	85.2	13.0
4th quarter	1 918.4	1 313.7	325.8	298.4	929.7	439.8	398.3	91.5	58.2	22.9	101.8	85.9	13.0
2008													
1st quarter	1 922.9	1 317.0	333.7	306.7	929.9	438.5	401.5	89.9	53.3	23.3	102.9	87.0	12.8
2nd quarter	1 955.4	1 343.3	346.4	319.0	942.4	436.9	403.8	101.7	54.5	23.6	103.9	88.2	12.9
3rd quarter	1 944.9	1 330.2	329.0	301.3	949.4	440.2	405.9	103.4	51.9	23.9	103.2	87.3	13.1
4th quarter	1 917.3	1 283.7	324.3	296.7	928.7	429.8	407.0	91.9	30.7	24.2	105.0	88.2	13.6

¹Includes components not shown separately.

Table 6-8. State and Local Government Current Receipts and Expenditures—*Continued*

(National income and product accounts, calendar years, billions of dollars, quarterly data are at seasonally adjusted annual rates.)

NIPA Table 3.3

Year and quarter	Current receipts—Continued					Current expenditures					Net state and local government saving, NIPA (surplus + / deficit -)		
	Current transfer receipts				Current surplus of government enterprises	Total [1]	Consumption expenditures	Government social benefits to persons	Interest payments	Subsidies	Total	Social insurance funds	Other
	Total	Federal grants-in-aid	From business, net	From persons									
1950	2.3	1.9	0.1	0.3	0.4	18.6	14.9	3.2	0.6	...	1.3	0.1	1.2
1951	2.5	2.0	0.1	0.3	0.5	19.4	16.1	2.6	0.6	...	2.6	0.1	2.5
1952	2.6	2.2	0.1	0.3	0.5	20.7	17.1	2.9	0.7	...	3.0	0.1	2.9
1953	2.8	2.3	0.1	0.3	0.6	22.0	18.2	3.0	0.8	...	3.5	0.1	3.4
1954	2.9	2.3	0.2	0.4	0.7	23.7	19.7	3.1	0.9	...	3.2	0.1	3.1
1955	3.0	2.4	0.2	0.4	0.8	25.9	21.6	3.3	1.1	...	3.5	0.1	3.4
1956	3.2	2.5	0.2	0.4	0.9	28.0	23.4	3.3	1.2	...	4.4	0.1	4.3
1957	3.6	2.9	0.2	0.5	0.9	30.8	25.8	3.6	1.4	...	4.2	0.1	4.1
1958	4.1	3.3	0.2	0.5	0.9	34.2	28.6	4.0	1.5	...	2.9	0.0	2.8
1959	4.2	3.8	0.1	0.3	1.1	36.9	30.7	4.3	1.8	0.0	3.8	0.0	3.8
1960	4.5	4.0	0.2	0.3	1.2	40.2	33.5	4.6	2.1	0.0	4.3	0.0	4.3
1961	5.2	4.5	0.2	0.4	1.3	43.8	36.6	5.0	2.2	0.0	4.3	0.0	4.3
1962	5.8	5.0	0.2	0.5	1.4	46.8	39.0	5.3	2.4	0.0	5.2	0.0	5.2
1963	6.4	5.6	0.3	0.5	1.6	50.3	41.9	5.7	2.7	0.0	5.7	0.0	5.7
1964	7.3	6.5	0.3	0.5	1.6	54.9	45.8	6.2	2.9	0.0	6.4	0.0	6.3
1965	8.0	7.2	0.3	0.5	1.7	60.0	50.2	6.7	3.1	0.0	6.5	0.1	6.4
1966	11.1	10.1	0.3	0.7	1.6	67.2	56.1	7.6	3.4	0.0	7.8	0.1	7.6
1967	13.1	11.7	0.5	0.9	1.5	75.5	62.6	9.2	3.7	0.0	7.0	0.1	6.9
1968	14.2	12.7	0.5	1.0	1.5	86.0	70.4	11.4	4.2	0.0	7.5	0.1	7.3
1969	16.2	14.6	0.5	1.1	1.5	97.5	79.9	13.2	4.4	0.0	8.0	0.2	7.8
1970	21.1	19.3	0.6	1.2	1.5	113.0	91.5	16.1	5.3	0.0	7.1	0.2	6.9
1971	25.2	23.2	0.6	1.4	1.4	128.5	102.7	19.3	6.5	0.0	6.5	0.2	6.2
1972	34.0	31.7	0.7	1.7	1.6	142.8	113.2	22.0	7.5	0.1	15.6	0.3	15.4
1973	37.3	34.8	0.9	1.7	1.5	158.6	126.0	24.1	8.5	0.1	15.7	0.3	15.4
1974	39.3	36.3	1.1	2.0	0.9	178.7	143.7	25.3	9.6	0.1	9.3	0.4	9.0
1975	48.7	45.1	1.2	2.4	0.4	207.1	165.1	30.8	11.1	0.2	2.5	0.5	2.0
1976	55.0	50.7	1.4	2.9	0.4	226.3	179.5	34.1	12.5	0.2	7.4	0.6	6.8
1977	61.4	56.6	1.6	3.3	0.3	246.8	195.9	37.0	13.7	0.2	13.1	1.0	12.2
1978	71.1	65.5	1.9	3.7	0.3	268.9	213.2	40.8	14.9	0.2	18.7	1.5	17.2
1979	72.7	66.3	2.2	4.1	-0.3	295.4	233.3	44.3	17.2	0.3	13.0	1.8	11.2
1980	79.5	72.3	2.5	4.7	-1.2	329.4	258.4	51.2	19.4	0.4	8.8	1.3	7.5
1981	81.0	72.5	2.9	5.7	-2.4	362.7	282.3	57.1	22.8	0.4	7.6	1.3	6.3
1982	79.1	69.5	3.2	6.4	-1.6	393.6	304.9	61.2	27.1	0.5	-2.2	1.2	-3.4
1983	82.4	71.6	3.6	7.2	-0.2	423.7	324.1	66.9	32.3	0.4	4.9	1.2	3.7
1984	89.0	76.7	4.2	8.1	1.5	456.2	347.7	71.2	37.0	0.4	23.9	1.4	22.5
1985	94.5	80.9	4.4	9.2	3.2	498.7	381.8	77.3	39.4	0.3	22.3	1.3	21.0
1986	105.0	87.6	6.7	10.6	2.8	540.7	417.9	84.3	38.2	0.3	21.0	1.9	19.1
1987	100.0	83.9	4.9	11.2	3.1	578.1	440.9	90.7	46.2	0.3	12.4	2.2	10.2
1988	109.0	91.6	5.4	12.0	4.8	617.6	470.4	98.5	48.4	0.4	17.9	2.5	15.4
1989	118.1	98.3	6.4	13.4	6.5	666.5	502.1	109.3	54.6	0.4	20.8	2.3	18.5
1990	133.5	111.4	7.1	14.9	6.7	730.5	544.6	127.7	57.9	0.4	7.2	2.0	5.3
1991	158.2	131.6	7.9	18.7	7.1	793.3	574.6	156.5	61.7	0.4	-4.2	2.4	-6.5
1992	180.3	149.1	9.2	21.9	7.7	845.0	602.7	180.0	61.9	0.4	0.7	3.1	-2.4
1993	197.7	163.7	10.5	23.5	9.0	886.0	630.3	195.2	60.2	0.4	0.9	4.2	-3.3
1994	211.9	174.7	12.0	25.2	9.0	932.4	663.3	206.7	62.0	0.3	10.5	4.6	5.8
1995	224.1	184.1	13.5	26.5	12.0	978.2	696.1	217.6	64.2	0.3	12.0	4.0	8.0
1996	234.1	191.2	15.2	27.8	13.9	1 017.5	724.8	224.3	68.1	0.3	25.8	2.8	23.0
1997	246.6	198.6	17.7	30.3	12.3	1 058.3	758.9	227.6	71.4	0.4	39.1	1.2	38.0
1998	266.8	212.8	22.1	31.9	10.2	1 111.2	801.4	235.8	73.6	0.4	52.0	1.7	50.3
1999	290.8	232.9	23.0	34.9	10.4	1 186.3	858.9	252.4	74.6	0.4	50.4	1.7	48.7
2000	315.4	247.3	28.8	39.2	7.7	1 269.5	917.8	271.7	79.5	0.5	50.0	2.0	47.9
2001	350.8	276.1	31.4	43.3	4.0	1 368.2	969.8	305.2	85.5	7.7	4.8	2.6	2.2
2002	384.7	304.6	32.6	47.5	2.5	1 444.3	1 025.3	332.0	86.0	0.9	-34.2	1.7	-35.9
2003	422.7	338.5	33.5	50.6	-0.6	1 514.5	1 073.8	353.0	87.7	0.1	-20.4	3.8	-24.1
2004	437.2	349.1	32.2	56.0	-3.0	1 592.8	1 120.3	383.8	88.4	0.4	1.5	7.1	-5.6
2005	450.3	360.9	31.7	57.6	-8.3	1 684.9	1 191.2	403.5	89.9	0.4	29.5	7.6	21.9
2006	456.5	358.0	38.3	60.2	-5.0	1 765.3	1 269.6	401.0	94.3	0.4	46.2	6.5	39.7
2007	481.3	376.3	40.9	64.1	-5.7	1 892.4	1 355.9	430.8	98.5	7.1	10.4	5.5	4.9
2008	496.7	388.3	42.0	66.5	-7.6	2 015.2	1 454.4	455.8	102.0	3.0	-80.1	5.6	-85.6
2006													
1st quarter	449.6	354.2	36.6	58.8	-4.7	1 724.2	1 240.8	390.3	92.7	0.4	57.5	6.9	50.6
2nd quarter	456.3	358.7	37.9	59.6	-4.8	1 752.2	1 260.2	397.7	93.9	0.4	63.1	6.6	56.5
3rd quarter	462.6	363.0	38.9	60.6	-5.5	1 788.1	1 281.8	410.6	95.3	0.4	32.2	6.3	25.9
4th quarter	457.6	356.2	39.7	61.7	-5.2	1 796.6	1 295.8	405.3	95.2	0.4	31.8	6.0	25.8
2007													
1st quarter	476.3	372.9	40.4	63.0	-5.8	1 854.3	1 318.7	436.8	96.9	1.9	23.2	5.7	17.5
2nd quarter	481.5	376.8	40.8	63.9	-5.7	1 874.0	1 344.4	420.7	98.2	10.7	35.8	5.5	30.3
3rd quarter	481.6	375.9	41.1	64.6	-5.3	1 900.7	1 365.3	427.6	99.1	8.8	4.7	5.4	-0.6
4th quarter	485.9	379.6	41.3	65.0	-5.9	1 940.7	1 395.2	438.3	100.0	7.3	-22.3	5.3	-27.6
2008													
1st quarter	486.4	379.9	41.4	65.2	-6.6	1 975.3	1 426.3	444.2	100.9	4.0	-52.4	5.4	-57.8
2nd quarter	491.8	384.4	41.6	65.8	-7.1	2 022.3	1 462.7	454.5	102.1	3.0	-66.9	5.5	-72.4
3rd quarter	495.4	386.6	42.1	66.8	-7.9	2 048.5	1 485.7	458.4	102.2	2.2	-103.6	5.6	-109.2
4th quarter	513.3	402.3	42.8	68.2	-8.9	2 014.8	1 443.0	466.1	102.8	2.8	-97.4	5.7	-103.1

[1] Includes components not shown separately.
. . . = Not available.

Table 6-9. State and Local Government Consumption Expenditures and Gross Investment

(National income and product accounts, calendar years, billions of dollars, quarterly data are at seasonally adjusted annual rates.)

NIPA Tables 3.9.5, 3.10.5

Year and quarter	Total	Consumption expenditures [1] — Total	Compensation of general government employees	Consumption of general government fixed capital	Intermediate goods and services purchased [2]	Less — Own-account investment	Less — Sales to other sectors — Total [3]	Tuition and related educational charges	Health and hospital charges	Gross investment — Total	Structures	Equipment and software
1950	20.7	14.9	10.1	1.7	4.9	0.3	1.6	0.1	0.3	5.9	5.4	0.5
1951	23.0	16.1	11.2	2.0	4.9	0.3	1.7	0.1	0.3	7.0	6.4	0.5
1952	24.4	17.1	12.3	2.2	4.9	0.4	1.8	0.2	0.3	7.3	6.7	0.6
1953	26.1	18.2	13.3	2.2	4.9	0.4	1.9	0.2	0.4	7.9	7.3	0.6
1954	28.9	19.7	14.7	2.2	5.2	0.4	2.0	0.2	0.4	9.2	8.5	0.7
1955	31.6	21.6	15.8	2.4	6.0	0.4	2.2	0.2	0.5	10.0	9.3	0.8
1956	34.7	23.4	17.6	2.8	5.9	0.5	2.4	0.2	0.6	11.3	10.4	0.9
1957	38.3	25.8	19.6	3.0	6.4	0.5	2.6	0.3	0.7	12.5	11.5	1.1
1958	42.2	28.6	21.6	3.1	7.5	0.6	3.0	0.3	0.9	13.5	12.5	1.1
1959	44.7	30.7	23.1	3.3	8.3	0.8	3.2	0.4	1.0	13.9	12.8	1.1
1960	47.5	33.5	25.5	3.5	8.9	0.8	3.5	0.4	1.0	13.9	12.7	1.2
1961	51.6	36.6	27.9	3.7	9.7	0.8	3.9	0.5	1.0	15.0	13.8	1.3
1962	54.9	39.0	30.2	3.9	10.1	0.9	4.4	0.6	1.3	15.9	14.5	1.3
1963	59.5	41.9	32.9	4.2	10.8	1.0	4.9	0.7	1.3	17.5	16.0	1.5
1964	64.8	45.8	35.9	4.5	11.9	1.0	5.5	0.8	1.5	19.0	17.2	1.8
1965	71.0	50.2	39.3	4.9	13.4	1.1	6.3	1.0	1.8	20.8	19.0	1.9
1966	79.2	56.1	44.1	5.5	14.9	1.2	7.2	1.2	2.1	23.1	21.0	2.1
1967	87.9	62.6	49.5	6.0	16.5	1.2	8.2	1.4	2.5	25.3	23.0	2.3
1968	98.0	70.4	55.9	6.6	18.7	1.3	9.5	1.6	3.2	27.7	25.2	2.4
1969	108.2	79.9	62.6	7.4	21.8	1.4	10.6	1.9	3.5	28.3	25.6	2.7
1970	120.3	91.5	71.1	8.4	25.4	1.5	11.8	2.4	3.8	28.7	25.8	3.0
1971	132.8	102.7	79.2	9.4	29.2	1.6	13.5	2.9	4.6	30.1	27.0	3.1
1972	143.8	113.2	87.7	10.2	32.2	1.7	15.2	3.2	5.6	30.6	27.1	3.5
1973	159.2	126.0	98.0	11.3	35.4	1.7	17.0	3.7	6.6	33.2	29.1	4.1
1974	183.4	143.7	107.7	14.1	42.7	2.1	18.7	4.0	7.4	39.6	34.7	4.9
1975	208.7	165.1	121.2	15.9	50.7	2.1	20.6	4.3	8.5	43.6	38.1	5.5
1976	223.3	179.5	133.0	16.6	55.2	2.0	23.3	4.7	9.9	43.8	38.1	5.7
1977	238.7	195.9	145.1	17.5	61.1	2.0	25.8	5.2	10.9	42.8	36.9	5.9
1978	262.6	213.2	158.9	18.9	66.9	2.3	29.2	5.8	12.7	49.5	42.8	6.6
1979	290.2	233.3	174.3	21.1	74.3	2.9	33.4	6.4	15.2	56.8	49.0	7.8
1980	322.4	258.4	193.0	24.3	82.0	3.3	37.6	7.2	17.3	64.0	55.1	8.9
1981	347.3	282.3	210.1	27.8	91.6	3.5	43.7	8.3	21.0	65.0	55.4	9.5
1982	369.7	304.9	227.4	30.3	100.6	3.7	49.7	9.4	24.5	64.8	54.2	10.6
1983	390.5	324.1	243.0	31.2	109.6	4.0	55.7	10.7	27.8	66.4	54.2	12.2
1984	422.6	347.7	261.1	32.0	119.0	4.6	59.8	11.7	29.4	75.0	60.5	14.4
1985	466.2	381.8	284.7	33.7	134.0	5.2	65.4	12.8	32.0	84.4	67.6	16.8
1986	510.7	417.9	307.3	36.2	151.6	5.7	71.5	13.9	34.8	92.8	74.2	18.6
1987	539.4	440.9	328.8	39.0	156.2	6.1	76.9	15.0	37.0	98.4	78.8	19.6
1988	576.7	470.4	353.7	41.5	166.0	6.7	84.1	16.6	40.3	106.3	84.8	21.5
1989	616.9	502.1	380.5	44.4	178.8	7.8	93.8	18.4	45.0	114.7	88.7	26.0
1990	671.9	544.6	414.6	48.0	194.0	8.6	103.5	20.3	50.0	127.2	98.5	28.7
1991	706.7	574.6	439.8	51.1	208.4	9.3	115.4	22.7	57.0	132.1	103.2	28.9
1992	737.0	602.7	463.9	53.4	224.0	9.5	129.1	25.5	65.3	134.3	104.2	30.1
1993	766.0	630.3	486.7	56.3	239.7	9.7	142.7	27.5	73.1	135.7	104.5	31.2
1994	806.3	663.3	511.2	59.5	256.0	10.1	153.3	29.4	78.8	143.0	108.7	34.3
1995	850.0	696.1	533.5	63.4	274.8	10.6	165.0	31.2	85.0	154.0	117.3	36.7
1996	888.6	724.8	552.7	66.7	289.6	11.0	173.2	33.0	86.6	163.8	126.8	36.9
1997	937.8	758.9	575.5	70.2	308.5	12.2	183.2	35.5	89.9	178.9	139.5	39.4
1998	987.9	801.4	603.3	73.9	331.4	12.6	194.6	38.1	95.9	186.5	143.6	43.0
1999	1 065.0	858.9	633.1	78.7	364.6	13.5	203.9	40.9	98.4	206.0	159.7	46.4
2000	1 142.8	917.8	669.4	84.8	399.0	14.9	220.6	44.3	105.5	225.0	176.0	49.0
2001	1 212.8	969.8	710.8	89.9	428.3	16.7	242.7	49.7	118.5	243.0	192.4	50.6
2002	1 281.5	1 025.3	754.2	94.8	452.9	17.0	259.5	53.6	128.4	256.1	205.9	50.2
2003	1 336.0	1 073.8	798.0	98.2	466.9	17.1	272.2	58.2	133.0	262.2	212.0	50.3
2004	1 391.2	1 120.3	831.9	103.9	489.5	18.1	286.9	61.4	138.3	270.9	220.3	50.6
2005	1 479.8	1 191.2	872.4	114.2	525.0	19.5	301.0	66.1	140.9	288.6	235.9	52.7
2006	1 575.9	1 269.6	913.0	124.1	565.9	19.9	313.5	71.0	142.9	306.3	250.2	56.1
2007	1 695.5	1 355.9	963.1	135.9	611.7	21.8	333.0	76.2	149.8	339.6	281.0	58.6
2008	1 810.4	1 454.4	1 010.1	146.7	673.5	22.7	353.2	82.2	157.3	356.0	295.6	60.4
2006												
1st quarter	1 535.5	1 240.8	895.9	119.7	552.6	19.5	307.9	69.1	141.4	294.8	239.7	55.1
2nd quarter	1 567.2	1 260.2	902.4	122.9	565.9	20.0	311.1	70.3	142.1	307.0	251.1	55.9
3rd quarter	1 591.4	1 281.8	919.8	125.3	572.2	20.0	315.4	71.6	143.4	309.6	253.2	56.4
4th quarter	1 609.7	1 295.8	934.1	128.6	572.9	20.3	319.6	72.9	144.7	313.9	256.9	57.0
2007												
1st quarter	1 646.8	1 318.7	945.0	132.0	588.3	20.9	325.7	74.4	146.8	328.0	270.2	57.8
2nd quarter	1 681.3	1 344.4	955.1	134.8	606.6	21.7	330.4	75.7	148.7	336.9	278.4	58.4
3rd quarter	1 709.5	1 365.3	969.4	137.3	615.7	22.1	335.0	76.7	150.4	344.2	285.4	58.8
4th quarter	1 744.6	1 395.2	982.8	139.6	636.4	22.5	341.1	78.1	153.3	349.4	290.0	59.4
2008												
1st quarter	1 771.6	1 426.3	993.3	142.3	659.3	22.1	346.5	79.8	154.7	345.3	285.2	60.1
2nd quarter	1 817.6	1 462.7	1 005.1	144.8	686.3	22.8	350.7	81.5	156.4	354.9	294.1	60.7
3rd quarter	1 848.1	1 485.7	1 017.6	147.9	699.3	23.1	356.1	83.0	158.3	362.4	301.8	60.7
4th quarter	1 804.4	1 443.0	1 024.3	151.9	649.2	22.8	359.7	84.5	159.8	361.4	301.2	60.2

[1]Excludes government sales to other sectors and government own-account investment (construction and software).
[2]Includes general government intermediate inputs for goods and services sold to other sectors and for own-account investment.
[3]Includes components not shown separately.

Table 6-10. State and Local Government Output, Lending and Borrowing, and Net Investment

(National income and product accounts, calendar years, billions of dollars, quarterly data are at seasonally adjusted annual rates.)

NIPA Tables 3.3, 3.10.5

| Year and quarter | Output | | | Net lending (net borrowing -) | | | | | | | Net investment |
| | Gross | Value added | Intermediate goods and services purchased[1] | Net saving, current (surplus +, deficit -) | Plus: Capital transfer receipts | Minus | | | Plus: consumption of fixed capital | Equals: Net lending (borrowing -) | |
						Gross investment	Capital transfer payments	Net purchases of nonproduced assets			
1950	16.7	11.8	4.9	1.3	0.6	5.9	. . .	0.3	2.1	-2.1	3.8
1951	18.1	13.2	4.9	2.6	0.7	7.0	. . .	0.3	2.6	-1.5	4.4
1952	19.3	14.4	4.9	3.0	0.7	7.3	. . .	0.3	2.7	-1.1	4.6
1953	20.5	15.5	4.9	3.5	0.8	7.9	. . .	0.3	2.8	-1.1	5.1
1954	22.1	16.9	5.2	3.2	0.8	9.2	. . .	0.4	2.9	-2.6	6.3
1955	24.2	18.2	6.0	3.5	1.0	10.0	. . .	0.6	3.1	-3.1	6.9
1956	26.3	20.4	5.9	4.4	1.1	11.3	. . .	0.7	3.5	-2.9	7.8
1957	29.0	22.6	6.4	4.2	1.6	12.5	. . .	0.7	3.9	-3.5	8.6
1958	32.2	24.7	7.5	2.9	2.7	13.5	. . .	0.8	4.0	-4.7	9.5
1959	34.8	26.5	8.3	3.8	3.5	13.9	. . .	0.8	4.2	-3.2	9.7
1960	37.9	28.9	8.9	4.3	3.0	13.9	. . .	0.9	4.4	-3.1	9.5
1961	41.3	31.6	9.7	4.3	3.3	15.0	. . .	1.0	4.7	-3.8	10.3
1962	44.3	34.2	10.1	5.2	3.5	15.9	. . .	1.1	5.0	-3.2	10.9
1963	47.9	37.1	10.8	5.7	4.1	17.5	. . .	1.2	5.4	-3.5	12.1
1964	52.3	40.4	11.9	6.4	4.7	19.0	. . .	1.3	5.7	-3.4	13.3
1965	57.6	44.2	13.4	6.5	4.7	20.8	. . .	1.3	6.2	-4.6	14.6
1966	64.5	49.6	14.9	7.8	5.1	23.1	. . .	1.4	6.9	-4.7	16.2
1967	72.0	55.5	16.5	7.0	5.1	25.3	. . .	1.4	7.5	-7.1	17.8
1968	81.2	62.5	18.7	7.5	6.8	27.7	. . .	1.4	8.3	-6.4	19.4
1969	91.9	70.0	21.8	8.0	6.8	28.3	. . .	1.0	9.3	-5.1	19.0
1970	104.9	79.5	25.4	7.1	6.2	28.7	. . .	1.1	10.6	-6.0	18.1
1971	117.9	88.6	29.2	6.5	7.0	30.1	. . .	1.6	11.8	-6.4	18.3
1972	130.0	97.9	32.2	15.6	7.3	30.6	. . .	1.7	12.8	3.4	17.8
1973	144.7	109.3	35.4	15.7	7.3	33.2	. . .	1.7	14.3	2.4	18.9
1974	164.5	121.8	42.7	9.3	9.2	39.6	. . .	1.9	17.7	-5.3	21.9
1975	187.9	137.1	50.7	2.5	11.0	43.6	. . .	1.9	20.2	-11.9	23.4
1976	204.8	149.7	55.2	7.4	12.0	43.8	. . .	1.7	21.3	-4.9	22.5
1977	223.7	162.6	61.1	13.1	13.1	42.8	. . .	1.6	22.6	4.5	20.2
1978	244.7	177.8	66.9	18.7	13.7	49.5	. . .	1.6	24.5	5.8	25.0
1979	269.6	195.4	74.3	13.0	16.2	56.8	. . .	1.7	27.5	-1.8	29.3
1980	299.3	217.3	82.0	8.8	18.6	64.0	. . .	1.8	31.8	-6.6	32.2
1981	329.5	237.9	91.6	7.6	17.8	65.0	. . .	2.0	36.3	-5.3	28.7
1982	358.3	257.7	100.6	-2.2	16.9	64.8	. . .	2.0	39.5	-12.6	25.3
1983	383.7	274.1	109.6	4.9	18.0	66.4	. . .	2.2	40.9	-4.9	25.5
1984	412.1	293.1	119.0	23.9	20.1	75.0	. . .	2.6	42.3	8.8	32.7
1985	452.4	318.4	134.0	22.3	22.0	84.4	. . .	3.1	44.6	1.5	39.8
1986	495.1	343.5	151.6	21.0	23.0	92.8	. . .	3.7	47.9	-4.6	44.9
1987	524.0	367.8	156.2	12.4	22.3	98.4	. . .	4.2	51.4	-16.4	47.0
1988	561.1	395.2	166.0	17.9	23.1	106.3	. . .	4.3	54.8	-14.8	51.5
1989	603.7	424.9	178.8	20.8	23.4	114.7	. . .	4.9	58.7	-16.6	56.0
1990	656.7	462.6	194.0	7.2	25.0	127.2	. . .	5.7	63.0	-37.7	64.2
1991	699.4	490.9	208.4	-4.2	25.8	132.1	. . .	5.8	66.9	-49.4	65.2
1992	741.3	517.3	224.0	0.7	26.9	134.3	. . .	5.9	69.9	-42.8	64.4
1993	782.7	543.0	239.7	0.9	28.6	135.7	. . .	5.8	73.8	-38.2	61.9
1994	826.7	570.7	256.0	10.5	29.9	143.0	. . .	6.2	78.5	-30.4	64.5
1995	871.7	596.9	274.8	12.0	32.4	154.0	. . .	6.6	83.1	-33.0	70.9
1996	908.9	619.3	289.6	25.8	33.9	163.8	. . .	6.1	87.2	-22.9	76.6
1997	954.3	645.8	308.5	39.1	35.3	178.9	. . .	5.8	91.6	-18.7	87.3
1998	1 008.6	677.2	331.4	52.0	36.0	186.5	. . .	7.5	96.2	-9.9	90.3
1999	1 076.4	711.8	364.6	50.4	39.9	206.0	. . .	8.6	102.1	-22.3	103.9
2000	1 153.2	754.2	399.0	50.0	43.7	225.0	. . .	8.8	109.8	-30.4	115.2
2001	1 229.1	800.8	428.3	4.8	48.6	243.0	. . .	9.2	117.8	-81.1	125.2
2002	1 301.8	848.9	452.9	-34.2	52.1	256.1	. . .	10.6	122.7	-126.1	133.4
2003	1 363.1	896.2	466.9	-20.4	51.6	262.2	. . .	10.9	127.8	-114.1	134.4
2004	1 425.3	935.8	489.5	1.5	52.1	270.9	. . .	10.5	136.1	-91.7	134.8
2005	1 511.7	986.6	525.0	29.5	54.2	288.6	. . .	9.4	153.2	-61.1	135.4
2006	1 603.1	1 037.2	565.9	46.2	57.2	306.3	. . .	9.6	162.3	-50.2	144.0
2007	1 710.7	1 099.0	611.7	10.4	58.7	339.6	. . .	11.0	177.6	-104.0	162.0
2008	1 830.3	1 156.8	673.5	-80.1	60.7	356.0	. . .	11.0	191.3	-195.1	164.7
2006											
1st quarter	1 568.2	1 015.6	552.6	57.5	56.5	294.8	. . .	9.2	156.5	-33.4	138.3
2nd quarter	1 591.2	1 025.3	565.9	63.1	55.9	307.0	. . .	9.4	160.8	-36.5	146.2
3rd quarter	1 617.3	1 045.1	572.2	32.2	59.7	309.6	. . .	9.7	163.9	-63.4	145.7
4th quarter	1 635.7	1 062.7	572.9	31.8	56.7	313.9	. . .	10.1	168.1	-67.4	145.8
2007											
1st quarter	1 665.3	1 077.1	588.3	23.2	52.4	328.0	. . .	10.6	172.5	-90.6	155.5
2nd quarter	1 696.5	1 089.9	606.6	35.8	58.2	336.9	. . .	10.9	176.0	-77.8	160.9
3rd quarter	1 722.3	1 106.6	615.7	4.7	64.1	344.2	. . .	11.1	179.3	-107.2	164.9
4th quarter	1 758.8	1 122.4	636.4	-22.3	60.1	349.4	. . .	11.2	182.4	-140.3	167.0
2008											
1st quarter	1 794.9	1 135.6	659.3	-52.4	56.9	345.3	. . .	11.1	185.5	-166.3	159.8
2nd quarter	1 836.2	1 149.9	686.3	-66.9	58.1	354.9	. . .	11.0	188.8	-185.8	166.1
3rd quarter	1 864.8	1 165.6	699.3	-103.6	63.8	362.4	. . .	11.0	192.9	-220.3	169.5
4th quarter	1 825.5	1 176.2	649.2	-97.4	64.0	361.4	. . .	11.0	197.9	-207.9	163.5

[1]Includes general government intermediate inputs for goods and services sold to other sectors and for own-account investment.
. . . = Not available.

Table 6-11. Chain-Type Quantity Indexes for State and Local Government Consumption Expenditures and Gross Investment

(Seasonally adjusted, 2000 = 100.)   **NIPA Tables 3.9.3, 3.10.3**

Year and quarter	State and local government consumption expenditures and gross investment											
		Consumption expenditures [1]								Gross investment		
							Less					
								Sales to other sectors				
	Total	Total	Compensation of general government employees	Consumption of general government fixed capital	Intermediate goods and services purchased [2]	Own-account investment	Total [3]	Tuition and related educational charges	Health and hospital charges	Total	Structures	Equipment and software
1955	21.9	20.6	27.0	14.9	9.3	23.3	11.7	7.7	7.7	25.9	36.6	3.5
1956	22.6	21.3	28.8	15.7	9.0	26.1	12.2	8.8	8.8	26.5	37.2	4.0
1957	24.0	22.4	30.3	16.7	9.4	26.4	12.9	10.1	10.0	28.4	39.3	4.9
1958	26.0	24.2	32.2	17.7	10.8	28.3	14.4	11.5	12.6	31.2	43.6	4.9
1959	27.0	25.2	33.4	18.7	11.6	38.3	15.2	12.3	13.2	32.1	44.8	5.2
1960	28.2	26.6	35.2	19.8	12.2	35.9	15.7	13.6	12.2	32.5	44.9	5.9
1961	29.9	28.1	37.0	20.9	13.1	37.6	16.8	14.9	12.5	35.1	48.6	6.0
1962	30.8	28.9	38.2	22.0	13.6	40.0	18.7	16.9	14.6	36.4	50.2	6.5
1963	32.7	30.3	40.2	23.3	14.5	44.9	20.5	19.3	15.2	39.6	54.4	7.4
1964	34.9	32.3	42.6	24.7	15.8	44.4	22.5	22.6	16.4	42.4	58.0	8.4
1965	37.3	34.4	45.2	26.3	17.4	45.6	25.0	26.2	18.7	45.4	62.1	9.0
1966	39.6	36.5	47.9	28.0	18.8	48.1	27.3	29.7	21.3	48.4	66.0	9.9
1967	41.6	38.2	49.7	29.8	20.3	46.7	30.1	33.1	24.2	51.4	70.2	10.3
1968	44.0	40.7	52.7	31.6	22.3	49.2	33.0	37.2	28.3	53.7	73.4	10.8
1969	45.5	43.3	55.1	33.3	24.7	49.5	34.5	41.0	29.3	51.5	69.5	11.6
1970	46.8	45.9	57.5	34.9	27.2	50.1	36.2	47.7	29.8	48.3	64.4	12.1
1971	48.2	48.1	59.8	36.3	29.7	50.1	39.5	53.7	34.7	46.9	62.2	12.3
1972	49.3	49.9	61.9	37.6	31.5	48.8	42.3	57.0	39.8	45.4	59.2	13.7
1973	50.7	51.7	64.1	38.9	32.6	47.4	44.2	61.5	44.1	45.6	58.7	15.3
1974	52.6	54.0	66.4	40.3	34.4	50.5	44.2	61.3	45.5	46.0	58.5	16.7
1975	54.5	56.7	68.4	41.6	37.1	47.6	44.6	61.4	46.7	45.6	58.1	16.4
1976	54.9	57.5	69.2	42.8	38.2	42.0	47.1	63.4	49.7	44.8	57.0	16.1
1977	55.1	58.6	70.2	43.8	39.3	38.3	48.6	66.0	50.6	42.1	53.2	15.8
1978	56.9	59.7	71.8	44.7	40.3	41.3	50.9	69.6	54.1	45.9	58.3	16.7
1979	57.8	60.1	73.0	45.8	40.3	47.7	53.2	71.5	58.7	48.2	60.8	18.3
1980	57.7	60.0	73.9	47.0	39.0	49.7	54.1	73.9	59.2	48.4	60.5	19.5
1981	56.6	59.8	73.7	48.0	39.3	47.5	56.4	75.5	62.9	44.3	54.6	19.4
1982	56.6	60.7	74.0	48.9	41.0	47.9	58.1	75.4	64.8	41.6	50.1	20.6
1983	57.3	61.4	73.5	49.8	43.6	47.5	60.2	77.8	66.4	42.1	49.6	23.5
1984	59.3	62.5	73.8	51.1	45.4	52.8	60.0	77.7	64.9	47.3	55.0	27.5
1985	63.0	65.8	75.8	52.9	50.1	57.0	62.0	77.7	66.4	52.4	60.3	31.9
1986	67.1	69.9	77.9	55.0	56.7	61.0	64.1	78.3	68.1	56.0	64.1	34.9
1987	68.0	70.8	79.2	57.1	56.6	62.3	65.1	78.8	68.1	57.4	65.5	36.4
1988	70.6	73.2	81.9	59.5	58.1	65.2	66.4	81.3	68.2	60.4	68.4	39.4
1989	73.0	75.4	84.2	62.4	59.9	72.8	68.2	83.8	68.7	63.7	69.8	46.8
1990	76.0	77.8	86.5	65.7	61.8	76.3	69.5	85.6	69.4	68.7	75.0	51.1
1991	77.6	79.4	87.3	68.9	64.7	79.7	71.8	87.0	72.4	70.3	77.5	50.5
1992	79.3	81.3	88.5	71.9	68.1	78.9	75.0	88.7	76.6	71.2	77.8	52.9
1993	80.5	83.0	89.5	74.7	71.4	78.5	78.6	87.6	81.1	70.5	76.0	54.7
1994	82.5	85.1	90.8	77.4	74.9	79.3	81.4	87.7	84.3	72.5	76.6	60.2
1995	84.7	87.0	92.4	80.3	77.7	80.4	84.4	88.0	88.1	75.7	79.2	64.7
1996	86.7	88.6	93.6	83.3	79.5	81.4	86.0	88.2	87.7	79.1	83.1	66.7
1997	89.8	91.0	95.3	86.8	83.4	89.0	88.9	90.3	89.8	84.9	88.5	73.7
1998	93.0	94.4	96.9	90.9	90.0	90.7	92.9	92.9	94.9	87.4	88.4	84.1
1999	97.4	98.1	98.3	95.4	96.6	94.6	95.2	96.1	95.6	94.6	94.9	93.7
2000	100.0	100.0	100.0	100.0	100.0	100.0	100.0	100.0	100.0	100.0	100.0	100.0
2001	103.2	102.6	102.1	104.5	105.5	109.1	106.8	106.6	108.9	105.7	105.7	105.5
2002	106.4	105.6	103.8	109.0	110.8	108.8	110.3	107.7	114.2	109.4	109.9	107.1
2003	106.6	105.7	104.1	112.2	109.3	105.5	110.0	107.9	112.4	110.2	110.6	108.9
2004	106.4	105.8	104.1	115.4	109.3	107.8	110.3	104.1	111.9	108.9	108.6	110.2
2005	106.3	105.9	104.6	118.6	108.5	110.6	111.0	104.2	110.2	107.7	106.2	114.7
2006	107.6	107.7	105.3	121.8	110.6	109.0	110.8	104.9	107.5	107.4	104.2	123.0
2007	110.2	109.8	106.8	125.1	113.7	114.8	112.8	106.0	109.1	111.5	108.0	128.6
2008	111.4	111.3	108.1	128.7	115.3	114.8	115.0	107.5	111.3	111.8	107.8	131.8
2006												
1st quarter	106.7	106.8	104.9	120.6	109.5	107.9	110.6	104.8	108.0	106.3	103.4	120.6
2nd quarter	107.5	107.3	105.0	121.4	110.2	109.7	110.6	104.7	107.4	108.4	105.5	122.4
3rd quarter	108.0	108.0	105.5	122.2	110.9	108.8	110.8	104.9	107.3	107.9	104.5	124.0
4th quarter	108.3	108.6	105.8	123.1	111.8	109.6	111.2	105.1	107.5	107.2	103.6	125.1
2007												
1st quarter	109.3	109.2	106.3	123.9	112.8	111.9	112.1	105.8	108.2	109.9	106.4	126.6
2nd quarter	110.0	109.6	106.6	124.7	113.5	114.8	112.6	105.9	108.9	111.2	107.8	128.1
3rd quarter	110.5	110.0	106.9	125.6	114.1	115.9	113.2	106.1	109.5	112.2	108.7	129.2
4th quarter	110.9	110.5	107.3	126.4	114.5	116.8	113.6	106.2	109.9	112.6	109.0	130.7
2008												
1st quarter	110.8	110.9	107.7	127.2	114.9	113.7	114.3	106.7	110.5	110.6	106.4	132.1
2nd quarter	111.5	111.2	108.1	128.3	115.1	115.6	114.7	107.3	111.0	112.7	108.7	132.9
3rd quarter	111.9	111.5	108.4	129.2	115.5	115.7	115.2	107.8	111.6	113.4	109.6	132.1
4th quarter	111.3	111.5	108.3	130.3	115.6	114.3	115.8	108.3	112.1	110.6	106.7	130.1

[1]Excludes government sales to other sectors and government own-account investment (construction and software).
[2]Includes general government intermediate inputs for goods and services sold to other sectors and for own-account investment.
[3]Includes components not shown separately.

Table 6-12. State Government Current Receipts and Expenditures

(National income and product accounts, calendar years, billions of dollars.)   **NIPA Table 3.20**

Year	Total [1]	Current tax receipts								Taxes on corporate income	Contributions for government social insurance	Income receipts on assets		
		Total	Personal current taxes		Taxes on production and imports							Total [1]	Interest receipts	Rents and royalties
			Total [1]	Income taxes	Total	Sales taxes	Property taxes	Other						
1959	21.8	16.7	3.1	2.0	12.5	10.0	0.5	2.0	1.1	0.4	0.5	0.3	0.2
1960	23.5	18.1	3.4	2.3	13.5	10.8	0.5	2.2	1.2	0.5	0.5	0.4	0.2
1961	25.2	19.3	3.7	2.5	14.4	11.6	0.5	2.3	1.3	0.5	0.6	0.4	0.2
1962	27.5	21.0	4.0	2.8	15.4	12.6	0.6	2.3	1.5	0.5	0.6	0.4	0.2
1963	29.6	22.4	4.3	3.1	16.4	13.4	0.6	2.4	1.6	0.6	0.6	0.4	0.2
1964	32.3	24.5	4.9	3.6	17.7	14.5	0.6	2.6	1.8	0.7	0.7	0.4	0.2
1965	35.8	26.9	5.4	3.9	19.6	16.1	0.7	2.8	1.9	0.8	0.8	0.5	0.3
1966	42.3	30.2	6.4	4.8	21.7	18.0	0.7	3.0	2.2	0.8	0.9	0.6	0.3
1967	46.5	32.7	7.0	5.3	23.3	19.4	0.7	3.1	2.5	0.9	1.1	0.8	0.3
1968	54.7	38.6	8.8	6.9	26.7	22.8	0.8	3.2	3.1	0.9	1.7	1.4	0.3
1969	62.6	44.0	10.8	8.6	29.9	25.7	0.9	3.3	3.4	1.0	2.1	1.8	0.3
1970	70.1	48.1	12.0	9.6	32.7	28.2	0.9	3.6	3.5	1.1	2.5	2.2	0.3
1971	79.4	53.8	13.4	11.0	36.3	31.4	1.0	3.9	4.0	1.2	2.7	2.3	0.4
1972	96.3	63.5	17.9	15.2	40.7	35.2	1.1	4.4	5.0	1.3	2.9	2.5	0.4
1973	104.5	70.2	19.8	16.8	44.7	38.8	1.2	4.7	5.7	1.5	3.9	3.3	0.5
1974	113.5	75.9	21.1	18.0	48.4	42.0	1.1	5.3	6.3	1.7	5.0	4.4	0.6
1975	127.4	81.9	23.2	19.9	51.8	44.7	1.4	5.6	6.9	1.8	5.6	5.0	0.6
1976	143.4	93.8	27.0	23.4	57.7	49.9	1.5	6.3	9.1	2.2	5.3	4.7	0.6
1977	160.0	105.1	30.9	27.2	63.4	55.0	1.5	6.9	10.8	2.8	6.1	5.4	0.6
1978	179.3	117.4	35.6	31.6	70.3	60.8	1.9	7.6	11.5	3.4	7.4	6.7	0.6
1979	197.3	128.9	38.9	34.6	77.1	65.7	2.3	9.0	12.9	3.9	10.3	9.2	1.1
1980	218.7	140.9	43.7	39.1	83.4	70.0	2.6	10.8	13.7	3.6	13.4	11.2	2.0
1981	239.5	155.6	48.5	43.6	92.7	76.5	2.7	13.6	14.5	3.9	15.6	13.2	2.2
1982	247.9	162.3	52.3	47.0	97.0	80.3	2.8	13.9	13.1	4.0	17.5	15.3	2.1
1983	272.9	180.5	58.9	53.2	106.8	90.0	3.0	13.8	14.9	4.1	19.5	17.2	2.2
1984	308.2	205.4	68.2	61.9	119.7	100.9	3.4	15.5	17.4	4.7	22.4	19.8	2.5
1985	333.1	220.9	73.2	66.1	129.0	109.0	3.5	16.5	18.7	4.9	25.9	23.1	2.6
1986	359.3	234.1	78.3	70.7	134.9	115.8	3.6	15.6	20.8	6.0	27.3	24.5	2.7
1987	380.4	253.6	87.5	79.1	144.3	124.6	3.7	16.0	21.8	7.2	28.2	25.5	2.6
1988	408.8	269.5	90.4	81.5	155.2	135.1	3.8	16.3	23.8	8.4	30.5	27.7	2.7
1989	441.4	288.1	102.4	92.9	163.5	142.3	4.3	17.0	22.2	9.0	32.4	29.8	2.4
1990	476.5	305.4	109.6	99.6	175.4	152.5	4.6	18.3	20.4	10.0	33.9	31.3	2.3
1991	512.3	314.1	111.8	101.4	180.8	157.5	4.9	18.3	21.5	11.6	34.4	31.4	2.6
1992	559.7	338.6	120.6	109.0	195.9	169.7	6.1	20.1	22.1	13.1	33.9	30.7	2.7
1993	593.9	356.9	126.3	114.9	206.3	179.4	5.9	21.0	24.3	14.1	32.6	29.5	2.5
1994	630.1	380.2	132.1	120.2	220.8	191.7	7.0	22.1	27.3	14.5	33.8	30.5	2.5
1995	662.8	401.4	140.9	128.4	231.3	200.5	7.2	23.6	29.1	13.6	36.6	33.1	2.6
1996	696.0	425.9	150.9	138.6	245.0	211.8	8.2	25.0	30.0	12.5	39.2	35.1	2.7
1997	731.1	449.0	162.7	149.7	255.4	221.3	8.1	26.0	30.8	10.8	41.6	37.4	2.7
1998	777.5	480.7	180.4	166.8	268.8	233.3	8.5	27.0	31.6	10.4	43.1	39.0	2.4
1999	826.2	508.0	192.5	178.4	283.0	245.9	9.1	27.9	32.5	9.8	46.7	42.4	2.6
2000	884.5	540.7	213.6	199.2	294.8	255.5	7.8	31.6	32.3	11.0	48.7	43.2	3.6
2001	922.0	547.2	219.9	205.5	300.1	259.6	7.9	32.6	27.2	13.6	46.6	41.0	3.7
2002	938.4	536.1	198.5	183.7	308.6	267.3	7.6	33.6	29.0	15.8	42.4	36.7	3.7
2003	990.2	562.6	202.2	186.2	328.6	281.8	9.3	37.5	31.8	19.8	41.6	34.9	4.5
2004	1 068.6	611.8	221.6	204.6	351.9	300.1	8.7	43.2	38.4	23.6	43.6	36.0	5.1
2005	1 152.7	679.5	247.0	229.5	382.2	322.7	9.1	50.4	50.3	24.2	49.3	40.8	6.1
2006	1 211.1	727.7	271.4	253.1	401.9	339.7	9.6	52.6	54.5	23.1	54.5	44.7	7.1
2007	1 269.6	761.0	291.2	272.6	414.7	351.1	9.8	53.8	55.1	22.8	58.4	47.3	8.3

[1]Includes components not shown separately.

Table 6-12. State Government Current Receipts and Expenditures—*Continued*

(National income and product accounts, calendar years, billions of dollars.)

NIPA Table 3.20

| Year | Current receipts—*Continued* | | | | | Current expenditures | | | | | Net state government saving, NIPA (surplus + / deficit -) | | |
| | Current transfer receipts | | | | | | | | | | | | |
	Total	Federal grants-in-aid	Local grants-in-aid	From business, net	From persons	Total [1]	Consumption expenditures	Government social benefits to persons	Grants-in-aid to local governments	Interest payments	Total	Social insurance funds	Other
1959	3.8	3.4	0.2	0.0	0.1	20.8	8.6	3.6	7.7	0.8	1.0	0.0	1.0
1960	3.9	3.5	0.2	0.0	0.1	22.6	9.3	3.8	8.6	0.9	0.9	0.0	0.9
1961	4.4	4.0	0.3	0.0	0.1	24.5	9.9	4.1	9.4	0.9	0.8	0.0	0.8
1962	4.9	4.4	0.3	0.1	0.2	26.6	10.7	4.4	10.3	1.0	0.9	0.0	0.9
1963	5.4	4.9	0.3	0.1	0.2	28.9	11.6	4.7	11.3	1.1	0.7	0.0	0.6
1964	5.9	5.4	0.3	0.1	0.2	31.4	12.5	5.1	12.4	1.2	0.9	0.0	0.9
1965	6.7	6.1	0.3	0.1	0.3	35.1	13.9	5.5	14.3	1.3	0.6	0.1	0.5
1966	9.6	8.9	0.4	0.1	0.3	40.2	15.6	6.4	16.7	1.4	2.1	0.1	2.0
1967	11.1	10.3	0.5	0.1	0.3	46.4	17.9	7.7	19.1	1.6	0.0	0.1	-0.1
1968	12.6	11.6	0.6	0.1	0.3	53.6	20.2	9.5	22.0	1.8	1.0	0.1	0.9
1969	14.6	13.3	0.8	0.1	0.4	61.4	23.2	10.8	25.4	1.8	1.1	0.2	1.0
1970	17.6	16.2	0.9	0.1	0.4	71.3	26.7	12.9	29.2	2.2	-1.2	0.2	-1.3
1971	21.0	19.4	1.0	0.1	0.4	81.1	29.8	15.3	33.0	2.8	-1.7	0.2	-2.0
1972	27.6	25.8	1.1	0.2	0.5	90.6	32.5	17.5	36.9	3.2	5.8	0.3	5.5
1973	27.9	25.8	1.2	0.2	0.7	101.2	36.5	19.4	41.1	3.6	3.3	0.3	3.0
1974	30.0	27.6	1.3	0.2	0.8	114.3	43.6	19.9	45.9	4.1	-0.8	0.4	-1.1
1975	36.9	33.9	1.7	0.2	1.0	132.3	51.0	24.2	51.4	4.7	-4.9	0.5	-5.4
1976	40.8	37.1	2.3	0.3	1.2	145.1	55.6	26.9	56.2	5.3	-1.8	0.6	-2.4
1977	44.6	40.6	2.4	0.3	1.4	157.4	60.6	29.1	60.7	5.8	2.5	1.0	1.6
1978	49.5	45.2	2.5	0.3	1.5	171.8	64.7	32.0	67.3	6.3	7.5	1.5	6.0
1979	52.4	48.3	2.2	0.4	1.6	191.9	72.0	35.4	75.4	7.3	5.3	1.8	3.6
1980	59.2	54.7	2.3	0.4	1.7	216.5	81.2	41.3	83.8	8.2	2.2	1.3	0.9
1981	62.8	57.7	2.7	0.5	2.0	238.7	89.8	46.7	90.4	9.4	0.8	1.3	-0.5
1982	61.9	56.0	3.1	0.6	2.3	255.9	96.6	51.0	94.5	11.3	-8.0	1.2	-9.2
1983	66.0	58.6	4.2	0.6	2.6	273.7	102.6	55.9	99.0	13.5	-0.8	1.2	-2.0
1984	72.1	63.3	5.0	0.8	3.0	297.3	110.2	59.8	108.7	15.5	10.9	1.4	9.5
1985	76.9	67.3	5.2	0.9	3.6	326.0	121.2	65.2	120.0	16.3	7.1	1.3	5.8
1986	86.7	74.5	5.3	2.8	4.1	350.2	131.3	71.4	128.9	15.0	9.0	1.9	7.2
1987	85.8	74.9	5.5	0.9	4.5	375.2	138.2	77.4	137.8	17.6	5.2	2.2	3.1
1988	93.9	82.1	5.6	1.1	5.2	404.6	148.8	84.4	148.1	18.4	4.3	2.5	1.7
1989	104.6	91.5	5.8	1.3	5.9	437.7	158.1	94.4	159.5	20.6	3.6	2.3	1.3
1990	119.5	104.7	6.2	1.6	6.9	479.6	171.4	111.0	169.4	22.3	-3.1	2.0	-5.1
1991	144.2	124.6	7.6	2.0	10.0	528.4	179.0	137.6	181.9	24.1	-16.1	2.4	-18.5
1992	165.4	141.8	9.0	2.6	12.1	570.4	186.1	159.5	194.8	24.0	-10.7	3.1	-13.8
1993	180.9	155.8	10.1	2.9	12.1	604.3	195.9	173.6	206.0	22.9	-10.4	4.2	-14.6
1994	191.7	164.9	11.0	3.4	12.4	639.5	206.5	184.4	218.9	23.5	-9.4	4.6	-14.0
1995	200.4	173.0	11.1	4.1	12.2	672.6	215.2	194.8	231.6	24.3	-9.8	4.0	-13.9
1996	206.8	177.7	12.0	5.0	12.0	699.4	221.2	202.5	242.4	25.6	-3.4	2.8	-6.2
1997	217.5	184.5	13.5	6.6	13.0	729.1	232.1	206.8	255.1	26.5	2.0	1.2	0.8
1998	231.3	194.9	13.3	9.8	13.2	773.5	249.0	214.6	273.9	27.1	4.0	1.7	2.3
1999	250.0	212.5	12.9	9.9	14.7	837.6	273.3	230.3	297.2	27.6	-11.4	1.7	-13.2
2000	273.4	227.4	14.0	14.7	17.3	898.7	291.5	248.7	319.4	29.3	-14.2	2.0	-16.2
2001	304.2	254.3	14.9	15.5	19.5	977.4	309.0	281.3	337.5	32.2	-55.4	2.6	-58.0
2002	334.3	280.6	15.5	16.3	21.9	1 029.3	326.2	306.6	352.6	32.2	-90.9	1.7	-92.6
2003	356.2	301.9	16.2	15.6	22.5	1 069.0	328.3	325.7	371.4	32.4	-78.8	3.8	-82.6
2004	378.6	321.8	18.0	14.8	24.1	1 123.3	335.5	354.9	386.8	33.9	-54.7	7.1	-61.8
2005	388.1	330.1	16.7	15.4	26.0	1 173.8	355.6	373.2	396.7	35.8	-21.1	7.6	-28.7
2006	392.1	331.8	15.2	17.3	27.8	1 220.9	379.0	370.2	419.9	38.4	-9.8	6.5	-16.3
2007	412.1	347.2	15.8	18.7	30.3	1 305.2	401.8	398.4	444.1	40.2	-35.7	5.5	-41.1

[1] Includes components not shown separately.

Table 6-13. Local Government Current Receipts and Expenditures

(National income and product accounts, calendar years, billions of dollars.)   **NIPA Table 3.21**

Year	Current receipts Total [1]	Current tax receipts Total	Personal current taxes Total [1]	Personal current taxes Income taxes	Taxes on production and imports Total	Sales taxes	Property taxes	Other	Taxes on corporate income	Contributions for government social insurance	Income receipts on assets Total [1]	Interest receipts	Rents and royalties
1959	26.9	17.1	0.8	0.2	16.4	1.2	14.3	0.9	0.0	. . .	0.7	0.5	0.1
1960	29.9	18.8	0.8	0.3	18.0	1.3	15.7	0.9	0.0	. . .	0.8	0.7	0.1
1961	32.6	20.3	0.9	0.3	19.4	1.4	17.0	1.0	0.0	. . .	0.9	0.7	0.2
1962	35.2	21.8	1.0	0.3	20.8	1.5	18.4	1.0	0.0	. . .	1.0	0.8	0.2
1963	38.2	23.4	1.1	0.4	22.3	1.6	19.7	1.0	0.0	. . .	1.0	0.9	0.2
1964	41.8	25.3	1.2	0.5	24.1	1.9	21.1	1.1	0.0	. . .	1.3	1.1	0.2
1965	45.5	27.0	1.2	0.5	25.7	2.1	22.5	1.1	0.0	. . .	1.4	1.2	0.2
1966	49.9	28.5	1.4	0.6	27.1	2.0	23.8	1.3	0.0	. . .	1.7	1.4	0.3
1967	55.8	31.3	1.6	0.8	29.5	1.9	26.2	1.3	0.2	. . .	2.0	1.6	0.3
1968	61.7	34.8	1.7	0.9	32.8	2.3	29.1	1.4	0.3	. . .	1.7	1.4	0.4
1969	69.2	38.4	2.0	1.1	36.1	2.9	31.9	1.4	0.3	. . .	2.2	1.8	0.4
1970	80.3	43.2	2.3	1.3	40.6	3.5	35.7	1.5	0.2	. . .	2.6	2.2	0.5
1971	89.8	47.9	2.5	1.5	45.2	4.0	39.5	1.8	0.3	. . .	2.8	2.3	0.5
1972	100.5	52.0	3.0	2.0	48.8	4.6	42.2	2.0	0.3	. . .	3.0	2.4	0.6
1973	112.8	56.1	3.0	2.0	52.7	5.2	45.2	2.3	0.3	. . .	3.9	3.3	0.6
1974	122.6	60.2	3.4	2.3	56.4	6.1	47.9	2.4	0.3	. . .	5.2	4.5	0.7
1975	136.5	65.5	3.7	2.5	61.4	7.0	51.9	2.5	0.4	. . .	5.6	4.9	0.7
1976	150.1	71.9	4.1	2.8	67.3	7.9	56.7	2.7	0.5	. . .	5.1	4.4	0.7
1977	164.5	78.6	4.5	3.2	73.6	9.0	61.7	2.9	0.6	. . .	5.6	4.9	0.7
1978	179.6	80.8	4.9	3.4	75.3	10.2	61.8	3.3	0.6	. . .	7.2	6.5	0.7
1979	190.4	83.1	5.1	3.6	77.3	11.5	62.1	3.7	0.6	. . .	9.8	8.9	0.9
1980	207.6	89.1	5.1	3.5	83.3	12.8	66.2	4.2	0.7	. . .	12.9	11.8	1.1
1981	226.1	100.2	6.2	4.3	93.0	14.3	74.4	4.3	1.0	. . .	16.4	15.3	1.1
1982	243.7	110.8	6.9	4.9	103.0	15.9	82.5	4.6	1.0	. . .	19.2	17.8	1.4
1983	261.7	120.4	7.2	5.1	112.1	17.7	88.9	5.5	1.0	. . .	21.9	19.8	2.1
1984	288.9	131.9	7.8	5.6	122.7	20.1	96.3	6.3	1.4	. . .	25.2	22.8	2.4
1985	316.8	142.8	8.2	6.0	133.1	22.1	104.0	7.0	1.5	. . .	29.0	26.2	2.7
1986	340.9	155.4	8.9	6.8	144.7	24.1	112.6	8.1	1.8	. . .	31.1	27.5	3.5
1987	358.5	168.5	9.1	6.8	157.3	25.7	122.7	8.9	2.1	. . .	29.9	27.2	2.7
1988	386.1	183.3	11.7	9.1	169.4	27.2	132.7	9.4	2.2	. . .	30.0	28.3	1.7
1989	417.2	199.9	12.3	9.4	185.6	30.1	145.6	10.0	2.1	. . .	33.3	31.6	1.7
1990	443.3	213.7	12.9	10.0	198.7	31.8	157.0	9.9	2.1	. . .	34.5	32.7	1.8
1991	473.1	230.2	13.5	10.3	214.5	33.2	171.1	10.2	2.2	. . .	33.6	31.6	1.9
1992	496.7	241.2	14.7	11.4	224.2	34.6	178.6	11.0	2.3	. . .	30.9	28.8	2.0
1993	516.1	247.8	14.8	11.3	230.5	37.0	181.3	12.1	2.6	. . .	28.7	26.7	2.1
1994	550.0	264.0	15.9	12.0	245.4	39.7	192.4	13.3	2.7	. . .	29.4	27.4	2.0
1995	577.9	270.7	17.2	13.3	251.0	42.2	195.3	13.4	2.6	. . .	31.8	29.8	2.0
1996	610.4	283.7	17.8	13.7	262.9	44.4	204.2	14.4	3.0	. . .	34.1	32.2	2.0
1997	644.6	300.9	19.3	14.9	278.4	47.4	215.5	15.6	3.3	. . .	36.2	34.2	2.1
1998	682.9	314.2	20.9	16.2	290.0	50.6	222.5	16.9	3.3	. . .	37.8	35.6	2.2
1999	730.9	332.4	21.9	17.1	307.1	55.6	233.7	17.8	3.3	. . .	38.6	36.0	2.5
2000	779.2	352.6	23.1	18.0	326.2	61.1	246.8	18.3	3.3	. . .	43.5	40.8	2.7
2001	814.9	368.6	22.9	17.6	342.7	61.6	261.4	19.8	3.0	. . .	42.1	39.3	2.8
2002	851.9	392.9	22.8	17.1	366.9	62.8	282.6	21.5	3.2	. . .	35.8	32.9	2.9
2003	903.8	416.9	24.5	18.3	388.9	65.9	298.5	24.4	3.5	. . .	31.3	27.9	3.4
2004	943.6	449.3	27.4	20.4	417.3	69.9	318.9	28.5	4.7	. . .	31.8	28.2	3.5
2005	988.8	482.8	30.1	22.5	446.8	76.4	338.4	32.0	5.9	. . .	36.6	32.6	3.9
2006	1 050.4	514.5	31.9	23.9	476.3	81.8	360.0	34.5	6.2	. . .	40.1	35.8	4.3
2007	1 108.8	543.1	34.2	25.7	503.1	85.4	381.2	36.5	5.8	. . .	41.9	37.3	4.5

[1]Includes components not shown separately.
. . . = Not available.

Table 6-13. Local Government Current Receipts and Expenditures—*Continued*

(National income and product accounts, calendar years, billions of dollars.)   **NIPA Table 3.21**

Year	Total	Federal grants-in-aid	State grants-in-aid	From business, net	From persons	Total ¹	Consumption expenditures	Government social benefits to persons	Grants-in-aid to state governments	Interest payments	Total	Social insurance funds	Other
1959	8.3	0.4	7.7	0.1	0.1	24.1	22.1	0.7	0.2	1.0	2.8	...	2.8
1960	9.4	0.5	8.6	0.1	0.2	26.4	24.2	0.8	0.2	1.2	3.4	...	3.4
1961	10.4	0.6	9.4	0.2	0.3	29.1	26.6	0.9	0.3	1.3	3.5	...	3.5
1962	11.5	0.6	10.3	0.2	0.3	30.9	28.3	0.9	0.3	1.4	4.3	...	4.3
1963	12.6	0.8	11.3	0.2	0.3	33.2	30.4	1.0	0.3	1.5	5.0	...	5.0
1964	14.0	1.1	12.4	0.2	0.3	36.3	33.3	1.0	0.3	1.7	5.5	...	5.5
1965	15.9	1.1	14.3	0.3	0.3	39.6	36.3	1.1	0.3	1.8	5.9	...	5.9
1966	18.6	1.2	16.7	0.2	0.4	44.2	40.5	1.3	0.4	2.0	5.7	...	5.7
1967	21.6	1.5	19.1	0.4	0.6	48.9	44.7	1.6	0.5	2.1	7.0	...	7.0
1968	24.2	1.1	22.0	0.4	0.7	55.2	50.2	2.0	0.6	2.4	6.5	...	6.5
1969	27.7	1.3	25.4	0.4	0.7	62.4	56.6	2.4	0.8	2.5	6.8	...	6.8
1970	33.6	3.2	29.2	0.4	0.8	72.0	64.9	3.2	0.9	3.1	8.3	...	8.3
1971	38.2	3.8	33.0	0.5	0.9	81.6	72.9	4.0	1.0	3.8	8.2	...	8.2
1972	44.4	5.9	36.9	0.5	1.1	90.6	80.6	4.5	1.1	4.3	9.9	...	9.9
1973	51.8	9.0	41.1	0.7	1.0	100.4	89.5	4.7	1.2	4.9	12.4	...	12.4
1974	56.6	8.7	45.9	0.9	1.1	112.5	100.1	5.4	1.3	5.6	10.1	...	10.1
1975	65.0	11.2	51.4	1.0	1.4	129.1	114.1	6.6	1.7	6.4	7.4	...	7.4
1976	72.6	13.6	56.2	1.1	1.7	140.9	123.9	7.3	2.3	7.2	9.1	...	9.1
1977	79.9	16.0	60.7	1.3	1.9	153.9	135.3	8.0	2.4	7.9	10.6	...	10.6
1978	91.4	20.4	67.3	1.5	2.2	168.5	148.5	8.7	2.5	8.6	11.1	...	11.1
1979	97.8	18.1	75.4	1.8	2.6	182.8	161.3	8.9	2.2	9.9	7.7	...	7.7
1980	106.4	17.6	83.8	2.0	3.0	201.0	177.2	9.9	2.3	11.2	6.6	...	6.6
1981	111.3	14.8	90.4	2.4	3.7	219.4	192.6	10.4	2.7	13.4	6.8	...	6.8
1982	114.8	13.5	94.5	2.7	4.1	237.9	208.2	10.2	3.1	15.8	5.8	...	5.8
1983	119.5	13.0	99.0	3.0	4.5	256.0	221.5	11.0	4.2	18.8	5.7	...	5.7
1984	130.6	13.3	108.7	3.4	5.2	275.9	237.4	11.4	5.0	21.5	13.1	...	13.1
1985	142.7	13.6	120.0	3.5	5.7	301.6	260.6	12.1	5.2	23.0	15.2	...	15.2
1986	152.4	13.2	128.9	3.9	6.5	329.0	286.6	12.9	5.3	23.1	11.9	...	11.9
1987	157.4	9.0	137.8	4.0	6.7	351.3	302.7	13.4	5.5	28.6	7.2	...	7.2
1988	168.8	9.5	148.1	4.3	6.9	372.4	321.5	14.1	5.6	30.0	13.6	...	13.6
1989	178.8	6.8	159.5	5.1	7.5	400.0	344.1	15.0	5.8	34.0	17.2	...	17.2
1990	189.6	6.7	169.4	5.5	8.0	433.0	373.2	16.6	6.2	35.6	10.3	...	10.3
1991	203.5	7.0	181.9	5.9	8.7	461.2	395.6	18.9	7.6	37.7	11.9	...	11.9
1992	218.6	7.4	194.8	6.7	9.8	485.3	416.5	20.5	9.0	37.9	11.4	...	11.4
1993	232.9	7.9	206.0	7.7	11.4	504.7	434.4	21.6	10.1	37.2	11.4	...	11.4
1994	250.2	9.8	218.9	8.6	12.9	530.1	456.8	22.4	11.0	38.6	19.8	...	19.8
1995	266.4	11.1	231.6	9.4	14.3	556.0	480.8	22.9	11.1	39.9	21.9	...	21.9
1996	281.7	13.4	242.4	10.2	15.7	581.3	503.6	21.8	12.0	42.5	29.2	...	29.2
1997	297.7	14.1	255.1	11.1	17.3	607.5	526.8	20.8	13.5	44.9	37.1	...	37.1
1998	322.7	17.8	273.9	12.3	18.7	634.9	552.4	21.1	13.3	46.5	48.0	...	48.0
1999	350.9	20.3	297.2	13.1	20.2	669.1	585.6	22.1	12.9	47.0	61.8	...	61.8
2000	375.4	19.9	319.4	14.2	21.9	715.0	626.3	23.0	14.0	50.2	64.2	...	64.2
2001	399.0	21.7	337.5	15.8	23.9	754.7	660.7	24.0	14.9	53.4	60.2	...	60.2
2002	418.5	23.9	352.6	16.4	25.6	795.2	699.2	25.4	15.5	53.8	56.7	...	56.7
2003	454.0	36.6	371.4	17.9	28.1	845.4	745.5	27.3	16.2	55.3	58.5	...	58.5
2004	463.4	27.3	386.8	17.4	31.9	887.4	784.8	28.9	18.0	54.4	56.2	...	56.2
2005	475.5	30.8	396.7	16.3	31.6	938.2	835.6	30.2	16.7	54.0	50.6	...	50.6
2006	499.5	26.2	419.9	21.0	32.4	994.4	890.7	30.7	15.2	55.8	55.9	...	55.9
2007	529.1	29.1	444.1	22.2	33.8	1 062.8	954.1	32.4	15.8	58.4	46.0	...	46.0

¹Includes components not shown separately.
. . . = Not available.

Section 6c: Federal Government Budget Accounts

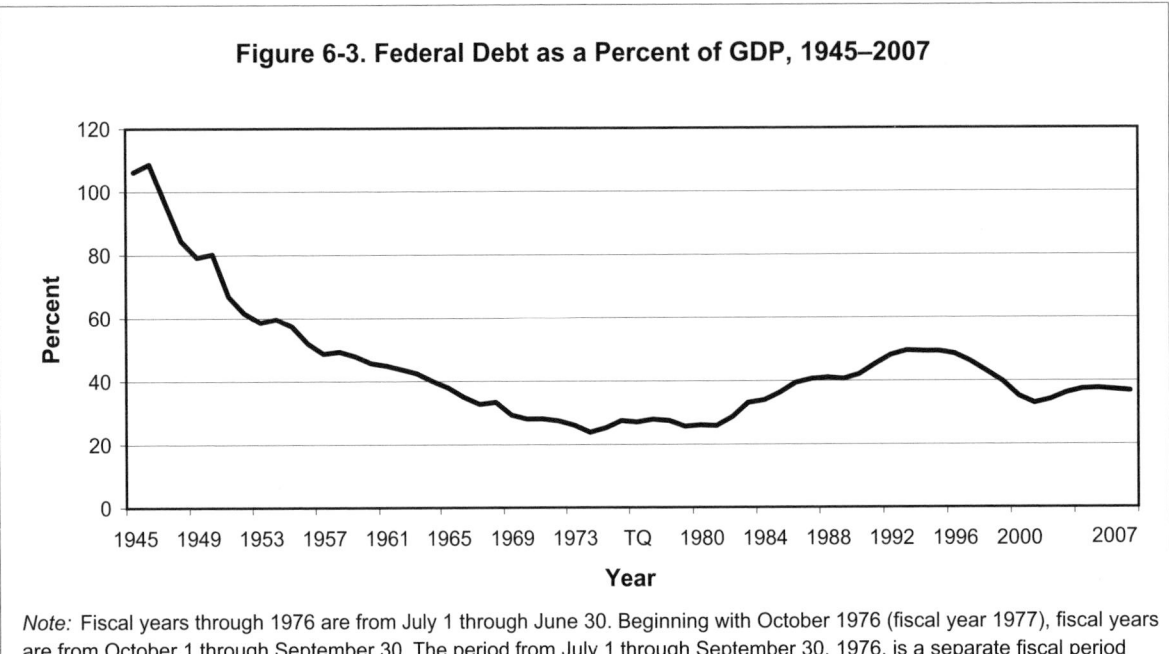

Figure 6-3. Federal Debt as a Percent of GDP, 1945–2007

Note: Fiscal years through 1976 are from July 1 through June 30. Beginning with October 1976 (fiscal year 1977), fiscal years are from October 1 through September 30. The period from July 1 through September 30, 1976, is a separate fiscal period known as the transition quarter (TQ) and is not included in any fiscal year.

- As fiscal year 2007 ended on September 30, 2007—shortly before the onset of the latest recession—the federal debt held by the public stood at 36.8 percent of GDP—slightly improved since 2005 but well above the most recent low achieved at the end of fiscal year 2001. (The "debt held by the public" is generally thought to be a more significant measure of the burden of the federal debt on credit markets than the gross debt, because it nets out the intragovernmental debt of the Social Security and other U.S. government trust funds.) (Table 6-15)

- This measure has increased since then and can be expected to continue to do so: the recession reduces revenues and increases spending, as a result of both automatic stabilizer programs, such as unemployment insurance, and the unprecedented level of spending for stimulus and financial rescue programs. The Congressional Budget Office has estimated that the debt held by the public was 40.8 percent of GDP at the end of fiscal year 2008 and could rise to 82.4 percent by the end of 2019 under the President's budget. This is not as high as the level reached at the end of World War II, and it has been argued that rapid economic progress was achieved after that war despite the huge initial debt overhang. But the rapid reduction in the debt/GDP ratio in those years was a result of balanced (on average) budgets—which will be much harder to achieve in coming years—and was helped by some episodes of inflation, which the public might prefer to avoid. (Tables 6-14, 6-15, 8-1 and 20-2)

- From the end of fiscal year 2001 through the end of fiscal year 2007, foreign investors bought 72 percent of the Treasury debt sold to the public to finance the deficits of 2002 through 2007. At the end of 2007, foreign residents held $2.24 trillion of Treasury debt, 44 percent of the $5.0 trillion total debt held by the public. (Table 6-15) At that time, foreign central banks held 69 percent of the federal debt held by foreign residents, according to U.S. budget documents (*Budget of the United States Government for Fiscal Year 2009, Analytical Perspectives,* p. 240).

Table 6-14. Federal Government Receipts and Outlays by Fiscal Year [1]

(Budget accounts, millions of dollars.)

| Year | Fiscal year GDP | Receipts, outlays, deficit, and financing | | | | | | | | Receipts by source | | | | |
| | | Total receipts, net | Total outlays, net | Budget surplus or deficit (-) | | | Sources of financing, total | | Individual income taxes | Corporate income taxes | Social insurance taxes and contributions | | |
				Total	On-budget	Off-budget	Borrowing from the public	Other financing			Employ-ment taxes and contri-butions	Unemploy-ment insurance	Other retirement contri-butions
1940	96 800	6 548	9 468	-2 920	-3 484	564	. . .	. . .	892	1 197	725	1 015	45
1941	114 100	8 712	13 653	-4 941	-5 594	653	5 451	-510	1 314	2 124	827	1 056	57
1942	144 300	14 634	35 137	-20 503	-21 333	830	19 530	973	3 263	4 719	1 064	1 299	89
1943	180 300	24 001	78 555	-54 554	-55 595	1 041	60 013	-5 459	6 505	9 557	1 338	1 477	229
1944	209 200	43 747	91 304	-47 557	-48 735	1 178	57 030	-9 473	19 705	14 838	1 557	1 644	272
1945	221 400	45 159	92 712	-47 553	-48 720	1 167	50 386	-2 833	18 372	15 988	1 592	1 568	291
1946	222 700	39 296	55 232	-15 936	-16 964	1 028	6 679	9 257	16 098	11 883	1 517	1 316	282
1947	233 200	38 514	34 496	4 018	2 861	1 157	-17 522	13 504	17 935	8 615	1 835	1 329	259
1948	256 000	41 560	29 764	11 796	10 548	1 248	-8 069	-3 727	19 315	9 678	2 168	1 343	239
1949	271 100	39 415	38 835	580	-684	1 263	-1 948	1 368	15 552	11 192	2 246	1 205	330
1950	273 000	39 443	42 562	-3 119	-4 702	1 583	4 701	-1 582	15 755	10 449	2 648	1 332	358
1951	320 600	51 616	45 514	6 102	4 259	1 843	-4 697	-1 405	21 616	14 101	3 688	1 609	377
1952	348 600	66 167	67 686	-1 519	-3 383	1 864	432	1 087	27 934	21 226	4 315	1 712	418
1953	372 900	69 608	76 101	-6 493	-8 259	1 766	3 625	2 868	29 816	21 238	4 722	1 675	423
1954	377 300	69 701	70 855	-1 154	-2 831	1 677	6 116	-4 962	29 542	21 101	5 192	1 561	455
1955	394 600	65 451	68 444	-2 993	-4 091	1 098	2 117	876	28 747	17 861	5 981	1 449	431
1956	427 200	74 587	70 640	3 947	2 494	1 452	-4 460	513	32 188	20 880	7 059	1 690	571
1957	450 300	79 990	76 578	3 412	2 639	773	-2 836	-576	35 620	21 167	7 405	1 950	642
1958	460 500	79 636	82 405	-2 769	-3 315	546	7 016	-4 247	34 724	20 074	8 624	1 933	682
1959	491 500	79 249	92 098	-12 849	-12 149	-700	8 365	4 484	36 719	17 309	8 821	2 131	770
1960	517 900	92 492	92 191	301	510	-209	2 139	-2 440	40 715	21 494	11 248	2 667	768
1961	530 800	94 388	97 723	-3 335	-3 766	431	1 517	1 818	41 338	20 954	12 679	2 903	857
1962	567 600	99 676	106 821	-7 146	-5 881	-1 265	9 653	-2 507	45 571	20 523	12 835	3 337	875
1963	598 700	106 560	111 316	-4 756	-3 966	-789	5 968	-1 212	47 588	21 579	14 746	4 112	946
1964	640 400	112 613	118 528	-5 915	-6 546	632	2 871	3 044	48 697	23 493	16 959	3 997	1 007
1965	687 100	116 817	118 228	-1 411	-1 605	194	3 929	-2 518	48 792	25 461	17 358	3 803	1 081
1966	752 900	130 835	134 532	-3 698	-3 068	-630	2 936	762	55 446	30 073	20 662	3 755	1 129
1967	811 800	148 822	157 464	-8 643	-12 620	3 978	2 912	5 731	61 526	33 971	27 823	3 575	1 221
1968	866 600	152 973	178 134	-25 161	-27 742	2 581	22 919	2 242	68 726	28 665	29 224	3 346	1 354
1969	948 600	186 882	183 640	3 242	-507	3 749	-11 437	8 195	87 249	36 678	34 236	3 328	1 451
1970	1 012 200	192 807	195 649	-2 842	-8 694	5 852	5 090	-2 248	90 412	32 829	39 133	3 464	1 765
1971	1 079 900	187 139	210 172	-23 033	-26 052	3 019	19 839	3 194	86 230	26 785	41 699	3 674	1 952
1972	1 178 300	207 309	230 681	-23 373	-26 068	2 695	19 340	4 033	94 737	32 166	46 120	4 357	2 097
1973	1 307 600	230 799	245 707	-14 908	-15 246	338	18 533	-3 625	103 246	36 153	54 876	6 051	2 187
1974	1 439 300	263 224	269 359	-6 135	-7 198	1 063	2 789	3 346	118 952	38 620	65 888	6 837	2 347
1975	1 560 700	279 090	332 332	-53 242	-54 148	906	51 001	2 241	122 386	40 621	75 199	6 771	2 565
1976	1 736 500	298 060	371 792	-73 732	-69 427	-4 306	82 704	-8 972	131 603	41 409	79 901	8 054	2 814
TQ[1]	456 700	81 232	95 975	-14 744	-14 065	-679	18 105	-3 361	38 801	8 460	21 801	2 698	720
1977	1 974 300	355 559	409 218	-53 659	-49 933	-3 726	53 595	64	157 626	54 892	92 199	11 312	2 974
1978	2 217 000	399 561	458 746	-59 185	-55 416	-3 770	58 022	1 163	180 988	59 952	103 881	13 850	3 237
1979	2 500 700	463 302	504 028	-40 726	-39 633	-1 093	33 180	7 546	217 841	65 677	120 058	15 387	3 494
1980	2 726 700	517 112	590 941	-73 830	-73 141	-689	71 617	2 213	244 069	64 600	138 748	15 336	3 719
1981	3 054 700	599 272	678 241	-78 968	-73 859	-5 109	77 487	1 481	285 917	61 137	162 973	15 763	3 984
1982	3 227 600	617 766	745 743	-127 977	-120 593	-7 384	135 165	-7 188	297 744	49 207	180 686	16 600	4 212
1983	3 440 700	600 562	808 364	-207 802	-207 692	-110	212 693	-4 891	288 938	37 022	185 766	18 799	4 429
1984	3 840 200	666 486	851 853	-185 367	-185 269	-98	169 707	15 660	298 415	56 893	209 658	25 138	4 580
1985	4 141 500	734 088	946 396	-212 308	-221 529	9 222	200 285	12 023	334 531	61 331	234 646	25 758	4 759
1986	4 412 400	769 215	990 441	-221 227	-237 915	16 688	233 363	-12 136	348 959	63 143	255 062	24 098	4 742
1987	4 647 100	854 353	1 004 083	-149 730	-168 357	18 627	149 130	600	392 557	83 926	273 028	25 575	4 715
1988	5 008 600	909 303	1 064 481	-155 178	-192 265	37 087	161 863	-6 685	401 181	94 508	305 093	24 584	4 658
1989	5 400 500	991 190	1 143 829	-152 639	-205 393	52 754	139 100	13 539	445 690	103 291	332 859	22 011	4 546
1990	5 735 400	1 032 094	1 253 130	-221 036	-277 626	56 590	220 842	194	466 884	93 507	353 891	21 635	4 522
1991	5 935 100	1 055 093	1 324 331	-269 238	-321 435	52 198	277 441	-8 203	467 827	98 086	370 526	20 922	4 568
1992	6 239 900	1 091 328	1 381 649	-290 321	-340 408	50 087	310 738	-20 417	475 964	100 270	385 491	23 410	4 788
1993	6 575 500	1 154 471	1 409 522	-255 051	-300 398	45 347	248 659	6 392	509 680	117 520	396 939	26 556	4 805
1994	6 961 300	1 258 721	1 461 907	-203 186	-258 840	55 654	184 669	18 517	543 055	140 385	428 810	28 004	4 661
1995	7 325 800	1 351 932	1 515 884	-163 952	-226 367	62 415	171 313	-7 361	590 244	157 004	451 045	28 878	4 550
1996	7 694 100	1 453 177	1 560 608	-107 431	-174 019	66 588	129 695	-22 264	656 417	171 824	476 361	28 584	4 469
1997	8 182 400	1 579 423	1 601 307	-21 884	-103 248	81 364	38 271	-16 387	737 466	182 293	506 751	28 202	4 418
1998	8 627 900	1 721 955	1 652 685	69 270	-29 925	99 195	-51 245	-18 025	828 586	188 677	540 014	27 484	4 333
1999	9 125 300	1 827 645	1 702 035	125 610	1 920	123 690	-88 736	-36 874	879 480	184 680	580 880	26 480	4 473
2000	9 709 800	2 025 457	1 789 216	236 241	86 422	149 819	-222 559	-13 682	1 004 462	207 289	620 451	27 640	4 761
2001	10 057 900	1 991 426	1 863 190	128 236	-32 445	160 681	-90 189	-38 047	994 339	151 075	661 442	27 812	4 713
2002	10 377 400	1 853 395	2 011 153	-157 758	-317 417	159 659	220 812	-63 054	858 345	148 044	668 547	27 619	4 594
2003	10 808 600	1 782 532	2 160 117	-377 585	-538 418	160 833	373 016	4 569	793 699	131 778	674 981	33 366	4 631
2004	11 499 900	1 880 279	2 293 006	-412 727	-567 961	155 234	382 101	30 626	808 959	189 371	689 360	39 453	4 594
2005	12 237 900	2 153 859	2 472 205	-318 346	-493 611	175 265	296 668	21 678	927 222	278 282	747 664	42 002	4 459
2006	13 015 500	2 407 254	2 655 435	-248 181	-434 494	186 313	236 760	11 421	1 043 908	353 915	790 043	43 420	4 358
2007	13 667 500	2 568 239	2 730 241	-162 002	-343 454	181 452	206 157	-44 155	1 163 472	370 243	824 258	41 091	4 258

[1]Fiscal years through 1976 are from July 1 through June 30. Beginning with October 1976 (fiscal year 1977), fiscal years are from October 1 through September 30. The period from July 1 through September 30, 1976, is a separate fiscal period known as the transition quarter (TQ) and is not included in any fiscal year.
. . . = Not available.

Table 6-14. Federal Government Receipts and Outlays by Fiscal Year [1]—Continued

(Budget accounts, millions of dollars.)

| Year | Receipts by source—Continued | | | | Outlays by function | | | | | | |
	Excise taxes	Estate and gift taxes	Customs deposits	Miscel-laneous receipts	National defense	International affairs	General science, space, and technology	Energy	Natural resources and environment	Agriculture	Commerce and housing credit
1940	1 977	353	331	14	1 660	51	0	88	997	369	550
1941	2 552	403	365	14	6 435	145	0	91	817	339	398
1942	3 399	420	369	11	25 658	968	4	156	819	344	1 521
1943	4 096	441	308	50	66 699	1 286	1	116	726	343	2 151
1944	4 759	507	417	48	79 143	1 449	48	65	642	1 275	624
1945	6 265	637	341	105	82 965	1 913	111	25	455	1 635	-2 630
1946	6 998	668	424	109	42 681	1 935	34	41	482	610	-1 857
1947	7 211	771	477	84	12 808	5 791	5	18	700	814	-923
1948	7 356	890	403	168	9 105	4 566	1	292	780	69	306
1949	7 502	780	367	241	13 150	6 052	48	341	1 080	1 924	800
1950	7 550	698	407	247	13 724	4 673	55	327	1 308	2 049	1 035
1951	8 648	708	609	261	23 566	3 647	51	383	1 310	-323	1 228
1952	8 852	818	533	359	46 089	2 691	49	474	1 233	176	1 278
1953	9 877	881	596	379	52 802	2 119	49	425	1 289	2 253	910
1954	9 945	934	542	429	49 266	1 596	46	432	1 007	1 817	-184
1955	9 131	924	585	341	42 729	2 223	74	325	940	3 514	92
1956	9 929	1 161	682	427	42 523	2 414	79	174	870	3 486	506
1957	10 534	1 365	735	573	45 430	3 147	122	240	1 098	2 288	1 424
1958	10 638	1 393	782	787	46 815	3 364	141	348	1 407	2 411	930
1959	10 578	1 333	925	662	49 015	3 144	294	382	1 632	4 509	1 933
1960	11 676	1 606	1 105	1 212	48 130	2 988	599	464	1 559	2 623	1 618
1961	11 860	1 896	982	918	49 601	3 184	1 042	510	1 779	2 641	1 203
1962	12 534	2 016	1 142	843	52 345	5 639	1 723	604	2 044	3 562	1 424
1963	13 194	2 167	1 205	1 022	53 400	5 308	3 051	530	2 251	4 384	62
1964	13 731	2 394	1 252	1 086	54 757	4 945	4 897	572	2 364	4 609	418
1965	14 570	2 716	1 442	1 594	50 620	5 273	5 823	699	2 531	3 954	1 157
1966	13 062	3 066	1 767	1 876	58 111	5 580	6 717	612	2 719	2 447	3 245
1967	13 719	2 978	1 901	2 107	71 417	5 566	6 233	782	2 869	2 990	3 979
1968	14 079	3 051	2 038	2 491	81 926	5 301	5 524	1 037	2 988	4 544	4 280
1969	15 222	3 491	2 319	2 909	82 497	4 600	5 020	1 010	2 900	5 826	-119
1970	15 705	3 644	2 430	3 424	81 692	4 330	4 511	997	3 065	5 166	2 112
1971	16 614	3 735	2 591	3 858	78 872	4 159	4 182	1 035	3 915	4 290	2 366
1972	15 477	5 436	3 287	3 632	79 174	4 781	4 175	1 296	4 241	5 227	2 222
1973	16 260	4 917	3 188	3 920	76 681	4 149	4 032	1 237	4 775	4 821	931
1974	16 844	5 035	3 334	5 368	79 347	5 710	3 980	1 303	5 697	2 194	4 705
1975	16 551	4 611	3 676	6 712	86 509	7 097	3 991	2 916	7 346	2 997	9 947
1976	16 963	5 216	4 074	8 027	89 619	6 433	4 373	4 204	8 184	3 109	7 619
TQ[1]	4 473	1 455	1 212	1 611	22 269	2 458	1 162	1 129	2 524	972	931
1977	17 548	7 327	5 150	6 531	97 241	6 353	4 736	5 770	10 032	6 734	3 093
1978	18 376	5 285	6 573	7 419	104 495	7 482	4 926	7 991	10 983	11 301	6 254
1979	18 745	5 411	7 439	9 252	116 342	7 459	5 234	9 179	12 135	11 176	4 686
1980	24 329	6 389	7 174	12 748	133 995	12 714	5 831	10 156	13 858	8 774	9 390
1981	40 839	6 787	8 083	13 790	157 513	13 104	6 468	15 166	13 568	11 241	8 206
1982	36 311	7 991	8 854	16 161	185 309	12 300	7 199	13 527	12 998	15 866	6 256
1983	35 300	6 053	8 655	15 600	209 903	11 848	7 934	9 353	12 672	22 814	6 681
1984	37 361	6 010	11 370	17 060	227 413	15 876	8 317	7 073	12 593	13 526	6 959
1985	35 992	6 422	12 079	18 571	252 748	16 176	8 626	5 608	13 357	25 477	4 337
1986	32 919	6 958	13 327	20 008	273 375	14 152	8 976	4 690	13 639	31 368	5 059
1987	32 457	7 493	15 085	19 518	281 999	11 649	9 215	4 072	13 363	26 513	6 435
1988	35 227	7 594	16 198	20 259	290 361	10 471	10 840	2 296	14 606	17 138	19 164
1989	34 386	8 745	16 334	23 328	303 559	9 585	12 837	2 705	16 182	16 861	29 710
1990	35 345	11 500	16 707	28 103	299 331	13 764	14 443	3 341	17 080	11 806	67 600
1991	42 402	11 138	15 949	23 675	273 292	15 851	16 110	2 436	18 559	15 056	76 271
1992	45 569	11 143	17 359	27 333	298 350	16 107	16 407	4 499	20 025	15 088	10 919
1993	48 057	12 577	18 802	19 535	291 086	17 248	17 029	4 319	20 239	20 246	-21 853
1994	55 225	15 225	20 099	23 258	281 642	17 083	16 226	5 218	21 026	14 915	-4 228
1995	57 484	14 763	19 301	28 663	272 066	16 434	16 723	4 936	21 915	9 672	-17 808
1996	54 014	17 189	18 670	25 649	265 753	13 496	16 708	2 839	21 524	9 036	-10 478
1997	56 924	19 845	17 928	25 596	270 505	15 228	17 173	1 475	21 227	8 890	-14 639
1998	57 673	24 076	18 297	32 815	268 207	13 109	18 217	1 270	22 300	12 078	1 008
1999	70 414	27 782	18 336	35 120	274 785	15 243	18 121	911	23 968	22 880	2 642
2000	68 865	29 010	19 914	43 065	294 394	17 216	18 633	-761	25 031	36 459	3 208
2001	66 232	28 400	19 369	38 044	304 759	16 493	19 784	9	25 623	26 253	5 732
2002	66 989	26 507	18 602	34 148	348 482	22 351	20 767	475	29 454	21 966	-406
2003	67 524	21 959	19 862	34 732	404 778	21 209	20 873	-736	29 703	22 497	728
2004	69 855	24 831	21 083	32 773	455 847	26 891	23 053	-166	30 725	15 440	5 266
2005	73 094	24 764	23 379	32 993	495 326	34 595	23 628	429	28 023	26 566	7 567
2006	73 961	27 877	24 810	44 962	521 840	29 549	23 616	782	33 055	25 970	6 188
2007	65 069	26 044	26 010	47 794	552 568	28 510	25 566	-860	31 772	17 663	488

[1]Fiscal years through 1976 are from July 1 through June 30. Beginning with October 1976 (fiscal year 1977), fiscal years are from October 1 through September 30. The period from July 1 through September 30, 1976, is a separate fiscal period known as the transition quarter (TQ) and is not included in any fiscal year.

Table 6-14. Federal Government Receipts and Outlays by Fiscal Year [1]—*Continued*

(Budget accounts, millions of dollars.)

Year	Outlays by function—*Continued*										
	Transpor-tation	Community and regional development	Education, employment, and social services	Health	Medicare	Income security	Social Security	Veterans benefits and services	Administra-tion of justice	General government	Net interest
1940	392	285	1 972	55	0	1 514	28	570	81	274	899
1941	353	123	1 592	60	0	1 855	91	560	92	306	943
1942	1 283	113	1 062	71	0	1 828	137	501	117	397	1 052
1943	3 220	219	375	92	0	1 739	177	276	154	673	1 529
1944	3 901	238	160	174	0	1 503	217	-126	192	900	2 219
1945	3 654	243	134	211	0	1 137	267	110	178	581	3 112
1946	1 970	200	85	201	0	2 384	358	2 465	176	825	4 111
1947	1 130	302	102	177	0	2 820	466	6 344	176	1 114	4 204
1948	787	78	191	162	0	2 499	558	6 457	170	1 045	4 341
1949	916	-33	178	197	0	3 174	657	6 599	184	824	4 523
1950	967	30	241	268	0	4 097	781	8 834	193	986	4 812
1951	956	47	235	323	0	3 352	1 565	5 526	218	1 097	4 665
1952	1 124	73	339	347	0	3 655	2 063	5 341	267	1 163	4 701
1953	1 264	117	441	336	0	3 823	2 717	4 519	243	1 209	5 156
1954	1 229	100	370	307	0	4 434	3 352	4 613	257	799	4 811
1955	1 246	129	445	291	0	5 071	4 427	4 675	256	651	4 850
1956	1 450	92	591	359	0	4 734	5 478	4 891	302	1 201	5 079
1957	1 662	135	590	479	0	5 427	6 661	5 005	303	1 360	5 354
1958	2 334	169	643	541	0	7 535	8 219	5 350	325	655	5 604
1959	3 655	211	789	685	0	8 239	9 737	5 443	356	926	5 762
1960	4 126	224	968	795	0	7 378	11 602	5 441	366	1 184	6 947
1961	3 987	275	1 063	913	0	9 683	12 474	5 705	400	1 354	6 716
1962	4 290	469	1 241	1 198	0	9 207	14 365	5 619	429	1 049	6 889
1963	4 596	574	1 458	1 451	0	9 311	15 788	5 514	465	1 230	7 740
1964	5 242	933	1 555	1 788	0	9 657	16 620	5 675	489	1 518	8 199
1965	5 763	1 114	2 140	1 791	0	9 469	17 460	5 716	536	1 499	8 591
1966	5 730	1 105	4 363	2 543	64	9 678	20 694	5 916	564	1 603	9 386
1967	5 936	1 108	6 453	3 351	2 748	10 261	21 725	6 735	618	1 719	10 268
1968	6 316	1 382	7 634	4 390	4 649	11 816	23 854	7 032	659	1 757	11 090
1969	6 526	1 552	7 548	5 162	5 695	13 076	27 298	7 631	766	1 939	12 699
1970	7 008	2 392	8 634	5 907	6 213	15 655	30 270	8 669	959	2 320	14 380
1971	8 052	2 917	9 849	6 843	6 622	22 946	35 872	9 768	1 307	2 442	14 841
1972	8 392	3 423	12 529	8 674	7 479	27 650	40 157	10 720	1 684	2 960	15 478
1973	9 066	4 605	12 745	9 356	8 052	28 276	49 090	12 003	2 174	9 774	17 349
1974	9 172	4 229	12 457	10 733	9 639	33 713	55 867	13 374	2 505	10 032	21 449
1975	10 918	4 322	16 022	12 930	12 875	50 176	64 658	16 584	3 028	10 374	23 244
1976	13 739	5 442	18 910	15 734	15 834	60 799	73 899	18 419	3 430	9 706	26 727
TQ[1]	3 358	1 569	5 169	3 924	4 264	14 985	19 763	3 960	918	3 878	6 949
1977	14 829	7 021	21 104	17 302	19 345	61 060	85 061	18 022	3 701	12 791	29 901
1978	15 521	11 841	26 710	18 524	22 768	61 505	93 861	18 961	3 923	11 961	35 458
1979	18 079	10 480	30 223	20 494	26 495	66 376	104 073	19 914	4 286	12 241	42 633
1980	21 329	11 252	31 843	23 169	32 090	86 557	118 547	21 169	4 702	12 975	52 533
1981	23 379	10 568	33 152	26 866	39 149	100 299	139 584	22 973	4 908	11 373	68 766
1982	20 625	8 347	26 612	27 445	46 567	108 155	155 964	23 938	4 842	10 861	85 032
1983	21 334	7 564	26 197	28 641	52 588	123 031	170 724	24 824	5 246	11 181	89 808
1984	23 669	7 673	26 922	30 417	57 540	113 352	178 223	25 588	5 811	11 756	111 102
1985	25 838	7 680	28 596	33 542	65 822	128 979	188 623	26 262	6 426	11 519	129 478
1986	28 117	7 233	29 779	35 936	70 164	120 633	198 757	26 327	6 735	12 493	136 017
1987	26 222	5 051	28 924	39 967	75 120	124 088	207 353	26 750	7 715	7 492	138 611
1988	27 272	5 294	30 936	44 487	78 878	130 377	219 341	29 386	9 397	9 401	151 803
1989	27 608	5 362	35 333	48 390	84 964	137 426	232 542	30 031	9 644	9 320	168 981
1990	29 485	8 531	37 179	57 716	98 102	148 668	248 623	29 058	10 185	10 488	184 347
1991	31 099	6 810	41 241	71 183	104 489	172 462	269 015	31 305	12 487	11 574	194 448
1992	33 332	6 836	42 751	89 497	119 024	199 562	287 585	34 064	14 650	12 888	199 344
1993	35 004	9 146	47 397	99 415	130 552	209 969	304 585	35 671	15 193	12 947	198 713
1994	38 066	10 620	43 295	107 122	144 747	217 166	319 565	37 584	15 516	11 183	202 932
1995	39 350	10 746	51 046	115 418	159 855	223 799	335 846	37 890	16 509	13 808	232 134
1996	39 565	10 741	48 336	119 378	174 225	229 736	349 671	36 985	17 898	11 762	241 053
1997	40 767	11 049	48 991	123 843	190 016	235 032	365 251	39 313	20 618	12 557	243 984
1998	40 343	9 771	50 532	131 442	192 822	237 750	379 215	41 781	23 360	15 556	241 118
1999	42 532	11 865	50 627	141 074	190 447	242 478	390 037	43 212	26 536	15 367	229 755
2000	46 853	10 623	53 789	154 533	197 113	253 724	409 423	47 083	28 499	13 028	222 949
2001	54 447	11 773	57 173	172 270	217 384	269 774	432 958	45 039	30 202	14 361	206 167
2002	61 833	12 981	70 581	196 544	230 855	312 720	455 980	50 984	35 061	16 968	170 949
2003	67 069	18 850	82 603	219 576	249 433	334 632	474 680	57 022	35 340	23 169	153 073
2004	64 627	15 822	87 990	240 134	269 360	333 059	495 548	59 779	45 576	22 347	160 245
2005	67 894	26 264	97 567	250 614	298 638	345 847	523 305	70 151	40 019	17 010	183 986
2006	70 244	54 531	118 560	252 780	329 868	352 477	548 549	69 842	41 016	18 215	226 603
2007	72 905	29 567	91 676	266 432	375 407	365 975	586 153	72 847	41 244	17 457	237 109

[1]Fiscal years through 1976 are from July 1 through June 30. Beginning with October 1976 (fiscal year 1977), fiscal years are from October 1 through September 30. The period from July 1 through September 30, 1976, is a separate fiscal period known as the transition quarter (TQ) and is not included in any fiscal year.

Table 6-15. Federal Government Debt by Fiscal Year [1]

(Billions of dollars, except as noted.)

Year	Federal government debt held by the public at end of fiscal year		Gross federal debt at end of fiscal year held by:						
	Debt held by the public	Debt/GDP ratio (percent)	Total	Social Security funds	Other U.S. government accounts	Federal Reserve System	Private investors		
							Total	Foreign residents	Domestic investors
1945	235	106.2	260	7	18	22	213	. . .	. . .
1946	242	108.6	271	8	21	24	218	. . .	. . .
1947	224	96.2	257	9	24	22	202	. . .	. . .
1948	216	84.5	252	10	26	21	195	. . .	. . .
1949	214	79.1	253	11	27	19	195	. . .	. . .
1950	219	80.2	257	13	25	18	201	. . .	. . .
1951	214	66.9	255	15	26	23	191	. . .	. . .
1952	215	61.6	259	17	28	23	192	. . .	. . .
1953	218	58.6	266	18	29	25	194	. . .	. . .
1954	224	59.5	271	20	26	25	199	. . .	. . .
1955	227	57.4	274	21	27	24	203	. . .	. . .
1956	222	52.0	273	23	28	24	198	. . .	. . .
1957	219	48.7	272	23	30	23	196	. . .	. . .
1958	226	49.2	280	24	29	25	201	. . .	. . .
1959	235	47.8	287	23	30	26	209	. . .	. . .
1960	237	45.7	291	23	31	27	210	. . .	. . .
1961	238	44.9	293	23	31	27	211	. . .	. . .
1962	248	43.7	303	22	33	30	218	. . .	. . .
1963	254	42.4	310	21	35	32	222	. . .	. . .
1964	257	40.1	316	22	37	35	222	. . .	. . .
1965	261	38.0	322	22	39	39	222	12	210
1966	264	35.0	328	22	43	42	222	12	210
1967	267	32.8	340	26	48	47	220	11	209
1968	290	33.4	369	28	51	52	237	11	226
1969	278	29.3	366	32	56	54	224	10	214
1970	283	28.0	381	38	60	58	225	14	211
1971	303	28.1	408	41	64	66	238	32	206
1972	322	27.4	436	44	70	71	251	49	202
1973	341	26.1	466	44	81	75	266	59	207
1974	344	23.9	484	46	94	81	263	57	206
1975	395	25.3	542	48	99	85	310	66	244
1976	477	27.5	629	45	107	95	383	70	313
TQ [1]	496	27.1	644	44	105	97	399	75	324
1977	549	27.8	706	40	118	105	444	96	348
1978	607	27.4	777	35	134	115	492	121	371
1979	640	25.6	829	33	156	116	525	120	405
1980	712	26.1	909	32	165	121	591	122	469
1981	789	25.8	995	27	178	124	665	131	534
1982	925	28.6	1 137	19	193	134	790	141	649
1983	1 137	33.1	1 372	32	202	156	982	160	822
1984	1 307	34.0	1 565	32	225	155	1 152	176	976
1985	1 507	36.4	1 817	40	270	170	1 337	223	1 114
1986	1 741	39.4	2 121	46	334	191	1 550	266	1 284
1987	1 890	40.7	2 346	65	391	212	1 678	280	1 398
1988	2 052	41.0	2 601	104	445	229	1 822	346	1 476
1989	2 191	40.6	2 868	157	520	220	1 971	395	1 576
1990	2 412	42.0	3 206	215	580	234	2 177	440	1 737
1991	2 689	45.3	3 598	268	641	259	2 430	477	1 953
1992	3 000	48.1	4 002	319	683	296	2 703	535	2 168
1993	3 248	49.4	4 351	366	737	326	2 923	591	2 331
1994	3 433	49.3	4 643	423	788	355	3 078	656	2 422
1995	3 604	49.2	4 921	483	833	374	3 230	800	2 430
1996	3 734	48.5	5 181	550	898	391	3 343	993	2 350
1997	3 772	46.1	5 369	631	966	425	3 348	1 231	2 117
1998	3 721	43.1	5 478	730	1 027	458	3 263	1 224	2 039
1999	3 632	39.8	5 606	855	1 118	497	3 136	1 281	1 854
2000	3 410	35.1	5 629	1 007	1 212	511	2 898	1 058	1 840
2001	3 320	33.0	5 770	1 170	1 280	534	2 785	1 006	1 780
2002	3 540	34.1	6 198	1 329	1 329	604	2 936	1 201	1 735
2003	3 913	36.2	6 760	1 485	1 362	656	3 257	1 454	1 803
2004	4 296	37.4	7 355	1 635	1 424	700	3 595	1 799	1 797
2005	4 592	37.5	7 905	1 809	1 504	736	3 856	1 931	1 925
2006	4 829	37.1	8 451	1 994	1 628	769	4 060	2 027	2 033
2007	5 035	36.8	8 951	2 181	1 735	780	4 255	2 240	2 015

[1]Fiscal years through 1976 are from July 1 through June 30. Beginning with October 1976 (fiscal year 1977), fiscal years are from October 1 through September 30. The period from July 1 through September 30, 1976, is a separate fiscal period known as the transition quarter (TQ) and is not included in any fiscal year.
. . . = Not available.

Section 6d: Government Output and Employment

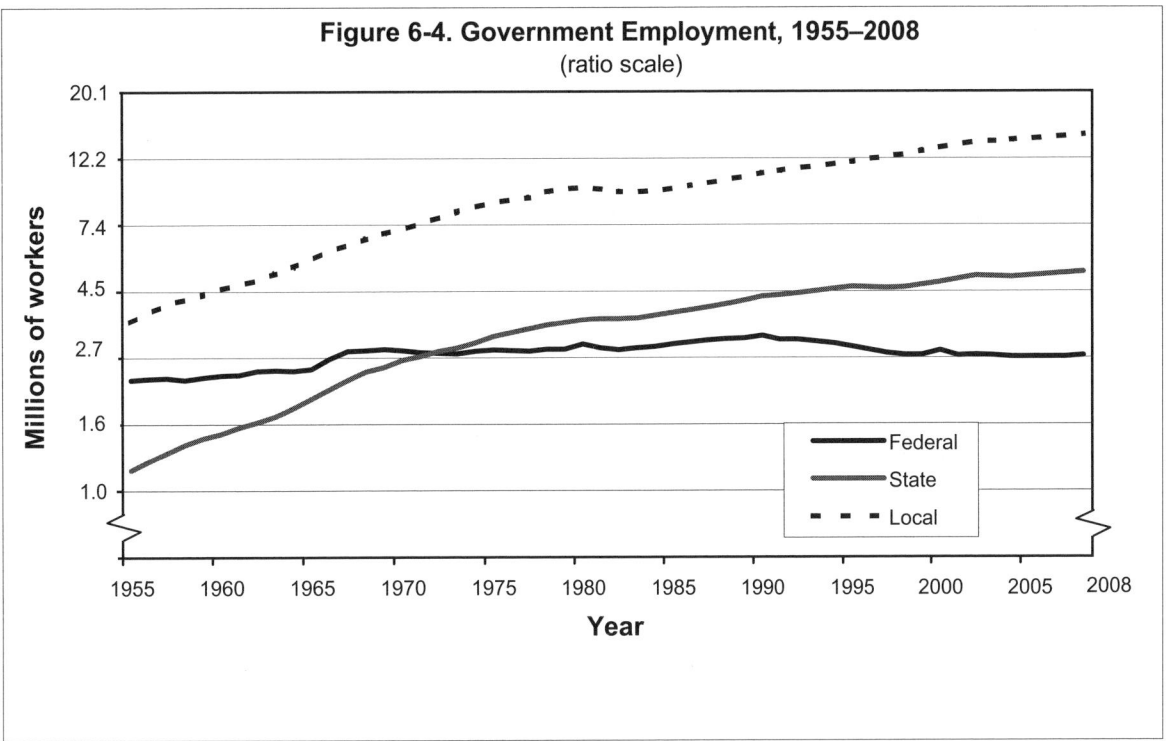

Figure 6-4. Government Employment, 1955–2008
(ratio scale)

- Since 1955, total reported employment of civilians by all levels of government has increased 220 percent—an annual rate of 2.2 percent per year—and its proportion of total nonfarm payroll employment has risen from 13.8 percent to 16.4 percent. Federal employment rose 20 percent; state government employment rose 343 percent, with half of this increase due to education; and local government rose 309 percent, with 58 percent of this increase due to education. (Tables 6-17, 10-7 and 20-4)

- Reported Department of Defense civilian employment has declined slightly since 2001, even as defense spending has been rising both absolutely and as a percentage of gross domestic product (GDP). It should be noted that the figures shown here are for civilian employees only, as compiled by the Bureau of Labor Statistics, and exclude the active-duty armed forces, defense contractors, and employees of the Central Intelligence Agency and the National Security Agency. (Table 6-17 and its notes and definitions)

- The real gross output of the federal government increased 94 percent from 1955 to 2008, with nondefense activity rising 268 percent and defense output rising 56 percent. The volume of intermediate goods and services purchased for nondefense purposes rose far faster than nondefense value added by government itself (where value added comprises the input of government employees and government-owned capital). For defense, government value added actually declined over that period, while purchases of intermediate goods and services rose 246 percent. (Table 6-16)

- Real gross output of state and local governments rose 480 percent over the same period, with value added rising 336 percent and goods and services purchased rising 1,140 percent. (Table 6-16)

Table 6-16. Chain-Type Quantity Indexes for Government Output

(Seasonally adjusted, 2000 = 100.)   NIPA Table 3.10.3

| Year and quarter | Federal government | | | | | | | | | State and local government | | |
| | Gross output of general government | | | Value added | | | Intermediate goods and services purchased [1] | | | Gross output of general government | Value added | Intermediate goods and services purchased [1] |
	Total	Defense	Nondefense	Total	Defense	Nondefense	Total	Defense	Nondefense			
1950	39.7	48.1	26.2	66.6	78.6	47.2	15.7	19.4	10.2	16.5	21.0	8.7
1951	60.0	82.6	21.9	87.6	112.1	44.1	32.7	50.9	6.1	16.4	21.5	8.1
1952	75.7	105.4	25.6	97.6	127.8	43.3	50.2	76.6	11.7	16.7	22.2	7.9
1953	81.4	110.2	32.8	98.0	130.0	40.2	58.9	82.8	23.6	17.3	23.2	7.9
1954	72.1	96.0	31.8	95.5	127.1	38.5	46.0	61.4	23.1	18.0	24.2	8.2
1955	69.0	90.3	32.9	93.3	123.5	38.8	42.6	54.7	24.5	19.3	25.3	9.3
1956	67.0	90.3	27.5	92.3	121.6	39.5	40.2	56.2	16.1	20.0	26.9	9.0
1957	71.1	96.6	27.8	92.0	120.7	40.4	47.1	67.5	16.1	21.0	28.4	9.4
1958	69.7	94.8	27.3	89.4	116.1	41.5	46.8	68.1	14.4	22.7	30.1	10.8
1959	69.2	87.1	38.9	88.6	114.9	41.5	46.6	55.3	33.1	23.8	31.4	11.6
1960	68.1	88.2	33.9	90.3	115.9	44.4	43.1	56.4	22.6	25.1	33.0	12.2
1961	69.3	90.2	33.6	92.1	118.2	45.5	43.6	58.0	21.3	26.5	34.8	13.1
1962	75.8	96.5	40.5	95.9	122.8	47.9	52.0	65.5	31.2	27.5	36.0	13.6
1963	77.8	97.4	44.2	96.8	122.4	51.0	54.8	67.5	35.3	29.0	37.9	14.5
1964	77.3	95.0	46.9	97.7	122.9	52.7	53.0	62.4	38.5	31.0	40.2	15.8
1965	78.4	95.6	48.8	98.4	122.9	54.5	54.4	63.5	40.4	33.1	42.6	17.4
1966	87.2	109.5	49.1	104.9	131.4	57.5	65.1	82.5	38.4	35.3	45.2	18.8
1967	96.4	122.6	51.6	111.7	140.2	60.7	76.0	99.5	40.1	37.0	47.1	20.3
1968	99.5	127.6	51.9	113.5	142.1	62.5	80.2	107.3	39.0	39.6	49.9	22.3
1969	97.4	122.6	54.4	113.8	142.1	63.3	75.7	97.2	42.8	42.0	52.2	24.7
1970	90.4	111.5	54.2	109.0	133.9	64.2	66.8	83.1	41.6	44.4	54.5	27.2
1971	85.9	102.8	56.7	103.9	125.0	66.1	63.1	74.9	44.5	46.8	56.7	29.7
1972	84.2	97.1	61.5	98.9	116.1	67.8	65.4	73.3	52.3	48.7	58.6	31.5
1973	79.7	90.6	60.5	95.2	110.3	68.1	59.9	65.7	50.1	50.4	60.7	32.6
1974	79.2	88.0	63.6	94.9	108.1	71.2	59.2	62.6	53.2	52.4	62.9	34.4
1975	78.2	85.4	65.5	94.3	106.6	72.4	57.6	58.6	55.6	54.7	64.8	37.1
1976	77.0	83.3	65.8	94.5	105.0	75.8	54.9	56.0	52.7	55.6	65.7	38.2
1977	78.8	84.3	69.0	94.7	104.4	77.6	58.5	58.9	57.4	56.7	66.7	39.3
1978	80.5	85.2	72.2	95.9	105.1	79.8	60.9	60.1	61.5	58.0	68.2	40.3
1979	81.9	86.3	74.0	95.8	104.7	80.2	63.9	62.9	64.9	58.8	69.4	40.3
1980	85.2	89.8	77.0	97.4	105.7	82.7	69.1	69.3	68.2	58.8	70.4	39.0
1981	88.7	94.9	77.6	98.9	108.8	81.3	74.9	76.7	71.0	58.9	70.3	39.3
1982	91.6	101.3	74.1	100.5	111.6	80.6	79.2	87.2	64.4	59.9	70.8	41.0
1983	95.9	106.4	77.1	102.8	114.2	82.5	85.8	95.0	68.7	60.8	70.5	43.6
1984	97.2	109.7	74.6	105.1	117.2	83.6	85.9	98.8	62.2	61.8	70.9	45.4
1985	103.0	116.3	78.8	108.1	121.1	84.8	95.0	108.8	69.7	64.8	73.0	50.1
1986	107.4	121.6	81.8	110.0	124.0	84.7	102.8	117.2	76.0	68.7	75.1	56.7
1987	110.1	126.1	80.9	112.9	127.2	86.9	105.2	123.6	71.6	69.6	76.5	56.6
1988	110.0	127.7	77.6	114.3	128.0	89.7	102.9	126.1	60.9	71.8	79.1	58.1
1989	111.6	126.7	83.9	115.7	129.4	91.0	104.8	121.8	73.7	74.0	81.6	59.9
1990	113.3	126.2	90.1	117.8	130.2	95.7	106.1	119.4	81.8	76.2	84.0	61.8
1991	113.8	126.0	91.8	118.5	130.9	96.4	106.2	118.0	84.7	78.0	85.1	64.7
1992	111.3	119.7	96.4	116.0	126.0	98.5	103.8	109.8	92.7	80.1	86.5	68.1
1993	107.4	114.7	94.5	113.8	122.3	99.0	97.4	103.0	87.3	82.1	87.7	71.4
1994	104.8	110.2	95.2	110.1	117.5	97.1	96.4	98.8	92.0	84.3	89.2	74.9
1995	101.2	105.5	93.7	106.0	112.6	94.4	93.7	94.5	92.3	86.4	91.0	77.7
1996	99.4	103.8	91.6	103.0	108.8	93.0	93.5	95.9	89.2	88.0	92.4	79.5
1997	99.1	102.3	93.5	101.1	105.6	93.4	95.8	97.0	93.7	90.6	94.3	83.4
1998	97.3	99.6	93.2	100.0	102.7	95.1	92.9	94.6	90.0	94.1	96.2	90.0
1999	98.5	101.0	94.1	99.1	100.7	96.5	97.4	101.4	90.2	97.5	97.9	96.6
2000	100.0	100.0	100.0	100.0	100.0	100.0	100.0	100.0	100.0	100.0	100.0	100.0
2001	103.8	104.0	103.6	100.5	100.5	100.7	109.3	109.6	108.7	103.5	102.4	105.5
2002	110.5	111.1	109.5	102.5	102.3	102.8	123.8	125.3	121.0	106.6	104.4	110.8
2003	118.0	120.6	113.4	105.3	105.2	105.3	139.6	146.1	127.6	106.5	105.0	109.3
2004	122.5	126.8	114.8	106.3	107.2	104.8	150.0	159.6	132.4	106.7	105.3	109.3
2005	123.6	128.1	115.7	107.0	108.1	105.1	152.1	161.7	134.3	106.9	106.1	108.5
2006	125.2	129.2	118.1	106.9	107.5	105.8	156.8	165.9	140.0	108.3	107.0	110.6
2007	127.3	132.6	117.6	107.7	108.0	107.1	161.1	174.5	136.2	110.5	108.7	113.7
2008	133.6	140.5	121.1	111.7	112.0	111.1	171.7	189.4	138.6	112.0	110.3	115.3
2006												
1st quarter	125.5	129.1	119.2	106.3	107.0	105.2	158.5	166.2	144.4	107.6	106.5	109.5
2nd quarter	124.9	129.1	117.3	106.4	106.9	105.6	156.7	166.7	138.2	107.9	106.8	110.2
3rd quarter	125.6	129.0	119.5	107.3	107.9	106.3	156.9	164.4	143.1	108.5	107.2	110.9
4th quarter	124.9	129.8	116.3	107.4	108.2	106.0	155.0	166.1	134.4	109.1	107.7	111.8
2007												
1st quarter	125.1	129.6	117.0	107.2	107.5	106.6	155.7	166.8	135.2	109.8	108.1	112.8
2nd quarter	126.5	131.4	117.7	107.0	107.3	106.6	160.1	172.4	137.3	110.3	108.5	113.5
3rd quarter	129.1	135.1	118.1	108.0	108.4	107.4	165.5	180.8	137.0	110.7	108.9	114.1
4th quarter	128.4	134.3	117.8	108.4	108.7	107.8	162.9	177.8	135.2	111.1	109.3	114.5
2008												
1st quarter	130.2	136.6	118.6	109.4	109.6	109.1	166.1	182.8	135.1	111.6	109.8	114.9
2nd quarter	131.3	137.7	119.8	110.6	110.7	110.5	167.2	184.0	136.0	111.9	110.2	115.1
3rd quarter	135.6	143.3	121.7	112.4	113.0	111.5	175.9	195.3	139.7	112.3	110.6	115.5
4th quarter	137.4	144.6	124.4	114.3	114.8	113.4	177.5	195.6	143.6	112.3	110.6	115.6

[1]Includes general government intermediate inputs for goods and services sold to other sectors and for own-account investment.

Table 6-17. Government Employment

(Calendar years, payroll employment in thousands.)

Year and month	Total government employment	Federal			State			Local		
		Total	Department of Defense	Postal Service	Total	Education	State government hospitals	Total	Education	Local government hospitals
1950	6 120	2 023	533	516	. . .	. . .	. . .	. . .	. . .	. . .
1951	6 502	2 415	797	521	. . .	. . .	. . .	. . .	. . .	. . .
1952	6 727	2 539	868	542	. . .	. . .	. . .	. . .	. . .	. . .
1953	6 758	2 418	818	530	. . .	. . .	. . .	. . .	. . .	. . .
1954	6 858	2 295	744	533	. . .	. . .	. . .	. . .	. . .	. . .
1955	7 021	2 295	744	534	1 168	308	. . .	3 558	1 751	. . .
1956	7 386	2 318	749	539	1 249	334	. . .	3 819	1 884	. . .
1957	7 724	2 326	729	555	1 328	363	. . .	4 071	2 026	. . .
1958	7 946	2 298	695	567	1 415	389	. . .	4 232	2 115	. . .
1959	8 192	2 342	699	578	1 484	420	. . .	4 366	2 198	. . .
1960	8 464	2 381	681	591	1 536	448	. . .	4 547	2 314	. . .
1961	8 706	2 391	683	601	1 607	474	. . .	4 708	2 411	. . .
1962	9 004	2 455	697	601	1 669	511	. . .	4 881	2 522	. . .
1963	9 341	2 473	687	603	1 747	557	. . .	5 121	2 674	. . .
1964	9 711	2 463	676	604	1 856	609	. . .	5 392	2 839	. . .
1965	10 191	2 495	679	619	1 996	679	. . .	5 700	3 031	. . .
1966	10 910	2 690	741	686	2 141	775	. . .	6 080	3 297	. . .
1967	11 525	2 852	802	719	2 302	873	. . .	6 371	3 490	. . .
1968	11 972	2 871	801	729	2 442	958	. . .	6 660	3 649	. . .
1969	12 330	2 893	815	737	2 533	1 042	. . .	6 904	3 785	. . .
1970	12 687	2 865	756	741	2 664	1 104	. . .	7 158	3 912	. . .
1971	13 012	2 828	731	731	2 747	1 149	. . .	7 437	4 091	. . .
1972	13 465	2 815	720	703	2 859	1 188	459	7 790	4 262	467
1973	13 862	2 794	696	698	2 923	1 205	472	8 146	4 433	477
1974	14 303	2 858	698	710	3 039	1 267	483	8 407	4 584	483
1975	14 820	2 882	704	699	3 179	1 323	503	8 758	4 722	489
1976	15 001	2 863	693	676	3 273	1 371	518	8 865	4 786	492
1977	15 258	2 859	676	657	3 377	1 385	538	9 023	4 859	494
1978	15 812	2 893	661	660	3 474	1 367	541	9 446	4 958	535
1979	16 068	2 894	649	673	3 541	1 378	538	9 633	4 989	571
1980	16 375	3 000	645	673	3 610	1 398	530	9 765	5 090	604
1981	16 180	2 922	655	675	3 640	1 420	515	9 619	5 095	622
1982	15 982	2 884	690	684	3 640	1 433	494	9 458	5 049	635
1983	16 011	2 915	699	685	3 662	1 450	471	9 434	5 020	644
1984	16 159	2 943	716	706	3 734	1 488	459	9 482	5 076	623
1985	16 533	3 014	738	750	3 832	1 540	449	9 687	5 221	608
1986	16 838	3 044	736	792	3 893	1 561	438	9 901	5 358	601
1987	17 156	3 089	736	815	3 967	1 586	439	10 100	5 469	606
1988	17 540	3 124	719	835	4 076	1 621	446	10 339	5 590	619
1989	17 927	3 136	735	838	4 182	1 668	442	10 609	5 740	632
1990	18 415	3 196	722	825	4 305	1 730	426	10 914	5 902	646
1991	18 545	3 110	702	813	4 355	1 768	417	11 081	5 994	653
1992	18 787	3 111	702	800	4 408	1 799	419	11 267	6 076	665
1993	18 989	3 063	670	793	4 488	1 834	414	11 438	6 206	673
1994	19 275	3 018	657	821	4 576	1 882	407	11 682	6 329	673
1995	19 432	2 949	627	850	4 635	1 919	395	11 849	6 453	669
1996	19 539	2 877	597	867	4 606	1 911	376	12 056	6 592	648
1997	19 664	2 806	588	866	4 582	1 904	360	12 276	6 759	632
1998	19 909	2 772	550	881	4 612	1 922	346	12 525	6 921	630
1999	20 307	2 769	525	890	4 709	1 983	344	12 829	7 120	626
2000	20 790	2 865	510	880	4 786	2 031	343	13 139	7 294	622
2001	21 118	2 764	504	873	4 905	2 113	345	13 449	7 479	628
2002	21 513	2 766	499	842	5 029	2 243	349	13 718	7 654	642
2003	21 583	2 761	486	809	5 002	2 255	348	13 820	7 709	651
2004	21 621	2 730	473	782	4 982	2 238	348	13 909	7 765	656
2005	21 804	2 732	488	774	5 032	2 260	350	14 041	7 856	655
2006	21 974	2 732	493	770	5 075	2 293	357	14 167	7 913	647
2007	22 218	2 734	491	769	5 122	2 318	360	14 362	7 987	654
2008	22 500	2 764	496	748	5 178	2 359	363	14 557	8 076	663

. . . = Not available.

NOTES AND DEFINITIONS

TABLES 6-1 THROUGH 6-13, 6-16, 19-10, AND 19-11 FEDERAL, STATE, AND LOCAL GOVERNMENT IN THE NATIONAL INCOME AND PRODUCT ACCOUNTS

SOURCE: U.S. DEPARTMENT OF COMMERCE, BUREAU OF ECONOMIC ANALYSIS (BEA)

These data are from the national income and product accounts (NIPAs), as published in the 2003 comprehensive NIPA revisions and as revised and updated through March 2009. For general information about the NIPAs and the 2003 revision, see the notes and definitions for Chapter 1.

Upcoming NIPA Revision

In July 2009 the Bureau of Economic Analysis will release a comprehensive, or benchmark, revision of the NIPAs.

Current-dollar estimates will be revised—especially for the most recent four years—because of data updating and classification and statistical changes. Users of the constant-dollar estimates and the quantity and price indexes will also, and immediately, notice a change in the reference year for the chain-type quantity and price indexes and the chained-dollar estimates, from 2000 (as used in the data in this volume) to 2005.

The change in the reference year will cause conspicuous differences in the *levels* of the constant-dollar measures and the price and quantity indexes, but this does not of itself affect the *rates of change*—the growth and inflation rates calculated from these data—which are based on chain-weighted indexes whatever the reference base year is. Significant changes are not expected in historical growth and inflation trends from those that can be derived from the data in this volume, other than the revisions occasioned by new data for the most recent several years.

BEA also plans changes in the treatment of disasters and a new classification system for personal consumption expenditures.

These and all of the other planned changes are described in "Preview of the 2009 Comprehensive Revision of the NIPAs: Changes in Definitions and Presentations," *Survey of Current Business*, March 2009, available at <http://www.bea.gov>.

THE FRAMEWORK FOR THE GOVERNMENT ACCOUNTS

In the 2003 revision, a new framework was introduced for government consumption expenditures—federal, state, and local—that explicitly recognizes the services produced by general government. Governments serve several functions in the economy. Three of these functions are recognized in the NIPAs: the production of nonmarket services; the consumption of these services, in that the value of the services provided to the general public is treated as government consumption expenditures; and the provision of transfer payments. These functions are financed through taxation, through contributions to social insurance funds, and in the world's capital markets.

In the new framework, the value of the government services produced and consumed (most of which are not sold in the market) is measured as the sum of the costs of the three major inputs: compensation of government employees, consumption of fixed capital (CFC), and intermediate goods and services purchased. The purchase from the private sector of goods and services by government, classified as final sales to government before the 2003 revision, was reclassified as intermediate purchases.

The value of government final purchases of consumption expenditures and gross investment, which constitutes the contribution of government demand to the gross domestic product (GDP), was not changed by this reclassification, since the previous definition of that contribution was the sum of compensation, CFC, and goods and services purchased. However, the distribution of GDP by type of product was changed—final sales of goods were reduced by the amount of goods purchased by government, and services were increased by the same amount.

In addition to this change in the conceptual framework, a number of the categories of government receipts and expenditures were redefined to make more precise distinctions. For example, items that used to be called "nontax payments" and included with taxes are now classified as transfer or fee payments and not included in taxes.

Finally, the concept previously known as "current surplus or deficit (-), national income and product accounts" was renamed "net government saving." This recognizes, in part, the role of government in the capital markets. When government runs a current surplus, net government saving is positive and funds are made available (for example, by repayment of outstanding debt) to finance investment—both private-sector capital spending and government investment. When government runs a current deficit, or "dis-saves," it must borrow funds that would otherwise be available to finance investment.

However, net government saving does not give a complete picture of governments' role in capital markets, because it is based on current receipts and expenditures alone and does not include government investment activity.

In the NIPAs, the capital spending of all levels of government is treated the same way as the accounts treat private investment spending. A depreciation, or more precisely "consumption of fixed capital" (CFC), entry for existing capital is calculated, using estimated replacement costs and realistic depreciation rates. In the government accounts this CFC value is entered as one element of current expenditures and output. Capital spending is excluded from government current expenditures but appears in the account for "net lending or borrowing (-)."

The basic concept expressed in the net lending section of the NIPAs is that when CFC exceeds actual investment expenditures, governments have a positive net cash flow and can lend (or repay debt); if gross investment exceeds CFC, government must borrow to finance the difference, indicating negative net cash flow and requiring borrowing. (As will be seen below in the definitions, capital transfer and purchase accounts also enter into the calculation of net lending.)

The federal *budget* accounts (see Tables 6-14 and 6-15) do not draw a distinction between current and capital spending. The budget accounts of individual state and local governments typically separate capital from current spending and allow capital spending to be financed by borrowing—even when deficit financing of current spending is constitutionally forbidden. However, neither federal nor state and local government budget accounts typically show depreciation as a current expense in the way that is standard to private-sector accounting or in the way adopted in the NIPAs.

Notes on the data

Government receipts and expenditures data are derived from the U.S. government accounts and from Census Bureau censuses and surveys of government finances, which cover state and local governments. However, BEA makes a number of adjustments to the data to convert them from fiscal year to calendar year and quarter bases and to agree with the concepts of national income accounting. Data are converted from the cash basis usually found in financial statements to the timing bases required for the NIPAs. In the NIPAs, receipts from businesses are generally on an accrual basis, purchases of goods and services are recorded when delivered, and receipts from and transfer payments to persons are on a cash basis. The federal receipts and expenditure data from the NIPAs in Table 6-1 therefore differ from the federal receipts and outlay data in Table 6-14. Among other differences, the latter are by fiscal year and are on a modified cash basis.

The NIPA data on government receipts and expenditures record transactions of governments (federal, state, and local) with other U.S. residents and foreigners. Each entry in the government receipts and expenditures account has a corresponding entry elsewhere in the NIPAs. Thus, for example, the sum of personal current taxes received by federal and state and local governments (Tables 6-1 and 6-8) is equal to personal current taxes paid, as shown in personal income (Table 4-1).

Definitions (general)

In the 2003 revision of the NIPAs, several items appear separately that were previously treated as "negative expenditures" and netted against other items on the expenditures side. This grossing-up of the accounts raises both receipts and outlays and has no effect on net saving. Grossing-up has been applied to taxes from the rest of the world, interest receipts (back to 1960 for the federal government and back to 1946 for state and local governments), dividends, and subsidies and the current surplus of government enterprises (back to 1959).

Definitions (current receipts)

Current tax receipts includes personal current taxes, taxes on production and imports, taxes on corporate income and (for the federal government only) taxes from the rest of the world. The taxes from the rest of the world are mostly income taxes and are not shown separately in the tables included in this chapter. The category *total tax receipts* does not include *contributions for government social insurance,* which are the taxes levied to finance Social Security, unemployment insurance, and Medicare, and are included in *receipts* in the budget accounts (Table 6-14). Analysts using NIPA data to analyze tax burdens as they are usually understood should add *contributions for government social insurance* to *tax receipts* for this purpose.

Personal current taxes is personal tax payments from residents of the United States that are not chargeable to business expense. Personal taxes consist of taxes on income, including on realized net capital gains, and on personal property. Personal contributions for social insurance are not included in this category. As of the 1999 revisions, estate and gift taxes are classified as capital transfers and are no longer included in personal current taxes. However, estate and gift taxes continue to be included in federal government receipts in Table 6-14.

Taxes on production and imports consists of federal excise taxes and customs duties and of state and local sales taxes, property taxes (including residential real estate taxes), motor vehicle licenses, severance taxes, other taxes, and special assessments. Before the 2003 revision, these taxes were a component of "indirect business tax and nontax liabilities."

Taxes on corporate income covers federal, state, and local government income taxes on all corporate income subject to taxes. This taxable income includes capital gains and other income excluded from the NIPA profits. The taxes are measured on an accrual basis, net of applicable tax credits.

Contributions for social insurance includes employer and personal contributions for Social Security, Medicare, unemployment insurance, and other government social insurance programs. As of the 1999 revisions, contributions to government employee retirement plans are no longer included in this category; these plans are now treated the same as private pension plans.

Income receipts on assets consists of *interest*, dividends (not shown separately here), and *rents and royalties*.

Interest receipts (1960 to the present for federal governments; 1946 to the present for state and local governments) consists of monetary and imputed interest received on loans and investments. In the NIPAs, this no longer includes interest received by government employee retirement plans, which is now credited to personal income. However, such interest received is still deducted from interest paid in the budget accounts that are shown in Table 6-14. Before the indicated years, receipts are deducted from aggregate interest payments in the NIPAs. Hence, they are not shown as receipts, and net interest is presented on the expenditure side. In the federal budget accounts in Table 6-14, net interest (total interest expenditures minus interest receipts) is the interest "expenditure" concept used throughout the period covered.

Current transfer receipts includes receipts in categories other than those specified above from persons and business. In the case of state and local government accounts (Table 6-8), it also includes *federal grants-in-aid*, a component of federal expenditures. Receipts from *business* and *persons* were previously included with income taxes in "tax and nontax payments." They consist of federal deposit insurance premiums and other nontaxes (largely fines and regulatory and inspection fees), state and local fines and other nontaxes (largely donations and tobacco settlements), and net insurance settlements paid to governments as policyholders.

The *current surplus of government enterprises* is the current operating revenue and subsidies received from other levels of government by such enterprises less their current expenses. No deduction is made for depreciation charges or net interest paid. Before 1959, this category of receipts is treated as a deduction from subsidies. In the *federal* NIPA accounts before 1959, there is no entry shown for the current surplus on the receipts side, and on the expenditure side, there is an entry for subsidies, which is net of the current surplus. (Subsidies are usually a larger amount than the enterprise surplus in the federal accounts.) In the *state and local* NIPA accounts before 1959, there is an entry for the surplus on the receipts side, which is net of subsidies. (Subsidies are typically smaller than the enterprise surplus in state and local finance.)

Definitions (consumption expenditures, saving, and gross investment)

Government consumption expenditures is expenditures by governments (federal or state and local) on services for current consumption. It includes *compensation of general gov-*

ernment employees (including employer contributions to government employee retirement plans, as of the 1999 revision); an allowance for *consumption of general government fixed capital (CFC),* including software (depreciation); and *intermediate goods and services purchased.* (See the general discussion above for an explanation.) The estimated value of *own-account investment*—investment goods, including software, produced by government resources and purchased inputs—is subtracted here, and added to *government gross investment. Sales to other sectors*—primarily tuition payments received from individuals for higher education and charges for medical care to individuals—are also deducted.

Government social benefits consists of payments to individuals for which the individuals do not render current services. Examples are Social Security benefits, Medicare, Medicaid, unemployment benefits, and public assistance. Retirement payments to retired government employees from their pension plans are no longer included in this category.

Government social benefits to persons consists of payments to persons residing in the United States (with a corresponding entry of an equal amount in the personal income receipts accounts). Government social benefits to the rest of the world—not shown separately here—appear only in the federal government account, and are transfers, mainly retirement benefits, to former residents of the United States.

Other current transfer payments (federal account only) includes *grants-in-aid to state and local governments* and military and nonmilitary grants to foreign governments, not shown separately here.

Federal grants-in-aid comprises net payments from federal to state and local governments that are made to help finance programs such as health (Medicaid), public assistance (the old Aid to Families with Dependent Children and the new Temporary Assistance for Needy Families), and education. Investment grants to state and local governments for highways, transit, air transportation, and water treatment plants are now classified as capital transfers and are no longer included in this category. However, such investment grants continue to be included as federal government outlays in Table 6-14.

Interest payments is monetary interest paid to U.S. and foreign persons and businesses and to foreign governments for public debt and other financial obligations. As noted above, from 1960 forward for the federal government and from 1946 forward for state and local governments, this represents gross total (not net) interest payments. Before those dates in the NIPAs, and throughout the federal budget accounts presented in Table 6-14, net instead of aggregate interest is shown; that is, gross total interest paid less interest received.

Subsidies are monetary grants paid by government to business, including to government enterprises at another level of government. Subsidies no longer include federal maritime construction subsidies, which are now classified as a capital transfer. For years prior to 1959, subsidies continue to be presented net of the *current surplus of government enterprises*, because detailed data to separate the series are not available for this period. See the entry for *current surplus of government enterprises*, described above, for explanation of the pre-1959 treatment of this item in the federal accounts in *Business Statistics*, which differs from the treatment in the state and local accounts.

Net saving, NIPA (surplus+/deficit-), is the sum of current receipts less the sum of current expenditures. This is shown separately for *social insurance funds* (which, in the case of the federal government, include Social Security and other trust funds) and *other* (all other government). As of the 1999 revision, net government saving—particularly that of state and local governments—is measured as being significantly smaller than before that revision, as the net accumulations of *government employee* retirement plans (not Social Security) are now classified as personal saving rather than in the government sector.

Gross government investment consists of general government and government enterprise expenditures for fixed assets—structures, equipment, and software. The expenditures include the compensation of government employees producing the assets and the purchase of goods and services as intermediate inputs to be incorporated in the assets. Government inventory investment is included in government consumption expenditures.

Capital consumption. Consumption of fixed capital (CFC; economic depreciation) is included in government consumption expenditures as a partial measure of the value of the services of general government fixed assets, including structures, equipment, and software.

Definitions (output, lending and borrowing, and net investment)

In Tables 6-5 and 6-10, current-dollar values of gross output and value added of government are presented, as described in the general discussion above. *Gross output* of government is the sum of the *intermediate goods and services purchased* by government and the value added by government as a producing industry. *Value added* consists of compensation of general government employees and consumption of general government fixed capital. Since this depreciation allowance is the only entry on the product side of the accounts measuring the output associated with such capital, a zero *net* return on these assets is implicitly assumed.

Gross output minus own-account investment and sales to other sectors (see the previous description) yields *government consumption expenditures*, which represents the contribution of government consumption spending to final demands in GDP.

Net lending (net borrowing -) consists of current *net saving* as defined above, plus the *consumption of fixed capital* (CFC, from the current expenditure account), minus *gross*

investment, plus *capital transfer receipts*, and minus *capital transfer payments* and *net purchases of non-produced assets*.

Capital transfer receipts and *payments* include grants between levels of government, or between government and the private sector, associated with acquisition or disposal of assets rather than with current consumption expenditures. Examples are federal grants to state and local government for highways, transit, air transportation, and water treatment plants; federal shipbuilding subsidies and other subsidies to businesses; and lump-sum payments to amortize the unfounded liability of the Uniformed Services Retiree Health Care Fund. Government capital transfer receipts include estate and gift taxes, which are no longer included in personal tax receipts. (Federal estate and gift taxes are shown in Table 6-14 and although on a fiscal year basis are almost identical to the annual values for federal capital transfer receipts in Table 6-5.)

Non-produced assets are land and radio spectrum. The unusually large negative entry for net purchases of non-produced assets in 2006 results from the negative purchase–that is, the sale–of spectrum. Since the sales receipts occurred entirely in the fourth quarter of the year, and are multiplied by 4 in the calculation of the annual rate, they appear as a very high number for that quarter.

The values of *net investment* shown in these tables are calculated by the editor, as gross investment minus the consumption of fixed capital.

Definitions (chain-type quantity indexes)

Chain-type quantity indexes represent changes over time in real values, removing the effects of inflation. Indexes for key categories in the government expenditure accounts, as well as for government gross output, value added, and intermediate goods and services purchased, use the chain formula described in the notes and definitions for Chapter 1 and are expressed as index numbers, with the average for the year 2000 equal to 100.

Data availability

The most recent data are published each month in the Survey of *Current Business*. Current and historical data may be obtained from the BEA Web site at <http://www.bea.gov> and the STAT-USA subscription Web site at <http://www.stat-usa.gov>.

References

See the references regarding the 2003 comprehensive revision of the NIPAs in the notes and definitions for Chapter 1. NIPA concepts and their differences from the budget estimates are discussed in "NIPA Estimates of the Federal Sector and the Federal Budget Estimates," *Survey of Current Business,* March 2007, p. 11.

For information about the classification of government expenditures into current consumption and gross investment, first undertaken in the 1996 comprehensive revisions, see the *Survey of Current Business* article, "Preview of the Comprehensive Revision of the National Income and Product Accounts: Recognition of Government Investment and Incorporation of a New Methodology for Calculating Depreciation" September 1995. Other sources of information about the NIPAs are listed in the notes and definitions for Chapter 1.

TABLES 6-12 AND 6-13
STATE GOVERNMENT CURRENT RECEIPTS AND EXPENDITURES; LOCAL GOVERNMENT CURRENT RECEIPTS AND EXPENDITURES

SOURCE: BUREAU OF ECONOMIC ANALYSIS (BEA)

In the standard presentation of the state and local sector of the national income and product accounts (NIPAs) such as in Tables 6-8 through 6-11 above, state and local governments are combined. Annual measures for aggregate state governments and aggregate local governments are now available on the BEA Web site for the years 1959 through 2007. These measures are shown in Tables 6-12 and 6-13. The definitions are the same as in the other NIPA tables described above.

Two new categories appear in each table, detailing the intergovernmental flows that are consolidated in Table 6-8. State government receipts include not only *federal grants-in-aid* but also *local grants-in-aid*, and state government expenditures include *grants-in-aid to local governments*. Local government receipts include not only *federal grants-in-aid* but also *state grants-in-aid*, and local government expenditures include *grants-in-aid to state governments*. To make room for these columns, the components *current surplus of government enterprises* and *subsidies* are not shown, though they are included in total current receipts and total current expenditures respectively.

These measures are described in "Receipts and Expenditures of State Governments and of Local Governments," *Survey of Current Business*, October 2005. Data back to 1959 are available on the BEA Web site at <http://www.bea.gov>.

TABLE 6-14
FEDERAL GOVERNMENT RECEIPTS AND OUTLAYS BY FISCAL YEAR

SOURCE: U.S. OFFICE OF MANAGEMENT AND BUDGET

These data on federal government receipts and outlays are on a modified cash basis and are from the *Budget of the United States Government: Historical Tables*. The data are by federal fiscal years, which are defined as July 1 through June 30 through 1976 and October 1 through September 30 for 1977 and subsequent years. The period July 1 through September 30, 1976, is a separate fiscal period known as the transition quarter (TQ) and is not included in any fiscal year.

There are numerous differences in both timing and definition between these estimates and the NIPA estimates in

Tables 6-1 through 6-7. See the notes and definitions for those tables for the definitional differences that were introduced with the 1999 comprehensive revision of the NIPAs.

Definitions

The definitions for this table are not affected by the 2003 or 1999 changes in the government sectors of the NIPAs.

Table references will be given indicating the source of each item in the *Historical Tables*; for example, "HT Table 1.1."

Receipts consist of gifts and other taxes or other compulsory payments to the government. Other types of payments to the government are netted against outlays. (HT Table 1.1)

Outlays occur when the federal government liquidates an obligation through a cash payment or when interest accrues on public debt issues. Beginning with the data for 1992, outlays include the subsidy cost of direct and guaranteed loans made. Before 1992, the costs and repayments associated with such loans are recorded on a cash basis. As noted previously, various types of nontax receipts are netted against cash outlays. These accounts do not distinguish between investment outlays and current consumption and do not include allowances for depreciation. (HT Table 1.1)

The *total surplus (deficit-)* is receipts minus outlays. (HT Table 1.1)

On-budget and off-budget. By law, two government programs that are included in the federal receipts and outlays totals are "off-budget"—old-age, survivors, and disability insurance (Social Security) and the Postal Service. The former accounts for nearly all of the off-budget activity. The *surplus (deficit-)* not accounted for by these two programs is the on-budget surplus or deficit. (HT Table 1.1)

Sources of financing is the means by which the total deficit is financed or the surplus is distributed. By definition, sources of financing sum to the total deficit or surplus with the sign reversed. The principal source is *borrowing from the public*, shown as a positive number, that is, the increase in the debt held by the public. (Calculated as the change in the debt held by the public as shown in HT Table 7.1.) When there is a budget surplus, as in fiscal years 1998 to 2001, debt can be reduced, indicated by a minus sign in this column. *Other financing* includes drawdown (or buildup, shown here with a minus sign) in Treasury cash balances, seigniorage on coins, direct and guaranteed loan account cash transactions, and miscellaneous other transactions. (Calculated by subtracting borrowing from the public from the total deficit or surplus with the sign reversed.)

Some of the categories of *receipts by source* are self-explanatory. *Employment taxes and contributions* includes taxes for old-age, survivors, and disability insurance (Social Security), hospital insurance (Medicare), and railroad retirement funds. *Other retirement contributions* includes the employee share of payments for retirement pensions, mainly those for federal employees. *Excise taxes* includes federal taxes on alcohol, tobacco, telephone service, and transportation fuels, as well as taxes funding smaller programs such as black lung disability and vaccine injury compensation. *Miscellaneous receipts* includes deposits of earnings by the Federal Reserve system and all other receipts. (HT Tables 2.1, 2.4, and 2.5)

Outlays by function presents outlays according to the major purpose of the spending. Functional classifications cut across departmental and agency lines. Most categories of offsetting receipts are netted against cash outlays in the appropriate function, which explains how recorded outlays in *energy* and *commerce and housing credit* (which, as its name suggests, includes loan programs) can be negative. There is also a category of "undistributed offsetting receipts" (not shown), always with a negative sign, that includes proceeds from the sale or lease of assets and payments from federal agencies to federal retirement funds and the Social Security and Medicare trust funds. Note that *Social Security* is recorded separately from other *income security* outlays, and *Medicare* separately from other *health* outlays. (HT Table 3.1) For further explanation, consult the *Budget of the United States Government.*

In order to provide authoritative comparisons of these budget values with the overall size of the economy, a special calculation of gross domestic product by fiscal year (supplied to the Office of Management and Budget by the BEA) is included in this table. (HT Table 1.2)

Data availability and references

Definitions and budget concepts are discussed in *Budget of the United States: Historical Tables,* available from the Government Printing Office (GPO) and on the Web site listed in the next paragraph.

Data availability

The annual data are from the *Budget of the United States Government for Fiscal Year 2009: Historical Tables* and are available on the GPO Web site at <http://www.gpo.gov/ usbudget>. Final data for 2008, along with projected estimates based on the President's budget, will be available on release of the complete President's Budget for Fiscal Year 2010, scheduled for release too late to be included in the volume.

Similarly defined data for the latest month, the year-ago month, and the current and year-ago fiscal year to date are published in the *Monthly Treasury Statement* prepared by the Financial Management Service, U.S. Department of the Treasury. For those who need up-to-date budget information, this publication is available on the Financial Management Service Web site at <http://www .fms.treas.gov>. As these monthly figures are never revised to agree with the final annual data, they are not published in this volume.

TABLE 6-15
FEDERAL GOVERNMENT DEBT BY FISCAL YEAR

SOURCE: U.S. OFFICE OF MANAGEMENT AND BUDGET

Debt outstanding at the end of each fiscal year is from the *Budget of the United States Government.* Most securities are recorded at sales price plus amortized discount or less amortized premium.

Definitions

Federal government debt held by the public consists of all federal debt held outside the federal government accounts—by individuals, financial institutions (including the Federal Reserve Banks), and foreign individuals, businesses, and central banks. It does not include federal debt held by federal government trust funds such as the Social Security trust fund. The level and change of the ratio of this debt to the value of gross domestic product (GDP) provide proportional measures of the impact of federal borrowing on credit markets. (HT Table 7.1) This measure of debt held by the public is very similar in concept and scope to the total federal government credit market debt outstanding in the flow-of-funds accounts, shown in *Business Statistics* in Table 12-5; however, it is not identical, being priced somewhat differently, and is shown here in Chapter 6 on a fiscal year rather than calendar year basis.

Gross federal debt—total. This is the total debt owed by the U.S. Treasury. It includes a small amount of matured debt. (HT Table 7.1)

Debt held by Social Security funds is the sum of the end-year funds for old age and survivors insurance and disability insurance. (HT Table 13.1)

Debt held by other U.S. government accounts is calculated by subtracting the Social Security debt holdings from the total debt held by federal government accounts, which is shown in HT Table 7.1. It includes the balances in all the other trust funds, including the Medicare funds, federal employee retirement funds, and the highway trust fund.

Debt held by the Federal Reserve System is the total value of Treasury securities held by the 12 Federal Reserve Banks, which are acquired in open market operations that carry out monetary policy. (HT Table 7.1)

Debt held by private investors is calculated by subtracting the Federal Reserve debt from the total debt held by the public.

Debt held by foreign residents is based on surveys by the Treasury Department. Every few years there is a benchmark revision, which renders year-to-year changes invalid as measures of the borrowing during the year; such revisions occurred in 1979, 1985, 1990, 1995, 1999, 2000, and 2002. (Table 16-6, *Budget of the United States for Fiscal Year 2008: Analytical Perspectives,* p. 235.)

Debt held by domestic investors is calculated by subtracting the foreign debt from the total debt held by private investors.

The "debt subject to statutory limitation," not shown here, is close to the gross federal debt in concept and size, but there are some relatively minor definitional differences specified by law. The debt limit can only be changed by an Act of Congress. For information about the debt subject to limit and other debt subjects, see the latest *Budget of the United States Government: Historical Statistics* and *Analytical Perspectives*.

Data availability

For the end-of-fiscal-year data, see *Historical Tables* and *Analytical Perspectives* in the *Budget of the United States Government*, which is available on the GPO Web site at <http://www.gpo.gov/usbudget>.

Recent quarterly data, measured on a somewhat different basis, are found in the *Treasury Bulletin* in the chapter on "Ownership of Federal Securities (OFS)," in Tables OFS-1 and OFS-2. The *Treasury Bulletin* can be accessed on the Internet at <http://www.fms.treas.gov/bulletin>. Holdings by Social Security funds are also available in the *Bulletin* in the

chapter on "Federal Debt," Table FD-3. The Disability Fund is listed separately from the Old-Age and Survivors Fund.

TABLE 6-17
GOVERNMENT EMPLOYMENT

SOURCE: U.S. DEPARTMENT OF LABOR, BUREAU OF LABOR STATISTICS (SEE NOTES AND DEFINITIONS FOR TABLE 10-7).

Government payroll employment includes federal, state, and local activities such as legislative, executive, and judicial functions, as well as all government-owned and government-operated business enterprises, establishments, and institutions (arsenals, navy yards, hospitals, etc.), and government force account construction. The figures relate to civilian employment only. The Bureau of Labor Statistics (BLS) considers regular full-time teachers (private and governmental) to be employed during the summer vacation period, regardless of whether they are specifically paid in those months.

Employment in federal government establishments reflects employee counts as of the pay period containing the 12th of the month. Federal government employment excludes employees of the Central Intelligence Agency and the National Security Agency.

CHAPTER 7: U.S. FOREIGN TRADE AND FINANCE

Section 7a: Foreign Transactions in the National Income and Product Accounts

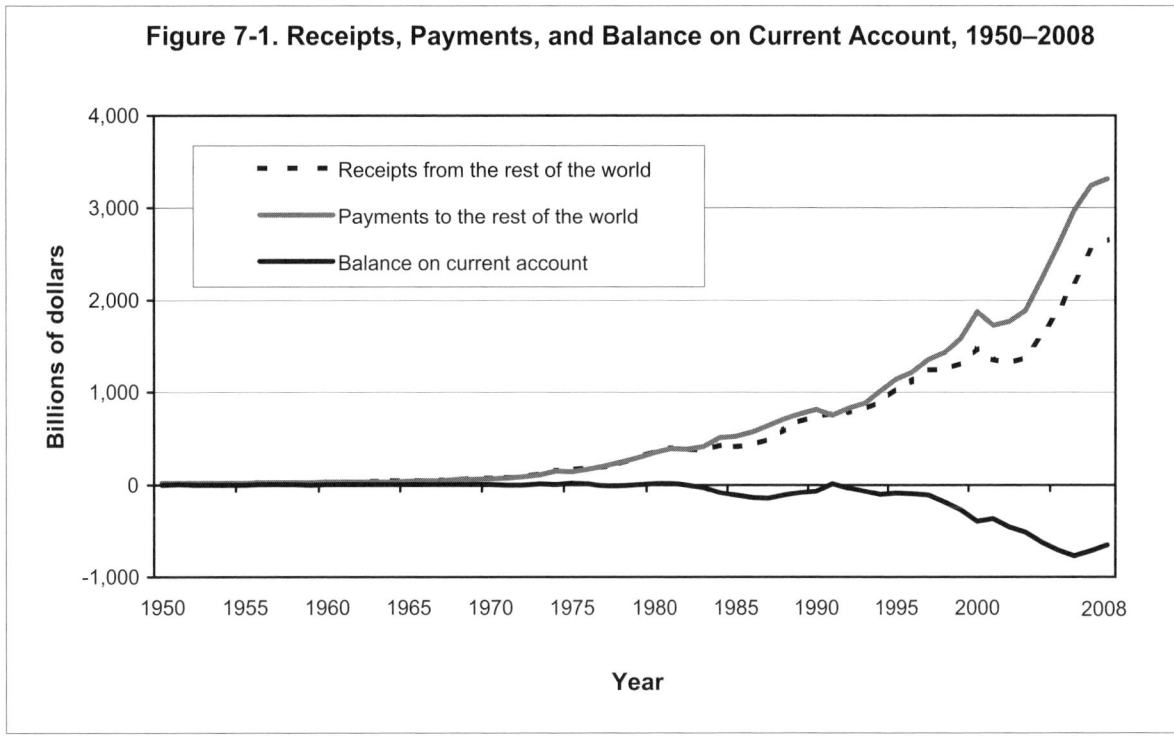

Figure 7-1. Receipts, Payments, and Balance on Current Account, 1950–2008

- For much of the early postwar period, U.S. current receipts from the rest of the world (exports and income receipts) and current payments to the rest of the world (imports, income payments, and net tax and transfer payments) were in rough balance. In most years through 1981, there was a surplus of receipts over payments—a positive balance on current account—that enabled the United States to invest in the economies of the rest of the world. (Table 7-1)

- However, beginning in 1983, large current-account deficits emerged, requiring net capital inflows from abroad to finance them. The only current-account surplus since then occurred in 1991, when payments from other countries financed most of the cost of the first Gulf War. (Table 7-1)

- U.S. current-account deficits typically diminish somewhat during recessions, as receipts hold up somewhat better than payments. The years 2007–2008 were no exception. (Table 7-1) In quantity terms, exports of goods and services continued to increase from 2006 to 2008, but goods imports declined. (Table 7-2)

- The NIPA current-account deficit of $656 billion in 2008 comprised a deficit of $832 billion on goods, a surplus of $163 billion on services, net income receipts of $133 billion, and net payments of $118 billion in taxes and transfer payments. (Table 7-1)

- All the major categories of goods and services in Table 7-5 show long-term growth in the quantity indexes for both exports and imports. Between 1967 and 2008, the slowest-growing category—imports of foods and feeds—grew at a 3.4 percent average annual rate in real terms, and the fastest-growing category—imports of capital goods, except automotive—grew at a 13.6 percent average annual rate. Generally, in the categories where both exports and imports grew relatively rapidly, such as autos and other consumer goods, capital goods, and financial and professional services, U.S. import growth exceeded export growth. (Table 7-5)

Table 7-1. Foreign Transactions in the National Income and Product Accounts

(Billions of dollars, quarterly data are at seasonally adjusted annual rates.)　　　　　　　　　　　　　　　　**NIPA Table 4.1**

Year and quarter	Current receipts from the rest of the world					Current payments to the rest of the world						Balance on current account, NIPAs	Net lending or net borrowing (-), NIPAs
	Total	Exports of goods and services			Income receipts	Total	Imports of goods and services			Income payments	Current taxes and transfer payments, net		
		Goods [1]		Services [1]			Goods [1]		Services [1]				
		Durable	Nondurable				Durable	Nondurable					
1950	14.5	5.1	5.1	2.1	2.2	16.4	3.0	6.1	2.5	0.7	4.0	-1.8	-1.8
1951	19.9	6.6	7.6	2.9	2.8	19.0	3.8	7.4	3.4	0.9	3.5	0.9	0.9
1952	19.3	6.9	6.5	3.0	2.9	18.7	4.1	6.7	4.5	0.9	2.5	0.6	0.6
1953	18.2	6.9	5.5	2.9	2.8	19.4	4.1	6.9	5.0	0.9	2.5	-1.3	-1.3
1954	18.9	7.1	5.8	2.9	3.0	18.6	3.6	6.7	5.1	0.9	2.3	0.2	0.2
1955	21.2	8.2	6.2	3.3	3.5	20.7	4.5	7.1	5.7	1.1	2.5	0.4	0.4
1956	25.2	9.8	7.8	3.7	3.9	22.5	5.2	7.6	6.1	1.1	2.4	2.8	2.8
1957	28.3	10.9	8.6	4.5	4.3	23.5	5.3	8.0	6.7	1.2	2.3	4.8	4.8
1958	24.4	9.0	7.4	4.1	3.9	23.5	5.0	8.0	7.1	1.2	2.3	0.9	0.9
1959	27.0	8.9	7.5	6.3	4.3	28.2	6.6	8.7	7.0	1.5	4.3	-1.2	-1.2
1960	31.9	11.3	9.2	6.6	4.9	28.7	6.4	8.9	7.6	1.8	4.1	3.2	3.2
1961	32.9	11.5	9.4	6.7	5.3	28.6	6.0	9.0	7.6	1.8	4.2	4.3	4.3
1962	35.0	12.0	9.7	7.4	5.9	31.1	6.9	9.9	8.1	1.8	4.3	3.9	3.9
1963	37.6	12.7	10.7	7.7	6.5	32.6	7.4	10.3	8.4	2.1	4.4	5.0	5.0
1964	42.3	14.7	12.0	8.3	7.2	34.7	8.4	11.0	8.7	2.3	4.3	7.5	7.5
1965	45.0	15.8	12.0	9.4	7.9	38.8	10.4	11.8	9.3	2.6	4.7	6.2	6.2
1966	49.0	17.5	13.2	10.2	8.1	45.1	13.3	13.1	10.7	3.0	5.0	3.9	3.9
1967	52.1	18.4	13.7	11.3	8.7	48.6	14.5	13.2	12.2	3.3	5.4	3.6	3.6
1968	58.0	21.0	14.3	12.6	10.1	56.3	18.8	15.1	12.6	4.0	5.7	1.7	1.7
1969	63.7	23.7	14.6	13.7	11.8	61.9	20.8	16.1	13.7	5.7	5.8	1.8	1.8
1970	72.5	27.1	17.4	15.2	12.8	68.5	22.8	18.1	14.9	6.4	6.3	4.0	4.0
1971	77.0	27.5	18.0	17.4	14.0	76.4	26.6	19.9	15.8	6.4	7.6	0.6	0.6
1972	87.1	31.0	20.8	19.0	16.3	90.7	33.3	23.6	17.3	7.7	8.8	-3.6	-3.6
1973	118.8	41.4	32.6	21.3	23.5	109.5	40.8	31.0	19.3	10.9	7.4	9.3	9.3
1974	156.5	56.5	44.5	25.7	29.8	149.8	50.3	54.2	22.9	14.3	8.1	6.6	6.6
1975	166.7	63.8	45.8	29.1	28.0	145.4	45.6	53.4	23.7	15.0	7.6	21.4	21.4
1976	181.9	69.0	48.7	31.7	32.4	173.0	56.8	67.8	26.5	15.5	6.3	8.9	8.9
1977	196.6	72.0	51.6	35.7	37.2	205.6	69.2	83.4	29.8	16.9	6.2	-9.0	-9.0
1978	233.1	85.3	60.1	41.5	46.3	243.6	89.0	88.4	34.8	24.7	6.7	-10.4	-10.4
1979	298.5	108.0	76.0	46.1	68.3	297.0	100.4	112.3	39.9	36.4	8.0	1.4	1.4
1980	359.9	133.3	92.5	55.0	79.1	348.5	111.9	136.6	45.3	44.9	9.8	11.4	11.4
1981	397.3	140.1	99.0	66.1	92.0	390.9	126.0	141.8	49.9	59.1	14.1	6.3	6.3
1982	384.2	124.7	90.3	68.2	101.0	384.4	125.1	125.4	52.6	64.5	16.7	-0.2	0.0
1983	378.9	120.4	86.9	69.7	101.9	410.9	147.3	125.4	56.0	64.8	17.5	-32.1	-31.8
1984	424.2	132.4	93.2	76.7	121.9	511.2	192.4	143.9	68.8	85.6	20.5	-86.9	-86.7
1985	414.5	137.2	85.0	79.8	112.4	525.3	204.2	139.1	73.9	85.9	22.2	-110.8	-110.5
1986	431.9	142.6	83.4	94.5	111.4	571.2	238.8	131.2	83.3	93.6	24.3	-139.2	-138.9
1987	487.1	162.9	94.6	106.4	123.2	637.9	264.2	150.6	94.3	105.3	23.5	-150.8	-150.4
1988	596.2	208.8	117.0	118.3	152.1	708.4	294.8	157.3	102.4	128.5	25.5	-112.2	-111.7
1989	681.0	239.8	129.5	134.0	177.7	769.3	310.4	174.4	106.7	151.5	26.4	-88.3	-88.0
1990	741.5	262.0	134.6	155.7	189.1	811.5	314.7	193.4	122.3	154.3	26.9	-70.1	-76.6
1991	765.7	282.3	141.3	173.3	168.9	752.3	315.7	185.0	123.6	138.5	-10.6	13.5	9.0
1992	788.0	300.6	147.4	187.4	152.7	824.9	346.9	198.1	123.6	123.0	33.4	-36.9	-37.5
1993	812.1	314.0	145.9	195.9	156.2	882.5	386.6	206.2	128.1	124.3	37.3	-70.4	-71.7
1994	907.3	349.7	160.4	210.8	186.4	1 012.5	454.2	222.6	137.7	160.2	37.8	-105.2	-106.9
1995	1 046.1	394.1	189.2	228.9	233.9	1 137.1	511.0	246.5	146.1	198.1	35.4	-91.0	-91.9
1996	1 117.3	421.8	196.6	250.2	248.7	1 217.6	533.6	273.8	157.4	213.7	39.1	-100.3	-101.0
1997	1 242.0	483.0	204.7	267.6	286.7	1 352.2	588.3	297.1	171.5	253.7	41.6	-110.2	-111.3
1998	1 243.1	487.1	193.8	275.1	287.1	1 430.5	636.5	292.5	186.9	265.8	48.8	-187.4	-188.1
1999	1 312.1	503.3	193.9	294.0	320.8	1 585.9	714.7	330.8	206.3	287.0	47.2	-273.9	-278.7
2000	1 478.9	569.2	215.1	311.9	382.7	1 875.6	820.7	422.8	232.3	343.7	56.1	-396.6	-397.4
2001	1 355.2	521.1	210.1	301.6	322.4	1 725.6	754.7	413.2	231.9	278.8	47.0	-370.4	-371.5
2002	1 311.6	487.2	210.4	308.4	305.7	1 769.9	770.0	419.4	241.0	275.0	64.5	-458.3	-459.7
2003	1 377.6	496.1	228.3	316.4	336.8	1 889.8	801.2	482.7	256.2	280.0	69.7	-512.3	-515.5
2004	1 619.9	563.8	254.5	364.1	437.5	2 244.0	934.1	565.4	298.3	361.3	84.9	-624.1	-626.5
2005	1 885.0	628.5	279.9	403.1	573.5	2 595.9	1 022.7	682.6	319.8	480.5	90.3	-710.9	-714.9
2006	2 206.1	718.2	313.9	448.7	725.4	2 977.0	1 127.6	755.1	355.4	647.1	92.5	-771.6	-775.5
2007	2 524.1	788.7	360.5	513.2	861.7	3 242.7	1 172.5	812.7	385.1	759.3	113.2	-718.6	-720.4
2008	2 657.7	836.2	447.0	576.3	798.3	3 311.3	1 156.5	958.6	413.4	665.1	117.7	-653.6	-656.1
2006													
1st quarter	2 085.1	692.3	298.6	432.4	661.9	2 853.9	1 098.9	739.7	346.3	582.4	86.6	-768.8	-775.6
2nd quarter	2 182.9	710.0	312.3	440.5	720.0	2 971.8	1 122.4	764.8	352.8	634.8	97.0	-788.9	-793.0
3rd quarter	2 238.4	723.1	321.5	448.0	745.9	3 064.0	1 140.6	789.2	355.4	679.4	99.4	-825.6	-827.7
4th quarter	2 318.2	747.3	323.4	473.8	773.7	3 021.5	1 148.5	726.6	367.2	691.8	87.2	-703.1	-705.6
2007													
1st quarter	2 348.8	752.8	332.2	475.5	788.2	3 126.4	1 157.4	759.9	372.0	715.8	121.2	-777.6	-779.8
2nd quarter	2 467.3	768.1	348.7	497.6	852.8	3 231.0	1 161.1	796.0	380.5	793.2	100.3	-763.8	-764.2
3rd quarter	2 613.4	807.6	373.6	533.8	898.5	3 295.4	1 189.5	815.8	392.1	786.3	111.7	-682.0	-684.5
4th quarter	2 667.1	826.4	387.3	546.0	907.4	3 318.1	1 181.9	878.9	395.6	742.0	119.6	-651.0	-653.3
2008													
1st quarter	2 664.0	829.2	427.7	563.9	843.2	3 357.0	1 173.2	944.8	408.5	705.1	125.4	-693.0	-695.4
2nd quarter	2 746.0	866.8	476.9	579.5	822.8	3 468.6	1 210.6	1 014.9	415.9	708.9	118.2	-722.6	-725.2
3rd quarter	2 784.5	882.1	492.1	594.6	815.6	3 480.9	1 194.3	1 056.7	425.6	688.7	115.6	-696.5	-699.1
4th quarter	2 436.3	766.5	391.1	567.1	711.6	2 938.9	1 048.1	818.0	403.6	557.7	111.4	-502.6	-504.8

[1] Exports and imports of certain goods, primarily military equipment purchased and sold by the federal government, are included in services. Beginning with 1986, repairs and alterations of equipment are reclassified from goods to services.

Table 7-2. Chain-Type Quantity Indexes for Exports and Imports of Goods and Services

(Index numbers, 2000 = 100.)

Year and quarter	Exports of goods and services					Imports of goods and services				
	Total	Goods [1]			Services [1]	Total	Goods [1]			Services [1]
		Total	Durable	Nondurable			Total	Durable	Nondurable	
1967	11.76	10.64	7.47	20.84	14.91	11.42	9.40	5.12	20.74	22.89
1968	12.68	11.48	8.17	22.05	16.05	13.12	11.34	6.52	23.50	23.30
1969	13.29	12.08	8.83	22.26	16.65	13.87	11.96	6.97	24.37	24.77
1970	14.72	13.46	9.66	25.53	18.13	14.46	12.43	7.16	25.70	26.06
1971	14.97	13.41	9.59	25.56	19.53	15.23	13.47	7.89	27.29	25.32
1972	16.10	14.85	10.60	28.42	19.40	16.94	15.31	9.07	30.48	26.39
1973	19.13	18.26	13.20	34.31	20.78	17.73	16.39	9.66	32.87	25.50
1974	20.64	19.71	15.24	33.99	22.40	17.33	15.93	9.70	30.82	25.47
1975	20.51	19.25	14.92	33.09	23.77	15.40	13.92	7.92	28.60	24.37
1976	21.41	20.17	15.13	36.27	24.48	18.41	17.07	9.71	35.09	26.05
1977	21.92	20.43	15.10	37.54	26.06	20.43	19.15	10.98	39.08	27.35
1978	24.23	22.71	16.83	41.57	28.23	22.20	20.87	12.70	40.35	29.30
1979	26.64	25.40	19.16	45.32	29.10	22.57	21.23	12.99	40.82	29.70
1980	29.51	28.42	21.37	50.97	30.92	21.07	19.65	13.09	35.15	29.04
1981	29.87	28.11	20.60	52.30	34.21	21.62	20.06	14.18	34.09	30.71
1982	27.59	25.57	17.91	50.72	33.26	21.35	19.55	14.34	32.10	32.35
1983	26.88	24.84	17.54	48.69	32.71	24.04	22.21	17.28	34.19	34.96
1984	29.07	26.80	19.43	50.61	35.63	29.89	27.58	23.00	38.94	43.72
1985	29.95	27.79	21.00	49.29	36.05	31.83	29.31	25.30	39.41	47.05
1986	32.26	29.22	22.22	51.26	41.33	34.56	32.31	27.64	44.06	47.64
1987	35.74	32.46	25.37	54.32	45.50	36.60	33.81	28.87	46.28	53.21
1988	41.47	38.57	31.48	59.87	49.62	38.04	35.18	30.07	48.05	55.01
1989	46.23	43.17	35.91	64.72	54.72	39.71	36.69	31.42	49.93	57.68
1990	50.39	46.81	39.75	67.46	60.48	41.14	37.77	32.25	51.65	61.43
1991	53.74	50.04	42.70	71.44	64.08	40.91	37.74	32.43	51.07	59.85
1992	57.44	53.79	46.11	76.06	67.59	43.75	41.26	35.82	54.85	58.32
1993	59.29	55.53	48.51	75.51	69.73	47.58	45.42	40.07	58.66	60.03
1994	64.45	60.94	54.38	79.09	74.10	53.26	51.47	46.69	62.93	63.42
1995	70.98	68.07	62.13	84.20	78.79	57.54	56.10	52.04	65.52	65.49
1996	76.93	74.09	69.37	86.81	84.48	62.54	61.34	57.61	69.82	69.09
1997	86.08	84.72	81.90	92.35	89.51	71.04	70.17	67.05	77.20	75.60
1998	88.16	86.61	84.53	92.28	92.08	79.30	78.36	75.77	84.14	84.22
1999	91.97	89.91	88.48	93.77	97.21	88.39	88.08	86.73	90.90	90.04
2000	100.00	100.00	100.00	100.00	100.00	100.00	100.00	100.00	100.00	100.00
2001	94.57	93.87	91.73	99.59	96.30	97.29	96.83	93.76	102.90	99.71
2002	92.43	90.14	86.29	100.46	98.10	100.60	100.38	97.61	105.83	101.82
2003	93.60	91.77	87.81	102.39	98.15	104.69	105.29	101.79	112.16	101.86
2004	102.72	100.01	98.13	105.58	109.45	116.55	117.17	116.29	119.49	113.59
2005	109.94	107.70	107.62	109.18	115.54	123.46	125.16	126.22	124.48	115.22
2006	119.94	118.41	119.98	116.30	123.83	130.82	132.61	137.42	126.62	122.15
2007	130.07	127.34	130.21	122.54	136.87	133.65	134.92	140.46	127.96	127.58
2008	138.11	134.95	136.20	133.22	145.92	129.04	129.33	134.39	122.86	127.86
2003										
1st quarter	91.52	89.97	85.09	102.88	95.39	102.36	102.56	98.70	110.07	101.49
2nd quarter	91.13	89.69	85.77	100.18	94.72	103.40	104.69	100.69	112.45	97.23
3rd quarter	93.61	91.60	87.41	102.78	98.62	104.35	104.85	100.90	112.51	102.02
4th quarter	98.14	95.83	92.96	103.74	103.87	108.67	109.09	106.85	113.63	106.69
2004										
1st quarter	100.50	97.54	95.31	103.95	107.84	111.87	112.10	109.39	117.53	110.84
2nd quarter	102.11	99.25	97.64	104.19	109.20	115.90	116.48	115.62	118.72	113.21
3rd quarter	102.90	100.75	99.31	105.27	108.24	117.28	118.03	118.33	118.34	113.71
4th quarter	105.39	102.50	100.27	108.92	112.53	121.14	122.09	121.82	123.37	116.60
2005										
1st quarter	107.45	104.28	102.46	109.69	115.29	122.08	123.58	122.64	125.98	114.89
2nd quarter	109.75	107.86	106.47	112.31	114.47	122.27	123.81	124.98	122.91	114.89
3rd quarter	109.85	107.63	108.10	107.83	115.39	122.51	124.15	126.66	121.31	114.59
4th quarter	112.72	111.02	113.43	106.91	117.00	126.96	129.11	130.60	127.72	116.50
2006										
1st quarter	117.15	115.73	117.31	113.56	120.75	130.12	131.94	135.49	127.72	121.34
2nd quarter	118.71	117.61	118.82	116.32	121.56	130.16	132.12	137.07	125.94	120.74
3rd quarter	119.73	118.66	120.07	116.94	122.53	131.16	133.34	138.22	127.25	120.66
4th quarter	124.15	121.62	123.72	118.40	130.47	131.82	133.06	138.92	125.59	125.87
2007										
1st quarter	124.34	122.25	124.53	118.64	129.59	134.29	135.77	139.83	130.85	127.17
2nd quarter	126.99	124.30	126.65	120.55	133.69	133.04	134.40	139.47	128.06	126.52
3rd quarter	133.75	130.57	133.43	125.81	141.62	134.03	135.20	142.05	126.49	128.46
4th quarter	135.19	132.22	136.24	125.16	142.57	133.25	134.32	140.49	126.45	128.19
2008										
1st quarter	136.88	133.69	135.48	130.92	144.79	132.99	133.65	138.22	127.69	129.91
2nd quarter	140.91	138.83	140.33	136.62	146.13	130.51	131.21	139.47	121.25	127.22
3rd quarter	141.94	140.08	142.01	137.13	146.64	129.37	129.65	136.91	120.73	128.25
4th quarter	132.71	127.20	126.97	128.19	146.10	123.28	122.79	122.94	121.79	126.04

[1]Exports and imports of certain goods, primarily military equipment purchased and sold by the federal government, are included in services. Beginning with 1986, repairs and alterations of equipment are reclassified from goods to services.

Table 7-3. Chain-Type Price Indexes for Exports and Imports of Goods and Services

(Index numbers, 2000 = 100.)   NIPA Table 4.2.4

Year and quarter	Exports of goods and services					Imports of goods and services				
	Total	Goods [1]			Services [1]	Total	Goods [1]			Services [1]
		Total	Durable	Nondurable			Total	Durable	Nondurable	
1967	33.73	38.56	43.39	30.65	24.29	23.69	23.75	34.60	15.07	22.86
1968	34.46	39.16	45.14	30.08	25.26	24.05	24.07	35.16	15.22	23.30
1969	35.63	40.37	47.11	30.44	26.31	24.68	24.75	36.28	15.58	23.78
1970	36.99	42.19	49.31	31.74	26.81	26.14	26.43	38.74	16.64	24.62
1971	38.36	43.32	50.45	32.76	28.58	27.74	27.78	41.10	17.29	26.85
1972	40.15	44.47	51.47	33.95	31.47	29.68	29.91	44.72	18.35	28.19
1973	45.43	51.62	55.04	44.13	32.94	34.84	35.26	51.48	22.33	32.61
1974	55.97	65.32	65.09	60.89	36.74	49.85	52.76	63.24	41.59	38.78
1975	61.68	72.60	75.12	64.38	39.21	54.00	57.18	70.19	44.14	41.92
1976	63.71	74.46	80.15	62.46	41.58	55.62	58.71	71.32	45.72	43.82
1977	66.30	77.17	83.82	63.92	43.92	60.52	64.08	76.76	50.50	46.93
1978	70.34	81.62	88.98	67.25	47.10	64.80	68.36	85.45	51.80	51.20
1979	78.81	92.40	99.03	77.99	50.77	75.88	80.61	94.25	65.09	57.82
1980	86.80	101.28	109.60	84.33	57.02	94.51	101.71	104.21	91.95	67.10
1981	93.22	108.43	119.47	87.98	61.97	99.59	107.38	108.33	98.36	70.01
1982	93.65	107.19	122.31	82.79	65.73	96.24	103.04	106.34	92.40	70.06
1983	94.02	106.41	120.58	82.98	68.31	92.63	98.73	103.87	86.72	68.91
1984	94.89	107.33	119.66	85.66	69.06	91.83	98.05	101.97	87.39	67.73
1985	91.98	101.96	114.83	80.17	70.94	88.81	94.19	98.34	83.51	67.65
1986	90.64	98.62	112.74	75.62	73.34	88.87	92.08	105.26	70.44	75.25
1987	92.87	101.17	112.81	80.98	74.94	94.25	98.65	111.52	76.97	76.32
1988	97.69	107.69	116.52	90.85	76.45	98.77	103.35	119.45	77.46	80.11
1989	99.31	109.08	117.32	93.04	78.50	100.94	106.27	120.39	82.61	79.66
1990	99.98	108.03	115.79	92.77	82.54	103.83	108.18	118.90	88.56	85.68
1991	101.31	107.91	116.12	91.94	86.69	103.42	106.70	118.63	85.70	88.88
1992	100.89	106.19	114.51	90.08	88.86	103.55	106.20	117.99	85.41	91.26
1993	100.90	105.59	113.73	89.83	90.07	102.67	104.95	117.56	83.14	91.87
1994	102.03	106.72	112.96	94.28	91.21	103.63	105.76	118.56	83.66	93.46
1995	104.38	109.25	111.44	104.46	93.14	106.41	108.57	119.65	88.98	96.06
1996	102.99	106.41	106.81	105.27	94.95	104.53	105.87	112.87	92.77	98.05
1997	101.23	103.50	103.60	103.05	95.86	100.82	101.47	106.90	91.01	97.69
1998	98.91	100.22	101.24	97.61	95.77	95.35	95.33	102.36	82.22	95.55
1999	98.31	98.87	99.94	96.11	96.97	95.96	95.46	100.41	86.07	98.63
2000	100.00	100.00	100.00	100.00	100.00	100.00	100.00	100.00	100.00	100.00
2001	99.62	99.32	99.80	98.08	100.39	97.50	97.00	98.09	94.98	100.13
2002	99.27	98.66	99.18	97.36	100.76	96.34	95.29	96.12	93.73	101.88
2003	101.43	100.64	99.26	103.64	103.33	99.69	98.06	95.92	101.80	108.29
2004	105.00	104.32	100.94	112.06	106.63	104.53	102.92	97.88	111.92	113.05
2005	108.81	107.54	102.59	119.19	111.86	111.15	109.57	98.73	129.71	119.50
2006	112.62	111.13	105.15	125.48	116.16	115.93	114.17	99.98	141.04	125.26
2007	116.59	115.06	106.41	136.75	120.21	120.17	118.33	101.72	150.22	129.93
2008	122.79	121.15	107.81	155.84	126.68	132.70	131.41	104.84	184.55	139.22
2003										
1st quarter	100.92	100.17	99.24	102.15	102.74	100.08	99.01	95.71	104.75	105.64
2nd quarter	101.19	100.58	99.37	103.18	102.69	99.09	97.31	95.70	100.10	108.63
3rd quarter	101.42	100.41	99.16	103.10	103.86	99.73	97.91	96.01	101.21	109.45
4th quarter	102.18	101.41	99.28	106.15	104.04	99.84	98.03	96.24	101.12	109.45
2004										
1st quarter	103.57	102.97	100.03	109.63	105.03	102.05	100.40	97.15	106.10	110.77
2nd quarter	104.79	104.29	100.66	112.61	106.02	103.87	102.33	97.90	110.16	112.04
3rd quarter	105.27	104.55	101.23	112.12	107.02	105.21	103.58	98.10	113.37	113.86
4th quarter	106.36	105.49	101.83	113.88	108.46	106.97	105.36	98.35	118.03	115.52
2005										
1st quarter	107.56	106.61	102.45	116.24	109.83	107.58	105.90	98.99	118.33	116.53
2nd quarter	108.49	107.41	102.64	118.58	111.06	110.10	108.45	99.04	125.69	118.78
3rd quarter	109.17	107.76	102.52	120.15	112.51	112.84	111.28	98.42	135.39	121.03
4th quarter	110.04	108.36	102.75	121.78	114.03	114.10	112.65	98.47	139.41	121.64
2006										
1st quarter	110.83	109.17	103.69	122.23	114.78	113.80	112.08	98.84	137.03	122.86
2nd quarter	112.42	110.84	105.00	124.83	116.17	116.62	114.88	99.79	143.65	125.80
3rd quarter	113.72	112.25	105.81	127.83	117.22	118.06	116.39	100.56	146.69	126.79
4th quarter	113.50	112.26	106.11	127.04	116.45	115.26	113.32	100.75	136.80	125.58
2007										
1st quarter	114.52	113.19	106.21	130.24	117.69	115.51	113.56	100.87	137.28	125.94
2nd quarter	116.01	114.59	106.54	134.58	119.39	119.05	117.09	101.44	146.90	129.48
3rd quarter	117.02	115.38	106.32	138.17	120.91	121.20	119.27	102.04	152.42	131.42
4th quarter	118.79	117.09	106.56	143.99	122.86	124.91	123.38	102.51	164.26	132.87
2008										
1st quarter	121.40	119.92	107.53	151.99	124.93	128.72	127.43	103.43	174.84	135.38
2nd quarter	124.56	123.46	108.52	162.41	127.21	137.14	136.39	105.77	197.80	140.74
3rd quarter	126.59	125.14	109.13	166.99	130.08	140.19	139.61	106.29	206.85	142.87
4th quarter	118.60	116.08	106.05	141.97	124.51	124.75	122.21	103.88	158.73	137.88

[1]Exports and imports of certain goods, primarily military equipment purchased and sold by the federal government, are included in services. Beginning with 1986, repairs and alterations of equipment are reclassified from goods to services.

Table 7-4. Exports and Imports of Selected NIPA Types of Product

(Billions of dollars, quarterly data are at seasonally adjusted annual rates.)   NIPA Table 4.2.5

Year and quarter	Exports							Imports							
	Goods					Services		Goods						Services	
	Foods, feeds, and beverages	Industrial supplies and materials	Capital goods, except auto-motive	Auto-motive vehicles, engines, and parts	Consumer goods, except auto-motive	Travel	Other private services (financial, profes-sional, etc.)	Foods, feeds, and beverages	Industrial supplies and materials, except petroleum and products	Petroleum and products	Capital goods, except auto-motive	Auto-motive vehicles, engines, and parts	Consumer goods, except auto-motive	Travel	Other private services (financial, profes-sional, etc.)
1967	5.0	10.0	9.9	2.8	2.1	1.6	0.7	4.6	9.9	2.1	2.5	2.4	4.2	3.2	0.4
1968	4.8	11.0	11.1	3.5	2.3	1.8	0.8	5.3	12.0	2.4	2.8	4.0	5.4	3.0	0.5
1969	4.7	11.7	12.4	3.9	2.6	2.0	0.9	5.2	11.7	2.6	3.4	5.1	6.5	3.4	0.6
1970	5.9	13.8	14.7	3.9	2.8	2.3	1.0	6.1	12.2	2.9	4.0	5.7	7.4	4.0	0.6
1971	6.1	12.6	15.4	4.7	2.9	2.5	1.3	6.4	13.6	3.7	4.3	7.6	8.4	4.4	0.7
1972	7.5	13.9	16.9	5.5	3.6	2.8	1.5	7.3	16.0	4.7	5.9	9.0	11.1	5.0	0.8
1973	15.2	19.7	22.0	7.0	4.8	3.4	1.7	9.1	19.2	8.4	8.3	10.7	12.9	5.5	0.9
1974	18.6	29.9	30.9	8.8	6.4	4.0	3.0	10.6	27.0	26.6	9.8	12.4	14.4	6.0	1.9
1975	19.2	29.3	36.6	10.8	6.6	4.7	3.7	9.6	23.6	27.0	10.2	12.1	13.2	6.4	2.3
1976	19.8	31.6	39.1	12.2	8.0	5.7	4.5	11.5	28.5	34.6	12.3	16.8	17.2	6.9	2.9
1977	19.7	33.2	39.8	13.5	8.9	6.2	4.9	14.0	33.4	45.0	14.0	19.4	21.8	7.5	3.2
1978	25.7	38.4	47.5	15.2	11.4	7.2	6.2	15.8	39.3	42.6	19.3	25.0	29.4	8.5	3.9
1979	30.5	53.3	60.2	17.9	14.0	8.4	7.3	18.0	45.0	60.4	24.6	26.6	31.3	9.4	4.6
1980	36.3	68.0	76.3	17.4	17.8	10.6	8.6	18.6	47.3	79.5	31.6	28.3	34.3	10.4	5.1
1981	38.8	65.7	84.2	19.7	17.7	12.9	13.2	18.6	52.0	78.4	37.1	31.0	38.4	11.5	6.3
1982	32.2	61.8	76.5	17.2	16.1	12.4	16.9	17.5	45.4	62.0	38.4	34.3	39.7	12.4	7.4
1983	32.1	57.1	71.7	18.5	14.9	10.9	17.6	18.8	51.1	55.1	43.7	43.0	47.3	13.2	7.3
1984	32.2	61.9	77.0	22.4	15.1	17.2	18.6	21.9	62.6	58.1	60.4	56.5	61.1	22.9	8.2
1985	24.6	59.4	79.3	24.9	14.6	17.8	19.4	21.8	59.2	51.4	61.3	64.9	66.3	24.6	9.4
1986	23.5	59.0	82.8	25.1	16.7	20.4	28.5	24.4	62.5	34.3	72.0	78.1	79.4	25.9	14.2
1987	25.2	67.4	92.7	27.6	20.3	23.6	29.8	24.8	66.1	42.9	85.1	85.2	88.8	29.3	17.7
1988	33.8	84.2	119.1	33.4	27.0	29.4	31.6	24.9	76.6	39.6	102.2	87.9	96.4	32.1	18.9
1989	36.3	95.3	136.9	35.0	36.0	36.2	37.2	24.9	78.8	50.9	112.4	87.2	103.6	33.4	20.4
1990	35.2	101.8	153.1	36.1	43.6	43.0	40.8	26.4	78.2	62.3	116.3	88.4	104.9	37.4	23.9
1991	35.8	106.1	166.6	39.7	46.7	48.4	48.3	26.2	75.6	51.7	121.0	85.7	107.6	35.3	27.6
1992	40.3	105.0	176.5	46.7	51.3	54.7	50.6	27.6	82.4	51.6	134.6	91.7	122.4	38.6	26.1
1993	40.6	102.8	182.9	51.3	54.6	57.9	53.8	27.9	88.7	51.5	152.9	102.4	133.7	40.7	28.7
1994	42.0	115.7	205.8	57.3	59.9	58.4	61.3	31.0	105.0	51.3	185.0	118.1	145.9	43.8	32.6
1995	50.5	141.3	234.5	61.3	64.3	63.4	65.5	33.2	119.9	56.0	222.2	123.6	159.4	44.9	36.2
1996	55.5	141.0	254.0	64.2	70.1	69.8	73.7	35.7	125.2	72.7	228.5	128.7	171.9	48.1	40.5
1997	51.5	152.6	295.9	73.3	78.0	73.4	84.5	39.7	135.3	71.7	253.4	139.5	194.1	52.1	44.6
1998	46.4	142.8	299.9	72.4	80.3	71.3	92.6	41.2	142.5	50.6	269.4	148.7	217.1	56.5	49.6
1999	46.0	142.4	311.2	75.3	80.9	74.8	105.2	43.6	147.9	67.8	295.7	179.0	242.0	59.0	58.1
2000	47.9	166.6	357.0	80.4	89.4	82.4	109.3	46.0	172.8	120.2	347.0	195.9	282.0	64.7	64.0
2001	49.4	155.3	321.7	75.4	88.3	71.9	116.3	46.6	164.8	103.6	298.0	189.8	284.5	60.2	70.9
2002	49.6	153.5	290.4	78.9	84.4	66.6	125.3	49.7	158.4	103.5	283.3	203.7	308.0	58.7	77.3
2003	55.0	168.3	293.7	80.6	89.9	64.3	130.7	55.8	174.4	133.1	295.9	210.1	334.0	57.4	80.2
2004	56.6	199.5	331.4	89.2	103.2	74.5	148.1	62.1	225.1	180.5	343.6	228.2	377.1	65.8	91.3
2005	59.0	227.5	363.3	98.4	115.3	81.8	160.0	68.1	264.8	251.9	379.3	239.4	411.5	69.0	97.8
2006	66.0	267.3	415.0	107.0	129.1	85.7	189.1	74.9	290.1	302.4	418.3	256.6	446.1	72.1	125.2
2007	84.3	303.1	447.4	121.0	146.1	96.7	223.5	81.7	294.4	331.0	444.5	258.9	478.5	76.2	144.4
2008	109.7	368.0	469.2	121.5	161.3	111.1	249.2	88.9	310.2	450.1	453.0	233.9	484.1	81.2	154.7
2003															
1st quarter	52.6	167.0	282.8	79.7	86.8	63.2	126.6	53.9	170.6	142.1	285.7	205.4	326.3	58.0	78.6
2nd quarter	53.0	165.5	283.2	82.0	87.8	57.3	129.0	54.9	170.9	125.9	292.1	211.7	327.9	52.0	77.9
3rd quarter	55.5	166.8	293.1	78.4	91.1	64.7	131.2	56.4	177.1	131.2	294.1	205.0	333.9	58.6	79.6
4th quarter	59.0	173.8	315.5	82.5	93.9	72.1	136.2	58.1	178.9	133.1	311.5	218.4	348.0	61.3	84.6
2004															
1st quarter	56.9	187.7	323.3	83.8	97.7	71.5	144.4	59.8	196.2	160.8	324.2	221.1	359.1	63.4	87.9
2nd quarter	56.0	196.4	329.5	87.7	102.7	74.7	146.6	62.5	221.8	166.5	340.4	229.6	379.8	65.8	89.1
3rd quarter	55.0	201.3	334.7	92.1	104.2	74.8	145.4	61.8	237.1	177.9	349.9	230.2	376.5	66.4	90.0
4th quarter	58.3	212.5	338.2	93.2	108.4	77.3	156.2	64.4	245.4	216.6	359.7	231.8	393.2	67.3	98.1
2005															
1st quarter	57.3	220.8	344.8	95.0	111.6	79.7	158.2	65.1	252.8	214.2	363.3	231.7	408.9	68.8	91.8
2nd quarter	60.5	230.9	363.0	95.5	114.2	83.7	153.4	67.5	255.2	230.1	381.3	234.5	413.2	70.0	95.7
3rd quarter	58.1	228.2	362.4	98.8	116.0	81.6	159.1	68.9	257.5	266.7	381.6	240.2	409.0	68.6	99.3
4th quarter	59.9	230.2	383.0	104.4	119.4	82.1	169.5	70.9	293.5	296.4	391.2	251.4	415.0	68.5	104.5
2006															
1st quarter	62.2	249.4	401.0	105.5	123.5	83.6	181.5	73.3	285.3	293.2	403.9	257.8	428.5	70.5	119.1
2nd quarter	64.9	267.8	411.9	104.7	127.0	85.1	184.0	73.3	288.1	313.7	415.4	258.0	438.9	71.8	123.3
3rd quarter	68.2	273.5	415.9	108.4	130.7	85.9	186.4	75.6	300.0	333.2	426.3	251.7	452.1	72.1	124.7
4th quarter	68.6	278.5	431.1	109.3	135.2	88.2	204.3	77.6	287.0	269.7	427.5	258.9	465.1	74.0	133.8
2007															
1st quarter	73.9	279.2	429.9	113.6	140.8	87.3	206.0	79.4	284.8	283.2	435.5	256.8	479.3	74.2	137.8
2nd quarter	78.7	296.3	433.3	118.6	143.4	92.6	218.1	80.4	299.9	312.5	439.7	254.0	475.9	75.4	141.7
3rd quarter	89.9	311.6	457.7	126.3	149.6	101.0	233.6	83.2	300.4	332.1	449.7	264.9	474.7	77.0	148.6
4th quarter	94.6	325.0	468.8	125.8	150.5	106.0	236.2	83.7	292.3	396.1	453.1	260.0	484.3	78.1	149.4
2008															
1st quarter	109.4	347.6	466.2	122.4	156.9	107.4	243.4	85.4	297.5	448.7	454.4	257.3	481.4	81.3	152.1
2nd quarter	119.7	395.4	480.6	124.2	163.9	112.1	249.0	90.1	325.5	494.5	469.3	249.9	496.3	81.9	154.3
3rd quarter	118.2	416.7	487.8	131.9	169.5	117.8	254.4	91.7	337.9	525.7	464.0	232.8	502.9	81.4	157.3
4th quarter	91.6	312.3	442.1	107.4	154.8	107.2	250.2	88.2	279.7	331.7	424.3	195.5	455.8	80.1	155.0

Table 7-5. Chain-Type Quantity Indexes for Exports and Imports of Selected NIPA Types of Product

(Index numbers, 2000 = 100.)   NIPA Table 4.2.3

	Exports							Imports							
	Goods					Services		Goods						Services	
Year and quarter	Foods, feeds, and beverages	Industrial supplies and materials	Capital goods, except automotive	Auto-motive vehicles, engines, and parts	Consumer goods, except auto-motive	Travel	Other private services (financial, profes-sional, etc.)	Foods, feeds, and beverages	Industrial supplies and materials, except petroleum and products	Petroleum and products	Capital goods, except auto-motive	Auto-motive vehicles, engines, and parts	Consumer goods, except auto-motive	Travel	Other private services (financial, profes-sional, etc.)
1967	26.36	23.08	4.04	17.27	7.81	9.91	2.54	35.29	24.28	20.44	0.77	8.39	5.92	17.14	1.75
1968	25.94	26.26	4.16	21.28	8.49	10.24	2.63	40.04	28.90	23.54	0.88	13.06	7.48	15.53	1.98
1969	25.40	27.46	4.41	23.00	9.09	11.18	2.89	37.94	27.35	26.27	1.03	15.95	8.82	16.85	2.20
1970	30.65	30.75	4.93	22.47	9.64	12.06	3.09	40.53	27.64	28.37	1.07	16.31	9.49	19.44	2.30
1971	29.84	27.80	5.15	25.47	9.67	12.59	3.59	41.84	30.12	32.45	1.06	19.89	9.98	19.42	2.54
1972	35.22	29.61	5.64	28.59	11.30	13.52	4.00	44.54	33.05	39.63	1.36	21.55	12.17	21.01	2.62
1973	45.60	36.43	7.16	33.56	13.78	15.53	4.36	45.67	33.27	56.30	1.68	22.24	12.49	19.82	2.93
1974	40.86	37.49	8.94	37.44	17.14	16.90	7.12	42.25	32.41	54.20	1.79	23.62	11.24	17.79	5.90
1975	43.23	32.79	9.08	39.42	15.80	18.27	8.26	37.37	27.30	53.30	1.70	18.75	8.71	17.16	6.67
1976	49.05	35.42	8.96	41.21	17.82	20.82	9.56	42.54	33.25	64.27	2.06	24.84	11.24	18.25	8.01
1977	49.01	35.71	8.81	41.51	19.27	20.86	9.85	42.11	35.77	77.32	2.20	26.31	13.58	18.81	8.39
1978	60.55	39.47	10.06	42.62	22.25	22.41	11.67	47.28	39.17	73.10	2.84	28.47	16.68	19.43	9.80
1979	64.23	45.20	12.08	42.89	23.39	24.03	13.00	48.53	37.63	73.94	3.47	27.53	16.81	18.95	11.10
1980	72.41	51.30	14.10	36.12	28.35	26.84	13.89	42.24	32.84	59.72	4.09	27.28	16.93	18.93	11.33
1981	73.93	47.84	14.15	35.71	27.18	29.62	19.87	43.95	35.65	52.33	4.82	26.40	18.54	20.02	13.35
1982	69.46	46.40	12.51	29.26	24.46	26.41	23.96	44.80	32.32	45.00	5.24	28.25	19.38	23.74	15.14
1983	66.39	44.14	12.07	30.27	22.37	22.30	23.67	48.62	38.38	44.54	6.34	34.58	23.32	26.89	14.18
1984	64.60	46.40	13.37	35.72	22.26	33.26	24.00	55.08	47.60	47.05	9.48	44.44	29.44	49.15	15.89
1985	55.91	46.67	14.69	38.87	21.60	32.93	23.96	57.46	47.87	44.18	10.68	49.79	32.14	54.25	17.71
1986	57.68	48.75	16.03	38.23	23.89	36.74	34.02	58.82	50.41	54.62	12.12	53.90	35.61	50.43	25.44
1987	61.73	49.97	18.51	41.21	28.11	40.54	34.06	60.29	49.92	57.05	13.84	55.31	36.76	59.80	28.93
1988	67.84	56.33	23.53	48.91	35.91	48.91	35.63	57.90	50.46	63.10	15.96	53.92	37.30	61.45	30.85
1989	70.75	62.58	27.29	50.14	46.21	58.46	41.11	59.22	49.33	68.06	18.07	52.45	39.03	63.32	35.90
1990	73.20	66.23	31.59	50.17	54.13	65.94	43.21	61.49	50.07	68.97	19.48	52.72	38.34	67.65	38.87
1991	74.65	70.80	34.55	53.75	56.05	69.86	49.12	58.71	49.15	65.55	20.94	49.18	38.99	61.26	43.16
1992	84.50	72.10	37.86	62.03	60.35	77.51	50.06	61.98	54.04	67.94	24.26	51.72	43.05	63.07	40.76
1993	83.96	70.20	40.34	67.60	63.43	81.30	52.14	62.70	58.63	74.98	28.29	56.86	46.63	66.16	43.70
1994	83.99	74.12	46.54	74.75	69.35	81.70	58.50	64.13	67.37	79.61	34.76	63.56	50.52	68.51	49.82
1995	93.15	79.87	55.43	78.89	73.51	87.60	61.25	65.71	70.74	78.21	42.80	64.62	54.40	69.05	55.29
1996	91.66	83.60	64.24	81.83	79.08	94.21	67.64	72.26	74.90	84.38	50.29	66.84	58.49	71.76	61.10
1997	91.84	90.83	78.76	92.64	87.29	96.90	76.58	79.60	81.05	88.20	63.05	72.30	66.85	77.95	67.28
1998	90.93	89.84	82.12	91.39	89.90	93.09	83.98	85.42	89.81	93.94	72.46	76.96	75.79	88.11	76.53
1999	94.44	90.89	86.65	94.43	90.91	95.14	96.91	93.39	93.67	94.46	83.19	92.01	85.08	89.82	89.56
2000	100.00	100.00	100.00	100.00	100.00	100.00	100.00	100.00	100.00	100.00	100.00	100.00	100.00	100.00	100.00
2001	102.86	96.10	90.18	93.56	99.19	86.93	106.32	104.61	96.37	103.71	88.60	96.96	101.70	95.26	110.85
2002	100.78	96.40	82.36	97.41	95.21	81.20	114.72	110.13	99.12	101.08	87.16	103.78	111.25	90.22	118.35
2003	102.52	98.85	84.21	98.80	100.90	76.98	118.10	118.67	100.81	107.64	92.37	106.46	120.90	81.49	122.34
2004	96.09	105.16	95.21	108.46	114.78	86.37	130.64	125.48	116.64	114.66	108.49	113.66	135.70	86.96	139.53
2005	101.49	108.03	104.15	118.30	126.76	91.13	136.44	130.06	124.52	117.24	120.58	118.03	146.81	85.42	145.26
2006	109.58	116.10	118.03	127.05	140.13	91.58	155.45	137.94	129.89	114.96	134.05	126.01	158.55	85.90	172.11
2007	119.27	122.48	127.53	142.11	155.34	99.73	178.02	139.69	124.90	112.67	141.96	125.86	167.79	84.47	193.48
2008	124.89	135.35	132.80	140.90	167.91	109.65	193.56	137.60	114.36	108.16	142.65	110.89	165.47	85.98	200.41
2003															
1st quarter	102.25	99.16	80.72	97.86	97.74	75.96	115.05	114.89	98.13	105.49	89.00	104.34	118.15	85.90	119.59
2nd quarter	100.55	97.44	80.90	100.55	98.69	69.24	116.81	117.11	99.47	108.61	91.07	107.39	118.68	72.15	118.56
3rd quarter	104.22	98.33	84.25	95.93	102.19	77.22	118.72	119.92	102.87	106.95	91.75	104.01	120.86	82.02	121.14
4th quarter	103.07	100.46	90.96	100.86	104.98	85.48	122.65	122.79	102.78	109.50	97.67	110.10	125.89	85.89	130.06
2004															
1st quarter	95.50	103.71	93.11	102.40	109.02	84.08	128.94	123.53	106.72	118.94	101.58	110.91	129.00	86.72	135.50
2nd quarter	88.81	105.45	94.70	106.74	114.46	86.79	129.68	126.49	115.66	110.20	107.42	114.70	136.64	87.79	136.36
3rd quarter	95.64	104.78	96.14	111.88	115.56	86.45	127.73	125.11	121.46	108.18	110.80	114.49	135.75	86.94	136.13
4th quarter	104.40	106.72	96.87	112.80	120.06	88.17	136.22	126.80	122.71	121.34	114.15	114.56	141.39	86.40	150.12
2005															
1st quarter	100.94	107.71	98.66	114.57	122.80	90.46	136.16	125.88	123.56	122.85	114.81	114.43	145.74	87.42	140.41
2nd quarter	103.31	110.58	103.88	114.97	125.52	94.40	130.96	128.50	122.95	113.50	120.44	115.48	147.22	85.55	143.51
3rd quarter	98.81	107.86	103.87	118.66	127.62	90.20	135.58	132.23	122.45	110.07	121.62	118.30	146.02	83.20	146.10
4th quarter	102.90	105.98	110.18	124.98	131.09	89.45	143.08	133.62	129.11	122.54	125.43	123.69	148.25	85.52	151.01
2006															
1st quarter	106.69	112.77	114.87	126.01	135.18	90.42	151.12	136.61	129.23	121.66	129.57	127.15	152.81	87.94	166.96
2nd quarter	110.35	116.29	117.36	124.48	138.17	90.71	151.70	136.70	130.18	112.41	133.31	126.90	156.47	85.01	170.23
3rd quarter	112.29	115.68	118.01	128.44	141.11	90.76	152.06	138.46	133.13	114.46	136.52	123.33	160.39	83.02	169.62
4th quarter	108.98	119.64	121.87	129.27	146.05	94.42	166.92	140.00	127.02	111.30	136.82	126.66	164.54	87.63	181.62
2007															
1st quarter	111.14	118.08	121.94	133.79	151.07	92.28	166.31	140.17	124.00	119.06	139.52	125.46	168.78	87.83	187.02
2nd quarter	115.97	120.12	123.55	139.37	152.70	96.11	174.83	139.39	126.41	111.79	141.18	123.93	167.49	82.88	190.63
3rd quarter	126.98	124.73	130.73	148.18	158.75	103.53	185.49	140.99	128.14	107.82	143.29	128.89	166.16	82.41	198.35
4th quarter	122.99	126.98	133.89	147.12	158.85	106.99	185.44	138.20	121.05	112.01	143.85	125.17	168.75	84.77	197.94
2008															
1st quarter	127.18	130.38	132.68	142.70	164.47	106.88	189.92	136.37	115.43	116.64	144.25	122.62	165.93	86.50	199.85
2nd quarter	129.85	138.94	136.26	144.20	170.41	110.08	193.27	137.96	115.32	103.47	147.34	118.53	169.22	83.98	200.09
3rd quarter	126.18	141.86	137.74	152.74	175.62	113.14	195.72	137.46	117.48	101.73	145.30	110.06	171.01	84.99	201.32
4th quarter	116.35	130.22	124.53	123.95	161.14	108.52	195.34	138.61	109.22	110.80	133.72	92.34	155.72	88.46	200.37

Section 7b: U.S. International Transactions Accounts

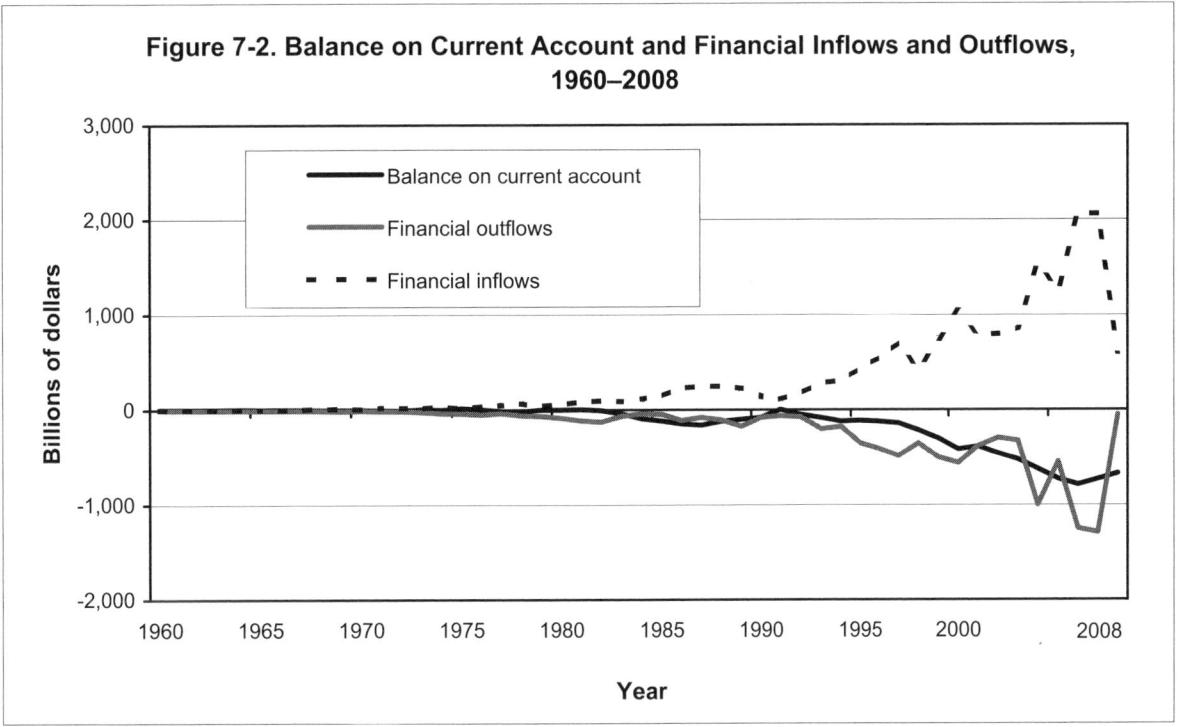

Figure 7-2. Balance on Current Account and Financial Inflows and Outflows, 1960–2008

- The U.S. current-account international balance is also recorded in the International Transactions Accounts (ITAs). The definitional differences between this balance and the balance in the NIPAs are minor, and the trends in the two measures are similar. The ITAs measure the current account surplus or deficit (commonly known as the "balance of payments") and directly measure the financial flows required to finance it. (Table 7-6)

- Figure 7-2 above shows the current-account balance since 1960, culminating in a $673 billion deficit in 2008. U.S. investment in assets abroad contributed a small further outflow, amounting to $52 billion in 2008. Financing the sum of these was a financial inflow, or an increase in foreign-owned assets in the United States, of $599 billion. The net of the financial flows does not equal the current-account balance because of a capital transactions item and the ITA statistical discrepancy. (Table 7-6)

- As Figure 7-2 suggests, the latest three years saw dramatic swings in international financial flows. U.S. private investors acquired foreign assets (indicated by a minus sign, because such investments represent an outflow) in the amount of over 1¼ trillion in both 2006 and 2007, then dumped such assets in 2008—while in the second half of 2008, the U.S. government acquired half a trillion in foreign currency and short-term assets. Foreigners' net acquisition of U.S. assets, over $2 trillion in 2006 and 2007, dropped to half a trillion in 2008. (Table 7-6)

- Before the 1980s, the United States was a net creditor with respect to the rest of the world. In other words, the value of the stock of U.S-owned assets abroad exceeded the value of foreign-owned assets in the United States. Since then, the persistent net financial inflows associated with current-account deficits have cumulated, resulting in a growing net debtor status, with the value of foreign-owned assets in the United States exceeding the value of U.S-owned assets abroad by $2.4 trillion as of the end of 2007. (Table 7-8)

Table 7-6. U.S. International Transactions

(Millions of dollars, seasonally adjusted.)

Year and quarter	Current account										
	Exports of goods and services and income receipts										
						Income receipts					
							Income receipts on U.S.-owned assets abroad				
	Total	Exports of goods and services	Exports of goods	Exports of services	Total	Total	Direct investment receipts	Other private receipts	U.S. government receipts	Compensation of employees
1960	30 556	25 940	19 650	6 290	4 616	4 616	3 621	646	349	. . .
1961	31 402	26 403	20 108	6 295	4 999	4 999	3 823	793	383	. . .
1962	33 340	27 722	20 781	6 941	5 618	5 618	4 241	904	473	. . .
1963	35 776	29 620	22 272	7 348	6 157	6 157	4 636	1 022	499	. . .
1964	40 165	33 341	25 501	7 840	6 824	6 824	5 106	1 256	462	. . .
1965	42 722	35 285	26 461	8 824	7 437	7 437	5 506	1 421	510	. . .
1966	46 454	38 926	29 310	9 616	7 528	7 528	5 260	1 669	599	. . .
1967	49 353	41 333	30 666	10 667	8 021	8 021	5 603	1 781	636	. . .
1968	54 911	45 543	33 626	11 917	9 367	9 367	6 591	2 021	756	. . .
1969	60 132	49 220	36 414	12 806	10 913	10 913	7 649	2 338	925	. . .
1970	68 387	56 640	42 469	14 171	11 748	11 748	8 169	2 671	907	. . .
1971	72 384	59 677	43 319	16 358	12 707	12 707	9 160	2 641	906	. . .
1972	81 986	67 222	49 381	17 841	14 765	14 765	10 949	2 949	866	. . .
1973	113 050	91 242	71 410	19 832	21 808	21 808	16 542	4 330	936	. . .
1974	148 484	120 897	98 306	22 591	27 587	27 587	19 157	7 356	1 074	. . .
1975	157 936	132 585	107 088	25 497	25 351	25 351	16 595	7 644	1 112	. . .
1976	172 090	142 716	114 745	27 971	29 375	29 375	18 999	9 043	1 332	. . .
1977	184 655	152 301	120 816	31 485	32 354	32 354	19 673	11 057	1 625	. . .
1978	220 516	178 428	142 075	36 353	42 088	42 088	25 458	14 788	1 843	. . .
1979	287 965	224 131	184 439	39 692	63 834	63 834	38 183	23 356	2 295	. . .
1980	344 440	271 834	224 250	47 584	72 606	72 606	37 146	32 898	2 562	. . .
1981	380 928	294 398	237 044	57 354	86 529	86 529	32 549	50 300	3 680	. . .
1982	366 983	275 236	211 157	64 079	91 747	91 747	29 469	58 160	4 118	. . .
1983	356 106	266 106	201 799	64 307	90 000	90 000	31 750	53 418	4 832	. . .
1984	399 913	291 094	219 926	71 168	108 819	108 819	35 325	68 267	5 227	. . .
1985	387 612	289 070	215 915	73 155	98 542	98 542	35 410	57 633	5 499	. . .
1986	407 098	310 033	223 344	86 689	97 064	96 156	36 938	52 806	6 413	908
1987	457 053	348 869	250 208	98 661	108 184	107 190	46 288	55 592	5 311	994
1988	567 862	431 149	320 230	110 919	136 713	135 718	58 445	70 571	6 703	995
1989	648 290	487 003	359 916	127 087	161 287	160 270	61 981	92 638	5 651	1 017
1990	706 975	535 233	387 401	147 832	171 742	170 570	65 973	94 072	10 525	1 172
1991	727 557	578 343	414 083	164 260	149 214	147 924	58 718	81 186	8 019	1 290
1992	750 648	616 882	439 631	177 251	133 767	131 971	57 539	67 316	7 115	1 796
1993	778 921	642 863	456 943	185 920	136 057	134 237	67 245	61 865	5 126	1 820
1994	869 775	703 254	502 859	200 395	166 521	164 578	77 344	83 106	4 128	1 943
1995	1 004 631	794 387	575 204	219 183	210 244	208 065	95 260	108 092	4 713	2 179
1996	1 077 731	851 602	612 113	239 489	226 129	223 948	102 505	116 852	4 591	2 181
1997	1 191 257	934 453	678 366	256 087	256 804	254 534	115 323	135 652	3 559	2 270
1998	1 194 993	933 174	670 416	262 758	261 819	259 382	103 963	151 818	3 601	2 437
1999	1 259 809	965 884	683 965	281 919	293 925	291 177	131 626	156 354	3 197	2 748
2000	1 421 515	1 070 597	771 994	298 603	350 918	348 083	151 839	192 398	3 846	2 835
2001	1 295 693	1 004 896	718 712	286 184	290 797	287 918	128 665	155 692	3 561	2 879
2002	1 255 663	974 721	682 422	292 299	280 942	278 131	145 590	129 238	3 303	2 811
2003	1 338 213	1 017 757	713 415	304 342	320 456	317 643	186 417	126 529	4 697	2 813
2004	1 574 326	1 160 588	807 516	353 072	413 739	410 917	250 606	157 313	2 998	2 822
2005	1 819 016	1 283 753	894 631	389 122	535 263	532 373	294 538	235 120	2 715	2 890
2006	2 142 164	1 457 015	1 023 109	433 905	685 150	682 270	328 543	351 327	2 400	2 880
2007	2 463 505	1 645 726	1 148 481	497 245	817 779	814 807	368 275	444 299	2 233	2 972
2008	2 591 254	1 835 786	1 291 371	544 414	755 468	752 421	371 268	376 249	4 904	3 048
2005										
1st quarter	434 701	310 048	214 857	95 191	124 653	123 948	71 552	51 691	705	705
2nd quarter	447 848	319 361	223 728	95 633	128 487	127 762	71 563	55 493	706	725
3rd quarter	457 508	321 370	223 603	97 767	136 138	135 411	73 952	60 832	627	727
4th quarter	478 958	332 973	232 443	100 530	145 986	145 253	77 472	67 104	677	733
2006										
1st quarter	504 862	349 179	244 679	104 500	155 683	154 962	78 178	76 194	590	721
2nd quarter	529 782	359 771	253 332	106 439	170 011	169 284	82 489	86 208	587	727
3rd quarter	543 893	367 643	259 277	108 365	176 251	175 539	82 911	92 034	594	712
4th quarter	563 627	380 422	265 821	114 600	183 205	182 485	84 965	96 891	629	720
2007										
1st quarter	572 182	385 436	270 318	115 118	186 746	186 013	83 391	102 063	559	733
2nd quarter	602 122	399 951	279 488	120 463	202 171	201 434	89 673	111 187	574	737
3rd quarter	638 393	424 873	295 494	129 378	213 520	212 774	94 953	117 275	546	746
4th quarter	650 808	435 465	303 180	132 285	215 343	214 587	100 259	113 774	554	756
2008										
1st quarter	651 416	451 517	317 548	133 969	199 900	199 137	97 346	101 088	703	763
2nd quarter	671 888	475 365	337 048	138 318	196 523	195 756	101 612	93 412	732	767
3rd quarter	678 258	485 911	346 272	139 639	192 347	191 603	95 708	94 583	1 312	745
4th quarter	589 692	422 993	290 505	132 489	166 699	165 925	76 603	87 166	2 156	774

. . . = Not available.

Table 7-6. U.S. International Transactions—*Continued*

(Millions of dollars, seasonally adjusted.)

Year and quarter	Current account—*Continued*									
	Imports of goods and services and income payments [1]									
					Income payments					
						Income payments on foreign-owned assets in the U.S.				
	Total	Imports of goods and services	Imports of goods	Imports of services	Total	Total	Direct investment payments	Other private payments	U.S. government payments	Compensation of employees
1960	-23 670	-22 432	-14 758	-7 674	-1 238	-1 238	-394	-511	-332	. . .
1961	-23 453	-22 208	-14 537	-7 671	-1 245	-1 245	-432	-535	-278	. . .
1962	-25 676	-24 352	-16 260	-8 092	-1 324	-1 324	-399	-586	-339	. . .
1963	-26 970	-25 410	-17 048	-8 362	-1 560	-1 560	-459	-701	-401	. . .
1964	-29 102	-27 319	-18 700	-8 619	-1 783	-1 783	-529	-802	-453	. . .
1965	-32 708	-30 621	-21 510	-9 111	-2 088	-2 088	-657	-942	-489	. . .
1966	-38 468	-35 987	-25 493	-10 494	-2 481	-2 481	-711	-1 221	-549	. . .
1967	-41 476	-38 729	-26 866	-11 863	-2 747	-2 747	-821	-1 328	-598	. . .
1968	-48 671	-45 293	-32 991	-12 302	-3 378	-3 378	-876	-1 800	-702	. . .
1969	-53 998	-49 129	-35 807	-13 322	-4 869	-4 869	-848	-3 244	-777	. . .
1970	-59 901	-54 386	-39 866	-14 520	-5 515	-5 515	-875	-3 617	-1 024	. . .
1971	-66 414	-60 979	-45 579	-15 400	-5 435	-5 435	-1 164	-2 428	-1 844	. . .
1972	-79 237	-72 665	-55 797	-16 868	-6 572	-6 572	-1 284	-2 604	-2 684	. . .
1973	-98 997	-89 342	-70 499	-18 843	-9 655	-9 655	-1 610	-4 209	-3 836	. . .
1974	-137 274	-125 190	-103 811	-21 379	-12 084	-12 084	-1 331	-6 491	-4 262	. . .
1975	-132 745	-120 181	-98 185	-21 996	-12 564	-12 564	-2 234	-5 788	-4 542	. . .
1976	-162 109	-148 798	-124 228	-24 570	-13 311	-13 311	-3 110	-5 681	-4 520	. . .
1977	-193 764	-179 547	-151 907	-27 640	-14 217	-14 217	-2 834	-5 841	-5 542	. . .
1978	-229 870	-208 191	-176 002	-32 189	-21 680	-21 680	-4 211	-8 795	-8 674	. . .
1979	-281 657	-248 696	-212 007	-36 689	-32 961	-32 961	-6 357	-15 481	-11 122	. . .
1980	-333 774	-291 241	-249 750	-41 491	-42 532	-42 532	-8 635	-21 214	-12 684	. . .
1981	-364 196	-310 570	-265 067	-45 503	-53 626	-53 626	-6 898	-29 415	-17 313	. . .
1982	-355 975	-299 391	-247 642	-51 749	-56 583	-56 583	-2 114	-35 187	-19 282	. . .
1983	-377 488	-323 874	-268 901	-54 973	-53 614	-53 614	-4 120	-30 501	-18 993	. . .
1984	-473 923	-400 166	-332 418	-67 748	-73 756	-73 756	-8 443	-44 158	-21 155	. . .
1985	-483 769	-410 950	-338 088	-72 862	-72 819	-72 819	-6 945	-42 745	-23 129	. . .
1986	-530 142	-448 572	-368 425	-80 147	-81 571	-78 893	-6 856	-47 412	-24 625	-2 678
1987	-594 443	-500 552	-409 765	-90 787	-93 891	-91 553	-7 676	-57 659	-26 218	-2 338
1988	-663 741	-545 715	-447 189	-98 526	-118 026	-116 179	-12 150	-72 314	-31 715	-1 847
1989	-721 607	-580 144	-477 665	-102 479	-141 463	-139 177	-7 045	-93 768	-38 364	-2 286
1990	-759 290	-616 097	-498 438	-117 659	-143 192	-139 728	-3 450	-95 508	-40 770	-3 464
1991	-734 564	-609 479	-491 020	-118 459	-125 085	-121 059	2 265	-82 452	-40 872	-4 026
1992	-765 626	-656 094	-536 528	-119 566	-109 532	-104 780	-2 190	-63 509	-39 081	-4 752
1993	-823 914	-713 174	-589 394	-123 780	-110 741	-105 609	-7 943	-58 290	-39 376	-5 132
1994	-951 122	-801 747	-668 690	-133 057	-149 375	-143 423	-22 150	-77 081	-44 192	-5 952
1995	-1 080 124	-890 771	-749 374	-141 397	-189 353	-183 090	-30 318	-97 149	-55 623	-6 263
1996	-1 159 478	-955 667	-803 113	-152 554	-203 811	-197 511	-33 093	-97 800	-66 618	-6 300
1997	-1 286 921	-1 042 726	-876 794	-165 932	-244 195	-237 529	-42 950	-112 878	-81 701	-6 666
1998	-1 356 868	-1 099 314	-918 637	-180 677	-257 554	-250 560	-38 418	-127 988	-84 154	-6 994
1999	-1 511 011	-1 230 974	-1 031 784	-199 190	-280 037	-272 082	-53 437	-138 120	-80 525	-7 955
2000	-1 780 296	-1 450 432	-1 226 684	-223 748	-329 864	-322 345	-56 910	-180 918	-84 517	-7 519
2001	-1 629 097	-1 370 022	-1 148 231	-221 791	-259 075	-250 989	-12 783	-159 825	-78 381	-8 086
2002	-1 651 990	-1 398 446	-1 167 377	-231 069	-253 544	-245 164	-43 244	-127 012	-74 908	-8 380
2003	-1 789 819	-1 514 672	-1 264 307	-250 365	-275 147	-266 635	-73 750	-119 051	-73 834	-8 512
2004	-2 114 837	-1 768 318	-1 477 094	-291 224	-346 519	-337 556	-99 754	-155 266	-82 536	-8 963
2005	-2 458 225	-1 995 320	-1 681 780	-313 540	-462 905	-453 615	-121 333	-228 408	-103 874	-9 290
2006	-2 838 254	-2 210 298	-1 861 380	-348 918	-627 956	-618 466	-144 397	-339 088	-134 981	-9 489
2007	-3 082 014	-2 345 984	-1 967 853	-378 130	-736 030	-726 031	-134 414	-426 515	-165 102	-9 999
2008	-3 144 807	-2 516 915	-2 112 196	-404 719	-627 891	-617 605	-103 381	-346 954	-167 270	-10 286
2005										
1st quarter	-580 114	-476 045	-399 862	-76 183	-104 069	-101 791	-28 997	-48 909	-23 885	-2 278
2nd quarter	-600 704	-490 090	-412 411	-77 679	-110 615	-108 315	-29 438	-53 765	-25 112	-2 300
3rd quarter	-617 311	-501 715	-422 752	-78 963	-115 595	-113 230	-27 013	-59 804	-26 413	-2 365
4th quarter	-660 097	-527 469	-446 754	-80 715	-132 627	-130 279	-35 885	-65 930	-28 464	-2 348
2006										
1st quarter	-679 297	-538 266	-453 286	-84 981	-141 031	-138 674	-33 882	-74 307	-30 485	-2 357
2nd quarter	-705 572	-551 612	-465 016	-86 596	-153 960	-151 608	-35 184	-83 504	-32 920	-2 352
3rd quarter	-730 083	-565 114	-477 900	-87 213	-164 969	-162 623	-39 927	-88 063	-34 633	-2 346
4th quarter	-723 303	-555 307	-465 178	-90 129	-167 996	-165 561	-35 404	-93 214	-36 943	-2 435
2007										
1st quarter	-738 938	-564 979	-473 681	-91 298	-173 959	-171 560	-33 128	-99 373	-39 059	-2 399
2nd quarter	-771 262	-578 770	-485 375	-93 395	-192 492	-189 991	-40 620	-107 963	-41 408	-2 501
3rd quarter	-783 548	-592 986	-496 698	-96 288	-190 562	-188 045	-35 243	-110 898	-41 904	-2 517
4th quarter	-788 264	-609 248	-512 099	-97 149	-179 016	-176 436	-25 424	-108 281	-42 731	-2 580
2008										
1st quarter	-796 593	-629 960	-530 126	-99 834	-166 633	-164 074	-27 020	-94 302	-42 752	-2 559
2nd quarter	-825 091	-656 784	-554 922	-101 862	-168 307	-165 760	-36 682	-86 115	-42 963	-2 547
3rd quarter	-829 558	-666 792	-562 526	-104 267	-162 766	-160 222	-31 635	-87 097	-41 490	-2 545
4th quarter	-693 564	-563 379	-464 624	-98 756	-130 185	-127 550	-8 045	-79 440	-40 065	-2 636

[1]A minus sign indicates imports of goods and services or payments of incomes.
. . . = Not available.

Table 7-6. U.S. International Transactions—*Continued*

(Millions of dollars, seasonally adjusted.)

Year and quarter	Current account—*Continued*				Capital account transactions, net [2]	Financial account					
	Unilateral current transfers, net [2]					U.S.-owned assets abroad, net, excluding financial derivatives [2]					
		U.S. government		Private remittances and other transfers				U.S. official reserve assets, net			
	Total	Grants	Pensions and other transfers			Total	Total	Gold	Special drawing rights	Reserve position in the IMF	Foreign currencies
1960	-4 062	-3 367	-273	-423	. . .	-4 099	2 145	1 703	0	442	0
1961	-4 127	-3 320	-373	-434	. . .	-5 538	607	857	0	-135	-115
1962	-4 277	-3 453	-347	-477	. . .	-4 174	1 535	890	0	626	19
1963	-4 392	-3 479	-339	-575	. . .	-7 270	378	461	0	29	-112
1964	-4 240	-3 227	-399	-614	. . .	-9 560	171	125	0	266	-220
1965	-4 583	-3 444	-463	-677	. . .	-5 716	1 225	1 665	0	-94	-346
1966	-4 955	-3 802	-499	-655	. . .	-7 321	570	571	0	537	-538
1967	-5 294	-3 844	-571	-879	. . .	-9 757	53	1 170	0	-94	-1 023
1968	-5 629	-4 256	-537	-836	. . .	-10 977	-870	1 173	0	-870	-1 173
1969	-5 735	-4 259	-537	-939	. . .	-11 585	-1 179	-967	0	-1 034	822
1970	-6 156	-4 449	-611	-1 096	. . .	-8 470	3 348	787	16	389	2 156
1971	-7 402	-5 589	-696	-1 117	. . .	-11 758	3 066	866	468	1 350	382
1972	-8 544	-6 665	-770	-1 109	. . .	-13 787	706	547	7	153	-1
1973	-6 913	-4 748	-915	-1 250	. . .	-22 874	158	0	9	-33	182
1974	-9 249	-7 293	-939	-1 017	. . .	-34 745	-1 467	0	-172	-1 265	-30
1975	-7 075	-5 101	-1 068	-906	. . .	-39 703	-849	0	-66	-466	-317
1976	-5 686	-3 519	-1 250	-917	. . .	-51 269	-2 558	0	-78	-2 212	-268
1977	-5 226	-2 990	-1 378	-859	. . .	-34 785	-375	-118	-121	-294	158
1978	-5 788	-3 412	-1 532	-844	. . .	-61 130	732	-65	1 249	4 231	-4 683
1979	-6 593	-4 015	-1 658	-920	. . .	-64 915	6	-65	3	-189	257
1980	-8 349	-5 486	-1 818	-1 044	. . .	-85 815	-7 003	0	1 136	-1 667	-6 472
1981	-11 702	-5 145	-2 041	-4 516	. . .	-113 054	-4 082	*	-730	-2 491	-861
1982	-16 544	-6 087	-2 251	-8 207	199	-127 882	-4 965	0	-1 371	-2 552	-1 041
1983	-17 310	-6 469	-2 207	-8 635	209	-66 373	-1 196	0	-66	-4 434	3 304
1984	-20 335	-8 696	-2 159	-9 479	235	-40 376	-3 131	0	-979	-995	-1 156
1985	-21 998	-11 268	-2 138	-8 593	315	-44 752	-3 858	0	-897	908	-3 869
1986	-24 132	-11 883	-2 372	-9 877	301	-111 723	312	0	-246	1 501	-942
1987	-23 265	-10 309	-2 409	-10 548	365	-79 296	9 149	0	-509	2 070	7 588
1988	-25 274	-10 537	-2 709	-12 028	493	-106 573	-3 912	0	127	1 025	-5 064
1989	-26 169	-10 860	-2 775	-12 534	336	-175 383	-25 293	0	-535	471	-25 229
1990	-26 654	-10 359	-3 224	-13 070	-6 579	-81 234	-2 158	0	-192	731	-2 697
1991	9 904	29 193	-3 775	-15 514	-4 479	-64 389	5 763	0	-176	-366	6 307
1992	-35 100	-16 319	-4 043	-14 738	-557	-74 410	3 901	0	2 316	-2 691	4 276
1993	-39 811	-17 035	-4 104	-18 672	-1 299	-200 551	-1 379	0	-537	-43	-798
1994	-40 265	-14 978	-4 556	-20 731	-1 723	-178 937	5 346	0	-441	494	5 293
1995	-38 074	-11 190	-3 451	-23 433	-927	-352 264	-9 742	0	-808	-2 466	-6 468
1996	-43 017	-15 401	-4 466	-23 150	-735	-413 409	6 668	0	370	-1 280	7 578
1997	-45 062	-12 472	-4 191	-28 399	-1 027	-485 475	-1 010	0	-350	-3 575	2 915
1998	-53 187	-13 270	-4 305	-35 612	-766	-353 829	-6 783	0	-147	-5 119	-1 517
1999	-50 428	-13 774	-4 406	-32 248	-4 939	-504 062	8 747	0	10	5 484	3 253
2000	-58 645	-16 714	-4 705	-37 226	-1 010	-560 523	-290	0	-722	2 308	-1 876
2001	-51 295	-11 517	-5 798	-33 980	-1 270	-382 616	-4 911	0	-630	-3 600	-681
2002	-64 948	-17 097	-5 125	-42 726	-1 470	-294 646	-3 681	0	-475	-2 632	-574
2003	-71 794	-22 173	-5 341	-44 280	-3 480	-325 424	1 523	0	601	1 494	-572
2004	-84 482	-23 634	-6 264	-54 584	-2 369	-1 000 870	2 805	0	-398	3 826	-623
2005	-89 784	-33 039	-6 303	-50 442	-4 036	-546 631	14 096	0	4 511	10 200	-615
2006	-92 027	-27 142	-6 508	-58 377	-3 880	-1 251 749	2 374	0	-223	3 331	-734
2007	-112 705	-33 237	-7 323	-72 145	-1 843	-1 289 854	-122	0	-154	1 021	-989
2008	-119 713	-34 603	-7 859	-77 251	-2 600	-52 459	-4 848	0	-106	-3 473	-1 269
2005											
1st quarter	-28 644	-9 403	-1 558	-17 683	-2 594	-129 175	5 331	0	1 713	3 763	-145
2nd quarter	-24 964	-5 893	-1 569	-17 502	-510	-222 397	-797	0	-97	-564	-136
3rd quarter	-9 090	-7 653	-1 584	147	-467	-204 361	4 766	0	2 976	1 951	-161
4th quarter	-27 085	-10 090	-1 592	-15 403	-465	9 302	4 796	0	-81	5 050	-173
2006											
1st quarter	-21 516	-5 671	-1 614	-14 231	-1 716	-359 608	513	0	-67	729	-149
2nd quarter	-24 116	-7 226	-1 627	-15 263	-1 005	-234 828	-560	0	-51	-351	-158
3rd quarter	-24 716	-7 741	-1 620	-15 355	-533	-286 769	1 006	0	-54	1 275	-215
4th quarter	-21 679	-6 504	-1 647	-13 528	-626	-370 543	1 415	0	-51	1 678	-212
2007											
1st quarter	-30 174	-10 567	-1 805	-17 802	-543	-442 065	-72	0	-43	212	-241
2nd quarter	-24 953	-5 611	-1 834	-17 508	-112	-523 556	26	0	-39	294	-229
3rd quarter	-27 796	-7 109	-1 837	-18 850	-617	-170 476	-54	0	-37	230	-247
4th quarter	-29 784	-9 950	-1 849	-17 985	-571	-153 757	-22	0	-35	285	-272
2008											
1st quarter	-31 731	-9 990	-1 951	-19 790	-600	-264 866	-276	0	-29	112	-359
2nd quarter	-29 034	-7 305	-1 966	-19 763	-631	99 910	-1 267	0	-22	-955	-290
3rd quarter	-29 998	-8 257	-1 969	-19 772	-735	28 056	-179	0	-30	256	-405
4th quarter	-28 949	-9 051	-1 973	-17 925	-633	84 441	-3 126	0	-25	-2 886	-215

[2]A minus sign indicates net unilateral transfers to foreigners, net capital or financial outflows, or increases in U.S. official assets.
. . . = Not available.
* = Less than $500,000 (+/-).

Table 7-6. U.S. International Transactions—Continued

(Millions of dollars, seasonally adjusted.)

Year and quarter	Financial account—Continued								
	U.S.-owned assets abroad, net, excluding financial derivatives 3—Continued								
	U.S. government assets other than official reserve assets, net				U.S. private assets, net				
								U.S. claims	
	Total	U.S. credits and other long-term assets	Repayments on U.S. credits and other long-term assets	U.S. foreign currency holdings and short-term assets, net	Total	Direct investment	Foreign securities	On unaffiliated foreigners reported by U.S. nonbanking concerns	Reported by U.S. banks, not included elsewhere
1960	-1 100	-1 214	642	-528	-5 144	-2 940	-663	-394	-1 148
1961	-910	-1 928	1 279	-261	-5 235	-2 653	-762	-558	-1 261
1962	-1 085	-2 128	1 288	-245	-4 623	-2 851	-969	-354	-450
1963	-1 662	-2 204	988	-447	-5 986	-3 483	-1 105	157	-1 556
1964	-1 680	-2 382	720	-19	-8 050	-3 760	-677	-1 108	-2 505
1965	-1 605	-2 463	874	-16	-5 336	-5 011	-759	341	93
1966	-1 543	-2 513	1 235	-265	-6 347	-5 418	-720	-442	233
1967	-2 423	-3 638	1 005	209	-7 386	-4 805	-1 308	-779	-495
1968	-2 274	-3 722	1 386	62	-7 833	-5 295	-1 569	-1 203	233
1969	-2 200	-3 489	1 200	89	-8 206	-5 960	-1 549	-126	-570
1970	-1 589	-3 293	1 721	-16	-10 229	-7 590	-1 076	-596	-967
1971	-1 884	-4 181	2 115	182	-12 940	-7 618	-1 113	-1 229	-2 980
1972	-1 568	-3 819	2 086	165	-12 925	-7 747	-618	-1 054	-3 506
1973	-2 644	-4 638	2 596	-602	-20 388	-11 353	-671	-2 383	-5 980
1974	366	-5 001	4 826	541	-33 643	-9 052	-1 854	-3 221	-19 516
1975	-3 474	-5 941	2 475	-9	-35 380	-14 244	-6 247	-1 357	-13 532
1976	-4 214	-6 943	2 596	133	-44 498	-11 949	-8 885	-2 296	-21 368
1977	-3 693	-6 445	2 719	33	-30 717	-11 890	-5 460	-1 940	-11 427
1978	-4 660	-7 470	2 941	-131	-57 202	-16 056	-3 626	-3 853	-33 667
1979	-3 746	-7 697	3 926	25	-61 176	-25 222	-4 726	-5 014	-26 213
1980	-5 162	-9 860	4 456	242	-73 651	-19 222	-3 568	-4 023	-46 838
1981	-5 097	-9 674	4 413	164	-103 875	-9 624	-5 699	-4 377	-84 175
1982	-6 131	-10 063	4 292	-360	-116 786	-4 556	-7 983	6 823	-111 070
1983	-5 006	-9 967	5 012	-51	-60 172	-12 528	-6 762	-10 954	-29 928
1984	-5 489	-9 599	4 490	-379	-31 757	-16 407	-4 756	533	-11 127
1985	-2 821	-7 657	4 719	117	-38 074	-18 927	-7 481	-10 342	-1 323
1986	-2 022	-9 084	6 089	973	-110 014	-23 995	-4 271	-21 773	-59 975
1987	1 006	-6 506	7 625	-113	-89 450	-35 034	-5 251	-7 046	-42 119
1988	2 967	-7 680	10 370	277	-105 628	-22 528	-7 980	-21 193	-53 927
1989	1 233	-5 608	6 725	115	-151 303	-43 447	-22 070	-27 646	-58 160
1990	2 317	-8 410	10 856	-130	-81 393	-37 183	-28 765	-27 824	12 379
1991	2 923	-12 880	16 777	-974	-73 075	-37 889	-45 673	11 097	-610
1992	-1 667	-7 408	5 807	-67	-76 644	-48 266	-49 166	-387	21 175
1993	-351	-6 311	6 270	-310	-198 823	-83 951	-146 253	766	30 615
1994	-390	-5 383	5 088	-95	-183 893	-80 167	-63 190	-36 336	-4 200
1995	-984	-4 859	4 125	-250	-341 538	-98 750	-122 394	-45 286	-75 108
1996	-989	-5 025	3 930	106	-419 088	-91 885	-149 315	-86 333	-91 555
1997	68	-5 417	5 438	47	-484 533	-104 803	-116 852	-121 760	-141 118
1998	-422	-4 678	4 111	145	-346 624	-142 644	-130 204	-38 204	-35 572
1999	2 750	-6 175	9 559	-634	-515 559	-224 934	-122 236	-97 704	-70 685
2000	-941	-5 182	4 265	-24	-559 292	-159 212	-127 908	-138 790	-133 382
2001	-486	-4 431	3 873	72	-377 219	-142 349	-90 644	-8 520	-135 706
2002	345	-5 251	5 701	-105	-291 310	-154 460	-48 568	-50 022	-38 260
2003	537	-7 279	7 981	-165	-327 484	-149 564	-146 722	-18 184	-13 014
2004	1 710	-3 044	4 716	38	-1 005 385	-316 223	-170 549	-152 566	-366 047
2005	5 539	-2 255	5 603	2 191	-566 266	-36 235	-251 199	-71 207	-207 625
2006	5 346	-2 992	8 329	9	-1 259 469	-241 244	-365 204	-164 597	-488 424
2007	-22 273	-2 475	4 104	-23 902	-1 267 459	-333 271	-288 731	-706	-644 751
2008	-529 510	-2 139	2 327	-529 698	481 899	-317 835	90 951	283 765	425 018
2005									
1st quarter	2 591	-519	1 083	2 027	-137 097	-58 799	-59 599	-64 051	45 352
2nd quarter	989	-708	1 586	111	-222 589	-41 548	-57 317	59 260	-182 984
3rd quarter	1 501	-518	1 957	62	-210 628	12 163	-66 383	-69 527	-86 881
4th quarter	459	-509	977	-9	4 047	51 948	-67 900	3 111	16 888
2006									
1st quarter	1 049	-1 517	2 558	8	-361 170	-55 969	-75 699	-24 771	-204 731
2nd quarter	1 765	-376	2 147	-6	-236 033	-47 902	-80 252	-48 334	-59 545
3rd quarter	1 570	-592	2 170	-8	-289 346	-65 992	-72 558	-57 000	-93 796
4th quarter	962	-507	1 454	15	-372 920	-71 381	-136 695	-34 492	-130 352
2007									
1st quarter	445	-608	1 091	-38	-442 438	-66 706	-99 541	-46 048	-230 143
2nd quarter	-596	-1 405	687	122	-522 985	-93 616	-84 671	-134 713	-209 985
3rd quarter	623	-182	780	25	-171 045	-62 043	-100 317	80 012	-88 697
4th quarter	-22 744	-279	1 546	-24 011	-130 990	-110 905	-4 202	100 043	-115 926
2008									
1st quarter	3 265	-179	487	2 957	-267 855	-93 321	-35 066	81 848	-221 316
2nd quarter	-41 592	-1 106	497	-40 983	142 769	-86 838	-33 576	49 324	213 859
3rd quarter	-225 990	-465	692	-226 217	254 226	-52 356	82 615	89 523	134 444
4th quarter	-265 193	-389	651	-265 455	352 760	-85 319	76 978	63 070	298 031

3A minus sign indicates financial outflows.

Table 7-6. U.S. International Transactions—*Continued*

(Millions of dollars, seasonally adjusted.)

Year and quarter	Total	Foreign-owned assets in the United States, net, excluding financial derivatives [4]											
		Foreign official assets in the United States, net							Other foreign assets in the United States, net				
		Total	U.S. government securities			Other U.S. govern- ment liabilities	U.S. liabilities reported by U.S. banks, not included elsewhere	Other foreign official assets	Total	Direct investment	U.S. Treasury securities	U.S. securities other than Treasury securities	U.S. currency
			Total	U.S. Treasury securities	Other								
1960	2 294	1 473	655	655	0	215	603	0	821	315	-364	282	. . .
1961	2 705	765	233	233	0	25	508	0	1 939	311	151	324	. . .
1962	1 911	1 270	1 409	1 410	-1	152	-291	0	641	346	-66	134	. . .
1963	3 217	1 986	816	803	12	429	742	0	1 231	231	-149	287	. . .
1964	3 643	1 660	432	434	-2	298	930	0	1 983	322	-146	-85	. . .
1965	742	134	-141	-134	-7	65	210	0	607	415	-131	-358	. . .
1966	3 661	-672	-1 527	-1 548	21	113	742	0	4 333	425	-356	906	. . .
1967	7 379	3 451	2 261	2 222	39	83	1 106	0	3 928	698	-135	1 016	. . .
1968	9 928	-774	-769	-798	29	-15	10	0	10 703	807	136	4 414	. . .
1969	12 702	-1 301	-2 343	-2 269	-74	251	792	0	14 002	1 263	-68	3 130	. . .
1970	6 359	6 908	9 439	9 411	28	-456	-2 075	0	-550	1 464	81	2 189	. . .
1971	22 970	26 879	26 570	26 578	-8	-510	819	0	-3 909	367	-24	2 289	. . .
1972	21 461	10 475	8 470	8 213	257	182	1 638	185	10 986	949	-39	4 507	. . .
1973	18 388	6 026	641	59	582	936	4 126	323	12 362	2 800	-216	4 041	. . .
1974	35 227	10 546	4 172	3 270	902	301	5 818	254	24 682	4 760	697	378	986
1975	16 870	7 027	5 563	4 658	905	1 517	-2 158	2 104	9 843	2 603	2 590	2 503	1 200
1976	37 839	17 693	9 892	9 319	573	4 627	969	2 205	20 147	4 347	2 783	1 284	1 321
1977	52 770	36 816	32 538	30 230	2 308	1 400	773	2 105	15 954	3 728	534	2 437	1 451
1978	66 275	33 678	24 221	23 555	666	2 476	5 551	1 430	32 597	7 897	2 178	2 254	2 239
1979	39 554	-13 665	-21 972	-22 435	463	-40	7 213	1 135	53 218	11 877	4 060	1 351	1 702
1980	60 885	15 497	11 895	9 708	2 187	615	-159	3 145	45 388	16 918	2 645	5 457	2 773
1981	84 591	4 960	6 322	5 019	1 303	-338	-3 670	2 646	79 631	25 195	2 927	6 905	1 559
1982	95 056	3 593	5 085	5 779	-694	605	-1 747	-350	91 464	12 635	7 027	6 085	2 467
1983	87 399	5 845	6 496	6 972	-476	602	545	-1 798	81 554	10 372	8 689	8 164	4 105
1984	116 048	3 140	4 703	4 690	13	739	555	-2 857	112 908	24 468	23 001	12 568	2 396
1985	144 231	-1 119	-1 139	-838	-301	844	645	-1 469	145 349	19 742	20 433	50 962	3 316
1986	228 330	35 648	33 150	34 364	-1 214	2 195	1 187	-884	192 681	35 420	3 809	70 969	2 421
1987	247 100	45 387	44 802	43 238	1 564	-2 326	3 918	-1 007	201 713	58 470	-7 643	42 120	3 866
1988	244 833	39 758	43 050	41 741	1 309	-467	-319	-2 506	205 075	57 735	20 239	26 353	4 111
1989	222 777	8 503	1 532	149	1 383	160	4 976	1 835	214 274	68 274	29 618	38 767	3 749
1990	139 357	33 910	30 243	29 576	667	1 868	3 385	-1 586	105 447	48 494	-2 534	1 592	16 586
1991	108 221	17 388	16 147	14 846	1 301	1 367	-1 484	1 359	90 833	23 171	18 826	35 144	12 813
1992	168 349	40 476	22 403	18 454	3 949	2 190	16 571	-688	127 872	19 822	37 131	30 043	11 086
1993	279 758	71 753	53 014	48 952	4 062	1 313	14 841	2 585	208 005	51 363	24 381	80 092	16 618
1994	303 174	39 583	36 827	30 750	6 077	1 564	3 665	-2 473	263 591	46 121	34 274	56 971	20 585
1995	435 102	109 880	72 712	68 977	3 735	-105	34 008	3 265	325 222	57 776	91 544	77 249	8 840
1996	547 885	126 724	120 679	115 671	5 008	-982	5 704	1 323	421 161	86 502	147 022	103 272	14 151
1997	704 452	19 036	-2 161	-6 690	4 529	-881	22 286	-208	685 416	105 603	130 435	161 409	22 425
1998	420 794	-19 903	-3 589	-9 921	6 332	-3 326	-9 501	-3 487	440 697	179 045	28 581	156 315	13 847
1999	742 210	43 543	32 527	12 177	20 350	-2 863	12 964	915	698 667	289 444	-44 497	298 834	24 407
2000	1 038 224	42 758	35 710	-5 199	40 909	-1 825	5 746	3 127	995 466	321 274	-69 983	459 889	-3 357
2001	782 870	28 059	54 620	33 700	20 920	-2 309	-29 978	5 726	754 811	167 021	-14 378	393 885	23 794
2002	795 161	115 945	90 971	60 466	30 505	137	21 221	3 616	679 216	84 372	100 403	283 299	18 861
2003	858 303	278 069	224 874	184 931	39 943	-723	48 643	5 275	580 234	63 750	91 455	220 705	10 591
2004	1 533 201	397 755	314 941	273 279	41 662	-134	69 245	13 703	1 135 446	145 966	93 608	381 493	13 301
2005	1 247 347	259 268	213 334	112 841	100 493	-421	26 260	20 095	988 079	112 638	132 300	450 386	8 447
2006	2 061 113	487 939	428 401	208 564	219 837	2 816	22 365	34 357	1 573 174	241 961	-58 204	683 363	2 227
2007	2 057 703	411 058	230 330	58 865	171 465	5 342	108 695	66 691	1 646 645	237 542	156 825	573 850	-10 675
2008	599 049	421 375	508 065	442 219	65 846	8 626	-153 656	58 340	177 674	325 254	307 631	-123 568	35 023
2005													
1st quarter	234 182	25 052	38 940	15 999	22 941	-698	-15 814	2 624	209 130	38 871	78 528	75 631	-1 709
2nd quarter	304 880	81 292	42 673	23 768	18 905	120	34 219	4 280	223 588	-9 004	-13 001	107 694	-196
3rd quarter	425 404	54 736	45 405	19 412	25 993	440	1 994	6 897	370 668	38 016	24 316	141 900	2 281
4th quarter	282 881	98 188	86 316	53 662	32 654	-283	5 861	6 294	184 693	44 755	42 457	125 161	8 071
2006													
1st quarter	537 649	130 427	117 579	65 573	52 006	-45	2 394	10 499	407 222	38 694	-25 913	167 614	35
2nd quarter	405 008	127 303	71 299	26 391	44 908	760	43 366	11 878	277 705	62 831	-24 019	139 710	-2 345
3rd quarter	524 858	121 843	121 907	60 641	61 266	913	-7 871	6 894	403 015	54 813	-21 586	197 908	-2 321
4th quarter	593 598	108 366	117 616	55 959	61 657	1 188	-15 524	5 086	485 232	85 623	13 314	178 131	6 858
2007													
1st quarter	692 713	163 270	121 640	40 337	81 303	366	30 329	10 935	529 443	14 026	42 882	183 507	-6 165
2nd quarter	718 112	88 822	61 641	1 610	60 031	-69	15 956	11 294	629 290	61 862	-13 522	310 340	-1 635
3rd quarter	266 476	13 469	-7 788	-25 810	18 022	913	9 873	10 471	253 007	105 908	67 406	-30 486	655
4th quarter	380 402	145 497	54 837	42 728	12 109	4 132	52 537	33 991	234 905	55 746	60 059	110 489	-3 530
2008													
1st quarter	460 105	173 533	167 883	88 649	79 234	1 645	-26 930	30 935	286 572	81 525	63 263	-20 475	-914
2nd quarter	23 208	145 391	151 288	58 143	93 145	2 439	-30 055	21 719	-122 183	105 793	65 692	17 068	230
3rd quarter	123 346	116 078	105 920	116 479	-10 559	1 642	10 302	-1 786	7 268	57 313	89 134	-91 398	5 845
4th quarter	-7 611	-13 627	82 974	178 948	-95 974	2 900	-106 973	7 472	6 016	80 622	89 542	-28 763	29 862

[4]A minus sign indicates financial outflows or a decrease in foreign official assets in the United States.
. . . = Not available.

Table 7-6. U.S. International Transactions—*Continued*

(Millions of dollars, seasonally adjusted.)

Year and quarter	Other foreign assets in the United States, net—Cont. / U.S. liabilities / To unaffiliated foreigners reported by U.S. nonbanking concerns	Reported by U.S. banks not included elsewhere	Financial derivatives, net	Statistical discrepancy 5 / Total	Seasonal adjustment discrepancy	Balance on goods	Balance on services	Balance on goods and services	Balance on income	Balance on goods, services, and income	Unilateral current transfers, net	Balance on current account
1960	-90	678	. . .	-1 019	0	4 892	-1 385	3 508	3 379	6 887	-4 062	2 824
1961	226	928	. . .	-989	0	5 571	-1 376	4 195	3 755	7 950	-4 127	3 822
1962	-110	336	. . .	-1 124	0	4 521	-1 151	3 370	4 294	7 664	-4 277	3 387
1963	-37	898	. . .	-360	0	5 224	-1 014	4 210	4 596	8 806	-4 392	4 414
1964	75	1 818	. . .	-907	0	6 801	-779	6 022	5 041	11 063	-4 240	6 823
1965	178	503	. . .	-457	0	4 951	-287	4 664	5 350	10 014	-4 583	5 431
1966	476	2 882	. . .	629	0	3 817	-877	2 940	5 047	7 987	-4 955	3 031
1967	584	1 765	. . .	-205	0	3 800	-1 196	2 604	5 274	7 878	-5 294	2 583
1968	1 475	3 871	. . .	438	0	635	-385	250	5 990	6 240	-5 629	611
1969	792	8 886	. . .	-1 516	0	607	-516	91	6 044	6 135	-5 735	399
1970	2 014	-6 298	. . .	-219	0	2 603	-349	2 254	6 233	8 487	-6 156	2 331
1971	369	-6 911	. . .	-9 779	0	-2 260	957	-1 303	7 272	5 969	-7 402	-1 433
1972	815	4 754	. . .	-1 879	0	-6 416	973	-5 443	8 192	2 749	-8 544	-5 795
1973	1 035	4 702	. . .	-2 654	0	911	989	1 900	12 153	14 053	-6 913	7 140
1974	1 844	16 017	. . .	-2 444	0	-5 505	1 213	-4 292	15 503	11 211	-9 249	1 962
1975	319	628	. . .	4 717	0	8 903	3 501	12 404	12 787	25 191	-7 075	18 116
1976	-578	10 990	. . .	9 134	0	-9 483	3 401	-6 082	16 063	9 981	-5 686	4 295
1977	1 086	6 719	. . .	-3 650	0	-31 091	3 845	-27 246	18 137	-9 109	-5 226	-14 335
1978	1 889	16 141	. . .	9 997	0	-33 927	4 164	-29 763	20 408	-9 355	-5 788	-15 143
1979	1 621	32 607	. . .	25 647	0	-27 568	3 003	-24 565	30 873	6 308	-6 593	-285
1980	6 852	10 743	. . .	22 613	0	-25 500	6 093	-19 407	30 073	10 666	-8 349	2 317
1981	917	42 128	. . .	23 433	0	-28 023	11 852	-16 172	32 903	16 731	-11 702	5 030
1982	-2 383	65 633	. . .	38 163	0	-36 485	12 329	-24 156	35 164	11 008	-16 544	-5 536
1983	-118	50 342	. . .	17 457	0	-67 102	9 335	-57 767	36 386	-21 381	-17 310	-38 691
1984	16 626	33 849	. . .	18 437	0	-112 492	3 419	-109 073	35 063	-74 010	-20 335	-94 344
1985	9 851	41 045	. . .	18 362	0	-122 173	294	-121 880	25 723	-96 157	-21 998	-118 155
1986	3 325	76 737	. . .	30 269	0	-145 081	6 543	-138 538	15 494	-123 044	-24 132	-147 177
1987	18 363	86 537	. . .	-7 514	0	-159 557	7 874	-151 684	14 293	-137 391	-23 265	-160 655
1988	32 893	63 744	. . .	-17 600	0	-126 959	12 393	-114 566	18 687	-95 879	-25 274	-121 153
1989	22 086	51 780	. . .	51 756	0	-117 749	24 607	-93 142	19 824	-73 318	-26 169	-99 486
1990	45 133	-3 824	. . .	27 425	0	-111 037	30 173	-80 864	28 550	-52 314	-26 654	-78 968
1991	-3 115	3 994	. . .	-42 252	0	-76 937	45 802	-31 136	24 131	-7 005	9 904	2 897
1992	13 573	16 216	. . .	-43 304	0	-96 897	57 685	-39 212	24 235	-14 977	-35 100	-50 078
1993	10 489	25 063	. . .	6 898	0	-132 451	62 141	-70 311	25 316	-44 995	-39 811	-84 805
1994	1 302	104 338	. . .	-902	0	-165 831	67 338	-98 493	17 146	-81 347	-40 265	-121 612
1995	59 637	30 176	. . .	31 656	0	-174 170	77 786	-96 384	20 891	-75 493	-38 074	-113 567
1996	53 736	16 478	. . .	-8 977	0	-191 000	86 935	-104 065	22 318	-81 747	-43 017	-124 764
1997	116 510	149 026	. . .	-77 224	0	-198 428	90 155	-108 273	12 609	-95 664	-45 062	-140 726
1998	23 140	39 769	. . .	148 863	0	-248 221	82 081	-166 140	4 265	-161 875	-53 187	-215 062
1999	76 247	54 232	. . .	68 421	0	-347 819	82 729	-265 090	13 888	-251 202	-50 428	-301 630
2000	170 672	116 971	. . .	-59 265	0	-454 690	74 855	-379 835	21 054	-358 781	-58 645	-417 426
2001	66 110	118 379	. . .	-14 285	0	-429 519	64 393	-365 126	31 722	-333 404	-51 295	-384 699
2002	95 871	96 410	. . .	-37 770	0	-484 955	61 230	-423 725	27 398	-396 327	-64 948	-461 275
2003	96 526	97 207	. . .	-6 000	0	-550 892	53 977	-496 915	45 309	-451 606	-71 794	-523 400
2004	165 872	335 206	. . .	95 030	0	-669 578	61 848	-607 730	67 219	-540 511	-84 482	-624 993
2005	69 572	214 736	. . .	32 313	0	-787 149	75 582	-711 567	72 358	-639 209	-89 784	-728 993
2006	242 727	461 100	29 710	-47 078	0	-838 270	84 987	-753 283	57 194	-696 089	-92 027	-788 116
2007	156 290	532 813	6 496	-41 287	0	-819 373	119 115	-700 258	81 749	-618 509	-112 705	-731 214
2008	-29 323	-337 343	. . .	129 275	0	-820 825	139 695	-681 130	127 577	-553 553	-119 713	-673 265
2005												
1st quarter	86 298	-68 489	. . .	71 644	12 224	-185 005	19 008	-165 997	20 584	-145 413	-28 644	-174 057
2nd quarter	-26 159	164 254	. . .	95 848	-1 323	-188 683	17 954	-170 729	17 872	-152 857	-24 964	-177 821
3rd quarter	51 727	112 428	. . .	-51 683	-21 122	-199 149	18 804	-180 345	20 543	-159 802	-9 090	-168 892
4th quarter	-42 294	6 543	. . .	-83 495	10 222	-214 312	19 815	-194 497	13 358	-181 139	-27 085	-208 223
2006												
1st quarter	63 888	162 904	1 633	17 994	10 054	-208 607	19 519	-189 087	14 652	-174 435	-21 516	-195 952
2nd quarter	59 875	41 653	14 090	16 641	587	-211 684	19 843	-191 841	16 051	-175 790	-24 116	-199 906
3rd quarter	69 984	104 217	15 134	-41 784	-19 426	-218 623	21 152	-197 471	11 282	-186 189	-24 716	-210 906
4th quarter	48 980	152 326	-1 147	-39 927	8 787	-199 356	24 471	-174 885	15 209	-159 676	-21 679	-181 355
2007												
1st quarter	90 061	205 132	14 795	-67 970	12 192	-203 363	23 820	-179 543	12 787	-166 756	-30 174	-196 930
2nd quarter	122 476	149 769	-1 007	656	722	-205 887	27 068	-178 819	9 679	-169 140	-24 953	-194 093
3rd quarter	55 599	53 925	5 942	71 627	-21 805	-201 204	33 090	-168 114	22 958	-145 156	-27 796	-172 952
4th quarter	-111 846	123 987	-13 234	-45 600	8 892	-208 919	35 136	-173 783	36 327	-137 456	-29 784	-167 241
2008												
1st quarter	84 085	79 088	-8 001	-9 729	13 673	-212 578	34 135	-178 443	33 266	-145 177	-31 731	-176 909
2nd quarter	-54 350	-256 616	-2 519	62 269	223	-217 874	36 455	-181 419	28 216	-153 203	-29 034	-182 237
3rd quarter	71 053	-124 679	-4 075	34 706	-28 548	-216 254	35 372	-180 882	29 581	-151 301	-29 998	-181 299
4th quarter	-130 111	-35 136	. . .	56 625	14 652	-174 119	33 733	-140 386	36 513	-103 873	-28 949	-132 822

4A minus sign indicates financial outflows or a decrease in foreign official assets in the United States.
5Sum of credits and debits with the sign reversed.
. . . = Not available.

Table 7-7. Foreigners' Transactions in Long-Term Securities with U.S. Residents

(Billions of dollars, not seasonally adjusted.)

Year and month	Gross purchases from U.S. residents	Gross sales to U.S. residents	Transactions in U.S. domestic securities between foreigners and U.S. residents							
			Net purchases							
				Private					Official	
			Total	Total	Treasury bonds and notes	Government agency bonds	Corporate bonds	Equities	Total	Treasury bonds and notes
1977	60.7	30.1	30.6	. . .	. . .	. . .	. . .	. . .	. . .	. . .
1978	60.5	51.1	9.4	3.6	1.0	0.6	0.3	1.7	5.8	3.7
1979	72.9	67.2	5.7	2.5	1.2	0.1	0.2	1.1	3.2	1.7
1980	106.9	91.1	15.8	6.6	1.0	0.4	0.9	4.3	9.2	3.9
1981	126.5	100.5	25.9	10.2	3.3	0.3	1.9	4.8	15.7	11.7
1982	159.5	136.8	22.7	9.2	2.8	0.3	2.5	3.6	13.5	14.6
1983	223.4	211.7	11.7	13.2	4.6	0.5	1.7	6.4	-1.5	0.8
1984	335.5	304.0	31.4	33.8	21.0	1.2	12.5	-0.9	-2.3	0.5
1985	667.2	588.9	78.3	71.9	21.1	4.6	41.4	4.8	6.4	8.1
1986	1 355.4	1 266.9	88.6	76.4	5.2	8.2	45.1	18.0	12.1	14.2
1987	1 692.1	1 623.0	69.1	37.5	-5.5	3.5	22.7	16.8	31.6	31.1
1988	1 827.9	1 753.1	74.8	49.4	22.2	5.4	21.3	0.4	25.4	26.6
1989	2 431.7	2 335.2	96.5	66.5	27.4	13.7	17.5	7.9	30.1	26.8
1990	2 111.2	2 092.4	18.7	-3.6	-5.3	5.6	9.8	-13.7	22.3	23.3
1991	2 382.1	2 324.0	58.1	54.3	18.7	8.9	16.5	10.1	3.8	1.2
1992	2 677.8	2 604.6	73.2	63.1	32.4	14.3	20.0	-3.7	10.1	6.9
1993	3 212.5	3 101.4	111.1	103.2	22.2	31.4	29.9	19.6	7.9	1.3
1994	3 351.1	3 210.7	140.4	94.9	37.0	15.6	38.0	4.3	45.4	41.8
1995	3 737.6	3 505.7	231.9	185.3	94.5	25.0	57.6	8.2	46.6	39.6
1996	4 667.6	4 297.4	370.2	278.1	146.4	36.7	82.2	12.7	92.1	85.8
1997	6 573.3	6 185.3	388.0	339.7	140.2	45.3	82.8	71.3	48.3	44.0
1998	7 633.5	7 355.7	277.8	270.8	44.9	50.5	121.7	53.7	7.0	4.1
1999	7 483.5	7 133.3	350.2	338.8	-0.1	71.9	158.8	108.2	11.4	-9.9
2000	8 684.1	8 226.3	457.8	420.1	-47.7	111.9	182.1	173.8	37.7	-6.3
2001	10 261.8	9 740.9	520.8	494.2	15.0	146.6	218.2	114.4	26.7	3.5
2002	13 022.9	12 475.4	547.6	508.3	112.8	166.6	176.7	52.2	39.3	7.1
2003	13 526.0	12 806.1	719.9	585.0	159.7	129.9	260.3	35.0	134.9	103.8
2004	15 178.9	14 262.4	916.5	680.9	150.9	205.7	298.0	26.2	235.6	201.1
2005	17 157.5	16 145.9	1 011.5	891.1	269.4	187.6	353.1	81.0	120.4	68.7
2006	21 077.1	19 933.9	1 143.2	946.6	125.9	193.8	482.2	144.6	196.6	69.6
2007	29 730.6	28 724.8	1 005.8	818.1	195.0	99.9	342.8	180.4	187.7	3.0
2008	30 673.4	30 260.9	412.5	309.1	239.4	-6.2	58.5	17.4	103.4	76.6
2006										
January	1 586.1	1 499.8	86.3	67.7	-4.7	20.2	27.8	24.3	18.7	6.4
February	1 621.3	1 516.4	105.0	85.1	5.2	27.2	34.1	18.5	19.9	14.1
March	1 824.5	1 728.2	96.3	94.9	15.7	11.3	46.7	21.2	1.4	-7.0
April	1 483.3	1 415.1	68.2	44.6	-15.9	12.1	39.4	9.0	23.6	12.4
May	2 066.9	1 959.2	107.7	107.3	27.9	26.8	39.8	12.8	0.3	-12.5
June	1 790.9	1 699.0	91.8	85.7	31.8	16.7	40.0	-2.8	6.1	-3.1
July	1 571.9	1 507.7	64.2	38.6	1.2	5.7	19.1	12.7	25.6	9.7
August	1 749.7	1 620.5	129.2	100.2	26.4	23.6	42.3	7.9	29.0	16.5
September	1 751.0	1 645.6	105.4	88.8	-5.3	17.6	61.2	15.4	16.6	7.6
October	1 869.8	1 763.6	106.1	80.8	6.9	8.5	37.9	27.5	25.3	18.5
November	1 918.5	1 798.5	120.0	113.9	32.3	11.8	60.6	9.2	6.1	1.0
December	1 843.4	1 780.4	63.0	39.0	4.3	12.3	33.5	-11.1	24.0	6.1
2007										
January	1 833.6	1 709.3	124.3	112.3	21.0	21.2	47.2	23.0	12.0	-4.9
February	2 047.6	1 962.5	85.1	72.5	15.5	0.7	44.1	12.2	12.6	2.2
March	2 719.3	2 617.4	101.9	81.1	29.7	-1.0	43.3	9.1	20.8	1.4
April	2 028.9	1 931.0	97.8	72.5	-8.9	22.4	30.7	28.3	25.3	9.4
May	2 429.8	2 259.7	170.1	158.6	27.2	14.3	74.4	42.7	11.5	-4.6
June	2 624.8	2 501.1	123.8	96.0	17.9	23.6	26.3	28.2	27.8	6.4
July	2 473.7	2 448.5	25.2	20.8	-2.4	1.2	3.7	18.4	4.4	-6.9
August	3 335.3	3 373.0	-37.7	-13.5	25.2	4.3	-3.9	-39.0	-24.2	-29.7
September	2 339.1	2 284.8	54.3	26.0	9.9	2.3	11.3	2.5	28.3	14.4
October	2 683.2	2 550.2	133.0	111.2	50.9	4.8	25.5	29.9	21.8	4.0
November	2 901.8	2 837.7	64.1	52.4	19.4	17.5	11.2	4.3	11.8	0.4
December	2 313.6	2 249.7	63.9	28.1	-10.6	-11.3	29.1	21.0	35.8	11.0
2008										
January	3 132.1	3 058.4	73.8	21.0	0.7	16.4	-0.6	4.5	52.8	36.1
February	2 913.1	2 846.0	67.1	60.4	15.8	32.4	14.9	-2.7	6.7	-3.6
March	3 066.5	2 992.7	73.8	25.4	23.0	0.2	-8.8	11.0	48.4	28.0
April	2 584.6	2 482.4	102.2	61.0	54.3	1.2	17.5	-12.0	41.3	22.3
May	2 599.2	2 496.1	103.1	86.7	5.5	14.5	50.8	15.9	16.4	-3.7
June	2 794.1	2 733.8	60.2	45.4	26.9	20.2	0.6	-2.3	14.9	1.1
July	2 819.5	2 837.5	-18.0	-13.1	23.9	-25.9	-4.3	-6.8	-4.9	10.1
August	2 163.9	2 169.4	-5.5	4.8	28.0	-11.0	-12.6	0.4	-10.2	4.8
September	3 081.8	3 051.8	30.0	34.8	15.8	14.8	-7.3	11.5	-4.8	4.9
October	2 491.9	2 528.5	-36.6	-19.4	34.0	-33.5	-13.8	-6.1	-17.2	-1.1
November	1 546.4	1 606.5	-60.1	-22.9	0.4	-10.9	-15.3	2.8	-37.1	-26.2
December	1 480.2	1 457.9	22.4	25.2	11.1	-24.6	37.4	1.2	-2.8	3.9

. . . = Not available.

Table 7-7. Foreigners' Transactions in Long-Term Securities with U.S. Residents—*Continued*

(Billions of dollars, not seasonally adjusted.)

Year and month	Transactions in U.S. domestic securities between foreigners and U.S. residents—Continued			Transactions in foreign securities between foreigners and U.S. residents					Net long-term securities transactions	Other acquisitions of long-term securities, net	Net foreign acquisition of long-term securities
	Net purchases—Continued			Gross purchases from U.S. residents	Gross sales to U.S. residents	Net purchases ¹					
	Official—Continued					Total	Bonds	Equities			
	Government agency bonds	Corporate bonds	Equities								
1977	. . .	. . .	. . .	10.3	15.8	-5.5	-5.1	-0.4	25.1	. . .	. . .
1978	0.7	0.7	0.7	14.8	18.5	-3.7	-4.2	0.5	5.7	. . .	. . .
1979	0.5	0.4	0.6	17.3	22.1	-4.8	-4.0	-0.8	0.9	0.1	1.0
1980	2.2	2.0	1.1	25.0	28.1	-3.1	-1.0	-2.1	12.6	-1.6	11.0
1981	1.3	1.6	1.0	26.9	32.6	-5.7	-5.5	-0.2	20.2	-5.2	15.0
1982	-0.7	-0.7	0.3	34.3	42.3	-8.0	-6.6	-1.3	14.7	-5.4	9.3
1983	-0.5	-0.8	-1.0	49.6	56.6	-7.0	-3.2	-3.8	4.7	-3.2	1.5
1984	0.0	-0.8	-2.1	70.8	75.9	-5.0	-3.9	-1.1	26.4	-1.5	24.9
1985	-0.3	-1.6	0.1	102.1	110.0	-7.9	-4.0	-3.9	70.3	-2.3	68.1
1986	-1.2	-1.6	0.7	216.1	221.7	-5.5	-3.7	-1.9	83.0	-2.3	80.8
1987	1.6	-0.4	-0.6	294.5	301.4	-6.9	-8.0	1.1	62.3	-1.0	61.3
1988	1.3	-0.1	-2.4	293.9	303.3	-9.4	-7.4	-2.0	65.4	0.2	65.6
1989	1.4	-0.2	2.0	344.6	363.2	-18.6	-5.5	-13.1	78.0	0.0	78.0
1990	0.7	-0.1	-1.4	437.7	468.9	-31.2	-21.9	-9.2	-12.4	3.9	-8.5
1991	1.3	0.4	0.9	450.9	497.7	-46.8	-14.8	-32.0	11.3	0.4	11.7
1992	3.9	0.8	-1.5	663.6	711.5	-47.9	-15.6	-32.3	25.4	-0.3	25.0
1993	4.0	0.6	2.0	991.4	1 134.5	-143.1	-80.4	-62.7	-31.9	1.1	-30.8
1994	6.1	0.0	-2.5	1 234.5	1 291.8	-57.3	-9.2	-48.1	83.1	0.5	83.5
1995	3.7	0.2	3.0	1 235.1	1 333.8	-98.7	-48.4	-50.3	133.2	0.4	133.6
1996	5.0	1.5	-0.2	1 564.4	1 675.0	-110.6	-51.4	-59.3	259.6	-0.5	259.1
1997	4.5	1.5	-1.7	2 207.7	2 296.8	-89.1	-48.1	-40.9	298.9	0.0	298.9
1998	6.3	0.2	-3.7	2 257.8	2 269.0	-11.1	-17.3	6.2	266.7	0.1	266.7
1999	20.4	1.5	-0.6	1 975.6	1 965.6	10.0	-5.7	15.6	360.1	0.0	360.2
2000	40.9	2.0	1.1	2 761.1	2 778.3	-17.1	-4.1	-13.1	440.7	-59.8	380.8
2001	17.4	3.8	2.0	2 557.8	2 577.4	-19.6	30.5	-50.1	501.2	-41.5	459.8
2002	28.6	5.6	-2.0	2 640.0	2 613.0	27.0	28.5	-1.5	574.6	-39.3	535.2
2003	25.9	5.4	-0.3	2 761.8	2 818.4	-56.5	32.0	-88.6	663.3	-138.9	524.5
2004	20.8	11.5	2.2	3 123.1	3 276.0	-152.8	-67.9	-85.0	763.6	-38.8	724.8
2005	31.6	19.1	1.0	3 700.0	3 872.4	-172.4	-45.1	-127.3	839.1	-143.0	696.2
2006	92.6	28.6	5.8	5 515.9	5 766.8	-250.9	-144.5	-106.5	892.3	-174.6	717.7
2007	119.1	50.6	15.1	8 187.6	8 416.8	-229.2	-133.9	-95.3	776.6	-235.1	541.5
2008	-31.5	34.9	23.4	7 701.4	7 599.6	101.8	81.8	20.1	514.3	-196.7	317.6
2006											
January	8.9	2.4	0.9	400.5	415.9	-15.4	-4.0	-11.4	71.0	-15.6	55.4
February	2.8	3.6	-0.7	435.1	446.6	-11.5	0.0	-11.6	93.4	-9.8	83.6
March	4.2	2.6	1.6	482.0	503.3	-21.3	-8.5	-12.8	75.0	-11.3	63.7
April	5.9	1.9	3.4	416.1	435.3	-19.2	-7.6	-11.6	49.0	-14.1	34.9
May	9.2	2.5	1.2	569.0	595.8	-26.7	-18.8	-7.9	81.0	-10.2	70.7
June	6.3	1.8	1.2	458.7	467.1	-8.3	-11.0	2.7	83.5	-17.3	66.2
July	13.1	1.1	1.6	381.1	401.2	-20.0	-17.5	-2.5	44.2	-15.9	28.3
August	9.6	2.8	0.2	419.7	423.7	-3.9	-10.2	6.2	125.3	-12.8	112.4
September	7.9	1.8	-0.7	417.7	441.4	-23.7	-15.2	-8.6	81.7	-13.9	67.8
October	5.3	2.0	-0.4	498.8	515.6	-16.8	-9.0	-7.8	89.3	-12.4	76.9
November	4.0	3.2	-2.1	526.2	559.1	-32.8	-11.2	-21.7	87.1	-25.0	62.1
December	15.5	2.9	-0.5	510.8	561.9	-51.2	-31.6	-19.6	11.8	-16.3	-4.4
2007											
January	15.1	2.4	-0.6	548.8	561.8	-13.0	-0.5	-12.4	111.4	-18.9	92.4
February	4.5	5.6	0.3	587.6	606.2	-18.6	-4.1	-14.5	66.5	-20.8	45.8
March	16.1	2.9	0.4	697.2	739.9	-42.8	-32.7	-10.0	59.1	-17.9	41.3
April	13.7	2.9	-0.7	624.2	638.3	-14.0	-11.0	-3.0	83.8	-13.1	70.7
May	12.8	4.0	-0.7	735.1	769.4	-34.4	-21.8	-12.6	135.8	-19.7	116.1
June	16.0	3.7	1.7	721.7	736.8	-15.1	-6.7	-8.4	108.6	-20.2	88.4
July	7.5	1.0	2.8	743.8	757.9	-14.1	0.8	-14.9	11.2	-29.2	-18.0
August	4.1	3.0	-1.6	826.3	861.4	-35.1	-22.4	-12.8	-72.9	-20.6	-93.5
September	9.2	4.6	0.1	560.5	600.9	-40.4	-19.1	-21.3	13.9	-24.2	-10.3
October	10.0	7.4	0.4	811.1	815.1	-4.0	-9.1	5.0	128.9	-20.0	109.0
November	6.0	4.9	0.5	731.7	713.8	17.9	8.3	9.6	82.1	-16.8	65.2
December	4.1	8.2	12.5	599.6	615.3	-15.7	-15.7	0.0	48.2	-13.8	34.4
2008											
January	-0.6	3.9	13.3	771.4	792.9	-21.5	-19.2	-2.3	52.2	-17.9	34.3
February	1.2	4.4	4.8	684.0	698.4	-14.3	3.9	-18.3	52.8	-18.3	34.4
March	15.9	4.1	0.4	752.5	755.6	-3.1	-0.2	-2.9	70.7	-20.1	50.6
April	11.0	7.5	0.4	698.9	689.5	9.4	9.6	-0.2	111.6	-20.9	90.8
May	11.0	9.1	0.0	677.3	705.5	-28.3	-10.2	-18.1	74.9	-22.6	52.2
June	9.1	4.1	0.5	689.2	700.3	-11.1	-12.7	1.6	49.1	-18.8	30.3
July	-16.2	0.2	1.1	720.4	687.9	32.4	15.5	16.9	14.5	-14.5	-0.1
August	-13.1	-0.5	-1.4	585.7	565.5	20.2	17.4	2.9	14.8	-12.9	1.9
September	-8.7	-1.2	0.0	710.0	674.9	35.1	37.6	-2.5	65.1	-13.5	51.6
October	-16.7	0.7	-0.1	645.8	609.3	36.5	14.8	21.7	-0.1	-14.8	-14.9
November	-11.6	-0.9	1.6	412.2	377.9	34.3	12.9	21.3	-25.8	-12.0	-37.8
December	-12.9	3.5	2.6	354.1	341.8	12.3	12.2	0.1	34.6	-10.4	24.3

¹(-) indicates net U.S. acquisitions of foreign securities.
. . . = Not available.

Table 7-8. International Investment Position of the United States at Year-End

(Millions of dollars.)

Year	U.S. net international investment position	U.S.-owned assets abroad									
		Total	Financial derivatives	Official reserve assets	Other U.S. government assets	Direct investment		Foreign bonds	Foreign corporate stocks	U.S. nonbank claims	U.S. bank claims
						Current cost	Market value				
1976	165 374	456 964	. . .	44 094	44 978	222 283	. . .	34 704	9 453	20 317	81 135
1977	172 395	512 278	. . .	53 376	48 567	246 078	. . .	39 329	10 110	22 256	92 562
1978	208 052	621 227	. . .	69 450	53 187	285 005	. . .	42 148	11 236	29 385	130 816
1979	319 836	786 701	. . .	143 260	58 851	336 301	. . .	41 966	14 803	34 491	157 029
1980	365 502	929 806	. . .	171 412	65 573	388 072	. . .	43 524	18 930	38 429	203 866
1981	346 088	1 001 667	. . .	124 568	70 893	407 804	. . .	45 675	16 467	42 752	293 508
1982	336 778	1 108 436	. . .	143 445	76 903	374 059	226 638	56 604	17 442	35 405	404 578
1983	307 534	1 210 974	. . .	123 110	81 664	355 643	274 342	58 569	26 154	131 329	434 505
1984	171 550	1 204 900	. . .	105 040	86 945	348 342	270 574	62 810	25 994	130 138	445 631
1985	67 121	1 287 396	. . .	117 930	89 792	371 036	386 352	75 020	44 383	141 872	447 363
1986	-21 766	1 469 396	. . .	139 875	91 850	404 818	530 074	85 724	72 399	167 392	507 338
1987	-63 968	1 646 527	. . .	162 370	90 681	478 062	590 246	93 889	94 700	177 368	549 457
1988	-160 865	1 829 665	. . .	144 179	87 892	513 761	692 461	104 187	128 662	197 757	653 227
1989	-239 793	2 070 868	. . .	168 714	86 643	553 093	832 460	116 949	197 345	234 307	713 817
1990	-223 405	2 178 978	. . .	174 664	84 344	616 655	731 762	144 717	197 596	265 315	695 687
1991	-284 746	2 286 456	. . .	159 223	81 422	643 364	827 537	176 774	278 976	256 295	690 402
1992	-404 284	2 331 696	. . .	147 435	83 022	663 830	798 630	200 817	314 266	254 303	668 023
1993	-277 730	2 753 648	. . .	164 945	83 382	723 526	1 061 299	309 666	543 862	242 022	686 245
1994	-291 305	2 987 118	. . .	163 394	83 908	786 565	1 114 582	310 391	626 762	322 980	693 118
1995	-422 911	3 486 272	. . .	176 061	85 064	885 506	1 363 792	413 310	790 615	367 567	768 149
1996	-456 293	4 032 307	. . .	160 739	86 123	989 810	1 608 340	481 411	1 006 135	450 578	857 511
1997	-779 563	4 567 906	. . .	134 836	86 198	1 068 063	1 879 285	543 396	1 207 787	545 524	982 102
1998	-851 464	5 095 546	. . .	146 006	86 768	1 196 021	2 279 601	594 400	1 474 983	588 322	1 009 046
1999	-724 343	5 974 394	. . .	136 418	84 227	1 414 355	2 839 639	548 233	2 003 716	704 517	1 082 928
2000	-1 330 630	6 238 785	. . .	128 400	85 168	1 531 607	2 694 014	572 692	1 852 842	836 559	1 231 517
2001	-1 868 875	6 308 681	. . .	129 961	85 654	1 693 131	2 314 934	557 062	1 612 673	839 303	1 390 897
2002	-2 037 970	6 649 079	. . .	158 602	85 309	1 867 043	2 022 588	702 742	1 373 980	901 946	1 559 457
2003	-2 086 513	7 638 086	. . .	183 577	84 772	2 054 464	2 729 126	868 948	2 079 422	594 004	1 772 899
2004	-2 245 417	9 340 634	. . .	189 591	83 062	2 498 494	3 362 796	984 978	2 560 418	793 556	2 230 535
2005	-1 925 146	11 961 552	1 190 029	188 043	77 523	2 651 721	3 637 996	1 011 554	3 317 705	1 018 462	2 506 515
2006	-2 225 804	14 381 297	1 238 995	219 853	72 189	2 935 977	4 454 635	1 275 515	4 328 960	1 163 102	3 146 706
2007	-2 441 829	17 639 954	2 284 581	277 211	94 471	3 332 828	5 147 952	1 478 087	5 170 599	1 176 027	3 826 150

Year	Foreign-owned assets in the United States									
	Total	Financial derivatives	Foreign official assets	Direct investment in the United States		U.S. Treasury securities	Corporate and other bonds	Corporate stocks	U.S. currency	U.S. nonbank liabilities	U.S. bank liabilities
				Current cost	Market value						
1976	291 590	. . .	104 445	47 528	. . .	7 028	11 964	42 949	11 250	12 961	53 465
1977	339 883	. . .	140 867	55 413	. . .	7 562	11 456	39 779	12 701	11 921	60 184
1978	413 175	. . .	173 057	68 976	. . .	8 910	11 457	42 097	14 940	16 019	77 719
1979	466 865	. . .	159 852	88 579	. . .	14 210	10 269	48 318	16 642	18 669	110 326
1980	564 304	. . .	176 062	127 105	. . .	16 113	9 545	64 569	19 415	30 426	121 069
1981	655 579	. . .	180 425	164 623	. . .	18 505	10 694	64 391	20 974	30 606	165 361
1982	771 658	. . .	189 109	184 842	130 428	25 758	16 709	76 279	23 441	27 532	227 988
1983	903 440	. . .	194 468	193 708	153 318	33 846	17 454	96 357	27 546	61 731	278 330
1984	1 033 350	. . .	199 678	223 538	172 377	62 121	32 421	96 056	29 942	77 415	312 179
1985	1 220 275	. . .	202 482	247 223	219 996	87 954	82 290	125 578	33 258	86 993	354 497
1986	1 491 162	. . .	241 226	284 701	272 966	96 078	140 863	168 940	35 679	90 703	432 972
1987	1 710 495	. . .	283 058	334 552	316 200	82 588	166 089	175 643	39 545	110 187	518 833
1988	1 990 530	. . .	322 036	401 766	391 530	100 877	191 314	200 978	43 656	144 548	585 355
1989	2 310 661	. . .	341 746	467 886	534 734	166 541	231 673	251 191	47 405	167 093	637 126
1990	2 402 383	. . .	373 293	505 346	539 601	152 452	238 903	221 741	63 991	213 406	633 251
1991	2 571 202	. . .	398 538	533 404	669 137	170 295	274 136	271 872	76 804	208 908	637 245
1992	2 735 980	. . .	437 263	540 270	696 177	197 739	299 287	300 160	87 890	220 666	652 705
1993	3 031 378	. . .	509 422	593 313	768 398	221 501	355 822	340 627	104 508	229 038	677 147
1994	3 278 423	. . .	535 227	617 982	757 853	235 684	368 077	371 618	125 093	239 817	784 925
1995	3 909 183	. . .	682 873	680 066	1 005 726	326 995	459 080	510 769	133 933	300 424	815 043
1996	4 488 600	. . .	820 823	745 619	1 229 118	433 903	539 308	625 805	148 084	346 810	828 248
1997	5 347 469	. . .	873 716	824 136	1 637 408	538 137	618 837	893 888	170 509	459 407	968 839
1998	5 947 010	. . .	896 174	920 044	2 179 035	543 323	724 619	1 178 824	184 356	485 675	1 013 995
1999	6 698 737	. . .	951 088	1 101 709	2 798 193	440 685	825 175	1 526 116	208 763	578 046	1 067 155
2000	7 569 415	. . .	1 030 708	1 421 017	2 783 235	381 630	1 068 566	1 554 448	205 406	738 904	1 168 736
2001	8 177 556	. . .	1 109 072	1 518 473	2 560 294	375 059	1 343 071	1 478 301	229 200	798 314	1 326 066
2002	8 687 049	. . .	1 250 977	1 499 952	2 021 817	473 503	1 530 982	1 248 085	248 061	897 335	1 538 154
2003	9 724 599	. . .	1 562 564	1 580 994	2 454 877	527 223	1 710 787	1 712 069	258 652	450 884	1 921 426
2004	11 586 051	. . .	2 011 899	1 742 716	2 717 383	561 610	2 035 149	1 960 357	271 953	600 161	2 402 206
2005	13 886 698	1 132 114	2 306 292	1 905 979	2 817 970	643 793	2 243 135	2 109 863	280 400	658 177	2 606 945
2006	16 607 101	1 179 159	2 825 628	2 151 616	3 293 739	567 885	2 824 879	2 547 482	282 627	797 495	3 430 330
2007	20 081 783	2 201 052	3 337 030	2 422 796	3 523 600	734 776	3 299 325	2 833 113	271 952	959 544	4 022 195

Note: See notes and definitions.
. . . = Not available.

Section 7c: Exports and Imports

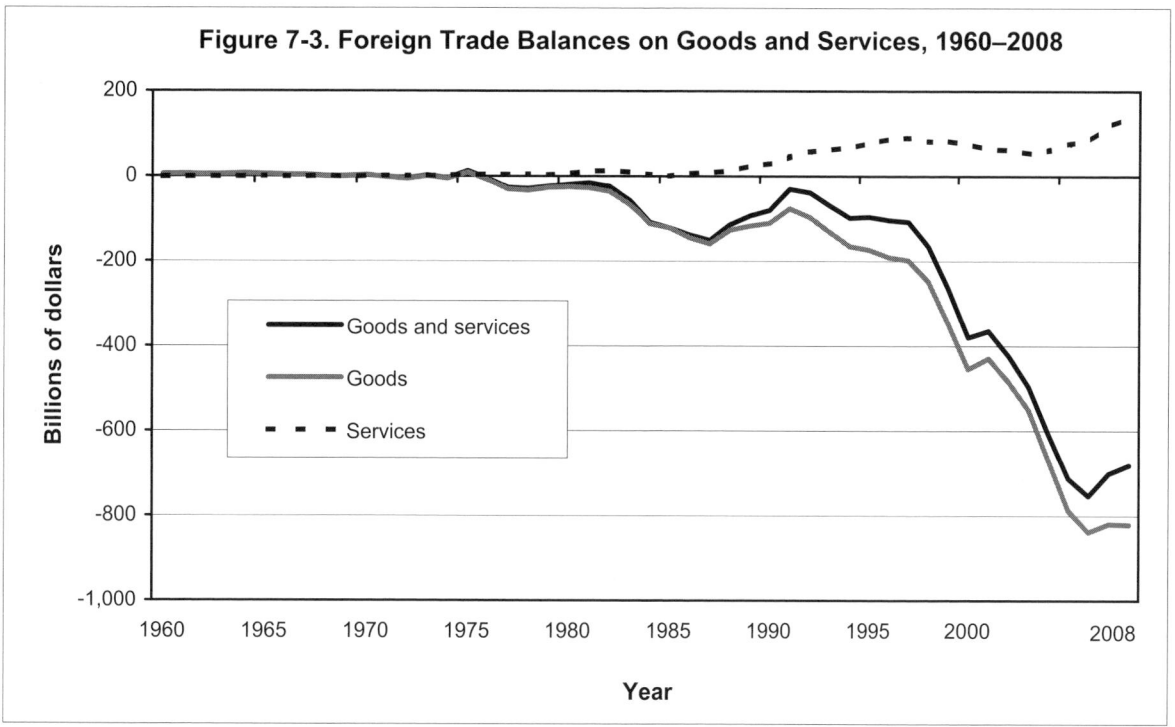

Figure 7-3. Foreign Trade Balances on Goods and Services, 1960–2008

- U.S. imports of goods and services exceeded exports by over $750 billion in 2006, setting yet another new record. After that, as the economy weakened, aggregate values of both exports and imports continued to increase, but the dollar increase in imports was somewhat smaller than that for exports and the trade deficit was diminished. (Table 7-9)

- Measured in constant dollars, exports of goods continued to rise in 2008, but real imports fell in a number of categories—foods, industrial supplies and materials, autos, and other consumer goods. (Table 7-12)

- Canada and Mexico are the principal trading partners of the United States, with relations governed by the North American Free Trade Agreement (NAFTA). In 2008, U.S. exports to those two countries brought in $413 billion, compared with $275 billion in exports to the European Union and $249 billion in exports to China, Japan, and the newly industrialized countries of Asia (the NICS—Hong Kong, South Korea, Singapore, and Taiwan). (Table 7-13)

- U.S. imports from Canada and Mexico in 2008 amounted to $551 billion, more than the $368 billion imported from the European Union but somewhat less than the $584 billion from China, Japan, and the Asian NICS. Growth in the value of imports from China, which averaged 23 percent per year from 2001 to 2006, slowed to 12 percent in 2007 and 5 percent in 2008. (Table 7-14)

- For U.S. services trade, "other private services" is the largest single category among both exports and imports. This includes such activities as education, financial services, and many other types of business and professional services. The United States had a surplus of $85 billion on "other private services" in 2008. The current-dollar value of this surplus has continued to increase and accounts for more than half of the total surplus on services. (Tables 7-9, 7-15 and 7-16)

Table 7-9. U.S. Exports and Imports of Goods and Services

(Balance of payments basis; millions of dollars, seasonally adjusted.)

Year and month	Goods and services			Goods			Services		
	Exports	Imports	Balance	Exports	Imports	Balance	Exports	Imports	Balance
1965	35 285	30 621	4 664	26 461	21 510	4 951	8 824	9 111	-287
1966	38 926	35 987	2 939	29 310	25 493	3 817	9 616	10 494	-878
1967	41 333	38 729	2 604	30 666	26 866	3 800	10 667	11 863	-1 196
1968	45 543	45 293	250	33 626	32 991	635	11 917	12 302	-385
1969	49 220	49 129	91	36 414	35 807	607	12 806	13 322	-516
1970	56 640	54 386	2 254	42 469	39 866	2 603	14 171	14 520	-349
1971	59 677	60 979	-1 302	43 319	45 579	-2 260	16 358	15 400	958
1972	67 222	72 665	-5 443	49 381	55 797	-6 416	17 841	16 868	973
1973	91 242	89 342	1 900	71 410	70 499	911	19 832	18 843	989
1974	120 897	125 190	-4 293	98 306	103 811	-5 505	22 591	21 379	1 212
1975	132 585	120 181	12 404	107 088	98 185	8 903	25 497	21 996	3 501
1976	142 716	148 798	-6 082	114 745	124 228	-9 483	27 971	24 570	3 401
1977	152 301	179 547	-27 246	120 816	151 907	-31 091	31 485	27 640	3 845
1978	178 428	208 191	-29 763	142 075	176 002	-33 927	36 353	32 189	4 164
1979	224 131	248 696	-24 565	184 439	212 007	-27 568	39 692	36 689	3 003
1980	271 834	291 241	-19 407	224 250	249 750	-25 500	47 584	41 491	6 093
1981	294 398	310 570	-16 172	237 044	265 067	-28 023	57 354	45 503	11 851
1982	275 236	299 391	-24 156	211 157	247 642	-36 485	64 079	51 749	12 329
1983	266 106	323 874	-57 767	201 799	268 901	-67 102	64 307	54 973	9 335
1984	291 094	400 166	-109 072	219 926	332 418	-112 492	71 168	67 748	3 420
1985	289 070	410 950	-121 880	215 915	338 088	-122 173	73 155	72 862	294
1986	310 033	448 572	-138 538	223 344	368 425	-145 081	86 689	80 147	6 543
1987	348 869	500 552	-151 684	250 208	409 765	-159 557	98 661	90 787	7 874
1988	431 149	545 715	-114 566	320 230	447 189	-126 959	110 919	98 526	12 393
1989	487 003	580 144	-93 141	359 916	477 665	-117 749	127 087	102 479	24 607
1990	535 233	616 097	-80 864	387 401	498 438	-111 037	147 832	117 659	30 173
1991	578 344	609 479	-31 135	414 083	491 020	-76 937	164 261	118 459	45 802
1992	616 882	656 094	-39 212	439 631	536 528	-96 897	177 251	119 566	57 685
1993	642 863	713 174	-70 311	456 943	589 394	-132 451	185 920	123 780	62 141
1994	703 254	801 747	-98 493	502 859	668 690	-165 831	200 395	133 057	67 338
1995	794 387	890 771	-96 384	575 204	749 374	-174 170	219 183	141 397	77 786
1996	851 602	955 667	-104 065	612 113	803 113	-191 000	239 489	152 554	86 935
1997	934 453	1 042 726	-108 273	678 366	876 794	-198 428	256 087	165 932	90 155
1998	933 174	1 099 314	-166 140	670 416	918 637	-248 221	262 758	180 677	82 081
1999	965 884	1 230 974	-265 090	683 965	1 031 784	-347 819	281 919	199 190	82 729
2000	1 070 597	1 450 432	-379 835	771 994	1 226 684	-454 690	298 603	223 748	74 855
2001	1 004 896	1 370 022	-365 126	718 712	1 148 231	-429 519	286 184	221 791	64 393
2002	974 721	1 398 446	-423 725	682 422	1 167 377	-484 955	292 299	231 069	61 230
2003	1 017 757	1 514 672	-496 915	713 415	1 264 307	-550 892	304 342	250 365	53 977
2004	1 160 588	1 768 318	-607 730	807 516	1 477 094	-669 578	353 072	291 244	61 848
2005	1 283 753	1 995 320	-711 567	894 631	1 681 780	-787 149	389 122	313 540	75 582
2006	1 457 014	2 210 298	-753 283	1 023 109	1 861 380	-838 270	433 905	348 918	84 987
2007	1 645 726	2 345 983	-700 258	1 148 481	1 967 853	-819 373	497 245	378 130	119 115
2008	1 835 785	2 516 915	-681 130	1 291 371	2 112 196	-820 825	544 414	404 719	139 695
2006									
January	115 225	180 763	-65 538	80 577	152 967	-72 390	34 648	27 796	6 852
February	116 026	178 324	-62 298	81 421	149 736	-68 315	34 605	28 588	6 017
March	117 929	179 179	-61 251	82 682	150 583	-67 902	35 247	28 596	6 651
April	117 882	180 572	-62 690	82 749	152 001	-69 252	35 133	28 571	6 562
May	119 928	185 094	-65 166	84 171	156 070	-71 899	35 757	29 024	6 733
June	121 960	185 945	-63 986	86 412	156 945	-70 534	35 548	29 000	6 548
July	120 314	187 278	-66 965	84 645	158 282	-73 638	35 669	28 996	6 673
August	123 244	189 965	-66 720	87 080	160 986	-73 905	36 164	28 979	7 185
September	124 086	187 872	-63 786	87 553	158 633	-71 080	36 533	29 239	7 294
October	125 640	183 365	-57 726	87 983	153 599	-65 617	37 657	29 766	7 891
November	127 268	184 118	-56 850	89 005	153 980	-64 975	38 263	30 138	8 125
December	127 514	187 823	-60 310	88 834	157 598	-68 765	38 680	30 225	8 455
2007									
January	128 315	186 726	-58 411	90 257	156 465	-66 208	38 058	30 261	7 797
February	126 987	185 797	-58 810	89 007	155 450	-66 443	37 980	30 347	7 633
March	130 134	192 456	-62 322	91 054	161 766	-70 712	39 080	30 690	8 390
April	130 520	190 779	-60 259	91 210	159 964	-68 754	39 310	30 815	8 495
May	133 687	193 122	-59 435	93 411	161 883	-68 472	40 276	31 239	9 037
June	135 744	194 869	-59 125	94 867	163 528	-68 661	40 877	31 341	9 536
July	139 982	197 299	-57 317	97 502	165 296	-67 794	42 480	32 003	10 477
August	142 113	197 446	-55 333	98 524	165 196	-66 672	43 589	32 250	11 339
September	142 778	198 243	-55 464	99 468	166 207	-66 738	43 310	32 036	11 274
October	144 108	200 441	-56 333	100 371	168 084	-67 713	43 737	32 357	11 380
November	145 214	205 084	-59 871	100 968	172 664	-71 697	44 246	32 420	11 826
December	146 144	203 722	-57 579	101 842	171 350	-69 509	44 302	32 372	11 930
2008									
January	149 346	208 503	-59 157	104 598	175 260	-70 662	44 748	33 243	11 505
February	152 507	214 388	-61 881	108 009	181 007	-72 998	44 498	33 381	11 117
March	149 664	207 069	-57 405	104 941	173 859	-68 918	44 723	33 210	11 513
April	155 192	217 011	-61 819	109 971	183 436	-73 465	45 221	33 575	11 646
May	157 138	217 604	-60 466	110 910	183 536	-72 626	46 228	34 068	12 160
June	163 035	222 170	-59 135	116 167	187 950	-71 783	46 868	34 220	12 648
July	167 465	229 969	-62 505	120 746	195 376	-74 631	46 719	34 593	12 126
August	164 671	224 915	-60 244	117 798	189 371	-71 573	46 873	35 544	11 329
September	153 774	211 908	-58 135	107 728	177 779	-70 052	46 046	34 129	11 917
October	149 813	207 849	-58 036	104 709	174 272	-69 563	45 104	33 577	11 527
November	140 663	183 114	-42 450	97 044	150 335	-53 290	43 619	32 779	10 840
December	132 517	172 416	-39 900	88 752	140 016	-51 265	43 765	32 400	11 365

Table 7-10. U.S. Exports of Goods by End-Use and Advanced Technology Categories

(Census basis, except as noted; billions of dollars; seasonally adjusted, except as noted.)

Year and month	Total exports of goods			Principal end-use category							Advanced technology products [1]
	Total, balance of payments basis	Net adjustments	Total, Census basis	Foods, feeds, and beverages	Industrial supplies and materials		Capital goods, except automotive	Automotive vehicles, engines, and parts	Consumer goods, except automotive	Other goods	
					Total	Petroleum and products					
1980	224.25	3.55	220.70	36.28	72.09	3.57	76.28	17.44	17.75	. . .	. . .
1981	237.04	3.31	233.74	38.84	70.19	4.56	84.17	19.69	17.70	. . .	. . .
1982	211.16	-1.12	212.28	32.20	64.05	6.87	76.50	17.23	16.13	. . .	. . .
1983	201.80	0.09	201.71	32.09	58.94	5.59	71.66	18.46	14.93	. . .	. . .
1984	219.93	1.18	218.74	32.20	64.12	5.43	77.01	22.42	15.09	. . .	. . .
1985	215.92	3.29	212.62	24.57	61.16	5.71	79.32	24.95	14.59	. . .	. . .
1986	223.34	-3.13	226.47	23.52	64.72	4.43	82.82	25.10	16.73	. . .	. . .
1987	250.21	-3.70	253.90	25.23	70.05	4.63	92.71	27.58	20.31	. . .	. . .
1988	320.23	-3.11	323.34	33.77	90.02	4.48	119.10	33.40	26.98	. . .	. . .
1989	359.92	-3.08	363.00	36.34	98.36	6.46	136.94	35.05	36.01	. . .	. . .
1990	387.40	-5.57	392.97	35.18	105.55	8.36	153.07	36.07	43.60	20.73	. . .
1991	414.08	-7.77	421.85	35.79	109.69	8.40	166.72	39.72	46.65	23.66	. . .
1992	439.63	-8.54	448.17	40.34	109.59	7.62	176.50	46.71	51.31	24.39	. . .
1993	456.94	-7.92	464.86	40.59	111.89	7.49	182.85	51.35	54.56	23.89	. . .
1994	502.86	-9.77	512.63	41.96	121.55	6.97	205.82	57.31	59.86	26.50	. . .
1995	575.20	-9.54	584.74	50.47	146.37	8.10	234.46	61.26	64.31	28.72	. . .
1996	612.11	-12.96	625.08	55.53	147.98	9.63	253.99	64.24	70.11	33.85	. . .
1997	678.37	-10.82	689.18	51.51	158.32	10.42	295.87	73.30	77.96	33.51	. . .
1998	670.42	-11.72	682.14	46.40	148.31	8.08	299.87	72.39	80.29	35.44	. . .
1999	683.97	-11.83	695.80	45.98	147.52	8.62	310.79	75.26	80.92	35.32	. . .
2000	771.99	-9.92	781.92	47.87	172.62	12.01	356.93	80.36	89.38	34.77	227.39
2001	718.71	-10.39	729.10	49.41	160.10	10.64	321.71	75.44	88.33	34.11	199.63
2002	682.42	-10.68	693.10	49.62	156.81	10.34	290.44	78.94	84.36	32.94	178.57
2003	713.42	-11.36	724.77	55.03	173.04	12.69	293.67	80.63	89.91	32.49	180.21
2004	807.52	-11.26	818.78	56.57	203.96	17.08	331.56	89.21	103.08	34.40	201.42
2005	894.63	-11.35	905.98	58.96	233.05	22.66	363.32	98.41	115.29	36.96	216.06
2006	1 023.11	-13.52	1 036.64	65.96	276.04	31.57	414.99	106.98	129.07	43.59	252.71
2007	1 148.48	-14.00	1 162.48	84.26	316.34	37.76	447.43	121.05	146.10	47.30	274.16
2008	1 291.37	-9.16	1 300.53	108.42	387.28	67.02	469.48	120.94	161.19	53.24	275.82
2005											
January	71.12	-0.76	71.88	4.68	18.47	1.45	28.53	8.12	9.16	2.93	15.27
February	71.59	-0.78	72.37	4.80	19.09	1.90	28.47	7.88	9.37	2.76	14.79
March	72.15	-0.93	73.08	4.86	19.01	2.02	29.21	7.75	9.36	2.89	19.53
April	75.09	-0.94	76.03	4.94	19.72	2.12	30.78	8.02	9.44	3.13	18.66
May	74.31	-1.04	75.35	5.23	19.88	2.30	29.68	7.92	9.58	3.07	17.11
June	74.33	-1.04	75.37	4.96	19.49	2.05	30.30	7.94	9.53	3.16	19.30
July	74.50	-0.71	75.21	4.84	19.53	1.99	30.45	8.02	9.53	2.84	17.44
August	75.78	-1.08	76.86	4.88	19.84	2.01	31.09	8.22	9.62	3.21	18.58
September	73.33	-1.00	74.33	4.80	19.00	1.66	29.06	8.46	9.85	3.16	17.17
October	75.78	-0.92	76.70	5.05	19.22	1.62	31.12	8.55	9.52	3.24	18.93
November	77.48	-0.97	78.45	4.93	19.56	1.73	32.14	8.66	9.94	3.21	18.95
December	79.19	-1.16	80.35	5.00	20.23	1.82	32.48	8.88	10.38	3.37	20.33
2006											
January	80.58	-0.83	81.41	5.18	20.92	2.04	32.96	8.91	10.14	3.29	18.31
February	81.42	-0.90	82.32	5.07	21.02	2.11	33.55	8.95	10.25	3.49	18.46
March	82.68	-0.91	83.59	5.30	22.34	2.42	33.74	8.52	10.47	3.22	22.83
April	82.75	-0.93	83.68	5.18	22.46	2.83	33.98	8.61	10.24	3.21	19.80
May	84.17	-1.03	85.20	5.46	23.12	2.59	34.06	8.59	10.66	3.32	19.94
June	86.41	-0.97	87.38	5.58	23.57	2.62	34.95	8.97	10.84	3.47	22.25
July	84.65	-1.10	85.75	5.57	22.95	2.79	33.77	9.11	10.85	3.48	19.58
August	87.08	-1.21	88.29	5.84	23.42	2.59	34.89	9.20	11.12	3.82	21.33
September	87.55	-1.28	88.84	5.64	24.37	3.57	35.32	8.79	10.69	4.04	22.02
October	87.98	-1.28	89.27	5.72	24.14	3.00	35.45	8.77	11.18	4.00	22.30
November	89.01	-1.61	90.62	5.56	23.99	2.66	36.45	9.03	11.32	4.27	22.93
December	88.83	-1.47	90.30	5.87	23.74	2.35	35.88	9.54	11.29	3.99	22.97
2007											
January	90.26	-1.25	91.50	6.09	23.78	2.63	36.76	9.20	11.73	3.94	20.94
February	89.01	-1.01	90.02	6.27	23.76	2.49	35.25	9.36	11.55	3.84	19.54
March	91.05	-1.37	92.43	6.11	24.87	2.60	35.47	9.84	11.93	4.20	24.31
April	91.21	-1.34	92.55	6.52	25.35	2.67	34.95	9.84	11.94	3.95	20.65
May	93.41	-1.25	94.66	6.48	25.87	2.85	36.66	9.86	12.09	3.71	22.44
June	94.87	-1.10	95.97	6.68	26.98	3.14	36.71	9.95	11.84	3.82	24.27
July	97.50	-1.17	98.67	6.91	26.47	3.23	38.23	10.85	12.35	3.86	22.17
August	98.52	-1.08	99.60	7.51	27.37	3.24	38.11	10.28	12.44	3.90	23.25
September	99.47	-0.90	100.37	8.05	27.64	3.20	38.10	10.43	12.61	3.54	22.93
October	100.37	-1.04	101.41	7.70	27.56	3.25	38.99	10.50	12.48	4.19	25.19
November	100.97	-1.43	102.40	7.97	27.99	4.21	38.82	10.84	12.35	4.44	23.65
December	101.84	-1.07	102.91	7.99	28.70	4.26	39.40	10.10	12.80	3.91	24.83
2008											
January	104.60	-0.80	105.39	8.52	29.78	4.47	39.40	10.28	13.27	4.13	22.13
February	108.01	-0.91	108.92	9.01	31.82	5.27	39.36	10.78	13.36	4.59	22.25
March	104.94	-0.51	105.45	9.49	31.60	4.83	37.86	9.40	12.58	4.53	24.65
April	109.97	-0.78	110.75	9.76	32.77	4.78	40.14	9.99	13.42	4.68	23.42
May	110.91	-0.55	111.46	9.55	34.23	6.02	39.47	10.17	13.41	4.62	24.08
June	116.17	-0.76	116.93	10.29	36.76	7.91	40.62	10.75	14.13	4.37	25.04
July	120.75	-0.83	121.57	10.25	38.32	8.05	41.53	12.12	14.88	4.48	23.31
August	117.80	-1.07	118.87	10.06	37.43	8.26	42.35	10.43	13.99	4.60	25.12
September	107.73	-0.46	108.19	8.91	33.01	4.67	38.16	10.29	13.47	4.36	21.56
October	104.71	-0.71	105.42	8.11	31.56	4.99	38.01	10.05	13.31	4.38	22.07
November	97.04	-0.92	97.97	7.58	27.28	4.26	36.56	8.97	13.08	4.50	20.13
December	88.75	-0.87	89.62	6.88	22.73	3.51	36.03	7.71	12.29	3.99	22.06

[1]Not seasonally adjusted.
. . . = Not available.

Table 7-11. U.S. Imports of Goods by End-Use and Advanced Technology Categories

(Census basis, except as noted; billions of dollars; seasonally adjusted, except as noted.)

Year and month	Total imports of goods			Principal end-use category							Advanced technology products [1]
	Total, balance of payments basis	Net adjustments	Total, Census basis	Foods, feeds, and beverages	Industrial supplies and materials		Capital goods, except automotive	Automotive vehicles, engines, and parts	Consumer goods, except automotive	Other goods	
					Total	Petroleum and products					
1980	249.75	4.23	245.52	18.55	124.96	...	30.72	28.13	34.22	...	...
1981	265.07	3.76	261.31	18.53	131.10	...	36.86	30.80	38.30	...	...
1982	247.64	3.70	243.94	17.47	107.82	...	38.22	34.26	39.66	...	...
1983	268.90	7.18	261.72	18.56	105.63	...	42.61	42.04	46.59	...	...
1984	332.42	1.91	330.51	21.92	122.72	...	60.15	56.77	61.19	...	...
1985	338.09	1.71	336.38	21.89	112.48	...	60.81	65.21	66.43	...	...
1986	368.43	2.75	365.67	24.40	101.37	...	71.86	78.25	79.43	...	...
1987	409.77	3.48	406.28	24.81	110.67	...	84.77	85.17	88.82	...	...
1988	447.19	5.26	441.93	24.93	118.06	...	101.79	87.95	96.42	...	...
1989	477.37	3.72	473.65	25.08	132.40	...	112.45	87.38	102.26	...	...
1990	498.34	2.36	495.98	26.65	143.41	62.16	116.04	87.69	105.29	16.09	...
1991	490.98	2.53	488.45	26.21	131.38	51.78	120.80	84.94	107.78	15.94	...
1992	536.46	3.80	532.66	27.61	138.64	51.60	134.25	91.79	122.66	17.71	...
1993	589.44	8.78	580.66	27.87	145.61	51.50	152.37	102.42	134.02	18.39	...
1994	668.59	5.33	663.26	27.87	145.61	51.28	152.37	102.42	134.02	18.39	...
1995	749.57	6.03	743.54	33.18	181.85	56.16	221.43	123.80	159.91	23.39	...
1996	803.33	8.04	796.77	35.74	204.43	72.75	228.07	128.95	172.00	26.11	...
1997	876.37	6.66	869.70	39.69	213.77	71.77	253.28	139.81	193.81	29.34	...
1998	917.18	5.28	911.90	41.24	200.14	50.90	269.56	149.05	216.52	35.39	...
1999	1 029.99	5.37	1 024.62	43.60	221.39	67.81	295.72	178.96	241.91	43.04	...
2000	1 224.42	6.40	1 218.02	45.98	298.98	120.28	347.03	195.88	281.83	48.33	222.08
2001	1 145.90	4.90	1 141.00	46.64	273.87	103.59	297.99	189.78	284.29	48.42	195.18
2002	1 164.72	3.35	1 161.37	49.69	267.69	103.51	283.32	203.74	307.84	49.08	195.15
2003	1 260.72	3.60	1 257.12	55.83	313.82	133.10	295.87	210.14	333.88	47.59	207.03
2004	1 477.09	7.39	1 469.70	62.14	412.83	180.46	343.49	228.20	372.94	50.11	238.28
2005	1 681.78	8.33	1 673.46	68.09	523.77	251.86	379.33	239.45	407.24	55.57	290.76
2006	1 861.38	7.44	1 853.94	74.94	601.99	302.43	418.26	256.63	442.64	59.49	290.76
2007	1 967.85	10.89	1 956.96	81.68	634.75	330.98	444.49	258.92	474.89	62.23	326.81
2008	2 112.20	12.07	2 100.13	89.01	775.49	453.32	453.90	233.55	482.16	66.03	331.37
2005											
January	132.74	0.68	132.07	5.44	38.62	17.02	30.72	19.57	33.30	4.42	18.95
February	135.50	0.57	134.92	5.42	40.05	18.16	30.17	19.55	35.34	4.38	18.10
March	131.63	0.72	130.90	5.42	39.81	18.37	29.92	18.80	32.48	4.47	21.09
April	137.87	0.74	137.13	5.55	41.78	19.54	31.80	19.22	33.90	4.88	20.89
May	136.33	0.67	135.67	5.62	40.02	18.20	31.27	19.90	34.14	4.72	21.01
June	138.21	0.60	137.61	5.70	41.18	19.79	32.25	19.51	34.28	4.69	22.87
July	138.16	0.74	137.42	5.58	42.09	20.43	31.69	19.76	33.68	4.63	21.45
August	139.88	0.70	139.19	5.73	43.77	22.23	31.53	20.15	33.47	4.55	21.73
September	144.71	0.75	143.96	5.92	46.95	24.03	32.17	20.12	34.01	4.79	22.68
October	149.42	0.74	148.68	5.78	50.71	25.45	32.31	20.85	34.31	4.73	23.67
November	147.35	0.70	146.65	5.92	49.37	24.84	32.29	20.68	33.64	4.75	23.84
December	149.99	0.72	149.26	6.03	49.44	23.81	33.21	21.32	34.69	4.56	23.46
2006											
January	152.97	0.70	152.27	6.13	50.44	25.20	33.79	22.06	34.94	4.91	21.65
February	149.74	0.57	149.17	5.92	49.63	25.41	32.72	21.38	34.75	4.76	19.80
March	150.58	0.67	149.91	6.26	46.78	22.69	34.46	21.01	36.53	4.86	25.35
April	152.00	0.56	151.44	6.16	48.86	24.07	34.47	21.38	35.69	4.89	21.52
May	156.07	0.59	155.48	6.06	52.34	27.60	34.70	21.27	36.24	4.88	23.09
June	156.95	0.57	156.38	6.11	51.71	26.76	34.69	21.86	37.01	5.00	24.53
July	158.28	0.63	157.65	6.16	53.58	28.11	35.28	20.82	36.89	4.92	24.15
August	160.99	0.70	160.29	6.38	54.88	28.70	35.69	21.07	37.34	4.94	24.92
September	158.63	0.61	158.03	6.35	52.12	26.48	35.60	21.04	37.91	5.01	26.20
October	153.60	0.66	152.94	6.45	46.99	22.13	35.57	20.79	37.96	5.18	27.24
November	153.98	0.63	153.35	6.43	46.68	21.95	35.65	21.07	38.47	5.05	27.21
December	157.60	0.57	157.03	6.53	47.99	23.33	35.65	22.87	38.90	5.09	25.11
2007											
January	156.47	0.54	155.92	6.52	48.74	24.67	36.10	21.13	38.50	4.94	25.37
February	155.45	0.48	154.98	6.56	45.60	21.35	36.45	21.19	40.04	5.13	23.46
March	161.77	1.42	160.35	6.78	49.81	24.77	36.32	21.87	40.51	5.06	27.34
April	159.96	1.17	158.79	6.62	50.54	25.21	36.07	21.35	39.24	4.98	25.22
May	161.88	1.12	160.76	6.72	52.04	26.38	36.67	20.73	39.43	5.17	25.36
June	163.53	0.64	162.89	6.76	52.83	26.55	37.19	21.43	39.49	5.21	27.63
July	165.30	1.08	164.22	6.88	53.55	27.24	37.23	22.23	39.06	5.27	27.12
August	165.20	1.04	164.16	6.96	53.48	27.65	37.28	21.93	39.23	5.27	27.90
September	166.21	1.09	165.11	6.96	53.51	28.13	37.91	22.08	39.38	5.28	28.07
October	168.08	0.88	167.21	6.92	55.14	29.98	37.70	22.17	39.98	5.30	31.77
November	172.66	0.63	172.03	7.10	59.20	33.94	37.85	22.10	40.31	5.47	30.02
December	171.35	0.80	170.55	6.91	60.31	35.12	37.71	20.72	39.73	5.17	27.56
2008											
January	175.26	0.79	174.47	7.09	64.22	39.53	37.52	21.20	39.16	5.28	25.61
February	181.01	1.66	179.35	7.20	64.77	38.15	38.35	22.77	41.06	5.21	25.59
March	173.86	1.58	172.28	7.10	61.78	35.29	37.96	20.27	39.63	5.54	27.93
April	183.44	1.59	181.85	7.39	67.76	39.81	39.19	21.45	40.29	5.77	28.73
May	183.54	0.75	182.78	7.65	67.33	39.11	39.86	20.44	41.94	5.56	27.62
June	187.95	0.71	187.24	7.51	73.63	45.50	38.51	20.50	41.43	5.66	28.91
July	195.38	1.03	194.35	7.56	80.12	51.25	39.09	20.42	41.17	6.00	30.40
August	189.37	0.65	188.73	7.81	74.03	44.14	38.33	19.26	43.67	5.62	28.33
September	177.78	1.46	176.32	7.61	65.51	36.83	38.81	18.44	40.31	5.65	29.31
October	174.27	0.78	173.49	7.70	65.00	37.50	37.40	17.57	40.44	5.38	29.94
November	150.34	0.72	149.61	7.28	48.49	23.92	35.14	16.42	36.93	5.35	24.71
December	140.02	0.34	139.67	7.11	42.84	22.30	33.76	14.81	36.14	5.01	24.29

[1] Not seasonally adjusted.
. . . = Not available.

Table 7-12. U.S. Exports and Imports of Goods by Principal End-Use Category in Constant Dollars

(Census basis; billions of 2000 chain-weighted dollars, except as noted; seasonally adjusted.)

Year and month	Exports							Imports						
	Total	Foods, feeds, and beverages	Industrial supplies and materials	Capital goods, except auto-motive	Auto-motive vehicles, engines, and parts	Consumer goods, except automotive	Other goods	Total	Foods, feeds, and beverages	Industrial supplies and materials	Capital goods, except auto-motive	Auto-motive vehicles, engines, and parts	Consumer goods, except automotive	Other goods
1986 ¹	227.20	22.30	57.30	75.80	21.70	. . .	. . .	365.40	24.40	101.30	71.80	78.20	79.40	. . .
1987 ¹	254.10	24.30	66.70	86.20	24.60	. . .	. . .	406.20	24.80	111.00	84.50	85.00	88.70	. . .
1988 ¹	322.40	32.30	85.10	109.20	29.30	. . .	. . .	441.00	24.80	118.30	101.40	87.70	95.90	. . .
1989 ¹	363.80	37.20	99.30	138.80	34.80	. . .	. . .	473.20	25.10	132.30	113.30	86.10	102.90	. . .
1990 ¹	393.60	35.10	104.40	152.70	37.40	39.22	18.70	495.30	26.60	146.20	116.40	87.30	105.70	14.46
1991 ¹	421.70	35.70	109.70	166.70	40.00	40.42	21.11	488.50	26.50	131.60	120.70	85.70	108.00	14.15
1992 ¹	448.20	40.30	109.10	175.90	47.00	43.60	21.71	532.70	27.60	138.60	134.30	91.80	122.70	15.46
1993 ¹	471.17	40.19	111.08	190.02	51.93	54.03	23.91	591.45	28.03	151.26	160.16	100.73	132.92	18.35
1994 ¹	522.29	40.43	114.17	225.76	56.54	58.97	26.41	675.05	29.52	168.80	199.56	112.13	144.22	20.82
1994	482.34	41.41	127.50	165.92	60.49	62.41	28.03	628.41	29.53	216.50	120.69	124.86	143.41	21.80
1995	531.74	45.70	136.13	192.70	64.02	66.02	28.79	682.73	30.28	222.84	145.53	126.99	154.37	23.01
1996	588.10	44.24	144.48	228.74	66.63	70.86	33.61	753.96	33.53	236.42	175.55	131.33	165.33	25.69
1997	666.61	44.12	156.35	280.22	75.18	77.82	33.38	858.67	36.75	252.73	219.82	141.98	188.23	29.06
1998	682.35	43.84	155.76	292.61	73.38	80.86	36.15	959.84	39.54	277.01	252.14	150.86	213.38	35.81
1999	704.29	45.35	156.88	308.44	75.99	81.42	36.12	1 075.39	43.18	281.43	289.21	180.17	239.60	43.70
2000	781.92	47.87	172.62	356.93	80.36	89.38	34.77	1 218.02	45.98	298.98	347.03	195.88	281.83	48.33
2001	733.58	49.14	164.85	321.92	75.13	88.38	34.15	1 177.64	47.76	297.51	306.31	189.86	286.48	48.79
2002	699.04	48.06	162.18	293.02	78.30	84.68	32.85	1 220.88	50.95	300.14	300.13	203.24	313.01	50.30
2003	716.76	48.90	169.20	298.57	79.57	89.30	31.49	1 284.63	55.65	312.13	317.04	208.48	339.95	47.88
2004	781.58	45.20	180.62	337.73	87.40	101.50	31.86	1 431.21	59.07	348.23	371.95	222.99	377.10	48.82
2005	837.32	47.30	186.07	368.89	95.41	112.03	32.79	1 534.77	61.23	367.87	413.49	231.62	407.79	52.48
2006	924.34	50.83	200.28	418.11	102.63	123.17	36.93	1 622.83	64.82	367.20	459.98	247.14	440.54	54.70
2007	998.07	54.06	213.82	450.57	114.93	135.98	38.09	1 652.86	65.46	356.45	487.43	246.84	465.68	55.63
2008	1 062.47	57.12	238.49	470.27	113.56	146.83	40.32	1 596.34	63.80	338.90	491.19	217.53	460.12	55.89
2005														
January	67.34	3.92	15.32	28.91	7.90	8.91	2.64	126.85	5.03	31.57	33.24	18.98	33.37	4.23
February	67.73	4.05	15.75	28.85	7.66	9.12	2.49	128.73	4.97	32.11	32.68	18.95	35.34	4.18
March	67.84	3.94	15.39	29.60	7.52	9.12	2.58	122.70	4.80	30.22	32.46	18.22	32.46	4.25
April	70.27	4.00	15.74	31.18	7.79	9.16	2.78	126.71	4.94	30.28	34.43	18.61	33.91	4.62
May	69.83	4.16	16.10	30.07	7.68	9.31	2.73	126.27	5.00	29.70	33.88	19.27	34.16	4.48
June	69.85	3.88	15.81	30.73	7.70	9.28	2.81	127.77	5.15	30.21	34.97	18.88	34.31	4.46
July	69.51	3.78	15.68	30.91	7.78	9.28	2.52	126.22	5.08	29.58	34.60	19.12	33.74	4.41
August	70.99	3.83	15.89	31.54	7.97	9.37	2.85	126.18	5.18	29.48	34.45	19.48	33.57	4.32
September	68.21	3.82	14.81	29.53	8.19	9.55	2.78	127.44	5.36	29.39	35.26	19.44	34.04	4.50
October	70.06	4.00	14.73	31.66	8.26	9.22	2.83	130.61	5.18	31.05	35.48	20.13	34.36	4.39
November	72.05	3.93	15.23	32.79	8.37	9.63	2.82	131.01	5.28	31.73	35.51	19.96	33.75	4.41
December	73.65	4.00	15.61	33.13	8.59	10.06	2.95	134.30	5.26	32.55	36.56	20.58	34.77	4.23
2006														
January	74.09	4.12	15.89	33.49	8.60	9.78	2.86	135.45	5.29	32.17	37.18	21.35	34.94	4.53
February	74.83	4.07	15.91	34.04	8.63	9.87	3.02	133.16	5.25	31.89	36.00	20.67	34.73	4.43
March	75.85	4.26	16.81	34.21	8.21	10.09	2.78	134.36	5.53	30.40	37.93	20.32	36.56	4.53
April	75.35	4.19	16.54	34.33	8.28	9.84	2.75	133.62	5.48	30.18	37.97	20.64	35.74	4.55
May	75.95	4.38	16.54	34.36	8.25	10.20	2.82	134.52	5.29	30.60	38.24	20.52	36.22	4.50
June	77.60	4.35	16.78	35.26	8.61	10.34	2.93	135.15	5.35	30.23	38.15	21.05	36.94	4.60
July	75.81	4.25	16.26	34.00	8.73	10.31	2.92	135.08	5.40	30.66	38.78	20.01	36.65	4.52
August	77.71	4.42	16.39	35.10	8.81	10.55	3.19	136.65	5.43	31.08	39.22	20.25	37.07	4.51
September	78.45	4.30	17.31	35.41	8.41	10.12	3.39	136.57	5.40	30.74	39.16	20.22	37.61	4.57
October	79.22	4.32	17.52	35.52	8.38	10.61	3.37	135.20	5.49	29.79	39.10	19.94	37.63	4.76
November	80.05	4.02	17.32	36.49	8.64	10.74	3.58	135.49	5.44	29.65	39.16	20.23	38.07	4.60
December	79.44	4.16	17.01	35.89	9.10	10.70	3.33	137.58	5.47	29.80	39.11	21.94	38.40	4.61
2007														
January	80.27	4.31	17.04	36.64	8.77	11.04	3.28	137.63	5.40	31.13	39.57	20.26	37.93	4.47
February	78.67	4.29	16.74	35.42	8.91	10.87	3.16	136.95	5.43	29.18	40.09	20.29	39.45	4.64
March	80.37	4.08	17.26	35.75	9.36	11.22	3.43	140.30	5.63	30.82	40.01	20.94	39.89	4.56
April	80.12	4.39	17.34	35.24	9.35	11.15	3.22	136.79	5.40	29.79	39.80	20.43	38.65	4.48
May	81.67	4.38	17.59	37.00	9.37	11.11	3.00	136.88	5.44	29.69	40.40	19.83	38.81	4.62
June	82.57	4.40	18.24	36.96	9.45	11.03	3.08	138.03	5.47	29.76	40.89	20.48	38.84	4.65
July	84.80	4.54	17.83	38.53	10.30	11.49	3.11	137.89	5.51	29.48	40.86	21.24	38.33	4.70
August	85.55	4.86	18.44	38.46	9.76	11.56	3.13	137.52	5.55	29.38	40.81	20.93	38.37	4.71
September	85.81	4.99	18.54	38.47	9.90	11.73	2.83	138.18	5.45	29.43	41.46	21.03	38.48	4.73
October	86.07	4.58	18.28	39.35	9.95	11.58	3.32	137.91	5.35	29.15	41.20	21.06	39.02	4.71
November	86.05	4.68	18.05	39.14	10.26	11.42	3.48	138.52	5.50	29.30	41.27	20.87	39.28	4.82
December	86.12	4.56	18.50	39.62	9.55	11.80	3.05	136.29	5.34	29.33	41.08	19.48	38.65	4.54
2008														
January	87.68	4.61	19.06	39.69	9.71	12.22	3.20	138.22	5.33	30.70	40.95	19.86	37.90	4.60
February	89.94	4.68	20.18	39.59	10.17	12.28	3.52	141.26	5.43	30.57	41.81	21.31	39.59	4.50
March	84.96	4.73	18.77	38.10	8.85	11.50	3.38	132.56	5.22	27.59	41.32	18.94	38.01	4.72
April	89.72	5.01	19.76	40.25	9.38	12.23	3.51	137.10	5.34	28.92	42.38	19.98	38.43	4.88
May	89.98	4.90	20.45	39.56	9.56	12.21	3.45	134.32	5.48	26.93	42.98	19.05	39.94	4.68
June	93.25	5.14	21.32	40.71	10.11	12.85	3.22	134.09	5.27	27.61	41.59	19.09	39.40	4.72
July	95.13	4.80	21.42	41.52	11.38	13.50	3.24	136.30	5.24	28.65	42.09	18.98	39.10	4.94
August	95.14	5.24	21.81	42.32	9.79	12.68	3.40	134.59	5.36	27.65	41.27	17.87	41.44	4.66
September	87.33	4.61	19.76	38.17	9.65	12.19	3.25	129.61	5.30	26.38	41.85	17.13	38.29	4.72
October	86.69	4.55	19.76	37.89	9.38	12.01	3.33	132.67	5.43	29.07	40.32	16.27	38.38	4.53
November	83.87	4.51	19.04	36.52	8.37	11.94	3.58	123.93	5.37	26.88	38.07	15.27	35.15	4.60
December	78.79	4.34	17.16	35.96	7.21	11.23	3.26	121.70	5.03	27.96	36.57	13.77	34.50	4.34

¹Data on the 2000 chain-weighted dollar basis are only available for 1994 to date. To provide more historical data, values in 1992 dollars are shown for the years 1986–1994.
. . . = Not available.

Table 7-13. U.S. Exports of Goods by Selected Regions and Countries

(Census f.a.s. basis; millions of dollars, not seasonally adjusted.)

| Year and month | Total, all countries | Selected regions [1] | | | | | Selected countries | | | | | |
		European Union, 15 countries	European Union, 25 countries	Euro area	Asian NICS	OPEC	Brazil	Canada	China	France	Germany, Federal Republic of	Hong Kong
1972	...	...	...	...	...	...	1 243	13 070	...	1 609	2 808	...
1973	...	...	...	...	...	...	1 916	16 146	...	2 263	3 756	...
1974	...	28 268	...	...	...	6 723	3 088	21 281	807	2 942	4 985	882
1975	...	22 862	...	...	...	10 767	3 056	22 948	304	3 031	5 194	808
1976	...	25 406	...	...	...	12 566	2 809	25 677	135	3 446	5 731	1 115
1977	...	26 476	...	...	...	14 019	2 490	27 738	171	3 503	5 989	1 292
1978	...	32 051	...	...	...	16 655	2 981	30 540	824	4 166	6 957	1 625
1979	...	42 582	...	...	...	15 051	3 442	37 599	1 724	5 587	8 478	2 083
1980	...	53 679	...	...	...	17 759	4 344	40 331	3 755	7 485	10 960	2 686
1981	...	52 363	...	...	...	21 533	3 798	44 602	3 603	7 341	10 277	2 635
1982	...	47 932	...	...	...	22 863	3 423	37 887	2 912	7 110	9 291	2 453
1983	201 708	44 311	...	...	...	16 905	2 557	43 345	2 173	5 961	8 737	2 564
1984	218 743	46 976	...	...	...	14 387	2 640	51 777	3 004	6 037	9 084	3 062
1985	212 621	48 994	...	...	16 918	12 480	3 140	53 287	3 856	6 096	9 050	2 786
1986	226 471	53 154	...	...	18 289	10 844	3 885	55 512	3 106	7 216	10 561	3 030
1987	253 904	60 575	...	...	23 548	11 058	4 040	59 814	3 497	7 943	11 748	3 983
1988	323 335	75 755	...	...	34 816	13 994	4 267	71 622	5 021	9 970	14 348	5 687
1989	363 836	86 331	...	...	38 404	13 196	4 804	78 809	5 755	11 579	16 862	6 246
1990	392 924	98 027	...	...	40 741	13 679	5 062	83 866	4 807	13 652	18 693	6 841
1991	421 764	103 123	...	...	45 628	19 054	6 148	85 150	6 278	15 346	21 302	8 137
1992	448 161	102 958	...	...	48 592	21 960	5 751	90 594	7 418	14 593	21 249	9 077
1993	465 090	96 973	...	...	52 502	19 500	6 058	100 444	8 763	13 267	18 932	9 874
1994	512 626	102 818	...	...	59 595	17 868	8 102	114 439	9 282	13 619	19 229	11 441
1995	584 742	123 671	...	...	74 234	19 533	11 439	127 226	11 754	14 245	22 394	14 232
1996	625 075	127 710	...	...	75 768	22 275	12 718	134 210	11 993	14 455	23 495	13 966
1997	689 182	140 773	...	...	78 225	25 526	15 915	151 767	12 862	15 965	24 458	15 117
1998	682 138	149 035	...	...	63 269	25 154	15 142	156 603	14 241	17 729	26 657	12 925
1999	695 797	151 814	...	...	70 989	20 166	13 203	166 600	13 111	18 877	26 800	12 652
2000	781 918	165 065	...	116 212	84 624	19 078	15 321	178 941	16 185	20 362	29 448	14 582
2001	729 100	158 768	...	112 903	71 982	20 053	15 880	163 424	19 182	19 865	29 995	14 028
2002	693 103	143 691	...	105 838	69 770	18 812	12 376	160 923	22 128	19 016	26 630	12 594
2003	724 771	151 731	...	113 132	71 601	17 279	11 211	169 924	28 368	17 053	28 832	13 521
2004	818 775	168 572	172 622	127 158	83 593	22 262	13 897	189 880	34 744	21 263	31 416	15 827
2005	905 978	...	186 437	137 497	86 828	32 074	15 372	211 899	41 925	22 410	34 184	16 351
2006	1 036 635	...	213 996	155 735	97 948	40 081	19 231	230 656	55 186	41 319	24 217	17 776
2007	1 162 479	...	247 242	180 232	107 356	49 603	24 626	248 888	65 236	27 413	49 651	20 118
2008	1 300 532	...	274 510	202 417	110 530	66 987	32 910	261 381	71 457	29 187	54 732	21 633
2006												
January	75 040	...	15 207	11 207	6 958	2 632	1 387	17 261	3 479	2 064	2 659	1 202
February	77 750	...	16 184	11 913	6 853	3 185	1 260	17 931	4 098	1 814	3 184	1 195
March	91 865	...	19 196	13 762	8 509	3 188	1 500	21 153	4 959	2 401	3 671	1 593
April	83 097	...	17 592	12 767	7 875	3 198	1 442	19 103	4 328	1 795	3 403	1 416
May	87 746	...	18 400	13 180	7 654	3 337	1 514	20 490	4 501	2 082	3 402	1 450
June	90 622	...	19 312	13 783	8 826	3 279	1 398	20 875	4 348	2 512	3 407	1 621
July	80 023	...	15 866	11 364	7 611	3 068	1 572	16 621	5 060	1 679	3 225	1 391
August	89 228	...	17 540	12 805	8 306	3 641	1 775	20 288	4 758	2 028	3 554	1 429
September	88 408	...	18 413	13 499	8 652	3 588	1 795	19 249	4 645	1 862	3 633	1 786
October	92 468	...	18 886	13 974	8 216	3 822	1 768	19 975	4 991	2 136	3 884	1 486
November	91 367	...	18 681	13 729	8 729	3 357	1 851	19 730	4 809	1 893	3 561	1 546
December	89 021	...	18 721	13 753	9 759	3 787	1 969	17 981	5 209	1 952	3 738	1 660
2007												
January	85 918	...	19 577	14 609	8 076	2 986	2 176	17 804	4 442	2 396	3 619	1 610
February	84 921	...	19 247	13 954	7 826	2 890	1 540	18 335	4 634	2 269	3 690	1 253
March	100 512	...	23 003	16 448	9 206	4 170	1 862	22 007	5 574	2 336	4 567	1 756
April	91 665	...	20 168	14 440	8 669	3 446	1 845	20 220	4 758	2 178	4 030	1 494
May	97 902	...	21 141	14 905	8 561	3 545	1 833	21 793	5 238	2 390	4 008	1 540
June	99 122	...	20 763	15 043	9 764	4 001	1 868	21 768	5 911	2 429	4 305	1 766
July	91 857	...	18 877	13 733	8 668	3 881	2 087	18 772	4 793	2 205	3 836	1 559
August	101 143	...	20 257	15 026	9 321	4 562	2 206	21 379	5 883	2 049	4 325	1 658
September	98 068	...	20 724	15 397	8 715	4 207	2 169	21 055	5 609	2 243	4 377	2 022
October	106 563	...	21 801	16 080	9 625	4 834	2 335	23 300	5 684	2 506	4 523	2 079
November	103 363	...	20 934	15 165	8 933	5 158	2 120	22 652	5 848	2 252	4 254	1 677
December	101 448	...	20 751	15 432	9 993	5 923	2 584	19 806	6 863	2 161	4 117	1 707
2008												
January	99 549	...	21 279	15 389	8 711	4 575	2 304	20 417	5 855	2 145	4 062	1 551
February	105 930	...	23 778	17 316	9 202	4 596	2 219	21 193	5 774	2 243	4 611	1 798
March	112 085	...	24 072	17 963	10 517	4 570	2 401	22 900	6 354	2 630	4 641	1 766
April	111 131	...	24 065	14 461	9 848	5 250	2 517	23 648	5 681	2 668	4 761	1 809
May	114 291	...	24 153	17 722	10 227	5 010	2 606	24 536	6 614	2 934	4 815	1 924
June	118 184	...	25 125	18 317	10 857	5 351	2 796	23 683	6 414	2 410	5 041	2 300
July	115 718	...	23 835	17 648	9 998	5 417	2 984	22 436	6 437	2 364	4 774	1 758
August	118 082	...	23 624	17 447	9 542	6 994	3 894	22 065	6 507	2 508	4 723	1 759
September	106 699	...	20 929	15 571	9 258	5 728	2 945	22 315	5 320	2 232	4 264	2 319
October	111 586	...	22 900	16 847	8 718	6 611	3 147	22 106	6 072	2 570	4 765	1 760
November	97 410	...	20 700	15 671	7 244	6 326	2 605	19 172	5 223	2 199	4 388	1 507
December	89 866	...	20 051	15 049	6 408	6 559	2 494	16 909	5 206	2 285	3 887	1 382

[1]See notes and definitions for definitions of regions.
. . . = Not available.

Table 7-13. U.S. Exports of Goods by Selected Regions and Countries—*Continued*

(Census f.a.s. basis; millions of dollars, not seasonally adjusted.)

Year and month	Indonesia	Italy	Japan	Malaysia	Mexico	Netherlands	Singapore	South Korea	Taiwan	United Kingdom	Venezuela
1972	...	1 434	4 963	...	1 982	...	...	...	...	2 658	924
1973	...	2 119	8 313	...	2 937	...	...	...	...	3 564	1 033
1974	...	2 752	10 679	...	4 855	3 979	988	...	1 427	4 574	1 768
1975	...	2 867	9 563	...	5 141	4 183	994	...	1 660	4 527	2 243
1976	...	3 071	10 145	...	4 990	4 645	965	...	1 635	4 801	2 628
1977	...	2 790	10 529	...	4 806	4 796	1 172	...	1 798	5 951	3 171
1978	...	3 361	12 885	...	6 680	5 683	1 462	...	2 340	7 116	3 728
1979	...	4 362	17 581	...	9 847	6 907	2 331	...	3 271	10 635	3 934
1980	1 545	5 511	20 790	...	15 145	8 669	3 033	...	4 337	12 694	4 573
1981	1 302	5 360	21 823	...	17 789	8 595	3 003	...	4 305	12 439	5 445
1982	2 025	4 616	20 966	...	11 817	8 604	3 214	...	4 367	10 645	5 206
1983	1 466	3 908	21 894	...	9 082	7 767	3 759	...	4 667	10 621	2 811
1984	1 216	4 375	23 575	...	11 992	7 554	3 675	...	5 003	12 210	3 377
1985	795	4 625	22 631	...	13 635	7 269	3 476	5 956	4 700	11 273	3 399
1986	946	4 838	26 882	...	12 392	7 848	3 380	6 355	5 524	11 418	3 141
1987	767	5 530	28 249	...	14 582	8 217	4 053	8 099	7 413	14 114	3 586
1988	1 059	6 775	37 725	...	20 628	10 117	5 768	11 232	12 129	18 364	4 612
1989	1 247	7 215	44 494	...	24 982	11 364	7 345	13 478	11 335	20 837	3 025
1990	1 897	7 987	48 585	...	28 375	13 016	8 019	14 399	11 482	23 484	3 107
1991	1 891	8 570	48 125	3 900	33 277	13 511	8 804	15 505	13 182	22 046	4 656
1992	2 779	8 721	47 813	4 363	40 592	13 752	9 626	14 639	15 250	22 800	5 444
1993	2 770	6 464	47 892	6 064	41 581	12 839	11 678	14 782	16 168	26 438	4 590
1994	2 809	7 183	53 488	6 969	50 844	13 582	13 020	18 025	17 109	26 900	4 039
1995	3 360	8 862	64 343	8 816	46 292	16 558	15 333	25 380	19 290	28 857	4 640
1996	3 977	8 797	67 607	8 546	56 792	16 662	16 720	26 621	18 460	30 962	4 750
1997	4 522	8 995	65 549	10 780	71 388	19 827	17 696	25 046	20 366	36 425	6 602
1998	2 299	8 991	57 831	8 957	78 773	18 978	15 694	16 486	18 165	39 058	6 516
1999	2 038	10 091	57 466	9 060	86 909	19 437	16 247	22 958	19 131	38 407	5 354
2000	2 402	11 060	64 924	10 938	111 349	21 836	17 806	27 830	24 406	41 570	5 550
2001	2 521	9 916	57 452	9 358	101 297	19 485	17 652	22 181	18 122	40 714	5 642
2002	2 556	10 057	51 449	10 344	97 470	18 311	16 218	22 576	18 382	33 205	4 430
2003	2 516	10 561	52 004	10 914	97 412	20 695	16 560	24 073	17 448	33 828	2 831
2004	2 671	10 685	54 243	10 921	110 835	24 289	19 609	26 413	21 744	36 000	4 767
2005	3 054	11 524	55 485	10 461	120 365	26 485	20 642	27 765	22 069	38 588	6 421
2006	3 079	12 546	59 613	12 544	133 979	31 129	24 684	32 442	23 047	45 410	9 002
2007	4 235	14 150	62 704	11 680	136 092	32 963	26 284	34 645	26 309	50 229	10 201
2008	5 913	15 479	66 579	12 963	151 539	40 223	28 810	34 807	25 279	53 775	12 611
2006											
January	232	973	4 381	883	10 503	2 179	1 624	2 552	1 581	3 152	591
February	224	1 011	4 509	871	10 051	2 360	1 741	2 378	1 539	3 435	633
March	237	1 032	5 400	1 372	11 968	2 553	2 021	3 017	1 878	4 326	676
April	265	1 131	4 454	1 067	10 773	2 682	2 008	2 729	1 721	3 762	724
May	290	1 080	4 794	1 244	11 570	2 794	1 980	2 412	1 813	4 024	700
June	250	1 187	5 401	1 071	11 715	2 660	1 815	2 789	2 601	4 385	750
July	276	950	4 960	1 013	10 408	2 253	1 784	2 556	1 881	3 642	813
August	246	867	5 093	1 107	11 735	2 504	2 083	2 925	1 869	3 722	738
September	251	1 096	5 127	1 005	11 009	2 840	2 106	2 878	1 882	3 797	771
October	297	1 057	5 480	967	12 410	2 731	1 985	2 632	2 113	3 748	932
November	248	1 027	5 074	1 034	11 777	2 845	2 468	2 619	2 097	3 875	913
December	263	1 136	4 940	912	10 061	2 729	3 071	2 956	2 073	3 543	761
2007											
January	279	1 130	4 997	932	10 702	3 016	2 023	2 691	1 753	3 685	696
February	242	1 072	4 793	939	9 980	2 531	2 202	2 541	1 831	4 132	679
March	329	1 296	5 729	1 049	11 494	3 147	2 585	2 955	1 911	5 105	854
April	374	1 110	5 230	921	10 893	2 859	1 911	2 990	2 275	4 226	821
May	340	1 181	5 293	924	11 956	2 610	1 979	2 772	2 270	4 758	898
June	427	1 197	5 431	964	11 623	2 592	2 407	3 106	2 485	4 409	1 017
July	371	1 139	4 859	889	11 220	2 471	2 022	2 789	2 298	3 699	907
August	414	1 035	5 077	930	12 304	2 727	2 175	2 984	2 504	3 807	900
September	273	1 140	5 262	1 014	11 385	2 564	2 155	2 582	1 957	4 101	858
October	359	1 283	5 540	1 048	12 330	2 569	2 258	3 189	2 099	4 348	945
November	323	1 276	5 179	1 005	12 127	2 702	2 172	2 941	2 142	4 043	884
December	506	1 290	5 313	1 065	10 078	3 176	2 395	3 106	2 785	3 917	741
2008											
January	463	1 212	5 161	1 060	11 878	3 199	2 154	2 740	2 266	4 734	768
February	443	1 295	5 665	1 034	12 220	3 576	2 526	2 741	2 137	4 797	875
March	532	1 370	5 603	1 170	11 718	3 606	2 935	3 169	2 646	4 674	830
April	582	1 363	5 403	1 063	12 542	3 276	2 768	3 124	2 148	4 962	854
May	434	1 480	6 187	1 103	12 274	3 210	2 655	3 154	2 494	4 897	971
June	487	1 623	5 991	1 256	13 348	3 367	2 740	3 456	2 362	5 103	1 176
July	539	1 278	5 644	1 227	13 802	3 620	2 322	3 180	2 738	4 809	1 099
August	629	1 288	6 366	1 271	13 728	3 718	2 444	3 115	2 224	4 443	1 204
September	589	1 164	5 530	1 030	13 040	2 868	2 248	2 932	1 758	3 890	1 103
October	497	1 276	5 385	1 096	14 856	3 224	2 283	2 911	1 764	4 333	1 403
November	330	1 127	5 094	904	11 965	3 323	1 859	2 424	1 455	3 548	1 237
December	387	1 004	4 549	749	10 168	3 237	1 876	1 861	1 288	3 586	1 092

. . . = Not available.

Table 7-14. U.S. Imports of Goods by Selected Regions and Countries

(Census Customs basis; millions of dollars, not seasonally adjusted.)

Year and month	Total, all countries	Selected regions [1]					Selected countries					
		European Union, 15 countries	European Union, 25 countries	Euro area	Asian NICS	OPEC	Brazil	Canada	China	France	Germany, Federal Republic of	Hong Kong
1972	. . .	. . .	. . .	. . .	. . .	. . .	942	14 927	. . .	1 369	4 250	. . .
1973	. . .	. . .	. . .	. . .	. . .	. . .	1 189	17 715	. . .	1 732	5 345	. . .
1974	. . .	19 035	. . .	. . .	. . .	. . .	1 700	21 924	. . .	2 257	6 324	. . .
1975	. . .	16 610	. . .	. . .	. . .	. . .	1 464	21 747	. . .	2 137	5 382	. . .
1976	. . .	17 848	. . .	. . .	. . .	. . .	1 737	26 237	. . .	2 509	5 592	. . .
1977	. . .	22 087	. . .	. . .	. . .	. . .	2 241	29 599	. . .	3 032	7 238	. . .
1978	. . .	29 009	. . .	. . .	. . .	. . .	2 826	33 525	. . .	4 051	9 962	. . .
1979	. . .	33 295	. . .	. . .	. . .	. . .	3 118	38 046	. . .	4 768	10 955	. . .
1980	. . .	35 958	. . .	. . .	. . .	. . .	3 715	41 455	. . .	5 247	11 681	. . .
1981	. . .	41 624	. . .	. . .	. . .	. . .	4 475	46 414	. . .	5 851	11 379	. . .
1982	. . .	42 509	. . .	. . .	. . .	. . .	4 285	46 477	. . .	5 545	11 975	. . .
1983	261 723	43 892	. . .	. . .	. . .	. . .	4 946	52 130	. . .	6 025	12 695	. . .
1984	330 510	57 360	. . .	. . .	. . .	. . .	7 621	66 478	. . .	8 113	16 996	. . .
1985	336 383	67 822	. . .	. . .	. . .	22 800	7 526	69 006	3 862	9 482	20 239	8 396
1986	365 672	75 736	. . .	. . .	. . .	19 750	6 813	68 253	4 771	10 129	25 124	8 891
1987	406 283	81 188	. . .	. . .	. . .	23 953	7 865	71 085	6 294	10 730	27 069	9 854
1988	441 926	84 939	. . .	. . .	. . .	22 962	9 294	81 398	8 511	12 509	26 362	10 238
1989	473 647	85 153	. . .	. . .	. . .	30 601	8 410	87 953	11 989	13 013	24 832	9 739
1990	495 980	91 868	. . .	. . .	. . .	38 017	7 976	91 372	15 224	13 124	28 109	9 488
1991	488 452	86 481	. . .	. . .	59 277	32 644	6 717	91 064	18 969	13 333	26 137	9 279
1992	532 663	93 993	. . .	. . .	62 384	33 200	7 609	98 630	25 728	14 797	28 820	9 793
1993	580 658	97 941	. . .	. . .	64 572	31 739	7 479	111 216	31 540	15 279	28 562	9 554
1994	663 256	110 875	. . .	. . .	71 388	31 685	8 683	128 406	38 787	16 699	31 744	9 696
1995	743 543	131 871	. . .	. . .	82 008	35 197	8 830	145 349	45 543	17 209	36 844	10 291
1996	795 289	142 947	. . .	. . .	82 770	44 285	8 773	155 893	51 513	18 646	38 945	9 865
1997	869 704	157 528	. . .	. . .	86 164	44 025	9 626	168 201	62 558	20 636	43 122	10 288
1998	911 896	176 380	. . .	. . .	85 961	33 925	10 102	173 256	71 169	24 016	49 842	10 538
1999	1 024 618	195 227	. . .	. . .	95 102	41 978	11 314	198 711	81 788	25 709	55 228	10 528
2000	1 218 022	220 019	. . .	163 520	111 438	67 090	13 853	230 838	100 018	29 800	58 513	11 449
2001	1 140 999	220 057	. . .	166 373	93 202	59 754	14 466	216 268	102 278	30 408	59 077	9 646
2002	1 161 366	225 771	. . .	172 573	91 850	53 245	15 781	209 088	125 193	28 240	62 506	9 328
2003	1 257 121	244 826	. . .	187 204	92 818	68 344	17 910	221 595	152 436	29 219	68 113	8 851
2004	1 469 704	272 439	281 959	209 606	105 476	94 105	21 160	256 360	196 682	31 606	77 266	9 314
2005	1 673 455	298 879	308 776	228 881	102 609	124 940	24 436	290 384	243 470	33 842	84 751	8 892
2006	1 853 938	319 590	330 482	246 667	109 730	145 370	26 367	302 438	287 774	37 040	37 040	7 947
2007	1 956 962	. . .	354 409	266 074	111 260	173 818	25 644	317 057	321 443	41 553	94 164	7 026
2008	2 100 129	. . .	367 927	277 972	106 772	242 600	30 459	335 555	337 790	43 997	97 553	6 485
2006												
January	144 562	. . .	24 878	18 662	9 136	11 172	2 006	25 966	21 383	2 883	6 611	755
February	134 702	. . .	24 114	18 068	7 908	10 648	1 858	23 750	17 905	2 838	6 880	554
March	154 040	. . .	29 298	21 854	8 944	11 350	2 218	26 478	20 531	3 240	8 059	640
April	146 919	. . .	27 055	19 907	8 714	11 130	2 061	24 837	21 459	3 059	7 745	586
May	159 164	. . .	29 602	21 687	9 316	13 951	1 944	26 459	22 318	3 123	7 412	611
June	160 487	. . .	28 398	21 340	9 313	13 209	2 259	26 544	23 990	3 269	7 402	700
July	157 768	. . .	28 875	21 656	9 477	14 329	2 551	22 927	24 632	3 079	7 406	696
August	167 558	. . .	28 458	21 457	9 952	14 559	2 650	26 299	26 713	3 002	7 687	733
September	158 470	. . .	25 539	18 750	9 299	12 764	2 309	24 966	27 571	2 918	6 755	772
October	164 028	. . .	28 223	21 010	9 762	11 392	2 367	25 081	29 389	3 316	7 383	746
November	157 289	. . .	28 400	21 306	9 163	10 197	2 285	25 242	27 775	3 147	7 819	625
December	148 952	. . .	27 643	20 970	8 748	10 669	1 858	23 889	24 109	3 166	7 923	527
2007												
January	150 833	. . .	26 094	19 645	9 544	12 315	2 046	25 115	25 641	2 961	6 854	529
February	139 793	. . .	25 379	19 135	8 276	9 944	1 645	23 679	23 039	2 976	6 991	490
March	161 363	. . .	31 284	23 693	9 330	12 830	2 223	27 238	22 723	3 711	8 352	493
April	156 584	. . .	29 325	22 017	9 061	13 268	2 195	26 084	24 242	3 495	7 858	500
May	163 324	. . .	29 714	22 013	9 832	14 603	2 038	26 920	25 291	3 208	7 703	573
June	164 462	. . .	30 373	22 758	9 246	13 950	2 203	27 837	27 071	3 541	7 734	611
July	166 765	. . .	31 396	23 621	9 776	14 693	2 254	24 610	28 601	3 966	8 385	635
August	170 766	. . .	30 193	22 976	9 273	15 928	2 387	26 903	28 425	3 437	8 480	601
September	162 772	. . .	27 175	20 078	8 828	15 254	2 213	26 391	29 419	3 400	7 205	632
October	182 044	. . .	33 777	25 323	9 705	15 847	2 439	28 714	31 555	4 148	8 487	751
November	175 663	. . .	31 182	23 316	9 843	16 982	1 939	28 011	29 781	3 636	8 115	634
December	162 594	. . .	28 517	21 500	8 546	18 203	2 063	25 556	25 657	3 073	8 001	577
2008												
January	167 362	. . .	27 332	15 389	9 428	20 106	2 289	26 274	26 168	3 326	6 966	614
February	165 081	. . .	30 647	23 319	8 557	17 828	2 051	27 653	24 129	3 601	8 026	560
March	170 539	. . .	31 563	24 152	8 966	18 699	2 328	29 317	22 432	3 724	9 123	536
April	181 880	. . .	32 605	24 944	9 256	20 868	2 372	31 031	25 919	3 884	9 199	451
May	182 136	. . .	32 047	24 220	9 178	22 951	2 663	29 921	27 664	3 571	8 368	489
June	189 447	. . .	33 373	25 515	8 645	23 449	3 161	30 916	27 843	3 947	8 940	512
July	200 899	. . .	34 869	26 318	9 799	29 601	3 028	30 679	31 314	4 077	9 375	663
August	190 690	. . .	30 408	22 093	8 893	26 193	2 567	29 604	31 840	3 496	7 911	526
September	180 666	. . .	29 259	21 562	9 080	19 083	2 840	29 940	33 086	3 648	7 229	637
October	186 054	. . .	32 507	24 555	9 593	20 660	3 036	27 970	34 028	4 048	8 134	643
November	147 400	. . .	26 298	20 067	8 047	11 940	2 279	22 554	28 281	3 307	7 150	493
December	137 974	. . .	27 019	20 718	7 332	11 222	1 848	19 696	25 086	3 367	7 133	361

[1]See notes and definitions for definitions of regions.
. . . = Not available.

Table 7-14. U.S. Imports of Goods by Selected Regions and Countries—*Continued*

(Census Customs basis; millions of dollars, not seasonally adjusted.)

Year and month	Selected countries—*Continued*										
	Indonesia	Italy	Japan	Malaysia	Mexico	Netherlands	Singapore	South Korea	Taiwan	United Kingdom	Venezuela
1972	. . .	1 757	9 064	. . .	1 632	. . .	. . .	. . .	. . .	2 987	1 298
1973	. . .	2 002	9 676	. . .	2 306	. . .	. . .	. . .	. . .	3 657	1 787
1974	. . .	2 585	12 338	. . .	3 390	1 433	. . .	. . .	. . .	4 061	4 671
1975	. . .	2 397	11 268	. . .	3 059	1 083	. . .	. . .	. . .	3 784	3 624
1976	. . .	2 530	15 504	. . .	3 598	1 080	. . .	. . .	. . .	4 254	3 574
1977	. . .	3 037	18 550	. . .	4 694	1 477	. . .	. . .	. . .	5 141	4 084
1978	. . .	4 102	24 458	. . .	6 094	1 603	. . .	. . .	. . .	6 514	3 545
1979	. . .	4 918	26 248	. . .	8 800	1 852	. . .	. . .	. . .	8 028	5 166
1980	5 183	4 313	30 701	. . .	12 520	1 910	. . .	. . .	. . .	9 755	5 297
1981	6 022	5 189	37 612	. . .	13 765	2 366	. . .	. . .	. . .	12 835	5 566
1982	4 224	5 301	37 744	. . .	15 566	2 494	. . .	. . .	. . .	13 095	4 768
1983	5 285	5 455	41 183	. . .	16 776	2 970	. . .	. . .	. . .	12 470	4 938
1984	5 461	7 935	57 135	. . .	18 020	4 069	. . .	. . .	. . .	14 492	6 543
1985	4 569	9 674	68 783	. . .	19 132	4 081	4 260	10 031	16 396	14 937	6 537
1986	3 312	10 607	81 911	. . .	17 302	4 066	4 725	12 729	19 791	15 396	5 097
1987	3 394	11 040	84 575	. . .	20 271	3 964	6 201	16 987	24 622	17 341	5 579
1988	3 150	11 576	89 519	. . .	23 260	4 559	7 973	20 105	24 714	17 976	5 157
1989	3 529	11 933	93 586	. . .	27 162	4 810	8 950	19 742	24 326	18 319	6 771
1990	3 341	12 723	89 655	. . .	30 172	4 972	9 839	18 493	22 667	20 288	9 446
1991	3 241	11 764	91 511	6 102	31 130	4 811	9 957	17 019	23 023	18 413	8 179
1992	4 529	12 314	97 414	8 294	35 211	5 300	11 313	16 682	24 596	20 093	8 181
1993	5 435	13 216	107 246	10 563	39 917	5 443	12 798	17 118	25 102	21 730	8 140
1994	6 547	14 802	119 156	13 982	49 494	6 007	15 358	19 629	26 706	25 058	8 371
1995	7 435	16 348	123 479	17 455	61 684	6 405	18 560	24 184	28 972	26 930	9 721
1996	8 250	18 325	115 187	17 829	74 297	6 583	20 343	22 655	29 907	28 979	13 173
1997	9 188	19 408	121 663	18 027	85 938	7 293	20 075	23 173	32 629	32 659	13 477
1998	9 341	20 959	121 845	19 000	94 629	7 599	18 356	23 942	33 125	34 838	9 181
1999	9 525	22 357	130 864	21 424	109 721	8 475	18 191	31 179	35 204	39 237	11 335
2000	10 367	25 043	146 479	25 568	135 926	9 671	19 178	40 308	40 503	43 345	18 623
2001	10 104	23 790	126 473	22 340	131 338	9 515	15 000	35 181	33 375	41 369	15 251
2002	9 643	24 220	121 429	24 009	134 616	9 849	14 802	35 572	32 148	40 745	15 094
2003	9 515	25 414	118 037	25 440	138 060	10 953	15 138	37 229	31 599	42 795	17 136
2004	10 811	28 097	129 805	28 179	155 902	12 451	15 370	46 168	34 624	46 274	24 921
2005	12 014	31 009	138 004	33 685	170 109	14 862	15 110	43 781	34 826	51 033	33 978
2006	13 425	32 655	148 181	36 533	198 253	17 342	17 768	45 804	38 212	53 513	37 134
2007	14 301	35 028	145 463	32 629	210 714	18 403	18 394	47 562	38 278	56 858	39 910
2008	15 799	36 143	139 248	30 740	215 915	21 140	15 884	48 076	36 327	58 619	51 401
2006											
January	1 072	2 567	10 913	2 818	15 228	1 434	1 307	3 891	3 182	3 824	3 141
February	949	2 289	11 586	2 465	14 820	1 126	1 239	3 560	2 555	3 816	2 888
March	1 138	2 782	12 977	2 886	17 363	1 231	1 511	3 773	3 020	4 706	3 203
April	978	2 614	12 261	2 997	15 665	1 317	1 471	3 561	3 095	4 460	2 884
May	1 107	2 909	12 034	3 000	17 155	1 641	1 393	4 062	3 251	5 081	3 475
June	1 115	2 890	12 337	2 991	17 787	1 577	1 546	3 886	3 181	4 631	3 073
July	1 120	2 960	12 558	3 256	15 465	1 751	1 679	3 854	3 249	4 560	3 797
August	1 316	2 998	12 495	3 480	18 039	1 682	1 665	4 016	3 537	4 605	3 543
September	1 263	2 203	11 826	3 255	16 898	1 400	1 423	3 688	3 416	4 350	3 063
October	1 227	2 856	13 788	3 295	17 515	1 323	1 644	3 965	3 407	4 660	2 800
November	1 073	2 868	12 987	2 948	17 247	1 355	1 495	3 837	3 206	4 594	2 542
December	1 067	2 719	12 419	3 143	15 072	1 507	1 395	3 713	3 113	4 226	2 727
2007											
January	1 291	2 641	11 406	2 782	15 373	1 164	1 572	4 220	3 224	4 063	2 463
February	1 005	2 413	11 825	2 595	15 143	997	1 413	3 601	2 773	3 840	2 238
March	1 200	3 007	12 884	2 755	18 191	1 501	1 668	4 212	2 957	4 675	2 787
April	1 079	2 718	12 548	2 525	16 255	1 436	1 519	4 047	2 995	4 615	3 130
May	1 165	2 841	11 122	2 574	18 019	1 361	1 748	4 273	3 238	5 135	3 429
June	1 184	3 044	11 827	2 548	17 977	1 708	1 452	3 997	3 186	4 953	3 041
July	1 197	3 410	12 769	2 720	16 897	1 545	1 537	4 260	3 345	5 023	3 208
August	1 362	3 148	11 976	2 855	19 115	1 701	1 535	3 792	3 345	4 704	3 519
September	1 301	2 545	11 404	2 698	17 810	1 722	1 463	3 517	3 215	4 652	3 454
October	1 316	3 295	13 472	2 713	19 856	2 094	1 569	3 937	3 448	5 588	3 935
November	1 078	3 022	12 450	2 822	19 356	1 526	1 565	4 215	3 428	5 201	4 307
December	1 123	2 945	11 781	3 042	16 722	1 649	1 354	3 491	3 124	4 408	4 398
2008											
January	1 298	2 927	11 753	2 761	17 020	1 468	1 673	3 925	3 216	4 488	4 187
February	1 151	2 911	12 542	2 448	17 717	1 519	1 385	3 823	2 789	4 771	3 475
March	1 213	3 011	13 093	2 760	17 692	1 498	1 434	4 005	2 991	4 621	3 584
April	1 312	3 223	12 965	2 848	19 366	1 808	1 396	4 386	3 022	5 052	3 837
May	1 293	3 293	11 233	2 778	18 849	1 965	1 359	4 267	3 062	5 068	4 832
June	1 219	3 159	12 118	2 623	19 037	2 400	1 208	3 938	2 987	5 145	5 796
July	1 454	3 740	11 972	2 841	19 258	1 930	1 394	4 515	3 227	5 618	6 465
August	1 558	3 213	11 132	2 608	19 607	1 848	1 202	3 864	3 300	5 744	5 784
September	1 393	2 550	11 121	2 529	17 980	1 774	1 321	3 968	3 155	4 841	4 558
October	1 553	3 032	11 432	2 492	19 660	2 093	1 237	4 484	3 229	5 226	4 064
November	1 159	2 564	10 065	2 122	15 481	1 618	1 129	3 619	2 807	4 096	2 547
December	1 197	2 520	9 821	1 932	14 248	1 219	1 146	3 282	2 543	3 949	2 273

. . . = Not available.

Table 7-15. U.S. Exports of Services

(Balance of payments basis, millions of dollars, seasonally adjusted.)

Year and month	Total	Travel	Passenger fares	Other transportation	Royalties and license fees	Other private services (financial, professional, etc.)	Transfers under U.S. military sales contracts [1]	U.S. government miscellaneous services
1960	6 290	919	175	1 607	837	570	2 030	153
1961	6 295	947	183	1 620	906	607	1 867	164
1962	6 941	957	191	1 764	1 056	585	2 193	195
1963	7 348	1 015	205	1 898	1 162	613	2 219	236
1964	7 840	1 207	241	2 076	1 314	651	2 086	265
1965	8 824	1 380	271	2 175	1 534	714	2 465	285
1966	9 616	1 590	317	2 333	1 516	814	2 721	326
1967	10 667	1 646	371	2 426	1 747	951	3 191	336
1968	11 917	1 775	411	2 548	1 867	1 024	3 939	353
1969	12 806	2 043	450	2 652	2 019	1 160	4 138	343
1970	14 171	2 331	544	3 125	2 331	1 294	4 214	332
1971	16 358	2 534	615	3 299	2 545	1 546	5 472	347
1972	17 841	2 817	699	3 579	2 770	1 764	5 856	357
1973	19 832	3 412	975	4 465	3 225	1 985	5 369	401
1974	22 591	4 032	1 104	5 697	3 821	2 321	5 197	419
1975	25 497	4 697	1 039	5 840	4 300	2 920	6 256	446
1976	27 971	5 742	1 229	6 747	4 353	3 584	5 826	489
1977	31 485	6 150	1 366	7 090	4 920	3 848	7 554	557
1978	36 353	7 183	1 603	8 136	5 885	4 717	8 209	620
1979	39 692	8 441	2 156	9 971	6 184	5 439	6 981	520
1980	47 584	10 588	2 591	11 618	7 085	6 276	9 029	398
1981	57 354	12 913	3 111	12 560	7 284	10 250	10 720	517
1982	64 079	12 393	3 174	12 317	5 603	17 444	12 572	576
1983	64 307	10 947	3 610	12 590	5 778	18 192	12 524	666
1984	71 168	17 177	4 067	13 809	6 177	19 255	9 969	714
1985	73 155	17 762	4 411	14 674	6 678	20 035	8 718	878
1986	86 689	20 385	5 582	15 438	8 113	28 027	8 549	595
1987	98 661	23 563	7 003	17 027	10 174	29 263	11 106	526
1988	110 919	29 434	8 976	19 311	12 139	31 111	9 284	664
1989	127 087	36 205	10 657	20 526	13 818	36 729	8 564	587
1990	147 832	43 007	15 298	22 042	16 634	40 251	9 932	668
1991	164 261	48 385	15 854	22 631	17 819	47 748	11 135	690
1992	177 252	54 742	16 618	21 531	20 841	50 292	12 387	841
1993	185 920	57 875	16 528	21 958	21 695	53 510	13 471	883
1994	200 395	58 417	16 997	23 754	26 712	60 841	12 787	887
1995	219 183	63 395	18 909	26 081	30 289	65 048	14 643	818
1996	239 489	69 809	20 422	26 074	32 470	73 340	16 446	928
1997	256 087	73 426	20 868	27 006	33 228	83 929	16 675	955
1998	262 758	71 325	20 098	25 604	35 626	91 774	17 405	926
1999	281 919	74 801	19 785	26 916	39 670	103 934	15 928	885
2000	298 603	82 400	20 687	29 803	43 233	107 904	13 790	786
2001	286 184	71 893	17 926	28 442	40 696	113 857	12 539	831
2002	292 299	66 605	17 046	29 195	44 508	122 207	11 943	795
2003	302 681	64 348	15 693	31 512	46 988	130 561	12 769	810
2004	349 734	74 546	18 851	36 957	54 490	148 149	15 781	959
2005	389 122	81 799	20 970	41 281	64 395	160 051	19 539	1 087
2006	433 905	85 720	22 036	46 323	72 191	189 050	17 430	1 155
2007	497 245	96 712	25 586	51 586	82 614	223 483	16 052	1 212
2008	544 414	110 469	31 638	59 407	88 212	238 334	15 115	1 239
2007								
January	38 058	7 219	1 903	3 986	6 325	16 883	1 643	99
February	37 980	7 079	1 891	3 958	6 312	17 034	1 606	99
March	39 080	7 520	2 006	4 132	6 354	17 590	1 380	98
April	39 310	7 586	1 964	4 179	6 465	17 714	1 305	97
May	40 276	7 740	2 007	4 231	6 607	18 182	1 414	96
June	40 877	7 828	2 025	4 230	6 793	18 626	1 281	95
July	42 480	8 292	2 155	4 326	7 191	19 090	1 324	101
August	43 589	8 468	2 165	4 389	7 341	19 834	1 289	103
September	43 310	8 481	2 210	4 366	7 408	19 472	1 268	105
October	43 737	8 753	2 379	4 483	7 258	19 568	1 190	106
November	44 246	8 866	2 399	4 695	7 265	19 725	1 188	107
December	44 302	8 880	2 481	4 611	7 294	19 765	1 163	107
2008								
January	44 748	8 926	2 464	4 886	7 130	19 496	1 745	100
February	44 498	9 115	2 535	4 856	7 184	19 294	1 414	99
March	44 723	9 159	2 644	4 849	7 253	19 506	1 212	100
April	45 221	9 089	2 427	5 164	7 431	19 846	1 163	101
May	46 228	9 468	2 558	5 257	7 533	20 088	1 220	103
June	46 868	9 636	2 722	5 321	7 624	20 290	1 171	104
July	46 719	9 579	2 883	5 335	7 388	20 247	1 183	104
August	46 873	9 909	2 948	5 320	7 347	20 010	1 236	104
September	46 046	9 376	2 852	5 069	7 323	20 171	1 151	105
October	45 104	9 086	2 552	4 703	7 340	20 036	1 280	107
November	43 619	8 470	2 455	4 406	7 333	19 660	1 188	106
December	43 765	8 656	2 598	4 240	7 327	19 686	1 151	106

[1]Contains goods that cannot be separately identified.

Table 7-16. U.S. Imports of Services

(Balance of payments basis, millions of dollars, seasonally adjusted.)

Year and month	Total	Travel	Passenger fares	Other transportation	Royalties and license fees	Other private services (financial, professional, etc.)	Direct defense expenditures [1]	U.S. government miscellaneous services
1960	7 674	1 750	513	1 402	74	593	3 087	254
1961	7 671	1 785	506	1 437	89	588	2 998	268
1962	8 092	1 939	567	1 558	100	528	3 105	296
1963	8 362	2 114	612	1 701	112	493	2 961	370
1964	8 619	2 211	642	1 817	127	527	2 880	415
1965	9 111	2 438	717	1 951	135	461	2 952	457
1966	10 494	2 657	753	2 161	140	506	3 764	513
1967	11 863	3 207	829	2 157	166	565	4 378	561
1968	12 302	3 030	885	2 367	186	668	4 535	631
1969	13 322	3 373	1 080	2 455	221	751	4 856	586
1970	14 520	3 980	1 215	2 843	224	827	4 855	576
1971	15 400	4 373	1 290	3 130	241	956	4 819	592
1972	16 868	5 042	1 596	3 520	294	1 043	4 784	589
1973	18 843	5 526	1 790	4 694	385	1 180	4 629	640
1974	21 379	5 980	2 095	5 942	346	1 262	5 032	722
1975	21 996	6 417	2 263	5 708	472	1 551	4 795	789
1976	24 570	6 856	2 568	6 852	482	2 006	4 895	911
1977	27 640	7 451	2 748	7 972	504	2 190	5 823	951
1978	32 189	8 475	2 896	9 124	671	2 573	7 352	1 099
1979	36 689	9 413	3 184	10 906	831	2 822	8 294	1 239
1980	41 491	10 397	3 607	11 790	724	2 909	10 851	1 214
1981	45 503	11 479	4 487	12 474	650	3 562	11 564	1 287
1982	51 749	12 394	4 772	11 710	795	8 159	12 460	1 460
1983	54 973	13 149	6 003	12 222	943	8 001	13 087	1 568
1984	67 748	22 913	5 735	14 843	1 168	9 040	12 516	1 534
1985	72 862	24 558	6 444	15 643	1 170	10 203	13 108	1 735
1986	80 147	25 913	6 505	17 766	1 401	13 146	13 730	1 686
1987	90 787	29 310	7 283	19 010	1 857	16 485	14 950	1 893
1988	98 526	32 114	7 729	20 891	2 601	17 667	15 604	1 921
1989	102 479	33 416	8 249	22 172	2 528	18 930	15 313	1 871
1990	117 659	37 349	10 531	24 966	3 135	22 229	17 531	1 919
1991	118 459	35 322	10 012	24 975	4 035	25 590	16 409	2 116
1992	119 566	38 552	10 603	23 767	5 161	25 386	13 835	2 263
1993	123 779	40 713	11 410	24 524	5 032	27 760	12 086	2 255
1994	133 057	43 782	13 062	26 019	5 852	31 565	10 217	2 560
1995	141 397	44 916	14 663	27 034	6 919	35 199	10 043	2 623
1996	152 554	48 078	15 809	27 403	7 837	39 679	11 061	2 687
1997	165 932	52 051	18 138	28 959	9 161	43 154	11 707	2 762
1998	180 677	56 483	19 971	30 363	11 235	47 591	12 185	2 849
1999	199 190	58 963	21 315	34 139	13 107	55 510	13 335	2 821
2000	223 748	64 705	24 274	41 425	16 468	60 520	13 473	2 883
2001	221 791	60 200	22 633	38 682	16 538	66 021	14 835	2 882
2002	231 069	58 715	19 969	38 407	19 353	72 604	19 101	2 920
2003	250 276	57 444	20 957	44 705	19 033	79 710	25 296	3 131
2004	292 247	65 750	24 718	54 161	23 274	91 267	29 299	3 778
2005	313 540	68 970	26 149	61 937	24 612	97 818	30 075	3 979
2006	348 918	72 104	27 501	65 262	23 777	125 221	31 032	4 021
2007	378 130	76 167	28 486	67 050	25 048	144 375	32 820	4 184
2008	404 719	80 000	32 429	71 840	26 468	153 044	36 542	4 396
2007								
January	30 261	6 163	2 210	5 385	2 211	11 346	2 610	336
February	30 347	6 130	2 236	5 310	2 223	11 469	2 640	339
March	30 690	6 245	2 275	5 328	2 208	11 628	2 665	341
April	30 815	6 248	2 296	5 495	2 115	11 638	2 682	340
May	31 239	6 286	2 309	5 706	2 083	11 818	2 697	339
June	31 341	6 315	2 374	5 565	2 061	11 981	2 706	339
July	32 003	6 345	2 435	5 848	2 066	12 274	2 681	353
August	32 250	6 450	2 501	5 746	2 052	12 439	2 704	357
September	32 036	6 452	2 486	5 524	2 036	12 431	2 747	359
October	32 357	6 547	2 440	5 718	1 996	12 438	2 857	360
November	32 420	6 519	2 447	5 752	1 992	12 447	2 902	360
December	32 372	6 467	2 477	5 671	2 002	12 465	2 929	361
2008								
January	33 243	6 803	2 663	5 923	2 164	12 415	2 914	361
February	33 381	6 833	2 646	6 028	2 219	12 371	2 923	361
March	33 210	6 743	2 618	5 883	2 254	12 419	2 932	361
April	33 575	6 659	2 616	6 092	2 192	12 681	2 974	361
May	34 068	6 880	2 642	6 199	2 197	12 792	2 996	363
June	34 220	6 729	2 774	6 237	2 212	12 888	3 016	364
July	34 593	6 606	2 830	6 378	2 127	13 029	3 250	374
August	35 544	6 776	2 796	6 327	3 000	12 990	3 281	375
September	34 129	6 464	2 691	6 238	2 094	13 013	3 253	376
October	33 577	6 504	2 756	5 937	2 007	12 958	3 049	367
November	32 779	6 526	2 738	5 380	2 004	12 772	2 991	367
December	32 400	6 477	2 659	5 219	2 001	12 716	2 963	366

[1]Contains goods that cannot be separately identified.

Table 7-17. U.S. Export and Import Price Indexes by End-Use Category

(2000 = 100, not seasonally adjusted.)

Year and month	Exports			Imports		
	All commodities	Agricultural	Nonagricultural	All commodities	Petroleum [1]	Nonpetroleum
1989	94.7	110.5	92.7	91.1	61.2	96.0
1990	95.5	105.1	94.4	94.0	75.5	97.1
1991	96.3	103.4	95.4	94.2	67.3	98.7
1992	96.3	102.5	95.7	94.9	62.9	100.0
1993	96.9	104.4	96.2	94.6	57.7	100.6
1994	98.9	109.4	98.0	96.2	54.3	103.2
1995	103.9	119.0	102.5	100.6	59.8	107.2
1996	104.5	132.6	101.6	101.6	71.1	106.4
1997	103.1	120.6	101.3	99.1	66.0	104.1
1998	99.7	108.8	98.8	93.1	44.8	100.4
1999	98.4	101.1	98.2	93.9	60.1	99.0
2000	100.0	100.0	100.0	100.0	100.0	100.0
2001	99.2	101.2	99.0	96.5	82.8	98.5
2002	98.2	103.2	97.8	94.1	85.3	96.2
2003	99.7	112.3	98.8	96.9	103.2	97.3
2004	103.6	123.4	102.1	102.3	134.6	99.8
2005	106.9	121.0	105.9	110.0	185.1	102.5
2006	110.7	125.8	109.6	115.4	223.3	104.2
2007	116.1	150.9	113.6	120.2	249.1	107.0
2008	123.1	183.5	118.8	134.1	343.2	112.7
2004						
January	101.5	123.5	99.8	99.0	113.7	98.5
February	102.2	125.3	100.4	99.4	114.3	98.9
March	103.0	129.7	100.9	100.2	120.1	99.1
April	103.7	133.0	101.4	100.4	119.9	99.4
May	104.1	133.7	101.7	101.9	131.2	99.6
June	103.4	127.4	101.5	101.7	129.7	99.7
July	103.9	126.1	102.2	102.1	132.7	99.7
August	103.4	115.5	102.5	103.6	144.4	100.0
September	103.8	117.6	102.8	104.1	149.2	100.1
October	104.4	116.3	103.6	105.8	165.8	100.0
November	104.7	116.7	103.9	105.5	155.9	100.9
December	104.8	115.4	104.1	104.0	138.1	101.3
2005						
January	105.6	116.1	104.9	104.6	141.2	101.6
February	105.7	115.5	105.0	105.5	148.4	101.7
March	106.4	119.9	105.4	107.8	168.3	102.0
April	106.9	120.3	106.0	108.8	174.4	102.4
May	106.7	122.7	105.5	107.9	166.7	102.2
June	106.7	123.9	105.4	109.2	181.5	102.0
July	106.8	123.9	105.5	110.5	195.5	101.8
August	106.6	123.2	105.4	112.1	209.9	101.9
September	107.5	121.5	106.5	114.4	224.4	102.8
October	108.3	121.9	107.3	114.5	217.5	103.8
November	107.6	121.6	106.6	112.3	197.1	103.7
December	107.7	121.0	106.8	112.3	196.6	103.7
2006						
January	108.5	121.7	107.6	113.7	208.1	104.0
February	108.6	120.8	107.8	112.8	206.0	103.3
March	108.8	120.7	108.0	112.7	207.2	103.0
April	109.6	120.2	108.8	115.1	230.7	103.1
May	110.4	120.9	109.6	117.2	245.4	103.8
June	111.2	124.1	110.3	117.3	242.6	104.2
July	111.6	126.5	110.5	118.2	251.3	104.2
August	112.1	127.7	111.0	118.8	253.7	104.7
September	111.7	127.1	110.6	116.2	225.9	104.8
October	111.4	128.4	110.1	113.3	202.5	104.2
November	111.8	134.1	110.2	113.8	199.2	105.2
December	112.5	137.3	110.7	115.1	207.1	105.7
2007						
January	113.0	138.1	111.2	113.7	193.5	105.6
February	113.9	142.0	111.9	114.1	196.8	105.6
March	114.7	145.0	112.6	115.9	213.6	105.9
April	115.2	142.9	113.2	117.5	228.2	106.2
May	115.5	142.8	113.6	118.6	234.3	106.8
June	116.0	146.7	113.8	120.0	245.6	107.1
July	116.1	149.0	113.7	121.5	260.3	107.2
August	116.3	150.5	113.8	121.1	256.4	107.2
September	116.7	156.8	113.8	121.8	264.4	107.1
October	117.6	162.8	114.4	123.6	277.7	107.7
November	118.7	165.0	115.4	127.5	312.2	108.5
December	119.3	169.3	115.7	127.3	306.7	108.9
2008						
January	120.7	177.5	116.6	129.2	319.6	109.7
February	121.8	185.6	117.3	129.5	315.6	110.4
March	123.8	194.3	118.8	133.5	347.5	111.6
April	124.4	190.5	119.6	137.3	375.8	113.1
May	124.8	190.8	120.1	141.2	412.2	113.9
June	126.1	195.2	121.2	145.5	450.3	114.9
July	128.0	208.2	122.3	147.5	465.0	115.6
August	125.9	188.2	121.5	143.0	419.5	115.1
September	124.9	188.3	120.4	137.8	371.5	114.0
October	122.3	172.5	118.7	129.6	288.9	113.0
November	118.4	160.6	115.4	120.0	201.6	111.1
December	115.8	150.8	113.2	114.5	150.8	109.9

[1] Petroleum and petroleum products.

NOTES AND DEFINITIONS

This chapter presents data from two different data systems on international flows of goods, services, income payments, and financial transactions as they affect the U.S. economy. Tables 7-1 through 7-5 present data on the value, quantities, and prices of foreign transactions in the national income and product accounts (NIPAs). Tables 7-6 through 7-8 show foreign transactions and investment positions as depicted in the U.S. international transactions accounts (ITAs). Both sets of accounts are prepared by the Bureau of Economic Analysis (BEA) and draw on the same original source data. The Census Bureau source data for goods and services are presented in somewhat greater detail in Tables 7-9 through 7-16. Table 7-17 shows selected summary values for export and import price indexes compiled by the Bureau of Labor Statistics (BLS).

Further detail on U.S. foreign trade in goods and services by region, country, state, metropolitan area, product, and industry is published by Bernan online. For information, see: Diane Werneke. *United States Foreign Trade Highlights: Trends in the Global Market* (2nd edition). (Lanham, MD: Bernan Press, 2007.)

Due to a few differences in concept, scope, and definitions, the aggregate values of international transactions in the NIPAs (shown in Tables 7-1 and 7-4) are not exactly equal to the values for similar concepts in the ITAs or the Census values that serve as their sources, shown in Tables 7-6 through 7-16. The principal sources of differences are as follows:

- The NIPAs cover only the 50 states and the District of Columbia. The ITAs include the U.S. territories and Puerto Rico as part of the U.S. economy.
- Gold is treated differently.
- Services without payment by financial intermediaries except life insurance carriers (imputed interest) is treated differently.

A reconciliation of the two sets of international accounts is published regularly as part of the NIPAs. As of the time of writing, the most up-to-date reconciliation was Reconciliation Table 1, "Relation of Net Exports of Goods and Services and Net Receipts of Income in the NIPAs to Balance on Goods and Services and Income in the ITAs," which can be found in the *Survey of Current Business*, September 2008, page D-82.

In addition, certain conventions of presentation differ between the two sets of international accounts. In the NIPAs (Tables 7-1 through 7-5) and in Census tables of exports and imports of goods and services (Tables 7-9 through 7-16), values of imports are shown as positive values, even though they are in fact subtracted in the calculation of gross domestic product (GDP). In the ITA balance of payments (Table 7-6), however, values of imports of goods and services and of all other transactions that result in a payment to the rest of the world—income payments to foreigners, net transfers to foreigners, and net acquisition of assets from abroad—are presented with a minus sign.

TABLES 7-1 AND 7-4
FOREIGN TRANSACTIONS IN THE NATIONAL INCOME AND PRODUCT ACCOUNTS

SOURCE: U.S. DEPARTMENT OF COMMERCE, BUREAU OF ECONOMIC ANALYSIS

See the notes and definitions to Chapter 1 for an overview of the national income and product accounts (NIPAs).

In the 2003 comprehensive revision, the NIPA foreign transactions account was split into two accounts—the current account and the capital account. (This change had already been made in the ITAs.) Most international transactions fall into the current account, but occasionally there are substantial flows in the capital account when major already-existing assets are transferred. An example of this is the U.S. government's transfer of the Panama Canal to the Republic of Panama in 1999.

Upcoming NIPA Revision

In July 2009 the Bureau of Economic Analysis will release a comprehensive, or benchmark, revision of the NIPAs.

Current-dollar estimates will be revised—especially for the most recent four years—because of data updating and classification and statistical changes. Users of the constant-dollar estimates and the quantity and price indexes will also, and immediately, notice a change in the reference year for the chain-type quantity and price indexes and the chained-dollar estimates, from 2000 (as used in the data in this volume) to 2005.

The change in the reference year will cause conspicuous differences in the *levels* of the constant-dollar measures and the price and quantity indexes, but this does not of itself affect the *rates of change*—the growth and inflation rates calculated from these data—which are based on chain-weighted indexes whatever the reference base year is. Significant changes are not expected in historical growth and inflation trends from those that can be derived from the data in this volume, other than the revisions occasioned by new data for the most recent several years.

BEA also plans changes in the treatment of disasters and a new classification system for personal consumption expenditures.

These and all of the other planned changes are described in "Preview of the 2009 Comprehensive Revision of the NIPAs: Changes in Definitions and Presentations," *Survey of Current Business*, March 2009, available at <http://www.bea.gov>.

Definitions

In accordance with the split between current and capital account, there are now two NIPA measures of the balance of international transactions.

The *balance on current account, national income and product accounts* is *current receipts from the rest of the world* minus *current payments to the rest of the world*. A negative value indicates that current payments exceed current receipts.

Net lending or net borrowing (-), national income and product accounts is equal to the balance on current account less capital account transactions with the rest of the world (net). Capital account transactions with the rest of the world (net) is not shown separately in Table 7-1 but can be calculated from that table as the difference between net lending/borrowing and the current account balance. (A similar measure, a component of the ITAs, is shown explicitly in Table 7-6.) Capital account transactions with the rest of the world are cash or in-kind transfers linked to the acquisition or disposition of an existing, nonproduced, nonfinancial asset. In contrast, the current account is limited to flows associated with current production of goods and services.

Net lending or net borrowing provides an indirect measure of the net acquisition of foreign assets by U.S. residents less the net acquisition of U.S. assets by foreign residents. These asset flows are measured directly in the ITAs. See Table 7-6 and its notes and definitions for a more extensive discussion of the relationship between the balances on current and capital account and international asset flows.

Current receipts from the rest of the world is *exports of goods and services* plus *income receipts*.

Current payments to the rest of the world is *imports of goods and services* plus *income payments* plus *current taxes and transfer payments (net)*.

Exports and imports of goods and services. Goods, in general, are products that can be stored or inventoried. *Services*, in general, are products that cannot be stored and are consumed at the place and time of their purchase. Goods include expenditures abroad by U.S. residents, except for travel. Services include foreign travel by U.S. residents, expenditures in the United States by foreign travelers, and exports and imports of certain goods—primarily military equipment purchased and sold by the federal government. See the following paragraph for the definition of *travel*.

Table 7-4 shows values for selected components of total goods and services; the components shown will not add to the total because of omitted items. In the case of goods, a miscellaneous "other" category is not shown. In the case of services, only two components are shown in this table. One is *travel*, which does not include passenger fares but includes as exports spending by foreign tourists in the United States, and includes as imports all other spending abroad by tourists from the United States. The other com-

ponent shown here is a category called *other private services*, which includes the professional and financial services (for example, computer services) that have accounted for a large part of the long-term growth in the service category. The remaining components of total services are transfers under U.S. military agency sales contracts; passenger fares; other transportation; royalties and license fees; and a miscellaneous, smaller *other* category. They are shown separately in Tables 7-15 and 7-16.

Income receipts and payments. Income receipts—receipts from abroad of factor (labor or capital) income by U.S. residents—are analogous to exports and are combined with them to yield total *current receipts from the rest of the world. Income payments* by U.S. entities of factor income to entities abroad are analogous to imports.

Current taxes and transfer payments (net) consists of net payments between the United States and abroad that do not involve payment for the services of the labor or capital factors of production, purchase of currently-produced goods and services, or transfer of an existing asset. It includes net flows from persons, government, and business. The types of payments included are personal remittances from U.S. residents to the rest of the world, net of remittances from foreigners to U.S. residents; government grants; and transfer payments from businesses. Only the net payment to the rest of the world is shown. It usually appears in these accounts as a positive value, with transfers from the United States to abroad exceeding the reverse flow. An exception came in 1991, when U.S. allies in the Gulf War reimbursed the United States for the cost of the war. This resulted in net payments to the United States from the rest of the world and appears as a negative entry in the net transfer payments column of the NIPA accounts. (Note that these signs are reversed in the ITAs.)

TABLES 7-2, 7-3 AND 7-5
CHAIN-TYPE QUANTITY AND PRICE INDEXES FOR NIPA FOREIGN TRANSACTIONS

These indexes represent the separation of the current-dollar values in Tables 7-1 and 7-4 into their real quantity and price trends components. (See the notes and definitions to Chapter 1 for a general explanation of chained-dollar estimates of real output and prices.) As those notes explain, quantity indexes are shown instead of constant-dollar estimates, because BEA no longer publishes its real output estimates before 1990 in any detail in the constant-dollar form. Therefore, quantity indexes are the only comprehensive source of information about longer-term trends in real volumes.

TABLES 7-6 AND 19-12
U.S. INTERNATIONAL TRANSACTIONS

SOURCE: U.S. DEPARTMENT OF COMMERCE, BUREAU OF ECONOMIC ANALYSIS

The U.S. international transactions accounts (ITAs), or "balance of payments accounts," provide a comprehensive view of economic and financial transactions between the United States and foreign countries, measured in current dollars only (unlike the NIPAs, in which price and quantity trends are also estimated). Direct measurement of the values of financial asset flows further distinguishes this set of accounts from the NIPAs.

The ITAs are subdivided into three sets of accounts, with each comprising credit and debit items. In concept, all of these items together provide a complete accounting for U.S. international transactions and should therefore sum to zero. In practice, there are substantial discrepancies due to measurement problems. See the definitions below for an explanation of the *statistical discrepancy* in these accounts, which is different from the measure of the same name in the NIPAs.

The *balance on current account* is the most frequently quoted statistic from these accounts, and is often, but imprecisely, called the "trade balance." (See the definitions below for the correct definitions of "trade balance" and "merchandise trade balance," both of which differ from the current account balance.) The current account includes exports and imports of goods and of travel, transportation, and other services; receipts and payments of income between U.S. and foreign residents; and foreign aid and other current transfers. The *financial account* covers most international flows of private and official capital, including direct investment. The *capital account*, which is small relative to the other two accounts, includes certain transactions in existing assets.

More detailed data on exports and imports of goods and services as measured in these accounts are shown in Tables 7-9 through 7-16.

Definitions

Unlike the practice in the NIPA accounts, each category of transaction in the ITAs is presented either as a *credit,* with an implicit plus sign, or as a *debit,* with a clearly marked minus sign. The signs indicate the direction of the ultimate impact on the overall balance.

Credits (+): The following items are treated as credits in the international transactions accounts: exports of goods and services and income receipts; unilateral current transfers to the United States; capital account transactions receipts; and financial inflows, which are increases in foreign-owned assets (U.S. liabilities) and decreases in U.S.-owned assets (U.S. claims). Credits represent payments of funds to U.S. entities.

Debits (-): The following items are treated as debits in the international transactions accounts, indicated by minus signs in the data cells: imports of goods and services and income payments; unilateral current transfers to foreigners; capital accounts transactions payments; financial outflows, which are decreases in foreign-owned assets (U.S. liabilities) and increases in U.S.-owned assets (U.S. claims). Deb-

its represent requirements for U.S. entities to make payments to foreigners.

This convention of credits and debits is used only in the ITAs in Table 7-6 and the long-term flow data in Table 7-7 (see below). In Table 7-6, import values all have a negative sign. Import values are shown without negative signs both in the NIPA tables (Tables 7-1 and 7-4) and in the detailed tables from the Census Bureau on exports and imports of goods and services (Tables 7-9 through 7-16).

The *balance on goods* is the excess of exports of goods over imports of goods—the algebraic sum of the two, in ITA transactions accounting. A minus sign indicates an excess of imports over exports. A similar concept, which appears in monthly trade reports, is called the "merchandise trade balance."

The *balance on services* is the excess of service exports over service imports. A minus sign indicates an excess of imports over exports.

The *balance on goods and services* is the sum of the balance on goods and the balance on services. This concept is accurately described as the "balance of trade."

The *balance on income* is the excess of income receipts from abroad over income payments to foreigners. A minus sign indicates an excess of payments over receipts.

The *balance on goods, services, and income* is the excess of exports of goods, services, and income over imports of goods, services, and income. It is equal to the sum of the balance on goods and services and the balance on income. A minus sign indicates an excess of imports over exports.

The *balance on unilateral transfers* is equal to unilateral transfers, net, or transfers to the United States minus transfers from the United States. This category includes U.S. government grants, pensions, and other transfers, and private remittances and other transfers. It includes an adjustment for the difference between actual and normal insured losses. See the entry below, in the notes for Tables 7-9 through 7-16, concerning the measurement of insurance services.

The *balance on current account* is equal to the sum of the balance on goods, services, and income and the balance on unilateral transfers. It is the featured measure of the U.S. balance of payments.

The *capital account* covers net capital transfers and the acquisition and disposal of nonproduced nonfinancial assets. The major types of *capital transfers* are debt forgiveness and assets that accompany immigrants. *Nonproduced nonfinancial assets* include rights to natural resources, patents, copyrights, trademarks, franchises, and leases.

The *financial account* includes all other inflows and outflows of capital, or changes in U.S.-owned assets abroad and foreign-owned assets in the United States, including official reserve assets, direct investment, securities, currency, and bank deposits.

Direct investment financial flows are those associated with the acquisition of a significant interest (10 percent or more) in a business enterprise in one country by a resident of another country.

Foreign official assets in the United States. U.S. Treasury securities includes bills, certificates, marketable bonds and notes, and nonmarketable convertible and nonconvertible bonds and notes. *Other U.S. government securities* consists of U.S. Treasury and Export-Import Bank obligations, not included elsewhere, and of debt securities of U.S. government corporations and agencies. *Other U.S. government liabilities* primarily includes U.S. government liabilities to foreign official authorities associated with military agency sales contracts and other transactions arranged with or through foreign official agencies. *Other foreign official assets* consists of official investments in U.S. corporate stocks and in debt securities of private corporations and state and local governments.

In concept, the balance on current account is exactly offset by the net financial and capital inflow or outflow. For example, a U.S. current account deficit results in more dollars held by foreigners, which <u>must</u> be reflected in additional claims on the United States held by foreigners, whether in the form of U.S. currency, securities, loans, or other forms of ownership or obligation. However, because of different and incomplete data sources, the measured financial and capital accounts do not exactly offset the measured current account. The *statistical discrepancy* in the U.S. international accounts—the sum of all credits and debits, with the sign reversed—measures the amount by which the measured net financial and capital flow would have to be augmented (or diminished, in the case of a negative discrepancy) to exactly offset the current account balance. In the quarterly accounts, a part of this discrepancy, the *seasonal adjustment discrepancy*, results from separate seasonal adjustments of the components of the accounts. The statistical discrepancy in the international accounts is not the same as the statistical discrepancy in the national income and product accounts, which arises from measurement differences between domestic output and domestic income.

Notes on the data

There are "breaks" (discontinuities) in the historical series for several of the components of the balance of payments accounts. See Technical Notes in the June 1989–1990, 1992–1995, and July 1996–2007 issues of the *Survey of Current Business.*

Exports and imports of goods in the international transactions account excludes both exports of goods under U.S. military agency sales contracts identified in Census Bureau export documents and imports of goods under direct defense expenditures identified in import documents. They also reflect various other adjustments (for valuation, coverage, and timing) of Census Bureau statistics to a balance-of-payments basis. See the notes and definitions to Tables 7-9 through 7-16 for further information.

Services includes some goods, mainly military equipment (included in transfers under military agency sales contracts); major equipment, other materials, supplies, and petroleum products purchased abroad by U.S. military agencies (included in direct defense expenditures abroad); and fuels purchased by airline and steamship operators (included in other transportation).

U.S. government grants includes transfers of goods and services under U.S. military grant programs. The positive value in 1991 reflects net grants to the United States from other countries.

Beginning in 1982, *private remittances and other transfers* includes taxes paid by U.S. private residents to foreign governments and taxes paid by private nonresidents to the U.S. government.

At the present time, all U.S. Treasury-owned *gold* is held in the United States.

Repayments on U.S. credits and other long-term assets includes sales of foreign obligations to foreigners. The data for 1974 include extraordinary U.S. government transactions with India, as described in "Special U.S. Government Transactions," *Survey of Current Business,* June 1974, page 27.

Beginning with the data for 1982, *direct investment income payments* and the reinvested earnings component of *direct investment* financial flows are measured on a current-cost (replacement-cost) basis after adjustment to reported depreciation, depletion, and expensed exploration and development costs. For prior years, depreciation is valued in terms of the historical cost of assets and reflects a mix of prices for the various years in which capital investments were made. See *Survey of Current Business,* July 1999, pages 65–67, and *Survey of Current Business,* June 1992, pages 72ff.

The *U.S. Treasury securities* component of *other foreign assets in the United States* includes foreign-currency denominated notes sold to private residents abroad for 1978 through 1983.

Estimates of *U.S. currency flows abroad* were introduced for the first time as part of the July 1997 revisions. Data for 1974 and subsequent years were affected (see *Survey of Current Business,* July 1997). Beginning with the 1998 revisions, currency flows are published separately from U.S. Treasury securities.

Financial derivatives, net are estimated for the first time for 2006. (Previously, they were partly measured in other financial flow components and in part contributed to the statistical discrepancy.) They are reported on a net basis only, indicating net receipts (financial inflows) of $28.8 billion in 2006. See "References," below, for more explanation.

Revisions

The international transactions accounts are revised annually each July. Changes in definitions and methodology and newly available source data may be introduced in these revisions.

Data availability

Quarterly and annual data are available from BEA. Data first are reported in a press release and subsequently published in the *Survey of Current Business*, which can be found on the BEA Web site at <http://www.bea.gov/bea/pubs.htm>. Revisions to historical data are published on an annual basis. The most recent historical revisions appear in the July 2008 issue of the *Survey of Current Business*. Complete historical data are available on the BEA Web site at <http://www.bea.gov/>.

References

Discussions of the impact of changes in methodology and incorporation of new data sources are found in the July issues (the June issues for 1995 and earlier years) of the *Survey of Current Business*, with the most recent article entitled "Annual Revision of the U.S. International Accounts, 1974-2007" (July 2008). A similarly titled article in the July 2007 *Survey* includes an extensive discussion of the new data on financial derivatives and their role in the ITA financial account and investment position data.

The Balance of Payments of the United States: Concepts, Data Sources, and Estimating Procedures (May 1990), available on the BEA Web site or from the National Technical Information Service (Accession No. PB 90-268715), describes the methodology in detail and provides a list of data sources.

TABLE 7-7
FOREIGNERS' TRANSACTIONS IN LONG-TERM SECURITIES WITH U.S. RESIDENTS

SOURCE: U.S. DEPARTMENT OF THE TREASURY

Some of the transactions that go into the ITA financial account are collected monthly. Since December 2003, these transactions have been reported by the Treasury Department in a monthly press release. They are presented in Table 7-7.

These data cover transactions in long-term securities, measured at market value plus or minus commissions and fees, between foreigners and U.S. residents. They have more reporting gaps than the more comprehensive quarterly current account data in Table 7-6. These monthly data do not include direct investment, currency flows, changes in bank accounts, or transactions in short-term securities. They may be distorted by inappropriate reporting of repurchases and securities lending transactions. The data are more timely but less detailed than other information sources and are not reliable for country-by-country detail. They are based on a reporting panel of some 250 banks, securities dealers, and other enterprises with cross-border transactions of at least $50 million. This survey was designed to provide timely information for the balance of payments accounts, and its use for other applications—particularly those involving country detail—is less appropriate.

Definitions and notes on the data

U.S. residents includes any individual, corporation, or organization located in the United States (including branches, subsidiaries, and affiliates of foreign entities located in the United States) and any corporation incorporated in the United States, even if it has no physical presence in the country.

Gross purchases minus *gross sales* equals *net purchases*. As in the ITAs in Table 7-6, positive values for net purchases of U.S. securities by foreigners indicate capital inflows from foreigners to U.S. residents (and increased liabilities to foreigners on the part of the U.S. residents). Negative values for net purchases of foreign securities from U.S. residents indicate a capital outflow from U.S. residents to foreigners (and increased liabilities to U.S. residents on the part of foreigners). The algebraic sum of the two net purchases components gives *net long-term securities transactions*. When positive, this indicates that the net capital inflows on U.S. securities exceed the net U.S. acquisitions of foreign securities.

Other acquisitions of long-term securities, net consists of estimated foreign acquisitions of U.S. equity through stock swaps, plus the increase in nonmarketable treasury bonds and notes issued to official institutions and other residents of foreign countries, minus estimated unrecorded principal payments to foreigners on domestic corporate and agency asset-backed securities, minus estimated U.S. acquisitions of foreign equity through stock swaps.

Net foreign acquisition of long-term securities is the sum of *net long-term securities transactions* and *other acquisitions of long-term securities*.

Revisions

The monthly and annual data are revised frequently, when quarterly and annual benchmark data become available. The June release usually includes the final results from an annual survey of foreign holding of U.S. securities.

Data availability and references

Data for the latest month and recent historical data are published in a press release available around the middle of the second following month. The press release, supporting descriptions, references, and other relevant information concerning the Treasury International Capital System (TIC) can be found online at <http://www.treas.gov/tic>.

TABLE 7-8
INTERNATIONAL INVESTMENT POSITION OF THE UNITED STATES

Source: U.S. Department of Commerce, Bureau of Economic Analysis

The data presented in Tables 7-1 through 7-7 all represent *flows* of goods, services, and money over the designated time periods. Table 7-8, in contrast, is a measure of *stocks*, or total holdings of money and other claims. The data on the international investment position of the United States measure the extent to which the United States and its residents hold claims of ownership on foreigners or are creditors of foreigners; the extent to which foreigners, including foreign governments, hold claims of ownership on assets located in the United States or are creditors of U.S. residents and entities; and the net difference between the two amounts. This difference measures the amount by which the United States is a net creditor of the rest of the world or a net debtor to the rest of the world. A position of net U.S. indebtedness is represented by a minus sign in the net international investment position.

Changes in the net investment position can arise in two principal ways:

The first way is through inflows or outflows of capital. A net inflow of capital increases U.S. indebtedness to foreigners, while a net outflow increases foreigners' indebtedness to the United States. A deficit in the U.S. international current account requires an equivalent inflow of foreign capital, while a surplus would require an equivalent outflow of U.S. capital; see notes for Table 7-6 for further explanation.

The second way is through valuation adjustments, which are of several kinds: changes in market prices of assets; changes in exchange rates, which can cause revaluation of foreign-currency-denominated assets; and miscellaneous other adjustments due to changes in coverage, statistical discrepancies, and the like.

Two new features were introduced into the investment position accounts with the 2007 revision. First, only one version of the net position is now published, the one in which direct investment is measured at current cost. (See definitions below.) However, alternative measures of direct investment measured at market prices are also published, so that the user can calculate the position with market valuation of direct investment. Second, for the years 2005 forward, assets and the net position include financial derivatives, which introduces a break in the series. The values for financial derivatives are shown separately so that the user can eliminate them from the calculation if desired. The net value of derivatives amounted to $84 billion in 2007, shrinking the U.S. negative international investment position by 3.4 percent.

Definitions: direct investment, current cost, and market value

Direct investment occurs when an individual or business in one country (the parent) obtains a lasting interest in, and a degree of influence over the management of, a business enterprise in another country (the affiliate). The U.S. data define this degree of interest to be ownership of at least 10 percent of the voting securities of an incorporated business enterprise or the equivalent interest in an unincorporated business enterprise.

When direct investment positions are valued at the historical costs carried on the books of the affiliated companies, much of the investment will reflect the price levels of earlier time periods. Therefore, before calculating the overall U.S. position, BEA re-estimates the aggregate direct investment totals using two alternative valuation bases. *Detailed direct investment data by country and industry are available only on a historical cost basis.*

At *current cost*, the portion of the direct investment position representing the parents' shares of their affiliates' tangible assets (property, plant, equipment, and inventories) is revalued to replacement cost in today's money, using a perpetual inventory model, appropriate price indexes, and appropriate depreciation allowances. (The same methodology is used for the U.S. stock of fixed assets; see the notes and definitions to Tables 5-5 and 5-6 for further information.) This is an adjustment made to the asset side of the balance sheet and reflects prices of tangible assets only.

The *market value* method revalues the owners' equity portion of the direct investment positions using general country indexes of stock market prices. This adjustment is made on the liability and owner's equity side of the balance sheet. Stock price changes reflect changes not only in the value of tangible assets, but also in the value of intangible assets and in the outlook for a country or industry.

Market values are more volatile than current cost, reflecting the nature of stock markets and the additional uncertainties concerning the intangibles included in the valuation. Typically, the total market value of direct investment is greater than the current replacement cost, though by varying proportions. However, in a few years (such as 1982 through 1984) aggregate market values fell below the estimated replacement cost.

Definitions: net international investment position

U.S. net international investment position is defined as the value of *U.S.-owned assets abroad* minus the value of *foreign-owned assets in the United States.*

U.S.-owned assets abroad is the sum of *financial derivatives, official reserve assets, other U.S. government assets, direct investment at current cost, foreign bonds, foreign corporate stocks, U.S. nonblank claims,* and *U.S. bank claims.*

As a component of U.S.-owned assets, the *financial derivatives* category is the sum of derivatives positions with a positive "fair value" to U.S. residents. The fair value of a derivatives contract is the amount for which the contract could be exchanged between willing parties. A derivatives contract between a U.S. and a foreign resident with a positive fair value represents the amount that the foreign resident would have to pay to the U.S. resident if the contract was terminated.

U.S. official reserve assets includes gold, valued at the current market price; special drawing rights; the U.S. reserve position in the International Monetary Fund; and official holdings of foreign currencies.

Other U.S. government assets includes other U.S. government claims on foreigners and holdings of foreign currency and short-term assets.

U.S. nonbank claims includes U.S. claims on affiliated foreigners reported by U.S. nonbanking concerns.

U.S. bank claims consists of claims on foreigners, such as loans and commercial paper, held by U.S. banks and not reported elsewhere in the accounts.

Foreign-owned assets in the United States includes *financial derivatives, foreign official assets, direct investment in the United States at current cost, U.S. Treasury securities, U.S. currency, corporate and other bonds, corporate stocks, U.S. nonbank liabilities,* and *U.S. bank liabilities.*

As a component of foreign-owned assets in the United States, *financial derivatives* consists of derivatives positions with a negative "fair value" to U.S. residents. A contract with a negative fair value represents the amount that the U.S. resident would have to pay to the foreign resident if the contract was terminated.

Foreign official assets includes foreign government holdings of claims on the United States, including U.S. government securities and other liabilities and deposits held by such governments in U.S. banks.

Foreign-owned assets in the United States, other than official assets, also include *U.S. Treasury securities, U.S. currency, corporate and other bonds, corporate stocks, U.S. liabilities (to foreigners) reported by U.S. nonbanking concerns,* and *U.S. bank liabilities to foreigners* (such as deposits).

Data availability

The annual (year-end) data, along with revisions for earlier years and a descriptive article, are presented each year in the July issue of the *Survey of Current Business*. The articles and the data are available on the BEA Web site at <http://www.bea.gov>.

References

Relevant articles in the July 2008 *Survey of Current Business* include: "The International Investment Position of the United States at Yearend 2007;" "Direct Investment Positions for 2007: Country and Industry Detail;" and "Annual Revision of the U.S. International Accounts, 1974–2007." Comparable articles from the July 2007 *Survey* include extensive data and discussion of the new coverage of financial derivatives. For background on the valuation of direct investment and other components, see "Valuation of the U.S. Net International Investment Position," *Survey of Current Business*, May 1991. Also see the references for Table 7-6.

TABLES 7-9 THROUGH 7-16
EXPORTS AND IMPORTS OF GOODS AND SERVICES

SOURCES: U.S. DEPARTMENT OF COMMERCE, CENSUS BUREAU AND BUREAU OF ECONOMIC ANALYSIS

These tables present the source data used to build up the aggregate measures of goods and services flows shown in Tables 7-1 through 7-6. These data are compiled and published monthly, making trends evident before the publication of the quarterly aggregate estimates. They also provide more detail than the quarterly aggregates.

Monthly and annual data on exports and imports of *goods* are compiled by the Census Bureau from documents collected by the U.S. Customs Service. The Bureau of Economic Analysis (BEA) makes certain adjustments to these data (as described below) to place the estimates on a *balance of payments* basis—a basis consistent with the national and international accounts.

Data on exports and imports of *services* are prepared by BEA from a variety of sources. Monthly data on services are available from January 1992. Annual and quarterly data for earlier years are available as part of the international transactions accounts. Current data on goods and services are available each month in a joint Census Bureau-BEA press release.

In the case of some of the detailed breakdowns of exports and imports, such as by end-use categories, monthly data may not sum exactly to annual totals. This is due to later revisions, which are made only to annual data and are not allocated to monthly data. Also, the constant-dollar figures expressed in 2000 dollars are now calculated using chain weights. Therefore, the 2000-dollar detail will not add to the 2000-dollar totals.

In addition, monthly and annual data on exports and imports of goods for individual countries and various country groupings do not reflect subsequent revisions of annual total data. These country data are compiled by the Census Bureau for all countries, although this volume includes only a selection of the most significant ones. The full set of data can be accessed on the Census Web site at <http://www.census.gov>.

Definitions: Goods

Goods: Census basis. The Census basis goods data are compiled from documents collected by the U.S. Customs Service. They reflect the movement of goods between foreign countries and the 50 states, the District of Columbia, Puerto Rico, the U.S. Virgin Islands, and U.S. Foreign Trade Zones. They include government and nongovernment shipments of goods, and exclude shipments between the United States and its territories and possessions; transactions with U.S. military, diplomatic, and consular installations abroad; U.S. goods returned to the United States by its armed forces; personal and household effects of travelers; and in-transit shipments. The general import values reflect the total arrival of merchandise from foreign countries that immediately enters consumption channels, warehouses, or Foreign Trade Zones.

For *imports,* the value reported is the U.S. Customs Service appraised value of merchandise (generally, the price paid for merchandise for export to the United States). Import duties, freight, insurance, and other charges incurred in bringing merchandise to the United States are excluded.

Exports are valued at the f.a.s. (free alongside ship) value of merchandise at the U.S. port of export, based on the transaction price including inland freight, insurance, and other charges incurred in placing the merchandise alongside the carrier at the U.S. port of exportation.

Goods: balance of payments (BOP) basis. Goods on a Census basis are adjusted by BEA to goods on a BOP basis to bring the data in line with the concepts and definitions used to prepare the international and national accounts. In general, the adjustments include changes in ownership that occur without goods passing into or out of the customs territory of the United States. These adjustments are necessary to supplement coverage of the Census basis data, to eliminate duplication of transactions recorded elsewhere in the international accounts, and to value transactions according to a standard definition.

The *export* adjustments include the following: (1) The deduction of *U.S. military sales contracts.* The Census Bureau has included these contracts in the goods data, but BEA includes them in the service category "Transfers Under U.S. Military Sales Contracts." BEA's source material for these contracts is more comprehensive but does not distinguish between goods and services. (2) The addition of *private gift parcels* mailed to foreigners by individuals through the U.S. Postal Service. Only commercial shipments are covered in Census goods exports. (3) The addition to *nonmonetary gold exports* of gold purchased by foreign official agencies from private dealers in the United States and held at the Federal Reserve Bank of New York. The Census data include only gold that leaves the customs territory. (4) *Smaller adjustments* includes deductions for repairs of goods, exposed motion picture film, and military grant aid, and additions for sales of fish in U.S. territorial waters, exports of electricity to Mexico, and vessels and oil

rigs that change ownership without export documents being filed.

The *import* adjustments include the following: (1) On *inland freight in Canada,* the customs value for imports for certain Canadian goods is the point of origin in Canada. BEA makes an addition for the inland freight charges of transporting these Canadian goods to the U.S. border. (2) An addition is made to *nonmonetary gold imports* for gold sold by foreign official agencies to private purchasers out of stock held at the Federal Reserve Bank of New York. The Census Bureau data include only gold that enters the customs territory. (3) A deduction is made for *imports by U.S. military agencies.* The Census Bureau has included these contracts in the goods data, but BEA includes them in the service category "Direct Defense Expenditures." BEA's source material is more comprehensive but does not distinguish between goods and services. (4) *Smaller adjustments* includes deductions for repairs of goods and for exposed motion picture film and additions for imported electricity from Mexico, conversion of vessels for commercial use, and repairs to U.S. vessels abroad.

Definitions: Services

The statistics are estimates of service transactions between foreign countries and the 50 states, the District of Columbia, Puerto Rico, the U.S. Virgin Islands, and other U.S. territories and possessions. Transactions with U.S. military, diplomatic, and consular installations abroad are excluded because they are considered to be part of the U.S. economy. Services are shown in the broad categories described below. For six of these categories, the definitions are the same for imports and exports. For the seventh, the export category is "Transfers under U.S. Military Sales Contracts," while for imports, the category is "Direct Defense Expenditures."

Travel includes purchases of services and goods by U.S. travelers abroad and by foreign visitors to the United States. A traveler is defined as a person who stays for a period of less than one year in a country where the person is not a resident. Included are expenditures for food, lodging, recreation, gifts, and other items incidental to a foreign visit. Not included are the international costs of the travel itself, which are covered in *passenger fares* (see below).

Passenger fares consists of fares paid by residents of one country to residents in other countries. Receipts consist of fares received by U.S. carriers from foreign residents for travel between the United States and foreign countries and between two foreign points. Payments consist of fares paid by U.S. residents to foreign carriers for travel between the United States and foreign countries.

Break in series: travel and passenger fares. Beginning with data for 1984, these items incorporate results from a survey administered by the U.S. Travel and Tourism Administration. See *Survey of Current Business,* June 1989, pages 57ff.

Other transportation includes charges for the transportation of goods by ocean, air, waterway, pipeline, and rail carriers to and from the United States. Included are freight charges, operating expenses that transportation companies incur in foreign ports, and payments for vessel charter and aircraft and freight car rentals. (*Break in series*: Estimates of freight charges for the transportation of goods by truck between the United States and Canada are included in the data beginning with 1986. Reliable estimates for earlier years are not available. See *Survey of Current Business*, June 1994, pages 70ff.)

Royalties and license fees consists of transactions with foreign residents involving intangible assets and proprietary rights, such as the use of patents, techniques, processes, formulas, designs, know-how, trademarks, copyrights, franchises, and manufacturing rights. The term *royalties* generally refers to payments for the utilization of copyrights or trademarks, and the term *license fees* generally refers to payments for the use of patents or industrial processes.

Other private services includes transactions with "affiliated" foreigners for which no identification by type is available and transactions with unaffiliated foreigners.

The term "affiliated" refers to a direct investment relationship, which exists when a U.S. person has ownership or control (directly or indirectly) of 10 percent or more of a foreign business enterprise, or when a foreign person has a similar interest in a U.S. enterprise.

Transactions with "unaffiliated" foreigners in this "other private services" category consist of education services, financial services, insurance services, telecommunications services, and business, professional, and technical services. Included in the last group are advertising services; computer and data processing services; database and other information services; research, development, and testing services; management, consulting, and public relations services; legal services; construction, engineering, architectural, and mining services; industrial engineering services; installation, maintenance, and repair of equipment; and other services, including medical services and film and tape rental.

The insurance component of "other private services" was previously measured as premiums less actual losses paid or recovered. Furthermore, catastrophic losses were entered immediately when the loss occurred, rather than when the insurance claim was actually paid out. This led to sharp swings for any month in which catastrophic losses occurred, such as Hurricane Katrina in August 2005 or the September 11, 2001, terror attacks. In the accounts as revised in July 2003 and presented here, insurance services are now measured as premiums less "normal" losses. Normal losses consist of a measure of expected regularly occurring losses based on six years of past experience <u>plus</u> an additional allowance for catastrophic loss. Catastrophic losses, when they occur, are added in equal increments to the estimate of regularly occurring losses over the 20 years following the occurrence. As adoption of this methodology introduces a difference between actual and normal losses, an amount equal to the difference is entered in the international accounts as a current unilateral transfer.

BEA conducts surveys of international transactions in financial services and "selected services" (largely business, professional, and technical services). Beginning with data for 1986, *other private services* includes estimates of business, professional, and technical services from the BEA surveys of selected services. (See *Survey of Current Business*, June 1989, pages 57ff.)

Breaks in series: royalties and license fees and other private services. These items are presented on a gross basis beginning in 1982. The definition of exports is revised to exclude U.S. parents' payments to foreign affiliates and to include U.S. affiliates' receipts from foreign parents. The definition of imports is revised to include U.S. parents' payments to foreign affiliates and to exclude U.S. affiliates' receipts from foreign parents.

Transfers under U.S. military sales contracts (exports only) includes exports of goods and services in which U.S. government military agencies participate. This category includes both goods, such as equipment, and services, such as repair services and training, that cannot be separately identified. Transfers of goods and services under U.S. military grant programs are included.

Direct defense expenditures (imports only) consists of expenditures incurred by U.S. military agencies abroad, including expenditures by U.S. personnel, payments of wages to foreign residents, construction expenditures, payments for foreign contractual services, and procurement of foreign goods. Included are both goods and services that cannot be separately identified.

U.S. government miscellaneous services includes transactions of U.S. government nonmilitary agencies with foreign residents. Most of these transactions involve the provision of services to, or purchases of services from, foreigners. Transfers of some goods are also included.

Services estimates are based on quarterly, annual, and benchmark surveys and partial information generated from monthly reports. Service transactions are estimated at market prices. Estimates are seasonally adjusted when statistically significant seasonal patterns are present.

Definitions: Area groupings

The *European Union* originally included Austria, Belgium, Denmark, Finland, France, Germany, Greece, Ireland, Italy, Luxembourg, the Netherlands, Portugal, Spain, Sweden, and the United Kingdom. On May 1, 2004, the European Union expanded from 15 countries to 25 countries. The 10 countries added included Cyprus, the Czech Republic, Estonia, Hungary, Latvia, Lithuania, Malta, Poland, Slovakia, and Slovenia. For 2004, data are shown here for both the 15-country original group and the full 25-nation group.

The *Euro area* originally included Austria, Belgium, Finland, France, Germany, Greece, Ireland, Italy, Luxembourg, the Netherlands, Portugal, and Spain. Greece entered the European Monetary Union (EMU) beginning in January 2001. Greece is included in the data for 2001 and later years but not in the data for 2000. Slovenia entered the EMU in January 2007 and will be included in this group beginning at that time. See the notes and definitions to Table 13-8 for further information about the euro.

The *Asian Newly Industrialized Countries (NICS)* includes Hong Kong SAR, South Korea, Singapore, and Taiwan.

The *Organization of Petroleum Exporting Countries (OPEC)* consists of Algeria, Gabon, Indonesia, Iran, Iraq, Kuwait, Libya, Nigeria, Qatar, Saudi Arabia, the United Arab Emirates, and Venezuela.

Notes on the data

U.S./Canada data exchange and substitution. The data for U.S. exports to Canada are derived from import data compiled by Canada. The use of Canada's import data to produce U.S. export data requires several alignments in order to compare the two series.

Coverage: Canadian imports are based on country of origin. U.S. goods shipped from a third country are included, but U.S. exports exclude these foreign shipments. U.S. export coverage also excludes certain Canadian postal shipments.

Valuation: Canadian imports are valued at their point of origin in the United States. However, U.S. exports are valued at the port of exit in the United States and include inland freight charges, making the U.S. export value slightly larger. Canada requires inland freight to be reported.

Reexports: U.S. exports include re-exports of foreign goods. Again, the aggregate U.S. export figure is slightly larger.

Exchange Rate: Average monthly exchange rates are applied to convert the published data to U.S. currency.

End-use categories and seasonal adjustment of trade in goods. Goods are initially classified under the Harmonized System, which describes and measures the characteristics of goods traded. Combining trade into approximately 140 export and 140 import end-use categories makes it possible to examine goods according to their principal uses. These categories are used as the basis for computing the seasonal and working-day adjusted data. Adjusted data are then summed to the six end-use aggregates for publication.

The seasonal adjustment procedure is based on a model that estimates the monthly movements as percentages above or below the general level of each end-use commodity series (unlike other methods that redistribute the actual series values over the calendar year). Imports of petroleum and petroleum products are adjusted for the length of the month.

Data availability

Data are released monthly in a joint Census Bureau-BEA press release (FT-900), which is published about six weeks after the end of the month to which the data pertain. The release and historical data are available on the Census Bureau Web site at <http://www.census.gov/foreign-trade/www/>.

Revisions

Data for recent years are normally revised annually. In some cases, revisions to annual totals are not distributed to monthly data; therefore, monthly data may not sum to the revised total shown. Data on trade in services may be subject to extensive revision as part of BEA's annual revision of the international transactions accounts (ITAs), usually released in July.

References

Discussion of the impact of changes in methodology and incorporation of new data sources are found in the discussions of annual revisions of the ITAs in the July issues of BEA's *Survey of Current Business*. The most recent pertinent article is "Annual Revision of the U.S. International Accounts, 1974–2007" (July 2008).

TABLE 7-17
EXPORT AND IMPORT PRICE INDEXES

SOURCE: U.S. DEPARTMENT OF LABOR, BUREAU OF LABOR STATISTICS

The International Price Program of the Bureau of Labor Statistics (BLS) collects price data for nonmilitary goods traded between the United States and the rest of the world and for selected transportation services in international markets. BLS aggregates the goods price data into export and import price indexes. Summary values of these price indexes for goods are presented in *Business Statistics*. For product and locality detail on international prices for both goods and services, see the *Handbook of U.S. Labor Statistics*, also published by Bernan Press.

Definitions

The *export* price index provides a measure of price change for all goods sold by U.S. residents (businesses and individuals located within the geographic boundaries of the United States, whether or not owned by U.S. citizens) to foreign buyers.

The *import* price index provides a measure of price change for goods purchased from other countries by U.S. residents.

Notes on the data

Published index series use a base year of 2000 = 100 whenever possible.

The product universe for both the import and export indexes includes raw materials, agricultural products, and manufactures. Price data are primarily collected by mail questionnaire, and directly from the exporter or importer in all but a few cases.

To the greatest extent possible, the data refer to prices at the U.S. border for exports and at either the foreign border or the U.S. border for imports. For nearly all products, the prices refer to transactions completed during the first week of the month and represent the actual price for which the product was bought or sold, including discounts, allowances, and rebates.

For the export price indexes, the preferred pricing basis is f.a.s. (free alongside ship) U.S. port of exportation. Where necessary, adjustments are made to reported prices to place them on this basis. An attempt is made to collect two prices for imports: f.o.b. (free on board) at the port of exportation and c.i.f. (cost, insurance, and freight) at the U.S. port of importation. Adjustments are made to account for changes in product characteristics in order to obtain a pure measure of price change.

The indexes are weighted indexes of the Laspeyres type. (See "General Notes" at the beginning of this volume for further explanation.) The values assigned to each weight category are based on trade value figures compiled by the Census Bureau. They are reweighted annually, with a two-year lag (as concurrent value data are not available) in revisions.

The merchandise price indexes are published using three different classification systems: the Harmonized System, the Bureau of Economic Analysis End-Use System, and the Standard International Trade Classification (SITC) system. The aggregate indexes shown here are from the End-Use System.

Data availability

Indexes are published monthly in a press release and a more detailed report. Indexes are published for detailed product categories, as well as for all commodities. Aggregate import indexes by country or region of origin also are available, as are indexes for selected categories of internationally traded services. Additional information is available from the Division of International Prices in the Bureau of Labor Statistics. Complete historical data are available on the BLS Web site at <http://www.bls.gov>.

References

The indexes are described in "BLS to Produce Monthly Indexes of Export and Import Prices," *Monthly Labor Review* (December 1988), and Chapter 15, "International Price Indexes," *BLS Handbook of Methods* Bulletin 2490 (April 1997).

CHAPTER 8: PRICES

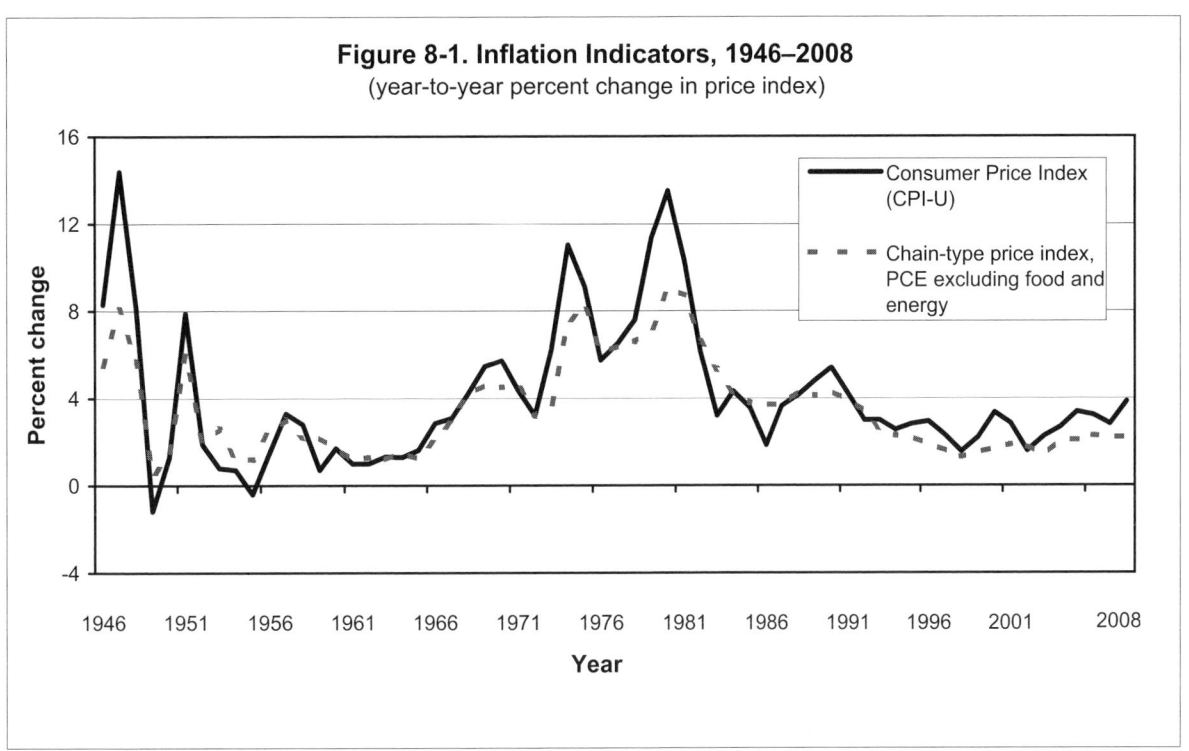

Figure 8-1. Inflation Indicators, 1946–2008
(year-to-year percent change in price index)

- Figure 8-1 shows annual rates of change in the Consumer Price Index for All Urban Consumers (CPI-U), the most widely used measure of the general price level. It also shows changes in the chain-type price index for personal consumption expenditures (PCE) excluding food and energy, which provides one widely used measure of the underlying rate of inflation. (Tables 8-1, 8-2, 8-3, 19-5, and 20-2)

- There was far more turbulence in prices during 2008 than can be seen in the annual average data. The CPI rose 3.5 percent from December 2007 to July 2008, then fell 3.5 percent from July to December. Food prices rose throughout the year, while energy prices soared and then collapsed. Weighting made more of a difference than usual, because one of the most volatile components—gasoline—has greater weight in the CPI-W than in the CPI-U, and greater weight in the CPI-U than the CPI-E (the experimental index for persons 62 and older). (Tables 8-1, 8-2, and 8-3)

- From 1965 to 2008, commodity prices in the CPI-U rose at an average rate of 3.8 percent per year, but service prices increased at an average annual rate of 5.4 percent. (Table 8-1)

- The Producer Price Index (PPI) measures prices at the point of production, rather than at the consumer level. The most widely used product of the PPI system—the PPI for Finished Goods—only covers commodities, whereas the CPI covers both commodities and services. For these reasons, the PPI for Finished Goods fluctuates more (both up and down) than the aggregate CPI-U, but has a less inflationary trend. (Table 8-4)

- The PPI data set also includes prices for intermediate materials, supplies, and components and crude materials for further processing. Intermediate materials prices fluctuate more than those of finished goods, and crude materials prices fluctuate most of all. (Table 8-4)

Table 8-1. Consumer Price Indexes, All Urban Consumers (CPI-U)

(1982–1984 = 100; seasonally adjusted, except as noted.)

Year and month	All items — Not seasonally adjusted	Seasonally adjusted — Index	Seasonally adjusted — Percent change from previous period	Total	Total food	Food at home — Total	Cereals and bakery products	Meats, poultry, fish, and eggs	Dairy and related products	Fruits and vege-tables	Non-alcoholic beverages	Other food at home	Food away from home [1]	Alcoholic bever-ages
1965	31.5	31.5	1.6	. . .	32.2	33.5	31.9	. . .	36.0	32.6	23.4	. . .	28.4	44.6
1966	32.4	32.4	2.9	. . .	33.8	35.2	33.3	. . .	38.3	33.3	23.3	. . .	29.7	45.4
1967	33.4	33.4	3.1	35.0	34.1	35.1	34.0	38.0	40.0	33.3	23.1	29.3	31.3	46.4
1968	34.8	34.8	4.2	36.2	35.3	36.3	34.2	39.1	41.3	35.9	23.5	29.8	32.9	48.0
1969	36.7	36.7	5.5	38.1	37.1	38.0	35.2	42.6	42.7	36.4	24.2	30.7	34.9	49.7
1970	38.8	38.8	5.7	40.1	39.2	39.9	37.1	44.6	44.7	37.8	27.1	32.9	37.5	52.1
1971	40.5	40.5	4.4	41.4	40.4	40.9	38.8	44.1	46.1	39.7	28.1	34.3	39.4	54.2
1972	41.8	41.8	3.2	43.1	42.1	42.7	39.0	48.0	46.8	41.6	28.0	34.6	41.0	55.4
1973	44.4	44.4	6.2	48.8	48.2	49.7	43.5	60.9	51.2	47.4	30.1	36.7	44.2	56.8
1974	49.3	49.3	11.0	55.5	55.1	57.1	56.5	62.2	60.7	55.2	35.9	47.8	49.8	61.1
1975	53.8	53.8	9.1	60.2	59.8	61.8	62.9	67.0	62.6	56.9	41.3	55.4	54.5	65.9
1976	56.9	56.9	5.8	62.1	61.6	63.1	61.5	68.0	67.7	58.4	49.4	56.4	58.2	68.1
1977	60.6	60.6	6.5	65.8	65.5	66.8	62.5	67.4	69.5	63.8	74.4	68.4	62.6	70.0
1978	65.2	65.2	7.6	72.2	72.0	73.8	68.1	77.6	74.2	70.9	78.7	73.6	68.3	74.1
1979	72.6	72.6	11.3	79.9	79.9	81.8	74.9	89.0	82.8	76.6	82.6	79.0	75.9	79.9
1980	82.4	82.4	13.5	86.7	86.8	88.4	83.9	92.0	90.9	82.1	91.4	88.4	83.4	86.4
1981	90.9	90.9	10.3	93.5	93.6	94.8	92.3	96.0	97.4	92.0	95.3	94.9	90.9	92.5
1982	96.5	96.5	6.2	97.3	97.4	98.1	96.5	99.6	98.8	97.0	97.9	97.3	95.8	96.7
1983	99.6	99.6	3.2	99.5	99.4	99.1	99.6	99.2	100.0	97.3	99.8	99.5	100.0	100.4
1984	103.9	103.9	4.3	103.2	103.2	102.8	103.9	101.3	101.3	105.7	102.3	103.1	104.2	103.0
1985	107.6	107.6	3.6	105.6	105.6	104.3	107.9	100.1	103.2	108.4	104.3	105.7	108.3	106.4
1986	109.6	109.6	1.9	109.1	109.0	107.3	110.9	104.5	103.3	109.4	110.4	109.4	112.5	111.1
1987	113.6	113.6	3.6	113.5	113.5	111.9	114.8	110.5	105.9	119.1	107.5	110.5	117.0	114.1
1988	118.3	118.3	4.1	118.2	118.2	116.6	122.1	114.3	108.4	128.1	107.5	113.1	121.8	118.6
1989	124.0	124.0	4.8	124.9	125.1	124.2	132.4	121.3	115.6	138.0	111.3	119.1	127.4	123.5
1990	130.7	130.7	5.4	132.1	132.4	132.3	140.0	130.0	126.5	149.0	113.5	123.4	133.4	129.3
1991	136.2	136.2	4.2	136.8	136.3	135.8	145.8	132.6	125.1	155.8	114.1	127.3	137.9	142.8
1992	140.3	140.3	3.0	138.7	137.9	136.8	151.5	130.9	128.5	155.4	114.3	128.8	140.7	147.3
1993	144.5	144.5	3.0	141.6	140.9	140.1	156.6	135.5	129.4	159.0	114.6	130.5	143.2	149.6
1994	148.2	148.2	2.6	144.9	144.3	144.1	163.0	137.2	131.7	165.0	123.2	135.6	145.7	151.5
1995	152.4	152.4	2.8	148.9	148.4	148.8	167.5	138.8	132.8	177.7	131.7	140.8	149.0	153.9
1996	156.9	156.9	3.0	153.7	153.3	154.3	174.0	144.8	142.1	183.9	128.6	142.9	152.7	158.5
1997	160.5	160.5	2.3	157.7	157.3	158.1	177.6	148.5	145.5	187.5	133.4	147.3	157.0	162.8
1998	163.0	163.0	1.6	161.1	160.7	161.1	181.1	147.3	150.8	198.2	133.0	150.8	161.1	165.7
1999	166.6	166.6	2.2	164.6	164.1	164.2	185.0	147.9	159.6	203.1	134.3	153.5	165.1	169.7
2000	172.2	172.2	3.4	168.4	167.8	167.9	188.3	154.5	160.7	204.6	137.8	155.6	169.0	174.7
2001	177.1	177.1	2.8	173.6	173.1	173.4	193.8	161.3	167.1	212.2	139.2	159.6	173.9	179.3
2002	179.9	179.9	1.6	176.8	176.2	175.6	198.0	162.1	168.1	220.9	139.2	160.8	178.3	183.6
2003	184.0	184.0	2.3	180.5	180.0	179.4	202.8	169.3	167.9	225.9	139.8	162.6	182.1	187.2
2004	188.9	188.9	2.7	186.6	186.2	186.2	206.0	181.7	180.2	232.7	140.4	164.9	187.5	192.1
2005	195.3	195.3	3.4	191.2	190.7	189.8	209.0	184.7	182.4	241.4	144.4	167.0	193.4	195.9
2006	201.6	201.6	3.2	195.7	195.2	193.1	212.8	186.6	181.4	252.9	147.4	169.6	199.4	200.7
2007	207.3	207.3	2.8	203.3	202.9	201.2	222.1	195.6	194.8	262.6	153.4	173.3	206.7	207.0
2008	215.3	215.3	3.9	214.2	214.1	214.1	244.9	204.7	210.4	278.9	160.0	184.2	215.8	214.5
2007														
January	202.4	203.6	0.1	198.7	198.2	195.7	216.8	189.5	182.4	256.3	150.2	170.9	203.2	203.3
February	203.5	204.4	0.4	200.0	199.6	197.5	218.9	190.5	183.1	264.9	150.7	171.5	203.9	203.9
March	205.4	205.3	0.5	200.7	200.3	198.6	218.5	192.4	185.2	264.3	153.0	171.7	204.1	205.0
April	206.7	205.9	0.3	201.4	201.0	199.3	220.1	194.3	186.1	263.2	151.9	172.4	204.7	205.6
May	207.9	206.7	0.4	202.1	201.7	200.1	220.3	196.4	187.3	262.4	153.0	172.4	205.2	206.2
June	208.4	207.0	0.2	203.1	202.7	201.4	221.8	197.4	193.2	262.1	153.5	173.2	205.9	207.0
July	208.3	207.3	0.2	203.7	203.4	201.8	222.3	196.8	198.4	259.5	153.8	173.7	206.9	207.6
August	207.9	207.5	0.1	204.6	204.3	202.8	223.0	197.1	202.3	260.3	155.1	173.9	207.8	208.4
September	208.5	208.4	0.4	205.6	205.3	203.7	224.1	197.9	204.0	262.9	155.1	174.4	208.8	208.6
October	208.9	209.1	0.4	206.0	205.6	204.1	225.0	198.4	204.5	262.0	155.4	174.7	209.3	209.3
November	210.2	211.2	1.0	206.7	206.4	205.0	226.6	198.4	205.6	267.2	154.9	175.1	209.9	209.6
December	210.0	211.7	0.3	206.9	206.6	205.0	227.9	198.3	205.3	266.3	154.5	175.4	210.2	209.8
2008														
January	211.1	212.5	0.4	208.3	208.0	206.9	229.2	199.7	205.7	272.1	156.9	176.2	211.1	210.8
February	211.7	212.9	0.2	209.1	208.8	207.6	233.3	199.5	207.3	268.6	156.7	178.0	211.9	211.5
March	213.5	213.7	0.4	209.5	209.3	208.0	236.3	199.5	205.6	268.9	157.2	178.2	212.5	211.7
April	214.8	214.0	0.2	211.4	211.2	211.1	239.6	201.4	208.0	274.1	159.9	181.5	213.1	212.8
May	216.6	215.0	0.5	212.1	211.9	211.6	243.5	201.6	207.8	274.1	158.4	182.4	214.0	213.1
June	218.8	217.0	0.9	213.6	213.5	213.7	244.8	203.3	211.1	281.9	158.7	183.1	215.0	213.6
July	220.0	218.6	0.7	215.5	215.5	216.2	249.2	205.4	214.5	285.4	159.8	185.0	216.4	214.4
August	219.1	218.6	0.0	216.8	216.8	217.9	249.0	207.5	215.4	291.5	160.4	186.2	217.1	215.2
September	218.8	218.7	0.0	218.0	218.0	219.2	251.8	209.5	214.1	290.0	161.6	188.1	218.2	216.3
October	216.6	216.9	-0.8	218.6	218.6	219.4	253.2	210.7	211.9	283.8	163.5	189.3	219.3	217.1
November	212.4	213.3	-1.7	219.0	218.9	219.4	253.7	209.3	212.8	282.6	163.7	190.5	220.0	218.2
December	210.2	211.6	-0.8	218.9	218.8	218.6	254.6	208.3	210.8	275.7	163.6	191.7	220.7	219.2

[1] Not seasonally adjusted.
. . . = Not available.

Table 8-1. Consumer Price Indexes, All Urban Consumers (CPI-U)—*Continued*

(1982–1984 = 100, except as noted; seasonally adjusted, except as noted.)

Year and month	Total	Housing — Shelter Total	Rent of shelter [2]	Rent of primary residence	Lodging away from home [3]	Owners' equivalent rent of primary residence [2]	Tenants' and household insur- ance [1,3]	Fuels and utilities Total	Fuel oil and other fuels	Gas (piped) and electricity	Water and sewer and trash collection services [3]	Household furnishings and operations Total	Household oper- ations [1,3]
1965	. . .	27.0	. . .	40.9	. . .	. . .	. . .	26.6	14.6	23.5	. . .	. . .	. . .
1966	. . .	27.8	. . .	41.5	. . .	. . .	. . .	26.7	15.0	23.6	. . .	. . .	. . .
1967	30.8	28.8	. . .	42.2	. . .	. . .	. . .	27.1	15.5	23.7	. . .	42.0	. . .
1968	32.0	30.1	. . .	43.3	. . .	. . .	. . .	27.4	16.0	23.9	. . .	43.6	. . .
1969	34.0	32.6	. . .	44.7	. . .	. . .	. . .	28.0	16.3	24.3	. . .	45.2	. . .
1970	36.4	35.5	. . .	46.5	. . .	. . .	. . .	29.1	17.0	25.4	. . .	46.8	. . .
1971	38.0	37.0	. . .	48.7	. . .	. . .	. . .	31.1	18.2	27.1	. . .	48.6	. . .
1972	39.4	38.7	. . .	50.4	. . .	. . .	. . .	32.5	18.3	28.5	. . .	49.7	. . .
1973	41.2	40.5	. . .	52.5	. . .	. . .	. . .	34.3	21.1	29.9	. . .	51.1	. . .
1974	45.8	44.4	. . .	55.2	. . .	. . .	. . .	40.7	33.2	34.5	. . .	56.8	. . .
1975	50.7	48.8	. . .	58.0	. . .	. . .	. . .	45.4	36.4	40.1	. . .	63.4	. . .
1976	53.8	51.5	. . .	61.1	. . .	. . .	. . .	49.4	38.8	44.7	. . .	67.3	. . .
1977	57.4	54.9	. . .	64.8	. . .	. . .	. . .	54.7	43.9	50.5	. . .	70.4	. . .
1978	62.4	60.5	. . .	69.3	. . .	. . .	. . .	58.5	46.2	55.0	. . .	74.7	. . .
1979	70.1	68.9	. . .	74.3	. . .	. . .	. . .	64.8	62.4	61.0	. . .	79.9	. . .
1980	81.1	81.0	. . .	80.9	. . .	. . .	. . .	75.4	86.1	71.4	. . .	86.3	. . .
1981	90.4	90.5	. . .	87.9	. . .	. . .	. . .	86.4	104.6	81.9	. . .	93.0	. . .
1982	96.9	96.9	. . .	94.6	. . .	. . .	. . .	94.9	103.4	93.2	. . .	98.0	. . .
1983	99.5	99.1	102.7	100.1	. . .	102.5	. . .	100.2	97.2	101.5	. . .	100.2	. . .
1984	103.6	104.0	107.7	105.3	. . .	107.3	. . .	104.8	99.4	105.4	. . .	101.9	. . .
1985	107.7	109.8	113.9	111.8	. . .	113.2	. . .	106.5	95.9	107.1	. . .	103.8	. . .
1986	110.9	115.8	120.2	118.3	. . .	119.4	. . .	104.1	77.6	105.7	. . .	105.2	. . .
1987	114.2	121.3	125.9	123.1	. . .	124.8	. . .	103.0	77.9	103.8	. . .	107.1	. . .
1988	118.5	127.1	132.0	127.8	. . .	131.1	. . .	104.4	78.1	104.6	. . .	109.4	. . .
1989	123.0	132.8	138.0	132.8	. . .	137.4	. . .	107.8	81.7	107.5	. . .	111.2	. . .
1990	128.5	140.0	145.5	138.4	. . .	144.8	. . .	111.6	99.3	109.3	. . .	113.3	. . .
1991	133.6	146.3	152.1	143.3	. . .	150.4	. . .	115.3	94.6	112.6	. . .	116.0	. . .
1992	137.5	151.2	157.3	146.9	. . .	155.5	. . .	117.8	90.7	114.8	. . .	118.0	. . .
1993	141.2	155.7	162.0	150.3	. . .	160.5	. . .	121.3	90.3	118.5	. . .	119.3	. . .
1994	144.8	160.5	167.0	154.0	. . .	165.8	. . .	122.8	88.8	119.2	. . .	121.0	. . .
1995	148.5	165.7	172.4	157.8	. . .	171.3	. . .	123.7	88.1	119.2	. . .	123.0	. . .
1996	152.8	171.0	178.0	162.0	. . .	176.8	. . .	127.5	99.2	122.1	. . .	124.7	. . .
1997	156.8	176.3	183.4	166.7	. . .	181.9	. . .	130.8	99.8	125.1	. . .	125.4	. . .
1998	160.4	182.1	189.6	172.1	109.0	187.8	99.8	128.5	90.0	121.2	101.6	126.6	101.5
1999	163.9	187.3	195.0	177.5	112.3	192.9	101.3	128.8	91.4	120.9	104.0	126.7	104.5
2000	169.6	193.4	201.3	183.9	117.5	198.7	103.7	137.9	129.7	128.0	106.5	128.2	110.5
2001	176.4	200.6	208.9	192.1	118.6	206.3	106.2	150.2	129.3	142.4	109.6	129.1	115.6
2002	180.3	208.1	216.7	199.7	118.3	214.7	108.7	143.6	115.5	134.4	113.0	128.3	119.0
2003	184.8	213.1	221.9	205.5	119.3	219.9	114.8	154.5	139.5	145.0	117.2	126.1	121.8
2004	189.5	218.8	227.9	211.0	125.9	224.9	116.2	161.9	160.5	150.6	124.0	125.5	125.0
2005	195.7	224.4	233.7	217.3	130.3	230.2	117.6	179.0	208.6	166.5	130.3	126.1	130.3
2006	203.2	232.1	241.9	225.1	136.0	238.2	116.5	194.7	234.9	182.1	136.8	127.0	136.6
2007	209.6	240.6	250.8	234.7	142.8	246.2	117.0	200.6	251.5	186.3	143.7	126.9	140.6
2008	216.3	246.7	257.2	243.3	143.7	252.4	118.8	220.0	334.4	202.2	152.1	127.8	147.5
2007													
January	206.7	237.4	247.4	230.7	139.8	243.3	117.4	194.8	227.4	181.7	140.5	127.1	139.5
February	207.5	238.0	248.1	231.6	140.0	244.0	117.3	197.1	227.4	184.3	140.9	127.3	139.7
March	207.9	238.2	248.3	232.4	137.2	244.6	117.3	199.4	232.8	186.5	141.6	127.4	139.9
April	208.5	239.0	249.2	233.0	140.0	245.0	117.6	199.8	236.9	186.6	142.2	127.2	140.3
May	209.0	239.6	249.8	233.7	141.9	245.3	116.4	200.6	242.1	187.1	142.7	127.1	140.5
June	209.6	240.5	250.7	234.3	144.4	245.8	117.1	201.3	245.7	187.6	143.1	127.1	140.5
July	209.9	241.0	251.3	234.9	145.4	246.3	116.6	201.1	249.1	186.9	144.0	126.9	140.7
August	210.1	241.5	251.7	235.4	144.9	246.8	116.9	200.0	251.5	185.2	144.7	126.7	141.0
September	210.6	242.2	252.5	236.1	146.1	247.5	116.8	200.6	255.6	185.5	145.3	126.5	140.7
October	211.1	242.6	252.9	237.1	144.9	248.0	116.6	202.6	264.7	187.2	145.7	126.4	141.0
November	211.9	243.3	253.6	238.1	144.6	248.8	117.0	204.9	288.2	188.3	146.6	126.4	141.6
December	212.4	244.0	254.3	238.9	145.1	249.4	117.0	205.6	295.3	188.5	147.3	126.4	142.1
2008													
January	212.9	244.7	255.2	239.7	146.7	250.1	117.4	205.6	306.2	187.5	148.1	126.5	142.8
February	213.3	244.8	255.3	240.2	145.0	250.4	117.6	208.2	302.5	190.7	148.6	126.5	143.5
March	214.2	245.2	255.7	240.8	144.1	250.9	117.7	212.3	326.4	194.2	149.1	127.2	145.0
April	214.9	245.3	255.7	241.5	141.5	251.5	118.4	216.9	338.2	199.0	149.5	127.1	145.8
May	215.9	245.8	256.3	241.9	143.4	251.7	118.4	222.1	364.8	203.6	150.2	127.4	147.0
June	216.9	246.6	257.0	242.8	144.4	252.3	119.1	226.2	396.0	206.6	150.8	127.4	148.0
July	218.3	247.1	257.6	243.5	145.4	252.6	118.8	233.5	401.3	214.9	151.9	127.9	148.3
August	218.1	247.3	257.7	244.3	143.8	253.0	118.6	230.9	375.2	212.5	153.8	128.2	149.2
September	217.9	248.0	258.5	245.0	145.2	253.5	119.9	224.4	353.3	205.8	154.3	128.9	150.2
October	217.8	248.1	258.6	245.8	142.8	253.9	119.9	223.1	322.2	205.5	155.8	128.9	150.1
November	217.6	248.5	259.1	246.6	141.2	254.6	120.2	219.5	278.4	203.5	156.4	128.7	150.0
December	217.5	248.6	259.2	247.1	140.2	254.8	120.0	218.4	252.8	203.4	156.8	128.9	150.7

[1] Not seasonally adjusted.
[2] December 1982 = 100.
[3] December 1997 = 100.
. . . = Not available.

Table 8-1. Consumer Price Indexes, All Urban Consumers (CPI-U)—*Continued*

(1982–1984 = 100; seasonally adjusted, except as noted.)

Year and month	Apparel					Transportation									
							Private transportation							Motor vehicle parts and equipment [1]	Motor vehicle maintenance and repair
								New and used motor vehicles			Motor fuel				
	Total	Men's and boys' apparel	Women's and girls' apparel	Infants' and toddlers' apparel	Footwear	Total	Total	Total [3]	New vehicles	Used cars and trucks [1]	Total	Gasoline (all types)		
1965	47.8	49.9	58.1	35.1	43.4	31.9	32.5	...	49.8	29.8	25.1	25.1	...	28.7
1966	49.0	51.2	59.2	35.4	46.0	32.3	32.9	...	48.9	29.0	25.6	25.6	...	29.2
1967	51.0	53.1	61.9	35.8	48.2	33.3	33.8	...	49.3	29.9	26.4	26.4	...	30.4
1968	53.7	56.1	65.6	37.3	50.8	34.3	34.8	...	50.7	...	26.8	26.8	...	32.1
1969	56.8	59.7	69.2	38.4	53.9	35.7	36.0	...	51.5	30.9	27.6	27.7	...	34.1
1970	59.2	62.2	71.8	39.2	56.8	37.5	37.5	...	53.1	31.2	27.9	27.9	...	36.6
1971	61.1	63.9	74.4	40.0	58.6	39.5	39.4	...	55.3	33.0	28.1	28.1	...	39.3
1972	62.3	64.7	76.2	41.1	60.3	39.9	39.7	...	54.8	33.1	28.4	28.4	...	41.1
1973	64.6	67.1	78.8	42.5	62.8	41.2	41.0	...	54.8	35.2	31.2	31.2	...	43.2
1974	69.4	72.4	83.5	54.2	66.6	45.8	46.2	...	58.0	36.7	42.2	42.2	...	47.6
1975	72.5	75.5	85.5	64.5	69.6	50.1	50.6	...	63.0	43.8	45.1	45.1	...	53.7
1976	75.2	78.1	87.9	68.0	72.3	55.1	55.6	...	67.0	50.3	47.0	47.0	...	57.6
1977	78.6	81.7	90.6	74.6	75.7	59.0	59.7	...	70.5	54.7	49.7	49.7	...	61.9
1978	81.4	83.5	92.4	77.4	79.0	61.7	62.5	...	75.9	55.8	51.8	51.8	77.6	67.0
1979	84.9	85.4	94.0	79.0	85.3	70.5	71.7	...	81.9	60.2	70.1	70.2	85.1	73.7
1980	90.9	89.4	96.0	85.5	91.8	83.1	84.2	...	88.5	62.3	97.4	97.5	95.3	81.5
1981	95.3	94.2	97.5	92.9	96.7	93.2	93.8	...	93.9	76.9	108.5	108.5	101.0	89.2
1982	97.8	97.6	98.5	96.3	99.1	97.0	97.1	...	97.5	88.8	102.8	102.8	103.6	96.0
1983	100.2	100.3	100.2	101.1	99.8	99.3	99.3	...	99.9	98.7	99.4	99.4	100.7	100.3
1984	102.1	102.1	101.3	102.6	101.1	103.7	103.6	...	102.6	112.5	97.9	97.8	95.6	103.8
1985	105.0	105.0	104.9	107.2	102.3	106.4	106.2	...	106.1	113.7	98.7	98.6	95.9	106.8
1986	105.9	106.2	104.0	111.8	101.9	102.3	101.2	...	110.6	108.8	77.1	77.0	95.4	110.3
1987	110.6	109.1	110.4	112.1	105.1	105.4	104.2	...	114.4	113.1	80.2	80.1	96.1	114.8
1988	115.4	113.4	114.9	116.4	109.9	108.7	107.6	...	116.5	118.0	80.9	80.8	97.9	119.7
1989	118.6	117.0	116.4	119.1	114.4	114.1	112.9	...	119.2	120.4	88.5	88.5	100.2	124.9
1990	124.1	120.4	122.6	125.8	117.4	120.5	118.8	...	121.4	117.6	101.2	101.0	100.9	130.1
1991	128.7	124.2	127.6	128.9	120.9	123.8	121.9	...	126.0	118.1	99.4	99.2	102.2	136.0
1992	131.9	126.5	130.4	129.3	125.0	126.5	124.6	...	129.2	123.2	99.0	99.0	103.1	141.3
1993	133.7	127.5	132.6	127.1	125.9	130.4	127.5	91.8	132.7	133.9	98.0	97.7	101.6	145.9
1994	133.4	126.4	130.9	128.1	126.0	134.3	131.4	95.5	137.6	141.7	98.5	98.2	101.4	150.2
1995	132.0	126.2	126.9	127.2	125.4	139.1	136.3	99.4	141.0	156.5	100.0	99.8	102.1	154.0
1996	131.7	127.7	124.7	129.7	126.6	143.0	140.0	101.0	143.7	157.0	106.3	105.9	102.2	158.4
1997	132.9	130.1	126.1	129.0	127.6	144.3	141.0	100.5	144.3	151.1	106.2	105.8	101.9	162.7
1998	133.0	131.8	126.0	126.1	128.0	141.6	137.9	100.1	143.4	150.6	92.2	91.6	101.1	167.1
1999	131.3	131.1	123.3	129.0	125.7	144.4	140.5	100.1	142.9	152.0	100.7	100.1	100.5	171.9
2000	129.6	129.7	121.5	130.6	123.8	153.3	149.1	100.8	142.8	155.8	129.3	128.6	101.5	177.3
2001	127.3	125.7	119.3	129.2	123.0	154.3	150.0	101.3	142.1	158.7	124.7	124.0	104.8	183.5
2002	124.0	121.7	115.8	126.4	121.4	152.9	148.8	99.2	140.0	152.0	116.6	116.0	106.9	190.2
2003	120.9	118.0	113.1	122.1	119.6	157.6	153.6	96.5	137.9	142.9	135.8	135.1	107.8	195.6
2004	120.4	117.5	113.0	118.5	119.3	163.1	159.4	94.2	137.1	133.3	160.4	159.7	108.7	200.2
2005	119.5	116.1	110.8	116.7	122.6	173.9	170.2	95.6	137.9	139.4	195.7	194.7	111.9	206.9
2006	119.5	114.1	110.7	116.5	123.5	180.9	177.0	95.6	137.6	140.0	221.0	219.9	117.3	215.6
2007	119.0	112.4	110.3	113.9	122.4	184.7	180.8	94.3	136.3	135.7	239.1	238.0	121.6	223.0
2008	118.9	113.0	107.5	113.8	124.2	195.5	191.0	93.3	134.2	134.0	279.7	277.5	128.7	233.9
2007														
January	120.0	112.6	112.3	114.6	123.0	177.9	173.9	94.3	136.4	135.3	210.6	209.6	119.8	219.3
February	120.6	112.5	113.0	115.3	122.9	177.5	173.5	94.1	136.2	134.6	209.1	208.1	120.2	220.2
March	119.4	112.0	111.5	115.6	122.3	180.8	176.8	94.2	136.5	134.4	223.1	222.1	120.5	221.0
April	119.1	112.3	111.1	113.5	121.8	181.9	178.0	94.2	136.6	134.4	228.3	227.3	120.7	221.6
May	118.7	112.1	110.7	112.5	121.8	184.5	180.8	94.1	136.3	134.5	241.1	240.1	121.0	222.1
June	118.3	112.0	109.2	112.9	121.5	184.8	181.0	94.2	136.3	135.1	241.3	240.2	120.9	222.7
July	118.7	113.0	109.2	112.2	122.9	185.3	181.6	94.4	136.3	136.0	242.1	240.9	121.5	223.5
August	118.1	112.2	109.0	112.4	122.3	184.3	180.4	94.6	136.4	137.1	235.9	234.7	121.7	224.2
September	118.3	112.8	108.8	113.3	121.9	185.6	181.7	94.4	136.1	137.1	241.3	240.2	122.3	224.5
October	118.4	112.4	108.7	114.8	122.2	186.1	182.1	94.4	136.0	137.0	243.6	242.5	123.0	224.8
November	119.1	112.3	109.6	115.7	123.5	192.7	188.8	94.4	136.0	136.6	272.3	271.1	123.5	225.4
December	119.2	112.2	110.4	114.6	122.5	194.7	190.7	94.4	136.0	136.9	279.9	278.6	123.9	226.1
2008														
January	119.8	112.9	110.7	116.0	123.2	195.7	191.8	94.3	135.6	137.2	283.0	281.9	124.3	227.7
February	119.4	114.2	108.4	115.6	123.3	194.4	190.4	94.2	135.2	137.2	277.4	276.1	125.2	228.4
March	117.8	113.3	105.5	113.7	123.2	195.8	191.6	94.1	135.0	137.2	282.0	279.8	126.3	229.6
April	118.4	113.8	105.5	114.4	124.3	194.5	190.3	93.9	134.8	136.8	276.6	274.3	126.0	230.7
May	118.0	114.2	105.2	113.4	124.3	198.5	194.1	93.8	134.7	136.3	292.2	289.9	126.8	231.8
June	118.1	113.1	105.7	112.9	124.5	205.9	201.5	93.9	135.0	136.0	321.6	319.1	127.8	233.3
July	119.6	113.1	107.9	112.6	126.0	209.4	204.9	94.1	135.3	135.8	334.7	332.2	129.1	234.8
August	120.2	113.4	110.1	111.7	124.0	206.3	201.6	93.7	134.5	135.4	320.6	318.3	130.3	236.3
September	120.0	113.1	109.7	113.2	123.6	205.0	200.4	92.9	133.6	132.9	318.0	316.4	131.0	237.3
October	118.8	112.5	107.3	113.8	123.9	194.0	189.3	92.2	132.9	129.7	273.7	271.6	131.9	238.1
November	119.2	111.8	108.0	114.4	125.3	175.1	169.9	91.4	132.2	126.9	194.3	191.4	132.9	238.8
December	118.0	110.9	106.4	113.4	124.3	167.4	162.0	91.1	131.6	125.9	161.7	158.5	133.1	239.4

[1]Not seasonally adjusted.
[3]December 1997 = 100.
. . . = Not available.

Table 8-1. Consumer Price Indexes, All Urban Consumers (CPI-U)—*Continued*

(1982–1984 = 100, except as noted; seasonally adjusted, except as noted.)

Year and month	Transportation—Continued		Medical care					Recreation	Video and audio [3]	Education and communication			
	Public transportation	Transportation services	Medical care, total	Medical care commodities	Medical care services			Total [3]		Total [3]	Education		
					Total	Professional services	Hospital and related services				Total [3]	Educational books and supplies	Tuition, other school fees, and childcare
1965	25.2	30.3	25.2	45.0	22.7	. . .	. . .	. . .	. . .	. . .	. . .	. . .	. . .
1966	26.1	31.6	26.3	45.1	23.9	. . .	. . .	. . .	. . .	. . .	. . .	. . .	. . .
1967	27.4	32.6	28.2	44.9	26.0	30.9	. . .	. . .	. . .	. . .	. . .	33.7	. . .
1968	28.7	33.9	29.9	45.0	27.9	32.5	. . .	. . .	. . .	. . .	. . .	35.4	. . .
1969	30.9	36.3	31.9	45.4	30.2	34.7	. . .	. . .	. . .	. . .	. . .	37.4	. . .
1970	35.2	40.2	34.0	46.5	32.3	37.0	. . .	. . .	. . .	. . .	. . .	38.8	. . .
1971	37.8	43.4	36.1	47.3	34.7	39.4	. . .	. . .	. . .	. . .	. . .	41.4	. . .
1972	39.3	44.4	37.3	47.4	35.9	40.8	. . .	. . .	. . .	. . .	. . .	44.2	. . .
1973	39.7	44.7	38.8	47.5	37.5	42.2	. . .	. . .	. . .	. . .	. . .	45.6	. . .
1974	40.6	46.3	42.4	49.2	41.4	45.8	. . .	. . .	. . .	. . .	. . .	47.2	. . .
1975	43.5	49.8	47.5	53.3	46.6	50.8	. . .	. . .	. . .	. . .	. . .	50.3	. . .
1976	47.8	56.9	52.0	56.5	51.3	55.5	. . .	. . .	. . .	. . .	. . .	53.7	. . .
1977	50.0	61.5	57.0	60.2	56.4	60.0	. . .	. . .	. . .	. . .	. . .	56.9	. . .
1978	51.5	64.4	61.8	64.4	61.2	64.5	55.1	. . .	. . .	. . .	. . .	61.6	59.8
1979	54.9	69.5	67.5	69.0	67.2	70.1	61.0	. . .	. . .	. . .	. . .	65.7	64.7
1980	69.0	79.2	74.9	75.4	74.8	77.9	69.2	. . .	. . .	. . .	. . .	71.4	71.2
1981	85.6	88.6	82.9	83.7	82.8	85.9	79.1	. . .	. . .	. . .	. . .	80.3	79.9
1982	94.9	96.1	92.5	92.3	92.6	93.2	90.3	. . .	. . .	. . .	. . .	91.0	90.5
1983	99.5	99.1	100.6	100.2	100.7	99.8	100.5	. . .	. . .	. . .	. . .	100.3	99.7
1984	105.7	104.8	106.8	107.5	106.7	107.0	109.2	. . .	. . .	. . .	. . .	108.7	109.8
1985	110.5	110.0	113.5	115.2	113.2	113.5	116.1	. . .	. . .	. . .	. . .	118.2	119.7
1986	117.0	116.3	122.0	122.8	121.9	120.8	123.1	. . .	. . .	. . .	. . .	128.1	129.6
1987	121.1	121.9	130.1	131.0	130.0	128.8	131.6	. . .	. . .	. . .	. . .	138.1	140.0
1988	123.3	128.0	138.6	139.9	138.3	137.5	143.9	. . .	. . .	. . .	. . .	148.1	151.0
1989	129.5	135.6	149.3	150.8	148.9	146.4	160.5	. . .	. . .	. . .	. . .	158.0	162.7
1990	142.6	144.2	162.8	163.4	162.7	156.1	178.0	. . .	. . .	. . .	. . .	171.3	175.7
1991	148.9	151.2	177.0	176.8	177.1	165.7	196.1	. . .	. . .	. . .	. . .	180.3	191.4
1992	151.4	155.7	190.1	188.1	190.5	175.8	214.0	. . .	. . .	. . .	. . .	190.3	208.5
1993	167.0	162.9	201.4	195.0	202.9	184.7	231.9	90.7	96.5	85.5	78.4	197.6	225.3
1994	172.0	168.6	211.0	200.7	213.4	192.5	245.6	92.7	95.4	88.8	83.3	205.5	239.8
1995	175.9	175.9	220.5	204.5	224.2	201.0	257.8	94.5	95.1	92.2	88.0	214.4	253.8
1996	181.9	180.5	228.2	210.4	232.4	208.3	269.5	97.4	96.6	95.3	92.7	226.9	267.1
1997	186.7	185.0	234.6	215.3	239.1	215.4	278.4	99.6	99.4	98.4	97.3	238.4	280.4
1998	190.3	187.9	242.1	221.8	246.8	222.2	287.5	101.1	101.1	100.3	102.1	250.8	294.2
1999	197.7	190.7	250.6	230.7	255.1	229.2	299.5	102.0	100.7	101.2	107.0	261.7	308.4
2000	209.6	196.1	260.8	238.1	266.0	237.7	317.3	103.3	101.0	102.5	112.5	279.9	324.0
2001	210.6	201.9	272.8	247.6	278.8	246.5	338.3	104.9	101.5	105.2	118.5	295.9	341.1
2002	207.4	209.1	285.6	256.4	292.9	253.9	367.8	106.2	102.8	107.9	126.0	317.6	362.1
2003	209.3	216.3	297.1	262.8	306.0	261.2	394.8	107.5	103.6	109.8	134.4	335.4	386.7
2004	209.1	220.6	310.1	269.3	321.3	271.5	417.9	108.6	104.2	111.6	143.7	351.0	414.3
2005	217.3	225.7	323.2	276.0	336.7	281.7	439.9	109.4	104.2	113.7	152.7	365.6	440.9
2006	226.6	230.8	336.2	285.9	350.6	289.3	468.1	110.9	104.6	116.8	162.1	388.9	468.1
2007	230.0	233.7	351.1	290.0	369.3	300.8	498.9	111.4	102.9	119.6	171.4	420.4	494.1
2008	250.5	244.1	364.1	296.0	384.9	311.0	534.0	113.3	102.6	123.6	181.3	450.2	522.1
2007													
January	226.2	232.1	343.8	288.5	360.1	295.7	481.9	111.2	103.1	117.6	167.1	404.6	482.2
February	227.3	232.4	345.5	287.7	362.6	297.6	484.8	111.2	103.1	117.9	167.9	405.3	484.5
March	227.9	232.6	345.9	287.0	363.4	297.8	487.0	111.2	102.7	118.5	168.8	411.5	486.9
April	227.5	232.5	347.3	288.3	364.8	298.2	490.5	111.2	102.7	118.8	169.6	413.8	489.0
May	226.7	231.9	348.5	288.5	366.4	299.0	493.7	111.4	103.0	119.5	170.3	415.6	491.1
June	227.9	232.7	349.5	288.4	367.8	299.8	495.8	111.4	103.3	119.5	170.8	416.7	492.7
July	228.1	233.5	351.5	289.9	370.0	300.9	500.0	111.3	102.8	119.8	171.7	421.6	495.0
August	229.4	234.2	353.2	290.9	371.9	302.4	502.9	111.2	102.4	120.2	172.4	427.9	496.7
September	230.9	234.8	354.5	291.1	373.6	303.1	506.8	111.5	102.9	120.4	172.9	429.0	498.2
October	233.3	235.2	356.4	292.1	375.8	304.2	511.7	111.8	103.1	120.7	174.1	430.2	501.5
November	236.4	236.0	357.7	293.4	377.2	304.9	514.7	112.0	103.0	120.8	175.0	432.7	504.2
December	238.6	236.9	358.9	294.2	378.3	305.9	517.5	112.0	103.3	121.1	175.9	436.3	506.5
2008													
January	239.4	238.2	360.8	295.8	380.5	307.0	522.9	112.2	103.3	121.6	176.9	436.6	509.7
February	239.1	238.4	361.2	296.2	380.8	307.2	524.6	112.4	103.1	121.7	177.4	436.4	511.3
March	245.1	240.1	361.7	297.4	381.0	307.5	525.7	112.7	103.4	122.1	178.1	437.6	513.5
April	244.1	240.4	362.2	296.9	382.0	308.1	528.5	112.6	102.9	122.6	179.2	441.7	516.5
May	249.9	242.4	362.8	294.7	383.8	310.2	530.6	112.7	102.4	123.0	180.0	443.7	518.6
June	258.5	245.1	363.6	295.1	384.7	311.1	532.6	112.8	102.2	123.6	180.7	444.5	521.0
July	261.3	246.4	363.9	294.4	385.4	311.7	534.2	113.3	102.2	124.2	181.6	447.8	523.3
August	264.2	248.3	364.7	294.7	386.5	312.6	537.5	113.9	102.7	124.5	182.7	459.5	525.8
September	261.6	248.4	365.8	295.2	387.8	313.3	540.5	114.1	102.8	124.6	183.5	461.6	527.9
October	252.9	247.4	366.5	295.7	388.5	313.6	542.7	114.2	102.2	124.9	184.3	462.5	530.3
November	246.1	246.7	367.3	297.5	388.9	314.5	542.5	114.2	102.1	125.2	184.9	463.9	532.2
December	242.9	246.8	368.4	299.0	389.7	315.0	545.5	114.0	102.2	125.6	185.8	466.7	534.6

[3]December 1997 = 100.
. . . = Not available.

Table 8-1. Consumer Price Indexes, All Urban Consumers (CPI-U)—*Continued*

(1982–1984 = 100; seasonally adjusted, except as noted.)

Year and month	Education and communication—Continued					Other goods and services					Commodity and service groups of CPI-U		
	Communication							Personal care					
		Information and information processing											
				Information technology, hardware, and services			Tobacco and smoking products [1]						Energy
	Total [3]	Total [1,3]	Telephone services [1,3]	Total [1,4]	Personal computers and peripheral equipment [1,5]	Total		Total	Personal care products [1]	Personal care services [1]	Commodities	Services	
1965	...	...	...	...	...	...	32.6	36.6	38.4	34.8	35.2	26.6	22.9
1966	...	...	...	...	...	...	34.2	37.3	38.0	36.4	36.1	27.6	23.3
1967	...	...	...	...	...	35.1	35.5	38.4	38.6	38.1	36.8	28.8	23.8
1968	...	...	...	...	...	36.9	37.8	40.0	39.8	40.1	38.1	30.3	24.2
1969	...	...	...	...	...	38.7	39.8	42.0	41.6	42.2	39.9	32.4	24.8
1970	...	...	...	...	...	40.9	43.1	43.5	42.7	44.2	41.7	35.0	25.5
1971	...	...	...	...	...	42.9	44.9	44.9	44.0	45.7	43.2	37.0	26.5
1972	...	...	...	...	...	44.7	47.4	46.0	45.2	46.8	44.5	38.4	27.2
1973	...	...	...	...	...	46.4	48.7	48.1	46.4	49.7	47.8	40.1	29.4
1974	...	...	...	...	...	49.8	51.1	52.8	51.5	53.9	53.5	43.8	38.1
1975	...	...	...	...	...	53.9	54.7	57.9	58.0	57.7	58.2	48.0	42.1
1976	...	...	...	...	...	57.0	57.0	61.7	61.3	61.9	60.7	52.0	45.1
1977	...	...	...	...	...	60.4	59.8	65.7	64.7	66.4	64.2	56.0	49.4
1978	...	...	...	...	...	64.3	63.0	69.9	68.2	71.3	68.8	60.8	52.5
1979	...	...	...	...	...	68.9	66.8	75.2	72.9	77.2	76.6	67.5	65.7
1980	...	...	...	...	...	75.2	72.0	81.9	79.6	83.7	86.0	77.9	86.0
1981	...	...	...	...	...	82.6	77.8	89.1	87.8	90.2	93.2	88.1	97.7
1982	...	...	...	...	...	91.1	86.5	95.4	95.1	95.7	97.0	96.0	99.2
1983	...	...	...	...	...	101.1	103.4	100.3	100.7	100.0	99.8	99.4	99.9
1984	...	...	...	...	...	107.9	110.1	104.3	104.2	104.4	103.2	104.6	100.9
1985	...	...	...	...	...	114.5	116.7	108.3	107.6	108.9	105.4	109.9	101.6
1986	...	...	...	...	...	121.4	124.7	111.9	111.3	112.5	104.4	115.4	88.2
1987	...	...	...	...	...	128.5	133.6	115.1	113.9	116.2	107.7	120.2	88.6
1988	...	...	...	...	...	137.0	145.8	119.4	118.1	120.7	111.5	125.7	89.3
1989	...	...	...	96.3	...	147.7	164.4	125.0	123.2	126.8	116.7	131.9	94.3
1990	...	...	...	93.5	...	159.0	181.5	130.4	128.2	132.8	122.8	139.2	102.1
1991	...	...	...	88.6	...	171.6	202.7	134.9	132.8	137.0	126.6	146.3	102.5
1992	...	...	...	83.7	...	183.3	219.8	138.3	136.5	140.0	129.1	152.0	103.0
1993	96.7	97.7	...	78.8	...	192.9	228.4	141.5	139.0	144.0	131.5	157.9	104.2
1994	97.6	98.6	...	72.0	...	198.5	220.0	144.6	141.5	147.9	133.8	163.1	104.6
1995	98.8	98.7	...	63.8	...	206.9	225.7	147.1	143.1	151.5	136.4	168.7	105.2
1996	99.6	99.5	...	57.2	...	215.4	232.8	150.1	144.3	156.6	139.9	174.1	110.1
1997	100.3	100.4	...	50.1	...	224.8	243.7	152.7	144.2	162.4	141.8	179.4	111.5
1998	98.7	98.5	100.7	39.9	875.1	237.7	274.8	156.7	148.3	166.0	141.9	184.2	102.9
1999	96.0	95.5	100.1	30.5	598.7	258.3	355.8	161.1	151.8	171.4	144.4	188.8	106.6
2000	93.6	92.8	98.5	25.9	459.9	271.1	394.9	165.6	153.7	178.1	149.2	195.3	124.6
2001	93.3	92.3	99.3	21.3	330.1	282.6	425.2	170.5	155.1	184.3	150.7	203.4	129.3
2002	92.3	90.8	99.7	18.3	248.4	293.2	461.5	174.7	154.7	188.4	149.7	209.8	121.7
2003	89.7	87.8	98.3	16.1	196.9	298.7	469.0	178.0	153.5	193.2	151.2	216.5	136.5
2004	86.7	84.6	95.8	14.8	171.2	304.7	478.0	181.7	153.9	197.6	154.7	222.8	151.4
2005	84.7	82.6	94.9	13.6	143.2	313.4	502.8	185.6	154.4	203.9	160.2	230.1	177.1
2006	84.1	81.7	95.8	12.5	120.9	321.7	519.9	190.2	155.8	209.7	164.0	238.9	196.9
2007	83.4	80.7	98.2	10.6	108.4	333.3	554.2	195.6	158.3	216.6	167.5	246.8	207.7
2008	84.2	81.4	100.5	10.1	94.9	345.4	588.7	201.3	159.3	223.7	174.8	255.5	236.7
2007													
January	82.8	80.2	96.9	10.9	114.8	329.2	543.5	193.6	157.7	214.0	163.6	243.2	191.6
February	82.8	80.3	97.1	10.9	113.9	330.1	548.9	193.8	158.0	214.6	164.0	244.1	192.2
March	83.1	80.6	97.5	10.9	114.0	330.7	550.0	194.1	158.6	215.1	165.3	244.6	199.9
April	83.2	80.7	97.6	10.9	113.8	331.4	547.7	194.8	158.7	215.4	165.9	245.3	202.4
May	83.8	81.2	98.5	10.8	111.6	332.4	549.7	195.3	158.6	216.2	167.2	245.9	208.8
June	83.6	80.9	98.5	10.6	108.6	333.2	552.3	195.7	158.8	215.9	167.5	246.7	209.2
July	83.6	80.8	98.6	10.5	107.4	333.6	554.0	195.8	158.5	216.7	167.9	247.2	209.4
August	83.7	80.9	98.8	10.5	106.6	334.0	555.2	196.0	157.8	217.0	167.5	247.6	205.7
September	83.7	81.0	98.9	10.5	105.8	335.2	559.6	196.5	157.6	217.6	168.3	248.4	208.5
October	83.7	80.9	99.0	10.4	104.3	335.8	560.6	196.9	158.4	217.9	168.7	249.1	210.7
November	83.3	80.5	98.8	10.2	100.1	336.7	562.0	197.4	158.6	218.6	171.7	249.8	225.2
December	83.3	80.5	98.8	10.2	100.0	337.6	566.7	197.6	158.2	219.7	172.5	250.5	229.1
2008													
January	83.4	80.6	98.9	10.2	101.0	339.1	572.7	198.1	158.2	219.9	173.4	251.3	230.6
February	83.4	80.6	98.8	10.3	100.5	339.9	575.2	198.5	157.7	220.8	173.0	251.8	229.4
March	83.5	80.8	99.0	10.2	100.4	341.4	574.9	199.6	158.4	222.8	173.6	252.7	233.8
April	83.7	80.9	99.5	10.2	98.9	343.1	576.4	200.8	159.4	222.8	173.7	253.5	233.8
May	83.9	81.1	99.9	10.1	97.0	344.3	581.2	201.2	158.8	223.6	175.3	254.6	244.1
June	84.4	81.5	100.7	10.1	95.7	345.7	589.9	201.4	158.9	223.5	178.6	255.9	260.3
July	84.8	82.0	101.3	10.1	94.7	347.0	596.8	201.7	159.0	223.7	180.7	257.3	270.6
August	84.7	81.8	101.3	10.0	92.9	347.7	597.4	202.2	159.3	224.2	179.7	257.6	262.1
September	84.5	81.6	101.3	9.9	90.8	348.5	597.6	202.8	159.6	224.6	179.5	257.7	257.1
October	84.5	81.7	101.4	9.9	89.9	349.4	599.7	203.2	159.8	225.6	175.3	257.7	235.1
November	84.6	81.7	101.5	9.9	89.0	349.3	599.8	203.1	161.0	226.2	168.1	257.8	195.1
December	84.7	81.9	101.7	9.9	88.5	349.2	602.6	202.8	161.4	226.3	164.8	258.0	178.9

[1]Not seasonally adjusted.
[3]December 1997 = 100.
[4]December 1988 = 100.
[5]December 2007 = 100.
... = Not available.

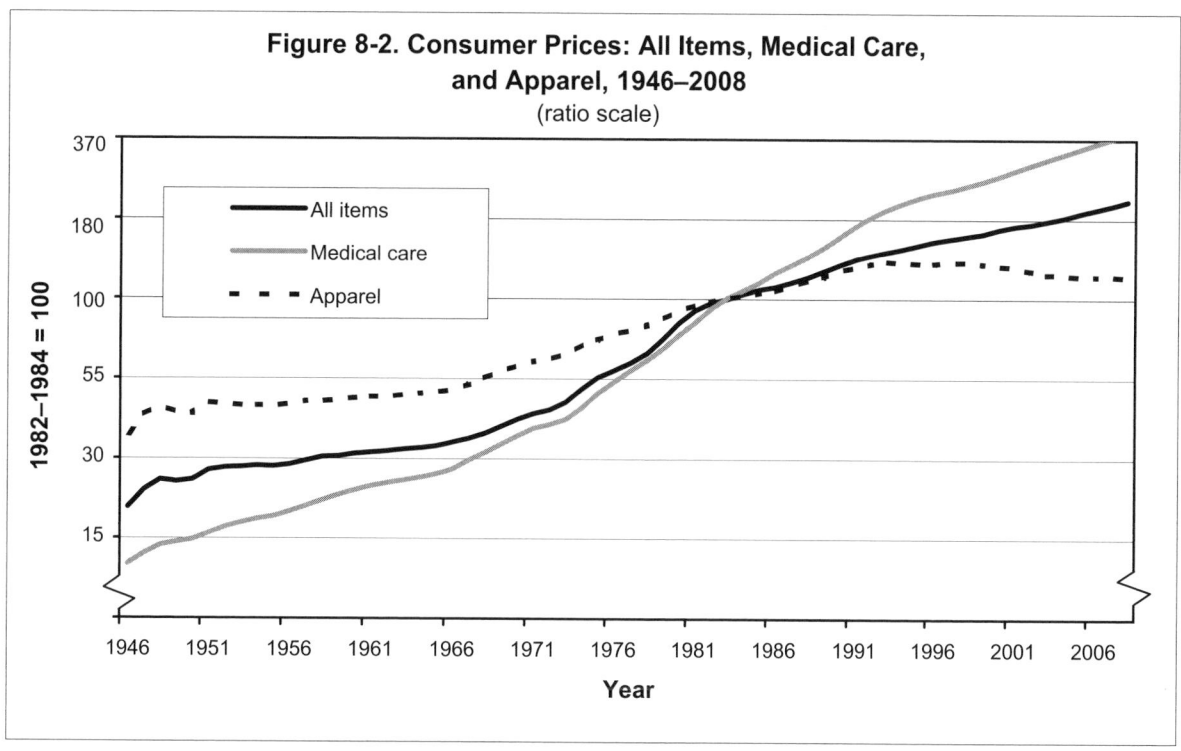

Figure 8-2. Consumer Prices: All Items, Medical Care, and Apparel, 1946–2008
(ratio scale)

- Figure 8-2 charts two components of the Consumer Price Index for All Urban Consumers (CPI-U) along with the all-items total. Since all three indexes have the base years 1982–1984, they converge around 100 in those years. However, over the entire postwar period, the trends of the two components are very different. (Tables 8-1 and 20-2)

- Apparel has been one of the areas most subject to international competition, and the apparel index shows far less growth than the overall average of prices.

- Medical care, on the other hand, has little price competition from producers in other countries. It is often paid for by third-party insurers, both government and private, rather than directly by consumers. Furthermore, it is characterized by trend growth in demand, due to rising income and expectations and to technological progress. All of these economic factors cause medical care prices to rise faster than the general price level.

- Medical care has arguably been overstated in the CPI due to the difficulties of making quality adjustments. Quality adjustments have been much improved in recent years, although such improvements are not retroactively introduced into the official CPIs. But even since 1997, when a major improvement was introduced into the hospital cost component of the CPI, measured medical care prices have increased at a 4.1 percent annual rate, while the total CPI rose at a 2.7 percent average annual rate. (Table 8-1)

- Medical care spending accounts for a greater proportion of out-of-pocket spending by senior citizens than for the public in general. This is true even though the Consumer Expenditure Survey, which determines the weights for the CPIs, does not include spending by government and private insurance companies. For this reason, when the CPI is re-weighted to reflect the out-of-pocket spending patterns of persons age 62 years and over, the resulting "CPI-E" rises an average of 0.2 percentage points per year more rapidly than the CPI-U from 1983 to 2008—and 0.3 percentage points faster than the CPI-W, which is the index actually used to escalate Social Security payments. (Table 8-3)

Table 8-2. Alternative Measures of Total and Core Consumer Prices: Index Levels

(Various bases; monthly data seasonally adjusted, except as noted.)

Year and month	CPIs, all items						CPIs, all items less food and energy			Chain-type price indexes for personal consumption expenditures (PCE), 2000 = 100			
												Excluding food and energy	
	CPI-U, 1982–1984 = 100	CPI-W, 1982–1984 = 100	CPI-U-X1, 1982–1984 = 100	CPI-E, Dec. 1982 = 100, not seasonally adjusted	CPI-U-RS, Dec. 1977 = 100, not seasonally adjusted	C-CPI-U, Dec. 1999 = 100, not seasonally adjusted	CPI-U, 1982–1984 = 100	CPI-U-RS, Dec. 1977 = 100, not seasonally adjusted	C-CPI-U, Dec. 1999 = 100, not seasonally adjusted	PCE, total	PCE, market-based	PCE, total	PCE, market-based
1960	29.6	29.8	32.2	. . .	. . .	. . .	30.6	. . .	. . .	20.8	. . .	21.4	. . .
1961	29.9	30.1	32.5	. . .	. . .	. . .	31.0	. . .	. . .	21.0	. . .	21.6	. . .
1962	30.2	30.4	32.8	. . .	. . .	. . .	31.4	. . .	. . .	21.2	. . .	21.9	. . .
1963	30.6	30.8	33.3	. . .	. . .	. . .	31.8	. . .	. . .	21.5	. . .	22.2	. . .
1964	31.0	31.2	33.7	. . .	. . .	. . .	32.3	. . .	. . .	21.8	. . .	22.5	. . .
1965	31.5	31.7	34.2	. . .	. . .	. . .	32.7	. . .	. . .	22.1	. . .	22.8	. . .
1966	32.4	32.6	35.2	. . .	. . .	. . .	33.5	. . .	. . .	22.7	. . .	23.2	. . .
1967	33.4	33.6	36.3	. . .	. . .	. . .	34.7	. . .	. . .	23.2	. . .	23.9	. . .
1968	34.8	35.0	37.7	. . .	. . .	. . .	36.3	. . .	. . .	24.2	. . .	24.9	. . .
1969	36.7	36.9	39.4	. . .	. . .	. . .	38.4	. . .	. . .	25.3	. . .	26.1	. . .
1970	38.8	39.0	41.3	. . .	. . .	. . .	40.8	. . .	. . .	26.4	. . .	27.3	. . .
1971	40.5	40.7	43.1	. . .	. . .	. . .	42.7	. . .	. . .	27.6	. . .	28.5	. . .
1972	41.8	42.1	44.4	. . .	. . .	. . .	44.0	. . .	. . .	28.5	. . .	29.5	. . .
1973	44.4	44.7	47.2	. . .	. . .	. . .	45.6	. . .	. . .	30.1	. . .	30.5	. . .
1974	49.3	49.6	51.9	. . .	. . .	. . .	49.4	. . .	. . .	33.2	. . .	32.8	. . .
1975	53.8	54.1	56.2	. . .	. . .	. . .	53.9	. . .	. . .	36.0	. . .	35.5	. . .
1976	56.9	57.2	59.4	. . .	. . .	. . .	57.4	. . .	. . .	37.9	. . .	37.7	. . .
1977	60.6	60.9	63.2	. . .	. . .	. . .	61.0	. . .	. . .	40.4	. . .	40.1	. . .
1978	65.2	65.6	67.5	. . .	104.4	. . .	65.5	103.6	. . .	43.2	. . .	42.8	. . .
1979	72.6	73.1	74.0	. . .	114.4	. . .	71.9	111.0	. . .	47.1	. . .	45.7	. . .
1980	82.4	82.9	82.3	. . .	127.1	. . .	80.8	120.9	. . .	52.1	. . .	49.9	. . .
1981	90.9	91.4	90.1	. . .	139.2	. . .	89.2	132.2	. . .	56.7	. . .	54.2	. . .
1982	96.5	96.9	95.6	. . .	147.6	. . .	95.8	142.4	. . .	59.9	. . .	57.8	. . .
1983	99.6	99.8	99.6	102.1	153.9	. . .	99.6	150.4	. . .	62.4	. . .	60.8	. . .
1984	103.9	103.3	103.9	106.5	160.2	. . .	104.6	157.9	. . .	64.8	. . .	63.4	. . .
1985	107.6	106.9	107.6	110.5	165.7	. . .	109.1	164.8	. . .	66.9	. . .	65.8	. . .
1986	109.6	108.6	109.6	113.3	168.7	. . .	113.5	171.4	. . .	68.6	. . .	68.2	. . .
1987	113.6	112.5	113.6	117.7	174.4	. . .	118.2	178.1	. . .	70.9	. . .	70.8	. . .
1988	118.3	117.0	118.3	122.7	180.8	. . .	123.4	185.2	. . .	73.8	. . .	73.8	. . .
1989	124.0	122.6	124.0	128.9	188.6	. . .	129.0	192.6	. . .	77.0	. . .	76.9	. . .
1990	130.7	129.0	130.7	136.6	198.0	. . .	135.5	201.4	. . .	80.5	. . .	80.2	. . .
1991	136.2	134.3	136.2	143.0	205.1	. . .	142.1	209.9	. . .	83.4	. . .	83.3	. . .
1992	140.3	138.2	140.3	147.6	210.3	. . .	147.3	216.4	. . .	85.8	. . .	86.1	. . .
1993	144.5	142.1	144.5	152.2	215.5	. . .	152.2	222.5	. . .	87.8	. . .	88.3	. . .
1994	148.2	145.6	148.2	156.6	220.1	. . .	156.5	227.7	. . .	89.7	. . .	90.4	. . .
1995	152.4	149.8	152.4	161.2	225.4	. . .	161.2	233.4	. . .	91.6	. . .	92.4	. . .
1996	156.9	154.1	156.9	166.1	231.4	. . .	165.6	239.1	. . .	93.5	. . .	94.1	. . .
1997	160.5	157.6	160.5	170.1	236.4	. . .	169.5	244.4	. . .	95.1	95.8	95.6	96.6
1998	163.0	159.7	163.0	173.2	239.7	. . .	173.4	249.7	. . .	96.0	96.4	96.9	97.6
1999	166.6	163.2	166.6	177.3	244.7	. . .	177.0	254.8	. . .	97.6	97.7	98.3	98.6
2000	172.2	168.9	172.2	183.5	252.9	102.0	181.3	260.8	101.4	100.0	100.0	100.0	100.0
2001	177.1	173.5	177.1	189.2	260.0	104.3	186.1	267.8	103.5	102.1	101.9	101.9	101.7
2002	179.9	175.9	179.9	192.7	264.2	105.6	190.5	273.9	105.4	103.5	103.1	103.7	103.2
2003	184.0	179.8	184.0	197.4	270.1	107.8	193.2	277.9	106.6	105.6	105.0	105.2	104.3
2004	188.9	184.5	188.9	203.3	277.4	110.5	196.6	282.9	108.4	108.4	107.4	107.3	105.9
2005	195.3	191.0	195.3	210.4	286.7	113.7	200.9	289.0	110.4	111.6	110.3	109.6	107.7
2006	201.6	197.1	201.6	217.3	296.1	117.0	205.9	296.2	112.9	114.7	113.2	112.1	109.7
2007	207.3	202.8	207.3	223.8	304.5	120.0	210.7	303.1	115.0	117.7	115.9	114.5	111.7
2008	215.3	211.1	215.3	232.4	316.2	¹123.9	215.6	310.1	¹117.2	121.6	119.8	117.0	113.8
2007													
January	203.6	198.8	203.6	218.8	297.2	117.3	208.6	299.2	113.8	115.9	114.2	113.5	110.9
February	204.4	199.6	204.4	220.1	298.8	117.9	209.1	300.8	114.3	116.2	114.5	113.7	111.2
March	205.3	200.8	205.3	221.8	301.6	118.9	209.3	302.0	114.6	116.6	114.9	113.8	111.2
April	205.9	201.3	205.9	223.1	303.5	119.7	209.7	302.5	114.8	116.9	115.2	114.0	111.3
May	206.7	202.2	206.7	224.2	305.4	120.3	210.1	302.5	114.8	117.3	115.6	114.2	111.4
June	207.0	202.4	207.0	224.8	306.0	120.4	210.5	302.8	114.8	117.6	115.8	114.4	111.6
July	207.3	202.7	207.3	224.9	305.9	120.4	210.9	303.2	114.9	117.8	116.0	114.6	111.7
August	207.5	202.9	207.5	224.6	305.3	120.3	211.2	303.7	115.2	117.9	116.0	114.8	111.8
September	208.4	203.8	208.4	224.9	306.2	120.6	211.6	304.4	115.5	118.3	116.4	115.1	112.0
October	209.1	204.6	209.1	225.4	306.8	120.9	212.1	305.4	115.8	118.6	116.7	115.3	112.3
November	211.2	206.9	211.2	226.6	308.6	121.5	212.6	305.6	115.8	119.3	117.5	115.5	112.4
December	211.7	207.5	211.7	226.5	308.4	121.3	213.2	305.5	115.6	119.7	117.9	115.7	112.6
2008													
January	212.5	208.3	212.5	227.9	310.0	¹121.9	213.7	306.6	¹116.0	120.1	118.3	116.0	112.9
February	212.9	208.7	212.9	228.7	310.9	¹122.2	213.9	307.6	¹116.4	120.2	118.4	116.1	113.0
March	213.7	209.5	213.7	230.7	313.6	¹123.2	214.3	309.1	¹116.9	120.6	118.7	116.4	113.1
April	214.0	209.8	214.0	231.8	315.5	¹123.8	214.5	309.4	¹117.0	120.9	119.0	116.5	113.3
May	215.0	210.9	215.0	233.5	318.1	¹124.6	215.0	309.5	¹117.1	121.4	119.6	116.7	113.5
June	217.0	213.1	217.0	235.8	321.3	¹125.6	215.6	310.1	¹117.2	122.3	120.6	117.1	113.8
July	218.6	214.8	218.6	237.2	323.0	¹126.1	216.2	310.8	¹117.4	123.0	121.3	117.3	114.0
August	218.6	214.7	218.6	236.2	321.7	¹125.8	216.5	311.4	¹117.6	123.0	121.3	117.5	114.2
September	218.7	214.8	218.7	235.5	321.3	¹125.7	216.8	311.9	¹117.8	123.1	121.4	117.7	114.4
October	216.9	212.6	216.9	233.5	318.0	¹124.8	216.8	312.2	¹117.9	122.6	120.8	117.7	114.5
November	213.3	208.1	213.3	229.8	311.9	¹122.3	216.9	311.7	¹117.5	121.3	119.2	117.8	114.5
December	211.6	206.1	211.6	227.8	308.7	¹120.6	216.9	310.9	¹117.2	120.7	118.5	117.7	114.5

¹Interim values.
. . . = Not available.

Table 8-3. Alternative Measures of Total and Core Consumer Prices: Inflation Rates

(Percent changes from year earlier, except as noted; monthly data seasonally adjusted, except as noted.)

Year and month	CPIs, all items						CPIs, all items less food and energy			Chain-type price indexes for personal consumption expenditures (PCE), 2000 = 100			
	CPI-U, 1982–1984 = 100	CPI-W, 1982–1984 = 100	CPI-U-X1, 1982–1984 = 100	CPI-E, Dec. 1982 = 100, not seasonally adjusted	CPI-U-RS, Dec. 1977 = 100, not seasonally adjusted	C-CPI-U, Dec. 1999 = 100, not seasonally adjusted	CPI-U, 1982–1984 = 100	CPI-U-RS, Dec. 1977 = 100, not seasonally adjusted	C-CPI-U, Dec. 1999 = 100, not seasonally adjusted	PCE, total	PCE, market-based	Excluding food and energy PCE, total	Excluding food and energy PCE, market-based
1960	1.7	1.7	1.9	...	...	...	1.3	...	...	1.6	...	1.7	...
1961	1.0	1.0	0.9	...	...	...	1.3	...	...	1.0	...	1.2	...
1962	1.0	1.0	0.9	...	...	...	1.3	...	...	1.2	...	1.3	...
1963	1.3	1.3	1.5	...	...	...	1.3	...	...	1.2	...	1.2	...
1964	1.3	1.3	1.2	...	...	...	1.6	...	...	1.4	...	1.5	...
1965	1.6	1.6	1.5	...	...	...	1.2	...	...	1.5	...	1.2	...
1966	2.9	2.8	2.9	...	...	...	2.4	...	...	2.5	...	2.1	...
1967	3.1	3.1	3.1	...	...	...	3.6	...	...	2.5	...	2.9	...
1968	4.2	4.2	3.9	...	...	...	4.6	...	...	3.9	...	4.2	...
1969	5.5	5.4	4.5	...	...	...	5.8	...	...	4.6	...	4.6	...
1970	5.7	5.7	4.8	...	...	...	6.3	...	...	4.7	...	4.5	...
1971	4.4	4.4	4.4	...	...	...	4.7	...	...	4.3	...	4.6	...
1972	3.2	3.4	3.0	...	...	...	3.0	...	...	3.5	...	3.2	...
1973	6.2	6.2	6.3	...	...	...	3.6	...	...	5.4	...	3.6	...
1974	11.0	11.0	10.0	...	...	...	8.3	...	...	10.3	...	7.5	...
1975	9.1	9.1	8.3	...	...	...	9.1	...	...	8.3	...	8.3	...
1976	5.8	5.7	5.7	...	...	...	6.5	...	...	5.5	...	6.1	...
1977	6.5	6.5	6.4	...	...	...	6.3	...	...	6.5	...	6.4	...
1978	7.6	7.7	6.8	...	...	...	7.4	...	...	7.0	...	6.6	...
1979	11.3	11.4	9.6	...	9.6	...	9.8	7.1	...	8.8	...	7.0	...
1980	13.5	13.4	11.2	...	11.1	...	12.4	8.9	...	10.7	...	9.0	...
1981	10.3	10.3	9.5	...	9.5	...	10.4	9.3	...	8.9	...	8.7	...
1982	6.2	6.0	6.1	...	6.0	...	7.4	7.7	...	5.5	...	6.6	...
1983	3.2	3.0	4.2	...	4.3	...	4.0	5.6	...	4.3	...	5.3	...
1984	4.3	3.5	4.3	4.3	4.1	...	5.0	5.0	...	3.8	...	4.2	...
1985	3.6	3.5	3.6	3.8	3.4	...	4.3	4.4	...	3.3	...	3.8	...
1986	1.9	1.6	1.9	2.5	1.8	...	4.0	4.0	...	2.4	...	3.7	...
1987	3.6	3.6	3.6	3.9	3.4	...	4.1	3.9	...	3.5	...	3.7	...
1988	4.1	4.0	4.1	4.2	3.7	...	4.4	4.0	...	4.0	...	4.3	...
1989	4.8	4.8	4.8	5.1	4.3	...	4.5	4.0	...	4.4	...	4.1	...
1990	5.4	5.2	5.4	6.0	5.0	...	5.0	4.6	...	4.6	...	4.3	...
1991	4.2	4.1	4.2	4.7	3.6	...	4.9	4.2	...	3.6	...	3.9	...
1992	3.0	2.9	3.0	3.2	2.5	...	3.7	3.1	...	2.9	...	3.4	...
1993	3.0	2.8	3.0	3.1	2.5	...	3.3	2.8	...	2.3	...	2.6	...
1994	2.6	2.5	2.6	2.9	2.1	...	2.8	2.3	...	2.1	...	2.3	...
1995	2.8	2.9	2.8	2.9	2.4	...	3.0	2.5	...	2.1	...	2.2	...
1996	3.0	2.9	3.0	3.0	2.7	...	2.7	2.4	...	2.2	...	1.9	...
1997	2.3	2.3	2.3	2.4	2.2	...	2.4	2.2	...	1.7	...	1.6	...
1998	1.6	1.3	1.6	1.8	1.4	...	2.3	2.2	...	0.9	0.6	1.3	1.0
1999	2.2	2.2	2.2	2.4	2.1	...	2.1	2.0	...	1.7	1.4	1.5	1.1
2000	3.4	3.5	3.4	3.5	3.4	...	2.4	2.4	...	2.5	2.4	1.7	1.4
2001	2.8	2.7	2.8	3.1	2.8	2.3	2.6	2.7	2.1	2.1	1.9	1.9	1.7
2002	1.6	1.4	1.6	1.8	1.6	1.2	2.4	2.3	1.8	1.4	1.1	1.8	1.5
2003	2.3	2.2	2.3	2.4	2.2	2.1	1.4	1.5	1.1	2.0	1.9	1.4	1.1
2004	2.7	2.6	2.7	3.0	2.7	2.5	1.8	1.8	1.7	2.6	2.3	2.1	1.5
2005	3.4	3.5	3.4	3.5	3.4	2.9	2.2	2.2	1.8	2.9	2.7	2.1	1.7
2006	3.2	3.2	3.2	3.3	3.3	2.9	2.5	2.5	2.3	2.8	2.6	2.3	1.9
2007	2.8	2.9	2.8	3.0	2.8	2.5	2.3	2.3	1.8	2.6	2.4	2.2	1.8
2008	3.8	4.1	3.8	3.8	3.8	I3.3	2.3	2.3	I1.9	3.3	3.3	2.2	1.9
Percent change, annual rate:													
1978–2008	4.1	4.0	3.9	...	3.8	...	4.1	3.7	...	3.5	...	3.4	...
1983–2008	3.1	3.0	3.1	3.3	2.9	...	3.1	2.9	...	2.7	...	2.7	...
2000–2008	2.8	2.8	2.8	3.0	2.8	2.5	2.2	2.2	1.8	2.5	2.3	2.0	1.6
2008													
January	4.4	4.8	4.4	4.1	4.3	I3.9	2.5	2.5	I2.0	3.6	3.5	2.2	1.8
February	4.2	4.6	4.2	3.9	4.0	I3.7	2.3	2.3	I1.9	3.5	3.4	2.1	1.7
March	4.1	4.4	4.1	4.0	4.0	I3.6	2.4	2.4	I2.0	3.4	3.3	2.2	1.7
April	3.9	4.2	3.9	3.9	4.0	I3.5	2.3	2.3	I1.9	3.4	3.3	2.2	1.8
May	4.0	4.3	4.0	4.2	4.2	I3.6	2.3	2.3	I2.0	3.5	3.5	2.2	1.9
June	4.8	5.3	4.8	4.9	5.0	I4.2	2.4	2.4	I2.1	4.1	4.1	2.3	2.0
July	5.4	6.0	5.4	5.4	5.6	I4.7	2.5	2.5	I2.2	4.5	4.6	2.4	2.1
August	5.3	5.9	5.3	5.2	5.4	I4.6	2.5	2.5	I2.1	4.4	4.6	2.4	2.2
September	4.9	5.4	4.9	4.7	4.9	I4.2	2.5	2.5	I2.0	4.1	4.3	2.3	2.1
October	3.7	3.9	3.7	3.6	3.7	I3.2	2.2	2.2	I1.8	3.3	3.5	2.1	2.0
November	1.0	0.6	1.0	1.4	1.1	I0.6	2.0	2.0	I1.5	1.6	1.5	2.0	1.9
December	-0.1	-0.7	-0.1	0.5	0.1	I-0.5	1.7	1.8	I1.3	0.8	0.6	1.8	1.7

I Interim values.
. . . = Not available.

Table 8-4. Producer Price Indexes and Purchasing Power of the Dollar

(1982 = 100, seasonally adjusted.)

Year and month	Finished goods		Finished consumer goods	Finished consumer foods			Finished consumer goods, except foods			Capital equipment		
	Total	Percent change from previous period	Total	Total	Crude	Processed	Total	Durable goods	Nondurable goods less foods	Total	Manu-facturing industries	Nonmanu-facturing industries
1960	33.4	0.9	33.6	35.5	39.8	35.2	33.5	43.8	28.4	32.8	30.2	34.8
1961	33.4	0.0	33.6	35.4	38.0	35.3	33.4	43.6	28.4	32.9	30.3	34.8
1962	33.5	0.3	33.7	35.7	38.4	35.6	33.4	43.4	28.4	33.0	30.5	34.9
1963	33.4	-0.3	33.5	35.3	37.8	35.2	33.4	43.1	28.5	33.1	30.6	34.8
1964	33.5	0.3	33.6	35.4	38.9	35.2	33.3	43.3	28.4	33.4	31.0	35.1
1965	34.1	1.8	34.2	36.8	39.0	36.8	33.6	43.2	28.8	33.8	31.5	35.4
1966	35.2	3.2	35.4	39.2	41.5	39.2	34.1	43.4	29.3	34.6	32.5	36.0
1967	35.6	1.1	35.6	38.5	39.6	38.8	34.7	44.1	30.0	35.8	33.8	37.0
1968	36.6	2.8	36.5	40.0	42.5	40.0	35.5	45.1	30.6	37.0	35.0	38.2
1969	38.0	3.8	37.9	42.4	45.9	42.3	36.3	45.9	31.5	38.3	36.2	39.5
1970	39.3	3.4	39.1	43.8	46.0	43.9	37.4	47.2	32.5	40.1	38.1	41.3
1971	40.5	3.1	40.2	44.5	45.8	44.7	38.7	48.9	33.5	41.7	39.6	43.0
1972	41.8	3.2	41.5	46.9	48.0	47.2	39.4	50.0	34.1	42.8	40.5	44.2
1973	45.6	9.1	46.0	56.5	63.6	55.8	41.2	50.9	36.1	44.2	42.2	45.3
1974	52.6	15.4	53.1	64.4	71.6	63.9	48.2	55.5	44.0	50.5	48.8	51.2
1975	58.2	10.6	58.2	69.8	71.7	70.3	53.2	61.0	48.9	58.2	56.5	58.9
1976	60.8	4.5	60.4	69.6	76.7	69.0	56.5	63.7	52.4	62.1	60.3	62.9
1977	64.7	6.4	64.3	73.3	79.5	72.7	60.6	67.4	56.8	66.1	64.5	66.8
1978	69.8	7.9	69.4	79.9	85.8	79.4	64.9	73.6	60.0	71.3	70.1	71.8
1979	77.6	11.2	77.5	87.3	92.3	86.8	73.5	80.8	69.3	77.5	77.1	77.7
1980	88.0	13.4	88.6	92.4	93.9	92.3	87.1	91.0	85.1	85.8	86.0	85.7
1981	96.1	9.2	96.6	97.8	104.4	97.2	96.1	96.4	95.8	94.6	94.9	94.4
1982	100.0	4.1	100.0	100.0	100.0	100.0	100.0	100.0	100.0	100.0	100.0	100.0
1983	101.6	1.6	101.3	101.0	102.4	100.9	101.2	102.8	100.5	102.8	102.3	103.0
1984	103.7	2.1	103.3	105.4	111.4	104.9	102.2	104.5	101.1	105.2	104.9	105.4
1985	104.7	1.0	103.8	104.6	102.9	104.8	103.3	106.5	101.7	107.5	107.4	107.6
1986	103.2	-1.4	101.4	107.3	105.6	107.4	98.5	108.9	93.3	109.7	109.7	109.7
1987	105.4	2.1	103.6	109.5	107.1	109.6	100.7	111.5	94.9	111.7	111.8	111.6
1988	108.0	2.5	106.2	112.6	109.8	112.7	103.1	113.8	97.3	114.3	115.5	113.9
1989	113.6	5.2	112.1	118.7	119.6	118.6	108.9	117.6	103.8	118.8	120.3	118.2
1990	119.2	4.9	118.2	124.4	123.0	124.4	115.3	120.4	111.5	122.9	124.5	122.2
1991	121.7	2.1	120.5	124.1	119.3	124.4	118.7	123.9	115.0	126.7	127.8	126.3
1992	123.2	1.2	121.7	123.3	107.6	124.4	120.8	125.7	117.3	129.1	129.3	129.0
1993	124.7	1.2	123.0	125.7	114.4	126.5	121.7	128.0	117.6	131.4	131.2	131.4
1994	125.5	0.6	123.3	126.8	111.3	127.9	121.6	130.9	116.2	134.1	133.2	134.3
1995	127.9	1.9	125.6	129.0	118.8	129.8	124.0	132.7	118.8	136.7	135.8	137.0
1996	131.3	2.7	129.5	133.6	129.2	133.8	127.6	134.2	123.3	138.3	137.3	138.6
1997	131.8	0.4	130.2	134.5	126.6	135.1	128.2	133.7	124.3	138.2	137.7	138.4
1998	130.7	-0.8	128.9	134.3	127.2	134.8	126.4	132.9	122.2	137.6	137.9	137.4
1999	133.0	1.8	132.0	135.1	125.5	135.9	130.5	133.0	127.9	137.6	138.5	137.3
2000	138.0	3.8	138.2	137.2	123.5	138.3	138.4	133.9	138.7	138.8	139.5	138.6
2001	140.7	2.0	141.5	141.3	127.7	142.4	141.4	134.0	142.8	139.7	140.4	139.4
2002	138.9	-1.3	139.4	140.1	128.5	141.0	138.8	133.0	139.8	139.1	140.0	138.7
2003	143.3	3.2	145.3	145.9	130.0	147.2	144.7	133.1	148.4	139.5	139.9	139.3
2004	148.5	3.6	151.7	152.7	138.2	153.9	150.9	135.0	156.6	141.4	142.4	141.0
2005	155.7	4.8	160.4	155.7	140.2	156.9	161.9	136.6	172.0	144.6	146.0	144.1
2006	160.4	3.0	166.0	156.7	151.3	157.1	169.2	136.9	182.6	146.9	149.2	145.9
2007	166.6	3.9	173.5	167.0	170.2	166.7	175.6	138.3	191.7	149.5	152.5	148.3
2008¹	177.1	6.3	186.3	178.4	175.5	178.8	189.0	141.1	210.5	153.7	157.3	152.4
2007												
January	160.8	0.1	166.0	161.5	162.0	161.3	167.3	137.6	179.4	148.6	151.6	147.5
February	162.8	2.5	168.5	164.3	178.5	162.7	169.8	137.9	182.9	149.0	152.0	147.9
March	164.3	3.1	170.5	166.5	187.2	164.3	171.6	137.9	185.8	149.1	152.1	147.9
April	165.4	3.2	171.9	167.6	186.8	165.5	173.2	137.7	188.2	149.2	152.4	148.0
May	166.4	3.7	173.3	166.6	164.4	166.7	175.5	138.0	191.5	149.4	152.5	148.2
June	166.1	3.2	172.8	166.0	149.1	167.6	175.0	138.6	190.5	149.7	152.5	148.5
July	167.2	4.0	174.2	166.2	158.2	166.8	176.9	139.0	193.1	149.9	152.8	148.8
August	166.2	2.4	172.8	166.1	150.9	167.5	175.0	138.7	190.5	149.9	152.8	148.7
September	167.4	4.5	174.4	168.0	163.6	168.3	176.6	138.6	192.7	149.9	153.1	148.7
October	168.6	6.3	176.0	170.1	186.2	168.4	177.9	138.3	194.9	149.9	153.1	148.7
November	172.6	7.6	181.1	170.0	178.2	169.0	185.1	139.1	205.0	150.5	153.5	149.3
December	171.8	6.4	180.2	172.3	192.7	170.1	182.9	138.8	201.9	150.4	153.5	149.2
2008												
January	173.4	7.8	182.0	174.8	197.8	172.4	184.4	139.4	203.8	151.1	154.4	149.9
February	174.1	6.9	182.9	173.9	180.5	173.1	186.0	139.8	206.0	151.7	155.1	150.4
March	175.6	6.9	184.8	176.0	194.1	174.1	187.9	139.8	209.0	151.8	155.2	150.5
April	176.0	6.4	185.1	176.3	184.5	175.3	188.1	140.6	208.8	152.6	156.0	151.3
May	178.6	7.3	188.5	177.6	177.6	177.4	192.4	140.7	215.2	153.0	156.3	151.7
June	181.0	9.0	191.7	179.8	188.6	178.8	195.9	140.8	220.6	153.4	156.9	152.0
July	183.4	9.7	194.6	180.8	172.8	181.4	199.7	141.1	226.0	154.2	158.2	152.7
August	182.5	9.8	193.1	181.2	168.2	182.3	197.3	141.8	222.1	154.8	158.7	153.3
September	182.3	8.9	192.7	181.2	173.0	181.9	196.8	142.3	221.1	155.4	159.2	153.9
October	177.6	5.3	185.9	181.3	177.5	181.4	187.2	143.3	205.9	156.3	159.8	154.9
November	172.9	0.1	179.6	181.5	177.5	181.7	178.4	142.5	192.9	156.2	159.8	154.8
December¹	169.7	-1.2	175.1	179.0	158.1	180.8	173.0	143.1	184.5	156.4	159.7	155.1

¹Data are preliminary.

Table 8-4. Producer Price Indexes and Purchasing Power of the Dollar—Continued

(1982 = 100, seasonally adjusted.)

Year and month	Total	Materials and components for manufacturing					Materials and components for construction	Processed fuels and lubricants			Containers, nonreturnable	Supplies	
		Total	Materials for food manufacturing	Materials for nondurable manufacturing	Materials for durable manufacturing	Components for manufacturing		Total	Manufacturing industries	Nonmanufacturing industries		Total	Manufacturing industries
1960	30.8	33.3	35.7	35.9	30.4	34.0	32.7	16.6	19.7	14.6	33.4	33.3	36.2
1961	30.6	32.9	36.9	35.1	30.0	33.7	32.2	16.8	19.9	14.8	33.2	33.7	35.8
1962	30.6	32.7	36.1	34.9	30.0	33.4	32.1	16.7	19.9	14.7	33.6	34.5	36.0
1963	30.7	32.7	37.9	34.6	30.0	33.4	32.2	16.6	19.8	14.5	33.2	35.0	35.8
1964	30.8	33.1	37.3	34.8	30.6	33.7	32.5	16.2	19.4	14.1	32.9	34.7	35.9
1965	31.2	33.6	38.3	35.2	31.2	34.2	32.8	16.5	19.6	14.4	33.5	35.0	36.1
1966	32.0	34.3	40.0	35.4	31.8	35.4	33.6	16.8	19.9	14.7	34.5	36.5	37.1
1967	32.2	34.5	39.2	35.2	32.3	36.5	34.0	16.9	20.1	14.8	35.0	36.8	37.6
1968	33.0	35.3	39.8	35.6	33.4	37.3	35.7	16.5	19.8	14.2	35.9	37.1	38.7
1969	34.1	36.5	42.0	36.0	35.2	38.5	37.7	16.6	20.0	14.4	37.2	37.8	39.8
1970	35.4	38.0	44.3	36.5	37.0	40.6	38.3	17.7	21.5	15.2	39.0	39.7	41.4
1971	36.8	38.9	45.7	37.0	38.1	41.9	40.8	19.5	23.6	16.6	40.8	40.8	42.5
1972	38.2	40.4	47.0	38.5	39.9	42.9	43.0	20.1	24.5	16.9	42.7	42.5	43.3
1973	42.4	44.1	57.2	42.6	43.1	44.3	46.5	22.2	26.4	19.4	45.2	51.7	45.6
1974	52.5	56.0	82.0	54.6	55.4	51.1	55.0	33.6	35.5	32.7	53.3	56.8	53.3
1975	58.0	61.7	82.1	61.4	60.8	57.8	60.1	39.4	41.9	38.0	60.0	61.8	59.4
1976	60.9	64.0	70.6	64.8	64.8	60.8	64.1	42.3	44.8	41.1	63.1	65.8	62.6
1977	64.9	67.4	71.9	66.8	70.2	64.5	69.3	47.7	51.0	46.2	65.9	69.3	66.6
1978	69.5	72.0	81.0	69.2	76.2	69.2	76.5	49.9	53.7	48.1	71.0	72.9	71.2
1979	78.4	80.9	89.9	78.3	87.3	75.8	84.2	61.6	64.3	60.4	79.4	80.2	78.1
1980	90.3	91.7	103.7	91.2	97.1	84.6	91.3	85.0	85.5	84.7	89.1	89.9	87.2
1981	98.6	98.7	102.1	100.5	100.7	94.7	97.9	100.6	100.2	101.0	96.7	96.9	95.2
1982	100.0	100.0	100.0	100.0	100.0	100.0	100.0	100.0	100.0	100.0	100.0	100.0	100.0
1983	100.6	101.2	101.3	98.5	103.0	102.4	102.8	95.4	96.2	94.9	100.4	101.8	101.5
1984	103.1	104.1	106.3	102.1	104.9	105.0	105.6	95.7	97.1	94.6	105.9	104.1	105.0
1985	102.7	103.3	101.5	100.5	103.3	106.4	107.3	92.8	93.8	92.0	109.0	104.4	107.3
1986	99.1	102.2	98.4	98.1	101.2	107.5	108.1	72.7	75.1	71.2	110.3	105.6	108.3
1987	101.5	105.3	100.8	102.2	106.2	108.8	109.8	73.3	75.9	71.7	114.5	107.7	110.0
1988	107.1	113.2	106.0	112.9	118.7	112.3	116.1	71.2	73.3	69.9	120.1	113.7	114.8
1989	112.0	118.1	112.7	118.5	123.6	116.4	121.3	76.4	78.3	75.3	125.4	118.1	119.8
1990	114.5	118.7	117.9	118.0	120.7	119.0	122.9	85.9	87.3	85.0	127.7	119.4	122.1
1991	114.4	118.1	115.3	116.7	117.2	121.0	124.5	85.3	88.4	83.4	128.1	121.4	124.4
1992	114.7	117.9	113.9	115.4	117.2	122.0	126.5	84.5	87.5	82.6	127.7	122.7	125.9
1993	116.2	118.9	115.6	115.5	119.1	123.0	132.0	84.7	88.1	82.6	126.4	125.0	128.5
1994	118.5	122.1	118.5	119.2	125.2	124.3	136.6	83.1	86.1	81.1	129.7	127.0	130.7
1995	124.9	130.4	119.5	135.1	135.6	126.5	142.1	84.2	87.1	82.3	148.8	132.1	137.0
1996	125.7	128.6	125.3	130.5	131.3	126.9	143.6	90.0	92.4	88.4	141.1	135.9	138.7
1997	125.6	128.3	123.2	129.6	132.8	126.4	146.5	89.3	92.0	87.6	136.0	135.9	139.4
1998	123.0	126.1	123.2	126.7	128.0	125.9	146.8	81.1	85.8	78.1	140.8	134.8	140.6
1999	123.2	124.6	120.8	124.9	125.1	125.7	148.9	84.6	87.9	82.5	142.5	134.2	140.7
2000	129.2	128.1	119.2	132.6	129.0	126.2	150.7	102.0	100.9	102.3	151.6	136.9	143.5
2001	129.7	127.4	124.3	131.8	125.1	126.4	150.6	104.5	105.7	103.5	153.1	138.7	145.4
2002	127.8	126.1	123.2	129.2	124.7	126.1	151.3	96.3	98.7	94.8	152.1	138.9	144.7
2003	133.7	129.7	134.4	137.2	127.9	125.9	153.6	112.6	116.0	110.5	153.7	141.5	146.5
2004	142.6	137.9	145.0	147.8	146.6	127.4	166.4	124.3	125.1	123.8	159.3	146.7	149.2
2005	154.0	146.0	146.0	163.2	158.3	129.9	176.6	150.0	148.6	150.9	167.1	151.9	155.7
2006	164.0	155.9	146.2	175.0	180.5	134.5	188.4	162.8	158.1	165.7	175.0	157.0	161.1
2007	170.7	162.4	161.4	184.0	189.8	136.3	192.5	173.9	172.6	175.0	180.3	161.7	162.9
2008¹	188.6	177.6	180.6	215.5	203.4	140.3	205.4	206.4	199.3	209.9	191.9	174.1	170.7
2007													
January	164.0	157.5	150.7	174.1	183.5	136.4	190.4	155.5	153.9	156.9	178.0	159.6	161.9
February	165.4	157.7	153.0	174.6	184.2	136.0	190.7	161.3	161.4	162.1	178.2	160.2	161.7
March	166.9	158.8	155.5	176.4	186.6	135.8	191.3	165.5	162.4	167.7	178.4	160.5	161.9
April	168.6	160.7	157.6	177.8	193.0	135.9	192.1	169.0	164.7	171.6	179.5	160.7	162.2
May	170.1	162.8	159.9	182.9	195.1	136.0	192.8	171.1	169.2	172.7	179.9	160.7	162.2
June	170.6	163.6	162.2	185.1	194.9	136.2	193.2	170.9	168.2	172.9	179.8	161.3	162.6
July	171.9	164.5	162.5	187.3	195.2	136.3	193.5	174.5	170.2	177.1	180.3	161.8	163.0
August	170.5	163.4	163.6	185.3	192.0	136.5	193.5	169.9	167.9	171.6	180.5	161.9	163.4
September	170.9	163.4	166.0	186.3	189.3	136.5	193.2	171.8	170.3	173.2	180.7	162.2	163.5
October	172.0	164.5	166.3	189.7	189.3	136.6	193.4	173.7	172.0	175.3	181.9	163.0	163.9
November	177.1	166.4	167.3	195.4	189.0	136.7	193.4	192.7	186.0	196.4	182.9	164.0	164.3
December	177.2	166.6	170.7	195.4	188.5	136.9	193.7	191.9	183.8	196.1	183.3	164.7	165.0
2008													
January	179.2	168.5	174.0	199.5	189.9	137.4	194.5	194.5	186.3	198.8	185.0	166.9	166.4
February	181.0	170.2	176.8	201.6	193.5	137.8	195.8	197.0	187.9	201.7	185.8	168.3	166.9
March	185.0	173.2	179.8	206.1	200.7	137.9	197.4	207.4	196.7	212.7	186.2	170.1	167.6
April	186.9	175.5	180.2	209.6	205.8	138.6	200.3	208.1	196.2	214.0	187.3	171.3	168.5
May	191.6	179.1	181.8	215.9	212.0	139.4	203.4	220.0	205.6	226.9	188.0	173.0	169.1
June	195.5	182.3	184.4	222.9	215.5	140.0	206.6	228.3	208.8	237.3	189.3	174.6	170.2
July	200.9	187.3	186.3	235.0	219.3	141.3	209.8	238.0	220.1	246.4	191.9	178.2	171.9
August	198.3	188.8	186.3	239.1	219.0	141.9	212.8	218.5	210.2	222.9	194.9	178.8	172.9
September	197.1	186.9	184.4	235.2	214.7	142.4	213.9	216.0	208.6	220.0	198.0	178.9	173.7
October	188.9	180.5	179.4	222.9	202.4	142.5	212.3	192.2	189.5	194.1	198.7	176.9	173.5
November	181.4	171.4	178.3	207.3	192.0	142.4	210.4	172.5	170.1	174.3	199.0	176.1	173.7
December¹	173.7	164.9	173.0	188.4	178.1	142.0	207.8	157.8	159.2	158.0	198.0	174.1	173.1

¹Data are preliminary.

Table 8-4. Producer Price Indexes and Purchasing Power of the Dollar—*Continued*

(1982 = 100, seasonally adjusted.)

Year and month	Intermediate materials, supplies, and components—Continued — Supplies—Continued — Nonmanufacturing industries — Total	Feeds	Other supplies	Crude materials for further processing — Total	Foodstuffs and feedstuffs	Crude nonfood materials — Total	Crude nonfood materials except fuel [2] — Total [2]	Manufacturing [2]	Construction	Crude fuel [3] — Total	Manufacturing industries	Nonmanufacturing industries
1960	32.1	37.2	33.2	30.4	38.4	. . .	26.9	26.3	35.9	10.5	9.0	11.8
1961	32.9	40.9	32.9	30.2	37.9	. . .	27.2	26.6	35.9	10.5	9.0	11.8
1962	33.8	43.6	33.2	30.5	38.6	. . .	27.1	26.5	36.1	10.4	8.9	11.8
1963	34.6	45.9	33.2	29.9	37.5	. . .	26.7	26.1	36.0	10.5	9.0	11.9
1964	34.1	45.0	32.9	29.6	36.6	. . .	27.2	26.6	35.9	10.5	9.0	11.9
1965	34.5	45.9	33.0	31.1	39.2	. . .	27.7	27.2	36.1	10.6	9.0	11.9
1966	36.2	50.0	33.8	33.1	42.7	. . .	28.3	27.8	36.3	10.9	9.3	12.3
1967	36.3	48.3	34.5	31.3	40.3	21.1	26.5	25.8	37.0	11.3	9.7	12.8
1968	36.4	46.5	35.4	31.8	40.9	21.6	27.1	26.3	38.4	11.5	9.9	13.1
1969	36.9	46.4	36.0	33.9	44.1	22.5	28.4	27.6	39.8	12.0	10.2	13.8
1970	38.9	49.9	37.6	35.2	45.2	23.8	29.1	28.3	42.1	13.8	11.3	16.6
1971	39.9	50.4	38.9	36.0	46.1	24.7	29.4	28.4	44.1	15.7	12.6	19.3
1972	42.0	56.1	39.8	39.9	51.5	27.0	32.3	31.5	45.0	16.8	13.5	20.6
1973	54.7	97.3	42.7	54.5	72.6	34.3	42.9	42.7	46.2	18.6	14.8	22.9
1974	58.4	90.2	50.5	61.4	76.4	44.1	54.5	55.0	50.0	24.8	19.1	31.8
1975	62.9	84.0	58.9	61.6	77.4	43.7	50.0	49.7	55.9	30.6	24.4	38.0
1976	67.3	95.1	62.0	63.4	76.8	48.2	54.9	54.7	59.6	34.5	29.0	40.5
1977	70.7	99.3	65.2	65.5	77.5	51.7	56.3	56.0	63.1	42.0	37.2	47.4
1978	73.8	95.5	69.7	73.4	87.3	57.5	61.9	61.5	68.7	48.2	43.1	53.8
1979	81.2	106.9	76.3	85.9	100.0	69.6	75.5	75.6	76.6	57.3	53.1	62.0
1980	91.1	110.6	87.5	95.3	104.6	84.6	91.8	92.3	87.9	69.4	66.7	72.5
1981	97.8	111.3	95.4	103.0	103.9	101.8	109.8	110.9	96.8	84.8	83.6	86.2
1982	100.0	100.0	100.0	100.0	100.0	100.0	100.0	100.0	100.0	100.0	100.0	100.0
1983	102.0	109.1	101.0	101.3	101.8	100.7	98.8	98.6	100.1	105.1	105.8	104.4
1984	103.7	104.2	103.7	103.5	104.7	102.2	101.0	100.8	103.1	105.1	105.6	104.6
1985	103.0	86.6	105.3	95.8	94.8	96.9	94.3	93.1	105.7	102.7	102.7	102.5
1986	104.2	90.5	106.2	87.7	93.2	81.6	76.0	72.6	106.5	92.2	91.1	93.6
1987	106.6	94.6	108.3	93.7	96.2	87.9	88.5	84.7	114.8	84.1	82.1	86.3
1988	113.2	115.0	112.7	96.0	106.1	85.5	85.9	81.5	126.5	82.1	80.1	84.5
1989	117.2	114.4	117.5	103.1	111.2	93.4	95.8	91.0	136.9	85.3	83.9	87.0
1990	118.0	102.8	120.2	108.9	113.1	101.5	107.3	102.5	145.2	84.8	82.9	87.0
1991	119.9	101.3	122.5	101.2	105.5	94.6	97.5	92.2	147.5	82.9	82.3	84.1
1992	121.1	103.0	123.7	100.4	105.1	93.5	94.2	87.9	162.1	84.0	83.1	85.2
1993	123.2	105.4	125.8	102.4	108.4	94.7	94.1	85.6	193.6	87.1	85.9	88.6
1994	125.1	105.8	127.9	101.8	106.5	94.8	97.0	88.3	199.1	82.4	81.7	83.6
1995	129.5	103.4	133.2	102.7	105.8	96.8	105.8	97.3	201.7	72.1	72.5	72.9
1996	134.4	133.1	134.6	113.8	121.5	104.5	105.7	97.6	195.7	92.6	90.7	94.3
1997	134.1	129.1	134.8	111.1	112.2	106.4	103.5	95.0	201.4	101.3	98.4	103.3
1998	132.2	100.2	136.2	96.8	103.9	88.4	84.5	76.7	196.0	86.7	84.8	88.5
1999	131.4	89.2	136.5	98.2	98.7	94.3	91.1	83.0	195.7	91.2	90.0	92.9
2000	134.1	94.6	138.8	120.6	100.2	130.4	118.0	108.7	193.4	136.9	136.9	139.3
2001	135.8	96.8	140.5	121.0	106.1	126.8	101.5	93.2	181.7	151.4	150.2	154.2
2002	136.3	98.1	140.9	108.1	99.5	111.4	101.0	92.5	181.4	117.3	113.4	119.8
2003	139.0	106.6	143.1	135.3	113.5	148.2	116.9	107.5	180.8	185.7	176.4	189.9
2004	144.9	119.1	148.4	159.0	127.0	179.2	149.2	137.7	191.8	211.4	200.5	216.2
2005	149.7	107.4	154.9	182.2	122.7	223.4	176.7	163.4	199.3	279.7	263.9	286.3
2006	154.7	110.9	160.1	184.8	119.3	230.6	210.0	194.5	201.1	241.5	229.2	247.0
2007	160.1	138.4	163.2	207.1	146.7	246.3	238.7	221.6	201.7	236.8	224.9	242.2
2008[1]	173.5	183.7	173.5	251.7	163.5	313.5	309.0	287.7	198.8	296.7	282.0	303.4
2007												
January	157.8	125.3	162.0	181.6	131.9	212.8	199.5	184.7	197.8	212.4	202.3	217.1
February	158.4	133.4	161.8	197.9	140.7	234.9	209.6	194.2	201.4	253.2	240.0	258.9
March	158.8	135.7	161.9	202.8	143.9	241.0	217.7	201.8	204.6	255.1	241.8	260.9
April	159.1	135.4	162.3	204.8	145.6	243.3	225.3	208.8	205.7	247.7	234.9	253.3
May	159.0	131.4	162.7	206.7	146.2	246.1	223.9	207.5	205.5	257.7	244.2	263.6
June	159.6	135.2	162.9	208.0	145.4	249.5	227.5	210.9	203.6	260.3	246.6	266.2
July	160.2	138.5	163.2	208.5	146.7	249.3	243.7	226.2	202.4	237.0	225.1	242.3
August	160.2	137.8	163.3	201.6	145.5	238.0	242.6	225.2	201.4	212.1	202.0	216.7
September	160.6	139.1	163.6	203.6	149.7	237.9	255.7	237.5	201.3	193.5	184.8	197.7
October	161.4	144.7	164.1	211.9	150.0	252.6	262.7	244.1	200.1	217.8	207.4	222.7
November	162.5	150.3	164.9	226.3	154.2	274.7	280.8	261.1	197.6	243.9	231.6	249.4
December	163.3	153.5	165.4	230.1	160.4	276.3	277.8	258.3	198.0	251.7	238.9	257.4
2008												
January	165.6	163.3	166.9	236.6	165.4	283.7	288.1	268.0	198.5	253.5	240.7	259.2
February	167.2	170.2	168.0	245.8	166.8	299.6	295.4	274.9	197.5	283.1	268.1	289.5
March	169.4	179.4	169.3	262.1	170.5	327.1	324.3	302.0	200.4	306.0	289.3	313.0
April	170.6	179.3	170.7	274.4	169.4	351.6	349.0	325.3	199.2	328.1	310.9	335.5
May	172.6	186.1	172.2	290.8	170.3	381.8	372.0	346.9	200.0	368.4	348.2	376.8
June	174.2	187.3	173.9	298.6	174.0	392.8	383.2	357.4	201.0	378.1	357.3	386.8
July	178.3	208.5	176.1	310.3	174.1	415.0	398.6	371.9	199.7	410.3	387.3	419.7
August	178.8	205.2	177.0	273.0	167.8	350.4	357.8	333.5	200.2	309.8	294.6	316.7
September	178.7	197.4	177.8	253.1	165.6	314.8	324.3	302.0	199.9	273.4	261.1	279.4
October	176.2	179.1	177.1	212.3	148.2	254.7	253.6	235.5	200.2	236.3	226.9	241.4
November	175.2	172.5	176.6	183.0	146.5	200.7	193.2	178.7	196.0	197.8	191.4	201.8
December[1]	173.0	165.5	174.9	173.3	138.4	190.4	164.1	151.4	193.6	220.8	212.7	225.5

[1]Data are preliminary.
[2]Includes crude petroleum.
[3]Excludes crude petroleum.
. . . = Not available.

Table 8-4. Producer Price Indexes and Purchasing Power of the Dollar—*Continued*

(1982 = 100, seasonally adjusted.)

Year and month	Finished energy goods	Finished goods excluding: Foods	Finished goods excluding: Energy	Finished goods excluding: Foods and energy	Finished consumer goods excluding: Energy	Finished consumer goods excluding: Foods and energy	Intermediate foods and feeds	Intermediate energy goods	Intermediate materials less: Foods and feeds	Intermediate materials less: Energy	Intermediate materials less: Foods and energy	Crude energy materials [2]	Crude materials less energy	Crude nonfood materials less energy [3]
1960	...	...	...	...	...	...	...	...	30.7	...	...	...	...	...
1961	...	...	...	...	...	...	...	...	30.3	...	...	...	...	...
1962	...	...	...	...	...	...	...	...	30.2	...	...	...	...	...
1963	...	...	...	...	...	...	...	...	30.1	...	...	...	...	...
1964	...	...	...	...	...	...	...	...	30.3	...	...	...	...	...
1965	...	...	...	...	...	...	...	...	30.7	...	...	...	...	...
1966	...	...	...	...	...	...	...	...	31.3	...	...	...	...	...
1967	...	35.0	...	...	...	...	41.8	...	31.7	...	...	...	...	...
1968	...	35.9	...	...	...	...	41.5	...	32.5	...	...	...	...	...
1969	...	36.9	...	...	...	...	42.9	...	33.6	...	...	...	...	...
1970	...	38.2	...	...	...	...	45.6	...	34.8	...	...	...	...	...
1971	...	39.6	...	...	...	...	46.7	...	36.2	...	...	...	...	...
1972	...	40.4	...	...	...	...	49.5	...	37.7	...	...	...	...	...
1973	...	42.0	...	48.1	...	50.4	70.3	...	40.6	...	44.3	...	...	70.8
1974	26.2	48.8	...	53.6	58.7	55.5	83.6	33.1	50.5	56.2	54.0	27.8	78.4	83.3
1975	30.7	54.7	62.4	59.7	63.9	60.6	81.6	38.7	56.6	61.7	60.2	33.3	75.9	69.3
1976	34.3	58.1	64.8	63.1	65.7	63.7	77.4	41.5	60.0	64.7	63.8	35.3	77.6	80.2
1977	39.7	62.2	68.6	66.9	69.4	67.3	79.6	46.8	64.1	68.5	67.6	40.4	78.1	79.8
1978	42.3	66.7	74.0	71.9	74.9	72.2	84.8	49.1	68.6	73.4	72.5	45.2	87.5	87.8
1979	57.1	74.6	80.7	78.3	81.7	78.8	94.5	61.1	77.4	81.7	80.7	54.9	101.5	106.2
1980	85.2	86.7	88.4	87.1	89.3	87.8	105.5	84.9	89.4	91.4	90.3	73.1	106.5	113.1
1981	101.5	95.6	95.4	94.6	95.7	94.6	104.6	100.5	98.2	98.2	97.7	97.7	105.7	111.7
1982	100.0	100.0	100.0	100.0	100.0	100.0	100.0	100.0	100.0	100.0	100.0	100.0	100.0	100.0
1983	95.2	101.8	102.5	103.0	102.4	103.1	103.6	95.3	100.5	101.7	101.6	98.7	102.6	105.3
1984	91.2	103.2	105.5	105.5	105.6	105.7	105.7	95.5	103.0	104.6	104.7	98.0	106.3	111.7
1985	87.6	104.6	107.2	108.1	107.0	108.4	97.3	92.6	103.0	104.7	105.2	93.3	97.0	104.9
1986	63.0	101.9	109.7	110.6	109.7	111.1	96.2	72.6	99.3	104.5	104.9	71.8	95.4	103.1
1987	61.8	104.0	112.3	113.3	112.5	114.2	99.2	73.0	101.7	107.3	107.8	75.0	100.9	115.7
1988	59.8	106.5	115.8	117.0	116.3	118.5	109.5	70.9	106.9	114.6	115.2	67.7	112.6	133.0
1989	65.7	111.8	121.2	122.1	122.1	124.0	113.8	76.1	111.9	119.5	120.2	75.9	117.7	137.9
1990	75.0	117.4	126.0	126.6	127.2	128.8	113.3	85.5	114.5	120.4	120.9	85.9	118.6	136.3
1991	78.1	120.9	129.1	131.1	130.0	133.7	111.1	85.1	114.6	120.8	121.4	80.4	110.9	128.2
1992	77.8	123.1	131.1	134.2	131.8	137.3	110.7	84.3	114.9	121.3	122.0	78.8	110.7	128.4
1993	78.0	124.4	132.9	135.8	133.5	138.5	112.7	84.6	116.4	123.2	123.8	76.7	116.3	140.2
1994	77.0	125.1	134.2	137.1	134.2	139.0	114.8	83.0	118.7	126.3	127.1	72.1	119.3	156.2
1995	78.1	127.5	136.9	140.0	136.9	141.9	114.8	84.1	125.5	134.0	135.2	69.4	123.5	173.6
1996	83.2	130.5	139.6	142.0	140.1	144.3	128.1	89.8	125.6	133.6	134.0	85.0	130.0	155.8
1997	83.4	130.9	140.2	142.4	141.0	145.1	125.4	89.0	125.7	133.7	134.2	87.3	123.5	156.5
1998	75.1	129.5	141.1	143.7	142.5	147.7	116.2	80.8	123.4	132.4	133.5	68.6	113.6	142.1
1999	78.8	132.3	143.0	146.1	145.2	151.7	111.1	84.3	123.9	131.7	133.1	78.5	107.9	135.2
2000	94.1	138.1	144.9	148.0	147.4	154.0	111.7	101.7	130.1	135.0	136.6	122.1	111.7	145.2
2001	96.7	140.4	147.6	150.0	150.8	156.9	115.9	104.1	130.5	135.1	136.4	122.3	112.2	130.7
2002	88.8	138.3	147.3	150.2	150.8	157.6	115.5	95.9	128.5	134.5	135.8	102.0	108.7	135.7
2003	102.0	142.4	149.0	150.5	153.1	157.9	125.9	111.9	134.2	137.7	138.5	147.2	123.4	152.5
2004	113.0	147.2	152.4	152.7	157.2	160.3	137.1	123.2	143.0	145.8	146.5	174.6	144.0	193.0
2005	132.6	155.5	155.9	156.4	160.8	164.3	133.8	149.2	155.1	153.3	154.6	234.0	143.5	202.4
2006	145.9	161.0	157.9	158.7	162.7	166.7	135.2	162.8	165.4	162.1	163.8	226.9	152.3	244.5
2007	156.3	166.2	162.8	161.7	168.7	170.0	154.4	174.6	171.5	167.6	168.4	232.8	182.6	282.6
2008 [1]	178.6	176.5	169.8	167.2	176.9	176.3	182.2	208.3	189.0	181.2	181.2	308.5	205.7	325.4
2007														
January	139.2	160.4	160.2	160.2	165.4	168.1	143.0	155.1	165.1	164.2	165.6	195.8	164.6	255.9
February	143.7	162.1	161.4	160.9	166.9	168.9	147.3	160.7	166.3	164.5	165.6	223.8	173.8	265.5
March	148.3	163.4	162.0	160.9	167.8	168.8	149.8	164.9	167.8	165.4	166.3	224.3	180.8	284.2
April	151.8	164.5	162.4	161.0	168.3	169.0	151.1	168.0	169.5	166.7	167.7	226.1	182.9	287.6
May	156.2	166.0	162.5	161.5	168.3	169.7	151.1	171.7	171.1	167.6	168.6	232.7	182.1	282.3
June	154.4	165.8	162.6	161.9	168.4	170.1	154.0	172.2	171.5	168.1	169.0	238.0	181.3	281.5
July	158.3	167.2	162.9	162.2	168.7	170.6	155.1	175.9	172.8	168.7	169.6	236.9	183.0	284.4
August	153.3	165.9	163.0	162.4	168.8	170.8	155.7	171.8	171.3	168.1	168.9	221.9	182.3	285.8
September	156.6	167.0	163.6	162.5	169.7	171.1	157.8	173.0	171.6	168.3	169.0	220.1	187.0	291.5
October	159.6	167.9	164.2	162.6	170.6	171.2	159.7	175.6	172.7	169.0	169.6	238.1	188.0	294.8
November	175.9	173.0	164.6	163.2	170.9	171.8	162.0	194.0	178.0	170.3	170.9	267.5	190.7	291.5
December	170.2	171.4	165.3	163.3	171.9	172.0	165.3	193.3	177.9	170.7	171.1	268.9	196.3	293.5
2008														
January	172.4	172.6	166.6	164.1	173.4	172.9	170.9	196.3	179.7	172.4	172.6	273.4	203.5	307.8
February	174.8	173.9	166.9	164.9	173.6	173.9	175.1	199.3	181.4	173.8	173.8	291.5	207.3	319.7
March	179.0	175.2	167.6	165.1	174.6	174.1	180.3	209.8	185.3	176.2	175.9	324.9	212.9	331.8
April	178.2	175.6	168.3	165.9	175.2	175.0	180.5	209.8	187.3	178.4	178.4	345.5	219.5	365.8
May	187.4	178.6	169.0	166.4	176.1	175.5	184.0	221.6	192.1	181.4	181.3	385.7	221.6	371.9
June	195.5	181.0	169.8	166.7	177.2	175.9	186.1	230.6	196.1	183.9	183.8	400.2	225.1	373.9
July	202.9	183.8	170.8	167.7	178.2	176.9	194.8	241.8	201.4	187.9	187.5	426.5	228.1	386.7
August	196.0	182.5	171.4	168.5	178.8	177.7	193.6	224.7	198.6	188.9	188.7	339.3	220.5	375.9
September	193.4	182.3	172.0	169.2	179.4	178.6	189.6	219.2	197.6	188.9	188.9	303.9	210.7	339.5
October	168.7	176.2	172.7	170.1	180.0	179.6	180.0	195.7	189.4	184.6	184.9	244.8	182.9	278.6
November	147.8	170.3	172.6	170.1	179.9	179.3	176.9	171.0	181.8	181.6	181.9	190.5	170.1	227.0
December [1]	134.3	166.9	172.2	170.3	179.2	179.8	171.0	154.2	173.9	176.2	176.6	179.2	162.5	222.1

[1] Data are preliminary.
[2] Includes crude petroleum.
[3] Excludes crude petroleum.
. . . = Not available.

Table 8-4. Producer Price Indexes and Purchasing Power of the Dollar—*Continued*

(1982 = 100, except as noted; not seasonally adjusted.)

Year and month	Finished goods						Capital equipment	Intermediate materials, supplies, and components	Crude materials for further processing	Purchasing power of the dollar	
	Total	Finished consumer goods								Producer prices for finished goods (1982–1984 = $1.00)	Consumer prices (CPI-U, 1982–1984 = $1.00)
		Total	Foods	Finished consumer goods except foods							
				Total	Durable goods	Nondurable goods less foods					
1960	33.4	33.6	35.5	33.5	43.8	28.4	32.8	30.8	30.4	3.047	3.373
1961	33.4	33.6	35.4	33.4	43.6	28.4	32.9	30.6	30.2	3.047	3.340
1962	33.5	33.7	35.7	33.4	43.4	28.4	33.0	30.6	30.5	3.038	3.304
1963	33.4	33.5	35.3	33.4	43.1	28.5	33.1	30.7	29.9	3.047	3.265
1964	33.5	33.6	35.4	33.3	43.3	28.4	33.4	30.8	29.6	3.038	3.220
1965	34.1	34.2	36.8	33.6	43.2	28.8	33.8	31.2	31.1	2.984	3.166
1966	35.2	35.4	39.2	34.1	43.4	29.3	34.6	32.0	33.1	2.891	3.080
1967	35.6	35.6	38.5	34.7	44.1	30.0	35.8	32.2	31.3	2.859	2.993
1968	36.6	36.5	40.0	35.5	45.1	30.6	37.0	33.0	31.8	2.781	2.873
1969	38.0	37.9	42.4	36.3	45.9	31.5	38.3	34.1	33.9	2.678	2.726
1970	39.3	39.1	43.8	37.4	47.2	32.5	40.1	35.4	35.2	2.589	2.574
1971	40.5	40.2	44.5	38.7	48.9	33.5	41.7	36.8	36.0	2.513	2.466
1972	41.8	41.5	46.9	39.4	50.0	34.1	42.8	38.2	39.9	2.435	2.391
1973	45.6	46.0	56.5	41.2	50.9	36.1	44.2	42.4	54.5	2.232	2.251
1974	52.6	53.1	64.4	48.2	55.5	44.0	50.5	52.5	61.4	1.935	2.029
1975	58.2	58.2	69.8	53.2	61.0	48.9	58.2	58.0	61.6	1.749	1.859
1976	60.8	60.4	69.6	56.5	63.7	52.4	62.1	60.9	63.4	1.674	1.757
1977	64.7	64.3	73.3	60.6	67.4	56.8	66.1	64.9	65.5	1.573	1.649
1978	69.8	69.4	79.9	64.9	73.6	60.0	71.3	69.5	73.4	1.458	1.532
1979	77.6	77.5	87.3	73.5	80.8	69.3	77.5	78.4	85.9	1.311	1.380
1980	88.0	88.6	92.4	87.1	91.0	85.1	85.8	90.3	95.3	1.156	1.215
1981	96.1	96.6	97.8	96.1	96.4	95.8	94.6	98.6	103.0	1.059	1.098
1982	100.0	100.0	100.0	100.0	100.0	100.0	100.0	100.0	100.0	1.018	1.035
1983	101.6	101.3	101.0	101.2	102.8	100.5	102.8	100.6	101.3	1.002	1.003
1984	103.7	103.3	105.4	102.2	104.5	101.1	105.2	103.1	103.5	0.981	0.961
1985	104.7	103.8	104.6	103.3	106.5	101.7	107.5	102.7	95.8	0.972	0.928
1986	103.2	101.4	107.3	98.5	108.9	93.3	109.7	99.1	87.7	0.986	0.913
1987	105.4	103.6	109.5	100.7	111.5	94.9	111.7	101.5	93.7	0.966	0.880
1988	108.0	106.2	112.6	103.1	113.8	97.3	114.3	107.1	96.0	0.942	0.846
1989	113.6	112.1	118.7	108.9	117.6	103.8	118.8	112.0	103.1	0.896	0.807
1990	119.2	118.2	124.4	115.3	120.4	111.5	122.9	114.5	108.9	0.854	0.766
1991	121.7	120.5	124.1	118.7	123.9	115.0	126.7	114.4	101.2	0.836	0.734
1992	123.2	121.7	123.3	120.8	125.7	117.3	129.1	114.7	100.4	0.826	0.713
1993	124.7	123.0	125.7	121.7	128.0	117.6	131.4	116.2	102.4	0.816	0.692
1994	125.5	123.3	126.8	121.6	130.9	116.2	134.1	118.5	101.8	0.811	0.675
1995	127.9	125.6	129.0	124.0	132.7	118.8	136.7	124.9	102.7	0.796	0.656
1996	131.3	129.5	133.6	127.6	134.2	123.3	138.3	125.7	113.8	0.775	0.638
1997	131.8	130.2	134.5	128.2	133.7	124.3	138.2	125.6	111.1	0.772	0.623
1998	130.7	128.9	134.3	126.4	132.9	122.2	137.6	123.0	96.8	0.779	0.614
1999	133.0	132.0	135.1	130.5	133.0	127.9	137.6	123.2	98.2	0.765	0.600
2000	138.0	138.2	137.2	138.4	133.9	138.7	138.8	129.2	120.6	0.737	0.581
2001	140.7	141.5	141.3	141.4	134.0	142.8	139.7	129.7	121.0	0.723	0.565
2002	138.9	139.4	140.1	138.8	133.0	139.8	139.1	127.8	108.1	0.733	0.556
2003	143.3	145.3	145.9	144.7	133.1	148.4	139.5	133.7	135.3	0.710	0.544
2004	148.5	151.7	152.7	150.9	135.0	156.6	141.4	142.6	159.0	0.685	0.530
2005	155.7	160.4	155.7	161.9	136.6	172.0	144.6	154.0	182.2	0.654	0.512
2006	160.4	166.0	156.7	169.2	136.9	182.6	146.9	164.0	184.8	0.634	0.496
2007	166.6	173.5	167.0	175.6	138.3	191.7	149.5	170.7	207.1	0.611	0.482
2008[1]	177.1	186.3	178.4	189.0	141.1	210.5	153.7	188.6	251.7	0.575	0.465
2007											
January	160.1	164.9	161.1	166.0	138.3	177.1	148.9	163.3	180.0	0.636	0.494
February	161.8	167.1	163.9	167.9	138.4	180.0	149.2	164.3	197.0	0.629	0.491
March	164.1	170.2	166.3	171.2	138.2	185.2	149.1	166.6	202.1	0.620	0.487
April	165.9	172.7	166.8	174.5	137.7	190.4	149.1	169.1	204.2	0.613	0.484
May	167.5	174.8	166.8	177.6	137.7	195.0	149.1	171.1	208.0	0.608	0.481
June	167.2	174.4	166.3	177.2	137.7	194.5	149.0	172.0	209.7	0.609	0.480
July	168.5	176.2	166.4	179.7	137.6	198.1	149.1	173.6	210.3	0.604	0.480
August	166.1	173.0	166.3	175.3	137.2	191.8	149.0	171.5	202.8	0.613	0.481
September	167.4	174.8	168.4	177.0	136.7	194.6	148.9	172.2	204.6	0.608	0.480
October	168.6	175.9	169.7	177.9	139.8	194.5	150.6	172.2	211.8	0.604	0.479
November	171.4	179.4	169.5	182.9	140.2	201.5	151.0	176.2	225.6	0.594	0.476
December	170.4	178.2	172.2	180.1	139.5	197.9	150.7	175.7	229.0	0.597	0.476
2008											
January	172.0	180.1	174.5	181.9	140.1	200.3	151.4	177.8	235.5	0.592	0.474
February	172.3	180.4	173.6	182.7	140.2	201.4	151.8	179.1	245.5	0.591	0.472
March	175.1	184.2	176.0	187.1	139.9	208.2	151.8	184.5	262.1	0.581	0.468
April	176.5	185.8	175.5	189.6	140.5	211.7	152.4	187.3	274.6	0.577	0.465
May	179.8	190.3	177.6	195.0	140.3	220.0	152.7	192.8	293.1	0.566	0.462
June	182.4	193.8	180.0	199.0	139.7	226.4	152.7	197.2	301.2	0.558	0.457
July	185.1	197.2	181.0	203.4	139.6	233.1	153.3	203.1	313.3	0.550	0.455
August	182.2	193.2	181.3	197.5	140.2	223.9	153.9	199.4	274.6	0.559	0.456
September	182.2	193.0	181.5	197.2	140.3	223.4	154.3	198.6	254.2	0.559	0.457
October	177.4	185.5	180.7	187.0	144.8	205.4	157.0	189.0	212.0	0.574	0.462
November	172.0	178.2	179.8	177.0	144.2	190.6	156.9	179.2	183.3	0.592	0.471
December[1]	168.8	173.8	178.5	171.4	143.9	182.3	156.7	172.7	171.7	0.603	0.476

[1]Data are preliminary.

Table 8-5. Producer Price Indexes by Major Commodity Groups

(1982 = 100, not seasonally adjusted.)

Year and month	All commodities	Farm products	Processed foods and feeds	Industrial commodities Total	Textile products and apparel	Hides, leather, and related products	Fuels and related products and power	Chemicals and allied products	Rubber and plastics products	Lumber and wood products	Pulp, paper, and allied products	Metals and metal products	Machinery and metal equipment	Furniture and household durables	Nonmetallic mineral products	Transportation equipment	Miscellaneous products
1950	27.3	44.0	33.2	25.0	50.2	32.9	12.6	30.4	35.6	31.4	25.7	22.0	22.6	40.9	23.5	. . .	28.6
1951	30.4	51.2	36.9	27.6	56.0	37.7	13.0	34.8	43.7	34.1	30.5	24.5	25.3	44.4	25.0	. . .	30.3
1952	29.6	48.4	36.4	26.9	50.5	30.5	13.0	33.0	39.6	33.2	29.7	24.5	25.3	43.5	25.0	. . .	30.2
1953	29.2	43.8	34.8	27.2	49.3	31.0	13.4	33.4	36.9	33.1	29.6	25.3	25.9	44.4	26.0	. . .	31.0
1954	29.3	43.2	35.4	27.2	48.2	29.5	13.2	33.8	37.5	32.5	29.6	25.5	26.3	44.9	26.6	. . .	31.3
1955	29.3	40.5	33.8	27.8	48.2	29.4	13.2	33.7	42.4	34.1	30.4	27.2	27.2	45.1	27.3	. . .	31.3
1956	30.3	40.0	33.8	29.1	48.2	31.2	13.6	33.9	43.0	34.6	32.4	29.6	29.3	46.3	28.5	. . .	31.7
1957	31.2	41.1	34.8	29.9	48.3	31.2	14.3	34.6	42.8	32.8	33.0	30.2	31.4	47.5	29.6	. . .	32.6
1958	31.6	42.9	36.5	30.0	47.4	31.6	13.7	34.9	42.8	32.5	33.4	30.0	32.1	47.9	29.9	. . .	33.3
1959	31.7	40.2	35.6	30.5	48.1	35.9	13.7	34.8	42.6	34.7	33.7	30.6	32.8	48.0	30.3	. . .	33.4
1960	31.7	40.1	35.6	30.5	48.6	34.6	13.9	34.8	42.7	33.5	34.0	30.6	33.0	47.8	30.4	. . .	33.6
1961	31.6	39.7	36.2	30.4	47.8	34.9	14.0	34.5	41.1	32.0	33.0	30.5	33.0	47.5	30.5	. . .	33.7
1962	31.7	40.4	36.5	30.4	48.2	35.3	14.0	33.9	39.9	32.2	33.4	30.2	33.0	47.2	30.5	. . .	33.9
1963	31.6	39.6	36.8	30.3	48.2	34.3	13.9	33.5	40.1	32.8	33.1	30.3	33.1	46.9	30.3	. . .	34.2
1964	31.6	39.0	36.7	30.5	48.5	34.4	13.5	33.6	39.6	33.5	33.0	31.1	33.3	47.1	30.4	. . .	34.4
1965	32.3	40.7	38.0	30.9	48.8	35.9	13.8	33.9	39.7	33.7	33.3	32.0	33.7	46.8	30.4	. . .	34.7
1966	33.3	43.7	40.2	31.5	48.9	39.4	14.1	34.0	40.5	35.2	34.2	32.8	34.7	47.4	30.7	. . .	35.3
1967	33.4	41.3	39.8	32.0	48.9	38.1	14.4	34.2	41.4	35.1	34.6	33.2	35.9	48.3	31.2	. . .	36.2
1968	34.2	42.3	40.6	32.8	50.7	39.3	14.3	34.1	42.8	39.8	35.0	34.0	37.0	49.7	32.4	. . .	37.0
1969	35.6	45.0	42.7	33.9	51.8	41.5	14.6	34.2	43.6	44.0	36.0	36.0	38.2	50.7	33.6	40.4	38.1
1970	36.9	45.8	44.6	35.2	52.4	42.0	15.3	35.0	44.9	39.9	37.5	38.7	40.0	51.9	35.3	41.9	39.8
1971	38.1	46.6	45.5	36.5	53.3	43.4	16.6	35.6	45.2	44.7	38.1	39.4	41.4	53.1	38.2	44.2	40.8
1972	39.8	51.6	48.0	37.8	55.5	50.0	17.1	35.6	45.3	50.7	39.3	40.9	42.3	53.8	39.4	45.5	41.5
1973	45.0	72.7	58.9	40.3	60.5	54.5	19.4	37.6	46.6	62.2	42.3	44.0	43.7	55.7	40.7	46.1	43.3
1974	53.5	77.4	68.0	49.2	68.0	55.2	30.1	50.2	56.4	64.5	52.5	57.0	50.0	61.8	47.8	50.3	48.1
1975	58.4	77.0	72.6	54.9	67.4	56.5	35.4	62.0	62.2	62.1	59.0	61.5	57.9	67.5	54.4	56.7	53.4
1976	61.1	78.8	70.8	58.4	72.4	63.9	38.3	64.0	66.0	72.2	62.1	65.0	61.3	70.3	58.2	60.5	55.6
1977	64.9	79.4	74.0	62.5	75.3	68.3	43.6	65.9	69.4	83.0	64.6	69.3	65.2	73.2	62.6	64.6	59.4
1978	69.9	87.7	80.6	67.0	78.1	76.1	46.5	68.0	72.4	96.9	67.7	75.3	70.3	77.5	69.6	69.5	66.7
1979	78.7	99.6	88.5	75.7	82.5	96.1	58.9	76.0	80.5	105.5	75.9	86.0	76.7	82.8	77.6	75.3	75.5
1980	89.8	102.9	95.9	88.0	89.7	94.7	82.8	89.0	90.1	101.5	86.3	95.0	86.0	90.7	88.4	82.9	93.6
1981	98.0	105.2	98.9	97.4	97.6	99.3	100.2	98.4	96.4	102.8	94.8	99.6	94.4	95.9	96.7	94.3	96.1
1982	100.0	100.0	100.0	100.0	100.0	100.0	100.0	100.0	100.0	100.0	100.0	100.0	100.0	100.0	100.0	100.0	100.0
1983	101.3	102.4	101.8	101.1	100.3	103.2	95.9	100.3	100.8	107.9	103.3	101.8	102.7	103.4	101.6	102.8	104.8
1984	103.7	105.5	105.4	103.3	102.7	109.0	94.8	102.9	102.3	108.0	110.3	104.8	105.1	105.7	105.4	105.2	107.0
1985	103.2	95.1	103.5	103.7	102.9	108.9	91.4	103.7	101.9	106.6	113.3	104.4	107.2	107.1	108.6	107.9	109.4
1986	100.2	92.9	105.4	100.0	103.2	113.0	69.8	102.6	101.9	107.2	116.1	103.2	108.8	108.2	110.0	110.5	111.6
1987	102.8	95.5	107.9	102.6	105.1	120.4	70.2	106.4	103.0	112.8	121.8	107.1	110.4	109.9	110.0	112.5	114.9
1988	106.9	104.9	112.7	106.3	109.2	131.4	66.7	116.3	109.3	118.9	130.4	118.7	113.2	113.1	111.2	114.3	120.2
1989	112.2	110.9	117.8	111.6	112.3	136.3	72.9	123.0	112.6	126.7	137.8	124.1	117.4	116.9	112.6	117.7	126.5
1990	116.3	112.2	121.9	115.8	115.0	141.7	82.3	123.6	113.6	129.7	141.2	122.9	120.7	119.2	114.7	121.5	134.2
1991	116.5	105.7	121.9	116.5	116.3	138.9	81.2	125.6	115.1	132.1	142.9	120.2	123.0	121.2	117.2	126.4	140.8
1992	117.2	103.6	122.1	117.4	117.8	140.4	80.4	125.9	115.1	146.6	145.2	119.2	123.4	122.2	117.3	130.4	145.3
1993	118.9	107.1	124.0	119.0	118.0	143.7	80.0	128.2	116.0	174.0	147.3	119.2	124.0	123.7	120.0	133.7	145.4
1994	120.4	106.3	125.5	120.7	118.3	148.5	77.8	132.1	117.6	180.0	152.5	124.8	125.1	126.1	124.2	137.2	141.9
1995	124.7	107.4	127.0	125.5	120.8	153.7	78.0	142.5	124.3	178.1	172.2	134.5	126.6	128.2	129.0	139.7	145.4
1996	127.7	122.4	133.3	127.3	122.4	150.5	85.8	142.1	123.8	176.1	168.7	131.0	126.5	130.4	131.0	141.7	147.7
1997	127.6	112.9	134.0	127.7	122.6	154.2	86.1	143.6	123.2	183.8	167.9	131.8	125.9	130.8	133.2	141.6	150.9
1998	124.4	104.6	131.6	124.8	122.9	148.0	75.3	143.9	122.6	179.1	171.7	127.8	124.9	131.3	135.4	141.2	156.0
1999	125.5	98.4	131.1	126.5	121.1	146.0	80.5	144.2	122.5	183.6	174.1	124.6	124.3	131.7	138.9	141.8	166.6
2000	132.7	99.5	133.1	134.8	121.4	151.5	103.5	151.0	125.5	178.2	183.7	128.1	124.0	132.6	142.5	143.8	170.8
2001	134.2	103.8	137.3	135.7	121.3	158.4	105.3	151.8	127.2	174.4	184.8	125.4	123.7	133.2	144.3	145.2	181.3
2002	131.1	99.0	136.2	132.4	119.9	157.6	93.2	151.9	126.8	173.3	185.9	125.9	122.9	133.5	146.2	144.6	182.4
2003	138.1	111.5	143.4	139.1	119.8	162.3	112.9	161.8	130.1	177.4	190.0	129.2	121.9	133.9	148.2	145.7	179.6
2004	146.7	123.3	151.2	147.6	121.0	164.5	126.9	174.4	133.8	195.6	195.7	149.6	122.1	135.1	153.2	148.6	183.2
2005	157.4	118.5	153.1	160.2	122.8	165.4	156.4	192.0	143.8	196.5	202.6	160.8	123.7	139.4	164.2	151.0	195.1
2006	164.7	117.0	153.8	168.8	124.5	168.4	166.7	205.8	153.8	194.4	209.8	181.6	126.2	142.6	179.9	152.6	205.6
2007	172.6	143.4	165.1	175.1	125.8	173.6	177.6	214.8	155.0	192.4	216.9	193.5	127.3	144.7	186.2	155.0	210.3
2008[1]	189.7	161.4	180.8	192.4	128.8	173.7	214.4	246.7	166.0	191.3	226.7	213.2	129.8	148.9	197.1	158.5	216.7
2008																	
January	181.0	164.2	172.7	182.8	126.9	172.2	195.9	229.2	159.2	189.3	222.3	197.5	127.8	145.7	188.5	157.5	212.7
February	182.7	164.4	174.6	184.6	127.1	172.5	199.5	231.3	159.9	189.1	223.4	201.8	128.3	146.1	188.8	157.5	213.3
March	187.9	169.6	176.9	190.2	127.2	172.5	217.1	235.6	160.6	189.9	224.0	208.0	128.5	146.4	189.5	156.8	214.8
April	190.9	166.7	177.8	193.8	127.6	172.9	224.7	240.4	161.3	190.5	224.9	217.6	128.7	147.2	191.0	157.6	214.9
May	196.6	169.7	180.8	200.0	128.2	172.9	243.2	246.5	162.8	193.8	225.2	223.4	129.2	147.3	192.1	157.5	216.4
June	200.5	176.2	182.4	204.0	128.2	174.8	254.8	252.7	164.0	194.6	225.7	226.9	129.6	148.0	194.4	156.7	217.1
July	205.5	174.3	187.0	209.5	129.1	175.0	268.7	262.8	167.4	193.5	227.0	231.8	130.4	149.3	198.8	156.7	218.3
August	199.0	164.7	187.3	202.4	130.1	174.9	237.9	263.3	169.7	193.5	229.6	230.9	130.5	150.3	202.7	157.6	218.4
September	196.9	163.5	185.9	200.1	131.0	175.2	230.2	264.2	171.6	193.7	231.1	223.7	130.7	151.0	204.4	157.8	218.3
October	186.4	145.3	182.5	189.3	130.7	175.1	194.5	252.5	172.5	191.1	230.9	209.1	130.9	151.8	205.0	162.8	218.8
November	177.5	143.3	181.3	179.0	130.3	174.6	162.5	245.5	172.9	188.9	227.8	196.8	131.2	152.4	205.8	161.8	218.5
December[1]	171.3	134.3	178.9	172.6	129.4	171.7	146.3	230.9	170.1	187.6	228.0	188.9	131.0	152.3	203.9	162.2	217.7

[1]Data are preliminary
. . . = Not available.

Table 8-6. Producer Price Indexes for the Net Output of Selected NAICS Industry Groups

(Various index bases, not seasonally adjusted.)

Year and month	Mining		Manufacturing (Dec. 1984 = 100)									
	Total (Dec. 1984 = 100)	Oil and gas extraction (Dec. 1985 = 100)	Total	Food manu-facturing	Leather and products	Petroleum and coal products	Chemicals	Plastics and rubber products	Nonmetallic mineral products	Primary metals	Fabricated metal products	Furniture and related products
1990	81.8	82.7	114.5	116.2	122.6	91.4	121.0	111.3	110.0	116.5	115.1	119.1
1991	78.4	77.9	115.9	116.5	124.8	83.1	124.4	113.7	112.3	113.1	116.6	121.6
1992	76.9	76.5	117.4	116.9	127.0	80.3	125.8	114.2	112.8	111.7	117.2	122.9
1993	76.4	76.2	119.1	118.7	129.0	77.6	127.2	115.4	115.4	111.4	118.2	125.4
1994	73.3	71.1	120.7	120.1	130.6	74.8	130.0	117.1	119.6	117.0	120.3	129.7
1995	71.0	66.6	124.2	121.7	134.1	77.2	143.4	123.3	124.3	128.2	124.8	133.3
1996	84.4	84.8	127.1	127.1	134.7	87.4	145.8	123.1	125.8	123.7	126.2	136.2
1997	86.1	87.5	127.5	127.9	137.1	85.6	147.1	122.8	127.4	124.7	127.6	138.2
1998	70.8	68.3	126.2	126.3	137.1	66.3	148.7	122.1	129.3	120.9	128.7	139.7
1999	78.0	78.5	128.3	126.3	136.5	76.8	149.7	122.2	132.6	115.8	129.1	141.3
2000	113.5	126.8	133.5	128.5	137.9	112.8	156.7	124.6	134.7	119.8	130.3	143.3
2001	114.3	127.5	134.6	132.8	141.3	105.3	158.4	125.9	136.0	116.1	131.0	145.1
2002	96.6	107.0	133.7	132.0	141.1	98.8	157.3	125.5	137.1	116.2	131.7	146.3
2003	131.3	160.1	137.1	137.4	142.8	122.0	164.6	128.4	138.0	118.4	132.9	147.4
2004	153.4	192.7	142.9	144.3	143.6	149.9	172.8	131.7	142.7	142.8	141.3	151.5
2005	201.0	262.0	150.8	146.1	144.5	200.4	187.3	141.2	152.0	156.3	149.5	157.8
2006	208.7	252.5	156.9	146.8	146.6	235.5	196.8	149.7	163.4	179.3	155.7	162.5
2007	220.1	267.1	162.9	158.6	149.7	260.3	203.3	150.6	166.8	190.5	162.3	165.7
2008[1]	274.2	346.1	175.8	174.1	153.5	329.4	228.4	161.4	170.9	212.1	174.5	171.5
2008												
January	254.2	321.9	168.5	165.8	152.0	294.9	213.6	154.8	168.1	190.4	165.6	167.1
February	263.8	335.0	169.6	167.5	152.4	298.4	215.8	155.6	168.2	194.2	166.8	167.8
March	287.2	371.6	173.4	169.8	152.6	337.1	218.4	156.4	168.6	202.4	168.3	168.3
April	301.6	390.8	175.3	171.2	152.7	347.7	221.1	156.8	169.1	211.5	171.1	169.5
May	329.0	436.2	179.4	174.0	152.4	384.1	224.5	158.3	169.6	221.1	173.0	170.2
June	341.4	456.0	182.0	176.1	153.4	406.0	228.5	159.4	170.0	227.8	174.7	171.3
July	363.8	490.4	185.6	180.3	153.8	429.6	234.5	162.9	171.0	232.7	177.2	172.3
August	299.2	383.6	182.6	180.5	154.1	382.2	238.2	165.2	171.9	233.5	178.8	173.5
September	273.4	341.2	182.9	179.2	154.8	382.6	240.4	166.9	172.5	228.9	179.6	174.3
October	223.3	259.4	176.8	176.4	154.6	300.0	239.3	167.8	173.3	214.9	179.6	175.1
November	183.4	194.9	169.5	174.6	155.1	222.3	235.4	167.9	174.0	201.8	179.4	175.6
December[1]	171.5	177.9	164.2	172.2	154.7	169.1	230.1	165.1	174.3	184.7	178.4	175.2

Year and month	Transportation and warehousing					Health care and social assistance			Other services industries (Dec. 1996 = 100)			
	Air transpor-tation (Dec. 1992 = 100)	Rail transpor-tation (Dec. 1996 = 100)	Pipeline transportation (June 1986 = 100)		Postal service (June 1989 = 100)	Offices of physicians (Dec. 1996 = 100)	Home health care (Dec. 1996 = 100)	Hospitals (Dec. 1992 = 100)	Legal services	Architec-tural, engineering, and related services	Employment services	Accom-modation
			Crude oil	Refined petr. products								
1990	. . .	. . .	94.2	100.8	100.0	. . .	. . .	. . .	. . .	. . .	. . .	. . .
1991	. . .	. . .	94.4	101.1	117.9	. . .	. . .	. . .	. . .	. . .	. . .	. . .
1992	. . .	. . .	94.8	101.2	119.8	. . .	. . .	. . .	. . .	. . .	. . .	. . .
1993	105.6	. . .	95.0	101.3	119.8	. . .	. . .	102.5	. . .	. . .	. . .	. . .
1994	108.5	. . .	102.5	103.4	119.8	. . .	. . .	106.2	. . .	. . .	. . .	. . .
1995	113.7	. . .	113.4	104.6	132.2	. . .	. . .	110.0	. . .	. . .	. . .	. . .
1996	121.1	. . .	104.7	104.3	132.3	. . .	. . .	112.6	. . .	. . .	. . .	. . .
1997	125.3	100.5	96.0	105.3	132.3	101.0	103.3	113.6	102.5	102.2	101.0	104.2
1998	124.5	101.7	96.8	104.8	132.3	103.2	106.2	114.4	106.1	105.1	103.2	108.1
1999	130.8	101.3	95.5	104.9	135.3	105.5	107.1	116.4	108.7	108.5	105.2	112.7
2000	147.7	102.6	101.0	105.3	135.2	107.3	111.1	119.4	112.5	111.8	107.3	116.2
2001	157.2	104.5	111.1	108.5	143.4	110.4	114.0	123.0	117.9	115.9	108.2	121.3
2002	157.8	106.6	112.3	111.0	150.2	110.3	116.6	127.5	121.7	121.1	108.9	121.3
2003	162.1	108.8	111.1	112.7	155.0	112.1	117.0	134.9	125.6	124.3	111.4	122.0
2004	162.3	113.4	115.2	116.0	155.0	114.3	119.8	141.5	131.8	126.8	113.9	125.2
2005	171.0	125.2	125.5	120.3	155.0	116.4	121.1	146.9	138.5	129.2	116.3	131.9
2006	180.4	135.9	135.3	123.8	164.7	117.5	121.8	153.3	145.2	134.4	119.2	136.7
2007	183.7	140.9	138.9	131.7	171.9	122.3	124.0	158.6	153.6	140.0	121.7	142.9
2008[1]	204.3	157.5	151.8	139.0	178.9	123.5	126.0	163.2	161.5	141.1	123.2	146.5
2008												
January	192.0	152.1	144.8	136.0	175.5	123.3	125.4	162.4	159.9	139.2	122.3	145.4
February	191.8	151.6	144.9	136.0	175.5	123.3	125.5	162.6	160.3	140.3	123.0	145.2
March	198.6	152.0	145.1	136.1	175.5	123.3	125.5	162.9	160.7	140.3	123.0	145.3
April	199.5	152.9	149.9	135.7	175.5	123.2	125.4	162.7	161.1	140.5	122.9	145.6
May	203.7	156.4	149.9	136.5	180.5	123.2	125.4	162.7	160.9	140.5	122.7	144.9
June	213.5	159.6	149.9	136.5	180.5	123.2	125.4	162.6	161.1	141.3	122.8	147.0
July	213.6	162.5	156.1	141.9	180.5	123.5	125.6	163.2	161.5	141.6	123.0	149.9
August	213.0	164.3	156.1	141.8	180.5	123.6	126.3	163.2	161.5	141.6	123.4	150.9
September	208.6	163.7	156.8	142.0	180.5	123.7	126.5	163.0	162.6	141.6	123.1	146.9
October	209.3	160.9	156.8	142.7	180.5	124.0	127.3	164.9	163.2	141.8	123.6	145.6
November	206.7	158.5	156.8	141.8	180.5	123.9	127.3	164.3	163.2	142.1	124.1	146.5
December[1]	198.0	154.6	156.1	142.4	180.5	124.2	127.1	164.3	163.1	142.1	124.2	144.3

[1]Data are preliminary.
. . . = Not available.

NOTES AND DEFINITIONS

TABLES 8-1 THROUGH 8-3 AND 20-2
CONSUMER PRICE INDEXES

SOURCES: U.S. DEPARTMENT OF LABOR, BUREAU OF LABOR STATISTICS (BLS) AND U.S. DEPARTMENT OF COMMERCE, BUREAU OF ECONOMIC ANALYSIS (BEA)

The Consumer Price Index (CPI), which is compiled by the Bureau of Labor Statistics (BLS), was originally conceived as a statistical measure of the average change in the cost to consumers of a market basket of goods and services purchased by urban wage earners and clerical workers. In 1978, its scope was broadened to also provide a measure of the change in the cost of the average market basket for all urban consumers. There was still a demand for a wage-earner index, so both versions have been calculated and published since then. The most commonly cited measure in this system is the Consumer Price Index for All Urban Consumers (CPI-U). The wage-earner alternative, used for calculating cost of living adjustments in many government programs, including Social Security, and in wage contracts, is called the Consumer Price Index for Urban Wage Earners and Clerical Workers (CPI-W). Both are presented by the BLS back to 1919; however, the *movements* (percent changes) in the two indexes before 1978 are identical and are based on the wage-earner market basket.

These CPIs have typically been called "cost-of-living" indexes, even though the original fixed market basket concept does not correspond to economists' definition of a cost-of-living index. In recent years, the concept measured in practice in the CPI has developed into something intended to be closer to the theoretical definition of a cost-of-living index—that is, the cost of maintaining a constant standard of living or level of satisfaction rather than the cost of a fixed market basket. In addition, a new variation of the CPI—the Chained Consumer Price Index for All Urban Consumers (C-CPI-U)—is intended to provide an even closer approximation of a cost-of-living index.

The reference base for the total BLS Consumer Price Index and most of its components is currently 1982–1984 = 100. However, new products that have been introduced into the index since January 1982 are shown on later reference bases, as is the entire C-CPI-U.

Price indexes for personal consumption expenditures (PCE) are calculated and published by the Bureau of Economic Analysis (BEA) as a part of the national income and product accounts (NIPAs). (See Chapters 1 and 4 and their notes and definitions.) The reference base for these indexes is the average in the NIPA base year, 2000. These indexes differ in a number of other respects from the CPIs, and are often emphasized by the Federal Reserve in its analyses of the nation's economy. NIPA data are also available monthly and are shown in Tables 8-2 and 8-3 for convenient comparison with the CPIs. See the definitions for those tables for more information.

The CPI-U and the CPI-W

All of the BLS consumer price indexes in Table 8-1 are components of the *CPI-U*. This index uses the consumption patterns for all urban consumers, who comprised about 87 percent of the population in the 1993–1995 period.

A slightly different index that is widely used for adjusting wages and government benefits is the *CPI-W*, of which the all-items total is shown in Tables 8-2 and 8-3. It represents the buying habits of only urban wage earners and clerical workers—about 32 percent of the population in the 1993–1995 period. The weights are derived from the same Consumer Expenditure Surveys (CES) used for the CPI-U weights, and are changed on the same schedule. However, they include only consumers from the specified categories instead of all urban consumers.

Beginning with January 2008, the weights in both indexes are based on consumer expenditures in the 2005–2006 period. From January 2006 to December 2007, the weights represented expenditures in the 2003–2004 period. From January 2004 to December 2005, the weights represented expenditures in the 2001–2002 period. From January 2002 to December 2003, the weights represented consumer expenditures in the 1999–2000 period. Between January 1998 and December 2001, weights from the 1993–1995 period were used. The weights will continue to be updated at two-year intervals, with new weights introduced in the January indexes of each even-numbered year. Previously, new weights were introduced only at the time of a major revision, which translated into a lag of a decade or more.

Specifically, the CPI weights for 1964 through 1977 were derived from reported expenditures of a sample of wage-earner and clerical-worker families and individuals in 1960–1961 and adjusted for price changes between the survey dates and 1963. Weights for the 1978–1986 period were derived from a survey undertaken during the 1972–1974 period and adjusted for price change between the survey dates and December 1977. For 1987 through 1997, the spending patterns reflected in the CPI were derived from a survey undertaken during the 1982–1984 period. The reported expenditures were adjusted for price change between the survey dates and December 1986.

The CPI was overhauled and updated in the latest major revision, which took effect in January 1998. In addition, new products and improved methods are regularly introduced into the index, usually in January.

The latest change in methods was the introduction of a geometric mean formula for calculating many of the basic components of the index. Beginning with the index for January 1999, this formula is used for categories comprising approximately 61 percent of total consumer spending. The new formula allows for the possibility that some consumers may react to changing relative prices within a category by substituting items whose relative prices have declined for products whose relative prices have risen, while maintaining their overall level of satisfaction. The geometric mean formula is not used for categories in which consumer substitution in the short term is not feasible, notably housing rent, utilities, and hospital services.

The CPI-U was introduced in 1978. Before that time, only CPI-W data were available. The movements of the CPI-U before 1978 are therefore based on the changes in the CPI-W. However, the index <u>levels</u> are different because the two indexes differed in the 1982–1984 base period.

Because the official CPI-U and CPI-W are so widely used in "escalation"—the calculation of cost-of-living adjustments for wages and for government payments and tax parameters—these price indexes are not retrospectively revised to incorporate new information and methods. (An exception is occasionally made for outright error, which happened in September 2000 and affected the data for January through August of that year.) Instead, the new information and methods of calculation are introduced in the current index and affect future index changes only. In Tables 8-2 and 8-3, special CPI and PCE indexes that are subject to retrospective revision are presented. These indexes can be used by researchers to provide more consistent historical information.

Notes on the CPI data

The CPI is based on prices of food, clothing, shelter, fuel, utilities, transportation, medical care, and other goods and services that people buy for day-to-day living. The quantity and quality of these priced items are kept essentially constant between revisions to ensure that only price changes will be measured. All taxes directly associated with the purchase and use of these items, such as sales and property taxes, are included in the index; the effects of income and payroll tax changes are not included.

Data are collected from about 23,000 retail establishments and about 50,000 housing units in 87 urban areas across the country. These data are used to develop the U.S. city average.

Periodic major revisions of the indexes update the content and weights of the market basket of goods and services; update the statistical sample of urban areas, outlets, and unique items used in calculating the CPI; and improve the statistical methods used. In addition, retail outlets and items are resampled on a rotating 5-year basis. Adjustments for changing quality are made at times of major product changes, such as the annual auto model changeover. Other methodological changes are introduced from time to time.

The CES provides the weights—that is, the relative importance—used to combine the individual price changes into subtotals and totals. This survey is composed of two separate surveys: an interview survey and a diary survey, both of which are conducted by the Census Bureau for BLS. Each expenditure reported in the two surveys is classified into a series of detailed categories, which are then combined into expenditure classes and ultimately into major expenditure groups. CPI data as of 1998 are grouped into eight such categories: (1) food and beverages, (2) housing, (3) apparel, (4) transportation, (5) medical care, (6) recreation, (7) education and communication, and (8) other goods and services.

Seasonally adjusted national CPI indexes are published for selected series for which there is a significant seasonal pattern of price change. The factors currently in use were derived by the X-12-ARIMA seasonal adjustment method. Some series with extreme or sharp movements are seasonally adjusted using X-12-ARIMA Intervention Analysis Seasonal Adjustment. Seasonally adjusted indexes and seasonal factors for the preceding five years are updated annually based on data through the previous December. Due to these revisions, BLS advises against the use of seasonally adjusted data for escalation. Detailed descriptions of seasonal adjustment procedures are available upon request from BLS.

CPI Definitions

Definitions of the major CPI groupings were modified beginning with the data for January 1998. These modifications were carried back to 1993. The following definitions are the current definitions currently used for the CPI components.

The *food and beverage index* includes both food at home and food away from home (restaurant meals and other food bought and eaten away from home).

The *housing index* measures changes in rental costs and expenses connected with the acquisition and operation of a home. The CPI-U, beginning with data for January 1983, and the CPI-W, beginning with data for January 1985, reflect a change in the methodology used to compute the homeownership component. A rental equivalence measure replaced an asset-price approach. The central purpose of the change was to separate shelter costs from the investment component of homeownership, so that the index would only reflect the cost of shelter services provided by owner-occupied homes. In addition to measures of the cost of shelter, the housing category includes insurance, fuel, utilities, and household furnishings and operations.

The *apparel index* includes the purchase of apparel and footwear.

The *private transportation index* includes prices paid by urban consumers for such items as new and used automobiles and other vehicles, gasoline, motor oil, tires, repairs and maintenance, insurance, registration fees, driver's licenses, parking fees, and the like. Auto finance charges, like mortgage interest payments, are considered to be a cost of asset acquisition, not of current consumption. Therefore, they are no longer included in the CPI. City bus, streetcar, subway, taxicab, intercity bus, airplane, and railroad coach fares are some of the components of the *public transportation index*.

The *medical care index* includes prices for professional medical services, hospital and related services, prescription and nonprescription drugs, and other medical care commodities. The portion of health insurance premiums used to cover the costs of these medical goods and services is distributed among the items; the portion of health insurance costs attributable to administrative expenses and profits of insurance providers constitutes a separate health insurance item. Effective with the January 1997 data, the method of calculating the hospital cost component was changed from the pricing of individual commodities and services to a more comprehensive cost-of-treatment approach.

Recreation includes components formerly listed in housing, apparel, entertainment, and "other goods and services."

Education and communication is a new group including components formerly categorized in housing and "other goods and services," such as telephone services and computers.

Other goods and services now includes tobacco, personal care, and miscellaneous.

Alternative price measures in Tables 8-2 and 8-3

Table 8-2 shows the all-items CPI-U and CPI-W, along with a number of other indexes that various analysts of price trends have preferred as measures of the price level. Table 8-3 shows the inflation rates (percent changes in price levels) implied by each of the indexes in Table 8-2.

As food and energy prices are volatile and frequently determined by forces separate from monetary aggregate demand pressures, many analysts prefer an index of prices excluding those components. Indexes *excluding food and energy* are known as *core* indexes, and inflation rates calculated from them are known as *core inflation rates*.

The *CPI-U-X1* is a special experimental version of the CPI that researchers have used to provide a more historically consistent series. As explained above, the official CPI-U treated homeownership on an asset-price basis until January 1983. It then changed to a rental equivalence method. The CPI-U-X1 incorporates a rental equivalence approach to homeowners' costs for the years 1967–1982 as well. It is rebased to the December 1982 value of the CPI-U (1982–1984 = 100); thus, it is identical to the CPI-U in December 1982 and all subsequent periods, as can be seen in Table 8-2. For this reason, it is not updated or published in the CPI news release or on the BLS Web site.

Newly introduced in the 13th edition of *Business Statistics* is the *CPI-E,* an experimental re-weighting of components of the CPI-U to represent price change for the goods and services purchased by Americans age 62 years and over,

who accounted for 16.5 percent of the total number of urban consumer units in the 2001–2002 CES.

This index is not an ideal measure of price change for older Americans. Because the sample is small, the sampling error in the weights is greater than the error in the all-urban index. The products and outlets sampled are those characteristic of the general urban population rather than older residents. In addition, senior discounts are not included in the prices collected. Such discounts are included—appropriately—in the weights, which are based on the expenditures reported by the older consumers' households, and are thus only a problem if they do not move proportionately to general prices.

The *CPI-U-RS* is a "research series" CPI that retroactively incorporates estimates of the effects of most of the methodological changes implemented since 1978, including the rental equivalence method, new or improved quality adjustments, and improvement of formulas to eliminate bias and allow for some consumer substitution within categories. This index is calculated from 1977 onward. Its reference base is December 1977 = 100. Thus, although it generally shows less *increase* than the official index, its current *levels* are considerably higher because the earlier reference base period had lower prices. Unlike the official CPIs and the CPI-U-X1, its historical values will be revised each time a significant change is made in the calculation of the current index. This index is not seasonally adjusted and is not included in the CPI news release. It is available on the BLS Web site, along with an explanation and background material. The CPI-U-RS is used by BLS in the calculation of historical trends in real compensation per hour in its Productivity and Costs system; see Table 9-3 and its notes and definitions. It is also now used by the Census Bureau to convert household incomes into constant dollars, as seen in Chapter 3.

The *C-CPI-U* (Chained Consumer Price Index for All Urban Consumers) is a new, supplemental index that has been published in the monthly CPI news release since August 2002. It is available only from December 1999 to date and is calculated with the base December 1999 = 100; it is not seasonally adjusted. It is designed to be a still-closer approximation to a true cost-of-living index than the CPI-U and the CPI-W, in that it assumes that consumers substitute between and within categories in response to changes in relative prices in order to maintain a fixed basket of "consumer satisfaction."

The C-CPI-U is a "superlative" index, using a method known as the "Tornqvist formula" to incorporate the composition of consumer spending in the current period as well as in the earlier base period. As it requires consumer expenditure data for the current as well as the earlier period, its final version can only be calculated after the expenditure data become available—about two years before the current period—and is approximated in more recent periods by making more extensive use of the geometric mean formula (see above). With the release of January 2009 data, the indexes for 2007 were revised to their final form, and the initial indexes for 2008 were revised to "interim" levels.

Personal consumption expenditure (PCE) chain-type price indexes are calculated by the Bureau of Economic Analysis (BEA) in the framework of the national income and product accounts (NIPAs). (See the notes and definitions for Chapters 1 and 4.) The scope of NIPA PCE is broader than the scope of the CPI. PCE includes the rural as well as the urban population and the consumption spending of nonprofit entities. The CPI includes only consumer out-of-pocket cash spending, whereas PCE includes some imputed services and includes expenditures financed by government and private insurance, particularly in the medical care area. For this reason, there is a large difference between the relatively small weight of medical care spending in the CPI and the markedly greater percentage of PCE that is accounted for by total medical care spending. Housing, on the other hand, has a somewhat smaller weight in PCE and all non-housing components have a higher weight. It is believed that the CES tends to report housing expenditures accurately and somewhat underestimate other spending, which suggests that the weight of housing relative to all other products may be overestimated in the CPI but measured more correctly in the PCE price index.

PCE chain-type indexes use the expenditure weights of both the earlier and the later period to determine the aggregate price change between the two periods. (See the notes and definitions for Chapter 1.) Thus, they are subject to revision as improved data on the composition of consumption spending become available, and in this respect resemble the C-CPI-U.

For a large share of PCE, the price movements for basic individual spending categories are determined by CPI components. The differences between the rates of change in the aggregate CPI and PCE indexes are largely the result of the different weights, but also reflect some alternative methodologies and the previously mentioned differences in scope.

Market-based PCE indexes are based on household expenditures for which there are observable price measures. They exclude most implicit prices (for example, the services furnished without payment by financial intermediaries) and they exclude items not deflated by a detailed component of either the Consumer Price Index (CPI) or the Producer Price Index (PPI). This means that the price observations that make up these new aggregate measures are all based on observed market transactions. The new price measures are therefore known as "market-based price indexes." The imputed rent for owner-occupied housing is included in the market-based price index, since it is based on observed rentals of comparable homes. Household insurance premiums are also included in the market-based index, since they are deflated by the CPI for tenants' and household insurance. Excluded are services furnished without payment by financial intermediaries, most insurance purchases, expenses of NPISHs (nonprofit institutions serving house-

holds), gambling, margins on used light motor vehicles, and expenditures by U.S. residents working and traveling abroad. Also excluded are medical, hospitalization, and income loss insurance; expense of handling life insurance; motor vehicle insurance; and workers' compensation.

The *inflation rates* shown in Table 8-3 are percent changes in the price indexes introduced in Table 8-2. For annual indexes, the rate is the percent change from the previous year. For monthly indexes, the rate is the percent change from the same month a year earlier. To give an indication of the longer-run implications of use of these different price indicators, compound annual inflation rates are also shown as calculated by the editor for the 1978–2008, 1983–2008, and 2000–2008 periods, using the growth rate formula presented in the article at the beginning of this volume.

Data availability and references

The CPI-U, CPI-W, and C-CPI-U are initially issued in a press release two to three weeks after the end of the month for which the data were collected. This release and detailed and complete current and historical data on the CPI and its variants and components, along with extensive documentation, are available on the BLS Web site at <http://www.bls.gov/cpi>.

Information available on the BLS Web site includes "Common Misconceptions about the Consumer Price Index: Questions and Answers;" another fact sheet on frequently asked questions; a fact sheet on seasonal adjustment; Chapter 17 of the *BLS Handbook of Methods*, entitled "The Consumer Price Index"; a section entitled "Note on Chained Consumer Price Index for All Urban Consumers"; and a number of explanatory CPI fact sheets on specific subjects.

As previously indicated, the CPI-U-X1 is not currently published because its recent values are identical to the CPI-U. The CPI-E is presented in articles in the CPI section of the BLS Web site, the most recent of which is "Experimental Consumer Price Index for Americans 62 Years of Age and Older, 1998–2005"; recent values are available by request from BLS. The CPI-U-RS is updated each month in a report entitled "CPI Research Series Using Current Methods" on the site. In both cases, the reports describe the indexes and provide references.

The monthly PCE indexes are included in the personal income report issued by BEA, which is published near the end of the following month. These indexes are revised month-by-month to reflect new information and annually to reflect the annual and quinquennial benchmarking of the NIPAs. They can be found on the BEA Web site at <http://www.bea.gov> by selecting "Gross Domestic Product," "Supplemental Estimates," and "Underlying Detail Tables."

Two special editions of the *Monthly Labor Review* were devoted to CPI issues. The December 1996 issue describes the subsequently implemented 1997 and 1998 revisions in a series of articles, and the December 1993 issue, entitled *The Anatomy of Price Change*, includes the following articles: "The Consumer Price Index: Underlying Concepts and Caveats"; "Basic Components of the CPI: Estimation of Price Changes"; "The Commodity Substitution Effect in CPI Data, 1982–1991"; and "Quality Adjustment of Price Indexes."

The new formula for calculating basic components is described in "Incorporating a Geometric Mean Formula into the CPI," *Monthly Labor Review* (October 1998). For a detailed discussion of the treatment of homeownership, see "Changing the Homeownership Component of the Consumer Price Index to Rental Equivalence," *CPI Detailed Report* (January 1983).

For a comprehensive, up-to-date professional review of CPI concepts and methodology, see Charles Schultze and Christopher Mackie, ed., *At What Price? Conceptualizing and Measuring Cost-of-Living and Price Indexes* (Washington, DC: National Academy Press, 2001). Earlier references include: "Using Survey Data to Assess Bias in the Consumer Price Index," *Monthly Labor Review* (April 1998); Joel Popkin, "Improving the CPI: The Record and Suggested Next Steps," *Business Economics*, Vol. XXXII, No. 3 (July 1997), pages 42–47; *Measurement Issues in the Consumer Price Index* (Bureau of Labor Statistics, U.S. Department of Labor, June 1997); *Toward a More Accurate Measure of the Cost of Living* (Final Report to the Senate Finance Committee from the Advisory Commission to Study the Consumer Price Index, December 4, 1996)—also known as the "Boskin Commission" report; and *Government Price Statistics* (U.S. Congress Joint Economic Committee, 87th Congress, 1st Session, January 24, 1961)—also known as the "Stigler Committee" report.

For an explanation of the differences between the CPI-U and the PCE index, see Clinton P. McCully, Brian C. Moyer, and Kenneth J. Stewart, "Comparing the Consumer Price Index and the Personal Consumption Expenditures Price Index," *Survey of Current Business*, November 2007, pp. 26-33.

TABLES 8-4 THROUGH 8-6 AND 20-2 PRODUCER PRICE INDEXES

SOURCE: U.S. DEPARTMENT OF LABOR, BUREAU OF LABOR STATISTICS (BLS)

Producer Price Indexes (PPI) measure average changes in prices received by domestic producers. The prices of individual commodities are organized into three different, separate systems: stage of processing, commodity group, and industry. Most of the indexes currently are published on a base of 1982 = 100. However, there are a number of exceptions for products and industries introduced into the index system since 1982. In this book, alternative base periods are identified in the column headings for the individual series.

Table 8-4 presents price indexes for commodities by stage of processing. Table 8-5 presents data by major commodity groups; these are the groupings that have the longest continuous history. In recent years, the major commodity groups—particularly the totals for all commodities and industrial commodities—have been de-emphasized, as they aggregate successive stages of processing and thus often exaggerate price trends. This effect was particularly acute in the energy price crisis of the early 1970s. To avoid this problem, the stage-of-processing groups were introduced in 1978. However, the individual commodity groups (for example, textile products and apparel) provide a much longer historical perspective on individual industrial sectors than the current industry groupings, and are presented here for that reason.

Table 8-6 presents PPIs for the net output of selected industry groups. As the coverage of the PPI is expanded, indexes for additional industries are frequently introduced, and new industries may only go back to December of the most recent year. This volume includes only those industry groupings with at least 10 years of historical data.

Definitions

The *stage-of-processing* PPI indexes (Table 8-4) organize commodities by class of buyer and degree of fabrication. These have been the featured measures since 1978. The three major indexes are: (1) *finished goods*, or commodities that will not undergo further processing and are ready for sale to the ultimate user (such as automobiles, meats, apparel, and machine tools, and also unprocessed foods such as eggs and fresh vegetables, that are ready for the consumer); (2) *intermediate materials, supplies, and components*, or commodities that have been processed but require further processing before they become finished goods (such as steel mill products, cotton yarns, lumber, and flour), as well as physically complete goods that are purchased by business firms as inputs for their operations (such as diesel fuel and paper boxes); and (3) *crude materials* for further processing, or products entering the market for the first time that have not been manufactured or fabricated and are not sold directly to consumers (such as ores, scrap metals, crude petroleum, raw cotton, and livestock).

PPIs for the *net output* of industries and their products (Table 8-6) are grouped according to the North American Industry Classification System (NAICS). For each industry, they include both measures of price change for the products "primary" to that industry (products made primarily but not necessarily exclusively by that industry), and measures of changes in prices received by establishments classified in the industry for products or services chiefly made in some other industry. Thus, they are designed to be compatible with other economic time series organized by industry, such as data on shipments, employment, wages, and productivity.

Notes on the data

The probability sample used for calculating the PPI provides more than 100,000 price quotations per month, selected to represent the movement of prices of all commodities produced in the manufacturing; agriculture, forestry, and fishing; mining; and gas, electricity, and public utility sectors.

In addition, new PPIs are gradually being introduced for the products and services produced by industries in the construction, transportation, trade, finance, and services sectors. These are only used for industry indexes and are not incorporated in the commodity indexes or the commodity by stage of processing indexes.

To the greatest extent possible, prices used in calculating the PPI represent prices received by domestic producers in the first important commercial transaction for each commodity. These indexes attempt to measure only price changes (changes in receipts per unit of measurement not influenced by changes in quality, quantity sold, terms of sale, or level of distribution). Most quotations are the selling prices of selected manufacturers or other producers, although a few prices are those quoted on organized exchanges or markets. Transaction prices are sought instead of list or book prices.

Price data are generally collected monthly, primarily by mail questionnaire. Most prices are obtained directly from producing companies on a voluntary and confidential basis. Prices are generally reported for the Tuesday of the week containing the 13th day of the month.

The name "Producer Price Index" became effective with the release of March 1978 data and replaced the term "Wholesale Price Index." The change was made to more accurately reflect the coverage of the data. At the same time, there was a shift in analytical emphasis from the All Commodities Index and other traditional commodity grouping indexes (as shown in Table 8-5) to the Finished Goods Index and other stage-of-processing indexes.

The BLS revises the PPI weighting structure when data from economic censuses become available. Beginning with data for January 2007, the weights used to construct the PPI reflect 2002 shipments values as measured by the 2002 Economic Censuses. Data for 2002 through 2006 use 1997 shipments values. Data for 1996 through 2001 reflect 1992 shipments values; 1992 through 1995 reflect 1987 shipments values; 1987 through 1991 reflect 1982 values; 1976 through 1986 reflect 1972 values; and 1967 through 1975 reflect 1963 values.

BLS has been working for a number of years on a comprehensive overhaul of the theory, methodology, and procedures used to construct the PPI. One aspect of this overhaul was the previously mentioned shift in emphasis to the stage-of-processing measures, which began in 1978. Other changes phased in since 1978 include the replacement of

judgment sampling with probability sampling techniques; expansion to systematic coverage of the net output of virtually all industries in the mining and manufacturing sectors; introduction of measures for selected services industries, including retail trade; a shift from a commodity to an industry orientation; and the exclusion of imports from, and the inclusion of exports in, the survey universe.

The commodity components of the stage-of-processing indexes, in addition to being available in unadjusted form, are also adjusted for seasonal variation using the X-12-ARIMA method. Since January 1988, BLS has also used X-12-ARIMA Intervention Analysis Seasonal Adjustment for a small number of series to remove unusual values that might distort seasonal patterns before calculating the seasonal adjustment factors. Seasonal factors for the PPI are revised annually to take into account the most recent 12 months of data. Seasonally adjusted data for the previous 5 years are subject to these annual revisions. The industry net output indexes are not seasonally adjusted.

Data availability and references

The indexes are initially issued in a press release two to three weeks after the end of the month for which the data were collected. Data are subsequently published in greater detail in a monthly BLS publication, *PPI Detailed Report*. Each month, data for the fourth previous month (both unadjusted and seasonally adjusted) are revised to reflect late reports and corrections.

The press release, the *PPI Detailed Report*, detailed and complete current and historical data, and extensive documentation are available at <http://www.bls.gov/ppi>. The items available on this Web site include Chapter 14 of the *BLS Handbook of Methods*, "Producer Price Indexes"; a selection of *Monthly Labor Review* articles on the PPI; and fact sheets on a number of issues and index components.

TABLE 8-4
PURCHASING POWER OF THE DOLLAR

SOURCE: U.S. DEPARTMENT OF LABOR, BUREAU OF LABOR STATISTICS (BLS); CALCULATIONS BY THE EDITOR

The purchasing power of the dollar measures changes in the quantity of goods and services a dollar will buy at a particular date compared with a selected base date. It must be defined in terms of the following: (1) the specific commodities and services that are to be purchased with the dollar; (2) the market level (producer, retail, etc.) at which they are purchased; and (3) the dates for which the comparison is to be made. Thus, the purchasing power of the dollar for a selected period, compared with another period, may be measured in terms of a single commodity or a large group of commodities (such as all goods and services purchased by consumers at retail or all finished commodities sold in primary markets).

Broad price indexes calculated by BLS that have been used to measure the purchasing power of the dollar in the United States include: (1) the Producer Price Index (PPI) for Finished Goods, which relates to prices received by the producers of finished commodities at the primary market level; and (2) two versions of the Consumer Price Index (the CPI-U and CPI-W), which measure average changes in retail prices of goods and services. These indexes are described above in the sections of the notes and definitions pertaining to the Producer Price Index and the Consumer Price Index, respectively.

The purchasing power of the dollar is computed by dividing the price index number for the base period by the price index number for the comparison date and expressing the result in dollars and cents. The base period is the period in which the price index equals 100; the purchasing power in that base period is therefore $1.00. In this book, 1982–1984 is used as the base period for both purchasing power measures.

Purchasing power estimates in terms of both the CPI-U and the CPI-W are calculated by BLS and published in the CPI press release. The CPI-U version is shown here. The comparable purchasing power in terms of the finished goods PPI is calculated by the editor of *Business Statistics* after rebasing the index from its published 1982 base to 1982–1984 = 100. In all cases, the purchasing power measure is based on indexes not adjusted for seasonal variation.

CHAPTER 9: EMPLOYMENT COSTS, PRODUCTIVITY, AND PROFITS

Section 9a: Employment Cost Indexes

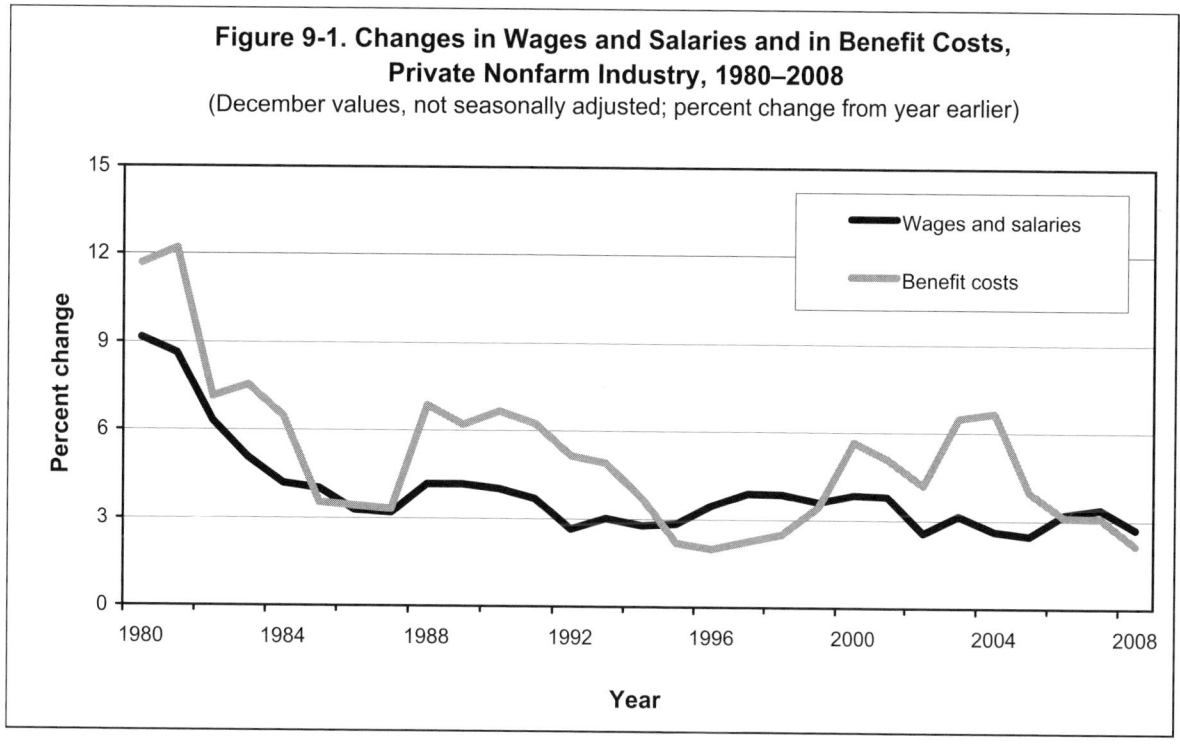

Figure 9-1. Changes in Wages and Salaries and in Benefit Costs, Private Nonfarm Industry, 1980–2008
(December values, not seasonally adjusted; percent change from year earlier)

- In most of the years since 1979 in which ECI data have been collected, benefit costs have risen faster than wages and salaries, driven by the rising costs of medical benefits. Figure 9-1 shows that like the late 1990s, the years 2006 through 2008 were an exception, as wages and salaries strengthened slightly and benefit growth slowed. (Tables 9-1 and 9-2)

- Between December 2001 and December 2008, total compensation per hour (wages, salaries, and benefits combined) as measured in the ECI—which holds the composition of employment constant in order to isolate increases in compensation for individual workers and excludes stock options—rose at an average annual rate of 3.2 percent. (Table 9-1) The consumer price index for all urban consumers (CPI-U) rose at a 2.5 percent annual rate over the same period (Tables 8-1 and 20-2), implying an increase in real worker compensation of 0.7 percent per year.

- Real worker compensation is said to track worker productivity—but over the same 7-year period, the output per hour of nonfarm industry workers rose 2.3 percent per year (Tables 9-3 and 19-13), exceeding the rate of real compensation increase by 1.6 percentage points. Of this gap, 0.3 percentage points reflects a difference between the CPI and the price index used in calculating productivity, leaving a real gap between productivity growth and compensation growth of 1.3 percentage points per year. (Tables 9-3, 19-13, 8-1, and 20-2)

Table 9-1. Employment Cost Indexes, NAICS Basis

(December 2005 [not seasonally adjusted] = 100; annual values are for December, not seasonally adjusted; quarterly values, seasonally adjusted, except as noted.)

Year and month	All civilian workers [1]	State and local government workers	All private industry workers	Excluding incentive paid occupations [2]	Management, professional, and related	Sales and office	Natural resources, construction, and maintenance	Production, transportation, and material moving	Service occupations [3]	Goods-producing industries Total	Goods-producing industries Manufacturing	Service-providing	Union [2]	Non-union [2]
TOTAL COMPENSATION														
2001	87.1	86.2	87.3	. . .	87.4	86.9	86.6	87.4	89.4	86.0	85.5	87.8	84.8	87.8
2002	90.0	89.7	90.0	. . .	89.7	89.8	89.7	90.3	92.0	89.0	88.7	90.4	88.2	90.3
2003	93.5	92.8	93.6	. . .	93.8	93.1	93.3	93.6	95.0	92.6	92.4	94.0	92.3	93.9
2004	97.0	96.1	97.2	. . .	97.1	96.8	97.1	97.8	97.7	96.9	96.9	97.3	97.3	97.2
2005	100.0	100.0	100.0	100.0	100.0	100.0	100.0	100.0	100.0	100.0	100.0	100.0	100.0	100.0
2006	103.3	104.1	103.2	103.2	103.5	102.9	103.6	102.3	103.1	102.5	101.8	103.4	103.0	103.2
2007	106.7	108.4	106.3	106.4	106.8	106.1	106.7	104.5	107.0	105.0	103.8	106.7	105.1	106.5
2008	109.5	111.6	108.9	109.5	109.9	107.9	109.6	106.9	109.8	107.5	105.9	109.4	108.0	109.1
2001														
March	84.7	83.6	85.0	. . .	. . .	. . .	. . .	. . .	. . .	84.0	83.7	85.3	82.0	85.5
June	85.5	84.5	85.8	. . .	. . .	. . .	. . .	. . .	. . .	84.7	84.4	86.1	82.9	86.3
September	86.4	85.5	86.7	. . .	. . .	. . .	. . .	. . .	. . .	85.4	84.9	87.1	83.7	87.2
December	87.2	86.1	87.5	. . .	. . .	. . .	. . .	. . .	. . .	86.2	85.8	87.9	84.8	87.8
2002														
March	87.9	86.8	88.2	. . .	88.2	87.8	87.6	88.5	90.3	87.1	86.8	88.6	85.7	88.7
June	88.8	87.5	89.1	. . .	89.0	88.9	88.6	89.1	90.7	87.7	87.5	89.6	86.5	89.6
September	89.5	88.7	89.6	. . .	89.4	89.3	89.3	89.8	91.6	88.2	88.0	90.1	87.5	90.0
December	90.1	89.6	90.2	. . .	90.0	90.1	90.2	90.5	92.1	89.2	89.0	90.5	88.2	90.3
2003														
March	91.2	90.4	91.4	. . .	91.5	90.9	91.0	91.6	93.0	90.6	90.6	91.7	89.5	91.8
June	92.0	91.3	92.2	. . .	92.2	91.7	92.0	92.4	93.5	91.4	91.3	92.4	90.7	92.5
September	92.9	92.0	93.2	. . .	93.2	92.8	92.8	93.2	94.4	92.1	92.0	93.5	91.6	93.5
December	93.6	92.7	93.8	. . .	94.1	93.4	93.7	93.7	95.1	92.8	92.6	94.1	92.3	93.9
2004														
March	94.6	93.5	94.9	. . .	94.8	94.5	95.0	95.5	95.9	94.5	94.7	95.0	94.5	95.0
June	95.5	94.4	95.8	. . .	95.5	95.5	95.9	96.5	96.7	95.4	95.6	96.0	95.9	95.9
September	96.4	95.1	96.7	. . .	96.4	96.5	96.4	97.4	97.2	96.4	96.7	96.8	96.7	96.7
December	97.0	95.9	97.3	. . .	97.4	97.0	97.3	97.9	97.8	97.1	97.1	97.4	97.3	97.2
2005														
March	98.0	97.0	98.2	. . .	98.4	97.9	98.0	98.5	98.4	98.0	98.2	98.3	97.9	98.3
June	98.6	97.8	98.8	. . .	99.0	98.4	98.7	99.0	99.0	98.9	99.0	98.8	98.8	98.9
September	99.3	98.7	99.5	. . .	99.6	99.2	99.4	99.7	99.6	99.7	99.7	99.4	99.6	99.5
December	100.1	99.8	100.2	100.0	100.3	100.2	100.2	100.1	100.1	100.2	100.2	100.1	100.0	100.0
2006														
March	100.7	100.5	100.8	100.9	101.0	100.6	101.0	100.5	100.8	100.3	100.0	100.9	100.5	100.9
June	101.6	101.5	101.6	101.7	101.8	101.5	102.0	101.1	101.5	101.3	100.9	101.7	101.8	101.7
September	102.6	102.8	102.5	102.5	102.9	102.1	102.9	101.7	102.3	101.9	101.4	102.7	102.4	102.6
December	103.4	103.9	103.3	103.2	103.8	103.1	103.7	102.3	103.1	102.6	101.9	103.5	103.0	103.2
2007														
March	104.2	105.1	104.0	104.0	104.5	103.8	104.1	102.5	104.4	102.9	101.9	104.3	102.7	104.2
June	105.1	106.2	104.8	105.0	105.4	104.5	104.8	103.3	105.2	103.8	102.8	105.2	103.9	105.1
September	105.9	107.2	105.6	105.8	106.3	105.2	105.8	103.9	106.4	104.3	103.1	106.1	104.4	105.9
December	106.8	108.2	106.5	106.4	107.1	106.2	106.8	104.5	107.1	105.2	103.9	106.9	105.1	106.5
2008														
March	107.6	108.9	107.3	107.6	108.0	106.8	107.8	105.5	107.8	106.1	104.7	107.6	105.9	107.5
June	108.3	109.9	107.9	108.3	108.8	107.3	108.2	106.0	108.7	106.7	105.1	108.4	106.7	108.3
September	109.1	110.9	108.6	109.0	109.6	107.7	108.9	106.6	109.5	107.1	105.6	109.1	107.4	108.9
December	109.6	111.5	109.1	109.5	110.2	108.0	109.7	106.9	109.8	107.7	106.0	109.5	108.0	109.1

[1] Excludes farm workers, private household workers, and federal government employees.
[2] Not seasonally adjusted.
[3] Wages and salaries not seasonally adjusted.
. . . = Not available.

Table 9-1. Employment Cost Indexes, NAICS Basis—*Continued*

(December 2005 [not seasonally adjusted] = 100; annual values are for December, not seasonally adjusted; quarterly values, seasonally adjusted, except as noted.)

Year and month	All civilian workers [1]	State and local government workers	All private industry workers	Excluding incentive paid occupations [2]	Private industry workers								Union [2]	Non-union [2]
					By occupational group					By industry				
					Management, professional, and related	Sales and office	Natural resources, construction, and maintenance	Production, transportation, and material moving	Service occupations [3]	Goods-producing industries		Service-providing		
										Total	Manufacturing			
WAGES AND SALARIES														
2001	89.9	90.2	89.9	. . .	89.5	89.1	90.0	91.0	91.7	90.0	90.2	89.8	89.6	89.9
2002	92.4	93.0	92.2	. . .	91.7	91.7	92.6	93.3	93.9	92.6	92.8	92.1	92.6	92.2
2003	95.1	95.0	95.1	. . .	95.3	94.3	95.2	95.4	96.1	94.9	95.1	95.2	94.9	95.1
2004	97.5	97.0	97.6	. . .	97.8	97.2	97.5	97.8	97.9	97.2	97.4	97.7	97.6	97.6
2005	100.0	100.0	100.0	100.0	100.0	100.0	100.0	100.0	100.0	100.0	100.0	100.0	100.0	100.0
2006	103.2	103.5	103.2	103.2	103.6	103.0	103.4	102.4	102.9	102.9	102.3	103.3	102.3	103.3
2007	106.7	107.1	106.6	106.7	107.2	106.2	107.1	105.0	107.1	106.0	104.9	106.8	104.7	106.9
2008	109.6	110.4	109.4	110.1	110.5	108.0	110.5	107.8	110.1	109.0	107.7	109.6	108.1	109.6
2001														
March	87.6	87.6	87.6	. . .	. . .	. . .	. . .	. . .	89.7	87.9	88.2	87.4	86.5	87.7
June	88.4	88.4	88.4	. . .	. . .	. . .	. . .	. . .	90.2	88.7	89.0	88.3	87.4	88.6
September	89.2	89.4	89.2	. . .	. . .	. . .	. . .	. . .	90.6	89.3	89.5	89.1	88.3	89.3
December	90.0	90.0	90.0	. . .	. . .	. . .	. . .	. . .	91.7	90.1	90.3	90.0	89.6	89.9
2002														
March	90.7	90.5	90.7	. . .	90.4	91.1	90.7	91.9	92.5	90.8	91.2	90.7	90.2	90.8
June	91.5	91.2	91.6	. . .	91.2	91.1	91.6	92.4	92.8	91.3	91.7	91.6	91.1	91.7
September	92.0	92.1	92.0	. . .	91.5	91.3	92.2	92.8	93.4	91.8	92.2	92.0	91.9	92.0
December	92.4	92.8	92.3	. . .	91.9	92.0	92.8	93.3	93.9	92.7	93.0	92.2	92.6	92.2
2003														
March	93.3	93.5	93.3	. . .	93.3	92.5	93.4	94.1	94.5	93.3	93.8	93.2	93.0	93.3
June	93.9	94.1	93.8	. . .	93.9	93.2	94.0	94.6	94.8	94.0	94.4	93.8	93.8	94.0
September	94.6	94.4	94.7	. . .	94.8	94.1	94.6	95.1	95.6	94.5	94.8	94.7	94.4	94.9
December	95.1	94.9	95.2	. . .	95.4	94.5	95.3	95.4	96.1	95.0	95.3	95.2	94.9	95.1
2004														
March	95.7	95.5	95.8	. . .	95.9	95.3	95.9	96.0	96.4	95.6	95.7	95.8	95.6	95.8
June	96.3	96.0	96.4	. . .	96.4	96.0	96.6	96.7	96.9	96.2	96.4	96.5	96.4	96.5
September	97.0	96.3	97.2	. . .	97.2	97.0	96.9	97.6	97.4	97.2	97.4	97.2	97.1	97.3
December	97.5	96.9	97.7	. . .	97.9	97.3	97.6	97.8	97.9	97.4	97.6	97.8	97.6	97.6
2005														
March	98.2	97.6	98.3	. . .	98.6	98.0	98.0	98.4	98.6	97.9	98.2	98.4	97.9	98.3
June	98.7	98.3	98.8	. . .	99.1	98.4	98.6	98.9	99.0	98.6	98.8	98.9	98.7	98.9
September	99.3	98.8	99.4	. . .	99.5	99.1	99.3	99.5	99.6	99.5	99.6	99.4	99.5	99.5
December	100.1	99.8	100.1	100.0	100.2	100.1	100.1	100.0	100.0	100.2	100.2	100.1	100.0	100.0
2006														
March	100.7	100.3	100.8	100.8	101.0	100.6	100.8	100.6	100.6	100.7	100.6	100.8	100.3	100.8
June	101.6	101.2	101.6	101.7	101.9	101.5	101.8	101.2	101.3	101.7	101.6	101.6	101.2	101.8
September	102.5	102.5	102.5	102.5	102.9	102.2	102.7	101.8	102.0	102.2	101.8	102.6	101.7	102.7
December	103.3	103.3	103.3	103.2	103.8	103.0	103.5	102.4	102.9	103.0	102.5	103.4	102.3	103.3
2007														
March	104.3	104.2	104.3	104.3	104.9	104.0	104.4	103.2	104.6	103.9	103.2	104.4	102.8	104.5
June	105.1	105.1	105.1	105.2	105.7	104.7	105.0	103.8	105.3	104.6	103.8	105.2	103.7	105.3
September	105.9	106.0	105.9	106.1	106.6	105.2	106.1	104.5	106.5	105.4	104.4	106.1	104.4	106.2
December	106.7	106.9	106.7	106.7	107.4	106.2	107.1	105.0	107.1	106.1	105.1	106.9	104.7	106.9
2008														
March	107.6	107.7	107.6	107.9	108.4	106.9	108.3	106.0	107.9	107.2	105.9	107.7	105.5	107.9
June	108.4	108.7	108.4	108.7	109.2	107.5	108.9	106.8	108.8	107.8	106.6	108.5	106.7	108.7
September	109.2	109.8	109.0	109.5	110.0	107.8	109.6	107.5	109.7	108.5	107.3	109.2	107.4	109.4
December	109.7	110.2	109.6	110.1	110.7	108.1	110.6	107.8	110.1	109.1	107.8	109.7	108.1	109.6

[1]Excludes farm workers, private household workers, and federal government employees.
[2]Not seasonally adjusted.
[3]Wages and salaries not seasonally adjusted.
. . . = Not available.

Table 9-1. Employment Cost Indexes, NAICS Basis—*Continued*

(December 2005 [not seasonally adjusted] = 100; annual values are for December, not seasonally adjusted; quarterly values, seasonally adjusted, except as noted.)

Year and month	All civilian workers [1]	State and local government workers	Private industry workers — All private industry workers	Excluding incentive paid occupations [2]	By occupational group — Management, professional, and related	Sales and office	Natural resources, construction, and maintenance	Production, transportation, and material moving	Service occupations [3]	By industry — Goods-producing industries Total	Goods-producing industries Manufacturing	Service-providing	Union [2]	Non-union [2]
TOTAL BENEFITS														
2001	80.6	78.1	81.3	. . .	82.0	81.1	79.8	80.7	82.5	78.5	77.2	82.4	77.3	82.2
2002	84.3	83.0	84.7	. . .	84.7	84.7	84.1	84.5	86.5	82.3	81.3	85.8	81.2	85.5
2003	89.7	88.2	90.2	. . .	90.1	90.0	89.8	90.2	91.7	88.2	87.3	91.0	88.1	90.6
2004	95.7	94.1	96.2	. . .	95.4	95.8	96.4	97.7	97.0	96.3	96.0	96.1	96.8	96.0
2005	100.0	100.0	100.0	. . .	100.0	100.0	100.0	100.0	100.0	100.0	100.0	100.0	100.0	100.0
2006	103.6	105.2	103.1	. . .	103.4	102.9	104.0	102.0	103.6	101.7	100.8	103.7	104.2	102.9
2007	106.8	111.0	105.6	. . .	106.0	106.0	105.9	103.7	106.7	103.2	101.7	106.6	105.8	105.6
2008	109.1	114.2	107.7	. . .	108.5	107.8	107.7	105.1	108.8	104.7	102.5	108.9	107.8	107.6
2001														
March	78.0	75.2	78.8	. . .	. . .	. . .	. . .	. . .	. . .	76.5	75.4	79.7	74.8	79.9
June	78.8	76.3	79.5	. . .	. . .	. . .	. . .	. . .	. . .	77.0	75.8	80.5	75.7	80.5
September	79.9	77.4	80.6	. . .	. . .	. . .	. . .	. . .	. . .	77.8	76.4	81.7	76.6	81.6
December	80.8	78.0	81.5	. . .	. . .	. . .	. . .	. . .	. . .	78.7	77.4	82.6	77.3	82.2
2002														
March	81.5	78.8	82.3	. . .	82.7	81.8	81.2	81.8	83.5	79.9	78.8	83.2	78.6	83.2
June	82.5	79.9	83.3	. . .	83.7	83.2	82.1	82.7	84.4	80.6	79.7	84.4	79.3	84.3
September	83.5	81.4	84.1	. . .	84.2	84.2	83.3	83.7	86.0	81.2	80.3	85.2	80.5	84.9
December	84.6	82.9	85.0	. . .	85.2	85.1	84.6	84.8	86.8	82.5	81.5	86.0	81.2	85.5
2003														
March	86.3	84.1	87.0	. . .	87.1	86.6	86.0	86.7	88.5	85.2	84.7	87.7	83.9	87.8
June	87.5	85.4	88.1	. . .	88.0	88.0	87.6	88.1	89.4	86.5	85.7	88.8	85.7	88.8
September	88.9	86.9	89.4	. . .	89.5	89.3	88.7	89.4	90.8	87.5	86.8	90.2	87.2	89.9
December	90.0	88.0	90.5	. . .	90.7	90.4	90.3	90.4	92.0	88.4	87.5	91.4	88.1	90.6
2004														
March	92.1	89.5	92.9	. . .	91.9	92.5	92.9	94.4	94.3	92.4	92.7	93.0	92.8	93.0
June	93.7	91.1	94.4	. . .	93.4	94.2	94.5	96.0	95.9	93.8	94.1	94.6	95.0	94.5
September	94.8	92.5	95.4	. . .	94.5	95.2	95.3	97.1	96.7	95.0	95.3	95.5	96.0	95.2
December	95.9	94.0	96.5	. . .	96.0	96.1	96.8	98.0	97.3	96.5	96.1	96.4	96.8	96.0
2005														
March	97.5	95.5	98.0	. . .	97.8	97.5	98.0	98.7	98.0	98.2	98.2	97.9	98.0	98.2
June	98.4	96.8	98.8	. . .	98.8	98.3	98.9	99.1	98.8	99.5	99.4	98.6	98.9	99.0
September	99.4	98.4	99.7	. . .	99.8	99.4	99.7	100.0	99.5	100.3	100.0	99.4	99.8	99.6
December	100.2	99.9	100.3	. . .	100.5	100.3	100.3	100.1	100.3	100.2	100.1	100.3	100.0	100.0
2006														
March	100.8	100.7	100.8	. . .	100.9	100.7	101.2	100.1	101.2	99.5	98.9	101.3	100.8	101.0
June	101.7	102.0	101.6	. . .	101.6	101.4	102.4	100.8	102.1	100.4	99.7	102.1	102.7	101.5
September	102.7	103.6	102.5	. . .	102.8	102.1	103.4	101.5	103.0	101.2	100.5	103.0	103.4	102.3
December	103.7	105.2	103.4	. . .	103.9	103.1	104.2	102.1	103.9	101.8	100.9	104.0	104.2	102.9
2007														
March	103.9	107.0	103.1	. . .	103.5	103.3	103.6	101.2	104.0	101.0	99.6	104.0	102.4	103.4
June	105.2	108.7	104.2	. . .	104.8	104.2	104.5	102.3	105.0	102.2	101.0	105.0	104.1	104.3
September	106.0	109.7	105.0	. . .	105.6	105.2	105.2	102.7	106.0	102.3	100.7	106.0	104.3	105.1
December	106.9	111.0	105.8	. . .	106.5	106.2	106.0	103.7	106.9	103.3	101.7	106.8	105.8	105.6
2008														
March	107.5	111.3	106.4	. . .	106.9	106.5	106.8	104.5	107.4	104.1	102.3	107.4	106.6	106.5
June	108.1	112.5	106.9	. . .	107.7	106.9	106.7	104.5	108.4	104.4	102.2	108.0	106.6	107.1
September	108.8	113.3	107.5	. . .	108.5	107.5	107.4	104.8	108.7	104.5	102.3	108.7	107.2	107.6
December	109.2	114.2	107.9	. . .	109.0	108.0	107.8	105.1	109.0	104.8	102.5	109.1	107.8	107.6

[1] Excludes farm workers, private household workers, and federal government employees.
[2] Not seasonally adjusted.
[3] Wages and salaries not seasonally adjusted.
. . . = Not available.

Table 9-2. Employment Cost Indexes, SIC Basis

(Not seasonally adjusted, December 2005 = 100; annual values are for December.)

Year	All civilian workers [1,2]	State and local government workers [2]	All private industry workers [2]	Private industry workers excluding sales occupations	By occupational group				By industry division								
									Goods-producing industries			Service-providing industries					
					Production and nonsupervisory occupations	White-collar occupations	Blue-collar occupations	Service occupations [2]	Total [2]	Construction [2]	Manufacturing [2]	Total [2]	Transportation and utilities	Wholesale trade	Retail trade	Finance, insurance, and real estate [2]	Services
TOTAL COMPENSATION																	
1979	...	...	32.8	32.5	...	31.2	35.0	33.9	33.7	...	33.1	32.0	...	...	...	...	...
1980	...	...	35.9	35.9	...	34.2	38.5	37.1	37.0	...	36.4	35.1	...	...	...	...	...
1981	39.0	36.8	39.5	39.4	40.1	37.6	42.2	40.5	40.7	...	40.0	38.6	...	...	...	...	...
1982	41.5	39.4	42.0	42.0	42.8	40.1	44.7	43.9	43.2	...	42.4	41.1	...	...	...	...	...
1983	43.9	41.8	44.4	44.4	45.2	42.7	47.0	46.3	45.3	...	44.6	43.8	...	...	...	...	...
1984	46.2	44.6	46.6	46.7	47.3	44.8	49.0	49.4	47.4	...	46.9	46.0	...	...	...	...	...
1985	48.2	47.1	48.4	48.3	49.1	47.0	50.5	50.9	49.0	50.8	48.4	48.1	50.6	...	52.4	44.7	46.1
1986	49.9	49.6	49.9	49.9	50.5	48.6	51.9	52.4	50.5	52.3	50.0	49.6	51.8	48.5	53.5	46.1	48.1
1987	51.7	51.8	51.6	51.7	52.2	50.4	53.5	53.7	52.1	54.2	51.5	51.4	53.3	50.4	54.8	47.0	50.5
1988	54.2	54.7	54.1	54.1	54.8	52.9	55.9	56.5	54.4	56.5	53.8	54.0	54.9	52.5	58.0	50.0	53.5
1989	56.9	58.1	56.7	56.5	57.6	55.7	58.2	59.0	56.7	59.0	56.3	56.8	56.9	57.1	59.9	52.7	56.4
1990	59.7	61.5	59.3	59.3	60.1	58.4	60.7	61.8	59.4	60.9	59.1	59.4	59.1	58.2	62.5	54.9	59.9
1991	62.3	63.7	61.9	62.0	62.7	61.0	63.4	64.7	62.1	63.3	61.9	61.9	61.7	60.7	65.2	57.2	62.5
1992	64.4	66.0	64.1	64.2	64.9	63.1	65.6	66.7	64.5	65.6	64.3	63.9	63.9	62.5	66.9	57.9	65.2
1993	66.7	67.9	66.4	66.6	67.3	65.4	68.1	68.8	67.0	67.1	66.9	66.2	66.1	64.4	68.9	60.5	67.5
1994	68.7	69.9	68.5	68.6	69.2	67.5	70.0	70.8	69.0	69.6	69.0	68.1	68.7	66.4	70.8	61.8	69.4
1995	70.6	72.0	70.2	70.4	71.0	69.4	71.7	72.1	70.7	71.1	70.8	70.0	71.2	69.4	72.3	64.0	70.9
1996	72.6	73.9	72.4	72.4	73.1	71.7	73.6	74.2	72.7	72.9	72.9	72.3	73.4	71.5	75.1	65.5	73.1
1997	75.0	75.6	74.9	74.9	75.4	74.4	75.5	77.2	74.5	74.8	74.6	75.1	75.5	73.8	77.7	69.9	75.9
1998	77.6	77.8	77.5	77.2	78.1	77.3	77.6	79.4	76.5	77.4	76.6	78.0	78.4	78.0	80.0	74.1	78.2
1999	80.2	80.5	80.2	80.0	80.4	79.9	80.2	82.1	79.1	79.9	79.2	80.6	80.1	81.1	83.0	77.1	80.9
2000	83.6	82.9	83.6	83.6	84.0	83.6	83.6	85.3	82.6	84.6	82.3	84.2	83.5	84.4	86.4	81.0	84.5
2001	87.0	86.4	87.1	87.0	87.4	87.1	86.7	89.1	85.7	88.2	85.3	87.8	87.5	87.2	90.3	83.9	88.3
2002	90.0	89.9	90.0	89.9	90.2	89.9	89.8	92.0	88.9	91.0	88.5	90.5	91.0	91.1	91.9	87.6	90.7
2003	93.5	92.9	93.6	93.6	93.6	93.6	93.4	94.9	92.4	94.1	92.2	94.2	94.0	94.0	94.9	94.1	94.0
2004	96.9	96.1	97.1	97.2	97.2	96.9	97.5	97.7	96.8	96.4	96.7	97.3	97.6	96.5	97.1	96.7	97.5
2005	100.0	100.0	100.0	100.0	100.0	100.0	100.0	100.0	100.0	100.0	100.0	100.0	100.0	100.0	100.0	100.0	100.0
WAGES AND SALARIES																	
1979	...	...	36.1	36.1	36.8	34.1	39.4	37.9	38.2	41.4	37.5	34.9	39.1	33.7	39.7	32.8	31.7
1980	...	...	39.4	39.3	40.3	37.1	43.1	41.0	41.8	45.0	41.0	38.0	43.5	37.1	42.5	35.2	34.5
1981	42.3	40.1	42.8	42.9	43.9	40.4	46.8	44.4	45.4	49.0	44.5	41.4	47.1	40.0	45.6	38.8	38.1
1982	45.0	42.7	45.5	45.6	46.7	43.1	49.4	48.2	48.0	51.5	47.0	44.2	50.5	42.5	47.5	41.3	41.2
1983	47.3	45.0	47.8	47.9	48.9	45.7	51.3	50.4	49.9	53.0	49.0	46.7	53.0	45.1	49.5	44.3	43.9
1984	49.4	47.7	49.8	50.1	50.8	47.6	53.1	53.5	51.8	53.7	51.2	48.7	54.8	47.6	52.0	43.9	46.7
1985	51.5	50.3	51.8	51.9	52.9	50.0	55.0	54.8	53.6	55.3	53.0	51.0	56.9	49.7	54.5	47.9	48.4
1986	53.3	53.0	53.5	53.6	54.3	51.7	56.4	56.2	55.3	56.7	54.8	52.5	57.9	51.5	55.7	49.2	50.3
1987	55.2	55.2	55.2	55.5	56.0	53.6	58.1	57.6	57.1	58.6	56.6	54.3	59.1	53.6	57.2	49.8	53.0
1988	57.5	57.9	57.5	57.5	58.4	56.1	59.9	60.1	58.9	60.7	58.3	56.9	60.6	55.6	60.1	52.9	55.6
1989	60.1	61.0	59.9	59.8	61.0	58.7	62.0	62.3	61.2	62.8	60.6	59.5	62.2	60.7	62.0	55.7	58.3
1990	62.6	64.2	62.3	62.4	63.2	61.2	64.2	64.8	63.4	64.1	63.1	61.8	64.3	61.2	64.2	57.6	61.6
1991	64.9	66.4	64.6	64.7	65.4	63.5	66.4	67.4	65.8	66.0	65.6	64.1	66.6	63.6	66.6	59.6	63.8
1992	66.6	68.4	66.3	66.5	67.2	65.2	68.1	68.8	67.6	67.3	67.6	65.7	68.7	65.5	68.2	59.5	66.0
1993	68.7	70.2	68.3	68.5	69.2	67.4	70.0	70.3	69.6	68.6	69.7	67.8	70.9	67.1	70.2	62.1	68.0
1994	70.6	72.4	70.2	70.5	71.1	69.3	72.0	72.4	71.7	70.8	71.8	69.6	73.5	69.1	71.9	62.8	70.0
1995	72.7	74.7	72.2	72.5	73.0	71.3	74.1	74.0	73.7	72.5	73.9	71.7	76.0	72.4	73.6	65.1	71.7
1996	75.1	76.8	74.7	74.9	75.5	73.8	76.3	76.6	76.0	74.6	76.3	74.2	78.1	74.7	76.8	67.2	74.2
1997	77.9	78.9	77.6	77.7	78.3	77.0	78.8	79.9	78.3	77.1	78.6	77.4	80.7	77.0	79.7	71.8	77.5
1998	80.8	81.3	80.6	80.4	81.4	80.3	81.3	82.4	81.1	79.9	81.3	80.5	83.0	81.5	82.2	76.9	80.1
1999	83.6	84.2	83.5	83.4	83.8	83.1	84.0	85.1	83.8	82.5	84.1	83.4	84.8	84.5	85.2	79.8	83.0
2000	86.7	87.0	86.7	86.7	87.1	86.4	87.1	88.3	87.1	86.9	87.1	86.6	87.5	87.4	88.6	83.4	86.3
2001	90.0	90.2	90.0	90.0	90.4	89.6	90.5	91.8	90.2	90.4	90.2	89.9	91.7	89.3	91.9	85.8	90.0
2002	92.6	93.1	92.4	92.5	92.6	92.0	93.0	94.1	92.9	92.8	93.0	92.3	94.7	92.8	93.2	89.4	92.0
2003	95.2	95.0	95.2	95.4	95.1	95.2	95.2	96.2	95.1	95.1	95.2	95.3	96.2	95.3	95.5	95.9	94.8
2004	97.5	97.0	97.5	97.8	97.5	97.5	97.6	97.9	97.4	97.0	97.5	97.7	98.6	96.6	97.2	97.7	97.8
2005	100.0	100.0	100.0	100.0	100.0	100.0	100.0	100.0	100.0	100.0	100.0	100.0	100.0	100.0	100.0	100.0	100.0

[1]Excludes farm workers, private household workers, and federal government employees.
[2]Roughly continuous and comparable with new NAICS-based series. See notes and definitions for more information.
. . . = Not available.

Table 9-2. Employment Cost Indexes, SIC Basis—*Continued*

(Not seasonally adjusted, December 2005 = 100; annual values are for December.)

Year	All civilian workers [1,2]	State and local government workers [2]	All private industry workers [2]	Private industry workers excluding sales occupations	Production and nonsupervisory occupations	White-collar occupations	Blue-collar occupations	Service occupations [2]	Goods-producing industries Total [2]	Construction [2]	Manufacturing [2]	Service-providing industries Total [2]	Transportation and utilities	Wholesale trade	Retail trade	Finance, insurance, and real estate [2]	Services
TOTAL BENEFITS																	
1979	. . .	. . .	25.7	. . .	. . .	24.7	27.4	. . .	26.0	. . .	25.8	25.4	. . .	. . .	. . .	. . .	. . .
1980	. . .	. . .	28.7	. . .	. . .	27.7	30.4	. . .	28.8	. . .	28.5	28.6	. . .	. . .	. . .	. . .	. . .
1981	31.8	. . .	32.2	. . .	. . .	31.1	34.0	. . .	32.4	. . .	32.1	31.9	. . .	. . .	. . .	. . .	. . .
1982	34.2	. . .	34.5	. . .	. . .	33.3	36.5	. . .	34.8	. . .	34.4	34.1	. . .	. . .	. . .	. . .	. . .
1983	36.8	. . .	37.1	. . .	. . .	35.8	39.1	. . .	37.2	. . .	36.9	36.8	. . .	. . .	. . .	. . .	. . .
1984	39.3	. . .	39.5	. . .	. . .	38.3	41.4	. . .	39.6	. . .	39.3	39.4	. . .	. . .	. . .	. . .	. . .
1985	40.8	. . .	40.9	. . .	. . .	40.0	42.5	41.2	40.8	. . .	40.4	40.9	. . .	. . .	. . .	. . .	. . .
1986	42.4	. . .	42.3	. . .	. . .	41.4	43.8	42.9	42.0	. . .	41.6	42.5	. . .	. . .	. . .	. . .	. . .
1987	44.0	. . .	43.7	. . .	. . .	42.9	45.3	43.9	43.2	. . .	42.7	44.2	. . .	. . .	. . .	. . .	. . .
1988	47.0	. . .	46.7	. . .	. . .	45.6	48.6	47.4	46.3	. . .	46.0	47.1	. . .	. . .	. . .	. . .	. . .
1989	50.1	52.2	49.6	. . .	. . .	48.6	51.2	50.5	48.8	. . .	48.7	50.2	. . .	. . .	. . .	. . .	. . .
1990	53.5	55.8	52.9	. . .	. . .	52.0	54.4	53.8	52.3	. . .	52.1	53.4	. . .	. . .	. . .	. . .	. . .
1991	56.5	58.0	56.2	. . .	. . .	55.2	57.8	57.7	55.5	. . .	55.2	56.7	. . .	. . .	. . .	. . .	. . .
1992	59.5	61.1	59.1	. . .	. . .	57.8	61.0	61.0	58.7	. . .	58.3	59.4	. . .	. . .	. . .	. . .	. . .
1993	62.2	62.9	62.0	. . .	. . .	60.5	64.4	64.4	62.0	. . .	61.8	62.0	. . .	. . .	. . .	. . .	. . .
1994	64.4	64.6	64.3	. . .	. . .	63.2	66.2	66.0	64.1	. . .	63.9	64.4	. . .	. . .	. . .	. . .	. . .
1995	65.8	66.3	65.7	. . .	. . .	64.8	67.2	66.6	65.2	. . .	65.0	66.0	. . .	. . .	. . .	. . .	. . .
1996	67.1	67.8	67.0	. . .	. . .	66.2	68.4	67.3	66.4	. . .	66.5	67.3	. . .	. . .	. . .	. . .	. . .
1997	68.5	68.6	68.5	. . .	. . .	68.0	69.4	69.6	67.3	. . .	67.4	69.2	. . .	. . .	. . .	. . .	. . .
1998	70.3	70.7	70.2	. . .	. . .	69.9	70.7	70.9	68.1	. . .	67.9	71.4	. . .	. . .	. . .	. . .	. . .
1999	72.6	72.7	72.6	. . .	. . .	72.3	73.0	73.4	70.5	. . .	70.3	73.8	. . .	. . .	. . .	. . .	. . .
2000	76.2	74.4	76.7	. . .	. . .	76.5	76.9	76.6	74.3	. . .	73.6	78.1	. . .	. . .	. . .	. . .	. . .
2001	80.2	78.5	80.6	. . .	. . .	81.1	79.5	81.3	77.3	. . .	76.3	82.5	. . .	. . .	. . .	. . .	. . .
2002	84.2	83.3	84.4	. . .	. . .	84.6	83.8	85.7	81.3	. . .	80.4	86.1	. . .	. . .	. . .	. . .	. . .
2003	89.5	88.4	89.8	. . .	. . .	89.7	89.8	91.3	87.4	. . .	86.7	91.2	. . .	. . .	. . .	. . .	. . .
2004	95.7	94.3	96.0	. . .	. . .	95.3	97.3	97.1	95.7	. . .	95.3	96.2	. . .	. . .	. . .	. . .	. . .
2005	100.0	100.0	100.0	. . .	. . .	100.0	100.0	100.0	100.0	. . .	100.0	100.0	. . .	. . .	. . .	. . .	. . .

[1]Excludes farm workers, private household workers, and federal government employees.
[2]Roughly continuous and comparable with new NAICS-based series. See notes and definitions for more information.
. . . = Not available.

Section 9b: Productivity and Related Data

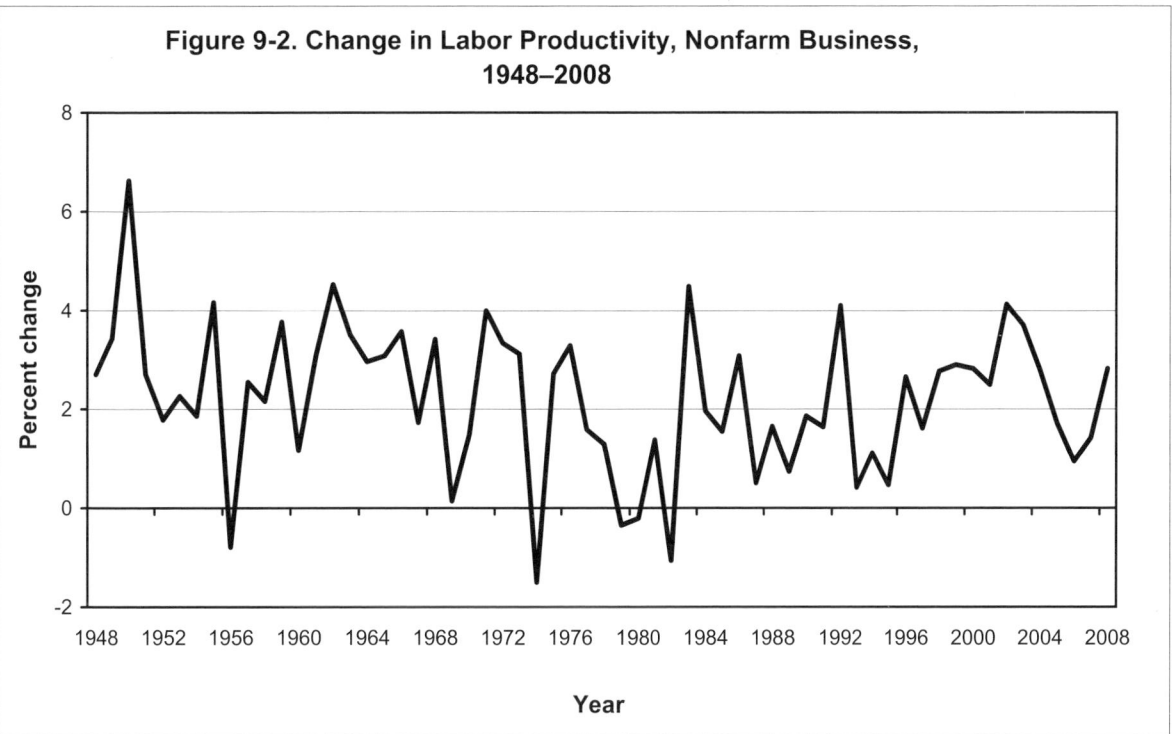

Figure 9-2. Change in Labor Productivity, Nonfarm Business, 1948–2008

- As Figure 9-2 demonstrates, the rate of change in U.S. nonfarm labor productivity is quite variable from year to year, and up through the 1980s tended to decline in recession years and rebound in recovery. One explanation of this was that firms expected that declines in demand would be temporary, and therefore held on to their experienced workers in order to be prepared for the recovery. (Tables 9-3 and 19-13)

- On average, measuring between cyclically high growth years, productivity grew at a 2.8 percent annual rate from 1948 to 1973. Productivity growth slowed between 1973 and 1989, averaging just 1.3 percent. Since 1989, productivity growth averaged 2.2 percent per year; growth was still variable but did not drop in recession years. (Tables 9-3 and 19-13)

- The productivity and costs accounts also include a measure of labor compensation. Unlike the ECI (Tables 9-1 and 9-2), these compensation data include the value of exercised stock options and other transitory payments. (See the notes and definitions for further explanation and other differences.) The rate of increase of compensation per hour minus the rate of increase of output per hour (productivity) equals the rate of increase in unit labor costs. For nonfinancial corporations, the accounts also provide separate measures for "nonlabor costs"—depreciation, interest, and indirect taxes—and corporate profits per unit of output. (Table 9-3)

- Between 2000 and 2007—comparable business cycle peak years—unit labor costs at nonfinancial corporations rose 1.1 percent per year and unit non-labor costs 1.8 percent per year. Neither rate was higher than the 1.8 percent rate of increase in the "implicit deflator" (the price of the sector's output), hence neither was exerting cost-push upward inflationary pressure. Unit profits rose at a 6.4 percent annual rate. (Table 9-3)

Table 9-3. Productivity and Related Data

(1992 = 100, seasonally adjusted.)

Year and quarter	Business sector Output per hour of all persons	Output	Hours of all persons	Compensation per hour	Real compensation per hour	Unit labor costs	Unit nonlabor payments	Implicit price deflator	Nonfarm business sector Output per hour of all persons	Output	Hours of all persons	Compensation per hour	Real compensation per hour	Unit labor costs	Unit nonlabor payments	Implicit price deflator
1950	37.3	23.4	62.6	8.3	44.7	22.1	21.5	21.9	41.9	22.9	54.7	8.8	47.9	21.1	20.8	21.0
1951	38.5	24.9	64.6	9.0	45.4	23.5	23.7	23.6	43.0	24.6	57.2	9.6	48.3	22.3	22.5	22.4
1952	39.6	25.7	64.8	9.6	47.3	24.2	23.2	23.8	43.8	25.3	57.9	10.1	49.9	23.1	22.3	22.8
1953	41.0	26.9	65.6	10.2	50.0	24.9	22.6	24.0	44.8	26.6	59.3	10.7	52.3	23.9	22.2	23.3
1954	41.9	26.6	63.4	10.5	51.2	25.2	22.5	24.2	45.6	26.1	57.3	11.0	53.6	24.2	22.3	23.5
1955	43.6	28.7	65.8	10.8	52.7	24.8	24.0	24.5	47.5	28.3	59.6	11.4	55.8	24.1	23.7	23.9
1956	43.6	29.1	66.8	11.5	55.3	26.4	23.5	25.3	47.2	28.8	61.1	12.1	58.3	25.8	23.1	24.8
1957	45.0	29.6	65.8	12.3	57.0	27.2	24.2	26.1	48.4	29.4	60.7	12.8	59.7	26.6	23.8	25.6
1958	46.3	29.1	62.9	12.8	57.9	27.7	24.7	26.6	49.4	28.7	58.2	13.4	60.4	27.0	24.1	26.0
1959	48.0	31.4	65.5	13.3	59.9	27.8	25.2	26.8	51.3	31.2	60.9	13.9	62.3	27.1	25.0	26.3
1960	48.9	32.0	65.6	13.9	61.3	28.4	24.9	27.1	51.9	31.8	61.2	14.5	63.9	27.9	24.3	26.6
1961	50.6	32.7	64.6	14.4	63.1	28.5	25.3	27.3	53.5	32.4	60.6	15.0	65.3	28.0	24.8	26.8
1962	52.9	34.8	65.8	15.1	65.2	28.5	26.1	27.6	55.9	34.6	61.9	15.6	67.3	27.8	25.8	27.1
1963	55.0	36.4	66.2	15.6	66.6	28.4	26.6	27.7	57.8	36.2	62.6	16.1	68.7	27.8	26.3	27.3
1964	56.8	38.7	68.1	16.2	68.3	28.5	27.3	28.1	59.6	38.7	64.9	16.6	69.9	27.9	27.2	27.6
1965	58.8	41.4	70.4	16.8	69.7	28.6	28.4	28.5	61.4	41.4	67.4	17.1	71.1	27.9	28.1	28.0
1966	61.2	44.2	72.3	17.9	72.3	29.3	29.0	29.2	63.6	44.4	69.8	18.2	73.2	28.6	28.7	28.6
1967	62.5	45.1	72.1	19.0	74.1	30.3	29.5	30.0	64.7	45.1	69.7	19.2	75.2	29.7	29.2	29.5
1968	64.7	47.3	73.2	20.5	76.9	31.7	30.4	31.2	66.9	47.5	71.0	20.7	77.8	31.0	30.2	30.7
1969	65.0	48.8	75.0	21.9	78.0	33.7	30.8	32.6	67.0	48.9	73.0	22.1	78.8	33.0	30.5	32.1
1970	66.3	48.7	73.5	23.6	79.5	35.6	31.5	34.1	68.0	48.9	71.9	23.7	79.8	34.9	31.2	33.5
1971	69.0	50.6	73.3	25.1	80.9	36.3	34.1	35.5	70.7	50.7	71.7	25.2	81.4	35.7	33.8	35.0
1972	71.2	53.9	75.6	26.7	83.3	37.4	35.7	36.8	73.1	54.1	74.0	26.9	84.0	36.8	34.9	36.1
1973	73.4	57.6	78.5	28.9	85.1	39.4	37.5	38.7	75.3	58.0	77.0	29.1	85.5	38.6	35.3	37.4
1974	72.3	56.8	78.7	31.7	84.0	43.9	40.0	42.4	74.2	57.3	77.2	31.9	84.5	43.0	38.1	41.2
1975	74.8	56.3	75.3	34.9	84.8	46.7	46.3	46.6	76.2	56.3	73.9	35.1	85.2	46.0	44.9	45.6
1976	77.1	60.0	77.8	38.0	87.1	49.2	48.7	49.0	78.7	60.2	76.5	38.1	87.4	48.3	47.8	48.1
1977	78.5	63.3	80.7	41.0	88.3	52.2	51.5	52.0	80.0	63.6	79.5	41.2	88.7	51.5	50.7	51.2
1978	79.3	67.3	84.9	44.5	89.7	56.2	54.8	55.6	81.0	67.8	83.7	44.8	90.3	55.3	53.4	54.6
1979	79.3	69.6	87.7	48.9	89.9	61.6	58.2	60.4	80.7	70.0	86.6	49.1	90.2	60.8	56.5	59.2
1980	79.2	68.8	87.0	54.1	89.6	68.4	61.3	65.8	80.6	69.2	85.9	54.4	90.0	67.5	60.4	64.9
1981	80.8	70.7	87.6	59.3	89.6	73.5	69.1	71.8	81.7	70.7	86.6	59.7	90.2	73.1	67.7	71.1
1982	80.1	68.6	85.6	63.6	90.6	79.4	70.1	75.9	80.8	68.4	84.7	63.9	91.1	79.1	69.3	75.5
1983	83.0	72.3	87.1	66.3	90.6	79.8	76.3	78.5	84.5	72.9	86.3	66.6	91.1	78.9	76.1	77.9
1984	85.2	78.6	92.2	69.1	90.8	81.1	80.2	80.8	86.1	78.9	91.6	69.5	91.2	80.7	79.2	80.1
1985	87.1	82.2	94.3	72.5	92.0	83.2	82.0	82.7	87.5	82.2	94.0	72.6	92.2	83.0	81.5	82.5
1986	89.7	85.3	95.1	76.1	94.9	84.9	82.6	84.1	90.2	85.4	94.7	76.4	95.2	84.7	82.4	83.9
1987	90.1	88.3	97.9	79.0	95.2	87.6	83.1	85.9	90.6	88.4	97.6	79.2	95.5	87.4	82.8	85.7
1988	91.5	92.1	100.6	83.0	96.5	90.7	85.1	88.6	92.1	92.4	100.4	83.1	96.7	90.2	85.0	88.3
1989	92.4	95.4	103.3	85.2	95.0	92.2	91.3	91.9	92.8	95.7	103.1	85.3	95.1	91.9	90.9	91.5
1990	94.4	96.9	102.7	90.6	96.2	96.0	93.7	95.1	94.5	97.1	102.7	90.4	96.0	95.7	93.5	94.9
1991	95.9	96.1	100.2	95.1	97.5	99.1	96.7	98.2	96.1	96.3	100.2	95.0	97.4	98.9	96.8	98.1
1992	100.0	100.0	100.0	100.0	100.0	100.0	100.0	100.0	100.0	100.0	100.0	100.0	100.0	100.0	100.0	100.0
1993	100.4	103.1	102.7	102.2	99.8	101.8	102.6	102.1	100.4	103.4	102.9	102.0	99.5	101.6	103.1	102.1
1994	101.4	108.2	106.8	103.7	99.0	102.3	106.7	103.9	101.5	108.3	106.6	103.7	99.1	102.1	107.3	104.0
1995	101.5	111.4	109.7	105.8	98.7	104.2	108.3	105.7	102.0	111.8	109.6	105.9	98.8	103.8	109.3	105.8
1996	104.5	116.5	111.5	109.5	99.5	104.8	111.9	107.4	104.7	116.8	111.5	109.4	99.5	104.5	112.1	107.3
1997	106.5	122.7	115.2	113.0	100.5	106.1	113.8	109.0	106.4	122.8	115.4	112.8	100.4	106.0	114.5	109.1
1998	109.5	128.6	117.5	119.9	105.2	109.5	110.0	109.7	109.4	128.9	117.9	119.6	104.9	109.3	111.0	109.9
1999	112.8	135.2	119.8	125.8	108.1	111.5	109.4	110.7	112.5	135.6	120.5	125.2	107.6	111.3	110.9	111.1
2000	116.1	140.5	121.0	134.7	112.0	116.0	107.2	112.7	115.7	140.8	121.7	134.2	111.6	116.0	108.7	113.3
2001	119.1	141.0	118.4	140.3	113.5	117.9	110.0	114.9	118.6	141.3	119.2	139.5	112.8	117.7	111.6	115.4
2002	123.9	143.1	115.4	145.3	115.7	117.3	114.2	116.1	123.5	143.4	116.1	144.6	115.1	117.1	116.0	116.7
2003	128.7	147.5	114.6	151.2	117.7	117.5	118.3	117.8	128.0	147.8	115.4	150.4	117.1	117.5	119.6	118.3
2004	132.4	153.7	116.1	157.0	119.0	118.5	124.6	120.8	131.6	153.9	116.9	156.0	118.2	118.5	125.5	121.1
2005	134.8	159.1	118.0	163.2	119.7	121.0	130.5	124.6	133.9	159.2	118.9	162.1	118.9	121.1	132.1	125.1
2006	136.1	163.9	120.5	169.4	120.3	124.5	134.8	128.3	135.1	164.2	121.5	168.3	119.5	124.5	136.8	129.1
2007	138.2	167.3	121.1	176.5	121.9	127.7	137.7	131.4	137.0	167.5	122.2	175.2	121.0	127.9	138.4	131.7
2008	141.9	168.6	118.8	182.9	121.7	128.9	142.0	133.8	140.9	168.8	119.8	181.8	120.9	129.0	143.2	134.2
2006																
1st quarter	135.9	162.8	119.8	167.8	120.5	123.5	133.4	127.2	134.8	163.2	121.0	166.5	119.6	123.5	135.5	127.9
2nd quarter	136.5	164.0	120.1	168.1	119.6	123.1	136.3	128.8	135.6	164.3	121.1	167.0	118.9	123.3	138.6	128.8
3rd quarter	136.0	164.1	120.7	169.0	119.1	124.3	136.3	128.8	135.1	164.4	121.7	168.0	118.4	124.3	138.4	129.5
4th quarter	135.9	164.8	121.3	172.6	122.1	127.0	133.3	129.4	134.9	165.0	122.3	171.7	121.4	127.2	134.7	130.0
2007																
1st quarter	135.7	164.5	121.3	174.3	122.2	128.5	134.3	130.7	134.7	164.7	122.2	173.4	121.6	128.7	135.1	131.1
2nd quarter	137.5	166.8	121.3	175.4	121.6	127.5	137.5	131.2	136.3	167.0	122.5	174.0	120.6	127.6	138.3	131.5
3rd quarter	140.0	169.0	120.8	177.4	122.1	126.7	139.8	131.6	138.7	169.2	122.0	175.8	121.1	126.8	140.5	131.8
4th quarter	139.6	168.8	120.9	178.9	121.7	128.2	139.0	132.2	138.5	168.9	122.0	177.8	120.9	128.4	139.7	132.5
2008																
1st quarter	140.4	169.1	120.4	180.5	121.5	128.6	140.2	132.9	139.4	169.3	121.5	179.4	120.8	128.7	141.0	133.2
2nd quarter	142.0	170.2	119.9	181.3	120.6	127.7	142.4	133.5	141.0	170.5	120.9	180.2	119.8	127.8	143.3	133.5
3rd quarter	142.8	169.4	118.6	183.9	120.3	128.8	144.3	134.6	141.7	169.7	119.7	182.7	119.5	128.9	145.6	135.0
4th quarter	142.6	165.7	116.2	186.1	124.7	130.5	141.3	134.5	141.6	165.8	117.1	185.0	124.0	130.7	142.9	135.2

Table 9-3. Productivity and Related Data—*Continued*

(1992 = 100, seasonally adjusted.)

Year and quarter	Nonfinancial corporations										Manufacturing					
	Output per hour of all employees	Output	Employee hours	Compensation per hour	Real compensation per hour	Unit costs			Unit profits	Implicit price deflator	Output per hour of all persons	Output	Hours of all persons	Compensation per hour	Real compensation per hour	Unit labor costs
						Total	Labor costs	Nonlabor costs								
1950	...	...	...	...	...	...	...	...	...	...	...	...	...	...	...	...
1951	...	...	...	...	...	...	...	...	...	...	...	...	...	...	...	...
1952	...	...	...	...	...	...	...	...	...	...	...	...	...	...	...	...
1953	...	...	...	...	...	...	...	...	...	...	...	...	...	...	...	...
1954	...	...	...	...	...	...	...	...	...	...	...	...	...	...	...	...
1955	...	...	...	...	...	...	...	...	...	...	...	...	...	...	...	...
1956	...	...	...	...	...	...	...	...	...	...	...	...	...	...	...	...
1957	...	...	...	...	...	...	...	...	...	...	...	...	...	...	...	...
1958	52.8	25.4	48.0	15.0	67.8	27.1	28.4	23.5	47.2	28.9	...	...	...	...	...	...
1959	55.3	28.2	50.9	15.6	69.9	26.6	28.1	22.3	55.8	29.2	...	...	...	...	...	...
1960	56.2	29.1	51.7	16.2	71.4	27.3	28.8	23.3	50.2	29.4	...	...	...	...	...	...
1961	57.9	29.7	51.3	16.7	73.0	27.5	28.8	23.8	50.3	29.5	...	...	...	...	...	...
1962	60.4	32.2	53.3	17.4	75.1	27.3	28.7	23.4	54.5	29.7	...	...	...	...	...	...
1963	62.6	34.1	54.5	17.9	76.4	27.2	28.6	23.4	57.3	29.9	...	...	...	...	...	...
1964	63.5	36.5	57.5	18.2	76.8	27.2	28.7	23.3	59.7	30.1	...	...	...	...	...	...
1965	65.1	39.5	60.7	18.8	77.8	27.3	28.8	23.1	64.1	30.6	...	...	...	...	...	...
1966	66.2	42.3	63.9	19.8	79.9	28.2	29.9	23.3	63.6	31.3	...	...	...	...	...	...
1967	67.1	43.4	64.6	20.9	81.8	29.4	31.2	24.7	59.9	32.2	...	...	...	...	...	...
1968	69.5	46.1	66.4	22.5	84.5	30.7	32.4	26.2	60.0	33.4	...	...	...	...	...	...
1969	69.5	47.9	69.0	24.0	85.6	33.0	34.6	28.6	54.0	34.8	...	...	...	...	...	...
1970	69.8	47.4	67.9	25.7	86.6	35.6	36.9	32.2	44.4	36.4	...	...	...	...	...	...
1971	72.7	49.3	67.8	27.3	88.1	36.5	37.6	33.6	50.5	37.8	...	...	...	...	...	...
1972	74.2	53.1	71.6	28.8	90.0	37.5	38.8	33.9	54.1	39.0	...	...	...	...	...	...
1973	74.8	56.3	75.2	31.0	91.2	39.9	41.4	35.7	54.9	41.2	...	...	...	...	...	...
1974	73.3	55.3	75.5	33.9	89.9	44.9	46.3	41.1	48.4	45.2	...	...	...	...	...	...
1975	76.2	54.6	71.7	37.3	90.5	48.3	49.0	46.6	63.1	49.6	...	...	...	...	...	...
1976	78.6	58.9	75.0	40.3	92.6	50.0	51.3	46.4	71.4	51.9	...	...	...	...	...	...
1977	80.6	63.2	78.4	43.5	93.8	52.5	54.0	48.4	77.3	54.7	...	...	...	...	...	...
1978	81.7	67.4	82.5	47.6	95.8	56.4	58.2	51.2	79.1	58.4	...	...	...	...	...	...
1979	81.0	69.5	85.8	51.9	95.5	61.9	64.1	55.8	74.0	62.9	...	...	...	...	...	...
1980	80.8	68.8	85.2	57.2	94.7	69.2	70.8	64.9	66.9	69.0	...	...	...	...	...	...
1981	82.9	71.6	86.4	62.4	94.3	74.8	75.3	73.5	81.0	75.4	...	...	...	...	...	...
1982	83.1	69.9	84.1	66.5	94.7	80.4	80.0	81.3	75.2	79.9	...	...	...	...	...	...
1983	85.7	73.1	85.3	68.9	94.3	80.7	80.4	81.6	91.2	81.7	...	...	...	...	...	...
1984	87.8	79.7	90.8	71.9	94.4	81.7	81.9	81.3	107.6	84.1	...	...	...	...	...	...
1985	89.6	83.2	92.9	75.2	95.4	83.8	83.9	83.6	102.3	85.5	...	...	...	...	...	...
1986	91.4	85.2	93.2	78.9	98.4	86.3	86.3	86.3	90.2	86.6	...	...	...	...	...	...
1987	93.3	89.7	96.1	81.6	98.4	87.0	87.4	85.8	100.1	88.1	89.1	92.4	103.8	81.3	98.0	91.3
1988	95.7	94.9	99.1	84.9	98.8	88.2	88.7	86.8	111.6	90.3	90.9	97.2	106.9	84.1	97.8	92.5
1989	94.6	96.6	102.2	87.0	97.0	92.4	92.0	93.3	101.2	93.2	91.9	98.8	107.6	86.6	96.6	94.3
1990	95.4	97.8	102.5	91.1	96.8	96.0	95.5	97.3	96.9	96.1	93.9	98.5	104.9	90.5	96.1	96.4
1991	97.4	97.0	99.6	95.5	97.9	99.3	98.0	102.7	93.2	98.7	96.3	96.8	100.5	95.6	98.0	99.2
1992	100.0	100.0	100.0	100.0	100.0	100.0	100.0	100.0	100.0	100.0	100.0	100.0	100.0	100.0	100.0	100.0
1993	100.3	102.8	102.4	101.8	99.3	101.0	101.4	99.9	114.1	102.2	102.6	103.9	101.3	102.0	99.6	99.5
1994	102.2	109.2	106.8	103.5	98.9	101.2	101.3	100.8	131.7	103.9	106.2	110.1	103.7	105.3	100.6	99.2
1995	103.3	114.3	110.6	105.3	98.3	101.7	101.9	101.2	136.9	104.9	111.0	115.9	104.4	107.3	100.1	96.7
1996	107.1	120.6	112.6	108.5	98.6	100.9	101.3	100.0	150.0	105.3	115.0	119.8	104.2	109.3	99.4	95.1
1997	109.9	128.4	116.9	111.7	99.4	101.1	101.7	99.7	154.3	105.9	121.3	128.7	106.0	112.2	99.8	92.5
1998	113.7	135.8	119.5	118.3	103.8	102.9	104.1	99.5	137.0	105.9	127.9	135.3	105.8	118.7	104.2	92.8
1999	117.9	144.0	122.2	124.2	106.7	104.0	105.3	100.4	129.1	106.2	133.7	140.4	105.1	123.5	106.1	92.4
2000	122.5	151.5	123.7	133.0	110.6	107.4	108.6	104.2	108.7	107.5	139.1	144.2	103.7	134.7	112.0	96.9
2001	124.7	150.2	120.4	138.6	112.1	111.6	111.2	112.6	82.2	108.9	141.2	136.9	96.9	137.8	111.5	97.6
2002	129.7	151.5	116.8	143.6	114.3	110.7	110.7	110.8	98.0	109.6	151.0	136.0	90.1	147.8	117.7	97.9
2003	134.6	154.8	115.0	149.5	116.4	111.0	111.0	111.1	109.9	110.9	160.4	137.3	85.6	158.2	123.2	98.7
2004	139.7	162.7	116.5	154.0	116.8	110.0	110.3	109.3	144.8	113.1	164.0	139.7	85.2	161.5	122.5	98.5
2005	143.4	170.0	118.5	159.6	117.1	111.7	111.3	112.7	163.0	116.3	171.9	144.8	84.3	164.5	120.7	95.7
2006	146.0	176.9	121.2	165.4	117.5	113.6	113.3	114.6	183.5	119.9	173.7	147.5	84.9	171.2	121.6	98.6
2007	147.1	179.4	122.0	172.2	118.9	117.4	117.1	118.3	167.3	121.9	179.7	149.9	83.4	177.4	122.5	98.7
2008	...	...	...	...	...	...	...	...	...	...	182.4	146.2	80.2	184.5	122.7	101.2
2006																
1st quarter	146.0	176.1	120.6	164.2	117.9	112.6	112.5	113.0	182.6	118.8	172.3	147.2	85.4	170.7	122.5	99.0
2nd quarter	145.7	176.2	120.9	164.4	117.0	113.3	112.8	114.6	183.4	119.5	172.6	147.4	85.4	169.4	120.6	98.2
3rd quarter	146.7	178.1	121.4	165.1	116.4	113.1	112.5	114.5	193.4	120.3	174.6	148.0	84.8	170.4	120.1	97.6
4th quarter	145.6	177.3	121.8	167.8	118.7	115.6	115.3	116.5	174.4	120.8	175.3	147.4	84.1	174.4	123.4	99.5
2007																
1st quarter	145.4	177.2	121.9	170.0	119.2	117.1	116.9	117.6	172.4	122.1	176.6	147.8	83.7	176.6	123.8	100.0
2nd quarter	146.7	179.1	122.0	171.1	118.6	116.9	116.6	117.9	173.1	122.0	178.6	149.6	83.8	176.3	122.2	98.7
3rd quarter	147.8	180.2	121.9	172.8	119.0	117.2	116.9	118.2	167.4	121.7	181.2	151.2	83.4	177.0	121.8	97.6
4th quarter	148.3	181.2	122.2	174.9	119.0	118.3	117.9	119.3	156.4	121.7	182.4	151.0	82.8	179.6	122.2	98.5
2008																
1st quarter	148.1	180.6	121.9	176.1	118.5	119.0	118.9	119.4	150.8	121.8	183.7	150.7	82.0	181.1	121.9	98.6
2nd quarter	151.2	183.2	121.2	177.4	118.0	118.0	117.3	119.8	147.8	120.6	183.2	149.3	81.5	182.7	121.4	99.7
3rd quarter	153.6	184.2	120.0	180.0	117.8	118.3	117.3	121.3	156.7	121.8	182.2	145.9	80.1	185.1	121.1	101.6
4th quarter	...	...	...	...	...	...	...	...	...	...	180.3	139.0	77.1	189.6	127.0	105.1

. . . = Not available.

Section 9c: Returns and Profits by Industry

Figure 9-3. Rates of Return, Nonfinancial Industry Groups, 1997–2006

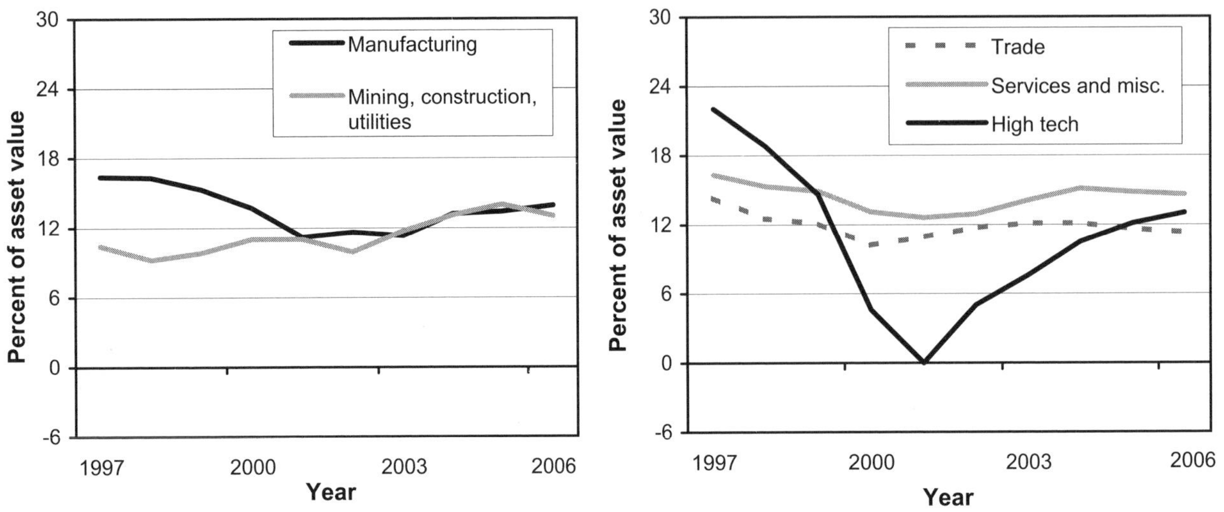

- Corporate profits reached a high point in 1997 and began to decline well before the business cycle peak in early 2001. However, by 2003, aggregate profits measures recovered to surpass their 1997 highs, and they continued to increase through 2006. Measuring between the high points for profits, profits of domestic industries as a share of gross domestic income increased from 9.2 percent in 1997 to 10.5 percent in 2006. (Table 1-11)

- New measures of rates of return on physical capital in nonfinancial industry groups are shown in Figure 9-3. The rate of return is the net operating surplus—the sum of corporate profits, net interest, transfer payments, and proprietors' income—as a percentage of the value of the net stock of capital plus inventories. The net operating surplus is a more comprehensive measure of the return to capital than corporate profits. As the figure indicates, rates of return declined from 1997 through 2001 or 2002. Only the mining, construction, and utilities group was above its 1997 rate as of 2006. (Table 9-4)

- The high-tech or "ICT-producing" industries—a small group of industries, one of which is a component of manufacturing and the rest of which are components of the services and miscellaneous group ("other" in BEA terminology)—had a more extreme swing, going from a 22 percent rate of return in 1997 to a loss in 2001, then recovering to 13.0 percent in 2006. (Table 9-4)

- BEA rate of return data are not available for financial industries, presumably because of greater difficulty in identifying and measuring the capital base. Aggregate profits of financial industries (leaving out the Federal Reserve System) rose 11.3 percent per year from 1997 to 2006, much faster than aggregate profits of nonfinancial industries, which rose 8.8 percent. However, financial profits declined nearly twice as fast as nonfinancial profits from 2006 to 2008, and for the full 11-year period from 1997 to 2008, profits for both groups were up at a rate of about 4½ percent. (Tables 9-5 and 9-6)

Table 9-4. Rates of Return and Related Data for Major Nonfinancial Industry Groups, NAICS Basis

Year	Nonfinancial corporations	Nonfinancial industries					
		Total	Mining, construction, and utilities	Manufacturing	Wholesale and retail trade	Other industries [1]	ICT-producing industries [2]
NET OPERATING SURPLUS (Billions of dollars)							
1997	736.3	1 278.1	164.0	320.1	202.9	591.1	71.3
1998	717.4	1 257.5	151.7	331.3	188.1	586.4	65.8
1999	742.7	1 288.5	166.7	322.4	192.4	607.0	55.4
2000	716.5	1 243.7	194.5	300.2	174.2	574.9	19.2
2001	611.8	1 243.9	208.5	251.1	192.5	591.8	-3.2
2002	650.8	1 301.6	197.5	261.5	210.4	632.3	22.5
2003	709.2	1 435.7	240.4	255.1	225.3	714.9	33.8
2004	879.9	1 646.6	291.9	306.0	240.9	807.8	47.3
2005	940.0	1 776.4	353.5	325.4	247.5	850.1	56.5
2006	1 015.0	1 888.1	368.7	354.8	260.6	904.0	63.5
2007	981.6	. . .	. . .	. . .	. . .	. . .	. . .
PRODUCED ASSETS, AVERAGE OF YEAR-END VALUES (Billions of dollars)							
1997	7 056.0	8 580.9	1 584.2	1 951.6	1 422.5	3 622.8	323.7
1998	7 419.0	9 011.4	1 649.8	2 030.7	1 500.7	3 830.3	349.3
1999	7 809.2	9 483.3	1 694.8	2 112.6	1 595.2	4 080.8	378.5
2000	8 295.2	10 074.4	1 776.0	2 195.8	1 702.5	4 400.3	417.5
2001	8 705.2	10 587.0	1 897.3	2 236.9	1 762.6	4 690.2	448.8
2002	8 950.8	10 919.2	1 985.8	2 247.2	1 801.0	4 885.2	451.8
2003	9 185.0	11 252.7	2 057.6	2 255.9	1 867.4	5 071.8	445.3
2004	9 682.7	11 896.2	2 231.8	2 314.1	1 985.6	5 364.1	452.2
2005	10 474.0	12 871.5	2 533.0	2 434.4	2 141.7	5 755.7	467.6
2006	11 261.6	13 868.6	2 826.4	2 551.5	2 300.2	6 184.4	487.9
2007	11 906.4	. . .	. . .	. . .	. . .	. . .	. . .
RATES OF RETURN (Percent)							
1997	10.4	14.9	10.4	16.4	14.3	16.3	22.0
1998	9.7	14.0	9.2	16.3	12.5	15.3	18.8
1999	9.5	13.6	9.8	15.3	12.1	14.9	14.6
2000	8.6	12.3	11.0	13.7	10.2	13.1	4.6
2001	7.0	11.7	11.0	11.2	10.9	12.6	-0.7
2002	7.3	11.9	9.9	11.6	11.7	12.9	5.0
2003	7.7	12.8	11.7	11.3	12.1	14.1	7.6
2004	9.1	13.8	13.1	13.2	12.1	15.1	10.5
2005	9.0	13.8	14.0	13.4	11.6	14.8	12.1
2006	9.0	13.6	13.0	13.9	11.3	14.6	13.0
2007	8.2	. . .	. . .	. . .	. . .	. . .	. . .
NET OPERATING SURPLUS AS A SHARE OF NET VALUE ADDED (Percent)							
1997	18.7	20.2	32.1	28.1	19.7	16.2	22.7
1998	17.2	22.0	28.8	27.8	17.5	20.1	18.9
1999	16.8	21.3	29.2	26.5	16.9	19.4	14.5
2000	15.2	19.5	30.6	23.8	14.8	17.4	4.6
2001	13.2	19.3	31.2	21.5	15.8	17.4	-0.9
2002	13.8	19.7	29.4	22.2	16.8	18.0	6.2
2003	14.5	20.7	32.9	21.4	17.3	19.3	9.2
2004	16.7	22.2	35.9	24.3	17.6	20.3	12.3
2005	16.9	22.5	38.4	24.9	17.3	20.1	13.7
2006	17.2	22.3	37.4	24.9	16.8	20.1	14.2
2007	16.0	. . .	. . .	. . .	. . .	. . .	. . .

[1]Consists of agriculture, forestry, fishing and hunting; transportation and warehousing; information; rental and leasing services and lessors of intangible assets; professional, scientific, and technical services; administrative and waste management services; educational services; health care and social assistance; arts, entertainment, and recreation; accommodation and food services; and "other services, except government."
[2]Information-communication-technology (ICT) producing industries consists of computer and electronic products; publishing industries (includes software); information and data processing services; and computer systems design and related services. Computer and electronic products are included in manufacturing; the other ICT-producing industries are included in "other" industries.
. . . = Not available.

Table 9-5. Corporate Profits with Inventory Valuation Adjustment by Industry Group, NAICS Basis

(Billions of dollars.)

NIPA Table 6.16D

Year and quarter	Total	Domestic industries												
		Financial			Nonfinancial									
								Manufacturing						
									Durable goods					
		Total	Federal Reserve banks	Other financial	Total	Utilities	Total	Fabricated metal products	Machinery	Computer and electronic products	Electrical equipment, appliances, and components	Motor vehicles, bodies and trailers, and parts	Other durable goods
1998	738.5	635.5	25.2	140.2	470.1	32.7	157.0	16.7	15.6	3.9	6.1	6.4	34.6
1999	776.8	655.3	26.3	168.0	461.1	33.1	150.6	16.5	12.4	-6.5	6.3	7.3	36.4
2000	759.3	613.6	30.8	169.4	413.4	24.4	144.3	15.5	8.2	4.0	5.6	-1.0	27.7
2001	719.2	549.5	28.3	199.3	322.0	24.7	52.6	9.9	2.7	-48.5	1.9	-9.2	17.8
2002	766.2	610.4	23.7	252.7	334.0	10.6	48.2	8.9	1.7	-35.3	-0.1	-5.0	20.0
2003	894.5	729.0	20.1	297.2	411.8	11.6	76.0	7.9	1.5	-15.6	2.1	-12.3	10.5
2004	1 161.6	968.2	20.0	328.9	619.3	18.6	152.7	11.9	7.2	-4.9	0.3	-7.6	31.3
2005	1 582.8	1 343.3	26.6	398.7	918.1	28.9	243.8	17.8	14.9	7.9	-1.6	0.1	54.2
2006	1 834.2	1 566.7	33.8	445.0	1 087.9	55.6	304.3	19.2	20.0	14.1	8.4	-8.4	62.6
2007	1 835.1	1 490.5	37.7	412.2	1 040.6	58.5	316.6	21.7	22.3	13.5	10.9	-5.9	64.9
2008	1 548.2	1 161.7	35.5	273.4	852.7	54.6	239.8	16.5	18.9	8.1	6.1	-23.9	43.3
2006													
1st quarter	1 778.7	1 528.3	31.0	439.0	1 058.3	44.9	279.2	20.8	19.6	10.5	4.1	-5.9	61.7
2nd quarter	1 841.6	1 571.9	33.6	459.5	1 078.8	53.5	305.8	17.8	19.8	15.1	7.6	-9.1	48.5
3rd quarter	1 887.2	1 626.7	35.8	437.5	1 153.4	62.5	333.5	17.6	19.7	17.6	10.2	-9.8	71.7
4th quarter	1 829.3	1 540.0	34.9	443.8	1 061.2	61.4	298.9	20.7	20.8	13.3	11.8	-9.0	68.5
2007													
1st quarter	1 794.7	1 496.6	38.2	415.9	1 042.5	57.2	317.0	21.5	22.7	16.4	11.6	-8.7	63.7
2nd quarter	1 859.5	1 556.7	38.5	454.2	1 064.0	54.7	350.8	20.0	22.4	9.0	9.6	-2.7	64.8
3rd quarter	1 866.1	1 509.7	37.5	422.8	1 049.3	58.7	306.6	22.5	22.2	13.2	10.7	-4.4	66.8
4th quarter	1 820.2	1 398.9	36.5	355.9	1 006.5	63.2	292.1	22.8	22.0	15.4	11.5	-7.7	64.3
2008													
1st quarter	1 641.5	1 243.1	35.8	377.1	830.2	46.2	240.5	18.9	19.2	14.4	6.9	-19.9	46.1
2nd quarter	1 596.0	1 222.5	31.0	352.2	839.3	56.7	214.9	15.1	14.8	6.6	5.9	-27.4	39.3
3rd quarter	1 602.8	1 224.4	34.4	274.3	915.6	59.1	272.6	14.7	12.3	4.0	5.6	-20.2	52.0
4th quarter	1 352.6	956.7	41.0	89.9	825.8	56.3	231.2	17.2	29.2	7.6	6.2	-28.0	35.8

Year and quarter	Domestic industries—Continued										Rest of the world, net
	Nonfinancial—Continued										
	Manufacturing—Continued										
	Nondurable goods					Wholesale trade	Retail trade	Transportation and warehousing	Information	Other nonfinancial	
	Total	Food and beverage and tobacco products	Petroleum and coal products	Chemical products	Other nondurable goods						
1998	73.6	21.8	4.9	25.1	21.8	53.2	66.4	21.0	20.1	119.8	103.0
1999	78.3	30.7	1.8	23.0	22.7	55.5	65.2	16.1	10.5	130.1	121.5
2000	84.3	25.4	26.9	14.2	17.8	59.7	59.6	14.9	-17.6	128.2	145.7
2001	78.0	28.0	29.6	12.6	7.8	52.1	71.0	1.3	-25.6	145.9	169.7
2002	58.1	24.9	1.6	18.4	13.2	49.3	79.4	-0.9	-8.5	155.8	155.8
2003	81.9	23.6	23.3	19.5	15.5	55.2	86.8	7.3	3.2	171.7	165.5
2004	114.5	24.2	48.9	25.4	16.0	79.2	91.1	14.1	43.9	219.7	193.4
2005	150.5	26.2	78.9	25.8	19.6	97.3	120.4	29.1	79.7	318.9	239.4
2006	188.4	33.8	77.5	53.8	23.4	107.5	132.3	42.5	91.1	354.7	267.5
2007	189.3	38.5	66.9	66.4	17.5	102.6	132.3	42.7	103.0	284.9	344.7
2008	170.8	37.7	61.3	66.4	5.4	76.5	91.7	24.7	101.9	263.7	386.6
2006											
1st quarter	168.4	28.1	75.4	46.3	18.6	102.3	133.5	39.3	87.2	371.8	250.5
2nd quarter	206.0	31.5	91.5	59.0	24.1	94.5	126.0	44.2	91.3	363.7	269.7
3rd quarter	206.4	36.9	88.1	61.4	20.0	128.3	132.1	42.2	95.8	359.1	260.5
4th quarter	172.9	38.7	54.8	48.4	30.9	104.9	137.5	44.4	89.9	324.2	289.4
2007											
1st quarter	189.8	33.5	71.7	62.1	22.5	108.2	132.8	40.7	100.8	285.8	298.1
2nd quarter	227.8	42.7	106.7	64.6	13.8	112.7	145.9	45.4	85.0	269.4	302.9
3rd quarter	175.7	39.2	55.6	65.1	15.9	109.1	126.0	47.0	108.4	293.5	356.4
4th quarter	163.8	38.7	33.6	73.8	17.8	80.2	124.5	37.7	117.9	290.9	421.3
2008											
1st quarter	155.0	34.8	48.8	60.2	11.1	49.2	112.0	24.4	106.0	252.0	398.5
2nd quarter	160.7	40.9	36.6	78.5	4.7	59.4	92.7	24.8	115.0	275.8	373.5
3rd quarter	204.2	40.8	92.0	70.8	0.6	92.1	86.2	25.2	103.8	276.6	378.4
4th quarter	163.3	34.2	67.7	56.1	5.3	105.2	75.8	24.4	82.6	250.4	395.9

Table 9-6. Corporate Profits with Inventory Valuation Adjustment by Industry Group, SIC Basis

(Billions of dollars.)   NIPA Tables 6.16B, 6.16C

		Domestic industries										
		Financial			Nonfinancial							
							Manufacturing					
								Durable goods				
Classification basis, year, and quarter	Total	Total	Federal Reserve banks	Other financial	Total	Total	Primary metal industries	Fabricated metal products	Industrial machinery and equipment	Electronic and other electric equipment	Motor vehicles and equipment	Other durable goods
1972 SIC Basis												
1948	33.7	32.5	0.2	2.5	29.7	17.5	1.6	0.8	1.3	0.6	1.4	1.8
1949	31.5	30.3	0.2	3.1	27.0	16.2	1.5	0.7	1.3	0.8	2.1	1.7
1950	38.3	37.0	0.2	3.1	33.7	21.0	2.3	1.1	1.6	1.2	3.1	2.6
1951	43.6	41.8	0.3	3.4	38.1	24.7	3.1	1.3	2.3	1.3	2.4	2.8
1952	41.2	39.3	0.3	4.1	34.9	21.7	1.9	1.0	2.3	1.5	2.4	2.6
1953	40.7	38.9	0.4	4.4	34.0	22.0	2.5	1.0	1.9	1.4	2.6	2.6
1954	39.0	37.1	0.3	4.8	32.0	19.9	1.7	0.9	1.7	1.2	2.1	2.9
1955	48.1	45.8	0.3	5.0	40.5	26.1	2.9	1.1	1.7	1.1	4.1	3.5
1956	47.8	44.9	0.5	5.2	39.3	24.8	3.0	1.1	2.1	1.2	2.2	3.1
1957	47.5	44.4	0.6	5.4	38.5	24.1	3.1	1.1	2.0	1.5	2.6	3.1
1958	42.7	40.2	0.6	5.9	33.7	19.5	1.9	0.9	1.5	1.3	0.9	2.9
1959	53.5	50.8	0.7	6.9	43.2	26.5	2.3	1.1	2.2	1.7	3.0	3.5
1960	51.5	48.3	0.9	7.5	39.9	23.8	2.0	0.8	1.8	1.3	3.0	2.7
1961	51.8	48.5	0.8	7.6	40.2	23.4	1.6	1.0	1.9	1.3	2.5	2.9
1962	57.0	53.3	0.9	7.7	44.7	26.3	1.6	1.2	2.4	1.5	4.0	3.4
1963	62.1	58.1	1.0	7.3	49.8	29.7	2.0	1.3	2.6	1.6	4.9	4.0
1964	68.6	64.1	1.1	7.6	55.4	32.6	2.5	1.5	3.3	1.7	4.6	4.4
1965	78.9	74.2	1.3	8.0	64.9	39.8	3.1	2.1	4.0	2.7	6.2	5.2
1966	84.6	80.1	1.7	9.1	69.3	42.6	3.6	2.4	4.6	3.0	5.2	5.2
1967	82.0	77.2	2.0	9.2	66.0	39.2	2.7	2.5	4.2	3.0	4.0	4.9
1968	88.8	83.2	2.5	10.3	70.4	41.9	1.9	2.3	4.2	2.9	5.5	5.6
1969	85.5	78.9	3.1	10.5	65.3	37.3	1.4	2.0	3.8	2.3	4.8	4.9
1970	74.4	67.3	3.5	11.9	52.0	27.5	0.8	1.1	3.1	1.3	1.3	2.9
1971	88.3	80.4	3.3	14.3	62.8	35.1	0.8	1.5	3.1	2.0	5.2	4.1
1972	101.2	91.7	3.3	15.8	72.6	41.9	1.7	2.2	4.5	2.9	6.0	5.6
1973	115.3	100.4	4.5	16.0	79.9	47.2	2.3	2.7	4.9	3.2	5.9	6.2
1974	109.5	92.1	5.7	14.5	71.9	41.4	5.0	1.8	3.3	0.6	0.7	4.0
1975	135.0	120.4	5.6	14.6	100.2	55.2	2.8	3.3	5.1	2.6	2.3	4.7
1976	165.6	149.0	5.9	19.1	124.1	71.3	2.1	3.9	6.9	3.8	7.4	7.3
1977	194.7	175.6	6.1	25.8	143.7	79.3	1.0	4.5	8.6	5.9	9.4	8.5
1978	222.4	199.6	7.6	31.9	160.0	90.5	3.6	5.0	10.7	6.7	9.0	10.5
1979	231.8	197.2	9.4	30.9	156.8	89.6	3.5	5.3	9.5	5.6	4.7	8.5
1980	211.4	175.9	11.8	22.2	141.9	78.3	2.7	4.4	8.0	5.2	-4.3	2.7
1981	219.1	189.4	14.4	14.7	160.3	91.1	3.1	4.5	9.0	5.2	0.3	-2.6
1982	191.0	158.5	15.2	10.8	132.4	67.1	-4.7	2.7	3.1	1.7	0.0	2.1
1983	226.5	191.4	14.6	20.9	155.9	76.2	-4.9	3.1	4.0	3.5	5.3	8.4
1984	264.6	228.1	16.4	18.0	193.7	91.8	-0.4	4.7	6.0	5.1	9.2	14.6
1985	257.5	219.4	16.3	29.5	173.5	84.3	-0.9	4.9	5.7	2.6	7.4	10.1
1986	253.0	213.5	15.5	41.2	156.8	57.9	0.9	5.2	0.8	2.7	4.6	12.1
1987	301.4	253.4	15.7	44.1	193.5	86.3	2.6	5.5	5.4	5.9	3.7	17.6
1987 SIC Basis												
1987	301.4	253.4	15.7	44.1	193.5	86.3	2.6	5.5	5.4	5.9	3.7	17.6
1988	363.9	306.9	17.6	51.1	238.2	121.2	6.0	6.5	11.1	7.7	6.2	16.5
1989	367.4	300.3	20.2	57.8	222.3	110.9	6.4	6.4	12.2	9.3	2.7	14.2
1990	396.6	320.5	21.4	73.0	226.1	113.1	3.5	6.0	11.8	8.5	-1.9	15.9
1991	427.9	351.4	20.3	103.9	227.3	98.0	1.5	5.3	5.7	10.0	-5.4	17.3
1992	458.3	385.2	17.8	111.9	255.4	99.5	0.0	6.2	7.5	10.4	-1.0	17.4
1993	513.1	436.1	16.2	120.6	299.3	115.6	0.4	7.4	7.5	15.2	6.0	19.4
1994	564.6	487.6	18.1	101.8	367.7	147.0	2.3	11.1	9.1	22.8	7.8	21.3
1995	656.0	563.2	22.5	139.7	401.0	173.7	7.1	11.8	14.8	21.5	0.0	25.8
1996	736.1	634.2	22.1	150.5	461.6	188.8	5.6	14.5	16.9	20.1	4.2	29.2
1997	812.3	701.4	23.8	169.2	508.4	209.0	6.3	17.0	16.7	25.3	4.8	33.0
1998	738.5	635.5	25.2	140.7	469.6	173.5	6.5	16.4	19.5	8.9	5.9	30.1
1999	776.8	655.3	26.3	170.1	458.9	175.2	2.4	16.2	12.4	5.3	7.3	35.3
2000	759.3	613.6	30.8	173.0	409.8	166.3	1.2	15.4	16.3	4.7	-1.5	28.8
1998												
1st quarter	752.0	643.1	25.0	147.9	470.2	178.5	6.9	14.9	14.4	12.2	6.4	28.8
2nd quarter	732.5	626.3	25.2	136.4	464.7	170.1	6.2	16.7	19.5	8.3	3.5	27.4
3rd quarter	743.5	647.3	25.4	136.9	485.0	176.6	6.1	18.5	20.4	6.6	4.5	31.3
4th quarter	725.9	625.3	25.1	141.8	458.4	168.8	6.8	15.7	23.7	8.3	9.3	32.9
1999												
1st quarter	771.3	657.3	24.9	163.0	469.5	175.0	3.8	15.9	9.8	4.3	8.9	33.9
2nd quarter	773.2	656.5	25.5	157.8	473.2	182.5	3.1	15.7	12.8	4.9	6.1	37.8
3rd quarter	766.8	648.3	26.2	175.3	446.8	174.2	1.5	16.2	12.3	6.9	7.3	34.3
4th quarter	796.1	659.1	28.6	184.5	446.0	169.1	1.2	17.1	14.7	4.9	6.7	35.3
2000												
1st quarter	766.8	635.7	30.0	179.5	426.2	172.6	2.1	18.8	12.6	2.5	1.2	33.3
2nd quarter	773.5	634.9	30.5	164.5	440.0	186.1	2.0	16.2	16.1	8.7	0.3	33.7
3rd quarter	756.3	611.7	31.1	171.1	409.5	164.9	0.5	15.2	18.1	3.4	-2.4	27.3
4th quarter	740.7	572.1	31.7	176.8	363.6	141.6	0.3	11.3	18.1	4.1	-5.2	21.0

Table 9-6. Corporate Profits with Inventory Valuation Adjustment by Industry Group, SIC Basis —Continued

(Billions of dollars.)

NIPA Tables 6.16B, 6.16C

Classification basis, year, and quarter	Manufacturing—Continued Nondurable goods Total	Food and kindred products	Chemicals and allied products	Petroleum and coal products	Other nondurable goods	Transportation and public utilities Total	Transportation	Communications	Electric, gas, and sanitary services	Wholesale trade	Retail trade	Other nonfinancial	Rest of the world
1972 SIC Basis													
1948	10.0	1.9	1.7	2.8	3.7	3.0	1.5	0.4	1.1	2.4	3.2	3.5	1.3
1949	8.1	1.6	1.8	1.9	2.8	3.0	1.2	0.5	1.4	1.9	2.8	3.1	1.1
1950	9.0	1.6	2.3	2.3	2.7	4.1	1.9	0.7	1.5	2.1	3.0	3.5	1.3
1951	11.4	1.4	2.8	2.8	4.4	4.7	1.9	1.0	1.8	2.6	2.6	3.6	1.7
1952	10.0	1.8	2.3	2.3	3.6	5.0	1.9	1.1	2.0	2.3	2.7	3.3	1.9
1953	10.0	1.8	2.2	2.7	3.3	5.0	1.6	1.2	2.2	1.8	2.3	3.0	1.8
1954	9.5	1.6	2.2	2.8	2.9	4.7	1.0	1.3	2.4	1.7	2.3	3.3	2.0
1955	11.8	2.2	3.0	3.0	3.6	5.7	1.5	1.7	2.5	2.4	2.9	3.5	2.4
1956	12.0	1.8	2.8	3.3	4.1	5.9	1.4	1.8	2.7	2.2	2.6	3.9	2.8
1957	10.8	1.8	2.8	2.6	3.6	5.9	1.1	2.0	2.7	2.2	2.6	3.8	3.1
1958	10.2	2.1	2.5	2.1	3.4	5.9	0.9	2.3	2.7	2.2	2.6	3.5	2.5
1959	12.9	2.5	3.5	2.6	4.3	7.1	1.1	2.8	3.1	2.9	3.3	3.4	2.7
1960	12.2	2.2	3.1	2.6	4.2	7.5	0.9	3.0	3.6	2.5	2.8	3.3	3.1
1961	12.1	2.4	3.3	2.3	4.2	7.9	1.0	3.2	3.7	2.5	3.0	3.4	3.3
1962	12.3	2.4	3.2	2.2	4.4	8.5	1.0	3.6	3.9	2.8	3.4	3.6	3.8
1963	13.3	2.7	3.7	2.2	4.7	9.5	1.4	3.9	4.2	2.8	3.6	4.1	4.1
1964	14.5	2.7	4.1	2.4	5.3	10.2	1.6	4.0	4.6	3.4	4.5	4.7	4.5
1965	16.5	2.9	4.6	2.9	6.1	11.0	2.1	4.3	4.6	3.8	4.9	5.4	4.7
1966	18.6	3.3	4.9	3.4	6.9	12.0	2.3	4.8	4.9	4.0	4.9	5.9	4.5
1967	18.0	3.3	4.3	4.0	6.4	10.9	1.3	4.8	4.8	4.1	5.7	6.1	4.8
1968	19.4	3.2	5.3	3.8	7.1	11.0	1.0	5.1	4.9	4.6	6.4	6.6	5.6
1969	18.1	3.1	4.6	3.4	7.0	10.7	0.7	5.4	4.6	4.9	6.4	6.1	6.6
1970	17.0	3.2	3.9	3.7	6.1	8.3	-0.1	4.8	3.6	4.4	6.0	5.8	7.1
1971	18.5	3.6	4.5	3.8	6.6	8.9	0.7	4.1	4.1	5.2	7.2	6.4	7.9
1972	19.2	3.0	5.3	3.3	7.6	9.5	1.5	3.9	4.0	6.9	7.4	7.0	9.5
1973	22.0	2.5	6.2	5.4	7.9	9.1	1.3	4.3	3.4	8.2	6.6	8.7	14.9
1974	26.1	2.6	5.3	10.9	7.3	7.6	2.0	4.1	1.5	11.5	2.3	9.1	17.5
1975	34.5	8.6	6.4	10.1	9.5	11.0	1.0	4.3	5.7	13.8	8.2	12.0	14.6
1976	39.9	7.1	8.2	13.5	11.1	15.3	3.0	5.7	6.5	12.9	10.5	14.0	16.5
1977	41.4	6.9	7.8	13.1	13.6	18.6	3.7	6.6	8.3	15.6	12.4	17.8	19.1
1978	45.1	6.2	8.3	15.8	14.8	21.8	4.1	8.6	9.1	15.6	12.3	19.8	22.9
1979	52.5	5.8	7.2	24.8	14.7	17.0	3.5	7.5	6.0	18.8	9.8	21.6	34.6
1980	59.5	6.1	5.7	34.7	13.1	18.4	2.7	7.7	8.0	17.2	6.2	21.8	35.5
1981	71.6	9.2	8.0	40.0	14.5	20.3	1.7	8.6	10.0	22.4	9.9	16.7	29.7
1982	62.1	7.3	5.1	34.7	15.0	23.1	-0.1	8.6	14.6	19.6	13.4	9.2	32.6
1983	56.7	6.3	7.4	23.9	19.1	29.5	3.2	9.9	16.4	21.0	18.7	10.4	35.1
1984	52.6	6.8	8.2	17.6	20.1	40.1	6.1	12.8	21.3	29.5	21.1	11.1	36.6
1985	54.6	8.8	6.6	18.7	20.5	33.8	1.8	14.2	17.8	23.9	22.2	9.2	38.1
1986	31.7	7.5	7.5	-4.7	21.3	35.8	3.4	17.6	14.7	24.1	23.5	15.5	39.5
1987	45.6	11.4	14.4	-1.5	21.3	41.9	3.4	19.4	19.1	18.6	23.4	23.4	48.0
1987 SIC Basis													
1987	45.6	11.4	14.4	-1.5	21.3	41.9	3.4	19.4	19.1	18.6	23.4	23.4	48.0
1988	67.1	12.0	18.6	12.7	23.7	48.4	7.9	19.5	21.1	20.1	20.3	28.3	57.0
1989	59.7	11.1	18.2	6.5	23.9	43.3	1.3	18.2	23.9	21.8	20.8	25.5	67.1
1990	69.2	14.3	16.8	16.4	21.7	44.2	-0.4	20.1	24.5	19.2	20.7	29.0	76.1
1991	63.6	18.1	16.2	7.3	22.0	53.3	2.3	23.5	27.5	21.7	26.7	27.5	76.5
1992	59.0	18.2	16.0	-0.9	25.6	58.4	2.3	27.7	28.4	25.1	32.6	39.7	73.1
1993	59.7	16.4	15.9	2.7	24.7	69.5	7.0	32.9	29.6	26.3	39.1	48.9	76.9
1994	72.6	19.9	23.2	1.2	28.3	83.2	10.5	36.7	36.1	30.9	46.2	60.4	77.1
1995	92.8	27.1	27.9	7.1	30.6	85.8	11.5	33.6	40.8	27.3	43.1	71.2	92.8
1996	98.2	22.1	26.4	15.0	34.7	91.3	15.7	35.0	40.7	39.8	51.9	89.7	101.9
1997	105.9	24.6	32.3	17.3	31.7	84.2	19.0	25.5	39.7	47.6	64.2	103.4	110.9
1998	86.2	21.9	26.5	6.7	31.1	78.9	21.6	21.4	35.8	52.3	73.4	91.5	103.0
1999	96.4	28.1	25.2	4.3	38.9	56.8	15.8	4.6	36.3	52.6	74.6	99.7	121.5
2000	101.5	25.7	16.0	29.1	30.7	43.8	15.2	1.3	27.3	56.9	70.1	72.8	145.7
1998													
1st quarter	94.9	23.6	30.5	9.4	31.3	76.8	20.6	22.1	34.1	50.2	71.3	93.4	108.8
2nd quarter	88.5	24.6	22.9	8.9	32.1	81.0	21.5	24.0	35.5	52.6	72.5	88.6	106.2
3rd quarter	89.2	25.8	24.9	7.3	31.3	86.7	24.2	25.1	37.4	57.5	73.8	90.4	96.2
4th quarter	72.0	13.6	27.6	1.3	29.6	71.0	20.3	14.5	36.3	48.8	76.0	93.8	100.5
1999													
1st quarter	98.5	28.5	31.8	0.6	37.6	62.6	16.8	9.2	36.6	54.8	79.4	97.7	113.9
2nd quarter	102.1	28.6	31.8	4.0	37.7	52.1	16.0	3.4	32.8	53.1	79.0	106.6	116.6
3rd quarter	95.8	27.0	22.1	8.2	38.5	52.5	13.5	1.3	37.6	49.3	69.6	101.2	118.5
4th quarter	89.1	28.2	14.9	4.4	41.6	59.9	17.0	4.5	38.4	53.3	70.5	93.2	137.0
2000													
1st quarter	102.1	28.3	20.0	15.3	38.6	47.5	14.7	-0.3	33.0	52.4	75.5	78.3	131.1
2nd quarter	109.2	25.4	17.4	33.8	32.7	42.4	19.4	-3.4	26.4	63.2	70.8	77.4	138.5
3rd quarter	102.8	28.2	13.3	33.9	27.4	43.2	15.7	0.4	27.1	62.9	70.3	68.3	144.6
4th quarter	91.9	21.0	13.2	33.4	24.3	42.2	11.2	8.4	22.6	48.9	63.9	67.0	168.6

NOTES AND DEFINITIONS

GENERAL NOTE ON DATA ON COMPENSATION PER HOUR

This chapter includes two data series with similar names—the Employment Cost Index for total compensation and the index of compensation per hour—that often display different behavior. Both are compiled and published by the Bureau of Labor Statistics (BLS), but the definitions, sources, and methods of compilation are different. Users should be aware of these differences and of the consequent differences in the appropriate uses and interpretations for each of the two series.

The *Employment Cost Index (ECI)* (Tables 9-1 and 9-2) measures changes in hourly compensation for "all civilian workers", which is not quite as broad as it sounds, as it excludes federal government workers, farm workers, and private household workers. Indexes are also published for subgroups including state and local workers, "all private industry" (again excluding farm and private household workers), and a number of industry and occupational subgroups.

The ECI is calculated and published separately for *total compensation* and for the two major components of hourly compensation, *wages and salaries* and the employer cost of employee *benefits*. It is constructed by analogy with the Consumer Price Index (CPI); that is, it *holds the composition of employment constant* in order to isolate hourly compensation trends that take place for individual occupations, which are then aggregated, using relative importance weights. The ECI is based on a sample survey and may be revised from time to time, due to updated classification, weighting, and seasonal adjustments. However, it is not subject to major benchmark revision of the underlying wage, salary, and benefit rate observations. By design, it excludes any representation of employee stock options. As it is based on a sample survey, the ECI is measured "from the bottom up," aggregating from individual employers' reports to higher levels. The ECI is frequently and appropriately used as the best available measure of the general trend of wages and of the extent of inflationary pressure exerted on prices by labor costs.

The *compensation per hour* component of the report on "Productivity and Costs" (Table 9-3) is calculated and published for total compensation in total business, nonfarm business, nonfinancial corporations, and manufacturing. The nonfarm business category is similar in scope to the "all private industry" category in the ECI. The measures in Table 9-3, however, are compiled "from the top down," starting with aggregate estimates of compensation and hours, then dividing the former by the latter. Compensation per hour *is affected by changes in the composition of employment*. If the composition of employment shifts toward higher-paid employees and/or industries, compensation per hour will

rise even if there is no increase in hourly compensation for *any* individual worker.

In addition, *compensation per hour* includes the value of exercised stock options as expensed by companies. Also included are other transitory payments, many of which may be of little relevance to the typical worker or to ongoing production costs. These values are not reported immediately. Instead, they are incorporated when later, more comprehensive reports are received. This process can lead to dramatic revisions. For example, the fourth-quarter 2004 increase in compensation per hour in nonfarm business was initially reported at an annual rate of 3.1 percent. Four months later, the reported rate for the same time period was 10.2 percent. The rate of increase from a year earlier was revised from 3.6 to 5.9 percent. According to then-Federal Reserve Chairman Alan Greenspan, in testimony before the Joint Economic Committee on June 9, 2005, this reflected "a large but apparently transitory surge in bonuses and the proceeds of stock option exercises," not a potentially inflationary acceleration in the rate of labor compensation increase.

These characteristics suggest that *compensation per hour* should not be considered a reliable or appropriate indicator of wage or compensation trends for typical workers. It is useful in conjunction with the productivity series, because aggregate productivity is subject to the same composition shifts—higher-productivity industries also tend to have higher-paid employees. Hence, the measure of *unit labor costs* (derived by dividing compensation per hour by output per hour in this system) is not distorted when the composition of output shifts toward higher-productivity industries. The shift affects the numerator and denominator of the ratio similarly. However, both compensation and unit labor costs can still be distorted by transitory payments, such as those discussed above.

There are other, probably less important differences between the two measures. Compensation per hour refers to the entire quarter, while the ECI is observed in the terminal month of each quarter. Tips and other forms of compensation not provided by employers are included in hourly compensation but not in the ECI. The ECI excludes persons working for token wages, business owners and others who set their own wage, and family workers who do not earn a market wage; all of these workers are included in the productivity and cost accounts. Hourly compensation excludes employees of nonprofit institutions serving individuals—about 10 percent of private workers (mostly in education and medical care) who are within the scope of the ECI. Hourly compensation measures include an estimate for the unincorporated self-employed, who are assumed to earn the same hourly compensation as other employees in the sector. Implicitly, unpaid family workers also are included in the hourly compensation measures with the assumption that their hourly compensation is zero. Both of these groups are also excluded from the ECI.

TABLES 9-1 AND 9-2
EMPLOYMENT COST INDEXES

SOURCE: U.S. DEPARTMENT OF LABOR, BUREAU OF LABOR STATISTICS (BLS)

The Employment Cost Index (ECI) is a quarterly measure of the change in the cost of labor, independent of the influence of employment shifts among occupations and industries. It uses a fixed market basket of labor—similar in concept to the Consumer Price Index's fixed market basket of goods and services—to measure changes over time in employer costs of employing labor. Data are quarterly in all cases and are reported for the final month of each quarter. These measures are expressed as indexes, with the not-seasonally-adjusted value for December 2005 set at 100.

Care should be used in comparing the ECI with other data sets. The "all private industry" category in the ECI excludes farm and household workers (it is sometimes, and more precisely, called "private nonfarm industry"), and the "all civilian workers" category excludes federal government, farm, and household workers, all of whom fall outside the scope of the ECI survey.

The data for 1979 through 2005, which are presented in Table 9-2 and are the official ECI measures for that time period, were based on the 1987 Standard Industrial Classification (SIC) and 1990 Occupational Classification System (OCS).

Currently the ECI is compiled based on the 2007 North American Industry Classification System (NAICS) and the 2000 Standard Occupational Classification Manual (SOC). These data, along with comparable data for 2001 through 2005, are shown in Table 9-1.

For certain broad categories shown in this volume—indicated by footnote 2 in Table 9-2—the old SIC categories are roughly comparable and continuous with the data for 2006 and subsequent years. (However, they differ slightly on overlap dates, and should be "linked" if a continuous time series is desired.) Many of the new industry and occupational categories are not continuous with the old series shown here, and some of the old categories are not being continued because BLS finds them obsolete and no longer meaningful.

Definitions

Total compensation comprises wages, salaries, and the employer's costs for employee benefits. Excluded from wages and salaries and employee benefits are the value of stock option exercises and items such as payment-in-kind, free room and board, and tips.

Wages and salaries consists of straight-time earnings per hour before payroll deductions, including production bonuses, incentive earnings, commissions, and cost-of-living adjustments. These wage rates exclude premium pay for overtime and for work on weekends and holidays, shift differentials, and nonproduction bonuses such as lump-sum payments provided in lieu of wage increases.

Benefits includes the cost to employers for paid leave—vacations, holidays, sick leave, and other leave; for supplemental pay—premium pay for work in addition to the regular work schedule (such as overtime, weekends, and holidays), shift differentials, and nonproduction bonuses (such as referral bonuses and lump-sum payments provided in lieu of wage increases); for insurance benefits—life, health, short-term disability, and long-term disability; for retirement and savings benefits—defined benefit and defined contribution plans; and for legally required benefits—Social Security, Medicare, federal and state unemployment insurance, and workers' compensation. Severance pay and supplemental unemployment benefit (SUB) plans are included in the data through December 2005 but were dropped beginning with the March 2006 data. The combined cost of these two benefits accounted for less than one-tenth of one percent of compensation, and according to BLS, dropping these benefits has had virtually no impact on the index.

Civilian workers are private industry workers, as defined below, and workers in state and local government. Federal workers are not included.

Private industry workers are paid workers in private industry excluding farms and private households. To be included in the ECI, employees in occupations must receive cash payments from the establishment for services performed and the establishment must pay the employer's portion of Medicare taxes on that individual's wages. Major exclusions from the survey are the self-employed, individuals who set their own pay (for example, proprietors, owners, major stockholders, and partners in unincorporated firms), volunteers, unpaid workers, family members being paid token wages, individuals receiving long-term disability compensation, and U.S. citizens working overseas.

Private industry workers excluding incentive paid occupations is a new category introduced in the 2006 revision to eliminate the quarter-to-quarter variability related to the way workers are paid. (The category *private industry workers excluding sales occupations* was intended to serve a similar purpose in the previous SIC-based classification system, but was much less accurate in separately identifying workers with highly variable compensation.)

Goods-producing industries include mining, construction, and manufacturing.

Service-providing industries include the following NAICS industries: wholesale trade; retail trade; transportation and warehousing; utilities; information; finance and insurance; real estate and rental and leasing; professional, scientific, and technical services; management of companies and enterprises; administrative and support and waste management and remediation services; education services; health care and social assistance; arts, entertainment, and recreation; accommodation and food services; and other services, except public administration.

Notes on the data

Employee benefit costs are calculated as cents per hour worked.

The December 2008 data were collected from probability samples of approximately 64,700 occupational observations in about 13,600 sample establishments in private industry, and approximately 11,800 occupations within about 1,900 establishments in state and local governments. The private industry sample is rotated over approximately five years. The state and local government sample is replaced less frequently; the latest sample was introduced in September 2007.

Currently, the sample establishments are classified in industry categories based on the NAICS. Within an establishment, specific job categories are selected and classified into approximately 800 occupational classifications according to the SOC. Similar procedures were followed under the previous classification systems. Data are collected each quarter for the pay periods including the 12th day of March, June, September, and December.

Aggregate indexes are calculated using fixed employment weights. Beginning with March 2006, ECI weights are based on fixed employment counts for 2002 from the BLS Occupational Employment Statistics survey. ECI measures were based on 1990 employment counts from March 1995 through December 2005 and 1980 census employment counts from June 1986 through December 1994. Prior to June 1986, they were based on 1970 census employment counts. Use of fixed weights ensures that changes in the indexes reflect only changes in hourly compensation, not employment shifts among industries or occupations with different levels of wages and compensation. This feature distinguishes the ECI from other compensation series such as average hourly earnings (see Table 10-11 and its notes and definitions) and the compensation per hour component of the productivity series (see Table 9-3 and its notes and definitions, and the general note above), each of which is affected by such employment shifts.

Data availability

Data for wages and salaries for the private nonfarm economy are available beginning with the data for 1975; data for compensation begin with the 1980 data. The series for state and local government and for the civilian nonfarm economy begin with the 1981 data. All series are available on the BLS Web site at <http://www.bls.gov>.

Wage and salary change and compensation cost change data also are available by major occupational and industry groups, as well as by region and collective bargaining status. Information on wage and salary change is available from 1975 to the present for most of these series. Compensation cost change data are available from 1980 to the present for most series. For 10 occupational and industry series, benefit cost change data are available from the early 1980s to the present. For state and local governments and the civilian economy (state and local governments plus private industry), wage and salary change and compensation cost change data are available for major occupational and industry series. BLS provides data for all these series from June 1981 to the present.

Updates are available about four weeks after the end of the reference quarter. Reference quarters end in March, June, September, and December.

References

Explanatory notes, including references, are included in a Technical Note in each quarter's ECI news release, and can be found on the BLS Web site, in the PDF version of the release.

More detailed information on the ECI is available from a chapter, "National compensation measures," (www.bls.gov/opub/hom/pdf/homch8.pdf) from the *BLS Handbook of Methods*, and several articles published in the Monthly Labor Review and Compensation and Working Conditions. The articles and other descriptive pieces are available at www.bls.gov/ect/#publications, by calling (202) 691-6199, or sending e-mail to NCSinfo@bls.gov.

TABLES 9-3 AND 19-13
PRODUCTIVITY AND RELATED DATA

SOURCE: U.S. DEPARTMENT OF LABOR, BUREAU OF LABOR STATISTICS (BLS)

Productivity measures relate real physical output to real input. They encompass a family of measures that includes single-factor input measures, such as output per unit of labor input or output per unit of capital input, as well as measures of multifactor productivity (output per unit of combined labor and capital inputs). The indexes published in this book are indexes of labor productivity expressed in terms of output per hour of labor input. (A larger group of BLS productivity measures can be found in Bernan Press's *Handbook of U.S. Labor Statistics*.) Data are provided here for four sectors of the economy: business, nonfarm business, the nonfinancial corporate sector, and manufacturing. All data are presented as indexes with a base of 1992 = 100.

Definitions

Output per hour of all persons (labor productivity) is the value of goods and services in constant prices produced per hour of labor input. By definition, nonfinancial corporations include no self-employed persons. Productivity in this sector is expressed as *output per hour of all employees*.

Compensation per hour is the wages and salaries of employees plus employers' contributions for social insurance and private benefit plans and wages, salaries, and supplementary payments for the self-employed—the sum of these divided by hours at work. Included in compensation is the value of exercised stock options that companies report as a charge against earnings. Stock option values are reported with a delay; consequently, recent values are estimated based on extrapolation. They are revised to actual values when the data become available. The labor compensation of proprietors cannot be explicitly identified and must be estimated. This is done by assuming that proprietors have the same hourly compensation as employees in the same sector. The quarterly labor productivity and cost measures do not contain estimates of compensation for unpaid family workers.

Real compensation per hour is compensation per hour deflated by the CPI-U for recent quarters and the Consumer Price Index Research Series (CPI-U-RS) for the period 1978 through 2007. Changes in the Consumer Price Index for Urban Wage Earners and Clerical Workers (CPI-W) are used for data before 1978, as there was no CPI-U for that period. See the Notes and Definitions to Chapter 8 for explanation of the CPI-U, the CPI-W, and the CPI-U-RS.

Unit labor costs are the current-dollar labor costs expended in the production of a unit of output. They are derived by dividing compensation by output.

Unit nonlabor payments include profits, depreciation, interest, rental income of persons, and indirect taxes per unit of output. They are computed by subtracting current-dollar compensation of all persons from current-dollar value of output and dividing by output.

Unit nonlabor costs are available for nonfinancial corporations only. They contain all the components of unit nonlabor payments except unit profits (and rental income of persons, which is zero by definition for nonfinancial corporations).

Unit profits, the other component of unit nonlabor payments, are also only available for nonfinancial corporations.

Hours of all persons consists of the total hours at work (employment multiplied by the average workweek) of payroll workers, self-employed persons, and unpaid family workers. For the nonfinancial corporations data, there are no self-employed persons; the data represent *employee hours.*

Notes on the data

Output for the business sector is equal to constant-dollar gross domestic product minus: the rental value of owner-occupied dwellings, the output of nonprofit institutions, the output of paid employees of private households, and general government output. The measures are derived from national income and product account (NIPA) data supplied by the U.S. Department of Commerce's Bureau of Economic Analysis (BEA). For manufacturing, BLS produces annual estimates of sectoral output. Quarterly manufacturing output indexes derived from the Federal Reserve

Board of Governors' monthly indexes of industrial production (see Chapter 2) are adjusted to these annual measures by the BLS, and are also used to project the quarterly values in the current period.

Nonfinancial corporate output excludes unincorporated businesses and financial corporations from business sector output and accounted for approximately 54 percent of the value of GDP in 2000. Unit profits and unit nonlabor costs can be calculated separately for this sector and are shown in this table.

Compensation and hours data are developed from BLS and BEA data. The primary source for hours and employment is BLS's Current Employment Statistics (CES) program (see the notes and definitions for Tables 10-7 through 10-12). The CES provides data on total nonfarm industry employment and on hours paid for production or nonsupervisory workers. The BLS Office of Productivity and Technology estimates the paid hours of nonproduction and supervisory workers, using data from the Current Population Survey (CPS), the National Compensation Survey (NCS), and the CES. Weekly paid hours are adjusted to hours at work using the NCS. For paid employees, hours at work differ from hours paid, in that they exclude paid vacation and holidays, paid sick leave, and other paid personal or administrative leave. Data from the CPS are used for farm employment, nonfarm proprietors, and unpaid family workers.

Although the labor productivity measures relate output to labor input, they do not measure the contribution of labor or any other specific factor of production. Instead, they reflect the joint effect of many influences, including changes in technology; capital investment; level of output; utilization of capacity, energy, and materials; the organization of production; managerial skill; and the characteristics and efforts of the work force.

Revisions

Data for recent years are revised frequently to take account of revisions in the output and labor input measures that underlie the estimates. Customarily, all revisions to source data are reflected in the release following the source data revision. Data in this volume were released March 5, 2009, and reflect the midyear 2008 revisions to the NIPAs and all revisions in labor input and compensation available up to that release date.

Data availability

Series are available quarterly and annually. Quarterly measures are based entirely on seasonally adjusted data. For some detailed manufacturing series (not shown here), only annual averages are available. Productivity indexes are published early in the second and third months of each quarter, reflecting new data for preceding quarters. Complete historical data are available on the BLS Web site at <http://www.bls.gov>.

BLS also publishes productivity estimates for a number of individual industries. A release entitled "Productivity and Costs by Industry" is available on the BLS Web site at <http://www.bls.gov>.

References

Further information is available in the Technical Notes and footnotes on the most current monthly release, available on the Web site, and from the following sources: Chapter 10, "Productivity Measures: Business Sector and Major Subsectors," *BLS Handbook of Methods*—Bulletin 2490 (April 1997) and the following *Monthly Labor Review* articles: "Alternative Measures of Supervisory Employee Hours and Productivity Growth" (April 2004); "Possible Measurement Bias in Aggregate Productivity Growth" (February 1999); "Improvements to the Quarterly Productivity Measures" (October 1995); "Hours of Work: A New Base for BLS Productivity Statistics" (February 1990); and "New Sector Definitions for Productivity Series" (October 1976).

TABLE 9-4
RATES OF RETURN AND RELATED DATA FOR MAJOR NONFINANCIAL INDUSTRY GROUPS

SOURCE: U.S. DEPARTMENT OF COMMERCE, BUREAU OF ECONOMIC ANALYSIS

This table presents data on the net operating surplus and rate of return for five major nonfinancial industry groups from 1997 through 2006, based on the NAICS. The industry groups include both corporations and proprietors. Therefore, their data differ from the data for nonfinancial corporations alone, which are available through 2007 and shown for comparison purposes in the first column of this table. (Nonfinancial corporation rates of return and related data for 1960 through 2006 can be found in Table 1-15.)

Definitions

Net operating surplus for the nonfinancial industries includes corporate profits, net interest, business current transfer payments, and proprietors' income (mainly the income of unincorporated self-employed workers).

Produced assets is the average of the end-year values for the current and previous year of the net stock of capital plus inventories, valued at current cost.

Rate of return is net operating surplus as a percent of the average value of produced assets at the beginning and end of the year.

Share of net value added is the net operating surplus as a percent of total value added in the industry. Value added is the portion of total national gross domestic product (GDP) produced in the industry and includes the net operating surplus, compensation of employees, taxes on production and imports less subsidies, and consumption of fixed capital.

Data availability, revisions, and references

These data were presented for the first time and described in "Returns for Domestic Nonfinancial Business," *Survey of Current Business,* May 2007, pp. 6-10. The data were revised and updated in the May 2008 *Survey of Current Business.*

TABLE 9-5 AND 9-6
CORPORATE PROFITS WITH INVENTORY VALUATION ADJUSTMENT BY INDUSTRY GROUP

SOURCE: U.S. DEPARTMENT OF COMMERCE, BUREAU OF ECONOMIC ANALYSIS

These profits measures are derived from the NIPAs. See the notes and definitions to Chapter 1 for definitions, data availability, and references. Note that this industry breakdown of profits incorporates the inventory valuation adjustment (IVA), which eliminates any capital gain element in profits arising from changes in the prices at which inventories are valued, but does <u>not</u> incorporate the capital consumption adjustment (CCAdj), which adjusts historical costs of fixed capital to replacement costs and uses actual rather than tax-based service lives. This is because the CCAdj is calculated at an aggregate level, whereas the IVA is calculated at an industry level.

Beginning with 1998, data are compiled on the NAICS basis, as shown in Table 9-5. Data for earlier years based on the December 2003 revision—including an overlap for the years 1998 through 2000—are based on the older Standard Industrial Classification system (SIC) and are shown back to 1948 in Table 9-6 on that basis; these have not been revised and are as shown in previous years' *Business Statistics.* See Chapter 14 for an outline and discussion of NAICS and its relation to SIC.

CHAPTER 10: EMPLOYMENT, HOURS, AND EARNINGS

Section 10a: Labor Force, Employment, and Unemployment

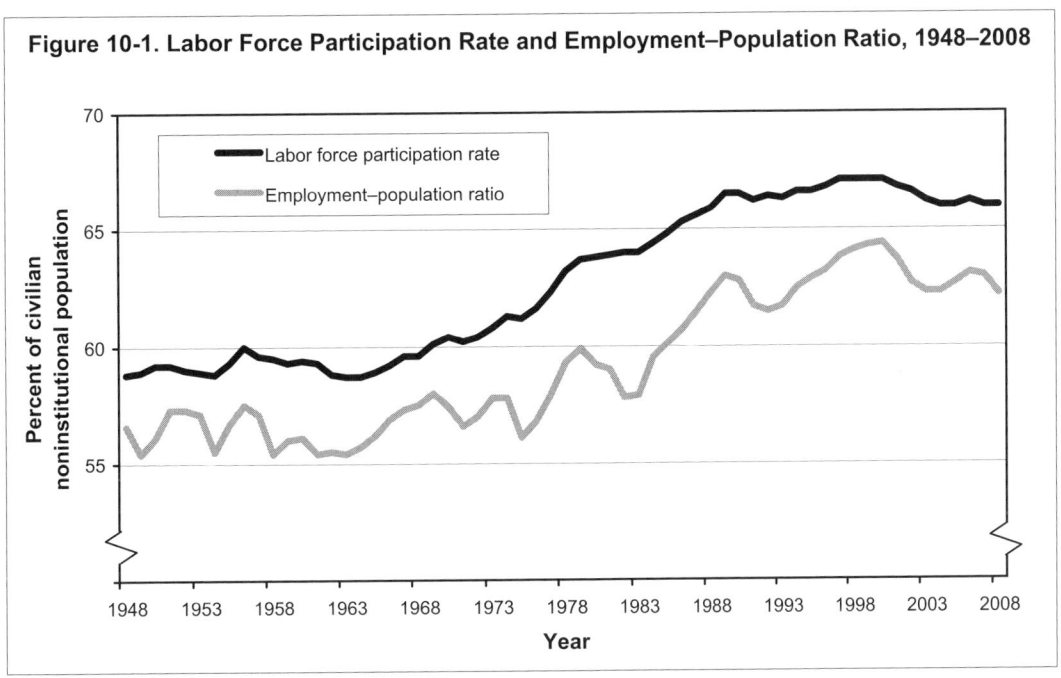

Figure 10-1. Labor Force Participation Rate and Employment–Population Ratio, 1948–2008

- The employment-population ratio, which peaked at 64.4 percent in 2000, was down to 61.0 percent by December 2008. (Tables 10-3 and 20-3)

- The labor force participation rate edged down in 2007 and 2008. Its high point of 67.1 percent was reached in 1997 through 2000. By the end of 2008 it was down further, to 65.7 percent. (Tables 10-1 and 20-3)

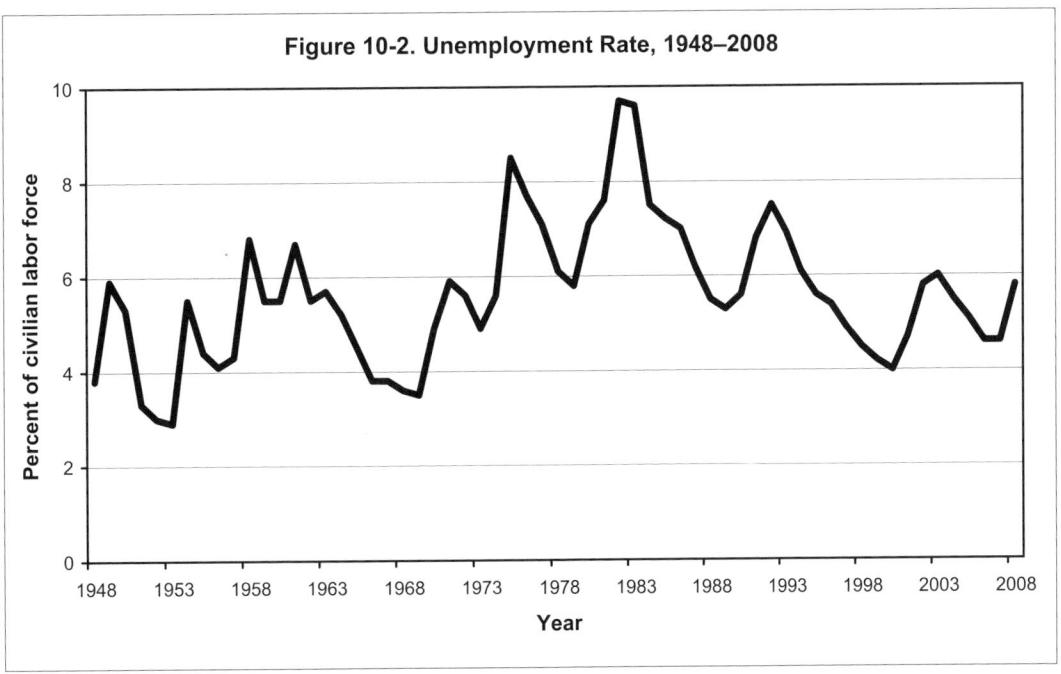

Figure 10-2. Unemployment Rate, 1948–2008

- The unemployment rate got down to 4.6 percent in 2006 and 2007—not as low as the 4.0 percent achieved in 2000—rose to 7.2 percent by December 2008, and continued upward in early 2009. (Tables 10-4 and 20-3)

Table 10-1. Civilian Population and Labor Force [1]

(Thousands of persons, 16 years of age and over; percent.)

Year and month	Civilian noninstitutional population	Not seasonally adjusted — Civilian labor force — Total	Employed	Unemployed	Seasonally adjusted — Civilian labor force (thousands) — Total	Men, 20 years and over	Women, 20 years and over	Both sexes, 16 to 19 years	Participation rate (percent) [2] — Total	Men, 20 years and over	Women, 20 years and over	Both sexes, 16 to 19 years
1965	126 513	74 455	71 088	3 366	74 455	44 857	23 686	5 910	58.9	83.9	39.4	45.7
1966	128 058	75 770	72 895	2 875	75 770	44 788	24 431	6 558	59.2	83.6	40.1	48.2
1967	129 874	77 347	74 372	2 975	77 347	45 354	25 475	6 521	59.6	83.4	41.1	48.4
1968	132 028	78 737	75 920	2 817	78 737	45 852	26 266	6 619	59.6	83.1	41.6	48.3
1969	134 335	80 734	77 902	2 832	80 734	46 351	27 413	6 970	60.1	82.8	42.7	49.4
1970	137 085	82 771	78 678	4 093	82 771	47 220	28 301	7 249	60.4	82.6	43.3	49.9
1971	140 216	84 382	79 367	5 016	84 382	48 009	28 904	7 470	60.2	82.1	43.3	49.7
1972	144 126	87 034	82 153	4 882	87 034	49 079	29 901	8 054	60.4	81.6	43.7	51.9
1973	147 096	89 429	85 064	4 365	89 429	49 932	30 991	8 507	60.8	81.3	44.4	53.7
1974	150 120	91 949	86 794	5 156	91 949	50 879	32 201	8 871	61.3	81.0	45.3	54.8
1975	153 153	93 775	85 846	7 929	93 775	51 494	33 410	8 870	61.2	80.3	46.0	54.0
1976	156 150	96 158	88 752	7 406	96 158	52 288	34 814	9 056	61.6	79.8	47.0	54.5
1977	159 033	99 009	92 017	6 991	99 009	53 348	36 310	9 351	62.3	79.7	48.1	56.0
1978	161 910	102 251	96 048	6 202	102 251	54 471	38 128	9 652	63.2	79.8	49.6	57.8
1979	164 863	104 962	98 824	6 137	104 962	55 615	39 708	9 638	63.7	79.8	50.6	57.9
1980	167 745	106 940	99 303	7 637	106 940	56 455	41 106	9 378	63.8	79.4	51.3	56.7
1981	170 130	108 670	100 397	8 273	108 670	57 197	42 485	8 988	63.9	79.0	52.1	55.4
1982	172 271	110 204	99 526	10 678	110 204	57 980	43 699	8 526	64.0	78.7	52.7	54.1
1983	174 215	111 550	100 834	10 717	111 550	58 744	44 636	8 171	64.0	78.5	53.1	53.5
1984	176 383	113 544	105 005	8 539	113 544	59 701	45 900	7 943	64.4	78.3	53.7	53.9
1985	178 206	115 461	107 150	8 312	115 461	60 277	47 283	7 901	64.8	78.1	54.7	54.5
1986	180 587	117 834	109 597	8 237	117 834	61 320	48 589	7 926	65.3	78.1	55.5	54.7
1987	182 753	119 865	112 440	7 425	119 865	62 095	49 783	7 988	65.6	78.0	56.2	54.7
1988	184 613	121 669	114 968	6 701	121 669	62 768	50 870	8 031	65.9	77.9	56.8	55.3
1989	186 393	123 869	117 342	6 528	123 869	63 704	52 212	7 954	66.5	78.1	57.7	55.9
1990	189 164	125 840	118 793	7 047	125 840	64 916	53 131	7 792	66.5	78.2	58.0	53.7
1991	190 925	126 346	117 718	8 628	126 346	65 374	53 708	7 265	66.2	77.7	57.9	51.6
1992	192 805	128 105	118 492	9 613	128 105	66 213	54 796	7 096	66.4	77.7	58.5	51.3
1993	194 838	129 200	120 259	8 940	129 200	66 642	55 388	7 170	66.3	77.3	58.5	51.5
1994	196 814	131 056	123 060	7 996	131 056	66 921	56 655	7 481	66.6	76.8	59.3	52.7
1995	198 584	132 304	124 900	7 404	132 304	67 324	57 215	7 765	66.6	76.7	59.4	53.5
1996	200 591	133 943	126 708	7 236	133 943	68 044	58 094	7 806	66.8	76.8	59.9	52.3
1997	203 133	136 297	129 558	6 739	136 297	69 166	59 198	7 932	67.1	77.0	60.5	51.6
1998	205 220	137 673	131 463	6 210	137 673	69 715	59 702	8 256	67.1	76.8	60.4	52.8
1999	207 753	139 368	133 488	5 880	139 368	70 194	60 840	8 333	67.1	76.7	60.7	52.0
2000	212 577	142 583	136 891	5 692	142 583	72 010	62 301	8 271	67.1	76.7	60.6	52.0
2001	215 092	143 734	136 933	6 801	143 734	72 816	63 016	7 902	66.8	76.5	60.6	49.6
2002	217 570	144 863	136 485	8 378	144 863	73 630	63 648	7 585	66.6	76.3	60.5	47.4
2003	221 168	146 510	137 736	8 774	146 510	74 623	64 716	7 170	66.2	75.9	60.6	44.5
2004	223 357	147 401	139 252	8 149	147 401	75 364	64 923	7 114	66.0	75.8	60.3	43.9
2005	226 082	149 320	141 730	7 591	149 320	76 443	65 714	7 164	66.0	75.8	60.4	43.7
2006	228 815	151 428	144 427	7 001	151 428	77 562	66 585	7 281	66.2	75.9	60.5	43.7
2007	231 867	153 124	146 047	7 078	153 124	78 596	67 516	7 012	66.0	75.9	60.6	41.3
2008	233 788	154 287	145 362	8 924	154 287	79 047	68 382	6 858	66.0	75.7	60.9	40.2
2007												
January	230 650	151 924	144 275	7 649	153 012	78 447	67 347	7 218	66.3	76.2	60.8	42.7
February	230 834	151 879	144 479	7 400	152 879	78 430	67 316	7 133	66.2	76.1	60.7	42.2
March	231 034	152 236	145 323	6 913	153 004	78 448	67 507	7 050	66.2	76.1	60.8	41.6
April	231 253	151 829	145 297	6 532	152 522	78 485	67 019	7 018	66.0	76.0	60.3	41.4
May	231 480	152 350	145 864	6 486	152 759	78 536	67 304	6 919	66.0	76.0	60.5	40.8
June	231 713	154 252	146 958	7 295	153 085	78 528	67 442	7 114	66.1	75.9	60.6	41.9
July	231 958	154 871	147 315	7 556	153 101	78 569	67 552	6 980	66.0	75.8	60.7	41.1
August	232 211	153 493	146 406	7 088	152 855	78 496	67 623	6 736	65.8	75.7	60.7	39.6
September	232 461	153 400	146 448	6 952	153 424	78 634	67 794	6 996	66.0	75.7	60.8	41.1
October	232 715	153 516	146 743	6 773	153 162	78 555	67 580	7 027	65.8	75.6	60.5	41.2
November	232 939	154 035	147 118	6 917	153 877	79 068	67 804	7 005	66.1	76.0	60.6	41.1
December	233 156	153 705	146 334	7 371	153 836	78 943	67 888	7 005	66.0	75.8	60.7	41.1
2008												
January	232 616	152 828	144 607	8 221	153 873	78 907	67 982	6 984	66.1	76.0	60.8	41.1
February	232 809	152 503	144 550	7 953	153 498	78 806	67 879	6 813	65.9	75.8	60.7	40.0
March	232 995	153 135	145 108	8 027	153 843	78 866	68 174	6 803	66.0	75.8	60.9	39.9
April	233 198	153 208	145 921	7 287	153 932	78 820	68 118	6 993	66.0	75.7	60.8	41.0
May	233 405	154 003	145 927	8 076	154 510	78 913	68 367	7 231	66.2	75.7	61.0	42.4
June	233 627	155 582	146 649	8 933	154 400	79 055	68 421	6 924	66.1	75.7	61.0	40.6
July	233 864	156 300	146 867	9 433	154 506	79 286	68 273	6 947	66.1	75.9	60.8	40.7
August	234 107	155 387	145 909	9 479	154 823	79 308	68 666	6 849	66.1	75.8	61.1	40.1
September	234 360	154 509	145 310	9 199	154 621	79 392	68 385	6 844	66.0	75.8	60.8	40.0
October	234 612	155 012	145 543	9 469	154 878	79 380	68 700	6 799	66.0	75.7	61.0	39.7
November	234 828	154 624	144 609	10 015	154 620	79 335	68 753	6 531	65.8	75.6	61.0	38.2
December	235 035	154 349	143 350	10 999	154 447	78 998	68 891	6 557	65.7	75.2	61.1	38.3

[1]Changes in survey design, population estimates, and methodology in 1994 and several other years affect year-to-year comparisons. See notes and definitions for more information.
[2]Labor force as a percent of the demographic group's civilian noninstitutional population.

Table 10-2. Civilian Employment [1]

(Thousands of persons, 16 years of age and over; seasonally adjusted, except as noted.)

Year and month	Total	By age and sex			Agricultural	By class of worker						
		Men, 20 years and over	Women, 20 years and over	Both sexes, 16 to 19 years		Nonagricultural industries					Self-employed	Unpaid family workers [2]
						Total	Wage and salary					
							Total	Government	Private industries			
									Private house-holds [2]	Other private industries		
1965	71 088	43 422	22 630	5 036	4 361	66 726	60 031	9 608	. . .	. . .	6 097	600
1966	72 895	43 668	23 510	5 721	3 979	68 915	62 362	10 323	. . .	. . .	5 991	564
1967	74 372	44 294	24 397	5 682	3 844	70 527	64 848	11 146	. . .	. . .	5 174	505
1968	75 920	44 859	25 281	5 781	3 817	72 103	66 519	11 590	. . .	. . .	5 102	485
1969	77 902	45 388	26 397	6 117	3 606	74 296	68 528	12 025	. . .	. . .	5 252	517
1970	78 678	45 581	26 952	6 144	3 463	75 215	69 491	12 431	. . .	. . .	5 221	502
1971	79 367	45 912	27 246	6 208	3 394	75 972	70 120	12 799	. . .	. . .	5 327	522
1972	82 153	47 130	28 276	6 746	3 484	78 669	72 785	13 393	. . .	. . .	5 365	519
1973	85 064	48 310	29 484	7 271	3 470	81 594	75 580	13 655	. . .	. . .	5 474	540
1974	86 794	48 922	30 424	7 448	3 515	83 279	77 094	14 124	. . .	. . .	5 697	489
1975	85 846	48 018	30 726	7 104	3 408	82 438	76 249	14 675	. . .	. . .	5 705	483
1976	88 752	49 190	32 226	7 336	3 331	85 421	79 175	15 132	. . .	. . .	5 783	464
1977	92 017	50 555	33 775	7 688	3 283	88 734	82 121	15 361	. . .	. . .	6 114	498
1978	96 048	52 143	35 836	8 070	3 387	92 661	85 753	15 525	. . .	. . .	6 429	479
1979	98 824	53 308	37 434	8 083	3 347	95 477	88 222	15 635	. . .	. . .	6 791	463
1980	99 303	53 101	38 492	7 710	3 364	95 938	88 525	15 912	. . .	. . .	7 000	413
1981	100 397	53 582	39 590	7 225	3 368	97 030	89 543	15 689	. . .	. . .	7 097	390
1982	99 526	52 891	40 086	6 549	3 401	96 125	88 462	15 516	. . .	. . .	7 262	401
1983	100 834	53 487	41 004	6 342	3 383	97 450	89 500	15 537	. . .	. . .	7 575	376
1984	105 005	55 769	42 793	6 444	3 321	101 685	93 565	15 770	. . .	. . .	7 785	335
1985	107 150	56 562	44 154	6 434	3 179	103 971	95 871	16 031	. . .	. . .	7 811	289
1986	109 597	57 569	45 556	6 472	3 163	106 434	98 299	16 342	. . .	. . .	7 881	255
1987	112 440	58 726	47 074	6 640	3 208	109 232	100 771	16 800	. . .	. . .	8 201	260
1988	114 968	59 781	48 383	6 805	3 169	111 800	103 021	17 114	. . .	. . .	8 519	260
1989	117 342	60 837	49 745	6 759	3 199	114 142	105 259	17 469	. . .	. . .	8 605	279
1990	118 793	61 678	50 535	6 581	3 223	115 570	106 598	17 769	. . .	. . .	8 719	253
1991	117 718	61 178	50 634	5 906	3 269	114 449	105 373	17 934	. . .	. . .	8 851	226
1992	118 492	61 496	51 328	5 669	3 247	115 245	106 437	18 136	. . .	. . .	8 575	233
1993	120 259	62 355	52 099	5 805	3 115	117 144	107 966	18 579	. . .	. . .	8 959	218
1994	123 060	63 294	53 606	6 161	3 409	119 651	110 517	18 293	. . .	. . .	9 003	131
1995	124 900	64 085	54 396	6 419	3 440	121 460	112 448	18 362	. . .	. . .	8 902	110
1996	126 708	64 897	55 311	6 500	3 443	123 264	114 171	18 217	. . .	. . .	8 971	122
1997	129 558	66 284	56 613	6 661	3 399	126 159	116 983	18 131	. . .	. . .	9 056	120
1998	131 463	67 135	57 278	7 051	3 378	128 085	119 019	18 383	. . .	. . .	8 962	103
1999	133 488	67 761	58 555	7 172	3 281	130 207	121 323	18 903	. . .	. . .	8 790	95
2000	136 891	69 634	60 067	7 189	2 464	134 427	125 114	19 248	718	105 148	9 205	108
2001	136 933	69 776	60 417	6 740	2 299	134 635	125 407	19 335	694	105 378	9 121	107
2002	136 485	69 734	60 420	6 332	2 311	134 174	125 156	19 636	757	104 764	8 923	95
2003	137 736	70 415	61 402	5 919	2 275	135 461	126 015	19 634	764	105 616	9 344	101
2004	139 252	71 572	61 773	5 907	2 232	137 020	127 463	19 983	779	106 701	9 467	90
2005	141 730	73 050	62 702	5 978	2 197	139 532	129 931	20 357	812	108 761	9 509	93
2006	144 427	74 431	63 834	6 162	2 206	142 221	132 449	20 337	803	111 309	9 685	87
2007	146 047	75 337	64 799	5 911	2 095	143 952	134 283	21 003	813	112 467	9 557	112
2008	145 362	74 750	65 039	5 573	2 168	143 194	133 882	21 258	805	111 819	9 219	93
2007												
January	145 983	75 199	64 633	6 152	2 213	143 731	133 976	21 000	749	112 220	9 630	111
February	145 992	75 193	64 728	6 070	2 305	143 679	133 888	20 884	856	112 132	9 603	117
March	146 267	75 330	64 928	6 010	2 189	144 046	134 124	20 901	859	112 326	9 766	121
April	145 647	75 310	64 408	5 929	2 069	143 613	133 817	20 987	819	111 985	9 685	103
May	145 915	75 386	64 706	5 823	2 095	143 798	134 053	21 148	810	112 041	9 663	94
June	146 057	75 308	64 781	5 968	1 957	144 071	134 188	21 126	837	112 262	9 783	143
July	145 972	75 278	64 771	5 923	2 019	144 046	134 345	21 088	856	112 559	9 593	132
August	145 732	75 245	64 843	5 644	1 857	143 902	134 283	21 120	819	112 388	9 528	114
September	146 203	75 305	65 028	5 870	2 072	144 160	134 504	21 128	823	112 566	9 521	116
October	145 867	75 177	64 774	5 917	2 103	143 843	134 454	20 914	760	112 744	9 315	115
November	146 665	75 781	65 024	5 861	2 143	144 473	135 016	20 945	759	113 273	9 330	97
December	146 294	75 496	64 976	5 822	2 211	143 992	134 659	20 807	803	113 005	9 291	81
2008												
January	146 317	75 474	65 101	5 742	2 205	144 097	134 764	20 946	787	113 015	9 233	76
February	146 075	75 395	64 993	5 688	2 208	143 878	134 277	21 219	763	112 283	9 418	100
March	146 023	75 216	65 079	5 729	2 191	143 821	134 449	21 245	744	112 422	9 242	99
April	146 257	75 147	65 196	5 914	2 111	144 219	134 698	21 309	780	112 585	9 371	125
May	145 974	74 992	65 114	5 868	2 136	143 830	134 328	21 253	774	112 271	9 383	132
June	145 738	74 949	65 169	5 620	2 134	143 563	134 094	21 190	862	112 080	9 396	120
July	145 596	74 973	65 103	5 520	2 142	143 453	133 894	21 129	873	112 036	9 483	106
August	145 273	74 737	65 003	5 533	2 138	143 111	133 727	21 257	799	111 721	9 313	84
September	145 029	74 503	65 008	5 518	2 199	142 851	133 582	21 183	820	111 591	9 178	81
October	144 657	74 292	64 975	5 390	2 177	142 566	133 694	21 539	840	111 279	8 852	69
November	144 144	74 045	64 902	5 196	2 206	141 901	132 983	21 431	836	110 677	8 816	65
December	143 338	73 285	64 860	5 194	2 191	141 047	132 082	21 395	782	109 863	8 940	62

[1]Changes in survey design, population estimates, and methodology in 1994 and several other years affect year-to-year comparisons. See notes and definitions for more information.
[2]Not seasonally adjusted.
. . . = Not available.

Table 10-3. Civilian Employment and Unemployment [1]

(Thousands of persons; percent; seasonally adjusted.)

Year and month	Employment-population ratio, percent				Multiple jobholders		Employed and at work part time		Unemployment (thousands)				
	Total	Men, 20 years and over	Women, 20 years and over	Both sexes, 16 to 19 years	Total (thousands)	Percent of total employed	Economic reasons	Non-economic reasons	Total	Long-term [2]	Men, 20 years and over	Women, 20 years and over	Both sexes, 16 to 19 years
1965	56.2	81.2	37.6	38.9	. . .	. . .	2 209	8 466	3 366	755	1 435	1 056	874
1966	56.9	81.5	38.6	42.1	. . .	. . .	1 960	8 112	2 875	526	1 120	921	837
1967	57.3	81.5	39.3	42.2	. . .	. . .	2 163	8 701	2 975	448	1 060	1 078	839
1968	57.5	81.3	40.0	42.2	. . .	. . .	1 970	9 075	2 817	412	993	985	838
1969	58.0	81.1	41.1	43.4	. . .	. . .	2 056	9 652	2 832	375	963	1 015	853
1970	57.4	79.7	41.2	42.3	. . .	. . .	2 446	9 999	4 093	663	1 638	1 349	1 106
1971	56.6	78.5	40.9	41.3	. . .	. . .	2 688	10 152	5 016	1 187	2 097	1 658	1 262
1972	57.0	78.4	41.3	43.5	. . .	. . .	2 648	10 612	4 882	1 167	1 948	1 625	1 308
1973	57.8	78.6	42.2	45.9	. . .	. . .	2 554	10 972	4 365	826	1 624	1 507	1 235
1974	57.8	77.9	42.8	46.0	. . .	. . .	2 988	11 153	5 156	955	1 957	1 777	1 422
1975	56.1	74.8	42.3	43.3	. . .	. . .	3 804	11 228	7 929	2 505	3 476	2 684	1 767
1976	56.8	75.1	43.5	44.2	. . .	. . .	3 607	11 607	7 406	2 366	3 098	2 588	1 719
1977	57.9	75.6	44.8	46.1	. . .	. . .	3 608	12 120	6 991	1 942	2 794	2 535	1 663
1978	59.3	76.4	46.6	48.3	. . .	. . .	3 516	12 650	6 202	1 414	2 328	2 292	1 583
1979	59.9	76.5	47.7	48.5	. . .	. . .	3 577	12 893	6 137	1 241	2 308	2 276	1 555
1980	59.2	74.6	48.1	46.6	. . .	. . .	4 321	13 067	7 637	1 871	3 353	2 615	1 669
1981	59.0	74.0	48.6	44.6	. . .	. . .	4 768	13 025	8 273	2 285	3 615	2 895	1 763
1982	57.8	71.8	48.4	41.5	. . .	. . .	6 170	12 953	10 678	3 485	5 089	3 613	1 977
1983	57.9	71.4	48.8	41.5	. . .	. . .	6 266	12 911	10 717	4 210	5 257	3 632	1 829
1984	59.5	73.2	50.1	43.7	. . .	. . .	5 744	13 169	8 539	2 737	3 932	3 107	1 499
1985	60.1	73.3	51.0	44.4	. . .	. . .	5 590	13 489	8 312	2 305	3 715	3 129	1 468
1986	60.7	73.3	52.0	44.6	. . .	. . .	5 588	13 935	8 237	2 232	3 751	3 032	1 454
1987	61.5	73.8	53.1	45.5	. . .	. . .	5 401	14 395	7 425	1 983	3 369	2 709	1 347
1988	62.3	74.2	54.0	46.8	. . .	. . .	5 206	14 963	6 701	1 610	2 987	2 487	1 226
1989	63.0	74.5	54.9	47.5	. . .	. . .	4 894	15 393	6 528	1 375	2 867	2 467	1 194
1990	62.8	74.3	55.2	45.3	. . .	. . .	5 204	15 341	7 047	1 525	3 239	2 596	1 212
1991	61.7	72.7	54.6	42.0	. . .	. . .	6 161	15 172	8 628	2 357	4 195	3 074	1 359
1992	61.5	72.1	54.8	41.0	. . .	. . .	6 520	14 918	9 613	3 408	4 717	3 469	1 427
1993	61.7	72.3	55.0	41.7	. . .	. . .	6 481	15 240	8 940	3 094	4 287	3 288	1 365
1994	62.5	72.6	56.2	43.4	7 260	5.9	4 625	17 638	7 996	2 860	3 627	3 049	1 320
1995	62.9	73.0	56.5	44.2	7 693	6.2	4 473	17 734	7 404	2 363	3 239	2 819	1 346
1996	63.2	73.2	57.0	43.5	7 832	6.2	4 315	17 770	7 236	2 316	3 146	2 783	1 306
1997	63.8	73.7	57.8	43.4	7 955	6.1	4 068	18 149	6 739	2 062	2 882	2 585	1 271
1998	64.1	73.9	58.0	45.1	7 926	6.0	3 665	18 530	6 210	1 637	2 580	2 424	1 205
1999	64.3	74.0	58.5	44.7	7 802	5.8	3 357	18 758	5 880	1 480	2 433	2 285	1 162
2000	64.4	74.2	58.4	45.2	7 604	5.6	3 227	18 814	5 692	1 318	2 376	2 235	1 081
2001	63.7	73.3	58.1	42.3	7 357	5.4	3 715	18 790	6 801	1 752	3 040	2 599	1 162
2002	62.7	72.3	57.5	39.6	7 291	5.3	4 213	18 843	8 378	2 904	3 896	3 228	1 253
2003	62.3	71.7	57.5	36.8	7 315	5.3	4 701	19 014	8 774	3 378	4 209	3 314	1 251
2004	62.3	71.9	57.4	36.4	7 473	5.4	4 567	19 380	8 149	3 072	3 791	3 150	1 208
2005	62.7	72.4	57.6	36.5	7 546	5.3	4 350	19 491	7 591	2 619	3 392	3 013	1 186
2006	63.1	72.9	58.0	36.9	7 576	5.2	4 162	19 591	7 001	2 266	3 131	2 751	1 119
2007	63.0	72.8	58.2	34.8	7 655	5.2	4 401	19 756	7 078	2 303	3 259	2 718	1 101
2008	62.2	71.6	57.9	32.6	7 620	5.2	5 875	19 343	8 924	3 188	4 297	3 342	1 285
2007													
January	63.3	73.0	58.3	36.4	7 703	5.3	4 200	19 766	7 029	2 116	3 248	2 714	1 067
February	63.2	73.0	58.4	35.9	7 750	5.3	4 222	19 991	6 887	2 184	3 237	2 587	1 063
March	63.3	73.0	58.5	35.5	7 772	5.3	4 288	20 104	6 737	2 227	3 118	2 579	1 040
April	63.0	72.9	58.0	35.0	7 900	5.4	4 340	19 864	6 874	2 266	3 175	2 610	1 089
May	63.0	72.9	58.2	34.3	7 745	5.3	4 482	19 706	6 844	2 244	3 150	2 598	1 096
June	63.0	72.8	58.2	35.2	7 625	5.2	4 315	19 990	7 028	2 309	3 221	2 661	1 146
July	62.9	72.7	58.2	34.9	7 621	5.2	4 338	19 923	7 128	2 392	3 291	2 780	1 057
August	62.8	72.5	58.2	33.2	7 512	5.2	4 598	19 683	7 123	2 349	3 251	2 780	1 092
September	62.9	72.5	58.3	34.5	7 505	5.1	4 557	19 755	7 221	2 374	3 329	2 765	1 127
October	62.7	72.3	58.0	34.7	7 583	5.2	4 400	19 427	7 295	2 355	3 378	2 807	1 110
November	63.0	72.8	58.2	34.4	7 670	5.2	4 491	19 598	7 212	2 378	3 287	2 781	1 144
December	62.7	72.5	58.1	34.1	7 479	5.1	4 638	19 536	7 541	2 484	3 446	2 912	1 183
2008													
January	62.9	72.7	58.3	33.8	7 585	5.2	4 738	19 563	7 555	2 477	3 433	2 881	1 241
February	62.7	72.5	58.1	33.4	7 607	5.2	4 890	19 317	7 423	2 400	3 412	2 886	1 125
March	62.7	72.3	58.2	33.6	7 478	5.1	4 937	19 402	7 820	2 444	3 650	3 095	1 075
April	62.7	72.2	58.2	34.7	7 671	5.2	5 240	19 792	7 675	2 652	3 673	2 923	1 079
May	62.5	71.9	58.1	34.4	7 685	5.3	5 290	19 396	8 536	2 808	3 921	3 252	1 363
June	62.4	71.8	58.1	32.9	7 780	5.3	5 495	19 428	8 662	2 966	4 106	3 252	1 304
July	62.3	71.8	58.0	32.3	7 727	5.3	5 813	19 348	8 910	3 168	4 313	3 170	1 427
August	62.1	71.4	57.8	32.4	8 013	5.5	5 879	19 690	9 550	3 447	4 572	3 662	1 316
September	61.9	71.1	57.8	32.3	7 612	5.2	6 292	19 275	9 592	3 662	4 889	3 377	1 326
October	61.7	70.8	57.7	31.5	7 551	5.2	6 848	19 083	10 221	4 109	5 088	3 725	1 408
November	61.4	70.5	57.6	30.4	7 410	5.1	7 323	18 886	10 476	3 964	5 290	3 851	1 335
December	61.0	69.7	57.5	30.3	7 352	5.1	8 038	18 922	11 108	4 517	5 714	4 031	1 363

[1] Changes in survey design, population estimates, and methodology in 1994 and several other years affect year-to-year comparisons. See notes and definitions for more information.
[2] Fifteen weeks and over.
. . . = Not available.

Table 10-4. Unemployment Rates [1]

(Unemployment as a percent of the civilian labor force in group; seasonally adjusted, except as noted.)

Year and month	All civilian workers	By age and sex			By race				Hispanic or Latino ethnicity	By marital status		
		Men, 20 years and over	Women, 20 years and over	Both sexes, 16 to 19 years	White	Black and other	Black or African American	Asian [2]		Married men, spouse present	Married women, spouse present	Women who maintain families [2]
1965	4.5	3.2	4.5	14.8	4.1	8.1	. . .	. . .	. . .	2.4	4.5	. . .
1966	3.8	2.5	3.8	12.8	3.4	7.3	. . .	. . .	. . .	1.9	3.7	. . .
1967	3.8	2.3	4.2	12.9	3.4	7.4	. . .	. . .	. . .	1.8	4.5	4.9
1968	3.6	2.2	3.8	12.7	3.2	6.7	. . .	. . .	. . .	1.6	3.9	4.4
1969	3.5	2.1	3.7	12.2	3.1	6.4	. . .	. . .	. . .	1.5	3.9	4.4
1970	4.9	3.5	4.8	15.3	4.5	8.2	. . .	. . .	. . .	2.6	4.9	5.4
1971	5.9	4.4	5.7	16.9	5.4	9.9	. . .	. . .	. . .	3.2	5.7	7.3
1972	5.6	4.0	5.4	16.2	5.1	10.0	10.4	. . .	. . .	2.8	5.4	7.2
1973	4.9	3.3	4.9	14.5	4.3	9.0	9.4	. . .	7.5	2.3	4.7	7.1
1974	5.6	3.8	5.5	16.0	5.0	9.9	10.5	. . .	8.1	2.7	5.3	7.0
1975	8.5	6.8	8.0	19.9	7.8	13.8	14.8	. . .	12.2	5.1	7.9	10.0
1976	7.7	5.9	7.4	19.0	7.0	13.1	14.0	. . .	11.5	4.2	7.1	10.1
1977	7.1	5.2	7.0	17.8	6.2	13.1	14.0	. . .	10.1	3.6	6.5	9.4
1978	6.1	4.3	6.0	16.4	5.2	11.9	12.8	. . .	9.1	2.8	5.5	8.5
1979	5.8	4.2	5.7	16.1	5.1	11.3	12.3	. . .	8.3	2.8	5.1	8.3
1980	7.1	5.9	6.4	17.8	6.3	13.1	14.3	. . .	10.1	4.2	5.8	9.2
1981	7.6	6.3	6.8	19.6	6.7	14.2	15.6	. . .	10.4	4.3	6.0	10.4
1982	9.7	8.8	8.3	23.2	8.6	17.3	18.9	. . .	13.8	6.5	7.4	11.7
1983	9.6	8.9	8.1	22.4	8.4	17.8	19.5	. . .	13.7	6.5	7.0	12.2
1984	7.5	6.6	6.8	18.9	6.5	14.4	15.9	. . .	10.7	4.6	5.7	10.3
1985	7.2	6.2	6.6	18.6	6.2	13.7	15.1	. . .	10.5	4.3	5.6	10.4
1986	7.0	6.1	6.2	18.3	6.0	13.1	14.5	. . .	10.6	4.4	5.2	9.8
1987	6.2	5.4	5.4	16.9	5.3	11.6	13.0	. . .	8.8	3.9	4.3	9.2
1988	5.5	4.8	4.9	15.3	4.7	10.4	11.7	. . .	8.2	3.3	3.9	8.1
1989	5.3	4.5	4.7	15.0	4.5	10.0	11.4	. . .	8.0	3.0	3.7	8.1
1990	5.6	5.0	4.9	15.5	4.8	10.1	11.4	. . .	8.2	3.4	3.8	8.3
1991	6.8	6.4	5.7	18.7	6.1	11.1	12.5	. . .	10.0	4.4	4.5	9.3
1992	7.5	7.1	6.3	20.1	6.6	12.7	14.2	. . .	11.6	5.1	5.0	10.0
1993	6.9	6.4	5.9	19.0	6.1	11.7	13.0	. . .	10.8	4.4	4.6	9.7
1994	6.1	5.4	5.4	17.6	5.3	10.5	11.5	. . .	9.9	3.7	4.1	8.9
1995	5.6	4.8	4.9	17.3	4.9	9.6	10.4	. . .	9.3	3.3	3.9	8.0
1996	5.4	4.6	4.8	16.7	4.7	9.3	10.5	. . .	8.9	3.0	3.6	8.2
1997	4.9	4.2	4.4	16.0	4.2	8.8	10.0	. . .	7.7	2.7	3.1	8.1
1998	4.5	3.7	4.1	14.6	3.9	7.8	8.9	. . .	7.2	2.4	2.9	7.2
1999	4.2	3.5	3.8	13.9	3.7	7.0	8.0	. . .	6.4	2.2	2.7	6.4
2000	4.0	3.3	3.6	13.1	3.5	6.7	7.6	3.6	5.7	2.0	2.7	5.9
2001	4.7	4.2	4.1	14.7	4.2	7.7	8.6	4.5	6.6	2.7	3.1	6.6
2002	5.8	5.3	5.1	16.5	5.1	9.2	10.2	5.9	7.5	3.6	3.7	8.0
2003	6.0	5.6	5.1	17.5	5.2	. . .	10.8	6.0	7.7	3.8	3.7	8.5
2004	5.5	5.0	4.9	17.0	4.8	. . .	10.4	4.4	7.0	3.1	3.5	8.0
2005	5.1	4.4	4.6	16.6	4.4	. . .	10.0	4.0	6.0	2.8	3.3	7.8
2006	4.6	4.0	4.1	15.4	4.0	. . .	8.9	3.0	5.2	2.4	2.9	7.1
2007	4.6	4.1	4.0	15.7	4.1	. . .	8.3	3.2	5.6	2.5	2.8	6.5
2008	5.8	5.4	4.9	18.7	5.2	. . .	10.1	4.0	7.6	3.4	3.6	8.0
2007												
January	4.6	4.1	4.0	14.8	4.1	. . .	8.0	3.2	5.7	2.5	2.7	6.6
February	4.5	4.1	3.8	14.9	4.0	. . .	8.1	2.7	5.3	2.7	2.7	6.5
March	4.4	4.0	3.8	14.8	3.8	. . .	8.3	3.0	5.2	2.4	2.6	6.7
April	4.5	4.0	3.9	15.5	4.0	. . .	8.4	3.3	5.5	2.6	2.7	6.2
May	4.5	4.0	3.9	15.8	3.9	. . .	8.4	2.9	5.9	2.6	2.8	6.3
June	4.6	4.1	3.9	16.1	4.1	. . .	8.5	3.1	5.6	2.4	2.7	6.8
July	4.7	4.2	4.1	15.1	4.2	. . .	8.0	3.0	5.9	2.7	2.9	6.8
August	4.7	4.1	4.1	16.2	4.2	. . .	7.7	3.4	5.5	2.5	3.1	6.2
September	4.7	4.2	4.1	16.1	4.2	. . .	8.1	3.2	5.8	2.5	2.9	6.4
October	4.8	4.3	4.2	15.8	4.2	. . .	8.5	3.7	5.6	2.5	2.9	6.3
November	4.7	4.2	4.1	16.3	4.2	. . .	8.4	3.6	5.7	2.5	3.0	6.6
December	4.9	4.4	4.3	16.9	4.4	. . .	8.9	3.7	6.2	2.6	3.0	6.9
2008												
January	4.9	4.4	4.2	17.8	4.4	. . .	9.2	3.2	6.4	2.7	3.0	7.0
February	4.8	4.3	4.3	16.5	4.4	. . .	8.4	3.0	6.3	2.7	3.1	6.7
March	5.1	4.6	4.5	15.8	4.5	. . .	9.0	3.6	7.0	2.8	3.4	7.1
April	5.0	4.7	4.3	15.4	4.4	. . .	8.8	3.2	7.0	2.8	3.0	6.8
May	5.5	5.0	4.8	18.9	4.9	. . .	9.7	3.8	7.0	3.0	3.2	6.9
June	5.6	5.2	4.8	18.8	5.0	. . .	9.4	4.5	7.7	3.1	3.4	7.9
July	5.8	5.4	4.6	20.5	5.2	. . .	9.9	4.0	7.5	3.3	3.4	8.5
August	6.2	5.8	5.3	19.2	5.5	. . .	10.7	4.4	8.1	3.7	3.7	9.6
September	6.2	6.2	4.9	19.4	5.5	. . .	11.4	3.8	7.9	3.9	3.5	8.2
October	6.6	6.4	5.4	20.7	6.0	. . .	11.3	3.8	8.8	4.1	4.2	8.8
November	6.8	6.7	5.6	20.4	6.2	. . .	11.3	4.8	8.6	4.2	4.3	9.3
December	7.2	7.2	5.9	20.8	6.6	. . .	11.9	5.1	9.2	4.4	4.5	9.5

[1]Changes in survey design, population estimates, and methodology in 1994 and several other years affect year-to-year comparisons. See notes and definitions for more information.
[2]Not seasonally adjusted.
. . . = Not available.

Table 10-5. Unemployment Rates and Related Data [1]

(Seasonally adjusted.)

Year and month	Unemployment rates by reason for unemployment (percent of total civilian labor force)					Duration of unemployment		Alternative measures of labor underutilization		
	Total	Job losers and persons who completed temporary jobs	Job leavers	Reentrants	New entrants	Average (mean) weeks unemployed	Median weeks unemployed	Including discouraged workers (U-4)	Including all marginally attached workers (U-5)	Including marginally attached and underemployed (U-6)
1965	4.5	...	...	...	...	11.8	...	...	...	...
1966	3.8	...	...	...	...	10.4	...	...	...	...
1967	3.8	1.6	0.6	1.2	0.5	8.7	2.3	...	...	...
1968	3.6	1.4	0.5	1.2	0.5	8.4	4.5	...	...	...
1969	3.5	1.3	0.5	1.2	0.5	7.8	4.4	...	...	...
1970	4.9	2.2	0.7	1.5	0.6	8.6	4.9	...	...	...
1971	5.9	2.8	0.7	1.7	0.7	11.3	6.3	...	...	...
1972	5.6	2.4	0.7	1.7	0.8	12.0	6.2	...	...	...
1973	4.9	1.9	0.8	1.5	0.7	10.0	5.2	...	...	...
1974	5.6	2.4	0.8	1.6	0.7	9.8	5.2	...	...	...
1975	8.5	4.7	0.9	2.0	0.9	14.2	8.4	...	...	...
1976	7.7	3.8	0.9	2.0	0.9	15.8	8.2	...	...	...
1977	7.1	3.2	0.9	2.0	1.0	14.3	7.0	...	...	...
1978	6.1	2.5	0.9	1.8	0.9	11.9	5.9	...	...	...
1979	5.8	2.5	0.8	1.7	0.8	10.8	5.4	...	...	...
1980	7.1	3.7	0.8	1.8	0.8	11.9	6.5	...	...	...
1981	7.6	3.9	0.8	1.9	0.9	13.7	6.9	...	...	...
1982	9.7	5.7	0.8	2.2	1.1	15.6	8.7	...	...	...
1983	9.6	5.6	0.7	2.2	1.1	20.0	10.1	...	...	...
1984	7.5	3.9	0.7	1.9	1.0	18.2	7.9	...	...	...
1985	7.2	3.6	0.8	2.0	0.9	15.6	6.8	...	...	...
1986	7.0	3.4	0.9	1.8	0.9	15.0	6.9	...	...	...
1987	6.2	3.0	0.8	1.6	0.8	14.5	6.5	...	...	...
1988	5.5	2.5	0.8	1.5	0.7	13.5	5.9	...	...	...
1989	5.3	2.4	0.8	1.5	0.5	11.9	4.8	...	...	...
1990	5.6	2.7	0.8	1.5	0.5	12.0	5.3	...	...	...
1991	6.8	3.7	0.8	1.7	0.6	13.7	6.8	...	...	...
1992	7.5	4.2	0.8	1.8	0.7	17.7	8.7	...	...	...
1993	6.9	3.8	0.8	1.7	0.7	18.0	8.3	...	...	...
1994	6.1	2.9	0.6	2.1	0.5	18.8	9.2	6.5	7.4	10.9
1995	5.6	2.6	0.6	1.9	0.4	16.6	8.3	5.9	6.7	10.1
1996	5.4	2.5	0.6	1.9	0.4	16.7	8.3	5.7	6.5	9.7
1997	4.9	2.2	0.6	1.7	0.4	15.8	8.0	5.2	5.9	8.9
1998	4.5	2.1	0.5	1.5	0.4	14.5	6.7	4.7	5.4	8.0
1999	4.2	1.9	0.6	1.4	0.3	13.4	6.4	4.4	5.0	7.4
2000	4.0	1.8	0.5	1.4	0.3	12.6	5.9	4.2	4.8	7.0
2001	4.7	2.4	0.6	1.4	0.3	13.1	6.8	4.9	5.6	8.1
2002	5.8	3.2	0.6	1.6	0.4	16.6	9.1	6.0	6.7	9.6
2003	6.0	3.3	0.6	1.7	0.4	19.2	10.1	6.3	7.0	10.1
2004	5.5	2.8	0.6	1.6	0.5	19.6	9.8	5.8	6.5	9.6
2005	5.1	2.5	0.6	1.6	0.4	18.4	8.9	5.4	6.1	8.9
2006	4.6	2.2	0.5	1.5	0.4	16.8	8.3	4.9	5.5	8.2
2007	4.6	2.3	0.5	1.4	0.4	16.8	8.5	4.9	5.5	8.3
2008	5.8	3.1	0.6	1.6	0.5	17.9	9.4	6.1	6.8	10.5
2007										
January	4.6	2.2	0.5	1.4	0.4	16.3	8.1	4.9	5.6	8.3
February	4.5	2.2	0.5	1.3	0.4	16.5	8.3	4.7	5.4	8.1
March	4.4	2.1	0.5	1.4	0.4	17.5	8.7	4.6	5.3	8.0
April	4.5	2.2	0.5	1.4	0.4	17.0	8.6	4.8	5.4	8.2
May	4.5	2.2	0.5	1.4	0.4	16.8	8.4	4.7	5.4	8.3
June	4.6	2.2	0.5	1.4	0.4	16.8	8.3	4.8	5.5	8.3
July	4.7	2.4	0.5	1.3	0.4	17.4	8.8	4.9	5.5	8.3
August	4.7	2.4	0.5	1.3	0.4	17.0	8.7	4.9	5.5	8.5
September	4.7	2.4	0.5	1.4	0.4	16.4	8.8	4.9	5.5	8.4
October	4.8	2.4	0.5	1.4	0.5	16.9	8.5	5.0	5.6	8.5
November	4.7	2.4	0.5	1.4	0.4	17.3	8.7	4.9	5.5	8.4
December	4.9	2.5	0.5	1.5	0.5	16.5	8.4	5.1	5.7	8.7
2008										
January	4.9	2.5	0.5	1.4	0.4	17.5	8.7	5.2	6.0	9.0
February	4.8	2.5	0.5	1.4	0.4	16.6	8.4	5.1	5.8	9.0
March	5.1	2.7	0.5	1.4	0.5	16.1	8.2	5.3	5.9	9.1
April	5.0	2.6	0.6	1.4	0.4	17.0	9.3	5.2	5.9	9.2
May	5.5	2.8	0.6	1.6	0.5	16.8	8.3	5.8	6.4	9.8
June	5.6	2.9	0.5	1.7	0.5	17.6	10.1	5.9	6.6	10.1
July	5.8	3.0	0.6	1.7	0.5	17.3	9.8	6.0	6.7	10.4
August	6.2	3.2	0.6	1.7	0.5	17.6	9.3	6.4	7.2	10.9
September	6.2	3.5	0.6	1.7	0.5	18.7	10.3	6.5	7.2	11.2
October	6.6	3.8	0.6	1.7	0.5	19.8	10.6	6.9	7.6	12.0
November	6.8	4.0	0.6	1.7	0.5	18.9	10.0	7.1	7.9	12.6
December	7.2	4.2	0.7	1.8	0.5	19.7	10.6	7.6	8.3	13.5

[1]Changes in survey design, population estimates, and methodology in 1994 and several other years affect year-to-year comparisons. See notes and definitions for more information.
. . . = Not available.

Table 10-6. Insured Unemployment

(Averages of weekly data; thousands of persons, except as noted.)

Year and month	State programs, seasonally adjusted			Federal programs, not seasonally adjusted					
				Initial claims		Persons claiming benefits			
	Initial claims	Insured unemployment	Insured unemployment rate (percent) I	Federal employees	Newly discharged veterans	Federal employees	Newly discharged veterans	Railroad retirement	Extended benefits
1967	227	1 206	...	...	...	...	...	...	...
1968	197	1 088	...	...	...	...	...	...	...
1969	196	1 092	...	...	...	...	...	...	...
1970	297	1 848	...	...	...	...	...	...	...
1971	296	2 152	4.1	...	...	...	...	...	...
1972	263	1 844	3.5	...	...	...	...	...	...
1973	244	1 629	2.7	...	...	...	...	...	...
1974	352	2 278	3.5	...	...	...	...	...	...
1975	474	3 965	6.0	...	...	...	...	...	...
1976	383	2 978	4.5	...	...	...	...	...	...
1977	374	2 644	3.9	...	...	...	...	...	...
1978	341	2 337	3.3	...	...	...	...	...	...
1979	383	2 428	3.0	...	...	...	...	...	...
1980	488	3 365	3.9	...	...	...	...	...	...
1981	451	3 032	3.5	...	...	...	...	...	...
1982	586	4 094	4.7	...	...	...	...	...	...
1983	441	3 337	3.9	...	...	...	...	...	...
1984	374	2 452	2.8	...	...	...	...	...	...
1985	392	2 584	2.9	...	...	...	...	...	...
1986	378	2 632	2.8	2.13	2.52	20.24	17.11	...	...
1987	325	2 273	2.4	2.19	2.57	21.29	17.71	...	9.51
1988	309	2 075	2.1	2.32	2.74	22.91	18.13	13.28	1.17
1989	330	2 174	2.1	2.14	2.31	22.17	15.09	10.37	0.61
1990	385	2 539	2.4	2.45	2.54	23.89	18.43	10.56	2.36
1991	447	3 338	3.2	2.55	2.93	30.50	22.12	10.73	32.16
1992	409	3 208	3.1	2.75	4.95	32.10	60.25	8.77	4.61
1993	344	2 768	2.6	2.55	3.94	32.06	54.90	7.40	7.59
1994	340	2 667	2.5	2.54	3.02	32.21	37.65	6.21	31.09
1995	359	2 590	2.4	4.57	2.51	31.68	29.78	5.48	14.27
1996	352	2 552	2.3	7.33	2.13	29.84	24.30	5.40	5.53
1997	322	2 300	2.0	2.01	1.75	23.58	19.66	4.00	5.35
1998	317	2 213	1.9	1.64	1.41	19.60	15.68	3.19	6.43
1999	298	2 186	1.8	1.48	1.18	16.85	14.25	3.24	3.05
2000	299	2 112	1.7	1.73	1.05	18.60	12.54	3.92	0.58
2001	406	3 016	2.4	1.47	1.15	18.57	13.98	...	0.57
2002	404	3 570	2.8	1.46	1.22	17.54	16.07	...	10.79
2003	402	3 532	2.8	1.56	1.46	18.22	19.68	...	22.30
2004	342	2 930	2.3	1.50	1.89	18.14	26.90	...	4.22
2005	331	2 662	2.1	1.46	2.03	16.92	27.58	...	1.69
2006	313	2 460	1.9	1.34	1.96	15.51	26.37	...	1.38
2007	321	2 552	1.9	1.30	1.68	14.90	22.80	...	0.00
2008	420	3 357	2.5	1.26	1.63	14.53	22.16	...	5.71
2006									
January	294	2 515	2.0	1.77	2.50	21.24	29.32	...	4.17
February	291	2 460	1.9	1.03	1.98	18.82	29.41	...	4.56
March	303	2 437	1.9	0.92	1.83	16.55	28.51	...	3.41
April	305	2 416	1.9	0.94	1.67	13.80	26.65	...	0.58
May	335	2 424	1.9	1.01	2.00	11.71	25.91	...	3.50
June	308	2 450	1.9	1.31	1.89	11.69	25.43	...	0.43
July	319	2 478	1.9	1.69	2.16	13.69	25.41	...	0.06
August	318	2 494	1.9	1.16	2.11	15.12	25.87	...	0.03
September	317	2 474	1.9	1.08	1.89	14.39	25.05	...	0.01
October	317	2 463	1.9	1.47	1.93	15.02	25.09	...	0.02
November	324	2 470	1.9	1.72	1.75	15.56	24.76	...	0.01
December	321	2 443	1.9	1.82	1.88	18.72	25.74	...	0.00
2007									
January	316	2 462	1.9	1.89	1.91	19.71	25.77	...	0.00
February	320	2 499	2.3	1.07	1.69	17.87	24.52	...	0.01
March	310	2 489	2.2	0.93	1.70	15.75	23.47	...	0.00
April	323	2 515	2.0	0.96	1.55	13.19	22.50	...	0.00
May	308	2 501	1.7	0.87	1.56	11.06	21.45	...	0.00
June	320	2 538	1.7	1.30	1.61	11.49	20.97	...	0.00
July	314	2 579	2.0	1.49	1.68	14.03	21.38	...	0.00
August	325	2 591	1.8	1.14	1.83	14.20	21.45	...	0.00
September	316	2 581	1.6	1.13	1.80	14.05	22.12	...	0.01
October	330	2 589	1.7	1.55	1.86	15.28	23.06	...	0.00
November	333	2 614	1.8	1.53	1.53	15.36	23.44	...	0.00
December	341	2 658	2.1	1.71	1.51	17.40	23.86	...	0.00
2008									
January	334	2 700	2.0	1.65	1.56	18.89	24.23	...	0.00
February	344	2 726	2.1	0.98	2.22	16.92	23.08	...	0.00
March	363	2 859	2.1	0.83	1.45	14.91	22.20	...	0.00
April	365	2 985	2.3	0.93	1.42	12.50	21.19	...	0.00
May	374	3 091	2.3	0.96	1.34	10.95	19.93	...	0.00
June	394	3 154	2.4	1.30	1.56	11.41	19.28	...	1.16
July	402	3 247	2.5	1.39	1.58	13.32	20.60	...	1.59
August	442	3 450	2.6	1.09	1.70	13.74	21.40	...	1.36
September	470	3 607	2.7	1.05	1.71	13.46	22.24	...	1.50
October	478	3 786	2.8	1.51	1.75	14.12	22.93	...	10.10
November	513	4 086	3.1	1.70	1.61	15.70	23.99	...	21.31
December	544	4 422	3.3	1.82	1.81	19.12	25.16	...	1.96

I Insured unemployed as a percent of employment covered by state programs.
. . . = Not available.

Section 10b: Payroll Employment, Hours, and Earnings

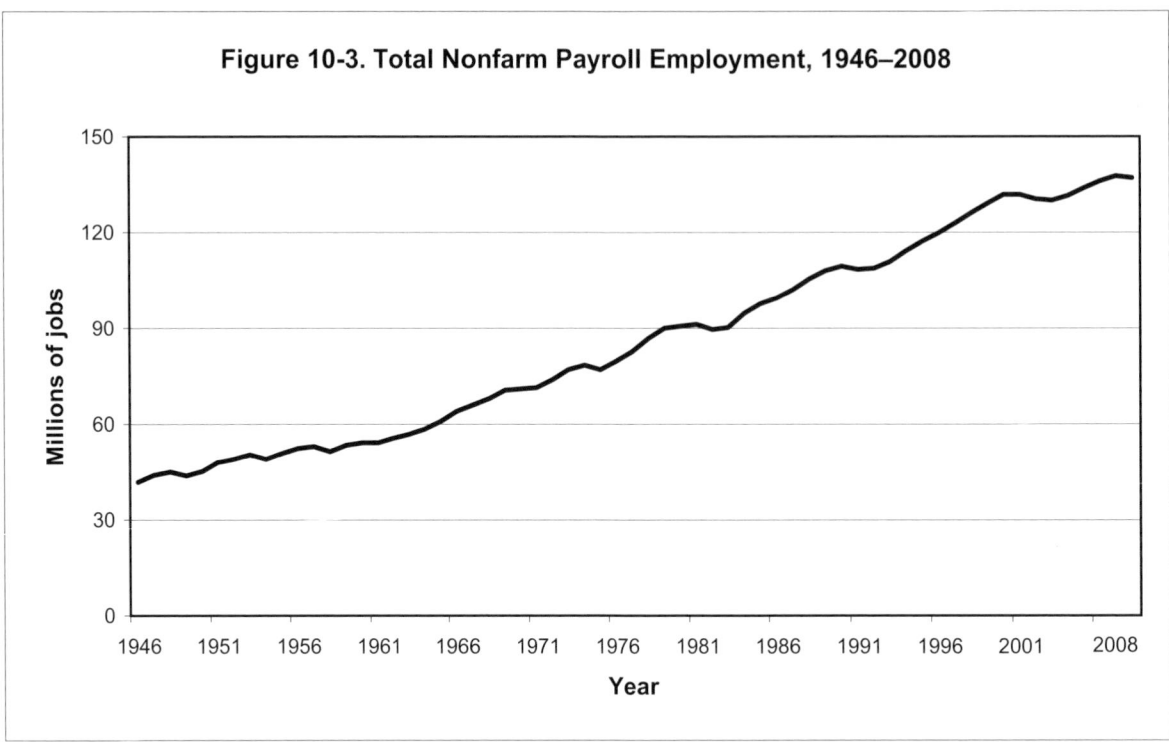

Figure 10-3. Total Nonfarm Payroll Employment, 1946–2008

- The 2001–2007 economic expansion ended in December 2007, according to the National Bureau of Economic Research. Payroll employment peaked in the same month, declined 2.2 percent from December 2007 to December 2008 (Table 10-7), and continued to plunge in the early months of 2009.

- Based on annual average data, payroll employment grew by 5.8 million jobs between the 2000 and 2007 business cycle high points, an average growth rate of 0.6 percent per year during the latest completed cycle. The previous business cycle lasted 10 years between high points, from 1990 to 2000. During that period, 22.3 million jobs were added to U.S. nonfarm payrolls, for an annual average growth rate of 1.9 percent per year. (Table 10-7)

- The diffusion index shows the percentage of industries in which employment is higher than six months earlier. Diffusion indexes measure the extent to which expansion and contraction spread throughout the economy; indexes below 50 percent indicate recession. By December 2008, this index had dropped to 24.4 percent—lower than the lowest points reached in any of the previous four recessions (1980, 1981–1982, 1990–1991, and 2001), and thus indicating the most widespread and pervasive decline in 30 years or more. (Table 10-7)

Table 10-7. Nonfarm Payroll Employment by NAICS Supersector

(Thousands; seasonally adjusted, except as noted.)

Year and month	Total	Private							Service-providing				
		Total	Goods-producing						Total	Private			
			Total	Mining and logging	Construc- tion	Manufacturing				Total	Trade, transportation, and utilities		
						Total	Durable	Nondurable			Total	Wholesale trade	Retail trade
1965	60 874	50 683	20 595	694	3 284	16 617	9 973	6 644	40 279	30 089	12 139	2 967	6 262
1966	64 020	53 110	21 740	690	3 371	17 680	10 803	6 878	42 280	31 370	12 611	3 080	6 530
1967	65 931	54 406	21 882	679	3 305	17 897	10 952	6 945	44 049	32 524	12 950	3 158	6 711
1968	68 023	56 050	22 292	671	3 410	18 211	11 137	7 074	45 731	33 759	13 334	3 236	6 977
1969	70 512	58 181	22 893	683	3 637	18 573	11 396	7 177	47 619	35 288	13 853	3 344	7 295
1970	71 006	58 318	22 179	677	3 654	17 848	10 762	7 086	48 827	36 139	14 144	3 418	7 463
1971	71 335	58 323	21 602	658	3 770	17 174	10 229	6 944	49 734	36 721	14 318	3 424	7 657
1972	73 798	60 333	22 299	672	3 957	17 669	10 630	7 039	51 499	38 034	14 788	3 547	8 038
1973	76 912	63 050	23 450	693	4 167	18 589	11 414	7 176	53 462	39 600	15 349	3 688	8 371
1974	78 389	64 086	23 364	755	4 095	18 514	11 432	7 082	55 025	40 721	15 693	3 823	8 536
1975	77 069	62 250	21 318	802	3 608	16 909	10 266	6 643	55 751	40 932	15 606	3 810	8 600
1976	79 502	64 501	22 025	832	3 662	17 531	10 640	6 891	57 477	42 476	16 128	3 920	8 966
1977	82 593	67 334	22 972	865	3 940	18 167	11 132	7 035	59 620	44 362	16 765	4 055	9 359
1978	86 826	71 014	24 156	902	4 322	18 932	11 770	7 162	62 670	46 858	17 658	4 280	9 879
1979	89 932	73 864	24 997	1 008	4 562	19 426	12 220	7 206	64 935	48 868	18 303	4 485	10 180
1980	90 528	74 154	24 263	1 077	4 454	18 733	11 679	7 054	66 265	49 891	18 413	4 557	10 244
1981	91 289	75 109	24 118	1 180	4 304	18 634	11 611	7 023	67 172	50 991	18 604	4 634	10 364
1982	89 677	73 695	22 550	1 163	4 024	17 363	10 610	6 753	67 127	51 145	18 457	4 575	10 372
1983	90 280	74 269	22 110	997	4 065	17 048	10 326	6 722	68 171	52 160	18 668	4 559	10 635
1984	94 530	78 371	23 435	1 014	4 501	17 920	11 050	6 870	71 095	54 936	19 653	4 788	11 223
1985	97 511	80 978	23 585	974	4 793	17 819	11 034	6 784	73 926	57 393	20 379	4 915	11 733
1986	99 474	82 636	23 318	829	4 937	17 552	10 795	6 757	76 156	59 318	20 795	4 935	12 078
1987	102 088	84 932	23 470	771	5 090	17 609	10 767	6 842	78 618	61 462	21 302	5 003	12 419
1988	105 345	87 806	23 909	770	5 233	17 906	10 969	6 938	81 436	63 897	21 974	5 153	12 808
1989	108 014	90 087	24 045	750	5 309	17 985	11 004	6 981	83 969	66 042	22 510	5 284	13 108
1990	109 487	91 072	23 723	765	5 263	17 695	10 737	6 958	85 764	67 349	22 666	5 268	13 182
1991	108 375	89 829	22 588	739	4 780	17 068	10 220	6 848	85 787	67 241	22 281	5 185	12 896
1992	108 726	89 940	22 095	689	4 608	16 799	9 946	6 853	86 631	67 845	22 125	5 110	12 828
1993	110 844	91 855	22 219	666	4 779	16 774	9 901	6 872	88 625	69 636	22 378	5 093	13 021
1994	114 291	95 016	22 774	659	5 095	17 020	10 132	6 889	91 517	72 242	23 128	5 247	13 491
1995	117 298	97 865	23 156	641	5 274	17 241	10 373	6 868	94 142	74 710	23 834	5 433	13 897
1996	119 708	100 169	23 409	637	5 536	17 237	10 486	6 751	96 299	76 760	24 239	5 522	14 143
1997	122 776	103 113	23 886	654	5 813	17 419	10 705	6 714	98 890	79 227	24 700	5 664	14 389
1998	125 930	106 021	24 354	645	6 149	17 560	10 911	6 649	101 576	81 667	25 186	5 795	14 609
1999	128 993	108 686	24 465	598	6 545	17 322	10 831	6 491	104 528	84 221	25 771	5 893	14 970
2000	131 785	110 995	24 649	599	6 787	17 263	10 877	6 386	107 136	86 346	26 225	5 933	15 280
2001	131 826	110 708	23 873	606	6 826	16 441	10 336	6 105	107 952	86 834	25 983	5 773	15 239
2002	130 341	108 828	22 557	583	6 716	15 259	9 485	5 774	107 784	86 271	25 497	5 652	15 025
2003	129 999	108 416	21 816	572	6 735	14 510	8 964	5 546	108 183	86 600	25 287	5 608	14 917
2004	131 435	109 814	21 882	591	6 976	14 315	8 925	5 390	109 553	87 932	25 533	5 663	15 058
2005	133 703	111 899	22 190	628	7 336	14 226	8 956	5 271	111 513	89 709	25 959	5 764	15 280
2006	136 086	114 113	22 531	684	7 691	14 155	8 981	5 174	113 556	91 582	26 276	5 905	15 353
2007	137 598	115 380	22 233	724	7 630	13 879	8 808	5 071	115 366	93 147	26 630	6 015	15 520
2008	137 066	114 566	21 419	774	7 215	13 431	8 476	4 955	115 646	93 146	26 385	5 964	15 356
2007													
January	137 180	115 068	22 465	707	7 737	14 021	8 901	5 120	114 715	92 603	26 500	5 967	15 450
February	137 216	115 091	22 347	713	7 636	13 998	8 890	5 108	114 869	92 744	26 539	5 983	15 476
March	137 400	115 250	22 392	716	7 710	13 966	8 871	5 095	115 008	92 858	26 594	5 986	15 526
April	137 435	115 260	22 333	720	7 680	13 933	8 855	5 078	115 102	92 927	26 598	6 002	15 514
May	137 591	115 388	22 307	720	7 670	13 917	8 837	5 080	115 284	93 081	26 628	6 009	15 535
June	137 645	115 400	22 289	723	7 677	13 889	8 813	5 076	115 356	93 111	26 620	6 022	15 512
July	137 580	115 415	22 251	727	7 647	13 877	8 806	5 071	115 329	93 164	26 630	6 028	15 514
August	137 552	115 339	22 151	726	7 599	13 826	8 775	5 051	115 401	93 188	26 629	6 030	15 511
September	137 652	115 389	22 099	726	7 577	13 796	8 753	5 043	115 553	93 290	26 649	6 029	15 509
October	137 817	115 521	22 069	728	7 567	13 774	8 733	5 041	115 748	93 452	26 664	6 040	15 512
November	138 032	115 707	22 072	737	7 555	13 780	8 740	5 040	115 960	93 635	26 749	6 048	15 590
December	138 152	115 783	22 043	743	7 523	13 777	8 728	5 049	116 109	93 740	26 725	6 045	15 568
2008													
January	138 080	115 689	21 981	748	7 489	13 744	8 710	5 034	116 099	93 708	26 717	6 034	15 572
February	137 936	115 515	21 887	750	7 445	13 692	8 673	5 019	116 049	93 628	26 655	6 021	15 526
March	137 814	115 373	21 800	756	7 401	13 643	8 637	5 006	116 014	93 573	26 629	6 013	15 506
April	137 654	115 203	21 679	756	7 337	13 586	8 587	4 999	115 975	93 524	26 562	5 996	15 458
May	137 517	115 029	21 612	763	7 293	13 556	8 567	4 989	115 905	93 417	26 503	5 989	15 420
June	137 356	114 834	21 507	770	7 232	13 505	8 533	4 972	115 849	93 327	26 467	5 983	15 404
July	137 228	114 691	21 432	777	7 201	13 454	8 502	4 952	115 796	93 259	26 425	5 967	15 380
August	137 053	114 497	21 351	787	7 177	13 387	8 439	4 948	115 702	93 146	26 354	5 954	15 335
September	136 732	114 197	21 247	794	7 131	13 322	8 392	4 930	115 485	92 950	26 257	5 947	15 278
October	136 352	113 813	21 063	794	7 066	13 203	8 300	4 903	115 289	92 750	26 157	5 920	15 217
November	135 755	113 212	20 814	793	6 939	13 082	8 216	4 866	114 941	92 398	26 005	5 890	15 126
December	135 074	112 542	20 532	789	6 841	12 902	8 085	4 817	114 542	92 010	25 843	5 851	15 038

Table 10-7. Nonfarm Payroll Employment by NAICS Supersector—*Continued*

(Thousands; seasonally adjusted, except as noted.)

Year and month	Information	Financial activities	Professional and business services	Education and health services	Leisure and hospitality	Other services	Government Total	Federal Total	Federal Department of Defense [1]	State Total	State Education	Local Total	Local Education	Diffusion index, 6-month span, private nonfarm [2]
1965	1 824	2 878	4 306	3 587	3 951	1 404	10 191	2 495	679	1 996	679	5 700	3 031	. . .
1966	1 908	2 961	4 517	3 770	4 127	1 475	10 910	2 690	741	2 141	775	6 080	3 297	. . .
1967	1 955	3 087	4 720	3 986	4 269	1 558	11 525	2 852	802	2 302	873	6 371	3 490	. . .
1968	1 991	3 234	4 918	4 191	4 453	1 638	11 972	2 871	801	2 442	958	6 660	3 649	. . .
1969	2 048	3 404	5 156	4 428	4 670	1 731	12 330	2 893	815	2 533	1 042	6 904	3 785	. . .
1970	2 041	3 532	5 267	4 577	4 789	1 789	12 687	2 865	756	2 664	1 104	7 158	3 912	. . .
1971	2 009	3 651	5 328	4 675	4 914	1 827	13 012	2 828	731	2 747	1 149	7 437	4 091	. . .
1972	2 056	3 784	5 523	4 863	5 121	1 900	13 465	2 815	720	2 859	1 188	7 790	4 262	. . .
1973	2 135	3 920	5 774	5 092	5 341	1 990	13 862	2 794	696	2 923	1 205	8 146	4 433	. . .
1974	2 160	4 023	5 974	5 322	5 471	2 078	14 303	2 858	698	3 039	1 267	8 407	4 584	. . .
1975	2 061	4 047	6 034	5 497	5 544	2 144	14 820	2 882	704	3 179	1 323	8 758	4 722	. . .
1976	2 111	4 155	6 287	5 756	5 794	2 244	15 001	2 863	693	3 273	1 371	8 865	4 786	. . .
1977	2 185	4 348	6 587	6 052	6 065	2 359	15 258	2 859	676	3 377	1 385	9 023	4 859	77.5
1978	2 287	4 599	6 972	6 427	6 411	2 505	15 812	2 893	661	3 474	1 367	9 446	4 958	75.6
1979	2 375	4 843	7 312	6 767	6 631	2 637	16 068	2 894	649	3 541	1 378	9 633	4 989	57.7
1980	2 361	5 025	7 544	7 072	6 721	2 755	16 375	3 000	645	3 610	1 398	9 765	5 090	61.2
1981	2 382	5 163	7 782	7 357	6 840	2 865	16 180	2 922	655	3 640	1 420	9 619	5 095	39.0
1982	2 317	5 209	7 848	7 515	6 874	2 924	15 982	2 884	690	3 640	1 433	9 458	5 049	34.8
1983	2 253	5 334	8 039	7 766	7 078	3 021	16 011	2 915	699	3 662	1 450	9 434	5 020	78.2
1984	2 398	5 553	8 464	8 193	7 489	3 186	16 159	2 943	716	3 734	1 488	9 482	5 076	64.9
1985	2 437	5 815	8 871	8 657	7 869	3 366	16 533	3 014	738	3 832	1 540	9 687	5 221	59.5
1986	2 445	6 128	9 211	9 061	8 156	3 523	16 838	3 044	736	3 893	1 561	9 901	5 358	62.4
1987	2 507	6 385	9 608	9 515	8 446	3 699	17 156	3 089	736	3 967	1 586	10 100	5 469	73.5
1988	2 585	6 500	10 090	10 063	8 778	3 907	17 540	3 124	719	4 076	1 621	10 339	5 590	66.3
1989	2 622	6 562	10 555	10 616	9 062	4 116	17 927	3 136	735	4 182	1 668	10 609	5 740	54.6
1990	2 688	6 614	10 848	10 984	9 288	4 261	18 415	3 196	722	4 305	1 730	10 914	5 902	36.7
1991	2 677	6 558	10 714	11 506	9 256	4 249	18 545	3 110	702	4 355	1 768	11 081	5 994	45.0
1992	2 641	6 540	10 970	11 891	9 437	4 240	18 787	3 111	702	4 408	1 799	11 267	6 076	62.9
1993	2 668	6 709	11 495	12 303	9 732	4 350	18 989	3 063	670	4 488	1 834	11 438	6 206	72.1
1994	2 738	6 867	12 174	12 807	10 100	4 428	19 275	3 018	657	4 576	1 882	11 682	6 329	80.8
1995	2 843	6 827	12 844	13 289	10 501	4 572	19 432	2 949	627	4 635	1 919	11 849	6 453	68.5
1996	2 940	6 969	13 462	13 683	10 777	4 690	19 539	2 877	597	4 606	1 911	12 056	6 592	77.7
1997	3 084	7 178	14 335	14 087	11 018	4 825	19 664	2 806	588	4 582	1 904	12 276	6 759	80.1
1998	3 218	7 462	15 147	14 446	11 232	4 976	19 909	2 772	550	4 612	1 922	12 525	6 921	69.2
1999	3 419	7 648	15 957	14 798	11 543	5 087	20 307	2 769	525	4 709	1 983	12 829	7 120	69.0
2000	3 630	7 687	16 666	15 109	11 862	5 168	20 790	2 865	510	4 786	2 031	13 139	7 294	58.1
2001	3 629	7 808	16 476	15 645	12 036	5 258	21 118	2 764	504	4 905	2 113	13 449	7 479	32.7
2002	3 395	7 847	15 976	16 199	11 986	5 372	21 513	2 766	499	5 029	2 243	13 718	7 654	36.3
2003	3 188	7 977	15 987	16 588	12 173	5 401	21 583	2 761	486	5 002	2 255	13 820	7 709	39.7
2004	3 118	8 031	16 394	16 953	12 493	5 409	21 621	2 730	473	4 982	2 238	13 909	7 765	60.0
2005	3 061	8 153	16 954	17 372	12 816	5 395	21 804	2 732	488	5 032	2 260	14 041	7 856	61.6
2006	3 038	8 328	17 566	17 826	13 110	5 438	21 974	2 732	493	5 075	2 293	14 167	7 913	57.9
2007	3 032	8 301	17 942	18 322	13 427	5 494	22 218	2 734	491	5 122	2 318	14 362	7 987	56.6
2008	2 997	8 146	17 778	18 855	13 459	5 528	22 500	2 764	496	5 178	2 359	14 557	8 076	30.6
2007														
January	3 028	8 354	17 854	18 077	13 322	5 468	22 112	2 730	491	5 109	2 314	14 273	7 956	60.3
February	3 035	8 351	17 887	18 115	13 341	5 476	22 125	2 731	490	5 117	2 317	14 277	7 953	57.2
March	3 031	8 337	17 896	18 163	13 354	5 483	22 150	2 731	491	5 118	2 318	14 301	7 961	60.5
April	3 035	8 312	17 910	18 212	13 371	5 489	22 175	2 732	489	5 119	2 320	14 324	7 970	58.3
May	3 039	8 319	17 941	18 250	13 408	5 496	22 203	2 730	489	5 119	2 316	14 354	7 989	55.5
June	3 037	8 309	17 930	18 294	13 421	5 500	22 245	2 725	493	5 129	2 324	14 391	8 008	56.5
July	3 034	8 317	17 935	18 330	13 419	5 499	22 165	2 734	493	5 114	2 306	14 317	7 937	52.8
August	3 028	8 293	17 935	18 388	13 418	5 497	22 213	2 734	492	5 106	2 299	14 373	7 986	52.4
September	3 033	8 272	17 938	18 438	13 468	5 492	22 263	2 733	490	5 127	2 318	14 403	8 004	56.6
October	3 030	8 263	18 005	18 488	13 507	5 495	22 296	2 734	490	5 134	2 324	14 428	8 019	54.4
November	3 029	8 248	18 039	18 519	13 544	5 507	22 325	2 738	492	5 138	2 324	14 449	8 030	56.8
December	3 025	8 243	18 109	18 570	13 551	5 517	22 369	2 746	492	5 142	2 328	14 481	8 048	59.0
2008														
January	3 022	8 229	18 069	18 613	13 534	5 524	22 391	2 737	488	5 157	2 340	14 497	8 050	56.6
February	3 025	8 211	18 018	18 657	13 529	5 533	22 421	2 746	487	5 153	2 334	14 522	8 070	53.0
March	3 023	8 204	17 954	18 698	13 528	5 537	22 441	2 751	487	5 152	2 335	14 538	8 076	50.7
April	3 017	8 190	17 950	18 752	13 512	5 541	22 451	2 758	489	5 159	2 340	14 534	8 066	47.4
May	3 013	8 179	17 887	18 798	13 495	5 542	22 488	2 763	491	5 167	2 348	14 558	8 085	40.2
June	3 006	8 162	17 824	18 843	13 490	5 535	22 522	2 765	497	5 175	2 355	14 582	8 101	33.4
July	2 995	8 154	17 788	18 888	13 473	5 536	22 537	2 776	501	5 184	2 365	14 577	8 088	31.0
August	2 990	8 141	17 727	18 950	13 454	5 530	22 556	2 768	502	5 204	2 380	14 584	8 085	33.4
September	2 986	8 115	17 675	18 957	13 428	5 532	22 535	2 771	499	5 192	2 373	14 572	8 075	30.6
October	2 982	8 088	17 612	18 981	13 395	5 535	22 539	2 775	504	5 194	2 373	14 570	8 072	29.0
November	2 965	8 043	17 488	19 044	13 344	5 509	22 543	2 783	505	5 197	2 380	14 563	8 068	26.0
December	2 940	8 010	17 356	19 080	13 304	5 477	22 532	2 778	506	5 196	2 381	14 558	8 061	24.4

[1]Not seasonally adjusted.
[2]See notes and definitions for explanation. September value used to represent year.
. . . = Not available.

Table 10-8. Production or Nonsupervisory Workers on Private Nonfarm Payrolls by NAICS Supersector

(Thousands, seasonally adjusted.)

| Year and month | Total private | Mining and logging | Construc-tion | Manu-facturing | Trade, transportation, and utilities | | | Information | Financial activities | Profes-sional and business services | Education and health services | Leisure and hospitality | Other services |
					Total	Wholesale trade	Retail trade						
1965	42 302	523	2 906	12 905	10 702	. . .	. . .	1 268	2 434	3 515	3 443	3 443	1 161
1966	44 292	517	2 977	13 703	11 095	. . .	. . .	1 334	2 492	3 715	3 623	3 607	1 230
1967	45 185	501	2 903	13 714	11 369	. . .	. . .	1 365	2 585	3 890	3 818	3 734	1 306
1968	46 519	491	2 986	13 908	11 688	. . .	. . .	1 394	2 700	4 067	4 008	3 898	1 379
1969	48 246	501	3 177	14 147	12 152	. . .	. . .	1 438	2 841	4 252	4 196	4 089	1 452
1970	48 180	496	3 158	13 490	12 388	. . .	. . .	1 422	2 922	4 321	4 305	4 185	1 494
1971	48 151	474	3 238	13 034	12 502	. . .	. . .	1 392	2 978	4 354	4 372	4 286	1 521
1972	49 971	494	3 425	13 497	12 954	2 920	7 257	1 437	3 066	4 518	4 531	4 467	1 583
1973	52 235	502	3 576	14 227	13 437	3 041	7 551	1 504	3 164	4 748	4 747	4 664	1 666
1974	52 846	550	3 469	14 040	13 700	3 148	7 673	1 516	3 217	4 907	4 941	4 766	1 740
1975	51 010	581	2 990	12 576	13 578	3 121	7 714	1 416	3 227	4 939	5 088	4 821	1 795
1976	52 916	606	2 999	13 127	14 038	3 212	8 048	1 459	3 300	5 153	5 309	5 046	1 880
1977	55 207	636	3 209	13 591	14 579	3 323	8 396	1 514	3 452	5 404	5 561	5 284	1 978
1978	58 188	658	3 544	14 150	15 329	3 509	8 861	1 586	3 645	5 717	5 874	5 588	2 099
1979	60 403	737	3 760	14 458	15 843	3 667	9 113	1 650	3 825	5 993	6 157	5 772	2 209
1980	60 372	785	3 623	13 667	15 907	3 708	9 158	1 626	3 957	6 197	6 442	5 850	2 318
1981	60 960	861	3 469	13 492	16 004	3 753	9 238	1 633	4 052	6 396	6 694	5 944	2 414
1982	59 465	834	3 208	12 315	15 821	3 662	9 254	1 564	4 055	6 421	6 812	5 976	2 458
1983	60 005	698	3 240	12 121	15 999	3 639	9 494	1 502	4 128	6 581	7 032	6 161	2 542
1984	63 316	714	3 614	12 821	16 797	3 821	9 964	1 631	4 289	6 918	7 368	6 491	2 672
1985	65 436	686	3 868	12 648	17 427	3 935	10 399	1 660	4 476	7 258	7 770	6 817	2 827
1986	66 802	577	3 984	12 449	17 769	3 941	10 704	1 663	4 698	7 532	8 107	7 066	2 957
1987	68 700	541	4 088	12 537	18 196	3 989	10 986	1 717	4 861	7 859	8 488	7 310	3 104
1988	71 029	545	4 199	12 765	18 771	4 132	11 306	1 775	4 894	8 256	8 956	7 587	3 280
1989	72 927	526	4 257	12 805	19 230	4 235	11 565	1 807	4 931	8 648	9 432	7 833	3 459
1990	73 684	538	4 115	12 669	19 032	4 198	11 308	1 866	4 973	8 889	9 748	8 299	3 555
1991	72 520	515	3 674	12 164	18 640	4 122	11 008	1 871	4 911	8 748	10 212	8 247	3 539
1992	72 786	478	3 546	12 200	18 506	4 071	10 931	1 871	4 908	8 971	10 555	8 406	3 526
1993	74 591	462	3 704	12 070	18 752	4 072	11 104	1 896	5 057	9 451	10 908	8 667	3 623
1994	77 382	461	3 973	12 361	19 392	4 196	11 502	1 928	5 183	10 078	11 338	8 979	3 689
1995	79 845	458	4 113	12 567	19 984	4 361	11 841	2 007	5 165	10 645	11 765	9 330	3 812
1996	81 773	461	4 325	12 532	20 325	4 423	12 057	2 096	5 279	11 161	12 123	9 565	3 907
1997	84 158	479	4 546	12 673	20 698	4 523	12 274	2 181	5 415	11 896	12 478	9 780	4 013
1998	86 316	473	4 807	12 729	21 059	4 605	12 440	2 217	5 605	12 566	12 791	9 947	4 124
1999	88 430	438	5 105	12 524	21 576	4 673	12 772	2 351	5 728	13 184	13 089	10 216	4 219
2000	90 336	446	5 295	12 428	21 965	4 686	13 040	2 502	5 737	13 790	13 362	10 516	4 296
2001	89 983	457	5 332	11 677	21 709	4 555	12 952	2 531	5 810	13 588	13 846	10 662	4 373
2002	88 393	436	5 196	10 768	21 337	4 474	12 774	2 398	5 872	13 049	14 311	10 576	4 449
2003	87 658	420	5 123	10 189	21 078	4 396	12 655	2 347	5 967	12 911	14 532	10 666	4 426
2004	88 937	440	5 309	10 072	21 319	4 444	12 788	2 371	5 989	13 287	14 771	10 955	4 425
2005	91 135	473	5 611	10 060	21 830	4 584	13 030	2 386	6 090	13 854	15 129	11 263	4 438
2006	93 451	519	5 903	10 137	22 166	4 724	13 110	2 399	6 281	14 446	15 539	11 568	4 494
2007	94 903	547	5 883	9 975	22 546	4 851	13 317	2 403	6 326	14 784	15 999	11 861	4 578
2008	94 509	580	5 562	9 649	22 415	4 839	13 197	2 398	6 271	14 622	16 503	11 893	4 617
2007													
January	94 413	533	5 922	10 047	22 382	4 788	13 221	2 391	6 335	14 716	15 769	11 769	4 549
February	94 417	542	5 815	10 036	22 432	4 802	13 260	2 394	6 339	14 730	15 791	11 784	4 554
March	94 609	543	5 912	10 007	22 487	4 805	13 322	2 391	6 339	14 742	15 847	11 782	4 559
April	94 689	545	5 900	9 996	22 491	4 820	13 312	2 400	6 323	14 762	15 897	11 804	4 571
May	94 863	547	5 903	9 999	22 533	4 833	13 339	2 410	6 330	14 781	15 935	11 847	4 578
June	94 940	548	5 943	9 982	22 527	4 848	13 311	2 407	6 332	14 765	15 990	11 861	4 585
July	95 011	551	5 928	9 980	22 552	4 869	13 316	2 405	6 342	14 774	16 024	11 867	4 588
August	94 962	546	5 884	9 942	22 551	4 876	13 312	2 404	6 327	14 780	16 071	11 870	4 587
September	95 050	547	5 867	9 936	22 589	4 881	13 318	2 406	6 322	14 786	16 112	11 902	4 583
October	95 183	546	5 867	9 918	22 609	4 895	13 317	2 408	6 316	14 841	16 152	11 937	4 589
November	95 329	555	5 845	9 933	22 680	4 900	13 373	2 410	6 307	14 863	16 180	11 963	4 593
December	95 473	560	5 816	9 947	22 704	4 903	13 384	2 414	6 310	14 930	16 226	11 963	4 603
2008													
January	95 432	564	5 788	9 930	22 696	4 895	13 381	2 418	6 307	14 905	16 274	11 942	4 608
February	95 299	565	5 750	9 886	22 654	4 889	13 344	2 418	6 302	14 849	16 317	11 939	4 619
March	95 208	569	5 727	9 853	22 640	4 889	13 334	2 416	6 304	14 777	16 360	11 938	4 624
April	95 091	567	5 668	9 795	22 582	4 872	13 293	2 411	6 301	14 794	16 404	11 944	4 625
May	94 931	569	5 633	9 770	22 540	4 866	13 269	2 409	6 290	14 727	16 448	11 920	4 625
June	94 765	572	5 580	9 723	22 495	4 858	13 248	2 401	6 284	14 680	16 491	11 920	4 619
July	94 636	578	5 546	9 672	22 457	4 844	13 224	2 395	6 276	14 647	16 536	11 908	4 621
August	94 470	590	5 538	9 608	22 392	4 833	13 190	2 389	6 273	14 569	16 593	11 897	4 621
September	94 217	597	5 489	9 543	22 310	4 819	13 138	2 390	6 261	14 523	16 601	11 879	4 624
October	93 825	592	5 430	9 425	22 202	4 800	13 064	2 392	6 249	14 433	16 623	11 851	4 628
November	93 286	595	5 323	9 322	22 051	4 770	12 982	2 373	6 213	14 318	16 687	11 803	4 601
December	92 759	591	5 246	9 174	21 933	4 739	12 915	2 358	6 184	14 212	16 719	11 764	4 578

. . . = Not available.

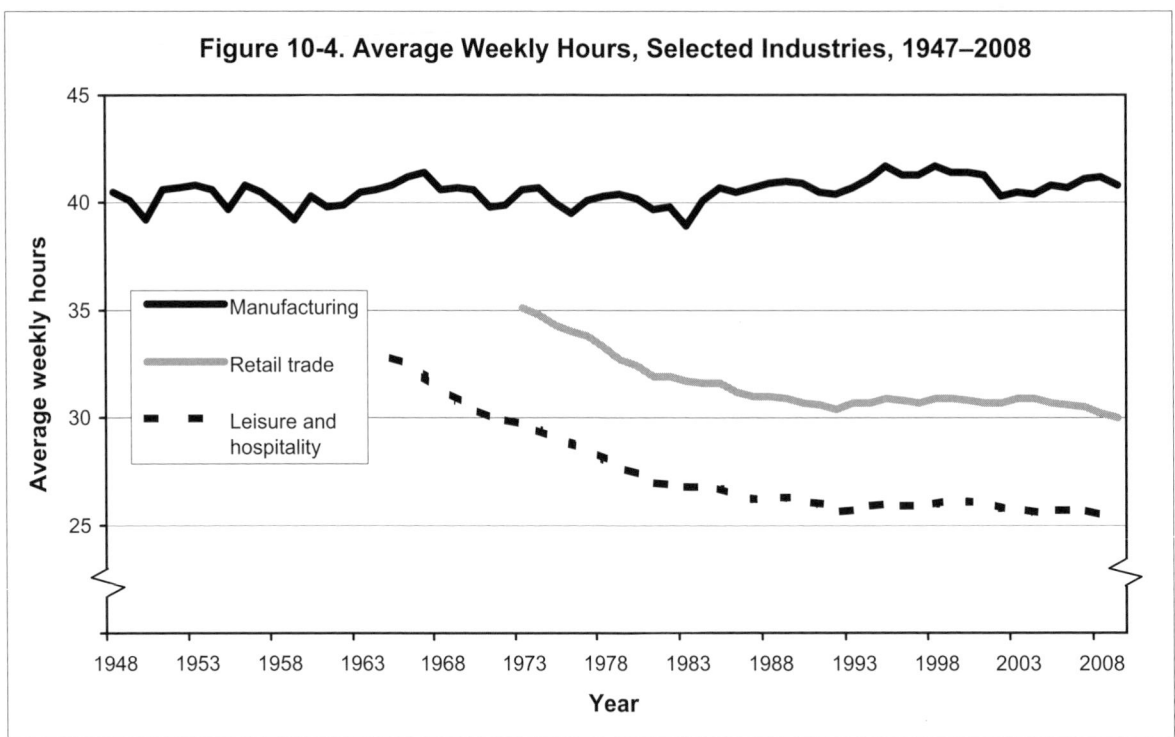

Figure 10-4. Average Weekly Hours, Selected Industries, 1947–2008

- The hours worked per week at the average private nonfarm production or nonsupervisory job have trended downward over the past four decades, falling from 38.5 hours in 1964 to 33.6 hours in 2008. It should be noted that these are hours per job, not hours per person. A worker with two half-time jobs enters this average as two workers with 20-hour workweeks, not as one worker with a 40-hour workweek. (Tables 10-9 and 20-4)

- The downtrend in the all-industry average reflects increases in the number of part-time jobs, as well as the increasing importance of retail trade, leisure and hospitality (restaurants, hotels, and motels), and other service-providing industries in which such jobs are often found. As shown by Figure 10-4 above, manufacturing—which accounts for a steadily declining share of employment—displays no long-term downtrend in the workweek; if anything, factory workers have worked longer hours on average since the early 1980s. There was also no downtrend for construction or for mining and logging. Workweeks declined in retail trade and leisure and hospitality up until about 1991, leveled off until 2006, and then declined again as the recession began to take hold. These industries already had shorter workweeks, and have recently accounted for an increasing share of total employment, which can continue to pull down the average even if the workweek is constant within the industry. (Tables 10-7, 10-9, and 20-4)

- The manufacturing workweek and manufacturing overtime hours are both considered leading indicators of the general state of the economy. In Table 10-9, the sharp decline in the workweek beginning in August 2008 and the drop in overtime beginning even earlier can be seen. These declines continued into early 2009.

Table 10-9. Average Weekly Hours of Production or Nonsupervisory Workers on Private Nonfarm Payrolls by NAICS Supersector

(Hours per week, seasonally adjusted.)

Year and month	Total private	Mining and logging	Construc-tion	Manufacturing Average weekly hours	Manufacturing Overtime hours	Trade, transportation, and utilities Total	Trade, transportation, and utilities Wholesale trade	Trade, transportation, and utilities Retail trade	Informa-tion	Financial activities	Profes-sional and business services	Education and health services	Leisure and hospitality	Other services
1965	38.6	43.7	37.9	41.2	3.6	39.6	. . .	. . .	38.3	37.1	37.3	35.2	32.5	36.1
1966	38.5	44.1	38.1	41.4	3.9	39.1	. . .	. . .	38.3	37.2	37.0	34.9	31.9	35.8
1967	37.9	43.9	38.1	40.6	3.3	38.5	. . .	. . .	37.6	36.9	36.6	34.5	31.3	35.4
1968	37.7	44.0	37.8	40.7	3.5	38.2	. . .	. . .	37.6	36.8	36.3	34.1	30.8	35.0
1969	37.5	44.3	38.4	40.6	3.6	37.9	. . .	. . .	37.6	36.9	36.3	34.1	30.4	35.0
1970	37.0	43.9	37.8	39.8	2.9	37.6	. . .	. . .	37.2	36.6	35.9	33.8	30.0	34.7
1971	36.8	43.7	37.6	39.9	2.9	37.4	. . .	. . .	37.0	36.4	35.5	33.3	29.9	34.2
1972	36.9	44.0	37.0	40.6	3.4	37.4	39.8	35.1	37.3	36.4	35.5	33.3	29.7	34.2
1973	36.9	43.8	37.2	40.7	3.8	37.2	39.6	34.8	37.3	36.4	35.5	33.3	29.4	34.1
1974	36.4	43.7	37.1	40.0	3.2	36.8	39.2	34.3	37.0	36.3	35.3	33.1	29.1	33.9
1975	36.0	43.7	36.9	39.5	2.6	36.4	39.1	34.0	36.6	36.2	35.1	33.0	28.8	33.8
1976	36.1	44.2	37.3	40.1	3.1	36.3	39.1	33.8	36.7	36.2	34.9	32.7	28.5	33.6
1977	35.9	44.7	37.0	40.3	3.4	36.0	39.2	33.3	36.8	36.2	34.7	32.5	28.1	33.4
1978	35.8	44.9	37.3	40.4	3.6	35.6	39.2	32.7	36.8	36.1	34.6	32.3	27.7	33.2
1979	35.6	44.7	37.5	40.2	3.3	35.4	39.2	32.4	36.6	35.9	34.4	32.2	27.4	33.0
1980	35.2	44.9	37.5	39.7	2.8	35.0	38.8	31.9	36.3	36.0	34.3	32.1	27.0	33.0
1981	35.2	45.1	37.4	39.8	2.8	34.9	38.9	31.9	36.3	36.0	34.3	32.1	26.9	33.0
1982	34.7	44.1	37.2	38.9	2.3	34.6	38.7	31.7	35.8	36.0	34.2	32.1	26.8	33.0
1983	34.9	43.9	37.6	40.1	2.9	34.6	38.8	31.6	36.2	35.9	34.4	32.1	26.8	33.0
1984	35.1	44.6	38.2	40.7	3.4	34.7	38.9	31.6	36.6	36.2	34.3	32.0	26.7	32.9
1985	34.9	44.6	38.2	40.5	3.3	34.4	38.8	31.2	36.5	36.1	34.2	31.9	26.4	32.8
1986	34.7	43.6	37.9	40.7	3.4	34.1	38.7	31.0	36.4	36.1	34.3	32.0	26.2	32.9
1987	34.7	43.5	38.2	40.9	3.7	34.1	38.5	31.0	36.5	36.0	34.3	32.0	26.3	32.8
1988	34.6	43.3	38.2	41.0	3.8	33.8	38.5	30.9	36.1	35.6	34.2	32.0	26.3	32.9
1989	34.5	44.1	38.3	40.9	3.8	33.8	38.4	30.7	36.1	35.6	34.2	32.0	26.1	32.9
1990	34.3	45.0	38.3	40.5	3.9	33.7	38.4	30.6	35.8	35.5	34.2	31.9	26.0	32.8
1991	34.1	45.3	38.1	40.4	3.8	33.7	38.4	30.4	35.6	35.5	34.0	31.9	25.6	32.7
1992	34.2	44.6	38.0	40.7	4.0	33.8	38.5	30.7	35.8	35.6	34.0	32.0	25.7	32.6
1993	34.3	44.9	38.4	41.1	4.4	34.1	38.5	30.7	36.0	35.5	34.0	32.0	25.9	32.6
1994	34.5	45.3	38.8	41.7	5.0	34.3	38.8	30.9	36.0	35.5	34.1	32.0	26.0	32.7
1995	34.3	45.3	38.8	41.3	4.7	34.1	38.6	30.8	36.0	35.5	34.0	32.0	25.9	32.6
1996	34.3	46.0	38.9	41.3	4.8	34.1	38.6	30.7	36.4	35.5	34.1	31.9	25.9	32.5
1997	34.5	46.2	38.9	41.7	5.1	34.3	38.8	30.9	36.3	35.7	34.3	32.2	26.0	32.7
1998	34.5	44.9	38.8	41.4	4.9	34.2	38.6	30.9	36.6	36.0	34.3	32.2	26.2	32.6
1999	34.3	44.2	39.0	41.4	4.9	33.9	38.6	30.8	36.7	35.8	34.4	32.1	26.1	32.5
2000	34.3	44.4	39.2	41.3	4.7	33.8	38.8	30.7	36.8	35.9	34.5	32.2	26.1	32.5
2001	34.0	44.6	38.7	40.3	4.0	33.5	38.4	30.7	36.9	35.8	34.2	32.3	25.8	32.3
2002	33.9	43.2	38.4	40.5	4.2	33.6	38.0	30.9	36.5	35.6	34.2	32.4	25.8	32.0
2003	33.7	43.6	38.4	40.4	4.2	33.6	37.9	30.9	36.2	35.5	34.1	32.3	25.6	31.4
2004	33.7	44.5	38.3	40.8	4.6	33.5	37.8	30.7	36.3	35.5	34.2	32.4	25.7	31.0
2005	33.8	45.6	38.6	40.7	4.6	33.4	37.7	30.6	36.5	35.9	34.2	32.6	25.7	30.9
2006	33.9	45.6	39.0	41.1	4.4	33.4	38.0	30.5	36.6	35.7	34.6	32.5	25.7	30.9
2007	33.9	45.9	39.0	41.2	4.2	33.3	38.2	30.2	36.5	35.9	34.8	32.6	25.5	30.9
2008	33.6	45.1	38.5	40.8	3.7	33.2	38.2	30.0	36.7	35.8	34.8	32.5	25.2	30.8
2007														
January	33.8	45.1	38.8	41.0	4.1	33.4	37.9	30.3	36.6	35.9	34.6	32.5	25.7	30.8
February	33.8	45.9	38.7	40.9	4.1	33.3	38.1	30.2	36.6	36.0	34.7	32.4	25.4	30.9
March	33.9	45.9	39.1	41.2	4.3	33.4	38.2	30.2	36.7	36.0	34.8	32.6	25.6	31.1
April	33.8	46.2	38.9	41.2	4.1	33.2	38.2	30.1	36.6	35.9	34.7	32.6	25.6	31.0
May	33.9	45.8	39.0	41.1	4.2	33.4	38.4	30.2	36.4	35.8	34.8	32.6	25.6	31.1
June	33.9	46.0	39.1	41.3	4.3	33.4	38.3	30.2	36.4	36.0	34.8	32.6	25.5	31.0
July	33.8	45.9	38.9	41.3	4.1	33.2	38.1	30.1	36.6	35.9	34.8	32.6	25.3	30.9
August	33.8	45.5	38.7	41.2	4.1	33.3	38.2	30.1	36.4	35.8	34.7	32.6	25.4	30.8
September	33.8	46.3	38.9	41.3	4.1	33.3	38.2	30.2	36.5	35.7	34.8	32.6	25.4	30.9
October	33.8	46.0	39.0	41.2	4.1	33.3	38.1	30.2	36.3	35.7	34.7	32.6	25.4	30.8
November	33.8	46.0	39.2	41.4	4.2	33.3	38.1	30.2	36.2	35.8	34.8	32.7	25.4	30.9
December	33.8	45.9	39.3	41.2	4.1	33.3	38.3	30.2	36.3	35.8	34.8	32.6	25.3	30.9
2008														
January	33.7	45.6	38.8	41.1	4.1	33.3	38.3	30.2	36.3	35.7	34.7	32.6	25.3	30.7
February	33.8	45.6	38.8	41.2	4.1	33.3	38.2	30.2	36.3	35.8	34.7	32.6	25.4	30.8
March	33.8	46.2	38.9	41.2	4.0	33.3	38.4	30.2	36.5	35.8	34.8	32.7	25.3	30.9
April	33.8	45.0	38.9	41.0	4.0	33.3	38.3	30.2	36.6	35.9	34.8	32.6	25.4	30.8
May	33.7	44.6	38.5	40.9	3.9	33.2	38.3	30.1	36.6	35.9	34.9	32.7	25.3	30.8
June	33.6	44.9	38.7	40.9	3.8	33.2	38.3	30.0	36.7	35.8	34.8	32.5	25.3	30.7
July	33.6	44.8	38.7	41.0	3.7	33.2	38.4	30.0	36.7	35.7	34.8	32.5	25.2	30.8
August	33.7	45.3	38.6	40.8	3.7	33.2	38.3	30.0	36.8	36.1	34.9	32.6	25.2	30.9
September	33.6	44.5	38.3	40.5	3.5	33.2	38.1	30.1	36.9	36.0	34.8	32.5	25.2	30.7
October	33.5	44.7	38.3	40.4	3.5	33.1	38.2	29.9	36.9	35.9	34.9	32.5	25.1	30.7
November	33.4	45.3	37.7	40.2	3.2	33.0	38.1	29.8	37.0	36.1	34.9	32.4	25.0	30.7
December	33.3	44.3	38.0	39.9	2.9	32.9	37.8	29.7	37.0	35.9	34.8	32.4	25.0	30.6

. . . = Not available.

Table 10-10. Indexes of Aggregate Weekly Hours of Production or Nonsupervisory Workers on Private Nonfarm Payrolls by NAICS Supersector

(2002 = 100, seasonally adjusted.)

Year and month	Total private	Mining and logging	Construc-tion	Manu-facturing	Trade, transportation, and utilities			Information	Financial activities	Profes-sional and business services	Education and health services	Leisure and hospitality	Other services
					Total	Wholesale trade	Retail trade						
1965	54.6	121.6	55.2	122.0	59.0	. . .	. . .	55.5	43.3	29.4	26.2	41.0	29.4
1966	56.9	121.1	56.8	130.1	60.5	. . .	. . .	58.3	44.3	30.8	27.3	42.2	30.9
1967	57.2	117.0	55.4	127.8	61.1	. . .	. . .	58.6	45.7	31.9	28.4	42.9	32.4
1968	58.5	114.9	56.5	130.1	62.2	. . .	. . .	59.9	47.6	33.1	29.5	44.1	33.9
1969	60.5	118.1	61.0	131.9	64.3	. . .	. . .	61.7	50.2	34.6	30.9	45.6	35.6
1970	59.5	115.7	59.8	123.3	64.9	. . .	. . .	60.4	51.1	34.7	31.3	46.1	36.3
1971	59.1	109.9	61.0	119.2	65.1	. . .	. . .	58.7	51.9	34.7	31.4	46.9	36.5
1972	61.6	115.6	63.4	125.7	67.5	68.4	64.4	61.1	53.4	36.0	32.6	48.6	37.9
1973	64.3	117.0	66.7	132.9	69.6	71.0	66.4	64.1	55.1	37.8	34.1	50.3	39.9
1974	64.3	127.7	64.5	128.9	70.2	72.7	66.7	64.0	55.8	38.8	35.3	50.8	41.4
1975	61.3	134.9	55.2	113.9	68.9	71.8	66.4	59.1	55.9	38.9	36.2	50.9	42.6
1976	63.8	142.4	56.0	120.8	70.9	73.9	68.8	61.1	57.1	40.3	37.5	52.8	44.3
1977	66.3	151.1	59.4	125.8	73.1	76.7	70.7	63.5	59.7	42.1	39.0	54.4	46.3
1978	69.5	156.9	66.2	131.2	76.1	81.0	73.4	66.6	63.0	44.3	40.9	56.6	48.8
1979	71.8	175.2	70.6	133.3	78.3	84.6	74.7	69.0	65.8	46.3	42.7	57.9	51.2
1980	71.0	187.2	68.0	124.4	77.6	84.8	74.0	67.4	68.1	47.7	44.6	57.9	53.6
1981	71.6	206.2	64.9	123.1	78.0	86.0	74.5	67.6	69.8	49.2	46.3	58.7	55.8
1982	69.0	195.5	59.7	109.9	76.4	83.4	74.2	64.0	69.8	49.2	47.1	58.7	56.8
1983	70.0	162.8	61.0	111.6	77.2	83.3	76.0	62.1	70.9	50.7	48.8	60.5	58.9
1984	74.3	169.3	69.1	119.6	81.2	87.5	79.8	68.0	74.2	53.2	50.9	63.6	61.7
1985	76.2	162.7	73.9	117.5	83.5	89.9	82.2	69.1	77.3	55.6	53.5	66.1	65.1
1986	77.5	133.5	75.5	116.3	84.5	89.8	83.9	69.1	81.2	57.8	55.9	68.0	68.2
1987	79.7	125.2	78.1	117.8	86.5	90.5	86.3	71.4	83.7	60.3	58.5	70.5	71.5
1988	82.1	125.6	80.4	120.2	88.6	93.6	88.5	73.1	83.4	63.3	61.8	73.0	75.7
1989	84.1	123.2	81.7	120.3	90.5	95.9	90.0	74.4	83.9	66.3	65.2	74.9	79.8
1990	84.4	128.6	78.8	117.7	89.5	94.9	87.5	76.2	84.5	68.0	67.2	78.9	81.8
1991	82.6	123.8	70.1	112.8	87.4	93.3	84.8	76.1	83.3	66.7	70.2	77.3	81.2
1992	83.1	113.3	67.5	112.4	87.3	92.4	85.1	76.5	83.5	68.4	72.9	79.3	80.6
1993	85.5	110.3	71.3	113.9	89.0	92.4	86.3	78.0	85.9	71.9	75.4	82.2	82.8
1994	89.2	111.0	77.3	118.3	92.7	95.8	89.8	79.2	88.0	77.0	78.3	85.6	84.5
1995	91.6	110.2	79.9	119.0	95.1	99.2	92.3	82.5	87.8	81.2	81.2	88.5	87.1
1996	93.8	112.7	84.3	118.8	96.6	100.7	93.7	87.0	89.8	85.2	83.4	90.8	89.1
1997	97.1	117.6	88.6	121.4	98.8	103.4	95.9	90.4	92.6	91.5	86.7	93.4	91.9
1998	99.4	112.8	93.4	121.0	100.3	104.8	97.2	92.6	96.5	96.7	88.9	95.5	94.3
1999	101.5	102.9	99.7	118.9	101.9	106.2	99.5	98.5	98.0	101.7	90.6	97.9	96.3
2000	103.6	105.1	104.0	117.7	103.5	107.1	101.3	105.0	98.5	106.6	92.8	100.6	97.8
2001	102.1	108.3	103.2	108.1	101.5	102.9	100.5	106.6	99.5	104.0	96.6	100.7	99.1
2002	100.0	100.0	100.0	100.0	100.0	100.0	100.0	100.0	100.0	100.0	100.0	100.0	100.0
2003	98.7	97.4	98.4	94.5	98.6	98.0	98.9	97.0	101.5	98.7	101.4	100.1	97.5
2004	100.2	104.0	101.7	94.3	99.6	98.9	99.4	98.3	101.9	101.8	103.3	103.0	96.1
2005	102.8	114.7	108.3	93.9	101.6	101.8	100.8	99.4	104.7	106.3	106.4	106.3	96.2
2006	105.8	125.8	115.3	95.6	103.3	105.7	101.1	100.2	107.4	112.1	109.0	108.9	97.5
2007	107.3	133.5	114.8	94.4	104.8	109.2	101.8	100.2	108.7	115.3	112.5	110.9	99.4
2008	106.2	138.9	107.3	90.4	103.6	109.0	100.3	100.4	107.6	114.2	115.8	109.9	99.7
2007													
January	106.6	127.7	115.0	94.5	104.2	106.9	101.4	99.9	108.8	114.1	110.6	110.9	98.3
February	106.6	132.2	112.7	94.2	104.1	107.7	101.4	100.0	109.2	114.6	110.4	109.7	98.7
March	107.2	132.4	115.7	94.6	104.7	108.1	101.8	100.2	109.2	115.0	111.4	110.6	99.5
April	106.9	133.8	114.9	94.5	104.1	108.4	101.4	100.3	108.6	114.8	111.8	110.8	99.4
May	107.4	133.1	115.3	94.3	104.9	109.3	102.0	100.1	108.4	115.3	112.1	111.2	99.9
June	107.5	134.0	116.3	94.6	104.9	109.3	101.8	100.0	109.1	115.2	112.4	110.9	99.7
July	107.3	134.4	115.5	94.6	104.4	109.3	101.5	100.5	109.0	115.2	112.7	110.0	99.5
August	107.2	132.0	114.0	94.0	104.7	109.7	101.4	99.9	108.4	114.9	113.0	110.5	99.1
September	107.3	134.6	114.3	94.2	104.9	109.8	101.8	100.3	108.0	115.3	113.3	110.8	99.3
October	107.5	133.5	114.6	93.8	105.0	109.8	101.8	99.8	107.9	115.4	113.6	111.1	99.1
November	107.7	135.7	114.7	94.4	105.3	109.9	102.2	99.6	108.1	115.9	114.1	111.4	99.6
December	107.8	136.6	114.4	94.1	105.4	110.6	102.3	100.0	108.1	116.4	114.1	110.9	99.8
2008													
January	107.5	136.7	112.4	93.7	105.4	110.4	102.3	100.2	107.8	115.9	114.4	110.7	99.2
February	107.6	136.9	111.7	93.5	105.2	110.0	102.0	100.2	108.0	115.5	114.7	111.2	99.8
March	107.5	139.7	111.5	93.2	105.1	110.5	101.9	100.7	108.0	115.2	115.4	110.7	100.2
April	107.4	135.6	110.4	92.2	104.8	109.9	101.6	100.7	108.3	115.4	115.4	111.2	99.9
May	106.9	134.9	108.6	91.7	104.3	109.7	101.1	100.7	108.1	115.2	116.0	110.5	99.9
June	106.4	136.5	108.1	91.3	104.1	109.6	100.6	100.6	107.7	114.5	115.6	110.5	99.5
July	106.2	137.6	107.5	91.0	103.9	109.5	100.4	100.3	107.2	114.2	115.9	110.0	99.8
August	106.4	142.0	107.0	90.0	103.6	109.0	100.2	100.4	108.4	114.0	116.7	109.9	100.2
September	105.8	141.2	105.3	88.7	103.3	108.1	100.1	100.7	107.9	113.3	116.4	109.7	99.6
October	105.0	140.6	104.1	87.4	102.4	108.0	98.9	100.8	107.4	112.9	116.5	109.0	99.7
November	104.1	143.2	100.5	86.0	101.4	107.0	97.9	100.2	107.3	112.0	116.6	108.2	99.1
December	103.2	139.1	99.8	84.0	100.6	105.5	97.1	99.6	106.2	110.8	116.9	107.8	98.3

. . . = Not available.

Table 10-11. Average Hourly Earnings of Production or Nonsupervisory Workers on Private Nonfarm Payrolls by NAICS Supersector

(Dollars, seasonally adjusted.)

| Year and month | Total private | Mining and logging | Construc-tion | Manu-facturing | Trade, transportation, and utilities | | | Information | Financial activities | Profes-sional and business services | Education and health services | Leisure and hospitality | Other services |
					Total	Wholesale trade	Retail trade						
1965	2.63	2.87	3.23	2.49	2.94	. . .	. . .	4.47	2.38	3.28	2.12	1.17	1.25
1966	2.73	3.00	3.41	2.60	3.04	. . .	. . .	4.56	2.47	3.39	2.23	1.26	1.37
1967	2.85	3.14	3.63	2.71	3.15	. . .	. . .	4.68	2.58	3.51	2.36	1.37	1.49
1968	3.02	3.30	3.92	2.89	3.32	. . .	. . .	4.85	2.75	3.65	2.49	1.53	1.62
1969	3.22	3.54	4.30	3.07	3.48	. . .	. . .	5.05	2.92	3.84	2.68	1.69	1.81
1970	3.40	3.77	4.74	3.23	3.65	. . .	. . .	5.25	3.07	4.04	2.88	1.82	2.01
1971	3.63	3.99	5.17	3.45	3.86	. . .	. . .	5.53	3.23	4.26	3.11	1.95	2.24
1972	3.90	4.28	5.55	3.70	4.23	4.58	3.52	5.87	3.37	4.50	3.33	2.08	2.46
1973	4.14	4.59	5.89	3.97	4.45	4.80	3.69	6.17	3.55	4.72	3.54	2.20	2.67
1974	4.43	5.09	6.29	4.31	4.74	5.11	3.92	6.52	3.80	5.01	3.82	2.40	2.95
1975	4.73	5.68	6.78	4.71	5.02	5.45	4.14	6.92	4.08	5.29	4.09	2.58	3.21
1976	5.06	6.19	7.17	5.09	5.31	5.75	4.36	7.37	4.30	5.60	4.39	2.78	3.51
1977	5.44	6.70	7.56	5.55	5.67	6.12	4.65	7.84	4.58	5.95	4.72	3.03	3.84
1978	5.88	7.44	8.11	6.05	6.10	6.61	5.00	8.34	4.93	6.32	5.07	3.33	4.19
1979	6.34	8.20	8.71	6.57	6.55	7.12	5.34	8.86	5.31	6.71	5.44	3.63	4.56
1980	6.85	8.97	9.37	7.15	7.04	7.68	5.71	9.47	5.82	7.22	5.93	3.98	5.05
1981	7.44	9.89	10.24	7.86	7.55	8.28	6.09	10.21	6.34	7.80	6.49	4.36	5.61
1982	7.87	10.64	11.04	8.36	7.91	8.81	6.34	10.76	6.82	8.30	7.00	4.63	6.11
1983	8.20	11.14	11.36	8.70	8.23	9.27	6.60	11.18	7.32	8.70	7.39	4.89	6.51
1984	8.49	11.54	11.56	9.05	8.45	9.61	6.73	11.50	7.65	8.98	7.67	4.99	6.79
1985	8.74	11.87	11.75	9.40	8.60	9.88	6.83	11.81	7.97	9.28	7.98	5.10	7.10
1986	8.93	12.14	11.92	9.59	8.74	10.07	6.93	12.08	8.37	9.55	8.25	5.20	7.38
1987	9.14	12.17	12.15	9.77	8.92	10.32	7.02	12.36	8.73	9.85	8.57	5.30	7.69
1988	9.44	12.45	12.52	10.05	9.15	10.71	7.23	12.63	9.07	10.22	8.96	5.50	8.08
1989	9.80	12.91	12.98	10.35	9.46	11.12	7.46	12.99	9.54	10.69	9.46	5.76	8.58
1990	10.20	13.40	13.42	10.78	9.83	11.58	7.71	13.40	9.99	11.14	10.00	6.02	9.08
1991	10.52	13.82	13.65	11.13	10.08	11.95	7.89	13.90	10.42	11.50	10.49	6.22	9.39
1992	10.77	14.09	13.81	11.40	10.30	12.21	8.12	14.29	10.86	11.78	10.87	6.36	9.66
1993	11.05	14.12	14.04	11.70	10.55	12.57	8.36	14.86	11.36	11.96	11.21	6.48	9.90
1994	11.34	14.41	14.38	12.04	10.80	12.93	8.61	15.32	11.82	12.15	11.50	6.62	10.18
1995	11.65	14.78	14.73	12.34	11.10	13.34	8.85	15.68	12.28	12.53	11.80	6.79	10.51
1996	12.04	15.10	15.11	12.75	11.46	13.80	9.21	16.30	12.71	13.00	12.17	6.99	10.85
1997	12.51	15.57	15.67	13.14	11.90	14.41	9.59	17.14	13.22	13.57	12.56	7.32	11.29
1998	13.01	16.20	16.23	13.45	12.39	15.07	10.05	17.67	13.93	14.27	13.00	7.67	11.79
1999	13.49	16.33	16.80	13.85	12.82	15.62	10.45	18.40	14.47	14.85	13.44	7.96	12.26
2000	14.02	16.55	17.48	14.32	13.31	16.28	10.86	19.07	14.98	15.52	13.95	8.32	12.73
2001	14.54	17.00	18.00	14.76	13.70	16.77	11.29	19.80	15.59	16.33	14.64	8.57	13.27
2002	14.97	17.19	18.52	15.29	14.02	16.98	11.67	20.20	16.17	16.81	15.21	8.81	13.72
2003	15.37	17.56	18.95	15.74	14.34	17.36	11.90	21.01	17.14	17.21	15.64	9.00	13.84
2004	15.69	18.07	19.23	16.14	14.58	17.65	12.08	21.40	17.52	17.48	16.15	9.15	13.98
2005	16.13	18.72	19.46	16.56	14.92	18.16	12.36	22.06	17.95	18.08	16.71	9.38	14.34
2006	16.76	19.90	20.02	16.81	15.39	18.91	12.57	23.23	18.80	19.13	17.38	9.75	14.77
2007	17.43	20.97	20.95	17.26	15.78	19.59	12.75	23.96	19.64	20.15	18.11	10.41	15.42
2008	18.08	22.50	21.87	17.74	16.16	20.14	12.87	24.77	20.27	21.19	18.88	10.84	16.08
2007													
January	17.12	20.58	20.57	17.02	15.59	19.27	12.68	23.77	19.33	19.69	17.74	10.10	15.09
February	17.18	20.74	20.59	17.05	15.60	19.24	12.70	23.81	19.41	19.82	17.79	10.17	15.16
March	17.23	20.82	20.68	17.10	15.64	19.36	12.70	23.83	19.49	19.84	17.87	10.21	15.27
April	17.29	20.90	20.77	17.20	15.67	19.41	12.71	23.85	19.49	19.91	17.91	10.31	15.29
May	17.34	20.96	20.91	17.23	15.69	19.42	12.72	23.87	19.56	20.04	17.99	10.33	15.32
June	17.42	20.97	20.95	17.29	15.77	19.56	12.74	23.95	19.65	20.12	18.07	10.39	15.39
July	17.48	20.97	20.96	17.30	15.80	19.59	12.77	23.92	19.66	20.23	18.14	10.47	15.45
August	17.51	20.97	20.99	17.35	15.83	19.64	12.77	23.96	19.72	20.29	18.21	10.50	15.50
September	17.57	20.87	21.10	17.37	15.88	19.71	12.80	24.03	19.77	20.37	18.28	10.55	15.56
October	17.60	21.04	21.09	17.34	15.91	19.77	12.83	24.11	19.81	20.40	18.34	10.59	15.61
November	17.66	20.87	21.22	17.41	15.93	19.86	12.81	24.17	19.86	20.46	18.43	10.63	15.67
December	17.71	21.53	21.30	17.42	15.98	19.94	12.80	24.26	19.90	20.51	18.49	10.66	15.73
2008													
January	17.77	21.83	21.38	17.52	16.00	19.97	12.80	24.40	19.99	20.58	18.56	10.68	15.79
February	17.83	21.80	21.48	17.58	16.04	20.03	12.81	24.48	20.04	20.69	18.60	10.75	15.85
March	17.90	22.28	21.58	17.64	16.07	20.04	12.83	24.58	20.12	20.78	18.69	10.75	15.94
April	17.94	21.77	21.62	17.64	16.08	20.05	12.84	24.56	20.17	20.90	18.74	10.81	16.00
May	17.99	21.79	21.72	17.68	16.13	20.07	12.87	24.71	20.23	20.96	18.80	10.83	16.04
June	18.04	22.04	21.77	17.73	16.16	20.11	12.87	24.78	20.24	21.08	18.84	10.85	16.09
July	18.10	22.54	21.85	17.80	16.17	20.15	12.88	24.87	20.26	21.19	18.92	10.87	16.13
August	18.18	23.01	22.02	17.78	16.23	20.28	12.92	24.95	20.37	21.38	18.96	10.89	16.17
September	18.21	23.08	22.09	17.81	16.20	20.20	12.91	24.90	20.43	21.47	19.04	10.90	16.20
October	18.28	23.03	22.17	17.89	16.23	20.22	12.89	24.99	20.43	21.63	19.08	10.92	16.24
November	18.34	23.28	22.28	17.94	16.29	20.29	12.93	24.94	20.41	21.78	19.13	10.90	16.29
December	18.40	23.23	22.41	17.96	16.31	20.31	12.94	24.91	20.53	21.97	19.20	10.94	16.29

. . . = Not available.

Table 10-12. Average Weekly Earnings of Production or Nonsupervisory Workers on Private Nonfarm Payrolls by NAICS Supersector

(Dollars, seasonally adjusted.)

Year and month	Total private	Mining and logging	Construc-tion	Manu-facturing	Trade, transportation, and utilities			Information	Financial activities	Profes-sional and business services	Education and health services	Leisure and hospitality	Other services
					Total	Wholesale trade	Retail trade						
1965	101.52	125.42	122.42	102.59	116.42	. . .	. . .	171.20	88.30	122.34	74.62	38.03	45.13
1966	105.11	132.30	129.92	107.64	118.86	. . .	. . .	174.65	91.88	125.43	77.83	40.19	49.05
1967	108.02	137.85	138.30	110.03	121.28	. . .	. . .	175.97	95.20	128.47	81.42	42.88	52.75
1968	113.85	145.20	148.18	117.62	126.82	. . .	. . .	182.36	101.20	132.50	84.91	47.12	56.70
1969	120.75	156.82	165.12	124.64	131.89	. . .	. . .	189.88	107.75	139.39	91.39	51.38	63.35
1970	125.80	165.50	179.17	128.55	137.24	. . .	. . .	195.30	112.36	145.04	97.34	54.60	69.75
1971	133.58	174.36	194.39	137.66	144.36	. . .	. . .	204.61	117.57	151.23	103.56	58.31	76.61
1972	143.91	188.32	205.35	150.22	158.20	182.28	123.55	218.95	122.67	159.75	110.89	61.78	84.13
1973	152.77	201.04	219.11	161.58	165.54	190.08	128.41	230.14	129.22	167.56	117.88	64.68	91.05
1974	161.25	222.43	233.36	172.40	174.43	200.31	134.46	241.24	137.94	176.85	126.44	69.84	100.01
1975	170.28	248.22	250.18	186.05	182.73	213.10	140.76	253.27	147.70	185.68	134.97	74.30	108.50
1976	182.67	273.60	267.44	204.11	192.75	224.83	147.37	270.48	155.66	195.44	143.55	79.23	117.94
1977	195.30	299.49	279.72	223.67	204.12	239.90	154.85	288.51	165.80	206.47	153.40	85.14	128.26
1978	210.50	334.06	302.50	244.42	217.16	259.11	163.50	306.91	177.97	218.67	163.76	92.24	139.11
1979	225.70	366.54	326.63	264.11	231.87	279.10	173.02	324.28	190.63	230.82	175.17	99.46	150.48
1980	241.12	402.75	351.38	283.86	246.40	297.98	182.15	343.76	209.52	247.65	190.35	107.46	166.65
1981	261.89	446.04	382.98	312.83	263.50	322.09	194.27	370.62	228.24	267.54	208.33	117.28	185.13
1982	273.09	469.22	410.69	325.20	273.69	340.95	200.98	385.21	245.52	283.86	224.70	124.08	201.63
1983	286.18	489.05	427.14	348.87	284.76	359.68	208.56	404.72	262.79	299.28	237.22	131.05	214.83
1984	298.00	514.68	441.59	368.34	293.22	373.83	212.67	420.90	276.93	308.01	245.44	133.23	223.39
1985	305.03	529.04	448.85	380.70	295.84	383.34	213.10	431.07	287.72	317.38	254.56	134.64	232.88
1986	309.87	529.30	451.77	390.31	298.03	389.71	214.83	439.71	302.16	327.57	264.00	136.24	242.80
1987	317.16	529.40	464.13	399.59	304.17	397.32	217.62	451.14	314.28	337.86	274.24	139.39	252.23
1988	326.62	539.09	478.26	412.05	309.27	412.34	223.41	455.94	322.89	349.52	286.72	144.65	265.83
1989	338.10	569.33	497.13	423.32	319.75	427.01	229.02	468.94	339.62	365.60	302.72	150.34	282.28
1990	349.75	602.54	513.43	436.16	331.55	444.48	235.62	479.50	354.66	380.52	319.27	156.32	297.91
1991	358.51	625.42	520.41	449.73	339.19	459.27	240.15	495.17	369.57	391.09	334.55	159.15	306.91
1992	368.25	629.02	525.13	464.43	348.68	470.41	249.63	512.20	386.01	400.64	348.29	163.70	315.08
1993	378.91	634.77	539.81	480.83	359.33	484.46	256.89	535.19	403.02	406.20	359.08	167.56	322.69
1994	391.22	653.14	558.53	502.05	370.38	501.17	265.77	551.21	419.20	414.16	368.14	172.33	332.44
1995	400.07	670.32	571.57	509.26	378.79	515.14	272.56	564.92	436.12	426.44	377.73	175.74	342.36
1996	413.28	695.07	588.48	526.55	390.64	533.29	282.76	592.72	451.49	442.81	388.27	180.98	352.62
1997	431.86	720.11	609.48	548.22	407.54	559.39	295.97	622.37	472.37	465.51	404.65	190.52	368.63
1998	448.56	727.28	629.75	557.12	423.30	582.21	310.34	646.34	500.98	490.00	418.82	200.82	384.25
1999	463.15	721.74	655.11	573.14	434.31	602.77	321.63	675.47	517.57	510.99	431.35	208.05	398.77
2000	481.01	734.92	685.78	590.77	449.88	631.40	333.38	700.86	537.37	535.07	449.29	217.20	413.41
2001	493.79	757.92	695.89	595.19	459.53	643.45	346.16	730.88	557.92	557.84	473.39	220.73	428.64
2002	506.75	741.97	711.82	618.75	471.27	644.38	360.81	737.77	575.54	574.66	492.74	227.17	439.76
2003	518.06	765.94	726.83	635.99	481.14	657.29	367.15	760.45	609.08	587.02	505.69	230.42	434.41
2004	529.09	803.82	735.55	658.49	488.42	667.09	371.13	777.25	622.87	597.56	523.78	234.86	433.04
2005	544.33	853.71	750.22	673.30	498.43	685.00	377.58	805.08	644.99	618.87	544.59	241.36	443.37
2006	567.87	907.95	781.21	691.02	514.34	718.63	383.02	850.42	672.21	662.27	564.94	250.34	456.50
2007	590.04	962.64	816.66	711.56	526.07	748.94	385.11	874.65	705.13	700.82	590.09	265.52	477.06
2008	607.99	1 013.78	842.36	724.23	535.79	769.91	386.39	908.44	726.37	738.25	614.30	273.27	494.99
2007													
January	578.66	928.16	798.12	697.82	520.71	730.33	384.20	869.98	693.95	681.27	576.55	259.57	464.77
February	580.68	951.97	796.83	697.35	519.48	733.04	383.54	871.45	698.76	687.75	576.40	258.32	468.44
March	584.10	955.64	808.59	704.52	522.38	739.55	383.54	874.56	701.64	690.43	582.56	261.38	474.90
April	584.40	965.58	807.95	708.64	520.24	741.46	382.57	872.91	699.69	690.88	583.87	263.94	473.99
May	587.83	959.97	815.49	708.15	524.05	745.73	384.14	868.87	700.25	697.39	586.47	264.45	476.45
June	590.54	964.62	819.15	714.08	526.72	749.15	384.75	871.78	707.40	700.18	589.08	264.95	477.09
July	590.82	962.52	815.34	714.49	524.56	746.38	384.38	875.47	705.79	704.00	591.36	264.89	477.41
August	591.84	954.14	812.31	714.82	527.14	750.25	384.38	872.14	705.98	704.06	593.65	266.70	477.40
September	593.87	966.28	820.79	717.38	528.80	752.92	386.56	877.10	705.79	708.88	595.93	267.97	480.80
October	594.88	967.84	822.51	714.41	529.80	753.24	387.47	875.19	707.22	707.88	597.88	268.99	480.79
November	596.91	960.02	831.82	720.77	530.47	756.67	386.86	874.95	710.99	712.01	602.66	270.00	484.20
December	598.60	988.23	837.09	717.70	532.13	763.70	386.56	880.64	712.42	713.75	602.77	269.70	486.06
2008													
January	598.85	995.45	829.54	720.07	532.80	764.85	386.56	885.72	713.64	714.13	605.06	270.20	484.75
February	602.65	994.08	833.42	724.30	534.13	765.15	386.86	888.62	717.43	717.94	606.36	273.05	488.18
March	605.02	1 029.34	839.46	726.77	535.13	769.54	387.47	897.17	720.30	723.14	611.16	271.98	492.55
April	606.37	979.65	841.02	723.24	535.46	767.92	387.77	898.90	724.10	727.32	610.92	274.57	492.80
May	606.26	971.83	836.22	723.11	535.52	768.68	387.39	904.39	726.26	731.50	614.76	274.00	494.03
June	606.14	989.60	842.50	725.16	536.51	770.21	386.10	909.43	724.59	733.58	612.30	274.51	493.96
July	608.16	1 009.79	845.60	729.80	536.84	773.76	386.40	912.73	723.28	737.41	614.90	273.92	496.80
August	612.67	1 042.35	849.97	725.42	538.84	776.72	387.60	918.16	735.36	746.16	618.10	274.43	499.65
September	611.86	1 027.06	846.05	721.31	537.84	769.62	388.59	918.81	735.48	747.16	618.80	274.68	497.34
October	612.38	1 029.44	849.11	722.76	537.21	772.40	385.41	922.13	733.44	754.89	620.10	274.09	498.57
November	612.56	1 054.58	839.96	721.19	537.57	773.05	385.31	922.78	736.80	760.12	619.81	272.50	500.10
December	612.72	1 029.09	851.58	716.60	536.60	767.72	384.32	921.67	737.03	764.56	622.08	273.50	498.47

. . . = Not available.

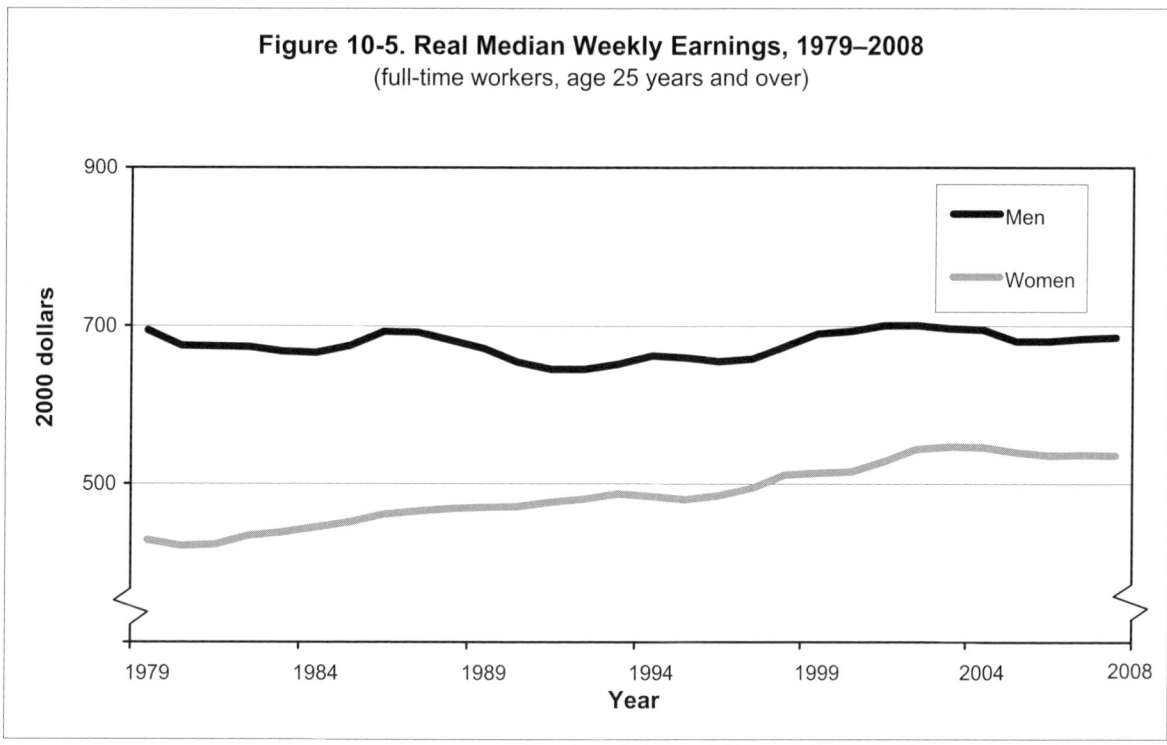

Figure 10-5. Real Median Weekly Earnings, 1979–2008
(full-time workers, age 25 years and over)

- "Median usual weekly earnings of full-time wage and salary workers," as shown in Table 10-13, are derived quarterly from the Current Population Survey, not from the payroll survey that provides the weekly earnings shown in Table 10-12. That is, they are collected from individual households in the CPS sample, instead of from employers. This makes it possible to tabulate earnings by sex and other demographic characteristics, to identify full-time workers and measure them separately from part-time workers, and to identify the median worker. As a result, this data set provides better approximations of the paychecks of typical breadwinners than the payroll data on average weekly earnings (AWE).

- The 2008 median earnings of all full-time workers in Table 10-13 are significantly higher than AWE for all private industry as shown in Table 10-12, because part-time jobs are included in the latter measure. (Tables 10-13 and 10-12)

- Women's earnings were moving closer to men's over most of the period covered in this survey, rising from 61.8 percent in 1979 to a high of 79.4 percent in 2005. Since then the ratio has edged down, and the median female full-time worker earned 78.2 cents for every dollar earned by the median male worker in 2008. (Table 10-13)

- In Figure 10-5 above, median weekly earnings for men and women over 25 years of age have been converted to constant year-2000 dollars using the CPI-U-RS—a price index developed to measure price changes more consistently than the official Consumer Price Index (CPI). (See the notes and definitions to Chapters 8, 3, and 9.) (Tables 10-13 and 8-2)

- As Figure 10-5 shows, typical workers of both sexes lost ground in real terms in recent years. In 2008, median earnings for adult men in 2000 dollars were down 2.3 percent from the 2002 level, and median earnings for adult women were down 2.0 percent from their 2003 high. (Labor productivity in nonfarm business rose 14.1 percent from 2002 to 2008. See the article at the beginning of this book for a discussion of the relationship between productivity and compensation, in the section entitled "Comparison of the last two completed business cycles.") Men's earnings have been essentially stagnant for the entire 29 years—down 1.3 percent from 1979—while women's earnings have increased 24.9 percent. (Tables 10-13 and 9-3)

Table 10-13. Median Usual Weekly Earnings of Full-Time Wage and Salary Workers

(Current dollars, except as noted; not seasonally adjusted.)

Year and quarter	Total, 16 years and over	Sex and age									Race and ethnicity			
		Men, 16 years and over				Women, 16 years and over					White	Black or African American	Asian	Hispanic or Latino ethnicity
		Total	16 to 24 years	25 years and over		Total	16 to 24 years	25 years and over						
				Current dollars	2000 dollars [1]			Current dollars	2000 dollars [1]					
1979	240	291	196	314	694	182	154	194	429	247	198	. . .	. . .	
1980	261	312	208	339	675	201	167	212	422	268	212	. . .	. . .	
1981	283	339	218	371	674	219	180	233	423	290	234	. . .	. . .	
1982	302	364	224	393	673	238	191	254	435	309	245	. . .	. . .	
1983	313	378	223	406	667	252	197	267	439	319	261	. . .	. . .	
1984	326	391	231	422	666	265	203	282	445	336	269	. . .	. . .	
1985	343	406	240	442	675	277	210	296	452	355	277	. . .	. . .	
1986	358	419	245	462	693	290	218	308	462	370	291	. . .	277	
1987	373	433	257	477	692	303	226	321	465	383	301	. . .	284	
1988	385	449	261	487	681	315	235	335	469	394	314	. . .	290	
1989	399	468	271	500	670	328	246	351	471	409	319	. . .	298	
1990	412	481	282	512	654	346	254	369	471	424	329	. . .	304	
1991	426	493	285	523	645	366	266	387	477	442	348	. . .	312	
1992	440	501	284	536	645	380	267	400	481	458	357	. . .	322	
1993	459	510	288	555	651	393	273	415	487	475	369	. . .	331	
1994	467	522	294	576	662	399	276	421	484	484	371	. . .	324	
1995	479	538	303	588	660	406	275	428	480	494	383	. . .	329	
1996	490	557	307	599	655	418	284	444	485	506	387	. . .	339	
1997	503	579	317	615	658	431	292	462	494	519	400	. . .	351	
1998	523	598	334	639	674	456	305	485	512	545	426	. . .	370	
1999	549	618	356	668	690	473	324	497	514	573	445	. . .	385	
2000	576	641	375	693	693	493	344	516	516	590	474	615	399	
2001	596	670	391	720	700	512	353	543	528	610	491	639	417	
2002	608	679	391	732	701	529	367	568	544	623	498	658	424	
2003	620	695	398	744	697	552	371	584	547	636	514	693	440	
2004	638	713	400	762	695	573	375	599	546	657	525	708	456	
2005	651	722	409	771	680	585	381	612	540	672	520	753	471	
2006	671	743	418	797	681	600	395	627	536	690	554	784	486	
2007	695	766	443	823	684	614	409	646	537	716	569	830	503	
2008	722	798	461	857	685	638	420	670	536	742	589	861	529	
2000														
1st quarter	573	641	372	687	696	489	340	510	517	588	469	602	399	
2nd quarter	569	639	373	691	693	486	332	510	511	585	475	613	394	
3rd quarter	574	631	372	691	687	494	340	522	519	587	469	625	403	
4th quarter	585	652	381	702	695	503	367	523	518	600	480	617	400	
2001														
1st quarter	589	659	385	708	694	509	356	533	522	605	482	612	408	
2nd quarter	592	664	391	715	694	511	348	541	525	606	495	637	419	
3rd quarter	596	676	392	729	706	507	349	540	523	610	490	666	421	
4th quarter	606	681	398	726	706	522	358	556	540	620	498	649	419	
2002														
1st quarter	611	682	405	730	707	530	375	568	550	624	512	653	426	
2nd quarter	605	677	398	732	701	520	355	559	535	622	500	648	420	
3rd quarter	603	671	376	729	695	527	360	570	544	620	484	665	420	
4th quarter	613	686	390	737	700	542	384	576	547	630	495	667	435	
2003														
1st quarter	620	695	396	741	697	551	384	581	547	636	516	718	447	
2nd quarter	616	692	391	743	697	547	366	582	546	631	509	678	430	
3rd quarter	618	689	396	742	692	550	366	585	546	633	509	692	444	
4th quarter	625	704	409	750	700	561	372	588	549	646	522	680	441	
2004														
1st quarter	634	711	410	757	700	567	387	592	547	652	521	712	450	
2nd quarter	639	714	397	763	696	572	370	601	548	655	536	720	451	
3rd quarter	632	704	400	759	689	571	371	602	547	651	531	701	458	
4th quarter	647	722	396	768	693	578	371	603	544	671	519	698	467	
2005														
1st quarter	653	729	401	775	696	586	380	610	547	677	513	738	470	
2nd quarter	643	713	407	762	675	580	374	608	538	663	518	743	473	
3rd quarter	649	716	407	768	672	585	379	615	538	667	520	761	462	
4th quarter	659	731	418	778	677	588	389	614	534	682	533	767	479	
2006														
1st quarter	668	744	417	793	686	600	388	624	540	688	560	766	487	
2nd quarter	659	731	421	783	667	593	395	619	527	678	534	765	485	
3rd quarter	675	749	409	808	684	599	393	629	532	692	555	798	485	
4th quarter	682	749	429	800	683	609	403	638	545	702	569	809	489	
2007														
1st quarter	693	759	451	811	686	615	414	646	546	714	561	798	502	
2nd quarter	690	763	436	819	679	607	404	635	527	713	562	827	503	
3rd quarter	695	767	430	831	687	616	398	654	541	713	578	842	502	
4th quarter	700	774	459	831	682	618	421	649	533	722	574	856	507	
2008														
1st quarter	719	790	466	848	688	637	419	666	541	742	582	842	520	
2nd quarter	719	800	469	862	685	634	415	668	531	738	591	855	537	
3rd quarter	720	796	446	857	673	631	406	666	523	739	589	854	529	
4th quarter	728	807	462	859	694	650	449	679	549	748	593	889	535	

[1]Converted to 2000 dollars by the editor using CPI-U-RS. See notes and definitions.
. . . = Not available.

NOTES AND DEFINITIONS

GENERAL NOTE ON EMPLOYMENT DATA

This chapter includes two different data sets that measure employment. Both are compiled and published by the Bureau of Labor Statistics (BLS), but each set has different characteristics. Users should be aware of these dissimilarities and the consequent differences in the appropriate uses and interpretations of data from the two systems.

One set of employment estimates comes from the Current Population Survey (CPS), a large sample survey of U.S. households. The numbers in the sample are expanded to match the latest estimates of the total U.S. population. These are the most comprehensive estimates in their scope—that is, in the universe that they are designed to measure. These estimates represent all civilian workers, including the following groups that are excluded by definition from the other set of estimates: all farm workers, household workers (domestic servants), nonagricultural self-employed workers, and nonagricultural unpaid family workers.

However, official CPS data are characterized by periodic discontinuities, which occur when new benchmarks for Census measures of the total population are introduced. These updates take place in a single month—usually January—and the official data for previous months are typically <u>not</u> modified to provide a smooth transition. Therefore, shorter-term comparisons (for a year or two or for a business cycle phase) will be misleading if such a discontinuity is included in the period. Two recent examples will illustrate. Beginning with January 2006, the estimates for population, labor force, employment, and unemployment were all adjusted downward; if the same population controls had been used for December 2005, employment would have been lower by 123,000 persons. Beginning with January 2007, new controls were introduced that would have raised employment in December 2006 by 153,000 persons. Such discontinuities occur throughout the history of the series.

> For users who would like to examine monthly CPS data in which these discontinuities have been smoothed, BLS now provides unofficial smoothed estimates of total labor force and total employment from January 1990 through December 2008 on its Web site, <http://www.bls.gov>. In this edition of *Business Statistics*, these two series are included in Table 20-3A in Chapter 20, Selected Historical Data.

The CPS is a count of persons employed, rather than a count of jobs. A person is counted as employed in this data set only once, no matter how many jobs he or she may hold. The CPS count is limited to persons 16 years of age and over.

The second set of employment estimates—the payroll survey—comes from a very large sample survey of employers, the Current Employment Statistics (CES) survey. It is benchmarked annually to a survey of all employers. Benchmark data are introduced with a smooth adjustment back to the previous benchmark, thus preserving the continuity of the series and making it more appropriate for measurement of employment change over a year or two, a business cycle, or other short- to medium-length periods. The sample is much larger than the CPS sample, and consequently the threshold of statistical significance for changes is lower.

The scope of the CES survey is wage and salary workers on nonfarm payrolls, and it is a count of jobs. Thus, a person with more than one nonfarm wage or salary job is counted as employed in each job. Workers are not classified by age; as a result, there may be some workers younger than 16 years old in the job count.

Persons with a job but not at work (absent due to bad weather, work stoppages, personal reasons, and the like) are included in the household survey. However, they are excluded from the payroll survey if on leave without pay for the entire payroll period.

In addition to the differences in definitions and scope between the two series, there are also differences in sample design, collection methodology, and the sampling variability inherent in the surveys.

The payroll survey provides the most reliable and detailed information on the breakdown of employment by industry (for example, the data shown in Table 16-1).

The CPS employment estimates provide information not collected in the CES on the breakdown of employment by demographic characteristics, such as age, race, and Hispanic ethnicity; by education levels; and by occupation. A few of these breakdowns are shown in *Business Statistics*. Many more breakdowns, in richer detail, can be found in the *Handbook of U.S. Labor Statistics*, also published by Bernan Press.

The differences between these two employment measures are discussed in an article by Mary Bowler and Teresa L. Morisi entitled "Understanding the employment measures from the CPS and CES survey" in *Monthly Labor Review*, February 2006, available on the BLS Web site http://www.bls.gov.

TABLES 10-1 THROUGH 10-5 AND 20-3
LABOR FORCE, EMPLOYMENT, AND UNEMPLOYMENT

SOURCE: U.S. DEPARTMENT OF LABOR, BUREAU OF LABOR STATISTICS (BLS)

Labor force, employment, and unemployment data are derived from the Current Population Survey (CPS), a sample survey of households conducted each month by the Census Bureau for the Bureau of Labor Statistics (BLS).

The data pertain to the U.S. civilian noninstitutional population age 16 years and over.

Due to changes in questionnaire design and survey methodology, data for 1994 and subsequent years are not fully comparable with data for 1993 and earlier years. Additionally, discontinuities in the reported number of persons in the population, and consequently in the estimated numbers of employed and unemployed persons and the number of persons in the labor force, are introduced whenever periodic updates are made to U.S. population estimates.

For example, population controls based on Census 2000 were introduced beginning with the data for January 2000. These data are therefore not comparable with data for December 1999 and earlier. Data for 1990 through 1999 incorporate 1990 census–based population controls and are not comparable with the preceding years. An additional large population adjustment was introduced in January 2004, making the data from that time forward not comparable with data for December 2003 and earlier; further adjustments have been made in each subsequent January and other discontinuities have been introduced in various earlier years, usually with January data. See "Notes on the Data," below, for additional information.

For the most part, these population adjustments distort comparisons involving the *numbers of persons* in the population, labor force, and employment. They generally have negligible effects on the *percentages* that comprise the most important features of the CPS: the unemployment rates, the labor force participation rates, and the employment-population ratios.

BLS now makes available unofficial smoothed data for the total number of persons in the civilian labor force and the number of persons employed for 1990 through 2008, which introduce the population adjustments gradually within the period shown. These data are shown in Table 20-3A.

Beginning with the data for January 2000, data classified by industry and occupation use the 2002 North American Industry Classification System (NAICS—see Chapter 14 for more information) and the 2000 Standard Occupational Classification System. This creates breaks in the time series between December 1999 and January 2000 for occupational and industry data at all levels of aggregation. Since the recent history is so short, most industry and occupation data have been dropped from *Business Statistics* in favor of other important and economically meaningful data for which a longer consistent history can be supplied. However, detailed employment data by occupation and industry can be found in Bernan Press's *Handbook of U.S. Labor Statistics*.

Race and ethnic origin

Data for two broad racial categories were made available beginning in 1954: *White* and *Black and other*. The latter included Asians and all other "nonwhite" races, and was discontinued after 2002. Data for *Blacks* only are available beginning with 1972; this category is now called *Black or African American*. Data for *Asians* are shown beginning with 2000. Persons in the remaining race categories—American Indian or Alaska Native, Native Hawaiian or Other Pacific Islanders, and persons who selected more than one race category beginning in 2003 (see below)—are included in the estimates of total employment and unemployment, but are not shown separately because their numbers are too small to yield quality estimates.

Hispanic or Latino ethnicity, previously labeled *Hispanic origin*, is not a racial category and is established in a survey question separate from the question about race. Persons of Hispanic or Latino ethnicity may be of any race.

In January 2003, changes that affected classification by race and Hispanic ethnicity were introduced. These changes caused discontinuities in race and ethnic group data between December 2002 and January 2003.

Individuals in the sample are now asked whether they are of Hispanic ethnicity *before* being asked about their race. Prior to 2003, individuals were asked their ethnic origin *after* they were asked about their race. Furthermore, respondents are now asked directly if they are Spanish, Hispanic, or Latino. Previously, they were identified based on their or their ancestors' country of origin.

Individuals in the sample are now allowed to choose more than one race category. Before 2003, they were required to select a single primary race. This change had no impact on the size of the overall civilian noninstitutional population and labor force. It did reduce the population and labor force levels of Whites and Blacks beginning in January 2003, as individuals who reported more than one race are now excluded from those groups.

BLS has estimated, based on a special survey, that these changes reduced the population and labor force levels for Whites by about 950,000 and 730,000 persons, respectively, and for Blacks by about 320,000 and 240,000 persons, respectively, while having little or no impact on either of their unemployment rates. The changes did not affect the size of the Hispanic population or labor force, but they did cause an increase of about half a percentage point in the Hispanic unemployment rate.

Definitions

The employment status of the civilian population is surveyed each month with respect to a specific week in mid-month—not for the entire month. This is known as the "reference week." For a precise definition and explanation of the reference week, see Notes on the Data, which follows these definitions.

The *civilian noninstitutional population* comprises all civilians 16 years of age and over who are not inmates of penal or mental institutions, sanitariums, or homes for the aged, infirm, or needy.

Civilian employment includes those civilians who (1) worked for pay or profit at any time during the week that includes the 12th day of the month (the reference week), or who worked for 15 hours or more as an unpaid worker in a family-operated enterprise; or (2) were temporarily absent from regular jobs because of vacation, illness, industrial dispute, bad weather, or similar reasons. Each employed person is counted only once; those who hold more than one job are counted as being in the job at which they worked the greatest number of hours during the reference week.

Unemployed persons are all civilians who were not employed (according to the above definition) during the reference week, but who were available for work—except for temporary illness—and who had made specific efforts to find employment sometime during the previous four weeks. Persons who did not look for work because they were on layoff are also counted as unemployed.

The *civilian labor force* comprises all civilians classified as employed or unemployed.

Civilians 16 years of age and over in the noninstitutional population who are not classified as employed or unemployed are defined as *not in the labor force*. This group includes those engaged in own-home housework; in school; unable to work because of long-term illness, retirement, or age; seasonal workers for whom the reference week fell in an "off" season (if not qualifying as unemployed by looking for a job); persons who became discouraged and gave up the search for work; and the voluntarily idle. Also included are those doing only incidental work (less than 15 hours) in a family-operated business during the reference week.

The civilian *labor force participation rate* represents the percentage of the civilian noninstitutional population (age 16 years and over) that is in the civilian labor force.

The *employment-population ratio* represents the percentage of the civilian noninstitutional population (age 16 years and over) that is employed. This is traditionally called a "ratio," although it is traditionally expressed as a percent and therefore would be more appropriately called a "rate," as is the case with the labor force participation rate.

Employment is shown by *class of worker*, including a breakdown of total employment into *agricultural* and *nonagricultural* industries. Employment in *nonagricultural industries* includes *wage and salary workers*, the *self-employed*, and *unpaid family workers*.

Wage and salary workers receive wages, salaries, commissions, tips, and/or pay-in-kind. This category includes owners of self-owned incorporated businesses.

Self-employed workers are those who work for profit or for fees in their own business, profession, trade, or farm. This category includes only the unincorporated; those whose businesses are incorporated are considered wage and salary workers since they are paid employees of a corporation, even if they are the corporation's president and sole employee.

Wage and salary employment comprises *government* and *private industry* wage and salary workers. Domestic workers and other employees of *private households*, who are not included in the payroll employment series, are shown separately from *all other private industries*. The series for *government* and *other private industries* wage and salary workers are the closest in scope to similar categories in the payroll employment series.

Multiple jobholders are employed persons who, during the reference week, either had two or more jobs as a wage and salary worker, were self-employed and also held a wage and salary job, or worked as an unpaid family worker and also held a wage and salary job. Excluded are self-employed persons with multiple businesses and persons with multiple jobs as unpaid family workers. Multiple jobholders are counted as being in the job at which they worked the greatest number of hours during the reference week.

Employed and at work part time excludes employed persons who were absent from their jobs during the entire reference week for reasons such as vacation, illness, or industrial dispute.

At work part time for economic reasons ("involuntary" part time) refers to individuals who worked 1 to 34 hours during the reference week because of slack work, unfavorable business conditions, an inability to find full-time work, or seasonal declines in demand. To be included in this category, workers must also indicate that they want and are available for full-time work.

At work part time for noneconomic reasons ("voluntary" part time) refers to persons who usually work part time and were at work for 1 to 34 hours during the reference week for reasons such as illness, other medical limitations, family obligations, education, retirement, Social Security limits on earnings, or working in an industry where the workweek is less than 35 hours. It also includes respondents who gave an economic reason but were not available for, or did not want, full-time work. At work part time for noneconomic reasons excludes persons who usually work full time, but who worked only 1 to 34 hours during the reference week for reasons such as holidays, illnesses, and bad weather.

The *long-term unemployed* are persons currently unemployed (searching or on layoff) who have been unemployed for 15 consecutive weeks or longer. If a person ceases to look for work for two weeks or more, or becomes temporarily employed, the continuity of long-term unemployment is broken. If he or she starts searching for work or is laid off again, the monthly CPS will record the length of his or her unemployment from the time the search recommenced or since the latest layoff.

The civilian *unemployment rate* is the number of unemployed as a percentage of the civilian labor force. The unemployment rates for groups within the civilian population (such as males age 20 years and over) are the number of unemployed in a group as a percent of that group's labor force.

Unemployment rates by reason provides a breakdown of the total unemployment rate. Each unemployed person is classified into one of four groups.

Job losers and persons who completed temporary jobs includes persons on temporary layoff, permanent job losers, and persons who completed temporary jobs and began looking for work after those jobs ended. These three categories are shown separately without seasonal adjustment in the BLS's "Employment Situation" news release and on its Web site. They are combined, under the title shown here, for the purpose of seasonal adjustment. This is the category of unemployment that responds most strongly to the business cycle.

Job leavers terminated their employment voluntarily and immediately began looking for work.

Reentrants are persons who previously worked, but were out of the labor force prior to beginning their current job search.

New entrants are persons searching for a first job who have never worked.

Each of these categories is expressed as a proportion of the entire civilian labor force, so that the sum of the four rates equals the unemployment rate for all civilian workers (except for possible discrepancies due to rounding or separate seasonal adjustment).

Median and average weeks unemployed are summary measures of the length of time that persons classified as unemployed have been looking for work. For persons on layoff, the duration represents the number of full weeks of the layoff. The *average (mean)* number of weeks is computed by aggregating all the weeks of unemployment experienced by all unemployed persons during their current spell of unemployment and dividing by the number of unemployed. The *median* number of weeks unemployed is the number of weeks of unemployment experienced by the person at the midpoint of the distribution of all unemployed persons, as ranked by duration of unemployment.

Alternative measures of labor underutilization are calculated by BLS and published in the monthly Employment Situation release. They measure alternative concepts of unused working capacity, and are numbered "U-1" through "U-6" in order of increasing breadth of the definition of underutilization.

"U-1" is persons unemployed 15 weeks or longer, as a percent of the civilian labor force. It is not shown in *Business Statistics*.

"U-2" is job losers and persons who completed temporary jobs, as a percent of the civilian labor force; it is shown in *Business Statistics* in the second column of Table 10-5.

"U-3" is the official rate, described above and shown in the first columns of Tables 10-4 and 10-5.

"U-4" through "U-6" are shown in the last three columns of Table 10-5. They are based on additional labor force status questions, now included in the CPS survey, that were introduced beginning in 1994. U-4 and U-5 are increasingly broader rates of unemployment, while U-6 can be described as an "unemployment and underemployment rate."

"U-4" adds discouraged workers to unemployment and the labor force. Discouraged workers are persons not in the officially defined labor force who have given a job-market-related reason for not looking currently for a job—for example, they have not looked for a job because they believed that no jobs were available.

"U-5" adds both discouraged workers and all other "marginally attached" workers to unemployment and the labor force. "Marginally attached" workers are all persons who currently are neither working nor looking for work but indicate that they want and are available for a job and have looked for work some time in the recent past.

"U-6" adds persons employed part time for economic reasons, as shown in Table 10-3, to the number of persons counted as unemployed in "U-5", with the same labor force definition as in "U-5." Recently this statistic, measuring combined unemployment and underemployment, has been cited in press reports on the employment situation.

For more information, see "BLS introduced new range of alternative unemployment measures" in the October 1995 issue of the *Monthly Labor Review*.

Notes on the data

The CPS data are collected by trained interviewers from about 60,000 sample households selected to represent the U.S. civilian noninstitutional population. Sample size was about 60,000 households from mid-1989 to mid-1995, but was reduced for budgetary reasons in two stages to about 50,000 households, beginning in January 1996. This sample size was maintained from 1996 through 2000. The sample size was increased back to 60,000 households, beginning with the data for July 2001, as part of a plan to meet the requirements of the State Children's Health Insurance Program legislation. The CPS provides data for other data series in addition to the BLS employment status data, such as household income and poverty (see Chapter 3) and health insurance.

The employment status data are based on the activity or status reported for the calendar week, Sunday through Saturday, that includes the 12th day of the month (the reference week). Households are interviewed in the week following the reference week. Sample households are phased in and out of the sample on a rotating basis. Consequently, three-fourths of the sample is the same for any two consecutive months. One-half of the sample is the same as the sample in the same month a year earlier.

Data relating to 1994 and subsequent years are not strictly comparable with data for 1993 and earlier years because of a major redesign of the survey questionnaire and collection methodology. The redesign includes new and revised questions for the classification of individuals as employed or unemployed, the collection of new data on multiple job-holding, a change in the definition of discouraged workers, and the implementation of a more completely automated data collection.

The 1994 redesign of the CPS was the most extensive since 1967. However, there are many other significant periods of year-to-year noncomparability in the labor force data. These typically result from the introduction of new decennial census data into the CPS estimation procedures, expansions of the sample, or other improvements made to increase the reliability of the estimates. Each change introduces a new discontinuity, usually between December of the previous year and January of the newly altered year. The discontinuities are usually minor or negligible with respect to figures expressed as nationwide percentages (such as the unemployment rate or the labor force participation rate), but can be significant with respect to levels (such as labor force and employment in thousands of persons). A list of the dates of the major discontinuities follows, with BLS estimates of their quantitative impact on the national totals. (There are likely to be larger impacts on population subgroups.) The discontinuities occur in January unless otherwise indicated. Note that some of the changes caused adjustments that were carried back to an earlier year.

- 1953: 1950 census data introduced. Labor force and employment were raised by about 350,000.
- 1960: Alaska and Hawaii included. The labor force was increased by about 300,000, mainly in nonagricultural employment.
- 1962: 1960 census data introduced. Labor force and employment were reduced by about 200,000.
- 1972: 1970 census data introduced. Labor force and employment were raised by about 300,000.
- March 1973: Further 1970 census data were introduced, reducing White labor force and employment by about 150,000 and raising Black and other labor force and employment by approximately 210,000.
- July 1975: Adjustment for Vietnamese refugee inflow, raising total and Black and other population by 76,000.
- 1978: Sample expansion and revised estimation procedures increased labor force and employment by about 250,000.
- 1982: Change in estimation procedures introduced. To avoid major breaks, many series were reestimated back to

1970. This did not smooth the breaks occurring between 1972 and 1979.
- 1986, with revisions carried back to 1980: Adjustment for better estimates of immigration, raising labor force by nearly 400,000 and employment by 350,000, mainly among Hispanics.
- 1994: 1990 census data introduced and carried back to 1990, when employment was increased by about 880,000 and the unemployment rate was raised by about 0.1 percentage point.
- 1997: New estimates of immigration and emigration, raising labor force and employment by about 300,000, again mainly among Hispanics.
- 1998: New population estimates and estimation procedures, reducing labor force and employment by around 250,000.
- 1999: New information on immigration, raising labor force and employment by around 60,000, but lowering Hispanic employment by about 200,000.
- 2000: Census 2000 data introduced, using the 2002 NAICS and the 2000 Standard Occupational Classification System. The labor force was increased by about 1.6 million in January 2000, growing to around 2.5 million by December 2002.
- 2003: Further population estimates introduced (based on an annual population update and therefore not carried back to 2000), raising the labor force by 614,000.
- 2004: Population controls updated to reflect revised migration estimates, reducing labor force and employment by around 400,000, mostly among Hispanics.
- 2005: Updated migration and vital statistics data decreased labor force and employment by around 45,000.
- 2006: Updated migration and vital statistics data decreased labor force and employment by about 125,000.
- 2007: Updated migration and vital statistics data increased labor force and employment by about 150,000.
- 2008: Updated migration and vital statistics data decreased labor force by 637,000 and employment by 598,000.
- 2009: Updated migration adjustments, new vital statistics data, and methodological changes decreased labor force by 449,000 and employment by 407,000.

For further information on these changes, see the BLS publications *Employment and Earnings* for February of each year. The most recent information is posted on <http://www.bls.gov/cps> under "Publications and Other Documentation."

The monthly labor force, employment, and unemployment data are seasonally adjusted by the X-12-ARIMA method. All seasonally adjusted civilian labor force and unemployment rate statistics, as well as major employment and unemployment estimates, are computed by aggregating independently adjusted series. For example, the seasonally adjusted level of total unemployment is the sum of the seasonally adjusted levels of unemployment for the four age/sex groups (men and women age 16 to 19 years, and men and women age 20 years and over). Seasonally adjusted employment is the sum of the seasonally adjusted levels of employment for the same four groups. The seasonally adjusted civilian labor force is the sum of all eight components. Finally, the seasonally adjusted civilian worker unemployment rate is calculated by taking total seasonally adjusted unemployment as a percent of the total seasonally adjusted civilian labor force. Seasonal adjustment factors are revised at the end of each year to reflect recent experience. The revisions also affect the preceding four years. An article describing the seasonal adjustment methodology for the household survey data and revised data for January 2008–November 2008 is available at http://www.bls.gov/cps/cpsrs2009.pdf.

Breakdowns other than the basic age/sex classification described above—such as the employment data by class of worker in Table 10-2—will not necessarily add to totals because of independent seasonal adjustment.

Data availability

Data for each month are usually released on the first Friday of the following month in the "Employment Situation" press release, which also includes data from the establishment survey (Tables 10-7 through 10-12 and Chapter 16). The press release and data are available on the BLS Web site at <http://www.bls.gov>. Data are subsequently published in the BLS monthly periodical *Employment and Earnings*, which contains detailed explanatory notes. The last paper issue of *Employment and Earnings* was for April 2007; subsequent issues are available on the BLS Web site. Selected data are published each month in the *Monthly Labor Review*, also available online at the BLS Web site, which also features frequent articles analyzing developments in the labor force, employment, and unemployment.

Monthly and annual data are available beginning with 1948. Historical unadjusted data are published in *Labor Force Statistics Derived from the Current Population Survey* (BLS Bulletin 2307). Historical seasonally adjusted data are available from BLS upon request. Complete historical data are available on the BLS Web site at <http://www.bls.gov/cps>.

Seasonal adjustment factors are revised each year for the five previous years, with the release of December data in early January. New population controls are introduced with the release of January data in early February.

References

Comprehensive descriptive material can be found at <http://www.bls.gov/cps> under the "Publications and Other Documentation" section. Historical background on the CPS, as well as a description of the 1994 redesign, can be found in three articles from the September 1993 edition of *Monthly Labor Review*: "Why Is It Necessary to Change?"; "Redesigning the Questionnaire"; and "Evaluating Changes in the Estimates." The redesign is also described in the February 1994 issue of *Employment and Earnings*. See also Chapter 1, "Labor Force Data Derived from the Current Population Survey," *BLS Handbook of Methods*, Bulletin 2490 (April 1997).

TABLE 20-3A
LABOR FORCE AND EMPLOYMENT ESTIMATES SMOOTHED FOR POPULATION ADJUSTMENTS

SOURCE: U.S. DEPARTMENT OF LABOR, BUREAU OF LABOR STATISTICS

This table presents seasonally adjusted monthly estimates of total civilian labor force and total civilian employment in which discontinuities caused by the introduction of new population controls in the official series—as described above—have been smoothed. They are taken from "Labor Force and Employment Estimates Smoothed for Population Adjustments, 1990–2008," posted on February 6, 2009 <http://www.bls.gov/cps/cpspopsm.pdf>. The method of smoothing is described in Marisa L. Di Natale, "Creating Comparability in CPS Employment Series," on the BLS Web site at <http://www.bls.gov/cps/cpscomp.pdf>. BLS notes that these series do not match the official estimates in BLS publications, which are also the data shown in all other tables in this volume.

TABLE 10-6
INSURED UNEMPLOYMENT

SOURCE: U.S. DEPARTMENT OF LABOR, EMPLOYMENT AND TRAINING ADMINISTRATION

Definitions

State programs of unemployment insurance cover operations of regular programs under state unemployment insurance laws. In 1976, the law was amended to extend coverage to include virtually all state and local government employees, as well as many agricultural and domestic workers. (This took effect on January 1, 1978.) Benefits under state programs are financed by taxes levied by the states on employers.

Federal programs are those directly financed by the federal government. They include unemployment benefits for *federal employees* (Unemployment Compensation for Federal Employees, or UCFE), *newly discharged veterans* (Unemployment Compensation for Ex-Service Members, or UCX), *railroad retirement,* and *extended benefits,* which are sometimes enacted by Congress in times of widespread or protracted unemployment.

UCX pays benefits, based on service, to veterans who were on active duty and honorably separated. In the case of both UCFE and UCX, state laws determine the benefit amounts, number of weeks benefits can be paid, and other eligibility conditions.

An *initial claim* is the first claim in a benefit year filed by a worker after losing his or her job, or the first claim filed at the beginning of a subsequent period of unemployment in the same benefit year. The initial claim establishes the starting date for any insured unemployment that may result if the claimant is unemployed for one week or longer. Transitional claims (filed by claimants as they start a new benefit year in a continuing spell of unemployment) are excluded; therefore, these data more closely represent instances of new unemployment and are widely followed as a leading indicator of job market conditions.

Insured unemployment and *persons claiming benefits* both describe the average number of persons receiving benefits in the indicated month or year.

The *insured unemployment rate* for state programs is the level of insured unemployment as a percentage of employment covered by state programs.

Monthly averages in this book are averages, calculated by the editor, of the weekly data published by the Employment and Training Administration. Annual data are averages of the monthly data.

Data availability

Data are published in weekly press releases from the Employment and Training Administration. These releases are available on their Web site at <http://www.doleta.gov> under "Labor Market Data." Historical data on weekly claims are available at the Department of Labor's Information Technology Support Center at <http://www.itsc.state .md.us>.

TABLES 10-7, 10-8, 16-1, 16-2, AND 20-4 NONFARM PAYROLL EMPLOYMENT

SOURCE: U.S. DEPARTMENT OF LABOR, BUREAU OF LABOR STATISTICS (BLS)

These nonfarm employment data, as well as the hours and earnings data in Tables 10-9 through 10-12, 16-3 through 16-7, and 20-4, are compiled from payroll records. Information is reported monthly on a voluntary basis to BLS and its cooperating state agencies by a large sample of establishments, representing all industries except farming. These data, formally known as the Current Employment Statistics (CES) survey, are often referred to as the "establishment data" or the "payroll data." They are also known as the BLS-790 survey.

The survey, originally based on a stratified quota sample, has been replaced on a phased-in basis by a stratified probability sample. The new sampling procedure went into effect for wholesale trade in June 2000; for mining, construction, and manufacturing in June 2001; and for retail trade, transportation and public utilities, and finance, insurance, and real estate in June 2002. The phase-in was completed in June 2003, upon its extension to the service industries. The phase-in schedule was slightly different for the state and area series.

The sample has always been very large. Currently, it includes approximately 160,000 businesses and government agencies covering about 390,000 individual worksites, which account for about one-third of total benchmark employment of payroll workers. The sample is drawn from a sampling frame of over 8 million unemployment insurance tax accounts.

With the release of January 2008 data on February 1, 2008, the CES National Nonfarm Payroll series was updated to the 2007 North American Industry Classification System (NAICS) from the 2002 NAICS basis. For further details on the 2007 NAICS update, visit the CES NAICS web page. The previous revision to CES industry classification was the June 2003 replacement of the 1987 Standard Industrial Classification (SIC) with 2002 NAICS. Information on the SIC to NAICS conversion can be found at CES NAICS conversion web page.

BLS has reconstructed historical time series to conform with NAICS, to ensure that all published series have a NAICS-based history extending back to at least January 1990. NAICS-based history extends back to January 1939 for total nonfarm and other high-level aggregates. For more detailed series, the starting date for NAICS data varies depending on the extent of the definitional changes between the old Standard Industrial Classification (SIC) and NAICS.

Definitions

An *establishment* is an economic unit, such as a factory, store, or professional office, that produces goods or services at a single location and is engaged in one type of economic activity.

Employment comprises all persons who received pay (including holiday and sick pay) for any part of the payroll period that includes the 12th day of the month. Included are all full-time and part-time workers in nonfarm establishments, including salaried officers of corporations. Persons holding more than one job are counted in each establishment that reports them. Not covered are proprietors, the self-employed, unpaid volunteer and family workers, farm workers, domestic workers in households, and military personnel. Employees of the Central Intelligence Agency, the Defense Intelligence Agency, the National Geospatial-Intelligence Agency, and the National Security Agency are not included.

Persons on an establishment payroll who are on paid sick leave (when pay is received directly from the employer), on paid holiday or vacation, or who work during a portion of the pay period despite being unemployed or on strike during the rest of the period, are counted as employed. Not counted as employed are persons who are laid off, on leave without pay, on strike for the entire period, or hired but not paid during the period.

Intermittent workers are counted if they performed any service during the month. BLS considers regular full-time teachers (private and government) to be employed during the summer vacation period, regardless of whether they are specifically paid during those months.

The *government* division includes federal, state, and local activities such as legislative, executive, and judicial functions, as well as the U.S. Postal Service and all government-owned and government-operated business enterprises, establishments, and institutions (arsenals, navy yards, hospitals, state-owned utilities, etc.), and government force account construction. However, as indicated earlier, members of the armed forces and employees of certain national-security-related agencies are not included.

The monthly *diffusion index of employment change*, currently based on 271 private nonfarm NAICS industries, represents the percentage of those industries in which the seasonally adjusted level of employment in that month was higher than six months earlier, plus one-half of the percentage of industries with unchanged employment. Therefore, the diffusion index reported for September represents the change from March to September. *Business Statistics* uses the September value to represent the year as a whole, since it spans the year's midpoint. Diffusion indexes measure the dispersion of economic gains and losses, with values below 50 percent associated with recessions. The current NAICS-based series begins with January 1991. For October 1976 through December 1990, an earlier series is available based on 347 SIC industries (there are more industries using the older classification system because in SIC manufacturing industries were represented in greater detail). September values from this series are used to represent the years 1977 through 1990.

Production or nonsupervisory workers include all production and related workers in mining and manufacturing; construction workers in construction; and nonsupervisory workers in transportation, communication, electric, gas, and sanitary services; wholesale and retail trade; finance, insurance, and real estate; and services. These groups account for about four-fifths of the total employment on private nonagricultural payrolls.

Production and related workers include working supervisors and all nonsupervisory workers (including group leaders and trainees) engaged in fabricating, processing, assembling, inspecting, receiving, storing, handling, packing, warehousing, shipping, trucking, hauling, maintenance, repair, janitorial, guard services, product development, auxiliary production for plant's own use (such as a power plant), record keeping, and other services closely associated with these production operations.

Construction workers include the following employees in the construction division of the NAICS: working supervisors, qualified craft workers, mechanics, apprentices, laborers, and the like, who are engaged in new work, alterations, demolition, repair, maintenance, and other tasks, whether working at the site of construction or working in shops or yards at jobs (such as precutting and preassembling) ordinarily performed by members of the construction trades.

Nonsupervisory employees include employees (not above the working supervisory level) such as office and clerical workers, repairers, salespersons, operators, drivers, physicians, lawyers, accountants, nurses, social workers, research aides, teachers, drafters, photographers, beauticians, musicians, restaurant workers, custodial workers, attendants, line installers and repairers, laborers, janitors, guards, and other employees at similar occupational levels whose services are closely associated with those of the employees listed.

Notes on the data

Benchmark adjustments. The establishment survey data are adjusted annually to comprehensive counts of employment, called "benchmarks." Benchmark information on employment by industry is compiled by state agencies from reports of establishments covered under state unemployment insurance laws; these form an annual compilation of administrative data known as the ES-202. These tabulations cover about 97 percent of all employees on nonfarm payrolls. Benchmark data for the residual are obtained from alternate sources, primarily from Railroad Retirement Board records and the Census Bureau's *County Business Patterns*. The latest benchmark adjustment, which is incorporated into the data in this volume, reduced the not seasonally adjusted employment level in March 2008 by 89,000 jobs — less than 0.1 percent.

The estimates for the benchmark month are compared with new benchmark levels for each industry. If revisions are necessary, the monthly series of estimates between benchmark periods are adjusted by graduated amounts between the new benchmark and the preceding one ("wedged back"), and the new benchmark level for each industry is then carried forward month by month based on the sample.

More specifically, the month-to-month changes for each estimation cell are based on changes in a matched sample for that cell, plus an estimate of net business births and deaths. The matched sample for each pair of months consists of establishments that have reported data for both months (which automatically excludes establishments that have gone out of business by the second month). Since new businesses are not immediately incorporated into the sample, a model-based estimate of net business births and deaths in that estimating cell is added. The model-based estimate is based on past benchmark revisions.

Not-seasonally-adjusted data for all months since the last benchmark to which the series has been adjusted are subject to revision.

Beginning in 1959, the data include Alaska and Hawaii. This inclusion resulted in an increase of 212,000 (0.4 percent) in total nonfarm employment for the March 1959 benchmark month.

Seasonal adjustment. The seasonal movements that recur periodically—such as warm and cold weather, holidays, and vacations—are generally the largest single component of month-to-month changes in employment. After adjusting the data to remove such seasonal variation, the basic trends are more evident. BLS uses X-12-ARIMA software to produce the seasonal factors and perform concurrent seasonal adjustment, using the most recent 10 years of data. New factors are developed each month adding the most current data.

For most series, a special procedure called REGARIMA (regression with autocorrelated errors) is used before calculating the seasonal factors; this adjusts for the length of the interval (which can be either four or five weeks) between the survey weeks. REGARIMA has also been used to isolate extreme weather effects that distorted the measurement of seasonal patterns in the construction industry, and to identify variations in local government employment due to the presence or absence of election poll workers.

Seasonal adjustment factors are directly applied to the component levels. Seasonally adjusted totals for employment series are then obtained by aggregating the seasonally adjusted components directly, while hours and earnings series represent weighted averages of the seasonally adjusted component series. Seasonally adjusted data are not published for a small number of series characterized by small seasonal components relative to their trend and/or irregular components. However, these series are used in aggregating to broader seasonally adjusted levels.

Revisions of the seasonally adjusted data, usually for the most recent five-year period, are made once a year coincident with the benchmark revisions. This means that these revisions typically extend back farther than the benchmark revisions.

Data availability

Employment data by industry division are available beginning with 1919. Data for each month usually are released on the first Friday of the following month in a press release that also contains data from the household survey (Tables 10-1 through 10-5). Data are subsequently published in the BLS monthly periodical *Employment and Earnings*, which features detailed explanatory notes. Selected data are published each month in the *Monthly Labor Review*, which frequently contains articles analyzing developments in the labor force, employment, and unemployment. *Employment and Earnings*, the *Monthly Labor Review*, press releases, and complete historical data are available on the BLS Web site at <http://www.bls.gov>.

Benchmark revisions and revised seasonally adjusted data for recent years are made each year with the release of January data in early February. Before 2004, the benchmark revisions were not made until June; the acceleration is due to earlier availability of the benchmark UI (ES-202) data.

References

References can be found at <http://www.bls.gov/ces> under the headings "Special Notices," "Benchmark Information," and "Technical Notes." The extensive changes incorporated in June 2003 are described in "Recent Changes in the

National Current Employment Statistics Survey," the *Monthly Labor Review*, June 2003; and in the "Explanatory Notes" in any subsequent issue of *Employment and Earnings*. The latest benchmark revision is discussed in an article available on the BLS Web site. See also Chapter 2, "Employment, Hours, and Earnings from the Establishment Survey," *BLS Handbook of Methods*, Bulletin 2490 (April 1997).

**TABLES 10-9, 10-10, 16-3, 16-6, AND 20-4
AVERAGE HOURS PER WEEK; AGGREGATE EMPLOYEE HOURS**

SOURCE: U.S. DEPARTMENT OF LABOR, BUREAU OF LABOR STATISTICS (BLS)

See the notes and definitions to Tables 10-7 and 10-8 for an overall description of the "establishment" or "payroll" survey that is the source of hours data.

BLS PLANS NEW DATA ON ALL-EMPLOYEE HOURS AND EARNINGS

The Current Employment Statistics (CES) program began work in 2005 to measure the average hourly earnings and average weekly hours of all nonfarm private-sector employees. Additionally, CES is adding average overtime hours in manufacturing. Historically, the CES program has published average hours and earnings series for production workers in the goods-producing industries and non-supervisory workers in the service-providing industries, accounting for about 80 percent of total private nonfarm employment.

The new hours and earnings series are more comprehensive in coverage, thereby providing improved information for analyzing economic trends and for constructing other major economic indicators, including nonfarm productivity and personal income.

The new series are now being released as experimental estimates on the same date as the Employment Situation news release (typically the first Friday of the month). By the end of 2009, BLS should have sufficient historical data to seasonally adjust the all employee payroll and hours series and is planning to publish them as official CES data in the Employment Situation news release and other BLS publications beginning in February 2010.

Currently, and contrary to plans announced two years earlier, BLS plans to continue issuing the hours and earnings data for production and nonsupervisory workers, as presented in this volume and described below, as well as the new all-employee data.

For further information and the latest experimental estimates, see <http://www.bls.gov/ces/cesaepp.htm>.

Definitions

Average weekly hours represents the average hours paid per production or nonsupervisory worker during the pay period that includes the 12th of the month. Included are hours paid for holidays and vacations, as well as those paid for sick leave when pay is received directly from the firm.

Average weekly hours are different from standard or scheduled hours. Factors such as unpaid absenteeism, labor turnover, part-time work, and work stoppages can cause average weekly hours to be lower than scheduled hours of work for an establishment.

Average weekly hours pertain to jobs, not to persons; thus, a person with half-time jobs in two different establishments is represented in this series as two jobs that have 20-hour workweeks, not as one person with a 40-hour workweek.

Overtime hours represent the portion of average weekly hours worked in excess of regular hours, for which overtime premiums were paid. Weekend and holiday hours are included only if overtime premiums were paid. Hours for which only shift differential, hazard, incentive, or other similar types of premiums were paid are excluded.

Production or nonsupervisory workers. See the notes and definitions to Tables 10-7 and 10-8.

Aggregate hours provide a partial measure of changes over time in labor input to the industry, in index-number form. Data pertain to production or nonsupervisory workers in nonfarm establishments. The indexes are obtained by multiplying seasonally adjusted production or non-supervisory worker employment by seasonally adjusted average weekly hours, dividing the resulting series by their monthly averages for the 2002 period, and multiplying the results by 100, so that the annual average for 2002 equals 100. For total private, goods-producing, service-providing, and major industry divisions, the indexes are obtained by summing the seasonally adjusted aggregate weekly employee hours for the component industries, dividing by the monthly average for the 2002 period, and multiplying by 100.

Notes on the data

Benchmark adjustments. Independent benchmarks are not available for the hours and earnings series. At the time of the annual adjustment of the employment series to new benchmarks, the levels of hours and earnings may be affected by the revised employment weights (which are used in computing the industry averages for hours and earnings), as well as by the changes in seasonal adjustment factors introduced with the benchmark revision.

Method of computing industry series. "Average weekly hours" for individual industries are computed by dividing production or nonsupervisory worker hours (reported by establishments classified in each industry) by the number

of production or nonsupervisory workers reported for the same establishments. Estimates for divisions and major industry groups are averages (weighted by employment) of the figures for component industries.

Seasonal adjustment. Hours and earnings series are seasonally adjusted by applying factors directly to the corresponding unadjusted series. Data for some industries are not seasonally adjusted because the seasonal component is small relative to the trend-cycle and/or irregular components. Consequently, they cannot be separated with sufficient precision.

Special adjustments are made to average weekly hours to account for the presence or absence of religious holidays in the April survey reference period and the occasional occurrence of Labor Day in the September reference period. In addition, REGARIMA modeling is used prior to seasonal adjustment to correct for reporting and processing errors associated with the number of weekdays in a month (rather than to correct for the 4- and 5-week effect, which is less significant for hours than it is for employment). This is of particular importance for average weekly hours in the service-providing industries other than retail trade. For this reason, BLS advises that calculations of over-the-year changes (for example, the change for the current month from a year earlier) should use seasonally adjusted data, since the actual not-seasonally-adjusted monthly data may be distorted.

Data availability

See data availability for Tables 10-7 and 10-8.

References

See references for Tables 10-7 and 10-8.

TABLES 10-11, 10-12, 16-4, 16-5, AND 20-4 HOURLY AND WEEKLY EARNINGS

SOURCE: U.S. DEPARTMENT OF LABOR, BUREAU OF LABOR STATISTICS (BLS)

See the notes and definitions to Tables 10-7 and 10-8 for an overall description of the "establishment" or "payroll" survey that is the source of these earnings data.

> See the box on the previous page concerning BLS plans to publish hours and earnings for all employees beginning in 2010.

Definitions

Earnings are the payments that production or nonsupervisory workers receive during the survey period (before deductions for taxes and other items), including premium pay for overtime or late-shift work but excluding irregular bonuses and other special payments. After being previously excluded, tips were asked to be reported beginning in September 2005. This made little difference in most industries, and BLS asserts that many respondents had already been including tips. In two industries, full-service restaurants and cafeterias, there was a substantial difference, and the historical earnings data for those industries have been reconstructed to reflect the new higher level of earnings. These effects can be seen beginning with the data for 1974.

Production or nonsupervisory workers. See the notes and definitions to Tables 10-7 and 10-8.

Notes on the data

The hours and earnings series are based on reports of gross payroll and corresponding paid hours for full- and part-time production and related workers, construction workers, or nonsupervisory workers who received pay for any part of the pay period that included the 12th of the month.

Total payrolls are before deductions, such as for the employee share of old-age and unemployment insurance, group insurance, withholding taxes, bonds, and union dues. The payroll figures also include pay for overtime, holidays, vacations, and sick leave (paid directly by the employer for the period reported). Excluded from the payroll figures are fringe benefits (health and other types of insurance and contributions to retirement, paid by the employer, and the employer share of payroll taxes), bonuses (unless earned and paid regularly each pay period), other pay not earned in the pay period reported (retroactive pay), and the value of free rent, fuel, meals, or other payment-in-kind.

Average hourly earnings data reflect not only changes in basic hourly and incentive wage rates, but also such variable factors as premium pay for overtime and late-shift work and changes in output of workers paid on an incentive basis. Shifts in the volume of employment between relatively high-paid and low-paid work also affect the general average of hourly earnings.

Averages of hourly earnings should not be confused with wage rates, which represent the rates stipulated for a given unit of work or time, while earnings refer to the actual return to the worker for a stated period of time. The earnings series do not represent total labor cost to the employer because of the inclusion of tips and the exclusion of irregular bonuses, retroactive items, the cost of employer-provided benefits, payroll taxes paid by employers, and earnings for those employees not covered under the production-worker or nonsupervisory-worker definition.

Average weekly earnings are not the amounts available to workers for spending, since they do not reflect deductions, such as those for income taxes and Social Security taxes. It should also be noted that they represent earnings per job, not per worker (since a worker may have more than one job) and not per family (since a family may have more than

one worker). A person with two half-time jobs will be reflected as two earners with low weekly earnings rather than as one person with the total earnings from his or her two jobs.

Method of computing industry series. Average hourly earnings are obtained by dividing the reported total production or nonsupervisory worker payroll by the total production or nonsupervisory worker hours. Estimates for both hours and hourly earnings for nonfarm divisions and major industry groups are employment-weighted averages of the figures for component industries.

Average weekly earnings are computed by multiplying average hourly earnings by average weekly hours. In addition to the factors mentioned above, which exert varying influences upon average hourly earnings, average weekly earnings are affected by changes in the length of the workweek, part-time work, work stoppages, labor turnover, and absenteeism. Persistent long-term uptrends in the proportion of part-time workers in retail trade and many of the service industries have reduced average workweeks (as measured here), and have similarly affected the average weekly earnings series.

Benchmark adjustments. Independent benchmarks are not available for the hours and earnings series. At the time of the annual adjustment of the employment series to new benchmarks, the levels of hours and earnings may be affected by the revised employment weights (which are used in computing the industry averages for hours and earnings), as well as by the changes in seasonal adjustment factors that were also introduced with the benchmark revision.

Seasonal adjustment. Hours and earnings series are seasonally adjusted by applying factors directly to the corresponding unadjusted series; seasonally adjusted average weekly earnings are the product of seasonally adjusted hourly earnings and weekly hours.

REGARIMA modeling is used to correct for reporting and processing errors associated with variations in the number of weekdays in a month (rather than for the 4- and 5-week effect, which is less significant for earnings than for employment). This is of particular importance for average hourly earnings in wholesale trade, financial activities, professional and business services, and other services. For this reason, BLS advises that calculations of over-the-year changes, for example the change for the current month from a year earlier, should use seasonally adjusted data, since the actual not seasonally adjusted monthly data may be distorted.

Data availability

See data availability for Tables 10-7 and 10-8.

References

See references for Tables 10-7 and 10-8.

TABLE 10-13
MEDIAN USUAL WEEKLY EARNINGS OF FULL-TIME WAGE AND SALARY WORKERS

SOURCE: U.S. DEPARTMENT OF LABOR, BUREAU OF LABOR STATISTICS

These data are from the Current Population Survey, which was described in the notes to Tables 10-1 through 10-5. Because they are earnings per worker, not per job, and are limited to full-time workers, the data are not distorted by the increasing proportion of part-time workers, as the CES earnings data are.

Definitions

Full-time wage and salary workers are those who receive wages, salaries, commissions, tips, pay in kind, or piece rates, and usually work 35 hours or more per week at their sole or principal job. Both private-sector and public-sector employees are included. All self-employed persons are excluded (even those whose businesses are incorporated). The number of full-time wage and salary workers was about 103.5 million in the first quarter of 2006; these workers made up 73 percent of total civilian employment.

Usual weekly earnings are earnings before taxes and other deductions and include any overtime pay, commissions, or tips usually received. In the case of multiple jobholders they refer to the main job. The wording of the question was changed in January 1994 to better deal with persons who found it easier to report earnings on other than a weekly basis. Such reports are then converted to the weekly equivalent. According to BLS, "the term 'usual' is as perceived by the respondent. If the respondent asks for a definition of usual, interviewers are instructed to define the term as more than half the weeks worked during the past 4 or 5 months."

The *median* is the amount that divides a given earnings distribution into two equal groups, one having earnings above the median and the other having earnings below the median.

2000 dollars. For men 25 and older and women 25 and older, median usual weekly earnings are shown on both a current-dollar and a constant-dollar basis. The editor has converted the current-dollar figures to 2000 dollars using the CPI-U-RS, which is shown and described in Chapter 8. The CPI-U-RS was chosen because it is the deflator used by the Census Bureau to convert household income and earnings to constant dollars and by the Bureau of Labor Statistics to convert compensation per hour to constant dollars. It corrects historical values of the CPI to be consistent with current CPI methodology.

Race and ethnicity. See the notes to Tables 10-1 through 10-5 for the definitions of these categories.

Data availability

These data become available about 3 weeks after the end of each quarter in the "Usual Weekly Earnings of Wage and Salary Workers" press release, available on the BLS Web site at <http://www.bls.gov/cps>. Recent data are available at that location. Also available are greater detail by demographic and age groups, by occupation, by union status, and by education; distributional data, by deciles and quartiles; and earnings for part-time workers. Also available are earnings in 1982 dollars using the CPI-U. Historical data are available upon request from BLS by telephone at (202) 691-6378.

CHAPTER 11: ENERGY

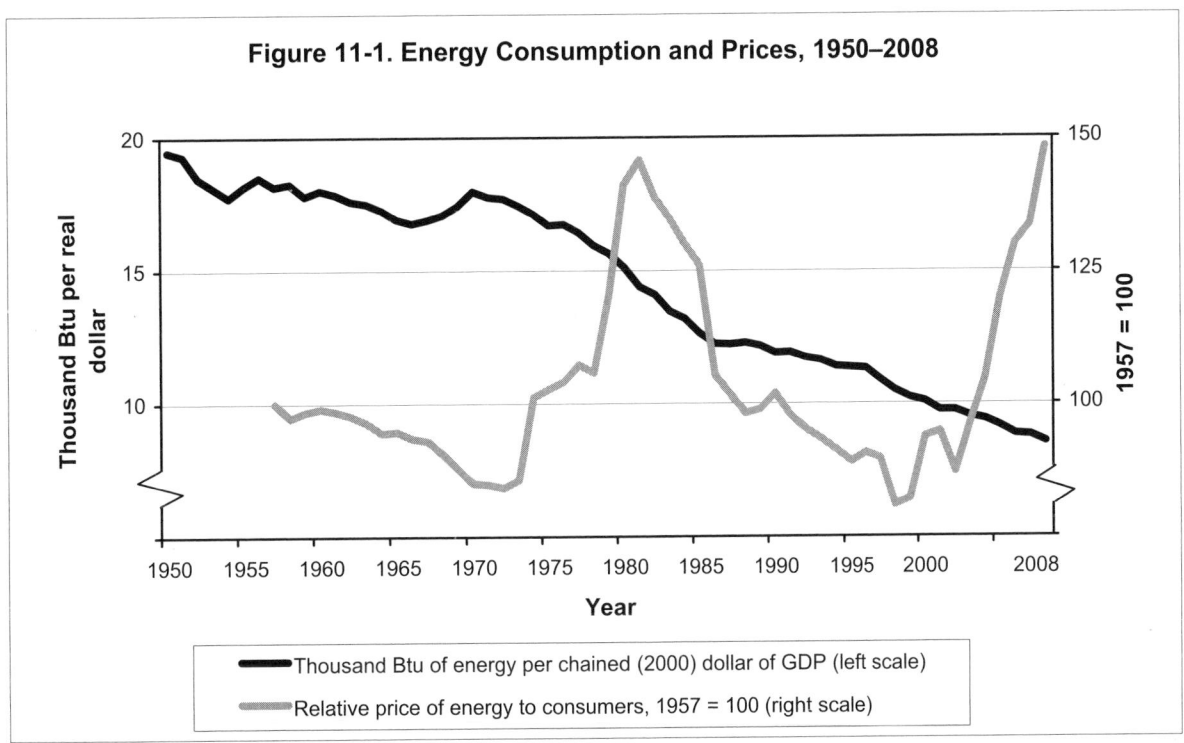

Figure 11-1. Energy Consumption and Prices, 1950–2008

Thousand Btu of energy per chained (2000) dollar of GDP (left scale)

Relative price of energy to consumers, 1957 = 100 (right scale)

- U.S. energy consumption has nearly tripled since 1950, but real gross domestic product (GDP) is more than six times what it was in that year. Consequently, there has been a downward trend in energy use per dollar of real GDP, which can also be described as an increase in the energy efficiency of national production. (Table 11-2 and Figure 11-1) This trend may seem surprising in light of increases in motor vehicle use, air conditioning, air travel, and other consumer uses of energy. Evidently, these increases are more than offset by factors such as the rising share of services and high-tech goods in GDP and the declining relative importance of energy-intensive materials production processes such as primary metals production.

- As Figure 11-1 also indicates, there have been dramatic ups and downs in relative energy prices—measured as the ratio of the CPI for energy to the total CPI—over the last half-century. (Tables 8-1 and 20-2) These swings appear to affect the rate of decline in the energy/GDP trend. Energy use per dollar of GDP declined 2.4 percent per year between 1973 and 1981 with the first sharp rise in energy prices; the decline in energy use in these years was much faster than the 0.5 percent per year trend from 1950 to 1973. Energy use per dollar declined more slowly, 1.8 percent per year from 1981 to 1998, when relative energy prices were falling. With the latest energy price increase, energy use declined by 2.0 percent per year between 1998 and 2008. (Table 11-2)

- Between 1973 and 2008, the greatest savings in energy relative to GDP were achieved in industrial use—which actually fell slightly, despite increases of 168 percent in real GDP and 121 percent in industrial production (Tables 1-2 and 2-1). More modest economies were achieved in the use of energy for residential and commercial purposes, which rose 65 percent, and in transportation use, which rose 51 percent. (Table 11-1)

- Consumption of petroleum and natural gas per dollar of real GDP rose between 1950 and the early 1970s, but has declined 61 percent since then. Use of other forms of energy per real dollar leveled off during the 1970s and 1980s but then resumed its decline, and is down 62 percent over the entire postwar period. (Table 11-2)

- Net imports supplied 26 percent of total U.S. energy consumption in 2006, compared with 17 percent in 1973 and 1 percent in 1955. In 2008, nuclear electric power supplied 8½ percent of total consumption; hydroelectric about 2½ percent; and biomass (wood, waste, and ethanol) about 4 percent. (Table 11-1)

267

Table 11-1. Energy Supply and Consumption

(Quadrillion Btu.)

Year and month	Imports	Exports	Production, by source								Consumption, by end-use sector			
			Total[I]	Coal	Natural gas	Crude oil	Natural gas plant liquids	Nuclear electric power	Hydroelectric power	Biomass	Total	Residential and commercial	Industrial	Transportation
1955	2.790	2.286	40.148	12.370	9.345	14.410	1.240	0.000	1.360	1.424	40.208	11.185	19.472	9.551
1956	3.207	2.945	42.622	13.306	10.002	15.180	1.283	0.000	1.435	1.416	41.754	11.698	20.196	9.860
1957	3.529	3.439	42.983	13.061	10.605	15.178	1.289	0.000	1.516	1.334	41.787	11.686	20.205	9.897
1958	3.884	2.050	40.133	10.783	10.942	14.204	1.287	0.002	1.592	1.323	41.645	12.333	19.307	10.005
1959	4.076	1.534	41.949	10.778	11.952	14.933	1.383	0.002	1.548	1.353	43.466	12.800	20.316	10.349
1960	4.188	1.477	42.804	10.817	12.656	14.935	1.461	0.006	1.608	1.320	45.087	13.667	20.823	10.597
1961	4.437	1.377	43.280	10.447	13.105	15.206	1.549	0.020	1.656	1.295	45.739	14.032	20.937	10.770
1962	4.994	1.473	44.877	10.901	13.717	15.522	1.593	0.026	1.816	1.300	47.828	14.839	21.768	11.221
1963	5.087	1.835	47.174	11.849	14.513	15.966	1.709	0.038	1.771	1.323	49.646	15.261	22.730	11.655
1964	5.447	1.815	49.056	12.524	15.298	16.164	1.803	0.040	1.886	1.337	51.817	15.730	24.090	11.998
1965	5.892	1.829	50.676	13.055	15.775	16.521	1.883	0.043	2.059	1.335	54.017	16.509	25.075	12.434
1966	6.146	1.829	53.534	13.468	17.011	17.561	1.996	0.064	2.062	1.369	57.017	17.517	26.397	13.102
1967	6.159	2.115	56.379	13.825	17.943	18.651	2.177	0.088	2.347	1.340	58.908	18.541	26.616	13.752
1968	6.905	1.998	58.225	13.609	19.068	19.308	2.321	0.142	2.349	1.419	62.419	19.665	27.888	14.866
1969	7.676	2.126	60.541	13.863	20.446	19.556	2.420	0.154	2.648	1.440	65.621	21.000	29.114	15.506
1970	8.342	2.632	63.501	14.607	21.666	20.401	2.512	0.239	2.634	1.431	67.844	22.105	29.641	16.098
1971	9.535	2.151	62.723	13.186	22.280	20.033	2.544	0.413	2.824	1.432	69.289	22.959	29.601	16.729
1972	11.387	2.118	63.920	14.092	22.208	20.041	2.598	0.584	2.864	1.503	72.704	24.036	30.953	17.716
1973	14.613	2.033	63.585	13.992	22.187	19.493	2.569	0.910	2.861	1.529	75.708	24.437	32.653	18.612
1974	14.304	2.203	62.372	14.074	21.210	18.575	2.471	1.272	3.177	1.540	73.991	24.046	31.819	18.119
1975	14.032	2.323	61.357	14.989	19.640	17.729	2.374	1.900	3.155	1.499	71.999	24.308	29.447	18.244
1976	16.760	2.172	61.602	15.654	19.480	17.262	2.327	2.111	2.976	1.713	76.012	25.476	31.430	19.099
1977	19.948	2.052	62.052	15.755	19.565	17.454	2.327	2.702	2.333	1.838	78.000	25.866	32.307	19.820
1978	19.106	1.920	63.137	14.910	19.485	18.434	2.245	3.024	2.937	2.038	79.986	26.637	32.733	20.615
1979	19.460	2.855	65.948	17.540	20.076	18.104	2.286	2.776	2.931	2.152	80.903	26.469	33.962	20.471
1980	15.796	3.695	67.232	18.598	19.908	18.249	2.254	2.739	2.900	2.476	78.122	26.350	32.077	19.696
1981	13.719	4.307	67.014	18.377	19.699	18.146	2.307	3.008	2.758	2.597	76.168	25.897	30.756	19.513
1982	11.861	4.608	66.623	18.639	18.319	18.309	2.191	3.131	3.266	2.664	73.153	26.405	27.657	19.088
1983	11.752	3.693	64.181	17.247	16.593	18.392	2.184	3.203	3.527	2.906	73.039	26.380	27.481	19.175
1984	12.471	3.786	68.925	19.719	18.008	18.848	2.274	3.553	3.386	2.973	76.715	27.434	29.625	19.654
1985	11.781	4.196	67.801	19.325	16.980	18.992	2.241	4.076	2.970	3.018	76.493	27.532	28.877	20.087
1986	14.151	4.021	67.180	19.509	16.541	18.376	2.149	4.380	3.071	2.934	76.759	27.633	28.333	20.789
1987	15.398	3.812	67.662	20.141	17.136	17.675	2.215	4.754	2.635	2.877	79.175	28.265	29.444	21.469
1988	17.296	4.366	69.032	20.738	17.599	17.279	2.260	5.587	2.334	3.019	82.822	29.762	30.739	22.318
1989	18.766	4.661	69.479	21.360	17.847	16.117	2.158	5.602	2.837	3.162	84.946	31.061	31.398	22.479
1990	18.817	4.752	70.872	22.488	18.326	15.571	2.175	6.104	3.046	2.737	84.654	30.348	31.895	22.420
1991	18.335	5.141	70.534	21.636	18.229	15.701	2.306	6.422	3.016	2.784	84.609	31.003	31.487	22.118
1992	19.372	4.937	70.129	21.694	18.375	15.223	2.363	6.479	2.617	2.935	85.958	30.881	32.661	22.416
1993	21.273	4.258	68.497	20.336	18.584	14.494	2.408	6.410	2.892	2.912	87.605	32.125	32.721	22.770
1994	22.390	4.061	70.895	22.202	19.348	14.103	2.391	6.694	2.683	3.031	89.261	32.292	33.607	23.367
1995	22.260	4.511	71.320	22.130	19.082	13.887	2.442	7.075	3.205	3.103	91.174	33.276	34.047	23.849
1996	23.702	4.633	72.642	22.790	19.344	13.723	2.530	7.087	3.590	3.158	94.176	34.744	34.989	24.439
1997	25.215	4.514	72.635	23.310	19.394	13.658	2.495	6.597	3.640	3.112	94.766	34.720	35.288	24.752
1998	26.581	4.299	73.041	24.045	19.613	13.235	2.420	7.068	3.297	2.933	95.183	35.000	34.928	25.258
1999	27.252	3.715	71.907	23.295	19.341	12.451	2.528	7.610	3.268	2.969	96.817	36.004	34.855	25.951
2000	28.973	4.006	71.490	22.735	19.662	12.358	2.611	7.862	2.811	3.010	98.975	37.664	34.758	26.552
2001	30.157	3.771	71.892	23.547	20.166	12.282	2.547	8.033	2.242	2.629	96.326	37.247	32.806	26.279
2002	29.408	3.669	70.935	22.732	19.439	12.163	2.559	8.143	2.689	2.712	97.858	38.241	32.764	26.849
2003	31.061	4.054	70.264	22.094	19.661	12.026	2.346	7.959	2.825	2.815	98.209	38.559	32.650	27.002
2004	33.544	4.434	70.384	22.852	19.093	11.503	2.466	8.222	2.690	3.010	100.350	38.842	33.609	27.899
2005	34.711	4.562	69.646	23.185	18.574	10.963	2.334	8.160	2.703	3.140	100.500	39.593	32.545	28.361
2006	34.679	4.872	71.052	23.790	19.022	10.801	2.356	8.214	2.869	3.322	99.888	38.514	32.534	28.841
2007	34.703	5.482	71.535	23.501	19.643	10.721	2.409	8.458	2.455	3.578	101.580	39.964	32.537	29.075
2008	32.894	7.137	73.922	24.003	21.168	10.519	2.415	8.485	2.478	3.901	99.587	40.406	31.127	28.042
2007														
January	2.984	0.447	6.157	2.042	1.606	0.921	0.192	0.776	0.258	0.299	9.300	4.087	2.834	2.378
February	2.464	0.350	5.490	1.815	1.470	0.832	0.177	0.684	0.184	0.269	8.824	4.003	2.626	2.196
March	3.047	0.422	6.050	2.003	1.652	0.918	0.204	0.674	0.240	0.294	8.615	3.481	2.712	2.424
April	2.915	0.419	5.774	1.907	1.579	0.903	0.195	0.601	0.237	0.287	7.969	2.931	2.655	2.386
May	3.057	0.451	6.094	1.987	1.668	0.934	0.206	0.682	0.258	0.295	8.054	2.819	2.736	2.500
June	2.873	0.426	5.969	1.959	1.623	0.887	0.198	0.723	0.226	0.291	8.136	3.023	2.663	2.449
July	3.032	0.503	6.022	1.908	1.658	0.903	0.205	0.763	0.223	0.305	8.531	3.288	2.695	2.544
August	3.035	0.478	6.147	2.063	1.669	0.883	0.203	0.763	0.198	0.305	8.856	3.516	2.774	2.561
September	2.879	0.439	5.786	1.894	1.627	0.850	0.199	0.709	0.146	0.296	7.983	2.987	2.621	2.374
October	2.809	0.442	6.004	2.026	1.688	0.907	0.211	0.647	0.147	0.309	8.017	2.838	2.717	2.462
November	2.766	0.564	5.944	1.987	1.665	0.873	0.209	0.681	0.156	0.307	8.137	3.065	2.698	2.374
December	2.844	0.542	6.096	1.911	1.737	0.909	0.210	0.755	0.182	0.322	9.159	3.927	2.805	2.426
2008														
January	2.932	0.541	6.288	2.021	1.758	0.916	0.205	0.770	0.227	0.315	9.509	4.356	2.815	2.336
February	2.591	0.573	5.868	1.917	1.668	0.860	0.197	0.684	0.173	0.296	8.679	3.918	2.585	2.176
March	2.750	0.616	6.210	1.984	1.801	0.924	0.212	0.679	0.210	0.318	8.646	3.584	2.674	2.389
April	2.763	0.601	6.035	1.989	1.728	0.898	0.209	0.601	0.211	0.313	7.895	2.962	2.572	2.362
May	2.736	0.631	6.267	1.978	1.785	0.929	0.219	0.680	0.262	0.326	7.962	2.841	2.675	2.447
June	2.762	0.635	6.131	1.849	1.764	0.889	0.201	0.738	0.283	0.320	8.104	3.170	2.595	2.337
July	2.805	0.616	6.442	2.032	1.838	0.919	0.213	0.779	0.246	0.338	8.472	3.427	2.623	2.418
August	2.828	0.595	6.358	2.058	1.833	0.880	0.211	0.762	0.202	0.343	8.308	3.282	2.605	2.418
September	2.438	0.527	5.731	2.036	1.585	0.689	0.171	0.703	0.155	0.328	7.405	2.874	2.340	2.190
October	2.831	0.598	6.176	2.138	1.777	0.835	0.200	0.659	0.150	0.337	7.849	2.818	2.644	2.389
November	2.688	0.601	6.019	1.955	1.781	0.859	0.193	0.665	0.154	0.332	7.873	3.103	2.519	2.250
December	2.772	0.604	6.396	2.044	1.850	0.921	0.184	0.765	0.204	0.335	8.885	4.073	2.477	2.329

[I]Includes categories not shown separately: geothermal, solar thermal and photovoltaic, and wind.

Table 11-2. Energy Consumption Per Dollar of Real Gross Domestic Product

Year	Energy consumption (quadrillion Btu)			Gross domestic product (billions of chained [2000] dollars)	Energy consumption per real dollar of GDP (thousand Btu per chained [2000] dollar)		
	Total	Petroleum and natural gas	Other energy		Total	Petroleum and natural gas	Other energy
1950	34.616	19.284	15.332	1 777.3	19.48	10.85	8.63
1951	36.974	21.477	15.497	1 915.0	19.31	11.21	8.09
1952	36.748	22.505	14.243	1 988.3	18.48	11.32	7.16
1953	37.664	23.462	14.202	2 079.5	18.11	11.28	6.83
1954	36.639	24.169	12.470	2 065.4	17.74	11.70	6.04
1955	40.208	26.253	13.955	2 212.8	18.17	11.86	6.31
1956	41.754	27.551	14.203	2 255.8	18.51	12.21	6.30
1957	41.787	28.122	13.665	2 301.1	18.16	12.22	5.94
1958	41.645	29.190	12.455	2 279.2	18.27	12.81	5.46
1959	43.466	31.040	12.426	2 441.3	17.80	12.71	5.09
1960	45.087	32.305	12.782	2 501.8	18.02	12.91	5.11
1961	45.739	33.143	12.596	2 560.0	17.87	12.95	4.92
1962	47.828	34.780	13.048	2 715.2	17.61	12.81	4.81
1963	49.646	36.104	13.542	2 834.0	17.52	12.74	4.78
1964	51.817	37.589	14.228	2 998.6	17.28	12.54	4.74
1965	54.017	39.014	15.003	3 191.1	16.93	12.23	4.70
1966	57.017	41.396	15.621	3 399.1	16.77	12.18	4.60
1967	58.908	43.228	15.680	3 484.6	16.91	12.41	4.50
1968	62.419	46.189	16.230	3 652.7	17.09	12.65	4.44
1969	65.621	49.016	16.605	3 765.4	17.43	13.02	4.41
1970	67.844	51.315	16.529	3 771.9	17.99	13.60	4.38
1971	69.289	53.030	16.259	3 898.6	17.77	13.60	4.17
1972	72.704	55.645	17.059	4 105.0	17.71	13.56	4.16
1973	75.708	57.352	18.356	4 341.5	17.44	13.21	4.23
1974	73.991	55.187	18.804	4 319.6	17.13	12.78	4.35
1975	71.999	52.678	19.321	4 311.2	16.70	12.22	4.48
1976	76.012	55.520	20.492	4 540.9	16.74	12.23	4.51
1977	78.000	57.053	20.947	4 750.5	16.42	12.01	4.41
1978	79.986	57.966	22.021	5 015.0	15.95	11.56	4.39
1979	80.903	57.789	23.114	5 173.4	15.64	11.17	4.47
1980	78.122	54.438	23.684	5 161.7	15.13	10.55	4.59
1981	76.168	51.678	24.490	5 291.7	14.39	9.77	4.63
1982	73.153	48.588	24.566	5 189.3	14.10	9.36	4.73
1983	73.039	47.275	25.764	5 423.8	13.47	8.72	4.75
1984	76.715	49.445	27.271	5 813.6	13.20	8.51	4.69
1985	76.493	48.626	27.867	6 053.7	12.64	8.03	4.60
1986	76.759	48.787	27.971	6 263.6	12.25	7.79	4.47
1987	79.175	50.505	28.670	6 475.1	12.23	7.80	4.43
1988	82.822	52.670	30.151	6 742.7	12.28	7.81	4.47
1989	84.946	53.813	31.133	6 981.4	12.17	7.71	4.46
1990	84.654	53.156	31.498	7 112.5	11.90	7.47	4.43
1991	84.609	52.878	31.731	7 100.5	11.92	7.45	4.47
1992	85.958	54.240	31.718	7 336.6	11.72	7.39	4.32
1993	87.605	54.973	32.632	7 532.7	11.63	7.30	4.33
1994	89.261	56.290	32.972	7 835.5	11.39	7.18	4.21
1995	91.174	57.108	34.066	8 031.7	11.35	7.11	4.24
1996	94.176	58.758	35.418	8 328.9	11.31	7.05	4.25
1997	94.766	59.382	35.383	8 703.5	10.89	6.82	4.07
1998	95.183	59.647	35.536	9 066.9	10.50	6.58	3.92
1999	96.817	60.747	36.070	9 470.3	10.22	6.41	3.81
2000	98.975	62.089	36.887	9 817.0	10.08	6.32	3.76
2001	96.326	60.959	35.367	9 890.7	9.74	6.16	3.58
2002	97.858	61.785	36.073	10 048.8	9.74	6.15	3.59
2003	98.209	61.706	36.502	10 301.0	9.53	5.99	3.54
2004	100.350	63.226	37.125	10 675.8	9.40	5.92	3.48
2005	100.505	62.977	37.528	10 989.5	9.15	5.73	3.41
2006	99.888	62.182	37.706	11 294.8	8.84	5.51	3.34
2007	101.581	63.424	38.158	11 523.9	8.81	5.50	3.31
2008	99.587	61.008	38.579	11 652.0	8.55	5.24	3.31

NOTES AND DEFINITIONS

TABLES 11-1 AND 11-2
ENERGY SUPPLY AND CONSUMPTION

SOURCES: U.S. DEPARTMENT OF ENERGY, ENERGY INFORMATION ADMINISTRATION; U.S. DEPARTMENT OF COMMERCE, BUREAU OF ECONOMIC ANALYSIS

Definitions

The *British thermal unit (Btu)* is a measure used to combine data for different energy sources into a consistent aggregate. It is the amount of energy required to raise the temperature of 1 pound of water 1 degree Fahrenheit when the water is near a temperature of 39.2 degrees Fahrenheit. To illustrate one of the factors used to convert volumes to Btu, conventional motor gasoline has a heat content of 5.253 million Btu per barrel. For further information, see the Energy Information Administration's *Monthly Energy Review*, Appendix A.

Production: Crude oil includes lease condensates.

Hydroelectric power includes conventional electrical utility and industrial generation.

Biomass includes wood, waste, and alcohol fuels (ethanol blended into motor gasoline).

Energy production components not shown in this volume, which account for the difference between total production and the sum of the categories shown, include energy generated for distribution from geothermal, solar, and wind sources and an allowance for net hydroelectric energy losses related to pumped storage.

The sum of domestic energy *production* and net imports of energy (*imports* minus *exports*) does not exactly equal domestic energy *consumption*. The difference is attributed to inventory changes; losses and gains in conversion, transportation, and distribution; the addition of blending compounds; shipments of anthracite to U.S. armed forces in Europe; and adjustments to account for discrepancies between reporting systems.

Consumption by end-use sector is based on total, not net, consumption. Components may not add to totals because of different sector-specific conversion factors.

References and notes on the data

These data are published each month in Tables 1.1, 1.2, 1.7, and 2.1 in the *Monthly Energy Review*. Annual data before 1973 are published in the *Annual Energy Review*. These two publications are no longer published in printed form but are available on the EIA Web site at <http://www.eia.doe.gov/emeu/mer> along with all current and historical data. The real gross domestic product (GDP) data used to calculate energy consumption per dollar of real GDP are from the Bureau of Economic Analysis; see Table 1-2 and the applicable notes and definitions in this volume of *Business Statistics*.

CHAPTER 12: MONEY, INTEREST, ASSETS, LIABILITIES, AND ASSET PRICES

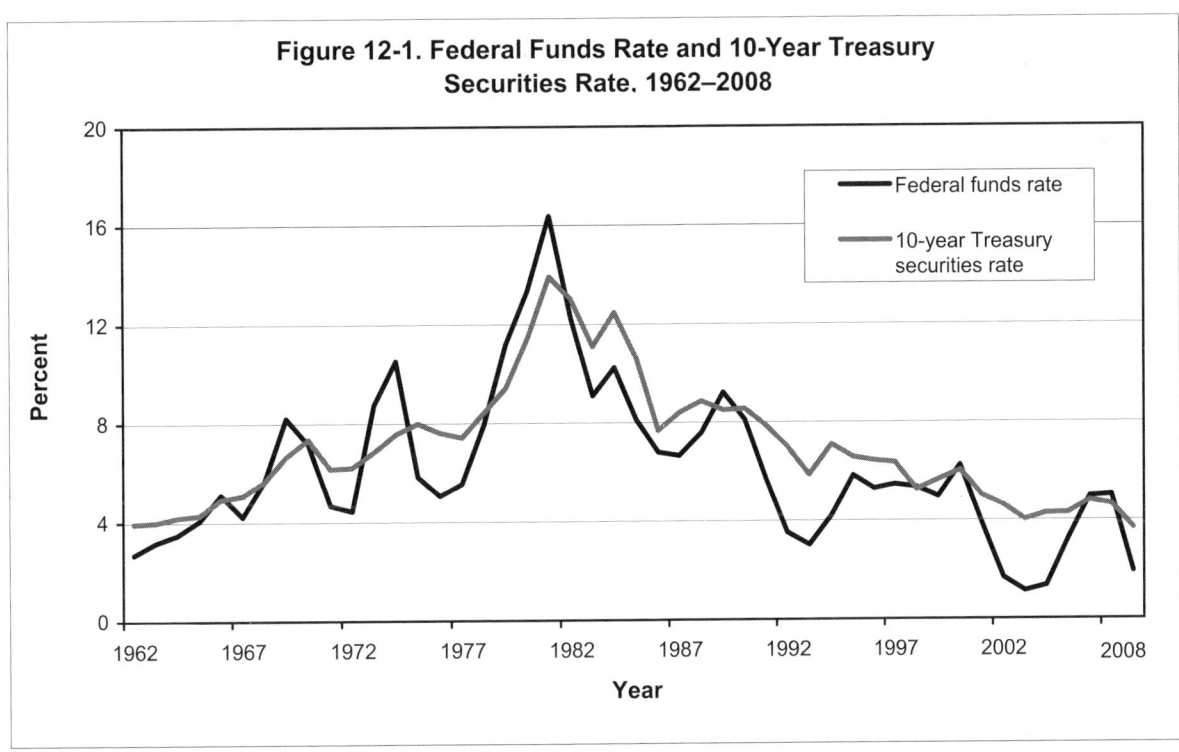

Figure 12-1. Federal Funds Rate and 10-Year Treasury Securities Rate. 1962–2008

- At times in recent years, the short-term interest rates established by Federal Reserve monetary policy have been lower than at any time since the Great Depression, World War II, and its aftermath. The federal funds rate—shown in Figure 12-1—averaged just 2 percent in 2008 and was 0.16 percent in December 2008. This represented negative "real" rates (subtracting out the current underlying inflation rate of around 2 percent). The rate on short-term Treasury bills was equally low. (Tables 12-9, 20-6, and 18-3)

- Longer-term rates have also declined dramatically. The rate on Treasury 10-year securities, the ultimate in safe longer-term investments, is also shown in Figure 12-1. It was down to 2.42 percent in December 2008, the lowest value seen since 1954. (Tables 12-9 and 20-6)

- The rate spread between Aaa-rated and Baa-rated corporate bonds, representing a market evaluation of risk, was more than 3 percentage points (300 "basis points") in December 2008. This exceeded the previous record postwar spreads seen in 1982. (Table 12-9)

- Quantitative measures demonstrate extraordinary monetary easing during 2008. The narrowly defined money supply, M1, grew 17 percent from December 2007 to December 2008, compared with essentially no growth during the previous year. M2 grew 9.4 percent during 2008 compared with 5.6 percent during 2007. (Table 12-1) The monetary base, which grew only slightly during 2007, doubled in 2008, and the Federal Reserve added $1.3 trillion in assets to its balance sheet during 2008. (Table 12-3)

Table 12-1. Money Stock Measures and Components of M1

(Billions of dollars, monthly data are averages of daily figures, annual data are for December.)

Year and month	Not seasonally adjusted		Seasonally adjusted							
	M1	M2	M1	M2	Currency	Traveler's checks	Demand deposits	Other checkable deposits		
								At commercial banks	At thrift institutions	Total
1960	144.5	315.3	140.7	312.4	28.7	0.3	111.6	0.0	0.0	0.0
1961	149.2	338.5	145.2	335.5	29.3	0.4	115.5	0.0	0.0	0.0
1962	151.9	365.8	147.8	362.7	30.3	0.4	117.1	0.0	0.0	0.0
1963	157.5	396.4	153.3	393.2	32.2	0.4	120.6	0.0	0.1	0.1
1964	164.9	428.3	160.3	424.7	33.9	0.5	125.8	0.0	0.1	0.1
1965	172.6	463.1	167.8	459.2	36.0	0.5	131.3	0.0	0.1	0.1
1966	176.9	483.7	172.0	480.2	38.0	0.6	133.4	0.0	0.1	0.1
1967	188.4	528.0	183.3	524.8	40.0	0.6	142.5	0.0	0.1	0.1
1968	202.8	569.7	197.4	566.8	43.0	0.7	153.6	0.0	0.1	0.1
1969	209.4	590.1	203.9	587.9	45.7	0.8	157.3	0.0	0.1	0.2
1970	220.1	627.8	214.4	626.5	48.6	0.9	164.7	0.0	0.1	0.1
1971	234.5	711.2	228.3	710.3	52.0	1.0	175.1	0.0	0.2	0.2
1972	256.1	803.1	249.2	802.3	56.2	1.2	191.6	0.0	0.2	0.2
1973	270.2	856.5	262.9	855.5	60.8	1.4	200.3	0.0	0.3	0.3
1974	281.8	903.5	274.2	902.1	67.0	1.7	205.1	0.2	0.4	0.4
1975	295.3	1 017.8	287.1	1 016.2	72.8	2.1	211.3	0.4	0.5	0.9
1976	314.5	1 153.5	306.2	1 152.0	79.5	2.6	221.5	1.3	1.4	2.7
1977	340.0	1 273.0	330.9	1 270.3	87.4	2.9	236.4	1.8	2.3	4.2
1978	367.9	1 370.8	357.3	1 366.0	96.0	3.3	249.5	5.3	3.1	8.5
1979	393.2	1 479.0	381.8	1 473.7	104.8	3.5	256.6	12.7	4.2	16.8
1980	419.5	1 604.8	408.5	1 599.8	115.3	3.9	261.2	20.8	7.3	28.1
1981	447.0	1 760.3	436.7	1 755.5	122.5	4.1	231.4	63.0	15.6	78.7
1982	485.8	1 917.2	474.8	1 909.3	132.5	4.1	234.1	80.5	23.6	104.1
1983	533.3	2 136.2	521.4	2 125.7	146.2	4.7	238.5	97.3	34.8	132.1
1984	564.6	2 320.9	551.6	2 308.8	156.1	5.0	243.4	104.7	42.4	147.1
1985	633.3	2 506.6	619.8	2 494.6	167.7	5.6	266.9	124.7	54.9	179.5
1986	739.8	2 744.1	724.7	2 731.4	180.4	6.1	302.9	161.0	74.2	235.2
1987	765.4	2 842.7	750.2	2 830.8	196.7	6.6	287.7	178.2	81.0	259.2
1988	803.1	3 006.3	786.7	2 993.9	212.0	7.0	287.1	192.5	88.1	280.6
1989	810.6	3 171.4	792.9	3 158.4	222.3	6.9	278.6	197.4	87.7	285.1
1990	842.7	3 290.2	824.7	3 276.8	246.5	7.7	276.8	208.7	85.0	293.7
1991	915.6	3 391.2	897.0	3 377.1	267.1	7.7	289.6	241.6	90.9	332.5
1992	1 045.6	3 446.9	1 024.9	3 430.4	292.2	8.2	340.0	280.8	103.8	384.6
1993	1 153.3	3 501.5	1 129.6	3 481.0	321.6	8.0	385.4	302.6	112.0	414.6
1994	1 174.5	3 518.0	1 150.7	3 496.8	354.5	8.6	383.6	297.4	106.6	404.0
1995	1 152.7	3 664.3	1 127.4	3 640.8	372.8	9.0	389.0	249.0	107.6	356.6
1996	1 105.8	3 839.9	1 081.6	3 819.9	394.6	8.8	402.3	172.1	103.8	275.9
1997	1 097.5	4 053.5	1 072.7	4 033.0	425.3	8.4	393.8	148.3	96.9	245.3
1998	1 121.2	4 398.4	1 095.8	4 376.5	460.5	8.5	376.8	143.9	106.1	250.0
1999	1 148.2	4 657.1	1 122.6	4 630.1	517.8	8.6	353.0	139.7	103.7	243.3
2000	1 111.7	4 939.9	1 087.7	4 909.4	531.2	8.3	309.9	133.2	105.2	238.4
2001	1 208.3	5 450.7	1 182.3	5 416.1	581.1	8.0	335.7	142.0	115.4	257.5
2002	1 245.1	5 792.9	1 220.4	5 763.5	626.3	7.8	306.8	154.3	125.3	279.6
2003	1 332.0	6 082.1	1 306.8	6 054.7	662.5	7.7	326.4	175.3	135.0	310.3
2004	1 401.3	6 427.4	1 376.4	6 398.4	697.5	7.5	343.2	187.0	141.1	328.2
2005	1 396.5	6 685.3	1 374.2	6 659.1	723.6	7.2	324.6	180.7	138.1	318.9
2006	1 387.3	7 046.8	1 365.6	7 019.1	748.3	6.7	304.8	177.2	128.6	305.8
2007	1 386.1	7 442.5	1 364.5	7 414.9	757.6	6.3	292.9	174.3	133.5	307.8
2008	1 624.1	8 140.6	1 595.4	8 123.8	812.1	5.5	464.8	178.9	134.2	313.0
2007										
January	1 368.8	7 040.7	1 373.6	7 067.1	749.8	6.7	307.8	179.0	130.3	309.3
February	1 347.2	7 048.3	1 366.0	7 073.8	750.2	6.7	304.1	176.1	129.0	305.1
March	1 378.7	7 145.5	1 368.2	7 109.4	751.8	6.6	300.8	177.4	131.7	309.0
April	1 392.1	7 232.3	1 378.8	7 158.2	754.5	6.6	306.2	178.6	132.9	311.5
May	1 384.0	7 172.8	1 379.7	7 186.7	755.8	6.5	306.5	179.0	131.9	310.9
June	1 368.4	7 215.1	1 364.6	7 209.9	756.0	6.5	302.2	168.2	131.7	299.9
July	1 365.6	7 217.3	1 366.5	7 236.9	757.9	6.5	301.5	169.3	131.3	300.5
August	1 368.7	7 276.4	1 368.1	7 284.9	759.0	6.4	300.3	171.3	130.9	302.2
September	1 350.9	7 302.5	1 366.1	7 320.1	760.5	6.4	295.8	170.9	132.5	303.4
October	1 361.6	7 314.7	1 371.7	7 350.5	762.8	6.4	296.8	173.6	132.1	305.6
November	1 361.6	7 374.0	1 366.6	7 382.0	761.0	6.3	296.6	173.0	129.6	302.6
December	1 386.1	7 442.5	1 364.5	7 414.9	757.6	6.3	292.9	174.3	133.5	307.8
2008										
January	1 364.3	7 436.1	1 368.3	7 461.7	756.6	6.2	295.2	175.1	135.1	310.2
February	1 351.3	7 515.4	1 370.8	7 536.9	757.6	6.2	294.7	176.9	135.5	312.4
March	1 384.7	7 650.1	1 372.8	7 598.6	760.7	6.2	294.6	176.6	134.8	311.4
April	1 387.3	7 696.0	1 373.6	7 618.4	760.1	6.1	295.1	177.1	135.3	312.3
May	1 376.8	7 631.3	1 373.6	7 637.0	763.4	6.1	292.0	175.1	137.1	312.2
June	1 388.1	7 651.2	1 383.6	7 647.7	769.0	6.0	294.3	176.4	137.7	314.2
July	1 399.6	7 665.2	1 400.0	7 692.2	774.5	5.9	303.5	176.8	139.3	316.1
August	1 392.0	7 668.8	1 391.9	7 673.2	777.0	5.8	300.6	172.4	136.0	308.4
September	1 434.8	7 747.5	1 451.8	7 782.1	781.6	5.8	350.2	176.9	137.3	314.2
October	1 464.6	7 863.6	1 475.0	7 900.7	796.5	5.7	360.7	176.3	135.8	312.1
November	1 517.7	7 947.4	1 523.5	7 951.5	804.3	5.6	406.7	173.5	133.4	306.9
December	1 624.1	8 140.6	1 595.4	8 123.8	812.1	5.5	464.8	178.9	134.2	313.0

Table 12-2. Components of Non-M1 M2

(Billions of dollars, seasonally adjusted; monthly data are averages of daily figures, annual data are for December.)

Year and month	Savings deposits			Small-denomination time deposits			Retail money funds	Total non-M1 M2	Memorandum: Institutional money funds
	At commercial banks	At thrift institutions	Total	At commercial banks	At thrift institutions	Total			
1960	58.3	100.8	159.1	9.7	2.8	12.5	0.0	171.7	0.0
1961	64.2	111.3	175.5	11.1	3.7	14.8	0.0	190.3	0.0
1962	71.3	123.4	194.8	15.5	4.6	20.1	0.0	214.9	0.0
1963	76.8	137.6	214.4	19.9	5.7	25.5	0.0	240.0	0.0
1964	82.9	152.4	235.2	22.4	6.8	29.2	0.0	264.4	0.0
1965	92.4	164.5	256.9	26.7	7.8	34.5	0.0	291.3	0.0
1966	89.9	163.3	253.1	38.7	16.3	55.0	0.0	308.1	0.0
1967	94.1	169.6	263.7	50.7	27.1	77.8	0.0	341.5	0.0
1968	96.1	172.8	268.9	63.5	37.1	100.5	0.0	369.4	0.0
1969	93.8	169.8	263.7	71.6	48.8	120.4	0.0	384.0	0.0
1970	98.6	162.3	261.0	79.3	71.9	151.2	0.0	412.1	0.0
1971	112.8	179.4	292.2	94.7	95.1	189.7	0.0	481.9	0.0
1972	124.8	196.6	321.4	108.2	123.5	231.6	0.0	553.0	0.0
1973	128.0	198.7	326.8	116.8	149.0	265.8	0.1	592.6	0.0
1974	136.8	201.8	338.6	123.1	164.8	287.9	1.4	627.9	0.2
1975	161.2	227.6	388.9	142.3	195.5	337.9	2.4	729.1	0.5
1976	201.8	251.4	453.2	155.5	235.2	390.7	1.8	845.8	0.6
1977	218.8	273.4	492.2	167.5	278.0	445.5	1.8	939.4	1.0
1978	216.5	265.4	481.9	185.1	335.8	521.0	5.8	1 008.7	3.5
1979	195.0	228.8	423.8	235.5	398.7	634.3	33.9	1 092.0	10.4
1980	185.7	214.5	400.3	286.2	442.3	728.5	62.5	1 191.3	16.0
1981	159.0	184.9	343.9	347.7	475.4	823.1	151.7	1 318.8	38.2
1982	190.1	210.0	400.1	379.9	471.0	850.9	183.4	1 434.4	48.8
1983	363.2	321.7	684.9	350.9	433.1	784.1	135.3	1 604.3	40.9
1984	389.3	315.4	704.7	387.9	500.9	888.8	163.8	1 757.2	63.7
1985	456.6	358.6	815.3	386.4	499.3	885.7	173.8	1 874.8	66.7
1986	533.5	407.4	940.9	369.4	489.0	858.4	207.5	2 006.7	87.5
1987	534.8	402.6	937.4	391.7	529.3	921.0	222.1	2 080.6	94.6
1988	542.4	383.9	926.4	451.2	585.9	1 037.1	243.7	2 207.2	94.7
1989	541.1	352.6	893.7	533.8	617.6	1 151.3	320.5	2 365.5	112.5
1990	581.3	341.6	922.9	610.7	562.6	1 173.3	356.0	2 452.1	141.5
1991	664.8	379.6	1 044.5	602.2	463.1	1 065.3	370.3	2 480.1	190.7
1992	754.2	433.1	1 187.2	508.1	359.7	867.7	350.5	2 405.5	215.2
1993	785.3	434.0	1 219.3	467.9	313.6	781.5	350.6	2 351.3	219.6
1994	752.8	398.5	1 151.3	503.6	313.9	817.5	377.4	2 346.1	214.5
1995	774.8	361.0	1 135.9	575.8	356.5	932.4	445.1	2 513.3	267.6
1996	906.4	368.9	1 275.4	594.2	353.7	947.9	515.1	2 738.3	328.1
1997	1 023.2	378.9	1 402.1	625.5	342.2	967.6	590.4	2 960.2	402.6
1998	1 188.7	416.6	1 605.3	626.4	324.9	951.3	724.2	3 280.8	554.0
1999	1 288.4	451.0	1 739.5	636.9	318.3	955.2	812.8	3 507.5	660.3
2000	1 424.3	454.0	1 878.3	700.8	345.2	1 046.0	897.3	3 821.7	815.4
2001	1 738.3	570.7	2 309.0	636.1	338.5	974.5	950.3	4 233.8	1 219.0
2002	2 060.2	713.7	2 774.0	591.2	303.4	894.7	874.5	4 543.1	1 268.4
2003	2 337.9	824.7	3 162.7	541.7	276.1	817.8	767.4	4 747.9	1 129.2
2004	2 631.1	875.3	3 506.4	551.4	276.4	827.8	687.7	5 021.9	1 080.0
2005	2 773.9	828.4	3 602.3	645.3	347.2	992.5	690.1	5 284.9	1 149.3
2006	2 909.7	783.0	3 692.7	759.3	408.0	1 167.3	793.5	5 653.5	1 350.8
2007	3 041.3	827.3	3 868.7	822.9	391.5	1 214.4	967.3	6 050.4	1 899.8
2008	3 328.7	771.8	4 100.5	1 018.1	351.0	1 369.2	1 058.7	6 528.3	2 385.5
2007									
January	2 927.4	790.7	3 718.1	761.0	409.8	1 170.8	804.6	5 693.5	1 351.3
February	2 929.2	794.1	3 723.3	765.3	410.0	1 175.3	809.2	5 707.7	1 363.9
March	2 921.0	818.4	3 739.5	756.0	423.6	1 179.6	822.1	5 741.2	1 388.5
April	2 928.4	836.1	3 764.4	758.5	427.3	1 185.8	829.3	5 779.5	1 420.8
May	2 930.3	847.0	3 777.3	760.5	428.8	1 189.3	840.4	5 807.0	1 460.2
June	2 946.3	853.1	3 799.4	762.5	428.2	1 190.7	855.3	5 845.4	1 491.8
July	2 965.1	842.6	3 807.7	768.5	424.3	1 192.8	869.9	5 870.4	1 536.0
August	2 990.4	838.3	3 828.8	770.3	424.5	1 194.8	893.3	5 916.8	1 614.0
September	3 007.9	828.6	3 836.5	778.0	427.0	1 205.0	912.5	5 954.0	1 715.5
October	3 013.5	831.2	3 844.8	804.8	405.2	1 210.0	924.0	5 978.8	1 800.5
November	3 029.8	829.2	3 859.0	821.3	391.6	1 213.0	943.4	6 015.4	1 864.9
December	3 041.3	827.3	3 868.7	822.9	391.5	1 214.4	967.3	6 050.4	1 899.8
2008									
January	3 050.1	835.7	3 885.8	824.1	395.6	1 219.8	987.8	6 093.4	1 936.7
February	3 081.5	839.9	3 921.4	825.4	395.6	1 221.0	1 023.7	6 166.1	2 060.3
March	3 120.7	855.2	3 975.9	820.5	391.6	1 212.1	1 037.7	6 225.8	2 129.0
April	3 122.0	859.2	3 981.2	817.5	391.2	1 208.6	1 055.0	6 244.8	2 174.7
May	3 126.5	883.6	4 010.1	818.8	388.6	1 207.4	1 045.9	6 263.4	2 210.3
June	3 123.9	897.3	4 021.2	823.3	383.5	1 206.8	1 036.2	6 264.2	2 242.2
July	3 130.9	902.2	4 033.1	838.4	379.2	1 217.6	1 041.5	6 292.2	2 259.3
August	3 116.5	889.4	4 005.9	861.5	380.6	1 242.2	1 033.2	6 281.3	2 280.9
September	3 170.8	862.0	4 032.8	889.5	377.0	1 266.5	1 031.1	6 330.3	2 245.5
October	3 250.3	784.7	4 034.9	979.0	345.1	1 324.1	1 066.7	6 425.7	2 227.6
November	3 246.4	769.2	4 015.6	1 003.2	350.9	1 354.1	1 058.3	6 428.0	2 322.5
December	3 328.7	771.8	4 100.5	1 018.1	351.0	1 369.2	1 058.7	6 528.3	2 385.5

Table 12-3. Aggregate Reserves, Monetary Base, and FR Balance Sheet

(Millions of dollars; reserves and monetary base adjusted for seasonality and changes in reserve requirements, except as noted; annual data are for December.)

Year and month	Reserves					Monetary base	Federal Reserve balance sheet: total assets
	Total	Nonborrowed	Nonborrowed plus extended credit [1]	Required	Excess reserves, not seasonally adjusted		
1960	11 247	11 172	11 172	10 503	743	40 977	. . .
1961	11 499	11 366	11 366	10 915	584	41 853	. . .
1962	11 604	11 344	11 344	11 033	572	42 957	. . .
1963	11 730	11 397	11 397	11 239	490	45 003	. . .
1964	12 011	11 747	11 747	11 605	406	47 161	. . .
1965	12 316	11 872	11 872	11 892	423	49 620	. . .
1966	12 223	11 690	11 690	11 884	339	51 565	. . .
1967	13 180	12 952	12 952	12 805	375	54 579	. . .
1968	13 767	13 021	13 021	13 341	426	58 357	. . .
1969	14 168	13 049	13 049	13 882	286	61 569	. . .
1970	14 558	14 225	14 225	14 309	249	65 013	. . .
1971	15 230	15 104	15 104	15 049	182	69 108	. . .
1972	16 645	15 595	15 595	16 361	284	75 167	. . .
1973	17 021	15 723	15 723	16 717	304	81 073	. . .
1974	17 550	16 823	16 970	17 292	258	87 535	. . .
1975	17 822	17 692	17 704	17 556	266	93 887	. . .
1976	18 388	18 335	18 335	18 115	274	101 515	. . .
1977	18 990	18 420	18 420	18 800	190	110 324	. . .
1978	19 753	18 885	18 885	19 521	232	120 445	. . .
1979	20 720	19 248	19 248	20 279	442	131 143	. . .
1980	22 015	20 325	20 328	21 501	514	142 004	. . .
1981	22 443	21 807	21 956	22 124	319	149 021	. . .
1982	23 600	22 966	23 152	23 100	500	160 127	. . .
1983	25 367	24 593	24 595	24 806	561	175 467	. . .
1984	26 913	23 727	26 331	26 078	835	187 252	. . .
1985	31 569	30 250	30 749	30 505	1 063	203 555	. . .
1986	38 840	38 014	38 317	37 667	1 173	223 416	. . .
1987	38 913	38 135	38 618	37 893	1 019	239 829	. . .
1988	40 453	38 738	39 982	39 392	1 061	256 897	. . .
1989	40 486	40 221	40 241	39 545	941	267 766	. . .
1990	41 766	41 440	41 463	40 101	1 665	293 287	. . .
1991	45 516	45 324	45 325	44 526	990	317 546	. . .
1992	54 421	54 298	54 298	53 267	1 154	350 912	. . .
1993	60 566	60 484	60 484	59 497	1 069	386 600	. . .
1994	59 466	59 257	59 257	58 295	1 171	418 345	. . .
1995	56 483	56 226	56 226	55 193	1 290	434 586	. . .
1996	50 185	50 030	50 030	48 766	1 418	452 032	. . .
1997	46 875	46 551	46 551	45 189	1 687	479 909	. . .
1998	45 170	45 053	45 053	43 658	1 512	513 887	. . .
1999	42 183	41 862	41 862	40 889	1 294	593 842	. . .
2000	38 717	38 507	38 507	37 391	1 325	584 929	. . .
2001	41 442	41 376	41 376	39 799	1 643	635 559	. . .
2002	40 400	40 320	40 320	38 392	2 008	681 631	. . .
2003	42 757	42 711	. . .	41 710	1 047	720 402	. . .
2004	46 552	46 489	. . .	44 643	1 909	759 072	. . .
2005	45 139	44 970	. . .	43 238	1 901	786 976	. . .
2006	43 338	43 147	. . .	41 475	1 863	811 126	. . .
2007	42 674	27 244	. . .	40 905	1 769	822 357	917 922
2008	820 942	167 376	. . .	53 530	767 412	1 651 175	2 240 946
2007							
January	42 309	42 098	. . .	40 764	1 545	812 903	. . .
February	42 454	42 425	. . .	41 001	1 453	812 618	. . .
March	42 290	42 236	. . .	40 673	1 617	814 101	. . .
April	42 576	42 497	. . .	40 989	1 587	817 123	. . .
May	43 188	43 084	. . .	41 734	1 453	819 087	. . .
June	43 374	43 187	. . .	41 623	1 751	819 842	. . .
July	41 821	41 559	. . .	40 183	1 638	821 019	. . .
August	45 022	44 047	. . .	40 196	4 826	825 296	874 472
September	42 667	41 101	. . .	40 934	1 733	823 289	882 076
October	42 436	42 181	. . .	40 977	1 459	825 915	886 929
November	42 623	42 258	. . .	40 928	1 696	825 405	883 726
December	42 674	27 244	. . .	40 905	1 769	822 357	917 922
2008							
January	42 150	-3 510	. . .	40 509	1 640	820 174	882 218
February	42 826	-17 331	. . .	41 100	1 726	821 355	893 069
March	44 299	-50 224	. . .	41 321	2 978	825 910	899 335
April	43 561	-91 848	. . .	41 716	1 846	824 631	889 693
May	44 128	-111 652	. . .	42 115	2 013	827 170	894 711
June	43 364	-127 914	. . .	41 089	2 275	832 490	919 188
July	43 330	-122 334	. . .	41 353	1 977	838 062	915 702
August	44 559	-123 520	. . .	42 568	1 991	842 815	913 223
September	102 784	-187 321	. . .	42 733	60 051	905 174	1 510 704
October	315 516	-332 803	. . .	47 612	267 904	1 130 304	2 082 321
November	609 937	-88 849	. . .	50 883	559 053	1 433 490	2 138 975
December	820 942	167 376	. . .	53 530	767 412	1 651 175	2 240 946

[1]Extended credit program discontinued January 9, 2003. See notes and definitions for more information.
. . . = Not available.

Table 12-4. Commercial Banks: Bank Credit and Selected Liabilities

(All commercial banks in the United States, billions of dollars, seasonally adjusted, annual data are for December.)

Year and month	Bank credit									
	Total	Securities in bank credit			Loans and leases in bank credit					
		Total	U.S. Treasury and agency securities	Other securities	Total	Commercial and industrial	Real estate			
							Total	Revolving home equity	Other residential	Commercial
1955	152.2	76.5	65.6	10.9	75.7	27.2	19.9	. . .	. . .	. . .
1956	158.0	73.2	62.1	11.1	84.9	33.0	21.7	. . .	. . .	. . .
1957	162.7	73.5	61.0	12.4	89.2	34.7	22.3	. . .	. . .	. . .
1958	184.1	85.9	70.5	15.4	98.2	35.4	25.1	. . .	. . .	. . .
1959	189.5	77.4	61.9	15.5	112.1	39.5	28.1	. . .	. . .	. . .
1960	197.6	79.5	63.9	15.6	118.1	42.4	28.7	. . .	. . .	. . .
1961	213.1	88.2	70.4	17.9	124.8	44.1	30.2	. . .	. . .	. . .
1962	231.0	92.2	70.7	21.5	138.8	47.7	34.0	. . .	. . .	. . .
1963	250.7	92.6	67.4	25.2	158.1	52.5	38.9	. . .	. . .	. . .
1964	270.4	94.7	66.7	28.1	175.6	58.7	43.5	. . .	. . .	. . .
1965	297.1	96.1	64.3	31.9	201.0	69.5	48.9	. . .	. . .	. . .
1966	318.6	97.2	61.0	36.2	221.4	79.3	53.8	. . .	. . .	. . .
1967	350.5	111.4	70.7	40.6	239.2	86.5	58.2	. . .	. . .	. . .
1968	390.5	121.9	73.8	48.1	268.6	96.5	64.8	. . .	. . .	. . .
1969	401.6	112.4	64.2	48.2	289.2	106.9	69.9	. . .	. . .	. . .
1970	434.4	129.7	73.4	56.3	304.6	111.6	72.9	. . .	. . .	. . .
1971	485.2	147.5	79.8	67.7	337.6	118.0	81.7	. . .	. . .	. . .
1972	555.3	160.6	85.4	75.2	394.7	133.6	98.8	. . .	. . .	. . .
1973	638.6	168.4	89.7	78.7	470.1	162.8	119.4	. . .	. . .	. . .
1974	701.7	173.8	87.9	85.9	527.9	193.0	132.5	. . .	. . .	. . .
1975	732.9	206.7	117.9	88.9	526.2	184.3	137.2	. . .	. . .	. . .
1976	790.7	228.6	137.3	91.3	562.1	186.3	151.3	. . .	. . .	. . .
1977	876.0	236.3	137.4	98.9	639.7	205.8	178.0	. . .	. . .	. . .
1978	989.4	242.2	138.4	103.8	747.2	239.0	213.5	. . .	. . .	. . .
1979	1 111.4	260.7	147.2	113.4	850.7	282.2	245.0	. . .	. . .	. . .
1980	1 207.1	296.8	173.2	123.6	910.3	314.5	265.7	. . .	. . .	. . .
1981	1 302.7	311.1	181.8	129.3	991.6	353.3	287.5	. . .	. . .	. . .
1982	1 412.3	338.6	204.7	133.9	1 073.7	396.4	303.8	. . .	. . .	. . .
1983	1 566.7	403.8	263.4	140.4	1 163.0	419.1	334.8	. . .	. . .	. . .
1984	1 733.4	406.6	262.9	143.7	1 326.9	479.4	380.8	. . .	. . .	. . .
1985	1 922.2	455.9	273.8	182.2	1 466.3	506.5	431.0	. . .	. . .	. . .
1986	2 106.6	510.0	312.8	197.2	1 596.5	544.0	499.9	. . .	. . .	. . .
1987	2 255.3	535.0	338.9	196.1	1 720.2	575.0	595.7	32.2	. . .	. . .
1988	2 432.2	559.3	364.3	195.0	1 873.0	612.5	678.3	43.0	. . .	. . .
1989	2 602.0	582.9	399.6	183.3	2 019.1	642.7	771.4	54.0	. . .	. . .
1990	2 750.4	633.9	456.0	177.9	2 116.5	645.4	858.0	67.2	. . .	. . .
1991	2 854.6	745.4	565.5	179.9	2 109.2	624.0	883.7	75.2	. . .	. . .
1992	2 954.0	842.6	666.5	176.1	2 111.4	600.2	906.2	79.3	. . .	. . .
1993	3 112.9	917.9	733.7	184.2	2 195.0	591.1	946.9	78.8	. . .	. . .
1994	3 319.8	942.3	723.1	219.2	2 377.5	650.6	1 010.4	81.1	. . .	. . .
1995	3 601.4	987.4	703.6	283.8	2 614.0	720.7	1 090.8	85.1	. . .	. . .
1996	3 751.1	983.6	702.5	281.1	2 767.5	780.0	1 142.8	91.4	. . .	. . .
1997	4 088.5	1 094.1	754.5	339.6	2 994.4	847.8	1 245.5	105.3	. . .	. . .
1998	4 517.0	1 229.3	796.6	432.7	3 287.7	939.6	1 337.3	104.2	. . .	. . .
1999	4 743.4	1 270.0	811.3	458.7	3 473.4	990.2	1 476.0	101.7	. . .	. . .
2000	5 200.4	1 336.2	789.5	546.8	3 864.2	1 078.4	1 660.5	130.4	. . .	. . .
2001	5 409.6	1 480.5	849.2	631.3	3 929.1	1 018.0	1 790.4	156.0	. . .	. . .
2002	5 888.2	1 719.7	1 033.1	686.5	4 168.5	955.7	2 038.4	213.8	. . .	. . .
2003	6 260.8	1 851.0	1 107.7	743.4	4 409.8	896.1	2 235.4	281.1	. . .	. . .
2004	6 811.5	1 944.5	1 165.5	779.0	4 867.1	918.5	2 574.8	399.2	1 093.9	1 081.7
2005	7 531.8	2 063.0	1 159.7	903.4	5 468.8	1 035.8	2 942.0	445.6	1 223.3	1 273.0
2006	8 359.3	2 240.4	1 211.7	1 028.7	6 118.9	1 187.5	3 378.8	469.9	1 456.6	1 452.2
2007	9 206.0	2 412.0	1 128.5	1 283.5	6 794.0	1 430.8	3 607.9	486.0	1 519.6	1 602.3
2008	9 965.9	2 771.7	1 262.3	1 509.4	7 194.2	1 582.8	3 828.1	590.7	1 500.5	1 736.9
2007										
January	8 419.0	2 248.8	1 210.5	1 038.3	6 170.2	1 196.2	3 406.0	471.2	1 470.7	1 464.1
February	8 480.6	2 253.6	1 208.0	1 045.6	6 227.0	1 209.3	3 434.6	472.5	1 480.8	1 481.3
March	8 450.5	2 265.0	1 205.1	1 059.9	6 185.5	1 222.4	3 371.1	462.6	1 423.1	1 485.5
April	8 508.1	2 269.7	1 186.8	1 082.9	6 238.5	1 230.1	3 390.5	460.3	1 435.3	1 494.9
May	8 569.7	2 282.4	1 174.1	1 108.3	6 287.3	1 246.2	3 414.8	462.0	1 447.5	1 505.3
June	8 627.8	2 303.6	1 170.4	1 133.2	6 324.2	1 267.2	3 434.8	463.3	1 456.5	1 515.0
July	8 699.3	2 317.0	1 169.1	1 147.9	6 382.3	1 287.9	3 445.7	464.2	1 446.0	1 535.5
August	8 808.2	2 339.9	1 172.1	1 167.8	6 468.3	1 311.9	3 468.0	468.2	1 452.3	1 547.6
September	8 926.2	2 375.5	1 167.9	1 207.6	6 550.7	1 351.6	3 495.2	472.0	1 461.6	1 561.5
October	9 048.1	2 400.3	1 147.9	1 252.4	6 647.8	1 384.5	3 554.0	477.0	1 503.6	1 573.5
November	9 169.0	2 441.1	1 129.8	1 311.2	6 728.0	1 403.8	3 588.5	481.8	1 518.8	1 588.0
December	9 206.0	2 412.0	1 128.5	1 283.5	6 794.0	1 430.8	3 607.9	486.0	1 519.6	1 602.3
2008										
January	9 307.2	2 435.4	1 101.0	1 334.4	6 871.8	1 448.3	3 626.2	489.8	1 522.5	1 613.9
February	9 361.7	2 465.3	1 097.8	1 367.5	6 896.4	1 456.4	3 641.7	494.9	1 518.9	1 627.9
March	9 495.5	2 554.1	1 106.3	1 447.9	6 941.4	1 480.0	3 658.9	500.1	1 519.0	1 639.8
April	9 417.8	2 524.9	1 099.6	1 425.3	6 893.0	1 487.9	3 643.6	506.2	1 486.4	1 651.0
May	9 422.4	2 503.6	1 109.4	1 394.2	6 918.8	1 494.1	3 639.8	511.1	1 467.9	1 660.8
June	9 401.2	2 496.8	1 125.9	1 370.9	6 904.4	1 505.5	3 631.7	516.7	1 442.8	1 672.2
July	9 426.0	2 507.2	1 123.4	1 383.8	6 918.9	1 516.1	3 620.8	522.4	1 423.0	1 675.3
August	9 415.0	2 487.7	1 131.6	1 356.1	6 927.3	1 516.5	3 623.1	526.8	1 418.9	1 677.5
September	9 572.6	2 538.3	1 155.6	1 382.7	7 034.3	1 537.0	3 660.5	540.2	1 432.5	1 687.8
October	9 982.9	2 720.2	1 236.0	1 484.3	7 262.7	1 602.3	3 820.8	579.7	1 512.2	1 728.9
November	9 924.7	2 712.3	1 264.5	1 447.7	7 212.4	1 600.2	3 826.8	585.0	1 509.5	1 732.2
December	9 965.9	2 771.7	1 262.3	1 509.4	7 194.2	1 582.8	3 828.1	590.7	1 500.5	1 736.9

. . . = Not available.

Table 12-4. Commercial Banks: Bank Credit and Selected Liabilities—*Continued*

(All commercial banks in the United States, billions of dollars, seasonally adjusted, annual data are for December.)

Year and month	Bank credit—*Continued*				Selected liabilities			
	Loans and leases in bank credit—*Continued*			Deposits	Borrowings			
	Consumer	Security	Other loans and leases		Total	From banks in the United States	From others
1955	17.3	5.1	6.1	. . .	. . .	. . .	. . .
1956	19.1	4.8	6.2	. . .	. . .	. . .	. . .
1957	20.0	4.6	7.6	. . .	. . .	. . .	. . .
1958	20.4	4.7	12.7	. . .	. . .	. . .	. . .
1959	24.1	5.0	15.4	. . .	. . .	. . .	. . .
1960	26.3	5.2	15.6	. . .	. . .	. . .	. . .
1961	27.6	6.1	16.8	. . .	. . .	. . .	. . .
1962	30.3	6.6	20.2	. . .	. . .	. . .	. . .
1963	34.2	7.9	24.6	. . .	. . .	. . .	. . .
1964	39.5	8.3	25.7	. . .	. . .	. . .	. . .
1965	45.0	8.0	29.7	. . .	. . .	. . .	. . .
1966	47.7	8.3	32.4	. . .	. . .	. . .	. . .
1967	51.2	9.6	33.8	. . .	. . .	. . .	. . .
1968	57.7	10.5	39.2	. . .	. . .	. . .	. . .
1969	62.6	10.0	39.8	. . .	. . .	. . .	. . .
1970	65.3	10.4	44.5	. . .	. . .	. . .	. . .
1971	73.3	10.9	53.9	. . .	. . .	. . .	. . .
1972	85.4	14.4	62.5	. . .	. . .	. . .	. . .
1973	98.3	11.2	78.4	651.6	70.5	44.1	26.4
1974	102.1	10.6	89.6	718.9	76.3	47.8	28.6
1975	104.6	12.7	87.5	759.3	72.1	45.1	27.0
1976	115.9	17.7	91.0	815.3	95.5	56.3	39.2
1977	138.1	20.7	97.2	899.4	111.7	61.8	49.9
1978	164.6	19.1	110.9	996.7	138.4	72.6	65.8
1979	184.5	17.4	121.6	1 069.3	176.6	97.4	79.2
1980	179.2	17.2	133.6	1 181.6	212.3	118.1	94.2
1981	182.7	20.2	148.0	1 247.4	256.0	142.3	113.7
1982	188.2	23.6	161.7	1 365.5	282.2	153.9	128.3
1983	213.2	26.5	169.4	1 478.8	282.8	149.1	133.7
1984	253.6	34.1	179.0	1 607.0	316.9	165.8	151.1
1985	294.5	42.9	191.4	1 752.1	372.6	192.4	180.1
1986	314.5	38.6	199.5	1 911.2	410.2	213.3	196.9
1987	327.7	34.8	187.0	1 971.7	427.2	222.2	204.9
1988	354.9	39.9	187.3	2 114.4	492.0	251.6	240.4
1989	375.2	40.8	189.0	2 240.0	552.7	281.4	271.3
1990	380.7	44.8	187.7	2 340.6	575.6	294.5	281.2
1991	363.7	50.6	187.2	2 467.7	496.9	220.8	276.1
1992	355.8	59.9	189.2	2 498.5	498.8	211.9	286.9
1993	387.1	79.6	190.4	2 531.4	537.4	213.4	324.0
1994	447.7	67.8	201.0	2 531.5	637.4	256.4	381.1
1995	490.9	73.3	238.2	2 663.4	717.1	287.5	429.6
1996	511.9	64.4	268.4	2 852.8	730.2	296.1	434.1
1997	502.5	83.8	314.8	3 083.4	853.6	304.0	549.6
1998	496.9	126.6	387.3	3 273.9	1 017.5	318.5	699.1
1999	491.7	128.6	386.8	3 457.5	1 118.5	343.5	775.0
2000	541.2	153.1	431.0	3 755.0	1 236.4	382.1	854.3
2001	558.7	119.8	442.2	4 115.7	1 245.5	408.4	837.1
2002	589.7	161.2	423.5	4 377.5	1 408.2	423.0	985.2
2003	645.8	187.9	444.5	4 646.4	1 462.5	389.3	1 073.2
2004	698.3	188.7	486.8	5 171.8	1 591.4	398.5	1 192.9
2005	707.6	236.4	547.0	5 609.6	1 752.7	366.3	1 386.4
2006	742.8	257.4	552.5	6 134.1	1 988.6	403.4	1 585.2
2007	806.8	285.4	663.0	6 676.2	2 297.9	477.2	1 820.7
2008	881.4	244.7	657.1	7 301.3	2 548.3	373.8	2 174.5
2007							
January	743.4	262.4	562.2	6 175.5	2 018.6	398.4	1 620.3
February	747.4	268.5	567.3	6 200.1	2 030.1	394.8	1 635.3
March	746.3	274.3	571.3	6 213.3	2 047.9	402.0	1 645.9
April	751.6	274.2	592.0	6 251.5	2 067.5	401.0	1 666.5
May	755.5	278.5	592.3	6 295.0	2 053.6	397.9	1 655.7
June	766.2	264.4	591.6	6 305.9	2 100.5	411.1	1 689.4
July	775.8	277.2	595.6	6 339.5	2 133.2	419.6	1 713.6
August	777.2	283.7	627.4	6 402.2	2 189.6	431.6	1 758.0
September	785.1	276.6	642.2	6 458.8	2 226.8	433.0	1 793.7
October	788.1	265.1	656.0	6 574.0	2 216.7	439.7	1 777.1
November	796.6	278.2	660.8	6 660.8	2 234.5	444.6	1 790.0
December	806.8	285.4	663.0	6 676.2	2 297.9	477.2	1 820.7
2008							
January	807.5	307.2	682.7	6 716.1	2 296.0	471.0	1 825.1
February	810.7	298.4	689.2	6 770.2	2 301.0	472.0	1 829.0
March	818.1	300.7	683.7	6 857.2	2 334.4	468.8	1 865.6
April	824.8	287.5	649.1	6 839.5	2 315.1	463.1	1 852.1
May	828.8	304.7	651.4	6 863.0	2 335.1	472.7	1 862.4
June	834.0	290.1	643.1	6 900.1	2 330.5	467.5	1 863.0
July	843.0	297.7	641.2	6 904.6	2 358.1	465.4	1 892.7
August	847.8	303.6	636.2	6 903.4	2 376.6	460.1	1 916.5
September	853.8	327.4	655.7	7 092.2	2 415.3	465.3	1 950.0
October	872.2	293.6	673.8	7 162.7	2 670.2	443.8	2 226.4
November	878.3	263.3	643.9	7 115.8	2 655.2	390.2	2 265.0
December	881.4	244.7	657.1	7 301.3	2 548.3	373.8	2 174.5

. . . = Not available.

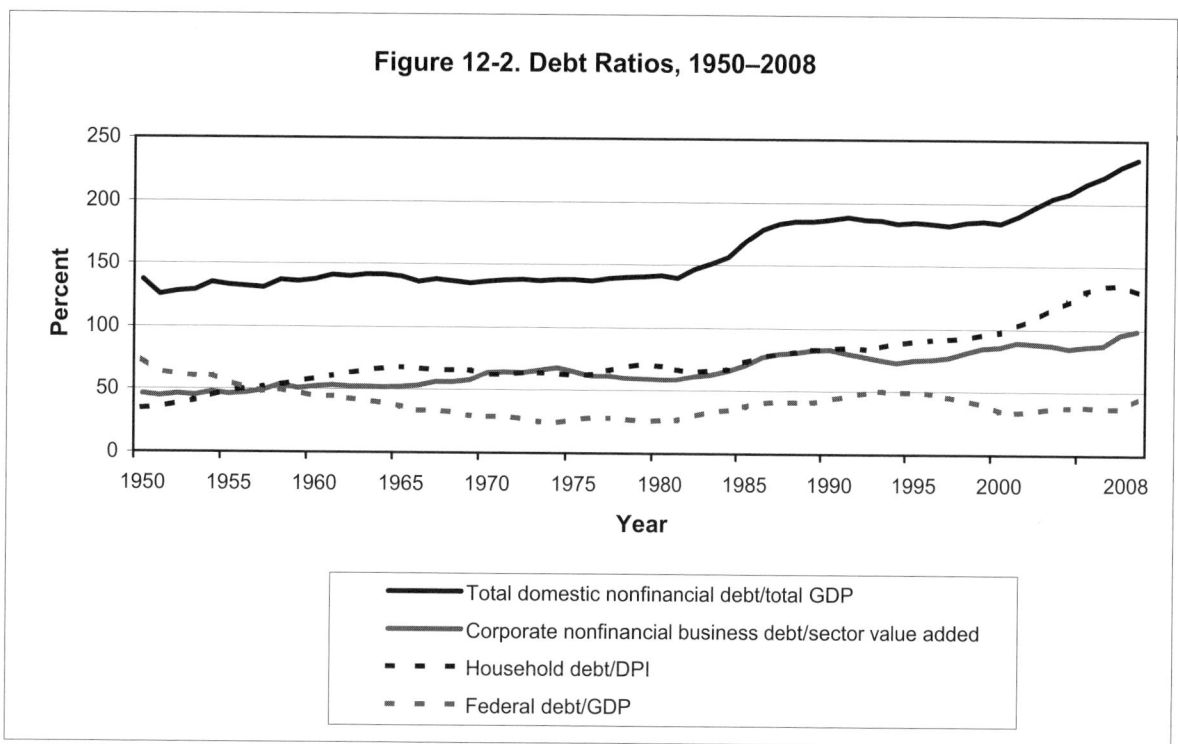

Figure 12-2. Debt Ratios, 1950–2008

- Unsustainable debt growth was the source of the credit crisis and economic decline in 2007 and 2008. Among the major nonfinancial divisions of the economy, the most striking expansion in debt relative to income occurred in the household sector. Household debt averaged less than 70 percent of aggregate disposable personal income (DPI) from the 1950s through the mid-1980s, then began a rapid and uninterrupted expansion. In 2001, debt rose above 100 percent of the annual rate of income, and it reached 135 percent at the end of 2007. In 2008, household debt leveled off, and fell back to 130 percent of DPI. (Table 12-5)

- Nonfinancial corporations also went increasingly into debt, but did not become as deeply indebted as households; at the end of 2008 their aggregate debt was still under 100 percent of their annual value added. (Table 12-5)

- Financial sector debt—much of it reflecting the securitization of nonfinancial sector debt, especially mortgages—grew more rapidly than nonfinancial sector debt. Between 1985 and 2008, financial sector debt rose from 30 percent to 121 percent of GDP, while total nonfinancial sector debt grew from 169 to 235 percent. Through 2004, more than half of all financial sector debt was owed by federal government-related entities—government-sponsored enterprises (GSEs) such as "Fannie Mae" and "Freddie Mac"—and mortgage pools backed by federal agencies and GSEs. Since then, private financial debt grew faster, but the federal government-related sector still accounted for nearly half of all financial sector debt. (Table 12-5)

- Debt of the federal government itself—that is, Treasury securities issued to fund budget deficits—contributed little, on balance, to the rising trend of aggregate debt—until the recession struck in 2008, revenues fell, and spending rose because of both recession-sensitive programs like unemployment insurance and new moves to stabilize credit markets and the economy. (Tables 12-5 and 6-1)

Table 12-5. Credit Market Debt Outstanding, by Borrower and Lender

(Billions of dollars, except as noted; end of period; not seasonally adjusted.)

Year and quarter	Total	Domestic financial sectors			Domestic nonfinancial sectors									
					Total		Federal government			Households		Nonfinancial business		
		Total	Federal govern-ment-related	Private	Billions of dollars	Percent of GDP	Total	Treasury securities	Budget agency securities and mortgages	Billions of dollars	Percent of DPI	Total	Corporate	
													Total	Percent of sector value added
1950	425.3	8.5	1.8	6.7	402.8	137.1	216.5	216.1	0.4	72.9	34.7	92.1	70.3	45.9
1951	449.2	9.6	2.1	7.5	425.0	125.3	216.1	215.8	0.2	81.5	35.3	103.9	78.7	44.8
1952	484.7	11.1	2.2	8.9	458.5	128.0	221.4	220.8	0.6	93.9	38.6	112.4	84.8	46.2
1953	516.7	12.7	2.2	10.5	487.8	128.6	228.4	226.2	2.3	106.1	41.0	117.5	88.9	45.4
1954	541.8	12.3	2.1	10.1	513.0	134.8	230.8	228.5	2.3	117.4	44.4	123.6	92.4	47.9
1955	582.0	15.3	3.1	12.1	550.2	132.6	230.0	228.4	1.6	138.0	48.7	136.0	100.9	46.3
1956	611.3	17.9	3.6	14.3	576.0	131.7	224.1	222.8	1.4	152.9	50.5	148.6	110.3	47.4
1957	642.5	20.8	5.0	15.7	602.9	130.8	221.9	220.1	1.8	165.3	51.7	160.7	119.9	49.3
1958	681.2	21.0	5.1	15.9	639.5	136.9	231.1	229.0	2.1	176.1	53.3	171.6	126.9	53.5
1959	738.0	27.7	7.3	20.4	688.9	136.0	238.0	236.2	1.8	198.1	56.5	186.1	135.3	50.9
1960	779.2	32.5	8.1	24.5	723.4	137.4	236.0	234.0	1.9	215.6	59.0	199.7	143.9	52.1
1961	827.2	34.9	8.8	26.1	766.9	140.8	243.2	240.7	2.5	232.3	60.8	213.6	151.1	53.3
1962	886.5	39.4	10.4	29.0	819.5	139.9	250.0	246.8	3.3	254.3	62.8	231.4	161.2	52.0
1963	952.2	46.6	12.0	34.6	874.8	141.6	253.8	250.7	3.2	281.2	66.1	250.6	171.5	52.0
1964	1 026.0	53.0	12.6	40.4	938.1	141.4	259.9	255.9	4.0	310.3	67.1	272.3	184.8	51.9
1965	1 104.0	61.9	14.7	47.2	1 004.6	139.7	261.5	257.0	4.5	338.7	68.0	301.2	204.2	52.2
1966	1 183.9	72.9	20.2	52.6	1 071.6	136.0	265.1	259.3	5.8	361.2	67.2	335.2	228.2	53.2
1967	1 264.3	73.6	20.3	53.2	1 147.4	137.8	278.1	268.2	9.9	380.4	66.1	371.5	254.0	56.3
1968	1 369.3	84.0	24.1	59.9	1 239.3	136.2	290.6	277.6	13.0	412.8	66.1	409.7	281.1	56.5
1969	1 487.0	111.5	33.8	77.7	1 326.2	134.7	287.4	276.8	10.6	442.7	65.7	457.8	313.6	58.0
1970	1 595.8	127.8	43.6	84.1	1 416.0	136.4	299.5	289.9	9.6	457.1	62.1	509.1	357.9	64.1
1971	1 747.0	138.9	49.5	89.3	1 551.6	137.7	324.4	315.9	8.5	499.4	62.3	561.1	386.9	64.2
1972	1 932.4	162.8	57.9	104.8	1 708.5	138.0	339.4	330.1	9.3	555.4	63.9	633.0	427.1	63.8
1973	2 170.3	209.8	77.9	131.9	1 893.1	136.9	346.3	336.7	9.6	624.9	63.9	727.1	493.2	65.7
1974	2 407.1	258.3	97.9	160.4	2 067.6	137.8	358.2	348.8	9.4	680.3	63.5	820.9	549.2	67.8
1975	2 616.7	260.4	107.3	153.2	2 259.4	137.9	443.9	434.9	8.9	734.3	61.8	861.8	568.9	64.9
1976	2 902.5	283.9	121.9	162.0	2 502.9	137.1	513.1	503.7	9.3	818.9	62.9	933.1	609.7	61.6
1977	3 290.5	337.8	145.0	192.8	2 824.1	139.1	569.4	560.9	8.4	946.7	65.9	1 051.8	684.6	61.2
1978	3 776.7	412.5	181.7	230.8	3 208.5	139.8	621.9	614.9	7.0	1 105.4	68.7	1 185.7	758.7	59.6
1979	4 273.2	504.9	230.3	274.6	3 599.8	140.4	657.7	652.1	5.6	1 276.1	71.1	1 343.9	840.6	59.4
1980	4 721.5	578.1	273.9	304.2	3 950.0	141.6	735.0	730.0	5.0	1 396.0	69.5	1 474.5	906.6	59.0
1981	5 254.1	682.4	319.4	362.9	4 357.8	139.3	820.5	815.9	4.5	1 507.2	67.1	1 658.1	1 023.4	58.6
1982	5 761.9	778.1	383.9	394.2	4 775.7	146.7	981.8	978.1	3.7	1 576.4	65.1	1 803.7	1 109.6	61.4
1983	6 455.9	882.7	451.6	431.1	5 349.1	151.2	1 167.0	1 163.4	3.6	1 732.0	66.4	1 989.0	1 220.3	63.1
1984	7 421.7	1 052.4	526.2	526.2	6 136.5	156.0	1 364.2	1 360.8	3.4	1 943.3	66.7	2 315.3	1 428.6	65.9
1985	8 621.7	1 257.3	625.7	631.7	7 121.9	168.8	1 589.9	1 586.6	3.3	2 276.5	73.2	2 577.6	1 617.9	70.3
1986	9 811.2	1 593.6	804.6	789.0	7 965.7	178.5	1 805.9	1 802.2	3.6	2 536.0	77.2	2 871.7	1 840.8	77.1
1987	10 823.9	1 895.5	972.6	922.9	8 669.4	182.9	1 949.6	1 944.6	5.2	2 753.8	79.6	3 123.2	2 034.5	79.6
1988	11 865.8	2 145.8	1 093.4	1 052.4	9 450.3	185.2	2 104.9	2 082.3	22.6	3 042.2	81.2	3 410.1	2 234.3	80.6
1989	12 838.7	2 399.3	1 242.9	1 156.4	10 151.5	185.1	2 251.2	2 227.0	24.2	3 335.5	82.9	3 624.4	2 401.3	82.5
1990	13 766.6	2 613.6	1 413.6	1 200.1	10 834.7	186.7	2 498.1	2 465.8	32.4	3 595.9	83.9	3 753.3	2 535.8	83.4
1991	14 421.4	2 769.6	1 559.4	1 210.2	11 301.4	188.5	2 776.4	2 757.8	18.6	3 784.1	84.8	3 662.3	2 480.7	80.0
1992	15 213.5	3 024.1	1 715.7	1 308.4	11 817.0	186.5	3 080.3	3 061.6	18.8	3 983.1	83.8	3 658.5	2 506.6	77.5
1993	16 185.0	3 321.0	1 880.9	1 440.1	12 395.7	186.2	3 336.5	3 309.9	26.6	4 221.1	85.9	3 685.0	2 551.6	75.1
1994	17 204.7	3 791.1	2 173.4	1 617.7	12 970.5	183.4	3 492.3	3 465.6	26.7	4 541.4	88.2	3 829.5	2 684.5	73.2
1995	18 475.2	4 233.5	2 377.7	1 855.8	13 674.1	184.8	3 636.7	3 608.5	28.2	4 856.7	89.8	4 133.9	2 940.4	75.8
1996	19 812.6	4 747.5	2 609.1	2 138.4	14 407.9	184.3	3 781.7	3 755.1	26.6	5 193.1	91.3	4 406.9	3 140.3	76.4
1997	21 245.0	5 301.4	2 822.8	2 478.6	15 219.9	183.3	3 804.8	3 778.3	26.5	5 494.3	91.7	4 843.9	3 472.4	78.9
1998	23 338.3	6 328.2	3 294.4	3 033.8	16 226.9	185.5	3 752.2	3 723.7	28.5	5 920.3	92.6	5 410.7	3 855.6	82.8
1999	25 406.3	7 349.9	3 887.7	3 462.2	17 308.2	186.7	3 681.0	3 652.7	28.3	6 416.1	95.8	6 030.1	4 276.5	86.4
2000	27 156.8	8 158.2	4 319.6	3 838.6	18 184.0	185.2	3 385.1	3 357.8	27.3	7 010.7	97.5	6 590.4	4 638.4	88.0
2001	29 343.8	9 158.6	4 962.4	4 196.2	19 319.8	190.8	3 379.5	3 352.7	26.8	7 682.9	102.6	6 954.0	4 834.2	91.3
2002	31 842.8	10 037.8	5 509.0	4 528.8	20 732.1	198.0	3 637.0	3 609.8	27.3	8 513.7	108.7	7 133.9	4 857.1	90.4
2003	34 622.5	10 927.9	5 928.0	4 999.9	22 441.9	204.7	4 033.1	4 008.2	24.9	9 500.1	116.4	7 341.1	4 974.4	89.5
2004	37 808.4	11 920.5	6 050.9	5 869.6	24 450.2	209.2	4 395.0	4 370.7	24.3	10 576.0	121.8	7 796.3	5 178.4	86.9
2005	41 269.3	12 980.1	6 134.1	6 846.0	26 776.8	215.6	4 701.9	4 678.0	23.8	11 747.1	129.6	8 473.2	5 510.9	86.2
2006	45 324.7	14 278.6	6 465.1	7 813.5	29 166.3	221.3	4 885.3	4 861.7	23.5	12 916.3	134.0	9 358.9	5 977.1	87.1
2007	49 865.7	16 176.5	7 373.7	8 802.8	31 672.8	229.4	5 122.3	5 099.2	23.1	13 765.1	135.3	10 593.7	6 784.9	95.9
2008	52 592.7	17 216.5	8 189.2	9 027.3	33 517.9	235.0	6 361.5	6 338.2	23.3	13 821.0	129.9	11 095.8	7 103.7	99.1
2006														
1st quarter	42 334.8	13 316.5	6 209.1	7 107.5	27 453.0	211.8	4 858.0	4 834.4	23.6	12 030.4	127.1	8 684.0	5 621.6	83.0
2nd quarter	43 351.5	13 720.9	6 320.1	7 400.8	28 021.4	213.3	4 783.2	4 759.6	23.6	12 386.9	129.4	8 929.1	5 757.0	84.4
3rd quarter	44 271.2	13 964.8	6 380.7	7 584.1	28 547.5	215.5	4 826.6	4 803.2	23.4	12 693.9	130.9	9 081.4	5 805.7	83.8
4th quarter	45 324.7	14 278.6	6 465.1	7 813.5	29 166.3	218.1	4 885.3	4 861.7	23.5	12 916.3	131.5	9 358.9	5 977.1	86.2
2007														
1st quarter	46 479.2	14 773.3	6 600.2	8 173.1	29 800.0	220.6	5 037.4	5 014.3	23.2	13 092.7	130.8	9 607.0	6 150.8	87.9
2nd quarter	47 464.4	15 155.8	6 760.6	8 395.2	30 336.9	220.8	4 927.4	4 904.0	23.2	13 341.0	132.2	9 947.1	6 393.4	90.5
3rd quarter	48 765.0	15 775.5	7 067.1	8 708.4	31 016.6	222.3	5 032.9	5 010.0	23.0	13 577.8	132.7	10 261.6	6 573.2	92.6
4th quarter	49 865.7	16 176.5	7 373.7	8 802.8	31 672.8	225.7	5 122.3	5 099.2	23.1	13 765.1	133.0	10 593.7	6 784.9	95.1
2008														
1st quarter	50 602.0	16 388.8	7 542.6	8 846.2	32 132.1	227.1	5 322.6	5 299.1	23.5	13 819.0	132.5	10 777.1	6 886.1	96.7
2nd quarter	51 050.8	16 645.0	7 865.5	8 779.5	32 305.2	226.0	5 274.1	5 250.6	23.5	13 841.8	128.1	10 964.8	7 017.8	98.1
3rd quarter	51 839.1	16 911.8	8 049.7	8 862.1	32 962.4	228.7	5 800.6	5 777.5	23.1	13 897.1	129.9	11 038.4	7 054.5	97.2
4th quarter	52 592.7	17 216.5	8 189.2	9 027.3	33 517.9	236.0	6 361.5	6 338.2	23.3	13 821.0	129.9	11 095.8	7 103.7	99.4

Table 12-5. Credit Market Debt Outstanding, by Borrower and Lender—*Continued*

(Billions of dollars, except as noted; end of period; not seasonally adjusted.)

Year and quarter	Credit market debt outstanding owed by: —Continued / Domestic nonfinancial sectors —Continued / Nonfinancial business—Continued / Nonfarm non-corporate	Farm	State and local govern-ments	Foreign credit market debt held in United States	Credit market assets held by: Total	Selected government-related sectors Total	Federal govern-ment	Govern-ment-sponsored enter-prises	Federally related mortgage pools	State and local govern-ments	State and local retirement funds	Federal govern-ment retirement funds	Selected domestic financial sectors Total, selected sectors	Monetary authority
1950	12.3	9.5	21.2	14.0	425.3	33.2	16.0	3.1	0.0	9.4	4.7	0.0	262.3	20.7
1951	14.3	10.8	23.6	14.7	449.2	36.2	17.2	3.5	0.0	10.1	5.4	0.0	280.9	23.6
1952	16.1	11.6	30.8	15.1	484.7	40.6	18.8	3.6	0.1	11.7	6.4	0.0	303.6	24.1
1953	17.1	11.5	35.8	16.3	516.7	44.9	20.8	3.7	0.1	12.6	7.7	0.0	323.3	25.3
1954	18.9	12.3	41.1	16.6	541.8	47.3	20.5	4.0	0.1	13.5	9.2	0.0	346.7	25.0
1955	21.5	13.7	46.1	16.6	582.0	51.4	21.1	5.0	0.1	14.7	10.5	0.0	369.5	24.4
1956	23.7	14.6	50.4	17.4	611.3	55.6	21.8	6.0	0.1	15.9	11.7	0.0	390.9	24.7
1957	25.2	15.6	55.0	18.8	642.5	59.1	22.4	7.3	0.2	15.9	13.3	0.0	411.1	23.8
1958	27.7	17.0	60.7	20.8	681.2	62.8	23.9	7.7	0.2	16.1	15.0	0.0	444.7	26.3
1959	31.9	18.9	66.7	21.4	738.0	70.1	25.7	9.9	0.2	17.5	16.8	0.0	471.5	26.7
1960	35.8	20.0	72.2	23.2	779.2	76.0	26.7	11.1	0.2	19.1	18.9	0.0	502.8	27.0
1961	41.0	21.6	77.8	25.5	827.2	82.0	28.4	12.1	0.3	20.1	21.1	0.0	541.4	28.8
1962	46.4	23.9	83.8	27.5	886.5	89.4	30.4	13.7	0.4	21.7	23.2	0.0	587.3	30.5
1963	52.6	26.4	89.2	30.8	952.2	96.6	31.9	15.3	0.5	23.3	25.6	0.0	638.4	33.7
1964	58.5	29.0	95.6	35.0	1 026.0	104.7	34.7	16.0	0.6	25.0	28.3	0.0	695.3	36.6
1965	64.7	32.3	103.2	37.5	1 104.0	115.5	37.6	18.3	0.9	27.5	31.3	0.0	758.1	40.6
1966	71.5	35.5	110.0	39.5	1 183.9	129.8	42.7	23.3	1.3	27.5	34.9	0.0	803.9	43.7
1967	78.7	38.8	117.4	43.3	1 264.3	138.5	47.3	23.3	2.0	27.6	38.3	0.0	869.3	49.1
1968	87.1	41.6	126.1	46.1	1 369.3	154.4	52.3	26.5	2.5	31.4	41.6	0.0	943.0	53.0
1969	99.6	44.6	138.3	49.2	1 487.0	175.6	55.4	35.1	3.2	36.4	45.5	0.0	1 000.2	57.2
1970	103.6	47.6	150.3	52.1	1 595.8	191.5	58.2	43.9	4.8	35.1	49.6	0.0	1 074.6	62.2
1971	122.6	51.6	166.7	56.6	1 747.0	201.1	60.3	45.0	9.5	33.4	52.9	0.0	1 186.9	69.6
1972	149.0	56.8	180.7	61.1	1 932.4	223.0	62.2	49.0	14.4	40.1	57.4	0.0	1 331.9	71.2
1973	168.5	65.4	194.8	67.4	2 170.3	260.2	64.9	64.4	18.0	49.8	63.1	0.0	1 498.4	80.5
1974	198.4	73.3	208.2	81.2	2 407.1	304.7	72.2	85.3	21.5	56.4	69.4	0.0	1 633.9	85.3
1975	210.7	82.1	219.4	96.9	2 616.7	347.5	87.1	89.8	28.5	63.8	78.3	0.0	1 761.9	93.5
1976	231.2	92.2	237.8	115.7	2 902.5	398.6	93.7	94.5	40.7	82.0	87.7	0.0	1 955.4	100.3
1977	261.3	105.9	256.2	128.6	3 290.5	471.6	103.6	101.4	56.8	110.6	99.2	0.0	2 214.0	108.9
1978	304.8	122.2	295.6	155.7	3 776.7	582.6	120.6	128.1	70.4	147.5	116.0	0.0	2 512.2	117.4
1979	357.5	145.7	322.2	168.5	4 273.2	696.0	141.4	158.1	94.8	175.2	126.6	0.0	2 822.7	124.5
1980	406.4	161.5	344.4	193.4	4 721.5	804.5	165.5	184.5	114.0	193.4	147.2	0.0	3 085.5	128.0
1981	456.8	177.8	372.1	214.0	5 254.1	931.1	189.9	217.7	129.0	225.6	169.0	0.0	3 387.0	136.9
1982	509.5	184.5	413.8	208.1	5 761.9	1 058.9	205.8	233.7	178.5	250.1	190.7	0.0	3 635.8	144.5
1983	580.3	188.4	461.1	224.1	6 455.9	1 177.7	215.3	236.4	244.8	282.4	198.8	0.0	4 038.5	159.2
1984	698.8	187.9	513.6	232.8	7 421.7	1 339.7	232.6	265.9	289.0	319.0	233.2	0.0	4 595.2	167.6
1985	798.0	161.7	677.9	242.5	8 621.7	1 618.0	251.2	291.0	367.9	455.6	252.4	0.0	5 202.4	186.0
1986	886.0	144.9	752.1	251.9	9 811.2	1 920.0	258.0	307.6	531.6	525.8	297.1	0.0	5 917.1	205.5
1987	956.3	132.4	842.6	259.0	10 823.9	2 156.6	242.8	330.9	669.4	583.6	328.8	1.1	6 459.6	226.5
1988	1 054.2	121.6	893.0	269.8	11 865.8	2 298.7	217.4	364.2	745.3	618.6	350.5	2.7	7 000.3	240.6
1989	1 100.5	122.7	940.4	287.9	12 838.7	2 489.2	209.4	359.9	869.5	664.1	381.5	4.9	7 439.7	233.3
1990	1 093.3	124.1	987.4	318.2	13 766.6	2 749.6	243.1	373.9	1 019.9	703.4	402.0	7.4	7 801.9	241.4
1991	1 058.5	123.1	1 078.6	350.4	14 421.4	2 961.6	251.0	388.9	1 156.5	750.6	404.6	10.0	8 060.5	272.5
1992	1 028.4	123.4	1 095.1	372.4	15 213.5	3 176.3	239.0	458.1	1 272.0	752.3	441.8	13.1	8 439.7	300.4
1993	1 007.9	125.6	1 153.1	468.2	16 185.0	3 402.7	229.6	546.7	1 356.8	784.9	468.6	16.2	9 031.3	336.7
1994	1 015.9	129.2	1 107.3	443.1	17 204.7	3 583.6	214.8	667.9	1 472.4	729.9	478.7	19.9	9 506.9	368.2
1995	1 062.1	131.4	1 046.7	567.6	18 475.2	3 702.8	197.6	762.8	1 570.7	638.6	509.8	23.3	10 325.2	380.8
1996	1 131.1	135.5	1 026.2	657.2	19 812.6	3 915.9	201.6	833.8	1 711.7	604.8	538.4	25.6	10 936.8	393.1
1997	1 228.8	142.8	1 076.9	723.6	21 245.0	4 204.4	213.1	934.2	1 826.3	605.0	598.3	27.5	11 780.6	431.4
1998	1 404.2	150.9	1 143.8	783.2	23 338.3	4 895.6	218.8	1 251.5	2 019.0	714.6	661.5	30.2	12 957.6	452.5
1999	1 599.4	154.2	1 181.0	748.2	25 406.3	5 645.2	256.3	1 538.8	2 293.5	816.5	707.0	33.1	14 093.7	478.1
2000	1 795.8	156.1	1 197.9	814.5	27 156.8	6 217.5	264.3	1 794.4	2 493.2	887.3	743.2	35.1	15 011.5	511.8
2001	1 957.3	162.6	1 303.4	865.4	29 343.8	6 914.5	268.2	2 099.1	2 831.8	981.2	689.4	44.8	16 162.2	551.7
2002	2 107.1	169.7	1 447.5	1 072.8	31 842.8	7 521.7	276.2	2 323.2	3 158.6	1 067.4	638.7	57.6	17 457.3	629.4
2003	2 198.7	168.0	1 567.6	1 252.7	34 622.5	8 011.2	273.6	2 564.2	3 326.7	1 125.6	657.5	63.6	18 814.3	666.7
2004	2 443.8	174.0	1 683.0	1 437.7	37 808.4	8 205.1	275.9	2 613.0	3 374.6	1 198.1	675.3	68.2	20 512.0	717.8
2005	2 775.4	186.9	1 854.7	1 512.3	41 269.3	8 482.2	275.0	2 543.9	3 541.9	1 352.0	693.4	76.0	22 557.8	744.2
2006	3 184.1	197.7	2 005.9	1 879.8	45 324.7	9 033.6	281.2	2 590.5	3 837.3	1 470.6	769.7	84.3	24 711.4	778.9
2007	3 594.9	214.0	2 191.6	2 016.5	49 865.7	9 988.4	287.5	2 829.5	4 463.5	1 512.0	799.8	96.1	26 715.5	740.6
2008	3 766.8	225.3	2 239.6	1 858.3	52 592.7	10 652.1	364.7	2 992.4	4 965.1	1 413.5	796.1	120.3	27 793.9	986.7
2006														
1st quarter	2 876.7	185.7	1 880.7	1 565.3	42 334.8	8 621.2	278.1	2 552.5	3 619.3	1 375.7	718.2	77.3	23 116.4	758.5
2nd quarter	2 981.0	191.0	1 922.2	1 609.2	43 351.5	8 800.2	279.6	2 591.2	3 681.6	1 410.8	755.1	81.8	23 707.7	766.4
3rd quarter	3 081.6	194.1	1 945.6	1 759.0	44 271.2	8 899.8	281.1	2 579.0	3 763.1	1 434.2	758.7	83.7	24 211.4	768.9
4th quarter	3 184.1	197.7	2 005.9	1 879.8	45 324.7	9 033.5	281.2	2 590.5	3 837.3	1 470.6	769.7	84.3	24 711.4	778.9
2007														
1st quarter	3 257.0	199.2	2 062.8	1 905.9	46 479.2	9 157.4	285.8	2 558.4	3 955.7	1 501.9	767.5	88.1	25 157.7	780.9
2nd quarter	3 349.4	204.2	2 121.6	1 971.7	47 464.4	9 357.4	286.6	2 596.7	4 075.8	1 537.2	772.2	88.9	25 741.0	790.5
3rd quarter	3 479.9	208.5	2 144.2	1 973.0	48 765.0	9 699.7	288.7	2 758.9	4 243.1	1 528.2	787.5	93.3	26 309.0	779.6
4th quarter	3 594.9	214.0	2 191.6	2 016.5	49 865.7	9 988.4	287.5	2 829.5	4 463.5	1 512.0	799.8	96.1	26 715.5	740.6
2008														
1st quarter	3 673.7	217.2	2 213.4	2 081.1	50 602.0	10 181.3	292.9	2 893.4	4 602.4	1 484.7	801.8	106.1	27 104.3	631.0
2nd quarter	3 720.7	226.3	2 224.5	2 100.6	51 050.8	10 427.5	296.4	2 987.8	4 761.5	1 473.2	800.5	108.1	27 070.5	509.1
3rd quarter	3 760.1	223.8	2 226.3	1 964.9	51 839.1	10 611.6	301.6	3 021.2	4 894.9	1 479.9	798.9	115.1	27 303.4	780.9
4th quarter	3 766.8	225.3	2 239.6	1 858.3	52 592.7	10 652.1	364.7	2 992.4	4 965.1	1 413.5	796.1	120.3	27 793.9	986.7

Table 12-5. Credit Market Debt Outstanding, by Borrower and Lender—*Continued*

(Billions of dollars, except as noted; end of period; not seasonally adjusted.)

Year and quarter	Commercial banks	Savings institutions	Credit unions	Life insurance companies	Property-casualty insurance companies	Private pension funds	Money market mutual funds	Mutual funds	Asset-backed security issuers	Finance companies	Households	Foreign holdings in United States	All other financial and non-financial sectors
1950	125.6	36.7	0.7	57.9	7.2	5.3	0.0	0.4	0.0	7.8	96.2	4.8	28.8
1951	132.8	39.5	0.8	61.6	7.8	6.0	0.0	0.5	0.0	8.3	96.9	4.9	30.3
1952	141.4	44.1	1.1	65.9	8.7	7.0	0.0	0.5	0.0	10.8	104.6	5.1	30.7
1953	145.2	49.5	1.4	70.6	9.9	8.3	0.0	0.5	0.0	12.5	109.6	5.8	33.1
1954	154.9	55.5	1.6	75.4	10.8	9.6	0.0	0.7	0.0	13.2	109.5	6.4	31.9
1955	159.2	63.2	2.0	80.5	11.5	10.8	0.0	0.8	0.0	17.0	117.6	6.7	36.8
1956	164.8	70.2	2.4	85.6	11.9	12.3	0.0	1.1	0.0	18.0	124.9	7.3	32.7
1957	170.1	77.0	2.9	90.5	12.6	13.9	0.0	1.2	0.0	19.3	131.9	7.5	32.9
1958	185.0	85.5	3.1	95.5	13.4	15.4	0.0	1.5	0.0	19.0	132.7	7.5	33.5
1959	189.7	95.1	3.8	100.5	14.6	16.9	0.0	1.8	0.0	22.4	142.8	11.7	41.8
1960	199.7	104.2	4.5	105.6	15.5	18.4	0.0	2.0	0.0	25.9	150.9	12.6	36.8
1961	215.9	115.3	4.9	110.9	16.5	19.6	0.0	2.4	0.0	27.0	154.9	13.1	35.9
1962	235.2	128.3	5.6	116.9	18.0	21.0	0.0	2.6	0.0	29.2	158.2	14.8	36.8
1963	252.8	144.5	6.3	123.3	18.7	22.6	0.0	2.8	0.0	33.7	159.8	15.9	41.4
1964	276.1	160.2	7.2	130.3	19.5	24.4	0.0	3.2	0.0	37.9	166.2	16.9	42.9
1965	305.1	173.5	8.2	137.8	20.6	25.7	0.0	3.9	0.0	42.7	170.0	17.4	43.0
1966	323.1	181.7	9.4	145.9	22.0	28.0	0.0	5.1	0.0	44.9	190.0	17.3	42.9
1967	359.8	195.0	10.2	153.3	23.5	28.7	0.0	4.3	0.0	45.5	195.2	20.0	41.3
1968	398.7	208.9	11.7	160.7	25.4	29.8	0.0	4.1	0.0	50.6	203.5	22.6	45.8
1969	418.3	221.5	13.8	167.6	27.0	30.4	0.0	5.1	0.0	59.2	241.4	23.2	46.6
1970	455.3	236.8	15.2	174.6	30.9	32.5	0.0	5.7	0.0	61.5	242.4	35.0	52.3
1971	506.5	271.7	17.2	182.8	34.6	31.3	0.0	5.5	0.0	67.6	233.2	62.8	63.0
1972	575.7	314.5	20.1	192.5	38.3	36.1	0.0	6.0	0.0	77.5	230.0	73.2	74.3
1973	662.4	348.0	23.7	204.8	41.8	41.3	0.0	6.6	0.0	89.4	254.7	74.7	82.3
1974	737.5	369.7	26.4	217.7	46.4	47.9	0.8	7.4	0.0	94.8	299.5	79.8	89.2
1975	768.8	415.2	31.7	234.6	53.7	59.8	1.5	8.0	0.0	95.0	320.7	88.3	98.3
1976	833.2	477.5	38.4	258.3	66.2	64.4	2.1	8.4	0.0	106.6	331.3	99.4	117.8
1977	924.6	548.1	45.6	285.8	83.7	74.4	1.9	12.3	0.0	128.6	358.0	135.8	111.1
1978	1 052.6	614.4	52.0	318.9	100.2	84.8	5.1	12.5	0.0	154.2	405.6	162.3	113.9
1979	1 181.8	671.9	53.8	352.0	113.7	102.2	24.9	14.5	0.0	183.4	485.0	150.8	118.7
1980	1 289.9	722.7	53.0	385.1	123.5	128.3	42.0	17.1	0.0	195.8	519.6	171.1	140.8
1981	1 398.2	748.7	55.0	419.8	132.0	150.2	107.5	20.2	0.0	218.6	544.9	198.7	192.4
1982	1 482.9	756.7	57.3	463.2	137.0	202.4	137.6	25.4	0.0	228.9	610.8	242.0	214.5
1983	1 626.1	879.5	69.4	513.8	138.6	240.2	119.7	34.9	3.0	254.0	703.4	265.8	270.5
1984	1 800.1	1 018.6	85.0	570.1	150.3	276.6	164.1	53.9	19.8	289.0	821.3	344.0	321.5
1985	1 989.5	1 097.6	98.4	646.6	176.5	329.0	178.2	129.9	34.8	335.9	978.8	428.2	394.3
1986	2 187.6	1 191.0	113.9	734.5	219.2	333.6	213.1	259.9	71.4	387.6	1 009.9	552.8	411.3
1987	2 323.0	1 310.3	131.3	823.1	258.6	347.2	215.0	291.1	113.2	420.2	1 187.6	606.5	413.6
1988	2 479.5	1 409.3	148.8	927.2	287.9	369.2	225.5	304.5	147.6	460.4	1 393.7	714.4	458.7
1989	2 647.4	1 316.0	156.0	1 028.3	317.5	420.8	293.7	327.2	201.1	498.3	1 483.2	854.8	571.8
1990	2 772.5	1 176.5	166.6	1 134.5	344.0	464.3	371.3	360.1	250.3	520.4	1 745.5	926.4	543.3
1991	2 853.3	1 013.2	179.4	1 218.9	376.6	489.7	403.9	440.2	299.5	513.3	1 834.7	963.2	601.4
1992	2 948.6	937.4	197.1	1 304.4	389.4	515.7	408.6	566.4	357.9	513.8	1 885.2	1 051.0	661.3
1993	3 090.8	914.1	218.7	1 415.5	422.7	551.9	429.0	725.9	437.8	488.3	1 870.0	1 194.2	686.8
1994	3 254.3	920.8	246.8	1 487.5	446.4	591.5	459.0	718.8	501.0	512.7	2 178.4	1 277.6	658.2
1995	3 520.1	913.3	263.0	1 587.5	468.7	608.4	545.5	771.3	612.0	654.6	2 241.7	1 464.8	740.7
1996	3 707.7	933.2	288.5	1 657.0	491.2	602.3	634.3	820.2	712.2	697.1	2 424.2	1 795.6	740.1
1997	4 031.9	928.5	305.3	1 751.5	515.3	646.8	721.9	901.1	826.5	720.8	2 402.5	2 035.6	821.9
1998	4 336.1	965.5	324.2	1 828.0	521.1	639.7	970.5	1 028.4	1 078.8	812.8	2 455.6	2 202.0	827.5
1999	4 648.3	1 032.6	351.7	1 886.0	518.2	746.9	1 155.3	1 076.8	1 253.2	946.6	2 590.8	2 196.1	880.5
2000	5 019.8	1 088.8	379.7	1 943.9	509.4	621.9	1 317.5	1 103.1	1 413.7	1 101.9	2 481.2	2 451.1	995.5
2001	5 226.0	1 133.5	421.2	2 074.8	518.4	585.8	1 584.9	1 229.7	1 665.5	1 170.7	2 392.9	2 850.2	1 024.0
2002	5 630.8	1 166.9	465.4	2 307.8	558.3	577.3	1 567.1	1 368.4	1 893.4	1 292.5	2 552.0	3 303.0	1 008.8
2003	6 010.9	1 294.2	516.6	2 488.3	625.2	646.5	1 471.3	1 506.4	2 119.5	1 468.7	2 783.9	3 836.1	1 177.0
2004	6 621.2	1 417.7	556.4	2 661.4	698.8	646.1	1 346.3	1 623.0	2 547.4	1 675.9	3 102.4	4 634.7	1 354.2
2005	7 278.4	1 617.1	592.6	2 765.4	765.8	690.6	1 340.8	1 747.1	3 275.2	1 740.6	3 452.1	5 188.3	1 588.9
2006	8 040.5	1 519.2	622.7	2 806.1	813.5	751.6	1 560.8	1 932.0	4 074.5	1 811.6	3 625.6	6 198.2	1 755.9
2007	8 785.2	1 584.9	657.9	2 888.6	839.8	852.9	1 945.7	2 203.1	4 388.6	1 828.2	3 942.5	7 369.3	1 850.0
2008	9 439.5	1 310.4	700.4	2 891.1	827.0	941.0	2 672.3	2 278.1	3 968.0	1 779.4	3 876.4	7 830.7	2 439.6
2006													
1st quarter	7 452.2	1 649.5	604.1	2 806.3	780.8	693.5	1 353.5	1 805.4	3 469.2	1 743.4	3 580.3	5 378.7	1 638.3
2nd quarter	7 666.2	1 680.1	615.6	2 827.9	792.9	708.5	1 375.9	1 839.5	3 670.6	1 764.2	3 616.1	5 624.0	1 603.5
3rd quarter	7 718.1	1 745.1	618.9	2 842.5	800.8	737.2	1 461.2	1 874.0	3 852.8	1 791.7	3 611.3	5 867.1	1 681.7
4th quarter	8 040.5	1 519.2	622.7	2 806.1	813.5	751.6	1 560.8	1 932.0	4 074.5	1 811.6	3 625.6	6 198.2	1 756.0
2007													
1st quarter	8 048.9	1 578.1	629.2	2 831.3	821.7	776.3	1 649.5	2 005.4	4 230.0	1 806.4	3 753.7	6 533.6	1 876.8
2nd quarter	8 239.0	1 595.8	641.0	2 855.4	830.4	807.2	1 699.2	2 093.5	4 382.0	1 807.0	3 718.0	6 827.5	1 820.5
3rd quarter	8 490.3	1 629.5	652.6	2 882.4	838.9	831.7	1 801.8	2 141.6	4 428.7	1 831.9	3 912.0	6 963.3	1 881.0
4th quarter	8 785.2	1 584.9	657.9	2 888.6	839.8	852.9	1 945.7	2 203.1	4 388.6	1 828.2	3 942.5	7 369.3	1 850.0
2008													
1st quarter	8 915.4	1 599.2	665.0	2 916.5	836.6	871.2	2 253.4	2 256.7	4 312.4	1 846.9	3 880.3	7 549.5	1 886.6
2nd quarter	8 980.8	1 607.0	684.7	2 929.1	835.0	888.1	2 356.6	2 356.6	4 212.3	1 835.1	3 845.3	7 777.0	1 930.5
3rd quarter	9 401.0	1 325.9	697.7	2 911.6	826.4	902.9	2 186.6	2 340.9	4 112.6	1 816.9	3 945.4	7 828.1	2 150.6
4th quarter	9 439.5	1 310.4	700.4	2 891.1	827.0	941.0	2 672.3	2 278.1	3 968.0	1 779.4	3 876.4	7 830.7	2 439.6

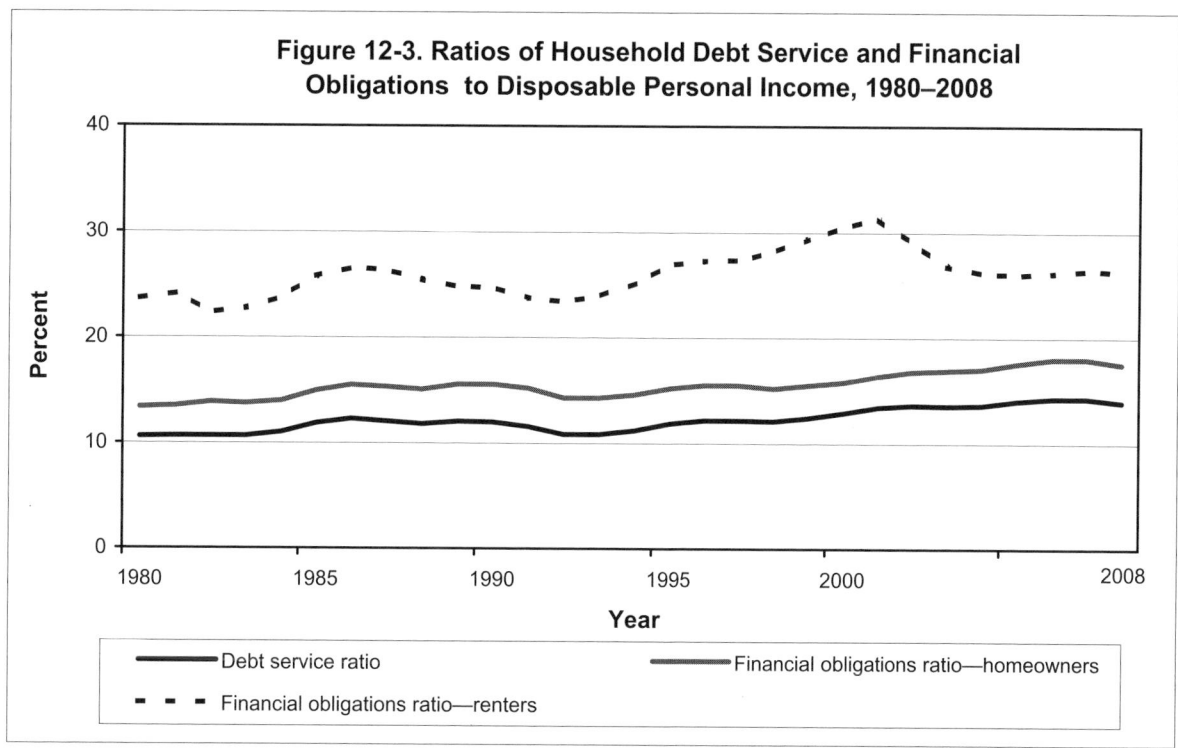

Figure 12-3. Ratios of Household Debt Service and Financial Obligations to Disposable Personal Income, 1980–2008

- The Federal Reserve calculates aggregate household debt service (payments of principal and interest) and total financial obligations as a percentage of aggregate disposable personal income (DPI) for the period 1980 to the present. These measures provide supplements to the ratio of the total level of household debt to DPI (shown in Figure 12-2 and Table 12-5), and are important because lengthening maturities and lower interest rates can mitigate much of the burden of a high level of debt. Unlike the debt/income ratio, the debt service ratio leveled off between 2002 and 2004, reflecting the decline in interest rates. However, the debt service ratio rose to a new record high of 14.3 percent in mid-2006 and remained there until the second quarter of 2008, when it dropped back to 13.9 percent. (Tables 12-5, 12-6, and 12-9)

- The financial obligations ratios are calculated separately for homeowners and renters and include all debt service, rental payments on primary residences, property taxes, homeowners' insurance, and automobile lease payments. The financial obligations ratio for homeowners is, of course, higher than the ratio for debt service alone. It stood at a record 18 percent of income through the first quarter of 2008, but has dropped back slightly since then. (Table 12-6)

- Reflecting the lower average incomes of the renters' group, the financial obligations ratio for renters is about double the ratio for homeowners. But the renters' ratio peaked in the fourth quarter of 2001. It then declined through 2004 and has remained stable since then. (Table 12-6)

- Additional evidence of the trend toward more debt is seen in the ratio of aggregate household debt to aggregate household financial and tangible assets, which rose from around 10 percent in 1960 to 21 percent at the end of 2008. (Table 12-6) Narrowing the comparison to mortgage debt alone, home mortgage debt as a percent of the value of real estate has increased from a range of 30 to 35 percent that prevailed from 1960 through 1987 to 60 percent in the fourth quarter of 2008; in other words, homeowners as a group now have only 40 percent equity in their homes, compared with the nearly 70 percent that they had as recently as 1982. (Table 12-7)

Table 12-6. Household Assets, Liabilities, Net Worth, Financial Obligations, and Delinquency Rates

(Billions of dollars, except as noted; end of period; not seasonally adjusted, except as noted.)

| Year and quarter | Financial assets of the household sector [1] | | | | | | | | | | | | | |
	Total [2]	Checkable deposits and currency	Time and savings deposits	Money market fund shares	U.S. savings bonds	Other Treasury securities	Agency- and GSE- backed securities	Municipal securities	Corporate and foreign bonds	Mortgages	Corporate equities	Mutual fund shares	Security credit	Life insurance reserves
1950	736.0	56.9	67.4	0.0	49.6	16.9	0.1	5.5	6.0	17.6	128.7	3.3	1.0	55.0
1951	801.1	61.0	72.2	0.0	49.1	16.3	0.1	5.7	6.3	18.6	151.1	3.5	0.9	57.8
1952	828.9	63.4	80.0	0.0	49.2	18.2	0.0	11.0	6.0	19.2	151.0	3.9	0.7	60.7
1953	846.6	64.6	88.3	0.0	49.4	18.7	0.2	13.9	6.0	20.2	145.8	4.1	0.7	63.6
1954	924.8	66.4	97.5	0.0	50.0	16.1	0.1	16.0	4.9	21.4	198.8	6.1	1.0	66.3
1955	1 013.6	67.4	106.1	0.0	50.2	18.6	0.6	19.2	5.0	22.7	248.2	7.8	0.9	69.3
1956	1 081.8	69.2	115.5	0.0	50.1	20.1	1.0	21.9	6.1	24.3	271.0	9.0	0.9	72.7
1957	1 093.9	68.3	127.4	0.0	48.2	23.3	1.5	23.9	7.2	26.2	244.5	8.7	0.9	75.5
1958	1 221.5	70.6	141.3	0.0	47.7	20.9	0.8	24.6	7.9	28.8	322.3	13.2	1.2	78.5
1959	1 297.4	72.9	152.7	0.0	45.9	25.7	2.3	28.4	8.2	30.7	357.3	15.8	1.0	82.0
1960	1 345.0	74.7	164.8	0.0	45.6	26.6	1.0	31.0	10.6	33.5	359.8	17.0	1.1	85.2
1961	1 488.6	73.6	183.2	0.0	46.4	25.5	0.6	32.5	10.8	36.8	443.2	22.9	1.2	88.6
1962	1 529.6	73.2	209.3	0.0	47.0	26.8	0.2	32.1	10.2	39.0	431.2	21.1	1.2	92.4
1963	1 627.4	78.1	235.5	0.0	48.1	24.7	0.0	32.1	10.1	40.5	469.9	25.0	1.2	96.6
1964	1 780.0	80.8	261.8	0.0	49.1	24.5	0.2	34.9	10.3	42.0	544.1	28.8	1.7	101.1
1965	1 944.9	87.5	289.7	0.0	49.7	25.1	1.1	36.5	9.0	42.6	616.1	34.8	2.5	105.9
1966	1 965.9	89.6	308.9	0.0	50.2	28.8	5.9	41.2	11.1	44.6	548.3	34.3	2.7	110.6
1967	2 214.5	100.2	344.4	0.0	51.2	27.8	6.3	38.2	15.1	46.5	682.1	43.5	4.9	115.5
1968	2 477.5	109.7	375.5	0.0	51.9	29.9	6.1	36.5	18.0	49.0	815.3	50.1	7.0	120.3
1969	2 421.3	108.1	385.5	0.0	51.8	41.4	11.3	47.2	22.0	49.1	667.4	46.3	5.2	125.4
1970	2 512.0	115.4	427.9	0.0	52.1	31.0	15.9	47.1	29.7	50.0	650.2	45.3	4.4	130.7
1971	2 797.1	128.9	493.8	0.0	54.4	19.8	14.6	46.0	37.4	47.3	743.7	54.2	4.9	137.1
1972	3 196.0	140.9	566.6	0.0	57.7	19.7	8.9	47.7	38.5	48.2	921.4	57.9	5.0	143.9
1973	3 199.1	149.5	629.6	0.0	60.4	28.1	8.3	55.1	41.5	47.2	693.9	45.4	4.9	151.3
1974	3 165.9	155.0	686.5	2.4	63.3	32.9	13.7	62.2	54.4	50.5	445.0	33.7	3.9	158.4
1975	3 610.1	156.6	766.7	3.7	67.4	44.4	7.6	66.8	64.3	50.4	584.6	41.5	4.5	168.6
1976	4 088.5	166.7	870.2	3.4	72.0	30.7	11.7	72.9	74.3	52.8	731.6	45.0	5.7	177.8
1977	4 355.2	181.1	975.9	3.3	76.8	27.8	8.4	78.8	79.4	55.3	631.3	44.1	5.7	187.8
1978	4 873.4	195.3	1 080.3	9.3	80.7	29.6	9.5	104.2	73.0	62.4	640.0	44.8	8.5	199.4
1979	5 584.9	212.7	1 154.4	40.6	79.9	76.0	12.4	123.6	65.6	71.6	768.1	49.9	10.4	210.3
1980	6 448.0	225.5	1 276.7	67.0	72.5	101.3	18.8	130.1	57.4	87.2	1 010.4	59.2	16.2	220.6
1981	6 833.0	266.9	1 350.0	161.2	68.2	100.6	14.7	160.3	57.8	101.4	905.2	56.7	14.7	230.1
1982	7 423.9	279.9	1 473.0	192.8	68.3	117.4	14.6	201.1	49.8	110.9	966.3	70.9	17.8	238.0
1983	8 159.3	286.3	1 684.0	160.7	71.5	161.3	15.9	246.7	53.1	111.2	1 088.6	104.9	20.6	246.7
1984	8 675.2	299.3	1 917.0	206.2	74.5	205.9	29.5	290.4	52.8	102.5	1 008.7	125.4	21.6	252.8
1985	9 947.4	309.9	1 981.3	204.6	79.8	206.0	26.1	395.1	101.2	114.2	1 229.5	213.8	35.1	264.3
1986	11 061.3	423.7	2 072.1	243.4	93.3	181.1	27.0	410.9	130.8	110.6	1 494.0	378.7	44.0	282.6
1987	11 720.6	426.4	2 194.1	264.6	101.1	210.8	34.3	516.6	151.3	118.2	1 462.6	424.5	39.1	309.5
1988	12 855.5	423.8	2 373.7	282.7	109.6	288.1	54.1	586.0	141.8	120.5	1 757.1	439.1	40.9	335.7
1989	14 181.0	423.0	2 454.1	360.9	117.7	281.3	77.3	613.3	176.2	129.4	2 147.5	513.0	53.2	365.3
1990	14 573.5	411.2	2 485.2	390.6	126.2	382.4	118.7	647.7	238.0	138.8	1 961.4	511.5	62.4	391.7
1991	16 115.3	460.2	2 409.8	407.7	138.1	401.4	117.0	701.8	276.9	141.0	2 759.2	645.0	87.0	418.6
1992	16 917.4	569.5	2 302.4	365.5	157.3	475.0	113.2	672.2	279.7	135.2	3 094.2	799.4	76.2	447.7
1993	18 164.5	615.7	2 192.7	363.5	171.9	506.1	57.2	640.8	300.8	128.1	3 437.0	1 098.0	102.3	484.8
1994	18 830.9	582.2	2 167.2	373.1	179.9	695.5	175.2	594.1	345.2	118.8	3 294.2	1 096.6	109.0	520.3
1995	21 510.2	561.9	2 299.7	472.4	185.0	648.6	223.0	533.4	466.5	113.3	4 434.2	1 253.0	127.6	566.2
1996	23 390.0	494.7	2 441.8	527.9	187.0	707.2	340.8	493.0	514.6	105.8	4 712.2	1 561.5	162.9	610.6
1997	26 656.1	448.1	2 578.5	602.3	186.5	616.6	398.9	497.6	526.9	98.7	6 144.3	1 948.8	215.5	665.0
1998	29 942.5	463.8	2 674.1	706.6	186.6	552.8	452.3	498.7	590.5	94.3	7 511.2	2 351.8	276.7	718.3
1999	34 372.3	417.7	2 776.2	816.1	186.4	628.0	552.0	528.1	509.4	101.6	9 769.9	2 894.9	323.9	783.9
2000	33 181.6	335.1	3 034.1	959.8	184.8	400.1	608.7	531.2	553.9	103.4	8 147.3	2 704.2	412.4	819.1
2001	32 035.4	407.2	3 307.8	1 113.2	190.3	254.6	441.5	580.8	717.0	108.7	6 829.5	2 614.6	454.3	880.0
2002	30 093.7	414.5	3 618.3	1 071.7	194.9	93.4	299.9	678.4	1 056.4	116.0	5 161.2	2 218.4	412.7	920.9
2003	35 071.0	399.0	3 939.4	960.2	203.8	237.7	437.3	703.8	971.1	121.3	6 787.7	2 904.3	475.4	1 013.2
2004	38 940.3	370.3	4 410.7	904.1	204.4	331.0	405.4	742.4	1 145.1	132.1	7 495.9	3 417.4	578.3	1 060.4
2005	42 895.1	256.8	4 887.8	949.2	205.1	306.2	501.1	821.0	1 303.7	142.2	8 004.4	3 839.3	575.3	1 082.6
2006	47 370.7	236.4	5 363.0	1 114.5	202.4	238.1	434.2	873.6	1 563.9	117.4	9 198.6	4 410.1	655.7	1 163.7
2007	49 754.1	101.3	5 803.8	1 346.7	196.4	-5.2	739.7	906.8	1 842.0	97.0	9 158.2	4 873.4	866.4	1 201.5
2008	40 814.2	156.2	5 891.4	1 577.9	194.0	79.2	920.4	959.8	1 600.9	94.2	5 502.4	3 254.1	742.7	1 156.4
2006														
1st quarter	44 829.5	271.9	5 069.2	952.7	205.9	417.3	443.2	823.0	1 373.7	139.4	8 673.6	4 108.6	598.6	1 102.4
2nd quarter	44 574.6	252.2	5 147.8	988.2	205.2	382.2	378.9	865.1	1 465.9	134.5	8 332.9	4 069.9	646.3	1 110.1
3rd quarter	45 486.1	239.2	5 271.0	1 010.4	203.6	339.9	426.7	867.2	1 457.4	126.9	8 540.4	4 165.9	654.8	1 133.5
4th quarter	47 370.7	236.4	5 363.0	1 114.5	202.4	238.1	434.2	873.6	1 563.9	117.4	9 198.7	4 410.1	655.7	1 163.7
2007														
1st quarter	48 517.5	247.6	5 602.6	1 113.6	200.3	222.8	486.1	877.6	1 655.9	109.2	9 530.0	4 594.4	690.1	1 172.7
2nd quarter	49 941.7	183.9	5 627.1	1 169.7	198.6	199.8	542.3	911.3	1 547.9	107.1	9 856.9	4 885.8	745.3	1 191.1
3rd quarter	50 495.2	87.4	5 716.8	1 248.8	197.1	166.0	664.2	907.0	1 694.7	101.1	9 805.0	4 992.2	757.8	1 199.6
4th quarter	49 754.1	101.3	5 803.8	1 346.7	196.4	-5.2	739.7	906.8	1 842.0	97.0	9 158.2	4 873.4	866.4	1 201.5
2008														
1st quarter	48 049.8	57.1	5 942.7	1 468.9	195.3	61.8	736.2	900.5	1 759.3	93.3	8 406.8	4 605.4	984.5	1 187.2
2nd quarter	47 330.6	42.8	5 872.2	1 411.0	194.9	79.9	706.6	918.4	1 747.8	98.1	7 980.4	4 685.1	992.1	1 196.4
3rd quarter	45 351.1	12.1	5 950.2	1 446.4	194.2	117.9	870.7	921.4	1 689.0	95.9	7 168.8	4 111.0	998.6	1 184.7
4th quarter	40 814.2	156.2	5 891.4	1 577.9	194.0	79.2	920.4	959.8	1 600.9	94.2	5 502.4	3 254.1	742.7	1 156.4

[1] Includes nonprofit organizations.
[2] Includes components not shown separately.

Table 12-6. Household Assets, Liabilities, Net Worth, Financial Obligations, and Delinquency Rates
—Continued

(Billions of dollars, except as noted; end of period; not seasonally adjusted, except as noted.)

Year and quarter	Financial assets of the household sector [1] —Continued Pension fund reserves	Equity in non-corporate business	Tangible assets of the household sector Total [1]	House-hold real estate [3]	Debt as a percent of total assets [1]	Total liabilities [1]	Net worth [1]	Ratios to disposable personal income (percent, seasonally adjusted) House-hold debt service	Household financial obligations Total	Home-owners	Renters	Consumer credit card accounts held at banks (percent, seasonally adjusted) Delinquency rate	Charge-off rate
1950	27.9	294.5	378.9	243.3	6.5	76.3	1 038.6	. . .	. . .	. . .	. . .	. . .	. . .
1951	33.5	320.6	420.3	270.9	6.7	85.3	1 136.1	. . .	. . .	. . .	. . .	. . .	. . .
1952	31.7	322.3	453.4	294.8	7.3	97.6	1 184.7	. . .	. . .	. . .	. . .	. . .	. . .
1953	36.5	322.1	482.4	315.1	8.0	110.4	1 218.5	. . .	. . .	. . .	. . .	. . .	. . .
1954	41.6	325.8	509.3	337.6	8.2	122.6	1 311.4	. . .	. . .	. . .	. . .	. . .	. . .
1955	49.3	334.9	553.8	367.4	8.8	143.9	1 423.6	. . .	. . .	. . .	. . .	. . .	. . .
1956	55.0	351.1	596.4	394.3	9.1	159.2	1 519.0	. . .	. . .	. . .	. . .	. . .	. . .
1957	60.8	363.1	631.3	417.2	9.6	171.6	1 553.7	. . .	. . .	. . .	. . .	. . .	. . .
1958	70.7	377.8	657.4	438.4	9.4	183.6	1 695.3	. . .	. . .	. . .	. . .	. . .	. . .
1959	80.0	379.2	692.5	463.7	10.0	206.2	1 783.7	. . .	. . .	. . .	. . .	. . .	. . .
1960	87.9	389.2	723.6	486.9	10.4	223.8	1 844.7	. . .	. . .	. . .	. . .	. . .	. . .
1961	100.3	405.8	755.2	511.1	10.4	241.9	2 001.8	. . .	. . .	. . .	. . .	. . .	. . .
1962	105.4	422.0	788.4	533.2	11.0	264.0	2 054.0	. . .	. . .	. . .	. . .	. . .	. . .
1963	118.5	426.6	823.6	553.3	11.5	292.9	2 158.0	. . .	. . .	. . .	. . .	. . .	. . .
1964	132.9	445.6	867.7	579.8	11.7	322.1	2 325.7	. . .	. . .	. . .	. . .	. . .	. . .
1965	148.2	471.7	913.1	605.6	11.9	351.5	2 506.6	. . .	. . .	. . .	. . .	. . .	. . .
1966	156.6	505.0	986.3	649.0	12.2	374.7	2 577.5	. . .	. . .	. . .	. . .	. . .	. . .
1967	177.4	529.5	1 053.6	685.7	11.6	397.8	2 870.3	. . .	. . .	. . .	. . .	. . .	. . .
1968	198.5	573.9	1 177.9	768.2	11.3	433.8	3 221.6	. . .	. . .	. . .	. . .	. . .	. . .
1969	208.8	607.5	1 283.4	832.4	11.9	461.4	3 243.3	. . .	. . .	. . .	. . .	. . .	. . .
1970	229.4	637.8	1 363.4	874.5	11.8	475.6	3 399.8	. . .	. . .	. . .	. . .	. . .	. . .
1971	266.9	703.5	1 487.9	957.2	11.7	521.6	3 763.4	. . .	. . .	. . .	. . .	. . .	. . .
1972	311.8	784.5	1 681.7	1 098.6	11.4	582.6	4 295.0	. . .	. . .	. . .	. . .	. . .	. . .
1973	313.5	919.3	1 905.9	1 251.4	12.2	649.1	4 455.9	. . .	. . .	. . .	. . .	. . .	. . .
1974	312.1	1 029.3	2 018.6	1 261.1	13.1	704.8	4 479.7	. . .	. . .	. . .	. . .	. . .	. . .
1975	390.4	1 128.7	2 237.4	1 413.7	12.6	760.9	5 086.6	. . .	. . .	. . .	. . .	. . .	. . .
1976	449.1	1 257.8	2 486.8	1 590.0	12.5	850.5	5 724.8	. . .	. . .	. . .	. . .	. . .	. . .
1977	490.6	1 420.1	2 885.7	1 886.8	13.1	981.6	6 259.4	. . .	. . .	. . .	. . .	. . .	. . .
1978	575.2	1 650.5	3 339.7	2 210.9	13.5	1 144.7	7 068.4	. . .	. . .	. . .	. . .	. . .	. . .
1979	665.7	1 915.6	3 882.2	2 603.3	13.5	1 317.8	8 149.2	. . .	. . .	. . .	. . .	. . .	. . .
1980	817.0	2 156.4	4 359.8	2 943.2	12.9	1 447.5	9 360.3	10.6	15.4	13.3	23.6	. . .	. . .
1981	902.0	2 313.8	4 823.0	3 293.0	12.9	1 559.7	10 096.2	10.6	15.6	13.5	24.1	. . .	. . .
1982	1 116.9	2 358.9	5 052.5	3 447.4	12.6	1 633.4	10 843.0	10.6	15.6	13.8	22.3	. . .	. . .
1983	1 326.0	2 418.6	5 307.2	3 602.8	12.9	1 800.3	11 666.2	10.6	15.6	13.7	22.7	. . .	. . .
1984	1 482.9	2 417.7	5 946.2	4 110.1	13.3	2 011.4	12 609.9	11.0	16.0	14.0	23.8	. . .	. . .
1985	2 088.6	2 487.1	6 634.0	4 658.4	13.7	2 366.8	14 214.6	11.9	17.1	14.9	25.7	. . .	2.98
1986	2 326.8	2 609.7	7 242.1	5 088.2	13.9	2 633.9	15 669.4	12.3	17.7	15.5	26.5	. . .	3.42
1987	2 504.8	2 701.9	7 814.3	5 502.4	14.1	2 842.0	16 692.8	12.0	17.5	15.3	26.3	. . .	3.26
1988	2 738.3	2 843.0	8 474.7	5 977.8	14.3	3 142.6	18 187.7	11.8	17.1	15.1	25.4	. . .	3.22
1989	3 169.0	2 966.2	9 139.0	6 474.0	14.3	3 451.9	19 868.0	12.1	17.4	15.5	24.8	. . .	3.27
1990	3 308.0	3 038.8	9 358.8	6 584.2	15.0	3 717.9	20 214.3	12.0	17.4	15.5	24.7	. . .	3.84
1991	3 824.8	2 989.2	9 592.1	6 784.3	14.7	3 931.1	21 776.2	11.5	17.0	15.2	23.7	5.30	4.66
1992	4 130.2	2 948.6	9 954.1	7 114.7	14.8	4 134.4	22 737.1	10.8	16.2	14.3	23.4	4.69	4.54
1993	4 605.6	3 083.1	10 317.4	7 364.9	14.8	4 401.6	24 080.2	10.8	16.2	14.2	23.9	3.90	3.35
1994	4 888.4	3 291.9	10 751.1	7 629.5	15.4	4 726.5	24 855.5	11.2	16.7	14.5	25.2	3.27	3.07
1995	5 715.3	3 486.6	11 242.5	7 984.3	14.8	5 053.9	27 698.9	11.9	17.5	15.2	26.9	3.93	3.93
1996	6 377.5	3 702.2	11 772.5	8 363.0	14.8	5 414.9	28 947.6	12.1	17.7	15.5	27.3	4.59	4.63
1997	7 354.8	3 907.7	12 388.1	8 775.2	14.1	5 762.1	33 282.2	12.1	17.7	15.5	27.3	4.78	5.48
1998	8 264.5	4 121.4	13 411.8	9 553.7	13.7	6 217.0	37 137.3	12.1	17.5	15.2	28.2	4.70	5.14
1999	9 265.2	4 320.5	14 538.8	10 443.0	13.1	6 794.4	42 116.7	12.4	17.9	15.5	29.3	4.50	4.45
2000	9 166.0	4 695.3	16 237.4	11 840.7	14.2	7 400.1	42 018.8	12.9	18.3	15.8	30.5	4.56	4.49
2001	8 766.4	4 822.9	17 744.9	13 204.0	15.4	8 031.2	41 749.1	13.4	18.9	16.4	31.3	4.69	6.22
2002	8 198.0	5 041.7	19 262.5	14 506.9	17.2	8 833.9	40 522.3	13.6	18.9	16.8	29.1	4.84	5.43
2003	9 722.4	5 544.4	21 162.1	16 176.8	16.9	9 860.3	46 372.8	13.6	18.6	16.9	26.8	4.42	5.90
2004	10 632.6	6 369.3	23 969.3	18 619.3	16.8	11 035.7	51 873.9	13.6	18.5	17.0	26.1	4.02	4.57
2005	11 368.9	7 827.6	27 391.2	21 380.7	16.7	12 188.2	58 098.0	14.0	19.0	17.6	26.0	3.52	5.97
2006	12 612.6	8 294.2	28 360.1	21 887.2	17.1	13 431.2	62 299.6	14.3	19.3	18.0	26.1	3.92	3.97
2007	13 247.4	8 436.3	27 264.8	20 488.4	17.9	14 329.0	62 689.8	14.3	19.4	18.0	26.4	4.54	4.10
2008	10 280.0	7 537.7	24 904.7	18 334.8	21.0	14 242.0	51 476.9	13.9	19.0	17.5	26.3	5.56	6.25
2006													
1st quarter	11 773.9	8 031.9	27 711.6	21 557.9	16.6	12 492.1	60 049.0	14.0	19.0	17.7	25.8	3.88	3.13
2nd quarter	11 703.4	8 024.8	27 792.5	21 567.1	17.1	12 846.4	59 520.7	14.2	19.2	17.9	25.9	4.15	3.49
3rd quarter	12 033.7	8 133.9	28 006.2	21 657.4	17.3	13 167.5	60 324.8	14.3	19.3	18.0	26.0	4.11	3.96
4th quarter	12 612.6	8 294.2	28 360.1	21 887.3	17.1	13 431.2	62 299.6	14.3	19.3	18.0	26.1	3.92	3.97
2007													
1st quarter	12 758.3	8 341.0	28 396.3	21 821.7	17.0	13 598.6	63 315.2	14.2	19.2	17.9	25.9	4.03	3.94
2nd quarter	13 278.6	8 536.6	28 325.6	21 603.6	17.0	13 905.6	64 361.7	14.3	19.4	18.0	26.3	4.03	3.84
3rd quarter	13 427.1	8 576.9	27 898.6	21 131.7	17.3	14 109.0	64 285.0	14.3	19.4	18.0	26.3	4.38	4.10
4th quarter	13 247.4	8 436.3	27 264.8	20 488.4	17.9	14 329.0	62 689.8	14.3	19.4	18.0	26.4	4.54	4.10
2008													
1st quarter	12 437.7	8 283.7	26 573.3	19 803.5	18.5	14 427.9	60 195.3	14.3	19.3	18.0	26.4	4.86	4.72
2nd quarter	12 341.5	8 157.3	26 358.4	19 660.7	18.8	14 381.1	59 308.0	13.8	18.8	17.4	25.7	4.91	5.47
3rd quarter	11 672.5	8 030.0	25 786.3	19 074.4	19.5	14 550.9	56 586.4	13.9	19.0	17.6	26.2	4.83	5.64
4th quarter	10 280.0	7 537.7	24 904.7	18 334.8	21.0	14 242.0	51 476.9	13.9	19.0	17.5	26.3	5.56	6.25

[1]Includes nonprofit organizations.
[3]Excludes nonprofit organizations.
. . . = Not available.

Table 12-7. Mortgage Debt Outstanding

(Billions of dollars, except as noted; end of period; not seasonally adjusted.)

Year and quarter	Total	By type of property					By type of holder							
		Home		Multi-family residences	Commercial	Farm	Commercial banks	Savings institutions	Life insurance companies	Federal and related agencies	Mortgage pools or trusts			Other
		Billions of dollars	Percent of value of real estate								Total [1]	Federally related agencies	ABS issuers	
1950	73	45	18	9	12	6	14	22	16	3	0	0	0	19
1951	83	52	19	11	13	7	15	25	19	3	0	0	0	20
1952	91	58	20	11	14	7	16	29	21	4	0	0	0	21
1953	101	66	21	12	15	8	17	34	23	5	0	0	0	22
1954	113	75	22	13	17	8	19	40	26	5	0	0	0	24
1955	129	88	24	13	19	9	21	48	29	5	0	0	0	26
1956	144	99	25	14	21	10	23	55	33	6	0	0	0	27
1957	156	107	26	15	24	10	23	60	35	7	0	0	0	29
1958	171	117	27	17	26	11	26	68	37	8	0	0	0	33
1959	190	130	28	19	29	12	28	77	39	10	0	0	0	36
1960	207	141	29	21	32	13	29	86	42	11	0	0	0	39
1961	227	154	30	24	36	14	30	96	44	12	0	0	0	44
1962	251	168	32	27	40	15	34	109	47	12	0	0	0	47
1963	277	185	33	30	45	17	39	125	51	11	1	1	0	51
1964	304	202	35	35	48	19	44	140	55	12	1	1	0	53
1965	331	219	36	38	52	21	50	153	60	13	1	1	0	55
1966	355	233	36	41	58	23	54	160	65	16	1	1	0	58
1967	378	246	36	45	62	25	59	170	68	19	2	2	0	60
1968	407	263	34	48	69	27	65	182	70	23	3	3	0	65
1969	436	279	33	53	75	29	71	194	72	28	3	3	0	68
1970	465	292	33	60	82	30	73	205	74	34	5	5	0	74
1971	514	318	33	70	93	32	83	231	75	37	10	10	0	79
1972	587	357	33	83	111	35	99	268	77	40	14	14	0	89
1973	664	400	32	93	131	40	119	300	81	47	18	18	0	99
1974	726	435	35	100	146	45	132	321	86	61	21	21	0	104
1975	783	474	34	101	159	50	136	351	89	73	29	29	0	106
1976	868	535	34	106	172	55	151	398	92	76	41	41	0	111
1977	997	628	33	114	191	64	179	459	97	84	57	57	0	121
1978	1 148	738	33	125	212	73	214	517	106	100	70	70	0	140
1979	1 314	856	33	135	236	87	245	565	118	121	95	95	0	169
1980	1 454	958	33	143	256	97	263	594	131	143	114	114	0	209
1981	1 576	1 030	31	142	296	107	284	612	138	160	129	129	0	252
1982	1 653	1 070	31	146	326	111	301	576	142	177	179	179	0	279
1983	1 840	1 186	33	161	379	114	331	627	151	188	245	245	0	299
1984	2 082	1 321	32	186	462	112	381	710	157	202	300	289	11	332
1985	2 367	1 525	33	206	542	94	431	766	172	213	393	368	25	392
1986	2 654	1 728	34	239	603	84	505	785	194	202	550	532	19	419
1987	2 955	1 926	35	259	694	76	595	824	212	189	702	669	32	434
1988	3 273	2 161	36	275	766	71	677	888	233	192	787	745	41	496
1989	3 543	2 385	37	288	801	69	771	873	254	198	923	870	53	525
1990	3 798	2 621	40	288	821	68	849	802	268	239	1 088	1 020	68	552
1991	3 948	2 789	41	285	807	67	881	705	260	266	1 271	1 156	115	565
1992	4 058	2 954	42	272	763	68	901	628	242	286	1 442	1 272	170	559
1993	4 191	3 114	42	269	740	68	948	598	224	326	1 565	1 357	208	530
1994	4 358	3 292	43	270	727	70	1 013	596	216	316	1 703	1 472	231	515
1995	4 547	3 461	43	276	739	72	1 090	597	213	308	1 819	1 571	248	520
1996	4 817	3 685	44	288	770	74	1 145	628	208	294	1 997	1 712	286	543
1997	5 130	3 919	45	300	833	79	1 245	632	207	285	2 175	1 826	349	587
1998	5 617	4 276	45	333	925	83	1 337	644	214	292	2 497	2 019	478	633
1999	6 228	4 702	45	375	1 064	87	1 495	668	231	320	2 845	2 294	552	669
2000	6 789	5 129	43	405	1 171	85	1 660	723	236	341	3 111	2 493	618	718
2001	7 498	5 681	43	447	1 282	89	1 790	758	243	373	3 572	2 832	740	762
2002	8 400	6 438	44	485	1 382	95	2 058	781	250	434	4 009	3 159	851	868
2003	9 399	7 232	45	565	1 509	94	2 256	871	261	695	4 350	3 327	1 023	967
2004	10 666	8 272	44	618	1 680	97	2 596	1 057	273	704	4 830	3 375	1 456	1 206
2005	12 108	9 387	44	689	1 930	102	2 958	1 153	286	667	5 684	3 542	2 142	1 057
2006	13 488	10 434	48	744	2 209	102	3 403	1 074	304	689	6 607	3 837	2 770	1 109
2007	14 562	11 122	54	843	2 489	108	3 646	1 095	326	727	7 414	4 464	2 951	1 038
2008	14 640	11 030	60	900	2 599	111	3 841	860	338	786	7 550	4 965	2 585	904
2006														
1st quarter	12 508	9 704	45	705	1 997	102	3 033	1 192	289	672	5 931	3 619	2 311	1 391
2nd quarter	12 906	10 023	46	715	2 066	101	3 140	1 221	296	678	6 159	3 682	2 478	1 412
3rd quarter	13 242	10 279	47	727	2 135	101	3 181	1 249	300	682	6 395	3 763	2 632	1 434
4th quarter	13 488	10 434	48	744	2 209	101	3 403	1 074	304	689	6 607	3 837	2 770	1 412
2007														
1st quarter	13 761	10 640	49	762	2 256	103	3 386	1 117	306	694	6 852	3 956	2 897	1 404
2nd quarter	14 079	10 850	50	785	2 339	105	3 472	1 113	312	702	7 089	4 076	3 013	1 391
3rd quarter	14 337	10 995	52	811	2 425	106	3 525	1 147	317	713	7 249	4 243	3 006	1 386
4th quarter	14 562	11 122	54	843	2 489	108	3 646	1 095	326	727	7 414	4 464	2 951	1 354
2008														
1st quarter	14 686	11 184	56	858	2 535	109	3 686	1 112	330	742	7 478	4 602	2 876	1 338
2nd quarter	14 725	11 170	57	875	2 571	109	3 662	1 116	334	757	7 542	4 762	2 780	1 315
3rd quarter	14 707	11 121	58	895	2 581	110	3 855	884	338	753	7 584	4 895	2 689	1 294
4th quarter	14 640	11 030	60	900	2 599	111	3 841	860	338	786	7 550	4 965	2 585	1 265

[1] Outstanding principal balances of mortgage-backed securities issued or guaranteed by the holder indicated.

Table 12-8. Consumer Credit

(Outstanding at end of period, billions of dollars.)

Year and month	Seasonally adjusted			Not seasonally adjusted							
	Total	By major credit type		Total	By major holder						
		Revolving	Non-revolving		Commercial banks	Finance companies	Credit unions	Federal government and Sallie Mae	Savings institutions	Nonfinancial businesses	Securitized pools [1]
1960	60.0	. . .	60.0	61.2	26.4	15.4	3.4	0.0	2.4	13.5	0.0
1961	62.2	. . .	62.2	63.4	27.9	15.5	3.6	0.0	2.9	13.6	0.0
1962	68.1	. . .	68.1	69.3	30.6	17.3	4.1	0.0	3.0	14.3	0.0
1963	76.6	. . .	76.6	77.9	34.7	19.6	4.5	0.0	3.6	15.5	0.0
1964	86.0	. . .	86.0	87.4	39.8	21.6	5.4	0.0	3.7	16.8	0.0
1965	96.0	. . .	96.0	97.5	45.2	23.9	6.5	0.0	3.9	18.1	0.0
1966	101.8	. . .	101.8	103.4	48.2	24.8	7.5	0.0	4.0	19.0	0.0
1967	106.8	. . .	106.8	108.6	51.7	24.6	8.3	0.0	4.1	19.9	0.0
1968	117.4	2.0	115.4	119.3	58.5	26.1	9.7	0.0	4.3	20.8	0.0
1969	127.2	3.6	123.6	129.2	63.4	27.8	11.7	0.0	4.4	21.9	0.0
1970	131.6	5.0	126.6	133.7	65.6	27.6	13.0	0.0	4.4	23.0	0.0
1971	146.9	8.2	138.7	149.2	74.3	29.2	14.8	0.0	4.7	26.2	0.0
1972	166.2	9.4	156.8	168.8	87.0	31.9	17.0	0.0	5.1	27.8	0.0
1973	190.1	11.3	178.7	193.0	99.6	35.4	19.6	0.0	8.5	29.8	0.0
1974	198.9	13.2	185.7	201.9	103.0	36.1	21.9	0.0	9.1	31.8	0.0
1975	204.0	14.5	189.5	207.0	106.1	32.6	25.7	0.0	10.1	32.6	0.0
1976	225.7	16.5	209.2	229.0	118.0	33.7	31.2	0.0	10.8	35.2	0.0
1977	260.6	37.4	223.1	264.9	140.3	37.3	37.6	0.5	11.8	37.4	0.0
1978	306.1	45.7	260.4	311.3	166.5	44.4	45.2	0.9	13.1	41.2	0.0
1979	348.6	53.6	295.0	354.6	185.7	55.4	47.4	1.5	20.0	44.6	0.0
1980	351.9	55.0	297.0	358.0	180.2	62.2	44.1	2.6	22.7	46.2	0.0
1981	371.3	60.9	310.4	377.9	184.2	70.1	46.7	4.8	24.0	48.1	0.0
1982	389.8	66.3	323.5	396.7	190.9	75.3	48.8	6.4	26.6	48.7	0.0
1983	437.1	79.0	358.0	444.9	213.7	83.3	56.1	4.6	31.5	55.7	0.0
1984	517.3	100.4	416.9	526.6	258.8	89.9	67.9	5.6	44.2	60.2	0.0
1985	599.7	124.5	475.2	610.6	297.2	111.7	74.0	6.8	57.6	63.3	0.0
1986	654.8	141.1	513.7	666.4	320.2	134.0	77.1	8.2	62.9	64.0	0.0
1987	686.3	160.9	525.5	698.6	334.1	140.0	81.0	10.0	65.3	68.1	0.0
1988	731.9	184.6	547.3	745.2	360.8	144.7	88.3	13.2	66.8	71.4	0.0
1989	794.6	211.2	583.4	809.3	383.3	138.9	91.7	16.0	62.5	69.6	47.3
1990	808.2	238.6	569.6	824.4	382.0	133.4	91.6	19.2	49.6	71.9	76.7
1991	798.0	263.8	534.3	815.6	370.2	121.6	90.3	21.1	42.2	67.3	103.0
1992	806.1	278.4	527.7	824.8	362.9	118.1	91.7	24.2	37.4	70.3	120.3
1993	865.7	309.9	555.7	886.2	395.7	116.1	101.6	27.2	37.9	77.2	130.5
1994	997.3	365.6	631.7	1 021.2	458.8	134.4	119.6	37.2	38.5	86.6	146.1
1995	1 140.7	443.9	696.8	1 168.2	502.3	152.1	131.9	43.5	40.1	85.1	213.1
1996	1 253.4	507.5	745.9	1 273.9	527.5	154.9	144.1	51.4	44.7	77.7	273.5
1997	1 324.8	540.0	784.8	1 344.2	515.1	167.5	152.4	57.2	47.2	84.4	320.5
1998	1 421.0	581.4	839.6	1 441.3	512.0	183.3	155.4	64.9	52.4	79.3	393.9
1999	1 532.4	610.7	921.7	1 553.6	507.8	201.6	167.9	81.8	61.7	76.1	456.7
2000	1 717.7	683.7	1 034.0	1 741.3	551.1	234.4	184.4	96.7	64.8	81.5	528.4
2001	1 867.3	716.6	1 150.7	1 892.0	568.4	280.0	189.6	111.9	71.1	73.1	598.0
2002	1 974.3	748.8	1 225.5	1 999.9	602.6	307.5	195.7	117.3	68.7	74.8	633.3
2003	2 078.3	770.4	1 307.9	2 104.4	669.4	393.0	205.9	102.9	77.9	58.5	596.8
2004	2 191.6	799.8	1 391.8	2 219.4	704.3	492.3	215.4	86.1	91.3	58.6	571.5
2005	2 285.2	824.5	1 460.7	2 313.9	707.0	516.5	228.6	89.8	109.1	58.8	604.0
2006	2 387.7	874.6	1 513.1	2 418.3	741.2	534.4	234.5	91.7	95.5	56.8	664.2
2007	2 519.0	939.5	1 579.5	2 551.9	804.1	584.1	235.7	98.4	90.8	55.2	683.7
2008	2 563.3	961.6	1 601.7	2 596.9	878.5	575.8	235.0	111.0	86.3	55.6	654.7
2007											
January	2 392.8	876.6	1 516.2	2 415.2	742.4	531.9	234.3	94.9	95.2	55.0	661.4
February	2 403.1	881.3	1 521.9	2 400.3	725.9	527.1	232.8	95.1	94.9	53.4	671.1
March	2 417.0	888.7	1 528.3	2 399.0	723.3	532.0	232.3	95.1	94.6	53.0	668.8
April	2 421.8	889.8	1 532.0	2 405.3	729.1	535.2	233.4	94.9	95.4	53.0	664.1
May	2 439.0	898.8	1 540.2	2 422.1	735.7	540.5	234.7	94.8	96.3	53.4	666.7
June	2 449.5	903.3	1 546.2	2 432.2	737.9	542.6	233.0	94.9	97.2	53.5	673.2
July	2 462.1	910.1	1 552.0	2 447.7	748.6	554.0	234.9	94.6	86.9	53.4	675.3
August	2 480.9	917.2	1 563.8	2 486.8	763.9	566.5	237.7	96.7	86.9	54.0	681.2
September	2 493.5	921.9	1 571.6	2 502.2	771.5	567.6	236.9	98.0	87.0	53.8	687.3
October	2 501.1	929.2	1 571.8	2 506.3	771.3	569.7	236.8	98.3	87.1	53.7	689.4
November	2 513.8	936.1	1 577.7	2 527.1	788.0	574.0	236.6	98.5	87.2	55.3	687.5
December	2 519.0	939.5	1 579.5	2 551.9	804.1	584.1	235.7	98.4	90.8	55.2	683.7
2008											
January	2 526.0	945.8	1 580.3	2 549.8	808.7	579.5	233.9	102.4	89.7	53.2	682.5
February	2 536.9	951.4	1 585.5	2 533.9	800.0	577.0	232.0	103.1	88.6	51.9	681.3
March	2 549.0	957.3	1 591.7	2 529.8	796.3	580.7	230.1	103.5	87.5	51.2	680.4
April	2 558.8	957.3	1 601.5	2 541.3	807.4	583.9	231.1	103.9	88.3	51.1	675.5
May	2 565.5	963.0	1 602.5	2 547.7	807.9	584.5	231.7	104.2	89.2	51.3	678.9
June	2 574.1	965.8	1 608.3	2 555.9	813.0	581.8	231.1	104.6	90.0	51.3	684.1
July	2 581.8	972.1	1 609.7	2 566.7	820.3	586.5	233.5	105.3	89.7	51.5	679.8
August	2 575.8	974.2	1 601.6	2 581.8	832.9	592.4	235.5	106.5	89.4	52.0	673.0
September	2 582.8	976.8	1 606.0	2 591.6	844.1	596.3	236.1	106.9	79.3	51.9	677.0
October	2 578.3	973.9	1 604.4	2 583.6	850.6	585.8	236.6	108.6	82.5	52.0	667.5
November	2 568.9	968.2	1 600.7	2 582.6	863.1	580.7	236.9	109.6	83.1	52.9	656.2
December	2 563.3	961.6	1 601.7	2 596.9	878.5	575.8	235.0	111.0	86.3	55.6	654.7

[1]Outstanding balances of pools upon which securities have been issued; these balances are no longer carried on the balance sheets of the loan originators.
. . . = Not available.

Table 12-9. Selected Interest Rates and Bond Yields

(Percent per annum; interest rates are nominal [not adjusted for inflation], except as noted.)

Year and month	Short-term rates								Inflation: percent change from year earlier in PCE chain-type price index excluding food and energy	Real federal funds rate (nominal rate minus inflation)	Interest rate swaps	
	Federal funds	Federal Reserve discount rate[1]	Eurodollar deposits, 1-month	U.S. Treasury bills, secondary market, 3-month	U.S. Treasury bills, secondary market, 6-month	Commercial paper, 3-month[2]	CDs (secondary market), 3-month	Bank prime rate			1-year	30-year
1960	3.21	3.53	. . .	2.87	3.20	. . .	. . .	4.82	1.67	1.54	. . .	. . .
1961	1.95	3.00	. . .	2.35	2.59	. . .	. . .	4.50	1.21	0.74	. . .	. . .
1962	2.71	3.00	. . .	2.77	2.90	. . .	. . .	4.50	1.25	1.46	. . .	. . .
1963	3.18	3.23	. . .	3.16	3.26	. . .	. . .	4.50	1.20	1.98	. . .	. . .
1964	3.50	3.55	. . .	3.55	3.68	. . .	3.92	4.50	1.45	2.05	. . .	. . .
1965	4.07	4.04	. . .	3.95	4.05	. . .	4.36	4.54	1.22	2.85	. . .	. . .
1966	5.11	4.50	. . .	4.86	5.06	. . .	5.45	5.63	2.09	3.02	. . .	. . .
1967	4.22	4.19	. . .	4.29	4.61	. . .	4.99	5.63	2.88	1.34	. . .	. . .
1968	5.66	5.17	. . .	5.34	5.47	. . .	5.82	6.31	4.25	1.41	. . .	. . .
1969	8.21	5.87	. . .	6.67	6.86	. . .	7.23	7.96	4.64	3.57	. . .	. . .
1970	7.17	5.95	. . .	6.39	6.51	. . .	7.55	7.91	4.53	2.64	. . .	. . .
1971	4.67	4.88	6.40	4.33	4.52	5.25	5.00	5.73	4.65	0.02	. . .	. . .
1972	4.44	4.50	5.00	4.06	4.47	4.66	4.66	5.25	3.24	1.20	. . .	. . .
1973	8.74	6.45	9.19	7.04	7.20	8.21	9.30	8.03	3.64	5.10	. . .	. . .
1974	10.51	7.83	10.79	7.85	7.95	10.05	10.29	10.81	7.51	3.00	. . .	. . .
1975	5.82	6.25	6.35	5.79	6.10	6.26	6.44	7.86	8.28	-2.46	. . .	. . .
1976	5.05	5.50	5.26	4.98	5.26	5.24	5.27	6.84	6.11	-1.06	. . .	. . .
1977	5.54	5.46	5.75	5.26	5.52	5.54	5.63	6.83	6.35	-0.81	. . .	. . .
1978	7.94	7.46	8.33	7.18	7.58	7.93	8.21	9.06	6.59	1.35	. . .	. . .
1979	11.20	10.29	11.66	10.05	10.04	10.95	11.20	12.67	6.97	4.23	. . .	. . .
1980	13.35	11.77	13.77	11.39	11.32	12.61	13.02	15.26	9.04	4.31	. . .	. . .
1981	16.39	13.42	16.72	14.04	13.81	15.34	15.93	18.87	8.71	7.68	. . .	. . .
1982	12.24	11.01	12.74	10.60	11.06	11.90	12.27	14.85	6.57	5.67	. . .	. . .
1983	9.09	8.50	9.38	8.62	8.74	8.88	9.07	10.79	5.27	3.82	. . .	. . .
1984	10.23	8.80	10.45	9.54	9.78	10.12	10.39	12.04	4.16	6.07	. . .	. . .
1985	8.10	7.69	8.12	7.47	7.65	7.95	8.04	9.93	3.83	4.27	. . .	. . .
1986	6.80	6.32	6.78	5.97	6.02	6.49	6.51	8.33	3.75	3.05	. . .	. . .
1987	6.66	5.66	6.88	5.78	6.03	6.82	6.87	8.21	3.70	2.96	. . .	. . .
1988	7.57	6.20	7.69	6.67	6.91	7.66	7.73	9.32	4.33	3.24	. . .	. . .
1989	9.21	6.93	9.16	8.11	8.03	8.99	9.09	10.87	4.13	5.08	. . .	. . .
1990	8.10	6.98	8.15	7.50	7.46	8.06	8.15	10.01	4.26	3.84	. . .	. . .
1991	5.69	5.45	5.81	5.38	5.44	5.87	5.83	8.46	3.91	1.78	. . .	. . .
1992	3.52	3.25	3.62	3.43	3.54	3.75	3.68	6.25	3.41	0.11	. . .	. . .
1993	3.02	3.00	3.07	3.00	3.12	3.22	3.17	6.00	2.56	0.46	. . .	. . .
1994	4.21	3.60	4.34	4.25	4.64	4.66	4.63	7.15	2.31	1.90	. . .	. . .
1995	5.83	5.21	5.86	5.49	5.56	5.93	5.92	8.83	2.23	3.60	. . .	. . .
1996	5.30	5.02	5.32	5.01	5.08	5.41	5.39	8.27	1.88	3.42	. . .	. . .
1997	5.46	5.00	5.52	5.06	5.18	5.52	5.62	8.44	1.61	3.85	. . .	. . .
1998	5.35	4.92	5.45	4.78	4.83	5.37	5.47	8.35	1.31	4.04	. . .	. . .
1999	4.97	4.62	5.15	4.64	4.75	5.21	5.33	8.00	1.49	3.48	. . .	. . .
2000	6.24	5.73	6.33	5.82	5.90	6.33	6.46	9.23	1.68	4.56	6.73	6.93
2001	3.88	3.40	3.81	3.40	3.34	3.65	3.71	6.91	1.90	1.98	3.87	6.20
2002	1.67	1.17	1.71	1.61	1.68	1.70	1.73	4.67	1.77	-0.10	2.21	5.80
2003	1.13	. . .	1.14	1.01	1.05	1.13	1.15	4.12	1.42	-0.29	1.36	5.24
2004	1.35	2.34	1.43	1.37	1.58	1.52	1.57	4.34	2.06	-0.71	2.13	5.38
2005	3.22	4.19	3.33	3.15	3.39	3.44	3.51	6.19	2.15	1.07	4.04	5.03
2006	4.97	5.96	5.09	4.73	4.81	5.07	5.16	7.96	2.27	2.70	5.33	5.44
2007	5.02	5.86	5.28	4.36	4.44	5.13	5.27	8.05	2.16	2.86	5.09	5.45
2008	1.92	2.39	3.03	1.37	1.62	2.83	2.97	5.09	2.18	-0.26	2.75	4.57
2007												
January	5.25	6.25	5.32	4.98	4.95	5.24	5.32	8.25	2.39	2.86	5.38	5.37
February	5.26	6.25	5.32	5.03	4.96	5.23	5.31	8.25	2.42	2.84	5.38	5.37
March	5.26	6.25	5.32	4.94	4.89	5.22	5.30	8.25	2.23	3.03	5.22	5.28
April	5.25	6.25	5.31	4.87	4.78	5.23	5.31	8.25	2.14	3.11	5.30	5.42
May	5.25	6.25	5.32	4.73	4.78	5.23	5.31	8.25	2.06	3.19	5.36	5.48
June	5.25	6.25	5.32	4.61	4.76	5.25	5.33	8.25	2.01	3.24	5.46	5.86
July	5.26	6.25	5.32	4.82	4.83	5.25	5.32	8.25	2.03	3.23	5.40	5.84
August	5.02	6.01	5.53	4.20	4.38	5.30	5.49	8.25	1.96	3.06	5.09	5.62
September	4.94	5.53	5.50	3.89	4.05	5.19	5.46	8.03	2.05	2.89	4.91	5.41
October	4.76	5.24	5.01	3.90	4.01	4.91	5.08	7.74	2.11	2.65	4.79	5.38
November	4.49	5.00	4.83	3.27	3.46	4.75	4.97	7.50	2.22	2.27	4.42	5.18
December	4.24	4.83	5.23	3.00	3.23	4.76	5.02	7.33	2.28	1.96	4.29	5.10
2008												
January	3.94	4.48	3.93	2.75	2.75	3.70	3.84	6.98	2.18	1.76	3.33	4.82
February	2.98	3.50	3.17	2.12	2.04	3.03	3.06	6.00	2.13	0.85	2.69	4.99
March	2.61	3.04	2.87	1.26	1.48	2.70	2.79	5.66	2.23	0.38	2.41	4.78
April	2.28	2.49	2.97	1.29	1.55	2.72	2.85	5.24	2.19	0.09	2.71	4.80
May	1.98	2.25	2.63	1.73	1.82	2.61	2.66	5.00	2.24	-0.26	2.88	4.92
June	2.00	2.25	2.66	1.86	2.13	2.70	2.76	5.00	2.34	-0.34	3.22	5.12
July	2.01	2.25	2.65	1.63	1.93	2.72	2.79	5.00	2.38	-0.37	3.09	5.02
August	2.00	2.25	2.61	1.72	1.92	2.76	2.79	5.00	2.38	-0.38	3.03	4.95
September	1.81	2.25	4.01	1.13	1.61	2.91	3.59	5.00	2.25	-0.44	3.03	4.65
October	0.97	1.81	4.93	0.67	1.20	3.19	4.32	4.56	2.09	-1.12	2.86	4.30
November	0.39	1.25	2.08	0.19	0.73	1.54	2.36	4.00	1.96	-1.57	2.11	3.83
December	0.16	0.86	1.75	0.03	0.26	1.09	1.77	3.61	1.77	-1.61	1.62	2.69

[1]Federal Reserve Bank of New York. Through 2002, represents the rate for adjustment credit. Beginning in 2003, represents the rate for primary credit. See notes and definitions for more information.
[2]Prior to September 1997, this series represents both nonfinancial and financial commercial paper rates. Beginning September 1997, rates for financial companies only are shown. See notes and definitions for more information.
. . . = Not available.

Table 12-9. Selected Interest Rates and Bond Yields—*Continued*

(Percent per annum; interest rates are nominal [not adjusted for inflation], except as noted.)

Year and month	U.S. Treasury securities, constant maturities								Bond yields			Fixed-rate first mortgages
	Nominal yields					Inflation-indexed yields			Domestic corporate (Moody's)		State and local bonds (Bond Buyer)	
	1-year	5-year	10-year	20-year	30-year	5-year	20-year	Long-term average	Aaa	Baa		
1960	...	...	...	...	...	...	...	...	4.41	5.19	3.52	...
1961	...	...	...	...	...	...	...	...	4.35	5.08	3.45	...
1962	3.10	3.70	3.95	...	...	...	...	...	4.33	5.02	3.15	...
1963	3.36	3.83	4.00	...	...	...	...	...	4.26	4.86	3.17	...
1964	3.85	4.07	4.19	...	...	...	...	...	4.41	4.83	3.21	...
1965	4.15	4.25	4.28	...	...	...	...	...	4.49	4.87	3.26	...
1966	5.20	5.11	4.93	...	...	...	...	...	5.13	5.67	3.81	...
1967	4.88	5.10	5.07	...	...	...	...	...	5.51	6.23	3.94	...
1968	5.69	5.70	5.64	...	...	...	...	...	6.18	6.94	4.45	...
1969	7.12	6.93	6.67	...	...	...	...	...	7.03	7.81	5.72	...
1970	6.90	7.38	7.35	...	...	...	...	...	8.04	9.11	6.33	...
1971	4.89	5.99	6.16	...	...	...	...	...	7.39	8.56	5.47	...
1972	4.95	5.98	6.21	...	...	...	...	...	7.21	8.16	5.26	7.38
1973	7.32	6.87	6.85	...	...	...	...	...	7.44	8.24	5.19	8.04
1974	8.20	7.82	7.56	...	...	...	...	...	8.57	9.50	6.17	9.19
1975	6.78	7.78	7.99	...	...	...	...	...	8.83	10.61	7.05	9.04
1976	5.88	7.18	7.61	...	...	...	...	...	8.43	9.75	6.64	8.86
1977	6.08	6.99	7.42	...	7.75	...	...	...	8.02	8.97	5.68	8.84
1978	8.34	8.32	8.41	...	8.49	...	...	...	8.73	9.49	6.02	9.63
1979	10.65	9.51	9.43	...	9.28	...	...	...	9.63	10.69	6.52	11.19
1980	12.00	11.45	11.43	...	11.27	...	...	...	11.94	13.67	8.59	13.77
1981	14.80	14.25	13.92	...	13.45	...	...	...	14.17	16.04	11.33	16.63
1982	12.27	13.01	13.01	...	12.76	...	...	...	13.79	16.11	11.66	16.08
1983	9.58	10.79	11.10	...	11.18	...	...	...	12.04	13.55	9.51	13.23
1984	10.91	12.26	12.46	...	12.41	...	...	...	12.71	14.19	10.10	13.87
1985	8.42	10.12	10.62	...	10.79	...	...	...	11.37	12.72	9.10	12.42
1986	6.45	7.30	7.67	...	7.78	...	...	...	9.02	10.39	7.32	10.18
1987	6.77	7.94	8.39	...	8.59	...	...	...	9.38	10.58	7.64	10.20
1988	7.65	8.48	8.85	...	8.96	...	...	...	9.71	10.83	7.68	10.34
1989	8.53	8.50	8.49	...	8.45	...	...	...	9.26	10.18	7.23	10.32
1990	7.89	8.37	8.55	...	8.61	...	...	...	9.32	10.36	7.27	10.13
1991	5.86	7.37	7.86	...	8.14	...	...	...	8.77	9.80	6.92	9.25
1992	3.89	6.19	7.01	...	7.67	...	...	...	8.14	8.98	6.44	8.40
1993	3.43	5.14	5.87	6.29	6.59	...	...	...	7.22	7.93	5.60	7.33
1994	5.32	6.69	7.09	7.49	7.37	...	...	...	7.97	8.63	6.18	8.35
1995	5.94	6.38	6.57	6.95	6.88	...	...	...	7.59	8.20	5.95	7.95
1996	5.52	6.18	6.44	6.83	6.71	...	...	...	7.37	8.05	5.76	7.80
1997	5.63	6.22	6.35	6.69	6.61	...	...	...	7.27	7.87	5.52	7.60
1998	5.05	5.15	5.26	5.72	5.58	...	...	...	6.53	7.22	5.09	6.94
1999	5.08	5.55	5.65	6.20	5.87	...	...	...	7.05	7.88	5.43	7.43
2000	6.11	6.16	6.03	6.23	5.94	...	...	...	7.62	8.37	5.71	8.06
2001	3.49	4.56	5.02	5.63	5.49	...	...	...	7.08	7.95	5.15	6.97
2002	2.00	3.82	4.61	5.43	5.43	...	...	...	6.49	7.80	5.04	6.54
2003	1.24	2.97	4.01	4.96	...	1.27	...	2.54	5.66	6.76	4.75	5.82
2004	1.89	3.43	4.27	5.04	...	1.04	2.14	2.21	5.63	6.39	4.68	5.84
2005	3.62	4.05	4.29	4.64	...	1.50	1.97	1.94	5.23	6.06	4.40	5.86
2006	4.94	4.75	4.80	5.00	4.91	2.28	2.31	2.27	5.59	6.48	4.40	6.41
2007	4.53	4.43	4.63	4.91	4.84	2.15	2.36	2.34	5.56	6.48	4.40	6.34
2008	1.83	2.80	3.66	4.36	4.28	1.30	2.18	2.20	5.63	7.44	4.86	6.04
2007												
January	5.06	4.75	4.76	4.95	4.85	2.47	2.42	2.40	5.40	6.34	4.23	6.22
February	5.05	4.71	4.72	4.93	4.82	2.34	2.38	2.36	5.39	6.28	4.22	6.29
March	4.92	4.48	4.56	4.81	4.72	2.04	2.27	2.25	5.30	6.27	4.15	6.16
April	4.93	4.59	4.69	4.95	4.87	2.12	2.35	2.34	5.47	6.39	4.26	6.18
May	4.91	4.67	4.75	4.98	4.90	2.29	2.45	2.43	5.47	6.39	4.31	6.26
June	4.96	5.03	5.10	5.29	5.20	2.65	2.67	2.65	5.79	6.70	4.60	6.66
July	4.96	4.88	5.00	5.19	5.11	2.60	2.62	2.60	5.73	6.65	4.56	6.70
August	4.47	4.43	4.67	5.00	4.93	2.39	2.47	2.46	5.79	6.65	4.64	6.57
September	4.14	4.20	4.52	4.84	4.79	2.14	2.30	2.29	5.74	6.59	4.51	6.38
October	4.10	4.20	4.53	4.83	4.77	2.01	2.26	2.25	5.66	6.48	4.39	6.38
November	3.50	3.67	4.15	4.56	4.52	1.35	1.99	1.98	5.44	6.40	4.46	6.21
December	3.26	3.49	4.10	4.57	4.53	1.27	2.08	2.06	5.49	6.65	4.42	6.10
2008												
January	2.71	2.98	3.74	4.35	4.33	0.86	1.81	1.80	5.33	6.54	4.27	5.76
February	2.05	2.78	3.74	4.49	4.52	0.65	1.87	1.87	5.53	6.82	4.64	5.92
March	1.54	2.48	3.51	4.36	4.39	0.23	1.76	1.76	5.51	6.89	4.93	5.97
April	1.74	2.84	3.68	4.44	4.44	0.62	1.91	1.90	5.55	6.97	4.70	5.92
May	2.06	3.15	3.88	4.60	4.60	0.79	2.00	2.00	5.57	6.93	4.58	6.04
June	2.42	3.49	4.10	4.74	4.69	0.97	2.19	2.20	5.68	7.07	4.69	6.32
July	2.28	3.30	4.01	4.62	4.57	0.84	2.09	2.08	5.67	7.16	4.68	6.43
August	2.18	3.14	3.89	4.53	4.50	1.15	2.15	2.13	5.64	7.15	4.69	6.48
September	1.91	2.88	3.69	4.32	4.27	1.55	2.25	2.25	5.65	7.31	4.86	6.04
October	1.42	2.73	3.81	4.45	4.17	2.75	2.87	2.92	6.28	8.88	5.50	6.20
November	1.07	2.29	3.53	4.27	4.00	3.69	3.00	3.09	6.12	9.21	5.23	6.09
December	0.49	1.52	2.42	3.18	2.87	1.76	2.32	2.43	5.05	8.43	5.56	5.33

. . . = Not available.

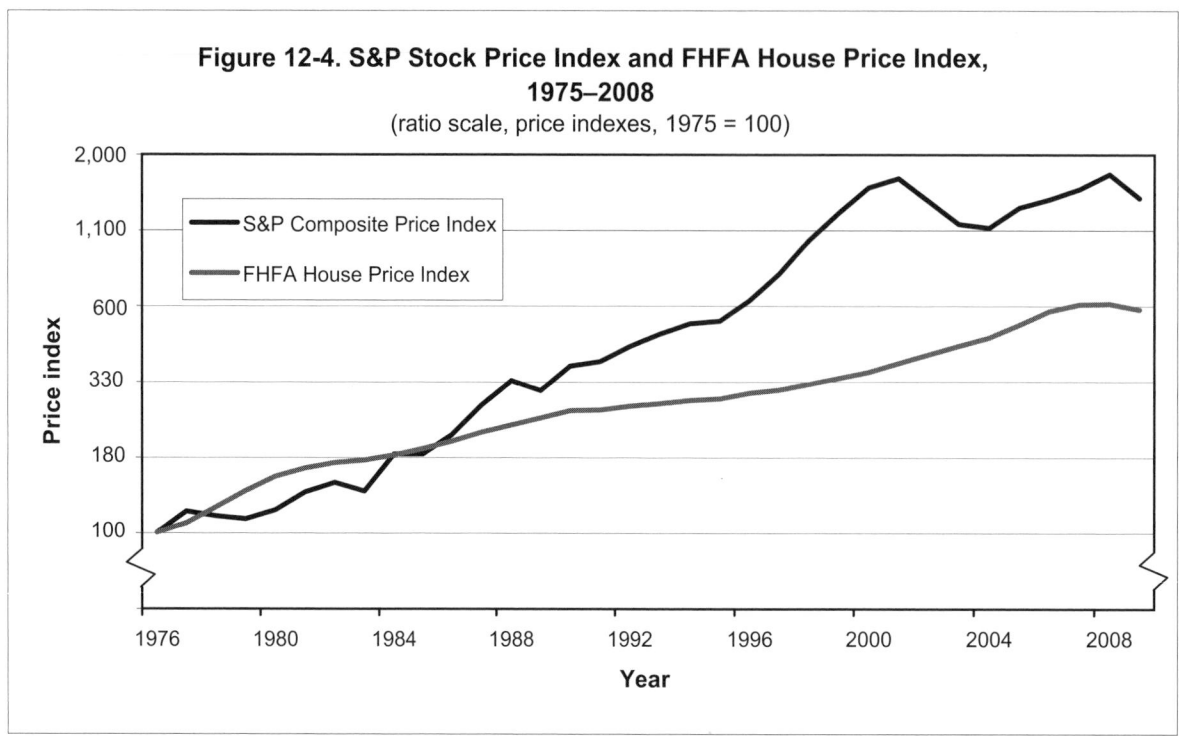

Figure 12-4. S&P Stock Price Index and FHFA House Price Index, 1975–2008
(ratio scale, price indexes, 1975 = 100)

- The rise in prices of existing homes sold and refinanced, as measured by the total Federal Housing Finance Agency (FHFA) House Price Index, ended in 2007, having already slowed from an annual rate of 11 percent in 2005. From the peak in the second quarter of 2007 through the fourth quarter of 2008, prices for this broad category of housing declined 4.6 percent. A separate FHFA index for purchases only, excluding refinancings, has declined 10.8 percent; this is probably more typical of the price declines facing distressed borrowers. See the notes and definitions for the limitations of both of these indexes. The total index is shown in Figure 12-4 because it has the longest history. (Table 12-10)

- The long-terms gains in housing prices have been no match for those in the prices of common stocks. This is demonstrated in Figure 12-4 above, where the house price index is compared with the S&P 500 stock index. Neither set of numbers is graphed as published: instead, both are rebased to 1975 = 100 so that their growth since then can be directly compared. Over the 33 years, house prices rose at an average 5.5 percent annual rate, while the index of stock prices, though more volatile than home prices, rose at an 8.4 percent rate. (This price increase comparison does not take account of tax considerations, stock dividends, or the value of shelter provided by the owner-occupied home. Past history is no guarantee of future results.) (Table 12-10)

- Based on current dividends, the S&P stocks at the end of 2008 were as good a buy as they had been since the early 1990s. Based on earnings, however, the earnings/price ratio was at a record low, meaning that the price/earnings ratio was at a record high. (Table 12-10)

Table 12-10. Common Stock Prices and Yields; Existing House Prices

Year and month	Stock price indexes			Yields based on Standard and Poor's composite (percent)		FHFA House Price Indexes			
						House Price Index (purchases and refinance)		Purchase-Only Index	
	Dow Jones industrials (30 stocks)	Standard and Poor's composite (500 stocks) (1941–1943 = 10)	Nasdaq composite (Feb. 5, 1971 = 100)	Dividend-price ratio	Earnings-price ratio	Level at end of period (1980:I = 100)	Appreciation from same quarter one year earlier (percent)	Level at end of period (1991:I = 100)	Appreciation from same quarter one year earlier (percent)
1955	442.72	40.49	...	4.08	7.95	...	...	...	...
1956	493.01	46.62	...	4.09	7.55	...	...	...	...
1957	475.71	44.38	...	4.35	7.89	...	...	...	...
1958	491.66	46.24	...	3.97	6.23	...	...	...	...
1959	632.12	57.38	...	3.23	5.78	...	...	...	...
1960	618.04	55.85	...	3.47	5.90	...	...	...	...
1961	691.55	66.27	...	2.98	4.62	...	...	...	...
1962	639.76	62.38	...	3.37	5.82	...	...	...	...
1963	714.81	69.87	...	3.17	5.50	...	...	...	...
1964	834.05	81.37	...	3.01	5.32	...	...	...	...
1965	910.88	88.17	...	3.00	5.59	...	...	...	...
1966	873.60	85.26	...	3.40	6.63	...	...	...	...
1967	879.12	91.93	...	3.20	5.73	...	...	...	...
1968	906.00	98.70	...	3.07	5.67	...	...	...	...
1969	876.72	97.84	...	3.24	6.08	...	...	...	...
1970	753.19	83.22	...	3.83	6.45	...	...	...	...
1971	884.76	98.29	107.44	3.14	5.41	...	...	...	...
1972	950.71	109.20	128.52	2.84	5.50	...	...	...	...
1973	923.88	107.43	109.90	3.06	7.12	...	...	...	...
1974	759.37	82.85	76.29	4.47	11.59	...	...	...	...
1975	802.49	86.16	77.20	4.31	9.15	62.86	...	...	...
1976	974.92	102.01	89.90	3.77	8.90	67.81	7.87	...	...
1977	894.63	98.20	98.71	4.62	10.79	76.98	13.52	...	...
1978	820.23	96.02	117.53	5.28	12.03	87.59	13.78	...	...
1979	844.40	103.01	136.57	5.47	13.46	98.08	11.98	...	...
1980	891.41	118.78	168.61	5.26	12.66	104.72	6.77	...	...
1981	932.92	128.05	203.18	5.20	11.96	109.47	4.54	...	...
1982	884.36	119.71	188.97	5.81	11.60	111.44	1.80	...	...
1983	1 190.34	160.41	285.43	4.40	8.03	116.14	4.22	...	...
1984	1 178.48	160.46	248.88	4.64	10.02	122.10	5.13	...	...
1985	1 328.23	186.84	290.19	4.25	8.12	129.50	6.06	...	...
1986	1 792.76	236.34	366.96	3.49	6.09	139.11	7.42	...	...
1987	2 275.99	286.83	402.57	3.08	5.48	147.22	5.83	...	...
1988	2 060.82	265.79	374.43	3.64	8.01	155.83	5.85	...	...
1989	2 508.91	322.84	437.81	3.45	7.42	165.05	5.92	...	...
1990	2 678.94	334.59	409.17	3.61	6.47	166.03	0.59	...	...
1991	2 929.33	376.18	491.69	3.24	4.79	170.89	2.93	101.16	...
1992	3 284.29	415.74	599.26	2.99	4.22	174.67	2.21	103.82	2.63
1993	3 522.06	451.41	715.16	2.78	4.46	178.92	2.43	106.76	2.83
1994	3 793.77	460.42	751.65	2.82	5.83	181.26	1.31	109.85	2.89
1995	4 493.76	541.72	925.19	2.56	6.09	189.62	4.61	112.82	2.70
1996	5 742.89	670.50	1 164.96	2.19	5.24	194.80	2.73	116.28	3.07
1997	7 441.15	873.43	1 469.49	1.77	4.57	203.72	4.58	120.26	3.42
1998	8 625.52	1 085.50	1 794.91	1.49	3.46	213.78	4.94	126.96	5.57
1999	10 464.88	1 327.33	2 728.15	1.25	3.17	224.33	4.93	134.62	6.03
2000	10 734.90	1 427.22	3 783.67	1.15	3.63	240.56	7.23	143.92	6.91
2001	10 189.13	1 194.18	2 035.00	1.32	2.95	258.04	7.27	153.66	6.77
2002	9 226.43	993.94	1 539.73	1.61	2.92	275.72	6.85	165.35	7.61
2003	8 993.59	965.23	1 647.17	1.77	3.84	295.12	7.04	177.84	7.55
2004	10 317.39	1 130.65	1 986.53	1.72	4.89	326.34	10.58	194.26	9.23
2005	10 547.67	1 207.23	2 099.32	1.83	5.36	363.67	11.44	212.40	9.34
2006	11 408.67	1 310.46	2 263.41	1.87	5.78	383.05	5.33	220.32	3.73
2007	13 169.98	1 477.19	2 578.47	1.86	5.29	385.50	0.64	218.57	-0.79
2008	11 252.62	1 220.04	2 161.65	2.37	3.55	368.28	-4.47	200.50	-8.27
2007									
January	12 512.89	1 424.16	2 453.19	1.81	...	...	...	...	...
February	12 631.48	1 444.79	2 479.86	1.82	...	...	...	...	...
March	12 268.53	1 406.95	2 401.49	1.89	5.85	385.57	4.13	221.50	2.94
April	12 754.80	1 463.65	2 499.57	1.84	...	...	...	...	...
May	13 407.76	1 511.14	2 562.14	1.81	...	...	...	...	...
June	13 480.21	1 514.49	2 595.40	1.81	5.65	386.14	3.26	224.80	2.51
July	13 677.89	1 520.70	2 655.08	1.80	...	...	...	...	...
August	13 239.71	1 454.62	2 539.50	1.92	...	...	...	...	...
September	13 557.69	1 497.12	2 634.47	1.88	5.15	383.96	1.69	223.34	1.37
October	13 901.28	1 539.66	2 780.42	1.84	...	...	...	...	...
November	13 200.58	1 463.39	2 662.80	1.95	...	...	...	...	...
December	13 406.99	1 479.23	2 661.55	1.93	4.51	385.50	0.64	218.60	-0.79
2008									
January	12 538.12	1 378.76	2 418.09	2.06	...	...	...	...	...
February	12 419.57	1 354.87	2 325.83	2.10	...	...	...	...	...
March	12 193.88	1 316.94	2 254.82	2.17	4.57	384.80	-0.20	214.55	-3.14
April	12 656.63	1 370.47	2 368.10	2.09	...	...	...	...	...
May	12 812.48	1 403.22	2 483.24	2.07	...	...	...	...	...
June	12 056.67	1 341.25	2 427.45	2.15	4.01	378.65	-1.94	213.99	-4.81
July	11 322.38	1 257.33	2 278.14	2.27	...	...	...	...	...
August	11 530.75	1 281.47	2 389.27	2.23	...	...	...	...	...
September	11 114.08	1 217.01	2 205.20	2.36	3.94	369.00	-3.90	209.63	-6.14
October	9 176.71	968.80	1 730.32	2.83	...	...	...	...	...
November	8 614.55	883.04	1 542.70	3.11	...	...	...	...	...
December	8 595.56	877.56	1 525.89	3.00	1.66	368.28	-4.47	200.50	-8.27

. . . = Not available.

NOTES AND DEFINITIONS

Most of the data in this chapter are found on the Federal Reserve Board Web site, <http://www.federalreserve.gov>. Current releases and most historical data are found at that site by selecting Economic Research & Data/Statistical Releases and Historical Data and then selecting the appropriate report. This is the location for all data not otherwise specified.

TABLES 12-1, 12-2, AND 20-5B
MONEY STOCK MEASURES AND COMPONENTS

SOURCE: BOARD OF GOVERNORS OF THE FEDERAL RESERVE SYSTEM

Estimates of two monetary aggregates (M1 and M2) and the components of these measures are published weekly. The monthly data are averages of daily figures.

The Federal Reserve Board ceased publication of the M3 aggregate on March 23, 2006. Weekly publication was also discontinued for the following components of M3: large-denomination time deposits, repurchase agreements (RPs), and Eurodollars. The Board continues to publish institutional money market mutual funds as a memorandum item in this release. Measures of large-denomination time deposits continue to be published in the flow of funds accounts (Z.1 release) and in the H.8 release weekly for commercial banks.

The Board stated that "M3 does not appear to convey any additional information about economic activity that is not already embodied in M2 and has not played a role in the monetary policy process for many years. Consequently, the Board judged that the costs of collecting the underlying data and publishing M3 outweigh the benefits." ("Discontinuance of M3," H.6, Money Stock Measures [November 10, 2005, revised March 9, 2006]. [Accessed November 6, 2006.]

Definitions

M1 consists of (1) currency, (2) traveler's checks of nonbank issuers, (3) demand deposits, and (4) other checkable deposits.

M2 consists of M1 plus savings deposits (including money market deposit accounts), small-denomination time deposits, and balances in retail money market mutual funds.

Currency consists of currency outside the U.S. Treasury, the Federal Reserve Banks, and the vaults of depository institutions.

Traveler's checks is the outstanding amount of U.S. dollar-denominated traveler's checks of nonbank issuers. Traveler's checks issued by depository institutions are included in demand deposits.

Demand deposits consists of demand deposits at domestically chartered commercial banks, U.S. branches and agencies of foreign banks, and Edge Act corporations (excluding those amounts held by depository institutions, the U.S. government, and foreign banks and official institutions) less cash items in the process of collection and Federal Reserve float. A "demand deposit" is a deposit that the depositor has a right to withdraw at any time without prior notice to the depository institution—most commonly, a checking account. "Federal Reserve float" is Federal Reserve credit that appears on the books of the depository institution of both the check writer and the check receiver while a check is being processed. This and cash items in the process of collection are subtracted to avoid double counting of deposits, so that they will not be counted both at the bank in which the check is deposited and at the bank on which the check is drawn.

Other checkable deposits at commercial banks consists of negotiable order of withdrawal (NOW) and automatic transfer service (ATS) balances at domestically chartered commercial banks, U.S. branches and agencies of foreign banks, and Edge Act corporations.

Other checkable deposits at thrift institutions consists of NOW and ATS balances at thrift institutions, credit union share draft balances, and demand deposits at thrift institutions.

Savings deposits includes money market deposit accounts and other savings deposits at *commercial banks* and *thrift institutions*.

Small time deposits are deposits issued at *commercial banks* and *thrift institutions* in amounts less than $100,000. All Individual Retirement Account (IRA) and Keogh account balances at commercial banks and thrift institutions are subtracted from small time deposits.

Retail money funds exclude IRA and Keogh account balances at money market mutual funds.

Institutional money funds are included in the money stock report for informational purposes. They are not part of M1 or M2.

Notes on the data

Seasonal adjustment. Seasonally adjusted M1 is calculated by summing currency, traveler's checks, demand deposits, and other checkable deposits (each seasonally adjusted separately). Seasonally adjusted M2 is computed by adjusting each of its non-M1 components and then adding this result to seasonally adjusted M1.

Revisions. Money stock measures are revised frequently and have a benchmark and seasonal factor review in the middle of the year; this review typically extends back a number of years. The monetary aggregates were redefined in major revisions introduced in 1980.

Data availability

Estimates are released weekly in Federal Reserve Statistical Release H.6, "Money Stock Measures." Current and historical data are available on the Federal Reserve Web site.

References

Board of Governors of the Federal Reserve System, *The Federal Reserve System: Purposes and Functions,* available online at <http://www.federalreserve.gov> in the category "About the Fed/Features," includes a chapter discussing monetary policy and the monetary aggregates and a glossary of terms as an appendix.

An explanation of the 1980 redefinition of the monetary aggregates is found in the *Federal Reserve Bulletin* for February 1980.

TABLES 12-3 AND 20-5B
AGGREGATE RESERVES, MONETARY BASE, AND FR BALANCE SHEET

SOURCE: BOARD OF GOVERNORS OF THE FEDERAL RESERVE SYSTEM

The data on reserves and the monetary base presented here are in millions of dollars, seasonally adjusted (with one exception), and adjusted for changes in reserve requirements ("break-adjusted") in order to provide a consistent gauge of the effect of Federal Reserve open-market operations. Break adjustment is required because an observed increase in reserves will not represent an easing in monetary conditions if it is simply equal to the increase in reserves required by the Federal Reserve. Therefore, the mandated increases and decreases are deducted to provide the break-adjusted series. Monthly data are averages of daily figures. Annual data are for December.

The series "Federal Reserve balance sheet: total assets" is new in this edition of *Business Statistics*, having only recently become a subject of public attention. It demonstrates the extent to which the Federal Reserve has, beginning in 2007, undertaken "quantitative easing"—direct purchases of financial assets—in addition to conventional easing, which has consisted of reducing short-term interest rates to near zero. The balance sheet data are accessed on a different part of the Federal Reserve Web site—"Monetary Policy" instead of "Economic Research and Data"—which features an extensive explanation and discussion of the meaning and importance of this indicator. The balance sheet is reported in millions of dollars for each Wednesday, and is shown here with the last Wednesday of the month representing the month and the last Wednesday of December representing the year. These values are not adjusted for seasonal variation.

Definitions

Total reserves consists of reserve balances with the Federal Reserve Banks plus vault cash used to satisfy reserve requirements. Seasonally adjusted, break-adjusted total reserves equal seasonally adjusted, break-adjusted required reserves plus unadjusted excess reserves.

Seasonally adjusted, break-adjusted *nonborrowed reserves* equal seasonally adjusted, break-adjusted total reserves less unadjusted total borrowings of depository institutions from the Federal Reserve.

Extended credit consisted of borrowing at the discount window under the terms and conditions established for the extended credit program to help depository institutions deal with sustained liquidity pressures. Since there was not the same need to repay such borrowing promptly as there was with traditional short-term adjustment credit, the money market impact of extended credit was similar to that of nonborrowed reserves. The extended credit program was significant in the 1980s but used infrequently in subsequent years. It ended with the 2002 revision of the discount window program, effective January 9, 2003. See the explanation of the discount rate in the notes and definitions for Table 12-9.

To adjust *required reserves* for discontinuities due to regulatory changes in reserve requirements, a multiplicative procedure is used to estimate what required reserves would have been in past periods, had current reserve requirements been in effect. Break-adjusted required reserves include required reserves against transactions deposits and personal time and savings deposits (but not reservable nondeposit liabilities).

Excess reserves, not seasonally adjusted equals unadjusted total reserves less unadjusted required reserves.

The seasonally adjusted, break-adjusted *monetary base* consists of (1) seasonally adjusted, break-adjusted total reserves; plus (2) the seasonally adjusted currency component of the money stock; plus (3) the seasonally adjusted, break-adjusted difference between current vault cash and the amount applied to satisfy current reserve requirements for all quarterly reporters on the "Report of Transaction Accounts, Other Deposits and Vault Cash" and for all weekly reporters whose vault cash exceeds their required reserves.

Federal Reserve balance sheet: total assets is total assets from the Consolidated Statement of Condition of All Federal Reserve Banks, which is reported each Wednesday. The last Wednesday of the month is used to represent the month, and the last Wednesday in December is used to represent the year. Currently, the principal components of total assets are Treasury, federal agency, and mortgage-backed securities; repurchase agreements; term auction credit; portfolio holdings of various limited liability companies (LLCs) set up to manage assets taken over from other institutions; liquidity swaps with foreign central banks; and other loans, including traditional loans to member commercial banks made at the discount rate (see the definitions for Table 12-9). Total assets are equal to the sum of Federal Reserve liabilities and capital. The principal components of liabilities are Federal Reserve notes and the deposits of member banks representing their reserves.

Revisions

The data on reserves and the monetary base are revised annually around midyear to reflect the result of annual reviews of seasonal factors and break factors. The Federal Reserve balance sheet is not subject to revision.

Data availability

Reserve and monetary base data are released weekly in Federal Reserve Release H.3, "Aggregate Reserves of Depository Institutions and the Monetary Base." Current and historical data are available on the Federal Reserve Web site.

The Federal Reserve balance sheet appears each week in the H.4.1 release, Factors Affecting Reserve Balances, released each Thursday at 4:30 p.m., and available on the Federal Reserve Web site under Economic Research and Data/Statistical Releases and Historical Data. However, to obtain the full historical data for total assets, the user must go to Monetary policy/Credit and liquidity programs and the balance sheet/Recent balance sheet trends/Total assets/View as table/All/Copy data.

TABLE 12-4
COMMERCIAL BANKS: BANK CREDIT AND SELECTED LIABILITIES

SOURCE: BOARD OF GOVERNORS OF THE FEDERAL RESERVE SYSTEM.

Definitions and notes on the data

The data are for all commercial banks in the United States. This category covers the following types of institutions in the 50 states and the District of Columbia: domestically chartered commercial banks that report weekly (large domestic), other domestically chartered commercial banks (small domestic), branches and agencies of foreign banks, and Edge Act and Agreement corporations (foreign related institutions). International Banking Facilities are excluded.

Data are collected weekly for Wednesday values, and monthly data are pro rata averages of Wednesday values. Annual data represent December figures.

Data are complete for large domestic banks. Data for other institutions are estimated on the basis of weekly samples and end-of-quarter condition reports. Data are adjusted for breaks caused by the reclassifications of assets and liabilities.

Data before 1988 are based on previous versions of this survey—the G.7 release, "Loans and Securities at Commercial Banks," and the G.10 release, "Major Nondeposit Funds of Commercial Banks."

Most of the categories of credit and liabilities are self-explanatory.

U.S. Treasury and agency securities includes liabilities of the U.S. Treasury, liabilities of U.S. government agencies, and liabilities of U.S. government-sponsored enterprises.

Loans and leases in bank credit excludes various forms of credit extended to other commercial banks in the United States.

Security loans consists of loans to purchase and carry securities and reverse repurchase agreements (RPs) with brokers, dealers, and others. In a reverse RP, a bank has provided liquidity to a borrower by buying a security, which the borrower promises to repurchase at a certain date.

Interbank loans, cash assets, and other assets are not components of bank credit and are omitted from Table 12-4. Interbank loans include loans made to commercial banks, reverse RPs with commercial banks, and federal funds sold to commercial banks.

Selected liabilities show *deposits* and *borrowings*. Two components of total liabilities, "net due to foreign offices" and "other liabilities," are omitted.

Revisions

Data are revised annually around midyear to reflect new benchmark information and revised seasonal factors.

Data availability

Federal Reserve Statistical Release H.8, "Assets and Liabilities of Commercial Banks in the United States," is issued each Friday around 4:30 p.m. (EST). Current and historical data are available on the Federal Reserve Web site.

TABLE 12-5
CREDIT MARKET DEBT OUTSTANDING, BY BORROWER AND LENDER

SOURCE: BOARD OF GOVERNORS OF THE FEDERAL RESERVE SYSTEM

The flow of funds accounts, compiled quarterly by the Federal Reserve Board, supplement the national income and product accounts (NIPAs) by providing a comprehensive and detailed accounting of financial transactions with a balance sheet for each financial and nonfinancial sector of the economy. Table 12-5 is taken from these accounts. It shows the *credit market debt outstanding owed* by the major sectors in the economy, and it shows the major lending sectors in the credit markets under *credit market assets held*. One purpose of these statistics is to show the comparative growth of the various lending sectors.

Aggregates of these data can include multiple layers of financial intermediation, such as banks making advances to finance companies that subsequently lend to households. Adding bank data to finance company data would involve duplication of such debt. In macroeconomic analysis, the most widely used flow of funds measure is the total debt of domestic nonfinancial sectors. By eliminating the financial sectors, this measure has little duplication due to financial intermediation. The Federal Reserve uses this along with the monetary aggregates as an indicator of monetary conditions.

Definitions and notes on the data

Quarterly data on debt outstanding are shown on an end-of-period basis, not adjusted for seasonal variation or for "breaks" or discontinuities in the series. Due to these discontinuities, caution should be used in interpreting *changes* in debt levels. Break-adjusted values of changes, representing best estimates of actual fund flows, can be found in the quarterly flow of funds report, along with a suggested method for calculating percentage changes.

The data on credit market debt exclude corporate equities and mutual fund shares. However, these values of these instruments held by households and nonprofits appear as assets in the household sector accounts in Table 12-6.

Data for the current and several preceding years are revised each year to reflect revisions in source data, including the NIPAs; the revisions are issued about a month after the release of the annual NIPA revisions.

Sectors owing debt

Domestic financial sectors

Federal government-related sectors include government-sponsored enterprises (GSEs) such as Fannie Mae (originally the Federal National Mortgage Association), Freddie Mac (originally the Federal Home Loan Mortgage Corporation), and Ginnie Mae (originally the Government National Mortgage Association); agency and GSE-backed mortgage pools; and the monetary authority (Federal Reserve). However, the Federal Reserve usually owes no credit market debt.

The *private* sector includes commercial banks and bank holding companies, savings institutions, credit unions, life insurance companies, asset-backed securities (ABS) issuers, brokers and dealers, finance and mortgage companies, REITs (real estate investment trusts), and funding corporations.

Domestic nonfinancial sectors

Federal government consists of all federal government agencies and funds included in the unified budget. However, the District of Columbia government is included in the state and local sector.

Treasury securities as shown here *excludes* securities issued by the Treasury but held by agencies within the U.S. government (e.g., in the Social Security trust funds). In this respect, it corresponds to the "Federal debt" shown in

Table 6-15, except that the latter table uses a fiscal-year basis rather than a calendar-year basis. Federal government debt as shown here is smaller than the official total public debt and the "debt subject to limit." Both of those *include* the securities held by U.S. government agencies. The value shown here is considered to be a more accurate measure of the effect of government borrowing in relation to the economy and credit markets than those obtained from the larger aggregates.

Budget agency securities and mortgages are those issued by government-owned corporations and agencies, such as the Export-Import Bank, that issue securities individually. There are no mortgages currently included in the debt of agencies.

Households also includes personal trusts and nonprofit organizations.

State and local governments represent operating funds only. State and local government retirement funds are included in the financial sector.

Foreign credit market debt held in the United States shows the foreign credit market debt owed to U.S. residents. This debt is included along with the debt of domestic financial and nonfinancial sectors in total credit market debt outstanding.

Percentage measures

Table 12-5 includes three measures of relative debt burdens, calculated by the editor.

Domestic nonfinancial debt as a percent of GDP is the total debt owed by domestic nonfinancial sectors as a percent of the current-dollar value of total Gross Domestic Product. (Table 1-1)

Household debt as a percent of DPI is the value of debt owed by households as a percent of the current-dollar value of disposable personal income. (Table 4-1)

Corporate nonfinancial business debt as a percent of sector value added is the total debt owed by domestic corporate nonfinancial business as a percent of the current-dollar gross value added of domestic corporate nonfinancial business. (Table 1-13)

For the annual ratios, debt outstanding at the end of the year is taken as a percent of the product or income data for the full preceding year. For the quarterly ratios, the debt outstanding at the end of the quarter is taken as a percent of the annual rate of the product or income flow for that quarter. This means that the end-year ratios will almost inevitably be higher than the corresponding end-quarter ratios and should therefore not be compared with them.

Credit market assets held by sector

Selected government-related sectors

This grouping includes two nonfinancial and four financial sectors. The nonfinancial sectors are the *federal government,* as reflected in the U.S. Budget accounts, and the operations of *state and local governments,* including the District of Columbia. *State and local employee retirement funds* and *federal government retirement funds* are shown separately and considered to be financial sectors. The other two government-related financial sectors are *government-sponsored enterprises (GSEs)* and *federally related mortgage pools.*

Government-sponsored enterprises (GSEs) are financial institutions that provide credit to housing, agriculture, and other specific areas of the economy, such as Federal Home Loan Banks, Fannie Mae, and Freddie Mac (see above for explanation of the latter two terms).

Federally related mortgage pools are entities established for bookkeeping purposes that record the issuance of pooled securities representing an interest in mortgages backed by federal agencies and GSEs. Rather than being composed of a group of institutions, the sector is made up of a set of contractual arrangements in regard to pooled mortgages.

Selected domestic financial sectors

This grouping includes major financial sectors, such as *commercial banks, savings institutions,* and *credit unions.* The *monetary authority* (the Federal Reserve) has been put in this group because it is sometimes included in banking sector totals. Other important financial sectors are *life insurance companies, property-casualty insurance companies,* and *private pension funds.* Additional private financial sectors are *money market mutual funds,* which issue shares and invest in short-term liquid assets; *mutual funds,* whose investments are not restricted to the short-term area; *asset-backed security (ABS) issuers,* which issue debt obligations that are backed by pooled assets, a financial procedure similar to that of federally related mortgage pools; and *finance companies,* which provide credit to businesses and individuals.

Private domestic nonfinancial sectors

Households were the dominant private domestic nonfinancial lenders in earlier years, but lending by domestic households has now been surpassed by *foreign holdings* of assets representing claims on U.S. entities.

A number of lending sectors of smaller importance are included in the category "*All other financial and nonfinancial.*" One of those is nonfinancial business, a sector that is important on the borrowing side but not on the lending side. The financial sectors included in this total are closed-end funds, exchange-traded funds, real estate investment trusts (REITs), brokers and dealers, and funding corporations.

Data availability

Debt estimates are released quarterly, about nine weeks following the end of the quarter. The data can be found in Federal Reserve Statistical Release Z.1, "Flow of Funds of the United States," available on the Federal Reserve Web site. The data in Table 12-5 are found in Tables L.1 and L.2 of that release. Current and historical data are also available on the same Federal Reserve Web site.

References

A *Guide to the Flow of Funds Accounts* can be ordered; ordering information is available on the Federal Reserve Web site along with the Z.1 release. Individual table descriptions can be accessed at the same location. The *Federal Reserve Bulletin* for July 2001 includes an article entitled "The U.S. Flow of Funds Accounts and Their Uses." To access *Bulletin* articles on the Federal Reserve Web site, select Economic Research & Data/Federal Reserve Bulletin and select the year.

TABLE 12-6
HOUSEHOLD ASSETS, LIABILITIES, NET WORTH, FINANCIAL OBLIGATIONS, AND DELINQUENCY RATES

SOURCE: BOARD OF GOVERNORS OF THE FEDERAL RESERVE SYSTEM

The quarterly data on household sector assets, liabilities, and net worth are also obtained from the Federal Reserve Board's flow of funds accounts, which are described above. These data appear in Table B.100 of the Z.1 statistical release, also cited above.

The household credit ratios and rates are also compiled by the Federal Reserve. The household debt service ratio relates required debt service (interest and principal) payments to disposable personal income (DPI). The financial obligations ratios include not only required debt payments, but also rental payments, automobile lease payments, homeowners' insurance, and property taxes. They are also expressed as a percentage of DPI. Unlike the debt service ratio, the financial obligations ratios are not distorted by the trend toward debt-financed homeownership in preference to rental or the trend toward auto leasing in preference to loan financing.

The delinquency and charge-off rates relate delinquent (past due 30 days or more) and charged-off consumer credit card credit at commercial banks to total bank holdings of that type of credit.

Definitions and notes on the data

Quarterly data on holdings of *financial assets* are shown on an end-of-period basis, not adjusted for seasonal variations. Data for the current and preceding years are revised annually to reflect revisions in source data.

It is important to note that for most categories in this reporting system, the values for the household sector are calculated as residuals. That is, starting with a known total (such as total Treasury securities outstanding), the amounts in that category reported or estimated to be held by other sectors are subtracted and the remainder is assigned to the household sector. This means that any error in one of the other sectors causes an equal and opposite error in the household sector. As an example of how far off track the household data can go, household holdings of demand deposits and currency in 2006 are revised sharply upward from those estimated by the Federal Reserve two years ago and shown in the previous edition of *Business Statistics*. The precipitous decline in such holdings shown in this volume for 2007 and much of 2008 may be similarly revised away at a later date.

Financial assets of the household sector include holdings of nonprofit organizations, which are difficult to estimate separately. Household sector assets exclude holdings by unincorporated businesses.

The table shows total household ownership of *checkable deposits and currency, time and savings deposits, money market fund shares, U.S. savings bonds, other Treasury securities, agency- and GSE-backed securities, municipal securities, corporate and foreign bonds, mortgages, corporate equities* (at market value), *mutual fund shares* (with equities at market value and other assets at book value), *security credit, life insurance reserves, pension fund reserves,* and *equity in noncorporate business.* Note that the reserves of life insurance companies and pension funds, though held by institutions, are counted here as assets of the household sector. *Pension fund reserves* includes insurance and pension fund reserves of federal, state, and local government employee funds—but not the Social Security system—as well as private industry funds. Bank personal trusts were formerly included as a type of household financial asset. However, in the latest revision of the flow of funds accounts, the various assets in these trusts were instead included in the appropriate categories, such as bonds, equities, and so forth. Included in total *financial assets,* but not shown separately, are foreign deposits, open market paper, and claims on insurance companies, such as unearned premium reserves of other insurance companies and health insurance reserves of life insurance companies.

Tangible assets complete the asset side of the household balance sheet. Tangible assets comprise equipment and software owned by nonprofit organizations, real estate, and consumer durable goods. *Household real estate* includes farm homes, mobile homes, second homes not rented, vacant homes for sale, vacant land, and owner-occupied housing. It is valued at market value, while equipment, software, and consumer durables are valued at replacement (current) cost.

Debt as a percent of total assets is calculated by the editor as household credit market debt outstanding, from Table 12-5, as a percent of the total of tangible and financial assets in this table. It covers both households and nonprofit organizations.

Total liabilities consists of household credit market debt, as shown in Table 12-5, plus security credit, trade payables of nonprofit organizations, and deferred and unpaid life insurance premiums.

Net worth is the sum of the value of financial and tangible assets minus total liabilities.

The *household debt-service* and *financial obligations ratios* are estimated on a quarterly basis by the Federal Reserve based on aggregate and consumer survey data. They are seasonally adjusted, unlike almost all of the other data in Table 12-6. Fourth-quarter values are shown to represent the calendar year. The denominator for the aggregate ratio is disposable personal income (DPI) from the NIPAs. (See Chapter 4.) The allocation of the NIPA data between *renters* and *homeowners* is estimated by the Federal Reserve based on data from its triennial Survey of Consumer Finances and the Census Bureau's Current Population Survey (CPS). (For more information on the CPS, see the notes and definitions to Chapters 3 and 10.)

Debt service payments are the minimum required monthly payments of principal and interest on mortgage debt (including home equity loans), revolving credit (credit card debt), and auto, student, mobile home, recreational vehicle, marine, and personal loans.

The *financial obligations ratios* include, in addition to debt service, rental payments on primary residences, property taxes, homeowners' insurance, and automobile lease payments.

Delinquency and *charge-off rates of credit card accounts held at banks* are compiled from the quarterly FFIEC (Federal Financial Institutions Examination Council) Consolidated Reports of Condition and Income (FFIEC 031 through 034) and pertain to all insured U.S.-chartered commercial banks. The *delinquency rate* concerns loans past due 30 days or more and still accruing interest as well as those in nonaccrual status, measured as a percentage of end-of-period loans. The *charge-off rate* is the value of net charge-offs (loans removed from the books and charged against loss reserves, minus recoveries) as a percentage of average loans outstanding over the quarter, annualized.

Data availability

Household balance sheet estimates are released quarterly, about nine weeks following the end of a quarter, in the Federal Reserve Statistical Release Z.1, "Flow of Funds Accounts of the United States." Further information on data availability is given in the notes to Table 12-5, a table which is also based on the flow of funds accounts.

The revised debt service ratio and the new obligations ratios are described in "Recent Changes to a Measure of U.S. Household Debt Service," *Federal Reserve Bulletin*, October 2003. The data are estimated by the Federal Reserve about three months after the end of each quarter. Current and historical data and articles from the *Bulletin* are available on the Federal Reserve Web site by selecting Economic Research and Data and either Statistical Releases and Historical Data or Federal Reserve Bulletin, then selecting the year.

Delinquency and charge-off rates of credit card accounts held at banks are also available on the Federal Reserve Web site, listed under "Charge-off and Delinquency Rates on Loans at Commercial Banks." Rates are posted approximately 60 days after the end of the quarter.

TABLE 12-7
MORTGAGE DEBT OUTSTANDING

SOURCE: BOARD OF GOVERNORS OF THE FEDERAL RESERVE SYSTEM

These data are also published in the Federal Reserve's Statistical Release Z.1, "Flow of Funds Accounts," Table L.217. They are based on reports from various government and private organizations.

Definitions and notes on the data

By type of property:

Home mortgages includes home equity loans; these are also shown separately in the flow of funds accounts.

Multifamily residences refers to mortgages on structures of five or more units.

By type of holder:

Federal and related agencies shows mortgages held directly by the federal government and GSEs (see notes and definitions for Table 12-5 above).

Mortgage pools or trusts show mortgages that were refinanced by their holders through the issuance of mortgage-backed securities. They are shown in two columns: refinancings by *federally related agencies*—mainly the GSEs Fannie Mae, Freddie Mac, and Ginnie Mae (see above)—and refinancings by private conduits (these are referred to as *ABS issuers* in the flow of funds accounts, which stands for issuers of asset-backed securities).

Other holders encompasses a variety of groups, including finance companies, individuals, state and local governments, credit unions, and others.

Home mortgage debt as a percentage of the value of real estate is calculated by the editor, using total home mortgage debt as a percentage of the value of household real estate, which is shown in Table 12-6.

Data availability

Mortgage debt data are compiled quarterly about nine weeks following the end of the quarter in Federal Reserve Statistical Release Z.1, "Flow of Funds Accounts of the United States." The release and current and historical data are available on the Federal Reserve Web site.

TABLE 12-8
CONSUMER CREDIT

SOURCE: BOARD OF GOVERNORS OF THE FEDERAL RESERVE SYSTEM

The consumer credit series cover most short- and intermediate-term credit extended to individuals through regular business channels, excluding loans secured by real estate (such as first and second mortgages and home equity credit). In October 2003, the scope of this survey was expanded to incorporate student loans extended by the federal government and by SLM Holding Corporation (SLM), the parent company of Sallie Mae (Student Loan Marketing Association). The historical data have been revised back to 1977 to reflect this inclusion.

The failure to include home equity credit is an important limitation of this data set. The household debt series presented in Table 12-5 are more comprehensive, comprising both mortgage and consumer debt.

Consumer credit is categorized by major types of credit and by major holders.

Definitions and notes on the data

The major types of consumer credit are *revolving* and *nonrevolving*. *Revolving credit* includes credit arising from purchases on credit card plans of retail stores and banks, cash advances and check credit plans of banks, and some overdraft credit arrangements. *Nonrevolving credit* includes automobile loans, mobile home loans, and all other loans not included in revolving credit, such as loans for education, boats, trailers, or vacations. These loans may be secured or unsecured.

Debt secured by real estate (including first liens, junior liens, and home equity loans) is excluded. Credit extended to governmental agencies and nonprofit or charitable organizations, as well as credit extended to business or to individuals exclusively for business purposes, is excluded.

Categories of *holders* include *commercial banks, finance companies, credit unions, federal government and Sallie Mae, savings institutions, nonfinancial businesses,* and *pools of securitized assets.* Retailers and gasoline companies are included in the nonfinancial businesses category. *Pools of securitized assets* comprises the outstanding balances of pools upon which securities have been issued; these balances are no longer carried on the balance sheets of the loan originators.

The consumer credit series are benchmarked to comprehensive data that periodically become available. Current monthly estimates are brought forward from the latest benchmarks in accordance with weighted changes indicated by sample data. Classifications are made on a "holder" basis. Thus, installment paper sold by retail outlets is included in the figures for the banks and finance companies that purchased the paper.

The amount of outstanding credit represents the sum of the balances in the installment receivable accounts of financial institutions and retail outlets at the end of each month.

The estimates of the amount of credit outstanding include any finance and insurance charges included as part of the installment contract. Unearned income on loans is included in some cases when lenders cannot separate the components.

The seasonally-adjusted data are adjusted for differences in the number of trading days and for seasonal influences.

Data availability

Current data are available monthly in the Federal Reserve Statistical Release G.19, "Consumer Credit," available along with all current and historical data on the Federal Reserve Web site. In the autumn of each year there is a revision of several years of past data reflecting benchmarking and seasonal factor review.

TABLES 12-9, 12-10 AND 20-6
INTEREST RATES, BOND YIELDS, STOCK PRICES AND YIELDS, AND EXISTING HOUSE PRICES

Sources: Board of Governors of the Federal Reserve System; Bureau of Economic Analysis; Moody's Investors Service; The Bond Buyer; Dow Jones, Inc.; Standard and Poor's Corporation; New York Stock Exchange; Federal Housing Finance Agency (FHFA), previously OFHEO (Office of Federal Housing Enterprise Oversight)

Definitions and notes on the data

Interest rates and bond yields are percents per year and are averages of business day figures, except as noted. With four exceptions, they are nominal rates or yields not adjusted for inflation.

The daily effective *federal funds rate* is a weighted average of rates on trades through New York brokers. Monthly figures include each calendar day in the month. Annualized figures use a 360-day year.

The *Federal Reserve discount rate* is the rate for discount window borrowing at the Federal Reserve Bank of New York. Monthly figures include each calendar day in the month. Annualized figures use a 360-day year.

Beginning in January 2003, the rules governing the discount window programs were revised. "Adjustment credit," which

had been extended at a below-market rate (as can be seen in the average discount rates from 1978 through 2002 shown in Table 12-9, which are below the federal funds rate), was replaced by a new type of credit called "primary credit." Primary credit is available for very short terms as a backup source of liquidity to depository institutions in generally sound financial condition, as judged by the lending Federal Reserve Bank. Primary credit is extended at a rate *above* the federal funds rate, eliminating the incentive for institutions to exploit the spread of money market rates over the discount rate.

Through December 2002, Table 12-9 displays the adjustment credit rate. Beginning in February 2003, the new primary credit rate is shown. The rule change, and the change in discount rates shown, did not entail a change in the stance of monetary policy at that time. The overall stance of monetary policy is consistently measured by the level of the federal funds rate.

The *Eurodollar deposits* rate shown is the bid rate at about 9:30 a.m. (EST) for 1-month Eurodollar deposits. Annualized figures use a 360-day year.

The *U.S. Treasury bills, 3-month rate* and the *U.S. Treasury bills, 6-month rate* are the yields on these securities based on their prices as traded in the secondary market. The rates are quoted on a discount basis. Annualized figures use a 360-day year.

Commercial paper, 3-month rates are interpolated from data on certain commercial paper trades settled by the Depository Trust Company. This company is a clearinghouse and custodian for nearly all domestic commercial paper activity. The trades, which are on a discount basis, represent sales of commercial paper by dealers or direct issuers. Annualized figures use a 360-day year. Prior to September 1997, the series represented both nonfinancial and financial commercial paper. Since September 1997, rates have been reported separately for nonfinancial and financial companies; only rates for financial companies are shown here. This introduces a slight discontinuity in this series between August and September 1997.

CDs (secondary market), 3-month rates are averages of dealer offering rates on nationally traded certificates of deposit. Annualized figures use a 360-day year.

The *bank prime rate* is one of several base rates used by banks to price short-term business loans. It is the rate posted by a majority of the top 25 (by amount of assets in domestic offices) insured U.S.-chartered commercial banks. Monthly figures include each calendar day in the month. Annualized figures use a 360-day year. Before 1949, the data are not on the Federal Reserve Web site but have been reproduced from the Federal Reserve publication *Banking and Monetary Statistics, 1941-1970*, Washington: Board of Governors of the Federal Reserve System, 1976. In that volume, the prime rate is described as "the rate that banks charge their most creditworthy business customers on short-term loans," as posted by the largest banks.

The *inflation* column is the rate of change in the PCE chain-type price index, excluding food and energy. For monthly entries, it is the change from the same month a year earlier. This price index is calculated by the Bureau of Economic Analysis (BEA) and shown in Table 8-2. The inflation rate is shown along with other rates in Table 8-3; see the notes and definitions for that table.

Real federal funds rate. There is no directly observable real short-term rate, but it can be approximated by subtracting some measure of the current inflation rate from the nominal rate. For Table 12-9, the editor has selected one widely-followed measure—the rate of change in the core PCE (personal consumption expenditures, excluding food and energy) chain price index, shown in the previous column of the table—and calculated a "real" federal funds rate by subtracting the core inflation rate from the nominal rate. In the annual data, the inflation rate is the percentage change in the price index from the previous year; in the monthly data, it is the percentage change from the same month a year earlier. As noted in Chapter 8, which includes and defines several different measures of inflation, other price indexes could be used as inflation indicators.

Interest rate swaps. An interest rate swap is a type of financial market derivative in which two parties, known as "counterparties," exchange two streams of cash flows. The rates shown here are the results of transactions in which streams of fixed-rate interest flows are exchanged for streams of floating-rate interest flows. The rates shown are the fixed interest rates which are exchanged for floating-rate flows paying the three-month LIBOR (London Interbank Offered Rate, a rate at which highly-rated banks can borrow short-term). They are International Swaps and Derivatives Association (ISDA ®) mid-market par swap rates, collected at 11 a.m. EST by Garban Intercapital plc and published on Reuters Page ISDAFIX ®1. ISDAFIX is a registered service mark of ISDA. Reprinted by the Federal Reserve from Reuters Limited.

U.S. Treasury securities, constant maturities. The rates shown for 1-year, 5-year, 10-year, 20-year, and 30-year securities are yields on actively traded issues adjusted to constant maturities. Yields on Treasury securities at "constant maturity" are interpolated by the Treasury Department from the daily yield curve. This curve, which relates the yield on a security to its time to maturity, is based on the closing market bid yields on actively traded Treasury securities in the over-the-counter market. These market yields are calculated from composites of quotations reported by U.S. Gov-

ernment securities dealers to the Federal Reserve Bank of New York. The constant maturity yield values are read from the yield curve at fixed maturities. For example, this method provides a yield for a 10-year maturity, even if no outstanding security has exactly 10 years remaining to maturity. The 30-year series was discontinued as of February 2002, because the Treasury Department was no longer issuing such bonds at that time. However, issuance of 30-year bonds was resumed in 2005 as an additional means of financing rising deficits, and the 30-year interest rate series resumes in 2006.[1] The current 20-year series begins with 1993 and is not comparable with an earlier 20-year series. For further information, see the historical data series on the Federal Reserve Web site.

Inflation-indexed yields. In recent years, the Treasury Department has issued Treasury Inflation-Protected Securities (TIPS), which are marketable long-term bonds whose redemption value is increased by the change in the CPI-U from the date of purchase. (See notes and definitions to Chapter 8.) The purchaser of these bonds, unlike with ordinary securities, is guaranteed that the real value of his or her principal will remain intact. He or she need not estimate future inflation in order to make a rational bid. Therefore, the observed purchase price represents a real rate of interest that purchasers and sellers are mutually willing to accept. Inflation-indexed yields are shown here for 5 and 20 years (adjusted to constant maturities by the Treasury) and for the long-term average, which is the unweighted average of the bid yields for all TIPS with remaining terms to maturity over 10 years.

Domestic corporate bond yields, Aaa and Baa. The rates shown are for general obligation bonds based on Thursday figures, and are provided by Moody's Investors Service and republished by the Federal Reserve. The Aaa rates through December 6, 2001 are averages of Aaa utility and Aaa industrial bond rates. As of December 7, 2001, these rates are averages of Aaa industrial bonds only.

The *state and local bond yields* are the Bond Buyer index as republished by the Federal Reserve. The index is based on 20 state and local government general obligation bonds of mixed quality maturing in 20 years or less. Quotes are as of the Thursday of each week. These rates are normally lower than those on U.S. Treasury or private long-term bonds because the interest on them is exempt from U.S. income taxes, but the most recent data display different patterns because of changing assessments of credit risks relative to Treasury securities.

The *fixed-rate first mortgage* rates are primary market contract interest rates on commitments for fixed-rate conventional 30-year first mortgages. The rates are obtained by the

---

[1] From February 18, 2002, to February 9, 2006, the U.S. Treasury published a factor for adjusting the daily nominal 20-year constant maturity in order to estimate a 30-year nominal rate. The historical adjustment factor can be found at www.treas.gov/offices/domestic-finance/debt-management/interest-rate/ltcompositeindex_historical.shtml.

Federal Reserve from the Federal Home Loan Mortgage Corporation (FHLMC, or Freddie Mac).

Stock price indexes and yields. The *Dow Jones industrial* average is an average price of 30 stocks compiled by Dow Jones, Inc. The *Standard and Poor's composite* is an index of the prices of 500 stocks that are weighted by the volume of shares outstanding, accounting for about 90 percent of New York Stock Exchange value, with a base of 1941–1943 = 10, compiled by Standard and Poor's Corporation. (Before February 1957, these data are based on a conversion of an earlier 90-stock index.) The *dividend-price ratio* is compiled by Standard and Poor's, covering the 500 stocks in the S&P index. It represents aggregate cash dividends (based on the latest known annual rate) divided by aggregate market value based on Wednesday closing prices. The *earnings/price ratio* measures earnings (after taxes) for four quarters, ending with the indicated quarter, as a ratio to stock prices for the last day of that quarter. Monthly data are averages of weekly figures; annual data are averages of monthly or quarterly figures. The *Nasdaq composite index* is an average price of over 5,000 stocks traded on the Nasdaq exchange.

FHFA (formerly OFHEO) House Price Indexes. The value of single-family owner-occupied houses has been an increasingly important element in household wealth and credit expansion and the subsequent collapse. The Federal Housing Finance Agency (FHFA), a government agency charged with regulation of the government-sponsored mortgage finance institutions Fannie Mae and Freddie Mac and the 12 Federal Home Loan Banks, uses data from those institutions to compile a quarterly House Price Index of the value of existing single-family homes. Not included are condominiums, cooperatives, multi-unit properties, and planned unit developments. This index was developed by the predecessor agency, the Office of Federal Housing Enterprise Oversight (OFHEO), and has been published since the fourth quarter of 1995.

The data come from all properties for which a conventional, "conforming" mortgage has been purchased or securitized by Fannie Mae or Freddie Mac since January 1975. (Conventional mortgages are those not insured or guaranteed by the FHA, VA, or other federal government entities. A conforming mortgage is one no larger than the maximum that the insuring institution will insure. The limit has increased over time and is $417,000 in 2006 and 2007.) Every new mortgage transaction that can be matched against a previous transaction for that property yields a rate of price change over the period between the two transactions, which enters into the calculation of the index. This data set is very large, with about 32 million repeat transactions over the 32-year span. Due to the size of this data set, the index can be calculated not only for the United States as a whole but also for regions, states, metropolitan statistical areas (MSAs) and metropolitan divisions (subdivisions of MSAs). The index is computed using a modified version of the Case-Shiller geometric weighted repeat-sales procedure.

In addition, FHFA now publishes a Purchase-Only Index for the house purchase subgroup of new mortgage transactions, excluding refinancing transactions. This index is based on 4.7 million transactions over the latest 16 years. While this is still a very large statistical base, it is subject to somewhat greater revision and is less reliable for smaller geographical areas.

The FHFA price indexes are subject to revision for preceding quarters and years, because each new transaction, when reported, affects the rate of price change since the last time that the property involved in the new transaction changed hands or was refinanced.

Seasonally adjusted data are also available for the purchase-only indexes. Seasonal price patterns appear to have some significance, especially for regional indexes. The seasonally adjusted indexes are not shown here because the year-over-change, calculated from not-seasonally-adjusted data, is the main focus of attention in these data.

The FHFA indexes do not come from a random sample of house prices, and users need to consider possible sources of bias. Expensive houses are under-represented in general because the transactions are limited to conforming mortgages. This is important if the price *trends* for expensive houses are different. It is also suspected that houses that are refinanced may be those that have appreciated in price more than other houses. In fact, the new purchase-only indexes showed little difference from the combined House Price Index for the period of appreciation between 1991 and the peak in the second quarter of 2007: total house prices rose 126 percent while purchased houses rose 122 percent. However, since then the total index declined 4.6 percent but the prices of purchased houses fell 10.8 percent.

New nongovernmental house price indexes are now receiving regular media attention, and even provide the basis for a futures contract trading on the Chicago Mercantile Exchange. Standard & Poor's now issues S&P/Case-Shiller® Home Price Indexes each month. They cover resales only for houses at all price ranges, based on information obtained from county assessor and recorder offices. They are value-weighted, meaning that price trends for more expensive homes have greater influence on changes in the index. The FHFA index weights price trends equally for all properties. S&P/Case-Shiller data are only collected for 20 major metropolitan statistical areas. Series description and data can be found at <http://www.homeprice.standardandpoors.com>.

Data availability and references

Interest rates and bond yields are published weekly in the Federal Reserve's H.15 release, "Selected Interest Rates"; the release and current and historical data are available on the Federal Reserve Web site. The starting dates for individual interest rate series vary; some date back to 1911, and many begin in the 1950s and 1960s. See the notes and definitions to Chapters 18 and 20 for sources for data for earlier years not available on the Web site.

Stock market data are published monthly in *Economic Indicators,* and annually in *Economic Report of the President,* available online at <http://www.gpo.gov/> select "Economic Indicators" or "Economic Report of the President" from the A-Z Resource List. Some historical interest rate data that are not available on the Federal Reserve Web site were also taken from the *Economic Report of the President.*

The FHFA house price indexes for the United States as a whole, regions, states, and metropolitan and sub-metropolitan groups are published every 3 months, approximately 2 months after the end of the previous quarter. The release and supporting data and explanatory material are available at <http://www.ofheo.gov/hpi>.

The OFHEO (now (FHFA) and other price indexes for houses are discussed and compared in Jordan Rappaport, "Comparing Aggregate Housing Price Measures," *Business Economics,* October 2007, pp. 55-65.

CHAPTER 13: INTERNATIONAL COMPARISONS

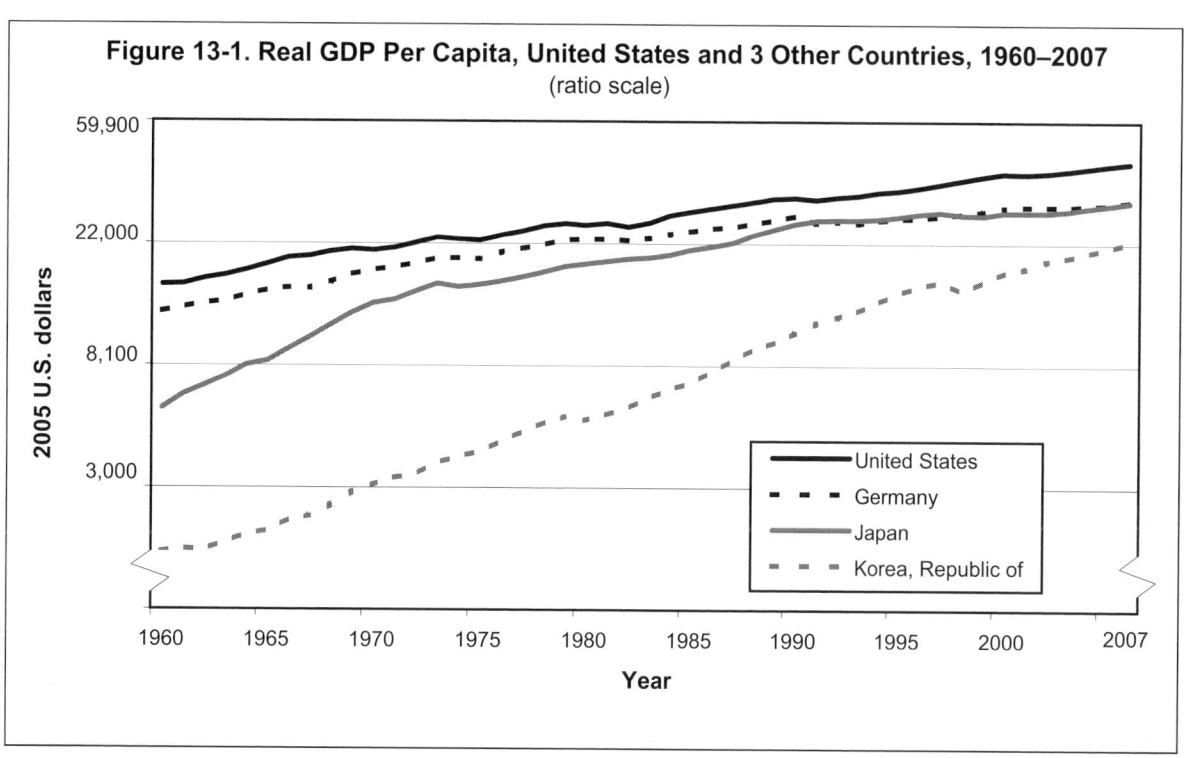

Figure 13-1. Real GDP Per Capita, United States and 3 Other Countries, 1960–2007
(ratio scale)

- In the United States, gross domestic product (GDP) per capita grew at an annual rate of 2.2 percent between 1960 and 2007. The major industrial nations with the next-highest average levels of living in 1960 grew at similar rates of 2.0 to 2.4 percent. The industrial nations that were further behind in 1960—France, Italy, Japan, and Korea—grew at faster rates: 2.5 percent, 2.7 percent, 3.7 percent, and 5.7 percent, respectively. The growth paths of the United States, Germany, Japan, and Korea are compared in Figure 13-1. (Table 13-2)

- In France, Germany, Italy, Japan, and the United Kingdom, the growth rate in GDP per employed person—a measure of labor productivity—was very similar to the growth rate in GDP per capita. In other words, growth in productivity and in potential living standards was the same. In contrast, growth in GDP per employee was significantly less than per capita output growth in the United States and the other countries shown. In these countries, a significant fraction of the growth in GDP per capita was obtained from putting a larger proportion of the population to work, instead of from greater efficiency. The growth rates in output per employee in the United States, Australia, and Canada were 1.4 to 1.6 percent, significantly lower than in the other countries shown. (Tables 13-2 and 13-3)

- In 2007, inflation in the 10 countries shown in Table 13-4 ranged from zero in Japan to 4.3 percent in the United Kingdom. (Table 13-4)

- The portion of the civilian working-age population employed is markedly lower in France, Germany, and Italy than in the Netherlands and the English-speaking countries, with Japan in between. (Table 13-6)

Table 13-1. International Comparisons: Growth Rates in Real Gross Domestic Product (GDP)

(Percent change at annual rate.)

Area and country	1990–1999	2000	2001	2002	2003	2004	2005	2006	2007	2008 [1]	2009 [1]
World	2.9	4.7	2.2	2.8	3.6	4.9	4.5	5.1	5.0	3.7	2.2
Advanced economies	2.7	4.0	1.2	1.6	1.9	3.2	2.6	3.0	2.6	1.4	-0.3
United States	3.1	3.7	0.8	1.6	2.5	3.6	2.9	2.8	2.0	1.4	-0.7
Japan	1.5	2.9	0.2	0.3	1.4	2.7	1.9	2.4	2.1	0.5	-0.2
United Kingdom	2.2	3.9	2.5	2.1	2.8	2.8	2.1	2.8	3.0	0.8	-1.3
Canada	2.4	5.2	1.8	2.9	1.9	3.1	2.9	3.1	2.7	0.6	0.3
Euro area [2]	. . .	3.8	1.9	0.9	0.8	2.1	1.6	2.8	2.6	1.2	-0.5
Germany	2.3	3.2	1.2	(3)	-0.2	1.2	0.8	3.0	2.5	1.7	-0.8
France	1.9	3.9	1.9	1.0	1.1	2.5	1.9	2.2	2.2	0.8	-0.5
Italy	1.4	3.7	1.8	0.5	(3)	1.5	0.6	1.8	1.5	-0.2	-0.6
Spain	2.8	5.1	3.6	2.7	3.1	3.3	3.6	3.9	3.7	1.4	-0.7
Memorandum:											
Newly industrialized Asian economies [4]	6.1	7.7	1.2	5.5	3.2	5.9	4.8	5.6	5.6	3.9	2.1
Emerging and developing economies	3.2	5.9	3.8	4.8	6.3	7.5	7.1	7.9	8.0	6.6	5.1
Regional groups:											
Africa	2.3	3.5	4.9	6.2	5.4	6.5	5.8	6.1	6.1	5.2	4.7
Central and eastern Europe	1.2	4.9	0.4	4.2	4.8	6.9	6.1	6.7	5.7	4.2	2.5
Commonwealth of Independent States [5]	. . .	9.1	6.1	5.2	7.8	8.2	6.8	8.2	8.6	6.9	3.2
Russia	. . .	10.0	5.1	4.7	7.3	7.2	6.4	7.4	8.1	6.8	3.5
Developing Asia	7.2	7.0	5.8	6.9	8.2	8.6	9.0	9.8	10.0	8.3	7.1
China	9.9	8.4	8.3	9.1	10.0	10.1	10.4	11.6	11.9	9.7	8.5
India	5.6	5.7	3.9	4.6	6.9	7.9	9.1	9.8	9.3	7.8	6.3
Middle East	4.3	5.5	2.6	3.8	7.1	5.8	5.7	5.7	6.0	6.1	5.3
Western Hemisphere	2.9	4.1	0.7	0.5	2.2	6.1	4.7	5.5	5.6	4.5	2.5
Brazil	1.7	4.3	1.3	2.7	1.1	5.7	3.2	3.8	5.4	5.2	3.0
Mexico	3.3	6.6	-0.2	0.8	1.7	4.0	3.1	4.9	3.2	1.9	0.9

[1] All figures are forecasts as published by the International Monetary Fund.
[2] Euro area consists of: Austria, Belgium, Cyprus, Finland, France, Germany, Greece, Ireland, Italy, Luxembourg, Malta, Netherlands, Portugal, Slovenia, and Spain.
[3] Figure is zero or negligible.
[4] Includes Hong Kong SAR (Special Administrative Region of China), Korea (Republic of), Singapore, and Taiwan Province of China.
[5] Includes Mongolia, which is not a member of the Commonwealth of Independent States, but is included for reasons of geography and similarities in economic structure.
. . . = Not available.

Table 13-2. International Comparisons: Real Gross Domestic Product (GDP) Per Capita

(2005 U.S. dollars.)

Year	United States	Australia	Canada	France	Germany [1]	Italy	Japan	Korea, Republic of	Netherlands	Spain	United Kingdom
1960	15 640	13 245	13 002	9 540	12 553	8 291	5 698	1 750	12 086	. . .	12 191
1961	15 744	12 832	13 144	9 907	12 961	8 912	6 375	1 798	12 272	. . .	12 370
1962	16 443	13 322	13 804	10 398	13 408	9 401	6 858	1 785	12 621	. . .	12 386
1963	16 917	13 843	14 268	10 865	13 652	9 856	7 385	1 895	12 860	. . .	12 836
1964	17 655	14 470	14 908	11 449	14 415	10 049	8 124	2 024	13 781	8 843	13 447
1965	18 554	14 875	15 573	11 895	15 019	10 291	8 409	2 087	14 313	9 296	13 657
1966	19 537	15 043	16 301	12 417	15 300	10 822	9 287	2 283	14 522	9 863	13 845
1967	19 812	15 792	16 477	12 927	15 218	11 515	10 197	2 362	15 119	10 169	14 105
1968	20 561	16 387	17 017	13 398	15 990	12 192	11 284	2 569	15 969	10 731	14 628
1969	20 988	17 144	17 620	14 244	17 021	12 862	12 484	2 859	16 860	11 551	14 866
1970	20 783	17 906	17 901	14 980	17 706	13 474	13 488	3 043	17 684	11 896	15 152
1971	21 211	17 787	18 097	15 615	18 059	13 655	13 889	3 229	18 223	12 285	15 377
1972	22 097	17 884	18 863	16 196	18 708	14 078	14 849	3 311	18 490	13 128	15 878
1973	23 148	18 414	19 931	17 120	19 503	14 980	15 820	3 644	19 402	13 994	16 971
1974	22 820	18 413	20 380	17 770	19 517	15 701	15 418	3 840	20 071	14 649	16 737
1975	22 556	18 596	20 451	17 516	19 343	15 281	15 701	4 000	19 923	14 595	16 635
1976	23 529	19 079	21 233	18 216	20 471	16 288	16 158	4 353	20 706	14 903	17 077
1977	24 368	19 194	21 712	18 779	21 098	16 634	16 710	4 714	20 977	15 114	17 494
1978	25 455	19 390	22 347	19 437	21 757	17 112	17 434	5 074	21 338	15 135	18 065
1979	25 970	19 981	22 968	20 037	22 664	18 080	18 237	5 337	21 623	15 030	18 530
1980	25 613	20 309	23 164	20 270	22 809	18 661	18 606	5 176	21 920	15 145	18 115
1981	25 998	20 826	23 682	20 343	22 789	18 796	19 015	5 410	21 673	15 039	17 843
1982	25 252	20 474	22 733	20 714	22 591	18 860	19 405	5 717	21 313	15 145	18 205
1983	26 155	20 104	23 121	20 850	23 069	19 074	19 584	6 241	21 655	15 340	18 838
1984	27 790	21 108	24 235	21 057	23 814	19 685	20 066	6 664	22 319	15 551	19 288
1985	28 682	22 027	25 162	21 311	24 358	20 230	20 956	7 047	22 722	15 853	19 919
1986	29 408	22 173	25 517	21 724	24 912	20 807	21 468	7 718	23 349	16 319	20 663
1987	30 130	22 789	26 252	22 145	25 275	21 469	22 177	8 491	23 670	17 182	21 565
1988	31 091	23 338	27 202	23 031	26 058	22 359	23 580	9 303	24 325	18 018	22 598
1989	31 889	24 001	27 416	23 849	26 735	23 099	24 735	9 833	25 253	18 851	23 028
1990	32 125	23 995	27 056	24 348	27 728	23 553	25 936	10 628	26 132	19 535	23 141
1991	31 648	23 428	26 176	24 475	26 084	23 891	26 699	11 512	26 554	19 986	22 744
1992	32 268	23 614	26 092	24 688	26 463	24 066	26 858	12 062	26 805	20 105	22 735
1993	32 703	24 300	26 409	24 359	26 062	23 838	26 844	12 673	26 950	19 836	23 198
1994	33 608	25 256	27 375	24 808	26 674	24 346	27 070	13 617	27 584	20 254	24 138
1995	34 045	25 872	27 853	25 245	27 099	25 034	27 534	14 717	28 298	20 764	24 778
1996	34 895	26 589	28 008	25 437	27 290	25 301	28 225	15 597	29 138	21 217	25 408
1997	36 031	27 394	28 903	25 916	27 729	25 761	28 600	16 171	30 226	21 980	26 129
1998	37 101	28 445	29 838	26 728	28 300	26 115	27 944	14 954	31 220	22 881	26 930
1999	38 312	29 385	31 233	27 472	28 849	26 492	27 862	16 256	32 464	23 775	27 651
2000	39 277	30 022	32 562	28 357	29 738	27 458	28 600	17 489	33 503	24 696	28 604
2001	39 165	30 232	32 788	28 679	30 052	27 940	28 565	18 026	33 891	25 184	29 170
2002	39 398	31 115	33 368	28 770	30 000	27 979	28 602	19 175	33 699	25 375	29 663
2003	40 006	31 643	33 671	28 883	29 921	27 757	28 959	19 671	33 653	25 747	30 365
2004	41 083	32 490	34 359	29 405	30 245	27 906	29 732	20 525	34 294	26 165	31 203
2005	41 954	32 953	35 065	29 785	30 496	27 854	30 312	21 342	34 724	26 650	31 570
2006	42 751	33 391	35 660	30 250	31 407	28 205	31 046	22 364	35 715	27 342	32 306
2007	43 267	34 154	36 243	30 724	32 228	28 434	31 696	23 399	36 783	28 079	33 191

[1]Data prior to 1991 are for West Germany only. In 1991, real GDP per capita in West Germany alone was $28,754 (2005 U.S. dollars).
. . . = Not available.

Table 13-3. International Comparisons: Real Gross Domestic Product (GDP) Per Employed Person

(2005 U.S. dollars.)

Year	United States	Australia	Canada	France	Germany [1]	Italy	Japan	Korea, Republic of	Netherlands	Spain	United Kingdom
1960	41 396	32 747	37 337	22 267	26 700	19 891	11 429	. . .	30 113	. . .	26 448
1961	42 343	32 474	37 934	23 379	27 552	21 388	12 616	. . .	30 540	. . .	26 777
1962	44 128	33 531	39 469	24 990	28 737	22 781	13 544	. . .	31 228	. . .	26 928
1963	45 425	34 529	40 622	26 364	29 476	24 465	14 610	6 830	31 825	. . .	28 019
1964	47 033	35 592	41 771	27 775	31 412	25 237	16 006	7 359	33 965	. . .	29 166
1965	48 855	36 149	42 861	29 048	32 907	26 713	16 656	7 384	35 464	. . .	29 522
1966	50 528	35 661	43 918	30 361	33 929	28 782	17 975	8 071	36 175	. . .	30 026
1967	50 600	37 184	43 827	31 790	34 964	30 469	19 564	8 251	38 211	. . .	31 126
1968	51 949	38 300	45 049	33 306	36 839	32 479	21 485	8 743	40 396	. . .	32 584
1969	52 267	39 916	45 873	35 179	38 981	34 709	23 821	9 714	42 436	. . .	33 262
1970	52 064	40 869	46 704	36 852	40 432	36 383	25 974	10 200	44 532	. . .	34 101
1971	53 605	41 506	47 459	38 621	41 500	37 033	26 924	10 676	46 185	29 336	34 818
1972	54 829	41 801	48 578	40 193	43 093	38 499	29 038	10 688	47 757	31 341	35 954
1973	56 138	42 466	49 444	42 257	44 659	40 667	30 677	11 358	50 498	32 939	37 933
1974	54 830	42 667	49 172	43 772	45 295	42 247	30 429	11 663	52 142	34 663	37 334
1975	55 344	43 715	49 161	43 731	45 962	41 332	31 448	12 071	52 610	35 556	37 249
1976	56 452	44 870	50 703	45 318	48 667	43 834	32 432	12 572	54 832	37 137	38 460
1977	57 016	44 914	51 565	46 553	49 981	44 819	33 455	13 397	54 739	38 440	39 352
1978	57 729	45 832	52 020	48 161	51 063	46 118	34 878	13 987	55 471	39 992	40 424
1979	57 931	46 928	51 751	49 608	52 339	48 329	36 417	14 727	55 618	40 934	41 096
1980	57 519	46 953	51 366	50 314	52 049	49 274	37 188	14 422	55 113	42 468	40 404
1981	58 316	47 906	51 661	50 973	52 157	49 730	37 989	14 940	54 573	43 453	40 868
1982	57 656	47 932	51 825	52 149	52 289	49 834	38 723	15 637	54 189	44 376	42 486
1983	59 485	48 573	52 854	52 936	53 977	50 255	38 760	17 171	56 315	45 319	44 306
1984	61 268	50 099	54 556	54 059	55 407	51 879	39 834	18 661	57 544	47 183	44 492
1985	62 539	51 395	55 564	55 188	56 114	52 830	41 633	19 210	57 233	48 778	45 492
1986	63 285	50 359	55 214	56 331	56 645	53 970	42 646	20 516	58 211	49 225	47 013
1987	63 793	51 408	55 947	57 295	57 070	55 566	44 090	21 611	59 363	49 580	48 217
1988	65 015	51 569	57 004	59 387	58 736	57 282	46 532	23 181	59 691	50 342	49 026
1989	65 989	51 717	57 211	60 836	59 992	58 821	48 283	23 771	61 080	50 927	48 843
1990	66 445	51 541	56 929	61 951	61 583	59 087	49 961	25 194	61 617	50 919	49 002
1991	66 955	52 141	56 729	62 513	54 020	58 891	50 606	26 727	61 510	51 595	49 639
1992	68 824	53 465	57 799	63 737	56 038	59 780	50 527	27 761	61 306	52 810	50 965
1993	69 727	55 308	58 871	63 979	56 335	60 884	50 461	29 119	62 152	53 791	52 622
1994	70 960	56 355	60 459	65 301	57 892	63 236	50 962	30 627	63 560	55 334	53 828
1995	71 735	56 243	61 070	66 097	58 853	65 154	51 890	32 508	63 681	55 798	55 444
1996	73 378	57 812	61 505	66 580	59 601	65 493	53 094	34 051	64 535	56 338	56 468
1997	75 036	59 666	62 793	67 773	60 733	66 511	53 554	35 029	65 221	56 858	57 210
1998	77 063	61 361	63 794	69 096	61 234	66 783	53 082	34 716	65 859	57 169	58 530
1999	79 302	63 085	65 645	69 963	61 632	67 034	53 747	37 348	67 131	57 788	59 506
2000	80 198	63 612	67 417	70 800	62 440	68 187	55 630	38 860	67 954	58 661	61 061
2001	80 753	64 241	67 782	70 853	62 938	68 053	56 157	39 573	67 509	58 925	61 996
2002	82 260	65 650	68 101	71 138	63 292	67 213	57 200	41 192	66 756	59 216	62 786
2003	83 495	66 066	68 785	71 821	63 758	66 209	58 199	42 525	67 369	59 190	63 907
2004	85 598	67 297	68 669	73 517	64 178	66 928	59 667	43 711	69 003	59 075	65 316
2005	86 724	67 052	69 800	74 497	64 737	66 914	60 591	44 950	70 019	58 840	65 862
2006	87 601	67 521	70 356	75 392	66 181	66 815	61 789	46 655	70 828	58 790	67 215
2007	88 540	68 228	70 589	76 012	66 718	67 026	62 788	48 386	71 532	59 279	68 783

[1]Data prior to 1991 are for West Germany only. In 1991, real GDP per employed person in West Germany alone was $63,120 (2005 U.S. dollars).
. . . = Not available.

Table 13-4. International Comparisons: Consumer Price Indexes

(1982–1984 = 100.)

Year	United States Index	United States Percent change	Australia Index	Australia Percent change	Canada Index	Canada Percent change	France Index	France Percent change	Germany [1] Index	Germany [1] Percent change	Italy Index	Italy Percent change	Japan Index	Japan Percent change	Netherlands Index	Netherlands Percent change	Spain Index	Spain Percent change	United Kingdom Index	United Kingdom Percent change
1950	24.1	. . .	12.6	. . .	21.6	. . .	11.2	. . .	. . .	. . .	. . .	. . .	14.7	. . .	. . .	. . .	5.5	. . .	9.8	. . .
1951	26.0	7.9	15.1	19.8	23.8	10.2	13.1	17.0	. . .	. . .	. . .	. . .	17.2	17.0	. . .	. . .	6.0	9.1	10.7	9.2
1952	26.5	1.9	17.7	17.2	24.5	2.9	14.7	12.2	. . .	. . .	. . .	. . .	18.0	4.7	. . .	. . .	5.9	-1.7	11.7	9.3
1953	26.7	0.8	18.4	4.0	24.2	-1.2	14.5	-1.4	. . .	. . .	10.3	. . .	19.2	6.7	. . .	. . .	6.0	1.7	12.1	3.4
1954	26.9	0.7	18.6	1.1	24.4	0.8	14.4	-0.7	. . .	. . .	10.6	2.9	20.4	6.3	. . .	. . .	6.1	1.7	12.3	1.7
1955	26.8	-0.4	19.0	2.2	24.4	0.0	14.6	1.4	. . .	. . .	10.9	2.8	20.2	-1.0	. . .	. . .	6.3	3.3	12.8	4.1
1956	27.2	1.5	20.1	5.8	24.7	1.2	14.9	2.1	. . .	. . .	11.2	2.8	20.3	0.5	. . .	. . .	6.7	6.3	13.5	5.5
1957	28.1	3.3	20.6	2.5	25.6	3.6	15.3	2.7	. . .	. . .	11.4	1.8	20.9	3.0	. . .	. . .	7.4	10.4	14.0	3.7
1958	28.9	2.8	20.9	1.5	26.3	2.7	17.6	15.0	. . .	. . .	11.7	2.6	20.8	-0.5	. . .	. . .	8.4	13.5	14.4	2.9
1959	29.1	0.7	21.3	1.9	26.4	0.4	18.7	6.2	. . .	. . .	11.7	0.0	21.0	1.0	. . .	. . .	9.0	7.1	14.5	0.7
1960	29.6	1.7	22.1	3.8	26.8	1.5	19.4	3.7	. . .	. . .	11.9	1.7	21.8	3.8	. . .	. . .	9.1	1.1	14.6	0.7
1961	29.9	1.0	22.6	2.3	27.1	1.1	20.0	3.1	. . .	. . .	12.2	2.5	23.0	5.5	. . .	. . .	9.2	1.1	15.1	3.4
1962	30.2	1.0	22.6	0.0	27.5	1.5	21.0	5.0	43.1	. . .	12.7	4.1	24.5	6.5	. . .	. . .	9.7	5.4	15.8	4.6
1963	30.6	1.3	22.7	0.4	27.8	1.1	22.0	4.8	44.4	3.0	13.7	7.9	26.4	7.8	. . .	. . .	10.6	9.3	16.1	1.9
1964	31.0	1.3	23.2	2.2	28.3	1.8	22.7	3.2	45.5	2.5	14.5	5.8	27.4	3.8	. . .	. . .	11.3	6.6	16.6	3.1
1965	31.5	1.6	24.1	3.9	29.0	2.5	23.3	2.6	46.9	3.1	15.2	4.8	29.5	7.7	. . .	. . .	12.8	13.3	17.4	4.8
1966	32.4	2.9	24.9	3.3	30.2	4.1	23.9	2.6	48.5	3.4	15.5	2.0	31.0	5.1	. . .	. . .	13.6	6.2	18.1	4.0
1967	33.4	3.1	25.7	3.2	31.3	3.6	24.6	2.9	49.4	1.9	16.1	3.9	32.2	3.9	. . .	. . .	14.5	6.6	18.6	2.8
1968	34.8	4.2	26.4	2.7	32.5	3.8	25.7	4.5	50.2	1.6	16.3	1.2	33.9	5.3	. . .	. . .	15.2	4.8	19.4	4.3
1969	36.7	5.5	27.2	3.0	34.0	4.6	27.3	6.2	51.1	1.8	16.7	2.5	35.7	5.3	40.6	. . .	15.5	2.0	20.5	5.7
1970	38.8	5.7	28.2	3.7	35.1	3.2	28.8	5.5	52.9	3.5	17.5	4.8	38.4	7.6	42.1	3.7	16.4	5.8	21.8	6.3
1971	40.5	4.4	29.8	5.7	36.1	2.8	30.3	5.2	55.7	5.3	18.4	5.1	40.9	6.5	45.3	7.6	17.7	7.9	23.8	9.2
1972	41.8	3.2	31.7	6.4	37.8	4.7	32.2	6.3	58.7	5.4	19.4	5.4	42.9	4.9	48.9	7.9	19.2	8.5	25.5	7.1
1973	44.4	6.2	34.6	9.1	40.8	7.9	34.6	7.5	62.8	7.0	21.6	11.3	47.9	11.7	52.9	8.2	21.4	11.5	27.8	9.0
1974	49.3	11.0	39.9	15.3	45.3	11.0	39.3	13.6	67.2	7.0	25.7	19.0	59.0	23.2	58.1	9.8	24.8	15.9	32.3	16.2
1975	53.8	9.1	45.9	15.0	50.1	10.6	43.9	11.7	71.2	6.0	30.0	16.7	65.9	11.7	63.8	9.8	29.0	16.9	40.1	24.1
1976	56.9	5.8	52.0	13.3	53.7	7.2	48.2	9.8	74.2	4.2	35.1	17.0	72.2	9.6	69.6	9.1	34.1	17.6	46.8	16.7
1977	60.6	6.5	58.5	12.5	58.1	8.2	52.7	9.3	77.0	3.8	41.0	16.8	78.1	8.2	74.1	6.5	42.4	24.3	54.2	15.8
1978	65.2	7.6	63.1	7.9	63.2	8.8	57.5	9.1	79.1	2.7	46.0	12.2	81.4	4.2	77.2	4.2	50.8	19.8	58.7	8.3
1979	72.6	11.3	68.8	9.0	69.1	9.3	63.6	10.6	82.3	4.0	52.8	14.8	84.3	3.6	80.5	4.3	58.8	15.7	66.6	13.5
1980	82.4	13.5	75.8	10.2	76.0	10.0	72.3	13.7	86.8	5.5	64.0	21.2	91.0	7.9	86.1	7.0	67.9	15.5	78.5	17.9
1981	90.9	10.3	83.1	9.6	85.5	12.5	82.0	13.4	92.2	6.2	75.4	17.8	95.3	4.7	91.9	6.7	77.8	14.6	87.9	12.0
1982	96.5	6.2	92.5	11.3	94.9	11.0	91.6	11.7	97.1	5.3	87.8	16.4	98.1	2.9	97.2	5.8	89.0	14.4	95.4	8.5
1983	99.6	3.2	101.8	10.1	100.4	5.8	100.5	9.7	100.2	3.2	100.7	14.7	99.8	1.7	99.8	2.7	99.9	12.2	99.8	4.6
1984	103.9	4.3	105.8	3.9	104.7	4.3	107.9	7.4	102.7	2.5	111.5	10.7	102.1	2.3	103.0	3.2	111.1	11.2	104.8	5.0
1985	107.6	3.6	112.9	6.7	108.9	4.0	114.2	5.8	104.8	2.0	121.8	9.2	104.2	2.1	105.3	2.2	120.9	8.8	111.1	6.0
1986	109.6	1.9	123.2	9.1	113.4	4.1	117.2	2.6	104.7	-0.1	129.0	5.9	104.8	0.6	105.6	0.3	131.6	8.9	114.9	3.4
1987	113.6	3.6	133.6	8.4	118.4	4.4	120.9	3.2	104.9	0.2	135.1	4.7	104.9	0.1	105.1	-0.5	138.5	5.2	119.7	4.2
1988	118.3	4.1	143.3	7.3	123.0	3.9	124.2	2.7	106.2	1.2	141.9	5.0	105.6	0.7	106.1	1.0	145.2	4.8	125.6	4.9
1989	124.0	4.8	154.1	7.5	129.3	5.1	128.6	3.5	109.2	2.8	150.8	6.3	108.0	2.3	107.1	0.9	155.0	6.7	135.4	7.8
1990	130.7	5.4	165.3	7.3	135.5	4.8	133.0	3.4	112.1	2.7	160.5	6.4	111.3	3.1	109.9	2.6	165.4	6.7	148.2	9.5
1991	136.2	4.2	170.7	3.3	143.1	5.6	137.3	3.2	116.3	3.7	170.6	6.3	115.1	3.4	113.3	3.1	175.2	5.9	156.9	5.9
1992	140.3	3.0	172.4	1.0	145.2	1.5	140.5	2.3	122.3	5.2	179.6	5.3	117.0	1.7	116.9	3.2	185.6	5.9	162.7	3.7
1993	144.5	3.0	175.5	1.8	147.9	1.9	143.5	2.1	127.6	4.3	187.8	4.6	118.5	1.3	120.0	2.7	194.1	4.6	165.3	1.6
1994	148.2	2.6	178.8	1.9	148.1	0.1	145.8	1.6	131.2	2.8	195.5	4.1	119.2	0.6	123.3	2.8	203.3	4.7	169.3	2.4
1995	152.4	2.8	187.1	4.6	151.4	2.2	148.4	1.8	133.4	1.7	205.8	5.3	119.1	-0.1	125.7	1.9	212.8	4.7	175.2	3.5
1996	156.9	3.0	192.0	2.6	153.6	1.5	151.3	2.0	135.3	1.4	214.0	4.0	119.2	0.1	128.2	2.0	220.3	3.5	179.4	2.4
1997	160.5	2.3	192.5	0.3	156.2	1.7	153.2	1.3	137.9	1.9	218.3	2.0	121.5	1.9	131.0	2.2	224.7	2.0	185.1	3.2
1998	163.0	1.6	194.1	0.8	157.8	1.0	154.3	0.7	139.3	1.0	222.6	2.0	122.2	0.6	133.6	2.0	228.8	1.8	191.4	3.4
1999	166.6	2.2	197.0	1.5	160.5	1.7	155.0	0.5	140.0	0.5	226.3	1.7	121.8	-0.3	136.5	2.2	234.1	2.3	194.3	1.5
2000	172.2	3.4	205.8	4.5	164.9	2.7	157.7	1.7	142.0	1.4	232.1	2.6	120.9	-0.7	139.7	2.3	242.1	3.4	200.1	3.0
2001	177.1	2.8	214.8	4.4	169.0	2.5	160.3	1.6	144.8	2.0	238.5	2.8	120.1	-0.7	145.5	4.2	250.8	3.6	207.0	1.7
2002	179.9	1.6	221.2	3.0	172.8	2.2	163.4	1.9	146.9	1.5	244.5	2.5	119.0	-0.9	150.3	3.3	259.7	3.5	207.0	1.7
2003	184.0	2.3	227.4	2.8	177.6	2.8	166.8	2.1	148.5	1.1	251.0	2.7	118.7	-0.3	153.5	2.1	267.6	3.0	213.0	2.9
2004	188.9	2.7	232.7	2.3	180.9	1.9	170.3	2.1	150.9	1.6	256.6	2.2	118.7	0.0	155.4	1.2	275.7	3.0	219.4	3.0
2005	195.3	3.4	238.9	2.7	184.9	2.2	173.4	1.8	153.2	1.5	261.6	1.9	118.3	-0.3	158.0	1.7	285.0	3.4	225.6	2.8
2006	201.6	3.2	247.4	3.6	188.5	1.9	176.2	1.6	155.7	1.6	267.1	2.1	118.7	0.3	159.8	1.1	295.0	3.5	232.8	3.2
2007	207.3	2.8	253.1	2.3	192.7	2.2	178.9	1.5	159.2	2.2	272.0	1.8	118.7	0.0	162.4	1.6	303.3	2.8	242.7	4.3

[1]Data prior to 1991 are for West Germany only.
. . . = Not available.

Table 13-5. International Comparisons: Civilian Working Age Population

(Approximating U.S. concepts, thousands of persons.)

Year	United States	Australia	Canada	France	Germany [1]	Italy	Japan	Netherlands	United Kingdom
1960	117 245	. . .	11 494	31 369	43 436	37 130	64 990	. . .	38 952
1961	118 771	. . .	11 708	31 596	43 647	37 358	65 820	. . .	39 287
1962	120 153	. . .	11 940	32 319	43 972	37 815	67 330	. . .	39 804
1963	122 416	. . .	12 179	33 166	44 232	38 083	69 170	. . .	40 036
1964	124 485	7 668	12 453	33 717	44 525	38 515	71 000	. . .	40 281
1965	126 513	7 830	12 755	34 219	44 909	38 724	72 650	. . .	40 481
1966	128 058	8 023	13 083	34 606	45 174	39 276	74 090	. . .	40 631
1967	129 874	8 208	13 444	34 995	45 111	39 456	75 340	. . .	40 779
1968	132 028	8 403	13 805	35 362	45 163	39 833	76 550	. . .	40 874
1969	134 335	8 612	14 162	35 742	45 570	39 781	77 580	. . .	41 006
1970	137 085	8 819	14 528	36 151	46 094	40 279	78 610	. . .	41 101
1971	140 216	9 036	14 872	36 578	46 687	40 385	79 560	. . .	40 397
1972	144 126	9 238	15 186	36 965	47 100	40 780	80 470	. . .	40 564
1973	147 096	9 425	15 526	37 352	47 594	41 186	82 150	9 750	40 741
1974	150 120	9 614	15 924	37 711	47 904	41 745	83 170	9 885	40 912
1975	153 153	9 763	16 323	38 020	48 018	42 131	84 190	9 803	41 103
1976	156 150	9 957	16 582	38 330	48 128	42 312	85 160	9 960	41 331
1977	159 033	10 136	16 964	38 679	48 418	42 529	86 070	10 103	41 608
1978	161 910	10 406	17 302	39 008	48 788	43 000	87 020	10 256	41 904
1979	164 863	10 575	17 663	39 371	49 255	43 436	88 000	10 415	42 228
1980	167 745	10 778	18 032	39 750	49 849	43 860	89 080	10 588	42 570
1981	170 130	10 994	18 398	40 114	50 344	44 184	89 930	10 744	42 868
1982	172 271	11 204	18 716	40 476	50 714	44 847	90 920	10 871	43 083
1983	174 215	11 401	18 981	40 828	50 928	45 457	92 080	10 996	43 327
1984	176 383	11 602	19 220	41 165	51 112	45 853	93 230	11 131	43 596
1985	178 206	11 826	19 459	41 500	51 261	46 174	94 410	11 271	43 863
1986	180 587	12 074	19 715	41 846	51 467	46 628	95 630	11 403	44 087
1987	182 753	12 323	19 985	42 217	51 643	46 986	96 960	11 561	44 296
1988	184 613	12 593	20 257	42 605	51 893	47 778	98 250	11 667	44 456
1989	186 393	12 823	20 540	43 008	52 279	47 660	99 500	11 766	44 602
1990	189 164	13 051	20 852	43 343	53 135	48 016	100 650	11 865	44 705
1991	190 925	13 227	21 176	43 623	66 487	48 044	101 750	11 979	44 825
1992	192 805	13 391	21 459	43 892	67 083	48 203	102 590	12 077	44 854
1993	194 838	13 561	21 731	44 138	67 709	47 130	103 460	12 162	44 887
1994	196 814	13 729	21 994	44 377	68 022	47 430	104 200	12 246	44 960
1995	198 584	13 936	22 274	44 609	68 240	47 702	104 860	12 319	45 104
1996	200 591	14 117	22 575	44 856	68 498	47 909	105 470	12 387	45 266
1997	203 133	14 321	22 866	45 147	68 797	48 096	106 370	12 455	45 432
1998	205 220	14 525	23 130	45 446	68 914	48 277	107 040	12 538	45 610
1999	207 753	14 698	23 390	45 771	69 187	48 388	107 590	12 614	45 828
2000	212 577	14 902	23 692	46 129	69 365	48 567	108 120	12 703	46 086
2001	215 092	15 138	24 033	46 522	69 599	48 750	108 620	12 803	46 395
2002	217 570	15 385	24 395	46 909	69 900	48 894	109 030	12 892	46 679
2003	221 168	15 613	24 714	47 281	70 160	48 896	109 380	12 962	46 975
2004	223 357	15 825	25 046	47 621	70 431	49 080	109 660	13 019	47 338
2005	226 082	16 083	25 381	47 959	70 705	49 606	109 830	13 075	47 767
2006	228 815	16 303	25 760	48 280	70 844	49 913	109 960	13 128	48 167
2007	231 867	16 589	26 134	48 550	70 925	50 301	110 190	13 184	48 580

[1] Data prior to 1991 are for West Germany only.
. . . = Not available.

Table 13-6. International Comparisons: Civilian Employment-Population Ratios

(Approximating U.S. concepts. Civilian employment as a percent of civilian working-age population.)

Year	United States	Australia	Canada	France	Germany [1]	Italy	Japan	Netherlands	United Kingdom
1960	56.1	. . .	52.6	58.6	59.2	54.0	66.7	. . .	60.6
1961	55.4	. . .	52.4	58.2	59.6	54.0	66.8	. . .	60.8
1962	55.5	. . .	52.8	57.1	59.3	53.2	66.0	. . .	60.4
1963	55.4	. . .	53.0	56.6	59.2	51.9	64.9	. . .	60.2
1964	55.7	58.6	53.7	56.9	58.8	51.1	64.1	. . .	60.7
1965	56.2	59.1	54.4	56.4	58.5	49.6	63.6	. . .	61.0
1966	56.9	59.6	55.4	56.4	58.0	48.1	63.7	. . .	60.9
1967	57.3	60.0	55.4	56.2	56.3	48.5	64.0	. . .	60.0
1968	57.5	60.1	55.0	55.5	56.2	47.9	64.1	. . .	59.6
1969	58.0	60.2	55.3	55.9	56.6	47.6	63.9	. . .	59.5
1970	57.4	61.1	54.5	56.0	56.6	47.4	63.8	. . .	59.2
1971	56.6	61.0	54.5	55.8	56.2	47.1	63.4	. . .	60.2
1972	57.0	60.6	54.9	55.5	55.8	45.9	62.9	. . .	60.1
1973	57.8	61.2	56.4	55.8	55.9	45.8	63.2	51.8	60.8
1974	57.8	61.3	57.3	55.7	54.8	46.2	62.2	51.6	60.7
1975	56.1	60.1	56.9	54.8	53.2	46.0	61.2	51.7	60.2
1976	56.8	59.7	58.2	54.8	52.8	46.1	61.1	51.2	59.5
1977	57.9	59.2	57.9	54.8	52.5	46.2	61.3	51.6	59.2
1978	59.3	58.0	58.5	54.6	52.6	45.9	61.3	51.3	59.1
1979	59.9	57.8	59.8	54.2	52.9	45.9	61.4	51.4	59.3
1980	59.2	58.3	60.3	53.8	53.1	46.0	61.3	52.1	58.5
1981	59.0	58.4	60.8	53.1	52.5	45.9	61.2	51.7	56.6
1982	57.8	57.3	58.0	52.7	51.6	45.1	61.2	50.8	55.2
1983	57.9	55.3	57.6	52.3	50.6	44.7	61.4	49.3	54.5
1984	59.5	56.0	58.3	51.4	50.5	44.5	61.0	49.3	55.3
1985	60.1	56.6	59.2	50.9	50.7	44.4	60.7	50.1	55.7
1986	60.7	57.8	60.2	50.7	51.3	44.2	60.4	50.3	55.7
1987	61.5	58.0	61.2	50.4	51.5	43.8	60.1	49.8	56.6
1988	62.3	58.9	62.2	50.4	51.6	43.7	60.4	50.7	58.3
1989	63.0	60.3	62.7	50.7	52.0	43.6	60.8	51.4	59.6
1990	62.8	60.4	62.2	50.9	52.6	43.9	61.3	52.7	59.8
1991	61.7	58.2	60.2	50.7	55.5	44.5	61.8	53.6	57.2
1992	61.5	57.2	58.9	50.1	54.2	44.0	62.0	54.3	56.4
1993	61.7	56.8	58.5	49.2	53.2	43.6	61.7	53.9	56.1
1994	62.5	57.8	59.0	49.0	52.6	42.5	61.3	54.0	56.4
1995	62.9	59.2	59.3	49.2	52.4	42.0	60.9	55.4	57.0
1996	63.2	59.3	59.1	49.1	52.0	42.0	60.9	56.2	57.3
1997	63.8	59.0	59.6	49.1	51.6	41.9	61.0	57.7	58.1
1998	64.1	59.3	60.4	49.7	52.3	42.2	60.2	59.1	58.5
1999	64.3	59.6	61.3	50.4	52.1	42.6	59.4	60.3	59.0
2000	64.4	60.3	62.0	51.4	52.2	43.2	59.0	61.5	59.4
2001	63.7	60.0	61.9	51.9	52.2	43.8	58.4	62.6	59.5
2002	62.7	60.2	62.4	51.8	51.5	44.3	57.5	62.9	59.6
2003	62.3	60.7	63.1	51.5	50.8	44.9	57.1	62.2	59.8
2004	62.3	61.1	63.3	51.1	50.6	45.1	57.1	61.8	60.0
2005	62.7	62.0	63.4	51.1	51.2	44.9	57.3	61.6	60.0
2006	63.1	62.5	63.6	51.2	52.2	45.5	57.5	62.5	60.1
2007	63.0	63.1	64.2	51.8	53.3	45.6	57.6	63.8	60.0

[1]Data prior to 1991 are for West Germany only.
. . . = Not available.

Table 13-7. International Comparisons: Civilian Unemployment Rates

(Approximating U.S. concepts. Civilian unemployment as a percent of civilian labor force.)

Year	United States	Australia	Canada	France	Germany [1]	Italy	Japan	Netherlands	United Kingdom
1960	5.5	1.6	6.5	1.5	1.1	3.7	1.7	. . .	2.2
1961	6.7	3.0	6.7	1.2	0.6	3.2	1.5	. . .	2.0
1962	5.5	2.9	5.5	1.4	0.6	2.8	1.3	. . .	2.7
1963	5.7	2.3	5.2	1.6	0.5	2.4	1.3	. . .	3.3
1964	5.2	1.4	4.4	1.2	0.4	2.7	1.2	. . .	2.5
1965	4.5	1.3	3.6	1.6	0.3	3.5	1.2	. . .	2.1
1966	3.8	1.6	3.3	1.6	0.3	3.7	1.4	. . .	2.3
1967	3.8	1.9	3.8	2.1	1.3	3.4	1.3	. . .	3.3
1968	3.6	1.8	4.5	2.7	1.1	3.5	1.2	. . .	3.2
1969	3.5	1.8	4.4	2.3	0.6	3.5	1.1	. . .	3.1
1970	4.9	1.7	5.7	2.5	0.5	3.2	1.2	. . .	3.1
1971	5.9	1.9	6.2	2.8	0.6	3.3	1.3	. . .	4.2
1972	5.6	2.6	6.2	2.9	0.7	3.8	1.4	. . .	4.4
1973	4.9	2.3	5.6	2.8	0.7	3.7	1.3	3.1	3.7
1974	5.6	2.7	5.3	2.9	1.6	3.1	1.4	3.6	3.7
1975	8.5	4.9	6.9	4.2	3.4	3.4	1.9	5.1	4.5
1976	7.7	4.8	6.9	4.6	3.4	3.9	2.0	5.4	5.4
1977	7.1	5.6	7.8	5.2	3.4	4.1	2.0	4.9	5.6
1978	6.1	6.3	8.1	5.4	3.3	4.1	2.3	5.1	5.5
1979	5.8	6.3	7.3	6.1	2.9	4.4	2.1	5.1	5.4
1980	7.1	6.1	7.3	6.5	2.8	4.4	2.0	6.0	6.9
1981	7.6	5.8	7.3	7.6	4.0	4.9	2.2	8.9	9.7
1982	9.7	7.2	10.7	8.3	5.6	5.4	2.4	10.2	10.8
1983	9.6	10.0	11.6	8.6	6.9	5.9	2.7	11.4	11.5
1984	7.5	9.0	10.9	10.0	7.1	5.9	2.8	11.5	11.8
1985	7.2	8.3	10.2	10.5	7.2	6.0	2.7	9.6	11.4
1986	7.0	7.9	9.3	10.6	6.6	7.5	2.8	10.0	11.4
1987	6.2	7.9	8.4	10.8	6.3	7.9	2.9	9.8	10.5
1988	5.5	7.0	7.4	10.3	6.3	7.9	2.5	9.3	8.6
1989	5.3	6.0	7.1	9.6	5.7	7.8	2.3	8.4	7.3
1990	5.6	6.7	7.7	8.6	5.0	7.0	2.1	7.6	7.1
1991	6.8	9.3	9.8	9.1	5.6	6.9	2.1	7.1	9.5
1992	7.5	10.5	10.6	10.0	6.7	7.3	2.2	6.8	10.2
1993	6.9	10.6	10.8	11.3	8.0	9.8	2.5	6.3	10.4
1994	6.1	9.4	9.6	11.9	8.5	10.7	2.9	6.9	9.5
1995	5.6	8.2	8.6	11.3	8.2	11.3	3.2	7.1	8.7
1996	5.4	8.2	8.8	11.8	9.0	11.3	3.4	6.6	8.1
1997	4.9	8.3	8.4	11.7	9.9	11.4	3.4	5.6	7.0
1998	4.5	7.7	7.7	11.2	9.3	11.5	4.1	4.4	6.3
1999	4.2	6.9	7.0	10.5	8.5	11.0	4.7	3.5	6.0
2000	4.0	6.3	6.1	9.1	7.8	10.2	4.8	3.0	5.5
2001	4.7	6.8	6.5	8.4	7.9	9.2	5.1	2.3	5.1
2002	5.8	6.4	7.0	8.8	8.6	8.7	5.4	2.8	5.2
2003	6.0	5.9	6.9	9.2	9.3	8.5	5.3	3.7	5.0
2004	5.5	5.4	6.4	9.6	10.3	8.1	4.8	4.6	4.8
2005	5.1	5.1	6.0	9.6	11.2	7.8	4.5	4.8	4.9
2006	4.6	4.8	5.5	9.5	10.4	6.9	4.2	3.9	5.5
2007	4.6	4.4	5.3	8.6	8.7	6.2	3.9	3.2	5.4

[1]Data prior to 1991 are for West Germany only.
. . . = Not available.

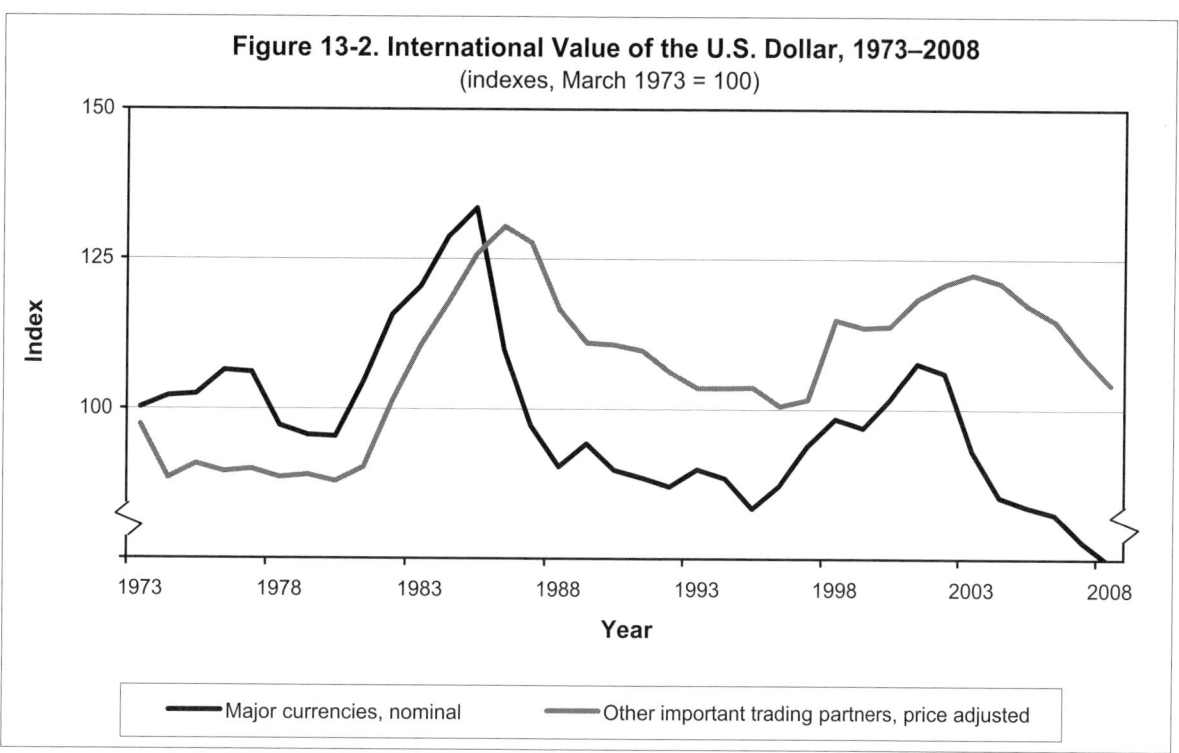

Figure 13-2. International Value of the U.S. Dollar, 1973–2008
(indexes, March 1973 = 100)

- Aggregate indexes of the value of the dollar based on annual averages, such as the two shown in the above figure, indicate a further decline in 2008. The monthly data shown in Table 13-8, however, indicate some unusual cross-currents in the last three months of 2008 as the financial crisis took hold worldwide. The dollar suddenly strengthened noticeably against the Canadian dollar and against European currencies—the euro, the Swiss franc, and the British pound—while weakening dramatically relative to the Japanese yen. (Table 13-8)

- Figure 13-2 above displays two indexes of the dollar's value. One is relative to a weighted average of seven major currencies—the euro, the British pound, the Canadian dollar, the Japanese yen, the Swiss franc, the Australian dollar, and the Swedish krona. These are all major industrial countries whose currencies are freely traded on world markets. Measured against these major currencies in terms of annual averages, the dollar depreciated 31 percent from 2001 to 2008, comparable to the 32 percent drop from 1985 to 1988. Dollar depreciation seems unsurprising in light of the large current-account deficits detailed in Chapter 7. (Table 13-8 and Chapter 7)

- The major-currency index is not relevant to the emerging-market currencies ("Other important trading partners" or OITP) that account for much of the U.S. trade deficit. Many emerging-market countries, especially China, are able to control the international values of their currencies (through, for example, direct capital controls) and keep their currencies from appreciating relative to the dollar to maintain their competitiveness in the U.S. market. In recent years, however, the Chinese have allowed some yuan appreciation and there has been a 12 percent decline in the price-adjusted OITP index from 2001 to 2008. (Table 13-8)

Table 13-8. Foreign Exchange Rates

(Not seasonally adjusted.)

Year and month	Foreign currency per U.S. dollar						Trade-weighted exchange indexes of value of U.S. dollar [1]					
							Nominal				Price-adjusted	
	European currency unit	Japanese yen	German mark	Swiss franc	British pound	Canadian dollar	G-10 countries (March 1973 = 100)	Broad (January 1997 = 100)	Major currencies (March 1973 = 100)	Other important trading partners (January 1997 = 100)	Broad (March 1973 = 100)	Other important trading partners (March 1973 = 100)
1971	. . .	346.62	3.4673	4.1171	0.4092	1.0099	117.81	. . .	. . .	. . .	. . .	. . .
1972	. . .	303.11	3.1889	3.8186	0.4005	0.9908	109.07	. . .	. . .	. . .	. . .	. . .
1973	. . .	271.40	2.6719	3.1688	0.4084	1.0002	99.14	31.70	100.23	2.03	98.94	97.25
1974	. . .	291.94	2.5873	2.9805	0.4277	0.9781	101.41	32.58	102.05	2.14	95.52	88.45
1975	. . .	296.77	2.4614	2.5839	0.4521	1.0173	98.50	33.68	102.39	2.39	94.50	90.78
1976	. . .	296.48	2.5184	2.5002	0.5567	0.9861	105.63	35.83	106.42	2.70	94.48	89.55
1977	. . .	268.38	2.3225	2.4065	0.5733	1.0635	103.35	36.88	106.08	3.02	92.75	89.89
1978	. . .	210.46	2.0089	1.7907	0.5214	1.1408	92.39	35.09	97.21	3.18	87.16	88.60
1979	. . .	219.21	1.8331	1.6644	0.4720	1.1716	88.07	35.36	95.60	3.40	88.23	88.94
1980	. . .	226.58	1.8183	1.6772	0.4304	1.1694	87.39	36.35	95.35	3.75	89.55	87.91
1981	. . .	220.45	2.2606	1.9675	0.4978	1.1989	103.26	40.34	104.67	4.27	96.61	90.20
1982	. . .	249.05	2.4281	2.0319	0.5727	1.2339	116.50	46.83	115.76	5.52	106.12	101.19
1983	. . .	237.45	2.5545	2.1007	0.6601	1.2326	125.32	52.81	120.45	7.44	110.59	110.48
1984	. . .	237.59	2.8483	2.3500	0.7521	1.2952	138.34	60.11	128.75	9.78	118.07	117.77
1985	. . .	238.47	2.9443	2.4552	0.7792	1.3659	143.24	67.16	133.60	13.14	123.04	125.80
1986	. . .	168.50	2.1711	1.7979	0.6821	1.3898	112.27	62.35	109.86	16.49	107.65	130.46
1987	. . .	144.63	1.7976	1.4918	0.6117	1.3261	96.95	60.42	97.16	19.92	98.89	127.73
1988	. . .	128.14	1.7561	1.4643	0.5621	1.2309	92.75	60.92	90.41	24.07	92.29	116.60
1989	. . .	138.00	1.8792	1.6369	0.6111	1.1841	98.52	66.90	94.24	29.61	94.04	111.08
1990	. . .	144.82	1.6159	1.3901	0.5630	1.1670	89.05	71.41	89.87	40.10	91.50	110.73
1991	. . .	134.51	1.6585	1.4356	0.5667	1.1460	89.73	74.35	88.52	46.69	89.97	109.82
1992	. . .	126.75	1.5624	1.4064	0.5699	1.2088	86.64	76.91	87.02	53.13	88.08	106.17
1993	. . .	111.23	1.6537	1.4781	0.6662	1.2902	93.17	83.78	89.92	63.37	89.43	103.52
1994	. . .	102.19	1.6219	1.3667	0.6531	1.3659	91.32	90.87	88.42	80.54	89.25	103.52
1995	. . .	94.11	1.4331	1.1812	0.6337	1.3727	84.30	92.65	83.46	92.51	86.80	103.59
1996	. . .	108.81	1.5049	1.2361	0.6410	1.3637	87.34	97.46	87.24	98.24	88.81	100.55
1997	. . .	121.06	1.7339	1.4514	0.6106	1.3849	96.35	104.43	93.92	104.64	93.54	101.61
1998	. . .	130.99	1.7593	1.4506	0.6034	1.4836	98.82	115.89	98.41	125.89	101.54	114.92
1999	0.9387	113.73	1.8359	1.5045	0.6184	1.4858	. . .	116.04	96.84	129.20	100.92	113.63
2000	1.0864	107.80	. . .	1.6904	0.6611	1.4855	. . .	119.45	101.57	129.84	104.79	113.81
2001	1.1180	121.57	. . .	1.6891	0.6948	1.5487	. . .	125.93	107.65	135.91	110.82	118.38
2002	1.0612	125.22	. . .	1.5567	0.6667	1.5704	. . .	126.67	106.01	140.36	110.97	120.86
2003	0.8833	115.94	. . .	1.3450	0.6117	1.4008	. . .	119.11	93.01	143.52	104.24	122.48
2004	0.8040	108.15	. . .	1.2428	0.5456	1.3017	. . .	113.63	85.36	143.38	99.61	121.11
2005	0.8033	110.11	. . .	1.2459	0.5493	1.2115	. . .	110.71	83.72	138.89	97.98	117.40
2006	0.7960	116.31	. . .	1.2532	0.5425	1.1340	. . .	108.52	82.48	135.38	96.87	114.69
2007	0.7293	117.76	. . .	1.1999	0.4995	1.0734	. . .	103.40	77.87	130.28	92.28	109.06
2008	0.6791	103.39	. . .	1.0816	0.5392	1.0660	. . .	99.83	74.41	127.23	88.60	104.13
2006												
January	0.8247	115.48	. . .	1.2773	0.5654	1.1572	. . .	110.01	84.29	136.05	97.41	114.64
February	0.8375	117.86	. . .	1.3052	0.5721	1.1489	. . .	110.26	85.05	135.38	97.44	113.39
March	0.8314	117.28	. . .	1.3050	0.5733	1.1573	. . .	110.43	85.01	135.87	98.18	114.64
April	0.8148	117.07	. . .	1.2830	0.5656	1.1441	. . .	109.64	83.88	135.80	98.19	115.57
May	0.7833	111.73	. . .	1.2190	0.5351	1.1100	. . .	107.34	80.63	135.60	96.57	115.99
June	0.7898	114.63	. . .	1.2321	0.5424	1.1137	. . .	108.62	81.51	137.35	97.89	117.80
July	0.7886	115.77	. . .	1.2376	0.5422	1.1294	. . .	108.37	81.94	135.92	97.77	116.70
August	0.7806	115.92	. . .	1.2318	0.5280	1.1182	. . .	107.64	81.18	135.39	97.09	116.24
September	0.7860	117.21	. . .	1.2455	0.5308	1.1161	. . .	107.92	81.59	135.37	96.70	115.06
October	0.7926	118.61	. . .	1.2602	0.5329	1.1285	. . .	108.21	82.36	134.79	96.20	113.39
November	0.7759	117.32	. . .	1.2356	0.5229	1.1359	. . .	107.34	81.48	134.06	94.91	111.95
December	0.7573	117.32	. . .	1.2099	0.5095	1.1532	. . .	106.53	80.89	133.03	94.07	110.89
2007												
January	0.7696	120.45	. . .	1.2431	0.5105	1.1763	. . .	107.59	82.37	133.18	95.12	111.15
February	0.7645	120.50	. . .	1.2393	0.5105	1.1710	. . .	107.23	82.07	132.77	94.72	110.25
March	0.7549	117.26	. . .	1.2178	0.5135	1.1682	. . .	106.67	81.23	132.80	95.03	111.38
April	0.7400	118.93	. . .	1.2124	0.5030	1.1350	. . .	105.30	79.87	131.64	94.44	111.34
May	0.7398	120.77	. . .	1.2211	0.5040	1.0951	. . .	104.40	79.20	130.48	94.08	110.91
June	0.7451	122.69	. . .	1.2330	0.5033	1.0651	. . .	104.12	78.93	130.23	93.86	110.63
July	0.7285	121.41	. . .	1.2069	0.4913	1.0502	. . .	102.77	77.51	129.26	92.29	109.01
August	0.7339	116.73	. . .	1.2027	0.4973	1.0579	. . .	103.33	77.51	130.72	92.32	109.39
September	0.7189	115.04	. . .	1.1852	0.4954	1.0267	. . .	101.93	75.91	129.94	91.02	108.49
October	0.7026	115.87	. . .	1.1741	0.4890	0.9754	. . .	99.80	73.93	127.98	88.85	106.16
November	0.6811	111.07	. . .	1.1233	0.4831	0.9672	. . .	98.37	72.20	127.40	87.54	105.35
December	0.6869	112.45	. . .	1.1402	0.4960	1.0021	. . .	99.27	73.69	126.99	88.04	104.72
2008												
January	0.6790	107.82	. . .	1.1006	0.5076	1.0099	. . .	98.48	73.06	126.08	87.47	103.93
February	0.6776	107.03	. . .	1.0890	0.5090	0.9986	. . .	97.67	72.57	124.83	86.15	101.40
March	0.6443	100.76	. . .	1.0126	0.4996	1.0029	. . .	95.77	70.32	123.96	85.11	101.53
April	0.6348	102.68	. . .	1.0138	0.5046	1.0137	. . .	95.48	70.47	122.91	85.22	101.13
May	0.6429	104.36	. . .	1.0448	0.5089	0.9993	. . .	95.83	70.75	123.33	85.94	102.18
June	0.6426	106.92	. . .	1.0371	0.5085	1.0166	. . .	96.09	71.42	122.78	86.55	102.26
July	0.6346	106.85	. . .	1.0283	0.5028	1.0130	. . .	95.40	70.91	121.89	85.98	101.43
August	0.6687	109.36	. . .	1.0841	0.5301	1.0535	. . .	97.93	74.09	122.94	87.88	101.90
September	0.6973	106.57	. . .	1.1102	0.5564	1.0582	. . .	100.30	75.51	126.53	89.72	104.48
October	0.7538	99.97	. . .	1.1429	0.5930	1.1847	. . .	106.95	80.42	135.09	94.58	109.86
November	0.7847	96.97	. . .	1.1910	0.6524	1.2171	. . .	109.63	82.74	137.95	95.13	109.79
December	0.7401	91.28	. . .	1.1404	0.6732	1.2337	. . .	108.47	80.69	138.51	93.51	109.63

[1]See notes and definitions for explanation of index categories.
. . . = Not available.

NOTES AND DEFINITIONS

TABLE 13-1
INTERNATIONAL COMPARISONS: GROWTH RATES IN REAL GROSS DOMESTIC PRODUCT

SOURCE: ECONOMIC REPORT OF THE PRESIDENT, ANNUAL REPORT OF THE COUNCIL OF ECONOMIC ADVISERS, FEBRUARY 2009

Table 13-1 is reprinted from the 2009 *Annual Report of the U.S. Council of Economic Advisers*, where it appears as Table B-112. It is based on data from the Department of Commerce's Bureau of Economic Analysis (BEA) and the International Monetary Fund.

TABLES 13-2 AND 13-3
INTERNATIONAL COMPARISONS: REAL GROSS DOMESTIC PRODUCT PER CAPITA, REAL GROSS DOMESTIC PRODUCT PER EMPLOYED PERSON

SOURCE: U.S. DEPARTMENT OF LABOR, BUREAU OF LABOR STATISTICS (BLS)

Definitions and notes on the data

Real gross domestic product (GDP) per capita can be taken as a rough measure of potential economic welfare; that is, the potential standard of living available to each of a country's residents. Because income distributions are typically "skewed," GDP per capita (which is an average or "mean") should not be taken as a representation of the standard of living actually enjoyed by a typical ("median") individual. See the subsection entitled "Whose standard of living?" in the article "Using the Data: The U.S. Economy in the New Century," which can be found at the beginning of this volume.

Real gross domestic product per employed person is a rough measure of productivity (ignoring any differences in hours worked by employees).

The GDP, population, and employment measures for each country come from the country's own national accounts and population sources. Not all countries use annual chain-weighted methods such as those incorporated in U.S. GDP. (See notes and definitions to Chapter 1.) Some of the employment and population figures have been recalculated for greater comparability by BLS. GDP figures are converted from national currency values to U.S. dollar equivalents using purchasing power parities (PPPs) published by the OECD (Organisation for Economic Co-operation and Development) in the OECD-Eurostat PPP Program.

PPPs are currency conversion rates that allow output in different currency units to be expressed in a common unit of value (in this case, U.S. dollars). They are preferable to international market exchange rates for this purpose. According to BLS, "At best, market exchange rates represent only the relative prices of goods and services that are traded internationally, not the relative value of total domestic output, which also consists of goods, and particularly services, that are not traded internationally, or which are isolated from the effects of foreign trade. Market exchange rates also are affected by... currency traders' views of the stability of governments in various countries, relative interest rates among countries, and other incentives for holding financial assets in one currency rather than another."

Measuring PPPs is difficult and subject to error, and BLS emphasizes that statistics using PPPs should be used with caution: "The per capita GDPs of most OECD countries fall within a relatively narrow range, and changes in rankings can occur as a result of relatively minor adjustments to PPP estimates."

In addition to the 11 countries shown here, BLS also calculates and publishes similar data for Austria, Belgium, Denmark, Norway, and Sweden. In the latest report, referenced below, there are also discussion and graphs dealing with GDP per hour worked for 13 countries, and with gross national income and GDP per capita for 17 countries including Ireland.

References

For additional data and information, see: Department of Labor, Bureau of Labor Statistics, Office of Productivity and Technology. "Comparative Real Gross Domestic Product Per Capita and Per Employed Person, Sixteen Countries, 1960–2007" (July 7, 2008), available online at <http://www.bls.gov/fls>.

TABLE 13-4
INTERNATIONAL COMPARISONS: CONSUMER PRICE INDEXES

SOURCE: U.S. DEPARTMENT OF LABOR, BUREAU OF LABOR STATISTICS

Notes on the data

These data are prepared by the BLS Division of Foreign Labor Statistics, based on national consumer price indexes as published by each country. The update presented here was issued June 27, 2008. The data are not adjusted for comparability across countries. National differences exist with respect to population coverage, frequency of market basket weight changes, and treatment of homeowner costs. For some countries, BLS publishes indexes for all households and for workers' households; in such cases, *Business Statistics* shows the all-households index.

BLS links published indexes together to form historical series and rebases the foreign indexes to the U.S. base 1982–1984 = 100.

References

For a description of the U.S. index, see the notes and definitions for Table 8-1.

The indexes for the other countries are presented and described in "Consumer Price Indexes, Sixteen Countries, 1950–2007" (June 27, 2008), available at <http://www.bls.gov/fls>. In addition to the 10 countries shown here, price indexes for Austria, Belgium, Denmark, Norway, Sweden, and Switzerland are also presented and described.

TABLES 13-5 THROUGH 13-7
INTERNATIONAL COMPARISONS: WORKING-AGE POPULATION, EMPLOYMENT-POPULATION RATIOS, AND UNEMPLOYMENT RATES

SOURCE: U.S. DEPARTMENT OF LABOR, BUREAU OF LABOR STATISTICS

Notes on the data

Current and historical data on working-age population, labor force, employment, and unemployment for 10 industrial countries are collected and adjusted by BLS to approximate U.S. concepts and definitions. (For the U.S. concepts and definitions, see the notes and definitions for Tables 10-1 through 10-5.) Nine of those countries are shown in Tables 13-5 through 13-7; the tenth is Sweden. The German data are for the former West Germany through 1990, and for unified Germany from 1991 to the present. Adding the former East Germany raised the 1991 unemployment rate from 4.3 percent (for West Germany alone) to 5.6 percent for unified Germany.

It should be noted that there is also a set of employment-population ratios, quite different from the ones shown here, published by BLS in the report for "Comparative Real Gross Domestic Product Per Capita" that is referenced above in the notes for Tables 13-2 and 13-3. The ratios in that report are for employment divided by the *total resident population* (including children). The ratios shown and described here are for employment divided by the *working-age population*.

Historically, there were large differences between published and BLS-adjusted unemployment rates; however, in recent years, the two unemployment rate series have nearly converged for most countries. Major differences between the country's own official unemployment rates and those adjusted by BLS remain for Canada, Germany, the Netherlands, and Sweden.

There are many qualifications to the adjustments for comparability. Many of the adjusted measures still use a lower age limit than the U.S. limit of 16 years, if the age at which compulsory schooling ends in that country is lower than 16. Currently, however, no country's age limit is lower than 15 years. In Japan and Germany, the institutional population is included. In some countries where the customary significance of layoffs is different, workers on layoff are counted as employed, although in the United States they are considered unemployed. In addition, each country except Japan has some break in historical continuity because of methodological change. The source document includes documentation of each country's series breaks and deviations from exact comparability.

Data availability and references

In addition to the series shown here, BLS calculates and publishes comparative labor force participation rates, employment-population ratios, and unemployment rates by sex; employment by sex and by economic sector; and unemployment rates by age. All data and documentation are presented by the BLS Division of Foreign Labor Statistics in "International comparisons of annual labor force statistics: 10 countries, 1960–2007" (October 21, 2008). The compendium is updated annually. This report and monthly updates to unemployment rates are available on the Foreign Labor Statistics Web site at <http://www.bls.gov/fls>.

TABLE 13-8
FOREIGN EXCHANGE RATES

SOURCE: BOARD OF GOVERNORS OF THE FEDERAL RESERVE SYSTEM

Definitions and notes on the data

This table shows measures of the U.S. dollar relative to the currencies of some important individual countries and also relative to average values for major groups of countries. In *Business Statistics,* all of these measures are defined as the foreign currency price of the U.S. dollar. When the measure is relatively high, the dollar is relatively strong—but less competitive (in the sense of price competition)—and the other currency or group of currencies named in the measure is relatively weak and more competitive.

For consistency, this definition is used in *Business Statistics* even in the case of currencies that are commonly quoted in the financial press and elsewhere as dollars per foreign currency unit instead of foreign currency units per dollar. Notably, this is the case for the new euro and for the British pound. Where *Business Statistics* shows the December 2006 value of the dollar as 0.7573 euros, the more usual statement—and the one found on the Federal Reserve release used as a source for this information—is that in December 2006, the euro was worth $1.3205 (1 divided by 0.7573). Where *Business Statistics* shows the December 2006 value of the dollar as 0.5095 British pounds, the more usual statement is that the pound was worth $1.9627. The Canadian dollar is also sometimes quoted relative to the U.S. dollar, rather than as shown here and in documents from the Federal Reserve.

(This definition of the dollar's value is the most useful for economic analysis from the U.S. point of view and for foreign tourists in the United States. For American tourists overseas, it is easier to use the inverse of this measure, the value of the other currency; for example, the traveler in Paris can more easily translate prices into dollars by multiplying by the dollar value of the euro than by dividing by the euro value of the dollar.)

The foreign exchange rates shown are averages of the daily noon buying rates in New York City for cable transfers payable in foreign currencies. Annual figures are averages of monthly data.

The introduction of the euro in January 1999 as the common currency for 11 European countries—Austria, Belgium, Finland, France, Germany, Ireland, Italy, Luxembourg, Netherlands, Portugal, and Spain—marked a major change in the international currency system, and the use of the euro continues to spread. Greece entered the European Monetary Union (EMU) in January 2001 and Slovenia entered in January 2007. Cyprus and Malta join in January 2008. The euro is also the national currency in Monaco, the Vatican City and San Marino, and is the de facto currency in Andorra, Kosovo, and Montenegro. The values of the currencies of these countries no longer fluctuate relative to each other, but the value of the euro still fluctuates relative to the dollar and to currencies for countries outside the EMU. The currency and coins of the individual countries continued to circulate from 1999 through the end of 2001, but in January 2002, new euro currency and coins were introduced, replacing the currency and coins of the individual countries. Once a country has entered the monetary union, its values relative to the dollar will continue to fluctuate—but only due to fluctuations in the value of the euro relative to the dollar.

There is no fully satisfactory historical equivalent to the euro. For comparisons over time, the Federal Reserve Board uses a "restated German mark," derived simply by dividing each historical value of the mark by the euro conversion factor, 1.95583. The G-10 dollar index described below includes five of the currencies that later merged into the euro, but also includes the currencies of Canada, Japan, the United Kingdom, Switzerland, and Sweden.

Trade-weighted indexes of the value of the dollar against groups of foreign currencies also appear in this table. In each case, weighted averages of the individual currency values of the dollar are set at 100 in a base period. The weights are based on goods trade only and exclude trade in services. Base periods differ for different indexes.

The first four columns show the more familiar type of foreign exchange indexes, which use *nominal* values of each currency. The last two columns are *price-adjusted* (indexes of "real" exchange rates), aggregating values of the dollar in terms of each currency that have been adjusted for inflation, using each country's consumer price index.

Where any currency has had an episode of hyperinflation with consequent huge depreciation in terms of the dollar, the nominal index will not reflect the actual competitiveness of the dollar in terms of that currency over the longer term. As there have been hyperinflations in some of the countries making up the broad index and its "other important trading partners" component (see below), price-adjusted indexes are also shown for those two groupings in the final two columns.

The *G-10 Index (March 1973 = 100)*. This measure is an index of the exchange value of the U.S. dollar in terms of the weighted average currencies of the G-10 ("Other industrialized") countries, which are Belgium, Canada, France, Germany, Italy, Japan, the Netherlands, Sweden, Switzerland, and the United Kingdom. Unlike the three indexes that follow, the weights in this index—which represented "multilateral" (world market) trade shares—were fixed. The Federal Reserve stopped calculating this index as of December 1998.

The three newer indexes, introduced in December 1998, use weights that focus more directly on U.S. competitiveness and that change as trade flows shift. Each country's weight is based on an average of the country's share of U.S. imports, the country's share of U.S. exports, and the country's share of exports that go to other countries that are large importers of U.S. goods. The weights are updated each year; the latest weights were introduced on January 2, 2007, with the previous weights having been in effect from December 15, 2005 to December 29, 2006. The index formula uses geometric averaging.

The *broad index (January 1997 = 100)*. The new overall index includes currencies of all economies that have a share of U.S. non-oil goods imports or goods exports of at least 0.5 percent. These economies encompass the euro area and 25 other countries. The list of currencies is updated each year, though no changes have been made in the list of included countries. These countries are then classified in either the major currency index or the other important trading partners as outlined below.

The *major currency index (March 1973 = 100)*. This index serves purposes similar to those of the discontinued G-10 index, and its level and movements are similar. It is a measure of the competitiveness of U.S. products in the major industrial countries and a gauge of financial pressure on the dollar. The index includes countries whose currencies are traded in deep and relatively liquid financial markets and circulate widely outside the country of issue. These are also countries for which information on short and long-term interest rates is readily available. As of January 2007, this index includes the currencies of the euro countries, Canada, Japan, the United Kingdom, Switzerland, Australia, and Sweden. This list has not changed since the introduction of the new indexes in 1998.

The *other important trading partners (OITP) index (January 1997 = 100)*. This index captures the competitiveness of U.S. products in key emerging markets in Latin America, Asia, the Middle East, and Eastern Europe, whose currencies do not circulate widely outside the country of issue. Hyperinflations and large depreciations for some of these countries have led to a persistent upward trend in the nominal version of this index. Hence, the nominal OITP index is mainly useful for analysis of short-term developments, and the price-adjusted index is shown to give a more appropriate measure of longer-term competitiveness.

As of January 2007, this index includes the countries of Mexico, China, Taiwan, South Korea, Singapore, Hong Kong, Malaysia, Brazil, Thailand, Philippines, Indonesia, India, Israel, Saudi Arabia, Russia, Argentina, Venezuela, Chile, and Colombia.

Data availability and references

Current press releases, historical data, and information on weights and methods for exchange rates and exchange rate indexes are available on the Federal Reserve Web site at <http://www.federalreserve.gov/releases/H10>. The dollar value indexes are described in the article "Indexes of the Foreign Exchange Value of the Dollar," *Federal Reserve Bulletin* (Winter 2005), available via a link in the "Currency Weights" area of the Federal Reserve Web site.

Additional information on exchange rates can be found on the Federal Reserve Bank of St. Louis Web site at <http://www.stls.frb.org/fred/data/exchange.html>.

PART B

INDUSTRY PROFILES

CHAPTER 14: INDUSTRY DEFINITION AND STRUCTURE

THE STRUCTURE OF U.S. INDUSTRY:
AN INTRODUCTION TO THE NORTH AMERICAN INDUSTRY CLASSIFICATION SYSTEM (NAICS)

This volume of *Business Statistics* incorporates data based on the new North American Industry Classification System (NAICS) for all of the major government statistical series that use classification by industry and have incorporated the new classification system.

Industry data collection is important because demands for goods and services are channeled into demands for labor and capital through the industries responsible for producing the requested goods and services. NAICS delineates industries that are better defined in relation to today's demands. It also groups together industries that are more closely related to each other by technology. Notable examples of these new features of NAICS include the more detailed data available on service industries, the more rational grouping of the Computer and electronic product manufacturing subsector, and the creation of the Information sector.

The editor has prepared a table of NAICS industry definitions to use as a guide to the contents of the new categories, which shows the NAICS two-digit industry sectors and their component three-digit subsectors. The table follows this introduction and precedes the chapters of statistical tables. Parenthetical listings of the component activities are shown in places where the short NAICS sector titles are not sufficiently self-explanatory.

For the user needing information as to how the new classifications do (and do not) relate to the old Standard Industrial Classification System (SIC), a column showing a rough match between the 2002 NAICS and the 1987 SIC has been added to the table. It must be emphasized that this match is approximate, not exact, and does not reflect every aspect of the change in the classification systems. However, this column indicates just how thoroughly some SIC industries have been mixed and rematched; it therefore explains why it has been difficult for the statistical agencies to produce longer spans of historical data on the new basis.

As a further illustration, the reader will note frequent references in this table to parts of SIC industries that have been parceled out among different NAICS industries. In some cases, the editor has included, in parentheses, the part of the old SIC industry contained in the new NAICS industry. See the entry of new NAICS subsector 711, Performing arts and spectator sports, for an example. This subsector now contains dinner theaters, which used to be included in eating places (a subdivision of retail trade in the old system).

NAICS industries are groupings of producing units—not of products as such—and are grouped according to similarity of production processes. This is done in order to collect consistent data on inputs and outputs, which are then used to measure important concepts, such as productivity and input-output parameters. Emphasis on the production process helps to explain a number of ways in which the NAICS differs from the SIC.

Manufacturing activities at retail locations, such as bakeries, have been classified separately from retail activity and put into the Food manufacturing industry.

Central administrative offices of companies have a new sector of their own, Management of companies and enterprises (sector 55). For example, the headquarters office of a food-producing corporation is considered part of the new sector instead of part of the Food manufacturing industry.

Reproduction of packaged software, classified as a business service in the SIC, is now classified in sector 334, Computer and electronic product manufacturing, as a manufacturing process.

Electronic markets and agents and brokers, formerly undifferentiated components of wholesale trade industries, have a sector of their own (425).

Retail trade in NAICS (sectors 44 and 45) now includes establishments such as office supply stores, computer and software stores, building materials dealers, plumbing supply stores, and electrical supply stores, that display merchandise and use mass-media advertising to sell to individuals as well as to businesses, and that were formerly classified in wholesale trade.

References

The NAICS is explained and laid out in *North American Industry Classification System: United States, 2007*, from the Executive Office of the President, Office of Management and Budget. This presents the second five-year updating of the system, which was first introduced in 1997. Changes introduced in these updatings have been minor and have not affected the definitions of industries presented in *Business Statistics*.

More precise information on differences between NAICS and SIC can be found in *North American Industry Classification System: United States, 1997*, from the Executive Office of the President, Office of Management and Budget (which contains matches between the 1997 NAICS and the 1987 SIC); and *North American Industry Classification System: United States, 2002* (which contains matches that show the relatively few changes from the 1997 NAICS to the 2002 NAICS).

The 2002 and 2007 edition of these volumes are available from Bernan Press. These volumes fully describe the development and application of the new classification system and are the sources for the material presented in this volume. Information is also available on the NAICS Web site at <http://www.census.gov/naics>. Additional background information can also be found in Bernan Press's *Business Statistics of the United States: 2002* (8th edition), pp. xxiv–xxviii.

Table 14-1. NAICS Industry Definitions, with Rough Derivation from SIC

NAICS code	NAICS 2-digit industry sector and 3-digit industry subsector	Roughly corresponding major component SIC industry group or industry
11	**AGRICULTURE, FORESTRY, FISHING, AND HUNTING**	Division A – Agriculture, forestry, and fishing; 241 – Logging
111	Crop production	
112	Animal production	
113	Forestry and logging	
114	Fishing, hunting, and trapping	
115	Agriculture and forestry support activities	
21	**MINING**	Division B – Mining
211	Oil and gas extraction	
212	Mining, except oil and gas (includes coal mining, mining for ores, and mining and quarrying of nonmetallic minerals)	
213	Support activities for mining (includes oil and gas well drilling and other support activities)	
22	**UTILITIES**	49 – Electric, gas, and sanitary services (with some exclusions)
221	Utilities (includes electric power generation, transmission, and distribution; natural gas distribution; and water, sewage, irrigation, steam, and air-conditioning systems)	
23	**CONSTRUCTION**	Division C – Construction
236	Construction of buildings	
237	Heavy and civil engineering construction	
238	Specialty trade contractors	
31-33	**MANUFACTURING**	Division D – Manufacturing (excluding 241 – Logging; 271, 272, 273, and 274 – Publishing; and with other exclusions and inclusions)
311	Food manufacturing	20 – Food and kindred products (excluding 208 – Beverages)
312	Beverage and tobacco product manufacturing	208 – Beverages; 21 – Tobacco products
313	Textile mills	221-4, 226, 228 – Yarns, fabrics, and finishing

Table 14-1. NAICS Industry Definitions, with Rough Derivation from SIC—*Continued*

NAICS code	NAICS 2-digit industry sector and 3-digit industry subsector	Roughly corresponding major component SIC industry group or industry
314	Textile product mills (including household and miscellaneous products)	227 – Carpets and rugs; 229 – Miscellaneous textile products
315	Apparel manufacturing	23 – Apparel; 225 – Knitting mills
316	Leather and allied product manufacturing	31 – Leather and leather products
321	Wood product manufacturing	24 – Lumber and wood products (excluding 241 – Logging)
322	Paper manufacturing	26 – Paper and allied products
323	Printing and related support activities, including quick and instant	275-9 – Commercial printing and miscellaneous printing and trade services
324	Petroleum and coal products manufacturing (includes refineries, asphalt, oil and grease, and coke manufacturing)	29 – Petroleum and coal products
325	Chemical manufacturing (includes basic organic and inorganic chemicals; plastics materials; synthetic fibers and rubber; agricultural chemicals; pharmaceuticals and medicine; paint, adhesives, cleaning, and toilet preparations; and ink, explosives, and miscellaneous)	28 – Chemicals and allied products
326	Plastics and rubber products	30 – Rubber and miscellaneous plastics products
327	Nonmetallic mineral product manufacturing (includes pottery; plumbing fixtures; bricks and structural clay products; glass and products; cement and concrete; and lime, gypsum, and stone products)	32 – Stone, clay, and glass products
331	Primary metal manufacturing (primary and secondary ferrous and nonferrous metals; rolling, drawing, and extruding; and foundries)	33 – Primary metal industries
332	Fabricated metal product manufacturing (includes forging and stamping, cutlery, hardware, structural metal work, boilers, containers, machine shops, valves, fixtures, bearings, metal testing, small arms, ordnance, and ammunition)	34 – Fabricated metal products
333	Machinery manufacturing (includes machinery for agriculture, construction, mining, manufacturing, commercial, and service industries; metalworking machinery; turbine and power transmission; pumps and compressors; elevators and material handling; cranes; and miscellaneous general purpose machinery)	Parts of 35 – Industrial machinery and equipment, 36 – Electronic and other electric equipment, and 38 – Instruments and related products
334	Computer and electronic product manufacturing (includes electronic computers and equipment; communications equipment; audio and video equipment; semiconductors and other electronic components; electromedical equipment; navigation, measuring, and controlling instruments; reproducing software; and media manufacturing and reproducing)	Parts of 357 – Computer and office equipment, 36 – Electronic and other electric equipment, 38 – Instruments and related products, 73 – Business services, and 78 – Motion picture services
335	Electrical equipment and appliance manufacturing (includes electrical lighting, household appliances, electrical equipment, batteries, and wire and cable manufacturing)	Parts of 36 – Electronic and other electric equipment, and 335 – Nonferrous wire drawing
336	Transportation equipment manufacturing (includes motor vehicles and parts, truck trailers, aerospace products and parts, railroad rolling stock, ship and boat building and repairing, motorcycles, bicycles, military armored vehicles, and parts)	37 – Transportation equipment
337	Furniture and related product manufacturing	25 – Furniture and fixtures; parts of other industries
339	Miscellaneous manufacturing (includes medical equipment and supplies, jewelry, silverware, sporting goods, toys, games, office supplies, art supplies, burial caskets, and other goods)	Parts of 38 – Instruments, 39 – Miscellaneous, 25 – Furniture, and other industries

Table 14-1.   NAICS Industry Definitions, with Rough Derivation from SIC—*Continued*

NAICS code	NAICS 2-digit industry sector and 3-digit industry subsector	Roughly corresponding major component SIC industry group or industry
42	**WHOLESALE TRADE**	
423	Merchant wholesalers, durable goods	Parts of 50 – Wholesale trade—durable goods, and other industries
424	Merchant wholesalers, nondurable goods	Parts of 51 – Wholesale trade—nondurable goods, and other industries
425	Electronic markets and agents and brokers	Parts of 50 and 51 – Wholesale trade
44-45	**RETAIL TRADE**	
441	Motor vehicle and parts dealers	Parts of 55 – Automotive dealers and service stations, wholesale trade, and other industries
442	Furniture and home furnishings stores	Parts of 57 – Furniture and home furnishing stores, wholesale trade, and other industries
443	Electronics and appliance stores	5722 – Household appliance stores; 5734 – Computer and software stores; 5946 – Camera and photo supply stores; and parts of wholesale trade and other industries
444	Building material and garden supply stores	52 – Retail building materials and garden supplies, and parts of wholesale trade
445	Food and beverage stores	54 – Food stores, and 5921 – Liquor stores
446	Health and personal care stores	5912 – Drug stores and proprietary stores; and parts of wholesale trade, food stores, and miscellaneous stores
447	Gasoline stations (including stations with convenience stores)	Parts of 55 – Automotive dealers and service stations, and 54 – Food stores
448	Clothing and clothing accessories stores	56 – Apparel and accessory stores; 5944 – Jewelry stores; and 5948 – Luggage and leather goods stores
451	Sporting goods, hobby, book, and music stores	Parts of 59 – Miscellaneous retail, 57 – Furniture and home furnishing stores, and other industries
452	General merchandise stores (includes department stores, warehouse clubs, superstores, and other general merchandise)	53 – General merchandise, and parts of other retail
453	Miscellaneous store retailers (includes florists and office supply and stationery, gift, used merchandise, pet, manufactured and mobile home, tobacco, and miscellaneous other store retailers)	Parts of 59 – Miscellaneous retail, and other industries
454	Nonstore retailers (includes electronic shopping and auctions, mail order, vending machines, fuel, and other direct selling)	Parts of 59 – Miscellaneous retail, and 517 – Wholesale petroleum
48-49	**TRANSPORTATION AND WAREHOUSING**	
481	Air transportation	Parts of 45 – Transportation by air
482	Rail transportation	Parts of 40 – Railroad transportation
483	Water transportation	Parts of 44 – Water transportation
484	Truck transportation	Parts of 42 – Trucking and warehousing
485	Transit and ground passenger transportation	Parts of 41 – Local and suburban transportation

Table 14-1.   NAICS Industry Definitions, with Rough Derivation from SIC—*Continued*

NAICS code	NAICS 2-digit industry sector and 3-digit industry subsector	Roughly corresponding major component SIC industry group or industry
486	Pipeline transportation	46 – Pipelines, except natural gas; and parts of 492 – Gas production and distribution
487	Scenic and sightseeing transportation	Parts of 41 – Local and suburban, 44 – Water, 45 – Air, 47 – Transportation services, and 7999 – Amusement and recreation n.e.c.
488	Support activities for transportation	Parts of industries in transportation, communications, manufacturing, government (air traffic control), and services
491	Postal service	4311 – U.S. Postal Service, and part of 7389 – Business services n.e.c.
492	Couriers and messengers	4513 – Air couriers, and 4215 – Courier services except air
493	Warehousing and storage	Parts of 422 – Public warehousing and storage
51	**INFORMATION**	
511	Publishing industries, except Internet	
5111	Newspaper, book, and directory publishers	Parts of 271 – Newspapers, 272 – Periodicals, 273 – Books, 274 – Miscellaneous publishing, 277 – Greeting cards, and 733 – Mailing, reproduction, and stenographic services
5112	Software publishers	Part of 7372 – Prepackaged software
512	Motion picture and sound recording industries (includes music books and sheet music)	781 – Motion picture production and services; 783 – Motion picture theaters; and parts of 782 – Motion picture distribution and services, and other manufacturing and service industries
515	Broadcasting, except Internet	483 – Radio and television broadcasting; and part of 484 – Cable and other pay TV services
516	Internet publishing and broadcasting	Parts of publishing and service industries
517	Telecommunications	Parts of 481 – Telephone communications, 482 – Telegraph and other communications, and 484 – Cable and other pay TV services
518	ISPs, search portals, and data processing	7374 – Data processing and preparation; 7375 – Information retrieval services; and parts of other service industries
519	Other information services (includes news syndicates, libraries, archives, and other information services)	8231 – Libraries; and parts of other service industries
52	**FINANCE AND INSURANCE**	
521	Monetary authorities—central bank	6011 – Federal Reserve Banks
522	Credit intermediation and related activities (includes commercial banking, savings institutions, credit unions, credit card issuing, sales financing, consumer lending, real estate credit, trade financing, loan brokers, and processing and clearing)	Parts of 60 – Depository institutions, and 61 – Nondepository institutions
523	Securities, commodity contracts, and investments	62 – Security and commodity brokers, and parts of 60 – Depository institutions, 61 – Nondepository institutions, 63 – Insurance carriers, and 67 – Holding and other investment offices
524	Insurance carriers and related activities	64 – Insurance agents, brokers, and service; and parts of 63 – Insurance carriers
525	Funds, trusts, and other financial vehicles	672 – Investment offices; 6798 – Real estate investment trusts; and parts of 63 – Insurance carriers, and 673 – Trusts

n.e.c. = Not elsewhere classified.

Table 14-1. NAICS Industry Definitions, with Rough Derivation from SIC—*Continued*

NAICS code	NAICS 2-digit industry sector and 3-digit industry subsector	Roughly corresponding major component SIC industry group or industry
53	**REAL ESTATE AND RENTAL AND LEASING**	
531	Real estate	Parts of 65 – Real estate, and 4225 – General warehousing and storage (mini-warehouses and self-storage units)
532	Rental and leasing services	7352 – Medical equipment rental; 7377 – Computer rental and leasing; 751 – Automotive rentals, no drivers; 7841 – Video tape rental; and parts of 4499 – Water transportation n.e.c., 4741 – Rental of railroad cars, 7299 – Miscellaneous personal services n.e.c., 735 – Miscellaneous equipment rental, 7922 – Theatrical producers and services, and 7999 – Amusement and recreation n.e.c.
533	Lessors of nonfinancial intangible assets (except copyrighted)	6794 – Patent owners and lessors, and part of 6792 – Oil royalty traders
54	**PROFESSIONAL AND TECHNICAL SERVICES** (includes legal, accounting, bookkeeping, architectural, engineering, design, computer design and programming, management and other consulting, scientific research and development, advertising and public relations, market research, polling, and other services)	741 – Veterinary services; 6541 – Title abstract offices, 731 – Advertising, 7221 – Photographic studios, portrait, 7921 – Tax return preparation, 7336 – Commercial art and graphic design, 7361 – Employment agencies, 7371 – Computer programming; 7373 – Computer systems design, 7376 – Computer facilities management, 8111 – Legal services, 871 – Engineering and architectural services, 873 – Research and testing; and parts of mining, 37 – Aircraft and guided missiles, 73 – Business services, 87 – Engineering and management services, and other industries
55	**MANAGEMENT OF COMPANIES AND ENTERPRISES**	671 – Holding companies, and establishments classified as auxilaries in producing industries
56	**ADMINISTRATIVE AND WASTE SERVICES**	
561	Administrative and support services (includes office administrative, employment placement, temporary help, telephone call centers, collection agencies, credit bureaus, court reporting, travel arrangement, investigation and security, services to buildings, and other support services)	782 – Lawn and garden services, 783 – Ornamental shrub and tree services, 4724 – Travel agencies, 4725 – Tour operators, 7217 – Carpet and upholstery cleaning, 732 – Credit reporting and collection, 7338 – Secretarial and court reporting, 734 – Services to buildings, 7363 – Help supply services, 7381 – Detective and armored car services, 7382 – Security systems, 8744 – Facilities support, and parts of 458 – Airfields, 472 – Passenger transportation arrangement, 495 – Sanitary services, 729 – Miscellaneous personal services, 73, Business services, 769 – Miscellaneous repair shops, 7819 – Services allied to motion pictures, 79 – Amusement and recreation services, 86 – Membership organizations, and 8741 – Management services
562	Waste management and remediation services	4953 – Refuse systems, and parts of 1799 – Special trade contractors, 4212 – Local trucking, 4959 – Sanitary services, 735 – Miscellaneous equipment rental and leasing (portable toilet rental), and 769 – Miscellaneous repair shops
61	**EDUCATIONAL SERVICES**	82 – Educational services, except 823 – Libraries; and parts of 7231 – Beauty shops, 7241 – Barber shops, 7911 – Dance studios, 7999 – Amusement and recreation n.e.c., and 8748 – Business consulting n.e.c. (educational testing services)
62	**HEALTH CARE AND SOCIAL ASSISTANCE**	
621	Ambulatory health care services	Offices and clinics for: 801 – Doctors, 802 – Dentists, 803 – Osteopaths, and 804 – Other health practitioners, 8071 – Medical laboratories, 8082 – Home health care services, 4119 – Ambulances; 4522 – Air ambulances, and parts of 809 – Health and allied services n.e.c.
622	Hospitals	806 – Hospitals
623	Nursing and residential care facilities	805 – Nursing and personal care facilities, and 836 – Residential care
624	Social assistance	8322 – Individual and family services, except parole and probation offices; 8331 – Job training; and 8351 – Child day care services

n.e.c. = Not elsewhere classified.

Table 14-1. NAICS Industry Definitions, with Rough Derivation from SIC—*Continued*

NAICS code	NAICS 2-digit industry sector and 3-digit industry subsector	Roughly corresponding major component SIC industry group or industry
71	**ARTS, ENTERTAINMENT, AND RECREATION**	
711	Performing arts and spectator sports	7929 – Bands and other entertainment groups; 7941 – Professional sports clubs and promoters; 7948 – Racing; parts of 5812 – Eating places (dinner theaters) and 6512 – Building operators (stadium and arena owners); and agents, artists, writers, performers, correspondents, taxidermists, and antique restorers, previously classified as part of 738 – Miscellaneous business services; 76 – Miscellaneous repair services; 7819 – Motion picture services; 7999 – Amusement and recreation n.e.c.; and 8999 – Membership organizations, n.e.c.
712	Museums, historical sites, zoos, and parks	84 – Museums and botanical and zoological gardens; and part of 7999 – Amusement and recreation n.e.c. (caverns and miscellaneous commercial parks)
713	Amusements, gambling, and recreation	4493 – Marinas, 793 – Bowling centers, 7991 – Physical fitness facilities, 7992 – Public golf courses, 7995 – Coin operated amusments, 7996 – Amusement parks, 7997 – Membership sports and recreation clubs, and parts of 7911 – Dance studios, and 7999 – Amusement and recreation n.e.c.
72	**ACCOMMODATION AND FOOD SERVICES**	
721	Accommodation (includes hotels, motels, bed-and-breakfast inns, RV parks, camps, and rooming and boarding houses)	70 – Hotels and other lodging places
722	Food services and drinking places	5812 – Eating places (other than dinner theaters), 5813 – Drinking places, and parts of 4789 – Transportation services n.e.c. (contract dining car operations), 5641 – Retail bakeries, and 5963 – Direct selling (mobile food wagons)
81	**OTHER SERVICES, EXCEPT PUBLIC ADMINISTRATION**	
811	Repair and maintenance	753 – Automotive repair shops (other than tire retreading); 7542 – Carwashes; 7631 – Watch, clock, and jewelery repair; 7692 – Welding repair; and parts of 3732 – Boat repair, 7219 – Clothing alteration and repair, 7251 – Shoe repair, 7378 – Computer repair, 7549 – auto window tinting, 7622 – Radio and TV repair, 7623 – Refrigeration repair, 7629 – Electrical repair n.e.c., 7641 – Reupholstery and furniture repair, 7694 – Armature (rewinding), and 7699 – Repair services n.e.c.
812	Personal and laundry services	6553 – Cemetery subdividers and developers; 7211 – Power laundries; 7212 – Garment pressing and cleaners' agents; 7213 – Linen supply; 7215 – Coin-operated laundries and cleaning; 7216 – Drycleaning, except rugs; 7218 – Industrial launderers; 7261 – Funeral service and crematories; 7384 – Photofinishing laboratories; 7521 – Auto parking; and parts of 0752 – Pet care, 6531 – Real estate agents and managers (cemetery management), 7219 – Diaper and miscellaneous services, 7231 – Beauty shops, 7241 – Barber shops, 7251 – Shoe shine parlors, and 7389 – Business services n.e.c. (apparel pressing for the trade, bail bonding)
813	Membership associations and organizations	6732 – Educational, religious and charitable trusts; 8399 – Social services n.e.c. (voluntary health organizations, human rights organizations, environment, conservation, and wildlife, and other grant making, giving, and social advocacy organizations); 8611 – Business associations; 8621 – Professional organizations; 8631 – Labor organizations; 8651 – Political organizations; 8661 – Religious organizations; and parts of 6531 – Real estate agents and managers (condominium associations), 8641 – Civic and social organizations (all except tribal governments), and 8699 – Membership organizations n.e.c. (all except motor travel clubs)
814	Private households	8811 – Private households

n.e.c. = Not elsewhere classified.

Table 14-1. NAICS Industry Definitions, with Rough Derivation from SIC—*Continued*

NAICS code	NAICS 2-digit industry sector and 3-digit industry subsector	Roughly corresponding major component SIC industry group or industry
92	**PUBLIC ADMINISTRATION**	
921	Executive, legislative, and general government	91 – Executive, legislative, and general; 9311 – Finance, taxation, and monetary policy; and part of 8641 – Civic and social associations (tribal governments)
922	Justice, public order, and safety activities	92 – Justice, public order, and safety; and part of 8322 – Individual and family services (parole and probation)
923	Administration of human resource programs	94 – Administration of human resources
924	Administration of environmental programs	951 – Environmental quality
925	Community and housing program administration	953 – Housing and urban development
926	Administration of economic programs	9611 – Administration of general economic programs; 9631 – Regulation and administration of utilities; 9641 – Regulation of agricultural marketing; 9651 – Miscellaneous commercial regulation; and parts of 9621 – Regulation and administration of transportation (all except air traffic control)
927	Space research and technology	9661 – Space research and technology
928	National security and international affairs	97 – National security and international affairs

CHAPTER 15: PRODUCT AND INCOME BY INDUSTRY

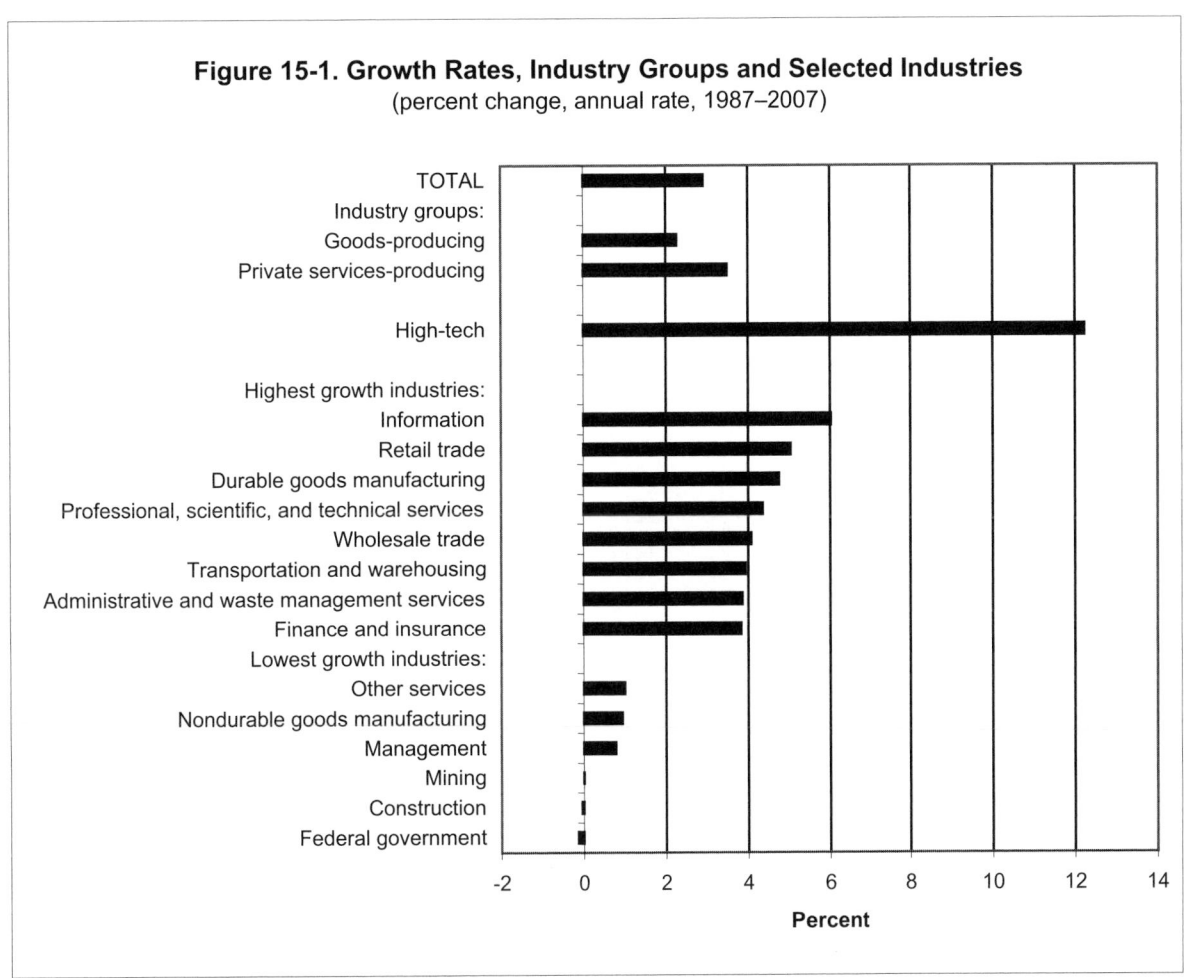

Figure 15-1. Growth Rates, Industry Groups and Selected Industries
(percent change, annual rate, 1987–2007)

- Between 1987 and 2007, total real gross domestic product (GDP) rose at an average annual rate of 2.9 percent. The goods-producing sector grew at a 2.3 percent rate, while private service-producing industries grew at a 3.5 percent rate. The high-tech sector (information-communications-technology-producing industries), which accounted for just 3.3 percent of total GDP in 1987, grew at a 12.2 percent annual rate over the subsequent 20 years, but still only accounts for 3.7 percent of total GDP. (Tables 15-1 and 15-2)

- Of the 22 industries reported in this chapter, 8 experienced annual average growth of 3.8 percent or better per year. The fastest-growing was the information industry, and durable goods manufacturing and professional, scientific, and technical services, which also have high-tech components, also had high growth rates. But three goods-handling industries—retail trade, wholesale trade, and transportation and warehousing—also were in the high-growth category, despite the below-average performance of the U.S. goods-producing sector. This reflects the fact that the increasing share of imports in U.S. consumption flows through these sectors. Rounding out the list of high-growth industries were administrative and waste management services, which includes the temporary help industry, and the finance and insurance sector. (Table 15-2)

- Table 15-3 can be used to assess the share of each industry group in total domestic factor income and the shares paid to employees and accruing to land and capital in each private industry. In 2007, the highest labor share was in education (91 percent), and labor shares exceeding 70 percent were also found in construction, durable goods manufacturing, retail trade, management, administrative and waste management (which includes temporary help), health care and social assistance, accommodation and food services, and other services. The high-tech grouping also falls into this labor-intensive category.

Table 15-1. Gross Domestic Product (Value Added) by NAICS Industry Group

(Billions of dollars.)

Year	Total gross domestic product	Private industries					Manufacturing							
		Total	Agriculture, forestry, fishing, and hunting	Mining	Utilities	Construc-tion	Durable goods	Nondurable goods	Wholesale trade	Retail trade	Transpor-tation and ware-housing	Information	Finance and insurance	Real estate and rental and leasing
1947	244.2	213.7	19.9	5.7	3.3	9.0	31.7	30.8	15.5	22.9	14.6	6.2	5.7	19.8
1948	269.2	239.2	23.2	7.6	3.7	11.2	35.8	34.2	17.1	24.3	16.1	6.9	6.5	21.6
1949	267.3	235.9	18.6	6.5	4.3	11.3	35.4	33.0	16.6	24.7	15.6	7.4	7.3	23.2
1950	293.8	262.2	19.9	7.6	4.7	12.9	43.5	35.9	18.6	25.8	17.3	8.0	7.9	25.5
1951	339.3	300.4	23.0	8.4	5.4	15.4	53.2	41.4	21.3	28.2	19.6	8.9	9.0	28.4
1952	358.3	313.8	22.1	8.2	5.9	16.6	56.3	42.0	21.5	29.7	20.3	9.6	10.0	31.0
1953	379.4	332.8	20.1	8.6	6.5	17.2	63.4	44.0	22.0	30.6	21.1	10.5	11.2	34.0
1954	380.4	332.1	19.6	8.7	7.2	17.4	58.4	43.2	22.3	31.2	19.6	10.7	12.0	36.9
1955	414.8	363.8	18.8	9.9	7.8	18.6	67.5	47.5	25.1	33.2	21.4	11.6	13.0	39.9
1956	437.5	383.1	18.6	10.7	8.3	20.5	69.7	49.6	27.0	34.4	22.4	12.4	14.0	42.4
1957	461.1	403.0	18.4	10.8	9.0	21.5	74.1	50.2	28.5	36.4	23.3	13.2	15.1	45.3
1958	467.2	405.4	20.6	9.9	9.6	21.2	66.6	50.8	29.2	37.1	22.1	13.8	16.3	48.5
1959	506.6	441.4	19.0	9.7	10.6	23.0	77.2	54.8	33.5	40.4	23.2	15.2	17.5	51.9
1960	526.4	457.1	19.9	10.0	11.5	23.4	77.7	55.7	34.9	41.3	23.4	16.0	18.9	55.5
1961	544.7	471.2	20.1	10.1	12.2	24.4	77.0	57.0	36.0	42.4	23.6	16.9	20.0	59.1
1962	585.6	506.8	20.4	10.2	12.9	26.2	86.9	60.4	38.5	45.5	25.1	18.1	20.5	63.7
1963	617.7	533.2	20.5	10.5	13.5	28.0	92.6	63.1	40.0	47.5	26.0	19.5	21.3	67.7
1964	663.6	572.9	19.6	10.8	14.4	30.7	100.1	67.1	43.2	52.2	27.5	21.2	23.4	72.0
1965	719.1	622.2	22.5	11.0	15.0	33.7	112.5	72.3	46.6	55.9	29.8	22.9	25.5	76.7
1966	787.8	680.2	23.5	11.7	16.1	37.1	125.4	79.4	51.1	60.3	32.4	25.1	28.1	81.8
1967	832.6	714.2	22.9	11.9	16.9	38.7	128.0	81.5	54.1	64.7	33.1	26.9	31.3	86.8
1968	910.0	778.3	23.7	12.7	18.4	42.4	139.2	89.0	59.4	71.4	35.7	29.2	35.1	93.5
1969	984.6	840.8	26.4	13.3	19.7	47.3	146.2	93.0	64.1	77.4	38.0	32.2	39.7	101.6
1970	1 038.5	880.2	27.3	14.9	21.0	50.2	139.2	96.3	68.0	82.8	40.1	35.0	42.9	109.1
1971	1 127.1	954.8	29.4	15.0	23.8	55.2	147.1	101.9	73.8	90.5	44.1	38.1	47.3	121.7
1972	1 238.3	1 051.0	34.4	15.8	26.1	61.0	164.1	109.6	82.0	98.1	48.4	42.6	51.5	133.4
1973	1 382.7	1 180.5	52.3	18.9	28.0	69.1	185.4	117.3	92.2	107.9	53.4	47.0	55.3	147.9
1974	1 500.0	1 277.3	50.1	29.3	29.2	74.0	192.5	125.7	104.7	113.4	58.5	50.9	62.9	160.5
1975	1 638.3	1 391.5	51.4	33.8	37.1	74.8	198.5	138.6	114.6	127.3	59.4	56.5	71.6	176.6
1976	1 825.3	1 556.2	50.2	37.5	41.5	85.5	230.2	156.5	122.7	144.0	68.8	63.5	78.3	193.8
1977	2 030.9	1 739.4	51.3	43.4	45.9	94.2	265.0	173.6	134.9	158.5	76.2	71.1	92.3	211.7
1978	2 294.7	1 977.0	59.8	49.5	50.4	111.5	303.4	186.5	153.4	177.6	86.7	81.4	109.7	237.7
1979	2 563.3	2 217.7	70.6	58.4	51.9	127.0	331.1	212.7	175.8	193.2	96.6	90.3	121.6	268.7
1980	2 789.5	2 405.8	62.0	91.3	60.0	130.3	333.9	222.7	188.7	200.9	102.3	99.0	136.8	305.6
1981	3 128.4	2 702.5	75.4	122.9	70.7	131.8	370.4	246.1	208.3	221.0	109.9	112.7	154.5	343.9
1982	3 255.0	2 792.6	71.3	120.0	81.7	128.8	353.4	249.8	207.9	229.9	105.9	123.6	167.6	372.3
1983	3 536.7	3 043.5	57.1	103.1	91.6	139.8	379.3	273.8	222.9	261.6	117.8	140.0	190.5	414.2
1984	3 933.2	3 395.1	77.1	107.2	102.3	164.4	443.5	280.5	249.4	293.6	131.4	147.1	209.3	460.9
1985	4 220.3	3 637.0	77.1	105.4	109.2	184.6	449.2	291.1	268.3	318.7	136.3	162.9	225.9	503.8
1986	4 462.8	3 842.9	74.2	68.9	114.4	207.7	459.3	306.7	278.5	336.6	145.6	173.1	255.7	539.4
1987	4 739.5	4 080.4	79.8	71.5	123.0	218.2	483.8	327.5	285.3	349.9	151.1	185.0	274.4	565.9
1988	5 103.8	4 399.1	80.2	71.4	122.8	232.7	519.0	357.9	318.1	366.0	161.1	194.0	295.8	614.3
1989	5 484.4	4 732.3	92.8	76.0	135.9	244.8	543.2	384.1	337.4	389.0	164.1	210.4	316.2	659.2
1990	5 803.1	4 997.8	96.7	84.9	142.9	248.5	542.7	404.7	347.7	398.8	169.4	225.1	340.1	702.0
1991	5 995.9	5 138.7	89.2	76.0	152.5	230.2	540.9	416.6	360.5	405.5	178.2	235.2	376.5	727.1
1992	6 337.7	5 440.4	99.6	71.3	157.4	232.5	562.8	433.8	378.9	430.0	186.6	250.9	407.5	769.8
1993	6 657.4	5 729.3	93.1	72.1	165.3	248.3	593.1	446.8	401.2	458.0	201.0	272.6	437.8	803.7
1994	7 072.2	6 110.5	105.6	73.6	174.6	274.4	647.7	471.1	442.7	493.3	218.0	294.0	450.1	847.7
1995	7 397.6	6 407.2	93.1	74.1	181.5	287.0	677.2	500.0	457.0	514.9	226.3	307.6	490.9	892.1
1996	7 816.9	6 795.2	113.8	87.5	183.3	311.7	706.5	502.9	489.1	543.8	235.2	335.7	530.7	940.0
1997	8 304.3	7 247.5	110.7	92.6	179.6	337.6	755.5	524.3	521.2	574.2	253.7	347.8	595.5	997.8
1998	8 747.0	7 652.5	102.4	74.8	180.8	374.4	806.9	537.0	542.9	598.6	273.7	381.6	641.1	1 043.5
1999	9 268.4	8 127.2	93.8	85.4	185.4	406.6	820.4	552.7	577.7	635.5	287.4	439.3	679.8	1 118.6
2000	9 817.0	8 614.3	98.0	121.3	189.3	435.9	865.3	560.9	591.7	662.4	301.6	458.3	740.5	1 190.5
2001	10 128.0	8 869.7	97.9	118.7	202.3	469.5	778.9	562.5	607.1	691.6	296.9	476.9	782.6	1 276.6
2002	10 469.6	9 131.2	95.4	106.5	207.3	482.3	774.8	577.9	615.4	719.6	304.6	483.0	822.7	1 319.2
2003	10 960.8	9 542.3	114.4	143.3	220.0	496.2	771.8	587.5	637.0	751.5	316.6	489.1	864.6	1 380.0
2004	11 685.9	10 194.3	142.2	171.3	240.3	539.2	807.5	620.4	686.7	776.9	344.6	530.6	907.9	1 470.9
2005	12 421.9	10 853.1	133.3	223.8	239.5	605.4	845.1	635.5	722.4	824.7	364.7	557.8	989.5	1 538.5
2006	13 178.4	11 529.3	121.6	262.4	272.7	646.0	899.4	678.0	773.2	866.5	387.4	559.6	1 060.9	1 624.8
2007	13 807.5	12 064.6	167.9	275.0	281.4	610.8	922.0	694.9	805.3	892.5	407.2	586.3	1 091.4	1 719.8

Table 15-1. Gross Domestic Product (Value Added) by NAICS Industry Group—*Continued*

(Billions of dollars.)

Year	Profes-sional, scientific, and technical services	Manage-ment of companies and enterprises	Adminis-trative and waste manage-ment services	Educational services	Health care and social assistance	Arts, entertain-ment, and recreation	Accom-modation and food services	Other services except govern-ment	Total govern-ment	Federal	State and local	Private goods-producing industries	Private services-producing industries	Information-communi-cations-technology-producing industries[1]
1947	3.6	4.0	1.4	0.8	3.8	1.5	6.3	7.2	30.4	20.4	10.0	97.1	116.6	. . .
1948	4.0	4.5	1.5	0.9	4.3	1.6	6.6	7.6	30.0	18.5	11.5	112.0	127.2	. . .
1949	4.2	4.5	1.6	1.0	4.5	1.6	6.8	7.8	31.3	18.7	12.6	104.9	131.1	. . .
1950	4.7	5.0	1.8	1.1	4.9	1.7	7.1	8.3	31.6	18.2	13.4	119.8	142.4	. . .
1951	5.4	5.8	2.1	1.1	5.5	1.8	7.7	9.0	38.9	23.9	15.0	141.3	159.1	. . .
1952	5.9	6.1	2.3	1.2	6.0	1.9	8.1	9.3	44.5	28.0	16.5	145.2	168.7	. . .
1953	6.5	6.5	2.6	1.2	6.6	2.1	8.3	9.8	46.6	28.8	17.8	153.3	179.5	. . .
1954	6.9	6.4	2.7	1.3	6.8	2.1	8.5	10.1	48.3	28.9	19.3	147.3	184.8	. . .
1955	7.6	7.1	3.0	1.5	8.1	2.3	9.0	11.0	50.9	30.0	20.9	162.4	201.5	. . .
1956	8.4	7.4	3.3	1.6	8.5	2.4	9.4	12.0	54.3	31.1	23.2	169.1	214.0	. . .
1957	9.3	7.8	3.6	1.8	9.4	2.5	10.0	12.7	58.1	32.6	25.5	175.0	228.0	. . .
1958	9.7	7.7	3.9	1.9	10.3	2.7	10.1	13.2	61.8	34.0	27.8	169.2	236.2	. . .
1959	10.9	8.6	4.3	2.1	11.5	3.0	11.0	14.1	65.2	35.1	30.1	183.7	257.6	. . .
1960	11.4	8.8	4.6	2.3	12.1	3.3	11.2	15.1	69.4	36.4	32.9	186.7	270.3	. . .
1961	12.4	9.0	4.9	2.6	12.8	3.5	11.6	15.8	73.6	37.8	35.7	188.6	282.6	. . .
1962	13.5	9.8	5.3	2.9	14.0	3.6	12.4	16.7	78.8	40.2	38.6	204.1	302.7	. . .
1963	14.5	10.2	5.8	3.2	15.0	3.9	13.1	17.4	84.6	42.6	42.0	214.6	318.6	. . .
1964	16.0	11.0	6.3	3.5	16.6	4.2	14.3	18.6	90.7	45.1	45.6	228.4	344.5	. . .
1965	17.6	11.9	7.0	3.9	18.0	4.5	15.5	19.5	96.9	47.2	49.7	251.9	370.3	. . .
1966	20.0	13.1	7.8	4.5	20.2	4.7	16.8	21.2	107.5	52.2	55.3	277.1	403.2	. . .
1967	21.8	13.8	8.4	4.9	23.1	4.9	18.2	22.5	118.4	56.9	61.5	282.9	431.2	. . .
1968	23.6	15.1	9.1	5.5	26.0	5.3	20.0	24.1	131.7	62.6	69.1	306.9	471.3	. . .
1969	26.2	16.1	10.2	6.4	29.7	5.5	21.8	25.9	143.8	66.8	77.1	326.2	514.5	. . .
1970	28.6	16.6	11.0	7.3	33.6	6.0	23.5	27.0	158.4	71.2	87.2	327.9	552.3	. . .
1971	31.1	17.8	11.9	8.2	37.2	6.4	25.5	28.9	172.3	75.5	96.9	348.7	606.1	. . .
1972	34.8	19.4	13.3	9.3	41.8	6.8	27.8	30.8	187.3	80.5	106.8	384.8	666.1	. . .
1973	40.0	21.4	15.3	10.2	47.0	7.8	30.6	33.4	202.2	83.0	119.2	443.0	737.5	. . .
1974	44.0	23.3	17.3	10.8	53.5	8.6	32.3	35.8	222.6	90.4	132.2	471.7	805.6	. . .
1975	48.6	25.6	18.7	11.8	62.5	9.5	36.2	38.4	246.9	98.2	148.7	497.2	894.3	. . .
1976	54.5	29.0	21.6	12.2	71.8	10.7	41.2	42.8	269.1	107.4	161.7	559.8	996.4	. . .
1977	64.5	32.7	25.5	12.7	81.1	12.8	45.9	46.1	291.5	116.2	175.4	627.5	1 111.9	. . .
1978	74.8	37.0	30.0	13.9	92.5	14.2	53.7	53.2	317.7	125.9	191.8	710.6	1 266.4	. . .
1979	88.0	40.6	35.4	15.3	105.2	16.0	61.1	58.2	345.7	135.6	210.1	799.7	1 417.9	. . .
1980	102.0	44.6	39.8	17.5	122.3	17.4	66.1	62.6	383.7	150.7	233.0	840.2	1 565.6	. . .
1981	117.5	49.9	45.8	19.1	140.8	19.4	74.1	68.5	425.9	171.4	254.5	946.6	1 755.9	. . .
1982	130.0	52.1	48.8	20.7	157.2	20.4	80.5	70.7	462.4	186.2	276.2	923.3	1 869.3	. . .
1983	147.9	58.5	56.1	23.7	174.6	22.8	89.2	79.2	493.1	197.6	295.6	953.1	2 090.5	. . .
1984	170.6	66.7	66.5	26.0	188.0	24.1	97.0	89.3	538.1	220.0	318.1	1 072.7	2 322.3	. . .
1985	193.1	72.9	74.8	27.9	203.4	27.9	106.4	98.0	583.3	236.2	347.1	1 107.4	2 529.5	. . .
1986	216.7	78.8	83.3	29.6	222.4	29.7	115.1	107.2	620.0	245.2	374.8	1 116.7	2 726.1	. . .
1987	238.6	81.3	94.1	32.7	253.7	31.6	120.5	112.3	659.1	257.8	401.3	1 180.8	2 899.5	157.9
1988	273.0	87.0	106.3	34.7	274.4	33.8	132.1	124.4	704.7	272.3	432.4	1 261.3	3 137.8	174.0
1989	305.9	92.6	119.5	37.6	309.4	39.1	141.1	133.9	752.0	286.5	465.6	1 341.0	3 391.4	186.4
1990	338.3	98.2	133.3	40.0	346.7	45.5	149.8	142.6	805.3	299.4	505.9	1 377.4	3 620.4	195.8
1991	341.8	103.8	133.7	44.1	380.7	47.9	154.3	144.2	857.2	321.4	535.8	1 352.8	3 785.9	204.2
1992	369.9	110.0	146.7	47.4	416.1	54.8	161.4	153.0	897.3	333.2	564.1	1 400.0	4 040.5	216.5
1993	386.8	116.2	156.1	50.1	437.9	55.5	170.0	163.7	928.1	335.5	592.6	1 453.4	4 275.9	228.4
1994	405.1	123.4	169.9	53.2	457.9	56.9	178.1	173.2	961.8	339.2	622.6	1 572.4	4 538.0	255.4
1995	428.0	127.7	187.4	56.0	477.4	62.4	185.9	180.9	990.4	338.7	651.7	1 631.4	4 775.8	275.3
1996	467.5	134.7	207.8	58.8	493.7	66.6	197.8	188.1	1 021.6	343.7	678.0	1 722.4	5 072.8	306.5
1997	518.1	145.7	232.7	62.2	510.8	74.0	215.8	197.4	1 056.8	349.3	707.5	1 820.8	5 426.8	347.7
1998	565.3	156.8	254.0	67.6	533.9	76.8	229.1	211.1	1 094.5	352.9	741.6	1 895.4	5 757.1	385.0
1999	613.9	170.5	280.1	72.8	561.7	83.8	244.0	217.8	1 141.2	361.9	779.4	1 958.9	6 168.3	425.9
2000	675.1	183.4	282.4	79.2	599.2	88.7	261.4	229.1	1 202.7	378.7	823.9	2 081.5	6 532.8	465.8
2001	698.8	177.6	289.4	85.1	654.2	95.7	265.8	241.5	1 258.3	385.7	872.6	2 027.5	6 842.2	424.2
2002	705.2	183.8	300.0	93.3	706.3	102.4	279.1	252.5	1 338.4	417.3	921.1	2 036.9	7 094.3	416.6
2003	733.1	195.5	320.3	100.1	757.2	107.2	291.7	265.3	1 418.4	448.6	969.8	2 113.3	7 429.1	421.2
2004	792.7	210.1	335.3	108.3	808.0	113.7	313.7	273.9	1 491.6	479.4	1 012.3	2 280.6	7 913.7	440.5
2005	859.4	236.2	368.3	113.6	856.1	118.1	333.6	287.5	1 568.8	501.9	1 066.9	2 443.2	8 409.9	473.6
2006	930.6	246.9	388.9	121.1	904.8	126.9	358.0	299.5	1 649.1	527.6	1 121.5	2 607.4	8 921.8	496.5
2007	1 007.8	271.3	415.1	129.5	957.4	133.8	379.5	315.6	1 742.9	554.0	1 188.9	2 670.6	9 394.0	516.0

[1]Consists of computer and electronic products manufacturing; publishing, including software; information and data processing services; and computer systems design and related services.
. . . = Not available.

Table 15-2. Chain-Type Quantity Indexes for Value Added by NAICS Industry Group

(2000 = 100.)

Year	Total gross domestic product	Private industries												
							Manufacturing				Transpor-tation and ware-housing	Information	Finance and insurance	Real estate and rental and leasing
		Total	Agriculture, forestry, fishing, and hunting	Mining	Utilities	Construc-tion	Durable goods	Nondurable goods	Wholesale trade	Retail trade				
1947	16.0	15.0	25.2	49.6	8.8	35.1	12.2	20.7	8.7	14.2	22.6	5.8	12.0	11.9
1948	16.7	15.7	28.9	50.7	9.8	40.7	12.9	22.2	8.9	14.4	21.8	6.2	12.1	12.3
1949	16.7	15.6	27.6	44.3	11.1	40.9	12.1	22.0	9.0	15.1	19.5	6.5	12.6	12.9
1950	18.1	17.0	29.1	49.7	12.0	45.6	14.4	24.1	10.0	16.4	21.2	6.6	13.0	13.8
1951	19.5	18.2	27.6	54.5	14.0	50.9	16.5	25.7	10.3	16.6	23.8	7.1	14.0	14.6
1952	20.3	18.8	29.0	53.0	15.0	53.0	17.4	25.9	10.7	17.0	23.0	7.3	14.7	15.6
1953	21.2	19.7	30.3	54.7	16.2	55.0	19.0	26.9	11.0	17.7	23.2	7.8	15.3	16.5
1954	21.0	19.4	31.3	52.8	17.8	57.0	17.0	26.5	11.1	17.8	21.7	7.9	15.6	17.4
1955	22.5	21.0	32.1	59.4	18.6	60.7	19.2	28.4	12.2	19.2	23.9	8.4	17.1	18.5
1956	23.0	21.4	32.1	61.5	19.8	64.1	18.7	29.0	12.7	19.3	24.5	8.7	18.1	19.3
1957	23.4	21.9	30.8	61.1	21.3	64.3	19.0	29.3	13.0	19.7	24.4	9.1	19.0	20.3
1958	23.2	21.5	31.8	56.1	22.2	66.8	16.4	29.3	13.2	19.7	22.4	9.3	18.7	21.3
1959	24.9	23.3	31.8	58.1	24.2	72.4	18.7	31.9	15.0	20.9	23.7	9.9	19.0	22.8
1960	25.5	23.8	33.3	59.4	25.9	73.2	18.7	32.0	15.6	21.2	24.0	10.3	20.0	24.1
1961	26.1	24.3	33.6	59.9	27.3	74.3	18.4	32.7	16.1	21.2	24.0	10.7	21.0	25.3
1962	27.7	25.8	33.0	61.6	28.8	77.9	20.6	34.8	17.1	22.6	25.3	11.4	21.6	26.9
1963	28.9	27.2	34.3	64.3	30.2	80.0	22.3	37.5	17.8	23.3	26.7	12.2	22.1	28.1
1964	30.5	28.8	33.6	66.6	32.4	84.1	24.3	39.4	18.9	24.9	27.7	13.1	23.2	29.4
1965	32.5	30.8	35.8	69.5	33.8	87.7	27.2	41.9	20.4	26.4	30.1	14.0	23.8	31.1
1966	34.6	32.7	34.7	73.7	36.2	88.6	29.8	45.0	21.7	27.8	32.9	15.2	24.6	32.5
1967	35.5	33.3	37.2	74.6	38.1	86.7	29.7	44.5	22.7	28.1	32.7	16.1	26.0	33.5
1968	37.2	34.9	36.2	76.9	41.5	86.2	31.2	47.4	24.2	29.5	34.3	17.1	27.3	35.2
1969	38.4	36.0	37.3	79.2	44.0	83.2	31.9	48.9	25.2	29.7	35.5	18.5	29.9	37.2
1970	38.4	35.9	38.3	82.2	45.5	76.4	29.1	48.4	25.9	30.2	35.0	19.7	30.8	38.1
1971	39.7	37.1	40.2	80.2	49.0	74.2	29.5	50.6	27.4	31.5	35.6	20.5	31.4	40.7
1972	41.8	39.4	40.7	79.8	50.1	75.2	32.4	54.5	29.5	33.5	38.4	22.0	33.1	43.1
1973	44.2	42.0	40.4	82.5	56.1	78.0	36.3	58.6	30.5	35.5	40.9	23.5	35.0	45.1
1974	44.0	41.6	39.5	79.0	57.1	75.2	35.1	55.0	30.2	34.0	41.3	24.3	37.8	46.9
1975	43.9	41.5	45.9	80.3	60.8	68.1	31.6	53.7	30.9	34.2	38.5	25.2	40.3	48.9
1976	46.3	43.9	44.6	80.1	60.2	73.1	34.9	59.6	32.0	36.9	41.7	26.5	40.4	50.7
1977	48.4	46.1	46.4	86.3	59.9	74.1	37.7	64.0	33.6	38.4	43.5	28.5	41.0	51.4
1978	51.1	48.8	45.1	88.9	59.6	78.4	40.2	66.1	37.1	40.7	45.7	31.5	44.8	53.9
1979	52.7	50.6	48.6	79.7	54.7	81.2	40.8	70.3	39.9	40.7	48.3	34.2	46.5	57.1
1980	52.6	50.3	47.5	90.0	52.0	74.6	38.5	67.2	39.8	38.9	47.2	36.4	49.8	59.1
1981	53.9	51.7	59.7	90.3	51.7	67.9	39.6	72.3	42.1	40.0	46.2	38.3	51.2	60.2
1982	52.9	50.4	63.0	86.3	50.7	59.5	35.6	69.9	42.1	40.0	43.9	38.2	52.6	60.1
1983	55.2	52.8	43.3	81.2	52.7	62.8	38.0	76.7	43.8	44.1	49.5	41.0	52.4	62.9
1984	59.2	56.8	57.1	88.8	57.3	72.2	44.0	76.5	47.1	48.3	52.1	40.7	54.2	65.9
1985	61.7	59.4	69.6	93.1	60.9	79.0	45.2	78.7	49.5	51.2	52.7	42.0	54.1	68.3
1986	63.8	61.1	68.6	87.5	64.4	81.8	45.6	77.5	54.5	54.2	53.0	42.7	56.1	69.0
1987	66.0	63.4	71.5	91.7	72.3	82.4	48.9	83.6	53.1	52.1	55.7	45.8	60.2	69.8
1988	68.7	66.3	64.7	100.0	70.6	85.4	52.8	85.4	56.4	56.5	58.0	47.6	62.4	72.8
1989	71.1	68.7	71.1	97.1	79.0	87.6	53.7	86.1	58.6	58.8	59.5	51.2	63.4	74.9
1990	72.5	69.9	74.7	96.2	84.4	86.5	53.0	85.4	57.3	59.8	62.3	53.4	65.2	76.3
1991	72.3	69.8	75.4	97.6	85.3	79.1	51.5	85.8	59.4	59.5	65.1	54.4	67.4	76.9
1992	74.7	72.4	83.1	95.7	85.4	80.0	52.7	89.7	65.0	63.0	68.8	57.6	67.3	79.9
1993	76.7	74.3	72.8	97.0	85.8	82.0	55.2	92.9	67.1	65.4	72.0	61.4	70.3	81.3
1994	79.8	77.8	84.6	105.3	89.5	86.6	60.2	98.4	71.3	69.8	77.8	65.2	70.5	83.8
1995	81.8	79.7	73.1	105.7	93.8	86.3	65.2	97.8	70.8	73.0	80.5	68.0	72.9	86.0
1996	84.8	83.2	80.0	98.9	95.4	90.7	69.1	98.4	77.3	79.4	84.6	72.7	74.9	88.2
1997	88.7	87.4	88.3	102.5	91.2	93.3	75.3	100.4	85.6	86.0	88.4	74.6	80.1	91.2
1998	92.4	91.7	86.3	101.7	90.5	97.1	84.4	99.8	95.4	90.4	91.5	82.3	85.7	93.1
1999	96.5	96.2	89.2	104.3	94.7	99.4	89.6	101.3	100.4	95.7	95.3	95.5	91.6	97.2
2000	100.0	100.0	100.0	100.0	100.0	100.0	100.0	100.0	100.0	100.0	100.0	100.0	100.0	100.0
2001	100.8	100.9	93.7	94.7	95.1	100.2	94.0	95.0	107.0	107.0	97.4	104.0	104.4	103.5
2002	102.4	102.4	98.8	88.7	99.1	98.2	95.7	99.1	108.1	109.3	99.5	106.3	106.7	103.6
2003	104.9	105.1	106.2	87.9	106.0	96.2	98.2	98.3	110.4	113.6	101.5	109.4	110.5	105.4
2004	108.7	109.2	113.3	88.8	112.1	96.4	103.9	103.5	112.6	116.5	110.8	122.2	111.6	109.7
2005	111.9	113.1	122.9	85.4	105.4	96.0	109.6	98.3	116.3	126.9	115.3	132.9	120.2	111.9
2006	115.1	116.6	116.4	91.8	106.6	92.0	118.5	100.4	117.0	134.0	117.6	136.5	127.7	115.0
2007	117.4	119.0	124.5	91.8	107.9	81.8	124.2	100.8	118.0	140.1	120.6	147.5	127.8	118.8

Table 15-2. Chain-Type Quantity Indexes for Value Added by NAICS Industry Group—*Continued*

(2000 = 100.)

Year	Profes-sional, scientific, and technical services	Manage-ment of companies and enterprises	Adminis-trative and waste manage-ment services	Educational services	Health care and social assistance	Arts, entertain-ment, and recreation	Accom-modation and food services	Other services except govern-ment	Total govern-ment	Federal	State and local	Private goods-producing industries	Private services-producing industries	Information-communi-cations-technology-producing industries[1]
1947	8.8	18.7	6.4	19.4	10.8	15.8	20.0	41.1	35.4	67.7	20.6	19.7	12.8	. . .
1948	8.9	19.4	6.5	22.4	11.3	15.5	20.1	42.0	34.1	63.5	21.0	21.4	13.1	. . .
1949	8.9	19.2	6.6	23.0	11.7	15.3	20.6	41.8	34.0	61.2	22.0	20.5	13.3	. . .
1950	9.3	21.0	7.2	23.2	12.3	15.4	22.0	42.9	34.4	61.3	22.6	23.0	14.2	. . .
1951	9.8	22.5	7.5	23.3	12.8	16.2	22.2	43.4	40.6	79.7	23.1	25.0	15.0	. . .
1952	10.1	23.4	7.9	23.1	13.5	16.1	22.7	43.2	43.8	88.7	23.7	25.8	15.4	. . .
1953	10.4	24.6	8.2	23.6	14.2	16.5	23.6	43.7	44.6	89.1	24.6	27.4	16.1	. . .
1954	10.5	23.9	8.2	23.9	15.1	16.5	23.7	43.2	44.4	86.8	25.4	26.2	16.2	. . .
1955	11.0	25.9	8.8	24.8	15.5	17.1	25.3	46.1	44.6	85.1	26.4	28.6	17.5	. . .
1956	11.3	26.3	9.3	25.2	16.1	17.8	25.6	47.8	45.4	84.2	27.9	28.7	18.0	. . .
1957	12.2	26.8	9.9	27.1	17.1	18.1	26.5	49.2	46.3	84.1	29.3	28.8	18.7	. . .
1958	12.5	25.9	10.4	28.4	18.4	18.5	26.3	50.4	46.8	82.1	30.8	27.3	18.9	. . .
1959	13.5	28.4	11.2	29.1	19.5	19.8	27.7	52.0	47.5	81.6	32.2	29.8	20.2	. . .
1960	13.6	28.9	11.6	30.3	20.3	20.8	28.2	54.1	49.2	83.4	33.9	30.1	20.9	. . .
1961	14.4	29.3	12.3	31.9	21.2	21.5	28.1	55.3	50.9	85.2	35.5	30.2	21.5	. . .
1962	15.1	31.4	12.9	33.7	23.0	22.0	30.0	56.7	52.8	88.6	36.7	32.4	22.8	. . .
1963	15.9	33.3	13.5	35.1	24.4	22.9	31.2	57.7	54.4	89.5	38.7	34.6	23.8	. . .
1964	16.8	35.2	14.4	36.3	27.2	24.1	33.1	59.8	56.4	90.8	40.9	36.7	25.2	. . .
1965	17.8	38.0	15.4	38.8	28.3	24.6	35.3	61.3	58.5	92.2	43.3	39.8	26.7	. . .
1966	19.5	40.9	16.8	41.2	29.9	24.9	37.0	64.2	62.1	98.6	45.7	42.4	28.3	. . .
1967	20.5	41.3	17.2	43.4	31.1	25.1	38.0	65.7	65.2	104.6	47.4	42.3	29.2	. . .
1968	21.3	43.6	18.1	45.2	33.2	25.8	39.3	66.4	67.9	107.2	50.1	43.9	30.7	. . .
1969	22.4	45.0	19.4	46.9	35.8	25.4	39.8	67.2	69.6	107.6	52.3	44.7	32.0	. . .
1970	23.1	44.5	19.8	49.0	38.0	26.1	40.8	66.4	69.7	103.0	54.4	42.5	32.8	. . .
1971	23.5	46.1	20.1	51.8	40.5	26.6	42.2	66.8	69.9	99.0	56.5	43.2	34.3	. . .
1972	25.0	49.4	21.8	52.5	42.9	27.4	44.7	69.0	70.2	95.5	58.5	46.1	36.4	. . .
1973	27.0	53.5	23.5	53.5	45.9	30.3	47.3	70.7	70.4	91.7	60.6	49.7	38.5	. . .
1974	27.7	50.6	24.8	55.5	47.8	30.8	45.7	68.4	72.3	92.5	62.9	47.6	38.9	. . .
1975	27.2	49.8	23.7	56.8	51.1	31.5	45.9	68.2	73.1	91.1	64.9	45.5	39.7	. . .
1976	28.4	53.9	25.0	57.4	53.8	33.8	49.5	71.0	74.3	92.8	65.8	49.1	41.5	. . .
1977	31.1	57.6	27.2	57.8	57.8	38.2	52.0	71.2	75.0	92.8	66.8	52.3	43.3	. . .
1978	33.8	60.7	30.0	60.4	60.6	40.1	56.0	75.1	76.7	94.9	68.4	54.6	46.2	. . .
1979	36.6	61.4	32.9	60.6	63.5	42.4	57.1	75.7	77.7	94.9	69.9	56.1	48.1	. . .
1980	38.4	60.3	34.2	62.7	67.4	43.7	55.2	74.4	79.0	96.6	71.0	53.9	48.8	. . .
1981	39.9	59.5	35.3	61.7	69.3	46.2	56.7	72.3	79.3	97.6	70.9	55.8	49.9	. . .
1982	39.9	59.9	34.3	61.9	69.8	46.4	58.6	69.1	79.5	97.1	71.4	52.0	49.8	. . .
1983	42.0	65.2	37.2	66.8	71.7	49.1	63.2	72.5	80.2	99.5	71.3	53.4	52.6	. . .
1984	45.9	72.5	42.4	70.0	72.6	49.5	66.2	77.5	81.0	101.1	71.8	59.5	55.7	. . .
1985	49.7	77.1	46.0	71.5	73.8	55.6	69.5	80.9	83.2	103.5	73.8	62.6	58.1	. . .
1986	53.7	82.1	49.8	71.9	75.5	56.9	73.7	82.9	85.1	105.0	76.0	62.5	60.6	. . .
1987	56.5	83.7	54.9	75.7	80.8	58.3	72.0	84.2	86.8	107.3	77.3	66.2	62.3	16.8
1988	61.4	86.6	58.8	75.6	81.2	60.3	75.1	89.0	88.8	108.2	79.9	69.1	65.2	18.8
1989	65.8	89.5	63.8	77.3	84.8	66.4	76.2	92.2	91.0	109.8	82.4	70.4	68.0	20.4
1990	69.0	92.2	67.5	77.5	88.2	73.3	76.9	94.4	93.2	111.9	84.6	69.9	69.9	21.6
1991	66.4	91.8	65.0	80.9	90.3	73.4	74.5	91.3	93.7	111.9	85.3	68.2	70.3	22.3
1992	68.7	91.8	68.2	83.5	92.8	81.9	75.8	92.5	94.1	111.2	86.3	70.3	73.1	24.2
1993	69.6	92.0	70.9	85.8	93.0	81.0	78.1	95.2	94.1	108.7	87.3	72.1	75.0	26.4
1994	70.8	94.2	75.6	87.7	93.0	80.6	80.6	98.6	94.4	106.8	88.7	77.8	77.7	30.9
1995	71.7	93.5	81.8	90.1	93.9	85.9	82.8	99.7	94.3	102.2	90.6	79.6	79.8	36.9
1996	75.7	97.5	88.6	90.5	94.6	88.2	86.3	99.1	94.8	100.3	92.2	82.6	83.4	44.3
1997	80.4	103.1	95.6	92.3	95.1	95.0	88.8	99.3	95.9	99.7	94.1	87.2	87.4	53.8
1998	86.8	100.4	99.5	95.4	95.6	95.5	92.8	101.9	96.9	99.2	95.9	91.9	91.6	68.3
1999	92.4	101.2	105.1	97.3	97.3	99.1	96.1	100.2	98.0	98.5	97.8	95.4	96.4	83.7
2000	100.0	100.0	100.0	100.0	100.0	100.0	100.0	100.0	100.0	100.0	100.0	100.0	100.0	100.0
2001	100.6	98.1	97.2	99.8	103.6	103.1	98.0	98.3	100.8	98.4	101.9	95.7	102.6	99.6
2002	99.1	101.1	98.4	102.4	108.2	106.8	99.1	98.7	102.5	100.3	103.5	96.9	104.1	101.6
2003	103.0	103.9	104.7	106.1	113.1	108.8	102.5	100.6	103.8	102.8	104.2	97.4	107.5	108.9
2004	111.1	98.9	105.8	108.2	117.0	112.1	106.8	100.8	104.3	103.7	104.5	101.3	111.7	121.3
2005	117.3	101.4	113.7	107.9	120.8	113.0	109.5	102.8	105.0	104.0	105.4	101.9	116.6	136.4
2006	124.0	100.0	114.8	109.8	124.9	117.6	113.0	102.4	105.5	103.8	106.3	104.6	120.4	149.2
2007	132.8	97.8	117.2	113.3	127.3	119.8	114.9	102.8	106.9	104.5	108.1	103.9	123.9	168.5

[1]Consists of computer and electronic products manufacturing; publishing, including software; information and data processing services; and computer systems design and related services.
. . . = Not available.

Table 15-3. Gross Domestic Factor Income by NAICS Industry Group

(Billions of current dollars.)

NAICS industry	1998	1999	2000	2001	2002	2003	2004	2005	2006	2007
Gross domestic factor income, total	8 142.5	8 638.6	9 152.4	9 454.6	9 745.2	10 201.5	10 866.7	11 553.0	12 251.9	12 844.4
Compensation of employees	5 023.9	5 362.3	5 787.3	5 947.2	6 096.6	6 331.1	6 662.5	7 037.2	7 440.4	7 819.4
Gross operating surplus	3 118.6	3 276.3	3 365.1	3 507.4	3 648.6	3 870.4	4 204.2	4 515.8	4 811.5	5 025.0
Private industries	7 037.0	7 486.2	7 939.2	8 185.2	8 393.7	8 769.1	9 360.4	9 969.3	10 587.5	11 085.6
Compensation of employees	4 107.7	4 407.0	4 776.4	4 882.4	4 957.6	5 118.7	5 382.2	5 692.4	6 035.3	6 342.0
Gross operating surplus	2 929.3	3 079.2	3 162.8	3 302.8	3 436.1	3 650.4	3 978.2	4 276.9	4 552.2	4 743.6
Agriculture, forestry, fishing, and hunting	107.9	106.8	112.1	110.6	99.2	123.5	148.0	148.6	128.1	170.5
Compensation of employees	31.2	33.0	34.6	36.1	36.4	36.1	38.7	39.6	40.3	42.4
Gross operating surplus	76.7	73.8	77.5	74.5	62.8	87.4	109.3	109.0	87.8	128.1
Mining	63.8	74.6	108.2	104.5	93.8	128.6	154.7	204.4	240.9	251.8
Compensation of employees	34.6	33.4	36.0	38.8	37.7	39.4	44.0	49.4	57.6	64.2
Gross operating surplus	29.2	41.2	72.2	65.7	56.1	89.2	110.7	155.0	183.3	187.6
Utilities	152.0	155.5	158.4	176.5	172.6	182.8	200.9	197.8	228.5	235.2
Compensation of employees	41.2	42.6	46.3	48.4	51.2	51.8	57.4	55.7	56.1	59.8
Gross operating surplus	110.8	112.9	112.1	128.1	121.4	131.0	143.5	142.1	172.4	175.4
Construction	370.0	401.8	430.9	464.3	476.5	489.9	532.2	597.6	637.9	603.0
Compensation of employees	254.3	282.8	309.2	327.6	332.7	341.0	356.3	390.7	424.2	442.8
Gross operating surplus	115.7	119.0	121.7	136.7	143.8	148.9	175.9	206.9	213.7	160.2
Durable goods manufacturing	794.2	807.5	851.7	764.9	760.0	756.2	790.6	827.1	880.3	901.7
Compensation of employees	546.2	570.4	621.2	584.2	570.8	583.6	588.4	598.0	628.5	641.2
Gross operating surplus	248.0	237.1	230.5	180.7	189.2	172.6	202.2	229.1	251.8	260.5
Nondurable goods manufacturing	512.4	527.7	533.8	534.7	548.2	556.8	588.8	601.2	642.4	657.9
Compensation of employees	279.1	283.8	297.6	292.6	303.5	305.0	314.3	310.8	325.1	328.2
Gross operating surplus	233.3	243.9	236.2	242.1	244.7	251.8	274.5	290.4	317.3	329.7
Wholesale trade	416.1	446.4	456.3	471.8	477.5	492.7	532.0	559.2	603.2	630.4
Compensation of employees	291.0	313.9	328.6	334.1	333.4	344.8	363.2	387.1	413.3	438.2
Gross operating surplus	125.1	132.5	127.7	137.7	144.1	147.9	168.8	172.1	189.9	192.2
Retail trade	474.4	502.6	522.0	549.0	572.6	596.5	612.1	646.5	677.5	696.8
Compensation of employees	342.3	368.2	396.6	410.5	422.3	432.6	446.4	466.0	481.4	496.0
Gross operating surplus	132.1	134.4	125.4	138.5	150.3	163.9	165.7	180.5	196.1	200.8
Transportation and warehousing	259.6	272.5	285.6	287.1	288.7	302.4	327.2	345.3	367.2	385.4
Compensation of employees	174.9	186.1	199.3	203.5	204.1	204.1	222.2	229.0	237.3	249.1
Gross operating surplus	84.7	86.4	86.3	83.6	84.6	98.3	105.0	116.3	129.9	136.3
Information	349.9	405.1	421.9	439.9	445.0	450.4	490.1	515.8	517.9	545.2
Compensation of employees	185.6	217.5	248.0	244.4	227.9	225.6	231.6	236.9	247.1	258.4
Gross operating surplus	164.3	187.6	173.9	195.5	217.1	224.8	258.5	278.9	270.8	286.8
Finance and insurance	613.3	650.7	710.4	751.2	789.2	827.9	866.6	945.7	1 015.3	1 044.1
Compensation of employees	344.5	370.7	409.3	437.0	448.0	472.3	508.1	546.4	587.6	617.1
Gross operating surplus	268.8	280.0	301.1	314.2	341.2	355.6	358.5	399.3	427.7	427.0
Real estate and rental and leasing	904.7	972.2	1 036.0	1 111.4	1 139.8	1 189.0	1 265.9	1 320.9	1 392.4	1 481.1
Compensation of employees	66.2	70.7	77.4	81.3	84.1	87.7	94.4	102.4	110.0	113.7
Gross operating surplus	838.5	901.5	958.6	1 030.1	1 055.7	1 101.3	1 171.5	1 218.5	1 282.4	1 367.4
Professional, scientific, and technical services	555.9	603.8	664.2	687.5	693.3	720.6	779.2	844.6	914.9	991.5
Compensation of employees	378.3	422.0	486.9	499.6	489.1	497.4	526.4	579.1	629.9	679.5
Gross operating surplus	177.6	181.8	177.3	187.9	204.2	223.2	252.8	265.5	285.0	312.0
Management of companies and enterprises	153.8	167.3	179.9	174.5	180.7	192.3	206.6	232.4	243.0	266.9
Compensation of employees	127.5	136.1	147.4	139.9	139.5	148.2	162.6	180.7	188.6	206.6
Gross operating surplus	26.3	31.2	32.5	34.6	41.2	44.1	44.0	51.7	54.4	60.3
Administrative and waste management services	247.7	273.3	274.8	281.7	292.0	312.0	326.5	359.0	378.9	404.7
Compensation of employees	193.9	213.1	211.7	217.0	222.9	232.9	242.2	265.6	284.1	301.8
Gross operating surplus	53.8	60.2	63.1	64.7	69.1	79.1	84.3	93.4	94.8	102.9
Educational services	66.6	71.8	78.2	83.9	92.0	98.8	106.9	112.0	119.5	127.7
Compensation of employees	61.2	65.9	72.0	78.1	85.5	90.9	96.9	101.9	108.1	115.8
Gross operating surplus	5.4	5.9	6.2	5.8	6.5	7.9	10.0	10.1	11.4	11.9
Health care and social assistance	527.3	554.7	591.9	646.4	697.8	748.0	798.1	845.1	892.8	944.7
Compensation of employees	425.9	447.1	478.8	516.2	553.8	590.9	628.0	672.2	709.5	753.6
Gross operating surplus	101.4	107.6	113.1	130.2	144.0	157.1	170.1	172.9	183.3	191.1
Arts, entertainment, and recreation	69.1	75.1	79.7	86.2	92.5	96.6	102.4	106.2	114.0	119.6
Compensation of employees	44.5	48.4	53.6	56.9	59.9	63.1	67.1	69.1	73.5	77.3
Gross operating surplus	24.6	26.7	26.1	29.3	32.6	33.5	35.3	37.1	40.5	42.3
Accommodation and food services	201.2	214.0	229.5	233.7	246.2	256.6	276.6	293.1	314.9	334.7
Compensation of employees	143.7	152.8	164.7	170.6	177.8	186.8	199.6	211.3	224.6	236.9
Gross operating surplus	57.5	61.2	64.8	63.1	68.4	69.8	77.0	81.8	90.3	97.8
Other services, except government	197.2	203.0	213.5	225.5	235.7	247.6	255.0	266.8	277.7	293.0
Compensation of employees	141.5	148.5	157.2	165.6	176.7	184.6	194.4	200.4	208.5	219.7
Gross operating surplus	55.7	54.5	56.3	59.9	59.0	63.0	60.6	66.4	69.2	73.3
Government	1 105.5	1 152.3	1 213.1	1 269.3	1 351.5	1 432.3	1 506.2	1 583.6	1 664.4	1 758.8
Compensation of employees	916.2	955.3	1 010.8	1 064.8	1 139.0	1 212.4	1 280.3	1 344.7	1 405.1	1 477.3
Gross operating surplus	189.3	197.0	202.3	204.5	212.5	219.9	225.9	238.9	259.3	281.5
Addenda:										
Private goods-producing industries	1 848.3	1 918.3	2 036.8	1 979.0	1 978.0	2 055.0	2 214.4	2 378.8	2 529.7	2 584.9
Compensation of employees	1 145.4	1 203.4	1 298.7	1 279.3	1 281.2	1 305.1	1 341.7	1 388.5	1 475.8	1 518.8
Gross operating surplus	702.9	714.9	738.1	699.7	696.8	749.9	872.7	990.3	1 053.9	1 066.1
Private services-producing industries	5 188.7	5 567.9	5 902.5	6 206.2	6 415.8	6 714.2	7 146.1	7 590.5	8 057.9	8 500.7
Compensation of employees	2 962.3	3 203.6	3 477.8	3 603.1	3 676.4	3 813.6	4 040.5	4 303.9	4 559.6	4 823.3
Gross operating surplus	2 226.4	2 364.3	2 424.7	2 603.1	2 739.4	2 900.6	3 105.6	3 286.6	3 498.3	3 677.4
Information-communications-technology-producing industries [1]	378.5	418.9	458.1	416.3	408.5	412.7	431.3	463.9	486.1	505.0
Compensation of employees	275.2	320.3	388.8	364.1	330.2	323.5	327.9	351.0	380.4	396.6
Gross operating surplus	103.3	98.6	69.3	52.2	78.3	89.2	103.4	112.9	105.7	108.4

[1] Consists of computer and electronic products manufacturing; publishing, including software; information and data processing services; and computer systems design and related services.

NOTES AND DEFINITIONS

TABLES 15-1 THROUGH 15-3
GROSS DOMESTIC PRODUCT (VALUE ADDED) AND GROSS FACTOR INCOME BY INDUSTRY

SOURCE: U.S. DEPARTMENT OF COMMERCE, BUREAU OF ECONOMIC ANALYSIS (BEA)

In the introduction to the notes and definitions for Chapter 1, it was observed that gross domestic product (GDP), while primarily measured as the sum of final demands for goods and services, is also the sum of the values created by each industry in the economy. In this chapter, selected data are presented from the industry accounts in the national income and product accounts (NIPAs). The industry accounts measure the contribution of each major industry to GDP. They are only calculated on an annual basis; no quarterly data are available.

In recent years, estimates of GDP by industry have been prepared using a methodology integrated with annual input-output accounts in order to produce estimates of gross industry output, industry input, and the difference between the two—industry value added—with greater consistency and timeliness than was previously possible. The current integrated industry accounts also include a wealth of related information too extensive for inclusion here, such as quantity and price indexes for gross output and intermediate inputs, cost per unit of real value added allocated to the three components of value added, and components of domestic supply (domestic output, imports, exports, and inventory change).

The estimates of GDP by NAICS industry have been extended back to 1947, using approximations of current methods in earlier years when the source data were less comprehensive. Table 15-1 presents current-dollar GDP for NAICS industry groups. Table 15-2 presents indexes of real value added for each industry group.

In Table 15-3, the editor presents a measure derived from the components of current-dollar value added as published by BEA. This measure, "gross domestic factor income," enables users to obtain a clearer picture of the quantitative impact of each industry on the economy and of the shares of capital and labor in each industry.

The 2004 revision incorporated a change in terminology. An industry's contribution to total GDP, formerly referred to as "gross product originating" (GPO) or "gross product by industry," is now called "value added." This is consistent with the use of the term "value added" in most economic writing. However, it should not be confused with a concept known as "Census value added," which is used in U.S. censuses and surveys of manufactures. Census value added is calculated at the individual establishment level and does not exclude purchased business services. This means that census value added is not a true measure of economic value added.

Definitions and notes on the data

An industry's *gross domestic product (value added)*, formerly *GPO*, is equal to the market value of its gross output (which consists of the value, including taxes, of sales or receipts and other operating income plus the value of inventory change) minus the value of its intermediate inputs (energy, raw materials, semifinished goods, and services that are purchased from domestic industries or from foreign sources).

In concept, this is also equal to the sum of *compensation of employees, taxes on production and imports less subsidies,* and *gross operating surplus*. (See Chapter 1 and its notes and definitions for more information.)

Compensation of employees consists of wage and salary accruals and supplements to wages and salaries. This approximates the labor share of production, subject to the note below about proprietors' income.

Taxes on production and imports less subsidies. Although this is shown in BEA source data as a single net line item, it represents two separate components.

Taxes on production and imports are included in the market value of the goods and services sold to final consumers and therefore in the consumer valuation of those goods. Since they are not part of the payments to the labor and capital inputs in the producing industries, they must be *added* to the sum of the returns to those inputs in order to account for the total value to consumers. Taxes that fall into this classification include property taxes, sales and excise taxes, and Customs duties.

BEA allocates these taxes to the industry level at which they are assessed by law. Most sales taxes are considered by BEA to be part of the value added by retail trade. Some sales taxes, most fuel taxes, and all customs duties are allocated by BEA to wholesale trade. Residential real property taxes, including those on owner-occupied dwellings, are allocated by BEA to the real estate industry.

Subsidies to business by government are included in the labor and/or capital payments made by that industry. Since they are payments to the industry in addition to the market values paid by consumers, they are *subtracted* from the values of the labor and capital inputs to make them consistent with the market values as defined in value added. The role of subsidies is obvious in the source data for the agricultural sector, where the net "taxes on production and imports less subsidies" has a negative sign: farm subsidies more than offset this industry's taxes on production and imports, which mainly consist of property taxes, since sales, excise, and import taxes are not levied on farms.

For private sector businesses, *gross operating surplus* consists of business income (corporate profits before tax, proprietors' income, and rental income of persons), net interest and miscellaneous payments, business current transfer payments (net), and capital consumption allowances. For government, households, and institutions, it consists of consumption of fixed capital and (for government) government enterprises' current surplus. This approximates the share of the value of production ascribable to capital and land as measured in the NIPAs accounts; however, as BEA notes, "an unknown portion [of proprietors' income] reflects the labor contribution of proprietors." (*Survey of Current Business*, June 2004, p. 27, footnote 7.) Another aspect to be noted is that gross operating surplus includes the return to owner-occupied housing in the real estate sector. Because there is in the NIPAs no employee compensation attributed to owner-occupied housing, the capital share in that industry as measured by gross operating surplus is very large.

Quantity indexes for value added. Measures of the constant-dollar change in each industry's gross output minus its intermediate input use are calculated by BEA, using a Fisher index-number formula which incorporates weights from two adjacent years. The changes for successive years are chained together in indexes, with the value for the year 2000 set at 100. The indexes are multiplied by the 2000 current-dollar to provide estimates of value added in "chained 2000 dollars," but because the actual weights used change from year to year, components in chained 2000 dollars typically do not add up to total GDP in 2000 dollars—and do not contain any information not already summarized in the indexes. For that reason, only the indexes are published here.

Gross domestic factor income (not a category published as such in the NIPAs) is calculated by the editor as value added minus "taxes on production and imports less subsidies." The effect of this procedure is to take out the specified taxes, and to leave in the subsidies embedded in the employee compensation and gross operating surplus components. The editor believes that this provides a valuable alternative basis for assessing the importance of different industries in the economy and the shares of labor and capital in each industry's output.

The editor's reasoning is based on the facts that more than half of these taxes are sales, excise, and import taxes, and the assignment of these taxes to industries is economically arbitrary. BEA assigns them to the industry with the legal liability to pay, not to the entity bearing the major incidence of the tax. Yet economists have demonstrated that most of the burdens of sales and excise taxes and import duties are not borne by the factors in the legally liable industry;

instead, they are passed on to consumers. In addition, because the wholesale and retail trade industries are classified as "services-producing," BEA's allocation of those taxes has a very peculiar result: taxes on goods are represented as paid by "service" industries. The process adopted instead by the editor in Table 15-3, which excludes these taxes and focuses on "gross domestic factor income," has the effect (for example) of keeping the wholesale trade industry from appearing to be both larger and more heavily taxed than it really is.

Private goods-producing industries consists of agriculture, forestry, fishing, and hunting; mining; construction; and manufacturing.

Private services-producing industries consists of utilities; wholesale trade; retail trade; transportation and warehousing; information; finance, insurance, real estate, rental, and leasing; professional and business services; educational services, health care, and social assistance; arts, entertainment, recreation, accommodation, and food services; and other services, except government.

Information-communications-technology-producing industries is a category that cuts across the goods and services framework, consisting of computer and electronic products manufacturing; publishing industries (which includes software) from the information sector; information and data processing services; and computer systems design and related services.

Data availability and references

The industry estimates shown here are those published in "Annual Industry Accounts: Revised Statistics for 2005–2007" in the December 2008 *Survey of Current Business.* Information on concepts, methodology, and previous references can be found in that article.

Advance estimates for 2008, with considerably less detail and using approximations of the detailed methods, are to be published late in April 2009.

All data and *Survey of Current Business* articles are available on the BEA Web site at <http://www.bea.gov>. Click on "Annual Industry Accounts." For the tables, click on "Interactive Tables" under "Gross Domestic Product (GDP) by Industry."

CHAPTER 16: EMPLOYMENT, HOURS, AND EARNINGS BY NAICS INDUSTRY

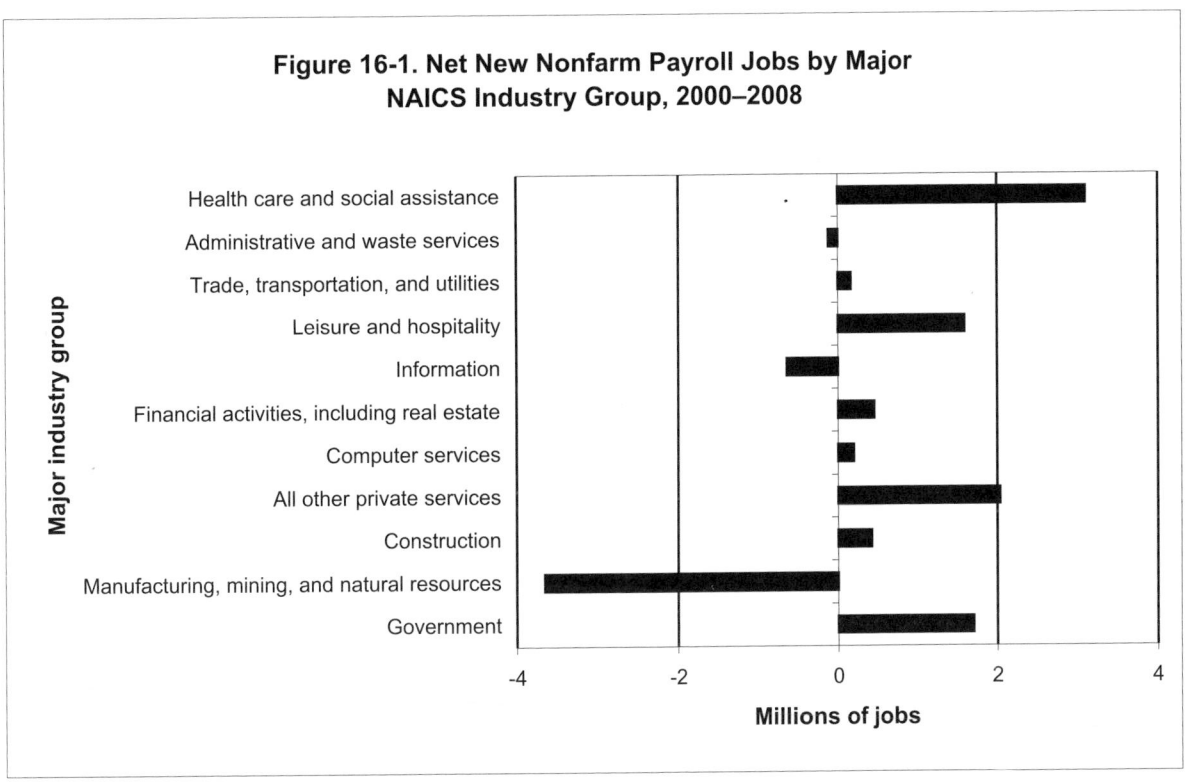

Figure 16-1. Net New Nonfarm Payroll Jobs by Major NAICS Industry Group, 2000–2008

- Between 2000 and 2008, U.S. nonfarm employers added a net total of 5.3 million jobs. This period includes the beginning of the latest recession, and also encompasses an entire business cycle, from the peak in 2000 to the peak in 2007. (Table 16-1)

- A large portion of the job gains occurred in two of the categories shown in Figure 16-1: health care and social assistance and "all other private services," a catchall category, created by the editors for the graph, that includes most professional and technical services, private educational services, personal and repair services, and membership associations and organizations. Temporary help services, which are included in "administrative and waste services" and which had grown strongly in the 1990s, showed no gains from 2000 to 2007 and fell in 2008. (Table 16-1)

- Government provided 1.7 million net new jobs—1.4 million at the local government level and 0.4 million at the state government level, partly offset by a reported loss of 0.1 million jobs at the federal government level. (Table 16-1) However, federal government employment in this survey excludes the armed forces and several intelligence agencies. It also excludes contract employees, who are reported in private services categories. See the notes and definitions to Chapter 10 for more information.

- Leisure and hospitality provided 1.6 million net new jobs, of which 1.4 million were at food services and drinking places. (Table 16-1)

- Manufacturing, mining, and natural resources lost 3.7 million jobs, all of them in manufacturing, and most of them gone even before the recession began in 2008. (Table 16-1)

- In 2008, the average workweek for production and nonsupervisory workers fell in many industries as the recession began to take hold. (Table 16-3)

- Average hourly earnings for production or nonsupervisory workers in 2008 ranged from just over $10 in the leisure and hospitality sector to over $25 in petroleum and coal products manufacturing and utilities. (Table 16-4)

Table 16-1. Nonfarm Employment by NAICS Sector and Industry

(Wage and salary workers on nonfarm payrolls, thousands.)

Industry	1990	1991	1992	1993	1994	1995	1996	1997	1998	1999
TOTAL NONFARM	109 487	108 375	108 726	110 844	114 291	117 298	119 708	122 776	125 930	128 993
Total Private	91 072	89 829	89 940	91 855	95 016	97 865	100 169	103 113	106 021	108 686
Goods-Producing	23 723	22 588	22 095	22 219	22 774	23 156	23 409	23 886	24 354	24 465
Mining and logging	765	739	689	666	659	641	637	654	645	598
Logging	84.6	78.7	78.7	81.0	82.0	82.5	80.7	82.1	80.0	80.8
Mining	680.1	660.5	609.8	584.9	576.5	558.1	556.4	571.3	564.7	517.4
Oil and gas extraction	190.2	191.0	182.2	170.9	162.4	151.7	146.9	144.1	140.8	131.2
Mining, except oil and gas [1]	302.2	285.1	271.8	250.9	255.2	252.4	249.4	249.5	243.1	234.5
Coal mining	136.0	125.6	117.5	100.2	103.5	96.7	90.5	89.4	85.3	78.6
Support activities for mining	187.6	184.5	155.7	163.1	158.8	154.0	160.1	177.7	180.8	151.7
Construction	5 263	4 780	4 608	4 779	5 095	5 274	5 536	5 813	6 149	6 545
Construction of buildings	1 413.0	1 252.9	1 187.3	1 227.4	1 300.8	1 325.4	1 380.2	1 435.4	1 508.8	1 586.3
Heavy and civil engineering	813.0	759.1	734.2	738.4	761.7	774.7	800.1	824.9	865.3	908.7
Specialty trade contractors	3 037.3	2 768.4	2 686.0	2 813.6	3 032.5	3 174.1	3 355.1	3 552.6	3 775.1	4 049.6
Manufacturing	17 695	17 068	16 799	16 774	17 020	17 241	17 237	17 419	17 560	17 322
Durable goods	10 737	10 220	9 946	9 901	10 132	10 373	10 486	10 705	10 911	10 831
Wood products	540.6	498.5	501.9	524.1	560.6	573.7	582.8	595.4	609.2	620.3
Nonmetallic mineral products	528.4	494.7	487.3	491.1	505.3	513.1	517.3	525.7	535.3	540.8
Primary metals	688.6	656.1	630.3	618.4	630.4	641.7	639.3	638.8	641.5	625.0
Fabricated metal products	1 610.0	1 541.3	1 497.2	1 509.5	1 565.3	1 623.4	1 647.5	1 695.8	1 739.5	1 728.4
Machinery	1 409.8	1 347.9	1 311.2	1 330.9	1 381.4	1 442.3	1 468.9	1 495.9	1 514.1	1 468.3
Computer and electronic products [1]	1 902.5	1 809.3	1 707.3	1 655.9	1 651.1	1 688.4	1 746.6	1 803.3	1 830.9	1 780.5
Computer and peripheral equipment	367.4	348.6	328.5	305.7	297.7	295.6	304.6	316.7	322.1	310.1
Communications equipment	223.0	212.5	202.0	202.6	210.0	224.3	228.9	235.0	237.4	228.7
Semiconductors and electronic components	574.0	546.6	519.4	519.4	535.4	571.0	606.6	639.8	649.8	630.5
Electronic instruments	634.8	598.0	556.2	525.3	501.4	490.5	497.8	502.8	509.2	498.3
Electrical equipment and appliances	633.1	597.7	579.4	575.8	588.5	592.8	591.0	586.3	591.6	588.0
Transportation equipment [1]	2 134.5	2 029.3	1 978.1	1 915.0	1 937.4	1 978.5	1 975.1	2 027.6	2 078.4	2 088.6
Motor vehicles and parts	1 054.2	1 017.6	1 047.0	1 077.8	1 168.5	1 241.5	1 240.3	1 253.9	1 271.5	1 312.5
Furniture and related products	604.0	563.6	565.5	578.1	602.8	609.4	606.5	617.8	643.9	667.6
Miscellaneous manufacturing	685.7	681.8	687.7	702.5	709.0	709.7	710.7	718.2	726.8	724.0
Nondurable goods	6 958	6 848	6 853	6 872	6 889	6 868	6 751	6 714	6 649	6 491
Food manufacturing	1 507.3	1 515.2	1 518.3	1 534.6	1 539.2	1 560.0	1 562.0	1 557.9	1 554.9	1 549.8
Beverage and tobacco products	217.7	214.7	208.5	207.1	204.6	202.6	204.4	206.3	208.9	208.3
Textile mills	491.8	479.9	479.0	478.7	477.6	468.5	443.2	436.2	424.5	397.1
Textile product mills	235.6	225.1	228.0	232.6	242.9	242.1	237.1	236.4	234.7	232.4
Apparel	902.8	876.9	879.3	857.3	831.9	791.1	722.3	680.8	621.4	540.5
Leather and allied products	133.2	124.4	120.8	118.1	113.9	104.9	94.2	89.5	82.9	74.9
Paper and paper products	647.2	638.5	639.6	639.7	639.4	639.5	631.4	630.6	624.9	615.6
Printing and related support activities	808.6	792.3	780.2	785.2	802.2	817.3	815.8	821.1	827.9	814.6
Petroleum and coal products	152.8	154.8	152.3	146.2	144.0	140.4	137.3	136.0	134.5	127.8
Chemicals	1 035.7	1 024.1	1 028.9	1 024.9	1 004.7	987.9	984.5	986.8	992.6	982.5
Plastics and rubber products	824.8	802.1	817.9	847.8	888.1	913.7	918.7	932.7	941.4	947.0
Service-Providing	85 764	85 787	86 631	88 625	91 517	94 142	96 299	98 890	101 576	104 528
Private Service-Providing	67 349	67 241	67 845	69 636	72 242	74 710	76 760	79 227	81 667	84 221
Trade, transportation, and utilities	22 666	22 281	22 125	22 378	23 128	23 834	24 239	24 700	25 186	25 771
Wholesale trade	5 268.4	5 185.3	5 109.7	5 093.2	5 247.3	5 433.1	5 522.0	5 663.9	5 795.2	5 892.5
Durable goods	2 833.7	2 766.6	2 698.8	2 687.0	2 786.0	2 908.8	2 977.8	3 071.9	3 162.4	3 219.6
Nondurable goods	1 900.2	1 891.3	1 891.5	1 888.3	1 927.0	1 969.3	1 977.5	2 007.9	2 032.7	2 061.1
Electronic markets, agents, and brokers	534.5	527.4	519.4	517.9	534.4	555.0	566.7	584.1	600.1	611.8

[1]Includes other industries, not shown separately.

Table 16-1. Nonfarm Employment by NAICS Sector and Industry—*Continued*

(Wage and salary workers on nonfarm payrolls, thousands.)

Industry	2000	2001	2002	2003	2004	2005	2006	2007	2008
TOTAL NONFARM	131 785	131 826	130 341	129 999	131 435	133 703	136 086	137 598	137 066
Total Private	110 995	110 708	108 828	108 416	109 814	111 899	114 113	115 380	114 566
Goods-Producing	24 649	23 873	22 557	21 816	21 882	22 190	22 531	22 233	21 419
Mining and logging	599	606	583	572	591	628	684	724	774
Logging	79.0	73.5	70.4	69.4	67.6	65.2	64.4	60.1	57.0
Mining	520.2	532.5	512.2	502.7	523.0	562.2	619.7	663.8	717.0
Oil and gas extraction	124.9	123.7	121.9	120.2	123.4	125.7	134.5	146.2	161.6
Mining, except oil and gas [1]	224.8	218.7	210.6	202.7	205.1	212.8	220.3	223.4	227.7
Coal mining	72.2	74.3	74.4	70.0	70.6	73.9	78.0	77.2	80.6
Support activities for mining	170.6	190.1	179.8	179.8	194.6	223.7	264.9	294.3	327.7
Construction	6 787	6 826	6 716	6 735	6 976	7 336	7 691	7 630	7 215
Construction of buildings	1 632.5	1 588.9	1 574.8	1 575.8	1 630.0	1 711.9	1 804.9	1 774.2	1 659.3
Heavy and civil engineering	937.0	953.0	930.6	903.1	907.4	951.2	985.1	1 005.4	970.2
Specialty trade contractors	4 217.0	4 283.9	4 210.4	4 255.7	4 438.6	4 673.1	4 901.1	4 850.2	4 585.3
Manufacturing	17 263	16 441	15 259	14 510	14 315	14 226	14 155	13 879	13 431
Durable goods	10 877	10 336	9 485	8 964	8 925	8 956	8 981	8 808	8 476
Wood products	613.0	574.1	554.9	537.6	549.6	559.2	558.8	515.3	459.6
Nonmetallic mineral products	554.2	544.5	516.0	494.2	505.5	505.3	509.6	500.5	468.1
Primary metals	621.8	570.9	509.4	477.4	466.8	466.0	464.0	455.8	443.3
Fabricated metal products	1 752.6	1 676.4	1 548.5	1 478.9	1 497.1	1 522.0	1 553.1	1 562.8	1 528.3
Machinery	1 457.0	1 370.6	1 231.8	1 151.6	1 145.2	1 165.5	1 183.2	1 187.1	1 185.6
Computer and electronic products [1]	1 820.0	1 748.8	1 507.2	1 355.2	1 322.8	1 316.4	1 307.5	1 272.5	1 247.6
Computer and peripheral equipment	301.9	286.2	250.0	224.0	210.0	205.1	196.2	186.2	182.8
Communications equipment	238.6	225.4	179.0	149.2	143.0	141.4	136.2	128.1	129.0
Semiconductors and electronic components	676.3	645.4	524.5	461.1	454.1	452.0	457.9	447.5	432.4
Electronic instruments	487.7	483.6	456.8	435.4	436.9	441.0	444.5	443.2	441.6
Electrical equipment and appliances	590.9	556.9	496.5	459.6	445.1	433.5	432.7	429.4	424.9
Transportation equipment [1]	2 057.1	1 939.1	1 830.0	1 775.1	1 766.7	1 772.3	1 768.9	1 711.9	1 606.5
Motor vehicles and parts	1 313.6	1 212.9	1 151.2	1 125.3	1 112.8	1 096.7	1 070.0	994.2	876.9
Furniture and related products	682.5	645.1	606.9	575.7	576.1	568.2	560.1	531.1	481.0
Miscellaneous manufacturing	728.0	709.5	683.3	658.3	650.6	647.2	643.7	641.7	630.8
Nondurable goods	6 386	6 105	5 774	5 546	5 390	5 271	5 174	5 071	4 955
Food manufacturing	1 553.1	1 551.2	1 525.7	1 517.5	1 493.7	1 477.6	1 479.4	1 484.1	1 484.8
Beverage and tobacco products	207.0	209.0	207.4	199.6	194.6	191.9	194.2	198.2	199.0
Textile mills	378.2	332.9	290.9	261.3	236.9	217.6	195.0	169.7	151.0
Textile product mills	229.6	217.0	204.2	187.7	183.2	176.4	166.7	157.7	147.5
Apparel	483.5	415.2	350.0	303.9	278.0	250.5	232.4	214.6	198.4
Leather and allied products	68.8	58.0	50.2	44.5	41.8	39.6	36.8	33.8	33.6
Paper and paper products	604.7	577.6	546.6	516.2	495.5	484.2	470.5	458.2	445.8
Printing and related support activities	806.8	768.4	706.6	680.5	662.6	646.3	634.4	622.1	594.1
Petroleum and coal products	123.2	121.1	118.1	114.3	111.7	112.1	113.2	114.5	117.1
Chemicals	980.4	959.0	927.5	906.1	887.0	872.1	865.9	860.9	849.8
Plastics and rubber products	950.9	896.2	846.8	814.3	804.7	802.3	785.5	757.2	734.2
Service-Providing	107 136	107 952	107 784	108 183	109 553	111 513	113 556	115 366	115 646
Private Service-Providing	86 346	86 834	86 271	86 600	87 932	89 709	91 582	93 147	93 146
Trade, transportation, and utilities	26 225	25 983	25 497	25 287	25 533	25 959	26 276	26 630	26 385
Wholesale trade	5 933.2	5 772.7	5 652.3	5 607.5	5 662.9	5 764.4	5 904.5	6 015.2	5 963.7
Durable goods	3 250.7	3 130.4	3 007.9	2 940.6	2 950.5	2 999.2	3 074.8	3 121.5	3 060.7
Nondurable goods	2 064.8	2 031.3	2 015.0	2 004.6	2 010.0	2 022.4	2 041.3	2 062.2	2 053.0
Electronic markets, agents, and brokers	617.7	611.1	629.4	662.2	702.4	742.8	788.5	831.5	850.1

[1]Includes other industries, not shown separately.

Table 16-1. Nonfarm Employment by NAICS Sector and Industry—*Continued*

(Wage and salary workers on nonfarm payrolls, thousands.)

Industry	2008, seasonally adjusted											
	January	February	March	April	May	June	July	August	September	October	November	December
TOTAL NONFARM	138 080	137 936	137 814	137 654	137 517	137 356	137 228	137 053	136 732	136 352	135 755	135 074
Total Private	115 689	115 515	115 373	115 203	115 029	114 834	114 691	114 497	114 197	113 813	113 212	112 542
Goods-Producing	21 981	21 887	21 800	21 679	21 612	21 507	21 432	21 351	21 247	21 063	20 814	20 532
Mining and logging	748	750	756	756	763	770	777	787	794	794	793	789
Logging	59.0	58.2	57.8	58.6	57.3	56.0	55.8	56.1	56.5	56.6	56.6	55.7
Mining	689.1	691.7	697.7	697.8	705.5	713.8	721.3	730.6	737.7	737.7	736.8	733.3
Oil and gas extraction	155.0	154.9	156.2	155.1	158.8	160.7	162.7	164.7	166.3	166.5	167.4	169.4
Mining, except oil and gas [1]	224.7	223.7	223.6	222.9	226.3	226.9	227.6	230.0	230.2	230.5	230.7	229.2
Coal mining	77.5	77.6	77.9	78.1	79.2	79.6	79.5	81.7	82.5	83.1	84.3	84.5
Support activities for mining	309.4	313.1	317.9	319.8	320.4	326.2	331.0	335.9	341.2	340.7	338.7	334.7
Construction	7 489	7 445	7 401	7 337	7 293	7 232	7 201	7 177	7 131	7 066	6 939	6 841
Construction of buildings	1 728.8	1 716.5	1 712.6	1 693.8	1 676.9	1 660.6	1 655.5	1 647.5	1 625.0	1 609.9	1 588.4	1 572.9
Heavy and civil engineering	1 001.7	997.3	993.6	980.5	982.1	972.2	970.9	966.1	960.2	952.6	942.5	933.2
Specialty trade contractors	4 758.4	4 731.4	4 694.5	4 662.3	4 633.6	4 598.7	4 574.6	4 563.1	4 545.4	4 503.9	4 408.5	4 335.2
Manufacturing	13 744	13 692	13 643	13 586	13 556	13 505	13 454	13 387	13 322	13 203	13 082	12 902
Durable goods	8 710	8 673	8 637	8 587	8 567	8 533	8 502	8 439	8 392	8 300	8 216	8 085
Wood products	492.7	486.2	479.8	477.3	468.3	462.9	458.4	451.9	446.4	438.8	429.8	416.2
Nonmetallic mineral products	487.5	484.2	479.4	477.2	473.0	469.7	466.4	464.5	460.2	458.2	450.1	441.2
Primary metals	452.0	450.8	450.9	449.7	447.9	446.6	444.8	440.8	441.1	438.6	429.8	419.6
Fabricated metal products	1 560.0	1 558.6	1 557.5	1 546.0	1 544.8	1 534.8	1 528.4	1 530.6	1 519.4	1 505.0	1 486.3	1 461.5
Machinery	1 192.3	1 190.5	1 193.8	1 193.1	1 192.2	1 190.8	1 191.1	1 187.5	1 183.1	1 179.3	1 162.7	1 150.2
Computer and electronic products [1]	1 258.9	1 254.7	1 257.9	1 255.7	1 252.8	1 248.5	1 247.3	1 248.3	1 246.5	1 239.8	1 233.3	1 223.7
Computer and peripheral equipment	183.5	184.0	183.8	184.0	183.6	182.1	182.5	182.6	182.8	182.4	181.8	180.0
Communications equipment	128.5	127.5	128.3	129.1	129.1	130.2	129.1	129.1	129.2	128.6	129.5	129.1
Semiconductors and electronic components	441.4	439.2	439.2	437.0	434.4	431.2	431.9	432.3	431.0	428.4	423.2	417.4
Electronic instruments	442.0	440.1	443.6	442.9	443.1	442.4	441.8	442.6	442.5	440.2	438.8	437.5
Electrical equipment and appliances	428.1	427.9	427.4	428.5	428.5	428.3	428.4	425.5	422.6	421.3	417.5	412.0
Transportation equipment [1]	1 686.2	1 676.7	1 653.8	1 632.1	1 636.6	1 634.3	1 625.7	1 584.5	1 572.6	1 531.3	1 532.5	1 501.8
Motor vehicles and parts	951.2	945.2	918.3	898.0	897.2	895.1	892.9	856.7	839.7	829.7	809.6	781.5
Furniture and related products	512.6	507.3	501.4	495.2	491.6	488.0	483.4	475.7	470.3	458.8	449.6	440.6
Miscellaneous manufacturing	639.6	636.4	635.2	632.5	631.4	629.0	627.9	630.1	629.4	628.5	624.2	618.4
Nondurable goods	5 034	5 019	5 006	4 999	4 989	4 972	4 952	4 948	4 930	4 903	4 866	4 817
Food manufacturing	1 489.5	1 489.7	1 485.7	1 483.2	1 483.1	1 482.1	1 478.1	1 482.7	1 484.3	1 484.7	1 489.0	1 477.6
Beverage and tobacco products	198.3	196.7	198.9	201.6	201.4	200.6	200.0	199.2	199.3	197.2	196.4	195.8
Textile mills	162.2	161.2	158.5	155.9	154.3	150.7	149.0	149.5	147.5	145.6	140.6	136.8
Textile product mills	152.1	150.7	151.0	150.1	149.1	147.1	146.2	145.2	145.5	144.5	143.5	141.2
Apparel	207.0	205.7	203.8	202.5	200.8	200.0	199.5	200.4	197.3	192.8	187.1	183.5
Leather and allied products	34.3	33.2	33.2	33.6	33.6	34.2	33.0	34.5	34.3	33.9	32.6	32.6
Paper and paper products	452.7	451.0	449.9	450.6	449.8	448.2	447.1	444.7	441.9	439.7	437.1	433.4
Printing and related support activities	614.8	608.2	607.4	605.6	601.2	594.8	591.5	591.5	587.6	582.3	574.1	567.0
Petroleum and coal products	115.8	116.4	116.3	115.9	117.1	117.6	118.1	118.0	117.9	117.8	117.2	116.9
Chemicals	857.2	855.8	854.0	854.1	854.2	852.8	850.0	847.3	844.3	843.4	842.6	837.1
Plastics and rubber products	750.0	750.1	747.3	745.5	744.3	743.4	739.3	734.7	729.7	721.1	705.9	694.9
Service-Providing	116 099	116 049	116 014	115 975	115 905	115 849	115 796	115 702	115 485	115 289	114 941	114 542
Private Service-Providing	93 708	93 628	93 573	93 524	93 417	93 327	93 259	93 146	92 950	92 750	92 398	92 010
Trade, transportation, and utilities	26 717	26 655	26 629	26 562	26 503	26 467	26 425	26 354	26 257	26 157	26 005	25 843
Wholesale trade	6 033.9	6 021.2	6 012.5	5 995.9	5 989.3	5 983.1	5 966.9	5 954.3	5 947.2	5 920.1	5 890.3	5 850.7
Durable goods	3 113.5	3 101.0	3 099.8	3 087.2	3 078.2	3 071.7	3 062.5	3 052.4	3 047.2	3 026.1	3 004.9	2 978.6
Nondurable goods	2 073.3	2 067.9	2 063.0	2 060.9	2 063.7	2 061.5	2 053.2	2 049.0	2 044.1	2 040.5	2 033.6	2 025.1
Electronic markets, agents, and brokers	847.1	852.3	849.7	847.8	847.4	849.9	851.2	852.9	855.9	853.5	851.8	847.0

[1]Includes other industries, not shown separately.

Table 16-1. Nonfarm Employment by NAICS Sector and Industry—*Continued*

(Wage and salary workers on nonfarm payrolls, thousands.)

Industry	1990	1991	1992	1993	1994	1995	1996	1997	1998	1999
Retail trade	13 182	12 896	12 828	13 021	13 491	13 897	14 143	14 389	14 609	14 970
Motor vehicle and parts dealers [1]	1 494.4	1 435.1	1 428.1	1 475.3	1 564.7	1 627.1	1 685.6	1 723.4	1 740.9	1 796.6
Automobile dealers	983.3	938.3	934.8	970.4	1 031.8	1 071.6	1 113.0	1 134.5	1 142.0	1 179.7
Furniture and home furnishings stores	431.5	412.8	410.3	418.6	441.6	461.2	474.2	484.7	499.1	524.4
Electronics and appliance stores	382.3	381.1	378.1	386.9	417.0	448.7	470.2	494.0	510.2	542.2
Building material and garden supply stores	890.9	863.0	872.1	891.9	946.2	981.8	1 007.2	1 043.1	1 062.3	1 101.0
Food and beverage stores	2 778.8	2 767.9	2 743.9	2 774.8	2 825.0	2 879.8	2 927.8	2 956.9	2 965.7	2 984.5
Health and personal care stores	792.0	788.5	780.2	778.6	797.0	811.9	826.4	853.3	876.0	898.2
Gasoline stations	910.2	889.3	876.4	881.2	902.3	922.3	946.4	956.2	961.3	943.5
Clothing and clothing accessories stores	1 313.0	1 275.8	1 249.1	1 259.9	1 261.7	1 246.3	1 220.6	1 235.9	1 268.6	1 306.6
Sporting goods, hobby, book, and music stores	532.0	527.7	534.4	545.2	577.6	605.8	614.0	626.2	635.4	664.3
General merchandise stores [1]	2 499.8	2 416.7	2 414.2	2 450.2	2 541.0	2 635.4	2 657.3	2 657.6	2 686.5	2 751.8
Department stores	1 493.9	1 440.8	1 445.2	1 486.8	1 560.4	1 629.8	1 645.0	1 653.5	1 679.2	1 709.2
Miscellaneous store retailers	738.2	734.7	736.8	752.9	795.7	841.1	874.3	913.2	950.3	985.5
Nonstore retailers	419.2	403.7	404.5	404.9	421.2	435.4	438.5	444.5	453.0	471.6
Transportation and warehousing	3 475.6	3 462.8	3 461.8	3 553.8	3 701.0	3 837.8	3 935.3	4 026.5	4 168.0	4 300.3
Air transportation	529.2	525.4	519.6	516.6	511.2	510.9	525.7	542.0	562.7	586.3
Rail transportation	271.8	255.6	248.1	242.2	234.6	232.5	225.2	221.0	225.0	228.8
Water transportation	56.8	57.4	56.7	52.8	52.3	50.8	51.0	50.7	50.5	51.7
Truck transportation	1 122.4	1 104.6	1 107.4	1 154.8	1 206.2	1 249.1	1 282.4	1 308.2	1 354.4	1 391.5
Transit and ground passenger transportation	274.2	283.9	287.9	299.9	316.6	327.9	339.1	349.6	362.7	371.0
Pipeline transportation	59.8	60.7	60.1	58.7	57.0	53.6	51.4	49.7	48.1	46.9
Scenic and sightseeing transportation	15.7	16.5	17.7	19.3	21.3	22.0	23.2	24.5	25.4	26.1
Support activities for transportation	364.1	376.6	369.9	381.8	404.7	430.4	445.8	473.4	496.8	518.1
Couriers and messengers	375.0	378.9	388.8	414.3	466.2	516.8	539.9	546.0	568.2	585.9
Warehousing and storage	406.6	403.2	405.6	413.4	431.0	443.8	451.8	461.5	474.2	494.1
Utilities	740.0	736.1	726.0	710.7	689.3	666.2	639.6	620.9	613.4	608.5
Information	2 688	2 677	2 641	2 668	2 738	2 843	2 940	3 084	3 218	3 419
Publishing industries, except Internet	870.6	863.4	854.2	873.1	891.0	910.7	927.2	955.5	982.3	1 004.8
Motion picture and sound recording industries	254.6	258.9	254.3	259.6	278.4	311.1	334.7	353.0	369.5	384.4
Broadcasting, except Internet	283.8	281.2	279.7	284.0	290.1	298.1	309.1	313.0	321.2	329.4
Internet publishing and broadcasting	29.4	28.3	28.2	28.7	29.7	33.7	39.6	45.4	53.9	78.1
Telecommunications	1 008.5	999.9	972.9	969.5	989.5	1 009.3	1 038.1	1 108.0	1 167.4	1 270.8
Data processing, hosting, and related services	211.4	212.8	219.6	223.4	226.9	242.6	252.0	268.4	282.8	307.1
Other information services	59.3	61.2	60.5	58.1	62.5	71.8	79.0	85.5	95.3	121.9
Financial activities	6 614	6 558	6 540	6 709	6 867	6 827	6 969	7 178	7 462	7 648
Finance and insurance	4 976.4	4 935.1	4 912.4	5 033.0	5 132.5	5 069.0	5 151.4	5 302.1	5 528.6	5 664.9
Monetary authorities–central bank	24.0	24.2	23.7	23.4	23.4	23.0	22.8	22.1	21.7	22.6
Credit intermediation and related activities [1]	2 424.8	2 352.4	2 317.3	2 360.7	2 375.7	2 314.4	2 368.2	2 433.6	2 531.9	2 591.0
Depository credit intermediation [1]	1 908.5	1 830.7	1 769.0	1 760.5	1 736.7	1 700.2	1 691.4	1 696.6	1 708.9	1 709.7
Commercial banking	1 361.8	1 333.7	1 302.8	1 308.7	1 297.4	1 281.7	1 275.1	1 277.9	1 286.0	1 281.2
Securities, commodity contracts, investments	457.9	455.0	475.7	507.9	553.4	562.2	589.6	636.1	692.2	737.3
Insurance carriers and related activities	2 016.1	2 048.2	2 039.5	2 082.5	2 118.8	2 108.2	2 108.0	2 143.6	2 209.4	2 236.1
Funds, trusts, and other financial vehicles	53.5	55.3	56.2	58.5	61.2	61.2	62.8	66.8	73.4	78.0
Real estate and rental and leasing	1 637.1	1 623.0	1 627.7	1 676.3	1 734.2	1 758.1	1 817.1	1 875.9	1 933.7	1 982.5
Real estate	1 109.0	1 109.8	1 116.7	1 148.6	1 185.9	1 181.7	1 208.6	1 243.8	1 277.7	1 302.6
Rental and leasing services	514.2	499.4	496.4	511.0	529.9	557.4	587.7	609.5	630.8	653.1
Lessors of nonfinancial intangible assets	13.9	13.9	14.6	16.7	18.4	19.0	20.8	22.6	25.3	26.8

[1]Includes other industries, not shown separately.

Table 16-1. Nonfarm Employment by NAICS Sector and Industry—*Continued*

(Wage and salary workers on nonfarm payrolls, thousands.)

Industry	2000	2001	2002	2003	2004	2005	2006	2007	2008
Retail trade	15 280	15 239	15 025	14 917	15 058	15 280	15 353	15 520	15 356
Motor vehicle and parts dealers [1]	1 846.9	1 854.6	1 879.4	1 882.9	1 902.3	1 918.6	1 909.7	1 908.3	1 844.5
Automobile dealers	1 216.5	1 225.1	1 252.8	1 254.4	1 257.3	1 261.4	1 246.7	1 242.2	1 186.0
Furniture and home furnishings stores	543.5	541.2	538.7	547.3	563.4	576.1	586.9	574.6	542.8
Electronics and appliance stores	564.4	554.5	525.3	512.2	516.2	535.8	541.1	549.4	549.6
Building material and garden supply stores	1 142.1	1 151.8	1 176.5	1 185.0	1 227.1	1 276.1	1 324.1	1 309.3	1 253.1
Food and beverage stores	2 993.0	2 950.5	2 881.6	2 838.4	2 821.6	2 817.8	2 821.1	2 843.6	2 858.4
Health and personal care stores	927.6	951.5	938.8	938.1	941.1	953.7	961.1	993.1	1 002.4
Gasoline stations	935.7	925.3	895.9	882.0	875.6	871.1	864.1	861.5	843.4
Clothing and clothing accessories stores	1 321.6	1 321.1	1 312.5	1 304.5	1 364.3	1 414.6	1 450.9	1 500.0	1 484.2
Sporting goods, hobby, book, and music stores	685.7	679.2	661.3	646.5	641.3	647.0	645.5	656.3	646.7
General merchandise stores [1]	2 819.8	2 842.2	2 812.0	2 822.4	2 863.1	2 934.3	2 935.0	3 020.6	3 047.1
Department stores	1 755.0	1 768.3	1 684.0	1 620.6	1 605.3	1 595.1	1 557.2	1 591.5	1 557.0
Miscellaneous store retailers	1 007.1	993.3	959.5	930.7	913.5	899.9	881.0	865.4	847.8
Nonstore retailers	492.4	473.5	443.7	427.3	428.8	434.6	432.8	437.9	436.3
Transportation and warehousing	4 410.3	4 372.0	4 223.6	4 185.4	4 248.6	4 360.9	4 469.6	4 540.9	4 505.0
Air transportation	614.4	615.3	563.5	528.3	514.5	500.8	487.0	491.8	492.6
Rail transportation	231.7	226.7	217.8	217.7	225.7	227.8	227.5	233.7	229.5
Water transportation	56.0	54.0	52.6	54.5	56.4	60.6	62.7	65.5	65.2
Truck transportation	1 405.8	1 386.8	1 339.3	1 325.6	1 351.7	1 397.6	1 435.8	1 439.2	1 391.1
Transit and ground passenger transportation	372.1	374.8	380.8	382.2	384.9	389.2	399.3	412.1	418.1
Pipeline transportation	46.0	45.4	41.7	40.2	38.4	37.8	38.7	39.9	42.0
Scenic and sightseeing transportation	27.5	29.1	25.6	26.6	27.2	28.8	27.5	28.6	28.0
Support activities for transportation	537.4	539.2	524.7	520.3	535.1	552.2	570.6	584.2	589.9
Couriers and messengers	605.0	587.0	560.9	561.7	556.6	571.4	582.4	580.7	575.9
Warehousing and storage	514.4	513.8	516.7	528.3	558.1	594.7	638.1	665.2	672.8
Utilities	601.3	599.4	596.2	577.0	563.8	554.0	548.5	553.4	559.5
Information	3 630	3 629	3 395	3 188	3 118	3 061	3 038	3 032	2 997
Publishing industries, except Internet	1 035.0	1 020.7	964.1	924.8	909.1	904.1	902.4	901.2	882.6
Motion picture and sound recording industries	382.6	376.8	387.9	376.2	385.0	377.5	375.7	380.6	381.6
Broadcasting, except Internet	343.5	344.6	334.1	324.3	325.0	327.7	328.3	325.2	315.9
Internet publishing and broadcasting	110.8	100.4	76.3	67.2	66.1	67.2	69.1	72.9	80.3
Telecommunications	1 396.6	1 423.9	1 280.9	1 166.8	1 115.1	1 071.3	1 047.6	1 030.6	1 021.4
Data processing, hosting, and related services	315.7	316.8	303.9	280.0	267.1	262.5	263.2	267.8	261.6
Other information services	157.1	146.5	123.6	115.9	116.9	117.7	120.8	126.3	133.6
Financial activities	7 687	7 808	7 847	7 977	8 031	8 153	8 328	8 301	8 146
Finance and insurance	5 676.7	5 769.2	5 813.6	5 919.1	5 945.3	6 018.9	6 156.0	6 132.0	6 015.2
Monetary authorities–central bank	22.8	23.0	23.4	22.6	21.8	20.8	21.2	21.6	22.2
Credit intermediation and related activities [1]	2 547.8	2 597.7	2 686.0	2 792.4	2 817.0	2 869.0	2 924.9	2 866.3	2 735.8
Depository credit intermediation [1]	1 681.2	1 701.2	1 733.0	1 748.5	1 751.5	1 769.2	1 802.0	1 823.5	1 819.5
Commercial banking	1 250.5	1 258.4	1 278.1	1 280.1	1 280.8	1 296.0	1 322.9	1 351.4	1 359.9
Securities, commodity contracts, investments	804.5	830.5	789.4	757.7	766.1	786.1	818.3	848.6	858.1
Insurance carriers and related activities	2 220.6	2 233.7	2 233.2	2 266.0	2 258.6	2 259.3	2 303.7	2 306.8	2 308.8
Funds, trusts, and other financial vehicles	81.1	84.4	81.7	80.4	81.7	83.7	87.9	88.7	90.3
Real estate and rental and leasing	2 010.6	2 038.4	2 033.3	2 057.5	2 085.5	2 133.5	2 172.5	2 169.1	2 130.2
Real estate	1 316.0	1 343.4	1 356.6	1 387.1	1 418.7	1 460.8	1 499.0	1 500.4	1 481.1
Rental and leasing services	666.8	666.3	649.1	643.1	641.1	645.8	645.5	640.3	620.9
Lessors of nonfinancial intangible assets	27.8	28.7	27.6	27.3	25.7	26.9	28.1	28.4	28.2

[1] Includes other industries, not shown separately.

Table 16-1. Nonfarm Employment by NAICS Sector and Industry—*Continued*

(Wage and salary workers on nonfarm payrolls, thousands.)

Industry	2008, seasonally adjusted											
	January	February	March	April	May	June	July	August	September	October	November	December
Retail trade	15 572	15 526	15 506	15 458	15 420	15 404	15 380	15 334	15 278	15 217	15 126	15 038
Motor vehicle and parts dealers [1]	1 901.2	1 894.6	1 890.9	1 885.1	1 877.4	1 866.2	1 851.4	1 832.6	1 818.4	1 792.7	1 770.5	1 745.6
Automobile dealers	1 238.4	1 229.8	1 227.6	1 220.9	1 214.6	1 204.7	1 191.5	1 176.2	1 164.8	1 141.7	1 121.2	1 099.9
Furniture and home furnishings stores	564.7	558.5	550.4	549.5	547.6	546.5	545.8	542.3	538.4	532.4	522.6	514.2
Electronics and appliance stores	551.0	551.2	552.9	554.5	555.0	552.9	553.0	551.0	547.1	545.1	541.5	538.6
Building material and garden supply stores	1 277.5	1 271.9	1 264.9	1 254.5	1 256.0	1 252.2	1 244.1	1 245.9	1 248.4	1 245.9	1 235.8	1 227.8
Food and beverage stores	2 870.3	2 872.0	2 874.7	2 866.7	2 864.0	2 863.2	2 863.4	2 853.8	2 846.5	2 851.9	2 843.5	2 835.1
Health and personal care stores	1 013.0	1 006.7	1 007.7	1 006.9	1 004.8	1 003.6	1 005.4	999.0	998.9	995.9	989.4	991.2
Gasoline stations	853.4	854.6	854.2	848.5	838.1	845.8	843.0	840.9	834.8	836.1	836.9	834.4
Clothing and clothing accessories stores	1 500.3	1 497.7	1 498.2	1 495.0	1 490.9	1 487.2	1 483.6	1 483.3	1 478.5	1 471.5	1 462.2	1 448.5
Sporting goods, hobby, book, and music stores	666.2	660.0	653.8	646.2	649.2	646.9	642.2	645.8	641.6	641.2	633.1	624.3
General merchandise stores [1]	3 067.8	3 058.1	3 060.7	3 052.9	3 043.2	3 052	3 062.3	3 058.2	3 045.8	3 025.5	3 024.5	3 029.2
Department stores	1 602.8	1 588.2	1 583.5	1 576.4	1 564.0	1 561.8	1 563.2	1 554.4	1 541.9	1 523.9	1 517.5	1 521.2
Miscellaneous store retailers	863.5	857.0	854.5	855.0	851.8	849.4	848.3	845.6	844.3	845.0	838.3	825.0
Nonstore retailers	442.8	443.8	443.1	442.8	441.9	438.5	437.7	436.1	435.5	433.6	427.7	424.0
Transportation and warehousing	4 554.4	4 551.6	4 553.4	4 551.7	4 536.3	4 521.1	4 518.0	4 506.0	4 471.3	4 456.9	4 424.4	4 389.9
Air transportation	503.5	506.2	505.4	501.9	498.3	494.9	492.9	488.1	483.2	482.1	481.6	477.8
Rail transportation	231.7	231.4	231.4	231.1	230.3	227.1	230.1	228.8	227.6	229.5	229.0	226.8
Water transportation	67.6	66.7	66.0	66.2	65.8	66.1	66.4	64.9	64.5	63.9	62.6	60.3
Truck transportation	1 418.4	1 411.9	1 414.6	1 410.4	1 405.1	1 393.1	1 391.2	1 390.3	1 378.1	1 370.3	1 358.0	1 340.8
Transit and ground passenger transportation	419.1	419.9	420.0	423.0	418.8	421.9	420.8	422.7	414.4	413.8	411.7	410.1
Pipeline transportation	40.3	40.6	40.8	40.9	41.7	42.3	42.7	42.5	43.1	43.3	43.2	43.3
Scenic and sightseeing transportation	29.0	28.9	28.7	28.4	28.1	28.1	27.6	27.3	27.1	27.1	27.2	27.2
Support activities for transportation	589.9	590.9	591.2	593.0	591.5	590.9	592.8	592.1	589.5	588.0	582.2	579.5
Couriers and messengers	581.5	581.2	577.5	577.8	578.9	579.2	577.7	575.7	572.9	570.5	565.7	564.6
Warehousing and storage	673.4	673.9	677.8	679.0	677.8	677.5	675.8	673.6	670.9	668.4	663.2	659.5
Utilities	556.8	556.4	557.4	557.1	557.0	558.2	559.7	559.3	560.5	562.8	564.0	564.6
Information	3 022	3 025	3 023	3 017	3 013	3 006	2 995	2 990	2 986	2 982	2 965	2 940
Publishing industries, except Internet	897.6	895.7	893.3	893.2	890.4	886.8	882.9	879.4	876.6	872.6	863.6	857.8
Motion picture and sound recording industries	374.6	381.9	385.2	384.5	383.3	383.5	380.1	380.0	381.7	388.7	385.0	377.2
Broadcasting, except Internet	320.2	319.3	319.0	317.3	317.7	315.7	315.9	313.8	313.0	312.9	313.1	308.1
Internet publishing and broadcasting	77.3	79.4	80.1	79.7	79.1	80.2	81.1	81.1	80.7	81.1	81.4	82.7
Telecommunications	1 032.1	1 029.3	1 028.0	1 025.5	1 025.3	1 025.5	1 022.8	1 023.1	1 021.6	1 014.5	1 010.2	1 004.0
Data processing, hosting, and related services	265.7	265.6	263.4	263.2	263.3	261.8	260.5	259.8	259.6	258.9	257.5	256.4
Other information services	131.7	133.1	134.2	132.9	132.5	132.2	133.0	133.6	133.6	134.1	135.1	136.5
Financial activities	8 229	8 211	8 204	8 190	8 179	8 162	8 154	8 141	8 115	8 088	8 043	8 010
Finance and insurance	6 069.8	6 059.3	6 055.8	6 050.8	6 039.7	6 026.1	6 019.9	6 010.6	5 994.3	5 978.7	5 948.7	5 924.0
Monetary authorities–central bank	22.1	22.3	22.4	22.7	22.5	22.3	22.3	22.3	22.3	22.1	21.5	21.3
Credit intermediation and related activities [1]	2 784.8	2 775.6	2 763.3	2 756.6	2 746.7	2 738.5	2 730.9	2 724.4	2 722.4	2 706.4	2 692.8	2 680.8
Depository credit intermediation [1]	1 825.4	1 826.3	1 824.9	1 827.9	1 824.8	1 822.2	1 820.0	1 818.4	1 814.8	1 811.1	1 806.9	1 804.9
Commercial banking	1 359.5	1 362.0	1 362.0	1 363.4	1 363.0	1 362.1	1 361.1	1 360.1	1 359.0	1 356.0	1 352.7	1 351.8
Securities, commodity contracts, investments	861.5	864.4	867.5	867.4	865.8	864.4	860.4	861.4	851.4	847.8	842.1	839.9
Insurance carriers and related activities	2 311.6	2 307.2	2 313.3	2 313.4	2 314.7	2 310.6	2 316.1	2 312.0	2 307.6	2 311.0	2 300.9	2 292.0
Funds, trusts, and other financial vehicles	89.8	89.8	89.3	90.7	90.0	90.3	90.2	90.5	90.6	91.4	91.4	90.0
Real estate and rental and leasing	2 159.4	2 151.3	2 148.5	2 139.6	2 138.9	2 135.9	2 134.4	2 130.0	2 120.6	2 109.0	2 093.8	2 085.8
Real estate	1 494.9	1 491.2	1 489.4	1 486.9	1 486.2	1 485.5	1 481.5	1 482.4	1 474.5	1 471.2	1 461.7	1 458.2
Rental and leasing services	636.1	631.7	630.6	624.3	624.8	622.5	624.4	619.4	617.7	609.7	603.8	599.3
Lessors of nonfinancial intangible assets	28.4	28.4	28.5	28.4	27.9	27.9	28.5	28.2	28.4	28.1	28.3	28.3

[1] Includes other industries, not shown separately.

Table 16-1. Nonfarm Employment by NAICS Sector and Industry—*Continued*

(Wage and salary workers on nonfarm payrolls, thousands.)

Industry	1990	1991	1992	1993	1994	1995	1996	1997	1998	1999
Professional and business services	10 848	10 714	10 970	11 495	12 174	12 844	13 462	14 335	15 147	15 957
Professional and technical services [1]	4 538.2	4 509.2	4 575.6	4 689.1	4 823.3	5 078.4	5 312.7	5 628.8	5 992.3	6 345.4
Legal services	943.6	946.0	949.8	963.9	965.6	959.2	968.4	987.5	1 021.1	1 051.4
Accounting and bookkeeping services	664.1	655.4	657.8	654.2	670.1	706.3	729.8	761.2	802.0	837.6
Architectural and engineering services	941.5	906.2	901.8	922.7	952.0	997.1	1 024.5	1 063.4	1 114.8	1 168.1
Computer systems design and related services	409.7	419.9	444.9	484.8	531.4	611.2	701.4	826.7	974.9	1 132.9
Management and technical consulting services	305.1	314.3	340.2	366.2	396.5	451.8	492.7	541.7	590.4	619.0
Management of companies and enterprises	1 667.4	1 638.1	1 623.4	1 640.1	1 665.9	1 685.8	1 702.7	1 729.7	1 756.1	1 773.8
Administrative and waste services	4 642.8	4 566.6	4 770.5	5 165.6	5 684.4	6 079.7	6 446.5	6 976.6	7 398.0	7 837.5
Administrative and support services [1]	4 413.3	4 334.3	4 533.8	4 917.0	5 423.7	5 806.4	6 164.5	6 686.0	7 098.7	7 527.0
Employment services [1]	1 512.1	1 466.0	1 610.4	1 884.3	2 246.8	2 448.1	2 625.3	2 953.9	3 245.8	3 581.6
Temporary help services	1 155.8	1 123.3	1 212.5	1 388.8	1 632.2	1 743.8	1 849.0	2 059.7	2 245.2	2 469.6
Business support services	504.6	503.3	524.5	549.0	574.4	629.8	678.3	733.9	772.2	780.5
Services to buildings and dwellings	1 174.6	1 150.9	1 159.7	1 197.9	1 267.2	1 302.4	1 361.5	1 424.1	1 460.0	1 534.7
Waste management and remediation services	229.4	232.4	236.7	248.6	260.7	273.3	282.0	290.5	299.3	310.5
Education and health services	10 984	11 506	11 891	12 303	12 807	13 289	13 683	14 087	14 446	14 798
Educational services	1 688.0	1 736.6	1 713.1	1 755.4	1 894.9	2 010.2	2 077.6	2 155.0	2 232.9	2 320.4
Health care and social assistance	9 295.8	9 769.8	10 178.0	10 548.1	10 911.7	11 278.4	11 604.9	11 932.2	12 213.5	12 477.1
Health care	8 210.7	8 617.7	8 954.8	9 253.6	9 529.7	9 808.9	10 092.6	10 358.0	10 540.9	10 690.9
Ambulatory health care services [1]	2 841.6	3 028.4	3 199.9	3 385.5	3 578.8	3 767.5	3 939.9	4 093.0	4 161.2	4 226.6
Offices of physicians	1 278.0	1 345.2	1 401.1	1 442.0	1 480.9	1 540.4	1 603.8	1 660.5	1 723.6	1 786.6
Outpatient care centers	260.5	271.4	286.5	303.1	314.5	328.8	340.2	352.1	363.3	375.4
Home health care services	287.5	340.7	393.4	463.8	553.2	621.8	667.2	702.8	659.5	629.6
Hospitals	3 512.6	3 617.3	3 711.4	3 740.0	3 724.0	3 733.7	3 772.8	3 821.6	3 892.4	3 935.5
Nursing and residential care facilities [1]	1 856.4	1 972.0	2 043.5	2 128.1	2 227.0	2 307.7	2 379.9	2 443.4	2 487.3	2 528.8
Nursing care facilities	1 169.8	1 240.2	1 273.4	1 319.3	1 377.1	1 413.0	1 448.4	1 474.6	1 489.3	1 501.0
Social assistance [1]	1 085.1	1 152.2	1 223.3	1 294.4	1 381.9	1 469.5	1 512.3	1 574.2	1 672.6	1 786.2
Child day care services	387.8	413.2	446.5	468.9	510.0	557.1	559.2	570.4	615.1	673.7
Leisure and hospitality	9 288	9 256	9 437	9 732	10 100	10 501	10 777	11 018	11 232	11 543
Arts, entertainment, and recreation	1 132.0	1 177.0	1 236.3	1 301.9	1 375.6	1 459.4	1 522.1	1 599.9	1 645.2	1 709.1
Performing arts and spectator sports	273.0	283.0	290.0	287.0	296.0	308.0	329.0	350.0	350.0	361.0
Museums, historical sites, zoos, and parks	68.0	71.0	75.0	78.3	81.8	83.9	88.9	93.8	97.4	103.1
Amusements, gambling, and recreation	791.3	823.4	871.8	936.8	997.7	1 067.8	1 104.5	1 156.5	1 197.9	1 244.9
Accommodation and food services	8 155.6	8 078.9	8 200.5	8 430.4	8 724.1	9 041.6	9 254.3	9 417.9	9 586.2	9 833.7
Accommodation	1 616.0	1 574.3	1 561.5	1 580.5	1 615.3	1 652.5	1 698.9	1 729.5	1 773.5	1 831.7
Food services and drinking places	6 539.6	6 504.6	6 639.0	6 849.9	7 108.7	7 389.1	7 555.4	7 688.5	7 812.7	8 002.0
Other services	4 261	4 249	4 240	4 350	4 428	4 572	4 690	4 825	4 976	5 087
Repair and maintenance	1 009.0	960.0	964.0	998.0	1 023.5	1 078.9	1 135.5	1 169.3	1 189.2	1 222.0
Personal and laundry services	1 119.9	1 109.2	1 098.9	1 116.0	1 120.3	1 143.9	1 165.7	1 180.4	1 205.6	1 220.3
Membership associations and organizations	2 132.2	2 179.5	2 177.1	2 236.4	2 284.5	2 348.9	2 389.1	2 474.9	2 581.3	2 644.4
Government	18 415	18 545	18 787	18 989	19 275	19 432	19 539	19 664	19 909	20 307
Federal	3 196	3 110	3 111	3 063	3 018	2 949	2 877	2 806	2 772	2 769
Federal, except U.S. Postal Service	2 370.5	2 296.2	2 310.7	2 269.4	2 197.2	2 098.8	2 009.8	1 940.2	1 891.3	1 879.5
U.S. Postal Service	825.1	813.2	800.0	793.2	820.6	849.9	867.2	866.0	880.5	889.7
State government	4 305	4 355	4 408	4 488	4 576	4 635	4 606	4 582	4 612	4 709
State government education	1 729.9	1 767.6	1 798.6	1 834.1	1 881.9	1 919.0	1 910.7	1 904.0	1 922.2	1 983.2
State government, excluding education	2 574.6	2 587.3	2 609.7	2 653.8	2 693.6	2 715.5	2 695.1	2 677.9	2 690.2	2 725.6
Local government	10 914	11 081	11 267	11 438	11 682	11 849	12 056	12 276	12 525	12 829
Local government education	5 902.1	5 994.1	6 075.9	6 206.3	6 329.4	6 453.1	6 592.3	6 758.5	6 920.9	7 120.4
Local government, excluding education	5 012.4	5 086.9	5 191.6	5 231.9	5 352.2	5 396.0	5 464.1	5 516.9	5 603.9	5 708.6

[1]Includes other industries, not shown separately.

Table 16-1. Nonfarm Employment by NAICS Sector and Industry—*Continued*

(Wage and salary workers on nonfarm payrolls, thousands.)

Industry	2000	2001	2002	2003	2004	2005	2006	2007	2008
Professional and business services	16 666	16 476	15 976	15 987	16 394	16 954	17 566	17 942	17 778
Professional and technical services [1]	6 701.7	6 871.1	6 648.8	6 602.7	6 747.1	7 024.6	7 356.7	7 659.5	7 829.7
Legal services	1 065.7	1 091.3	1 115.3	1 142.1	1 163.1	1 168.0	1 173.2	1 175.4	1 163.7
Accounting and bookkeeping services	866.4	872.2	837.3	815.3	805.9	849.3	889.0	935.9	950.1
Architectural and engineering services	1 237.9	1 274.7	1 246.1	1 226.9	1 258.2	1 310.9	1 385.7	1 432.2	1 444.8
Computer systems design and related services	1 254.3	1 297.8	1 152.8	1 116.6	1 148.6	1 195.2	1 284.6	1 372.1	1 450.3
Management and technical consulting services	672.7	715.1	707.7	718.0	763.0	824.2	886.4	952.7	1 008.9
Management of companies and enterprises	1 796.0	1 779.0	1 705.4	1 687.2	1 724.4	1 758.9	1 810.9	1 866.4	1 894.6
Administrative and waste services	8 168.3	7 826.0	7 621.9	7 696.8	7 922.9	8 170.2	8 398.3	8 416.3	8 053.7
Administrative and support services [1]	7 855.4	7 508.7	7 303.6	7 374.7	7 594.4	7 832.5	8 050.2	8 061.3	7 693.5
Employment services [1]	3 849.3	3 468.2	3 273.2	3 326.4	3 455.5	3 606.9	3 680.9	3 545.9	3 144.4
Temporary help services	2 635.6	2 337.7	2 193.7	2 224.2	2 387.2	2 549.4	2 637.4	2 597.4	2 342.6
Business support services	786.7	779.7	756.6	749.7	757.8	766.4	792.9	817.4	823.2
Services to buildings and dwellings	1 570.5	1 606.2	1 606.1	1 636.1	1 693.7	1 737.5	1 801.4	1 849.5	1 847.0
Waste management and remediation services	312.9	317.3	318.3	322.1	328.6	337.6	348.1	355.0	360.2
Education and health services	15 109	15 645	16 199	16 588	16 953	17 372	17 826	18 322	18 855
Educational services	2 390.4	2 510.6	2 642.8	2 695.1	2 762.5	2 835.8	2 900.9	2 941.4	3 036.6
Health care and social assistance	12 718.0	13 134.0	13 555.7	13 892.6	14 190.2	14 536.3	14 925.3	15 380.2	15 818.5
Health care	10 857.8	11 188.1	11 536.0	11 817.1	12 055.3	12 313.9	12 601.8	12 946.8	13 309.8
Ambulatory health care services [1]	4 320.3	4 461.5	4 633.2	4 786.4	4 952.3	5 113.5	5 285.8	5 473.5	5 660.7
Offices of physicians	1 839.9	1 911.2	1 967.8	2 002.5	2 047.8	2 093.5	2 147.8	2 201.6	2 265.7
Outpatient care centers	386.4	399.7	413.0	426.8	450.5	473.2	492.6	512.0	532.5
Home health care services	633.3	638.6	679.8	732.6	776.6	821.0	865.6	913.8	958.0
Hospitals	3 954.3	4 050.9	4 159.6	4 244.6	4 284.7	4 345.4	4 423.4	4 515.0	4 641.1
Nursing and residential care facilities [1]	2 583.2	2 675.8	2 743.3	2 786.2	2 818.4	2 855.0	2 892.5	2 958.3	3 008.1
Nursing care facilities	1 513.6	1 546.8	1 573.2	1 579.8	1 576.9	1 577.4	1 581.4	1 602.6	1 613.7
Social assistance [1]	1 860.2	1 945.9	2 019.7	2 075.4	2 134.8	2 222.3	2 323.5	2 433.4	2 508.7
Child day care services	695.8	714.6	744.1	755.3	764.7	789.7	818.3	850.4	859.2
Leisure and hospitality	11 862	12 036	11 986	12 173	12 493	12 816	13 110	13 427	13 459
Arts, entertainment, and recreation	1 787.9	1 824.4	1 782.6	1 812.9	1 849.6	1 892.3	1 928.5	1 969.2	1 969.3
Performing arts and spectator sports	382.0	382.0	364.0	372.0	368.0	376.0	399.0	405.0	406.0
Museums, historical sites, zoos, and parks	110.4	115.0	114.0	114.7	118.3	120.7	123.8	130.3	131.8
Amusements, gambling, and recreation	1 295.7	1 327.1	1 305.0	1 326.5	1 363.8	1 395.3	1 406.3	1 433.9	1 431.2
Accommodation and food services	10 073.5	10 211.3	10 203.2	10 359.8	10 643.2	10 923.0	11 181.1	11 457.4	11 489.3
Accommodation	1 884.4	1 852.2	1 778.6	1 775.4	1 789.5	1 818.6	1 832.1	1 866.9	1 857.3
Food services and drinking places	8 189.1	8 359.1	8 424.6	8 584.4	8 853.7	9 104.4	9 349.0	9 590.4	9 632.0
Other services	5 168	5 258	5 372	5 401	5 409	5 395	5 438	5 494	5 528
Repair and maintenance	1 241.5	1 256.5	1 246.9	1 233.6	1 228.8	1 236.0	1 248.5	1 253.4	1 228.2
Personal and laundry services	1 242.9	1 255.0	1 257.2	1 263.5	1 272.9	1 276.6	1 288.4	1 309.7	1 326.6
Membership associations and organizations	2 683.3	2 746.4	2 867.8	2 903.6	2 907.5	2 882.2	2 901.2	2 931.1	2 973.3
Government	20 790	21 118	21 513	21 583	21 621	21 804	21 974	22 218	22 500
Federal	2 865	2 764	2 766	2 761	2 730	2 732	2 732	2 734	2 764
Federal, except U.S. Postal Service	1 984.8	1 891.0	1 923.8	1 952.4	1 947.5	1 957.3	1 962.6	1 964.7	2 016.8
U.S. Postal Service	879.7	873.0	842.4	808.6	782.1	774.2	769.7	769.1	747.5
State government	4 786	4 905	5 029	5 002	4 982	5 032	5 075	5 122	5 178
State government education	2 030.6	2 112.9	2 242.8	2 254.7	2 238.1	2 259.9	2 292.5	2 317.5	2 359.0
State government, excluding education	2 755.9	2 791.8	2 786.3	2 747.6	2 743.9	2 771.6	2 782.0	2 804.3	2 818.9
Local government	13 139	13 449	13 718	13 820	13 909	14 041	14 167	14 362	14 557
Local government education	7 293.9	7 479.3	7 654.4	7 709.4	7 765.2	7 856.1	7 913.0	7 986.8	8 075.6
Local government, excluding education	5 844.6	5 970.0	6 063.2	6 110.2	6 144.1	6 184.6	6 253.8	6 375.5	6 481.8

[1]Includes other industries, not shown separately.

Table 16-1. Nonfarm Employment by NAICS Sector and Industry—*Continued*

(Wage and salary workers on nonfarm payrolls, thousands.)

Industry	2008, seasonally adjusted											
	January	February	March	April	May	June	July	August	September	October	November	December
Professional and business services	18 069	18 018	17 954	17 950	17 887	17 824	17 788	17 727	17 675	17 612	17 488	17 356
Professional and technical services [1]	7 819.7	7 823.1	7 818.8	7 833.7	7 821.5	7 828.9	7 833.6	7 833.0	7 834.4	7 844.0	7 827.7	7 797.2
Legal services	1 169.8	1 171.2	1 168.8	1 166.6	1 165.2	1 164.5	1 163.0	1 161.0	1 160.2	1 160.2	1 157.7	1 156.8
Accounting and bookkeeping services	965.9	958.7	948.8	954.1	944.9	948.3	947.5	947.9	945.6	946.4	941.0	933.7
Architectural and engineering services	1 452.0	1 453.6	1 450.9	1 451.7	1 449.3	1 450.5	1 449.2	1 447.2	1 441.4	1 437.1	1 428.6	1 419.4
Computer systems design and related services	1 425.7	1 429.9	1 432.4	1 441.7	1 445.8	1 446.2	1 456.2	1 460.6	1 461.6	1 466.1	1 467.9	1 466.8
Management and technical consulting services	990.8	993.1	997.1	999.2	1 002.3	1 010.1	1 011.3	1 011.6	1 021.0	1 022.9	1 024.9	1 020.5
Management of companies and enterprises	1 903.5	1 905.9	1 906.7	1 903.8	1 902.1	1 900.6	1 895.3	1 895.2	1 887.1	1 882.8	1 882.0	1 872.1
Administrative and waste services	8 345.5	8 289.3	8 228.2	8 212.0	8 163.3	8 094.9	8 058.6	7 998.6	7 953.2	7 884.8	7 778.3	7 686.3
Administrative and support services [1]	7 985.1	7 933.2	7 870.7	7 853.6	7 804.4	7 736.4	7 699.3	7 637.0	7 591.9	7 522.0	7 414.2	7 324.4
Employment services [1]	3 420.3	3 370.7	3 304.7	3 285.6	3 242.7	3 184.0	3 146.9	3 089.5	3 049.8	2 987.7	2 896.7	2 829.5
Temporary help services	2 558.5	2 520.3	2 486.8	2 464.0	2 426.7	2 383.5	2 349.1	2 301.1	2 264.2	2 218.9	2 128.5	2 055.6
Business support services	828.1	829.9	831.1	828.4	822.6	818.1	817.4	814.9	818.1	820.8	823.7	816.0
Services to buildings and dwellings	1 859.4	1 858.0	1 853.7	1 853.8	1 853.5	1 851.4	1 848.6	1 847.0	1 843.3	1 837.4	1 829.4	1 818.1
Waste management and remediation services	360.4	356.1	357.5	358.4	358.9	358.5	359.3	361.6	361.3	362.8	364.1	361.9
Education and health services	18 613	18 657	18 698	18 752	18 798	18 843	18 888	18 950	18 957	18 981	19 044	19 080
Educational services	2 990.7	3 000.1	3 006.5	3 017.4	3 025.4	3 049.2	3 062.4	3 083.7	3 055.1	3 047.3	3 066.0	3 063.1
Health care and social assistance	15 622.6	15 657.0	15 691.1	15 734.1	15 772.3	15 794.1	15 825.9	15 865.9	15 901.9	15 934.1	15 977.8	16 017.0
Health care	13 139.8	13 171.7	13 199.7	13 239.1	13 268.3	13 291.7	13 329.4	13 354.4	13 376.0	13 401.2	13 442.4	13 475.9
Ambulatory health care services [1]	5 575.0	5 588.9	5 599.3	5 622.6	5 634.9	5 652.0	5 676.3	5 683.8	5 699.5	5 706.1	5 727.7	5 742.6
Offices of physicians	2 234.7	2 241.2	2 243.7	2 251.8	2 256.8	2 264.6	2 272.7	2 272.7	2 279.0	2 283.3	2 289.8	2 294.5
Outpatient care centers	524.9	526.4	527.5	530.4	531.5	531.2	535.4	537.2	534.8	536.6	536.9	536.7
Home health care services	937.4	940.6	943.3	948.7	951.8	955.3	961.1	963.4	966.8	968.6	975.6	980.7
Hospitals	4 574.0	4 587.5	4 599.1	4 610.4	4 627.2	4 634.0	4 646.8	4 660.7	4 668.9	4 681.9	4 692.4	4 703.7
Nursing and residential care facilities [1]	2 990.8	2 995.3	3 001.3	3 006.1	3 006.2	3 005.7	3 006.3	3 009.9	3 007.6	3 013.2	3 022.3	3 029.6
Nursing care facilities	1 613.5	1 616.0	1 614.7	1 615.0	1 615.1	1 613.0	1 612.3	1 612.6	1 608.9	1 611.0	1 614.5	1 617.3
Social assistance [1]	2 482.8	2 485.3	2 491.4	2 495.0	2 504.0	2 502.4	2 496.5	2 511.5	2 525.9	2 532.9	2 535.4	2 541.1
Child day care services	860.6	859.7	861.7	859.9	863.3	853.8	844.6	851.6	862.5	862.3	863.2	864.3
Leisure and hospitality	13 534	13 529	13 528	13 512	13 495	13 490	13 473	13 454	13 428	13 395	13 344	13 304
Arts, entertainment, and recreation	1 992.8	1 993.0	1 996.1	1 984.9	1 978.3	1 975.1	1 966.6	1 964.7	1 955.3	1 952.0	1 944.0	1 947.1
Performing arts and spectator sports	411.7	410.4	409.3	409.5	409.4	409.7	406.9	406.2	402.9	402.5	398.8	401.4
Museums, historical sites, zoos, and parks	132.9	132.0	133.2	132.9	133.9	132.2	132.1	132.1	130.6	129.6	130.6	130.8
Amusements, gambling, and recreation	1 448.2	1 450.6	1 453.6	1 442.5	1 435.0	1 433.2	1 427.6	1 426.4	1 421.8	1 419.9	1 414.6	1 414.9
Accommodation and food services	11 540.9	11 535.9	11 532.0	11 527.5	11 516.7	11 515.3	11 506.3	11 489.3	11 472.4	11 442.7	11 399.6	11 356.5
Accommodation	1 890.8	1 888.7	1 883.9	1 881.1	1 872.1	1 865.0	1 854.6	1 843.6	1 841.3	1 827.9	1 812.1	1 794.3
Food services and drinking places	9 650.1	9 647.2	9 648.1	9 646.4	9 644.6	9 650.3	9 651.7	9 645.7	9 631.1	9 614.8	9 587.5	9 562.2
Other services	5 524	5 533	5 537	5 541	5 542	5 535	5 536	5 530	5 532	5 535	5 509	5 477
Repair and maintenance	1 247.1	1 246.2	1 242.2	1 242.2	1 239.6	1 233.6	1 230.6	1 220.6	1 221.2	1 216.4	1 204.7	1 189.9
Personal and laundry services	1 319.4	1 320.5	1 324.2	1 324.9	1 325.3	1 327.4	1 328.9	1 331.7	1 333.9	1 330.1	1 323.2	1 320.9
Membership associations and organizations	2 957.3	2 966.6	2 970.2	2 973.5	2 976.9	2 973.8	2 976.6	2 977.6	2 977.1	2 988.3	2 980.7	2 965.7
Government	22 391	22 421	22 441	22 451	22 488	22 522	22 537	22 556	22 535	22 539	22 543	22 532
Federal	2 737	2 746	2 751	2 758	2 763	2 765	2 776	2 768	2 771	2 775	2 783	2 778
Federal, except U.S. Postal Service	1 977.7	1 984.7	1 989.6	1 996.4	2 007.7	2 014.6	2 020.2	2 027.1	2 034.3	2 043.5	2 052.4	2 057.3
U.S. Postal Service	759.7	761.2	761.5	761.3	755.7	750.5	755.8	740.6	736.5	731.9	730.1	720.9
State government	5 157	5 153	5 152	5 159	5 167	5 175	5 184	5 204	5 192	5 194	5 197	5 196
State government education	2 339.7	2 334.4	2 334.7	2 340.0	2 348.0	2 355.4	2 365.1	2 379.5	2 373.3	2 372.8	2 380.3	2 381.3
State government, excluding education	2 817.7	2 818.3	2 817.3	2 819.4	2 818.5	2 819.4	2 819.1	2 824.6	2 818.9	2 820.7	2 816.4	2 814.8
Local government	14 497	14 522	14 538	14 534	14 558	14 582	14 577	14 584	14 572	14 570	14 563	14 558
Local government education	8 050.1	8 069.7	8 076.4	8 066.2	8 085.2	8 101.3	8 088.3	8 084.5	8 075.4	8 071.6	8 067.6	8 060.5
Local government, excluding education	6 446.4	6 451.8	6 461.5	6 467.6	6 472.9	6 481.1	6 488.2	6 499.4	6 496.4	6 498.3	6 495.6	6 497.7

[1] Includes other industries, not shown separately.

Table 16-2. Production or Nonsupervisory Workers on Private Nonfarm Payrolls by NAICS Industry

(Wage and salary workers on nonfarm payrolls, thousands.)

Industry	1990	1991	1992	1993	1994	1995	1996	1997	1998	1999
Total Private	73 684	72 520	72 786	74 591	77 382	79 845	81 773	84 158	86 316	88 430
Goods-Producing	17 322	16 352	16 043	16 236	16 795	17 137	17 318	17 698	18 008	18 067
Mining and logging	538	515	478	462	461	458	461	479	473	438
Construction	4 115	3 674	3 546	3 704	3 973	4 113	4 325	4 546	4 807	5 105
Manufacturing	12 669	12 164	12 020	12 070	12 361	12 567	12 532	12 673	12 729	12 524
Durable goods	7 397	7 001	6 853	6 880	7 134	7 352	7 426	7 599	7 721	7 651
Wood products	449.9	412.8	417.0	436.8	468.7	477.5	484.9	496.6	507.9	514.4
Nonmetallic mineral products	413.2	384.1	378.4	380.7	392.3	399.7	404.8	412.5	420.6	426.0
Primary metals	525.1	496.9	478.7	473.3	487.4	500.3	500.3	501.6	505.3	491.9
Fabricated metal products	1 190.1	1 131.6	1 101.0	1 116.9	1 172.0	1 223.0	1 241.6	1 285.3	1 319.6	1 304.9
Machinery	938.9	884.9	857.7	875.5	922.5	969.9	984.5	1 006.9	1 016.1	978.4
Computer and electronic products	980.2	925.6	876.3	856.4	864.0	890.3	915.3	951.1	964.7	932.9
Electrical equipment and appliances	465.2	435.6	425.0	421.8	434.7	438.4	433.9	427.7	431.8	433.2
Transportation equipment [1]	1 473.4	1 406.4	1 388.6	1 367.1	1 415.6	1 472.2	1 481.0	1 521.9	1 530.2	1 526.5
Motor vehicles and parts	869.5	840.1	868.0	896.4	978.4	1 048.9	1 052.4	1 062.4	1 050.2	1 075.8
Furniture and related products	476.9	441.7	444.5	456.0	477.4	481.7	479.7	491.5	513.9	534.3
Miscellaneous manufacturing	484.2	481.2	486.0	495.1	499.0	499.1	500.1	503.4	511.0	508.9
Nondurable goods	5 272	5 163	5 167	5 191	5 227	5 214	5 106	5 075	5 008	4 872
Food manufacturing	1 165.0	1 174.2	1 182.0	1 195.3	1 200.4	1 221.0	1 227.7	1 227.7	1 227.6	1 228.7
Beverage and tobacco products	117.2	116.9	116.2	117.6	118.2	117.3	120.1	121.4	122.5	120.1
Textile mills	417.9	407.2	406.0	403.9	403.3	393.2	371.7	367.1	357.2	333.7
Textile product mills	194.9	185.0	187.4	191.0	199.0	197.9	192.5	192.6	189.7	186.8
Apparel	805.2	781.0	785.3	764.2	740.1	697.9	631.1	593.7	534.0	458.3
Leather and allied products	116.6	107.5	104.4	101.4	97.2	88.5	78.5	73.6	67.0	59.9
Paper and paper products	493.2	488.4	489.9	490.9	492.8	493.8	487.5	488.7	484.1	474.0
Printing and related support activities	597.6	581.7	573.6	579.7	591.4	599.1	594.0	597.0	598.4	585.1
Petroleum and coal products	97.5	97.4	96.8	93.0	90.9	88.8	87.2	87.8	87.1	84.6
Chemicals	620.3	599.7	586.2	590.1	595.6	598.4	595.1	593.3	600.6	595.2
Plastics and rubber products	646.7	623.9	638.9	663.8	698.5	718.7	720.3	731.7	739.3	746.0
Private Service-Providing	56 362	56 168	56 743	58 355	60 587	62 708	64 455	66 460	68 308	70 363
Trade, transportation, and utilities	19 032	18 640	18 506	18 752	19 392	19 984	20 325	20 698	21 059	21 576
Wholesale trade	4 198.3	4 122.2	4 070.7	4 072.2	4 196.4	4 360.8	4 423.2	4 523.2	4 605.0	4 673.1
Retail trade	11 308.4	11 007.9	10 931.4	11 104.0	11 502.1	11 841.0	12 056.7	12 273.6	12 439.8	12 771.5
Transportation and warehousing	2 940.8	2 928.4	2 934.3	3 019.4	3 152.8	3 260.2	3 339.3	3 406.8	3 521.6	3 641.9
Utilities	584.9	581.5	569.5	556.5	540.9	521.8	505.5	493.8	492.2	489.2
Information	1 866	1 871	1 871	1 896	1 928	2 007	2 096	2 181	2 217	2 351
Financial activities	4 973	4 911	4 908	5 057	5 183	5 165	5 279	5 415	5 605	5 728
Professional and business services	8 889	8 748	8 971	9 451	10 078	10 645	11 161	11 896	12 566	13 184
Education and health services	9 748	10 212	10 555	10 908	11 338	11 765	12 123	12 478	12 791	13 089
Leisure and hospitality	8 299	8 247	8 406	8 667	8 979	9 330	9 565	9 780	9 947	10 216
Other services	3 555	3 539	3 526	3 623	3 689	3 812	3 907	4 013	4 124	4 219

[1]Includes other industries, not shown separately.

Table 16-2. Production or Nonsupervisory Workers on Private Nonfarm Payrolls by NAICS Industry
—Continued

(Wage and salary workers on nonfarm payrolls, thousands.)

Industry	2000	2001	2002	2003	2004	2005	2006	2007	2008
Total Private	90 336	89 983	88 393	87 658	88 937	91 135	93 451	94 903	94 509
Goods-Producing	18 169	17 466	16 400	15 732	15 821	16 145	16 559	16 405	15 791
Mining and logging	446	457	436	420	440	473	519	547	580
Construction	5 295	5 332	5 196	5 123	5 309	5 611	5 903	5 883	5 562
Manufacturing	12 428	11 677	10 768	10 189	10 072	10 060	10 137	9 975	9 649
Durable goods	7 659	7 164	6 530	6 152	6 140	6 220	6 355	6 250	5 986
Wood products	505.6	468.3	448.7	433.0	443.9	453.0	449.9	405.7	359.0
Nonmetallic mineral products	439.5	427.1	398.8	374.7	387.8	387.0	391.2	383.6	365.9
Primary metals	490.0	446.9	396.2	370.3	363.7	362.7	362.6	357.5	348.9
Fabricated metal products	1 325.8	1 253.5	1 147.0	1 092.5	1 108.6	1 129.3	1 161.8	1 170.9	1 143.4
Machinery	961.4	890.7	786.9	732.3	729.7	748.9	769.8	774.0	770.5
Computer and electronic products	949.3	875.8	744.1	672.7	655.8	700.1	755.6	743.8	732.1
Electrical equipment and appliances	433.1	402.2	351.9	319.5	307.2	300.1	302.9	305.2	305.9
Transportation equipment [1]	1 497.8	1 398.7	1 310.2	1 269.3	1 265.2	1 276.8	1 303.7	1 274.5	1 176.5
Motor vehicles and parts	1 073.0	986.8	931.0	906.3	902.9	893.7	872.7	804.2	696.5
Furniture and related products	546.2	510.9	476.7	446.0	445.7	437.1	434.2	410.4	366.4
Miscellaneous manufacturing	509.8	489.8	469.2	442.1	432.2	424.4	423.4	424.6	417.0
Nondurable goods	4 769	4 513	4 238	4 037	3 932	3 841	3 782	3 725	3 663
Food manufacturing	1 227.9	1 221.3	1 202.3	1 192.5	1 177.8	1 170.0	1 172.2	1 183.5	1 187.3
Beverage and tobacco products	116.9	115.6	119.5	106.4	106.5	111.5	114.6	118.1	112.1
Textile mills	315.2	275.8	242.2	216.9	193.9	174.2	157.8	137.3	122.0
Textile product mills	183.4	173.7	162.0	148.3	147.1	143.0	134.9	123.2	115.5
Apparel	403.8	341.4	286.0	241.5	218.6	192.7	182.0	173.4	162.9
Leather and allied products	55.4	46.8	40.0	34.9	32.7	30.9	28.6	27.3	28.0
Paper and paper products	467.5	446.3	421.4	392.7	373.7	365.2	357.4	350.5	344.4
Printing and related support activities	575.7	544.4	492.6	471.2	459.5	447.3	446.6	442.6	424.5
Petroleum and coal products	83.1	80.9	78.0	74.4	76.7	75.4	72.2	72.6	76.8
Chemicals	587.7	562.2	531.9	524.9	520.2	510.0	507.7	504.4	514.4
Plastics and rubber products	752.6	704.4	661.9	633.4	625.6	620.4	607.6	592.3	575.3
Private Service-Providing	72 167	72 517	71 993	71 926	73 116	74 990	76 893	78 498	78 718
Trade, transportation, and utilities	21 965	21 709	21 337	21 078	21 319	21 830	22 166	22 546	22 415
Wholesale trade	4 686.4	4 555.1	4 473.5	4 395.9	4 443.5	4 583.6	4 724.3	4 850.9	4 839.2
Retail trade	13 039.8	12 952.3	12 774.0	12 654.9	12 788.1	13 029.6	13 110.2	13 317.1	13 196.5
Transportation and warehousing	3 753.2	3 718.2	3 611.3	3 563.1	3 637.1	3 774.0	3 889.1	3 934.6	3 927.8
Utilities	485.1	482.8	478.4	463.7	449.9	443.0	442.6	443.5	450.9
Information	2 502	2 531	2 398	2 347	2 371	2 386	2 399	2 403	2 398
Financial activities	5 737	5 810	5 872	5 967	5 989	6 090	6 281	6 326	6 271
Professional and business services	13 790	13 588	13 049	12 911	13 287	13 854	14 446	14 784	14 622
Education and health services	13 362	13 846	14 311	14 532	14 771	15 129	15 539	15 999	16 503
Leisure and hospitality	10 516	10 662	10 576	10 666	10 955	11 263	11 568	11 861	11 893
Other services	4 296	4 373	4 449	4 426	4 425	4 438	4 494	4 578	4 617

[1]Includes other industries, not shown separately.

Table 16-2. Production or Nonsupervisory Workers on Private Nonfarm Payrolls by NAICS Industry
—Continued

(Wage and salary workers on nonfarm payrolls, thousands.)

Industry	2008, seasonally adjusted											
	January	February	March	April	May	June	July	August	September	October	November	December
Total Private	95 432	95 299	95 208	95 091	94 931	94 765	94 636	94 470	94 217	93 825	93 286	92 759
Goods-Producing	16 282	16 201	16 149	16 030	15 972	15 875	15 796	15 736	15 629	15 447	15 240	15 011
Mining and logging	564	565	569	567	569	572	578	590	597	592	595	591
Construction	5 788	5 750	5 727	5 668	5 633	5 580	5 546	5 538	5 489	5 430	5 323	5 246
Manufacturing	9 930	9 886	9 853	9 795	9 770	9 723	9 672	9 608	9 543	9 425	9 322	9 174
Durable goods	6 209	6 176	6 146	6 099	6 077	6 040	6 006	5 948	5 898	5 805	5 741	5 633
Wood products	385.3	380.1	375.5	373.9	365.7	360.6	358.4	353.6	348.4	341.5	335.8	324.5
Nonmetallic mineral products	379.1	375.6	373.6	372.8	369.5	367.5	363.3	364.3	360.3	359.3	353.7	344.2
Primary metals	356.9	357.0	357.3	356.7	354.3	353.0	350.8	346.4	346.1	343.5	334.4	323.8
Fabricated metal products	1 174.9	1 171.3	1 169.8	1 160.1	1 159.5	1 149.5	1 142.3	1 144.9	1 135.1	1 120.4	1 103.6	1 085.1
Machinery	783.5	781.6	781.5	780.5	778.6	775.0	775.8	771.3	764.3	760.4	744.8	735.5
Computer and electronic products	744.3	744.4	745.7	743.9	739.5	735.3	732.2	730.9	725.6	718.8	713.2	707.9
Electrical equipment and appliances	305.9	306.1	307.0	307.8	308.5	308.4	308.8	307.0	304.9	304.9	302.2	297.9
Transportation equipment [1]	1 258.9	1 249.7	1 229.9	1 204.9	1 209.0	1 203.8	1 192.1	1 150.4	1 138.3	1 093.3	1 104.1	1 076.2
Motor vehicles and parts	767.6	762.0	740.3	718.2	718.4	714.2	708.9	671.5	660.6	647.5	633.9	609.5
Furniture and related products	394.4	389.5	384.8	379.9	375.0	371.1	367.2	360.9	358.1	347.8	338.4	330.8
Miscellaneous manufacturing	426.0	420.4	420.9	418.4	417.4	415.3	414.8	417.9	417.3	414.7	410.5	406.9
Nondurable goods	3 721	3 710	3 707	3 696	3 693	3 683	3 666	3 660	3 645	3 620	3 581	3 541
Food manufacturing	1 193.1	1 191.5	1 191.6	1 187.2	1 188.2	1 186.4	1 182.0	1 184.2	1 186.1	1 185.9	1 184.8	1 179.7
Beverage and tobacco products	107.5	106.9	110.1	110.1	111.8	113.9	113.5	113.1	113.0	113.0	113.8	114.6
Textile mills	131.4	130.8	129.1	126.7	125.1	123.0	121.4	121.5	118.3	116.2	111.3	108.3
Textile product mills	117.7	116.6	117.9	117.9	117.3	115.6	115.0	113.2	114.1	113.8	112.5	110.7
Apparel	170.4	169.0	166.5	165.7	164.2	163.9	164.2	165.7	162.7	158.7	152.7	149.5
Leather and allied products	28.1	27.5	27.1	27.7	27.8	28.3	27.9	29.0	28.7	28.2	27.1	27.1
Paper and paper products	347.7	346.2	346.3	347.8	347.7	346.1	345.8	343.8	342.2	341.0	339.1	336.0
Printing and related support activities	440.8	437.4	436.9	433.9	430.7	424.9	421.6	422.1	418.6	414.3	408.4	401.0
Petroleum and coal products	76.6	77.7	77.5	76.8	77.0	76.8	77.4	77.7	77.7	76.3	74.5	72.9
Chemicals	517.3	516.4	517.1	517.9	519.6	520.1	516.1	513.5	510.5	509.3	508.3	502.3
Plastics and rubber products	590.7	590.4	587.3	583.9	583.8	583.6	580.7	576.6	572.6	562.9	548.7	538.8
Private Service-Providing	79 150	79 098	79 059	79 061	78 959	78 890	78 840	78 734	78 588	78 378	78 046	77 748
Trade, transportation, and utilities	22 696	22 654	22 640	22 582	22 540	22 495	22 457	22 392	22 310	22 202	22 051	21 933
Wholesale trade	4 894.8	4 888.5	4 888.5	4 872.1	4 865.8	4 857.9	4 844.0	4 833.3	4 818.9	4 800.3	4 770.2	4 738.7
Retail trade	13 381.0	13 344.5	13 334.1	13 293.0	13 269.4	13 248.5	13 224.3	13 190.5	13 137.9	13 064.3	12 981.5	12 914.9
Transportation and warehousing	3 972.1	3 975.2	3 969.8	3 968.4	3 956.4	3 937.9	3 936.7	3 917.1	3 900.2	3 883.1	3 844.3	3 823.0
Utilities	447.6	445.9	447.7	448.4	448.7	450.4	451.6	451.4	453.3	454.6	455.2	456.6
Information	2 418	2 418	2 416	2 411	2 409	2 401	2 395	2 389	2 390	2 392	2 373	2 358
Financial activities	6 307	6 302	6 304	6 301	6 290	6 284	6 276	6 273	6 261	6 249	6 213	6 184
Professional and business services	14 905	14 849	14 777	14 794	14 727	14 680	14 647	14 569	14 523	14 433	14 318	14 212
Education and health services	16 274	16 317	16 360	16 404	16 448	16 491	16 536	16 593	16 601	16 623	16 687	16 719
Leisure and hospitality	11 942	11 939	11 938	11 944	11 920	11 920	11 908	11 897	11 879	11 851	11 803	11 764
Other services	4 608	4 619	4 624	4 625	4 625	4 619	4 621	4 621	4 624	4 628	4 601	4 578

[1]Includes other industries, not shown separately.

Table 16-3. Average Weekly Hours of Production or Nonsupervisory Workers on Private Nonfarm Payrolls by NAICS Industry

(Hours.)

Industry	1990	1991	1992	1993	1994	1995	1996	1997	1998	1999
Total Private	34.3	34.1	34.2	34.3	34.5	34.3	34.3	34.5	34.5	34.3
Goods-Producing	40.1	40.1	40.2	40.6	41.1	40.8	40.8	41.1	40.8	40.8
Mining and logging	45.0	45.3	44.6	44.9	45.3	45.3	46.0	46.2	44.9	44.2
Construction	38.3	38.1	38.0	38.4	38.8	38.8	38.9	38.9	38.8	39.0
Manufacturing	40.5	40.4	40.7	41.1	41.7	41.3	41.3	41.7	41.4	41.4
Overtime hours	3.9	3.8	4.0	4.4	5.0	4.7	4.8	5.1	4.9	4.9
Durable goods	41.1	40.9	41.3	41.9	42.6	42.1	42.1	42.6	42.1	41.9
Overtime hours	3.9	3.7	3.9	4.5	5.3	5.0	5.0	5.4	5.0	5.0
Wood products	40.4	40.2	40.9	41.2	41.7	41.0	41.2	41.4	41.4	41.3
Nonmetallic mineral products	40.9	40.5	41.0	41.5	42.2	41.8	42.0	41.9	42.2	42.1
Primary metals	42.1	41.5	42.4	43.1	44.1	43.4	43.6	44.3	43.5	43.8
Fabricated metal products	41.0	40.8	41.2	41.6	42.3	41.9	41.9	42.3	41.9	41.7
Machinery	42.1	41.9	42.4	43.2	43.9	43.5	43.3	44.0	43.1	42.3
Computer and electronic products	41.3	40.9	41.4	41.8	42.2	42.2	41.9	42.5	41.9	41.5
Electrical equipment and appliances	41.2	41.4	41.8	42.4	43.0	41.9	42.1	42.1	41.8	41.8
Transportation equipment	42.0	41.9	41.9	43.0	44.3	43.7	43.8	44.2	43.2	43.6
Motor vehicles and parts	41.4	41.5	41.6	43.3	44.8	43.8	43.8	43.9	42.6	43.8
Furniture and related products	38.0	37.8	38.7	39.0	39.3	38.5	38.2	39.1	39.4	39.3
Miscellaneous manufacturing	39.0	39.1	39.3	39.2	39.4	39.2	39.1	39.7	39.2	39.3
Nondurable goods	39.6	39.7	40.0	40.1	40.5	40.1	40.1	40.5	40.5	40.4
Overtime hours	3.9	4.0	4.2	4.3	4.6	4.3	4.4	4.7	4.6	4.6
Food manufacturing	39.3	39.2	39.2	39.3	39.8	39.6	39.5	39.8	40.1	40.2
Beverage and tobacco products	38.9	38.8	38.7	38.3	39.3	39.3	39.7	40.0	40.3	41.0
Textile mills	40.2	40.7	41.3	41.6	41.9	40.9	40.8	41.6	41.0	41.0
Textile product mills	38.5	38.6	38.7	39.2	39.4	38.6	38.7	39.2	39.2	39.1
Apparel	34.7	35.4	35.6	35.5	35.7	35.3	35.2	35.6	35.6	35.4
Leather and allied products	37.4	37.6	37.9	38.4	38.2	37.7	37.8	38.2	37.4	37.2
Paper and paper products	43.6	43.6	43.8	43.8	44.2	43.4	43.5	43.9	43.6	43.6
Printing and related support activities	38.7	38.6	39.0	39.2	39.6	39.1	39.1	39.5	39.3	39.1
Petroleum and coal products	44.4	43.9	43.6	44.0	44.3	43.7	43.7	43.1	43.6	42.6
Chemicals	42.8	43.1	43.3	43.2	43.4	43.3	43.3	43.4	43.2	42.7
Plastics and rubber products	40.6	40.5	41.2	41.4	41.8	41.1	41.0	41.4	41.3	41.3
Private Service-Providing	32.5	32.4	32.5	32.5	32.7	32.6	32.6	32.8	32.8	32.7
Trade, transportation, and utilities	33.7	33.7	33.8	34.1	34.3	34.1	34.1	34.3	34.2	33.9
Wholesale trade	38.4	38.4	38.5	38.5	38.8	38.6	38.6	38.8	38.6	38.6
Retail trade	30.6	30.4	30.7	30.7	30.9	30.8	30.7	30.9	30.9	30.8
Transportation and warehousing	37.7	37.4	37.4	38.9	39.5	38.9	39.1	39.4	38.7	37.6
Utilities	41.5	41.5	41.7	42.1	42.3	42.3	42.0	42.0	42.0	42.0
Information	35.8	35.6	35.8	36.0	36.0	36.0	36.4	36.3	36.6	36.7
Financial activities	35.5	35.5	35.6	35.5	35.5	35.5	35.5	35.7	36.0	35.8
Professional and business services	34.2	34.0	34.0	34.0	34.1	34.0	34.1	34.3	34.3	34.4
Education and health services	31.9	31.9	32.0	32.0	32.0	32.0	31.9	32.2	32.2	32.1
Leisure and hospitality	26.0	25.6	25.7	25.9	26.0	25.9	25.9	26.0	26.2	26.1
Other services	32.8	32.7	32.6	32.6	32.7	32.6	32.5	32.7	32.6	32.5

Table 16-3. Average Weekly Hours of Production or Nonsupervisory Workers on Private Nonfarm Payrolls by NAICS Industry—*Continued*

(Hours.)

Industry	2000	2001	2002	2003	2004	2005	2006	2007	2008
Total Private	34.3	34.0	33.9	33.7	33.7	33.8	33.9	33.9	33.6
Goods-Producing	40.7	39.9	39.9	39.8	40.0	40.1	40.5	40.6	40.2
Mining and logging	44.4	44.6	43.2	43.6	44.5	45.6	45.6	45.9	45.1
Construction	39.2	38.7	38.4	38.4	38.3	38.6	39.0	39.0	38.5
Manufacturing	41.3	40.3	40.5	40.4	40.8	40.7	41.1	41.2	40.8
Overtime hours	4.7	4.0	4.2	4.2	4.6	4.6	4.4	4.2	3.7
Durable goods	41.8	40.6	40.8	40.8	41.3	41.1	41.4	41.5	41.1
Overtime hours	4.8	3.9	4.2	4.3	4.7	4.6	4.4	4.2	3.7
Wood products	41.0	40.2	39.9	40.4	40.7	40.0	39.8	39.4	38.6
Nonmetallic mineral products	41.6	41.6	42.0	42.2	42.4	42.2	43.0	42.3	42.1
Primary metals	44.2	42.4	42.4	42.3	43.1	43.1	43.6	42.9	42.2
Fabricated metal products	41.9	40.6	40.6	40.7	41.1	41.0	41.4	41.6	41.3
Machinery	42.3	40.9	40.5	40.8	42.0	42.1	42.4	42.6	42.3
Computer and electronic products	41.4	39.8	39.7	40.4	40.4	40.0	40.5	40.6	41.0
Electrical equipment and appliances	41.6	39.8	40.1	40.6	40.7	40.6	41.0	41.2	40.9
Transportation equipment	43.3	41.9	42.5	41.9	42.5	42.4	42.7	42.8	42.0
Motor vehicles and parts	43.4	41.6	42.6	42.0	42.6	42.3	42.2	42.3	41.4
Furniture and related products	39.2	38.3	39.2	38.9	39.5	39.2	38.8	39.2	38.1
Miscellaneous manufacturing	39.0	38.8	38.6	38.4	38.5	38.7	38.7	38.9	38.9
Nondurable goods	40.3	39.9	40.0	39.8	40.0	39.9	40.6	40.8	40.4
Overtime hours	4.5	4.1	4.2	4.1	4.4	4.4	4.4	4.1	3.7
Food manufacturing	40.1	39.6	39.6	39.3	39.3	39.0	40.1	40.7	40.5
Beverage and tobacco products	42.0	40.9	39.4	39.1	39.2	40.1	40.8	40.7	38.8
Textile mills	41.4	40.0	40.6	39.1	40.1	40.3	40.6	40.3	38.7
Textile product mills	38.7	38.4	39.0	39.3	38.7	38.9	39.8	39.7	38.6
Apparel	35.7	36.0	36.7	35.6	36.1	35.8	36.5	37.2	36.4
Leather and allied products	37.5	36.4	37.5	39.3	38.4	38.4	38.9	38.2	37.5
Paper and paper products	42.8	42.1	41.9	41.5	42.1	42.5	42.9	43.1	42.9
Printing and related support activities	39.2	38.7	38.4	38.2	38.4	38.4	39.2	39.1	38.3
Petroleum and coal products	42.7	43.8	43.0	44.5	44.9	45.5	45.0	44.1	44.6
Chemicals	42.2	41.9	42.3	42.4	42.8	42.3	42.5	41.9	41.5
Plastics and rubber products	40.8	40.0	40.6	40.4	40.4	40.0	40.6	41.3	41.0
Private Service-Providing	32.7	32.5	32.5	32.3	32.3	32.4	32.5	32.4	32.3
Trade, transportation, and utilities	33.8	33.5	33.6	33.6	33.5	33.4	33.4	33.3	33.2
Wholesale trade	38.8	38.4	38.0	37.9	37.8	37.7	38.0	38.2	38.2
Retail trade	30.7	30.7	30.9	30.9	30.7	30.6	30.5	30.2	30.0
Transportation and warehousing	37.4	36.7	36.8	36.8	37.2	37.0	36.9	37.0	36.4
Utilities	42.0	41.4	40.9	41.1	40.9	41.1	41.4	42.4	42.7
Information	36.8	36.9	36.5	36.2	36.3	36.5	36.6	36.5	36.7
Financial activities	35.9	35.8	35.6	35.5	35.5	35.9	35.7	35.9	35.8
Professional and business services	34.5	34.2	34.2	34.1	34.2	34.2	34.6	34.8	34.8
Education and health services	32.2	32.3	32.4	32.3	32.4	32.6	32.5	32.6	32.5
Leisure and hospitality	26.1	25.8	25.8	25.6	25.7	25.7	25.7	25.5	25.2
Other services	32.5	32.3	32.0	31.4	31.0	30.9	30.9	30.9	30.8

Table 16-3. Average Weekly Hours of Production or Nonsupervisory Workers on Private Nonfarm Payrolls by NAICS Industry—*Continued*

(Hours.)

Industry	2008, seasonally adjusted											
	January	February	March	April	May	June	July	August	September	October	November	December
Total Private	33.7	33.8	33.8	33.8	33.7	33.6	33.6	33.7	33.6	33.5	33.4	33.3
Goods-Producing	40.5	40.5	40.6	40.4	40.2	40.3	40.3	40.2	39.9	39.8	39.5	39.4
Mining and logging	45.6	45.6	46.2	45.0	44.6	44.9	44.8	45.3	44.5	44.7	45.3	44.3
Construction	38.8	38.8	38.9	38.9	38.5	38.7	38.7	38.6	38.3	38.3	37.7	38.0
Manufacturing	41.1	41.2	41.2	41.0	40.9	40.9	41.0	40.8	40.5	40.4	40.2	39.9
Overtime hours	4.1	4.1	4.0	4.0	3.9	3.8	3.7	3.7	3.5	3.5	3.2	2.9
Durable goods	41.5	41.5	41.5	41.4	41.2	41.2	41.2	41.1	40.6	40.6	40.4	40.0
Overtime hours	4.2	4.2	4.1	4.0	3.9	3.8	3.7	3.7	3.4	3.4	3.1	2.8
Wood products	39.2	39.1	38.7	38.6	39.0	39.1	38.8	38.8	38.4	38.1	37.6	36.8
Nonmetallic mineral products	42.3	42.3	43.2	42.3	42.3	42.0	42.6	42.2	41.9	41.8	40.9	40.9
Primary metals	42.6	42.7	43.0	42.6	42.4	42.5	42.2	42.5	41.8	41.4	40.9	40.5
Fabricated metal products	41.8	41.8	41.8	41.6	41.5	41.2	41.2	41.1	40.9	40.8	40.8	40.3
Machinery	42.9	43.0	42.8	42.5	42.2	42.1	42.1	42.5	42.1	41.8	41.4	41.1
Computer and electronic products	40.4	40.5	41.0	41.1	41.1	41.2	41.1	41.0	40.8	40.8	41.3	40.4
Electrical equipment and appliances	41.4	41.1	41.3	41.0	41.1	40.9	40.8	40.8	41.0	40.4	40.2	39.7
Transportation equipment	42.7	43.0	42.4	42.5	41.9	42.1	42.6	41.7	40.9	41.3	40.9	40.9
Motor vehicles and parts	42.3	42.7	41.9	42.1	41.4	41.4	42.0	40.5	40.9	40.6	40.0	39.9
Furniture and related products	38.5	38.3	38.7	38.7	38.8	38.7	38.3	37.9	37.4	37.4	37.2	37.3
Miscellaneous manufacturing	39.1	38.8	39.2	39.3	39.2	39.0	39.1	39.4	38.7	38.9	38.5	38.3
Nondurable goods	40.6	40.6	40.7	40.5	40.5	40.4	40.6	40.4	40.2	40.2	39.9	39.7
Overtime hours	4.0	3.9	3.9	3.9	3.8	3.8	3.7	3.8	3.6	3.6	3.4	3.1
Food manufacturing	40.5	40.7	40.8	40.8	40.8	40.6	40.6	40.5	40.3	40.3	39.9	39.8
Beverage and tobacco products	40.3	39.9	40.1	39.4	39.5	38.8	38.7	38.2	38.2	38.1	37.9	36.7
Textile mills	38.9	38.9	38.8	38.4	38.9	38.8	39.2	39.5	38.9	38.4	37.7	37.0
Textile product mills	38.7	39.4	39.3	38.3	38.7	38.9	39.1	38.7	38.1	37.9	37.9	37.1
Apparel	36.7	36.7	36.7	36.6	36.0	36.4	37.0	36.5	35.9	36.3	36.2	36.0
Leather and allied products	38.3	38.2	38.6	38.6	38.8	38.4	38.2	37.5	37.5	36.9	34.4	34.7
Paper and paper products	44.0	43.9	43.6	43.3	42.6	42.7	42.6	42.9	42.4	42.2	42.1	41.9
Printing and related support activities	38.3	38.2	38.6	38.5	38.6	38.1	38.0	38.2	38.3	38.3	38.2	38.0
Petroleum and coal products	43.9	43.9	43.7	43.2	44.1	44.6	45.5	45.6	45.2	45.2	44.4	45.3
Chemicals	41.6	41.4	41.9	41.3	41.2	41.6	41.9	41.4	41.3	41.5	41.3	41.1
Plastics and rubber products	41.1	41.3	41.2	41.0	40.9	41.0	41.3	41.0	40.7	40.6	40.6	40.0
Private Service-Providing	32.4	32.4	32.4	32.4	32.4	32.3	32.3	32.4	32.3	32.3	32.2	32.2
Trade, transportation, and utilities	33.3	33.3	33.3	33.3	33.2	33.2	33.2	33.2	33.2	33.1	33.0	32.9
Wholesale trade	38.3	38.2	38.4	38.3	38.3	38.3	38.4	38.3	38.1	38.2	38.1	37.8
Retail trade	30.2	30.2	30.2	30.2	30.1	30.0	30.0	30.0	30.1	29.9	29.8	29.7
Transportation and warehousing	36.6	36.7	36.6	36.6	36.4	36.4	36.4	36.4	36.4	36.3	36.1	36.2
Utilities	43.2	42.8	43.2	42.6	42.5	43.0	42.4	42.3	42.7	42.5	42.4	42.9
Information	36.3	36.3	36.5	36.6	36.6	36.7	36.7	36.8	36.9	36.9	37.0	37.0
Financial activities	35.7	35.8	35.8	35.9	35.9	35.8	35.7	36.1	36.0	35.9	36.1	35.9
Professional and business services	34.7	34.7	34.8	34.8	34.9	34.8	34.8	34.9	34.8	34.9	34.9	34.8
Education and health services	32.6	32.6	32.7	32.6	32.7	32.5	32.5	32.6	32.5	32.5	32.4	32.4
Leisure and hospitality	25.3	25.4	25.3	25.4	25.3	25.3	25.2	25.2	25.2	25.1	25.0	25.0
Other services	30.7	30.8	30.9	30.8	30.8	30.7	30.8	30.9	30.7	30.7	30.7	30.6

Table 16-4. Average Hourly Earnings of Production or Nonsupervisory Workers on Private Nonfarm Payrolls by NAICS Industry

(Dollars.)

Industry	1990	1991	1992	1993	1994	1995	1996	1997	1998	1999
Total Private	10.20	10.52	10.77	11.05	11.34	11.65	12.04	12.51	13.01	13.49
Goods-Producing	11.46	11.76	11.99	12.28	12.63	12.96	13.38	13.82	14.23	14.71
Mining and logging	13.40	13.82	14.09	14.12	14.41	14.78	15.10	15.57	16.20	16.33
Construction	13.42	13.65	13.81	14.04	14.38	14.73	15.11	15.67	16.23	16.80
Manufacturing	10.78	11.13	11.40	11.70	12.04	12.34	12.75	13.14	13.45	13.85
Excluding overtime [1]	10.28	10.63	10.86	11.10	11.36	11.68	12.05	12.37	12.70	13.08
Durable goods	11.40	11.81	12.09	12.41	12.78	13.05	13.45	13.83	14.07	14.46
Wood products	8.82	9.03	9.24	9.41	9.66	9.92	10.24	10.52	10.85	11.18
Nonmetallic mineral products	11.11	11.34	11.57	11.83	12.11	12.38	12.80	13.17	13.59	13.97
Primary metals	12.97	13.37	13.72	14.08	14.47	14.75	15.12	15.39	15.66	16.00
Fabricated metal products	10.64	10.97	11.16	11.40	11.64	11.91	12.26	12.64	12.97	13.34
Machinery	11.73	12.12	12.40	12.72	12.94	13.13	13.49	13.94	14.23	14.77
Computer and electronic products	10.89	11.35	11.64	11.95	12.19	12.29	12.75	13.24	13.85	14.37
Electrical equipment and appliances	10.00	10.30	10.50	10.65	10.94	11.25	11.80	12.24	12.51	12.90
Transportation equipment	14.44	15.12	15.59	16.21	16.93	17.21	17.66	17.99	17.91	18.24
Motor vehicles and parts	15.00	15.67	15.92	16.56	17.38	17.72	18.14	18.43	18.21	18.49
Furniture and related products	8.53	8.74	9.01	9.25	9.52	9.75	10.09	10.50	10.88	11.28
Miscellaneous manufacturing	8.87	9.15	9.43	9.64	9.90	10.23	10.59	10.88	11.17	11.55
Nondurable goods	9.87	10.18	10.45	10.70	10.96	11.30	11.68	12.04	12.45	12.85
Food manufacturing	9.04	9.32	9.59	9.82	10.00	10.27	10.50	10.77	11.09	11.40
Beverage and tobacco products	13.24	13.65	14.07	14.30	14.97	15.40	15.73	16.00	16.03	16.54
Textile mills	8.17	8.49	8.82	9.12	9.35	9.63	9.88	10.22	10.58	10.90
Textile product mills	7.37	7.60	7.85	8.09	8.29	8.60	8.95	9.30	9.61	10.04
Apparel	6.22	6.43	6.60	6.74	6.95	7.22	7.45	7.76	8.05	8.35
Leather and allied products	7.18	7.43	7.68	7.88	8.23	8.50	8.94	9.31	9.68	9.93
Paper and paper products	12.06	12.45	12.78	13.13	13.49	13.94	14.38	14.76	15.20	15.58
Printing and related support activities	11.11	11.32	11.53	11.67	11.89	12.08	12.41	12.78	13.20	13.67
Petroleum and coal products	17.00	17.90	18.83	19.43	19.96	20.24	20.18	21.10	21.75	22.22
Chemicals	12.85	13.30	13.70	13.97	14.33	14.86	15.37	15.78	16.23	16.40
Plastics and rubber products	9.76	10.07	10.35	10.55	10.66	10.86	11.17	11.48	11.79	12.25
Private Service-Providing	9.72	10.07	10.35	10.62	10.89	11.21	11.59	12.07	12.61	13.09
Trade, transportation, and utilities	9.83	10.08	10.30	10.55	10.80	11.10	11.46	11.90	12.39	12.82
Wholesale trade	11.58	11.95	12.21	12.57	12.93	13.34	13.80	14.41	15.07	15.62
Retail trade	7.71	7.89	8.12	8.36	8.61	8.85	9.21	9.59	10.05	10.45
Transportation and warehousing	12.50	12.61	12.77	12.71	12.84	13.18	13.45	13.78	14.12	14.55
Utilities	16.14	16.70	17.17	17.95	18.66	19.19	19.78	20.59	21.48	22.03
Information	13.40	13.90	14.29	14.86	15.32	15.68	16.30	17.14	17.67	18.40
Financial activities	9.99	10.42	10.86	11.36	11.82	12.28	12.71	13.22	13.93	14.47
Professional and business services	11.14	11.50	11.78	11.96	12.15	12.53	13.00	13.57	14.27	14.85
Education and health services	10.00	10.49	10.87	11.21	11.50	11.80	12.17	12.56	13.00	13.44
Leisure and hospitality	6.02	6.22	6.36	6.48	6.62	6.79	6.99	7.32	7.67	7.96
Other services	9.08	9.39	9.66	9.90	10.18	10.51	10.85	11.29	11.79	12.26

[1]Derived by assuming that overtime hours are paid at the rate of time and one-half.

Table 16-4. Average Hourly Earnings of Production or Nonsupervisory Workers on Private Nonfarm Payrolls by NAICS Industry—*Continued*

(Dollars.)

Industry	2000	2001	2002	2003	2004	2005	2006	2007	2008
Total Private	14.02	14.54	14.97	15.37	15.69	16.13	16.76	17.43	18.08
Goods-Producing	15.27	15.78	16.33	16.80	17.19	17.60	18.02	18.67	19.33
Mining and logging	16.55	17.00	17.19	17.56	18.07	18.72	19.90	20.97	22.50
Construction	17.48	18.00	18.52	18.95	19.23	19.46	20.02	20.95	21.87
Manufacturing	14.32	14.76	15.29	15.74	16.14	16.56	16.81	17.26	17.74
Excluding overtime [1]	13.55	14.06	14.54	14.96	15.29	15.68	15.96	16.43	16.97
Durable goods	14.92	15.38	16.02	16.45	16.82	17.33	17.68	18.20	18.70
Wood products	11.63	11.99	12.33	12.71	13.03	13.16	13.39	13.68	14.20
Nonmetallic mineral products	14.53	14.86	15.40	15.76	16.25	16.61	16.59	16.93	16.90
Primary metals	16.64	17.06	17.68	18.13	18.57	18.94	19.36	19.66	20.18
Fabricated metal products	13.77	14.19	14.68	15.01	15.31	15.80	16.17	16.53	16.99
Machinery	15.21	15.48	15.92	16.29	16.67	17.02	17.20	17.72	17.97
Computer and electronic products	14.73	15.42	16.20	16.69	17.27	18.39	18.94	19.94	21.03
Electrical equipment and appliances	13.23	13.78	13.98	14.36	14.90	15.24	15.53	15.93	15.78
Transportation equipment	18.89	19.48	20.63	21.22	21.48	22.09	22.41	23.04	23.83
Motor vehicles and parts	19.11	19.66	21.09	21.68	21.71	22.26	22.14	22.00	22.19
Furniture and related products	11.73	12.14	12.62	12.99	13.16	13.45	13.80	14.32	14.54
Miscellaneous manufacturing	11.93	12.45	12.91	13.30	13.84	14.07	14.36	14.66	15.19
Nondurable goods	13.31	13.75	14.15	14.63	15.05	15.27	15.33	15.67	16.15
Food manufacturing	11.77	12.18	12.55	12.80	12.98	13.04	13.13	13.55	14.00
Beverage and tobacco products	17.40	17.67	17.73	17.96	19.14	18.76	18.18	18.54	19.35
Textile mills	11.23	11.40	11.73	11.99	12.13	12.38	12.55	13.00	13.57
Textile product mills	10.31	10.49	10.85	11.15	11.31	11.61	11.86	11.78	11.73
Apparel	8.61	8.83	9.11	9.58	9.77	10.26	10.65	11.05	11.40
Leather and allied products	10.35	10.69	11.00	11.66	11.63	11.50	11.44	12.04	12.96
Paper and paper products	15.91	16.38	16.85	17.33	17.91	17.99	18.01	18.44	18.88
Printing and related support activities	14.09	14.48	14.93	15.37	15.71	15.74	15.80	16.15	16.75
Petroleum and coal products	22.80	22.90	23.04	23.63	24.39	24.47	24.11	25.21	27.46
Chemicals	17.09	17.57	17.97	18.50	19.17	19.67	19.60	19.55	19.49
Plastics and rubber products	12.70	13.21	13.55	14.18	14.59	14.80	14.97	15.39	15.85
Private Service-Providing	13.62	14.18	14.59	14.99	15.29	15.74	16.42	17.11	17.77
Trade, transportation, and utilities	13.31	13.70	14.02	14.34	14.58	14.92	15.39	15.78	16.16
Wholesale trade	16.28	16.77	16.98	17.36	17.65	18.16	18.91	19.59	20.14
Retail trade	10.86	11.29	11.67	11.90	12.08	12.36	12.57	12.75	12.87
Transportation and warehousing	15.05	15.33	15.76	16.25	16.52	16.70	17.28	17.72	18.41
Utilities	22.75	23.58	23.96	24.77	25.61	26.68	27.40	27.88	28.84
Information	19.07	19.80	20.20	21.01	21.40	22.06	23.23	23.96	24.77
Financial activities	14.98	15.59	16.17	17.14	17.52	17.95	18.80	19.64	20.27
Professional and business services	15.52	16.33	16.81	17.21	17.48	18.08	19.13	20.15	21.19
Education and health services	13.95	14.64	15.21	15.64	16.15	16.71	17.38	18.11	18.88
Leisure and hospitality	8.32	8.57	8.81	9.00	9.15	9.38	9.75	10.41	10.84
Other services	12.73	13.27	13.72	13.84	13.98	14.34	14.77	15.42	16.08

[1]Derived by assuming that overtime hours are paid at the rate of time and one-half.

Table 16-4. Average Hourly Earnings of Production or Nonsupervisory Workers on Private Nonfarm Payrolls by NAICS Industry—Continued

(Dollars.)

Industry	2008, seasonally adjusted											
	January	February	March	April	May	June	July	August	September	October	November	December
Total Private	17.77	17.83	17.90	17.94	17.99	18.04	18.10	18.18	18.21	18.28	18.34	18.40
Goods-Producing	19.00	19.07	19.17	19.16	19.20	19.27	19.36	19.43	19.48	19.56	19.63	19.69
Mining and logging	21.83	21.80	22.28	21.77	21.79	22.04	22.54	23.01	23.08	23.03	23.28	23.23
Construction	21.38	21.48	21.58	21.62	21.72	21.77	21.85	22.02	22.09	22.17	22.28	22.41
Manufacturing	17.52	17.58	17.64	17.64	17.68	17.73	17.80	17.78	17.81	17.89	17.94	17.96
Excluding overtime [1]	16.69	16.75	16.82	16.82	16.88	16.94	17.03	17.01	17.07	17.15	17.25	17.33
Durable goods	18.45	18.53	18.58	18.61	18.63	18.70	18.78	18.74	18.74	18.84	18.91	18.94
Wood products	...	...	...	...	...	...	...	...	...	...	...	...
Nonmetallic mineral products	...	...	...	...	...	...	...	...	...	...	...	...
Primary metals	...	...	...	...	...	...	...	...	...	...	...	...
Fabricated metal products	...	...	...	...	...	...	...	...	...	...	...	...
Machinery	...	...	...	...	...	...	...	...	...	...	...	...
Computer and electronic products	...	...	...	...	...	...	...	...	...	...	...	...
Electrical equipment and appliances	...	...	...	...	...	...	...	...	...	...	...	...
Transportation equipment	...	...	...	...	...	...	...	...	...	...	...	...
Motor vehicles and parts	...	...	...	...	...	...	...	...	...	...	...	...
Furniture and related products	...	...	...	...	...	...	...	...	...	...	...	...
Miscellaneous manufacturing	...	...	...	...	...	...	...	...	...	...	...	...
Nondurable goods	15.93	15.95	16.05	16.01	16.08	16.11	16.16	16.19	16.28	16.35	16.37	16.39
Food manufacturing	...	...	...	...	...	...	...	...	...	...	...	...
Beverage and tobacco products	...	...	...	...	...	...	...	...	...	...	...	...
Textile mills	...	...	...	...	...	...	...	...	...	...	...	...
Textile product mills	...	...	...	...	...	...	...	...	...	...	...	...
Apparel	...	...	...	...	...	...	...	...	...	...	...	...
Leather and allied products	...	...	...	...	...	...	...	...	...	...	...	...
Paper and paper products	...	...	...	...	...	...	...	...	...	...	...	...
Printing and related support activities	...	...	...	...	...	...	...	...	...	...	...	...
Petroleum and coal products	...	...	...	...	...	...	...	...	...	...	...	...
Chemicals	...	...	...	...	...	...	...	...	...	...	...	...
Plastics and rubber products	...	...	...	...	...	...	...	...	...	...	...	...
Private Service-Providing	17.46	17.51	17.58	17.63	17.69	17.74	17.79	17.87	17.90	17.97	18.03	18.10
Trade, transportation, and utilities	16.00	16.04	16.07	16.08	16.13	16.16	16.17	16.23	16.20	16.23	16.29	16.31
Wholesale trade	19.97	20.03	20.04	20.05	20.07	20.11	20.15	20.28	20.20	20.22	20.29	20.31
Retail trade	12.80	12.81	12.83	12.84	12.87	12.87	12.88	12.92	12.91	12.89	12.93	12.94
Transportation and warehousing	18.11	18.21	18.25	18.31	18.39	18.41	18.42	18.48	18.47	18.58	18.66	18.66
Utilities	28.62	28.62	28.79	28.54	28.81	29.12	28.67	28.89	28.86	28.91	28.91	29.16
Information	24.40	24.48	24.58	24.56	24.71	24.78	24.87	24.95	24.90	24.99	24.94	24.91
Financial activities	19.99	20.04	20.12	20.17	20.23	20.24	20.26	20.37	20.43	20.43	20.41	20.53
Professional and business services	20.58	20.69	20.78	20.90	20.96	21.08	21.19	21.38	21.47	21.63	21.78	21.97
Education and health services	18.56	18.60	18.69	18.74	18.80	18.84	18.92	18.96	19.04	19.08	19.13	19.20
Leisure and hospitality	10.68	10.75	10.75	10.81	10.83	10.85	10.87	10.89	10.90	10.92	10.90	10.94
Other services	15.79	15.85	15.94	16.00	16.04	16.09	16.13	16.17	16.20	16.24	16.29	16.29

[1]Derived by assuming that overtime hours are paid at the rate of time and one-half.
. . . = Not available.

Table 16-5. Average Weekly Earnings of Production or Nonsupervisory Workers on Private Nonfarm Payrolls by NAICS Industry

(Dollars.)

Industry	1990	1991	1992	1993	1994	1995	1996	1997	1998	1999
Total Private	349.75	358.51	368.25	378.91	391.22	400.07	413.28	431.86	448.56	463.15
Goods-Producing	459.55	471.32	482.58	498.82	519.58	528.62	546.48	568.43	580.99	599.99
Mining and logging	602.54	625.42	629.02	634.77	653.14	670.32	695.07	720.11	727.28	721.74
Construction	513.43	520.41	525.13	539.81	558.53	571.57	588.48	609.48	629.75	655.11
Manufacturing	436.16	449.73	464.43	480.83	502.05	509.26	526.55	548.22	557.12	573.14
Durable goods	468.43	483.28	499.60	519.81	544.52	549.49	566.53	589.06	591.77	606.55
Wood products	356.38	362.69	377.76	387.34	402.86	406.51	422.32	435.74	449.78	461.61
Nonmetallic mineral products	453.91	459.21	474.46	490.73	510.92	517.69	538.03	551.70	573.00	587.42
Primary metals	545.36	555.34	581.45	606.49	637.73	639.70	658.81	681.52	681.68	700.93
Fabricated metal products	436.12	447.98	459.64	474.21	492.07	498.48	513.57	534.48	543.20	555.86
Machinery	493.22	507.79	525.26	549.73	567.90	571.04	584.59	613.31	613.69	625.19
Computer and electronic products	449.96	464.25	482.09	499.09	514.78	518.26	534.39	562.80	579.90	596.49
Electrical equipment and appliances	412.42	426.81	439.04	451.44	470.24	471.72	496.69	515.77	522.54	538.98
Transportation equipment	606.71	633.69	652.68	697.18	750.26	751.78	773.51	795.60	774.42	795.73
Motor vehicles and parts	621.68	650.36	662.82	717.68	779.29	776.41	794.09	808.28	775.56	809.31
Furniture and related products	324.30	330.65	348.22	360.82	374.03	375.13	385.75	410.45	428.66	443.61
Miscellaneous manufacturing	345.86	358.31	370.56	378.14	389.79	400.96	414.03	431.77	437.83	454.20
Nondurable goods	390.73	404.17	417.95	429.15	443.88	452.77	467.88	487.04	504.02	519.95
Food manufacturing	355.61	364.90	375.72	386.04	398.50	406.75	414.70	428.58	444.81	458.63
Beverage and tobacco products	515.73	530.09	544.25	547.60	588.39	605.00	624.82	639.69	646.26	679.06
Textile mills	328.11	345.48	364.45	379.74	391.64	394.17	403.08	425.53	434.15	447.38
Textile product mills	283.66	293.45	303.69	317.63	326.47	332.30	346.80	364.16	376.16	392.41
Apparel	215.97	227.82	235.29	239.59	248.42	255.12	261.95	276.01	286.26	295.68
Leather and allied products	268.32	279.41	291.11	302.85	314.18	319.98	337.86	355.63	361.87	369.80
Paper and paper products	525.71	542.26	560.27	575.49	596.19	604.74	625.38	647.55	662.20	679.24
Printing and related support activities	429.93	437.00	450.02	457.91	470.74	472.37	484.99	504.46	518.32	534.15
Petroleum and coal products	754.13	786.05	821.72	855.36	883.81	883.68	881.24	908.50	949.28	947.60
Chemicals	550.25	573.27	593.17	603.67	622.50	644.37	666.10	685.39	700.70	700.55
Plastics and rubber products	396.22	408.28	426.60	436.82	445.90	445.88	458.29	474.94	487.04	505.42
Private Service-Providing	316.03	325.90	336.08	345.65	355.63	364.80	377.37	395.51	413.50	427.98
Trade, transportation, and utilities	331.55	339.19	348.68	359.33	370.38	378.79	390.64	407.54	423.30	434.31
Wholesale trade	444.48	459.27	470.41	484.46	501.17	515.14	533.29	559.39	582.21	602.77
Retail trade	235.62	240.15	249.63	256.89	265.77	272.56	282.76	295.97	310.34	321.63
Transportation and warehousing	471.72	471.12	478.02	494.36	507.27	513.37	525.64	542.55	546.86	547.97
Utilities	670.40	693.40	716.36	756.35	789.98	811.52	830.74	865.26	902.94	924.59
Information	479.50	495.17	512.20	535.19	551.21	564.92	592.72	622.37	646.34	675.47
Financial activities	354.66	369.57	386.01	403.02	419.20	436.12	451.49	472.37	500.98	517.57
Professional and business services	380.52	391.09	400.64	406.20	414.16	426.44	442.81	465.51	490.00	510.99
Education and health services	319.27	334.55	348.29	359.08	368.14	377.73	388.27	404.65	418.82	431.35
Leisure and hospitality	156.32	159.15	163.70	167.56	172.33	175.74	180.98	190.52	200.82	208.05
Other services	297.91	306.91	315.08	322.69	332.44	342.36	352.62	368.63	384.25	398.77

Table 16-5. Average Weekly Earnings of Production or Nonsupervisory Workers on Private Nonfarm Payrolls by NAICS Industry—*Continued*

(Dollars.)

Industry	2000	2001	2002	2003	2004	2005	2006	2007	2008
Total Private	481.01	493.79	506.75	518.06	529.09	544.33	567.87	590.04	607.99
Goods-Producing	621.86	630.01	651.61	669.13	688.13	705.31	730.16	757.34	776.60
Mining and logging	734.92	757.92	741.97	765.94	803.82	853.71	907.95	962.64	1 013.78
Construction	685.78	695.89	711.82	726.83	735.55	750.22	781.21	816.66	842.36
Manufacturing	590.77	595.19	618.75	635.99	658.49	673.30	691.02	711.56	724.23
Durable goods	624.22	624.47	652.94	671.21	694.06	712.95	732.00	754.77	767.56
Wood products	477.13	481.36	492.00	514.10	530.16	526.62	533.11	539.34	547.81
Nonmetallic mineral products	604.87	618.91	646.87	664.92	688.30	700.64	712.67	716.78	711.30
Primary metals	734.79	723.82	749.32	767.45	799.77	815.90	843.63	843.26	850.84
Fabricated metal products	576.68	576.60	596.38	610.37	628.80	647.34	668.98	687.20	701.47
Machinery	643.81	632.56	645.38	664.48	699.42	716.42	728.84	754.19	759.92
Computer and electronic products	609.73	613.22	642.90	674.72	697.86	735.75	766.96	808.80	861.43
Electrical equipment and appliances	550.48	548.03	560.33	583.27	607.00	618.88	637.04	656.46	645.60
Transportation equipment	817.52	816.90	877.66	889.03	912.56	937.78	957.65	986.79	999.94
Motor vehicles and parts	828.73	818.68	898.54	910.02	924.72	940.64	934.41	930.51	919.46
Furniture and related products	459.95	464.69	494.17	505.47	519.72	527.43	535.90	560.84	554.20
Miscellaneous manufacturing	464.86	483.04	498.84	510.62	533.30	545.04	555.90	569.99	591.73
Nondurable goods	536.82	548.41	566.72	582.61	602.53	609.24	621.97	639.99	652.20
Food manufacturing	472.06	481.67	496.94	502.92	509.52	508.55	525.99	551.32	566.91
Beverage and tobacco products	730.35	721.68	698.39	702.45	751.20	751.54	741.34	755.22	750.18
Textile mills	464.51	456.64	476.52	469.33	486.68	498.47	509.39	524.40	524.93
Textile product mills	399.13	402.47	423.08	438.58	438.08	451.14	472.24	467.77	453.12
Apparel	307.69	317.74	334.24	340.95	352.21	366.71	389.17	411.39	415.17
Leather and allied products	388.46	388.83	412.99	457.83	446.66	441.96	445.47	459.50	486.49
Paper and paper products	681.34	690.06	705.62	719.73	754.14	764.04	772.39	795.58	809.21
Printing and related support activities	552.15	560.89	573.05	587.58	603.97	604.73	618.92	632.02	642.50
Petroleum and coal products	973.53	1 003.34	990.88	1 052.32	1 095.00	1 114.51	1 085.50	1 112.73	1 224.26
Chemicals	721.87	735.42	759.53	784.07	819.66	831.76	833.51	819.54	808.80
Plastics and rubber products	517.84	528.73	550.03	572.32	590.06	591.71	608.41	635.63	649.04
Private Service-Providing	445.74	461.08	473.80	484.68	494.22	509.58	532.78	554.89	574.31
Trade, transportation, and utilities	449.88	459.53	471.27	481.14	488.42	498.43	514.34	526.07	535.79
Wholesale trade	631.40	643.45	644.38	657.29	667.09	685.00	718.63	748.94	769.91
Retail trade	333.38	346.16	360.81	367.15	371.13	377.58	383.02	385.11	386.39
Transportation and warehousing	562.31	562.70	579.88	598.41	614.96	618.58	636.97	654.95	670.33
Utilities	955.66	977.18	979.09	1 017.27	1 048.44	1 095.90	1 135.34	1 182.65	1 231.19
Information	700.86	730.88	737.77	760.45	777.25	805.08	850.42	874.65	908.44
Financial activities	537.37	557.92	575.54	609.08	622.87	644.99	672.21	705.13	726.37
Professional and business services	535.07	557.84	574.66	587.02	597.56	618.87	662.27	700.82	738.25
Education and health services	449.29	473.39	492.74	505.69	523.78	544.59	564.94	590.09	614.30
Leisure and hospitality	217.20	220.73	227.17	230.42	234.86	241.36	250.34	265.52	273.27
Other services	413.41	428.64	439.76	434.41	433.04	443.37	456.50	477.06	494.99

Table 16-5. Average Weekly Earnings of Production or Nonsupervisory Workers on Private Nonfarm Payrolls by NAICS Industry—*Continued*

(Dollars.)

Industry	2008, seasonally adjusted											
	January	February	March	April	May	June	July	August	September	October	November	December
Total Private	598.85	602.65	605.02	606.37	606.26	606.14	608.16	612.67	611.86	612.38	612.56	612.72
Goods-Producing	769.50	772.34	778.30	774.06	771.84	776.58	780.21	781.09	777.25	778.49	775.39	775.79
Mining and logging	995.45	994.08	1 029.34	979.65	971.83	989.60	1 009.79	1 042.35	1 027.06	1 029.44	1 054.58	1 029.09
Construction	829.54	833.42	839.46	841.02	836.22	842.50	845.60	849.97	846.05	849.11	839.96	851.58
Manufacturing	720.07	724.30	726.77	723.24	723.11	725.16	729.80	725.42	721.31	722.76	721.19	716.60
Durable goods	765.68	769.00	771.07	770.45	767.56	770.44	773.74	770.21	760.84	764.90	763.96	757.60
Wood products	. . .	. . .	. . .	. . .	. . .	. . .	. . .	. . .	. . .	. . .	. . .	. . .
Nonmetallic mineral products	. . .	. . .	. . .	. . .	. . .	. . .	. . .	. . .	. . .	. . .	. . .	. . .
Primary metals	. . .	. . .	. . .	. . .	. . .	. . .	. . .	. . .	. . .	. . .	. . .	. . .
Fabricated metal products	. . .	. . .	. . .	. . .	. . .	. . .	. . .	. . .	. . .	. . .	. . .	. . .
Machinery	. . .	. . .	. . .	. . .	. . .	. . .	. . .	. . .	. . .	. . .	. . .	. . .
Computer and electronic products	. . .	. . .	. . .	. . .	. . .	. . .	. . .	. . .	. . .	. . .	. . .	. . .
Electrical equipment and appliances	. . .	. . .	. . .	. . .	. . .	. . .	. . .	. . .	. . .	. . .	. . .	. . .
Transportation equipment	. . .	. . .	. . .	. . .	. . .	. . .	. . .	. . .	. . .	. . .	. . .	. . .
Motor vehicles and parts	. . .	. . .	. . .	. . .	. . .	. . .	. . .	. . .	. . .	. . .	. . .	. . .
Furniture and related products	. . .	. . .	. . .	. . .	. . .	. . .	. . .	. . .	. . .	. . .	. . .	. . .
Miscellaneous manufacturing	. . .	. . .	. . .	. . .	. . .	. . .	. . .	. . .	. . .	. . .	. . .	. . .
Nondurable goods	646.76	647.57	653.24	648.41	651.24	650.84	656.10	654.08	654.46	657.27	653.16	650.68
Food manufacturing	. . .	. . .	. . .	. . .	. . .	. . .	. . .	. . .	. . .	. . .	. . .	. . .
Beverage and tobacco products	. . .	. . .	. . .	. . .	. . .	. . .	. . .	. . .	. . .	. . .	. . .	. . .
Textile mills	. . .	. . .	. . .	. . .	. . .	. . .	. . .	. . .	. . .	. . .	. . .	. . .
Textile product mills	. . .	. . .	. . .	. . .	. . .	. . .	. . .	. . .	. . .	. . .	. . .	. . .
Apparel	. . .	. . .	. . .	. . .	. . .	. . .	. . .	. . .	. . .	. . .	. . .	. . .
Leather and allied products	. . .	. . .	. . .	. . .	. . .	. . .	. . .	. . .	. . .	. . .	. . .	. . .
Paper and paper products	. . .	. . .	. . .	. . .	. . .	. . .	. . .	. . .	. . .	. . .	. . .	. . .
Printing and related support activities	. . .	. . .	. . .	. . .	. . .	. . .	. . .	. . .	. . .	. . .	. . .	. . .
Petroleum and coal products	. . .	. . .	. . .	. . .	. . .	. . .	. . .	. . .	. . .	. . .	. . .	. . .
Chemicals	. . .	. . .	. . .	. . .	. . .	. . .	. . .	. . .	. . .	. . .	. . .	. . .
Plastics and rubber products	. . .	. . .	. . .	. . .	. . .	. . .	. . .	. . .	. . .	. . .	. . .	. . .
Private Service-Providing	565.70	567.32	569.59	571.21	573.16	573.00	574.62	578.99	578.17	580.43	580.57	582.82
Trade, transportation, and utilities	532.80	534.13	535.13	535.46	535.52	536.51	536.84	538.84	537.84	537.21	537.57	536.60
Wholesale trade	764.85	765.15	769.54	767.92	768.68	770.21	773.76	776.72	769.62	772.40	773.05	767.72
Retail trade	386.56	386.86	387.47	387.77	387.39	386.10	386.40	387.60	388.59	385.41	385.31	384.32
Transportation and warehousing	662.83	668.31	667.95	670.15	669.40	670.12	670.49	672.67	672.31	674.45	673.63	675.49
Utilities	1 236.38	1 224.94	1 243.73	1 215.80	1 224.43	1 252.16	1 215.61	1 222.05	1 232.32	1 228.68	1 225.78	1 250.96
Information	885.72	888.62	897.17	898.90	904.39	909.43	912.73	918.16	918.81	922.13	922.78	921.67
Financial activities	713.64	717.43	720.30	724.10	726.26	724.59	723.28	735.36	735.48	733.44	736.80	737.03
Professional and business services	714.13	717.94	723.14	727.32	731.50	733.58	737.41	746.16	747.16	754.89	760.12	764.56
Education and health services	605.06	606.36	611.16	610.92	614.76	612.30	614.90	618.10	618.80	620.10	619.81	622.08
Leisure and hospitality	270.20	273.05	271.98	274.57	274.00	274.51	273.92	274.43	274.68	274.09	272.50	273.50
Other services	484.75	488.18	492.55	492.80	494.03	493.96	496.80	499.65	497.34	498.57	500.10	498.47

. . . = Not available.

Table 16-6. Indexes of Aggregate Weekly Hours of Production or Nonsupervisory Workers on Private Nonfarm Payrolls by NAICS Industry

(2002 = 100.)

Industry	1990	1991	1992	1993	1994	1995	1996	1997	1998	1999
Total Private	84.4	82.6	83.1	85.5	89.2	91.6	93.8	97.1	99.4	101.5
Goods-Producing	106.1	100.1	98.7	100.8	105.6	106.8	108.1	111.2	112.3	112.6
Mining and logging	128.6	123.8	113.3	110.3	111.0	110.2	112.7	117.6	112.8	102.9
Construction	78.8	70.1	67.5	71.3	77.3	79.9	84.3	88.6	93.4	99.7
Manufacturing	117.7	112.8	112.4	113.9	118.3	119.0	118.8	121.4	121.0	118.9
Durable goods	114.2	107.6	106.4	108.2	114.2	116.3	117.5	121.6	122.0	120.5
Wood products	101.5	92.6	95.2	100.5	109.1	109.3	111.6	114.8	117.5	118.6
Nonmetallic mineral products	100.8	92.8	92.6	94.3	98.8	99.7	101.5	103.1	105.8	106.9
Primary metals	131.5	122.9	120.8	121.5	128.0	129.3	129.9	132.3	131.1	128.4
Fabricated metal products	104.7	99.1	97.3	99.7	106.3	109.9	111.6	116.6	118.6	116.7
Machinery	123.8	116.2	113.9	118.6	126.9	132.2	133.7	138.9	137.3	129.8
Computer and electronic products	137.1	128.1	122.9	121.1	123.5	127.1	129.9	136.8	136.7	131.1
Electrical equipment and appliances	136.0	127.9	125.9	126.8	132.4	130.3	129.4	127.7	127.8	128.3
Transportation equipment	111.1	105.8	104.3	105.5	112.5	115.4	116.4	120.7	118.7	119.5
Motor vehicles and parts	90.9	87.9	91.1	97.9	110.6	115.9	116.1	117.5	112.8	118.7
Furniture and related products	97.1	89.5	92.1	95.3	100.5	99.2	98.3	102.9	108.4	112.6
Miscellaneous manufacturing	104.2	103.9	105.3	107.0	108.4	107.9	107.8	110.1	110.4	110.3
Nondurable goods	123.0	120.8	121.7	122.7	124.7	123.1	120.5	120.9	119.4	116.1
Food manufacturing	96.2	96.6	97.3	98.7	100.5	101.6	101.8	102.6	103.4	103.8
Beverage and tobacco products	96.9	96.4	95.4	95.6	98.7	97.9	101.4	103.1	104.9	104.7
Textile mills	170.4	168.4	170.3	170.8	171.6	163.5	154.1	155.2	148.9	139.1
Textile product mills	118.8	113.1	114.8	118.7	124.0	121.0	118.0	119.4	117.6	115.5
Apparel	266.6	263.6	266.8	258.8	252.0	235.0	211.5	201.3	181.0	154.6
Leather and allied products	290.0	268.9	263.5	259.1	246.9	221.8	197.5	187.1	166.6	148.3
Paper and paper products	121.8	120.6	121.7	121.9	123.5	121.4	120.1	121.5	119.5	117.1
Printing and related support activities	122.3	118.7	118.4	120.3	123.8	123.9	122.8	124.6	124.3	120.9
Petroleum and coal products	128.9	127.5	126.0	122.0	120.0	115.5	113.5	112.7	113.4	107.6
Chemicals	118.2	115.0	112.9	113.4	115.1	115.4	114.7	114.7	115.4	113.1
Plastics and rubber products	97.7	94.1	98.0	102.3	108.7	109.8	110.0	112.7	113.7	114.6
Private Service-Providing	78.3	77.8	78.8	81.2	84.6	87.3	89.7	93.1	95.8	98.4
Trade, transportation, and utilities	89.5	87.4	87.3	89.0	92.7	95.1	96.6	98.8	100.3	101.9
Wholesale trade	94.9	93.3	92.4	92.4	95.8	99.2	100.7	103.4	104.8	106.2
Retail trade	87.5	84.8	85.1	86.3	89.8	92.3	93.7	95.9	97.2	99.5
Transportation and warehousing	83.5	82.3	82.7	88.4	93.7	95.6	98.2	101.0	102.6	103.2
Utilities	124.3	123.5	121.6	119.9	117.1	112.9	108.6	106.1	105.8	105.0
Information	76.2	76.1	76.5	78.0	79.2	82.5	87.0	90.4	92.6	98.5
Financial activities	84.5	83.3	83.5	85.9	88.0	87.8	89.8	92.6	96.5	98.0
Professional and business services	68.0	66.7	68.4	71.9	77.0	81.2	85.2	91.5	96.7	101.7
Education and health services	67.2	70.2	72.9	75.4	78.3	81.2	83.4	86.7	88.9	90.6
Leisure and hospitality	78.9	77.3	79.3	82.2	85.6	88.5	90.8	93.4	95.5	97.9
Other services	81.8	81.2	80.6	82.8	84.5	87.1	89.1	91.9	94.3	96.3

Table 16-6. Indexes of Aggregate Weekly Hours of Production or Nonsupervisory Workers on Private Nonfarm Payrolls by NAICS Industry—*Continued*

(2002 = 100.)

Industry	2000	2001	2002	2003	2004	2005	2006	2007	2008
Total Private	103.6	102.1	100.0	98.7	100.2	102.8	105.8	107.3	106.2
Goods-Producing	113.1	106.6	100.0	95.7	96.8	98.9	102.5	101.7	96.9
Mining and logging	105.1	108.3	100.0	97.4	104.0	114.7	125.8	133.5	138.9
Construction	104.0	103.2	100.0	98.4	101.7	108.3	115.3	114.8	107.3
Manufacturing	117.7	108.1	100.0	94.5	94.3	93.9	95.6	94.4	90.4
Durable goods	120.3	109.3	100.0	94.3	95.2	96.1	98.9	97.4	92.3
Wood products	115.8	105.0	100.0	97.8	100.9	101.3	100.0	89.3	77.4
Nonmetallic mineral products	109.1	106.1	100.0	94.3	98.0	97.4	100.3	96.9	91.9
Primary metals	128.9	113.0	100.0	93.4	93.3	93.1	94.1	91.4	87.6
Fabricated metal products	119.1	109.3	100.0	95.3	97.7	99.3	103.1	104.5	101.3
Machinery	127.5	114.1	100.0	93.6	96.0	98.8	102.2	103.2	102.1
Computer and electronic products	133.0	117.9	100.0	92.1	89.7	94.8	103.6	102.1	101.5
Electrical equipment and appliances	127.7	113.4	100.0	92.0	88.7	86.4	88.0	89.1	88.7
Transportation equipment	116.3	105.3	100.0	95.4	96.4	97.3	99.9	98.0	88.6
Motor vehicles and parts	117.3	103.6	100.0	95.9	97.0	95.2	92.9	85.8	72.8
Furniture and related products	114.7	104.7	100.0	93.0	94.3	91.8	90.3	86.1	74.8
Miscellaneous manufacturing	109.6	104.8	100.0	93.6	91.8	90.6	90.4	91.0	89.5
Nondurable goods	113.3	106.0	100.0	94.7	92.7	90.3	90.4	89.6	87.1
Food manufacturing	103.5	101.5	100.0	98.4	97.1	95.8	98.6	101.2	101.0
Beverage and tobacco products	104.2	100.3	100.0	88.4	88.8	94.8	99.3	102.2	92.3
Textile mills	132.4	112.2	100.0	86.3	79.0	71.3	65.1	56.3	47.9
Textile product mills	112.4	105.5	100.0	92.4	90.2	88.0	85.0	77.5	70.6
Apparel	137.6	117.1	100.0	82.0	75.1	65.7	63.4	61.5	56.6
Leather and allied products	138.4	113.3	100.0	91.3	83.6	79.0	74.1	69.3	69.8
Paper and paper products	113.4	106.6	100.0	92.4	89.2	87.9	86.9	85.7	83.6
Printing and related support activities	119.4	111.5	100.0	95.3	93.4	90.9	92.5	91.6	86.1
Petroleum and coal products	105.8	105.6	100.0	98.7	102.6	102.4	96.9	95.6	102.1
Chemicals	110.4	104.7	100.0	99.0	99.0	95.9	96.1	94.1	94.9
Plastics and rubber products	114.3	104.9	100.0	95.2	94.2	92.4	91.9	91.1	87.7
Private Service-Providing	101.0	100.8	100.0	99.5	101.1	103.8	106.7	108.9	108.8
Trade, transportation, and utilities	103.5	101.5	100.0	98.6	99.6	101.6	103.3	104.8	103.6
Wholesale trade	107.1	102.9	100.0	98.0	98.9	101.8	105.7	109.2	109.0
Retail trade	101.3	100.5	100.0	98.9	99.4	100.8	101.1	101.8	100.3
Transportation and warehousing	105.6	102.7	100.0	98.8	101.9	105.2	107.9	109.4	107.6
Utilities	104.2	102.4	100.0	97.4	94.2	93.1	93.8	96.2	98.5
Information	105.0	106.6	100.0	97.0	98.3	99.4	100.2	100.2	100.4
Financial activities	98.5	99.5	100.0	101.5	101.9	104.7	107.4	108.7	107.6
Professional and business services	106.6	104.0	100.0	98.7	101.8	106.3	112.1	115.3	114.2
Education and health services	92.8	96.6	100.0	101.4	103.3	106.4	109.0	112.5	115.8
Leisure and hospitality	100.6	100.7	100.0	100.1	103.0	106.3	108.9	110.9	109.9
Other services	97.8	99.1	100.0	97.5	96.1	96.2	97.5	99.4	99.7

Table 16-6. Indexes of Aggregate Weekly Hours of Production or Nonsupervisory Workers on Private Nonfarm Payrolls by NAICS Industry—*Continued*

(2002 = 100.)

Industry	2008, seasonally adjusted											
	January	February	March	April	May	June	July	August	September	October	November	December
Total Private	107.5	107.6	107.5	107.4	106.9	106.4	106.2	106.4	105.8	105.0	104.1	103.2
Goods-Producing	100.8	100.3	100.2	99.0	98.1	97.8	97.3	96.7	95.3	93.9	92.0	90.4
Mining and logging	136.7	136.9	139.7	135.6	134.9	136.5	137.6	142.0	141.2	140.6	143.2	139.1
Construction	112.4	111.7	111.5	110.4	108.6	108.1	107.5	107.0	105.3	104.1	100.5	99.8
Manufacturing	93.7	93.5	93.2	92.2	91.7	91.3	91.0	90.0	88.7	87.4	86.0	84.0
Durable goods	96.8	96.3	95.8	94.9	94.1	93.5	93.0	91.8	90.0	88.5	87.1	84.6
Wood products	84.4	83.0	81.2	80.6	79.7	78.7	77.7	76.6	74.7	72.7	70.5	66.7
Nonmetallic mineral products	95.7	94.8	96.3	94.1	93.3	92.1	92.4	91.7	90.1	89.6	86.3	84.0
Primary metals	90.6	90.8	91.5	90.5	89.5	89.4	88.2	87.7	86.2	84.7	81.5	78.1
Fabricated metal products	105.4	105.1	104.9	103.6	103.2	101.6	101.0	101.0	99.6	98.1	96.6	93.8
Machinery	105.4	105.4	104.8	104.0	103.0	102.3	102.4	102.8	100.9	99.6	96.7	94.8
Computer and electronic products	101.8	102.1	103.5	103.5	102.9	102.6	101.9	101.5	100.2	99.3	99.7	96.8
Electrical equipment and appliances	89.8	89.2	89.9	89.5	89.9	89.4	89.3	88.8	88.6	87.3	86.1	83.8
Transportation equipment	96.5	96.4	93.6	91.9	90.9	90.9	91.1	86.1	83.5	81.0	81.0	79.0
Motor vehicles and parts	81.9	82.0	78.2	76.2	75.0	74.6	75.1	68.6	68.1	66.3	63.9	61.3
Furniture and related products	81.3	79.9	79.8	78.7	77.9	76.9	75.3	73.3	71.7	69.7	67.4	66.1
Miscellaneous manufacturing	91.9	89.9	91.0	90.7	90.2	89.3	89.4	90.8	89.1	89.0	87.1	85.9
Nondurable goods	89.0	88.7	88.9	88.2	88.1	87.7	87.7	87.1	86.3	85.7	84.2	82.8
Food manufacturing	101.5	101.9	102.1	101.7	101.8	101.2	100.8	100.7	100.4	100.4	99.3	98.6
Beverage and tobacco products	92.0	90.6	93.8	92.1	93.8	93.9	93.3	91.8	91.7	91.4	91.6	89.3
Textile mills	51.9	51.7	50.9	49.4	49.4	48.5	48.3	48.8	46.7	45.3	42.6	40.7
Textile product mills	72.1	72.7	73.3	71.5	71.9	71.2	71.2	69.4	68.8	68.3	67.5	65.0
Apparel	59.6	59.1	58.2	57.8	56.3	56.9	57.9	57.6	55.7	54.9	52.7	51.3
Leather and allied products	71.6	69.9	69.6	71.1	71.8	72.3	70.9	72.4	71.6	69.3	62.0	62.5
Paper and paper products	86.7	86.1	85.6	85.3	83.9	83.7	83.5	83.6	82.2	81.5	80.9	79.8
Printing and related support activities	89.3	88.4	89.2	88.3	87.9	85.6	84.7	85.3	84.8	83.9	82.5	80.6
Petroleum and coal products	100.3	101.7	101.0	98.9	101.3	102.1	105.0	105.6	104.7	102.8	98.6	98.4
Chemicals	95.7	95.1	96.4	95.2	95.2	96.2	96.2	94.6	93.8	94.0	93.4	91.8
Plastics and rubber products	90.4	90.8	90.1	89.1	88.9	89.1	89.3	88.0	86.8	85.1	82.9	80.2
Private Service-Providing	109.7	109.6	109.5	109.5	109.4	109.0	108.9	109.1	108.5	108.2	107.5	107.0
Trade, transportation, and utilities	105.4	105.2	105.1	104.8	104.3	104.1	103.9	103.6	103.3	102.4	101.4	100.6
Wholesale trade	110.4	110.0	110.5	109.9	109.7	109.6	109.5	109.0	108.1	108.0	107.0	105.5
Retail trade	102.3	102.0	101.9	101.6	101.1	100.6	100.4	100.2	100.1	98.9	97.9	97.1
Transportation and warehousing	109.4	109.8	109.4	109.3	108.4	107.9	107.9	107.3	106.9	106.1	104.5	104.2
Utilities	98.9	97.6	98.9	97.7	97.5	99.1	97.9	97.7	99.0	98.8	98.7	100.2
Information	100.2	100.2	100.7	100.7	100.7	100.6	100.3	100.4	100.7	100.8	100.2	99.6
Financial activities	107.8	108.0	108.0	108.3	108.1	107.7	107.2	108.4	107.9	107.4	107.3	106.2
Professional and business services	115.9	115.5	115.2	115.4	115.2	114.5	114.2	114.0	113.3	112.9	112.0	110.8
Education and health services	114.4	114.7	115.4	115.4	116.0	115.6	115.9	116.7	116.4	116.5	116.6	116.9
Leisure and hospitality	110.7	111.2	110.7	111.2	110.5	110.5	110.0	109.9	109.7	109.0	108.2	107.8
Other services	99.2	99.8	100.2	99.9	99.9	99.5	99.8	100.2	99.6	99.7	99.1	98.3

NOTES AND DEFINITIONS

TABLES 16-1 THROUGH 16-6
EMPLOYMENT, HOURS, AND EARNINGS
BY NAICS INDUSTRY

SOURCE: U.S. DEPARTMENT OF LABOR, BUREAU OF LABOR STATISTICS

See the notes and definitions for Tables 10-7 through 10-12 regarding definitions of *employment, production or nonsupervisory workers, average weekly hours, overtime hours, average hourly earnings, average weekly earnings,* and the *indexes of aggregate weekly hours.* Availability and reference information is also provided in those notes and definitions.

See Chapter 14 for information on the North American Industry Classification System (NAICS).

CHAPTER 17: KEY SECTOR STATISTICS

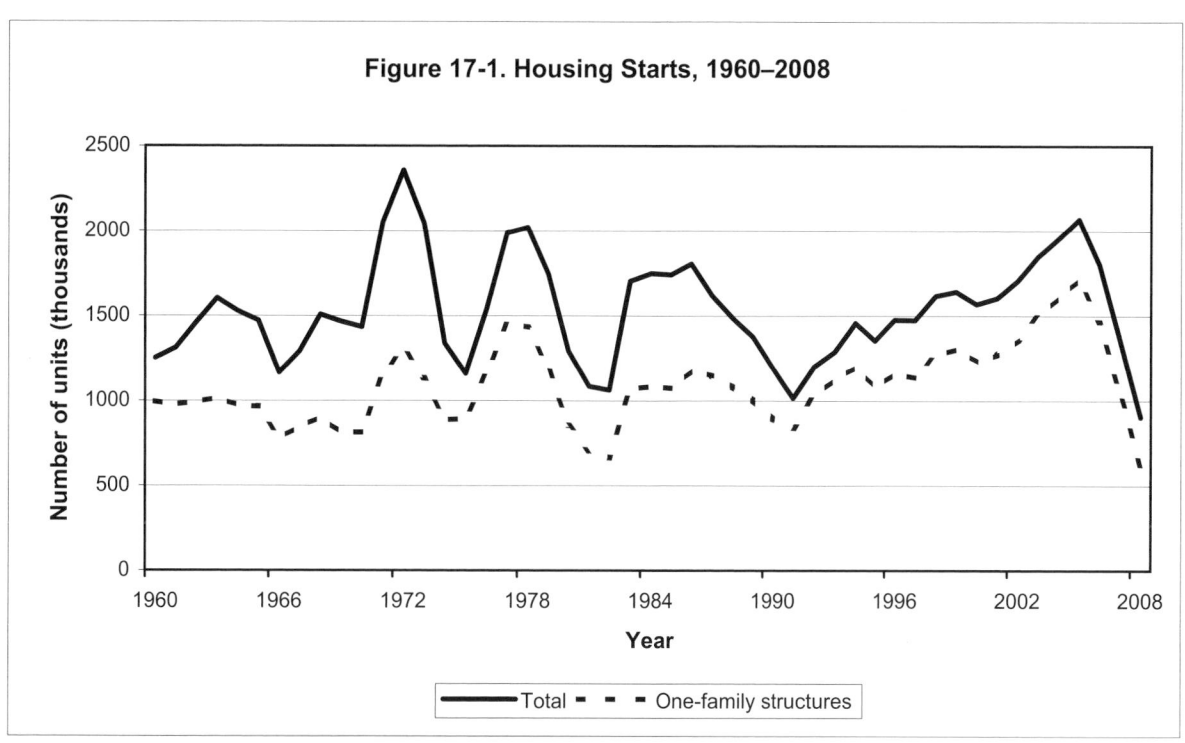

Figure 17-1. Housing Starts, 1960–2008

- The housing sector was the source of the boom and bust cycle of 2001–2009. In 2005, as shown in Figure 17-1, 2.1 million housing units were started, the highest since 1972. Of those, 1.7 million were one-family homes, an all-time record. By 2008, however, both total and single-family starts plunged to the lowest levels of their 50-year history. (Table 17-3)

- Associated with this dramatic swing in real activity was an unsustainable speculative "bubble" in the prices of new and existing homes. Home prices were collapsing by 2008, as can be seen in Table 17-3, Table 12-10, and Figure 12-4. The price bubble encouraged excessive growth in home mortgage debt, which is now weighing heavily on household incomes and net worth, as can be seen in Tables 12-4 through 12-6.

- New orders for nondefense capital goods at U.S. manufacturing firms declined 28 percent from December 2007 to December 2008. Even excluding the volatile aircraft sector, they were down 12 percent. (Table 17-6)

- Sales of cars and light trucks plunged 36 percent from December 2007 to December 2008. For the full year 2008, 13.1 million units were sold, down 24 percent from the record high of 17.3 million units in 2000. (Table 17-8)

- Some service industries were also affected by the recession. New seasonally adjusted revenue estimates show marked declines in the fourth quarter of 2008 in the information, legal services, and employment services (temporary help) industries. More detailed industry estimates that are not seasonally adjusted show declines from a year earlier for print and radio and TV broadcasting, partly offset by gains at wireless and cable industries. Health care and some professional industries also showed gains over the year. (Table 17-14)

- As a percentage of the total supply of petroleum and products (domestic crude oil and natural gas liquids production plus net imports), net imports have increased from 10.4 percent in 1955 to 62.1 percent in 2008. (Table 17-1)

- Sales by electronic shopping and mail order grew from 1.9 percent of total retail sales in 1992 to 5.4 percent in 2008. (Table 17-9) E-commerce alone grew from 0.6 percent of total retail sales at the end of 1999 to 3.4 percent at the end of 2008. (Table 17-10)

Table 17-1. Petroleum and Petroleum Products—Prices, Imports, Domestic Production, and Stocks

(Not seasonally adjusted.)

Year and month	Crude oil futures price (dollars per barrel) Current dollars	Crude oil futures price 2000 dollars	Imports Total energy-related petroleum products (thousands of barrels)	Imports Crude petroleum Thousands of barrels Total	Imports Crude petroleum Thousands of barrels Average per day	Imports Crude petroleum Unit price (dollars per barrel)	Supply Petroleum and products Exports	Supply Petroleum and products Imports	Supply Petroleum and products Net imports	Supply Domestic production Crude oil	Supply Domestic production Natural gas plant liquids	Stocks Crude oil and petroleum products	Stocks Crude petroleum Total	Stocks Crude petroleum Strategic petroleum reserve
1955	...	...	...	...	...	...	368	1 248	880	6 807	771	715	266	...
1956	...	...	...	...	...	...	430	1 436	1 006	7 151	800	780	266	...
1957	...	...	...	...	...	...	568	1 574	1 006	7 170	808	841	282	...
1958	...	...	...	...	...	...	276	1 700	1 424	6 710	808	789	263	...
1959	...	...	...	...	...	...	211	1 780	1 569	7 054	879	809	257	...
1960	...	...	...	...	...	...	202	1 815	1 613	7 035	929	785	240	...
1961	...	...	...	...	...	...	174	1 917	1 743	7 183	991	825	245	...
1962	...	...	...	...	...	...	168	2 082	1 914	7 332	1 021	834	252	...
1963	...	...	...	...	...	...	208	2 123	1 915	7 542	1 098	836	237	...
1964	...	...	...	...	...	...	202	2 259	2 057	7 614	1 154	839	230	...
1965	...	...	...	...	...	...	187	2 468	2 281	7 804	1 210	836	220	...
1966	...	...	...	...	...	...	198	2 573	2 375	8 295	1 284	874	238	...
1967	...	...	...	...	...	...	307	2 537	2 230	8 810	1 409	944	249	...
1968	...	...	...	...	...	...	231	2 840	2 609	9 096	1 504	1 000	272	...
1969	...	...	...	...	...	...	233	3 166	2 933	9 238	1 590	980	265	...
1970	...	...	...	...	...	...	259	3 419	3 160	9 637	1 660	1 018	276	...
1971	...	...	...	...	...	...	224	3 926	3 702	9 463	1 693	1 044	260	...
1972	...	...	...	...	...	...	222	4 741	4 519	9 441	1 744	959	246	...
1973	...	...	...	1 392 970	3 816	3.30	231	6 256	6 025	9 208	1 738	1 008	242	...
1974	...	...	...	1 367 081	3 745	11.17	221	6 112	5 892	8 774	1 688	1 074	265	...
1975	...	...	...	1 584 730	4 342	11.59	209	6 056	5 846	8 375	1 633	1 133	271	...
1976	...	...	...	2 050 424	5 618	12.43	223	7 313	7 090	8 132	1 604	1 112	285	...
1977	...	...	...	2 519 806	6 904	13.33	243	8 807	8 565	8 245	1 618	1 312	348	7
1978	...	...	...	2 392 350	6 554	13.43	362	8 363	8 002	8 707	1 567	1 278	376	67
1979	...	...	...	2 467 315	6 760	18.68	471	8 456	7 985	8 552	1 584	1 341	430	91
1980	...	...	...	1 977 247	5 417	31.36	544	6 909	6 365	8 597	1 573	1 392	466	108
1981	...	...	...	1 763 072	4 830	35.13	595	5 996	5 401	8 572	1 609	1 484	594	230
1982	...	...	...	1 420 753	3 892	33.39	815	5 113	4 298	8 649	1 550	1 430	644	294
1983	30.66	49.11	...	1 293 819	3 545	29.51	739	5 051	4 312	8 688	1 559	1 454	723	379
1984	29.44	45.44	...	1 319 683	3 616	27.68	722	5 437	4 715	8 879	1 630	1 556	796	451
1985	27.89	41.67	...	1 260 856	3 454	26.20	781	5 067	4 286	8 971	1 609	1 519	814	493
1986	15.05	21.95	...	1 634 567	4 478	13.90	785	6 224	5 439	8 680	1 551	1 593	843	512
1987	19.15	26.99	...	1 744 977	4 781	16.80	764	6 678	5 914	8 349	1 595	1 607	890	541
1988	15.96	21.64	...	1 887 860	5 172	13.69	815	7 402	6 587	8 140	1 625	1 597	890	560
1989	19.58	25.44	...	2 146 552	5 881	16.49	859	8 061	7 202	7 613	1 546	1 581	921	580
1990	24.50	30.44		2 216 604	6 073	19.75	857	8 018	7 161	7 355	1 559	1 621	908	586
1991	21.50	25.77	2 828 953	2 146 064	5 880	17.46	1 001	7 627	6 626	7 417	1 659	1 617	893	569
1992	20.58	23.98	2 947 582	2 294 570	6 269	16.80	950	7 888	6 938	7 171	1 697	1 592	893	575
1993	18.48	21.05	3 257 008	2 543 374	6 968	15.13	1 003	8 620	7 618	6 847	1 736	1 647	922	587
1994	17.19	19.17	3 416 045	2 704 196	7 409	14.23	942	8 996	8 054	6 662	1 727	1 653	929	592
1995	18.40	20.09	3 361 882	2 767 312	7 582	15.81	949	8 835	7 886	6 560	1 762	1 563	895	592
1996	22.03	23.55	3 622 385	2 893 647	7 906	18.98	981	9 478	8 498	6 465	1 830	1 507	850	566
1997	20.61	21.67	3 802 574	3 734 226	8 409	17.67	1 003	10 162	9 158	6 452	1 817	1 560	868	563
1998	14.40	15.00	4 088 027	3 242 711	8 884	11.49	945	10 708	9 764	6 252	1 759	1 647	895	571
1999	19.30	19.78	4 081 181	3 228 092	8 844	15.76	940	10 852	9 912	5 881	1 850	1 493	852	567
2000	30.26	30.26	4 314 825	3 399 239	9 288	26.44	1 040	11 459	10 419	5 822	1 911	1 468	826	541
2001	25.95	25.42	4 475 026	3 471 067	9 510	21.40	971	11 871	10 900	5 801	1 868	1 586	862	550
2002	26.15	25.26	4 337 075	3 418 022	9 364	22.61	984	11 530	10 546	5 746	1 880	1 548	877	599
2003	30.99	29.35	4 654 638	3 676 005	10 071	26.98	1 027	12 264	11 238	5 681	1 719	1 568	907	638
2004	41.47	38.26	4 917 591	3 820 979	10 440	34.48	1 048	13 145	12 097	5 419	1 809	1 645	961	676
2005	56.70	50.82	5 004 339	3 754 671	10 287	46.81	1 165	13 714	12 549	5 178	1 717	1 698	1 008	685
2006	66.25	57.77	4 880 734	3 734 226	10 231	58.01	1 317	13 707	12 390	5 102	1 739	1 720	1 001	689
2007	72.41	61.54	4 807 811	3 690 568	10 111	64.28	1 433	13 468	12 036	5 064	1 783	1 662	983	697
2008	99.75	82.07	4 613 626	3 591 136	9 812	95.23	1 789	12 890	11 101	4 950	1 811	1 718	1 026	702
2008														
January	92.93	77.41	420 916	322 206	10 394	84.09	1 623	13 493	11 869	5 093	1 783	1 677	995	698
February	95.35	79.32	367 098	286 483	9 879	84.76	2 072	12 604	10 531	5 113	1 830	1 662	1 000	699
March	105.42	87.42	363 252	278 571	8 986	89.85	1 823	12 550	10 728	5 139	1 847	1 653	1 013	700
April	112.46	93.04	388 145	303 050	10 102	96.81	1 754	13 252	11 498	5 162	1 880	1 665	1 020	701
May	125.46	103.33	373 287	293 995	9 484	106.28	1 806	12 862	11 056	5 166	1 908	1 673	1 007	704
June	134.02	109.54	382 675	297 532	9 918	117.13	2 165	13 367	11 202	5 109	1 810	1 686	1 001	706
July	133.48	108.51	424 467	342 024	11 033	124.66	2 069	13 064	10 995	5 110	1 856	1 699	1 002	707
August	116.69	94.87	388 670	308 380	9 948	119.99	2 068	13 060	10 992	4 895	1 839	1 710	1 009	707
September	103.76	84.29	339 044	253 276	8 443	107.58	1 338	11 512	10 174	3 960	1 537	1 705	1 006	702
October	76.72	62.67	413 766	324 185	10 458	92.02	1 669	13 217	11 548	4 645	1 745	1 712	1 014	702
November	57.44	47.45	341 870	261 600	8 720	66.72	1 694	12 831	11 137	5 008	1 839	1 716	1 022	702
December	42.04	34.91	410 426	319 834	10 317	49.93	1 395	12 830	11 435	4 989	1 851	1 718	1 026	702

... = Not available.

Table 17-2. New Construction Put in Place

(Billions of dollars, monthly data are at seasonally adjusted annual rates.)

Year and month	Total	Private											
		Total [1]	Residential	Office	Commercial		Health care	Educational	Amusement and recreation	Transportation	Communication	Power	Manufacturing
					Total [1]	Multi-retail							
1975	152.6	109.3	51.6	. . .	. . .	. . .	. . .	. . .	. . .	. . .	. . .	. . .	. . .
1976	172.1	128.2	68.3	. . .	. . .	. . .	. . .	. . .	. . .	. . .	. . .	. . .	. . .
1977	200.5	157.4	92.0	. . .	. . .	. . .	. . .	. . .	. . .	. . .	. . .	. . .	. . .
1978	239.9	189.7	109.8	. . .	. . .	. . .	. . .	. . .	. . .	. . .	. . .	. . .	. . .
1979	272.9	216.2	116.4	. . .	. . .	. . .	. . .	. . .	. . .	. . .	. . .	. . .	. . .
1980	273.9	210.3	100.4	. . .	. . .	. . .	. . .	. . .	. . .	. . .	. . .	. . .	. . .
1981	289.1	224.4	99.2	. . .	. . .	. . .	. . .	. . .	. . .	. . .	. . .	. . .	. . .
1982	279.3	216.3	84.7	. . .	. . .	. . .	. . .	. . .	. . .	. . .	. . .	. . .	. . .
1983	311.9	248.4	125.8	. . .	. . .	. . .	. . .	. . .	. . .	. . .	. . .	. . .	. . .
1984	370.2	300.0	155.0	. . .	. . .	. . .	. . .	. . .	. . .	. . .	. . .	. . .	. . .
1985	403.4	325.6	160.5	. . .	. . .	. . .	. . .	. . .	. . .	. . .	. . .	. . .	. . .
1986	433.5	348.9	190.7	. . .	. . .	. . .	. . .	. . .	. . .	. . .	. . .	. . .	. . .
1987	446.6	356.0	199.7	. . .	. . .	. . .	. . .	. . .	. . .	. . .	. . .	. . .	. . .
1988	462.0	367.3	204.5	. . .	. . .	. . .	. . .	. . .	. . .	. . .	. . .	. . .	. . .
1989	477.5	379.3	204.3	. . .	. . .	. . .	. . .	. . .	. . .	. . .	. . .	. . .	. . .
1990	476.8	369.3	191.1	. . .	. . .	. . .	. . .	. . .	. . .	. . .	. . .	. . .	. . .
1991	432.6	322.5	166.3	. . .	. . .	. . .	. . .	. . .	. . .	. . .	. . .	. . .	. . .
1992	463.7	347.8	199.4	. . .	. . .	. . .	. . .	. . .	. . .	. . .	. . .	. . .	. . .
1993	485.5	358.2	208.2	20.0	34.4	11.5	14.9	4.8	4.6	4.7	9.8	23.6	23.4
1994	531.9	401.5	241.0	20.4	39.6	12.2	15.4	5.0	5.1	4.7	10.1	21.0	28.8
1995	548.7	408.7	228.1	23.0	44.1	12.0	15.3	5.7	5.9	4.8	11.1	22.0	35.4
1996	599.7	453.0	257.5	26.5	49.4	13.3	15.4	7.0	7.0	5.8	11.8	17.4	38.1
1997	631.9	478.4	264.7	32.8	53.1	12.2	17.4	8.8	8.5	6.2	12.5	16.4	37.6
1998	688.5	533.7	296.3	40.4	55.7	13.3	17.7	9.8	8.6	7.3	12.5	21.7	40.5
1999	744.6	575.5	326.3	45.1	59.4	15.2	18.4	9.8	9.6	6.5	18.4	22.0	35.1
2000	802.8	621.4	346.1	52.4	64.1	14.9	19.5	11.7	8.8	6.9	18.8	29.3	37.6
2001	840.2	638.3	364.4	49.7	63.6	16.4	19.5	12.8	7.8	7.1	19.6	31.5	37.8
2002	847.9	634.4	396.7	35.3	59.0	15.6	22.4	13.1	7.5	6.8	18.4	32.6	22.7
2003	891.5	675.4	446.0	30.6	57.5	15.4	24.2	13.4	7.8	6.6	14.5	33.6	21.4
2004	991.6	771.4	532.9	32.9	63.2	18.8	26.3	12.7	8.4	6.8	15.5	27.4	23.7
2005	1 102.7	868.5	611.9	37.3	66.6	22.8	28.5	12.8	7.5	7.1	18.8	26.3	29.9
2006	1 167.6	912.2	613.7	45.7	73.4	29.2	32.0	13.8	9.3	8.7	22.2	31.2	35.1
2007	1 137.2	850.0	492.5	53.4	85.0	34.2	34.8	17.1	10.4	9.4	26.9	41.5	42.2
2008	1 074.1	766.6	355.9	57.5	81.9	32.3	37.9	18.8	10.9	10.1	24.7	60.1	63.2
2006													
January	1 186.0	943.4	663.9	38.9	73.5	28.0	29.8	13.4	7.8	8.7	21.8	31.1	32.2
February	1 201.5	954.8	672.7	41.2	71.3	27.3	30.2	13.5	8.3	9.3	21.3	32.2	31.2
March	1 213.5	962.0	676.4	41.6	71.8	27.8	30.5	13.6	8.4	9.1	21.3	30.9	33.1
April	1 183.9	928.6	640.6	43.9	70.5	27.9	30.8	13.7	9.2	8.4	21.5	28.7	34.9
May	1 180.7	926.9	633.3	45.0	72.5	29.5	31.3	13.8	9.7	8.7	21.2	30.2	34.5
June	1 173.0	915.3	615.9	46.5	73.1	29.7	32.6	13.6	9.0	9.0	21.6	30.6	35.7
July	1 165.7	907.6	605.7	48.3	73.2	30.5	32.3	13.4	9.5	8.8	21.9	31.8	34.7
August	1 159.1	904.2	596.7	48.6	73.4	31.0	33.0	13.2	9.9	8.0	22.3	31.6	39.2
September	1 151.2	896.4	589.2	47.8	74.6	30.2	33.1	13.9	10.2	8.3	23.4	30.5	37.2
October	1 139.0	882.1	577.8	47.3	72.7	29.3	32.8	14.4	10.2	8.4	23.3	30.5	35.4
November	1 136.8	876.2	564.7	48.5	75.6	29.3	33.2	14.7	9.9	8.6	23.0	33.0	35.1
December	1 152.3	882.1	563.1	50.5	77.6	29.2	34.7	15.1	9.6	8.8	23.9	33.3	35.9
2007													
January	1 149.1	872.3	553.3	51.7	78.4	30.8	33.9	15.2	8.9	9.3	23.2	31.5	36.6
February	1 149.0	875.0	545.3	51.3	80.9	31.5	34.4	15.6	8.6	9.8	25.7	33.7	38.7
March	1 162.4	887.3	552.1	52.1	81.7	33.2	34.2	15.3	9.8	9.0	25.9	35.8	38.0
April	1 148.2	869.4	528.5	50.8	83.4	33.4	34.1	16.0	9.6	8.9	25.5	36.6	41.1
May	1 154.6	868.5	520.9	50.6	84.6	33.8	33.4	15.9	10.0	9.0	27.3	40.8	40.0
June	1 149.4	863.0	508.2	51.1	85.4	33.5	33.6	17.3	10.2	9.1	27.6	43.3	40.1
July	1 139.4	852.9	493.6	52.1	84.6	33.8	34.6	17.7	10.6	9.3	26.7	42.5	42.9
August	1 138.8	848.5	480.2	54.1	86.5	34.1	35.2	18.2	11.7	9.7	27.5	44.2	42.6
September	1 134.9	837.7	465.1	55.4	87.9	35.6	35.8	18.0	10.6	9.9	27.8	45.0	42.8
October	1 124.2	829.9	447.0	57.6	88.6	35.7	36.2	18.1	10.8	9.8	28.0	47.7	44.8
November	1 115.3	816.9	428.7	57.8	89.1	38.2	36.1	18.4	11.4	9.6	28.3	48.9	47.2
December	1 093.5	797.5	413.9	56.1	85.1	35.6	36.0	18.6	11.6	9.9	28.7	46.0	51.2
2008													
January	1 085.4	794.6	404.9	58.4	86.7	35.6	35.1	18.7	11.6	9.8	27.4	51.5	48.8
February	1 075.3	783.7	392.0	57.0	87.0	34.5	35.5	18.8	11.8	10.0	26.8	53.1	49.5
March	1 090.5	789.6	391.6	57.3	86.9	33.7	36.6	18.8	11.4	10.1	27.8	54.8	51.1
April	1 085.2	783.7	383.5	57.7	87.5	34.2	36.7	18.5	11.4	10.2	26.5	54.5	52.0
May	1 088.3	784.1	371.4	57.8	85.6	32.8	36.9	18.6	11.1	10.3	26.9	55.3	63.3
June	1 086.6	780.4	356.4	57.4	84.8	33.8	37.5	18.2	11.2	10.0	26.2	58.4	72.4
July	1 060.0	751.5	334.5	58.1	82.9	33.2	37.6	18.4	11.3	10.3	24.5	60.4	66.1
August	1 085.7	769.1	352.9	58.2	81.6	32.8	37.6	18.7	11.1	10.1	23.0	62.2	65.3
September	1 089.4	777.0	350.2	59.7	78.4	30.5	39.8	19.8	10.8	10.4	23.0	66.1	71.6
October	1 082.3	766.9	343.8	58.2	77.8	31.1	39.4	19.4	10.9	10.2	22.1	63.5	74.0
November	1 044.6	728.0	314.1	56.3	74.5	29.8	39.8	19.0	9.8	10.3	21.3	66.4	70.4
December	1 012.0	705.3	298.4	52.0	71.6	28.1	39.3	18.6	9.4	9.8	22.3	69.0	72.6

[1]Includes categories not shown separately.
. . . = Not available.

Table 17-2. New Construction Put in Place—*Continued*

(Billions of dollars, monthly data are at seasonally adjusted annual rates.)

| Year and month | Total | Public | | | | | | | | | | | | Federal |
| | | State and local | | | | | | | | | | | | |
		Total [1]	Residential	Office	Health care	Educational	Public safety	Amusement and recreation	Transportation	Power	Highway and street	Sewage and waste disposal	Water supply	
1975	43.3	37.2	. . .	. . .	. . .	. . .	. . .	. . .	. . .	. . .	. . .	. . .	. . .	6.1
1976	44.0	37.2	. . .	. . .	. . .	. . .	. . .	. . .	. . .	. . .	. . .	. . .	. . .	6.8
1977	43.1	36.0	. . .	. . .	. . .	. . .	. . .	. . .	. . .	. . .	. . .	. . .	. . .	7.1
1978	50.1	42.0	. . .	. . .	. . .	. . .	. . .	. . .	. . .	. . .	. . .	. . .	. . .	8.1
1979	56.6	48.1	. . .	. . .	. . .	. . .	. . .	. . .	. . .	. . .	. . .	. . .	. . .	8.6
1980	63.6	54.0	. . .	. . .	. . .	. . .	. . .	. . .	. . .	. . .	. . .	. . .	. . .	9.6
1981	64.7	54.3	. . .	. . .	. . .	. . .	. . .	. . .	. . .	. . .	. . .	. . .	. . .	10.4
1982	63.1	53.1	. . .	. . .	. . .	. . .	. . .	. . .	. . .	. . .	. . .	. . .	. . .	10.0
1983	63.5	52.9	. . .	. . .	. . .	. . .	. . .	. . .	. . .	. . .	. . .	. . .	. . .	10.6
1984	70.2	59.0	. . .	. . .	. . .	. . .	. . .	. . .	. . .	. . .	. . .	. . .	. . .	11.2
1985	77.8	65.8	. . .	. . .	. . .	. . .	. . .	. . .	. . .	. . .	. . .	. . .	. . .	12.0
1986	84.6	72.2	. . .	. . .	. . .	. . .	. . .	. . .	. . .	. . .	. . .	. . .	. . .	12.4
1987	90.6	76.6	. . .	. . .	. . .	. . .	. . .	. . .	. . .	. . .	. . .	. . .	. . .	14.1
1988	94.7	82.5	. . .	. . .	. . .	. . .	. . .	. . .	. . .	. . .	. . .	. . .	. . .	12.3
1989	98.2	86.0	. . .	. . .	. . .	. . .	. . .	. . .	. . .	. . .	. . .	. . .	. . .	12.2
1990	107.5	95.4	. . .	. . .	. . .	. . .	. . .	. . .	. . .	. . .	. . .	. . .	. . .	12.1
1991	110.1	97.3	. . .	. . .	. . .	. . .	. . .	. . .	. . .	. . .	. . .	. . .	. . .	12.8
1992	115.8	101.5	. . .	. . .	. . .	. . .	. . .	. . .	. . .	. . .	. . .	. . .	. . .	14.4
1993	127.4	112.9	3.4	2.8	2.3	24.2	4.6	4.3	9.8	7.4	34.5	11.2	6.4	14.4
1994	130.4	116.0	4.2	3.0	2.4	25.3	4.5	4.7	9.2	5.1	37.3	12.0	6.4	14.4
1995	140.0	124.3	4.5	3.3	2.6	27.5	5.0	5.1	9.6	5.7	38.6	13.0	7.3	15.8
1996	146.7	131.4	3.7	3.6	2.8	31.0	5.5	5.0	10.4	4.8	40.6	13.6	7.7	15.3
1997	153.4	139.4	3.3	3.8	2.9	34.3	5.6	5.7	10.3	4.4	44.4	13.1	8.1	14.1
1998	154.8	140.5	3.2	3.7	2.3	35.1	6.1	6.2	10.5	2.8	45.4	13.2	8.9	14.3
1999	169.1	155.1	3.2	3.6	2.5	39.8	6.2	7.2	11.4	2.9	51.0	14.5	9.6	14.0
2000	181.3	167.2	3.0	4.5	2.8	46.8	5.9	7.6	13.0	5.5	51.6	14.0	9.5	14.2
2001	201.9	186.8	3.5	5.6	2.9	52.8	6.1	9.1	15.9	5.3	56.4	14.2	11.4	15.1
2002	213.4	196.9	3.8	6.3	3.5	59.5	6.0	9.2	17.3	3.8	56.7	15.3	11.7	16.6
2003	216.1	198.2	3.7	6.1	4.0	59.3	5.8	8.4	16.5	6.8	56.3	15.6	11.7	17.9
2004	220.2	201.8	4.1	6.0	5.0	59.7	5.5	7.8	16.4	7.0	57.4	17.1	12.0	18.3
2005	234.2	216.9	4.0	5.2	5.1	65.8	6.0	7.3	16.3	8.3	63.2	18.3	13.5	17.3
2006	255.4	237.8	4.3	5.6	5.6	69.8	6.6	9.4	17.7	7.8	71.0	21.5	14.3	17.6
2007	287.1	266.8	5.1	7.1	7.0	77.6	8.4	11.0	21.2	11.4	74.8	23.1	14.9	20.3
2008	307.5	283.5	4.9	9.5	7.2	83.6	9.5	11.5	22.6	10.8	79.5	24.2	15.7	24.0
2006														
January	242.6	226.1	4.1	5.3	5.0	68.8	6.2	8.2	16.3	7.3	65.9	20.9	14.1	16.5
February	246.8	230.0	4.3	5.2	5.3	69.0	6.5	8.4	16.3	8.5	67.6	21.4	13.7	16.8
March	251.5	234.3	4.4	4.9	5.4	69.8	6.4	8.6	17.4	8.0	69.4	21.8	14.4	17.2
April	255.3	237.4	4.7	5.4	5.5	68.4	6.5	8.7	17.5	8.6	72.9	21.1	14.2	17.9
May	253.8	236.7	4.4	5.4	5.6	68.2	6.6	9.1	17.5	8.1	72.7	20.8	14.6	17.1
June	257.7	241.2	4.5	5.7	5.6	70.1	6.4	9.7	18.2	8.3	73.2	21.4	14.3	16.6
July	258.0	240.9	3.8	5.7	5.7	70.2	6.4	9.8	17.9	5.9	75.4	21.8	14.5	17.1
August	254.9	238.1	4.1	5.8	5.7	69.1	6.1	9.9	18.0	7.1	72.2	21.9	14.1	16.8
September	254.8	237.9	4.2	5.9	5.8	69.2	6.8	10.2	18.0	7.7	69.9	21.7	14.2	16.9
October	256.9	236.6	4.3	5.8	5.8	69.5	6.9	9.8	17.6	7.2	69.0	21.9	14.6	20.3
November	260.6	241.6	4.6	5.8	6.0	71.7	7.0	10.0	17.9	7.7	69.9	21.7	14.6	19.0
December	270.2	250.7	4.8	5.8	5.9	75.0	7.3	10.5	18.9	9.4	71.4	22.0	14.7	19.5
2007														
January	276.8	256.3	4.4	6.0	6.3	72.0	7.7	10.0	19.5	10.5	77.4	22.9	14.7	20.5
February	274.0	255.2	4.6	6.2	6.3	71.2	7.7	9.9	19.2	11.0	75.7	23.6	15.0	18.8
March	275.1	256.6	4.9	7.0	6.5	73.3	8.1	10.3	18.6	12.8	73.2	21.7	15.5	18.5
April	278.8	259.9	5.1	6.4	6.8	75.9	8.1	10.3	19.5	12.5	73.0	22.5	15.4	18.9
May	286.1	266.5	5.2	7.1	7.2	77.9	8.4	11.7	20.5	11.9	73.1	22.4	16.1	19.7
June	286.4	265.9	5.6	7.1	6.8	79.2	8.5	10.6	20.7	10.5	73.6	22.7	15.3	20.5
July	286.6	266.1	5.5	7.2	7.0	79.6	8.7	11.5	22.4	11.5	70.3	22.5	14.5	20.4
August	290.3	268.8	5.5	7.7	7.6	79.0	8.5	11.7	21.8	10.3	74.3	22.7	14.8	21.5
September	297.2	277.1	5.2	7.4	7.0	79.6	8.7	12.0	22.6	12.0	77.8	23.7	15.0	20.1
October	294.3	273.0	5.2	7.7	7.4	78.3	8.4	11.3	22.7	10.9	76.1	24.4	14.7	21.3
November	298.4	276.8	4.8	7.6	7.5	82.1	9.2	10.8	22.5	11.4	76.7	24.5	14.2	21.6
December	296.0	274.1	4.8	7.4	7.1	80.5	9.1	11.1	22.7	11.9	77.0	23.9	13.3	21.9
2008														
January	290.8	268.5	4.7	7.9	7.0	80.5	9.0	11.1	21.6	11.4	73.8	23.5	13.0	22.3
February	291.6	269.4	4.5	8.4	7.1	78.3	9.0	11.2	22.4	11.0	74.6	23.5	14.2	22.2
March	300.8	278.6	4.5	8.8	7.5	82.2	9.3	11.5	22.5	11.5	77.0	23.9	14.7	22.3
April	301.5	278.9	4.5	9.1	7.2	83.0	9.2	11.5	22.3	11.2	78.0	23.6	14.8	22.6
May	304.1	281.5	4.7	9.7	7.2	85.0	9.6	12.2	22.4	11.9	75.4	23.6	15.5	22.6
June	306.2	283.3	4.8	9.9	6.8	85.0	9.4	11.7	23.5	12.3	75.6	23.2	16.2	22.9
July	308.5	284.6	5.3	10.1	7.0	84.7	9.7	11.4	22.9	10.3	77.6	24.4	16.8	23.9
August	316.7	291.4	5.2	10.1	7.4	85.6	9.7	11.6	22.8	11.3	82.7	23.8	16.7	25.3
September	312.4	288.7	5.4	10.1	7.2	84.1	9.8	11.6	23.2	10.3	81.8	24.5	16.5	23.6
October	315.4	290.3	5.4	10.0	7.4	84.3	9.9	11.3	23.2	9.9	82.8	25.3	16.5	25.0
November	316.6	290.1	5.1	10.1	7.0	85.1	9.8	11.5	22.8	10.0	83.2	25.1	16.6	26.4
December	306.7	279.1	4.7	10.4	7.0	82.5	9.6	11.4	21.7	7.9	78.6	25.1	16.2	27.6

[1] Includes categories not shown separately.
. . . = Not available.

Table 17-3. Housing Starts and Building Permits; New House Sales and Prices

Year and month	Housing starts and building permits										New house sales and prices			
	New private housing units (thousands)									Shipments of manufactured homes (thousands, seasonally adjusted annual rate)	Seasonally adjusted		Median sales price (dollars)	Price index (2005 = 100)
	Started (not seasonally adjusted)			Seasonally adjusted annual rate										
				Started			Authorized by building permits ²				Sold (thousands, annual rate)	For sale, end-of-period (thousands)		
	Total ¹	One-family structures	Five units or more	Total ¹	One-family structures	Five units or more	Total ¹	One-family structures	Five units or more					
1975	1 160	892	204	1 160	892	204	939	676	200	213	549	316	. . .	22.1
1976	1 538	1 162	289	1 538	1 162	289	1 296	894	310	246	646	358	. . .	24.0
1977	1 987	1 451	414	1 987	1 451	414	1 690	1 126	443	266	819	408	27.0	27.0
1978	2 020	1 433	462	2 020	1 433	462	1 801	1 183	487	276	817	419	55 700	30.9
1979	1 745	1 194	429	1 745	1 194	429	1 552	982	445	277	709	402	62 900	35.3
1980	1 292	852	330	1 292	852	331	1 191	710	366	222	530	342	64 600	38.9
1981	1 084	705	288	1 084	705	288	986	564	319	241	437	278	68 900	42.0
1982	1 062	663	320	1 062	663	320	1 001	546	366	240	412	255	69 300	43.0
1983	1 703	1 068	522	1 703	1 068	522	1 605	902	570	296	623	304	75 300	43.9
1984	1 750	1 084	544	1 750	1 084	544	1 682	922	617	295	639	358	79 900	45.7
1985	1 742	1 072	576	1 742	1 072	576	1 733	957	657	284	687	350	84 300	46.2
1986	1 805	1 179	542	1 805	1 179	542	1 769	1 078	584	244	750	361	92 000	48.0
1987	1 620	1 146	409	1 621	1 146	409	1 535	1 024	421	233	671	370	104 500	50.6
1988	1 488	1 081	348	1 488	1 081	348	1 456	994	386	218	676	371	112 500	52.5
1989	1 376	1 003	318	1 376	1 003	318	1 338	932	340	198	650	366	120 000	54.6
1990	1 193	895	260	1 193	895	260	1 111	794	263	188	534	321	122 900	55.7
1991	1 014	840	138	1 014	840	138	949	754	152	171	509	284	120 000	56.4
1992	1 200	1 030	139	1 200	1 030	139	1 095	911	138	211	610	267	121 500	57.2
1993	1 288	1 126	133	1 288	1 126	133	1 199	987	160	254	666	295	126 500	59.4
1994	1 457	1 198	224	1 457	1 198	224	1 372	1 069	241	304	670	340	130 000	62.9
1995	1 354	1 076	244	1 354	1 076	244	1 333	997	272	340	667	374	133 900	64.3
1996	1 477	1 161	271	1 477	1 161	271	1 426	1 070	290	363	757	326	140 000	66.0
1997	1 474	1 134	296	1 474	1 134	296	1 441	1 062	310	354	804	287	146 000	67.5
1998	1 617	1 271	303	1 617	1 271	303	1 612	1 188	356	373	886	300	152 500	69.2
1999	1 641	1 302	307	1 641	1 302	307	1 664	1 247	351	348	880	315	161 000	72.8
2000	1 569	1 231	299	1 569	1 231	299	1 592	1 198	329	250	877	301	169 000	75.6
2001	1 603	1 273	293	1 603	1 273	293	1 637	1 236	335	193	908	310	175 200	77.9
2002	1 705	1 359	308	1 705	1 359	308	1 748	1 333	341	169	973	344	187 600	81.4
2003	1 848	1 499	315	1 848	1 499	315	1 889	1 461	346	131	1 086	377	195 000	86.0
2004	1 956	1 611	303	1 956	1 611	303	2 070	1 613	366	131	1 203	431	221 000	92.8
2005	2 068	1 716	311	2 068	1 716	311	2 155	1 682	389	147	1 283	511	240 900	100.0
2006	1 801	1 465	293	1 801	1 465	293	1 839	1 378	384	117	1 051	536	246 500	104.8
2007	1 355	1 046	277	1 355	1 046	277	1 398	980	359	96	776	496	247 900	104.9
2008	904	622	265	904	622	265	893	570	290	82	482	359	230 600	99.6
2006														
January	153	121	30	2 273	1 823	423	2 212	1 689	422	163	1 174	523	244 900	. . .
February	145	124	19	2 119	1 804	280	2 141	1 643	413	146	1 061	539	250 800	104.1
March	166	138	25	1 969	1 601	331	2 118	1 551	484	135	1 116	552	238 800	. . .
April	160	135	21	1 821	1 511	254	1 998	1 496	424	126	1 123	565	257 000	. . .
May	190	158	28	1 942	1 570	320	1 905	1 450	374	122	1 086	565	238 200	105.7
June	170	140	26	1 802	1 451	307	1 867	1 393	402	116	1 074	566	243 200	. . .
July	161	133	20	1 737	1 424	230	1 763	1 307	378	110	965	572	238 100	. . .
August	147	120	23	1 650	1 364	246	1 722	1 282	363	108	1 035	566	243 900	104.8
September	150	119	28	1 720	1 384	306	1 655	1 218	365	102	1 016	559	226 700	. . .
October	131	104	23	1 491	1 212	242	1 570	1 175	326	98	941	554	250 400	. . .
November	115	92	22	1 570	1 290	261	1 535	1 163	314	97	1 003	543	240 100	103.8
December	112	82	26	1 649	1 249	350	1 638	1 198	368	97	998	536	244 700	. . .
2007														
January	95	75	18	1 382	1 106	254	1 585	1 138	373	94	872	537	254 400	. . .
February	103	83	18	1 486	1 188	268	1 580	1 118	389	93	820	544	250 800	107.2
March	124	101	20	1 492	1 196	259	1 578	1 135	371	95	823	546	262 600	. . .
April	136	111	21	1 487	1 198	253	1 489	1 078	350	97	907	549	242 500	. . .
May	136	111	22	1 436	1 146	256	1 522	1 063	395	98	857	545	245 000	105.9
June	138	110	24	1 458	1 136	284	1 433	1 016	361	101	793	543	235 500	. . .
July	128	100	24	1 371	1 055	276	1 386	997	332	99	796	539	246 200	. . .
August	121	87	31	1 337	968	332	1 343	928	360	96	702	533	236 500	103.0
September	102	79	20	1 185	936	220	1 277	870	357	94	694	528	240 300	. . .
October	115	77	34	1 275	884	351	1 182	811	323	94	723	513	234 300	. . .
November	89	59	28	1 179	816	342	1 187	767	367	93	629	502	249 100	102.1
December	69	52	16	1 000	779	211	1 111	714	341	92	600	496	227 700	. . .
2008														
January	71	48	20	1 064	750	287	1 052	675	334	91	597	488	232 400	. . .
February	78	52	24	1 107	722	356	981	646	295	94	572	475	245 300	98.8
March	82	62	20	988	711	261	932	621	274	90	513	465	229 300	. . .
April	90	63	26	1 004	681	308	982	649	295	92	542	463	246 400	. . .
May	92	66	24	982	682	280	978	635	309	87	515	458	229 300	102.0
June	102	65	35	1 089	663	404	1 138	616	489	84	499	445	234 300	. . .
July	87	60	26	949	644	291	937	584	320	84	505	434	237 300	. . .
August	76	54	21	854	615	224	857	553	273	81	448	427	221 000	101.0
September	74	49	23	824	551	254	805	538	233	76	434	418	225 200	. . .
October	68	46	21	767	536	221	730	470	231	70	406	407	213 500	. . .
November	47	32	14	651	460	175	615	414	180	68	388	395	219 700	96.3
December	37	26	10	550	398	145	547	364	166	65	331	359	206 500	. . .

¹Includes structures with 2 to 4 units, not shown separately.
²Data beginning with 2004 cover 20,000 permit-issuing places; 1994 through 2003: 19,000 places; 1984 through 1993: 17,000 places; 1978 through 1983: 16,000 places; 1972 through 1977: 14,000 places; 1971: 13,000 places.
. . . = Not available.

Table 17-4. Manufacturers' Shipments

(Millions of dollars, adjusted for trading-day and calendar-month variation, but without seasonal adjustment.)

Year and month	Total	NAICS durable goods industries									
		Total[1]	Nonmetallic mineral products	Primary metals		Fabricated metal products	Machinery	Computers and electronic products	Electrical equipment, appliances, and components	Transportation equipment	
				Total	Iron and steel mills					Total	Motor vehicles and parts
1992	2 904 024	1 518 862	61 902	123 789	55 947	170 403	186 589	273 728	81 813	433 611	279 197
1993	3 020 497	1 604 544	64 957	126 988	59 632	177 967	201 076	286 457	87 646	453 437	310 178
1994	3 238 112	1 764 061	70 598	142 976	67 087	194 113	224 920	320 769	95 531	494 745	364 840
1995	3 479 677	1 902 815	74 865	160 774	72 019	212 444	246 277	370 679	101 051	508 271	379 551
1996	3 597 188	1 978 597	81 308	157 638	71 814	222 995	257 459	399 516	105 283	516 030	387 394
1997	3 834 699	2 147 384	86 465	168 118	76 900	242 812	270 687	439 380	112 116	575 307	421 573
1998	3 899 813	2 231 588	92 501	166 109	75 871	253 720	280 651	443 768	116 024	612 882	439 590
1999	4 031 887	2 326 736	96 153	156 648	70 087	257 071	276 904	467 059	118 313	676 328	498 716
2000	4 208 584	2 373 688	97 329	156 598	70 470	268 213	291 548	510 639	125 443	639 861	471 180
2001	3 970 499	2 174 406	94 861	138 246	60 559	253 113	266 554	429 471	114 068	602 495	427 175
2002	3 914 723	2 123 621	95 064	139 436	62 543	246 847	255 321	357 324	102 845	636 711	469 561
2003	4 015 388	2 142 589	96 945	138 270	63 116	245 340	257 429	352 273	99 906	655 871	491 713
2004	4 308 970	2 264 667	102 880	181 602	94 629	261 101	272 123	365 545	105 084	662 000	494 567
2005	4 742 077	2 424 844	114 849	203 264	103 429	289 433	302 650	372 882	111 977	690 743	501 486
2006	5 019 962	2 560 691	126 015	232 558	112 922	317 224	326 430	390 776	120 040	698 348	500 137
2007	5 081 075	2 562 863	119 189	241 511	114 967	326 685	331 451	386 897	126 995	693 036	479 703
2008	5 184 609	2 493 817	109 132	255 701	130 185	330 421	347 165	379 683	124 933	618 884	387 032
2004											
January	311 513	160 909	7 101	12 385	5 856	18 562	18 787	26 110	7 269	48 354	37 989
February	331 185	178 175	7 185	13 188	6 273	19 638	19 871	28 249	7 982	58 126	43 463
March	379 089	209 320	8 624	15 380	7 470	22 928	25 607	33 945	9 300	66 318	50 033
April	350 032	185 466	8 791	14 905	7 470	21 460	23 374	27 672	8 435	55 186	42 936
May	356 451	186 388	8 576	14 861	7 597	21 842	22 177	28 469	8 660	55 807	41 450
June	379 971	204 343	9 117	15 892	8 410	22 951	25 002	33 613	9 428	60 276	44 308
July	332 132	164 096	8 839	14 602	7 969	21 024	21 723	26 910	8 178	38 062	26 447
August	371 658	192 938	9 491	16 444	8 919	23 130	21 921	29 411	9 017	56 114	42 337
September	381 093	203 985	9 093	16 555	8 965	23 370	24 271	34 178	9 829	59 026	43 532
October	377 248	194 120	9 212	16 384	8 799	22 833	23 293	29 920	8 780	56 991	43 517
November	367 064	188 003	8 785	15 742	8 523	22 084	21 355	30 832	9 033	53 442	39 825
December	371 534	196 924	8 066	15 264	8 378	21 279	24 742	36 236	9 173	54 298	38 730
2005											
January	346 290	175 787	7 973	16 674	8 886	21 081	21 987	26 972	7 956	48 775	37 496
February	359 346	187 281	8 050	16 777	8 928	22 045	22 980	28 069	8 553	54 896	41 783
March	407 749	214 095	9 349	18 393	9 688	24 346	27 052	35 074	9 562	61 162	43 939
April	385 838	197 458	9 508	17 411	9 004	23 845	25 785	27 591	8 895	56 906	42 183
May	396 154	201 786	9 830	17 130	8 790	24 650	25 391	28 718	9 212	58 805	43 492
June	416 913	218 679	10 174	17 186	8 554	25 636	27 348	34 984	9 969	63 219	45 675
July	362 283	172 159	9 462	14 753	7 231	22 415	23 362	26 356	8 510	40 739	27 748
August	416 109	208 699	10 627	17 265	8 492	25 850	25 011	30 197	9 777	60 841	45 781
September	424 253	219 965	10 293	17 488	8 670	25 901	26 466	35 738	10 513	63 550	47 565
October	414 920	210 694	10 503	17 699	8 678	25 710	25 809	30 013	9 718	61 846	46 775
November	402 704	203 504	9 997	16 728	8 299	24 345	24 305	30 807	9 742	58 298	40 442
December	409 518	214 737	9 083	15 760	8 209	23 609	27 154	38 363	9 570	61 706	38 607
2006											
January	382 939	189 076	9 633	18 131	9 098	24 126	24 044	26 995	8 669	50 663	38 702
February	390 277	202 935	9 642	17 879	8 938	24 933	24 737	30 980	8 999	57 779	42 076
March	448 153	237 910	10 963	20 123	9 971	27 870	30 518	37 335	10 528	69 276	49 921
April	405 289	202 590	10 331	18 596	9 006	25 677	27 590	28 823	9 441	54 147	39 625
May	441 804	222 532	11 309	20 815	9 943	27 754	28 117	30 858	10 559	63 229	46 834
June	455 070	237 699	11 535	21 254	10 218	28 611	30 249	37 438	10 988	65 939	47 496
July	393 925	184 938	10 456	18 830	9 148	24 889	25 628	28 581	9 328	39 962	26 749
August	445 015	223 323	11 483	21 466	10 358	28 674	27 301	31 872	10 667	61 835	45 511
September	426 514	223 816	10 655	20 137	9 734	27 559	27 833	36 909	10 908	59 617	41 018
October	419 564	216 357	11 161	19 981	9 610	27 449	27 808	31 221	10 179	59 418	43 743
November	403 682	206 962	9 940	18 173	8 632	25 235	25 180	32 759	9 801	57 759	39 839
December	407 730	212 753	8 907	17 173	8 266	24 447	27 425	37 005	9 973	58 724	38 623
2007											
January	378 924	190 569	9 128	19 509	9 454	25 277	23 183	28 396	9 305	50 288	36 865
February	385 519	198 725	8 990	18 801	9 018	25 292	24 634	29 612	9 618	55 927	40 237
March	440 501	231 607	10 392	21 008	10 251	28 042	30 090	35 715	11 342	65 914	46 046
April	414 836	210 551	10 357	20 809	9 983	27 292	28 991	30 137	10 630	55 168	39 434
May	441 067	222 421	10 964	21 921	10 383	28 843	28 874	30 382	10 873	61 888	43 866
June	448 561	232 417	10 675	21 283	9 991	28 855	30 112	36 258	11 343	63 662	43 680
July	403 222	193 082	10 151	19 481	9 054	26 748	26 800	27 410	9 974	45 322	29 910
August	444 427	225 962	10 891	20 940	9 661	30 028	27 712	30 981	11 167	64 507	45 730
September	431 529	220 448	9 814	19 902	9 288	27 704	28 461	35 920	11 331	58 477	39 221
October	444 046	220 960	10 556	21 257	9 975	28 589	28 150	31 529	10 953	60 605	43 121
November	427 915	208 074	9 415	19 060	9 088	25 900	25 941	32 427	10 340	57 238	38 391
December	420 528	208 047	7 856	17 540	8 821	24 115	28 503	38 130	10 119	54 040	33 202
2008											
January	404 937	195 064	8 229	20 550	10 023	25 271	25 892	29 997	9 592	50 286	35 045
February	417 428	207 105	8 414	21 228	10 478	26 066	28 313	29 690	10 112	56 604	38 486
March	447 025	222 176	9 009	22 113	10 905	27 404	31 856	35 514	10 976	57 352	35 789
April	447 052	213 520	9 623	23 298	11 956	28 535	30 316	30 524	10 597	53 008	34 255
May	460 851	215 193	9 805	23 487	12 144	28 841	29 615	30 431	10 926	53 842	34 012
June	479 381	229 644	10 045	24 441	13 060	29 564	31 657	34 809	11 375	57 974	35 145
July	448 540	199 721	9 856	23 312	12 521	28 286	28 204	29 928	10 581	42 267	24 236
August	456 897	210 847	9 883	23 845	12 684	29 590	27 975	29 516	10 823	51 133	31 827
September	448 947	220 680	9 640	22 850	11 927	29 301	30 832	34 668	11 374	53 749	32 634
October	431 372	208 711	9 843	20 628	10 313	28 906	28 759	31 304	10 588	51 120	33 256
November	372 138	181 580	7 798	15 928	7 531	25 034	25 441	28 637	8 959	44 357	27 219
December	370 041	189 576	6 987	14 021	6 643	23 623	28 305	34 665	9 030	47 192	25 128

[1]Includes categories not shown separately.

Table 17-4. Manufacturers' Shipments—*Continued*

(Millions of dollars, adjusted for trading-day and calendar-month variation, but without seasonal adjustment.)

Year and month	Total [1]	Food products	Beverage and tobacco products	Textile mills	Textile products	Apparel	Paper products	Chemical products	Petroleum and coal products	Plastics and rubber products
					NAICS nondurable goods industries					
1992	1 385 162	358 494	85 687	52 923	24 763	61 535	127 122	319 501	150 095	113 827
1993	1 415 953	373 612	79 227	55 375	25 623	63 210	126 982	330 760	144 731	122 807
1994	1 474 051	379 786	83 434	58 607	27 233	64 894	136 922	350 098	143 339	134 288
1995	1 576 862	393 204	88 945	59 885	27 976	65 214	166 051	376 995	151 431	145 084
1996	1 618 591	404 173	94 033	59 796	28 515	64 237	152 860	385 919	174 181	149 773
1997	1 687 315	421 737	96 971	58 707	31 052	68 018	150 296	415 617	177 394	159 161
1998	1 668 225	428 479	102 359	57 416	31 137	64 932	154 984	416 742	137 957	163 736
1999	1 705 151	426 001	106 920	54 306	32 689	62 305	156 915	420 321	162 620	171 885
2000	1 834 896	435 229	111 692	52 112	33 654	60 339	165 298	449 159	235 134	178 236
2001	1 796 093	451 385	118 786	45 681	31 971	54 598	155 845	438 410	219 074	170 717
2002	1 791 102	458 206	105 456	45 497	32 082	41 901	153 755	462 499	215 513	174 675
2003	1 872 799	488 518	109 080	42 653	31 256	38 645	151 098	487 742	247 119	178 328
2004	2 044 303	512 339	113 737	40 898	33 636	32 873	155 380	540 884	330 439	184 710
2005	2 317 233	532 403	124 085	42 328	35 022	31 401	161 928	610 873	475 787	200 303
2006	2 459 071	537 788	124 693	38 795	33 220	30 462	170 360	657 747	548 954	211 345
2007	2 518 212	573 563	132 251	36 587	30 487	29 814	168 500	664 057	564 114	210 734
2008	2 690 792	610 555	137 668	33 578	26 748	31 134	172 331	689 921	674 586	210 781
2004										
January	150 604	39 177	8 123	3 074	2 517	2 526	12 435	39 738	21 625	13 915
February	153 010	39 745	8 316	3 402	2 792	2 916	12 203	40 268	21 646	14 034
March	169 769	41 628	9 737	3 529	2 896	2 955	13 025	46 903	24 265	16 425
April	164 566	41 291	9 294	3 377	2 779	2 553	12 413	43 841	25 407	15 731
May	170 063	42 188	9 893	3 450	2 777	2 633	12 683	44 560	28 411	15 599
June	175 628	43 051	10 418	3 491	2 919	2 674	13 787	46 946	27 474	16 428
July	168 036	41 119	9 668	3 190	2 833	2 717	12 896	43 983	28 808	14 931
August	178 720	44 569	10 116	3 525	3 021	2 866	13 571	46 203	30 275	16 118
September	177 108	44 575	9 796	3 680	2 840	2 788	13 213	46 200	29 339	15 844
October	183 128	46 106	9 572	3 548	2 947	3 045	13 140	47 691	32 182	15 915
November	179 061	45 439	9 414	3 358	2 816	2 844	12 939	47 584	30 824	15 058
December	174 610	43 451	9 390	3 274	2 499	2 356	13 075	46 967	30 183	14 712
2005										
January	170 503	42 036	8 649	3 299	2 591	2 355	13 146	46 198	29 237	14 958
February	172 065	42 382	8 901	3 640	2 826	2 645	13 004	46 004	29 234	15 378
March	193 654	44 567	9 694	3 700	2 955	2 594	13 995	53 383	36 697	17 217
April	188 380	42 016	10 084	3 711	2 955	2 377	13 401	51 312	37 369	16 827
May	194 368	44 605	11 258	3 696	2 896	2 480	13 905	51 584	38 358	17 238
June	198 234	45 082	11 278	3 906	3 050	2 753	14 364	51 785	40 012	17 467
July	190 124	42 229	10 798	3 330	2 936	2 614	13 083	49 178	42 331	15 683
August	207 410	45 350	11 651	3 558	3 112	2 735	13 692	53 437	47 317	17 644
September	204 288	46 106	10 528	3 549	3 146	2 680	13 099	51 347	47 150	17 449
October	204 226	46 295	10 529	3 507	3 069	2 900	13 449	51 911	45 650	17 649
November	199 200	46 647	10 493	3 347	2 932	2 913	13 366	53 299	40 290	16 999
December	194 781	45 088	10 222	3 085	2 554	2 355	13 424	51 435	42 142	15 794
2006										
January	193 863	42 859	9 438	3 091	2 602	2 180	13 887	52 541	42 634	16 561
February	187 342	42 784	9 488	3 363	2 830	2 469	13 310	50 579	37 705	16 687
March	210 243	45 141	10 299	3 576	2 983	2 786	14 618	58 648	44 621	18 602
April	202 699	42 774	10 058	3 306	2 832	2 374	13 577	54 851	47 120	17 324
May	219 272	44 550	11 577	3 285	2 855	2 624	14 956	58 337	53 239	19 033
June	217 371	44 698	11 276	3 436	2 983	2 597	14 985	57 225	51 992	19 266
July	208 987	42 493	10 350	3 045	2 825	2 502	13 821	54 501	54 284	16 879
August	221 692	46 267	11 348	3 324	2 862	2 618	14 649	58 223	54 100	19 213
September	202 698	45 883	10 120	3 306	2 776	2 580	14 089	53 999	42 966	17 752
October	203 207	47 434	10 456	3 279	2 753	2 838	14 305	54 766	40 042	17 887
November	196 720	47 099	10 532	3 063	2 560	2 646	13 634	52 374	38 982	16 576
December	194 977	45 806	9 751	2 721	2 359	2 248	14 529	51 703	41 269	15 565
2007										
January	188 355	44 109	9 412	2 959	2 354	2 176	13 984	51 821	36 591	16 532
February	186 794	44 324	9 609	3 125	2 524	2 480	13 178	50 772	36 447	16 011
March	208 894	47 106	10 745	3 223	2 677	2 480	14 145	58 035	43 102	18 138
April	204 285	44 670	10 602	3 069	2 577	2 307	13 625	55 851	45 187	17 716
May	218 646	47 706	12 130	3 151	2 622	2 354	14 387	58 197	50 388	18 896
June	216 144	47 887	11 779	3 233	2 794	2 299	14 458	57 110	49 061	18 604
July	210 140	46 266	11 174	2 887	2 588	2 370	13 978	55 169	49 879	17 367
August	218 465	50 233	12 262	3 163	2 708	2 761	14 450	56 853	47 804	18 913
September	211 081	49 920	10 852	3 113	2 534	2 624	13 969	53 727	47 741	17 276
October	223 086	51 314	11 737	3 132	2 570	2 809	14 548	57 961	50 214	18 809
November	219 841	50 599	11 353	2 884	2 412	2 859	13 995	54 265	54 728	17 126
December	212 481	49 429	10 596	2 648	2 127	2 295	13 783	54 296	52 972	15 346
2008										
January	209 873	48 249	10 067	2 734	2 125	2 285	14 360	54 893	50 155	16 772
February	210 323	48 625	10 163	2 951	2 348	2 636	13 909	55 068	49 478	16 920
March	224 849	50 131	11 144	2 974	2 392	2 574	14 310	59 180	55 610	17 598
April	233 532	49 055	11 316	2 936	2 375	2 494	14 303	60 650	63 344	18 276
May	245 658	51 046	12 612	2 873	2 432	2 572	14 397	60 736	71 672	18 814
June	249 737	51 263	12 080	3 012	2 524	2 602	14 758	62 337	73 292	19 260
July	248 819	51 102	12 001	2 815	2 334	2 707	14 577	61 489	74 957	18 492
August	246 050	53 033	12 260	3 002	2 408	2 849	14 983	60 380	69 916	18 433
September	228 267	53 324	11 612	2 891	2 150	2 751	14 975	57 375	56 092	18 153
October	222 661	53 688	11 821	2 825	2 136	2 791	14 790	58 576	48 582	18 161
November	190 558	51 435	11 425	2 456	1 908	2 707	13 495	49 629	33 809	15 270
December	180 465	49 604	11 167	2 109	1 616	2 166	13 474	49 608	27 679	14 632

[1] Includes categories not shown separately.

Table 17-4. Manufacturers' Shipments—*Continued*

(Millions of dollars, seasonally adjusted.)

Year and month	Total	NAICS durable goods industries									
		Total ¹	Nonmetallic mineral products	Primary metals		Fabricated metal products	Machinery	Computers and electronic products	Electrical equipment, appliances, and components	Transportation equipment	
				Total	Iron and steel mills					Total	Motor vehicles and parts
1992	2 904 024	1 518 862	61 902	123 789	55 947	170 403	186 589	273 728	81 813	433 611	279 197
1993	3 020 497	1 604 544	64 957	126 988	59 632	177 967	201 076	286 457	87 646	453 437	310 178
1994	3 238 112	1 764 061	70 598	142 976	67 087	194 113	224 920	320 769	95 531	494 745	364 840
1995	3 479 677	1 902 815	74 865	160 774	72 019	212 444	246 277	370 679	101 051	508 271	379 551
1996	3 597 188	1 978 597	81 308	157 638	71 814	222 995	257 459	399 516	105 283	516 030	387 394
1997	3 834 699	2 147 384	86 465	168 118	76 900	242 812	270 687	439 380	112 116	575 307	421 573
1998	3 899 813	2 231 588	92 501	166 109	75 871	253 720	280 651	443 768	116 024	612 882	439 590
1999	4 031 887	2 326 736	96 153	156 648	70 087	257 071	276 904	467 059	118 313	676 328	498 716
2000	4 208 584	2 373 688	97 329	156 598	70 470	268 213	291 548	510 639	125 443	639 861	471 180
2001	3 970 499	2 174 406	94 861	138 246	60 559	253 113	266 554	429 471	114 068	602 495	427 175
2002	3 914 723	2 123 621	95 064	139 436	62 543	246 847	255 321	357 324	102 845	636 711	469 561
2003	4 015 388	2 142 589	96 945	138 270	63 116	245 340	257 429	352 273	99 906	655 871	491 713
2004	4 308 970	2 264 667	102 880	181 602	94 629	261 101	272 123	365 545	105 084	662 000	494 567
2005	4 742 077	2 424 844	114 849	203 264	103 429	289 433	302 650	372 882	111 977	690 743	501 486
2006	5 019 962	2 560 891	126 015	232 558	112 922	317 224	326 430	390 776	120 040	698 348	500 137
2007	5 081 075	2 562 863	119 189	241 511	114 967	326 685	331 451	386 897	126 995	693 036	479 703
2008	5 184 609	2 493 817	109 132	255 701	130 185	330 421	347 165	379 683	124 933	618 884	387 032
2004											
January	339 559	179 198	7 891	12 658	5 992	20 189	20 796	30 129	8 427	54 099	40 831
February	339 254	181 691	7 872	13 145	6 292	20 065	20 541	29 994	8 350	56 970	41 872
March	354 351	189 931	8 542	14 199	6 794	21 797	22 673	29 966	8 575	58 459	44 275
April	352 424	186 733	8 521	14 276	7 107	21 417	22 283	30 359	8 720	55 155	41 912
May	352 370	185 081	8 305	14 317	7 315	21 448	21 638	30 444	8 682	54 165	39 864
June	356 599	187 221	8 471	14 963	7 887	21 441	22 909	30 051	8 608	54 729	40 728
July	357 137	185 776	8 682	15 729	8 611	22 016	22 841	30 560	8 916	51 253	37 558
August	362 297	189 453	8 735	15 998	8 747	21 918	22 523	30 800	8 820	54 089	39 940
September	363 220	190 998	8 686	16 305	8 886	22 273	23 634	30 090	8 906	54 772	40 861
October	368 982	190 679	8 667	16 166	8 812	22 104	23 546	30 985	8 784	54 295	40 000
November	373 078	192 470	8 978	16 697	9 095	22 829	23 151	30 735	9 047	54 330	41 005
December	375 496	196 156	9 165	17 085	9 182	22 870	24 685	30 537	8 995	55 085	41 855
2005											
January	380 836	198 031	9 055	17 256	9 162	23 130	24 436	31 184	9 220	56 176	41 807
February	379 951	196 877	9 088	17 217	9 149	23 266	24 457	30 690	9 229	55 276	41 368
March	387 240	197 830	9 255	17 193	8 934	23 588	24 418	30 853	9 014	55 604	40 803
April	387 625	198 378	9 341	16 705	8 615	23 602	24 361	30 696	9 026	56 716	40 609
May	388 071	198 501	9 311	16 195	8 292	23 837	24 821	30 924	9 117	56 417	41 019
June	391 171	199 658	9 439	16 224	8 077	23 983	24 921	30 971	9 225	56 794	41 575
July	391 130	197 377	9 444	16 001	7 927	23 651	24 868	30 412	9 274	55 736	40 341
August	398 861	201 473	9 676	16 537	8 224	24 108	25 296	31 258	9 391	57 227	41 868
September	404 787	205 517	9 796	17 142	8 567	24 663	25 796	31 312	9 567	58 758	44 230
October	406 903	207 681	9 921	17 584	8 758	24 983	25 891	30 990	9 702	59 715	43 495
November	409 711	208 819	10 245	17 794	8 914	25 270	26 595	31 063	9 789	58 727	41 670
December	416 683	214 897	10 457	17 987	9 108	25 743	27 225	32 241	9 605	62 032	42 594
2006											
January	418 485	211 448	10 775	18 413	9 144	26 116	26 567	31 593	9 853	58 152	42 432
February	415 090	214 614	10 902	18 408	9 133	26 455	26 354	33 971	9 740	58 845	42 065
March	419 491	214 350	10 696	18 499	9 025	26 418	26 927	33 070	9 753	59 324	42 986
April	417 258	210 903	10 415	18 427	8 915	26 254	26 980	32 008	9 868	57 751	41 973
May	426 125	215 811	10 587	19 384	9 242	26 458	27 224	32 937	10 281	59 542	43 335
June	426 294	216 094	10 625	19 892	9 608	26 721	27 538	33 020	10 166	58 692	42 668
July	422 650	210 431	10 480	20 433	10 067	26 314	27 024	32 684	10 119	54 485	38 624
August	426 221	215 189	10 412	20 615	10 106	26 617	27 674	33 159	10 234	57 633	41 137
September	410 821	212 088	10 375	19 986	9 769	26 517	27 406	32 418	9 996	56 551	39 477
October	408 628	211 305	10 334	19 519	9 514	26 377	27 563	32 314	10 039	56 835	39 948
November	410 829	212 101	10 167	19 522	9 356	26 381	27 380	32 732	9 980	57 706	40 665
December	419 663	216 381	10 406	19 897	9 278	26 914	27 896	31 049	10 188	60 727	43 401
2007											
January	408 610	210 501	10 181	19 568	9 345	27 030	25 247	32 775	10 374	57 253	39 582
February	411 584	211 161	10 190	19 433	9 198	26 983	26 387	32 708	10 422	57 328	40 501
March	417 629	212 648	10 298	19 714	9 498	26 990	26 872	31 667	10 617	58 514	41 390
April	422 726	215 748	10 209	20 211	9 607	27 528	28 004	33 211	10 971	57 484	40 279
May	426 330	216 056	10 213	20 450	9 708	27 468	28 251	32 625	10 619	58 181	40 526
June	422 938	213 400	10 030	20 097	9 528	27 217	27 715	31 790	10 481	57 804	40 315
July	431 756	219 187	9 974	20 626	9 765	27 846	28 187	31 973	10 695	61 434	42 843
August	423 435	215 802	9 859	19 991	9 413	27 676	27 945	32 116	10 683	58 959	40 296
September	422 225	212 453	9 722	20 122	9 508	27 023	28 466	31 706	10 600	56 907	39 108
October	427 623	213 240	9 674	20 492	9 731	27 208	27 661	32 231	10 660	57 127	38 546
November	435 555	212 950	9 559	20 443	9 808	27 119	28 183	32 363	10 538	56 892	38 710
December	433 063	211 274	9 210	20 512	9 952	26 643	29 016	31 821	10 477	55 739	37 620
2008											
January	437 643	215 917	9 204	20 744	9 990	27 043	28 074	34 806	10 712	57 566	37 689
February	429 531	211 772	9 160	21 012	10 203	26 815	29 216	31 733	10 548	55 702	36 766
March	434 378	209 778	9 174	21 346	10 439	27 249	29 040	31 476	10 540	53 404	34 567
April	446 031	213 591	9 243	21 978	11 111	27 803	28 816	33 333	10 657	53 886	33 497
May	447 411	211 049	9 254	22 291	11 547	27 691	28 837	32 417	10 693	51 840	32 260
June	455 873	212 947	9 397	23 124	12 347	28 025	29 469	31 257	10 699	52 965	32 904
July	462 379	217 549	9 433	23 933	12 944	28 578	29 143	33 147	11 063	54 184	33 167
August	445 455	208 339	9 226	23 118	12 374	27 943	28 955	31 283	10 554	49 765	30 152
September	431 492	208 240	9 188	22 260	11 694	27 848	30 105	30 574	10 527	50 827	31 131
October	415 900	201 119	8 925	19 843	9 926	27 563	28 441	31 260	10 330	48 073	29 519
November	388 928	192 772	8 315	17 975	8 579	26 990	28 305	29 694	9 399	45 936	29 056
December	377 642	190 845	8 153	16 622	7 619	25 921	28 943	29 565	9 462	46 540	27 680

¹Includes categories not shown separately.

Table 17-4. Manufacturers' Shipments—*Continued*

(Millions of dollars, seasonally adjusted.)

Year and month	NAICS nondurable goods industries									
	Total [1]	Food products	Beverage and tobacco products	Textile mills	Textile products	Apparel	Paper products	Chemical products	Petroleum and coal products	Plastics and rubber products
1992	1 385 162	358 494	85 687	52 923	24 763	61 535	127 122	319 501	150 095	113 827
1993	1 415 953	373 612	79 227	55 375	25 623	63 210	126 982	330 760	144 731	122 807
1994	1 474 051	379 786	83 434	58 607	27 233	64 894	136 922	350 098	143 339	134 288
1995	1 576 862	393 204	88 945	59 885	27 976	65 214	166 051	376 995	151 431	145 084
1996	1 618 591	404 173	94 033	59 796	28 515	64 237	152 860	385 919	174 181	149 773
1997	1 687 315	421 737	96 971	58 707	31 052	68 018	150 296	415 617	177 394	159 161
1998	1 668 225	428 479	102 359	57 416	31 137	64 932	154 984	416 742	137 957	163 736
1999	1 705 151	426 001	106 920	54 306	32 689	62 305	156 915	420 321	162 620	171 885
2000	1 834 896	435 229	111 692	52 112	33 654	60 339	165 298	449 159	235 134	178 236
2001	1 796 093	451 385	118 786	45 681	31 971	54 598	155 845	438 410	219 074	170 717
2002	1 791 102	458 206	105 456	45 497	32 082	41 901	153 755	462 499	215 513	174 675
2003	1 872 799	488 518	109 080	42 653	31 256	38 645	151 098	487 742	247 119	178 328
2004	2 044 303	512 339	113 737	40 898	33 636	32 873	155 380	540 884	330 439	184 710
2005	2 317 233	532 403	124 085	42 328	35 022	31 401	161 928	610 873	475 787	200 303
2006	2 459 071	537 788	124 693	38 795	33 220	30 462	170 360	657 747	548 954	211 345
2007	2 518 212	573 563	132 251	36 587	30 487	29 814	168 500	664 057	564 114	210 734
2008	2 690 792	610 555	137 668	33 578	26 748	31 134	172 331	689 921	674 586	210 781
2004										
January	160 361	41 065	8 964	3 430	2 880	2 900	12 737	41 810	23 606	14 916
February	157 563	39 968	8 736	3 340	2 785	2 787	12 415	41 554	23 719	14 290
March	164 420	40 839	9 750	3 341	2 807	2 873	12 633	43 540	25 008	15 476
April	165 691	42 846	9 329	3 419	2 760	2 792	12 646	43 027	25 442	15 305
May	167 289	42 590	9 299	3 383	2 730	2 765	12 619	43 870	26 823	15 063
June	169 378	42 692	9 858	3 241	2 731	2 679	13 200	44 840	26 232	15 396
July	171 361	43 342	9 451	3 407	2 785	2 706	13 104	45 344	27 418	15 374
August	172 844	43 726	9 669	3 395	2 808	2 638	13 253	45 777	27 958	15 437
September	172 222	43 199	9 676	3 444	2 782	2 662	13 082	45 655	27 768	15 561
October	178 303	43 892	9 606	3 388	2 829	2 667	12 997	47 591	31 454	15 519
November	180 608	44 004	9 552	3 462	2 844	2 649	13 140	48 602	32 268	15 719
December	179 340	42 930	9 624	3 635	2 853	2 673	13 163	48 107	31 752	16 134
2005										
January	182 805	44 102	9 564	3 646	2 931	2 700	13 530	49 197	32 196	16 259
February	183 074	44 237	9 513	3 697	2 928	2 647	13 660	48 822	32 684	16 245
March	189 410	43 489	9 710	3 596	2 901	2 601	13 754	50 003	38 190	16 545
April	189 247	44 101	10 148	3 631	2 895	2 556	13 646	50 245	37 140	16 296
May	189 570	44 826	10 599	3 656	2 850	2 560	13 628	50 034	36 436	16 397
June	191 513	44 736	10 660	3 630	2 859	2 790	13 798	49 907	38 198	16 328
July	193 753	44 384	10 688	3 513	2 879	2 599	13 378	50 748	40 787	16 289
August	197 388	44 218	11 056	3 415	2 926	2 542	13 208	52 051	42 887	16 484
September	199 270	44 778	10 441	3 378	3 065	2 553	12 962	51 188	44 933	17 220
October	199 222	44 179	10 546	3 364	2 948	2 574	13 356	51 783	44 562	17 272
November	200 892	44 955	10 584	3 428	2 988	2 685	13 594	54 273	42 228	17 665
December	201 786	44 790	10 490	3 446	2 881	2 639	13 662	53 218	44 523	17 628
2006										
January	207 037	44 728	10 440	3 404	2 920	2 476	14 099	55 326	47 237	17 748
February	200 476	44 758	10 170	3 410	2 938	2 478	14 034	53 918	42 224	17 794
March	205 141	44 644	10 328	3 371	2 893	2 705	14 711	54 715	46 035	17 555
April	206 355	44 509	10 222	3 307	2 816	2 626	14 156	54 958	47 592	17 352
May	210 314	44 516	10 765	3 231	2 835	2 690	14 438	55 662	49 419	17 774
June	210 200	44 489	10 670	3 206	2 770	2 639	14 349	55 338	49 818	17 975
July	212 219	44 713	10 271	3 210	2 771	2 543	14 144	56 076	52 042	17 570
August	211 032	44 939	10 738	3 207	2 688	2 446	14 251	56 658	49 437	17 857
September	198 733	44 643	10 077	3 163	2 708	2 470	14 059	54 354	40 774	17 729
October	197 323	45 197	10 457	3 172	2 646	2 510	14 058	53 861	39 395	17 282
November	198 728	45 469	10 563	3 132	2 622	2 429	13 930	53 827	40 658	17 256
December	203 282	45 568	10 103	3 031	2 662	2 472	14 885	54 003	44 097	17 574
2007										
January	198 109	45 719	10 318	3 203	2 650	2 468	13 971	53 744	39 663	17 396
February	200 423	46 465	10 340	3 168	2 622	2 496	13 946	54 367	40 790	17 238
March	204 981	46 556	10 785	3 055	2 564	2 433	13 882	54 593	44 641	17 430
April	206 978	46 855	10 784	3 069	2 577	2 517	14 002	55 250	45 364	17 564
May	210 274	47 510	11 236	3 106	2 596	2 424	13 981	55 600	47 191	17 641
June	209 538	47 739	11 160	3 007	2 587	2 360	13 938	55 469	46 852	17 487
July	212 569	48 434	11 102	3 059	2 542	2 421	14 137	55 886	48 205	17 765
August	207 633	48 645	11 582	3 023	2 542	2 547	14 005	55 400	43 342	17 530
September	209 772	48 772	10 931	3 011	2 482	2 525	14 183	55 134	46 246	17 554
October	214 383	48 759	11 621	3 013	2 492	2 492	14 121	56 323	48 513	17 873
November	222 605	48 927	11 354	2 954	2 449	2 588	14 258	56 052	57 027	17 846
December	221 789	49 379	10 972	2 978	2 406	2 547	14 137	56 915	56 159	17 399
2008										
January	221 726	49 802	11 056	2 938	2 385	2 592	14 430	57 228	54 854	17 631
February	217 759	49 254	10 696	2 872	2 351	2 535	14 133	56 770	53 001	17 576
March	224 600	49 771	11 285	2 894	2 344	2 587	14 314	56 771	58 381	17 455
April	232 440	51 119	11 454	2 875	2 356	2 601	14 362	58 032	63 112	17 553
May	236 362	50 960	11 632	2 809	2 366	2 643	14 133	58 683	66 612	17 801
June	242 926	51 421	11 569	2 841	2 351	2 690	14 290	60 483	70 431	18 135
July	244 830	52 436	11 805	2 918	2 296	2 712	14 606	60 730	70 255	18 257
August	237 116	51 751	11 681	2 864	2 226	2 653	14 759	60 213	64 621	17 746
September	223 252	51 691	11 613	2 813	2 147	2 629	14 704	57 542	53 755	17 792
October	214 781	51 103	11 712	2 701	2 077	2 505	14 383	57 585	46 956	17 242
November	196 156	50 308	11 380	2 545	1 982	2 493	14 048	52 788	35 887	16 526
December	186 797	49 824	11 486	2 437	1 877	2 467	13 716	51 026	29 340	16 334

[1] Includes categories not shown separately.

Table 17-4. Manufacturers' Shipments—Continued

(Millions of dollars, seasonally adjusted.)

Year and month	Construction materials and supplies	Information technology industries	By topical categories						
			Capital goods				Consumer goods		
				Nondefense					
			Total	Total	Excluding aircraft and parts	Defense	Total	Durable	Nondurable
1992	281 232	236 015	566 268	471 485	435 696	94 783	1 098 480	253 111	845 369
1993	303 391	241 680	580 859	493 875	463 753	86 984	1 127 629	274 813	852 816
1994	332 734	264 092	616 435	538 203	512 327	78 232	1 192 098	314 931	877 167
1995	353 198	291 885	666 167	590 578	565 729	75 589	1 256 611	324 036	932 575
1996	371 401	311 028	704 635	630 932	605 295	73 703	1 292 955	328 402	964 553
1997	399 880	349 846	779 232	702 971	665 074	76 261	1 358 516	360 193	998 323
1998	418 756	362 564	821 736	747 046	695 717	74 690	1 351 812	373 404	978 408
1999	434 138	374 384	839 754	768 799	713 042	70 955	1 424 828	412 646	1 012 182
2000	444 812	399 751	875 396	808 345	757 617	67 051	1 500 532	391 463	1 109 069
2001	424 517	353 237	801 999	728 466	678 229	73 533	1 480 495	367 522	1 112 973
2002	424 008	284 799	728 585	652 500	609 654	76 085	1 494 575	395 953	1 098 622
2003	429 183	274 829	719 602	633 878	600 699	85 724	1 584 329	418 821	1 165 508
2004	463 148	287 837	752 905	661 217	629 207	91 688	1 700 835	419 182	1 281 653
2005	509 865	295 447	821 906	729 862	686 827	92 044	1 895 119	422 555	1 472 564
2006	545 973	320 307	885 526	795 525	745 209	90 001	1 988 697	421 854	1 566 843
2007	533 380	322 058	889 599	796 439	739 632	93 160	2 037 553	418 456	1 619 097
2008	520 305	320 479	907 457	800 074	748 783	107 383	2 121 030	354 120	1 766 910
2004									
January	35 414	23 733	59 763	52 342	49 991	7 421	134 976	34 575	100 401
February	35 396	23 375	61 099	52 348	49 533	8 751	134 071	35 640	98 431
March	38 627	23 642	62 206	54 573	51 742	7 633	139 529	37 474	102 055
April	38 749	23 985	61 636	54 157	51 818	7 479	139 120	35 269	103 851
May	38 411	23 849	61 737	53 891	50 972	7 846	139 046	33 721	105 325
June	38 037	23 631	62 281	54 946	52 479	7 335	140 769	34 348	106 421
July	38 748	24 188	62 656	54 970	52 680	7 686	138 849	31 005	107 844
August	39 450	24 323	63 152	55 470	52 718	7 682	142 687	33 875	108 812
September	39 255	23 813	63 578	56 146	53 465	7 432	141 882	34 452	107 430
October	38 808	24 658	64 461	56 843	53 989	7 618	146 789	34 145	112 644
November	39 762	24 137	63 044	55 578	53 384	7 466	149 080	34 985	114 095
December	40 686	23 771	64 899	57 547	54 627	7 352	147 148	35 789	111 359
2005									
January	40 745	24 350	65 721	58 407	56 121	7 314	148 711	34 622	114 089
February	40 862	24 228	65 393	57 876	55 753	7 517	149 187	34 931	114 256
March	41 507	24 319	65 917	58 513	55 635	7 404	154 417	34 761	119 656
April	41 566	24 030	66 944	59 115	55 676	7 829	154 009	34 229	119 780
May	41 455	24 442	67 627	59 754	56 867	7 873	154 473	34 364	120 109
June	42 083	24 607	67 938	59 943	56 950	7 995	156 600	34 903	121 697
July	41 646	24 250	66 948	59 398	56 537	7 550	158 139	34 367	123 772
August	42 338	24 718	68 583	60 872	57 511	7 711	161 732	34 905	126 827
September	43 502	24 617	68 241	60 368	58 078	7 873	165 440	37 198	128 242
October	44 193	25 152	70 373	62 666	58 404	7 707	164 276	36 195	128 081
November	44 977	24 955	71 809	64 240	59 266	7 569	162 829	35 541	127 288
December	45 772	25 399	75 068	67 229	60 113	7 839	164 655	36 326	128 329
2006									
January	46 324	26 226	71 832	64 232	60 541	7 600	167 340	36 163	131 177
February	46 821	26 582	73 131	66 000	61 233	7 131	161 625	35 861	125 764
March	46 413	26 691	73 828	66 318	62 115	7 510	167 304	36 397	130 907
April	45 296	26 740	73 103	65 439	62 056	7 664	167 913	35 639	132 274
May	45 669	27 122	74 368	66 896	62 791	7 472	171 674	36 616	135 058
June	45 775	27 167	74 236	66 629	62 413	7 607	171 299	36 438	134 861
July	45 120	26 969	73 625	66 379	62 491	7 246	169 367	32 212	137 155
August	45 475	27 310	74 901	67 323	63 211	7 578	169 209	33 939	135 270
September	45 040	26 793	74 481	67 102	62 393	7 379	158 358	33 313	125 045
October	44 583	25 851	73 520	65 852	61 597	7 668	157 726	33 411	124 315
November	44 275	27 027	74 526	66 905	62 716	7 621	159 985	33 898	126 087
December	45 968	26 020	74 182	66 602	62 419	7 580	165 937	36 501	129 436
2007									
January	44 470	25 937	71 680	64 004	59 220	7 676	158 918	33 637	125 281
February	44 397	27 416	73 116	65 178	60 836	7 938	161 547	34 501	127 046
March	44 717	26 737	73 023	65 521	61 034	7 502	166 564	35 128	131 436
April	44 967	26 510	73 561	65 960	61 421	7 601	168 188	35 633	132 555
May	45 335	27 054	74 343	66 591	62 138	7 752	170 386	35 483	134 903
June	44 851	26 801	73 834	66 300	61 521	7 534	170 257	35 400	134 857
July	45 606	26 408	74 383	66 263	61 200	8 120	173 360	36 554	136 806
August	44 586	27 000	75 469	67 514	62 279	7 955	167 843	35 530	132 313
September	44 002	27 117	75 612	67 859	63 029	7 753	168 933	34 328	134 605
October	44 033	27 074	74 832	67 140	62 042	7 692	172 222	34 508	137 714
November	43 626	27 100	75 185	67 186	62 414	7 999	180 040	34 272	145 768
December	42 657	26 990	75 605	67 798	63 101	7 807	179 751	33 700	146 051
2008									
January	42 976	27 755	77 505	68 947	62 834	8 558	178 420	33 946	144 474
February	43 748	26 861	74 879	66 455	62 023	8 424	174 960	33 134	141 826
March	43 444	26 891	75 338	66 680	62 500	8 658	178 994	31 018	147 976
April	43 634	27 156	77 135	67 879	63 121	9 256	185 308	30 690	154 618
May	43 595	27 631	76 753	67 712	63 260	9 041	187 681	30 067	157 614
June	44 406	27 128	77 267	68 194	63 663	9 073	192 033	29 959	162 074
July	44 885	27 684	78 153	69 045	63 850	9 108	193 506	30 268	163 238
August	44 070	26 722	75 853	66 795	62 504	9 058	185 131	28 746	156 385
September	43 563	26 628	76 747	67 540	63 567	9 207	174 757	28 731	146 026
October	42 812	26 175	73 765	64 469	61 218	9 296	165 659	27 496	138 163
November	41 000	25 687	72 244	63 155	60 425	9 089	152 359	26 513	125 846
December	40 056	25 088	73 620	65 134	60 790	8 486	144 203	25 272	118 931

Table 17-5. Manufacturers' Inventories

(Current cost basis, end of period; seasonally adjusted, except as noted; millions of dollars.)

Year, and month	Total, not seasonally adjusted	Total	NAICS durable goods industries											Durables total by stage of fabrication		
			Total ¹	Non-metallic mineral products	Primary metals		Fabricated metal products	Machinery	Computers and electronic products	Electrical equipment, appliances, and components	Transportation equipment		Materials and supplies	Work in process	Finished goods
					Total	Iron and steel mills					Total	Motor vehicles and parts			
1992	369 673	378 709	238 102	8 002	17 972	9 620	26 101	36 260	44 551	12 218	66 415	17 101	69 737	104 211	64 154
1993	370 775	379 660	238 737	7 580	17 973	9 597	26 287	37 091	43 965	12 455	64 345	18 221	72 657	101 999	64 081
1994	390 540	399 910	253 141	7 831	20 112	10 435	28 194	40 845	47 070	13 760	64 915	20 186	78 573	106 556	68 012
1995	414 969	424 772	267 358	8 437	21 457	11 292	30 298	44 576	53 554	14 177	63 178	20 749	85 473	106 658	75 227
1996	420 680	430 446	272 495	8 741	21 787	11 701	31 298	45 300	50 852	13 946	68 136	21 137	86 226	110 563	75 706
1997	433 451	443 566	281 074	9 010	22 552	12 302	32 439	45 857	55 181	14 093	68 902	20 736	92 292	109 960	78 822
1998	438 845	449 065	290 700	9 037	22 123	12 432	32 869	47 099	52 014	14 023	79 961	21 229	93 629	115 235	81 836
1999	452 803	463 625	296 553	9 448	22 139	12 152	33 468	47 421	54 894	14 011	79 720	22 654	97 959	114 111	84 483
2000	470 084	481 673	306 727	9 993	22 047	12 443	34 805	50 585	65 364	15 028	71 913	22 918	106 214	111 196	89 317
2001	417 487	428 113	267 829	9 488	19 619	10 525	31 521	43 223	51 205	13 072	64 571	20 491	91 291	93 924	82 614
2002	412 328	423 133	260 582	9 725	19 554	10 869	31 387	42 202	46 171	12 558	63 657	21 599	88 575	92 386	79 621
2003	397 631	408 304	246 963	9 416	18 541	9 846	29 908	38 822	41 085	11 801	62 204	21 595	82 354	88 719	75 890
2004	428 960	440 697	265 070	10 001	24 194	14 008	34 110	41 935	38 982	12 346	65 918	22 935	92 207	91 207	81 656
2005	459 893	472 860	283 598	10 400	25 984	14 593	36 941	44 787	44 995	12 766	67 562	24 143	98 271	98 929	86 398
2006	497 426	511 487	309 914	11 658	31 025	17 170	41 377	49 563	45 421	14 410	74 131	25 766	108 819	105 340	95 755
2007	515 952	530 664	320 757	11 855	30 682	16 375	42 292	52 226	45 059	14 857	81 653	24 526	109 305	113 969	97 483
2008	529 521	544 301	343 484	11 948	32 182	18 733	43 714	55 310	48 125	14 925	95 466	21 741	115 956	130 621	96 907
2005															
January	445 114	447 366	268 973	10 083	25 006	14 612	34 557	42 511	39 819	12 407	66 443	23 501	94 108	92 139	82 726
February	454 413	451 939	272 178	10 202	25 353	15 002	35 199	42 837	39 998	12 447	67 624	23 824	94 405	93 730	84 043
March	454 374	455 665	274 115	10 208	25 986	15 316	35 603	42 970	39 911	12 579	67 946	24 330	95 131	93 687	85 297
April	458 995	456 878	274 728	10 213	26 073	15 308	35 941	43 348	40 175	12 684	67 109	24 370	95 584	93 270	85 874
May	460 210	456 706	275 924	10 257	26 223	15 382	36 313	43 722	40 676	12 638	67 064	24 312	95 730	93 966	86 228
June	455 649	457 820	275 459	10 326	26 011	15 189	36 125	43 720	40 903	12 572	66 653	24 535	96 012	93 815	85 632
July	464 735	461 583	278 175	10 412	25 859	15 033	36 223	44 416	41 847	12 529	67 577	24 132	96 026	95 659	86 490
August	464 941	461 411	277 971	10 396	25 748	14 805	36 158	44 676	42 168	12 495	66 641	24 223	95 965	95 191	86 815
September	462 562	462 324	278 147	10 308	25 570	14 504	36 066	44 653	42 766	12 638	66 546	23 749	96 521	95 876	85 750
October	469 992	466 827	280 150	10 291	25 633	14 581	36 168	44 479	43 658	12 646	67 520	24 345	96 801	97 068	86 281
November	469 570	469 304	282 762	10 294	25 754	14 558	36 708	44 688	44 813	12 678	67 823	24 532	97 914	97 961	86 887
December	459 893	472 860	283 598	10 400	25 984	14 593	36 941	44 787	44 995	12 766	67 562	24 143	98 271	98 929	86 398
2006															
January	475 971	478 608	285 540	10 513	26 463	14 738	37 509	45 229	45 572	13 000	67 218	24 097	97 986	99 581	87 973
February	480 899	478 575	285 614	10 551	26 845	14 989	37 777	45 339	44 434	13 033	67 333	24 169	98 903	98 551	88 160
March	481 512	482 900	288 271	10 620	26 863	14 897	38 109	45 862	45 286	13 228	67 861	24 310	100 303	99 658	88 310
April	490 143	487 600	291 477	10 829	27 308	15 066	38 396	46 276	45 727	13 329	68 749	24 514	101 284	100 945	89 248
May	495 427	491 256	293 701	10 858	27 957	15 131	38 701	46 761	45 647	13 333	69 321	24 612	102 388	101 307	90 006
June	494 320	496 334	296 386	10 967	28 207	15 257	39 189	46 968	45 678	13 616	70 443	24 886	103 211	102 120	91 055
July	504 739	500 974	300 325	11 139	28 710	15 614	39 600	47 303	45 976	13 818	72 089	25 200	105 179	102 983	92 163
August	508 113	504 079	302 077	11 249	29 277	15 966	40 124	47 711	46 237	14 153	71 230	25 335	106 467	101 674	93 936
September	507 873	507 632	305 427	11 440	30 299	16 700	40 525	48 503	45 865	13 977	72 477	25 210	107 459	103 306	94 662
October	513 071	510 028	308 289	11 575	30 936	17 026	40 865	48 814	45 897	14 043	73 813	25 621	108 683	104 354	95 252
November	511 666	511 609	309 252	11 633	30 977	17 064	41 066	48 655	46 025	14 120	74 531	26 039	108 755	104 142	96 355
December	497 426	511 487	309 914	11 658	31 025	17 170	41 377	49 563	45 421	14 410	74 131	25 766	108 819	105 340	95 755
2007															
January	509 521	512 189	311 878	11 627	30 893	16 888	41 951	49 865	45 996	14 347	74 834	25 986	109 085	106 344	96 449
February	515 209	512 706	312 453	11 655	30 786	16 780	41 884	50 247	45 749	14 281	75 271	26 059	108 863	106 371	97 219
March	511 660	512 988	312 312	11 623	30 802	16 873	41 910	50 208	45 357	14 303	75 489	25 759	108 642	106 176	97 494
April	517 561	514 686	313 015	11 645	31 121	16 960	41 972	50 466	45 230	14 355	76 490	25 494	109 083	106 879	97 053
May	521 240	516 996	313 421	11 617	30 884	17 025	41 829	50 567	45 355	14 259	76 785	25 434	109 099	107 808	96 514
June	515 930	517 956	313 371	11 567	31 257	17 207	41 802	50 811	44 636	14 227	76 959	25 121	108 988	107 988	96 395
July	522 281	518 644	313 495	11 512	31 444	17 132	41 836	51 150	43 398	14 376	77 494	25 087	108 988	108 400	96 107
August	521 865	518 057	313 236	11 558	31 347	16 994	41 455	51 245	43 591	14 394	77 537	24 797	108 732	109 137	95 367
September	522 192	521 995	314 636	11 621	31 134	16 813	41 689	51 620	44 269	14 217	77 917	24 712	107 972	109 712	96 952
October	525 845	522 777	315 650	11 664	30 791	16 520	41 892	51 850	44 499	14 518	78 168	24 635	108 567	110 980	96 103
November	526 508	526 439	317 534	11 707	30 616	16 408	41 883	52 015	44 773	14 721	79 554	24 417	108 943	111 928	96 663
December	515 952	530 664	320 757	11 855	30 682	16 375	42 292	52 226	45 059	14 857	81 653	24 526	109 305	113 969	97 483
2008															
January	534 311	537 497	322 384	11 862	30 785	16 591	42 338	52 550	45 158	15 035	82 502	24 176	110 161	115 144	97 079
February	542 782	540 675	323 841	11 880	30 979	16 689	42 288	52 839	45 503	15 213	83 435	23 979	110 644	116 407	96 790
March	544 108	545 791	327 066	11 972	31 693	17 185	42 443	53 549	46 045	15 119	84 809	24 026	111 560	118 227	97 279
April	548 589	545 633	328 911	12 019	32 282	17 607	42 860	53 407	46 363	15 285	85 596	23 720	112 097	119 869	96 945
May	553 028	548 825	330 426	11 913	32 971	18 090	42 976	53 562	46 388	15 122	86 360	23 653	112 275	121 109	97 042
June	553 170	555 627	333 127	11 880	33 515	18 510	43 553	53 849	46 336	15 243	87 294	23 693	113 575	122 118	97 434
July	563 051	559 070	336 185	11 881	34 040	19 030	44 332	54 246	46 523	15 145	88 318	23 470	115 462	123 189	97 534
August	567 598	562 781	339 033	11 975	35 073	20 053	44 791	54 435	46 999	15 262	88 780	23 272	115 897	124 479	98 657
September	559 375	558 296	339 728	12 024	35 168	20 335	44 942	54 629	47 022	15 366	88 576	22 904	116 330	124 799	98 599
October	559 181	554 990	341 168	12 069	34 793	20 272	44 726	54 869	47 419	15 172	90 136	22 837	116 603	126 385	98 180
November	552 910	552 253	342 259	12 025	33 651	19 721	44 410	55 190	47 478	14 940	92 707	22 372	116 700	128 071	97 488
December	529 521	544 301	343 484	11 948	32 182	18 733	43 714	55 310	48 125	14 925	95 466	21 741	115 956	130 621	96 907

¹Includes categories not shown separately.

Table 17-5. Manufacturers' Inventories—*Continued*

(Current cost basis, end of period; seasonally adjusted, except as noted; millions of dollars.)

Year, and month	NAICS nondurable goods industries										Nondurables total by stage of fabrication		
	Total [1]	Food products	Beverage and tobacco products	Textile mills	Textile products	Apparel	Paper products	Chemical products	Petroleum and coal products	Plastics and rubber products	Materials and supplies	Work in process	Finished goods
1992	140 607	26 439	11 627	6 468	3 515	8 914	13 435	37 530	11 659	12 646	53 179	23 304	64 124
1993	140 923	26 607	11 282	6 840	3 641	10 084	13 451	37 817	10 471	12 833	54 289	23 305	63 329
1994	146 769	27 541	10 951	7 192	3 931	10 478	13 734	38 861	11 302	14 287	57 161	24 383	65 225
1995	157 414	29 243	11 418	7 623	4 112	10 469	16 596	42 014	11 482	15 302	60 725	25 755	70 934
1996	157 951	29 561	12 367	7 237	4 092	8 764	15 283	43 322	12 772	15 795	59 101	26 438	72 412
1997	162 492	29 919	13 798	6 884	4 543	9 635	15 192	45 259	12 178	16 165	60 160	28 478	73 854
1998	158 365	29 187	13 923	6 925	4 214	9 443	14 823	45 565	9 690	16 185	58 223	27 044	73 098
1999	167 072	30 465	13 849	6 881	4 411	9 778	15 166	48 513	12 174	17 226	61 098	28 741	77 233
2000	174 946	31 754	14 091	6 459	4 901	9 488	15 342	52 457	13 821	18 021	61 509	30 015	83 422
2001	160 284	30 253	14 555	5 318	4 533	5 958	14 176	48 792	13 672	15 816	55 726	27 073	77 485
2002	162 551	31 319	14 754	4 918	3 528	5 678	14 451	49 238	15 542	16 084	56 536	27 828	78 187
2003	161 341	31 487	14 631	4 393	3 348	4 658	13 608	49 282	17 231	16 017	56 847	27 047	77 447
2004	175 627	32 185	15 408	4 307	3 373	4 328	14 318	55 169	21 619	17 791	61 713	29 953	83 961
2005	189 262	33 089	14 485	4 157	3 415	4 014	14 381	59 435	29 865	19 151	66 394	32 889	89 979
2006	201 573	34 988	14 758	4 032	3 489	4 078	15 050	64 775	32 020	20 572	69 638	36 247	95 688
2007	209 907	36 586	14 981	3 783	3 344	4 363	15 346	65 926	35 742	21 719	72 911	38 405	98 591
2008	200 817	36 945	15 189	3 658	3 218	4 249	15 284	66 274	26 755	21 253	68 159	36 997	95 661
2005													
January	178 393	31 986	15 447	4 289	3 465	4 432	14 607	55 167	23 595	18 426	62 573	29 469	86 351
February	179 761	32 143	15 236	4 255	3 487	4 434	14 685	55 669	24 211	18 556	62 761	30 382	86 618
March	181 550	32 376	15 031	4 212	3 497	4 425	14 662	56 328	24 997	18 829	63 553	31 070	86 927
April	182 150	32 988	15 014	4 222	3 457	4 436	14 736	56 134	25 198	18 768	63 656	30 584	87 910
May	180 782	32 672	14 875	4 241	3 435	4 410	14 751	56 227	24 076	18 862	63 616	30 232	86 934
June	182 361	32 688	14 721	4 181	3 416	4 352	14 822	56 803	25 330	18 779	63 536	30 809	88 016
July	183 408	32 796	14 771	4 157	3 366	4 293	14 800	56 319	26 918	18 683	63 769	31 081	88 558
August	183 440	32 770	14 616	4 071	3 374	4 279	14 694	56 209	27 461	18 752	63 977	31 443	88 020
September	184 177	32 940	14 423	4 093	3 339	4 247	14 579	56 655	28 168	18 385	64 161	32 137	87 879
October	186 677	32 969	14 704	4 142	3 375	4 219	14 592	56 934	29 829	18 634	64 911	32 918	88 848
November	186 542	33 045	14 687	4 134	3 318	4 113	14 433	57 147	29 348	18 995	64 509	33 064	88 969
December	189 262	33 089	14 485	4 157	3 415	4 014	14 381	59 435	29 865	19 151	66 394	32 889	89 979
2006													
January	193 068	33 665	14 492	4 195	3 408	4 027	14 457	60 949	30 829	19 695	66 734	34 670	91 664
February	192 961	33 655	14 499	4 191	3 426	4 040	14 655	60 534	30 789	19 861	67 274	33 021	92 666
March	194 629	33 556	14 345	4 218	3 443	4 091	14 822	61 849	30 946	20 000	67 976	33 079	93 574
April	196 123	33 428	14 385	4 178	3 452	4 088	14 931	61 560	32 385	20 252	68 293	34 229	93 601
May	197 555	33 366	14 278	4 106	3 416	4 113	14 976	61 930	33 617	20 271	70 152	33 376	94 027
June	199 948	33 610	14 245	4 147	3 504	4 078	14 901	63 179	34 316	20 346	69 922	35 668	94 358
July	200 649	33 602	14 353	4 166	3 554	4 157	14 993	63 322	34 245	20 569	70 074	36 011	94 564
August	202 002	33 603	14 508	4 163	3 558	4 226	15 020	63 876	34 592	20 777	70 634	36 472	94 896
September	202 205	33 849	14 457	4 193	3 554	3 893	15 087	65 053	33 327	20 995	70 995	35 905	95 305
October	201 739	34 418	14 625	4 095	3 548	3 951	15 080	65 345	31 607	21 234	69 490	36 187	96 062
November	202 357	34 764	14 693	4 050	3 515	4 070	15 188	65 268	31 793	21 209	69 955	36 560	95 842
December	201 573	34 988	14 758	4 032	3 489	4 078	15 050	64 775	32 020	20 572	69 638	36 247	95 688
2007													
January	200 311	34 754	14 869	3 963	3 454	4 096	15 139	64 720	30 843	20 656	69 687	35 863	94 761
February	200 253	34 654	14 858	3 943	3 435	4 097	15 148	64 416	31 244	20 599	70 147	35 861	94 245
March	200 676	34 707	14 917	3 857	3 391	4 108	15 031	64 604	31 556	20 692	70 049	36 163	94 464
April	201 671	35 061	15 002	3 829	3 352	4 159	15 003	64 727	32 130	20 666	70 523	35 873	95 275
May	203 575	35 641	15 109	3 806	3 385	4 182	14 999	65 346	32 479	20 916	71 132	36 392	96 051
June	204 585	35 848	15 057	3 820	3 373	4 262	14 950	65 552	32 870	21 115	71 545	36 359	96 681
July	205 149	36 341	15 108	3 772	3 355	4 437	14 967	65 777	32 426	21 297	71 772	35 812	97 565
August	204 821	36 794	15 072	3 794	3 347	4 314	15 016	65 621	31 809	21 394	72 246	35 273	97 302
September	207 359	36 924	14 929	3 783	3 351	4 328	15 027	65 926	33 828	21 493	73 731	35 546	98 082
October	207 127	36 365	15 008	3 784	3 343	4 349	15 039	65 941	33 996	21 366	73 175	36 333	97 619
November	208 905	36 355	14 979	3 780	3 348	4 329	15 087	66 450	35 136	21 517	72 998	37 281	98 626
December	209 907	36 586	14 981	3 783	3 344	4 363	15 346	65 926	35 742	21 719	72 911	38 405	98 591
2008													
January	215 113	37 014	15 064	3 778	3 365	4 387	15 116	67 718	39 368	21 719	75 343	40 346	99 424
February	216 834	37 284	15 189	3 765	3 353	4 428	15 128	68 002	40 019	21 880	75 458	41 346	100 030
March	218 725	37 425	15 135	3 749	3 349	4 427	15 292	67 739	41 580	22 094	75 215	41 550	101 960
April	216 722	37 564	15 193	3 710	3 322	4 444	15 334	67 950	39 134	22 182	75 045	40 515	101 162
May	218 399	37 822	15 141	3 645	3 250	4 485	15 412	68 311	40 191	22 212	76 167	42 033	100 199
June	222 500	38 006	15 100	3 604	3 222	4 503	15 470	68 255	44 055	22 433	76 810	41 533	104 157
July	222 885	37 858	15 042	3 669	3 290	4 534	15 391	69 069	43 394	22 882	76 685	42 641	103 559
August	223 748	37 390	15 089	3 666	3 295	4 495	15 493	69 952	43 443	23 236	76 770	42 683	104 295
September	218 568	37 151	15 136	3 702	3 301	4 448	15 541	68 778	39 863	22 905	76 309	41 327	100 932
October	213 822	37 215	15 145	3 711	3 302	4 396	15 775	68 995	34 773	22 813	73 784	39 283	100 755
November	209 994	37 109	15 166	3 706	3 265	4 335	15 706	68 439	31 916	22 476	71 592	38 278	100 124
December	200 817	36 945	15 189	3 658	3 218	4 249	15 284	66 274	26 755	21 253	68 159	36 997	95 661

[1]Includes categories not shown separately.

Table 17-5. Manufacturers' Inventories—Continued

(Current cost basis, end of period; seasonally adjusted, except as noted; millions of dollars.)

Year, and month	Construction materials and supplies	Information technology industries	Capital goods Total	Nondefense Total	Nondefense Excluding aircraft and parts	Defense	Consumer goods Total	Durable	Nondurable
1992	36 729	40 236	120 589	97 442	78 978	23 147	103 237	20 892	82 345
1993	38 275	39 180	118 499	97 175	79 595	21 324	104 761	21 868	82 893
1994	40 894	41 551	123 438	103 396	85 733	20 042	109 516	23 980	85 536
1995	43 444	46 832	129 674	111 508	94 556	18 166	116 392	25 283	91 109
1996	44 149	43 530	132 808	115 225	93 383	17 583	116 378	24 788	91 590
1997	45 740	48 112	137 621	122 593	98 784	15 028	119 680	24 936	94 744
1998	46 506	45 384	145 203	127 187	97 386	18 016	117 437	24 928	92 509
1999	48 508	46 178	146 439	126 353	99 634	20 086	124 285	26 097	98 188
2000	50 526	52 735	149 298	131 850	110 244	17 448	130 943	27 225	103 718
2001	46 369	42 939	128 849	115 143	93 366	13 706	121 668	25 377	96 291
2002	46 595	39 022	122 632	108 442	88 593	14 190	124 782	25 680	99 102
2003	45 333	35 214	115 159	99 841	82 089	15 318	124 946	25 011	99 935
2004	51 147	33 154	118 035	99 617	84 067	18 418	133 750	26 249	107 501
2005	54 576	39 245	127 542	111 379	93 344	16 163	144 468	28 138	116 330
2006	59 945	39 925	137 777	120 999	100 488	16 778	152 618	29 244	123 374
2007	59 671	40 417	146 970	128 234	103 670	18 736	158 364	29 502	128 862
2008	59 876	43 190	167 259	147 646	109 919	19 613	150 122	28 320	121 802
2005									
January	52 001	33 853	119 051	100 896	85 179	18 155	135 912	26 354	109 558
February	52 995	34 245	120 417	102 483	85 950	17 934	136 756	26 529	110 227
March	53 777	34 544	120 547	103 427	86 767	17 120	137 721	26 746	110 975
April	53 999	35 000	120 314	103 478	87 526	16 836	138 716	27 108	111 608
May	54 254	35 605	121 179	104 474	88 092	16 705	137 179	27 314	109 865
June	53 818	35 548	120 723	104 427	88 565	16 296	138 818	27 322	111 496
July	53 830	36 320	123 449	106 878	90 035	16 571	140 308	27 363	112 945
August	53 663	36 843	123 992	107 875	90 862	16 117	141 554	27 980	113 574
September	53 253	37 246	125 042	108 877	91 413	16 165	141 787	27 560	114 227
October	53 533	37 782	125 538	109 343	91 676	16 195	144 217	28 020	116 197
November	53 856	38 930	126 810	110 667	92 917	16 143	143 702	28 300	115 402
December	54 576	39 245	127 542	111 379	93 344	16 163	144 468	28 138	116 330
2006									
January	55 127	39 629	127 962	112 343	93 900	15 619	147 170	28 256	118 914
February	55 592	39 698	128 197	112 432	94 128	15 765	146 721	28 347	118 374
March	55 970	39 716	129 000	112 954	94 732	16 046	147 417	28 217	119 200
April	56 695	39 968	130 279	114 245	95 586	16 034	148 984	28 309	120 675
May	57 301	39 597	130 354	114 161	95 628	16 193	150 238	28 412	121 826
June	57 977	39 218	131 374	115 240	96 277	16 134	151 650	28 373	123 277
July	58 507	39 640	133 393	116 842	97 129	16 551	152 390	28 807	123 583
August	59 408	40 094	133 107	116 437	98 112	16 670	153 169	29 227	123 942
September	60 005	40 153	135 234	118 375	99 044	16 859	152 186	28 910	123 276
October	60 195	40 113	136 342	119 420	99 631	16 922	151 797	29 322	122 475
November	60 277	40 307	136 361	119 369	99 578	16 992	152 745	29 628	123 117
December	59 945	39 925	137 777	120 999	100 488	16 778	152 618	29 244	123 374
2007									
January	60 067	40 695	138 179	120 998	101 148	17 181	151 541	29 382	122 159
February	60 110	40 486	138 665	121 621	101 312	17 044	152 081	29 570	122 511
March	59 959	40 223	138 962	122 026	101 016	16 936	152 107	29 489	122 618
April	60 012	40 014	139 414	122 097	100 732	17 317	152 612	29 172	123 440
May	59 736	40 356	140 725	123 627	101 638	17 098	154 071	29 252	124 819
June	59 540	39 957	140 519	123 289	101 294	17 230	154 851	29 191	125 660
July	59 503	39 127	140 763	123 391	101 026	17 372	155 141	29 219	125 922
August	59 345	39 385	141 160	123 910	101 383	17 250	154 017	28 721	125 296
September	59 483	40 075	142 270	124 686	101 948	17 584	156 700	28 966	127 734
October	59 505	40 310	143 297	125 473	102 758	17 824	156 441	29 148	127 293
November	59 391	40 468	144 933	126 962	103 233	17 971	157 803	29 233	128 570
December	59 671	40 417	146 970	128 234	103 670	18 736	158 364	29 502	128 862
2008									
January	59 734	40 541	148 583	129 993	104 220	18 590	163 451	29 354	134 097
February	59 560	40 746	149 941	131 025	104 837	18 916	164 289	29 247	135 042
March	59 202	41 541	152 616	133 603	106 149	19 013	165 924	29 227	136 697
April	59 445	41 879	153 972	134 612	106 620	19 360	163 008	28 589	134 419
May	59 358	41 714	154 810	135 505	106 683	19 305	164 371	28 467	135 904
June	59 783	41 730	155 830	136 602	107 184	19 228	168 363	28 556	139 807
July	60 415	41 799	157 838	138 532	107 802	19 306	167 433	28 408	139 025
August	60 901	42 214	158 991	139 920	108 517	19 071	167 403	28 471	138 932
September	61 174	42 369	159 247	140 368	108 679	18 879	163 554	28 725	134 829
October	61 017	42 404	161 112	141 864	108 972	19 248	158 668	28 731	129 937
November	60 490	42 293	163 341	143 768	108 983	19 573	155 389	28 586	126 803
December	59 876	43 190	167 259	147 646	109 919	19 613	150 122	28 320	121 802

Table 17-6. Manufacturers' New Orders

(Net, millions of dollars, seasonally adjusted.)

Year and month	Total [1]	NAICS durable goods industries Total [1]	Primary metals Total [1]	Iron and steel mills	Aluminum and nonferrous metal products	Fabricated metal products	Machinery	Computers and electronic products	Electrical equipment, appliances, and components	Transportation equipment Total [1]	Motor vehicles and parts	Nondefense aircraft and parts	Defense aircraft and parts
1993	2 960 015	1 544 062	128 895	62 580	53 733	175 990	202 848	248 104	88 263	427 966	311 928	38 427	32 569
1994	3 199 686	1 725 635	146 503	67 619	64 594	196 567	232 226	274 776	96 919	487 253	367 306	39 309	31 524
1995	3 426 503	1 849 641	159 957	72 600	72 264	214 488	251 307	311 275	101 409	508 133	378 886	57 454	27 736
1996	3 567 384	1 948 793	158 066	71 301	70 657	227 447	258 405	327 288	104 837	552 024	385 712	72 094	32 520
1997	3 779 835	2 092 520	171 407	78 577	74 974	247 839	272 998	363 635	113 411	581 780	422 427	85 797	23 280
1998	3 808 143	2 139 918	160 743	72 378	71 274	253 847	278 100	372 433	115 711	600 205	440 934	84 150	23 854
1999	3 957 242	2 252 091	156 968	70 924	68 469	258 116	278 277	402 216	120 774	660 215	499 527	81 619	25 717
2000	4 161 472	2 326 576	153 625	68 181	67 122	270 021	294 608	436 415	126 196	663 326	468 470	99 249	31 326
2001	3 872 952	2 076 859	136 758	60 185	59 873	248 512	264 327	354 668	110 968	593 618	425 510	74 200	36 284
2002	3 801 705	2 010 603	138 016	62 512	60 706	242 338	244 338	272 217	102 402	625 767	470 028	63 768	39 156
2003	3 964 425	2 091 626	140 636	65 323	60 573	246 224	261 970	287 311	99 346	661 288	493 586	55 295	44 549
2004	4 255 431	2 211 128	185 893	97 643	71 147	265 932	274 091	297 239	106 521	663 443	495 280	73 191	31 759
2005	4 744 813	2 427 580	207 707	106 649	82 182	297 252	312 885	296 761	114 590	745 402	504 251	118 750	29 893
2006	5 037 520	2 578 449	233 056	112 155	100 048	324 084	341 606	336 962	124 051	742 903	502 736	127 873	38 173
2007	5 131 164	2 612 952	241 829	115 247	106 563	330 855	343 454	330 062	128 209	781 392	477 855	184 484	40 855
2008	5 153 328	2 462 536	246 897	123 189	102 181	327 648	354 992	324 410	123 639	649 363	384 052	124 002	60 701
2004													
January	332 340	171 979	13 203	6 258	5 679	21 422	20 610	23 894	8 295	51 435	40 701	3 592	2 019
February	334 748	177 185	14 091	6 870	5 877	20 999	21 057	24 518	8 553	55 714	42 175	5 046	3 461
March	353 560	189 140	15 107	7 372	6 285	22 478	23 994	25 738	8 938	58 571	44 478	5 404	2 504
April	347 897	182 206	14 382	7 372	5 652	22 430	21 921	24 415	9 324	55 318	42 124	4 779	2 676
May	348 145	180 856	15 026	7 868	5 732	21 264	22 254	25 355	8 822	53 450	40 240	6 096	2 551
June	352 293	182 915	15 225	8 050	5 803	21 677	22 820	24 289	8 397	55 956	40 953	5 265	5 099
July	356 370	185 009	16 838	9 497	5 868	21 665	22 229	23 346	8 912	57 819	37 438	11 767	2 631
August	355 241	182 397	16 561	9 274	5 832	22 541	22 215	23 822	9 057	52 851	40 325	5 474	2 245
September	358 497	186 275	16 339	8 938	5 927	21 716	24 045	26 630	9 228	53 205	41 005	5 323	1 963
October	361 655	183 352	15 523	8 099	5 962	22 922	23 720	25 193	8 644	52 336	39 399	5 247	2 669
November	371 871	191 263	16 585	9 025	6 060	23 278	23 385	24 344	9 391	57 951	40 823	8 929	2 492
December	368 733	189 393	16 966	9 109	6 366	23 082	25 011	24 874	8 769	53 819	41 743	5 418	1 355
2005													
January	372 812	190 007	16 684	8 524	6 560	23 659	25 013	24 622	9 334	54 744	41 639	3 663	1 725
February	377 085	194 011	17 310	9 333	6 533	23 866	25 729	24 690	9 289	56 329	41 539	5 473	2 199
March	378 782	189 372	17 067	8 691	6 881	23 665	24 702	25 521	8 998	52 297	40 796	3 106	1 333
April	380 848	191 601	16 022	7 811	6 616	23 995	25 222	23 725	9 052	56 434	40 807	5 061	2 155
May	393 875	204 305	15 897	7 852	6 429	24 450	24 982	24 151	9 307	68 019	41 333	16 831	2 127
June	399 829	208 316	15 874	7 703	6 673	25 101	25 503	26 582	9 543	67 382	41 628	11 827	2 069
July	390 052	196 299	16 287	8 202	6 523	24 087	25 167	23 627	9 221	60 548	40 518	9 432	1 982
August	400 198	202 810	17 572	9 220	6 891	25 242	26 263	25 619	9 970	59 921	42 285	8 856	2 027
September	402 912	203 641	18 907	9 747	7 500	25 648	26 637	24 708	10 213	59 210	44 870	5 129	2 056
October	408 999	209 777	18 947	10 177	7 082	25 777	26 723	24 297	9 899	64 937	44 093	9 383	5 319
November	420 178	219 286	19 104	9 905	7 529	25 980	28 152	24 330	9 933	72 405	41 455	20 423	2 836
December	419 154	217 368	18 630	9 809	7 183	26 345	28 206	24 427	10 109	70 517	43 133	17 432	3 981
2006													
January	408 350	201 313	18 621	9 290	7 557	26 677	28 244	25 608	10 440	51 089	42 893	5 429	3 529
February	413 922	213 446	18 340	8 972	7 583	26 949	27 301	27 282	10 080	62 367	42 239	9 629	3 266
March	426 610	221 469	18 482	8 945	7 805	26 698	28 210	30 137	9 894	68 009	43 322	14 865	2 937
April	419 229	212 874	18 849	9 353	7 763	27 035	27 848	27 939	10 546	60 912	42 645	10 769	2 047
May	423 108	212 794	20 016	9 642	8 647	27 230	29 146	26 847	10 898	58 591	43 290	8 831	2 426
June	429 311	219 111	20 180	9 782	8 570	28 089	28 710	28 546	10 923	62 797	42 775	9 558	2 658
July	423 937	211 718	20 764	10 228	8 713	26 853	28 371	29 196	10 573	56 318	38 971	8 997	2 580
August	419 738	208 706	20 124	9 601	8 819	27 278	27 888	28 186	9 628	56 452	41 159	4 556	2 710
September	429 000	230 267	19 773	9 387	8 701	27 309	28 899	29 192	10 305	75 500	39 899	19 273	2 426
October	408 514	211 191	19 550	9 391	8 547	26 292	29 987	26 704	10 439	59 259	40 083	11 288	2 980
November	415 722	216 994	19 096	8 836	8 561	26 613	27 690	29 506	10 388	65 135	40 480	10 967	4 757
December	421 690	218 408	19 665	8 958	8 937	27 543	29 525	28 030	10 235	64 001	43 492	12 555	5 714
2007													
January	405 820	207 711	19 716	9 572	8 415	28 042	26 124	25 825	11 021	58 413	39 763	7 693	2 459
February	412 981	212 558	19 075	9 029	8 451	26 938	27 572	28 596	10 619	61 899	40 609	12 703	3 094
March	422 322	217 341	19 866	9 615	8 611	26 603	28 495	25 961	10 855	67 467	41 091	18 592	1 797
April	428 894	221 916	21 127	10 439	9 001	27 884	27 783	26 839	11 396	68 219	40 116	17 031	2 306
May	427 149	216 875	20 507	9 762	9 028	27 290	28 115	28 533	10 828	62 701	40 655	13 349	2 670
June	427 369	217 831	18 848	8 350	8 845	27 671	28 204	26 626	10 825	67 208	40 120	17 485	3 078
July	442 069	229 500	20 489	9 528	9 270	28 154	30 448	28 231	10 365	73 306	42 628	20 502	3 403
August	426 512	218 879	19 768	9 191	8 926	27 949	29 147	28 448	10 579	64 779	39 633	11 043	5 866
September	425 399	215 627	20 086	9 477	8 907	27 022	29 625	28 847	10 329	62 097	38 820	15 072	3 705
October	430 254	215 871	20 650	9 953	9 064	27 897	28 971	27 453	10 446	62 494	38 296	14 357	3 517
November	437 808	215 203	20 964	10 312	8 984	27 537	28 489	27 049	10 607	63 130	38 753	17 374	2 694
December	445 917	224 128	20 883	10 167	9 048	28 052	31 023	27 622	10 569	69 005	37 383	18 361	6 376
2008													
January	435 415	213 689	21 036	10 497	8 866	26 892	30 675	27 226	11 148	59 894	37 245	13 099	3 888
February	433 860	216 101	21 331	10 312	9 244	26 969	28 126	27 640	11 429	64 208	36 398	14 721	4 344
March	440 216	215 616	21 855	10 887	9 198	28 368	30 526	27 889	9 279	60 913	34 613	16 000	4 638
April	445 915	213 475	22 408	11 603	9 000	27 694	32 006	27 330	10 956	55 857	33 448	12 058	4 510
May	450 033	213 671	22 008	11 358	8 847	27 771	30 748	28 093	11 078	56 852	32 183	12 783	5 174
June	459 576	216 650	23 734	12 833	9 073	28 041	31 553	28 372	11 629	55 805	32 855	10 055	4 723
July	462 993	218 163	24 418	13 661	8 806	28 241	32 740	27 099	10 658	57 313	33 042	12 294	5 881
August	443 200	206 084	21 371	10 786	8 645	27 731	30 578	27 626	10 302	51 934	30 116	7 658	5 189
September	429 286	206 034	20 113	9 866	8 307	27 470	30 643	26 949	10 190	54 809	30 828	9 866	5 839
October	403 315	188 534	16 834	7 436	7 725	26 667	27 206	25 627	9 155	47 772	29 214	9 003	5 356
November	377 203	181 047	15 966	6 667	7 561	26 058	26 449	26 646	8 662	43 065	28 585	4 840	4 982
December	362 437	175 640	14 831	6 204	7 102	24 987	24 948	24 903	9 397	42 992	27 020	2 720	5 793

[1]Includes categories not shown separately.

Table 17-6. Manufacturers' New Orders—Continued

(Net, millions of dollars, seasonally adjusted.)

Year and month	Construction materials and supplies	Information technology industries	By topical categories						
			Capital goods				Consumer goods		
			Total	Nondefense		Defense	Total	Durable	Nondurable
				Total	Excluding aircraft and parts				
1993	304 264	239 387	561 097	488 166	466 433	72 931	1 128 447	275 631	852 816
1994	335 962	265 010	616 252	542 094	523 461	74 158	1 192 584	315 417	877 167
1995	355 161	297 605	680 857	612 132	576 769	68 725	1 256 721	324 146	932 575
1996	373 536	310 074	737 268	648 797	607 174	88 471	1 293 537	328 984	964 553
1997	403 860	352 700	792 859	728 362	676 119	64 497	1 360 010	361 687	998 323
1998	419 330	365 723	809 727	745 600	698 279	64 127	1 352 708	374 300	978 408
1999	435 034	389 160	840 603	772 703	728 089	67 900	1 425 617	413 435	1 012 182
2000	446 792	409 500	910 933	831 335	767 754	79 598	1 501 810	392 741	1 109 069
2001	419 920	344 402	782 700	698 956	665 460	83 744	1 478 648	365 675	1 112 973
2002	422 093	265 375	692 742	621 805	582 747	70 937	1 494 706	396 084	1 098 622
2003	429 286	276 833	731 556	634 722	609 135	96 834	1 585 289	419 781	1 165 508
2004	466 369	293 621	765 326	673 126	630 522	92 200	1 701 298	419 645	1 281 653
2005	517 655	296 540	882 158	789 245	702 052	92 913	1 893 962	421 398	1 472 564
2006	549 140	337 686	948 873	860 705	775 897	88 168	1 988 746	421 903	1 566 843
2007	540 104	327 798	988 684	891 459	755 394	97 225	2 037 940	418 843	1 619 097
2008	520 164	323 284	945 825	830 481	754 133	115 344	2 119 772	352 862	1 766 910
2004									
January	36 127	23 209	57 703	50 174	48 656	7 529	134 938	34 537	100 401
February	36 252	23 975	61 010	52 230	49 638	8 780	133 701	35 270	98 431
March	39 177	25 350	65 390	56 867	54 509	8 523	139 674	37 619	102 055
April	40 062	23 971	61 609	53 633	51 158	7 976	138 763	34 912	103 851
May	38 405	24 716	61 374	54 773	51 394	6 601	139 458	34 133	105 325
June	37 762	23 782	64 143	55 292	52 328	8 851	140 729	34 308	106 421
July	38 084	23 673	68 439	61 514	52 550	6 925	138 700	30 856	107 844
August	39 989	23 359	61 195	54 235	51 167	6 960	142 831	34 019	108 812
September	38 376	26 661	65 833	57 823	55 388	8 010	142 075	34 645	107 430
October	39 386	25 496	64 752	55 478	52 883	9 274	146 798	34 154	112 644
November	40 056	24 249	67 745	60 493	54 049	7 252	149 791	35 696	114 095
December	40 992	24 337	63 625	58 228	55 225	5 397	146 967	35 608	111 359
2005									
January	40 827	24 393	65 310	58 841	57 598	6 469	148 117	34 028	114 089
February	41 555	24 281	67 344	60 073	57 205	7 271	149 200	34 944	114 256
March	41 897	25 176	64 292	57 138	56 563	7 154	154 121	34 465	119 656
April	41 845	23 617	66 912	59 353	57 016	7 559	154 104	34 324	119 780
May	41 859	23 924	79 116	71 129	56 985	7 987	154 901	34 792	120 109
June	42 890	26 630	78 660	68 853	59 308	9 807	156 265	34 568	121 697
July	41 858	23 753	72 080	64 106	57 420	7 974	158 177	34 405	123 772
August	43 521	25 574	73 077	65 877	59 696	7 200	162 287	35 460	126 827
September	44 444	25 082	69 330	61 784	59 357	7 546	165 390	37 148	128 242
October	44 924	24 837	75 762	66 141	59 719	9 621	164 437	36 356	128 081
November	46 460	24 464	85 920	78 275	60 290	7 645	162 559	35 271	127 288
December	46 538	24 445	82 009	75 456	60 950	6 553	163 760	35 431	128 329
2006									
January	46 642	26 149	65 841	65 123	62 769	718	167 260	36 083	131 177
February	47 129	27 238	75 936	68 343	63 046	7 593	161 936	36 172	125 764
March	47 270	30 058	83 793	75 318	65 446	8 475	166 846	35 939	130 907
April	45 953	27 785	77 181	70 451	63 355	6 730	168 125	35 851	132 274
May	46 604	27 452	75 711	70 063	64 540	5 648	171 773	36 715	135 058
June	45 946	28 495	80 865	71 211	65 027	9 654	171 144	36 283	134 861
July	45 554	28 942	77 855	70 627	64 833	7 228	169 759	32 604	137 155
August	45 241	28 402	74 521	66 276	64 758	8 245	168 963	33 693	135 270
September	44 996	29 108	96 447	83 250	67 806	13 197	158 161	33 116	125 045
October	44 663	26 513	78 602	72 876	65 255	5 726	158 113	33 798	124 315
November	44 047	29 655	81 982	72 445	65 462	9 537	160 209	34 122	126 087
December	45 876	28 181	80 327	74 759	64 845	5 568	165 468	36 032	129 436
2007									
January	44 928	25 740	73 056	65 148	61 369	7 908	159 195	33 914	125 281
February	45 657	28 008	78 532	69 914	61 088	8 618	161 507	34 461	127 046
March	44 529	25 887	83 462	77 522	63 150	5 940	166 427	34 991	131 436
April	44 826	27 060	85 594	78 168	64 342	7 426	168 616	36 061	132 555
May	45 556	28 549	80 913	73 057	63 431	7 856	170 622	35 719	134 903
June	45 720	26 442	82 486	75 720	62 596	6 766	170 190	35 333	134 857
July	45 797	27 726	89 529	80 464	63 560	9 065	173 531	36 725	136 806
August	45 024	27 942	80 814	70 219	63 737	10 595	167 609	35 296	132 313
September	45 167	28 665	81 838	74 677	63 602	7 161	168 909	34 304	134 605
October	44 540	26 853	81 128	72 501	62 189	8 627	172 244	34 530	137 714
November	44 294	26 907	81 583	75 585	62 189	5 998	179 914	34 146	145 768
December	43 923	27 959	89 606	78 238	64 997	11 368	179 637	33 586	146 051
2008									
January	43 557	27 150	82 029	73 271	64 459	8 758	178 125	33 651	144 474
February	43 260	27 309	83 976	74 408	63 860	9 568	174 737	32 911	141 826
March	43 556	27 121	83 738	75 431	63 222	8 307	179 019	31 043	147 976
April	44 629	27 276	82 188	73 609	65 174	8 579	185 454	30 836	154 618
May	43 947	28 456	83 427	73 639	65 001	9 788	187 380	29 766	157 614
June	45 563	28 336	83 256	71 958	66 070	11 298	192 091	30 017	162 074
July	45 938	27 397	83 583	74 498	66 300	9 085	193 526	30 288	163 238
August	44 202	27 397	78 537	68 694	64 774	9 843	184 744	28 359	156 385
September	43 047	26 769	80 062	67 923	62 547	12 139	174 750	28 724	146 026
October	42 236	25 500	71 326	63 487	58 373	7 839	165 382	27 219	138 163
November	39 942	26 538	68 653	60 140	58 995	8 513	152 342	26 496	125 846
December	38 533	24 948	67 757	56 363	57 110	11 394	144 150	25 219	118 931

Table 17-7. Manufacturers' Unfilled Orders, Durable Goods Industries

(End of period, millions of dollars, seasonally adjusted, except as noted.)

Year and month	Not seasonally adjusted, total	Total [1]	Primary metals			Fabricated metal products	Machinery	Computers and electronic products	Electrical equipment, appliances, and components
			Total [1]	Iron and steel mills	Aluminum and nonferrous metal products				
1992	447 770	451 273	18 658	9 155	7 250	29 719	41 146	84 657	12 170
1993	422 314	425 979	20 701	12 267	6 401	27 767	42 965	81 327	12 815
1994	430 982	434 979	24 260	12 780	9 336	30 261	50 494	82 522	14 288
1995	443 497	447 411	23 376	13 329	7 989	32 331	55 703	88 901	14 638
1996	484 865	488 726	23 759	12 748	8 724	36 875	56 765	87 940	14 132
1997	508 480	512 916	27 173	14 495	9 957	42 052	59 240	90 912	15 475
1998	491 858	496 083	21 643	10 841	8 293	42 204	56 517	94 848	15 164
1999	500 749	505 498	22 020	11 712	8 226	43 345	57 860	113 911	17 728
2000	544 517	549 445	18 930	9 300	7 189	45 219	60 882	130 910	18 554
2001	510 143	514 349	17 364	8 868	6 021	40 536	58 316	119 109	15 347
2002	458 560	462 122	15 836	8 766	4 814	35 961	47 339	95 154	14 874
2003	474 205	477 608	18 185	10 960	4 798	36 944	51 782	96 845	14 287
2004	493 022	496 343	22 493	13 972	5 830	42 051	53 823	100 765	15 787
2005	570 355	572 835	26 959	17 219	6 983	50 042	64 037	99 208	18 496
2006	657 878	660 406	27 424	16 447	7 947	57 066	79 323	115 421	22 628
2007	771 816	773 297	27 744	16 781	7 970	61 374	91 385	122 336	23 930
2008	798 503	801 887	19 403	10 068	6 502	58 794	100 219	124 995	22 629
2005									
January	498 840	494 758	21 921	13 334	5 914	42 580	54 400	100 642	15 901
February	504 807	497 952	22 014	13 518	5 903	43 180	55 672	100 702	15 961
March	505 082	495 425	21 888	13 275	6 039	43 257	55 956	101 301	15 945
April	503 550	494 901	21 205	12 471	6 084	43 650	56 817	100 583	15 971
May	512 492	506 868	20 907	12 031	6 118	44 263	56 978	99 973	16 161
June	522 914	521 648	20 557	11 657	6 164	45 381	58 560	101 706	16 479
July	525 117	526 765	20 843	11 932	6 138	45 817	58 859	101 116	16 426
August	529 609	534 449	21 878	12 928	6 277	46 951	59 826	101 824	17 005
September	530 398	539 073	23 643	14 108	6 800	47 936	60 667	101 720	17 651
October	536 936	546 980	25 006	15 527	6 741	48 730	61 499	100 838	17 848
November	552 694	563 554	26 316	16 518	7 032	49 440	63 056	100 212	17 992
December	570 355	572 835	26 959	17 219	6 983	50 042	64 037	99 208	18 496
2006									
January	573 570	568 234	27 167	17 365	7 009	50 603	65 714	98 757	19 083
February	582 286	574 322	27 099	17 204	7 003	51 097	66 661	99 324	19 423
March	598 657	587 745	27 082	17 124	7 034	51 377	67 944	102 695	19 564
April	604 582	595 079	27 504	17 562	6 974	52 158	68 812	103 989	20 242
May	604 352	598 148	28 136	17 962	7 217	52 930	70 734	103 985	20 859
June	608 233	607 100	28 424	18 136	7 249	54 298	71 906	105 446	21 616
July	611 993	614 072	28 755	18 297	7 354	54 837	73 253	107 643	22 070
August	607 910	613 391	28 264	17 792	7 423	55 498	73 467	108 472	21 464
September	626 919	637 063	28 051	17 410	7 614	56 290	74 960	110 739	21 773
October	631 387	643 221	28 082	17 287	7 864	56 205	77 384	111 401	22 173
November	641 131	653 650	27 656	16 767	7 961	56 437	77 694	113 711	22 581
December	657 878	660 406	27 424	16 447	7 947	57 066	79 323	115 421	22 628
2007									
January	671 060	664 272	27 572	16 674	7 822	58 078	80 200	115 127	23 275
February	680 324	670 877	27 214	16 505	7 673	58 033	81 385	116 223	23 472
March	692 814	680 483	27 366	16 622	7 713	57 646	83 008	115 430	23 710
April	703 846	693 329	28 282	17 454	7 787	58 002	82 787	115 736	24 135
May	706 184	699 668	28 339	17 508	7 739	57 824	82 651	117 164	24 344
June	709 949	708 841	27 090	16 330	7 708	58 278	83 140	116 742	24 688
July	721 800	724 733	26 953	16 093	7 817	58 586	85 401	118 579	24 358
August	726 261	732 889	26 730	15 871	7 823	58 859	86 603	119 990	24 254
September	729 237	740 534	26 694	15 840	7 818	58 858	87 762	121 602	23 983
October	734 765	748 304	26 852	16 062	7 747	59 547	89 072	121 963	23 769
November	741 403	755 712	27 373	16 566	7 775	59 965	89 378	121 804	23 838
December	771 816	773 297	27 744	16 781	7 970	61 374	91 385	122 336	23 930
2008									
January	786 882	777 859	28 036	17 288	7 799	61 223	93 986	121 546	24 366
February	797 537	786 860	28 355	17 397	7 961	61 377	92 896	122 125	25 247
March	811 015	797 114	28 864	17 845	8 032	62 496	94 382	122 954	23 986
April	815 034	802 972	29 294	18 287	7 992	62 387	97 572	122 925	24 285
May	817 565	810 293	29 011	18 098	7 950	62 467	99 483	123 300	24 670
June	819 678	818 023	29 621	18 584	8 084	62 483	101 567	124 442	25 600
July	821 604	824 232	30 106	19 301	7 803	62 146	105 164	123 989	25 195
August	819 953	826 529	28 359	17 713	7 600	61 934	106 787	124 884	24 943
September	816 475	828 225	26 212	15 885	7 268	61 556	107 325	125 161	24 606
October	806 675	820 672	23 203	13 395	6 885	60 660	106 070	124 560	23 431
November	797 367	812 879	21 194	11 483	6 728	59 728	104 214	125 444	22 694
December	798 503	801 887	19 403	10 068	6 502	58 794	100 219	124 995	22 629

[1]Includes categories not shown separately.

Table 17-7. Manufacturers' Unfilled Orders, Durable Goods Industries—*Continued*

(End of period, millions of dollars, seasonally adjusted, except as noted.)

Year and month	Transportation equipment				By topical categories						
							Capital goods				
								Nondefense			
	Total [1]	Motor vehicles and parts	Non-defense aircraft and parts	Defense aircraft and parts	Construction materials and supplies	Information technology industries	Total	Total	Excluding aircraft and parts	Defense	Consumer durable goods
1992	259 282	11 591	127 556	49 508	20 951	80 429	318 867	179 562	92 692	139 305	3 868
1993	233 723	13 366	110 908	46 574	21 843	78 157	299 168	173 915	95 478	125 253	4 706
1994	226 072	15 889	101 069	44 570	25 177	79 170	299 111	177 963	106 847	121 148	5 256
1995	225 620	15 191	109 318	42 222	27 226	84 979	313 830	199 565	118 050	114 265	5 354
1996	261 332	13 481	130 420	45 093	29 466	84 135	346 373	217 425	120 101	128 948	5 892
1997	267 568	14 328	143 330	40 811	33 590	87 260	360 246	242 973	131 551	117 273	7 428
1998	254 755	15 606	137 436	37 667	34 219	90 634	348 173	241 333	134 087	106 840	8 334
1999	238 504	16 355	126 443	35 541	35 174	105 748	349 430	245 578	149 553	103 852	9 166
2000	261 796	13 649	138 296	42 385	37 271	115 762	384 973	268 541	159 929	116 432	10 498
2001	252 988	11 986	122 051	50 875	32 568	106 768	365 291	238 526	146 652	126 765	8 646
2002	241 863	12 464	111 104	55 860	30 634	87 120	329 146	207 407	119 447	121 739	8 743
2003	247 090	14 339	102 550	61 237	30 747	89 163	340 957	208 228	127 868	132 729	9 694
2004	248 114	15 042	111 178	51 296	34 072	94 836	353 263	220 157	129 415	133 106	10 173
2005	301 679	17 759	153 097	43 111	42 044	95 945	412 513	278 802	144 611	133 711	9 023
2006	345 866	20 296	194 911	42 462	45 206	113 425	475 841	343 867	175 777	131 974	9 043
2007	432 962	18 447	276 946	43 614	51 920	119 019	573 739	437 766	191 792	135 973	9 435
2008	463 688	15 606	304 633	48 468	52 141	121 810	613 012	469 182	197 922	143 830	8 124
2005											
January	246 682	14 874	109 716	49 661	34 154	94 879	352 852	220 591	130 892	132 261	9 579
February	247 735	15 045	110 426	48 707	34 847	94 932	354 803	222 788	132 344	132 015	9 592
March	244 428	15 038	107 713	46 818	35 237	95 789	353 178	221 413	133 272	131 765	9 296
April	244 146	15 236	106 294	45 649	35 516	95 376	353 146	221 651	134 612	131 495	9 391
May	255 748	15 550	117 420	44 559	35 920	94 858	364 635	233 026	134 730	131 609	9 819
June	266 336	15 603	123 499	43 458	36 727	96 881	375 357	241 936	137 088	133 421	9 484
July	271 148	15 780	127 032	42 495	36 939	96 384	380 489	246 644	137 971	133 845	9 522
August	273 842	16 197	130 155	41 313	38 122	97 240	384 983	251 649	140 156	133 334	10 077
September	274 294	16 837	130 527	40 171	39 064	97 705	386 072	253 065	141 435	133 007	10 027
October	279 516	17 435	132 814	42 569	39 795	97 390	391 461	256 540	142 750	134 921	10 188
November	293 194	17 220	145 529	42 294	41 278	96 899	405 572	270 575	143 774	134 997	9 918
December	301 679	17 759	153 097	43 111	42 044	95 945	412 513	278 802	144 611	133 711	9 023
2006											
January	294 616	18 220	152 006	43 596	42 362	95 868	406 522	279 693	146 839	126 829	8 943
February	298 138	18 394	153 974	43 754	42 670	96 524	409 327	282 036	148 652	127 291	9 254
March	306 823	18 730	162 031	43 542	43 527	99 891	419 292	291 036	151 983	128 256	8 796
April	309 984	19 402	166 531	42 481	44 184	100 936	423 370	296 048	153 282	127 322	9 008
May	309 033	19 357	168 405	41 682	45 119	101 266	424 713	299 215	155 031	125 498	9 107
June	313 138	19 464	170 816	41 303	45 290	102 594	431 342	303 797	157 645	127 545	8 952
July	314 971	19 811	173 050	40 742	45 724	104 567	435 572	308 045	159 987	127 527	9 344
August	313 790	19 833	170 534	40 134	45 490	105 659	435 192	306 998	161 534	128 194	9 098
September	332 739	20 255	182 050	39 380	45 446	107 974	457 158	323 146	166 947	134 012	8 901
October	335 163	20 390	186 036	38 953	45 526	108 636	462 240	330 170	170 605	132 070	9 288
November	342 592	20 205	189 642	40 260	45 298	111 264	469 696	335 710	173 351	133 986	9 512
December	345 866	20 296	194 911	42 462	45 206	113 425	475 841	343 867	175 777	131 974	9 043
2007											
January	347 026	20 477	194 403	41 567	45 664	113 228	477 217	345 011	177 926	132 206	9 320
February	351 597	20 585	199 286	41 317	46 924	113 820	482 633	349 747	178 178	132 886	9 280
March	360 550	20 286	209 695	39 961	46 736	112 970	493 072	361 748	180 294	131 324	9 143
April	371 285	20 123	218 728	39 033	46 595	113 520	505 105	373 956	183 215	131 149	9 571
May	375 805	20 252	223 972	38 307	46 816	115 015	511 675	380 422	184 508	131 253	9 807
June	385 209	20 057	233 004	38 243	47 685	114 656	520 327	389 842	185 583	130 485	9 740
July	397 081	19 842	244 646	37 989	47 876	115 974	535 473	404 043	187 943	131 430	9 911
August	402 901	19 179	246 458	40 515	48 314	116 916	540 818	406 748	189 401	134 070	9 677
September	408 091	18 891	253 148	41 037	49 479	118 464	547 044	413 566	189 974	133 478	9 653
October	413 458	18 641	258 623	41 081	49 986	118 243	553 340	418 927	190 121	134 413	9 675
November	419 696	18 684	267 311	40 431	50 654	118 050	559 738	427 326	189 896	132 412	9 549
December	432 962	18 447	276 946	43 614	51 920	119 019	573 739	437 766	191 792	135 973	9 435
2008											
January	435 290	18 003	280 108	44 006	52 501	118 414	578 263	442 090	193 417	136 173	9 140
February	443 796	17 635	286 620	43 757	52 013	118 862	587 360	450 043	195 254	137 317	8 917
March	451 305	17 681	294 712	43 895	52 125	119 092	595 760	458 794	195 976	136 966	8 942
April	453 276	17 632	298 123	43 777	53 120	119 212	600 813	464 524	198 029	136 289	9 088
May	458 288	17 555	302 698	44 446	53 472	120 037	607 487	470 451	199 770	137 036	8 787
June	461 128	17 506	304 297	44 522	54 629	121 245	613 476	474 215	202 177	139 261	8 845
July	464 257	17 381	307 408	45 350	55 682	120 958	618 906	479 668	204 627	139 238	8 865
August	466 426	17 345	306 936	45 832	55 814	121 633	621 590	481 567	206 897	140 023	8 478
September	470 408	17 042	309 107	46 470	55 298	121 774	624 905	481 950	205 877	142 955	8 471
October	470 107	16 737	311 249	47 069	54 722	121 099	622 466	480 968	203 032	141 498	8 194
November	467 236	16 266	309 955	47 512	53 664	121 950	618 875	477 953	201 602	140 922	8 177
December	463 688	15 606	304 633	48 468	52 141	121 810	613 012	469 182	197 922	143 830	8 124

[1]Includes categories not shown separately.

Table 17-8. Motor Vehicle Sales and Inventories

(Units.)

Year and month	Retail sales of new passenger cars						Retail inventories of new domestic passenger cars (thousands of units, end of period)		
	Thousands of units, not seasonally adjusted			Millions of units, seasonally adjusted annual rate			Not seasonally adjusted	Seasonally adjusted	Inventory to sales ratio
	Total	Domestic	Foreign	Total	Domestic	Foreign			
1970	8 402.6	7 119.4	1 283.2	8.403	7.119	1.283	. . .	. . .	. . .
1971	10 227.8	8 661.9	1 566.0	10.228	8.662	1.566	. . .	. . .	. . .
1972	10 873.3	9 252.7	1 620.7	10.873	9.253	1.621	1 311.0	1 379.0	1.700
1973	11 350.1	9 588.7	1 761.5	11.350	9.589	1.762	1 600.0	1 654.0	2.500
1974	8 773.7	7 361.8	1 411.9	8.774	7.362	1.412	1 672.0	1 730.0	3.400
1975	8 537.8	6 951.0	1 586.9	8.538	6.951	1.587	1 419.0	1 468.0	2.200
1976	9 994.0	8 492.3	1 502.0	9.994	8.492	1.502	1 465.0	1 494.0	1.900
1977	11 046.0	8 971.2	2 074.8	11.046	8.971	2.075	1 731.0	1 743.0	2.300
1978	11 164.0	9 163.8	2 000.1	11.164	9.164	2.000	1 729.0	1 731.0	2.300
1979	10 558.8	8 230.1	2 328.7	10.559	8.230	2.329	1 691.0	1 667.0	2.400
1980	8 981.8	6 581.3	2 400.4	8.982	6.581	2.401	1 448.0	1 440.0	2.600
1981	8 534.3	6 208.8	2 325.5	8.534	6.209	2.326	1 471.0	1 495.0	3.600
1982	7 979.4	5 758.2	2 221.2	7.980	5.758	2.221	1 126.0	1 127.0	2.200
1983	9 178.6	6 793.2	2 385.6	9.179	6.793	2.386	1 352.0	1 350.0	2.000
1984	10 390.2	7 951.5	2 438.5	10.390	7.952	2.439	1 415.0	1 411.0	2.100
1985	10 978.4	8 204.6	2 773.7	10.978	8.205	2.774	1 630.0	1 619.0	2.500
1986	11 405.7	8 214.9	3 190.7	11.406	8.215	3.191	1 499.0	1 515.0	2.000
1987	10 170.9	7 080.8	3 090.0	10.171	7.081	3.090	1 680.0	1 716.0	2.800
1988	10 545.6	7 539.3	3 006.2	10.546	7.539	3.006	1 601.0	1 601.0	2.300
1989	9 776.8	7 078.1	2 698.7	9.777	7.078	2.699	1 669.0	1 687.0	3.100
1990	9 300.2	6 896.9	2 403.3	9.300	6.897	2.403	1 408.0	1 418.0	2.600
1991	8 175.0	6 136.8	2 038.1	8.175	6.137	2.038	1 283.0	1 296.0	2.600
1992	8 214.4	6 276.5	1 937.8	8.214	6.277	1.938	1 276.0	1 288.0	2.300
1993	8 517.7	6 734.2	1 783.7	8.518	6.734	1.784	1 345.5	1 392.3	2.489
1994	8 990.4	7 255.3	1 735.2	8.990	7.255	1.735	1 378.6	1 409.6	2.335
1995	8 636.2	7 129.1	1 507.4	8.637	7.129	1.508	1 639.2	1 665.9	2.810
1996	8 526.8	7 253.8	1 273.1	8.527	7.254	1.273	1 441.4	1 485.4	2.463
1997	8 272.5	6 906.5	1 366.3	8.273	6.907	1.366	1 316.8	1 356.4	2.360
1998	8 142.1	6 764.3	1 378.2	8.143	6.764	1.378	1 270.5	1 336.0	2.381
1999	8 696.5	6 981.8	1 714.8	8.697	6.982	1.715	1 318.1	1 392.3	2.394
2000	8 852.1	6 832.8	2 019.3	8.852	6.833	2.019	1 330.5	1 360.8	2.400
2001	8 422.1	6 322.7	2 099.4	8.422	6.323	2.099	1 108.2	1 147.3	2.198
2002	8 102.4	5 871.3	2 231.1	8.102	5.871	2.231	1 105.6	1 156.2	2.368
2003	7 614.5	5 527.3	2 087.4	7.615	5.527	2.087	1 143.6	1 251.5	2.720
2004	7 504.5	5 349.9	2 154.6	7.505	5.350	2.155	1 096.2	1 219.9	2.741
2005	7 667.2	5 480.5	2 186.8	7.667	5.481	2.187	947.8	1 078.3	2.365
2006	7 780.5	5 435.8	2 344.6	7.780	5.436	2.345	971.3	1 109.5	2.460
2007	7 588.1	5 220.9	2 367.2	7.588	5.221	2.367	990.8	1 141.7	2.628
2008	6 806.2	4 487.8	2 278.2	6.731	4.488	2.243	921.1	1 103.3	3.068
2006									
January	558.2	419.0	139.2	8.537	6.390	2.147	974.3	1 059.8	1.990
February	568.8	421.6	147.2	7.540	5.462	2.078	1 021.9	1 074.0	2.359
March	691.2	494.7	196.5	7.486	5.348	2.138	1 091.6	1 105.9	2.481
April	711.9	502.1	209.8	7.968	5.622	2.346	1 033.6	1 111.0	2.371
May	732.2	508.6	223.6	7.749	5.359	2.390	1 005.4	1 113.9	2.494
June	716.8	498.3	218.5	7.698	5.299	2.399	997.7	1 107.1	2.507
July	715.6	485.7	229.9	8.131	5.552	2.579	796.9	1 060.2	2.291
August	719.6	493.3	226.3	7.728	5.293	2.435	810.8	1 077.8	2.443
September	635.3	442.5	192.8	7.662	5.306	2.356	866.7	1 114.5	2.520
October	546.5	376.1	170.4	7.469	5.137	2.332	967.4	1 142.9	2.670
November	536.5	359.9	176.6	7.367	5.008	2.359	1 045.7	1 169.5	2.803
December	647.9	434.1	213.8	8.029	5.453	2.576	1 043.6	1 177.6	2.592
2007									
January	508.0	346.6	161.4	7.644	5.192	2.452	1 101.9	1 188.2	2.746
February	561.7	390.6	171.1	7.528	5.099	2.429	1 114.9	1 165.1	2.742
March	720.8	488.0	232.8	7.556	5.116	2.440	1 119.1	1 158.7	2.718
April	624.4	427.4	197.0	7.400	5.086	2.314	1 071.5	1 153.8	2.723
May	778.7	538.8	239.9	7.918	5.478	2.440	988.3	1 121.6	2.457
June	719.3	498.3	221.0	7.622	5.242	2.380	977.8	1 121.0	2.566
July	620.1	417.8	202.3	7.317	4.993	2.324	884.4	1 159.5	2.787
August	682.4	475.0	207.4	7.426	5.170	2.256	871.6	1 154.6	2.680
September	612.7	428.1	184.6	7.490	5.188	2.302	866.8	1 144.0	2.646
October	561.2	384.7	176.5	7.524	5.170	2.354	960.5	1 147.8	2.664
November	566.4	390.2	176.2	7.873	5.513	2.360	1 012.6	1 119.8	2.438
December	632.4	435.4	197.0	7.760	5.404	2.356	920.1	1 066.5	2.368
2008									
January	496.9	347.8	149.1	7.345	5.105	2.240	945.2	1 036.8	2.437
February	557.4	389.2	168.2	7.393	5.039	2.354	979.8	1 020.9	2.431
March	682.6	451.3	231.3	7.525	4.955	2.570	931.6	1 001.4	2.425
April	660.5	426.0	234.5	7.479	4.877	2.602	911.9	984.9	2.423
May	798.7	523.8	274.9	7.879	5.173	2.706	795.7	944.8	2.192
June	664.2	427.7	236.5	7.537	4.796	2.741	791.2	959.4	2.400
July	622.2	391.4	230.8	6.911	4.429	2.482	738.7	1 043.2	2.826
August	631.0	418.4	212.6	6.764	4.492	2.272	758.1	1 094.7	2.925
September	480.9	338.1	142.8	6.207	4.321	1.886	853.5	1 160.4	3.222
October	429.4	289.2	140.2	5.570	3.763	1.807	1 042.8	1 272.3	4.057
November	359.7	235.7	124.0	4.960	3.286	1.674	1 149.5	1 356.8	4.955
December	422.7	289.4	133.3	5.198	3.618	1.580	1 154.9	1 363.4	4.522

. . . = Not available.

Table 17-8. Motor Vehicle Sales and Inventories—*Continued*

(Units.)

Year and month	Retail sales of new trucks and buses								Unit sales of cars and light trucks (millions of units, seasonally adjusted annual rate)		
	Thousands of units, not seasonally adjusted				Millions of units, seasonally adjusted annual rate						
	Total	0–14,000 pounds		14,001 pounds and over	Total	0–14,000 pounds		14,001 pounds and over	Total	Domestic	Foreign
		Domestic	Foreign			Domestic	Foreign				
1970	. . .	1 408.5	. . .	337.3	. . .	1.408	. . .	0.335	. . .	8.528	. . .
1971	. . .	1 693.0	. . .	338.9	. . .	1.700	. . .	0.339	. . .	10.362	. . .
1972	. . .	2 122.5	. . .	437.4	. . .	2.116	. . .	0.437	. . .	11.369	. . .
1973	. . .	2 509.4	. . .	495.7	. . .	2.513	. . .	0.495	. . .	12.102	. . .
1974	. . .	2 180.1	. . .	423.9	. . .	2.176	. . .	0.424	. . .	9.538	. . .
1975	. . .	2 052.6	. . .	298.3	. . .	2.055	. . .	0.298	. . .	9.006	. . .
1976	3 300.5	2 738.3	237.5	324.7	3.296	2.733	0.239	0.324	12.966	11.225	1.741
1977	3 813.0	3 112.8	323.1	377.1	3.818	3.116	0.324	0.378	14.486	12.088	2.398
1978	4 256.8	3 481.1	335.9	439.8	4.249	3.469	0.340	0.440	14.973	12.633	2.340
1979	3 589.7	2 730.2	469.4	390.1	3.599	2.740	0.469	0.390	13.768	10.970	2.798
1980	2 487.4	1 731.1	484.6	271.7	2.482	1.731	0.480	0.271	11.192	8.312	2.881
1981	2 255.6	1 581.7	447.6	226.3	2.255	1.585	0.444	0.226	10.564	7.794	2.770
1982	2 562.8	1 967.5	410.4	184.9	2.569	1.971	0.413	0.185	10.363	7.729	2.634
1983	3 117.3	2 465.2	463.3	188.8	3.130	2.480	0.461	0.189	12.120	9.273	2.846
1984	4 093.1	3 207.2	607.7	278.2	4.085	3.199	0.609	0.278	14.197	11.150	3.047
1985	4 741.7	3 618.4	828.3	295.0	4.759	3.634	0.831	0.295	15.443	11.838	3.604
1986	4 912.1	3 671.4	967.2	273.5	4.918	3.676	0.969	0.273	16.051	11.891	4.160
1987	4 991.5	3 792.0	912.2	287.3	4.977	3.783	0.907	0.288	14.861	10.864	3.997
1988	5 231.9	4 199.7	697.9	334.3	5.225	4.194	0.697	0.334	15.436	11.733	3.703
1989	5 055.9	4 113.6	630.3	312.0	5.065	4.123	0.629	0.313	14.529	11.201	3.328
1990	4 837.0	3 956.8	602.7	277.5	4.841	3.960	0.602	0.278	13.863	10.857	3.006
1991	4 355.4	3 605.6	528.8	221.0	4.360	3.612	0.528	0.221	12.314	9.748	2.566
1992	4 892.2	4 247.0	395.9	249.3	4.894	4.247	0.398	0.248	12.860	10.524	2.336
1993	5 667.8	5 000.5	364.5	302.8	5.658	4.991	0.365	0.302	13.874	11.725	2.148
1994	6 407.3	5 658.2	396.3	352.8	6.408	5.659	0.395	0.354	15.044	12.914	2.130
1995	6 469.8	5 690.9	390.5	388.4	6.486	5.703	0.393	0.390	14.732	12.832	1.900
1996	6 921.8	6 131.8	430.9	359.1	6.914	6.127	0.429	0.357	15.083	13.381	1.702
1997	7 217.8	6 270.4	571.2	376.2	7.229	6.283	0.570	0.376	15.126	13.190	1.936
1998	7 815.8	6 745.3	646.2	424.3	7.788	6.720	0.644	0.425	15.506	13.484	2.022
1999	8 704.2	7 420.0	762.9	521.3	8.713	7.429	0.763	0.521	16.888	14.411	2.478
2000	8 953.5	7 650.8	840.8	461.9	8.951	7.649	0.841	0.461	17.342	14.481	2.861
2001	9 046.3	7 718.4	977.8	350.1	9.043	7.715	0.978	0.350	17.115	14.038	3.078
2002	9 035.6	7 646.9	1 066.3	322.4	9.035	7.647	1.066	0.322	16.816	13.518	3.298
2003	9 357.0	7 801.4	1 227.2	328.4	9.356	7.802	1.227	0.328	16.643	13.329	3.315
2004	9 792.4	8 114.6	1 246.2	431.6	9.790	8.115	1.246	0.429	16.865	13.465	3.401
2005	9 777.4	8 065.4	1 215.5	496.5	9.778	8.065	1.215	0.497	16.948	13.546	3.402
2006	9 267.8	7 376.8	1 346.6	544.4	9.269	7.377	1.347	0.545	16.504	12.813	3.691
2007	8 872.2	7 113.0	1 388.1	371.1	8.874	7.113	1.388	0.373	16.089	12.334	3.755
2008	6 686.8	5 291.9	1 096.4	298.5	6.694	5.302	1.094	0.298	13.127	9.790	3.337
2006											
January	617.9	491.3	90.4	36.2	9.491	7.687	1.292	0.512	17.516	14.077	3.439
February	729.3	590.4	98.0	40.9	9.466	7.587	1.326	0.553	16.453	13.049	3.404
March	885.4	711.1	123.3	51.0	9.576	7.681	1.342	0.553	16.509	13.029	3.480
April	777.9	614.8	117.1	46.0	9.248	7.275	1.421	0.552	16.664	12.897	3.767
May	801.5	638.1	114.6	48.8	9.035	7.161	1.321	0.553	16.231	12.520	3.711
June	828.5	669.0	110.2	49.3	9.124	7.306	1.267	0.551	16.271	12.605	3.666
July	815.4	658.3	115.6	41.5	9.419	7.565	1.328	0.526	17.024	13.117	3.907
August	810.4	647.5	115.4	47.5	8.916	7.154	1.211	0.551	16.093	12.447	3.646
September	758.8	605.2	109.9	43.7	9.359	7.460	1.350	0.549	16.472	12.766	3.706
October	714.1	553.6	113.0	47.5	9.259	7.238	1.470	0.551	16.177	12.375	3.802
November	700.1	547.9	110.5	41.7	9.125	7.182	1.409	0.534	15.958	12.190	3.768
December	828.5	649.6	128.6	50.3	9.207	7.225	1.423	0.559	16.677	12.678	3.999
2007											
January	616.3	475.9	103.6	36.8	9.187	7.246	1.449	0.492	16.339	12.438	3.901
February	723.4	585.5	103.9	34.0	9.404	7.542	1.405	0.457	16.475	12.641	3.834
March	854.0	680.7	135.3	38.0	9.086	7.237	1.426	0.423	16.219	12.353	3.866
April	741.6	598.7	109.3	33.6	9.282	7.480	1.407	0.395	16.287	12.566	3.721
May	811.5	659.2	120.8	31.5	8.741	7.041	1.339	0.361	16.298	12.519	3.779
June	762.0	610.0	120.9	31.1	8.439	6.707	1.376	0.356	15.705	11.949	3.756
July	711.0	570.6	113.6	26.8	8.455	6.779	1.341	0.335	15.437	11.772	3.665
August	818.1	664.9	124.0	29.2	9.139	7.498	1.303	0.338	16.227	12.668	3.559
September	723.1	587.8	109.9	25.4	8.971	7.236	1.402	0.333	16.128	12.424	3.704
October	695.3	552.5	112.9	29.9	8.785	7.025	1.430	0.330	15.979	12.195	3.784
November	634.1	498.8	110.2	25.1	8.474	6.762	1.391	0.321	16.026	12.275	3.751
December	781.8	628.4	123.7	29.7	8.521	6.803	1.388	0.330	15.951	12.207	3.744
2008											
January	566.5	446.5	95.7	24.3	8.278	6.637	1.318	0.323	15.300	11.742	3.558
February	639.0	513.0	101.2	24.8	8.214	6.581	1.317	0.316	15.291	11.620	3.671
March	696.0	554.7	114.2	27.1	7.829	6.212	1.302	0.315	15.039	11.167	3.872
April	612.5	480.9	102.1	29.5	7.316	5.739	1.244	0.333	14.462	10.616	3.846
May	621.9	487.0	107.2	27.7	6.659	5.189	1.145	0.325	14.213	10.362	3.851
June	548.4	438.6	82.5	27.3	6.414	5.062	1.032	0.320	13.631	9.858	3.773
July	533.7	421.4	88.6	23.7	5.887	4.618	0.982	0.287	12.511	9.047	3.464
August	638.1	519.0	96.8	22.3	7.207	5.931	0.999	0.277	13.694	10.423	3.271
September	503.6	404.1	77.2	22.3	6.526	5.209	1.042	0.275	12.458	9.530	2.928
October	429.6	330.2	75.0	24.4	5.213	4.043	0.903	0.267	10.516	7.806	2.710
November	404.1	313.2	70.6	20.3	5.455	4.266	0.912	0.277	10.138	7.552	2.586
December	493.4	383.3	85.3	24.8	5.327	4.135	0.935	0.257	10.268	7.753	2.515

. . . = Not available.

Table 17-9. Retail and Food Services Sales

(All retail establishments and food services; millions of dollars; not seasonally adjusted.)

Year and month	Retail and food services, total [1]	Retail (NAICS industry categories)											Food services and drinking places
		GAFO (department store type goods), total [2]	Motor vehicles and parts	Furniture and home furnishings	Electronics and appliances	Building materials and garden	Food and beverages	Health and personal care	Gasoline	Clothing and accessories	General merchandise	Nonstore retailers	
1992	2 019 131	534 367	419 353	52 467	42 763	131 244	371 451	89 782	156 556	120 346	247 968	78 657	203 415
1993	2 158 299	571 790	473 948	55 587	48 760	141 220	375 440	92 671	162 587	125 001	266 088	85 977	216 051
1994	2 335 650	617 379	542 235	60 551	57 413	157 497	385 265	96 442	171 416	129 341	285 278	96 460	225 629
1995	2 456 129	651 071	580 842	63 601	64 919	164 831	391 312	101 719	181 294	131 593	300 589	103 705	233 625
1996	2 609 561	683 678	628 687	67 848	68 515	176 972	402 020	109 646	194 601	136 851	315 398	117 963	242 896
1997	2 732 043	714 453	655 013	72 863	70 211	191 345	410 288	118 769	199 856	140 565	331 454	126 397	258 040
1998	2 859 332	759 063	689 679	77 569	74 686	202 724	417 433	129 699	191 887	149 433	351 186	134 113	272 227
1999	3 093 569	816 827	765 549	84 451	79 138	218 611	434 599	142 829	212 682	160 043	380 291	152 022	285 013
2000	3 294 217	863 903	797 568	91 328	82 363	229 320	445 666	155 372	249 975	167 968	404 344	180 688	305 461
2001	3 385 577	883 866	816 941	91 644	80 395	239 707	463 330	166 678	251 537	167 583	427 586	180 805	317 852
2002	3 466 136	913 925	820 269	94 610	83 897	248 888	465 794	180 143	250 770	172 617	446 648	189 535	331 814
2003	3 615 170	948 246	841 215	97 528	86 957	265 052	477 130	192 224	273 566	178 778	468 734	203 902	349 693
2004	3 846 316	1 007 195	864 541	105 303	94 811	298 782	494 966	198 933	320 435	190 079	497 174	224 002	371 976
2005	4 081 692	1 062 366	885 997	111 763	101 609	327 192	514 998	209 008	373 855	201 534	525 248	246 656	393 633
2006	4 307 730	1 120 147	898 624	117 659	108 362	344 728	533 779	224 752	416 246	214 876	552 109	275 654	420 367
2007	4 482 668	1 162 719	919 252	118 657	111 359	337 173	560 649	237 437	445 212	224 651	576 426	303 423	442 257
2008	4 474 970	1 165 318	807 659	109 104	110 618	325 262	589 392	247 141	489 340	219 945	595 639	314 888	459 289
2006													
January	318 567	78 837	65 483	8 876	8 531	23 924	41 716	17 940	30 363	12 965	38 447	22 526	32 173
February	314 313	79 485	67 206	8 755	8 006	23 433	39 826	17 294	28 836	14 542	39 346	21 311	31 421
March	362 536	87 449	82 497	9 761	8 432	30 490	43 503	19 135	33 418	16 479	43 068	24 340	35 640
April	352 657	86 526	76 023	8 898	7 580	32 107	43 111	17 880	35 565	16 961	44 045	20 489	34 925
May	374 805	89 852	81 349	9 597	8 211	35 290	45 573	19 180	38 504	17 218	45 206	21 944	35 987
June	367 919	89 152	80 432	9 863	8 361	32 789	44 781	18 599	38 610	16 625	44 566	21 239	35 639
July	363 425	87 674	80 719	9 654	8 315	29 133	45 662	18 137	40 068	16 392	43 752	19 923	36 133
August	377 184	93 898	82 850	10 401	8 935	30 280	45 563	18 953	40 508	17 961	45 009	22 696	36 460
September	347 750	88 093	72 962	9 971	8 277	27 330	43 909	18 251	34 352	16 906	42 448	21 764	35 213
October	350 536	89 499	70 378	9 638	8 008	28 796	44 486	18 991	32 725	17 414	44 568	24 078	35 598
November	358 545	103 592	67 574	10 689	10 362	26 794	45 408	19 000	31 096	19 622	51 751	25 533	33 573
December	419 493	146 090	71 151	11 556	15 344	24 362	50 241	21 392	32 201	31 791	69 903	29 811	37 605
2007													
January	331 239	83 078	66 897	9 292	8 770	22 922	44 263	19 634	30 489	14 114	40 771	25 226	33 342
February	326 042	82 275	69 808	8 911	8 390	21 799	41 827	18 512	29 332	15 342	40 818	24 364	32 836
March	377 547	93 296	84 435	9 997	8 630	28 657	46 184	20 308	35 077	18 244	46 215	25 588	37 973
April	362 087	88 362	77 935	9 107	7 759	30 415	44 512	19 296	36 181	17 363	44 836	23 333	36 271
May	395 495	95 021	86 034	9 877	8 487	35 979	48 105	20 240	40 841	18 772	47 678	23 991	38 079
June	380 587	93 141	80 756	9 792	8 468	31 779	47 254	19 526	39 974	17 550	46 908	22 759	38 302
July	376 319	91 434	80 019	9 839	8 501	29 948	47 536	19 418	40 167	17 123	45 636	23 019	38 450
August	392 108	99 584	85 633	10 605	9 243	29 663	47 856	20 127	39 799	19 091	48 156	24 400	38 800
September	357 452	89 132	74 317	9 541	8 347	26 494	45 860	18 796	37 126	17 016	43 796	23 047	36 565
October	372 495	92 525	75 367	9 787	8 377	28 862	46 742	20 131	38 757	17 913	46 110	26 407	37 395
November	381 344	108 704	68 187	10 737	11 095	27 226	48 040	19 610	39 111	20 888	54 156	28 596	35 748
December	429 953	146 167	69 864	11 172	15 292	23 429	52 470	21 839	38 358	31 235	71 346	32 693	38 496
2008													
January	346 951	84 711	66 840	8 858	8 832	21 906	46 981	20 219	37 914	14 459	42 052	27 657	34 931
February	348 876	87 385	70 240	8 822	8 857	21 783	45 351	20 078	36 789	16 128	44 205	25 942	35 632
March	378 755	93 727	78 183	9 136	8 659	25 703	48 557	20 779	41 281	18 119	47 929	26 017	38 519
April	375 400	89 438	75 416	8 812	8 117	31 011	46 930	20 081	42 637	17 384	45 576	25 734	37 941
May	405 376	99 696	78 108	9 454	8 973	34 385	51 398	20 917	47 418	19 409	51 427	25 386	40 836
June	385 737	94 384	71 479	8 942	8 778	31 597	48 876	20 076	48 825	17 344	49 273	25 453	39 010
July	391 683	95 039	71 907	9 429	8 948	30 879	51 077	20 396	50 341	17 722	48 567	25 018	39 982
August	390 352	100 785	71 827	9 450	9 161	27 401	50 921	20 247	47 639	19 370	50 333	24 467	40 857
September	357 661	87 343	62 461	8 619	8 188	27 087	47 803	19 986	43 714	16 215	44 161	25 291	37 537
October	357 686	91 213	57 034	8 675	7 949	27 865	49 540	20 865	39 155	17 165	47 675	26 606	38 791
November	343 376	103 990	49 765	9 071	10 277	23 374	49 444	19 879	28 674	19 185	54 754	25 453	36 887
December	393 117	137 607	54 399	9 836	13 879	22 271	52 514	23 618	24 953	27 445	69 687	32 864	38 366

[1]Includes store categories not shown separately.
[2]Includes furniture, home furnishings, electronics, appliances, clothing, sporting goods, hobby, book, music, general merchandise, office supplies, stationery, and gifts.

Table 17-9. Retail and Food Services Sales—*Continued*

(All retail establishments and food services; millions of dollars; seasonally adjusted.)

Year and month	Total	Retail and food services										
		Retail (NAICS industry categories)										
		Total	GAFO (department store type goods) 2	Motor vehicles and parts	Furniture and home furnishings	Electronics and appliances	Building materials and garden	Food and beverages			Health and personal care	Gasoline
								Total 1	Groceries	Beer, wine, and liquor		
1992	2 019 131	1 815 716	534 367	419 353	52 467	42 763	131 244	371 451	337 925	21 825	89 782	156 556
1993	2 158 299	1 942 248	571 790	473 948	55 587	48 760	141 220	375 440	341 855	21 675	92 671	162 587
1994	2 335 650	2 110 021	617 379	542 235	60 551	57 413	157 497	385 265	351 056	22 240	96 442	171 416
1995	2 456 129	2 222 504	651 071	580 842	63 601	64 919	164 831	391 312	356 932	22 145	101 719	181 294
1996	2 609 561	2 366 665	683 678	628 687	67 848	68 515	176 972	402 020	366 075	23 300	109 646	194 601
1997	2 732 043	2 474 003	714 453	655 013	72 863	70 211	191 345	410 288	373 072	24 222	118 769	199 856
1998	2 859 332	2 587 105	759 063	689 679	77 569	74 686	202 724	417 433	378 675	25 533	129 699	191 887
1999	3 093 569	2 808 556	816 827	765 549	84 451	79 138	218 611	434 599	394 724	26 635	142 829	212 682
2000	3 294 217	2 988 756	863 903	797 568	91 328	82 363	229 320	445 666	402 988	28 668	155 372	249 975
2001	3 385 577	3 067 725	883 866	816 941	91 644	80 395	239 707	463 330	418 596	29 783	166 678	251 537
2002	3 466 136	3 134 322	913 925	820 269	94 610	83 897	248 888	465 794	420 288	30 061	180 143	250 770
2003	3 615 170	3 265 477	948 246	841 215	97 528	86 957	265 052	477 130	429 962	30 676	192 224	273 566
2004	3 846 316	3 474 340	1 007 195	864 541	105 303	94 811	298 782	494 966	444 610	32 434	198 933	320 435
2005	4 081 692	3 688 059	1 062 366	885 997	111 763	101 609	327 192	514 998	462 568	33 902	209 008	373 855
2006	4 307 730	3 887 363	1 120 147	898 624	117 659	108 362	344 728	533 779	477 736	36 737	224 752	416 246
2007	4 482 668	4 040 411	1 162 719	919 252	118 657	111 359	337 173	560 649	501 077	39 584	237 437	445 212
2008	4 474 970	4 015 681	1 165 318	807 659	109 104	110 618	325 262	589 392	527 447	42 233	247 141	489 340
2006												
January	357 997	323 215	92 359	77 222	9 797	9 111	29 976	43 461	38 859	2 988	18 103	34 077
February	355 346	320 931	92 206	74 330	9 815	8 807	29 991	43 968	39 312	3 070	18 185	33 726
March	356 766	322 130	92 053	75 038	9 820	8 921	30 218	43 767	39 223	2 994	18 381	33 586
April	359 389	324 707	93 057	75 360	9 778	8 951	29 708	44 005	39 406	3 032	18 376	35 318
May	358 461	323 691	92 554	73 600	9 763	8 927	29 086	44 321	39 703	3 040	18 603	36 120
June	358 115	323 514	92 996	73 526	9 913	8 981	28 403	44 462	39 852	3 031	18 749	36 152
July	361 048	326 438	93 141	75 504	9 851	9 013	28 345	44 594	39 948	3 053	18 737	36 929
August	361 877	326 718	93 279	74 521	9 849	9 023	28 335	44 956	40 262	3 073	18 934	37 129
September	359 224	323 763	94 811	74 520	9 991	9 045	27 847	44 535	39 826	3 090	18 992	33 678
October	359 706	324 179	94 361	75 185	9 785	8 976	28 055	45 522	40 730	3 102	19 241	32 241
November	360 428	324 826	93 912	75 754	9 771	9 127	27 720	45 201	40 409	3 141	19 408	33 151
December	365 338	328 864	95 265	76 920	9 777	9 339	28 150	45 500	40 718	3 146	19 447	33 896
2007												
January	365 610	329 526	96 372	76 352	10 024	9 277	28 097	45 678	40 867	3 162	19 440	33 690
February	368 271	332 267	95 486	77 290	10 012	9 199	27 952	46 183	41 320	3 214	19 486	34 427
March	371 322	334 880	97 276	77 188	10 037	9 161	28 765	45 997	41 059	3 254	19 602	35 218
April	370 568	334 151	96 114	77 319	10 030	9 157	27 804	46 133	41 277	3 213	19 690	36 037
May	376 206	339 627	96 881	77 876	9 987	9 191	29 093	46 393	41 431	3 311	19 746	38 312
June	372 603	335 739	96 642	75 999	9 901	9 103	28 096	46 601	41 631	3 336	19 763	37 013
July	374 270	337 120	97 543	75 800	10 009	9 190	28 125	46 996	42 017	3 346	19 916	36 716
August	374 253	337 195	97 504	77 244	9 967	9 276	27 966	46 687	41 732	3 318	19 987	36 214
September	378 404	341 093	97 686	79 032	9 887	9 306	27 929	47 140	42 084	3 340	20 017	37 388
October	379 623	342 153	97 853	79 259	9 866	9 425	27 581	47 525	42 481	3 321	20 031	38 072
November	384 163	346 809	98 487	77 680	9 797	9 718	28 316	47 813	42 773	3 333	19 969	41 830
December	380 968	343 078	98 066	76 528	9 690	9 435	27 454	48 018	42 930	3 388	19 854	40 633
2008												
January	381 673	343 910	98 425	75 427	9 670	9 444	27 608	48 265	43 320	3 397	20 179	41 894
February	378 106	340 599	97 551	74 416	9 476	9 372	27 020	48 179	43 217	3 397	20 220	41 243
March	380 020	342 367	97 982	74 044	9 477	9 372	26 740	48 592	43 563	3 434	20 272	42 296
April	380 788	342 733	98 619	71 759	9 455	9 504	27 339	48 960	43 865	3 449	20 408	42 552
May	383 769	345 425	99 675	71 116	9 502	9 657	28 017	48 891	43 775	3 468	20 407	43 946
June	384 069	345 636	99 542	69 205	9 315	9 548	27 840	49 405	44 188	3 527	20 570	45 334
July	381 578	343 097	99 475	66 303	9 253	9 497	27 938	49 527	44 253	3 578	20 581	45 352
August	378 966	340 422	98 348	67 234	8 983	9 243	27 367	49 836	44 547	3 593	20 597	43 988
September	373 033	334 415	96 729	63 351	8 804	9 164	27 168	49 662	44 377	3 579	20 711	43 934
October	360 296	321 965	95 170	59 623	8 658	8 935	26 571	49 422	44 106	3 611	20 741	38 163
November	351 777	313 152	95 394	58 925	8 525	9 013	25 657	49 447	44 227	3 582	20 838	31 201
December	341 072	302 935	93 334	57 724	8 392	8 486	25 059	48 293	43 174	3 528	20 938	26 322

1 Includes store categories not shown separately.
2 Includes furniture, home furnishings, electronics, appliances, clothing, sporting goods, hobby, book, music, general merchandise, office supplies, stationery, and gifts.

Table 17-9. Retail and Food Services Sales—*Continued*

(All retail establishments and food services; millions of dollars; seasonally adjusted, except as noted.)

Year and month	Retail and food services—*Continued*												
	Retail (NAICS industry categories)—*Continued*												Food services and drinking places
	Clothing and accessories					Sporting goods, hobby, book, and music	General merchandise			Miscellaneous store retailers	Nonstore retailers		
	Total [1]	Men's clothing [3]	Women's clothing	Family clothing [3]	Shoes		Total	Department stores [4]	Other general merchandise		Total [1]	Electronic shopping and mail order	
1992	120 346	10 185	31 840	33 159	18 630	49 296	247 968	177 089	70 879	55 833	78 657	35 252	203 415
1993	125 001	9 968	32 377	35 311	19 042	52 368	266 088	187 685	78 403	62 601	85 977	40 725	216 051
1994	129 341	10 039	30 611	38 118	19 921	57 538	285 278	198 945	86 333	70 585	96 460	47 093	225 629
1995	131 593	9 322	28 723	40 014	20 354	60 922	300 589	205 920	94 669	77 177	103 705	52 741	233 625
1996	136 851	9 554	28 266	42 275	21 248	64 055	315 398	212 203	103 195	84 109	117 963	61 174	242 896
1997	140 565	10 077	27 851	45 259	21 463	65 573	331 454	220 108	111 346	91 669	126 397	70 136	258 040
1998	149 433	10 204	28 363	50 169	22 251	68 939	351 186	223 290	127 896	99 757	134 113	80 366	272 227
1999	160 043	9 675	29 581	55 333	22 704	72 764	380 291	230 304	149 987	105 577	152 022	94 361	285 013
2000	167 968	9 515	31 480	58 928	22 888	76 112	404 344	232 475	171 869	108 052	180 688	113 877	305 461
2001	167 583	8 632	31 487	60 165	22 897	77 138	427 586	228 377	199 209	104 381	180 805	114 844	317 852
2002	172 617	8 119	31 280	64 305	23 215	76 988	446 648	220 743	225 905	104 163	189 535	122 313	331 814
2003	178 778	8 488	32 525	67 272	23 219	77 335	468 734	214 427	254 307	103 056	203 902	131 171	349 693
2004	190 079	9 051	34 734	71 963	23 740	80 061	497 174	215 657	281 517	105 253	224 002	147 199	371 976
2005	201 534	9 479	36 823	77 441	25 315	81 801	525 248	214 346	310 902	108 398	246 656	164 345	393 633
2006	214 876	9 903	39 100	82 031	26 686	84 772	552 109	212 749	339 360	115 802	275 654	190 865	420 367
2007	224 651	10 527	40 383	85 313	26 506	87 324	576 426	209 892	366 534	118 848	303 423	210 431	442 257
2008	219 945	10 088	38 924	84 472	26 642	88 184	595 639	200 574	395 065	118 509	314 888	217 177	459 289
2006													
January	17 463	627	3 294	4 688	2 255	7 284	45 345	17 993	27 352	9 632	21 744	15 146	34 782
February	17 509	613	3 172	5 036	2 237	7 184	45 376	17 917	27 459	9 716	22 324	15 350	34 415
March	17 395	728	3 201	6 247	2 127	7 141	45 356	17 755	27 601	9 638	22 869	15 835	34 636
April	17 719	766	3 273	6 486	2 218	7 179	46 009	17 820	28 189	9 681	22 623	15 568	34 682
May	17 632	768	3 229	6 295	2 186	7 070	45 740	17 731	28 009	9 630	23 199	15 617	34 770
June	17 797	783	3 268	6 367	2 188	7 059	45 795	17 796	27 999	9 582	23 095	15 762	34 601
July	17 962	696	3 322	6 577	2 180	6 965	45 836	17 558	28 278	9 569	23 133	15 593	34 610
August	17 900	802	3 211	7 037	2 214	6 989	45 986	17 565	28 421	9 518	23 578	16 137	35 159
September	18 430	809	3 305	6 541	2 339	7 185	46 581	17 789	28 792	9 576	23 383	16 247	35 461
October	18 294	884	3 258	6 954	2 290	7 056	46 555	17 669	28 886	9 699	23 570	16 406	35 527
November	17 988	937	3 194	7 959	2 243	6 938	46 425	17 622	28 803	9 761	23 582	16 399	35 602
December	18 494	1 490	3 354	11 844	2 241	7 018	46 968	17 713	29 255	9 864	23 491	16 725	36 474
2007													
January	18 752	735	3 345	5 191	2 242	7 030	47 658	17 993	29 665	9 573	23 955	16 808	36 084
February	18 579	710	3 308	5 385	2 166	7 058	46 957	17 631	29 326	9 684	25 440	17 264	36 004
March	19 008	807	3 377	7 150	2 274	7 295	47 950	17 807	30 143	9 950	24 709	17 306	36 442
April	18 495	874	3 298	6 545	2 159	7 221	47 470	17 458	30 012	9 751	25 044	17 149	36 417
May	18 948	888	3 469	6 934	2 185	7 384	47 659	17 618	30 041	9 964	25 074	17 468	36 579
June	18 730	863	3 351	6 668	2 180	7 353	47 787	17 386	30 401	10 196	25 197	17 539	36 864
July	18 928	760	3 391	6 785	2 227	7 495	48 173	17 533	30 640	10 000	25 772	18 129	37 150
August	18 791	769	3 399	7 540	2 236	7 385	48 346	17 528	30 818	10 065	25 267	17 653	37 058
September	18 974	794	3 393	6 492	2 218	7 418	48 350	17 397	30 953	10 155	25 497	17 727	37 311
October	18 886	867	3 405	6 955	2 187	7 432	48 504	17 413	31 091	9 964	25 608	17 847	37 470
November	19 125	969	3 409	8 385	2 238	7 440	48 707	17 367	31 340	9 922	26 492	18 373	37 354
December	18 777	1 491	3 387	11 283	2 221	7 308	49 274	17 330	31 944	9 948	26 159	17 894	37 890
2008													
January	19 141	731	3 368	5 325	2 245	7 539	48 979	17 118	31 861	9 984	25 780	17 613	37 763
February	18 752	722	3 359	5 680	2 224	7 346	49 065	17 050	32 015	9 762	25 748	17 673	37 507
March	18 872	816	3 339	6 751	2 210	7 404	49 285	16 986	32 299	9 829	26 184	17 893	37 653
April	18 973	851	3 404	6 395	2 257	7 453	49 615	17 018	32 597	9 912	26 803	18 258	38 055
May	19 094	908	3 369	7 173	2 275	7 509	50 306	17 128	33 178	9 904	27 076	18 397	38 344
June	19 071	860	3 351	6 582	2 286	7 543	50 508	17 131	33 377	10 092	27 205	18 504	38 433
July	19 151	751	3 327	7 156	2 282	7 504	50 503	17 031	33 472	10 302	27 186	18 312	38 481
August	19 014	794	3 332	7 673	2 294	7 498	50 126	16 668	33 458	9 950	26 586	18 231	38 544
September	18 241	770	3 247	6 191	2 171	7 325	49 764	16 423	33 341	9 928	26 363	18 125	38 618
October	17 776	807	3 103	6 757	2 142	7 104	49 323	16 189	33 134	9 905	25 744	17 871	38 331
November	17 617	863	3 091	7 984	2 154	7 184	49 765	16 467	33 298	9 540	25 440	17 925	38 625
December	16 910	1 215	2 946	10 805	2 113	7 113	49 167	16 128	33 039	9 384	25 147	18 101	38 137

[1]Includes store categories not shown separately.
[3]Not seasonally adjusted.
[4]Excluding leased departments.

Table 17-10. Quarterly U.S. Retail Sales: Total and E-Commerce

Year and quarter	Retail sales (millions of dollars)		E-commerce as a percent of total sales	Percent change from prior quarter		Percent change from same quarter a year ago	
	Total	E-commerce		Total sales	E-commerce sales	Total sales	E-commerce sales
NOT SEASONALLY ADJUSTED							
2003							
1st quarter	741 060	12 313	1.7	-11.1	-13.4	3.3	27.2
2nd quarter	819 232	12 880	1.6	10.5	4.6	3.6	27.0
3rd quarter	830 692	13 769	1.7	1.4	6.9	4.8	27.3
4th quarter	874 493	17 653	2.0	5.3	28.2	4.9	24.2
2004							
1st quarter	794 720	15 911	2.0	-9.1	-9.9	7.2	29.2
2nd quarter	870 834	16 151	1.9	9.6	1.5	6.3	25.4
3rd quarter	872 340	17 009	1.9	0.2	5.3	5.0	23.5
4th quarter	936 446	21 867	2.3	7.3	28.6	7.1	23.9
2005							
1st quarter	834 847	19 408	2.3	-10.8	-11.2	5.0	22.0
2nd quarter	930 532	20 075	2.2	11.5	3.4	6.9	24.3
3rd quarter	938 131	21 196	2.3	0.8	5.6	7.5	24.6
4rd quarter	984 549	26 718	2.7	4.9	26.1	5.1	22.2
2006							
1st quarter	896 182	24 131	2.7	-9.0	-9.7	7.3	24.3
2nd quarter	988 830	24 448	2.5	10.3	1.3	6.3	21.8
3rd quarter	980 553	25 233	2.6	-0.8	3.2	4.5	19.0
4rd quarter	1 021 798	32 771	3.2	4.2	29.9	3.8	22.7
2007							
1st quarter	930 677	28 594	3.1	-8.9	-12.7	3.8	18.5
2nd quarter	1 025 517	29 894	2.9	10.2	4.5	3.7	22.3
3rd quarter	1 012 064	30 210	3.0	-1.3	1.1	3.2	19.7
4rd quarter	1 072 153	38 992	3.6	5.9	29.1	4.9	19.0
2008							
1st quarter	965 500	32 383	3.4	-9.9	-16.9	3.7	13.3
2nd quarter	1 048 726	32 509	3.1	8.6	0.4	2.3	8.7
3rd quarter	1 021 320	31 613	3.1	-2.6	-2.8	0.9	4.6
4th quarter	980 135	37 073	3.8	-4.0	17.3	-8.6	-4.9
SEASONALLY ADJUSTED							
1999							
4th quarter	724 737	4 600	0.6	2.2	. . .	9.0	. . .
2000							
1st quarter	742 622	5 795	0.8	2.5	26.0	9.3	. . .
2nd quarter	741 410	6 454	0.9	-0.2	11.4	7.0	. . .
3rd quarter	748 083	7 362	1.0	0.9	14.1	5.5	. . .
4th quarter	753 134	7 856	1.0	0.7	6.7	3.9	70.8
2001							
1st quarter	756 971	8 209	1.1	0.5	4.5	1.9	41.7
2nd quarter	765 448	8 340	1.1	1.1	1.6	3.2	29.2
3rd quarter	759 291	8 300	1.1	-0.8	-0.5	1.5	12.7
4th quarter	786 127	9 354	1.2	3.5	12.7	4.4	19.1
2002							
1st quarter	773 200	10 050	1.3	-1.6	7.4	2.1	22.4
2nd quarter	779 478	10 785	1.4	0.8	7.3	1.8	29.3
3rd quarter	789 941	11 543	1.5	1.3	7.0	4.0	39.1
4th quarter	792 471	12 274	1.5	0.3	6.3	0.8	31.2
2003							
1st quarter	799 911	12 764	1.6	0.9	4.0	3.5	27.0
2nd quarter	805 286	13 665	1.7	0.7	7.1	3.3	26.7
3rd quarter	828 124	14 631	1.8	2.8	7.1	4.8	26.8
4th quarter	830 826	15 361	1.8	0.3	5.0	4.8	25.2
2004							
1st quarter	847 184	16 462	1.9	2.0	7.2	5.9	29.0
2nd quarter	856 086	17 129	2.0	1.1	4.1	6.3	25.3
3rd quarter	868 399	18 052	2.1	1.4	5.4	4.9	23.4
4th quarter	890 268	19 088	2.1	2.5	5.7	7.2	24.3
2005							
1st quarter	898 783	20 083	2.2	1.0	5.2	6.1	22.0
2nd quarter	917 012	21 253	2.3	2.0	5.8	7.1	24.1
3rd quarter	932 108	22 580	2.4	1.6	6.2	7.3	25.1
4rd quarter	937 149	23 236	2.5	0.5	2.9	5.3	21.7
2006							
1st quarter	966 276	25 012	2.6	3.1	7.6	7.5	24.5
2nd quarter	971 912	25 824	2.7	0.6	3.2	6.0	21.5
3rd quarter	976 919	26 989	2.8	0.5	4.5	4.8	19.5
4rd quarter	977 869	28 311	2.9	0.1	4.9	4.3	21.8
2007							
1st quarter	996 673	29 758	3.0	1.9	5.1	3.1	19.0
2nd quarter	1 009 517	31 602	3.1	1.3	6.2	3.9	22.4
3rd quarter	1 015 408	32 504	3.2	0.6	2.9	3.9	20.4
4th quarter	1 032 040	33 793	3.3	1.6	4.0	5.5	19.4
2008							
1st quarter	1 026 876	33 645	3.3	-0.5	-0.4	3.0	13.1
2nd quarter	1 033 794	34 237	3.3	0.7	1.8	2.4	8.3
3rd quarter	1 017 934	33 873	3.3	-1.5	-1.1	0.2	4.2
4rd quarter	938 052	31 946	3.4	-7.8	-5.7	-9.1	-5.5

. . . = Not available.

Table 17-11. Retail Inventories

(All retail stores; end of period, millions of dollars.)

Year and month	Not seasonally adjusted			Seasonally adjusted (NAICS industry categories)								
	Total	Excluding motor vehicles and parts	Motor vehicles and parts	Total	Excluding motor vehicles and parts	Motor vehicles and parts	Furniture, home furnishings, electronics, and appliances	Building materials and garden	Food and beverages	Clothing and accessories	General merchandise	
											Total	Department stores [1]
1992	256 810	185 195	71 615	261 369	192 066	69 303	16 208	21 144	27 467	27 467	49 783	38 333
1993	274 748	196 932	77 816	279 526	204 233	75 293	18 138	22 667	27 558	28 193	53 700	40 854
1994	300 517	211 758	88 759	305 442	219 514	85 928	20 421	24 905	28 171	29 602	56 830	42 136
1995	318 021	221 462	96 559	322 925	229 379	93 546	21 839	26 384	28 776	29 382	59 550	43 455
1996	328 912	228 456	100 456	334 010	236 601	97 409	22 300	27 497	29 718	29 864	60 611	44 124
1997	339 565	234 858	104 707	344 609	243 120	101 489	22 157	28 947	29 949	31 167	60 735	44 309
1998	351 996	245 964	106 032	357 269	254 466	102 803	22 705	30 966	30 901	32 383	61 566	43 438
1999	379 626	260 483	119 143	385 009	269 181	115 828	24 139	33 124	32 705	33 820	64 306	43 840
2000	401 305	269 653	131 652	406 853	278 514	128 339	25 665	34 462	32 186	36 855	64 915	42 677
2001	388 818	267 061	121 757	394 713	275 501	119 212	24 537	34 499	33 250	35 738	64 746	40 478
2002	410 347	272 489	137 858	416 159	280 854	135 305	25 921	36 428	32 967	37 526	65 855	38 727
2003	426 609	278 270	148 339	432 359	286 500	145 859	27 323	37 969	32 684	38 598	66 554	36 895
2004	455 568	298 468	157 100	461 405	306 923	154 482	30 358	42 438	33 709	41 584	70 845	37 370
2005	465 874	310 365	155 509	471 956	318 989	152 967	31 138	46 268	34 038	43 386	73 274	37 392
2006	482 153	325 687	156 466	488 591	334 645	153 946	31 893	48 117	34 969	47 757	75 851	37 403
2007	494 978	334 770	160 208	502 777	344 249	158 528	33 063	49 490	36 595	47 282	76 280	37 033
2008	480 352	329 403	150 949	486 517	338 216	148 301	31 223	50 053	37 889	45 982	74 126	33 776
2005												
January	452 816	297 673	155 143	461 586	308 790	152 796	30 003	43 519	33 885	42 061	71 073	37 396
February	458 652	300 884	157 768	463 659	310 150	153 509	29 955	43 439	33 862	42 655	71 334	37 488
March	469 052	307 877	161 175	465 023	311 310	153 713	29 980	43 307	33 820	42 843	72 665	38 513
April	470 796	308 461	162 335	465 059	311 818	153 241	30 167	43 077	33 921	42 859	72 626	37 671
May	465 087	306 997	158 090	466 079	312 910	153 169	30 611	43 496	33 919	42 782	72 824	37 524
June	457 874	306 742	151 132	462 018	314 305	147 713	30 835	43 698	33 964	43 342	72 813	37 583
July	439 642	306 707	132 935	453 748	313 766	139 982	30 722	43 790	33 794	43 374	72 469	37 665
August	442 613	312 357	130 256	456 530	315 725	140 805	30 736	44 024	33 866	43 539	73 334	37 696
September	458 586	323 866	134 720	461 628	316 478	145 150	30 568	44 582	33 452	43 601	73 367	37 589
October	482 696	339 944	142 752	463 340	316 140	147 200	30 475	44 728	33 795	43 758	72 945	37 316
November	497 476	345 595	151 881	467 717	317 230	150 487	30 617	45 468	33 975	43 449	72 947	37 134
December	465 874	310 365	155 509	471 956	318 989	152 967	31 138	46 268	34 038	43 386	73 274	37 392
2006												
January	465 322	309 405	155 917	474 227	320 499	153 728	31 330	46 985	34 258	43 050	72 706	36 706
February	468 102	311 016	157 086	473 183	320 172	153 011	31 603	46 411	34 411	43 560	72 127	36 207
March	482 852	319 865	162 987	478 944	323 183	155 761	31 700	47 581	34 478	44 193	72 525	36 216
April	482 412	319 826	162 586	477 041	323 273	153 768	31 872	47 877	34 582	44 569	71 270	35 989
May	483 196	319 453	163 743	484 095	325 313	158 782	32 094	47 867	34 769	44 920	72 020	35 965
June	483 783	319 557	164 226	487 356	326 851	160 505	32 173	48 229	34 841	45 138	72 167	35 617
July	472 330	320 559	151 771	487 839	327 941	159 898	32 212	48 827	34 913	45 184	73 125	35 970
August	474 189	326 992	147 197	489 368	330 502	158 866	32 135	49 570	34 959	45 366	73 898	36 289
September	484 849	338 491	146 358	488 245	331 129	157 116	32 088	49 096	35 098	45 757	74 146	36 501
October	508 175	356 625	151 550	488 239	332 117	156 122	31 928	48 741	35 095	46 124	75 057	36 803
November	517 515	362 436	155 079	486 849	333 324	153 525	31 862	48 686	35 016	46 770	75 580	37 219
December	482 153	325 687	156 466	488 591	334 645	153 946	31 893	48 117	34 969	47 757	75 851	37 403
2007												
January	479 779	323 051	156 728	489 024	334 478	154 546	32 222	47 803	34 896	47 782	76 082	37 533
February	484 751	327 532	157 219	490 533	337 120	153 413	32 523	48 262	34 833	48 477	76 557	37 595
March	490 358	332 233	158 125	488 131	336 605	151 526	32 295	47 922	35 056	47 890	76 582	37 352
April	493 391	333 149	160 242	489 524	337 167	152 357	32 271	49 264	34 775	47 613	76 680	37 572
May	490 371	332 923	157 448	492 560	339 350	153 210	32 148	49 056	35 166	47 774	76 966	37 472
June	489 962	332 058	157 904	494 960	340 099	154 861	32 345	49 256	35 410	47 544	76 977	37 703
July	483 471	332 472	150 999	498 711	340 007	158 704	32 574	49 114	35 481	47 390	76 470	37 565
August	486 280	336 494	149 786	501 726	340 441	161 285	32 553	49 106	35 824	47 344	76 431	37 415
September	498 184	347 978	150 206	501 531	340 449	161 082	32 860	48 735	35 979	47 359	76 330	37 477
October	523 878	368 303	155 575	503 046	342 939	160 107	33 594	49 235	36 310	47 178	76 785	37 804
November	532 353	370 412	161 941	502 475	341 698	160 777	33 344	49 281	36 383	47 037	75 773	36 909
December	494 978	334 770	160 208	502 777	344 249	158 528	33 063	49 490	36 595	47 282	76 280	37 033
2008												
January	494 118	333 424	160 694	504 564	345 830	158 734	33 101	50 146	36 652	47 237	76 951	37 068
February	498 312	335 342	162 970	505 447	345 655	159 792	32 897	50 133	36 858	46 921	77 133	37 178
March	501 926	338 210	163 716	499 972	342 663	157 309	32 542	50 113	37 019	46 288	75 563	36 442
April	505 106	340 739	164 367	501 054	344 600	156 454	32 947	50 191	37 302	46 463	76 196	36 349
May	497 623	337 756	159 867	499 667	344 089	155 578	32 716	49 925	37 413	46 148	76 016	36 312
June	494 305	336 680	157 625	500 100	345 074	155 026	33 007	49 983	37 525	46 260	75 930	35 931
July	492 166	339 797	152 369	506 863	347 038	159 825	33 444	50 479	37 591	46 519	75 886	35 696
August	488 437	342 313	146 124	503 330	346 447	156 883	33 456	51 083	37 732	46 465	75 191	35 380
September	501 464	355 162	146 302	504 102	347 800	156 302	33 608	51 446	38 062	46 570	76 047	35 789
October	525 412	373 229	152 183	502 955	347 311	155 644	33 682	51 271	38 211	46 672	76 017	35 605
November	524 519	371 502	153 017	493 785	342 257	151 528	31 637	50 997	38 109	46 393	75 120	34 459
December	480 352	329 403	150 949	486 517	338 216	148 301	31 223	50 053	37 889	45 982	74 126	33 776

[1] Excluding leased departments.

Table 17-12. Merchant Wholesalers—Sales and Inventories

(Millions of dollars.)

| Year and month | Not seasonally adjusted | | | | | | Seasonally adjusted | | | | | |
| | Sales | | | Inventories (current cost, end of period) | | | Sales | | | Inventories (current cost, end of period) | | |
	Total	Durable goods establishments	Nondurable goods establishments	Total	Durable goods establishments	Nondurable goods establishments	Total	Durable goods establishments	Nondurable goods establishments	Total	Durable goods establishments	Nondurable goods establishments
1992	1 767 130	861 182	905 948	197 793	121 809	75 984	1 767 130	861 182	905 948	196 914	123 435	73 479
1993	1 848 215	939 945	908 270	205 815	127 094	78 721	1 848 215	939 945	908 270	204 842	128 851	75 991
1994	1 974 899	1 037 638	937 261	222 826	139 941	82 885	1 974 899	1 037 638	937 261	221 978	141 975	80 003
1995	2 158 980	1 141 701	1 017 279	239 275	151 709	87 566	2 158 980	1 141 701	1 017 279	238 392	154 089	84 303
1996	2 284 343	1 190 342	1 094 001	241 396	154 207	87 189	2 284 343	1 190 342	1 094 001	241 050	156 664	84 386
1997	2 377 845	1 256 384	1 121 461	258 900	165 371	93 529	2 377 845	1 256 384	1 121 461	258 575	168 079	90 496
1998	2 427 120	1 306 545	1 120 575	272 575	175 994	96 581	2 427 120	1 306 545	1 120 575	272 404	178 893	93 511
1999	2 599 159	1 406 371	1 192 788	290 482	188 122	102 360	2 599 159	1 406 371	1 192 788	290 318	191 280	99 038
2000	2 814 554	1 486 673	1 327 881	309 977	199 336	110 641	2 814 554	1 486 673	1 327 881	309 462	202 625	106 837
2001	2 785 152	1 422 195	1 362 957	299 009	183 710	115 299	2 785 152	1 422 195	1 362 957	297 927	186 719	111 208
2002	2 835 528	1 421 503	1 414 025	303 359	183 721	119 638	2 835 528	1 421 503	1 414 025	301 891	186 624	115 267
2003	2 962 284	1 448 944	1 513 340	309 628	186 600	123 028	2 962 284	1 448 944	1 513 340	307 642	189 545	118 097
2004	3 296 520	1 654 621	1 641 899	339 550	212 122	127 428	3 296 520	1 654 621	1 641 899	287 435	145 788	141 647
2005	3 574 976	1 771 835	1 803 141	363 887	227 991	135 896	3 574 976	1 771 835	1 803 141	362 451	231 399	131 052
2006	3 880 751	1 929 281	1 951 470	393 839	247 560	146 279	3 880 751	1 929 281	1 951 470	392 291	251 149	141 142
2007	4 150 455	1 997 552	2 152 903	418 759	251 548	167 211	4 150 455	1 997 552	2 152 903	416 632	255 389	161 243
2008	4 500 703	2 049 340	2 451 363	429 769	267 853	161 916	4 500 703	2 049 340	2 451 363	429 572	272 000	157 572
2005												
January	263 086	128 298	134 788	345 518	217 134	128 384	289 957	145 137	144 820	342 599	218 089	124 510
February	263 761	130 150	133 611	346 242	220 344	125 898	290 385	145 057	145 328	344 121	219 657	124 464
March	311 088	156 345	154 743	347 428	220 259	127 169	289 256	144 024	145 232	346 121	220 370	125 751
April	291 189	144 379	146 810	348 602	222 540	126 062	293 505	145 918	147 587	348 931	221 405	127 526
May	295 567	146 211	149 356	345 017	222 106	122 911	291 644	145 414	146 230	349 158	221 935	127 223
June	306 164	154 953	151 211	348 576	224 437	124 139	292 459	145 143	147 316	350 532	223 722	126 810
July	284 372	140 035	144 337	350 485	226 911	123 574	295 270	145 918	149 352	351 267	224 612	126 655
August	316 233	156 329	159 904	348 927	224 418	124 509	299 089	147 639	151 450	352 042	224 320	127 722
September	313 561	155 694	157 867	352 301	223 769	128 532	305 254	149 062	156 192	353 302	223 848	129 454
October	315 180	154 927	160 253	357 893	227 620	130 273	311 789	152 313	159 476	356 125	227 179	128 946
November	306 257	151 201	155 056	359 164	228 235	130 929	308 673	152 633	156 040	357 813	228 804	129 009
December	308 518	153 313	155 205	363 887	227 991	135 896	313 279	156 504	156 775	362 451	231 399	131 052
2006												
January	294 567	143 664	150 903	366 125	230 949	135 176	316 222	157 497	158 725	363 363	232 018	131 345
February	286 297	141 744	144 553	368 949	234 713	134 236	317 337	159 061	158 276	366 765	234 150	132 615
March	339 434	171 137	168 297	369 388	235 071	134 317	318 044	158 302	159 742	368 666	235 485	133 181
April	308 384	150 345	158 039	372 219	240 390	131 829	319 394	157 090	162 304	372 795	239 520	133 275
May	337 846	166 965	170 881	371 486	241 229	130 257	323 186	160 883	162 303	375 750	241 197	134 553
June	342 391	172 088	170 303	376 565	243 334	133 231	325 041	160 209	164 832	378 021	242 571	135 450
July	315 582	154 307	161 275	380 595	247 352	133 243	326 517	160 890	165 627	380 948	244 967	135 981
August	349 164	172 184	176 980	381 770	246 794	134 976	328 443	161 814	166 629	384 226	246 374	137 852
September	325 228	164 485	160 743	386 214	249 582	136 632	324 566	162 077	162 489	386 199	248 996	137 203
October	338 705	171 511	167 194	390 780	252 318	138 462	324 588	162 616	161 972	388 826	251 408	137 418
November	323 845	162 334	161 511	395 369	251 917	143 452	327 530	164 392	163 138	393 600	252 200	141 400
December	319 308	158 517	160 791	393 839	247 560	146 279	334 816	167 321	167 495	392 291	251 149	141 142
2007												
January	316 213	155 830	160 383	396 135	251 141	144 994	331 110	166 113	164 997	393 488	252 552	140 936
February	300 307	146 063	154 244	397 421	253 278	144 143	334 869	164 987	169 882	395 164	253 135	142 029
March	350 248	174 545	175 703	397 362	252 181	145 181	338 367	166 703	171 664	397 094	253 202	143 892
April	337 939	164 101	173 838	396 496	251 771	144 725	340 974	166 438	174 536	397 519	251 379	146 140
May	359 568	171 128	188 440	393 748	252 084	141 664	342 363	164 543	177 820	398 469	252 278	146 191
June	352 275	171 782	180 493	397 345	252 422	144 923	342 150	164 182	177 968	399 147	251 891	147 256
July	340 604	162 483	178 121	399 314	252 804	146 510	340 456	163 486	176 970	399 782	250 284	149 498
August	364 966	176 893	188 073	397 975	251 491	146 484	343 061	165 841	177 220	400 642	250 655	149 987
September	339 698	163 444	176 254	403 763	253 070	150 693	348 836	166 186	182 650	404 360	251 688	152 672
October	380 292	182 638	197 654	408 564	253 339	155 225	355 112	167 689	187 423	406 200	251 872	154 328
November	361 881	169 734	192 147	413 297	253 286	160 011	365 947	171 456	194 491	410 917	253 245	157 672
December	346 464	158 911	187 553	418 759	251 548	167 211	365 171	168 388	196 783	416 632	255 389	161 243
2008												
January	359 257	161 950	197 307	426 318	257 169	169 149	377 100	173 417	203 683	422 416	258 876	163 540
February	347 593	156 512	191 081	430 218	260 566	169 652	372 986	170 017	202 969	426 580	261 044	165 536
March	378 023	174 934	203 089	426 592	260 151	166 441	378 230	173 309	204 921	425 868	261 635	164 233
April	390 686	180 670	210 016	429 982	264 775	165 207	382 513	177 087	205 426	431 059	264 646	166 413
May	397 439	178 644	218 795	427 499	266 327	161 172	387 371	176 436	210 935	433 432	266 638	166 794
June	408 484	185 785	222 699	433 954	268 402	165 552	396 165	177 546	218 619	436 648	267 809	168 839
July	406 740	182 277	224 463	440 533	273 841	166 692	392 898	177 223	215 675	441 145	271 013	170 132
August	391 378	175 409	215 969	441 139	275 841	165 298	386 401	174 022	212 379	443 937	274 585	169 352
September	391 316	180 009	211 307	442 785	278 653	164 132	378 625	170 950	207 675	442 528	276 544	165 984
October	387 762	178 075	209 687	440 930	278 082	162 848	362 539	163 429	199 110	438 249	276 165	162 084
November	314 621	143 400	171 221	436 970	275 488	161 482	337 615	155 187	182 428	434 986	275 414	159 572
December	327 404	151 675	175 729	429 769	267 853	161 916	325 672	151 407	174 265	429 572	272 000	157 572

Table 17-13. Selected Service Industries—Revenue, by NAICS Industry

(Millions of dollars; employer and nonemployer firms, except as noted.)

NAICS code	Kind of business	1998	1999	2000	2001	2002	2003	2004	2005	2006	2007
	Total for Selected Service Industries [1, 2]	3 759 984	4 082 942	4 442 227	4 539 960	4 643 495	4 851 593	5 273 151	5 666 791	6 074 675	6 433 269
484	Truck transportation	170 762	181 000	192 523	190 387	192 943	200 443	223 348	249 829	268 524	276 044
492	Couriers and messengers	51 250	54 178	60 268	61 113	60 980	62 945	65 684	70 611	75 621	78 840
493	Warehousing and storage	13 177	14 011	14 929	15 586	16 945	17 896	18 246	19 510	21 209	22 243
51	Information	707 049	789 663	871 491	891 678	899 396	916 728	964 552	1 013 418	1 068 204	1 126 388
	1997 NAICS, Employer Firms Only									...	...
511	Publishing industries	212 688	231 687	246 800	247 090	246 043	247 635	...	...	...	...
512	Motion picture and sound recording industries	60 389	66 720	71 560	72 904	78 250	83 113	...	...	...	...
513	Broadcasting and telecommunications	383 457	428 460	473 503	487 451	485 607	492 997	...	...	...	...
514	Information services and data processing services	44 302	55 777	72 009	76 531	81 946	84 464	...	...	...	...
	2002 NAICS, Employer and Employee Firms										
511	Publishing industries except Internet	...	...	...	...	...	...	258 618	272 113	285 304	300 271
512	Motion picture and sound recording industries	...	...	...	...	...	...	90 524	96 041	100 912	104 811
515	Broadcasting (except Internet)	...	...	...	...	...	...	84 072	88 300	93 763	97 377
516	Internet publishing and broadcasting	...	...	...	...	...	...	9 090	10 877	13 456	16 226
517	Telecommunications	...	...	...	...	...	...	430 698	447 529	464 643	492 250
518	Internet service providers, web search portals, and data processing servers	...	...	...	...	...	...	83 770	90 015	101 085	105 664
519	Other information services	...	...	...	...	...	...	7 780	8 543	9 041	9 789
5231	Securities and commodity contracts intermediation and brokerage	213 055	256 534	302 440	252 870	217 669	230 627	254 737	284 118	340 687	317 694
532	Rental and leasing services	88 061	96 222	103 945	102 599	100 626	102 194	108 964	115 106	125 894	131 080
54	Professional, scientific, and technical services (except notaries) [1]	758 515	829 733	911 320	947 450	961 540	1 002 014	1 099 966	1 195 866	1 289 193	1 409 625
56	Administrative and support and waste management and remediation services [2]	344 658	380 852	415 933	410 942	419 179	438 173	523 540	570 802	609 672	644 341
561	Administrative and support services [2]	297 930	330 363	363 839	358 379	366 785	382 434	463 651	506 242	539 552	571 635
562	Waste management and remediation services	46 728	50 489	52 094	52 564	52 394	55 739	59 889	64 560	70 120	72 706
62	Health care and social assistance	971 521	1 013 111	1 072 561	1 157 852	1 253 127	1 334 868	1 427 450	1 528 705	1 611 265	1 721 209
621	Ambulatory health care services	403 295	420 346	446 946	483 312	520 680	560 641	604 368	648 851	687 490	734 902
622	Hospitals	391 557	406 717	423 888	455 261	500 113	529 202	569 463	611 522	644 904	687 135
623	Nursing and residential care facilities	104 927	107 544	114 169	122 030	128 650	134 877	140 002	147 575	151 813	162 228
624	Social assistance	71 742	78 504	87 558	97 249	103 684	110 149	113 617	120 757	127 058	136 944
71	Arts, entertainment, and recreation	129 005	136 507	145 113	152 224	161 904	170 356	181 006	190 264	205 165	216 238
711	Performing arts, spectator sports, and related industries	56 785	60 098	64 163	67 632	73 094	75 891	79 432	82 975	90 098	94 662
712	Museums, historical sites, and similar institutions	8 358	8 757	9 402	9 282	8 674	9 150	9 768	10 347	12 055	13 078
713	Amusement, gambling, and recreation industries	63 862	67 652	71 548	75 310	80 136	85 315	91 806	96 942	103 012	108 498
81	Other services (except public administration; religious, labor, and political organizations; and private households)	312 932	331 132	351 707	357 259	359 187	375 349	405 658	428 562	459 241	489 567
811	Repair and maintenance	122 254	127 832	134 133	139 783	141 123	147 209	153 405	159 948	165 547	170 934
812	Personal and laundry services	86 724	92 032	97 973	101 655	105 100	109 859	118 339	126 022	131 022	136 578
813	Religious, grantmaking, civic, professional, and similar organizations (except religious, labor, and political organizations)	103 954	111 268	119 601	115 822	112 964	118 281	133 913	142 590	162 671	182 054

. . . = Not available.
[1] 1998 through 2003 excludes landscape architectural services.
[2] 1998 through 2003 excludes landscaping services.

Table 17-14. Selected Services—Quarterly Estimated Revenue for Employer Firms

(Millions of dollars.)

NAICS code	Kind of business	2003 4th quarter	2004 1st quarter	2004 2nd quarter	2004 3rd quarter	2004 4th quarter	2005 1st quarter	2005 2nd quarter	2005 3rd quarter	2005 4th quarter
NOT SEASONALLY ADJUSTED										
51	**Information**	242 106	228 097	237 871	237 720	251 395	241 014	249 443	250 483	262 322
511	Publishing industries (except Internet)	. . .	. . .	. . .	. . .	. . .	. . .	. . .	. . .	. . .
51111	Newspaper publishers	. . .	. . .	. . .	. . .	. . .	. . .	. . .	. . .	. . .
51112	Periodical publishers	. . .	. . .	. . .	. . .	. . .	. . .	. . .	. . .	. . .
5111pt	Book, directory and mailing list, and other publishers	. . .	. . .	. . .	. . .	. . .	. . .	. . .	. . .	. . .
5112	Software publishers	31 130	26 827	27 183	27 287	30 964	28 254	29 839	29 582	33 659
512	Motion pictures and sound recording industries	24 981	20 949	22 224	20 121	24 975	22 680	22 876	22 344	25 755
515	Broadcasting (except Internet)	. . .								
5151	Radio and television broadcasting	12 787	11 522	13 484	12 900	14 187	12 548	13 252	12 240	14 268
5152	Cable and other subscription programming	. . .	. . .	. . .	. . .	. . .	. . .	. . .	. . .	. . .
516, 5181, 519	Internet publishing and broadcasting, Internet service providers and web search portals, and other information services	. . .	. . .	. . .	. . .	. . .	. . .	. . .	. . .	. . .
517	Telecommunications	. . .	. . .	. . .	. . .	. . .	. . .	. . .	. . .	. . .
5171	Wired telecommunications carriers	53 863	53 159	52 811	52 481	52 725	52 181	51 959	51 463	51 019
5172	Wireless telecommunications carriers (except satellite)	29 397	29 934	31 506	33 062	33 100	33 160	34 648	35 720	36 497
5175	Cable and other program distribution	. . .	. . .	. . .	. . .	. . .	. . .	. . .	. . .	. . .
517pt	Other telecommunications	4 255	4 086	4 347	4 361	4 541	4 935	4 874	4 629	4 643
5182	Data processing, hosting, and related services	15 036	13 826	14 499	14 395	14 610	14 503	15 325	16 110	16 691
54	**Professional, Scientific, and Technical Services**	. . .	. . .	. . .	. . .	. . .	. . .	. . .	. . .	. . .
54 pt	Professional, scientific, and technical services (except landscape architectural services and veterinary services)	230 941	230 637	243 738	235 596	256 038	252 679	263 558	257 209	278 727
5411	Legal services	55 376	46 274	52 427	51 970	61 220	52 140	56 038	53 370	62 830
5412	Accounting, tax preparation, bookkeeping, and payroll services	21 254	27 594	23 990	19 767	21 533	30 952	26 280	20 953	22 765
5413	Architectural, engineering, and related services	. . .	. . .	. . .	. . .	. . .	. . .	. . .	. . .	. . .
5413pt	Architectural and related services	. . .	. . .	. . .	. . .	. . .	. . .	. . .	. . .	. . .
54133	Engineering services	. . .	. . .	. . .	. . .	. . .	. . .	. . .	. . .	. . .
5415	Computer systems design and related services	41 697	43 089	42 447	43 101	44 888	45 150	47 540	47 281	48 295
5416	Management, scientific, and technical consulting services	28 145	28 040	30 676	30 562	32 431	32 472	34 184	34 075	36 633
5417	Scientific research and development services	. . .	. . .	. . .	. . .	. . .	. . .	. . .	. . .	. . .
5418	Advertising and related services	15 653	14 874	15 738	15 742	17 231	15 453	16 960	16 644	17 988
541pt	Other professional, scientific, and technical services [1]	. . .	. . .	. . .	. . .	. . .	. . .	. . .	. . .	. . .
541pt	Other professional, scientific, and technical services [2]	. . .	. . .	. . .	. . .	. . .	. . .	. . .	. . .	. . .
56	**Administrative and Support and Waste Management and Remediation Services**	. . .	. . .	. . .	. . .	. . .	. . .	. . .	. . .	. . .
56pt	Administrative and support and waste management and remediation services except landscaping services	101 874	103 094	109 450	112 964	118 418	113 934	120 110	122 179	126 615
561	Administrative and support services	. . .	. . .	. . .	. . .	. . .	. . .	. . .	. . .	. . .
5613	Employment services	33 235	32 644	35 971	37 056	40 046	37 836	38 923	40 526	41 859
5615	Travel arrangement and reservation services	6 255	6 706	7 574	7 110	6 810	7 100	7 825	7 147	7 045
561pt	Other administrative and support services	. . .	. . .	. . .	. . .	. . .	. . .	. . .	. . .	. . .
561 pt	Other administrative and support services (except landscaping services)	48 759	50 493	51 812	53 178	55 883	55 069	58 259	57 822	60 231
562	Waste management and remediation services	13 625	13 251	14 093	15 620	15 679	13 929	15 103	16 684	17 480
62pt	**Selected Health Care Services**	. . .	. . .	. . .	. . .	183 777	187 192	188 421	190 136	191 351
622	Hospitals	. . .	. . .	. . .	. . .	147 631	151 594	152 066	153 581	154 281
623	Nursing and residential care facilities	. . .	. . .	. . .	. . .	36 146	35 598	36 355	36 555	37 070
SEASONALLY ADJUSTED										
51	**Information**	233 468	234 909	237 396	239 879	243 129	247 448	249 194	252 503	254 188
54 (pt)	**Professional, Scientific, and Technical Services (Except Landscape Architectural Services and Veterinary Services)**	225 528	232 263	239 193	244 394	250 037	254 460	259 663	265 712	271 929
5411	Legal services	48 962	50 462	52 479	54 192	54 758	56 185	56 207	55 710	56 098
5412	Accounting, tax preparation, bookkeeping, and payroll services	23 589	22 600	23 001	23 645	23 979	25 308	25 197	25 063	25 323
56 pt	**Administrative and Support and Waste Management and Remediation Services (Except Landscaping Services)**	100 563	105 165	109 268	112 432	117 004	116 063	119 849	121 735	125 310
5613	Employment services	31 987	33 688	36 079	37 168	38 767	38 846	39 079	40 648	40 640
5615	Travel arrangement and reservation services	6 640	6 857	7 026	7 139	7 161	7 267	7 286	7 176	7 385
562	Waste management and remediation services	13 177	14 127	14 351	14 947	15 193	14 881	15 225	16 089	17 054

. . . = Not available.

[1]Including 5417, scientific research and development.
[2]Excluding 5417.

Table 17-14. Selected Services—Quarterly Estimated Revenue for Employer Firms—*Continued*

(Millions of dollars.)

NAICS code	Kind of business	2006 1st quarter	2006 2nd quarter	2006 3rd quarter	2006 4th quarter	2007 1st quarter	2007 2nd quarter	2007 3rd quarter	2007 4th quarter
NOT SEASONALLY ADJUSTED									
51	**Information**	251 648	262 328	263 445	280 009	268 035	277 705	278 122	291 021
511	Publishing industries (except Internet)	...	...	70 999	76 306	71 079	73 178	73 977	79 475
51111	Newspaper publishers	...	...	11 754	13 295	11 516	12 359	11 917	12 482
51112	Periodical publishers	...	...	12 117	12 581	11 369	12 431	12 598	12 894
5111pt	Book, directory and mailing list, and other publishers	...	...	14 847	13 790	12 361	13 087	15 975	15 016
5112	Software publishers	31 057	32 279	32 281	36 640	35 833	35 301	33 487	39 083
512	Motion pictures and sound recording industries	22 804	24 526	23 228	27 834	24 462	25 879	24 520	27 305
515	Broadcasting (except Internet)	...	...	22 220	24 974	22 863	24 375	23 652	25 838
5151	Radio and television broadcasting	13 434	13 858	12 877	14 984	13 580	14 266	13 204	14 808
5152	Cable and other subscription programming	...	...	9 343	9 990	9 283	10 109	10 448	11 030
516, 5181, 519	Internet publishing and broadcasting, Internet service providers and web search portals, and other information services	...	...	12 105	13 014	13 086	13 177	13 518	14 856
517	Telecommunications	...	...	116 920	119 344	118 906	122 264	124 159	125 432
5171	Wired telecommunications carriers	49 056	48 507	48 686	48 843	47 606	48 372	48 761	48 040
5172	Wireless telecommunications carriers (except satellite)	37 609	38 998	40 591	41 379	41 982	42 788	44 213	45 102
5175	Cable and other program distribution	...	...	22 338	23 630	23 737	25 298	25 282	26 532
517pt	Other telecommunications	4 882	5 117	5 305	5 492	5 581	5 806	5 903	5 758
5182	Data processing, hosting, and related services	16 542	17 745	17 973	18 537	17 639	18 832	18 296	18 115
54	**Professional, Scientific, and Technical Services**	...	...	286 175	307 870	308 622	319 166	313 878	334 902
54 pt	Professional, scientific, and technical services (except landscape architectural services and veterinary services)	275 282	283 901	278 102	300 311	301 085	311 369	306 557	327 709
5411	Legal services	52 254	58 453	58 125	69 619	60 268	61 972	60 846	71 238
5412	Accounting, tax preparation, bookkeeping, and payroll services	33 159	27 595	22 881	25 501	34 458	31 682	26 095	29 055
5413	Architectural, engineering, and related services	...	...	56 813	58 203	58 497	59 535	61 783	64 028
5413pt	Architectural and related services	...	...	16 055	16 353	17 350	17 386	17 718	18 645
54133	Engineering services	...	...	40 758	41 850	41 147	42 149	44 065	45 383
5415	Computer systems design and related services	48 779	50 317	49 955	53 230	53 595	57 027	58 020	59 981
5416	Management, scientific, and technical consulting services	37 542	37 654	37 235	37 336	39 269	42 242	41 419	42 318
5417	Scientific research and development services	...	...	...	...	24 343	25 146	25 467	26 402
5418	Advertising and related services	17 238	18 030	17 912	19 731	18 366	19 809	19 745	21 113
541pt	Other professional, scientific, and technical services [1]	...	...	43 254	44 250	44 169	46 899	45 970	47 169
541pt	Other professional, scientific, and technical services [2]	...	...	...	...	19 826	21 753	20 503	20 767
56	**Administrative and support and waste management and remediation services**	...	...	145 901	147 736	141 720	150 872	151 581	150 649
56pt	Administrative and support and waste management and remediation services except landscaping services	124 602	128 803	129 719	132 738	130 164	136 622	138 295	138 177
561	Administrative and support services	...	...	128 224	130 231	124 980	133 092	133 276	132 263
5613	Employment services	41 330	42 362	42 421	44 906	42 587	44 276	44 535	47 269
5615	Travel arrangement and reservation services	6 939	7 828	7 663	7 771	7 950	8 594	8 018	7 510
561pt	Other administrative and support services	...	...	78 140	77 554	74 443	80 222	80 723	77 484
561 pt	Other administrative and support services (except landscaping services)	60 268	61 165	61 958	62 556	62 887	65 972	67 437	65 012
562	Waste management and remediation services	16 065	17 448	17 677	17 505	16 740	17 780	18 305	18 386
62pt	**Selected Health Care Services**	196 263	198 149	198 113	202 164	208 712	210 824	211 714	215 922
622	Hospitals	158 922	160 724	160 681	164 577	169 985	171 290	171 301	174 559
623	Nursing and residential care facilities	37 341	37 425	37 432	37 587	38 727	39 534	40 413	41 363
SEASONALLY ADJUSTED									
51	**Information**	258 101	262 066	265 302	271 590	274 908	277 428	279 520	283 094
54 (pt)	**Professional, Scientific, and Technical Services (Except Landscape Architectural Services and Veterinary Services)**	277 502	280 535	285 819	293 272	304 126	307 981	313 453	320 655
5411	Legal services	56 369	58 747	60 421	62 890	64 389	62 472	62 922	64 527
5412	Accounting, tax preparation, bookkeeping, and payroll services	27 224	26 356	27 337	28 334	28 431	30 116	31 214	32 248
56 pt	**Administrative and Support and Waste Management and Remediation Services (Except Landscaping Services)**	126 674	128 384	129 425	131 528	132 158	136 008	138 013	137 255
5613	Employment services	42 260	42 532	42 634	43 640	43 501	44 409	44 714	46 071
5615	Travel arrangement and reservation services	7 110	7 309	7 671	8 120	8 112	8 092	7 986	7 914
562	Waste management and remediation services	17 036	17 378	17 162	17 212	17 658	17 535	17 876	18 258

. . . = Not available.
[1] Including 5417, scientific research and development.
[2] Excluding 5417.

Table 17-14. Selected Services—Quarterly Estimated Revenue for Employer Firms—*Continued*

(Millions of dollars.)

NAICS code	Kind of business	2008			
		1st quarter	2nd quarter	3rd quarter	4th quarter
NOT SEASONALLY ADJUSTED					
51	Information	276 923	283 552	281 685	285 890
511	Publishing industries (except Internet)	72 795	74 358	73 856	74 816
51111	Newspaper publishers	10 748	10 779	10 473	10 677
51112	Periodical publishers	11 739	11 800	12 268	11 801
5111pt	Book, directory and mailing list, and other publishers	13 295	13 787	15 766	14 173
5112	Software publishers	37 013	37 992	35 349	38 165
512	Motion pictures and sound recording industries	24 694	26 203	23 844	25 201
515	Broadcasting (except Internet)	24 292	25 389	25 136	25 799
5151	Radio and television broadcasting	13 717	13 949	13 530	13 207
5152	Cable and other subscription programming	10 575	11 440	11 606	12 592
516, 5181, 519	Internet publishing and broadcasting, Internet service providers and web search portals, and other information services	14 322	14 331	14 827	15 136
517	Telecommunications	123 511	125 212	126 738	126 854
5171	Wired telecommunications carriers	46 710	46 505	46 689	45 755
5172	Wireless telecommunications carriers (except satellite)	45 116	45 947	47 123	47 589
5175	Cable and other program distribution	26 341	27 113	27 389	28 145
517pt	Other telecommunications	5 344	5 647	5 537	5 365
5182	Data processing, hosting, and related services	17 309	18 059	17 284	18 084
54	**Professional, Scientific, and Technical Services**	327 843	340 849	334 466	343 603
54 pt	Professional, scientific, and technical services (except landscape architectural services and veterinary services)	320 639	332 849	326 467	336 210
5411	Legal services	58 082	63 670	62 327	68 168
5412	Accounting, tax preparation, bookkeeping, and payroll services	38 661	34 273	26 969	28 569
5413	Architectural, engineering, and related services	62 563	66 462	68 440	69 289
5413pt	Architectural and related services	18 100	18 837	19 174	18 424
54133	Engineering services	44 463	47 625	49 266	50 865
5415	Computer systems design and related services	61 714	63 612	63 693	64 702
5416	Management, scientific, and technical consulting services	40 851	42 812	42 663	43 192
5417	Scientific research and development services	25 503	27 419	27 998	28 146
5418	Advertising and related services	20 240	20 765	21 286	21 270
541pt	Other professional, scientific, and technical services [1]	45 732	49 255	49 088	48 413
541pt	Other professional, scientific, and technical services [2]	20 229	21 836	21 090	20 267
56	**Administrative and support and waste management and remediation services**	148 024	153 540	154 028	151 473
56pt	Administrative and support and waste management and remediation services except landscaping services	138 222	141 290	141 014	139 733
561	Administrative and support services	130 046	133 751	134 516	132 156
5613	Employment services	45 992	46 634	46 917	46 953
5615	Travel arrangement and reservation services	7 948	8 485	8 170	7 361
561pt	Other administrative and support services	76 106	78 632	79 429	77 842
561 pt	Other administrative and support services (except landscaping services)	66 304	66 382	66 415	66 102
562	Waste management and remediation services	17 978	19 789	19 512	19 317
62pt	**Selected Health Care Services**	223 760	224 456	221 984	226 320
622	Hospitals	181 581	181 400	179 208	182 957
623	Nursing and residential care facilities	42 179	43 056	42 776	43 363
SEASONALLY ADJUSTED					
51	Information	284 024	283 269	282 249	278 917
54 (pt)	**Professional, Scientific, and Technical Services (Except Landscape Architectural Services and Veterinary Services)**	325 192	329 227	331 775	329 618
5411	Legal services	62 387	64 054	64 122	61 746
5412	Accounting, tax preparation, bookkeeping, and payroll services	31 978	32 517	32 221	31 849
56 pt	**Administrative and Support and Waste Management and Remediation Services (Except Landscaping Services)**	140 117	140 535	140 718	139 059
5613	Employment services	46 883	46 774	47 058	45 853
5615	Travel arrangement and reservation services	8 085	7 997	8 097	7 806
562	Waste management and remediation services	18 845	19 382	19 148	19 298

[1]Including 5417, scientific research and development.
[2]Excluding 5417.

NOTES AND DEFINITIONS

TABLE 17-1
PETROLEUM AND PETROLEUM PRODUCTS—PRICES, IMPORTS, DOMESTIC PRODUCTION, AND STOCKS

SOURCES: FUTURES PRICES—U.S. DEPARTMENT OF ENERGY, ENERGY INFORMATION ADMINISTRATION (EIA), AND U.S. DEPARTMENT OF COMMERCE, BUREAU OF ECONOMIC ANALYSIS; IMPORTS—U.S. DEPARTMENT OF COMMERCE, CENSUS BUREAU (SEE NOTES AND DEFINITIONS FOR TABLES 7-9 THROUGH 7-14); SUPPLY (NET IMPORTS AND DOMESTIC PRODUCTION) AND STOCKS—EIA.

Definitions and notes on the data

The *crude oil futures price* in *current dollars per barrel* is the price for next-month delivery in Cushing, Oklahoma (a pipeline hub), of light, sweet crude oil, as determined by trading on the New York Mercantile Exchange (NYMEX). Official daily closing prices are reported each day at 2:30 p.m., and are tabulated weekly in Table 16 of *EIA's Weekly Petroleum Status Report*. The monthly averages shown in this volume are the average prices for the nearest future from each trading day of the month. For example, for most days in January, the futures contract priced will be for February; for the last few days in January, the February contract will have expired and the March contract will be quoted. The annual averages are averages of the monthly averages.

The *crude oil futures price* in *2000 dollars* is calculated by the editor and divides the current-dollar price by the chain price index for total personal consumption expenditures (PCE), with the price index average for the year 2000 set at 1.0000. The PCE chain price index is compiled by the Bureau of Economic Analysis (BEA). It is described in the notes and definitions for Chapter 1 and is also presented in Chapter 8 and discussed in its notes and definitions.

The import data in Columns 3 through 6 of this table are those published as Exhibit 17, "Imports of Energy-related Petroleum Products, including Crude Petroleum," in the monthly Census-BEA foreign trade press release, FT900. *Total energy-related petroleum products* includes the following Standard International Trade Classification (SITC) commodity groupings: crude oil, petroleum preparations, and liquefied propane and butane gas.

The data in Columns 7 through 11, on exports, imports, and net imports (imports minus exports) of petroleum and products and domestic production of crude oil and natural gas plant liquids (all expressed as thousands of barrels per day), and in Columns 12 through 14, depicting stocks of crude oil in millions of barrels, are derived from the Department of Energy's weekly petroleum supply reporting system. They are published in EIA's *Monthly Energy Review* and can be found in Tables 3.1 and 3.4. Stock totals are as of the end of the period. Geographic coverage includes the 50 states and the District of Columbia.

Data availability

Data on futures prices, petroleum supply and stocks are available from the EIA Web site at <http://www.eia.doe.gov>, under the categories "Publications and Reports/Monthly Energy Review" and "Petroleum/Weekly Petroleum Status Report." The *Monthly Energy Review* is no longer published in printed form.

See the notes and definitions for Tables 7-9 through 7-14 for information about the availability of import data.

TABLE 17-2
CONSTRUCTION PUT IN PLACE

SOURCE: U.S. DEPARTMENT OF COMMERCE, CENSUS BUREAU

The Census Bureau's estimates of the value of new construction put in place are intended to provide monthly estimates of the total dollar value of construction work done in the United States.

Definitions and notes on the data

The estimates cover all construction work done each month on new private residential and nonresidential buildings and structures, public construction, and improvements to existing buildings and structures. Included are the cost of labor, materials, and equipment rental; cost of architectural and engineering work; overhead costs assigned to the project; interest and taxes paid during construction; and contractor's profits.

The total value put in place for a given period is the sum of the value of work done on all projects underway during this period, regardless of when work on each individual project was started or when payment was made to the contractors. For some categories, estimates are derived by distributing the total construction cost of the project by means of historic construction progress patterns. Published estimates represent payments made during a period for some categories.

The statistics on the value of construction put in place result from direct measurement and indirect estimation. A series results from direct measurement when it is based on reports of the actual value of construction progress or construction expenditures obtained in a complete census or a sample survey. All other series are developed by indirect estimation using related construction statistics. On an annual basis, estimates for series directly measured monthly, quarterly, or annually accounted for about 71 percent of total construction in 1998 (private multifamily residential, private residential improvements, private nonresidential buildings, farm nonresidential construction, public utility construction, all other private construction, and virtually all of public construction). On a monthly basis, directly measured data are available for about 55 percent of the value in place estimates.

Beginning in 1993, the Construction Expenditures Branch of the Census Bureau's Manufacturing and Construction Division began collecting these data using a new classification system, which bases project types on their end usage instead of on building/nonbuilding types. Data collection on this system for federal construction began in January 2002.

With the changes in project classifications, data presented in these tables for 1993 to date are not directly comparable with data for previous years, except at aggregate levels. For that reason, *Business Statistics* shows earlier historical data only at these aggregate levels. Although some categories, such as lodging, office, education, and religion, have the same names as categories in previously published data, there have been changes within the classifications that make these values noncomparable. For example, private medical office buildings were classified as "office" buildings previously, but are categorized as "health care" under the new classification.

The seasonally adjusted data are obtained by removing normal seasonal movement from the unadjusted data to bring out underlying trends and business cycles, which is accomplished by using the Census X-12-ARIMA method. Seasonal adjustment accounts for month-to-month variations resulting from normal or average changes in any phenomena affecting the data, such as weather conditions, the differing lengths of months, and the varying number of holidays, weekdays, and weekends within each month. It does not adjust for abnormal conditions within each month or for year-to-year variations in weather. The seasonally adjusted annual rate is the seasonally adjusted monthly rate multiplied by 12.

Residential consists of new houses, town houses, apartments, and condominiums for sale or rent; these dwellings are built by the owner or for the owner on contract. It includes improvements inside and outside residential structures, such as remodeling, additions, major replacements, and additions of swimming pools and garages. Manufactured housing, houseboats, and maintenance and repair work are not included.

Office includes general office buildings, administration buildings, professional buildings, and financial institution buildings. Office buildings at manufacturing sites are classified as *manufacturing,* but office buildings owned by manufacturing companies but not at such a site are included in the *office* category. In the state and local government category, *office* includes capitols, city halls, courthouses, and similar buildings.

Commercial includes buildings and structures used by the retail, wholesale, farm, and selected service industries. One of the subgroups of this category is *multi-retail,* which consists of department and variety stores, shopping centers and malls, and warehouse-type retail stores.

Health care includes hospitals, medical buildings, nursing homes, adult day-care centers, and similar institutions.

Educational includes schools at all levels, higher education facilities, trade schools, libraries, museums, and similar institutions.

Amusement and recreation includes theme and amusement parks, sports structures not located at educational institutions, fitness centers and health clubs, neighborhood centers, camps, movie theaters, and similar establishments.

Transportation includes airport facilities; rail facilities, track, and bridges; bus, rail, maritime, and air terminals; and docks, marinas, and similar structures.

Communication includes telephone, television, and radio distribution and maintenance structures.

Power includes electricity production and distribution and gas and crude oil transmission, storage, and distribution.

Manufacturing includes all buildings and structures at manufacturing sites but not the installation of production machinery or special-purpose equipment.

Included in *total private construction,* but not shown separately in these pages, are lodging facilities (hotels and motels), religious structures, and private public safety, sewage and waste disposal, water supply, highway and street, and conservation and development spending.

Included in *total state and local construction,* but not shown separately in these pages, are state and local construction of commercial buildings, conservation and development (dams, levees, jetties, and dredging), lodging, religious facilities, and communication structures.

Public safety includes correctional facilities, police and sheriffs' stations, fire stations, and similar establishments.

Highway and street includes pavement, lighting, retaining walls, bridges, tunnels, toll facilities, and maintenance and rest facilities.

Sewage and waste disposal includes sewage systems, solid waste disposal, and recycling.

Water supply includes water supply, transmission, and storage facilities.

Among the data sources for construction expenditures are the Census Bureau's Survey of Construction, Building Permits Survey, Consumer Expenditure Survey (conducted for the Bureau of Labor Statistics), Annual Capital Expenditures Survey, and Construction Progress Reporting Survey; also included are data from the F.W. Dodge Division of the McGraw-Hill Information Systems Company, the U.S. Department of Agriculture, and utility regulatory agencies.

Data availability

Each month's "Construction Spending" press release is released on the last workday of the following month. The release, more detailed data, and a discussion of methodologies can be found on the Census Bureau's Web site at <http://www.census.gov/constructionspending>.

TABLE 17-3
HOUSING STARTS AND BUILDING PERMITS;
NEW HOUSE SALES AND PRICES

SOURCE: U.S. DEPARTMENT OF COMMERCE, CENSUS BUREAU

These data are mainly found in two major Census Bureau reports, "New Residential Construction" and "New Residential Sales." They cover new housing units intended for occupancy and maintained by the occupants, excluding hotels, motels, and group residential structures. Manufactured home units are reported in a separate survey.

Definitions

A *housing unit* is a house, an apartment, or a group of rooms or single room intended for occupancy as separate living quarters. Occupants must live separately from other individuals in the building and have direct access to the housing unit from the outside of the building or through a common hall. Each apartment unit in an apartment building is counted as one housing unit. As of January 2000, a previous requirement for residents to have the capability to eat separately has been eliminated. (Based on the old definition, some senior housing projects were excluded from the multifamily housing statistics because individual units did not have their own eating facilities.) Housing starts exclude group quarters such as dormitories or rooming houses, transient accommodations such as motels, and manufactured homes. Publicly owned housing units are excluded, but units in structures built by private developers with subsidies or for sale to local public housing authorities are both classified as private housing.

The *start* of construction of a privately owned housing unit is when excavation begins for the footings or foundation of a building primarily intended as a housekeeping residential structure and designed for nontransient occupancy. All housing units in a multifamily building are defined as being started when excavation for the building begins.

One-family structures includes fully detached, semi-detached, row houses, and townhouses. In the case of attached units, each must be separated from the adjacent unit by a ground-to-roof wall to be classified as a one-unit structure and must not share facilities such as heating or water supply. Units built one on top of another and those built side-by-side without a ground-to-roof wall and/or with common facilities are classified by the number of units in the structure.

Apartment buildings are defined as buildings containing *five units or more.* The type of ownership is not the criterion—a condominium apartment building is not classified as one-family structures but as a multifamily structure.

A *manufactured* home is a moveable dwelling, 8 feet or more wide and 40 feet or more long, designed to be towed on its own chassis with transportation gear integral to the unit when it leaves the factory, and without need of a permanent foundation. Multiwides and expandable manufactured homes are included. Excluded are travel trailers, motor homes, and modular housing. The shipments figures are based on reports submitted by manufacturers on the number of homes actually shipped during the survey month. Shipments to dealers may not necessarily be placed for residential use in the same month as they are shipped. The number of manufactured "homes" used for nonresidential purposes (for example, those used for offices) is not known.

Units authorized by building permits represents the approximately 97 percent of housing in permit-requiring areas.

The *start* occurs when excavation begins for the footing or foundation. Starts are estimated for all areas, regardless of whether permits are required.

New house *sales* are reported only for new single-family residential structures. The sales transaction must intend to include both house and land. Excluded are houses built for rent, houses built by the owner, and houses built by a contractor on the owner's land. A sale is reported when a deposit is taken or a sales agreement is signed; this can occur prior to a permit being issued.

Once the sale is reported, the sold housing unit drops out of the survey. Consequently the Census Bureau does not find out if the sales contract is cancelled or if the house is ever resold. As a result, if conditions are worsening and cancellations are high, sales are temporarily overestimated. When conditions improve and the cancelled sales materialize as actual sales, the Census sales estimates are then underestimated because the case did not re-enter the survey. In the long run, cancellations do not cause the survey to overestimate or underestimate sales; but in the short run, cancellations and ultimate resales are not reflected in this survey, and fluctuations can appear less severe than in reality.

A house is *for sale* when a permit to build has been issued (or work begun in non-permit areas) and a sales contract has not been signed nor a deposit accepted.

The *sales price* used in this survey is the price agreed upon between the purchaser and the seller at the time the first sales contract is signed or deposit made. It includes the price of the improved lot. The *median sales price* is the sales price of the house that falls on the middle point of a distribution by price of the total number of houses sold. Half of the houses sold have a sales lower than the median; half have a price higher than the median. Changes in the *sales price* data reflect changes in the distribution of houses by region, size, and the like, as well as changes in the prices of houses with identical characteristics.

The *price index* measures the change in price of a new single-family house of constant physical characteristics, using the characteristics of houses built in 1996. Characteristics held constant include floor area, whether inside or outside a metropolitan area, number of bedrooms, number of bathrooms, number of fireplaces, type of parking facility, type of foundation, presence of a deck, construction method, exterior wall material, type of heating, and presence of air-conditioning. The indexes are calculated separately for attached and detached houses and combined with base period weights. The price measured includes the value of the lot.

See the notes and definitions to Table 12-10 for a discussion of the characteristics of the various price indexes for single-family houses.

Notes on the data

Monthly permit authorizations are based on data collected by a mail survey from a sample of about 9,000 permit-issuing places, selected from and representing a universe of 20,000 such places in the United States. The remaining places are surveyed annually. Data for 1994 through 2003 represented 19,000 places; data for 1984 through 1993 represented 17,000 places; data for 1978 through 1983 represented 16,000 places; data for 1972 through 1977 represented 14,000 places; data for 1967 through 1971 represented 13,000 places; data for 1963 through 1966 represented 12,000 places; and data for 1959 through 1962 represented 10,000 places.

Housing starts and sales data are obtained from the Survey of Construction, for which Census Bureau field representatives sample both permit-issuing and non-permit-issuing places.

Effective with the January 2005 data release, the Survey of Construction implemented a new sample of building permit offices, replacing a previous sample selected in 1985. As a result, writes the Census Bureau, "Data users should uses caution when analyzing year over year changes in housing prices and characteristics between 2004 and 2005." In the newer sample, land may be more abundant, lot sizes larger, and sales prices lower.

For 2004, the permit data were compiled for both the new 20,000 place universe and the old 19,000 place universe. Ratios of the new estimates to the old were calculated by state for total housing units, structures by number of units, and valuation. For the United States as a whole, the new estimate was 100.9 percent of the old estimate. The complete table of ratios can be found on the Census Bureau Web site at <http://www.census.gov/const/www/permitsindex>.

Effective with the data for April 2001, the Census Bureau made changes to the methodology used for new house sales, including discontinuing an adjustment for con-

struction in areas in which building permits are required without a permit being issued. It was believed that such unauthorized construction has virtually ceased. The upward adjustment was not phased out but dropped completely in revised estimates as of January 1999. The total effect of these changes was to lower the number of sales by about 2.9 percent relative to those published for earlier years.

The data used in the price index are collected in the Survey of Construction, through monthly interviews with the builders or owners. The size of the sample is currently about 20,000 observations per year.

Data availability and references

Housing starts and building permit data have been collected monthly by the Bureau of the Census since 1959.

The monthly report for "New Residential Construction" (permits, starts, and completions) is issued in the middle of the following month. The monthly report and associated descriptions and historical data can be found at <http://www.census.gov/newresconst>.

The monthly report for "New Residential Sales" (sales, houses for sale, and prices) is issued toward the end of the following month. The monthly report and associated descriptions and historical data can be found at <http://www.census.gov/newhomesales>.

The manufactured housing data (not seasonally adjusted) and background information can be found at <http://www.manufacturedhousing.org/statistics>. Data with and without seasonal adjustment can be found at <http://www.census.gov/const/mhs/shiphist>.

Data and background on the price index for new one-family houses can be found at <http://www.census.gov/const/price_sold>.

TABLES 17-4 THROUGH 17-7
MANUFACTURERS' SHIPMENTS, INVENTORIES, AND ORDERS

SOURCE: U.S. DEPARTMENT OF COMMERCE, CENSUS BUREAU

These data are from the Census Bureau's monthly M3 survey, a sample-based survey that provides measures of changes in the value of domestic manufacturing activity and indications of future production commitments. The sample includes approximately 4,300 reporting units, including most companies with $500 million or more in annual shipments and a selection of smaller companies. Currently, reported monthly data represent approximately 61 percent of shipments at the total manufacturing level.

One important technology industry, semiconductors, is represented in the shipments and inventories data in this report but not in new or unfilled orders. This affects the new and unfilled orders totals for computers and electronic products, durable goods industries, and total manufacturing. Based on shipments data, semiconductors accounted for about 15 percent of computers and electronic products, 3 percent of durable goods industries, and 1.5 percent of total manufacturing. Since semiconductors are intermediate materials and components rather than finished final products, the absence of these data does not distort new and unfilled orders data for important final demand categories, such as capital goods and information technology.

Definitions and notes on the data

Shipments. The value of shipments data represent net selling values, f.o.b. (free on board) plant, after discounts and allowances and excluding freight charges and excise taxes. For multi-establishment companies, the M3 reports are typically company- or division-level reports that encompass groups of plants or products. The data reported are usually net sales and receipts from customers and do not include the value of interplant transfers. The reported sales are used to calculate month-to-month changes that bring forward the estimates for the entire industry (that is, estimates of the statistical "universe") that have been developed from the Annual Survey of Manufactures (ASM). The value of products made elsewhere under contract from materials owned by the plant is also included in shipments, along with receipts for contract work performed for others, resales, miscellaneous activities such as the sale of scrap and refuse, and installation and repair work performed by employees of the plant.

Inventories. Inventories in the M3 survey are collected on a current cost or pre-LIFO (last in, first out) basis. As different inventory valuation methods are reflected in the reported data, the estimates differ slightly from replacement cost estimates. Companies using the LIFO method for valuing inventories report their pre-LIFO value; the adjustment to their base-period prices is excluded. In the ASM, inventories are collected according to this same definition. However, there are discontinuities in the historical data in both surveys. Inventory data prior to 1982 are not comparable to later years because of changes in valuation methods. Until 1982, respondents were asked in the ASM to report their inventories at book values—that is, according to whatever method they used for tax purposes (LIFO, FIFO [first in, first out], and so forth). Because of this, the value of aggregate inventories for an industry was not precise. The change in instructions for reporting current cost inventories was carried to the monthly survey beginning in January 1987. The data for 1982 to 1987 were redefined (but not re-collected by survey) on a pre-LIFO, or current cost, basis.

Inventory data are requested from respondents by three stages of fabrication: finished goods, work in process, and raw materials and supplies. Response to the stage of fabrication inquiries is lower than for total inventories; not all companies keep their monthly data at this level of detail. It should be noted that a product considered to be a finished

good in one industry, such as steel mill shapes, may be reported as a raw material in another industry, such as stamping plants. For some purposes, this difference in definitions is an advantage. When a factory accumulates inventory that it considers to be raw materials, it can be expected that that accumulation is intentional. But when a factory—whether a materials-making or a final-product producer—has a buildup of finished goods inventories, it may indicate involuntary accumulation as a result of sales falling short of expectations. Hence, the two types of accumulation can have different economic interpretations, even if they represent identical types of goods.

Like total inventories, stage of fabrication inventories are benchmarked to the ASM data. Stage of fabrication data are benchmarked at the major group level, as opposed to the level of total inventories, which is benchmarked at the individual industry level.

New orders, as reported in the monthly survey, are net of order cancellations and includes orders received and filled during the month as well as orders received for future delivery. They also include the value of contract changes that increase or decrease the value of the unfilled orders to which they relate. Orders are defined to include those supported by binding legal documents such as signed contracts, letters of award, or letters of intent, although this definition may not be strictly applicable in some industries.

Unfilled orders includes new orders (as defined above) that have not been reflected as shipments. Generally, unfilled orders at the end of the reporting period are equal to unfilled orders at the beginning of the period plus net new orders received less net shipments.

Series are adjusted for seasonal variation and variation in the number of trading days in the month using the X-12-ARIMA version of the Census Bureau's seasonal adjustment program.

Benchmarking and revisions

The M3 series are periodically benchmarked and their seasonal adjustment factors recalculated. In the latest benchmark, published in May 2008 and available on the Census Bureau Web site, the shipments and inventory data were benchmarked to the 2006 ASM, new and unfilled orders were adjusted to be consistent with the benchmarked shipments and inventory data, and other corrections were made. Seasonal adjustment factors were also revised and updated for all series.

Data availability and references

Data have been collected monthly since 1958.

The "Advance Report on Durable Goods Manufacturers' Shipments, Inventories and Orders" is available as a press release about 18 working days after the end of each month. It includes seasonally adjusted and not seasonally adjusted estimates of shipments, new orders, unfilled orders, and inventories for durable goods industries.

The monthly "Manufacturers' Shipments, Inventories, and Orders" report is released on the 23rd working day after the end of the month. Content includes revisions to the advance durable goods data, estimates for nondurable goods industries, tabulations by market category, and ratios of shipments to inventories and to unfilled orders. Revisions may affect selected data for the two previous months.

Press releases, historical data, descriptions of the survey, and extensive documentation of the new NAICS including comparisons with the SIC are available on the Census Bureau Web site at <http://www.census.gov>, under the category "Economic Indicators."

TABLE 17-8
MOTOR VEHICLE SALES AND INVENTORIES

Source: U.S. Department of Commerce, Bureau of Economic Analysis

Retail sales and *inventories of cars, trucks, and buses.* These estimates are prepared by the Bureau of Economic Analysis (BEA), based on data from the American Automobile Manufacturers Association, Ward's Automotive Reports, and other sources. Seasonal adjustments are recalculated annually. Data are available on the BEA Web site at <http://www.bea.gov> as a part of the national income and product accounts data set; they are found under the "Supplemental Estimates" heading. They are also available on the STAT-USA subscription Web site at <http://www.stat-usa.gov>.

In this table, unlike in some other tables that include inventories in *Business Statistics,* the yearly values shown for inventories and the inventory to sales ratio are annual averages of monthly figures.

TABLES 17-9 AND 17-11
RETAIL AND FOOD SERVICES SALES; RETAIL INVENTORIES

Source: U.S. Department of Commerce, Census Bureau

Every month, the Census Bureau prepares estimates of retail sales and inventories by kind of business, based on a mail-out/mail-back survey of about 12,500 retail businesses with paid employees.

Retail sales and inventories are now compiled using the new NAICS classification system, which replaced the old SIC system. Historical data have been restated on the NAICS basis back to January 1992. In NAICS, Eating and drinking places and Mobile food services have been reclassified out of retail trade and into sector 72, Accommodation and food services, which also includes Hotels. The retail sales survey still collects and publishes sales data for Food services and drinking places. It no longer includes them in the Retail total, but they are included in a new Retail and food services total.

Subtotals of durable and nondurable goods are no longer published. They were always imprecise for retail sales, since general merchandise stores (including department stores) were included in nondurable goods, yet obviously sold substantial quantities of durable goods.

For further information about SIC and NAICS, see Chapter 14.

Definitions

Sales is the value of merchandise sold for cash or credit at retail or wholesale. Services that are incidental to the sale of merchandise, and excise taxes that are paid by the manufacturer or wholesaler and passed along to the retailer, are also included. Sales are net, after deductions for refunds and merchandise returns. They exclude sales taxes collected directly from customers and paid directly to a local, state, or federal tax agency. The sales estimates include only sales by establishments primarily engaged in retail trade, and are not intended to measure the total sales for a given commodity or merchandise line.

Inventories is the value of stocks of goods held for sale through retail stores, valued at cost, as of the last day of the report period. Stocks may be held either at the store or at warehouses that maintain supplies primarily intended for distribution to retail stores within the organization.

Inventory data prior to 1980 are not comparable to later years, due to changes in valuation methods. Prior to 1980, inventories are the book values of merchandise on hand at the end of the period. They are valued according to the valuation method used by each respondent. Thus the aggregates are a mixture of LIFO (last in, first out) and non-LIFO values. Beginning with 1980, inventories are valued using methods other than LIFO in order to better reflect the current costs of goods held as inventory.

Leased departments consists of the operations of one company conducted within the establishment of another company, such as jewelry counters or optical centers within department stores. The values for sales and inventories at department stores in Tables 17-9 and 17-10 exclude sales of leased departments.

GAFO (department store type goods) is a special aggregate grouping of sales at general merchandise stores and at other stores that sell merchandise normally sold in department stores—clothing and accessories, furniture and home furnishings, electronics, appliances, sporting goods, hobby, book, music, office supplies, stationery, and gifts.

Notes on the data

The new NAICS-based data have been benchmarked to the 2002, 1997, and 1992 Economic Censuses and the Annual Retail Trade Surveys for 2006 and previous years. Each year, the monthly series are benchmarked to the latest annual survey and new factors are incorporated to adjust for seasonal, trading-day, and holiday variations, using the Census Bureau's X-12-ARIMA program. The data shown here incorporate the 2006 benchmark revision issued in April 2008.

The survey sample is stratified by kind of business and estimated sales. All firms with sales above applicable size cut-offs are included. Firms are selected randomly from the remaining strata. The sample used for the end-of-month inventory estimates is a sub-sample of the monthly sales sample, about one-third of the size of the whole sample.

New samples, designed to produce NAICS estimates, were introduced with the 1999 Annual Retail Trade Survey and the March 2001 Monthly Retail Trade Survey. On November 30, 2006, another new sample was introduced, affecting the data for September 2006 and the following months. The sample is updated quarterly to take account of business births and deaths.

Data availability and references

An "Advance Monthly Retail Sales" report is released about nine working days after the close of the reference month, based on responses from a sub-sample of the complete retail sample.

The revised and more complete monthly "Retail Trade, Sales, and Inventories" reports are released six weeks after the close of the reference month. They contain preliminary figures for the current month and final figures for the prior 12 months. Statistics include retail sales, inventories, and ratios of inventories to sales. Data are both seasonally adjusted and unadjusted.

The "Annual Benchmark Report for Retail Trade" is released each spring. It includes updated seasonal adjustment factors; revised and benchmarked monthly estimates of sales and inventories; monthly data for the most recent 10 or more years; detailed annual estimates and ratios for the United States by kind of business; and comparable prior-year statistics and year-to-year changes. The latest such report available when *Business Statistics* was compiled was U.S. Census Bureau, *Annual Revision of Monthly Retail and Food Services: Sales and inventories—January 1992 through February 2008,* issued in April 2008 and available on the Census Bureau Web site at <http://www.census.gov/mrts>, along with the latest data releases and complete historical data.

TABLE 17-10
QUARTERLY RETAIL SALES: TOTAL AND E-COMMERCE

SOURCE: U.S. DEPARTMENT OF COMMERCE, CENSUS BUREAU

Beginning with the fourth quarter of 1999, the Census Bureau has conducted a quarterly survey of retail e-commerce sales from the Monthly Retail Trade Survey sample. (The monthly survey does not report electronic shopping separately; it is combined with mail order.) E-commerce sales are the sales of goods and services in which an order is placed by the buyer or the price and terms of sale are negotiated over the Internet or an extranet, Electronic Data Interchange (EDI) network, electronic mail, or other online system. Payment may or may not be made online. The quarterly release is issued around the 20th of February, May, August, and November, and is available along with full historical data on the Census Bureau Web site at <http://www.census.gov>. It can be located under the heading "Retail" in the alphabetical Web site index, under "E" for "Economic data and information."

These estimates reflect the NAICS definition of retail sales, which excludes food service. Online travel services, financial brokers and dealers, and ticket sales agencies are not classified as retail and are not included in these estimates; they are, however, included in the annual survey of selected services. See Table 17-16 for more information.

TABLE 17-12
MERCHANT WHOLESALERS—SALES AND INVENTORIES

SOURCE: U.S. DEPARTMENT OF COMMERCE, CENSUS BUREAU

These data are based on a monthly mail-out/mail-back sample survey conducted by the Census Bureau.

These data are now based on the new NAICS classification system, which replaced the old SIC system. Historical data have been restated on the NAICS basis back to January 1992.

Classification changes in NAICS

NAICS shifts a significant number of businesses from the Wholesale to the Retail sector. An important new criterion for classification concerns whether or not the establishment is intended to solicit walk-in traffic. If it is, and if it uses mass-media advertising, it is now classified as Retail, even if it also serves business and institutional clients. (See notes on retail trade, above, for the major categories involved in this shift.)

Definitions

Merchant wholesalers includes merchant wholesalers that take title of the goods they sell, as well as jobbers, industrial distributors, exporters, and importers. Excluded are non-merchant wholesalers such as manufacturer sales branches and offices and agents, merchandise or commodity brokers, and commission merchants.

Notes on the data

Inventories are valued using methods other than LIFO (last in, first out) in order to better reflect the current costs of goods held as inventory.

A survey has been conducted monthly since 1946. New samples are drawn every 5 years, most recently in 2006. The samples are updated every quarter to add new businesses and to drop companies that are no longer active.

Data availability and references

"Monthly Wholesale Trade, Sales and Inventories" reports are released six weeks after the close of the reference month. They contain preliminary current-month figures and final figures for the previous month. Statistics include sales, inventories, and stock/sale ratios, along with standard errors. Data are both seasonally adjusted and unadjusted.

The "Annual Benchmark Report for Wholesale Trade" is released each spring. It contains estimated annual sales, monthly and year-end inventories, inventory/sales ratios, purchases, gross margins, and gross margin/sales ratios by kind of business. Annual estimates are benchmarked to the most recent census of wholesale trade. This report also presents the results of a benchmarking operation that revises monthly sales and inventories estimates. Seasonal adjustment factors are revised at the same time, and revised data for both seasonally adjusted and unadjusted values are published.

Data and documentation are available on the Census Bureau Web site at <http://www.census.gov>.

TABLE 17-13
SELECTED SERVICE INDUSTRIES—REVENUE

SOURCE: U.S. DEPARTMENT OF COMMERCE, CENSUS BUREAU

The Census Service Annual Survey provides annual estimates of revenues for selected service industries. The survey is based on a sample of establishments, selected from a universe of firms having paid employees. Firms without paid employees are included in the estimates through administrative data provided by other federal agencies and through imputation.

Data are collected using the North American Industry Classification System (NAICS), and the data for each industry include both taxable and nontaxable firms. They have been adjusted to reflect the results of the 2002 Economic Census.

Notes on the data

There are some discontinuities in the data between 2003 and 2004 reflecting expanded industry coverage and a revision of the classifications within the Information sector, both effective with the data for 2004 and 2005. The discontinuities are noted in the tables. The newly covered industries are landscape architectural services in sector 54, landscaping services in sector 56, and pet care (except veterinary) services in sector 81.

Data availability and references

Data for the latest year and revisions of previous years are published annually as *Current Business Reports, Service Annual Survey*. They are available on the Census Bureau Web site at <http://www.census.gov>.

TABLE 17-14
SELECTED SERVICES, QUARTERLY: ESTIMATED REVENUE FOR EMPLOYER FIRMS

SOURCE: U.S. DEPARTMENT OF COMMERCE, CENSUS BUREAU

New Census data on quarterly revenue for selected service industries are based on information collected from a probability sample of approximately 6,000 employer firms (firms with employees) chosen from the sample from the larger Service Annual Survey (see notes on Table 17-13) and expanded to represent totals—for employer firms only—for the selected industries. Industries are defined according to the 2007 NAICS. An expansion of the survey's scope effective with the second quarter of 2006, to include landscape architectural, landscaping, veterinary, and legal services, is reflected in some discontinuities in the data, noted in the table.

Data for selected industry groups are adjusted for seasonal variation using the X-12 ARIMA program.

Data availability and references

The quarterly release "U.S. Government Estimates of Quarterly Revenue for Selected Services" is available on the Census Web site at <http://www.census.gov/qss> around the middle of the third month following the end of the quarter. Information about the survey and its reliability is included in this release. Also available on the Web site are historical data adjusted to the results of the latest Service Annual Survey.

PART C

HISTORICAL DATA

CHAPTER 18: THE U.S. ECONOMY, 1929–1948

- In this chapter, summary annual statistics for the years 1929 through 1948 are presented, depicting the economy during two of its most tumultuous decades. This period encompasses the "great contraction," the economic collapse that began in August 1929 and lasted until March 1933; a subsequent period of recovery, which failed to return many important economic indicators to their expected trend levels and was interrupted by a new, though less severe, recession; apprehension of coming war, then the outbreak of war in Europe in September 1939, leading to increased war-related production; United States participation in all-out war, beginning with the Japanese attack on Pearl Harbor on December 7, 1941, and ending in 1945, with supercharged production and employment rates; then, rapid demobilization, and return to a high peacetime rate of economic activity by 1948.

- For a first overall view of the economy during these decades, Figure 18-1 shows total U.S. employment as calculated by the Bureau of Economic Analysis, including all private and government jobs, both civilian and military. In this graph a "trend" line is shown connecting the two peacetime high employment levels of 1929 and 1948.

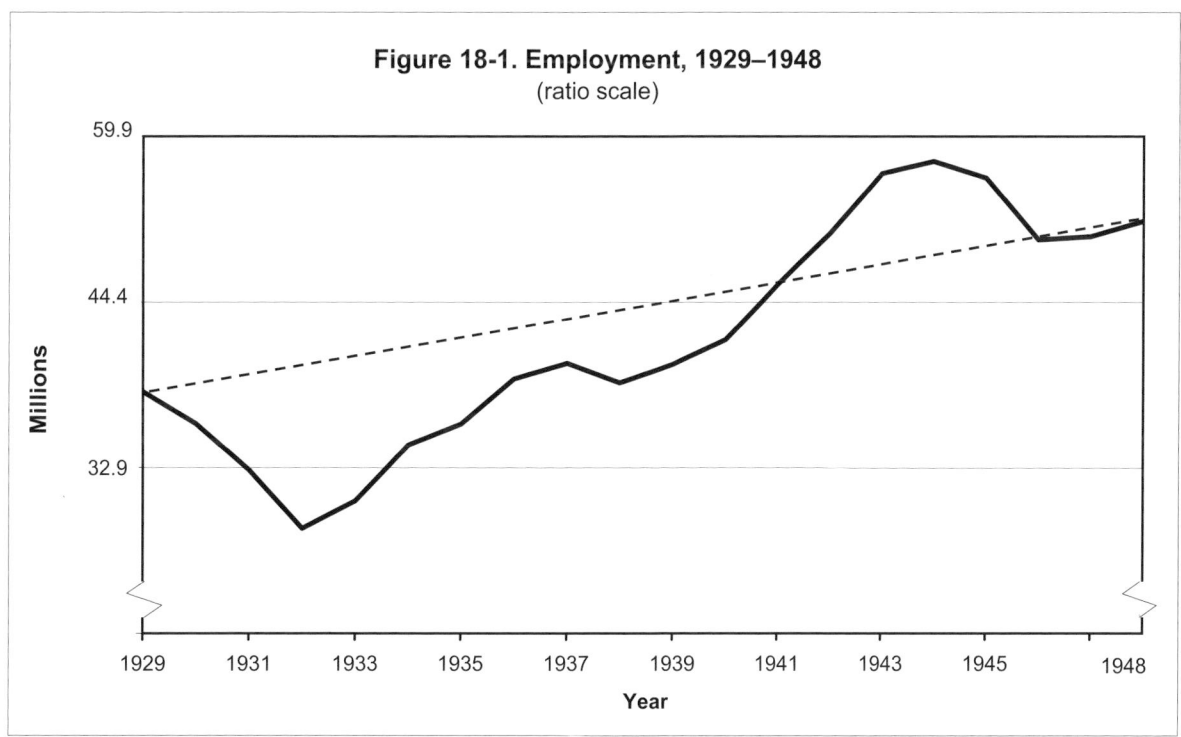

Figure 18-1. Employment, 1929–1948
(ratio scale)

EMPLOYMENT, 1929–1948

- More than one-fifth of all the jobs held in the U.S. in economy in 1929 were gone by 1932. In the subsequent recovery, total employment was back at the 1929 level by 1936, but only because of government employment, including over 3½ million work relief jobs; private industry employment would not recover to its 1929 level until 1941. (Table 18-2)

- Because the recovery was incomplete and economic activity did not recover to a trend level until after the decade's end, the entire decade of the 1930s is often described as "The Great Depression."

- During the war, men were drafted into the armed forces, practically all of the unemployed were put back to work, and women were drawn into the labor force, resulting in a period of what might be called "super-employment." After the war, employment fell back to a more normal trend level. (Tables 18-2 and 18-4)

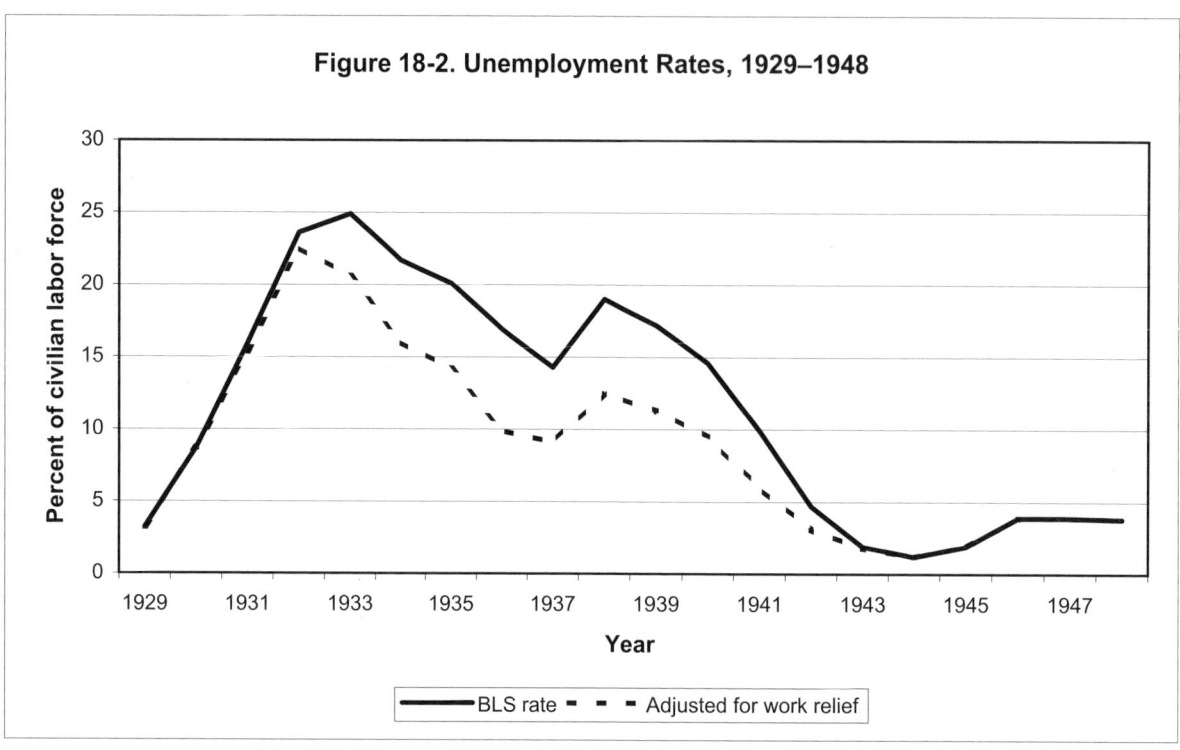

Figure 18-2. Unemployment Rates, 1929–1948

UNEMPLOYMENT RATES, 1929–1947

- The unemployment rates for the prewar period calculated by the Bureau of Labor Statistics, unlike the employment data used in Figure 18-1, count people on government work relief programs as unemployed. By this reckoning, unemployment rose from 3.2 percent of the civilian labor force in 1929 to a peak of 24.9 percent in 1933, and got no lower than 14.3 percent for the rest of the 1930s, as shown in Figure 18-2. (Table 18-4)

- State and local governments started hiring people for work relief in 1930. The Federal government's programs began in 1933, and in 1936 and 1938 agencies such as the WPA and the CCC employed over 3½ million people. When workers in these programs are counted as employed rather than unemployed, the high point for unemployment was 22.5 percent in 1932, and it was reduced to 9.1 percent in 1937, as shown by the dashed line in Figure 18-2. (Table 18-4; see Notes and Definitions for further explanation.)

- By 1943, the economy reached a state of over-full employment, which would have been associated with runaway inflation if not for comprehensive price, wage, and production controls; the years of full wartime production, 1943 through 1945, all saw unemployment rates below 2 percent. After demobilization, the unemployment rate returned to just under 4 percent. (Tables 18-4 and 20-3)

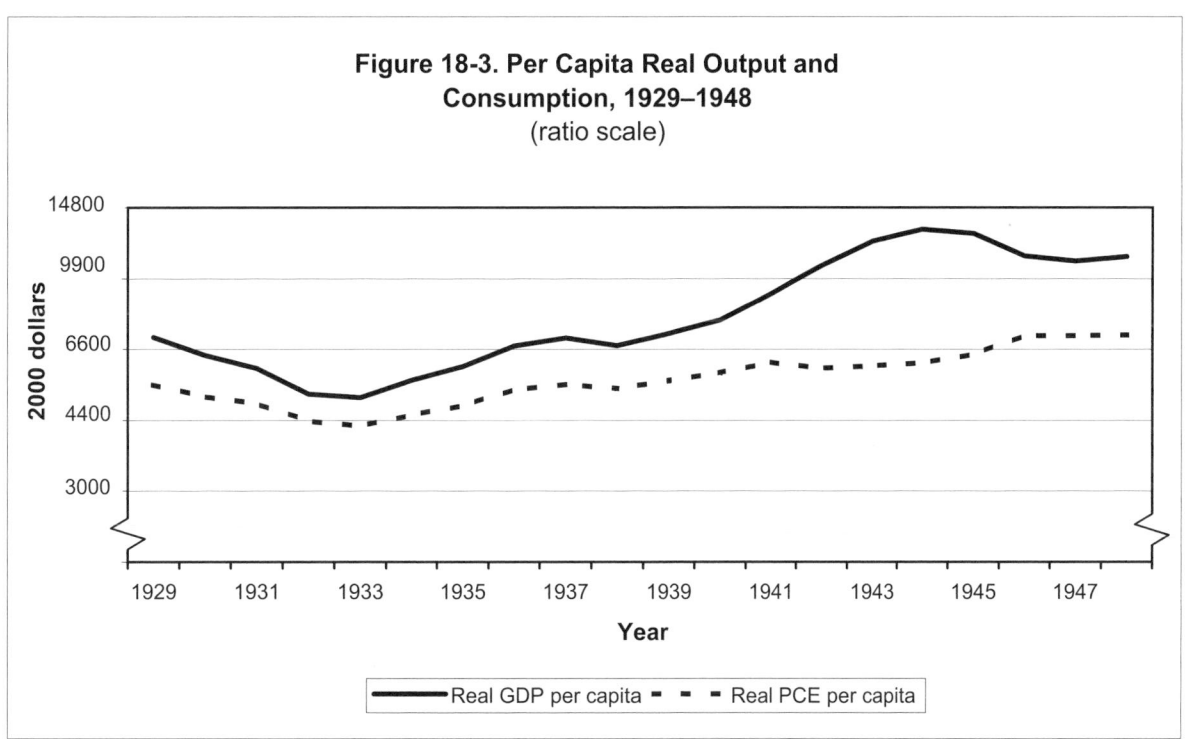

Figure 18-3. Per Capita Real Output and Consumption, 1929–1948
(ratio scale)

PER CAPITA REAL OUTPUT AND CONSUMPTION, 1929–1948

- Real GDP declined 26.5 percent from 1929 to 1933—28.7 percent on a per capita basis. Per capita output recovered almost to the 1929 level in 1937 but fell back 4.2 percent in the 1938 recession. Output then nearly doubled from 1939 to the peak war production year, 1944; the per capita annual growth rate was 12.5 percent. Output fell back during the demobilization, but in 1948 was still at a per capita level representing a 4.9 percent growth rate since 1939. (Table 18-2)

- Per capita personal consumption expenditures fell 20.6 percent from 1929 to 1933. The decline would have been greater if consumers had not dipped into their assets to keep their living standards from declining as steeply as their incomes; the personal saving rate was negative in 1932 and 1933. Per capita consumption recovered to the 1929 level by 1937. Despite rationing and shortages, real per capita consumption spending declined little during the war years. In 1948, it was 29.2 percent above the 1939 level. (Tables 18-1 and 18-2)

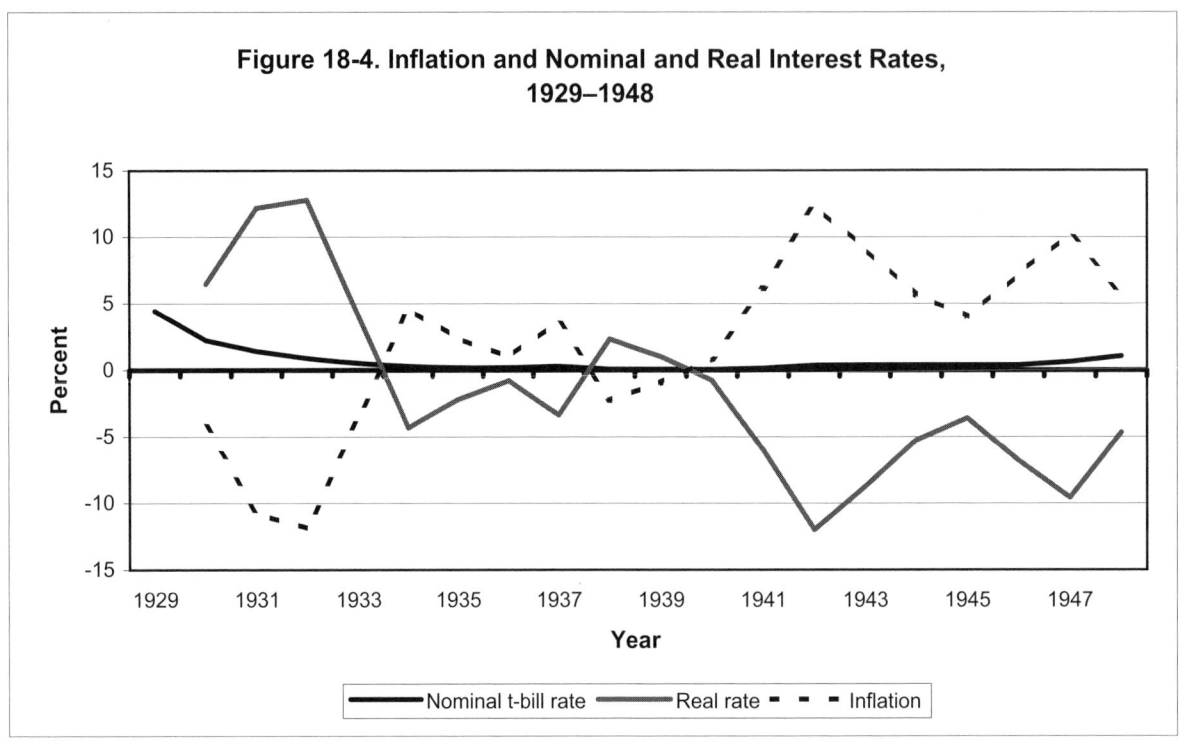

Figure 18-4. Inflation and Nominal and Real Interest Rates, 1929–1948

INFLATION AND NOMINAL AND REAL INTEREST RATES, 1929–1948

- Why was the 1929–1933 contraction so deep and long-lasting? Often, blame is placed on U.S. government tax increases and imposition of new trade barriers (the Smoot-Hawley Tariff), which undoubtedly made their contribution. A substantial number of well-regarded economists, however, point primarily to deflation and its interaction with debt. The price index for personal consumption expenditures, whose rate of change is shown in Figure 18-4, declined 27 percent from 1929 to 1933, for an annual average *deflation* rate of 7.7 percent. Current and prospective price declines make debt more burdensome and debtors more likely to default, as interest payments remain fixed while incomes and asset values decline. (Table 18-2)

- Current and prospective price declines also make borrowing prohibitively expensive; a low nominal interest rate becomes high in real terms (since the real rate is the nominal rate *minus* the inflation rate, and subtraction means changing the sign and adding). A dollar in the hands of a prospective lender will be worth more in terms of purchasing power if he simply holds on to it than if he invests it in some real economic asset or activity whose price will be lower at the end of the year. There is no feasible way for a central bank to lower interest rates below zero in order to reduce real rates in the presence of deflation. As Table 18-5 and Figure 18-4 show, real rates were high from 1930 through 1933 despite near-zero market nominal rates on Treasury bills. (Table 18-5)

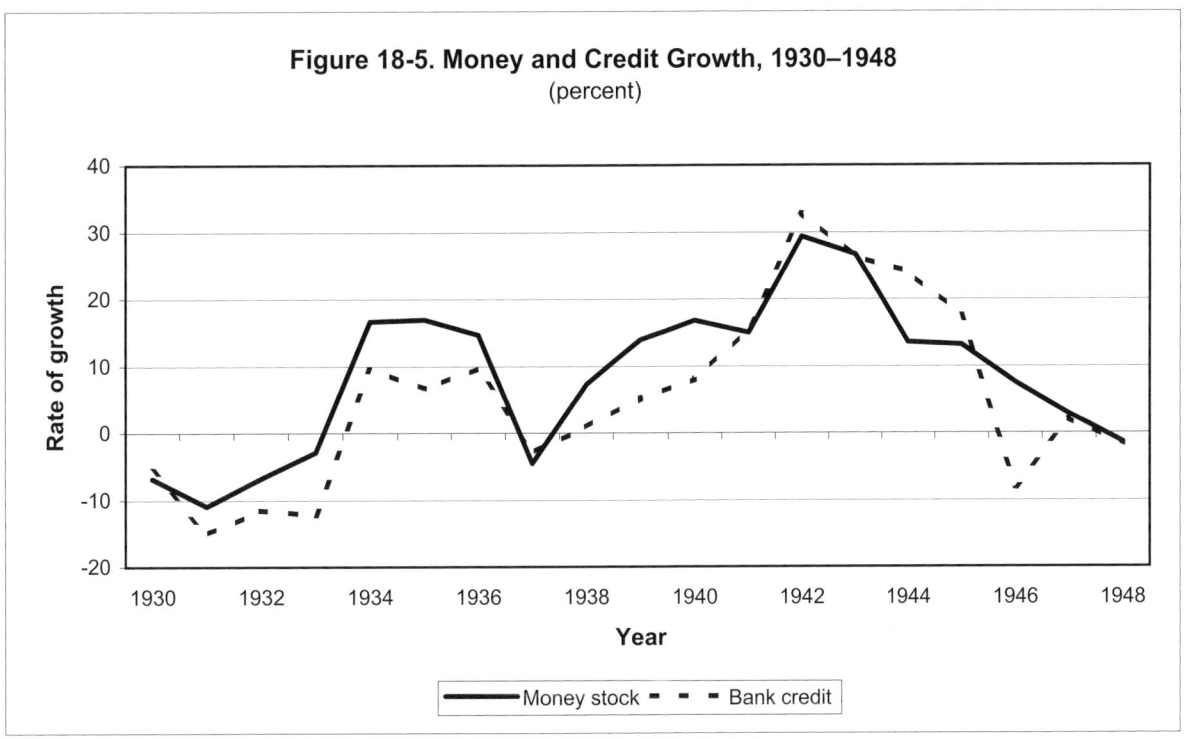

Figure 18-5. Money and Credit Growth, 1930–1948
(percent)

MONEY AND CREDIT GROWTH, 1930–1948

- Deflation was rooted in deep and sustained declines in the dollar volume of money and credit, as shown in Table 18-3 and illustrated in Figure 18-5. The money stock (currency and demand deposits) declined 27 percent from June 30, 1929, to June 30, 1933. Loans and investments at all commercial banks declined 29 percent over the same period. Commercial paper outstanding plunged 76 percent between December 1929 and December 1932, and bankers' acceptances were down 59 percent. (Table 18-3)

- Positive money and credit growth after 1933 was reflected in moderate rates of price increase and moderately negative—which means stimulative—real interest rates. As can be seen in Figures 18-4 and 18-5, there was a monetary component to the 1937–1938 recession (Tables 18-3 and 18-5). There was also a premature federal budget retrenchment at that time. (Table 18-6)

- During the war, monetary policy was pre-empted by wartime needs. Interest rates were held low to facilitate the financing of huge federal deficits. (Tables 18-3 and 18-6)

- Worker incomes increased during the wartime boom as employment, average hours, and hourly wages all rose. But inflation and consumer spending were held down by price and production controls and rationing. Personal saving rates soared when there was little to buy and the government emphasized the sale of "war bonds"; the saving rate reached 26 percent in 1943 and 1944, then fell back to 4.3 percent in 1947, almost equal to its 1929 level. (Tables 18-1 and 18-4)

Table 18-1. National Income and Product Accounts, 1929–1948

(Billions of current dollars, except as noted.)

Classification	1929	1930	1931	1932	1933	1934	1935	1936	1937	1938
Gross domestic product, total	103.6	91.2	76.5	58.7	56.4	66.0	73.3	83.8	91.9	86.1
Personal consumption expenditures, total	77.4	70.1	60.7	48.7	45.9	51.5	55.9	62.2	66.8	64.3
Durable goods	9.2	7.2	5.5	3.6	3.5	4.2	5.1	6.3	6.9	5.7
Nondurable goods	37.7	34.0	29.0	22.7	22.3	26.7	29.3	32.9	35.2	34.0
Services	30.5	29.0	26.2	22.3	20.2	20.5	21.5	23.0	24.7	24.6
Gross private domestic fixed investment, total	14.9	11.0	7.0	3.6	3.1	4.3	5.6	7.5	9.5	7.7
Nonresidential, total	11.0	8.6	5.3	2.9	2.5	3.3	4.3	5.8	7.5	5.5
Structures	5.5	4.4	2.6	1.4	1.1	1.2	1.4	1.9	2.7	2.1
Equipment and software	5.5	4.2	2.6	1.5	1.4	2.1	2.8	3.9	4.8	3.4
Residential	4.0	2.4	1.8	0.8	0.6	0.9	1.3	1.7	2.1	2.1
Change in private inventories	1.5	-0.2	-1.1	-2.4	-1.4	-0.6	1.1	1.2	2.6	-0.6
Net exports of goods and services	0.4	0.3	0.0	0.0	0.1	0.3	-0.2	-0.1	0.1	1.0
Exports	5.9	4.4	2.9	2.0	2.0	2.6	2.8	3.0	4.0	3.8
Imports	5.6	4.1	2.9	1.9	1.9	2.2	3.0	3.2	4.0	2.8
Government consumption expenditures and gross investment, total	9.4	10.0	9.9	8.7	8.7	10.5	10.9	13.1	12.8	13.8
Federal	1.7	1.8	1.9	1.8	2.3	3.3	3.4	5.6	5.1	5.7
National defense	0.9	0.9	0.9	0.9	0.9	0.8	1.0	1.2	1.3	1.4
State and local	7.6	8.2	8.0	6.9	6.4	7.2	7.5	7.5	7.7	8.1
Gross national product	104.4	91.9	77.0	59.1	56.7	66.3	73.6	84.0	92.2	86.5
National income, total	94.2	83.1	67.6	51.3	48.9	58.3	66.3	75.0	83.6	76.8
Compensation of employees	51.1	46.9	39.8	31.1	29.6	34.3	37.4	42.9	45.0	45.0
Proprietors' income with IVA and CCAdj	14.2	11.1	8.5	5.1	5.4	7.1	10.2	10.4	12.6	10.6
Farm	5.8	4.0	3.1	1.8	2.3	2.7	5.0	4.0	5.7	4.1
Nonfarm	8.4	7.0	5.3	3.3	3.1	4.4	5.2	6.4	6.9	6.6
Rental income of persons with CCAdj	6.2	5.5	4.5	3.6	2.9	2.6	2.6	2.8	3.0	3.6
Corporate profits with IVA and CCAdj	10.8	7.5	2.9	-0.2	-0.1	2.5	4.0	6.2	7.1	5.0
Net interest and miscellaneous payments	4.6	4.8	4.8	4.5	4.0	4.0	4.1	3.8	3.7	3.6
Taxes on production and imports	6.8	7.0	6.7	6.6	6.9	7.6	8.0	8.5	8.9	8.9
Less: Subsidies less current surplus of government enterprises	0.0	0.0	0.1	0.1	0.1	0.4	0.5	0.2	0.2	0.4
Business current transfer payments (net)	0.5	0.5	0.5	0.6	0.5	0.5	0.5	0.5	0.5	0.4
Personal income, total	85.1	76.3	65.3	49.9	46.9	53.7	60.4	68.7	74.1	68.4
Less: Personal current taxes	1.7	1.6	1.0	0.7	0.8	0.9	1.1	1.3	1.9	1.9
Equals: Disposable personal income (DPI)	83.4	74.7	64.3	49.2	46.1	52.8	59.3	67.4	72.2	66.6
Less: Personal outlays	79.6	71.6	61.8	49.7	46.8	52.3	56.7	63.1	67.9	65.3
Equals: Personal saving	3.8	3.1	2.5	-0.5	-0.7	0.5	2.6	4.3	4.3	1.3
As a percentage of DPI	4.5	4.1	3.9	-0.9	-1.5	1.0	4.3	6.3	6.0	2.0
Gross saving	19.3	15.0	8.3	3.3	3.3	6.4	9.6	11.5	16.2	11.7
Net saving	9.9	5.8	-0.3	-4.2	-3.9	-1.2	2.1	3.6	7.5	2.8
Net private saving	7.4	4.2	0.9	-3.6	-3.4	-0.2	2.8	4.5	5.2	2.1
Net government saving, federal	1.0	0.2	-2.1	-1.3	-0.9	-2.2	-1.9	-3.2	0.2	-1.3
Net government saving, state and local	1.5	1.3	1.0	0.7	0.4	1.2	1.1	2.3	2.0	2.0
Consumption of fixed capital, private	8.4	8.3	7.7	6.7	6.3	6.5	6.5	6.6	7.4	7.6
Consumption of fixed capital, government	1.0	0.9	0.9	0.8	0.9	1.1	1.1	1.2	1.3	1.4
Gross domestic investment, total	19.3	13.9	8.9	3.4	3.7	6.4	9.5	12.8	15.9	11.3
Private	16.5	10.8	5.9	1.3	1.7	3.7	6.7	8.6	12.2	7.1
Government	2.8	3.2	3.0	2.1	1.9	2.7	2.8	4.1	3.8	4.2
Net lending or net borrowing (-), NIPAs	0.8	0.7	0.2	0.2	0.2	0.4	-0.1	-0.1	0.2	1.2
Net domestic investment	9.9	4.7	0.3	-4.1	-3.5	-1.2	1.9	4.9	7.3	2.3
Gross saving as a percentage of gross national income	18.6	16.3	10.9	5.6	5.8	9.7	13.0	13.9	17.5	13.7
Net saving as a percentage of gross national income	9.6	6.3	-0.3	-7.2	-7.0	-1.8	2.8	4.4	8.1	3.2

Table 18-1. National Income and Product Accounts, 1929–1948—*Continued*

(Billions of current dollars, except as noted.)

Classification	1939	1940	1941	1942	1943	1944	1945	1946	1947	1948
Gross domestic product, total	92.2	101.4	126.7	161.9	198.6	219.8	223.1	222.3	244.2	269.2
Personal consumption expenditures, total	67.2	71.3	81.1	89.0	99.9	108.7	120.0	144.3	162.0	175.0
Durable goods	6.7	7.8	9.7	6.9	6.5	6.7	8.0	15.8	20.4	22.9
Nondurable goods	35.1	37.0	42.9	50.8	58.6	64.3	71.9	82.7	90.9	96.6
Services	25.4	26.5	28.5	31.4	34.8	37.6	40.1	45.8	50.7	55.6
Gross private domestic fixed investment, total	9.1	11.2	13.8	8.5	6.9	8.7	12.3	25.1	35.5	42.4
Nonresidential, total	6.1	7.7	9.7	6.3	5.4	7.4	10.6	17.3	23.5	26.8
Structures	2.2	2.6	3.3	2.2	1.8	2.4	3.3	7.4	8.1	9.5
Equipment and software	3.9	5.2	6.4	4.1	3.7	5.0	7.3	9.9	15.3	17.3
Residential	3.0	3.5	4.1	2.2	1.4	1.4	1.7	7.8	12.1	15.6
Change in private inventories	0.2	2.4	4.3	1.9	-0.7	-0.9	-1.5	6.0	-0.6	5.7
Net exports of goods and services	0.8	1.5	1.0	-0.3	-2.2	-2.0	-0.8	7.2	10.8	5.5
Exports	4.0	4.9	5.5	4.4	4.0	4.9	6.8	14.2	18.7	15.5
Imports	3.1	3.4	4.4	4.6	6.3	6.9	7.5	7.0	7.9	10.1
Government consumption expenditures and gross investment, total ...	14.8	15.0	26.5	62.7	94.8	105.3	93.0	39.6	36.4	40.6
Federal	6.0	6.5	18.0	54.1	86.5	97.0	84.1	28.9	22.7	24.2
National defense	1.5	2.5	14.3	51.1	84.2	94.5	82.0	25.2	18.2	18.3
State and local	8.8	8.6	8.6	8.6	8.4	8.4	9.0	10.8	13.7	16.3
Gross national product	92.5	101.7	127.2	162.3	198.9	220.1	223.4	222.9	245.3	270.6
National income, total	82.2	91.2	116.0	149.8	184.5	198.2	198.4	198.5	216.6	243.0
Compensation of employees	48.1	52.2	64.8	85.3	109.6	121.3	123.3	119.6	130.1	142.0
Proprietors' income with IVA and CCAdj	11.2	12.3	16.7	23.4	28.3	29.4	30.8	35.6	34.5	39.3
Farm	4.1	4.1	6.1	9.7	11.6	11.5	11.8	14.2	14.4	16.7
Nonfarm	7.1	8.2	10.6	13.7	16.7	18.0	19.0	21.4	20.2	22.6
Rental income of persons with CCAdj	3.8	3.9	4.5	5.5	6.1	6.5	6.7	7.1	7.2	7.9
Corporate profits with IVA and CCAdj	6.6	9.8	15.5	20.6	24.9	24.9	20.3	17.8	23.7	31.2
Net interest and miscellaneous payments	3.6	3.3	3.3	3.2	2.9	2.4	2.3	1.9	2.5	2.6
Taxes on production and imports	9.1	9.8	11.1	11.5	12.4	13.7	15.1	16.8	18.1	19.7
Less: Subsidies less current surplus of government enterprises	0.7	0.6	0.3	0.4	0.4	0.9	1.0	1.2	0.2	0.3
Business current transfer payments (net)	0.4	0.5	0.5	0.5	0.6	0.8	0.9	0.7	0.7	0.7
Personal income, total	72.9	78.5	96.1	123.5	152.2	166.0	171.7	178.6	191.0	209.8
Less: Personal current taxes	1.5	1.7	2.3	4.9	16.7	17.7	19.4	17.2	19.8	19.2
Equals: Disposable personal income (DPI)	71.4	76.8	93.8	118.6	135.4	148.3	152.2	161.4	171.2	190.6
Less: Personal outlays	68.2	72.4	82.3	90.0	100.8	109.7	121.2	145.9	163.8	177.3
Equals: Personal saving	3.2	4.4	11.5	28.6	34.6	38.7	31.1	15.5	7.4	13.4
As a percentage of DPI	4.5	5.7	12.2	24.1	25.6	26.1	20.4	9.6	4.3	7.0
Gross saving	13.6	18.5	29.8	39.8	44.9	39.9	29.8	38.4	46.6	58.0
Net saving	4.6	9.0	19.0	26.4	28.6	20.5	8.7	15.1	20.2	29.9
Net private saving	4.6	7.4	14.9	33.6	41.2	45.8	36.1	18.6	13.5	25.1
Net government saving, federal	-2.1	-0.3	2.2	-8.7	-14.1	-26.9	-29.0	-5.0	5.3	3.6
Net government saving, state and local	2.0	2.0	1.9	1.5	1.5	1.6	1.6	1.5	1.4	1.2
Consumption of fixed capital, private	7.6	7.9	8.8	9.9	10.0	10.5	10.9	12.5	15.7	18.4
Consumption of fixed capital, government	1.4	1.5	2.0	3.5	6.2	8.9	10.1	10.8	10.7	9.7
Gross domestic investment, total	13.8	18.0	28.9	39.0	45.2	44.4	35.0	34.6	39.6	55.1
Private	9.3	13.6	18.1	10.4	6.1	7.8	10.8	31.1	35.0	48.1
Government	4.5	4.4	10.8	28.5	39.1	36.6	24.1	3.5	4.6	7.0
Net lending or net borrowing (-), NIPAs	1.0	1.5	1.3	-0.1	-2.1	-2.0	-1.3	4.9	9.3	2.4
Net domestic investment	4.8	8.6	18.1	25.6	28.9	25.1	13.9	11.3	13.2	27.0
Gross saving as a percentage of gross national income	14.9	18.4	23.5	24.4	22.4	18.3	13.6	17.3	19.2	21.4
Net saving as a percentage of gross national income	5.0	9.0	15.0	16.2	14.3	9.4	4.0	6.8	8.3	11.0

Table 18-2. NIPA Data on Real Output, Prices, and Employment, 1929–1948

Classification	1929	1930	1931	1932	1933	1934	1935	1936	1937	1938
POPULATION										
Population (midperiod, thousands)	121 878	123 188	124 149	124 949	125 690	126 485	127 362	128 181	128 961	129 969
BILLIONS OF CHAINED (2000) DOLLARS (except as noted)										
Real gross domestic product, total	865.2	790.7	739.9	643.7	635.5	704.2	766.9	866.6	911.1	879.7
Per capita (2000 dollars)	7 099	6 418	5 960	5 152	5 056	5 567	6 021	6 761	7 065	6 769
Personal consumption expenditures	661.4	626.1	606.9	553.0	541.0	579.3	614.8	677.0	702.0	690.7
Per capita (2000 dollars)	5 427	5 082	4 888	4 426	4 305	4 580	4 827	5 282	5 444	5 314
Gross private domestic investment	91.3	60.9	38.3	11.5	17.0	30.7	56.9	72.9	91.1	60.2
Exports	34.9	28.9	24.0	18.8	18.9	21.0	22.2	23.3	29.3	29.0
Imports	44.3	38.5	33.6	27.9	29.1	29.7	38.9	38.4	43.3	33.6
Government	120.6	132.9	138.5	133.8	129.2	145.7	149.7	174.7	167.3	180.2
Disposable personal income	712.7	666.8	643.5	558.4	542.3	594.5	652.2	733.6	758.6	715.5
Per capita (2000 dollars)	5 848	5 413	5 183	4 469	4 315	4 700	5 121	5 723	5 882	5 505
CHAIN-TYPE PRICE INDEXES, 2000 = 100										
Gross domestic product	11.94	11.48	10.33	9.15	8.91	9.35	9.53	9.64	10.00	9.81
Percent change	. . .	-3.9	-10.0	-11.5	-2.6	4.9	2.0	1.2	3.7	-1.9
Personal consumption expenditures	11.70	11.20	10.00	8.81	8.49	8.88	9.10	9.18	9.52	9.30
Percent change	. . .	-4.2	-10.8	-11.9	-3.6	4.6	2.4	1.0	3.6	-2.3
EMPLOYMENT										
Total	37 699	35 590	32 724	29 445	30 940	34 238	35 577	38 599	39 701	38 322
Domestic industries	37 699	35 590	32 723	29 444	30 939	34 237	35 576	38 598	39 700	38 321
Private industries	34 088	31 811	28 590	25 071	25 038	27 417	28 426	30 548	32 508	30 124
Agriculture, forestry, and fisheries	3 556	3 337	3 252	3 028	2 995	2 986	3 013	3 106	3 083	2 949
Mining	993	932	813	672	693	822	840	897	955	859
Contract construction	1 484	1 366	1 198	907	703	806	866	1 104	1 082	1 055
Manufacturing	10 428	9 309	7 895	6 678	7 204	8 364	8 904	9 645	10 591	9 131
Durable goods	5 238	4 457	3 497	2 724	2 893	3 587	3 941	4 460	5 130	4 085
Nondurable goods	5 190	4 852	4 398	3 954	4 311	4 777	4 963	5 185	5 461	5 046
Transportation and public utilities	3 989	3 742	3 282	2 826	2 684	2 774	2 808	2 973	3 140	2 837
Wholesale trade	1 757	1 693	1 530	1 380	1 377	1 492	1 507	1 612	1 770	1 767
Retail trade and automobile services	4 684	4 469	4 148	3 688	3 699	4 075	4 200	4 543	4 904	4 780
Finance, insurance, and real estate	1 520	1 491	1 423	1 358	1 309	1 332	1 352	1 401	1 445	1 436
Services	5 677	5 472	5 049	4 534	4 374	4 766	4 936	5 267	5 538	5 310
Government	3 611	3 779	4 133	4 373	5 901	6 820	7 150	8 050	7 192	8 197
Federal	981	1 034	1 019	1 006	1 470	2 227	2 209	4 993	4 085	4 987
General government	644	695	683	673	1 135	1 868	1 835	4 612	3 698	4 583
Civilian, except work relief	267	310	296	290	294	357	449	521	517	507
Military[1]	377	385	387	383	370	371	396	438	474	504
Work relief	. . .	. . .	. . .	. . .	471	1 140	990	3 653	2 707	3 572
Government enterprises	337	339	336	333	335	359	374	381	387	404
State and local	2 630	2 745	3 114	3 367	4 431	4 593	4 941	3 057	3 107	3 210
General government	2 509	2 618	2 984	3 249	4 317	4 473	4 815	2 922	2 967	3 070
Public education	1 067	1 095	1 105	1 093	1 069	1 069	1 097	1 118	1 149	1 180
Nonschool, except work relief	1 442	1 503	1 580	1 564	1 524	1 570	1 621	1 713	1 762	1 871
Work relief	. . .	20	299	592	1 724	1 834	2 097	91	56	19
Government enterprises	121	127	130	118	114	120	126	135	140	140
Rest of the world	0	0	1	1	1	1	1	1	1	1

[1]Includes Coast Guard.
. . . = Not available.

Table 18-2. NIPA Data on Real Output, Prices, and Employment, 1929–1948—*Continued*

Classification	1939	1940	1941	1942	1943	1944	1945	1946	1947	1948
POPULATION										
Population (midperiod, thousands)	131 028	132 122	133 402	134 860	136 739	138 397	139 928	141 389	144 126	146 631
BILLIONS OF CHAINED (2000) DOLLARS (except as noted)										
Real gross domestic product, total	950.7	1 034.1	1 211.1	1 435.4	1 670.9	1 806.5	1 786.3	1 589.4	1 574.5	1 643.2
Per capita (2000 dollars)	7 256	7 827	9 079	10 644	12 220	13 053	12 766	11 241	10 925	11 206
Personal consumption expenditures	729.1	767.1	821.9	803.1	826.1	850.2	902.7	1 012.9	1 031.6	1 054.4
Per capita (2000 dollars)	5 565	5 806	6 161	5 955	6 042	6 143	6 451	7 164	7 158	7 191
Gross private domestic investment	77.4	107.9	131.7	69.6	41.1	50.8	67.0	172.1	165.3	211.2
Exports	30.6	34.8	35.7	23.6	19.9	21.4	29.9	64.6	73.7	58.0
Imports	35.3	36.2	44.5	40.4	50.9	53.3	56.7	47.0	44.6	52.0
Government	196.0	201.5	335.1	788.6	1 173.3	1 320.5	1 152.9	396.8	337.2	361.7
Disposable personal income	774.9	826.5	950.7	1 069.9	1 119.9	1 160.7	1 145.3	1 132.7	1 090.3	1 148.4
Per capita (2000 dollars)	5 914	6 255	7 127	7 934	8 190	8 387	8 185	8 011	7 565	7 832
CHAIN-TYPE PRICE INDEXES, 2000 = 100										
Gross domestic product	9.69	9.77	10.40	11.26	11.88	12.16	12.48	13.93	15.49	16.37
Percent change	-1.2	0.9	6.5	8.2	5.6	2.4	2.6	11.7	11.2	5.7
Personal consumption expenditures	9.22	9.29	9.86	11.08	12.09	12.78	13.29	14.25	15.70	16.60
Percent change	-0.9	0.8	6.1	12.3	9.1	5.7	4.0	7.2	10.2	5.7
EMPLOYMENT										
Total	39 633	41 437	45 785	50 219	55 995	57 221	55 548	49 643	49 936	51 332
Domestic industries	39 632	41 435	45 782	50 214	56 016	57 276	55 614	49 690	49 941	51 325
Private industries	31 612	33 518	37 210	39 728	40 723	39 749	38 183	40 379	42 458	43 431
Agriculture, forestry, and fisheries	2 859	2 809	2 779	2 692	2 563	2 372	2 259	2 343	2 427	2 498
Mining	832	927	975	985	917	879	829	871	933	981
Contract construction	1 219	1 285	1 774	2 131	1 566	1 110	1 135	1 739	2 062	2 278
Manufacturing	9 967	10 882	13 137	15 284	17 402	17 050	15 186	14 493	15 205	15 276
Durable goods	4 609	5 367	6 999	8 846	10 924	10 722	8 933	7 742	8 330	8 309
Nondurable goods	5 358	5 515	6 138	6 438	6 478	6 328	6 253	6 751	6 875	6 967
Transportation and public utilities	2 943	3 064	3 311	3 458	3 652	3 822	3 926	4 113	4 173	4 212
Wholesale trade	1 833	1 899	2 014	1 916	1 808	1 828	1 927	2 286	2 480	2 573
Retail trade and automobile services	4 992	5 321	5 754	5 623	5 570	5 529	5 717	6 769	7 061	7 223
Finance, insurance, and real estate	1 470	1 518	1 559	1 531	1 475	1 447	1 477	1 692	1 744	1 811
Services	5 497	5 813	5 907	6 108	5 770	5 712	5 727	6 073	6 373	6 579
Government	8 020	7 917	8 572	10 486	15 293	17 527	17 431	9 311	7 483	7 894
Federal	4 754	4 652	5 281	7 252	12 155	14 405	14 258	5 902	3 808	4 007
General government	4 342	4 227	4 829	6 765	11 611	13 885	13 722	5 294	3 268	3 437
Civilian, except work relief	560	642	944	1 702	2 497	2 520	2 420	1 822	1 436	1 428
Military[1]	566	793	1 693	4 154	9 029	11 365	11 302	3 472	1 832	2 009
Work relief	3 216	2 792	2 192	909	85	. . .	. . .	. . .	. . .	. . .
Government enterprises	412	425	452	487	544	520	536	608	540	570
State and local	3 266	3 265	3 291	3 234	3 138	3 122	3 173	3 409	3 675	3 887
General government	3 123	3 104	3 119	3 063	2 965	2 956	3 007	3 236	3 481	3 657
Public education	1 207	1 194	1 256	1 264	1 256	1 256	1 273	1 347	1 445	1 504
Nonschool, except work relief	1 877	1 872	1 846	1 794	1 709	1 700	1 734	1 889	2 036	2 153
Work relief	39	38	17	5	. . .	. . .	. . .	. . .	. . .	. . .
Government enterprises	143	161	172	171	173	166	166	173	194	230
Rest of the world	1	2	3	5	-21	-55	-66	-47	-5	7

[1]Includes Coast Guard.
. . . = Not available.

Table 18-3. Fixed Assets, Money and Credit, and Interest Rates, 1929–1948

Classification	1929	1930	1931	1932	1933	1934	1935	1936	1937	1938
CURRENT-COST NET STOCK OF FIXED ASSETS (billions of dollars, year end)										
Total	274.3	263.0	226.2	208.6	225.1	231.6	235.7	260.7	275.5	277.9
Private, total	233.5	223.4	190.1	173.0	183.3	185.7	187.0	206.5	218.4	218.7
Nonresidential										
Equipment and software	33.1	31.7	29.0	26.0	25.8	26.0	25.4	27.5	29.8	29.7
Structures	80.6	77.3	67.6	63.1	65.7	67.1	67.4	74.4	77.2	75.9
Residential	119.8	114.3	93.5	83.9	91.7	92.7	94.2	104.7	111.3	113.1
Government, total	40.8	39.7	36.1	35.7	41.8	45.9	48.7	54.2	57.2	59.2
Nonresidential										
Equipment and software	2.4	2.3	2.3	2.3	2.3	2.6	2.8	3.0	3.2	3.3
Structures	38.4	37.3	33.8	33.4	39.4	43.2	45.8	51.1	53.8	55.6
Residential	0.0	0.0	0.0	0.0	0.0	0.0	0.0	0.1	0.2	0.2
Private and government fixed assets, total	274.3	263.0	226.2	208.6	225.1	231.6	235.7	260.7	275.5	277.9
Nonresidential										
Equipment and software	35.5	34.0	31.3	28.3	28.2	28.6	28.3	30.5	33.0	33.0
Structures	119.0	114.7	101.4	96.4	105.2	110.3	113.2	125.4	131.0	131.5
Residential	119.8	114.3	93.5	84.0	91.7	92.7	94.2	104.8	111.5	113.4
Government, by level										
Federal	7.9	7.4	6.8	6.7	7.6	8.6	9.8	11.4	12.6	13.3
State and local	32.9	32.2	29.3	29.0	34.2	37.2	38.8	42.8	44.6	45.9
CHAIN-TYPE QUANTITY INDEXES FOR NET STOCK OF FIXED ASSETS (index numbers, 2000 = 100)										
Total	14.04	14.32	14.44	14.37	14.26	14.24	14.31	14.54	14.80	14.97
Private, total	15.58	15.80	15.80	15.58	15.34	15.19	15.14	15.23	15.40	15.43
Nonresidential										
Equipment and software	6.58	6.64	6.45	6.09	5.76	5.57	5.53	5.67	5.92	5.90
Structures	20.73	21.29	21.42	21.26	21.00	20.81	20.65	20.64	20.77	20.76
Residential	17.57	17.69	17.75	17.67	17.56	17.50	17.52	17.60	17.70	17.80
Government, total	9.74	10.29	10.86	11.31	11.62	12.03	12.47	13.18	13.78	14.45
Nonresidential										
Equipment and software	2.47	2.47	2.50	2.48	2.47	2.62	2.81	2.92	3.04	3.23
Structures	12.68	13.44	14.22	14.85	15.29	15.80	16.35	17.28	18.03	18.89
Residential	0.03	0.06	0.09	0.12	0.14	0.17	0.25	0.70	1.33	1.57
Private and government fixed assets, total	14.04	14.32	14.44	14.37	14.26	14.24	14.31	14.54	14.80	14.97
Nonresidential										
Equipment and software	5.53	5.58	5.44	5.16	4.90	4.77	4.77	4.90	5.12	5.13
Structures	17.08	17.72	18.13	18.31	18.36	18.48	18.65	19.07	19.47	19.85
Residential	17.47	17.58	17.64	17.57	17.46	17.40	17.42	17.51	17.62	17.73
Government, by level										
Federal	6.68	6.73	6.86	7.09	7.52	8.13	8.98	9.78	10.50	11.20
State and local	10.97	11.72	12.46	13.01	13.26	13.59	13.88	14.56	15.10	15.77
MONEY STOCK AND BANK CREDIT (millions of dollars)										
June 30										
Currency outside banks	3 639	3 369	3 651	4 616	4 761	4 659	4 783	5 222	5 489	5 417
Demand deposits adjusted	22 540	21 706	19 832	15 625	14 411	16 694	20 433	23 780	25 198	24 313
Total	26 179	25 075	23 483	20 241	19 172	21 353	25 216	29 002	30 687	29 730
Time deposits	28 611	28 992	28 961	24 756	21 656	22 875	23 854	24 908	25 905	26 236
Loans and investments, all commercial banks	49 424	48 892	44 853	36 091	30 357	32 742	34 588	38 540	39 472	37 109
December 31										
Currency outside banks	3 557	3 605	4 470	4 669	4 782	4 655	4 917	5 516	5 638	5 775
Demand deposits adjusted	22 809	20 967	17 412	15 728	15 035	18 459	22 115	25 483	23 959	25 986
Total	26 366	24 572	21 882	20 397	19 817	23 114	27 032	30 999	29 597	31 761
Time deposits	28 189	28 676	25 979	24 457	21 715	23 156	24 241	25 361	26 218	26 305
Loans and investments, all commercial banks	49 467	46 700	39 653	35 083	30 789	33 735	35 982	39 472	38 333	38 669
COMMERCIAL PAPER AND BANKERS' ACCEPTANCES (millions of dollars outstanding, year end)										
Commercial paper	334	358	120	81	109	166	171	215	279	187
Bankers' acceptances	1 732	1 556	974	710	764	543	397	373	343	270
INTEREST RATES AND YIELDS										
Federal Reserve discount rate	5.17	3.04	2.11	2.82	2.56	1.54	1.50	1.50	1.33	1.00
U.S. Treasury 3-month bills	4.42	2.23	1.40	0.88	0.52	0.28	0.17	0.17	0.28	0.07
Bank prime rate	5.5–6	3.5–6	2.75–5	3.25–4	1.5–4	1.50	1.50	1.50	1.50	1.50
Prime commercial paper, 4- to 6-months	5.85	3.59	2.64	2.73	1.73	1.02	0.76	0.75	0.94	0.81
Bond yields:										
United States government, long-term	3.60	3.29	3.34	3.68	3.31	3.12	2.79	2.65	2.68	2.56
Corporate:										
Moodys Aaa	4.73	4.55	4.58	5.01	4.49	4.00	3.60	3.24	3.26	3.19
Moodys Baa	5.90	5.90	7.62	9.30	7.76	6.32	5.75	4.77	5.03	5.80
State and local	4.27	4.07	4.01	4.65	4.71	4.03	3.41	3.07	3.10	2.91

Table 18-3. Fixed Assets, Money and Credit, and Interest Rates, 1929–1948—*Continued*

Classification	1939	1940	1941	1942	1943	1944	1945	1946	1947	1948
CURRENT-COST NET STOCK OF FIXED ASSETS (billions of dollars, year end)										
Total	283.9	308.9	353.2	403.7	451.3	484.7	526.2	616.8	709.5	753.6
Private, total	222.4	241.3	268.6	286.7	302.0	314.8	337.8	416.5	495.0	539.0
Nonresidential										
Equipment and software	30.3	32.7	38.1	38.6	38.9	39.1	44.5	53.6	65.2	79.1
Structures	75.3	80.5	90.7	97.5	99.6	101.0	109.0	135.8	162.4	171.9
Residential	116.7	128.1	139.9	150.6	163.5	174.7	184.3	227.1	267.4	288.0
Government, total	61.6	67.6	84.5	117.0	149.3	169.9	188.4	200.3	214.4	214.6
Nonresidential										
Equipment and software	3.6	4.0	7.7	20.9	45.4	65.5	75.8	70.7	62.0	52.2
Structures	57.7	63.1	75.8	94.4	101.3	101.6	109.6	125.7	146.8	157.4
Residential	0.3	0.5	1.0	1.7	2.6	2.8	3.0	4.0	5.6	5.0
Private and government fixed assets, total	283.9	308.9	353.2	403.7	451.3	484.7	526.2	616.8	709.5	753.6
Nonresidential										
Equipment and software	33.9	36.7	45.8	59.5	84.3	104.6	120.3	124.2	127.2	131.3
Structures	133.0	143.5	166.5	191.9	201.0	202.6	218.6	261.5	309.2	329.3
Residential	117.0	128.7	140.9	152.3	166.0	177.6	187.3	231.1	273.0	293.0
Government, by level										
Federal	14.0	15.7	24.4	49.7	80.8	103.0	118.9	122.4	121.1	113.0
State and local	47.6	51.9	60.2	67.4	68.5	66.9	69.5	77.9	93.3	101.6
CHAIN-TYPE QUANTITY INDEXES FOR NET STOCK OF FIXED ASSETS (index numbers, 2000 = 100)										
Total	15.25	15.58	16.23	17.29	18.48	19.46	19.87	19.78	19.90	20.21
Private, total	15.57	15.81	16.12	16.07	15.94	15.89	15.98	16.53	17.23	18.02
Nonresidential										
Equipment and software	5.96	6.19	6.52	6.42	6.28	6.33	6.71	7.29	8.18	9.04
Structures	20.79	20.90	21.07	20.96	20.71	20.57	20.60	21.13	21.57	22.13
Residential	18.04	18.33	18.66	18.71	18.65	18.59	18.52	19.02	19.72	20.58
Government, total	15.21	15.91	17.81	22.77	28.75	33.63	35.31	32.67	30.41	28.75
Nonresidential										
Equipment and software	3.43	3.63	6.71	19.63	44.68	68.64	76.94	63.16	50.31	39.61
Structures	19.85	20.69	22.10	24.78	25.85	26.16	26.31	26.09	26.11	26.37
Residential	2.04	3.42	6.20	9.26	13.16	14.10	14.32	15.89	16.38	16.68
Private and government fixed assets, total	15.25	15.58	16.23	17.29	18.48	19.46	19.87	19.78	19.90	20.21
Nonresidential										
Equipment and software	5.21	5.42	6.17	8.02	11.42	14.71	16.15	14.83	13.89	13.21
Structures	20.30	20.73	21.45	22.57	22.92	22.98	23.06	23.26	23.52	23.96
Residential	17.97	18.26	18.61	18.71	18.74	18.69	18.64	19.15	19.85	20.71
Government, by level										
Federal	11.83	12.80	18.70	37.17	60.75	80.43	87.48	77.16	67.76	60.14
State and local	16.58	17.17	17.50	17.53	17.37	17.19	17.04	17.05	17.25	17.59
MONEY STOCK AND BANK CREDIT (millions of dollars)										
June 30										
Currency outside banks	6 005	6 699	8 204	10 936	15 814	20 881	25 097	26 516	. . .	. . .
Demand deposits adjusted	27 355	31 962	37 317	41 870	56 039	60 065	69 053	79 476	. . .	. . .
Total	33 360	38 661	45 521	52 806	71 853	80 946	94 150	105 992	. . .	. . .
Time deposits	26 791	27 463	27 879	27 320	30 260	35 720	44 253	51 829	. . .	. . .
Loans and investments, all commercial banks	39 367	41 148	47 627	53 652	76 633	95 731	114 505	119 448	112 756	113 855
December 31										
Currency outside banks	6 401	7 325	9 615	13 946	18 837	23 505	26 490	26 730	. . .	. . .
Demand deposits adjusted	29 793	34 945	38 992	48 922	60 803	66 930	75 851	83 814	. . .	. . .
Total	36 194	42 270	48 607	62 868	79 640	90 435	102 341	110 044	. . .	. . .
Time deposits	27 059	27 738	27 729	28 431	32 748	39 790	48 452	53 960	. . .	. . .
Loans and investments, all commercial banks	40 667	43 922	50 746	67 393	85 095	105 530	124 019	113 993	116 284	114 298
COMMERCIAL PAPER AND BANKERS' ACCEPTANCES (millions of dollars outstanding, year end)										
Commercial paper	210	218	375	230	202	166	159	228	287	269
Bankers' acceptances	233	209	194	118	117	129	154	227	261	259
INTEREST RATES AND YIELDS										
Federal Reserve discount rate	1.00	1.00	1.00	1.00	1.00	1.00	1.00	1.00	1.00	1.34
U.S. Treasury 3-month bills	0.05	0.04	0.13	0.34	0.38	0.38	0.38	0.38	0.61	1.05
Bank prime rate	1.50	1.50	1.50	1.50	1.50	1.50	1.50	1.50	1.63	1.88
Prime commercial paper, 4- to 6-months	0.59	0.56	0.53	0.66	0.69	0.73	0.75	0.81	1.03	1.44
Bond yields:										
United States government, long-term	2.36	2.21	2.12	2.46	2.47	2.48	2.37	2.19	2.25	2.44
Corporate:										
Moodys Aaa	3.01	2.84	2.77	2.83	2.73	2.72	2.62	2.53	2.61	2.82
Moodys Baa	4.96	4.75	4.33	4.28	3.91	3.61	3.29	3.05	3.24	3.47
State and local	2.76	2.50	2.10	2.36	2.06	1.86	1.67	1.64	2.01	2.40

. . . = Not available.

Table 18-4. Price and Production Indexes, Labor Force Data, and Stock Prices and Yields, 1929–1948

Classification	1929	1930	1931	1932	1933	1934	1935	1936	1937	1938
CONSUMER AND PRODUCER PRICE INDEXES										
Consumer prices, all items; 1982–1984 = 100:										
All urban consumers (CPI-U)	17.1	16.7	15.2	13.7	13.0	13.4	13.7	13.9	14.4	14.1
Percent change	0.0	-2.3	-9.0	-9.9	-5.1	3.1	2.2	1.5	3.6	-2.1
Urban wage earners and clerical workers (CPI-W)	17.2	16.8	15.3	13.7	13.0	13.5	13.8	13.9	14.4	14.2
Producer prices, 1982 = 100:										
All commodities	16.4	14.9	12.6	11.2	11.4	12.9	13.8	13.9	14.9	13.5
Farm products	26.4	22.4	16.4	12.2	13.0	16.5	19.8	20.4	21.8	17.3
Industrial commodities	15.6	14.5	12.8	11.9	12.1	13.3	13.3	13.5	14.5	13.9
INDEXES OF INDUSTRIAL PRODUCTION (2002 = 100)										
Total	8.5	7.1	5.8	4.6	5.4	5.9	6.8	8.0	8.8	6.9
Products	...	...	...	...	...	...	...	...	...	...
Consumer goods	...	...	...	...	...	...	...	...	...	...
Materials	...	...	...	...	...	...	...	...	...	...
Manufacturing (SIC)	8.2	6.8	5.5	4.3	5.1	5.6	6.5	7.8	8.5	6.5
EMPLOYMENT STATUS OF THE CIVILIAN NONINSTITUTIONAL POPULATION, 14 YEARS AND OVER (Thousands of persons, except as noted)										
Civilian noninstitutional population	...	...	...	...	...	...	...	...	...	...
Civilian labor force	49 180	49 820	50 420	51 000	51 590	52 230	52 870	53 440	54 000	54 610
Participation rate, percent	...	...	...	...	...	...	...	...	...	...
Employment, total	47 630	45 480	42 400	38 940	38 760	40 890	42 260	44 410	46 300	44 220
Ratio, employment to population, percent	...	...	...	...	...	...	...	...	...	...
Agricultural	10 450	10 340	10 290	10 170	10 090	9 900	10 110	10 000	9 820	9 690
Nonagricultural	37 180	35 140	32 110	28 770	28 670	30 990	32 150	34 410	36 480	34 530
Unemployment	1 550	4 340	8 020	12 060	12 830	11 340	10 610	9 030	7 700	10 390
Percent of civilian labor force	3.2	8.7	15.9	23.6	24.9	21.7	20.1	16.9	14.3	19.0
Unemployment rate counting persons on work relief as employed, percent of civilian labor force [1]	3.2	8.7	15.3	22.5	20.6	16.0	14.2	9.9	9.1	12.5
NONFARM PAYROLL EMPLOYMENT (NAICS) (Thousands of persons, except as noted)										
Total	...	...	...	...	...	...	...	...	...	...
Private, total	...	...	...	...	...	...	...	...	...	...
Goods-producing, total	...	...	...	...	...	...	...	...	...	...
Natural resources and mining	...	...	...	...	...	...	...	...	...	...
Construction	...	...	...	...	...	...	...	...	...	...
Manufacturing, total	...	...	...	...	...	...	...	...	...	...
Durable goods	...	...	...	...	...	...	...	...	...	...
Nondurable goods, total	...	...	...	...	...	...	...	...	...	...
Private service-providing, total	...	...	...	...	...	...	...	...	...	...
Trade, transportation, and utilities, total	...	...	...	...	...	...	...	...	...	...
Wholesale trade	...	...	...	...	...	...	...	...	...	...
Retail trade	...	...	...	...	...	...	...	...	...	...
Information	...	...	...	...	...	...	...	...	...	...
Financial activities	...	...	...	...	...	...	...	...	...	...
Professional and business services	...	...	...	...	...	...	...	...	...	...
Education and health services	...	...	...	...	...	...	...	...	...	...
Leisure and hospitality	...	...	...	...	...	...	...	...	...	...
Other services	...	...	...	...	...	...	...	...	...	...
Government, total	...	...	...	...	...	...	...	...	...	...
Federal, total	...	...	...	...	...	...	...	...	...	...
Department of Defense, total	...	...	...	...	...	...	...	...	...	...
Service-providing	...	...	...	...	...	...	...	...	...	...
Manufacturing, production workers:										
Total (thousands)	...	...	...	...	...	...	...	...	...	...
Average weekly hours (number of hours per week)	...	...	...	...	...	...	...	...	...	...
Index of aggregate weekly hours (2002 = 100)	...	...	...	...	...	...	...	...	...	...
Average hourly earnings (dollars)	...	...	...	...	...	...	...	...	...	...
Average weekly earnings (dollars)	...	...	...	...	...	...	...	...	...	...
CORPORATE COMMON STOCKS (STANDARD AND POOR'S CORPORATION)										
Price index, 500 stocks, 1941–1943 = 10	26.02	21.03	13.66	6.93	8.96	9.84	10.60	15.47	15.41	11.49
Dividend-price ratio	3.47	4.51	6.15	7.43	4.21	3.72	3.82	3.44	4.86	5.18
Earnings-price ratio	7.51	6.33	7.51	5.95	4.36	5.16	7.23	6.57	8.25	5.55

[1]Michael Darby, "Three-and-a-Half Million U.S. Employees Have Been Mislaid." *Journal of Political Economy*, February 1976, v. 84, no. 1
... = Not available.

Table 18-4. Price and Production Indexes, Labor Force Data, and Stock Prices and Yields, 1929–1948
—Continued

Classification	1939	1940	1941	1942	1943	1944	1945	1946	1947	1948
CONSUMER AND PRODUCER PRICE INDEXES										
Consumer prices, all items; 1982–1984 = 100:										
All urban consumers (CPI-U)	13.9	14.0	14.7	16.3	17.3	17.6	18.0	19.5	22.3	24.1
Percent change	-1.4	0.7	5.0	10.9	6.1	1.7	2.3	8.3	14.4	8.1
Urban wage earners and clerical workers (CPI-W)	14.0	14.1	14.8	16.4	17.4	17.7	18.1	19.6	22.5	24.2
Producer prices, 1982 = 100:										
All commodities	13.3	13.5	15.1	17.0	17.8	17.9	18.2	20.8	25.6	27.7
Farm products	16.5	17.1	20.8	26.7	30.9	31.2	32.4	37.5	45.1	48.5
Industrial commodities	13.9	14.1	15.1	16.2	16.5	16.7	17.0	18.6	22.7	24.6
INDEXES OF INDUSTRIAL PRODUCTION (2002 = 100)										
Total	8.5	9.8	12.4	14.2	17.3	18.6	16.0	13.8	15.5	16.1
Products	8.5	9.6	12.1	13.8	17.1	18.7	15.8	13.8	15.4	16.1
Consumer goods	11.6	12.3	14.8	13.7	13.9	14.6	15.0	18.0	19.1	19.7
Materials	8.3	10.0	12.5	14.5	17.1	18.0	15.8	13.4	15.2	15.8
Manufacturing (SIC)	7.8	9.2	11.7	13.7	17.0	18.4	15.4	12.8	14.3	14.8
EMPLOYMENT STATUS OF THE CIVILIAN NONINSTITUTIONAL POPULATION, 14 YEARS AND OVER (Thousands of persons, except as noted)										
Civilian noninstitutional population	. . .	99 840	99 900	98 640	94 640	93 220	94 090	103 070	106 018	. . .
Civilian labor force	55 230	55 640	55 910	56 410	55 540	54 630	53 860	57 520	60 168	. . .
Participation rate, percent	. . .	55.7	56.0	57.2	58.7	58.6	57.2	55.8	56.8	. . .
Employment, total	45 750	47 520	50 350	53 750	54 470	53 960	52 820	55 250	57 812	. . .
Ratio, employment to population, percent	. . .	47.6	50.4	54.5	57.6	57.9	56.1	53.6	54.5	. . .
Agricultural	9 610	9 540	9 100	9 250	9 080	8 950	8 580	8 320	8 256	. . .
Nonagricultural	36 140	37 980	41 250	44 500	45 390	45 010	44 240	46 930	49 557	. . .
Unemployment	9 480	8 120	5 560	2 660	1 070	670	1 040	2 270	2 356	. . .
Percent of civilian labor force	17.2	14.6	9.9	4.7	1.9	1.2	1.9	3.9	3.9	. . .
Unemployment rate counting persons on work relief as employed, percent of civilian labor force [1]	11.3	9.5	6.0	3.1	1.8	. . .	. . .	. . .	. . .	. . .
NONFARM PAYROLL EMPLOYMENT (NAICS) (Thousands of persons, except as noted)										
Total	30 645	32 407	36 600	40 213	42 574	42 006	40 510	41 759	43 945	44 954
Private, total	26 606	28 156	31 874	34 621	36 353	35 819	34 428	36 054	38 379	39 213
Goods-producing, total	11 511	12 378	14 940	17 275	18 738	17 981	16 308	16 122	17 314	17 579
Natural resources and mining	856	927	967	1 010	958	926	864	885	976	1 014
Construction	1 205	1 352	1 852	2 234	1 627	1 152	1 190	1 724	2 051	2 241
Manufacturing, total	9 450	10 099	12 121	14 030	16 153	15 903	14 255	13 513	14 287	14 324
Durable goods	4 654	5 261	6 778	8 502	10 583	10 372	8 732	7 535	8 079	8 028
Nondurable goods, total	4 796	4 839	5 343	5 528	5 570	5 531	5 523	5 978	6 208	6 296
Private service-providing, total	15 094	15 778	16 934	17 347	17 615	17 839	18 121	19 932	21 064	21 634
Trade, transportation, and utilities, total	6 739	7 043	7 550	7 607	7 628	7 805	8 048	8 945	9 452	9 716
Wholesale trade	1 507.6	1 570.9	1 678.7	1 635.0	1 565.8	1 585.0	1 671.9	1 962.4	2 115.7	2 229.7
Retail trade	3 157.5	3 324.4	3 551.7	3 521.5	3 479.2	3 515.5	3 623.5	4 118.3	4 392.7	4 523.6
Information	1 141	1 196	1 342	1 470	1 605	1 635	1 581	1 594	1 658	1 669
Financial activities	1 386	1 424	1 466	1 455	1 431	1 414	1 435	1 619	1 674	1 742
Professional and business services	1 976	2 073	2 265	2 410	2 518	2 523	2 495	2 666	2 828	2 893
Education and health services	1 405	1 470	1 566	1 632	1 660	1 667	1 698	1 885	2 015	2 077
Leisure and hospitality	1 896	1 995	2 130	2 133	2 122	2 142	2 200	2 485	2 650	2 726
Other services	553	578	616	641	652	654	664	737	788	812
Government, total	4 040	4 251	4 726	5 592	6 222	6 187	6 082	5 705	5 567	5 742
Federal, total	950	1 045	1 406	2 322	3 047	3 071	2 945	2 365	1 985	1 954
Department of Defense, total	132.5	181.6	374.9	920.4	1 361.2	1 352.3	1 233.8	745.8	498.6	511.4
Service-providing	19 134	20 029	21 660	22 938	23 837	24 026	24 203	25 637	26 631	27 376
Manufacturing, production workers:										
Total (thousands)	8 163	8 737	10 641	12 447	14 407	14 031	12 445	11 781	12 453	12 383
Average weekly hours (number of hours per week)	37.7	38.2	40.7	43.2	45.1	45.4	43.6	40.4	40.5	40.1
Index of aggregate weekly hours (2002 = 100)	70.5	76.4	99.2	123.1	148.8	145.6	124.3	108.9	115.7	114.0
Average hourly earnings (dollars)	0.49	0.53	0.61	0.74	0.86	0.91	0.90	0.95	1.10	1.20
Average weekly earnings (dollars)	18.47	20.25	24.83	31.97	38.79	41.31	39.24	38.38	44.55	48.12
CORPORATE COMMON STOCKS (STANDARD AND POOR'S CORPORATION)										
Price index, 500 stocks, 1941–1943 = 10	12.06	11.02	9.82	8.67	11.50	12.47	15.16	17.08	15.17	15.53
Dividend-price ratio	4.05	5.59	6.82	7.24	4.93	4.86	4.17	3.85	4.93	5.54
Earnings-price ratio	7.34	9.80	12.14	11.42	7.82	7.34	6.39	6.31	10.69	14.60

[1]Michael Darby, "Three-and-a-Half Million U.S. Employees Have Been Mislaid." *Journal of Political Economy*, February 1976, v. 84, no. 1
. . . = Not available.

Table 18-5. Money, Credit, and Real Interest Rates, 1930–1948

(Percent.)

Classification	1930	1931	1932	1933	1934	1935	1936	1937	1938	1939
Change in money stock, December 31 from year earlier	-6.8	-10.9	-6.8	-2.8	16.6	17.0	14.7	-4.5	7.3	14.0
Change in bank credit (loans and investments), December 31 from year earlier	-5.6	-15.1	-11.5	-12.2	9.6	6.7	9.7	-2.9	0.9	5.2
Nominal Treasury bill rate	2.23	1.40	0.88	0.52	0.28	0.17	0.17	0.28	0.07	0.05
Inflation (PCE price index)	-4.2	-10.8	-11.9	-3.6	4.6	2.4	1.0	3.6	-2.3	-0.9
Real treasury bill rate	6.5	12.2	12.8	4.1	-4.3	-2.2	-0.8	-3.4	2.3	1.0

Classification	1940	1941	1942	1943	1944	1945	1946	1947	1948
Change in money stock, December 31 from year earlier	16.8	15.0	29.3	26.7	13.6	13.2	7.5	2.8	-1.4
Change in bank credit (loans and investments), December 31 from year earlier	8.0	15.5	32.8	26.3	24.0	17.5	-8.1	2.0	-1.7
Nominal Treasury bill rate	0.04	0.13	0.34	0.38	0.38	0.38	0.38	0.61	1.05
Inflation (PCE price index)	0.8	6.1	12.3	9.1	5.7	4.0	7.2	10.2	5.7
Real treasury bill rate	-0.8	-6.0	-12.0	-8.8	-5.3	-3.6	-6.8	-9.6	-4.7

Table 18-6. Federal Budget, 1929–1948

(Fiscal years, billions of dollars, percent.)

Classification	1929	1930	1931	1932	1933	1934	1935	1936	1937	1938
Receipts	3.9	4.1	3.1	1.9	2.0	3.0	3.6	3.9	5.4	6.8
Outlays	3.1	3.3	3.6	4.7	4.6	6.5	6.4	8.2	7.6	6.8
National defense	. . .	. . .	. . .	. . .	. . .	. . .	. . .	. . .	. . .	. . .
Surplus or deficit (-)	0.7	0.7	-0.5	-2.7	-2.6	-3.6	-2.8	-4.3	-2.2	-0.1
Fiscal year GDP	. . .	97.4	83.8	67.6	57.6	61.2	69.6	78.5	87.8	89.0
As percent of GDP:										
Receipts	. . .	4.2	3.7	2.8	3.5	4.8	5.2	5.0	6.1	7.6
Outlays	. . .	3.4	4.3	6.9	8.0	10.7	9.2	10.5	8.6	7.7
National defense	. . .	. . .	. . .	. . .	. . .	. . .	. . .	. . .	. . .	. . .
Surplus or deficit (-)	. . .	0.8	-0.6	-4.0	-4.5	-5.9	-4.0	-5.5	-2.5	-0.1
Debt held by the public, end of year:										
Billions of dollars	. . .	. . .	. . .	. . .	. . .	. . .	. . .	. . .	. . .	. . .
Percent of GDP	. . .	. . .	. . .	. . .	. . .	. . .	. . .	. . .	. . .	. . .

Classification	1939	1940	1941	1942	1943	1944	1945	1946	1947	1948
Receipts	6.3	6.6	8.7	14.6	24.0	43.8	45.2	39.3	38.5	41.6
Outlays	9.1	9.5	13.6	35.1	78.6	91.3	92.7	55.2	34.5	29.8
National defense	. . .	1.7	6.4	25.7	66.7	79.1	83.0	42.7	12.8	9.1
Surplus or deficit (-)	-2.8	-2.9	-4.9	-20.5	-54.6	-47.6	-47.6	-15.9	4.0	11.8
Fiscal year GDP	89.1	96.8	114.1	144.3	180.3	209.2	221.4	222.7	233.2	256.0
As percent of GDP:										
Receipts	7.1	6.8	7.6	10.1	13.3	20.9	20.4	17.6	16.5	16.2
Outlays	10.3	9.8	12.0	24.3	43.6	43.6	41.9	24.8	14.8	11.6
National defense	. . .	1.7	5.6	17.8	37.0	37.8	37.5	19.2	5.5	3.6
Surplus or deficit (-)	-3.2	-3.0	-4.3	-14.2	-30.3	-22.7	-21.5	-7.2	1.7	4.6
Debt held by the public, end of year:										
Billions of dollars	. . .	42.8	48.2	67.8	127.8	184.8	235.2	241.9	224.3	216.3
Percent of GDP	. . .	44.2	42.3	47.0	70.9	88.3	106.2	108.6	96.2	84.5

. . . = Not available.

NOTES AND DEFINITIONS

GENERAL NOTE ON THE CHRONOLOGY OF THE 1930S AND 1940S

See the article at the beginning of this book, "Business Statistics in Turbulent Times," for the business cycle peaks and troughs occurring in this period, as determined by the National Bureau of Economic Research (NBER).

The NBER chronology may surprise readers who are looking for "The Great Depression" and are not familiar with the NBER approach to business cycles. As NBER perceives it, a downtrend in economic activity began in August 1929 (*before* the stock market crash) and lasted until March 1933. This 43-month period has been called the "Great Contraction": it was the longest period of economic decline since the 1870s, and nearly three times as long as the longest recession identified and completed since that time (16 months). For the rest of the 1930s—except a 13-month recession in 1937–1938—the economy is viewed by the NBER as being in an expansion phase. The NBER chronology does not use the term "depression."

However, the term "Great Depression" is often colloquially used for the entire 1929–1939 period, even though the economy was expanding for most of the period following March 1933. This is because economic activity during that time, though increasing, remained below the likely capacity of the economy, as is indicated in Figures 18-1 and 18-2.

It should also be noted that NBER construes the entire period from June 1938 through February 1945 as a business cycle expansion. The recovery from the 1937–1938 recession merged into a further, continued rise in activity that reflected the outbreak of war in Europe in September 1939 and a consequent preparedness effort in the United States. The United States entered the war after being attacked by Japan in December 1941, launching an all-out war production effort at that time.

The February 1945 end of the "wartime expansion" (as NBER terms the period June 1938–February 1945) preceded the end of the war, as the European war ended in May 1945 and the Pacific war concluded in August 1945. A brief demobilization recession occurred from February to October 1945, followed by the first postwar expansion, which lasted from October 1945 to November 1948.

TABLES 18-1 AND 18-2
NATIONAL INCOME AND PRODUCT ACCOUNTS (NIPAS) AND RELATED DATA, 1929–1948

For most of these data, the sources, definitions, and availability are the same as for the identically titled series in Part A. Specific references to the appropriate chapter's notes and definitions are given below.

Gross domestic product and its components in current and constant dollars, gross national product, national income and its components, population and per capita data, and chain-type price indexes: See the notes and definitions for Chapter 1.

Personal income and its disposition and disposable personal income: See the notes and definitions for Chapter 4.

Saving and investment: See the notes and definitions for Chapter 5.

Employment, NIPA data, full-time and part-time employees: As seen in Table 18-4, payroll employment data from the Bureau of Labor Statistics (BLS) are not available for the years before 1939, and the BLS civilian employment estimates do not include work-relief employees. In order to provide more complete information on employment, this table presents NIPA estimates for the total number of full-time and part-time employees. Like the BLS payroll data, these estimates are a count of jobs rather than of persons employed, and persons with two jobs will appear as two persons employed in these data. These estimates include members of the armed forces and employees of Depression-era work-relief programs in the total, and also show them as separate categories. The issue of counting work-relief jobs is discussed below.

References

The data published here have been calculated after the fact and differ from what was actually available during the 1930s and 1940s. For an article on what was available at that time and the history of the NIPAs during that period, see Rosemary D. Marcuss and Richard E. Kane, "U.S. National Income and Product Statistics: Born of the Great Depression and World War II," *Survey of Current Business*, February 2007, pp. 32-46.

TABLE 18-3
FIXED ASSETS, MONEY AND CREDIT, AND INTEREST RATES, 1929–1948

For the data on the *net stock of fixed assets*, see the notes and definitions for Tables 5-5 and 5-6.

All of the other data in this table are taken from two volumes of statistical data issued by the Board of Governors of the Federal Reserve System: *Banking and Monetary Statistics,* Washington, D.C., Board of Governors of the Federal Reserve System, 1943, and *Banking and Monetary Statistics, 1941–1970,* Washington: Board of Governors of the Federal Reserve System, 1976. None of these data are included in the online data banks made available by the Federal Reserve on its Web site.

Federal Reserve *money stock* data for these years pertain only to the last day of June and the last day of December. These are the "call dates" on which banks report to the federal government. For more data and analysis covering monetary developments in this period, including monthly money supply estimates, see Milton Friedman and Anna Jacobson

Schwartz, *A Monetary History of the United States, 1867–1960,* Princeton, Princeton University Press, 1963.

Federal Reserve calculation of money stock data based on monthly averages of daily figures begins with the data for January 1947, shown in Table 20-5A and described in its notes and definitions. The definitions for the money stock data in Table 18-3 are the same as for the data in 20-5A, although the terms used in the source documents are slightly different.

Currency outside banks is defined the same as the *currency component* of Table 20-5A: currency in circulation outside the Treasury and Federal Reserve Banks less vault cash held by commercial banks.

Demand deposits adjusted is defined the same as the *demand deposit component* of Table 20-5A: demand deposits at commercial banks in the continental United States except interbank and U.S. Government deposits, less cash items in process of collection. The term "adjusted" in this context refers to the elimination of these three items, which represent double counting—not to seasonal adjustment, which is not applicable to call report data.

The *total* of currency outside banks and demand deposits adjusted is the concept labeled *money stock, total* in Table 20-5A, and corresponds to M1.

Time deposits are the same as *time deposits adjusted* in Table 20-5A: they include time deposits at commercial banks, mutual savings banks, and the Postal Savings System, except interbank deposits, postal savings redeposited in banks, and U.S. Government time deposits. This item could be added to the money stock total to yield an approximation of the current concept of M2.

Bank credit. Loans and investments, all commercial banks is the sum of these items from commercial bank balance sheets, including total loans, holdings of U.S. Government securities, and holdings of other securities, which according to the 1976 Federal Reserve source book "consist mainly of State and municipal issues."

Data are also shown for the outstanding values of two forms of securities used by businesses for short-term borrowing, *commercial paper* and *bankers' acceptances.* Figures for bankers' acceptances represent amounts reported by banks and dealers in the United States as well as by agencies of foreign banks located in the United States. From 1929 through 1934, acceptances includes acceptances held by Federal Reserve Banks, both for their own account ($391 million in December 1929) and for account of foreign correspondent banks ($548 million in December 1929). These Federal Reserve holdings declined rapidly after 1931 and amounted to zero by December 1934. By then, most of the outstanding acceptances were held by banks.

Federal Reserve discount rate is the rate set by the New York Federal Reserve Bank for bank borrowing secured by eligible paper, in percent per annum. Annual averages calculated by editor.

U.S. Treasury 3-month bills, yield in percent per annum, based on dealers' quotations from 1934 through 1948. For 1931 through 1933, the average rate on new issues of bills offered within the period. For 1929 and 1930, the rate on 3- to 6-month Treasury notes and certificates.

Bank prime rate is the rate that banks charge their most creditworthy business customers on short-term loans. According to the 1976 source document cited above, "A nationally publicized and uniform prime rate did not emerge until the depression of the 1930's. The rate in that period—1½ percent—represented a floor below which banks were said to regard lending as unprofitable…The date shown [for the beginning of a changed rate] is that on which the new rate was put into effect by the first bank to make the change. The table shows a range of rates for 1929–1933 because no information is available to indicate when the rate changed in that period." For further information, the source document cites "The Prime Rate," *Monthly Review,* Federal Reserve Bank of New York, April and May 1962, pp. 54-59 and 70-73, respectively.

Prime commercial paper, 4- to 6-months. Prevailing rate in New York City, percent per annum.

U.S. government bond yields, long-term. Yield in percent per annum. Before 1941, yields on bonds that were partly tax-exempt. The 1941 yield for the partly tax-exempt series was 1.95 percent.

Corporate bond yields, Moody's Investors Service. See Notes and Definitions for Table 12-9.

State and local bond yields on high-grade municipal bonds were provided by Standard and Poor's.

TABLE 18-4
PRICE AND PRODUCTION INDEXES, LABOR FORCE DATA, AND STOCK PRICES AND YIELDS, 1929–1948

Consumer and producer price indexes: See the notes and definitions for Chapter 8.

Indexes of industrial production: See the notes and definitions for Chapter 2.

Civilian noninstitutional population, labor force, employment, and unemployment are as defined in the notes and definitions to Chapter 10 with the following exceptions:

The data for 1929 to 1947 in Chapter 18 pertain to persons 14 years of age and over. The data in Chapter 10 from 1947 to the present are for persons 16 years of age and over. The differences made by this change in definitions can be observed in the two different sets of data—one from this table, the other from Tables 10-1 through 10-5—for the overlap year, 1947. In that year, the unemployment rates are the same (3.9 percent) for both age definitions. However, the labor force participation rate and the employment/population ratio are higher when the 14- and 15-year-olds are excluded.

The Census Bureau began the monthly survey of households that provides labor force data in 1942, and the Census of Population supplied data for 1940. For earlier years, data for the labor force, employment, and unemployment are retrospective estimates made by BLS.

The 1940 Census and the BLS data for 1931 through 1942 did not treat government work relief employment as employment; persons engaged in such work were counted as unemployed. In the labor force survey used today, anyone who worked for pay or profit is counted as employed (see the notes and definitions for Chapter 10). Therefore, today's survey would count work relief as employment and not unemployment, and the BLS figures for the period before 1942 are not consistent with today's unemployment rates. Michael Darby calculated an alternative unemployment rate in which such workers are counted as employed, and this rate is also shown in Table 18-4. It would appear that the Darby rate is more consistent with the NIPA total employment data. Furthermore, the NIPA data on GDP include, as output, the work done by relief workers, and the buildings they constructed are included in investment and capital stock.

BLS data for 1940 through 1947 are published on their Web site at <http://www.bls.gov>. The data for 1929 through 1939 were published in *Employment and Earnings,* May 1972, and in U.S. Commerce Department, Bureau of Economic Analysis, *Long-Term Economic Growth, 1860–1970,* June 1973, p. 163.

The Darby alternative unemployment rate is found in Michael Darby, "Three-and-a-Half Million U.S. Employees Have Been Mislaid," *Journal of Political Economy,* February 1976, v. 84, no. 1. It is also displayed and discussed in Robert A. Margo, "Employment and Unemployment in the 1930s," *Journal of Economic Perspectives,* v. 7, no. 2, Spring 1993.

Nonfarm employment and its components, and number, hours, and earnings for manufacturing production workers:

See the notes and definitions for Chapter 10. Note that because age is not specified in the Current Employment Survey that is the source of these data, this measure of employment includes any payroll workers that are under 16 years of age and has always done so.

Corporate common stock price index, dividend-price ratio, and earnings-price ratio (Standard and Poor's Corporation). See Notes and Definitions for Table 12-9. Before 1957, these measures represent a conversion of an earlier 90-stock index to the current 500-stock index. They are obtained from the Federal Reserve volumes of *Banking and Monetary Statistics* cited above in the notes to Table 18-3.

TABLE 18-5
MONEY, CREDIT, AND REAL INTEREST RATES, 1930–1948

These data are derived from data in preceding tables.

Change in money stock is the percent change from a year earlier in the December 31 value of the total of currency outside banks and demand deposits adjusted, usually known as M1, from Table 18-3.

Change in bank credit is the percent change from a year earlier in the December 31 value of loans and investments at all commercial banks, from Table 18-3.

The *nominal Treasury bill rate* is the interest rate on U.S. Treasury 3-month bills from Table 18-3.

Inflation is the percent change in the chain-type price index for personal consumption expenditures (PCE) from Table 18-2.

The *real Treasury bill rate* is the nominal rate minus the inflation rate. Note that subtraction means changing the sign and adding—hence negative inflation (deflation, price decline) contributes to large positive real rates.

TABLE 18-6
FEDERAL BUDGET, 1929–1948

See notes and definitions for Tables 6-14 and 6-15.

CHAPTER 19: SELECTED HISTORICAL DATA FOR QUARTERLY SERIES

Table 19-1. Gross Domestic Product

(Billions of dollars, quarterly data are at seasonally adjusted annual rates.)

NIPA Tables 1.1.5, 1.4.5

Year and quarter	Gross domestic product	Personal consump-tion expen-ditures	Gross private domestic investment				Exports and imports of goods and services			Government consumption expenditures and gross investment			Addendum: Final sales of domestic product
			Total	Fixed investment		Change in private inventories	Net exports	Exports	Imports	Total	Federal	State and local	
				Nonresi-dential	Residential								
1946	222.3	144.3	31.1	17.3	7.8	6.0	7.2	14.2	7.0	39.6	28.9	10.8	216.3
1947	244.2	162.0	35.0	23.5	12.1	-0.6	10.8	18.7	7.9	36.4	22.7	13.7	244.7
1948	269.2	175.0	48.1	26.8	15.6	5.7	5.5	15.5	10.1	40.6	24.2	16.3	263.5
1949	267.3	178.5	36.9	24.9	14.6	-2.7	5.2	14.5	9.2	46.7	27.7	19.0	270.0
1947													
1st quarter	237.2	156.3	33.7	22.8	10.4	0.5	10.9	18.4	7.5	36.3	23.4	13.0	236.7
2nd quarter	240.5	160.2	32.4	23.2	10.4	-1.2	11.3	19.5	8.2	36.6	23.3	13.4	241.7
3rd quarter	244.6	163.7	32.7	23.3	12.3	-2.9	11.8	19.4	7.7	36.4	22.4	14.0	247.5
4th quarter	254.4	167.8	41.0	24.5	15.1	1.5	9.3	17.6	8.3	36.3	21.6	14.7	252.9
1948													
1st quarter	260.4	170.5	45.0	26.2	15.2	3.6	7.3	16.9	9.6	37.6	22.4	15.2	256.7
2nd quarter	267.3	174.3	48.1	26.0	16.3	5.9	5.2	15.2	10.0	39.7	23.8	15.9	261.5
3rd quarter	273.9	177.2	50.2	27.0	16.1	7.2	4.9	15.4	10.5	41.4	24.6	16.8	266.7
4th quarter	275.2	178.1	49.1	28.1	15.0	6.0	4.5	14.6	10.1	43.5	26.0	17.5	269.2
1949													
1st quarter	270.0	177.0	40.9	26.6	14.0	0.4	6.5	16.1	9.6	45.6	27.6	18.0	269.6
2nd quarter	266.2	178.6	34.0	25.5	13.7	-5.1	6.3	15.6	9.4	47.3	28.6	18.7	271.4
3rd quarter	267.7	178.0	37.3	24.1	14.5	-1.3	5.2	14.1	8.9	47.2	27.7	19.5	269.0
4th quarter	265.2	180.4	35.2	23.5	16.3	-4.7	3.0	12.1	9.1	46.6	26.9	19.7	269.9
1950													
1st quarter	275.2	183.1	44.4	24.2	18.1	2.0	2.2	11.7	9.5	45.6	25.5	20.0	273.2
2nd quarter	284.6	187.0	49.9	26.6	20.4	2.8	1.6	11.9	10.2	46.1	25.7	20.4	281.7
3rd quarter	302.0	200.7	56.1	29.6	22.3	4.2	-0.7	12.3	13.0	45.9	24.9	21.0	297.8
4th quarter	313.4	198.1	65.9	30.6	21.3	14.0	-0.2	13.5	13.7	49.5	27.9	21.6	299.3
1951													
1st quarter	329.0	209.4	62.1	30.9	20.8	10.4	0.2	15.0	14.9	57.4	35.2	22.1	318.6
2nd quarter	336.7	205.1	64.8	31.8	18.2	14.8	1.9	17.1	15.2	64.7	41.8	22.9	321.9
3rd quarter	343.6	207.8	59.4	32.5	17.2	9.7	3.7	18.1	14.3	72.6	49.2	23.4	333.8
4th quarter	348.0	211.8	54.4	32.2	17.5	4.7	4.2	18.2	14.0	77.6	53.9	23.7	343.3
1952													
1st quarter	351.3	213.1	55.2	32.4	18.0	4.7	3.7	18.7	15.0	79.2	55.4	23.8	346.5
2nd quarter	352.2	217.3	49.9	32.9	18.5	-1.5	2.0	16.6	14.6	83.1	58.5	24.6	353.7
3rd quarter	358.5	219.8	53.9	29.8	18.5	5.6	0.0	15.2	15.3	84.9	60.5	24.4	353.0
4th quarter	371.4	227.9	57.1	32.5	19.4	5.3	-1.0	15.3	16.3	87.4	62.4	25.0	366.1
1953													
1st quarter	378.4	231.5	57.9	34.3	19.7	3.9	-0.7	15.1	15.8	89.7	63.9	25.8	374.5
2nd quarter	382.0	233.3	58.1	34.8	19.8	3.6	-1.3	15.2	16.4	91.8	66.2	25.6	378.4
3rd quarter	381.1	234.0	57.4	35.9	19.2	2.3	-0.6	15.8	16.3	90.3	64.0	26.3	378.8
4th quarter	375.9	233.5	52.3	35.4	18.9	-2.0	-0.3	15.2	15.5	90.5	63.6	26.9	377.9
1954													
1st quarter	375.3	235.5	51.5	34.5	19.0	-2.0	-0.4	14.4	14.8	88.6	60.8	27.8	377.3
2nd quarter	376.0	238.3	51.2	34.3	20.3	-3.4	0.3	16.4	16.2	86.2	57.7	28.5	379.4
3rd quarter	380.8	240.7	54.7	35.0	21.8	-2.1	0.6	15.9	15.3	84.8	55.4	29.5	382.9
4th quarter	389.5	245.5	57.8	34.9	23.2	-0.3	1.1	16.6	15.5	85.0	55.2	29.8	389.8
1955													
1st quarter	402.6	251.8	64.2	35.4	25.0	3.8	1.1	17.3	16.2	85.4	54.6	30.8	398.8
2nd quarter	410.9	256.9	68.1	37.9	25.6	4.6	-0.2	16.9	17.1	86.0	54.7	31.3	406.3
3rd quarter	419.5	261.1	70.0	40.4	25.2	4.3	0.7	18.1	17.4	87.7	55.8	31.8	415.2
4th quarter	426.0	265.1	73.9	42.5	24.2	7.2	0.2	18.3	18.1	86.8	54.4	32.4	418.8
1956													
1st quarter	428.3	266.7	73.0	42.9	23.7	6.4	0.4	19.4	18.9	88.2	54.7	33.5	421.9
2nd quarter	434.2	269.4	71.4	43.9	23.9	3.6	1.9	20.9	19.0	91.5	57.1	34.4	430.6
3rd quarter	439.3	272.6	72.5	45.4	23.5	3.6	2.6	21.8	19.3	91.6	56.4	35.1	435.7
4th quarter	448.1	278.0	71.2	45.9	23.0	2.2	4.5	23.1	18.5	94.4	58.5	35.8	445.9
1957													
1st quarter	457.2	282.4	71.8	47.0	22.6	2.2	4.8	24.9	20.1	98.2	61.1	37.1	455.1
2nd quarter	459.2	284.7	71.9	47.1	22.2	2.7	4.1	24.4	20.3	98.4	60.5	38.0	456.5
3rd quarter	466.4	289.3	73.2	48.4	22.0	2.8	4.0	23.8	19.8	99.9	61.2	38.7	463.6
4th quarter	461.5	291.0	64.9	47.5	21.9	-4.5	3.4	23.0	19.6	102.3	62.7	39.6	466.1
1958													
1st quarter	454.0	290.5	60.5	43.6	20.9	-4.0	1.1	20.5	19.5	101.8	61.2	40.6	458.0
2nd quarter	458.1	293.4	58.7	42.0	21.0	-4.2	0.5	20.5	20.1	105.4	63.9	41.6	462.3
3rd quarter	471.7	298.5	65.5	41.4	22.5	1.5	0.9	20.6	19.7	106.9	64.2	42.7	470.2
4th quarter	485.0	302.3	73.2	43.1	24.9	5.2	-0.3	20.6	20.8	109.7	66.0	43.7	479.8
1959													
1st quarter	495.4	310.0	76.2	44.5	27.8	3.9	0.4	21.8	21.4	108.9	64.3	44.5	491.5
2nd quarter	508.4	316.0	82.2	46.1	28.8	7.3	0.0	22.6	22.5	110.2	65.5	44.7	501.2
3rd quarter	509.3	321.2	76.4	47.8	28.3	0.4	0.6	23.5	22.9	111.0	66.2	44.8	508.9
4th quarter	513.2	323.3	79.3	47.7	27.5	4.1	0.6	23.1	22.5	110.0	65.4	44.6	509.1
1960													
1st quarter	526.9	326.9	89.1	49.5	28.4	11.2	2.7	26.0	23.3	108.3	62.4	45.8	515.7
2nd quarter	526.1	332.7	79.7	50.3	26.1	3.2	4.2	27.6	23.5	109.5	62.4	47.2	522.9
3rd quarter	528.9	332.7	78.7	49.0	25.3	4.3	4.2	27.0	22.9	113.4	65.3	48.1	524.6
4th quarter	523.6	334.6	68.1	48.6	25.3	-5.8	5.8	27.5	21.7	115.1	66.3	48.8	529.4
1961													
1st quarter	527.9	335.1	70.3	47.5	25.3	-2.5	5.8	27.5	21.7	116.7	66.0	50.7	530.5
2nd quarter	539.0	340.1	75.8	48.4	25.5	1.8	5.5	27.4	21.9	117.6	66.8	50.8	537.2
3rd quarter	549.4	343.0	82.4	48.8	26.9	6.7	3.9	27.2	23.3	120.2	68.6	51.6	542.8
4th quarter	562.5	350.3	84.2	50.4	27.8	6.0	4.4	28.3	23.9	123.6	70.2	53.4	556.6

Table 19-1. Gross Domestic Product—Continued

(Billions of dollars, quarterly data are at seasonally adjusted annual rates.)   **NIPA Tables 1.1.5, 1.4.5**

| Year and quarter | Gross domestic product | Personal consumption expenditures | Gross private domestic investment | | | | Exports and imports of goods and services | | | Government consumption expenditures and gross investment | | | Addendum: Final sales of domestic product |
| | | | Total | Fixed investment | | Change in private inventories | Net exports | Exports | Imports | Total | Federal | State and local | |
				Nonresidential	Residential								
1962													
1st quarter	576.0	355.6	89.4	51.6	28.4	9.4	4.0	28.3	24.3	127.2	73.4	53.8	566.6
2nd quarter	583.2	361.2	87.9	53.2	29.2	5.4	5.8	30.7	24.9	128.3	73.9	54.4	577.8
3rd quarter	590.0	365.1	89.3	53.9	29.2	6.2	3.8	29.0	25.1	131.8	76.6	55.2	583.8
4th quarter	593.3	371.3	86.0	53.5	29.1	3.4	2.8	28.4	25.6	133.2	77.1	56.1	589.9
1963													
1st quarter	602.4	374.9	90.5	53.4	30.2	6.9	3.9	29.1	25.2	133.2	75.5	57.6	595.6
2nd quarter	611.2	379.0	92.2	55.1	32.2	4.8	6.5	32.4	25.9	133.4	74.9	58.5	606.3
3rd quarter	623.9	386.0	95.0	56.8	32.5	5.7	3.9	30.6	26.7	139.0	78.8	60.2	618.2
4th quarter	633.5	390.7	97.4	58.7	33.7	5.1	5.4	32.2	26.8	139.9	78.4	61.5	628.4
1964													
1st quarter	649.6	400.3	100.7	60.1	35.4	5.1	7.3	34.2	27.0	141.3	78.6	62.7	644.5
2nd quarter	658.8	408.3	100.6	61.9	34.2	4.5	7.1	34.8	27.7	142.9	78.4	64.5	654.4
3rd quarter	670.5	417.2	102.5	64.1	33.7	4.7	6.4	34.8	28.4	144.4	78.9	65.5	665.8
4th quarter	675.6	419.8	104.6	65.7	33.8	5.0	6.9	36.2	29.3	144.3	77.8	66.5	670.6
1965													
1st quarter	695.7	430.5	115.7	70.3	33.9	11.5	4.6	33.1	28.5	144.9	77.1	67.8	684.1
2nd quarter	708.1	437.4	115.8	73.1	34.2	8.6	7.5	39.1	31.7	147.4	77.5	69.9	699.6
3rd quarter	725.2	446.6	119.7	76.1	34.3	9.3	4.9	36.9	32.0	154.0	81.6	72.5	715.9
4th quarter	747.5	460.6	121.8	79.7	34.5	7.6	5.5	39.5	33.9	159.6	85.5	74.1	739.9
1966													
1st quarter	770.8	471.0	131.7	83.0	34.8	13.9	4.4	39.4	35.0	163.6	87.6	76.0	756.9
2nd quarter	779.9	476.1	130.7	85.2	33.2	12.3	5.2	41.5	36.2	167.9	90.0	77.9	767.6
3rd quarter	793.4	485.3	130.2	86.4	31.9	11.9	2.2	40.4	38.2	175.7	95.8	79.9	781.5
4th quarter	807.1	491.1	132.7	87.0	29.2	16.5	3.6	42.4	38.8	179.8	96.8	83.0	790.6
1967													
1st quarter	817.9	495.4	129.3	85.6	28.3	15.4	4.6	44.0	39.4	188.7	103.2	85.4	802.5
2nd quarter	822.5	504.5	123.7	85.7	31.6	6.3	4.5	43.5	39.0	189.7	102.9	86.8	816.1
3rd quarter	837.1	511.8	128.5	85.8	33.4	9.3	2.9	42.4	39.5	194.0	105.6	88.3	827.9
4th quarter	852.8	519.3	132.9	88.4	36.0	8.4	2.2	43.9	41.7	198.4	107.4	90.9	844.4
1968													
1st quarter	879.9	537.3	137.2	91.9	36.9	8.4	1.1	45.5	44.4	204.3	110.3	94.0	871.5
2nd quarter	904.2	551.2	143.4	91.2	38.2	14.1	1.9	47.4	45.4	207.7	110.7	97.0	890.2
3rd quarter	919.4	567.4	139.7	93.2	38.9	7.7	1.3	49.5	48.2	211.1	111.8	99.2	911.7
4th quarter	936.3	576.3	144.4	97.4	40.9	6.0	1.1	49.2	48.2	214.6	112.7	102.0	930.3
1969													
1st quarter	961.0	588.5	155.7	101.0	43.2	11.5	0.2	44.0	43.8	216.6	112.2	104.4	949.5
2nd quarter	976.3	599.9	155.7	103.0	43.4	9.2	1.2	53.9	52.7	219.5	112.1	107.4	967.0
3rd quarter	996.5	610.2	160.3	106.9	43.2	10.2	1.0	53.3	52.4	224.9	115.4	109.5	986.3
4th quarter	1 004.6	622.2	154.1	107.6	40.7	5.8	3.3	56.5	53.1	225.0	113.7	111.3	998.9
1970													
1st quarter	1 017.3	633.3	150.7	108.1	40.7	1.8	3.4	56.9	53.5	229.9	115.0	114.9	1 015.5
2nd quarter	1 033.2	643.3	153.9	109.4	39.4	5.1	5.4	60.6	55.2	230.7	112.7	118.0	1 028.2
3rd quarter	1 050.7	655.3	156.1	110.6	40.4	5.1	3.8	60.3	56.4	235.6	112.8	122.7	1 045.6
4th quarter	1 052.9	662.0	148.9	107.9	45.0	-4.0	3.2	61.1	57.9	238.9	113.3	125.6	1 056.9
1971													
1st quarter	1 098.3	681.0	171.3	110.4	48.6	12.3	4.4	63.1	58.7	241.6	112.9	128.7	1 086.1
2nd quarter	1 119.1	695.1	178.8	113.4	54.6	10.9	-0.2	63.1	63.3	245.3	113.5	131.8	1 108.2
3rd quarter	1 139.3	707.5	183.4	114.8	58.3	10.2	-0.1	65.4	65.5	248.5	114.7	133.8	1 129.1
4th quarter	1 151.7	723.8	179.2	118.0	61.5	-0.3	-1.7	60.3	61.9	250.3	113.6	136.8	1 152.0
1972													
1st quarter	1 190.6	741.2	193.2	123.3	66.6	3.2	-3.5	68.6	72.2	259.7	119.8	139.9	1 187.3
2nd quarter	1 225.9	759.8	206.5	126.3	68.2	12.0	-4.3	67.2	71.4	263.9	122.6	141.3	1 213.9
3rd quarter	1 249.7	778.3	212.4	129.1	69.6	13.7	-2.6	71.5	74.1	261.6	116.9	144.8	1 236.0
4th quarter	1 287.0	803.1	218.4	136.6	74.3	7.5	-3.1	76.1	79.2	268.6	119.4	149.2	1 279.5
1973													
1st quarter	1 335.5	827.7	232.5	144.1	77.9	10.6	-1.4	84.0	85.4	276.7	123.4	153.3	1 325.0
2nd quarter	1 371.9	843.3	246.0	152.1	75.8	18.2	2.5	91.9	89.5	280.1	123.3	156.8	1 353.7
3rd quarter	1 391.2	861.8	241.8	157.0	75.0	9.8	6.4	97.6	91.1	281.2	120.4	160.8	1 381.4
4th quarter	1 432.3	876.9	257.6	159.9	72.7	25.0	9.0	107.6	98.7	288.8	122.9	165.9	1 407.3
1974													
1st quarter	1 447.0	895.1	244.1	162.6	69.0	12.5	6.4	116.7	110.3	301.4	128.6	172.8	1 434.5
2nd quarter	1 485.3	923.7	252.3	167.4	67.5	17.4	-2.7	126.7	129.4	312.1	131.1	180.9	1 467.9
3rd quarter	1 514.2	952.5	245.4	172.5	67.4	5.6	-7.0	126.6	133.6	323.2	136.1	187.1	1 508.6
4th quarter	1 553.4	962.4	255.8	175.4	60.0	20.4	0.0	136.6	136.6	335.1	142.5	192.6	1 532.9
1975													
1st quarter	1 570.0	988.6	218.7	171.0	57.7	-10.0	16.5	141.4	124.9	346.3	144.0	202.2	1 580.0
2nd quarter	1 605.6	1 017.4	216.8	170.8	59.9	-14.0	21.6	136.8	115.2	349.8	144.9	204.9	1 619.6
3rd quarter	1 663.1	1 051.3	237.8	174.6	64.6	-1.4	12.0	134.1	122.1	362.0	151.4	210.6	1 664.5
4th quarter	1 714.6	1 080.2	247.6	178.6	68.7	0.3	13.8	142.5	128.7	372.9	156.0	216.9	1 714.2
1976													
1st quarter	1 772.6	1 114.0	274.8	183.9	76.2	14.7	4.7	143.6	138.9	379.1	156.3	222.8	1 757.9
2nd quarter	1 804.9	1 133.7	291.6	188.5	80.7	22.4	-0.5	146.6	147.1	380.1	157.8	222.3	1 782.4
3rd quarter	1 838.3	1 163.1	296.5	195.1	80.6	20.8	-4.1	151.8	155.8	382.8	159.9	223.0	1 817.5
4th quarter	1 885.3	1 196.9	304.9	201.9	92.5	10.5	-6.6	156.1	162.7	390.0	164.9	225.2	1 874.8

Table 19-1. Gross Domestic Product—*Continued*

(Billions of dollars, quarterly data are at seasonally adjusted annual rates.)   **NIPA Tables 1.1.5, 1.4.5**

| Year and quarter | Gross domestic product | Personal consumption expenditures | Gross private domestic investment | | | | Exports and imports of goods and services | | | Government consumption expenditures and gross investment | | | Addendum: Final sales of domestic product |
| | | | Total | Fixed investment | | Change in private inventories | Net exports | Exports | Imports | Total | Federal | State and local | |
				Nonresidential	Residential								
1977													
1st quarter	1 939.3	1 232.5	326.6	214.2	97.6	14.8	-21.1	155.4	176.4	401.4	169.8	231.5	1 924.5
2nd quarter	2 006.0	1 260.4	354.9	223.8	111.7	19.5	-21.1	161.9	183.0	411.8	174.8	237.0	1 986.6
3rd quarter	2 066.8	1 291.7	378.4	232.5	115.0	30.9	-20.6	162.3	182.9	417.3	176.5	240.8	2 035.9
4th quarter	2 111.6	1 329.8	385.5	244.5	116.9	24.1	-29.6	157.8	187.4	425.8	180.6	245.3	2 087.5
1978													
1st quarter	2 150.0	1 359.9	396.8	250.4	121.0	25.5	-38.7	164.6	203.3	431.9	183.0	249.0	2 124.5
2nd quarter	2 275.6	1 417.6	430.9	276.0	130.6	24.3	-22.6	186.2	208.8	449.8	189.2	260.6	2 251.4
3rd quarter	2 336.2	1 448.7	451.4	290.6	135.8	25.0	-23.8	191.3	215.1	459.9	192.4	267.4	2 311.2
4th quarter	2 417.0	1 487.9	472.8	305.3	139.0	28.5	-16.4	205.4	221.8	472.7	199.1	273.6	2 388.5
1979													
1st quarter	2 464.4	1 523.6	481.1	318.8	138.5	23.9	-18.2	211.7	229.8	477.8	202.3	275.5	2 440.5
2nd quarter	2 527.6	1 564.3	493.0	324.9	140.6	27.4	-22.2	220.9	243.1	492.5	207.9	284.6	2 500.2
3rd quarter	2 600.7	1 618.6	497.9	342.3	143.5	12.1	-23.0	234.3	257.3	507.3	211.8	295.5	2 588.6
4th quarter	2 660.5	1 662.2	499.5	349.6	141.4	8.6	-26.8	253.7	280.5	525.5	220.5	305.0	2 651.9
1980													
1st quarter	2 725.3	1 709.1	505.2	361.3	134.0	9.9	-35.8	268.5	304.3	546.8	231.7	315.1	2 715.4
2nd quarter	2 729.3	1 711.2	470.4	350.9	111.7	7.8	-15.2	277.4	292.6	562.8	243.0	319.8	2 721.5
3rd quarter	2 786.6	1 770.1	443.5	361.1	116.3	-33.9	5.5	284.7	279.2	567.6	243.6	324.0	2 820.5
4th quarter	2 916.9	1 838.1	497.9	376.2	130.8	-9.1	-6.7	292.5	299.2	587.5	256.8	330.8	2 926.0
1981													
1st quarter	3 052.7	1 893.7	563.1	393.1	131.3	38.8	-14.3	305.5	319.7	610.1	266.5	343.6	3 014.0
2nd quarter	3 085.9	1 925.5	551.4	410.8	128.9	11.7	-13.5	308.4	322.0	622.5	278.7	343.8	3 074.2
3rd quarter	3 178.7	1 965.1	592.8	428.4	120.4	44.0	-7.6	302.3	309.9	628.4	281.4	347.0	3 134.8
4th quarter	3 196.4	1 979.9	582.2	447.8	109.6	24.8	-14.8	304.7	319.4	649.0	294.2	354.8	3 171.6
1982													
1st quarter	3 186.8	2 018.0	526.4	443.1	104.8	-21.5	-16.3	293.2	309.5	658.6	298.7	359.9	3 208.2
2nd quarter	3 242.7	2 044.4	530.8	432.0	102.9	-4.2	-4.4	294.7	299.1	671.9	305.1	366.8	3 246.9
3rd quarter	3 276.2	2 092.4	528.7	419.5	103.5	5.8	-29.7	279.6	309.3	684.7	312.3	372.4	3 270.4
4th quarter	3 314.4	2 154.2	483.0	411.3	111.5	-39.8	-29.6	265.3	294.9	706.8	327.1	379.7	3 354.2
1983													
1st quarter	3 382.9	2 194.1	496.6	400.5	131.2	-35.1	-24.6	270.7	295.3	716.7	332.9	383.8	3 417.9
2nd quarter	3 484.1	2 258.2	542.2	402.9	147.0	-7.7	-45.4	272.5	318.0	729.1	342.1	387.0	3 491.8
3rd quarter	3 589.3	2 328.6	577.7	419.5	162.4	-4.2	-65.2	278.2	343.4	748.2	354.2	394.0	3 593.5
4th quarter	3 690.4	2 381.3	640.7	446.0	170.8	23.9	-71.4	286.6	358.0	739.8	342.5	397.3	3 666.5
1984													
1st quarter	3 809.6	2 427.6	709.7	460.1	176.6	73.0	-95.0	293.0	388.0	767.4	359.3	408.0	3 736.6
2nd quarter	3 908.6	2 486.3	735.1	484.4	181.4	69.3	-104.3	302.2	406.5	791.5	374.0	417.4	3 839.3
3rd quarter	3 978.2	2 524.9	753.5	500.7	181.4	71.3	-103.9	305.7	409.6	803.6	375.3	428.4	3 906.8
4th quarter	4 036.3	2 574.3	744.3	513.3	183.0	48.0	-107.8	308.6	416.4	825.5	388.8	436.7	3 988.3
1985													
1st quarter	4 119.5	2 645.7	720.0	520.5	183.3	16.2	-91.9	305.4	397.3	845.7	398.1	447.6	4 103.3
2nd quarter	4 178.4	2 690.1	735.3	528.5	185.1	21.6	-115.4	303.1	418.6	868.5	407.7	460.8	4 156.8
3rd quarter	4 261.3	2 758.7	727.2	522.2	188.8	16.3	-118.6	295.6	414.2	894.0	420.8	473.2	4 245.0
4th quarter	4 321.8	2 786.7	762.2	533.6	195.5	33.1	-134.9	304.0	438.9	907.8	424.7	483.1	4 288.7
1986													
1st quarter	4 385.6	2 830.3	763.8	527.2	206.3	30.3	-127.6	312.2	439.8	919.2	421.5	497.7	4 355.3
2nd quarter	4 425.7	2 862.0	753.0	517.5	219.8	15.7	-130.0	314.4	444.4	940.7	434.8	505.9	4 410.0
3rd quarter	4 493.9	2 933.5	732.5	513.5	226.1	-7.0	-139.5	320.4	459.8	967.4	452.1	515.3	4 500.9
4th quarter	4 546.1	2 973.2	736.7	521.2	228.3	-12.7	-133.8	335.2	469.0	970.0	446.2	523.9	4 558.8
1987													
1st quarter	4 613.8	3 008.0	765.0	506.8	230.1	28.0	-141.3	336.8	478.1	982.1	451.9	530.2	4 585.8
2nd quarter	4 690.0	3 075.3	767.6	518.2	232.9	16.5	-147.6	355.1	502.7	994.6	459.1	535.5	4 673.5
3rd quarter	4 767.8	3 141.6	769.5	534.2	234.2	1.0	-146.0	371.7	517.7	1 002.7	461.0	541.7	4 766.8
4th quarter	4 886.3	3 176.0	837.8	537.2	237.5	63.1	-145.9	392.0	537.9	1 018.4	468.2	550.2	4 823.2
1988													
1st quarter	4 951.9	3 256.8	797.6	546.2	234.4	17.0	-124.7	418.5	543.2	1 022.2	460.9	561.3	4 934.9
2nd quarter	5 062.8	3 316.4	820.4	562.3	238.4	19.7	-107.4	439.1	546.6	1 033.5	459.7	573.8	5 043.2
3rd quarter	5 146.6	3 384.0	825.7	567.5	240.0	18.2	-100.5	452.9	553.3	1 037.4	456.8	580.5	5 128.5
4th quarter	5 253.7	3 457.2	842.6	579.1	244.4	19.1	-109.0	465.8	574.8	1 062.9	471.8	591.1	5 234.7
1989													
1st quarter	5 367.1	3 511.3	884.1	591.3	244.6	48.2	-98.2	484.0	582.3	1 070.0	470.1	599.9	5 318.9
2nd quarter	5 454.1	3 573.9	878.2	601.9	240.2	36.0	-91.6	505.7	597.3	1 093.6	482.2	611.5	5 418.1
3rd quarter	5 531.9	3 630.9	870.3	621.9	238.4	10.0	-79.3	508.4	587.7	1 109.9	489.7	620.2	5 521.9
4th quarter	5 584.3	3 677.8	867.3	615.8	234.8	16.6	-83.5	515.2	598.7	1 122.7	486.9	635.8	5 567.7
1990													
1st quarter	5 716.4	3 762.6	880.0	626.9	239.2	13.9	-83.6	537.6	621.1	1 157.4	501.4	655.9	5 702.4
2nd quarter	5 797.7	3 815.9	882.5	617.9	230.9	33.7	-70.9	546.3	617.2	1 170.2	506.7	663.5	5 764.0
3rd quarter	5 849.4	3 879.6	866.8	626.1	218.8	21.9	-78.5	555.9	634.3	1 181.5	505.8	675.7	5 827.6
4th quarter	5 848.8	3 901.7	814.6	618.9	207.0	-11.3	-79.0	569.7	648.7	1 211.5	519.2	692.3	5 860.1
1991													
1st quarter	5 888.0	3 914.2	787.9	608.2	195.2	-15.6	-41.5	574.6	616.1	1 227.4	530.4	697.0	5 903.5
2nd quarter	5 964.3	3 970.3	784.0	601.4	200.7	-18.1	-24.3	592.3	616.6	1 234.3	532.9	701.4	5 982.4
3rd quarter	6 035.6	4 015.7	805.2	594.1	210.3	0.8	-22.7	602.6	625.3	1 237.5	527.3	710.2	6 034.8
4th quarter	6 095.8	4 044.1	834.4	589.0	214.2	31.2	-21.4	617.8	639.2	1 238.6	520.5	718.1	6 064.5

Table 19-1. Gross Domestic Product—*Continued*

(Billions of dollars, quarterly data are at seasonally adjusted annual rates.)   **NIPA Tables 1.1.5, 1.4.5**

Year and quarter	Gross domestic product	Personal consumption expenditures	Gross private domestic investment				Exports and imports of goods and services			Government consumption expenditures and gross investment			Addendum: Final sales of domestic product
			Total	Fixed investment		Change in private inventories	Net exports	Exports	Imports	Total	Federal	State and local	
				Nonresidential	Residential								
1992													
1st quarter	6 196.1	4 142.5	810.2	585.6	224.4	0.2	-14.2	627.4	641.6	1 257.6	526.8	730.7	6 195.9
2nd quarter	6 290.1	4 193.1	865.4	607.1	235.1	23.2	-33.7	628.0	661.7	1 265.3	530.0	735.3	6 266.9
3rd quarter	6 380.5	4 264.3	876.8	619.0	237.3	20.5	-39.6	641.8	681.4	1 278.9	539.6	739.3	6 360.0
4th quarter	6 484.3	4 341.1	906.6	636.7	248.6	21.3	-45.5	644.1	689.6	1 282.1	539.3	742.8	6 463.0
1993													
1st quarter	6 542.7	4 379.3	931.3	642.8	252.6	35.9	-50.0	645.1	695.1	1 282.1	528.9	753.2	6 506.8
2nd quarter	6 612.1	4 446.7	942.3	660.3	257.9	24.1	-65.2	654.3	719.6	1 288.3	524.7	763.6	6 588.0
3rd quarter	6 674.6	4 510.7	943.4	667.5	269.3	6.6	-70.9	651.6	722.5	1 291.5	521.7	769.8	6 668.0
4th quarter	6 800.2	4 574.9	996.5	695.7	284.1	16.7	-74.0	672.3	746.3	1 302.8	525.7	777.2	6 783.5
1994													
1st quarter	6 911.0	4 643.9	1 043.2	704.8	293.1	45.3	-77.6	681.2	758.8	1 301.5	513.3	788.2	6 865.7
2nd quarter	7 030.6	4 702.8	1 106.7	720.5	304.7	81.5	-94.6	706.3	801.0	1 315.7	516.2	799.5	6 949.1
3rd quarter	7 115.1	4 778.6	1 092.9	734.7	304.8	53.4	-99.7	737.2	836.9	1 343.4	528.6	814.8	7 061.7
4th quarter	7 232.2	4 847.9	1 145.5	765.6	304.8	75.1	-102.4	758.8	861.2	1 341.3	518.5	822.8	7 157.1
1995													
1st quarter	7 298.3	4 879.0	1 160.6	797.7	301.7	61.2	-102.7	780.7	883.4	1 361.4	523.5	837.9	7 237.1
2nd quarter	7 337.7	4 946.7	1 132.6	805.5	293.4	33.7	-114.3	797.7	912.0	1 372.7	523.3	849.3	7 304.0
3rd quarter	7 432.1	5 011.0	1 126.2	811.2	303.8	11.2	-78.2	830.9	909.1	1 373.0	520.3	852.7	7 420.8
4th quarter	7 522.5	5 066.4	1 156.6	825.8	312.4	18.3	-70.3	839.6	909.8	1 369.8	509.7	860.1	7 504.2
1996													
1st quarter	7 624.1	5 142.8	1 170.0	841.4	321.8	6.8	-84.2	848.2	932.4	1 395.6	527.8	867.8	7 617.3
2nd quarter	7 776.6	5 232.0	1 227.9	860.5	336.9	30.5	-97.0	859.6	956.6	1 413.7	533.6	880.0	7 746.2
3rd quarter	7 866.2	5 286.4	1 279.9	889.0	339.7	51.1	-116.7	860.8	977.5	1 416.6	522.8	893.8	7 815.1
4th quarter	8 000.4	5 366.1	1 283.3	910.7	337.9	34.7	-87.1	905.6	992.7	1 438.1	525.3	912.8	7 965.8
1997													
1st quarter	8 113.8	5 448.8	1 315.4	930.1	340.8	44.4	-103.0	919.7	1 022.7	1 452.7	523.5	929.2	8 069.4
2nd quarter	8 250.4	5 484.6	1 385.2	950.0	346.8	88.5	-88.3	955.5	1 043.8	1 468.9	535.6	933.3	8 162.0
3rd quarter	8 381.9	5 589.8	1 419.5	995.7	351.3	72.5	-99.6	975.6	1 075.2	1 472.2	532.8	939.4	8 309.4
4th quarter	8 471.2	5 666.4	1 439.1	998.9	357.5	82.7	-115.3	970.6	1 085.9	1 481.1	531.7	949.4	8 388.6
1998													
1st quarter	8 586.7	5 733.4	1 505.5	1 024.0	365.9	115.5	-129.2	965.2	1 094.4	1 477.0	520.3	956.7	8 471.2
2nd quarter	8 657.9	5 834.2	1 474.6	1 049.1	378.6	46.9	-162.4	949.6	1 112.0	1 511.5	534.4	977.1	8 611.0
3rd quarter	8 789.5	5 924.2	1 507.8	1 054.3	392.8	60.7	-174.2	938.3	1 112.5	1 531.7	530.5	1 001.2	8 728.8
4th quarter	8 953.8	6 026.2	1 548.6	1 082.7	406.0	59.9	-174.0	970.6	1 144.6	1 553.1	536.6	1 016.4	8 893.9
1999													
1st quarter	9 066.6	6 101.7	1 596.7	1 101.0	413.5	82.2	-207.5	960.1	1 167.6	1 575.6	540.6	1 035.0	8 984.4
2nd quarter	9 174.1	6 237.2	1 589.9	1 130.1	421.7	38.1	-252.1	972.8	1 224.9	1 599.1	545.9	1 053.2	9 136.0
3rd quarter	9 313.5	6 337.2	1 628.3	1 151.5	427.8	49.1	-285.2	1 000.5	1 285.7	1 633.2	560.0	1 073.2	9 264.4
4th quarter	9 519.5	6 453.7	1 687.7	1 153.0	436.5	98.2	-297.2	1 031.6	1 328.8	1 675.3	576.8	1 098.5	9 421.3
2000													
1st quarter	9 629.4	6 613.9	1 672.3	1 193.9	448.5	29.9	-346.4	1 055.1	1 401.5	1 689.6	565.3	1 124.3	9 599.6
2nd quarter	9 822.8	6 688.1	1 781.7	1 236.5	448.8	96.3	-366.9	1 091.8	1 458.7	1 720.0	586.6	1 133.4	9 726.5
3rd quarter	9 862.1	6 783.9	1 749.0	1 247.5	443.1	58.4	-400.7	1 122.4	1 523.1	1 729.9	581.2	1 148.6	9 803.7
4th quarter	9 953.6	6 871.6	1 738.9	1 250.3	447.2	41.4	-403.9	1 115.8	1 519.7	1 746.9	582.0	1 164.9	9 912.2
2001													
1st quarter	10 021.5	6 955.8	1 675.3	1 229.6	455.6	-9.9	-392.9	1 100.7	1 493.7	1 783.3	596.2	1 187.2	10 031.4
2nd quarter	10 128.9	7 017.5	1 647.7	1 187.1	467.6	-7.0	-361.7	1 060.5	1 422.2	1 825.4	610.9	1 214.5	10 136.0
3rd quarter	10 135.1	7 058.5	1 613.0	1 167.2	477.6	-31.8	-361.9	1 003.5	1 365.3	1 825.6	614.3	1 211.2	10 166.9
4th quarter	10 226.3	7 188.4	1 521.4	1 123.2	476.3	-78.2	-351.6	966.6	1 318.2	1 868.2	630.1	1 238.1	10 304.5
2002													
1st quarter	10 333.3	7 230.3	1 564.1	1 085.2	487.2	-8.3	-373.1	976.4	1 349.5	1 912.0	654.9	1 257.2	10 341.6
2nd quarter	10 426.6	7 323.0	1 571.4	1 067.8	501.0	2.6	-416.1	1 008.2	1 424.3	1 948.3	675.2	1 273.1	10 424.0
3rd quarter	10 527.4	7 396.6	1 592.9	1 061.4	505.4	26.0	-433.8	1 022.9	1 456.7	1 971.8	682.0	1 289.8	10 501.4
4th quarter	10 591.1	7 453.1	1 600.1	1 050.7	522.1	27.3	-474.6	1 016.2	1 490.8	2 012.5	706.6	1 305.9	10 563.9
2003													
1st quarter	10 705.6	7 548.1	1 606.4	1 044.0	539.3	23.0	-499.3	1 012.4	1 511.7	2 050.3	725.9	1 324.4	10 682.6
2nd quarter	10 831.8	7 628.4	1 617.1	1 067.4	553.2	-3.5	-501.3	1 010.8	1 512.1	2 087.7	762.2	1 325.5	10 835.4
3rd quarter	11 086.1	7 782.6	1 690.5	1 093.3	585.4	11.8	-495.2	1 040.7	1 535.9	2 108.2	764.8	1 343.3	11 074.3
4th quarter	11 219.5	7 855.3	1 742.3	1 104.8	611.6	25.9	-501.8	1 099.1	1 600.9	2 123.7	772.8	1 350.9	11 193.6
2004													
1st quarter	11 405.5	8 010.1	1 769.6	1 100.4	632.2	37.0	-543.2	1 140.9	1 684.1	2 169.1	806.2	1 362.9	11 368.6
2nd quarter	11 610.3	8 135.0	1 875.6	1 135.4	671.1	69.0	-603.1	1 172.8	1 775.8	2 202.8	821.9	1 381.0	11 541.3
3rd quarter	11 779.4	8 245.1	1 929.7	1 172.7	692.0	65.0	-632.6	1 187.3	1 820.0	2 237.3	839.4	1 397.9	11 714.4
4th quarter	11 948.5	8 393.3	1 979.5	1 209.5	706.6	63.4	-682.6	1 228.6	1 911.2	2 258.2	835.0	1 423.2	11 885.0
2005													
1st quarter	12 155.4	8 480.9	2 046.0	1 233.6	729.7	82.6	-670.7	1 266.8	1 937.5	2 299.2	861.0	1 438.2	12 072.7
2nd quarter	12 297.5	8 610.8	2 039.7	1 261.0	759.3	19.4	-680.9	1 305.1	1 986.0	2 328.0	867.1	1 460.9	12 278.1
3rd quarter	12 538.2	8 791.1	2 084.2	1 286.1	787.1	11.0	-725.1	1 314.5	2 039.6	2 388.0	894.2	1 493.8	12 527.2
4th quarter	12 696.4	8 893.7	2 174.6	1 311.8	802.5	60.3	-777.7	1 359.6	2 137.4	2 405.9	879.5	1 526.4	12 636.1
2006													
1st quarter	12 959.6	9 026.3	2 236.7	1 375.5	808.1	53.1	-761.7	1 423.2	2 184.9	2 458.4	922.8	1 535.5	12 906.5
2nd quarter	13 134.1	9 161.9	2 253.7	1 408.3	779.6	65.9	-777.2	1 462.8	2 240.0	2 495.7	928.5	1 567.2	13 068.3
3rd quarter	13 249.6	9 283.7	2 231.7	1 433.0	736.2	62.5	-792.7	1 492.5	2 285.2	2 526.9	935.5	1 591.4	13 187.1
4th quarter	13 370.1	9 357.0	2 159.5	1 439.6	704.0	15.8	-697.7	1 544.5	2 242.2	2 551.4	941.7	1 609.7	13 354.3

Table 19-2. Real Gross Domestic Product

(Billions of chained [2000] dollars, quarterly data are at seasonally adjusted annual rates.)   **NIPA Tables 1.1.6, 1.4.6**

Year and quarter	Gross domestic product	Personal consumption expenditures	Gross private domestic investment				Exports and imports of goods and services			Government consumption expenditures and gross investment			Addendum: Final sales of domestic product
			Total	Fixed investment		Change in private inventories	Net exports	Exports	Imports	Total	Federal	State and local	
				Nonresidential	Residential								
1946	1 589.4	1 012.9	172.1	. . .	. . .	22.9	. . .	64.6	47.0	396.8	. . .	. . .	1 566.4
1947	1 574.5	1 031.6	165.3	. . .	. . .	-3.2	. . .	73.7	44.6	337.2	. . .	. . .	1 598.5
1948	1 643.2	1 054.4	211.2	. . .	. . .	17.4	. . .	58.0	52.0	361.7	. . .	. . .	1 628.1
1949	1 634.6	1 083.5	161.2	. . .	. . .	-9.2	. . .	57.5	50.2	404.9	. . .	. . .	1 666.7
1947													
1st quarter	1 570.5	1 017.2	170.2	. . .	. . .	4.7	. . .	78.3	46.0	335.4	. . .	. . .	1 584.0
2nd quarter	1 568.7	1 034.0	156.7	. . .	. . .	-3.1	. . .	77.5	46.9	337.4	. . .	. . .	1 594.5
3rd quarter	1 568.0	1 037.5	151.6	. . .	. . .	-12.3	. . .	73.7	41.6	340.5	. . .	. . .	1 607.6
4th quarter	1 590.9	1 037.7	182.6	. . .	. . .	-2.1	. . .	65.3	43.9	335.4	. . .	. . .	1 607.8
1948													
1st quarter	1 616.1	1 042.6	202.6	. . .	. . .	10.0	. . .	62.3	49.5	342.0	. . .	. . .	1 614.6
2nd quarter	1 644.6	1 054.3	215.8	. . .	. . .	19.4	. . .	56.4	51.4	358.4	. . .	. . .	1 625.6
3rd quarter	1 654.1	1 056.1	218.3	. . .	. . .	22.7	. . .	57.7	54.1	365.5	. . .	. . .	1 628.8
4th quarter	1 658.0	1 064.8	207.9	. . .	. . .	17.5	. . .	55.7	53.2	381.0	. . .	. . .	1 643.4
1949													
1st quarter	1 633.2	1 066.1	174.8	. . .	. . .	-1.8	. . .	62.3	51.6	391.7	. . .	. . .	1 649.4
2nd quarter	1 628.4	1 082.6	150.9	. . .	. . .	-15.8	. . .	61.8	50.9	409.5	. . .	. . .	1 671.2
3rd quarter	1 646.7	1 085.0	164.3	. . .	. . .	-3.5	. . .	56.7	48.8	413.7	. . .	. . .	1 670.4
4th quarter	1 629.9	1 100.2	154.9	. . .	. . .	-15.7	. . .	49.1	49.5	404.7	. . .	. . .	1 675.7
1950													
1st quarter	1 696.8	1 118.9	194.2	. . .	. . .	6.6	. . .	48.3	50.9	397.9	. . .	. . .	1 703.0
2nd quarter	1 747.3	1 136.8	215.5	. . .	. . .	9.5	. . .	48.9	53.7	404.3	. . .	. . .	1 748.1
3rd quarter	1 815.8	1 195.3	234.8	. . .	. . .	12.7	. . .	50.1	66.3	396.7	. . .	. . .	1 811.4
4th quarter	1 848.9	1 160.1	266.2	. . .	. . .	40.7	. . .	54.1	66.4	422.3	. . .	. . .	1 792.7
1951													
1st quarter	1 871.3	1 187.4	237.9	. . .	. . .	25.2	. . .	56.9	66.4	467.2	. . .	. . .	1 844.6
2nd quarter	1 903.1	1 154.5	244.0	. . .	. . .	36.7	. . .	62.5	64.2	531.4	. . .	. . .	1 854.0
3rd quarter	1 941.1	1 167.9	225.3	. . .	. . .	24.1	. . .	64.0	58.8	591.5	. . .	. . .	1 915.3
4th quarter	1 944.4	1 174.9	206.1	. . .	. . .	10.3	. . .	63.4	57.2	623.9	. . .	. . .	1 943.7
1952													
1st quarter	1 964.7	1 178.1	210.9	. . .	. . .	13.0	. . .	66.8	63.9	643.7	. . .	. . .	1 960.4
2nd quarter	1 966.0	1 200.7	193.3	. . .	. . .	-3.2	. . .	59.4	63.6	665.3	. . .	. . .	1 991.3
3rd quarter	1 978.8	1 206.0	203.5	. . .	. . .	14.5	. . .	54.7	67.4	672.0	. . .	. . .	1 971.5
4th quarter	2 043.8	1 248.3	218.1	. . .	. . .	14.4	. . .	55.2	73.4	684.1	. . .	. . .	2 036.6
1953													
1st quarter	2 082.3	1 263.4	222.5	. . .	. . .	11.7	. . .	54.2	71.7	707.1	. . .	. . .	2 080.8
2nd quarter	2 098.1	1 271.2	223.3	. . .	. . .	11.4	. . .	54.5	75.4	722.6	. . .	. . .	2 097.4
3rd quarter	2 085.4	1 268.2	218.0	. . .	. . .	7.0	. . .	56.7	75.1	713.9	. . .	. . .	2 092.3
4th quarter	2 052.5	1 259.7	201.0	. . .	. . .	-6.0	. . .	54.8	71.4	711.9	. . .	. . .	2 080.4
1954													
1st quarter	2 042.4	1 264.3	199.1	. . .	. . .	-5.3	. . .	52.4	67.3	692.6	. . .	. . .	2 068.1
2nd quarter	2 044.3	1 280.1	198.5	. . .	. . .	-8.5	. . .	59.9	73.3	668.0	. . .	. . .	2 075.7
3rd quarter	2 066.9	1 297.1	208.7	. . .	. . .	-6.8	. . .	58.0	68.9	651.9	. . .	. . .	2 095.9
4th quarter	2 107.8	1 324.0	218.2	. . .	. . .	-2.6	. . .	60.6	69.6	647.8	. . .	. . .	2 130.4
1955													
1st quarter	2 168.5	1 353.5	241.6	. . .	. . .	10.1	. . .	62.9	73.7	647.1	. . .	. . .	2 170.9
2nd quarter	2 204.0	1 379.1	256.8	. . .	. . .	14.9	. . .	61.4	77.9	640.5	. . .	. . .	2 199.1
3rd quarter	2 233.4	1 396.1	260.4	. . .	. . .	13.6	. . .	65.5	79.1	644.5	. . .	. . .	2 231.1
4th quarter	2 245.3	1 413.3	266.0	. . .	. . .	18.8	. . .	65.8	82.0	630.5	. . .	. . .	2 235.5
1956													
1st quarter	2 234.8	1 415.5	257.1	. . .	. . .	15.9	. . .	68.9	85.4	630.0	. . .	. . .	2 230.3
2nd quarter	2 252.5	1 420.2	254.1	. . .	. . .	11.0	. . .	73.5	85.0	643.3	. . .	. . .	2 255.1
3rd quarter	2 249.8	1 423.4	251.2	. . .	. . .	8.5	. . .	76.0	85.8	637.3	. . .	. . .	2 255.9
4th quarter	2 286.5	1 442.8	248.4	. . .	. . .	7.5	. . .	79.4	81.9	653.6	. . .	. . .	2 294.6
1957													
1st quarter	2 300.3	1 452.7	244.3	. . .	. . .	4.0	. . .	84.6	88.4	667.2	. . .	. . .	2 314.8
2nd quarter	2 294.6	1 455.1	244.1	. . .	. . .	5.9	. . .	82.1	89.1	662.8	. . .	. . .	2 305.9
3rd quarter	2 317.0	1 467.0	249.9	. . .	. . .	8.6	. . .	79.8	87.3	668.0	. . .	. . .	2 323.6
4th quarter	2 292.5	1 467.8	228.7	. . .	. . .	-8.0	. . .	77.3	87.5	680.2	. . .	. . .	2 323.4
1958													
1st quarter	2 230.2	1 447.3	211.9	. . .	. . .	-10.0	. . .	69.7	88.8	672.5	. . .	. . .	2 263.4
2nd quarter	2 243.4	1 458.9	206.7	. . .	. . .	-8.7	. . .	70.0	92.5	689.4	. . .	. . .	2 274.9
3rd quarter	2 295.2	1 482.2	223.8	. . .	. . .	4.4	. . .	70.2	91.3	693.6	. . .	. . .	2 307.2
4th quarter	2 348.0	1 500.9	244.5	. . .	. . .	11.5	. . .	70.1	96.4	708.3	. . .	. . .	2 350.4
1959													
1st quarter	2 392.9	1 525.9	258.0	. . .	. . .	9.2	. . .	74.7	98.3	703.7	. . .	. . .	2 396.9
2nd quarter	2 455.8	1 551.7	279.8	. . .	. . .	23.4	. . .	77.2	103.3	714.4	. . .	. . .	2 440.3
3rd quarter	2 453.9	1 569.2	260.1	. . .	. . .	2.7	. . .	79.6	104.5	723.4	. . .	. . .	2 471.1
4th quarter	2 462.6	1 571.4	268.8	. . .	. . .	14.0	. . .	77.4	101.8	715.6	. . .	. . .	2 462.3
1960													
1st quarter	2 517.4	1 585.6	298.5	. . .	. . .	34.2	. . .	87.2	105.6	701.3	. . .	. . .	2 488.1
2nd quarter	2 504.8	1 605.1	268.0	. . .	. . .	9.7	. . .	92.7	106.3	707.0	. . .	. . .	2 511.5
3rd quarter	2 508.7	1 598.5	266.4	. . .	. . .	14.0	. . .	90.4	103.1	724.1	. . .	. . .	2 507.9
4th quarter	2 476.2	1 600.3	233.6	. . .	. . .	-16.3	. . .	92.2	98.3	729.1	. . .	. . .	2 519.8

. . . = Not available.

Table 19-2. Real Gross Domestic Product—*Continued*

(Billions of chained [2000] dollars, quarterly data are at seasonally adjusted annual rates.) **NIPA Tables 1.1.6, 1.4.6**

Year and quarter	Gross domestic product	Personal consumption expenditures	Gross private domestic investment				Exports and imports of goods and services			Government consumption expenditures and gross investment			Addendum: Final sales of domestic product
			Total	Fixed investment		Change in private inventories	Net exports	Exports	Imports	Total	Federal	State and local	
				Nonresidential	Residential								
1961													
1st quarter	2 491.2	1 600.2	239.4	. . .	. . .	-7.2	. . .	91.6	97.8	738.6	. . .	. . .	2 522.0
2nd quarter	2 538.0	1 624.2	257.3	. . .	. . .	6.2	. . .	90.3	99.0	740.3	. . .	. . .	2 549.1
3rd quarter	2 579.1	1 632.1	279.0	. . .	. . .	21.3	. . .	89.8	105.6	754.9	. . .	. . .	2 568.9
4th quarter	2 631.8	1 664.9	283.7	. . .	. . .	17.6	. . .	92.6	108.1	771.4	. . .	. . .	2 627.3
1962													
1st quarter	2 679.1	1 682.7	300.6	. . .	. . .	27.9	. . .	92.4	111.4	785.2	. . .	. . .	2 659.5
2nd quarter	2 708.4	1 703.1	297.7	. . .	. . .	17.5	. . .	101.3	113.8	789.4	. . .	. . .	2 704.5
3rd quarter	2 733.3	1 717.0	302.9	. . .	. . .	20.5	. . .	95.6	115.2	807.3	. . .	. . .	2 725.6
4th quarter	2 740.0	1 741.5	292.6	. . .	. . .	12.0	. . .	93.5	116.6	808.5	. . .	. . .	2 744.5
1963													
1st quarter	2 775.9	1 753.1	308.9	. . .	. . .	24.1	. . .	95.7	113.9	803.6	. . .	. . .	2 762.8
2nd quarter	2 810.6	1 770.0	313.4	. . .	. . .	16.0	. . .	106.9	116.6	802.6	. . .	. . .	2 809.7
3rd quarter	2 863.5	1 794.0	323.7	. . .	. . .	18.5	. . .	101.2	119.6	837.0	. . .	. . .	2 859.4
4th quarter	2 885.8	1 809.3	327.8	. . .	. . .	13.3	. . .	106.3	119.2	829.4	. . .	. . .	2 889.5
1964													
1st quarter	2 950.5	1 845.2	341.2	. . .	. . .	14.5	. . .	112.8	119.1	832.3	. . .	. . .	2 952.7
2nd quarter	2 984.8	1 877.9	339.7	. . .	. . .	13.9	. . .	114.7	121.8	837.8	. . .	. . .	2 988.1
3rd quarter	3 025.5	1 912.6	347.7	. . .	. . .	16.7	. . .	113.8	125.0	838.3	. . .	. . .	3 025.4
4th quarter	3 033.6	1 918.0	350.3	. . .	. . .	16.5	. . .	117.2	128.4	835.9	. . .	. . .	3 033.2
1965													
1st quarter	3 108.2	1 960.3	385.8	. . .	. . .	36.8	. . .	104.5	123.8	834.0	. . .	. . .	3 081.0
2nd quarter	3 150.2	1 982.0	385.7	. . .	. . .	26.5	. . .	124.2	138.4	844.6	. . .	. . .	3 136.6
3rd quarter	3 214.1	2 016.0	399.5	. . .	. . .	30.0	. . .	117.1	139.0	873.8	. . .	. . .	3 195.5
4th quarter	3 291.8	2 072.7	401.4	. . .	. . .	24.0	. . .	125.5	145.8	892.7	. . .	. . .	3 282.4
1966													
1st quarter	3 372.3	2 103.2	435.2	. . .	. . .	42.4	. . .	123.3	149.5	908.7	. . .	. . .	3 337.0
2nd quarter	3 384.0	2 109.0	427.3	. . .	. . .	40.3	. . .	128.7	153.2	924.8	. . .	. . .	3 352.4
3rd quarter	3 406.3	2 133.1	423.1	. . .	. . .	36.3	. . .	123.9	161.8	949.7	. . .	. . .	3 380.2
4th quarter	3 433.7	2 142.0	425.2	. . .	. . .	49.4	. . .	128.0	163.7	965.1	. . .	. . .	3 389.6
1967													
1st quarter	3 464.1	2 154.6	413.4	. . .	. . .	45.8	. . .	130.4	166.1	1 006.1	. . .	. . .	3 424.2
2nd quarter	3 464.3	2 183.4	395.8	. . .	. . .	21.0	. . .	129.3	164.8	1 000.6	. . .	. . .	3 460.2
3rd quarter	3 491.8	2 194.5	407.2	. . .	. . .	27.8	. . .	126.1	167.1	1 011.0	. . .	. . .	3 477.8
4th quarter	3 518.2	2 207.8	416.0	. . .	. . .	26.4	. . .	129.7	175.9	1 018.0	. . .	. . .	3 508.2
1968													
1st quarter	3 590.7	2 260.3	425.2	. . .	. . .	24.4	. . .	133.5	186.2	1 035.6	. . .	. . .	3 581.7
2nd quarter	3 651.6	2 295.1	442.3	. . .	. . .	43.8	. . .	136.1	189.1	1 040.3	. . .	. . .	3 617.7
3rd quarter	3 676.5	2 338.2	427.9	. . .	. . .	23.3	. . .	144.1	200.4	1 042.6	. . .	. . .	3 669.4
4th quarter	3 692.0	2 348.6	432.3	. . .	. . .	18.1	. . .	142.3	198.7	1 043.3	. . .	. . .	3 692.2
1969													
1st quarter	3 750.2	2 375.0	460.8	. . .	. . .	33.2	. . .	125.2	180.0	1 044.4	. . .	. . .	3 730.5
2nd quarter	3 760.9	2 390.0	457.1	. . .	. . .	28.0	. . .	153.3	215.5	1 040.0	. . .	. . .	3 748.6
3rd quarter	3 784.2	2 401.0	467.8	. . .	. . .	30.8	. . .	149.6	212.7	1 041.4	. . .	. . .	3 767.6
4th quarter	3 766.3	2 419.8	442.7	. . .	. . .	16.0	. . .	154.8	210.3	1 026.0	. . .	. . .	3 768.1
1970													
1st quarter	3 760.0	2 434.4	428.7	. . .	. . .	3.9	. . .	156.1	209.7	1 020.5	. . .	. . .	3 778.0
2nd quarter	3 767.1	2 445.7	430.2	. . .	. . .	14.8	. . .	163.0	213.8	1 007.3	. . .	. . .	3 771.0
3rd quarter	3 800.5	2 467.1	437.5	. . .	. . .	14.4	. . .	162.5	213.3	1 011.8	. . .	. . .	3 804.6
4th quarter	3 759.8	2 460.1	411.9	. . .	. . .	-12.9	. . .	164.0	216.7	1 011.8	. . .	. . .	3 797.2
1971													
1st quarter	3 864.1	2 507.4	465.6	. . .	. . .	34.0	. . .	164.6	214.1	995.4	. . .	. . .	3 844.7
2nd quarter	3 885.9	2 530.5	479.9	. . .	. . .	29.9	. . .	164.3	230.2	992.3	. . .	. . .	3 871.3
3rd quarter	3 916.7	2 550.7	486.3	. . .	. . .	27.9	. . .	171.0	235.3	991.5	. . .	. . .	3 905.2
4th quarter	3 927.9	2 593.2	471.3	. . .	. . .	-2.7	. . .	156.7	219.3	984.1	. . .	. . .	3 952.5
1972													
1st quarter	3 997.7	2 627.6	504.4	. . .	. . .	9.9	. . .	173.3	251.4	987.7	. . .	. . .	4 006.9
2nd quarter	4 092.1	2 677.3	535.4	. . .	. . .	34.0	. . .	168.2	242.5	993.8	. . .	. . .	4 073.0
3rd quarter	4 131.1	2 718.4	542.9	. . .	. . .	35.0	. . .	178.4	247.5	973.3	. . .	. . .	4 109.6
4th quarter	4 198.7	2 781.7	545.5	. . .	. . .	13.3	. . .	185.9	258.7	979.4	. . .	. . .	4 204.8
1973													
1st quarter	4 305.3	2 832.0	580.4	. . .	. . .	20.9	. . .	199.6	270.6	988.9	. . .	. . .	4 296.4
2nd quarter	4 355.1	2 830.5	607.4	. . .	. . .	47.2	. . .	209.2	262.8	983.1	. . .	. . .	4 317.4
3rd quarter	4 331.9	2 840.6	583.6	. . .	. . .	21.4	. . .	209.9	255.6	970.5	. . .	. . .	4 322.6
4th quarter	4 373.3	2 832.2	606.2	. . .	. . .	50.5	. . .	220.2	257.5	977.6	. . .	. . .	4 327.3
1974													
1st quarter	4 335.4	2 807.8	566.9	. . .	. . .	24.0	. . .	223.0	248.7	998.1	. . .	. . .	4 322.7
2nd quarter	4 347.9	2 819.0	564.7	. . .	. . .	33.1	. . .	233.9	261.9	1 004.7	. . .	. . .	4 328.7
3rd quarter	4 305.8	2 831.6	533.0	. . .	. . .	11.7	. . .	221.3	257.4	1 006.2	. . .	. . .	4 316.3
4th quarter	4 288.9	2 790.8	537.9	. . .	. . .	34.9	. . .	227.0	254.8	1 009.8	. . .	. . .	4 254.5
1975													
1st quarter	4 237.6	2 814.6	443.8	. . .	. . .	-13.8	. . .	228.7	229.3	1 022.1	. . .	. . .	4 287.8
2nd quarter	4 268.6	2 860.5	427.7	. . .	. . .	-25.9	. . .	222.0	210.9	1 014.2	. . .	. . .	4 331.0
3rd quarter	4 340.9	2 901.2	463.9	. . .	. . .	-5.2	. . .	218.2	228.4	1 032.2	. . .	. . .	4 370.1
4th quarter	4 397.8	2 931.4	477.2	. . .	. . .	-0.4	. . .	230.6	240.6	1 040.9	. . .	. . .	4 421.1

. . . = Not available.

Table 19-2. Real Gross Domestic Product—*Continued*

(Billions of chained [2000] dollars, quarterly data are at seasonally adjusted annual rates.)   **NIPA Tables 1.1.6, 1.4.6**

Year and quarter	Gross domestic product	Personal consumption expenditures	Gross private domestic investment Total	Fixed investment Nonresidential	Fixed investment Residential	Change in private inventories	Net exports	Exports	Imports	Government Total	Federal	State and local	Addendum: Final sales of domestic product
1976													
1st quarter	4 496.8	2 989.7	526.4	...	...	28.2	...	229.0	255.7	1 043.4	...	...	4 482.1
2nd quarter	4 530.3	3 016.3	549.3	...	...	41.9	...	231.3	266.8	1 032.0	...	...	4 496.3
3rd quarter	4 552.0	3 047.9	550.0	...	...	39.4	...	238.0	277.6	1 026.6	...	...	4 523.7
4th quarter	4 584.6	3 088.0	553.1	...	...	13.4	...	240.4	286.8	1 025.8	...	...	4 587.1
1977													
1st quarter	4 640.0	3 124.6	580.9	...	...	26.5	...	236.6	300.4	1 035.1	...	...	4 631.5
2nd quarter	4 731.1	3 141.5	625.5	...	...	32.6	...	243.0	303.2	1 045.8	...	...	4 705.5
3rd quarter	4 815.8	3 171.4	659.8	...	...	60.6	...	244.8	299.0	1 047.7	...	...	4 755.2
4th quarter	4 815.3	3 219.1	641.9	...	...	34.2	...	237.0	303.2	1 044.4	...	...	4 794.1
1978													
1st quarter	4 830.8	3 237.3	654.0	...	...	39.2	...	242.6	323.5	1 046.1	...	...	4 799.5
2nd quarter	5 021.2	3 306.4	699.3	...	...	38.6	...	267.8	324.5	1 074.3	...	...	4 989.9
3rd quarter	5 070.7	3 320.8	720.6	...	...	40.4	...	270.8	328.8	1 082.9	...	...	5 036.0
4th quarter	5 137.4	3 347.8	736.6	...	...	46.2	...	281.6	333.4	1 092.7	...	...	5 100.6
1979													
1st quarter	5 147.4	3 365.3	737.1	...	...	36.6	...	281.8	332.4	1 082.9	...	...	5 117.8
2nd quarter	5 152.3	3 364.0	735.1	...	...	40.0	...	282.5	334.2	1 094.4	...	...	5 117.9
3rd quarter	5 189.4	3 397.3	720.6	...	...	15.3	...	292.7	329.1	1 095.9	...	...	5 192.3
4th quarter	5 204.7	3 407.1	707.2	...	...	8.5	...	311.0	336.3	1 103.1	...	...	5 216.9
1980													
1st quarter	5 221.3	3 401.7	701.6	...	...	11.3	...	319.8	336.6	1 120.8	...	...	5 227.3
2nd quarter	5 115.9	3 325.8	638.7	...	...	10.0	...	325.8	312.1	1 124.3	...	...	5 126.2
3rd quarter	5 107.4	3 362.0	590.3	...	...	-42.6	...	325.1	289.6	1 108.8	...	...	5 193.5
4th quarter	5 202.1	3 406.8	650.6	...	...	-10.7	...	323.2	305.2	1 107.7	...	...	5 239.7
1981													
1st quarter	5 307.5	3 421.3	716.0	...	...	48.7	...	329.2	318.2	1 122.5	...	...	5 261.7
2nd quarter	5 266.1	3 422.1	682.2	...	...	13.4	...	331.1	318.7	1 124.9	...	...	5 272.8
3rd quarter	5 329.8	3 435.7	724.7	...	...	52.1	...	324.0	315.1	1 122.3	...	...	5 278.5
4th quarter	5 263.4	3 409.7	696.4	...	...	25.4	...	325.5	324.2	1 132.7	...	...	5 247.4
1982													
1st quarter	5 177.1	3 432.2	623.7	...	...	-24.4	...	311.4	314.9	1 131.5	...	...	5 232.9
2nd quarter	5 204.9	3 444.3	622.9	...	...	-4.6	...	313.3	309.8	1 138.2	...	...	5 230.5
3rd quarter	5 185.2	3 470.8	615.8	...	...	6.6	...	299.4	324.1	1 146.0	...	...	5 196.6
4th quarter	5 189.8	3 533.9	561.5	...	...	-47.5	...	285.7	311.4	1 165.8	...	...	5 273.3
1983													
1st quarter	5 253.8	3 568.5	581.3	...	...	-42.3	...	290.3	318.5	1 174.6	...	...	5 329.2
2nd quarter	5 372.3	3 639.5	637.7	...	...	-5.8	...	291.2	343.0	1 184.6	...	...	5 404.6
3rd quarter	5 478.4	3 704.1	680.1	...	...	-4.9	...	295.6	369.7	1 205.2	...	...	5 505.1
4th quarter	5 590.5	3 762.5	750.7	...	...	27.4	...	301.5	387.9	1 184.8	...	...	5 577.0
1984													
1st quarter	5 699.8	3 794.9	830.1	...	...	81.0	...	307.8	419.0	1 196.6	...	...	5 614.4
2nd quarter	5 797.9	3 849.3	858.0	...	...	75.6	...	315.5	436.6	1 222.4	...	...	5 717.5
3rd quarter	5 854.3	3 879.1	878.3	...	...	78.7	...	322.4	447.9	1 231.4	...	...	5 770.2
4th quarter	5 902.4	3 930.2	864.3	...	...	49.9	...	329.0	461.1	1 257.9	...	...	5 854.6
1985													
1st quarter	5 956.9	3 996.2	835.2	...	...	16.3	...	329.2	450.9	1 272.2	...	...	5 953.0
2nd quarter	6 007.8	4 032.6	849.8	...	...	23.3	...	328.0	473.1	1 300.8	...	...	5 998.5
3rd quarter	6 101.7	4 109.1	840.5	...	...	18.8	...	323.2	468.5	1 334.6	...	...	6 095.8
4th quarter	6 148.6	4 118.4	873.5	...	...	36.2	...	332.9	486.7	1 342.6	...	...	6 121.2
1986													
1st quarter	6 207.4	4 152.7	871.6	...	...	33.7	...	343.6	486.5	1 357.1	...	...	6 184.1
2nd quarter	6 232.0	4 196.7	852.2	...	...	17.4	...	347.3	507.1	1 385.9	...	...	6 230.5
3rd quarter	6 291.7	4 269.5	825.4	...	...	-7.6	...	355.2	521.2	1 417.5	...	...	6 317.8
4th quarter	6 323.4	4 296.7	826.6	...	...	-10.4	...	368.5	525.4	1 409.6	...	...	6 355.0
1987													
1st quarter	6 365.0	4 298.6	852.0	...	...	33.4	...	368.7	522.0	1 413.2	...	...	6 344.4
2nd quarter	6 435.0	4 357.3	853.2	...	...	18.7	...	383.6	535.1	1 423.1	...	...	6 431.4
3rd quarter	6 493.4	4 406.3	854.1	...	...	0.5	...	400.1	545.5	1 425.6	...	...	6 510.8
4th quarter	6 606.8	4 417.1	920.6	...	...	68.7	...	414.9	558.0	1 445.1	...	...	6 542.5
1988													
1st quarter	6 639.1	4 490.6	868.8	...	...	16.9	...	437.8	555.6	1 436.7	...	...	6 637.2
2nd quarter	6 723.5	4 522.7	889.9	...	...	20.5	...	450.0	549.1	1 439.9	...	...	6 716.4
3rd quarter	6 759.4	4 560.5	895.6	...	...	20.0	...	458.3	561.9	1 438.0	...	...	6 749.5
4th quarter	6 848.6	4 614.0	907.5	...	...	23.6	...	472.4	578.8	1 465.9	...	...	6 835.1
1989													
1st quarter	6 918.1	4 631.2	942.3	...	...	49.7	...	485.9	577.2	1 456.7	...	...	6 873.3
2nd quarter	6 963.5	4 653.0	931.3	...	...	37.5	...	507.1	585.8	1 479.2	...	...	6 933.6
3rd quarter	7 013.1	4 697.3	920.4	...	...	10.2	...	513.0	586.5	1 493.0	...	...	7 015.3
4th quarter	7 030.9	4 718.8	910.8	...	...	15.9	...	521.4	594.2	1 501.0	...	...	7 026.8
1990													
1st quarter	7 112.1	4 757.1	920.0	603.9	321.0	14.1	-63.8	543.6	607.3	1 524.2	659.9	861.9	7 110.6
2nd quarter	7 130.3	4 773.0	920.1	593.5	308.6	33.9	-63.6	550.5	614.1	1 526.8	660.7	863.6	7 103.8
3rd quarter	7 130.8	4 792.6	898.4	597.2	291.1	22.8	-58.1	555.1	613.2	1 526.7	654.9	869.4	7 118.3
4th quarter	7 076.9	4 758.3	841.8	585.8	275.0	-9.3	-33.2	560.7	593.8	1 542.2	660.7	878.9	7 101.3

. . . = Not available.

Table 19-2. Real Gross Domestic Product—*Continued*

(Billions of chained [2000] dollars, quarterly data are at seasonally adjusted annual rates.)　　　　　　　　　　**NIPA Tables 1.1.6, 1.4.6**

Year and quarter	Gross domestic product	Personal consumption expenditures	Gross private domestic investment				Exports and imports of goods and services			Government consumption expenditures and gross investment			Addendum: Final sales of domestic product
			Total	Fixed investment		Change in private inventories	Net exports	Exports	Imports	Total	Federal	State and local	
				Nonresidential	Residential								
1991													
1st quarter	7 040.8	4 738.1	807.3	570.7	258.6	-14.4	-18.3	563.2	581.5	1 548.4	665.8	880.0	7 071.5
2nd quarter	7 086.5	4 779.4	803.5	565.3	264.7	-18.1	-14.3	583.8	598.1	1 553.7	667.7	883.5	7 120.2
3rd quarter	7 120.7	4 800.1	823.5	559.9	275.7	-0.1	-16.0	597.8	613.9	1 546.6	655.5	888.6	7 134.6
4th quarter	7 154.1	4 795.9	854.7	556.9	281.7	30.7	-9.6	611.6	621.2	1 540.4	642.8	895.2	7 133.8
1992													
1st quarter	7 228.2	4 875.0	835.8	554.5	296.1	1.8	-4.7	621.9	626.6	1 552.3	643.1	906.9	7 239.3
2nd quarter	7 297.9	4 903.0	890.7	576.5	307.4	22.9	-20.2	622.2	642.4	1 550.7	642.6	905.8	7 284.3
3rd quarter	7 369.5	4 951.8	900.2	588.2	308.2	19.6	-15.9	635.6	651.4	1 559.0	650.1	906.6	7 360.5
4th quarter	7 450.7	5 009.4	929.1	606.0	318.6	21.5	-23.0	639.1	662.1	1 559.3	650.4	906.6	7 440.3
1993													
1st quarter	7 459.7	5 027.3	950.3	609.6	320.1	36.7	-37.4	639.9	677.2	1 543.0	630.5	910.4	7 431.2
2nd quarter	7 497.5	5 071.9	957.8	625.9	323.8	24.3	-48.6	647.4	696.0	1 541.4	621.4	918.0	7 483.7
3rd quarter	7 536.0	5 127.3	957.8	632.8	335.0	7.0	-59.4	645.7	705.1	1 537.0	612.5	922.7	7 540.6
4th quarter	7 637.4	5 172.9	1 007.3	659.3	351.9	14.5	-63.0	667.0	730.1	1 542.7	614.1	926.9	7 633.7
1994													
1st quarter	7 715.1	5 230.3	1 050.6	665.9	358.8	46.3	-73.8	672.8	746.5	1 527.1	595.8	929.6	7 677.5
2nd quarter	7 815.7	5 268.0	1 112.0	679.3	370.9	83.0	-83.0	695.0	778.1	1 533.7	592.6	939.6	7 737.2
3rd quarter	7 859.5	5 305.7	1 092.4	692.0	367.0	51.7	-79.0	721.0	800.0	1 558.8	606.8	950.4	7 814.3
4th quarter	7 951.6	5 358.7	1 143.2	722.6	362.3	73.4	-81.9	737.3	819.2	1 545.5	590.5	953.7	7 882.3
1995													
1st quarter	7 973.7	5 367.2	1 154.6	752.1	354.2	60.8	-86.0	750.5	836.5	1 551.9	589.4	961.2	7 918.7
2nd quarter	7 988.0	5 411.7	1 123.8	757.4	342.9	34.6	-87.7	761.0	848.7	1 558.2	588.3	968.7	7 962.3
3rd quarter	8 053.1	5 458.8	1 113.1	762.5	353.6	7.9	-57.1	794.5	851.7	1 553.2	582.7	969.2	8 055.0
4th quarter	8 112.0	5 496.1	1 144.4	777.9	361.6	16.2	-53.1	806.6	859.7	1 535.5	560.6	974.1	8 104.8
1996													
1st quarter	8 169.2	5 544.6	1 160.2	797.1	371.1	3.0	-68.2	816.4	884.6	1 544.9	572.3	971.6	8 175.4
2nd quarter	8 303.1	5 604.9	1 220.0	820.0	386.8	24.5	-81.2	830.3	911.4	1 570.3	583.6	985.6	8 285.8
3rd quarter	8 372.7	5 640.7	1 280.8	847.3	385.7	57.5	-104.3	837.3	941.6	1 565.1	569.6	994.7	8 319.9
4th quarter	8 470.6	5 687.6	1 276.1	870.1	381.8	29.9	-64.9	889.5	954.4	1 579.2	568.5	1 010.0	8 444.7
1997													
1st quarter	8 536.1	5 749.1	1 302.9	892.2	383.1	34.7	-89.0	905.7	994.7	1 581.6	561.2	1 019.8	8 507.3
2nd quarter	8 665.8	5 775.8	1 389.6	914.3	387.9	94.2	-93.1	941.8	1 034.8	1 598.1	573.6	1 024.0	8 574.6
3rd quarter	8 773.7	5 870.7	1 417.5	961.1	389.7	72.3	-108.8	964.2	1 073.0	1 598.5	569.9	1 028.0	8 705.7
4th quarter	8 838.4	5 931.4	1 440.7	969.0	393.6	83.4	-127.6	963.2	1 090.9	1 597.9	565.7	1 031.8	8 758.6
1998													
1st quarter	8 936.2	5 996.8	1 515.8	1 001.6	401.8	116.9	-163.7	967.4	1 131.1	1 589.1	551.9	1 037.0	8 821.1
2nd quarter	8 995.3	6 092.1	1 491.7	1 032.5	412.9	50.4	-205.1	957.0	1 162.1	1 621.4	565.9	1 055.2	8 948.7
3rd quarter	9 098.9	6 165.7	1 525.8	1 042.4	424.1	64.2	-223.9	952.9	1 176.9	1 636.0	561.1	1 074.9	9 038.4
4th quarter	9 237.1	6 248.8	1 563.0	1 074.7	434.3	58.9	-222.3	988.7	1 211.0	1 651.1	566.1	1 084.9	9 182.2
1999													
1st quarter	9 315.5	6 311.3	1 606.6	1 094.0	438.1	79.5	-262.1	980.1	1 242.2	1 662.2	562.9	1 099.3	9 239.7
2nd quarter	9 392.6	6 409.7	1 607.8	1 127.3	441.8	41.7	-295.2	991.2	1 286.4	1 672.3	565.3	1 107.0	9 353.7
3rd quarter	9 502.2	6 476.7	1 647.4	1 154.4	444.5	50.8	-313.9	1 017.4	1 331.3	1 693.1	576.7	1 116.3	9 453.5
4th quarter	9 671.1	6 556.8	1 708.4	1 157.3	449.9	103.5	-313.7	1 044.1	1 357.9	1 720.2	589.9	1 130.2	9 569.3
2000													
1st quarter	9 695.6	6 661.3	1 678.0	1 196.7	454.5	26.9	-350.6	1 060.9	1 411.5	1 707.3	568.2	1 139.2	9 668.8
2nd quarter	9 847.9	6 703.3	1 788.6	1 238.6	450.4	99.3	-374.5	1 092.0	1 466.5	1 730.5	591.2	1 139.3	9 748.4
3rd quarter	9 836.6	6 768.0	1 742.6	1 245.2	441.2	56.2	-395.6	1 120.0	1 515.6	1 721.5	578.6	1 142.9	9 780.4
4th quarter	9 887.7	6 825.0	1 732.7	1 247.9	441.6	43.5	-397.2	1 112.3	1 509.5	1 727.1	577.2	1 149.9	9 844.3
2001													
1st quarter	9 875.6	6 853.1	1 670.3	1 234.4	444.0	-7.8	-398.2	1 097.2	1 495.4	1 749.6	588.5	1 161.1	9 883.2
2nd quarter	9 905.9	6 870.3	1 637.4	1 190.2	450.1	-2.5	-385.2	1 060.6	1 445.8	1 783.0	601.4	1 181.6	9 908.7
3rd quarter	9 871.1	6 900.5	1 592.6	1 169.3	452.1	-29.9	-398.4	1 008.7	1 407.1	1 776.1	601.5	1 174.6	9 899.9
4th quarter	9 910.0	7 017.6	1 493.4	1 128.2	447.8	-86.7	-414.5	980.3	1 394.9	1 812.7	614.2	1 198.5	9 992.3
2002													
1st quarter	9 977.3	7 042.2	1 541.7	1 090.3	459.0	-10.2	-441.3	992.8	1 434.0	1 832.0	623.2	1 208.9	9 986.8
2nd quarter	10 031.6	7 083.5	1 549.0	1 073.3	469.5	2.6	-458.9	1 018.0	1 476.9	1 853.4	641.7	1 211.8	10 028.4
3rd quarter	10 090.7	7 123.2	1 570.9	1 068.0	471.8	28.0	-472.2	1 025.2	1 497.4	1 863.9	646.5	1 217.5	10 063.5
4th quarter	10 095.8	7 148.2	1 567.0	1 054.5	479.3	29.5	-513.0	1 017.2	1 530.2	1 885.8	662.3	1 223.6	10 067.3
2003													
1st quarter	10 126.0	7 184.9	1 561.8	1 047.5	484.1	24.3	-507.2	1 003.3	1 510.5	1 879.3	662.5	1 216.9	10 100.9
2nd quarter	10 212.7	7 254.8	1 574.4	1 074.5	496.3	-2.7	-526.9	999.0	1 525.9	1 907.5	693.0	1 214.4	10 213.7
3rd quarter	10 398.7	7 352.9	1 639.7	1 098.8	521.8	10.5	-513.8	1 026.3	1 540.0	1 914.5	693.7	1 220.8	10 385.9
4th quarter	10 467.0	7 394.3	1 676.5	1 106.5	535.2	25.0	-527.8	1 075.8	1 603.6	1 918.0	699.0	1 219.0	10 440.0
2004													
1st quarter	10 543.6	7 475.1	1 685.3	1 099.1	540.5	35.0	-549.1	1 101.8	1 650.9	1 925.4	709.5	1 215.9	10 507.1
2nd quarter	10 634.2	7 520.5	1 766.3	1 127.5	561.7	64.9	-591.1	1 119.4	1 710.5	1 931.8	713.7	1 218.1	10 568.5
3rd quarter	10 728.7	7 585.5	1 800.5	1 160.7	567.5	60.1	-602.7	1 128.0	1 730.8	1 939.4	724.5	1 214.7	10 666.6
4th quarter	10 796.4	7 664.3	1 828.8	1 189.7	570.9	57.2	-632.3	1 155.3	1 787.7	1 930.6	716.0	1 214.4	10 737.0
2005													
1st quarter	10 875.8	7 697.5	1 869.1	1 200.4	582.1	74.6	-623.7	1 177.9	1 801.7	1 929.6	718.0	1 211.4	10 799.3
2nd quarter	10 946.1	7 766.4	1 844.8	1 219.0	595.8	16.7	-601.3	1 203.1	1 804.4	1 934.0	720.1	1 213.8	10 925.9
3rd quarter	11 050.0	7 838.1	1 862.8	1 237.1	601.7	11.0	-603.6	1 204.3	1 807.9	1 950.4	736.8	1 213.6	11 035.5
4th quarter	11 086.1	7 864.9	1 917.3	1 248.2	602.0	53.5	-637.8	1 235.7	1 873.6	1 941.9	723.2	1 218.5	11 028.4
2006													
1st quarter	11 217.3	7 947.4	1 946.3	1 295.2	596.5	45.9	-636.0	1 284.3	1 920.2	1 960.5	740.6	1 219.9	11 167.6
2nd quarter	11 291.8	8 002.1	1 944.3	1 315.4	570.1	56.9	-619.4	1 301.4	1 920.9	1 966.6	737.7	1 228.8	11 232.1
3rd quarter	11 314.1	8 046.3	1 917.8	1 332.7	536.7	53.3	-623.0	1 312.6	1 935.7	1 974.9	741.1	1 233.7	11 257.8
4th quarter	11 356.4	8 119.9	1 841.6	1 329.3	508.4	13.1	-584.3	1 361.1	1 945.3	1 982.7	744.4	1 238.2	11 339.7

Table 19-3. Contributions to Percent Change in Real Gross Domestic Product

(Percent; percentage points.)   NIPA Table 1.1.2

Year and quarter	Percent change at seasonally adjusted annual rate, real GDP	Personal consump-tion expen-ditures	Gross private domestic investment				Exports and imports of goods and services			Government consumption expenditures and gross investment		
							Percentage points at seasonally adjusted annual rates					
			Total	Fixed investment		Change in private inventories	Net exports	Exports	Imports	Total	Federal	State and local
				Nonresi-dential	Residential							
1946	-11.0	6.36	7.46	2.24	2.39	2.84	3.82	3.25	0.57	-28.67	-29.06	0.39
1947	-0.9	1.20	-0.57	1.31	1.06	-2.93	1.08	0.91	0.17	-2.65	-3.32	0.68
1948	4.4	1.47	4.00	0.51	0.98	2.50	-2.18	-1.63	-0.55	1.08	0.71	0.37
1949	-0.5	1.79	-4.22	-0.93	-0.44	-2.85	0.08	-0.05	0.13	1.83	0.90	0.93
1947												
1st quarter	...	...	...	...	...	...	...	...	...	...	...	0.31
2nd quarter	-0.5	4.55	-4.65	-0.58	-0.84	-3.24	-0.68	-0.43	-0.25	0.36	0.04	0.31
3rd quarter	-0.2	1.07	-1.65	-0.73	2.78	-3.70	-0.19	-1.75	1.56	0.66	0.00	0.66
4th quarter	6.0	-0.06	11.09	1.32	4.20	5.57	-4.15	-3.48	-0.67	-0.86	-1.24	0.39
1948												
1st quarter	6.5	1.32	6.71	2.72	-0.27	4.26	-2.74	-1.24	-1.50	1.25	1.28	-0.03
2nd quarter	7.3	3.04	4.21	-1.40	1.36	4.26	-2.94	-2.35	-0.59	2.97	2.24	0.73
3rd quarter	2.3	0.36	0.96	0.14	-0.74	1.56	-0.30	0.48	-0.78	1.31	0.83	0.49
4th quarter	1.0	1.94	-2.95	1.08	-1.74	-2.30	-0.58	-0.82	0.24	2.54	1.95	0.59
1949												
1st quarter	-5.8	0.28	-10.72	-2.04	-1.78	-6.90	2.75	2.33	0.41	1.70	0.74	0.96
2nd quarter	-1.2	3.69	-7.96	-1.54	-0.34	-6.08	0.05	-0.17	0.22	3.02	1.54	1.48
3rd quarter	4.6	0.18	4.97	-1.86	1.75	5.08	-1.33	-1.91	0.59	0.75	-0.42	1.17
4th quarter	-4.0	3.32	-2.95	-0.60	2.67	-5.02	-2.88	-2.70	-0.18	-1.50	-2.05	0.56
1950												
1st quarter	17.4	4.16	14.93	1.12	3.10	10.72	-0.55	-0.22	-0.33	-1.08	-1.86	0.78
2nd quarter	12.5	4.18	7.64	3.40	2.76	1.47	-0.50	0.23	-0.73	1.18	0.91	0.27
3rd quarter	16.6	14.05	6.52	3.53	1.66	1.32	-2.80	0.44	-3.25	-1.13	-1.15	0.02
4th quarter	7.5	-7.70	9.90	-0.06	-1.36	11.32	1.26	1.31	-0.05	4.04	4.02	0.01
1951												
1st quarter	4.9	6.42	-9.05	-1.04	-1.46	-6.55	0.76	0.81	-0.05	6.78	7.06	-0.28
2nd quarter	7.0	-6.92	1.76	0.54	-3.43	4.65	2.38	1.82	0.56	9.75	9.29	0.46
3rd quarter	8.2	2.95	-5.78	0.45	-1.38	-4.85	2.05	0.52	1.53	9.02	8.89	0.13
4th quarter	0.7	1.39	-5.75	-0.75	0.18	-5.17	0.22	-0.15	0.37	4.81	4.86	-0.04
1952												
1st quarter	4.2	0.24	1.51	0.21	0.59	0.71	-0.63	1.23	-1.85	3.11	3.02	0.10
2nd quarter	0.3	4.54	-5.15	0.44	0.37	-5.97	-2.16	-2.18	0.02	3.06	2.46	0.60
3rd quarter	2.6	0.92	3.08	-3.29	-0.21	6.58	-2.31	-1.31	-1.00	0.93	1.67	-0.74
4th quarter	13.8	8.94	4.38	3.20	1.17	0.01	-1.26	0.22	-1.48	1.75	1.07	0.68
1953												
1st quarter	7.7	3.03	1.17	1.95	0.34	-1.11	0.25	-0.18	0.42	3.28	2.67	0.61
2nd quarter	3.1	1.39	0.19	0.26	0.06	-0.13	-0.68	0.17	-0.85	2.18	2.23	-0.04
3rd quarter	-2.4	-0.74	-1.29	0.84	-0.78	-1.34	0.73	0.71	0.03	-1.10	-1.84	0.74
4th quarter	-6.2	-1.78	-4.35	-0.42	-0.16	-3.77	0.25	-0.55	0.80	-0.26	-0.93	0.67
1954												
1st quarter	-2.0	0.66	-0.30	-1.09	0.21	0.58	0.14	-0.76	0.90	-2.45	-3.50	1.05
2nd quarter	0.4	2.99	-0.08	-0.37	1.31	-1.03	0.70	2.16	-1.46	-3.25	-3.37	0.12
3rd quarter	4.5	3.25	3.00	1.04	1.36	0.60	0.38	-0.61	0.99	-2.13	-2.99	0.86
4th quarter	8.2	5.35	2.83	-0.09	1.49	1.43	0.54	0.73	-0.20	-0.54	-0.68	0.15
1955												
1st quarter	12.0	5.84	6.68	0.69	1.86	4.13	-0.38	0.58	-0.96	-0.12	-1.41	1.28
2nd quarter	6.7	4.79	4.11	2.32	0.35	1.44	-1.35	-0.43	-0.91	-0.83	-1.24	0.41
3rd quarter	5.4	3.17	0.93	1.93	-0.55	-0.45	0.78	1.08	-0.31	0.56	0.61	-0.05
4th quarter	2.2	3.07	1.40	1.06	-1.05	1.39	-0.57	0.04	-0.61	-1.74	-1.92	0.19
1956												
1st quarter	-1.9	0.31	-2.16	-0.69	-0.57	-0.90	0.05	0.79	-0.74	-0.03	-0.37	0.33
2nd quarter	3.2	0.75	-0.76	0.63	-0.15	-1.24	1.34	1.28	0.06	1.87	1.46	0.41
3rd quarter	-0.5	0.47	-0.70	0.33	-0.44	-0.59	0.48	0.66	-0.18	-0.73	-0.90	0.16
4th quarter	6.7	3.43	-0.69	-0.09	-0.33	-0.27	1.73	0.93	0.80	2.22	1.88	0.34
1957												
1st quarter	2.4	1.59	-0.89	0.30	-0.30	-0.90	-0.01	1.35	-1.36	1.77	0.94	0.83
2nd quarter	-1.0	0.33	-0.09	-0.10	-0.48	0.49	-0.73	-0.57	-0.16	-0.51	-0.80	0.29
3rd quarter	4.0	2.06	1.46	0.91	-0.25	0.80	-0.26	-0.57	0.32	0.72	0.22	0.49
4th quarter	-4.2	0.07	-5.24	-1.03	-0.03	-4.19	-0.64	-0.57	-0.07	1.65	0.80	0.85
1958												
1st quarter	-10.4	-3.29	-4.21	-2.72	-0.69	-0.80	-2.05	-1.81	-0.24	-0.87	-1.84	0.98
2nd quarter	2.4	2.01	-1.33	-1.61	0.05	0.23	-0.64	0.11	-0.75	2.34	1.80	0.53
3rd quarter	9.6	4.14	4.58	-0.54	1.36	3.76	0.29	0.10	0.20	0.55	-0.26	0.82
4th quarter	9.5	3.13	5.44	1.35	2.10	1.99	-0.97	-0.01	-0.96	1.94	1.24	0.69
1959												
1st quarter	7.9	3.94	3.89	1.11	2.37	0.41	0.76	1.18	-0.42	-0.72	-1.02	0.30
2nd quarter	10.9	4.26	5.69	1.14	0.83	3.73	-0.31	0.63	-0.94	1.32	1.21	0.11
3rd quarter	-0.3	2.72	-4.42	1.14	-0.43	-5.13	0.37	0.59	-0.23	1.03	0.99	0.04
4th quarter	1.4	0.33	2.07	-0.15	-0.63	2.86	-0.04	-0.49	0.45	-0.95	-0.77	-0.18
1960												
1st quarter	9.2	2.47	6.70	1.49	0.65	4.57	1.70	2.30	-0.60	-1.63	-2.24	0.62
2nd quarter	-2.0	3.13	-6.92	0.58	-1.76	-5.74	1.15	1.26	-0.10	0.66	-0.20	0.85
3rd quarter	0.6	-0.99	-0.46	-0.94	-0.60	1.08	0.01	-0.54	0.54	2.07	1.52	0.55
4th quarter	-5.1	0.31	-7.21	-0.18	-0.03	-7.00	1.26	0.43	0.83	0.58	0.16	0.42
1961												
1st quarter	2.4	-0.03	1.40	-0.76	0.07	2.08	-0.07	-0.14	0.07	1.12	-0.08	1.20
2nd quarter	7.7	3.89	4.14	0.77	0.07	3.30	-0.48	-0.28	-0.20	0.19	0.45	-0.26
3rd quarter	6.6	1.25	4.84	0.30	1.03	3.51	-1.17	-0.11	-1.06	1.74	1.41	0.32
4th quarter	8.4	5.15	1.11	1.20	0.66	-0.75	0.21	0.62	-0.40	1.95	0.88	1.07

. . . = Not available.

Table 19-3. Contributions to Percent Change in Real Gross Domestic Product—*Continued*

(Percent; percentage points.)   **NIPA Table 1.1.2**

Year and quarter	Percent change at seasonally adjusted annual rate, real GDP	Personal consumption expenditures	Gross private domestic investment				Exports and imports of goods and services			Government consumption expenditures and gross investment		
			Total	Fixed investment		Change in private inventories	Net exports	Exports	Imports	Total	Federal	State and local
				Nonresidential	Residential							
1962												
1st quarter	7.4	2.69	3.66	0.82	0.36	2.48	-0.56	-0.05	-0.51	1.59	1.86	-0.27
2nd quarter	4.4	3.02	-0.56	1.05	0.62	-2.23	1.51	1.88	-0.37	0.47	0.20	0.27
3rd quarter	3.7	2.03	1.10	0.46	-0.02	0.65	-1.38	-1.17	-0.21	1.99	1.52	0.48
4th quarter	1.0	3.53	-2.05	-0.26	-0.03	-1.77	-0.63	-0.42	-0.21	0.13	-0.28	0.41
1963												
1st quarter	5.3	1.74	3.30	-0.06	0.73	2.63	0.88	0.46	0.41	-0.53	-1.25	0.72
2nd quarter	5.1	2.43	0.88	1.13	1.44	-1.70	1.90	2.29	-0.38	-0.12	-0.46	0.35
3rd quarter	7.7	3.45	2.02	1.11	0.39	0.52	-1.53	-1.11	-0.42	3.80	2.76	1.04
4th quarter	3.1	2.10	0.80	1.19	0.63	-1.02	1.05	0.99	0.06	-0.81	-1.35	0.54
1964												
1st quarter	9.3	5.00	2.64	0.93	1.32	0.38	1.30	1.27	0.02	0.33	-0.25	0.58
2nd quarter	4.7	4.42	-0.25	0.95	-1.10	-0.09	-0.02	0.35	-0.37	0.58	-0.31	0.89
3rd quarter	5.6	4.66	1.46	1.29	-0.33	0.50	-0.60	-0.16	-0.44	0.06	-0.36	0.43
4th quarter	1.1	0.71	0.44	0.81	-0.36	0.00	0.17	0.62	-0.45	-0.24	-0.66	0.42
1965												
1st quarter	10.2	5.68	6.36	2.72	0.07	3.56	-1.65	-2.29	0.64	-0.18	-0.56	0.38
2nd quarter	5.5	2.83	-0.09	1.52	0.15	-1.77	1.68	3.59	-1.91	1.10	0.08	1.02
3rd quarter	8.4	4.36	2.34	1.59	0.08	0.67	-1.31	-1.23	-0.07	2.96	1.82	1.14
4th quarter	10.0	7.18	0.32	1.77	-0.41	-1.04	0.62	1.48	-0.86	1.91	1.31	0.60
1966												
1st quarter	10.1	3.74	5.68	1.88	0.42	3.38	-0.82	-0.36	-0.46	1.55	1.05	0.50
2nd quarter	1.4	0.67	-1.22	0.65	-1.47	-0.40	0.45	0.89	-0.45	1.49	1.19	0.31
3rd quarter	2.7	2.80	-0.65	0.51	-0.55	-0.61	-1.82	-0.80	-1.02	2.33	1.86	0.46
4th quarter	3.3	1.02	0.32	-0.12	-1.70	2.14	0.48	0.68	-0.20	1.44	0.38	1.06
1967												
1st quarter	3.6	1.44	-1.83	-0.91	-0.43	-0.49	0.16	0.41	-0.25	3.82	3.30	0.52
2nd quarter	0.0	3.25	-2.69	-0.15	1.58	-4.11	-0.03	-0.20	0.17	-0.51	-0.74	0.23
3rd quarter	3.2	1.27	1.73	-0.21	0.77	1.17	-0.74	-0.51	-0.24	0.97	0.80	0.17
4th quarter	3.1	1.49	1.32	0.84	0.94	-0.46	-0.41	0.58	-0.99	0.65	-0.09	0.74
1968												
1st quarter	8.5	5.97	1.38	1.34	0.11	-0.06	-0.54	0.60	-1.15	1.70	0.93	0.77
2nd quarter	7.0	3.85	2.57	-0.73	0.43	2.87	0.10	0.42	-0.31	0.45	-0.39	0.84
3rd quarter	2.7	4.59	-2.06	0.52	0.30	-2.89	0.01	1.22	-1.21	0.22	-0.40	0.62
4th quarter	1.7	1.09	0.63	1.18	0.21	-0.77	-0.10	-0.27	0.17	0.07	-0.30	0.37
1969												
1st quarter	6.5	2.80	4.16	1.23	0.65	2.28	-0.58	-2.53	1.94	0.10	-0.26	0.36
2nd quarter	1.1	1.54	-0.49	0.45	-0.19	-0.75	0.50	4.08	-3.58	-0.39	-0.75	0.36
3rd quarter	2.5	1.13	1.51	1.14	-0.14	0.52	-0.25	-0.53	0.28	0.12	0.03	0.09
4th quarter	-1.9	1.92	-3.44	-0.25	-1.27	-1.92	0.98	0.74	0.24	-1.34	-1.25	-0.09
1970												
1st quarter	-0.7	1.46	-1.90	-0.23	0.03	-1.70	0.26	0.19	0.08	-0.50	-0.91	0.41
2nd quarter	0.8	1.17	0.20	-0.23	-1.08	1.51	0.57	0.98	-0.41	-1.18	-1.43	0.25
3rd quarter	3.6	2.23	1.00	0.20	0.81	-0.01	-0.03	-0.08	0.05	0.40	-0.64	1.04
4th quarter	-4.2	-0.66	-3.42	-1.61	1.61	-3.43	-0.12	0.21	-0.33	0.00	-0.24	0.24
1971												
1st quarter	11.6	5.09	7.60	0.32	0.96	6.33	0.36	0.09	0.26	-1.42	-1.64	0.22
2nd quarter	2.3	2.34	1.86	0.57	1.80	-0.51	-1.63	-0.05	-1.59	-0.28	-0.60	0.32
3rd quarter	3.2	2.03	0.83	0.18	0.97	-0.32	0.43	0.92	-0.49	-0.08	-0.19	0.12
4th quarter	1.1	4.14	-1.98	0.92	0.79	-3.69	-0.35	-1.93	1.57	-0.67	-1.27	0.60
1972												
1st quarter	7.3	3.34	4.54	1.49	1.44	1.62	-0.89	2.23	-3.12	0.31	0.15	0.16
2nd quarter	9.8	4.83	4.22	0.78	0.45	2.99	0.21	-0.68	0.89	0.55	0.65	-0.10
3rd quarter	3.9	3.77	1.05	0.68	0.05	0.32	0.82	1.30	-0.48	-1.78	-2.16	0.38
4th quarter	6.7	5.83	0.45	2.17	0.80	-2.53	-0.11	0.95	-1.07	0.55	-0.11	0.66
1973												
1st quarter	10.6	4.61	4.47	2.02	0.80	1.65	0.59	1.73	-1.14	0.88	0.67	0.22
2nd quarter	4.7	-0.14	3.36	1.75	-1.19	2.80	1.96	1.20	0.75	-0.47	-0.55	0.08
3rd quarter	-2.1	0.87	-2.72	0.73	-0.95	-2.50	0.78	0.06	0.71	-1.04	-1.52	0.48
4th quarter	3.9	-0.72	2.84	0.34	-1.03	3.53	1.17	1.39	-0.22	0.59	0.02	0.57
1974												
1st quarter	-3.4	-2.09	-4.40	-0.07	-1.48	-2.84	1.38	0.37	1.01	1.69	1.07	0.62
2nd quarter	1.2	1.07	-0.34	-0.11	-0.82	0.59	-0.15	1.56	-1.71	0.58	-0.07	0.65
3rd quarter	-3.8	1.15	-3.85	-0.51	-0.58	-2.76	-1.24	-1.85	0.61	0.12	0.18	-0.06
4th quarter	-1.6	-3.45	0.33	-1.27	-2.33	3.93	1.26	0.90	0.36	0.31	0.29	0.03
1975												
1st quarter	-4.7	2.15	-11.74	-2.70	-0.93	-8.11	3.84	0.23	3.61	1.08	-0.40	1.48
2nd quarter	3.0	4.21	-2.11	-1.13	0.32	-1.30	1.52	-1.05	2.56	-0.65	-0.28	-0.37
3rd quarter	6.9	3.69	4.53	0.39	1.06	3.08	-2.86	-0.57	-2.29	1.59	0.94	0.65
4th quarter	5.4	2.68	1.64	0.37	0.69	0.58	0.26	1.81	-1.56	0.77	0.11	0.67
1976												
1st quarter	9.3	5.03	6.17	0.73	1.63	3.80	-2.12	-0.23	-1.89	0.24	-0.33	0.56
2nd quarter	3.0	2.23	2.76	0.47	0.50	1.79	-1.04	0.33	-1.37	-0.93	-0.06	-0.86
3rd quarter	1.9	2.63	0.12	0.89	-0.29	-0.47	-0.39	0.94	-1.33	-0.43	-0.09	-0.34
4th quarter	2.9	3.39	0.34	0.83	2.24	-2.73	-0.77	0.34	-1.11	-0.06	0.10	-0.15

Table 19-3. Contributions to Percent Change in Real Gross Domestic Product—*Continued*

(Percent; percentage points.)

NIPA Table 1.1.2

Year and quarter	Percent change at seasonally adjusted annual rate, real GDP	Personal consumption expenditures	Gross private domestic investment				Exports and imports of goods and services			Government consumption expenditures and gross investment		
			Total	Fixed investment		Change in private inventories	Net exports	Exports	Imports	Total	Federal	State and local
				Nonresidential	Residential							
1977												
1st quarter	4.9	3.14	3.07	1.74	0.62	0.71	-2.08	-0.51	-1.57	0.78	0.31	0.47
2nd quarter	8.1	1.43	5.23	1.33	2.40	1.50	0.55	0.87	-0.33	0.89	0.60	0.29
3rd quarter	7.4	2.46	3.98	0.99	-0.07	3.06	0.77	0.25	0.53	0.15	0.20	-0.05
4th quarter	0.0	3.69	-1.94	1.56	-0.30	-3.20	-1.53	-1.03	-0.50	-0.27	-0.34	0.07
1978												
1st quarter	1.3	1.35	1.63	0.51	0.10	1.02	-1.83	0.67	-2.50	0.12	0.11	0.01
2nd quarter	16.7	5.68	5.56	4.18	1.14	0.23	3.23	3.34	-0.11	2.27	0.85	1.42
3rd quarter	4.0	1.06	2.45	1.71	0.31	0.43	-0.12	0.35	-0.48	0.61	0.11	0.50
4th quarter	5.4	2.01	1.85	1.62	-0.08	0.31	0.80	1.31	-0.50	0.71	0.29	0.43
1979												
1st quarter	0.8	1.34	-0.03	1.04	-0.54	-0.53	0.14	0.03	0.10	-0.67	0.04	-0.71
2nd quarter	0.4	-0.12	-0.18	-0.21	-0.43	0.46	-0.10	0.09	-0.19	0.78	0.39	0.40
3rd quarter	2.9	2.42	-1.50	1.56	-0.27	-2.79	1.87	1.24	0.63	0.12	-0.05	0.16
4th quarter	1.2	0.68	-1.40	0.10	-0.86	-0.64	1.39	2.22	-0.84	0.51	0.01	0.50
1980												
1st quarter	1.3	-0.45	-0.49	0.55	-1.65	0.61	1.02	0.97	0.05	1.19	1.00	0.19
2nd quarter	-7.8	-5.56	-6.62	-2.68	-3.61	-0.33	4.09	0.75	3.35	0.26	0.87	-0.61
3rd quarter	-0.7	2.72	-5.29	0.38	0.28	-5.95	3.04	-0.07	3.10	-1.14	-0.47	-0.67
4th quarter	7.6	3.44	6.58	1.11	1.66	3.82	-2.30	-0.20	-2.10	-0.08	0.12	-0.20
1981												
1st quarter	8.4	1.15	7.08	0.86	-0.31	6.53	-0.92	0.83	-1.75	1.09	0.74	0.36
2nd quarter	-3.1	0.07	-3.50	1.06	-0.58	-3.99	0.18	0.26	-0.08	0.18	1.04	-0.86
3rd quarter	4.9	1.01	4.46	1.32	-1.28	4.43	-0.36	-0.82	0.46	-0.17	-0.03	-0.14
4th quarter	-4.9	-1.83	-2.89	1.33	-1.55	-2.67	-0.92	0.17	-1.09	0.76	0.40	0.36
1982												
1st quarter	-6.4	1.64	-7.46	-1.28	-0.78	-5.40	-0.52	-1.67	1.15	-0.06	0.08	-0.13
2nd quarter	2.2	0.88	-0.05	-1.98	-0.42	2.35	0.83	0.20	0.63	0.50	0.36	0.14
3rd quarter	-1.5	1.93	-0.68	-1.82	-0.04	1.18	-3.32	-1.62	-1.70	0.57	0.57	0.00
4th quarter	0.4	4.60	-5.61	-1.07	0.92	-5.46	-0.08	-1.56	1.48	1.44	1.13	0.31
1983												
1st quarter	5.0	2.48	2.20	-1.00	2.26	0.94	-0.29	0.51	-0.80	0.63	0.47	0.16
2nd quarter	9.3	5.25	5.88	0.52	1.86	3.50	-2.53	0.10	-2.63	0.73	0.85	-0.11
3rd quarter	8.1	4.71	4.26	2.05	1.70	0.51	-2.31	0.47	-2.79	1.47	1.11	0.36
4th quarter	8.4	4.22	6.83	3.03	0.79	3.01	-1.21	0.63	-1.84	-1.39	-1.36	-0.03
1984												
1st quarter	8.1	2.34	7.29	1.59	0.54	5.17	-2.35	0.66	-3.01	0.82	0.31	0.51
2nd quarter	7.1	3.83	2.34	2.44	0.35	-0.45	-0.91	0.77	-1.68	1.80	1.22	0.58
3rd quarter	3.9	2.06	1.65	1.67	-0.17	0.15	-0.38	0.67	-1.05	0.61	-0.15	0.76
4th quarter	3.3	3.42	-1.28	1.22	0.02	-2.52	-0.58	0.61	-1.19	1.77	1.28	0.49
1985												
1st quarter	3.8	4.30	-2.40	0.61	-0.06	-2.95	0.90	0.01	0.89	0.95	0.42	0.52
2nd quarter	3.5	2.35	1.24	0.73	0.14	0.36	-2.00	-0.12	-1.87	1.86	0.96	0.90
3rd quarter	6.4	4.95	-0.72	-0.76	0.23	-0.18	-0.02	-0.44	0.42	2.19	1.33	0.86
4th quarter	3.1	0.57	2.71	0.84	0.42	1.45	-0.68	0.81	-1.49	0.50	-0.01	0.51
1986												
1st quarter	3.9	2.10	-0.06	-0.68	0.78	-0.16	0.95	0.85	0.10	0.89	-0.21	1.10
2nd quarter	1.6	2.69	-1.50	-1.22	1.05	-1.33	-1.37	0.28	-1.65	1.77	1.22	0.55
3rd quarter	3.9	4.48	-2.08	-0.70	0.31	-1.68	-0.47	0.63	-1.10	1.95	1.51	0.44
4th quarter	2.0	1.65	0.12	0.44	-0.04	-0.28	0.72	1.06	-0.33	-0.46	-0.59	0.13
1987												
1st quarter	2.7	0.10	2.09	-1.26	-0.06	3.41	0.23	0.02	0.21	0.25	0.27	-0.02
2nd quarter	4.5	3.64	0.09	1.03	0.09	-1.02	0.11	1.19	-1.08	0.63	0.60	0.03
3rd quarter	3.7	3.00	0.06	1.40	-0.06	-1.29	0.45	1.31	-0.86	0.17	0.08	0.09
4th quarter	7.2	0.66	5.17	-0.11	0.10	5.18	0.15	1.16	-1.02	1.21	0.62	0.58
1988												
1st quarter	2.0	4.33	-3.88	0.34	-0.42	-3.80	1.98	1.78	0.20	-0.46	-1.01	0.55
2nd quarter	5.2	1.92	1.57	1.11	0.15	0.31	1.48	0.96	0.52	0.21	-0.35	0.56
3rd quarter	2.1	2.20	0.40	0.23	0.01	0.15	-0.35	0.64	-1.00	-0.09	-0.25	0.16
4th quarter	5.4	3.15	0.85	0.47	0.17	0.21	-0.22	1.07	-1.29	1.61	1.10	0.51
1989												
1st quarter	4.1	0.99	2.48	0.75	-0.12	1.85	1.15	1.02	0.12	-0.49	-0.72	0.23
2nd quarter	2.6	1.25	-0.78	0.62	-0.54	-0.86	0.92	1.57	-0.64	1.25	0.80	0.45
3rd quarter	2.9	2.51	-0.76	1.26	-0.19	-1.84	0.38	0.43	-0.05	0.76	0.35	0.41
4th quarter	1.0	1.20	-0.66	-0.67	-0.36	0.37	0.05	0.60	-0.55	0.43	-0.17	0.60
1990												
1st quarter	4.7	2.19	0.60	0.58	0.17	-0.16	0.64	1.57	-0.93	1.28	0.54	0.74
2nd quarter	1.0	0.85	0.03	-0.77	-0.64	1.43	0.02	0.48	-0.47	0.14	0.05	0.09
3rd quarter	0.0	1.06	-1.42	0.25	-0.92	-0.76	0.39	0.31	0.08	0.00	-0.30	0.30
4th quarter	-3.0	-1.92	-3.70	-0.84	-0.83	-2.03	1.81	0.39	1.42	0.82	0.31	0.51
1991												
1st quarter	-2.0	-1.18	-2.25	-1.14	-0.87	-0.24	1.08	0.18	0.90	0.33	0.27	0.06
2nd quarter	2.6	2.29	-0.22	-0.41	0.31	-0.12	0.26	1.43	-1.16	0.29	0.11	0.18
3rd quarter	1.9	1.14	1.31	-0.40	0.56	1.15	-0.12	0.95	-1.07	-0.38	-0.65	0.27
4th quarter	1.9	-0.24	2.02	-0.23	0.30	1.94	0.43	0.92	-0.49	-0.32	-0.67	0.35

Table 19-3. Contributions to Percent Change in Real Gross Domestic Product—*Continued*

(Percent; percentage points.)   NIPA Table 1.1.2

Year and quarter	Percent change at seasonally adjusted annual rate, real GDP	Personal consumption expenditures	Gross private domestic investment				Exports and imports of goods and services			Government consumption expenditures and gross investment		
			Total	Fixed investment		Change in private inventories	Net exports	Exports	Imports	Total	Federal	State and local
				Nonresidential	Residential							
1992												
1st quarter	4.2	4.50	-1.26	-0.19	0.72	-1.79	0.32	0.68	-0.37	0.65	0.02	0.64
2nd quarter	3.9	1.56	3.45	1.50	0.56	1.39	-1.01	0.02	-1.03	-0.08	-0.03	-0.06
3rd quarter	4.0	2.70	0.58	0.78	0.03	-0.24	0.26	0.86	-0.60	0.44	0.40	0.04
4th quarter	4.5	3.14	1.80	1.18	0.51	0.11	-0.47	0.22	-0.70	0.02	0.02	0.00
1993												
1st quarter	0.5	0.92	1.34	0.25	0.07	1.03	-0.93	0.05	-0.98	-0.85	-1.04	0.19
2nd quarter	2.0	2.37	0.48	1.04	0.18	-0.75	-0.72	0.46	-1.18	-0.08	-0.47	0.38
3rd quarter	2.1	2.95	0.01	0.44	0.54	-0.96	-0.67	-0.10	-0.56	-0.22	-0.46	0.24
4th quarter	5.5	2.47	2.97	1.69	0.83	0.45	-0.25	1.29	-1.53	0.29	0.08	0.21
1994												
1st quarter	4.1	3.07	2.47	0.39	0.34	1.74	-0.65	0.34	-0.99	-0.76	-0.90	0.14
2nd quarter	5.3	1.98	3.56	0.81	0.58	2.17	-0.56	1.31	-1.86	0.33	-0.16	0.49
3rd quarter	2.3	1.94	-1.11	0.75	-0.18	-1.68	0.20	1.49	-1.29	1.23	0.71	0.52
4th quarter	4.8	2.71	2.89	1.82	-0.22	1.29	-0.19	0.93	-1.12	-0.64	-0.80	0.16
1995												
1st quarter	1.1	0.39	0.69	1.68	-0.38	-0.61	-0.26	0.72	-0.98	0.28	-0.06	0.34
2nd quarter	0.7	2.21	-1.68	0.29	-0.53	-1.44	-0.11	0.59	-0.70	0.31	-0.05	0.36
3rd quarter	3.3	2.37	-0.58	0.29	0.50	-1.37	1.75	1.92	-0.17	-0.24	-0.27	0.03
4th quarter	3.0	1.87	1.70	0.88	0.38	0.44	0.21	0.68	-0.47	-0.82	-1.06	0.24
1996												
1st quarter	2.9	2.46	0.76	1.09	0.44	-0.77	-0.85	0.56	-1.42	0.49	0.59	-0.10
2nd quarter	6.7	3.02	3.17	1.29	0.73	1.15	-0.71	0.77	-1.48	1.23	0.56	0.67
3rd quarter	3.4	1.74	3.14	1.48	-0.05	1.71	-1.23	0.38	-1.61	-0.25	-0.66	0.40
4th quarter	4.8	2.28	-0.25	1.20	-0.18	-1.27	2.09	2.75	-0.66	0.64	-0.05	0.69
1997												
1st quarter	3.1	2.89	1.40	1.14	0.06	0.21	-1.22	0.82	-2.03	0.06	-0.34	0.40
2nd quarter	6.2	1.27	4.39	1.14	0.22	3.03	-0.18	1.81	-1.99	0.73	0.57	0.16
3rd quarter	5.1	4.42	1.38	2.34	0.08	-1.04	-0.73	1.10	-1.83	0.01	-0.15	0.16
4th quarter	3.0	2.78	1.12	0.37	0.17	0.57	-0.87	-0.04	-0.83	0.01	-0.15	0.16
1998												
1st quarter	4.5	2.98	3.53	1.57	0.35	1.61	-1.65	0.20	-1.85	-0.41	-0.66	0.25
2nd quarter	2.7	4.25	-1.12	1.44	0.47	-3.04	-1.86	-0.48	-1.38	1.40	0.61	0.79
3rd quarter	4.7	3.29	1.57	0.45	0.48	0.64	-0.82	-0.19	-0.63	0.66	-0.19	0.85
4th quarter	6.2	3.71	1.71	1.49	0.44	-0.22	0.13	1.59	-1.46	0.64	0.20	0.44
1999												
1st quarter	3.4	2.68	1.96	0.87	0.16	0.93	-1.67	-0.39	-1.28	0.46	-0.14	0.60
2nd quarter	3.4	4.23	0.05	1.47	0.16	-1.57	-1.35	0.48	-1.83	0.41	0.09	0.32
3rd quarter	4.8	2.90	1.72	1.19	0.11	0.42	-0.75	1.12	-1.87	0.88	0.49	0.39
4th quarter	7.3	3.47	2.65	0.12	0.23	2.30	0.01	1.13	-1.11	1.17	0.58	0.59
2000												
1st quarter	1.0	4.38	-1.30	1.64	0.19	-3.13	-1.53	0.70	-2.23	-0.56	-0.93	0.36
2nd quarter	6.4	1.78	4.65	1.76	-0.16	3.05	-0.98	1.30	-2.27	0.96	0.96	0.01
3rd quarter	-0.5	2.62	-1.84	0.28	-0.38	-1.74	-0.87	1.14	-2.01	-0.37	-0.51	0.15
4th quarter	2.1	2.29	-0.36	0.11	0.02	-0.49	-0.07	-0.31	0.24	0.22	-0.07	0.29
2001												
1st quarter	-0.5	1.07	-2.44	-0.52	0.10	-2.01	-0.04	-0.59	0.56	0.92	0.46	0.46
2nd quarter	1.2	0.67	-1.28	-1.76	0.25	0.23	0.49	-1.45	1.94	1.35	0.52	0.83
3rd quarter	-1.4	1.20	-1.76	-0.83	0.08	-1.02	-0.56	-2.04	1.48	-0.28	0.00	-0.28
4th quarter	1.6	4.71	-3.95	-1.63	-0.18	-2.14	-0.66	-1.11	0.45	1.48	0.51	0.97
2002												
1st quarter	2.7	1.01	1.92	-1.50	0.46	2.95	-0.97	0.47	-1.44	0.79	0.36	0.43
2nd quarter	2.2	1.64	0.30	-0.66	0.43	0.53	-0.62	0.96	-1.58	0.88	0.76	0.12
3rd quarter	2.4	1.57	0.87	-0.21	0.09	0.98	-0.49	0.27	-0.76	0.43	0.20	0.23
4th quarter	0.2	0.97	-0.14	-0.52	0.30	0.08	-1.52	-0.31	-1.21	0.89	0.64	0.25
2003												
1st quarter	1.2	1.41	-0.16	-0.24	0.20	-0.12	0.21	-0.53	0.74	-0.26	0.01	-0.27
2nd quarter	3.5	2.53	0.51	1.01	0.51	-1.01	-0.73	-0.16	-0.57	1.16	1.26	-0.10
3rd quarter	7.5	4.13	2.56	0.92	1.08	0.56	0.51	1.02	-0.51	0.29	0.03	0.26
4th quarter	2.7	1.59	1.39	0.29	0.55	0.56	-0.47	1.81	-2.29	0.14	0.21	-0.07
2004												
1st quarter	3.0	3.12	0.30	-0.28	0.21	0.37	-0.75	0.95	-1.70	0.29	0.41	-0.12
2nd quarter	3.5	1.73	3.00	1.00	0.89	1.12	-1.50	0.64	-2.14	0.25	0.17	0.09
3rd quarter	3.6	2.46	1.26	1.16	0.24	-0.14	-0.42	0.31	-0.73	0.30	0.43	-0.13
4th quarter	2.5	2.93	1.04	1.00	0.14	-0.11	-1.07	0.97	-2.04	-0.35	-0.33	-0.01
2005												
1st quarter	3.0	1.25	1.48	0.37	0.48	0.63	0.28	0.80	-0.52	-0.04	0.08	-0.12
2nd quarter	2.6	2.50	-0.86	0.64	0.57	-2.07	0.79	0.89	-0.10	0.17	0.08	0.10
3rd quarter	3.8	2.59	0.69	0.64	0.25	-0.19	-0.07	0.04	-0.11	0.65	0.66	-0.01
4th quarter	1.3	0.94	1.98	0.40	0.01	1.56	-1.26	1.09	-2.35	-0.34	-0.53	0.19
2006												
1st quarter	4.8	2.86	1.15	1.62	-0.23	-0.24	0.09	1.70	-1.61	0.72	0.66	0.06
2nd quarter	2.7	1.88	-0.02	0.71	-1.11	0.38	0.59	0.58	0.01	0.23	-0.11	0.34
3rd quarter	0.8	1.52	-0.92	0.59	-1.40	-0.11	-0.12	0.39	-0.51	0.32	0.13	0.19
4th quarter	1.5	2.55	-2.68	-0.09	-1.18	-1.41	1.33	1.66	-0.33	0.30	0.12	0.18

Table 19-4. Chain-Type Quantity Indexes for Gross Domestic Product and Domestic Purchases

(Index numbers, 2000 = 100.)   NIPA Tables 1.1.3, 1.4.3, 2.3.3

Year and quarter	Gross domestic product, total	Personal consumption expenditures		Private fixed investment			Exports and imports of goods and services		Government consumption expenditures and gross investment			Gross domestic purchases
		Total	Excluding food and energy	Total	Nonresidential	Residential	Exports	Imports	Total	Federal	State and local	
1946	16.2	15.0	11.2	9.0	7.1	16.6	5.9	3.2	23.0	43.0	11.6	15.4
1947	16.0	15.3	11.7	10.8	8.2	21.3	6.7	3.0	19.6	31.8	13.2	15.1
1948	16.7	15.6	12.2	11.9	8.7	25.5	5.3	3.5	21.0	34.3	14.0	16.1
1949	16.7	16.1	12.6	10.9	7.9	23.6	5.2	3.4	23.5	37.6	16.2	16.0
1947												
1st quarter	16.0	15.1	. . .	10.6	8.3	19.6	7.1	3.1	19.5	32.0	12.9	15.0
2nd quarter	16.0	15.3	. . .	10.3	8.2	18.6	7.1	3.2	19.6	32.1	13.0	15.0
3rd quarter	16.0	15.4	. . .	10.7	8.0	21.5	6.7	2.8	19.8	32.1	13.3	15.0
4th quarter	16.2	15.4	. . .	11.6	8.3	25.6	6.0	3.0	19.5	31.0	13.6	15.4
1948												
1st quarter	16.5	15.5	. . .	12.0	8.8	25.3	5.7	3.4	19.9	32.0	13.5	15.8
2nd quarter	16.8	15.6	. . .	12.0	8.5	26.8	5.1	3.5	20.8	33.9	13.9	16.2
3rd quarter	16.8	15.7	. . .	11.9	8.5	26.0	5.3	3.7	21.2	34.7	14.2	16.3
4th quarter	16.9	15.8	. . .	11.7	8.8	24.1	5.1	3.6	22.1	36.5	14.5	16.3
1949												
1st quarter	16.6	15.8	. . .	11.0	8.3	22.2	5.7	3.5	22.8	37.3	15.1	16.0
2nd quarter	16.6	16.1	. . .	10.7	8.0	21.9	5.6	3.4	23.8	38.7	16.0	15.9
3rd quarter	16.8	16.1	. . .	10.7	7.6	23.7	5.2	3.3	24.0	38.3	16.6	16.1
4th quarter	16.6	16.3	. . .	11.0	7.5	26.6	4.5	3.4	23.5	36.3	17.0	16.1
1950												
1st quarter	17.3	16.6	. . .	11.8	7.7	29.7	4.4	3.4	23.1	34.6	17.4	16.8
2nd quarter	17.8	16.9	. . .	12.8	8.4	32.5	4.5	3.6	23.5	35.4	17.5	17.3
3rd quarter	18.5	17.7	. . .	13.8	9.1	34.3	4.6	4.5	23.0	34.1	17.5	18.1
4th quarter	18.8	17.2	. . .	13.5	9.1	32.7	4.9	4.5	24.5	38.2	17.6	18.4
1951												
1st quarter	19.1	17.6	. . .	13.0	8.9	31.0	5.2	4.5	27.1	45.6	17.4	18.6
2nd quarter	19.4	17.1	. . .	12.4	9.0	26.8	5.7	4.4	30.9	55.4	17.7	18.8
3rd quarter	19.8	17.3	. . .	12.2	9.1	25.1	5.8	4.0	34.4	64.9	17.8	19.1
4th quarter	19.8	17.4	. . .	12.1	8.9	25.3	5.8	3.9	36.2	70.1	17.7	19.1
1952												
1st quarter	20.0	17.5	. . .	12.2	9.0	26.0	6.1	4.3	37.4	73.3	17.8	19.3
2nd quarter	20.0	17.8	. . .	12.4	9.1	26.5	5.4	4.3	38.6	76.2	18.2	19.5
3rd quarter	20.2	17.9	. . .	11.6	8.2	26.2	5.0	4.6	39.0	78.2	17.7	19.7
4th quarter	20.8	18.5	. . .	12.5	9.0	27.6	5.0	5.0	39.7	79.4	18.1	20.4
1953												
1st quarter	21.2	18.7	. . .	13.0	9.5	28.0	4.9	4.9	41.1	82.4	18.5	20.8
2nd quarter	21.4	18.9	. . .	13.1	9.5	28.1	5.0	5.1	42.0	85.0	18.4	21.0
3rd quarter	21.2	18.8	. . .	13.1	9.7	27.0	5.2	5.1	41.5	82.7	18.9	20.8
4th quarter	20.9	18.7	. . .	13.0	9.6	26.8	5.0	4.8	41.4	81.6	19.4	20.5
1954												
1st quarter	20.8	18.8	. . .	12.8	9.3	27.1	4.8	4.6	40.2	77.2	20.1	20.4
2nd quarter	20.8	19.0	. . .	13.0	9.2	28.9	5.5	5.0	38.8	73.0	20.2	20.4
3rd quarter	21.1	19.2	. . .	13.5	9.5	30.6	5.3	4.7	37.9	69.4	20.7	20.6
4th quarter	21.5	19.6	. . .	13.8	9.5	32.5	5.5	4.7	37.6	68.6	20.8	20.9
1955												
1st quarter	22.1	20.1	. . .	14.3	9.6	35.0	5.7	5.0	37.6	66.9	21.7	21.6
2nd quarter	22.5	20.5	. . .	15.0	10.2	35.5	5.6	5.3	37.2	65.4	22.0	22.0
3rd quarter	22.8	20.7	. . .	15.3	10.8	34.7	6.0	5.4	37.4	66.1	22.0	22.2
4th quarter	22.9	21.0	. . .	15.3	11.1	33.3	6.0	5.6	36.6	63.6	22.1	22.4
1956												
1st quarter	22.8	21.0	. . .	15.0	10.9	32.4	6.3	5.8	36.6	63.1	22.3	22.3
2nd quarter	22.9	21.1	. . .	15.1	11.0	32.2	6.7	5.8	37.4	64.8	22.6	22.4
3rd quarter	22.9	21.1	. . .	15.1	11.1	31.5	6.9	5.8	37.0	63.6	22.7	22.3
4th quarter	23.3	21.4	. . .	15.0	11.1	31.1	7.2	5.5	38.0	65.9	22.9	22.6
1957												
1st quarter	23.4	21.6	. . .	15.0	11.2	30.6	7.7	6.0	38.8	67.1	23.5	22.7
2nd quarter	23.4	21.6	. . .	14.8	11.1	29.9	7.5	6.0	38.5	66.0	23.7	22.7
3rd quarter	23.6	21.8	. . .	15.0	11.4	29.5	7.3	5.9	38.8	66.3	24.1	22.9
4th quarter	23.4	21.8	. . .	14.7	11.1	29.4	7.1	5.9	39.5	67.2	24.6	22.7
1958												
1st quarter	22.7	21.5	. . .	13.8	10.3	28.3	6.4	6.0	39.1	64.8	25.3	22.2
2nd quarter	22.9	21.6	. . .	13.4	9.8	28.3	6.4	6.3	40.0	66.9	25.7	22.4
3rd quarter	23.4	22.0	. . .	13.6	9.7	30.4	6.4	6.2	40.3	66.6	26.3	22.9
4th quarter	23.9	22.3	. . .	14.4	10.1	33.6	6.4	6.5	41.1	68.1	26.8	23.5
1959												
1st quarter	24.4	22.6	18.2	15.3	10.4	37.5	6.8	6.7	40.9	67.0	27.0	23.9
2nd quarter	25.0	23.0	18.6	15.8	10.7	38.8	7.0	7.0	41.5	68.6	27.0	24.5
3rd quarter	25.0	23.3	18.8	16.0	11.0	38.1	7.3	7.1	42.0	70.0	27.1	24.5
4th quarter	25.1	23.3	18.8	15.8	11.0	37.0	7.1	6.9	41.6	69.0	26.9	24.6
1960												
1st quarter	25.6	23.5	19.0	16.3	11.4	38.0	8.0	7.2	40.7	65.9	27.4	25.0
2nd quarter	25.5	23.8	19.3	16.0	11.6	34.9	8.5	7.2	41.1	65.6	28.1	24.8
3rd quarter	25.6	23.7	19.3	15.6	11.3	33.8	8.2	7.0	42.1	67.7	28.5	24.9
4th quarter	25.2	23.7	19.3	15.5	11.2	33.8	8.4	6.7	42.3	67.9	28.8	24.5
1961												
1st quarter	25.4	23.7	19.2	15.3	11.0	33.9	8.4	6.6	42.9	67.8	29.7	24.6
2nd quarter	25.9	24.1	19.6	15.6	11.2	34.0	8.2	6.7	43.0	68.4	29.5	25.1
3rd quarter	26.3	24.2	19.7	15.9	11.3	35.9	8.2	7.2	43.8	70.4	29.8	25.6
4th quarter	26.8	24.7	20.3	16.5	11.7	37.1	8.4	7.3	44.8	71.6	30.6	26.1

. . . = Not available.

Table 19-4. Chain-Type Quantity Indexes for Gross Domestic Product and Domestic Purchases—*Continued*

(Index numbers, 2000 = 100.)   **NIPA Tables 1.1.3, 1.4.3, 2.3.3**

Year and quarter	Gross domestic product, total	Personal consumption expenditures		Private fixed investment			Exports and imports of goods and services		Government consumption expenditures and gross investment			Gross domestic purchases
		Total	Excluding food and energy	Total	Nonresidential	Residential	Exports	Imports	Total	Federal	State and local	
1962												
1st quarter	27.3	25.0	20.5	16.8	12.0	37.7	8.4	7.5	45.6	74.3	30.4	26.6
2nd quarter	27.6	25.3	20.8	17.3	12.3	38.9	9.2	7.7	45.9	74.6	30.6	26.8
3rd quarter	27.8	25.5	21.0	17.5	12.5	38.9	8.7	7.8	46.9	76.8	31.0	27.2
4th quarter	27.9	25.8	21.4	17.4	12.4	38.8	8.5	7.9	47.0	76.4	31.3	27.3
1963												
1st quarter	28.3	26.0	21.6	17.6	12.4	40.2	8.7	7.7	46.7	74.5	31.9	27.6
2nd quarter	28.6	26.3	21.9	18.4	12.8	43.1	9.8	7.9	46.6	73.8	32.2	27.8
3rd quarter	29.2	26.6	22.2	18.9	13.2	43.9	9.2	8.1	48.6	77.9	33.1	28.4
4th quarter	29.4	26.8	22.4	19.5	13.6	45.3	9.7	8.1	48.2	75.9	33.5	28.6
1964												
1st quarter	30.1	27.4	23.0	20.2	13.9	48.1	10.3	8.1	48.3	75.5	34.0	29.1
2nd quarter	30.4	27.9	23.4	20.2	14.3	45.6	10.5	8.3	48.7	75.0	34.8	29.5
3rd quarter	30.8	28.4	23.8	20.5	14.8	44.9	10.4	8.5	48.7	74.4	35.2	29.9
4th quarter	30.9	28.5	23.9	20.6	15.1	44.1	10.7	8.7	48.6	73.3	35.6	30.0
1965												
1st quarter	31.7	29.1	24.5	21.6	16.1	44.2	9.5	8.4	48.4	72.4	35.9	30.9
2nd quarter	32.1	29.4	24.7	22.2	16.7	44.6	11.3	9.4	49.1	72.5	36.8	31.2
3rd quarter	32.7	29.9	25.2	22.8	17.3	44.7	10.7	9.4	50.8	75.5	37.9	31.9
4th quarter	33.5	30.8	25.9	23.3	18.0	43.8	11.5	9.9	51.9	77.6	38.4	32.7
1966												
1st quarter	34.4	31.2	26.4	24.2	18.8	44.8	11.2	10.1	52.8	79.3	38.9	33.5
2nd quarter	34.5	31.3	26.4	23.9	19.1	41.2	11.7	10.4	53.7	81.4	39.2	33.6
3rd quarter	34.7	31.7	26.8	23.8	19.4	39.8	11.3	11.0	55.2	84.7	39.6	34.0
4th quarter	35.0	31.8	27.0	23.1	19.3	35.7	11.7	11.1	56.1	85.4	40.7	34.2
1967												
1st quarter	35.3	32.0	27.1	22.6	18.9	34.6	11.9	11.3	58.4	91.3	41.2	34.5
2nd quarter	35.3	32.4	27.5	23.2	18.8	38.5	11.8	11.2	58.1	90.0	41.4	34.5
3rd quarter	35.6	32.6	27.8	23.4	18.7	40.5	11.5	11.3	58.7	91.4	41.5	34.9
4th quarter	35.8	32.8	27.8	24.1	19.1	42.8	11.8	11.9	59.1	91.2	42.3	35.2
1968												
1st quarter	36.6	33.5	28.6	24.7	19.7	43.1	12.2	12.6	60.2	92.8	43.0	35.9
2nd quarter	37.2	34.1	29.0	24.6	19.4	44.2	12.4	12.8	60.4	92.0	43.8	36.5
3rd quarter	37.5	34.7	29.6	24.9	19.6	45.0	13.1	13.6	60.6	91.2	44.5	36.8
4th quarter	37.6	34.8	29.8	25.5	20.2	45.5	13.0	13.5	60.6	90.7	44.9	37.0
1969												
1st quarter	38.2	35.2	30.1	26.3	20.8	47.1	11.4	12.2	60.7	90.2	45.2	37.6
2nd quarter	38.3	35.5	30.3	26.5	21.0	46.6	14.0	14.6	60.4	88.7	45.6	37.7
3rd quarter	38.5	35.6	30.5	26.9	21.6	46.3	13.6	14.4	60.5	88.8	45.7	37.9
4th quarter	38.4	35.9	30.7	26.2	21.5	42.9	14.1	14.3	59.6	86.4	45.6	37.6
1970												
1st quarter	38.3	36.1	30.8	26.1	21.4	43.0	14.2	14.2	59.3	84.7	46.0	37.6
2nd quarter	38.4	36.3	30.9	25.6	21.3	40.1	14.9	14.5	58.5	82.0	46.3	37.6
3rd quarter	38.7	36.6	31.2	26.0	21.4	42.2	14.8	14.5	58.8	80.8	47.3	37.9
4th quarter	38.3	36.5	31.0	26.0	20.6	46.7	15.0	14.7	58.8	80.4	47.6	37.5
1971												
1st quarter	39.4	37.2	31.8	26.6	20.8	49.2	15.0	14.5	57.8	77.3	47.8	38.5
2nd quarter	39.6	37.5	32.2	27.7	21.1	54.1	15.0	15.6	57.6	76.2	48.1	38.9
3rd quarter	39.9	37.8	32.6	28.2	21.1	56.8	15.6	15.9	57.6	75.8	48.2	39.2
4th quarter	40.0	38.5	33.3	29.0	21.6	59.0	14.3	14.9	57.2	73.5	48.8	39.3
1972												
1st quarter	40.7	39.0	33.8	30.3	22.3	63.0	15.8	17.0	57.4	73.8	49.0	40.1
2nd quarter	41.7	39.7	34.4	30.9	22.7	64.2	15.3	16.4	57.7	74.9	48.9	41.0
3rd quarter	42.1	40.3	35.0	31.2	23.0	64.3	16.3	16.8	56.5	70.9	49.3	41.3
4th quarter	42.8	41.3	35.9	32.6	24.2	66.6	17.0	17.5	56.9	70.7	50.0	42.0
1973												
1st quarter	43.9	42.0	36.8	34.0	25.4	68.9	18.2	18.3	57.4	71.8	50.2	43.0
2nd quarter	44.4	42.0	36.9	34.3	26.4	65.4	19.1	17.8	57.1	70.7	50.3	43.3
3rd quarter	44.1	42.1	37.0	34.2	26.9	62.6	19.1	17.3	56.4	67.7	50.8	43.0
4th quarter	44.5	42.0	37.0	33.9	27.1	59.6	20.1	17.5	56.8	67.8	51.4	43.3
1974												
1st quarter	44.2	41.7	37.0	33.1	27.0	55.2	20.3	16.9	58.0	69.9	52.1	42.7
2nd quarter	44.3	41.8	37.1	32.6	27.0	52.8	21.3	17.8	58.4	69.8	52.8	42.8
3rd quarter	43.9	42.0	37.1	32.0	26.7	51.1	20.2	17.4	58.4	70.1	52.7	42.6
4th quarter	43.7	41.4	36.4	30.2	25.9	44.4	20.7	17.3	58.7	70.7	52.8	42.3
1975												
1st quarter	43.2	41.8	36.8	28.4	24.3	41.6	20.9	15.5	59.4	69.9	54.3	41.4
2nd quarter	43.5	42.4	37.3	28.0	23.7	42.5	20.2	14.3	58.9	69.3	53.9	41.5
3rd quarter	44.2	43.0	38.0	28.7	23.9	45.5	19.9	15.5	60.0	71.0	54.6	42.6
4th quarter	44.8	43.5	38.6	29.2	24.1	47.5	21.0	16.3	60.5	71.2	55.3	43.1
1976												
1st quarter	45.8	44.4	39.3	30.4	24.6	52.3	20.9	17.3	60.6	70.6	55.9	44.3
2nd quarter	46.1	44.8	39.6	30.9	24.9	53.8	21.1	18.1	59.9	70.4	54.9	44.7
3rd quarter	46.4	45.2	40.0	31.2	25.4	52.9	21.7	18.8	59.6	70.2	54.5	45.0
4th quarter	46.7	45.8	40.5	32.8	25.9	59.7	21.9	19.4	59.6	70.4	54.4	45.4

Table 19-4. Chain-Type Quantity Indexes for Gross Domestic Product and Domestic Purchases—*Continued*

(Index numbers, 2000 = 100.)

NIPA Tables 1.1.3, 1.4.3, 2.3.3

| Year and quarter | Gross domestic product | | | | | | | | | | | Gross domestic purchases |
| | Gross domestic product, total | Personal consumption expenditures | | Private fixed investment | | | Exports and imports of goods and services | | Government consumption expenditures and gross investment | | | |
		Total	Excluding food and energy	Total	Nonresidential	Residential	Exports	Imports	Total	Federal	State and local	
1977												
1st quarter	47.3	46.4	41.0	34.0	26.9	61.5	21.6	20.4	60.1	71.0	54.9	46.2
2nd quarter	48.2	46.6	41.5	35.9	27.7	68.5	22.2	20.5	60.7	72.1	55.2	47.1
3rd quarter	49.1	47.1	42.0	36.4	28.3	68.3	22.3	20.3	60.9	72.6	55.2	47.8
4th quarter	49.1	47.8	42.8	37.1	29.3	67.4	21.6	20.5	60.7	71.8	55.3	48.0
1978												
1st quarter	49.2	48.0	43.0	37.4	29.5	67.8	22.1	21.9	60.8	72.1	55.3	48.3
2nd quarter	51.1	49.1	44.3	40.1	32.0	71.0	24.4	22.0	62.4	73.8	56.9	49.8
3rd quarter	51.7	49.3	44.5	41.2	33.2	72.0	24.7	22.3	62.9	74.1	57.5	50.3
4th quarter	52.3	49.7	44.8	42.1	34.2	71.7	25.7	22.6	63.5	74.7	58.1	50.9
1979												
1st quarter	52.4	49.9	45.0	42.4	35.0	70.1	25.7	22.5	62.9	74.8	57.1	51.0
2nd quarter	52.5	49.9	45.2	42.1	34.9	68.8	25.8	22.6	63.6	75.8	57.6	51.0
3rd quarter	52.9	50.4	45.8	42.9	36.0	67.9	26.7	22.3	63.7	75.6	57.8	51.2
4th quarter	53.0	50.6	45.8	42.5	36.1	65.4	28.4	22.8	64.1	75.6	58.5	51.1
1980												
1st quarter	53.2	50.5	45.7	41.9	36.5	60.4	29.2	22.8	65.1	78.0	58.8	51.2
2nd quarter	52.1	49.3	44.5	38.2	34.6	49.2	29.7	21.1	65.3	80.0	58.0	49.6
3rd quarter	52.0	49.9	45.3	38.6	34.9	50.0	29.7	19.6	64.4	78.9	57.2	49.2
4th quarter	53.0	50.6	46.2	40.1	35.6	54.9	29.5	20.7	64.3	79.2	57.0	50.4
1981												
1st quarter	54.1	50.8	46.5	40.4	36.2	53.9	30.0	21.6	65.2	80.8	57.4	51.6
2nd quarter	53.6	50.8	46.3	40.7	36.9	52.1	30.2	21.6	65.3	83.2	56.3	51.1
3rd quarter	54.3	51.0	46.7	40.7	37.8	48.1	29.6	21.4	65.2	83.1	56.1	51.8
4th quarter	53.6	50.6	46.1	40.6	38.7	43.2	29.7	22.0	65.8	84.0	56.5	51.3
1982												
1st quarter	52.7	50.9	46.5	39.3	37.8	40.7	28.4	21.3	65.7	84.2	56.4	50.5
2nd quarter	53.0	51.1	46.6	37.9	36.4	39.4	28.6	21.0	66.1	84.9	56.6	50.7
3rd quarter	52.8	51.5	47.1	36.9	35.2	39.3	27.3	22.0	66.6	86.2	56.6	50.9
4th quarter	52.9	52.4	48.2	36.8	34.5	42.2	26.1	21.1	67.7	88.8	56.9	51.0
1983												
1st quarter	53.5	53.0	48.8	37.6	33.9	49.3	26.5	21.6	68.2	89.8	57.2	51.6
2nd quarter	54.7	54.0	49.9	39.1	34.3	55.2	26.6	23.2	68.8	91.7	57.0	53.1
3rd quarter	55.8	55.0	50.8	41.4	35.8	60.6	27.0	25.1	70.0	94.3	57.5	54.5
4th quarter	56.9	55.8	51.9	43.8	38.1	63.2	27.5	26.3	68.8	91.0	57.4	55.7
1984												
1st quarter	58.1	56.3	52.6	45.2	39.4	65.0	28.1	28.4	69.5	91.8	58.1	57.1
2nd quarter	59.1	57.1	53.3	47.1	41.3	66.2	28.8	29.6	71.0	94.7	58.8	58.2
3rd quarter	59.6	57.6	53.8	48.1	42.7	65.5	29.4	30.4	71.5	94.3	59.9	58.8
4th quarter	60.1	58.3	54.7	49.0	43.7	65.6	30.0	31.2	73.1	97.4	60.5	59.4
1985												
1st quarter	60.7	59.3	55.7	49.3	44.2	65.4	30.0	30.6	73.9	98.5	61.3	59.8
2nd quarter	61.2	59.8	56.4	49.9	44.9	65.9	29.9	32.1	75.6	100.9	62.5	60.6
3rd quarter	62.2	61.0	57.7	49.5	44.2	66.8	29.5	31.7	77.5	104.3	63.7	61.5
4th quarter	62.6	61.1	57.7	50.5	44.9	68.3	30.4	33.0	78.0	104.2	64.5	62.0
1986												
1st quarter	63.2	61.6	58.3	50.6	44.3	71.3	31.3	33.0	78.8	103.7	66.1	62.5
2nd quarter	63.5	62.3	59.0	50.4	43.2	75.2	31.7	34.4	80.5	107.0	66.9	62.9
3rd quarter	64.1	63.4	60.3	50.1	42.6	76.4	32.4	35.3	82.3	111.0	67.5	63.6
4th quarter	64.4	63.8	60.6	50.5	43.0	76.2	33.6	35.6	81.9	109.3	67.7	63.8
1987												
1st quarter	64.8	63.8	60.7	49.5	41.8	76.0	33.6	35.4	82.1	110.0	67.7	64.1
2nd quarter	65.6	64.7	61.6	50.4	42.8	76.4	35.0	36.3	82.7	111.6	67.8	64.8
3rd quarter	66.1	65.4	62.5	51.4	44.2	76.1	36.5	37.0	82.8	111.7	67.9	65.3
4th quarter	67.3	65.5	62.6	51.4	44.1	76.5	37.8	37.8	83.9	113.4	68.8	66.4
1988												
1st quarter	67.6	66.6	63.6	51.4	44.5	74.9	39.9	37.6	83.4	110.3	69.6	66.4
2nd quarter	68.5	67.1	64.0	52.4	45.6	75.5	41.0	37.2	83.6	109.2	70.5	67.0
3rd quarter	68.9	67.7	64.5	52.6	45.8	75.5	41.8	38.1	83.5	108.4	70.7	67.4
4th quarter	69.8	68.5	65.3	53.1	46.3	76.2	43.1	39.2	85.1	111.6	71.5	68.3
1989												
1st quarter	70.5	68.7	65.6	53.6	47.1	75.7	44.3	39.1	84.6	109.4	71.9	68.8
2nd quarter	70.9	69.0	66.1	53.7	47.7	73.4	46.3	39.7	85.9	111.8	72.6	69.1
3rd quarter	71.4	69.7	66.8	54.6	49.1	72.6	46.8	39.7	86.7	112.9	73.3	69.5
4th quarter	71.6	70.0	66.9	53.7	48.4	71.1	47.6	40.3	87.2	112.3	74.2	69.7
1990												
1st quarter	72.4	70.6	67.8	54.4	49.0	71.8	49.6	41.2	88.5	114.0	75.4	70.3
2nd quarter	72.6	70.8	67.8	53.2	48.2	69.1	50.2	41.6	88.7	114.2	75.6	70.5
3rd quarter	72.6	71.1	68.0	52.6	48.5	65.1	50.6	41.6	88.7	113.2	76.1	70.5
4th quarter	72.1	70.6	67.6	51.1	47.5	61.5	51.1	40.2	89.6	114.2	76.9	69.6
1991												
1st quarter	71.7	70.3	67.4	49.3	46.3	57.9	51.4	39.4	89.9	115.0	77.0	69.1
2nd quarter	72.2	70.9	67.8	49.3	45.9	59.2	53.3	40.5	90.2	115.4	77.3	69.5
3rd quarter	72.5	71.2	68.2	49.4	45.4	61.7	54.5	41.6	89.8	113.3	77.8	69.9
4th quarter	72.9	71.2	68.3	49.5	45.2	63.0	55.8	42.1	89.5	111.1	78.3	70.1

Table 19-4. Chain-Type Quantity Indexes for Gross Domestic Product and Domestic Purchases—*Continued*

(Index numbers, 2000 = 100.)

NIPA Tables 1.1.3, 1.4.3, 2.3.3

| Year and quarter | Gross domestic product | | | | | | | | | | | Gross domestic purchases |
| | Gross domestic product, total | Personal consumption expenditures | | Private fixed investment | | | Exports and imports of goods and services | | Government consumption expenditures and gross investment | | | |
		Total	Excluding food and energy	Total	Nonresidential	Residential	Exports	Imports	Total	Federal	State and local	
1992												
1st quarter	73.6	72.3	69.6	50.0	45.0	66.3	56.7	42.5	90.2	111.1	79.4	70.8
2nd quarter	74.3	72.8	70.2	52.0	46.8	68.8	56.8	43.5	90.1	111.0	79.3	71.6
3rd quarter	75.1	73.5	71.0	52.8	47.7	69.0	58.0	44.1	90.6	112.3	79.3	72.3
4th quarter	75.9	74.3	71.7	54.4	49.2	71.3	58.3	44.9	90.6	112.4	79.3	73.2
1993												
1st quarter	76.0	74.6	72.1	54.7	49.5	71.6	58.4	45.9	89.6	108.9	79.7	73.4
2nd quarter	76.4	75.3	72.8	56.0	50.8	72.5	59.1	47.2	89.5	107.4	80.3	73.9
3rd quarter	76.8	76.1	73.5	57.0	51.4	75.0	58.9	47.8	89.3	105.8	80.7	74.4
4th quarter	77.8	76.8	74.3	59.5	53.5	78.7	60.8	49.5	89.6	106.1	81.1	75.5
1994												
1st quarter	78.6	77.6	75.3	60.3	54.0	80.3	61.4	50.6	88.7	102.9	81.3	76.3
2nd quarter	79.6	78.2	75.7	61.7	55.1	83.0	63.4	52.7	89.1	102.4	82.2	77.4
3rd quarter	80.1	78.7	76.4	62.3	56.2	82.1	65.8	54.2	90.5	104.8	83.2	77.8
4th quarter	81.0	79.5	77.4	64.0	58.7	81.1	67.3	55.5	89.8	102.0	83.5	78.8
1995												
1st quarter	81.2	79.6	77.5	65.5	61.0	79.3	68.5	56.7	90.1	101.8	84.1	79.0
2nd quarter	81.4	80.3	78.2	65.2	61.5	76.7	69.4	57.5	90.5	101.6	84.8	79.2
3rd quarter	82.0	81.0	79.0	66.1	61.9	79.1	72.5	57.7	90.2	100.7	84.8	79.5
4th quarter	82.6	81.6	79.7	67.5	63.1	80.9	73.6	58.3	89.2	96.9	85.2	80.0
1996												
1st quarter	83.2	82.3	80.4	69.2	64.7	83.0	74.5	59.9	89.7	98.9	85.0	80.7
2nd quarter	84.6	83.2	81.4	71.5	66.6	86.5	75.7	61.8	91.2	100.8	86.2	82.2
3rd quarter	85.3	83.7	82.2	73.1	68.8	86.3	76.4	63.8	90.9	98.4	87.0	83.1
4th quarter	86.3	84.4	82.9	74.3	70.6	85.4	81.1	64.7	91.7	98.2	88.4	83.7
1997												
1st quarter	87.0	85.3	83.9	75.8	72.4	85.7	82.6	67.4	91.9	97.0	89.2	84.6
2nd quarter	88.3	85.7	84.4	77.4	74.2	86.8	85.9	70.1	92.8	99.1	89.6	85.9
3rd quarter	89.4	87.1	86.0	80.4	78.0	87.2	87.9	72.7	92.8	98.5	90.0	87.1
4th quarter	90.0	88.0	87.0	81.1	78.7	88.1	87.9	73.9	92.8	97.7	90.3	87.9
1998												
1st quarter	91.0	89.0	88.1	83.5	81.3	89.9	88.2	76.6	92.3	95.4	90.7	89.3
2nd quarter	91.6	90.4	89.5	86.0	83.8	92.4	87.3	78.7	94.2	97.8	92.3	90.3
3rd quarter	92.7	91.5	90.7	87.3	84.6	94.9	86.9	79.7	95.0	96.9	94.1	91.5
4th quarter	94.1	92.7	92.2	89.8	87.2	97.2	90.2	82.1	95.9	97.8	94.9	92.8
1999												
1st quarter	94.9	93.6	93.2	91.2	88.8	98.0	89.4	84.2	96.6	97.2	96.2	94.0
2nd quarter	95.7	95.1	94.7	93.4	91.5	98.9	90.4	87.2	97.1	97.7	96.9	95.0
3rd quarter	96.8	96.1	95.8	95.2	93.7	99.5	92.8	90.2	98.3	99.6	97.7	96.3
4th quarter	98.5	97.3	97.0	95.7	93.9	100.7	95.2	92.0	99.9	101.9	98.9	97.9
2000												
1st quarter	98.8	98.8	98.9	98.3	97.1	101.7	96.8	95.6	99.2	98.2	99.7	98.5
2nd quarter	100.3	99.5	99.4	100.6	100.5	100.8	99.6	99.4	100.5	102.1	99.7	100.3
3rd quarter	100.2	100.4	100.5	100.4	101.1	98.7	102.2	102.7	100.0	100.0	100.0	100.4
4th quarter	100.7	101.3	101.2	100.6	101.3	98.8	101.5	102.3	100.3	99.7	100.6	100.9
2001												
1st quarter	100.6	101.7	101.7	100.0	100.2	99.3	100.1	101.3	101.6	101.7	101.6	100.8
2nd quarter	100.9	101.9	102.3	97.7	96.6	100.7	96.7	98.0	103.6	103.9	103.4	100.9
3rd quarter	100.6	102.4	102.8	96.6	94.9	101.2	92.0	95.3	103.2	103.9	102.8	100.7
4th quarter	100.9	104.1	104.7	93.9	91.6	100.2	89.4	94.5	105.3	106.1	104.9	101.3
2002												
1st quarter	101.6	104.5	105.1	92.4	88.5	102.7	90.6	97.2	106.4	107.7	105.8	102.2
2nd quarter	102.2	105.1	105.6	92.1	87.1	105.1	92.9	100.1	107.7	110.9	106.0	102.9
3rd quarter	102.8	105.7	106.3	91.9	86.7	105.6	93.5	101.5	108.3	111.7	106.5	103.6
4th quarter	102.8	106.1	106.6	91.6	85.6	107.2	92.8	103.7	109.5	114.4	107.1	104.0
2003												
1st quarter	103.1	106.6	107.1	91.5	85.0	108.3	91.5	102.4	109.2	114.5	106.5	104.2
2nd quarter	104.0	107.6	108.3	93.8	87.2	111.1	91.1	103.4	110.8	119.7	106.3	105.3
3rd quarter	105.9	109.1	109.9	96.9	89.2	116.8	93.6	104.4	111.2	119.9	106.8	107.0
4th quarter	106.6	109.7	110.6	98.2	89.8	119.8	98.1	108.7	111.4	120.8	106.7	107.8
2004												
1st quarter	107.4	110.9	111.8	98.1	89.2	120.9	100.5	111.9	111.8	122.6	106.4	108.7
2nd quarter	108.3	111.6	112.6	101.2	91.5	125.7	102.1	115.9	112.2	123.3	106.6	110.0
3rd quarter	109.3	112.6	113.7	103.4	94.2	127.0	102.9	117.3	112.6	125.2	106.3	111.0
4th quarter	110.0	113.7	114.8	105.3	96.6	127.7	105.4	121.1	112.1	123.7	106.3	112.0
2005												
1st quarter	110.8	114.2	115.3	106.6	97.4	130.3	107.4	122.1	112.1	124.1	106.0	112.7
2nd quarter	111.5	115.2	116.4	108.6	98.9	133.3	109.7	122.3	112.3	124.4	106.2	113.2
3rd quarter	112.6	116.3	117.4	110.0	100.4	134.6	109.9	122.5	113.3	127.3	106.2	114.2
4th quarter	112.9	116.7	117.7	110.7	101.3	134.7	112.7	127.0	112.8	125.0	106.6	114.9
2006												
1st quarter	114.3	117.9	119.3	112.9	105.1	133.5	117.1	130.1	113.9	128.0	106.7	116.2
2nd quarter	115.0	118.7	120.0	112.2	106.8	127.6	118.7	130.2	114.2	127.5	107.5	116.8
3rd quarter	115.3	119.4	120.7	110.8	108.2	120.1	119.7	131.2	114.7	128.0	108.0	117.0
4th quarter	115.7	120.5	122.0	108.6	107.9	113.8	124.2	131.8	115.2	128.6	108.3	117.1

Table 19-5. Chain-Type Price Indexes for Gross Domestic Product and Domestic Purchases

(Index numbers, 2000 = 100.)

NIPA Tables 1.1.4, 1.6.4, 2.3.4

Year and quarter	Gross domestic product, total	Personal consumption expenditures Total	Personal consumption expenditures Excluding food and energy	Private fixed investment Total	Private fixed investment Nonresidential	Private fixed investment Residential	Exports and imports of goods and services Exports	Exports and imports of goods and services Imports	Government consumption expenditures and gross investment Total	Government consumption expenditures and gross investment Federal	Government consumption expenditures and gross investment State and local	Gross domestic purchases
1946	13.9	14.2	14.4	16.7	19.9	10.6	21.9	14.9	10.0	11.6	8.1	13.6
1947	15.5	15.7	15.6	19.6	23.2	12.6	25.4	17.8	10.8	12.3	9.1	15.1
1948	16.4	16.6	16.5	21.3	25.2	13.7	26.8	19.3	11.2	12.2	10.2	16.0
1949	16.4	16.5	16.6	21.7	25.8	13.9	25.2	18.4	11.5	12.7	10.3	16.1
1947												
1st quarter	15.1	15.4	...	18.7	22.2	11.9	23.4	16.3	10.8	12.6	8.8	14.8
2nd quarter	15.3	15.5	...	19.4	22.9	12.6	25.1	17.5	10.9	12.5	9.0	15.0
3rd quarter	15.6	15.8	...	19.9	23.6	12.9	26.3	18.4	10.7	12.1	9.2	15.2
4th quarter	15.9	16.2	...	20.3	24.0	13.2	27.0	19.0	10.8	12.1	9.5	15.5
1948												
1st quarter	16.1	16.4	...	20.6	24.1	13.4	27.2	19.5	11.0	12.1	9.8	15.7
2nd quarter	16.3	16.5	...	21.0	24.8	13.6	27.0	19.5	11.1	12.1	10.0	15.9
3rd quarter	16.6	16.8	...	21.7	25.7	13.9	26.7	19.3	11.3	12.3	10.4	16.2
4th quarter	16.6	16.7	...	21.9	26.1	13.9	26.3	19.0	11.4	12.3	10.5	16.2
1949												
1st quarter	16.5	16.6	...	21.9	25.9	14.1	25.8	18.6	11.6	12.8	10.4	16.2
2nd quarter	16.4	16.5	...	21.8	25.8	14.0	25.3	18.4	11.6	12.8	10.3	16.1
3rd quarter	16.3	16.4	...	21.6	25.7	13.7	24.9	18.3	11.4	12.5	10.2	16.0
4th quarter	16.3	16.4	...	21.5	25.6	13.7	24.7	18.4	11.5	12.8	10.2	16.0
1950												
1st quarter	16.2	16.4	...	21.5	25.6	13.7	24.3	18.7	11.5	12.8	10.1	15.9
2nd quarter	16.3	16.5	...	21.9	25.8	14.1	24.3	19.1	11.4	12.6	10.2	16.0
3rd quarter	16.6	16.8	...	22.5	26.4	14.6	24.5	19.8	11.6	12.6	10.5	16.4
4th quarter	16.9	17.1	...	22.9	27.3	14.6	25.0	20.7	11.7	12.6	10.8	16.6
1951												
1st quarter	17.5	17.6	...	23.7	28.2	15.0	26.5	22.4	12.3	13.4	11.1	17.2
2nd quarter	17.6	17.8	...	24.0	28.7	15.2	27.4	23.6	12.2	13.1	11.3	17.3
3rd quarter	17.6	17.8	...	24.2	29.0	15.3	28.3	24.3	12.3	13.1	11.6	17.4
4th quarter	17.8	18.0	...	24.5	29.3	15.4	28.7	24.4	12.4	13.3	11.7	17.6
1952												
1st quarter	17.9	18.1	...	24.6	29.4	15.5	28.0	23.4	12.3	13.1	11.7	17.6
2nd quarter	17.9	18.1	...	24.7	29.5	15.6	27.9	23.0	12.5	13.3	11.8	17.7
3rd quarter	18.1	18.2	...	24.7	29.4	15.8	27.8	22.6	12.6	13.4	12.1	17.8
4th quarter	18.1	18.3	...	24.7	29.4	15.7	27.8	22.2	12.8	13.6	12.1	17.9
1953												
1st quarter	18.2	18.3	...	24.7	29.4	15.7	27.9	22.0	12.7	13.4	12.2	17.9
2nd quarter	18.2	18.4	...	24.8	29.7	15.7	27.9	21.8	12.7	13.5	12.2	17.9
3rd quarter	18.3	18.5	...	25.0	29.9	15.9	27.8	21.7	12.6	13.4	12.2	18.0
4th quarter	18.3	18.5	...	25.0	29.9	15.8	27.7	21.7	12.7	13.5	12.1	18.0
1954												
1st quarter	18.4	18.6	...	25.0	30.0	15.7	27.5	22.0	12.8	13.6	12.1	18.1
2nd quarter	18.4	18.6	...	25.1	30.1	15.8	27.4	22.1	12.9	13.6	12.4	18.2
3rd quarter	18.4	18.6	...	25.1	29.9	15.9	27.4	22.2	13.0	13.8	12.4	18.2
4th quarter	18.5	18.5	...	25.1	30.0	15.9	27.4	22.2	13.1	13.9	12.5	18.2
1955												
1st quarter	18.5	18.6	...	25.1	29.9	16.0	27.5	21.9	13.2	14.1	12.4	18.2
2nd quarter	18.6	18.6	...	25.3	30.0	16.1	27.6	22.0	13.4	14.5	12.5	18.3
3rd quarter	18.8	18.7	...	25.6	30.5	16.3	27.7	22.0	13.6	14.6	12.7	18.5
4th quarter	18.9	18.8	...	26.0	31.2	16.3	27.9	22.1	13.8	14.8	12.8	18.6
1956												
1st quarter	19.1	18.8	...	26.5	32.1	16.4	28.1	22.1	14.0	15.0	13.1	18.8
2nd quarter	19.3	19.0	...	26.8	32.3	16.6	28.4	22.3	14.2	15.2	13.3	18.9
3rd quarter	19.5	19.2	...	27.2	33.2	16.7	28.7	22.4	14.4	15.3	13.5	19.2
4th quarter	19.6	19.3	...	27.4	33.6	16.6	29.1	22.7	14.4	15.4	13.7	19.3
1957												
1st quarter	19.8	19.4	...	27.7	34.2	16.6	29.5	22.7	14.7	15.7	13.8	19.5
2nd quarter	20.0	19.6	...	27.8	34.3	16.6	29.7	22.8	14.9	15.8	14.0	19.6
3rd quarter	20.1	19.7	...	28.0	34.6	16.7	29.8	22.6	15.0	16.0	14.1	19.8
4th quarter	20.2	19.8	...	28.1	34.9	16.6	29.8	22.4	15.0	16.1	14.1	19.9
1958												
1st quarter	20.4	20.1	...	27.9	34.5	16.6	29.5	21.9	15.1	16.3	14.0	20.0
2nd quarter	20.5	20.1	...	28.0	34.7	16.6	29.3	21.7	15.3	16.5	14.1	20.1
3rd quarter	20.6	20.1	...	28.0	34.7	16.6	29.3	21.6	15.4	16.7	14.2	20.2
4th quarter	20.6	20.1	...	28.1	34.8	16.6	29.4	21.6	15.5	16.8	14.3	20.2
1959												
1st quarter	20.7	20.3	20.9	28.1	34.9	16.6	29.2	21.8	15.5	16.6	14.5	20.3
2nd quarter	20.7	20.4	21.0	28.2	35.1	16.6	29.2	21.8	15.4	16.5	14.5	20.3
3rd quarter	20.8	20.5	21.1	28.3	35.2	16.6	29.5	21.9	15.3	16.3	14.5	20.4
4th quarter	20.9	20.6	21.2	28.4	35.3	16.6	29.8	22.1	15.4	16.4	14.5	20.5
1960												
1st quarter	20.9	20.6	21.3	28.4	35.3	16.7	29.8	22.1	15.4	16.4	14.6	20.5
2nd quarter	21.0	20.7	21.3	28.5	35.3	16.8	29.8	22.1	15.5	16.4	14.7	20.6
3rd quarter	21.1	20.8	21.4	28.4	35.3	16.8	29.9	22.2	15.7	16.7	14.8	20.7
4th quarter	21.2	20.9	21.5	28.4	35.2	16.8	29.8	22.1	15.8	16.9	14.8	20.8
1961												
1st quarter	21.2	20.9	21.5	28.3	35.1	16.7	30.0	22.2	15.8	16.8	14.9	20.8
2nd quarter	21.2	20.9	21.6	28.3	35.1	16.8	30.4	22.1	15.9	16.9	15.0	20.8
3rd quarter	21.3	21.0	21.7	28.3	35.0	16.8	30.3	22.1	15.9	16.8	15.1	20.9
4th quarter	21.4	21.0	21.7	28.3	35.1	16.8	30.5	22.1	16.0	16.9	15.3	20.9

. . . = Not available.

Table 19-5. Chain-Type Price Indexes for Gross Domestic Product and Domestic Purchases—*Continued*

(Index numbers, 2000 = 100.)   **NIPA Tables 1.1.4, 1.6.4, 2.3.4**

| Year and quarter | Gross domestic product, total | Personal consumption expenditures | | Private fixed investment | | | Exports and imports of goods and services | | Government consumption expenditures and gross investment | | | Gross domestic purchases |
		Total	Excluding food and energy	Total	Nonresidential	Residential	Exports	Imports	Total	Federal	State and local	
1962												
1st quarter	21.5	21.1	21.8	28.3	35.1	16.8	30.6	21.8	16.2	17.1	15.5	21.0
2nd quarter	21.5	21.2	21.9	28.4	35.1	16.8	30.3	21.9	16.3	17.1	15.5	21.1
3rd quarter	21.6	21.3	22.0	28.4	35.1	16.8	30.3	21.8	16.3	17.2	15.6	21.2
4th quarter	21.7	21.3	22.0	28.3	35.1	16.8	30.3	21.9	16.5	17.4	15.7	21.2
1963												
1st quarter	21.7	21.4	22.1	28.3	35.1	16.8	30.4	22.1	16.6	17.5	15.8	21.3
2nd quarter	21.8	21.4	22.1	28.3	35.1	16.7	30.3	22.2	16.6	17.5	15.9	21.3
3rd quarter	21.8	21.5	22.2	28.2	35.1	16.5	30.3	22.3	16.6	17.5	15.9	21.4
4th quarter	21.9	21.6	22.3	28.3	35.1	16.6	30.3	22.5	16.9	17.9	16.0	21.5
1964												
1st quarter	22.0	21.7	22.4	28.2	35.1	16.5	30.4	22.7	17.0	18.0	16.1	21.6
2nd quarter	22.1	21.7	22.5	28.4	35.3	16.7	30.4	22.8	17.1	18.1	16.2	21.7
3rd quarter	22.2	21.8	22.5	28.4	35.3	16.8	30.6	22.7	17.2	18.3	16.3	21.8
4th quarter	22.3	21.9	22.6	28.8	35.5	17.2	30.9	22.8	17.3	18.3	16.3	21.9
1965												
1st quarter	22.4	22.0	22.7	28.8	35.5	17.1	31.6	23.0	17.4	18.4	16.5	21.9
2nd quarter	22.5	22.1	22.7	28.8	35.6	17.2	31.5	22.9	17.5	18.5	16.6	22.0
3rd quarter	22.6	22.2	22.8	28.9	35.7	17.1	31.5	23.1	17.6	18.7	16.7	22.1
4th quarter	22.7	22.2	22.9	29.2	35.9	17.6	31.4	23.3	17.9	19.1	16.9	22.3
1966												
1st quarter	22.9	22.4	23.0	29.1	35.8	17.4	32.0	23.4	18.0	19.1	17.1	22.4
2nd quarter	23.1	22.6	23.1	29.6	36.2	18.0	32.2	23.7	18.2	19.1	17.4	22.6
3rd quarter	23.3	22.8	23.3	29.6	36.3	17.9	32.6	23.6	18.5	19.6	17.6	22.8
4th quarter	23.5	22.9	23.5	29.9	36.6	18.3	33.2	23.7	18.6	19.6	17.9	23.0
1967												
1st quarter	23.6	23.0	23.6	30.1	36.8	18.3	33.7	23.7	18.8	19.5	18.2	23.1
2nd quarter	23.8	23.1	23.8	30.2	37.0	18.4	33.7	23.7	19.0	19.8	18.4	23.3
3rd quarter	24.0	23.3	24.0	30.4	37.2	18.5	33.7	23.7	19.2	20.0	18.6	23.5
4th quarter	24.2	23.5	24.2	30.8	37.6	18.9	33.8	23.7	19.5	20.4	18.8	23.7
1968												
1st quarter	24.5	23.8	24.5	31.1	37.8	19.2	34.1	23.8	19.7	20.5	19.1	24.0
2nd quarter	24.8	24.0	24.8	31.4	38.2	19.4	34.8	24.0	20.0	20.8	19.4	24.2
3rd quarter	25.0	24.3	25.1	31.6	38.5	19.4	34.4	24.1	20.2	21.2	19.5	24.5
4th quarter	25.4	24.5	25.4	32.3	39.1	20.1	34.6	24.2	20.6	21.5	19.9	24.8
1969												
1st quarter	25.6	24.8	25.6	32.6	39.4	20.5	35.1	24.3	20.7	21.5	20.2	25.1
2nd quarter	26.0	25.1	25.9	33.0	39.8	20.8	35.2	24.5	21.1	21.8	20.6	25.4
3rd quarter	26.3	25.4	26.2	33.3	40.2	20.9	35.7	24.6	21.6	22.5	21.0	25.8
4th quarter	26.7	25.7	26.5	33.7	40.7	21.2	36.5	25.3	21.9	22.7	21.4	26.1
1970												
1st quarter	27.1	26.0	26.8	33.9	41.1	21.2	36.5	25.5	22.5	23.5	21.8	26.5
2nd quarter	27.4	26.3	27.1	34.7	41.8	22.0	37.2	25.8	22.9	23.7	22.3	26.8
3rd quarter	27.7	26.6	27.4	34.6	42.1	21.4	37.1	26.5	23.3	24.1	22.7	27.1
4th quarter	28.0	26.9	27.8	35.0	42.6	21.6	37.2	26.7	23.6	24.4	23.1	27.4
1971												
1st quarter	28.4	27.2	28.1	35.6	43.2	22.1	38.3	27.4	24.3	25.2	23.6	27.9
2nd quarter	28.8	27.5	28.4	36.1	43.8	22.6	38.4	27.5	24.7	25.7	24.0	28.2
3rd quarter	29.1	27.7	28.7	36.6	44.1	23.0	38.2	27.8	25.1	26.1	24.3	28.5
4th quarter	29.3	27.9	28.9	36.9	44.4	23.4	38.5	28.2	25.4	26.7	24.5	28.8
1972												
1st quarter	29.8	28.2	29.2	37.4	44.9	23.7	39.6	28.7	26.3	28.1	25.0	29.2
2nd quarter	30.0	28.4	29.4	37.6	45.2	23.8	39.9	29.5	26.6	28.3	25.3	29.4
3rd quarter	30.3	28.6	29.6	38.0	45.5	24.2	40.1	29.9	26.9	28.5	25.7	29.7
4th quarter	30.6	28.9	29.8	38.5	45.8	24.9	41.0	30.6	27.4	29.2	26.1	30.1
1973												
1st quarter	31.0	29.2	30.0	38.9	46.2	25.3	42.1	31.5	28.0	29.7	26.7	30.5
2nd quarter	31.5	29.8	30.4	39.6	46.8	25.9	44.0	34.0	28.5	30.1	27.3	31.1
3rd quarter	32.1	30.3	30.7	40.4	47.5	26.8	46.6	35.6	29.0	30.7	27.7	31.6
4th quarter	32.7	31.0	31.1	40.9	48.0	27.2	49.0	38.2	29.5	31.3	28.2	32.2
1974												
1st quarter	33.4	31.9	31.6	41.7	48.8	27.9	52.4	44.3	30.2	31.8	29.0	33.1
2nd quarter	34.1	32.8	32.4	42.9	50.4	28.5	54.2	49.4	31.1	32.5	30.0	34.0
3rd quarter	35.2	33.6	33.3	44.6	52.5	29.4	57.2	52.0	32.1	33.5	31.0	35.0
4th quarter	36.2	34.5	34.1	46.4	54.9	30.2	60.1	53.7	33.2	34.9	31.9	36.1
1975												
1st quarter	37.1	35.1	34.7	48.1	57.1	31.0	61.8	54.5	33.9	35.6	32.6	36.8
2nd quarter	37.6	35.6	35.3	49.2	58.6	31.5	61.6	54.6	34.5	36.1	33.3	37.4
3rd quarter	38.3	36.2	35.8	49.8	59.3	31.8	61.5	53.4	35.1	36.8	33.8	38.1
4th quarter	39.0	36.9	36.4	50.5	60.1	32.4	61.8	53.5	35.8	37.9	34.3	38.7
1976												
1st quarter	39.4	37.3	36.9	51.0	60.8	32.6	62.7	54.4	36.3	38.3	34.9	39.2
2nd quarter	39.9	37.6	37.4	51.9	61.6	33.6	63.4	55.2	36.8	38.7	35.4	39.6
3rd quarter	40.4	38.2	38.0	52.6	62.4	34.1	63.8	56.2	37.3	39.3	35.8	40.2
4th quarter	41.1	38.8	38.6	53.5	63.3	34.7	64.9	56.8	38.0	40.5	36.2	40.8

Table 19-5. Chain-Type Price Indexes for Gross Domestic Product and Domestic Purchases—*Continued*

(Index numbers, 2000 = 100.)   **NIPA Tables 1.1.4, 1.6.4, 2.3.4**

Year and quarter	Gross domestic product, total	Personal consumption expenditures		Private fixed investment			Exports and imports of goods and services		Government consumption expenditures and gross investment			Gross domestic purchases
		Total	Excluding food and energy	Total	Nonresi-dential	Residential	Exports	Imports	Total	Federal	State and local	
1977												
1st quarter	41.8	39.5	39.2	54.6	64.6	35.5	65.7	58.7	38.8	41.4	36.9	41.6
2nd quarter	42.5	40.1	39.8	55.7	65.6	36.5	66.6	60.4	39.4	41.9	37.6	42.3
3rd quarter	43.0	40.7	40.4	56.9	66.8	37.7	66.3	61.2	39.8	42.1	38.2	43.0
4th quarter	43.8	41.3	41.0	58.1	67.9	38.8	66.6	61.8	40.8	43.4	38.8	43.7
1978												
1st quarter	44.5	42.0	41.7	59.3	68.9	40.0	67.9	62.8	41.3	43.9	39.4	44.4
2nd quarter	45.4	42.9	42.4	60.5	70.1	41.2	69.6	64.4	41.9	44.3	40.1	45.3
3rd quarter	46.1	43.6	43.1	61.7	71.2	42.2	70.8	65.4	42.5	44.9	40.7	46.0
4th quarter	47.1	44.5	43.8	62.9	72.5	43.4	73.1	66.6	43.3	46.1	41.2	46.9
1979												
1st quarter	47.9	45.3	44.4	64.2	74.0	44.2	75.2	69.1	44.1	46.7	42.2	47.8
2nd quarter	49.1	46.5	45.3	65.9	75.7	45.7	78.3	72.7	45.0	47.4	43.2	49.0
3rd quarter	50.1	47.7	46.1	67.5	77.3	47.2	80.1	78.2	46.3	48.4	44.7	50.3
4th quarter	51.1	48.8	47.1	68.9	78.7	48.3	81.6	83.4	47.6	50.4	45.6	51.5
1980												
1st quarter	52.2	50.2	48.2	70.5	80.5	49.6	84.0	90.4	48.8	51.3	46.9	52.9
2nd quarter	53.4	51.5	49.3	72.1	82.4	50.8	85.2	93.6	50.1	52.5	48.2	54.2
3rd quarter	54.6	52.7	50.4	73.7	84.1	51.9	87.6	96.2	51.2	53.3	49.5	55.4
4th quarter	56.1	54.0	51.6	75.3	85.8	53.2	90.5	97.8	53.0	56.1	50.8	56.9
1981												
1st quarter	57.6	55.3	52.7	77.3	88.3	54.4	92.8	100.4	54.4	57.0	52.4	58.4
2nd quarter	58.6	56.3	53.7	79.1	90.5	55.2	93.2	101.0	55.3	57.9	53.4	59.4
3rd quarter	59.7	57.2	54.7	80.4	92.1	55.9	93.3	98.4	56.0	58.5	54.1	60.4
4th quarter	60.7	58.1	55.7	81.9	94.0	56.8	93.6	98.6	57.3	60.5	54.9	61.4
1982												
1st quarter	61.6	58.8	56.5	83.1	95.3	57.6	94.2	98.3	58.2	61.4	55.9	62.2
2nd quarter	62.3	59.4	57.3	84.0	96.3	58.5	94.1	96.6	59.0	62.1	56.7	62.9
3rd quarter	63.2	60.3	58.2	84.5	96.8	59.0	93.4	95.4	59.8	62.6	57.6	63.7
4th quarter	63.9	61.0	59.1	84.6	96.8	59.2	92.9	94.7	60.6	63.7	58.3	64.4
1983												
1st quarter	64.4	61.5	59.9	84.2	96.1	59.5	93.3	92.7	61.0	64.0	58.8	64.8
2nd quarter	64.9	62.1	60.3	83.9	95.5	59.7	93.6	92.7	61.6	64.4	59.4	65.2
3rd quarter	65.5	62.9	61.3	83.7	95.1	60.0	94.1	92.9	62.1	64.9	60.0	65.8
4th quarter	66.0	63.3	61.8	83.9	95.0	60.5	95.0	92.3	62.4	65.0	60.5	66.2
1984												
1st quarter	66.8	64.0	62.4	83.9	94.9	60.9	95.2	92.6	64.1	67.7	61.5	67.1
2nd quarter	67.4	64.6	63.1	84.3	95.2	61.3	95.8	93.1	64.8	68.3	62.1	67.6
3rd quarter	68.0	65.1	63.7	84.6	95.3	61.9	94.8	91.4	65.3	68.8	62.6	68.1
4th quarter	68.4	65.5	64.2	84.8	95.4	62.4	93.8	90.3	65.6	69.0	63.1	68.5
1985												
1st quarter	69.2	66.2	65.0	85.1	95.6	62.7	92.8	88.1	66.5	69.9	63.9	69.1
2nd quarter	69.5	66.7	65.5	85.2	95.7	62.9	92.4	88.5	66.8	69.8	64.5	69.5
3rd quarter	69.9	67.1	66.0	85.5	96.0	63.3	91.4	88.4	67.0	69.7	65.0	69.9
4th quarter	70.3	67.7	66.6	86.1	96.4	64.0	91.3	90.2	67.6	70.4	65.6	70.5
1986												
1st quarter	70.7	68.2	67.3	86.5	96.6	64.8	90.9	90.4	67.7	70.3	65.9	70.9
2nd quarter	71.0	68.2	67.9	87.1	97.3	65.4	90.5	87.6	67.9	70.3	66.2	71.0
3rd quarter	71.5	68.7	68.6	87.9	98.0	66.3	90.2	88.2	68.3	70.4	66.8	71.5
4th quarter	72.0	69.2	69.2	88.5	98.4	67.0	91.0	89.3	68.8	70.5	67.7	72.0
1987												
1st quarter	72.5	70.0	69.8	88.8	98.4	67.7	91.4	91.6	69.5	71.0	68.5	72.7
2nd quarter	72.9	70.6	70.4	88.9	98.3	68.2	92.6	94.0	69.9	71.1	69.1	73.2
3rd quarter	73.5	71.3	71.1	89.0	98.2	68.8	93.0	95.0	70.3	71.3	69.8	73.8
4th quarter	73.9	71.9	71.8	89.8	98.9	69.4	94.5	96.4	70.5	71.4	70.0	74.3
1988												
1st quarter	74.6	72.5	72.6	90.6	99.8	70.1	95.6	97.8	71.2	72.2	70.6	75.0
2nd quarter	75.3	73.3	73.5	91.1	100.3	70.7	97.6	99.5	71.8	72.7	71.2	75.7
3rd quarter	76.2	74.2	74.3	91.6	100.7	71.1	98.8	98.5	72.1	72.8	71.8	76.4
4th quarter	76.8	74.9	75.1	92.4	101.7	71.8	98.6	99.3	72.5	73.0	72.3	77.1
1989												
1st quarter	77.6	75.8	75.9	92.9	102.1	72.3	99.6	100.9	73.5	74.3	73.0	77.9
2nd quarter	78.3	76.8	76.6	93.5	102.5	73.2	99.7	102.0	73.9	74.5	73.7	78.8
3rd quarter	78.9	77.3	77.2	93.9	102.9	73.4	99.1	100.2	74.4	75.0	74.1	79.2
4th quarter	79.4	77.9	77.9	94.3	103.4	73.9	98.8	100.7	74.8	74.9	74.9	79.8
1990												
1st quarter	80.4	79.1	78.8	94.9	103.9	74.5	98.9	102.2	75.9	76.0	76.1	80.9
2nd quarter	81.3	79.9	79.9	95.2	104.2	74.8	99.2	100.5	76.7	76.7	76.8	81.6
3rd quarter	82.1	81.0	80.6	95.8	104.9	75.1	100.2	103.4	77.4	77.3	77.7	82.5
4th quarter	82.7	82.0	81.3	96.4	105.7	75.3	101.6	109.2	78.6	78.6	78.8	83.5
1991												
1st quarter	83.7	82.6	82.2	97.1	106.7	75.5	102.0	105.9	79.3	79.7	79.2	84.2
2nd quarter	84.2	83.1	82.9	97.1	106.5	75.8	101.4	103.1	79.4	79.8	79.4	84.5
3rd quarter	84.8	83.7	83.6	97.0	106.2	76.3	100.8	101.8	80.0	80.5	79.9	85.1
4th quarter	85.2	84.3	84.4	96.7	105.9	76.0	101.0	102.9	80.4	81.0	80.2	85.6

Table 19-5. Chain-Type Price Indexes for Gross Domestic Product and Domestic Purchases—*Continued*

(Index numbers, 2000 = 100.)

NIPA Tables 1.1.4, 1.6.4, 2.3.4

Year and quarter	Gross domestic product, total	Personal consumption expenditures		Private fixed investment			Exports and imports of goods and services		Government consumption expenditures and gross investment			Gross domestic purchases
		Total	Excluding food and energy	Total	Nonresidential	Residential	Exports	Imports	Total	Federal	State and local	
1992												
1st quarter	85.8	85.0	85.2	96.5	105.7	75.8	100.9	102.4	81.0	81.9	80.6	86.1
2nd quarter	86.2	85.5	85.8	96.6	105.4	76.5	100.9	103.0	81.6	82.5	81.2	86.6
3rd quarter	86.6	86.1	86.4	96.7	105.3	77.0	101.0	104.6	82.0	83.0	81.5	87.1
4th quarter	87.0	86.7	87.0	96.9	105.2	78.0	100.8	104.2	82.2	82.9	81.9	87.5
1993												
1st quarter	87.7	87.1	87.5	97.4	105.5	78.9	100.8	102.6	83.1	83.9	82.7	88.1
2nd quarter	88.2	87.7	88.2	97.7	105.5	79.7	101.1	103.4	83.6	84.4	83.2	88.6
3rd quarter	88.6	88.0	88.6	98.0	105.5	80.4	100.9	102.5	84.0	85.2	83.4	88.9
4th quarter	89.0	88.4	89.0	98.1	105.5	80.8	100.8	102.2	84.5	85.6	83.8	89.3
1994												
1st quarter	89.6	88.8	89.5	98.6	105.8	81.7	101.3	101.7	85.2	86.2	84.8	89.8
2nd quarter	90.0	89.3	90.1	99.0	106.1	82.2	101.6	103.0	85.8	87.1	85.1	90.3
3rd quarter	90.5	90.1	90.8	99.3	106.2	83.0	102.3	104.7	86.2	87.1	85.7	90.9
4th quarter	91.0	90.5	91.2	99.6	106.0	84.1	102.9	105.2	86.8	87.8	86.3	91.3
1995												
1st quarter	91.6	90.9	91.7	100.0	106.1	85.2	104.0	105.6	87.7	88.8	87.2	91.9
2nd quarter	91.9	91.4	92.2	100.3	106.4	85.6	104.8	107.5	88.1	89.0	87.7	92.3
3rd quarter	92.3	91.8	92.6	100.4	106.4	85.9	104.6	106.7	88.4	89.3	88.0	92.7
4th quarter	92.7	92.2	93.1	100.4	106.2	86.4	104.1	105.8	89.2	90.9	88.3	93.1
1996												
1st quarter	93.3	92.8	93.5	100.1	105.6	86.7	103.9	105.4	90.3	92.2	89.3	93.6
2nd quarter	93.6	93.4	93.9	99.8	104.9	87.1	103.5	105.0	90.0	91.5	89.3	93.9
3rd quarter	94.1	93.7	94.3	100.1	104.9	88.1	102.8	103.8	90.5	91.8	89.9	94.3
4th quarter	94.5	94.4	94.8	100.1	104.7	88.5	101.8	104.0	91.1	92.4	90.4	94.8
1997												
1st quarter	95.0	94.8	95.1	99.9	104.2	89.0	101.5	102.8	91.8	93.3	91.1	95.2
2nd quarter	95.3	95.0	95.6	99.8	103.9	89.4	101.5	100.8	91.9	93.4	91.1	95.3
3rd quarter	95.5	95.2	95.8	99.8	103.6	90.2	101.2	100.2	92.1	93.5	91.4	95.5
4th quarter	95.9	95.5	96.1	99.6	103.1	90.8	100.8	99.5	92.7	94.0	92.1	95.8
1998												
1st quarter	96.1	95.6	96.4	99.1	102.2	91.1	99.8	96.7	93.0	94.3	92.3	95.8
2nd quarter	96.3	95.8	96.7	98.8	101.6	91.7	99.2	95.7	93.2	94.4	92.6	95.9
3rd quarter	96.6	96.1	97.0	98.8	101.1	92.6	98.5	94.5	93.6	94.6	93.2	96.1
4th quarter	96.9	96.4	97.4	98.7	100.7	93.5	98.2	94.5	94.1	94.8	93.7	96.4
1999												
1st quarter	97.3	96.7	97.7	98.9	100.6	94.4	98.0	94.0	94.8	96.1	94.2	96.8
2nd quarter	97.7	97.3	98.2	98.9	100.2	95.4	98.1	95.3	95.6	96.6	95.2	97.3
3rd quarter	98.0	97.9	98.5	98.8	99.7	96.3	98.3	96.6	96.5	97.1	96.1	97.8
4th quarter	98.5	98.4	99.0	98.9	99.6	97.0	98.8	97.9	97.4	97.8	97.2	98.4
2000												
1st quarter	99.3	99.3	99.6	99.5	99.8	98.7	99.5	99.3	99.0	99.5	98.7	99.3
2nd quarter	99.8	99.8	99.9	99.8	99.8	99.6	100.0	99.5	99.4	99.2	99.5	99.7
3rd quarter	100.2	100.2	100.1	100.3	100.2	100.4	100.2	100.5	100.5	100.4	100.5	100.3
4th quarter	100.7	100.7	100.5	100.5	100.2	101.3	100.3	100.7	101.1	100.8	101.3	100.7
2001												
1st quarter	101.5	101.5	101.2	100.4	99.6	102.6	100.3	99.9	101.9	101.3	102.2	101.4
2nd quarter	102.3	102.1	101.7	100.9	99.7	103.9	100.0	98.4	102.4	101.6	102.8	102.0
3rd quarter	102.7	102.3	102.1	101.4	99.8	105.6	99.5	97.1	102.8	102.1	103.1	102.2
4th quarter	103.1	102.4	102.7	101.4	99.6	106.4	98.6	94.6	103.1	102.6	103.3	102.4
2002												
1st quarter	103.6	102.7	103.0	101.3	99.5	106.2	98.4	94.1	104.4	105.1	104.0	102.8
2nd quarter	103.9	103.4	103.5	101.5	99.5	106.7	99.0	96.5	105.1	105.2	105.1	103.4
3rd quarter	104.3	103.8	104.0	101.5	99.4	107.1	99.8	97.3	105.8	105.5	105.9	103.8
4th quarter	104.9	104.3	104.3	102.3	99.6	109.0	99.9	97.4	106.7	106.7	106.7	104.4
2003												
1st quarter	105.7	105.1	104.6	103.1	99.7	111.4	100.9	100.1	109.1	109.6	108.8	105.4
2nd quarter	106.1	105.2	104.9	102.9	99.3	111.5	101.2	99.1	109.4	110.0	109.1	105.6
3rd quarter	106.6	105.9	105.4	103.2	99.5	112.2	101.4	99.7	110.1	110.3	110.0	106.2
4th quarter	107.2	106.2	105.8	104.1	99.8	114.3	102.2	99.8	110.7	110.6	110.8	106.7
2004												
1st quarter	108.2	107.2	106.4	105.2	100.1	117.0	103.6	102.0	112.7	113.6	112.1	107.8
2nd quarter	109.2	108.2	107.1	106.4	100.7	119.5	104.8	103.9	114.0	115.2	113.4	108.9
3rd quarter	109.8	108.7	107.6	107.4	101.0	122.0	105.3	105.2	115.4	115.9	115.1	109.6
4th quarter	110.7	109.5	108.2	108.4	101.7	123.8	106.4	107.0	117.0	116.6	117.2	110.6
2005												
1st quarter	111.8	110.2	108.8	109.7	102.8	125.4	107.6	107.6	119.2	119.9	118.7	111.6
2nd quarter	112.4	110.9	109.4	110.8	103.5	127.5	108.5	110.1	120.4	120.4	120.4	112.5
3rd quarter	113.5	112.2	109.8	112.2	104.0	130.9	109.2	112.8	122.4	121.4	123.1	113.9
4th quarter	114.5	113.1	110.5	113.8	105.1	133.3	110.0	114.1	123.9	121.6	125.3	115.0
2006												
1st quarter	115.5	113.6	111.1	115.2	106.2	135.4	110.8	113.8	125.4	124.6	125.9	115.8
2nd quarter	116.3	114.5	111.9	116.2	107.1	136.7	112.4	116.6	126.9	125.9	127.5	116.9
3rd quarter	117.1	115.4	112.5	116.6	107.5	137.1	113.7	118.1	128.0	126.2	129.0	117.7
4th quarter	117.7	115.2	113.0	117.5	108.3	138.4	113.5	115.3	128.7	126.5	130.0	117.9

Table 19-6. Personal Income and Its Disposition

(Billions of current dollars, except as noted; quarterly data are at seasonally adjusted annual rates.)   **NIPA Table 2.1**

| Year and quarter | Personal income | | | | | | | Less: Personal current taxes | Equals: Disposable personal income | Less: Personal outlays | Equals: Personal saving | | Disposable personal income, billions of chained (2000) dollars |
	Total	Compensation of employees, received	Proprietors' income with IVA and CCAdj	Rental income of persons with CCAdj	Personal income receipts on assets	Personal current transfer receipts	Less: Contributions for government social insurance				Billions of dollars	Percent of disposable personal income	
1946	178.6	119.6	35.6	7.1	12.3	10.6	6.6	17.2	161.4	145.9	15.5	9.6	1 132.7
1947	191.0	130.1	34.5	7.2	13.9	10.8	5.6	19.8	171.2	163.8	7.4	4.3	1 090.3
1948	209.8	141.9	39.3	7.9	15.1	10.3	4.6	19.2	190.6	177.3	13.4	7.0	1 148.4
1949	207.1	141.9	34.7	8.2	16.0	11.2	4.9	16.7	190.4	180.9	9.5	5.0	1 155.8
1947													
1st quarter	187.6	127.2	36.6	7.0	13.4	9.7	6.3	19.2	168.4	158.1	10.3	6.1	1 096.0
2nd quarter	185.7	128.7	32.4	7.1	13.8	9.6	6.0	19.5	166.2	161.9	4.3	2.6	1 072.8
3rd quarter	193.7	130.0	33.9	7.3	14.2	13.5	5.2	19.7	174.0	165.6	8.4	4.8	1 102.8
4th quarter	197.0	134.3	35.3	7.5	14.2	10.5	4.8	20.8	176.2	169.7	6.5	3.7	1 089.7
1948													
1st quarter	202.3	137.8	36.1	7.7	14.9	10.7	4.8	21.2	181.1	172.7	8.4	4.6	1 107.3
2nd quarter	208.3	139.4	40.4	7.9	14.7	10.4	4.6	18.9	189.3	176.5	12.8	6.8	1 145.3
3rd quarter	214.3	144.6	41.0	7.9	15.2	10.1	4.6	18.2	196.1	179.5	16.6	8.5	1 168.4
4th quarter	214.4	145.8	39.7	8.0	15.6	9.8	4.5	18.4	196.0	180.4	15.6	8.0	1 171.9
1949													
1st quarter	208.3	143.9	35.5	7.9	15.7	10.5	5.2	17.8	190.5	179.2	11.3	5.9	1 147.6
2nd quarter	207.0	142.2	34.9	8.0	15.9	11.0	5.1	17.0	190.0	181.0	9.0	4.7	1 151.4
3rd quarter	206.3	141.0	34.2	8.3	16.0	11.5	4.8	16.3	190.0	180.4	9.6	5.0	1 158.1
4th quarter	207.0	140.5	34.2	8.5	16.5	11.8	4.5	15.8	191.2	183.0	8.2	4.3	1 165.7
1950													
1st quarter	221.6	144.6	35.7	8.8	17.7	20.2	5.3	16.6	205.0	185.7	19.3	9.4	1 252.8
2nd quarter	222.4	150.6	36.3	9.0	18.0	13.8	5.3	17.6	204.8	189.7	15.1	7.4	1 245.4
3rd quarter	231.3	159.0	38.8	9.2	19.0	10.8	5.5	18.9	212.4	203.6	8.8	4.1	1 264.8
4th quarter	240.7	166.8	39.5	9.5	19.6	11.1	5.8	22.5	218.2	201.1	17.1	7.8	1 277.4
1951													
1st quarter	249.6	174.8	42.1	9.7	18.6	11.1	6.6	24.4	225.2	212.4	12.8	5.7	1 276.9
2nd quarter	256.9	180.7	42.5	10.0	19.1	11.4	6.7	26.4	230.6	208.1	22.5	9.8	1 297.5
3rd quarter	260.1	183.0	42.7	10.3	19.2	11.6	6.6	27.8	232.4	210.8	21.6	9.3	1 305.9
4th quarter	265.5	187.0	43.6	10.5	19.5	11.6	6.7	29.6	235.8	214.8	21.1	8.9	1 308.5
1952													
1st quarter	267.5	191.3	41.9	10.8	19.1	11.4	6.9	30.9	236.7	216.2	20.4	8.6	1 308.1
2nd quarter	271.4	192.7	43.1	11.1	19.8	11.5	6.8	31.8	239.6	220.5	19.1	8.0	1 323.9
3rd quarter	278.2	196.6	44.9	11.4	20.0	12.3	6.9	32.3	246.0	223.2	22.8	9.3	1 349.7
4th quarter	284.3	204.1	42.7	11.7	20.5	12.3	7.1	33.1	251.2	231.5	19.7	7.8	1 376.0
1953													
1st quarter	289.0	208.0	43.1	12.0	20.6	12.4	7.1	33.4	255.6	235.3	20.3	7.9	1 395.0
2nd quarter	293.0	211.4	42.4	12.3	21.7	12.3	7.1	33.4	259.6	237.3	22.2	8.6	1 414.5
3rd quarter	293.1	211.6	41.7	12.6	21.9	12.5	7.2	33.2	259.9	238.2	21.8	8.4	1 408.7
4th quarter	292.4	210.1	41.4	12.9	22.1	12.9	7.1	32.9	259.4	237.7	21.7	8.4	1 399.8
1954													
1st quarter	292.4	208.1	42.7	13.2	23.0	13.5	8.1	30.2	262.2	239.7	22.5	8.6	1 407.5
2nd quarter	291.9	207.7	42.0	13.4	22.7	14.1	8.0	30.0	262.0	242.5	19.5	7.4	1 407.4
3rd quarter	294.0	208.3	42.4	13.6	23.4	14.5	8.1	30.0	264.0	245.2	18.8	7.1	1 422.7
4th quarter	299.4	212.6	42.2	13.7	23.9	15.2	8.1	30.5	269.0	249.9	19.1	7.1	1 450.6
1955													
1st quarter	305.3	216.9	43.5	13.8	24.7	15.3	8.9	31.4	273.9	256.3	17.5	6.4	1 471.9
2nd quarter	313.2	223.1	44.5	13.8	25.2	15.6	9.0	32.4	280.7	261.6	19.1	6.8	1 506.9
3rd quarter	320.5	229.1	44.7	13.9	26.1	15.9	9.2	33.4	287.2	266.1	21.1	7.3	1 535.3
4th quarter	325.5	233.6	44.5	14.0	26.7	16.0	9.3	34.2	291.3	270.3	21.0	7.2	1 552.7
1956													
1st quarter	330.9	238.0	44.9	14.1	27.4	16.3	9.9	35.4	295.5	272.1	23.4	7.9	1 568.4
2nd quarter	336.7	242.6	45.4	14.1	27.9	16.6	10.0	36.2	300.4	274.9	25.5	8.5	1 583.9
3rd quarter	341.6	245.7	46.2	14.2	28.3	17.1	10.0	36.9	304.7	278.2	26.5	8.7	1 590.6
4th quarter	349.2	251.6	46.9	14.3	29.2	17.3	10.1	37.9	311.3	283.7	27.7	8.9	1 615.9
1957													
1st quarter	353.3	255.3	47.0	14.4	29.8	18.2	11.4	38.6	314.7	288.3	26.5	8.4	1 618.9
2nd quarter	357.8	257.0	47.8	14.5	30.5	19.4	11.4	39.0	318.9	290.6	28.2	8.9	1 629.5
3rd quarter	362.1	259.7	48.7	14.6	31.0	19.6	11.5	39.2	322.9	295.3	27.7	8.6	1 637.5
4th quarter	361.5	258.1	47.9	14.9	31.1	20.8	11.3	38.8	322.7	297.0	25.8	8.0	1 628.2
1958													
1st quarter	362.0	254.6	50.2	15.2	31.3	22.1	11.3	38.2	323.8	296.6	27.3	8.4	1 613.2
2nd quarter	364.3	254.2	50.3	15.3	31.8	23.9	11.3	37.7	326.6	299.4	27.2	8.3	1 623.7
3rd quarter	372.6	262.2	50.0	15.5	32.1	24.2	11.4	38.9	333.6	304.4	29.2	8.8	1 656.8
4th quarter	377.2	267.2	50.1	15.6	32.2	23.7	11.5	39.4	337.8	308.3	29.5	8.7	1 677.1
1959													
1st quarter	383.8	274.5	50.4	15.6	33.0	24.0	13.7	40.8	343.0	315.9	27.1	7.9	1 688.6
2nd quarter	392.4	281.6	50.7	16.0	34.0	23.9	13.9	42.0	350.5	322.1	28.4	8.1	1 721.0
3rd quarter	394.6	282.3	50.5	16.4	35.1	24.2	13.9	42.7	352.0	327.6	24.4	6.9	1 719.5
4th quarter	400.3	285.5	50.9	16.7	36.3	24.8	13.9	43.7	356.6	329.9	26.7	7.5	1 733.2
1960													
1st quarter	406.7	294.0	50.2	16.9	37.4	24.6	16.4	45.3	361.4	333.6	27.8	7.7	1 753.2
2nd quarter	411.2	296.9	50.9	17.0	37.5	25.3	16.5	46.0	365.2	339.7	25.5	7.0	1 761.8
3rd quarter	413.4	297.6	50.9	17.2	38.1	26.0	16.5	46.5	366.9	339.8	27.0	7.4	1 762.8
4th quarter	414.7	297.1	51.2	17.4	38.5	27.0	16.4	46.4	368.3	342.0	26.3	7.1	1 761.2
1961													
1st quarter	418.8	298.0	52.4	17.6	38.7	28.8	16.7	46.5	372.3	342.6	29.8	8.0	1 777.6
2nd quarter	424.8	302.2	52.6	17.8	39.5	29.7	16.9	46.9	377.9	347.5	30.4	8.0	1 804.6
3rd quarter	431.8	307.2	53.4	18.0	40.5	29.9	17.1	47.4	384.4	350.5	33.9	8.8	1 829.2
4th quarter	440.6	313.8	54.6	18.2	41.9	29.4	17.3	48.1	392.5	357.9	34.5	8.8	1 865.4

Table 19-6. Personal Income and Its Disposition—*Continued*

(Billions of current dollars, except as noted; quarterly data are at seasonally adjusted annual rates.)   **NIPA Table 2.1**

| Year and quarter | Personal income | | | | | | | Less: Personal current taxes | Equals: Disposable personal income | Less: Personal outlays | Equals: Personal saving | | Disposable personal income, billions of chained (2000) dollars |
	Total	Compensation of employees, received	Proprietors' income with IVA and CCAdj	Rental income of persons with CCAdj	Personal income receipts on assets	Personal current transfer receipts	Less: Contributions for government social insurance				Billions of dollars	Percent of disposable personal income	
1962													
1st quarter	447.4	320.4	55.4	18.5	42.0	30.0	18.9	49.4	398.0	363.3	34.7	8.7	1 883.4
2nd quarter	454.8	326.4	55.2	18.7	43.6	30.0	19.1	50.9	403.8	369.1	34.7	8.6	1 904.1
3rd quarter	459.4	329.2	55.2	18.9	44.9	30.4	19.2	52.3	407.1	373.2	33.9	8.3	1 914.7
4th quarter	465.2	332.6	55.7	19.1	45.9	31.2	19.3	53.6	411.6	379.7	31.9	7.8	1 930.4
1963													
1st quarter	470.2	337.5	56.0	19.3	46.1	32.6	21.3	54.1	416.1	383.6	32.6	7.8	1 946.0
2nd quarter	475.0	342.4	55.8	19.5	47.1	31.7	21.5	54.3	420.7	387.9	32.7	7.8	1 964.3
3rd quarter	482.0	347.4	56.3	19.6	48.4	32.0	21.8	54.6	427.4	395.3	32.1	7.5	1 986.4
4th quarter	491.3	353.6	57.7	19.6	49.9	32.5	22.0	55.2	436.1	400.3	35.8	8.2	2 019.6
1964													
1st quarter	500.8	360.0	58.1	19.6	51.5	33.6	22.0	53.8	447.1	410.1	37.0	8.3	2 060.6
2nd quarter	510.0	367.4	59.0	19.6	53.1	33.2	22.3	49.7	460.3	418.4	41.9	9.1	2 116.8
3rd quarter	519.4	374.6	59.6	19.7	54.6	33.5	22.5	51.6	467.8	427.7	40.1	8.6	2 144.6
4th quarter	528.1	380.8	60.8	19.6	55.8	33.7	22.7	53.2	474.8	430.5	44.4	9.3	2 169.4
1965													
1st quarter	538.6	387.3	62.2	19.9	57.1	35.0	22.9	57.0	481.7	441.3	40.4	8.4	2 193.3
2nd quarter	547.8	394.1	63.4	20.1	58.8	34.6	23.2	58.4	489.4	448.7	40.7	8.3	2 217.4
3rd quarter	561.7	402.3	64.2	20.3	60.3	38.1	23.6	57.0	504.7	458.1	46.6	9.2	2 278.4
4th quarter	574.8	414.3	65.9	20.3	61.4	36.9	24.0	58.3	516.5	472.2	44.3	8.6	2 324.3
1966													
1st quarter	586.9	426.7	69.4	20.7	62.6	37.8	30.4	61.5	525.3	482.8	42.5	8.1	2 345.9
2nd quarter	596.5	437.8	67.4	20.6	63.6	37.9	30.8	65.6	530.9	488.3	42.6	8.0	2 351.7
3rd quarter	609.6	449.0	67.6	20.9	64.5	39.6	31.9	67.9	541.7	497.6	44.1	8.1	2 381.3
4th quarter	622.8	457.2	68.3	20.9	65.5	43.1	32.2	70.6	552.2	503.6	48.5	8.8	2 408.6
1967													
1st quarter	633.3	463.3	69.1	21.1	67.5	46.1	33.6	71.2	562.2	508.2	53.9	9.6	2 445.0
2nd quarter	640.4	469.0	68.9	21.2	68.7	47.2	34.6	70.9	569.5	517.9	51.6	9.1	2 464.5
3rd quarter	654.1	478.7	71.0	21.2	69.8	48.7	35.2	73.8	580.3	524.9	55.3	9.5	2 488.1
4th quarter	665.4	489.7	70.5	21.1	70.1	50.0	36.0	75.9	589.5	532.6	57.0	9.7	2 506.1
1968													
1st quarter	684.7	504.5	72.2	20.9	72.4	52.4	37.6	78.6	606.2	550.9	55.3	9.1	2 549.8
2nd quarter	704.2	517.6	73.6	20.9	74.7	55.9	38.4	81.7	622.5	565.1	57.4	9.2	2 592.3
3rd quarter	722.0	531.4	75.4	21.0	76.0	57.3	39.1	91.9	630.2	581.9	48.3	7.7	2 597.1
4th quarter	737.2	543.8	76.0	20.8	77.6	58.7	39.7	95.9	641.3	591.2	50.2	7.8	2 613.7
1969													
1st quarter	751.2	555.9	76.2	21.1	80.5	60.4	42.9	102.6	648.6	603.9	44.7	6.9	2 617.5
2nd quarter	769.2	569.8	77.4	21.1	83.0	61.5	43.7	105.7	663.5	616.0	47.5	7.2	2 643.5
3rd quarter	789.5	586.6	78.1	21.3	85.3	62.9	44.6	104.1	685.4	626.7	58.7	8.6	2 696.6
4th quarter	804.0	598.2	77.9	21.2	87.7	64.3	45.3	105.6	698.4	639.2	59.2	8.5	2 716.1
1970													
1st quarter	814.7	606.1	77.6	21.2	89.6	66.1	46.0	104.6	710.1	650.7	59.4	8.4	2 729.4
2nd quarter	836.1	616.3	77.1	20.9	91.9	76.1	46.3	105.5	730.5	660.9	69.6	9.5	2 777.4
3rd quarter	848.2	622.5	79.1	21.5	95.4	76.3	46.7	100.7	747.5	673.2	74.4	10.0	2 814.6
4th quarter	856.1	623.9	79.7	21.8	97.1	80.1	46.5	101.5	754.6	680.2	74.5	9.9	2 804.4
1971													
1st quarter	876.1	641.6	81.8	21.7	99.5	82.0	50.5	98.3	777.8	699.6	78.2	10.1	2 863.6
2nd quarter	898.6	653.5	83.9	22.3	100.3	89.6	51.0	100.7	797.9	714.1	83.7	10.5	2 904.6
3rd quarter	911.3	663.5	85.2	22.7	101.7	89.6	51.3	102.3	809.0	727.1	81.9	10.1	2 916.4
4th quarter	928.0	674.8	88.3	23.1	102.4	91.3	51.9	105.5	822.5	743.9	78.5	9.5	2 946.8
1972													
1st quarter	956.1	702.6	88.5	23.7	105.2	94.3	58.1	119.8	836.4	761.8	74.6	8.9	2 965.0
2nd quarter	972.3	716.2	91.8	20.7	107.6	94.9	58.8	123.4	848.9	780.9	68.0	8.0	2 991.5
3rd quarter	998.6	729.9	96.5	24.6	111.1	96.0	59.5	124.3	874.3	799.8	74.5	8.5	3 053.6
4th quarter	1 043.8	751.9	106.7	24.6	114.6	106.4	60.4	127.1	916.7	825.0	91.6	10.0	3 175.0
1973													
1st quarter	1 064.8	781.6	106.0	24.5	117.2	109.1	73.6	126.4	938.4	849.9	88.5	9.4	3 210.5
2nd quarter	1 094.6	801.1	111.1	24.5	121.1	111.5	74.7	129.2	965.4	866.0	99.4	10.3	3 240.3
3rd quarter	1 122.6	819.9	114.4	23.5	127.6	113.3	76.1	134.1	988.5	884.9	103.6	10.5	3 258.3
4th quarter	1 161.0	842.5	122.4	24.5	132.6	116.5	77.6	140.0	1 021.0	901.6	119.4	11.7	3 297.6
1974													
1st quarter	1 177.8	860.7	115.9	24.7	137.7	121.9	83.1	142.8	1 035.0	918.7	116.3	11.2	3 246.6
2nd quarter	1 203.9	881.9	108.8	24.0	144.0	129.9	84.7	148.9	1 055.0	947.8	107.2	10.2	3 219.9
3rd quarter	1 241.8	904.6	112.9	24.4	149.1	137.1	86.4	154.9	1 086.9	977.4	109.4	10.1	3 231.1
4th quarter	1 267.1	915.7	114.7	24.2	154.7	144.3	86.6	157.6	1 109.5	987.9	121.5	11.0	3 217.3
1975													
1st quarter	1 284.0	919.4	113.2	24.1	159.0	155.9	87.6	158.0	1 126.0	1 015.5	110.5	9.8	3 205.7
2nd quarter	1 314.2	931.7	115.4	23.8	159.9	171.5	88.0	121.1	1 193.2	1 044.5	148.6	12.5	3 354.6
3rd quarter	1 351.9	957.6	122.4	23.7	163.1	174.8	89.8	152.8	1 199.1	1 079.1	120.0	10.0	3 309.1
4th quarter	1 390.1	987.5	126.9	23.2	166.7	177.6	91.8	158.5	1 231.5	1 108.3	123.2	10.0	3 342.0
1976													
1st quarter	1 425.6	1 022.3	127.6	22.9	170.4	181.4	98.9	162.1	1 263.5	1 141.8	121.7	9.6	3 390.9
2nd quarter	1 453.5	1 046.0	129.9	21.9	176.3	179.7	100.4	169.0	1 284.5	1 161.6	122.9	9.6	3 417.5
3rd quarter	1 491.5	1 070.7	133.7	22.1	180.8	186.4	102.2	175.8	1 315.8	1 191.4	124.4	9.5	3 448.0
4th quarter	1 528.5	1 098.0	137.4	22.2	186.2	188.5	103.8	182.4	1 346.1	1 225.9	120.2	8.9	3 473.0

Table 19-6. Personal Income and Its Disposition—*Continued*

(Billions of current dollars, except as noted; quarterly data are at seasonally adjusted annual rates.)   **NIPA Table 2.1**

Year and quarter	Personal income Total	Compensation of employees, received	Proprietors' income with IVA and CCAdj	Rental income of persons with CCAdj	Personal income receipts on assets	Personal current transfer receipts	Less: Contributions for government social insurance	Less: Personal current taxes	Equals: Disposable personal income	Less: Personal outlays	Equals: Personal saving Billions of dollars	Equals: Personal saving Percent of disposable personal income	Disposable personal income, billions of chained (2000) dollars
1977													
1st quarter	1 561.0	1 126.9	140.4	22.2	190.2	190.6	109.3	188.4	1 372.5	1 262.7	109.8	8.0	3 479.7
2nd quarter	1 606.6	1 164.3	141.6	20.6	201.0	191.1	112.1	195.3	1 411.3	1 291.8	119.5	8.5	3 517.4
3rd quarter	1 652.4	1 196.8	143.3	20.0	210.5	196.2	114.3	198.2	1 454.3	1 323.9	130.3	9.0	3 570.6
4th quarter	1 712.8	1 233.7	157.5	19.8	219.5	199.0	116.7	208.1	1 504.6	1 363.2	141.4	9.4	3 642.1
1978													
1st quarter	1 750.7	1 269.6	157.8	21.4	224.9	203.1	126.2	211.7	1 538.9	1 394.9	144.0	9.4	3 663.5
2nd quarter	1 811.9	1 318.3	167.3	20.9	230.6	204.9	130.1	222.8	1 589.0	1 454.2	134.8	8.5	3 706.3
3rd quarter	1 866.5	1 355.2	170.4	22.7	237.4	213.6	132.8	236.0	1 630.5	1 486.7	143.8	8.8	3 737.6
4th quarter	1 921.7	1 400.2	171.2	23.3	246.2	216.9	136.0	247.0	1 674.8	1 527.3	147.5	8.8	3 768.3
1979													
1st quarter	1 979.1	1 445.2	178.2	25.0	257.1	222.5	148.8	253.4	1 725.8	1 563.8	162.0	9.4	3 811.7
2nd quarter	2 021.9	1 478.4	178.2	22.1	267.0	227.1	150.9	261.8	1 760.2	1 605.5	154.6	8.8	3 785.2
3rd quarter	2 088.5	1 519.0	181.3	21.8	277.7	242.7	154.2	274.6	1 813.9	1 661.3	152.6	8.4	3 807.2
4th quarter	2 159.2	1 561.2	182.7	26.3	297.2	248.9	157.1	285.0	1 874.2	1 706.8	167.4	8.9	3 841.5
1980													
1st quarter	2 228.2	1 602.7	176.1	29.8	324.0	258.7	163.1	284.2	1 944.0	1 759.2	184.9	9.5	3 869.4
2nd quarter	2 246.8	1 625.1	161.0	25.4	334.6	263.9	163.2	291.6	1 955.2	1 761.2	194.0	9.9	3 800.0
3rd quarter	2 322.8	1 657.4	173.5	26.6	336.0	295.9	166.6	301.6	2 021.2	1 819.7	201.6	10.0	3 839.0
4th quarter	2 433.7	1 722.1	185.9	38.2	360.1	299.3	171.8	318.2	2 115.5	1 890.1	225.4	10.7	3 920.8
1981													
1st quarter	2 492.2	1 774.5	188.5	36.7	378.2	305.9	191.6	330.3	2 161.9	1 950.2	211.6	9.8	3 905.7
2nd quarter	2 544.9	1 808.0	179.6	36.5	405.6	309.3	194.1	342.1	2 202.8	1 984.6	218.3	9.9	3 915.0
3rd quarter	2 645.9	1 846.2	186.3	37.8	445.5	327.9	197.7	356.3	2 289.6	2 027.5	262.2	11.5	4 003.1
4th quarter	2 682.1	1 874.2	177.4	41.0	458.5	330.4	199.4	352.1	2 330.1	2 044.9	285.1	12.2	4 012.8
1982													
1st quarter	2 711.6	1 898.0	170.2	40.1	474.7	335.7	207.2	351.9	2 359.7	2 086.6	273.1	11.6	4 013.3
2nd quarter	2 758.2	1 917.2	175.1	37.6	491.7	344.9	208.4	359.1	2 399.1	2 116.4	282.7	11.8	4 041.9
3rd quarter	2 796.7	1 937.0	176.1	39.6	492.3	361.5	209.8	349.5	2 447.2	2 167.1	280.1	11.4	4 059.3
4th quarter	2 834.7	1 951.1	183.9	38.0	494.7	377.3	210.2	356.0	2 478.7	2 231.5	247.2	10.0	4 066.2
1983													
1st quarter	2 871.5	1 979.2	188.0	38.0	506.4	380.2	220.4	350.3	2 521.2	2 274.0	247.2	9.8	4 100.4
2nd quarter	2 923.3	2 018.5	189.4	38.3	514.4	386.4	223.6	359.0	2 564.3	2 341.0	223.3	8.7	4 132.7
3rd quarter	2 980.0	2 059.9	190.2	35.8	539.3	381.9	227.2	344.9	2 635.1	2 414.5	220.6	8.4	4 191.6
4th quarter	3 068.0	2 114.6	202.4	39.0	558.2	386.5	232.6	355.1	2 712.9	2 469.6	243.3	9.0	4 286.5
1984													
1st quarter	3 166.0	2 184.6	231.6	37.8	569.7	393.4	251.0	360.7	2 805.3	2 517.2	288.2	10.3	4 385.5
2nd quarter	3 255.3	2 235.2	245.9	36.3	596.0	397.8	255.8	370.0	2 885.4	2 578.9	306.5	10.6	4 467.0
3rd quarter	3 338.6	2 281.5	248.7	40.8	627.1	400.5	259.9	383.6	2 955.0	2 620.5	334.5	11.3	4 539.8
4th quarter	3 397.9	2 320.3	247.1	45.8	638.9	408.9	263.1	395.5	3 002.4	2 672.5	330.0	11.0	4 583.9
1985													
1st quarter	3 464.0	2 366.0	263.3	44.1	646.4	419.6	275.4	431.8	3 032.2	2 748.5	283.7	9.4	4 580.0
2nd quarter	3 505.6	2 403.3	261.2	43.3	654.5	422.1	278.8	388.1	3 117.5	2 798.6	318.9	10.2	4 673.4
3rd quarter	3 536.5	2 441.1	261.1	41.0	648.6	427.5	282.8	421.1	3 115.4	2 869.7	245.7	7.9	4 640.4
4th quarter	3 600.6	2 489.2	263.6	39.3	666.6	430.4	288.4	428.5	3 172.2	2 900.4	271.8	8.6	4 688.0
1986													
1st quarter	3 659.1	2 522.7	264.5	38.3	688.9	442.7	297.9	425.8	3 233.4	2 945.6	287.7	8.9	4 744.2
2nd quarter	3 698.0	2 545.3	271.3	36.2	697.5	448.5	300.7	428.9	3 269.1	2 978.6	290.5	8.9	4 793.8
3rd quarter	3 746.2	2 581.4	283.9	31.7	698.7	455.4	305.1	438.9	3 307.2	3 050.8	256.4	7.8	4 813.6
4th quarter	3 786.2	2 631.1	282.9	27.9	697.1	457.3	310.1	455.5	3 330.7	3 091.8	238.9	7.2	4 813.4
1987													
1st quarter	3 847.3	2 678.6	291.7	31.7	699.3	462.5	316.5	450.3	3 397.1	3 124.0	273.0	8.0	4 854.6
2nd quarter	3 900.6	2 721.1	298.5	29.3	704.3	467.6	320.2	511.2	3 389.4	3 191.3	198.1	5.8	4 802.3
3rd quarter	3 973.0	2 767.3	304.7	34.7	722.1	468.7	324.5	488.5	3 484.5	3 258.9	225.6	6.5	4 887.3
4th quarter	4 068.6	2 833.9	313.9	38.1	742.3	471.7	331.2	506.5	3 562.1	3 293.4	268.7	7.5	4 954.1
1988													
1st quarter	4 139.6	2 883.1	333.4	39.1	747.1	489.0	352.1	501.1	3 638.5	3 376.1	262.4	7.2	5 016.9
2nd quarter	4 208.2	2 945.5	339.5	37.2	752.5	492.6	359.1	496.9	3 711.3	3 437.6	273.7	7.4	5 061.3
3rd quarter	4 292.6	2 994.2	350.2	38.4	775.3	498.8	364.4	505.7	3 786.9	3 506.8	280.0	7.4	5 103.3
4th quarter	4 374.5	3 045.9	343.2	47.6	802.1	506.0	370.3	516.3	3 858.2	3 582.7	275.5	7.1	5 149.2
1989													
1st quarter	4 506.2	3 092.8	367.0	46.1	849.9	530.2	379.8	551.3	3 954.9	3 640.9	314.0	7.9	5 216.3
2nd quarter	4 558.5	3 122.1	360.1	46.5	875.1	537.6	382.8	565.1	3 993.4	3 708.1	285.3	7.1	5 199.1
3rd quarter	4 608.8	3 158.3	359.0	41.5	888.3	548.0	386.4	570.0	4 038.8	3 769.0	269.7	6.7	5 224.9
4th quarter	4 677.8	3 207.7	367.0	38.3	898.6	557.9	391.8	578.2	4 099.5	3 820.1	279.5	6.8	5 259.9
1990													
1st quarter	4 778.8	3 272.8	376.4	44.5	911.4	577.8	404.1	580.6	4 198.2	3 905.6	292.6	7.0	5 307.9
2nd quarter	4 860.8	3 330.5	379.7	47.7	922.3	588.8	408.3	592.7	4 268.1	3 960.9	307.2	7.2	5 338.7
3rd quarter	4 924.5	3 370.2	385.1	54.0	930.9	598.4	414.1	598.8	4 325.7	4 027.8	297.8	6.9	5 343.6
4th quarter	4 950.2	3 379.2	381.1	56.4	931.3	616.1	413.9	598.9	4 351.3	4 051.3	300.0	6.9	5 306.6
1991													
1st quarter	4 965.7	3 394.4	367.9	55.9	932.0	640.0	424.5	578.5	4 387.1	4 066.7	320.4	7.3	5 310.5
2nd quarter	5 025.5	3 426.9	374.2	58.3	934.1	659.8	427.7	583.7	4 441.8	4 124.1	317.7	7.2	5 347.1
3rd quarter	5 071.7	3 461.5	377.2	61.6	935.0	669.1	432.6	588.0	4 483.7	4 170.0	313.7	7.0	5 359.6
4th quarter	5 140.9	3 498.5	389.2	65.3	927.0	696.9	435.9	596.4	4 544.5	4 199.8	344.7	7.6	5 389.4

Table 19-6. Personal Income and Its Disposition—*Continued*

(Billions of current dollars, except as noted; quarterly data are at seasonally adjusted annual rates.)   **NIPA Table 2.1**

Year and quarter	Personal income							Less: Personal current taxes	Equals: Disposable personal income	Less: Personal outlays	Equals: Personal saving		Disposable personal income, billions of chained (2000) dollars
	Total	Compensation of employees, received	Proprietors' income with IVA and CCAdj	Rental income of persons with CCAdj	Personal income receipts on assets	Personal current transfer receipts	Less: Contributions for government social insurance				Billions of dollars	Percent of disposable personal income	
1992													
1st quarter	5 238.0	3 566.8	409.5	71.6	914.1	724.8	448.7	586.6	4 651.4	4 292.0	359.4	7.7	5 473.9
2nd quarter	5 321.0	3 617.0	425.3	79.8	909.3	743.2	453.7	604.9	4 716.1	4 342.3	373.8	7.9	5 514.6
3rd quarter	5 382.5	3 659.9	432.4	70.8	907.2	769.9	457.8	613.9	4 768.6	4 418.5	350.1	7.3	5 537.4
4th quarter	5 506.5	3 761.0	443.1	89.9	912.7	759.4	459.6	636.9	4 869.6	4 488.7	380.9	7.8	5 619.2
1993													
1st quarter	5 419.5	3 666.6	444.6	90.9	907.7	777.8	468.1	617.9	4 801.6	4 529.2	272.4	5.7	5 512.1
2nd quarter	5 542.3	3 780.5	456.3	95.3	903.8	782.3	475.9	641.2	4 901.1	4 596.9	304.3	6.2	5 590.2
3rd quarter	5 579.6	3 821.2	448.9	94.3	897.5	797.8	480.1	655.3	4 924.3	4 659.8	264.5	5.4	5 597.4
4th quarter	5 692.8	3 911.4	465.5	101.7	898.4	802.4	486.6	672.1	5 020.8	4 725.7	295.1	5.9	5 677.2
1994													
1st quarter	5 668.9	3 873.2	460.9	105.7	905.2	822.6	498.7	670.2	4 998.7	4 795.4	203.3	4.1	5 629.9
2nd quarter	5 813.7	3 973.4	475.1	120.9	931.0	819.6	506.5	695.6	5 118.1	4 859.3	258.8	5.1	5 733.1
3rd quarter	5 891.0	4 009.0	475.9	126.2	967.1	823.3	510.5	693.5	5 197.5	4 941.2	256.3	4.9	5 770.8
4th quarter	5 996.5	4 062.8	481.3	125.9	999.8	843.8	517.1	703.4	5 293.1	5 013.7	279.4	5.3	5 850.9
1995													
1st quarter	6 072.3	4 118.6	483.1	122.6	1 006.7	867.2	525.9	721.4	5 350.9	5 048.1	302.9	5.7	5 886.4
2nd quarter	6 119.2	4 153.2	484.9	122.3	1 012.2	876.8	530.1	742.9	5 376.3	5 123.3	253.0	4.7	5 881.7
3rd quarter	6 174.6	4 197.5	493.9	119.6	1 014.7	884.1	535.2	747.5	5 427.1	5 196.8	230.3	4.2	5 912.1
4th quarter	6 243.0	4 238.7	506.7	124.1	1 032.0	881.6	540.0	764.4	5 478.6	5 260.9	217.6	4.0	5 943.3
1996													
1st quarter	6 371.1	4 291.7	526.0	131.1	1 056.1	910.7	544.4	796.6	5 574.5	5 338.0	236.5	4.2	6 010.0
2nd quarter	6 490.5	4 359.0	547.9	130.7	1 073.2	931.9	552.2	833.9	5 656.6	5 433.6	223.0	3.9	6 059.8
3rd quarter	6 566.0	4 419.1	545.5	132.1	1 100.2	928.0	558.9	838.5	5 727.5	5 492.6	234.9	4.1	6 111.3
4th quarter	6 654.6	4 477.8	553.4	132.0	1 127.4	929.4	565.3	859.4	5 795.3	5 576.0	219.2	3.8	6 142.5
1997													
1st quarter	6 773.1	4 556.4	569.6	130.0	1 146.7	946.2	575.8	895.7	5 877.4	5 663.7	213.7	3.6	6 201.3
2nd quarter	6 847.0	4 617.9	566.8	129.5	1 168.7	946.4	582.2	910.4	5 936.7	5 706.0	230.6	3.9	6 251.9
3rd quarter	6 956.7	4 693.4	579.9	128.2	1 192.4	952.9	590.0	935.9	6 020.8	5 816.1	204.7	3.4	6 323.3
4th quarter	7 083.7	4 790.8	587.9	127.4	1 219.0	959.4	600.7	963.3	6 120.5	5 896.2	224.3	3.7	6 406.6
1998													
1st quarter	7 247.1	4 894.1	606.2	131.0	1 257.6	969.7	611.5	991.2	6 255.9	5 964.2	291.7	4.7	6 543.4
2nd quarter	7 376.0	4 977.6	619.2	135.7	1 287.6	975.8	619.9	1 018.3	6 357.7	6 072.3	285.4	4.5	6 638.6
3rd quarter	7 485.8	5 062.2	632.6	141.6	1 298.8	979.1	628.5	1 037.7	6 448.1	6 167.6	280.5	4.3	6 710.9
4th quarter	7 583.0	5 146.4	653.3	141.6	1 288.8	989.8	636.8	1 061.0	6 522.1	6 272.5	249.6	3.8	6 763.0
1999													
1st quarter	7 658.4	5 242.8	664.3	145.2	1 249.4	1 009.5	652.8	1 071.7	6 586.7	6 346.3	240.4	3.6	6 812.9
2nd quarter	7 728.8	5 297.3	672.0	147.6	1 255.4	1 013.3	656.8	1 090.2	6 638.6	6 489.5	149.1	2.2	6 822.1
3rd quarter	7 823.7	5 371.2	680.6	144.5	1 262.3	1 027.4	662.4	1 115.5	6 708.2	6 593.2	115.0	1.7	6 856.0
4th quarter	7 998.8	5 496.5	696.1	152.1	1 289.7	1 038.1	673.8	1 152.5	6 846.2	6 716.6	129.7	1.9	6 955.6
2000													
1st quarter	8 266.2	5 694.1	709.3	153.8	1 349.9	1 054.6	695.5	1 207.0	7 059.2	6 888.0	171.2	2.4	7 109.7
2nd quarter	8 372.3	5 727.2	726.5	148.5	1 385.6	1 080.8	696.3	1 231.1	7 141.2	6 970.0	171.3	2.4	7 157.5
3rd quarter	8 514.4	5 837.4	735.6	148.2	1 406.2	1 094.8	707.7	1 248.0	7 266.4	7 076.3	190.1	2.6	7 249.3
4th quarter	8 565.8	5 871.9	742.1	150.5	1 406.5	1 106.0	711.2	1 256.6	7 309.3	7 168.1	141.2	1.9	7 259.6
2001													
1st quarter	8 688.7	5 946.2	769.4	155.3	1 397.4	1 149.6	729.2	1 296.6	7 392.1	7 253.5	138.6	1.9	7 283.0
2nd quarter	8 719.9	5 944.6	770.6	161.7	1 388.7	1 185.7	731.5	1 312.3	7 407.6	7 318.8	88.7	1.2	7 252.1
3rd quarter	8 733.1	5 939.3	773.4	176.4	1 373.3	1 202.6	731.9	1 110.3	7 622.8	7 361.2	261.6	3.4	7 452.2
4th quarter	8 754.8	5 938.3	774.2	176.2	1 360.3	1 237.8	731.9	1 230.0	7 524.8	7 484.4	40.5	0.5	7 346.0
2002													
1st quarter	8 814.7	6 025.3	763.0	172.1	1 340.6	1 260.9	747.1	1 063.2	7 751.5	7 526.1	225.4	2.9	7 549.9
2nd quarter	8 892.0	6 091.5	763.5	167.7	1 336.5	1 284.0	751.1	1 050.3	7 841.7	7 620.5	221.2	2.8	7 585.2
3rd quarter	8 895.4	6 114.5	769.1	142.9	1 327.4	1 292.7	751.1	1 050.0	7 845.4	7 692.4	153.0	2.0	7 555.5
4th quarter	8 925.5	6 133.4	778.1	129.2	1 328.5	1 307.1	750.9	1 043.8	7 881.7	7 742.4	139.3	1.8	7 559.3
2003													
1st quarter	8 998.2	6 191.0	779.1	137.4	1 329.1	1 327.0	765.4	1 022.7	7 975.5	7 826.4	149.1	1.9	7 591.7
2nd quarter	9 111.3	6 275.4	801.6	130.5	1 334.9	1 344.0	775.0	1 023.7	8 087.6	7 913.7	173.9	2.2	7 685.7
3rd quarter	9 203.6	6 340.8	823.5	116.3	1 339.5	1 365.5	782.1	942.6	8 261.0	8 067.0	194.0	2.3	7 804.8
4th quarter	9 341.3	6 434.3	840.8	147.6	1 343.1	1 367.6	791.9	1 015.4	8 326.0	8 143.5	182.5	2.2	7 837.3
2004													
1st quarter	9 482.8	6 509.1	879.3	140.4	1 359.8	1 404.9	810.8	1 008.1	8 474.7	8 299.5	175.1	2.1	7 908.7
2nd quarter	9 629.6	6 618.2	908.7	126.0	1 384.4	1 415.3	822.9	1 024.5	8 605.1	8 432.9	172.2	2.0	7 955.1
3rd quarter	9 770.9	6 734.7	914.1	105.5	1 420.1	1 432.7	836.1	1 062.1	8 708.9	8 553.7	155.2	1.8	8 012.2
4th quarter	10 025.5	6 823.6	944.4	101.7	1 564.1	1 437.1	845.5	1 090.7	8 934.8	8 710.6	224.2	2.5	8 158.8
2005													
1st quarter	10 044.5	6 884.4	936.3	90.1	1 513.6	1 479.7	859.6	1 163.8	8 880.7	8 808.1	72.5	0.8	8 060.4
2nd quarter	10 184.4	6 957.4	948.1	72.2	1 564.7	1 508.8	866.9	1 192.7	8 991.7	8 945.9	45.8	0.5	8 110.0
3rd quarter	10 289.1	7 090.2	960.4	-56.9	1 616.9	1 559.6	881.1	1 222.3	9 066.9	9 129.8	-62.9	-0.7	8 084.0
4th quarter	10 561.0	7 171.0	994.5	58.0	1 692.3	1 534.7	889.5	1 252.5	9 308.6	9 234.2	74.4	0.8	8 231.8
2006													
1st quarter	10 781.6	7 338.0	1 004.7	52.8	1 735.4	1 567.6	917.1	1 316.0	9 465.6	9 371.2	94.4	1.0	8 334.2
2nd quarter	10 913.2	7 364.2	1 018.3	45.6	1 809.5	1 594.5	918.9	1 341.1	9 572.1	9 518.0	54.2	0.6	8 360.4
3rd quarter	11 056.1	7 441.9	1 013.4	40.4	1 865.8	1 620.1	925.5	1 356.2	9 699.9	9 651.8	48.1	0.5	8 407.1
4th quarter	11 224.7	7 586.1	1 022.4	38.2	1 888.6	1 629.8	940.4	1 399.6	9 825.1	9 739.0	86.1	0.9	8 526.2

Table 19-7. Per Capita Product and Income, Population, and Inventories to Sales Ratios

(Seasonally adjusted.)   NIPA Tables 5.7.5A, 5.7.5B, 5.7.6A, 5.7.6B, 7.1

Year and quarter	Chained (2000) dollars per capita		Population (mid-period, thousands)	Ratio, inventories at end of quarter to monthly rate of sales during the quarter					
	Gross domestic product	Disposable personal income		Total private inventories to final sales of domestic business		Nonfarm inventories to final sales of domestic business		Nonfarm inventories to final sales of goods and structures	
				Current dollars	Chained (2000) dollars	Current dollars	Chained (2000) dollars	Current dollars	Chained (2000) dollars
1946	11 241	8 011	141 389	. . .	. . .	. . .	. . .	. . .	. . .
1947	10 925	7 565	144 126	6.16	3.60	2.77	2.19	3.38	3.34
1948	11 206	7 832	146 631	5.62	3.77	2.96	2.30	3.63	3.51
1949	10 957	7 747	149 188	5.12	3.60	2.73	2.17	3.36	3.30
1947									
1st quarter	10 971	7 656	143 156	5.81	3.73	2.78	2.21	3.43	3.38
2nd quarter	10 908	7 460	143 803	5.77	3.70	2.78	2.21	3.42	3.38
3rd quarter	10 854	7 634	144 462	5.89	3.62	2.72	2.17	3.34	3.33
4th quarter	10 962	7 508	145 135	6.16	3.60	2.77	2.19	3.38	3.34
1948									
1st quarter	11 087	7 597	145 761	5.87	3.62	2.83	2.22	3.45	3.37
2nd quarter	11 238	7 826	146 341	5.89	3.67	2.86	2.24	3.49	3.42
3rd quarter	11 254	7 950	146 973	5.75	3.74	2.93	2.28	3.59	3.49
4th quarter	11 228	7 937	147 659	5.62	3.77	2.96	2.30	3.63	3.51
1949									
1st quarter	11 013	7 739	148 298	5.54	3.76	2.93	2.30	3.61	3.52
2nd quarter	10 937	7 733	148 891	5.27	3.68	2.79	2.24	3.44	3.42
3rd quarter	11 013	7 745	149 529	5.28	3.67	2.78	2.23	3.43	3.40
4th quarter	10 851	7 760	150 211	5.12	3.60	2.73	2.17	3.36	3.30
1950									
1st quarter	11 248	8 305	150 852	5.15	3.56	2.72	2.16	3.36	3.27
2nd quarter	11 542	8 226	151 385	5.17	3.49	2.71	2.14	3.33	3.24
3rd quarter	11 943	8 319	152 039	5.11	3.34	2.69	2.07	3.27	3.10
4th quarter	12 106	8 364	152 724	5.70	3.53	3.00	2.24	3.68	3.39
1951									
1st quarter	12 204	8 328	153 336	5.84	3.55	3.08	2.27	3.73	3.42
2nd quarter	12 362	8 428	153 947	5.88	3.67	3.21	2.39	3.93	3.64
3rd quarter	12 551	8 444	154 655	5.79	3.65	3.16	2.40	3.87	3.64
4th quarter	12 513	8 421	155 389	5.76	3.62	3.11	2.40	3.78	3.61
1952									
1st quarter	12 591	8 384	156 033	5.68	3.66	3.13	2.43	3.81	3.66
2nd quarter	12 551	8 452	156 644	5.54	3.62	3.04	2.38	3.72	3.60
3rd quarter	12 578	8 579	157 324	5.54	3.71	3.11	2.45	3.82	3.71
4th quarter	12 932	8 706	158 043	5.16	3.61	3.02	2.39	3.69	3.59
1953									
1st quarter	13 125	8 793	158 648	4.99	3.56	2.99	2.36	3.65	3.54
2nd quarter	13 176	8 883	159 234	4.92	3.57	3.02	2.38	3.71	3.57
3rd quarter	13 037	8 806	159 963	4.92	3.59	3.06	2.39	3.76	3.59
4th quarter	12 771	8 710	160 713	4.96	3.61	3.04	2.39	3.75	3.59
1954									
1st quarter	12 655	8 721	161 389	4.95	3.59	3.01	2.37	3.72	3.57
2nd quarter	12 616	8 685	162 044	4.84	3.54	2.95	2.32	3.65	3.50
3rd quarter	12 696	8 739	162 792	4.78	3.47	2.90	2.27	3.61	3.43
4th quarter	12 885	8 868	163 585	4.67	3.40	2.85	2.23	3.54	3.35
1955									
1st quarter	13 201	8 960	164 266	4.61	3.34	2.82	2.20	3.51	3.31
2nd quarter	13 364	9 137	164 926	4.50	3.33	2.84	2.21	3.48	3.27
3rd quarter	13 480	9 267	165 674	4.41	3.30	2.85	2.21	3.52	3.29
4th quarter	13 487	9 327	166 481	4.36	3.33	2.91	2.24	3.61	3.36
1956									
1st quarter	13 367	9 381	167 190	4.43	3.36	2.97	2.28	3.69	3.43
2nd quarter	13 418	9 436	167 869	4.51	3.37	3.00	2.30	3.72	3.45
3rd quarter	13 339	9 431	168 654	4.44	3.36	2.99	2.31	3.71	3.47
4th quarter	13 490	9 533	169 497	4.41	3.33	2.99	2.30	3.74	3.48
1957									
1st quarter	13 514	9 511	170 218	4.38	3.33	2.99	2.30	3.71	3.46
2nd quarter	13 425	9 534	170 915	4.42	3.36	3.01	2.33	3.74	3.51
3rd quarter	13 496	9 538	171 684	4.39	3.35	2.99	2.33	3.72	3.50
4th quarter	13 292	9 441	172 463	4.39	3.36	2.98	2.32	3.74	3.52
1958									
1st quarter	12 883	9 319	173 116	4.60	3.44	3.00	2.36	3.78	3.58
2nd quarter	12 909	9 343	173 781	4.58	3.44	2.96	2.33	3.73	3.55
3rd quarter	13 150	9 492	174 535	4.51	3.37	2.88	2.27	3.65	3.47
4th quarter	13 391	9 565	175 340	4.44	3.33	2.87	2.25	3.62	3.42
1959									
1st quarter	13 592	9 592	176 045	4.31	3.25	2.80	2.21	3.54	3.36
2nd quarter	13 896	9 738	176 727	4.28	3.24	2.83	2.23	3.59	3.40
3rd quarter	13 827	9 689	177 481	4.19	3.21	2.81	2.22	3.57	3.38
4th quarter	13 814	9 722	178 268	4.20	3.26	2.87	2.27	3.67	3.48
1960									
1st quarter	14 009	9 756	179 694	4.24	3.27	2.90	2.30	3.70	3.51
2nd quarter	13 890	9 770	180 335	4.16	3.26	2.88	2.30	3.68	3.51
3rd quarter	13 853	9 734	181 094	4.22	3.30	2.92	2.33	3.73	3.55
4th quarter	13 612	9 682	181 915	4.17	3.27	2.86	2.29	3.67	3.51
1961									
1st quarter	13 640	9 733	182 634	4.14	3.25	2.83	2.27	3.63	3.48
2nd quarter	13 843	9 843	183 337	4.06	3.23	2.80	2.25	3.63	3.48
3rd quarter	14 009	9 936	184 103	4.12	3.25	2.82	2.27	3.63	3.50
4th quarter	14 234	10 089	184 894	4.07	3.20	2.78	2.24	3.58	3.45

. . . = Not available.

Table 19-7. Per Capita Product and Income, Population, and Inventories to Sales Ratios—*Continued*

(Seasonally adjusted.)

NIPA Tables 5.7.5A, 5.7.5B, 5.7.6A, 5.7.6B, 7.1

| Year and quarter | Chained (2000) dollars per capita | | Population (mid-period, thousands) | Ratio, inventories at end of quarter to monthly rate of sales during the quarter | | | | | |
| | Gross domestic product | Disposable personal income | | Total private inventories to final sales of domestic business | | Nonfarm inventories to final sales of domestic business | | Nonfarm inventories to final sales of goods and structures | |
				Current dollars	Chained (2000) dollars	Current dollars	Chained (2000) dollars	Current dollars	Chained (2000) dollars
1962									
1st quarter	14 439	10 150	185 553	4.10	3.22	2.79	2.27	3.60	3.48
2nd quarter	14 545	10 226	186 203	4.04	3.19	2.77	2.26	3.58	3.48
3rd quarter	14 623	10 243	186 926	4.12	3.21	2.80	2.29	3.61	3.50
4th quarter	14 599	10 286	187 680	4.09	3.21	2.79	2.29	3.60	3.51
1963									
1st quarter	14 742	10 334	188 299	4.07	3.23	2.80	2.30	3.61	3.53
2nd quarter	14 878	10 398	188 906	4.00	3.19	2.76	2.27	3.58	3.50
3rd quarter	15 100	10 475	189 631	3.95	3.17	2.76	2.28	3.56	3.49
4th quarter	15 160	10 609	190 362	3.91	3.15	2.75	2.27	3.56	3.49
1964									
1st quarter	15 451	10 791	190 954	3.81	3.09	2.71	2.24	3.50	3.44
2nd quarter	15 581	11 051	191 560	3.75	3.07	2.70	2.24	3.50	3.45
3rd quarter	15 737	11 155	192 256	3.74	3.05	2.70	2.24	3.49	3.43
4th quarter	15 723	11 244	192 938	3.75	3.07	2.73	2.26	3.54	3.49
1965									
1st quarter	16 066	11 337	193 467	3.77	3.07	2.74	2.28	3.55	3.50
2nd quarter	16 238	11 430	193 994	3.78	3.05	2.73	2.27	3.54	3.49
3rd quarter	16 512	11 705	194 647	3.74	3.04	2.73	2.27	3.53	3.48
4th quarter	16 857	11 903	195 279	3.73	2.99	2.70	2.24	3.47	3.42
1966									
1st quarter	17 227	11 983	195 763	3.76	3.00	2.71	2.26	3.47	3.43
2nd quarter	17 241	11 981	196 277	3.83	3.06	2.77	2.33	3.58	3.56
3rd quarter	17 302	12 096	196 877	3.87	3.09	2.82	2.37	3.63	3.61
4th quarter	17 387	12 197	197 481	3.88	3.16	2.89	2.44	3.74	3.75
1967									
1st quarter	17 498	12 351	197 967	3.91	3.22	2.95	2.50	3.84	3.85
2nd quarter	17 456	12 418	198 455	3.90	3.21	2.93	2.49	3.80	3.83
3rd quarter	17 546	12 502	199 012	3.89	3.24	2.95	2.52	3.83	3.88
4th quarter	17 629	12 557	199 572	3.87	3.25	2.96	2.54	3.86	3.92
1968									
1st quarter	17 954	12 749	199 995	3.85	3.22	2.92	2.51	3.80	3.86
2nd quarter	18 217	12 932	200 452	3.84	3.24	2.90	2.52	3.79	3.90
3rd quarter	18 291	12 921	200 997	3.79	3.22	2.87	2.51	3.75	3.87
4th quarter	18 319	12 969	201 538	3.76	3.23	2.87	2.53	3.76	3.91
1969									
1st quarter	18 569	12 961	201 955	3.77	3.22	2.88	2.53	3.75	3.90
2nd quarter	18 580	13 060	202 419	3.81	3.25	2.88	2.56	3.78	3.95
3rd quarter	18 643	13 285	202 986	3.80	3.28	2.92	2.59	3.82	4.01
4th quarter	18 500	13 341	203 584	3.85	3.30	2.95	2.62	3.89	4.08
1970									
1st quarter	18 424	13 374	204 086	3.83	3.29	2.94	2.61	3.88	4.06
2nd quarter	18 401	13 567	204 721	3.83	3.31	2.94	2.62	3.89	4.10
3rd quarter	18 501	13 702	205 419	3.82	3.29	2.94	2.62	3.91	4.10
4th quarter	18 240	13 605	206 130	3.78	3.29	2.94	2.63	3.92	4.13
1971									
1st quarter	18 688	13 850	206 763	3.81	3.28	2.93	2.63	3.91	4.12
2nd quarter	18 739	14 008	207 362	3.81	3.29	2.92	2.63	3.90	4.12
3rd quarter	18 830	14 021	208 000	3.76	3.29	2.90	2.63	3.88	4.11
4th quarter	18 826	14 124	208 642	3.73	3.24	2.86	2.59	3.83	4.07
1972									
1st quarter	19 115	14 177	209 142	3.69	3.20	2.82	2.57	3.77	4.02
2nd quarter	19 520	14 270	209 637	3.72	3.18	2.81	2.55	3.74	3.98
3rd quarter	19 655	14 528	210 181	3.73	3.17	2.81	2.55	3.76	3.99
4th quarter	19 924	15 066	210 737	3.72	3.09	2.75	2.50	3.66	3.90
1973									
1st quarter	20 386	15 202	211 192	3.81	3.02	2.77	2.47	3.65	3.83
2nd quarter	20 576	15 309	211 663	4.00	3.06	2.84	2.50	3.74	3.88
3rd quarter	20 415	15 356	212 191	4.07	3.08	2.85	2.51	3.77	3.91
4th quarter	20 560	15 503	212 708	4.18	3.13	2.96	2.57	3.91	4.01
1974									
1st quarter	20 340	15 232	213 144	4.25	3.18	3.10	2.63	4.10	4.10
2nd quarter	20 355	15 074	213 602	4.27	3.22	3.26	2.67	4.33	4.18
3rd quarter	20 107	15 088	214 147	4.46	3.25	3.37	2.70	4.49	4.24
4th quarter	19 976	14 985	214 700	4.49	3.37	3.52	2.82	4.73	4.50
1975									
1st quarter	19 697	14 901	215 135	4.28	3.33	3.38	2.76	4.56	4.41
2nd quarter	19 794	15 555	215 652	4.24	3.26	3.28	2.70	4.44	4.32
3rd quarter	20 070	15 299	216 289	4.17	3.22	3.22	2.66	4.34	4.24
4th quarter	20 281	15 412	216 848	4.02	3.17	3.14	2.62	4.24	4.17
1976									
1st quarter	20 692	15 604	217 314	3.96	3.14	3.12	2.60	4.21	4.13
2nd quarter	20 803	15 693	217 776	4.08	3.17	3.19	2.64	4.31	4.20
3rd quarter	20 849	15 792	218 338	4.01	3.19	3.21	2.66	4.37	4.23
4th quarter	20 942	15 864	218 917	3.93	3.14	3.17	2.63	4.32	4.21

Table 19-7. Per Capita Product and Income, Population, and Inventories to Sales Ratios—*Continued*

(Seasonally adjusted.)   **NIPA Tables 5.7.5A, 5.7.5B, 5.7.6A, 5.7.6B, 7.1**

Year and quarter	Chained (2000) dollars per capita		Population (mid-period, thousands)	Ratio, inventories at end of quarter to monthly rate of sales during the quarter					
	Gross domestic product	Disposable personal income		Total private inventories to final sales of domestic business		Nonfarm inventories to final sales of domestic business		Nonfarm inventories to final sales of goods and structures	
				Current dollars	Chained (2000) dollars	Current dollars	Chained (2000) dollars	Current dollars	Chained (2000) dollars
1977									
1st quarter	21 146	15 858	219 427	3.66	3.14	3.18	2.63	4.34	4.20
2nd quarter	21 509	15 991	219 956	3.69	3.11	3.14	2.61	4.26	4.14
3rd quarter	21 833	16 188	220 573	3.75	3.13	3.14	2.62	4.28	4.18
4th quarter	21 769	16 465	221 201	3.86	3.13	3.14	2.62	4.29	4.18
1978									
1st quarter	21 788	16 523	221 719	4.01	3.18	3.20	2.67	4.41	4.28
2nd quarter	22 589	16 674	222 281	3.90	3.06	3.10	2.58	4.21	4.08
3rd quarter	22 745	16 766	222 933	3.92	3.06	3.11	2.58	4.20	4.07
4th quarter	22 978	16 854	223 583	3.95	3.06	3.12	2.58	4.20	4.06
1979									
1st quarter	22 964	17 005	224 152	4.13	3.09	3.20	2.61	4.30	4.10
2nd quarter	22 926	16 843	224 737	4.17	3.13	3.27	2.64	4.42	4.18
3rd quarter	23 021	16 890	225 418	4.15	3.08	3.26	2.60	4.38	4.07
4th quarter	23 018	16 989	226 117	4.17	3.08	3.33	2.60	4.47	4.08
1980									
1st quarter	23 026	17 064	226 754	4.23	3.09	3.43	2.61	4.63	4.10
2nd quarter	22 499	16 711	227 389	4.38	3.20	3.55	2.71	4.84	4.29
3rd quarter	22 394	16 833	228 070	4.32	3.10	3.48	2.64	4.75	4.18
4th quarter	22 748	17 145	228 689	4.23	3.05	3.42	2.60	4.69	4.13
1981									
1st quarter	23 161	17 044	229 155	4.24	3.09	3.46	2.63	4.73	4.15
2nd quarter	22 929	17 046	229 674	4.23	3.10	3.45	2.63	4.74	4.18
3rd quarter	23 143	17 382	230 301	4.18	3.15	3.46	2.67	4.76	4.23
4th quarter	22 795	17 379	230 903	4.15	3.20	3.47	2.71	4.80	4.31
1982									
1st quarter	22 373	17 344	231 395	4.17	3.20	3.45	2.70	4.79	4.31
2nd quarter	22 444	17 429	231 906	4.13	3.20	3.41	2.70	4.76	4.31
3rd quarter	22 302	17 460	232 498	4.10	3.25	3.41	2.73	4.82	4.40
4th quarter	22 267	17 446	233 074	3.95	3.15	3.28	2.64	4.67	4.26
1983									
1st quarter	22 496	17 557	233 546	3.87	3.08	3.18	2.58	4.56	4.18
2nd quarter	22 956	17 659	234 028	3.80	3.02	3.13	2.54	4.49	4.11
3rd quarter	23 352	17 867	234 603	3.72	2.95	3.11	2.51	4.46	4.05
4th quarter	23 774	18 228	235 153	3.68	2.91	3.07	2.49	4.39	3.98
1984									
1st quarter	24 192	18 614	235 605	3.76	2.95	3.13	2.53	4.48	4.04
2nd quarter	24 559	18 922	236 082	3.74	2.96	3.14	2.53	4.49	4.04
3rd quarter	24 737	19 183	236 657	3.73	2.99	3.16	2.57	4.53	4.09
4th quarter	24 880	19 322	237 232	3.70	2.98	3.14	2.56	4.50	4.07
1985									
1st quarter	25 064	19 270	237 673	3.59	2.93	3.05	2.52	4.40	4.02
2nd quarter	25 224	19 622	238 176	3.53	2.93	3.03	2.51	4.38	4.02
3rd quarter	25 553	19 433	238 789	3.45	2.90	2.97	2.48	4.30	3.98
4th quarter	25 685	19 584	239 387	3.49	2.92	2.99	2.50	4.36	4.03
1986									
1st quarter	25 879	19 779	239 861	3.40	2.91	2.92	2.50	4.27	4.01
2nd quarter	25 927	19 944	240 368	3.36	2.91	2.90	2.50	4.25	4.02
3rd quarter	26 111	19 976	240 962	3.28	2.86	2.84	2.46	4.15	3.95
4th quarter	26 180	19 928	241 539	3.23	2.84	2.80	2.44	4.12	3.92
1987									
1st quarter	26 301	20 059	242 009	3.30	2.87	2.85	2.48	4.22	4.02
2nd quarter	26 534	19 802	242 520	3.28	2.83	2.84	2.46	4.20	3.97
3rd quarter	26 709	20 102	243 120	3.24	2.79	2.81	2.42	4.14	3.90
4th quarter	27 108	20 327	243 721	3.31	2.84	2.88	2.47	4.25	3.99
1988									
1st quarter	27 186	20 543	244 208	3.28	2.80	2.84	2.44	4.22	3.94
2nd quarter	27 475	20 682	244 716	3.27	2.77	2.84	2.43	4.20	3.91
3rd quarter	27 549	20 800	245 354	3.28	2.76	2.84	2.44	4.22	3.94
4th quarter	27 844	20 934	245 966	3.27	2.75	2.84	2.43	4.22	3.92
1989									
1st quarter	28 070	21 165	246 460	3.30	2.76	2.87	2.44	4.28	3.94
2nd quarter	28 190	21 048	247 017	3.27	2.77	2.86	2.45	4.25	3.94
3rd quarter	28 313	21 094	247 698	3.20	2.73	2.81	2.43	4.16	3.89
4th quarter	28 308	21 177	248 374	3.22	2.75	2.82	2.44	4.22	3.94
1990									
1st quarter	28 570	21 322	248 936	3.16	2.72	2.77	2.42	4.11	3.88
2nd quarter	28 554	21 379	249 711	3.16	2.75	2.76	2.45	4.16	3.97
3rd quarter	28 455	21 324	250 595	3.19	2.76	2.81	2.46	4.24	4.00
4th quarter	28 141	21 101	251 482	3.21	2.77	2.81	2.46	4.27	4.02
1991									
1st quarter	27 911	21 052	252 258	3.16	2.79	2.76	2.48	4.21	4.05
2nd quarter	28 003	21 129	253 063	3.07	2.76	2.69	2.45	4.12	4.02
3rd quarter	28 038	21 104	253 965	3.03	2.75	2.68	2.45	4.12	4.03
4th quarter	28 074	21 149	254 835	3.04	2.77	2.69	2.46	4.17	4.07

Table 19-7. Per Capita Product and Income, Population, and Inventories to Sales Ratios—*Continued*

(Seasonally adjusted.)   NIPA Tables 5.7.5A, 5.7.5B, 5.7.6A, 5.7.6B, 7.1

| Year and quarter | Chained (2000) dollars per capita | | Population (mid-period, thousands) | Ratio, inventories at end of quarter to monthly rate of sales during the quarter | | | | | |
| | | | | Total private inventories to final sales of domestic business | | Nonfarm inventories to final sales of domestic business | | Nonfarm inventories to final sales of goods and structures | |
	Gross domestic product	Disposable personal income		Current dollars	Chained (2000) dollars	Current dollars	Chained (2000) dollars	Current dollars	Chained (2000) dollars
1992									
1st quarter	28 281	21 417	255 585	2.98	2.72	2.61	2.41	4.07	3.98
2nd quarter	28 459	21 505	256 439	2.97	2.71	2.61	2.40	4.08	3.98
3rd quarter	28 632	21 514	257 386	2.95	2.69	2.59	2.39	4.06	3.95
4th quarter	28 848	21 757	258 277	2.90	2.67	2.55	2.36	3.99	3.90
1993									
1st quarter	28 798	21 279	259 039	2.93	2.69	2.57	2.39	4.04	3.96
2nd quarter	28 856	21 515	259 826	2.91	2.68	2.56	2.39	4.02	3.94
3rd quarter	28 905	21 469	260 714	2.87	2.66	2.53	2.38	4.00	3.93
4th quarter	29 201	21 706	261 547	2.83	2.63	2.50	2.35	3.92	3.86
1994									
1st quarter	29 419	21 468	262 250	2.84	2.64	2.49	2.35	3.92	3.87
2nd quarter	29 715	21 797	263 020	2.84	2.66	2.52	2.37	3.96	3.89
3rd quarter	29 785	21 870	263 870	2.84	2.66	2.52	2.36	3.96	3.88
4th quarter	30 043	22 106	264 678	2.87	2.67	2.54	2.38	3.99	3.88
1995									
1st quarter	30 046	22 180	265 388	2.91	2.69	2.59	2.40	4.07	3.91
2nd quarter	30 014	22 100	266 142	2.92	2.69	2.62	2.41	4.13	3.95
3rd quarter	30 161	22 143	267 000	2.88	2.65	2.58	2.39	4.08	3.91
4th quarter	30 289	22 191	267 820	2.86	2.63	2.56	2.38	4.05	3.88
1996									
1st quarter	30 427	22 385	268 487	2.82	2.61	2.53	2.35	3.99	3.84
2nd quarter	30 838	22 506	269 251	2.79	2.58	2.49	2.33	3.93	3.79
3rd quarter	30 995	22 624	270 128	2.79	2.59	2.48	2.33	3.92	3.79
4th quarter	31 258	22 667	270 991	2.74	2.56	2.45	2.30	3.87	3.74
1997									
1st quarter	31 416	22 823	271 709	2.72	2.56	2.43	2.31	3.83	3.73
2nd quarter	31 803	22 944	272 487	2.71	2.59	2.42	2.33	3.84	3.78
3rd quarter	32 092	23 129	273 391	2.68	2.57	2.39	2.32	3.78	3.74
4th quarter	32 228	23 361	274 246	2.68	2.60	2.41	2.34	3.82	3.78
1998									
1st quarter	32 501	23 798	274 950	2.68	2.63	2.41	2.38	3.84	3.84
2nd quarter	32 627	24 079	275 703	2.64	2.62	2.39	2.37	3.79	3.82
3rd quarter	32 900	24 265	276 564	2.60	2.62	2.36	2.37	3.74	3.81
4th quarter	33 299	24 380	277 400	2.56	2.59	2.33	2.35	3.67	3.75
1999									
1st quarter	33 497	24 498	278 103	2.56	2.61	2.33	2.37	3.69	3.80
2nd quarter	33 682	24 464	278 864	2.55	2.59	2.32	2.35	3.67	3.77
3rd quarter	33 967	24 507	279 751	2.56	2.59	2.34	2.36	3.71	3.78
4th quarter	34 467	24 789	280 592	2.59	2.60	2.37	2.37	3.76	3.79
2000									
1st quarter	34 467	25 274	281 304	2.58	2.58	2.36	2.36	3.75	3.76
2nd quarter	34 921	25 381	282 007	2.60	2.60	2.38	2.38	3.79	3.81
3rd quarter	34 784	25 635	282 787	2.61	2.61	2.40	2.40	3.83	3.84
4th quarter	34 871	25 602	283 554	2.63	2.62	2.41	2.40	3.85	3.86
2001									
1st quarter	34 746	25 624	284 220	2.62	2.61	2.38	2.39	3.82	3.84
2nd quarter	34 770	25 455	284 902	2.58	2.61	2.35	2.39	3.76	3.84
3rd quarter	34 555	26 088	285 659	2.54	2.61	2.32	2.39	3.72	3.84
4th quarter	34 603	25 650	286 396	2.44	2.55	2.23	2.33	3.57	3.74
2002									
1st quarter	34 761	26 304	287 028	2.45	2.56	2.24	2.34	3.61	3.77
2nd quarter	34 871	26 367	287 673	2.45	2.55	2.25	2.34	3.64	3.78
3rd quarter	34 988	26 197	288 406	2.48	2.56	2.26	2.35	3.68	3.79
4th quarter	34 920	26 146	289 113	2.51	2.58	2.28	2.37	3.73	3.85
2003									
1st quarter	34 952	26 204	289 714	2.53	2.57	2.30	2.36	3.78	3.83
2nd quarter	35 173	26 470	290 356	2.48	2.54	2.26	2.33	3.71	3.78
3rd quarter	35 725	26 814	291 076	2.44	2.49	2.21	2.28	3.59	3.66
4th quarter	35 874	26 861	291 770	2.45	2.49	2.22	2.28	3.62	3.67
2004									
1st quarter	36 067	27 054	292 332	2.48	2.48	2.24	2.28	3.67	3.68
2nd quarter	36 299	27 154	292 965	2.51	2.49	2.26	2.28	3.70	3.69
3rd quarter	36 531	27 281	293 687	2.52	2.49	2.28	2.28	3.74	3.67
4th quarter	36 671	27 712	294 409	2.53	2.49	2.30	2.28	3.77	3.68
2005									
1st quarter	36 865	27 321	295 020	2.56	2.50	2.33	2.30	3.82	3.71
2nd quarter	37 025	27 432	295 639	2.51	2.47	2.29	2.27	3.75	3.63
3rd quarter	37 283	27 276	296 378	2.52	2.45	2.30	2.25	3.76	3.59
4th quarter	37 313	27 706	297 109	2.56	2.47	2.33	2.27	3.84	3.64
2006									
1st quarter	37 674	27 991	297 743	2.52	2.45	2.31	2.25	3.78	3.60
2nd quarter	37 841	28 018	298 399	2.56	2.45	2.35	2.26	3.85	3.61
3rd quarter	37 818	28 101	299 175	2.58	2.47	2.36	2.28	3.88	3.66
4th quarter	37 859	28 424	299 965	2.56	2.45	2.34	2.26	3.87	3.65

Table 19-8. National Income by Type of Income

(Billions of dollars, quarterly data are at seasonally adjusted annual rates.)   **NIPA Tables 1.7.5, 1.12**

Year and quarter	National income, total	Compensation of employees — Total	Wage and salary accruals	Supplements to wages and salaries	Proprietors' income with IVA and CCAdj — Farm	Nonfarm	Rental income of persons with CCAdj	Corporate profits with IVA and CCAdj	Net interest and miscellaneous payments	Taxes on production and imports	Less: Subsidies	Business current transfer payments, net	Addendum: Net national factor income
1946	198.5	119.6	112.0	7.6	14.2	21.4	7.1	17.8	1.9	16.8	1.2	0.7	182.1
1947	216.6	130.1	123.1	7.0	14.4	20.2	7.2	23.7	2.5	18.1	0.2	0.7	198.0
1948	243.0	142.0	135.6	6.4	16.7	22.6	7.9	31.2	2.6	19.7	0.3	0.7	222.9
1949	238.0	141.9	134.7	7.1	12.0	22.7	8.2	29.1	2.9	20.9	0.3	0.7	216.6
1947													
1st quarter	211.7	127.2	119.7	7.5	16.0	20.6	7.0	20.6	2.3	17.7	0.3	0.7	193.7
2nd quarter	213.0	128.7	121.5	7.2	12.4	20.0	7.1	24.1	2.4	17.7	0.2	0.7	194.7
3rd quarter	216.6	130.1	123.4	6.6	14.1	19.8	7.3	24.2	2.6	18.0	0.2	0.7	198.0
4th quarter	225.2	134.3	127.8	6.5	14.9	20.3	7.5	25.9	2.6	19.0	0.1	0.7	205.5
1948													
1st quarter	233.7	137.9	131.4	6.5	14.5	21.6	7.7	29.9	2.5	19.0	0.2	0.7	214.1
2nd quarter	242.3	139.6	133.2	6.4	18.0	22.5	7.9	31.6	2.6	19.7	0.1	0.7	222.0
3rd quarter	247.2	144.5	138.1	6.4	17.9	23.1	7.9	30.8	2.6	20.0	0.4	0.7	226.9
4th quarter	248.9	145.9	139.5	6.4	16.4	23.2	8.0	32.3	2.6	20.3	0.6	0.7	228.5
1949													
1st quarter	241.9	144.1	137.0	7.1	12.7	22.8	7.9	31.0	2.7	20.4	0.3	0.7	221.2
2nd quarter	237.6	141.9	134.6	7.2	12.1	22.7	8.0	28.7	2.8	20.8	0.2	0.7	216.2
3rd quarter	238.1	141.0	133.9	7.1	11.6	22.6	8.3	29.9	2.9	21.3	0.3	0.7	216.4
4th quarter	234.5	140.5	133.4	7.0	11.5	22.7	8.5	26.7	3.0	21.2	0.2	0.8	212.8
1950													
1st quarter	244.2	144.6	137.1	7.5	12.2	23.4	8.8	30.2	3.1	21.6	0.4	0.7	222.4
2nd quarter	255.7	150.6	142.9	7.8	12.2	24.1	9.0	33.8	3.2	22.5	0.6	0.8	233.0
3rd quarter	273.4	159.0	150.8	8.2	13.1	25.7	9.2	38.5	3.2	24.4	0.5	0.9	248.6
4th quarter	284.3	166.9	158.3	8.6	13.9	25.6	9.5	41.6	3.2	23.4	0.8	1.0	260.7
1951													
1st quarter	295.9	175.0	165.5	9.4	15.0	27.1	9.7	40.4	3.4	25.1	0.9	1.1	270.5
2nd quarter	301.7	180.6	170.8	9.7	15.4	27.1	10.0	40.6	3.6	24.1	0.8	1.2	277.2
3rd quarter	306.9	183.7	173.8	9.9	15.1	27.6	10.3	41.2	3.8	24.5	0.6	1.2	281.7
4th quarter	312.9	186.5	176.2	10.2	15.6	27.9	10.5	42.5	3.8	25.3	0.7	1.3	286.9
1952													
1st quarter	314.8	191.5	181.2	10.3	13.7	28.2	10.8	39.8	3.9	26.1	0.5	1.3	287.9
2nd quarter	316.5	192.8	182.4	10.4	14.5	28.6	11.1	37.8	4.0	26.9	0.4	1.3	288.8
3rd quarter	322.4	196.3	185.7	10.6	15.9	28.9	11.4	37.6	4.1	27.3	0.4	1.2	294.2
4th quarter	333.6	204.1	193.3	10.8	13.0	29.6	11.7	41.9	4.2	28.2	0.3	1.2	304.5
1953													
1st quarter	339.9	208.0	196.9	11.1	13.0	30.1	12.0	42.6	4.5	28.8	0.3	1.3	310.2
2nd quarter	342.9	211.3	200.1	11.3	12.4	30.0	12.3	41.8	4.6	29.2	0.1	1.3	312.5
3rd quarter	341.5	211.5	200.3	11.2	11.7	30.0	12.6	40.7	4.8	29.3	0.3	1.2	311.3
4th quarter	333.7	210.0	198.7	11.3	11.5	29.9	12.9	33.8	5.0	29.2	-0.2	1.1	303.1
1954													
1st quarter	335.4	208.1	196.4	11.7	12.8	29.9	13.2	36.1	5.2	28.7	-0.3	1.0	305.3
2nd quarter	335.5	207.7	196.0	11.7	11.6	30.4	13.4	37.3	5.5	28.8	0.3	1.0	306.0
3rd quarter	338.9	208.3	196.3	11.9	11.7	30.6	13.6	39.2	5.7	28.8	-0.1	1.0	309.1
4th quarter	347.9	212.6	200.4	12.2	10.6	31.6	13.7	42.8	6.0	29.3	-0.3	1.0	317.3
1955													
1st quarter	360.0	217.1	204.2	12.9	10.9	32.6	13.8	48.0	6.1	30.3	-0.2	1.2	328.4
2nd quarter	370.1	223.6	210.3	13.3	11.2	33.3	13.8	49.3	6.3	31.2	-0.1	1.3	337.5
3rd quarter	377.0	228.6	214.7	13.9	10.6	34.1	13.9	49.9	6.2	32.0	-0.4	1.5	343.2
4th quarter	383.6	233.6	219.5	14.1	9.9	34.7	14.0	51.0	6.3	32.5	-0.2	1.6	349.4
1956													
1st quarter	387.2	238.0	223.3	14.8	10.1	34.8	14.1	48.9	6.6	33.1	-0.1	1.7	352.5
2nd quarter	392.9	242.6	227.5	15.1	10.3	35.2	14.1	48.8	6.8	33.6	0.2	1.7	357.7
3rd quarter	397.0	245.7	230.0	15.8	10.8	35.4	14.2	47.9	7.1	34.6	0.5	1.8	361.1
4th quarter	405.2	251.6	235.4	16.2	10.8	36.1	14.3	48.6	7.0	35.7	0.8	1.8	368.4
1957													
1st quarter	412.1	255.3	238.3	17.1	9.8	37.1	14.4	50.4	7.7	36.2	0.9	1.9	374.9
2nd quarter	414.4	257.0	239.6	17.4	10.4	37.4	14.5	49.4	8.0	36.6	0.8	1.9	376.7
3rd quarter	418.4	259.7	241.8	17.8	10.9	37.8	14.6	48.8	8.2	37.0	0.6	1.9	380.0
4th quarter	412.1	258.1	240.1	18.1	10.6	37.3	14.9	44.8	8.2	36.8	0.5	1.9	373.9
1958													
1st quarter	407.2	255.2	237.4	17.9	13.2	37.0	15.2	39.5	9.0	36.8	0.6	1.9	369.0
2nd quarter	408.4	254.8	236.9	17.9	12.9	37.4	15.3	40.0	9.5	37.4	0.8	1.8	370.0
3rd quarter	418.9	260.9	242.6	18.3	12.0	38.0	15.5	44.2	9.8	37.8	1.0	1.8	380.4
4th quarter	432.5	267.2	248.4	18.8	11.2	38.9	15.6	50.4	9.9	39.0	1.2	1.7	393.1
1959													
1st quarter	445.0	274.5	254.0	20.5	10.8	39.6	15.6	54.5	8.8	39.8	1.1	1.7	403.7
2nd quarter	459.8	281.6	260.6	21.1	9.8	40.9	16.0	59.6	9.8	40.3	0.9	1.8	417.7
3rd quarter	456.6	282.3	260.9	21.4	9.3	41.2	16.4	54.2	9.8	41.8	1.1	1.8	413.2
4th quarter	461.9	285.5	263.9	21.6	10.0	40.9	16.7	54.4	10.1	42.5	1.1	1.8	417.6
1960													
1st quarter	474.8	294.1	270.8	23.3	9.5	40.6	16.9	58.0	10.2	43.7	1.0	1.8	429.3
2nd quarter	474.8	296.9	273.4	23.5	10.4	40.5	17.0	53.9	10.1	44.4	1.3	1.8	428.9
3rd quarter	475.8	297.6	274.0	23.7	10.8	40.1	17.2	52.8	10.7	44.9	1.0	1.9	429.3
4th quarter	474.0	297.1	273.3	23.8	11.1	40.0	17.4	50.4	11.2	45.3	1.2	1.9	427.2
1961													
1st quarter	476.1	298.0	273.8	24.2	11.3	41.0	17.6	49.5	11.6	45.8	1.6	2.0	429.1
2nd quarter	485.8	302.2	277.6	24.6	10.7	41.9	17.8	53.8	12.2	46.5	2.0	2.0	438.6
3rd quarter	495.2	307.2	282.3	24.9	10.8	42.5	18.0	56.1	12.6	47.3	2.2	2.0	447.3
4th quarter	509.2	313.8	288.4	25.4	11.3	43.3	18.2	60.0	13.4	48.4	2.3	2.1	460.0

Table 19-8. National Income by Type of Income—*Continued*

(Billions of dollars, quarterly data are at seasonally adjusted annual rates.)

NIPA Tables 1.7.5, 1.12

| Year and quarter | National income, total | Compensation of employees | | | Proprietors' income with IVA and CCAdj | | Rental income of persons with CCAdj | Corporate profits with IVA and CCAdj | Net interest and miscellaneous payments | Taxes on production and imports | Less: Subsidies | Business current transfer payments, net | Addendum: Net national factor income |
		Total	Wage and salary accruals	Supplements to wages and salaries	Farm	Nonfarm							
1962													
1st quarter	520.2	320.4	293.3	27.2	11.7	43.7	18.5	62.6	13.1	49.4	2.3	2.2	470.0
2nd quarter	526.9	326.4	298.7	27.6	10.9	44.3	18.7	61.9	14.1	50.0	2.4	2.2	476.3
3rd quarter	532.9	329.2	301.2	28.0	10.5	44.8	18.9	63.2	14.6	50.9	2.2	2.3	481.1
4th quarter	540.3	332.6	304.2	28.4	11.0	44.7	19.1	65.4	15.0	51.4	2.2	2.3	487.9
1963													
1st quarter	546.7	337.5	308.0	29.5	11.2	44.8	19.3	65.4	14.6	52.1	2.0	2.6	492.8
2nd quarter	556.1	342.4	312.4	30.0	10.6	45.3	19.5	68.7	14.8	53.0	2.2	2.6	501.3
3rd quarter	564.6	347.4	316.8	30.6	10.4	45.9	19.6	70.1	15.3	54.0	2.3	2.7	508.9
4th quarter	574.9	353.6	322.2	31.3	10.9	46.8	19.6	71.7	15.8	54.7	2.4	2.8	518.4
1964													
1st quarter	587.7	360.0	328.2	31.8	9.6	48.5	19.6	76.1	16.6	55.7	2.7	2.9	530.4
2nd quarter	597.4	367.4	334.8	32.5	9.3	49.7	19.6	76.1	17.1	56.8	2.9	2.9	539.2
3rd quarter	608.9	374.7	341.4	33.3	9.1	50.5	19.7	77.3	17.9	57.9	2.6	3.3	549.1
4th quarter	616.7	380.7	346.7	34.0	10.2	50.6	19.6	76.4	18.1	58.8	2.7	3.4	555.6
1965													
1st quarter	635.1	387.3	352.8	34.5	11.2	51.0	19.9	84.3	19.0	60.2	2.9	3.6	572.8
2nd quarter	646.1	394.1	358.9	35.2	11.8	51.6	20.1	86.4	19.5	60.4	3.0	3.6	583.5
3rd quarter	657.0	402.3	366.2	36.1	12.0	52.2	20.3	87.6	20.0	60.6	3.0	3.6	594.5
4th quarter	675.6	414.3	377.1	37.2	12.3	53.6	20.3	91.6	20.0	61.9	3.1	3.6	612.1
1966													
1st quarter	695.1	426.7	385.8	40.9	14.6	54.7	20.7	94.7	21.1	61.4	3.6	3.6	632.6
2nd quarter	704.6	437.8	395.9	41.9	12.4	55.0	20.6	93.4	21.9	62.9	3.9	3.5	641.1
3rd quarter	715.9	449.0	406.1	42.8	12.1	55.5	20.9	91.7	22.7	63.8	4.1	3.5	651.8
4th quarter	728.3	457.1	413.5	43.7	12.0	56.3	20.9	93.0	23.8	65.0	4.2	3.5	663.1
1967													
1st quarter	734.7	463.3	418.8	44.4	11.7	57.3	21.1	90.5	24.7	65.6	4.0	3.6	668.5
2nd quarter	741.8	469.0	423.6	45.4	10.9	57.9	21.2	89.5	25.5	66.9	3.9	3.7	674.1
3rd quarter	757.6	478.7	432.0	46.6	11.8	59.2	21.2	91.0	25.8	68.8	3.7	3.8	687.6
4th quarter	773.4	489.7	441.6	48.1	11.4	59.1	21.1	94.3	26.2	70.7	3.7	3.9	701.7
1968													
1st quarter	794.3	504.5	454.2	50.3	11.5	60.7	20.9	95.5	26.6	73.5	4.0	4.1	719.6
2nd quarter	815.1	517.6	465.9	51.7	11.1	62.5	20.9	99.4	27.0	75.5	4.2	4.3	738.3
3rd quarter	833.6	531.4	478.3	53.1	11.6	63.7	21.0	99.6	27.1	77.8	4.2	4.4	754.4
4th quarter	849.6	543.8	489.4	54.4	11.8	64.2	20.8	100.7	27.7	79.2	4.2	4.6	769.0
1969													
1st quarter	866.2	555.9	499.1	56.8	11.4	64.8	21.1	100.4	30.5	80.7	4.3	4.9	784.0
2nd quarter	882.1	569.8	511.4	58.4	12.4	65.1	21.1	97.2	32.1	83.0	4.5	5.0	797.6
3rd quarter	900.7	586.6	526.4	60.1	12.9	65.1	21.3	94.5	33.7	85.3	4.7	5.0	814.1
4th quarter	909.7	598.2	536.5	61.8	13.9	64.0	21.2	89.5	34.6	86.8	4.7	5.0	821.4
1970													
1st quarter	914.5	608.6	545.1	63.5	13.4	64.3	21.2	82.0	36.0	88.6	4.7	4.8	825.4
2nd quarter	926.1	614.2	549.1	65.1	12.2	64.9	20.9	85.7	38.1	90.6	4.8	4.6	836.0
3rd quarter	941.3	622.2	555.7	66.4	13.0	66.2	21.5	85.8	40.5	92.6	4.7	4.4	849.1
4th quarter	941.8	623.9	556.3	67.6	12.3	67.4	21.8	80.9	41.9	94.2	4.8	4.3	848.3
1971													
1st quarter	979.3	641.6	570.2	71.4	13.2	68.6	21.7	94.4	43.1	97.8	4.8	4.3	882.6
2nd quarter	999.0	653.7	580.3	73.4	13.1	70.8	22.3	96.6	44.0	99.1	4.8	4.3	900.5
3rd quarter	1 016.3	664.1	588.8	75.3	12.7	72.5	22.7	98.9	44.1	101.8	4.5	4.3	915.0
4th quarter	1 037.6	676.3	599.0	77.3	13.9	74.4	23.1	102.2	44.3	103.8	4.6	4.4	934.2
1972													
1st quarter	1 069.0	701.1	618.0	83.2	12.9	75.7	23.7	107.2	45.2	104.7	6.1	4.7	965.7
2nd quarter	1 088.7	715.8	630.5	85.3	15.1	76.6	20.7	108.0	46.5	106.9	6.2	4.8	982.7
3rd quarter	1 120.0	729.7	642.4	87.3	17.0	79.5	24.6	113.0	48.9	109.0	7.2	5.0	1 012.6
4th quarter	1 167.2	753.9	664.3	89.7	22.2	84.5	24.6	120.2	51.1	111.6	7.1	5.2	1 056.4
1973													
1st quarter	1 205.3	781.7	683.4	98.3	21.7	84.3	24.5	127.2	51.3	114.7	5.9	5.7	1 090.7
2nd quarter	1 229.4	800.8	700.1	100.7	27.1	84.0	24.5	123.8	52.8	116.3	5.7	6.1	1 113.0
3rd quarter	1 257.8	819.9	716.2	103.7	29.4	85.0	23.5	124.0	56.8	118.5	4.7	5.9	1 138.6
4th quarter	1 297.0	842.5	735.4	107.1	37.4	85.0	24.5	127.0	60.0	119.8	4.6	6.1	1 176.5
1974													
1st quarter	1 308.9	860.7	748.2	112.5	28.4	87.5	24.7	120.0	64.4	120.9	3.6	6.6	1 185.6
2nd quarter	1 329.6	881.4	765.3	116.1	19.8	89.0	24.0	118.3	69.1	124.2	2.9	6.9	1 201.6
3rd quarter	1 357.6	903.1	783.1	120.0	21.2	91.7	24.4	114.5	72.4	127.2	3.2	7.3	1 227.3
4th quarter	1 372.5	915.8	792.5	123.3	23.4	91.4	24.2	110.4	77.3	127.8	3.6	7.7	1 242.4
1975													
1st quarter	1 380.6	919.5	791.9	127.6	19.4	93.8	24.1	112.4	80.7	129.0	4.2	8.7	1 249.9
2nd quarter	1 412.3	931.7	800.4	131.4	19.9	95.5	23.8	125.3	80.8	133.2	4.3	9.5	1 277.0
3rd quarter	1 473.2	957.7	821.3	136.4	23.5	98.9	23.7	147.3	82.2	138.4	4.6	9.7	1 333.3
4th quarter	1 517.4	987.6	845.8	141.9	24.1	102.8	23.2	154.3	82.8	141.3	4.9	9.8	1 374.8
1976													
1st quarter	1 567.4	1 022.4	871.2	151.1	19.2	108.4	22.9	167.1	82.5	141.9	5.1	9.8	1 422.4
2nd quarter	1 593.2	1 046.1	889.4	156.8	16.7	113.2	21.9	161.8	85.2	145.1	4.8	9.8	1 445.0
3rd quarter	1 626.0	1 070.8	908.4	162.4	15.9	117.8	22.1	162.4	86.6	147.9	5.1	9.5	1 475.6
4th quarter	1 660.7	1 098.1	929.9	168.1	16.1	121.3	22.2	162.1	87.9	151.5	5.5	9.0	1 507.7

Table 19-8. National Income by Type of Income—*Continued*

(Billions of dollars, quarterly data are at seasonally adjusted annual rates.)   **NIPA Tables 1.7.5, 1.12**

| Year and quarter | National income, total | Compensation of employees | | | Proprietors' income with IVA and CCAdj | | Rental income of persons with CCAdj | Corporate profits with IVA and CCAdj | Net interest and miscellaneous payments | Taxes on production and imports | Less: Subsidies | Business current transfer payments, net | Addendum: Net national factor income |
		Total	Wage and salary accruals	Supplements to wages and salaries	Farm	Nonfarm							
1977													
1st quarter	1 706.2	1 127.0	950.0	177.0	15.7	124.6	22.2	170.7	90.5	155.0	5.8	8.6	1 550.7
2nd quarter	1 775.3	1 164.4	980.9	183.5	13.9	127.8	20.6	191.9	98.6	158.2	5.9	8.2	1 617.2
3rd quarter	1 833.1	1 196.9	1 007.5	189.4	11.5	131.8	20.0	207.1	105.1	161.7	6.4	8.3	1 672.4
4th quarter	1 881.1	1 233.7	1 038.2	195.6	21.7	135.8	19.8	200.1	110.1	164.5	10.3	8.6	1 721.2
1978													
1st quarter	1 917.3	1 269.7	1 064.2	205.5	18.3	139.5	21.4	191.7	111.3	167.2	8.7	9.6	1 751.9
2nd quarter	2 012.2	1 318.4	1 106.4	212.0	20.6	146.7	20.9	218.7	113.9	173.3	8.4	10.2	1 839.1
3rd quarter	2 058.2	1 355.7	1 138.0	217.7	20.4	150.0	22.7	222.8	115.3	170.0	8.3	10.9	1 886.8
4th quarter	2 121.9	1 400.6	1 176.2	224.3	19.1	152.1	23.3	233.3	119.6	174.2	10.4	11.5	1 948.0
1979													
1st quarter	2 177.9	1 445.3	1 210.2	235.1	23.3	154.8	25.0	223.8	126.6	176.7	8.4	12.5	1 998.8
2nd quarter	2 216.0	1 477.5	1 236.3	241.2	21.4	156.8	22.1	224.8	132.8	178.8	8.8	12.9	2 035.3
3rd quarter	2 269.9	1 518.9	1 270.9	248.1	21.9	159.4	21.8	223.7	140.8	181.2	8.1	13.3	2 086.6
4th quarter	2 332.4	1 561.4	1 305.8	255.5	20.5	162.2	26.3	220.7	155.4	184.9	8.9	13.4	2 146.5
1980													
1st quarter	2 386.8	1 602.5	1 338.4	264.1	12.9	163.2	29.8	216.7	171.3	189.9	9.2	13.5	2 196.5
2nd quarter	2 371.2	1 625.1	1 354.9	270.3	2.7	158.3	25.4	185.8	176.9	197.2	9.6	13.8	2 174.2
3rd quarter	2 434.0	1 657.9	1 381.0	276.9	11.5	162.0	26.6	192.3	180.1	204.7	10.1	14.1	2 230.5
4th quarter	2 565.3	1 721.6	1 436.3	285.3	18.3	167.6	38.2	209.7	199.0	211.0	10.3	16.1	2 354.3
1981													
1st quarter	2 656.9	1 774.5	1 474.7	299.8	17.3	171.2	36.7	223.7	201.9	231.2	10.6	16.9	2 425.3
2nd quarter	2 702.3	1 808.0	1 502.4	305.7	17.8	161.8	36.5	218.8	221.4	235.9	10.7	17.1	2 464.3
3rd quarter	2 798.7	1 846.4	1 535.1	311.3	23.0	163.3	37.8	238.6	251.0	237.8	11.1	17.8	2 560.1
4th quarter	2 811.5	1 874.2	1 557.8	316.4	16.7	160.7	41.0	223.3	255.1	239.2	13.5	18.4	2 571.0
1982													
1st quarter	2 815.6	1 897.9	1 573.2	324.6	14.1	156.1	40.1	201.1	266.4	237.8	14.0	19.5	2 575.7
2nd quarter	2 864.2	1 917.3	1 587.1	330.2	12.6	162.5	37.6	214.4	278.3	238.7	13.6	20.1	2 622.7
3rd quarter	2 883.8	1 937.1	1 602.3	334.8	11.8	164.3	39.6	214.8	271.4	242.2	13.0	20.4	2 639.0
4th quarter	2 893.7	1 951.1	1 612.2	338.9	13.8	170.1	38.0	208.4	268.4	246.7	19.4	20.6	2 649.7
1983													
1st quarter	2 959.1	1 979.2	1 629.5	349.7	12.8	175.2	38.0	230.4	274.8	251.1	19.8	21.0	2 710.4
2nd quarter	3 040.0	2 017.2	1 661.8	355.4	7.6	181.8	38.3	260.9	275.6	261.6	21.5	21.6	2 781.4
3rd quarter	3 117.8	2 059.5	1 699.0	360.6	-0.1	190.2	35.8	277.3	290.0	267.9	22.1	22.7	2 852.8
4th quarter	3 219.9	2 114.5	1 748.1	366.4	3.5	198.9	39.0	288.3	300.8	274.2	21.5	24.6	2 945.0
1984													
1st quarter	3 358.1	2 184.8	1 794.0	390.8	19.2	212.4	37.8	314.3	303.3	282.1	21.2	27.6	3 071.7
2nd quarter	3 458.5	2 235.4	1 837.9	397.5	20.9	225.0	36.3	324.2	321.7	288.2	20.9	29.6	3 163.6
3rd quarter	3 526.4	2 281.5	1 877.3	404.1	20.1	228.6	40.8	314.5	340.0	292.7	20.8	31.1	3 225.5
4th quarter	3 586.2	2 320.9	1 911.1	409.7	22.2	225.0	45.8	321.4	343.2	298.0	21.1	32.1	3 278.5
1985													
1st quarter	3 652.6	2 366.2	1 946.2	419.9	22.6	240.7	44.1	322.7	343.2	301.5	21.0	33.1	3 339.5
2nd quarter	3 700.1	2 402.2	1 976.3	426.0	20.3	240.9	43.3	326.7	341.3	306.1	20.9	39.0	3 374.7
3rd quarter	3 746.8	2 441.1	2 009.3	431.8	19.1	242.0	41.0	343.3	334.5	312.2	21.2	33.5	3 421.0
4th quarter	3 794.1	2 489.2	2 050.1	439.1	21.2	242.4	39.3	328.5	346.3	314.3	21.9	33.8	3 466.8
1986													
1st quarter	3 856.3	2 522.7	2 076.3	446.4	19.4	245.2	38.3	327.1	365.1	317.8	23.0	42.8	3 517.7
2nd quarter	3 874.1	2 545.3	2 093.8	451.5	19.8	251.5	36.2	320.6	368.6	319.8	24.1	35.1	3 542.1
3rd quarter	3 916.8	2 581.4	2 124.0	457.4	25.6	258.3	31.7	313.7	369.9	326.5	25.4	33.8	3 580.7
4th quarter	3 962.1	2 631.1	2 165.2	466.0	25.6	257.3	27.9	316.6	363.4	330.7	26.7	34.6	3 621.9
1987													
1st quarter	4 035.8	2 678.6	2 207.7	470.8	26.5	265.1	31.7	327.9	361.9	336.3	28.2	34.3	3 691.8
2nd quarter	4 124.5	2 721.1	2 244.9	476.2	28.6	269.9	29.3	363.6	361.5	344.7	30.4	34.8	3 774.0
3rd quarter	4 218.3	2 767.6	2 285.4	482.2	28.8	275.9	34.7	387.5	368.2	352.7	31.2	33.1	3 862.7
4th quarter	4 316.4	2 833.7	2 344.9	488.7	30.7	283.3	38.1	396.3	373.8	357.8	31.0	33.1	3 955.8
1988													
1st quarter	4 410.8	2 883.1	2 381.5	501.6	33.3	300.1	39.1	408.2	379.8	365.5	30.3	32.3	4 043.6
2nd quarter	4 503.2	2 945.5	2 435.5	510.0	27.5	312.0	37.2	427.5	373.9	373.0	29.7	33.0	4 123.6
3rd quarter	4 591.3	2 994.2	2 476.0	518.3	28.9	321.3	38.4	436.0	385.6	378.1	29.1	34.5	4 204.5
4th quarter	4 692.2	3 045.9	2 518.8	527.1	17.6	325.5	47.6	458.8	402.1	383.0	28.4	36.2	4 297.5
1989													
1st quarter	4 775.4	3 092.8	2 555.5	537.3	36.7	330.3	46.1	437.1	425.8	391.6	27.8	38.1	4 368.8
2nd quarter	4 803.9	3 122.1	2 576.9	545.2	32.4	327.7	46.5	428.1	433.0	397.8	27.2	38.3	4 389.7
3rd quarter	4 840.7	3 158.3	2 605.0	553.3	30.0	329.0	41.5	421.0	437.1	404.3	26.9	40.9	4 417.0
4th quarter	4 886.6	3 207.7	2 648.1	559.7	32.9	334.1	38.3	420.3	432.5	403.7	27.1	39.7	4 465.8
1990													
1st quarter	4 999.4	3 272.8	2 701.2	571.6	34.7	341.8	44.5	433.6	436.6	419.9	26.9	39.4	4 563.9
2nd quarter	5 090.7	3 330.5	2 749.8	580.7	32.5	347.3	47.7	457.8	441.1	420.0	26.7	39.1	4 656.8
3rd quarter	5 121.3	3 370.2	2 781.3	588.9	31.3	353.8	54.0	430.4	440.7	427.4	26.7	39.1	4 680.4
4th quarter	5 145.2	3 379.4	2 783.7	595.6	29.0	352.0	56.4	429.4	450.3	434.7	26.8	40.0	4 696.6
1991													
1st quarter	5 165.9	3 394.5	2 786.7	607.9	26.0	341.9	55.9	456.0	429.8	444.7	26.9	40.6	4 704.1
2nd quarter	5 199.7	3 426.5	2 809.6	616.9	27.7	346.5	58.3	449.4	420.6	452.0	27.0	39.7	4 729.0
3rd quarter	5 246.9	3 461.5	2 834.3	627.2	24.5	352.7	61.6	447.8	418.8	461.6	27.3	39.6	4 766.8
4th quarter	5 298.9	3 498.5	2 861.4	637.2	28.8	360.4	65.3	451.6	403.8	471.7	27.9	39.6	4 808.3

Table 19-8. National Income by Type of Income—*Continued*

(Billions of dollars, quarterly data are at seasonally adjusted annual rates.)

NIPA Tables 1.7.5, 1.12

Year and quarter	National income, total	Compensation of employees			Proprietors' income with IVA and CCAdj		Rental income of persons with CCAdj	Corporate profits with IVA and CCAdj	Net interest and miscellaneous payments	Taxes on production and imports	Less: Subsidies	Business current transfer payments, net	Addendum: Net national factor income
		Total	Wage and salary accruals	Supplements to wages and salaries	Farm	Nonfarm							
1992													
1st quarter	5 432.6	3 566.8	2 911.7	655.0	33.0	376.5	71.6	492.4	397.5	476.7	28.4	39.3	4 937.7
2nd quarter	5 506.4	3 617.0	2 950.1	666.9	35.5	389.8	79.8	494.8	390.4	481.5	29.0	38.9	5 007.3
3rd quarter	5 486.7	3 659.9	2 982.3	677.6	35.2	397.2	70.8	428.5	382.7	486.3	30.2	48.0	4 974.3
4th quarter	5 625.3	3 698.0	3 014.0	684.0	34.3	408.8	89.9	501.6	383.3	490.7	31.9	43.5	5 115.9
1993													
1st quarter	5 663.8	3 738.7	3 042.7	696.0	28.8	415.9	90.9	505.1	381.0	490.1	35.2	42.3	5 160.4
2nd quarter	5 750.9	3 782.5	3 074.2	708.3	35.1	421.2	95.3	536.2	371.6	498.3	37.3	40.2	5 241.9
3rd quarter	5 779.8	3 823.2	3 105.5	717.6	25.5	423.4	94.3	539.3	359.2	505.3	37.4	39.8	5 264.8
4th quarter	5 898.9	3 861.2	3 134.3	727.0	35.5	429.9	101.7	587.0	351.1	520.1	35.7	40.3	5 366.6
1994													
1st quarter	5 931.9	3 929.6	3 190.9	738.7	40.9	420.0	105.7	526.7	353.9	532.3	33.3	48.5	5 376.8
2nd quarter	6 091.1	3 978.1	3 231.5	746.6	35.9	439.3	120.9	597.1	357.9	544.6	32.1	40.3	5 529.2
3rd quarter	6 181.8	4 013.7	3 262.9	750.8	31.4	444.5	126.2	625.2	370.9	550.6	31.6	42.0	5 611.9
4th quarter	6 284.2	4 067.5	3 313.7	753.8	27.6	453.7	125.9	652.2	382.9	555.1	31.7	42.3	5 709.8
1995													
1st quarter	6 356.3	4 134.9	3 379.2	755.7	20.9	462.2	122.6	657.4	379.1	555.2	33.3	45.4	5 777.2
2nd quarter	6 408.0	4 169.5	3 412.6	757.0	19.0	465.9	122.3	683.9	369.2	554.0	33.8	46.7	5 829.8
3rd quarter	6 492.1	4 213.8	3 455.1	758.7	22.0	471.8	119.6	720.6	360.1	559.5	34.3	47.6	5 908.0
4th quarter	6 559.3	4 255.1	3 495.7	759.4	28.8	477.9	124.1	724.9	359.8	564.2	34.6	47.8	5 970.6
1996													
1st quarter	6 677.0	4 295.3	3 532.7	762.6	36.7	489.3	131.1	768.1	359.9	571.1	34.6	48.0	6 080.4
2nd quarter	6 796.6	4 362.7	3 596.7	765.9	43.9	504.0	130.7	780.9	370.2	578.1	34.5	48.4	6 192.4
3rd quarter	6 876.8	4 422.7	3 653.9	768.8	33.4	512.1	132.1	787.1	379.8	582.0	34.2	48.8	6 267.2
4th quarter	7 010.0	4 481.5	3 709.5	772.0	35.2	518.2	132.0	808.5	394.9	593.3	33.9	67.0	6 370.3
1997													
1st quarter	7 114.6	4 553.5	3 777.7	775.8	39.1	530.5	130.0	835.2	404.3	596.0	33.4	46.8	6 492.6
2nd quarter	7 220.0	4 615.0	3 833.7	781.3	29.8	537.0	129.5	861.2	409.0	610.6	32.7	47.3	6 581.5
3rd quarter	7 361.1	4 690.5	3 900.5	790.0	34.5	545.3	128.2	895.5	416.9	616.9	32.5	53.3	6 710.9
4th quarter	7 473.0	4 787.8	3 986.8	801.0	33.4	554.5	127.4	881.9	432.3	624.3	32.9	52.1	6 817.4
1998													
1st quarter	7 573.3	4 893.4	4 075.7	817.6	29.6	576.6	131.0	811.9	464.7	629.2	33.5	59.8	6 907.3
2nd quarter	7 687.5	4 976.9	4 146.4	830.5	27.7	591.5	135.7	794.0	488.5	635.8	34.2	60.8	7 014.3
3rd quarter	7 823.1	5 061.5	4 218.3	843.2	27.4	605.1	141.6	807.1	498.8	643.4	35.7	63.3	7 141.6
4th quarter	7 927.3	5 145.7	4 290.4	855.3	32.8	620.4	141.6	793.5	496.2	651.0	38.2	75.1	7 230.2
1999													
1st quarter	8 074.2	5 248.0	4 380.9	867.0	34.9	629.4	145.2	844.2	480.6	657.9	41.3	64.2	7 382.2
2nd quarter	8 161.3	5 302.5	4 425.4	877.1	29.3	642.7	147.6	849.3	490.6	667.5	44.0	65.4	7 462.0
3rd quarter	8 254.7	5 376.3	4 486.1	890.2	25.6	655.1	144.5	842.3	498.8	679.6	45.6	68.1	7 542.6
4th quarter	8 456.4	5 501.7	4 593.2	908.5	24.6	671.5	152.1	869.3	511.5	691.2	45.8	71.8	7 730.7
2000													
1st quarter	8 680.5	5 694.1	4 760.0	934.1	23.2	686.1	153.8	832.6	548.3	697.6	44.4	81.3	7 938.1
2nd quarter	8 750.4	5 727.2	4 783.2	944.0	23.8	702.7	148.5	833.0	560.6	706.9	44.4	85.0	7 995.8
3rd quarter	8 858.3	5 837.4	4 874.9	962.5	23.0	712.6	148.2	811.8	564.3	712.2	44.3	88.9	8 097.2
4th quarter	8 891.7	5 871.9	4 898.8	973.1	20.7	721.4	150.5	794.3	563.0	718.7	44.1	93.1	8 121.9
2001													
1st quarter	8 987.6	5 946.2	4 961.1	985.1	21.9	747.5	155.3	778.7	565.2	725.1	52.3	98.3	8 214.7
2nd quarter	9 001.5	5 944.6	4 951.4	993.2	19.2	751.5	161.7	783.1	569.9	726.3	58.4	104.8	8 229.9
3rd quarter	8 890.3	5 939.3	4 935.2	1 004.1	17.7	755.7	176.4	714.5	565.5	725.6	67.3	65.7	8 169.1
4th quarter	9 039.9	5 938.3	4 923.4	1 014.8	20.0	754.1	176.2	793.0	564.8	737.6	43.1	102.5	8 246.4
2002													
1st quarter	9 131.1	6 025.3	4 961.2	1 064.2	8.9	754.1	172.1	829.4	545.8	746.0	39.9	91.1	8 335.6
2nd quarter	9 211.7	6 091.5	4 989.4	1 102.1	4.0	759.4	167.7	864.3	519.3	757.9	37.0	85.8	8 406.2
3rd quarter	9 247.5	6 114.5	4 988.5	1 126.0	11.0	758.1	142.9	895.4	507.0	771.6	38.3	81.4	8 428.9
4th quarter	9 326.7	6 133.4	4 984.5	1 148.9	18.4	759.7	129.2	956.1	511.5	775.5	38.3	78.8	8 508.4
2003													
1st quarter	9 406.7	6 202.4	5 032.4	1 170.0	21.8	757.4	137.4	923.6	529.1	787.5	42.0	84.1	8 571.7
2nd quarter	9 537.9	6 289.7	5 098.7	1 190.3	30.5	771.2	130.5	956.2	529.6	800.2	55.6	83.8	8 706.9
3rd quarter	9 699.3	6 365.8	5 159.3	1 206.6	32.1	791.5	116.3	1 016.2	526.4	812.9	46.5	84.1	8 848.4
4th quarter	9 885.4	6 444.3	5 220.4	1 223.9	32.5	808.3	147.6	1 076.5	513.7	828.0	47.3	83.3	9 022.8
2004													
1st quarter	10 090.0	6 505.6	5 257.4	1 248.2	40.3	839.1	140.4	1 184.0	497.3	844.8	43.7	84.8	9 206.6
2nd quarter	10 248.0	6 596.7	5 329.7	1 266.9	39.6	869.1	126.0	1 227.4	491.8	857.1	42.9	86.6	9 350.6
3rd quarter	10 317.8	6 709.7	5 422.8	1 286.9	33.0	881.1	105.5	1 218.7	483.9	867.8	44.2	67.0	9 431.9
4th quarter	10 571.3	6 813.6	5 508.1	1 305.5	36.5	908.0	101.7	1 294.8	491.8	885.5	47.6	93.6	9 646.3
2005													
1st quarter	10 826.3	6 884.4	5 553.1	1 331.4	33.2	903.0	90.1	1 438.2	537.0	904.5	54.5	97.4	9 886.0
2nd quarter	10 958.9	6 957.4	5 611.5	1 346.0	38.3	909.8	72.2	1 472.4	554.8	924.0	58.6	97.9	10 004.9
3rd quarter	10 779.5	7 090.2	5 725.6	1 364.7	37.1	923.3	-56.9	1 342.6	583.9	937.4	60.7	8.5	9 920.2
4th quarter	11 331.3	7 191.0	5 816.5	1 374.5	27.7	966.7	58.0	1 538.6	600.8	946.8	63.3	76.1	10 383.0
2006													
1st quarter	11 611.1	7 318.0	5 926.4	1 391.6	17.3	987.5	52.8	1 634.2	615.5	962.7	54.2	85.1	10 625.3
2nd quarter	11 738.5	7 364.2	5 966.2	1 398.0	9.8	1 008.4	45.6	1 681.6	629.7	973.6	49.8	83.5	10 739.4
3rd quarter	11 848.6	7 441.9	6 034.2	1 407.8	13.8	999.6	40.4	1 713.8	630.1	980.1	48.2	86.0	10 839.7
4th quarter	11 984.7	7 611.1	6 187.2	1 423.9	23.7	998.7	38.2	1 644.5	649.3	988.3	46.8	86.8	10 965.6

Table 19-9. Saving and Investment

(Billions of dollars, except as noted; quarterly data are at seasonally adjusted annual rates.) **NIPA Tables 1.7.5, 5.1**

Year and quarter	Gross saving									Gross domestic investment and net lending, NIPAs				Net domestic invest-ment	Gross national income	Net saving as a percent-age of gross national income
	Total	Net saving			Consumption of fixed capital				Gross domestic investment			Net lending or net borrow-ing (-), NIPAs				
		Private	Government		Total	Private	Government		Total	Private	Govern-ment					
			Federal	State and local			Federal	State and local								
1946	38.4	18.6	-5.0	1.5	23.3	12.5	9.3	1.5	34.6	31.1	3.5	4.9	11.3	221.8	6.8
1947	46.6	13.5	5.3	1.4	26.4	15.7	8.8	1.8	39.6	35.0	4.6	9.3	13.2	243.0	8.3
1948	58.0	25.1	3.6	1.2	28.1	18.4	7.6	2.1	55.1	48.1	7.0	2.4	27.0	271.1	11.0
1949	45.6	21.1	-5.7	1.5	28.7	20.0	6.6	2.1	46.6	36.9	9.7	0.9	17.9	266.7	6.3
1947															
1st quarter	46.6	13.4	5.9	1.6	25.6	14.6	9.3	1.7	38.0	33.7	4.3	9.4	12.3	237.4	8.8
2nd quarter	44.0	11.2	5.2	1.6	26.0	15.4	8.9	1.8	36.7	32.4	4.3	9.9	10.6	239.0	7.5
3rd quarter	45.1	15.3	2.0	1.1	26.7	16.1	8.7	1.9	37.4	32.7	4.7	10.1	10.7	243.3	7.6
4th quarter	50.7	14.2	7.9	1.3	27.2	16.9	8.4	1.9	46.2	41.0	5.1	7.8	19.0	252.3	9.3
1948															
1st quarter	55.4	19.3	7.7	1.0	27.4	17.4	8.0	2.0	51.2	45.0	6.2	4.9	23.9	261.0	10.7
2nd quarter	59.1	25.1	5.1	1.2	27.8	18.1	7.6	2.1	54.8	48.1	6.7	3.0	27.0	270.1	11.6
3rd quarter	58.6	27.6	1.4	1.2	28.4	18.8	7.5	2.1	57.4	50.2	7.1	0.9	28.9	275.7	11.0
4th quarter	58.9	28.5	0.2	1.5	28.8	19.4	7.2	2.2	57.1	49.1	8.0	0.8	28.3	277.7	10.8
1949															
1st quarter	51.1	24.1	-3.4	1.5	28.9	19.6	7.1	2.2	49.5	40.9	8.6	2.2	20.6	270.8	8.2
2nd quarter	44.0	20.4	-6.5	1.4	28.7	19.8	6.8	2.1	43.6	34.0	9.5	1.7	14.8	266.4	5.7
3rd quarter	46.0	22.3	-6.5	1.6	28.6	20.1	6.4	2.1	47.6	37.3	10.3	0.6	19.1	266.7	6.5
4th quarter	41.3	17.5	-6.2	1.3	28.6	20.3	6.2	2.1	45.5	35.2	10.4	-1.0	16.9	263.1	4.8
1950															
1st quarter	48.7	27.6	-8.4	1.0	28.5	20.6	5.9	2.0	53.4	44.4	9.0	-1.0	24.9	272.8	7.4
2nd quarter	56.6	24.3	2.8	0.7	28.8	21.0	5.8	2.1	59.2	49.9	9.4	-1.3	30.4	284.6	9.8
3rd quarter	63.0	18.2	13.5	1.8	29.6	21.7	5.7	2.1	66.4	56.1	10.2	-2.7	36.8	302.9	11.0
4th quarter	74.1	27.4	14.2	1.8	30.8	22.6	5.9	2.3	76.5	65.9	10.6	-2.5	45.7	315.1	13.7
1951															
1st quarter	70.8	18.8	17.2	2.7	32.1	23.7	6.0	2.4	75.0	62.1	13.0	-1.7	42.9	328.0	11.8
2nd quarter	77.4	32.0	10.0	2.5	32.9	24.3	6.0	2.5	81.1	64.8	16.2	0.3	48.2	334.6	13.3
3rd quarter	75.5	34.2	5.3	2.4	33.6	24.9	6.1	2.6	78.4	59.4	19.0	2.2	44.8	340.5	12.3
4th quarter	76.4	33.4	6.0	2.7	34.3	25.4	6.3	2.7	76.7	54.4	22.3	2.7	42.3	347.2	12.1
1952															
1st quarter	77.1	32.4	6.9	2.9	34.9	25.8	6.5	2.6	77.1	55.2	21.9	3.6	42.1	349.7	12.0
2nd quarter	70.8	29.6	3.4	2.4	35.5	26.0	6.7	2.7	71.8	49.9	22.0	1.2	36.4	352.0	10.0
3rd quarter	73.1	32.8	1.1	3.3	36.0	26.2	7.0	2.8	76.4	53.9	22.5	-1.0	40.4	358.3	10.4
4th quarter	75.7	32.2	3.5	3.4	36.5	26.5	7.2	2.8	80.1	57.1	22.9	-1.2	43.6	370.1	10.6
1953															
1st quarter	77.0	32.9	4.3	2.9	37.0	26.7	7.4	2.8	81.8	57.9	23.9	-1.3	44.8	376.8	10.6
2nd quarter	77.4	33.2	2.6	4.0	37.6	27.1	7.6	2.8	82.8	58.1	24.6	-1.8	45.2	380.5	10.5
3rd quarter	77.2	32.2	3.5	3.5	38.1	27.6	7.7	2.8	81.7	57.4	24.3	-1.1	43.6	379.6	10.3
4th quarter	68.8	30.1	-3.2	3.6	38.4	27.7	7.8	2.8	75.4	52.3	23.1	-0.9	37.1	372.1	8.2
1954															
1st quarter	71.9	32.7	-3.3	3.6	38.9	28.1	8.0	2.8	75.3	51.5	23.8	-0.4	36.4	374.3	8.8
2nd quarter	72.0	31.0	-1.9	3.3	39.7	28.6	8.2	2.9	74.4	51.2	23.2	0.4	34.7	375.2	8.6
3rd quarter	72.6	30.8	-1.3	3.0	40.2	28.9	8.3	2.9	76.4	54.7	21.7	0.0	36.2	379.1	8.6
4th quarter	77.0	33.2	0.0	3.1	40.7	29.3	8.5	3.0	79.2	57.8	21.4	1.0	38.5	388.6	9.3
1955															
1st quarter	81.7	34.2	3.6	3.0	40.9	29.4	8.6	2.9	85.2	64.2	21.0	0.6	44.3	401.0	10.2
2nd quarter	88.1	36.6	6.7	3.3	41.4	29.9	8.6	3.0	90.0	68.1	21.9	-0.2	48.5	411.5	11.3
3rd quarter	89.1	38.0	4.9	3.8	42.5	30.6	8.7	3.2	90.7	70.0	20.7	0.9	48.3	419.4	11.1
4th quarter	93.1	38.0	7.8	3.9	43.4	31.3	8.9	3.2	94.1	73.9	20.3	0.5	50.7	427.1	11.6
1956															
1st quarter	96.7	39.0	8.5	4.3	44.8	32.4	9.1	3.4	94.7	73.0	21.8	1.0	49.9	432.1	12.0
2nd quarter	97.7	40.6	6.7	4.5	45.9	33.2	9.2	3.5	93.7	71.4	22.2	2.3	47.8	438.7	11.8
3rd quarter	101.3	42.0	7.8	4.5	47.0	34.1	9.3	3.6	96.4	72.5	23.9	3.1	49.4	444.0	12.2
4th quarter	101.9	42.4	7.3	4.3	47.9	34.8	9.4	3.7	94.9	71.2	23.7	4.6	47.0	453.1	11.9
1957															
1st quarter	102.1	42.5	6.1	4.8	48.6	35.2	9.6	3.7	96.0	71.8	24.2	5.6	47.4	460.7	11.6
2nd quarter	102.0	44.0	4.3	4.3	49.4	35.8	9.7	3.9	95.8	71.9	23.9	4.9	46.4	463.8	11.3
3rd quarter	101.9	43.1	4.4	4.1	50.3	36.5	9.8	3.9	97.9	73.2	24.6	5.0	47.6	468.7	11.0
4th quarter	92.6	39.3	-1.5	3.6	51.2	37.4	9.9	3.9	89.6	64.9	24.7	3.7	38.4	463.3	8.9
1958															
1st quarter	88.8	38.3	-3.2	2.7	51.1	37.5	9.8	3.9	85.6	60.5	25.1	1.6	34.5	458.3	8.2
2nd quarter	84.4	38.2	-8.3	2.6	51.9	38.2	9.8	4.0	84.0	58.7	25.3	0.9	32.0	460.3	7.1
3rd quarter	91.1	42.4	-6.4	2.6	52.5	38.5	9.9	4.1	92.8	65.5	27.3	1.2	40.3	471.5	8.2
4th quarter	99.0	46.2	-3.5	3.6	52.6	38.5	10.0	4.1	101.5	73.2	28.2	0.0	48.8	485.2	9.6
1959															
1st quarter	104.7	46.1	3.2	3.1	52.4	38.1	10.1	4.2	106.7	76.2	30.5	-1.4	54.3	497.4	10.5
2nd quarter	111.3	49.8	5.2	3.6	52.7	38.3	10.2	4.2	111.7	82.2	29.5	-2.0	59.0	512.6	11.4
3rd quarter	103.0	42.8	2.9	4.2	53.2	38.7	10.3	4.3	105.8	76.4	29.3	-0.5	52.6	509.8	9.8
4th quarter	105.8	45.6	2.1	4.3	53.8	39.1	10.4	4.3	107.1	79.3	27.8	-0.8	53.3	515.7	10.1
1960															
1st quarter	118.3	47.6	11.7	4.3	54.7	39.9	10.5	4.3	116.8	89.1	27.7	1.8	62.0	529.6	12.0
2nd quarter	110.8	43.0	8.2	4.2	55.3	40.4	10.6	4.4	107.2	79.7	27.5	2.5	51.9	530.2	10.5
3rd quarter	111.0	44.2	6.6	4.3	55.9	40.8	10.6	4.5	107.7	78.7	29.0	3.8	51.8	531.7	10.4
4th quarter	105.2	42.3	2.2	4.4	56.3	41.1	10.7	4.5	97.0	68.1	28.9	4.8	40.7	530.3	9.2
1961															
1st quarter	108.2	45.0	2.5	4.1	56.6	41.3	10.8	4.6	101.7	70.3	31.4	5.4	45.1	532.7	9.7
2nd quarter	110.2	48.4	0.8	4.0	57.0	41.5	10.8	4.6	105.7	75.8	30.0	4.1	48.8	542.8	9.8
3rd quarter	117.1	52.7	2.5	4.5	57.4	41.7	10.9	4.7	113.5	82.4	31.2	3.8	56.2	552.6	10.8
4th quarter	121.8	54.7	4.7	4.6	57.8	42.0	11.0	4.8	117.0	84.2	32.8	3.8	59.2	567.1	11.3

Table 19-9. Saving and Investment—*Continued*

(Billions of dollars, except as noted; quarterly data are at seasonally adjusted annual rates.)   **NIPA Tables 1.7.5, 5.1**

Year and quarter	Gross saving								Gross domestic investment and net lending, NIPAs				Net domestic invest-ment	Gross national income	Net saving as a percent-age of gross national income
	Total	Net saving			Consumption of fixed capital				Gross domestic investment			Net lending or net borrow-ing (-), NIPAs			
		Private	Government		Total	Private	Government		Total	Private	Govern-ment				
			Federal	State and local			Federal	State and local							
1962															
1st quarter	124.5	58.8	2.4	4.9	58.3	42.2	11.3	4.9	122.4	89.4	33.0	3.1	64.1	578.5	11.4
2nd quarter	123.9	57.9	2.2	5.0	58.8	42.5	11.3	5.0	120.6	87.9	32.7	4.9	61.8	585.7	11.1
3rd quarter	125.7	57.5	3.1	5.5	59.6	42.9	11.6	5.1	123.0	89.3	33.7	4.2	63.5	592.5	11.2
4th quarter	125.7	57.5	2.4	5.5	60.4	43.4	11.8	5.1	119.7	86.0	33.7	3.3	59.3	600.7	10.9
1963															
1st quarter	128.5	57.6	4.2	5.4	61.4	44.2	12.0	5.2	123.5	90.5	33.0	4.0	62.1	608.0	11.0
2nd quarter	133.1	59.1	6.3	5.5	62.1	44.7	12.1	5.3	125.0	92.2	32.8	5.4	62.9	618.2	11.5
3rd quarter	133.6	58.9	5.9	6.0	62.8	45.2	12.2	5.4	129.8	95.0	34.8	4.7	67.0	627.4	11.3
4th quarter	137.6	63.1	5.2	5.9	63.4	45.7	12.2	5.5	131.3	97.4	33.9	6.0	67.9	638.3	11.6
1964															
1st quarter	140.0	67.7	2.0	6.4	63.8	46.0	12.3	5.6	134.9	100.7	34.2	8.3	71.0	651.5	11.7
2nd quarter	140.3	72.0	-2.6	6.3	64.6	46.5	12.3	5.7	135.2	100.6	34.6	6.8	70.6	662.0	11.4
3rd quarter	143.5	70.4	1.3	6.5	65.3	47.2	12.4	5.8	137.2	102.5	34.8	7.6	71.9	674.2	11.6
4th quarter	149.7	73.7	3.3	6.4	66.4	48.0	12.4	5.9	139.5	104.6	34.9	7.4	73.1	683.1	12.2
1965															
1st quarter	157.1	75.9	7.6	6.2	67.4	48.9	12.5	6.0	149.9	115.7	34.2	5.8	82.5	702.5	12.8
2nd quarter	158.7	76.7	6.8	6.5	68.7	49.9	12.6	6.2	150.6	115.8	34.8	7.1	81.9	714.7	12.6
3rd quarter	158.8	82.6	-0.4	6.6	70.0	51.0	12.7	6.3	156.1	119.7	36.5	6.0	86.2	727.0	12.2
4th quarter	159.2	81.6	-0.6	6.8	71.4	52.2	12.8	6.4	158.5	121.8	36.7	6.0	87.1	747.0	11.8
1966															
1st quarter	167.5	81.8	5.0	7.7	73.0	53.5	12.9	6.6	170.4	131.7	38.7	4.8	97.4	768.1	12.3
2nd quarter	167.3	81.0	3.5	8.0	74.8	54.9	13.0	6.8	168.9	130.7	38.2	4.0	94.1	779.4	11.9
3rd quarter	167.3	81.4	1.4	8.0	76.5	56.1	13.4	7.0	170.4	130.2	40.3	2.8	93.9	792.4	11.5
4th quarter	172.7	88.2	-0.9	7.3	78.1	57.4	13.6	7.2	174.7	132.7	42.0	4.0	96.6	806.4	11.7
1967															
1st quarter	168.0	90.9	-9.7	7.5	79.3	58.3	13.7	7.3	172.8	129.3	43.4	4.4	93.5	814.0	10.9
2nd quarter	164.3	87.2	-10.4	6.9	80.6	59.3	13.9	7.4	165.7	123.7	42.0	3.6	85.1	822.5	10.2
3rd quarter	171.8	91.7	-8.5	6.4	82.2	60.4	14.1	7.6	171.7	128.5	43.2	3.2	89.5	839.7	10.7
4th quarter	177.9	95.7	-8.8	7.2	83.8	61.7	14.4	7.8	176.2	132.9	43.3	2.9	92.3	857.2	11.0
1968															
1st quarter	176.1	89.5	-6.0	7.2	85.4	62.8	14.6	8.1	180.3	137.2	43.1	1.8	94.9	879.7	10.3
2nd quarter	181.9	93.9	-7.4	8.2	87.2	64.3	14.7	8.2	187.4	143.4	44.0	2.4	100.3	902.3	10.5
3rd quarter	182.3	84.2	1.5	7.4	89.1	65.9	14.9	8.3	183.6	139.7	43.8	1.7	94.4	922.7	10.1
4th quarter	187.6	86.1	2.7	7.2	91.6	68.0	15.1	8.6	187.9	144.4	43.6	1.0	96.3	941.3	10.2
1969															
1st quarter	196.0	79.7	14.6	7.4	94.4	70.2	15.2	8.9	201.1	155.7	45.4	1.8	106.7	960.5	10.6
2nd quarter	196.3	80.2	11.5	7.8	96.8	72.2	15.4	9.2	199.1	155.7	43.4	0.8	102.2	978.9	10.2
3rd quarter	202.9	89.8	5.6	8.5	99.0	74.1	15.5	9.4	203.9	160.3	43.6	1.6	104.9	999.7	10.4
4th quarter	198.1	85.3	3.2	8.2	101.4	76.0	15.7	9.7	194.8	154.1	40.7	2.9	93.4	1 011.0	9.6
1970															
1st quarter	191.9	82.5	-2.3	8.2	103.5	77.6	15.9	10.0	193.5	150.7	42.8	4.0	90.0	1 018.0	8.7
2nd quarter	194.1	96.4	-15.8	7.7	105.8	79.4	16.0	10.4	196.5	153.9	42.6	5.5	90.7	1 031.9	8.6
3rd quarter	195.7	100.2	-19.4	7.1	107.7	80.8	16.2	10.7	200.1	156.1	44.1	3.8	92.4	1 049.0	8.4
4th quarter	189.0	97.0	-23.1	5.4	109.8	82.3	16.3	11.1	193.7	148.9	44.8	2.7	84.0	1 051.5	7.5
1971															
1st quarter	203.1	109.7	-23.6	5.0	112.0	84.1	16.5	11.4	212.9	171.3	41.7	4.6	100.9	1 091.3	8.3
2nd quarter	206.9	117.0	-30.1	6.0	113.9	85.7	16.6	11.7	220.6	178.8	41.8	0.3	106.7	1 113.0	8.4
3rd quarter	211.4	118.0	-29.1	6.5	116.0	87.6	16.5	11.9	225.7	183.4	42.3	-0.1	109.6	1 132.4	8.4
4th quarter	214.3	118.4	-30.6	8.4	118.1	89.5	16.4	12.2	220.5	179.2	41.3	-2.5	102.4	1 155.7	8.3
1972															
1st quarter	222.1	114.5	-22.6	9.1	121.1	92.0	16.6	12.4	235.5	193.2	42.3	-4.7	114.4	1 190.0	8.5
2nd quarter	229.4	108.7	-27.7	18.7	122.9	100.5	16.5	12.6	249.4	206.5	42.9	-4.3	119.7	1 218.4	8.2
3rd quarter	237.8	118.1	-16.6	10.1	126.1	96.6	16.6	12.9	253.5	212.4	41.1	-3.1	127.3	1 246.1	9.0
4th quarter	260.8	137.7	-30.7	24.6	129.2	99.2	16.8	13.3	262.7	218.4	44.3	-2.3	133.5	1 296.4	10.2
1973															
1st quarter	274.0	137.6	-14.7	18.9	132.2	101.7	16.8	13.7	280.0	232.5	47.5	2.6	147.8	1 337.6	10.6
2nd quarter	283.4	143.5	-14.7	15.7	138.9	107.8	17.0	14.1	292.8	246.0	46.7	5.9	153.9	1 368.3	10.6
3rd quarter	293.9	148.7	-10.1	14.6	140.8	109.2	17.2	14.5	287.4	241.8	45.6	13.0	146.6	1 398.6	10.9
4th quarter	316.7	163.5	-5.7	13.6	145.2	113.0	17.2	15.0	305.1	257.6	47.5	15.8	159.9	1 442.3	11.9
1974															
1st quarter	308.2	154.0	-8.3	11.8	150.8	117.5	17.4	15.9	295.6	244.1	51.5	17.0	144.7	1 459.7	10.8
2nd quarter	298.6	140.1	-10.8	10.6	158.7	123.8	17.8	17.1	308.8	252.3	56.5	3.2	150.1	1 488.3	9.4
3rd quarter	298.8	133.0	-10.5	10.0	166.3	129.4	18.5	18.4	303.4	245.4	58.0	1.0	137.1	1 523.8	8.7
4th quarter	300.2	146.5	-25.4	4.9	174.2	135.9	19.0	19.3	314.9	255.8	59.0	5.3	140.7	1 546.7	8.1
1975															
1st quarter	280.4	146.2	-47.2	0.6	180.7	141.6	19.3	19.9	281.3	218.7	62.6	19.2	100.6	1 561.3	6.4
2nd quarter	278.7	194.4	-104.2	2.6	185.9	146.3	19.5	20.1	274.8	216.8	58.1	23.0	88.9	1 598.2	5.8
3rd quarter	308.9	177.3	-62.0	3.6	190.1	149.8	19.9	20.3	301.7	237.8	63.9	20.0	111.6	1 663.3	7.1
4th quarter	320.0	185.4	-62.8	3.1	194.3	153.3	20.4	20.6	315.5	247.6	67.8	23.3	121.2	1 711.7	7.3
1976															
1st quarter	337.3	186.0	-52.4	5.7	198.0	156.3	20.8	20.9	345.2	274.8	70.4	14.9	147.2	1 765.4	7.9
2nd quarter	342.9	181.4	-48.1	6.5	203.0	160.7	21.2	21.2	357.4	291.6	65.8	10.8	154.4	1 796.2	7.8
3rd quarter	343.7	181.9	-51.7	6.3	207.1	164.2	21.6	21.3	361.8	296.5	65.3	4.2	154.7	1 833.1	7.4
4th quarter	344.6	176.0	-54.8	11.0	212.5	168.8	22.0	21.6	368.9	304.9	64.0	5.6	156.5	1 873.2	7.1

Table 19-9. Saving and Investment—*Continued*

(Billions of dollars, except as noted; quarterly data are at seasonally adjusted annual rates.)   **NIPA Tables 1.7.5, 5.1**

Year and quarter	Gross saving Total	Net saving Private	Net saving Government Federal	Net saving Government State and local	Consumption of fixed capital Total	Consumption of fixed capital Private	Consumption of fixed capital Government Federal	Consumption of fixed capital Government State and local	Gross domestic investment Total	Gross domestic investment Private	Gross domestic investment Government	Net lending or net borrowing (-), NIPAs	Net domestic investment	Gross national income	Net saving as a percentage of gross national income
1977															
1st quarter	353.5	169.0	-45.3	9.6	220.2	175.6	22.6	22.0	393.5	326.6	66.9	-6.3	173.3	1 926.4	6.9
2nd quarter	392.9	193.1	-39.4	11.8	227.4	182.1	23.0	22.4	424.0	354.9	69.1	-7.0	196.6	2 002.7	8.3
3rd quarter	418.0	215.0	-45.2	15.7	232.5	186.6	23.1	22.8	446.0	378.4	67.6	-5.9	213.5	2 065.6	9.0
4th quarter	425.8	216.9	-46.5	15.5	239.9	193.1	23.7	23.2	452.0	385.5	66.5	-16.9	212.0	2 121.1	8.8
1978															
1st quarter	434.5	215.0	-46.3	16.9	249.0	201.1	24.3	23.6	463.2	396.8	66.4	-23.0	214.2	2 166.3	8.6
2nd quarter	472.8	217.4	-25.5	23.0	257.8	208.8	24.8	24.2	507.9	430.9	77.0	-10.7	250.1	2 270.0	9.5
3rd quarter	490.8	227.4	-19.4	16.1	266.8	216.8	25.3	24.8	532.0	451.4	80.7	-9.2	265.2	2 325.0	9.6
4th quarter	514.0	234.3	-14.7	18.7	275.6	224.7	25.6	25.4	557.0	472.8	84.2	1.1	281.3	2 397.5	9.9
1979															
1st quarter	533.1	240.2	-6.1	14.5	284.4	232.5	25.9	26.1	560.2	481.1	79.1	0.6	275.8	2 462.3	10.1
2nd quarter	533.2	231.5	-6.2	11.9	296.0	242.4	26.6	27.0	578.4	493.0	85.4	-0.1	282.4	2 512.0	9.4
3rd quarter	536.5	227.7	-11.9	13.9	306.7	251.3	27.4	27.9	591.6	497.9	93.7	5.1	284.9	2 576.6	8.9
4th quarter	544.3	240.0	-20.8	11.6	313.4	256.5	28.0	28.9	595.2	499.5	95.7	0.1	281.8	2 645.9	8.7
1980															
1st quarter	548.6	242.8	-30.9	10.6	326.0	267.4	28.7	30.0	606.9	505.2	101.7	-7.9	280.9	2 712.8	8.2
2nd quarter	526.9	238.3	-54.7	5.5	337.8	276.9	29.7	31.1	570.3	470.4	99.9	12.7	232.6	2 709.0	7.0
3rd quarter	533.4	246.6	-68.7	7.5	348.1	285.3	30.4	32.4	541.3	443.5	97.9	31.0	193.3	2 782.1	6.7
4th quarter	588.8	277.6	-60.2	11.5	359.9	294.9	31.4	33.6	599.4	497.9	101.5	9.6	239.5	2 925.2	7.8
1981															
1st quarter	619.5	275.6	-39.3	11.7	371.5	304.3	32.4	34.8	670.7	563.1	107.6	4.5	299.2	3 028.4	8.2
2nd quarter	629.5	281.8	-43.4	8.0	383.2	313.9	33.4	35.9	656.9	551.4	105.5	3.1	273.7	3 085.5	8.0
3rd quarter	688.8	338.7	-51.1	7.7	393.5	322.4	34.3	36.8	698.0	592.8	105.2	10.0	304.4	3 192.3	9.3
4th quarter	680.7	353.2	-79.4	2.8	404.1	331.1	35.2	37.7	691.5	582.2	109.3	7.6	287.4	3 215.6	8.6
1982															
1st quarter	644.0	330.8	-100.4	-0.7	414.3	339.5	36.3	38.5	633.2	526.4	106.7	4.0	218.9	3 229.9	7.1
2nd quarter	668.6	352.1	-105.9	-1.4	423.8	347.2	37.3	39.3	643.6	530.8	112.8	20.8	219.8	3 288.0	7.4
3rd quarter	633.4	349.1	-143.8	-2.6	430.7	352.6	38.1	40.0	641.0	528.7	112.3	-10.7	210.3	3 314.5	6.1
4th quarter	570.3	312.8	-177.3	-4.0	438.8	359.8	38.7	40.3	600.4	483.0	117.4	-14.0	161.6	3 332.5	3.9
1983															
1st quarter	587.7	332.4	-173.2	-7.4	436.0	356.0	39.4	40.6	614.5	496.6	117.9	-4.7	178.5	3 395.1	4.5
2nd quarter	595.8	322.9	-169.4	3.0	439.4	358.5	40.2	40.7	662.0	542.2	119.7	-24.5	222.6	3 479.4	4.5
3rd quarter	598.3	325.2	-185.7	9.8	449.0	366.6	41.4	41.0	703.5	577.7	125.8	-44.7	254.5	3 566.8	4.2
4th quarter	655.6	354.4	-163.8	14.2	450.8	367.4	42.1	41.3	768.7	640.7	128.0	-53.5	317.9	3 670.7	5.6
1984															
1st quarter	738.4	410.0	-153.9	22.5	459.8	374.9	43.3	41.6	842.6	709.7	133.0	-75.3	382.8	3 817.9	7.3
2nd quarter	768.6	437.0	-164.0	26.7	468.9	382.6	44.2	42.1	872.2	735.1	137.1	-84.6	403.3	3 927.4	7.6
3rd quarter	792.9	466.8	-171.7	21.1	476.7	389.2	45.0	42.6	892.6	753.5	139.1	-87.0	415.9	4 003.1	7.9
4th quarter	793.9	466.4	-182.8	25.4	484.9	395.8	46.1	43.0	892.5	744.3	148.3	-99.9	407.7	4 071.1	7.6
1985															
1st quarter	783.6	412.3	-147.0	24.7	493.6	403.1	46.9	43.7	869.2	720.0	149.1	-85.8	375.5	4 146.3	7.0
2nd quarter	779.6	451.7	-197.3	24.0	501.2	409.4	47.5	44.3	893.3	735.3	157.9	-107.6	392.1	4 201.3	6.6
3rd quarter	748.2	388.4	-174.3	21.7	512.5	419.0	48.6	44.9	892.2	727.2	165.0	-117.4	379.8	4 259.3	5.5
4th quarter	758.5	401.1	-181.3	19.0	519.6	424.4	49.5	45.7	925.3	762.2	163.1	-131.3	405.7	4 313.7	5.5
1986															
1st quarter	771.5	405.0	-180.7	26.7	520.5	424.1	50.0	46.4	928.9	763.8	165.1	-124.5	408.4	4 376.8	5.7
2nd quarter	744.4	398.5	-202.1	20.5	527.5	428.9	51.2	47.4	923.5	753.0	170.5	-138.1	396.0	4 401.6	4.9
3rd quarter	705.8	355.4	-207.1	22.8	534.8	434.3	52.2	48.3	913.6	732.5	181.1	-146.5	378.8	4 451.6	3.8
4th quarter	712.4	329.4	-173.3	13.8	542.5	440.0	53.1	49.4	913.0	736.7	176.2	-146.6	370.5	4 504.6	3.8
1987															
1st quarter	754.6	378.4	-180.5	6.0	550.7	446.3	54.2	50.1	943.8	765.0	178.9	-147.2	393.1	4 586.5	4.4
2nd quarter	773.6	322.6	-126.0	19.4	557.7	451.9	54.7	51.0	951.3	767.6	183.7	-150.7	393.6	4 682.2	4.6
3rd quarter	803.6	361.1	-134.4	12.2	564.8	457.3	55.5	51.9	957.4	769.5	187.9	-150.4	392.6	4 783.0	5.0
4th quarter	855.4	407.7	-139.1	12.1	574.6	465.4	56.5	52.7	1 024.4	837.8	186.7	-153.3	449.8	4 891.0	5.7
1988															
1st quarter	872.8	417.6	-142.4	13.6	584.0	472.8	57.7	53.6	979.1	797.6	181.5	-123.1	395.0	4 994.8	5.8
2nd quarter	909.9	434.8	-131.0	13.2	592.9	479.8	58.7	54.4	1 006.7	820.4	186.3	-106.0	413.8	5 096.1	6.2
3rd quarter	933.7	439.3	-128.0	21.2	601.2	486.3	59.7	55.2	1 012.0	825.7	186.3	-102.4	410.8	5 192.6	6.4
4th quarter	943.7	444.4	-136.4	23.6	612.2	495.1	60.9	56.1	1 033.1	842.6	190.4	-115.4	420.9	5 304.3	6.3
1989															
1st quarter	982.0	445.7	-111.4	26.6	621.2	502.3	62.0	57.0	1 075.2	884.1	191.1	-98.3	454.0	5 396.6	6.7
2nd quarter	938.6	409.7	-128.6	27.2	630.4	509.5	62.9	58.0	1 073.2	878.2	195.1	-91.0	442.9	5 434.3	5.7
3rd quarter	933.0	392.0	-139.5	22.8	657.7	534.7	63.9	59.1	1 072.5	870.3	202.2	-79.7	414.8	5 498.4	5.0
4th quarter	925.0	391.4	-140.9	6.7	667.8	541.8	65.1	60.9	1 069.6	867.3	202.3	-82.9	401.8	5 554.3	4.6
1990															
1st quarter	929.7	418.2	-168.6	15.8	664.2	536.7	66.2	61.2	1 092.4	880.0	212.4	-79.5	428.2	5 663.6	4.7
2nd quarter	963.1	448.9	-171.4	10.1	675.5	545.8	67.2	62.5	1 096.2	882.5	213.7	-69.5	420.7	5 766.2	5.0
3rd quarter	935.0	405.2	-164.9	6.1	688.5	556.5	68.3	63.8	1 082.6	866.8	215.8	-80.4	394.1	5 809.8	4.2
4th quarter	934.0	418.5	-183.1	-3.1	701.7	567.2	69.8	64.7	1 035.6	814.6	221.0	-77.0	333.9	5 846.9	4.0
1991															
1st quarter	1 017.3	465.9	-158.4	-7.0	716.8	580.2	70.9	65.6	1 004.3	787.9	216.4	52.9	287.6	5 882.6	5.1
2nd quarter	954.6	449.2	-211.7	-6.2	723.3	585.0	71.7	66.6	1 005.3	784.0	221.3	18.3	282.0	5 923.0	3.9
3rd quarter	932.1	437.1	-232.7	-0.2	727.8	587.7	72.7	67.4	1 027.2	805.2	222.0	-25.3	299.4	5 974.7	3.4
4th quarter	952.5	472.1	-252.1	-3.3	735.9	594.5	73.4	68.0	1 055.9	834.4	221.5	-10.0	320.1	6 034.8	3.6

Table 19-9. Saving and Investment—*Continued*

(Billions of dollars, except as noted; quarterly data are at seasonally adjusted annual rates.)   NIPA Tables 1.7.5, 5.1

Year and quarter	Gross saving									Gross domestic investment and net lending, NIPAs				Net domestic invest-ment	Gross national income	Net saving as a percent-age of gross national income
	Total	Net saving			Consumption of fixed capital				Gross domestic investment			Net lending or net borrow-ing (-), NIPAs			
		Private	Government		Total	Private	Government		Total	Private	Govern-ment				
			Federal	State and local			Federal	State and local							
1992																
1st quarter	959.0	520.8	-288.5	-0.3	726.9	584.7	73.7	68.5	1 037.3	810.2	227.1	-11.2	310.4	6 159.6	3.8
2nd quarter	971.1	530.6	-291.7	2.1	730.2	586.3	74.4	69.5	1 090.1	865.4	224.6	-35.3	359.9	6 236.6	3.9
3rd quarter	942.3	454.7	-316.1	-3.8	807.5	662.4	74.9	70.2	1 098.2	876.8	221.3	-42.4	290.7	6 294.2	2.1
4th quarter	920.5	466.0	-293.4	4.8	743.1	596.0	75.9	71.2	1 126.0	906.6	219.4	-60.9	382.9	6 368.4	2.8
1993																
1st quarter	954.2	498.6	-300.6	-9.9	766.1	616.7	77.1	72.4	1 148.0	931.3	216.7	-46.9	381.9	6 430.0	2.9
2nd quarter	970.8	472.7	-268.0	-1.7	767.8	616.7	77.7	73.4	1 163.4	942.3	221.1	-68.8	395.5	6 518.8	3.1
3rd quarter	943.5	432.5	-274.0	-0.3	785.3	632.8	78.3	74.2	1 160.9	943.4	217.6	-71.6	375.6	6 565.1	2.4
4th quarter	981.3	430.4	-251.3	15.7	786.5	632.6	78.7	75.2	1 217.2	996.5	220.7	-99.5	430.6	6 685.4	2.9
1994																
1st quarter	1 040.4	395.3	-232.2	4.2	873.1	716.3	79.1	77.7	1 255.1	1 043.2	211.9	-80.1	382.0	6 805.0	2.5
2nd quarter	1 064.1	441.4	-190.3	6.4	806.6	649.2	79.9	77.4	1 324.9	1 106.7	218.2	-106.1	518.3	6 897.7	3.7
3rd quarter	1 070.7	444.0	-211.3	17.8	820.2	661.1	80.3	78.8	1 321.6	1 092.9	228.7	-114.8	501.4	7 002.0	3.6
4th quarter	1 107.7	474.8	-215.5	13.5	834.9	673.6	81.3	79.9	1 372.1	1 145.5	226.6	-126.7	537.2	7 119.0	3.8
1995																
1st quarter	1 166.1	516.9	-215.2	10.2	854.3	691.2	81.7	81.4	1 392.1	1 160.6	231.5	-101.4	537.8	7 210.6	4.3
2nd quarter	1 161.3	485.7	-195.3	0.4	870.6	706.2	81.8	82.6	1 368.7	1 132.6	236.1	-107.3	498.1	7 278.5	4.0
3rd quarter	1 187.1	488.8	-198.7	13.4	883.6	718.1	81.8	83.7	1 357.0	1 126.2	230.8	-89.5	473.4	7 375.7	4.1
4th quarter	1 223.7	473.2	-178.7	24.3	904.9	737.9	82.1	84.9	1 389.1	1 156.6	232.5	-69.6	484.2	7 464.3	4.3
1996																
1st quarter	1 238.9	495.0	-182.1	23.7	902.2	734.3	82.0	85.9	1 409.1	1 170.0	239.1	-84.0	506.9	7 579.2	4.4
2nd quarter	1 273.8	483.6	-143.1	21.9	911.5	742.8	82.0	86.7	1 473.4	1 227.9	245.5	-98.4	561.9	7 708.1	4.7
3rd quarter	1 308.3	491.0	-133.1	27.2	923.2	753.4	82.1	87.7	1 526.2	1 279.9	246.3	-123.1	603.0	7 800.0	4.9
4th quarter	1 343.6	486.3	-108.7	30.4	935.5	764.7	82.1	88.7	1 532.0	1 283.3	248.7	-98.4	596.5	7 945.5	5.1
1997																
1st quarter	1 380.9	489.3	-89.2	29.6	951.2	779.1	82.3	89.8	1 567.9	1 315.4	252.5	-110.9	616.7	8 065.8	5.3
2nd quarter	1 450.5	516.5	-69.1	36.4	966.7	793.1	82.5	91.1	1 640.0	1 385.2	254.7	-87.1	673.3	8 186.7	5.9
3rd quarter	1 495.1	503.5	-35.0	44.4	982.1	807.6	82.5	92.0	1 672.7	1 419.5	253.3	-106.1	690.7	8 343.2	6.1
4th quarter	1 517.8	503.9	-30.0	46.1	997.8	821.4	82.9	93.5	1 687.2	1 439.1	248.1	-141.0	689.4	8 470.8	6.1
1998																
1st quarter	1 573.5	503.7	13.0	48.6	1 008.2	831.4	82.4	94.4	1 751.7	1 505.5	246.2	-145.4	743.5	8 581.5	6.6
2nd quarter	1 577.2	480.0	28.9	46.7	1 021.6	843.6	82.7	95.3	1 733.5	1 474.6	258.9	-181.8	711.9	8 709.1	6.4
3rd quarter	1 629.4	482.1	60.4	49.7	1 037.3	857.6	82.8	96.8	1 780.9	1 507.8	273.1	-210.0	743.7	8 860.4	6.7
4th quarter	1 614.8	445.2	53.0	63.0	1 053.6	872.2	83.2	98.2	1 819.8	1 548.6	271.2	-215.4	766.3	8 980.9	6.2
1999																
1st quarter	1 696.7	498.8	79.4	49.0	1 069.5	886.1	83.9	99.6	1 871.1	1 596.7	274.4	-221.6	801.6	9 143.7	6.9
2nd quarter	1 650.6	413.7	104.6	45.3	1 087.0	901.2	84.5	101.3	1 874.2	1 589.9	284.4	-262.7	787.2	9 248.3	6.1
3rd quarter	1 648.1	368.1	107.8	52.0	1 120.3	932.3	85.1	102.8	1 916.6	1 628.3	288.3	-300.8	796.4	9 375.0	5.6
4th quarter	1 701.6	395.3	122.7	55.3	1 128.3	937.6	85.8	104.8	1 987.8	1 687.7	300.1	-329.9	859.5	9 584.7	6.0
2000																
1st quarter	1 784.5	362.8	212.7	55.9	1 153.1	959.6	86.7	106.8	1 975.6	1 672.3	303.3	-363.6	822.6	9 833.6	6.4
2nd quarter	1 772.4	354.5	181.4	59.5	1 177.0	981.0	87.0	109.0	2 085.7	1 781.7	304.0	-381.9	908.7	9 927.4	6.0
3rd quarter	1 795.1	355.0	191.2	49.0	1 199.9	1 001.6	87.4	110.9	2 054.0	1 749.0	305.0	-423.3	854.1	10 058.2	5.9
4th quarter	1 730.0	300.8	172.5	35.4	1 221.3	1 021.1	87.6	112.5	2 044.5	1 738.9	305.6	-419.9	823.3	10 113.0	5.0
2001																
1st quarter	1 745.3	315.7	156.6	32.5	1 240.5	1 038.4	87.9	114.2	1 988.5	1 675.3	313.2	-412.0	748.0	10 228.0	4.9
2nd quarter	1 704.0	283.8	123.6	25.8	1 270.8	1 067.0	88.3	115.6	1 981.6	1 647.7	333.9	-377.4	710.7	10 272.3	4.2
3rd quarter	1 647.9	412.4	-88.6	-8.6	1 332.7	1 121.3	88.4	122.9	1 929.3	1 613.0	316.3	-353.7	596.6	10 223.0	3.1
4th quarter	1 533.1	286.5	-4.7	-30.6	1 281.8	1 075.2	88.2	118.4	1 854.0	1 521.4	332.7	-342.9	572.2	10 321.8	2.4
2002																
1st quarter	1 535.7	497.4	-208.5	-35.3	1 282.0	1 073.1	88.6	120.3	1 903.1	1 564.1	339.0	-422.2	621.1	10 413.1	2.4
2nd quarter	1 512.6	500.9	-241.4	-35.1	1 288.2	1 077.5	88.6	122.1	1 915.4	1 571.4	343.9	-460.7	627.2	10 499.9	2.1
3rd quarter	1 461.5	445.4	-247.3	-31.4	1 294.9	1 082.4	88.8	123.7	1 939.7	1 592.9	346.8	-465.1	644.8	10 542.4	1.6
4th quarter	1 446.6	473.3	-294.6	-34.9	1 302.7	1 088.4	89.4	124.9	1 947.4	1 600.1	347.4	-490.7	644.7	10 629.4	1.4
2003																
1st quarter	1 402.6	436.9	-290.2	-61.2	1 317.0	1 101.1	89.7	126.2	1 954.6	1 606.4	348.2	-532.5	637.6	10 723.7	0.8
2nd quarter	1 435.6	498.9	-365.5	-27.2	1 329.5	1 111.7	90.6	127.2	1 969.6	1 617.1	352.5	-519.2	640.1	10 867.3	1.0
3rd quarter	1 445.6	562.6	-451.4	-8.2	1 342.6	1 123.6	90.7	128.3	2 053.4	1 690.5	362.8	-513.2	710.7	11 041.9	0.9
4th quarter	1 552.2	561.5	-381.5	15.2	1 357.0	1 136.7	90.7	129.5	2 102.6	1 742.3	360.3	-496.9	745.6	11 242.4	1.7
2004																
1st quarter	1 552.4	597.8	-411.1	-7.9	1 373.7	1 150.9	92.0	130.8	2 129.9	1 769.6	360.3	-541.3	756.2	11 463.7	1.6
2nd quarter	1 590.0	571.8	-374.1	-1.9	1 394.3	1 166.8	93.7	133.7	2 247.1	1 875.6	371.5	-618.0	852.8	11 642.3	1.7
3rd quarter	1 678.3	517.9	-361.9	-12.3	1 534.5	1 302.3	94.3	137.9	2 307.5	1 929.7	377.8	-623.0	773.0	11 852.4	1.2
4th quarter	1 651.7	516.9	-335.4	28.3	1 442.0	1 203.8	96.1	142.1	2 361.2	1 979.5	381.6	-723.6	919.2	12 013.3	1.7
2005																
1st quarter	1 780.3	550.5	-278.7	41.2	1 467.2	1 225.3	97.3	144.6	2 427.9	2 046.0	381.9	-693.5	960.7	12 293.5	2.5
2nd quarter	1 807.5	544.6	-269.5	38.3	1 494.1	1 248.0	98.2	147.9	2 433.2	2 039.7	393.5	-691.1	939.1	12 453.0	2.5
3rd quarter	1 873.4	311.9	-364.7	19.3	1 907.0	1 641.1	99.8	166.0	2 487.0	2 084.2	402.9	-660.8	580.1	12 686.5	-0.3
4th quarter	1 915.5	570.4	-253.8	19.1	1 579.8	1 324.4	101.0	154.4	2 587.5	2 174.6	412.9	-814.2	1 007.6	12 911.1	2.6
2006																
1st quarter	2 034.2	601.9	-207.9	57.5	1 582.7	1 323.1	103.0	156.5	2 648.4	2 236.7	411.7	-775.6	1 065.7	13 193.8	3.4
2nd quarter	2 022.8	572.1	-225.0	63.1	1 612.5	1 346.8	105.0	160.8	2 680.1	2 253.7	426.3	-793.0	1 067.5	13 351.0	3.1
3rd quarter	2 005.9	553.8	-218.4	32.2	1 638.3	1 367.8	106.7	163.9	2 660.6	2 231.7	428.9	-827.7	1 022.3	13 486.9	2.7
4th quarter	2 090.9	550.1	-153.2	31.8	1 662.2	1 386.2	107.8	168.1	2 599.1	2 159.5	439.6	-705.6	936.9	13 646.9	3.1

Table 19-10. Federal Government Current Receipts and Expenditures

(National income and product accounts, calendar years, billions of dollars, quarterly data are at seasonally adjusted annual rates.)

NIPA Table 3.2

Year and quarter	Total	Current receipts												
		Tax receipts							Contributions for government social insurance	Income receipts on assets			Current transfer receipts	Current surplus of government enterprises
		Total [1]	Personal current taxes	Taxes on production and imports		Taxes on corporate income				Total	Interest receipts	Rents and royalties		
				Total [1]	Excise taxes	Total	Federal Reserve banks	Other						
1946	39.5	32.7	16.4	7.7	7.2	8.6	0.0	8.6	6.5	. . .	. . .	. . .	0.3	. . .
1947	42.8	37.1	18.8	7.7	7.2	10.7	0.1	10.6	5.4	. . .	. . .	. . .	0.3	. . .
1948	42.4	37.6	18.1	7.8	7.4	11.8	0.2	11.6	4.4	. . .	. . .	. . .	0.3	. . .
1949	37.9	32.8	15.4	7.9	7.5	9.6	0.2	9.4	4.7	. . .	. . .	. . .	0.3	. . .
1947														
1st quarter	43.4	36.9	18.2	7.8	. . .	10.9	0.1	10.9	6.2	. . .	. . .	. . .	0.3	. . .
2nd quarter	42.5	36.4	18.5	7.5	. . .	10.4	0.1	10.3	5.8	. . .	. . .	. . .	0.3	. . .
3rd quarter	41.6	36.3	18.7	7.4	. . .	10.2	0.1	10.1	5.0	. . .	. . .	. . .	0.3	. . .
4th quarter	43.8	38.9	19.8	7.9	. . .	11.1	0.1	11.0	4.6	. . .	. . .	. . .	0.3	. . .
1948														
1st quarter	44.0	39.1	20.1	7.5	. . .	11.5	0.1	11.4	4.6	. . .	. . .	. . .	0.3	. . .
2nd quarter	42.5	37.8	17.8	7.9	. . .	12.1	0.1	12.0	4.3	. . .	. . .	. . .	0.3	. . .
3rd quarter	41.6	36.9	17.1	7.9	. . .	11.9	0.2	11.7	4.4	. . .	. . .	. . .	0.3	. . .
4th quarter	41.4	36.7	17.3	7.9	. . .	11.5	0.2	11.3	4.3	. . .	. . .	. . .	0.3	. . .
1949														
1st quarter	39.9	34.6	16.5	7.8	. . .	10.4	0.2	10.2	5.0	. . .	. . .	. . .	0.3	. . .
2nd quarter	37.9	32.7	15.6	7.9	. . .	9.1	0.2	8.9	4.9	. . .	. . .	. . .	0.3	. . .
3rd quarter	37.4	32.5	14.9	8.1	. . .	9.5	0.2	9.3	4.6	. . .	. . .	. . .	0.3	. . .
4th quarter	36.2	31.5	14.5	7.7	. . .	9.3	0.2	9.2	4.3	. . .	. . .	. . .	0.3	. . .
1950														
1st quarter	41.4	36.1	15.2	7.9	. . .	13.0	0.2	12.9	5.1	. . .	. . .	. . .	0.2	. . .
2nd quarter	45.5	40.2	16.1	8.5	. . .	15.6	0.2	15.4	5.1	. . .	. . .	. . .	0.2	. . .
3rd quarter	51.8	46.3	17.4	9.8	. . .	19.1	0.2	18.9	5.3	. . .	. . .	. . .	0.2	. . .
4th quarter	56.5	50.7	21.0	8.8	. . .	20.9	0.2	20.7	5.6	. . .	. . .	. . .	0.2	. . .
1951														
1st quarter	64.5	57.9	22.8	9.8	. . .	25.3	0.2	25.0	6.4	. . .	. . .	. . .	0.3	. . .
2nd quarter	61.6	54.9	24.7	8.8	. . .	21.4	0.3	21.1	6.5	. . .	. . .	. . .	0.3	. . .
3rd quarter	60.9	54.3	26.1	8.8	. . .	19.4	0.3	19.1	6.3	. . .	. . .	. . .	0.3	. . .
4th quarter	64.6	57.9	27.9	9.3	. . .	20.7	0.3	20.4	6.4	. . .	. . .	. . .	0.3	. . .
1952														
1st quarter	64.7	57.8	29.1	9.8	. . .	19.0	0.3	18.7	6.7	. . .	. . .	. . .	0.3	. . .
2nd quarter	64.8	58.0	30.0	10.1	. . .	17.9	0.3	17.6	6.6	. . .	. . .	. . .	0.3	. . .
3rd quarter	65.3	58.4	30.4	10.1	. . .	17.8	0.3	17.5	6.6	. . .	. . .	. . .	0.3	. . .
4th quarter	68.4	61.4	31.2	10.5	. . .	19.7	0.3	19.3	6.8	. . .	. . .	. . .	0.3	. . .
1953														
1st quarter	70.1	63.1	31.5	10.8	. . .	20.8	0.3	20.4	6.8	. . .	. . .	. . .	0.3	. . .
2nd quarter	70.5	63.3	31.5	11.0	. . .	20.9	0.3	20.5	6.8	. . .	. . .	. . .	0.3	. . .
3rd quarter	69.5	62.4	31.2	10.7	. . .	20.4	0.4	20.0	6.9	. . .	. . .	. . .	0.3	. . .
4th quarter	64.3	57.3	31.0	10.4	. . .	15.9	0.3	15.6	6.7	. . .	. . .	. . .	0.3	. . .
1954														
1st quarter	61.6	53.6	28.1	9.7	. . .	15.7	0.3	15.4	7.8	. . .	. . .	. . .	0.3	. . .
2nd quarter	61.7	53.7	27.9	9.6	. . .	16.2	0.3	15.9	7.7	. . .	. . .	. . .	0.3	. . .
3rd quarter	62.3	54.3	27.9	9.3	. . .	17.1	0.3	16.9	7.7	. . .	. . .	. . .	0.3	. . .
4th quarter	64.4	56.3	28.3	9.5	. . .	18.4	0.2	18.2	7.8	. . .	. . .	. . .	0.3	. . .
1955														
1st quarter	68.3	59.5	29.0	10.0	. . .	20.4	0.2	20.2	8.5	. . .	. . .	. . .	0.3	. . .
2nd quarter	70.3	61.3	30.1	10.5	. . .	20.7	0.2	20.4	8.7	. . .	. . .	. . .	0.3	. . .
3rd quarter	72.0	62.8	31.0	10.6	. . .	21.2	0.3	20.9	8.9	. . .	. . .	. . .	0.3	. . .
4th quarter	73.7	64.5	31.8	10.6	. . .	22.0	0.3	21.7	8.9	. . .	. . .	. . .	0.3	. . .
1956														
1st quarter	74.2	64.3	32.7	10.6	. . .	21.0	0.4	20.6	9.5	. . .	. . .	. . .	0.4	. . .
2nd quarter	75.6	65.6	33.6	10.6	. . .	21.4	0.4	21.0	9.6	. . .	. . .	. . .	0.4	. . .
3rd quarter	75.4	65.4	34.2	11.0	. . .	20.1	0.4	19.7	9.6	. . .	. . .	. . .	0.4	. . .
4th quarter	78.2	68.1	35.2	11.7	. . .	21.2	0.4	20.8	9.8	. . .	. . .	. . .	0.4	. . .
1957														
1st quarter	80.4	69.0	35.7	11.6	. . .	21.7	0.5	21.3	11.0	. . .	. . .	. . .	0.4	. . .
2nd quarter	79.9	68.5	36.1	11.6	. . .	20.8	0.5	20.3	11.0	. . .	. . .	. . .	0.4	. . .
3rd quarter	79.9	68.4	36.3	11.7	. . .	20.4	0.6	19.8	11.1	. . .	. . .	. . .	0.4	. . .
4th quarter	77.1	65.8	35.9	11.3	. . .	18.6	0.6	18.0	10.9	. . .	. . .	. . .	0.4	. . .
1958														
1st quarter	73.6	62.2	35.2	11.1	. . .	16.0	0.6	15.4	10.9	. . .	. . .	. . .	0.4	. . .
2nd quarter	73.5	62.2	34.7	11.2	. . .	16.3	0.6	15.8	10.9	. . .	. . .	. . .	0.4	. . .
3rd quarter	76.7	65.3	35.9	11.1	. . .	18.4	0.5	17.9	11.0	. . .	. . .	. . .	0.4	. . .
4th quarter	80.4	68.9	36.2	11.5	. . .	21.1	0.5	20.7	11.1	. . .	. . .	. . .	0.4	. . .
1959														
1st quarter	84.9	71.4	37.2	11.9	10.9	22.3	0.7	21.6	13.3	0.0	. . .	0.0	0.4	-0.1
2nd quarter	88.6	74.9	38.3	12.1	11.0	24.4	0.8	23.6	13.5	0.0	. . .	0.0	0.4	-0.1
3rd quarter	86.8	73.2	38.7	12.5	11.4	21.9	1.0	20.9	13.4	0.0	. . .	0.0	0.4	-0.2
4th quarter	87.4	73.7	39.7	12.5	11.4	21.4	1.2	20.2	13.5	0.0	. . .	0.0	0.4	-0.1
1960														
1st quarter	95.6	78.2	41.1	13.3	12.1	23.6	0.9	22.7	16.0	1.3	1.3	0.0	0.4	-0.2
2nd quarter	94.3	76.8	41.8	13.2	12.1	21.7	0.9	20.8	16.0	1.3	1.2	0.0	0.4	-0.2
3rd quarter	93.7	76.2	42.3	13.1	12.1	20.7	0.9	19.8	16.0	1.5	1.4	0.0	0.4	-0.4
4th quarter	92.2	74.8	42.1	12.9	11.9	19.7	0.8	18.9	15.9	1.4	1.4	0.0	0.4	-0.4

[1]Includes components not shown separately.
. . . = Not available.

Table 19-10. Federal Government Current Receipts and Expenditures—*Continued*

(National income and product accounts, calendar years, billions of dollars, quarterly data are at seasonally adjusted annual rates.)

NIPA Table 3.2

| Year and quarter | Current expenditures [1] | | | | | | | | | | Net federal government saving, NIPA (surplus + / deficit -) | | |
| | Total | Con-sumption expend-itures | Government social benefits | | Other current transfer payments | | Interest payments | | | Subsidies | Total | Social insurance funds | Other |
			Total [1]	To persons	Total [1]	Grants-in-aid to state and local governments	Total	To persons and business	To the rest of the world				
1946	44.5	27.0	8.7	8.7	3.3	1.0	4.0	...	0.0	1.6	-5.0	3.2	-8.2
1947	37.6	20.9	8.4	8.4	3.6	1.6	4.1	...	0.0	0.6	5.3	3.2	2.1
1948	38.8	21.2	7.2	7.2	5.6	1.7	4.2	...	0.0	0.6	3.6	2.4	1.2
1949	43.5	23.3	8.2	8.2	7.0	1.9	4.3	...	0.0	0.7	-5.7	1.5	-7.2
1947													
1st quarter	37.5	21.7	7.7	7.7	3.2	1.4	4.2	...	0.0	0.7	5.9	...	...
2nd quarter	37.3	21.6	7.3	7.3	3.6	1.7	4.1	...	0.0	0.6	5.2	...	...
3rd quarter	39.7	20.6	10.7	10.7	3.8	1.6	4.1	...	0.0	0.5	2.0	...	...
4th quarter	35.8	19.6	7.8	7.8	3.8	1.6	4.1	...	0.0	0.5	7.9	...	...
1948													
1st quarter	36.3	19.6	7.5	7.5	4.6	1.6	4.1	...	0.0	0.5	7.7	...	...
2nd quarter	37.4	21.0	7.2	7.2	4.6	1.7	4.1	...	0.0	0.4	5.1	...	...
3rd quarter	40.2	21.8	7.0	7.0	6.6	1.8	4.1	...	0.0	0.7	1.4	...	...
4th quarter	41.2	22.5	7.0	7.0	6.4	1.9	4.2	...	0.0	1.0	0.2	...	...
1949													
1st quarter	43.3	23.8	7.7	7.7	6.9	1.7	4.3	...	0.0	0.7	-3.4	...	...
2nd quarter	44.4	24.4	8.2	8.2	7.1	1.7	4.3	...	0.0	0.5	-6.5	...	...
3rd quarter	43.9	23.0	8.5	8.5	7.4	2.1	4.3	...	0.0	0.7	-6.5	...	...
4th quarter	42.3	22.2	8.5	8.5	6.6	1.9	4.4	...	0.0	0.7	-6.2	...	...
1950													
1st quarter	49.8	22.1	16.6	16.6	5.8	1.9	4.4	...	0.0	0.9	-8.4	...	...
2nd quarter	42.8	22.1	9.6	9.6	5.7	1.9	4.4	...	0.0	1.0	2.8	...	...
3rd quarter	38.3	20.6	7.2	7.2	5.0	1.9	4.5	...	0.0	0.9	13.5	...	...
4th quarter	42.3	23.6	7.5	7.5	5.4	1.9	4.5	...	0.0	1.3	14.2	...	...
1951													
1st quarter	47.3	28.8	7.5	7.5	5.1	2.0	4.6	...	0.0	1.3	17.2	...	...
2nd quarter	51.6	32.7	7.9	7.9	5.2	2.1	4.6	...	0.0	1.3	10.0	...	...
3rd quarter	55.5	37.4	8.1	8.1	5.1	1.9	4.6	...	0.0	1.1	5.3	...	...
4th quarter	58.7	38.7	8.0	8.0	5.4	2.1	4.7	...	0.0	1.2	6.0	...	...
1952													
1st quarter	57.8	40.8	7.7	7.7	3.8	2.0	4.6	...	0.0	1.0	6.9	...	...
2nd quarter	61.4	43.8	7.6	7.6	4.5	2.1	4.6	...	0.0	0.9	3.4	...	...
3rd quarter	64.2	45.3	8.5	8.5	4.8	2.3	4.6	...	0.1	0.9	1.1	...	...
4th quarter	64.9	46.9	8.5	8.5	3.9	2.3	4.7	...	0.1	0.8	3.5	...	...
1953													
1st quarter	65.8	47.7	8.6	8.6	3.9	1.8	4.7	...	0.1	0.9	4.3	...	...
2nd quarter	67.8	49.2	8.4	8.4	4.8	2.7	4.7	...	0.1	0.6	2.6	...	...
3rd quarter	66.1	47.6	8.6	8.6	4.2	2.3	4.7	...	0.1	0.8	3.5	...	...
4th quarter	67.5	48.8	9.2	9.2	4.2	2.3	4.8	...	0.1	0.4	-3.2	...	...
1954													
1st quarter	65.0	45.9	9.9	9.9	4.1	2.3	4.8	...	0.1	0.3	-3.3	...	...
2nd quarter	63.6	43.6	10.5	10.5	3.7	2.3	4.8	...	0.1	0.9	-1.9	...	...
3rd quarter	63.7	43.1	10.9	10.9	4.3	2.4	4.8	...	0.1	0.6	-1.3	...	...
4th quarter	64.3	43.2	11.4	11.4	4.4	2.3	4.8	...	0.1	0.4	0.0	...	...
1955													
1st quarter	64.7	43.3	11.4	11.4	4.8	2.3	4.7	...	0.1	0.6	3.6	...	...
2nd quarter	63.6	42.8	11.4	11.4	4.4	2.4	4.6	...	0.1	0.8	6.7	...	...
3rd quarter	67.1	45.2	11.6	11.6	4.4	2.5	4.8	...	0.1	0.5	4.9	...	...
4th quarter	65.9	44.4	11.6	11.6	4.3	2.4	4.9	...	0.1	0.7	7.8	...	...
1956													
1st quarter	65.7	43.9	11.9	11.9	4.2	2.4	4.9	...	0.1	0.8	8.5	...	...
2nd quarter	68.8	46.1	12.1	12.1	4.4	2.5	5.1	...	0.1	1.0	6.7	...	...
3rd quarter	67.6	43.9	12.5	12.5	4.5	2.6	5.2	...	0.2	1.4	7.8	...	...
4th quarter	70.9	46.3	12.6	12.6	4.6	2.7	5.7	...	0.2	1.7	7.3	...	...
1957													
1st quarter	74.3	49.1	13.4	13.4	4.6	2.9	5.4	...	0.2	1.7	6.1	...	...
2nd quarter	75.5	49.0	14.5	14.5	4.8	2.8	5.6	...	0.2	1.6	4.3	...	...
3rd quarter	75.5	49.1	14.6	14.6	4.7	2.9	5.7	...	0.2	1.5	4.4	...	...
4th quarter	78.6	50.7	15.7	15.7	4.9	3.1	5.9	...	0.2	1.4	-1.5	...	...
1958													
1st quarter	76.8	49.1	16.8	16.8	4.6	2.9	5.4	...	0.2	1.5	-3.2	-1.3	-1.9
2nd quarter	81.8	51.8	18.6	18.6	5.1	3.3	5.2	...	0.1	1.7	-8.3	-3.6	-4.7
3rd quarter	83.1	50.6	19.0	19.0	5.1	3.2	5.3	...	0.1	1.9	-6.4	-3.5	-3.0
4th quarter	83.9	52.0	18.3	18.3	5.9	4.0	5.6	...	0.2	2.0	-3.5	-2.4	-1.1
1959													
1st quarter	81.7	48.3	18.4	18.4	7.5	3.5	6.4	...	0.2	1.1	3.2	-0.6	3.8
2nd quarter	83.4	50.2	18.3	18.3	8.1	3.9	5.9	...	0.2	0.9	5.2	-0.3	5.5
3rd quarter	83.9	50.7	18.5	18.5	7.2	3.8	6.3	...	0.3	1.1	2.9	-0.7	3.6
4th quarter	85.3	50.7	19.1	19.1	7.8	3.8	6.7	...	0.4	1.1	2.1	-1.2	3.3
1960													
1st quarter	83.9	48.1	19.1	18.9	7.1	3.9	8.6	8.2	0.4	1.0	11.7	1.3	10.3
2nd quarter	86.0	48.6	19.6	19.5	8.0	4.0	8.5	8.2	0.3	1.3	8.2	0.8	7.4
3rd quarter	87.1	50.6	20.3	20.1	6.9	4.0	8.2	7.9	0.3	1.0	6.6	0.2	6.4
4th quarter	90.0	51.7	21.2	21.0	7.7	4.2	8.1	7.8	0.3	1.2	2.2	-0.8	3.0

[1]Includes components not shown separately.
. . . = Not available.

Table 19-10. Federal Government Current Receipts and Expenditures—*Continued*

(National income and product accounts, calendar years, billions of dollars, quarterly data are at seasonally adjusted annual rates.)

NIPA Table 3.2

Year and quarter		Current receipts												
			Tax receipts							Contribu-tions for govern-ment social insurance	Income receipts on assets			Current transfer receipts	Current surplus of govern-ment enter-prises
	Total	Total ¹	Personal current taxes	Taxes on production and imports		Taxes on corporate income					Total	Interest receipts	Rents and royalties		
				Total ¹	Excise taxes	Total	Federal Reserve banks	Other							
1961															
1st quarter	92.2	74.6	42.2	12.9	11.9	19.4	0.7	18.7	16.3	1.4	1.4	0.1	0.5	-0.5
2nd quarter	94.1	76.4	42.5	13.1	12.1	20.7	0.7	20.1	16.4	1.5	1.4	0.1	0.5	-0.6
3rd quarter	96.0	78.0	42.8	13.2	12.1	22.0	0.7	21.3	16.6	1.4	1.4	0.1	0.5	-0.5
4th quarter	99.5	81.0	43.4	13.6	12.5	23.9	0.7	23.2	16.8	1.6	1.5	0.1	0.5	-0.3
1962															
1st quarter	101.0	80.9	44.6	14.0	12.8	22.3	0.8	21.5	18.4	1.6	1.5	0.1	0.5	-0.4
2nd quarter	102.5	82.2	46.0	14.0	12.8	22.1	0.8	21.3	18.6	1.8	1.7	0.1	0.5	-0.5
3rd quarter	104.9	84.5	47.2	14.4	13.2	22.7	0.8	21.9	18.6	1.7	1.6	0.1	0.5	-0.5
4th quarter	106.1	85.7	48.4	14.3	13.1	22.8	0.8	22.0	18.7	1.7	1.6	0.1	0.5	-0.5
1963															
1st quarter	109.1	86.3	48.8	14.4	13.2	22.9	0.8	22.0	20.7	1.7	1.7	0.1	0.6	-0.3
2nd quarter	111.4	88.4	49.0	14.7	13.5	24.5	0.9	23.6	20.9	1.7	1.7	0.1	0.6	-0.3
3rd quarter	112.5	89.3	49.1	14.8	13.6	25.2	0.9	24.3	21.1	1.8	1.7	0.1	0.6	-0.3
4th quarter	114.1	90.5	49.6	15.0	13.7	25.8	0.9	24.8	21.4	1.8	1.7	0.1	0.6	-0.2
1964															
1st quarter	112.7	89.1	48.0	15.0	13.8	25.9	1.5	24.4	21.4	1.9	1.8	0.1	0.6	-0.2
2nd quarter	109.0	85.3	43.7	15.4	14.1	26.0	1.6	24.4	21.6	1.8	1.7	0.1	0.5	-0.2
3rd quarter	111.7	87.6	45.4	15.5	14.2	26.5	1.6	24.9	21.8	2.0	1.9	0.1	0.9	-0.6
4th quarter	113.6	89.1	46.9	15.9	14.5	26.1	1.7	24.5	22.0	1.6	1.5	0.1	1.0	-0.2
1965															
1st quarter	119.5	94.6	50.5	16.4	15.0	27.5	1.2	26.3	22.2	2.0	1.9	0.1	1.0	-0.3
2nd quarter	121.4	96.2	51.9	15.7	14.1	28.4	1.3	27.1	22.4	2.0	1.9	0.1	1.0	-0.2
3rd quarter	119.8	94.3	50.4	14.8	13.1	28.9	1.3	27.6	22.8	2.0	1.9	0.1	1.1	-0.4
4th quarter	123.1	97.6	51.5	15.0	13.3	30.8	1.4	29.4	23.2	1.7	1.6	0.1	1.1	-0.5
1966															
1st quarter	132.5	100.2	54.4	13.9	12.1	31.7	1.5	30.2	29.6	2.0	1.9	0.1	1.1	-0.5
2nd quarter	137.3	104.6	58.0	14.7	12.8	31.7	1.6	30.2	30.0	2.0	1.9	0.1	1.1	-0.6
3rd quarter	139.7	106.1	59.8	14.6	12.7	31.4	1.7	29.7	31.1	2.1	2.0	0.1	1.2	-0.8
4th quarter	142.3	108.2	62.2	14.9	13.0	30.9	1.8	29.0	31.4	2.3	2.1	0.1	1.2	-0.7
1967															
1st quarter	143.2	107.7	62.9	15.0	13.0	29.7	1.9	27.8	32.8	2.3	2.2	0.2	1.0	-0.7
2nd quarter	144.3	107.5	62.6	15.2	13.3	29.4	1.9	27.5	33.7	2.5	2.4	0.2	1.1	-0.6
3rd quarter	147.8	110.3	65.2	15.3	13.5	29.6	1.9	27.8	34.4	2.5	2.4	0.2	1.1	-0.5
4th quarter	152.2	114.0	66.9	15.5	13.5	31.4	2.0	29.4	35.1	2.6	2.4	0.2	1.2	-0.8
1968															
1st quarter	160.9	120.6	68.8	16.2	14.1	35.2	2.3	33.0	36.7	2.9	2.7	0.2	1.1	-0.4
2nd quarter	165.6	124.4	71.4	16.8	14.6	35.9	2.4	33.5	37.5	2.9	2.7	0.2	1.1	-0.3
3rd quarter	176.8	134.8	81.0	17.3	15.0	36.1	2.5	33.5	38.1	3.1	2.9	0.2	1.1	-0.3
4th quarter	181.5	139.3	84.5	17.5	15.1	37.0	2.6	34.4	38.7	2.8	2.6	0.2	1.1	-0.4
1969															
1st quarter	191.0	145.9	90.7	17.4	15.4	37.4	2.8	34.6	41.9	2.6	2.4	0.2	1.1	-0.5
2nd quarter	194.1	148.1	93.3	17.9	15.3	36.5	3.0	33.5	42.7	2.6	2.5	0.2	1.1	-0.5
3rd quarter	191.9	144.8	90.8	18.3	15.8	35.3	3.1	32.2	43.6	2.7	2.5	0.2	1.2	-0.4
4th quarter	193.3	145.4	91.9	18.0	15.6	35.1	3.3	31.8	44.2	2.8	2.6	0.2	1.2	-0.3
1970															
1st quarter	187.2	139.2	90.6	18.0	15.5	30.3	3.4	27.0	44.9	2.9	2.7	0.2	1.2	-1.0
2nd quarter	188.1	140.5	91.4	18.2	15.8	30.5	3.5	27.0	45.2	3.1	2.8	0.2	1.2	-1.8
3rd quarter	184.7	136.5	86.3	18.3	15.8	31.5	3.6	27.9	45.6	3.1	2.8	0.3	1.1	-1.5
4th quarter	183.8	135.9	87.2	18.3	15.7	30.1	3.5	26.6	45.4	3.1	2.9	0.3	1.1	-1.7
1971															
1st quarter	188.5	136.8	83.6	19.5	16.9	33.3	3.4	29.9	49.3	3.2	2.9	0.3	1.1	-2.0
2nd quarter	191.4	138.2	85.1	18.8	16.1	33.9	3.3	30.7	49.9	3.5	3.1	0.3	1.1	-1.3
3rd quarter	191.8	138.7	86.3	19.0	15.8	33.1	3.4	29.8	50.1	3.5	3.1	0.4	1.1	-1.6
4th quarter	195.1	141.1	88.2	19.1	15.1	33.5	3.4	30.1	50.7	3.7	3.3	0.4	1.1	-1.5
1972															
1st quarter	214.1	154.0	100.3	18.3	15.2	35.0	3.2	31.8	56.9	3.5	3.2	0.4	1.2	-1.5
2nd quarter	217.5	156.4	102.4	18.4	15.6	35.2	3.2	32.0	57.5	3.5	3.2	0.4	1.3	-1.2
3rd quarter	220.4	158.4	103.1	18.6	15.7	36.3	3.2	33.1	58.2	3.7	3.3	0.4	1.3	-1.1
4th quarter	228.2	164.7	105.3	19.1	15.9	39.9	3.3	36.6	59.0	3.7	3.3	0.4	1.3	-0.6
1973															
1st quarter	243.5	167.6	104.5	19.7	16.2	43.0	3.7	39.3	72.2	3.8	3.4	0.4	1.4	-1.4
2nd quarter	247.6	170.7	106.9	20.0	16.7	43.5	4.2	39.4	73.3	3.8	3.4	0.4	1.5	-1.8
3rd quarter	250.8	173.4	111.0	19.8	16.7	42.2	4.6	37.6	74.5	3.7	3.3	0.4	1.1	-1.9
4th quarter	259.6	180.9	116.0	20.2	17.0	44.3	4.9	39.4	76.0	3.8	3.3	0.5	1.1	-2.2
1974															
1st quarter	267.2	182.3	119.5	19.9	16.5	42.5	5.1	37.4	81.5	4.0	3.5	0.5	1.3	-2.0
2nd quarter	277.6	190.2	124.8	20.2	16.7	44.8	5.5	39.3	83.1	4.2	3.6	0.5	1.4	-1.2
3rd quarter	288.4	199.8	129.7	20.4	16.5	49.3	5.8	43.5	84.7	4.2	3.7	0.6	1.5	-1.8
4th quarter	284.9	196.6	132.0	20.3	16.5	43.9	5.8	38.1	84.8	4.3	3.8	0.6	1.5	-2.3
1975															
1st quarter	278.3	189.6	132.3	19.9	15.8	37.0	5.5	31.5	85.9	4.5	3.9	0.6	1.5	-3.1
2nd quarter	245.1	156.1	94.6	21.5	16.3	39.6	5.4	34.2	86.2	4.8	4.2	0.6	1.5	-3.4
3rd quarter	288.5	198.0	125.7	23.5	16.6	48.3	5.2	43.2	87.9	5.1	4.5	0.6	1.5	-3.9
4th quarter	296.8	204.4	130.4	24.1	16.8	49.4	5.5	43.9	89.9	5.2	4.5	0.6	1.5	-4.1

¹Includes components not shown separately.

Table 19-10. Federal Government Current Receipts and Expenditures—*Continued*

(National income and product accounts, calendar years, billions of dollars, quarterly data are at seasonally adjusted annual rates.)

NIPA Table 3.2

Year and quarter	Current expenditures [1]										Net federal government saving, NIPA (surplus + / deficit -)		
	Total	Con-sumption expend-itures	Government social benefits		Other current transfer payments		Interest payments			Subsidies	Total	Social insurance funds	Other
			Total [1]	To persons	Total [1]	Grants-in-aid to state and local governments	Total	To persons and business	To the rest of the world				
1961													
1st quarter	89.7	49.8	22.9	22.7	7.5	4.2	7.9	7.6	0.3	1.6	2.5	-2.1	4.6
2nd quarter	93.4	51.2	23.7	23.4	8.7	4.5	7.8	7.6	0.3	2.0	0.8	-2.7	3.5
3rd quarter	93.5	52.2	23.7	23.5	7.5	4.6	7.9	7.6	0.3	2.2	2.5	-2.7	5.2
4th quarter	94.9	53.3	23.1	22.9	8.1	4.7	8.0	7.7	0.3	2.3	4.7	-1.8	6.5
1962													
1st quarter	98.6	56.0	23.6	23.3	8.5	4.9	8.2	7.9	0.3	2.3	2.4	-0.6	3.1
2nd quarter	100.3	56.9	23.4	23.1	9.1	4.9	8.6	8.2	0.3	2.4	2.2	-0.3	2.5
3rd quarter	101.7	58.9	23.7	23.5	8.1	5.2	8.8	8.5	0.3	2.2	3.1	-0.5	3.6
4th quarter	103.7	59.6	24.3	24.1	8.6	5.2	9.0	8.6	0.4	2.2	2.4	-0.8	3.2
1963													
1st quarter	104.9	59.5	25.5	25.3	8.8	5.3	9.0	8.7	0.4	2.0	4.2	-0.2	4.3
2nd quarter	105.0	59.1	24.4	24.2	10.1	5.5	9.2	8.8	0.4	2.2	6.3	1.1	5.2
3rd quarter	106.7	61.8	24.6	24.3	8.6	5.8	9.4	9.0	0.4	2.3	5.9	1.2	4.7
4th quarter	108.9	62.7	25.0	24.8	9.2	6.1	9.6	9.2	0.4	2.4	5.2	1.2	4.0
1964													
1st quarter	110.7	62.7	25.8	25.5	9.6	6.5	9.8	9.4	0.4	2.7	2.0	0.5	1.5
2nd quarter	111.6	62.9	25.2	24.9	10.7	6.5	9.9	9.5	0.4	2.9	-2.6	1.3	-3.9
3rd quarter	110.4	63.4	25.3	25.1	9.0	6.2	10.1	9.7	0.4	2.6	1.3	1.5	-0.2
4th quarter	110.3	62.1	25.4	25.1	9.8	6.6	10.2	9.7	0.5	2.7	3.3	1.7	1.6
1965													
1st quarter	111.9	62.3	26.5	26.2	9.8	6.5	10.3	9.9	0.5	2.9	7.6	0.9	6.7
2nd quarter	114.6	63.1	26.2	25.7	11.8	7.1	10.5	10.1	0.5	3.0	6.8	1.6	5.1
3rd quarter	120.2	66.7	29.5	29.2	10.5	7.5	10.6	10.1	0.5	3.0	-0.4	-1.2	0.8
4th quarter	123.7	70.8	28.2	27.9	10.8	7.6	10.8	10.3	0.5	3.1	-0.6	0.5	-1.1
1966													
1st quarter	127.4	71.3	29.0	28.7	12.6	9.0	11.0	10.5	0.5	3.5	5.0	6.4	-1.4
2nd quarter	133.8	74.5	28.6	28.3	15.3	10.1	11.5	10.9	0.5	3.9	3.5	6.7	-3.2
3rd quarter	138.3	78.6	30.2	29.8	13.6	10.5	11.8	11.2	0.6	4.0	1.4	6.2	-4.8
4th quarter	143.2	79.1	33.1	32.8	14.5	10.7	12.3	11.7	0.6	4.2	-0.9	4.7	-5.6
1967													
1st quarter	152.9	85.2	35.9	35.6	15.3	11.1	12.5	12.0	0.5	4.0	-9.7	3.7	-13.4
2nd quarter	154.7	86.2	36.4	36.1	15.8	11.6	12.4	11.8	0.6	3.8	-10.4	4.3	-14.7
3rd quarter	156.3	87.3	37.5	36.9	15.3	11.6	12.6	12.0	0.6	3.7	-8.5	4.0	-12.5
4th quarter	161.0	89.9	37.9	37.6	16.4	12.7	13.1	12.5	0.7	3.7	-8.8	4.6	-13.4
1968													
1st quarter	166.9	93.7	39.6	39.3	15.6	11.8	13.8	13.1	0.7	4.0	-6.0	4.6	-10.5
2nd quarter	173.0	94.5	42.2	41.8	17.6	13.3	14.5	13.8	0.7	4.2	-7.4	2.9	-10.3
3rd quarter	175.2	95.9	43.2	42.8	17.0	12.6	14.9	14.3	0.7	4.2	1.5	2.6	-1.1
4th quarter	178.9	97.5	43.9	43.5	18.2	13.2	15.1	14.4	0.7	4.2	2.7	2.7	0.0
1969													
1st quarter	176.4	95.4	44.9	44.6	16.6	13.1	15.1	14.3	0.8	4.3	14.6	5.1	9.4
2nd quarter	182.5	97.6	45.7	45.3	19.2	14.0	15.6	14.8	0.8	4.4	11.5	5.5	6.1
3rd quarter	186.2	100.2	46.5	46.1	19.0	15.1	15.9	15.1	0.8	4.6	5.6	6.0	-0.3
4th quarter	190.1	100.3	47.4	47.0	21.0	16.1	16.7	15.9	0.8	4.6	3.2	6.2	-3.0
1970													
1st quarter	189.5	99.8	48.6	48.3	21.5	17.5	17.3	16.4	0.8	4.7	-2.3	6.6	-8.8
2nd quarter	204.0	98.0	57.9	57.5	23.6	18.8	17.5	16.6	1.0	4.8	-15.8	-1.3	-14.5
3rd quarter	204.1	98.4	57.4	56.9	25.0	20.1	18.2	17.0	1.1	4.7	-19.4	0.5	-19.9
4th quarter	206.9	98.3	60.3	59.8	25.5	20.8	18.0	16.9	1.2	4.8	-23.1	-1.7	-21.4
1971													
1st quarter	212.0	101.0	61.5	61.0	27.0	21.6	17.9	16.5	1.3	4.7	-23.6	1.3	-24.9
2nd quarter	221.5	101.9	68.4	67.9	28.8	23.2	17.6	16.0	1.6	4.8	-30.1	-5.1	-25.0
3rd quarter	221.0	102.0	67.7	67.2	28.7	23.5	18.0	15.9	2.1	4.5	-29.1	-4.1	-25.1
4th quarter	225.7	103.0	68.7	68.2	31.3	24.7	18.2	15.9	2.4	4.6	-30.6	-4.2	-26.4
1972													
1st quarter	236.6	108.3	70.7	70.2	33.2	25.7	18.3	15.8	2.5	6.1	-22.6	0.1	-22.7
2nd quarter	245.2	109.4	70.7	70.2	40.3	33.9	18.6	16.0	2.6	6.2	-27.7	0.8	-28.5
3rd quarter	237.0	105.9	70.7	70.3	34.4	26.8	18.8	16.1	2.7	7.1	-16.6	2.0	-18.5
4th quarter	258.9	107.0	81.2	80.6	46.4	40.4	19.4	16.5	2.9	7.0	-30.7	-5.4	-25.3
1973													
1st quarter	258.2	108.5	82.8	82.2	40.1	35.6	21.0	17.6	3.5	5.9	-14.7	6.1	-20.8
2nd quarter	262.3	109.2	84.2	83.6	40.8	34.7	22.4	18.5	3.9	5.6	-14.7	5.7	-20.4
3rd quarter	260.9	107.8	85.7	85.1	39.2	33.9	23.5	19.5	4.0	4.6	-10.1	5.7	-15.8
4th quarter	265.3	109.9	87.9	87.3	38.7	34.9	24.3	20.3	4.0	4.5	-5.7	5.6	-11.3
1974													
1st quarter	275.5	114.0	94.5	94.1	38.9	34.6	24.8	20.8	4.0	3.5	-8.3	9.1	-17.4
2nd quarter	288.4	114.6	101.3	100.7	43.5	35.4	25.6	21.4	4.2	2.8	-10.8	4.1	-14.8
3rd quarter	298.9	119.0	107.1	106.4	41.7	36.8	26.7	22.4	4.3	3.1	-10.5	1.8	-12.3
4th quarter	310.4	124.3	112.6	112.0	43.1	38.2	26.9	22.4	4.5	3.5	-25.4	-2.2	-23.3
1975													
1st quarter	325.5	125.8	121.2	120.5	47.1	40.7	27.3	22.4	4.9	4.1	-47.2	-9.1	-38.1
2nd quarter	349.3	128.2	134.9	134.2	54.1	45.8	28.1	23.7	4.4	4.1	-104.2	-14.9	-89.3
3rd quarter	350.5	130.2	137.4	136.8	49.3	46.5	29.3	24.8	4.5	4.4	-62.0	-21.1	-40.8
4th quarter	359.6	134.0	138.6	137.8	51.5	47.5	31.0	26.6	4.4	4.8	-62.8	-19.6	-43.2

[1] Includes components not shown separately.

Table 19-10. Federal Government Current Receipts and Expenditures—*Continued*

(National income and product accounts, calendar years, billions of dollars, quarterly data are at seasonally adjusted annual rates.)

NIPA Table 3.2

Year and quarter	Total	Current receipts													
		Tax receipts							Contributions for government social insurance	Income receipts on assets			Current transfer receipts	Current surplus of government enterprises
		Total [1]	Personal current taxes	Taxes on production and imports		Taxes on corporate income				Total	Interest receipts	Rents and royalties		
				Total [1]	Excise taxes	Total	Federal Reserve banks	Other						
1976														
1st quarter	312.1	210.0	132.7	21.0	16.7	55.7	5.8	49.9	96.9	5.7	5.0	0.7	1.5	-2.0
2nd quarter	319.0	215.4	138.4	21.5	17.0	54.8	5.8	49.0	98.3	5.9	5.2	0.7	1.6	-2.2
3rd quarter	326.6	221.2	144.2	21.9	17.1	54.4	5.9	48.5	100.0	6.1	5.4	0.7	1.6	-2.3
4th quarter	332.5	225.9	149.7	21.9	17.3	53.5	6.0	47.5	101.4	5.8	5.1	0.7	1.7	-2.3
1977														
1st quarter	347.0	234.7	154.9	22.2	17.1	56.9	5.9	51.0	106.8	6.5	5.6	0.8	1.7	-2.6
2nd quarter	360.8	245.7	160.6	22.7	17.4	61.7	6.0	55.7	109.4	6.7	5.8	0.9	1.8	-2.7
3rd quarter	367.4	250.2	162.3	23.4	17.6	63.8	5.9	57.9	111.5	6.9	5.9	1.0	2.1	-3.2
4th quarter	378.5	259.1	170.8	23.4	17.9	64.1	6.0	58.1	113.6	6.8	5.8	1.0	2.1	-3.2
1978														
1st quarter	388.7	258.9	173.1	24.2	17.8	60.7	6.3	54.4	123.0	7.6	6.6	1.0	2.3	-3.1
2nd quarter	417.1	282.1	182.7	25.6	18.5	72.8	6.6	66.2	126.8	8.4	7.3	1.1	2.4	-2.5
3rd quarter	434.7	295.7	195.1	25.8	18.5	73.9	7.2	66.7	129.3	8.7	7.6	1.1	2.5	-1.5
4th quarter	453.5	310.7	204.9	26.6	19.1	78.2	7.9	70.3	132.4	9.4	8.2	1.2	2.6	-1.5
1979														
1st quarter	469.1	313.3	211.3	26.2	18.6	74.8	8.2	66.6	145.0	9.9	8.6	1.3	2.7	-1.8
2nd quarter	480.3	322.4	219.7	26.2	18.7	75.4	8.8	66.5	147.0	10.2	8.7	1.4	2.8	-2.1
3rd quarter	492.4	330.9	229.2	25.7	18.4	74.8	9.5	65.3	150.3	10.9	9.4	1.6	2.9	-2.6
4th quarter	503.1	338.3	238.3	25.9	18.6	72.7	10.6	62.1	153.2	11.6	9.9	1.7	3.0	-2.9
1980														
1st quarter	517.2	345.7	237.6	28.0	20.7	78.6	11.6	67.0	159.5	12.1	10.2	2.0	3.1	-3.2
2nd quarter	514.3	341.2	243.6	33.9	27.0	62.1	12.3	49.8	160.3	13.0	10.8	2.2	3.2	-3.4
3rd quarter	533.6	357.3	252.2	36.5	29.3	67.0	11.0	56.0	162.8	14.2	11.8	2.5	3.2	-3.8
4th quarter	563.3	379.5	266.6	37.7	30.4	73.6	11.9	61.7	167.9	15.3	12.5	2.8	4.6	-3.9
1981														
1st quarter	606.6	401.9	277.8	51.0	43.2	71.5	13.0	58.5	187.9	16.6	13.5	3.1	3.9	-3.7
2nd quarter	616.1	406.4	288.4	52.2	43.8	64.3	13.6	50.7	190.3	17.5	14.2	3.4	3.5	-1.7
3rd quarter	631.9	419.0	300.8	49.5	40.7	67.2	14.5	52.7	193.7	18.8	15.2	3.6	3.7	-3.3
4th quarter	623.2	405.0	295.3	48.5	39.1	59.8	15.0	44.8	195.5	20.2	16.4	3.8	3.9	-1.4
1982														
1st quarter	616.5	388.4	294.6	43.9	34.8	48.6	15.1	33.5	203.2	21.6	17.7	3.9	4.9	-1.5
2nd quarter	622.7	393.2	301.1	40.4	31.7	50.4	15.7	34.7	204.3	22.0	18.1	3.9	5.2	-2.0
3rd quarter	611.9	381.7	289.1	40.5	32.2	50.8	15.4	35.4	205.8	22.4	18.5	3.8	5.4	-3.3
4th quarter	615.2	383.7	295.2	40.7	32.4	46.3	14.6	31.7	206.1	22.7	19.0	3.7	5.5	-2.8
1983														
1st quarter	622.1	379.8	289.0	41.5	33.8	48.2	13.9	34.3	216.3	23.2	19.7	3.5	5.5	-2.8
2nd quarter	647.7	401.8	294.7	45.7	36.7	60.2	13.9	46.3	219.6	23.3	19.8	3.4	5.8	-2.8
3rd quarter	641.1	391.5	276.8	45.9	36.2	67.6	14.3	53.3	223.1	24.0	20.6	3.4	6.1	-3.5
4th quarter	658.4	401.2	284.4	46.2	36.1	69.4	14.8	54.6	228.3	24.9	21.4	3.5	6.6	-2.6
1984														
1st quarter	692.5	416.4	287.4	47.4	36.5	80.3	15.4	64.8	246.5	25.5	21.7	3.8	7.1	-3.0
2nd quarter	705.2	423.0	294.1	48.0	35.8	79.5	15.7	63.8	251.2	27.0	23.1	3.9	7.3	-3.1
3rd quarter	711.8	426.1	306.9	47.9	35.7	70.1	16.3	53.8	255.2	26.8	22.9	3.9	7.3	-3.7
4th quarter	726.6	437.4	317.3	47.8	35.5	71.0	16.7	54.3	258.4	27.3	23.5	3.9	7.3	-3.8
1985														
1st quarter	779.8	476.7	352.6	46.8	34.5	75.9	18.2	57.7	270.7	27.7	23.9	3.8	7.9	-3.2
2nd quarter	743.6	429.5	307.1	46.0	34.4	74.5	18.2	56.3	274.1	28.3	24.7	3.6	13.6	-2.0
3rd quarter	781.1	467.3	339.6	47.2	35.1	78.4	17.5	60.8	277.9	30.0	26.6	3.4	8.0	-2.1
4th quarter	788.6	469.1	344.7	45.8	33.1	76.3	17.3	59.0	283.2	30.5	27.4	3.1	7.9	-2.2
1986														
1st quarter	799.2	469.3	341.3	44.8	32.0	81.7	18.7	63.0	292.4	31.5	28.8	2.7	8.0	-2.0
2nd quarter	802.6	470.1	343.9	43.3	29.8	81.4	17.9	63.4	294.9	31.1	28.6	2.5	8.2	-1.7
3rd quarter	816.8	479.2	351.4	44.1	29.8	81.9	17.3	64.6	298.9	32.9	30.6	2.3	7.3	-1.5
4th quarter	842.2	499.9	363.7	43.9	29.7	90.3	17.2	73.1	303.6	30.1	27.8	2.2	9.4	-0.8
1987														
1st quarter	842.3	494.3	357.9	44.4	29.5	90.2	17.2	73.0	309.7	29.3	26.9	2.4	10.0	-1.0
2nd quarter	911.8	560.1	409.7	46.1	30.3	102.3	17.7	84.6	313.2	28.8	26.4	2.4	11.2	-1.5
3rd quarter	906.2	552.6	394.4	46.7	31.3	109.5	18.0	91.5	317.2	27.9	25.5	2.3	10.7	-2.1
4th quarter	926.2	568.9	408.0	47.7	31.8	110.7	18.1	92.7	323.5	25.9	23.6	2.3	11.0	-3.2
1988														
1st quarter	940.0	556.5	401.7	50.0	33.7	102.7	16.7	85.9	344.1	33.9	31.7	2.2	10.1	-4.5
2nd quarter	949.9	561.6	399.6	49.8	33.6	109.5	16.6	92.8	350.8	28.2	26.2	2.0	10.5	-1.3
3rd quarter	961.3	568.1	401.6	50.7	34.2	113.4	17.5	95.9	355.9	27.9	26.0	1.9	11.1	-1.7
4th quarter	981.8	580.5	408.7	50.7	33.9	119.0	18.6	100.4	361.6	29.9	28.0	1.9	11.6	-1.7
1989														
1st quarter	1 028.2	618.5	437.9	51.3	34.2	126.3	21.2	105.1	371.1	28.4	26.5	1.9	11.8	-1.6
2nd quarter	1 030.8	618.1	446.8	49.7	32.2	119.1	22.1	97.0	374.0	28.2	26.2	2.0	12.0	-1.4
3rd quarter	1 038.5	619.2	455.5	50.5	32.8	110.5	21.5	89.0	377.4	30.3	28.1	2.2	13.1	-1.5
4th quarter	1 052.0	630.9	465.8	49.4	31.8	113.0	21.8	91.1	382.6	27.4	25.1	2.3	12.8	-1.7
1990														
1st quarter	1 057.5	626.9	461.3	50.8	33.1	112.1	22.6	89.6	394.6	27.5	25.1	2.5	12.3	-3.8
2nd quarter	1 075.8	643.0	470.1	51.3	33.5	118.7	23.2	95.5	398.5	26.8	24.3	2.6	12.7	-5.1
3rd quarter	1 093.2	653.9	475.1	51.6	34.2	124.2	24.7	99.5	403.9	27.2	24.6	2.7	13.7	-5.5
4th quarter	1 099.5	647.3	474.3	52.0	35.0	117.5	24.0	93.5	403.4	39.3	36.6	2.7	15.5	-6.0

[1] Includes components not shown separately.

Table 19-10. Federal Government Current Receipts and Expenditures—*Continued*

(National income and product accounts, calendar years, billions of dollars, quarterly data are at seasonally adjusted annual rates.)

NIPA Table 3.2

| Year and quarter | Current expenditures [1] | | | | | | | | | | Net federal government saving, NIPA (surplus + / deficit -) | | |
| | Total | Consumption expenditures | Government social benefits | | Other current transfer payments | | Interest payments | | | Subsidies | Total | Social insurance funds | Other |
			Total [1]	To persons	Total [1]	Grants-in-aid to state and local governments	Total	To persons and business	To the rest of the world				
1976													
1st quarter	364.5	134.2	141.8	141.0	51.3	48.7	32.4	28.0	4.4	5.0	-52.4	-14.9	-37.5
2nd quarter	367.1	136.5	140.1	139.3	52.7	49.5	33.2	28.8	4.4	4.7	-48.1	-12.5	-35.6
3rd quarter	378.3	136.6	145.8	145.0	57.0	50.4	34.1	29.5	4.6	4.9	-51.7	-17.3	-34.3
4th quarter	387.3	141.4	148.1	147.3	57.2	54.4	35.4	30.7	4.7	5.3	-54.8	-17.9	-37.0
1977													
1st quarter	392.3	145.3	150.3	149.4	55.6	52.5	35.6	30.8	4.8	5.6	-45.3	-14.4	-30.9
2nd quarter	400.2	149.5	149.3	148.6	59.4	55.5	36.4	31.3	5.1	5.7	-39.4	-12.0	-27.3
3rd quarter	412.6	151.6	154.9	154.1	62.8	59.1	37.2	31.6	5.6	6.2	-45.2	-14.7	-30.5
4th quarter	425.0	156.5	157.1	156.2	62.2	59.2	39.2	32.6	6.6	10.1	-46.5	-14.2	-32.3
1978													
1st quarter	435.1	158.3	159.1	158.3	67.3	63.5	41.9	34.1	7.8	8.5	-46.3	-5.6	-40.7
2nd quarter	442.6	162.1	158.6	157.7	70.1	66.1	43.8	35.4	8.4	8.1	-25.5	-1.4	-24.1
3rd quarter	454.2	164.0	166.5	165.6	69.3	65.5	46.4	37.8	8.6	8.0	-19.4	-6.3	-13.2
4th quarter	468.1	168.9	169.0	168.0	70.9	67.1	49.2	39.3	9.8	10.1	-14.7	-5.0	-9.7
1979													
1st quarter	475.3	173.2	173.1	172.2	68.4	64.4	52.3	41.2	11.1	8.1	-6.1	4.9	-11.0
2nd quarter	486.5	178.0	176.4	175.4	69.3	65.0	54.4	43.4	11.0	8.5	-6.2	4.5	-10.7
3rd quarter	504.2	177.3	190.8	189.8	72.0	67.6	56.4	45.3	11.1	7.8	-11.9	-4.2	-7.6
4th quarter	524.0	187.5	194.6	193.6	73.7	68.4	59.7	48.4	11.3	8.5	-20.8	-4.5	-16.3
1980													
1st quarter	548.1	195.8	202.5	201.5	75.8	69.3	65.3	52.9	12.3	8.9	-30.9	-2.3	-28.6
2nd quarter	569.0	207.1	207.6	206.6	75.2	70.8	69.7	57.8	11.9	9.3	-54.7	-7.6	-47.0
3rd quarter	602.4	208.1	235.9	234.8	78.7	73.4	70.0	57.8	12.1	9.7	-68.7	-27.7	-41.0
4th quarter	623.5	219.0	236.9	235.7	83.8	75.8	73.9	59.5	14.4	9.9	-60.2	-24.3	-35.9
1981													
1st quarter	645.8	228.1	241.1	239.9	79.5	74.4	87.0	70.8	16.2	10.2	-39.3	-7.3	-32.0
2nd quarter	659.5	237.1	242.2	241.0	79.8	74.5	90.1	72.7	17.4	10.3	-43.4	-6.2	-37.2
3rd quarter	683.0	238.3	260.0	258.7	78.2	71.9	96.0	78.3	17.7	10.7	-51.1	-19.9	-31.2
4th quarter	702.6	249.7	262.2	260.9	75.2	69.2	102.4	84.6	17.9	13.1	-79.4	-22.0	-57.4
1982													
1st quarter	716.8	255.2	265.5	264.6	76.0	68.8	106.5	87.7	18.8	13.5	-100.4	-18.8	-81.6
2nd quarter	728.7	256.5	272.8	271.6	76.1	70.4	110.2	91.9	18.3	13.1	-105.9	-25.5	-80.4
3rd quarter	755.7	265.1	288.2	286.9	75.2	69.0	114.9	94.9	19.9	12.5	-143.8	-38.9	-104.9
4th quarter	792.6	276.6	303.3	301.9	78.3	69.8	115.5	95.4	20.1	18.9	-177.3	-52.0	-125.3
1983													
1st quarter	795.3	280.5	302.9	301.6	75.5	70.6	117.0	98.2	18.9	19.4	-173.2	-41.7	-131.5
2nd quarter	817.2	287.3	308.2	306.9	78.4	72.7	121.0	102.3	18.7	21.0	-169.4	-44.2	-125.3
3rd quarter	826.8	296.3	302.1	300.8	78.8	71.8	127.5	108.5	19.0	21.7	-185.7	-33.5	-152.2
4th quarter	822.2	282.0	304.2	302.9	82.0	71.2	132.8	113.4	19.4	21.0	-163.8	-29.8	-134.0
1984													
1st quarter	846.3	297.2	307.1	305.9	82.0	75.4	139.6	119.8	19.8	20.7	-153.9	-13.0	-140.8
2nd quarter	869.2	310.5	309.2	307.9	84.3	77.4	145.0	124.7	20.3	20.5	-164.0	-9.5	-154.5
3rd quarter	883.5	313.2	309.8	308.6	84.8	75.1	155.2	133.5	21.6	20.4	-171.7	-5.2	-166.5
4th quarter	909.4	319.1	315.8	314.6	92.9	78.8	161.5	138.6	22.9	20.7	-182.8	-7.2	-175.6
1985													
1st quarter	926.8	329.3	324.0	322.7	88.6	79.1	164.3	141.3	23.0	20.7	-147.0	-1.9	-145.1
2nd quarter	940.9	334.5	324.9	323.7	90.9	80.0	169.0	146.1	22.9	20.6	-197.3	1.1	-198.4
3rd quarter	955.5	342.1	328.3	327.1	94.1	81.2	170.1	146.8	23.3	20.9	-174.3	1.7	-176.0
4th quarter	969.9	347.7	329.3	328.0	97.1	83.1	174.2	150.9	23.3	21.6	-181.3	6.1	-187.4
1986													
1st quarter	979.9	347.2	339.2	337.7	93.6	84.8	177.2	152.7	24.5	22.7	-180.7	6.8	-187.5
2nd quarter	1 004.7	357.1	342.9	341.4	102.5	89.0	178.5	154.2	24.2	23.8	-202.1	6.1	-208.2
3rd quarter	1 023.9	365.8	348.6	347.2	106.1	91.8	178.4	153.7	24.8	25.1	-207.1	4.8	-211.9
4th quarter	1 015.6	362.9	350.4	348.3	97.3	84.9	178.5	153.5	25.0	26.5	-173.3	8.0	-181.4
1987													
1st quarter	1 022.8	369.6	354.5	353.0	91.1	82.1	179.7	153.9	25.8	27.9	-180.5	11.2	-191.7
2nd quarter	1 037.8	372.3	358.5	357.1	95.4	85.8	181.5	155.5	26.0	30.1	-126.0	11.5	-137.5
3rd quarter	1 040.5	372.3	358.9	357.4	93.4	83.9	185.2	159.1	26.1	30.9	-134.4	15.7	-150.1
4th quarter	1 065.3	382.8	360.7	359.2	99.0	83.8	191.8	164.9	26.9	30.7	-139.1	22.2	-161.3
1988													
1st quarter	1 082.4	381.5	375.6	374.0	99.4	89.5	195.9	167.0	28.9	29.9	-142.4	31.4	-173.8
2nd quarter	1 080.9	379.9	376.7	375.1	98.6	90.0	196.2	165.3	30.9	29.4	-131.0	38.5	-169.5
3rd quarter	1 089.3	377.0	380.1	378.5	103.3	93.1	200.1	167.2	32.9	28.7	-128.0	42.1	-170.1
4th quarter	1 118.2	391.4	383.9	382.3	109.9	93.8	205.0	170.9	34.1	28.0	-136.4	46.7	-183.2
1989													
1st quarter	1 139.6	389.0	404.4	402.8	105.3	94.9	213.5	176.6	36.9	27.4	-111.4	41.8	-153.2
2nd quarter	1 159.4	400.5	408.8	407.2	104.2	95.6	219.1	181.0	38.1	26.8	-128.6	42.6	-171.3
3rd quarter	1 178.0	403.0	414.3	412.6	113.3	101.4	220.9	181.8	39.1	26.5	-139.5	42.9	-182.4
4th quarter	1 192.9	404.5	421.4	419.7	116.5	101.4	223.9	184.6	39.3	26.7	-140.9	45.2	-186.1
1990													
1st quarter	1 226.0	414.9	437.6	435.9	117.7	106.5	229.2	189.2	40.1	26.5	-168.6	43.8	-212.4
2nd quarter	1 247.2	418.1	443.5	441.7	125.7	110.3	233.6	193.1	40.5	26.4	-171.4	43.5	-214.9
3rd quarter	1 258.1	416.4	448.0	446.2	125.9	112.6	241.5	200.6	40.9	26.4	-164.9	45.8	-210.7
4th quarter	1 282.6	429.7	459.5	457.8	121.7	116.3	245.5	203.9	41.6	26.4	-183.1	39.0	-222.2

[1]Includes components not shown separately.

Table 19-10. Federal Government Current Receipts and Expenditures—*Continued*

(National income and product accounts, calendar years, billions of dollars, quarterly data are at seasonally adjusted annual rates.)

NIPA Table 3.2

Year and quarter	Current receipts														
	Total	Tax receipts							Contribu-tions for govern-ment social insurance	Income receipts on assets			Current transfer receipts	Current surplus of govern-ment enter-prises
		Total [1]	Personal current taxes	Taxes on production and imports		Taxes on corporate income				Total	Interest receipts	Rents and royalties		
				Total [1]	Excise taxes	Total	Federal Reserve banks	Other						
1991														
1st quarter	1 087.0	627.5	457.3	60.1	43.6	107.4	21.5	85.9	413.5	32.4	29.6	2.8	17.1	-3.5
2nd quarter	1 095.7	632.6	459.2	61.7	45.6	109.0	20.8	88.2	416.3	30.1	27.3	2.8	17.7	-1.0
3rd quarter	1 107.1	638.5	461.9	62.2	45.5	111.8	20.5	91.3	420.8	30.4	27.7	2.8	18.3	-0.9
4th quarter	1 115.3	645.6	467.0	64.6	46.7	111.6	20.3	91.2	423.7	27.5	24.8	2.7	18.6	-0.1
1992														
1st quarter	1 126.8	645.8	459.1	64.0	46.3	120.0	17.8	102.2	436.1	26.5	23.9	2.6	18.4	0.1
2nd quarter	1 143.7	658.8	468.0	63.5	45.5	124.7	17.4	107.3	440.7	25.8	23.2	2.5	18.2	0.2
3rd quarter	1 137.6	649.2	477.2	62.3	43.6	107.1	16.2	90.9	444.5	25.0	22.5	2.5	18.6	0.3
4th quarter	1 180.6	687.8	496.8	65.0	46.1	123.3	15.7	107.5	446.0	25.5	23.0	2.5	22.3	-1.1
1993														
1st quarter	1 174.4	674.6	481.4	62.5	43.9	127.8	16.4	111.4	454.3	26.9	24.3	2.6	21.0	-2.5
2nd quarter	1 218.1	709.6	502.8	65.1	44.9	139.0	16.0	123.1	461.9	26.9	24.2	2.7	20.8	-1.1
3rd quarter	1 226.8	715.5	511.7	65.7	45.2	135.4	15.7	119.7	465.8	26.5	23.8	2.7	20.8	-1.9
4th quarter	1 270.9	753.9	526.1	73.4	53.5	151.6	15.8	135.8	472.2	24.6	21.8	2.7	21.9	-1.6
1994														
1st quarter	1 272.4	741.0	523.3	75.9	55.3	138.9	18.6	120.3	484.1	23.9	21.1	2.8	23.3	0.1
2nd quarter	1 326.8	789.4	553.7	79.0	57.8	153.5	19.5	134.0	491.9	23.4	20.6	2.8	22.0	0.1
3rd quarter	1 331.0	789.4	542.3	80.9	58.9	163.1	20.9	142.1	496.0	23.4	20.7	2.7	22.7	-0.5
4th quarter	1 353.0	807.8	551.4	81.7	59.8	171.4	22.9	148.6	502.7	22.8	20.2	2.6	21.1	-1.4
1995														
1st quarter	1 373.8	817.7	564.6	76.9	56.9	172.6	22.8	149.8	511.9	22.9	20.6	2.3	20.5	0.8
2nd quarter	1 407.3	848.1	590.6	76.1	56.1	177.7	23.8	154.0	516.3	23.8	21.5	2.3	19.5	-0.4
3rd quarter	1 415.2	852.5	586.8	75.8	56.1	185.8	23.6	162.1	521.8	23.1	20.6	2.5	18.9	-1.1
4th quarter	1 429.8	862.0	601.8	74.8	55.1	181.2	23.3	157.8	526.8	25.0	22.2	2.8	17.6	-1.6
1996														
1st quarter	1 470.5	896.1	631.3	73.0	52.9	187.2	19.9	167.3	531.4	26.4	22.9	3.5	18.1	-1.6
2nd quarter	1 519.0	936.4	668.1	71.5	52.2	192.0	20.0	172.0	539.6	26.4	22.6	3.8	18.3	-1.7
3rd quarter	1 529.5	937.5	669.2	72.1	52.4	190.9	20.1	170.8	546.6	27.7	23.5	4.2	18.8	-1.1
4th quarter	1 577.0	959.6	685.2	76.3	58.6	192.4	20.3	172.0	553.5	27.2	22.8	4.4	37.2	-0.5
1997														
1st quarter	1 600.2	990.0	718.0	72.3	53.3	194.9	20.0	174.9	564.5	27.0	22.5	4.5	19.3	-0.6
2nd quarter	1 636.3	1 017.7	733.5	80.1	59.6	199.3	20.5	178.8	571.3	27.0	22.4	4.5	19.6	0.8
3rd quarter	1 672.8	1 046.8	751.8	80.3	60.5	209.6	20.9	188.8	579.4	25.7	21.3	4.5	20.4	0.5
4th quarter	1 703.1	1 067.9	774.0	80.1	60.8	208.2	21.3	186.9	590.2	23.9	19.6	4.4	20.4	0.7
1998														
1st quarter	1 731.4	1 086.0	796.1	79.9	60.5	205.2	26.4	178.9	600.9	22.5	18.3	4.1	21.2	1.0
2nd quarter	1 758.1	1 104.9	816.5	80.5	60.9	202.8	26.6	176.2	609.4	21.8	17.9	3.9	21.4	0.7
3rd quarter	1 792.4	1 131.4	836.3	81.8	62.0	207.7	26.8	181.0	618.2	20.9	17.2	3.7	21.8	0.1
4th quarter	1 813.2	1 145.1	854.5	82.1	62.6	201.3	26.6	174.7	626.7	20.8	17.4	3.5	21.8	-1.4
1999														
1st quarter	1 843.6	1 157.5	864.1	81.7	63.5	206.3	24.0	182.3	643.0	20.8	17.7	3.2	21.9	0.4
2nd quarter	1 869.5	1 179.2	879.7	82.1	64.2	211.4	24.6	186.8	647.1	21.2	17.9	3.4	22.1	-0.2
3rd quarter	1 900.2	1 203.9	899.5	84.2	64.5	213.9	25.3	188.5	652.6	21.5	18.0	3.5	22.5	-0.4
4th quarter	1 951.6	1 242.4	928.7	87.5	66.5	220.2	27.7	192.5	663.9	22.3	18.4	3.8	24.2	-1.2
2000														
1st quarter	2 035.7	1 301.9	975.4	86.7	66.7	233.0	24.7	208.3	685.3	24.5	20.1	4.4	24.8	-0.8
2nd quarter	2 044.9	1 309.4	987.4	88.9	67.0	225.5	25.0	200.6	685.6	25.5	20.7	4.8	25.3	-0.9
3rd quarter	2 066.8	1 322.6	1 011.7	88.1	66.5	215.6	25.6	189.9	696.5	25.0	19.6	5.4	25.8	-3.1
4th quarter	2 068.0	1 320.4	1 021.7	87.5	66.5	203.7	26.1	177.6	699.4	25.9	19.9	6.0	26.7	-4.5
2001														
1st quarter	2 089.2	1 323.0	1 047.3	87.6	65.8	180.7	29.6	151.1	716.4	26.4	19.8	6.6	27.2	-3.8
2nd quarter	2 080.5	1 315.6	1 045.7	86.9	66.3	176.6	28.0	148.7	718.1	25.2	18.6	6.7	27.3	-5.7
3rd quarter	1 895.4	1 132.0	881.0	84.2	64.3	159.7	26.6	133.2	717.9	24.4	17.9	6.5	27.1	-6.1
4th quarter	1 999.6	1 238.1	1 004.1	84.6	64.4	141.6	24.3	117.4	717.6	23.5	17.3	6.2	26.6	-6.2
2002														
1st quarter	1 845.9	1 071.3	843.1	84.9	66.3	136.3	25.0	111.3	732.1	21.1	15.8	5.3	25.7	-4.3
2nd quarter	1 854.1	1 077.5	835.2	87.7	68.0	147.4	25.3	122.1	735.5	20.1	15.0	5.1	24.9	-3.9
3rd quarter	1 856.1	1 075.4	825.8	88.5	67.9	153.9	24.4	129.5	735.0	19.8	15.2	4.7	24.5	1.4
4th quarter	1 856.6	1 078.0	818.0	88.0	67.2	164.2	23.2	141.0	734.4	19.9	15.5	4.4	24.0	0.3
2003														
1st quarter	1 888.9	1 092.7	804.4	90.0	68.5	190.8	23.9	166.9	747.6	19.8	15.0	4.7	24.2	4.6
2nd quarter	1 903.3	1 097.0	810.4	89.5	68.3	186.5	22.8	163.7	755.9	23.0	16.6	6.4	24.7	2.7
3rd quarter	1 817.3	1 004.5	708.2	88.8	67.3	199.6	21.4	178.2	761.7	24.2	16.9	7.3	25.4	1.5
4th quarter	1 910.2	1 089.1	774.7	90.3	68.8	214.3	20.0	194.3	770.3	24.8	17.2	7.6	25.7	0.4
2004														
1st quarter	1 939.5	1 100.7	767.5	93.8	71.5	229.7	17.2	212.5	788.3	23.6	16.7	6.9	27.6	-0.6
2nd quarter	1 989.7	1 139.0	785.8	94.3	71.3	249.8	17.2	232.6	799.6	23.4	16.9	6.5	28.5	-0.8
3rd quarter	2 023.5	1 159.4	809.6	95.1	71.7	246.4	18.1	228.2	812.1	23.9	17.5	6.4	29.4	-1.4
4th quarter	2 082.8	1 209.9	826.6	95.3	71.0	275.3	19.8	255.5	820.9	24.2	17.6	6.6	29.9	-2.1
2005														
1st quarter	2 225.7	1 338.8	894.9	97.1	72.1	335.4	18.5	316.9	835.0	24.1	17.2	6.9	31.0	-3.2
2nd quarter	2 264.1	1 369.2	917.8	101.2	75.9	339.8	20.6	319.2	842.5	25.0	17.2	7.7	31.8	-4.4
3rd quarter	2 214.5	1 375.8	944.2	100.0	74.6	318.0	21.6	296.4	857.0	23.8	16.8	7.0	-35.8	-6.4
4th quarter	2 363.3	1 448.0	965.8	98.5	72.9	370.6	25.1	345.5	865.7	23.1	16.4	6.7	32.8	-6.2

[1]Includes components not shown separately.

Table 19-10. Federal Government Current Receipts and Expenditures—*Continued*

(National income and product accounts, calendar years, billions of dollars, quarterly data are at seasonally adjusted annual rates.)

NIPA Table 3.2

Year and quarter	Current expenditures [1]										Net federal government saving, NIPA (surplus + / deficit -)		
	Total	Con-sumption expend-itures	Government social benefits		Other current transfer payments		Interest payments			Subsidies	Total	Social insurance funds	Other
			Total [1]	To persons	Total [1]	Grants-in-aid to state and local governments	Total	To persons and business	To the rest of the world				
1991													
1st quarter	1 245.4	443.8	480.9	479.1	46.1	122.8	248.2	206.4	41.8	26.5	-158.4	29.7	-188.1
2nd quarter	1 307.4	442.2	491.2	489.3	96.0	128.1	251.0	210.1	40.9	26.6	-211.7	25.0	-236.6
3rd quarter	1 339.8	438.1	495.0	493.1	129.0	134.9	250.7	209.7	41.1	26.9	-232.7	27.1	-259.7
4th quarter	1 367.4	433.9	509.5	506.5	142.7	140.6	253.9	214.1	39.7	27.5	-252.1	20.9	-273.1
1992													
1st quarter	1 415.3	439.2	539.5	538.0	156.9	143.2	251.7	212.6	39.2	28.0	-288.5	8.8	-297.3
2nd quarter	1 435.4	441.1	551.2	548.5	161.9	146.2	252.6	213.3	39.3	28.6	-291.7	4.5	-296.3
3rd quarter	1 453.7	450.1	555.5	553.5	166.6	152.4	251.8	212.6	39.1	29.8	-316.1	6.5	-322.6
4th quarter	1 473.9	450.3	560.7	559.1	182.5	154.6	248.9	210.2	38.8	31.6	-293.4	6.2	-299.6
1993													
1st quarter	1 475.0	442.7	574.1	572.7	169.9	156.3	253.4	214.6	38.8	34.8	-300.6	3.6	-304.3
2nd quarter	1 486.1	440.0	580.4	578.4	174.8	159.3	253.9	215.2	38.7	36.9	-268.0	5.8	-273.8
3rd quarter	1 500.8	441.2	585.4	583.4	183.0	165.0	254.2	214.3	39.8	37.0	-274.0	4.9	-278.9
4th quarter	1 522.2	443.7	589.5	587.5	201.6	174.1	252.0	211.9	40.1	35.4	-251.3	8.3	-259.5
1994													
1st quarter	1 504.6	437.8	600.4	599.0	183.0	171.2	250.4	209.7	40.7	32.9	-232.2	13.4	-245.5
2nd quarter	1 517.2	438.4	604.3	602.9	185.3	171.6	257.5	215.1	42.3	31.7	-190.3	18.1	-208.4
3rd quarter	1 542.3	446.7	610.0	606.3	190.1	174.9	264.3	219.8	44.6	31.2	-211.3	18.0	-229.3
4th quarter	1 568.6	440.4	615.7	613.9	207.9	181.2	273.2	224.0	49.1	31.4	-215.5	22.4	-237.9
1995													
1st quarter	1 589.0	442.9	631.9	630.7	198.0	185.0	283.1	234.8	48.3	33.0	-215.2	20.7	-235.9
2nd quarter	1 602.6	442.6	640.3	638.2	196.0	184.9	290.2	237.5	52.7	33.5	-195.3	17.9	-213.2
3rd quarter	1 613.9	443.5	646.0	643.9	197.1	185.1	293.4	237.4	56.0	34.0	-198.7	18.6	-217.3
4th quarter	1 608.5	432.8	652.6	650.5	194.0	181.6	294.9	236.6	58.3	34.3	-178.7	18.8	-197.5
1996													
1st quarter	1 652.6	443.6	672.0	669.7	205.8	186.1	296.9	237.2	59.7	34.3	-182.1	8.6	-190.6
2nd quarter	1 662.1	447.6	678.5	676.4	207.0	195.0	294.8	232.0	62.8	34.2	-143.1	11.7	-154.9
3rd quarter	1 662.6	442.2	682.2	680.1	206.0	193.2	298.3	231.2	67.2	33.9	-133.1	16.3	-149.4
4th quarter	1 685.7	451.7	687.4	685.3	214.2	190.3	298.9	227.6	71.4	33.5	-108.7	19.2	-127.8
1997													
1st quarter	1 689.4	453.2	702.8	700.7	202.9	192.4	297.5	223.1	74.4	33.0	-89.2	20.9	-110.1
2nd quarter	1 705.4	461.7	706.0	703.7	206.1	195.5	299.3	221.6	77.7	32.3	-69.1	25.6	-94.7
3rd quarter	1 707.8	457.2	707.7	705.7	209.7	198.4	301.1	220.4	80.7	32.1	-35.0	33.0	-68.0
4th quarter	1 733.1	458.5	708.9	706.7	231.2	208.2	302.0	220.3	81.7	32.4	-30.0	42.8	-72.8
1998													
1st quarter	1 718.4	447.7	716.7	714.4	218.7	207.9	302.3	220.9	81.3	33.1	13.0	46.2	-33.2
2nd quarter	1 729.2	457.9	718.0	715.6	218.2	208.1	301.2	220.1	81.2	33.7	28.9	54.8	-25.8
3rd quarter	1 732.0	451.0	720.5	718.3	225.9	213.0	299.3	220.1	79.2	35.3	60.4	62.1	-1.7
4th quarter	1 760.2	461.8	721.4	719.1	246.6	222.0	292.6	217.1	75.5	37.7	53.0	72.9	-19.9
1999													
1st quarter	1 764.2	467.0	733.4	731.0	238.5	227.0	284.4	210.6	73.8	40.9	79.4	85.5	-6.1
2nd quarter	1 764.8	463.9	736.5	734.2	237.4	223.7	283.3	210.4	72.9	43.6	104.6	89.5	15.1
3rd quarter	1 792.4	477.6	739.3	736.9	250.2	237.6	280.1	205.2	75.0	45.2	107.8	95.3	12.5
4th quarter	1 828.9	491.8	742.9	740.6	265.9	243.2	282.8	206.2	76.5	45.4	122.7	105.9	16.9
2000													
1st quarter	1 823.0	485.7	756.1	753.7	252.1	239.0	285.1	205.6	79.6	43.9	212.7	117.7	95.0
2nd quarter	1 863.5	505.1	771.8	769.3	257.0	242.8	285.7	203.5	82.2	43.8	181.4	105.3	76.1
3rd quarter	1 875.5	501.5	776.8	774.2	271.1	255.0	282.5	198.6	83.9	43.7	191.2	114.1	77.1
4th quarter	1 895.5	505.0	785.1	782.6	282.2	252.6	279.6	193.5	86.2	43.5	172.5	112.2	60.2
2001													
1st quarter	1 932.6	518.4	817.3	814.6	278.1	266.5	274.5	188.6	85.9	44.3	156.6	102.6	54.0
2nd quarter	1 956.9	528.0	831.2	828.5	290.1	278.3	263.7	178.7	85.0	44.0	123.6	95.2	28.4
3rd quarter	1 984.0	532.7	849.4	846.7	286.1	272.8	253.3	173.4	80.0	62.5	-88.6	80.9	-169.5
4th quarter	2 004.3	548.4	867.6	865.0	305.8	286.6	242.8	164.0	78.8	39.7	-4.7	69.3	-74.1
2002													
1st quarter	2 054.4	571.3	896.4	893.7	318.7	291.4	229.9	150.8	79.1	38.1	-208.5	64.9	-273.4
2nd quarter	2 095.5	585.0	922.8	920.1	317.9	303.1	233.3	155.6	77.7	36.5	-241.4	46.1	-287.5
3rd quarter	2 103.4	591.4	927.0	924.3	320.6	306.6	227.7	151.8	76.0	36.7	-247.3	44.0	-291.3
4th quarter	2 151.1	618.5	932.2	929.5	336.3	317.2	225.4	151.5	73.9	38.7	-294.6	40.6	-335.1
2003													
1st quarter	2 179.0	636.9	948.0	945.3	337.0	311.9	216.6	144.1	72.5	41.9	-290.2	42.4	-332.6
2nd quarter	2 268.8	668.4	964.0	961.1	367.4	342.2	212.4	141.2	71.2	55.2	-365.5	37.4	-402.9
3rd quarter	2 268.8	669.1	972.7	969.8	369.4	345.9	210.0	135.3	74.7	47.5	-451.4	36.7	-488.1
4th quarter	2 291.7	676.5	981.5	978.6	374.8	354.2	212.5	135.4	77.1	46.4	-381.5	39.4	-420.8
2004													
1st quarter	2 350.6	709.6	1 007.8	1 004.8	375.1	341.3	216.3	141.5	74.9	43.3	-411.1	44.2	-455.3
2nd quarter	2 363.8	721.2	1 010.0	1 007.0	373.2	350.6	215.3	133.6	81.8	42.6	-374.1	56.0	-430.1
3rd quarter	2 385.4	734.6	1 015.4	1 012.4	367.1	344.6	224.4	140.0	84.4	43.9	-361.9	64.3	-426.2
4th quarter	2 418.2	729.6	1 028.2	1 025.0	385.5	359.8	227.8	138.7	89.0	47.2	-335.4	62.6	-398.0
2005													
1st quarter	2 504.4	758.2	1 060.1	1 057.1	398.6	358.5	233.4	137.8	95.5	54.2	-278.7	52.7	-331.3
2nd quarter	2 533.6	760.3	1 074.5	1 071.4	387.2	361.1	253.4	152.9	100.4	58.2	-269.5	48.1	-317.6
3rd quarter	2 579.2	782.1	1 090.1	1 087.0	392.8	359.7	253.8	148.1	105.7	60.4	-364.7	57.1	-421.8
4th quarter	2 617.1	764.5	1 101.5	1 098.3	407.2	364.3	281.0	167.2	113.9	62.9	-253.8	58.4	-312.2

[1]Includes components not shown separately.

Table 19-11. State and Local Government Current Receipts and Expenditures

(National income and product accounts, calendar years, billions of dollars, quarterly data are at seasonally adjusted annual rates.)

NIPA Table 3.3

Year and quarter	Current receipts												
	Total	Current tax receipts							Taxes on corporate income	Contributions for government social insurance	Income receipts on assets		
		Total	Personal current taxes		Taxes on production and imports						Total [1]	Interest receipts	Rents and royalties
			Total [1]	Income taxes	Total	Sales taxes	Property taxes	Other					
1946	12.6	10.5	0.9	0.4	9.1	2.9	4.8	1.4	0.5	0.2	0.4	0.3	0.1
1947	14.9	12.0	1.0	0.5	10.4	3.5	5.3	1.6	0.6	0.2	0.4	0.3	0.1
1948	16.8	13.7	1.1	0.6	11.9	4.1	5.9	1.8	0.7	0.2	0.5	0.3	0.2
1949	18.3	15.0	1.4	0.7	13.0	4.3	6.6	2.1	0.6	0.2	0.5	0.3	0.2
1947													
1st quarter	14.1	11.5	1.0	. . .	9.9	. . .	. . .	. . .	0.6	0.2	0.4	. . .	0.1
2nd quarter	14.7	11.8	1.0	. . .	10.2	. . .	. . .	. . .	0.6	0.2	0.4	. . .	0.1
3rd quarter	15.1	12.2	1.0	. . .	10.6	. . .	. . .	. . .	0.6	0.2	0.4	. . .	0.1
4th quarter	15.6	12.7	1.0	. . .	11.1	. . .	. . .	. . .	0.6	0.2	0.4	. . .	0.1
1948													
1st quarter	16.1	13.2	1.1	. . .	11.4	. . .	. . .	. . .	0.7	0.2	0.5	. . .	0.2
2nd quarter	16.6	13.6	1.1	. . .	11.7	. . .	. . .	. . .	0.7	0.2	0.5	. . .	0.2
3rd quarter	17.0	13.9	1.1	. . .	12.1	. . .	. . .	. . .	0.7	0.2	0.5	. . .	0.2
4th quarter	17.3	14.1	1.1	. . .	12.3	. . .	. . .	. . .	0.7	0.2	0.5	. . .	0.2
1949													
1st quarter	17.7	14.6	1.3	. . .	12.6	. . .	. . .	. . .	0.7	0.2	0.5	. . .	0.2
2nd quarter	17.9	14.8	1.4	. . .	12.9	. . .	. . .	. . .	0.6	0.2	0.5	. . .	0.2
3rd quarter	18.7	15.2	1.4	. . .	13.2	. . .	. . .	. . .	0.6	0.2	0.5	. . .	0.2
4th quarter	18.8	15.4	1.4	. . .	13.4	. . .	. . .	. . .	0.6	0.2	0.5	. . .	0.2
1950													
1st quarter	19.2	15.8	1.5	. . .	13.7	. . .	. . .	. . .	0.6	0.2	0.5	. . .	0.2
2nd quarter	19.7	16.1	1.5	. . .	14.0	. . .	. . .	. . .	0.7	0.2	0.5	. . .	0.2
3rd quarter	20.4	16.9	1.5	. . .	14.6	. . .	. . .	. . .	0.9	0.2	0.5	. . .	0.2
4th quarter	20.6	17.1	1.5	. . .	14.6	. . .	. . .	. . .	0.9	0.2	0.6	. . .	0.2
1951													
1st quarter	21.7	17.9	1.6	. . .	15.3	. . .	. . .	. . .	1.0	0.2	0.6	. . .	0.2
2nd quarter	21.6	17.8	1.7	. . .	15.3	. . .	. . .	. . .	0.9	0.2	0.6	. . .	0.2
3rd quarter	21.9	18.1	1.7	. . .	15.6	. . .	. . .	. . .	0.8	0.2	0.6	. . .	0.2
4th quarter	22.5	18.6	1.7	. . .	16.0	. . .	. . .	. . .	0.8	0.2	0.6	. . .	0.2
1952													
1st quarter	22.9	19.0	1.8	. . .	16.3	. . .	. . .	. . .	0.8	0.3	0.6	. . .	0.2
2nd quarter	23.4	19.4	1.8	. . .	16.8	. . .	. . .	. . .	0.8	0.3	0.7	. . .	0.2
3rd quarter	24.0	19.8	1.8	. . .	17.2	. . .	. . .	. . .	0.8	0.3	0.7	. . .	0.2
4th quarter	24.6	20.4	1.8	. . .	17.7	. . .	. . .	. . .	0.9	0.3	0.7	. . .	0.2
1953													
1st quarter	24.6	20.7	1.9	. . .	18.0	. . .	. . .	. . .	0.9	0.3	0.7	. . .	0.3
2nd quarter	25.8	21.0	1.9	. . .	18.2	. . .	. . .	. . .	0.9	0.3	0.7	. . .	0.3
3rd quarter	25.8	21.4	2.0	. . .	18.6	. . .	. . .	. . .	0.8	0.3	0.7	. . .	0.3
4th quarter	25.9	21.4	2.0	. . .	18.8	. . .	. . .	. . .	0.7	0.3	0.7	. . .	0.3
1954													
1st quarter	26.4	21.7	2.1	. . .	19.0	. . .	. . .	. . .	0.7	0.3	0.8	. . .	0.3
2nd quarter	26.6	22.0	2.1	. . .	19.2	. . .	. . .	. . .	0.7	0.3	0.8	. . .	0.3
3rd quarter	27.1	22.4	2.1	. . .	19.5	. . .	. . .	. . .	0.8	0.3	0.8	. . .	0.3
4th quarter	27.6	22.8	2.1	. . .	19.9	. . .	. . .	. . .	0.8	0.3	0.8	. . .	0.3
1955													
1st quarter	28.3	23.6	2.4	. . .	20.3	. . .	. . .	. . .	0.9	0.3	0.8	. . .	0.3
2nd quarter	29.0	24.0	2.4	. . .	20.7	. . .	. . .	. . .	0.9	0.3	0.8	. . .	0.3
3rd quarter	29.8	24.7	2.4	. . .	21.3	. . .	. . .	. . .	1.0	0.3	0.9	. . .	0.3
4th quarter	30.4	25.3	2.4	. . .	21.9	. . .	. . .	. . .	1.0	0.3	0.9	. . .	0.3
1956													
1st quarter	31.3	26.1	2.7	. . .	22.4	. . .	. . .	. . .	1.0	0.4	0.9	. . .	0.3
2nd quarter	32.0	26.8	2.7	. . .	23.0	. . .	. . .	. . .	1.1	0.4	1.0	. . .	0.3
3rd quarter	32.8	27.3	2.7	. . .	23.6	. . .	. . .	. . .	1.0	0.4	1.0	. . .	0.3
4th quarter	33.4	27.8	2.7	. . .	24.1	. . .	. . .	. . .	1.1	0.4	1.0	. . .	0.3
1957													
1st quarter	34.4	28.5	2.9	. . .	24.6	. . .	. . .	. . .	1.1	0.4	1.1	. . .	0.3
2nd quarter	34.7	28.9	2.9	. . .	25.0	. . .	. . .	. . .	1.0	0.4	1.1	. . .	0.3
3rd quarter	35.3	29.3	2.9	. . .	25.4	. . .	. . .	. . .	1.0	0.4	1.1	. . .	0.3
4th quarter	35.6	29.3	2.9	. . .	25.5	. . .	. . .	. . .	0.9	0.4	1.1	. . .	0.3
1958													
1st quarter	35.7	29.7	3.0	1.8	25.8	9.8	13.4	2.7	0.9	0.4	1.1	0.7	0.4
2nd quarter	36.5	30.1	3.0	1.8	26.1	9.8	13.6	2.7	0.9	0.4	1.1	0.8	0.4
3rd quarter	37.2	30.8	3.1	1.8	26.7	10.0	13.9	2.8	1.0	0.4	1.1	0.8	0.4
4th quarter	38.9	31.7	3.1	1.8	27.4	10.3	14.2	3.0	1.2	0.4	1.2	0.8	0.4
1959													
1st quarter	39.1	32.7	3.6	2.0	27.9	10.7	14.4	2.8	1.2	0.4	1.1	0.8	0.3
2nd quarter	40.1	33.2	3.7	2.1	28.2	10.9	14.5	2.9	1.3	0.4	1.1	0.8	0.3
3rd quarter	41.3	34.4	4.0	2.4	29.3	11.4	14.9	2.9	1.1	0.4	1.1	0.9	0.3
4th quarter	42.1	35.1	4.0	2.4	30.0	11.5	15.4	3.0	1.1	0.4	1.2	0.9	0.3
1960													
1st quarter	43.3	36.0	4.2	2.5	30.4	11.8	15.6	3.1	1.4	0.4	1.3	1.1	0.3
2nd quarter	44.2	36.7	4.2	2.5	31.2	12.1	16.0	3.1	1.3	0.4	1.4	1.1	0.3
3rd quarter	44.8	37.3	4.3	2.6	31.8	12.3	16.5	3.1	1.2	0.5	1.3	1.0	0.3
4th quarter	45.5	37.9	4.3	2.6	32.4	12.4	16.9	3.1	1.1	0.5	1.3	1.0	0.3

[1] Includes components not shown separately.
. . . = Not available.

Table 19-11. State and Local Government Current Receipts and Expenditures—*Continued*

(National income and product accounts, calendar years, billions of dollars, quarterly data are at seasonally adjusted annual rates.)

NIPA Table 3.3

| Year and quarter | Current receipts—*Continued* | | | | Current surplus of government enterprises | Current expenditures | | | | | Net state and local government saving, NIPA (surplus + / deficit -) | | |
| | Current transfer receipts | | | | | | | | | | | | |
	Total	Federal grants-in-aid	From business, net	From persons		Total ¹	Consumption expenditures	Government social benefits to persons	Interest payments	Subsidies	Total	Social insurance funds	Other
1946	1.2	1.0	0.1	0.2	0.4	11.1	9.2	1.5	0.5	...	1.5	0.1	1.4
1947	1.8	1.6	0.1	0.2	0.4	13.5	10.9	2.0	0.5	...	1.4	0.1	1.4
1948	2.0	1.7	0.1	0.2	0.3	15.5	12.3	2.7	0.5	...	1.2	0.1	1.1
1949	2.2	1.9	0.1	0.3	0.4	16.8	13.7	2.7	0.5	...	1.5	0.1	1.4
1947													
1st quarter	1.6	1.4	0.1	0.2	0.4	12.5	10.3	1.6	0.5	...	1.6	...	...
2nd quarter	1.9	1.7	0.1	0.2	0.4	13.1	10.7	1.9	0.5	...	1.6	...	...
3rd quarter	1.9	1.6	0.1	0.2	0.4	14.0	11.1	2.4	0.5	...	1.1	...	...
4th quarter	1.9	1.6	0.1	0.2	0.4	14.3	11.5	2.3	0.5	...	1.3	...	...
1948													
1st quarter	1.9	1.6	0.1	0.2	0.4	15.1	11.8	2.8	0.5	...	1.0	...	...
2nd quarter	2.0	1.7	0.1	0.2	0.3	15.4	12.0	2.8	0.5	...	1.2	...	...
3rd quarter	2.1	1.8	0.1	0.3	0.3	15.8	12.5	2.7	0.5	...	1.2	...	...
4th quarter	2.2	1.9	0.1	0.3	0.3	15.8	13.0	2.4	0.5	...	1.5	...	...
1949													
1st quarter	2.1	1.7	0.1	0.3	0.4	16.2	13.3	2.5	0.5	...	1.5	...	...
2nd quarter	2.0	1.7	0.1	0.3	0.4	16.5	13.4	2.6	0.5	...	1.4	...	...
3rd quarter	2.5	2.1	0.1	0.3	0.4	17.1	13.8	2.7	0.5	...	1.6	...	...
4th quarter	2.3	1.9	0.1	0.3	0.4	17.5	14.1	2.9	0.5	...	1.3	...	...
1950													
1st quarter	2.3	1.9	0.1	0.3	0.4	18.2	14.5	3.2	0.6	...	1.0	...	...
2nd quarter	2.3	1.9	0.1	0.3	0.4	18.9	14.7	3.7	0.6	...	0.7	...	...
3rd quarter	2.3	1.9	0.1	0.3	0.4	18.6	15.0	3.0	0.6	...	1.8	...	...
4th quarter	2.3	1.9	0.1	0.3	0.4	18.8	15.3	2.9	0.6	...	1.8	...	...
1951													
1st quarter	2.5	2.0	0.1	0.3	0.5	19.0	15.6	2.8	0.6	...	2.7	...	...
2nd quarter	2.5	2.1	0.1	0.3	0.5	19.1	15.9	2.6	0.6	...	2.5	...	...
3rd quarter	2.4	1.9	0.1	0.3	0.5	19.5	16.2	2.6	0.6	...	2.4	...	...
4th quarter	2.6	2.1	0.1	0.3	0.5	19.8	16.6	2.6	0.7	...	2.7	...	...
1952													
1st quarter	2.5	2.0	0.1	0.3	0.5	20.0	16.5	2.8	0.7	...	2.9	...	...
2nd quarter	2.5	2.1	0.1	0.3	0.5	21.0	17.3	3.0	0.7	...	2.4	...	...
3rd quarter	2.7	2.3	0.1	0.3	0.5	20.7	17.1	2.9	0.7	...	3.3	...	...
4th quarter	2.7	2.3	0.1	0.3	0.5	21.2	17.5	2.9	0.7	...	3.4	...	...
1953													
1st quarter	2.3	1.8	0.1	0.3	0.5	21.7	18.0	2.9	0.7	...	2.9	...	...
2nd quarter	3.2	2.7	0.1	0.3	0.5	21.8	18.0	3.0	0.8	...	4.0	...	...
3rd quarter	2.8	2.3	0.1	0.4	0.6	22.3	18.4	3.1	0.8	...	3.5	...	...
4th quarter	2.8	2.3	0.2	0.4	0.6	22.3	18.5	2.9	0.8	...	3.6	...	...
1954													
1st quarter	2.9	2.3	0.2	0.4	0.6	22.8	18.9	3.0	0.9	...	3.6	...	...
2nd quarter	2.8	2.3	0.2	0.4	0.7	23.4	19.4	3.0	0.9	...	3.3	...	...
3rd quarter	2.9	2.4	0.2	0.4	0.7	24.1	20.1	3.1	0.9	...	3.0	...	...
4th quarter	2.9	2.3	0.2	0.4	0.7	24.5	20.4	3.1	1.0	...	3.1	...	...
1955													
1st quarter	2.8	2.3	0.2	0.4	0.8	25.3	21.1	3.2	1.0	...	3.0	...	...
2nd quarter	2.9	2.4	0.2	0.4	0.8	25.7	21.3	3.3	1.1	...	3.3	...	...
3rd quarter	3.1	2.5	0.2	0.4	0.9	26.0	21.7	3.3	1.1	...	3.8	...	...
4th quarter	3.0	2.4	0.2	0.4	0.9	26.5	22.1	3.2	1.1	...	3.9	...	...
1956													
1st quarter	3.0	2.4	0.2	0.4	0.9	27.0	22.6	3.3	1.2	...	4.3	...	...
2nd quarter	3.1	2.5	0.2	0.4	0.9	27.6	23.1	3.2	1.2	...	4.5	...	...
3rd quarter	3.3	2.6	0.2	0.4	0.9	28.3	23.8	3.3	1.3	...	4.5	...	...
4th quarter	3.3	2.7	0.2	0.5	0.9	29.0	24.4	3.4	1.3	...	4.3	...	...
1957													
1st quarter	3.6	2.9	0.2	0.5	0.9	29.6	24.8	3.5	1.3	...	4.8	...	...
2nd quarter	3.5	2.8	0.2	0.5	0.9	30.4	25.5	3.5	1.4	...	4.3	...	...
3rd quarter	3.7	2.9	0.2	0.5	0.9	31.3	26.2	3.6	1.4	...	4.1	...	...
4th quarter	3.8	3.1	0.2	0.5	0.9	32.0	26.8	3.7	1.5	...	3.6	...	...
1958													
1st quarter	3.6	2.9	0.2	0.5	0.9	33.0	27.6	4.0	1.5	...	2.7	0.1	2.6
2nd quarter	4.1	3.3	0.2	0.5	0.9	33.9	28.4	4.0	1.5	...	2.6	0.0	2.5
3rd quarter	3.9	3.2	0.2	0.5	0.9	34.6	29.0	4.0	1.6	...	2.6	0.0	2.6
4th quarter	4.7	4.0	0.2	0.5	0.9	35.3	29.5	4.1	1.6	...	3.6	0.0	3.6
1959													
1st quarter	3.9	3.5	0.1	0.3	1.0	36.1	30.0	4.3	1.7	0.0	3.1	0.0	3.0
2nd quarter	4.3	3.9	0.1	0.3	1.1	36.5	30.5	4.3	1.7	0.0	3.6	0.0	3.5
3rd quarter	4.2	3.8	0.1	0.3	1.2	37.1	30.9	4.3	1.8	0.0	4.2	0.0	4.1
4th quarter	4.2	3.8	0.1	0.3	1.2	37.8	31.5	4.4	1.9	0.0	4.3	0.0	4.3
1960													
1st quarter	4.3	3.9	0.2	0.3	1.2	39.0	32.5	4.4	2.1	0.0	4.3	0.0	4.3
2nd quarter	4.4	4.0	0.2	0.3	1.3	40.0	33.4	4.5	2.1	0.0	4.2	0.0	4.2
3rd quarter	4.5	4.0	0.2	0.3	1.3	40.5	33.8	4.6	2.0	0.0	4.3	0.0	4.3
4th quarter	4.7	4.2	0.2	0.3	1.3	41.2	34.5	4.7	2.0	0.0	4.4	0.0	4.3

¹Includes components not shown separately.
. . . = Not available.

Table 19-11. State and Local Government Current Receipts and Expenditures—*Continued*

(National income and product accounts, calendar years, billions of dollars, quarterly data are at seasonally adjusted annual rates.)

NIPA Table 3.3

Year and quarter	Current receipts												
		Current tax receipts							Taxes on corporate income	Contributions for government social insurance	Income receipts on assets		
	Total	Total	Personal current taxes		Taxes on production and imports						Total ¹	Interest receipts	Rents and royalties
			Total ¹	Income taxes	Total	Sales taxes	Property taxes	Other					
1961													
1st quarter	46.5	38.4	4.3	2.6	32.9	12.6	17.2	3.2	1.2	0.5	1.4	1.0	0.4
2nd quarter	47.6	39.2	4.5	2.7	33.4	12.8	17.5	3.2	1.2	0.5	1.4	1.1	0.4
3rd quarter	48.6	40.1	4.6	2.9	34.1	13.2	17.7	3.2	1.3	0.5	1.4	1.1	0.4
4th quarter	49.6	41.0	4.7	3.0	34.8	13.6	18.0	3.2	1.4	0.5	1.4	1.1	0.4
1962													
1st quarter	50.7	41.8	4.9	3.1	35.5	13.9	18.3	3.2	1.5	0.5	1.5	1.1	0.4
2nd quarter	51.5	42.4	5.0	3.1	36.0	13.9	18.7	3.3	1.5	0.5	1.5	1.1	0.4
3rd quarter	52.5	43.1	5.1	3.2	36.5	14.0	19.2	3.3	1.5	0.6	1.6	1.2	0.4
4th quarter	53.3	43.8	5.2	3.3	37.1	14.2	19.6	3.3	1.5	0.6	1.5	1.1	0.4
1963													
1st quarter	54.1	44.4	5.3	3.3	37.6	14.3	19.9	3.4	1.5	0.6	1.5	1.1	0.4
2nd quarter	55.3	45.2	5.3	3.3	38.3	14.7	20.1	3.5	1.6	0.6	1.6	1.2	0.4
3rd quarter	56.8	46.3	5.5	3.5	39.1	15.3	20.4	3.5	1.7	0.6	1.7	1.3	0.4
4th quarter	57.9	47.1	5.6	3.6	39.8	15.6	20.6	3.5	1.7	0.7	1.7	1.3	0.4
1964													
1st quarter	59.7	48.3	5.8	3.7	40.7	16.1	21.0	3.6	1.8	0.7	1.8	1.4	0.4
2nd quarter	60.7	49.2	6.0	4.0	41.4	16.3	21.4	3.7	1.8	0.7	2.0	1.5	0.4
3rd quarter	61.7	50.5	6.2	4.1	42.4	16.7	21.9	3.7	1.9	0.7	1.9	1.5	0.4
4th quarter	62.9	51.1	6.4	4.2	42.9	16.7	22.4	3.8	1.8	0.7	2.0	1.5	0.4
1965													
1st quarter	64.1	52.2	6.5	4.3	43.8	17.2	22.8	3.8	1.9	0.7	2.1	1.6	0.4
2nd quarter	65.9	53.2	6.5	4.4	44.7	17.8	23.1	3.9	1.9	0.8	2.2	1.8	0.4
3rd quarter	67.3	54.4	6.6	4.4	45.8	18.5	23.3	4.0	2.0	0.8	2.2	1.7	0.4
4th quarter	68.9	55.7	6.8	4.5	46.8	19.2	23.6	4.0	2.1	0.8	2.3	1.8	0.4
1966													
1st quarter	71.8	56.9	7.1	4.8	47.5	19.5	23.9	4.1	2.3	0.8	2.5	2.0	0.5
2nd quarter	74.1	58.0	7.6	5.2	48.2	19.7	24.3	4.2	2.3	0.8	2.6	2.0	0.5
3rd quarter	76.1	59.5	8.0	5.6	49.2	20.2	24.7	4.3	2.2	0.8	2.7	2.2	0.5
4th quarter	77.7	60.6	8.4	6.0	50.1	20.4	25.2	4.5	2.2	0.8	2.7	2.2	0.5
1967													
1st quarter	79.2	61.6	8.3	5.9	50.7	20.4	25.8	4.4	2.6	0.9	2.8	2.2	0.6
2nd quarter	80.7	62.5	8.3	5.9	51.7	20.7	26.6	4.4	2.6	0.9	2.8	2.2	0.6
3rd quarter	83.3	64.8	8.7	6.2	53.5	21.8	27.3	4.5	2.6	0.9	3.1	2.5	0.6
4th quarter	86.8	67.0	9.0	6.5	55.2	22.7	28.1	4.4	2.7	0.9	3.3	2.7	0.6
1968													
1st quarter	89.3	70.2	9.7	7.1	57.2	23.8	28.9	4.5	3.2	0.9	3.4	2.6	0.7
2nd quarter	92.9	72.3	10.3	7.6	58.7	24.6	29.6	4.6	3.3	0.9	3.4	2.7	0.7
3rd quarter	94.6	74.6	10.8	8.1	60.4	25.6	30.3	4.6	3.3	1.0	3.5	2.8	0.7
4th quarter	97.3	76.5	11.4	8.5	61.8	26.2	30.9	4.6	3.4	1.0	3.7	3.0	0.7
1969													
1st quarter	100.1	79.0	11.9	8.9	63.3	27.1	31.6	4.7	3.8	1.0	4.0	3.2	0.8
2nd quarter	103.4	81.1	12.3	9.3	65.1	28.1	32.3	4.7	3.7	1.0	4.2	3.5	0.8
3rd quarter	107.5	83.9	13.4	10.3	67.0	29.1	33.1	4.7	3.5	1.0	4.5	3.7	0.8
4th quarter	110.9	85.9	13.7	10.5	68.8	29.9	34.1	4.8	3.4	1.1	4.7	3.9	0.8
1970													
1st quarter	115.1	88.4	14.0	10.8	70.6	30.6	35.1	4.9	3.8	1.1	4.9	4.1	0.8
2nd quarter	118.6	90.3	14.1	10.9	72.4	31.3	36.2	4.9	3.7	1.1	5.1	4.3	0.8
3rd quarter	122.2	92.5	14.3	11.0	74.3	32.1	37.2	5.0	3.8	1.1	5.2	4.4	0.8
4th quarter	124.5	94.0	14.4	11.0	76.0	32.6	38.2	5.2	3.6	1.1	5.3	4.5	0.8
1971													
1st quarter	128.5	97.1	14.7	11.3	78.3	33.6	39.2	5.5	4.1	1.1	5.4	4.5	0.9
2nd quarter	133.2	100.0	15.6	12.2	80.2	34.5	40.1	5.6	4.2	1.2	5.5	4.6	0.9
3rd quarter	136.7	103.2	16.0	12.5	82.8	36.1	40.9	5.8	4.4	1.2	5.5	4.6	0.9
4th quarter	141.3	106.5	17.3	13.8	84.7	37.3	41.6	5.9	4.5	1.2	5.5	4.6	0.9
1972													
1st quarter	147.2	110.9	19.5	15.9	86.4	38.1	42.2	6.1	5.0	1.3	5.7	4.7	1.0
2nd quarter	159.4	114.5	21.0	17.3	88.5	39.4	42.8	6.3	5.0	1.3	5.8	4.8	1.0
3rd quarter	154.9	116.8	21.2	17.5	90.4	40.3	43.6	6.5	5.2	1.3	6.0	5.0	1.0
4th quarter	172.3	120.1	21.8	18.1	92.5	41.4	44.4	6.7	5.7	1.4	6.3	5.3	1.0
1973													
1st quarter	171.0	123.0	21.9	18.0	95.1	43.0	45.3	6.8	6.0	1.4	6.9	5.8	1.1
2nd quarter	172.4	124.7	22.3	18.4	96.3	43.3	46.1	6.9	6.1	1.5	7.4	6.3	1.1
3rd quarter	175.1	127.6	23.1	19.1	98.7	44.9	46.8	7.0	5.9	1.5	8.0	6.9	1.1
4th quarter	178.9	129.7	24.0	19.9	99.6	45.1	47.3	7.2	6.1	1.6	8.7	7.5	1.1
1974													
1st quarter	180.4	130.6	23.3	19.2	101.0	45.7	47.8	7.5	6.3	1.6	9.4	8.1	1.3
2nd quarter	185.8	134.7	24.1	19.9	104.0	47.8	48.5	7.7	6.6	1.6	10.0	8.7	1.3
3rd quarter	192.0	139.3	25.2	21.0	106.8	49.7	49.3	7.8	7.3	1.7	10.5	9.2	1.3
4th quarter	194.0	139.6	25.6	21.3	107.5	49.4	50.3	7.8	6.5	1.7	10.8	9.5	1.3
1975													
1st quarter	198.3	140.9	25.7	21.4	109.0	49.5	51.6	7.9	6.1	1.8	11.2	9.9	1.3
2nd quarter	207.6	144.8	26.5	22.1	111.7	50.8	52.8	8.1	6.6	1.8	11.3	9.9	1.3
3rd quarter	213.8	150.3	27.2	22.7	114.9	52.6	54.0	8.3	8.2	1.9	11.2	9.8	1.3
4th quarter	218.6	153.9	28.2	23.6	117.3	53.8	55.2	8.2	8.4	2.0	11.0	9.6	1.3

¹Includes components not shown separately.

Table 19-11. State and Local Government Current Receipts and Expenditures—*Continued*

(National income and product accounts, calendar years, billions of dollars, quarterly data are at seasonally adjusted annual rates.)

NIPA Table 3.3

Year and quarter	Current receipts—*Continued*					Current expenditures					Net state and local government saving, NIPA (surplus + / deficit -)		
	Current transfer receipts				Current surplus of government enterprises	Total [1]	Consumption expenditures	Government social benefits to persons	Interest payments	Subsidies	Total	Social insurance funds	Other
	Total	Federal grants-in-aid	From business, net	From persons									
1961													
1st quarter	4.9	4.2	0.2	0.4	1.3	42.4	35.5	4.9	2.0	0.0	4.1	0.0	4.1
2nd quarter	5.2	4.5	0.2	0.4	1.4	43.6	36.5	4.9	2.2	0.0	4.0	0.0	4.0
3rd quarter	5.3	4.6	0.2	0.4	1.3	44.1	36.8	5.0	2.3	0.0	4.5	0.0	4.4
4th quarter	5.4	4.7	0.2	0.5	1.4	45.0	37.5	5.1	2.4	0.0	4.6	0.0	4.6
1962													
1st quarter	5.6	4.9	0.2	0.5	1.3	45.8	38.1	5.2	2.4	0.0	4.9	0.0	4.9
2nd quarter	5.6	4.9	0.2	0.5	1.4	46.5	38.7	5.3	2.4	0.0	5.0	0.0	5.0
3rd quarter	5.9	5.2	0.2	0.5	1.4	47.0	39.2	5.3	2.5	0.0	5.5	0.0	5.5
4th quarter	5.9	5.2	0.2	0.5	1.5	47.8	39.9	5.5	2.4	0.0	5.5	0.0	5.5
1963													
1st quarter	6.0	5.3	0.3	0.5	1.6	48.7	40.7	5.6	2.5	0.0	5.4	0.0	5.3
2nd quarter	6.2	5.5	0.3	0.5	1.6	49.7	41.5	5.7	2.6	0.0	5.5	0.0	5.5
3rd quarter	6.5	5.8	0.3	0.5	1.7	50.8	42.3	5.7	2.7	0.0	6.0	0.0	6.0
4th quarter	6.8	6.1	0.3	0.5	1.6	52.0	43.3	5.8	2.9	0.0	5.9	0.0	5.8
1964													
1st quarter	7.3	6.5	0.3	0.5	1.6	53.2	44.4	6.0	2.9	0.0	6.4	0.0	6.4
2nd quarter	7.3	6.5	0.3	0.5	1.6	54.5	45.3	6.1	3.0	0.0	6.3	0.0	6.2
3rd quarter	7.0	6.2	0.3	0.5	1.7	55.3	46.2	6.2	2.8	0.0	6.5	0.1	6.4
4th quarter	7.4	6.6	0.3	0.5	1.7	56.5	47.2	6.4	2.9	0.0	6.4	0.1	6.3
1965													
1st quarter	7.4	6.5	0.3	0.5	1.7	57.8	48.3	6.5	3.0	0.0	6.2	0.1	6.1
2nd quarter	7.9	7.1	0.3	0.5	1.7	59.3	49.5	6.6	3.2	0.0	6.5	0.1	6.4
3rd quarter	8.3	7.5	0.3	0.5	1.7	60.8	50.9	6.7	3.2	0.0	6.6	0.1	6.5
4th quarter	8.5	7.6	0.3	0.6	1.7	62.1	52.1	6.8	3.2	0.0	6.8	0.1	6.7
1966													
1st quarter	10.0	9.0	0.3	0.6	1.6	64.0	53.7	7.0	3.3	0.0	7.7	0.1	7.6
2nd quarter	11.1	10.1	0.3	0.7	1.6	66.1	55.2	7.5	3.4	0.0	8.0	0.1	7.9
3rd quarter	11.5	10.5	0.3	0.8	1.6	68.2	56.9	7.7	3.5	0.0	8.0	0.1	7.9
4th quarter	11.8	10.7	0.3	0.8	1.6	70.4	58.7	8.2	3.5	0.0	7.3	0.1	7.1
1967													
1st quarter	12.4	11.1	0.5	0.9	1.6	71.7	60.0	8.4	3.3	0.0	7.5	0.1	7.4
2nd quarter	12.9	11.6	0.5	0.9	1.6	73.9	61.5	8.9	3.4	0.0	6.9	0.1	6.7
3rd quarter	13.0	11.6	0.5	0.9	1.5	76.9	63.5	9.5	3.8	0.0	6.4	0.1	6.2
4th quarter	14.2	12.7	0.5	1.0	1.5	79.6	65.3	10.1	4.3	0.0	7.2	0.1	7.1
1968													
1st quarter	13.2	11.8	0.5	1.0	1.6	82.1	67.4	10.6	4.0	0.0	7.2	0.1	7.0
2nd quarter	14.8	13.3	0.5	1.0	1.5	84.7	69.2	11.4	4.1	0.0	8.2	0.1	8.1
3rd quarter	14.1	12.6	0.5	1.0	1.5	87.2	71.3	11.7	4.2	0.0	7.4	0.1	7.3
4th quarter	14.7	13.2	0.5	1.0	1.5	90.1	73.6	12.1	4.3	0.0	7.2	0.2	7.1
1969													
1st quarter	14.7	13.1	0.5	1.0	1.5	92.7	75.9	12.6	4.2	0.0	7.4	0.1	7.3
2nd quarter	15.6	14.0	0.5	1.1	1.5	95.6	78.4	12.8	4.3	0.0	7.8	0.2	7.6
3rd quarter	16.7	15.1	0.5	1.1	1.5	99.0	81.2	13.4	4.4	0.0	8.5	0.2	8.3
4th quarter	17.7	16.1	0.5	1.1	1.5	102.6	83.9	14.0	4.6	0.0	8.2	0.2	8.1
1970													
1st quarter	19.2	17.5	0.6	1.1	1.5	106.9	87.3	14.7	4.9	0.0	8.2	0.2	8.0
2nd quarter	20.6	18.8	0.6	1.2	1.5	110.8	90.0	15.6	5.2	0.0	7.7	0.2	7.5
3rd quarter	21.9	20.1	0.6	1.2	1.5	115.1	93.0	16.6	5.4	0.0	7.1	0.2	7.0
4th quarter	22.6	20.8	0.6	1.3	1.5	119.1	95.8	17.5	5.8	0.0	5.4	0.2	5.2
1971													
1st quarter	23.5	21.6	0.6	1.3	1.4	123.5	99.0	18.3	6.2	0.0	5.0	0.2	4.8
2nd quarter	25.1	23.2	0.6	1.4	1.3	127.1	101.6	19.1	6.4	0.0	6.0	0.2	5.8
3rd quarter	25.5	23.5	0.6	1.4	1.4	130.2	104.2	19.6	6.7	0.0	6.5	0.2	6.2
4th quarter	26.8	24.7	0.6	1.5	1.4	132.9	106.1	20.3	6.9	0.0	8.4	0.2	8.2
1972													
1st quarter	28.0	25.7	0.7	1.6	1.5	138.1	109.1	21.2	7.2	0.0	9.1	0.2	8.8
2nd quarter	36.2	33.9	0.7	1.6	1.6	140.7	111.6	21.6	7.4	0.1	18.7	0.3	18.4
3rd quarter	29.1	26.8	0.7	1.7	1.6	144.8	114.6	22.5	7.6	0.1	10.1	0.3	9.9
4th quarter	42.8	40.4	0.7	1.7	1.6	147.6	117.3	22.5	7.8	0.1	24.6	0.3	24.4
1973													
1st quarter	38.1	35.6	0.9	1.7	1.6	152.1	120.7	23.2	8.1	0.1	18.9	0.3	18.7
2nd quarter	37.2	34.7	0.9	1.7	1.5	156.6	124.2	24.0	8.3	0.1	15.7	0.3	15.4
3rd quarter	36.5	33.9	0.9	1.7	1.4	160.5	127.7	24.2	8.6	0.1	14.6	0.3	14.3
4th quarter	37.6	34.9	0.9	1.8	1.3	165.3	131.4	25.0	8.8	0.1	13.6	0.3	13.3
1974													
1st quarter	37.6	34.6	1.1	1.8	1.2	168.6	136.0	23.4	9.1	0.1	11.8	0.4	11.4
2nd quarter	38.4	35.4	1.1	1.9	1.0	175.2	140.9	24.7	9.4	0.1	10.6	0.4	10.3
3rd quarter	39.9	36.8	1.1	2.0	0.7	182.0	146.3	25.9	9.8	0.1	10.0	0.4	9.6
4th quarter	41.4	38.2	1.1	2.1	0.5	189.1	151.8	27.1	10.1	0.1	4.9	0.4	4.5
1975													
1st quarter	44.1	40.7	1.2	2.2	0.3	197.7	157.8	29.2	10.5	0.1	0.6	0.4	0.2
2nd quarter	49.4	45.8	1.2	2.3	0.4	205.0	163.5	30.5	10.9	0.2	2.6	0.5	2.1
3rd quarter	50.2	46.5	1.2	2.4	0.3	210.3	167.9	31.0	11.3	0.2	3.6	0.5	3.1
4th quarter	51.3	47.5	1.2	2.6	0.5	215.5	171.1	32.6	11.6	0.2	3.1	0.5	2.6

[1]Includes components not shown separately.

Table 19-11. State and Local Government Current Receipts and Expenditures—*Continued*

(National income and product accounts, calendar years, billions of dollars, quarterly data are at seasonally adjusted annual rates.)

NIPA Table 3.3

Year and quarter	Current receipts Total	Current tax receipts Total	Personal current taxes Total¹	Personal current taxes Income taxes	Taxes on production and imports Total	Taxes on production and imports Sales taxes	Taxes on production and imports Property taxes	Taxes on production and imports Other	Taxes on corporate income	Contributions for government social insurance	Income receipts on assets Total¹	Income receipts on assets Interest receipts	Income receipts on assets Rents and royalties
1976													
1st quarter	225.8	160.0	29.5	24.8	120.9	55.9	56.4	8.5	9.7	2.0	10.5	9.1	1.3
2nd quarter	230.2	163.7	30.6	25.8	123.5	57.2	57.7	8.7	9.6	2.1	10.4	9.0	1.3
3rd quarter	234.9	167.3	31.6	26.7	126.0	58.0	58.9	9.2	9.7	2.2	10.3	9.0	1.3
4th quarter	243.8	171.9	32.6	27.7	129.6	60.0	60.0	9.6	9.6	2.3	10.5	9.1	1.3
1977													
1st quarter	247.9	176.9	33.5	28.6	132.9	61.8	61.5	9.5	10.5	2.5	10.9	9.6	1.3
2nd quarter	256.3	181.6	34.7	29.8	135.5	63.1	62.8	9.6	11.4	2.7	11.4	10.1	1.3
3rd quarter	265.2	186.1	35.9	30.9	138.3	64.7	63.8	9.8	11.8	2.9	11.9	10.6	1.3
4th quarter	270.4	190.3	37.3	32.2	141.1	66.4	64.6	10.0	12.0	3.0	12.5	11.2	1.3
1978													
1st quarter	277.7	192.1	38.6	33.4	143.0	67.3	65.3	10.4	10.5	3.2	13.2	11.8	1.3
2nd quarter	289.5	200.2	40.1	34.7	147.7	70.8	66.1	10.9	12.4	3.3	14.1	12.7	1.3
3rd quarter	287.5	197.6	40.9	35.4	144.2	72.0	61.3	10.9	12.5	3.5	15.1	13.7	1.3
4th quarter	295.5	202.7	42.1	36.5	147.6	74.0	62.3	11.3	13.1	3.6	16.2	14.9	1.3
1979													
1st quarter	298.8	206.3	42.0	36.3	150.6	75.4	63.2	12.0	13.7	3.8	18.2	16.2	1.9
2nd quarter	302.8	208.4	42.1	36.3	152.6	76.3	64.0	12.3	13.8	3.9	19.5	17.5	1.9
3rd quarter	312.8	214.6	45.4	39.6	155.6	77.9	64.8	12.8	13.6	3.9	20.8	18.8	1.9
4th quarter	319.0	218.8	46.6	40.7	159.0	79.6	65.6	13.8	13.2	4.0	22.0	20.0	1.9
1980													
1st quarter	328.0	224.5	46.6	40.4	161.9	81.2	66.5	14.2	16.1	3.6	24.3	21.1	3.1
2nd quarter	329.5	224.1	48.0	41.7	163.3	80.8	67.8	14.7	12.8	2.9	25.6	22.4	3.1
3rd quarter	341.5	231.5	49.4	43.0	168.2	83.5	69.5	15.2	14.0	3.8	26.9	23.7	3.1
4th quarter	353.7	240.0	51.6	45.2	173.3	86.0	71.5	15.8	15.1	4.0	28.3	25.1	3.1
1981													
1st quarter	363.5	249.5	52.5	46.0	180.2	89.6	73.9	16.7	16.8	3.7	29.9	26.5	3.3
2nd quarter	368.1	252.5	53.7	47.0	183.7	89.6	76.2	17.9	15.2	3.8	31.4	27.9	3.3
3rd quarter	374.0	259.5	55.5	48.8	188.3	91.8	78.0	18.5	15.7	3.9	32.7	29.2	3.3
4th quarter	375.3	261.6	56.8	49.9	190.7	92.1	80.2	18.4	14.1	4.0	33.9	30.4	3.3
1982													
1st quarter	380.8	265.4	57.3	50.2	193.9	92.9	82.4	18.5	14.1	4.0	35.2	31.6	3.5
2nd quarter	389.1	270.6	58.1	50.9	198.3	95.5	84.5	18.3	14.3	4.0	36.3	32.6	3.5
3rd quarter	395.0	276.5	60.4	53.1	201.7	97.0	86.3	18.4	14.4	4.1	37.3	33.6	3.5
4th quarter	400.8	280.1	60.8	53.4	206.0	99.3	87.9	18.7	13.3	4.1	38.1	34.5	3.5
1983													
1st quarter	407.6	283.7	61.3	53.7	209.6	101.5	89.3	18.8	12.8	4.0	39.5	35.4	4.0
2nd quarter	423.6	295.9	64.3	56.5	216.0	106.2	90.9	18.9	15.7	4.1	40.7	36.4	4.2
3rd quarter	436.4	307.5	68.1	60.2	222.0	109.9	92.7	19.5	17.4	4.1	42.0	37.5	4.4
4th quarter	446.9	316.4	70.7	62.7	228.0	113.1	94.6	20.3	17.7	4.3	43.5	38.8	4.6
1984													
1st quarter	465.3	328.0	73.3	65.0	234.7	116.8	96.8	21.1	20.1	4.5	44.9	40.0	4.7
2nd quarter	478.1	336.0	75.8	67.4	240.3	119.9	98.8	21.6	19.9	4.7	46.7	41.7	4.9
3rd quarter	481.6	339.0	76.8	68.1	244.7	122.0	100.7	22.0	17.5	4.8	48.6	43.4	5.0
4th quarter	495.6	346.1	78.2	69.3	250.2	125.3	102.5	22.3	17.7	4.8	50.5	45.3	5.1
1985													
1st quarter	506.6	353.9	79.3	70.2	254.7	127.3	104.5	22.9	20.0	4.7	52.9	47.6	5.1
2nd quarter	516.4	360.6	80.9	71.8	260.0	130.6	106.5	23.0	19.6	4.8	54.5	49.1	5.2
3rd quarter	526.1	367.5	81.5	72.2	265.1	132.8	108.5	23.8	20.9	4.9	55.4	49.8	5.4
4th quarter	535.2	372.7	83.7	74.3	268.5	133.8	110.6	24.1	20.5	5.2	56.7	50.9	5.7
1986													
1st quarter	552.7	378.9	84.5	75.0	273.0	136.1	112.6	24.3	21.4	5.5	57.7	51.3	6.2
2nd quarter	554.8	383.6	85.0	75.4	276.6	137.8	114.9	23.8	22.0	5.8	58.3	51.9	6.3
3rd quarter	567.1	392.2	87.5	77.7	282.3	142.0	117.3	23.0	22.4	6.1	58.7	52.3	6.3
4th quarter	572.0	403.5	91.8	81.8	286.8	143.5	119.8	23.5	24.8	6.4	58.9	52.6	6.2
1987													
1st quarter	570.8	405.0	92.4	82.1	291.9	145.1	122.5	24.2	20.7	6.7	58.5	52.4	6.0
2nd quarter	593.2	423.7	101.5	90.9	298.5	148.6	125.1	24.8	23.7	7.0	58.0	52.2	5.6
3rd quarter	594.1	425.5	94.1	83.4	306.0	152.9	127.7	25.4	25.5	7.3	58.0	52.7	5.2
4th quarter	604.1	434.2	98.4	87.5	310.0	154.7	130.3	25.1	25.7	7.7	58.1	53.3	4.6
1988													
1st quarter	616.4	438.9	99.4	88.3	315.5	157.8	132.4	25.3	24.0	8.0	59.0	54.2	4.7
2nd quarter	626.2	446.3	97.2	85.8	323.3	162.3	134.9	26.1	25.8	8.3	59.9	55.2	4.5
3rd quarter	643.4	458.1	104.1	92.5	327.4	163.7	137.7	25.9	26.6	8.5	61.0	56.5	4.3
4th quarter	656.2	467.7	107.6	95.8	332.4	165.8	141.0	25.6	27.8	8.7	62.2	57.8	4.2
1989													
1st quarter	673.4	480.2	113.4	101.3	340.3	168.7	145.0	26.6	26.6	8.8	64.1	59.7	4.2
2nd quarter	687.0	491.0	118.2	105.8	348.1	172.9	148.4	26.9	24.6	8.9	65.2	60.9	4.1
3rd quarter	694.5	491.0	114.5	102.1	353.8	174.6	151.5	27.7	22.7	9.0	66.3	62.0	4.1
4th quarter	694.3	489.8	112.4	99.8	354.3	173.2	154.5	26.6	23.1	9.3	67.2	63.0	4.0
1990													
1st quarter	721.5	509.9	119.3	106.6	369.1	183.7	156.6	28.7	21.5	9.5	67.5	63.5	3.8
2nd quarter	730.6	514.0	122.6	109.5	368.7	181.2	159.7	27.9	22.7	9.9	68.4	64.4	3.8
3rd quarter	744.3	523.0	123.7	110.8	375.7	185.3	163.1	27.3	23.6	10.2	69.6	64.3	5.0
4th quarter	754.7	529.6	124.6	111.5	382.7	186.9	166.7	29.1	22.2	10.5	68.3	64.0	4.0

¹Includes components not shown separately.

Table 19-11. State and Local Government Current Receipts and Expenditures—*Continued*

(National income and product accounts, calendar years, billions of dollars, quarterly data are at seasonally adjusted annual rates.)

NIPA Table 3.3

Year and quarter	Current receipts—*Continued*				Current surplus of government enterprises	Current expenditures					Net state and local government saving, NIPA (surplus + / deficit -)		
	Current transfer receipts					Total [1]	Consumption expenditures	Government social benefits to persons	Interest payments	Subsidies	Total	Social insurance funds	Other
	Total	Federal grants-in-aid	From business, net	From persons									
1976													
1st quarter	52.7	48.7	1.4	2.7	0.5	220.1	174.5	33.4	12.0	0.2	5.7	0.5	5.2
2nd quarter	53.6	49.5	1.4	2.8	0.4	223.7	177.8	33.4	12.4	0.2	6.5	0.6	5.9
3rd quarter	54.7	50.4	1.4	2.9	0.3	228.6	180.9	34.7	12.7	0.2	6.3	0.6	5.7
4th quarter	58.8	54.4	1.4	3.0	0.3	232.8	184.6	35.0	13.0	0.2	11.0	0.7	10.3
1977													
1st quarter	57.2	52.5	1.6	3.2	0.3	238.3	189.2	35.7	13.3	0.2	9.6	0.8	8.8
2nd quarter	60.3	55.5	1.6	3.3	0.3	244.5	193.3	37.5	13.5	0.2	11.8	0.9	10.9
3rd quarter	64.1	59.1	1.6	3.3	0.3	249.5	198.2	37.3	13.8	0.2	15.7	1.1	14.7
4th quarter	64.2	59.2	1.6	3.4	0.4	254.9	202.8	37.7	14.1	0.2	15.5	1.2	14.3
1978													
1st quarter	68.8	63.5	1.9	3.5	0.4	260.9	207.2	39.2	14.3	0.2	16.9	1.3	15.5
2nd quarter	71.6	66.1	1.9	3.6	0.3	266.5	210.7	41.0	14.6	0.2	23.0	1.4	21.6
3rd quarter	71.1	65.5	1.9	3.7	0.2	271.4	215.2	41.3	15.1	0.2	16.1	1.5	14.5
4th quarter	72.8	67.1	1.9	3.8	0.1	276.8	219.6	41.7	15.6	0.3	18.7	1.7	17.1
1979													
1st quarter	70.5	64.4	2.2	4.0	0.0	284.3	225.5	42.4	16.4	0.3	14.5	1.7	12.9
2nd quarter	71.2	65.0	2.2	4.1	-0.2	290.9	229.2	43.5	17.0	0.3	11.9	1.8	10.1
3rd quarter	74.0	67.6	2.2	4.2	-0.4	298.9	236.3	44.5	17.6	0.3	13.9	1.8	12.1
4th quarter	74.9	68.4	2.2	4.3	-0.6	307.4	242.4	46.9	18.0	0.3	11.6	1.8	9.8
1980													
1st quarter	76.2	69.3	2.5	4.4	-0.7	317.3	249.3	49.1	18.4	0.3	10.6	1.4	9.2
2nd quarter	77.9	70.8	2.5	4.6	-0.9	324.0	255.8	49.0	19.0	0.3	5.5	0.7	4.8
3rd quarter	80.7	73.4	2.5	4.8	-1.4	334.0	261.6	52.4	19.6	0.4	7.5	1.5	6.0
4th quarter	83.3	75.8	2.5	5.0	-1.9	342.2	267.0	54.3	20.4	0.4	11.5	1.6	9.9
1981													
1st quarter	82.6	74.4	2.9	5.4	-2.3	351.8	274.4	55.6	21.4	0.4	11.7	1.3	10.4
2nd quarter	83.0	74.5	2.9	5.6	-2.6	360.0	279.9	57.4	22.3	0.4	8.0	1.3	6.7
3rd quarter	80.5	71.9	2.9	5.8	-2.5	366.4	284.9	57.7	23.3	0.4	7.7	1.3	6.4
4th quarter	78.1	69.2	2.9	6.0	-2.2	372.5	290.1	57.7	24.3	0.4	2.8	1.3	1.5
1982													
1st quarter	78.2	68.8	3.2	6.1	-2.0	381.5	296.6	59.0	25.4	0.4	-0.7	1.3	-2.0
2nd quarter	79.9	70.4	3.2	6.3	-1.7	390.6	302.6	61.0	26.5	0.5	-1.4	1.2	-2.7
3rd quarter	78.7	69.0	3.3	6.4	-1.5	397.7	307.4	62.1	27.7	0.5	-2.6	1.2	-3.9
4th quarter	79.7	69.8	3.3	6.6	-1.2	404.8	312.8	62.6	29.0	0.5	-4.0	1.2	-5.2
1983													
1st quarter	81.1	70.6	3.6	6.8	-0.8	415.0	318.4	65.8	30.4	0.5	-7.4	1.2	-8.6
2nd quarter	83.3	72.7	3.6	7.0	-0.4	420.6	322.1	66.3	31.7	0.4	3.0	1.2	1.8
3rd quarter	82.7	71.8	3.6	7.3	0.0	426.6	326.0	67.2	33.0	0.4	9.8	1.2	8.5
4th quarter	82.4	71.2	3.7	7.5	0.2	432.7	329.8	68.3	34.1	0.4	14.2	1.3	12.9
1984													
1st quarter	87.1	75.4	4.0	7.8	0.7	442.8	337.2	69.9	35.2	0.4	22.5	1.4	21.1
2nd quarter	89.6	77.4	4.2	8.0	1.1	451.4	343.9	70.6	36.4	0.4	26.7	1.5	25.3
3rd quarter	87.7	75.1	4.3	8.3	1.6	460.5	351.3	71.3	37.6	0.4	21.1	1.5	19.7
4th quarter	91.6	78.8	4.3	8.5	2.5	470.2	358.2	72.8	38.8	0.4	25.4	1.4	24.0
1985													
1st quarter	92.2	79.1	4.3	8.7	2.9	481.9	367.3	74.9	39.4	0.3	24.7	1.3	23.4
2nd quarter	93.4	80.0	4.4	9.1	3.2	492.4	376.0	76.3	39.8	0.3	24.0	1.2	22.8
3rd quarter	95.0	81.2	4.4	9.4	3.4	504.5	386.9	78.1	39.2	0.3	21.7	1.3	20.4
4th quarter	97.4	83.1	4.5	9.7	3.3	516.2	397.0	79.8	39.2	0.3	19.0	1.5	17.6
1986													
1st quarter	107.6	84.8	12.6	10.2	3.1	526.0	406.9	81.6	37.2	0.3	26.7	1.6	25.0
2nd quarter	104.2	89.0	4.7	10.5	2.9	534.3	413.1	83.6	37.2	0.3	20.5	1.8	18.7
3rd quarter	107.4	91.8	4.8	10.8	2.7	544.3	420.5	85.3	38.3	0.3	22.8	2.0	20.8
4th quarter	100.7	84.9	4.8	11.0	2.5	558.2	430.9	86.9	40.1	0.3	13.8	2.1	11.8
1987													
1st quarter	97.9	82.1	4.8	11.0	2.6	564.8	433.7	88.3	42.6	0.3	6.0	2.1	3.9
2nd quarter	101.7	85.8	4.8	11.1	2.8	573.8	438.7	89.9	44.9	0.3	19.4	2.1	17.3
3rd quarter	100.1	83.9	4.9	11.2	3.1	581.9	442.5	91.6	47.6	0.3	12.2	2.2	9.9
4th quarter	100.2	83.8	5.0	11.4	3.9	592.0	448.9	93.1	49.7	0.3	12.1	2.3	9.8
1988													
1st quarter	106.2	89.5	5.1	11.6	4.2	602.8	459.2	95.3	48.0	0.3	13.6	2.4	11.2
2nd quarter	107.1	90.0	5.2	11.9	4.6	613.0	467.2	97.3	48.1	0.3	13.2	2.5	10.7
3rd quarter	110.7	93.1	5.5	12.1	5.0	622.2	474.0	99.5	48.3	0.4	21.2	2.6	18.6
4th quarter	112.0	93.8	5.7	12.5	5.6	632.6	481.1	101.9	49.3	0.4	23.6	2.6	21.0
1989													
1st quarter	114.0	94.9	6.1	13.0	6.3	646.8	489.8	104.2	52.3	0.4	26.6	2.5	24.1
2nd quarter	115.2	95.6	6.3	13.3	6.6	659.8	498.1	107.3	54.0	0.4	27.2	2.4	24.8
3rd quarter	121.5	101.4	6.5	13.5	6.8	671.7	504.8	111.0	55.6	0.4	22.8	2.3	20.6
4th quarter	121.9	101.4	6.7	13.9	6.2	687.6	515.9	114.8	56.5	0.4	6.7	2.1	4.5
1990													
1st quarter	127.8	106.5	7.2	14.0	6.8	705.7	530.0	118.8	56.5	0.4	15.8	2.0	13.8
2nd quarter	131.7	110.3	6.9	14.5	6.7	720.5	538.5	124.2	57.5	0.4	10.1	2.0	8.2
3rd quarter	134.9	112.6	7.0	15.2	6.6	738.2	549.3	130.3	58.3	0.4	6.1	2.0	4.1
4th quarter	139.6	116.3	7.2	16.0	6.7	757.8	560.8	137.4	59.2	0.4	-3.1	2.0	-5.0

[1] Includes components not shown separately.

Table 19-11. State and Local Government Current Receipts and Expenditures—*Continued*

(National income and product accounts, calendar years, billions of dollars, quarterly data are at seasonally adjusted annual rates.)

NIPA Table 3.3

Year and quarter	Current receipts	Current tax receipts	Personal current taxes		Taxes on production and imports				Taxes on corporate income	Contributions for government social insurance	Income receipts on assets		
	Total	Total	Total [1]	Income taxes	Total	Sales taxes	Property taxes	Other			Total [1]	Interest receipts	Rents and royalties
1991													
1st quarter	763.0	528.5	121.2	108.0	384.6	184.8	171.2	28.6	22.7	11.0	68.8	64.1	4.3
2nd quarter	778.8	538.2	124.5	111.2	390.3	187.9	174.7	27.7	23.4	11.4	68.3	63.5	4.5
3rd quarter	798.2	549.7	126.1	112.2	399.3	193.1	177.8	28.4	24.2	11.8	67.7	62.7	4.6
4th quarter	816.6	560.8	129.4	115.5	407.1	196.9	180.5	29.7	24.2	12.2	67.1	62.0	4.7
1992													
1st quarter	824.3	564.4	127.5	112.7	412.6	200.6	182.9	29.1	24.4	12.6	66.9	61.1	5.3
2nd quarter	842.7	580.4	136.9	122.3	418.0	201.6	184.4	32.0	25.5	13.0	65.0	60.0	4.6
3rd quarter	851.7	582.6	136.7	121.9	424.0	207.4	185.4	31.3	21.8	13.3	64.1	59.1	4.6
4th quarter	863.9	591.6	140.2	124.6	425.7	207.7	186.0	32.0	25.8	13.6	63.1	58.1	4.6
1993													
1st quarter	862.5	588.6	136.5	121.8	427.6	210.9	184.8	31.8	24.6	13.8	62.0	57.0	4.6
2nd quarter	875.9	598.5	138.3	123.9	433.2	214.7	185.9	32.6	27.0	14.1	61.4	56.3	4.5
3rd quarter	893.2	609.5	143.6	128.7	439.6	217.4	187.8	34.4	26.3	14.2	61.0	55.8	4.5
4th quarter	916.1	622.3	145.9	130.5	446.7	222.5	190.5	33.7	29.7	14.4	60.9	55.8	4.5
1994													
1st quarter	920.9	629.9	146.9	131.4	456.4	225.7	196.0	34.7	26.5	14.6	61.6	56.4	4.5
2nd quarter	931.4	636.9	141.9	125.8	465.5	230.9	198.8	35.8	29.5	14.6	62.4	57.1	4.5
3rd quarter	952.3	652.1	151.2	135.1	469.7	233.1	200.8	35.8	31.2	14.5	63.8	58.5	4.5
4th quarter	966.9	658.0	152.0	136.7	473.4	235.9	201.9	35.6	32.6	14.4	65.0	59.6	4.5
1995													
1st quarter	980.9	665.6	156.8	140.6	478.3	240.4	200.8	37.2	30.5	14.0	66.5	61.1	4.5
2nd quarter	979.1	661.6	152.4	136.1	477.9	239.6	201.6	36.8	31.3	13.7	67.6	62.3	4.5
3rd quarter	997.6	677.2	160.6	144.2	483.7	243.7	203.0	37.0	32.8	13.5	69.1	63.5	4.5
4th quarter	1 003.3	684.1	162.6	146.0	489.4	247.3	204.9	37.2	32.0	13.2	70.4	64.7	4.5
1996													
1st quarter	1 021.7	695.8	165.3	149.0	498.1	252.4	208.1	37.6	32.4	13.0	71.4	65.6	4.6
2nd quarter	1 042.6	705.7	165.9	149.6	506.5	255.7	210.9	40.0	33.3	12.7	72.6	66.7	4.6
3rd quarter	1 049.1	712.4	169.3	152.8	509.9	256.8	213.7	39.4	33.1	12.3	73.9	67.8	4.7
4th quarter	1 059.7	724.5	174.2	157.8	517.0	259.9	216.7	40.5	33.3	11.9	75.1	69.0	4.7
1997													
1st quarter	1 073.4	734.3	177.8	160.7	523.7	262.8	220.0	40.9	32.8	11.3	76.5	70.3	4.8
2nd quarter	1 084.0	741.0	176.9	159.6	530.5	266.8	222.6	41.2	33.5	10.9	77.4	71.1	4.8
3rd quarter	1 106.5	756.0	184.1	166.8	536.6	270.5	224.8	41.3	35.3	10.6	78.3	71.9	4.8
4th quarter	1 125.8	768.5	189.2	171.6	544.3	274.5	226.8	43.0	34.9	10.5	79.1	72.8	4.7
1998													
1st quarter	1 137.5	779.5	195.1	177.2	549.3	277.5	227.7	44.1	35.2	10.6	79.8	73.5	4.6
2nd quarter	1 150.5	791.8	201.8	183.6	555.3	281.4	229.7	44.2	34.7	10.4	80.3	74.1	4.6
3rd quarter	1 165.3	798.6	201.4	183.2	561.6	285.4	232.0	44.2	35.5	10.3	81.2	74.9	4.6
4th quarter	1 199.4	809.7	206.5	188.0	568.9	291.1	234.7	43.1	34.3	10.1	82.4	76.0	4.7
1999													
1st quarter	1 205.1	818.6	207.6	188.8	576.1	292.9	238.3	45.0	34.9	9.8	83.0	76.5	4.8
2nd quarter	1 217.1	831.4	210.4	191.6	585.4	298.8	241.3	45.3	35.6	9.7	84.4	77.7	5.0
3rd quarter	1 249.6	847.3	216.0	196.9	595.4	305.4	244.3	45.7	35.9	9.7	86.0	79.0	5.2
4th quarter	1 275.0	864.3	223.8	204.7	603.7	309.3	247.2	47.1	36.8	9.9	87.7	80.4	5.5
2000													
1st quarter	1 294.4	880.3	231.6	212.2	610.9	313.3	249.9	47.7	37.8	10.3	90.4	82.7	5.9
2nd quarter	1 319.0	898.4	243.7	224.5	618.0	315.7	252.9	49.4	36.7	10.7	91.9	83.9	6.2
3rd quarter	1 330.5	895.4	236.3	216.6	624.1	317.0	256.1	51.1	35.0	11.2	92.8	84.5	6.4
4th quarter	1 333.9	898.8	234.8	215.7	631.2	320.3	259.5	51.5	32.8	11.8	93.7	85.1	6.7
2001													
1st quarter	1 367.2	919.1	249.2	230.1	637.5	322.8	262.6	52.1	32.4	12.7	91.6	83.1	6.6
2nd quarter	1 397.4	937.9	266.6	246.9	639.4	320.5	266.5	52.4	31.9	13.5	89.9	81.4	6.6
3rd quarter	1 354.6	899.9	229.3	209.5	641.4	317.7	271.3	52.4	29.2	14.0	87.7	79.3	6.5
4th quarter	1 372.5	906.2	225.8	205.9	652.9	323.5	276.7	52.7	27.4	14.4	85.9	77.5	6.4
2002													
1st quarter	1 379.7	910.3	220.1	200.3	661.1	324.2	282.9	54.0	29.1	15.0	82.3	73.8	6.4
2nd quarter	1 396.4	916.5	215.1	194.6	670.2	328.1	288.3	53.8	31.2	15.6	79.0	70.5	6.5
3rd quarter	1 422.7	940.1	224.2	203.5	683.2	333.9	292.9	56.4	32.8	16.1	76.5	67.9	6.6
4th quarter	1 441.7	949.0	225.8	204.9	687.5	334.5	296.5	56.6	35.6	16.5	75.0	66.2	6.8
2003													
1st quarter	1 435.8	949.2	218.3	197.1	697.5	338.3	300.7	58.5	33.3	17.8	74.0	64.5	7.3
2nd quarter	1 474.2	956.8	213.2	191.4	710.7	344.7	305.2	60.7	32.9	19.1	73.0	63.1	7.7
3rd quarter	1 516.8	994.4	234.4	211.7	724.1	350.5	310.1	63.5	35.9	20.4	72.5	62.2	8.1
4th quarter	1 549.9	1 017.4	240.6	217.7	737.7	357.3	315.4	65.0	39.1	21.7	72.2	61.7	8.3
2004													
1st quarter	1 555.2	1 031.0	240.6	217.1	751.0	362.8	320.3	67.8	39.4	22.5	73.0	62.5	8.4
2nd quarter	1 582.5	1 044.6	238.6	215.1	762.9	367.3	325.2	70.4	43.1	23.3	74.6	63.8	8.6
3rd quarter	1 584.8	1 067.5	252.5	228.4	772.7	370.0	330.0	72.8	42.3	24.0	75.9	64.8	8.7
4th quarter	1 654.8	1 101.6	264.1	239.5	790.1	379.8	334.7	75.7	47.3	24.6	78.0	66.0	8.9
2005													
1st quarter	1 685.7	1 132.1	268.9	244.2	807.4	389.4	339.6	78.4	55.8	24.6	81.1	69.3	9.4
2nd quarter	1 711.3	1 153.9	274.9	250.1	822.8	397.1	344.8	81.0	56.2	24.4	84.6	72.2	9.8
3rd quarter	1 716.5	1 167.6	278.0	252.9	837.4	404.4	350.1	82.9	52.2	24.1	87.6	74.8	10.2
4th quarter	1 743.8	1 195.8	286.7	261.0	848.3	405.4	355.6	87.3	60.8	23.8	90.2	77.1	10.5

[1]Includes components not shown separately.

Table 19-11. State and Local Government Current Receipts and Expenditures—*Continued*

(National income and product accounts, calendar years, billions of dollars, quarterly data are at seasonally adjusted annual rates.)

NIPA Table 3.3

Year and quarter	Current receipts—Continued					Current expenditures					Net state and local government saving, NIPA (surplus + / deficit -)		
	Current transfer receipts				Current surplus of government enterprises	Total 1	Con-sumption expen-ditures	Govern-ment social benefits to persons	Interest payments	Subsidies	Total	Social insurance funds	Other
	Total	Federal grants-in-aid	From business, net	From persons									
1991													
1st quarter	147.8	122.8	7.8	17.2	6.9	769.9	567.1	141.5	60.9	0.4	-7.0	2.1	-9.1
2nd quarter	153.9	128.1	7.6	18.2	7.0	785.0	570.8	152.2	61.6	0.4	-6.2	2.3	-8.5
3rd quarter	162.0	134.9	7.9	19.2	7.1	798.4	577.4	158.6	62.0	0.4	-0.2	2.4	-2.6
4th quarter	169.2	140.6	8.5	20.1	7.3	819.9	583.2	173.8	62.5	0.4	-3.3	2.6	-5.9
1992													
1st quarter	173.1	143.2	8.9	21.0	7.3	824.6	591.3	170.5	62.4	0.4	-0.3	2.8	-3.0
2nd quarter	176.8	146.2	8.9	21.7	7.5	840.6	599.5	178.6	62.0	0.4	2.1	3.0	-0.9
3rd quarter	183.8	152.4	9.2	22.2	7.9	855.5	607.5	185.8	61.9	0.4	-3.8	3.3	-7.1
4th quarter	187.3	154.6	10.0	22.7	8.2	859.1	612.4	185.0	61.3	0.4	4.8	3.5	1.3
1993													
1st quarter	189.4	156.3	10.1	23.0	8.7	872.5	622.6	188.9	60.6	0.4	-9.9	3.8	-13.7
2nd quarter	193.0	159.3	10.4	23.3	8.9	877.6	627.3	189.7	60.3	0.4	-1.7	4.1	-5.8
3rd quarter	199.3	165.0	10.6	23.7	9.2	893.6	632.8	200.6	59.9	0.4	-0.3	4.3	-4.7
4th quarter	209.2	174.1	11.0	24.1	9.2	900.5	638.5	201.7	59.9	0.4	15.7	4.5	11.1
1994													
1st quarter	207.3	171.2	11.4	24.7	7.5	916.7	651.8	203.6	60.9	0.4	4.2	4.6	-0.4
2nd quarter	208.5	171.6	11.8	25.1	9.0	925.0	659.1	203.9	61.6	0.3	6.4	4.7	1.7
3rd quarter	212.5	174.9	12.1	25.4	9.4	934.5	668.0	203.7	62.5	0.3	17.8	4.7	13.1
4th quarter	219.5	181.2	12.5	25.8	10.0	953.4	674.3	215.7	63.1	0.3	13.5	4.6	8.9
1995													
1st quarter	223.9	185.0	12.9	26.0	11.0	970.8	687.0	220.4	63.1	0.3	10.2	4.4	5.8
2nd quarter	224.5	184.9	13.3	26.3	11.7	978.7	694.0	220.7	63.7	0.3	0.4	4.2	-3.8
3rd quarter	225.5	185.1	13.7	26.6	12.4	984.3	698.7	220.7	64.5	0.3	13.4	3.9	9.4
4th quarter	222.7	181.6	14.1	27.0	13.0	979.0	704.5	208.8	65.4	0.3	24.3	3.7	20.6
1996													
1st quarter	227.8	186.1	14.5	27.2	13.7	998.1	712.9	218.2	66.6	0.3	23.7	3.4	20.2
2nd quarter	237.6	195.0	15.0	27.6	14.0	1 020.7	720.5	232.2	67.7	0.3	21.9	3.0	18.8
3rd quarter	236.5	193.2	15.4	27.9	14.0	1 021.9	728.2	224.8	68.5	0.3	27.2	2.6	24.6
4th quarter	234.4	190.3	15.8	28.3	13.8	1 029.3	737.7	221.7	69.5	0.4	30.4	2.2	28.3
1997													
1st quarter	238.1	192.4	16.3	29.5	13.2	1 043.8	747.0	226.0	70.4	0.4	29.6	1.5	28.1
2nd quarter	242.2	195.5	16.6	30.1	12.6	1 047.7	752.5	223.7	71.1	0.4	36.4	1.2	35.2
3rd quarter	249.6	198.4	20.6	30.6	12.0	1 062.0	761.7	228.0	71.8	0.4	44.4	1.0	43.4
4th quarter	256.5	208.2	17.2	31.0	11.3	1 079.7	774.4	232.4	72.4	0.5	46.1	1.0	45.1
1998													
1st quarter	257.9	207.9	18.8	31.2	9.7	1 088.9	783.1	232.2	73.1	0.5	48.6	1.5	47.1
2nd quarter	257.7	208.1	18.0	31.6	10.2	1 103.7	794.7	235.2	73.4	0.5	46.7	1.7	45.1
3rd quarter	264.8	213.0	19.6	32.1	10.5	1 115.6	807.6	233.9	73.7	0.4	49.7	1.8	47.9
4th quarter	286.6	222.0	31.8	32.8	10.6	1 136.4	820.0	241.7	74.2	0.4	63.0	1.8	61.2
1999													
1st quarter	282.8	227.0	22.4	33.5	10.8	1 156.1	834.3	247.7	73.8	0.4	49.0	1.7	47.3
2nd quarter	280.9	223.7	22.8	34.3	10.7	1 171.8	850.8	246.3	74.2	0.4	45.3	1.7	43.6
3rd quarter	296.1	237.6	23.2	35.3	10.4	1 197.6	867.3	255.1	74.8	0.4	52.0	1.7	50.3
4th quarter	303.3	243.2	23.7	36.4	9.8	1 219.7	883.3	260.3	75.6	0.4	55.3	1.7	53.5
2000													
1st quarter	304.7	239.0	28.0	37.6	8.8	1 238.5	900.6	260.4	77.0	0.5	55.9	1.7	54.2
2nd quarter	310.0	242.8	28.6	38.7	8.0	1 259.5	910.8	269.6	78.5	0.5	59.5	1.9	57.7
3rd quarter	323.8	255.0	29.1	39.8	7.3	1 281.6	923.4	277.4	80.3	0.6	49.0	2.1	46.8
4th quarter	323.0	252.6	29.6	40.8	6.6	1 298.5	936.3	279.2	82.4	0.6	35.4	2.4	33.0
2001													
1st quarter	338.2	266.5	30.1	41.6	5.5	1 334.7	951.7	290.7	84.2	8.0	32.5	2.6	29.9
2nd quarter	351.5	278.3	30.5	42.7	4.6	1 371.6	963.6	308.3	85.3	14.4	25.8	2.7	23.1
3rd quarter	350.0	272.8	33.3	43.9	3.2	1 363.4	976.6	295.9	86.0	4.8	-8.6	2.6	-11.2
4th quarter	363.3	286.6	31.5	45.2	2.8	1 403.1	987.1	326.0	86.6	3.4	-30.6	2.4	-33.0
2002													
1st quarter	369.5	291.4	32.0	46.1	2.7	1 415.0	1 001.8	324.9	86.5	1.8	-35.3	2.1	-37.4
2nd quarter	382.5	303.1	32.4	47.0	2.7	1 431.5	1 019.4	325.4	86.2	0.6	-35.1	1.8	-36.9
3rd quarter	387.4	306.6	32.9	47.9	2.6	1 454.2	1 033.6	333.0	85.9	1.7	-31.4	1.6	-33.0
4th quarter	399.3	317.2	33.3	48.8	2.0	1 476.6	1 046.7	344.7	85.7	-0.4	-34.9	1.4	-36.2
2003													
1st quarter	394.0	311.9	32.6	49.5	0.7	1 497.0	1 065.2	345.3	86.4	0.1	-61.2	2.3	-63.5
2nd quarter	425.5	342.2	33.2	50.2	-0.2	1 501.4	1 066.7	347.2	87.1	0.3	-27.2	3.2	-30.4
3rd quarter	430.6	345.9	33.8	51.0	-1.1	1 525.0	1 076.2	361.8	88.1	-1.0	-8.2	4.3	-12.5
4th quarter	440.5	354.2	34.5	51.8	-1.8	1 534.8	1 086.9	357.8	89.2	0.9	15.2	5.3	9.9
2004													
1st quarter	430.5	341.3	35.6	53.7	-1.9	1 563.1	1 099.2	375.0	88.6	0.4	-7.9	6.1	-14.0
2nd quarter	442.5	350.6	36.6	55.4	-2.5	1 584.5	1 110.2	385.6	88.3	0.4	-1.9	6.9	-8.8
3rd quarter	420.6	344.6	19.3	56.8	-3.3	1 597.0	1 124.8	383.7	88.1	0.4	-12.3	7.5	-19.8
4th quarter	455.1	359.8	37.2	58.0	-4.4	1 626.5	1 147.0	390.8	88.4	0.4	28.3	7.9	20.3
2005													
1st quarter	451.7	358.5	35.6	57.6	-3.9	1 644.5	1 159.1	396.3	88.7	0.4	41.2	7.9	33.3
2nd quarter	453.4	361.1	34.8	57.4	-4.9	1 673.1	1 174.1	409.4	89.2	0.4	38.3	7.8	30.5
3rd quarter	456.7	359.7	39.5	57.6	-19.5	1 697.3	1 203.1	403.7	90.2	0.4	19.3	7.5	11.8
4th quarter	439.2	364.3	16.9	58.0	-5.2	1 724.7	1 228.4	404.5	91.3	0.4	19.1	7.2	11.9

1Includes components not shown separately.

Table 19-12. U.S. International Transactions

(Millions of dollars, seasonally adjusted.)

Year and quarter	Exports of goods, services, and income				Imports of goods, services, and income [1]				Unilateral current transfers, net [2]	U.S.-owned assets abroad, net [3]					
										Total	U.S. official reserve assets, net	U.S. government assets other than official reserve assets, net	U.S. private assets, net		
	Total	Goods	Services	Income receipts	Total	Goods	Services	Income payments					Total	Direct investment	Foreign securities
1960															
1st quarter	7 355	4 685	1 543	1 127	-6 050	-3 812	-1 907	-331	-955	-1 066	159	-237	-988	-664	-266
2nd quarter	7 762	4 916	1 715	1 131	-6 078	-3 858	-1 906	-314	-1 154	-1 156	175	-339	-992	-586	-166
3rd quarter	7 650	5 031	1 453	1 166	-5 925	-3 648	-1 970	-307	-889	-956	740	-160	-1 536	-754	-111
4th quarter	7 791	5 018	1 580	1 193	-5 619	-3 440	-1 892	-287	-1 064	-923	1 071	-365	-1 629	-936	-120
1961															
1st quarter	7 827	5 095	1 481	1 251	-5 599	-3 394	-1 912	-293	-989	-1 320	371	-381	-1 310	-774	-135
2nd quarter	7 773	4 806	1 758	1 209	-5 659	-3 438	-1 922	-299	-1 208	-1 029	-320	471	-1 180	-551	-246
3rd quarter	7 757	5 038	1 468	1 251	-6 026	-3 809	-1 900	-317	-887	-1 928	-212	-486	-1 230	-737	-124
4th quarter	8 047	5 169	1 590	1 288	-6 171	-3 896	-1 939	-336	-1 043	-1 260	768	-513	-1 515	-592	-257
1962															
1st quarter	8 015	5 077	1 666	1 272	-6 256	-3 966	-1 971	-319	-1 113	-1 301	427	-406	-1 322	-545	-196
2nd quarter	8 719	5 336	2 004	1 379	-6 402	-4 080	-1 992	-330	-1 272	-1 461	-163	-381	-917	-716	-308
3rd quarter	8 295	5 331	1 567	1 397	-6 455	-4 116	-2 005	-334	-879	-279	881	8	-1 168	-811	-87
4th quarter	8 315	5 037	1 709	1 569	-6 567	-4 098	-2 126	-343	-1 016	-1 134	390	-306	-1 218	-779	-378
1963															
1st quarter	8 428	5 063	1 849	1 516	-6 478	-4 064	-2 057	-357	-1 107	-1 922	32	-482	-1 472	-980	-522
2nd quarter	9 244	5 599	2 150	1 495	-6 674	-4 226	-2 066	-382	-1 371	-2 631	124	-654	-2 101	-874	-536
3rd quarter	8 832	5 671	1 620	1 541	-6 893	-4 372	-2 122	-399	-918	-887	227	-86	-1 028	-721	-100
4th quarter	9 275	5 939	1 731	1 605	-6 926	-4 386	-2 118	-422	-999	-1 831	-5	-440	-1 386	-908	53
1964															
1st quarter	9 885	6 242	1 922	1 721	-6 982	-4 416	-2 140	-426	-993	-2 086	-51	-288	-1 747	-822	20
2nd quarter	9 975	6 199	2 088	1 688	-7 179	-4 598	-2 142	-439	-1 269	-2 018	303	-386	-1 935	-970	-206
3rd quarter	10 009	6 423	1 851	1 735	-7 349	-4 756	-2 153	-440	-935	-2 255	70	-414	-1 911	-1 018	2
4th quarter	10 299	6 637	1 982	1 680	-7 594	-4 930	-2 186	-478	-1 043	-3 200	-151	-592	-2 457	-949	-494
1965															
1st quarter	9 689	5 768	2 047	1 874	-7 395	-4 711	-2 187	-497	-1 037	-1 576	843	-374	-2 045	-1 606	-198
2nd quarter	11 263	6 876	2 448	1 939	-8 208	-5 428	-2 269	-511	-1 478	-1 270	69	-536	-803	-1 250	-147
3rd quarter	10 625	6 643	2 120	1 862	-8 307	-5 516	-2 263	-528	-1 013	-1 454	42	-254	-1 242	-1 030	-209
4th quarter	11 149	7 174	2 212	1 763	-8 802	-5 855	-2 393	-554	-1 058	-1 416	271	-441	-1 246	-1 125	-205
1966															
1st quarter	11 190	7 242	2 124	1 824	-9 068	-6 012	-2 483	-573	-1 140	-1 465	424	-321	-1 568	-1 115	-437
2nd quarter	11 726	7 169	2 705	1 852	-9 390	-6 195	-2 601	-594	-1 547	-1 967	68	-504	-1 531	-1 373	-115
3rd quarter	11 470	7 290	2 301	1 879	-9 912	-6 576	-2 693	-643	-1 073	-1 681	83	-339	-1 425	-1 314	-115
4th quarter	12 068	7 609	2 487	1 972	-10 098	-6 710	-2 717	-671	-1 194	-2 208	-5	-380	-1 823	-1 616	-53
1967															
1st quarter	12 439	7 751	2 731	1 957	-10 248	-6 708	-2 866	-674	-1 315	-1 203	1 027	-643	-1 587	-1 186	-265
2nd quarter	12 275	7 693	2 666	1 916	-10 136	-6 475	-2 986	-675	-1 472	-2 339	-419	-543	-1 377	-964	-261
3rd quarter	12 134	7 530	2 540	2 064	-10 262	-6 526	-3 059	-677	-1 309	-3 155	-375	-551	-2 229	-1 359	-419
4th quarter	12 506	7 692	2 731	2 083	-10 833	-7 157	-2 955	-721	-1 199	-3 060	-180	-685	-2 195	-1 297	-363
1968															
1st quarter	13 016	7 998	2 816	2 202	-11 571	-7 796	-2 997	-778	-1 249	-1 299	912	-706	-1 505	-981	-449
2nd quarter	13 577	8 324	2 936	2 317	-11 885	-8 051	-2 990	-844	-1 363	-2 427	-135	-632	-1 660	-1 172	-283
3rd quarter	14 195	8 745	3 039	2 411	-12 611	-8 612	-3 129	-870	-1 445	-3 447	-572	-568	-2 307	-1 573	-318
4th quarter	14 126	8 559	3 129	2 438	-12 604	-8 532	-3 185	-887	-1 573	-3 803	-1 075	-368	-2 360	-1 568	-519
1969															
1st quarter	12 921	7 468	2 884	2 569	-11 622	-7 444	-3 174	-1 004	-1 177	-2 595	-45	-406	-2 144	-1 556	-366
2nd quarter	15 492	9 536	3 283	2 673	-13 978	-9 527	-3 303	-1 148	-1 645	-3 428	-298	-632	-2 498	-1 663	-498
3rd quarter	15 439	9 400	3 245	2 794	-14 072	-9 380	-3 368	-1 324	-1 319	-3 361	-685	-703	-1 973	-1 548	-546
4th quarter	16 279	10 010	3 394	2 875	-14 329	-9 456	-3 481	-1 392	-1 593	-2 199	-151	-459	-1 589	-1 192	-139
1970															
1st quarter	16 461	10 258	3 235	2 968	-14 458	-9 587	-3 449	-1 422	-1 383	-2 611	481	-399	-2 693	-1 958	-306
2nd quarter	17 419	10 744	3 645	3 030	-14 861	-9 766	-3 690	-1 405	-1 586	-1 725	1 025	-348	-2 402	-2 144	80
3rd quarter	17 267	10 665	3 625	2 977	-15 141	-10 049	-3 715	-1 377	-1 611	-2 146	802	-423	-2 525	-1 718	-517
4th quarter	17 241	10 802	3 666	2 773	-15 443	-10 464	-3 668	-1 311	-1 576	-1 989	1 040	-419	-2 610	-1 771	-333
1971															
1st quarter	17 980	10 920	4 048	3 012	-15 551	-10 600	-3 724	-1 227	-1 746	-2 747	868	-573	-3 042	-2 033	-408
2nd quarter	18 163	10 878	4 087	3 198	-16 764	-11 614	-3 867	-1 283	-1 808	-2 534	839	-567	-2 806	-1 949	-368
3rd quarter	18 676	11 548	3 972	3 156	-17 460	-12 171	-3 861	-1 428	-1 752	-3 390	1 377	-387	-4 380	-2 308	-346
4th quarter	17 564	9 973	4 251	3 340	-16 639	-11 194	-3 948	-1 497	-2 098	-3 084	-18	-355	-2 711	-1 327	9
1972															
1st quarter	19 757	11 833	4 473	3 451	-19 153	-13 501	-4 173	-1 479	-2 297	-3 585	620	-212	-3 993	-2 187	-476
2nd quarter	19 427	11 618	4 233	3 576	-19 105	-13 254	-4 228	-1 623	-2 011	-2 125	-60	-271	-1 794	-1 481	-318
3rd quarter	20 788	12 351	4 634	3 803	-19 767	-14 022	-4 095	-1 650	-2 306	-3 952	96	-518	-3 530	-2 435	203
4th quarter	22 015	13 579	4 503	3 933	-21 212	-15 020	-4 371	-1 821	-1 933	-4 125	50	-566	-3 609	-1 644	-28
1973															
1st quarter	24 681	15 474	4 579	4 628	-23 000	-16 285	-4 613	-2 102	-1 536	-7 886	213	-572	-7 527	-3 785	55
2nd quarter	27 127	17 112	4 828	5 187	-24 301	-17 168	-4 741	-2 392	-1 953	-4 154	11	-423	-3 742	-2 691	-86
3rd quarter	29 329	18 271	5 145	5 913	-24 841	-17 683	-4 640	-2 518	-1 751	-3 189	-23	-608	-2 558	-2 159	-196
4th quarter	31 912	20 553	5 279	6 080	-26 855	-19 363	-4 849	-2 643	-1 674	-7 646	-43	-1 042	-6 561	-2 718	-445

[1]A minus sign indicates imports of goods or services or income payments.
[2]A minus sign indicates net unilateral transfers to foreigners.
[3]A minus sign indicates financial outflows or increases in U.S. official assets.

Table 19-12. U.S. International Transactions—*Continued*

(Millions of dollars, seasonally adjusted.)

Year and quarter	U.S.-owned assets abroad, net³—Continued / U.S. private assets, net—Continued / U.S. claims / On unaffiliated foreigners reported by U.S. nonbanking concerns	Reported by U.S. banks, not included elsewhere	Foreign-owned assets in the United States, net⁴ / Total	Foreign official assets in the United States, net	Other foreign assets in the United States, net / Total	Direct invest-ment	U.S. Treasury securities and U.S. currency flows	U.S. securities other than U.S. Treasury securities	U.S. liabilities / To unaffiliated foreigners reported by U.S. nonbanking concerns	Reported by U.S. banks, not included elsewhere	Statistical discrep-ancy⁵	Balance on goods and services	Balance on current account
1960													
1st quarter	38	-96	926	380	546	89	-100	170	-1	388	-210	509	350
2nd quarter	-100	-140	912	435	477	102	-143	118	-50	450	-286	867	530
3rd quarter	-51	-620	381	283	98	93	-99	5	-11	110	-261	866	836
4th quarter	-281	-292	77	377	-300	31	-22	-11	-28	-270	-262	1 266	1 108
1961													
1st quarter	-117	-284	435	438	-3	68	-82	104	73	-166	-354	1 270	1 239
2nd quarter	-164	-219	620	-307	927	86	-38	152	72	655	-497	1 204	906
3rd quarter	-149	-220	934	673	261	58	83	3	14	103	150	797	844
4th quarter	-128	-538	715	-41	756	99	188	66	67	336	-288	924	833
1962													
1st quarter	-186	-395	737	. . .	737	89	193	145	-14	324	-82	806	646
2nd quarter	-5	112	675	503	172	130	-51	7	-64	150	-259	1 268	1 045
3rd quarter	-181	-89	-277	178	-455	59	-109	-23	16	-398	-405	777	961
4th quarter	17	-78	779	591	188	68	-99	6	-47	260	-377	522	732
1963													
1st quarter	-27	57	1 191	946	245	40	25	14	-36	202	-112	791	843
2nd quarter	-108	-583	1 527	910	617	108	-109	119	69	430	-95	1 457	1 199
3rd quarter	47	-254	205	56	149	105	1	52	11	-20	-339	797	1 021
4th quarter	245	-776	295	75	220	-22	-66	102	-80	286	186	1 166	1 350
1964													
1st quarter	-206	-739	462	393	69	87	32	-42	0	-8	-286	1 608	1 910
2nd quarter	-166	-593	630	227	403	109	-108	14	19	369	-139	1 547	1 527
3rd quarter	-532	-363	769	275	494	56	-65	-30	37	496	-239	1 365	1 725
4th quarter	-204	-810	1 781	763	1 018	70	-5	-27	19	961	-243	1 503	1 662
1965													
1st quarter	286	-527	208	-202	410	184	60	57	3	106	111	917	1 257
2nd quarter	165	429	-330	-194	-136	-21	64	-243	63	1	23	1 627	1 577
3rd quarter	-19	16	587	115	472	147	-149	-227	49	652	-438	984	1 305
4th quarter	-91	175	280	421	-141	104	-106	54	63	-256	-153	1 138	1 289
1966													
1st quarter	-159	143	458	-164	622	143	-102	173	68	340	25	871	982
2nd quarter	-68	25	961	-57	1 018	133	-316	518	78	605	217	1 078	789
3rd quarter	-105	109	909	-342	1 251	-37	66	107	195	920	287	322	485
4th quarter	-110	-44	1 332	-111	1 443	187	-4	108	135	1 017	100	669	776
1967													
1st quarter	-107	-29	401	708	-307	169	-6	133	219	-822	-74	908	876
2nd quarter	-69	-83	1 884	1 100	784	174	-61	329	66	276	-212	898	667
3rd quarter	-40	-411	2 513	548	1 965	127	-36	520	164	1 190	79	485	563
4th quarter	-563	28	2 584	1 098	1 486	228	-32	34	135	1 121	2	311	474
1968													
1st quarter	-231	156	1 374	-533	1 907	367	22	855	207	456	-271	21	196
2nd quarter	-567	362	2 192	-2 007	4 199	133	86	1 122	478	2 380	-94	219	329
3rd quarter	-213	-203	2 809	442	2 367	148	-8	1 124	315	788	499	43	139
4th quarter	-191	-82	3 550	1 321	2 229	160	36	1 312	474	247	304	-29	-51
1969													
1st quarter	-132	-90	3 664	-1 117	4 781	359	-125	1 388	90	3 069	-1 191	-266	122
2nd quarter	-21	-316	3 896	-766	4 662	267	-35	365	181	3 884	-337	-11	-131
3rd quarter	141	-20	3 833	1 256	2 577	261	79	396	345	1 496	-520	-103	48
4th quarter	-114	-144	1 311	-672	1 983	376	13	981	176	437	531	467	357
1970													
1st quarter	-366	-63	2 160	2 830	-670	592	16	304	222	-1 804	-169	457	620
2nd quarter	-73	-265	848	694	154	212	-35	374	534	-931	-95	933	972
3rd quarter	-157	-133	1 940	1 411	529	357	1	720	510	-1 059	-309	526	515
4th quarter	0	-506	1 413	1 975	-562	303	99	792	748	-2 504	354	336	222
1971													
1st quarter	-355	-246	3 092	5 178	-2 086	196	179	559	-62	-2 958	-1 028	644	683
2nd quarter	-131	-358	5 154	5 630	-476	140	1 862	196	-34	-2 640	-2 211	-516	-409
3rd quarter	-337	-1 389	8 726	10 367	-1 641	-293	-795	626	79	-1 258	-4 800	-512	-536
4th quarter	-406	-987	5 997	5 704	293	324	-1 270	908	386	-55	-1 740	-918	-1 173
1972													
1st quarter	-248	-1 082	4 367	2 762	1 605	-136	-3	1 059	-14	699	911	-1 368	-1 693
2nd quarter	-185	190	4 277	1 103	3 174	373	-83	961	250	1 673	-463	-1 631	-1 689
3rd quarter	-241	-1 057	6 382	4 740	1 642	310	-12	718	216	410	-1 145	-1 132	-1 285
4th quarter	-380	-1 557	6 437	1 871	4 566	403	59	1 769	363	1 972	-1 182	-1 309	-1 130
1973													
1st quarter	-809	-2 988	10 743	9 937	806	631	-119	1 718	246	-1 670	-3 002	-845	145
2nd quarter	-202	-763	3 056	-403	3 458	835	-185	489	54	2 265	225	31	873
3rd quarter	-502	299	2 168	-772	2 940	539	-205	1 173	454	979	-1 716	1 093	2 737
4th quarter	-870	-2 528	2 423	-2 736	5 159	795	293	662	281	3 128	1 840	1 620	3 383

³A minus sign indicates financial outflows or increases in U.S. official assets.
⁴A minus sign indicates financial outflows or decreases in foreign official assets in the United States.
⁵Sum of credits and debits with the sign reversed.
. . . = Not available.

Table 19-12. U.S. International Transactions—*Continued*

(Millions of dollars, seasonally adjusted.)

Year and quarter	Exports of goods, services, and income				Imports of goods, services, and income [1]				Unilateral current transfers, net [2]	U.S.-owned assets abroad, net [3]					
										Total	U.S. official reserve assets, net	U.S. government assets other than official reserve assets, net	U.S. private assets, net		
	Total	Goods	Services	Income receipts	Total	Goods	Services	Income payments					Total	Direct investment	Foreign securities
1974															
1st quarter	34 698	22 614	5 189	6 895	-29 643	-21 952	-4 985	-2 706	-3 443	-5 914	-246	1 389	-7 057	900	-600
2nd quarter	37 295	24 500	5 691	7 104	-34 710	-26 346	-5 359	-3 005	-2 475	-10 318	-358	267	-10 227	-1 790	-272
3rd quarter	37 385	24 629	5 633	7 123	-36 004	-27 368	-5 360	-3 276	-1 676	-7 694	-1 002	-354	-6 338	-4 385	-282
4th quarter	39 105	26 563	6 078	6 464	-36 918	-28 145	-5 675	-3 098	-1 656	-10 818	139	-938	-10 019	-3 776	-699
1975															
1st quarter	40 047	27 480	6 454	6 113	-33 797	-24 980	-5 580	-3 237	-2 043	-10 576	-327	-877	-9 372	-4 022	-1 931
2nd quarter	38 675	25 866	6 807	6 002	-31 284	-22 832	-5 309	-3 143	-2 377	-9 591	-28	-875	-8 688	-3 990	-985
3rd quarter	38 347	26 109	5 886	6 352	-33 078	-24 487	-5 379	-3 212	-1 189	-5 099	-333	-745	-4 021	-1 495	-938
4th quarter	40 868	27 633	6 351	6 884	-34 588	-25 886	-5 729	-2 973	-1 467	-14 436	-161	-977	-13 298	-4 736	-2 393
1976															
1st quarter	41 183	27 575	6 556	7 052	-37 464	-28 176	-5 883	-3 405	-1 153	-12 364	-777	-749	-10 838	-3 923	-2 467
2nd quarter	42 309	28 256	6 660	7 393	-39 494	-30 182	-5 980	-3 332	-1 167	-11 701	-1 580	-914	-9 207	-2 017	-1 405
3rd quarter	43 818	29 056	7 311	7 451	-41 737	-32 213	-6 231	-3 293	-2 165	-10 618	-408	-1 428	-8 782	-3 327	-2 751
4th quarter	44 780	29 858	7 444	7 478	-43 416	-33 657	-6 478	-3 281	-1 201	-16 588	207	-1 124	-15 671	-2 682	-2 262
1977															
1st quarter	44 916	29 668	7 494	7 754	-46 360	-36 585	-6 676	-3 099	-1 243	-1 198	-420	-1 062	284	-1 880	-749
2nd quarter	46 796	30 852	7 901	8 043	-48 401	-38 063	-6 940	-3 398	-1 426	-12 182	-24	-885	-11 273	-3 783	-1 784
3rd quarter	47 125	30 752	7 991	8 382	-48 511	-38 005	-6 894	-3 612	-1 371	-6 297	112	-1 001	-5 408	-2 762	-2 177
4th quarter	45 818	29 544	8 098	8 176	-50 495	-39 254	-7 133	-4 108	-1 185	-15 109	-43	-746	-14 320	-3 466	-749
1978															
1st quarter	48 847	30 470	8 704	9 673	-54 471	-42 487	-7 612	-4 372	-1 396	-15 219	187	-1 009	-14 397	-4 771	-1 115
2nd quarter	54 213	35 674	8 772	9 767	-56 513	-43 419	-7 768	-5 326	-1 477	-5 606	248	-1 257	-4 597	-3 720	-1 094
3rd quarter	56 058	36 523	9 203	10 332	-58 300	-44 422	-8 248	-5 630	-1 425	-9 703	115	-1 394	-8 424	-2 753	-510
4th quarter	61 399	39 408	9 673	12 318	-60 587	-45 674	-8 561	-6 352	-1 491	-30 601	182	-999	-29 784	-4 812	-907
1979															
1st quarter	64 530	41 475	9 664	13 391	-63 492	-47 582	-8 649	-7 261	-1 462	-7 841	-2 446	-1 094	-4 301	-5 465	-908
2nd quarter	68 445	43 885	9 713	14 847	-67 584	-50 778	-8 960	-7 846	-1 552	-15 565	322	-970	-14 917	-7 220	-492
3rd quarter	74 411	47 104	9 936	17 371	-71 856	-54 002	-9 329	-8 525	-1 632	-27 156	2 779	-779	-29 156	-7 166	-2 331
4th quarter	80 577	51 975	10 378	18 224	-78 726	-59 645	-9 751	-9 330	-1 949	-14 353	-649	-904	-12 800	-5 370	-995
1980															
1st quarter	85 274	54 237	10 997	20 040	-86 559	-65 815	-10 335	-10 409	-2 174	-12 662	-2 116	-1 441	-9 105	-5 188	-787
2nd quarter	83 441	55 967	11 491	15 983	-82 734	-62 274	-10 106	-10 354	-1 648	-24 724	502	-1 159	-24 067	-2 659	-1 387
3rd quarter	86 148	55 830	12 543	17 775	-79 906	-59 010	-10 292	-10 604	-1 909	-19 666	-1 109	-1 382	-17 175	-4 156	-944
4th quarter	89 578	58 216	12 554	18 808	-84 577	-62 651	-10 760	-11 166	-2 618	-28 761	-4 279	-1 178	-23 304	-7 219	-450
1981															
1st quarter	94 665	60 317	13 684	20 664	-91 024	-67 004	-11 360	-12 660	-2 678	-21 922	-3 436	-1 361	-17 125	-2 044	-473
2nd quarter	96 294	60 141	14 392	21 761	-92 303	-67 181	-11 447	-13 675	-2 763	-24 158	-905	-1 491	-21 762	-5 709	-1 564
3rd quarter	95 013	58 031	14 835	22 147	-89 787	-64 407	-11 236	-14 144	-3 145	-17 945	-4	-1 268	-16 673	-1 124	-697
4th quarter	94 958	58 555	14 446	21 957	-91 082	-66 475	-11 460	-13 147	-3 117	-49 028	262	-976	-48 314	-745	-2 966
1982															
1st quarter	94 006	55 163	16 032	22 811	-90 336	-63 502	-12 749	-14 085	-3 955	-36 335	-1 089	-800	-34 446	. . .	-628
2nd quarter	96 060	55 344	16 187	24 529	-88 318	-60 580	-13 096	-14 642	-3 953	-42 754	-1 132	-1 727	-39 895	1 074	-471
3rd quarter	90 925	52 089	16 003	22 833	-90 938	-63 696	-12 794	-14 448	-4 027	-23 547	-794	-2 524	-20 229	903	-3 397
4th quarter	85 993	48 561	15 857	21 575	-86 379	-59 864	-13 109	-13 406	-4 611	-25 246	-1 950	-1 080	-22 217	-3 838	-3 488
1983															
1st quarter	86 146	49 198	16 239	20 709	-85 097	-59 757	-12 951	-12 389	-3 566	-28 890	-787	-1 136	-26 967	-862	-1 549
2nd quarter	87 214	49 340	16 093	21 781	-91 096	-64 783	-13 557	-12 756	-3 951	-2 974	16	-1 263	-1 727	-1 842	-2 813
3rd quarter	89 919	50 324	16 308	23 287	-98 481	-70 370	-14 133	-13 978	-4 339	-12 191	529	-1 171	-11 549	-4 861	-1 308
4th quarter	92 831	52 937	15 671	24 223	-102 822	-73 991	-14 337	-14 494	-5 453	-22 318	-953	-1 436	-19 929	-4 962	-1 093
1984															
1st quarter	96 000	52 991	17 353	25 656	-112 576	-79 740	-16 131	-16 705	-4 354	-8 338	-657	-2 033	-5 648	-1 837	758
2nd quarter	100 257	54 626	18 045	27 586	-119 220	-83 798	-16 885	-18 537	-4 476	-25 718	-566	-1 342	-23 811	-1 967	-764
3rd quarter	102 296	55 893	17 936	28 467	-120 533	-83 918	-17 168	-19 447	-5 147	15 298	-799	-1 392	17 489	-3 209	-1 106
4th quarter	101 361	56 416	17 834	27 111	-121 591	-84 962	-17 564	-19 065	-6 359	-21 618	-1 110	-720	-19 789	-9 396	-3 644
1985															
1st quarter	97 794	54 866	18 227	24 701	-116 249	-80 319	-17 707	-18 223	-5 064	-5 491	-233	-760	-4 498	-2 783	-2 474
2nd quarter	97 437	54 154	18 214	25 069	-120 891	-84 565	-18 276	-18 050	-5 235	-2 340	-356	-1 053	-931	-4 374	-2 219
3rd quarter	94 771	52 836	17 961	23 974	-120 285	-83 909	-18 151	-18 225	-5 789	-5 776	-121	-453	-5 202	-4 698	-1 572
4th quarter	97 612	54 059	18 756	24 797	-126 349	-89 295	-18 732	-18 322	-5 911	-31 146	-3 148	-555	-27 444	-7 073	-1 217
1986															
1st quarter	100 332	53 536	21 052	25 744	-129 342	-89 220	-19 855	-20 267	-5 199	-17 406	-115	-266	-17 025	-9 781	-5 930
2nd quarter	102 206	56 828	21 466	23 674	-131 690	-91 743	-19 066	-20 881	-6 208	-24 945	16	-230	-24 731	-7 298	-1 051
3rd quarter	101 288	55 645	21 969	23 674	-132 879	-92 801	-20 448	-19 630	-6 458	-32 615	280	-1 554	-31 341	-4 975	181
4th quarter	103 275	57 335	22 761	23 179	-136 232	-94 661	-20 778	-20 793	-6 269	-36 753	132	29	-36 914	-1 938	2 529
1987															
1st quarter	104 750	56 696	23 602	24 452	-138 887	-96 023	-21 273	-21 591	-5 128	8 177	1 956	-5	6 226	-6 547	-1 749
2nd quarter	111 642	60 202	24 740	26 700	-146 125	-100 648	-22 537	-22 940	-5 502	-26 738	3 419	-168	-29 989	-7 541	-287
3rd quarter	116 688	64 217	24 986	27 485	-151 111	-104 412	-22 833	-23 866	-5 706	-27 791	32	310	-28 133	-8 795	-1 159
4th quarter	123 968	69 093	25 329	29 546	-158 324	-108 682	-24 146	-25 496	-6 926	-32 943	3 742	868	-37 553	-12 150	-2 056

[1]A minus sign indicates imports of goods or services or income payments.
[2]A minus sign indicates net unilateral transfers to foreigners.
[3]A minus sign indicates financial outflows or increases in U.S. official assets.
. . . = Not available.

Table 19-12. U.S. International Transactions—*Continued*

(Millions of dollars, seasonally adjusted.)

Year and quarter	U.S.-owned assets abroad, net [3] —Continued — U.S. private assets, net—Continued — U.S. claims — On unaffiliated foreigners reported by U.S. nonbanking concerns	Reported by U.S. banks, not included elsewhere	Foreign-owned assets in the United States, net [4] — Total	Foreign official assets in the United States, net	Other foreign assets in the United States, net — Total	Direct investment	U.S. Treasury securities and U.S. currency flows	U.S. securities other than U.S. Treasury securities	U.S. liabilities — To unaffiliated foreigners reported by U.S. nonbanking concerns	Reported by U.S. banks, not included elsewhere	Statistical discrepancy [5]	Balance on goods and services	Balance on current account
1974													
1st quarter	-2 113	-5 244	6 444	-1 138	7 582	1 784	266	712	354	4 466	-2 142	866	1 612
2nd quarter	-588	-7 577	9 897	4 434	5 463	539	-5	363	390	4 176	311	-1 514	110
3rd quarter	273	-1 944	9 310	3 062	6 248	1 610	407	227	239	3 765	-1 321	-2 466	-295
4th quarter	-793	-4 751	9 577	4 188	5 389	828	1 015	-925	861	3 610	710	-1 179	531
1975													
1st quarter	353	-3 772	2 701	3 419	-718	278	805	344	359	-2 504	3 668	3 374	4 207
2nd quarter	112	-3 825	4 307	2 244	2 063	870	-54	385	55	807	270	4 532	5 014
3rd quarter	-939	-649	2 934	-1 731	4 665	86	2 367	737	-163	1 638	-1 915	2 129	4 080
4th quarter	-883	-5 286	6 929	3 095	3 834	1 369	672	1 038	68	687	2 694	2 369	4 813
1976													
1st quarter	-747	-3 701	7 709	3 699	4 010	1 471	677	1 036	154	672	2 089	72	2 566
2nd quarter	-999	-4 786	8 425	4 039	4 386	1 086	-119	134	-231	3 516	1 628	-1 246	1 648
3rd quarter	616	-3 320	9 062	2 958	6 104	999	3 267	64	-184	1 958	1 640	-2 077	-84
4th quarter	-1 166	-9 561	12 644	6 997	5 647	790	279	51	-317	4 844	3 781	-2 833	163
1977													
1st quarter	-771	3 684	2 968	5 554	-2 586	980	1 087	749	-98	-5 304	917	-6 099	-2 687
2nd quarter	-1 124	-4 582	14 673	7 888	6 785	965	-907	589	-102	6 240	540	-6 250	-3 031
3rd quarter	1 310	-1 779	14 585	8 257	6 328	1 023	1 560	337	768	2 640	-5 531	-6 156	-2 757
4th quarter	-1 355	-8 750	20 547	15 117	5 430	761	245	763	518	3 143	424	-8 745	-5 862
1978													
1st quarter	-2 241	-6 270	18 461	15 448	3 013	1 356	1 158	396	507	-404	3 778	-10 925	-7 020
2nd quarter	315	-98	1 412	-5 113	6 525	2 313	1 354	1 082	304	1 472	7 971	-6 741	-3 777
3rd quarter	-29	-5 132	17 390	4 903	12 487	2 620	-560	296	912	9 219	-4 020	-6 944	-3 667
4th quarter	-1 898	-22 167	29 013	18 440	10 573	1 608	2 465	480	166	5 854	2 267	-5 154	-679
1979													
1st quarter	-3 854	5 926	2 333	-8 697	11 030	1 554	2 590	409	-296	6 773	5 932	-5 092	-424
2nd quarter	716	-7 921	7 379	-9 775	17 154	3 354	459	524	799	12 018	8 877	-6 140	-691
3rd quarter	-1 826	-17 833	25 063	6 036	19 027	3 382	2 116	166	210	13 153	1 170	-6 291	923
4th quarter	-50	-6 385	4 780	-1 228	6 008	3 588	597	252	908	663	9 671	-7 043	-98
1980													
1st quarter	-1 927	-1 203	9 028	-7 413	16 441	3 321	3 746	2 435	340	6 599	7 093	-10 916	-3 459
2nd quarter	144	-20 165	10 994	7 731	3 264	5 756	-150	496	1 671	-4 509	14 671	-4 922	-941
3rd quarter	365	-12 440	14 599	7 564	7 035	4 713	-109	263	1 252	916	734	-929	4 333
4th quarter	-2 605	-13 030	26 263	7 614	18 649	3 128	1 931	2 263	3 590	7 737	115	-2 641	2 383
1981													
1st quarter	-2 944	-11 664	9 210	5 502	3 708	3 146	1 877	2 357	121	-3 793	11 749	-4 363	963
2nd quarter	513	-15 002	14 906	-3 159	18 065	5 294	1 183	3 512	13	8 063	8 024	-4 095	1 228
3rd quarter	458	-15 310	17 212	-5 992	23 204	5 505	-567	704	1 084	16 478	-1 348	-2 777	2 081
4th quarter	-2 404	-42 199	43 264	8 609	34 655	11 251	1 993	332	-301	21 380	5 005	-4 934	759
1982													
1st quarter	2 220	-33 343	26 797	-3 265	30 062	. . .	854	1 263	-65	25 856	9 768	-5 056	-285
2nd quarter	-1 095	-39 403	34 995	1 534	33 461	2 945	3 928	2 486	-2 023	26 125	3 918	-2 145	3 789
3rd quarter	3 670	-21 405	18 267	2 694	15 573	2 849	1 695	555	-282	10 756	9 272	-8 398	-4 040
4th quarter	2 028	-16 919	14 995	2 629	12 366	4 685	3 017	1 781	-13	2 896	15 204	-8 555	-4 997
1983													
1st quarter	-4 253	-20 303	15 870	-38	15 908	1 254	3 317	2 873	-2 763	11 227	15 486	-7 271	-2 517
2nd quarter	-590	3 518	16 049	1 612	14 437	3 287	4 340	2 470	-64	4 404	-5 294	-12 907	-7 833
3rd quarter	-1 764	-3 616	20 106	-2 689	22 795	4 059	1 994	1 777	1 311	13 654	4 933	-17 871	-12 901
4th quarter	-4 347	-9 527	35 373	6 960	28 413	1 771	3 143	1 044	1 398	21 057	2 336	-19 720	-15 444
1984													
1st quarter	-3 012	-1 557	22 780	-2 956	25 736	4 858	1 928	1 333	6 092	11 525	6 432	-25 527	-20 930
2nd quarter	-934	-20 146	42 415	-156	42 571	8 625	7 762	362	4 232	21 590	6 685	-28 012	-23 439
3rd quarter	3 987	17 817	7 158	-884	8 042	4 432	5 693	1 447	1 662	-5 192	868	-27 257	-23 384
4th quarter	492	-7 241	43 694	7 136	36 558	6 552	10 014	9 426	4 640	5 926	4 451	-28 276	-26 589
1985													
1st quarter	475	284	17 783	-10 962	28 745	4 913	2 831	9 615	-720	12 106	11 156	-24 933	-23 519
2nd quarter	2 337	3 325	28 903	8 502	20 401	4 376	6 457	7 194	1 724	650	2 050	-30 473	-28 689
3rd quarter	-2 779	3 847	37 802	2 506	35 296	4 839	8 675	11 669	2 801	7 312	-804	-31 263	-31 303
4th quarter	-10 375	-8 779	59 746	-1 165	60 911	5 618	5 786	22 484	6 046	20 977	5 961	-35 212	-34 648
1986													
1st quarter	-6 230	4 916	40 898	2 712	38 186	3 431	5 829	18 730	696	9 500	10 633	-34 487	-34 209
2nd quarter	-2 722	-13 660	53 279	15 918	37 361	5 520	4 189	22 752	1 635	3 265	7 282	-33 069	-35 692
3rd quarter	-7 638	-18 909	70 490	15 789	54 701	8 746	-1 240	17 107	1 947	28 141	104	-35 635	-38 049
4th quarter	-5 183	-32 322	63 662	1 229	62 433	17 723	-2 548	12 380	-953	35 831	12 246	-35 343	-39 226
1987													
1st quarter	-5 715	20 237	41 667	14 199	27 468	12 883	-2 906	18 372	6 151	-7 032	-10 666	-36 998	-39 265
2nd quarter	712	-22 873	57 020	10 444	46 576	8 593	-1 042	15 960	5 595	17 470	9 612	-38 243	-39 985
3rd quarter	-1 319	-16 860	82 791	764	82 027	20 763	-2 189	12 676	6 656	44 121	-14 965	-38 042	-40 129
4th quarter	-724	-22 623	65 621	19 980	45 641	16 230	2 360	-4 888	-39	31 978	8 511	-38 406	-41 282

[3]A minus sign indicates financial outflows or increases in U.S. official assets.
[4]A minus sign indicates financial outflows or decreases in foreign official assets in the United States.
[5]Sum of credits and debits with the sign reversed.
. . . = Not available.

Table 19-12. U.S. International Transactions—*Continued*

(Millions of dollars, seasonally adjusted.)

| Year and quarter | Exports of goods, services, and income | | | | Imports of goods, services, and income [1] | | | | Unilateral current transfers, net [2] | U.S.-owned assets abroad, net [3] | | | U.S. private assets, net | | |
	Total	Goods	Services	Income receipts	Total	Goods	Services	Income payments		Total	U.S. official reserve assets, net	U.S. government assets other than official reserve assets, net	Total	Direct investment	Foreign securities
1988															
1st quarter	134 932	75 655	26 598	32 679	-161 810	-109 963	-24 503	-27 344	-6 074	2 892	1 502	-1 597	2 987	-5 037	-4 504
2nd quarter	139 984	79 542	27 567	32 875	-163 265	-110 836	-24 282	-28 147	-5 615	-23 428	39	-854	-22 613	-2 594	1 318
3rd quarter	143 879	80 941	28 453	34 485	-165 901	-110 901	-24 588	-30 412	-5 902	-49 965	-7 380	1 960	-44 545	-7 791	-1 500
4th quarter	149 068	84 092	28 302	36 674	-172 770	-115 489	-25 157	-32 124	-7 685	-36 074	1 925	3 457	-41 456	-7 105	-3 294
1989															
1st quarter	155 853	86 322	30 576	38 955	-178 297	-118 709	-25 140	-34 448	-6 048	-53 703	-4 000	961	-50 664	-12 136	-2 225
2nd quarter	163 435	91 482	31 110	40 843	-182 850	-121 012	-25 241	-36 597	-5 753	-8 202	-12 095	-306	4 199	-7 686	-6 192
3rd quarter	163 560	90 743	32 316	40 501	-178 980	-117 459	-25 792	-35 729	-6 630	-51 678	-5 996	489	-46 171	-8 704	-9 149
4th quarter	165 444	91 369	33 087	40 988	-181 480	-120 485	-26 306	-34 689	-7 739	-61 803	-3 202	87	-58 688	-14 922	-4 504
1990															
1st quarter	171 856	95 070	35 016	41 770	-188 962	-124 947	-28 173	-35 842	-6 540	37 828	-3 177	-756	41 761	-10 391	-8 580
2nd quarter	174 266	96 273	35 988	42 005	-186 146	-121 782	-28 764	-35 600	-7 644	-37 204	371	-796	-36 779	-4 651	-11 037
3rd quarter	176 466	97 227	37 402	41 837	-190 664	-124 132	-29 923	-36 609	-7 339	-43 716	1 739	-338	-45 117	-17 898	-1 037
4th quarter	184 389	98 831	39 428	46 130	-193 514	-127 577	-30 795	-35 142	-5 133	-38 142	-1 092	4 205	-41 255	-4 240	-8 111
1991															
1st quarter	181 296	101 258	37 891	42 147	-186 167	-122 326	-29 801	-34 040	14 828	-10 570	-353	549	-10 766	-14 318	-9 960
2nd quarter	180 627	102 674	40 745	37 208	-181 695	-120 103	-29 660	-31 932	3 593	745	1 014	-423	154	-1 230	-12 021
3rd quarter	181 647	104 238	41 860	35 549	-182 800	-122 448	-29 200	-31 152	-3 033	-15 900	3 878	3 256	-23 034	-9 356	-12 550
4th quarter	183 993	105 913	43 766	34 314	-183 906	-126 143	-29 799	-27 964	-5 488	-38 664	1 226	-459	-39 431	-12 987	-11 142
1992															
1st quarter	186 444	108 062	44 164	34 218	-185 468	-127 962	-29 762	-27 744	-7 210	-11 428	-1 057	-259	-10 112	-20 695	-8 668
2nd quarter	186 873	107 941	44 133	34 799	-190 414	-132 484	-29 443	-28 487	-8 349	-16 235	1 464	-302	-17 397	-10 268	-8 196
3rd quarter	188 127	110 847	44 609	32 671	-193 313	-136 048	-30 175	-27 090	-7 982	-13 570	1 952	-392	-15 130	-5 157	-13 059
4th quarter	189 201	112 781	44 343	32 077	-196 427	-140 034	-30 182	-26 211	-11 561	-33 177	1 542	-715	-34 004	-12 145	-19 243
1993															
1st quarter	191 422	112 099	45 984	33 339	-197 860	-142 331	-29 996	-25 533	-8 339	-21 491	-983	487	-20 995	-14 982	-28 208
2nd quarter	193 169	113 257	46 457	33 455	-204 737	-146 800	-30 661	-27 276	-9 111	-45 843	822	-304	-46 361	-23 264	-29 833
3rd quarter	194 153	112 982	46 707	34 464	-205 549	-147 763	-30 922	-26 864	-9 906	-52 975	-544	-194	-52 237	-13 155	-51 940
4th quarter	200 170	118 605	46 766	34 799	-215 772	-152 500	-32 202	-31 070	-12 456	-80 243	-673	-340	-79 230	-32 550	-36 272
1994															
1st quarter	204 240	118 833	48 362	37 045	-220 726	-156 303	-32 809	-31 614	-8 495	-39 740	-59	399	-40 080	-28 554	-19 540
2nd quarter	211 812	122 251	49 978	39 583	-231 476	-163 200	-33 023	-35 253	-8 914	-45 677	3 537	477	-49 691	-14 932	-11 834
3rd quarter	222 795	132 828	50 667	43 181	-244 319	-171 342	-33 624	-39 353	-10 084	-31 948	-165	-323	-31 460	-17 316	-13 368
4th quarter	230 930	132 828	51 391	46 711	-254 602	-177 845	-33 603	-43 154	-12 773	-61 574	2 033	-943	-62 664	-19 367	-18 448
1995															
1st quarter	241 117	138 370	52 173	50 574	-263 108	-183 966	-34 426	-44 716	-9 443	-64 771	-5 318	-553	-58 900	-19 325	-8 596
2nd quarter	248 705	142 520	53 163	53 022	-271 587	-189 910	-35 097	-46 580	-9 131	-118 089	-2 722	-225	-115 142	-15 078	-27 964
3rd quarter	255 495	146 536	56 436	52 523	-272 929	-187 685	-35 604	-49 640	-9 543	-47 311	-1 893	252	-45 670	-21 772	-42 116
4th quarter	259 310	147 778	57 408	54 124	-272 501	-187 813	-36 272	-48 416	-9 956	-122 091	191	-458	-121 824	-42 573	-43 718
1996															
1st quarter	263 221	150 552	57 442	55 227	-279 419	-194 445	-37 090	-47 884	-11 242	-80 431	17	-210	-80 238	-23 759	-43 538
2nd quarter	266 995	152 861	59 350	54 784	-287 312	-200 070	-37 606	-49 636	-9 523	-68 123	-523	-568	-67 032	-15 096	-30 579
3rd quarter	266 854	151 856	58 664	56 334	-293 261	-202 367	-38 836	-52 058	-9 651	-91 580	7 489	105	-99 174	-23 129	-33 178
4th quarter	280 655	156 844	64 029	59 782	-299 487	-206 231	-39 023	-54 233	-12 603	-173 272	-315	-316	-172 641	-29 898	-42 020
1997															
1st quarter	287 279	162 670	62 515	62 094	-313 391	-214 209	-40 405	-58 777	-9 967	-152 729	4 480	-76	-157 133	-29 544	-24 352
2nd quarter	299 679	170 249	64 292	65 138	-318 210	-217 296	-40 879	-60 035	-10 267	-93 152	-236	-298	-92 618	-24 883	-31 275
3rd quarter	303 542	173 155	64 855	65 532	-325 593	-220 974	-42 078	-62 541	-10 666	-119 387	-730	377	-119 034	-21 217	-51 401
4th quarter	300 762	172 292	64 429	64 041	-329 728	-224 315	-42 571	-62 842	-14 160	-120 209	-4 524	65	-115 750	-29 161	-9 824
1998															
1st quarter	302 195	171 060	64 690	66 445	-334 146	-227 667	-43 304	-63 175	-12 053	-74 438	-444	-80	-73 914	-41 844	-19 451
2nd quarter	298 846	165 559	66 174	67 113	-337 834	-228 497	-44 627	-64 710	-12 361	-138 628	-1 945	-483	-136 200	-44 689	-42 961
3rd quarter	293 115	164 054	64 786	64 275	-338 864	-227 854	-45 784	-65 226	-13 140	-58 520	-2 025	188	-56 683	-20 479	7 783
4th quarter	300 835	169 743	67 106	63 986	-346 026	-234 619	-46 965	-64 442	-15 633	-82 245	-2 369	-47	-79 829	-35 634	-75 575
1999															
1st quarter	300 183	164 302	68 755	67 126	-351 564	-239 080	-47 703	-64 781	-11 885	-84 623	4 068	118	-88 809	-68 498	2 696
2nd quarter	307 288	166 144	70 138	71 006	-367 128	-250 480	-49 234	-67 414	-12 260	-182 426	1 159	-392	-183 193	-50 190	-69 682
3rd quarter	319 936	172 989	71 185	75 762	-388 656	-264 829	-50 818	-73 009	-11 987	-123 490	1 951	-686	-124 755	-64 062	-39 790
4th quarter	332 407	180 530	71 842	80 035	-403 662	-277 395	-51 435	-74 832	-14 295	-113 524	1 569	3 710	-118 803	-42 185	-15 460
2000															
1st quarter	341 683	185 253	73 127	83 303	-427 646	-294 137	-54 240	-79 269	-12 859	-207 606	-554	-127	-206 925	-34 934	-32 542
2nd quarter	355 307	191 227	75 335	88 745	-441 576	-302 219	-55 245	-84 112	-13 368	-107 301	2 020	-570	-108 751	-52 029	-38 171
3rd quarter	360 295	198 811	74 662	86 822	-454 243	-313 330	-57 353	-83 560	-14 208	-84 847	-346	114	-84 615	-39 618	-32 363
4th quarter	364 231	196 703	75 479	92 049	-456 835	-316 998	-56 914	-82 923	-18 212	-160 771	-1 410	-358	-159 003	-32 633	-24 832
2001															
1st quarter	350 489	193 976	74 564	81 949	-442 826	-309 885	-56 420	-76 521	-15 171	-216 194	190	77	-216 461	-35 381	-25 355
2nd quarter	334 968	185 030	74 110	75 828	-416 706	-290 729	-57 578	-68 399	-15 802	-86 702	-1 343	-783	-84 576	-26 783	-50 200
3rd quarter	312 094	172 648	70 579	68 867	-400 657	-278 526	-54 863	-67 268	-2 941	32 858	-3 559	77	36 340	-44 327	11 639
4th quarter	298 144	167 058	66 932	64 154	-368 912	-269 091	-52 930	-46 891	-17 374	-112 577	-199	143	-112 521	-35 857	-26 728

[1] A minus sign indicates imports of goods or services or income payments.
[2] A minus sign indicates net unilateral transfers to foreigners.
[3] A minus sign indicates financial outflows or increases in U.S. official assets.

Table 19-12. U.S. International Transactions—*Continued*

(Millions of dollars, seasonally adjusted.)

Year and quarter	U.S.-owned assets abroad, net [3]—Continued / U.S. private assets, net—Continued / U.S. claims / On unaffiliated foreigners reported by U.S. nonbanking concerns	Reported by U.S. banks, not included elsewhere	Foreign-owned assets in the United States, net [4] / Total	Foreign official assets in the United States, net	Other foreign assets in the United States, net / Total	Direct investment	U.S. Treasury securities and U.S. currency flows	U.S. securities other than U.S. Treasury securities	U.S. liabilities / To unaffiliated foreigners reported by U.S. nonbanking concerns	Reported by U.S. banks, not included elsewhere	Statistical discrepancy [5]	Balance on goods and services	Balance on current account
1988													
1st quarter	-3 454	15 982	31 524	24 925	6 599	8 425	6 007	2 423	12 593	-22 849	-1 573	-32 213	-32 952
2nd quarter	-9 954	-11 383	74 187	6 006	68 181	13 717	7 329	9 702	6 742	30 691	-21 981	-28 009	-28 896
3rd quarter	-5 217	-30 037	52 329	-1 974	54 303	13 778	4 275	7 464	6 399	22 387	25 430	-26 095	-27 924
4th quarter	-2 568	-28 489	86 793	10 801	75 992	21 815	6 739	6 764	7 159	33 515	-19 468	-28 252	-31 387
1989													
1st quarter	-9 293	-27 010	66 021	7 700	58 321	18 584	10 316	8 544	6 637	14 240	16 046	-26 951	-28 492
2nd quarter	-5 767	23 844	10 571	-5 114	15 685	15 325	4 380	9 365	12 000	-25 385	22 666	-23 661	-25 168
3rd quarter	-5 924	-22 394	73 526	13 060	60 466	11 519	12 202	10 270	-1 121	27 596	63	-20 192	-22 050
4th quarter	-6 662	-32 600	72 660	-7 142	79 802	22 846	6 469	10 588	4 570	35 329	12 982	-22 335	-23 775
1990													
1st quarter	3 019	57 713	-23 477	-6 421	-17 056	15 774	1 056	1 311	12 904	-48 101	9 314	-23 034	-23 646
2nd quarter	-5 069	-16 022	40 868	6 207	34 661	13 773	5 910	2 114	6 713	6 151	15 703	-18 285	-19 524
3rd quarter	-15 514	-10 668	62 621	13 937	48 684	8 313	5 434	-2 874	16 838	20 973	2 467	-19 426	-21 537
4th quarter	-10 260	-18 644	59 345	20 186	39 159	10 635	1 652	1 041	8 678	17 153	-63	-20 113	-14 258
1991													
1st quarter	-40	13 552	7 590	5 569	2 021	4 076	8 782	5 023	-586	-15 274	-6 036	-12 978	9 957
2nd quarter	7 902	5 503	12 016	-4 913	16 929	13 378	14 999	14 872	-2 549	-23 771	-15 359	-6 344	2 525
3rd quarter	3 341	-4 469	32 574	3 854	28 720	-1 354	2 342	10 310	4 761	12 661	-8 702	-5 550	-4 186
4th quarter	-106	-15 196	56 043	12 879	43 164	7 072	5 516	4 939	-4 741	30 378	-12 153	-6 263	-5 401
1992													
1st quarter	7 562	11 689	30 212	20 988	9 224	2 086	1 119	4 569	5 689	-4 239	-12 413	-5 498	-6 234
2nd quarter	-6 620	7 687	49 732	20 879	28 853	5 916	10 759	10 467	3 954	-2 243	-21 432	-9 853	-11 890
3rd quarter	-3 737	6 823	34 931	-7 524	42 455	2 898	10 470	2 531	4 854	21 702	-8 062	-10 767	-13 168
4th quarter	2 408	-5 024	53 472	6 133	47 339	8 922	25 869	12 476	-924	996	-1 394	-13 092	-18 787
1993													
1st quarter	-6 130	28 325	24 531	10 937	13 594	8 060	15 795	9 694	-215	-19 740	12 495	-14 244	-14 777
2nd quarter	-725	7 461	58 599	17 466	41 133	11 386	5 169	15 205	6 531	2 842	8 073	-17 747	-20 679
3rd quarter	5 896	6 962	84 967	19 073	65 894	11 688	8 931	17 782	288	27 205	-10 458	-18 996	-21 302
4th quarter	1 725	-12 133	111 662	24 277	87 385	20 229	11 104	37 411	3 885	14 756	-3 202	-19 331	-28 058
1994													
1st quarter	-2 215	10 229	89 488	10 568	78 920	5 883	14 620	21 070	5 856	31 491	-24 609	-21 917	-24 981
2nd quarter	-20 966	-1 959	56 279	9 455	46 824	5 767	-1 361	12 352	4 269	25 797	18 987	-23 994	-28 578
3rd quarter	-960	184	81 239	19 358	61 881	13 709	9 666	13 389	-1 620	26 737	-17 287	-25 352	-31 608
4th quarter	-12 195	-12 654	76 168	202	75 966	20 762	31 934	10 160	-7 203	20 313	22 009	-27 229	-36 445
1995													
1st quarter	-2 631	-28 348	96 842	21 956	74 886	9 924	33 337	12 400	17 764	1 461	-462	-27 849	-31 434
2nd quarter	-24 580	-47 520	121 385	37 072	84 313	11 888	29 574	15 851	11 864	15 136	28 763	-29 324	-32 013
3rd quarter	13 729	4 489	115 499	39 302	76 197	16 764	36 327	26 218	13 493	-16 605	-40 574	-20 317	-26 977
4th quarter	-31 804	-3 729	101 376	11 550	89 826	19 200	1 146	22 780	16 516	30 184	43 931	-18 899	-23 147
1996													
1st quarter	-15 210	2 269	84 335	51 771	32 564	28 518	12 726	20 356	4 350	-33 386	23 714	-23 541	-27 440
2nd quarter	-22 000	643	100 610	13 503	87 107	16 184	28 719	24 686	15 259	2 259	-2 469	-25 465	-29 840
3rd quarter	-9 090	-33 777	143 269	23 020	120 249	15 257	43 276	29 719	28 925	3 072	-15 445	-30 683	-36 058
4th quarter	-40 033	-60 690	219 670	38 430	181 240	26 542	76 452	28 511	5 202	44 533	-14 770	-24 381	-31 435
1997													
1st quarter	-38 112	-65 125	172 247	27 763	144 484	28 626	31 779	38 490	25 055	20 534	16 776	-29 429	-36 079
2nd quarter	-9 885	-26 575	140 222	-6 019	146 241	23 150	38 253	45 651	6 461	32 726	-17 992	-23 634	-28 798
3rd quarter	-22 173	-24 243	166 609	23 474	143 135	17 865	42 095	52 544	25 550	5 081	-14 205	-25 042	-32 717
4th quarter	-51 590	-25 175	225 372	-26 182	251 554	35 960	40 733	24 724	59 452	90 685	-61 805	-30 165	-43 126
1998													
1st quarter	-7 822	-4 797	78 365	11 072	67 293	19 759	-6 594	63 237	39 833	-48 942	40 271	-35 221	-44 004
2nd quarter	-20 363	-28 187	154 539	-10 235	164 774	20 391	23 647	56 146	30 722	33 868	35 629	-41 391	-51 349
3rd quarter	-15 658	-28 329	75 193	-46 640	121 833	23 490	1 425	6 628	14 976	75 314	42 413	-44 798	-58 889
4th quarter	5 639	25 741	112 697	25 900	86 797	115 405	23 950	30 304	-62 391	-20 471	30 556	-44 735	-60 824
1999													
1st quarter	-47 211	24 204	108 317	4 381	103 936	28 759	-11 853	49 157	51 307	-13 434	39 768	-53 726	-63 266
2nd quarter	-27 021	-36 300	247 211	-757	247 968	140 759	-9 004	70 205	16 928	29 080	7 506	-63 432	-72 100
3rd quarter	-13 663	-7 240	156 060	12 625	143 435	50 758	7 584	86 202	-8 777	7 668	48 326	-71 473	-80 707
4th quarter	-9 809	-51 349	230 623	27 294	203 329	69 169	-6 817	93 270	16 789	30 918	-27 186	-76 458	-85 550
2000													
1st quarter	-79 800	-59 649	242 782	22 542	220 240	52 094	-23 776	129 306	72 433	-9 817	63 869	-89 997	-98 822
2nd quarter	-25 287	6 736	246 564	6 952	239 612	91 669	-22 889	88 189	28 796	53 847	-39 388	-90 902	-99 637
3rd quarter	-14 121	1 487	245 064	11 354	233 710	79 979	-13 777	122 138	16 914	28 456	-51 791	-97 210	-108 156
4th quarter	-19 582	-81 956	303 816	1 910	301 906	97 534	-12 898	120 256	52 529	44 485	-31 950	-101 730	-110 816
2001													
1st quarter	-46 769	-108 956	330 767	21 333	309 434	59 145	-16 736	129 474	112 097	25 454	-6 764	-97 765	-107 508
2nd quarter	-7 507	-86	206 867	-19 965	226 832	59 338	-10 143	108 537	-173	69 273	-22 312	-89 167	-97 540
3rd quarter	1 824	67 204	24 226	15 653	8 573	13 783	1 495	60 748	-23 171	-44 282	34 753	-90 162	-91 504
4th quarter	43 932	-93 868	221 010	11 038	209 972	34 755	34 800	95 126	-22 643	67 934	-19 968	-88 031	-88 142

[3]A minus sign indicates financial outflows or increases in U.S. official assets.
[4]A minus sign indicates financial outflows or decreases in foreign official assets in the United States.
[5]Sum of credits and debits with the sign reversed.

Table 19-12. U.S. International Transactions—*Continued*

(Millions of dollars, seasonally adjusted.)

| Year and quarter | Exports of goods, services, and income | | | | Imports of goods, services, and income [1] | | | | Unilateral current transfers, net [2] | U.S.-owned assets abroad, net [3] | | | U.S. private assets, net | | |
	Total	Goods	Services	Income receipts	Total	Goods	Services	Income payments		Total	U.S. official reserve assets, net	U.S. government assets other than official reserve assets, net	Total	Direct investment	Foreign securities
2002															
1st quarter	302 429	165 171	70 799	66 459	-388 601	-273 665	-55 981	-58 955	-18 542	-84 841	390	133	-85 364	-48 155	-9 012
2nd quarter	314 174	172 131	72 292	69 751	-415 267	-291 790	-56 586	-66 891	-15 007	-139 712	-1 843	42	-137 911	-36 163	-20 735
3rd quarter	321 743	174 241	73 650	73 852	-423 307	-297 850	-57 979	-67 478	-15 005	892	-1 416	-27	2 335	-33 165	4 884
4th quarter	317 321	170 879	75 558	70 884	-424 810	-304 072	-60 522	-60 216	-16 394	-70 987	-812	197	-70 372	-36 979	-23 705
2003															
1st quarter	321 626	173 423	73 417	74 786	-439 095	-310 808	-60 683	-67 604	-18 219	-82 315	83	53	-82 451	-22 656	-31 947
2nd quarter	324 745	174 438	72 781	77 526	-437 889	-311 060	-59 848	-66 981	-17 600	-157 427	-170	310	-157 567	-46 512	-32 734
3rd quarter	335 183	177 796	76 996	80 391	-448 024	-314 727	-63 417	-69 880	-17 707	-755	-611	483	-627	-40 597	-27 677
4th quarter	356 654	187 758	81 147	87 749	-464 810	-327 712	-66 416	-70 682	-18 269	-84 924	2 221	-309	-86 836	-39 796	-54 364
2004															
1st quarter	375 712	194 110	85 435	96 167	-489 177	-345 176	-69 528	-74 474	-22 987	-353 976	557	727	-355 260	-77 283	-36 045
2nd quarter	387 382	200 045	87 323	100 014	-521 673	-365 168	-71 973	-84 532	-21 385	-170 502	1 122	-2	-171 622	-75 377	-44 702
3rd quarter	396 956	203 835	87 759	105 363	-534 133	-373 498	-73 461	-87 175	-17 289	-169 462	429	484	-170 375	-51 998	-53 988
4th quarter	414 275	209 526	92 555	112 194	-569 854	-393 252	-76 262	-100 339	-22 822	-306 929	697	501	-308 127	-111 564	-35 814
2005															
1st quarter	434 701	214 857	95 191	124 653	-580 114	-399 862	-76 183	-104 069	-28 644	-129 175	5 331	2 591	-137 097	-58 799	-59 599
2nd quarter	447 848	223 728	95 633	128 487	-600 704	-412 411	-77 679	-110 615	-24 964	-222 397	989	-222 589	-41 548	-57 317
3rd quarter	457 508	223 603	97 767	136 138	-617 311	-422 752	-78 963	-115 595	-9 090	-204 361	4 766	1 501	-210 628	12 163	-66 383
4th quarter	478 958	232 443	100 530	145 986	-660 097	-446 754	-80 715	-132 627	-27 085	9 302	4 796	459	4 047	51 948	-67 900
2006															
1st quarter	504 862	244 679	104 500	155 683	-679 297	-453 286	-84 981	-141 031	-21 516	-359 608	513	1 049	-361 170	-55 969	-75 699
2nd quarter	529 782	253 332	106 439	170 011	-705 572	-465 016	-86 596	-153 960	-24 116	-234 828	-560	1 765	-236 033	-47 902	-80 252
3rd quarter	543 893	259 277	108 365	176 251	-730 083	-477 900	-87 213	-164 969	-24 716	-286 769	1 006	1 570	-289 346	-65 992	-72 558
4th quarter	563 627	265 821	114 600	183 205	-723 303	-465 178	-90 129	-167 996	-21 679	-370 543	1 415	962	-372 920	-71 381	-136 695
2007															
1st quarter	572 182	270 318	115 118	186 746	-738 938	-473 681	-91 298	-173 959	-30 174	-442 065	-72	445	-442 438	-66 706	-99 541
2nd quarter	602 122	279 488	120 463	202 171	-771 262	-485 375	-93 395	-192 492	-24 953	-24 964	26	-596	-522 985	-93 616	-84 671
3rd quarter	638 393	295 494	129 378	213 520	-783 548	-496 698	-96 288	-190 562	-27 796	-170 476	-54	623	-171 045	-62 043	-100 317
4th quarter	650 808	303 180	132 285	215 343	-788 264	-512 099	-97 149	-179 016	-29 784	-153 757	-22	-22 744	-130 990	-110 905	-4 202
2008															
1st quarter	651 416	317 548	133 969	199 900	-796 593	-530 126	-99 834	-166 633	-31 731	-264 866	-276	3 265	-267 855	-93 321	-35 066
2nd quarter	671 888	337 048	138 318	196 523	-825 091	-554 922	-101 862	-168 307	-29 034	99 910	-1 267	-41 592	142 769	-86 838	-33 576
3rd quarter	678 258	346 272	139 639	192 347	-829 558	-562 526	-104 267	-162 766	-29 998	28 056	-179	-225 990	254 226	-52 356	82 615
4th quarter	589 692	290 505	132 489	166 699	-693 564	-464 624	-98 756	-130 185	-28 949	84 441	-3 126	-265 193	352 760	-85 319	76 978

[1]A minus sign indicates imports of goods or services or income payments.
[2]A minus sign indicates net unilateral transfers to foreigners.
[3]A minus sign indicates financial outflows or increases in U.S. official assets.

Table 19-12. U.S. International Transactions—*Continued*

(Millions of dollars, seasonally adjusted.)

| Year and quarter | U.S.-owned assets abroad, net [3] —Continued / U.S. private assets, net—Continued / U.S. claims | | Foreign-owned assets in the United States, net [4] | | | Other foreign assets in the United States, net | | | | | | Statistical discrep-ancy [5] | Balance on goods and services | Balance on current account |
	On unaffiliated foreigners reported by U.S. nonbanking concerns	Reported by U.S. banks, not included elsewhere	Total	Foreign official assets in the United States, net	Total	Direct invest-ment	U.S. Treasury securities and U.S. currency flows	U.S. securities other than U.S. Treasury securities	U.S. liabilities / To unaffiliated foreigners reported by U.S. nonbanking concerns	Reported by U.S. banks, not included elsewhere			
2002													
1st quarter	-27 798	-399	173 225	12 801	160 424	24 485	13 964	73 750	57 788	-9 563	16 651	-93 676	-104 714
2nd quarter	-13 680	-67 333	231 325	53 312	178 013	7 194	26 042	99 689	17 805	27 283	24 820	-103 953	-116 100
3rd quarter	-7 443	38 059	160 335	18 328	142 007	13 929	55 166	43 282	7 515	22 115	-44 259	-107 938	-116 569
4th quarter	-1 101	-8 587	230 275	31 504	198 771	38 763	24 092	66 578	12 763	56 575	-34 988	-118 157	-123 883
2003													
1st quarter	1 757	-29 605	240 908	50 531	190 377	37 169	10 894	52 209	68 460	21 645	-22 416	-124 651	-135 688
2nd quarter	-15 089	-63 232	217 732	66 877	150 855	-5 460	48 179	81 187	15 129	11 820	72 102	-123 689	-130 744
3rd quarter	21 261	46 386	129 177	64 397	64 780	-1 574	36 749	15 354	9 137	5 114	3 035	-123 352	-130 548
4th quarter	-26 113	33 437	270 487	96 264	174 223	33 616	6 224	71 955	3 800	58 628	-58 719	-125 223	-126 425
2004													
1st quarter	-67 088	-174 844	459 483	147 636	311 847	26 000	29 034	47 862	61 265	147 686	31 433	-135 159	-136 453
2nd quarter	-11 754	-39 789	331 630	79 949	251 681	32 658	73 376	87 270	21 013	37 364	-5 024	-149 773	-155 676
3rd quarter	-9 235	-55 154	274 147	76 120	198 027	34 113	-3 198	86 577	29 957	50 578	50 733	-155 365	-154 466
4th quarter	-64 489	-96 260	467 941	94 050	373 891	53 195	7 697	159 784	53 637	99 578	17 892	-167 434	-178 401
2005													
1st quarter	-64 051	45 352	234 182	25 052	209 130	38 871	76 819	75 631	86 298	-68 489	71 644	-165 997	-174 057
2nd quarter	59 260	-182 984	304 880	81 292	223 588	-9 004	-13 197	107 694	-26 159	164 254	95 848	-170 729	-177 821
3rd quarter	-69 527	-86 881	425 404	54 736	370 668	38 016	26 597	141 900	51 727	112 428	-51 683	-180 345	-168 892
4th quarter	3 111	16 888	282 881	98 188	184 693	44 755	50 528	125 161	-42 294	6 543	-83 495	-194 497	-208 223
2006													
1st quarter	-24 771	-204 731	537 649	130 427	407 222	38 694	-25 878	167 614	63 888	162 904	17 994	-189 087	-195 952
2nd quarter	-48 334	-59 545	405 008	127 303	277 705	62 831	-26 364	139 710	59 875	41 653	16 641	-191 841	-199 906
3rd quarter	-57 000	-93 796	524 858	121 843	403 015	54 813	-23 907	197 908	69 984	104 217	-41 784	-197 471	-210 906
4th quarter	-34 492	-130 352	593 598	108 366	485 232	85 623	20 172	178 131	48 980	152 326	-39 927	-174 885	-181 355
2007													
1st quarter	-46 048	-230 143	692 713	163 270	529 443	14 026	36 717	183 507	90 061	205 132	-67 970	-179 543	-196 930
2nd quarter	-134 713	-209 985	718 112	88 822	629 290	61 862	-15 157	310 340	122 476	149 769	656	-178 819	-194 093
3rd quarter	80 012	-88 697	266 476	13 469	253 007	105 908	68 061	-30 486	55 599	53 925	71 627	-168 114	-172 952
4th quarter	100 043	-115 926	380 402	145 497	234 905	55 746	56 529	110 489	-111 846	123 987	-45 600	-173 783	-167 241
2008													
1st quarter	81 848	-221 316	460 105	173 533	286 572	81 525	62 349	-20 475	84 085	79 088	-9 729	-178 443	-176 909
2nd quarter	49 324	213 859	23 208	145 391	-122 183	105 793	65 922	17 068	-54 350	-256 616	62 269	-181 419	-182 237
3rd quarter	89 523	134 444	123 346	116 078	7 268	57 313	94 979	-91 398	71 053	-124 679	34 706	-180 882	-181 299
4th quarter	63 070	298 031	-7 611	-13 627	6 016	80 622	119 404	-28 763	-130 111	-35 136	56 625	-140 386	-132 822

[3]A minus sign indicates financial outflows or increases in U.S. official assets.
[4]A minus sign indicates financial outflows or decreases in foreign official assets in the United States.
[5]Sum of credits and debits with the sign reversed.

Table 19-13. Productivity and Related Data

(1992 = 100, seasonally adjusted.)

Year and quarter	Business sector								Nonfarm business sector							
	Output per hour of all persons	Output	Hours of all persons	Compensation per hour	Real compensation per hour	Unit labor costs	Unit nonlabor payments	Implicit price deflator	Output per hour of all persons	Output	Hours of all persons	Compensation per hour	Real compensation per hour	Unit labor costs	Unit nonlabor payments	Implicit price deflator
1947	32.2	20.4	63.4	7.0	41.1	21.8	18.6	20.6	37.0	20.1	54.2	7.5	43.7	20.2	17.8	19.3
1948	33.7	21.5	63.8	7.6	41.2	22.6	20.6	21.8	38.0	20.9	55.1	8.1	43.9	21.3	19.4	20.6
1949	34.5	21.3	61.8	7.7	42.3	22.4	20.4	21.6	39.3	20.8	53.0	8.3	45.8	21.2	20.0	20.8
1947																
1st quarter	32.1	20.2	63.1	6.8	40.9	21.2	17.9	20.0	36.5	19.7	54.0	7.2	43.6	19.9	16.7	18.7
2nd quarter	32.3	20.3	63.0	7.0	41.3	21.5	18.0	20.2	37.4	20.2	54.0	7.4	43.7	19.7	17.7	19.0
3rd quarter	32.1	20.4	63.5	7.0	40.7	21.9	18.8	20.7	36.3	19.7	54.2	7.5	43.7	20.7	18.2	19.8
4th quarter	32.4	20.7	63.9	7.3	41.1	22.4	19.4	21.3	37.8	20.7	54.7	7.7	43.6	20.4	18.6	19.7
1948																
1st quarter	33.2	21.1	63.6	7.4	40.9	22.3	20.2	21.5	37.9	20.9	55.0	7.9	43.7	20.8	18.8	20.1
2nd quarter	33.9	21.6	63.6	7.5	40.7	22.1	21.0	21.7	37.9	20.9	55.0	8.0	43.7	21.2	19.2	20.4
3rd quarter	33.8	21.7	64.2	7.7	41.2	22.8	20.9	22.1	38.0	21.0	55.4	8.2	43.9	21.6	19.5	20.8
4th quarter	34.0	21.7	63.8	7.9	42.6	23.1	20.3	22.1	38.2	21.0	54.9	8.3	44.9	21.7	20.0	21.1
1949																
1st quarter	33.9	21.3	62.9	7.7	42.1	22.8	20.5	21.9	38.6	20.8	54.0	8.3	45.5	21.6	19.8	21.0
2nd quarter	34.0	21.2	62.4	7.6	41.5	22.3	20.5	21.6	39.0	20.7	53.1	8.3	45.4	21.3	19.8	20.8
3rd quarter	35.0	21.5	61.3	7.7	42.5	22.0	20.6	21.5	39.9	21.0	52.5	8.4	46.0	20.9	20.3	20.7
4th quarter	35.1	21.2	60.6	7.8	43.1	22.3	20.1	21.5	39.7	20.7	52.3	8.4	46.1	21.1	19.9	20.6
1950																
1st quarter	36.7	22.3	60.7	8.1	44.8	22.0	20.3	21.4	41.0	21.6	52.7	8.6	47.4	20.9	20.4	20.7
2nd quarter	37.0	23.0	62.1	8.2	44.8	22.0	20.7	21.5	41.5	22.4	54.0	8.7	47.9	21.0	20.4	20.8
3rd quarter	37.7	24.0	63.7	8.3	44.8	22.0	22.0	22.0	42.5	23.6	55.7	8.9	48.0	20.9	21.1	21.0
4th quarter	37.9	24.3	64.1	8.5	44.8	22.4	22.7	22.5	42.5	23.9	56.2	9.1	48.4	21.5	21.4	21.4
1951																
1st quarter	37.8	24.5	64.7	8.8	44.6	23.2	23.6	23.3	42.6	24.3	57.2	9.4	47.6	22.0	22.2	22.1
2nd quarter	38.0	24.8	65.1	9.0	45.3	23.7	23.4	23.6	42.5	24.5	57.6	9.5	48.1	22.5	22.1	22.3
3rd quarter	39.2	25.2	64.3	9.2	46.2	23.4	23.8	23.5	43.5	24.8	57.0	9.7	48.8	22.3	22.8	22.5
4th quarter	39.0	25.2	64.5	9.2	45.9	23.7	24.0	23.8	43.6	24.9	57.1	9.8	48.8	22.6	22.7	22.6
1952																
1st quarter	39.1	25.4	64.8	9.3	46.2	23.9	23.5	23.7	43.7	25.1	57.4	10.0	49.3	22.8	22.4	22.7
2nd quarter	39.5	25.3	64.1	9.5	47.0	24.1	23.0	23.7	43.7	25.0	57.2	10.0	49.5	23.0	22.1	22.6
3rd quarter	39.6	25.5	64.3	9.7	47.3	24.4	23.2	24.0	43.5	25.1	57.6	10.1	49.6	23.3	22.2	22.9
4th quarter	40.2	26.5	65.9	9.9	48.3	24.6	23.0	24.0	44.3	26.2	59.2	10.4	50.8	23.5	22.4	23.1
1953																
1st quarter	40.8	27.0	66.2	10.1	49.4	24.7	22.8	24.0	44.6	26.7	59.8	10.5	51.6	23.6	22.4	23.1
2nd quarter	41.1	27.2	66.1	10.2	49.7	24.7	22.7	24.0	44.8	26.8	59.9	10.7	52.1	23.8	22.3	23.3
3rd quarter	41.1	27.0	65.6	10.3	50.2	25.1	22.4	24.1	45.0	26.7	59.3	10.8	52.4	23.9	22.3	23.3
4th quarter	41.0	26.5	64.5	10.3	50.1	25.1	22.4	24.1	44.8	26.1	58.3	10.9	52.8	24.2	21.8	23.4
1954																
1st quarter	41.0	26.3	64.1	10.4	50.3	25.3	22.3	24.2	44.9	25.8	57.6	11.0	53.1	24.4	21.8	23.4
2nd quarter	41.6	26.3	63.2	10.5	51.1	25.3	22.1	24.1	45.2	25.8	57.1	11.0	53.3	24.3	22.1	23.5
3rd quarter	42.2	26.6	63.0	10.6	51.4	25.0	22.7	24.2	46.0	26.2	56.9	11.1	53.8	24.1	22.4	23.5
4th quarter	42.8	27.1	63.4	10.7	52.3	25.0	22.8	24.2	46.5	26.8	57.6	11.2	54.5	24.0	22.8	23.6
1955																
1st quarter	43.5	28.1	64.6	10.7	52.0	24.5	23.9	24.3	47.4	27.8	58.5	11.3	54.8	23.7	23.6	23.7
2nd quarter	43.8	28.6	65.2	10.8	52.8	24.7	23.8	24.3	47.5	28.2	59.3	11.4	55.5	23.9	23.5	23.8
3rd quarter	43.7	29.0	66.2	10.8	52.8	24.7	24.2	24.5	47.7	28.6	59.9	11.5	56.1	24.1	23.8	24.0
4th quarter	43.4	29.1	67.0	10.9	53.2	25.2	24.1	24.8	47.5	28.8	60.7	11.6	56.6	24.5	23.8	24.2
1956																
1st quarter	43.3	28.9	66.8	11.2	54.6	25.9	23.5	25.0	46.9	28.6	61.0	11.8	57.5	25.2	23.2	24.5
2nd quarter	43.5	29.1	67.0	11.5	55.3	26.3	23.1	25.1	47.1	28.8	61.2	12.1	58.3	25.6	22.9	24.6
3rd quarter	43.5	29.0	66.7	11.6	55.3	26.6	23.5	25.5	47.1	28.7	60.9	12.2	58.5	26.0	23.1	24.9
4th quarter	44.4	29.5	66.5	11.8	56.1	26.7	23.7	25.6	47.5	29.1	61.2	12.4	59.0	26.2	23.2	25.1
1957																
1st quarter	44.6	29.7	66.5	12.1	56.8	27.0	24.1	25.9	48.1	29.5	61.3	12.6	59.4	26.3	23.9	25.4
2nd quarter	44.7	29.5	66.1	12.2	56.8	27.3	24.1	26.1	47.9	29.3	61.2	12.8	59.5	26.6	23.7	25.5
3rd quarter	45.2	29.8	66.1	12.3	56.8	27.2	24.5	26.2	48.6	29.6	60.9	12.9	59.7	26.6	24.1	25.6
4th quarter	45.6	29.5	64.5	12.5	57.6	27.4	24.1	26.2	48.8	29.1	59.6	13.1	60.2	26.8	23.8	25.7
1958																
1st quarter	45.2	28.4	62.8	12.6	57.5	28.0	24.0	26.5	48.0	28.0	58.3	13.1	59.8	27.4	23.2	25.8
2nd quarter	45.9	28.5	62.3	12.7	57.2	27.6	24.5	26.5	48.9	28.1	57.4	13.3	59.8	27.1	23.8	25.9
3rd quarter	46.7	29.3	62.7	12.9	58.3	27.6	25.0	26.6	49.9	29.0	58.1	13.4	60.7	26.9	24.4	26.0
4th quarter	47.2	30.1	63.7	13.0	58.8	27.6	25.5	26.8	50.7	29.9	59.0	13.6	61.3	26.8	25.0	26.1
1959																
1st quarter	47.6	30.8	64.7	13.2	59.4	27.7	25.3	26.8	50.8	30.5	60.1	13.7	61.7	27.0	25.0	26.2
2nd quarter	47.9	31.7	66.2	13.2	59.4	27.6	25.4	26.8	51.5	31.5	61.3	13.8	62.2	26.9	25.1	26.2
3rd quarter	48.2	31.6	65.6	13.4	59.9	27.8	25.2	26.8	51.5	31.4	61.1	13.9	62.3	27.1	25.0	26.3
4th quarter	48.3	31.7	65.5	13.6	60.3	28.1	24.9	26.9	51.4	31.4	61.1	14.1	62.5	27.4	24.8	26.4
1960																
1st quarter	49.7	32.4	65.3	13.9	61.9	28.0	25.3	27.0	52.5	32.3	61.5	14.4	63.8	27.3	25.0	26.5
2nd quarter	48.7	32.1	66.0	13.9	61.2	28.5	24.8	27.1	51.8	31.9	61.6	14.4	63.8	27.9	24.2	26.5
3rd quarter	48.8	32.1	65.9	13.8	61.1	28.4	25.0	27.1	51.9	31.8	61.2	14.5	64.1	28.0	24.4	26.6
4th quarter	48.4	31.5	65.1	14.0	61.3	28.9	24.4	27.2	51.2	31.1	60.7	14.6	64.0	28.5	23.8	26.7

Table 19-13. Productivity and Related Data—*Continued*

(1992 = 100, seasonally adjusted.)

Year and quarter	Nonfinancial corporations										Manufacturing					
	Output per hour of all employees	Output	Employee hours	Compensation per hour	Real compensation per hour	Unit costs			Unit profits	Implicit price deflator	Output per hour of all persons	Output	Hours of all persons	Compensation per hour	Real compensation per hour	Unit labor costs
						Total	Labor costs	Nonlabor costs								
1947	...	...	...	...	...	...	...	...	...	...	...	...	...	...	...	...
1948	...	...	...	...	...	...	...	...	...	...	...	...	...	...	...	...
1949	...	...	...	...	...	...	...	...	...	...	...	...	...	...	...	...
1947																
1st quarter	...	...	...	...	...	...	...	...	...	...	...	...	...	...	...	...
2nd quarter	...	...	...	...	...	...	...	...	...	...	...	...	...	...	...	...
3rd quarter	...	...	...	...	...	...	...	...	...	...	...	...	...	...	...	...
4th quarter	...	...	...	...	...	...	...	...	...	...	...	...	...	...	...	...
1948																
1st quarter	...	...	...	...	...	...	...	...	...	...	...	...	...	...	...	...
2nd quarter	...	...	...	...	...	...	...	...	...	...	...	...	...	...	...	...
3rd quarter	...	...	...	...	...	...	...	...	...	...	...	...	...	...	...	...
4th quarter	...	...	...	...	...	...	...	...	...	...	...	...	...	...	...	...
1949																
1st quarter	...	...	...	...	...	...	...	...	...	...	...	...	...	...	...	...
2nd quarter	...	...	...	...	...	...	...	...	...	...	...	...	...	...	...	...
3rd quarter	...	...	...	...	...	...	...	...	...	...	...	...	...	...	...	...
4th quarter	...	...	...	...	...	...	...	...	...	...	...	...	...	...	...	...
1950																
1st quarter	...	...	...	...	...	...	...	...	...	...	...	...	...	...	...	...
2nd quarter	...	...	...	...	...	...	...	...	...	...	...	...	...	...	...	...
3rd quarter	...	...	...	...	...	...	...	...	...	...	...	...	...	...	...	...
4th quarter	...	...	...	...	...	...	...	...	...	...	...	...	...	...	...	...
1951																
1st quarter	...	...	...	...	...	...	...	...	...	...	...	...	...	...	...	...
2nd quarter	...	...	...	...	...	...	...	...	...	...	...	...	...	...	...	...
3rd quarter	...	...	...	...	...	...	...	...	...	...	...	...	...	...	...	...
4th quarter	...	...	...	...	...	...	...	...	...	...	...	...	...	...	...	...
1952																
1st quarter	...	...	...	...	...	...	...	...	...	...	...	...	...	...	...	...
2nd quarter	...	...	...	...	...	...	...	...	...	...	...	...	...	...	...	...
3rd quarter	...	...	...	...	...	...	...	...	...	...	...	...	...	...	...	...
4th quarter	...	...	...	...	...	...	...	...	...	...	...	...	...	...	...	...
1953																
1st quarter	...	...	...	...	...	...	...	...	...	...	...	...	...	...	...	...
2nd quarter	...	...	...	...	...	...	...	...	...	...	...	...	...	...	...	...
3rd quarter	...	...	...	...	...	...	...	...	...	...	...	...	...	...	...	...
4th quarter	...	...	...	...	...	...	...	...	...	...	...	...	...	...	...	...
1954																
1st quarter	...	...	...	...	...	...	...	...	...	...	...	...	...	...	...	...
2nd quarter	...	...	...	...	...	...	...	...	...	...	...	...	...	...	...	...
3rd quarter	...	...	...	...	...	...	...	...	...	...	...	...	...	...	...	...
4th quarter	...	...	...	...	...	...	...	...	...	...	...	...	...	...	...	...
1955																
1st quarter	...	...	...	...	...	...	...	...	...	...	...	...	...	...	...	...
2nd quarter	...	...	...	...	...	...	...	...	...	...	...	...	...	...	...	...
3rd quarter	...	...	...	...	...	...	...	...	...	...	...	...	...	...	...	...
4th quarter	...	...	...	...	...	...	...	...	...	...	...	...	...	...	...	...
1956																
1st quarter	...	...	...	...	...	...	...	...	...	...	...	...	...	...	...	...
2nd quarter	...	...	...	...	...	...	...	...	...	...	...	...	...	...	...	...
3rd quarter	...	...	...	...	...	...	...	...	...	...	...	...	...	...	...	...
4th quarter	...	...	...	...	...	...	...	...	...	...	...	...	...	...	...	...
1957																
1st quarter	...	...	...	...	...	...	...	...	...	...	...	...	...	...	...	...
2nd quarter	...	...	...	...	...	...	...	...	...	...	...	...	...	...	...	...
3rd quarter	...	...	...	...	...	...	...	...	...	...	...	...	...	...	...	...
4th quarter	...	...	...	...	...	...	...	...	...	...	...	...	...	...	...	...
1958																
1st quarter	51.5	24.8	48.2	14.8	67.2	27.4	28.7	23.7	42.8	28.7	...	...	...	...	...	...
2nd quarter	52.2	24.7	47.3	14.9	67.2	27.3	28.5	24.1	43.7	28.8	...	...	...	...	...	...
3rd quarter	53.2	25.5	47.9	15.1	68.2	27.1	28.4	23.6	48.1	29.0	...	...	...	...	...	...
4th quarter	54.3	26.5	48.8	15.3	68.8	26.7	28.1	22.8	53.8	29.1	...	...	...	...	...	...
1959																
1st quarter	54.8	27.4	50.1	15.3	69.1	26.4	28.0	22.1	56.9	29.1	...	...	...	...	...	...
2nd quarter	55.9	28.7	51.4	15.5	69.8	26.1	27.8	21.5	60.1	29.1	...	...	...	...	...	...
3rd quarter	55.1	28.1	51.1	15.6	69.9	26.8	28.4	22.5	53.6	29.2	...	...	...	...	...	...
4th quarter	55.5	28.4	51.2	15.8	70.3	27.0	28.4	22.9	52.6	29.3	...	...	...	...	...	...
1960																
1st quarter	56.5	29.4	52.1	16.1	71.4	26.8	28.4	22.5	54.8	29.3	...	...	...	...	...	...
2nd quarter	55.9	29.1	52.1	16.2	71.4	27.3	28.9	23.1	50.1	29.4	...	...	...	...	...	...
3rd quarter	56.1	29.1	51.8	16.2	71.5	27.4	28.9	23.6	49.2	29.4	...	...	...	...	...	...
4th quarter	56.3	28.8	51.1	16.3	71.6	27.7	29.0	24.1	46.6	29.4	...	...	...	...	...	...

. . . = Not available.

Table 19-13. Productivity and Related Data—*Continued*

(1992 = 100, seasonally adjusted.)

Year and quarter	Business sector								Nonfarm business sector							
	Output per hour of all persons	Output	Hours of all persons	Compensation per hour	Real compensation per hour	Unit labor costs	Unit nonlabor payments	Implicit price deflator	Output per hour of all persons	Output	Hours of all persons	Compensation per hour	Real compensation per hour	Unit labor costs	Unit nonlabor payments	Implicit price deflator
1961																
1st quarter	48.9	31.7	64.8	14.1	61.7	28.8	24.5	27.2	51.9	31.3	60.3	14.7	64.4	28.4	24.0	26.8
2nd quarter	50.6	32.4	64.0	14.4	63.1	28.5	25.2	27.3	53.3	32.1	60.2	14.9	65.3	28.0	24.8	26.8
3rd quarter	51.1	33.0	64.5	14.5	63.3	28.4	25.5	27.3	54.1	32.7	60.5	15.0	65.6	27.8	25.2	26.8
4th quarter	51.7	33.6	65.1	14.7	64.0	28.4	25.7	27.4	54.6	33.5	61.3	15.1	66.0	27.7	25.3	26.8
1962																
1st quarter	52.2	34.3	65.8	14.8	64.4	28.4	26.1	27.5	55.5	34.2	61.5	15.4	66.8	27.7	25.7	27.0
2nd quarter	52.5	34.7	66.1	15.0	64.9	28.6	25.8	27.6	55.4	34.5	62.3	15.5	66.9	27.9	25.6	27.1
3rd quarter	53.2	35.0	65.8	15.1	65.2	28.4	26.3	27.6	56.1	34.9	62.1	15.6	67.2	27.8	26.0	27.1
4th quarter	53.7	35.1	65.3	15.3	65.9	28.5	26.1	27.6	56.5	34.9	61.7	15.7	67.7	27.9	25.9	27.1
1963																
1st quarter	54.1	35.6	65.8	15.4	66.0	28.5	26.2	27.7	56.8	35.3	62.1	15.9	68.1	28.0	25.9	27.2
2nd quarter	54.4	36.1	66.2	15.5	66.2	28.4	26.4	27.7	57.4	35.9	62.5	16.0	68.4	27.8	26.1	27.2
3rd quarter	55.6	36.8	66.2	15.7	66.8	28.3	26.9	27.7	58.6	36.7	62.7	16.1	68.6	27.6	26.7	27.2
4th quarter	55.7	37.1	66.6	15.9	67.3	28.5	27.0	27.9	58.6	37.0	63.2	16.3	69.2	27.9	26.6	27.4
1964																
1st quarter	56.5	38.1	67.4	16.0	67.4	28.3	27.4	27.9	59.2	38.1	64.3	16.3	68.9	27.6	27.2	27.4
2nd quarter	56.6	38.5	68.0	16.1	67.8	28.4	27.3	28.0	59.6	38.5	64.6	16.5	69.5	27.7	27.3	27.5
3rd quarter	57.2	39.1	68.4	16.3	68.5	28.5	27.4	28.1	60.0	39.1	65.0	16.7	70.3	27.8	27.4	27.7
4th quarter	56.9	39.1	68.8	16.4	68.8	28.9	27.1	28.2	59.5	39.0	65.7	16.8	70.5	28.3	26.8	27.8
1965																
1st quarter	57.8	40.3	69.6	16.6	69.2	28.7	27.8	28.4	60.3	40.2	66.7	16.9	70.6	28.0	27.6	27.9
2nd quarter	57.9	40.8	70.5	16.7	69.1	28.8	27.9	28.5	60.6	40.8	67.4	17.0	70.6	28.1	27.7	27.9
3rd quarter	59.3	41.7	70.4	16.9	69.8	28.5	28.6	28.5	61.7	41.7	67.5	17.2	71.1	27.9	28.3	28.0
4th quarter	60.2	42.9	71.2	17.1	70.3	28.3	29.1	28.6	62.9	42.9	68.2	17.4	71.8	27.7	28.7	28.1
1966																
1st quarter	61.3	44.0	71.9	17.5	71.3	28.5	29.3	28.8	63.7	44.1	69.1	17.8	72.4	27.9	28.8	28.2
2nd quarter	61.0	44.1	72.4	17.8	71.9	29.2	28.8	29.0	63.3	44.2	69.8	18.0	72.8	28.5	28.5	28.5
3rd quarter	61.0	44.3	72.5	18.1	72.4	29.6	28.8	29.3	63.4	44.5	70.1	18.3	73.2	28.8	28.5	28.7
4th quarter	61.5	44.5	72.3	18.4	73.0	29.9	29.2	29.6	63.8	44.7	70.0	18.5	73.6	29.0	29.1	29.1
1967																
1st quarter	62.1	44.9	72.3	18.5	73.4	29.8	29.5	29.7	64.4	45.0	69.9	18.8	74.4	29.2	29.2	29.2
2nd quarter	62.6	44.8	71.6	18.9	74.3	30.1	29.3	29.8	64.6	44.8	69.4	19.1	75.2	29.6	29.1	29.4
3rd quarter	62.6	45.1	72.0	19.1	74.4	30.5	29.5	30.1	64.8	45.1	69.7	19.4	75.5	29.9	29.2	29.6
4th quarter	62.8	45.4	72.4	19.3	74.5	30.8	29.7	30.4	65.0	45.5	70.0	19.6	75.7	30.2	29.4	29.9
1968																
1st quarter	64.2	46.5	72.4	19.9	76.1	31.0	30.2	30.7	66.5	46.6	70.1	20.2	77.1	30.4	30.0	30.2
2nd quarter	64.9	47.3	73.0	20.3	76.7	31.3	30.7	31.0	67.1	47.5	70.8	20.5	77.6	30.6	30.5	30.6
3rd quarter	64.9	47.6	73.4	20.7	77.1	31.8	30.4	31.3	67.0	47.8	71.3	20.9	77.9	31.1	30.2	30.8
4th quarter	64.8	47.8	73.8	21.1	77.7	32.5	30.4	31.7	66.9	48.0	71.7	21.3	78.5	31.8	30.2	31.2
1969																
1st quarter	65.0	48.7	74.9	21.2	77.1	32.6	31.2	32.1	67.5	48.9	72.4	21.6	78.5	32.0	30.9	31.6
2nd quarter	64.9	48.7	75.0	21.7	77.8	33.4	30.9	32.5	66.9	48.9	73.1	21.9	78.6	32.7	30.5	31.9
3rd quarter	65.1	49.0	75.3	22.2	78.4	34.1	30.7	32.8	66.9	49.1	73.4	22.3	78.9	33.3	30.5	32.3
4th quarter	64.9	48.6	74.9	22.6	78.9	34.9	30.4	33.2	66.6	48.8	73.2	22.7	79.2	34.1	30.0	32.6
1970																
1st quarter	65.2	48.6	74.5	23.1	79.1	35.4	30.4	33.5	66.8	48.7	72.9	23.2	79.4	34.7	30.0	33.0
2nd quarter	66.0	48.7	73.8	23.4	79.1	35.4	31.5	34.0	67.9	48.8	71.9	23.6	79.6	34.7	31.3	33.4
3rd quarter	67.2	49.2	73.3	23.8	79.7	35.5	32.0	34.2	68.9	49.3	71.6	24.0	80.2	34.7	31.6	33.6
4th quarter	66.8	48.5	72.6	24.1	79.6	36.1	32.0	34.6	68.3	48.5	71.0	24.2	79.9	35.4	31.8	34.1
1971																
1st quarter	68.7	50.1	72.9	24.6	80.4	35.8	33.6	35.0	70.4	50.2	71.4	24.7	80.8	35.1	33.3	34.4
2nd quarter	68.8	50.4	73.4	24.9	80.6	36.2	34.1	35.4	70.6	50.5	71.6	25.1	81.3	35.5	33.7	34.9
3rd quarter	69.6	50.9	73.2	25.3	81.3	36.4	34.6	35.7	71.2	51.0	71.6	25.5	81.7	35.7	34.3	35.2
4th quarter	69.0	51.0	73.9	25.5	81.3	37.0	34.2	35.9	70.6	51.1	72.4	25.7	81.7	36.3	33.7	35.4
1972																
1st quarter	69.7	52.2	74.9	26.1	82.5	37.5	34.5	36.4	71.6	52.5	73.2	26.3	83.0	36.7	34.2	35.8
2nd quarter	71.4	53.7	75.3	26.4	83.0	37.1	35.7	36.5	73.1	53.9	73.8	26.6	83.6	36.4	35.1	35.9
3rd quarter	71.6	54.3	75.8	26.7	83.3	37.4	36.1	36.9	73.5	54.5	74.2	27.0	84.1	36.7	35.2	36.2
4th quarter	72.3	55.3	76.5	27.3	84.3	37.8	36.4	37.3	74.1	55.5	75.0	27.6	84.9	37.2	35.0	36.4
1973																
1st quarter	73.7	57.1	77.5	28.1	85.4	38.2	36.8	37.7	75.8	57.6	76.1	28.3	85.8	37.3	35.4	36.6
2nd quarter	73.9	57.9	78.4	28.6	85.0	38.7	37.5	38.2	75.8	58.3	76.9	28.7	85.4	37.9	35.5	37.0
3rd quarter	72.9	57.5	78.8	29.2	85.0	40.0	37.4	39.0	75.1	58.2	77.4	29.3	85.4	39.0	34.9	37.5
4th quarter	73.2	58.1	79.3	29.8	84.6	40.6	38.4	39.8	74.7	58.1	77.8	29.9	85.1	40.1	35.4	38.4
1974																
1st quarter	72.2	57.2	79.3	30.3	83.7	42.0	38.4	40.6	74.6	57.7	77.5	30.6	84.6	41.1	35.9	39.2
2nd quarter	72.5	57.4	79.1	31.3	84.1	43.1	39.2	41.7	74.4	57.8	77.7	31.4	84.6	42.3	37.7	40.6
3rd quarter	71.9	56.6	78.7	32.3	84.4	44.9	39.9	43.0	73.6	57.0	77.4	32.3	84.6	43.9	38.3	41.9
4th quarter	72.5	56.2	77.5	33.0	83.7	45.5	42.4	44.3	74.3	56.6	76.1	33.2	84.2	44.6	40.5	43.1
1975																
1st quarter	73.5	55.2	75.1	34.0	84.5	46.3	44.0	45.4	74.9	55.2	73.7	34.1	84.7	45.5	42.8	44.5
2nd quarter	74.7	55.6	74.5	34.7	85.1	46.4	45.5	46.1	76.1	55.6	73.0	34.8	85.4	45.7	44.4	45.2
3rd quarter	75.4	56.7	75.2	35.2	84.6	46.6	47.5	47.0	76.9	56.7	73.7	35.4	85.2	46.0	45.9	46.0
4th quarter	75.6	57.6	76.3	35.9	84.9	47.6	48.0	47.7	76.9	57.7	75.0	36.1	85.2	46.9	46.3	46.7

Table 19-13. Productivity and Related Data—*Continued*

(1992 = 100, seasonally adjusted.)

Year and quarter	Nonfinancial corporations										Manufacturing					
	Output per hour of all employees	Output	Employee hours	Compensation per hour	Real compensation per hour	Unit costs			Unit profits	Implicit price deflator	Output per hour of all persons	Output	Hours of all persons	Compensation per hour	Real compensation per hour	Unit labor costs
						Total	Labor costs	Nonlabor costs								
1961																
1st quarter	56.4	28.5	50.6	16.4	71.9	27.9	29.1	24.5	45.5	29.5	...	...	...	...	...	...
2nd quarter	57.8	29.4	50.8	16.6	72.9	27.5	28.8	23.9	49.8	29.5	...	...	...	...	...	...
3rd quarter	58.3	30.0	51.4	16.8	73.2	27.4	28.8	23.6	51.3	29.5	...	...	...	...	...	...
4th quarter	59.2	30.9	52.2	17.0	73.9	27.2	28.7	23.2	54.1	29.6	...	...	...	...	...	...
1962																
1st quarter	59.9	31.5	52.6	17.2	74.4	27.2	28.6	23.1	55.6	29.7	...	...	...	...	...	...
2nd quarter	60.0	32.0	53.4	17.3	74.7	27.3	28.8	23.3	53.4	29.7	...	...	...	...	...	...
3rd quarter	60.5	32.4	53.6	17.4	75.1	27.4	28.8	23.5	53.9	29.7	...	...	...	...	...	...
4th quarter	61.3	32.9	53.6	17.6	75.6	27.3	28.7	23.6	55.1	29.8	...	...	...	...	...	...
1963																
1st quarter	61.6	33.2	53.9	17.7	75.7	27.3	28.7	23.6	54.9	29.8	...	...	...	...	...	...
2nd quarter	62.3	34.0	54.5	17.8	76.0	27.1	28.5	23.4	57.5	29.8	...	...	...	...	...	...
3rd quarter	62.9	34.4	54.7	18.0	76.4	27.1	28.6	23.3	58.0	29.9	...	...	...	...	...	...
4th quarter	63.3	34.8	55.0	18.2	77.0	27.2	28.7	23.3	58.7	30.1	...	...	...	...	...	...
1964																
1st quarter	63.1	35.7	56.5	18.0	75.9	27.0	28.5	23.1	60.8	30.1	...	...	...	...	...	...
2nd quarter	63.4	36.2	57.1	18.2	76.6	27.2	28.6	23.2	59.9	30.1	...	...	...	...	...	...
3rd quarter	64.0	37.0	57.7	18.4	77.2	27.2	28.7	23.2	59.6	30.1	...	...	...	...	...	...
4th quarter	63.7	37.2	58.4	18.4	77.2	27.5	29.0	23.6	58.5	30.3	...	...	...	...	...	...
1965																
1st quarter	64.6	38.5	59.5	18.5	77.3	27.2	28.7	23.2	63.5	30.4	...	...	...	...	...	...
2nd quarter	64.7	39.0	60.4	18.6	77.2	27.3	28.8	23.2	64.1	30.6	...	...	...	...	...	...
3rd quarter	65.2	39.8	61.0	18.8	77.8	27.3	28.9	23.2	63.9	30.6	...	...	...	...	...	...
4th quarter	65.8	40.8	62.0	19.1	78.5	27.4	29.0	23.0	64.9	30.7	...	...	...	...	...	...
1966																
1st quarter	66.2	41.7	63.0	19.3	78.7	27.5	29.2	23.0	65.9	30.9	...	...	...	...	...	...
2nd quarter	66.1	42.2	63.8	19.6	79.3	28.0	29.7	23.2	64.2	31.2	...	...	...	...	...	...
3rd quarter	66.1	42.5	64.3	20.0	80.1	28.4	30.2	23.5	62.0	31.4	...	...	...	...	...	...
4th quarter	66.4	42.9	64.6	20.3	80.6	28.7	30.6	23.7	62.4	31.7	...	...	...	...	...	...
1967																
1st quarter	66.4	42.8	64.5	20.5	81.2	29.1	30.9	24.1	60.3	31.8	...	...	...	...	...	...
2nd quarter	67.1	43.0	64.1	20.8	81.9	29.2	31.0	24.5	59.3	31.9	...	...	...	...	...	...
3rd quarter	67.3	43.4	64.6	21.1	82.1	29.6	31.3	24.9	59.3	32.2	...	...	...	...	...	...
4th quarter	67.8	44.1	65.1	21.3	82.3	29.8	31.5	25.3	60.8	32.6	...	...	...	...	...	...
1968																
1st quarter	68.7	44.9	65.4	21.9	83.7	30.2	31.9	25.7	59.7	32.9	...	...	...	...	...	...
2nd quarter	69.4	45.9	66.1	22.3	84.3	30.5	32.1	26.0	60.8	33.2	...	...	...	...	...	...
3rd quarter	69.8	46.6	66.7	22.7	84.6	30.8	32.5	26.4	59.7	33.4	...	...	...	...	...	...
4th quarter	70.0	47.1	67.3	23.1	85.3	31.4	33.0	26.9	59.8	33.9	...	...	...	...	...	...
1969																
1st quarter	69.7	47.5	68.2	23.3	85.0	31.9	33.5	27.6	58.3	34.3	...	...	...	...	...	...
2nd quarter	69.5	47.9	68.9	23.8	85.3	32.6	34.2	28.2	55.7	34.6	...	...	...	...	...	...
3rd quarter	69.5	48.2	69.4	24.3	85.8	33.3	34.9	28.8	53.1	35.0	...	...	...	...	...	...
4th quarter	69.2	48.0	69.4	24.7	86.2	34.1	35.8	29.7	49.2	35.5	...	...	...	...	...	...
1970																
1st quarter	68.8	47.4	69.0	25.1	86.1	35.1	36.5	31.0	44.0	35.9	...	...	...	...	...	...
2nd quarter	69.6	47.4	68.2	25.5	86.3	35.4	36.7	31.8	46.4	36.4	...	...	...	...	...	...
3rd quarter	70.5	47.8	67.8	26.0	86.9	35.6	36.8	32.3	45.0	36.5	...	...	...	...	...	...
4th quarter	70.4	47.0	66.8	26.3	86.8	36.4	37.4	33.6	42.0	36.9	...	...	...	...	...	...
1971																
1st quarter	72.2	48.5	67.2	26.8	87.7	36.1	37.1	33.3	49.7	37.3	...	...	...	...	...	...
2nd quarter	72.4	49.0	67.6	27.2	88.1	36.5	37.5	33.6	50.2	37.7	...	...	...	...	...	...
3rd quarter	72.9	49.5	67.9	27.5	88.3	36.7	37.7	33.9	50.6	37.9	...	...	...	...	...	...
4th quarter	73.2	50.4	68.7	27.8	88.5	36.8	37.9	33.8	51.7	38.2	...	...	...	...	...	...
1972																
1st quarter	73.5	51.5	70.1	28.2	89.2	37.1	38.4	33.6	53.1	38.6	...	...	...	...	...	...
2nd quarter	74.0	52.6	71.2	28.6	89.7	37.4	38.6	34.1	52.0	38.7	...	...	...	...	...	...
3rd quarter	74.2	53.3	71.9	28.9	89.9	37.6	38.9	33.9	54.2	39.1	...	...	...	...	...	...
4th quarter	75.0	54.8	73.0	29.5	91.0	37.9	39.3	34.0	56.9	39.6	...	...	...	...	...	...
1973																
1st quarter	75.5	56.1	74.2	30.1	91.3	38.3	39.8	34.2	57.8	40.1	...	...	...	...	...	...
2nd quarter	75.0	56.2	75.0	30.6	91.1	39.4	40.9	35.3	54.1	40.7	...	...	...	...	...	...
3rd quarter	74.5	56.2	75.4	31.3	91.3	40.5	42.0	36.3	53.2	41.6	...	...	...	...	...	...
4th quarter	74.4	56.6	76.1	32.0	90.9	41.4	43.0	37.0	54.5	42.6	...	...	...	...	...	...
1974																
1st quarter	73.5	55.9	76.1	32.6	89.9	42.7	44.3	38.5	49.7	43.3	...	...	...	...	...	...
2nd quarter	73.7	56.0	76.0	33.5	90.0	43.9	45.4	39.8	49.2	44.4	...	...	...	...	...	...
3rd quarter	73.1	55.3	75.7	34.5	90.1	45.7	47.2	41.7	47.4	45.8	...	...	...	...	...	...
4th quarter	72.8	54.1	74.3	35.3	89.7	47.4	48.5	44.4	47.3	47.4	...	...	...	...	...	...
1975																
1st quarter	74.1	53.0	71.5	36.2	90.0	48.3	48.9	46.7	50.6	48.5	...	...	...	...	...	...
2nd quarter	76.0	53.7	70.7	36.9	90.6	48.2	48.6	47.0	59.3	49.2	...	...	...	...	...	...
3rd quarter	77.2	55.3	71.7	37.6	90.5	48.0	48.7	46.3	70.4	50.0	...	...	...	...	...	...
4th quarter	77.3	56.2	72.7	38.4	90.7	48.7	49.6	46.4	71.4	50.8	...	...	...	...	...	...

. . . = Not available.

Table 19-13. Productivity and Related Data—*Continued*

(1992 = 100, seasonally adjusted.)

Year and quarter	Business sector								Nonfarm business sector							
	Output per hour of all persons	Output	Hours of all persons	Compensation per hour	Real compensation per hour	Unit labor costs	Unit nonlabor payments	Implicit price deflator	Output per hour of all persons	Output	Hours of all persons	Compensation per hour	Real compensation per hour	Unit labor costs	Unit nonlabor payments	Implicit price deflator
1976																
1st quarter	76.6	59.3	77.4	36.8	86.0	48.0	48.3	48.2	78.1	59.5	76.2	36.9	86.1	47.2	47.2	47.2
2nd quarter	77.1	59.8	77.6	37.5	87.0	48.7	48.5	48.6	78.8	60.1	76.2	37.6	87.2	47.8	47.6	47.7
3rd quarter	77.2	60.1	77.9	38.3	87.3	49.6	48.7	49.3	78.9	60.4	76.5	38.5	87.7	48.7	47.8	48.4
4th quarter	77.7	60.7	78.1	39.2	88.1	50.5	49.5	50.1	79.1	60.9	77.0	39.3	88.2	49.6	48.6	49.3
1977																
1st quarter	78.0	61.6	78.9	39.9	88.0	51.1	50.5	50.9	79.6	61.9	77.8	40.0	88.2	50.2	49.6	50.0
2nd quarter	78.2	63.1	80.7	40.5	87.9	51.8	51.2	51.6	79.9	63.4	79.3	40.8	88.4	51.0	50.5	50.8
3rd quarter	79.2	64.4	81.3	41.4	88.5	52.2	52.0	52.1	80.8	64.7	80.1	41.6	88.9	51.5	51.5	51.5
4th quarter	78.3	64.3	82.1	42.1	88.7	53.8	52.4	53.2	79.7	64.4	80.9	42.3	89.2	53.1	51.2	52.4
1978																
1st quarter	78.0	64.4	82.5	43.3	89.8	55.5	51.6	54.0	79.7	64.8	81.3	43.5	90.4	54.6	50.4	53.1
2nd quarter	79.6	67.5	84.9	44.0	89.4	55.3	54.7	55.1	81.3	68.0	83.6	44.3	90.0	54.5	53.3	54.0
3rd quarter	79.7	68.2	85.6	44.9	89.6	56.3	55.6	56.0	81.3	68.6	84.3	45.1	90.1	55.5	54.3	55.1
4th quarter	80.0	69.2	86.5	46.0	90.0	57.5	56.9	57.3	81.8	69.8	85.4	46.2	90.4	56.5	55.6	56.2
1979																
1st quarter	79.5	69.2	87.1	47.3	90.4	59.5	56.2	58.3	81.0	69.6	86.0	47.5	90.8	58.6	54.4	57.1
2nd quarter	79.3	69.3	87.4	48.3	90.0	60.9	58.0	59.8	80.8	69.7	86.3	48.5	90.4	60.0	56.4	58.7
3rd quarter	79.3	69.9	88.1	49.4	89.6	62.3	59.1	61.1	80.7	70.2	87.0	49.6	90.0	61.5	57.4	60.0
4th quarter	79.1	69.9	88.4	50.5	89.5	63.9	59.4	62.2	80.6	70.3	87.2	50.8	90.0	63.1	57.8	61.1
1980																
1st quarter	79.6	70.0	88.0	52.1	89.5	65.5	60.3	63.6	80.9	70.4	87.0	52.3	89.8	64.7	59.3	62.7
2nd quarter	78.7	68.0	86.5	53.5	89.6	68.0	59.9	65.0	80.0	68.4	85.5	53.7	89.9	67.1	60.0	64.5
3rd quarter	78.8	67.9	86.2	54.8	89.7	69.6	61.1	66.4	80.3	68.3	85.1	55.1	90.1	68.6	60.2	65.5
4th quarter	79.6	69.4	87.3	56.2	89.8	70.6	63.8	68.1	81.2	69.9	86.2	56.6	90.4	69.7	62.1	66.9
1981																
1st quarter	81.1	71.1	87.7	57.7	89.6	71.1	67.9	69.9	82.4	71.4	86.6	58.1	90.2	70.5	66.5	69.0
2nd quarter	80.4	70.4	87.6	58.7	89.7	73.1	68.0	71.2	81.3	70.5	86.7	59.1	90.2	72.7	66.5	70.4
3rd quarter	81.4	71.3	87.6	60.0	89.8	73.7	70.5	72.5	82.0	71.1	86.6	60.4	90.4	73.6	68.9	71.9
4th quarter	80.2	70.1	87.3	60.9	89.6	75.9	70.0	73.7	81.0	69.9	86.3	61.3	90.1	75.7	69.0	73.2
1982																
1st quarter	79.8	68.5	85.9	62.5	90.7	78.3	68.3	74.6	80.5	68.3	84.9	62.9	91.3	78.1	67.4	74.2
2nd quarter	80.0	68.9	86.1	63.1	90.7	78.9	69.7	75.5	80.6	68.7	85.2	63.4	91.1	78.6	69.0	75.1
3rd quarter	80.0	68.5	85.6	64.0	90.5	80.0	70.5	76.5	80.8	68.4	84.6	64.4	90.9	79.7	69.6	76.0
4th quarter	80.8	68.5	84.8	64.9	90.6	80.3	71.8	77.1	81.5	68.3	83.9	65.2	91.1	80.0	71.3	76.8
1983																
1st quarter	81.6	69.5	85.2	65.4	90.9	80.2	73.4	77.7	82.5	69.6	84.4	65.8	91.4	79.8	72.6	77.2
2nd quarter	83.0	71.5	86.1	66.0	90.6	79.5	75.6	78.1	84.4	72.0	85.3	66.4	91.2	78.7	75.3	77.4
3rd quarter	83.3	73.2	87.8	66.3	90.2	79.6	77.7	78.9	85.2	74.1	87.0	66.8	90.8	78.3	77.8	78.1
4th quarter	84.0	75.0	89.2	67.2	90.6	80.0	78.3	79.4	85.6	75.9	88.6	67.5	90.9	78.8	78.3	78.6
1984																
1st quarter	84.4	76.8	91.0	68.0	90.4	80.6	79.0	80.0	85.5	77.2	90.3	68.3	90.8	79.9	77.9	79.2
2nd quarter	85.1	78.4	92.1	68.7	90.4	80.7	80.4	80.6	86.1	78.7	91.5	69.0	90.9	80.2	79.3	79.8
3rd quarter	85.5	79.2	92.6	69.6	91.0	81.4	80.5	81.1	86.4	79.4	91.9	70.0	91.4	81.0	79.6	80.5
4th quarter	85.8	79.8	93.1	70.2	90.9	81.9	80.8	81.5	86.5	80.0	92.5	70.5	91.3	81.5	79.8	80.9
1985																
1st quarter	86.1	80.7	93.8	71.1	91.3	82.6	81.6	82.3	86.6	80.8	93.3	71.4	91.7	82.4	80.7	81.8
2nd quarter	86.4	81.5	94.3	71.7	91.3	83.0	81.8	82.6	86.8	81.5	93.9	71.9	91.6	82.8	81.3	82.3
3rd quarter	87.9	83.0	94.4	72.8	92.1	82.9	82.6	82.8	88.0	82.8	94.1	72.9	92.3	82.9	82.5	82.8
4th quarter	88.2	83.6	94.8	74.2	92.9	84.1	81.8	83.2	88.4	83.6	94.6	74.2	93.0	84.0	81.4	83.0
1986																
1st quarter	89.1	84.5	94.8	75.0	93.5	84.2	82.5	83.6	89.5	84.5	94.5	75.2	93.8	84.0	82.4	83.4
2nd quarter	89.6	84.8	94.6	75.6	94.8	84.4	82.9	83.8	90.2	85.0	94.2	75.9	95.1	84.1	82.8	83.6
3rd quarter	90.1	85.7	95.1	76.3	95.1	84.7	83.1	84.1	90.6	85.8	94.7	76.6	95.4	84.6	82.7	83.9
4th quarter	89.8	86.1	95.8	77.6	96.0	86.4	81.9	84.7	90.3	86.2	95.4	77.9	96.4	86.2	81.6	84.5
1987																
1st quarter	89.4	86.6	96.9	77.7	95.1	86.9	82.1	85.1	89.9	86.8	96.6	78.0	95.4	86.8	81.8	84.9
2nd quarter	90.0	87.8	97.5	78.5	95.0	87.2	82.9	85.6	90.6	88.0	97.1	78.7	95.4	87.0	82.6	85.4
3rd quarter	90.1	88.4	98.1	79.3	95.1	88.0	83.4	86.3	90.6	88.6	97.8	79.6	95.4	87.8	83.1	86.1
4th quarter	91.0	90.2	99.1	80.3	95.5	88.3	83.9	86.7	91.4	90.3	98.8	80.5	95.8	88.1	83.6	86.4
1988																
1st quarter	91.2	90.5	99.2	81.6	96.4	89.5	83.9	87.4	91.6	90.6	98.9	81.8	96.7	89.3	83.4	87.1
2nd quarter	91.4	91.9	100.6	82.6	96.6	90.4	84.2	88.1	91.9	92.2	100.3	82.7	96.7	90.0	84.1	87.8
3rd quarter	91.6	92.3	100.7	83.6	96.7	91.3	85.6	89.1	92.2	92.7	100.6	83.7	96.8	90.8	85.2	88.7
4th quarter	91.8	93.6	101.9	84.1	96.3	91.5	86.8	89.8	92.7	94.3	101.7	84.2	96.5	90.8	87.1	89.4
1989																
1st quarter	92.0	94.6	102.9	84.3	95.7	91.7	89.2	90.8	92.4	94.8	102.7	84.5	95.8	91.5	88.4	90.3
2nd quarter	92.3	95.2	103.1	84.7	94.7	91.8	91.4	91.7	92.6	95.5	103.1	84.7	94.6	91.5	91.1	91.3
3rd quarter	92.6	95.9	103.5	85.3	94.7	92.1	92.4	92.2	93.0	96.1	103.3	85.4	94.7	91.8	92.3	92.0
4th quarter	92.8	96.0	103.5	86.4	95.1	93.2	92.2	92.8	93.2	96.3	103.4	86.5	95.1	92.8	91.7	92.4
1990																
1st quarter	93.8	97.2	103.6	88.3	95.6	94.1	93.4	93.8	94.0	97.4	103.6	88.1	95.4	93.7	93.0	93.5
2nd quarter	94.5	97.3	103.0	90.2	96.8	95.5	93.8	94.9	94.7	97.6	103.1	90.0	96.6	95.1	93.5	94.5
3rd quarter	95.0	97.1	102.2	91.6	96.7	96.4	94.2	95.6	95.0	97.3	102.4	91.4	96.5	96.2	93.9	95.4
4th quarter	94.2	96.0	101.9	92.3	95.9	98.0	93.5	96.3	94.3	96.1	101.9	92.2	95.8	97.7	93.6	96.2

Table 19-13. Productivity and Related Data—*Continued*

(1992 = 100, seasonally adjusted.)

Year and quarter	Nonfinancial corporations										Manufacturing					
	Output per hour of all employees	Output	Employee hours	Compensation per hour	Real compensation per hour	Unit costs			Unit profits	Implicit price deflator	Output per hour of all persons	Output	Hours of all persons	Compensation per hour	Real compensation per hour	Unit labor costs
						Total	Labor costs	Nonlabor costs								
1976																
1st quarter	78.4	58.2	74.3	39.1	91.3	48.7	49.9	45.4	75.7	51.1	...	...	...	...	...	...
2nd quarter	78.4	58.7	74.8	39.8	92.3	49.5	50.8	46.1	71.3	51.5	...	...	...	...	...	...
3rd quarter	78.8	59.3	75.3	40.7	92.8	50.3	51.7	46.5	70.3	52.1	...	...	...	...	...	...
4th quarter	78.7	59.5	75.6	41.6	93.6	51.5	52.9	47.5	68.5	53.0	...	...	...	...	...	...
1977																
1st quarter	78.8	60.4	76.6	42.1	93.0	52.1	53.5	48.2	70.2	53.7	...	...	...	...	...	...
2nd quarter	80.4	62.9	78.2	43.0	93.3	52.0	53.5	47.9	77.8	54.3	...	...	...	...	...	...
3rd quarter	82.1	64.9	79.0	44.0	94.0	52.0	53.6	47.9	82.4	54.7	...	...	...	...	...	...
4th quarter	81.1	64.8	79.9	44.9	94.6	53.8	55.3	49.6	78.5	56.0	...	...	...	...	...	...
1978																
1st quarter	81.0	64.8	80.1	46.0	95.5	55.4	56.8	51.4	71.0	56.8	...	...	...	...	...	...
2nd quarter	82.3	67.7	82.3	47.1	95.6	55.5	57.2	51.0	81.6	57.9	...	...	...	...	...	...
3rd quarter	81.6	67.9	83.2	48.0	95.8	56.6	58.8	50.7	81.0	58.8	...	...	...	...	...	...
4th quarter	81.9	69.0	84.3	49.2	96.2	57.8	60.1	51.7	82.3	60.0	...	...	...	...	...	...
1979																
1st quarter	81.5	69.4	85.1	50.3	96.2	59.4	61.7	53.1	77.2	61.0	...	...	...	...	...	...
2nd quarter	81.0	69.3	85.5	51.3	95.7	61.1	63.3	55.0	75.4	62.4	...	...	...	...	...	...
3rd quarter	80.7	69.5	86.2	52.4	95.1	62.8	65.0	56.7	72.3	63.6	...	...	...	...	...	...
4th quarter	80.8	69.8	86.4	53.6	94.9	64.2	66.4	58.2	71.1	64.8	...	...	...	...	...	...
1980																
1st quarter	80.9	69.8	86.2	55.1	94.6	66.1	68.1	60.7	69.4	66.4	...	...	...	...	...	...
2nd quarter	80.0	67.8	84.8	56.5	94.6	68.9	70.6	64.4	59.6	68.1	...	...	...	...	...	...
3rd quarter	80.6	67.9	84.3	57.8	94.6	70.4	71.8	66.4	65.0	69.9	...	...	...	...	...	...
4th quarter	81.6	69.8	85.5	59.4	94.9	71.5	72.8	68.2	73.4	71.7	...	...	...	...	...	...
1981																
1st quarter	82.1	70.7	86.1	60.7	94.3	72.8	73.9	69.9	78.7	73.4	...	...	...	...	...	...
2nd quarter	82.5	71.4	86.5	61.8	94.3	74.2	74.8	72.6	78.7	74.6	...	...	...	...	...	...
3rd quarter	83.9	72.8	86.7	63.1	94.4	74.9	75.2	74.2	87.2	76.0	...	...	...	...	...	...
4th quarter	82.9	71.5	86.3	64.1	94.2	77.2	77.3	77.1	79.1	77.4	...	...	...	...	...	...
1982																
1st quarter	83.1	70.5	84.8	65.5	95.1	79.0	78.8	79.5	73.5	78.5	...	...	...	...	...	...
2nd quarter	83.2	70.3	84.6	66.0	94.8	79.7	79.4	80.7	78.0	79.6	...	...	...	...	...	...
3rd quarter	83.0	69.7	84.0	66.8	94.4	80.9	80.6	81.8	78.0	80.6	...	...	...	...	...	...
4th quarter	83.0	69.0	83.0	67.5	94.4	81.9	81.3	83.5	71.2	81.0	...	...	...	...	...	...
1983																
1st quarter	84.2	70.2	83.4	67.9	94.3	81.2	80.6	82.7	79.6	81.0	...	...	...	...	...	...
2nd quarter	85.6	72.2	84.4	68.6	94.2	80.5	80.1	81.4	90.1	81.3	...	...	...	...	...	...
3rd quarter	86.3	74.2	85.9	69.1	93.9	80.4	80.0	81.4	96.2	81.8	...	...	...	...	...	...
4th quarter	86.7	75.9	87.6	70.1	94.5	80.9	80.9	81.0	98.0	82.5	...	...	...	...	...	...
1984																
1st quarter	87.1	77.8	89.3	70.6	93.8	80.8	81.0	80.3	108.5	83.3	...	...	...	...	...	...
2nd quarter	87.7	79.5	90.6	71.4	94.1	81.3	81.5	80.7	110.0	83.8	...	...	...	...	...	...
3rd quarter	88.0	80.2	91.2	72.5	94.7	82.2	82.4	81.9	105.9	84.3	...	...	...	...	...	...
4th quarter	88.3	81.2	92.0	73.1	94.7	82.6	82.8	82.2	106.0	84.7	...	...	...	...	...	...
1985																
1st quarter	88.6	81.8	92.4	73.9	94.9	83.4	83.4	83.3	103.4	85.2	...	...	...	...	...	...
2nd quarter	88.9	82.6	93.0	74.5	94.8	83.9	83.8	84.2	100.4	85.4	...	...	...	...	...	...
3rd quarter	90.5	84.1	93.0	75.5	95.5	83.3	83.5	83.0	107.1	85.5	...	...	...	...	...	...
4th quarter	90.7	84.4	93.1	76.9	96.3	84.6	84.8	84.0	98.2	85.8	...	...	...	...	...	...
1986																
1st quarter	91.2	85.0	93.2	77.7	96.9	85.3	85.2	85.8	93.3	86.1	...	...	...	...	...	...
2nd quarter	91.1	84.6	92.9	78.4	98.2	86.1	86.0	86.2	90.7	86.5	...	...	...	...	...	...
3rd quarter	91.3	84.9	93.0	79.2	98.7	86.7	86.8	86.6	88.3	86.9	...	...	...	...	...	...
4th quarter	92.1	86.1	93.5	80.3	99.4	87.0	87.2	86.5	88.4	87.1	...	...	...	...	...	...
1987																
1st quarter	91.9	87.1	94.7	80.5	98.6	87.3	87.6	86.5	91.5	87.7	87.3	90.0	103.1	80.6	98.6	92.3
2nd quarter	93.0	88.9	95.6	81.0	98.1	86.8	87.2	85.9	98.8	87.9	88.8	91.4	102.9	80.9	98.0	91.1
3rd quarter	94.0	90.7	96.5	81.8	98.1	86.5	87.0	85.1	105.9	88.2	89.6	92.9	103.7	81.7	98.0	91.2
4th quarter	94.3	91.9	97.4	82.8	98.6	87.2	87.8	85.7	104.1	88.7	90.5	95.4	105.5	82.0	97.5	90.7
1988																
1st quarter	95.5	93.2	97.7	83.7	98.8	87.2	87.6	85.8	109.5	89.2	90.4	95.8	106.1	82.9	97.9	91.8
2nd quarter	95.7	94.5	98.8	84.6	98.9	87.8	88.4	86.2	109.9	89.8	90.8	96.9	106.8	83.5	97.6	92.1
3rd quarter	95.6	95.0	99.4	85.5	98.9	88.9	89.5	87.2	110.9	90.8	90.9	97.4	107.1	84.4	97.6	92.9
4th quarter	96.2	96.8	100.6	85.9	98.4	88.9	89.3	87.9	116.0	91.3	91.7	98.8	107.8	85.6	98.1	93.3
1989																
1st quarter	95.0	96.6	101.6	86.3	97.9	90.8	90.8	90.8	105.1	92.1	92.3	99.7	108.1	85.9	97.5	93.1
2nd quarter	94.2	96.2	102.1	86.4	96.6	92.1	91.8	92.8	102.8	93.0	91.7	99.1	108.0	85.7	95.8	93.5
3rd quarter	94.5	96.7	102.3	87.0	96.6	92.8	92.1	94.6	101.3	93.5	91.4	98.3	107.7	86.6	96.1	94.9
4th quarter	94.7	97.1	102.6	88.3	97.1	93.8	93.3	95.2	95.8	94.0	92.0	98.1	106.7	88.2	97.0	95.8
1990																
1st quarter	94.1	97.4	103.5	88.8	96.2	94.7	94.4	95.4	98.1	95.0	93.2	98.6	105.9	88.3	95.7	94.9
2nd quarter	95.6	98.4	103.0	90.7	97.4	95.2	94.9	95.9	103.2	95.9	93.4	98.9	106.0	90.0	96.6	96.4
3rd quarter	95.7	97.9	102.3	92.1	97.3	96.7	96.3	98.0	94.9	96.6	94.5	99.0	104.7	91.2	96.2	96.5
4th quarter	96.2	97.6	101.4	92.9	96.5	97.4	96.5	99.9	91.5	96.9	94.4	97.4	103.1	92.4	96.0	97.8

. . . = Not available.

Table 19-13. Productivity and Related Data—*Continued*

(1992 = 100, seasonally adjusted.)

Year and quarter	Business sector								Nonfarm business sector							
	Output per hour of all persons	Output	Hours of all persons	Compensation per hour	Real compensation per hour	Unit labor costs	Unit nonlabor payments	Implicit price deflator	Output per hour of all persons	Output	Hours of all persons	Compensation per hour	Real compensation per hour	Unit labor costs	Unit nonlabor payments	Implicit price deflator
1991																
1st quarter	94.4	95.2	100.8	93.0	96.2	98.5	95.3	97.3	94.5	95.3	100.8	92.9	96.1	98.3	95.5	97.3
2nd quarter	95.8	95.9	100.2	94.7	97.5	98.9	96.2	97.9	95.9	96.1	100.2	94.7	97.4	98.7	96.3	97.8
3rd quarter	96.4	96.5	100.1	95.7	97.9	99.3	97.3	98.6	96.6	96.6	100.0	95.7	97.9	99.1	97.7	98.6
4th quarter	97.1	97.0	99.9	96.8	98.3	99.7	97.7	99.0	97.2	97.1	99.9	96.7	98.3	99.5	97.8	98.9
1992																
1st quarter	98.9	98.3	99.4	98.7	99.7	99.8	98.6	99.4	98.8	98.3	99.4	98.6	99.6	99.8	98.7	99.4
2nd quarter	99.5	99.4	99.9	99.3	99.6	99.8	99.6	99.7	99.5	99.3	99.8	99.4	99.7	99.9	99.5	99.7
3rd quarter	100.4	100.5	100.0	100.8	100.5	100.4	99.9	100.2	100.4	100.5	100.0	100.8	100.6	100.4	99.7	100.2
4th quarter	101.2	101.9	100.7	101.2	100.2	100.0	101.9	100.7	101.3	102.0	100.7	101.2	100.2	100.0	102.0	100.7
1993																
1st quarter	100.4	101.8	101.4	101.6	100.0	101.2	101.8	101.4	100.5	102.1	101.6	101.4	99.8	100.9	102.4	101.5
2nd quarter	100.0	102.5	102.5	102.0	99.8	102.1	101.7	101.9	99.9	102.7	102.8	101.8	99.5	101.9	102.0	101.9
3rd quarter	100.1	103.1	103.0	102.5	99.7	102.3	102.3	102.3	100.3	103.5	103.3	102.2	99.5	101.9	103.0	102.3
4th quarter	101.1	105.0	103.9	102.8	99.4	101.7	104.6	102.8	101.0	105.2	104.1	102.6	99.2	101.5	104.8	102.7
1994																
1st quarter	101.6	106.3	104.6	103.8	100.1	102.2	105.0	103.2	101.7	106.3	104.5	103.7	100.0	102.0	105.2	103.2
2nd quarter	101.4	107.9	106.5	103.4	99.2	102.0	106.1	103.6	101.6	108.0	106.3	103.5	99.3	101.9	106.5	103.6
3rd quarter	100.8	108.5	107.7	103.4	98.4	102.6	107.0	104.2	100.9	108.5	107.6	103.4	98.4	102.5	107.7	104.4
4th quarter	101.6	110.1	108.4	103.9	98.4	102.2	108.7	104.6	101.9	110.3	108.2	104.0	98.5	102.1	109.5	104.8
1995																
1st quarter	101.1	110.4	109.1	104.8	98.7	103.6	107.7	105.2	101.6	110.7	108.9	104.8	98.7	103.2	109.0	105.3
2nd quarter	101.2	110.5	109.3	105.3	98.4	104.1	107.9	105.5	101.8	110.9	109.0	105.5	98.6	103.6	109.3	105.7
3rd quarter	101.3	111.7	110.2	106.0	98.6	104.6	108.4	106.0	101.9	112.2	110.1	106.1	98.7	104.1	109.3	106.0
4th quarter	102.3	112.8	110.3	107.0	99.1	104.6	109.2	106.3	102.7	113.3	110.2	107.0	99.1	104.2	109.8	106.2
1996																
1st quarter	103.4	113.9	110.2	108.0	99.3	104.5	110.7	106.8	103.7	114.2	110.1	108.1	99.3	104.2	110.8	106.7
2nd quarter	104.6	116.0	111.0	109.1	99.4	104.4	112.2	107.3	104.8	116.3	111.0	109.2	99.5	104.2	112.0	107.0
3rd quarter	104.9	117.2	111.7	110.1	99.8	105.0	111.8	107.5	105.1	117.5	111.8	110.0	99.7	104.7	112.3	107.5
4th quarter	105.1	118.8	113.1	110.6	99.4	105.2	112.8	108.0	105.3	119.2	113.2	110.4	99.3	104.9	113.2	108.0
1997																
1st quarter	104.8	119.9	114.4	111.2	99.4	106.1	113.1	108.7	104.9	120.1	114.5	111.1	99.4	105.9	113.3	108.6
2nd quarter	106.2	122.1	115.0	112.0	100.0	105.5	114.3	108.8	106.2	122.2	115.1	112.0	99.9	105.5	115.1	109.0
3rd quarter	107.2	123.9	115.5	113.3	100.6	105.7	114.9	109.1	107.1	124.0	115.8	113.1	100.4	105.6	115.7	109.3
4th quarter	107.7	124.9	116.0	115.4	102.0	107.2	113.1	109.4	107.5	125.1	116.3	115.0	101.6	107.0	114.1	109.6
1998																
1st quarter	108.5	126.5	116.6	117.6	103.7	108.3	111.5	109.5	108.4	126.8	117.0	117.2	103.4	108.2	112.4	109.7
2nd quarter	108.7	127.4	117.2	119.1	104.8	109.6	109.4	109.5	108.7	127.7	117.5	118.8	104.5	109.3	110.5	109.8
3rd quarter	110.0	129.0	117.3	121.0	106.0	110.0	109.3	109.7	109.9	129.4	117.7	120.8	105.8	109.9	110.4	110.1
4th quarter	110.6	131.5	118.8	121.8	106.2	110.1	109.7	109.9	110.5	131.8	119.3	121.4	105.9	109.9	110.7	110.2
1999																
1st quarter	111.8	132.7	118.6	124.3	108.0	111.2	108.8	110.3	111.5	133.0	119.3	123.7	107.5	110.9	109.8	110.5
2nd quarter	112.0	133.9	119.5	124.7	107.6	111.3	109.1	110.5	111.7	134.3	120.2	124.1	107.1	111.1	110.7	111.0
3rd quarter	112.8	135.7	120.3	125.8	107.7	111.5	109.7	110.8	112.4	136.1	121.0	125.2	107.1	111.3	111.4	111.3
4th quarter	114.6	138.5	120.8	128.2	108.9	111.8	110.0	111.1	114.4	138.9	121.4	127.8	108.6	111.7	111.8	111.7
2000																
1st quarter	114.2	138.6	121.3	132.6	111.6	116.1	105.3	112.1	113.9	138.8	121.9	132.3	111.3	116.1	106.6	112.6
2nd quarter	116.4	141.1	121.3	133.1	111.2	114.4	109.5	112.6	115.9	141.4	121.9	132.6	110.8	114.4	111.0	113.1
3rd quarter	116.1	140.8	121.3	135.8	112.4	116.9	106.2	112.9	115.7	141.1	121.9	135.3	111.9	116.9	107.8	113.5
4th quarter	117.4	141.5	120.6	136.7	112.4	116.5	108.0	113.3	116.8	141.8	121.4	136.0	111.8	116.4	109.6	113.9
2001																
1st quarter	117.2	141.1	120.4	139.0	113.2	118.6	106.4	114.1	116.7	141.4	121.2	138.3	112.6	118.5	108.0	114.6
2nd quarter	118.8	141.4	119.1	140.0	113.1	117.9	109.9	114.4	118.3	141.9	119.9	139.1	112.4	117.6	111.7	115.4
3rd quarter	119.3	140.3	117.6	140.8	113.5	118.0	110.4	115.2	118.8	140.8	118.5	139.8	112.7	117.7	112.0	115.6
4th quarter	121.1	141.0	116.4	141.7	114.4	117.0	113.1	115.6	120.6	141.2	117.1	140.9	113.7	116.8	114.7	116.0
2002																
1st quarter	122.8	141.9	115.5	143.8	115.6	117.0	113.2	115.6	122.7	142.5	116.1	143.1	115.1	116.6	115.0	116.0
2nd quarter	123.3	142.6	115.6	145.3	116.0	117.9	112.6	115.9	122.9	143.0	116.3	144.6	115.4	117.7	114.8	116.6
3rd quarter	124.8	143.8	115.2	146.1	116.0	117.1	114.7	116.2	124.2	144.1	116.0	145.3	115.4	117.0	116.6	116.9
4th quarter	124.7	144.0	115.4	146.1	115.2	117.1	116.0	116.7	124.1	144.1	116.1	145.3	114.6	117.1	117.7	117.3
2003																
1st quarter	125.8	144.4	114.8	148.1	115.7	117.7	116.5	117.3	125.2	144.6	115.5	147.3	115.1	117.7	118.3	117.9
2nd quarter	127.9	146.0	114.2	150.7	117.9	117.9	116.7	117.4	126.9	146.1	115.1	149.7	117.1	118.0	118.1	118.0
3rd quarter	130.7	149.7	114.5	152.4	118.3	116.6	120.1	118.0	130.1	150.0	115.3	151.7	117.8	116.6	121.4	118.4
4th quarter	130.3	150.1	115.1	153.6	118.8	117.9	119.5	118.5	130.0	150.6	115.9	153.0	118.3	117.7	120.5	118.7
2004																
1st quarter	131.1	151.4	115.5	153.8	118.0	117.4	123.0	119.5	130.2	151.5	116.4	152.9	117.3	117.4	123.7	119.7
2nd quarter	132.3	153.1	115.7	155.8	118.6	117.7	125.3	120.5	131.7	153.4	116.5	154.9	117.9	117.6	125.9	120.6
3rd quarter	132.9	154.6	116.3	158.0	119.4	118.9	124.8	121.1	132.2	154.9	117.1	157.1	118.7	118.8	125.8	121.4
4th quarter	133.4	155.7	116.7	160.3	119.9	120.1	125.4	122.1	132.2	155.9	117.9	158.9	118.9	120.2	126.4	122.5
2005																
1st quarter	134.2	157.1	117.1	161.0	119.9	120.0	128.5	123.2	133.2	157.3	118.1	159.9	119.1	120.0	129.9	123.7
2nd quarter	134.2	158.4	118.0	161.6	119.5	120.4	129.4	123.8	133.4	158.4	118.8	160.8	118.9	120.5	130.8	124.3
3rd quarter	135.6	160.2	118.1	164.1	119.5	121.0	131.8	125.0	134.7	160.3	119.0	163.2	118.9	121.1	133.4	125.6
4th quarter	135.2	160.6	118.8	165.8	119.6	122.6	132.4	126.3	134.2	160.8	119.8	164.7	118.8	122.7	134.2	126.9

Table 19-13. Productivity and Related Data—*Continued*

(1992 = 100, seasonally adjusted.)

Year and quarter	Nonfinancial corporations										Manufacturing					
	Output per hour of all employees	Output	Employee hours	Compensation per hour	Real compensation per hour	Unit costs			Unit profits	Implicit price deflator	Output per hour of all persons	Output	Hours of all persons	Compensation per hour	Real compensation per hour	Unit labor costs
						Total	Labor costs	Nonlabor costs								
1991																
1st quarter	96.6	96.8	100.2	93.5	96.7	98.3	96.8	102.4	94.3	98.0	94.6	95.3	100.9	93.7	96.9	99.1
2nd quarter	97.5	96.8	99.3	95.2	98.0	99.1	97.7	102.9	93.7	98.6	95.8	96.0	100.2	95.3	98.0	99.4
3rd quarter	97.7	97.1	99.4	96.2	98.4	99.7	98.5	103.0	92.8	99.1	97.4	97.8	100.4	96.3	98.5	98.9
4th quarter	98.0	97.5	99.4	97.1	98.7	100.0	99.1	102.5	91.9	99.3	97.5	98.0	100.5	97.0	98.5	99.4
1992																
1st quarter	99.4	98.9	99.4	98.6	99.6	99.6	99.2	100.9	96.7	99.4	98.0	98.0	99.9	98.4	99.4	100.3
2nd quarter	99.7	99.8	100.1	99.4	99.7	99.7	99.7	99.9	100.6	99.8	99.4	99.7	100.3	99.5	99.8	100.1
3rd quarter	100.0	99.8	99.8	100.9	100.6	100.6	100.8	100.1	95.3	100.2	101.3	100.7	99.4	101.2	100.9	99.8
4th quarter	100.8	101.5	100.7	101.2	100.1	100.0	100.3	99.2	107.3	100.7	101.3	101.6	100.4	101.0	99.9	99.8
1993																
1st quarter	99.5	100.8	101.2	101.1	99.6	101.3	101.6	100.6	104.1	101.6	102.1	102.8	100.7	100.9	99.4	98.9
2nd quarter	100.3	102.4	102.1	101.6	99.3	100.8	101.3	99.4	113.4	101.9	102.1	103.3	101.3	101.5	99.2	99.5
3rd quarter	100.3	103.1	102.7	102.0	99.3	101.2	101.6	100.1	112.9	102.3	102.3	103.8	101.5	102.3	99.6	100.0
4th quarter	101.1	104.8	103.6	102.3	98.9	100.7	101.2	99.6	125.7	103.0	103.7	105.6	101.8	103.3	99.9	99.7
1994																
1st quarter	101.9	106.3	104.4	103.6	99.9	101.8	101.7	102.0	120.2	103.4	104.5	106.9	102.2	104.8	101.0	100.2
2nd quarter	102.1	108.5	106.3	103.3	99.1	100.9	101.2	99.9	131.5	103.6	105.9	109.2	103.1	104.9	100.6	99.0
3rd quarter	102.0	109.8	107.6	103.3	98.3	101.1	101.2	100.8	134.7	104.1	106.4	110.8	104.2	105.4	100.3	99.1
4th quarter	102.8	112.0	109.0	103.8	98.4	100.9	101.0	100.5	140.0	104.4	107.8	113.5	105.4	106.1	100.5	98.6
1995																
1st quarter	102.4	112.5	109.8	104.7	98.6	101.9	102.2	101.3	132.7	104.7	109.4	115.3	105.4	105.5	99.3	96.4
2nd quarter	102.8	113.4	110.3	105.0	98.1	102.0	102.2	101.6	132.4	104.7	110.6	115.3	104.3	107.0	99.9	96.8
3rd quarter	103.7	115.2	111.1	105.4	98.1	101.5	101.7	100.9	141.0	105.0	111.5	115.9	104.1	108.0	100.5	97.0
4th quarter	104.4	116.2	111.3	106.1	98.3	101.5	101.7	101.1	141.2	105.1	112.5	116.9	103.9	108.7	100.6	96.6
1996																
1st quarter	105.7	117.5	111.1	107.1	98.4	101.1	101.4	100.5	148.3	105.3	113.8	116.7	102.8	108.7	99.9	95.7
2nd quarter	106.7	119.6	112.1	108.2	98.6	101.1	101.4	100.0	149.9	105.4	114.1	119.0	104.3	109.0	99.3	95.5
3rd quarter	107.7	121.7	113.0	109.0	98.8	100.8	101.2	99.7	149.4	105.1	115.6	120.9	104.7	109.5	99.3	94.9
4th quarter	108.3	123.6	114.2	109.5	98.5	100.7	101.1	99.7	152.2	105.3	116.5	122.5	105.1	110.0	98.9	94.4
1997																
1st quarter	108.4	125.3	115.6	110.4	98.7	101.4	101.8	100.2	152.7	106.0	118.0	125.2	105.8	110.1	98.5	93.1
2nd quarter	109.2	127.2	116.5	110.9	99.0	101.1	101.6	99.9	152.9	105.8	120.0	126.9	105.7	111.5	99.5	92.9
3rd quarter	110.6	129.7	117.3	111.9	99.4	100.8	101.2	99.7	158.5	106.0	122.6	129.5	105.9	112.7	100.1	92.2
4th quarter	111.3	131.5	118.2	113.7	100.4	101.3	102.1	99.2	153.1	105.9	124.6	132.8	106.7	114.4	101.1	92.0
1998																
1st quarter	111.9	132.9	118.7	116.2	102.5	102.5	103.8	99.1	139.7	105.9	126.1	134.2	106.6	116.6	102.8	92.6
2nd quarter	113.1	134.7	119.1	117.7	103.5	102.7	104.0	99.1	136.6	105.8	126.9	134.4	106.0	118.3	104.0	93.3
3rd quarter	114.8	137.0	119.4	119.4	104.6	102.7	104.0	99.1	139.8	106.0	128.9	135.1	104.9	120.0	105.1	93.1
4th quarter	114.8	138.6	120.8	120.0	104.7	103.5	104.6	100.5	132.2	106.1	129.9	137.2	105.6	120.2	104.9	92.6
1999																
1st quarter	117.0	141.6	121.1	123.1	106.9	103.6	105.2	99.2	133.3	106.3	132.0	138.6	105.0	121.3	105.4	91.9
2nd quarter	117.6	143.2	121.8	123.4	106.4	103.5	104.9	99.7	133.6	106.2	133.1	139.7	105.1	122.1	105.3	91.9
3rd quarter	117.7	144.4	122.7	124.1	106.2	104.3	105.5	101.0	126.2	106.2	133.0	140.3	105.7	123.5	105.7	93.0
4th quarter	119.1	146.9	123.3	125.9	107.0	104.6	105.7	101.5	123.4	106.3	136.6	142.8	104.7	126.8	107.7	93.0
2000																
1st quarter	121.3	150.3	123.9	130.6	109.9	106.1	107.7	101.9	114.6	106.9	137.9	144.1	104.5	133.1	112.0	96.5
2nd quarter	122.0	151.1	123.9	131.4	109.8	106.6	107.7	103.5	115.9	107.4	138.9	145.2	104.5	132.5	110.7	95.4
3rd quarter	123.0	152.4	123.9	134.0	110.9	107.9	109.0	104.8	107.4	107.8	139.0	144.5	103.9	135.9	112.5	97.8
4th quarter	123.2	152.3	123.6	135.5	111.4	109.1	110.0	106.5	97.0	108.0	139.9	143.1	102.3	136.6	112.3	97.7
2001																
1st quarter	123.7	151.9	122.8	136.7	111.3	110.2	110.5	109.2	87.4	108.1	139.6	140.5	100.7	138.0	112.3	98.9
2nd quarter	124.6	151.1	121.3	138.0	111.6	111.0	110.8	111.5	86.9	108.9	140.6	138.2	98.3	137.4	111.0	97.7
3rd quarter	124.9	149.4	119.6	139.3	112.3	112.2	111.5	114.1	79.0	109.2	141.1	135.5	96.0	137.1	110.6	97.2
4th quarter	125.6	148.2	118.0	140.7	113.5	113.0	111.9	115.7	75.5	109.6	143.9	133.4	92.8	138.9	112.1	96.6
2002																
1st quarter	127.3	149.3	117.2	141.6	113.9	111.7	111.2	113.0	85.8	109.4	147.3	134.2	91.3	144.4	116.1	98.2
2nd quarter	129.3	151.3	117.0	143.5	114.5	110.9	111.0	110.7	94.5	109.4	150.2	136.1	90.7	147.6	117.8	98.3
3rd quarter	130.6	152.2	116.5	144.5	114.7	110.5	110.6	110.0	100.3	109.5	152.6	137.0	89.7	149.2	118.5	97.7
4th quarter	131.6	153.0	116.3	144.8	114.2	110.0	110.1	109.6	111.2	110.1	154.1	136.6	88.6	150.1	118.4	97.4
2003																
1st quarter	132.1	152.3	115.3	146.3	114.2	111.2	110.7	112.6	102.9	110.5	157.5	137.3	87.2	154.5	120.7	98.2
2nd quarter	133.8	153.6	114.8	148.8	116.4	111.2	111.2	111.0	105.7	110.7	159.3	136.6	85.7	157.2	123.0	98.7
3rd quarter	135.8	155.9	114.8	150.8	117.1	110.9	111.0	110.7	112.8	111.1	162.6	137.3	84.4	159.5	123.8	98.0
4th quarter	136.7	157.5	115.3	152.0	117.6	110.9	111.2	110.0	117.8	111.5	162.1	138.2	85.3	161.7	125.1	99.8
2004																
1st quarter	137.4	159.4	116.0	150.9	115.7	109.7	109.8	109.5	135.2	112.0	161.8	138.3	85.6	156.8	120.3	97.0
2nd quarter	139.1	161.6	116.2	152.9	116.4	109.8	109.9	109.3	145.7	113.0	163.0	138.9	85.3	159.9	121.7	98.1
3rd quarter	141.3	164.8	116.6	155.2	117.3	109.6	109.9	109.0	150.3	113.3	164.2	139.9	85.2	163.7	123.7	99.7
4th quarter	140.8	165.1	117.2	157.0	117.5	110.9	111.5	109.3	147.9	114.2	167.1	141.8	84.8	165.8	124.0	99.2
2005																
1st quarter	141.9	166.6	117.4	157.8	117.5	111.2	111.2	111.2	155.7	115.2	170.0	143.7	84.6	162.1	120.7	95.4
2nd quarter	144.0	170.2	118.2	158.6	117.3	110.4	110.2	111.2	166.5	115.5	172.0	144.5	84.0	164.1	121.4	95.5
3rd quarter	143.0	169.9	118.8	160.8	117.1	113.3	112.4	115.5	152.0	116.7	172.6	144.7	83.7	166.4	121.2	96.3
4th quarter	144.9	173.4	119.7	161.2	116.3	111.7	111.3	113.0	177.2	117.6	173.0	146.5	84.7	165.4	119.3	95.6

NOTES AND DEFINITIONS

TABLES 19-1 THROUGH 19-11
SELECTED NATIONAL INCOME AND PRODUCT ACCOUNT DATA

See the notes and definitions for Chapter 1.

For *personal income and its disposition* (Table 19-6), see the notes and definitions for Table 4-1.

For *inventories to sales ratios* (Table 19-7), see the notes and definitions for Table 5-7.

For *saving and investment* (Table 19-9), see the notes and definitions for Table 5-1.

For *federal* and *state and local government current receipts and expenditures* (Tables 19-10 and 19-11), see the notes and definitions for Tables 6-1 and 6-8. Some of the detailed data shown in Tables 6-1 and 6-8 is not available for earlier years, and is listed and explained below.

In Table 19-10, from 1947 through 1958, only total *taxes on production and imports* is available. Separate data on *excise taxes* and on customs duties (the other component of the total, not shown here) are not available.

In Table 19-10, prior to 1960, *interest receipts* are not shown separately, but have been subtracted from total *interest payments*, which therefore represent net interest in those years.

In Table 19-10, prior to 1959, the *current surplus of government enterprises* is not shown separately as a current receipt, and the expenditure category *subsidies* is presented net of the current surplus of government enterprises. In the case of the federal government, subsidies are substantial and government enterprise activity relatively minor.

In Table 19-11, prior to 1959, the *current surplus of government enterprises* category of current receipts is presented net of expenditures for *subsidies*, which are not shown separately. This is the reverse of the treatment in Table 19-10, reflecting the reality that subsidies by state and local governments are usually minor compared with their enterprise activities.

TABLE 19-12
U.S. INTERNATIONAL TRANSACTIONS

See the notes and definitions for Table 7-6.

TABLE 19-13
PRODUCTIVITY AND RELATED DATA

See the notes and definitions for Table 9-3.

CHAPTER 20: SELECTED HISTORICAL DATA FOR MONTHLY SERIES

Table 20-1. Industrial Production and Capacity Utilization

(Seasonally adjusted; 2002 = 100, except as noted.)

Year and month	Total industry	Manufac-turing (SIC)	Consumer goods Total	Consumer goods Durable	Consumer goods Nondurable	Business equipment	Defense and space equipment	Construction supplies	Business supplies	Materials	Capacity utilization Total industry	Capacity utilization Manufac-turing (SIC)
1947	15.5	14.3	19.1	12.5	22.6	7.8	9.1	23.1	12.8	15.5	. . .	. . .
1948	16.1	14.8	19.7	13.1	23.2	8.1	10.7	24.7	13.3	16.2	. . .	82.5
1949	15.2	14.0	19.6	12.4	23.4	7.1	11.1	22.7	13.2	14.7	. . .	74.2
1950	17.6	16.3	22.4	16.6	25.4	7.6	13.1	27.2	14.7	17.7	. . .	82.8
1951	19.1	17.6	22.2	14.4	26.3	9.2	32.2	28.4	15.6	19.5	. . .	85.8
1952	19.9	18.3	22.7	13.9	27.3	10.5	45.3	28.2	15.5	19.8	. . .	85.4
1953	21.5	19.9	24.0	16.3	28.1	10.9	54.2	30.3	16.5	22.0	. . .	89.3
1954	20.3	18.6	23.8	15.1	28.4	9.6	47.7	29.8	16.7	20.3	. . .	80.1
1955	22.9	21.0	26.6	18.6	30.6	10.4	43.6	34.2	18.7	24.0	. . .	87.0
1956	23.9	21.8	27.6	18.0	32.5	12.0	42.7	35.3	19.8	24.6	. . .	86.1
1957	24.3	22.1	28.3	18.0	33.6	12.5	44.6	34.8	20.1	24.6	. . .	83.6
1958	22.7	20.6	28.0	15.9	34.6	10.5	44.8	33.5	19.9	22.2	. . .	75.0
1959	25.4	23.1	30.7	19.0	37.0	11.8	47.2	37.6	21.7	25.5	. . .	81.6
1960	26.0	23.6	31.9	20.0	38.2	12.2	48.5	36.8	22.4	25.9	. . .	80.1
1961	26.1	23.7	32.6	19.7	39.4	11.8	49.2	37.0	23.1	25.9	. . .	77.3
1962	28.3	25.8	34.8	22.3	41.3	12.8	57.0	39.3	24.5	28.2	. . .	81.4
1963	30.1	27.4	36.7	24.3	43.2	13.5	61.5	41.1	26.1	30.1	. . .	83.5
1964	32.1	29.3	38.8	26.1	45.3	15.1	59.6	43.6	28.0	32.5	. . .	85.6
1965	35.3	32.4	41.8	30.5	47.2	17.3	65.9	46.3	29.8	36.2	. . .	89.5
1966	38.4	35.4	43.9	32.2	49.5	20.0	77.5	48.3	32.2	39.5	. . .	91.1
1967	39.2	36.1	45.1	31.0	52.1	20.4	88.4	49.5	33.8	39.1	87.0	87.2
1947												
January	15.3	14.1	19.0	11.9	22.8	7.5	9.4	21.9	12.7	15.2	. . .	. . .
February	15.4	14.2	18.9	12.2	22.5	7.6	9.2	22.6	12.7	15.4	. . .	. . .
March	15.4	14.2	19.0	12.5	22.4	7.6	9.0	22.8	12.7	15.9	. . .	. . .
April	15.3	14.3	18.9	12.6	22.3	7.7	9.1	23.0	12.9	15.5	. . .	. . .
May	15.4	14.1	18.8	12.5	22.1	7.8	9.0	23.3	12.8	15.5	. . .	. . .
June	15.4	14.1	18.8	12.6	22.1	7.8	8.9	23.4	12.7	15.4	. . .	. . .
July	15.3	14.1	18.9	12.3	22.3	7.7	8.9	22.8	12.8	15.2	. . .	. . .
August	15.4	14.1	19.0	12.2	22.6	7.8	8.8	23.1	12.6	15.2	. . .	. . .
September	15.5	14.2	19.2	12.6	22.7	7.9	8.8	23.3	12.7	15.4	. . .	. . .
October	15.7	14.4	19.5	12.8	23.0	8.0	9.1	23.3	12.7	15.5	. . .	. . .
November	15.9	14.6	19.8	13.2	23.3	8.0	9.2	23.7	13.0	15.9	. . .	. . .
December	15.9	14.6	19.8	13.3	23.2	8.0	9.4	23.8	13.2	15.7	. . .	. . .
1948												
January	16.0	14.7	19.7	13.2	23.1	8.1	9.5	24.9	13.2	15.8	. . .	84.4
February	16.1	14.7	19.8	13.0	23.4	8.1	9.9	24.6	13.3	15.9	. . .	84.0
March	15.9	14.7	19.6	13.1	23.0	8.1	10.1	24.7	13.3	15.7	. . .	83.4
April	15.9	14.7	19.7	13.0	23.3	8.1	10.3	24.5	13.2	15.6	. . .	82.8
May	16.2	14.8	19.6	12.7	23.3	8.0	10.1	24.7	13.3	16.4	. . .	83.3
June	16.4	15.0	20.0	13.3	23.5	8.1	10.5	24.4	13.4	16.4	. . .	83.6
July	16.4	15.0	19.9	13.6	23.2	8.2	10.7	25.1	13.3	16.6	. . .	83.4
August	16.3	14.9	19.8	13.4	23.1	8.2	10.9	25.0	13.5	16.4	. . .	82.7
September	16.2	14.8	19.6	13.0	23.1	8.1	11.2	24.7	13.3	16.4	. . .	81.5
October	16.3	14.9	19.9	13.4	23.2	8.0	11.4	25.2	13.4	16.4	. . .	81.7
November	16.1	14.7	19.6	12.9	23.3	8.0	11.6	24.5	13.4	16.3	. . .	80.2
December	16.0	14.6	19.4	12.4	23.1	7.9	11.6	24.3	13.4	16.2	. . .	79.3
1949												
January	15.8	14.4	19.2	12.0	23.0	7.7	11.4	23.6	13.2	15.9	. . .	77.9
February	15.7	14.3	19.1	11.9	23.1	7.7	11.4	23.1	13.0	15.8	. . .	76.9
March	15.4	14.1	19.3	11.9	23.3	7.5	11.4	22.8	13.0	15.2	. . .	75.9
April	15.3	13.9	19.2	11.9	23.2	7.4	11.2	22.5	13.0	14.9	. . .	74.2
May	15.1	13.7	19.2	11.8	23.3	7.2	11.4	22.2	13.1	14.5	. . .	73.2
June	15.0	13.8	19.5	12.1	23.3	7.1	11.4	22.2	13.1	14.3	. . .	73.1
July	15.0	13.8	19.6	12.5	23.4	7.0	11.4	21.9	13.0	14.2	. . .	73.1
August	15.1	13.9	19.8	12.7	23.7	6.9	11.0	22.1	13.1	14.5	. . .	73.6
September	15.3	14.2	20.1	13.1	23.7	6.9	11.0	22.8	13.3	14.7	. . .	74.8
October	14.7	13.7	20.2	13.3	23.8	6.6	10.7	22.1	13.5	13.2	. . .	71.7
November	15.1	13.8	19.9	12.6	23.7	6.4	10.6	22.8	13.4	14.5	. . .	72.0
December	15.4	14.1	19.7	12.5	23.6	6.4	10.5	23.8	13.5	15.1	. . .	73.6
1950												
January	15.7	14.4	20.5	13.9	24.0	6.5	10.5	23.5	13.6	15.3	. . .	74.9
February	15.7	14.6	20.5	13.9	24.0	6.7	10.5	24.4	14.0	15.0	. . .	75.4
March	16.2	14.8	21.0	14.5	24.3	6.8	10.6	25.0	14.0	16.0	. . .	76.4
April	16.8	15.4	21.6	15.5	24.7	7.0	10.8	26.3	14.3	16.7	. . .	79.2
May	17.2	15.8	22.0	16.3	24.9	7.3	11.2	26.6	14.4	17.2	. . .	81.0
June	17.7	16.3	22.6	17.7	25.1	7.6	11.6	27.5	14.5	17.8	. . .	83.1
July	18.2	16.8	23.3	18.4	25.6	7.8	12.2	28.2	14.9	18.3	. . .	85.5
August	18.8	17.5	24.1	19.0	26.6	8.3	13.4	28.8	15.2	18.8	. . .	88.4
September	18.7	17.3	23.5	18.1	26.2	8.1	14.8	28.8	15.1	19.1	. . .	87.2
October	18.8	17.4	23.3	17.7	26.0	8.2	15.9	29.1	15.3	19.3	. . .	87.5
November	18.8	17.4	23.2	17.4	26.1	8.3	17.0	29.1	15.4	19.1	. . .	87.0
December	19.1	17.6	23.5	17.2	26.8	8.4	18.5	29.2	15.6	19.4	. . .	88.1
1951												
January	19.2	17.8	23.7	16.9	27.2	8.5	20.5	29.4	15.8	19.2	. . .	88.3
February	19.3	17.8	23.7	16.9	27.2	8.6	23.7	29.1	15.6	19.3	. . .	88.3
March	19.4	17.9	23.3	16.8	26.6	8.8	26.9	29.3	15.9	19.7	. . .	88.4
April	19.4	17.9	22.9	16.0	26.5	9.0	29.5	29.1	16.2	19.8	. . .	88.2
May	19.4	17.8	22.5	15.2	26.2	9.1	30.5	28.9	16.0	20.0	. . .	87.4
June	19.3	17.7	22.2	14.5	26.2	9.2	32.1	28.7	15.8	20.1	. . .	86.6
July	19.0	17.4	21.4	13.0	26.0	9.2	33.9	28.0	15.6	19.7	. . .	84.9
August	18.8	17.2	21.0	12.1	25.7	9.4	35.0	27.9	15.4	19.4	. . .	83.6
September	18.9	17.3	21.2	12.6	25.7	9.6	36.1	27.9	15.3	19.5	. . .	83.7
October	18.9	17.2	21.0	12.5	25.7	9.7	37.7	27.6	15.0	19.2	. . .	83.1
November	19.0	17.4	21.4	12.8	26.0	9.9	39.8	27.4	15.1	19.3	. . .	83.6
December	19.1	17.5	21.6	12.9	26.2	10.0	40.7	27.4	15.1	19.3	. . .	83.9

. . . = Not available.

489

Table 20-1. Industrial Production and Capacity Utilization—*Continued*

(Seasonally adjusted; 2002 = 100, except as noted.)

Year and month	Total industry	Manufac-turing (SIC)	Consumer goods Total	Durable	Nondurable	Business equipment	Defense and space equipment	Construction supplies	Business supplies	Materials	Capacity util. Total industry	Manufac-turing (SIC)
1952												
January	19.4	17.7	21.7	12.9	26.5	10.3	41.4	27.8	15.2	19.8	. . .	84.4
February	19.5	17.8	21.9	12.8	26.8	10.4	41.8	28.0	15.2	19.6	. . .	84.6
March	19.5	17.9	22.0	13.1	26.8	10.5	41.9	27.9	15.2	19.6	. . .	84.7
April	19.4	17.7	22.0	13.0	26.8	10.5	42.4	27.4	15.1	19.2	. . .	83.6
May	19.2	17.7	22.0	13.4	26.5	10.5	43.8	27.0	15.0	19.0	. . .	83.1
June	19.0	17.5	22.6	13.5	27.5	10.6	45.1	26.8	15.3	17.9	. . .	81.9
July	18.7	17.1	22.2	12.2	27.6	10.1	45.4	26.8	15.5	17.5	. . .	79.8
August	19.9	18.3	22.6	13.4	27.7	10.2	46.1	28.6	15.6	19.7	. . .	85.1
September	20.6	19.0	23.2	14.8	27.7	10.5	46.8	28.9	15.8	21.0	. . .	87.7
October	20.8	19.3	23.6	15.3	27.9	10.6	48.4	29.3	16.0	20.9	. . .	88.8
November	21.3	19.7	24.1	16.3	28.2	10.7	49.4	29.8	16.2	21.5	. . .	90.2
December	21.4	19.8	24.1	16.3	28.1	10.8	50.9	29.9	16.1	21.6	. . .	90.5
1953												
January	21.4	19.9	24.3	17.0	28.1	10.9	51.6	30.4	15.9	21.5	. . .	90.5
February	21.6	20.1	24.5	17.1	28.3	11.0	52.7	30.9	16.2	22.0	. . .	91.1
March	21.7	20.2	24.5	17.3	28.1	11.0	53.7	30.9	16.5	22.2	. . .	91.4
April	21.8	20.3	24.4	17.1	28.3	11.1	54.5	31.1	16.6	22.4	. . .	91.5
May	21.9	20.4	24.5	17.2	28.4	11.0	55.4	30.4	16.7	22.9	. . .	91.7
June	21.9	20.2	24.2	16.6	28.3	10.9	55.8	30.2	16.7	22.9	. . .	90.7
July	22.1	20.4	24.2	16.5	28.2	11.1	56.2	30.6	16.8	23.2	. . .	91.0
August	22.0	20.3	24.1	16.3	28.1	11.0	55.8	30.5	16.8	22.6	. . .	90.6
September	21.6	19.9	23.7	15.7	27.9	10.9	55.8	29.9	16.7	22.0	. . .	88.3
October	21.4	19.7	23.7	15.5	28.1	10.9	55.2	30.0	16.5	21.3	. . .	87.2
November	20.9	19.2	23.4	15.0	27.8	10.5	51.6	29.5	16.5	20.8	. . .	84.7
December	20.3	18.7	23.0	14.4	27.5	10.4	52.1	28.8	16.2	20.3	. . .	82.3
1954												
January	20.2	18.6	23.1	14.2	27.9	10.1	51.0	29.3	16.2	20.0	. . .	81.3
February	20.3	18.5	23.4	14.6	28.1	9.9	50.6	29.4	16.4	20.0	. . .	80.8
March	20.1	18.4	23.4	14.6	28.1	9.8	50.0	29.2	16.4	19.8	. . .	80.2
April	20.0	18.3	23.4	14.7	27.9	9.6	49.1	29.2	16.4	19.8	. . .	79.4
May	20.1	18.4	23.5	15.0	28.0	9.6	48.4	29.6	16.4	20.0	. . .	79.8
June	20.2	18.5	23.7	15.1	28.1	9.5	47.6	28.9	16.6	20.3	. . .	79.9
July	20.2	18.4	23.8	15.0	28.4	9.5	47.4	28.8	16.4	20.4	. . .	79.4
August	20.2	18.4	23.8	15.1	28.4	9.4	46.5	28.7	16.5	20.3	. . .	78.8
September	20.2	18.5	24.0	15.2	28.7	9.3	46.0	30.1	17.0	20.1	. . .	79.2
October	20.5	18.7	24.1	15.4	28.7	9.3	45.5	31.1	17.1	20.5	. . .	79.7
November	20.8	19.0	24.6	15.8	29.2	9.4	45.3	31.4	17.4	20.9	. . .	80.9
December	21.1	19.3	25.0	16.4	29.5	9.5	44.6	31.7	17.6	21.3	. . .	81.8
1955												
January	21.6	19.8	25.6	17.6	29.6	9.5	44.3	32.1	17.7	22.0	. . .	83.5
February	21.8	20.0	25.7	17.8	29.6	9.7	44.3	32.6	18.0	22.6	. . .	84.1
March	22.3	20.4	26.2	18.3	30.1	9.8	44.1	33.7	18.5	23.2	. . .	85.8
April	22.6	20.7	26.4	18.6	30.3	10.1	44.0	33.9	18.4	23.6	. . .	86.7
May	23.0	21.1	26.7	19.1	30.5	10.3	44.0	34.0	18.7	24.1	. . .	87.9
June	23.0	21.1	26.5	18.7	30.4	10.4	43.6	34.6	18.8	24.1	. . .	87.6
July	23.2	21.2	26.6	18.9	30.4	10.4	43.5	34.7	18.8	24.4	. . .	87.7
August	23.1	21.2	26.7	18.9	30.4	10.5	43.2	34.7	18.6	24.4	. . .	87.3
September	23.3	21.3	26.8	19.0	30.7	10.5	43.3	34.9	19.1	24.7	. . .	87.5
October	23.7	21.6	27.3	19.1	31.5	11.0	43.1	34.9	19.2	24.9	. . .	88.4
November	23.7	21.7	27.4	18.9	31.7	11.1	43.1	35.3	19.5	24.8	. . .	88.3
December	23.8	22.0	27.5	18.8	32.0	11.3	43.2	35.5	19.4	25.0	. . .	89.0
1956												
January	24.0	21.8	27.6	18.6	32.2	11.3	42.7	36.1	19.6	25.1	. . .	88.2
February	23.8	21.7	27.5	18.3	32.2	11.5	42.3	36.0	19.6	24.6	. . .	87.4
March	23.8	21.7	27.5	18.3	32.2	11.6	41.4	35.9	19.7	24.6	. . .	87.0
April	24.0	22.0	27.6	18.6	32.2	12.0	41.7	35.7	19.9	24.7	. . .	87.8
May	23.7	21.7	27.4	18.2	32.3	11.9	41.8	35.2	19.8	24.3	. . .	86.3
June	23.5	21.6	27.4	17.7	32.4	12.0	41.8	34.8	19.7	24.0	. . .	85.3
July	22.8	20.7	27.4	17.8	32.5	12.0	41.8	33.0	19.8	22.0	. . .	81.5
August	23.7	21.7	27.6	17.8	32.8	12.1	42.3	34.7	19.9	24.0	. . .	84.9
September	24.3	22.0	27.5	17.5	32.8	12.2	42.7	35.6	19.8	25.3	. . .	86.0
October	24.5	22.2	27.8	17.7	33.0	12.3	43.8	35.3	20.0	25.7	. . .	86.5
November	24.3	22.1	27.6	17.5	32.9	12.5	44.5	35.1	20.0	25.2	. . .	85.8
December	24.6	22.5	27.8	18.2	32.8	12.6	45.5	35.7	20.1	25.6	. . .	86.8
1957												
January	24.6	22.4	28.0	18.3	33.0	12.8	45.7	35.2	20.2	25.1	. . .	86.2
February	24.8	22.7	28.4	18.6	33.4	13.1	45.9	36.3	20.2	25.3	. . .	87.0
March	24.8	22.6	28.4	18.5	33.6	13.0	45.8	35.7	20.1	25.2	. . .	86.4
April	24.4	22.3	28.1	18.0	33.5	12.8	46.0	34.9	20.2	24.9	. . .	85.0
May	24.3	22.2	28.2	17.9	33.5	12.5	45.3	34.7	20.3	24.7	. . .	84.2
June	24.4	22.3	28.3	18.2	33.6	12.6	45.5	35.0	20.1	24.9	. . .	84.6
July	24.6	22.3	28.4	18.0	33.9	12.6	45.0	35.1	20.2	25.0	. . .	84.3
August	24.6	22.4	28.6	18.5	33.8	12.6	45.1	34.8	20.2	25.1	. . .	84.2
September	24.3	22.2	28.6	18.4	33.9	12.5	44.2	34.6	20.2	24.7	. . .	83.2
October	24.0	21.8	28.1	17.7	33.6	12.1	43.1	34.2	20.0	24.3	. . .	81.4
November	23.4	21.3	28.1	17.7	33.5	11.8	41.7	33.7	19.8	23.5	. . .	79.4
December	23.0	20.9	27.9	16.9	33.8	11.4	41.4	33.2	19.7	22.7	. . .	77.5

. . . = Not available.

Table 20-1. Industrial Production and Capacity Utilization—*Continued*

(Seasonally adjusted; 2002 = 100, except as noted.)

Year and month	Total industry	Manufac-turing (SIC)	Market groups								Capacity utilization (output as percentage of capacity)	
			Consumer goods			Business equipment	Defense and space equipment	Construction supplies	Business supplies	Materials	Total industry	Manufac-turing (SIC)
			Total	Durable	Nondurable							
1958												
January	22.5	20.4	27.5	16.2	33.7	11.2	41.8	32.8	19.6	22.0	. . .	75.7
February	22.1	20.0	27.3	15.7	33.7	10.8	42.2	31.7	19.6	21.3	. . .	73.8
March	21.8	19.7	27.1	15.1	33.7	10.6	43.0	31.6	19.6	20.8	. . .	72.7
April	21.4	19.4	26.8	14.5	33.7	10.4	43.7	31.2	19.5	20.3	. . .	71.3
May	21.6	19.6	27.2	15.1	34.0	10.1	44.2	32.2	19.4	20.5	. . .	71.9
June	22.2	20.2	27.8	15.5	34.5	10.1	45.4	33.5	19.7	21.4	. . .	73.9
July	22.5	20.4	28.2	15.7	35.0	10.2	45.5	33.3	19.7	21.9	. . .	74.3
August	23.0	20.8	28.3	16.0	35.0	10.4	45.9	34.8	19.9	22.6	. . .	75.7
September	23.2	21.0	27.9	14.9	35.2	10.4	46.2	34.9	20.2	23.1	. . .	76.2
October	23.5	21.1	28.2	15.7	35.2	10.6	46.2	34.8	20.5	23.5	. . .	76.4
November	24.2	21.9	29.6	18.3	35.6	10.8	46.5	36.2	20.7	24.2	. . .	79.1
December	24.2	22.0	29.7	18.4	35.7	10.9	46.6	35.7	20.5	24.3	. . .	79.0
1959												
January	24.6	22.4	30.0	18.5	36.1	11.1	46.8	36.4	21.0	24.7	. . .	80.2
February	25.0	22.8	30.3	18.6	36.5	11.2	46.3	37.4	21.2	25.5	. . .	81.4
March	25.4	23.1	30.3	18.9	36.3	11.3	46.5	38.4	21.4	26.1	. . .	82.5
April	25.9	23.6	30.7	19.1	36.9	11.6	46.8	39.5	21.4	26.8	. . .	84.0
May	26.3	24.0	30.9	19.4	36.9	12.0	47.2	39.8	21.5	27.5	. . .	84.9
June	26.4	24.0	30.7	19.6	36.6	12.3	47.3	39.6	21.7	27.4	. . .	84.8
July	25.7	23.5	31.1	20.0	37.0	12.3	47.5	38.1	21.9	25.7	. . .	83.0
August	24.9	22.6	31.2	19.4	37.4	12.2	47.3	35.7	21.9	23.8	. . .	79.5
September	24.8	22.6	31.1	18.8	37.6	12.1	47.5	35.3	22.0	23.7	. . .	79.0
October	24.6	22.4	30.9	19.3	37.1	12.0	47.4	35.4	21.9	23.5	. . .	78.2
November	24.8	22.5	30.3	16.9	37.6	11.8	47.4	36.6	21.9	24.4	. . .	78.5
December	26.3	24.1	31.3	19.1	37.8	12.0	47.8	39.5	22.1	27.1	. . .	83.6
1960												
January	27.0	24.7	32.2	21.1	37.9	12.5	48.1	39.2	22.4	27.8	. . .	85.6
February	26.8	24.5	31.9	20.8	37.6	12.5	48.4	38.8	22.4	27.5	. . .	84.6
March	26.5	24.2	31.9	20.4	37.9	12.6	48.6	37.6	22.3	27.0	. . .	83.2
April	26.3	24.0	32.1	20.4	38.3	12.4	48.3	37.6	22.7	26.4	. . .	82.3
May	26.3	23.9	32.3	20.6	38.4	12.5	48.9	37.2	22.8	26.2	. . .	81.5
June	26.0	23.6	32.1	20.4	38.2	12.3	47.6	36.5	22.6	25.7	. . .	80.2
July	25.9	23.6	31.8	19.6	38.3	12.2	48.8	36.9	22.6	25.8	. . .	79.7
August	25.8	23.5	31.9	19.8	38.3	12.0	49.0	36.0	22.4	25.6	. . .	79.1
September	25.6	23.2	31.7	19.6	38.2	11.9	48.9	35.6	22.3	25.2	. . .	77.9
October	25.5	23.2	32.1	19.8	38.5	11.8	48.4	35.7	22.4	25.1	. . .	77.5
November	25.2	22.7	31.5	19.1	38.2	11.8	48.6	35.3	22.4	24.5	. . .	75.8
December	24.7	22.4	31.3	18.5	38.1	11.5	47.9	34.9	22.0	23.8	. . .	74.3
1961												
January	24.7	22.4	31.0	17.8	38.2	11.6	48.4	34.5	22.3	24.0	. . .	74.1
February	24.7	22.3	31.2	17.7	38.5	11.5	48.0	34.5	22.4	23.8	. . .	73.5
March	24.9	22.4	31.2	17.7	38.5	11.5	47.9	35.3	22.6	24.0	. . .	73.9
April	25.4	23.0	31.9	19.0	38.8	11.6	48.1	36.2	22.7	24.8	. . .	75.4
May	25.8	23.3	32.3	19.6	39.1	11.6	48.1	36.3	22.8	25.5	. . .	76.4
June	26.1	23.7	32.6	20.3	39.3	11.7	48.1	37.1	23.0	25.9	. . .	77.3
July	26.4	24.0	32.9	20.6	39.5	11.8	48.4	37.7	23.2	26.3	. . .	78.1
August	26.7	24.3	33.2	20.7	39.8	11.8	48.6	38.1	23.4	26.8	. . .	79.0
September	26.6	24.1	32.6	19.5	39.6	12.0	49.7	38.4	23.3	26.8	. . .	78.2
October	27.1	24.6	33.5	20.6	40.3	12.0	50.8	38.7	23.6	27.3	. . .	79.6
November	27.6	25.0	34.1	21.5	40.7	12.3	52.0	38.4	23.8	27.7	. . .	80.8
December	27.8	25.4	34.2	21.9	40.7	12.3	52.9	38.7	24.0	28.1	. . .	81.6
1962												
January	27.6	25.0	33.9	21.4	40.5	12.3	53.5	36.9	24.0	27.9	. . .	80.2
February	28.0	25.5	34.1	21.5	40.7	12.5	54.5	39.1	24.3	28.3	. . .	81.4
March	28.2	25.7	34.4	21.9	41.0	12.6	55.2	39.5	24.2	28.3	. . .	81.9
April	28.2	25.7	34.7	22.4	41.1	12.7	55.7	39.0	24.2	28.3	. . .	81.7
May	28.2	25.7	34.9	22.6	41.3	12.7	56.1	39.0	24.6	27.9	. . .	81.3
June	28.1	25.6	34.6	22.2	41.2	12.8	56.6	39.3	24.5	27.8	. . .	80.9
July	28.4	25.8	35.2	22.6	41.7	12.9	57.7	39.1	24.5	28.1	. . .	81.5
August	28.4	25.9	34.8	22.3	41.3	13.1	58.5	39.8	24.6	28.1	. . .	81.4
September	28.6	26.1	35.0	22.6	41.6	13.1	58.6	40.2	24.9	28.4	. . .	81.8
October	28.6	26.0	35.0	22.7	41.4	13.1	58.8	39.6	24.9	28.4	. . .	81.4
November	28.8	26.3	35.2	22.7	41.6	13.1	59.4	39.8	25.0	28.6	. . .	81.8
December	28.8	26.3	35.3	22.9	41.8	13.0	59.7	40.1	24.9	28.5	. . .	81.7
1963												
January	29.0	26.4	35.8	23.1	42.3	13.0	62.5	39.1	25.1	28.6	. . .	81.9
February	29.3	26.7	36.2	23.4	42.8	13.2	62.0	39.2	25.3	29.0	. . .	82.4
March	29.5	26.8	36.3	23.4	43.0	13.1	61.7	39.6	25.1	29.4	. . .	82.6
April	29.8	27.2	36.5	23.6	43.2	13.2	61.6	41.0	25.9	29.7	. . .	83.5
May	30.1	27.4	36.5	24.0	43.0	13.2	61.6	41.9	26.1	30.4	. . .	84.0
June	30.2	27.5	36.8	24.4	43.1	13.2	61.5	41.7	26.0	30.5	. . .	83.9
July	30.1	27.4	36.7	24.4	42.9	13.4	60.9	41.6	26.2	30.2	. . .	83.3
August	30.1	27.5	36.9	24.5	43.4	13.7	61.2	41.7	26.3	29.9	. . .	83.5
September	30.4	27.7	37.1	24.9	43.3	13.7	61.4	41.4	26.6	30.5	. . .	83.8
October	30.7	28.0	37.3	24.9	43.6	13.9	61.4	42.0	26.8	30.7	. . .	84.3
November	30.8	28.1	37.3	25.2	43.6	14.0	61.2	42.5	27.1	30.9	. . .	84.3
December	30.7	28.1	37.6	25.2	43.9	14.0	61.4	41.9	26.9	30.7	. . .	84.0

. . . = Not available.

Table 20-1. Industrial Production and Capacity Utilization—*Continued*

(Seasonally adjusted; 2002 = 100, except as noted.)

Year and month	Total industry	Manufac- turing (SIC)	Consumer goods Total	Durable	Nondurable	Business equipment	Defense and space equipment	Construction supplies	Business supplies	Materials	Capacity Total industry	Manufac- turing (SIC)
1964												
January	31.0	28.3	37.9	25.3	44.4	14.4	60.7	42.1	27.2	31.0	. . .	84.5
February	31.2	28.5	37.9	25.4	44.2	14.3	60.2	43.3	27.3	31.4	. . .	84.7
March	31.2	28.5	37.7	25.2	44.1	14.5	60.1	43.4	27.5	31.4	. . .	84.4
April	31.7	29.0	38.6	25.9	45.1	14.8	59.9	43.5	27.9	31.8	. . .	85.6
May	31.9	29.1	38.9	26.1	45.5	15.0	58.9	43.7	28.1	32.1	. . .	85.6
June	32.0	29.2	38.9	26.3	45.2	15.0	58.5	43.5	28.2	32.3	. . .	85.4
July	32.2	29.4	39.4	26.8	45.8	15.2	58.4	44.3	28.2	32.3	. . .	85.9
August	32.4	29.6	39.3	27.0	45.5	15.2	58.7	43.8	28.1	33.0	. . .	86.1
September	32.6	29.7	38.9	26.3	45.3	15.4	59.1	43.5	28.1	33.5	. . .	86.2
October	32.1	29.3	38.1	23.6	45.9	15.2	59.5	43.7	28.1	32.9	. . .	84.6
November	33.1	30.2	39.6	26.8	46.0	15.8	60.1	44.7	28.4	33.9	. . .	86.8
December	33.5	30.7	40.4	28.4	46.3	16.0	60.6	44.1	28.6	34.3	. . .	88.0
1965												
January	33.8	31.1	40.9	28.9	46.9	16.0	61.2	44.4	28.9	34.7	. . .	88.6
February	34.1	31.3	41.1	29.3	46.8	16.3	61.9	45.6	29.0	34.8	. . .	88.7
March	34.5	31.7	41.4	30.1	46.9	16.5	63.0	46.0	29.3	35.4	. . .	89.3
April	34.7	31.8	41.3	30.0	46.7	16.6	63.8	45.3	29.3	35.7	. . .	89.3
May	34.9	32.1	41.6	30.2	47.0	16.9	65.2	45.8	29.6	35.9	. . .	89.4
June	35.2	32.3	41.7	30.5	47.1	17.1	66.0	45.8	29.8	36.3	. . .	89.5
July	35.5	32.8	41.7	30.7	46.9	17.4	67.0	47.1	29.8	36.6	. . .	90.3
August	35.7	32.8	41.6	30.4	47.1	17.4	67.6	46.6	30.0	37.0	. . .	89.9
September	35.8	32.9	42.3	31.0	47.7	17.8	67.7	46.2	30.1	36.7	. . .	89.6
October	36.1	33.2	42.5	31.2	47.8	18.0	68.6	46.9	30.4	37.1	. . .	89.8
November	36.3	33.3	42.7	31.5	48.1	18.3	69.2	47.6	30.6	36.9	. . .	89.6
December	36.7	33.8	43.0	32.1	48.0	18.7	69.8	48.6	31.1	37.4	. . .	90.5
1966												
January	37.1	34.1	43.2	32.2	48.3	19.1	71.3	48.5	31.0	37.9	. . .	90.9
February	37.3	34.4	43.3	32.2	48.6	19.1	72.4	48.1	31.4	38.3	. . .	90.9
March	37.8	34.8	43.6	32.4	48.9	19.4	73.0	49.0	31.7	39.0	. . .	91.6
April	37.9	35.0	43.8	33.0	48.8	19.6	74.6	49.0	31.4	38.9	. . .	91.5
May	38.3	35.3	43.8	32.5	49.1	19.8	75.9	49.3	31.9	39.3	. . .	91.6
June	38.4	35.4	44.0	32.5	49.4	20.0	77.0	48.6	32.3	39.6	. . .	91.5
July	38.7	35.6	43.9	31.9	49.7	20.4	78.1	49.0	32.6	39.7	. . .	91.4
August	38.7	35.7	43.7	31.4	49.8	20.4	79.1	47.6	32.5	40.0	. . .	91.1
September	39.0	36.0	43.9	31.6	49.9	20.7	80.2	47.6	32.7	40.4	. . .	91.2
October	39.3	36.3	44.8	33.2	50.3	20.6	81.4	47.6	32.7	40.6	. . .	91.6
November	39.0	35.9	44.6	32.2	50.6	20.3	82.9	47.7	32.8	40.0	. . .	90.1
December	39.1	36.1	44.5	31.8	50.6	20.6	83.7	47.6	32.9	40.0	. . .	90.0
1967												
January	39.3	36.2	44.9	31.1	51.8	20.4	85.2	48.9	33.5	39.8	89.4	89.8
February	38.9	35.8	44.3	30.2	51.4	20.5	86.2	48.4	33.3	39.1	88.0	88.4
March	38.7	35.6	44.4	30.5	51.4	20.4	87.1	48.5	33.3	38.3	87.1	87.5
April	39.0	35.8	45.2	30.7	52.5	20.4	87.9	48.4	33.6	38.7	87.5	87.7
May	38.7	35.6	44.3	30.3	51.4	20.5	88.5	49.1	33.1	38.3	86.4	86.6
June	38.7	35.5	44.4	29.9	51.8	20.4	88.3	49.4	33.3	38.2	86.0	86.1
July	38.6	35.4	44.4	30.3	51.4	20.0	88.8	49.6	33.4	38.2	85.4	85.3
August	39.3	36.1	44.8	30.7	51.9	20.3	89.0	50.1	34.3	39.3	86.6	86.5
September	39.3	36.1	44.9	30.6	52.1	20.2	89.3	50.6	34.4	39.1	86.1	86.1
October	39.6	36.4	45.5	31.2	52.7	20.1	90.0	50.3	34.6	39.6	86.4	86.4
November	40.1	37.0	46.5	32.9	53.1	20.6	90.1	50.6	34.7	40.0	87.3	87.5
December	40.6	37.4	47.2	34.2	53.5	20.8	90.1	50.6	34.6	40.5	87.8	88.0
1968												
January	40.5	37.3	46.6	33.2	53.1	20.9	89.7	50.9	34.8	40.7	87.4	87.4
February	40.7	37.5	46.8	33.7	53.2	20.9	90.8	51.4	35.0	40.7	87.4	87.4
March	40.8	37.5	47.1	33.7	53.7	21.1	89.0	51.5	35.1	40.9	87.3	87.2
April	40.9	37.6	47.0	33.7	53.6	21.0	87.2	51.8	35.4	41.2	87.1	86.9
May	41.3	38.0	47.3	34.1	53.7	21.3	88.4	52.0	35.7	41.8	87.7	87.6
June	41.5	38.1	47.6	34.5	54.0	21.3	88.9	52.1	35.9	42.0	87.7	87.4
July	41.4	38.0	47.5	34.2	54.0	21.0	88.9	52.1	35.8	42.0	87.2	86.8
August	41.5	38.2	48.0	34.6	54.6	21.2	89.1	52.3	36.2	41.7	87.1	86.8
September	41.7	38.2	48.2	35.0	54.6	21.5	89.1	51.9	36.4	41.9	87.1	86.5
October	41.8	38.5	48.5	35.4	54.8	21.6	86.7	51.9	36.6	41.9	86.9	86.7
November	42.3	39.0	49.2	36.2	55.3	21.7	87.6	53.1	37.0	42.6	87.7	87.5
December	42.4	39.0	48.9	36.6	54.6	21.9	87.1	54.1	37.2	42.8	87.7	87.2
1969												
January	42.7	39.2	49.1	36.5	55.1	22.2	87.3	54.5	37.3	43.0	87.9	87.3
February	43.0	39.6	49.5	36.5	55.7	22.2	86.7	55.0	37.2	43.5	88.1	87.7
March	43.3	39.9	49.9	36.7	56.1	22.4	87.0	55.2	38.4	43.7	88.5	88.0
April	43.2	39.7	49.2	35.7	55.6	22.6	86.3	54.7	37.9	43.8	87.9	87.3
May	43.0	39.5	48.8	35.2	55.3	22.5	86.1	54.3	38.2	43.7	87.2	86.7
June	43.4	39.8	49.3	36.4	55.4	22.7	84.9	54.6	38.5	44.3	87.8	86.8
July	43.6	40.1	50.2	36.4	56.8	22.9	84.6	54.1	38.3	44.3	87.9	87.2
August	43.7	40.1	50.1	36.8	56.4	22.9	83.4	54.0	38.5	44.8	87.8	86.9
September	43.7	40.1	49.7	36.4	56.0	23.1	82.9	54.1	38.4	44.9	87.5	86.5
October	43.7	40.1	49.8	36.6	55.9	23.1	82.1	54.2	38.5	44.9	87.2	86.3
November	43.3	39.7	49.3	35.1	56.2	22.6	80.6	53.9	38.3	44.6	86.1	85.1
December	43.2	39.5	49.4	34.9	56.5	22.5	79.6	53.6	38.7	44.4	85.5	84.3

. . . = Not available.

Table 20-1. Industrial Production and Capacity Utilization—*Continued*

(Seasonally adjusted; 2002 = 100, except as noted.)

Year and month	Total industry	Manufac-turing (SIC)	Market groups								Capacity utilization (output as percentage of capacity)	
			Consumer goods			Business equipment	Defense and space equipment	Construction supplies	Business supplies	Materials	Total industry	Manufac-turing (SIC)
			Total	Durable	Nondurable							
1970												
January	42.4	38.6	48.6	33.1	56.4	22.2	78.5	51.9	38.7	43.4	83.7	82.2
February	42.4	38.6	49.0	33.6	56.8	22.3	77.2	51.8	38.4	43.1	83.4	82.0
March	42.3	38.5	49.0	33.9	56.5	22.4	75.5	52.2	38.6	43.0	83.0	81.5
April	42.2	38.4	49.2	33.9	56.8	22.3	73.8	52.7	38.4	42.7	82.5	80.9
May	42.2	38.3	49.5	33.9	57.2	22.3	72.2	52.8	38.3	42.6	82.2	80.5
June	42.0	38.2	49.6	34.6	57.0	22.2	71.0	52.6	38.3	42.4	81.7	80.0
July	42.1	38.3	49.7	34.6	57.2	22.1	69.8	53.2	38.4	42.6	81.6	80.0
August	42.1	38.1	48.9	33.6	56.5	22.1	69.2	52.9	38.1	43.1	81.2	79.2
September	41.8	37.7	48.7	32.7	56.8	21.6	68.5	52.8	38.4	42.8	80.4	78.3
October	40.9	36.9	48.1	30.7	57.1	20.9	67.6	52.3	38.2	41.7	78.6	76.3
November	40.7	36.7	47.7	30.8	56.6	20.8	67.1	51.6	38.3	41.4	77.9	75.6
December	41.6	37.6	49.8	34.4	57.5	21.0	66.3	52.2	38.3	42.4	79.4	77.4
1971												
January	41.9	37.9	50.5	35.8	57.8	20.6	66.8	52.3	38.5	43.0	79.8	77.8
February	41.9	38.0	50.5	36.6	57.2	20.7	65.2	52.6	38.9	42.7	79.4	77.7
March	41.8	37.9	50.7	36.6	57.4	20.5	64.7	52.4	38.6	42.8	79.1	77.3
April	42.1	38.1	51.1	36.9	57.9	20.4	64.7	52.9	39.0	43.1	79.4	77.5
May	42.3	38.3	51.1	37.4	57.6	20.2	65.5	53.1	39.0	43.6	79.6	77.8
June	42.4	38.4	51.5	37.7	58.0	20.3	64.5	53.7	38.9	43.8	79.7	77.8
July	42.3	38.5	52.3	38.4	58.8	20.4	64.0	54.2	39.9	42.7	79.3	77.8
August	42.1	38.0	51.7	38.1	58.1	20.7	64.0	53.3	39.4	42.5	78.6	76.7
September	42.8	38.8	52.2	38.0	58.9	21.1	63.4	55.2	40.0	43.3	79.7	78.0
October	43.1	39.4	52.9	38.7	59.6	21.4	63.0	56.0	40.3	43.4	80.1	79.0
November	43.3	39.5	53.3	39.1	60.1	21.5	62.5	56.2	40.7	43.5	80.3	79.1
December	43.8	39.9	53.7	39.2	60.5	21.6	61.5	57.2	40.9	44.4	81.0	79.6
1972												
January	44.8	40.9	54.5	40.4	61.1	22.3	61.3	58.7	41.6	45.8	82.7	81.4
February	45.2	41.2	54.8	40.6	61.4	22.6	61.6	58.9	42.3	46.2	83.3	81.8
March	45.6	41.5	54.8	40.3	61.7	22.9	62.1	59.4	42.8	46.7	83.7	82.2
April	46.0	42.0	55.4	41.5	61.9	23.3	62.4	60.0	42.8	47.1	84.3	82.9
May	46.0	42.1	55.2	41.1	61.7	23.3	61.9	60.3	43.0	47.2	84.1	82.8
June	46.2	42.2	55.2	41.1	61.7	23.4	61.9	60.9	43.4	47.3	84.2	82.9
July	46.2	42.3	55.6	42.0	61.8	23.5	61.9	61.7	43.4	47.0	83.9	82.7
August	46.8	42.8	56.2	42.4	62.6	23.9	61.9	62.2	44.0	47.7	84.8	83.6
September	47.1	43.1	56.5	42.8	62.7	24.1	62.2	62.7	43.9	48.2	85.2	83.9
October	47.7	43.7	57.3	43.8	63.4	24.5	62.4	63.6	44.7	48.7	86.0	84.9
November	48.3	44.3	57.8	44.8	63.4	24.9	64.1	64.1	44.8	49.4	86.8	85.7
December	48.8	44.9	58.2	45.7	63.5	25.2	65.2	63.9	44.9	50.2	87.5	86.6
1973												
January	49.2	45.2	58.1	45.5	63.4	25.8	66.0	64.7	45.3	50.6	87.8	86.9
February	49.9	46.0	58.8	46.4	64.0	26.3	67.6	65.9	45.7	51.4	88.8	88.1
March	49.9	46.0	59.0	46.4	64.3	26.4	67.2	66.3	45.8	51.2	88.5	87.9
April	49.8	45.9	58.4	45.7	63.8	26.6	66.7	66.0	45.7	51.3	88.1	87.4
May	50.2	46.2	58.8	45.6	64.5	26.9	67.1	66.4	46.0	51.6	88.4	87.7
June	50.2	46.2	58.4	45.5	63.9	27.2	67.7	66.5	46.1	51.7	88.1	87.4
July	50.4	46.4	58.3	45.5	63.7	27.6	69.2	67.0	46.3	51.9	88.2	87.5
August	50.3	46.3	57.7	44.1	63.8	27.6	69.2	67.1	46.3	52.0	87.8	87.0
September	50.8	46.7	58.7	45.6	64.3	28.1	69.2	67.0	46.4	52.2	88.2	87.4
October	51.1	47.1	58.9	45.3	64.9	28.5	70.7	66.9	46.9	52.6	88.6	87.9
November	51.4	47.5	59.1	45.3	65.2	28.7	70.1	67.4	46.9	52.9	88.7	88.3
December	51.3	47.5	58.0	44.3	64.0	28.9	69.6	68.0	46.5	53.2	88.3	88.1
1974												
January	50.9	47.1	57.2	42.1	64.3	28.9	69.2	68.1	46.5	52.8	87.4	87.1
February	50.7	46.9	57.0	41.9	64.1	28.6	70.1	67.3	46.3	52.7	86.8	86.4
March	50.7	46.9	57.1	42.0	64.2	29.0	69.9	67.4	46.4	52.5	86.6	86.1
April	50.6	46.7	56.9	41.7	64.1	28.7	69.7	66.8	46.4	52.5	86.2	85.6
May	51.0	47.0	57.4	41.8	64.8	29.1	70.1	67.1	46.7	52.7	86.6	85.9
June	50.9	47.1	57.7	42.4	64.9	29.1	69.2	66.8	46.9	52.5	86.3	85.7
July	50.9	47.0	57.5	42.2	64.8	29.1	70.0	65.5	46.5	52.8	86.1	85.3
August	50.4	46.6	57.5	42.2	64.7	29.1	71.4	64.7	46.3	51.8	85.1	84.5
September	50.5	46.7	57.0	42.1	64.0	29.6	71.6	64.3	46.1	52.0	85.0	84.4
October	50.3	46.3	57.1	41.6	64.4	29.6	72.6	63.2	45.9	51.7	84.5	83.5
November	48.7	44.9	55.4	39.6	63.1	29.3	72.2	61.1	44.9	49.5	81.6	80.9
December	46.9	42.9	53.7	36.3	62.5	28.0	71.6	58.3	44.0	47.6	78.6	77.1
1975												
January	46.3	42.1	52.5	34.8	61.5	27.5	72.1	58.1	43.3	47.2	77.4	75.4
February	45.2	40.9	51.7	33.8	61.0	26.6	68.4	56.2	42.4	46.0	75.4	73.1
March	44.8	40.3	51.9	34.3	61.0	26.1	69.0	54.1	41.8	45.3	74.5	72.0
April	44.8	40.3	53.0	35.5	61.8	25.8	68.5	53.6	41.9	45.0	74.4	71.7
May	44.7	40.3	53.2	36.5	61.6	25.6	71.7	53.7	41.7	44.8	74.1	71.6
June	45.0	40.6	54.0	36.9	62.7	25.3	72.8	53.4	41.9	45.1	74.5	72.1
July	45.5	41.2	55.4	38.7	63.6	25.5	71.8	54.2	42.3	45.3	75.1	73.0
August	45.9	41.6	55.7	39.3	63.8	25.3	71.2	54.7	42.7	46.1	75.7	73.6
September	46.5	42.3	56.5	40.1	64.5	25.7	73.3	55.4	42.8	46.7	76.5	74.6
October	46.7	42.5	56.6	39.9	64.7	25.7	73.2	55.7	43.0	46.9	76.6	74.8
November	46.8	42.6	56.8	40.0	65.1	25.7	70.2	56.0	43.1	47.1	76.7	74.9
December	47.4	43.2	57.3	40.7	65.4	26.1	72.2	56.0	43.6	47.8	77.5	75.7

Table 20-1. Industrial Production and Capacity Utilization—*Continued*

(Seasonally adjusted; 2002 = 100, except as noted.)

Year and month	Total industry	Manufac-turing (SIC)	Market groups								Capacity utilization (output as percentage of capacity)	
			Consumer goods			Business equipment	Defense and space equipment	Construction supplies	Business supplies	Materials	Total industry	Manufac-turing (SIC)
			Total	Durable	Nondurable							
1976												
January	48.1	43.8	58.1	41.4	66.2	26.4	72.3	57.5	44.0	48.6	78.5	76.6
February	48.5	44.4	58.2	41.8	66.1	26.6	72.2	58.3	44.2	49.3	79.0	77.5
March	48.6	44.5	58.1	41.8	65.9	26.7	72.2	57.4	44.4	49.5	78.9	77.5
April	48.9	44.8	58.2	41.8	66.2	27.0	70.8	58.2	44.6	49.8	79.3	77.9
May	49.1	45.0	58.7	41.9	66.9	27.3	70.1	58.9	44.8	49.9	79.5	78.1
June	49.1	45.0	58.5	41.7	66.7	27.3	69.3	59.3	44.5	50.0	79.3	77.9
July	49.3	45.3	58.9	41.9	67.1	27.5	67.5	60.6	45.2	50.1	79.6	78.3
August	49.7	45.6	59.0	42.5	66.9	28.0	67.6	59.9	45.3	50.6	80.0	78.7
September	49.8	45.7	59.0	42.2	67.1	27.9	67.3	60.3	46.2	50.7	80.0	78.6
October	49.8	45.7	59.5	42.7	67.6	28.0	67.1	60.3	46.5	50.5	79.9	78.5
November	50.6	46.3	60.6	44.1	68.4	28.9	66.8	60.6	46.7	51.1	80.9	79.3
December	51.1	46.8	61.2	45.2	68.7	29.4	65.4	60.9	47.2	51.6	81.5	79.9
1977												
January	50.8	46.7	61.0	45.1	68.5	29.5	64.5	60.0	47.0	51.2	80.9	79.5
February	51.6	47.5	61.8	45.6	69.4	30.2	64.3	61.3	47.6	52.0	82.0	80.8
March	52.2	48.2	61.8	46.9	68.6	30.6	63.0	62.7	47.9	53.0	82.8	81.7
April	52.7	48.7	62.2	47.2	69.0	31.0	63.4	64.2	48.5	53.5	83.3	82.4
May	53.1	49.1	62.3	47.4	68.9	31.5	63.3	65.1	49.0	53.9	83.8	82.8
June	53.5	49.5	62.7	48.3	69.1	32.1	63.2	65.6	49.4	54.1	84.1	83.2
July	53.6	49.5	62.8	48.3	69.3	32.5	63.0	65.6	49.5	54.1	84.1	83.0
August	53.7	49.8	62.9	48.3	69.4	32.7	62.5	66.1	49.8	54.0	83.9	83.3
September	53.9	49.9	63.0	48.6	69.4	33.0	62.6	65.9	50.0	54.4	84.1	83.1
October	54.1	50.0	63.6	48.6	70.3	32.9	57.0	65.9	50.0	54.6	84.1	83.1
November	54.1	50.0	63.5	48.5	70.3	32.8	56.5	66.2	50.0	54.7	83.8	82.9
December	54.1	50.6	64.1	48.7	71.0	33.4	60.2	66.8	50.4	54.1	83.7	83.5
1978												
January	53.4	49.9	62.5	46.2	70.1	32.9	61.0	65.5	50.3	53.6	82.3	82.1
February	53.7	50.0	63.5	47.3	71.0	33.5	57.9	65.4	50.4	53.5	82.5	82.1
March	54.7	50.9	64.8	48.8	72.0	34.3	63.1	66.5	51.1	54.3	83.7	83.2
April	55.8	51.7	65.3	49.7	72.3	34.9	62.7	68.1	51.3	56.0	85.2	84.2
May	56.0	51.9	64.8	49.0	71.9	35.2	63.0	68.0	51.6	56.5	85.3	84.3
June	56.4	52.3	65.2	49.3	72.4	35.8	63.7	68.6	52.0	56.8	85.7	84.8
July	56.4	52.3	64.9	49.4	71.8	36.2	63.6	68.6	52.0	56.8	85.4	84.5
August	56.6	52.5	64.8	49.2	71.9	36.8	64.4	68.7	52.0	56.9	85.5	84.6
September	56.8	52.8	64.9	48.9	72.2	37.0	64.6	69.0	52.1	57.0	85.5	84.7
October	57.2	53.2	64.9	49.0	72.1	37.7	64.0	69.6	52.4	57.7	85.9	85.1
November	57.6	53.6	65.1	49.2	72.3	38.4	63.7	70.1	52.7	58.1	86.3	85.6
December	58.0	54.1	65.2	49.3	72.4	38.9	64.6	71.3	53.1	58.4	86.6	86.1
1979												
January	57.6	53.6	65.0	49.7	71.9	39.3	64.7	69.5	53.1	57.6	85.8	85.0
February	57.9	53.9	64.6	49.1	71.6	39.9	66.1	70.0	53.6	58.1	86.1	85.2
March	58.1	54.1	64.9	49.0	72.1	40.1	65.5	70.8	53.8	58.2	86.1	85.3
April	57.5	53.3	63.7	46.6	71.8	39.3	63.9	69.6	53.5	57.8	85.0	83.8
May	57.9	53.9	64.1	47.9	71.5	40.4	65.1	70.0	53.7	58.1	85.5	84.6
June	57.9	54.0	63.8	47.4	71.5	40.6	65.7	70.3	53.4	58.2	85.3	84.5
July	57.8	54.0	63.3	46.7	71.0	41.0	66.9	70.3	53.5	58.0	84.9	84.4
August	57.4	53.3	62.6	44.7	71.2	40.4	67.7	69.5	53.7	57.6	84.1	83.1
September	57.5	53.5	63.0	46.3	70.8	41.6	68.4	69.7	53.0	57.3	84.1	83.1
October	57.8	53.7	63.1	46.0	71.2	41.1	70.4	70.2	53.6	57.8	84.4	83.2
November	57.8	53.5	62.9	45.2	71.4	41.2	72.0	70.0	53.8	57.7	84.1	82.8
December	57.8	53.7	62.9	44.9	71.6	41.4	73.7	70.3	53.8	57.6	84.0	82.8
1980												
January	58.0	53.9	62.6	44.1	71.7	42.0	74.7	70.1	53.4	58.1	84.2	83.0
February	58.1	53.9	62.9	43.9	72.3	42.3	77.9	69.1	53.5	58.0	84.1	82.8
March	57.9	53.5	62.5	43.1	72.1	42.0	78.6	68.2	53.4	57.9	83.7	82.0
April	56.8	52.4	61.5	41.3	71.7	41.6	79.2	65.0	52.5	56.5	81.9	80.1
May	55.3	50.8	60.2	38.6	71.2	40.9	79.4	62.4	51.4	54.8	79.7	77.5
June	54.6	50.0	59.9	38.1	71.2	40.3	80.1	61.1	50.8	53.9	78.5	76.1
July	54.3	49.5	60.0	38.0	71.3	40.4	80.8	60.7	51.0	53.0	77.8	75.1
August	54.5	49.9	60.2	38.3	71.5	40.4	81.0	61.5	51.3	53.2	77.9	75.5
September	55.3	50.7	60.8	40.2	71.2	41.1	81.2	63.1	52.0	54.2	79.0	76.5
October	56.1	51.6	61.2	40.9	71.5	41.9	82.5	64.4	52.1	55.0	79.8	77.7
November	57.0	52.6	61.6	41.9	71.3	42.6	83.5	65.8	52.7	56.3	81.0	78.9
December	57.3	52.7	61.5	41.3	71.6	42.7	83.6	65.8	53.2	56.9	81.3	78.9
1981												
January	57.0	52.6	61.5	41.1	71.8	42.9	83.0	65.6	53.4	56.2	80.7	78.4
February	56.7	52.3	61.3	40.9	71.6	42.4	82.6	64.9	52.8	56.0	80.1	77.8
March	57.1	52.5	61.3	41.5	71.2	42.9	82.8	65.1	52.8	56.3	80.3	77.8
April	56.7	52.6	61.5	42.0	71.2	42.9	83.0	65.2	53.1	55.5	79.7	77.9
May	57.1	52.9	62.2	42.7	71.8	43.0	83.9	65.1	53.8	55.9	80.0	78.1
June	57.4	52.7	61.7	42.4	71.3	42.8	84.7	64.1	54.0	56.6	80.2	77.6
July	57.8	52.8	62.1	42.6	71.8	43.0	86.0	64.2	54.3	57.0	80.6	77.5
August	57.8	52.9	62.2	42.3	72.1	43.1	87.2	64.1	54.0	57.0	80.4	77.5
September	57.4	52.6	61.6	41.3	71.7	43.0	89.0	63.7	54.0	56.6	79.7	76.9
October	57.0	52.1	61.9	41.1	72.5	42.9	91.0	61.7	53.6	55.8	79.0	76.0
November	56.4	51.5	61.9	40.3	72.8	42.4	93.3	60.8	53.4	54.8	77.9	74.9
December	55.8	50.7	61.3	38.6	73.0	41.7	95.9	59.7	53.3	54.1	76.9	73.5

Table 20-1. Industrial Production and Capacity Utilization—*Continued*

(Seasonally adjusted; 2002 = 100, except as noted.)

Year and month	Total industry	Manufac-turing (SIC)	Consumer goods Total	Consumer goods Durable	Consumer goods Nondurable	Business equipment	Defense and space equipment	Construction supplies	Business supplies	Materials	Capacity utilization Total industry	Capacity utilization Manufac-turing (SIC)
1982												
January	54.7	49.5	60.3	37.6	72.1	40.0	95.5	57.8	52.6	53.2	75.2	71.6
February	55.8	50.8	61.9	39.0	73.7	41.4	100.7	59.7	53.6	53.8	76.5	73.4
March	55.4	50.4	61.5	38.8	73.1	40.8	102.1	58.5	53.4	53.4	75.8	72.7
April	54.9	50.1	61.4	39.6	72.6	40.4	103.0	58.1	53.2	52.7	75.0	72.0
May	54.5	50.0	61.5	39.6	72.7	40.1	104.5	58.4	52.8	52.1	74.4	71.7
June	54.3	49.8	61.8	39.9	73.0	39.3	104.4	57.8	52.8	51.9	73.9	71.4
July	54.1	49.8	61.9	40.1	73.0	39.1	105.8	57.7	52.8	51.5	73.6	71.2
August	53.6	49.3	61.8	39.6	73.2	38.2	105.5	57.7	52.8	51.0	72.8	70.5
September	53.4	49.2	61.7	39.0	73.4	37.9	106.7	57.8	52.9	50.7	72.5	70.1
October	53.0	48.7	61.8	38.5	74.0	37.2	106.1	57.0	52.7	50.2	71.8	69.3
November	52.8	48.4	61.7	38.5	73.7	37.1	106.6	56.7	52.7	49.9	71.5	68.8
December	52.4	48.2	60.9	38.4	72.4	37.7	105.5	56.2	52.4	49.5	70.9	68.6
1983												
January	53.4	49.4	62.2	40.1	73.4	37.7	4.8	58.3	53.1	50.6	72.2	70.2
February	53.1	49.3	61.4	40.0	72.3	37.5	103.0	58.0	53.0	50.5	71.8	70.1
March	53.6	49.8	61.7	40.6	72.4	37.9	103.3	58.8	53.9	50.9	72.3	70.7
April	54.2	50.4	62.9	41.4	73.8	37.9	102.6	59.6	54.5	51.5	73.2	71.5
May	54.6	51.0	63.2	42.3	73.7	38.3	102.6	60.7	54.5	52.0	73.7	72.4
June	54.9	51.4	63.4	43.0	73.6	38.5	102.1	61.8	54.8	52.3	74.1	72.8
July	55.7	52.1	64.3	44.0	74.4	39.2	103.6	63.1	55.5	53.2	75.2	73.9
August	56.4	52.6	64.9	44.8	74.8	39.6	104.4	63.3	56.1	53.9	76.0	74.4
September	57.2	53.5	65.7	45.6	75.6	40.7	105.6	64.1	57.1	54.6	77.1	75.8
October	57.7	54.2	65.3	46.2	74.7	41.3	106.8	65.1	57.3	55.4	77.7	76.6
November	57.9	54.3	65.3	46.1	74.7	41.5	107.5	64.9	57.5	55.7	77.9	76.8
December	58.1	54.5	65.4	47.2	74.2	41.9	108.4	65.0	57.6	55.9	78.2	76.9
1984												
January	59.3	55.5	66.7	48.3	75.6	42.9	11.7	65.5	58.7	57.0	79.7	78.2
February	59.6	56.1	66.6	48.5	75.2	43.3	114.2	67.1	58.9	57.4	80.0	79.0
March	59.9	56.4	66.9	48.6	75.6	43.7	114.6	66.6	59.4	57.6	80.2	79.2
April	60.3	56.6	67.0	48.5	75.9	44.1	117.3	67.0	59.4	58.0	80.6	79.5
May	60.6	56.8	66.8	48.1	75.8	44.3	118.2	67.2	60.2	58.4	80.8	79.5
June	60.8	57.0	66.7	48.2	75.6	44.9	119.4	67.7	60.6	58.6	81.0	79.7
July	60.9	57.3	66.7	48.7	75.3	45.6	118.1	67.5	60.7	58.7	81.0	79.9
August	61.0	57.4	66.3	49.1	74.5	45.9	121.9	67.7	60.8	58.7	80.9	79.8
September	60.9	57.3	66.2	48.4	74.6	46.4	124.7	68.0	60.8	58.4	80.6	79.4
October	60.8	57.5	66.7	48.0	75.7	46.7	125.5	67.7	61.1	57.9	80.3	79.5
November	61.1	57.7	66.9	48.8	75.6	47.0	124.7	67.6	61.3	58.1	80.4	79.5
December	61.1	57.9	67.3	49.3	75.8	47.3	127.1	68.3	60.9	58.0	80.3	79.6
1985												
January	60.9	57.7	66.8	48.6	75.5	47.1	27.5	67.0	61.0	58.0	79.9	79.0
February	61.2	57.5	67.3	48.2	76.5	46.8	128.9	67.2	61.6	58.2	80.0	78.6
March	61.3	58.0	67.2	48.7	76.1	47.3	130.9	69.0	61.5	58.1	79.9	79.0
April	61.2	57.8	66.9	48.1	75.9	46.8	131.3	69.0	61.8	58.1	79.6	78.5
May	61.2	57.8	66.9	48.1	75.9	46.9	132.2	69.2	62.0	58.1	79.5	78.3
June	61.3	57.9	67.2	48.1	76.4	47.0	134.2	69.7	61.7	58.0	79.3	78.3
July	60.9	57.6	66.9	48.1	76.0	46.7	133.1	69.3	61.2	57.6	78.7	77.7
August	61.1	57.9	67.2	48.6	76.1	46.7	135.4	69.5	61.8	57.7	78.8	77.9
September	61.4	58.0	67.6	48.5	76.8	46.6	136.4	69.5	62.3	58.0	79.0	77.8
October	61.1	57.8	67.5	48.3	76.8	46.5	137.9	69.6	61.7	57.6	78.5	77.5
November	61.3	58.2	67.9	49.5	76.7	46.9	139.7	69.6	61.9	57.7	78.7	77.8
December	62.0	58.4	68.6	49.6	77.8	46.9	141.0	69.3	62.9	58.5	79.4	78.0
1986												
January	62.3	59.1	69.4	50.9	78.2	46.9	142.1	70.9	63.2	58.6	79.6	78.8
February	61.8	58.7	68.8	50.6	77.4	46.4	139.8	70.1	62.7	58.4	79.0	78.3
March	61.4	58.6	68.5	50.6	77.1	46.4	141.0	70.4	62.4	57.7	78.4	78.0
April	61.5	58.8	68.9	50.5	77.7	46.1	141.2	71.1	62.9	57.6	78.3	78.2
May	61.6	58.9	69.3	50.6	78.2	46.0	141.7	71.5	63.4	57.6	78.4	78.2
June	61.4	58.7	69.4	51.1	78.1	45.5	142.2	70.7	64.0	57.3	78.1	77.9
July	61.7	59.0	69.9	51.8	78.4	45.8	143.3	71.2	63.9	57.7	78.4	78.2
August	61.6	59.2	69.8	52.0	78.2	45.9	143.2	71.9	64.0	57.5	78.2	78.3
September	61.8	59.3	69.8	52.4	78.1	45.9	142.7	71.9	64.2	57.6	78.3	78.4
October	62.0	59.5	70.1	52.4	78.5	45.9	143.3	71.9	64.6	58.0	78.6	78.6
November	62.3	59.8	70.6	53.1	78.9	46.0	144.0	72.1	64.7	58.3	78.8	78.8
December	62.9	60.3	71.3	54.1	79.4	46.5	144.0	72.6	65.5	58.7	79.4	79.4
1987												
January	62.7	60.2	70.6	53.8	78.4	46.6	144.7	73.4	65.1	58.6	79.0	79.0
February	63.5	61.1	71.5	54.6	79.3	47.7	145.2	74.7	65.6	59.3	79.9	79.9
March	63.6	61.1	71.7	54.4	79.8	47.5	144.9	74.3	66.0	59.5	79.9	79.8
April	64.0	61.4	71.6	54.0	79.9	47.9	145.2	74.7	66.7	59.9	80.2	80.0
May	64.4	61.9	72.1	54.4	80.5	48.3	144.8	75.3	67.5	60.3	80.6	80.4
June	64.7	62.1	72.2	53.8	81.0	48.7	144.3	75.5	67.8	60.6	80.8	80.5
July	65.1	62.5	72.7	53.7	81.7	48.9	144.0	75.7	68.2	61.1	81.2	80.8
August	65.6	62.8	73.1	54.2	82.1	49.5	145.6	76.3	68.4	61.5	81.6	81.1
September	65.8	63.2	72.8	54.7	81.3	50.4	146.1	76.6	68.6	61.8	81.7	81.4
October	66.8	64.2	74.1	56.5	82.3	51.5	145.7	77.7	69.1	62.6	82.8	82.5
November	67.1	64.6	74.1	56.5	82.4	52.0	146.5	77.8	69.1	63.2	83.1	82.9
December	67.4	65.0	74.3	56.0	82.8	52.5	147.7	78.4	69.3	63.5	83.4	83.3

Table 20-1. Industrial Production and Capacity Utilization—*Continued*

(Seasonally adjusted; 2002 = 100, except as noted.)

Year and month	Total industry	Manufac-turing (SIC)	Market groups								Capacity utilization (output as percentage of capacity)	
			Consumer goods			Business equipment	Defense and space equipment	Construction supplies	Business supplies	Materials	Total industry	Manufac-turing (SIC)
			Total	Durable	Nondurable							
1988												
January	67.5	64.9	74.6	55.8	83.5	52.5	151.1	77.2	69.6	63.3	83.4	83.0
February	67.7	65.0	75.0	55.8	84.1	52.8	148.6	77.7	70.1	63.5	83.6	83.1
March	67.9	65.2	75.0	56.3	83.7	53.3	147.6	78.1	70.0	63.8	83.8	83.3
April	68.3	65.8	75.4	57.6	83.7	53.9	146.2	77.8	70.1	64.1	84.2	84.0
May	68.2	65.7	75.2	57.7	83.3	54.3	146.1	78.0	69.5	64.2	84.1	83.8
June	68.4	65.8	75.2	57.9	83.2	54.8	144.9	77.5	69.8	64.4	84.2	83.9
July	68.5	65.9	75.1	56.5	83.9	54.5	146.3	77.6	70.1	64.6	84.3	84.0
August	68.8	65.9	75.7	57.1	84.5	54.7	146.1	77.1	70.7	64.9	84.7	84.0
September	68.6	66.2	75.2	58.3	83.0	55.2	146.2	77.4	70.2	64.6	84.3	84.2
October	69.0	66.5	75.9	58.8	83.7	55.4	146.5	77.7	70.5	64.9	84.7	84.6
November	69.1	66.7	75.9	59.5	83.5	55.6	146.3	78.1	70.5	65.1	84.8	84.7
December	69.4	67.0	76.3	60.2	83.6	55.7	146.7	78.2	70.7	65.4	85.0	84.9
1989												
January	69.6	67.5	76.3	61.6	82.9	56.3	147.1	79.5	70.7	65.5	85.1	85.4
February	69.3	66.8	76.3	60.9	83.3	56.1	147.4	77.6	71.0	65.0	84.6	84.5
March	69.4	66.8	76.5	60.0	84.1	55.9	146.1	77.7	71.7	65.3	84.7	84.3
April	69.4	66.8	76.3	60.4	83.6	56.5	148.2	77.7	71.2	65.2	84.6	84.2
May	68.9	66.3	75.6	59.1	83.1	55.4	148.9	77.0	70.8	65.0	83.8	83.3
June	69.0	66.4	75.6	58.3	83.6	56.2	148.6	77.2	71.1	64.7	83.7	83.3
July	68.3	65.7	74.0	56.5	82.2	55.8	149.2	77.2	70.5	64.4	82.8	82.2
August	69.0	66.3	75.2	58.6	82.9	56.8	150.2	77.2	70.9	64.7	83.3	82.7
September	68.8	66.1	74.9	58.5	82.5	56.8	149.1	77.0	71.1	64.5	83.0	82.3
October	68.7	66.0	75.1	57.5	83.4	55.9	143.9	77.3	71.1	64.6	82.7	82.0
November	68.9	66.1	75.4	57.9	83.6	56.3	141.8	77.3	71.5	64.8	82.8	82.0
December	69.4	66.2	76.7	58.5	85.2	57.2	145.0	76.4	71.9	64.7	83.1	81.9
1990												
January	69.0	66.1	75.0	55.2	84.4	57.2	145.4	78.1	72.4	64.5	82.5	81.6
February	69.6	67.1	75.9	58.8	83.9	57.9	145.4	78.5	72.3	65.2	83.1	82.6
March	70.0	67.4	76.5	59.9	84.2	58.6	144.3	78.3	72.8	65.3	83.3	82.8
April	69.9	67.2	76.2	58.6	84.4	58.5	143.5	77.5	72.8	65.4	83.0	82.4
May	70.0	67.3	76.1	59.0	84.1	58.9	142.2	77.0	73.1	65.5	83.0	82.3
June	70.2	67.4	76.9	59.8	84.8	58.9	141.6	77.3	73.0	65.6	83.1	82.3
July	70.1	67.3	76.3	58.2	84.8	59.0	142.6	76.6	73.2	65.6	82.8	82.0
August	70.2	67.5	76.4	57.9	85.0	59.1	140.7	76.6	73.1	66.0	82.9	82.0
September	70.4	67.5	77.2	58.3	86.0	59.1	139.8	76.3	73.2	65.9	82.9	81.8
October	69.9	66.9	76.0	56.4	85.2	58.9	140.6	75.4	73.1	65.6	82.2	81.0
November	69.0	66.2	75.1	53.3	85.5	57.6	138.2	75.4	72.7	64.8	81.0	80.0
December	68.6	65.7	74.6	52.5	85.2	57.1	139.7	74.9	72.3	64.3	80.3	79.2
1991												
January	68.2	65.1	75.0	52.6	85.6	56.8	137.9	72.1	72.0	63.8	79.9	78.5
February	67.8	64.8	74.3	51.4	85.2	56.6	136.9	71.9	71.4	63.5	79.2	77.9
March	67.5	64.3	74.4	51.6	85.2	56.7	135.9	71.0	70.5	63.0	78.7	77.2
April	67.6	64.5	74.3	52.7	84.6	56.7	132.4	71.5	71.0	63.3	78.8	77.4
May	68.3	65.0	75.6	53.7	86.1	57.1	129.6	71.6	71.6	63.8	79.5	77.8
June	68.9	65.7	76.7	55.1	87.0	57.8	130.4	72.9	72.2	64.3	80.1	78.5
July	68.9	65.9	76.3	56.0	85.9	57.7	129.1	72.6	71.6	64.8	80.0	78.6
August	69.0	66.0	76.3	55.2	86.3	57.6	129.9	73.4	72.1	64.8	80.0	78.7
September	69.6	66.7	77.5	57.5	86.9	58.4	129.3	73.8	72.5	65.1	80.6	79.4
October	69.5	66.6	77.2	57.2	86.6	57.9	129.8	73.0	72.2	65.2	80.4	79.2
November	69.4	66.4	77.3	57.3	86.7	57.9	128.7	73.6	72.4	65.0	80.2	78.9
December	69.1	66.4	76.3	56.9	85.5	57.9	127.9	73.7	72.3	65.0	79.8	78.7
1992												
January	68.7	65.9	75.5	54.4	85.6	56.7	126.2	73.9	72.2	65.0	79.1	78.0
February	69.2	66.6	76.3	56.7	85.6	58.1	125.4	74.4	72.2	65.3	79.6	78.6
March	69.8	67.2	77.1	58.0	86.0	58.5	124.9	74.8	72.7	65.8	80.1	79.2
April	70.3	67.5	77.8	59.1	86.5	59.1	122.8	75.4	73.2	66.2	80.5	79.4
May	70.6	68.0	78.3	61.0	86.3	59.7	122.0	76.1	73.4	66.3	80.6	79.7
June	70.6	68.2	77.9	60.2	86.1	59.9	121.9	75.7	73.4	66.6	80.5	79.8
July	71.2	68.7	78.9	61.9	86.8	60.3	120.5	76.1	73.8	67.0	81.0	80.2
August	70.8	68.4	79.0	61.3	87.2	60.0	120.4	76.4	73.7	66.3	80.4	79.7
September	71.0	68.5	78.6	61.0	86.7	60.3	120.3	76.2	73.9	66.8	80.5	79.6
October	71.5	68.9	79.6	62.2	87.7	60.7	119.9	76.4	74.2	67.1	80.9	79.9
November	71.8	69.2	79.8	62.7	87.7	61.1	119.7	76.2	74.4	67.5	81.1	80.0
December	71.8	69.0	79.9	63.4	87.5	61.3	119.7	76.4	74.7	67.3	80.9	79.7
1993												
January	72.2	69.8	80.2	64.4	87.5	62.0	119.0	76.8	74.8	67.7	81.2	80.4
February	72.4	69.9	80.3	64.1	87.8	61.6	118.0	77.9	75.2	68.1	81.4	80.3
March	72.4	69.8	80.4	64.6	87.7	61.9	116.7	77.3	75.8	68.0	81.3	80.1
April	72.6	70.1	80.5	64.9	87.7	62.4	116.9	77.7	75.8	68.2	81.4	80.4
May	72.3	70.0	79.9	65.0	86.7	62.1	115.6	78.6	75.5	68.0	81.0	80.2
June	72.5	69.9	80.1	64.4	87.2	61.7	114.8	78.5	75.5	68.4	81.1	80.0
July	72.8	70.2	80.8	64.4	88.4	61.8	115.8	79.0	75.7	68.4	81.3	80.1
August	72.8	70.1	80.8	63.7	88.6	61.4	113.9	79.3	75.8	68.5	81.2	79.9
September	73.1	70.5	81.0	65.1	88.3	62.2	114.2	79.7	76.1	68.8	81.4	80.3
October	73.6	71.1	81.4	66.8	88.1	63.3	113.5	80.4	76.2	69.4	81.9	80.8
November	73.9	71.4	81.5	67.4	87.9	63.6	113.2	81.1	76.3	69.8	82.1	81.0
December	74.3	71.8	81.7	67.8	88.1	63.9	111.9	82.0	76.7	70.3	82.3	81.2

Table 20-1. Industrial Production and Capacity Utilization—*Continued*

(Seasonally adjusted; 2002 = 100, except as noted.)

Year and month	Total industry	Manufac- turing (SIC)	Market groups								Capacity utilization (output as percentage of capacity)	
			Consumer goods			Business equipment	Defense and space equipment	Construction supplies	Business supplies	Materials	Total industry	Manufac- turing (SIC)
			Total	Durable	Nondurable							
1994												
January	74.6	71.9	82.4	69.0	88.5	64.3	110.9	81.7	77.3	70.4	82.5	81.2
February	74.6	72.0	82.6	68.9	88.8	63.6	109.1	81.1	77.3	70.7	82.3	81.1
March	75.4	73.0	83.2	69.7	89.4	64.4	110.4	82.6	77.9	71.5	83.0	82.0
April	75.8	73.6	83.3	70.4	89.2	64.8	110.6	83.9	78.1	71.9	83.2	82.4
May	76.2	74.1	83.9	70.8	89.9	65.0	109.0	84.5	78.3	72.5	83.4	82.7
June	76.7	74.3	84.6	71.5	90.6	65.5	107.6	84.6	79.0	72.9	83.7	82.7
July	76.9	74.6	84.3	71.6	90.0	66.2	107.0	85.5	78.8	73.3	83.6	82.7
August	77.3	75.1	85.2	73.0	90.7	66.2	105.8	85.4	78.8	73.7	83.7	83.0
September	77.4	75.4	84.7	73.1	89.9	66.7	106.7	86.2	79.2	74.0	83.6	83.0
October	78.1	76.1	85.5	73.9	90.8	67.7	106.7	86.6	79.8	74.5	84.1	83.5
November	78.6	76.7	85.5	73.7	90.8	68.4	108.0	86.7	80.1	75.3	84.3	83.8
December	79.4	77.6	86.2	74.6	91.4	69.0	108.1	87.6	80.6	76.3	84.9	84.5
1995												
January	79.7	77.8	86.2	75.3	91.2	69.7	108.2	87.6	80.9	76.6	84.9	84.4
February	79.7	77.8	86.5	75.1	91.6	69.9	107.0	86.6	81.0	76.5	84.6	84.0
March	79.8	77.9	86.5	75.1	91.6	70.3	107.1	86.5	81.2	76.6	84.4	83.9
April	79.7	77.8	86.1	74.8	91.2	70.4	106.6	86.0	81.2	76.7	84.1	83.5
May	79.9	77.9	86.3	74.1	91.9	70.6	106.3	85.4	81.6	76.9	84.0	83.2
June	80.1	78.2	86.8	74.6	92.3	71.2	106.7	85.6	81.8	76.9	83.9	83.2
July	79.9	77.7	86.3	73.0	92.3	71.2	105.6	85.5	81.8	76.6	83.3	82.4
August	80.9	78.7	87.7	75.5	93.2	72.8	105.5	86.2	82.8	77.5	84.2	83.0
September	81.3	79.4	87.7	76.3	92.9	73.7	104.4	87.6	82.8	77.8	84.2	83.4
October	81.1	79.3	87.0	75.4	92.3	73.3	103.1	87.4	83.0	78.0	83.7	82.9
November	81.3	79.3	87.3	75.5	92.7	73.4	100.7	87.5	83.3	78.2	83.6	82.5
December	81.7	79.7	87.6	76.1	92.8	74.4	100.7	88.0	83.3	78.5	83.6	82.5
1996												
January	81.1	79.0	86.5	74.0	92.2	73.8	99.1	86.3	82.9	78.4	82.6	81.4
February	82.4	80.3	88.1	76.3	93.4	75.7	102.3	87.6	83.9	79.5	83.6	82.3
March	82.3	80.2	87.4	73.7	93.7	75.6	102.4	88.6	84.0	79.5	83.1	81.7
April	83.0	81.0	88.4	77.5	93.2	76.5	102.1	89.1	83.9	80.1	83.4	82.1
May	83.5	81.5	88.5	77.9	93.2	77.3	102.2	90.0	84.7	80.7	83.5	82.2
June	84.2	82.4	89.3	79.8	93.6	78.3	101.7	91.5	85.0	81.4	83.9	82.6
July	84.2	82.6	88.7	80.3	92.4	79.2	102.3	91.0	85.0	81.4	83.4	82.4
August	84.7	83.1	88.5	79.5	92.5	80.0	102.6	91.9	85.8	82.1	83.5	82.5
September	85.1	83.7	89.3	79.6	93.6	80.6	103.0	92.2	86.3	82.4	83.6	82.6
October	85.2	83.6	88.8	78.1	93.6	80.5	102.6	92.4	86.5	82.7	83.2	82.1
November	85.9	84.3	89.9	79.2	94.6	81.7	102.1	93.1	87.2	83.1	83.5	82.3
December	86.4	85.0	90.1	80.4	94.4	83.3	102.2	92.7	87.7	83.7	83.7	82.5
1997												
January	86.5	85.1	89.8	80.0	94.2	83.5	100.6	91.8	88.2	84.0	83.3	82.1
February	87.6	86.3	90.3	81.2	94.3	85.2	101.0	93.5	89.1	85.2	83.9	82.8
March	88.3	87.3	91.0	82.3	94.9	86.8	100.5	94.5	89.4	85.7	84.2	83.3
April	88.3	87.1	90.0	79.8	94.5	87.3	100.6	94.2	89.8	86.2	83.8	82.6
May	88.9	87.9	90.6	80.8	94.9	88.5	100.2	94.8	90.3	86.6	83.9	82.9
June	89.3	88.5	90.7	82.6	94.2	89.9	100.2	94.6	90.7	87.1	83.8	82.9
July	89.8	88.8	90.8	80.8	95.3	90.1	100.3	94.7	91.3	87.8	83.8	82.7
August	91.0	90.4	92.3	84.7	95.7	92.7	100.6	95.3	91.6	88.9	84.4	83.5
September	91.9	91.2	93.2	85.9	96.3	93.2	100.7	95.8	92.7	89.8	84.7	83.7
October	92.5	91.7	94.4	86.2	98.0	94.2	101.1	96.3	93.6	89.9	84.7	83.6
November	93.3	92.7	94.7	88.5	97.4	96.0	100.6	96.7	94.0	91.0	85.0	83.9
December	93.7	93.2	94.3	88.3	96.9	96.6	102.4	97.9	94.4	91.6	84.7	83.7
1998												
January	94.1	93.9	94.7	88.7	97.3	97.9	103.1	98.6	94.3	92.0	84.6	83.8
February	94.2	93.9	94.5	88.4	97.1	98.0	103.8	99.0	94.5	92.0	84.1	83.2
March	94.2	93.8	94.7	88.8	97.2	98.2	103.2	98.4	95.1	91.9	83.6	82.5
April	94.6	94.4	95.3	89.2	97.9	98.5	103.3	98.8	95.4	92.3	83.5	82.4
May	95.3	94.9	95.7	89.7	98.2	100.0	104.3	100.0	96.2	92.9	83.6	82.3
June	94.8	94.3	94.5	85.2	98.5	100.4	104.5	99.7	96.3	92.3	82.6	81.2
July	94.4	93.8	93.4	81.3	98.7	99.6	105.8	100.2	96.9	92.0	81.8	80.3
August	96.3	96.1	96.6	92.1	98.6	102.2	106.4	100.6	97.6	93.6	83.1	81.8
September	96.1	95.8	95.7	91.5	97.6	102.0	105.4	100.2	97.5	93.7	82.4	81.0
October	96.7	96.6	96.2	93.4	97.4	103.1	107.6	101.4	97.8	94.3	82.6	81.3
November	96.6	96.8	95.5	93.0	96.7	103.1	107.2	101.5	98.1	94.5	82.1	81.0
December	97.0	97.3	95.4	93.6	96.2	103.5	106.3	102.7	98.1	95.2	82.0	81.0
1999												
January	97.5	97.7	96.5	93.8	97.7	103.8	106.1	102.2	98.8	95.5	82.1	80.9
February	97.9	98.4	96.7	94.3	97.7	104.6	106.9	102.1	99.0	96.0	82.1	81.1
March	98.1	98.3	96.5	93.9	97.7	104.4	106.2	101.2	99.4	96.7	81.9	80.6
April	98.3	98.6	96.4	94.9	97.0	104.8	105.3	101.5	99.6	97.1	81.7	80.5
May	99.0	99.5	97.4	95.8	98.0	106.1	103.9	101.8	100.2	97.7	82.0	80.9
June	98.8	99.2	96.4	95.2	96.9	105.7	102.7	101.8	100.1	98.1	81.5	80.3
July	99.5	99.6	95.9	95.1	96.2	106.9	102.4	102.6	100.9	99.4	81.8	80.3
August	100.0	100.4	97.3	97.5	97.2	107.4	102.3	102.5	101.0	99.5	81.9	80.5
September	99.7	100.1	96.6	96.2	96.7	107.1	99.3	102.6	101.0	99.3	81.3	79.9
October	101.0	101.7	98.4	99.1	98.1	108.2	99.1	103.9	102.0	100.6	82.1	80.8
November	101.6	102.4	98.3	98.4	98.3	108.3	97.0	104.5	102.6	101.8	82.2	81.0
December	102.4	103.1	99.3	98.4	99.7	109.4	95.2	105.5	103.3	102.5	82.6	81.3

Table 20-1. Industrial Production and Capacity Utilization—*Continued*

(Seasonally adjusted; 2002 = 100, except as noted.)

Year and month	Total industry	Manufac-turing (SIC)	Market groups								Capacity utilization (output as percentage of capacity)	
			Consumer goods			Business equipment	Defense and space equipment	Construction supplies	Business supplies	Materials	Total industry	Manufac-turing (SIC)
			Total	Durable	Nondurable							
2000												
January	102.4	103.3	98.2	100.5	97.3	110.3	95.3	106.0	103.8	103.0	82.3	81.0
February	102.9	103.6	98.8	100.2	98.3	111.3	93.0	106.3	104.0	103.3	82.4	80.9
March	103.3	104.3	98.5	99.9	98.0	112.7	92.1	106.4	104.7	103.9	82.4	81.1
April	103.9	104.9	99.4	101.2	98.8	114.0	90.4	106.7	105.8	104.3	82.6	81.3
May	104.1	104.8	99.6	100.9	99.1	114.7	89.5	105.1	106.0	104.6	82.5	80.8
June	104.3	105.0	99.7	100.6	99.4	114.9	90.3	104.7	105.8	104.8	82.3	80.7
July	104.0	105.0	98.9	97.9	99.4	116.1	92.0	105.3	105.9	104.3	81.8	80.3
August	103.8	104.5	98.8	98.8	98.9	115.7	90.0	104.6	105.7	104.1	81.4	79.6
September	104.3	104.9	99.9	99.8	100.0	116.9	85.9	104.7	105.5	104.4	81.5	79.6
October	103.9	104.5	98.8	98.1	99.1	117.1	90.2	104.3	105.2	104.1	80.9	79.0
November	103.9	104.2	99.2	96.1	100.4	116.8	93.1	104.0	105.4	103.8	80.7	78.5
December	103.5	103.5	99.6	94.5	101.6	115.8	93.8	102.5	105.1	103.1	80.1	77.7
2001												
January	102.7	102.8	98.8	93.0	101.1	115.5	96.7	102.7	104.7	101.8	79.3	76.9
February	102.1	102.2	98.2	92.8	100.2	114.9	96.6	101.7	103.4	101.5	78.6	76.2
March	101.8	101.9	98.1	95.2	99.3	114.1	99.0	101.9	102.7	101.0	78.1	75.7
April	101.5	101.6	98.6	95.2	99.8	111.8	100.0	101.5	102.1	100.7	77.7	75.3
May	100.8	100.8	98.4	96.1	99.4	109.7	100.0	101.0	101.3	99.8	76.9	74.5
June	100.1	100.1	98.3	95.4	99.4	108.6	101.2	100.3	100.7	98.9	76.2	73.8
July	99.7	99.8	98.0	96.2	98.7	107.6	102.3	100.3	100.6	98.3	75.7	73.4
August	99.3	99.1	97.9	94.8	99.1	105.5	101.0	99.1	100.2	98.3	75.2	72.7
September	99.0	98.8	97.4	94.0	98.7	104.1	101.7	99.1	100.1	98.2	74.7	72.3
October	98.4	98.1	97.6	92.7	99.5	102.2	101.3	97.9	99.3	97.6	74.1	71.7
November	97.9	97.9	97.7	94.6	98.9	101.4	100.4	97.8	98.4	96.9	73.6	71.4
December	97.9	98.1	98.1	96.6	98.8	100.6	100.1	98.6	98.5	96.6	73.5	71.5
2002												
January	98.4	98.5	99.2	96.8	100.2	100.3	99.1	98.3	98.2	97.3	73.7	71.7
February	98.4	98.5	98.7	97.1	99.3	100.3	98.6	98.9	98.1	97.8	73.6	71.7
March	99.2	99.2	99.6	97.8	100.3	100.8	98.4	100.2	99.1	98.5	74.1	72.1
April	99.5	99.2	99.4	99.2	99.5	99.5	98.1	100.1	99.6	99.5	74.2	72.1
May	100.0	99.9	99.7	99.5	99.7	100.1	98.3	100.6	100.1	100.1	74.5	72.5
June	100.9	100.9	100.8	100.8	100.9	100.8	99.2	101.3	100.5	101.0	75.2	73.3
July	100.6	100.5	100.5	101.1	100.2	100.0	99.1	99.7	100.5	101.0	74.9	73.0
August	100.6	100.8	100.2	101.2	99.8	100.4	99.5	100.2	100.5	101.2	75.0	73.2
September	100.7	100.9	100.6	101.2	100.3	100.0	101.2	100.7	100.8	101.0	75.0	73.3
October	100.4	100.4	100.2	100.4	100.1	99.5	102.0	100.3	101.2	100.6	74.9	72.9
November	100.9	100.8	101.1	103.2	100.2	99.6	101.1	100.3	100.8	101.1	75.2	73.2
December	100.4	100.3	100.0	101.5	99.4	98.7	105.4	99.5	100.5	100.9	74.9	72.9
2003												
January	101.1	100.9	100.9	103.6	99.8	98.7	105.8	99.8	102.3	101.5	75.5	73.3
February	101.4	101.1	101.8	102.0	101.7	99.2	106.9	99.3	102.1	101.6	75.8	73.5
March	101.3	101.3	101.8	102.1	101.7	99.7	106.8	99.1	102.4	101.1	75.7	73.7
April	100.5	100.4	100.8	101.1	100.6	98.6	106.4	97.9	100.9	100.6	75.1	73.0
May	100.5	100.5	100.5	100.9	100.4	98.7	107.2	99.2	101.4	100.5	75.2	73.1
June	100.6	101.0	100.7	101.9	100.2	99.2	107.3	99.6	100.9	100.6	75.3	73.5
July	101.0	101.1	101.5	103.9	100.5	99.2	106.8	99.2	101.6	100.8	75.6	73.6
August	100.9	100.8	101.1	102.6	100.4	100.0	107.0	99.9	101.4	100.7	75.6	73.4
September	101.5	101.6	102.0	106.1	100.4	100.8	107.6	99.6	101.3	101.4	76.0	74.0
October	101.6	101.7	101.4	104.7	100.0	100.6	107.5	100.2	101.6	101.9	76.1	74.1
November	102.5	102.8	102.2	106.0	100.7	102.5	106.5	101.5	102.6	102.6	76.8	74.9
December	102.4	102.5	102.3	105.9	100.8	102.0	104.0	101.2	102.2	102.7	76.7	74.8
2004												
January	102.7	102.6	102.8	107.4	101.0	102.8	101.4	101.2	102.6	102.9	77.0	74.8
February	103.3	103.3	103.2	106.9	101.8	104.0	102.6	101.1	103.5	103.3	77.4	75.4
March	102.7	103.0	101.9	105.5	100.6	103.6	103.0	101.1	102.5	103.1	76.9	75.2
April	103.1	103.5	102.5	105.5	101.4	103.8	103.3	101.1	103.3	103.6	77.3	75.6
May	103.9	104.2	103.1	104.8	102.4	104.6	103.8	102.1	104.1	104.4	77.9	76.1
June	103.0	103.4	101.5	102.5	101.1	104.5	102.8	101.4	103.4	103.7	77.2	75.5
July	103.7	104.3	101.6	102.8	101.0	106.5	104.5	102.6	104.0	104.5	77.7	76.2
August	103.9	104.9	102.4	104.5	101.6	106.0	105.0	102.7	104.0	104.6	77.9	76.6
September	103.9	104.7	102.2	103.3	101.7	106.2	106.7	101.6	103.7	104.7	77.9	76.5
October	104.8	105.8	103.3	105.7	102.4	107.1	106.7	103.2	104.4	105.6	78.7	77.2
November	105.1	105.7	103.2	104.4	102.8	106.7	107.6	103.0	104.8	106.2	78.8	77.2
December	105.8	106.4	104.0	105.1	103.5	107.6	109.0	102.6	105.9	106.9	79.4	77.6
2005												
January	106.3	107.2	104.5	104.5	104.4	109.2	109.5	103.7	106.6	106.9	79.7	78.1
February	107.0	108.0	105.1	107.4	104.2	110.4	113.2	104.7	106.4	107.7	80.2	78.7
March	106.9	107.6	104.5	104.8	104.3	110.2	115.4	103.9	106.6	107.8	80.1	78.3
April	106.8	107.7	104.2	103.8	104.2	110.9	117.5	105.6	106.9	107.5	80.0	78.3
May	107.1	108.2	105.0	104.1	105.2	111.9	117.0	105.8	107.0	107.4	80.2	78.5
June	107.5	108.4	105.8	104.6	106.1	112.2	117.7	104.7	107.5	107.6	80.4	78.6
July	107.5	108.3	105.5	103.4	106.0	112.7	116.9	105.7	107.1	107.6	80.3	78.4
August	107.7	108.7	105.7	105.4	105.7	113.2	118.8	106.0	107.3	107.6	80.4	78.6
September	105.8	107.6	106.0	107.5	105.4	109.9	114.4	107.6	107.3	103.8	78.9	77.7
October	107.0	109.3	106.0	108.1	105.2	115.8	115.9	110.0	107.8	104.8	79.7	78.8
November	108.2	110.2	105.8	106.4	105.5	117.6	116.5	110.6	108.1	107.1	80.5	79.4
December	108.9	110.3	106.5	104.5	107.0	117.5	116.8	110.8	108.6	108.1	80.9	79.4

Table 20-1. Industrial Production and Capacity Utilization—*Continued*

(Seasonally adjusted; 2002 = 100, except as noted.)

Year and month	Total industry	Manufac-turing (SIC)	Consumer goods Total	Consumer goods Durable	Consumer goods Nondurable	Business equipment	Defense and space equipment	Construction supplies	Business supplies	Materials	Capacity utilization Total industry	Capacity utilization Manufac-turing (SIC)
2006												
January	108.9	111.1	105.3	106.2	104.9	119.0	115.1	111.5	108.4	108.8	80.9	79.8
February	108.9	110.8	105.1	105.5	104.9	119.3	115.2	111.0	108.1	108.9	80.8	79.5
March	109.1	110.6	105.9	105.8	105.8	119.9	112.6	110.8	108.4	108.7	80.8	79.3
April	109.5	111.2	105.7	105.4	105.7	122.1	112.9	110.3	108.7	109.2	81.0	79.6
May	109.4	110.9	105.6	104.7	105.7	122.0	112.0	109.4	108.5	109.3	80.8	79.3
June	109.9	111.3	106.1	105.2	106.2	123.1	112.0	108.9	108.7	109.8	81.1	79.5
July	110.1	111.3	105.4	102.4	106.2	125.2	113.4	109.5	108.9	110.2	81.1	79.5
August	110.3	111.7	106.2	104.4	106.7	125.4	112.4	108.5	108.7	110.3	81.2	79.6
September	110.0	111.5	105.9	103.6	106.5	125.2	112.7	107.9	108.1	110.0	80.8	79.4
October	109.8	110.9	106.0	101.8	107.2	125.2	113.4	106.8	108.6	109.5	80.6	78.9
November	109.6	110.8	106.1	102.6	107.1	125.1	113.9	105.8	108.2	109.1	80.3	78.7
December	110.5	112.1	106.5	104.6	107.0	126.8	115.1	107.8	108.9	110.1	80.9	79.5
2007												
January	109.9	111.4	106.1	102.3	107.3	124.4	116.6	106.1	109.2	109.6	80.3	78.8
February	110.8	111.7	107.7	103.9	108.8	124.4	115.8	106.2	110.1	110.4	80.8	78.9
March	110.6	112.2	106.7	104.0	107.4	124.9	112.8	107.5	109.8	110.6	80.6	79.1
April	111.1	112.5	107.1	105.7	107.4	124.8	114.4	107.6	110.1	111.2	80.7	79.2
May	111.1	112.5	106.9	105.4	107.3	124.9	115.9	107.7	109.8	111.5	80.7	79.1
June	111.2	112.9	106.9	106.3	107.0	125.7	117.4	108.1	109.7	111.3	80.6	79.1
July	111.5	113.5	107.1	106.8	107.1	127.3	118.1	108.0	109.5	111.7	80.7	79.4
August	111.6	113.0	107.0	105.5	107.4	126.8	118.5	107.1	109.9	112.1	80.6	78.9
September	112.0	113.4	107.2	104.5	108.0	128.5	120.1	107.0	110.3	112.4	80.7	79.1
October	111.4	112.9	106.1	104.0	106.7	128.1	119.4	106.0	109.8	112.2	80.2	78.6
November	112.1	113.3	106.3	104.2	106.9	128.3	121.1	105.7	110.1	113.3	80.5	78.7
December	112.4	113.7	106.6	104.2	107.3	129.4	121.4	105.6	110.1	113.7	80.6	78.8
2008												
January	112.3	113.4	106.9	102.7	108.2	130.2	122.3	105.0	110.2	113.2	80.5	78.5
February	112.0	112.8	106.7	101.6	108.2	129.8	120.5	104.0	109.9	113.1	80.2	78.0
March	111.6	112.7	105.6	98.7	107.6	130.8	120.7	103.3	109.4	112.9	79.8	77.8
April	111.0	111.7	105.0	96.0	107.7	128.4	120.8	102.1	109.1	112.4	79.2	77.0
May	110.7	111.5	104.7	96.0	107.3	128.4	120.2	102.2	108.3	112.1	78.9	76.7
June	110.4	111.0	104.8	97.1	107.1	128.2	121.9	101.7	107.6	111.7	78.7	76.3
July	110.4	110.8	104.5	97.8	106.6	127.4	120.2	102.4	107.3	111.9	78.6	76.1
August	109.2	109.7	102.7	92.2	105.9	126.2	120.8	101.2	106.6	110.9	77.6	75.3
September	104.8	105.7	101.4	91.5	104.3	117.7	118.9	99.1	104.3	104.3	74.5	72.5
October	106.2	106.0	103.0	89.5	107.0	114.8	120.4	97.8	104.3	106.9	75.4	72.7
November	104.8	103.7	102.1	86.6	106.7	117.8	120.1	93.7	102.8	104.8	74.5	71.1
December	102.5	100.9	100.7	82.7	106.1	121.4	120.0	89.2	100.2	101.1	72.8	69.2

Table 20-2. Summary Consumer and Producer Price Indexes

(Seasonally adjusted.)

Year and month	Consumer Price Index, all urban consumers, 1982–1984 = 100							Producer Price Index, 1982 = 100					
								Finished goods		Intermediate materials, supplies, and components		Crude materials for further processing	
	All items	All items less food and energy	Food	Energy	Apparel	Transportation	Medical care	Total	Less food and energy	Total	Less food and energy	Total	Crude nonfood less energy
1946	19.5	...	19.8	...	34.4	16.7	12.5	...	...	...	...	...	...
1947	22.3	...	24.1	...	39.9	18.5	13.5	26.4	...	23.3	...	31.7	...
1948	24.1	...	26.1	...	42.5	20.6	14.4	28.5	...	25.2	...	34.7	...
1949	23.8	...	25.0	...	40.8	22.1	14.8	27.7	...	24.2	...	30.1	...
1950	24.1	...	25.4	...	40.3	22.7	15.1	28.2	...	25.3	...	32.7	...
1951	26.0	...	28.2	...	43.9	24.1	15.9	30.8	...	28.4	...	37.6	...
1952	26.5	...	28.7	...	43.5	25.7	16.7	30.6	...	27.5	...	34.5	...
1953	26.7	...	28.3	...	43.1	26.5	17.3	30.3	...	27.7	...	31.9	...
1954	26.9	...	28.2	...	43.1	26.1	17.8	30.4	...	27.9	...	31.6	...
1955	26.8	...	27.8	...	42.9	25.8	18.2	30.5	...	28.4	...	30.4	...
1956	27.2	...	28.0	...	43.7	26.2	18.9	31.3	...	29.6	...	30.6	...
1957	28.1	28.9	28.9	21.5	44.5	27.7	19.7	32.5	...	30.3	...	31.2	...
1958	28.9	29.6	30.2	21.5	44.6	28.6	20.6	33.2	...	30.4	...	31.9	...
1959	29.1	30.2	29.7	21.9	45.0	29.8	21.5	33.1	...	30.8	...	31.1	...
1960	29.6	30.6	30.0	22.4	45.7	29.8	22.3	33.4	...	30.8	...	30.4	...
1961	29.9	31.0	30.4	22.5	46.1	30.1	22.9	33.4	...	30.6	...	30.2	...
1962	30.2	31.4	30.6	22.6	46.3	30.8	23.5	33.5	...	30.6	...	30.5	...
1963	30.6	31.8	31.1	22.6	46.9	30.9	24.1	33.4	...	30.7	...	29.9	...
1964	31.0	32.3	31.5	22.5	47.3	31.4	24.6	33.5	...	30.8	...	29.6	...
1947													
January	21.5	...	22.8	...	38.4	17.9	13.2	...	...	...	...	...	...
February	21.6	...	23.1	...	38.8	17.9	13.3	...	...	...	...	...	...
March	22.0	...	23.8	...	39.4	18.1	13.3	...	...	...	...	...	...
April	22.0	...	23.5	...	39.7	18.3	13.4	26.0	...	23.1	...	30.7	...
May	22.0	...	23.4	...	39.8	18.3	13.5	26.1	...	23.0	...	30.4	...
June	22.1	...	23.5	...	40.0	18.4	13.5	26.2	...	23.2	...	30.6	...
July	22.2	...	23.8	...	40.0	18.5	13.5	26.2	...	23.2	...	31.0	...
August	22.4	...	24.1	...	40.1	18.5	13.6	26.3	...	23.3	...	31.6	...
September	22.8	...	24.8	...	40.2	18.7	13.7	26.7	...	23.7	...	32.4	...
October	22.9	...	24.9	...	40.4	18.8	13.8	26.8	...	24.0	...	33.7	...
November	23.1	...	25.2	...	40.6	19.0	13.8	27.1	...	24.3	...	33.9	...
December	23.4	...	25.7	...	41.0	19.1	13.9	27.7	...	24.5	...	35.3	...
1948													
January	23.7	...	26.1	...	41.3	19.6	14.0	28.1	...	25.0	...	36.2	...
February	23.7	...	25.9	...	41.8	19.5	14.0	27.9	...	24.7	...	34.4	...
March	23.5	...	25.3	...	42.0	19.6	14.1	28.0	...	24.8	...	33.5	...
April	23.8	...	26.0	...	42.1	19.9	14.3	28.1	...	25.1	...	34.2	...
May	24.0	...	26.3	...	42.5	19.9	14.3	28.4	...	25.1	...	35.3	...
June	24.2	...	26.5	...	42.4	20.0	14.4	28.6	...	25.4	...	36.2	...
July	24.4	...	26.7	...	42.7	21.0	14.5	28.8	...	25.4	...	36.1	...
August	24.4	...	26.5	...	43.1	21.3	14.6	28.9	...	25.5	...	35.5	...
September	24.4	...	26.3	...	43.1	21.4	14.5	28.8	...	25.5	...	34.9	...
October	24.3	...	26.1	...	43.1	21.5	14.6	28.7	...	25.5	...	33.8	...
November	24.2	...	25.7	...	43.0	21.6	14.7	28.5	...	25.4	...	33.5	...
December	24.0	...	25.5	...	43.0	21.6	14.7	28.5	...	25.2	...	33.0	...
1949													
January	24.0	...	25.4	...	42.2	21.6	14.7	28.3	...	25.2	...	32.0	...
February	23.9	...	25.3	...	41.8	21.8	14.8	28.0	...	24.8	...	30.9	...
March	23.9	...	25.3	...	41.6	21.9	14.8	28.0	...	24.7	...	30.8	...
April	23.9	...	25.3	...	41.3	22.0	14.8	27.9	...	24.5	...	30.2	...
May	23.9	...	25.2	...	41.1	22.2	14.8	27.8	...	24.3	...	30.1	...
June	23.9	...	25.3	...	41.0	22.1	14.8	27.7	...	24.1	...	29.7	...
July	23.7	...	24.8	...	40.8	22.2	14.8	27.5	...	24.1	...	29.2	...
August	23.7	...	24.8	...	40.5	22.3	14.9	27.4	...	23.9	...	29.2	...
September	23.8	...	25.0	...	40.2	22.2	14.9	27.4	...	23.9	...	29.5	...
October	23.7	...	24.8	...	39.9	22.3	14.9	27.3	...	23.8	...	29.5	...
November	23.7	...	24.8	...	39.8	22.3	14.9	27.2	...	23.7	...	29.6	...
December	23.6	...	24.5	...	39.8	22.5	14.9	27.2	...	23.8	...	29.6	...
1950													
January	23.5	...	24.3	...	39.7	22.4	14.9	27.2	...	23.8	...	29.6	...
February	23.6	...	24.7	...	39.7	22.4	15.0	27.2	...	23.9	...	30.5	...
March	23.6	...	24.6	...	39.7	22.4	14.9	27.3	...	24.1	...	30.3	...
April	23.6	...	24.6	...	39.7	22.4	15.0	27.3	...	24.2	...	30.5	...
May	23.8	...	24.8	...	39.7	22.5	15.0	27.5	...	24.6	...	31.6	...
June	23.9	...	25.1	...	39.7	22.5	15.0	27.6	...	24.7	...	32.1	...
July	24.1	...	25.6	...	39.9	22.7	15.1	28.0	...	25.3	...	33.3	...
August	24.2	...	25.8	...	40.1	22.9	15.1	28.6	...	25.6	...	34.0	...
September	24.3	...	25.8	...	40.6	22.9	15.2	28.9	...	26.2	...	34.5	...
October	24.5	...	26.0	...	41.2	22.9	15.3	29.0	...	26.7	...	34.5	...
November	24.6	...	26.1	...	41.5	23.0	15.3	29.4	...	26.9	...	35.4	...
December	25.0	...	26.9	...	41.9	23.2	15.4	30.0	...	27.8	...	36.7	...

. . . = Not available.

Table 20-2. Summary Consumer and Producer Price Indexes—*Continued*

(Seasonally adjusted.)

Year and month	Consumer Price Index, all urban consumers, 1982–1984 = 100							Producer Price Index, 1982 = 100					
								Finished goods		Intermediate materials, supplies, and components		Crude materials for further processing	
	All items	All items less food and energy	Food	Energy	Apparel	Transportation	Medical care	Total	Less food and energy	Total	Less food and energy	Total	Crude nonfood less energy
1951													
January	25.4	...	27.6	...	42.6	23.3	15.4	30.5	...	28.5	...	38.2	...
February	25.8	...	28.5	...	43.3	23.6	15.5	30.8	...	28.7	...	39.6	...
March	25.9	...	28.4	...	43.5	23.8	15.7	30.9	...	28.8	...	39.1	...
April	25.9	...	28.2	...	43.8	23.9	15.7	30.9	...	28.8	...	39.1	...
May	26.0	...	28.3	...	43.9	24.0	15.8	31.1	...	28.8	...	38.4	...
June	25.9	...	28.0	...	43.9	24.1	15.8	31.0	...	28.7	...	38.1	...
July	25.9	...	27.9	...	44.0	24.1	15.8	30.8	...	28.4	...	36.8	...
August	25.9	...	27.8	...	44.0	24.2	15.9	30.7	...	28.0	...	36.2	...
September	26.0	...	27.9	...	44.8	24.4	15.9	30.6	...	28.0	...	35.9	...
October	26.2	...	28.4	...	44.7	24.5	16.0	30.8	...	27.9	...	36.7	...
November	26.3	...	28.6	...	44.4	24.8	16.1	30.9	...	27.9	...	36.4	...
December	26.5	...	28.9	...	44.3	24.9	16.3	30.9	...	27.8	...	36.6	...
1952													
January	26.4	...	28.9	...	43.9	25.0	16.3	30.8	...	27.8	...	35.8	...
February	26.4	...	28.6	...	43.9	25.2	16.4	30.7	...	27.7	...	35.5	...
March	26.4	...	28.5	...	43.7	25.3	16.5	30.9	...	27.6	...	35.0	...
April	26.5	...	28.7	...	43.6	25.5	16.5	30.7	...	27.5	...	34.9	...
May	26.5	...	28.7	...	43.6	25.6	16.5	30.7	...	27.5	...	34.8	...
June	26.5	...	28.6	...	43.5	25.8	16.8	30.7	...	27.6	...	34.6	...
July	26.7	...	28.9	...	43.5	26.0	16.9	30.8	...	27.5	...	34.6	...
August	26.7	...	28.9	...	43.4	25.9	16.9	30.7	...	27.6	...	34.7	...
September	26.6	...	28.7	...	43.3	26.0	16.9	30.6	...	27.6	...	33.8	...
October	26.7	...	28.8	...	43.1	26.1	16.9	30.5	...	27.5	...	33.8	...
November	26.7	...	28.8	...	43.0	26.2	16.9	30.4	...	27.4	...	33.7	...
December	26.7	...	28.6	...	43.0	26.2	17.0	30.2	...	27.3	...	32.9	...
1953													
January	26.6	...	28.4	...	43.0	26.3	17.0	30.3	...	27.4	...	32.5	...
February	26.6	...	28.3	...	43.0	26.2	17.0	30.2	...	27.4	...	32.4	...
March	26.6	...	28.3	...	43.0	26.3	17.0	30.3	...	27.5	...	32.4	...
April	26.7	...	28.1	...	43.1	26.4	17.1	30.2	...	27.5	...	31.6	...
May	26.7	...	28.2	...	43.2	26.4	17.2	30.3	...	27.6	...	31.8	...
June	26.8	...	28.4	...	43.3	26.5	17.3	30.4	...	27.7	...	31.4	...
July	26.8	...	28.2	...	43.3	26.6	17.3	30.5	...	28.0	...	32.3	...
August	26.8	...	28.3	...	43.2	26.7	17.4	30.4	...	27.9	...	31.8	...
September	26.9	...	28.4	...	43.2	26.7	17.5	30.4	...	27.9	...	32.0	...
October	27.0	...	28.4	...	43.2	26.6	17.5	30.4	...	27.9	...	31.4	...
November	26.8	...	28.1	...	43.3	26.3	17.6	30.3	...	27.8	...	31.2	...
December	26.9	...	28.3	...	43.2	26.2	17.6	30.4	...	27.8	...	31.7	...
1954													
January	26.9	...	28.5	...	43.3	26.5	17.6	30.5	...	27.9	...	32.0	...
February	27.0	...	28.5	...	43.2	26.3	17.7	30.4	...	27.9	...	32.0	...
March	26.9	...	28.4	...	43.0	26.3	17.7	30.4	...	27.9	...	32.1	...
April	26.9	...	28.4	...	43.0	26.4	17.8	30.6	...	27.9	...	32.2	...
May	26.9	...	28.4	...	43.1	26.4	17.8	30.6	...	27.9	...	32.1	...
June	26.9	...	28.4	...	43.2	26.4	17.8	30.4	...	27.8	...	31.5	...
July	26.9	...	28.4	...	43.1	26.0	17.8	30.5	...	27.9	...	31.4	...
August	26.8	...	28.3	...	43.0	25.9	17.9	30.4	...	27.9	...	31.3	...
September	26.8	...	28.0	...	42.9	25.9	17.9	30.3	...	27.8	...	31.5	...
October	26.7	...	27.9	...	42.9	25.4	17.9	30.2	...	27.8	...	31.2	...
November	26.8	...	27.9	...	42.9	25.8	18.0	30.3	...	27.9	...	31.4	...
December	26.8	...	27.8	...	42.9	25.8	18.0	30.3	...	27.9	...	30.8	...
1955													
January	26.8	...	27.8	...	42.8	25.9	18.0	30.4	...	27.9	...	31.1	...
February	26.8	...	28.0	...	42.8	25.9	18.1	30.5	...	28.0	...	31.0	...
March	26.8	...	28.0	...	42.7	25.9	18.1	30.3	...	28.0	...	30.7	...
April	26.8	...	28.0	...	42.8	25.6	18.1	30.4	...	28.1	...	31.0	...
May	26.8	...	27.9	...	42.8	25.7	18.2	30.4	...	28.1	...	30.2	...
June	26.7	...	27.7	...	42.8	25.8	18.2	30.5	...	28.2	...	30.7	...
July	26.8	...	27.7	...	42.8	25.7	18.2	30.4	...	28.4	...	30.4	...
August	26.7	...	27.6	...	42.9	25.6	18.3	30.4	...	28.5	...	30.1	...
September	26.8	...	27.8	...	43.0	25.7	18.3	30.5	...	28.8	...	30.4	...
October	26.8	...	27.7	...	43.0	25.8	18.4	30.6	...	28.9	...	30.4	...
November	26.9	...	27.6	...	43.0	26.0	18.5	30.6	...	28.9	...	29.4	...
December	26.9	...	27.6	...	43.1	25.8	18.6	30.7	...	29.0	...	29.5	...
1956													
January	26.8	...	27.5	...	43.2	25.8	18.6	30.7	...	29.1	...	29.4	...
February	26.9	...	27.5	...	43.5	25.8	18.7	30.8	...	29.2	...	29.9	...
March	26.9	...	27.5	...	43.5	25.8	18.7	30.9	...	29.4	...	29.8	...
April	26.9	...	27.6	...	43.6	25.8	18.8	31.0	...	29.5	...	30.3	...
May	27.0	...	27.8	...	43.6	26.0	18.8	31.2	...	29.6	...	30.7	...
June	27.2	...	28.1	...	43.6	26.0	18.8	31.4	...	29.6	...	30.5	...
July	27.3	...	28.4	...	43.8	26.2	18.9	31.3	...	29.4	...	30.5	...
August	27.3	...	28.2	...	43.9	26.3	19.0	31.4	...	29.7	...	31.0	...
September	27.4	...	28.2	...	44.0	26.4	19.1	31.6	...	29.8	...	31.0	...
October	27.5	...	28.3	...	44.0	27.0	19.1	31.8	...	30.0	...	31.0	...
November	27.5	...	28.4	...	44.1	26.9	19.1	31.9	...	30.0	...	31.1	...
December	27.6	...	28.5	...	44.3	27.0	19.2	31.9	...	30.1	...	31.7	...

. . . = Not available.

Table 20-2. Summary Consumer and Producer Price Indexes—*Continued*

(Seasonally adjusted.)

Year and month	Consumer Price Index, all urban consumers, 1982–1984 = 100							Producer Price Index, 1982 = 100					
								Finished goods		Intermediate materials, supplies, and components		Crude materials for further processing	
	All items	All items less food and energy	Food	Energy	Apparel	Transportation	Medical care	Total	Less food and energy	Total	Less food and energy	Total	Crude nonfood less energy
1957													
January	27.7	28.5	28.4	21.3	44.3	27.2	19.3	32.1	. . .	30.3	. . .	31.3	. . .
February	27.8	28.6	28.7	21.4	44.3	27.4	19.3	32.2	. . .	30.3	. . .	31.0	. . .
March	27.9	28.7	28.6	21.5	44.5	27.5	19.4	32.1	. . .	30.3	. . .	30.9	. . .
April	27.9	28.8	28.6	21.6	44.4	27.7	19.5	32.3	. . .	30.2	. . .	30.8	. . .
May	28.0	28.8	28.7	21.6	44.5	27.6	19.6	32.3	. . .	30.2	. . .	30.7	. . .
June	28.1	28.9	28.9	21.6	44.5	27.7	19.7	32.5	. . .	30.3	. . .	31.5	. . .
July	28.2	29.0	29.1	21.5	44.5	27.8	19.7	32.6	. . .	30.3	. . .	32.0	. . .
August	28.3	29.0	29.4	21.4	44.6	27.8	19.8	32.6	. . .	30.4	. . .	32.0	. . .
September	28.3	29.1	29.2	21.4	44.5	27.9	19.8	32.6	. . .	30.4	. . .	31.2	. . .
October	28.3	29.2	29.2	21.4	44.6	27.5	19.9	32.7	. . .	30.3	. . .	31.0	. . .
November	28.4	29.3	29.2	21.5	44.7	28.3	20.0	32.9	. . .	30.4	. . .	31.1	. . .
December	28.5	29.3	29.2	21.5	44.6	28.1	20.1	33.0	. . .	30.4	. . .	31.5	. . .
1958													
January	28.6	29.3	29.8	21.6	44.8	28.1	20.2	33.2	. . .	30.4	. . .	31.4	. . .
February	28.7	29.4	29.9	21.3	44.7	28.2	20.2	33.2	. . .	30.3	. . .	31.9	. . .
March	28.9	29.5	30.5	21.4	44.7	28.3	20.3	33.4	. . .	30.3	. . .	32.3	. . .
April	28.9	29.5	30.6	21.4	44.7	28.3	20.4	33.2	. . .	30.2	. . .	31.8	. . .
May	28.9	29.5	30.5	21.5	44.7	28.4	20.5	33.2	. . .	30.3	. . .	32.4	. . .
June	28.9	29.6	30.3	21.5	44.8	28.4	20.6	33.3	. . .	30.3	. . .	32.0	. . .
July	28.9	29.6	30.2	21.6	44.7	28.7	20.7	33.2	. . .	30.3	. . .	32.1	. . .
August	28.9	29.6	30.1	21.7	44.7	28.8	20.7	33.2	. . .	30.4	. . .	31.9	. . .
September	28.9	29.7	30.0	21.7	44.5	28.9	20.9	33.2	. . .	30.4	. . .	31.6	. . .
October	28.9	29.7	30.0	21.7	44.5	28.9	21.0	33.2	. . .	30.4	. . .	31.9	. . .
November	29.0	29.8	30.0	21.4	44.7	29.1	21.0	33.2	. . .	30.5	. . .	32.1	. . .
December	29.0	29.9	29.9	21.4	44.7	29.2	21.1	33.1	. . .	30.6	. . .	31.6	. . .
1959													
January	29.0	29.9	30.0	21.4	44.8	29.3	21.1	33.1	. . .	30.6	. . .	31.6	. . .
February	29.0	29.9	29.8	21.6	44.7	29.4	21.2	33.2	. . .	30.7	. . .	31.4	. . .
March	29.0	30.0	29.7	21.7	44.7	29.6	21.3	33.2	. . .	30.7	. . .	31.5	. . .
April	29.0	30.0	29.5	21.8	44.8	29.7	21.3	33.2	. . .	30.7	. . .	31.7	. . .
May	29.0	30.1	29.5	21.8	44.9	29.7	21.4	33.3	. . .	30.9	. . .	31.5	. . .
June	29.1	30.2	29.7	21.9	45.0	29.8	21.5	33.2	. . .	30.9	. . .	31.3	. . .
July	29.2	30.2	29.6	21.8	45.1	29.9	21.5	33.1	. . .	30.8	. . .	31.0	. . .
August	29.2	30.2	29.6	21.9	45.2	29.9	21.6	33.0	. . .	30.8	. . .	30.7	. . .
September	29.2	30.3	29.7	21.9	45.3	30.0	21.7	33.4	. . .	30.8	. . .	30.9	. . .
October	29.4	30.4	29.7	22.2	45.3	30.1	21.7	33.1	. . .	30.8	. . .	30.7	. . .
November	29.4	30.4	29.7	22.2	45.3	30.1	21.8	33.0	. . .	30.9	. . .	30.5	. . .
December	29.4	30.5	29.6	22.3	45.3	30.1	21.8	33.0	. . .	30.9	. . .	30.3	. . .
1960													
January	29.4	30.5	29.6	22.3	45.3	30.0	21.9	33.1	. . .	30.8	. . .	30.4	. . .
February	29.4	30.6	29.5	22.2	45.5	30.0	22.0	33.1	. . .	30.9	. . .	30.4	. . .
March	29.4	30.6	29.6	22.3	45.5	29.9	22.1	33.4	. . .	30.9	. . .	30.7	. . .
April	29.5	30.6	30.0	22.4	45.6	29.9	22.2	33.4	. . .	30.8	. . .	30.8	. . .
May	29.6	30.6	30.0	22.3	45.7	29.8	22.2	33.4	. . .	30.8	. . .	30.8	. . .
June	29.6	30.7	30.0	22.4	45.7	29.8	22.2	33.4	. . .	30.9	. . .	30.4	. . .
July	29.6	30.6	29.9	22.5	45.8	29.8	22.3	33.5	. . .	30.8	. . .	30.4	. . .
August	29.6	30.6	30.0	22.5	45.8	29.8	22.3	33.4	. . .	30.8	. . .	29.8	. . .
September	29.6	30.6	30.1	22.6	45.9	29.6	22.4	33.4	. . .	30.8	. . .	30.0	. . .
October	29.8	30.8	30.3	22.5	46.0	29.6	22.4	33.7	. . .	30.8	. . .	30.2	. . .
November	29.8	30.8	30.5	22.7	45.9	29.6	22.5	33.7	. . .	30.7	. . .	30.2	. . .
December	29.8	30.7	30.5	22.6	45.9	29.7	22.6	33.6	. . .	30.7	. . .	30.3	. . .
1961													
January	29.8	30.8	30.5	22.7	46.0	29.7	22.6	33.6	. . .	30.6	. . .	30.4	. . .
February	29.8	30.8	30.5	22.6	46.0	29.8	22.7	33.7	. . .	30.7	. . .	30.5	. . .
March	29.8	30.9	30.5	22.6	46.0	29.8	22.7	33.6	. . .	30.8	. . .	30.3	. . .
April	29.8	30.9	30.4	22.2	45.9	29.8	22.8	33.4	. . .	30.7	. . .	30.2	. . .
May	29.8	30.9	30.3	22.4	46.0	30.0	22.8	33.3	. . .	30.6	. . .	29.9	. . .
June	29.8	31.0	30.2	22.5	46.0	30.1	22.9	33.3	. . .	30.5	. . .	29.5	. . .
July	29.9	31.0	30.3	22.5	46.1	30.3	22.9	33.3	. . .	30.5	. . .	29.7	. . .
August	29.9	31.1	30.3	22.5	46.1	30.4	23.0	33.4	. . .	30.5	. . .	30.5	. . .
September	30.0	31.1	30.3	22.6	46.2	30.5	23.1	33.3	. . .	30.5	. . .	30.3	. . .
October	30.0	31.1	30.3	22.4	46.2	30.5	23.1	33.3	. . .	30.4	. . .	30.3	. . .
November	30.0	31.2	30.3	22.5	46.1	30.4	23.1	33.4	. . .	30.5	. . .	30.2	. . .
December	30.0	31.2	30.3	22.4	46.1	30.3	23.2	33.4	. . .	30.6	. . .	30.6	. . .
1962													
January	30.0	31.2	30.4	22.4	46.0	30.4	23.2	33.5	. . .	30.5	. . .	30.6	. . .
February	30.1	31.2	30.5	22.6	46.1	30.5	23.3	33.6	. . .	30.6	. . .	30.5	. . .
March	30.2	31.3	30.6	22.4	46.2	30.5	23.4	33.5	. . .	30.6	. . .	30.5	. . .
April	30.2	31.3	30.7	22.7	46.2	30.9	23.4	33.5	. . .	30.6	. . .	30.1	. . .
May	30.2	31.4	30.6	22.7	46.2	30.9	23.5	33.4	. . .	30.6	. . .	30.1	. . .
June	30.2	31.4	30.5	22.5	46.3	30.9	23.5	33.4	. . .	30.6	. . .	29.9	. . .
July	30.2	31.4	30.4	22.3	46.4	30.6	23.6	33.4	. . .	30.6	. . .	30.2	. . .
August	30.3	31.5	30.6	22.4	46.2	30.8	23.6	33.5	. . .	30.6	. . .	30.5	. . .
September	30.4	31.5	30.9	22.8	46.6	31.0	23.6	33.8	. . .	30.6	. . .	31.2	. . .
October	30.4	31.5	30.8	22.7	46.7	30.9	23.7	33.6	. . .	30.5	. . .	30.8	. . .
November	30.4	31.5	30.9	22.7	46.5	30.9	23.7	33.6	. . .	30.5	. . .	31.0	. . .
December	30.4	31.6	30.7	22.8	46.4	30.9	23.8	33.5	. . .	30.5	. . .	30.6	. . .

. . . = Not available.

Table 20-2. Summary Consumer and Producer Price Indexes—*Continued*

(Seasonally adjusted.)

Year and month	Consumer Price Index, all urban consumers, 1982–1984 = 100							Producer Price Index, 1982 = 100					
								Finished goods		Intermediate materials, supplies, and components		Crude materials for further processing	
	All items	All items less food and energy	Food	Energy	Apparel	Transportation	Medical care	Total	Less food and energy	Total	Less food and energy	Total	Crude nonfood less energy
1963													
January	30.4	31.5	31.0	22.8	46.6	30.6	23.9	33.4	. . .	30.5	. . .	30.3	. . .
February	30.5	31.6	31.1	22.7	46.7	30.7	23.9	33.4	. . .	30.5	. . .	30.0	. . .
March	30.5	31.7	31.0	22.7	46.7	30.8	23.9	33.3	. . .	30.5	. . .	29.6	. . .
April	30.5	31.7	30.9	22.6	46.8	30.8	23.9	33.3	. . .	30.5	. . .	29.8	. . .
May	30.5	31.7	30.9	22.6	46.7	30.9	24.0	33.4	. . .	30.7	. . .	29.6	. . .
June	30.6	31.8	31.0	22.5	46.8	30.9	24.1	33.5	. . .	30.7	. . .	29.9	. . .
July	30.7	31.8	31.2	22.7	46.9	30.9	24.1	33.4	. . .	30.7	. . .	30.0	. . .
August	30.8	31.9	31.2	22.6	47.0	31.0	24.2	33.4	. . .	30.7	. . .	29.9	. . .
September	30.7	31.9	31.1	22.5	47.0	31.0	24.2	33.4	. . .	30.7	. . .	29.8	. . .
October	30.8	32.0	31.0	22.7	47.1	31.2	24.2	33.5	. . .	30.8	. . .	29.9	. . .
November	30.8	32.0	31.2	22.6	47.2	31.1	24.3	33.5	. . .	30.8	. . .	30.2	. . .
December	30.9	32.1	31.3	22.6	47.2	31.2	24.3	33.4	. . .	30.8	. . .	29.4	. . .
1964													
January	30.9	32.2	31.4	22.8	47.2	31.4	24.4	33.5	. . .	30.8	. . .	29.8	. . .
February	30.9	32.2	31.4	22.2	47.2	31.3	24.4	33.5	. . .	30.8	. . .	29.4	. . .
March	30.9	32.2	31.4	22.6	47.2	31.4	24.4	33.4	. . .	30.8	. . .	29.5	. . .
April	31.0	32.2	31.4	22.5	47.3	31.3	24.5	33.5	. . .	30.8	. . .	29.5	. . .
May	31.0	32.2	31.4	22.5	47.3	31.3	24.5	33.5	. . .	30.7	. . .	29.4	. . .
June	31.0	32.3	31.4	22.6	47.3	31.4	24.6	33.5	. . .	30.6	. . .	29.0	. . .
July	31.0	32.3	31.5	22.5	47.4	31.3	24.6	33.5	. . .	30.7	. . .	29.2	. . .
August	31.0	32.3	31.4	22.6	47.4	31.4	24.7	33.6	. . .	30.6	. . .	29.4	. . .
September	31.1	32.3	31.6	22.5	47.2	31.3	24.7	33.6	. . .	30.7	. . .	30.1	. . .
October	31.1	32.4	31.6	22.5	47.2	31.3	24.7	33.6	. . .	30.8	. . .	29.8	. . .
November	31.2	32.5	31.7	22.5	47.3	31.4	24.8	33.6	. . .	30.8	. . .	29.9	. . .
December	31.2	32.5	31.7	22.6	47.4	31.7	24.8	33.6	. . .	30.9	. . .	29.8	. . .
1965													
January	31.3	32.6	31.6	22.8	47.5	31.9	24.8	33.6	. . .	30.9	. . .	29.5	. . .
February	31.3	32.6	31.5	22.7	47.5	31.8	24.9	33.7	. . .	30.9	. . .	29.9	. . .
March	31.3	32.6	31.7	22.6	47.5	31.8	25.0	33.7	. . .	31.0	. . .	30.0	. . .
April	31.4	32.7	31.8	22.9	47.6	31.9	25.0	34.0	. . .	31.1	. . .	30.4	. . .
May	31.5	32.7	32.1	23.0	47.7	32.0	25.1	34.1	. . .	31.1	. . .	30.8	. . .
June	31.6	32.7	32.6	23.1	47.8	31.9	25.1	34.2	. . .	31.2	. . .	31.6	. . .
July	31.6	32.7	32.5	23.0	47.7	31.9	25.3	34.1	. . .	31.2	. . .	31.2	. . .
August	31.6	32.7	32.4	23.0	47.8	31.9	25.3	34.2	. . .	31.3	. . .	31.5	. . .
September	31.6	32.8	32.3	23.1	47.8	31.9	25.3	34.3	. . .	31.3	. . .	31.4	. . .
October	31.6	32.8	32.5	23.0	47.9	31.8	25.4	34.4	. . .	31.3	. . .	31.8	. . .
November	31.8	32.9	32.6	23.1	48.0	31.9	25.5	34.5	. . .	31.4	. . .	32.1	. . .
December	31.8	33.0	32.8	23.1	48.1	32.0	25.5	34.7	. . .	31.4	. . .	32.7	. . .
1966													
January	31.9	33.0	33.0	23.1	48.3	31.9	25.6	34.7	. . .	31.4	. . .	33.1	. . .
February	32.1	33.1	33.5	23.2	48.4	32.0	25.6	35.0	. . .	31.6	. . .	33.7	. . .
March	32.2	33.1	33.8	23.2	48.5	32.1	25.8	35.0	. . .	31.7	. . .	33.5	. . .
April	32.3	33.3	33.8	23.2	48.7	32.2	25.9	35.1	. . .	31.8	. . .	33.3	. . .
May	32.4	33.4	33.7	23.2	48.8	32.1	26.0	35.1	. . .	32.0	. . .	33.0	. . .
June	32.4	33.5	33.7	23.3	48.9	32.2	26.1	34.9	. . .	32.0	. . .	33.0	. . .
July	32.4	33.6	33.5	23.4	49.1	32.5	26.3	35.1	. . .	32.2	. . .	33.4	. . .
August	32.6	33.7	34.0	23.3	49.1	32.6	26.4	35.4	. . .	32.3	. . .	33.5	. . .
September	32.8	33.8	34.1	23.4	49.4	32.6	26.7	35.6	. . .	32.2	. . .	33.4	. . .
October	32.8	34.0	34.2	23.4	49.6	32.7	26.9	35.5	. . .	32.1	. . .	32.9	. . .
November	32.9	34.0	34.1	23.5	49.7	32.8	27.1	35.5	. . .	32.2	. . .	32.3	. . .
December	32.9	34.1	34.0	23.5	49.9	32.6	27.2	35.4	. . .	32.2	. . .	32.1	. . .
1967													
January	32.9	34.2	33.9	23.6	50.1	32.6	27.4	35.4	. . .	32.2	. . .	32.2	. . .
February	33.0	34.2	33.8	23.7	50.3	32.8	27.5	35.3	. . .	32.1	. . .	31.5	. . .
March	33.0	34.3	33.8	23.6	50.4	32.8	27.6	35.3	. . .	32.1	. . .	31.1	. . .
April	33.1	34.4	33.7	23.9	50.6	33.0	27.8	35.3	. . .	32.1	. . .	30.7	. . .
May	33.1	34.5	33.7	23.9	50.7	33.1	27.9	35.4	. . .	32.1	. . .	31.1	. . .
June	33.3	34.6	34.0	23.8	50.9	33.1	28.1	35.7	. . .	32.2	. . .	31.4	. . .
July	33.4	34.7	34.1	23.8	51.1	33.3	28.2	35.7	. . .	32.2	. . .	31.3	. . .
August	33.5	34.9	34.3	23.9	51.3	33.4	28.3	35.8	. . .	32.2	. . .	31.3	. . .
September	33.6	35.0	34.3	24.0	51.3	33.7	28.5	35.8	. . .	32.3	. . .	31.2	. . .
October	33.7	35.1	34.4	23.9	51.5	33.6	28.7	35.9	. . .	32.3	. . .	31.3	. . .
November	33.9	35.2	34.5	24.0	51.6	33.9	28.8	35.9	. . .	32.4	. . .	31.1	. . .
December	34.0	35.4	34.6	23.9	51.9	33.9	29.0	36.0	. . .	32.6	. . .	31.5	. . .
1968													
January	34.1	35.5	34.6	24.0	52.1	34.1	29.1	36.1	. . .	32.6	. . .	31.4	. . .
February	34.2	35.7	34.8	24.1	52.4	34.2	29.2	36.2	. . .	32.7	. . .	31.5	. . .
March	34.3	35.8	34.9	24.1	52.7	34.2	29.4	36.3	. . .	32.8	. . .	31.6	. . .
April	34.4	35.9	35.0	24.0	53.0	34.1	29.5	36.5	. . .	32.8	. . .	31.7	. . .
May	34.5	36.0	35.1	24.1	53.3	34.1	29.6	36.5	. . .	32.8	. . .	31.5	. . .
June	34.7	36.2	35.2	24.2	53.5	34.3	29.7	36.6	. . .	32.9	. . .	31.3	. . .
July	34.9	36.4	35.3	24.2	53.9	34.3	29.9	36.7	. . .	33.0	. . .	31.6	. . .
August	35.0	36.5	35.4	24.3	54.2	34.4	30.0	36.8	. . .	33.0	. . .	31.7	. . .
September	35.1	36.7	35.6	24.3	54.5	34.4	30.2	37.0	. . .	33.1	. . .	31.9	. . .
October	35.3	36.9	35.9	24.3	54.8	34.5	30.4	37.0	. . .	33.2	. . .	32.1	. . .
November	35.4	37.1	35.9	24.4	54.9	34.7	30.6	37.1	. . .	33.2	. . .	32.8	. . .
December	35.6	37.2	36.0	24.3	55.2	34.5	30.8	37.1	. . .	33.4	. . .	32.4	. . .

. . . = Not available.

Table 20-2. Summary Consumer and Producer Price Indexes—*Continued*

(Seasonally adjusted.)

Year and month	Consumer Price Index, all urban consumers, 1982–1984 = 100							Producer Price Index, 1982 = 100					
								Finished goods		Intermediate materials, supplies, and components		Crude materials for further processing	
	All items	All items less food and energy	Food	Energy	Apparel	Transportation	Medical care	Total	Less food and energy	Total	Less food and energy	Total	Crude nonfood less energy
1969													
January	35.7	37.3	36.1	24.4	55.5	34.7	30.9	37.2	. . .	33.6	. . .	32.6	. . .
February	35.8	37.6	36.1	24.4	55.7	35.2	31.2	37.2	. . .	33.7	. . .	32.3	. . .
March	36.1	37.8	36.2	24.7	55.9	35.8	31.4	37.4	. . .	33.9	. . .	32.7	. . .
April	36.3	38.1	36.4	24.9	56.2	35.8	31.6	37.6	. . .	33.8	. . .	33.1	. . .
May	36.4	38.1	36.6	24.8	56.4	35.5	31.8	37.8	. . .	33.9	. . .	34.0	. . .
June	36.6	38.3	37.0	25.0	56.7	35.6	31.9	38.0	. . .	34.0	. . .	34.5	. . .
July	36.8	38.5	37.3	24.9	57.0	35.6	32.1	38.1	. . .	34.0	. . .	34.1	. . .
August	36.9	38.7	37.5	24.9	57.0	35.7	32.2	38.2	. . .	34.2	. . .	34.4	. . .
September	37.1	38.9	37.7	25.0	57.4	35.6	32.5	38.3	. . .	34.2	. . .	34.4	. . .
October	37.3	39.1	37.8	25.0	57.6	35.9	32.3	38.5	. . .	34.4	. . .	34.8	. . .
November	37.5	39.2	38.2	25.0	57.9	36.0	32.5	38.8	. . .	34.6	. . .	35.2	. . .
December	37.7	39.4	38.6	25.1	58.0	36.2	32.6	38.9	. . .	34.7	. . .	35.1	. . .
1970													
January	37.9	39.6	38.7	25.1	58.2	36.6	32.8	39.1	. . .	35.0	. . .	35.1	. . .
February	38.1	39.8	38.9	25.1	58.5	36.7	33.0	39.0	. . .	35.0	. . .	35.2	. . .
March	38.3	40.1	38.9	25.0	58.5	36.6	33.2	39.1	. . .	34.9	. . .	35.6	. . .
April	38.5	40.4	39.0	25.5	58.7	37.1	33.5	39.1	. . .	35.1	. . .	35.5	. . .
May	38.6	40.5	39.2	25.4	58.8	37.2	33.7	39.1	. . .	35.2	. . .	35.0	. . .
June	38.8	40.8	39.2	25.3	59.0	37.4	33.9	39.2	. . .	35.3	. . .	35.0	. . .
July	38.9	40.9	39.2	25.5	59.1	37.6	34.1	39.2	. . .	35.5	. . .	35.1	. . .
August	39.0	41.1	39.2	25.4	59.3	37.5	34.3	39.2	. . .	35.5	. . .	34.7	. . .
September	39.2	41.3	39.4	25.6	59.6	37.7	34.5	39.6	. . .	35.6	. . .	35.5	. . .
October	39.4	41.5	39.5	25.9	59.8	38.1	34.6	39.6	. . .	35.8	. . .	35.5	. . .
November	39.6	41.8	39.5	26.0	60.1	38.5	34.8	39.8	. . .	35.9	. . .	35.1	. . .
December	39.8	42.0	39.5	26.2	60.3	38.9	35.1	39.8	. . .	35.9	. . .	34.5	. . .
1971													
January	39.9	42.1	39.4	26.3	60.4	39.2	35.2	39.9	. . .	36.0	. . .	34.8	. . .
February	39.9	42.2	39.5	26.2	60.6	39.4	35.4	40.1	. . .	36.1	. . .	35.9	. . .
March	40.0	42.2	39.8	26.2	60.6	39.4	35.6	40.2	. . .	36.3	. . .	35.4	. . .
April	40.1	42.4	40.1	26.1	60.7	39.4	35.8	40.3	. . .	36.3	. . .	36.0	. . .
May	40.3	42.6	40.3	26.2	61.1	39.4	36.0	40.5	. . .	36.5	. . .	36.0	. . .
June	40.5	42.8	40.5	26.3	61.2	39.6	36.2	40.6	. . .	36.7	. . .	36.2	. . .
July	40.6	42.9	40.6	26.3	61.3	39.6	36.4	40.4	. . .	36.9	. . .	35.9	. . .
August	40.7	43.0	40.6	26.8	61.1	39.7	36.5	40.7	. . .	37.2	. . .	35.8	. . .
September	40.8	43.0	40.6	26.9	61.3	39.5	36.7	40.7	. . .	37.2	. . .	35.7	. . .
October	40.9	43.1	40.7	27.0	61.4	39.5	36.5	40.7	. . .	37.1	. . .	36.4	. . .
November	41.0	43.2	40.9	26.9	61.5	39.4	36.6	40.8	. . .	37.2	. . .	37.0	. . .
December	41.1	43.3	41.3	27.0	61.6	39.4	36.7	41.1	. . .	37.4	. . .	37.2	. . .
1972													
January	41.2	43.5	41.1	27.0	61.7	39.7	36.8	41.0	. . .	37.5	. . .	37.8	. . .
February	41.4	43.6	41.7	26.8	61.9	39.6	36.9	41.3	. . .	37.7	. . .	38.1	. . .
March	41.4	43.6	41.6	26.9	61.9	39.6	37.0	41.3	. . .	37.8	. . .	38.1	. . .
April	41.5	43.8	41.6	26.9	62.1	39.6	37.1	41.3	. . .	37.9	. . .	38.7	. . .
May	41.6	43.9	41.7	27.0	62.2	39.7	37.2	41.5	. . .	38.0	. . .	39.3	. . .
June	41.7	44.0	41.9	27.0	62.2	39.7	37.3	41.7	. . .	38.0	. . .	39.4	. . .
July	41.8	44.1	42.1	27.1	62.2	39.8	37.3	41.8	. . .	38.1	. . .	40.0	. . .
August	41.9	44.3	42.2	27.3	62.0	40.0	37.4	42.0	. . .	38.2	. . .	40.3	. . .
September	42.1	44.3	42.5	27.6	62.5	40.2	37.4	42.2	. . .	38.5	. . .	40.5	. . .
October	42.2	44.4	42.8	27.7	62.8	40.1	37.8	42.0	. . .	38.7	. . .	40.9	. . .
November	42.4	44.4	43.0	27.9	63.0	40.3	37.8	42.3	. . .	39.0	. . .	42.0	. . .
December	42.5	44.6	43.2	27.8	63.2	40.4	37.9	42.7	. . .	39.6	. . .	43.8	. . .
1973													
January	42.7	44.6	44.0	27.9	63.2	40.4	38.0	43.0	. . .	39.8	. . .	45.0	. . .
February	43.0	44.8	44.6	28.2	63.4	40.6	38.1	43.5	. . .	40.4	. . .	47.1	. . .
March	43.4	45.0	45.8	28.3	63.8	40.7	38.2	44.4	. . .	41.1	. . .	49.3	. . .
April	43.7	45.1	46.5	28.6	64.2	41.0	38.3	44.7	. . .	41.3	. . .	50.1	. . .
May	43.9	45.3	47.1	28.8	64.4	41.0	38.5	45.0	. . .	42.2	. . .	52.5	. . .
June	44.2	45.4	47.6	29.2	64.6	41.2	38.6	45.5	. . .	43.0	. . .	55.0	. . .
July	44.2	45.5	47.7	29.2	64.6	41.2	38.6	45.4	. . .	42.3	. . .	52.5	. . .
August	45.0	45.7	50.5	29.4	64.9	41.2	38.7	47.0	. . .	43.5	. . .	64.1	. . .
September	45.2	46.0	50.4	29.4	65.2	41.1	38.9	46.9	. . .	43.0	. . .	60.9	. . .
October	45.6	46.3	50.7	30.3	65.4	41.4	39.6	46.8	. . .	43.4	. . .	58.5	. . .
November	45.9	46.5	51.4	31.5	65.7	41.8	39.7	47.2	. . .	43.8	. . .	59.0	. . .
December	46.3	46.7	51.9	32.5	66.0	42.2	39.9	47.6	. . .	44.8	. . .	59.1	. . .
1974													
January	46.8	46.9	52.5	34.1	66.3	42.8	40.1	48.8	49.7	45.9	47.5	63.3	86.3
February	47.3	47.2	53.6	35.4	67.0	43.4	40.3	49.7	50.0	46.8	48.1	64.3	86.5
March	47.8	47.6	54.2	36.9	67.5	44.2	40.7	50.2	50.5	48.1	49.5	62.3	88.3
April	48.1	47.9	54.1	37.6	68.2	44.7	41.0	50.7	51.1	49.0	50.9	60.6	89.7
May	48.6	48.5	54.5	38.3	68.7	45.3	41.4	51.3	52.2	50.6	52.5	58.3	83.8
June	49.0	49.0	54.5	38.6	69.2	45.9	42.1	51.3	53.1	51.5	53.7	55.4	82.9
July	49.3	49.5	54.3	38.9	69.5	46.4	42.6	52.7	54.0	53.4	55.2	59.8	84.2
August	49.9	50.2	55.1	39.2	70.8	46.6	43.2	53.7	55.0	55.8	57.0	62.9	85.5
September	50.6	50.7	56.2	39.3	71.0	47.0	43.7	54.3	55.7	55.9	57.6	60.9	82.5
October	51.0	51.2	56.8	39.2	71.2	47.3	44.1	55.3	56.7	57.2	58.2	63.2	80.6
November	51.5	51.6	57.5	39.4	71.7	47.6	44.4	56.4	57.4	57.8	58.8	64.2	77.6
December	51.9	52.0	58.2	39.6	71.7	47.9	44.8	56.4	57.9	57.8	59.1	61.5	71.6

. . . = Not available.

Table 20-2. Summary Consumer and Producer Price Indexes—*Continued*

(Seasonally adjusted.)

Year and month	Consumer Price Index, all urban consumers, 1982–1984 = 100							Producer Price Index, 1982 = 100					
								Finished goods		Intermediate materials, supplies, and components		Crude materials for further processing	
	All items	All items less food and energy	Food	Energy	Apparel	Transportation	Medical care	Total	Less food and energy	Total	Less food and energy	Total	Crude nonfood less energy
1975													
January	52.3	52.3	58.4	40.0	71.8	48.0	45.3	56.7	58.3	58.0	59.6	59.6	69.8
February	52.6	52.8	58.5	40.3	72.0	48.3	45.8	56.6	58.7	57.8	59.8	57.9	69.2
March	52.8	53.0	58.4	40.6	72.1	48.7	46.3	56.6	59.0	57.4	59.7	57.1	68.2
April	53.0	53.3	58.3	41.0	72.1	48.8	46.7	57.1	59.2	57.5	59.7	59.5	67.7
May	53.1	53.5	58.6	41.3	72.2	48.9	47.0	57.4	59.3	57.3	59.7	61.2	68.8
June	53.5	53.8	59.2	41.7	72.2	49.4	47.4	57.9	59.5	57.3	59.8	61.5	66.5
July	54.0	54.0	60.3	42.5	72.6	50.2	47.8	58.4	59.8	57.5	59.9	62.4	66.5
August	54.2	54.2	60.3	42.8	72.6	50.6	48.1	58.9	59.9	58.0	60.1	63.0	67.7
September	54.6	54.5	60.7	43.2	72.7	51.4	48.5	59.3	60.2	58.2	60.3	64.5	71.2
October	54.9	54.8	61.3	43.5	73.0	51.7	48.9	59.8	60.6	58.8	61.0	65.1	71.5
November	55.3	55.2	61.7	43.9	73.2	52.4	48.8	60.0	61.0	59.0	61.4	64.4	71.9
December	55.6	55.5	62.1	44.1	73.4	52.6	49.3	60.1	61.4	59.2	61.8	64.0	73.1
1976													
January	55.8	55.9	61.9	44.5	73.7	53.0	49.7	60.0	61.7	59.4	62.1	63.0	72.4
February	55.9	56.2	61.3	44.4	74.0	53.3	50.2	59.9	61.9	59.6	62.3	62.1	73.8
March	56.0	56.5	60.9	44.1	74.2	53.8	50.7	60.0	62.2	59.8	62.6	61.5	74.5
April	56.1	56.7	60.9	43.9	74.3	54.0	51.0	60.3	62.3	60.0	62.8	63.9	78.1
May	56.4	57.0	61.1	44.1	74.6	54.3	51.4	60.4	62.4	60.3	63.2	63.6	80.6
June	56.7	57.2	61.3	44.4	74.9	54.8	51.8	60.5	62.8	60.8	63.6	65.2	82.8
July	57.0	57.6	61.6	44.8	75.3	55.1	52.3	60.7	63.1	61.1	63.9	64.8	87.3
August	57.3	57.9	61.8	45.2	75.8	55.4	52.6	60.9	63.5	61.3	64.3	63.6	84.1
September	57.6	58.2	62.1	45.7	76.1	56.0	53.0	61.1	63.9	61.9	64.7	63.4	84.4
October	57.9	58.5	62.4	46.1	76.2	56.6	53.2	61.4	64.1	62.0	65.0	63.0	82.2
November	58.1	58.7	62.3	46.8	76.5	57.0	53.9	61.9	64.6	62.4	65.3	63.4	81.8
December	58.4	58.9	62.5	47.5	76.8	57.3	54.2	62.4	64.9	62.8	65.6	64.5	81.1
1977													
January	58.7	59.3	62.7	48.1	77.2	57.8	54.6	62.5	65.1	63.0	65.8	64.3	78.7
February	59.3	59.7	63.9	48.1	77.6	58.2	54.9	63.2	65.4	63.3	65.9	65.7	79.7
March	59.6	60.0	64.2	48.4	77.5	58.7	55.5	63.7	65.7	63.9	66.4	66.6	81.5
April	60.0	60.3	65.0	48.6	77.6	59.0	56.0	64.0	65.9	64.4	66.7	68.3	82.1
May	60.2	60.6	65.3	48.9	78.1	59.1	56.5	64.4	66.1	64.9	67.1	67.6	82.5
June	60.5	61.0	65.7	48.9	78.5	59.1	57.0	64.6	66.5	64.9	67.4	65.5	79.7
July	60.8	61.2	65.9	49.1	79.1	59.0	57.3	64.8	66.8	65.1	67.9	64.7	78.8
August	61.1	61.5	66.2	49.5	79.2	58.9	57.7	65.2	67.3	65.4	68.2	63.9	79.2
September	61.3	61.8	66.4	49.8	79.1	59.1	58.2	65.5	67.8	65.7	68.7	63.7	79.2
October	61.6	62.0	66.6	50.5	79.3	59.3	58.4	65.9	68.2	65.8	68.8	64.0	78.5
November	62.0	62.3	67.1	51.3	79.8	59.5	58.6	66.4	68.8	66.3	69.1	65.4	78.4
December	62.3	62.7	67.4	51.6	80.1	59.8	59.0	66.7	69.0	66.6	69.4	66.4	80.1
1978													
January	62.7	63.1	67.9	51.1	80.1	60.1	59.3	67.0	69.2	66.9	69.8	67.3	80.3
February	63.0	63.4	68.6	50.6	79.5	60.2	59.9	67.5	69.5	67.4	70.3	68.4	80.6
March	63.4	63.8	69.5	51.0	79.9	60.3	60.2	67.8	69.9	67.8	70.6	69.8	80.3
April	63.9	64.3	70.6	51.4	80.7	60.4	60.7	68.6	70.6	68.1	71.1	72.1	82.2
May	64.5	64.7	71.6	51.7	81.3	60.7	61.1	69.1	71.1	68.7	71.6	72.8	84.6
June	65.0	65.2	72.7	51.9	81.6	61.1	61.5	69.7	71.7	69.2	72.2	74.6	87.4
July	65.5	65.6	73.0	52.1	81.5	61.6	61.9	70.3	72.3	69.4	72.5	74.2	89.6
August	65.9	66.1	73.3	52.6	81.7	62.0	62.4	70.4	72.8	69.9	73.2	73.7	90.4
September	66.5	66.7	73.6	53.2	81.9	62.6	62.8	71.1	73.5	70.5	73.7	75.1	92.3
October	67.1	67.2	74.2	54.1	82.4	63.3	63.3	71.4	73.4	71.3	74.5	77.0	94.7
November	67.5	67.6	74.7	54.9	82.6	63.9	63.8	72.0	74.1	71.9	75.2	77.4	96.3
December	67.9	68.0	75.1	55.9	82.6	64.5	64.1	72.8	74.7	72.4	75.6	78.0	96.8
1979													
January	68.5	68.5	76.4	55.8	83.0	64.6	64.8	73.7	75.3	73.1	76.3	80.1	96.4
February	69.2	69.2	77.7	55.9	83.3	65.2	65.2	74.4	75.9	73.7	77.0	82.1	99.6
March	69.9	69.8	78.4	57.4	83.6	66.4	65.7	75.0	76.4	74.6	77.8	83.8	104.2
April	70.6	70.3	79.0	59.5	84.0	67.8	66.1	75.8	77.0	75.7	78.9	84.4	105.1
May	71.4	70.8	79.7	62.0	84.5	69.1	66.6	76.2	77.4	76.6	79.6	84.7	106.7
June	72.2	71.3	80.0	64.7	84.7	70.5	67.1	76.6	78.0	77.5	80.1	85.6	111.6
July	73.0	71.9	80.5	67.3	84.8	71.7	67.7	77.4	78.5	78.7	81.1	86.5	109.4
August	73.7	72.7	80.4	69.7	85.0	72.7	68.2	78.2	78.8	79.8	81.8	85.5	106.4
September	74.4	73.3	80.9	71.9	85.6	73.5	68.7	79.5	79.7	81.1	82.7	87.9	106.5
October	75.2	74.0	81.5	73.5	86.1	74.0	69.2	80.4	80.4	82.4	83.9	88.8	108.9
November	76.0	74.8	82.0	74.8	86.6	74.7	69.8	81.4	81.0	83.2	84.5	90.0	111.3
December	76.9	75.7	82.8	76.8	87.3	75.8	70.6	82.2	81.7	84.0	85.2	91.2	111.3
1980													
January	78.0	76.7	83.3	79.1	88.1	78.0	71.4	83.4	83.3	86.0	87.2	90.9	112.6
February	79.0	77.5	83.4	81.9	88.7	79.8	72.3	84.6	84.2	87.6	88.2	92.6	115.3
March	80.1	78.6	84.1	84.5	89.7	81.8	73.0	85.5	84.7	88.2	88.6	90.8	111.7
April	80.9	79.5	84.7	85.4	90.1	82.2	73.6	86.2	85.5	88.5	88.8	88.3	109.9
May	81.7	80.1	85.2	86.4	90.3	82.8	74.2	86.6	85.7	89.0	89.1	89.5	107.2
June	82.5	81.0	85.7	86.5	90.6	82.7	74.7	87.3	86.6	89.8	89.8	90.1	106.1
July	82.6	80.8	86.6	86.7	90.9	83.1	75.2	88.7	87.7	90.5	90.3	94.6	109.6
August	83.2	81.3	88.0	87.2	91.4	83.7	75.6	89.7	88.4	91.5	91.1	99.0	112.4
September	83.9	82.1	89.1	87.5	92.0	84.6	76.3	90.1	88.8	91.9	91.4	100.4	116.2
October	84.7	83.0	89.8	88.0	92.7	85.3	76.9	90.8	89.6	92.8	92.1	102.2	118.2
November	85.6	83.9	90.8	88.8	93.1	86.1	77.3	91.4	90.1	93.5	92.6	103.5	119.8
December	86.4	84.9	91.3	90.7	93.3	86.8	77.8	91.8	90.4	94.4	93.7	102.7	119.3

Table 20-2. Summary Consumer and Producer Price Indexes—*Continued*

(Seasonally adjusted.)

Year and month	Consumer Price Index, all urban consumers, 1982–1984 = 100							Producer Price Index, 1982 = 100					
								Finished goods		Intermediate materials, supplies, and components		Crude materials for further processing	
	All items	All items less food and energy	Food	Energy	Apparel	Transportation	Medical care	Total	Less food and energy	Total	Less food and energy	Total	Crude nonfood less energy
1981													
January	87.2	85.4	91.6	92.1	93.4	88.5	78.6	92.8	91.4	95.6	94.7	103.4	113.3
February	88.0	85.9	92.1	95.2	93.9	90.7	79.2	93.6	92.0	96.1	94.9	104.2	106.2
March	88.6	86.4	92.6	97.4	94.3	91.8	79.9	94.7	92.6	97.1	95.6	103.8	108.9
April	89.1	87.0	92.8	97.6	94.7	91.7	80.7	95.7	93.5	98.3	96.6	104.2	111.9
May	89.7	87.8	92.8	97.9	94.8	92.2	81.4	96.0	94.0	98.7	97.1	103.8	113.7
June	90.5	88.6	93.2	97.3	95.0	92.7	82.3	96.5	94.6	99.0	97.7	104.9	115.5
July	91.5	89.8	93.9	97.3	95.4	93.5	83.4	96.7	94.8	99.2	98.4	105.0	116.4
August	92.2	90.7	94.4	97.8	95.9	93.9	84.3	96.8	95.3	99.7	98.9	104.0	115.5
September	93.1	91.8	94.8	98.6	96.1	94.6	85.1	97.2	95.9	99.7	99.3	102.7	112.6
October	93.4	92.1	95.0	99.2	96.4	95.5	85.9	97.6	96.5	99.8	99.5	101.2	110.8
November	93.8	92.5	95.1	100.5	96.4	96.2	86.8	97.9	97.0	99.9	99.7	99.7	107.5
December	94.1	93.0	95.3	101.5	96.7	96.4	87.5	98.3	97.6	100.0	99.8	98.8	106.0
1982													
January	94.4	93.3	95.6	100.6	96.7	96.7	88.2	98.9	98.1	100.4	99.9	99.7	101.2
February	94.7	93.8	96.3	98.0	97.0	96.2	88.8	98.8	98.1	100.3	100.0	100.0	100.7
March	94.7	93.9	96.2	96.6	97.3	95.8	89.6	98.8	98.7	99.9	99.9	99.7	100.0
April	95.0	94.7	96.4	94.2	97.5	94.5	90.5	99.0	99.0	99.7	99.8	100.2	101.1
May	95.9	95.4	97.2	95.7	97.6	95.1	91.3	99.0	99.4	99.7	100.1	101.9	102.2
June	97.0	96.1	98.1	98.4	97.7	97.2	92.2	99.8	99.9	99.8	100.0	101.8	101.0
July	97.5	96.7	98.2	99.3	98.1	98.1	93.0	100.2	100.1	100.0	99.8	100.7	101.4
August	97.7	97.1	98.0	99.8	98.1	98.2	93.9	100.6	100.6	99.9	99.7	99.8	100.0
September	97.7	97.2	98.2	100.3	98.1	98.0	94.7	100.7	100.8	100.0	100.2	99.2	98.9
October	98.1	97.5	98.2	101.7	98.3	98.2	95.5	101.0	101.3	99.9	100.2	98.7	97.7
November	98.0	97.3	98.2	102.5	98.3	98.2	96.5	101.4	101.6	100.1	100.2	99.2	96.3
December	97.7	97.2	98.2	102.8	98.2	97.7	97.2	101.8	102.2	100.1	100.3	98.8	95.9
1983													
January	97.9	97.6	98.1	99.6	98.6	97.6	97.9	101.0	101.8	99.8	100.3	98.8	97.3
February	98.0	98.0	98.2	97.7	99.1	96.9	98.8	101.1	102.2	100.0	100.8	100.0	99.8
March	98.1	98.2	98.8	96.8	99.1	96.5	99.0	101.0	102.5	99.7	100.8	100.5	102.2
April	98.8	98.6	99.2	98.9	99.3	97.8	99.4	101.1	102.4	99.5	100.9	101.2	102.1
May	99.2	98.9	99.5	100.4	99.9	98.6	99.9	101.4	102.6	99.8	101.0	100.9	103.4
June	99.4	99.2	99.6	100.6	100.3	99.0	100.4	101.6	102.8	100.2	101.3	100.5	104.8
July	99.8	99.8	99.6	100.9	100.9	99.6	100.8	101.6	103.1	100.5	101.8	99.5	106.2
August	100.1	100.1	99.7	101.2	101.0	100.4	101.4	101.9	103.5	100.9	102.0	102.2	108.4
September	100.4	100.5	100.0	101.0	100.8	100.7	101.8	102.2	103.5	101.6	102.3	103.3	109.0
October	100.8	101.0	100.3	100.8	100.6	101.1	102.3	102.2	103.6	101.7	102.5	103.2	109.1
November	101.1	101.5	100.3	100.5	100.9	101.5	102.8	102.0	103.8	101.8	102.8	102.3	109.9
December	101.4	101.8	100.6	100.0	101.1	101.5	103.4	102.3	104.1	101.9	103.1	103.5	111.2
1984													
January	102.1	102.5	102.0	100.2	101.5	102.0	104.0	103.0	104.5	102.1	103.4	104.6	111.5
February	102.6	102.8	102.7	101.4	101.2	102.2	105.0	103.4	104.7	102.5	103.8	103.8	113.8
March	102.9	103.2	102.9	101.4	101.3	102.9	105.2	103.8	105.2	103.0	104.4	105.7	114.8
April	103.3	103.7	102.9	101.7	101.2	103.3	105.8	103.9	105.3	103.2	104.5	105.2	115.1
May	103.5	104.1	102.7	101.6	101.4	103.7	106.2	103.8	105.3	103.4	104.6	104.5	115.7
June	103.7	104.5	103.1	100.8	101.3	103.9	106.7	103.8	105.5	103.6	104.8	103.3	114.1
July	104.1	105.0	103.3	100.5	101.9	103.7	107.2	104.0	105.7	103.4	104.9	104.0	112.0
August	104.4	105.4	103.9	100.1	102.5	103.8	107.7	103.8	105.9	103.2	105.1	103.3	109.6
September	104.7	105.8	103.8	100.6	102.7	104.1	108.1	103.8	106.2	103.1	105.0	102.8	110.5
October	105.1	106.2	104.0	101.1	103.0	104.8	108.7	103.6	105.9	103.2	105.1	101.5	108.5
November	105.3	106.4	104.1	100.8	103.0	104.9	109.3	104.0	106.2	103.3	105.3	101.9	107.7
December	105.5	106.8	104.5	100.1	103.1	104.7	109.8	104.0	106.3	103.2	105.3	101.4	107.3
1985													
January	105.7	107.1	104.7	100.3	103.2	105.1	110.2	104.0	106.9	103.1	105.3	99.9	107.4
February	106.3	107.7	105.2	100.3	104.1	105.6	110.8	104.1	107.3	102.8	105.3	99.4	107.2
March	106.8	108.1	105.5	101.3	104.5	106.3	111.4	104.1	107.6	102.7	105.2	97.6	107.0
April	107.0	108.4	105.4	102.3	104.5	106.8	112.0	104.6	107.6	102.9	105.2	96.7	107.4
May	107.2	108.8	105.2	102.2	104.4	106.5	112.6	104.9	107.8	103.2	105.3	95.8	105.3
June	107.5	109.1	105.5	102.2	105.1	106.5	113.3	104.6	108.2	102.6	105.5	95.2	103.6
July	107.7	109.4	105.5	102.2	105.2	106.6	113.9	104.7	108.4	102.3	105.3	94.9	104.3
August	107.9	109.8	105.6	101.2	105.3	106.2	114.6	104.5	108.5	102.3	105.3	92.9	103.6
September	108.1	110.0	105.8	101.2	105.5	106.2	115.2	103.8	107.9	102.2	105.2	91.8	103.3
October	108.5	110.5	105.8	101.2	105.7	106.5	115.8	104.9	108.9	102.3	105.1	94.1	103.7
November	109.0	111.1	106.5	101.8	106.0	107.0	116.5	105.5	109.1	102.5	105.1	95.7	103.0
December	109.5	111.4	107.3	102.4	106.1	107.5	117.1	106.0	109.1	102.9	105.1	95.5	102.4
1986													
January	109.9	111.9	107.5	102.6	106.1	108.0	118.0	105.5	109.3	102.4	105.0	94.2	103.6
February	109.7	112.2	107.3	99.5	105.4	107.0	118.8	104.1	109.5	101.2	104.9	90.5	103.5
March	109.1	112.5	107.5	92.6	105.0	103.6	119.7	102.8	109.6	99.9	105.0	88.2	103.8
April	108.7	112.9	107.7	87.2	105.0	101.0	120.4	102.3	110.1	98.9	104.7	85.6	103.9
May	109.0	113.1	108.2	87.2	104.9	101.4	121.2	102.8	110.2	98.7	104.6	86.5	104.1
June	109.4	113.4	108.3	88.8	104.9	102.3	121.8	103.1	110.5	98.6	104.7	86.2	104.7
July	109.5	113.8	109.1	85.6	105.5	101.1	122.5	102.3	110.7	98.0	104.8	86.4	105.3
August	109.6	114.2	110.1	83.6	106.4	100.1	123.2	102.7	110.8	98.0	104.9	86.7	99.7
September	110.0	114.6	110.2	84.4	106.9	100.6	124.0	102.9	110.7	98.5	105.1	86.6	100.3
October	110.2	115.0	110.5	82.8	106.6	100.5	124.7	103.5	111.8	98.3	105.1	87.4	102.0
November	110.4	115.3	111.1	82.1	106.9	100.8	125.5	103.4	112.0	98.3	105.2	87.6	102.8
December	110.8	115.6	111.4	82.5	107.2	101.1	126.2	103.6	112.1	98.5	105.3	86.9	104.1

Table 20-2. Summary Consumer and Producer Price Indexes—*Continued*

(Seasonally adjusted.)

Year and month	Consumer Price Index, all urban consumers, 1982–1984 = 100							Producer Price Index, 1982 = 100					
								Finished goods		Intermediate materials, supplies, and components		Crude materials for further processing	
	All items	All items less food and energy	Food	Energy	Apparel	Transpor-tation	Medical care	Total	Less food and energy	Total	Less food and energy	Total	Crude nonfood less energy
1987													
January	111.4	115.9	111.8	85.4	108.0	102.6	126.7	104.1	112.5	99.0	105.6	89.3	105.4
February	111.8	116.2	112.2	87.4	108.6	103.5	127.2	104.4	112.3	99.8	105.9	90.2	106.2
March	112.2	116.6	112.4	87.6	109.2	103.8	127.8	104.5	112.4	99.9	106.2	90.5	106.5
April	112.7	117.3	112.6	87.6	109.8	104.3	128.6	105.1	112.9	100.3	106.5	92.5	107.5
May	113.0	117.7	113.2	87.1	110.3	104.4	129.2	105.2	113.0	100.8	107.0	93.8	110.0
June	113.5	117.9	113.9	88.5	110.3	105.1	130.0	105.5	113.1	101.4	107.5	94.5	113.2
July	113.8	118.3	113.7	89.2	110.3	105.9	130.6	105.7	113.3	101.9	107.9	95.6	115.9
August	114.3	118.7	113.9	90.5	111.0	106.6	131.2	105.9	113.6	102.4	108.3	96.5	119.1
September	114.7	119.2	114.3	90.3	111.6	106.9	131.9	106.2	113.9	102.6	108.9	96.0	122.8
October	115.0	119.8	114.5	89.6	112.3	107.0	132.4	106.0	114.0	103.1	109.6	95.8	126.6
November	115.4	120.1	114.5	90.0	113.0	107.3	133.0	106.0	114.2	103.5	110.1	95.1	127.5
December	115.6	120.4	115.1	89.5	112.7	107.2	133.5	105.8	114.3	103.8	110.7	94.9	127.9
1988													
January	116.0	120.9	115.6	88.8	113.2	107.0	134.4	106.4	115.0	104.1	111.8	94.2	129.4
February	116.2	121.2	115.6	88.7	112.1	107.0	135.2	106.3	115.3	104.4	112.2	95.2	131.7
March	116.5	121.7	115.8	88.4	113.4	107.0	135.8	106.6	115.6	104.8	112.8	94.1	133.0
April	117.2	122.3	116.4	88.8	115.1	107.5	136.7	107.0	115.9	105.5	113.6	95.4	132.1
May	117.5	122.7	116.9	88.5	115.1	107.9	137.6	107.2	116.2	106.2	114.3	95.8	130.7
June	118.0	123.2	117.6	88.9	115.5	108.3	138.3	107.5	116.6	107.4	114.9	97.0	131.1
July	118.5	123.6	118.8	89.4	115.9	108.8	139.1	108.4	117.2	108.3	115.8	96.7	133.2
August	119.0	124.0	119.4	90.1	114.5	109.7	139.8	108.8	117.7	108.5	116.3	97.0	134.3
September	119.5	124.7	120.1	89.8	116.3	109.9	140.5	109.0	118.1	108.7	116.8	97.0	133.3
October	119.9	125.2	120.3	89.8	117.5	110.0	141.4	109.2	118.4	108.6	117.3	96.6	133.6
November	120.3	125.6	120.5	89.8	117.7	110.2	142.0	109.6	118.7	108.8	118.0	95.2	136.0
December	120.7	126.0	121.1	89.6	118.2	110.4	142.7	110.0	119.2	109.4	118.6	98.1	137.6
1989													
January	121.2	126.5	121.6	90.3	118.4	110.9	143.8	111.1	119.9	110.8	119.5	102.0	140.6
February	121.6	126.9	122.5	90.8	117.1	111.7	144.9	111.9	120.5	111.3	119.9	101.7	140.3
March	122.2	127.4	123.2	91.8	118.1	112.4	145.8	112.3	120.7	111.9	120.2	102.9	140.6
April	123.1	127.8	123.9	96.6	118.6	115.0	146.6	113.1	120.8	112.5	120.5	104.1	140.3
May	123.7	128.3	124.7	97.4	118.9	115.8	147.5	114.0	121.6	112.6	120.6	104.5	139.8
June	124.1	128.8	125.1	96.9	118.7	115.7	148.6	114.0	122.2	112.5	120.6	103.2	137.9
July	124.5	129.2	125.6	96.7	118.3	115.4	149.6	113.8	122.1	112.2	120.3	103.5	135.9
August	124.5	129.5	125.9	94.9	117.1	114.5	150.6	113.4	122.7	111.8	120.2	101.2	136.8
September	124.8	129.9	126.3	93.8	118.7	113.9	151.8	114.0	123.1	112.1	120.2	102.5	137.5
October	125.4	130.6	126.8	94.4	119.6	114.5	152.8	114.6	123.5	112.2	120.3	102.7	137.9
November	125.9	131.1	127.4	93.9	120.0	114.4	154.1	114.8	123.9	112.0	120.0	103.5	134.9
December	126.3	131.6	127.8	94.2	119.8	114.7	154.9	115.5	124.2	112.2	119.8	105.1	132.8
1990													
January	127.5	132.1	129.7	98.9	119.9	117.0	156.0	117.7	124.5	113.7	120.0	106.7	132.7
February	128.0	132.7	130.8	98.2	122.0	117.2	157.1	117.6	124.9	112.8	119.9	106.8	131.6
March	128.6	133.5	131.0	97.6	123.8	117.3	158.3	117.5	125.3	112.9	120.2	105.1	133.9
April	128.9	134.0	130.8	97.5	124.1	117.7	159.6	117.4	125.5	113.1	120.5	102.7	137.0
May	129.1	134.4	131.1	96.7	124.0	117.5	160.8	117.5	126.0	113.1	120.6	103.1	138.0
June	129.9	135.1	132.1	97.3	124.2	118.0	162.0	117.6	126.4	112.9	120.4	100.6	137.3
July	130.5	135.8	132.8	97.1	124.2	118.5	163.4	117.9	126.6	112.8	120.6	101.0	138.0
August	131.6	136.6	133.2	101.6	124.5	120.7	164.8	119.2	127.1	114.0	120.8	110.5	140.1
September	132.5	137.1	133.6	106.5	125.4	123.2	165.9	120.7	127.7	115.8	121.5	115.8	139.9
October	133.4	137.6	134.1	110.8	125.4	125.6	167.3	121.9	128.0	117.4	122.1	125.8	138.4
November	133.7	138.0	134.5	111.2	125.4	126.1	168.7	122.6	128.4	117.7	122.3	117.8	135.7
December	134.2	138.6	134.6	111.0	126.2	126.9	169.8	122.0	128.6	116.9	122.1	110.8	133.8
1991													
January	134.7	139.5	135.0	108.5	126.9	125.5	171.0	122.6	129.5	116.9	122.4	113.3	134.2
February	134.8	140.2	135.1	104.5	127.3	123.9	172.1	121.8	129.8	115.9	122.1	104.1	133.7
March	134.8	140.5	135.3	101.9	127.0	122.7	173.2	121.3	130.1	114.7	121.7	100.5	131.8
April	135.1	140.9	136.1	101.2	127.5	122.5	174.3	121.3	130.4	114.2	121.5	100.2	131.7
May	135.6	141.3	136.6	102.1	128.0	123.2	175.2	121.6	130.6	114.1	121.3	100.9	130.4
June	136.0	141.8	137.4	101.1	127.9	123.4	176.4	121.4	130.7	113.9	121.3	99.2	126.1
July	136.2	142.3	136.7	100.7	128.7	123.3	177.4	121.1	131.0	113.6	121.1	99.4	125.4
August	136.6	142.9	136.2	101.1	129.9	124.0	178.8	121.3	131.3	113.8	121.0	99.1	125.8
September	137.0	143.4	136.4	101.5	130.0	124.1	179.9	121.5	131.8	114.0	121.0	98.4	125.7
October	137.2	143.7	136.2	101.6	130.1	123.9	180.9	121.9	132.3	114.0	121.1	100.8	125.4
November	137.8	144.2	136.7	102.4	131.0	124.5	181.9	122.4	132.5	114.1	121.1	100.7	124.4
December	138.2	144.7	137.0	103.1	130.7	125.1	183.1	122.3	132.6	114.0	121.1	98.2	123.4
1992													
January	138.3	145.1	136.6	101.5	130.9	124.6	184.3	122.0	133.0	113.4	121.0	97.2	123.4
February	138.6	145.4	137.1	101.2	131.0	124.5	185.6	122.3	133.1	113.8	121.3	98.6	125.2
March	139.1	145.9	137.6	101.2	131.3	125.0	186.8	122.4	133.4	113.9	121.5	97.1	127.7
April	139.4	146.3	137.5	101.4	130.7	125.6	187.9	122.5	133.8	114.1	121.7	98.1	128.4
May	139.7	146.8	137.2	102.0	131.6	125.9	188.7	122.9	134.3	114.5	121.8	100.3	129.1
June	140.1	147.1	137.6	103.3	132.1	126.4	189.6	123.4	134.1	115.1	122.0	101.6	128.8
July	140.5	147.6	137.4	103.7	132.7	126.9	190.6	123.3	134.3	115.2	122.1	101.6	129.6
August	140.8	147.9	138.4	103.5	132.3	127.0	191.5	123.4	134.3	115.1	122.3	100.7	130.4
September	141.1	148.1	138.9	103.6	132.2	127.0	192.4	123.7	134.6	115.3	122.4	102.8	130.4
October	141.7	148.8	138.9	104.3	132.5	128.1	193.5	124.2	134.9	115.3	122.4	102.8	128.9
November	142.1	149.2	138.7	105.1	132.7	128.7	194.5	124.1	135.1	115.1	122.4	102.5	128.2
December	142.3	149.6	138.8	105.3	132.8	128.9	195.3	124.2	135.2	115.1	122.5	101.3	130.5

Table 20-2. Summary Consumer and Producer Price Indexes—*Continued*

(Seasonally adjusted.)

Year and month	Consumer Price Index, all urban consumers, 1982–1984 = 100							Producer Price Index, 1982 = 100					
								Finished goods		Intermediate materials, supplies, and components		Crude materials for further processing	
	All items	All items less food and energy	Food	Energy	Apparel	Transportation	Medical care	Total	Less food and energy	Total	Less food and energy	Total	Crude nonfood less energy
1993													
January	142.8	150.1	139.1	105.0	132.8	129.2	196.4	124.4	135.6	115.4	122.9	101.7	135.0
February	143.1	150.6	139.6	104.3	134.0	129.6	197.4	124.7	135.9	115.9	123.5	101.2	136.8
March	143.3	150.8	139.6	104.9	134.0	129.4	198.1	125.0	136.1	116.3	123.8	101.7	137.0
April	143.8	151.4	140.0	104.9	134.0	129.6	199.1	125.7	136.5	116.6	124.0	103.2	138.4
May	144.2	151.8	141.0	104.3	133.5	129.9	200.5	125.7	136.6	116.3	123.7	105.6	140.3
June	144.3	152.1	140.6	103.9	133.0	129.9	201.3	125.2	136.4	116.3	123.7	103.8	140.3
July	144.5	152.3	140.6	103.4	132.8	130.1	202.2	125.1	136.6	116.3	123.7	101.6	142.1
August	144.8	152.8	141.1	103.4	134.0	130.5	202.8	123.9	134.9	116.2	123.9	100.8	140.4
September	145.0	152.9	141.4	103.0	133.7	130.4	203.6	124.1	134.9	116.3	124.0	101.2	140.7
October	145.6	153.4	142.0	105.3	133.8	132.0	204.5	124.2	135.0	116.4	124.0	103.7	142.6
November	146.0	153.9	142.3	104.4	134.4	132.2	205.1	124.4	135.3	116.5	124.3	103.0	144.1
December	146.3	154.3	142.8	103.7	134.1	132.1	205.8	124.4	135.7	116.2	124.5	101.7	145.3
1994													
January	146.3	154.5	142.9	102.8	133.3	131.7	206.4	124.8	136.3	116.5	124.7	103.8	148.3
February	146.7	154.8	142.7	104.1	133.2	132.3	207.2	125.0	136.3	116.9	124.9	102.1	151.0
March	147.1	155.3	142.7	104.3	133.8	132.6	207.9	125.1	136.4	117.1	125.1	103.8	151.5
April	147.2	155.5	143.0	103.7	133.5	132.8	209.0	125.1	136.6	117.1	125.3	103.8	150.7
May	147.5	155.9	143.3	102.8	134.0	132.4	209.7	125.1	137.0	117.2	125.6	102.2	149.7
June	147.9	156.4	143.8	103.1	134.8	133.2	210.5	125.2	137.2	117.8	126.3	102.7	151.2
July	148.4	156.7	144.6	104.5	134.2	134.4	211.3	125.7	137.3	118.3	126.7	101.7	155.5
August	149.0	157.1	145.1	106.7	133.2	136.0	212.2	126.2	137.6	119.1	127.4	101.6	158.8
September	149.3	157.5	145.3	106.1	133.6	136.1	213.1	125.9	137.7	119.6	128.4	99.7	160.5
October	149.4	157.8	145.3	105.7	133.0	136.2	214.1	125.5	137.4	120.1	129.3	98.6	161.3
November	149.8	158.2	145.6	106.1	132.5	136.7	215.0	126.1	137.6	121.0	130.3	99.8	166.6
December	150.1	158.3	146.8	105.9	132.1	137.1	215.9	126.6	137.9	121.5	131.0	101.1	169.9
1995													
January	150.5	159.0	146.7	105.7	132.2	137.4	216.6	126.9	138.4	122.8	132.6	102.1	174.5
February	150.9	159.4	147.3	105.8	131.9	137.9	217.4	127.2	138.7	123.7	133.7	102.9	176.5
March	151.2	159.9	147.1	105.5	132.2	138.4	218.1	127.4	139.0	124.3	134.3	102.3	177.8
April	151.8	160.4	148.1	105.6	131.9	139.2	218.6	127.7	139.3	125.0	135.2	103.7	180.2
May	152.1	160.7	148.2	105.8	131.6	139.7	219.2	127.8	139.7	125.2	135.5	102.4	179.6
June	152.4	161.1	148.3	106.7	131.3	140.6	219.9	127.8	139.8	125.5	135.7	103.0	179.5
July	152.6	161.4	148.5	105.8	131.4	139.9	220.6	128.0	140.2	125.6	136.1	101.6	176.4
August	152.9	161.8	148.6	105.6	132.5	139.4	221.6	127.9	140.2	125.6	136.1	99.7	173.4
September	153.1	162.2	149.1	104.1	132.3	139.1	222.4	128.1	140.2	125.5	136.2	102.0	170.9
October	153.5	162.7	149.5	104.4	132.4	139.5	223.0	128.4	141.0	125.4	135.8	101.9	166.6
November	153.7	163.0	149.6	103.4	132.0	139.1	223.7	128.7	141.3	125.2	135.5	104.1	163.6
December	153.9	163.1	149.9	104.4	132.2	139.1	224.3	129.3	141.5	125.4	135.2	106.5	162.3
1996													
January	154.7	163.7	150.4	106.9	132.7	140.4	225.2	129.7	141.5	125.5	134.8	109.8	162.6
February	155.0	164.0	150.8	107.1	132.2	140.9	225.7	129.7	141.6	125.0	134.4	111.6	162.1
March	155.5	164.4	151.4	108.3	132.6	141.5	226.2	130.5	141.6	125.3	134.1	109.8	158.2
April	156.1	164.6	152.0	111.2	131.8	142.9	226.8	130.9	141.6	125.7	133.8	114.2	156.7
May	156.4	165.0	151.9	112.0	131.8	143.5	227.4	130.9	142.0	126.2	134.0	114.6	157.6
June	156.7	165.4	152.9	110.3	131.6	143.4	228.0	131.3	142.2	125.8	133.9	112.2	154.6
July	157.0	165.7	153.4	110.1	131.3	143.0	228.6	131.2	142.2	125.5	133.6	114.6	152.2
August	157.2	166.0	153.9	109.7	130.6	143.0	229.1	131.6	142.3	125.6	133.6	115.3	152.5
September	157.7	166.5	154.6	109.8	131.3	143.6	229.7	131.7	142.2	126.1	134.0	112.7	153.5
October	158.2	166.8	155.5	110.5	131.3	143.9	230.3	132.4	142.3	126.0	133.7	111.9	153.3
November	158.7	167.2	156.1	111.8	131.6	144.6	231.0	132.5	142.1	125.8	133.7	115.7	153.0
December	159.1	167.4	156.3	113.9	131.9	145.7	231.2	132.9	142.3	126.4	133.9	122.5	153.6
1997													
January	159.4	167.8	155.9	115.2	132.3	145.6	231.8	133.0	142.5	126.6	134.1	127.5	156.2
February	159.7	168.1	156.5	115.0	133.0	145.2	232.2	132.7	142.4	126.5	134.1	116.6	157.6
March	159.8	168.4	156.6	113.0	132.4	145.0	233.0	132.6	142.6	126.1	134.2	107.5	158.7
April	159.9	168.9	156.5	111.0	133.0	144.3	233.5	131.8	142.6	125.6	134.1	107.8	155.8
May	159.9	169.2	156.6	108.8	133.3	143.3	234.1	131.5	142.4	125.4	134.2	109.1	157.0
June	160.2	169.4	156.9	110.0	133.1	143.6	234.4	131.3	142.4	125.4	134.2	106.2	156.9
July	160.4	169.7	157.2	109.1	133.3	143.3	234.7	130.9	142.2	125.1	134.2	106.2	155.7
August	160.8	169.8	157.7	110.9	132.7	144.1	235.1	131.4	142.3	125.3	134.3	106.8	156.8
September	161.2	170.2	158.0	112.4	132.9	144.8	235.5	131.6	142.6	125.5	134.3	108.4	155.8
October	161.5	170.6	158.3	111.8	132.7	144.7	236.1	131.9	142.6	125.4	134.3	113.4	156.7
November	161.7	170.8	158.6	111.4	132.7	143.9	236.9	131.6	142.4	125.6	134.4	115.8	156.5
December	161.8	171.2	158.7	109.8	133.0	143.7	237.8	131.4	142.3	125.4	134.4	108.8	154.2
1998													
January	162.0	171.6	159.5	107.5	133.1	143.0	238.1	130.7	142.4	124.6	134.3	102.8	150.4
February	162.0	171.9	159.4	105.1	133.0	142.4	238.8	130.6	142.6	124.2	134.2	100.8	150.1
March	162.0	172.2	159.7	103.3	132.7	141.5	239.4	130.5	143.3	123.7	134.1	99.5	148.7
April	162.2	172.5	159.7	102.4	132.3	140.9	240.3	130.7	143.4	123.6	134.0	100.6	147.3
May	162.6	172.9	160.3	103.2	132.7	141.2	241.2	130.5	143.5	123.5	133.9	99.6	146.2
June	162.8	173.2	160.2	103.6	133.3	141.4	241.8	130.4	143.5	123.1	133.6	97.1	145.9
July	163.2	173.5	160.6	103.3	133.5	141.7	242.5	130.7	143.8	123.0	133.5	97.4	143.4
August	163.4	174.0	161.0	102.1	135.1	141.6	243.3	130.4	143.8	122.7	133.4	93.6	139.4
September	163.5	174.2	161.1	101.3	133.1	141.2	244.1	130.4	144.0	122.3	133.1	91.4	137.6
October	163.9	174.4	162.0	101.5	132.7	141.4	244.8	130.9	144.2	122.2	132.7	93.9	134.0
November	164.1	174.8	162.2	101.1	132.7	141.3	245.3	130.8	144.3	122.0	132.5	93.6	131.6
December	164.4	175.4	162.4	100.1	132.0	140.9	245.9	131.3	145.8	121.3	132.2	90.2	129.4

Table 20-2. Summary Consumer and Producer Price Indexes—*Continued*

(Seasonally adjusted.)

Year and month	Consumer Price Index, all urban consumers, 1982–1984 = 100							Producer Price Index, 1982 = 100					
								Finished goods		Intermediate materials, supplies, and components		Crude materials for further processing	
	All items	All items less food and energy	Food	Energy	Apparel	Transportation	Medical care	Total	Less food and energy	Total	Less food and energy	Total	Crude nonfood less energy
1999													
January	164.7	175.6	163.0	99.7	131.5	140.8	246.5	. . .	. . .	121.2	132.0	91.0	128.7
February	164.7	175.6	163.3	99.2	130.8	140.0	247.3	. . .	. . .	120.8	131.8	89.0	130.5
March	164.8	175.7	163.3	100.4	130.4	140.7	247.9	. . .	. . .	121.1	131.9	89.6	129.6
April	165.9	176.3	163.5	105.5	131.7	143.6	248.7	. . .	. . .	121.9	132.0	91.3	128.7
May	166.0	176.5	163.8	104.9	131.7	143.4	249.3	. . .	. . .	122.2	132.4	96.8	130.5
June	166.0	176.6	163.7	104.5	131.7	143.0	250.0	. . .	. . .	122.6	132.8	97.0	131.6
July	166.7	177.1	163.9	106.7	131.5	144.6	250.9	. . .	. . .	123.4	133.3	97.3	133.6
August	167.1	177.3	164.2	109.5	130.9	145.9	251.7	. . .	. . .	124.1	133.6	102.4	136.3
September	167.8	177.8	164.6	111.8	131.2	147.0	252.5	. . .	. . .	124.6	133.9	106.4	138.8
October	168.1	178.1	165.0	112.0	131.4	147.6	253.1	. . .	. . .	124.9	134.3	103.8	142.5
November	168.4	178.4	165.3	111.5	131.0	147.5	253.9	. . .	. . .	125.4	134.5	109.7	144.4
December	168.8	178.7	165.5	113.8	131.3	148.8	254.9	. . .	. . .	125.8	134.7	104.4	147.6
2000													
January	169.3	179.3	165.6	115.0	130.7	149.1	255.6	135.2	146.8	126.4	135.1	106.8	150.5
February	170.0	179.4	166.2	118.8	130.4	150.0	256.5	136.6	147.3	127.5	135.5	111.0	151.3
March	171.0	180.0	166.5	124.3	130.3	153.6	257.7	137.3	147.4	128.4	136.0	113.2	150.5
April	170.9	180.3	166.7	120.9	129.8	152.1	258.4	136.9	147.4	128.3	136.5	111.3	148.8
May	171.2	180.7	167.3	120.0	129.7	152.0	259.2	137.0	147.8	128.2	136.6	115.1	147.8
June	172.2	181.1	167.4	126.8	129.3	155.0	260.3	138.1	147.8	129.3	136.9	124.8	145.1
July	172.7	181.5	168.3	127.3	128.9	154.6	261.2	138.2	148.1	129.6	137.1	122.1	142.8
August	172.7	181.9	168.7	123.8	128.9	153.2	262.4	137.9	148.2	129.3	136.9	117.6	141.2
September	173.6	182.3	168.9	129.2	129.5	155.2	263.3	139.0	148.6	130.3	137.0	125.6	142.9
October	173.9	182.6	169.0	129.6	129.2	154.7	264.1	139.5	148.5	130.7	137.1	130.2	142.1
November	174.2	183.1	169.2	129.2	129.2	155.0	264.7	140.2	148.7	130.7	136.9	129.1	139.6
December	174.6	183.3	170.0	130.1	129.1	155.1	265.6	140.5	148.9	131.3	136.9	141.1	139.5
2001													
January	175.6	183.9	170.3	135.0	129.4	155.4	267.2	141.7	149.5	132.1	137.1	165.6	138.7
February	176.0	184.4	171.2	134.1	129.6	155.2	268.3	141.9	149.2	131.8	137.3	141.7	136.5
March	176.1	184.7	171.7	131.7	129.5	154.2	269.4	141.2	149.5	131.0	137.4	132.4	135.0
April	176.4	185.1	172.1	132.3	128.2	154.8	270.4	142.0	149.8	130.9	137.3	133.0	131.3
May	177.3	185.3	172.4	138.4	127.4	157.6	271.3	142.3	150.1	131.1	137.3	130.5	130.9
June	177.7	186.0	173.1	136.9	127.4	157.3	272.4	141.8	150.2	130.9	137.1	119.9	129.7
July	177.4	186.4	173.6	129.6	127.3	154.0	272.8	140.1	150.5	129.4	136.4	113.3	130.6
August	177.4	186.7	174.0	127.3	126.4	153.4	274.3	140.7	150.5	129.1	135.9	112.3	128.4
September	178.1	187.1	174.2	130.9	125.8	156.0	275.2	141.3	150.7	129.3	135.9	107.2	128.8
October	177.6	187.4	174.8	122.9	125.8	152.9	276.3	139.0	149.8	127.6	135.4	97.4	126.5
November	177.5	188.1	174.9	116.9	125.4	150.2	277.4	138.5	150.2	127.0	135.1	102.7	126.2
December	177.4	188.4	174.7	113.9	124.9	149.2	278.2	138.0	150.4	126.1	134.8	95.5	125.7
2002													
January	177.7	188.7	175.3	114.2	124.4	149.3	279.8	137.7	150.0	125.7	134.7	99.8	126.2
February	178.0	189.1	175.7	113.5	124.6	148.7	280.4	138.0	150.1	125.5	134.6	98.4	127.5
March	178.5	189.2	176.1	117.6	125.3	150.5	281.4	138.8	150.0	126.4	135.0	103.8	128.1
April	179.3	189.7	176.4	121.5	125.1	152.5	282.7	138.7	150.3	127.2	135.3	108.1	130.8
May	179.5	190.0	175.8	121.9	124.6	152.8	283.9	138.4	150.2	127.1	135.3	109.0	134.2
June	179.6	190.2	175.9	121.6	123.9	152.8	284.6	138.8	150.5	127.3	135.6	105.1	138.2
July	180.0	190.5	176.1	122.4	123.5	153.3	286.4	138.6	150.0	127.7	136.0	106.5	140.8
August	180.5	191.1	176.1	123.1	124.3	154.0	287.2	138.7	149.9	128.0	136.2	108.3	140.0
September	180.8	191.3	176.5	123.7	123.4	154.2	288.1	139.2	150.3	128.9	136.5	110.8	140.2
October	181.2	191.5	176.4	126.9	123.0	155.5	289.8	140.0	150.5	129.8	136.7	112.6	140.0
November	181.5	191.9	176.9	126.7	123.1	155.4	291.2	140.0	150.3	129.9	136.8	116.6	141.0
December	181.8	192.1	177.1	127.1	122.7	155.3	292.1	139.7	149.5	130.0	136.7	118.9	141.3
2003													
January	182.6	192.4	177.1	133.5	122.1	158.0	292.7	141.1	149.8	131.4	137.2	128.0	143.3
February	183.6	192.5	178.1	140.8	121.8	160.8	293.0	142.7	149.9	133.8	138.1	134.3	148.1
March	183.9	192.5	178.4	143.9	120.7	160.8	293.4	144.0	150.7	136.3	138.6	152.2	147.5
April	183.2	192.5	178.5	136.5	120.3	157.7	294.0	142.2	149.9	133.1	138.3	128.2	145.9
May	182.9	192.9	178.8	129.4	120.0	154.4	295.2	141.9	150.1	132.4	138.4	129.9	146.0
June	183.1	193.0	179.7	129.8	120.6	154.6	296.1	142.7	150.1	133.1	138.4	135.5	145.7
July	183.7	193.4	179.8	132.2	121.1	155.7	297.4	142.8	150.3	133.3	138.2	131.9	148.5
August	184.5	193.6	180.5	137.8	120.8	158.2	298.3	143.7	150.5	133.9	138.4	130.8	152.1
September	185.1	193.7	180.9	142.9	120.9	159.9	299.8	144.0	150.4	133.8	138.8	134.4	156.2
October	184.9	194.0	181.6	137.8	121.1	157.5	300.4	144.8	151.1	134.2	139.1	138.2	160.2
November	185.0	194.0	182.6	136.9	120.8	156.9	301.4	144.6	151.0	134.2	139.3	137.9	165.6
December	185.5	194.2	183.5	138.8	120.2	157.4	303.0	145.1	151.0	135.0	139.6	142.4	171.0
2004													
January	186.3	194.6	183.4	143.9	120.1	159.8	303.8	145.9	151.4	136.6	140.5	148.7	179.7
February	186.7	194.9	183.9	145.8	120.1	160.7	305.2	145.8	151.3	137.8	141.8	150.8	190.0
March	187.1	195.5	184.2	145.1	120.4	160.8	306.5	146.2	151.8	138.4	142.9	153.2	195.0
April	187.4	195.9	184.6	143.4	120.6	159.8	307.8	147.2	151.9	140.1	144.6	156.2	187.1
May	188.2	196.2	186.1	147.6	120.9	161.6	308.6	148.4	152.3	141.7	145.7	160.6	177.6
June	188.9	196.6	186.4	151.5	121.2	162.8	309.8	148.4	152.8	142.2	146.2	161.5	176.3
July	189.1	196.8	186.8	151.1	121.0	162.3	310.8	148.2	152.5	142.9	146.9	161.3	195.7
August	189.2	196.9	187.0	151.5	120.3	162.1	311.8	148.6	152.9	144.4	148.4	161.7	201.6
September	189.8	197.5	186.9	152.9	120.0	163.4	312.9	148.8	153.2	144.8	149.6	154.0	198.3
October	190.8	197.9	187.8	158.6	120.3	166.7	314.0	151.2	153.7	146.6	150.2	161.0	204.6
November	191.7	198.3	188.4	163.8	120.6	169.1	314.7	152.1	154.1	147.9	150.7	172.7	208.9
December	191.7	198.6	188.4	162.3	119.8	168.5	315.8	151.4	154.5	147.7	151.3	167.2	206.0

. . . = Not available.

Table 20-2. Summary Consumer and Producer Price Indexes—*Continued*

(Seasonally adjusted.)

Year and month	Consumer Price Index, all urban consumers, 1982–1984 = 100							Producer Price Index, 1982 = 100					
								Finished goods		Intermediate materials, supplies, and components		Crude materials for further processing	
	All items	All items less food and energy	Food	Energy	Apparel	Transportation	Medical care	Total	Less food and energy	Total	Less food and energy	Total	Crude nonfood less energy
2005													
January	191.8	199.0	188.6	159.0	120.2	167.2	317.1	152.0	155.4	148.5	152.4	164.2	203.7
February	192.4	199.4	188.6	161.7	120.1	168.6	318.4	152.8	155.4	149.6	153.2	163.2	200.3
March	193.1	200.1	189.0	163.5	120.4	169.4	319.6	153.6	155.6	150.7	153.9	170.8	199.6
April	193.8	200.3	190.3	167.4	119.9	170.8	320.7	154.1	156.0	151.4	153.9	175.5	203.5
May	193.5	200.5	190.6	162.0	119.9	168.2	321.8	153.8	156.5	150.7	153.5	169.5	196.5
June	193.6	200.6	190.5	162.2	119.4	168.4	322.7	153.8	156.3	151.0	153.3	165.7	188.9
July	194.7	200.9	190.9	171.4	118.9	172.0	324.0	155.0	156.8	152.4	153.5	174.3	190.6
August	196.0	201.1	191.1	182.5	119.6	176.7	324.2	156.3	156.8	153.4	153.4	181.2	200.9
September	198.7	201.3	191.5	207.4	119.2	187.2	325.2	158.9	157.1	157.3	155.0	199.9	211.3
October	199.2	202.0	192.0	206.6	119.0	184.7	327.0	160.4	156.8	162.6	157.2	212.1	207.7
November	198.4	202.5	192.6	193.4	119.2	177.9	328.8	158.8	156.7	160.4	157.9	209.7	213.9
December	198.3	202.9	192.9	189.0	118.6	176.5	329.5	159.7	156.8	160.5	158.5	202.1	216.8
2006													
January	199.4	203.2	193.7	198.1	118.9	179.6	329.7	160.6	157.5	162.3	159.8	200.2	216.5
February	199.5	203.6	193.8	195.2	117.9	179.0	331.2	158.9	158.0	161.7	160.4	183.5	224.0
March	199.8	204.3	194.0	192.5	119.0	178.3	332.6	159.3	158.3	161.6	161.1	178.8	227.4
April	200.7	204.9	193.8	197.6	119.7	181.4	333.8	160.2	158.5	163.0	162.0	183.3	238.6
May	201.3	205.4	194.1	199.1	119.8	182.4	335.0	160.4	158.9	164.4	163.8	185.9	258.9
June	201.7	206.0	194.7	198.5	120.1	182.5	336.0	161.0	159.1	165.1	164.7	180.3	255.4
July	202.7	206.3	195.1	205.2	119.0	185.7	336.9	160.8	158.2	165.5	165.6	185.0	259.8
August	203.6	206.8	195.7	210.0	119.8	187.6	338.1	162.3	158.7	166.8	166.3	190.5	251.9
September	202.8	207.2	196.3	198.0	120.2	181.4	339.1	160.2	159.2	164.7	166.2	183.3	255.1
October	201.9	207.6	196.9	184.0	119.7	175.8	340.0	158.6	158.4	163.0	166.1	167.6	249.5
November	202.3	207.8	197.0	186.6	119.4	176.0	340.8	160.4	159.8	163.9	165.4	187.8	249.4
December	203.3	208.1	197.1	194.5	119.8	179.1	341.3	161.4	159.9	165.0	165.5	192.7	253.8
2007													
January	203.6	208.6	198.3	191.9	120.0	177.8	343.7	160.8	160.2	164.0	165.6	181.6	255.9
February	204.4	209.1	199.8	193.9	120.3	178.3	345.4	162.8	160.9	165.4	165.6	197.9	265.5
March	205.3	209.3	200.4	201.8	119.7	181.7	345.9	164.3	160.9	166.9	166.3	202.8	284.2
April	205.9	209.7	200.9	203.7	119.2	182.7	347.3	165.4	161.0	168.6	167.7	204.8	287.6
May	206.7	210.1	201.7	207.8	119.0	184.3	348.5	166.4	161.5	170.1	168.6	206.7	282.3
June	207.0	210.5	202.6	206.7	118.5	183.8	349.6	166.1	161.9	170.6	169.0	208.0	281.5
July	207.3	210.9	203.2	206.2	118.7	183.9	351.7	167.2	162.2	171.9	169.6	208.5	284.4
August	207.5	211.2	204.1	204.5	118.0	183.5	353.3	166.2	162.4	170.5	168.9	201.6	285.8
September	208.4	211.6	205.0	208.7	118.0	185.4	354.6	167.4	162.5	170.9	169.0	203.6	291.5
October	209.1	212.1	205.6	211.9	118.4	186.6	356.3	168.6	162.6	172.0	169.6	211.9	294.8
November	211.2	212.6	206.5	227.5	118.9	193.9	357.7	172.6	163.2	177.1	170.9	226.3	291.5
December	211.7	213.2	206.8	228.8	119.4	194.5	358.8	171.8	163.3	177.2	171.1	230.1	293.5
2008													
January	212.5	213.7	208.1	230.7	119.7	195.5	360.5	173.4	164.1	179.2	172.6	236.6	307.8
February	212.9	213.9	208.9	232.2	119.0	195.6	361.0	174.1	164.9	181.0	173.8	245.8	319.7
March	213.7	214.3	209.4	236.9	118.1	197.3	361.8	175.6	165.1	185.0	175.9	262.1	331.8
April	214.0	214.5	211.2	235.8	118.5	195.7	362.3	176.0	165.9	186.9	178.4	274.4	365.8
May	215.0	215.0	212.0	242.1	118.4	197.9	362.8	178.6	166.4	191.6	181.3	290.8	371.9
June	217.0	215.6	213.4	256.2	118.4	204.2	363.7	181.0	166.7	195.5	183.8	298.6	373.9
July	218.6	216.2	215.4	265.3	119.5	207.1	364.1	183.4	167.7	200.9	187.5	310.3	386.7
August	218.6	216.5	216.6	260.1	120.0	205.2	364.8	182.5	168.5	198.3	188.7	273.0	375.9
September	218.7	216.8	217.7	257.4	119.6	204.9	365.8	182.3	169.2	197.1	188.9	253.1	339.5
October	216.9	216.8	218.6	237.3	118.8	195.0	366.4	177.6	170.1	188.9	184.9	212.3	278.6
November	213.3	216.9	219.0	197.1	118.9	176.1	367.3	172.8	170.1	179.9	180.4	184.5	226.2
December	211.6	216.9	219.1	178.8	118.2	167.4	368.3	169.7	170.3	173.7	176.6	173.3	222.1

Table 20-3. Summary Labor Force, Employment, and Unemployment

(Thousands of persons, percent, seasonally adjusted, except as noted.)

Year and month	Civilian noninstitutional population [1]	Civilian labor force		Employment, thousands of persons					Employment-population ratio, percent	Unemployment		
		Thousands of persons	Participation rate (percent)	By age and sex			By industry			Thousands of persons		Rate (percent)
				Men, 20 years and over	Women, 20 years and over	Both sexes, 16 to 19 years	Agricultural	Nonagricultural		Total	Unemployed 15 weeks and over	
1947	101 827	59 350	58.3		57 038		7 890	49 148	56.0	2 311	. . .	3.9
1948	103 068	60 621	58.8	39 382	14 936	4 026	7 629	50 714	56.6	2 276	309	3.8
1949	103 994	61 286	58.9	38 803	15 137	3 712	7 658	49 993	55.4	3 637	684	5.9
1950	104 995	62 208	59.2	39 394	15 824	3 703	7 160	51 758	56.1	3 288	782	5.3
1951	104 621	62 017	59.2	39 626	16 570	3 767	6 726	53 235	57.3	2 055	303	3.3
1952	105 231	62 138	59.0	39 578	16 958	3 719	6 500	53 749	57.3	1 883	232	3.0
1953	107 056	63 015	58.9	40 296	17 164	3 720	6 260	54 919	57.1	1 834	210	2.9
1954	108 321	63 643	58.8	39 634	17 000	3 475	6 205	53 904	55.5	3 532	812	5.5
1955	109 683	65 023	59.3	40 526	18 002	3 642	6 450	55 722	56.7	2 852	702	4.4
1956	110 954	66 552	60.0	41 216	18 767	3 818	6 283	57 514	57.5	2 750	533	4.1
1957	112 265	66 929	59.6	41 239	19 052	3 778	5 947	58 123	57.1	2 859	560	4.3
1958	113 727	67 639	59.5	40 411	19 043	3 582	5 586	57 450	55.4	4 602	1 452	6.8
1959	115 329	68 369	59.3	41 267	19 524	3 838	5 565	59 065	56.0	3 740	1 040	5.5
1960	117 245	69 628	59.4	41 543	20 105	4 129	5 458	60 318	56.1	3 852	957	5.5
1961	118 771	70 459	59.3	41 342	20 296	4 108	5 200	60 546	55.4	4 714	1 532	6.7
1962	120 153	70 614	58.8	41 815	20 693	4 195	4 944	61 759	55.5	3 911	1 119	5.5
1963	122 416	71 833	58.7	42 251	21 257	4 255	4 687	63 076	55.4	4 070	1 088	5.7
1964	124 485	73 091	58.7	42 886	21 903	4 516	4 523	64 782	55.7	3 786	973	5.2
1948												
January	102 603	60 095	58.6	39 386	14 556	4 119	8 077	49 984	56.6	2 034	311	3.4
February	102 698	60 524	58.9	39 480	14 621	4 095	7 696	50 500	56.7	2 328	283	3.8
March	102 771	60 070	58.5	39 098	14 481	4 092	7 333	50 338	56.1	2 399	292	4.0
April	102 831	60 677	59.0	39 157	15 001	4 133	7 557	50 734	56.7	2 386	324	3.9
May	102 923	59 972	58.3	39 139	14 712	4 003	7 141	50 713	56.2	2 118	329	3.5
June	102 992	60 957	59.2	39 392	15 213	4 138	7 591	51 152	57.0	2 214	322	3.6
July	103 216	61 181	59.3	39 607	15 348	4 013	7 602	51 366	57.1	2 213	295	3.6
August	103 240	60 806	58.9	39 510	14 994	3 952	7 562	50 894	56.6	2 350	332	3.9
September	103 291	60 815	58.9	39 324	15 207	3 982	7 865	50 648	56.6	2 302	298	3.8
October	103 361	60 646	58.7	39 522	14 956	3 909	7 626	50 761	56.5	2 259	324	3.7
November	103 424	60 702	58.7	39 459	15 054	3 904	7 624	50 793	56.5	2 285	282	3.8
December	103 468	61 169	59.1	39 539	15 137	4 064	7 984	50 756	56.8	2 429	305	4.0
1949												
January	103 529	60 771	58.7	39 233	14 991	3 951	7 790	50 385	56.2	2 596	315	4.3
February	103 559	61 057	59.0	39 117	15 117	3 974	8 022	50 186	56.2	2 849	374	4.7
March	103 665	61 073	58.9	39 015	15 069	3 959	8 008	50 035	56.0	3 030	414	5.0
April	103 739	61 007	58.8	38 993	14 978	3 776	7 911	49 836	55.7	3 260	483	5.3
May	103 845	61 259	59.0	38 701	15 066	3 785	8 067	49 485	55.4	3 707	602	6.1
June	103 930	60 948	58.6	38 632	15 003	3 537	7 802	49 370	55.0	3 776	705	6.2
July	104 042	61 301	58.9	38 405	15 244	3 541	8 021	49 169	55.0	4 111	848	6.7
August	104 121	61 590	59.2	38 610	15 181	3 606	7 604	49 793	55.1	4 193	917	6.8
September	104 219	61 633	59.1	38 744	15 129	3 711	7 297	50 287	55.3	4 049	973	6.6
October	104 338	62 185	59.6	38 394	15 260	3 615	6 814	50 455	54.9	4 916	1 000	7.9
November	104 421	62 005	59.4	38 860	15 422	3 727	7 497	50 512	55.6	3 996	1 056	6.4
December	104 524	61 908	59.2	38 908	15 300	3 637	7 379	50 466	55.3	4 063	961	6.6
1950												
January	104 619	61 661	58.9	38 780	15 255	3 600	7 065	50 570	55.1	4 026	947	6.5
February	104 737	61 687	58.9	38 818	15 339	3 594	7 057	50 694	55.1	3 936	947	6.4
March	104 844	61 604	58.8	38 851	15 366	3 511	7 116	50 612	55.1	3 876	912	6.3
April	104 943	62 158	59.2	39 100	15 831	3 652	7 264	51 319	55.8	3 575	920	5.8
May	105 014	62 083	59.1	39 416	15 628	3 605	7 277	51 372	55.8	3 434	890	5.5
June	105 104	62 419	59.4	39 476	15 953	3 623	7 285	51 767	56.2	3 367	868	5.4
July	105 194	62 121	59.1	39 517	15 793	3 691	7 126	51 875	56.1	3 120	769	5.0
August	105 282	62 596	59.5	39 879	16 124	3 794	7 248	52 549	56.8	2 799	633	4.5
September	105 269	62 349	59.2	39 865	15 902	3 808	6 992	52 583	56.6	2 774	648	4.4
October	105 096	62 428	59.4	39 737	16 175	3 891	7 371	52 432	56.9	2 625	545	4.2
November	104 979	62 286	59.3	39 668	16 195	3 834	7 163	52 534	56.9	2 589	507	4.2
December	104 872	62 068	59.2	39 536	16 149	3 744	6 760	52 669	56.7	2 639	482	4.3
1951												
January	104 844	61 941	59.1	39 595	16 279	3 762	6 828	52 808	56.9	2 305	438	3.7
February	104 604	61 778	59.1	39 695	16 257	3 709	6 738	52 923	57.0	2 117	386	3.4
March	104 629	62 526	59.8	40 013	16 557	3 831	6 858	53 543	57.7	2 125	355	3.4
April	104 541	61 808	59.1	39 804	16 426	3 659	6 722	53 167	57.3	1 919	294	3.1
May	104 491	62 044	59.4	39 752	16 581	3 855	6 752	53 436	57.6	1 856	269	3.0
June	104 488	61 615	59.0	39 538	16 368	3 714	6 529	53 091	57.1	1 995	258	3.2
July	104 504	62 106	59.4	39 483	16 898	3 775	6 601	53 555	57.6	1 950	260	3.1
August	104 536	61 927	59.2	39 508	16 665	3 821	6 790	53 204	57.4	1 933	249	3.1
September	104 588	61 780	59.1	39 416	16 504	3 793	6 558	53 155	57.1	2 067	223	3.3
October	104 690	62 204	59.4	39 555	16 674	3 781	6 636	53 374	57.3	2 194	269	3.5
November	104 740	62 014	59.2	39 504	16 669	3 663	6 699	53 137	57.1	2 178	316	3.5
December	104 810	62 457	59.6	39 691	16 946	3 860	7 065	53 432	57.7	1 960	269	3.1

[1] Not seasonally adjusted.
. . . = Not available.

Table 20-3. Summary Labor Force, Employment, and Unemployment—*Continued*

(Thousands of persons, percent, seasonally adjusted, except as noted.)

| Year and month | Civilian noninstitutional population [1] | Civilian labor force | | Employment, thousands of persons | | | | | Employment-population ratio, percent | Unemployment | | |
| | | Thousands of persons | Participation rate (percent) | By age and sex | | | By industry | | | Thousands of persons | | Rate (percent) |
				Men, 20 years and over	Women, 20 years and over	Both sexes, 16 to 19 years	Agricultural	Nonagricultural		Total	Unemployed 15 weeks and over	
1952												
January	104 862	62 432	59.5	39 714	17 001	3 745	7 148	53 312	57.7	1 972	282	3.2
February	104 868	62 419	59.5	39 772	16 935	3 755	7 020	53 442	57.7	1 957	248	3.1
March	104 860	61 721	58.9	39 580	16 627	3 701	6 468	53 440	57.1	1 813	234	2.9
April	104 906	61 720	58.8	39 542	16 659	3 708	6 525	53 384	57.1	1 811	242	2.9
May	104 996	62 058	59.1	39 588	16 844	3 763	6 334	53 861	57.3	1 863	219	3.0
June	105 118	62 103	59.1	39 558	16 837	3 824	6 529	53 690	57.3	1 884	210	3.0
July	105 246	61 962	58.9	39 496	16 778	3 697	6 334	53 637	57.0	1 991	194	3.2
August	105 346	61 877	58.7	39 289	16 867	3 634	6 174	53 616	56.8	2 087	211	3.4
September	105 436	62 457	59.2	39 386	17 477	3 658	6 537	53 984	57.4	1 936	249	3.1
October	105 591	61 971	58.7	39 451	17 032	3 649	6 363	53 769	56.9	1 839	230	3.0
November	105 706	62 491	59.1	39 549	17 450	3 749	6 509	54 239	57.5	1 743	216	2.8
December	105 812	62 621	59.2	40 011	17 181	3 762	6 361	54 593	57.6	1 667	238	2.7
1953												
January	106 594	63 439	59.5	40 256	17 482	3 862	6 642	54 958	57.8	1 839	263	2.9
February	106 678	63 520	59.5	40 546	17 321	4 017	6 463	55 421	58.0	1 636	208	2.6
March	106 744	63 657	59.6	40 648	17 397	3 965	6 420	55 590	58.1	1 647	213	2.6
April	106 826	63 167	59.1	40 346	17 242	3 856	6 362	55 082	57.5	1 723	180	2.7
May	106 910	62 615	58.6	40 323	16 983	3 713	5 937	55 082	57.1	1 596	176	2.5
June	106 978	63 063	58.9	40 358	17 301	3 797	6 361	55 095	57.4	1 607	213	2.5
July	107 034	63 057	58.9	40 378	17 341	3 678	6 267	55 130	57.4	1 660	168	2.6
August	107 132	62 816	58.6	40 352	17 108	3 691	6 319	54 832	57.1	1 665	177	2.7
September	107 253	62 727	58.5	40 192	17 063	3 651	6 198	54 708	56.8	1 821	178	2.9
October	107 383	62 867	58.5	40 155	17 236	3 502	6 096	54 797	56.7	1 974	190	3.1
November	107 504	62 949	58.6	40 163	16 974	3 601	6 345	54 393	56.5	2 211	259	3.5
December	107 623	62 795	58.3	39 885	16 599	3 493	5 929	54 048	55.7	2 818	309	4.5
1954												
January	107 763	63 101	58.6	39 834	16 574	3 616	6 073	53 951	55.7	3 077	372	4.9
February	107 880	63 994	59.3	39 899	17 162	3 602	6 590	54 073	56.2	3 331	532	5.2
March	107 987	63 793	59.1	39 497	17 022	3 667	6 395	53 791	55.7	3 607	765	5.7
April	108 080	63 934	59.2	39 613	17 015	3 557	6 142	54 043	55.7	3 749	774	5.9
May	108 184	63 675	58.9	39 467	16 975	3 466	6 210	53 698	55.4	3 767	879	5.9
June	108 267	63 343	58.5	39 476	16 894	3 422	6 162	53 630	55.2	3 551	880	5.6
July	108 344	63 302	58.4	39 467	16 777	3 399	6 222	53 421	55.0	3 659	932	5.8
August	108 440	63 707	58.7	39 582	16 868	3 403	6 087	53 766	55.2	3 854	1 002	6.0
September	108 546	64 209	59.2	39 702	17 133	3 447	6 453	53 829	55.5	3 927	1 017	6.1
October	108 668	63 936	58.8	39 618	17 209	3 443	6 242	54 028	55.5	3 666	1 009	5.7
November	108 798	63 759	58.6	39 745	17 213	3 399	5 934	54 423	55.5	3 402	975	5.3
December	108 892	63 312	58.1	39 763	17 121	3 232	5 848	54 268	55.2	3 196	827	5.0
1955												
January	109 059	63 910	58.6	39 937	17 375	3 441	6 113	54 640	55.7	3 157	882	4.9
February	109 078	63 696	58.4	39 964	17 413	3 350	5 854	54 873	55.7	2 969	826	4.7
March	109 254	63 882	58.5	40 111	17 415	3 438	6 242	54 722	55.8	2 918	816	4.6
April	109 377	64 564	59.0	40 120	17 867	3 528	6 363	55 152	56.2	3 049	811	4.7
May	109 544	64 381	58.8	40 410	17 665	3 559	6 327	55 307	56.3	2 747	734	4.3
June	109 680	64 482	58.8	40 444	17 837	3 500	6 243	55 538	56.3	2 701	668	4.2
July	109 792	65 145	59.3	40 751	18 123	3 639	6 438	56 075	56.9	2 632	640	4.0
August	109 882	65 581	59.7	40 747	18 377	3 673	6 575	56 222	57.1	2 784	535	4.2
September	109 977	65 628	59.7	40 920	18 285	3 745	6 819	56 131	57.2	2 678	558	4.1
October	110 085	65 821	59.8	40 858	18 327	3 806	6 728	56 263	57.2	2 830	572	4.3
November	110 177	66 037	59.9	40 936	18 422	3 899	6 655	56 602	57.4	2 780	564	4.2
December	110 296	66 445	60.2	41 063	18 630	3 991	6 653	57 031	57.7	2 761	581	4.2
1956												
January	110 390	66 419	60.2	41 203	18 691	3 859	6 590	57 163	57.8	2 666	561	4.0
February	110 478	66 124	59.9	41 175	18 582	3 761	6 457	57 061	57.5	2 606	545	3.9
March	110 582	66 175	59.8	41 199	18 496	3 716	6 221	57 190	57.3	2 764	521	4.2
April	110 650	66 264	59.9	41 289	18 629	3 696	6 460	57 154	57.5	2 650	476	4.0
May	110 810	66 722	60.2	41 166	18 844	3 851	6 375	57 486	57.6	2 861	506	4.3
June	110 903	66 702	60.1	41 196	18 748	3 876	6 335	57 485	57.5	2 882	516	4.3
July	111 019	66 752	60.1	41 216	18 718	3 866	6 320	57 480	57.5	2 952	523	4.4
August	111 099	66 673	60.0	41 265	18 864	3 843	6 280	57 692	57.6	2 701	543	4.1
September	111 222	66 714	60.0	41 221	19 019	3 839	6 375	57 704	57.6	2 635	577	3.9
October	111 335	66 546	59.8	41 261	18 928	3 786	6 137	57 838	57.5	2 571	530	3.9
November	111 432	66 657	59.8	41 208	18 846	3 742	5 997	57 799	57.3	2 861	575	4.3
December	111 526	66 700	59.8	41 192	18 859	3 859	5 806	58 104	57.3	2 790	567	4.2
1957												
January	111 626	66 428	59.5	41 168	18 740	3 724	5 790	57 842	57.0	2 796	509	4.2
February	111 711	66 879	59.9	41 341	19 115	3 801	6 125	58 132	57.5	2 622	530	3.9
March	111 824	66 913	59.8	41 500	19 066	3 838	5 963	58 441	57.6	2 509	514	3.7
April	111 933	66 647	59.5	41 345	18 937	3 765	5 836	58 211	57.2	2 600	516	3.9
May	112 031	66 695	59.5	41 334	18 897	3 754	5 999	57 986	57.1	2 710	538	4.1
June	112 172	67 052	59.8	41 411	18 973	3 812	6 002	58 194	57.2	2 856	526	4.3
July	112 317	67 336	60.0	41 472	19 262	3 806	6 401	58 139	57.5	2 796	535	4.2
August	112 421	66 706	59.3	41 243	19 020	3 696	5 898	58 061	56.9	2 747	542	4.1
September	112 554	67 064	59.6	41 116	19 116	3 792	5 728	58 393	57.0	2 943	559	4.4
October	112 710	67 066	59.5	41 069	19 160	3 817	5 875	58 171	56.8	3 020	650	4.5
November	112 874	67 123	59.5	40 853	19 082	3 734	5 686	57 983	56.4	3 454	674	5.1
December	113 013	67 398	59.6	40 884	19 285	3 753	6 037	57 885	56.6	3 476	731	5.2

[1] Not seasonally adjusted.

Table 20-3. Summary Labor Force, Employment, and Unemployment—*Continued*

(Thousands of persons, percent, seasonally adjusted, except as noted.)

Year and month	Civilian noninsti- tutional population [1]	Civilian labor force		Employment, thousands of persons					Employ- ment- population ratio, percent	Unemployment		
		Thousands of persons	Participa- tion rate (percent)	By age and sex			By industry			Thousands of persons		Rate (percent)
				Men, 20 years and over	Women, 20 years and over	Both sexes, 16 to 19 years	Agricultural	Nonagri- cultural		Total	Unem- ployed 15 weeks and over	
1958												
January	113 138	67 095	59.3	40 617	19 035	3 568	5 831	57 389	55.9	3 875	879	5.8
February	113 234	67 201	59.3	40 336	18 951	3 611	5 654	57 244	55.5	4 303	1 005	6.4
March	113 337	67 223	59.3	40 180	18 968	3 583	5 561	57 170	55.3	4 492	1 128	6.7
April	113 415	67 647	59.6	40 129	18 969	3 533	5 602	57 029	55.2	5 016	1 387	7.4
May	113 534	67 895	59.8	40 253	18 978	3 643	5 647	57 227	55.4	5 021	1 493	7.4
June	113 647	67 674	59.5	40 208	19 008	3 514	5 510	57 220	55.2	4 944	1 677	7.3
July	113 727	67 824	59.6	40 270	19 039	3 436	5 525	57 220	55.2	5 079	1 796	7.5
August	113 835	68 037	59.8	40 343	19 103	3 566	5 673	57 339	55.4	5 025	1 888	7.4
September	113 977	68 002	59.7	40 564	19 033	3 584	5 453	57 728	55.4	4 821	1 795	7.1
October	114 138	68 045	59.6	40 699	19 091	3 685	5 563	57 912	55.6	4 570	1 708	6.7
November	114 283	67 658	59.2	40 684	19 157	3 629	5 571	57 899	55.5	4 188	1 570	6.2
December	114 429	67 740	59.2	40 666	19 170	3 713	5 521	58 028	55.5	4 191	1 490	6.2
1959												
January	114 582	67 936	59.3	40 769	19 292	3 807	5 481	58 387	55.7	4 068	1 396	6.0
February	114 712	67 649	59.0	40 699	19 167	3 818	5 429	58 255	55.5	3 965	1 277	5.9
March	114 849	68 068	59.3	41 079	19 379	3 809	5 677	58 590	56.0	3 801	1 210	5.6
April	114 986	68 339	59.4	41 419	19 498	3 851	5 893	58 875	56.3	3 571	1 039	5.2
May	115 144	68 178	59.2	41 355	19 565	3 779	5 792	58 907	56.2	3 479	965	5.1
June	115 287	68 278	59.2	41 387	19 658	3 804	5 712	59 137	56.3	3 429	963	5.0
July	115 429	68 539	59.4	41 596	19 595	3 820	5 564	59 447	56.3	3 528	889	5.1
August	115 555	68 432	59.2	41 485	19 568	3 791	5 442	59 402	56.1	3 588	889	5.2
September	115 668	68 545	59.3	41 351	19 531	3 888	5 447	59 323	56.0	3 775	895	5.5
October	115 798	68 821	59.4	41 362	19 702	3 847	5 355	59 556	56.1	3 910	883	5.7
November	115 916	68 533	59.1	41 062	19 594	3 874	5 480	59 050	55.7	4 003	982	5.8
December	116 040	68 994	59.5	41 651	19 717	3 973	5 458	59 883	56.3	3 653	920	5.3
1960												
January	116 594	68 962	59.1	41 637	19 686	4 024	5 458	59 889	56.0	3 615	915	5.2
February	116 702	68 949	59.1	41 729	19 765	4 126	5 443	60 177	56.2	3 329	841	4.8
March	116 827	68 399	58.5	41 320	19 388	3 965	4 959	59 714	55.4	3 726	959	5.4
April	116 910	69 579	59.5	41 641	20 110	4 208	5 471	60 488	56.4	3 620	896	5.2
May	117 033	69 626	59.5	41 668	20 186	4 203	5 359	60 698	56.4	3 569	797	5.1
June	117 167	69 934	59.7	41 553	20 290	4 325	5 416	60 752	56.5	3 766	854	5.4
July	117 281	69 745	59.5	41 490	20 257	4 162	5 542	60 367	56.2	3 836	921	5.5
August	117 431	69 841	59.5	41 503	20 316	4 076	5 520	60 375	56.1	3 946	927	5.6
September	117 521	70 151	59.7	41 604	20 493	4 170	5 755	60 512	56.4	3 884	982	5.5
October	117 643	69 884	59.4	41 464	20 076	4 092	5 436	60 196	55.8	4 252	1 189	6.1
November	117 829	70 439	59.8	41 543	20 384	4 182	5 513	60 596	56.1	4 330	1 223	6.1
December	118 001	70 395	59.7	41 416	20 332	4 030	5 622	60 156	55.7	4 617	1 142	6.6
1961												
January	118 155	70 447	59.6	41 363	20 325	4 088	5 422	60 354	55.7	4 671	1 328	6.6
February	118 250	70 420	59.6	41 177	20 392	4 019	5 472	60 116	55.5	4 832	1 416	6.9
March	118 358	70 703	59.7	41 273	20 459	4 118	5 406	60 444	55.6	4 853	1 463	6.9
April	118 503	70 267	59.3	41 206	20 145	4 023	5 037	60 337	55.2	4 893	1 598	7.0
May	118 638	70 452	59.4	41 139	20 261	4 049	5 099	60 350	55.2	5 003	1 686	7.1
June	118 767	70 878	59.7	41 349	20 446	4 198	5 220	60 773	55.6	4 885	1 651	6.9
July	118 889	70 536	59.3	41 245	20 252	4 111	5 153	60 455	55.2	4 928	1 830	7.0
August	119 006	70 534	59.3	41 362	20 279	4 211	5 366	60 486	55.3	4 682	1 649	6.6
September	119 107	70 217	59.0	41 400	20 112	4 029	5 021	60 520	55.0	4 676	1 531	6.7
October	119 202	70 492	59.1	41 509	20 338	4 072	5 203	60 716	55.3	4 573	1 481	6.5
November	119 153	70 376	59.1	41 556	20 330	4 195	5 090	60 991	55.5	4 295	1 388	6.1
December	119 214	70 077	58.8	41 534	20 287	4 079	4 992	60 908	55.3	4 177	1 361	6.0
1962												
January	119 300	70 189	58.8	41 547	20 501	4 060	5 094	61 014	55.4	4 081	1 235	5.8
February	119 360	70 409	59.0	41 745	20 693	4 100	5 289	61 249	55.7	3 871	1 244	5.5
March	119 476	70 414	58.9	41 696	20 567	4 230	5 157	61 336	55.7	3 921	1 162	5.6
April	119 702	70 278	58.7	41 647	20 567	4 158	5 009	61 363	55.4	3 906	1 122	5.6
May	119 813	70 551	58.9	41 847	20 558	4 283	4 964	61 724	55.7	3 863	1 134	5.5
June	119 943	70 514	58.8	41 761	20 547	4 362	4 943	61 727	55.6	3 844	1 079	5.5
July	120 128	70 302	58.5	41 671	20 592	4 220	4 840	61 643	55.3	3 819	1 049	5.4
August	120 323	70 981	59.0	41 900	20 841	4 227	4 866	62 102	55.7	4 013	1 081	5.7
September	120 653	71 153	59.0	42 020	20 982	4 190	4 867	62 325	55.7	3 961	1 096	5.6
October	120 856	70 917	58.7	42 086	20 856	4 172	4 816	62 298	55.5	3 803	1 022	5.4
November	121 045	70 871	58.5	41 985	20 794	4 068	4 831	62 016	55.2	4 024	1 051	5.7
December	121 236	70 854	58.4	41 934	20 831	4 182	4 647	62 300	55.2	3 907	1 068	5.5
1963												
January	121 463	71 146	58.6	41 938	20 933	4 201	4 882	62 190	55.2	4 074	1 122	5.7
February	121 633	71 262	58.6	41 876	21 046	4 102	4 652	62 372	55.1	4 238	1 137	5.9
March	121 824	71 423	58.6	42 047	21 162	4 142	4 696	62 655	55.3	4 072	1 087	5.7
April	121 986	71 697	58.8	42 131	21 281	4 230	4 670	62 972	55.5	4 055	1 071	5.7
May	122 162	71 832	58.8	42 145	21 225	4 245	4 729	62 886	55.3	4 217	1 157	5.9
June	122 352	71 626	58.5	42 268	21 185	4 196	4 642	63 007	55.3	3 977	1 067	5.6
July	122 521	71 956	58.7	42 427	21 268	4 210	4 694	63 211	55.4	4 051	1 070	5.6
August	122 667	71 786	58.5	42 400	21 185	4 323	4 604	63 304	55.4	3 878	1 114	5.4
September	122 821	72 131	58.7	42 500	21 317	4 357	4 650	63 524	55.5	3 957	1 069	5.5
October	123 014	72 281	58.8	42 437	21 456	4 401	4 702	63 592	55.5	3 987	1 071	5.5
November	123 192	72 418	58.8	42 415	21 553	4 299	4 694	63 573	55.4	4 151	1 054	5.7
December	123 360	72 188	58.5	42 427	21 481	4 305	4 629	63 584	55.3	3 975	1 007	5.5

[1] Not seasonally adjusted.

Table 20-3. Summary Labor Force, Employment, and Unemployment—*Continued*

(Thousands of persons, percent, seasonally adjusted, except as noted.)

Year and month	Civilian noninsti-tutional population [1]	Civilian labor force		Employment, thousands of persons					Employ-ment-population ratio, percent	Unemployment		
		Thousands of persons	Participa-tion rate (percent)	By age and sex			By industry			Thousands of persons		Rate (percent)
				Men, 20 years and over	Women, 20 years and over	Both sexes, 16 to 19 years	Agricultural	Nonagri-cultural		Total	Unem-ployed 15 weeks and over	
1964												
January	123 560	72 356	58.6	42 510	21 462	4 355	4 603	63 724	55.3	4 029	1 057	5.6
February	123 707	72 683	58.8	42 579	21 652	4 520	4 563	64 188	55.6	3 932	1 015	5.4
March	123 857	72 713	58.7	42 600	21 685	4 478	4 366	64 397	55.5	3 950	1 039	5.4
April	124 019	73 274	59.1	42 885	22 110	4 361	4 414	64 942	55.9	3 918	934	5.3
May	124 204	73 395	59.1	43 025	22 103	4 503	4 603	65 028	56.1	3 764	975	5.1
June	124 386	73 032	58.7	42 760	21 995	4 463	4 556	64 662	55.6	3 814	1 047	5.2
July	124 567	73 007	58.6	42 998	21 846	4 555	4 591	64 808	55.7	3 608	1 002	4.9
August	124 731	73 118	58.6	42 963	22 002	4 498	4 573	64 890	55.7	3 655	934	5.0
September	124 920	73 290	58.7	43 009	21 863	4 706	4 619	64 959	55.7	3 712	917	5.1
October	125 108	73 308	58.6	43 023	21 984	4 575	4 550	65 032	55.6	3 726	903	5.1
November	125 291	73 286	58.5	43 171	21 954	4 610	4 496	65 239	55.7	3 551	922	4.8
December	125 468	73 465	58.6	43 109	22 136	4 569	4 322	65 492	55.6	3 651	873	5.0
1965												
January	125 647	73 569	58.6	43 237	22 282	4 478	4 271	65 726	55.7	3 572	793	4.9
February	125 810	73 857	58.7	43 279	22 276	4 572	4 322	65 805	55.7	3 730	919	5.1
March	125 985	73 949	58.7	43 370	22 373	4 696	4 318	66 121	55.9	3 510	796	4.7
April	126 155	74 228	58.8	43 397	22 416	4 820	4 424	66 209	56.0	3 595	796	4.8
May	126 320	74 466	59.0	43 579	22 494	4 961	4 724	66 310	56.2	3 432	736	4.6
June	126 499	74 412	58.8	43 487	22 759	4 779	4 444	66 581	56.1	3 387	786	4.6
July	126 573	74 761	59.1	43 489	22 841	5 130	4 390	67 070	56.5	3 301	683	4.4
August	126 756	74 616	58.9	43 447	22 783	5 132	4 355	67 007	56.3	3 254	733	4.4
September	126 906	74 502	58.7	43 371	22 684	5 231	4 271	67 015	56.2	3 216	732	4.3
October	127 043	74 838	58.9	43 461	22 819	5 415	4 418	67 277	56.4	3 143	672	4.2
November	127 171	74 797	58.8	43 447	22 892	5 448	4 093	67 631	56.4	3 073	645	4.1
December	127 294	75 093	59.0	43 513	22 983	5 566	4 159	67 903	56.6	3 031	659	4.0
1966												
January	127 394	75 186	59.0	43 495	23 098	5 605	4 077	68 121	56.7	2 988	623	4.0
February	127 514	74 954	58.8	43 528	23 089	5 517	4 078	68 056	56.6	2 820	594	3.8
March	127 626	75 075	58.8	43 576	23 109	5 503	4 069	68 119	56.6	2 887	583	3.8
April	127 744	75 338	59.0	43 679	23 227	5 604	4 108	68 402	56.8	2 828	575	3.8
May	127 879	75 447	59.0	43 710	23 282	5 505	3 930	68 567	56.7	2 950	534	3.9
June	127 983	75 647	59.1	43 662	23 359	5 754	3 967	68 808	56.9	2 872	475	3.8
July	128 102	75 736	59.1	43 574	23 422	5 864	3 920	68 940	56.9	2 876	427	3.8
August	128 240	76 046	59.3	43 636	23 605	5 905	3 921	69 225	57.0	2 900	464	3.8
September	128 359	76 056	59.3	43 718	23 881	5 659	3 952	69 306	57.1	2 798	488	3.7
October	128 494	76 199	59.3	43 776	23 881	5 744	3 912	69 489	57.1	2 798	494	3.7
November	128 627	76 610	59.6	43 804	24 130	5 906	3 945	69 895	57.4	2 770	464	3.6
December	128 730	76 641	59.5	43 820	24 025	5 884	3 906	69 823	57.3	2 912	488	3.8
1967												
January	128 909	76 639	59.5	44 029	23 872	5 770	3 890	69 781	57.1	2 968	489	3.9
February	129 032	76 521	59.3	43 997	23 919	5 690	3 723	69 883	57.0	2 915	459	3.8
March	129 190	76 328	59.1	43 922	23 832	5 685	3 757	69 682	56.8	2 889	436	3.8
April	129 344	76 777	59.4	44 061	24 161	5 660	3 748	70 134	57.1	2 895	428	3.8
May	129 515	76 773	59.3	44 100	24 172	5 572	3 658	70 186	57.0	2 929	417	3.8
June	129 722	77 270	59.6	44 230	24 303	5 745	3 689	70 589	57.3	2 992	422	3.9
July	129 918	77 464	59.6	44 364	24 416	5 740	3 833	70 687	57.4	2 944	412	3.8
August	130 187	77 712	59.7	44 410	24 600	5 757	3 963	70 804	57.4	2 945	441	3.8
September	130 392	77 812	59.7	44 535	24 683	5 636	3 851	71 003	57.4	2 958	448	3.8
October	130 582	78 194	59.9	44 610	24 802	5 639	4 008	71 043	57.5	3 143	472	4.0
November	130 754	78 191	59.8	44 625	24 914	5 586	3 933	71 192	57.5	3 066	490	3.9
December	130 936	78 491	59.9	44 719	25 104	5 650	4 076	71 397	57.6	3 018	485	3.8
1968												
January	131 112	77 578	59.2	44 606	24 581	5 513	3 908	70 792	57.0	2 878	503	3.7
February	131 277	78 230	59.6	44 659	24 881	5 689	3 959	71 270	57.3	3 001	468	3.8
March	131 412	78 256	59.6	44 663	25 019	5 697	3 904	71 475	57.4	2 877	447	3.7
April	131 553	78 270	59.5	44 753	25 072	5 736	3 875	71 686	57.4	2 709	393	3.5
May	131 712	78 847	59.9	44 841	25 513	5 753	3 814	72 293	57.8	2 740	395	3.5
June	131 872	79 120	60.0	44 914	25 466	5 802	3 806	72 376	57.8	2 938	405	3.7
July	132 053	78 970	59.8	44 935	25 347	5 805	3 820	72 267	57.6	2 883	426	3.7
August	132 251	78 811	59.6	44 897	25 201	5 945	3 736	72 307	57.5	2 768	393	3.5
September	132 446	78 858	59.5	44 893	25 445	5 834	3 758	72 414	57.5	2 686	375	3.4
October	132 617	78 913	59.5	44 884	25 475	5 865	3 741	72 483	57.5	2 689	386	3.4
November	132 903	79 209	59.6	44 996	25 674	5 824	3 758	72 736	57.6	2 715	357	3.4
December	133 120	79 463	59.7	45 262	25 712	5 804	3 746	73 032	57.7	2 685	351	3.4
1969												
January	133 324	79 523	59.6	45 154	25 777	5 874	3 704	73 101	57.6	2 718	339	3.4
February	133 465	80 019	60.0	45 339	26 092	5 896	3 770	73 557	57.9	2 692	358	3.4
March	133 639	80 079	59.9	45 305	26 115	5 947	3 668	73 699	57.9	2 712	353	3.4
April	133 821	80 281	60.0	45 262	26 233	6 028	3 629	73 894	57.9	2 758	386	3.4
May	134 027	80 125	59.8	45 278	26 283	5 851	3 706	73 706	57.8	2 713	387	3.4
June	134 213	80 696	60.1	45 313	26 429	6 138	3 663	74 217	58.0	2 816	368	3.5
July	134 414	80 827	60.1	45 305	26 516	6 138	3 548	74 411	58.0	2 868	377	3.5
August	134 597	81 106	60.3	45 513	26 556	6 181	3 613	74 637	58.1	2 856	373	3.5
September	134 774	81 290	60.3	45 447	26 572	6 231	3 551	74 699	58.1	3 040	391	3.7
October	135 012	81 494	60.4	45 488	26 658	6 299	3 517	74 928	58.1	3 049	374	3.7
November	135 239	81 397	60.2	45 505	26 652	6 384	3 477	75 064	58.1	2 856	392	3.5
December	135 489	81 624	60.2	45 577	26 832	6 331	3 409	75 331	58.1	2 884	413	3.5

[1]Not seasonally adjusted.

Table 20-3. Summary Labor Force, Employment, and Unemployment—*Continued*

(Thousands of persons, percent, seasonally adjusted, except as noted.)

Year and month	Civilian noninstitutional population [1]	Civilian labor force		Employment, thousands of persons					Employment-population ratio, percent	Unemployment		
				By age and sex			By industry			Thousands of persons		
		Thousands of persons	Participation rate (percent)	Men, 20 years and over	Women, 20 years and over	Both sexes, 16 to 19 years	Agricultural	Nonagricultural		Total	Unemployed 15 weeks and over	Rate (percent)
1970												
January	135 713	81 981	60.4	45 654	26 908	6 218	3 422	75 358	58.0	3 201	431	3.9
February	135 957	82 151	60.4	45 627	26 828	6 243	3 439	75 259	57.9	3 453	470	4.2
March	136 179	82 498	60.6	45 668	26 933	6 262	3 499	75 364	57.9	3 635	534	4.4
April	136 416	82 727	60.6	45 679	27 114	6 137	3 568	75 362	57.9	3 797	602	4.6
May	136 686	82 483	60.3	45 666	26 739	6 159	3 547	75 017	57.5	3 919	591	4.8
June	136 928	82 484	60.2	45 554	26 904	5 955	3 555	74 858	57.3	4 071	657	4.9
July	137 196	82 901	60.4	45 516	27 083	6 127	3 517	75 209	57.4	4 175	662	5.0
August	137 455	82 880	60.3	45 495	27 011	6 118	3 418	75 206	57.2	4 256	705	5.1
September	137 717	82 954	60.2	45 535	26 784	6 179	3 451	75 047	57.0	4 456	788	5.4
October	137 988	83 276	60.4	45 508	27 058	6 119	3 337	75 348	57.0	4 591	771	5.5
November	138 264	83 548	60.4	45 540	27 020	6 090	3 372	75 278	56.9	4 898	871	5.9
December	138 529	83 670	60.4	45 466	27 038	6 090	3 380	75 214	56.7	5 076	1 102	6.1
1971												
January	138 795	83 850	60.4	45 527	27 173	6 164	3 393	75 471	56.8	4 986	1 113	5.9
February	139 021	83 603	60.1	45 455	27 040	6 205	3 288	75 412	56.6	4 903	1 068	5.9
March	139 285	83 575	60.0	45 520	26 967	6 101	3 356	75 232	56.4	4 987	1 098	6.0
April	139 566	83 946	60.1	45 789	26 984	6 214	3 574	75 413	56.6	4 959	1 149	5.9
May	139 826	84 135	60.2	45 917	27 056	6 166	3 449	75 690	56.6	4 996	1 173	5.9
June	140 090	83 706	59.8	45 879	27 013	5 865	3 334	75 423	56.2	4 949	1 167	5.9
July	140 343	84 340	60.1	46 000	27 054	6 251	3 386	75 919	56.5	5 035	1 251	6.0
August	140 596	84 673	60.2	46 041	27 711	6 327	3 395	76 144	56.6	5 134	1 261	6.1
September	140 869	84 731	60.1	46 090	27 390	6 209	3 367	76 322	56.6	5 042	1 239	6.0
October	141 146	84 872	60.1	46 132	27 538	6 248	3 405	76 513	56.6	4 954	1 268	5.8
November	141 393	85 458	60.4	46 209	27 721	6 367	3 410	76 887	56.8	5 161	1 277	6.0
December	141 666	85 625	60.4	46 280	27 791	6 400	3 371	77 100	56.8	5 154	1 283	6.0
1972												
January	142 736	85 978	60.2	46 471	27 956	6 532	3 366	77 593	56.7	5 019	1 257	5.8
February	143 017	86 036	60.2	46 600	28 016	6 492	3 358	77 750	56.7	4 928	1 292	5.7
March	143 263	86 611	60.5	46 821	28 126	6 626	3 438	78 135	56.9	5 038	1 232	5.8
April	143 483	86 614	60.4	46 863	28 114	6 678	3 382	78 273	56.9	4 959	1 203	5.7
May	143 760	86 809	60.4	46 950	28 184	6 753	3 412	78 475	57.0	4 922	1 168	5.7
June	144 033	87 006	60.4	47 147	28 175	6 761	3 402	78 681	57.0	4 923	1 141	5.7
July	144 285	87 143	60.4	47 244	28 225	6 761	3 461	78 769	57.0	4 913	1 154	5.6
August	144 522	87 517	60.6	47 321	28 382	6 875	3 603	78 975	57.1	4 939	1 156	5.6
September	144 761	87 392	60.4	47 394	28 417	6 732	3 568	78 975	57.0	4 849	1 131	5.5
October	144 988	87 491	60.3	47 354	28 438	6 824	3 634	78 982	57.0	4 875	1 123	5.6
November	145 211	87 592	60.3	47 529	28 567	6 894	3 517	79 473	57.2	4 602	1 040	5.3
December	145 446	87 943	60.5	47 747	28 698	6 955	3 596	79 804	57.3	4 543	1 006	5.2
1973												
January	145 720	87 487	60.0	47 701	28 596	6 864	3 456	79 705	57.1	4 326	947	4.9
February	145 943	88 364	60.5	47 884	28 995	7 033	3 415	80 497	57.5	4 452	894	5.0
March	146 230	88 846	60.8	48 117	29 110	7 225	3 469	80 983	57.8	4 394	889	4.9
April	146 459	89 018	60.8	48 098	29 304	7 157	3 407	81 152	57.7	4 459	809	5.0
May	146 719	88 977	60.6	48 068	29 432	7 148	3 376	81 272	57.7	4 329	816	4.9
June	146 981	89 548	60.9	48 244	29 505	7 436	3 509	81 676	58.0	4 363	779	4.9
July	147 233	89 604	60.9	48 452	29 592	7 255	3 540	81 759	57.9	4 305	756	4.8
August	147 471	89 509	60.7	48 353	29 578	7 273	3 425	81 779	57.8	4 305	788	4.8
September	147 731	89 838	60.8	48 408	29 710	7 370	3 342	82 146	57.9	4 350	785	4.8
October	147 980	90 131	60.9	48 631	29 885	7 471	3 424	82 563	58.1	4 144	793	4.6
November	148 219	90 716	61.2	48 764	30 071	7 485	3 593	82 727	58.2	4 396	832	4.8
December	148 479	90 890	61.2	48 902	29 991	7 508	3 658	82 743	58.2	4 489	767	4.9
1974												
January	148 753	91 199	61.3	49 107	29 893	7 555	3 756	82 799	58.2	4 644	799	5.1
February	148 982	91 485	61.4	49 057	30 146	7 551	3 824	82 930	58.2	4 731	829	5.2
March	149 225	91 453	61.3	48 986	30 293	7 540	3 726	83 093	58.2	4 634	849	5.1
April	149 478	91 287	61.1	48 853	30 376	7 440	3 582	83 087	58.0	4 618	889	5.1
May	149 750	91 596	61.2	49 039	30 424	7 428	3 529	83 362	58.0	4 705	880	5.1
June	150 012	91 868	61.2	48 946	30 512	7 483	3 386	83 555	58.0	4 927	926	5.4
July	150 248	92 212	61.4	48 883	30 869	7 397	3 436	83 713	58.0	5 063	924	5.5
August	150 493	92 059	61.2	48 950	30 662	7 425	3 429	83 608	57.8	5 022	960	5.5
September	150 753	92 488	61.4	48 978	30 569	7 504	3 460	83 591	57.7	5 437	1 021	5.9
October	151 009	92 518	61.3	48 959	30 570	7 466	3 431	83 564	57.6	5 523	1 072	6.0
November	151 256	92 766	61.3	48 833	30 424	7 369	3 405	83 221	57.3	6 140	1 128	6.6
December	151 494	92 780	61.2	48 458	30 431	7 255	3 361	82 783	56.9	6 636	1 326	7.2
1975												
January	151 755	93 128	61.4	48 086	30 343	7 198	3 401	82 226	56.4	7 501	1 555	8.1
February	151 990	92 776	61.0	47 927	30 215	7 114	3 361	81 895	56.1	7 520	1 841	8.1
March	152 217	93 165	61.2	47 776	30 334	7 077	3 358	81 829	56.0	7 978	2 074	8.6
April	152 443	93 399	61.3	47 759	30 410	7 020	3 315	81 874	55.9	8 210	2 442	8.8
May	152 704	93 884	61.5	47 835	30 483	7 133	3 560	81 891	56.0	8 433	2 643	9.0
June	152 976	93 575	61.2	47 754	30 618	6 983	3 368	81 987	55.8	8 220	2 843	8.8
July	153 309	94 021	61.3	48 050	30 794	7 050	3 457	82 437	56.0	8 127	2 943	8.6
August	153 580	94 162	61.3	48 239	30 966	7 029	3 429	82 805	56.1	7 928	2 862	8.4
September	153 848	94 202	61.2	48 126	30 979	7 174	3 508	82 771	56.1	7 923	2 906	8.4
October	154 082	94 267	61.2	48 165	31 121	7 084	3 397	82 973	56.1	7 897	2 689	8.4
November	154 338	94 250	61.1	48 203	31 135	7 118	3 331	83 125	56.0	7 794	2 789	8.3
December	154 589	94 409	61.1	48 266	31 268	7 131	3 259	83 406	56.1	7 744	2 868	8.2

[1] Not seasonally adjusted.

Table 20-3. Summary Labor Force, Employment, and Unemployment—*Continued*

(Thousands of persons, percent, seasonally adjusted, except as noted.)

Year and month	Civilian noninstitutional population [1]	Civilian labor force		Employment, thousands of persons					Employment-population ratio, percent	Unemployment		
				By age and sex			By industry			Thousands of persons		Rate (percent)
		Thousands of persons	Participation rate (percent)	Men, 20 years and over	Women, 20 years and over	Both sexes, 16 to 19 years	Agricultural	Nonagricultural		Total	Unemployed 15 weeks and over	
1976												
January	154 853	94 934	61.3	48 592	31 595	7 213	3 387	84 013	56.4	7 534	2 713	7.9
February	155 066	94 998	61.3	48 721	31 680	7 271	3 304	84 368	56.5	7 326	2 519	7.7
March	155 306	95 215	61.3	48 836	31 842	7 307	3 296	84 689	56.7	7 230	2 441	7.6
April	155 529	95 746	61.6	49 097	31 951	7 368	3 438	84 978	56.8	7 330	2 210	7.7
May	155 765	95 847	61.5	49 193	32 147	7 454	3 367	85 427	57.0	7 053	2 115	7.4
June	156 027	95 885	61.5	49 010	32 267	7 286	3 310	85 253	56.8	7 322	2 332	7.6
July	156 276	96 583	61.8	49 236	32 334	7 523	3 358	85 735	57.0	7 490	2 316	7.8
August	156 525	96 741	61.8	49 417	32 437	7 369	3 380	85 843	57.0	7 518	2 378	7.8
September	156 779	96 553	61.6	49 485	32 390	7 298	3 278	85 895	56.9	7 380	2 296	7.6
October	156 993	96 704	61.6	49 524	32 412	7 338	3 316	85 958	56.9	7 430	2 292	7.7
November	157 235	97 254	61.9	49 561	32 753	7 320	3 263	86 371	57.0	7 620	2 354	7.8
December	157 438	97 348	61.8	49 599	32 914	7 290	3 251	86 552	57.0	7 545	2 375	7.8
1977												
January	157 688	97 208	61.6	49 738	32 872	7 318	3 185	86 743	57.0	7 280	2 200	7.5
February	157 913	97 785	61.9	49 838	32 997	7 507	3 222	87 120	57.2	7 443	2 174	7.6
March	158 131	98 115	62.0	50 031	33 246	7 531	3 212	87 596	57.4	7 307	2 057	7.4
April	158 371	98 330	62.1	50 185	33 470	7 616	3 313	87 958	57.6	7 059	1 936	7.2
May	158 657	98 665	62.2	50 280	33 851	7 623	3 432	88 322	57.8	6 911	1 928	7.0
June	158 929	99 093	62.4	50 544	33 678	7 737	3 340	88 619	57.9	7 134	1 918	7.2
July	159 185	98 913	62.1	50 597	33 749	7 738	3 247	88 837	57.8	6 829	1 907	6.9
August	159 430	99 366	62.3	50 745	33 809	7 887	3 260	89 181	58.0	6 925	1 836	7.0
September	159 674	99 453	62.3	50 825	34 218	7 659	3 201	89 501	58.1	6 751	1 853	6.8
October	159 915	99 815	62.4	51 046	34 187	7 819	3 272	89 780	58.2	6 763	1 789	6.8
November	160 129	100 576	62.8	51 316	34 536	7 909	3 375	90 386	58.6	6 815	1 804	6.8
December	160 377	100 491	62.7	51 492	34 668	7 945	3 320	90 785	58.7	6 386	1 717	6.4
1978												
January	160 617	100 873	62.8	51 542	34 948	7 894	3 434	90 950	58.8	6 489	1 643	6.4
February	160 831	100 837	62.7	51 578	35 118	7 823	3 320	91 199	58.8	6 318	1 584	6.3
March	161 038	101 092	62.8	51 635	35 310	7 810	3 351	91 404	58.8	6 337	1 531	6.3
April	161 263	101 574	63.0	51 912	35 546	7 936	3 349	92 045	59.2	6 180	1 502	6.1
May	161 518	101 896	63.1	52 050	35 597	8 122	3 325	92 444	59.3	6 127	1 420	6.0
June	161 795	102 371	63.3	52 240	35 828	8 275	3 483	92 860	59.5	6 028	1 352	5.9
July	162 034	102 399	63.2	52 190	35 764	8 136	3 441	92 649	59.3	6 309	1 373	6.2
August	162 259	102 511	63.2	52 228	35 856	8 347	3 401	93 030	59.4	6 080	1 242	5.9
September	162 502	102 795	63.3	52 284	36 274	8 112	3 400	93 270	59.5	6 125	1 308	6.0
October	162 783	103 080	63.3	52 448	36 525	8 160	3 409	93 724	59.7	5 947	1 319	5.8
November	163 017	103 562	63.5	52 802	36 559	8 124	3 284	94 201	59.8	6 077	1 242	5.9
December	163 272	103 809	63.6	52 807	36 686	8 088	3 396	94 185	59.8	6 228	1 269	6.0
1979												
January	163 516	104 057	63.6	53 072	36 697	8 179	3 305	94 643	59.9	6 109	1 250	5.9
February	163 726	104 502	63.8	53 233	36 904	8 192	3 373	94 956	60.1	6 173	1 297	5.9
March	164 027	104 589	63.8	53 120	37 159	8 201	3 368	95 112	60.0	6 109	1 365	5.8
April	164 162	104 172	63.5	53 085	36 944	8 074	3 291	94 812	59.8	6 069	1 272	5.8
May	164 459	104 171	63.3	53 178	37 134	8 019	3 272	95 059	59.8	5 840	1 239	5.6
June	164 721	104 638	63.5	53 309	37 221	8 149	3 331	95 348	59.9	5 959	1 171	5.7
July	164 970	105 002	63.6	53 384	37 514	8 108	3 335	95 671	60.0	5 996	1 123	5.7
August	165 198	105 096	63.6	53 336	37 548	7 892	3 374	95 402	59.8	6 320	1 203	6.0
September	165 431	105 530	63.8	53 510	37 798	8 032	3 371	95 969	60.0	6 190	1 172	5.9
October	165 813	105 700	63.7	53 478	37 931	7 995	3 325	96 079	59.9	6 296	1 219	6.0
November	166 051	105 812	63.7	53 435	38 065	8 074	3 436	96 138	60.0	6 238	1 239	5.9
December	166 300	106 258	63.9	53 555	38 259	8 119	3 400	96 533	60.1	6 325	1 277	6.0
1980												
January	166 544	106 562	64.0	53 501	38 367	8 011	3 316	96 563	60.0	6 683	1 353	6.3
February	166 759	106 697	64.0	53 686	38 389	7 920	3 397	96 598	60.0	6 702	1 358	6.3
March	166 984	106 442	63.7	53 353	38 406	7 954	3 418	96 295	59.7	6 729	1 457	6.3
April	167 197	106 591	63.8	53 035	38 427	7 771	3 326	95 907	59.4	7 358	1 694	6.9
May	167 407	106 929	63.9	52 915	38 335	7 695	3 382	95 563	59.1	7 984	1 740	7.5
June	167 643	106 780	63.7	52 712	38 312	7 658	3 296	95 386	58.9	8 098	1 760	7.6
July	167 932	107 159	63.8	52 733	38 374	7 689	3 319	95 477	58.8	8 363	1 995	7.8
August	168 103	107 105	63.7	52 815	38 511	7 498	3 234	95 590	58.8	8 281	2 162	7.7
September	168 297	107 098	63.6	52 866	38 595	7 616	3 443	95 634	58.9	8 021	2 309	7.5
October	168 503	107 405	63.7	53 094	38 620	7 603	3 372	95 945	58.9	8 088	2 306	7.5
November	168 695	107 568	63.8	53 210	38 795	7 540	3 396	96 149	59.0	8 023	2 329	7.5
December	168 883	107 352	63.6	53 333	38 737	7 564	3 492	96 142	59.0	7 718	2 406	7.2
1981												
January	169 104	108 026	63.9	53 392	39 042	7 521	3 429	96 526	59.1	8 071	2 389	7.5
February	169 280	108 242	63.9	53 445	39 280	7 466	3 345	96 846	59.2	8 051	2 344	7.4
March	169 453	108 553	64.1	53 662	39 464	7 445	3 365	97 206	59.4	7 982	2 276	7.4
April	169 641	108 925	64.2	53 886	39 628	7 542	3 529	97 527	59.6	7 869	2 231	7.2
May	169 829	109 222	64.3	53 879	39 759	7 410	3 369	97 679	59.5	8 174	2 221	7.5
June	170 042	108 396	63.7	53 576	39 682	7 040	3 334	96 964	59.0	8 098	2 250	7.5
July	170 246	108 556	63.8	53 814	39 683	7 196	3 296	97 397	59.1	7 863	2 166	7.2
August	170 399	108 725	63.8	53 718	39 723	7 248	3 379	97 310	59.1	8 036	2 241	7.4
September	170 593	108 294	63.5	53 625	39 342	7 097	3 361	96 703	58.7	8 230	2 261	7.6
October	170 809	109 024	63.8	53 482	39 843	7 053	3 412	96 966	58.8	8 646	2 303	7.9
November	170 996	109 236	63.9	53 335	39 908	6 964	3 415	96 792	58.6	9 029	2 345	8.3
December	171 166	108 912	63.6	53 149	39 708	6 788	3 227	96 418	58.2	9 267	2 374	8.5

[1] Not seasonally adjusted.

Table 20-3. Summary Labor Force, Employment, and Unemployment—*Continued*

(Thousands of persons, percent, seasonally adjusted, except as noted.)

Year and month	Civilian noninsti-tutional population [1]	Civilian labor force		Employment, thousands of persons					Employ-ment-population ratio, percent	Unemployment		
		Thousands of persons	Participa-tion rate (percent)	By age and sex			By industry			Thousands of persons		Rate (percent)
				Men, 20 years and over	Women, 20 years and over	Both sexes, 16 to 19 years	Agricultural	Nonagri-cultural		Total	Unem-ployed 15 weeks and over	
1982												
January	171 335	109 089	63.7	53 103	39 821	6 768	3 393	96 299	58.2	9 397	2 409	8.6
February	171 489	109 467	63.8	53 172	39 859	6 731	3 375	96 387	58.2	9 705	2 758	8.9
March	171 667	109 567	63.8	53 054	39 936	6 682	3 372	96 300	58.1	9 895	2 965	9.0
April	171 844	109 820	63.9	53 081	39 848	6 647	3 351	96 225	57.9	10 244	3 086	9.3
May	172 026	110 451	64.2	53 234	40 121	6 761	3 434	96 682	58.2	10 335	3 276	9.4
June	172 190	110 081	63.9	52 933	40 219	6 391	3 331	96 212	57.8	10 538	3 451	9.6
July	172 364	110 342	64.0	52 896	40 228	6 369	3 402	96 091	57.7	10 849	3 555	9.8
August	172 511	110 514	64.1	52 797	40 336	6 500	3 408	96 225	57.8	10 881	3 696	9.8
September	172 690	110 721	64.1	52 760	40 275	6 469	3 385	96 119	57.6	11 217	3 889	10.1
October	172 881	110 744	64.1	52 624	40 105	6 486	3 489	95 726	57.4	11 529	4 185	10.4
November	173 058	111 050	64.2	52 537	40 111	6 464	3 510	95 602	57.3	11 938	4 485	10.8
December	173 199	111 083	64.1	52 497	40 164	6 371	3 414	95 618	57.2	12 051	4 662	10.8
1983												
January	173 354	110 695	63.9	52 487	40 268	6 406	3 439	95 722	57.2	11 534	4 668	10.4
February	173 505	110 634	63.8	52 453	40 336	6 300	3 382	95 707	57.1	11 545	4 641	10.4
March	173 656	110 587	63.7	52 615	40 368	6 196	3 360	95 819	57.1	11 408	4 612	10.3
April	173 794	110 828	63.8	52 814	40 542	6 204	3 341	96 219	57.3	11 268	4 370	10.2
May	173 953	110 796	63.7	52 922	40 538	6 182	3 328	96 314	57.3	11 154	4 538	10.1
June	174 125	111 879	64.3	53 515	40 695	6 423	3 462	97 171	57.8	11 246	4 470	10.1
July	174 306	111 756	64.1	53 835	41 041	6 332	3 481	97 727	58.1	10 548	4 329	9.4
August	174 440	112 231	64.3	53 837	41 314	6 457	3 502	98 106	58.2	10 623	4 070	9.5
September	174 602	112 298	64.3	53 983	41 650	6 383	3 347	98 669	58.4	10 282	3 854	9.2
October	174 779	111 926	64.0	54 146	41 597	6 296	3 303	98 736	58.4	9 887	3 648	8.8
November	174 951	112 228	64.1	54 499	41 788	6 442	3 291	99 438	58.7	9 499	3 535	8.5
December	175 121	112 327	64.1	54 662	41 852	6 482	3 332	99 664	58.8	9 331	3 379	8.3
1984												
January	175 533	112 209	63.9	54 975	41 812	6 414	3 293	99 908	58.8	9 008	3 254	8.0
February	175 679	112 615	64.1	55 213	42 196	6 415	3 353	100 471	59.1	8 791	2 991	7.8
March	175 824	112 713	64.1	55 281	42 328	6 358	3 233	100 734	59.1	8 746	2 881	7.8
April	175 969	113 098	64.3	55 373	42 512	6 451	3 291	101 045	59.3	8 762	2 858	7.7
May	176 123	113 649	64.5	55 661	43 071	6 461	3 343	101 850	59.7	8 456	2 884	7.4
June	176 284	113 817	64.6	55 996	42 944	6 651	3 383	102 208	59.9	8 226	2 612	7.2
July	176 440	113 972	64.6	55 921	42 979	6 535	3 344	102 091	59.8	8 537	2 638	7.5
August	176 583	113 682	64.4	55 930	42 885	6 348	3 286	101 877	59.6	8 519	2 604	7.5
September	176 763	113 857	64.4	56 095	42 967	6 428	3 393	102 097	59.7	8 367	2 538	7.3
October	176 956	114 019	64.4	56 183	43 052	6 403	3 194	102 444	59.7	8 381	2 526	7.4
November	177 135	114 170	64.5	56 274	43 244	6 454	3 394	102 578	59.8	8 198	2 438	7.2
December	177 306	114 581	64.6	56 313	43 472	6 438	3 385	102 838	59.9	8 358	2 401	7.3
1985												
January	177 384	114 725	64.7	56 184	43 589	6 529	3 317	102 985	59.9	8 423	2 284	7.3
February	177 516	114 876	64.7	56 216	43 787	6 552	3 317	103 238	60.0	8 321	2 389	7.2
March	177 667	115 328	64.9	56 356	44 035	6 598	3 250	103 739	60.2	8 339	2 394	7.2
April	177 799	115 331	64.9	56 374	44 000	6 562	3 306	103 630	60.1	8 395	2 393	7.3
May	177 944	115 234	64.8	56 531	43 905	6 496	3 280	103 652	60.1	8 302	2 292	7.2
June	178 096	114 965	64.6	56 288	43 958	6 259	3 161	103 344	59.8	8 460	2 310	7.4
July	178 263	115 320	64.7	56 435	43 975	6 397	3 143	103 664	59.9	8 513	2 329	7.4
August	178 405	115 291	64.6	56 655	44 103	6 337	3 121	103 974	60.0	8 196	2 258	7.1
September	178 572	115 905	64.9	56 845	44 395	6 417	3 064	104 593	60.3	8 248	2 242	7.1
October	178 770	116 145	65.0	56 969	44 565	6 313	3 051	104 796	60.3	8 298	2 295	7.1
November	178 940	116 135	64.9	56 972	44 617	6 418	3 062	104 945	60.4	8 128	2 207	7.0
December	179 112	116 354	65.0	56 995	44 889	6 332	3 141	105 075	60.4	8 138	2 208	7.0
1986												
January	179 670	116 682	64.9	57 637	44 944	6 306	3 287	105 600	60.6	7 795	2 089	6.7
February	179 821	116 882	65.0	57 269	44 804	6 407	3 083	105 397	60.3	8 402	2 308	7.2
March	179 985	117 220	65.1	57 353	44 960	6 524	3 200	105 637	60.5	8 383	2 261	7.2
April	180 148	117 316	65.1	57 358	45 081	6 513	3 153	105 799	60.5	8 364	2 162	7.1
May	180 311	117 528	65.2	57 287	45 289	6 513	3 150	105 939	60.5	8 439	2 232	7.2
June	180 503	118 084	65.4	57 471	45 621	6 484	3 193	106 383	60.7	8 508	2 320	7.2
July	180 682	118 129	65.4	57 514	45 837	6 459	3 141	106 669	60.8	8 319	2 269	7.0
August	180 828	118 150	65.3	57 597	45 926	6 492	3 082	106 933	60.8	8 135	2 276	6.9
September	180 997	118 395	65.4	57 630	45 972	6 483	3 171	106 914	60.8	8 310	2 318	7.0
October	181 186	118 516	65.4	57 660	46 046	6 567	3 128	107 145	60.9	8 243	2 188	7.0
November	181 363	118 634	65.4	57 941	46 070	6 464	3 220	107 255	60.9	8 159	2 202	6.9
December	181 547	118 611	65.3	58 185	46 132	6 411	3 148	107 580	61.0	7 883	2 161	6.6
1987												
January	181 827	118 845	65.4	58 264	46 219	6 470	3 143	107 810	61.0	7 892	2 168	6.6
February	181 998	119 122	65.5	58 279	46 444	6 534	3 208	108 049	61.1	7 865	2 117	6.6
March	182 179	119 270	65.5	58 362	46 549	6 497	3 214	108 194	61.2	7 862	2 070	6.6
April	182 344	119 336	65.4	58 503	46 746	6 545	3 246	108 548	61.3	7 542	2 091	6.3
May	182 533	120 009	65.7	58 713	47 052	6 669	3 345	109 089	61.6	7 574	2 104	6.3
June	182 703	119 644	65.5	58 581	47 102	6 563	3 216	109 030	61.4	7 398	2 087	6.2
July	182 885	119 902	65.6	58 740	47 229	6 665	3 235	109 399	61.6	7 268	1 921	6.1
August	183 002	120 318	65.7	58 810	47 322	6 925	3 112	109 945	61.8	7 261	1 878	6.0
September	183 161	120 011	65.5	58 964	47 285	6 660	3 189	109 720	61.6	7 102	1 866	5.9
October	183 311	120 509	65.7	59 073	47 533	6 676	3 219	110 063	61.8	7 227	1 794	6.0
November	183 470	120 540	65.7	59 210	47 622	6 673	3 145	110 360	61.9	7 035	1 797	5.8
December	183 620	120 729	65.7	59 217	47 781	6 795	3 213	110 580	62.0	6 936	1 767	5.7

[1]Not seasonally adjusted.

Table 20-3. Summary Labor Force, Employment, and Unemployment—*Continued*

(Thousands of persons, percent, seasonally adjusted, except as noted.)

Year and month	Civilian noninsti-tutional population [1]	Civilian labor force		Employment, thousands of persons					Employ-ment-population ratio, percent	Unemployment		
		Thousands of persons	Participa-tion rate (percent)	By age and sex			By industry			Thousands of persons		Rate (percent)
				Men, 20 years and over	Women, 20 years and over	Both sexes, 16 to 19 years	Agricultural	Nonagri-cultural		Total	Unem-ployed 15 weeks and over	
1988												
January	183 822	120 969	65.8	59 346	47 862	6 808	3 247	110 769	62.0	6 953	1 714	5.7
February	183 969	121 156	65.9	59 535	47 919	6 773	3 201	111 026	62.1	6 929	1 738	5.7
March	184 111	120 913	65.7	59 393	48 090	6 554	3 169	110 868	61.9	6 876	1 744	5.7
April	184 232	121 251	65.8	59 832	48 147	6 671	3 224	111 426	62.2	6 601	1 563	5.4
May	184 374	121 071	65.7	59 644	47 946	6 702	3 121	111 171	62.0	6 779	1 647	5.6
June	184 562	121 473	65.8	59 751	48 146	7 030	3 111	111 816	62.3	6 546	1 531	5.4
July	184 729	121 665	65.9	59 888	48 186	6 986	3 060	112 000	62.3	6 605	1 601	5.4
August	184 830	122 125	66.1	59 877	48 467	6 938	3 119	112 163	62.4	6 843	1 639	5.6
September	184 962	121 960	65.9	59 980	48 511	6 865	3 165	112 191	62.4	6 604	1 569	5.4
October	185 114	122 206	66.0	60 023	48 859	6 756	3 231	112 407	62.5	6 568	1 562	5.4
November	185 244	122 637	66.2	60 042	49 254	6 804	3 241	112 859	62.7	6 537	1 468	5.3
December	185 402	122 622	66.1	60 059	49 257	6 788	3 194	112 910	62.6	6 518	1 490	5.3
1989												
January	185 644	123 390	66.5	60 477	49 529	6 702	3 287	113 421	62.9	6 682	1 480	5.4
February	185 777	123 135	66.3	60 588	49 497	6 691	3 234	113 542	62.9	6 359	1 304	5.2
March	185 897	123 227	66.3	60 795	49 503	6 724	3 198	113 824	62.9	6 205	1 353	5.0
April	186 024	123 565	66.4	60 764	49 565	6 768	3 162	113 935	62.9	6 468	1 397	5.2
May	186 181	123 474	66.3	60 795	49 583	6 721	3 125	113 974	62.9	6 375	1 348	5.2
June	186 329	123 995	66.5	61 054	49 542	6 822	3 068	114 350	63.0	6 577	1 300	5.3
July	186 483	123 967	66.5	60 947	49 693	6 832	3 227	114 245	63.0	6 495	1 435	5.2
August	186 598	124 166	66.5	60 915	49 804	6 936	3 284	114 371	63.1	6 511	1 302	5.2
September	186 726	123 944	66.4	60 668	50 015	6 671	3 219	114 135	62.8	6 590	1 360	5.3
October	186 871	124 211	66.5	60 958	49 871	6 752	3 215	114 366	62.9	6 630	1 392	5.3
November	187 017	124 637	66.6	60 958	50 221	6 733	3 132	114 780	63.0	6 725	1 418	5.4
December	187 165	124 497	66.5	61 068	50 116	6 646	3 188	114 642	63.0	6 667	1 375	5.4
1990												
January	188 413	125 833	66.8	61 742	50 436	6 903	3 210	115 871	63.2	6 752	1 412	5.4
February	188 516	125 710	66.7	61 805	50 438	6 816	3 188	115 871	63.2	6 651	1 350	5.3
March	188 630	125 801	66.7	61 832	50 463	6 908	3 260	115 943	63.2	6 598	1 331	5.2
April	188 778	125 649	66.6	61 579	50 457	6 816	3 231	115 621	63.0	6 797	1 376	5.4
May	188 913	125 893	66.6	61 778	50 646	6 727	3 266	115 885	63.1	6 742	1 415	5.4
June	189 058	125 573	66.4	61 762	50 550	6 671	3 245	115 738	62.9	6 590	1 436	5.2
July	189 188	125 732	66.5	61 683	50 514	6 613	3 192	115 618	62.8	6 922	1 534	5.5
August	189 342	125 990	66.5	61 715	50 635	6 452	3 197	115 605	62.7	7 188	1 607	5.7
September	189 528	125 892	66.4	61 608	50 587	6 329	3 206	115 318	62.5	7 368	1 695	5.9
October	189 710	125 995	66.4	61 606	50 616	6 314	3 270	115 266	62.5	7 459	1 689	5.9
November	189 872	126 070	66.4	61 545	50 541	6 220	3 189	115 117	62.3	7 764	1 831	6.2
December	190 017	126 142	66.4	61 506	50 530	6 205	3 245	114 996	62.2	7 901	1 804	6.3
1991												
January	190 163	125 955	66.2	61 383	50 472	6 085	3 208	114 732	62.0	8 015	1 866	6.4
February	190 271	126 020	66.2	61 117	50 523	6 115	3 270	114 485	61.9	8 265	1 955	6.6
March	190 381	126 238	66.3	61 144	50 422	6 086	3 177	114 475	61.8	8 586	2 137	6.8
April	190 517	126 548	66.4	61 280	50 760	6 069	3 241	114 868	62.0	8 439	2 206	6.7
May	190 650	126 176	66.2	61 052	50 457	5 931	3 275	114 165	61.6	8 736	2 252	6.9
June	190 800	126 331	66.2	61 147	50 585	5 907	3 300	114 339	61.7	8 692	2 533	6.9
July	190 946	126 154	66.1	61 179	50 636	5 753	3 319	114 249	61.6	8 586	2 388	6.8
August	191 116	126 150	66.0	61 122	50 601	5 761	3 313	114 171	61.5	8 666	2 460	6.9
September	191 302	126 650	66.2	61 279	50 864	5 785	3 319	114 609	61.6	8 722	2 497	6.9
October	191 497	126 642	66.1	61 174	50 811	5 815	3 289	114 511	61.5	8 842	2 638	7.0
November	191 657	126 701	66.1	61 201	50 759	5 810	3 296	114 474	61.4	8 931	2 718	7.0
December	191 798	126 664	66.0	61 074	50 728	5 664	3 146	114 320	61.2	9 198	2 892	7.3
1992												
January	191 953	127 261	66.3	61 116	51 095	5 767	3 155	114 823	61.5	9 283	3 060	7.3
February	192 067	127 207	66.2	61 062	51 033	5 658	3 239	114 514	61.3	9 454	3 182	7.4
March	192 204	127 604	66.4	61 363	51 204	5 577	3 236	114 908	61.5	9 460	3 196	7.4
April	192 354	127 841	66.5	61 468	51 323	5 635	3 245	115 181	61.6	9 415	3 130	7.4
May	192 503	128 119	66.6	61 513	51 245	5 617	3 213	115 162	61.5	9 744	3 444	7.6
June	192 663	128 459	66.7	61 537	51 383	5 499	3 297	115 122	61.5	10 040	3 758	7.8
July	192 826	128 563	66.7	61 641	51 458	5 614	3 285	115 428	61.6	9 850	3 614	7.7
August	193 018	128 613	66.6	61 681	51 386	5 759	3 279	115 547	61.6	9 787	3 579	7.6
September	193 229	128 501	66.5	61 663	51 359	5 698	3 274	115 446	61.4	9 781	3 504	7.6
October	193 442	128 026	66.2	61 550	51 373	5 705	3 254	115 374	61.3	9 398	3 505	7.3
November	193 621	128 441	66.3	61 644	51 535	5 697	3 207	115 669	61.4	9 565	3 397	7.4
December	193 784	128 554	66.3	61 721	51 524	5 752	3 259	115 738	61.4	9 557	3 651	7.4
1993												
January	193 962	128 400	66.2	61 895	51 505	5 675	3 222	115 853	61.4	9 325	3 346	7.3
February	194 108	128 458	66.2	61 963	51 573	5 739	3 125	116 150	61.4	9 183	3 190	7.1
March	194 248	128 598	66.2	61 808	51 808	5 727	3 119	116 423	61.5	9 056	3 115	7.0
April	194 398	128 584	66.1	62 032	51 732	5 710	3 074	116 400	61.5	9 110	3 014	7.1
May	194 549	129 264	66.4	62 309	51 996	5 810	3 100	117 015	61.7	9 149	3 101	7.1
June	194 719	129 411	66.5	62 409	52 183	5 698	3 108	117 182	61.8	9 121	3 141	7.0
July	194 882	129 397	66.4	62 497	52 088	5 882	3 126	117 341	61.8	8 930	3 046	6.9
August	195 063	129 619	66.4	62 634	52 294	5 928	3 026	117 830	62.0	8 763	3 026	6.8
September	195 259	129 268	66.2	62 437	52 241	5 876	3 174	117 380	61.7	8 714	3 042	6.7
October	195 444	129 573	66.3	62 614	52 379	5 830	3 084	117 739	61.8	8 750	3 029	6.8
November	195 625	129 711	66.3	62 732	52 531	5 906	3 157	118 012	61.9	8 542	2 986	6.6
December	195 794	129 941	66.4	62 760	52 813	5 891	3 116	118 348	62.0	8 477	2 968	6.5

[1] Not seasonally adjusted.

Table 20-3. Summary Labor Force, Employment, and Unemployment—*Continued*

(Thousands of persons, percent, seasonally adjusted, except as noted.)

Year and month	Civilian noninstitutional population [1]	Civilian labor force		Employment, thousands of persons					Employment-population ratio, percent	Unemployment		
		Thousands of persons	Participation rate (percent)	By age and sex			By industry			Thousands of persons		Rate (percent)
				Men, 20 years and over	Women, 20 years and over	Both sexes, 16 to 19 years	Agricultural	Nonagricultural		Total	Unemployed 15 weeks and over	
1994												
January	195 953	130 596	66.6	62 798	53 052	6 116	3 302	118 664	62.2	8 630	3 060	6.6
February	196 090	130 669	66.6	62 708	53 266	6 112	3 339	118 747	62.3	8 583	3 118	6.6
March	196 213	130 400	66.5	62 780	53 099	6 051	3 354	118 576	62.1	8 470	3 055	6.5
April	196 363	130 621	66.5	62 906	53 274	6 110	3 428	118 862	62.3	8 331	2 921	6.4
May	196 510	130 779	66.6	63 116	53 624	6 124	3 409	119 455	62.5	7 915	2 836	6.1
June	196 693	130 561	66.4	63 041	53 393	6 200	3 299	119 335	62.3	7 927	2 735	6.1
July	196 859	130 652	66.4	63 034	53 531	6 141	3 333	119 373	62.3	7 946	2 822	6.1
August	197 043	131 275	66.6	63 294	53 744	6 304	3 451	119 891	62.6	7 933	2 750	6.0
September	197 248	131 421	66.6	63 631	53 991	6 065	3 430	120 257	62.7	7 734	2 746	5.9
October	197 430	131 744	66.7	63 818	54 071	6 223	3 490	120 622	62.9	7 632	2 955	5.8
November	197 607	131 891	66.7	64 080	54 168	6 268	3 574	120 942	63.0	7 375	2 666	5.6
December	197 765	131 951	66.7	64 359	54 054	6 308	3 577	121 144	63.1	7 230	2 488	5.5
1995												
January	197 753	132 038	66.8	64 185	54 087	6 391	3 519	121 144	63.0	7 375	2 396	5.6
February	197 886	132 115	66.8	64 378	54 226	6 324	3 620	121 308	63.1	7 187	2 345	5.4
March	198 007	132 108	66.7	64 321	54 141	6 493	3 634	121 321	63.1	7 153	2 287	5.4
April	198 148	132 590	66.9	64 165	54 366	6 414	3 566	121 379	63.1	7 645	2 473	5.8
May	198 286	131 851	66.5	63 829	54 272	6 320	3 349	121 072	62.7	7 430	2 577	5.6
June	198 453	131 949	66.5	63 992	54 020	6 510	3 461	121 061	62.7	7 427	2 266	5.6
July	198 615	132 343	66.6	63 962	54 476	6 378	3 379	121 437	62.8	7 527	2 311	5.7
August	198 801	132 336	66.6	63 875	54 434	6 543	3 374	121 478	62.8	7 484	2 391	5.7
September	199 005	132 611	66.6	64 179	54 507	6 447	3 285	121 848	62.9	7 478	2 306	5.6
October	199 192	132 716	66.6	64 272	54 692	6 424	3 438	121 950	62.9	7 328	2 272	5.5
November	199 355	132 614	66.5	63 931	54 850	6 407	3 338	121 850	62.8	7 426	2 339	5.6
December	199 508	132 511	66.4	64 041	54 674	6 373	3 352	121 736	62.7	7 423	2 331	5.6
1996												
January	199 634	132 616	66.4	64 180	54 580	6 365	3 483	121 642	62.7	7 491	2 371	5.6
February	199 773	132 952	66.6	64 398	54 844	6 397	3 547	122 092	62.9	7 313	2 307	5.5
March	199 921	133 180	66.6	64 506	54 994	6 362	3 489	122 373	63.0	7 318	2 454	5.5
April	200 101	133 409	66.7	64 481	55 067	6 446	3 406	122 588	63.0	7 415	2 455	5.6
May	200 278	133 667	66.7	64 683	55 034	6 527	3 473	122 771	63.0	7 423	2 403	5.6
June	200 459	133 697	66.7	64 940	55 177	6 485	3 424	123 178	63.2	7 095	2 355	5.3
July	200 641	134 284	66.9	65 068	55 362	6 517	3 433	123 514	63.3	7 337	2 297	5.5
August	200 847	134 054	66.7	65 216	55 525	6 431	3 395	123 777	63.3	6 882	2 267	5.1
September	201 061	134 515	66.9	65 169	55 669	6 698	3 448	124 088	63.4	6 979	2 220	5.2
October	201 273	134 921	67.0	65 460	55 750	6 680	3 463	124 427	63.5	7 031	2 268	5.2
November	201 463	135 007	67.0	65 320	55 896	6 555	3 356	124 415	63.4	7 236	2 159	5.4
December	201 636	135 113	67.0	65 435	55 849	6 576	3 445	124 415	63.4	7 253	2 124	5.4
1997												
January	202 285	135 456	67.0	65 679	56 024	6 595	3 449	124 849	63.4	7 158	2 162	5.3
February	202 389	135 400	66.9	65 758	55 955	6 585	3 353	124 945	63.4	7 102	2 140	5.2
March	202 513	135 891	67.1	65 974	56 270	6 647	3 419	125 472	63.6	7 000	2 110	5.2
April	202 674	136 016	67.1	66 092	56 347	6 704	3 462	125 681	63.7	6 873	2 176	5.1
May	202 832	136 119	67.1	66 328	56 446	6 690	3 437	126 027	63.8	6 655	2 121	4.9
June	203 000	136 211	67.1	66 308	56 573	6 531	3 409	126 003	63.7	6 799	2 085	5.0
July	203 166	136 477	67.2	66 422	56 785	6 615	3 422	126 400	63.9	6 655	2 119	4.9
August	203 364	136 618	67.2	66 508	56 852	6 650	3 359	126 651	63.9	6 608	2 004	4.8
September	203 570	136 675	67.1	66 483	56 931	6 605	3 392	126 627	63.9	6 656	2 074	4.9
October	203 767	136 633	67.1	66 511	56 982	6 686	3 312	126 867	63.9	6 454	1 950	4.7
November	203 941	136 961	67.2	66 765	57 039	6 849	3 386	127 267	64.1	6 308	1 817	4.6
December	204 098	137 155	67.2	66 643	57 219	6 817	3 405	127 274	64.0	6 476	1 901	4.7
1998												
January	204 238	137 095	67.1	66 750	56 941	7 035	3 299	127 389	64.0	6 368	1 833	4.6
February	204 400	137 112	67.1	66 856	56 992	6 959	3 284	127 522	64.0	6 306	1 809	4.6
March	204 547	137 236	67.1	66 721	57 080	7 014	3 146	127 650	64.0	6 422	1 772	4.7
April	204 731	137 150	67.0	67 151	57 074	6 985	3 334	127 852	64.1	5 941	1 476	4.3
May	204 899	137 372	67.0	67 164	57 155	7 007	3 360	127 959	64.1	6 047	1 490	4.4
June	205 085	137 455	67.0	67 054	57 156	7 033	3 380	127 874	64.0	6 212	1 613	4.5
July	205 270	137 588	67.0	67 119	57 192	7 018	3 455	127 913	64.0	6 259	1 577	4.5
August	205 479	137 570	67.0	66 985	57 332	7 074	3 509	127 970	63.9	6 179	1 626	4.5
September	205 699	138 286	67.2	67 254	57 520	7 212	3 500	128 399	64.2	6 300	1 688	4.6
October	205 919	138 279	67.2	67 433	57 529	7 036	3 593	128 389	64.1	6 280	1 582	4.5
November	206 104	138 381	67.1	67 591	57 638	7 052	3 375	128 897	64.2	6 100	1 590	4.4
December	206 270	138 634	67.2	67 548	57 840	7 214	3 246	129 320	64.3	6 032	1 559	4.4
1999												
January	206 719	139 003	67.2	67 679	58 256	7 092	3 233	129 802	64.4	5 976	1 490	4.3
February	206 873	138 967	67.2	67 498	58 129	7 229	3 246	129 647	64.2	6 111	1 551	4.4
March	207 036	138 730	67.0	67 660	58 132	7 155	3 238	129 656	64.2	5 783	1 472	4.2
April	207 236	138 959	67.1	67 542	58 260	7 153	3 336	129 615	64.2	6 004	1 480	4.3
May	207 427	139 107	67.1	67 539	58 440	7 331	3 335	129 937	64.3	5 796	1 505	4.2
June	207 632	139 329	67.1	67 700	58 641	7 037	3 386	129 982	64.2	5 951	1 624	4.3
July	207 828	139 439	67.1	67 731	58 490	7 193	3 346	130 146	64.2	6 025	1 513	4.3
August	208 038	139 430	67.0	67 768	58 707	7 117	3 234	130 366	64.2	5 838	1 455	4.2
September	208 265	139 622	67.0	67 882	58 735	7 090	3 173	130 434	64.2	5 915	1 449	4.2
October	208 483	139 771	67.0	67 840	58 921	7 232	3 229	130 758	64.3	5 778	1 438	4.1
November	208 666	140 025	67.1	68 094	59 018	7 198	3 343	130 989	64.4	5 716	1 378	4.1
December	208 832	140 177	67.1	68 217	59 056	7 251	3 260	131 257	64.4	5 653	1 375	4.0

[1] Not seasonally adjusted.

Table 20-3. Summary Labor Force, Employment, and Unemployment—*Continued*

(Thousands of persons, percent, seasonally adjusted, except as noted.)

Year and month	Civilian noninstitutional population [1]	Civilian labor force		Employment, thousands of persons					Employment-population ratio, percent	Unemployment		
				By age and sex			By industry			Thousands of persons		
		Thousands of persons	Participation rate (percent)	Men, 20 years and over	Women, 20 years and over	Both sexes, 16 to 19 years	Agricultural	Nonagricultural		Total	Unemployed 15 weeks and over	Rate (percent)
2000												
January	211 410	142 267	67.3	69 419	59 842	7 298	2 613	133 863	64.6	5 708	1 380	4.0
February	211 576	142 456	67.3	69 505	59 887	7 206	2 731	133 912	64.6	5 858	1 300	4.1
March	211 772	142 434	67.3	69 482	59 977	7 241	2 579	134 022	64.6	5 733	1 312	4.0
April	212 018	142 751	67.3	69 519	60 358	7 393	2 505	134 806	64.7	5 481	1 261	3.8
May	212 242	142 388	67.1	69 399	59 951	7 280	2 480	134 144	64.4	5 758	1 325	4.0
June	212 466	142 591	67.1	69 629	60 027	7 284	2 445	134 528	64.5	5 651	1 242	4.0
July	212 677	142 278	66.9	69 525	60 011	6 995	2 408	134 196	64.2	5 747	1 343	4.0
August	212 916	142 514	66.9	69 823	59 719	7 120	2 433	134 311	64.2	5 853	1 394	4.1
September	213 163	142 518	66.9	69 700	60 083	7 110	2 384	134 489	64.2	5 625	1 290	3.9
October	213 405	142 622	66.8	69 762	60 238	7 088	2 319	134 808	64.2	5 534	1 337	3.9
November	213 540	142 962	66.9	69 910	60 269	7 143	2 330	134 921	64.3	5 639	1 315	3.9
December	213 736	143 248	67.0	69 939	60 503	7 172	2 389	135 194	64.4	5 634	1 329	3.9
2001												
January	213 888	143 800	67.2	70 064	60 609	7 104	2 360	135 304	64.4	6 023	1 372	4.2
February	214 110	143 701	67.1	69 959	60 615	7 038	2 370	135 291	64.3	6 089	1 491	4.2
March	214 305	143 924	67.2	69 881	60 902	7 001	2 350	135 372	64.3	6 141	1 521	4.3
April	214 525	143 569	66.9	69 916	60 523	6 860	2 336	135 036	64.0	6 271	1 499	4.4
May	214 732	143 318	66.7	69 865	60 509	6 717	2 353	134 735	63.8	6 226	1 502	4.3
June	214 950	143 357	66.7	69 690	60 371	6 812	2 082	134 755	63.7	6 484	1 532	4.5
July	215 180	143 654	66.8	69 808	60 480	6 784	2 295	134 858	63.7	6 583	1 653	4.6
August	215 420	143 284	66.5	69 585	60 301	6 356	2 305	133 944	63.2	7 042	1 861	4.9
September	215 665	143 989	66.8	69 933	60 265	6 649	2 322	134 558	63.5	7 142	1 950	5.0
October	215 903	144 086	66.7	69 621	60 168	6 602	2 327	134 098	63.2	7 694	2 082	5.3
November	216 117	144 240	66.7	69 444	60 174	6 620	2 203	133 955	63.0	8 003	2 318	5.5
December	216 315	144 305	66.7	69 551	60 095	6 400	2 293	133 751	62.9	8 258	2 444	5.7
2002												
January	216 506	143 883	66.5	69 308	60 032	6 361	2 385	133 233	62.7	8 182	2 578	5.7
February	216 663	144 653	66.8	69 534	60 479	6 425	2 397	134 127	63.0	8 215	2 608	5.7
March	216 823	144 481	66.6	69 480	60 190	6 507	2 368	133 816	62.8	8 304	2 719	5.7
April	217 006	144 725	66.7	69 574	60 204	6 349	2 371	133 833	62.7	8 599	2 852	5.9
May	217 198	144 938	66.7	69 981	60 226	6 332	2 260	134 278	62.9	8 399	2 967	5.8
June	217 407	144 808	66.6	69 769	60 297	6 348	2 161	134 135	62.7	8 393	3 023	5.8
July	217 630	144 803	66.5	69 806	60 290	6 317	2 324	134 107	62.7	8 390	2 966	5.8
August	217 866	145 009	66.6	69 937	60 560	6 208	2 127	134 593	62.7	8 304	2 887	5.7
September	218 107	145 552	66.7	70 207	60 679	6 416	2 285	135 102	63.0	8 251	2 971	5.7
October	218 340	145 314	66.6	69 948	60 663	6 397	2 471	134 580	62.7	8 307	3 042	5.7
November	218 548	145 041	66.4	69 615	60 697	6 209	2 261	134 171	62.5	8 520	3 062	5.9
December	218 741	145 066	66.3	69 620	60 667	6 139	2 352	134 071	62.4	8 640	3 271	6.0
2003												
January	219 897	145 937	66.4	69 919	61 406	6 091	2 337	135 045	62.5	8 520	3 166	5.8
February	220 114	146 100	66.4	70 262	61 159	6 060	2 234	135 306	62.5	8 618	3 161	5.9
March	220 317	146 022	66.3	70 243	61 317	5 874	2 263	135 232	62.4	8 588	3 161	5.9
April	220 540	146 474	66.4	70 311	61 374	5 948	2 150	135 561	62.4	8 842	3 348	6.0
May	220 768	146 500	66.4	70 215	61 393	5 936	2 183	135 370	62.3	8 957	3 318	6.1
June	221 014	147 056	66.5	70 159	61 747	5 884	2 185	135 419	62.3	9 266	3 552	6.3
July	221 252	146 485	66.2	70 190	61 437	5 847	2 187	135 242	62.1	9 011	3 633	6.2
August	221 507	146 445	66.1	70 237	61 442	5 870	2 313	135 200	62.1	8 896	3 557	6.1
September	221 779	146 530	66.1	70 631	61 119	5 860	2 349	135 355	62.0	8 921	3 486	6.1
October	222 039	146 716	66.1	70 685	61 451	5 848	2 479	135 571	62.1	8 732	3 451	6.0
November	222 279	147 000	66.1	70 935	61 494	5 995	2 373	136 003	62.3	8 576	3 420	5.8
December	222 509	146 729	65.9	71 170	61 396	5 845	2 243	136 145	62.2	8 317	3 366	5.7
2004												
January	222 161	146 842	66.1	71 318	61 183	5 971	2 196	136 228	62.3	8 370	3 364	5.7
February	222 357	146 709	66.0	71 122	61 514	5 906	2 210	136 362	62.3	8 167	3 248	5.6
March	222 550	146 944	66.0	71 155	61 534	5 764	2 180	136 302	62.2	8 491	3 314	5.8
April	222 757	146 850	65.9	71 121	61 647	5 912	2 241	136 474	62.3	8 170	2 971	5.6
May	222 967	147 065	66.0	71 180	61 762	5 911	2 300	136 556	62.3	8 212	3 103	5.6
June	223 196	147 460	66.1	71 562	61 793	5 819	2 237	136 748	62.4	8 286	3 130	5.6
July	223 422	147 692	66.1	71 780	61 884	5 891	2 222	137 354	62.5	8 136	2 918	5.5
August	223 677	147 564	66.0	71 808	61 836	5 930	2 333	137 230	62.4	7 990	2 846	5.4
September	223 941	147 415	65.8	71 744	61 859	5 884	2 251	137 323	62.3	7 927	2 910	5.4
October	224 192	147 793	65.9	71 860	61 942	5 931	2 216	137 598	62.3	8 061	3 041	5.5
November	224 422	148 162	66.0	72 110	62 088	6 033	2 206	137 978	62.5	7 932	2 960	5.4
December	224 640	148 059	65.9	72 058	62 136	5 931	2 171	137 947	62.4	7 934	2 927	5.4
2005												
January	224 837	148 005	65.8	72 068	62 259	5 920	2 112	138 108	62.4	7 759	2 835	5.2
February	225 041	148 349	65.9	72 293	62 252	5 831	2 129	138 255	62.4	7 972	2 888	5.4
March	225 236	148 366	65.9	72 463	62 209	5 954	2 180	138 434	62.4	7 740	2 808	5.2
April	225 441	148 926	66.1	72 842	62 487	5 914	2 245	139 012	62.7	7 683	2 674	5.2
May	225 670	149 273	66.1	73 114	62 557	5 929	2 226	139 366	62.7	7 672	2 686	5.1
June	225 911	149 262	66.1	73 207	62 517	5 987	2 304	139 240	62.7	7 551	2 426	5.1
July	226 153	149 445	66.1	73 331	62 692	6 006	2 309	139 786	62.8	7 415	2 458	5.0
August	226 421	149 794	66.2	73 511	62 848	6 075	2 183	140 291	62.9	7 360	2 579	4.9
September	226 693	149 977	66.2	73 339	63 038	6 030	2 181	140 292	62.8	7 570	2 545	5.0
October	226 959	150 007	66.1	73 464	63 121	5 966	2 190	140 446	62.8	7 457	2 506	5.0
November	227 204	150 095	66.1	73 397	63 141	6 017	2 174	140 346	62.7	7 541	2 479	5.0
December	227 425	150 002	66.0	73 495	63 219	6 069	2 094	140 661	62.8	7 219	2 416	4.8

[1] Not seasonally adjusted.

Table 20-3. Summary Labor Force, Employment, and Unemployment—*Continued*

(Thousands of persons, percent, seasonally adjusted, except as noted.)

Year and month	Civilian noninsti-tutional population [1]	Civilian labor force		Employment, thousands of persons					Employ-ment-population ratio, percent	Unemployment		
				By age and sex			By industry			Thousands of persons		
		Thousands of persons	Participa-tion rate (percent)	Men, 20 years and over	Women, 20 years and over	Both sexes, 16 to 19 years	Agricultural	Nonagri-cultural		Total	Unem-ployed 15 weeks and over	Rate (percent)
2006												
January	227 553	150 148	66.0	73 875	63 154	6 100	2 162	140 924	62.9	7 020	2 243	4.7
February	227 763	150 600	66.1	73 943	63 301	6 180	2 181	141 219	63.0	7 176	2 531	4.8
March	227 975	150 793	66.1	74 194	63 360	6 160	2 158	141 508	63.0	7 080	2 357	4.7
April	228 199	150 906	66.1	74 178	63 423	6 163	2 246	141 508	63.0	7 142	2 347	4.7
May	228 428	151 120	66.2	74 215	63 654	6 223	2 202	141 860	63.1	7 028	2 311	4.7
June	228 671	151 398	66.2	74 250	63 864	6 244	2 264	142 011	63.1	7 039	2 149	4.6
July	228 912	151 414	66.1	74 037	64 027	6 184	2 283	142 084	63.0	7 167	2 305	4.7
August	229 167	151 762	66.2	74 406	64 137	6 101	2 235	142 470	63.1	7 118	2 306	4.7
September	229 420	151 680	66.1	74 890	63 899	6 017	2 173	142 669	63.1	6 874	2 242	4.5
October	229 675	152 027	66.2	74 865	64 269	6 154	2 173	143 193	63.3	6 738	2 085	4.4
November	229 905	152 425	66.3	75 026	64 351	6 211	2 161	143 365	63.3	6 837	2 158	4.5
December	230 108	152 677	66.4	75 234	64 557	6 198	2 229	143 708	63.4	6 688	2 070	4.4
2007												
January	230 650	153 012	66.3	75 199	64 633	6 152	2 213	143 731	63.3	7 029	2 116	4.6
February	230 834	152 879	66.2	75 193	64 728	6 070	2 305	143 679	63.2	6 887	2 184	4.5
March	231 034	153 004	66.2	75 330	64 928	6 010	2 189	144 046	63.3	6 737	2 227	4.4
April	231 253	152 522	66.0	75 310	64 408	5 929	2 069	143 613	63.0	6 874	2 266	4.5
May	231 480	152 759	66.0	75 386	64 706	5 823	2 095	143 798	63.0	6 844	2 244	4.5
June	231 713	153 085	66.1	75 308	64 781	5 968	1 957	144 071	63.0	7 028	2 309	4.6
July	231 958	153 101	66.0	75 278	64 771	5 923	2 019	144 046	62.9	7 128	2 392	4.7
August	232 211	152 855	65.8	75 245	64 843	5 644	1 857	143 902	62.8	7 123	2 349	4.7
September	232 461	153 424	66.0	75 305	65 028	5 870	2 072	144 160	62.9	7 221	2 374	4.7
October	232 715	153 162	65.8	75 177	64 774	5 917	2 103	143 843	62.7	7 295	2 355	4.8
November	232 939	153 877	66.1	75 781	65 024	5 861	2 143	144 473	63.0	7 212	2 378	4.7
December	233 156	153 836	66.0	75 496	64 976	5 822	2 211	143 992	62.7	7 541	2 484	4.9
2008												
January	232 616	153 873	66.1	75 474	65 101	5 742	2 205	144 097	62.9	7 555	2 477	4.9
February	232 809	153 498	65.9	75 395	64 993	5 688	2 208	143 878	62.7	7 423	2 400	4.8
March	232 995	153 843	66.0	75 216	65 079	5 729	2 191	143 821	62.7	7 820	2 444	5.1
April	233 198	153 932	66.0	75 147	65 196	5 914	2 111	144 219	62.7	7 675	2 652	5.0
May	233 405	154 510	66.2	74 992	65 114	5 868	2 136	143 830	62.5	8 536	2 808	5.5
June	233 627	154 400	66.1	74 949	65 169	5 620	2 134	143 563	62.4	8 662	2 966	5.6
July	233 864	154 506	66.1	74 973	65 103	5 520	2 142	143 453	62.3	8 910	3 168	5.8
August	234 107	154 823	66.1	74 737	65 003	5 533	2 138	143 111	62.1	9 550	3 447	6.2
September	234 360	154 621	66.0	74 503	65 008	5 518	2 199	142 851	61.9	9 592	3 662	6.2
October	234 612	154 878	66.0	74 292	64 975	5 390	2 177	142 566	61.7	10 221	4 109	6.6
November	234 828	154 620	65.8	74 045	64 902	5 196	2 206	141 901	61.4	10 476	3 964	6.8
December	235 035	154 447	65.7	73 285	64 860	5 194	2 191	141 047	61.0	11 108	4 517	7.2

[1]Not seasonally adjusted.

Table 20-3A. Labor Force and Employment Estimates Smoothed for Population Adjustments

(Thousands of persons, seasonally adjusted.)

Year	January	February	March	April	May	June	July	August	September	October	November	December
CIVILIAN LABOR FORCE												
1990	125 845	125 734	125 837	125 697	125 953	125 645	125 816	126 087	126 001	126 116	126 203	126 287
1991	126 112	126 189	126 420	126 742	126 382	126 549	126 384	126 392	126 905	126 909	126 981	126 956
1992	127 566	127 524	127 934	128 184	128 475	128 829	128 945	129 008	128 908	128 444	128 872	128 998
1993	128 856	128 926	129 079	129 077	129 772	129 932	129 931	130 166	129 826	130 145	130 296	130 539
1994	131 210	131 296	131 038	131 272	131 444	131 237	131 341	131 980	132 139	132 477	132 637	132 710
1995	132 811	132 901	132 906	133 404	132 673	132 784	133 193	133 199	133 489	133 607	133 517	133 426
1996	133 545	133 896	134 138	134 381	134 654	134 697	135 302	135 083	135 560	135 982	136 082	136 202
1997	136 560	136 517	137 025	137 164	137 281	137 387	137 668	137 824	137 894	137 865	138 209	138 418
1998	138 370	138 401	138 539	138 465	138 703	138 800	138 947	138 942	139 679	139 685	139 801	140 070
1999	140 456	140 433	140 207	140 452	140 615	140 852	140 977	140 981	141 189	141 353	141 623	141 790
2000	142 264	142 450	142 426	142 740	142 374	142 574	142 258	142 492	142 493	142 594	142 931	143 214
2001	143 763	143 661	143 881	143 524	143 270	143 306	143 600	143 227	143 929	144 023	144 174	144 236
2002	143 812	144 578	144 403	144 644	144 854	144 721	144 714	144 916	145 456	145 215	144 940	144 962
2003	145 199	145 341	145 243	145 673	145 679	146 212	145 624	145 564	145 629	145 794	146 056	145 766
2004	146 303	146 160	146 383	146 278	146 481	146 864	147 084	146 945	146 786	147 151	147 507	147 394
2005	147 379	147 711	147 718	148 265	148 600	148 579	148 750	149 087	149 259	149 279	149 356	149 253
2006	149 519	149 961	150 144	150 248	150 452	150 721	150 728	151 066	150 975	151 312	151 699	151 941
2007	152 101	151 959	152 072	151 582	151 807	152 121	152 126	151 871	152 425	152 154	152 854	152 802
2008	153 471	153 093	153 433	153 517	154 090	153 976	154 077	154 389	154 184	154 436	154 174	153 998
CIVILIAN EMPLOYMENT, TOTAL												
1990	119 093	119 082	119 238	118 898	119 209	119 052	118 891	118 894	118 628	118 651	118 432	118 379
1991	118 089	117 915	117 823	118 293	117 634	117 845	117 785	117 712	118 169	118 052	118 033	117 740
1992	118 265	118 050	118 454	118 748	118 709	118 764	119 071	119 195	119 101	119 020	119 280	119 413
1993	119 503	119 715	119 995	119 938	120 594	120 781	120 970	121 373	121 081	121 363	121 722	122 031
1994	122 547	122 679	122 534	122 908	123 497	123 277	123 362	124 013	124 372	124 811	125 230	125 448
1995	125 402	125 681	125 720	125 722	125 207	125 321	125 629	125 677	125 972	126 241	126 052	125 963
1996	126 013	126 542	126 779	126 924	127 189	127 562	127 922	128 161	128 540	128 909	128 801	128 904
1997	129 358	129 370	129 981	130 247	130 584	130 544	130 970	131 172	131 194	131 368	131 859	131 898
1998	131 958	132 053	132 072	132 484	132 614	132 545	132 643	132 718	133 333	133 359	133 655	133 994
1999	134 436	134 276	134 381	134 402	134 775	134 855	134 905	135 097	135 227	135 529	135 862	136 092
2000	136 556	136 593	136 693	137 260	136 617	136 925	136 513	136 642	136 870	137 062	137 294	137 583
2001	137 745	137 576	137 744	137 258	137 048	136 827	137 022	136 190	136 792	136 336	136 179	135 986
2002	135 637	136 371	136 108	136 054	136 464	136 338	136 333	136 623	137 217	136 920	136 431	136 333
2003	136 731	136 777	136 711	136 890	136 783	137 009	136 676	136 732	136 773	137 128	137 546	137 515
2004	137 972	138 032	137 933	138 149	138 310	138 621	138 991	138 998	138 902	139 135	139 622	139 506
2005	139 662	139 783	140 021	140 626	140 972	141 072	141 379	141 773	141 736	141 870	141 864	142 081
2006	142 540	142 826	143 105	143 147	143 467	143 723	143 605	143 992	144 145	144 617	144 906	145 298
2007	145 130	145 129	145 392	144 766	145 022	145 153	145 059	144 810	145 268	144 924	145 707	145 328
2008	145 944	145 699	145 643	145 873	145 586	145 347	145 202	144 876	144 629	144 254	143 739	142 931

Table 20-4. Nonfarm Payroll Employment, Hours, and Earnings

(Wage and salary workers on nonfarm payrolls, seasonally adjusted.)

Year and month	All wage and salary workers (thousands)					Production or nonsupervisory workers on private payrolls							
	Total	Private			Service-providing	Number (thousands)		Average hours per week		Average hourly earnings, dollars		Average weekly earnings, dollars	
		Total	Goods-producing			Total private	Manufac-turing	Total private	Manufac-turing	Total private	Manufac-turing	Total private	Manufac-turing
			Total	Manufac-turing									
1946	41 759	36 054	16 122	13 513	25 637	. . .	11 781	. . .	40.4	. . .	0.95	. . .	38.38
1947	43 945	38 379	17 314	14 287	26 631	. . .	12 453	. . .	40.5	. . .	1.10	. . .	44.55
1948	44 954	39 213	17 579	14 324	27 376	. . .	12 383	. . .	40.1	. . .	1.20	. . .	48.12
1949	43 843	37 893	16 464	13 281	27 379	. . .	11 355	. . .	39.2	. . .	1.25	. . .	49.00
1950	45 287	39 167	17 343	14 013	27 945	. . .	12 032	. . .	40.6	. . .	1.32	. . .	53.59
1951	47 930	41 427	18 703	15 070	29 227	. . .	12 808	. . .	40.7	. . .	1.45	. . .	59.02
1952	48 909	42 182	18 928	15 291	29 981	. . .	12 797	. . .	40.8	. . .	1.53	. . .	62.42
1953	50 310	43 552	19 733	16 131	30 577	. . .	13 437	. . .	40.6	. . .	1.63	. . .	66.18
1954	49 093	42 235	18 515	15 002	30 578	. . .	12 300	. . .	39.7	. . .	1.66	. . .	65.90
1955	50 744	43 722	19 234	15 524	31 510	. . .	12 735	. . .	40.8	. . .	1.74	. . .	70.99
1956	52 473	45 087	19 799	15 858	32 674	. . .	12 869	. . .	40.5	. . .	1.84	. . .	74.52
1957	52 959	45 235	19 669	15 798	33 290	. . .	12 640	. . .	39.9	. . .	1.93	. . .	77.01
1958	51 426	43 480	18 319	14 656	33 107	. . .	11 532	. . .	39.2	. . .	1.99	. . .	78.01
1959	53 374	45 182	19 163	15 325	34 211	. . .	12 089	. . .	40.3	. . .	2.08	. . .	83.82
1960	54 296	45 832	19 182	15 438	35 114	. . .	12 074	. . .	39.8	. . .	2.15	. . .	85.57
1961	54 105	45 399	18 647	15 011	35 458	. . .	11 612	. . .	39.9	. . .	2.20	. . .	87.78
1962	55 659	46 655	19 203	15 498	36 455	. . .	11 986	. . .	40.5	. . .	2.27	. . .	91.94
1963	56 764	47 423	19 385	15 631	37 379	. . .	12 051	. . .	40.6	. . .	2.34	. . .	95.00
1964	58 391	48 680	19 733	15 888	38 658	40 575	12 298	38.5	40.8	2.53	2.41	97.41	98.33
1946													
January	39 839	34 054	15 031	12 719	24 808	. . .	10 990	. . .	40.9	. . .	0.86	. . .	35.17
February	39 250	33 472	14 308	11 922	24 942	. . .	10 292	. . .	40.4	. . .	0.85	. . .	34.34
March	40 192	34 434	15 017	12 545	25 175	. . .	10 989	. . .	40.6	. . .	0.89	. . .	36.13
April	40 908	35 147	15 439	13 200	25 469	. . .	11 616	. . .	40.4	. . .	0.92	. . .	37.17
May	41 348	35 616	15 875	13 389	25 473	. . .	11 758	. . .	39.8	. . .	0.93	. . .	37.01
June	41 732	36 052	16 206	13 598	25 526	. . .	11 905	. . .	40.0	. . .	0.94	. . .	37.60
July	42 153	36 471	16 461	13 771	25 692	. . .	12 065	. . .	40.2	. . .	0.96	. . .	38.59
August	42 642	36 961	16 728	13 981	25 914	. . .	12 241	. . .	40.6	. . .	0.98	. . .	39.79
September	42 908	37 239	16 912	14 135	25 996	. . .	12 311	. . .	40.4	. . .	0.99	. . .	40.00
October	43 094	37 430	17 002	14 182	26 092	. . .	12 302	. . .	40.4	. . .	1.00	. . .	40.40
November	43 396	37 757	17 157	14 310	26 239	. . .	12 421	. . .	40.3	. . .	1.02	. . .	41.11
December	43 379	37 751	17 164	14 301	26 215	. . .	12 419	. . .	40.5	. . .	1.02	. . .	41.31
1947													
January	43 545	37 926	17 213	14 328	26 332	. . .	12 445	. . .	40.5	. . .	1.03	. . .	41.72
February	43 563	37 957	17 200	14 278	26 363	. . .	12 487	. . .	40.4	. . .	1.04	. . .	42.02
March	43 605	38 017	17 196	14 259	26 409	. . .	12 518	. . .	40.3	. . .	1.06	. . .	42.72
April	43 491	37 933	17 178	14 240	26 313	. . .	12 531	. . .	40.5	. . .	1.06	. . .	42.93
May	43 637	38 086	17 176	14 189	26 461	. . .	12 449	. . .	40.4	. . .	1.08	. . .	43.63
June	43 808	38 284	17 253	14 200	26 555	. . .	12 389	. . .	40.4	. . .	1.10	. . .	44.44
July	43 742	38 218	17 106	14 076	26 636	. . .	12 265	. . .	40.4	. . .	1.10	. . .	44.44
August	43 958	38 439	17 280	14 200	26 678	. . .	12 370	. . .	40.0	. . .	1.11	. . .	44.40
September	44 201	38 662	17 398	14 315	26 803	. . .	12 430	. . .	40.5	. . .	1.11	. . .	44.96
October	44 415	38 849	17 499	14 393	26 916	. . .	12 464	. . .	40.5	. . .	1.13	. . .	45.77
November	44 486	38 901	17 517	14 414	26 969	. . .	12 494	. . .	40.5	. . .	1.14	. . .	46.17
December	44 578	38 973	17 563	14 428	27 015	. . .	12 526	. . .	40.8	. . .	1.16	. . .	47.33
1948													
January	44 686	39 062	17 625	14 438	27 061	. . .	12 520	. . .	40.5	. . .	1.16	. . .	46.98
February	44 537	38 922	17 447	14 339	27 090	. . .	12 437	. . .	40.2	. . .	1.16	. . .	46.63
March	44 680	39 057	17 544	14 364	27 136	. . .	12 489	. . .	40.4	. . .	1.16	. . .	46.86
April	44 369	38 726	17 302	14 183	27 067	. . .	12 304	. . .	40.1	. . .	1.17	. . .	46.92
May	44 795	39 114	17 508	14 235	27 287	. . .	12 344	. . .	40.2	. . .	1.18	. . .	47.44
June	45 032	39 296	17 633	14 318	27 399	. . .	12 402	. . .	40.3	. . .	1.19	. . .	47.96
July	45 160	39 386	17 649	14 359	27 511	. . .	12 417	. . .	40.2	. . .	1.21	. . .	48.64
August	45 175	39 384	17 655	14 353	27 520	. . .	12 397	. . .	40.2	. . .	1.23	. . .	49.45
September	45 294	39 489	17 741	14 441	27 553	. . .	12 450	. . .	40.1	. . .	1.24	. . .	49.72
October	45 250	39 421	17 683	14 390	27 567	. . .	12 364	. . .	39.8	. . .	1.25	. . .	49.75
November	45 194	39 325	17 599	14 292	27 595	. . .	12 302	. . .	39.8	. . .	1.26	. . .	50.15
December	45 028	39 140	17 417	14 086	27 611	. . .	12 127	. . .	39.6	. . .	1.26	. . .	49.90
1949													
January	44 675	38 781	17 170	13 867	27 505	. . .	11 905	. . .	39.4	. . .	1.26	. . .	49.64
February	44 500	38 607	17 019	13 734	27 481	. . .	11 792	. . .	39.4	. . .	1.26	. . .	49.64
March	44 238	38 323	16 848	13 581	27 390	. . .	11 654	. . .	39.1	. . .	1.26	. . .	49.27
April	44 230	38 282	16 685	13 439	27 545	. . .	11 517	. . .	38.8	. . .	1.25	. . .	48.50
May	43 982	38 020	16 492	13 269	27 490	. . .	11 352	. . .	38.9	. . .	1.25	. . .	48.63
June	43 739	37 783	16 351	13 178	27 388	. . .	11 266	. . .	39.0	. . .	1.26	. . .	49.14
July	43 530	37 568	16 222	13 067	27 308	. . .	11 168	. . .	39.2	. . .	1.26	. . .	49.39
August	43 621	37 636	16 327	13 158	27 294	. . .	11 251	. . .	39.2	. . .	1.25	. . .	49.00
September	43 784	37 794	16 403	13 225	27 381	. . .	11 284	. . .	39.4	. . .	1.25	. . .	49.25
October	42 950	36 980	15 739	12 891	27 211	. . .	10 940	. . .	39.6	. . .	1.24	. . .	49.10
November	43 244	37 294	16 040	12 882	27 204	. . .	10 964	. . .	39.1	. . .	1.24	. . .	48.48
December	43 516	37 564	16 217	13 062	27 299	. . .	11 173	. . .	39.4	. . .	1.25	. . .	49.25

. . . = Not available.

Table 20-4. Nonfarm Payroll Employment, Hours, and Earnings—*Continued*

(Wage and salary workers on nonfarm payrolls, seasonally adjusted.)

Year and month	All wage and salary workers (thousands)					Production or nonsupervisory workers on private payrolls							
	Total	Private			Service-providing	Number (thousands)		Average hours per week		Average hourly earnings, dollars		Average weekly earnings, dollars	
		Total	Goods-producing			Total private	Manufac-turing	Total private	Manufac-turing	Total private	Manufac-turing	Total private	Manufac-turing
			Total	Manufac-turing									
1950													
January	43 530	37 596	16 255	13 161	27 275	...	11 258	...	39.6	...	1.27	...	50.29
February	43 298	37 372	16 035	13 169	27 263	...	11 262	...	39.7	...	1.26	...	50.02
March	43 952	37 874	16 482	13 290	27 470	...	11 362	...	39.7	...	1.28	...	50.82
April	44 376	38 282	16 718	13 471	27 658	...	11 528	...	40.3	...	1.29	...	51.99
May	44 717	38 674	17 080	13 780	27 637	...	11 855	...	40.3	...	1.30	...	52.39
June	45 084	39 062	17 288	13 923	27 796	...	11 979	...	40.6	...	1.30	...	52.78
July	45 453	39 363	17 464	14 072	27 989	...	12 107	...	40.9	...	1.31	...	53.58
August	46 187	40 000	17 917	14 461	28 270	...	12 476	...	41.3	...	1.33	...	54.93
September	46 442	40 214	18 040	14 561	28 402	...	12 519	...	40.8	...	1.33	...	54.26
October	46 712	40 463	18 249	14 737	28 463	...	12 659	...	41.1	...	1.36	...	55.90
November	46 778	40 516	18 288	14 762	28 490	...	12 682	...	41.0	...	1.37	...	56.17
December	46 855	40 541	18 283	14 782	28 572	...	12 710	...	40.9	...	1.39	...	56.85
1951													
January	47 289	40 937	18 518	14 950	28 771	...	12 816	...	41.0	...	1.40	...	57.40
February	47 577	41 195	18 666	15 076	28 911	...	12 929	...	40.9	...	1.41	...	57.67
March	47 871	41 461	18 754	15 125	29 117	...	12 936	...	41.0	...	1.42	...	58.22
April	47 856	41 405	18 810	15 166	29 046	...	12 960	...	41.0	...	1.43	...	58.63
May	47 952	41 535	18 829	15 164	29 123	...	12 941	...	41.0	...	1.44	...	59.04
June	48 067	41 568	18 826	15 176	29 241	...	12 934	...	40.9	...	1.45	...	59.31
July	48 061	41 523	18 747	15 110	29 314	...	12 848	...	40.6	...	1.45	...	58.87
August	48 008	41 489	18 709	15 061	29 299	...	12 772	...	40.4	...	1.46	...	58.98
September	47 955	41 403	18 622	14 996	29 333	...	12 659	...	40.4	...	1.46	...	58.98
October	48 009	41 432	18 617	14 973	29 379	...	12 615	...	40.3	...	1.47	...	59.24
November	48 149	41 523	18 617	14 999	29 532	...	12 628	...	40.4	...	1.48	...	59.79
December	48 308	41 620	18 698	15 045	29 610	...	12 667	...	40.7	...	1.49	...	60.64
1952													
January	48 299	41 710	18 719	15 067	29 580	...	12 675	...	40.8	...	1.49	...	60.79
February	48 522	41 872	18 813	15 105	29 709	...	12 689	...	40.8	...	1.49	...	60.79
March	48 504	41 842	18 775	15 127	29 729	...	12 695	...	40.6	...	1.51	...	61.31
April	48 616	41 954	18 806	15 162	29 810	...	12 713	...	40.3	...	1.51	...	60.85
May	48 645	41 951	18 784	15 143	29 861	...	12 676	...	40.5	...	1.51	...	61.16
June	48 286	41 574	18 419	14 828	29 867	...	12 353	...	40.6	...	1.51	...	61.31
July	48 144	41 407	18 268	14 707	29 876	...	12 233	...	40.2	...	1.50	...	60.30
August	48 922	42 204	18 928	15 279	29 994	...	12 764	...	40.7	...	1.53	...	62.27
September	49 319	42 585	19 206	15 553	30 113	...	13 007	...	41.1	...	1.55	...	63.71
October	49 598	42 782	19 312	15 690	30 286	...	13 122	...	41.2	...	1.56	...	64.27
November	49 816	43 015	19 473	15 843	30 343	...	13 262	...	41.2	...	1.58	...	65.10
December	50 164	43 229	19 610	15 973	30 554	...	13 375	...	41.2	...	1.58	...	65.10
1953													
January	50 145	43 351	19 721	16 067	30 424	...	13 447	...	41.1	...	1.59	...	65.35
February	50 339	43 542	19 841	16 158	30 498	...	13 529	...	41.0	...	1.61	...	66.01
March	50 474	43 690	19 909	16 270	30 565	...	13 620	...	41.2	...	1.61	...	66.33
April	50 432	43 662	19 908	16 293	30 524	...	13 629	...	40.9	...	1.62	...	66.26
May	50 491	43 774	19 930	16 341	30 561	...	13 645	...	41.0	...	1.62	...	66.42
June	50 522	43 788	19 909	16 343	30 613	...	13 636	...	40.9	...	1.63	...	66.67
July	50 536	43 813	19 910	16 353	30 626	...	13 653	...	40.7	...	1.64	...	66.75
August	50 487	43 733	19 834	16 278	30 653	...	13 564	...	40.7	...	1.64	...	66.75
September	50 365	43 616	19 726	16 151	30 639	...	13 419	...	40.1	...	1.65	...	66.17
October	50 242	43 478	19 578	15 981	30 664	...	13 244	...	40.1	...	1.65	...	66.17
November	49 906	43 157	19 315	15 728	30 591	...	12 990	...	40.0	...	1.65	...	66.00
December	49 702	42 959	19 173	15 581	30 529	...	12 847	...	39.7	...	1.65	...	65.51
1954													
January	49 467	42 707	18 963	15 440	30 504	...	12 706	...	39.5	...	1.65	...	65.18
February	49 381	42 598	18 880	15 307	30 501	...	12 593	...	39.7	...	1.65	...	65.51
March	49 158	42 362	18 748	15 197	30 410	...	12 493	...	39.6	...	1.65	...	65.34
April	49 177	42 371	18 602	15 065	30 575	...	12 361	...	39.7	...	1.65	...	65.51
May	48 965	42 136	18 476	14 974	30 489	...	12 282	...	39.7	...	1.67	...	66.30
June	48 896	42 050	18 400	14 910	30 496	...	12 220	...	39.7	...	1.67	...	66.30
July	48 834	41 966	18 280	14 799	30 554	...	12 121	...	39.7	...	1.66	...	65.90
August	48 825	41 933	18 251	14 772	30 574	...	12 089	...	39.8	...	1.66	...	66.07
September	48 881	41 987	18 261	14 805	30 620	...	12 104	...	39.9	...	1.66	...	66.23
October	48 944	42 044	18 321	14 841	30 623	...	12 142	...	39.7	...	1.67	...	66.30
November	49 179	42 215	18 438	14 913	30 741	...	12 206	...	40.1	...	1.68	...	67.37
December	49 331	42 374	18 508	14 967	30 823	...	12 254	...	40.1	...	1.68	...	67.37
1955													
January	49 497	42 544	18 609	15 034	30 888	...	12 309	...	40.4	...	1.69	...	68.28
February	49 644	42 721	18 726	15 138	30 918	...	12 408	...	40.6	...	1.70	...	69.02
March	49 963	43 025	18 910	15 258	31 053	...	12 524	...	40.7	...	1.71	...	69.60
April	50 246	43 287	19 067	15 375	31 179	...	12 626	...	40.8	...	1.71	...	69.77
May	50 512	43 521	19 223	15 493	31 289	...	12 731	...	41.1	...	1.73	...	71.10
June	50 790	43 770	19 331	15 585	31 459	...	12 810	...	40.8	...	1.73	...	70.58
July	50 985	43 936	19 376	15 614	31 609	...	12 818	...	40.7	...	1.75	...	71.23
August	51 112	44 089	19 432	15 679	31 680	...	12 866	...	40.7	...	1.76	...	71.63
September	51 262	44 195	19 427	15 668	31 835	...	12 830	...	40.7	...	1.77	...	72.04
October	51 431	44 313	19 482	15 740	31 949	...	12 896	...	41.0	...	1.77	...	72.57
November	51 592	44 509	19 554	15 813	32 038	...	12 967	...	41.1	...	1.78	...	73.16
December	51 805	44 673	19 608	15 859	32 197	...	13 009	...	40.9	...	1.78	...	72.80

. . . = Not available.

Table 20-4. Nonfarm Payroll Employment, Hours, and Earnings—*Continued*

(Wage and salary workers on nonfarm payrolls, seasonally adjusted.)

Year and month	All wage and salary workers (thousands)					Production or nonsupervisory workers on private payrolls							
	Total	Private				Number (thousands)		Average hours per week		Average hourly earnings, dollars		Average weekly earnings, dollars	
		Total	Goods-producing		Service-providing	Total private	Manufac-turing	Total private	Manufac-turing	Total private	Manufac-turing	Total private	Manufac-turing
			Total	Manufac-turing									
1956													
January	51 975	44 808	19 665	15 882	32 310	...	13 011	...	40.8	...	1.78	...	72.62
February	52 167	44 955	19 731	15 889	32 436	...	12 986	...	40.7	...	1.79	...	72.85
March	52 295	45 043	19 691	15 829	32 604	...	12 905	...	40.6	...	1.80	...	73.08
April	52 375	45 099	19 811	15 909	32 564	...	12 970	...	40.5	...	1.82	...	73.71
May	52 506	45 139	19 825	15 893	32 681	...	12 925	...	40.4	...	1.83	...	73.93
June	52 583	45 216	19 905	15 835	32 678	...	12 836	...	40.3	...	1.83	...	73.75
July	51 954	44 549	19 390	15 468	32 564	...	12 435	...	40.3	...	1.82	...	73.35
August	52 632	45 181	19 922	15 893	32 710	...	12 860	...	40.3	...	1.85	...	74.56
September	52 600	45 119	19 860	15 863	32 740	...	12 822	...	40.5	...	1.87	...	75.74
October	52 781	45 262	19 918	15 937	32 863	...	12 908	...	40.6	...	1.88	...	76.33
November	52 822	45 269	19 886	15 916	32 936	...	12 864	...	40.4	...	1.88	...	75.95
December	52 930	45 346	19 926	15 957	33 004	...	12 882	...	40.6	...	1.91	...	77.55
1957													
January	52 888	45 268	19 833	15 970	33 055	...	12 881	...	40.4	...	1.90	...	76.76
February	53 098	45 452	19 933	15 998	33 165	...	12 885	...	40.5	...	1.91	...	77.36
March	53 156	45 484	19 936	15 994	33 220	...	12 855	...	40.4	...	1.92	...	77.57
April	53 238	45 537	19 887	15 970	33 351	...	12 811	...	40.0	...	1.91	...	76.40
May	53 149	45 436	19 834	15 931	33 315	...	12 762	...	40.0	...	1.92	...	76.80
June	53 066	45 364	19 777	15 873	33 289	...	12 697	...	40.0	...	1.92	...	76.80
July	53 122	45 368	19 735	15 854	33 387	...	12 669	...	40.0	...	1.93	...	77.20
August	53 128	45 371	19 728	15 867	33 400	...	12 673	...	40.0	...	1.94	...	77.60
September	52 932	45 183	19 545	15 710	33 387	...	12 528	...	39.7	...	1.95	...	77.42
October	52 765	44 997	19 421	15 599	33 344	...	12 437	...	39.4	...	1.96	...	77.22
November	52 557	44 788	19 260	15 466	33 297	...	12 301	...	39.2	...	1.96	...	76.83
December	52 385	44 539	19 111	15 332	33 274	...	12 170	...	39.1	...	1.95	...	76.25
1958													
January	52 077	44 256	18 902	15 130	33 175	...	11 969	...	38.9	...	1.95	...	75.86
February	51 576	43 744	18 529	14 908	33 047	...	11 757	...	38.7	...	1.95	...	75.47
March	51 300	43 452	18 335	14 670	32 965	...	11 532	...	38.8	...	1.96	...	76.05
April	51 026	43 158	18 120	14 506	32 906	...	11 373	...	38.9	...	1.96	...	76.24
May	50 913	43 019	18 008	14 414	32 905	...	11 294	...	38.9	...	1.97	...	76.63
June	50 912	42 986	17 984	14 408	32 928	...	11 300	...	39.1	...	1.98	...	77.42
July	51 037	43 065	18 038	14 450	32 999	...	11 349	...	39.3	...	1.98	...	77.81
August	51 233	43 221	18 147	14 524	33 086	...	11 412	...	39.5	...	2.01	...	79.40
September	51 506	43 490	18 331	14 658	33 175	...	11 556	...	39.5	...	2.00	...	79.00
October	51 485	43 454	18 218	14 503	33 267	...	11 394	...	39.6	...	2.00	...	79.20
November	51 943	43 915	18 610	14 827	33 333	...	11 702	...	39.9	...	2.03	...	81.00
December	52 088	43 988	18 592	14 877	33 496	...	11 743	...	39.9	...	2.04	...	81.40
1959													
January	52 481	44 376	18 796	14 998	33 685	...	11 849	...	40.2	...	2.04	...	82.01
February	52 687	44 571	18 890	15 115	33 797	...	11 950	...	40.3	...	2.05	...	82.62
March	53 016	44 884	19 069	15 259	33 947	...	12 078	...	40.4	...	2.07	...	83.63
April	53 320	45 178	19 269	15 385	34 051	...	12 185	...	40.5	...	2.08	...	84.24
May	53 549	45 396	19 378	15 487	34 171	...	12 277	...	40.7	...	2.08	...	84.66
June	53 678	45 535	19 462	15 554	34 216	...	12 330	...	40.6	...	2.09	...	84.85
July	53 803	45 630	19 529	15 623	34 274	...	12 366	...	40.3	...	2.09	...	84.23
August	53 337	45 156	19 049	15 202	34 288	...	11 936	...	40.4	...	2.07	...	83.63
September	53 428	45 189	19 052	15 254	34 376	...	11 984	...	40.4	...	2.08	...	84.03
October	53 359	45 094	18 925	15 158	34 434	...	11 864	...	40.1	...	2.07	...	83.01
November	53 635	45 351	19 108	15 300	34 527	...	11 991	...	39.9	...	2.07	...	82.59
December	54 175	45 807	19 425	15 573	34 750	...	12 254	...	40.3	...	2.11	...	85.03
1960													
January	54 274	45 967	19 491	15 687	34 783	...	12 362	...	40.6	...	2.13	...	86.48
February	54 513	46 187	19 605	15 765	34 908	...	12 434	...	40.3	...	2.14	...	86.24
March	54 458	45 933	19 373	15 707	35 085	...	12 362	...	40.0	...	2.14	...	85.60
April	54 812	46 278	19 446	15 654	35 366	...	12 299	...	40.0	...	2.14	...	85.60
May	54 472	46 040	19 374	15 575	35 098	...	12 218	...	40.1	...	2.14	...	85.81
June	54 347	45 915	19 240	15 466	35 107	...	12 102	...	39.9	...	2.14	...	85.39
July	54 303	45 861	19 170	15 413	35 133	...	12 047	...	39.9	...	2.14	...	85.39
August	54 272	45 800	19 105	15 360	35 167	...	11 986	...	39.7	...	2.15	...	85.36
September	54 228	45 734	19 057	15 330	35 171	...	11 956	...	39.4	...	2.16	...	85.10
October	54 144	45 642	18 952	15 231	35 192	...	11 846	...	39.7	...	2.16	...	85.75
November	53 962	45 446	18 799	15 112	35 163	...	11 726	...	39.3	...	2.15	...	84.50
December	53 743	45 146	18 548	14 947	35 195	...	11 556	...	38.4	...	2.16	...	82.94
1961													
January	53 683	45 119	18 508	14 863	35 175	...	11 473	...	39.3	...	2.16	...	84.89
February	53 556	44 969	18 418	14 801	35 138	...	11 414	...	39.4	...	2.16	...	85.10
March	53 662	45 051	18 438	14 802	35 224	...	11 410	...	39.5	...	2.16	...	85.32
April	53 626	44 997	18 432	14 825	35 194	...	11 444	...	39.5	...	2.18	...	86.11
May	53 783	45 119	18 523	14 932	35 260	...	11 544	...	39.7	...	2.19	...	86.94
June	53 977	45 289	18 618	14 981	35 359	...	11 593	...	40.0	...	2.20	...	88.00
July	54 124	45 400	18 640	15 029	35 484	...	11 639	...	40.0	...	2.21	...	88.40
August	54 299	45 535	18 725	15 093	35 574	...	11 701	...	40.1	...	2.22	...	89.02
September	54 387	45 591	18 730	15 080	35 657	...	11 679	...	39.5	...	2.20	...	86.90
October	54 521	45 716	18 805	15 143	35 716	...	11 731	...	40.3	...	2.23	...	89.87
November	54 743	45 931	18 927	15 259	35 816	...	11 842	...	40.7	...	2.23	...	90.76
December	54 871	46 035	18 981	15 309	35 890	...	11 872	...	40.4	...	2.24	...	90.50

. . . = Not available.

Table 20-4. Nonfarm Payroll Employment, Hours, and Earnings—*Continued*

(Wage and salary workers on nonfarm payrolls, seasonally adjusted.)

Year and month	All wage and salary workers (thousands)					Production or nonsupervisory workers on private payrolls							
	Total	Private			Service-providing	Number (thousands)		Average hours per week		Average hourly earnings, dollars		Average weekly earnings, dollars	
		Total	Goods-producing			Total private	Manufac-turing	Total private	Manufac-turing	Total private	Manufac-turing	Total private	Manufac-turing
			Total	Manufac-turing									
1962													
January	54 891	46 040	18 936	15 322	35 955	. . .	11 865	. . .	40.0	. . .	2.25	. . .	90.00
February	55 187	46 309	19 109	15 411	36 078	. . .	11 950	. . .	40.4	. . .	2.26	. . .	91.30
March	55 276	46 375	19 109	15 451	36 167	. . .	11 970	. . .	40.6	. . .	2.26	. . .	91.76
April	55 601	46 679	19 258	15 524	36 343	. . .	12 034	. . .	40.6	. . .	2.26	. . .	91.76
May	55 626	46 668	19 253	15 513	36 373	. . .	12 011	. . .	40.6	. . .	2.27	. . .	92.16
June	55 644	46 644	19 186	15 518	36 458	. . .	12 006	. . .	40.5	. . .	2.26	. . .	91.53
July	55 746	46 720	19 248	15 522	36 498	. . .	12 004	. . .	40.5	. . .	2.27	. . .	91.94
August	55 838	46 775	19 251	15 517	36 587	. . .	11 990	. . .	40.5	. . .	2.28	. . .	92.34
September	55 977	46 888	19 305	15 568	36 672	. . .	12 033	. . .	40.5	. . .	2.28	. . .	92.34
October	56 041	46 927	19 301	15 569	36 740	. . .	12 034	. . .	40.3	. . .	2.29	. . .	92.29
November	56 055	46 910	19 260	15 530	36 795	. . .	11 977	. . .	40.5	. . .	2.29	. . .	92.75
December	56 027	46 901	19 219	15 520	36 808	. . .	11 961	. . .	40.3	. . .	2.29	. . .	92.29
1963													
January	56 116	46 912	19 257	15 545	36 859	. . .	11 974	. . .	40.5	. . .	2.30	. . .	93.15
February	56 231	47 000	19 228	15 542	37 003	. . .	11 965	. . .	40.5	. . .	2.31	. . .	93.56
March	56 322	47 077	19 233	15 564	37 089	. . .	11 990	. . .	40.5	. . .	2.32	. . .	93.96
April	56 580	47 316	19 343	15 602	37 237	. . .	12 029	. . .	40.5	. . .	2.32	. . .	93.96
May	56 616	47 328	19 399	15 641	37 217	. . .	12 066	. . .	40.5	. . .	2.33	. . .	94.37
June	56 658	47 356	19 371	15 624	37 287	. . .	12 050	. . .	40.7	. . .	2.34	. . .	95.24
July	56 795	47 461	19 423	15 646	37 372	. . .	12 080	. . .	40.6	. . .	2.35	. . .	95.41
August	56 910	47 542	19 437	15 644	37 473	. . .	12 060	. . .	40.6	. . .	2.34	. . .	95.00
September	57 078	47 661	19 483	15 674	37 595	. . .	12 088	. . .	40.6	. . .	2.36	. . .	95.82
October	57 284	47 805	19 517	15 714	37 767	. . .	12 131	. . .	40.7	. . .	2.36	. . .	96.05
November	57 255	47 771	19 456	15 675	37 799	. . .	12 072	. . .	40.7	. . .	2.37	. . .	96.46
December	57 360	47 863	19 493	15 712	37 867	. . .	12 108	. . .	40.6	. . .	2.38	. . .	96.63
1964													
January	57 487	47 925	19 406	15 715	38 081	39 914	12 132	38.2	40.1	2.50	2.38	95.50	95.44
February	57 752	48 171	19 570	15 742	38 182	40 123	12 165	38.5	40.7	2.50	2.38	96.25	96.87
March	57 898	48 287	19 587	15 770	38 311	40 171	12 190	38.5	40.6	2.50	2.38	96.25	96.63
April	57 923	48 279	19 593	15 785	38 330	40 208	12 211	38.6	40.7	2.52	2.40	97.27	97.68
May	58 089	48 419	19 630	15 812	38 459	40 332	12 231	38.6	40.8	2.52	2.40	97.27	97.92
June	58 221	48 552	19 682	15 839	38 539	40 448	12 255	38.6	40.8	2.53	2.41	97.66	98.33
July	58 412	48 735	19 740	15 887	38 672	40 624	12 309	38.5	40.8	2.53	2.41	97.41	98.33
August	58 620	48 888	19 810	15 948	38 810	40 770	12 354	38.5	40.9	2.55	2.42	98.18	98.98
September	58 903	49 117	19 943	16 073	38 960	41 026	12 479	38.5	40.9	2.55	2.44	98.18	99.80
October	58 794	48 949	19 723	15 821	39 071	40 827	12 224	38.5	40.7	2.55	2.40	98.18	97.68
November	59 217	49 338	20 026	16 096	39 191	41 157	12 477	38.6	41.0	2.56	2.42	98.82	99.22
December	59 420	49 523	20 111	16 176	39 309	41 308	12 551	38.7	41.2	2.58	2.44	99.85	100.53
1965													
January	59 583	49 646	20 173	16 245	39 410	41 453	12 603	38.7	41.3	2.58	2.45	99.85	101.19
February	59 800	49 826	20 216	16 291	39 584	41 583	12 644	38.7	41.3	2.59	2.46	100.23	101.60
March	60 003	49 993	20 292	16 353	39 711	41 675	12 701	38.7	41.3	2.60	2.47	100.62	102.01
April	60 258	50 207	20 317	16 418	39 941	41 886	12 752	38.7	41.2	2.60	2.47	100.62	101.76
May	60 492	50 398	20 444	16 477	40 048	42 044	12 792	38.8	41.3	2.62	2.49	101.66	102.84
June	60 690	50 562	20 522	16 554	40 168	42 183	12 854	38.6	41.2	2.62	2.49	101.13	102.59
July	60 963	50 762	20 611	16 669	40 352	42 364	12 962	38.6	41.2	2.63	2.49	101.52	102.59
August	61 228	50 957	20 726	16 732	40 502	42 537	12 994	38.5	41.1	2.64	2.50	101.64	102.75
September	61 490	51 152	20 808	16 802	40 682	42 726	13 046	38.6	41.1	2.65	2.51	102.29	103.16
October	61 718	51 340	20 895	16 864	40 823	42 870	13 100	38.5	41.2	2.66	2.52	102.41	103.82
November	61 997	51 561	21 021	16 962	40 976	43 045	13 175	38.6	41.3	2.67	2.52	103.06	104.08
December	62 321	51 822	21 151	17 051	41 170	43 270	13 243	38.6	41.3	2.68	2.53	103.45	104.49
1966													
January	62 528	51 987	21 214	17 143	41 314	43 401	13 301	38.6	41.5	2.68	2.54	103.45	105.41
February	62 796	52 185	21 315	17 288	41 481	43 552	13 426	38.7	41.7	2.69	2.56	104.10	106.75
March	63 191	52 499	21 515	17 400	41 676	43 801	13 508	38.7	41.6	2.70	2.56	104.49	106.50
April	63 436	52 677	21 568	17 517	41 868	43 959	13 598	38.7	41.8	2.71	2.58	104.88	107.84
May	63 711	52 890	21 675	17 625	42 036	44 138	13 678	38.5	41.5	2.72	2.58	104.72	107.07
June	64 110	53 208	21 846	17 733	42 264	44 390	13 753	38.5	41.4	2.72	2.58	104.72	106.81
July	64 301	53 327	21 872	17 760	42 429	44 484	13 758	38.4	41.2	2.74	2.60	105.22	107.12
August	64 507	53 501	21 972	17 882	42 535	44 596	13 843	38.4	41.4	2.75	2.61	105.60	108.05
September	64 645	53 582	21 948	17 886	42 697	44 659	13 841	38.3	41.2	2.76	2.63	105.71	108.36
October	64 854	53 727	21 991	17 956	42 863	44 789	13 906	38.4	41.3	2.77	2.64	106.37	109.03
November	65 019	53 816	21 988	17 981	43 031	44 834	13 918	38.3	41.2	2.78	2.65	106.47	109.18
December	65 199	53 943	22 008	17 998	43 191	44 916	13 906	38.2	40.9	2.78	2.64	106.20	107.98
1967													
January	65 407	54 092	22 057	18 033	43 350	45 050	13 925	38.3	41.1	2.79	2.65	106.86	108.92
February	65 427	54 074	21 987	17 978	43 440	44 967	13 853	37.9	40.4	2.81	2.67	106.50	107.87
March	65 530	54 133	21 919	17 940	43 611	44 991	13 797	37.9	40.5	2.81	2.67	106.50	108.14
April	65 467	54 032	21 842	17 878	43 625	44 871	13 712	37.8	40.4	2.82	2.68	106.60	108.27
May	65 618	54 144	21 779	17 832	43 839	44 961	13 664	37.8	40.4	2.83	2.69	106.97	108.68
June	65 750	54 216	21 761	17 812	43 989	45 004	13 632	37.8	40.4	2.84	2.69	107.35	108.68
July	65 887	54 343	21 772	17 784	44 115	45 105	13 602	37.8	40.5	2.86	2.71	108.11	109.76
August	66 142	54 552	21 887	17 905	44 255	45 267	13 681	37.8	40.6	2.87	2.73	108.49	110.84
September	66 163	54 540	21 775	17 794	44 388	45 236	13 559	37.8	40.6	2.88	2.73	108.86	110.84
October	66 225	54 583	21 779	17 800	44 446	45 278	13 587	37.8	40.6	2.89	2.74	109.24	111.24
November	66 703	55 008	21 996	17 985	44 707	45 701	13 777	37.9	40.6	2.91	2.75	110.29	111.65
December	66 900	55 165	22 037	18 025	44 863	45 800	13 782	37.7	40.7	2.92	2.77	110.08	112.74

. . . = Not available.

Table 20-4. Nonfarm Payroll Employment, Hours, and Earnings—*Continued*

(Wage and salary workers on nonfarm payrolls, seasonally adjusted.)

Year and month	All wage and salary workers (thousands)					Production or nonsupervisory workers on private payrolls							
	Total	Private			Service-providing	Number (thousands)		Average hours per week		Average hourly earnings, dollars		Average weekly earnings, dollars	
		Total	Goods-producing			Total private	Manufac-turing	Total private	Manufac-turing	Total private	Manufac-turing	Total private	Manufac-turing
			Total	Manufac-turing									
1968													
January	66 805	55 011	21 917	18 040	44 888	45 655	13 798	37.6	40.4	2.94	2.81	110.54	113.52
February	67 214	55 395	22 117	18 054	45 097	45 980	13 793	37.8	40.8	2.95	2.82	111.51	115.06
March	67 296	55 454	22 119	18 067	45 177	46 041	13 803	37.7	40.8	2.97	2.84	111.97	115.87
April	67 555	55 677	22 207	18 131	45 348	46 239	13 858	37.6	40.3	2.98	2.85	112.05	114.86
May	67 652	55 747	22 255	18 190	45 397	46 267	13 900	37.7	40.9	3.00	2.87	113.10	117.38
June	67 904	55 917	22 264	18 228	45 640	46 402	13 921	37.8	40.9	3.01	2.88	113.78	117.79
July	68 126	56 108	22 329	18 265	45 797	46 562	13 953	37.7	40.8	3.03	2.89	114.23	117.91
August	68 328	56 286	22 350	18 254	45 978	46 669	13 903	37.7	40.7	3.03	2.89	114.23	117.62
September	68 487	56 420	22 390	18 252	46 097	46 792	13 914	37.7	40.9	3.06	2.92	115.36	119.43
October	68 720	56 619	22 419	18 293	46 301	46 989	13 974	37.7	41.0	3.07	2.94	115.74	120.54
November	68 985	56 878	22 512	18 346	46 473	47 244	14 028	37.5	40.9	3.09	2.96	115.88	121.06
December	69 245	57 100	22 617	18 410	46 628	47 384	14 044	37.5	40.7	3.11	2.97	116.63	120.88
1969													
January	69 438	57 229	22 644	18 432	46 794	47 528	14 086	37.7	40.8	3.12	2.99	117.62	121.99
February	69 698	57 474	22 755	18 502	46 943	47 697	14 134	37.5	40.4	3.14	3.00	117.75	121.20
March	69 906	57 677	22 813	18 558	47 093	47 852	14 169	37.6	40.8	3.15	3.01	118.44	122.81
April	70 072	57 827	22 815	18 554	47 257	47 959	14 144	37.7	41.0	3.17	3.03	119.51	124.23
May	70 328	58 044	22 899	18 588	47 429	48 122	14 161	37.6	40.7	3.19	3.04	119.94	123.73
June	70 636	58 277	22 981	18 640	47 655	48 330	14 206	37.5	40.7	3.20	3.05	120.00	124.14
July	70 730	58 390	22 990	18 642	47 740	48 434	14 194	37.5	40.6	3.22	3.08	120.75	125.05
August	71 005	58 632	23 111	18 767	47 894	48 616	14 287	37.5	40.6	3.24	3.10	121.50	125.86
September	70 918	58 539	22 988	18 620	47 930	48 524	14 159	37.5	40.6	3.26	3.12	122.25	126.67
October	71 119	58 689	22 976	18 613	48 143	48 669	14 174	37.4	40.5	3.28	3.13	122.67	126.77
November	71 088	58 640	22 840	18 467	48 248	48 589	14 035	37.5	40.5	3.29	3.14	123.38	127.17
December	71 240	58 763	22 884	18 485	48 356	48 638	14 013	37.5	40.6	3.30	3.15	123.75	127.89
1970													
January	71 176	58 680	22 726	18 424	48 450	48 564	13 964	37.3	40.4	3.31	3.16	123.46	127.66
February	71 302	58 784	22 747	18 361	48 555	48 600	13 897	37.3	40.2	3.33	3.17	124.21	127.43
March	71 453	58 850	22 738	18 360	48 715	48 690	13 917	37.2	40.1	3.35	3.19	124.62	127.92
April	71 348	58 643	22 552	18 207	48 796	48 479	13 785	37.0	39.8	3.36	3.19	124.32	126.96
May	71 122	58 454	22 336	18 029	48 786	48 287	13 616	37.0	39.8	3.38	3.22	125.06	128.16
June	71 028	58 361	22 241	17 930	48 787	48 226	13 554	36.9	39.8	3.39	3.24	125.09	128.95
July	71 055	58 358	22 195	17 877	48 860	48 242	13 527	37.0	40.0	3.41	3.25	126.17	130.00
August	70 932	58 221	22 105	17 779	48 827	48 089	13 449	37.0	39.8	3.43	3.26	126.91	129.75
September	70 949	58 208	21 988	17 692	48 961	48 101	13 401	36.8	39.6	3.45	3.29	126.96	130.28
October	70 519	57 726	21 477	17 173	49 042	47 619	12 905	36.8	39.5	3.46	3.26	127.33	128.77
November	70 409	57 579	21 345	17 024	49 064	47 466	12 781	36.7	39.5	3.47	3.26	127.35	128.77
December	70 790	57 945	21 673	17 309	49 117	47 778	13 062	36.8	39.5	3.50	3.32	128.80	131.14
1971													
January	70 866	57 988	21 594	17 280	49 272	47 859	13 069	36.8	39.9	3.52	3.36	129.54	134.06
February	70 805	57 928	21 514	17 216	49 291	47 779	13 033	36.7	39.7	3.54	3.39	129.92	134.58
March	70 859	57 951	21 491	17 154	49 368	47 819	12 984	36.7	39.8	3.56	3.39	130.65	134.92
April	71 037	58 092	21 552	17 149	49 485	47 966	12 993	36.8	39.9	3.57	3.41	131.38	136.06
May	71 247	58 277	21 645	17 225	49 602	48 153	13 081	36.8	40.0	3.60	3.43	132.12	137.20
June	71 253	58 245	21 568	17 139	49 685	48 109	13 012	36.8	39.9	3.62	3.45	133.22	137.66
July	71 316	58 305	21 564	17 126	49 752	48 167	13 001	36.7	40.0	3.63	3.46	133.22	138.40
August	71 368	58 327	21 570	17 115	49 798	48 164	12 993	36.7	39.8	3.66	3.48	134.32	138.50
September	71 620	58 552	21 650	17 154	49 970	48 362	13 038	36.7	39.7	3.67	3.48	134.69	138.16
October	71 642	58 527	21 604	17 126	50 038	48 305	13 027	36.8	39.9	3.68	3.50	135.42	139.65
November	71 844	58 696	21 684	17 166	50 160	48 442	13 064	36.9	40.0	3.69	3.49	136.16	139.60
December	72 108	58 918	21 741	17 202	50 367	48 613	13 078	36.9	40.2	3.73	3.55	137.64	142.71
1972													
January	72 445	59 179	21 865	17 283	50 580	49 035	13 173	36.9	40.2	3.80	3.57	140.22	143.51
February	72 652	59 354	21 915	17 361	50 737	49 143	13 235	36.9	40.4	3.82	3.61	140.96	145.84
March	72 945	59 616	22 036	17 447	50 909	49 437	13 316	36.9	40.4	3.84	3.63	141.70	146.65
April	73 163	59 805	22 099	17 508	51 064	49 561	13 373	36.9	40.5	3.86	3.65	142.43	147.83
May	73 467	60 051	22 222	17 602	51 245	49 745	13 451	36.8	40.5	3.87	3.67	142.42	148.64
June	73 760	60 355	22 282	17 641	51 478	49 997	13 475	36.9	40.6	3.88	3.68	143.17	149.41
July	73 709	60 227	22 162	17 556	51 547	49 842	13 387	36.8	40.5	3.90	3.69	143.52	149.45
August	74 137	60 607	22 400	17 741	51 737	50 156	13 562	36.8	40.6	3.92	3.73	144.26	151.44
September	74 268	60 693	22 456	17 774	51 812	50 224	13 572	36.9	40.6	3.94	3.75	145.39	152.25
October	74 672	61 066	22 613	17 893	52 059	50 552	13 681	37.0	40.7	3.97	3.78	146.89	153.85
November	74 965	61 322	22 688	18 005	52 277	50 790	13 783	36.9	40.7	3.98	3.79	146.86	154.25
December	75 270	61 586	22 772	18 158	52 498	51 054	13 902	36.8	40.6	4.01	3.83	147.57	155.50
1973													
January	75 620	61 930	22 955	18 276	52 665	51 349	14 006	36.8	40.4	4.03	3.86	148.30	155.94
February	76 017	62 306	23 160	18 410	52 857	51 686	14 127	36.9	40.9	4.04	3.87	149.08	158.28
March	76 286	62 541	23 262	18 493	53 024	51 901	14 181	37.0	40.9	4.06	3.88	150.22	158.69
April	76 456	62 679	23 316	18 530	53 140	51 982	14 192	36.9	40.8	4.08	3.91	150.55	159.53
May	76 646	62 829	23 382	18 564	53 264	52 082	14 217	36.9	40.7	4.10	3.93	151.29	159.95
June	76 886	63 014	23 485	18 606	53 401	52 234	14 253	36.9	40.7	4.12	3.95	152.03	160.77
July	76 911	63 046	23 522	18 598	53 389	52 238	14 232	36.9	40.7	4.15	3.98	153.14	161.99
August	77 166	63 262	23 559	18 629	53 607	52 393	14 251	36.9	40.6	4.16	4.00	153.50	162.40
September	77 281	63 389	23 548	18 609	53 733	52 410	14 213	36.8	40.7	4.19	4.03	154.19	164.02
October	77 605	63 628	23 641	18 702	53 964	52 655	14 289	36.7	40.6	4.21	4.05	154.51	164.43
November	77 909	63 874	23 719	18 773	54 190	52 847	14 342	36.9	40.6	4.23	4.07	156.09	165.24
December	78 035	63 965	23 779	18 820	54 256	52 954	14 386	36.7	40.6	4.25	4.09	155.98	166.05

Table 20-4. Nonfarm Payroll Employment, Hours, and Earnings—*Continued*

(Wage and salary workers on nonfarm payrolls, seasonally adjusted.)

Year and month	All wage and salary workers (thousands)					Production or nonsupervisory workers on private payrolls							
	Total	Private			Service-providing	Number (thousands)		Average hours per week		Average hourly earnings, dollars		Average weekly earnings, dollars	
		Total	Goods-producing			Total private	Manufac-turing	Total private	Manufac-turing	Total private	Manufac-turing	Total private	Manufac-turing
			Total	Manufac-turing									
1974													
January	78 104	64 014	23 709	18 788	54 395	52 896	14 340	36.6	40.5	4.26	4.10	155.92	166.05
February	78 253	64 118	23 718	18 727	54 535	52 971	14 269	36.6	40.4	4.29	4.13	157.01	166.85
March	78 295	64 143	23 687	18 700	54 608	52 951	14 223	36.6	40.4	4.31	4.15	157.75	167.66
April	78 384	64 193	23 670	18 702	54 714	53 003	14 225	36.4	39.5	4.34	4.16	157.98	164.32
May	78 547	64 326	23 635	18 688	54 912	53 095	14 199	36.5	40.3	4.39	4.25	160.24	171.28
June	78 602	64 363	23 591	18 690	55 011	53 107	14 197	36.5	40.2	4.43	4.30	161.70	172.86
July	78 634	64 346	23 462	18 656	55 172	53 044	14 152	36.5	40.1	4.45	4.33	162.43	173.63
August	78 619	64 291	23 396	18 570	55 223	53 025	14 089	36.5	40.2	4.49	4.38	163.89	176.08
September	78 614	64 192	23 274	18 492	55 340	52 915	14 025	36.4	40.0	4.53	4.42	164.89	176.80
October	78 627	64 143	23 118	18 364	55 509	52 836	13 884	36.3	40.0	4.56	4.48	165.53	179.20
November	78 259	63 727	22 773	18 077	55 486	52 413	13 607	36.1	39.5	4.57	4.49	164.98	177.36
December	77 657	63 098	22 303	17 693	55 354	51 856	13 259	36.1	39.3	4.61	4.52	166.42	177.64
1975													
January	77 297	62 673	21 974	17 344	55 323	51 439	12 933	36.1	39.2	4.61	4.54	166.42	177.97
February	76 919	62 172	21 512	17 004	55 407	50 934	12 622	35.9	38.9	4.63	4.58	166.22	178.16
March	76 649	61 895	21 274	16 853	55 375	50 666	12 483	35.7	38.8	4.66	4.63	166.36	179.64
April	76 463	61 668	21 109	16 759	55 354	50 439	12 407	35.8	39.0	4.66	4.63	166.83	180.57
May	76 623	61 796	21 097	16 746	55 526	50 558	12 406	35.9	39.0	4.68	4.65	168.01	181.35
June	76 519	61 735	21 018	16 690	55 501	50 537	12 371	35.9	39.2	4.72	4.68	169.45	183.46
July	76 768	61 907	20 981	16 678	55 787	50 726	12 374	35.9	39.4	4.73	4.71	169.81	185.57
August	77 154	62 284	21 176	16 824	55 978	51 070	12 538	36.1	39.7	4.77	4.75	172.20	188.58
September	77 232	62 408	21 284	16 904	55 948	51 183	12 617	36.1	39.8	4.79	4.78	172.92	190.24
October	77 535	62 635	21 384	16 984	56 151	51 376	12 687	36.1	39.9	4.81	4.80	173.64	191.52
November	77 679	62 776	21 442	17 025	56 237	51 458	12 700	36.1	39.9	4.85	4.83	175.09	192.72
December	78 017	63 071	21 602	17 140	56 415	51 759	12 811	36.2	40.2	4.87	4.86	176.29	195.37
1976													
January	78 506	63 537	21 799	17 287	56 707	52 182	12 945	36.3	40.3	4.90	4.90	177.87	197.47
February	78 817	63 836	21 893	17 384	56 924	52 430	13 030	36.3	40.4	4.94	4.94	179.32	199.58
March	79 049	64 062	21 980	17 470	57 069	52 615	13 092	36.0	40.2	4.96	4.98	178.56	200.20
April	79 293	64 308	22 050	17 541	57 243	52 810	13 160	36.0	39.6	4.98	4.98	179.28	197.21
May	79 311	64 340	21 988	17 513	57 323	52 802	13 130	36.1	40.3	5.02	5.04	181.22	203.11
June	79 376	64 413	21 982	17 521	57 394	52 830	13 121	36.1	40.2	5.04	5.07	181.94	203.81
July	79 546	64 553	21 988	17 524	57 558	52 973	13 124	36.1	40.3	5.07	5.11	183.03	205.93
August	79 704	64 697	22 038	17 596	57 666	53 072	13 195	36.0	40.2	5.12	5.16	184.32	207.43
September	79 892	64 921	22 142	17 665	57 750	53 268	13 253	36.0	40.2	5.15	5.20	185.40	209.04
October	79 905	64 877	22 037	17 548	57 868	53 165	13 109	35.9	40.0	5.17	5.19	185.60	207.60
November	80 237	65 164	22 207	17 682	58 030	53 362	13 199	35.9	40.1	5.21	5.25	187.04	210.53
December	80 448	65 373	22 261	17 719	58 187	53 543	13 230	35.9	39.9	5.23	5.29	187.76	211.07
1977													
January	80 692	65 636	22 320	17 803	58 372	53 756	13 305	35.6	39.4	5.26	5.35	187.26	210.79
February	80 987	65 931	22 478	17 843	58 509	54 016	13 331	36.0	40.2	5.30	5.36	190.80	215.47
March	81 391	66 341	22 672	17 941	58 719	54 390	13 424	35.9	40.3	5.33	5.40	191.35	217.62
April	81 730	66 655	22 807	18 024	58 923	54 670	13 490	36.0	40.4	5.37	5.45	193.32	220.18
May	82 089	66 957	22 919	18 107	59 170	54 940	13 567	36.0	40.5	5.40	5.49	194.40	222.35
June	82 488	67 281	23 046	18 192	59 442	55 195	13 622	36.0	40.5	5.43	5.54	195.48	224.37
July	82 836	67 537	23 106	18 259	59 730	55 395	13 670	35.9	40.4	5.46	5.58	196.01	225.43
August	83 074	67 746	23 124	18 276	59 950	55 543	13 679	35.9	40.4	5.48	5.61	196.73	226.64
September	83 532	68 129	23 244	18 334	60 288	55 859	13 714	35.9	40.4	5.51	5.65	197.81	228.26
October	83 794	68 331	23 279	18 356	60 515	56 004	13 722	36.0	40.6	5.56	5.69	200.16	231.01
November	84 173	68 658	23 371	18 419	60 802	56 281	13 771	35.9	40.5	5.59	5.72	200.68	231.66
December	84 408	68 870	23 371	18 531	61 037	56 466	13 861	35.8	40.4	5.61	5.75	200.84	232.30
1978													
January	84 595	68 984	23 374	18 593	61 221	56 547	13 917	35.3	39.5	5.66	5.83	199.80	230.29
February	84 948	69 277	23 453	18 639	61 495	56 768	13 950	35.6	39.9	5.69	5.86	202.56	233.81
March	85 461	69 730	23 649	18 699	61 812	57 176	13 992	35.8	40.5	5.73	5.88	205.13	238.14
April	86 163	70 366	24 008	18 772	62 155	57 709	14 037	35.8	40.4	5.79	5.93	207.28	239.57
May	86 509	70 675	24 082	18 848	62 427	57 941	14 096	35.8	40.4	5.82	5.96	208.36	240.78
June	86 951	71 099	24 238	18 919	62 713	58 263	14 129	35.9	40.6	5.87	6.01	210.73	244.01
July	87 205	71 304	24 300	18 951	62 905	58 422	14 152	35.9	40.6	5.90	6.06	211.81	246.04
August	87 481	71 590	24 374	19 006	63 107	58 626	14 187	35.8	40.5	5.93	6.09	212.29	246.65
September	87 618	71 799	24 444	19 068	63 174	58 819	14 241	35.8	40.5	5.97	6.15	213.73	249.08
October	87 954	72 096	24 548	19 142	63 406	59 017	14 291	35.8	40.5	6.03	6.20	215.87	251.10
November	88 391	72 497	24 678	19 257	63 713	59 377	14 388	35.7	40.6	6.06	6.26	216.34	254.16
December	88 674	72 763	24 758	19 334	63 916	59 599	14 459	35.7	40.5	6.10	6.31	217.77	255.56
1979													
January	88 811	72 874	24 740	19 388	64 071	59 659	14 497	35.6	40.4	6.14	6.36	218.58	256.94
February	89 054	73 107	24 784	19 409	64 270	59 840	14 501	35.7	40.5	6.18	6.40	220.63	259.20
March	89 480	73 524	24 998	19 453	64 482	60 216	14 526	35.8	40.6	6.22	6.45	222.68	261.87
April	89 441	73 441	24 958	19 450	64 460	60 067	14 515	35.3	39.3	6.22	6.43	219.57	252.70
May	89 790	73 800	25 071	19 509	64 719	60 368	14 551	35.6	40.2	6.28	6.52	223.57	262.10
June	90 108	74 063	25 161	19 553	64 947	60 583	14 566	35.6	40.2	6.32	6.56	224.99	263.71
July	90 214	74 064	25 163	19 531	65 051	60 558	14 536	35.6	40.2	6.36	6.59	226.42	264.92
August	90 296	74 067	25 059	19 406	65 237	60 516	14 397	35.6	40.1	6.40	6.63	227.84	265.86
September	90 323	74 195	25 088	19 442	65 235	60 629	14 440	35.6	40.1	6.45	6.67	229.62	267.47
October	90 480	74 344	25 038	19 390	65 442	60 746	14 384	35.6	40.2	6.47	6.71	230.33	269.74
November	90 574	74 401	24 947	19 299	65 627	60 778	14 295	35.6	40.1	6.51	6.74	231.76	270.27
December	90 669	74 489	24 970	19 301	65 699	60 860	14 300	35.5	40.1	6.57	6.80	233.24	272.68

Table 20-4. Nonfarm Payroll Employment, Hours, and Earnings—*Continued*

(Wage and salary workers on nonfarm payrolls, seasonally adjusted.)

Year and month	All wage and salary workers (thousands)					Production or nonsupervisory workers on private payrolls							
	Total	Private			Service-providing	Number (thousands)		Average hours per week		Average hourly earnings, dollars		Average weekly earnings, dollars	
		Total	Goods-producing			Total private	Manufac-turing	Total private	Manufac-turing	Total private	Manufac-turing	Total private	Manufac-turing
			Total	Manufac-turing									
1980													
January	90 800	74 599	24 949	19 282	65 851	60 896	14 241	35.4	40.0	6.57	6.82	232.58	272.80
February	90 879	74 653	24 874	19 219	66 005	60 964	14 170	35.4	40.1	6.63	6.88	234.70	275.89
March	90 991	74 695	24 818	19 217	66 173	60 987	14 165	35.3	39.9	6.70	6.95	236.51	277.31
April	90 846	74 263	24 507	18 973	66 339	60 540	13 914	35.2	39.8	6.72	6.97	236.54	277.41
May	90 415	73 961	24 234	18 726	66 181	60 194	13 632	35.1	39.3	6.76	7.02	237.28	275.89
June	90 095	73 654	23 968	18 490	66 127	59 892	13 405	35.0	39.2	6.82	7.10	238.70	278.32
July	89 832	73 414	23 698	18 276	66 134	59 693	13 227	34.9	39.1	6.86	7.16	239.41	279.96
August	90 092	73 682	23 860	18 414	66 232	59 908	13 349	35.1	39.5	6.91	7.24	242.54	285.98
September	90 205	73 875	23 931	18 445	66 274	60 075	13 396	35.1	39.6	6.95	7.30	243.95	289.08
October	90 485	74 099	24 012	18 506	66 473	60 239	13 437	35.2	39.8	7.02	7.38	247.10	293.72
November	90 741	74 350	24 123	18 601	66 618	60 449	13 528	35.3	39.9	7.09	7.47	250.28	298.05
December	90 936	74 563	24 182	18 640	66 754	60 606	13 550	35.3	40.1	7.13	7.52	251.69	301.55
1981													
January	91 031	74 671	24 152	18 639	66 879	60 710	13 545	35.4	40.1	7.19	7.58	254.53	303.96
February	91 098	74 752	24 118	18 613	66 980	60 736	13 518	35.2	39.8	7.23	7.62	254.50	303.28
March	91 202	74 910	24 203	18 647	66 999	60 875	13 550	35.3	40.0	7.29	7.68	257.34	307.20
April	91 276	75 016	24 151	18 711	67 125	60 973	13 594	35.3	40.1	7.33	7.76	258.75	311.18
May	91 286	75 088	24 148	18 766	67 138	60 973	13 633	35.3	40.2	7.37	7.81	260.16	313.96
June	91 482	75 323	24 290	18 789	67 192	61 134	13 632	35.2	40.0	7.42	7.85	261.18	314.00
July	91 594	75 419	24 302	18 785	67 292	61 222	13 629	35.2	39.9	7.46	7.89	262.59	314.81
August	91 558	75 448	24 258	18 748	67 300	61 216	13 573	35.2	40.0	7.53	7.97	265.06	318.80
September	91 471	75 440	24 210	18 712	67 261	61 235	13 565	35.0	39.6	7.57	8.03	264.95	317.99
October	91 371	75 302	24 051	18 566	67 320	61 066	13 399	35.1	39.6	7.59	8.06	266.41	319.18
November	91 162	75 084	23 875	18 409	67 287	60 817	13 235	35.1	39.4	7.64	8.08	268.16	318.35
December	90 884	74 811	23 656	18 223	67 228	60 511	13 033	34.9	39.2	7.64	8.09	266.64	317.13
1982													
January	90 557	74 516	23 362	18 047	67 195	60 206	12 874	34.1	37.3	7.72	8.26	263.25	308.10
February	90 551	74 540	23 361	17 981	67 190	60 277	12 831	35.1	39.6	7.73	8.21	271.32	325.12
March	90 422	74 398	23 214	17 857	67 208	60 140	12 727	34.9	39.1	7.76	8.24	270.82	322.18
April	90 141	74 131	22 996	17 683	67 145	59 867	12 566	34.8	39.1	7.77	8.28	270.40	323.75
May	90 096	74 093	22 884	17 588	67 212	59 840	12 506	34.8	39.1	7.83	8.33	272.48	325.70
June	89 853	73 837	22 643	17 430	67 210	59 589	12 365	34.8	39.2	7.85	8.37	273.18	328.10
July	89 510	73 620	22 434	17 278	67 076	59 411	12 261	34.8	39.2	7.89	8.40	274.57	329.28
August	89 352	73 422	22 268	17 160	67 084	59 203	12 153	34.7	39.0	7.94	8.43	275.52	328.77
September	89 171	73 248	22 126	17 074	67 025	59 069	12 104	34.8	39.0	7.94	8.45	276.31	329.55
October	88 894	72 938	21 879	16 853	67 015	58 750	11 880	34.6	38.9	7.96	8.44	275.42	328.32
November	88 770	72 793	21 736	16 722	67 034	58 613	11 766	34.6	39.0	7.98	8.46	276.11	329.94
December	88 756	72 775	21 688	16 690	67 068	58 585	11 746	34.7	39.0	8.02	8.49	278.29	331.11
1983													
January	88 981	72 958	21 757	16 705	67 224	58 813	11 783	34.8	39.3	8.06	8.52	280.49	334.84
February	88 903	72 899	21 676	16 706	67 227	58 792	11 794	34.5	39.3	8.10	8.59	279.45	337.59
March	89 076	73 071	21 649	16 711	67 427	58 958	11 817	34.7	39.6	8.10	8.59	281.07	340.16
April	89 352	73 362	21 729	16 794	67 623	59 201	11 894	34.8	39.7	8.13	8.61	282.92	341.82
May	89 629	73 624	21 829	16 885	67 800	59 444	11 987	34.9	40.0	8.17	8.64	285.13	345.60
June	90 007	73 987	21 949	16 960	68 058	59 806	12 054	34.9	40.1	8.19	8.66	285.83	347.27
July	90 425	74 414	22 103	17 059	68 322	60 189	12 155	34.9	40.3	8.23	8.71	287.23	351.01
August	90 117	74 101	22 207	17 118	67 910	59 820	12 200	34.9	40.3	8.20	8.71	286.18	351.01
September	91 231	75 189	22 381	17 255	68 850	60 849	12 318	35.0	40.6	8.26	8.76	289.10	355.66
October	91 502	75 516	22 546	17 367	68 956	61 095	12 408	35.2	40.6	8.31	8.80	292.51	357.28
November	91 854	75 857	22 698	17 479	69 156	61 378	12 503	35.1	40.6	8.32	8.84	292.03	358.90
December	92 210	76 202	22 803	17 551	69 407	61 664	12 553	35.1	40.5	8.33	8.87	292.38	359.24
1984													
January	92 657	76 647	22 942	17 630	69 715	61 906	12 617	35.1	40.6	8.38	8.91	294.14	361.75
February	93 136	77 111	23 146	17 728	69 990	62 329	12 703	35.3	41.1	8.37	8.92	295.46	366.61
March	93 411	77 381	23 209	17 806	70 202	62 516	12 768	35.1	40.7	8.41	8.96	295.19	364.67
April	93 774	77 699	23 305	17 872	70 469	62 801	12 814	35.2	40.8	8.45	8.98	297.44	366.38
May	94 082	77 979	23 389	17 916	70 693	63 012	12 840	35.1	40.7	8.44	8.99	296.24	365.89
June	94 461	78 334	23 497	17 967	70 964	63 296	12 871	35.1	40.6	8.48	9.03	297.65	366.62
July	94 773	78 601	23 571	18 013	71 202	63 517	12 901	35.1	40.6	8.52	9.05	299.05	367.43
August	95 014	78 790	23 608	18 034	71 406	63 654	12 906	35.0	40.5	8.52	9.09	298.20	368.15
September	95 325	79 070	23 617	18 019	71 708	63 874	12 880	35.1	40.5	8.56	9.12	300.46	369.36
October	95 611	79 337	23 626	18 024	71 985	64 083	12 868	34.9	40.5	8.55	9.15	298.40	370.58
November	95 960	79 649	23 639	18 016	72 321	64 325	12 846	35.0	40.4	8.57	9.19	299.95	371.28
December	96 087	79 805	23 673	18 023	72 414	64 441	12 848	35.1	40.5	8.61	9.22	302.21	373.41
1985													
January	96 353	80 017	23 672	18 009	72 681	64 657	12 833	34.9	40.3	8.61	9.27	300.49	373.58
February	96 477	80 128	23 621	17 966	72 856	64 758	12 784	34.8	40.1	8.64	9.29	300.67	372.53
March	96 823	80 428	23 661	17 939	73 162	65 007	12 758	34.9	40.4	8.67	9.32	302.58	376.53
April	97 018	80 588	23 644	17 886	73 374	65 113	12 701	34.9	40.5	8.69	9.35	303.28	378.68
May	97 292	80 818	23 632	17 855	73 660	65 307	12 673	34.9	40.4	8.70	9.37	303.63	378.55
June	97 437	80 939	23 592	17 819	73 845	65 382	12 635	34.9	40.5	8.74	9.39	305.03	380.30
July	97 626	81 006	23 549	17 776	74 077	65 432	12 596	34.8	40.4	8.74	9.42	304.15	380.57
August	97 819	81 200	23 546	17 756	74 273	65 615	12 593	34.8	40.6	8.77	9.43	305.20	382.86
September	98 023	81 385	23 528	17 718	74 495	65 750	12 556	34.8	40.6	8.80	9.44	306.24	383.26
October	98 210	81 556	23 529	17 708	74 681	65 917	12 556	34.8	40.7	8.79	9.46	305.89	385.02
November	98 419	81 745	23 520	17 697	74 899	66 069	12 545	34.8	40.7	8.82	9.49	306.94	386.24
December	98 587	81 893	23 518	17 693	75 069	66 197	12 550	34.9	40.9	8.87	9.55	309.56	390.60

Table 20-4. Nonfarm Payroll Employment, Hours, and Earnings—Continued

(Wage and salary workers on nonfarm payrolls, seasonally adjusted.)

Year and month	All wage and salary workers (thousands)					Production or nonsupervisory workers on private payrolls							
	Total	Private			Service-providing	Number (thousands)		Average hours per week		Average hourly earnings, dollars		Average weekly earnings, dollars	
		Total	Goods-producing			Total private	Manufac-turing	Total private	Manufac-turing	Total private	Manufac-turing	Total private	Manufac-turing
			Total	Manufac-turing									
1986													
January	98 710	81 995	23 530	17 686	75 180	66 293	12 546	35.0	40.7	8.85	9.53	309.75	387.87
February	98 817	82 058	23 485	17 663	75 332	66 365	12 530	34.8	40.7	8.88	9.56	309.02	389.09
March	98 910	82 155	23 428	17 624	75 482	66 403	12 498	34.8	40.7	8.89	9.58	309.37	389.91
April	99 098	82 333	23 427	17 616	75 671	66 531	12 495	34.7	40.5	8.89	9.56	308.48	387.18
May	99 223	82 433	23 349	17 593	75 874	66 606	12 474	34.8	40.7	8.90	9.59	309.72	390.31
June	99 130	82 351	23 263	17 530	75 867	66 533	12 424	34.7	40.7	8.91	9.58	309.18	389.91
July	99 448	82 669	23 235	17 497	76 213	66 810	12 389	34.6	40.6	8.92	9.60	308.63	389.76
August	99 561	82 761	23 225	17 489	76 336	66 909	12 399	34.7	40.7	8.94	9.61	310.22	391.13
September	99 907	82 997	23 216	17 498	76 691	67 108	12 411	34.6	40.7	8.94	9.60	309.32	390.72
October	100 094	83 125	23 208	17 477	76 886	67 206	12 396	34.6	40.6	8.96	9.62	310.02	390.57
November	100 280	83 275	23 204	17 472	77 076	67 344	12 407	34.7	40.7	9.00	9.64	312.30	392.35
December	100 484	83 463	23 237	17 478	77 247	67 493	12 425	34.6	40.8	9.01	9.66	311.75	394.13
1987													
January	100 655	83 610	23 232	17 465	77 423	67 614	12 405	34.7	40.8	9.02	9.67	312.99	394.54
February	100 887	83 851	23 296	17 499	77 591	67 845	12 438	34.9	41.2	9.05	9.69	315.85	399.23
March	101 136	84 072	23 307	17 507	77 829	67 991	12 446	34.7	41.0	9.07	9.71	314.73	398.11
April	101 474	84 365	23 342	17 525	78 132	68 237	12 465	34.7	40.8	9.08	9.71	315.08	396.17
May	101 701	84 589	23 390	17 542	78 311	68 426	12 481	34.8	41.0	9.11	9.73	317.03	398.93
June	101 872	84 748	23 390	17 537	78 482	68 552	12 482	34.7	40.9	9.11	9.74	316.12	398.37
July	102 218	85 058	23 455	17 593	78 763	68 798	12 521	34.7	41.0	9.12	9.74	316.46	399.34
August	102 388	85 216	23 506	17 630	78 882	68 926	12 560	34.9	40.9	9.18	9.80	320.38	400.82
September	102 617	85 482	23 566	17 691	79 051	69 139	12 614	34.7	40.8	9.19	9.85	318.89	401.88
October	103 109	85 840	23 655	17 729	79 454	69 416	12 637	34.8	41.1	9.22	9.84	320.86	404.42
November	103 340	86 041	23 711	17 775	79 629	69 594	12 678	34.8	41.0	9.27	9.87	322.60	404.67
December	103 634	86 287	23 772	17 809	79 862	69 826	12 707	34.6	41.0	9.28	9.89	321.09	405.49
1988													
January	103 728	86 363	23 668	17 790	80 060	69 833	12 684	34.6	41.1	9.29	9.91	321.43	407.30
February	104 180	86 791	23 769	17 823	80 411	70 228	12 706	34.7	41.1	9.29	9.92	322.36	407.71
March	104 456	87 009	23 824	17 844	80 632	70 371	12 712	34.5	40.9	9.31	9.94	321.20	406.55
April	104 701	87 249	23 880	17 874	80 821	70 578	12 733	34.6	41.0	9.36	9.99	323.86	409.59
May	104 928	87 447	23 896	17 892	81 032	70 693	12 747	34.6	41.0	9.41	10.02	325.59	410.82
June	105 291	87 776	23 951	17 916	81 340	71 000	12 767	34.6	41.1	9.42	10.04	325.93	412.64
July	105 514	88 020	23 966	17 926	81 548	71 210	12 774	34.7	41.1	9.45	10.05	327.92	413.06
August	105 635	88 091	23 926	17 891	81 709	71 273	12 752	34.5	40.9	9.46	10.07	326.37	411.86
September	105 975	88 341	23 942	17 914	82 033	71 456	12 764	34.5	41.0	9.51	10.12	328.10	414.92
October	106 243	88 573	23 987	17 966	82 256	71 649	12 812	34.7	41.1	9.56	10.16	331.73	417.58
November	106 582	88 836	24 030	18 003	82 552	71 872	12 851	34.5	41.1	9.58	10.19	330.51	418.81
December	106 871	89 135	24 054	18 025	82 817	72 144	12 864	34.6	40.9	9.60	10.20	332.16	417.18
1989													
January	107 133	89 359	24 097	18 057	83 036	72 361	12 882	34.7	41.1	9.65	10.23	334.86	420.45
February	107 391	89 579	24 080	18 055	83 311	72 545	12 880	34.5	41.2	9.68	10.26	333.96	422.71
March	107 583	89 761	24 069	18 060	83 514	72 663	12 878	34.5	41.1	9.70	10.29	334.65	422.92
April	107 756	89 916	24 100	18 055	83 656	72 788	12 867	34.6	41.1	9.75	10.28	337.35	422.51
May	107 874	89 998	24 089	18 040	83 785	72 826	12 852	34.4	41.0	9.73	10.30	334.71	422.30
June	107 991	90 079	24 052	18 013	83 939	72 906	12 822	34.4	40.9	9.77	10.33	336.09	422.50
July	108 030	90 125	24 027	17 980	84 003	72 943	12 790	34.5	40.9	9.82	10.36	338.79	423.72
August	108 077	90 088	24 048	17 964	84 029	72 931	12 790	34.5	40.9	9.83	10.39	339.14	424.95
September	108 326	90 299	24 000	17 922	84 326	73 080	12 745	34.4	40.8	9.87	10.41	339.53	424.73
October	108 437	90 404	23 997	17 895	84 440	73 176	12 723	34.6	40.8	9.93	10.43	343.58	425.54
November	108 714	90 657	24 009	17 886	84 705	73 392	12 713	34.4	40.7	9.93	10.44	341.59	424.91
December	108 809	90 734	23 949	17 881	84 860	73 468	12 705	34.3	40.5	9.98	10.49	342.31	424.85
1990													
January	109 151	91 000	23 984	17 799	85 167	73 700	12 741	34.4	40.5	10.01	10.51	344.34	425.66
February	109 396	91 219	24 074	17 896	85 322	73 901	12 850	34.3	40.6	10.08	10.64	345.74	431.98
March	109 611	91 317	24 025	17 870	85 586	73 964	12 823	34.4	40.7	10.11	10.70	347.78	435.49
April	109 651	91 274	23 968	17 847	85 683	73 928	12 805	34.3	40.6	10.13	10.68	347.46	433.61
May	109 800	91 201	23 887	17 796	85 913	73 840	12 755	34.3	40.6	10.16	10.74	348.49	436.04
June	109 817	91 261	23 848	17 775	85 969	73 823	12 738	34.4	40.7	10.20	10.77	350.88	438.34
July	109 775	91 215	23 745	17 703	86 030	73 773	12 674	34.3	40.6	10.22	10.81	350.55	438.89
August	109 567	91 110	23 647	17 648	85 920	73 707	12 624	34.2	40.5	10.24	10.80	350.21	437.40
September	109 485	91 048	23 572	17 610	85 913	73 602	12 597	34.2	40.5	10.28	10.86	351.58	439.83
October	109 324	90 881	23 471	17 575	85 853	73 466	12 576	34.1	40.4	10.30	10.92	351.23	441.17
November	109 180	90 730	23 283	17 428	85 897	73 315	12 437	34.2	40.2	10.32	10.89	352.94	437.78
December	109 120	90 652	23 202	17 394	85 918	73 248	12 413	34.2	40.3	10.35	10.93	353.97	440.48
1991													
January	109 001	90 527	23 062	17 331	85 939	73 101	12 352	34.1	40.2	10.37	10.97	353.62	440.99
February	108 695	90 213	22 903	17 214	85 792	72 816	12 245	34.1	40.1	10.39	10.98	354.30	440.30
March	108 535	90 047	22 780	17 141	85 755	72 665	12 191	34.0	40.0	10.41	11.00	353.94	440.00
April	108 324	89 839	22 689	17 095	85 635	72 495	12 157	34.0	40.1	10.45	11.04	355.30	442.70
May	108 196	89 698	22 617	17 069	85 579	72 401	12 147	34.0	40.1	10.49	11.08	356.66	444.31
June	108 283	89 722	22 569	17 042	85 714	72 418	12 135	34.1	40.5	10.52	11.13	358.73	450.77
July	108 236	89 638	22 508	17 016	85 728	72 382	12 130	34.1	40.5	10.55	11.17	359.76	452.39
August	108 251	89 684	22 493	17 025	85 758	72 439	12 154	34.1	40.6	10.56	11.18	360.10	453.91
September	108 286	89 743	22 467	17 011	85 819	72 451	12 140	34.1	40.6	10.58	11.22	360.78	455.53
October	108 298	89 705	22 417	16 998	85 881	72 422	12 138	34.2	40.6	10.59	11.25	362.18	456.75
November	108 240	89 613	22 315	16 960	85 925	72 348	12 101	34.1	40.6	10.61	11.26	361.80	457.16
December	108 263	89 622	22 274	16 916	85 989	72 393	12 074	34.1	40.7	10.64	11.26	362.82	458.28

Table 20-4. Nonfarm Payroll Employment, Hours, and Earnings—*Continued*

(Wage and salary workers on nonfarm payrolls, seasonally adjusted.)

Year and month	All wage and salary workers (thousands)					Production or nonsupervisory workers on private payrolls							
	Total	Private			Service-providing	Number (thousands)		Average hours per week		Average hourly earnings, dollars		Average weekly earnings, dollars	
		Total	Goods-producing			Total private	Manufac-turing	Total private	Manufac-turing	Total private	Manufac-turing	Total private	Manufac-turing
			Total	Manufac-turing									
1992													
January	108 312	89 624	22 214	16 840	86 098	72 429	12 011	34.1	40.6	10.65	11.24	363.17	456.34
February	108 246	89 557	22 144	16 831	86 102	72 407	12 018	34.1	40.7	10.67	11.30	363.85	459.91
March	108 296	89 581	22 127	16 805	86 169	72 422	12 007	34.1	40.7	10.70	11.33	364.87	461.13
April	108 454	89 715	22 131	16 830	86 323	72 570	12 029	34.3	41.0	10.72	11.36	367.70	465.76
May	108 580	89 827	22 134	16 834	86 446	72 684	12 045	34.2	40.9	10.74	11.39	367.31	465.85
June	108 640	89 878	22 096	16 825	86 544	72 726	12 042	34.1	40.8	10.77	11.41	367.26	465.53
July	108 711	89 894	22 075	16 820	86 636	72 734	12 047	34.2	40.8	10.79	11.43	369.02	466.34
August	108 852	89 969	22 045	16 783	86 807	72 815	12 020	34.2	40.8	10.82	11.47	370.04	467.98
September	108 887	90 058	22 020	16 761	86 867	72 919	12 002	34.3	40.8	10.82	11.46	371.13	467.57
October	109 064	90 236	22 028	16 750	87 036	73 074	12 000	34.2	40.8	10.86	11.47	371.41	467.98
November	109 204	90 363	22 042	16 758	87 162	73 221	12 010	34.2	40.9	10.88	11.49	372.10	469.94
December	109 415	90 537	22 074	16 767	87 341	73 411	12 031	34.2	40.9	10.89	11.51	372.44	470.76
1993													
January	109 725	90 824	22 133	16 791	87 592	73 683	12 058	34.3	41.1	10.93	11.55	374.90	474.71
February	109 967	91 065	22 189	16 806	87 778	73 941	12 075	34.3	41.1	10.95	11.58	375.59	475.94
March	109 916	91 009	22 142	16 795	87 774	73 855	12 074	34.1	40.8	10.99	11.58	374.76	472.46
April	110 225	91 287	22 130	16 771	88 095	74 079	12 056	34.4	41.5	10.99	11.63	378.06	482.65
May	110 490	91 539	22 189	16 766	88 301	74 331	12 055	34.3	41.1	11.02	11.66	377.99	479.23
June	110 663	91 694	22 165	16 742	88 498	74 440	12 039	34.3	40.9	11.03	11.67	378.33	477.30
July	110 958	91 898	22 184	16 740	88 774	74 618	12 042	34.4	41.1	11.05	11.69	380.12	480.46
August	111 119	92 091	22 203	16 741	88 916	74 793	12 049	34.3	41.2	11.08	11.72	380.04	482.86
September	111 360	92 319	22 252	16 769	89 108	74 981	12 080	34.4	41.3	11.10	11.77	381.84	486.10
October	111 637	92 595	22 305	16 777	89 332	75 227	12 092	34.4	41.3	11.13	11.79	382.87	486.93
November	111 898	92 830	22 347	16 800	89 551	75 443	12 118	34.4	41.3	11.15	11.83	383.56	488.58
December	112 206	93 097	22 413	16 815	89 793	75 662	12 141	34.4	41.4	11.18	11.88	384.59	491.83
1994													
January	112 474	93 327	22 464	16 854	90 010	75 871	12 181	34.4	41.4	11.21	11.89	385.62	492.25
February	112 675	93 525	22 452	16 863	90 223	76 076	12 199	34.2	40.9	11.25	11.98	384.75	489.98
March	113 137	93 947	22 549	16 896	90 588	76 436	12 234	34.5	41.7	11.25	11.95	388.13	498.32
April	113 490	94 267	22 640	16 932	90 850	76 734	12 276	34.5	41.7	11.27	11.96	388.82	498.73
May	113 821	94 557	22 703	16 961	91 118	77 012	12 304	34.5	41.8	11.30	11.98	389.85	500.76
June	114 136	94 862	22 765	17 011	91 371	77 262	12 352	34.5	41.8	11.31	12.00	390.20	501.60
July	114 499	95 198	22 807	17 026	91 692	77 566	12 369	34.6	41.8	11.34	12.02	392.36	502.44
August	114 799	95 493	22 877	17 082	91 922	77 801	12 427	34.5	41.7	11.36	12.06	391.92	502.90
September	115 153	95 816	22 946	17 113	92 207	78 067	12 458	34.4	41.6	11.39	12.09	391.82	502.94
October	115 360	96 016	22 973	17 143	92 387	78 252	12 489	34.5	41.8	11.43	12.12	394.34	506.62
November	115 783	96 416	23 051	17 187	92 732	78 601	12 528	34.5	41.8	11.45	12.16	395.03	508.29
December	116 057	96 669	23 096	17 218	92 961	78 840	12 559	34.5	41.8	11.48	12.17	396.06	508.71
1995													
January	116 378	96 981	23 146	17 261	93 232	79 085	12 594	34.5	41.8	11.49	12.19	396.41	509.54
February	116 587	97 180	23 103	17 265	93 484	79 239	12 602	34.4	41.7	11.53	12.25	396.63	510.83
March	116 809	97 382	23 150	17 262	93 659	79 423	12 600	34.4	41.5	11.55	12.24	397.32	507.96
April	116 971	97 537	23 174	17 278	93 797	79 559	12 608	34.3	41.2	11.57	12.26	396.85	505.11
May	116 955	97 537	23 120	17 259	93 835	79 573	12 589	34.2	41.2	11.59	12.28	396.38	505.94
June	117 186	97 741	23 139	17 249	94 047	79 739	12 575	34.3	41.2	11.63	12.31	398.91	507.17
July	117 265	97 828	23 119	17 218	94 146	79 813	12 539	34.3	41.1	11.68	12.38	400.62	508.82
August	117 536	98 107	23 163	17 239	94 373	80 058	12 566	34.3	41.2	11.69	12.39	400.97	510.47
September	117 781	98 351	23 207	17 246	94 574	80 252	12 565	34.3	41.2	11.72	12.41	402.00	511.29
October	117 928	98 464	23 205	17 215	94 723	80 373	12 535	34.3	41.2	11.76	12.44	403.37	512.53
November	118 076	98 613	23 198	17 207	94 878	80 449	12 514	34.3	41.3	11.78	12.45	404.05	514.19
December	118 207	98 741	23 207	17 229	95 000	80 604	12 550	34.2	40.9	11.81	12.49	403.90	510.84
1996													
January	118 188	98 738	23 196	17 208	94 992	80 525	12 519	33.8	39.7	11.86	12.60	400.87	500.22
February	118 622	99 137	23 281	17 230	95 341	80 912	12 532	34.3	41.3	11.87	12.56	407.14	518.73
March	118 885	99 353	23 275	17 192	95 610	81 092	12 489	34.3	41.1	11.89	12.50	407.83	513.75
April	119 046	99 531	23 316	17 204	95 730	81 258	12 504	34.2	41.2	11.95	12.69	408.69	522.83
May	119 369	99 840	23 358	17 222	96 011	81 518	12 517	34.3	41.4	11.98	12.70	410.91	525.78
June	119 647	100 119	23 400	17 227	96 247	81 731	12 523	34.4	41.5	12.04	12.76	414.18	529.54
July	119 879	100 332	23 417	17 222	96 462	81 922	12 517	34.3	41.4	12.06	12.78	413.66	529.09
August	120 075	100 571	23 479	17 255	96 596	82 121	12 545	34.4	41.5	12.09	12.82	415.90	532.03
September	120 295	100 728	23 497	17 252	96 798	82 243	12 543	34.4	41.6	12.14	12.84	417.62	534.14
October	120 538	100 984	23 546	17 268	96 992	82 476	12 558	34.4	41.4	12.16	12.84	418.30	531.58
November	120 834	101 269	23 583	17 276	97 251	82 662	12 558	34.4	41.5	12.21	12.89	420.02	534.94
December	121 001	101 430	23 597	17 283	97 404	82 832	12 571	34.4	41.7	12.25	12.95	421.40	540.02
1997													
January	121 231	101 638	23 620	17 299	97 611	82 978	12 581	34.3	41.4	12.29	13.00	421.55	538.20
February	121 532	101 934	23 687	17 317	97 845	83 252	12 592	34.5	41.6	12.32	13.00	425.04	540.80
March	121 844	102 236	23 738	17 339	98 106	83 478	12 613	34.5	41.8	12.37	13.03	426.77	544.65
April	122 135	102 532	23 767	17 351	98 368	83 727	12 618	34.6	41.8	12.38	13.04	428.35	545.07
May	122 391	102 790	23 810	17 363	98 581	83 947	12 633	34.6	41.7	12.43	13.06	430.08	544.60
June	122 644	102 984	23 835	17 388	98 809	84 080	12 648	34.4	41.6	12.47	13.08	428.97	544.13
July	122 927	103 241	23 861	17 388	99 066	84 319	12 644	34.5	41.6	12.50	13.09	431.25	544.54
August	122 909	103 292	23 951	17 451	98 958	84 266	12 699	34.6	41.6	12.57	13.17	434.92	547.87
September	123 417	103 738	23 996	17 465	99 421	84 661	12 711	34.6	41.6	12.59	13.17	435.61	547.87
October	123 756	104 018	24 053	17 513	99 703	84 866	12 745	34.5	41.8	12.67	13.28	437.12	555.10
November	124 059	104 298	24 112	17 556	99 947	85 055	12 776	34.6	41.8	12.72	13.33	440.11	557.19
December	124 358	104 592	24 183	17 587	100 175	85 289	12 800	34.6	42.0	12.75	13.35	441.15	560.70

Table 20-4. Nonfarm Payroll Employment, Hours, and Earnings—*Continued*

(Wage and salary workers on nonfarm payrolls, seasonally adjusted.)

Year and month	All wage and salary workers (thousands)					Production or nonsupervisory workers on private payrolls							
	Total	Private			Service-providing	Number (thousands)		Average hours per week		Average hourly earnings, dollars		Average weekly earnings, dollars	
		Total	Goods-producing			Total private	Manufac-turing	Total private	Manufac-turing	Total private	Manufac-turing	Total private	Manufac-turing
			Total	Manufac-turing									
1998													
January	124 628	104 858	24 266	17 623	100 362	85 442	12 820	34.6	41.9	12.79	13.35	442.53	559.37
February	124 817	105 031	24 283	17 627	100 534	85 606	12 828	34.6	41.7	12.84	13.39	444.26	558.36
March	124 961	105 169	24 264	17 637	100 697	85 630	12 823	34.5	41.6	12.88	13.44	444.36	559.10
April	125 238	105 422	24 338	17 635	100 900	85 846	12 814	34.5	41.3	12.92	13.41	445.74	553.83
May	125 639	105 764	24 360	17 623	101 279	86 124	12 789	34.5	41.5	12.96	13.46	447.12	558.59
June	125 851	105 972	24 388	17 609	101 463	86 272	12 770	34.4	41.4	12.99	13.43	446.86	556.00
July	125 970	106 040	24 237	17 421	101 733	86 278	12 557	34.5	41.4	13.01	13.34	448.85	552.28
August	126 322	106 363	24 420	17 563	101 902	86 571	12 702	34.5	41.4	13.09	13.47	451.61	557.66
September	126 540	106 555	24 419	17 557	102 121	86 737	12 714	34.4	41.3	13.11	13.53	450.98	558.79
October	126 733	106 732	24 405	17 511	102 328	86 879	12 673	34.5	41.4	13.14	13.52	453.33	559.73
November	127 017	106 973	24 394	17 465	102 623	87 041	12 634	34.5	41.4	13.18	13.54	454.71	560.56
December	127 359	107 280	24 452	17 447	102 907	87 307	12 624	34.5	41.5	13.21	13.56	455.75	562.74
1999													
January	127 480	107 396	24 406	17 432	103 074	87 359	12 607	34.4	41.3	13.27	13.60	456.49	561.68
February	127 890	107 746	24 434	17 395	103 456	87 680	12 575	34.4	41.4	13.30	13.63	457.52	564.28
March	127 996	107 828	24 378	17 368	103 618	87 732	12 562	34.3	41.3	13.34	13.69	457.56	565.40
April	128 372	108 135	24 424	17 343	103 948	87 961	12 540	34.4	41.3	13.38	13.75	460.27	567.88
May	128 585	108 356	24 445	17 333	104 140	88 154	12 533	34.4	41.4	13.43	13.80	461.99	571.32
June	128 851	108 579	24 435	17 296	104 416	88 331	12 503	34.4	41.3	13.47	13.86	463.37	572.42
July	129 142	108 803	24 474	17 308	104 668	88 520	12 526	34.4	41.4	13.52	13.91	465.09	575.87
August	129 334	108 959	24 466	17 286	104 868	88 642	12 502	34.4	41.5	13.55	13.93	466.12	578.10
September	129 536	109 132	24 483	17 279	105 053	88 766	12 494	34.4	41.5	13.61	13.99	468.18	580.59
October	129 944	109 487	24 506	17 273	105 438	89 084	12 483	34.4	41.4	13.64	13.99	469.22	579.19
November	130 238	109 742	24 560	17 281	105 678	89 310	12 488	34.4	41.4	13.66	14.00	469.90	579.60
December	130 532	109 992	24 579	17 277	105 953	89 525	12 491	34.4	41.4	13.70	14.06	471.28	582.08
2000													
January	130 781	110 210	24 636	17 292	106 145	89 685	12 496	34.4	41.5	13.75	14.13	473.00	586.40
February	130 902	110 303	24 608	17 284	106 294	89 770	12 482	34.4	41.6	13.80	14.15	474.72	588.64
March	131 374	110 641	24 705	17 302	106 669	90 037	12 490	34.3	41.4	13.85	14.18	475.06	587.05
April	131 660	110 858	24 688	17 298	106 972	90 260	12 477	34.4	41.5	13.91	14.24	478.50	590.96
May	131 885	110 738	24 647	17 279	107 238	90 165	12 463	34.3	41.3	13.94	14.22	478.14	587.29
June	131 839	110 952	24 674	17 298	107 165	90 329	12 468	34.3	41.3	13.98	14.29	479.51	590.18
July	132 002	111 135	24 716	17 321	107 286	90 482	12 475	34.3	41.5	14.03	14.31	481.23	593.87
August	132 005	111 168	24 682	17 286	107 323	90 498	12 431	34.2	41.0	14.07	14.36	481.19	588.76
September	132 127	111 392	24 638	17 226	107 489	90 650	12 381	34.2	41.0	14.12	14.40	482.90	590.40
October	132 116	111 373	24 636	17 215	107 480	90 631	12 356	34.3	41.1	14.18	14.48	486.37	595.13
November	132 347	111 587	24 623	17 202	107 724	90 760	12 337	34.2	41.1	14.23	14.52	486.67	596.77
December	132 485	111 681	24 572	17 178	107 913	90 805	12 306	34.0	40.4	14.28	14.51	485.52	586.20
2001													
January	132 469	111 634	24 543	17 114	107 926	90 759	12 236	34.2	40.7	14.29	14.48	488.72	589.34
February	132 530	111 624	24 475	17 029	108 055	90 688	12 156	34.0	40.5	14.38	14.56	488.92	589.68
March	132 500	111 555	24 410	16 939	108 090	90 655	12 084	34.1	40.5	14.42	14.58	491.72	590.49
April	132 219	111 227	24 255	16 803	107 964	90 432	11 980	34.0	40.5	14.45	14.64	491.30	592.92
May	132 175	111 146	24 120	16 662	108 055	90 344	11 858	34.0	40.4	14.50	14.69	493.00	593.48
June	132 047	110 910	23 966	16 516	108 081	90 148	11 737	34.0	40.3	14.55	14.74	494.70	594.02
July	131 922	110 737	23 833	16 378	108 089	90 042	11 631	34.0	40.6	14.56	14.80	495.04	600.88
August	131 762	110 544	23 660	16 225	108 102	89 886	11 493	33.9	40.3	14.60	14.85	494.94	598.46
September	131 518	110 276	23 533	16 113	107 985	89 618	11 398	33.8	40.2	14.64	14.90	494.83	598.98
October	131 193	109 918	23 377	15 971	107 816	89 329	11 286	33.7	40.1	14.66	14.88	494.04	596.69
November	130 901	109 575	23 209	15 825	107 692	88 999	11 175	33.8	40.1	14.72	14.96	497.54	599.90
December	130 723	109 368	23 093	15 710	107 630	88 898	11 079	33.9	40.3	14.75	15.02	500.03	605.31
2002													
January	130 591	109 214	22 972	15 598	107 619	88 857	11 004	33.8	40.2	14.76	15.06	498.89	605.41
February	130 444	109 054	22 879	15 518	107 565	88 799	10 953	33.8	40.3	14.79	15.12	499.90	609.34
March	130 420	108 989	22 789	15 446	107 631	88 756	10 900	33.9	40.5	14.82	15.15	502.40	613.58
April	130 335	108 892	22 691	15 394	107 644	88 601	10 859	33.9	40.5	14.83	15.17	502.74	614.39
May	130 328	108 814	22 605	15 338	107 723	88 475	10 822	33.9	40.6	14.88	15.23	504.43	618.34
June	130 373	108 824	22 577	15 297	107 796	88 387	10 795	33.9	40.7	14.95	15.26	506.81	621.08
July	130 276	108 732	22 515	15 250	107 761	88 240	10 760	33.8	40.4	14.98	15.27	506.32	616.91
August	130 260	108 671	22 442	15 164	107 818	88 163	10 696	33.9	40.5	15.02	15.34	509.18	621.27
September	130 205	108 659	22 393	15 115	107 812	88 141	10 666	33.9	40.5	15.07	15.38	510.87	622.89
October	130 331	108 772	22 324	15 059	108 007	88 217	10 630	33.8	40.3	15.12	15.45	511.06	622.64
November	130 339	108 758	22 282	14 992	108 057	88 167	10 581	33.8	40.4	15.15	15.48	512.07	625.39
December	130 183	108 595	22 187	14 910	107 996	87 973	10 522	33.8	40.5	15.21	15.54	514.10	629.37
2003													
January	130 266	108 640	22 147	14 867	108 119	88 020	10 483	33.8	40.3	15.22	15.59	514.44	628.28
February	130 108	108 484	22 022	14 780	108 086	87 873	10 417	33.6	40.2	15.29	15.62	513.74	627.92
March	129 896	108 286	21 946	14 722	107 950	87 572	10 355	33.8	40.4	15.29	15.64	516.80	631.86
April	129 847	108 252	21 863	14 608	107 984	87 539	10 255	33.6	40.0	15.28	15.63	513.41	625.20
May	129 841	108 274	21 831	14 556	108 010	87 506	10 220	33.7	40.2	15.34	15.67	516.96	629.93
June	129 839	108 233	21 788	14 493	108 051	87 478	10 166	33.6	40.3	15.36	15.72	516.10	633.52
July	129 864	108 231	21 707	14 401	108 157	87 462	10 093	33.6	40.0	15.40	15.74	517.44	629.60
August	129 822	108 266	21 708	14 378	108 114	87 524	10 085	33.7	40.2	15.42	15.78	519.65	634.36
September	129 925	108 421	21 700	14 347	108 225	87 635	10 058	33.6	40.5	15.42	15.82	518.11	640.71
October	130 128	108 570	21 691	14 334	108 437	87 721	10 055	33.7	40.6	15.43	15.83	519.99	642.70
November	130 146	108 611	21 687	14 315	108 459	87 778	10 040	33.7	40.9	15.47	15.90	521.34	650.31
December	130 270	108 724	21 703	14 300	108 567	87 859	10 029	33.6	40.7	15.48	15.92	520.13	647.94

Table 20-4. Nonfarm Payroll Employment, Hours, and Earnings—*Continued*

(Wage and salary workers on nonfarm payrolls, seasonally adjusted.)

Year and month	All wage and salary workers (thousands)					Production or nonsupervisory workers on private payrolls							
	Total	Private			Service-providing	Number (thousands)		Average hours per week		Average hourly earnings, dollars		Average weekly earnings, dollars	
		Total	Goods-producing			Total private	Manufac-turing	Total private	Manufac-turing	Total private	Manufac-turing	Total private	Manufac-turing
			Total	Manufac-turing									
2004													
January	130 420	108 882	21 717	14 292	108 703	87 940	10 029	33.7	40.9	15.52	15.94	523.02	651.95
February	130 463	108 913	21 691	14 277	108 772	87 958	10 014	33.8	41.0	15.52	15.97	524.58	654.77
March	130 801	109 213	21 759	14 288	109 042	88 217	10 025	33.7	40.9	15.57	16.02	524.71	655.22
April	131 051	109 437	21 803	14 316	109 248	88 465	10 058	33.7	40.8	15.60	16.07	525.72	655.66
May	131 361	109 747	21 881	14 342	109 480	88 780	10 091	33.8	41.0	15.64	16.06	528.63	658.46
June	131 442	109 841	21 884	14 331	109 558	88 927	10 085	33.6	40.7	15.67	16.11	526.51	655.68
July	131 489	109 883	21 903	14 333	109 586	89 034	10 100	33.7	40.8	15.71	16.18	529.43	660.14
August	131 610	109 984	21 942	14 343	109 668	89 170	10 115	33.7	40.9	15.75	16.20	530.78	662.58
September	131 770	110 135	21 956	14 330	109 814	89 363	10 103	33.7	40.7	15.79	16.29	532.12	663.00
October	132 121	110 465	22 006	14 334	110 115	89 678	10 104	33.7	40.6	15.82	16.26	533.13	660.16
November	132 185	110 493	21 995	14 305	110 190	89 707	10 077	33.7	40.5	15.85	16.30	534.15	660.15
December	132 317	110 624	22 003	14 285	110 314	89 877	10 063	33.8	40.6	15.87	16.35	536.41	663.81
2005													
January	132 499	110 741	21 968	14 266	110 531	89 980	10 050	33.7	40.7	15.91	16.38	536.17	666.67
February	132 720	110 968	22 038	14 272	110 682	90 209	10 057	33.7	40.6	15.94	16.44	537.18	667.46
March	132 841	111 096	22 066	14 270	110 775	90 361	10 056	33.7	40.4	15.98	16.43	538.53	663.77
April	133 153	111 388	22 122	14 253	111 031	90 670	10 050	33.8	40.5	16.02	16.47	541.48	667.04
May	133 365	111 576	22 166	14 252	111 199	90 821	10 058	33.7	40.4	16.05	16.53	540.89	667.81
June	133 624	111 824	22 174	14 220	111 450	91 090	10 044	33.7	40.4	16.08	16.53	541.90	667.81
July	133 946	112 087	22 187	14 213	111 759	91 308	10 037	33.7	40.4	16.15	16.57	544.26	669.43
August	134 136	112 281	22 214	14 199	111 922	91 487	10 041	33.7	40.5	16.18	16.63	545.27	673.52
September	134 223	112 379	22 228	14 175	111 995	91 581	10 045	33.8	40.8	16.21	16.59	547.90	676.87
October	134 321	112 504	22 300	14 198	112 021	91 723	10 077	33.8	41.0	16.29	16.68	550.60	683.88
November	134 701	112 842	22 373	14 193	112 328	92 068	10 093	33.8	40.9	16.32	16.68	551.62	682.21
December	134 861	112 989	22 393	14 202	112 468	92 260	10 118	33.8	40.8	16.37	16.68	553.31	680.54
2006													
January	135 155	113 293	22 490	14 219	112 665	92 569	10 159	33.9	41.1	16.43	16.71	556.98	686.78
February	135 429	113 556	22 555	14 214	112 874	92 832	10 168	33.8	41.2	16.50	16.70	557.70	688.04
March	135 711	113 805	22 579	14 217	113 132	93 115	10 175	33.8	41.1	16.55	16.71	559.39	686.78
April	135 862	113 940	22 620	14 224	113 242	93 301	10 185	33.9	41.2	16.64	16.75	564.10	690.10
May	135 886	113 958	22 590	14 198	113 296	93 356	10 174	33.8	41.2	16.66	16.76	563.11	690.51
June	135 956	114 007	22 579	14 202	113 377	93 416	10 183	33.9	41.2	16.73	16.77	567.15	690.92
July	136 142	114 157	22 566	14 176	113 576	93 530	10 168	33.9	41.3	16.78	16.78	568.84	693.01
August	136 291	114 292	22 559	14 153	113 732	93 678	10 156	33.9	41.2	16.83	16.83	570.54	693.40
September	136 438	114 384	22 537	14 128	113 901	93 712	10 122	33.8	41.1	16.88	16.83	570.54	691.71
October	136 520	114 461	22 467	14 084	114 053	93 774	10 077	33.9	41.1	16.94	16.90	574.27	694.59
November	136 781	114 707	22 433	14 052	114 348	94 003	10 054	33.9	41.0	16.99	16.92	575.96	693.72
December	137 000	114 919	22 455	14 035	114 545	94 266	10 059	34.0	41.2	17.07	17.00	580.38	700.40
2007													
January	137 180	115 068	22 465	14 021	114 715	94 413	10 047	33.8	41.0	17.12	17.02	578.66	697.82
February	137 216	115 091	22 347	13 998	114 869	94 417	10 036	33.8	40.9	17.18	17.05	580.68	697.35
March	137 400	115 250	22 392	13 966	115 008	94 609	10 007	33.9	41.2	17.23	17.10	584.10	704.52
April	137 435	115 260	22 333	13 933	115 102	94 689	9 996	33.8	41.2	17.29	17.20	584.40	708.64
May	137 591	115 388	22 307	13 917	115 284	94 863	9 999	33.9	41.1	17.34	17.23	587.83	708.15
June	137 645	115 400	22 289	13 889	115 356	94 940	9 982	33.9	41.3	17.42	17.29	590.54	714.08
July	137 580	115 415	22 251	13 877	115 329	95 011	9 980	33.8	41.3	17.48	17.30	590.82	714.49
August	137 552	115 339	22 151	13 826	115 401	94 962	9 942	33.8	41.2	17.51	17.35	591.84	714.82
September	137 652	115 389	22 099	13 796	115 553	95 050	9 936	33.8	41.3	17.57	17.37	593.87	717.38
October	137 817	115 521	22 069	13 774	115 748	95 183	9 918	33.8	41.2	17.60	17.34	594.88	714.41
November	138 032	115 707	22 072	13 780	115 960	95 329	9 933	33.8	41.4	17.66	17.41	596.91	720.77
December	138 152	115 783	22 043	13 777	116 109	95 473	9 947	33.8	41.2	17.71	17.42	598.60	717.70
2008													
January	138 080	115 689	21 981	13 744	116 099	95 432	9 930	33.7	41.1	17.77	17.52	598.85	720.07
February	137 936	115 515	21 887	13 692	116 049	95 299	9 886	33.8	41.2	17.83	17.58	602.65	724.30
March	137 814	115 373	21 800	13 643	116 014	95 208	9 853	33.8	41.2	17.90	17.64	605.02	726.77
April	137 654	115 203	21 679	13 586	115 975	95 091	9 795	33.8	41.0	17.94	17.64	606.37	723.24
May	137 517	115 029	21 612	13 556	115 905	94 931	9 770	33.7	40.9	17.99	17.68	606.26	723.11
June	137 356	114 834	21 507	13 505	115 849	94 765	9 723	33.6	40.9	18.04	17.73	606.14	725.16
July	137 228	114 691	21 432	13 454	115 796	94 636	9 672	33.6	41.0	18.10	17.80	608.16	729.80
August	137 053	114 497	21 351	13 387	115 702	94 470	9 608	33.7	40.8	18.18	17.78	612.67	725.42
September	136 732	114 197	21 247	13 322	115 485	94 217	9 543	33.6	40.5	18.21	17.81	611.86	721.31
October	136 352	113 813	21 063	13 203	115 289	93 825	9 425	33.5	40.4	18.28	17.89	612.38	722.76
November	135 755	113 212	20 814	13 082	114 941	93 286	9 322	33.4	40.2	18.34	17.94	612.56	721.19
December	135 074	112 542	20 532	12 902	114 542	92 759	9 174	33.3	39.9	18.40	17.96	612.72	716.60

Table 20-5A. Money Stock and Related Data, January 1947–January 1959

(Averages of daily figures; seasonally adjusted, billions of dollars.)

Year and month	Money stock			Time deposits adjusted
	Total	Currency component	Demand deposit component	
1947				
January	109.5	26.7	82.8	33.3
February	109.7	26.7	83.0	33.5
March	110.3	26.7	83.7	33.6
April	111.1	26.6	84.5	33.7
May	111.7	26.6	85.1	33.8
June	112.1	26.6	85.5	33.9
July	112.2	26.5	85.7	34.0
August	112.6	26.5	86.1	34.4
September	113.0	26.7	86.3	34.7
October	112.9	26.5	86.4	35.0
November	113.3	26.5	86.8	35.2
December	113.1	26.4	86.7	35.4
1948				
January	113.4	26.4	87.0	35.5
February	113.2	26.3	86.8	35.7
March	112.6	26.2	86.4	35.7
April	112.3	26.1	86.3	35.7
May	112.1	26.0	86.0	35.7
June	112.0	26.0	86.0	35.8
July	112.2	26.0	86.2	35.8
August	112.3	26.0	86.2	35.9
September	112.2	26.0	86.2	35.9
October	112.1	26.0	86.1	35.9
November	111.8	26.0	85.9	36.0
December	111.5	25.8	85.8	36.0
1949				
January	111.2	25.7	85.5	36.1
February	111.2	25.7	85.5	36.1
March	111.2	25.7	85.6	36.1
April	111.3	25.7	85.6	36.2
May	111.5	25.7	85.8	36.3
June	111.3	25.6	85.7	36.4
July	111.2	25.5	85.7	36.4
August	111.0	25.5	85.6	36.4
September	110.9	25.3	85.6	36.4
October	110.9	25.3	85.6	36.4
November	111.0	25.2	85.8	36.4
December	111.2	25.1	86.0	36.4
1950				
January	111.5	25.1	86.4	36.4
February	112.1	25.1	86.9	36.6
March	112.5	25.2	87.3	36.6
April	113.2	25.3	88.0	36.7
May	113.7	25.2	88.5	36.9
June	114.1	25.1	89.0	36.9
July	114.6	25.0	89.6	36.8
August	115.0	24.9	90.1	36.7
September	115.2	24.9	90.3	36.6
October	115.7	24.9	90.8	36.5
November	115.9	24.9	90.9	36.6
December	116.2	25.0	91.2	36.7
1951				
January	116.7	25.0	91.7	36.7
February	117.1	25.1	92.0	36.6
March	117.6	25.2	92.4	36.6
April	117.8	25.2	92.6	36.7
May	118.2	25.3	92.8	36.8
June	118.6	25.4	93.2	36.9
July	119.1	25.6	93.4	37.2
August	119.6	25.7	93.8	37.4
September	120.4	25.8	94.5	37.7
October	121.0	26.0	95.1	37.8
November	122.0	26.0	96.0	38.0
December	122.7	26.1	96.5	38.2
1952				
January	123.1	26.2	96.9	38.4
February	123.6	26.3	97.3	38.7
March	123.8	26.4	97.5	38.9
April	124.1	26.4	97.6	39.1
May	124.5	26.5	98.0	39.3
June	125.0	26.7	98.4	39.5
July	125.3	26.7	98.6	39.7
August	125.7	26.8	98.9	40.0
September	126.4	26.9	99.4	40.3
October	126.7	27.0	99.7	40.5
November	127.1	27.2	99.9	40.9
December	127.4	27.3	100.1	41.1

Table 20-5A. Money Stock and Related Data, January 1947–January 1959—*Continued*

(Averages of daily figures; seasonally adjusted, billions of dollars.)

Year and month	Money stock			Time deposits adjusted
	Total	Currency component	Demand deposit component	
1953				
January	127.3	27.4	99.9	41.4
February	127.4	27.5	99.9	41.6
March	128.0	27.6	100.4	41.9
April	128.3	27.7	100.7	42.1
May	128.5	27.7	100.7	42.4
June	128.5	27.7	100.7	42.6
July	128.6	27.8	100.8	42.9
August	128.7	27.8	100.9	43.2
September	128.6	27.8	100.8	43.5
October	128.7	27.8	100.9	43.9
November	128.7	27.8	100.9	44.2
December	128.8	27.7	101.1	44.5
1954				
January	129.0	27.7	101.3	44.8
February	129.1	27.7	101.5	45.2
March	129.2	27.6	101.6	45.6
April	128.6	27.6	101.0	46.1
May	129.7	27.6	102.1	46.5
June	129.9	27.5	102.3	46.8
July	130.3	27.5	102.8	47.3
August	130.7	27.5	103.2	47.8
September	130.9	27.4	103.5	47.9
October	131.5	27.4	104.1	48.1
November	132.1	27.4	104.7	48.2
December	132.3	27.4	104.9	48.3
1955				
January	133.0	27.4	105.6	48.5
February	133.9	27.5	106.4	48.7
March	133.6	27.5	106.0	48.8
April	133.9	27.5	106.3	49.0
May	134.6	27.6	107.0	49.0
June	134.4	27.6	106.8	49.2
July	134.8	27.7	107.2	49.3
August	134.8	27.7	107.0	49.3
September	135.0	27.7	107.3	49.6
October	135.2	27.8	107.4	49.7
November	134.9	27.8	107.1	49.9
December	135.2	27.8	107.4	50.0
1956				
January	135.5	27.9	107.7	49.9
February	135.5	27.9	107.7	49.9
March	135.7	27.9	107.8	50.1
April	136.0	27.9	108.1	50.3
May	135.8	27.9	107.9	50.4
June	136.0	27.9	108.1	50.7
July	136.0	28.0	108.0	50.9
August	135.7	28.0	107.8	51.2
September	136.2	28.0	108.2	51.5
October	136.3	28.0	108.2	51.6
November	136.6	28.1	108.4	51.8
December	136.9	28.2	108.7	51.9
1957				
January	136.9	28.2	108.6	52.6
February	136.8	28.2	108.6	53.1
March	136.9	28.2	108.7	53.7
April	136.9	28.2	108.7	54.0
May	137.0	28.2	108.8	54.5
June	136.9	28.3	108.6	54.8
July	137.0	28.3	108.7	55.3
August	137.1	28.3	108.8	55.7
September	136.8	28.3	108.4	56.1
October	136.5	28.3	108.2	56.6
November	136.3	28.3	108.0	57.0
December	135.9	28.3	107.6	57.4
1958				
January	135.5	28.3	107.2	57.6
February	136.2	28.2	107.9	59.2
March	136.5	28.2	108.3	60.5
April	137.0	28.2	108.7	61.5
May	137.5	28.3	109.2	62.3
June	138.4	28.3	110.1	63.2
July	138.4	28.4	110.0	64.0
August	139.1	28.4	110.7	64.6
September	139.5	28.5	111.1	64.8
October	140.1	28.5	111.6	64.9
November	140.9	28.5	112.4	65.2
December	141.1	28.6	112.6	65.4
1959				
January	142.2	28.7	113.5	66.3

Table 20-5B. Money Stock, Reserves, and Monetary Base

(Averages of daily figures; seasonally adjusted, except as noted.)

Year and month	Money stock measures, billions of dollars		Reserves and monetary base, adjusted for change in reserve requirements, millions of dollars					
	M1	M2	Total reserves	Nonborrowed reserves	Nonborrowed reserves plus extended credit [1]	Required reserves	Excess reserves, not seasonally adjusted	Monetary base
1959								
January	138.9	286.6	11 112	10 560	10 560	10 614	498	40 425
February	139.4	287.7	11 129	10 624	10 624	10 675	454	40 605
March	139.7	289.2	11 081	10 482	10 482	10 621	460	40 615
April	139.7	290.1	11 116	10 424	10 424	10 684	431	40 694
May	140.7	292.2	11 058	10 317	10 317	10 637	421	40 731
June	141.2	294.1	10 972	10 043	10 043	10 566	407	40 750
July	141.7	295.2	11 109	10 148	10 148	10 693	416	40 896
August	141.9	296.4	11 168	10 177	10 177	10 720	448	40 992
September	141.0	296.7	11 128	10 202	10 202	10 686	443	41 034
October	140.5	296.5	11 057	10 150	10 150	10 616	441	40 903
November	140.4	297.1	11 052	10 194	10 194	10 609	444	40 822
December	140.0	297.8	11 109	10 168	10 168	10 603	506	40 880
1960								
January	140.0	298.2	11 081	10 194	10 194	10 567	514	40 794
February	139.9	298.5	10 884	10 074	10 074	10 430	454	40 666
March	139.8	299.4	10 796	10 155	10 155	10 373	423	40 616
April	139.6	300.1	10 767	10 161	10 161	10 341	426	40 621
May	139.6	300.9	10 840	10 344	10 344	10 396	445	40 639
June	139.6	302.3	10 885	10 451	10 451	10 406	480	40 689
July	140.2	304.1	10 994	10 615	10 615	10 493	501	40 794
August	141.3	306.9	11 078	10 782	10 782	10 536	542	40 895
September	141.2	308.4	11 147	10 932	10 932	10 520	627	41 040
October	140.9	309.5	11 216	11 049	11 049	10 554	662	41 097
November	140.9	310.9	11 299	11 166	11 166	10 556	743	41 130
December	140.7	312.4	11 247	11 172	11 172	10 503	743	40 977
1961								
January	141.1	314.1	11 324	11 259	11 259	10 553	772	40 960
February	141.6	316.5	11 229	11 096	11 096	10 580	649	40 945
March	141.9	318.3	11 108	11 038	11 038	10 563	546	40 851
April	142.1	319.9	11 123	11 066	11 066	10 507	616	40 823
May	142.7	322.2	11 035	10 940	10 940	10 480	556	40 791
June	142.9	324.3	11 087	11 024	11 024	10 497	590	40 902
July	142.9	325.6	11 124	11 070	11 070	10 508	616	40 980
August	143.5	327.6	11 234	11 169	11 169	10 655	579	41 227
September	143.8	329.5	11 289	11 251	11 251	10 709	580	41 417
October	144.1	331.1	11 413	11 342	11 342	10 881	532	41 651
November	144.8	333.4	11 482	11 384	11 384	10 891	591	41 782
December	145.2	335.5	11 499	11 366	11 366	10 915	584	41 853
1962								
January	145.2	337.5	11 490	11 403	11 403	10 867	623	41 864
February	145.7	340.1	11 301	11 233	11 233	10 799	502	41 810
March	146.0	343.1	11 259	11 170	11 170	10 788	472	41 923
April	146.4	345.5	11 330	11 258	11 258	10 838	492	42 096
May	146.8	347.5	11 384	11 323	11 323	10 867	517	42 194
June	146.6	349.3	11 328	11 226	11 226	10 855	473	42 259
July	146.5	350.8	11 394	11 302	11 302	10 860	534	42 398
August	146.6	352.8	11 355	11 231	11 231	10 826	530	42 491
September	146.3	354.9	11 383	11 303	11 303	10 893	490	42 537
October	146.7	357.2	11 450	11 387	11 387	10 972	477	42 700
November	147.3	359.8	11 492	11 372	11 372	10 936	557	42 861
December	147.8	362.7	11 604	11 344	11 344	11 033	572	42 957
1963								
January	148.3	365.2	11 567	11 421	11 421	11 062	505	43 008
February	148.9	367.9	11 456	11 290	11 290	10 995	461	43 155
March	149.2	370.7	11 404	11 255	11 255	10 970	434	43 289
April	149.7	373.3	11 449	11 319	11 319	10 992	457	43 444
May	150.4	376.1	11 426	11 216	11 216	10 996	430	43 586
June	150.4	378.4	11 398	11 139	11 139	10 981	417	43 780
July	151.3	381.1	11 530	11 232	11 232	11 075	454	44 058
August	151.8	383.6	11 484	11 155	11 155	11 039	445	44 149
September	152.0	386.0	11 503	11 184	11 184	11 075	428	44 339
October	152.6	388.3	11 457	11 137	11 137	11 060	397	44 444
November	153.7	391.5	11 547	11 198	11 198	11 106	441	44 744
December	153.3	393.2	11 730	11 397	11 397	11 239	490	45 003
1964								
January	153.7	395.2	11 643	11 369	11 369	11 204	440	45 042
February	154.3	397.6	11 547	11 261	11 261	11 150	397	45 112
March	154.5	399.8	11 563	11 285	11 285	11 177	386	45 371
April	154.8	401.7	11 537	11 326	11 326	11 185	352	45 470
May	155.3	404.2	11 523	11 263	11 263	11 169	354	45 651
June	155.6	407.1	11 595	11 326	11 326	11 220	375	45 959
July	156.8	410.1	11 651	11 387	11 387	11 275	376	46 143
August	157.8	413.4	11 795	11 480	11 480	11 374	421	46 410
September	158.7	416.9	11 863	11 518	11 518	11 432	431	46 714
October	159.2	419.1	11 888	11 567	11 567	11 490	398	46 823
November	160.0	422.1	11 998	11 598	11 598	11 591	408	47 106
December	160.3	424.7	12 011	11 747	11 747	11 605	406	47 161

[1] Extended credit program discontinued January 9, 2003. See notes and definitions for more information.

Table 20-5B. Money Stock, Reserves, and Monetary Base—*Continued*

(Averages of daily figures; seasonally adjusted, except as noted.)

Year and month	Money stock measures, billions of dollars		Reserves and monetary base, adjusted for change in reserve requirements, millions of dollars					
	M1	M2	Total reserves	Nonborrowed reserves	Nonborrowed reserves plus extended credit [1]	Required reserves	Excess reserves, not seasonally adjusted	Monetary base
1965								
January	160.7	427.5	11 952	11 653	11 653	11 537	415	47 281
February	160.9	430.4	11 883	11 479	11 479	11 472	412	47 500
March	161.5	433.2	11 884	11 472	11 472	11 518	366	47 584
April	162.0	435.4	12 043	11 571	11 571	11 701	341	47 721
May	161.7	437.1	11 912	11 417	11 417	11 578	334	47 799
June	162.2	440.1	12 005	11 467	11 467	11 643	362	48 061
July	163.1	442.9	12 073	11 544	11 544	11 720	353	48 281
August	163.7	445.8	12 079	11 531	11 531	11 682	396	48 453
September	164.9	449.5	12 071	11 517	11 517	11 662	410	48 712
October	166.0	452.6	12 118	11 630	11 630	11 759	358	49 029
November	166.7	455.7	12 087	11 655	11 655	11 735	352	49 234
December	167.8	459.2	12 316	11 872	11 872	11 892	423	49 620
1966								
January	169.1	462.0	12 295	11 875	11 875	11 916	379	49 850
February	169.6	464.6	12 193	11 711	11 711	11 846	347	50 054
March	170.5	467.2	12 164	11 604	11 604	11 822	342	50 171
April	171.8	469.3	12 258	11 621	11 621	11 903	355	50 439
May	171.3	470.1	12 263	11 575	11 575	11 922	341	50 591
June	171.6	471.2	12 256	11 549	11 549	11 901	356	50 754
July	170.3	470.9	12 371	11 629	11 629	11 993	378	51 019
August	170.8	472.6	12 165	11 430	11 430	11 798	367	50 989
September	172.0	475.4	12 229	11 460	11 460	11 858	371	51 154
October	171.2	475.7	12 199	11 465	11 465	11 867	333	51 200
November	171.4	477.3	12 205	11 598	11 598	11 820	385	51 422
December	172.0	480.2	12 223	11 690	11 690	11 884	339	51 565
1967								
January	171.9	481.6	12 334	11 924	11 924	11 931	403	51 876
February	173.0	485.1	12 280	11 916	11 916	11 911	369	52 173
March	174.8	489.7	12 438	12 237	12 237	12 024	414	52 494
April	174.2	492.1	12 488	12 342	12 342	12 138	350	52 517
May	175.7	497.2	12 418	12 329	12 329	12 053	365	52 682
June	177.0	502.0	12 457	12 351	12 351	12 104	352	52 867
July	178.1	506.3	12 722	12 607	12 607	12 304	418	53 165
August	179.7	510.8	12 678	12 598	12 598	12 313	365	53 347
September	180.7	514.7	12 846	12 758	12 758	12 504	342	53 670
October	181.6	518.2	13 088	12 959	12 959	12 752	335	54 044
November	182.4	521.2	13 131	12 999	12 999	12 773	358	54 241
December	183.3	524.8	13 180	12 952	12 952	12 805	375	54 579
1968								
January	184.3	527.4	13 239	12 993	12 993	12 852	387	54 892
February	184.7	530.4	13 188	12 815	12 815	12 801	386	55 171
March	185.5	533.2	13 186	12 527	12 527	12 849	337	55 436
April	186.6	535.7	13 117	12 432	12 432	12 782	335	55 692
May	188.0	538.9	13 130	12 389	12 389	12 771	360	55 872
June	189.4	542.6	13 251	12 557	12 557	12 923	328	56 323
July	190.5	545.6	13 455	12 928	12 928	13 105	351	56 626
August	191.8	549.4	13 440	12 875	12 875	13 110	329	56 976
September	192.7	553.6	13 435	12 931	12 931	13 074	361	57 160
October	194.0	557.6	13 529	13 086	13 086	13 283	245	57 477
November	196.0	562.4	13 649	13 104	13 104	13 340	308	57 887
December	197.4	566.8	13 767	13 021	13 021	13 341	426	58 357
1969								
January	198.7	569.3	13 629	12 893	12 893	13 383	246	58 597
February	199.3	571.9	13 714	12 879	12 879	13 460	254	58 917
March	200.0	574.4	13 653	12 751	12 751	13 434	219	58 999
April	200.7	575.7	13 471	12 468	12 468	13 304	167	59 062
May	200.8	576.5	13 844	12 470	12 470	13 589	255	59 552
June	201.3	578.5	13 795	12 410	12 410	13 491	304	59 794
July	201.7	579.5	13 491	12 239	12 239	13 266	225	59 713
August	201.7	580.1	13 784	12 565	12 565	13 547	237	60 137
September	202.1	582.1	13 822	12 743	12 743	13 549	274	60 357
October	202.9	583.4	13 904	12 754	12 754	13 741	163	60 633
November	203.6	585.4	14 172	12 969	12 969	13 943	229	61 229
December	203.9	587.9	14 168	13 049	13 049	13 882	286	61 569
1970								
January	206.2	589.6	14 087	13 128	13 128	13 914	174	61 792
February	205.0	586.3	14 099	13 019	13 019	13 891	208	61 931
March	205.7	587.3	14 071	13 173	13 173	13 908	163	62 205
April	206.7	588.4	14 209	13 364	13 364	14 057	152	62 653
May	207.2	591.5	14 007	13 040	13 040	13 850	157	62 977
June	207.6	595.2	14 078	13 197	13 197	13 888	190	63 189
July	208.0	599.1	14 159	12 799	12 799	13 993	166	63 444
August	209.9	604.9	14 282	13 445	13 445	14 108	174	63 725
September	211.8	611.2	14 447	13 847	13 847	14 203	244	64 087
October	212.9	616.4	14 480	14 017	14 017	14 274	205	64 303
November	213.7	621.1	14 470	14 055	14 055	14 236	234	64 574
December	214.4	626.5	14 558	14 225	14 225	14 309	249	65 013

[1]Extended credit program discontinued January 9, 2003. See notes and definitions for more information.

Table 20-5B. Money Stock, Reserves, and Monetary Base—*Continued*

(Averages of daily figures; seasonally adjusted, except as noted.)

Year and month	Money stock measures, billions of dollars		Reserves and monetary base, adjusted for change in reserve requirements, millions of dollars					
	M1	M2	Total reserves	Nonborrowed reserves	Nonborrowed reserves plus extended credit [1]	Required reserves	Excess reserves, not seasonally adjusted	Monetary base
1971								
January	215.5	633.0	14 604	14 240	14 240	14 371	234	65 545
February	217.4	641.0	14 819	14 488	14 488	14 565	254	66 037
March	218.8	649.9	14 798	14 479	14 479	14 603	195	66 378
April	220.0	658.4	14 759	14 606	14 606	14 591	168	66 731
May	222.0	666.7	14 982	14 698	14 698	14 763	219	67 315
June	223.5	673.0	15 057	14 564	14 564	14 855	201	67 678
July	224.9	679.6	15 125	14 302	14 302	14 941	184	68 155
August	225.6	685.5	15 190	14 380	14 380	14 994	196	68 413
September	226.5	692.5	15 423	14 928	14 928	15 234	189	68 751
October	227.2	698.4	15 211	14 854	14 854	15 049	163	68 603
November	227.8	704.6	15 247	14 864	14 864	15 010	237	68 894
December	228.3	710.3	15 230	15 104	15 104	15 049	182	69 108
1972								
January	230.1	717.7	15 369	15 347	15 347	15 163	206	69 853
February	232.3	725.7	15 363	15 331	15 331	15 211	152	70 368
March	234.3	733.5	15 480	15 382	15 382	15 291	190	70 820
April	235.6	738.4	15 651	15 534	15 534	15 495	156	71 031
May	235.9	743.4	15 739	15 628	15 628	15 600	139	71 525
June	236.6	749.7	15 909	15 809	15 809	15 706	203	71 817
July	238.8	759.5	15 835	15 597	15 597	15 642	193	72 173
August	240.9	768.7	16 010	15 623	15 623	15 822	188	72 623
September	243.2	778.3	16 000	15 459	15 459	15 788	212	72 984
October	245.0	786.9	16 193	15 637	15 637	15 981	211	73 644
November	246.4	793.9	16 441	15 833	15 833	16 088	354	74 370
December	249.2	802.3	16 645	15 595	15 595	16 361	284	75 167
1973								
January	251.5	810.3	16 708	15 548	15 548	16 450	258	75 925
February	252.2	814.1	16 714	15 120	15 120	16 516	197	76 160
March	251.7	815.3	16 923	15 099	15 099	16 714	209	76 663
April	252.7	819.7	16 731	15 020	15 020	16 508	223	76 962
May	254.9	826.8	16 672	14 829	14 830	16 533	138	77 393
June	256.7	833.3	16 746	14 895	14 903	16 528	217	77 842
July	257.5	836.5	16 988	15 035	15 067	16 705	283	78 531
August	257.7	838.8	16 796	14 631	14 657	16 624	172	78 781
September	257.9	839.3	16 735	14 883	14 909	16 505	231	79 316
October	259.0	842.6	16 924	15 448	15 464	16 672	252	80 173
November	261.0	848.9	16 978	15 585	15 585	16 753	225	80 479
December	262.9	855.5	17 021	15 723	15 723	16 717	304	81 073
1974								
January	263.8	859.7	17 222	16 171	16 174	17 060	162	81 850
February	265.3	864.2	17 125	15 933	15 933	16 941	184	82 341
March	266.7	870.1	17 131	15 817	15 817	16 997	134	82 835
April	267.2	872.9	17 298	15 561	15 561	17 116	182	83 621
May	267.6	874.6	17 423	14 833	15 491	17 263	160	84 432
June	268.5	877.8	17 367	14 361	15 587	17 169	198	84 895
July	269.3	881.4	17 486	14 185	15 615	17 323	162	85 439
August	270.1	884.1	17 391	14 055	15 592	17 203	188	85 974
September	271.0	887.9	17 385	14 102	15 731	17 204	181	86 377
October	272.3	893.3	17 349	15 536	16 021	17 228	120	86 513
November	273.7	898.6	17 453	16 201	16 361	17 248	205	87 043
December	274.2	902.1	17 550	16 823	16 970	17 292	258	87 535
1975								
January	273.9	906.3	17 273	16 874	17 010	17 126	147	87 756
February	275.0	914.1	17 271	17 123	17 176	17 077	194	88 192
March	276.4	925.0	17 439	17 333	17 370	17 239	200	88 916
April	276.2	935.1	17 498	17 387	17 398	17 340	158	89 116
May	279.2	947.9	17 353	17 288	17 291	17 198	155	89 610
June	282.4	963.0	17 715	17 488	17 504	17 513	201	90 817
July	283.7	975.1	17 632	17 331	17 351	17 445	188	91 373
August	284.1	983.1	17 660	17 449	17 461	17 465	195	91 700
September	285.7	991.5	17 834	17 438	17 452	17 643	191	92 119
October	285.4	997.8	17 587	17 397	17 408	17 380	207	92 448
November	286.8	1 006.9	17 849	17 789	17 794	17 566	283	93 373
December	287.1	1 016.2	17 822	17 692	17 704	17 556	266	93 887
1976								
January	288.4	1 026.6	17 616	17 537	17 549	17 376	240	94 281
February	290.8	1 040.3	17 806	17 725	17 734	17 587	219	95 039
March	292.7	1 050.0	17 875	17 821	17 824	17 651	223	95 786
April	294.7	1 060.8	17 719	17 675	17 675	17 564	155	96 479
May	295.9	1 072.1	17 940	17 826	17 826	17 731	210	97 251
June	296.2	1 077.6	17 946	17 820	17 820	17 732	214	97 732
July	297.2	1 086.3	17 846	17 714	17 714	17 612	234	98 234
August	299.0	1 098.7	18 053	17 953	17 953	17 846	207	98 888
September	299.6	1 110.8	18 009	17 948	17 948	17 808	201	99 446
October	302.0	1 125.0	18 077	17 983	17 983	17 858	219	100 066
November	303.6	1 138.2	18 340	18 268	18 268	18 083	257	100 892
December	306.2	1 152.0	18 388	18 335	18 335	18 115	274	101 515

[1]Extended credit program discontinued January 9, 2003. See notes and definitions for more information.

Table 20-5B. Money Stock, Reserves, and Monetary Base—*Continued*

(Averages of daily figures; seasonally adjusted, except as noted.)

Year and month	Money stock measures, billions of dollars		Reserves and monetary base, adjusted for change in reserve requirements, millions of dollars					
	M1	M2	Total reserves	Nonborrowed reserves	Nonborrowed reserves plus extended credit [1]	Required reserves	Excess reserves, not seasonally adjusted	Monetary base
1977								
January	308.3	1 165.2	18 421	18 353	18 353	18 156	266	102 237
February	311.5	1 177.6	18 299	18 227	18 227	18 100	198	102 654
March	313.9	1 188.5	18 405	18 301	18 301	18 190	215	103 337
April	316.0	1 199.6	18 479	18 406	18 406	18 287	192	104 076
May	317.2	1 209.0	18 585	18 379	18 379	18 377	208	104 630
June	318.8	1 217.8	18 471	18 208	18 208	18 324	147	105 186
July	320.2	1 226.7	18 748	18 425	18 425	18 473	275	106 394
August	322.3	1 237.0	18 919	17 858	17 858	18 719	200	107 185
September	324.5	1 246.2	18 873	18 247	18 247	18 664	209	107 923
October	326.4	1 254.0	18 963	17 658	17 658	18 753	210	108 750
November	328.6	1 262.4	19 012	18 150	18 150	18 761	251	109 560
December	330.9	1 270.3	18 990	18 420	18 420	18 800	190	110 324
1978								
January	334.4	1 279.7	19 290	18 806	18 806	19 023	267	111 449
February	335.3	1 285.5	19 561	19 155	19 155	19 319	241	112 450
March	337.0	1 292.2	19 286	18 958	18 958	19 087	199	112 778
April	339.9	1 300.4	19 408	18 851	18 851	19 260	148	113 377
May	344.9	1 310.5	19 655	18 443	18 443	19 436	219	114 418
June	346.9	1 318.5	19 868	18 774	18 774	19 691	178	115 376
July	347.6	1 324.1	20 118	18 801	18 801	19 921	197	116 273
August	349.6	1 333.5	19 912	18 772	18 772	19 744	168	116 904
September	352.2	1 345.0	19 994	18 934	18 934	19 801	193	118 112
October	353.3	1 352.3	20 109	18 832	18 832	19 947	162	119 044
November	355.4	1 359.1	19 872	19 169	19 169	19 650	222	119 733
December	357.3	1 366.0	19 753	18 885	18 885	19 521	232	120 445
1979								
January	358.6	1 371.6	19 821	18 818	18 818	19 606	214	121 272
February	359.9	1 377.8	19 396	18 423	18 423	19 187	209	121 504
March	362.5	1 387.8	19 429	18 439	18 439	19 271	158	122 065
April	368.0	1 402.1	19 504	18 587	18 587	19 328	176	122 819
May	369.6	1 410.2	19 553	17 788	17 788	19 412	141	123 487
June	373.4	1 423.0	19 808	18 390	18 390	19 587	221	124 635
July	377.2	1 434.8	19 992	18 822	18 822	19 782	211	125 810
August	378.8	1 446.6	20 008	18 923	18 923	19 786	222	127 079
September	379.3	1 454.1	20 007	18 667	18 667	19 816	191	128 309
October	380.8	1 460.4	20 375	18 353	18 353	20 103	272	129 458
November	380.8	1 465.9	20 398	18 492	18 492	20 153	245	130 369
December	381.8	1 473.7	20 720	19 248	19 248	20 279	442	131 143
1980								
January	385.8	1 482.7	20 693	19 452	19 452	20 442	251	131 998
February	390.1	1 494.5	20 682	19 027	19 027	20 471	211	132 785
March	388.4	1 499.8	20 703	17 879	17 978	20 517	186	133 607
April	383.8	1 502.2	20 629	18 174	18 726	20 432	197	134 740
May	384.8	1 512.3	20 440	19 421	20 164	20 262	178	134 998
June	389.1	1 529.2	20 575	20 196	20 503	20 372	203	135 679
July	394.0	1 545.5	20 796	20 401	20 654	20 511	284	136 637
August	399.2	1 561.5	21 011	20 352	20 594	20 709	302	137 977
September	404.8	1 574.0	21 232	19 921	20 011	20 977	256	139 220
October	409.0	1 584.8	21 147	19 837	19 837	20 941	206	140 150
November	410.7	1 595.8	22 150	20 091	20 091	21 629	521	141 566
December	408.5	1 599.8	22 015	20 325	20 328	21 501	514	142 004
1981								
January	411.3	1 606.9	21 673	20 278	20 348	21 298	374	141 462
February	414.8	1 618.7	21 840	20 536	20 557	21 489	350	142 270
March	419.0	1 636.6	22 072	21 072	21 086	21 791	280	143 029
April	427.4	1 659.2	22 187	20 849	20 857	22 018	169	143 917
May	424.7	1 664.2	22 442	20 219	20 224	22 184	257	144 587
June	425.2	1 670.3	22 326	20 289	20 295	21 988	338	145 001
July	426.9	1 681.9	22 329	20 650	20 653	21 989	340	145 839
August	426.9	1 694.3	22 356	20 936	21 017	22 064	292	146 467
September	427.0	1 706.0	22 487	21 031	21 332	22 073	414	146 941
October	428.4	1 721.8	22 296	21 115	21 553	22 018	278	147 062
November	431.3	1 736.1	22 338	21 675	21 840	21 993	344	147 749
December	436.7	1 755.5	22 443	21 807	21 956	22 124	319	149 021
1982								
January	442.7	1 770.4	22 669	21 152	21 349	22 251	418	149 991
February	441.9	1 774.5	22 551	20 762	20 994	22 248	304	150 459
March	442.7	1 786.5	22 452	20 898	21 206	22 091	361	150 660
April	447.1	1 803.9	22 337	20 769	21 014	22 064	273	151 606
May	446.7	1 815.4	22 402	21 285	21 461	22 043	359	152 868
June	447.5	1 826.0	22 368	21 164	21 268	22 060	308	153 861
July	448.0	1 833.7	22 182	21 490	21 541	21 868	314	154 385
August	451.4	1 848.5	22 348	21 833	21 926	22 036	312	155 470
September	456.9	1 862.4	22 686	21 752	21 871	22 302	384	156 629
October	464.5	1 873.7	22 889	22 412	22 553	22 485	404	157 716
November	471.5	1 887.3	23 354	22 733	22 921	22 952	402	158 667
December	474.8	1 909.3	23 600	22 966	23 152	23 100	500	160 127

[1] Extended credit program discontinued January 9, 2003. See notes and definitions for more information.

Table 20-5B. Money Stock, Reserves, and Monetary Base—*Continued*

(Averages of daily figures; seasonally adjusted, except as noted.)

Year and month	Money stock measures, billions of dollars		Reserves and monetary base, adjusted for change in reserve requirements, millions of dollars					
	M1	M2	Total reserves	Nonborrowed reserves	Nonborrowed reserves plus extended credit [1]	Required reserves	Excess reserves, not seasonally adjusted	Monetary base
1983								
January	477.2	1 962.4	23 226	22 697	22 854	22 678	548	161 136
February	484.3	1 999.6	23 901	23 319	23 597	23 466	435	163 170
March	490.6	2 017.8	24 414	23 621	23 939	23 981	433	165 052
April	493.2	2 031.1	24 900	23 890	24 295	24 424	476	166 549
May	500.0	2 045.5	24 860	23 907	24 420	24 411	449	167 842
June	504.0	2 055.8	25 277	23 641	24 599	24 797	480	169 393
July	507.8	2 067.1	25 356	23 903	24 480	24 848	507	170 129
August	510.5	2 076.2	25 376	23 830	24 320	24 929	446	171 208
September	512.8	2 085.3	25 435	23 994	24 509	24 937	498	172 411
October	517.2	2 101.5	25 454	24 610	24 866	24 949	505	173 584
November	519.0	2 114.6	25 396	24 491	24 497	24 867	529	174 605
December	521.4	2 125.7	25 367	24 593	24 595	24 806	561	175 467
1984								
January	525.1	2 140.4	25 451	24 736	24 740	24 838	613	176 896
February	527.5	2 160.5	25 829	25 262	25 266	24 923	906	177 838
March	531.4	2 177.5	25 763	24 811	24 838	25 095	668	178 872
April	535.0	2 193.9	25 691	24 457	24 501	25 218	473	179 898
May	536.7	2 206.4	25 882	22 894	22 931	25 313	569	180 722
June	540.2	2 217.4	26 094	22 793	24 666	25 334	759	181 995
July	540.9	2 225.8	25 980	20 056	25 064	25 351	630	182 991
August	541.0	2 232.5	26 039	18 023	25 066	25 359	680	183 754
September	543.1	2 246.5	26 089	18 847	25 306	25 440	649	184 661
October	543.7	2 261.1	26 259	20 242	25 299	25 641	618	185 219
November	547.5	2 283.6	26 518	21 901	25 738	25 820	698	186 104
December	551.6	2 308.8	26 913	23 727	26 331	26 078	835	187 252
1985								
January	557.0	2 334.9	27 077	25 682	26 732	26 334	742	188 080
February	563.6	2 356.4	27 596	26 307	27 110	26 746	850	189 636
March	566.6	2 368.5	27 590	25 997	27 056	26 916	675	190 320
April	570.4	2 377.8	27 870	26 548	27 416	27 134	736	191 353
May	575.1	2 392.1	28 155	26 821	27 355	27 402	753	192 689
June	582.3	2 415.2	28 848	27 644	28 309	27 926	922	194 762
July	589.1	2 432.0	29 141	28 034	28 541	28 301	840	195 946
August	596.2	2 446.5	29 652	28 580	29 149	28 818	834	198 013
September	603.3	2 458.8	30 030	28 741	29 397	29 333	697	199 306
October	607.8	2 470.6	30 490	29 303	29 932	29 746	744	200 739
November	612.2	2 480.2	30 916	29 175	29 706	29 998	918	202 120
December	619.8	2 494.6	31 569	30 250	30 749	30 505	1 063	203 555
1986								
January	621.4	2 504.8	31 563	30 793	31 290	30 481	1 082	204 221
February	625.2	2 515.3	31 658	30 775	31 267	30 645	1 014	205 314
March	633.5	2 535.4	32 090	31 330	31 848	31 207	883	206 929
April	641.0	2 560.2	32 517	31 625	32 259	31 745	772	208 125
May	652.0	2 587.5	33 265	32 389	32 974	32 387	878	210 154
June	660.6	2 607.7	33 947	33 144	33 674	33 028	919	211 794
July	670.3	2 629.6	34 657	33 916	34 294	33 784	873	213 406
August	678.7	2 649.5	35 191	34 319	34 784	34 451	740	215 273
September	687.4	2 671.1	35 621	34 613	35 183	34 932	690	216 763
October	694.9	2 691.0	36 262	35 420	35 917	35 545	717	218 635
November	705.4	2 704.7	37 270	36 519	36 937	36 369	901	220 714
December	724.7	2 731.4	38 840	38 014	38 317	37 667	1 173	223 416
1987								
January	730.2	2 747.1	39 244	38 664	38 889	38 173	1 070	225 346
February	730.7	2 750.8	39 006	38 450	38 733	37 813	1 193	226 567
March	733.8	2 756.8	38 827	38 300	38 564	37 907	921	227 083
April	743.9	2 771.0	39 533	38 540	38 811	38 677	857	228 964
May	745.8	2 776.4	39 812	38 776	39 064	38 744	1 067	230 521
June	743.2	2 777.9	39 462	38 685	38 958	38 228	1 234	231 302
July	743.0	2 782.5	39 080	38 408	38 602	38 221	859	231 973
August	744.9	2 791.6	39 208	38 561	38 693	38 157	1 051	233 529
September	747.6	2 803.0	39 118	38 178	38 586	38 333	784	234 708
October	756.2	2 818.6	39 826	38 883	39 333	38 737	1 089	237 110
November	753.2	2 823.3	39 334	38 709	39 103	38 394	940	238 807
December	750.2	2 830.8	38 913	38 135	38 618	37 893	1 019	239 829
1988								
January	756.2	2 851.8	39 464	38 383	38 754	38 213	1 252	241 825
February	757.7	2 874.8	39 406	39 010	39 215	38 268	1 138	242 804
March	761.8	2 895.1	39 266	37 514	38 993	38 321	945	243 750
April	768.1	2 915.2	39 622	36 628	39 252	38 737	885	245 760
May	771.7	2 930.6	39 958	37 380	39 487	38 911	1 047	247 434
June	778.3	2 942.7	40 277	37 195	39 748	39 382	895	249 160
July	781.4	2 952.6	40 514	37 075	39 613	39 623	891	251 001
August	783.3	2 957.7	40 470	37 229	39 882	39 500	970	252 064
September	783.7	2 962.5	40 343	37 503	39 562	39 326	1 017	253 358
October	783.3	2 971.0	40 422	38 123	39 904	39 370	1 053	254 579
November	784.9	2 985.9	40 548	37 687	40 009	39 374	1 174	255 675
December	786.7	2 993.9	40 453	38 738	39 982	39 392	1 061	256 897

[1]Extended credit program discontinued January 9, 2003. See notes and definitions for more information.

Table 20-5B. Money Stock, Reserves, and Monetary Base—*Continued*

(Averages of daily figures; seasonally adjusted, except as noted.)

Year and month	Money stock measures, billions of dollars		Reserves and monetary base, adjusted for change in reserve requirements, millions of dollars					
	M1	M2	Total reserves	Nonborrowed reserves	Nonborrowed reserves plus extended credit [1]	Required reserves	Excess reserves, not seasonally adjusted	Monetary base
1989								
January	785.7	2 997.2	40 422	38 773	39 811	39 278	1 144	257 914
February	783.8	2 997.6	40 339	38 852	39 901	39 184	1 154	258 307
March	783.0	3 005.3	39 844	38 032	39 366	38 926	918	259 146
April	779.2	3 011.5	39 533	37 244	38 950	38 719	813	259 565
May	775.0	3 017.1	39 301	37 580	38 778	38 258	1 042	260 259
June	773.5	3 033.4	39 085	37 595	38 512	38 177	908	261 103
July	777.8	3 058.1	39 438	38 744	38 850	38 455	982	262 235
August	779.4	3 080.1	39 397	38 722	38 764	38 505	892	262 850
September	781.0	3 098.5	39 673	38 980	39 002	38 728	945	263 759
October	786.6	3 120.4	40 163	39 607	39 629	39 123	1 040	264 891
November	788.0	3 139.3	40 170	39 820	39 841	39 221	948	265 629
December	792.9	3 158.4	40 486	40 221	40 241	39 545	941	267 766
1990								
January	795.4	3 172.5	40 731	40 291	40 317	39 688	1 042	269 561
February	798.1	3 185.0	40 743	39 295	39 830	39 743	1 000	271 139
March	801.6	3 196.0	40 650	38 526	40 477	39 769	881	273 074
April	806.2	3 207.5	40 845	39 236	40 621	39 974	871	275 225
May	804.3	3 206.3	40 750	39 419	40 291	39 796	954	276 750
June	808.9	3 219.0	40 666	39 785	40 131	39 879	787	278 971
July	810.1	3 229.5	40 575	39 818	40 098	39 707	868	280 997
August	815.6	3 247.0	40 873	39 946	40 074	39 997	876	284 088
September	820.1	3 259.7	41 090	40 466	40 472	40 177	913	287 280
October	819.8	3 264.4	40 808	40 398	40 416	39 968	840	289 190
November	822.1	3 268.1	40 970	40 740	40 765	40 043	928	291 114
December	824.7	3 277.3	41 766	41 440	41 463	40 101	1 665	293 287
1991								
January	827.2	3 293.2	42 293	41 759	41 786	40 153	2 140	297 771
February	832.7	3 309.9	42 071	41 819	41 853	40 267	1 804	300 910
March	838.7	3 327.4	41 804	41 563	41 616	40 623	1 182	302 759
April	843.2	3 338.4	41 862	41 630	41 716	40 833	1 029	303 027
May	848.8	3 349.0	42 411	42 108	42 196	41 376	1 035	304 193
June	856.7	3 357.9	42 712	42 372	42 379	41 716	996	305 507
July	861.5	3 361.4	42 984	42 377	42 423	42 080	904	307 230
August	866.7	3 360.2	43 392	42 628	42 928	42 308	1 085	309 315
September	870.2	3 360.1	43 558	42 912	43 214	42 625	933	310 667
October	878.0	3 365.4	44 007	43 746	43 758	42 950	1 057	312 687
November	887.6	3 370.8	44 614	44 506	44 508	43 722	893	314 951
December	897.0	3 377.5	45 516	45 324	45 325	44 526	990	317 546
1992								
January	910.4	3 386.1	46 373	46 140	46 141	45 381	993	319 633
February	925.3	3 405.1	47 602	47 524	47 526	46 557	1 045	322 582
March	936.7	3 408.9	48 274	48 183	48 185	47 249	1 025	324 379
April	943.8	3 404.4	49 041	48 951	48 953	47 908	1 133	326 698
May	950.5	3 403.3	49 336	49 182	49 182	48 333	1 004	328 781
June	954.3	3 399.0	49 270	49 041	49 041	48 346	924	330 181
July	963.2	3 399.2	49 755	49 471	49 471	48 780	975	333 236
August	973.7	3 404.2	50 479	50 228	50 228	49 540	939	336 920
September	988.1	3 415.9	51 394	51 107	51 107	50 380	1 015	340 751
October	1 003.8	3 429.6	52 767	52 624	52 624	51 704	1 063	344 576
November	1 015.7	3 432.1	53 750	53 646	53 646	52 707	1 043	347 635
December	1 024.9	3 431.0	54 421	54 298	54 298	53 267	1 154	350 912
1993								
January	1 030.4	3 425.2	54 970	54 805	54 806	53 708	1 262	353 716
February	1 033.5	3 421.0	54 686	54 641	54 641	53 593	1 093	355 374
March	1 038.5	3 418.3	54 970	54 879	54 879	53 737	1 233	357 874
April	1 047.6	3 417.5	55 358	55 285	55 285	54 255	1 103	360 883
May	1 065.9	3 443.0	56 655	56 533	56 533	55 656	999	364 937
June	1 075.1	3 448.8	57 086	56 905	56 905	56 191	895	367 901
July	1 084.5	3 448.4	57 729	57 485	57 485	56 662	1 068	371 478
August	1 094.2	3 452.3	58 183	57 831	57 831	57 231	952	374 556
September	1 104.2	3 459.2	58 871	58 443	58 443	57 784	1 086	378 256
October	1 113.0	3 463.4	59 594	59 309	59 309	58 517	1 077	381 565
November	1 124.2	3 477.0	60 304	60 214	60 214	59 184	1 120	384 058
December	1 129.6	3 481.6	60 566	60 484	60 484	59 497	1 069	386 600
1994								
January	1 131.6	3 482.7	60 895	60 822	60 822	59 436	1 459	390 214
February	1 136.3	3 483.4	60 515	60 445	60 445	59 367	1 149	393 224
March	1 140.3	3 489.2	60 299	60 244	60 244	59 315	984	396 075
April	1 141.1	3 493.1	60 503	60 379	60 379	59 361	1 142	398 923
May	1 143.3	3 502.7	59 972	59 772	59 772	59 103	869	401 451
June	1 145.1	3 491.0	60 048	59 715	59 715	58 931	1 117	404 414
July	1 150.5	3 499.5	60 321	59 863	59 863	59 205	1 116	407 849
August	1 150.6	3 496.7	59 959	59 490	59 490	58 949	1 010	409 581
September	1 151.9	3 496.9	59 800	59 313	59 313	58 751	1 048	411 778
October	1 150.1	3 495.4	59 374	58 993	58 993	58 576	797	414 007
November	1 151.0	3 498.5	59 412	59 163	59 163	58 415	996	416 771
December	1 150.7	3 497.6	59 466	59 257	59 257	58 295	1 171	418 345

[1]Extended credit program discontinued January 9, 2003. See notes and definitions for more information.

Table 20-5B. Money Stock, Reserves, and Monetary Base—*Continued*

(Averages of daily figures; seasonally adjusted, except as noted.)

Year and month	Money stock measures, billions of dollars		Reserves and monetary base, adjusted for change in reserve requirements, millions of dollars					
	M1	M2	Total reserves	Nonborrowed reserves	Nonborrowed reserves plus extended credit [1]	Required reserves	Excess reserves, not seasonally adjusted	Monetary base
1995								
January	1 151.4	3 503.1	59 404	59 268	59 272	58 071	1 332	421 064
February	1 147.4	3 500.4	58 652	58 593	58 593	57 683	970	421 597
March	1 146.7	3 501.5	58 209	58 140	58 140	57 386	823	424 712
April	1 149.3	3 509.6	57 973	57 862	57 862	57 216	757	427 889
May	1 145.4	3 534.7	57 641	57 491	57 491	56 768	873	430 536
June	1 144.2	3 560.2	57 376	57 104	57 104	56 393	983	430 147
July	1 145.4	3 578.9	57 817	57 446	57 446	56 711	1 106	430 753
August	1 145.5	3 601.1	57 538	57 256	57 256	56 532	1 006	431 261
September	1 142.0	3 613.8	57 310	57 032	57 032	56 338	971	431 936
October	1 137.3	3 625.0	56 719	56 474	56 474	55 640	1 079	432 641
November	1 134.1	3 632.1	56 305	56 101	56 101	55 360	946	432 953
December	1 127.4	3 641.7	56 483	56 226	56 226	55 193	1 290	434 586
1996								
January	1 123.5	3 659.9	55 884	55 846	55 846	54 417	1 467	434 897
February	1 118.5	3 674.0	54 622	54 587	54 587	53 761	861	432 542
March	1 122.5	3 699.8	55 294	55 273	55 273	54 153	1 142	435 926
April	1 124.8	3 710.6	55 178	55 088	55 088	54 052	1 126	436 909
May	1 116.5	3 721.7	54 041	53 913	53 913	53 130	911	437 442
June	1 115.2	3 735.4	54 145	53 758	53 758	53 031	1 114	440 022
July	1 112.4	3 750.0	53 377	53 009	53 009	52 356	1 021	442 587
August	1 101.6	3 757.4	52 162	51 828	51 828	51 201	961	444 682
September	1 096.1	3 766.1	51 312	50 945	50 945	50 262	1 050	446 045
October	1 086.1	3 782.3	50 037	49 750	49 750	49 030	1 007	446 881
November	1 083.6	3 799.7	49 779	49 565	49 565	48 724	1 055	448 860
December	1 081.6	3 821.0	50 185	50 030	50 030	48 766	1 418	452 032
1997								
January	1 081.5	3 834.4	49 683	49 639	49 639	48 456	1 228	453 634
February	1 078.8	3 845.7	48 715	48 673	48 673	47 681	1 035	454 497
March	1 071.8	3 859.0	47 850	47 694	47 694	46 681	1 169	456 235
April	1 063.8	3 877.7	47 353	47 093	47 093	46 339	1 015	457 822
May	1 064.0	3 888.5	46 657	46 414	46 414	45 374	1 283	459 475
June	1 065.7	3 903.9	46 937	46 570	46 570	45 593	1 344	462 091
July	1 066.2	3 925.7	46 755	46 346	46 346	45 518	1 237	464 698
August	1 074.3	3 954.2	46 913	46 315	46 315	45 653	1 260	467 024
September	1 067.7	3 973.8	46 247	45 809	45 809	44 950	1 297	469 240
October	1 065.5	3 989.8	45 959	45 690	45 690	44 544	1 416	471 864
November	1 070.0	4 012.2	46 411	46 258	46 258	44 742	1 668	476 023
December	1 072.7	4 034.1	46 875	46 551	46 551	45 189	1 687	479 909
1998								
January	1 074.4	4 057.1	46 658	46 448	46 448	44 894	1 764	482 214
February	1 077.9	4 089.2	45 742	45 684	45 684	44 208	1 535	483 217
March	1 077.5	4 115.5	45 854	45 812	45 812	44 503	1 350	484 907
April	1 076.1	4 137.5	46 130	46 058	46 058	44 739	1 391	486 784
May	1 078.4	4 160.8	45 531	45 379	45 379	44 241	1 290	488 789
June	1 077.0	4 186.8	45 417	45 166	45 166	43 798	1 619	491 763
July	1 075.0	4 203.0	44 893	44 635	44 635	43 519	1 374	494 620
August	1 074.8	4 226.3	44 956	44 685	44 685	43 423	1 532	497 897
September	1 080.2	4 270.1	44 850	44 599	44 599	43 152	1 697	502 700
October	1 086.0	4 307.6	44 887	44 714	44 714	43 312	1 575	506 951
November	1 094.5	4 345.1	44 815	44 732	44 732	43 205	1 611	510 413
December	1 095.8	4 377.9	45 170	45 053	45 053	43 658	1 512	513 887
1999								
January	1 097.8	4 399.4	44 988	44 782	44 782	43 499	1 489	516 894
February	1 097.0	4 424.7	44 872	44 756	44 756	43 678	1 194	520 752
March	1 097.8	4 435.9	44 472	44 407	44 407	43 204	1 268	525 005
April	1 101.9	4 462.8	43 710	43 544	43 544	42 556	1 155	528 434
May	1 102.6	4 481.9	43 987	43 860	43 860	42 766	1 221	533 280
June	1 099.7	4 504.8	42 963	42 818	42 818	41 666	1 297	536 777
July	1 098.7	4 528.3	41 923	41 614	41 614	40 959	964	540 188
August	1 099.0	4 549.1	42 310	41 967	41 967	41 149	1 161	544 889
September	1 096.3	4 562.4	41 982	41 644	41 644	40 769	1 213	550 177
October	1 102.3	4 582.4	41 611	41 330	41 330	40 463	1 148	557 610
November	1 111.7	4 608.0	41 812	41 576	41 576	40 483	1 328	571 386
December	1 122.6	4 631.7	42 183	41 862	41 862	40 889	1 294	593 842
2000								
January	1 121.9	4 658.0	42 497	42 124	42 124	40 484	2 013	591 123
February	1 109.4	4 675.3	41 399	41 291	41 291	40 286	1 113	573 000
March	1 108.2	4 702.2	40 726	40 547	40 547	39 518	1 208	571 659
April	1 113.4	4 753.2	40 525	40 221	40 221	39 358	1 166	572 228
May	1 105.8	4 747.6	40 653	40 291	40 291	39 683	970	573 612
June	1 103.3	4 761.4	40 050	39 571	39 571	38 936	1 115	575 564
July	1 103.0	4 774.8	40 029	39 459	39 459	38 886	1 143	576 939
August	1 100.3	4 808.3	39 821	39 243	39 243	38 768	1 054	577 873
September	1 099.0	4 839.8	39 561	39 084	39 084	38 415	1 146	578 394
October	1 098.6	4 858.3	39 394	38 975	38 975	38 246	1 148	580 379
November	1 092.3	4 866.8	39 404	39 121	39 121	38 202	1 203	582 062
December	1 087.6	4 910.7	38 717	38 507	38 507	37 391	1 325	584 929

[1]Extended credit program discontinued January 9, 2003. See notes and definitions for more information.

Table 20-5B. Money Stock, Reserves, and Monetary Base—*Continued*

(Averages of daily figures; seasonally adjusted, except as noted.)

Year and month	Money stock measures, billions of dollars		Reserves and monetary base, adjusted for change in reserve requirements, millions of dollars					
	M1	M2	Total reserves	Nonborrowed reserves	Nonborrowed reserves plus extended credit [1]	Required reserves	Excess reserves, not seasonally adjusted	Monetary base
2001								
January	1 097.6	4 965.7	37 862	37 789	37 789	36 599	1 263	588 002
February	1 101.5	5 001.5	38 561	38 510	38 510	37 216	1 345	589 716
March	1 109.8	5 058.8	38 410	38 352	38 352	37 160	1 251	592 297
April	1 114.9	5 120.3	38 414	38 363	38 363	37 156	1 257	595 485
May	1 119.5	5 124.2	38 563	38 350	38 350	37 545	1 019	598 723
June	1 126.4	5 163.6	38 697	38 468	38 468	37 449	1 249	601 780
July	1 139.6	5 196.9	39 399	39 116	39 116	37 997	1 401	607 804
August	1 149.6	5 226.8	39 953	39 770	39 770	38 750	1 203	615 521
September	1 203.9	5 335.8	57 892	54 507	54 507	38 878	19 015	639 616
October	1 165.9	5 327.2	45 456	45 329	45 329	44 130	1 326	630 212
November	1 171.5	5 368.3	40 972	40 888	40 888	39 533	1 439	629 774
December	1 182.3	5 417.8	41 442	41 376	41 376	39 799	1 643	635 559
2002								
January	1 190.9	5 448.2	41 692	41 643	41 643	40 287	1 405	641 338
February	1 190.7	5 474.4	41 841	41 812	41 812	40 469	1 373	646 258
March	1 192.8	5 483.0	41 121	41 042	41 042	39 718	1 403	649 945
April	1 185.9	5 489.2	40 656	40 585	40 585	39 451	1 205	653 850
May	1 189.0	5 510.8	39 488	39 376	39 376	38 229	1 259	657 743
June	1 192.2	5 533.0	39 039	38 896	38 896	37 801	1 238	662 801
July	1 199.5	5 583.0	39 264	39 073	39 073	37 888	1 376	668 516
August	1 185.9	5 620.2	39 918	39 585	39 585	38 312	1 607	670 403
September	1 194.6	5 644.7	38 898	38 669	38 669	37 415	1 484	671 479
October	1 204.0	5 696.1	39 170	39 028	39 028	37 638	1 533	673 920
November	1 209.3	5 739.1	39 863	39 591	39 591	38 226	1 637	676 970
December	1 220.4	5 764.6	40 400	40 320	40 320	38 392	2 008	681 631
2003								
January	1 226.8	5 790.7	40 807	40 780	10 376	39 099	1 708	685 237
February	1 238.6	5 827.1	41 309	41 284	. . .	39 344	1 965	690 540
March	1 238.9	5 840.8	41 310	41 288	. . .	39 680	1 630	694 742
April	1 248.4	5 887.4	40 763	40 734	. . .	39 224	1 539	698 134
May	1 268.0	5 941.1	40 932	40 877	. . .	39 314	1 618	701 224
June	1 280.2	5 980.0	42 216	42 054	. . .	40 175	2 040	703 523
July	1 287.9	6 034.3	43 130	42 999	. . .	41 195	1 935	705 558
August	1 293.9	6 080.8	45 898	45 570	. . .	42 134	3 764	709 913
September	1 297.0	6 062.3	44 209	44 028	. . .	42 700	1 509	711 298
October	1 297.3	6 047.7	43 511	43 403	. . .	42 043	1 467	715 143
November	1 298.0	6 047.9	43 021	42 953	. . .	41 539	1 483	717 802
December	1 306.8	6 055.2	42 757	42 711	. . .	41 710	1 047	720 402
2004								
January	1 306.1	6 059.4	43 172	43 066	. . .	42 285	888	721 913
February	1 321.7	6 097.4	43 133	43 091	. . .	41 941	1 192	723 750
March	1 330.0	6 135.4	45 095	45 044	. . .	43 287	1 808	726 467
April	1 332.1	6 177.4	45 812	45 726	. . .	44 006	1 805	730 076
May	1 331.6	6 244.9	45 432	45 320	. . .	43 748	1 684	733 322
June	1 342.8	6 258.9	45 584	45 403	. . .	43 652	1 931	738 246
July	1 340.5	6 264.4	45 884	45 639	. . .	44 162	1 722	746 077
August	1 353.2	6 288.4	45 404	45 152	. . .	43 822	1 582	747 807
September	1 361.4	6 322.6	46 309	45 974	. . .	44 655	1 654	752 501
October	1 361.0	6 347.6	46 180	46 000	. . .	44 424	1 756	755 039
November	1 376.0	6 384.7	46 013	45 830	. . .	44 228	1 785	758 969
December	1 376.4	6 399.8	46 552	46 489	. . .	44 643	1 909	759 072
2005								
January	1 366.6	6 404.2	47 706	47 644	. . .	45 967	1 739	760 547
February	1 372.5	6 417.3	46 141	46 100	. . .	44 652	1 490	763 108
March	1 372.6	6 432.6	47 099	47 050	. . .	45 317	1 782	765 491
April	1 357.8	6 440.3	46 381	46 249	. . .	44 716	1 665	766 342
May	1 365.5	6 456.6	45 441	45 302	. . .	43 915	1 526	766 814
June	1 379.2	6 488.8	45 757	45 509	. . .	44 018	1 739	770 319
July	1 366.6	6 515.9	46 137	45 712	. . .	44 345	1 792	773 322
August	1 376.2	6 545.8	45 190	44 828	. . .	43 570	1 620	775 822
September	1 377.8	6 581.8	46 229	45 896	. . .	44 234	1 995	779 789
October	1 375.0	6 610.1	45 400	45 116	. . .	43 516	1 884	781 391
November	1 376.9	6 636.8	45 155	45 029	. . .	43 374	1 781	783 793
December	1 374.2	6 661.5	45 139	44 970	. . .	43 238	1 901	786 976
2006								
January	1 380.6	6 712.2	44 606	44 496	. . .	43 030	1 576	791 587
February	1 379.8	6 731.7	44 350	44 298	. . .	42 800	1 550	796 148
March	1 383.9	6 749.0	44 138	43 969	. . .	42 631	1 507	798 581
April	1 380.5	6 772.1	44 764	44 517	. . .	42 939	1 825	801 326
May	1 386.8	6 785.3	44 783	44 609	. . .	42 985	1 798	805 227
June	1 374.4	6 816.9	45 007	44 754	. . .	43 224	1 783	804 850
July	1 369.2	6 844.6	44 182	43 832	. . .	42 629	1 553	803 911
August	1 369.2	6 865.3	42 964	42 595	. . .	41 443	1 520	804 921
September	1 361.6	6 890.8	43 105	42 701	. . .	41 344	1 761	805 797
October	1 369.4	6 945.3	42 737	42 508	. . .	41 044	1 693	805 955
November	1 371.3	6 978.3	43 035	42 875	. . .	41 346	1 689	807 981
December	1 365.6	7 021.5	43 338	43 147	. . .	41 475	1 863	811 126

[1]Extended credit program discontinued January 9, 2003. See notes and definitions for more information.
. . . = Not available.

Table 20-6. Interest Rates, Bond Yields, and Stock Price Indexes

(Not seasonally adjusted.)

Year and month	Percent per annum											Stock price indexes		
	Short-term rates					U.S. Treasury securities		Bond yields			Fixed-rate first mortgages	Dow Jones industrials (30 stocks)	Standard and Poor's composite (500 stocks)[2]	Nasdaq composite[3]
	Federal funds	Federal Reserve discount rate[1]	U.S. Treasury bills, 3-month	U.S. Treasury bills, 6-month	Bank prime rate	1-year	10-year	Domestic corporate (Moody's)		State and local bonds (Bond Buyer)				
								Aaa	Baa					
1945	...	1.00	0.38	...	1.50	...	...	2.62	3.29	...	...	169.82	15.16	...
1946	...	1.00	0.38	...	1.50	...	...	2.53	3.05	...	...	191.65	17.08	...
1947	...	1.00	0.60	...	1.63	...	...	2.61	3.24	...	...	177.58	15.17	...
1948	...	1.34	1.04	...	1.88	...	...	2.82	3.47	...	...	179.95	15.53	...
1949	...	1.50	1.10	...	2.00	...	...	2.66	3.42	...	...	179.48	15.23	...
1950	...	1.59	1.22	...	2.07	...	...	2.62	3.24	...	...	216.31	18.40	...
1951	...	1.75	1.55	...	2.56	...	...	2.86	3.41	...	...	257.64	22.34	...
1952	...	1.75	1.77	...	3.00	...	...	2.96	3.52	...	...	270.76	24.50	...
1953	...	1.99	1.94	...	3.17	...	...	3.20	3.73	2.74	...	275.97	24.73	...
1954	...	1.60	0.95	...	3.05	1.05	2.40	2.90	3.51	2.39	...	333.94	29.69	...
1955	1.79	1.89	1.72	...	3.16	2.04	2.82	3.05	3.53	2.48	...	442.72	40.49	...
1956	2.73	2.77	2.62	...	3.77	2.99	3.18	3.36	3.88	2.76	...	493.01	46.62	...
1957	3.11	3.12	3.22	...	4.20	3.62	3.65	3.89	4.71	3.28	...	475.71	44.38	...
1958	1.57	2.15	1.77	3.01	3.83	2.27	3.32	3.79	4.73	3.16	...	491.66	46.24	...
1959	3.31	3.36	3.39	3.81	4.48	4.24	4.33	4.38	5.05	3.56	...	632.12	57.38	...
1945														
January	...	1.00	0.38	...	1.50	...	...	2.69	3.46	...	...	153.95	13.49	...
February	...	1.00	0.38	...	1.50	...	...	2.65	3.41	...	...	157.24	13.94	...
March	...	1.00	0.38	...	1.50	...	...	2.62	3.38	...	...	157.31	13.93	...
April	...	1.00	0.38	...	1.50	...	...	2.61	3.36	...	...	160.34	14.28	...
May	...	1.00	0.38	...	1.50	...	...	2.62	3.32	...	...	165.52	14.82	...
June	...	1.00	0.38	...	1.50	...	...	2.61	3.29	...	...	167.37	15.09	...
July	...	1.00	0.38	...	1.50	...	...	2.60	3.26	...	...	163.92	14.78	...
August	...	1.00	0.38	...	1.50	...	...	2.61	3.26	...	...	166.17	14.83	...
September	...	1.00	0.38	...	1.50	...	...	2.62	3.24	...	...	177.85	15.84	...
October	...	1.00	0.38	...	1.50	...	...	2.62	3.20	...	...	185.06	16.50	...
November	...	1.00	0.38	...	1.50	...	...	2.62	3.15	...	...	190.34	17.04	...
December	...	1.00	0.38	...	1.50	...	...	2.61	3.10	...	...	192.68	17.33	...
1946														
January	...	1.00	0.38	...	1.50	...	...	2.54	3.01	...	...	199.23	18.02	...
February	...	1.00	0.38	...	1.50	...	...	2.48	2.95	...	...	198.56	18.07	...
March	...	1.00	0.38	...	1.50	...	...	2.47	2.94	...	...	194.23	17.53	...
April	...	1.00	0.38	...	1.50	...	...	2.46	2.96	...	...	205.71	18.66	...
May	...	1.00	0.38	...	1.50	...	...	2.51	3.02	...	...	206.80	18.70	...
June	...	1.00	0.38	...	1.50	...	...	2.49	3.03	...	...	207.33	18.58	...
July	...	1.00	0.38	...	1.50	...	...	2.48	3.03	...	...	202.28	18.05	...
August	...	1.00	0.38	...	1.50	...	...	2.51	3.03	...	...	199.45	17.70	...
September	...	1.00	0.38	...	1.50	...	...	2.58	3.10	...	...	172.74	15.09	...
October	...	1.00	0.38	...	1.50	...	...	2.60	3.15	...	...	169.47	14.75	...
November	...	1.00	0.38	...	1.50	...	...	2.59	3.17	...	...	168.74	14.69	...
December	...	1.00	0.38	...	1.50	...	...	2.61	3.17	...	...	174.29	15.13	...
1947														
January	...	1.00	0.38	...	1.50	...	...	2.57	3.13	...	...	176.15	15.21	...
February	...	1.00	0.38	...	1.50	...	...	2.55	3.12	...	...	181.43	15.80	...
March	...	1.00	0.38	...	1.50	...	...	2.55	3.15	...	...	176.69	15.16	...
April	...	1.00	0.38	...	1.50	...	...	2.53	3.16	...	...	171.23	14.60	...
May	...	1.00	0.38	...	1.50	...	...	2.53	3.17	...	...	168.63	14.34	...
June	...	1.00	0.38	...	1.50	...	...	2.55	3.21	...	...	173.76	14.84	...
July	...	1.00	0.66	...	1.50	...	...	2.55	3.18	...	...	183.53	15.77	...
August	...	1.00	0.75	...	1.50	...	...	2.56	3.17	...	...	180.08	15.46	...
September	...	1.00	0.80	...	1.50	...	...	2.61	3.23	...	...	176.81	15.06	...
October	...	1.00	0.85	...	1.50	...	...	2.70	3.35	...	...	181.95	15.45	...
November	...	1.00	0.92	...	1.50	...	...	2.77	3.44	...	...	181.52	15.27	...
December	...	1.00	0.95	...	1.75	...	...	2.86	3.52	...	...	179.24	15.03	...
1948														
January	...	1.25	0.97	...	1.75	...	...	2.86	3.52	...	...	176.30	14.83	...
February	...	1.25	1.00	...	1.75	...	...	2.85	3.53	...	...	168.64	14.10	...
March	...	1.25	1.00	...	1.75	...	...	2.83	3.53	...	...	169.77	14.30	...
April	...	1.25	1.00	...	1.75	...	...	2.78	3.47	...	...	180.05	15.40	...
May	...	1.25	1.00	...	1.75	...	...	2.76	3.38	...	...	186.51	16.15	...
June	...	1.25	1.00	...	1.75	...	...	2.76	3.34	...	...	191.06	16.82	...
July	...	1.25	1.00	...	1.75	...	...	2.81	3.37	...	...	187.07	16.42	...
August	...	1.50	1.06	...	2.00	...	...	2.84	3.44	...	...	181.77	15.94	...
September	...	1.50	1.09	...	2.00	...	...	2.84	3.45	...	...	180.34	15.76	...
October	...	1.50	1.12	...	2.00	...	...	2.84	3.50	...	...	185.16	16.19	...
November	...	1.50	1.14	...	2.00	...	...	2.84	3.53	...	...	176.76	15.29	...
December	...	1.50	1.16	...	2.00	...	...	2.79	3.53	...	...	176.30	15.19	...

[1]Federal Reserve Bank of New York. Through 2002, represents the rate for adjustment credit. Beginning in 2003, represents the rate for primary credit. See notes and definitions for more information.
[2]1941–1943 = 10.
[3]February 5, 1971 = 100.
. . . = Not available.

Table 20-6. Interest Rates, Bond Yields, and Stock Price Indexes—*Continued*

(Not seasonally adjusted.)

Year and month	Percent per annum											Stock price indexes		
	Short-term rates					U.S. Treasury securities		Bond yields						
								Domestic corporate (Moody's)		State and local bonds (Bond Buyer)	Fixed-rate first mortgages	Dow Jones industrials (30 stocks)	Standard and Poor's composite (500 stocks) [2]	Nasdaq composite [3]
	Federal funds	Federal Reserve discount rate [1]	U.S. Treasury bills, 3-month	U.S. Treasury bills, 6-month	Bank prime rate	1-year	10-year	Aaa	Baa					
1949														
January	...	1.50	1.17	...	2.00	...	...	2.71	3.46	...	...	179.63	15.36	...
February	...	1.50	1.17	...	2.00	...	...	2.71	3.45	...	...	174.54	14.77	...
March	...	1.50	1.17	...	2.00	...	...	2.70	3.47	...	...	175.87	14.91	...
April	...	1.50	1.17	...	2.00	...	...	2.70	3.45	...	...	175.63	14.89	...
May	...	1.50	1.17	...	2.00	...	...	2.71	3.45	...	...	173.93	14.78	...
June	...	1.50	1.17	...	2.00	...	...	2.71	3.47	...	...	165.60	13.97	...
July	...	1.50	1.02	...	2.00	...	...	2.67	3.46	...	...	173.34	14.76	...
August	...	1.50	1.04	...	2.00	...	...	2.62	3.40	...	...	179.25	15.29	...
September	...	1.50	1.07	...	2.00	...	...	2.60	3.37	...	...	180.92	15.49	...
October	...	1.50	1.05	...	2.00	...	...	2.61	3.36	...	...	186.57	15.89	...
November	...	1.50	1.08	...	2.00	...	...	2.60	3.35	...	...	191.49	16.11	...
December	...	1.50	1.10	...	2.00	...	...	2.58	3.31	...	...	196.78	16.54	...
1950														
January	...	1.50	1.07	...	2.00	...	...	2.57	3.24	...	...	199.75	16.88	...
February	...	1.50	1.12	...	2.00	...	...	2.58	3.24	...	...	203.31	17.21	...
March	...	1.50	1.12	...	2.00	...	...	2.58	3.24	...	...	206.25	17.35	...
April	...	1.50	1.15	...	2.00	...	...	2.60	3.23	...	...	212.76	17.84	...
May	...	1.50	1.16	...	2.00	...	...	2.61	3.25	...	...	219.30	18.44	...
June	...	1.50	1.15	...	2.00	...	...	2.62	3.28	...	...	221.02	18.74	...
July	...	1.50	1.16	...	2.00	...	...	2.65	3.32	...	...	205.31	17.38	...
August	...	1.59	1.20	...	2.00	...	...	2.61	3.23	...	...	216.61	18.43	...
September	...	1.75	1.30	...	2.08	...	...	2.64	3.21	...	...	223.20	19.08	...
October	...	1.75	1.31	...	2.25	...	...	2.67	3.22	...	...	229.24	19.87	...
November	...	1.75	1.36	...	2.25	...	...	2.67	3.22	...	...	229.08	19.83	...
December	...	1.75	1.34	...	2.25	...	...	2.67	3.20	...	...	229.18	19.75	...
1951														
January	...	1.75	1.34	...	2.44	...	...	2.66	3.17	...	...	244.41	21.21	...
February	...	1.75	1.36	...	2.50	...	...	2.66	3.16	...	...	253.16	22.00	...
March	...	1.75	1.40	...	2.50	...	...	2.78	3.23	...	...	249.36	21.63	...
April	...	1.75	1.47	...	2.50	...	...	2.87	3.35	...	...	253.02	21.92	...
May	...	1.75	1.55	...	2.50	...	...	2.89	3.40	...	...	254.45	21.93	...
June	...	1.75	1.45	...	2.50	...	...	2.94	3.49	...	...	249.32	21.55	...
July	...	1.75	1.56	...	2.50	...	...	2.94	3.53	...	...	253.61	21.93	...
August	...	1.75	1.62	...	2.50	...	...	2.88	3.50	...	...	264.93	22.89	...
September	...	1.75	1.63	...	2.50	...	...	2.84	3.46	...	...	273.37	23.48	...
October	...	1.75	1.54	...	2.62	...	...	2.89	3.50	...	...	269.85	23.36	...
November	...	1.75	1.56	...	2.75	...	...	2.96	3.56	...	...	259.65	22.71	...
December	...	1.75	1.73	...	2.85	...	...	3.01	3.61	...	...	266.15	23.41	...
1952														
January	...	1.75	1.57	...	3.00	...	...	2.98	3.59	...	...	271.64	24.19	...
February	...	1.75	1.54	...	3.00	...	...	2.93	3.53	...	...	264.72	23.75	...
March	...	1.75	1.59	...	3.00	...	...	2.96	3.51	...	...	264.45	23.81	...
April	...	1.75	1.57	...	3.00	...	...	2.93	3.50	...	...	262.46	23.74	...
May	...	1.75	1.67	...	3.00	...	...	2.93	3.49	...	...	261.63	23.73	...
June	...	1.75	1.70	...	3.00	...	...	2.94	3.50	...	...	268.39	24.38	...
July	...	1.75	1.81	...	3.00	...	...	2.95	3.50	...	...	276.05	25.08	...
August	...	1.75	1.83	...	3.00	...	...	2.94	3.51	...	...	276.70	25.18	...
September	...	1.75	1.71	...	3.00	...	...	2.95	3.52	...	...	272.41	24.78	...
October	...	1.75	1.74	...	3.00	...	...	3.01	3.54	...	...	267.78	24.26	...
November	...	1.75	1.85	...	3.00	...	...	2.98	3.53	...	...	276.38	25.03	...
December	...	1.75	2.09	...	3.00	...	...	2.97	3.51	...	...	285.96	26.04	...
1953														
January	...	1.88	1.96	...	3.00	...	...	3.02	3.51	2.44	...	288.45	26.18	...
February	...	2.00	1.97	...	3.00	...	...	3.07	3.53	2.59	...	283.96	25.86	...
March	...	2.00	2.01	...	3.00	...	...	3.12	3.57	2.65	...	286.79	25.99	...
April	...	2.00	2.19	...	3.03	2.36	2.83	3.23	3.65	2.67	...	275.29	24.71	...
May	...	2.00	2.16	...	3.25	2.48	3.05	3.34	3.78	2.82	...	276.84	24.84	...
June	...	2.00	2.11	...	3.25	2.45	3.11	3.40	3.86	3.03	...	266.89	23.95	...
July	...	2.00	2.04	...	3.25	2.38	2.93	3.28	3.86	2.95	...	270.33	24.29	...
August	...	2.00	2.04	...	3.25	2.28	2.95	3.24	3.85	2.90	...	272.20	24.39	...
September	...	2.00	1.79	...	3.25	2.20	2.87	3.29	3.88	2.87	...	261.90	23.27	...
October	...	2.00	1.38	...	3.25	1.79	2.66	3.16	3.82	2.71	...	270.72	23.97	...
November	...	2.00	1.44	...	3.25	1.67	2.68	3.11	3.75	2.60	...	277.09	24.50	...
December	...	2.00	1.60	...	3.25	1.66	2.59	3.13	3.74	2.59	...	281.15	24.83	...
1954														
January	...	2.00	1.18	...	3.25	1.41	2.48	3.06	3.71	2.50	...	286.64	25.46	...
February	...	1.79	0.97	...	3.25	1.14	2.47	2.95	3.61	2.42	...	292.13	26.02	...
March	...	1.75	1.03	...	3.13	1.13	2.37	2.86	3.51	2.39	...	299.16	26.57	...
April	...	1.63	0.97	...	3.00	0.96	2.29	2.85	3.47	2.47	...	310.93	27.63	...
May	...	1.50	0.76	...	3.00	0.85	2.37	2.88	3.47	2.49	...	322.85	28.73	...
June	...	1.50	0.64	...	3.00	0.82	2.38	2.90	3.49	2.47	...	327.91	28.96	...
July	0.80	1.50	0.72	...	3.00	0.84	2.30	2.89	3.50	2.32	...	341.27	30.13	...
August	1.22	1.50	0.92	...	3.00	0.88	2.36	2.87	3.49	2.26	...	346.06	30.73	...
September	1.06	1.50	1.01	...	3.00	1.03	2.38	2.89	3.47	2.31	...	352.71	31.45	...
October	0.85	1.50	0.98	...	3.00	1.17	2.43	2.87	3.46	2.34	...	358.29	32.18	...
November	0.83	1.50	0.93	...	3.00	1.14	2.48	2.89	3.45	2.32	...	375.71	33.44	...
December	1.28	1.50	1.15	...	3.00	1.21	2.51	2.90	3.45	2.36	...	393.84	34.97	...

[1]Federal Reserve Bank of New York. Through 2002, represents the rate for adjustment credit. Beginning in 2003, represents the rate for primary credit. See notes and definitions for more information.
[2]1941–1943 = 10.
[3]February 5, 1971 = 100.
... = Not available.

Table 20-6. Interest Rates, Bond Yields, and Stock Price Indexes—Continued

(Not seasonally adjusted.)

Year and month	Percent per annum											Stock price indexes		
	Short-term rates					U.S. Treasury securities		Bond yields				Dow Jones industrials (30 stocks)	Standard and Poor's composite (500 stocks) [2]	Nasdaq composite [3]
	Federal funds	Federal Reserve discount rate [1]	U.S. Treasury bills, 3-month	U.S. Treasury bills, 6-month	Bank prime rate	1-year	10-year	Domestic corporate (Moody's)		State and local bonds (Bond Buyer)	Fixed-rate first mortgages			
								Aaa	Baa					
1955														
January	1.39	1.50	1.22	. . .	3.00	1.39	2.61	2.93	3.45	2.40	. . .	398.43	35.60	. . .
February	1.29	1.50	1.17	. . .	3.00	1.57	2.65	2.93	3.47	2.43	. . .	410.26	36.79	. . .
March	1.35	1.50	1.28	. . .	3.00	1.59	2.68	3.02	3.48	2.44	. . .	408.91	36.50	. . .
April	1.43	1.63	1.59	. . .	3.00	1.75	2.75	3.01	3.49	2.41	. . .	423.00	37.76	. . .
May	1.43	1.75	1.45	. . .	3.00	1.90	2.76	3.04	3.50	2.38	. . .	421.55	37.60	. . .
June	1.64	1.75	1.41	. . .	3.00	1.91	2.78	3.05	3.51	2.41	. . .	440.83	39.78	. . .
July	1.68	1.75	1.60	. . .	3.00	2.02	2.90	3.06	3.52	2.54	. . .	462.17	42.69	. . .
August	1.96	1.97	1.90	. . .	3.23	2.37	2.97	3.11	3.56	2.60	. . .	457.31	42.43	. . .
September	2.18	2.18	2.07	. . .	3.25	2.36	2.97	3.13	3.59	2.58	. . .	476.44	44.34	. . .
October	2.24	2.25	2.23	. . .	3.40	2.39	2.88	3.10	3.59	2.51	. . .	452.65	42.11	. . .
November	2.35	2.36	2.24	. . .	3.50	2.48	2.89	3.10	3.58	2.45	. . .	476.60	44.95	. . .
December	2.48	2.50	2.54	. . .	3.50	2.73	2.96	3.15	3.62	2.57	. . .	484.58	45.37	. . .
1956														
January	2.45	2.50	2.41	. . .	3.50	2.58	2.90	3.11	3.60	2.50	. . .	474.75	44.15	. . .
February	2.50	2.50	2.32	. . .	3.50	2.49	2.84	3.08	3.58	2.44	. . .	475.53	44.43	. . .
March	2.50	2.50	2.25	. . .	3.50	2.61	2.96	3.10	3.60	2.57	. . .	502.67	47.49	. . .
April	2.62	2.65	2.60	. . .	3.65	2.92	3.18	3.24	3.68	2.70	. . .	511.05	48.05	. . .
May	2.75	2.75	2.61	. . .	3.75	2.94	3.07	3.28	3.73	2.68	. . .	495.21	46.54	. . .
June	2.71	2.75	2.49	. . .	3.75	2.74	3.00	3.26	3.76	2.54	. . .	485.33	46.27	. . .
July	2.75	2.75	2.31	. . .	3.75	2.76	3.11	3.28	3.80	2.65	. . .	509.75	48.78	. . .
August	2.73	2.81	2.60	. . .	3.84	3.10	3.33	3.43	3.93	2.80	. . .	511.69	48.49	. . .
September	2.95	3.00	2.84	. . .	4.00	3.35	3.38	3.56	4.07	2.93	. . .	495.03	46.84	. . .
October	2.96	3.00	2.90	. . .	4.00	3.28	3.34	3.59	4.17	2.95	. . .	483.81	46.24	. . .
November	2.88	3.00	2.99	. . .	4.00	3.44	3.49	3.69	4.24	3.16	. . .	479.36	45.76	. . .
December	2.94	3.00	3.21	. . .	4.00	3.68	3.59	3.75	4.37	3.22	. . .	492.02	46.44	. . .
1957														
January	2.84	3.00	3.11	. . .	4.00	3.37	3.46	3.77	4.49	3.18	. . .	485.90	45.43	. . .
February	3.00	3.00	3.10	. . .	4.00	3.38	3.34	3.67	4.47	3.00	. . .	466.83	43.47	. . .
March	2.96	3.00	3.08	. . .	4.00	3.42	3.41	3.66	4.43	3.09	. . .	472.77	44.03	. . .
April	3.00	3.00	3.07	. . .	4.00	3.49	3.48	3.67	4.44	3.13	. . .	485.42	45.05	. . .
May	3.00	3.00	3.06	. . .	4.00	3.48	3.60	3.74	4.52	3.27	. . .	500.83	46.78	. . .
June	3.00	3.00	3.29	. . .	4.00	3.65	3.80	3.91	4.63	3.41	. . .	505.29	47.55	. . .
July	2.99	3.00	3.16	. . .	4.00	3.81	3.93	3.99	4.73	3.39	. . .	514.65	48.51	. . .
August	3.24	3.15	3.37	. . .	4.42	4.01	3.93	4.10	4.82	3.54	. . .	487.97	45.84	. . .
September	3.47	3.50	3.53	. . .	4.50	4.07	3.92	4.12	4.93	3.53	. . .	471.80	43.98	. . .
October	3.50	3.50	3.58	. . .	4.50	4.01	3.97	4.10	4.99	3.42	. . .	443.38	41.24	. . .
November	3.28	3.23	3.31	. . .	4.50	3.57	3.72	4.08	5.09	3.37	. . .	436.73	40.35	. . .
December	2.98	3.00	3.04	. . .	4.50	3.18	3.21	3.81	5.03	3.04	. . .	436.96	40.33	. . .
1958														
January	2.72	2.94	2.44	. . .	4.34	2.65	3.09	3.60	4.83	2.91	. . .	445.69	41.12	. . .
February	1.67	2.75	1.53	. . .	4.00	1.99	3.05	3.59	4.66	3.02	. . .	444.16	41.26	. . .
March	1.20	2.35	1.30	. . .	4.00	1.84	2.98	3.63	4.68	3.06	. . .	450.15	42.11	. . .
April	1.26	2.03	1.13	. . .	3.83	1.45	2.88	3.60	4.67	2.96	. . .	446.91	42.34	. . .
May	0.63	1.75	0.91	. . .	3.50	1.37	2.92	3.57	4.62	2.92	. . .	460.04	43.70	. . .
June	0.93	1.75	0.83	. . .	3.50	1.23	2.97	3.57	4.55	2.97	. . .	471.98	44.75	. . .
July	0.68	1.75	0.91	. . .	3.50	1.61	3.20	3.67	4.53	3.09	. . .	488.30	45.98	. . .
August	1.53	1.75	1.69	. . .	3.50	2.50	3.54	3.85	4.67	3.35	. . .	507.55	47.70	. . .
September	1.76	1.91	2.44	. . .	3.83	3.05	3.76	4.09	4.87	3.54	. . .	521.81	48.96	. . .
October	1.80	2.00	2.63	. . .	4.00	3.19	3.80	4.11	4.92	3.45	. . .	539.85	50.95	. . .
November	2.27	2.40	2.67	. . .	4.00	3.10	3.74	4.09	4.87	3.32	. . .	557.11	52.50	. . .
December	2.42	2.50	2.77	3.01	4.00	3.29	3.86	4.08	4.85	3.33	. . .	566.44	53.49	. . .
1959														
January	2.48	2.50	2.82	3.09	4.00	3.36	4.02	4.12	4.87	3.42	. . .	592.30	55.62	. . .
February	2.43	2.50	2.70	3.13	4.00	3.54	3.96	4.14	4.89	3.36	. . .	590.72	54.77	. . .
March	2.80	2.92	2.80	3.13	4.00	3.61	3.99	4.13	4.85	3.30	. . .	609.13	56.15	. . .
April	2.96	3.00	2.95	3.27	4.00	3.72	4.12	4.23	4.86	3.39	. . .	617.00	57.10	. . .
May	2.90	3.05	2.84	3.33	4.23	3.96	4.31	4.37	4.96	3.57	. . .	630.80	57.96	. . .
June	3.39	3.50	3.21	3.52	4.50	4.07	4.34	4.46	5.04	3.71	. . .	631.52	57.46	. . .
July	3.47	3.50	3.20	3.82	4.50	4.39	4.40	4.47	5.08	3.71	. . .	662.81	59.74	. . .
August	3.50	3.50	3.38	3.87	4.50	4.42	4.43	4.43	5.09	3.58	. . .	660.58	59.40	. . .
September	3.76	3.83	4.04	4.70	5.00	5.00	4.68	4.52	5.18	3.78	. . .	635.49	57.05	. . .
October	3.98	4.00	4.05	4.53	5.00	4.80	4.53	4.57	5.28	3.62	. . .	637.35	57.00	. . .
November	4.00	4.00	4.15	4.54	5.00	4.81	4.53	4.56	5.26	3.55	. . .	646.43	57.23	. . .
December	3.99	4.00	4.49	4.85	5.00	5.14	4.69	4.58	5.28	3.70	. . .	671.36	59.06	. . .
1960														
January	3.99	4.00	4.35	4.74	5.00	5.03	4.72	4.61	5.34	3.72	. . .	655.39	58.03	. . .
February	3.97	4.00	3.96	4.30	5.00	4.66	4.49	4.56	5.34	3.60	. . .	624.89	55.78	. . .
March	3.84	4.00	3.31	3.61	5.00	4.02	4.25	4.49	5.25	3.57	. . .	614.70	55.02	. . .
April	3.92	4.00	3.23	3.55	5.00	4.04	4.28	4.45	5.20	3.56	. . .	619.98	55.73	. . .
May	3.85	4.00	3.29	3.58	5.00	4.21	4.35	4.46	5.28	3.60	. . .	615.63	55.22	. . .
June	3.32	3.65	2.46	2.74	5.00	3.36	4.15	4.45	5.26	3.55	. . .	644.39	57.26	. . .
July	3.23	3.50	2.30	2.71	5.00	3.20	3.90	4.41	5.22	3.50	. . .	625.83	55.84	. . .
August	2.98	3.18	2.30	2.59	4.85	2.95	3.80	4.28	5.08	3.33	. . .	624.47	56.51	. . .
September	2.60	3.00	2.48	2.83	4.50	3.07	3.80	4.25	5.01	3.42	. . .	598.10	54.81	. . .
October	2.47	3.00	2.30	2.73	4.50	3.04	3.89	4.30	5.11	3.53	. . .	582.47	53.73	. . .
November	2.44	3.00	2.37	2.66	4.50	3.08	3.93	4.31	5.08	3.40	. . .	601.14	55.47	. . .
December	1.98	3.00	2.25	2.50	4.50	2.86	3.84	4.35	5.10	3.40	. . .	609.54	56.80	. . .

[1]Federal Reserve Bank of New York. Through 2002, represents the rate for adjustment credit. Beginning in 2003, represents the rate for primary credit. See notes and definitions for more information.
[2]1941–1943 = 10.
[3]February 5, 1971 = 100.
. . . = Not available.

Table 20-6. Interest Rates, Bond Yields, and Stock Price Indexes—*Continued*

(Not seasonally adjusted.)

Year and month	Percent per annum											Stock price indexes		
	Short-term rates					U.S. Treasury securities		Bond yields						
								Domestic corporate (Moody's)		State and local bonds (Bond Buyer)	Fixed-rate first mortgages	Dow Jones industrials (30 stocks)	Standard and Poor's composite (500 stocks) [2]	Nasdaq composite [3]
	Federal funds	Federal Reserve discount rate [1]	U.S. Treasury bills, 3-month	U.S. Treasury bills, 6-month	Bank prime rate	1-year	10-year	Aaa	Baa					
1961														
January	1.45	3.00	2.24	2.47	4.50	2.81	3.84	4.32	5.10	3.39	. . .	632.20	59.72	. . .
February	2.54	3.00	2.42	2.60	4.50	2.93	3.78	4.27	5.07	3.31	. . .	650.02	62.17	. . .
March	2.02	3.00	2.39	2.54	4.50	2.88	3.74	4.22	5.02	3.45	. . .	670.57	64.12	. . .
April	1.49	3.00	2.29	2.47	4.50	2.88	3.78	4.25	5.01	3.48	. . .	684.90	65.83	. . .
May	1.98	3.00	2.29	2.45	4.50	2.87	3.71	4.27	5.01	3.43	. . .	693.03	66.50	. . .
June	1.73	3.00	2.33	2.54	4.50	3.06	3.88	4.33	5.03	3.52	. . .	691.46	65.62	. . .
July	1.17	3.00	2.24	2.45	4.50	2.92	3.92	4.41	5.09	3.51	. . .	690.67	65.44	. . .
August	2.00	3.00	2.39	2.66	4.50	3.06	4.04	4.45	5.11	3.52	. . .	718.64	67.79	. . .
September	1.88	3.00	2.28	2.68	4.50	3.06	3.98	4.45	5.12	3.53	. . .	711.02	67.26	. . .
October	2.26	3.00	2.30	2.66	4.50	3.05	3.92	4.42	5.13	3.42	. . .	703.01	68.00	. . .
November	2.61	3.00	2.48	2.70	4.50	3.07	3.94	4.39	5.11	3.41	. . .	724.74	71.08	. . .
December	2.33	3.00	2.60	2.88	4.50	3.18	4.06	4.42	5.10	3.47	. . .	728.44	71.74	. . .
1962														
January	2.15	3.00	2.72	2.94	4.50	3.28	4.08	4.42	5.08	3.34	. . .	705.15	69.07	. . .
February	2.37	3.00	2.73	2.93	4.50	3.28	4.04	4.42	5.07	3.21	. . .	711.95	70.22	. . .
March	2.85	3.00	2.72	2.87	4.50	3.06	3.93	4.39	5.04	3.14	. . .	714.20	70.29	. . .
April	2.78	3.00	2.73	2.83	4.50	2.99	3.84	4.33	5.02	3.06	. . .	690.29	68.05	. . .
May	2.36	3.00	2.69	2.78	4.50	3.03	3.87	4.28	5.00	3.11	. . .	643.71	62.99	. . .
June	2.68	3.00	2.73	2.80	4.50	3.03	3.91	4.28	5.02	3.25	. . .	572.65	55.63	. . .
July	2.71	3.00	2.92	3.08	4.50	3.29	4.01	4.34	5.05	3.27	. . .	581.79	56.97	. . .
August	2.93	3.00	2.82	2.99	4.50	3.20	3.98	4.35	5.06	3.23	. . .	602.50	58.52	. . .
September	2.90	3.00	2.78	2.93	4.50	3.06	3.98	4.32	5.03	3.11	. . .	597.02	58.00	. . .
October	2.90	3.00	2.74	2.84	4.50	2.98	3.93	4.28	4.99	3.02	. . .	580.67	56.17	. . .
November	2.94	3.00	2.83	2.89	4.50	3.00	3.92	4.25	4.96	3.04	. . .	628.83	60.04	. . .
December	2.93	3.00	2.87	2.91	4.50	3.01	3.86	4.24	4.92	3.07	. . .	648.38	62.64	. . .
1963														
January	2.92	3.00	2.91	2.96	4.50	3.04	3.83	4.21	4.91	3.10	. . .	672.10	65.06	. . .
February	3.00	3.00	2.92	2.98	4.50	3.01	3.92	4.19	4.89	3.15	. . .	679.74	65.92	. . .
March	2.98	3.00	2.89	2.95	4.50	3.03	3.93	4.19	4.88	3.05	. . .	674.63	65.67	. . .
April	2.90	3.00	2.90	2.98	4.50	3.11	3.97	4.21	4.87	3.10	. . .	707.12	68.76	. . .
May	3.00	3.00	2.93	3.01	4.50	3.12	3.93	4.22	4.85	3.11	. . .	720.84	70.14	. . .
June	2.99	3.00	2.99	3.08	4.50	3.20	3.99	4.23	4.84	3.21	. . .	719.15	70.11	. . .
July	3.02	3.24	3.18	3.31	4.50	3.48	4.02	4.26	4.84	3.22	. . .	700.75	69.07	. . .
August	3.49	3.50	3.32	3.44	4.50	3.53	4.00	4.29	4.83	3.13	. . .	714.16	70.98	. . .
September	3.48	3.50	3.38	3.50	4.50	3.57	4.08	4.31	4.84	3.20	. . .	738.53	72.85	. . .
October	3.50	3.50	3.45	3.58	4.50	3.64	4.11	4.32	4.83	3.20	. . .	747.53	73.03	. . .
November	3.48	3.50	3.52	3.65	4.50	3.74	4.12	4.33	4.84	3.30	. . .	743.24	72.62	. . .
December	3.38	3.50	3.52	3.66	4.50	3.81	4.13	4.35	4.85	3.27	. . .	759.96	74.17	. . .
1964														
January	3.48	3.50	3.52	3.64	4.50	3.79	4.17	4.39	4.83	3.22	. . .	777.07	76.45	. . .
February	3.48	3.50	3.53	3.67	4.50	3.78	4.15	4.36	4.83	3.14	. . .	793.02	77.39	. . .
March	3.43	3.50	3.54	3.72	4.50	3.91	4.22	4.38	4.83	3.28	. . .	812.19	78.80	. . .
April	3.47	3.50	3.47	3.66	4.50	3.91	4.23	4.40	4.85	3.28	. . .	820.96	79.94	. . .
May	3.50	3.50	3.48	3.60	4.50	3.84	4.20	4.41	4.85	3.20	. . .	823.13	80.72	. . .
June	3.50	3.50	3.48	3.56	4.50	3.83	4.17	4.41	4.85	3.20	. . .	817.65	80.24	. . .
July	3.42	3.50	3.46	3.56	4.50	3.72	4.19	4.40	4.83	3.18	. . .	844.25	83.22	. . .
August	3.50	3.50	3.50	3.61	4.50	3.74	4.19	4.41	4.82	3.19	. . .	835.31	82.00	. . .
September	3.45	3.50	3.53	3.68	4.50	3.84	4.20	4.42	4.82	3.23	. . .	863.55	83.41	. . .
October	3.36	3.50	3.57	3.72	4.50	3.86	4.19	4.42	4.81	3.25	. . .	875.27	84.85	. . .
November	3.52	3.62	3.64	3.81	4.50	3.91	4.15	4.43	4.81	3.18	. . .	880.03	85.44	. . .
December	3.85	4.00	3.84	3.95	4.50	4.02	4.18	4.44	4.81	3.13	. . .	866.73	83.96	. . .
1965														
January	3.90	4.00	3.81	3.94	4.50	3.94	4.19	4.43	4.80	3.06	. . .	889.91	86.12	. . .
February	3.98	4.00	3.93	4.00	4.50	4.03	4.21	4.41	4.78	3.09	. . .	894.42	86.75	. . .
March	4.04	4.00	3.93	4.00	4.50	4.06	4.21	4.42	4.78	3.17	. . .	896.45	86.83	. . .
April	4.09	4.00	3.93	3.99	4.50	4.04	4.20	4.43	4.80	3.15	. . .	907.72	87.97	. . .
May	4.10	4.00	3.89	3.95	4.50	4.03	4.21	4.44	4.81	3.17	. . .	927.50	89.28	. . .
June	4.04	4.00	3.80	3.86	4.50	3.99	4.21	4.46	4.85	3.24	. . .	878.07	85.04	. . .
July	4.09	4.00	3.84	3.90	4.50	3.98	4.20	4.48	4.88	3.27	. . .	873.44	84.91	. . .
August	4.12	4.00	3.84	3.95	4.50	4.07	4.25	4.49	4.88	3.24	. . .	887.71	86.49	. . .
September	4.01	4.00	3.92	4.07	4.50	4.20	4.29	4.52	4.91	3.35	. . .	922.20	89.38	. . .
October	4.08	4.00	4.03	4.19	4.50	4.30	4.35	4.56	4.93	3.40	. . .	944.78	91.39	. . .
November	4.10	4.00	4.09	4.24	4.50	4.37	4.45	4.60	4.95	3.45	. . .	953.31	92.15	. . .
December	4.32	4.42	4.38	4.55	4.92	4.72	4.62	4.68	5.02	3.54	. . .	955.20	91.73	. . .
1966														
January	4.42	4.50	4.59	4.71	5.00	4.88	4.61	4.74	5.06	3.52	. . .	985.93	93.32	. . .
February	4.60	4.50	4.65	4.82	5.00	4.94	4.83	4.78	5.12	3.64	. . .	977.15	92.69	. . .
March	4.65	4.50	4.59	4.78	5.35	4.97	4.87	4.92	5.32	3.72	. . .	926.43	88.88	. . .
April	4.67	4.50	4.62	4.74	5.50	4.90	4.75	4.96	5.41	3.56	. . .	943.46	91.60	. . .
May	4.90	4.50	4.64	4.81	5.50	4.93	4.78	4.98	5.48	3.65	. . .	890.71	86.78	. . .
June	5.17	4.50	4.50	4.65	5.52	4.97	4.81	5.07	5.58	3.77	. . .	888.83	86.06	. . .
July	5.30	4.50	4.80	4.93	5.75	5.17	5.02	5.16	5.68	3.95	. . .	875.89	85.84	. . .
August	5.53	4.50	4.96	5.27	5.88	5.54	5.22	5.31	5.83	4.12	. . .	817.55	80.65	. . .
September	5.40	4.50	5.37	5.79	6.00	5.82	5.18	5.49	6.09	4.12	. . .	791.66	77.81	. . .
October	5.53	4.50	5.35	5.62	6.00	5.58	5.01	5.41	6.10	3.93	. . .	778.11	77.13	. . .
November	5.76	4.50	5.32	5.54	6.00	5.54	5.16	5.35	6.13	3.86	. . .	806.56	80.99	. . .
December	5.40	4.50	4.96	5.07	6.00	5.20	4.84	5.39	6.18	3.86	. . .	800.88	81.33	. . .

[1]Federal Reserve Bank of New York. Through 2002, represents the rate for adjustment credit. Beginning in 2003, represents the rate for primary credit. See notes and definitions for more information.
[2]1941–1943 = 10.
[3]February 5, 1971 = 100.
. . . = Not available.

Table 20-6. Interest Rates, Bond Yields, and Stock Price Indexes—*Continued*

(Not seasonally adjusted.)

Year and month	Percent per annum											Stock price indexes		
	Short-term rates					U.S. Treasury securities		Bond yields				Dow Jones industrials (30 stocks)	Standard and Poor's composite (500 stocks) [2]	Nasdaq composite [3]
	Federal funds	Federal Reserve discount rate [1]	U.S. Treasury bills, 3-month	U.S. Treasury bills, 6-month	Bank prime rate	1-year	10-year	Domestic corporate (Moody's)		State and local bonds (Bond Buyer)	Fixed-rate first mortgages			
								Aaa	Baa					
1967														
January	4.94	4.50	4.72	4.74	5.96	4.75	4.58	5.20	5.97	3.54	...	830.55	84.45	...
February	5.00	4.50	4.56	4.59	5.75	4.71	4.63	5.03	5.82	3.52	...	851.12	87.36	...
March	4.53	4.50	4.26	4.22	5.71	4.35	4.54	5.13	5.85	3.55	...	858.12	89.42	...
April	4.05	4.10	3.84	3.89	5.50	4.11	4.59	5.11	5.83	3.60	...	868.66	90.96	...
May	3.94	4.00	3.60	3.80	5.50	4.15	4.85	5.24	5.96	3.89	...	883.74	92.59	...
June	3.98	4.00	3.54	3.89	5.50	4.48	5.02	5.44	6.15	3.96	...	872.66	91.43	...
July	3.79	4.00	4.21	4.72	5.50	5.01	5.16	5.58	6.26	4.02	...	888.51	93.01	...
August	3.90	4.00	4.27	4.83	5.50	5.13	5.28	5.62	6.33	3.99	...	912.48	94.49	...
September	3.99	4.00	4.42	4.96	5.50	5.24	5.30	5.65	6.40	4.12	...	923.46	95.81	...
October	3.88	4.00	4.56	5.07	5.50	5.37	5.48	5.82	6.52	4.29	...	907.55	95.66	...
November	4.13	4.18	4.73	5.25	5.68	5.61	5.75	6.07	6.72	4.34	...	865.44	92.66	...
December	4.51	4.50	4.97	5.49	6.00	5.71	5.70	6.19	6.93	4.43	...	887.20	95.30	...
1968														
January	4.60	4.50	5.00	5.24	6.00	5.43	5.53	6.17	6.84	4.29	...	884.78	95.04	...
February	4.71	4.50	4.98	5.17	6.00	5.41	5.56	6.10	6.80	4.31	...	847.20	90.75	...
March	5.05	4.66	5.17	5.33	6.00	5.58	5.74	6.11	6.85	4.54	...	834.76	89.09	...
April	5.76	5.20	5.38	5.49	6.20	5.71	5.64	6.21	6.97	4.34	...	893.38	95.67	...
May	6.11	5.50	5.66	5.83	6.50	6.14	5.87	6.27	7.03	4.54	...	905.23	97.87	...
June	6.07	5.50	5.52	5.64	6.50	5.98	5.72	6.28	7.07	4.49	...	906.82	100.53	...
July	6.02	5.50	5.31	5.41	6.50	5.65	5.50	6.24	6.98	4.33	...	905.33	100.30	...
August	6.03	5.48	5.09	5.23	6.50	5.43	5.42	6.02	6.82	4.21	...	883.73	98.11	...
September	5.78	5.25	5.19	5.25	6.45	5.45	5.46	5.97	6.79	4.38	...	922.82	101.34	...
October	5.91	5.25	5.35	5.41	6.25	5.57	5.58	6.09	6.84	4.49	...	955.48	103.76	...
November	5.82	5.25	5.45	5.60	6.25	5.75	5.70	6.19	7.01	4.60	...	964.13	105.40	...
December	6.02	5.36	5.96	6.06	6.60	6.19	6.03	6.45	7.23	4.82	...	968.39	106.48	...
1969														
January	6.30	5.50	6.14	6.28	6.95	6.34	6.04	6.59	7.32	4.85	...	935.00	102.04	...
February	6.61	5.50	6.12	6.30	7.00	6.41	6.19	6.66	7.30	4.98	...	931.31	101.46	...
March	6.79	5.50	6.02	6.16	7.24	6.34	6.30	6.85	7.51	5.26	...	916.52	99.30	...
April	7.41	5.95	6.11	6.13	7.50	6.26	6.17	6.89	7.54	5.19	...	927.38	101.26	...
May	8.67	6.00	6.04	6.15	7.50	6.42	6.32	6.79	7.52	5.33	...	954.88	104.62	...
June	8.90	6.00	6.44	6.75	8.23	7.04	6.57	6.98	7.70	5.75	...	896.62	99.14	...
July	8.61	6.00	7.00	7.24	8.50	7.60	6.72	7.08	7.84	5.75	...	844.02	94.71	...
August	9.19	6.00	6.98	7.19	8.50	7.54	6.69	6.97	7.86	6.00	...	825.46	94.18	...
September	9.15	6.00	7.09	7.32	8.50	7.82	7.16	7.14	8.05	6.26	...	826.72	94.51	...
October	9.00	6.00	7.00	7.29	8.50	7.64	7.10	7.33	8.22	6.09	...	832.52	95.52	...
November	8.85	6.00	7.24	7.62	8.50	7.89	7.14	7.35	8.25	6.30	...	841.10	96.21	...
December	8.97	6.00	7.82	7.90	8.50	8.17	7.65	7.72	8.65	6.82	...	789.23	91.11	...
1970														
January	8.98	6.00	7.87	7.78	8.50	8.10	7.79	7.91	8.86	6.63	...	782.93	90.31	...
February	8.98	6.00	7.13	7.22	8.50	7.59	7.24	7.93	8.78	6.22	...	756.22	87.16	...
March	7.76	6.00	6.63	6.58	8.39	6.97	7.07	7.84	8.63	6.05	...	777.63	88.65	...
April	8.10	6.00	6.51	6.60	8.00	7.06	7.39	7.83	8.70	6.65	...	771.65	85.95	...
May	7.94	6.00	6.84	7.02	8.00	7.75	7.91	8.11	8.98	7.00	...	691.97	76.06	...
June	7.60	6.00	6.68	6.86	8.00	7.55	7.84	8.48	9.25	6.93	...	699.30	75.59	...
July	7.21	6.00	6.45	6.51	8.00	7.10	7.46	8.44	9.40	6.42	...	712.81	75.72	...
August	6.61	6.00	6.41	6.55	8.00	6.98	7.53	8.13	9.44	6.17	...	731.98	77.92	...
September	6.29	6.00	6.12	6.46	7.83	6.73	7.39	8.09	9.39	6.31	...	759.39	82.58	...
October	6.20	6.00	5.91	6.21	7.50	6.43	7.33	8.03	9.33	6.37	...	763.74	84.37	...
November	5.60	5.85	5.28	5.42	7.28	5.51	6.84	8.05	9.38	5.71	...	769.28	84.28	...
December	4.90	5.52	4.87	4.89	6.92	5.00	6.39	7.64	9.12	5.47	...	821.51	90.05	...
1971														
January	4.14	5.23	4.44	4.47	6.29	4.57	6.24	7.36	8.74	5.35	...	849.04	93.49	...
February	3.72	4.91	3.70	3.78	5.88	3.89	6.11	7.08	8.39	5.23	...	879.69	97.11	...
March	3.71	4.75	3.38	3.50	5.44	3.69	5.70	7.21	8.46	5.17	...	901.29	99.60	...
April	4.15	4.75	3.86	4.03	5.28	4.30	5.83	7.25	8.45	5.37	7.31	932.54	103.04	...
May	4.63	4.75	4.14	4.36	5.46	5.04	6.39	7.53	8.62	5.90	7.43	925.51	101.64	...
June	4.91	4.75	4.75	4.97	5.50	5.64	6.52	7.64	8.75	5.95	7.53	900.45	99.72	...
July	5.31	4.88	5.40	5.63	5.91	6.04	6.73	7.64	8.76	6.06	7.60	887.81	99.00	...
August	5.56	5.00	4.94	5.22	6.00	5.80	6.58	7.59	8.76	5.82	7.70	875.41	97.24	...
September	5.55	5.00	4.69	4.97	6.00	5.41	6.14	7.44	8.59	5.37	7.69	901.22	99.40	...
October	5.20	5.00	4.46	4.60	5.90	4.91	5.93	7.39	8.48	5.06	7.63	872.15	97.29	...
November	4.91	4.90	4.22	4.38	5.53	4.67	5.81	7.26	8.38	5.20	7.55	822.11	92.78	...
December	4.14	4.63	4.01	4.23	5.49	4.60	5.93	7.25	8.38	5.21	7.48	869.92	99.17	...
1972														
January	3.50	4.50	3.38	3.66	5.18	4.28	5.95	7.19	8.23	5.12	7.44	904.65	103.30	...
February	3.29	4.50	3.20	3.63	4.75	4.27	6.08	7.27	8.23	5.28	7.33	914.37	105.24	...
March	3.83	4.50	3.73	4.12	4.75	4.67	6.07	7.24	8.24	5.31	7.30	939.23	107.69	...
April	4.17	4.50	3.71	4.23	4.97	4.96	6.19	7.30	8.24	5.43	7.29	958.17	108.81	...
May	4.27	4.50	3.69	4.12	5.00	4.64	6.13	7.30	8.23	5.30	7.37	948.22	107.65	...
June	4.46	4.50	3.91	4.35	5.04	4.93	6.11	7.23	8.20	5.33	7.37	943.44	108.01	...
July	4.55	4.50	3.98	4.50	5.25	4.96	6.11	7.21	8.23	5.41	7.40	925.94	107.21	...
August	4.80	4.50	4.02	4.55	5.27	4.98	6.21	7.19	8.19	5.30	7.40	958.36	111.01	...
September	4.87	4.50	4.66	5.13	5.50	5.52	6.55	7.22	8.09	5.36	7.42	950.60	109.39	...
October	5.04	4.50	4.74	5.13	5.73	5.52	6.48	7.21	8.06	5.18	7.42	944.10	109.56	...
November	5.06	4.50	4.78	5.09	5.75	5.27	6.28	7.12	7.99	5.02	7.43	1 001.20	115.05	...
December	5.33	4.50	5.07	5.30	5.79	5.52	6.36	7.08	7.93	5.05	7.44	1 020.32	117.50	...

[1] Federal Reserve Bank of New York. Through 2002, represents the rate for adjustment credit. Beginning in 2003, represents the rate for primary credit. See notes and definitions for more information.
[2] 1941–1943 = 10.
[3] February 5, 1971 = 100.
. . . = Not available.

Table 20-6. Interest Rates, Bond Yields, and Stock Price Indexes—*Continued*

(Not seasonally adjusted.)

Year and month	Percent per annum											Stock price indexes		
	Short-term rates					U.S. Treasury securities		Bond yields						
								Domestic corporate (Moody's)		State and local bonds (Bond Buyer)	Fixed-rate first mortgages	Dow Jones industrials (30 stocks)	Standard and Poor's composite (500 stocks) [2]	Nasdaq com- posite [3]
	Federal funds	Federal Reserve discount rate [1]	U.S. Treasury bills, 3-month	U.S. Treasury bills, 6-month	Bank prime rate	1-year	10-year	Aaa	Baa					
1973														
January	5.94	4.77	5.41	5.62	6.00	5.89	6.46	7.15	7.90	5.05	7.44	1 026.82	118.42	...
February	6.58	5.05	5.60	5.83	6.02	6.19	6.64	7.22	7.97	5.13	7.44	974.05	114.16	...
March	7.09	5.50	6.09	6.51	6.30	6.85	6.71	7.29	8.03	5.29	7.46	957.36	112.42	...
April	7.12	5.50	6.26	6.52	6.61	6.85	6.67	7.26	8.09	5.15	7.54	944.12	110.27	...
May	7.84	5.90	6.36	6.62	7.01	6.89	6.85	7.29	8.06	5.15	7.65	922.41	107.22	...
June	8.49	6.33	7.19	7.23	7.49	7.31	6.90	7.37	8.13	5.17	7.73	893.90	104.75	...
July	10.40	6.98	8.01	8.12	8.30	8.39	7.13	7.45	8.24	5.40	8.05	903.61	105.83	...
August	10.50	7.29	8.67	8.65	9.23	8.82	7.40	7.68	8.53	5.48	8.50	883.73	103.80	...
September	10.78	7.50	8.29	8.45	9.86	8.31	7.09	7.63	8.63	5.10	8.82	909.99	105.61	...
October	10.01	7.50	7.22	7.32	9.94	7.40	6.79	7.60	8.41	5.05	8.77	967.63	109.84	...
November	10.03	7.50	7.83	7.96	9.75	7.57	6.73	7.67	8.42	5.18	8.58	878.99	102.03	...
December	9.95	7.50	7.45	7.56	9.75	7.27	6.74	7.68	8.48	5.12	8.54	824.08	94.78	...
1974														
January	9.65	7.50	7.77	7.65	9.73	7.42	6.99	7.83	8.48	5.22	8.54	857.25	96.11	...
February	8.97	7.50	7.12	6.96	9.21	6.88	6.96	7.85	8.53	5.20	8.46	831.33	93.45	...
March	9.35	7.50	7.96	7.83	8.85	7.76	7.21	8.01	8.62	5.40	8.41	874.01	97.44	...
April	10.51	7.60	8.33	8.32	10.02	8.62	7.51	8.25	8.87	5.73	8.58	847.79	92.46	...
May	11.31	8.00	8.23	8.40	11.25	8.78	7.58	8.37	9.05	6.02	8.97	830.26	89.67	...
June	11.93	8.00	7.90	8.12	11.54	8.67	7.54	8.47	9.27	6.13	9.09	831.45	89.79	...
July	12.92	8.00	7.55	7.94	11.97	8.80	7.81	8.72	9.48	6.68	9.28	783.01	82.82	...
August	12.01	8.00	8.96	9.11	12.00	9.36	8.04	9.00	9.77	6.71	9.59	729.30	76.03	...
September	11.34	8.00	8.06	8.53	12.00	8.87	8.04	9.24	10.18	6.76	9.96	651.29	68.12	...
October	10.06	8.00	7.46	7.74	11.68	8.05	7.90	9.27	10.48	6.57	9.98	638.62	69.44	...
November	9.45	8.00	7.47	7.52	10.83	7.66	7.68	8.89	10.60	6.61	9.79	642.11	71.74	...
December	8.53	7.81	7.15	7.11	10.50	7.31	7.43	8.89	10.63	7.05	9.62	596.50	67.07	...
1975														
January	7.13	7.40	6.26	6.36	10.05	6.83	7.50	8.83	10.81	6.82	9.43	659.09	72.56	...
February	6.24	6.82	5.50	5.62	8.96	5.98	7.39	8.62	10.65	6.39	9.11	724.89	80.10	...
March	5.54	6.40	5.49	5.62	7.93	6.11	7.73	8.67	10.48	6.73	8.90	765.06	83.78	...
April	5.49	6.25	5.61	6.00	7.50	6.90	8.23	8.95	10.58	6.95	8.82	790.94	84.72	...
May	5.22	6.12	5.23	5.59	7.40	6.39	8.06	8.90	10.69	6.97	8.91	836.55	90.10	...
June	5.55	6.00	5.34	5.61	7.07	6.29	7.86	8.77	10.62	6.94	8.89	845.70	92.40	...
July	6.10	6.00	6.13	6.50	7.15	7.11	8.06	8.84	10.55	7.07	8.89	856.29	92.49	...
August	6.14	6.00	6.44	6.94	7.66	7.70	8.40	8.95	10.59	7.17	8.94	815.52	85.71	...
September	6.24	6.00	6.42	6.92	7.88	7.75	8.43	8.95	10.61	7.44	9.13	818.29	84.67	...
October	5.82	6.00	5.96	6.25	7.96	6.95	8.14	8.86	10.62	7.39	9.22	831.27	88.57	...
November	5.22	6.00	5.48	5.80	7.53	6.49	8.05	8.78	10.56	7.43	9.15	845.52	90.07	...
December	5.20	6.00	5.44	5.85	7.26	6.60	8.00	8.79	10.56	7.31	9.10	840.80	88.70	...
1976														
January	4.87	5.79	4.87	5.14	7.00	5.81	7.74	8.60	10.41	7.07	9.02	929.34	96.86	...
February	4.77	5.50	4.88	5.20	6.75	5.91	7.79	8.55	10.24	6.94	8.81	971.72	100.64	...
March	4.84	5.50	5.00	5.44	6.75	6.21	7.73	8.52	10.12	6.91	8.76	988.55	101.08	...
April	4.82	5.50	4.86	5.18	6.75	5.92	7.56	8.40	9.94	6.60	8.73	992.52	101.93	...
May	5.29	5.50	5.20	5.62	6.75	6.40	7.90	8.58	9.86	6.87	8.77	988.82	101.16	...
June	5.48	5.50	5.41	5.77	7.20	6.52	7.86	8.62	9.89	6.87	8.85	985.60	101.77	...
July	5.31	5.50	5.23	5.53	7.25	6.20	7.83	8.56	9.82	6.79	8.93	993.20	104.20	...
August	5.29	5.50	5.14	5.40	7.01	6.00	7.77	8.45	9.64	6.61	9.00	981.63	103.29	...
September	5.25	5.50	5.08	5.30	7.00	5.84	7.59	8.38	9.40	6.51	8.98	994.38	105.45	...
October	5.02	5.50	4.92	5.06	6.77	5.50	7.41	8.32	9.29	6.30	8.93	951.96	101.89	...
November	4.95	5.43	4.75	4.88	6.50	5.29	7.29	8.25	9.23	6.29	8.81	944.58	101.19	...
December	4.65	5.25	4.35	4.51	6.35	4.89	6.87	7.98	9.12	5.94	8.79	976.87	104.66	...
1977														
January	4.61	5.25	4.62	4.83	6.25	5.29	7.21	7.96	9.08	5.87	8.72	970.63	103.81	...
February	4.68	5.25	4.67	4.90	6.25	5.47	7.39	8.04	9.12	5.88	8.67	941.75	100.96	...
March	4.69	5.25	4.60	4.88	6.25	5.50	7.46	8.10	9.12	5.89	8.69	946.10	100.57	...
April	4.73	5.25	4.54	4.80	6.25	5.44	7.37	8.04	9.07	5.72	8.75	929.12	99.05	...
May	5.35	5.25	4.96	5.20	6.41	5.84	7.46	8.05	9.01	5.75	8.82	926.30	98.76	...
June	5.39	5.25	5.02	5.21	6.75	5.80	7.28	7.95	8.91	5.62	8.86	916.57	99.29	...
July	5.42	5.25	5.19	5.40	6.75	5.94	7.33	7.94	8.87	5.63	8.94	908.21	100.18	...
August	5.90	5.27	5.49	5.83	6.83	6.37	7.40	7.98	8.82	5.62	8.94	872.27	97.75	...
September	6.14	5.75	5.81	6.04	7.13	6.53	7.34	7.92	8.80	5.51	8.90	853.37	96.23	...
October	6.47	5.80	6.16	6.43	7.52	6.97	7.52	8.04	8.89	5.64	8.92	823.96	93.74	...
November	6.51	6.00	6.10	6.41	7.75	6.95	7.58	8.08	8.95	5.49	8.92	828.52	94.28	...
December	6.56	6.00	6.07	6.40	7.75	6.96	7.69	8.19	8.99	5.57	8.96	818.80	93.82	...
1978														
January	6.70	6.37	6.44	6.70	7.93	7.28	7.96	8.41	9.17	5.71	9.02	781.08	90.25	...
February	6.78	6.50	6.45	6.74	8.00	7.34	8.03	8.47	9.20	5.62	9.16	763.58	88.98	...
March	6.79	6.50	6.29	6.63	8.00	7.31	8.04	8.47	9.22	5.61	9.20	756.37	88.82	...
April	6.89	6.50	6.29	6.73	8.00	7.45	8.15	8.56	9.32	5.79	9.36	794.66	92.71	...
May	7.36	6.84	6.41	7.02	8.27	7.82	8.35	8.69	9.49	6.03	9.58	838.56	97.41	...
June	7.60	7.00	6.73	7.23	8.63	8.09	8.46	8.76	9.60	6.22	9.71	840.25	97.66	...
July	7.81	7.23	7.01	7.44	9.00	8.39	8.64	8.88	9.60	6.28	9.74	831.72	97.19	...
August	8.04	7.43	7.08	7.37	9.01	8.31	8.41	8.69	9.48	6.12	9.79	887.93	103.92	...
September	8.45	7.83	7.85	7.99	9.41	8.64	8.42	8.69	9.42	6.09	9.76	878.64	103.86	...
October	8.96	8.26	7.99	8.55	9.94	9.14	8.64	8.89	9.59	6.13	9.86	857.70	100.58	...
November	9.76	9.50	8.64	9.24	10.94	10.01	8.81	9.03	9.83	6.19	10.11	804.30	94.71	...
December	10.03	9.50	9.08	9.36	11.55	10.30	9.01	9.16	9.94	6.50	10.35	807.96	96.11	...

[1]Federal Reserve Bank of New York. Through 2002, represents the rate for adjustment credit. Beginning in 2003, represents the rate for primary credit. See notes and definitions for more information.
[2]1941–1943 = 10.
[3]February 5, 1971 = 100.
. . . = Not available.

Table 20-6. Interest Rates, Bond Yields, and Stock Price Indexes—*Continued*

(Not seasonally adjusted.)

Year and month	Percent per annum											Stock price indexes		
	Short-term rates					U.S. Treasury securities		Bond yields				Dow Jones industrials (30 stocks)	Standard and Poor's composite (500 stocks) [2]	Nasdaq composite [3]
	Federal funds	Federal Reserve discount rate [1]	U.S. Treasury bills, 3-month	U.S. Treasury bills, 6-month	Bank prime rate	1-year	10-year	Domestic corporate (Moody's)		State and local bonds (Bond Buyer)	Fixed-rate first mortgages			
								Aaa	Baa					
1979														
January	10.07	9.50	9.35	9.47	11.75	10.41	9.10	9.25	10.13	6.46	10.39	837.39	99.71	. . .
February	10.06	9.50	9.32	9.41	11.75	10.24	9.10	9.26	10.08	6.31	10.41	825.18	98.23	. . .
March	10.09	9.50	9.48	9.47	11.75	10.25	9.12	9.37	10.26	6.33	10.43	847.85	100.11	. . .
April	10.01	9.50	9.46	9.49	11.75	10.12	9.18	9.38	10.33	6.28	10.50	864.97	102.07	. . .
May	10.24	9.50	9.61	9.54	11.75	10.12	9.25	9.50	10.47	6.25	10.69	837.41	99.73	. . .
June	10.29	9.50	9.06	9.06	11.65	9.57	8.91	9.29	10.38	6.12	11.04	838.65	101.73	. . .
July	10.47	9.69	9.24	9.24	11.54	9.64	8.95	9.20	10.29	6.13	11.09	836.96	102.71	. . .
August	10.94	10.24	9.52	9.49	11.91	9.98	9.03	9.23	10.35	6.20	11.09	873.55	107.36	. . .
September	11.43	10.70	10.26	10.20	12.90	10.84	9.33	9.44	10.54	6.52	11.30	878.51	108.60	. . .
October	13.77	11.77	11.70	11.66	14.39	12.44	10.30	10.13	11.40	7.08	11.64	840.52	104.47	. . .
November	13.18	12.00	11.79	11.82	15.55	12.39	10.65	10.76	11.99	7.30	12.83	815.79	103.66	. . .
December	13.78	12.00	12.04	11.84	15.30	11.98	10.39	10.74	12.06	7.22	12.90	836.14	107.78	. . .
1980														
January	13.82	12.00	12.00	11.84	15.25	12.06	10.80	11.09	12.42	7.35	12.88	860.75	110.87	. . .
February	14.13	12.52	12.86	12.86	15.63	13.92	12.41	12.38	13.57	8.16	13.04	878.22	115.34	. . .
March	17.19	13.00	15.20	15.03	18.31	15.82	12.75	12.96	14.45	9.16	15.28	803.57	104.69	. . .
April	17.61	13.00	13.20	12.88	19.77	13.30	11.47	12.04	14.19	8.63	16.33	786.35	102.97	. . .
May	10.98	12.94	8.58	8.65	16.57	9.39	10.18	10.99	13.17	7.59	14.26	828.20	107.69	. . .
June	9.47	11.40	7.07	7.30	12.63	8.16	9.78	10.58	12.71	7.63	12.71	869.86	114.55	. . .
July	9.03	10.87	8.06	8.06	11.48	8.65	10.25	11.07	12.65	8.13	12.19	909.79	119.83	. . .
August	9.61	10.00	9.13	9.41	11.12	10.24	11.10	11.64	13.15	8.67	12.56	947.33	123.50	. . .
September	10.87	10.17	10.27	10.57	12.23	11.52	11.51	12.02	13.70	8.94	13.20	946.68	126.51	. . .
October	12.81	11.00	11.62	11.63	13.79	12.49	11.75	12.31	14.23	9.11	13.79	949.17	130.22	. . .
November	15.85	11.47	13.73	13.50	16.06	14.15	12.68	12.97	14.64	9.56	14.21	971.09	135.65	. . .
December	18.90	12.87	15.49	14.64	20.35	14.88	12.84	13.21	15.14	10.20	14.79	945.97	133.48	. . .
1981														
January	19.08	13.00	15.02	14.08	20.16	14.08	12.57	12.81	15.03	9.66	14.90	962.14	132.97	. . .
February	15.93	13.00	14.79	14.05	19.43	14.57	13.19	13.35	15.37	10.09	15.13	945.51	128.40	. . .
March	14.70	13.00	13.36	12.81	18.05	13.71	13.12	13.33	15.34	10.16	15.40	987.18	133.19	. . .
April	15.72	13.00	13.69	13.45	17.15	14.32	13.68	13.88	15.56	10.62	15.58	1 004.86	134.43	. . .
May	18.52	13.87	16.30	15.29	19.61	16.20	14.10	14.32	15.95	10.77	16.40	979.53	131.73	. . .
June	19.10	14.00	14.73	14.09	20.03	14.86	13.47	13.75	15.80	10.67	16.70	996.27	132.28	. . .
July	19.04	14.00	14.95	14.74	20.39	15.72	14.28	14.38	16.17	11.14	16.83	947.95	129.13	. . .
August	17.82	14.00	15.51	15.52	20.50	16.72	14.94	14.89	16.34	12.26	17.29	926.26	129.63	. . .
September	15.87	14.00	14.70	14.92	20.08	16.52	15.32	15.49	16.92	12.92	18.16	853.39	118.27	. . .
October	15.08	14.00	13.54	13.82	18.45	15.38	15.15	15.40	17.11	12.83	18.45	853.26	119.80	. . .
November	13.31	13.03	10.86	11.30	16.84	12.41	13.39	14.22	16.39	11.89	17.83	860.43	122.92	. . .
December	12.37	12.10	10.85	11.52	15.75	12.85	13.72	14.23	16.55	12.91	16.92	878.29	123.79	. . .
1982														
January	13.22	12.00	12.28	12.83	15.75	14.32	14.59	15.18	17.10	13.28	17.40	853.42	117.28	. . .
February	14.78	12.00	13.48	13.61	16.56	14.73	14.43	15.27	17.18	12.97	17.60	833.16	114.50	. . .
March	14.68	12.00	12.68	12.77	16.50	13.95	13.86	14.58	16.82	12.82	17.16	812.34	110.84	. . .
April	14.94	12.00	12.70	12.80	16.50	13.98	13.87	14.46	16.78	12.58	16.89	844.93	116.31	. . .
May	14.45	12.00	12.09	12.16	16.50	13.34	13.62	14.26	16.64	11.95	16.68	846.74	116.35	. . .
June	14.15	12.00	12.47	12.70	16.50	14.07	14.30	14.81	16.92	12.44	16.70	804.37	109.70	. . .
July	12.59	11.81	11.35	11.88	16.26	13.24	13.95	14.61	16.80	12.28	16.82	818.41	109.38	. . .
August	10.12	10.68	8.68	9.88	14.39	11.43	13.06	13.71	16.32	11.23	16.27	832.11	109.65	. . .
September	10.31	10.00	7.92	9.37	13.50	10.85	12.34	12.94	15.63	10.66	15.43	917.27	122.43	. . .
October	9.71	9.68	7.71	8.29	12.52	9.32	10.91	12.12	14.73	9.68	14.61	988.73	132.66	. . .
November	9.20	9.35	8.07	8.34	11.85	9.16	10.55	11.68	14.30	10.06	13.83	1 027.76	138.10	. . .
December	8.95	8.73	7.94	8.16	11.50	8.91	10.54	11.83	14.14	9.96	13.62	1 033.10	139.37	. . .
1983														
January	8.68	8.50	7.86	7.93	11.16	8.62	10.46	11.79	13.94	9.50	13.25	1 064.31	144.27	. . .
February	8.51	8.50	8.11	8.23	10.98	8.92	10.72	12.01	13.95	9.58	13.04	1 087.40	146.80	. . .
March	8.77	8.50	8.35	8.37	10.50	9.04	10.51	11.73	13.61	9.20	12.80	1 129.58	151.88	. . .
April	8.80	8.50	8.21	8.30	10.50	8.98	10.40	11.51	13.29	9.04	12.78	1 168.43	157.71	. . .
May	8.63	8.50	8.19	8.22	10.50	8.90	10.38	11.46	13.09	9.11	12.63	1 212.86	164.10	. . .
June	8.98	8.50	8.79	8.89	10.50	9.66	10.85	11.74	13.37	9.52	12.87	1 221.47	166.39	. . .
July	9.37	8.50	9.08	9.26	10.50	10.20	11.38	12.15	13.39	9.53	13.42	1 213.94	166.96	. . .
August	9.56	8.50	9.34	9.51	10.89	10.53	11.85	12.51	13.64	9.72	13.81	1 189.22	162.42	. . .
September	9.45	8.50	9.00	9.15	11.00	10.16	11.65	12.37	13.55	9.58	13.73	1 237.04	167.16	. . .
October	9.48	8.50	8.64	8.83	11.00	9.81	11.54	12.25	13.46	9.66	13.54	1 252.20	167.65	. . .
November	9.34	8.50	8.76	8.93	11.00	9.94	11.69	12.41	13.61	9.74	13.44	1 250.00	165.23	. . .
December	9.47	8.50	9.00	9.17	11.00	10.11	11.83	12.57	13.75	9.89	13.42	1 257.65	164.36	. . .
1984														
January	9.56	8.50	8.90	9.01	11.00	9.90	11.67	12.20	13.65	9.63	13.37	1 258.89	166.39	. . .
February	9.59	8.50	9.09	9.18	11.00	10.04	11.84	12.08	13.59	9.64	13.23	1 164.45	157.25	. . .
March	9.91	8.50	9.52	9.66	11.21	10.59	12.32	12.57	13.99	9.94	13.39	1 161.98	157.44	. . .
April	10.29	8.87	9.69	9.84	11.93	10.90	12.63	12.81	14.31	9.96	13.65	1 152.72	157.60	. . .
May	10.32	9.00	9.83	10.31	12.39	11.66	13.41	13.28	14.74	10.49	13.94	1 143.42	156.55	. . .
June	11.06	9.00	9.87	10.51	12.60	12.08	13.56	13.55	15.05	10.67	14.42	1 121.14	153.12	. . .
July	11.23	9.00	10.12	10.52	13.00	12.03	13.36	13.44	15.15	10.42	14.67	1 113.29	151.08	. . .
August	11.64	9.00	10.47	10.61	13.00	11.82	12.72	12.87	14.63	9.99	14.47	1 212.82	164.42	. . .
September	11.30	9.00	10.37	10.47	12.97	11.58	12.52	12.66	14.35	10.10	14.35	1 213.52	166.11	. . .
October	9.99	9.00	9.74	9.87	12.58	10.90	12.16	12.63	13.94	10.25	14.13	1 199.30	164.82	. . .
November	9.43	8.83	8.61	8.81	11.77	9.82	11.57	12.29	13.48	10.17	13.64	1 211.31	166.27	247.00
December	8.38	8.37	8.06	8.28	11.06	9.33	11.50	12.13	13.40	9.95	13.18	1 188.96	164.48	242.53

[1]Federal Reserve Bank of New York. Through 2002, represents the rate for adjustment credit. Beginning in 2003, represents the rate for primary credit. See notes and definitions for more information.
[2]1941–1943 = 10.
[3]February 5, 1971 = 100.
. . . = Not available.

Table 20-6. Interest Rates, Bond Yields, and Stock Price Indexes—*Continued*

(Not seasonally adjusted.)

	Percent per annum											Stock price indexes		
	Short-term rates					U.S. Treasury securities		Bond yields						
								Domestic corporate (Moody's)		State and local bonds (Bond Buyer)	Fixed-rate first mortgages	Dow Jones industrials (30 stocks)	Standard and Poor's composite (500 stocks) [2]	Nasdaq composite [3]
Year and month	Federal funds	Federal Reserve discount rate [1]	U.S. Treasury bills, 3-month	U.S. Treasury bills, 6-month	Bank prime rate	1-year	10-year	Aaa	Baa					
1985														
January	8.35	8.00	7.76	8.00	10.61	9.02	11.38	12.08	13.26	9.51	13.08	1 238.16	171.61	260.85
February	8.50	8.00	8.27	8.39	10.50	9.29	11.51	12.13	13.23	9.65	12.92	1 283.23	180.88	285.52
March	8.58	8.00	8.52	8.90	10.50	9.86	11.86	12.56	13.69	9.77	13.17	1 268.84	179.42	280.43
April	8.27	8.00	7.95	8.23	10.50	9.14	11.43	12.23	13.51	9.42	13.20	1 266.38	180.62	280.90
May	7.97	7.81	7.48	7.65	10.31	8.46	10.85	11.72	13.15	9.01	12.91	1 279.41	184.90	287.51
June	7.53	7.50	6.95	7.09	9.78	7.80	10.16	10.94	12.40	8.69	12.22	1 314.00	188.89	290.45
July	7.88	7.50	7.08	7.20	9.50	7.86	10.31	10.97	12.43	8.81	12.03	1 343.17	192.54	302.04
August	7.90	7.50	7.14	7.32	9.50	8.05	10.33	11.05	12.50	9.08	12.19	1 326.19	188.31	298.25
September	7.92	7.50	7.10	7.27	9.50	8.07	10.37	11.07	12.48	9.27	12.19	1 317.95	184.06	287.94
October	7.99	7.50	7.16	7.33	9.50	8.01	10.24	11.02	12.36	9.08	12.14	1 351.58	186.18	285.37
November	8.05	7.50	7.24	7.30	9.50	7.88	9.78	10.55	11.99	8.54	11.78	1 432.89	197.45	304.36
December	8.27	7.50	7.10	7.14	9.50	7.67	9.26	10.16	11.58	8.42	11.26	1 517.02	207.26	320.24
1986														
January	8.14	7.50	7.07	7.16	9.50	7.73	9.19	10.05	11.44	8.08	10.88	1 534.85	208.19	328.54
February	7.86	7.50	7.06	7.11	9.50	7.61	8.70	9.67	11.11	7.44	10.71	1 652.74	219.37	348.79
March	7.48	7.10	6.56	6.57	9.10	7.03	7.78	9.00	10.50	7.08	10.08	1 757.36	232.33	368.28
April	6.99	6.83	6.06	6.08	8.83	6.44	7.30	8.79	10.19	7.19	9.94	1 807.06	237.98	382.54
May	6.85	6.50	6.15	6.19	8.50	6.65	7.71	9.09	10.29	7.54	10.14	1 801.81	238.46	388.49
June	6.92	6.50	6.21	6.27	8.50	6.73	7.80	9.13	10.34	7.87	10.68	1 867.71	245.30	398.60
July	6.56	6.16	5.83	5.86	8.16	6.27	7.30	8.88	10.16	7.51	10.51	1 809.92	240.18	385.90
August	6.17	5.82	5.53	5.55	7.90	5.93	7.17	8.72	10.18	7.21	10.20	1 843.45	245.00	375.62
September	5.89	5.50	5.21	5.35	7.50	5.77	7.45	8.89	10.20	7.11	10.01	1 813.48	238.27	358.26
October	5.85	5.50	5.18	5.26	7.50	5.72	7.43	8.86	10.24	7.08	9.97	1 817.06	237.36	355.05
November	6.04	5.50	5.35	5.41	7.50	5.80	7.25	8.68	10.07	6.84	9.70	1 883.65	245.09	358.08
December	6.91	5.50	5.53	5.55	7.50	5.87	7.11	8.49	9.97	6.87	9.31	1 924.09	248.61	354.90
1987														
January	6.43	5.50	5.43	5.44	7.50	5.78	7.08	8.36	9.72	6.66	9.20	2 065.13	264.51	384.24
February	6.10	5.50	5.59	5.59	7.50	5.96	7.25	8.38	9.65	6.61	9.08	2 202.34	280.93	411.71
March	6.13	5.50	5.59	5.60	7.50	6.03	7.25	8.36	9.61	6.65	9.04	2 292.61	292.47	432.19
April	6.37	5.50	5.64	5.90	7.75	6.50	8.02	8.85	10.04	7.55	9.83	2 302.66	289.32	422.75
May	6.85	5.50	5.66	6.05	8.14	7.00	8.61	9.33	10.51	8.00	10.60	2 291.12	289.12	416.64
June	6.73	5.50	5.67	5.99	8.25	6.80	8.40	9.32	10.52	7.79	10.54	2 384.02	301.38	423.70
July	6.58	5.50	5.69	5.76	8.25	6.68	8.45	9.42	10.61	7.72	10.28	2 481.73	310.09	429.01
August	6.73	5.50	6.04	6.15	8.25	7.03	8.76	9.67	10.80	7.82	10.33	2 655.02	329.36	448.45
September	7.22	5.95	6.40	6.64	8.70	7.67	9.42	10.18	11.31	8.26	10.89	2 570.81	318.66	442.82
October	7.29	6.00	6.13	6.69	9.07	7.59	9.52	10.52	11.62	8.70	11.26	2 224.58	280.16	385.05
November	6.69	6.00	5.69	6.19	8.78	6.96	8.86	10.01	11.23	7.95	10.65	1 931.88	245.01	318.65
December	6.77	6.00	5.77	6.36	8.75	7.17	8.99	10.11	11.29	7.96	10.65	1 910.07	240.96	314.55
1988														
January	6.83	6.00	5.81	6.25	8.75	6.99	8.67	9.88	11.07	7.69	10.43	1 947.35	250.48	339.29
February	6.58	6.00	5.66	5.93	8.51	6.64	8.21	9.40	10.62	7.49	9.89	1 980.65	258.13	353.58
March	6.58	6.00	5.70	5.91	8.50	6.71	8.37	9.39	10.57	7.74	9.93	2 044.32	265.74	375.55
April	6.87	6.00	5.91	6.21	8.50	7.01	8.72	9.67	10.90	7.81	10.20	2 036.14	262.61	377.23
May	7.09	6.00	6.26	6.56	8.84	7.40	9.09	9.90	11.04	7.91	10.46	1 988.91	256.12	371.88
June	7.51	6.00	6.46	6.71	9.00	7.49	8.92	9.86	11.00	7.78	10.46	2 104.95	270.68	385.99
July	7.75	6.00	6.73	6.99	9.29	7.75	9.06	9.96	11.11	7.76	10.43	2 104.23	269.05	391.43
August	8.01	6.37	7.06	7.39	9.84	8.17	9.26	10.11	11.21	7.79	10.60	2 051.28	263.73	379.60
September	8.19	6.50	7.24	7.43	10.00	8.09	8.98	9.82	10.90	7.66	10.48	2 080.07	267.97	382.17
October	8.30	6.50	7.35	7.50	10.00	8.11	8.80	9.51	10.41	7.46	10.30	2 144.33	277.40	385.02
November	8.35	6.50	7.76	7.86	10.05	8.48	8.96	9.45	10.48	7.46	10.27	2 099.04	271.02	372.90
December	8.76	6.50	8.07	8.22	10.50	8.99	9.11	9.57	10.65	7.61	10.61	2 148.59	276.51	375.80
1989														
January	9.12	6.50	8.27	8.36	10.50	9.05	9.09	9.62	10.65	7.35	10.73	2 234.68	285.41	389.33
February	9.36	6.59	8.53	8.55	10.93	9.25	9.17	9.64	10.61	7.44	10.65	2 304.31	294.01	404.09
March	9.85	7.00	8.82	8.85	11.50	9.57	9.36	9.80	10.67	7.59	11.03	2 283.10	292.71	404.00
April	9.84	7.00	8.65	8.65	11.50	9.36	9.18	9.79	10.61	7.49	11.05	2 348.92	302.25	417.14
May	9.81	7.00	8.43	8.41	11.50	8.98	8.86	9.57	10.46	7.25	10.77	2 439.57	313.93	435.99
June	9.53	7.00	8.15	7.93	11.07	8.44	8.28	9.10	10.03	7.02	10.20	2 494.89	323.73	447.63
July	9.24	7.00	7.88	7.61	10.98	7.89	8.02	8.93	9.87	6.96	9.88	2 554.04	331.93	446.70
August	8.99	7.00	7.90	7.74	10.50	8.18	8.11	8.96	9.88	7.06	9.99	2 691.12	346.61	461.83
September	9.02	7.00	7.75	7.74	10.50	8.22	8.19	9.01	9.91	7.26	10.13	2 693.41	347.33	469.28
October	8.84	7.00	7.64	7.62	10.50	7.99	8.01	8.92	9.81	7.22	9.95	2 692.01	347.40	469.69
November	8.55	7.00	7.69	7.49	10.50	7.77	7.87	8.89	9.81	7.14	9.77	2 642.50	340.22	454.69
December	8.45	7.00	7.63	7.42	10.50	7.72	7.84	8.86	9.82	6.98	9.74	2 728.47	348.57	449.02
1990														
January	8.23	7.00	7.64	7.55	10.11	7.92	8.21	8.99	9.94	7.10	9.90	2 679.24	339.97	439.35
February	8.24	7.00	7.74	7.70	10.00	8.11	8.47	9.22	10.14	7.22	10.20	2 614.19	330.45	424.53
March	8.28	7.00	7.90	7.85	10.00	8.35	8.59	9.37	10.21	7.29	10.27	2 700.13	338.47	436.10
April	8.26	7.00	7.77	7.84	10.00	8.40	8.79	9.46	10.30	7.39	10.37	2 708.27	338.18	429.00
May	8.18	7.00	7.74	7.76	10.00	8.32	8.76	9.47	10.41	7.35	10.48	2 793.82	350.25	442.60
June	8.29	7.00	7.73	7.63	10.00	8.10	8.48	9.26	10.22	7.24	10.16	2 894.84	360.39	462.31
July	8.15	7.00	7.62	7.52	10.00	7.94	8.47	9.24	10.20	7.19	10.04	2 934.23	360.03	455.83
August	8.13	7.00	7.45	7.38	10.00	7.78	8.75	9.41	10.41	7.32	10.10	2 681.89	330.75	396.33
September	8.20	7.00	7.36	7.32	10.00	7.76	8.89	9.56	10.64	7.43	10.18	2 550.69	315.41	368.57
October	8.11	7.00	7.17	7.16	10.00	7.55	8.72	9.53	10.74	7.49	10.18	2 460.54	307.12	338.02
November	7.81	7.00	7.06	7.03	10.00	7.31	8.39	9.30	10.62	7.18	10.01	2 518.58	315.29	347.72
December	7.31	6.79	6.74	6.70	10.00	7.05	8.08	9.05	10.43	7.09	9.67	2 610.92	328.75	370.21

[1]Federal Reserve Bank of New York. Through 2002, represents the rate for adjustment credit. Beginning in 2003, represents the rate for primary credit. See notes and definitions for more information.
[2]1941–1943 = 10.
[3]February 5, 1971 = 100.

Table 20-6. Interest Rates, Bond Yields, and Stock Price Indexes—*Continued*

(Not seasonally adjusted.)

Year and month	Percent per annum											Stock price indexes		
	Short-term rates					U.S. Treasury securities		Bond yields				Dow Jones industrials (30 stocks)	Standard and Poor's composite (500 stocks)[2]	Nasdaq composite[3]
	Federal funds	Federal Reserve discount rate[1]	U.S. Treasury bills, 3-month	U.S. Treasury bills, 6-month	Bank prime rate	1-year	10-year	Domestic corporate (Moody's)		State and local bonds (Bond Buyer)	Fixed-rate first mortgages			
								Aaa	Baa					
1991														
January	6.91	6.50	6.22	6.28	9.52	6.64	8.09	9.04	10.45	7.08	9.64	2 587.60	325.49	376.67
February	6.25	6.00	5.94	5.93	9.05	6.27	7.85	8.83	10.07	6.91	9.37	2 863.05	362.26	442.59
March	6.12	6.00	5.91	5.92	9.00	6.40	8.11	8.93	10.09	7.10	9.50	2 920.12	372.28	469.10
April	5.91	5.98	5.65	5.71	9.00	6.24	8.04	8.86	9.94	7.02	9.49	2 925.55	379.68	496.32
May	5.78	5.50	5.46	5.61	8.50	6.13	8.07	8.86	9.86	6.95	9.47	2 928.43	377.99	490.93
June	5.90	5.50	5.57	5.75	8.50	6.36	8.28	9.01	9.96	7.13	9.62	2 968.14	378.29	490.38
July	5.82	5.50	5.58	5.70	8.50	6.31	8.27	9.00	9.89	7.05	9.58	2 978.19	380.23	489.37
August	5.66	5.50	5.33	5.39	8.50	5.78	7.90	8.75	9.65	6.90	9.24	3 006.09	389.40	513.25
September	5.45	5.20	5.22	5.25	8.20	5.57	7.65	8.61	9.51	6.80	9.01	3 010.36	387.20	520.56
October	5.21	5.00	4.99	5.04	8.00	5.33	7.53	8.55	9.49	6.68	8.86	3 019.74	386.88	528.92
November	4.81	4.58	4.56	4.61	7.58	4.89	7.42	8.48	9.45	6.73	8.71	2 986.13	385.92	536.58
December	4.43	4.11	4.07	4.10	7.21	4.38	7.09	8.31	9.26	6.69	8.50	2 958.66	388.51	544.10
1992														
January	4.03	3.50	3.80	3.87	6.50	4.15	7.03	8.20	9.13	6.54	8.43	3 227.06	416.08	615.73
February	4.06	3.50	3.84	3.93	6.50	4.29	7.34	8.29	9.23	6.74	8.76	3 257.27	412.56	632.05
March	3.98	3.50	4.04	4.18	6.50	4.63	7.54	8.35	9.25	6.76	8.94	3 247.42	407.36	619.60
April	3.73	3.50	3.75	3.87	6.50	4.30	7.48	8.33	9.21	6.67	8.85	3 294.10	407.41	582.79
May	3.82	3.50	3.63	3.75	6.50	4.19	7.39	8.28	9.13	6.57	8.67	3 376.79	414.81	581.47
June	3.76	3.50	3.66	3.77	6.50	4.17	7.26	8.22	9.05	6.49	8.51	3 337.79	408.27	566.66
July	3.25	3.02	3.21	3.28	6.02	3.60	6.84	8.07	8.84	6.13	8.13	3 329.41	415.05	568.72
August	3.30	3.00	3.13	3.21	6.00	3.47	6.59	7.95	8.65	6.16	7.98	3 307.46	417.93	569.00
September	3.22	3.00	2.91	2.96	6.00	3.18	6.42	7.92	8.62	6.25	7.92	3 293.93	418.48	580.68
October	3.10	3.00	2.86	3.04	6.00	3.30	6.59	7.99	8.84	6.41	8.09	3 198.70	412.50	585.01
November	3.09	3.00	3.13	3.34	6.00	3.68	6.87	8.10	8.96	6.36	8.31	3 238.49	422.84	630.86
December	2.92	3.00	3.22	3.36	6.00	3.71	6.77	7.98	8.81	6.22	8.22	3 303.15	435.64	661.28
1993														
January	3.02	3.00	3.00	3.14	6.00	3.50	6.60	7.91	8.67	6.16	8.02	3 277.73	435.23	691.13
February	3.03	3.00	2.93	3.07	6.00	3.39	6.26	7.71	8.39	5.87	7.68	3 367.26	441.70	681.71
March	3.07	3.00	2.95	3.05	6.00	3.33	5.98	7.58	8.15	5.64	7.50	3 440.73	450.16	684.49
April	2.96	3.00	2.87	2.97	6.00	3.24	5.97	7.46	8.14	5.76	7.47	3 423.62	443.08	665.33
May	3.00	3.00	2.96	3.07	6.00	3.36	6.04	7.43	8.21	5.73	7.47	3 478.18	445.25	686.45
June	3.04	3.00	3.07	3.20	6.00	3.54	5.96	7.33	8.07	5.63	7.42	3 513.81	448.06	695.38
July	3.06	3.00	3.04	3.16	6.00	3.47	5.81	7.17	7.93	5.57	7.21	3 529.44	447.29	703.40
August	3.03	3.00	3.02	3.14	6.00	3.44	5.68	6.85	7.60	5.45	7.11	3 597.03	454.13	725.15
September	3.09	3.00	2.95	3.06	6.00	3.36	5.36	6.66	7.34	5.29	6.92	3 592.29	459.24	745.94
October	2.99	3.00	3.02	3.12	6.00	3.39	5.33	6.67	7.31	5.25	6.83	3 625.81	463.90	771.31
November	3.02	3.00	3.10	3.26	6.00	3.58	5.72	6.93	7.66	5.47	7.16	3 674.71	462.89	764.04
December	2.96	3.00	3.06	3.23	6.00	3.61	5.77	6.93	7.69	5.35	7.17	3 744.10	465.95	762.94
1994														
January	3.05	3.00	2.98	3.15	6.00	3.54	5.75	6.92	7.65	5.31	7.06	3 868.37	472.99	787.77
February	3.25	3.00	3.25	3.43	6.00	3.87	5.97	7.08	7.76	5.40	7.15	3 905.62	471.58	787.81
March	3.34	3.00	3.50	3.78	6.06	4.32	6.48	7.48	8.13	5.91	7.68	3 816.99	463.81	785.93
April	3.56	3.00	3.68	4.09	6.45	4.82	6.97	7.88	8.52	6.23	8.32	3 661.49	447.23	732.30
May	4.01	3.24	4.14	4.60	6.99	5.31	7.18	7.99	8.62	6.19	8.60	3 708.00	450.90	727.76
June	4.25	3.50	4.14	4.55	7.25	5.27	7.10	7.97	8.65	6.11	8.40	3 737.58	454.83	723.21
July	4.26	3.50	4.33	4.75	7.25	5.48	7.30	8.11	8.80	6.23	8.61	3 718.31	451.40	713.49
August	4.47	3.76	4.48	4.88	7.51	5.56	7.24	8.07	8.74	6.21	8.51	3 797.48	464.24	738.87
September	4.73	4.00	4.62	5.04	7.75	5.76	7.46	8.34	8.98	6.28	8.64	3 880.60	466.96	763.94
October	4.76	4.00	4.95	5.39	7.75	6.11	7.74	8.57	9.20	6.52	8.93	3 868.10	463.81	762.46
November	5.29	4.40	5.29	5.72	8.15	6.54	7.96	8.68	9.32	6.97	9.17	3 792.44	461.01	760.42
December	5.45	4.75	5.60	6.21	8.50	7.14	7.81	8.46	9.10	6.80	9.20	3 770.30	455.19	734.96
1995														
January	5.53	4.75	5.71	6.21	8.50	7.05	7.78	8.46	9.08	6.53	9.15	3 872.46	465.25	758.01
February	5.92	5.25	5.77	6.03	9.00	6.70	7.47	8.26	8.85	6.22	8.83	3 953.73	481.92	784.24
March	5.98	5.25	5.73	5.89	9.00	6.43	7.20	8.12	8.70	6.10	8.46	4 062.78	493.15	807.16
April	6.05	5.25	5.65	5.77	9.00	6.27	7.06	8.03	8.60	6.02	8.32	4 230.67	507.91	825.34
May	6.01	5.25	5.67	5.67	9.00	6.00	6.63	7.65	8.20	5.95	7.96	4 391.58	523.81	859.77
June	6.00	5.25	5.47	5.42	9.00	5.64	6.17	7.30	7.90	5.84	7.57	4 510.77	539.35	906.04
July	5.85	5.25	5.42	5.37	8.80	5.59	6.28	7.41	8.04	5.92	7.61	4 684.78	557.37	979.36
August	5.74	5.25	5.40	5.41	8.75	5.75	6.49	7.57	8.19	6.06	7.86	4 639.27	559.11	1 009.59
September	5.80	5.25	5.28	5.30	8.75	5.62	6.20	7.32	7.93	5.91	7.64	4 746.76	578.77	1 051.00
October	5.76	5.25	5.28	5.32	8.75	5.59	6.04	7.12	7.75	5.80	7.48	4 760.48	582.92	1 022.15
November	5.80	5.25	5.36	5.27	8.75	5.43	5.93	7.02	7.68	5.64	7.38	4 935.82	595.53	1 046.64
December	5.60	5.25	5.14	5.13	8.65	5.31	5.71	6.82	7.49	5.45	7.20	5 136.11	614.57	1 047.04
1996														
January	5.56	5.24	5.00	4.92	8.50	5.09	5.65	6.81	7.47	5.43	7.03	5 179.38	614.42	1 024.95
February	5.22	5.00	4.83	4.77	8.25	4.94	5.81	6.99	7.63	5.43	7.08	5 518.74	649.54	1 094.02
March	5.31	5.00	4.96	4.96	8.25	5.34	6.27	7.35	8.03	5.79	7.62	5 612.25	647.07	1 092.65
April	5.22	5.00	4.95	5.06	8.25	5.54	6.51	7.50	8.19	5.94	7.93	5 579.86	647.17	1 135.63
May	5.24	5.00	5.02	5.12	8.25	5.64	6.74	7.62	8.30	5.98	8.07	5 616.71	661.23	1 220.54
June	5.27	5.00	5.09	5.25	8.25	5.81	6.91	7.71	8.40	6.02	8.32	5 671.52	668.50	1 205.08
July	5.40	5.00	5.15	5.30	8.25	5.85	6.87	7.65	8.35	5.92	8.25	5 496.27	644.07	1 105.61
August	5.22	5.00	5.05	5.13	8.25	5.67	6.64	7.46	8.18	5.76	8.00	5 685.51	662.68	1 134.25
September	5.30	5.00	5.09	5.24	8.25	5.83	6.83	7.66	8.35	5.87	8.23	5 804.01	674.88	1 186.44
October	5.24	5.00	4.99	5.11	8.25	5.55	6.53	7.39	8.07	5.72	7.92	5 996.22	701.45	1 234.04
November	5.31	5.00	5.03	5.07	8.25	5.42	6.20	7.10	7.79	5.59	7.62	6 318.36	735.67	1 259.83
December	5.29	5.00	4.91	5.04	8.25	5.47	6.30	7.20	7.89	5.64	7.60	6 435.87	743.25	1 292.15

[1]Federal Reserve Bank of New York. Through 2002, represents the rate for adjustment credit. Beginning in 2003, represents the rate for primary credit. See notes and definitions for more information.
[2]1941–1943 = 10.
[3]February 5, 1971 = 100.

Table 20-6. Interest Rates, Bond Yields, and Stock Price Indexes—*Continued*

(Not seasonally adjusted.)

Year and month	Percent per annum											Stock price indexes		
	Short-term rates					U.S. Treasury securities		Bond yields			Fixed-rate first mortgages	Dow Jones industrials (30 stocks)	Standard and Poor's composite (500 stocks)[2]	Nasdaq composite[3]
	Federal funds	Federal Reserve discount rate[1]	U.S. Treasury bills, 3-month	U.S. Treasury bills, 6-month	Bank prime rate	1-year	10-year	Domestic corporate (Moody's)		State and local bonds (Bond Buyer)				
								Aaa	Baa					
1997														
January	5.25	5.00	5.03	5.10	8.25	5.61	6.58	7.42	8.09	5.72	7.82	6 707.05	766.22	1 345.41
February	5.19	5.00	5.01	5.06	8.25	5.53	6.42	7.31	7.94	5.63	7.65	6 917.46	798.39	1 349.17
March	5.39	5.00	5.14	5.26	8.30	5.80	6.69	7.55	8.18	5.76	7.90	6 901.14	792.16	1 282.86
April	5.51	5.00	5.16	5.37	8.50	5.99	6.89	7.73	8.34	5.88	8.14	6 657.51	763.93	1 225.00
May	5.50	5.00	5.05	5.30	8.50	5.87	6.71	7.58	8.20	5.70	7.94	7 242.33	833.09	1 352.56
June	5.56	5.00	4.93	5.13	8.50	5.69	6.49	7.41	8.02	5.53	7.69	7 599.61	876.29	1 422.45
July	5.52	5.00	5.05	5.12	8.50	5.54	6.22	7.14	7.75	5.35	7.50	7 990.65	925.29	1 531.14
August	5.54	5.00	5.14	5.19	8.50	5.56	6.30	7.22	7.82	5.41	7.48	7 948.42	927.74	1 596.74
September	5.54	5.00	4.95	5.09	8.50	5.52	6.21	7.15	7.70	5.39	7.43	7 866.59	937.02	1 660.15
October	5.50	5.00	4.97	5.09	8.50	5.46	6.03	7.00	7.57	5.38	7.29	7 875.82	951.16	1 682.17
November	5.52	5.00	5.14	5.17	8.50	5.46	5.88	6.87	7.42	5.33	7.21	7 677.35	938.92	1 600.97
December	5.50	5.00	5.16	5.24	8.50	5.53	5.81	6.76	7.32	5.19	7.10	7 909.82	962.37	1 567.00
1998														
January	5.56	5.00	5.04	5.03	8.50	5.24	5.54	6.61	7.19	5.06	6.99	7 808.36	963.36	1 570.23
February	5.51	5.00	5.09	5.07	8.50	5.31	5.57	6.67	7.25	5.10	7.04	8 323.62	1 023.74	1 714.87
March	5.49	5.00	5.03	5.04	8.50	5.39	5.65	6.72	7.32	5.21	7.13	8 709.48	1 076.83	1 781.27
April	5.45	5.00	4.95	5.06	8.50	5.38	5.64	6.69	7.33	5.23	7.14	9 037.43	1 112.20	1 852.30
May	5.49	5.00	5.00	5.14	8.50	5.44	5.65	6.69	7.30	5.20	7.14	9 080.09	1 108.42	1 836.39
June	5.56	5.00	4.98	5.12	8.50	5.41	5.50	6.53	7.13	5.12	7.00	8 872.96	1 108.39	1 795.74
July	5.54	5.00	4.96	5.03	8.50	5.36	5.46	6.55	7.15	5.14	6.95	9 097.15	1 156.58	1 941.58
August	5.55	5.00	4.90	4.95	8.50	5.21	5.34	6.52	7.14	5.10	6.92	8 478.54	1 074.63	1 784.75
September	5.51	5.00	4.61	4.63	8.49	4.71	4.81	6.40	7.09	4.99	6.72	7 909.80	1 020.64	1 663.43
October	5.07	4.86	3.96	4.05	8.12	4.12	4.53	6.37	7.18	4.93	6.71	8 164.47	1 032.47	1 615.69
November	4.83	4.63	4.41	4.42	7.89	4.53	4.83	6.41	7.34	5.03	6.87	9 005.78	1 144.43	1 888.72
December	4.68	4.50	4.39	4.40	7.75	4.52	4.65	6.22	7.23	4.98	6.72	9 018.68	1 190.05	2 071.03
1999														
January	4.63	4.50	4.34	4.33	7.75	4.51	4.72	6.24	7.29	5.01	6.79	9 345.86	1 248.77	2 357.80
February	4.76	4.50	4.44	4.44	7.75	4.70	5.00	6.40	7.39	5.03	6.81	9 322.94	1 246.58	2 356.99
March	4.81	4.50	4.44	4.47	7.75	4.78	5.23	6.62	7.53	5.10	7.04	9 753.64	1 281.66	2 391.14
April	4.74	4.50	4.29	4.37	7.75	4.69	5.18	6.64	7.48	5.08	6.92	10 443.50	1 334.76	2 537.89
May	4.74	4.50	4.50	4.56	7.75	4.85	5.54	6.93	7.72	5.18	7.15	10 853.88	1 332.07	2 512.60
June	4.76	4.50	4.57	4.82	7.75	5.10	5.90	7.23	8.02	5.37	7.55	10 704.03	1 322.55	2 520.96
July	4.99	4.50	4.55	4.58	8.00	5.03	5.79	7.19	7.95	5.36	7.63	11 052.22	1 380.99	2 741.26
August	5.07	4.56	4.72	4.87	8.06	5.20	5.94	7.40	8.15	5.58	7.94	10 935.48	1 327.49	2 642.45
September	5.22	4.75	4.68	4.88	8.25	5.25	5.92	7.39	8.20	5.69	7.82	10 714.03	1 318.17	2 807.95
October	5.20	4.75	4.86	4.98	8.25	5.43	6.11	7.55	8.38	5.92	7.85	10 396.89	1 300.01	2 815.28
November	5.42	4.86	5.07	5.20	8.37	5.55	6.03	7.36	8.15	5.86	7.74	10 809.80	1 391.00	3 230.55
December	5.30	5.00	5.20	5.44	8.50	5.84	6.28	7.55	8.19	5.95	7.91	11 246.37	1 428.68	3 739.88
2000														
January	5.45	5.00	5.32	5.50	8.50	6.12	6.66	7.78	8.33	6.08	8.21	11 281.27	1 425.59	4 013.49
February	5.73	5.24	5.55	5.72	8.73	6.22	6.52	7.68	8.29	6.00	8.33	10 541.93	1 388.87	4 410.87
March	5.85	5.34	5.69	5.85	8.83	6.22	6.26	7.68	8.37	5.83	8.24	10 483.38	1 442.21	4 802.99
April	6.02	5.50	5.66	5.81	9.00	6.15	5.99	7.64	8.40	5.75	8.15	10 944.32	1 461.36	3 863.64
May	6.27	5.71	5.79	6.10	9.24	6.33	6.44	7.99	8.90	6.00	8.52	10 580.28	1 418.48	3 528.42
June	6.53	6.00	5.69	5.97	9.50	6.17	6.10	7.67	8.48	5.80	8.29	10 582.93	1 461.96	3 865.48
July	6.54	6.00	5.96	6.00	9.50	6.08	6.05	7.65	8.35	5.63	8.15	10 662.98	1 473.00	4 017.69
August	6.50	6.00	6.09	6.07	9.50	6.18	5.83	7.55	8.26	5.51	8.03	11 014.51	1 485.46	3 909.60
September	6.52	6.00	6.00	5.98	9.50	6.13	5.80	7.62	8.35	5.56	7.91	10 967.88	1 468.05	3 875.82
October	6.51	6.00	6.11	6.04	9.50	6.01	5.74	7.55	8.34	5.59	7.80	10 440.96	1 390.14	3 333.82
November	6.51	6.00	6.17	6.06	9.50	6.09	5.72	7.45	8.28	5.54	7.75	10 666.08	1 375.04	3 055.42
December	6.40	6.00	5.77	5.68	9.50	5.60	5.24	7.21	8.02	5.22	7.38	10 652.52	1 330.93	2 657.81
2001														
January	5.98	5.52	5.15	4.95	9.05	4.81	5.16	7.15	7.93	5.10	7.03	10 682.76	1 335.63	2 656.86
February	5.49	5.00	4.88	4.71	8.50	4.68	5.10	7.10	7.87	5.18	7.05	10 774.58	1 305.75	2 449.57
March	5.31	4.81	4.42	4.28	8.32	4.30	4.89	6.98	7.84	5.13	6.95	10 081.33	1 185.85	1 986.66
April	4.80	4.28	3.87	3.85	7.80	3.98	5.14	7.20	8.07	5.27	7.08	10 234.52	1 189.84	1 933.93
May	4.21	3.73	3.62	3.62	7.24	3.78	5.39	7.29	8.07	5.29	7.15	11 004.95	1 270.37	2 181.13
June	3.97	3.47	3.49	3.45	6.98	3.58	5.28	7.18	7.97	5.20	7.16	10 767.19	1 238.71	2 112.05
July	3.77	3.25	3.51	3.45	6.75	3.62	5.24	7.13	7.97	5.20	7.13	10 444.50	1 204.45	2 033.98
August	3.65	3.16	3.36	3.29	6.67	3.47	4.97	7.02	7.85	5.03	6.95	10 314.70	1 178.50	1 929.71
September	3.07	2.77	2.64	2.63	6.28	2.82	4.73	7.17	8.03	5.09	6.82	9 042.57	1 044.64	1 573.31
October	2.49	2.02	2.16	2.12	5.53	2.33	4.57	7.03	7.91	5.05	6.62	9 220.75	1 076.59	1 656.43
November	2.09	1.58	1.87	1.88	5.10	2.18	4.65	6.97	7.81	5.04	6.66	9 721.83	1 129.68	1 870.06
December	1.82	1.33	1.69	1.78	4.84	2.22	5.09	6.77	8.05	5.25	7.07	9 979.89	1 144.93	1 977.71
2002														
January	1.73	1.25	1.65	1.73	4.75	2.16	5.04	6.55	7.87	5.16	7.00	9 923.81	1 140.21	1 976.77
February	1.74	1.25	1.73	1.82	4.75	2.23	4.91	6.51	7.89	5.11	6.89	9 891.05	1 100.67	1 799.72
March	1.73	1.25	1.79	2.01	4.75	2.57	5.28	6.81	8.11	5.29	7.01	10 500.96	1 153.79	1 863.05
April	1.75	1.25	1.72	1.93	4.75	2.48	5.21	6.76	8.03	5.22	6.99	10 165.18	1 112.03	1 758.80
May	1.75	1.25	1.73	1.86	4.75	2.35	5.16	6.75	8.09	5.19	6.81	10 080.49	1 079.27	1 660.31
June	1.75	1.25	1.70	1.79	4.75	2.20	4.93	6.63	7.95	5.09	6.65	9 492.44	1 014.05	1 505.49
July	1.73	1.25	1.68	1.70	4.75	1.96	4.65	6.53	7.90	5.02	6.49	8 616.53	903.59	1 346.09
August	1.74	1.25	1.62	1.60	4.75	1.76	4.26	6.37	7.58	4.95	6.29	8 685.48	912.55	1 327.36
September	1.75	1.25	1.63	1.60	4.75	1.72	3.87	6.15	7.40	4.74	6.09	8 160.79	867.81	1 251.07
October	1.75	1.25	1.58	1.56	4.75	1.65	3.94	6.32	7.73	4.88	6.11	8 048.12	854.63	1 241.91
November	1.34	0.83	1.23	1.27	4.35	1.49	4.05	6.31	7.62	4.95	6.07	8 625.73	909.93	1 409.15
December	1.24	0.75	1.19	1.24	4.25	1.45	4.03	6.21	7.45	4.85	6.05	8 526.67	899.18	1 387.15

[1]Federal Reserve Bank of New York. Through 2002, represents the rate for adjustment credit. Beginning in 2003, represents the rate for primary credit. See notes and definitions for more information.
[2]1941–1943 = 10.
[3]February 5, 1971 = 100.

Table 20-6. Interest Rates, Bond Yields, and Stock Price Indexes—*Continued*

(Not seasonally adjusted.)

Year and month	Percent per annum											Stock price indexes		
	Short-term rates					U.S. Treasury securities		Bond yields			Fixed-rate first mortgages	Dow Jones industrials (30 stocks)	Standard and Poor's composite (500 stocks) [2]	Nasdaq composite [3]
	Federal funds	Federal Reserve discount rate [1]	U.S. Treasury bills, 3-month	U.S. Treasury bills, 6-month	Bank prime rate	1-year	10-year	Domestic corporate (Moody's)		State and local bonds (Bond Buyer)				
								Aaa	Baa					
2003														
January	1.24	. . .	1.17	1.20	4.25	1.36	4.05	6.17	7.35	4.90	5.92	8 474.59	895.84	1 389.56
February	1.26	2.25	1.17	1.18	4.25	1.30	3.90	5.95	7.06	4.81	5.84	7 916.18	837.62	1 313.26
March	1.25	2.25	1.13	1.13	4.25	1.24	3.81	5.89	6.95	4.76	5.75	7 977.73	846.62	1 348.50
April	1.26	2.25	1.13	1.14	4.25	1.27	3.96	5.74	6.85	4.74	5.81	8 332.09	890.03	1 409.83
May	1.26	2.25	1.07	1.08	4.25	1.18	3.57	5.22	6.38	4.41	5.48	8 623.41	935.96	1 524.18
June	1.22	2.20	0.92	0.92	4.22	1.01	3.33	4.97	6.19	4.33	5.23	9 098.07	988.00	1 631.75
July	1.01	2.00	0.90	0.95	4.00	1.12	3.98	5.49	6.62	4.74	5.63	9 154.39	992.54	1 716.85
August	1.03	2.00	0.95	1.03	4.00	1.31	4.45	5.88	7.01	5.10	6.26	9 284.78	989.53	1 724.82
September	1.01	2.00	0.94	1.01	4.00	1.24	4.27	5.72	6.79	4.92	6.15	9 492.54	1 019.44	1 856.22
October	1.01	2.00	0.92	1.00	4.00	1.25	4.29	5.70	6.73	4.89	5.95	9 682.46	1 038.73	1 907.89
November	1.00	2.00	0.93	1.02	4.00	1.34	4.30	5.65	6.66	4.73	5.93	9 762.20	1 049.90	1 939.25
December	0.98	2.00	0.90	0.99	4.00	1.31	4.27	5.62	6.60	4.65	5.88	10 124.66	1 080.64	1 956.98
2004														
January	1.00	2.00	0.88	0.97	4.00	1.24	4.15	5.54	6.44	4.61	5.74	10 540.05	1 132.52	2 098.00
February	1.01	2.00	0.93	0.99	4.00	1.24	4.08	5.50	6.27	4.55	5.64	10 601.50	1 143.36	2 048.36
March	1.00	2.00	0.94	0.99	4.00	1.19	3.83	5.33	6.11	4.41	5.45	10 323.73	1 123.98	1 979.48
April	1.00	2.00	0.94	1.09	4.00	1.43	4.35	5.73	6.46	4.82	5.83	10 418.40	1 133.08	2 021.32
May	1.00	2.00	1.02	1.31	4.00	1.78	4.72	6.04	6.75	5.07	6.27	10 083.81	1 102.78	1 930.09
June	1.03	2.01	1.27	1.60	4.01	2.12	4.73	6.01	6.78	5.05	6.29	10 364.90	1 132.76	2 000.98
July	1.26	2.25	1.33	1.66	4.25	2.10	4.50	5.82	6.62	4.87	6.06	10 152.09	1 105.85	1 912.42
August	1.43	2.43	1.48	1.72	4.43	2.02	4.28	5.65	6.46	4.70	5.87	10 032.80	1 088.94	1 821.54
September	1.61	2.58	1.65	1.87	4.58	2.12	4.13	5.46	6.27	4.56	5.75	10 204.67	1 117.66	1 884.73
October	1.76	2.75	1.76	2.00	4.75	2.23	4.10	5.47	6.21	4.49	5.72	10 001.60	1 118.07	1 938.25
November	1.93	2.93	2.07	2.27	4.93	2.50	4.19	5.52	6.20	4.52	5.73	10 411.76	1 168.94	2 062.87
December	2.16	3.15	2.19	2.43	5.15	2.67	4.23	5.47	6.15	4.48	5.75	10 673.38	1 199.21	2 149.53
2005														
January	2.28	3.25	2.33	2.61	5.25	2.86	4.22	5.36	6.02	4.41	5.71	10 539.51	1 181.41	2 071.87
February	2.50	3.49	2.54	2.77	5.49	3.03	4.17	5.20	5.82	4.35	5.63	10 723.82	1 199.63	2 065.74
March	2.63	3.58	2.74	3.00	5.58	3.30	4.50	5.40	6.06	4.57	5.93	10 682.09	1 194.90	2 030.43
April	2.79	3.75	2.78	3.05	5.75	3.32	4.34	5.33	6.05	4.46	5.86	10 283.19	1 164.42	1 957.49
May	3.00	3.98	2.84	3.08	5.98	3.33	4.14	5.15	6.01	4.31	5.72	10 377.18	1 178.28	2 005.22
June	3.04	4.01	2.97	3.13	6.01	3.36	4.00	4.96	5.86	4.23	5.58	10 486.68	1 202.26	2 074.02
July	3.26	4.25	3.22	3.42	6.25	3.64	4.18	5.06	5.95	4.31	5.70	10 545.38	1 222.24	2 145.14
August	3.50	4.44	3.44	3.66	6.44	3.87	4.26	5.09	5.96	4.32	5.82	10 554.27	1 224.27	2 157.85
September	3.62	4.59	3.42	3.67	6.59	3.85	4.20	5.13	6.03	4.29	5.77	10 532.54	1 225.91	2 144.61
October	3.78	4.75	3.71	3.99	6.75	4.18	4.46	5.35	6.30	4.49	6.07	10 324.31	1 191.96	2 087.09
November	4.00	5.00	3.88	4.15	7.00	4.33	4.54	5.42	6.39	4.57	6.33	10 695.25	1 237.37	2 202.84
December	4.16	5.15	3.89	4.18	7.15	4.35	4.47	5.37	6.32	4.46	6.27	10 827.79	1 262.07	2 246.09
2006														
January	4.29	5.26	4.24	4.31	7.26	4.45	4.42	5.29	6.24	4.37	6.15	10 872.48	1 278.72	2 289.99
February	4.49	5.50	4.43	4.52	7.50	4.68	4.57	5.35	6.27	4.41	6.25	10 971.19	1 276.65	2 273.67
March	4.59	5.53	4.51	4.62	7.53	4.77	4.72	5.53	6.41	4.44	6.32	11 144.45	1 293.74	2 300.26
April	4.79	5.75	4.60	4.72	7.75	4.90	4.99	5.84	6.68	4.58	6.51	11 234.68	1 302.18	2 338.68
May	4.94	5.93	4.72	4.82	7.93	5.00	5.11	5.95	6.75	4.59	6.60	11 333.88	1 290.00	2 245.28
June	4.99	6.02	4.79	4.97	8.02	5.16	5.11	5.89	6.78	4.60	6.68	10 997.97	1 253.12	2 137.41
July	5.24	6.25	4.95	5.06	8.25	5.22	5.09	5.85	6.76	4.61	6.76	11 032.53	1 260.24	2 086.21
August	5.25	6.25	4.96	4.97	8.25	5.08	4.88	5.68	6.59	4.39	6.52	11 257.35	1 287.15	2 117.77
September	5.25	6.25	4.81	4.89	8.25	4.97	4.72	5.51	6.43	4.27	6.40	11 533.60	1 317.81	2 221.94
October	5.25	6.25	4.92	4.92	8.25	5.01	4.73	5.51	6.42	4.30	6.36	11 963.12	1 363.38	2 330.17
November	5.25	6.25	4.94	4.95	8.25	5.01	4.60	5.33	6.20	4.14	6.24	12 185.15	1 388.63	2 408.70
December	5.24	6.25	4.85	4.88	8.25	4.94	4.56	5.32	6.22	4.11	6.14	12 377.62	1 416.42	2 431.91
2007														
January	5.25	6.25	4.98	4.95	8.25	5.06	4.76	5.40	6.34	4.23	6.22	12 512.89	1 424.16	2 453.19
February	5.26	6.25	5.03	4.96	8.25	5.05	4.72	5.39	6.28	4.22	6.29	12 631.48	1 444.79	2 479.86
March	5.26	6.25	4.94	4.89	8.25	4.92	4.56	5.30	6.27	4.15	6.16	12 268.53	1 406.95	2 401.49
April	5.25	6.25	4.87	4.86	8.25	4.93	4.69	5.47	6.39	4.26	6.18	12 754.80	1 463.65	2 499.57
May	5.25	6.25	4.73	4.78	8.25	4.91	4.75	5.47	6.39	4.31	6.26	13 407.76	1 511.14	2 562.14
June	5.25	6.25	4.61	4.76	8.25	4.96	5.10	5.79	6.70	4.60	6.66	13 480.21	1 514.49	2 595.40
July	5.26	6.25	4.82	4.83	8.25	4.96	5.00	5.73	6.65	4.56	6.70	13 677.89	1 520.70	2 655.08
August	5.02	6.01	4.20	4.38	8.25	4.47	4.67	5.79	6.65	4.64	6.57	13 239.71	1 454.62	2 539.50
September	4.94	5.53	3.89	4.05	8.03	4.14	4.52	5.74	6.59	4.51	6.38	13 557.69	1 497.12	2 634.47
October	4.76	5.24	3.90	4.01	7.74	4.10	4.53	5.66	6.48	4.39	6.38	13 901.28	1 539.66	2 780.42
November	4.49	5.00	3.27	3.46	7.50	3.50	4.15	5.44	6.40	4.46	6.21	13 200.58	1 463.39	2 662.80
December	4.24	4.83	3.00	3.23	7.33	3.26	4.10	5.49	6.65	4.42	6.10	13 406.99	1 479.23	2 661.55
2008														
January	3.94	4.48	2.75	2.75	6.98	2.71	3.74	5.33	6.54	4.27	5.76	12 538.12	1 378.76	2 418.09
February	2.98	3.50	2.12	2.04	6.00	2.05	3.74	5.53	6.82	4.64	5.92	12 419.57	1 354.87	2 325.83
March	2.61	3.04	1.26	1.48	5.66	1.54	3.51	5.51	6.89	4.93	5.97	12 193.88	1 316.94	2 254.82
April	2.28	2.49	1.29	1.55	5.24	1.74	3.68	5.55	6.97	4.70	5.92	12 656.63	1 370.47	2 368.10
May	1.98	2.25	1.73	1.82	5.00	2.06	3.88	5.57	6.93	4.58	6.04	12 812.48	1 403.22	2 483.24
June	2.00	2.25	1.86	2.13	5.00	2.42	4.10	5.68	7.07	4.69	6.32	12 056.67	1 341.25	2 427.45
July	2.01	2.25	1.63	1.93	5.00	2.28	4.01	5.67	7.16	4.68	6.43	11 322.38	1 257.33	2 278.14
August	2.00	2.25	1.72	1.92	5.00	2.18	3.89	5.64	7.15	4.69	6.48	11 530.75	1 281.47	2 389.27
September	1.81	2.25	1.13	1.61	5.00	1.91	3.69	5.65	7.31	4.86	6.04	11 114.08	1 217.01	2 205.20
October	0.97	1.81	0.67	1.20	4.56	1.42	3.81	6.28	8.88	5.50	6.20	9 176.71	968.80	1 730.32
November	0.39	1.25	0.19	0.73	4.00	1.07	3.53	6.12	9.21	5.23	6.09	8 614.55	883.04	1 542.70
December	0.16	0.86	0.03	0.26	3.61	0.49	2.42	5.05	8.43	5.56	5.33	8 595.56	877.56	1 525.89

[1] Federal Reserve Bank of New York. Through 2002, represents the rate for adjustment credit. Beginning in 2003, represents the rate for primary credit. See notes and definitions for more information.
[2] 1941–1943 = 10.
[3] February 5, 1971 = 100.
. . . = Not available.

NOTES AND DEFINITIONS

TABLE 20-1
INDUSTRIAL PRODUCTION AND CAPACITY UTILIZATION

See the notes and definitions for Tables 2-1 through 2-3.

TABLE 20-2
SUMMARY CONSUMER AND PRODUCER PRICE INDEXES

See the notes and definitions for Tables 8-1 through 8-6.

TABLE 20-3
SUMMARY LABOR FORCE, EMPLOYMENT, AND UNEM-PLOYMENT

See the notes and definitions for Tables 10-1 through 10-5.

TABLE 20-3A
LABOR FORCE AND EMPLOYMENT ESTIMATES SMOOTHED FOR POPULATION ADJUSTMENTS

SOURCE: U.S. DEPARTMENT OF LABOR, BUREAU OF LABOR STATISTICS

This table presents seasonally adjusted monthly estimates of total civilian labor force and total civilian employment in which discontinuities caused by the introduction of new population controls in the official series—as described in the notes and definitions for Tables 10-1 through 10-5—have been smoothed. They are taken from the article "Labor force and employment estimates smoothed for population adjustments, 1990–2008," which was posted on the Bureau of Labor Statistics (BLS) Web site on February 6, 2009. The method of smoothing is described in Marisa L. Di Natale, "Creating Comparability in CPS Employment Series," on the BLS Web site at <http://www.bls.gov/cps/cpscomp.pdf>. BLS notes that these series do not match the official estimates in BLS publications, which are also the data shown in all other tables in this volume.

TABLE 20-4
NONFARM PAYROLL EMPLOYMENT, HOURS, AND EARNINGS

See the notes and definitions for Tables 10-7 through 10-12.

TABLE 20-5A
MONEY STOCK AND RELATED DATA, 1947–1958

SOURCE: BOARD OF GOVERNORS OF THE FEDERAL RESERVE SYSTEM

This table extends monthly data on money supply back to 1947. These figures are not currently maintained online by the Federal Reserve and are found in *Banking and Monetary Statistics, 1941-1970*, Washington: Board of Governors of the Federal Reserve System, 1976. They are not contin-uous with the currently maintained data for January 1959 forward that are shown in Table 20-5B. For that reason, the data on the 1976 basis for January 1959 are shown in Table 20-5A, for users who might need to calculate a factor to link the two sets of data.

Definitions and notes on the data

Money stock is the sum of the *currency component* and the *demand deposit component*. This is the narrowly defined money stock, best known as M1. As noted above, however, it is not continuous with the measure of M1 shown in Table 20-5B.

Currency component is all currency and coin outside the Treasury, Federal Reserve Banks, and commercial banks. Currency in circulation was reported by the U.S. Treasury Department. Member bank currency holdings were reported to the Federal Reserve, and nonmember bank holdings were estimated by the Federal Reserve.

Demand deposit component includes demand deposits held in commercial banks by individuals, partnerships, and cor-porations both domestic and foreign and demand deposits held by nonbank financial institutions and foreign banks. This measure also includes demand deposit liabilities to foreign governments, central banks, and international insti-tutions—said to be "relatively small" in the source docu-ment. (Deposits held by foreign banks and official institutions are excluded from the current measure of M1 shown in Tables 20-5B and 12-1.) U.S. government deposits are excluded but deposits of state and local governments are included. To eliminate double counting, the following are also excluded: domestic commercial interbank deposits, cash items in the process of collection, and Federal Reserve float. (See the notes and definitions to Chapter 12 for explanation.)

Time deposits adjusted is time and savings deposits at com-mercial banks, other than large negotiable certificates of deposit (CDs), and excluding all deposits due to the U.S. government and domestic commercial banks. This can be added to M1 to yield a measure of M2, although the source document does not publish such a measure for the years shown here.

TABLE 20-5B
MONEY STOCK, RESERVES, AND MONETARY BASE

See the notes and definitions for Tables 12-1 through 12-3. Note that these data are not precisely continuous with the data for earlier years in Table 20-5A; see notes above.

TABLE 20-6
INTEREST RATES, BOND YIELDS, AND STOCK PRICE INDEXES

See the notes and definitions for Tables 12-9 and 12-10.

PART D

REGIONAL AND STATE DATA

CHAPTER 21: REGIONAL AND STATE DATA

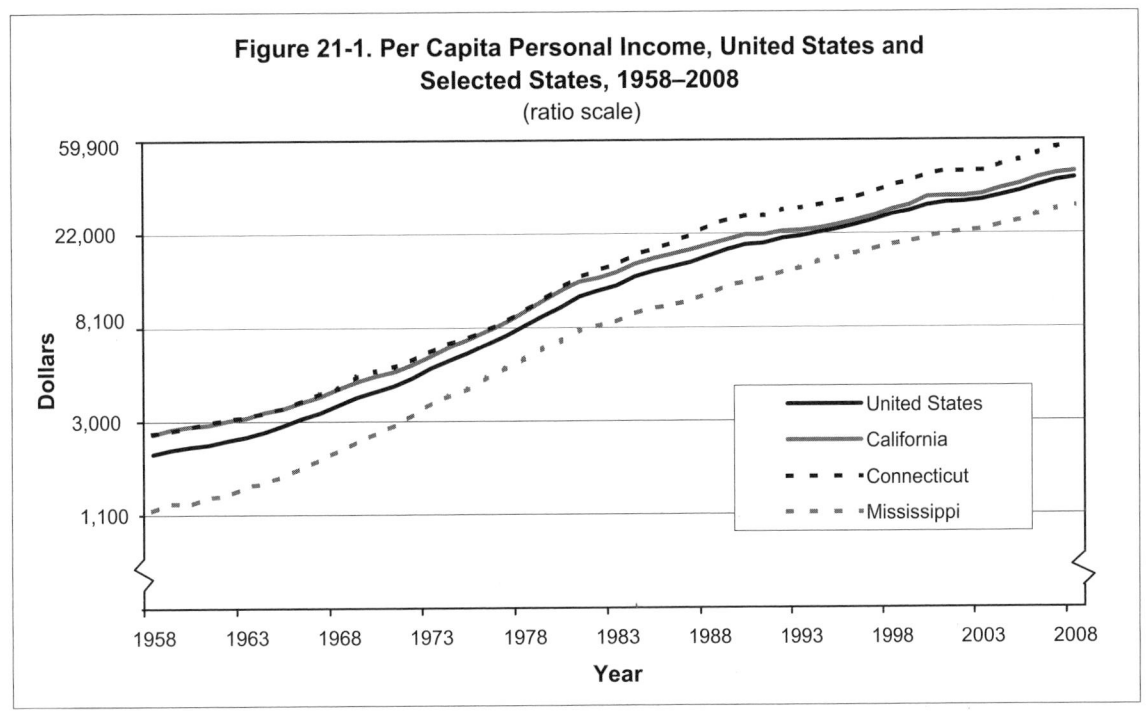

Figure 21-1. Per Capita Personal Income, United States and Selected States, 1958–2008
(ratio scale)

- Per capita personal income (total personal income divided by the size of the population) provides one measure of the affluence of states and regions and how it has changed over time. To provide examples, Figure 21-1 shows the time path since 1958 for the U.S. total; for the largest state in terms of both population and total income (California); for the state with the highest per capita income in 2008 (Connecticut); and for the state with the lowest per capita income in 2008 (Mississippi). (The District of Columbia, which is shown in Tables 21-1 and 21-2 in order to complete the coverage of the United States, has even higher per capita income than Connecticut. However, D.C. data are not really comparable with state data, since D.C. consists entirely of a central city area with an extremely large proportion of high-earning residents.) (Table 21-2)

- These data are not adjusted to remove the effects of inflation or the effects of different costs of living in different states or regions. In addition, they are averages ("means") and—due to the skewed distribution of income—do not necessarily approximate the income of the typical, or "median," person in the state. Inflation-adjusted state median household income data are shown in Table 3-6 of this volume. (See the article at the beginning of this volume for a discussion of means and medians, under the heading "Whose Standard of Living?" The District of Columbia provides an extreme example of the difference. Despite its high per capita income, the District's *median* income is low and its poverty rate is high.) However, per capita income data can be useful for assessing and comparing the economic and fiscal capacities of the states.

- Quantity indexes for state gross domestic product indicate that Nevada had the greatest output growth between 2000 and 2008—more than twice the national average—with Arizona as the runner-up. Output declined in Michigan, and Ohio had the lowest growth. The fastest-growing states in the late-expansion period from 1997 to 2000 were Arizona, California, and Colorado, while Alaska and Hawaii were the only states with declines over those three years. (Table 21-1)

Table 21-1. Gross Domestic Product by Region and State

(Billions of dollars; index numbers, 2000 = 100.)

Year	United States	New England							Mideast						
		Total	Connect-icut	Maine	Massa-chusetts	New Hamp-shire	Rhode Island	Vermont	Total	Delaware	District of Columbia	Maryland	New Jersey	New York	Pennsyl-vania
VALUE															
1977	1 986.1	103.4	29.3	7.6	49.6	6.3	7.3	3.4	402.8	6.0	15.1	35.4	66.6	179.2	100.4
1978	2 243.6	116.0	32.8	8.3	55.5	7.5	8.0	4.0	446.4	6.7	16.5	39.3	73.8	198.5	111.7
1979	2 491.4	128.7	36.4	9.2	61.4	8.4	8.9	4.5	488.6	7.3	18.0	43.2	82.1	215.7	122.3
1980	2 719.1	142.4	40.3	10.1	68.0	9.4	9.7	4.9	528.6	7.9	19.5	47.0	89.7	235.0	129.6
1981	3 064.6	159.3	45.1	11.1	76.2	10.6	10.8	5.5	585.6	8.9	21.4	52.7	99.9	261.3	141.4
1982	3 217.6	172.5	49.4	12.0	82.3	11.5	11.5	5.8	623.0	9.6	22.8	55.9	106.8	282.6	145.2
1983	3 451.3	190.4	54.4	13.1	91.4	12.7	12.4	6.4	676.2	10.7	24.3	61.8	119.0	305.2	155.2
1984	3 872.8	217.7	62.1	14.9	104.9	14.9	13.9	7.0	756.6	12.0	26.4	69.9	134.9	342.1	171.2
1985	4 155.0	239.0	67.4	16.1	115.6	16.9	15.3	7.7	814.6	13.2	28.5	77.3	147.6	366.8	181.2
1986	4 364.3	261.2	73.5	17.5	126.4	18.8	16.7	8.3	874.9	14.2	30.1	84.4	160.5	394.1	191.7
1987	4 663.3	287.7	81.3	19.3	138.5	21.5	17.9	9.3	945.8	15.6	32.2	92.1	175.7	423.8	206.5
1988	5 067.5	315.3	89.3	21.6	151.2	23.2	19.7	10.4	1 037.3	17.0	35.3	102.0	196.4	462.8	223.8
1989	5 385.8	331.2	94.6	22.8	157.7	23.9	20.9	11.3	1 089.7	19.0	37.7	108.5	206.4	481.3	236.7
1990	5 674.0	338.3	99.0	23.3	158.9	23.8	21.5	11.7	1 140.7	20.1	40.1	113.7	214.8	503.6	248.3
1991	5 857.3	341.9	100.2	23.4	160.2	24.8	21.6	11.7	1 168.7	21.9	41.8	116.2	221.7	508.9	258.1
1992	6 174.4	356.6	104.2	24.2	166.6	26.6	22.6	12.6	1 225.5	23.0	43.8	119.5	233.2	532.6	273.5
1993	6 453.5	368.8	106.3	25.0	173.2	27.6	23.6	13.1	1 271.7	23.6	45.7	124.7	243.4	549.2	285.0
1994	6 865.5	390.3	111.2	26.2	185.3	29.5	24.4	13.7	1 326.3	25.1	46.8	132.1	254.5	569.4	298.3
1995	7 232.7	415.4	120.8	27.6	195.3	32.1	25.7	13.9	1 387.7	27.5	47.1	137.4	266.7	594.4	314.5
1996	7 659.7	439.8	126.7	28.6	208.3	34.8	26.7	14.6	1 456.7	28.9	47.6	142.9	281.8	630.0	325.5
1997	8 171.0	472.0	137.5	29.9	223.0	37.1	29.0	15.5	1 539.2	31.3	49.4	152.3	296.1	668.1	342.0
1997 [1]	8 238.0	470.6	137.7	30.9	221.8	36.6	28.5	15.2	1 539.0	35.5	50.4	154.1	300.9	654.8	343.4
1998 [1]	8 679.7	497.8	145.4	31.7	236.1	39.1	29.5	15.9	1 613.3	36.8	51.7	162.0	314.1	686.9	361.8
1999 [1]	9 201.1	524.1	150.3	33.4	252.6	40.2	30.8	16.8	1 700.9	39.4	56.4	171.4	327.3	730.3	376.1
2000 [1]	9 749.1	565.8	160.4	35.5	274.9	43.5	33.6	17.8	1 792.1	41.5	58.7	180.4	344.8	777.2	389.6
2001 [1]	10 058.2	580.9	165.0	37.1	280.5	44.3	35.1	18.8	1 878.8	44.2	63.7	192.7	363.0	808.5	406.7
2002 [1]	10 398.4	591.7	166.1	38.6	284.4	46.2	36.9	19.6	1 934.6	45.3	67.7	204.1	372.8	821.6	423.1
2003 [1]	10 886.2	612.0	169.9	40.2	293.8	48.2	39.4	20.6	2 013.6	48.6	71.7	213.3	389.1	850.2	440.7
2004 [1]	11 607.0	647.5	182.1	43.2	306.8	51.4	42.1	21.8	2 124.9	52.3	77.9	228.2	410.1	896.4	459.9
2005 [1]	12 346.9	674.6	193.3	44.4	317.6	53.5	43.1	22.7	2 245.7	57.3	83.0	243.9	425.5	953.6	482.4
2006 [1]	13 119.9	712.1	205.0	46.3	335.3	56.1	45.7	23.6	2 390.9	59.6	88.2	257.6	448.4	1 028.3	508.8
2007 [1]	13 743.0	744.7	216.3	48.1	351.5	57.3	46.9	24.5	2 522.2	60.1	93.8	268.7	465.5	1 103.0	531.1
QUANTITY INDEX															
1977	47.7	42.3	43.6	51.4	41.7	29.4	51.0	41.3	54.2	44.3	80.8	49.4	45.7	54.9	59.9
1978	50.3	44.6	45.9	52.9	44.0	32.5	52.5	45.5	56.4	46.2	83.2	51.4	47.6	57.1	62.2
1979	51.8	46.3	47.7	54.3	45.6	34.4	54.2	47.5	57.7	46.5	84.3	52.7	49.5	58.2	63.4
1980	51.8	47.2	48.6	55.3	46.5	35.4	54.2	49.0	57.4	45.7	83.9	52.9	49.6	58.3	62.2
1981	53.2	48.4	49.7	55.9	47.8	36.7	55.5	50.6	58.3	46.6	82.7	54.1	50.7	59.3	62.4
1982	52.5	49.0	50.8	56.8	48.2	37.3	55.2	50.2	58.0	47.5	80.8	53.7	50.8	60.0	60:1
1983	54.0	51.6	53.2	59.2	51.1	39.7	56.7	52.3	60.0	51.0	81.4	56.3	54.2	61.4	61.6
1984	58.1	56.4	57.9	63.7	56.1	44.9	61.0	55.1	64.1	55.0	83.5	60.6	58.7	65.7	65.2
1985	60.6	59.9	60.9	67.0	59.8	49.2	64.8	58.7	66.3	58.7	85.1	64.5	61.9	67.5	66.9
1986	61.8	63.1	63.9	70.2	63.0	52.8	67.9	61.2	68.4	60.1	85.8	67.7	64.8	69.5	68.1
1987	64.4	67.8	69.1	74.9	67.3	58.9	70.6	66.3	72.0	64.4	88.6	71.4	69.0	72.9	71.7
1988	67.7	72.0	73.6	80.5	71.3	61.8	75.3	72.1	76.2	67.3	92.3	76.2	74.2	77.0	74.8
1989	69.2	72.7	74.7	82.0	71.6	61.3	77.1	75.1	77.0	72.2	94.4	78.0	75.1	77.2	76.1
1990	70.3	71.4	75.1	81.0	69.4	58.9	76.4	75.8	77.7	73.8	96.5	78.8	75.3	77.7	77.1
1991	70.0	69.5	73.2	78.4	67.3	59.2	73.6	73.4	76.5	76.3	94.6	77.3	74.8	75.4	77.3
1992	72.0	70.6	74.0	79.1	68.1	62.0	74.9	77.2	77.9	76.7	95.7	77.3	76.9	76.4	79.9
1993	73.3	71.0	73.3	79.3	68.9	62.9	76.0	78.2	78.7	76.7	96.7	78.4	78.0	76.7	81.0
1994	76.3	73.4	74.7	80.9	72.1	65.5	76.6	80.3	80.2	79.2	96.1	80.8	79.6	78.0	82.7
1995	78.8	76.4	79.2	82.5	74.4	70.5	78.9	80.2	81.9	83.5	93.2	81.8	81.5	79.6	85.3
1996	82.1	79.6	81.5	84.7	78.1	75.8	80.5	83.6	84.6	85.1	91.5	83.6	85.0	82.8	87.2
1997	86.3	84.0	86.7	87.5	82.2	80.1	85.6	87.3	87.7	88.6	92.4	87.3	87.7	86.3	90.2
1997 [1]	88.4	86.2	90.3	93.8	82.6	84.1	90.6	87.2	89.6	92.3	93.2	90.2	91.7	86.3	93.1
1998 [1]	92.4	90.4	94.0	93.9	87.5	90.9	92.0	91.1	92.8	93.7	93.9	93.7	94.5	89.9	96.6
1999 [1]	96.5	94.0	95.6	96.4	92.8	93.3	94.0	95.3	96.5	98.3	99.4	97.2	96.9	94.8	98.7
2000 [1]	100.0	100.0	100.0	100.0	100.0	100.0	100.0	100.0	100.0	100.0	100.0	100.0	100.0	100.0	100.0
2001 [1]	100.9	100.8	100.5	101.8	100.6	100.2	101.7	104.3	102.5	103.6	104.9	103.9	103.0	102.2	101.5
2002 [1]	102.4	100.5	98.9	103.3	100.0	102.4	103.9	106.3	103.3	103.5	107.0	107.3	103.8	101.9	103.4
2003 [1]	104.9	102.4	99.4	105.1	102.2	105.4	108.6	110.2	105.7	108.2	110.2	109.8	106.3	104.0	105.6
2004 [1]	108.5	105.5	103.4	109.5	104.2	109.7	112.6	114.0	108.4	112.5	115.1	114.0	109.0	106.8	106.8
2005 [1]	111.8	107.1	106.7	109.4	105.2	111.1	111.9	116.3	111.3	119.2	118.2	118.2	109.7	110.8	108.3
2006 [1]	115.3	110.1	110.3	110.7	108.4	113.1	114.9	117.7	115.1	119.8	121.5	121.0	112.2	116.7	110.5
2007 [1]	117.6	112.4	113.3	112.2	111.1	113.0	115.0	119.5	118.3	117.8	126.7	123.3	113.5	121.8	112.2

[1]NAICS basis, not continuous with previous years, which are based on the SIC. See notes and definitions.

Table 21-1. Gross Domestic Product by Region and State—*Continued*

(Billions of dollars; index numbers, 2000 = 100.)

Year	Great Lakes						Plains							
	Total	Illinois	Indiana	Michigan	Ohio	Wisconsin	Total	Iowa	Kansas	Minnesota	Missouri	Nebraska	North Dakota	South Dakota
VALUE														
1977	390.7	115.7	47.8	88.3	97.9	41.0	149.1	26.4	20.5	36.4	41.7	13.7	5.3	5.2
1978	434.9	128.8	53.7	98.0	108.6	45.8	169.1	30.1	22.8	41.1	46.9	15.7	6.5	6.0
1979	470.5	139.9	57.8	103.8	118.3	50.6	188.2	32.8	26.3	46.4	51.4	17.3	7.3	6.8
1980	483.6	146.4	58.7	102.4	122.7	53.4	198.1	34.0	28.2	49.7	53.4	18.1	7.7	6.9
1981	530.7	160.8	64.6	113.0	134.2	58.0	222.1	37.9	32.0	55.0	58.7	20.8	10.0	7.8
1982	539.2	165.2	64.7	113.4	135.9	60.0	228.0	36.9	33.5	57.0	61.6	21.2	10.0	7.8
1983	577.7	173.5	69.0	125.5	146.1	63.7	239.7	37.0	35.2	61.0	66.5	21.7	10.1	8.2
1984	650.8	194.7	78.6	141.5	165.4	70.7	270.3	41.0	38.4	70.3	75.9	24.6	10.7	9.3
1985	690.7	206.5	81.8	151.8	176.0	74.6	283.6	42.4	40.8	74.8	79.4	25.8	10.7	9.7
1986	729.2	218.5	86.1	161.5	184.5	78.5	293.8	43.1	41.7	78.2	84.7	26.1	9.8	10.2
1987	763.8	230.6	91.2	166.9	192.8	82.4	310.6	45.1	43.9	83.9	89.8	26.8	10.3	10.7
1988	823.4	251.1	98.7	177.4	206.3	89.9	331.9	48.9	46.3	90.0	96.5	29.3	9.7	11.2
1989	872.2	265.2	106.5	186.7	218.5	95.4	353.2	52.8	48.3	96.2	102.0	31.4	10.7	11.9
1990	905.7	277.2	110.1	189.7	228.3	100.3	369.7	55.9	51.3	100.3	104.1	33.8	11.5	12.8
1991	934.3	286.6	113.8	194.3	234.7	104.9	385.5	57.7	53.3	103.8	109.5	35.6	11.7	13.8
1992	997.9	304.0	123.6	207.4	250.2	112.8	410.2	61.3	56.1	111.9	115.2	38.0	12.8	14.9
1993	1 046.9	317.2	130.6	221.3	258.3	119.6	421.9	62.7	57.9	114.9	118.3	39.1	12.9	16.0
1994	1 137.5	343.4	141.2	246.1	278.5	128.4	458.0	69.2	61.8	124.7	128.5	42.8	14.0	17.0
1995	1 186.1	359.7	148.0	251.0	293.3	134.1	481.3	71.9	63.7	131.4	137.5	44.5	14.5	17.8
1996	1 243.8	377.3	155.5	263.9	305.4	141.8	515.4	77.2	68.0	141.7	145.0	48.3	16.1	19.1
1997	1 318.3	401.1	164.2	278.8	325.4	148.8	546.5	81.9	72.5	152.2	154.5	49.8	16.1	19.5
1997 [1]	1 354.8	404.0	168.1	299.0	332.1	151.5	554.8	81.9	72.1	155.9	158.2	50.5	16.3	19.8
1998 [1]	1 421.6	423.9	178.9	309.4	348.7	160.7	578.6	83.7	76.0	164.9	164.3	52.1	16.9	20.8
1999 [1]	1 485.3	443.8	185.7	326.2	360.6	169.0	598.5	86.1	78.7	172.9	169.0	53.4	16.9	21.6
2000 [1]	1 543.6	464.2	194.4	337.2	372.0	175.7	631.1	90.2	82.8	185.1	176.7	55.5	17.8	23.1
2001 [1]	1 562.7	476.5	195.2	334.4	374.7	181.9	650.8	91.9	86.4	190.2	182.4	57.4	18.5	23.9
2002 [1]	1 620.4	487.1	205.0	349.8	389.8	188.6	680.1	97.4	89.6	198.6	188.4	59.9	19.9	26.4
2003 [1]	1 683.1	510.3	215.4	359.0	402.4	195.9	713.2	102.2	93.6	208.2	195.5	64.6	21.7	27.4
2004 [1]	1 755.5	534.4	228.3	363.1	423.7	205.9	759.4	111.9	98.4	223.5	204.9	68.4	22.7	29.5
2005 [1]	1 812.4	554.1	232.8	372.2	439.3	214.1	790.2	115.6	103.3	232.0	213.0	71.2	24.6	30.5
2006 [1]	1 873.4	584.0	238.7	375.8	451.6	223.4	827.9	121.9	110.6	242.1	220.1	75.3	25.9	32.0
2007 [1]	1 936.6	609.6	246.4	382.0	466.3	232.3	872.5	129.0	117.3	255.0	229.5	80.1	27.7	33.9
QUANTITY INDEX														
1977	57.7	56.7	54.5	63.7	58.9	50.8	52.3	58.6	56.7	43.4	55.6	52.5	62.3	48.1
1978	60.1	59.2	57.1	66.1	61.1	53.2	55.1	62.0	58.2	45.7	58.4	55.7	69.8	51.5
1979	60.7	60.0	57.3	65.3	62.1	54.9	57.0	63.2	61.8	47.8	59.8	57.2	71.8	53.8
1980	57.8	58.1	54.2	59.4	59.6	54.1	55.8	62.0	61.0	47.7	57.6	56.6	69.0	51.6
1981	58.2	58.8	54.9	59.6	60.1	54.3	57.7	64.2	49.1	58.1	60.0	79.4	54.6	
1982	55.6	56.7	51.8	55.8	57.0	53.1	56.3	60.0	62.3	48.3	57.4	58.7	76.4	53.0
1983	57.3	57.2	52.9	59.5	59.2	54.0	56.5	57.2	62.4	49.6	59.1	57.0	74.5	52.2
1984	62.0	61.5	57.9	64.6	64.5	57.5	61.1	61.0	65.4	54.9	64.5	61.6	76.6	56.5
1985	64.1	63.2	59.1	67.6	66.9	59.6	63.0	62.6	68.2	57.3	65.5	64.3	77.2	58.9
1986	65.1	64.5	60.1	68.9	67.6	60.5	63.2	61.8	68.2	57.7	67.2	63.0	71.6	59.5
1987	66.8	66.6	62.3	69.5	69.3	61.9	65.2	63.1	70.3	60.5	69.5	63.2	73.3	60.8
1988	69.8	70.1	65.2	72.1	71.7	65.6	67.4	66.4	71.8	62.6	72.2	66.6	67.3	61.2
1989	71.2	71.4	67.7	73.0	73.1	66.9	69.1	68.9	72.3	64.4	73.6	68.7	71.2	62.2
1990	71.5	72.1	67.9	71.8	73.9	68.0	69.9	70.8	73.8	65.0	72.6	71.6	73.5	65.4
1991	71.1	71.9	67.9	70.6	73.3	68.9	70.7	71.1	74.5	65.0	73.6	73.7	73.3	68.7
1992	74.1	74.5	72.1	73.2	76.3	72.6	73.5	74.2	76.5	68.6	75.5	76.8	78.7	72.1
1993	75.8	75.7	74.3	75.9	76.8	75.3	73.7	74.2	76.8	68.6	75.5	77.1	77.5	75.8
1994	80.3	80.1	78.4	82.2	80.8	78.9	78.1	80.0	80.2	72.6	79.9	82.6	82.7	78.8
1995	82.2	82.3	80.8	82.3	83.5	80.4	80.4	82.1	81.1	74.6	83.8	84.1	84.0	80.9
1996	85.1	85.2	84.0	85.1	85.9	84.1	84.5	86.5	84.5	79.3	87.0	88.9	90.1	84.4
1997	89.0	89.2	87.7	88.9	90.4	87.6	88.8	91.6	89.2	84.3	91.3	91.2	90.0	86.3
1997 [1]	92.6	91.6	91.0	94.1	94.2	91.2	92.4	95.0	91.9	88.1	95.2	95.1	95.9	87.3
1998 [1]	95.7	94.8	95.2	95.8	97.5	95.0	95.1	95.8	95.9	92.2	97.1	96.8	98.7	91.2
1999 [1]	98.2	97.6	97.4	98.7	99.1	98.1	96.8	97.1	97.6	95.2	97.9	98.0	97.1	94.5
2000 [1]	100.0	100.0	100.0	100.0	100.0	100.0	100.0	100.0	100.0	100.0	100.0	100.0	100.0	100.0
2001 [1]	98.8	100.2	97.9	96.9	98.3	101.0	100.5	99.1	101.3	100.7	100.6	100.6	100.9	101.1
2002 [1]	100.7	100.4	101.2	99.9	100.4	102.6	103.0	102.9	103.0	103.3	101.8	102.6	106.0	109.6
2003 [1]	102.8	103.3	104.7	101.1	101.8	104.8	105.7	105.6	104.7	106.3	103.7	107.9	111.8	111.2
2004 [1]	104.3	105.0	107.8	100.2	104.1	107.0	109.0	111.9	106.6	110.8	105.5	109.8	112.5	115.0
2005 [1]	104.8	105.6	106.8	100.6	104.8	108.5	110.6	113.4	108.8	112.0	106.6	111.9	119.0	117.1
2006 [1]	105.3	107.9	106.5	99.2	104.5	110.1	112.9	116.7	113.3	113.7	107.0	116.1	121.4	119.9
2007 [1]	105.8	109.6	106.8	98.1	104.9	111.2	115.1	118.7	116.6	116.1	108.4	118.6	125.0	122.7

[1] NAICS basis, not continuous with previous years, which are based on the SIC. See notes and definitions.

Table 21-1. Gross Domestic Product by Region and State—*Continued*

(Billions of dollars; index numbers, 2000 = 100.)

Year	Southeast												
	Total	Alabama	Arkansas	Florida	Georgia	Kentucky	Louisiana	Mississippi	North Carolina	South Carolina	Tennessee	Virginia	West Virginia
VALUE													
1977	389.5	26.5	15.0	66.3	40.9	28.6	39.6	16.0	44.0	20.3	33.7	44.0	14.7
1978	443.5	30.4	17.3	77.1	46.3	32.1	45.2	17.9	50.2	23.2	38.4	49.2	16.3
1979	494.8	33.5	18.9	88.2	51.6	35.2	51.8	20.2	54.9	25.8	42.4	54.4	17.7
1980	546.9	36.0	20.1	100.6	56.3	36.6	64.0	21.5	59.3	28.0	45.4	60.0	19.0
1981	621.0	40.1	22.7	115.3	63.7	40.7	77.6	24.3	66.4	31.5	50.7	67.6	20.5
1982	651.7	41.5	23.3	124.8	68.3	41.7	78.5	24.9	69.4	32.8	52.4	72.9	21.3
1983	707.2	45.2	25.0	139.5	76.6	43.4	77.3	26.2	78.2	36.3	57.5	81.0	21.0
1984	796.8	49.7	28.2	158.8	88.6	48.8	83.0	29.1	89.3	41.9	64.6	91.8	22.8
1985	858.2	53.7	29.1	173.8	98.7	51.5	84.8	30.6	98.0	44.9	69.3	100.4	23.6
1986	906.3	56.0	30.4	188.1	108.4	53.3	75.9	31.3	106.2	48.5	74.1	110.0	24.0
1987	976.6	60.6	32.2	206.9	116.8	56.6	76.5	33.6	114.1	53.2	81.2	120.1	24.7
1988	1 058.7	65.4	34.5	226.6	126.1	60.7	82.3	35.7	125.2	58.0	87.5	130.4	26.2
1989	1 125.2	67.9	36.6	243.3	133.1	64.7	86.2	37.3	134.6	62.0	91.9	140.2	27.3
1990	1 181.7	71.1	38.1	257.2	139.5	67.5	93.6	38.8	140.3	65.7	94.6	147.0	28.3
1991	1 234.4	75.3	41.0	267.9	146.3	70.5	94.3	40.8	146.5	68.4	101.4	152.7	29.4
1992	1 309.7	80.5	44.3	283.8	158.3	76.6	88.9	43.7	159.2	71.6	111.3	160.5	31.0
1993	1 384.0	83.5	46.6	302.1	169.0	80.4	93.2	46.7	167.2	75.5	118.9	168.6	32.4
1994	1 485.3	88.6	50.2	322.1	184.3	86.3	101.9	50.6	179.6	81.0	128.9	177.0	34.9
1995	1 575.5	94.0	53.3	340.5	199.1	90.5	109.2	53.8	191.6	86.1	135.7	185.5	36.4
1996	1 664.3	97.9	56.5	363.0	215.1	95.0	115.0	56.0	201.3	89.3	141.3	196.6	37.3
1997	1 768.9	102.5	58.7	384.0	230.4	101.8	121.7	58.3	218.4	94.9	151.0	208.6	38.5
1997 [1]	1 797.9	102.4	59.2	391.5	237.5	105.7	113.3	58.0	228.9	97.4	153.4	211.9	38.8
1998 [1]	1 901.5	106.7	61.9	417.2	255.6	108.8	118.1	60.5	242.9	102.9	160.9	226.6	39.5
1999 [1]	2 022.5	111.9	65.6	442.6	277.1	113.5	124.0	63.0	262.7	108.7	169.6	242.7	41.1
2000 [1]	2 114.5	114.6	66.8	471.3	290.9	111.9	131.5	64.3	273.7	112.5	174.9	260.7	41.5
2001 [1]	2 202.9	118.7	68.9	497.4	299.4	115.1	133.7	66.0	285.7	117.3	180.6	276.8	43.4
2002 [1]	2 288.9	123.8	72.2	522.7	306.7	120.7	134.3	68.1	296.4	121.6	191.5	285.8	45.0
2003 [1]	2 409.9	130.2	75.7	559.0	317.9	124.9	146.7	72.3	306.0	127.9	200.3	302.5	46.5
2004 [1]	2 586.7	141.5	82.1	607.3	338.5	131.7	163.4	76.5	324.4	131.9	214.8	324.9	49.7
2005 [1]	2 783.9	150.5	86.1	670.2	359.7	138.5	184.0	79.5	349.2	138.6	224.2	350.3	53.0
2006 [1]	2 964.0	158.6	90.9	716.5	376.4	146.4	203.2	84.6	380.9	146.2	235.8	368.6	56.0
2007 [1]	3 087.9	165.8	95.4	734.5	396.5	154.2	216.1	88.5	399.4	152.8	243.9	383.0	57.7
QUANTITY INDEX													
1977	44.2	52.2	49.3	35.2	33.3	53.1	73.1	54.4	40.2	40.5	43.9	44.8	73.7
1978	46.9	55.6	52.9	38.3	35.3	55.5	76.6	56.2	42.7	43.5	46.9	46.9	75.2
1979	48.4	57.1	53.6	40.9	37.0	56.9	75.7	58.3	44.0	45.4	48.4	48.5	76.0
1980	49.0	56.8	52.8	43.1	37.4	55.3	78.0	57.3	44.2	45.7	47.9	49.3	75.8
1981	50.6	57.8	54.7	45.1	38.8	56.9	80.5	59.3	45.7	47.3	49.1	50.7	74.8
1982	50.0	56.3	53.2	45.8	39.3	54.9	77.4	57.4	44.7	46.4	48.0	50.9	72.9
1983	51.9	58.9	54.9	48.5	41.9	54.7	76.5	58.5	47.0	49.3	50.6	53.2	70.1
1984	56.1	62.0	59.3	52.6	46.2	59.3	81.1	62.7	51.3	54.3	54.5	57.1	74.1
1985	58.7	65.2	60.1	55.4	49.8	61.4	82.5	64.7	54.7	56.4	56.7	60.0	74.8
1986	60.4	65.9	61.1	57.6	52.7	61.2	80.5	64.5	56.8	58.9	58.5	63.1	75.3
1987	63.3	69.5	63.1	61.3	55.1	63.7	80.2	68.3	59.1	62.9	62.4	66.7	76.1
1988	66.4	72.4	65.5	64.8	57.4	66.3	84.3	70.0	62.5	66.1	64.9	69.9	78.5
1989	67.9	72.4	66.9	67.1	58.5	68.2	83.8	70.6	64.4	68.3	65.7	72.3	79.3
1990	68.8	73.6	67.5	68.4	59.3	69.0	85.3	70.7	64.7	70.3	65.3	73.1	80.5
1991	69.3	75.5	70.5	68.6	60.0	69.4	85.0	72.1	64.6	70.7	67.5	72.6	81.1
1992	71.7	78.8	74.6	70.9	63.3	73.4	79.2	75.5	68.1	72.4	72.4	74.0	84.1
1993	73.9	79.7	76.6	73.3	65.9	75.4	80.6	78.4	70.0	74.7	75.3	75.8	86.4
1994	77.9	82.6	80.6	76.3	70.4	80.0	87.1	83.2	74.9	78.5	79.7	78.4	91.0
1995	80.9	85.2	83.9	78.9	74.3	82.8	91.5	87.1	78.6	81.3	82.2	80.4	93.3
1996	84.1	87.8	87.5	82.7	79.2	85.7	92.3	89.3	81.4	83.5	84.6	83.7	95.2
1997	88.0	90.8	90.5	86.1	83.5	90.9	95.6	91.7	87.1	87.9	89.1	87.1	96.9
1997 [1]	90.3	93.9	93.5	88.0	86.2	99.7	98.0	95.9	87.6	91.8	93.2	86.7	97.9
1998 [1]	94.2	96.6	96.2	92.4	91.5	101.1	102.4	98.5	91.7	95.2	96.2	91.1	98.4
1999 [1]	98.2	99.9	100.4	96.2	97.2	103.4	104.2	100.6	97.6	98.6	99.3	95.4	101.3
2000 [1]	100.0	100.0	100.0	100.0	100.0	100.0	100.0	100.0	100.0	100.0	100.0	100.0	100.0
2001 [1]	101.5	100.9	100.3	102.9	100.7	100.2	98.3	99.5	101.7	101.4	100.8	103.4	101.1
2002 [1]	103.2	103.2	103.1	105.5	101.1	103.2	98.6	100.5	103.2	102.8	104.7	104.0	102.4
2003 [1]	106.3	106.1	105.9	110.4	103.0	104.8	100.3	103.6	104.6	106.3	107.8	107.9	102.8
2004 [1]	110.6	111.6	111.1	116.4	106.8	107.2	105.9	105.7	108.0	106.5	112.8	112.8	105.7
2005 [1]	115.2	115.1	113.6	124.9	110.7	109.7	107.4	106.2	113.2	108.9	114.9	118.2	107.7
2006 [1]	118.8	117.5	116.2	129.4	112.5	112.6	112.0	109.3	120.0	111.0	117.8	120.8	108.8
2007 [1]	120.6	119.6	117.9	129.4	115.7	115.1	114.8	111.2	122.7	113.2	118.8	123.1	108.9

[1]NAICS basis, not continuous with previous years, which are based on the SIC. See notes and definitions.

Table 21-1. Gross Domestic Product by Region and State—*Continued*

(Billions of dollars; index numbers, 2000 = 100.)

Year	Southwest					Rocky Mountain					
	Total	Arizona	New Mexico	Oklahoma	Texas	Total	Colorado	Idaho	Montana	Utah	Wyoming
VALUE											
1977	184.5	19.4	10.3	24.0	130.8	54.6	25.1	7.1	6.4	10.4	5.5
1978	211.6	23.0	11.7	27.2	149.7	63.9	29.2	8.4	7.5	12.1	6.7
1979	245.0	27.3	13.4	31.7	172.6	73.1	33.7	9.2	8.3	13.8	8.2
1980	288.9	30.4	16.0	37.8	204.6	83.1	38.2	9.8	9.0	15.4	10.6
1981	345.7	33.7	18.9	45.8	247.3	95.2	43.8	10.6	10.3	17.5	13.0
1982	367.0	35.0	19.7	49.8	262.5	99.8	47.4	10.6	10.4	18.5	12.9
1983	375.7	38.8	20.4	48.3	268.2	104.8	50.4	11.7	10.7	19.9	12.0
1984	412.8	45.2	22.1	52.0	293.5	114.7	55.9	12.5	11.2	22.4	12.7
1985	439.5	50.1	23.3	53.6	312.6	120.7	59.3	13.0	11.2	24.4	12.8
1986	425.6	55.2	22.4	49.2	298.8	120.1	60.1	13.1	11.2	24.6	11.1
1987	433.4	59.2	23.0	48.9	302.4	124.6	62.9	13.8	11.7	25.3	11.0
1988	471.7	63.6	23.8	52.7	331.6	132.0	66.3	15.1	11.9	27.4	11.3
1989	501.2	66.4	25.3	54.8	354.7	140.0	69.6	16.8	12.8	28.9	11.9
1990	538.0	69.3	26.9	57.7	384.1	150.0	74.2	17.8	13.4	31.4	13.2
1991	561.1	72.3	30.5	59.5	398.9	158.2	78.6	18.6	14.1	33.7	13.3
1992	596.3	79.7	32.6	62.0	422.1	169.5	85.1	20.3	15.0	35.7	13.3
1993	635.9	85.2	36.5	65.0	449.2	183.6	92.5	22.7	16.1	38.4	13.9
1994	681.7	95.3	41.1	67.1	478.1	198.5	100.4	24.8	17.0	42.2	14.1
1995	722.5	104.0	41.5	69.6	507.4	213.4	108.0	27.1	17.4	46.3	14.6
1996	781.7	113.1	43.7	74.9	550.0	229.4	116.0	28.2	18.0	51.4	15.7
1997	855.2	122.9	47.6	79.5	605.3	246.7	127.9	29.4	18.8	54.6	16.0
1997 [1]	852.3	127.4	47.4	78.0	599.5	252.0	132.9	28.5	19.1	56.6	14.9
1998 [1]	892.0	137.6	45.9	79.3	629.2	267.9	143.2	29.8	19.9	60.2	14.9
1999 [1]	949.7	148.5	49.0	83.2	669.0	289.1	156.3	32.7	20.4	63.8	15.9
2000 [1]	1 026.2	158.5	50.7	89.8	727.2	313.1	171.9	35.0	21.4	67.6	17.3
2001 [1]	1 073.3	165.4	51.4	94.3	762.2	325.2	178.1	35.6	22.5	70.1	18.9
2002 [1]	1 105.1	171.9	52.5	97.2	783.5	334.6	182.2	36.7	23.6	72.7	19.6
2003 [1]	1 171.7	182.0	57.5	103.5	828.8	348.2	187.4	38.1	25.5	75.4	21.7
2004 [1]	1 270.1	193.4	63.5	111.5	901.7	371.7	197.3	42.6	27.5	80.9	23.4
2005 [1]	1 384.1	215.8	68.2	120.8	979.3	405.2	213.3	46.4	30.0	88.9	26.6
2006 [1]	1 507.8	237.4	72.2	130.1	1 068.1	434.6	226.3	48.4	32.0	98.0	29.9
2007 [1]	1 604.5	247.0	76.2	139.3	1 142.0	458.9	236.3	51.1	34.3	105.7	31.5
QUANTITY INDEX											
1977	42.3	28.7	43.0	62.0	42.8	40.9	36.6	38.6	68.3	36.7	63.2
1978	44.8	31.7	45.4	64.8	45.2	44.2	39.6	41.9	73.3	39.6	69.3
1979	46.7	34.8	45.9	67.9	46.7	46.3	42.3	42.6	73.4	41.6	72.2
1980	48.5	35.7	47.5	71.2	48.5	47.8	43.7	43.0	73.7	42.6	79.5
1981	51.1	36.5	48.2	75.4	51.4	49.6	45.6	43.2	76.7	44.2	82.7
1982	51.3	35.5	47.6	77.7	51.7	49.2	46.6	41.4	73.6	43.9	78.0
1983	51.3	37.5	48.4	74.1	51.7	49.6	47.2	43.1	73.1	45.3	73.6
1984	54.7	41.8	51.0	77.8	55.0	52.4	50.0	44.2	74.1	49.0	77.6
1985	57.1	44.8	53.0	79.1	57.4	53.8	51.2	45.6	72.7	52.0	78.8
1986	55.8	47.5	52.1	74.0	55.6	52.8	50.5	44.5	71.9	51.2	74.9
1987	55.6	49.3	52.0	72.3	55.2	53.4	51.4	45.5	72.6	51.3	73.5
1988	58.8	51.2	52.4	76.0	58.8	54.9	52.6	48.0	71.4	53.8	76.1
1989	60.0	51.6	53.6	75.9	60.4	56.1	53.2	51.1	74.4	54.6	76.6
1990	61.5	52.1	54.6	76.4	62.3	57.9	54.6	52.7	75.4	57.5	80.3
1991	62.6	52.5	60.5	76.7	63.3	59.4	55.9	53.8	77.3	59.7	81.8
1992	65.4	56.6	63.7	78.4	65.8	62.3	59.1	57.5	81.0	61.8	82.0
1993	67.9	58.9	70.0	80.1	68.2	65.8	62.6	62.4	84.2	64.8	84.2
1994	71.6	64.4	78.2	81.3	71.5	69.7	66.5	66.8	86.6	69.5	85.5
1995	74.8	69.1	79.3	82.8	74.8	73.5	70.1	72.5	86.9	74.4	87.8
1996	79.2	74.6	82.5	86.9	79.0	77.5	73.8	74.7	88.4	81.5	90.3
1997	85.4	80.2	89.8	90.8	85.5	82.2	80.0	78.0	91.1	85.0	90.9
1997 [1]	86.1	80.4	90.2	92.3	86.3	83.9	80.2	82.3	94.1	88.9	92.3
1998 [1]	91.2	87.5	91.2	94.1	91.7	88.6	86.1	85.8	96.6	93.2	92.9
1999 [1]	96.0	94.4	98.7	96.8	96.1	94.4	92.7	93.6	97.9	97.1	98.0
2000 [1]	100.0	100.0	100.0	100.0	100.0	100.0	100.0	100.0	100.0	100.0	100.0
2001 [1]	102.5	103.1	100.4	102.3	102.5	101.6	101.7	100.7	101.4	101.0	104.5
2002 [1]	104.5	105.3	101.8	103.5	104.6	102.5	102.1	102.0	104.1	102.3	106.1
2003 [1]	106.5	109.9	105.8	105.1	106.0	103.9	102.7	104.2	109.1	103.8	108.8
2004 [1]	111.2	113.9	112.2	108.4	110.8	107.4	105.1	113.2	112.4	108.0	109.9
2005 [1]	114.8	123.9	113.7	110.5	113.5	112.9	109.8	121.8	118.4	114.7	112.1
2006 [1]	120.6	132.2	116.9	114.2	119.3	117.3	113.1	124.9	122.1	121.9	119.4
2007 [1]	125.1	134.6	120.2	118.8	124.2	120.7	115.4	127.9	126.4	128.3	121.6

[1]NAICS basis, not continuous with previous years, which are based on the SIC. See notes and definitions.

Table 21-1. Gross Domestic Product by Region and State—*Continued*

(Billions of dollars; index numbers, 2000 = 100.)

Year	Far West						
	Total	Alaska	California	Hawaii	Nevada	Oregon	Washington
VALUE							
1977	311.5	7.5	228.5	9.4	7.5	22.3	36.3
1978	358.2	9.1	261.5	10.5	9.1	25.9	42.2
1979	402.6	10.9	291.9	11.9	10.6	29.0	48.4
1980	447.6	15.1	324.4	13.3	12.0	30.5	52.2
1981	504.9	21.7	365.2	14.5	13.6	32.0	58.0
1982	536.4	23.3	389.9	15.4	14.3	31.9	61.6
1983	579.5	22.5	423.9	16.8	15.4	34.0	66.8
1984	653.1	23.8	483.2	18.6	17.0	37.9	72.6
1985	708.7	26.2	528.0	20.0	18.5	40.1	75.9
1986	753.2	18.8	568.4	21.5	20.2	42.3	81.9
1987	820.8	22.3	620.2	23.3	22.4	45.0	87.7
1988	897.2	21.3	678.8	25.7	25.5	49.6	96.2
1989	973.1	23.4	734.4	28.4	28.6	53.3	105.1
1990	1 050.0	25.0	788.3	31.9	31.8	57.3	115.7
1991	1 073.3	22.2	801.2	33.6	33.6	60.1	122.7
1992	1 108.5	22.6	819.4	35.2	36.5	63.7	131.1
1993	1 140.6	23.0	833.7	35.9	40.0	69.2	138.8
1994	1 187.9	23.1	862.5	36.3	44.9	74.4	146.7
1995	1 250.8	24.8	909.0	36.6	49.0	80.1	151.3
1996	1 328.5	26.1	958.5	37.0	54.1	91.2	161.8
1997	1 424.3	26.9	1 028.6	37.9	58.9	97.5	174.4
1997 [1]	1 416.6	25.0	1 019.2	37.5	59.9	96.6	178.3
1998 [1]	1 507.0	23.2	1 085.9	37.5	63.6	101.0	195.8
1999 [1]	1 631.0	24.3	1 180.6	38.6	68.8	104.3	214.4
2000 [1]	1 762.5	27.0	1 287.1	40.2	73.7	112.4	222.0
2001 [1]	1 783.5	26.6	1 301.1	41.8	77.3	110.9	225.8
2002 [1]	1 843.0	29.2	1 340.4	43.5	81.3	117.1	231.5
2003 [1]	1 934.5	31.2	1 406.5	46.4	87.8	121.6	240.8
2004 [1]	2 091.3	35.1	1 519.4	50.4	100.2	132.8	253.2
2005 [1]	2 250.7	39.3	1 632.8	54.9	112.5	138.1	273.3
2006 [1]	2 409.3	43.1	1 742.2	58.7	123.1	151.0	291.3
2007 [1]	2 515.7	44.5	1 813.0	61.5	127.2	158.2	311.3
QUANTITY INDEX							
1977	40.9	66.3	40.8	61.4	26.7	38.7	41.3
1978	43.8	72.4	43.6	64.0	30.0	41.2	44.7
1979	45.7	76.0	45.2	67.6	32.2	42.9	47.6
1980	46.8	87.3	46.3	69.3	33.2	42.5	47.7
1981	48.2	100.6	47.9	68.0	34.4	41.2	48.9
1982	48.1	103.6	47.9	68.0	33.9	38.9	48.9
1983	49.7	101.0	49.8	70.4	34.9	39.2	49.9
1984	53.6	105.5	54.3	72.9	36.8	41.8	51.6
1985	56.3	117.3	57.4	74.9	38.4	43.0	52.2
1986	58.1	96.0	59.7	77.2	40.3	43.7	54.3
1987	61.5	112.2	63.3	80.8	42.7	45.0	56.4
1988	65.0	109.0	67.1	85.7	46.4	47.9	59.6
1989	67.9	112.7	69.9	91.3	50.3	49.4	62.7
1990	70.5	112.0	72.2	98.9	54.4	51.4	66.6
1991	69.6	100.2	70.8	99.8	55.5	52.2	68.1
1992	70.2	101.3	70.7	101.9	59.0	53.9	70.8
1993	70.2	100.3	70.0	101.1	63.2	56.6	72.7
1994	71.5	100.1	70.8	99.6	68.9	59.5	74.9
1995	73.9	105.0	73.4	98.3	73.1	63.1	75.3
1996	77.2	103.6	76.1	97.4	79.7	71.7	79.1
1997	81.5	104.8	80.5	97.6	84.8	76.5	84.0
1997 [1]	82.8	104.0	81.1	100.5	87.5	85.0	84.9
1998 [1]	87.8	99.0	86.1	98.4	90.7	89.7	92.0
1999 [1]	94.1	100.1	93.0	98.9	95.8	92.8	98.9
2000 [1]	100.0	100.0	100.0	100.0	100.0	100.0	100.0
2001 [1]	99.5	95.3	99.6	101.1	101.9	98.3	99.2
2002 [1]	101.1	103.7	100.9	102.2	104.6	102.3	99.6
2003 [1]	104.0	101.4	103.9	105.9	110.7	104.9	101.4
2004 [1]	109.3	107.0	109.3	111.0	121.9	111.9	103.6
2005 [1]	114.3	108.5	114.2	116.8	131.9	114.9	109.0
2006 [1]	119.0	112.9	118.6	120.5	139.1	123.8	112.8
2007 [1]	121.2	113.3	120.3	124.0	139.9	127.8	117.6

[1]NAICS basis, not continuous with previous years, which are based on the SIC. See notes and definitions.

Table 21-2. Personal Income and Employment by Region and State

(Millions of dollars, except as noted.)

Region or state and year	Personal income, total	Earnings by place of work			Less: Contributions for government social insurance	Plus: Adjustment for residence	Equals: Net earnings by place of residence	Plus: Dividends, interest, and rent	Plus: Personal current transfer receipts	Per capita (dollars)		Population (thousands)	Total employment (thousands)
		Nonfarm	Farm	Total						Personal income	Disposable personal income		
UNITED STATES													
1958	367 249	292 629	15 252	307 881	11 371	-204	296 306	47 413	23 529	2 109	1 888	174 153	. . .
1959	391 286	317 047	13 034	330 081	13 824	-217	316 040	50 939	24 306	2 209	1 970	177 136	. . .
1960	408 376	330 712	13 561	344 273	16 349	-285	327 639	54 997	25 740	2 269	2 014	179 972	. . .
1961	425 829	341 270	14 265	355 535	16 905	-279	338 351	58 028	29 450	2 327	2 070	182 976	. . .
1962	453 276	364 933	14 329	379 262	19 011	-233	360 018	62 866	30 392	2 440	2 164	185 739	. . .
1963	476 109	384 082	14 167	398 249	21 548	-208	376 493	67 407	32 209	2 527	2 238	188 434	. . .
1964	510 599	413 156	13 017	426 173	22 247	-207	403 719	73 376	33 504	2 672	2 400	191 085	. . .
1965	551 432	443 773	15 369	459 142	23 268	-152	435 722	79 532	36 178	2 850	2 553	193 457	. . .
1966	598 615	489 059	16 397	505 456	31 127	-143	474 186	84 812	39 617	3 062	2 723	195 499	. . .
1967	642 212	523 648	15 077	538 725	34 558	-143	504 024	90 174	48 014	3 254	2 885	197 375	. . .
1968	705 105	576 211	15 276	591 487	38 338	-170	552 979	96 032	56 094	3 538	3 104	199 312	. . .
1969	772 235	631 338	17 243	648 581	43 792	-163	604 626	105 287	62 322	3 836	3 321	201 298	91 057
1970	832 429	671 582	17 463	689 045	46 012	-175	642 858	114 838	74 733	4 085	3 582	203 799	91 282
1971	897 952	719 396	17 970	737 366	50 859	-198	686 309	123 395	88 248	4 342	3 853	206 818	91 586
1972	987 137	793 438	21 733	815 171	58 897	-229	756 045	132 962	98 130	4 717	4 129	209 275	94 317
1973	1 105 605	884 639	34 658	919 297	75 183	-244	843 870	148 887	112 848	5 231	4 607	211 349	98 433
1974	1 217 556	968 564	29 813	998 377	84 873	-264	913 240	170 677	133 639	5 707	5 002	213 334	100 118
1975	1 329 892	1 034 062	28 873	1 062 935	88 975	-313	973 647	185 821	170 424	6 172	5 489	215 457	98 907
1976	1 469 467	1 160 623	24 993	1 185 616	100 987	-339	1 084 290	200 695	184 482	6 754	5 965	217 554	101 597
1977	1 627 310	1 295 462	24 254	1 319 716	112 699	-377	1 206 640	225 919	194 751	7 405	6 509	219 761	105 049
1978	1 831 117	1 467 160	28 073	1 495 233	130 827	-410	1 363 996	256 812	210 309	8 245	7 215	222 098	109 689
1979	2 053 827	1 641 985	29 875	1 671 860	152 274	-398	1 519 188	298 510	236 129	9 146	7 952	224 569	113 289
1980	2 298 255	1 795 158	20 392	1 815 550	165 669	-454	1 649 427	368 611	280 217	10 114	8 802	227 225	114 231
1981	2 580 600	1 969 935	27 169	1 997 104	195 066	-443	1 801 595	459 858	319 147	11 246	9 746	229 466	115 304
1982	2 764 886	2 066 560	24 558	2 091 118	208 173	-520	1 882 425	527 092	355 369	11 935	10 410	231 664	114 557
1983	2 949 883	2 206 755	17 235	2 223 990	225 148	-508	1 998 334	567 273	384 276	12 618	11 114	233 792	116 057
1984	3 275 805	2 452 535	31 814	2 484 349	256 554	-579	2 227 216	647 861	400 728	13 891	12 294	235 825	121 091
1985	3 511 344	2 639 477	31 950	2 671 427	280 384	-603	2 390 440	695 617	425 287	14 758	13 008	237 924	124 510
1986	3 708 199	2 798 353	33 079	2 831 432	302 395	-575	2 528 462	728 615	451 122	15 442	13 626	240 133	126 970
1987	3 934 655	2 997 457	39 409	3 036 866	322 010	-608	2 714 248	752 842	467 565	16 240	14 226	242 289	130 400
1988	4 237 460	3 253 621	39 109	3 292 730	360 256	-651	2 931 823	809 089	496 548	17 331	15 271	244 499	134 507
1989	4 571 133	3 446 466	45 677	3 492 143	383 938	-664	3 107 541	920 199	543 393	18 520	16 231	246 819	137 200
1990	4 861 936	3 655 379	46 760	3 702 139	408 654	-737	3 292 748	973 575	595 613	19 477	17 108	249 623	139 381
1991	5 032 196	3 762 522	41 579	3 804 101	428 560	-788	3 374 753	991 122	666 321	19 892	17 578	252 981	138 606
1992	5 349 384	4 017 224	49 550	4 066 774	453 745	-797	3 612 232	987 898	749 254	20 854	18 478	256 514	139 162
1993	5 548 121	4 191 800	47 244	4 239 044	476 585	-798	3 761 661	996 465	789 995	21 346	18 862	259 919	141 779
1994	5 833 906	4 395 182	49 932	4 445 114	507 172	-860	3 937 082	1 069 567	827 257	22 172	19 550	263 126	145 224
1995	6 144 741	4 622 731	39 675	4 662 406	531 848	-893	4 129 665	1 137 710	877 366	23 076	20 286	266 278	148 983
1996	6 512 485	4 868 019	54 906	4 922 925	554 248	-914	4 367 763	1 219 791	924 931	24 175	21 089	269 394	152 150
1997	6 907 332	5 180 807	52 982	5 233 789	586 178	-969	4 646 642	1 309 556	951 134	25 334	21 941	272 647	155 608
1998	7 415 709	5 591 837	49 748	5 641 585	623 147	-1 022	5 017 416	1 419 686	978 607	26 883	23 163	275 854	159 628
1999	7 796 137	5 975 196	49 774	6 024 970	660 395	-1 030	5 363 545	1 410 543	1 022 049	27 939	23 974	279 040	162 955
2000	8 422 074	6 460 197	44 482	6 504 679	701 650	-1 060	5 801 969	1 536 284	1 083 821	29 847	25 472	282 172	166 759
2001	8 716 992	6 665 188	42 811	6 707 999	730 005	-1 093	5 976 901	1 546 360	1 193 731	30 582	26 245	285 040	167 015
2002	8 872 871	6 817 857	33 461	6 851 318	748 787	-1 162	6 101 369	1 485 161	1 286 341	30 838	27 186	287 727	166 633
2003	9 150 320	7 060 393	48 530	7 108 923	777 556	-1 198	6 330 169	1 468 652	1 351 499	31 530	28 084	290 211	167 554
2004	9 711 363	7 510 105	57 358	7 567 463	827 415	-1 228	6 738 820	1 549 599	1 422 944	33 157	29 588	292 892	170 513
2005	10 252 973	7 915 453	54 457	7 969 910	872 860	-1 257	7 095 793	1 636 711	1 520 469	34 690	30 608	295 561	174 228
2006	10 978 053	8 394 381	38 369	8 432 750	924 059	-1 292	7 507 399	1 868 206	1 602 448	36 794	32 263	298 363	177 818
2007	11 634 322	8 793 506	54 734	8 848 240	964 574	-1 431	7 882 235	2 039 293	1 712 794	38 615	33 665	301 290	180 944
2008	12 086 534	9 054 634	56 192	9 110 826	995 910	-1 482	8 113 434	2 103 377	1 869 723	39 751	34 949	304 060	. . .

. . . = Not available.

Table 21-2. Personal Income and Employment by Region and State—*Continued*

(Millions of dollars, except as noted.)

Region or state and year	Personal income, total	Earnings by place of work — Nonfarm	Farm	Total	Less: Contributions for government social insurance	Plus: Adjustment for residence	Equals: Net earnings by place of residence	Plus: Dividends, interest, and rent	Plus: Personal current transfer receipts	Per capita (dollars) — Personal income	Disposable personal income	Population (thousands)	Total employment (thousands)
NEW ENGLAND													
1958	23 237	18 684	317	19 002	722	18	18 297	3 250	1 690	2 274	2 019	10 219	. . .
1959	24 798	20 248	248	20 496	872	20	19 644	3 468	1 686	2 376	2 103	10 437	. . .
1960	25 854	21 094	315	21 408	1 025	27	20 411	3 682	1 761	2 455	2 154	10 532	. . .
1961	27 111	21 999	266	22 265	1 073	28	21 220	3 914	1 977	2 542	2 241	10 666	. . .
1962	28 786	23 401	256	23 657	1 215	31	22 473	4 306	2 007	2 665	2 344	10 800	. . .
1963	30 043	24 325	248	24 573	1 357	36	23 252	4 665	2 126	2 735	2 400	10 986	. . .
1964	32 186	25 882	286	26 168	1 400	42	24 810	5 170	2 207	2 877	2 568	11 186	. . .
1965	34 527	27 608	337	27 945	1 450	44	26 539	5 658	2 330	3 048	2 712	11 329	. . .
1966	37 550	30 471	341	30 812	1 937	51	28 926	6 113	2 512	3 285	2 899	11 430	. . .
1967	40 858	32 904	237	33 141	2 133	58	31 066	6 710	3 082	3 534	3 107	11 562	. . .
1968	44 339	35 781	264	36 045	2 367	71	33 748	6 908	3 682	3 810	3 300	11 637	. . .
1969	49 110	38 952	292	39 244	2 634	850	37 460	7 541	4 110	4 185	3 580	11 735	5 516
1970	52 799	41 507	304	41 811	2 769	856	39 898	8 000	4 902	4 445	3 868	11 878	5 518
1971	56 146	43 683	281	43 964	3 008	884	41 840	8 432	5 874	4 680	4 130	11 996	5 454
1972	60 795	47 663	285	47 948	3 449	941	45 440	8 949	6 406	5 029	4 372	12 088	5 573
1973	66 585	52 617	395	53 013	4 355	997	49 655	9 734	7 195	5 481	4 795	12 148	5 783
1974	72 433	56 312	427	56 739	4 823	1 084	52 999	10 905	8 530	5 958	5 204	12 157	5 843
1975	77 693	58 564	310	58 874	4 913	1 171	55 131	11 426	11 135	6 381	5 657	12 176	5 685
1976	84 949	64 843	426	65 269	5 515	1 300	61 053	12 228	11 667	6 959	6 121	12 207	5 811
1977	93 075	71 649	382	72 030	6 127	1 453	67 356	13 611	12 109	7 593	6 663	12 257	6 007
1978	103 505	80 717	393	81 110	7 097	1 636	75 649	15 052	12 804	8 413	7 334	12 303	6 280
1979	115 950	90 631	376	91 006	8 287	1 868	84 587	17 099	14 264	9 392	8 123	12 345	6 515
1980	131 495	100 572	365	100 936	9 186	2 184	93 935	21 156	16 404	10 629	9 164	12 372	6 641
1981	147 313	110 056	468	110 524	10 801	2 360	102 084	26 458	18 771	11 846	10 151	12 436	6 692
1982	160 475	117 752	511	118 263	11 790	2 538	109 011	30 943	20 521	12 871	11 095	12 468	6 694
1983	173 474	128 988	477	129 465	13 042	2 671	119 094	32 462	21 918	13 829	12 050	12 544	6 828
1984	194 956	145 754	564	146 318	15 170	2 851	134 000	37 985	22 971	15 422	13 505	12 642	7 198
1985	210 807	159 769	554	160 324	16 763	3 009	146 570	40 070	24 166	16 546	14 396	12 741	7 447
1986	227 430	173 818	572	174 390	18 460	3 186	159 116	42 941	25 374	17 722	15 338	12 833	7 687
1987	247 610	191 880	637	192 517	20 144	3 353	175 726	45 790	26 095	19 119	16 431	12 951	7 828
1988	272 305	212 023	653	212 677	22 610	3 553	193 620	50 631	28 054	20 811	18 091	13 085	8 082
1989	291 087	221 728	601	222 329	23 600	3 478	202 207	57 540	31 340	22 083	19 157	13 182	8 072
1990	300 474	226 118	683	226 801	24 139	3 468	206 130	59 311	35 033	22 712	19 749	13 230	7 918
1991	304 280	225 468	629	226 097	24 576	3 464	204 986	58 851	40 443	22 969	20 068	13 248	7 585
1992	320 794	238 304	790	239 094	25 752	4 699	218 041	58 892	43 861	24 172	21 092	13 271	7 624
1993	330 058	247 633	733	248 366	26 959	4 136	225 544	59 163	45 351	24 752	21 510	13 334	7 748
1994	344 112	258 270	681	258 951	28 549	3 937	234 339	62 048	47 724	25 687	22 279	13 396	7 843
1995	361 504	270 708	604	271 313	30 077	4 736	245 972	64 974	50 558	26 832	23 136	13 473	7 938
1996	382 164	285 093	694	285 787	31 483	5 568	259 872	70 219	52 073	28 194	24 026	13 555	8 069
1997	404 990	304 268	598	304 867	33 623	5 185	276 428	74 302	54 260	29 687	25 007	13 642	8 228
1998	435 052	327 646	622	328 268	35 767	6 648	299 149	80 797	55 106	31 677	26 452	13 734	8 402
1999	458 387	351 831	674	352 505	38 053	6 557	321 009	80 582	56 796	33 126	27 510	13 838	8 562
2000	503 961	388 102	674	388 776	41 223	6 869	354 422	89 556	59 982	36 120	29 521	13 952	8 776
2001	524 402	402 212	596	402 808	42 658	6 275	366 425	92 812	65 165	37 332	30 818	14 047	8 835
2002	528 030	406 020	519	406 539	43 372	5 623	368 791	88 730	70 509	37 378	32 171	14 127	8 776
2003	538 413	415 677	549	416 226	44 302	5 279	377 203	86 996	74 214	37 966	33 007	14 181	8 755
2004	569 244	442 387	653	443 040	47 225	5 949	401 764	89 733	77 747	40 081	34 892	14 202	8 898
2005	592 994	460 485	558	461 044	49 038	6 053	418 059	92 348	82 588	41 736	35 882	14 208	9 022
2006	634 406	483 093	470	483 563	51 376	6 467	438 653	109 278	86 475	44 574	38 090	14 233	9 079
2007	673 337	506 516	635	507 151	53 713	6 614	460 052	121 041	92 245	47 221	40 029	14 259	9 155
2008	696 792	520 811	595	521 407	55 466	6 944	472 885	124 257	99 650	48 715	41 650	14 304	. . .

. . . = Not available.

Table 21-2. Personal Income and Employment by Region and State—*Continued*

(Millions of dollars, except as noted.)

Region or state and year	Personal income, total	Earnings by place of work Nonfarm	Farm	Total	Less: Contributions for government social insurance	Plus: Adjustment for residence	Equals: Net earnings by place of residence	Plus: Dividends, interest, and rent	Plus: Personal current transfer receipts	Per capita Personal income	Per capita Disposable personal income	Population (thousands)	Total employment (thousands)
MIDEAST													
1958	90 864	75 901	985	76 886	3 047	-582	73 256	11 892	5 715	2 409	2 124	37 721	. . .
1959	96 289	81 169	787	81 955	3 679	-623	77 653	12 702	5 935	2 521	2 212	38 202	. . .
1960	100 494	84 920	890	85 810	4 353	-749	80 708	13 666	6 119	2 604	2 279	38 597	. . .
1961	104 502	87 673	893	88 565	4 580	-780	83 205	14 303	6 994	2 670	2 338	39 133	. . .
1962	110 533	92 962	721	93 683	5 116	-792	87 775	15 607	7 150	2 795	2 440	39 552	. . .
1963	115 398	96 647	783	97 431	5 641	-828	90 962	16 844	7 593	2 879	2 512	40 083	. . .
1964	123 680	103 129	790	103 919	5 691	-887	97 341	18 478	7 861	3 050	2 701	40 555	. . .
1965	132 265	109 860	884	110 743	5 938	-926	103 879	19 981	8 405	3 224	2 844	41 025	. . .
1966	142 545	120 014	903	120 916	7 889	-1 004	112 023	21 121	9 401	3 446	3 021	41 360	. . .
1967	153 635	128 437	961	129 398	8 607	-1 171	119 620	22 413	11 602	3 692	3 220	41 617	. . .
1968	168 522	140 404	912	141 316	9 391	-1 292	130 633	24 017	13 872	4 020	3 474	41 924	. . .
1969	181 847	152 341	1 093	153 435	11 063	-1 763	140 609	25 972	15 266	4 318	3 681	42 111	19 435
1970	196 035	162 686	1 051	163 737	11 648	-1 676	150 413	27 506	18 116	4 611	3 985	42 517	19 469
1971	209 754	172 600	959	173 559	12 763	-1 757	159 039	28 964	21 751	4 893	4 285	42 870	19 304
1972	226 753	187 174	952	188 126	14 524	-1 928	171 674	30 644	24 435	5 274	4 553	42 992	19 526
1973	246 067	204 210	1 373	205 582	18 181	-2 067	185 334	33 415	27 318	5 744	4 988	42 837	19 973
1974	267 975	219 769	1 272	221 041	20 147	-2 304	198 590	37 559	31 826	6 274	5 427	42 709	19 960
1975	289 442	231 378	1 180	232 557	20 828	-2 632	209 098	39 856	40 487	6 774	5 949	42 728	19 485
1976	313 595	251 815	1 263	253 078	22 884	-2 988	227 206	42 683	43 707	7 350	6 424	42 667	19 568
1977	341 719	275 240	1 081	276 321	24 856	-3 397	248 068	47 609	46 041	8 032	6 982	42 547	19 855
1978	375 225	304 666	1 290	305 957	28 197	-3 929	273 831	52 546	48 848	8 845	7 660	42 421	20 412
1979	413 568	335 719	1 499	337 218	32 242	-4 599	300 377	59 582	53 610	9 764	8 395	42 358	20 900
1980	461 074	366 473	1 115	367 589	35 077	-5 472	327 039	72 378	61 657	10 907	9 373	42 272	20 962
1981	513 728	400 069	1 477	401 546	40 900	-6 096	354 550	89 636	69 543	12 137	10 351	42 329	21 061
1982	555 698	423 565	1 441	425 007	43 908	-6 361	374 738	103 732	77 228	13 112	11 214	42 382	20 945
1983	592 905	451 999	1 072	453 071	47 823	-6 483	398 764	110 628	83 513	13 936	12 083	42 544	21 140
1984	655 004	499 159	1 879	501 037	54 352	-6 832	439 853	128 241	86 910	15 345	13 339	42 687	21 891
1985	700 965	537 095	1 993	539 089	59 534	-7 145	472 409	137 210	91 346	16 380	14 176	42 794	22 485
1986	745 867	576 142	2 176	578 318	64 727	-7 570	506 021	143 331	96 515	17 349	15 010	42 991	22 996
1987	797 403	624 822	2 275	627 096	69 438	-8 069	549 589	148 639	99 174	18 463	15 832	43 190	23 505
1988	868 226	685 292	2 183	687 475	78 001	-8 776	600 698	162 243	105 285	19 989	17 295	43 435	24 124
1989	935 223	723 215	2 551	725 765	82 280	-9 049	634 436	186 854	113 933	21 457	18 486	43 585	24 412
1990	989 039	762 655	2 443	765 098	86 817	-9 850	668 431	195 844	124 764	22 601	19 569	43 762	24 476
1991	1 016 388	773 800	2 066	775 866	89 611	-10 425	675 831	199 744	140 813	23 063	20 110	44 071	23 904
1992	1 069 395	820 468	2 600	823 069	94 257	-12 216	716 596	195 997	156 802	24 090	21 021	44 392	23 796
1993	1 095 679	845 769	2 537	848 306	97 857	-12 146	738 302	192 182	165 194	24 502	21 308	44 717	23 915
1994	1 133 109	872 295	2 302	874 598	102 909	-11 974	759 714	202 048	171 348	25 197	21 864	44 970	24 084
1995	1 189 144	911 867	1 783	913 650	106 722	-13 142	793 786	213 982	181 376	26 317	22 793	45 186	24 376
1996	1 252 041	955 150	2 727	957 877	109 947	-13 630	834 300	226 610	191 130	27 588	23 716	45 384	24 602
1997	1 319 270	1 009 108	1 877	1 010 985	114 752	-14 012	882 222	243 551	193 498	28 944	24 665	45 580	24 971
1998	1 404 640	1 081 158	2 370	1 083 528	121 047	-15 313	947 168	259 099	198 373	30 654	25 973	45 822	25 416
1999	1 467 261	1 145 465	2 430	1 147 895	127 305	-16 820	1 003 770	257 372	206 119	31 824	26 804	46 106	25 900
2000	1 580 733	1 231 448	2 699	1 234 147	135 130	-15 670	1 083 347	279 930	217 456	34 080	28 579	46 383	26 540
2001	1 627 895	1 266 667	2 540	1 269 207	141 240	-15 191	1 112 776	278 002	237 117	34 925	29 222	46 612	26 653
2002	1 648 005	1 291 272	1 851	1 293 123	144 909	-16 065	1 132 149	262 297	253 559	35 191	30 378	46 830	26 615
2003	1 690 345	1 329 016	2 647	1 331 663	149 067	-16 152	1 166 445	257 176	266 724	35 946	31 360	47 025	26 732
2004	1 794 306	1 416 097	3 263	1 419 360	157 133	-17 126	1 245 101	268 074	281 131	38 014	33 176	47 202	27 167
2005	1 890 644	1 489 749	2 913	1 492 662	164 523	-17 501	1 310 638	290 358	289 649	39 955	34 473	47 319	27 651
2006	2 020 419	1 579 294	2 304	1 581 598	173 763	-18 764	1 389 071	324 952	306 396	42 595	36 483	47 433	27 952
2007	2 143 472	1 666 156	3 214	1 669 370	182 387	-19 796	1 467 187	353 475	322 810	45 058	38 271	47 571	28 273
2008	2 225 405	1 721 982	3 165	1 725 148	188 943	-20 801	1 515 403	361 690	348 312	46 635	39 903	47 720	. . .

. . . = Not available.

Table 21-2. Personal Income and Employment by Region and State—*Continued*

(Millions of dollars, except as noted.)

Region or state and year	Personal income, total	Derivation of personal income									Per capita (dollars)		Population (thousands)	Total employment (thousands)
		Earnings by place of work			Less: Contributions for government social insurance	Plus: Adjustment for residence	Equals: Net earnings by place of residence	Plus: Dividends, interest, and rent	Plus: Personal current transfer receipts		Personal income	Disposable personal income		
		Nonfarm	Farm	Total										
GREAT LAKES														
1958	79 768	64 987	2 400	67 388	2 492	-112	64 784	9 925	5 059		2 242	2 008	35 578	. . .
1959	85 126	70 816	1 903	72 719	3 045	-126	69 547	10 636	4 943		2 369	2 115	35 928	. . .
1960	88 445	73 432	1 976	75 408	3 656	-124	71 629	11 559	5 257		2 437	2 159	36 290	. . .
1961	90 551	73 553	2 402	75 954	3 617	-112	72 226	12 195	6 130		2 473	2 204	36 616	. . .
1962	96 107	78 602	2 309	80 911	4 043	-116	76 753	13 201	6 154		2 603	2 308	36 927	. . .
1963	100 629	82 530	2 311	84 842	4 561	-114	80 166	14 119	6 343		2 694	2 385	37 357	. . .
1964	108 246	89 273	1 999	91 273	4 762	-122	86 389	15 383	6 474		2 859	2 564	37 868	. . .
1965	118 260	97 093	2 587	99 680	4 946	-134	94 600	16 725	6 935		3 079	2 752	38 405	. . .
1966	128 663	107 168	2 921	110 089	6 742	-147	103 201	17 933	7 529		3 303	2 932	38 951	. . .
1967	135 549	112 492	2 495	114 987	7 271	-136	107 581	18 959	9 009		3 445	3 049	39 347	. . .
1968	147 984	123 164	2 399	125 563	7 985	-146	117 432	20 140	10 413		3 733	3 265	39 645	. . .
1969	161 216	134 765	2 823	137 588	9 310	287	128 564	21 319	11 332		4 040	3 475	39 904	17 785
1970	169 065	139 828	2 468	142 296	9 504	262	133 055	22 464	13 547		4 193	3 647	40 320	17 630
1971	181 621	149 081	2 856	151 936	10 425	334	141 845	23 673	16 103		4 471	3 941	40 622	17 549
1972	198 554	163 794	3 114	166 907	12 096	383	155 195	25 387	17 973		4 864	4 227	40 824	17 933
1973	222 988	183 726	5 158	188 884	15 629	435	173 689	28 362	20 937		5 446	4 759	40 947	18 710
1974	242 749	197 733	4 588	202 321	17 400	535	185 457	32 361	24 931		5 915	5 153	41 037	18 911
1975	261 436	205 408	5 752	211 160	17 671	628	194 118	35 288	32 030		6 360	5 614	41 105	18 399
1976	289 361	232 056	4 759	236 815	20 243	776	217 348	37 821	34 192		7 026	6 144	41 187	18 891
1977	321 800	260 950	4 757	265 707	22 759	959	243 908	42 176	35 716		7 782	6 770	41 353	19 508
1978	357 361	292 752	4 425	297 177	26 310	1 185	272 053	46 904	38 404		8 609	7 452	41 510	20 196
1979	394 863	321 395	5 134	326 529	29 955	1 405	297 979	53 456	43 428		9 489	8 182	41 611	20 520
1980	428 890	334 970	3 223	338 193	30 983	1 681	308 891	65 489	54 510		10 287	8 933	41 694	20 024
1981	468 448	357 480	3 605	361 085	35 487	1 440	327 038	80 802	60 608		11 248	9 729	41 648	19 862
1982	489 802	361 458	2 869	364 327	36 419	1 338	329 246	92 540	68 016		11 805	10 344	41 492	19 315
1983	514 149	380 781	-168	380 614	38 830	1 319	343 102	98 364	72 682		12 429	10 929	41 366	19 335
1984	568 589	421 539	4 319	425 858	44 244	1 423	383 037	111 096	74 456		13 736	12 136	41 393	20 120
1985	603 916	450 343	4 886	455 229	48 176	1 462	408 515	117 214	78 187		14 581	12 835	41 418	20 605
1986	634 420	475 878	4 409	480 287	51 707	1 531	430 111	122 456	81 853		15 304	13 487	41 455	21 050
1987	665 925	504 152	4 956	509 108	54 365	1 600	456 343	125 466	84 116		16 012	14 013	41 590	21 651
1988	711 001	546 216	3 304	549 520	60 533	1 724	490 711	132 499	87 791		17 042	14 974	41 721	22 219
1989	762 846	576 310	6 917	583 227	64 389	1 763	520 600	148 027	94 218		18 218	15 925	41 873	22 717
1990	804 166	605 942	5 825	611 767	68 063	1 966	545 671	155 614	102 881		19 105	16 725	42 091	23 093
1991	828 639	624 201	3 411	627 612	71 309	2 014	558 316	157 550	112 773		19 499	17 154	42 496	23 003
1992	884 713	669 058	5 717	674 776	75 713	2 245	601 308	159 796	123 609		20 621	18 213	42 903	23 126
1993	918 620	700 714	5 058	705 771	80 221	2 335	627 886	161 006	129 728		21 228	18 651	43 275	23 512
1994	975 700	745 488	5 695	751 183	86 536	2 549	667 196	174 775	133 729		22 384	19 607	43 590	24 215
1995	1 021 606	781 585	3 253	784 838	91 002	2 683	696 520	184 396	140 689		23 259	20 302	43 924	24 876
1996	1 073 297	812 452	6 713	819 165	93 998	2 994	728 161	197 605	147 531		24 261	21 032	44 239	25 274
1997	1 132 660	856 122	6 766	862 889	98 451	3 340	767 777	212 193	152 690		25 457	21 951	44 494	25 674
1998	1 207 487	916 993	5 562	922 556	103 148	3 466	822 873	229 877	154 737		26 996	23 179	44 728	26 131
1999	1 255 454	969 950	4 158	974 108	108 420	3 884	869 572	224 886	160 996		27 918	23 964	44 969	26 548
2000	1 333 971	1 024 233	4 264	1 028 498	111 902	4 245	920 840	242 503	170 627		29 498	25 334	45 222	26 986
2001	1 359 189	1 040 895	3 569	1 044 465	114 167	4 493	934 791	237 352	187 045		29 913	25 823	45 438	26 700
2002	1 386 117	1 068 457	1 999	1 070 457	116 016	4 570	959 010	228 113	198 993		30 394	26 789	45 605	26 454
2003	1 428 321	1 109 097	4 646	1 113 744	119 753	4 683	998 674	221 018	208 629		31 213	27 840	45 760	26 399
2004	1 476 856	1 149 095	7 523	1 156 617	125 925	5 042	1 035 735	225 172	215 949		32 161	28 772	45 921	26 714
2005	1 523 374	1 182 223	5 226	1 187 449	131 054	5 377	1 061 772	230 643	230 960		33 091	29 369	46 036	27 033
2006	1 594 771	1 224 783	4 628	1 229 412	136 356	5 706	1 098 761	253 625	242 384		34 545	30 487	46 165	27 133
2007	1 681 092	1 267 192	7 734	1 274 926	140 382	6 053	1 140 597	277 269	263 226		36 318	31 941	46 288	27 216
2008	1 735 439	1 290 753	9 615	1 300 368	143 380	6 463	1 163 451	285 670	286 319		37 405	33 143	46 396	. . .

. . . = Not available.

Table 21-2. Personal Income and Employment by Region and State—*Continued*

(Millions of dollars, except as noted.)

Region or state and year	Personal income, total	Earnings by place of work			Less: Contributions for government social insurance	Plus: Adjustment for residence	Equals: Net earnings by place of residence	Plus: Dividends, interest, and rent	Plus: Personal current transfer receipts	Per capita (dollars)		Population (thousands)	Total employment (thousands)
		Nonfarm	Farm	Total						Personal income	Disposable personal income		
PLAINS													
1958	30 375	21 265	3 831	25 097	826	7	24 278	4 140	1 957	2 026	1 830	14 994	. . .
1959	31 179	22 993	2 664	25 657	1 000	8	24 665	4 417	2 097	2 052	1 852	15 195	. . .
1960	32 729	23 903	3 071	26 974	1 156	7	25 825	4 687	2 218	2 122	1 902	15 424	. . .
1961	33 917	24 786	2 983	27 769	1 211	6	26 564	4 888	2 464	2 178	1 953	15 570	. . .
1962	36 235	26 311	3 484	29 795	1 317	7	28 485	5 191	2 560	2 314	2 073	15 657	. . .
1963	37 686	27 544	3 414	30 959	1 493	3	29 469	5 521	2 696	2 398	2 145	15 715	. . .
1964	39 277	29 455	2 733	32 187	1 554	5	30 638	5 851	2 788	2 488	2 254	15 787	. . .
1965	43 108	31 395	4 048	35 443	1 632	4	33 815	6 272	3 021	2 725	2 463	15 819	. . .
1966	46 359	34 470	4 240	38 710	2 197	0	36 513	6 583	3 263	2 918	2 617	15 888	. . .
1967	48 663	36 961	3 623	40 583	2 549	-5	38 030	6 739	3 894	3 053	2 730	15 942	. . .
1968	53 037	40 516	3 625	44 141	2 837	-14	41 291	7 241	4 505	3 305	2 934	16 047	. . .
1969	58 083	44 468	4 157	48 626	3 164	-414	45 048	8 096	4 940	3 585	3 134	16 202	7 506
1970	62 780	47 467	4 378	51 845	3 342	-358	48 145	8 844	5 791	3 840	3 394	16 350	7 516
1971	67 510	50 815	4 554	55 369	3 697	-355	51 317	9 541	6 651	4 098	3 665	16 475	7 544
1972	74 631	55 480	6 091	61 571	4 228	-361	56 982	10 399	7 250	4 506	3 979	16 563	7 731
1973	87 442	61 770	11 224	72 994	5 405	-399	67 190	11 804	8 448	5 259	4 681	16 628	8 065
1974	92 655	68 191	7 590	75 782	6 194	-432	69 156	13 651	9 848	5 558	4 866	16 672	8 219
1975	101 551	73 769	7 410	81 179	6 600	-423	74 155	15 275	12 120	6 065	5 380	16 743	8 181
1976	109 353	83 446	4 328	87 774	7 518	-521	79 735	16 453	13 165	6 485	5 716	16 864	8 438
1977	121 183	92 400	5 110	97 510	8 276	-659	88 574	18 694	13 914	7 150	6 291	16 950	8 657
1978	137 405	104 056	7 733	111 789	9 619	-819	101 350	20 900	15 155	8 069	7 080	17 028	8 958
1979	151 909	116 763	6 495	123 259	11 228	-989	111 041	23 892	16 975	8 885	7 731	17 097	9 247
1980	164 453	126 038	1 769	127 807	12 066	-1 146	114 596	29 583	20 275	9 557	8 314	17 208	9 250
1981	186 200	135 956	5 340	141 296	13 919	-1 338	126 039	37 048	23 113	10 785	9 363	17 264	9 212
1982	198 366	140 880	3 935	144 815	14 702	-1 344	128 769	43 844	25 753	11 472	9 977	17 292	9 082
1983	208 000	149 764	1 509	151 273	15 683	-1 434	134 156	46 139	27 705	12 006	10 597	17 325	9 196
1984	232 330	165 627	6 435	172 062	17 725	-1 604	152 733	50 727	28 870	13 366	11 911	17 382	9 512
1985	245 609	175 442	7 372	182 814	19 127	-1 714	161 973	53 060	30 576	14 114	12 556	17 402	9 664
1986	256 417	183 830	7 972	191 802	20 442	-1 829	169 531	54 841	32 046	14 743	13 149	17 393	9 754
1987	269 790	195 341	9 709	205 050	21 670	-1 940	181 440	55 378	32 971	15 480	13 717	17 428	10 009
1988	282 070	208 831	7 312	216 144	24 068	-2 103	189 972	57 506	34 591	16 088	14 260	17 533	10 221
1989	302 898	221 060	9 071	230 131	25 672	-2 186	202 274	63 155	37 469	17 215	15 193	17 595	10 427
1990	320 841	233 098	10 157	243 255	27 311	-2 429	213 515	66 828	40 499	18 129	15 987	17 698	10 617
1991	333 016	242 685	7 919	250 604	28 836	-2 481	219 286	69 176	44 554	18 663	16 544	17 843	10 667
1992	355 443	260 395	10 305	270 700	30 671	-2 726	237 302	69 859	48 282	19 718	17 507	18 026	10 778
1993	364 761	272 319	6 124	278 443	32 318	-2 813	243 312	70 294	51 155	20 031	17 720	18 210	11 004
1994	389 452	288 145	10 081	298 225	34 685	-3 032	260 509	75 507	53 436	21 188	18 730	18 381	11 301
1995	406 860	303 842	5 682	309 524	36 499	-3 171	269 854	80 406	56 600	21 934	19 298	18 550	11 611
1996	437 288	320 004	13 336	333 340	38 271	-3 394	291 675	86 163	59 450	23 378	20 468	18 705	11 836
1997	460 385	339 516	10 525	350 041	40 508	-3 805	305 728	93 219	61 438	24 422	21 257	18 851	12 054
1998	492 324	365 434	9 778	375 212	43 015	-4 066	328 132	100 976	63 216	25 928	22 520	18 988	12 316
1999	511 507	387 838	7 398	395 236	45 317	-4 402	345 517	99 915	66 075	26 737	23 251	19 131	12 510
2000	545 882	412 558	7 075	419 634	47 513	-4 695	367 426	107 850	70 606	28 327	24 565	19 270	12 696
2001	562 733	425 963	5 678	431 641	49 299	-4 827	377 515	107 646	77 572	29 055	25 268	19 368	12 692
2002	576 806	439 790	3 700	443 490	50 533	-4 963	387 994	105 060	83 752	29 650	26 320	19 454	12 662
2003	598 619	455 465	8 828	464 293	52 329	-4 994	406 970	104 367	87 282	30 637	27 495	19 539	12 665
2004	630 728	481 879	11 259	493 138	55 150	-5 195	432 793	107 073	90 862	32 105	28 916	19 646	12 880
2005	654 764	502 003	11 781	513 785	57 761	-5 511	450 513	108 185	96 066	33 153	29 562	19 750	13 084
2006	688 129	526 740	6 887	533 627	61 002	-5 735	466 889	117 663	103 577	34 608	30 615	19 883	13 245
2007	734 120	553 353	12 971	566 324	63 914	-6 041	496 369	127 808	109 942	36 661	32 292	20 025	13 413
2008	770 668	575 646	16 899	592 545	66 837	-6 329	519 379	132 356	118 933	38 217	33 902	20 166	. . .

. . . = Not available.

Table 21-2. Personal Income and Employment by Region and State—*Continued*

(Millions of dollars, except as noted.)

Region or state and year	Personal income, total	Derivation of personal income								Per capita (dollars)		Population (thousands)	Total employment (thousands)
		Earnings by place of work			Less: Contributions for government social insurance	Plus: Adjustment for residence	Equals: Net earnings by place of residence	Plus: Dividends, interest, and rent	Plus: Personal current transfer receipts	Personal income	Disposable personal income		
		Nonfarm	Farm	Total									
SOUTHEAST													
1958	58 253	45 299	3 569	48 868	1 738	465	47 595	6 595	4 063	1 556	1 423	37 435	. . .
1959	62 411	49 084	3 459	52 543	2 106	505	50 942	7 122	4 347	1 637	1 489	38 115	. . .
1960	64 713	50 920	3 318	54 238	2 445	552	52 345	7 765	4 603	1 664	1 508	38 885	. . .
1961	68 143	52 712	3 735	56 446	2 510	578	54 514	8 334	5 295	1 723	1 565	39 544	. . .
1962	72 754	56 795	3 495	60 290	2 803	634	58 122	9 076	5 556	1 811	1 634	40 179	. . .
1963	77 570	60 759	3 716	64 475	3 284	691	61 881	9 788	5 901	1 904	1 717	40 742	. . .
1964	83 864	66 215	3 584	69 798	3 441	752	67 109	10 598	6 158	2 028	1 848	41 349	. . .
1965	91 117	72 211	3 464	75 675	3 675	854	72 854	11 540	6 723	2 177	1 976	41 857	. . .
1966	99 915	80 502	3 667	84 170	4 912	951	80 209	12 366	7 340	2 364	2 130	42 257	. . .
1967	108 436	87 252	3 664	90 916	5 655	1 104	86 365	13 325	8 746	2 545	2 291	42 611	. . .
1968	120 221	97 328	3 544	100 871	6 394	1 202	95 679	14 442	10 100	2 793	2 489	43 042	. . .
1969	133 396	107 868	4 024	111 892	7 217	1 134	105 808	16 202	11 386	3 071	2 698	43 440	19 085
1970	146 106	116 499	4 011	120 510	7 781	1 014	113 743	18 589	13 773	3 323	2 949	43 974	19 254
1971	161 148	127 812	4 227	132 039	8 838	988	124 189	20 686	16 273	3 580	3 202	45 013	19 635
1972	181 308	144 522	4 922	149 444	10 454	1 049	140 039	22 857	18 412	3 940	3 482	46 019	20 523
1973	207 012	164 064	7 235	171 299	13 505	1 118	158 913	26 278	21 821	4 405	3 915	46 992	21 636
1974	231 338	181 835	6 604	188 439	15 476	1 237	174 199	30 756	26 383	4 824	4 270	47 955	22 069
1975	253 040	193 691	5 947	199 638	16 283	1 478	184 832	33 964	34 244	5 187	4 675	48 788	21 642
1976	282 944	219 142	6 323	225 465	18 670	1 667	208 462	37 160	37 323	5 714	5 112	49 514	22 351
1977	314 833	246 134	5 721	251 855	20 907	1 900	232 848	42 236	39 748	6 258	5 581	50 312	23 208
1978	358 185	281 063	6 871	287 935	24 367	2 207	265 774	48 856	43 555	7 008	6 217	51 113	24 309
1979	404 319	315 506	6 775	322 281	28 409	2 574	296 446	57 632	50 241	7 779	6 860	51 977	25 020
1980	457 351	349 106	4 103	353 209	31 472	3 121	324 858	72 622	59 871	8 649	7 623	52 881	25 378
1981	518 648	385 765	6 570	392 335	37 325	3 556	358 566	91 563	68 520	9 671	8 495	53 627	25 676
1982	556 499	405 718	6 722	412 439	40 014	3 774	376 199	104 262	76 038	10 258	9 056	54 249	25 579
1983	600 314	437 897	4 862	442 759	43 707	3 836	402 888	114 568	82 858	10 943	9 740	54 856	26 113
1984	671 395	490 730	8 332	499 062	49 941	4 023	453 144	130 915	87 337	12 094	10 838	55 515	27 396
1985	723 822	530 457	7 382	537 838	54 907	4 222	487 154	143 419	93 250	12 880	11 476	56 199	28 243
1986	769 051	565 084	6 887	571 971	59 646	4 445	516 769	152 882	99 400	13 525	12 057	56 861	28 986
1987	821 022	608 702	8 255	616 958	63 886	4 748	557 820	159 675	103 527	14 270	12 660	57 536	29 714
1988	887 860	658 337	10 858	669 195	71 716	5 205	602 684	174 165	111 012	15 276	13 616	58 120	30 732
1989	964 369	698 612	11 314	709 926	77 054	5 561	638 432	202 339	123 598	16 419	14 573	58 733	31 473
1990	1 027 597	742 219	10 581	752 800	82 334	6 324	676 790	215 541	135 266	17 266	15 364	59 516	32 068
1991	1 074 251	768 714	12 167	780 881	86 845	6 868	700 903	220 417	152 931	17 756	15 887	60 501	31 940
1992	1 148 896	827 937	13 040	840 977	92 810	7 344	755 511	217 769	175 616	18 679	16 736	61 508	32 402
1993	1 206 516	874 804	12 636	887 440	98 854	7 742	796 328	225 313	184 875	19 295	17 248	62 531	33 414
1994	1 278 747	924 517	13 835	938 352	106 194	7 667	839 825	243 165	195 757	20 114	17 930	63 574	34 368
1995	1 354 691	977 844	12 425	990 270	112 353	8 006	885 923	258 650	210 118	20 970	18 645	64 602	35 493
1996	1 437 179	1 031 269	14 127	1 045 396	117 639	7 546	935 303	278 888	222 988	21 904	19 354	65 611	36 336
1997	1 523 242	1 093 453	14 329	1 107 781	124 948	8 337	991 170	300 536	231 535	22 853	20 070	66 655	37 295
1998	1 633 535	1 178 179	12 881	1 191 060	133 230	8 240	1 066 071	328 652	238 811	24 155	21 113	67 627	38 306
1999	1 716 450	1 258 627	13 444	1 272 072	141 274	9 685	1 140 483	326 126	249 841	25 032	21 854	68 569	39 177
2000	1 840 460	1 347 513	12 238	1 359 751	148 752	8 106	1 219 106	354 362	266 993	26 485	23 091	69 490	39 981
2001	1 922 935	1 401 277	13 008	1 414 285	155 921	8 024	1 266 388	361 369	295 178	27 356	23 942	70 294	40 027
2002	1 973 853	1 448 066	7 699	1 455 765	161 078	9 523	1 304 209	349 999	319 646	27 759	24 783	71 107	40 072
2003	2 040 368	1 507 909	11 836	1 519 744	167 844	9 845	1 361 746	344 310	334 313	28 380	25 600	71 894	40 485
2004	2 183 763	1 612 436	12 980	1 625 416	179 519	9 952	1 455 849	368 397	359 517	29 970	27 055	72 864	41 572
2005	2 315 029	1 710 779	14 014	1 724 793	191 152	10 261	1 543 902	375 716	395 412	31 324	27 950	73 907	42 605
2006	2 500 697	1 821 233	9 296	1 830 530	203 797	11 068	1 637 801	456 904	405 993	33 457	29 725	74 743	43 683
2007	2 642 863	1 898 448	10 155	1 908 604	212 537	12 023	1 708 090	500 779	433 995	34 859	30 812	75 815	44 560
2008	2 736 883	1 941 928	9 865	1 951 794	218 352	12 609	1 746 051	515 160	475 672	35 706	31 824	76 651	. . .

. . . = Not available.

Table 21-2. Personal Income and Employment by Region and State—*Continued*

(Millions of dollars, except as noted.)

Region or state and year	Personal income, total	Earnings by place of work			Less: Contribu-tions for govern-ment social insurance	Plus: Adjust-ment for residence	Equals: Net earnings by place of residence	Plus: Dividends, interest, and rent	Plus: Personal current transfer receipts	Per capita (dollars)		Population (thou-sands)	Total employ-ment (thou-sands)
		Nonfarm	Farm	Total						Personal income	Disposable personal income		
SOUTHWEST													
1958	25 372	19 745	1 627	21 372	708	3	20 666	3 267	1 438	1 866	1 686	13 598	...
1959	26 926	21 132	1 477	22 608	847	4	21 766	3 604	1 556	1 941	1 750	13 874	...
1960	27 935	21 939	1 458	23 397	1 005	5	22 397	3 894	1 645	1 962	1 764	14 235	...
1961	29 462	22 931	1 610	24 541	1 039	6	23 508	4 103	1 851	2 022	1 817	14 572	...
1962	30 964	24 374	1 393	25 767	1 131	9	24 645	4 324	1 995	2 074	1 858	14 930	...
1963	32 317	25 667	1 175	26 842	1 276	12	25 579	4 586	2 152	2 139	1 916	15 108	...
1964	34 600	27 667	1 113	28 781	1 329	14	27 465	4 889	2 247	2 265	2 059	15 278	...
1965	37 086	29 492	1 330	30 821	1 399	16	29 438	5 197	2 451	2 406	2 182	15 414	...
1966	40 256	32 568	1 389	33 957	1 881	17	32 093	5 489	2 674	2 586	2 327	15 567	...
1967	43 804	35 693	1 278	36 971	2 180	19	34 809	5 752	3 242	2 784	2 499	15 734	...
1968	48 805	39 886	1 410	41 296	2 450	24	38 869	6 123	3 812	3 051	2 710	15 998	...
1969	54 214	44 504	1 499	46 003	2 889	-71	43 044	6 920	4 250	3 320	2 912	16 328	7 219
1970	59 884	48 244	1 824	50 069	3 105	-84	46 880	7 968	5 037	3 603	3 197	16 621	7 311
1971	65 468	52 674	1 670	54 344	3 502	-88	50 754	8 830	5 883	3 834	3 443	17 077	7 457
1972	72 894	58 803	2 002	60 805	4 087	-106	56 612	9 690	6 592	4 165	3 698	17 503	7 807
1973	83 245	66 442	3 284	69 726	5 309	-119	64 298	11 110	7 836	4 639	4 139	17 943	8 215
1974	94 055	75 785	2 119	77 904	6 216	-80	71 608	13 094	9 354	5 124	4 528	18 354	8 511
1975	106 022	84 534	2 094	86 628	6 833	-47	79 748	14 446	11 827	5 643	5 060	18 789	8 633
1976	119 729	96 956	2 068	99 024	7 905	24	91 143	15 644	12 942	6 213	5 537	19 270	9 001
1977	134 097	110 113	1 847	111 959	9 030	-222	102 707	17 649	13 741	6 803	6 017	19 710	9 467
1978	154 990	128 346	1 666	130 011	10 769	-359	118 884	20 872	15 235	7 680	6 778	20 180	10 043
1979	179 873	148 041	2 960	151 001	12 999	-351	137 651	24 817	17 406	8 658	7 569	20 777	10 539
1980	207 566	169 583	1 510	171 092	14 993	-456	155 643	31 513	20 410	9 688	8 443	21 426	10 944
1981	243 542	196 004	2 820	198 824	18 612	-188	180 023	40 197	23 321	11 077	9 553	21 985	11 485
1982	266 878	211 431	2 338	213 769	20 507	-250	193 012	47 492	26 373	11 710	10 171	22 791	11 717
1983	282 870	221 074	2 388	223 462	21 383	-180	201 899	51 515	29 455	12 086	10 706	23 405	11 747
1984	313 020	244 032	2 649	246 681	24 036	-180	222 465	59 312	31 243	13 165	11 737	23 776	12 310
1985	337 065	261 602	2 557	264 159	26 108	-147	237 904	65 691	33 470	13 948	12 430	24 166	12 686
1986	344 430	265 084	2 559	267 643	26 812	-32	240 799	67 158	36 473	14 010	12 609	24 585	12 551
1987	354 107	271 650	3 504	275 153	27 210	59	248 002	67 579	38 526	14 309	12 814	24 748	12 860
1988	375 506	289 186	4 149	293 336	29 947	156	263 545	71 110	40 851	15 105	13 591	24 860	13 137
1989	402 842	306 386	4 078	310 464	31 925	238	278 777	78 949	45 116	16 060	14 378	25 083	13 331
1990	433 473	329 983	4 921	334 904	34 487	336	300 752	82 704	50 017	17 058	15 253	25 411	13 646
1991	454 182	346 721	4 471	351 193	37 087	293	314 399	84 341	55 442	17 524	15 752	25 917	13 850
1992	487 472	372 640	5 286	377 926	39 441	332	338 816	84 232	64 424	18 401	16 609	26 491	13 978
1993	514 272	396 136	6 178	402 314	41 994	380	360 700	84 645	68 927	18 966	17 091	27 116	14 427
1994	546 291	419 859	5 256	425 116	45 155	401	380 362	92 027	73 902	19 670	17 702	27 772	14 943
1995	580 621	446 364	4 263	450 627	47 850	381	403 158	98 193	79 269	20 430	18 351	28 420	15 498
1996	622 613	479 691	3 922	483 613	51 087	383	432 909	105 301	84 403	21 455	19 136	29 020	15 990
1997	674 420	523 385	5 083	528 468	55 200	372	473 640	112 833	87 948	22 765	20 174	29 625	16 588
1998	732 215	572 873	4 924	577 797	59 764	378	518 411	122 915	90 889	24 214	21 371	30 240	17 179
1999	776 129	614 351	7 023	621 375	63 353	467	558 488	122 930	94 711	25 177	22 236	30 827	17 543
2000	850 326	676 366	4 669	681 035	67 860	527	613 701	135 901	100 723	27 091	23 841	31 387	18 052
2001	892 795	710 498	5 229	715 727	71 681	383	644 430	136 517	111 848	27 962	24 723	31 929	18 216
2002	905 918	720 256	5 386	725 642	73 109	393	652 926	130 339	122 653	27 879	25 203	32 495	18 243
2003	939 250	746 746	5 834	752 579	76 722	445	676 302	132 073	130 875	28 452	25 963	33 012	18 443
2004	1 009 685	807 751	6 176	813 927	81 390	501	733 038	138 946	137 701	30 071	27 554	33 577	18 767
2005	1 101 099	870 971	5 603	876 574	87 670	468	789 372	159 724	152 003	32 181	29 136	34 215	19 420
2006	1 194 853	949 903	2 961	952 864	95 693	403	857 574	174 263	163 016	34 088	30 629	35 052	20 242
2007	1 279 385	1 012 679	4 692	1 017 372	102 111	189	915 451	186 727	177 208	35 768	31 971	35 769	20 953
2008	1 350 689	1 064 849	3 010	1 067 859	107 550	98	960 407	192 502	197 780	37 052	33 384	36 454	...

... = Not available.

Table 21-2. Personal Income and Employment by Region and State—*Continued*

(Millions of dollars, except as noted.)

Region or state and year	Personal income, total	Earnings by place of work			Less: Contributions for government social insurance	Plus: Adjustment for residence	Equals: Net earnings by place of residence	Plus: Dividends, interest, and rent	Plus: Personal current transfer receipts	Per capita (dollars)		Population (thousands)	Total employment (thousands)
		Nonfarm	Farm	Total						Personal income	Disposable personal income		
ROCKY MOUNTAIN													
1958	8 406	6 292	704	6 995	252	-3	6 741	1 134	531	2 031	1 829	4 139	. . .
1959	8 885	6 793	578	7 372	291	-3	7 078	1 214	594	2 103	1 885	4 226	. . .
1960	9 390	7 247	580	7 827	354	-3	7 471	1 295	624	2 159	1 923	4 350	. . .
1961	9 938	7 744	525	8 269	382	-3	7 885	1 363	690	2 210	1 968	4 497	. . .
1962	10 720	8 224	711	8 935	412	-3	8 520	1 479	721	2 341	2 092	4 580	. . .
1963	11 050	8 605	623	9 228	478	-2	8 748	1 545	758	2 386	2 126	4 632	. . .
1964	11 554	9 109	509	9 617	491	-2	9 125	1 652	777	2 473	2 243	4 673	. . .
1965	12 423	9 584	726	10 310	499	-2	9 810	1 773	840	2 643	2 395	4 700	. . .
1966	13 175	10 328	693	11 022	646	-1	10 375	1 898	902	2 782	2 506	4 735	. . .
1967	14 009	10 942	707	11 650	720	-1	10 928	2 011	1 069	2 929	2 628	4 783	. . .
1968	15 230	11 979	747	12 726	803	-1	11 922	2 093	1 215	3 128	2 783	4 868	. . .
1969	16 945	13 223	881	14 104	884	15	13 235	2 364	1 345	3 428	3 003	4 943	2 216
1970	18 959	14 580	995	15 575	965	16	14 626	2 732	1 601	3 763	3 337	5 038	2 271
1971	21 075	16 293	959	17 252	1 105	19	16 166	3 038	1 871	4 058	3 621	5 194	2 343
1972	23 910	18 534	1 260	19 794	1 323	22	18 493	3 327	2 090	4 454	3 945	5 368	2 482
1973	27 460	21 163	1 742	22 905	1 732	22	21 195	3 823	2 442	4 968	4 399	5 527	2 646
1974	31 054	23 917	1 825	25 741	2 006	25	23 760	4 457	2 838	5 497	4 842	5 650	2 740
1975	34 301	26 568	1 373	27 942	2 181	37	25 797	4 974	3 529	5 933	5 293	5 782	2 778
1976	38 235	30 309	1 016	31 325	2 515	42	28 852	5 503	3 879	6 463	5 731	5 916	2 912
1977	42 875	34 583	675	35 258	2 873	44	32 429	6 301	4 146	7 053	6 225	6 079	3 060
1978	49 738	40 290	941	41 231	3 414	54	37 872	7 330	4 536	7 949	7 005	6 257	3 257
1979	56 617	46 043	731	46 773	4 095	54	42 733	8 734	5 150	8 793	7 695	6 439	3 406
1980	64 677	51 329	946	52 275	4 581	78	47 772	10 865	6 040	9 811	8 603	6 592	3 482
1981	73 822	57 702	1 039	58 740	5 544	49	53 245	13 518	7 059	10 949	9 552	6 743	3 571
1982	79 932	61 325	814	62 138	6 011	51	56 179	15 721	8 032	11 578	10 131	6 904	3 608
1983	85 115	64 682	1 132	65 814	6 402	53	59 465	16 820	8 830	12 099	10 771	7 035	3 654
1984	92 828	70 926	1 028	71 953	7 181	72	64 845	18 766	9 217	13 058	11 680	7 109	3 817
1985	97 850	74 902	831	75 733	7 736	90	68 087	19 988	9 775	13 651	12 184	7 168	3 882
1986	100 722	76 478	1 226	77 704	8 060	112	69 756	20 475	10 491	13 989	12 528	7 200	3 876
1987	104 000	78 751	1 569	80 320	8 246	137	72 212	20 659	11 129	14 433	12 871	7 206	3 908
1988	109 048	83 306	1 618	84 924	9 098	174	76 000	21 332	11 717	15 140	13 505	7 203	4 047
1989	118 433	88 587	2 194	90 781	9 785	209	81 205	24 296	12 932	16 372	14 524	7 234	4 142
1990	127 012	95 147	2 682	97 829	10 634	245	87 439	25 594	13 979	17 387	15 368	7 305	4 260
1991	134 339	101 315	2 427	103 742	11 630	275	92 386	26 574	15 379	17 967	15 926	7 477	4 364
1992	144 661	110 240	2 489	112 730	12 591	306	100 445	27 139	17 077	18 796	16 640	7 696	4 464
1993	156 042	119 490	3 211	122 701	13 759	338	109 281	28 341	18 420	19 656	17 367	7 939	4 657
1994	166 759	128 150	2 035	130 184	14 930	389	115 643	31 818	19 299	20 408	17 969	8 171	4 919
1995	179 084	136 956	1 965	138 920	15 894	453	123 479	34 611	20 994	21 371	18 790	8 380	5 080
1996	192 538	146 540	2 182	148 723	16 746	525	132 502	37 720	22 316	22 478	19 636	8 565	5 284
1997	206 054	157 536	2 191	159 727	17 842	595	142 480	40 740	22 835	23 560	20 448	8 746	5 475
1998	223 844	171 306	2 411	173 716	18 724	689	155 681	44 601	23 562	25 100	21 698	8 918	5 663
1999	239 693	186 425	2 798	189 223	20 083	791	169 932	44 939	24 822	26 356	22 713	9 094	5 815
2000	264 024	206 838	1 994	208 831	21 824	857	187 864	49 481	26 680	28 485	24 433	9 269	6 013
2001	279 678	218 558	2 523	221 082	22 884	922	199 120	51 284	29 275	29 619	25 671	9 442	6 057
2002	283 369	222 241	1 936	224 177	23 660	938	201 455	49 707	32 207	29 561	26 266	9 586	6 048
2003	289 654	227 034	2 091	229 126	24 349	978	205 755	50 093	33 806	29 838	26 776	9 708	6 075
2004	308 950	242 850	2 544	245 393	25 913	1 060	220 540	53 089	35 321	31 337	28 191	9 859	6 234
2005	333 093	260 265	2 449	262 714	27 890	1 096	235 920	59 090	38 083	33 213	29 505	10 029	6 443
2006	359 796	281 042	1 447	282 489	30 372	1 151	253 267	65 481	41 047	35 082	30 834	10 256	6 665
2007	383 085	296 634	2 346	298 980	32 119	1 225	268 086	71 150	43 848	36 527	31 828	10 488	6 874
2008	400 800	309 085	1 812	310 898	33 480	1 268	278 686	74 030	48 084	37 459	32 931	10 700	. . .

. . . = Not available.

Table 21-2. Personal Income and Employment by Region and State—*Continued*

(Millions of dollars, except as noted.)

Region or state and year	Personal income, total	Earnings by place of work			Less: Contributions for government social insurance	Plus: Adjustment for residence	Equals: Net earnings by place of residence	Plus: Dividends, interest, and rent	Plus: Personal current transfer receipts	Per capita (dollars)		Population (thousands)	Total employment (thousands)
		Nonfarm	Farm	Total						Personal income	Disposable personal income		
FAR WEST													
1958	50 973	40 455	1 819	42 274	1 584	-1	40 689	7 209	3 076	2 490	2 229	20 469	. . .
1959	55 671	44 813	1 917	46 730	1 984	-1	44 745	7 777	3 148	2 631	2 349	21 159	. . .
1960	58 816	47 258	1 953	49 211	2 356	-2	46 854	8 449	3 513	2 716	2 400	21 659	. . .
1961	62 206	49 873	1 852	51 725	2 494	-2	49 229	8 928	4 049	2 780	2 460	22 378	. . .
1962	67 177	54 264	1 961	56 225	2 976	-4	53 245	9 682	4 250	2 906	2 569	23 114	. . .
1963	71 416	58 004	1 897	59 900	3 458	-6	56 436	10 340	4 640	2 999	2 649	23 811	. . .
1964	77 190	62 426	2 004	64 430	3 580	-7	60 843	11 355	4 992	3 165	2 844	24 389	. . .
1965	82 647	66 529	1 995	68 524	3 730	-8	64 786	12 387	5 474	3 318	2 982	24 908	. . .
1966	90 151	73 538	2 243	75 781	4 925	-10	70 846	13 309	5 996	3 562	3 180	25 311	. . .
1967	97 258	78 966	2 113	81 078	5 443	-11	75 624	14 264	7 370	3 773	3 357	25 779	. . .
1968	106 969	87 154	2 375	89 529	6 111	-14	83 404	15 068	8 496	4 090	3 600	26 151	. . .
1969	117 424	95 215	2 474	97 689	6 630	-201	90 858	16 873	9 693	4 409	3 844	26 635	12 295
1970	126 801	100 771	2 433	103 204	6 899	-205	96 099	18 736	11 966	4 679	4 150	27 101	12 313
1971	135 230	106 438	2 464	108 902	7 521	-222	101 159	20 230	13 842	4 905	4 400	27 570	12 301
1972	148 290	117 467	3 108	120 575	8 736	-228	111 611	21 709	14 970	5 312	4 687	27 918	12 742
1973	164 806	130 648	4 247	134 895	11 068	-231	123 596	24 360	16 850	5 818	5 173	28 328	13 405
1974	185 296	145 021	5 388	150 410	12 611	-328	137 471	27 894	19 931	6 434	5 701	28 801	13 865
1975	206 409	160 150	4 808	164 958	13 666	-524	150 768	30 591	25 051	7 034	6 308	29 346	14 104
1976	231 301	182 055	4 812	186 867	15 736	-640	170 491	33 204	27 606	7 728	6 872	29 929	14 625
1977	257 728	204 392	4 682	209 074	17 871	-454	190 750	37 643	29 335	8 435	7 456	30 553	15 287
1978	294 707	235 270	4 753	240 023	21 055	-385	218 583	44 352	31 772	9 420	8 274	31 285	16 235
1979	336 728	267 888	5 905	273 793	25 059	-360	248 374	53 298	35 056	10 534	9 196	31 965	17 141
1980	382 747	297 087	7 361	304 449	27 313	-444	276 692	65 005	41 051	11 676	10 198	32 780	17 549
1981	428 897	326 903	5 851	332 754	32 478	-226	300 050	80 635	48 212	12 828	11 219	33 434	17 744
1982	457 237	344 431	5 928	350 359	34 820	-268	315 271	88 558	53 408	13 414	11 834	34 086	17 618
1983	493 057	371 570	5 962	377 532	38 277	-290	338 966	96 777	57 314	14 202	12 585	34 716	18 044
1984	547 683	414 770	6 608	421 378	43 906	-332	377 140	110 819	59 724	15 506	13 759	35 321	18 847
1985	591 310	449 866	6 376	456 241	48 033	-379	407 829	118 965	64 516	16 408	14 491	36 037	19 498
1986	629 862	482 039	7 279	489 318	52 540	-418	436 360	124 532	68 970	17 109	15 112	36 815	20 070
1987	674 798	522 159	8 505	530 664	57 052	-496	473 116	129 655	72 026	17 927	15 676	37 641	20 926
1988	731 443	570 428	9 031	579 459	64 283	-583	514 592	139 604	77 247	18 978	16 721	38 542	21 944
1989	793 435	610 569	8 951	619 521	69 234	-677	549 609	159 037	84 789	20 070	17 510	39 534	22 626
1990	859 336	660 218	9 468	669 686	74 869	-796	594 021	172 139	93 175	21 160	18 510	40 610	23 304
1991	887 101	679 618	8 488	688 106	78 666	-795	608 645	174 471	103 985	21 413	18 881	41 428	23 293
1992	938 010	718 181	9 322	727 503	82 509	-781	644 213	174 213	119 583	22 214	19 711	42 226	22 994
1993	962 172	734 935	10 767	745 702	84 623	-771	660 308	175 520	126 345	22 482	19 937	42 798	23 102
1994	999 736	758 458	10 047	768 505	88 214	-797	679 494	188 179	132 063	23 104	20 458	43 271	23 551
1995	1 051 231	793 565	9 699	803 264	91 451	-840	710 973	202 498	137 761	24 031	21 186	43 745	24 111
1996	1 115 366	837 819	11 205	849 024	95 077	-906	753 041	217 285	145 040	25 169	21 950	44 314	24 760
1997	1 186 310	897 418	11 612	909 031	100 854	-980	807 197	232 181	146 931	26 331	22 751	45 054	25 324
1998	1 286 611	978 248	11 199	989 447	108 453	-1 065	879 930	252 769	153 913	28 093	24 115	45 798	26 214
1999	1 371 257	1 060 709	11 848	1 072 557	116 590	-1 192	954 775	253 792	162 690	29 486	24 949	46 506	26 901
2000	1 502 717	1 173 138	10 869	1 184 007	127 447	-1 298	1 055 262	276 701	170 754	31 839	26 520	47 198	27 715
2001	1 547 366	1 199 117	9 667	1 208 784	132 156	-1 172	1 075 456	281 378	190 532	32 297	27 311	47 910	27 834
2002	1 570 773	1 221 754	10 372	1 232 126	136 110	-1 181	1 094 835	270 916	205 022	32 371	28 406	48 524	27 765
2003	1 625 348	1 269 448	12 099	1 281 547	143 191	-1 282	1 137 074	272 618	215 656	33 108	29 310	49 092	28 000
2004	1 737 831	1 357 611	12 961	1 370 572	155 159	-1 412	1 214 000	299 115	224 716	35 021	31 053	49 622	28 279
2005	1 841 974	1 438 977	11 913	1 450 890	163 773	-1 500	1 285 618	320 648	235 708	36 768	32 158	50 097	28 971
2006	1 984 981	1 528 293	10 375	1 538 668	171 700	-1 587	1 365 381	366 040	253 559	39 230	34 109	50 599	29 818
2007	2 096 968	1 592 528	12 986	1 605 514	177 411	-1 699	1 426 404	401 044	269 521	41 056	35 497	51 075	30 499
2008	2 169 858	1 629 579	11 230	1 640 809	181 902	-1 733	1 457 173	417 713	294 972	41 994	36 708	51 671	. . .

. . . = Not available.

Table 21-2. Personal Income and Employment by Region and State—*Continued*

(Millions of dollars, except as noted.)

| Region or state and year | Personal income, total | Derivation of personal income | | | | | | | | Per capita (dollars) | | Population (thou-sands) | Total employ-ment (thou-sands) |
| | | Earnings by place of work | | | Less: Contribu-tions for govern-ment social insurance | Plus: Adjust-ment for residence | Equals: Net earnings by place of residence | Plus: Dividends, interest, and rent | Plus: Personal current transfer receipts | Personal income | Disposable personal income | | |
		Nonfarm	Farm	Total									
ALABAMA													
1958	4 595	3 670	304	3 974	135	1	3 839	412	344	1 453	1 331	3 163	. . .
1959	4 837	3 934	248	4 181	159	1	4 024	451	363	1 510	1 382	3 204	. . .
1960	5 042	4 091	255	4 346	187	2	4 161	496	385	1 540	1 404	3 274	. . .
1961	5 199	4 193	245	4 438	194	2	4 247	523	429	1 568	1 435	3 316	. . .
1962	5 465	4 425	224	4 649	219	4	4 434	564	468	1 645	1 494	3 323	. . .
1963	5 821	4 695	271	4 966	259	6	4 713	613	496	1 734	1 577	3 358	. . .
1964	6 327	5 159	245	5 404	265	8	5 146	668	513	1 864	1 705	3 395	. . .
1965	6 884	5 625	254	5 879	273	10	5 616	718	551	1 999	1 825	3 443	. . .
1966	7 384	6 157	241	6 398	376	15	6 038	747	599	2 132	1 929	3 464	. . .
1967	7 801	6 524	206	6 730	429	21	6 323	787	690	2 256	2 040	3 458	. . .
1968	8 526	7 103	227	7 330	472	24	6 882	843	801	2 474	2 221	3 446	. . .
1969	9 384	7 734	277	8 011	551	137	7 597	895	891	2 728	2 412	3 440	1 411
1970	10 202	8 284	247	8 531	590	136	8 076	1 029	1 097	2 957	2 657	3 450	1 413
1971	11 199	9 013	276	9 289	655	144	8 778	1 136	1 284	3 202	2 889	3 497	1 423
1972	12 466	10 050	345	10 395	765	171	9 801	1 234	1 431	3 521	3 152	3 540	1 471
1973	14 103	11 284	532	11 816	983	188	11 021	1 401	1 681	3 939	3 527	3 581	1 526
1974	15 715	12 656	335	12 991	1 136	198	12 053	1 651	2 010	4 332	3 874	3 628	1 552
1975	17 537	13 669	410	14 079	1 221	204	13 061	1 876	2 600	4 765	4 307	3 681	1 543
1976	19 851	15 672	475	16 148	1 421	218	14 944	2 068	2 839	5 312	4 773	3 737	1 594
1977	21 914	17 571	380	17 951	1 595	247	16 603	2 317	2 995	5 793	5 199	3 783	1 651
1978	24 773	19 942	504	20 447	1 840	270	18 877	2 634	3 262	6 461	5 782	3 834	1 714
1979	27 615	22 041	516	22 557	2 102	297	20 753	3 061	3 801	7 137	6 355	3 869	1 739
1980	30 564	23 944	205	24 149	2 281	328	22 196	3 908	4 460	7 836	6 966	3 900	1 736
1981	34 004	25 812	485	26 297	2 648	427	24 076	4 920	5 008	8 678	7 698	3 919	1 724
1982	35 988	26 702	407	27 110	2 787	448	24 771	5 681	5 536	9 168	8 216	3 925	1 692
1983	38 491	28 731	289	29 020	3 053	441	26 409	6 087	5 996	9 784	8 766	3 934	1 722
1984	42 692	31 793	476	32 270	3 428	493	29 335	7 020	6 337	10 803	9 731	3 952	1 787
1985	45 944	34 347	462	34 809	3 740	503	31 572	7 678	6 694	11 566	10 352	3 973	1 831
1986	48 553	36 390	453	36 843	3 937	525	33 432	8 158	6 963	12 164	10 889	3 992	1 868
1987	51 502	38 824	537	39 361	4 163	533	35 731	8 652	7 119	12 826	11 419	4 015	1 923
1988	55 120	41 549	800	42 349	4 651	529	38 228	9 467	7 426	13 698	12 287	4 024	1 982
1989	59 911	43 962	934	44 896	4 972	548	40 472	11 047	8 391	14 865	13 266	4 030	2 019
1990	63 679	46 896	820	47 716	5 317	525	42 924	11 528	9 227	15 723	14 047	4 050	2 061
1991	67 250	49 183	1 097	50 280	5 674	555	45 161	11 899	10 191	16 406	14 714	4 099	2 073
1992	71 977	52 870	990	53 860	6 061	610	48 408	11 595	11 974	17 327	15 578	4 154	2 110
1993	74 863	55 245	1 001	56 246	6 437	659	50 468	12 097	12 298	17 764	15 941	4 214	2 172
1994	79 265	58 052	1 055	59 107	6 899	751	52 958	13 285	13 021	18 606	16 637	4 260	2 193
1995	83 534	60 851	798	61 649	7 276	827	55 200	14 302	14 033	19 441	17 344	4 297	2 256
1996	86 972	63 130	918	64 048	7 512	837	57 374	14 810	14 788	20 081	17 842	4 331	2 290
1997	91 419	65 943	998	66 940	7 863	938	60 015	15 979	15 425	20 930	18 528	4 368	2 335
1998	97 012	69 795	1 095	70 890	8 212	1 049	63 728	17 454	15 830	22 025	19 500	4 405	2 385
1999	100 662	73 138	1 307	74 445	8 569	1 116	66 992	17 154	16 517	22 722	20 095	4 430	2 405
2000	105 807	76 023	955	76 977	8 783	1 238	69 433	18 725	17 648	23 768	21 049	4 452	2 416
2001	110 421	79 205	1 242	80 448	9 146	1 252	72 554	18 739	19 129	24 742	22 017	4 463	2 393
2002	113 835	82 501	860	83 361	9 456	1 272	75 177	18 073	20 585	25 467	22 982	4 470	2 387
2003	118 356	85 880	1 247	87 127	9 850	1 299	78 576	18 033	21 747	26 380	24 014	4 487	2 397
2004	126 270	91 400	1 487	92 886	10 388	1 379	83 877	19 262	23 130	28 019	25 557	4 507	2 463
2005	133 706	96 749	1 507	98 256	11 082	1 428	88 602	20 091	25 013	29 468	26 672	4 537	2 527
2006	141 630	102 913	830	103 744	11 747	1 490	93 487	21 581	26 562	30 873	27 698	4 588	2 578
2007	149 991	106 885	843	107 728	12 246	1 587	97 070	24 548	28 373	32 419	28 977	4 627	2 618
2008	156 840	110 334	850	111 184	12 738	1 614	100 060	25 586	31 194	33 643	30 297	4 662	. . .

. . . = Not available.

Table 21-2. Personal Income and Employment by Region and State—*Continued*

(Millions of dollars, except as noted.)

Region or state and year	Personal income, total	Earnings by place of work			Less: Contributions for government social insurance	Plus: Adjustment for residence	Equals: Net earnings by place of residence	Plus: Dividends, interest, and rent	Plus: Personal current transfer receipts	Per capita (dollars)		Population (thousands)	Total employment (thousands)
		Nonfarm	Farm	Total						Personal income	Disposable personal income		
ALASKA													
1958	559	533	2	535	22	0	513	25	21	2 494	. . .	224	. . .
1959	592	566	1	567	24	0	544	27	21	2 645	. . .	224	. . .
1960	701	673	2	675	28	-2	646	33	22	3 062	2 703	229	. . .
1961	698	664	2	666	28	-3	635	36	27	2 931	2 611	238	. . .
1962	731	697	1	698	29	-5	665	40	26	2 970	2 622	246	. . .
1963	790	758	1	758	33	-8	717	45	27	3 086	2 714	256	. . .
1964	890	855	1	856	37	-13	806	55	29	3 385	3 047	263	. . .
1965	963	926	1	927	41	-18	869	63	31	3 554	3 149	271	. . .
1966	1 034	995	1	997	48	-23	926	74	34	3 814	3 392	271	. . .
1967	1 133	1 095	1	1 096	53	-30	1 012	82	39	4 075	3 620	278	. . .
1968	1 231	1 199	2	1 201	67	-38	1 096	87	48	4 319	3 822	285	. . .
1969	1 412	1 377	1	1 378	94	-26	1 258	100	54	4 769	4 071	296	144
1970	1 602	1 564	2	1 566	105	-47	1 414	116	72	5 263	4 573	304	149
1971	1 772	1 729	2	1 730	118	-61	1 551	130	91	5 600	4 901	316	153
1972	1 945	1 904	2	1 905	134	-76	1 695	146	103	5 956	5 141	326	158
1973	2 274	2 113	2	2 115	165	-94	1 856	171	247	6 823	5 978	333	167
1974	2 809	2 839	2	2 841	241	-210	2 391	210	209	8 148	6 964	345	189
1975	3 963	4 479	4	4 482	407	-614	3 462	264	237	10 683	9 055	371	227
1976	4 767	5 631	4	5 635	526	-885	4 224	309	233	12 125	10 279	393	243
1977	4 929	5 213	5	5 218	463	-454	4 301	350	278	12 405	10 554	397	237
1978	5 028	5 078	5	5 083	434	-326	4 324	406	299	12 501	10 819	402	237
1979	5 334	5 318	3	5 321	467	-289	4 565	477	293	13 219	11 291	404	241
1980	6 025	5 962	3	5 965	527	-329	5 109	573	343	14 866	12 947	405	244
1981	6 934	6 965	2	6 967	666	-473	5 827	701	406	16 569	14 127	418	253
1982	8 335	8 057	3	8 060	775	-565	6 720	891	724	18 538	16 050	450	278
1983	9 365	8 985	2	8 987	851	-623	7 513	1 061	791	19 174	16 869	488	298
1984	10 019	9 678	2	9 680	947	-639	8 094	1 243	682	19 503	17 375	514	310
1985	10 821	10 137	2	10 139	969	-632	8 539	1 396	886	20 321	18 184	532	318
1986	10 780	9 835	7	9 841	918	-571	8 353	1 431	996	19 807	17 938	544	311
1987	10 440	9 294	9	9 303	859	-533	7 911	1 490	1 038	19 357	17 373	539	312
1988	10 789	9 583	11	9 594	930	-556	8 108	1 564	1 117	19 907	17 972	542	318
1989	11 834	10 444	5	10 449	1 027	-618	8 804	1 793	1 237	21 628	19 231	547	330
1990	12 617	11 042	8	11 050	1 097	-654	9 299	1 950	1 369	22 804	20 147	553	341
1991	13 207	11 579	8	11 588	1 164	-700	9 724	2 020	1 463	23 161	20 666	570	349
1992	14 004	12 222	8	12 230	1 228	-734	10 268	2 109	1 627	23 786	21 320	589	353
1993	14 709	12 689	11	12 699	1 305	-753	10 641	2 253	1 814	24 538	22 023	599	361
1994	15 113	12 874	12	12 886	1 357	-771	10 759	2 499	1 855	25 050	22 402	603	366
1995	15 415	12 990	13	13 003	1 366	-778	10 859	2 624	1 932	25 504	22 822	604	367
1996	15 704	13 041	14	13 055	1 365	-793	10 897	2 728	2 079	25 805	23 003	609	371
1997	16 402	13 389	16	13 405	1 400	-783	11 222	2 928	2 252	26 759	23 765	613	377
1998	17 085	13 884	17	13 900	1 448	-834	11 619	3 015	2 451	27 560	24 401	620	383
1999	17 557	14 132	20	14 152	1 464	-832	11 856	2 970	2 730	28 100	24 932	625	384
2000	18 741	14 859	15	14 874	1 527	-887	12 461	3 191	3 090	29 870	26 429	627	395
2001	20 050	16 202	16	16 218	1 629	-937	13 652	3 148	3 249	31 666	28 114	633	402
2002	20 722	17 037	17	17 053	1 703	-1 000	14 350	3 022	3 351	32 258	29 085	642	411
2003	21 184	17 692	15	17 707	1 768	-1 014	14 925	2 966	3 293	32 570	29 626	650	411
2004	22 434	19 033	16	19 049	1 881	-1 076	16 093	3 107	3 234	33 941	31 107	661	421
2005	24 127	20 295	16	20 311	2 004	-1 137	17 170	3 403	3 553	36 084	32 887	669	430
2006	25 932	21 630	13	21 643	2 141	-1 256	18 246	3 781	3 905	38 344	34 783	676	440
2007	27 273	22 606	15	22 621	2 229	-1 364	19 028	3 878	4 367	40 042	36 126	681	445
2008	29 731	23 826	-4	23 823	2 363	-1 453	20 006	4 052	5 672	43 321	39 458	686	. . .

. . . = Not available.

Table 21-2. Personal Income and Employment by Region and State—*Continued*

(Millions of dollars, except as noted.)

Region or state and year	Personal income, total	Earnings by place of work			Less: Contributions for government social insurance	Plus: Adjustment for residence	Equals: Net earnings by place of residence	Plus: Dividends, interest, and rent	Plus: Personal current transfer receipts	Per capita (dollars)		Population (thousands)	Total employment (thousands)
		Nonfarm	Farm	Total						Personal income	Disposable personal income		
ARIZONA													
1958	2 258	1 771	130	1 901	79	-2	1 820	303	135	1 893	1 710	1 193	. . .
1959	2 496	1 975	124	2 099	95	-2	2 001	342	153	1 979	1 776	1 261	. . .
1960	2 728	2 165	127	2 293	117	-2	2 173	389	166	2 065	1 843	1 321	. . .
1961	2 970	2 329	134	2 462	125	-2	2 335	440	194	2 111	1 895	1 407	. . .
1962	3 198	2 527	136	2 664	139	-2	2 523	463	212	2 174	1 943	1 471	. . .
1963	3 358	2 680	111	2 790	162	0	2 628	499	231	2 208	1 974	1 521	. . .
1964	3 600	2 853	129	2 981	167	*	2 814	536	250	2 314	2 105	1 556	. . .
1965	3 816	3 008	127	3 134	174	1	2 961	572	282	2 409	2 191	1 584	. . .
1966	4 161	3 369	120	3 489	232	0	3 257	600	305	2 578	2 333	1 614	. . .
1967	4 524	3 620	148	3 767	265	0	3 502	644	377	2 748	2 473	1 646	. . .
1968	5 188	4 101	191	4 292	312	2	3 982	770	435	3 084	2 754	1 682	. . .
1969	6 039	4 715	203	4 918	322	-26	4 570	977	492	3 477	3 053	1 737	711
1970	6 884	5 320	180	5 499	362	-29	5 108	1 183	593	3 835	3 385	1 795	747
1971	7 855	6 070	201	6 270	430	-28	5 812	1 333	711	4 143	3 701	1 896	786
1972	9 010	7 060	205	7 265	525	-32	6 708	1 485	817	4 485	3 965	2 009	850
1973	10 450	8 237	239	8 476	695	-31	7 750	1 715	984	4 917	4 396	2 125	925
1974	11 814	9 076	384	9 460	791	-41	8 628	1 996	1 189	5 311	4 721	2 224	955
1975	12 679	9 474	217	9 691	816	-47	8 828	2 190	1 661	5 545	5 045	2 286	935
1976	14 254	10 665	329	10 994	916	-47	10 031	2 399	1 825	6 071	5 487	2 348	976
1977	16 080	12 261	266	12 527	1 061	-56	11 409	2 746	1 924	6 625	5 945	2 427	1 048
1978	18 974	14 559	317	14 876	1 292	-69	13 515	3 289	2 171	7 536	6 705	2 518	1 149
1979	22 475	17 302	398	17 700	1 606	-71	16 023	3 981	2 471	8 518	7 530	2 639	1 241
1980	26 073	19 463	476	19 939	1 810	-80	18 049	5 055	2 969	9 524	8 458	2 738	1 285
1981	29 889	21 780	414	22 194	2 178	-14	20 003	6 396	3 490	10 636	9 365	2 810	1 317
1982	31 598	22 582	397	22 979	2 300	-6	20 672	7 032	3 893	10 934	9 668	2 890	1 320
1983	34 656	24 757	327	25 083	2 581	4	22 506	7 886	4 263	11 673	10 413	2 969	1 383
1984	39 524	28 362	527	28 890	3 019	8	25 878	9 075	4 571	12 886	11 526	3 067	1 511
1985	43 833	31 695	492	32 187	3 436	21	28 772	10 101	4 961	13 769	12 250	3 184	1 632
1986	47 730	34 645	472	35 117	3 825	41	31 332	10 956	5 442	14 427	12 851	3 308	1 712
1987	51 506	37 301	636	37 937	4 093	68	33 912	11 648	5 946	14 985	13 324	3 437	1 777
1988	55 246	40 178	763	40 942	4 571	110	36 480	12 244	6 522	15 627	13 971	3 535	1 847
1989	59 413	41 787	690	42 477	4 863	168	37 781	14 075	7 557	16 403	14 598	3 622	1 880
1990	62 649	44 065	653	44 718	5 151	228	39 795	14 485	8 369	17 005	15 131	3 684	1 910
1991	65 390	46 059	729	46 787	5 487	224	41 524	14 561	9 304	17 260	15 379	3 789	1 918
1992	69 609	49 518	673	50 190	5 855	250	44 586	14 323	10 700	17 777	15 906	3 916	1 940
1993	74 370	53 127	796	53 923	6 325	268	47 866	14 923	11 580	18 293	16 325	4 065	2 026
1994	81 555	58 376	585	58 961	7 003	281	52 239	16 941	12 375	19 212	17 103	4 245	2 158
1995	88 333	63 463	833	64 296	7 298	302	57 300	17 890	13 143	19 929	17 717	4 432	2 275
1996	95 514	69 410	752	70 162	8 213	331	62 279	19 267	13 968	20 823	18 306	4 587	2 406
1997	103 557	75 371	745	76 116	8 833	365	67 648	21 308	14 601	21 861	19 157	4 737	2 515
1998	113 370	83 272	871	84 143	9 576	410	74 977	23 290	15 103	23 216	20 250	4 883	2 631
1999	120 857	90 179	926	91 105	10 295	469	81 279	23 414	16 165	24 057	20 966	5 024	2 722
2000	132 558	99 949	684	100 633	11 159	522	89 997	25 454	17 107	25 656	22 322	5 167	2 819
2001	138 854	104 250	836	105 085	11 709	564	93 940	25 454	19 460	26 181	22 918	5 304	2 857
2002	144 150	107 778	1 074	108 852	12 093	550	97 309	25 188	21 653	26 454	23 724	5 449	2 877
2003	150 582	112 922	787	113 710	12 683	571	101 598	25 637	23 347	26 959	24 354	5 586	2 953
2004	164 923	123 477	859	124 336	13 769	630	111 196	28 385	25 342	28 680	25 930	5 750	3 048
2005	182 533	136 106	760	136 866	15 221	656	122 301	32 154	28 078	30 620	27 285	5 961	3 224
2006	199 465	148 931	572	149 503	16 792	681	133 392	35 474	30 600	32 285	28 640	6 178	3 412
2007	208 603	153 893	758	154 651	17 512	725	137 864	37 711	33 029	32 833	29 006	6 353	3 521
2008	214 203	154 833	590	155 423	17 686	762	138 499	39 139	36 565	32 953	29 391	6 500	. . .

. . . = Not available.
* = Less than $50,000, but the estimates for this item are included in the total.

Table 21-2. Personal Income and Employment by Region and State—*Continued*

(Millions of dollars, except as noted.)

Region or state and year	Personal income, total	Earnings by place of work			Less: Contributions for government social insurance	Plus: Adjustment for residence	Equals: Net earnings by place of residence	Plus: Dividends, interest, and rent	Plus: Personal current transfer receipts	Per capita (dollars)		Population (thousands)	Total employment (thousands)
		Nonfarm	Farm	Total						Personal income	Disposable personal income		
ARKANSAS													
1958	2 254	1 606	283	1 889	66	-1	1 823	222	209	1 306	1 209	1 726	. . .
1959	2 476	1 727	364	2 091	79	-1	2 011	240	225	1 410	1 302	1 756	. . .
1960	2 503	1 785	310	2 095	92	-2	2 001	262	240	1 399	1 289	1 789	. . .
1961	2 715	1 894	365	2 258	95	-2	2 161	286	269	1 504	1 387	1 806	. . .
1962	2 893	2 082	320	2 402	109	-3	2 290	315	288	1 561	1 424	1 853	. . .
1963	3 073	2 228	318	2 546	126	-4	2 415	348	310	1 639	1 496	1 875	. . .
1964	3 338	2 416	356	2 772	137	-5	2 631	381	326	1 760	1 629	1 897	. . .
1965	3 525	2 598	283	2 881	147	-6	2 728	440	357	1 861	1 714	1 894	. . .
1966	3 920	2 849	388	3 238	191	-5	3 042	487	391	2 064	1 880	1 899	. . .
1967	4 158	3 097	297	3 394	221	-5	3 168	523	468	2 188	1 992	1 901	. . .
1968	4 512	3 413	334	3 747	251	-7	3 488	499	525	2 372	2 137	1 902	. . .
1969	4 978	3 744	342	4 086	279	30	3 837	557	584	2 602	2 320	1 913	800
1970	5 458	3 997	411	4 408	297	20	4 131	643	683	2 828	2 535	1 930	805
1971	6 072	4 470	404	4 874	341	19	4 552	719	801	3 079	2 795	1 972	831
1972	6 854	5 090	477	5 567	406	18	5 178	783	893	3 396	3 070	2 018	867
1973	8 167	5 770	909	6 679	526	14	6 166	918	1 083	3 967	3 575	2 058	902
1974	9 156	6 492	827	7 319	610	7	6 716	1 125	1 315	4 359	3 899	2 100	927
1975	10 066	6 943	789	7 733	640	6	7 099	1 298	1 669	4 664	4 250	2 158	905
1976	11 175	8 051	636	8 687	746	-4	7 938	1 415	1 823	5 153	4 636	2 169	941
1977	12 481	9 058	721	9 778	849	-8	8 921	1 625	1 935	5 655	5 104	2 207	981
1978	14 489	10 332	1 171	11 503	990	-14	10 499	1 863	2 127	6 466	5 834	2 241	1 022
1979	15 924	11 480	988	12 469	1 137	-15	11 317	2 168	2 439	7 018	6 284	2 269	1 033
1980	17 221	12 474	363	12 837	1 227	-3	11 607	2 726	2 888	7 524	6 704	2 289	1 035
1981	19 545	13 435	845	14 280	1 430	-22	12 828	3 446	3 270	8 523	7 605	2 293	1 030
1982	20 511	13 892	638	14 530	1 506	-18	13 006	3 949	3 556	8 940	7 927	2 294	1 014
1983	21 884	15 108	412	15 520	1 642	-48	13 830	4 205	3 849	9 491	8 520	2 306	1 043
1984	24 523	16 870	876	17 746	1 873	-68	15 806	4 682	4 035	10 571	9 564	2 320	1 084
1985	26 203	17 956	858	18 815	2 010	-72	16 733	5 197	4 273	11 260	10 163	2 327	1 104
1986	27 307	18 898	798	19 696	2 153	-94	17 449	5 356	4 502	11 710	10 593	2 332	1 116
1987	28 308	19 854	931	20 785	2 262	-112	18 411	5 264	4 634	12 085	10 882	2 342	1 143
1988	30 223	21 094	1 343	22 436	2 517	-146	19 774	5 587	4 862	12 901	11 639	2 343	1 177
1989	32 334	22 306	1 229	23 535	2 686	-146	20 703	6 261	5 371	13 781	12 395	2 346	1 197
1990	34 076	23 763	1 013	24 776	2 875	-210	21 692	6 572	5 813	14 460	12 987	2 357	1 211
1991	36 043	25 233	1 102	26 334	3 074	-236	23 024	6 611	6 408	15 124	13 625	2 383	1 238
1992	39 162	27 465	1 393	28 859	3 347	-259	25 252	6 771	7 139	16 209	14 621	2 416	1 263
1993	40 822	28 886	1 315	30 201	3 564	-289	26 348	6 946	7 528	16 619	14 977	2 456	1 309
1994	43 272	30 657	1 452	32 108	3 859	-312	27 937	7 420	7 915	17 350	15 563	2 494	1 337
1995	45 829	32 388	1 496	33 883	4 070	-282	29 531	7 802	8 497	18 076	16 170	2 535	1 391
1996	48 679	33 700	1 910	35 610	4 223	-273	31 114	8 536	9 028	18 926	16 920	2 572	1 414
1997	50 955	35 253	1 887	37 140	4 427	-272	32 441	9 102	9 411	19 590	17 424	2 601	1 435
1998	53 810	37 573	1 615	39 188	4 659	-275	34 254	9 853	9 703	20 489	18 146	2 626	1 462
1999	56 052	39 646	1 813	41 459	4 884	-301	36 274	9 738	10 040	21 137	18 749	2 652	1 482
2000	58 726	41 852	1 218	43 070	5 065	-346	37 659	10 411	10 656	21 927	19 377	2 678	1 504
2001	61 967	43 936	1 313	45 249	5 296	-350	39 604	10 558	11 805	23 039	20 459	2 690	1 499
2002	63 234	45 600	527	46 127	5 455	-381	40 292	10 184	12 758	23 404	21 066	2 702	1 497
2003	66 476	47 299	1 896	49 195	5 665	-373	43 157	9 981	13 339	24 459	22 261	2 718	1 500
2004	70 701	50 459	1 906	52 365	6 013	-382	45 970	10 513	14 218	25 801	23 529	2 740	1 530
2005	74 859	53 272	1 467	54 739	6 362	-370	48 008	11 616	15 235	27 035	24 471	2 769	1 564
2006	79 845	56 079	961	57 040	6 735	-355	49 950	13 287	16 609	28 473	25 675	2 804	1 590
2007	85 418	58 901	1 328	60 229	7 058	-292	52 880	14 683	17 856	30 177	27 114	2 831	1 606
2008	89 277	60 396	1 426	61 822	7 278	-275	54 269	15 399	19 609	31 266	28 270	2 855	. . .

. . . = Not available.

Table 21-2. Personal Income and Employment by Region and State—*Continued*

(Millions of dollars, except as noted.)

Region or state and year	Personal income, total	Earnings by place of work			Less: Contributions for government social insurance	Plus: Adjustment for residence	Equals: Net earnings by place of residence	Plus: Dividends, interest, and rent	Plus: Personal current transfer receipts	Per capita (dollars)		Population (thousands)	Total employment (thousands)
		Nonfarm	Farm	Total						Personal income	Disposable personal income		
CALIFORNIA													
1958	38 676	30 512	1 335	31 847	1 112	-4	30 731	5 721	2 223	2 599	2 312	14 880	. . .
1959	42 432	34 008	1 413	35 421	1 423	-5	33 992	6 167	2 273	2 743	2 432	15 467	. . .
1960	44 846	35 878	1 430	37 308	1 719	-6	35 583	6 679	2 584	2 826	2 497	15 870	. . .
1961	47 529	37 964	1 361	39 325	1 830	-6	37 488	7 042	2 999	2 881	2 549	16 497	. . .
1962	51 304	41 321	1 425	42 746	2 247	-7	40 492	7 633	3 179	3 005	2 655	17 072	. . .
1963	54 800	44 377	1 357	45 734	2 623	-7	43 104	8 179	3 517	3 102	2 740	17 668	. . .
1964	59 452	47 837	1 508	49 345	2 729	-8	46 608	9 031	3 812	3 275	2 945	18 151	. . .
1965	63 434	50 792	1 456	52 248	2 845	-10	49 393	9 829	4 213	3 413	3 069	18 585	. . .
1966	68 937	55 942	1 574	57 516	3 739	-12	53 765	10 519	4 653	3 656	3 268	18 858	. . .
1967	74 287	59 941	1 489	61 430	4 094	-14	57 323	11 210	5 755	3 874	3 450	19 176	. . .
1968	81 475	65 966	1 716	67 682	4 579	-16	63 087	11 744	6 643	4 201	3 699	19 394	. . .
1969	89 273	71 819	1 701	73 521	4 830	-132	68 559	13 099	7 616	4 529	3 958	19 711	9 033
1970	96 313	75 965	1 705	77 670	5 020	-116	72 534	14 479	9 300	4 810	4 275	20 023	9 057
1971	102 428	80 044	1 704	81 749	5 452	-126	76 170	15 564	10 694	5 034	4 526	20 346	9 036
1972	112 265	88 387	2 170	90 557	6 337	-129	84 090	16 654	11 520	5 454	4 815	20 585	9 369
1973	124 037	97 808	2 928	100 737	7 979	-116	92 642	18 638	12 757	5 944	5 298	20 868	9 844
1974	138 721	107 848	3 645	111 493	9 020	-131	102 342	21 263	15 116	6 552	5 819	21 173	10 163
1975	153 525	117 689	3 272	120 961	9 606	-21	111 333	23 200	18 992	7 129	6 411	21 537	10 287
1976	171 635	132 990	3 478	136 468	10 984	82	125 566	25 082	20 987	7 825	6 972	21 935	10 633
1977	191 542	149 938	3 545	153 483	12 566	-70	140 847	28 417	22 278	8 570	7 589	22 350	11 119
1978	218 788	172 547	3 490	176 037	14 800	-80	161 157	33 545	24 086	9 580	8 429	22 839	11 803
1979	250 061	196 345	4 575	200 920	17 658	-57	183 205	40 390	26 465	10 753	9 406	23 255	12 462
1980	284 455	218 407	5 591	223 999	19 245	-90	204 664	49 064	30 727	11 951	10 443	23 801	12 777
1981	319 962	241 392	4 357	245 749	23 075	248	222 921	60 883	36 159	13 175	11 537	24 286	12 969
1982	341 593	255 578	4 604	260 182	24 980	253	235 455	66 508	39 630	13 763	12 136	24 820	12 899
1983	369 132	277 336	4 235	281 571	27 658	261	254 174	72 635	42 324	14 556	12 871	25 360	13 219
1984	413 355	312 504	4 913	317 417	32 083	235	285 569	83 619	44 168	15 994	14 147	25 844	13 852
1985	448 335	340 854	4 952	345 807	35 345	182	310 644	89 931	47 760	16 956	14 918	26 441	14 359
1986	478 832	366 896	5 389	372 285	38 927	123	333 481	94 051	51 300	17 668	15 548	27 102	14 787
1987	515 252	399 627	6 612	406 238	42 578	40	363 700	98 032	53 520	18 549	16 142	27 777	15 394
1988	557 867	435 774	6 967	442 741	47 865	-3	394 873	105 733	57 261	19 599	17 202	28 464	16 133
1989	601 456	463 473	6 809	470 282	51 198	-20	419 064	119 685	62 706	20 585	17 899	29 218	16 550
1990	648 263	497 550	7 230	504 780	55 042	-79	449 660	129 702	68 901	21 638	18 871	29 960	16 965
1991	662 728	507 383	6 210	513 593	57 255	-69	456 269	129 807	76 651	21 750	19 154	30 471	16 870
1992	696 670	531 743	6 799	538 541	59 325	-71	479 146	128 895	88 629	22 492	19 957	30 975	16 510
1993	707 906	538 682	7 800	546 482	60 172	-3	486 306	128 042	93 558	22 635	20 067	31 275	16 484
1994	730 529	552 103	7 583	559 686	62 187	12	497 510	135 370	97 650	23 203	20 544	31 484	16 659
1995	765 806	576 839	7 281	584 120	64 041	-3	520 075	145 317	100 414	24 161	21 263	31 697	17 059
1996	810 448	607 170	8 183	615 354	66 134	-13	549 206	155 712	105 530	25 312	22 011	32 019	17 466
1997	860 545	650 342	8 753	659 095	70 388	-110	588 597	166 048	105 900	26 490	22 793	32 486	17 787
1998	936 009	711 197	8 260	719 456	75 771	-120	643 565	181 283	111 160	28 374	24 258	32 988	18 504
1999	999 228	772 928	9 163	782 091	82 306	-183	699 602	182 484	117 142	29 828	25 087	33 499	19 024
2000	1 103 842	866 034	8 089	874 122	91 271	-351	782 500	199 052	122 290	32 467	26 719	33 999	19 626
2001	1 135 304	883 356	7 168	890 523	95 774	-354	794 395	204 379	136 531	32 901	27 526	34 507	19 716
2002	1 147 716	896 771	7 778	904 549	98 694	-303	805 552	195 208	146 955	32 870	28 675	34 916	19 660
2003	1 187 040	931 629	8 964	940 593	103 993	-309	836 291	195 345	155 404	33 620	29 590	35 307	19 781
2004	1 265 970	996 977	9 829	1 006 806	113 080	-322	893 404	209 609	162 957	35 531	31 310	35 630	19 797
2005	1 342 754	1 054 746	8 978	1 063 724	118 875	-275	944 574	228 279	169 901	37 418	32 490	35 885	20 181
2006	1 445 581	1 116 077	7 695	1 123 773	123 500	-243	1 000 030	262 537	183 014	40 020	34 532	36 121	20 762
2007	1 520 755	1 156 638	9 664	1 166 302	126 865	-192	1 039 245	287 750	193 760	41 805	35 863	36 378	21 246
2008	1 569 370	1 180 461	8 277	1 188 738	129 720	-171	1 058 847	299 398	211 124	42 696	37 041	36 757	. . .

. . . = Not available.

Table 21-2. Personal Income and Employment by Region and State—*Continued*

(Millions of dollars, except as noted.)

| Region or state and year | Personal income, total | Earnings by place of work | | | Less: Contributions for government social insurance | Plus: Adjustment for residence | Equals: Net earnings by place of residence | Plus: Dividends, interest, and rent | Plus: Personal current transfer receipts | Per capita (dollars) | | Population (thousands) | Total employment (thousands) |
		Nonfarm	Farm	Total						Personal income	Disposable personal income		
COLORADO													
1958	3 583	2 756	177	2 932	95	1	2 839	524	220	2 149	1 917	1 667	...
1959	3 857	2 992	156	3 148	109	1	3 040	558	259	2 256	2 016	1 710	...
1960	4 130	3 226	171	3 397	133	1	3 266	589	275	2 335	2 058	1 769	...
1961	4 446	3 492	172	3 665	150	1	3 516	629	302	2 411	2 126	1 844	...
1962	4 680	3 686	153	3 839	163	1	3 676	685	319	2 465	2 176	1 899	...
1963	4 899	3 885	137	4 022	191	0	3 832	728	339	2 530	2 235	1 936	...
1964	5 186	4 129	135	4 264	197	*	4 066	776	343	2 632	2 374	1 970	...
1965	5 541	4 323	210	4 534	197	0	4 336	830	375	2 791	2 513	1 985	...
1966	5 960	4 735	188	4 924	263	-1	4 660	893	407	2 970	2 655	2 007	...
1967	6 431	5 089	184	5 272	294	-1	4 977	970	483	3 132	2 789	2 053	...
1968	7 147	5 658	242	5 900	333	-2	5 565	1 033	549	3 371	2 969	2 120	...
1969	7 967	6 340	249	6 589	388	2	6 204	1 158	605	3 678	3 191	2 166	1 001
1970	9 003	7 073	287	7 361	427	2	6 935	1 337	730	4 048	3 558	2 224	1 032
1971	10 164	8 031	300	8 331	499	3	7 835	1 478	850	4 412	3 902	2 304	1 072
1972	11 509	9 226	331	9 557	606	4	8 956	1 611	943	4 786	4 174	2 405	1 149
1973	13 217	10 612	438	11 051	797	3	10 256	1 853	1 108	5 296	4 640	2 496	1 243
1974	14 861	11 793	533	12 326	905	4	11 426	2 152	1 284	5 848	5 101	2 541	1 276
1975	16 379	12 907	462	13 369	966	8	12 411	2 357	1 611	6 333	5 602	2 586	1 285
1976	18 137	14 577	334	14 911	1 104	9	13 816	2 562	1 759	6 890	6 066	2 632	1 340
1977	20 343	16 562	263	16 825	1 260	12	15 578	2 900	1 865	7 546	6 598	2 696	1 411
1978	23 488	19 364	205	19 569	1 505	20	18 085	3 373	2 031	8 490	7 400	2 767	1 505
1979	27 101	22 430	213	22 643	1 837	20	20 827	3 992	2 282	9 512	8 242	2 849	1 594
1980	31 259	25 394	285	25 679	2 101	28	23 606	5 007	2 646	10 746	9 320	2 909	1 654
1981	36 126	29 007	302	29 309	2 592	6	26 723	6 295	3 108	12 131	10 462	2 978	1 722
1982	39 663	31 705	181	31 886	2 901	3	28 988	7 153	3 523	12 955	11 156	3 062	1 765
1983	42 631	33 698	356	34 055	3 128	0	30 926	7 807	3 898	13 604	12 016	3 134	1 794
1984	46 846	37 094	421	37 516	3 537	8	33 986	8 752	4 108	14 778	13 111	3 170	1 892
1985	49 537	39 247	391	39 639	3 833	17	35 823	9 414	4 300	15 438	13 661	3 209	1 926
1986	51 108	40 374	393	40 768	4 039	23	36 751	9 742	4 614	15 786	14 010	3 237	1 925
1987	53 063	41 724	475	42 199	4 136	35	38 098	9 992	4 974	16 275	14 392	3 260	1 915
1988	55 884	44 002	576	44 578	4 510	50	40 119	10 531	5 234	17 130	15 185	3 262	1 981
1989	60 652	46 648	615	47 263	4 834	66	42 495	12 314	5 844	18 515	16 307	3 276	2 017
1990	64 748	49 807	912	50 719	5 235	91	45 576	12 915	6 256	19 575	17 201	3 308	2 054
1991	68 283	52 974	630	53 604	5 731	103	47 976	13 357	6 950	20 160	17 740	3 387	2 101
1992	73 794	57 765	669	58 434	6 212	117	52 339	13 665	7 791	21 109	18 569	3 496	2 149
1993	79 697	62 827	812	63 639	6 819	130	56 949	14 405	8 344	22 054	19 345	3 614	2 249
1994	85 671	67 176	566	67 742	7 376	147	60 513	16 341	8 817	23 004	20 120	3 724	2 362
1995	92 704	72 272	535	72 807	7 887	169	65 088	17 858	9 758	24 226	21 175	3 827	2 441
1996	100 233	78 009	671	78 680	8 425	187	70 442	19 492	10 299	25 570	22 174	3 920	2 537
1997	107 873	84 641	685	85 326	9 109	207	76 424	21 010	10 439	26 846	23 068	4 018	2 647
1998	118 493	93 252	787	94 039	9 537	233	84 736	23 100	10 657	28 784	24 565	4 117	2 751
1999	128 860	103 383	934	104 318	10 435	262	94 145	23 323	11 392	30 492	25 948	4 226	2 840
2000	144 394	117 038	567	117 605	11 567	290	106 328	25 955	12 111	33 364	28 230	4 328	2 950
2001	152 700	123 456	768	124 224	12 146	336	112 414	26 990	13 296	34 455	29 553	4 432	2 969
2002	153 066	124 150	541	124 692	12 556	346	112 482	25 626	14 958	33 991	29 918	4 503	2 941
2003	154 829	125 729	639	126 368	12 737	357	113 987	25 229	15 612	34 041	30 315	4 548	2 934
2004	163 736	133 608	672	134 280	13 506	385	121 159	26 436	16 141	35 594	31 779	4 600	2 990
2005	175 371	142 349	653	143 002	14 411	397	128 989	28 981	17 401	37 611	33 221	4 663	3 065
2006	188 214	151 693	511	152 204	15 417	415	137 202	32 313	18 698	39 612	34 632	4 751	3 139
2007	199 483	158 809	681	159 490	16 210	443	143 723	35 746	20 014	41 192	35 697	4 843	3 216
2008	209 321	166 314	590	166 904	16 982	457	150 378	37 079	21 864	42 377	37 039	4 939	...

. . . = Not available.
* = Less than $50,000, but the estimates for this item are included in the total.

Table 21-2. Personal Income and Employment by Region and State—*Continued*

(Millions of dollars, except as noted.)

Region or state and year	Personal income, total	Derivation of personal income								Per capita (dollars)		Population (thousands)	Total employment (thousands)
		Earnings by place of work			Less: Contributions for government social insurance	Plus: Adjustment for residence	Equals: Net earnings by place of residence	Plus: Dividends, interest, and rent	Plus: Personal current transfer receipts	Personal income	Disposable personal income		
		Nonfarm	Farm	Total									
CONNECTICUT													
1958	6 396	5 121	67	5 188	184	-2	5 003	1 003	390	2 615	2 302	2 446	. . .
1959	6 839	5 552	58	5 610	230	-2	5 378	1 084	376	2 711	2 381	2 523	. . .
1960	7 117	5 787	63	5 849	278	3	5 575	1 154	389	2 798	2 437	2 544	. . .
1961	7 524	6 049	58	6 106	290	3	5 819	1 257	448	2 910	2 543	2 586	. . .
1962	8 042	6 479	59	6 538	320	3	6 221	1 381	441	3 038	2 652	2 647	. . .
1963	8 485	6 825	63	6 888	369	4	6 523	1 493	469	3 111	2 701	2 727	. . .
1964	9 112	7 299	61	7 360	379	5	6 985	1 632	495	3 257	2 883	2 798	. . .
1965	9 791	7 815	71	7 885	395	2	7 492	1 776	523	3 427	3 013	2 857	. . .
1966	10 753	8 747	73	8 820	553	0	8 267	1 923	564	3 704	3 230	2 903	. . .
1967	11 791	9 464	57	9 521	602	2	8 921	2 168	701	4 017	3 474	2 935	. . .
1968	12 576	10 196	67	10 264	671	7	9 600	2 122	854	4 243	3 604	2 964	. . .
1969	14 502	11 126	66	11 193	752	728	11 169	2 385	947	4 834	4 081	3 000	1 417
1970	15 432	11 725	71	11 796	783	722	11 735	2 552	1 146	5 078	4 405	3 039	1 414
1971	16 222	12 144	69	12 213	840	746	12 119	2 679	1 423	5 299	4 669	3 061	1 388
1972	17 478	13 231	68	13 299	968	785	13 115	2 857	1 505	5 694	4 943	3 070	1 416
1973	19 119	14 722	80	14 802	1 234	808	14 376	3 114	1 629	6 230	5 448	3 069	1 480
1974	20 906	15 985	83	16 068	1 395	841	15 514	3 474	1 918	6 797	5 942	3 076	1 511
1975	22 386	16 629	75	16 704	1 423	916	16 197	3 643	2 546	7 257	6 437	3 085	1 468
1976	24 327	18 206	82	18 289	1 577	1 011	17 723	3 895	2 708	7 883	6 908	3 086	1 493
1977	26 849	20 256	83	20 339	1 778	1 121	19 682	4 336	2 832	8 693	7 620	3 089	1 546
1978	29 896	22 830	80	22 910	2 062	1 273	22 121	4 855	2 920	9 660	8 383	3 095	1 616
1979	33 675	25 755	79	25 833	2 421	1 449	24 861	5 564	3 250	10 863	9 353	3 100	1 675
1980	38 470	28 754	83	28 837	2 682	1 695	27 850	6 884	3 737	12 357	10 587	3 113	1 709
1981	43 267	31 541	82	31 622	3 157	1 878	30 343	8 611	4 313	13 828	11 797	3 129	1 732
1982	46 731	33 642	108	33 750	3 431	2 035	32 354	9 582	4 796	14 887	12 683	3 139	1 731
1983	49 978	36 347	105	36 452	3 735	2 156	34 873	9 925	5 180	15 804	13 807	3 162	1 749
1984	55 880	40 799	129	40 928	4 304	2 309	38 932	11 532	5 416	17 572	15 437	3 180	1 831
1985	59 962	44 509	127	44 636	4 740	2 448	42 343	11 875	5 743	18 731	16 308	3 201	1 890
1986	64 552	48 289	140	48 429	5 210	2 609	45 827	12 650	6 075	20 024	17 335	3 224	1 948
1987	70 599	53 653	142	53 795	5 699	2 736	50 832	13 487	6 279	21 741	18 642	3 247	1 997
1988	77 821	59 457	156	59 613	6 394	2 923	56 142	14 902	6 777	23 784	20 660	3 272	2 053
1989	84 330	62 593	139	62 732	6 705	2 815	58 842	17 888	7 600	25 684	22 327	3 283	2 047
1990	87 251	64 508	182	64 689	6 927	2 780	60 542	18 214	8 495	26 504	23 121	3 292	2 018
1991	87 567	64 814	162	64 975	7 123	2 745	60 597	17 496	9 474	26 512	23 128	3 303	1 937
1992	93 615	68 000	187	68 187	7 344	3 958	64 801	17 646	11 168	28 362	24 471	3 301	1 917
1993	95 882	70 520	211	70 731	7 609	3 375	66 497	17 760	11 625	28 975	24 859	3 309	1 938
1994	98 467	72 709	187	72 896	7 970	3 139	68 065	18 343	12 059	29 693	25 468	3 316	1 920
1995	103 199	75 954	173	76 128	8 349	3 901	71 680	18 686	12 834	31 045	26 418	3 324	1 958
1996	108 189	79 217	162	79 379	8 695	4 689	75 373	19 607	13 210	32 424	27 105	3 337	1 989
1997	115 134	85 414	157	85 571	9 240	4 219	80 549	20 963	13 622	34 375	28 349	3 349	2 015
1998	123 918	91 518	182	91 699	9 733	5 609	87 575	22 535	13 807	36 822	30 068	3 365	2 043
1999	129 807	97 457	201	97 658	10 205	5 450	92 903	22 759	14 145	38 332	31 148	3 386	2 076
2000	141 570	106 464	191	106 655	10 785	5 678	101 549	25 164	14 858	41 495	33 388	3 412	2 114
2001	147 356	111 502	184	111 686	11 106	5 035	105 615	25 979	15 762	42 983	34 661	3 428	2 124
2002	146 997	112 370	169	112 540	11 641	4 379	105 277	24 790	16 930	42 629	35 906	3 448	2 118
2003	148 777	114 766	163	114 929	11 866	4 021	107 084	24 292	17 400	42 901	36 530	3 468	2 113
2004	159 337	122 401	172	122 573	12 433	4 547	114 687	26 330	18 319	45 848	39 064	3 475	2 153
2005	167 090	128 021	143	128 165	12 832	4 589	119 922	28 145	19 024	48 032	40 189	3 479	2 190
2006	179 974	134 065	144	134 209	13 346	4 940	125 803	33 909	20 262	51 600	42 882	3 488	2 211
2007	191 877	140 959	146	141 105	13 954	4 992	132 143	38 450	21 284	54 981	45 179	3 490	2 235
2008	196 939	143 591	137	143 728	14 251	5 315	134 792	39 238	22 909	56 248	46 775	3 501	. . .

. . . = Not available.

Table 21-2. Personal Income and Employment by Region and State—*Continued*

(Millions of dollars, except as noted.)

Region or state and year	Personal income, total	Derivation of personal income									Per capita (dollars)		Population (thousands)	Total employment (thousands)
		Earnings by place of work			Less: Contributions for government social insurance	Plus: Adjustment for residence	Equals: Net earnings by place of residence	Plus: Dividends, interest, and rent	Plus: Personal current transfer receipts		Personal income	Disposable personal income		
		Nonfarm	Farm	Total										
DELAWARE														
1958	1 156	917	35	952	32	-49	871	234	52		2 671	2 248	433	. . .
1959	1 207	974	30	1 004	42	-50	912	243	52		2 738	2 288	441	. . .
1960	1 264	1 023	34	1 057	53	-51	953	257	54		2 816	2 356	449	. . .
1961	1 300	1 049	29	1 079	51	-51	976	259	65		2 821	2 375	461	. . .
1962	1 377	1 114	32	1 147	58	-52	1 037	273	67		2 936	2 440	469	. . .
1963	1 475	1 209	26	1 234	69	-56	1 109	296	70		3 053	2 560	483	. . .
1964	1 598	1 308	26	1 333	68	-58	1 207	317	74		3 215	2 702	497	. . .
1965	1 762	1 444	35	1 478	69	-65	1 345	338	80		3 475	2 917	507	. . .
1966	1 860	1 584	26	1 609	99	-69	1 441	330	88		3 604	3 039	516	. . .
1967	1 983	1 683	32	1 715	117	-69	1 530	345	108		3 777	3 199	525	. . .
1968	2 173	1 848	29	1 878	119	-71	1 688	358	127		4 070	3 424	534	. . .
1969	2 382	1 992	55	2 047	139	-43	1 865	378	139		4 411	3 642	540	271
1970	2 530	2 132	35	2 167	147	-48	1 971	394	165		4 597	3 822	550	275
1971	2 765	2 349	38	2 387	168	-60	2 159	411	194		4 891	4 107	565	280
1972	3 040	2 606	49	2 655	196	-68	2 391	434	215		5 298	4 436	574	293
1973	3 392	2 928	96	3 023	253	-97	2 674	471	248		5 858	4 899	579	305
1974	3 695	3 171	82	3 253	282	-108	2 863	528	303		6 336	5 322	583	302
1975	3 969	3 340	91	3 432	293	-110	3 029	532	408		6 742	5 746	589	292
1976	4 355	3 693	84	3 776	325	-121	3 331	586	438		7 347	6 177	593	296
1977	4 696	3 989	56	4 045	352	-133	3 560	659	477		7 895	6 647	595	296
1978	5 155	4 431	60	4 492	402	-162	3 928	728	499		8 617	7 258	598	304
1979	5 677	4 876	54	4 929	460	-184	4 285	819	572		9 480	7 917	599	312
1980	6 394	5 412	12	5 424	512	-230	4 682	1 018	694		10 748	8 970	595	312
1981	7 051	5 814	42	5 856	592	-249	5 015	1 255	781		11 831	9 799	596	314
1982	7 593	6 231	65	6 296	648	-270	5 378	1 386	829		12 673	10 645	599	317
1983	8 172	6 723	78	6 801	704	-316	5 781	1 507	884		13 498	11 500	605	326
1984	9 046	7 399	96	7 495	780	-356	6 359	1 739	948		14 792	12 692	612	341
1985	9 884	8 096	104	8 200	865	-397	6 938	1 950	997		15 987	13 735	618	359
1986	10 484	8 526	143	8 669	926	-398	7 345	2 061	1 078		16 706	14 318	628	372
1987	11 293	9 338	114	9 452	1 007	-454	7 992	2 178	1 124		17 730	15 263	637	389
1988	12 308	10 204	181	10 386	1 144	-498	8 744	2 326	1 238		19 006	16 443	648	405
1989	13 655	11 136	192	11 327	1 255	-607	9 465	2 848	1 342		20 743	17 911	658	417
1990	14 343	11 826	139	11 966	1 333	-678	9 954	2 948	1 442		21 422	18 474	670	423
1991	15 089	12 312	130	12 442	1 406	-688	10 348	3 110	1 631		22 090	19 224	683	417
1992	15 754	13 178	114	13 292	1 448	-996	10 848	3 091	1 815		22 670	19 768	695	416
1993	16 224	13 504	109	13 613	1 510	-944	11 159	3 123	1 942		22 967	19 973	706	423
1994	16 884	14 216	120	14 337	1 611	-1 106	11 619	3 202	2 063		23 530	20 343	718	427
1995	17 811	14 687	87	14 774	1 701	-930	12 143	3 402	2 265		24 407	21 105	730	445
1996	19 063	15 455	120	15 575	1 790	-952	12 833	3 724	2 506		25 727	22 071	741	456
1997	19 895	16 449	95	16 544	1 895	-1 228	13 421	3 926	2 548		26 475	22 427	751	468
1998	21 565	17 776	140	17 916	1 983	-1 410	14 523	4 356	2 687		28 252	23 933	763	485
1999	22 416	19 089	139	19 228	2 131	-1 690	15 407	4 200	2 809		28 925	24 518	775	497
2000	24 277	20 358	122	20 480	2 233	-1 733	16 514	4 705	3 058		30 871	26 279	786	508
2001	25 537	21 620	184	21 804	2 370	-1 833	17 601	4 600	3 337		32 142	27 298	794	505
2002	26 530	22 457	139	22 595	2 439	-1 899	18 257	4 659	3 613		33 007	28 843	804	503
2003	27 395	23 344	206	23 551	2 546	-2 017	18 988	4 561	3 846		33 644	29 700	814	506
2004	29 331	24 958	242	25 201	2 701	-2 085	20 414	4 829	4 087		35 523	31 366	826	522
2005	30 852	26 572	267	26 838	2 882	-2 263	21 693	4 755	4 404		36 793	32 041	839	534
2006	32 947	27 899	169	28 068	3 042	-2 458	22 567	5 596	4 784		38 745	33 730	850	542
2007	34 575	28 536	211	28 747	3 103	-2 266	23 378	6 057	5 140		40 112	34 954	862	548
2008	35 667	28 954	216	29 170	3 160	-2 238	23 772	6 269	5 626		40 852	35 880	873	. . .

. . . = Not available.

Table 21-2. Personal Income and Employment by Region and State—Continued

(Millions of dollars, except as noted.)

Region or state and year	Personal income, total	Derivation of personal income								Per capita (dollars)		Population (thousands)	Total employment (thousands)
		Earnings by place of work			Less: Contributions for government social insurance	Plus: Adjustment for residence	Equals: Net earnings by place of residence	Plus: Dividends, interest, and rent	Plus: Personal current transfer receipts	Personal income	Disposable personal income		
		Nonfarm	Farm	Total									
DISTRICT OF COLUMBIA													
1958	2 057	2 751	0	2 751	79	-1 049	1 623	327	106	2 717	2 360	757	. . .
1959	2 123	2 902	0	2 902	89	-1 139	1 673	340	109	2 789	2 383	761	. . .
1960	2 147	3 088	0	3 088	101	-1 321	1 666	369	112	2 806	2 384	765	. . .
1961	2 265	3 281	0	3 281	107	-1 410	1 765	376	123	2 911	2 513	778	. . .
1962	2 445	3 536	0	3 536	114	-1 496	1 926	393	127	3 103	2 668	788	. . .
1963	2 601	3 805	0	3 805	138	-1 612	2 055	411	135	3 259	2 828	798	. . .
1964	2 765	4 086	0	4 086	135	-1 749	2 202	423	140	3 465	3 055	798	. . .
1965	2 995	4 443	0	4 443	140	-1 903	2 399	446	150	3 758	3 335	797	. . .
1966	3 126	4 792	0	4 792	186	-2 090	2 516	449	160	3 952	3 467	791	. . .
1967	3 349	5 418	0	5 418	213	-2 498	2 706	450	192	4 234	3 739	791	. . .
1968	3 524	5 840	0	5 840	234	-2 767	2 839	456	230	4 530	3 991	778	. . .
1969	3 423	6 168	0	6 168	252	-3 208	2 708	481	234	4 492	3 842	762	678
1970	3 755	6 720	0	6 720	274	-3 512	2 934	519	302	4 973	4 276	755	674
1971	4 129	7 309	0	7 309	299	-3 828	3 182	572	375	5 500	4 791	751	669
1972	4 482	7 918	0	7 918	343	-4 161	3 414	622	447	6 027	5 218	744	671
1973	4 748	8 441	0	8 441	414	-4 449	3 578	658	512	6 472	5 588	734	664
1974	5 228	9 285	0	9 285	472	-4 910	3 904	729	595	7 254	6 290	721	676
1975	5 709	10 269	0	10 269	521	-5 523	4 225	744	741	8 038	7 007	710	680
1976	6 080	11 186	0	11 186	573	-6 095	4 518	794	768	8 732	7 494	696	677
1977	6 577	12 269	0	12 269	609	-6 741	4 919	871	787	9 647	8 371	682	683
1978	6 949	13 370	0	13 370	668	-7 527	5 175	965	810	10 371	8 904	670	696
1979	7 366	14 631	0	14 631	770	-8 486	5 375	1 088	903	11 236	9 512	656	709
1980	7 845	16 125	0	16 125	859	-9 728	5 538	1 283	1 025	12 291	10 450	638	707
1981	8 610	17 541	0	17 541	1 002	-10 675	5 864	1 614	1 133	13 519	11 349	637	696
1982	9 352	18 647	0	18 647	1 074	-11 326	6 247	1 838	1 267	14 747	12 452	634	681
1983	9 796	19 582	0	19 582	1 292	-11 702	6 588	1 883	1 325	15 490	13 204	632	676
1984	10 829	21 323	0	21 323	1 463	-12 630	7 231	2 185	1 414	17 098	14 596	633	699
1985	11 516	22 794	0	22 794	1 678	-13 423	7 693	2 408	1 415	18 148	15 475	635	713
1986	12 135	24 283	0	24 283	1 845	-14 271	8 166	2 500	1 469	19 013	16 245	638	733
1987	12 829	26 112	0	26 112	2 015	-15 322	8 775	2 540	1 514	20 141	17 067	637	746
1988	14 042	28 785	0	28 785	2 312	-16 846	9 626	2 789	1 626	22 273	19 061	630	769
1989	15 063	30 522	0	30 522	2 550	-17 953	10 019	3 418	1 626	24 133	20 667	624	777
1990	16 025	32 860	0	32 860	2 813	-19 150	10 897	3 393	1 734	26 473	22 858	605	788
1991	16 564	34 558	0	34 558	2 987	-20 356	11 215	3 371	1 978	27 567	24 027	601	774
1992	17 279	36 614	0	36 614	3 172	-21 744	11 698	3 395	2 186	28 916	25 315	598	768
1993	17 857	38 062	0	38 062	3 319	-22 634	12 110	3 354	2 394	29 996	26 358	595	767
1994	18 169	38 961	0	38 961	3 470	-23 190	12 301	3 432	2 437	30 835	26 876	589	747
1995	18 151	39 471	0	39 471	3 530	-23 538	12 403	3 374	2 373	31 266	27 245	581	740
1996	18 766	39 820	0	39 820	3 567	-23 410	12 843	3 343	2 580	32 786	28 275	572	721
1997	19 580	41 000	0	41 000	3 676	-24 077	13 247	3 757	2 575	34 488	29 380	568	717
1998	20 562	42 956	0	42 956	3 907	-25 176	13 873	3 980	2 709	36 379	30 608	565	721
1999	21 115	46 459	0	46 459	4 268	-27 665	14 527	3 862	2 726	37 030	30 716	570	735
2000	23 102	48 999	0	48 999	4 493	-28 346	16 160	4 124	2 818	40 408	33 369	572	757
2001	25 525	52 256	0	52 256	4 921	-28 871	18 465	4 094	2 966	44 186	37 126	578	760
2002	25 786	55 075	0	55 075	5 258	-31 181	18 635	3 859	3 292	44 527	38 522	579	774
2003	26 914	57 451	0	57 451	5 466	-32 309	19 676	3 834	3 403	46 614	40 590	577	778
2004	29 203	62 288	0	62 288	5 842	-34 568	21 879	3 880	3 444	50 392	43 932	580	790
2005	31 847	66 062	0	66 062	6 140	-36 113	23 809	4 267	3 772	54 715	47 389	582	798
2006	34 440	69 670	0	69 670	6 488	-37 446	25 735	4 818	3 887	58 830	50 666	585	806
2007	36 732	72 997	0	72 997	6 823	-39 106	27 069	5 416	4 247	62 484	53 606	588	814
2008	38 464	76 475	0	76 475	7 181	-40 979	28 315	5 563	4 585	64 991	56 245	592	. . .

. . . = Not available.

Table 21-2. Personal Income and Employment by Region and State—*Continued*

(Millions of dollars, except as noted.)

Region or state and year	Personal income, total	Derivation of personal income								Per capita (dollars)		Population (thousands)	Total employment (thousands)
		Earnings by place of work			Less: Contributions for government social insurance	Plus: Adjustment for residence	Equals: Net earnings by place of residence	Plus: Dividends, interest, and rent	Plus: Personal current transfer receipts	Personal income	Disposable personal income		
		Nonfarm	Farm	Total									
FLORIDA													
1958	8 710	6 449	368	6 817	216	-1	6 600	1 531	580	1 881	1 708	4 630	. . .
1959	9 626	7 144	441	7 586	282	-1	7 302	1 668	655	2 002	1 811	4 808	. . .
1960	10 088	7 507	379	7 886	329	-1	7 556	1 817	715	2 016	1 822	5 004	. . .
1961	10 666	7 784	437	8 222	343	-1	7 877	1 959	829	2 034	1 839	5 243	. . .
1962	11 524	8 412	451	8 863	389	-1	8 474	2 122	928	2 111	1 907	5 458	. . .
1963	12 368	9 071	433	9 504	449	-1	9 055	2 302	1 011	2 198	1 985	5 628	. . .
1964	13 571	10 000	490	10 490	481	-1	10 008	2 508	1 055	2 347	2 137	5 781	. . .
1965	14 854	10 948	463	11 411	516	-1	10 894	2 788	1 171	2 495	2 265	5 954	. . .
1966	16 344	12 175	473	12 648	679	-1	11 967	3 071	1 306	2 678	2 426	6 104	. . .
1967	18 129	13 376	512	13 889	808	-2	13 079	3 422	1 628	2 904	2 608	6 242	. . .
1968	20 850	15 267	526	15 793	963	-4	14 826	4 089	1 936	3 241	2 875	6 433	. . .
1969	24 265	17 587	636	18 224	1 132	-22	17 070	5 002	2 194	3 654	3 215	6 641	2 857
1970	27 412	19 648	546	20 194	1 272	-20	18 903	5 865	2 645	4 004	3 566	6 845	2 966
1971	30 744	21 806	640	22 446	1 472	-14	20 960	6 598	3 187	4 292	3 846	7 163	3 082
1972	35 396	25 330	739	26 068	1 796	-11	24 261	7 382	3 753	4 707	4 148	7 520	3 338
1973	41 436	29 862	837	30 699	2 420	-10	28 269	8 608	4 559	5 227	4 634	7 927	3 666
1974	46 570	32 988	908	33 897	2 780	-1	31 116	9 957	5 496	5 599	4 981	8 317	3 766
1975	50 491	34 395	1 000	35 395	2 859	-9	32 527	10 783	7 181	5 911	5 362	8 542	3 676
1976	55 378	37 742	1 037	38 779	3 168	10	35 621	11 798	7 959	6 369	5 738	8 695	3 730
1977	62 064	42 319	1 035	43 354	3 570	22	39 806	13 548	8 710	6 982	6 273	8 889	3 929
1978	71 641	49 021	1 236	50 256	4 245	25	46 037	15 921	9 683	7 845	7 000	9 132	4 235
1979	82 755	56 229	1 312	57 541	5 105	22	52 458	19 076	11 221	8 738	7 743	9 471	4 457
1980	97 741	64 498	1 671	66 169	5 915	16	60 270	24 129	13 341	9 933	8 764	9 840	4 695
1981	113 537	73 001	1 405	74 406	7 194	111	67 323	30 619	15 595	11 139	9 811	10 193	4 881
1982	122 669	77 823	1 784	79 608	7 902	134	71 839	33 177	17 653	11 715	10 236	10 471	4 970
1983	136 037	85 908	2 474	88 382	8 777	160	79 765	36 964	19 309	12 655	11 331	10 750	5 185
1984	152 157	97 483	1 835	99 318	10 141	210	89 387	42 201	20 568	13 782	12 455	11 040	5 529
1985	166 837	107 129	1 841	108 970	11 349	255	97 876	46 765	22 196	14 698	13 130	11 351	5 809
1986	180 125	116 036	1 977	118 013	12 556	312	105 768	50 446	23 910	15 438	13 740	11 668	6 055
1987	194 991	127 575	2 145	129 719	13 658	373	116 434	53 207	25 351	16 253	14 440	11 997	6 140
1988	213 834	140 308	2 705	143 013	15 504	450	127 959	58 106	27 768	17 376	15 504	12 306	6 443
1989	238 049	149 588	2 484	152 072	16 800	531	135 803	70 930	31 317	18 836	16 792	12 638	6 654
1990	254 984	160 352	2 079	162 431	17 966	637	145 102	75 602	34 280	19 564	17 525	13 033	6 800
1991	264 449	165 073	2 458	167 531	18 866	683	149 348	76 318	38 783	19 780	17 842	13 370	6 775
1992	278 700	176 786	2 461	179 247	20 071	748	159 925	71 444	47 331	20 417	18 411	13 651	6 820
1993	293 167	188 108	2 534	190 641	21 391	803	170 054	75 621	47 492	21 050	18 942	13 927	7 061
1994	308 508	197 779	2 163	199 942	22 925	865	177 882	80 344	50 282	21 666	19 450	14 239	7 294
1995	329 885	210 690	2 183	212 873	24 318	933	189 489	86 064	54 333	22 691	20 321	14 538	7 554
1996	351 355	224 299	1 931	226 229	25 622	1 005	201 612	92 335	57 407	23 655	20 962	14 853	7 804
1997	372 094	236 991	2 117	239 108	27 216	1 101	212 993	99 454	59 647	24 502	21 513	15 186	8 068
1998	402 454	257 448	2 512	259 960	29 239	1 224	231 945	109 355	61 154	25 987	22 728	15 487	8 368
1999	423 834	277 556	2 928	280 484	31 118	1 351	250 717	109 423	63 693	26 894	23 509	15 759	8 656
2000	457 539	301 755	1 750	303 505	33 266	1 514	271 753	117 914	67 872	28 512	24 812	16 047	8 933
2001	478 637	313 257	2 053	315 310	35 508	1 572	281 373	74 367	74 367	29 291	25 633	16 341	9 112
2002	495.489	326 733	1 970	328 703	37 126	1 543	293 120	121 968	80 401	29 754	26 624	16 653	9 205
2003	514 378	344 549	1 767	346 316	39 065	1 531	308 782	120 125	85 471	30 369	27 567	16 937	9 411
2004	565 681	373 624	1 692	375 316	42 456	1 608	334 468	136 654	94 559	32 672	29 494	17 314	9 775
2005	614 433	407 074	1 470	408 544	46 357	1 653	363 840	152 071	98 523	34 709	30 837	17 702	10 148
2006	668 484	434 787	1 524	436 311	49 799	1 724	388 235	176 661	103 587	37 099	32 916	18 019	10 520
2007	699 176	445 813	1 620	447 433	51 048	1 891	398 276	190 467	110 434	38 417	33 920	18 200	10 680
2008	716 089	445 357	1 596	446 954	51 137	1 985	397 802	197 380	120 907	39 070	34 880	18 328	. . .

. . . = Not available.

Table 21-2. Personal Income and Employment by Region and State—*Continued*

(Millions of dollars, except as noted.)

Region or state and year	Personal income, total	Earnings by place of work			Less: Contributions for government social insurance	Plus: Adjustment for residence	Equals: Net earnings by place of residence	Plus: Dividends, interest, and rent	Plus: Personal current transfer receipts	Per capita (dollars)		Population (thousands)	Total employment (thousands)
		Nonfarm	Farm	Total						Personal income	Disposable personal income		
GEORGIA													
1958	5 974	4 845	359	5 204	186	-11	5 007	589	379	1 570	1 436	3 804	. . .
1959	6 378	5 261	310	5 571	224	-13	5 334	644	401	1 649	1 503	3 868	. . .
1960	6 670	5 485	323	5 808	261	-15	5 532	721	417	1 686	1 525	3 956	. . .
1961	6 954	5 641	343	5 985	266	-16	5 703	777	473	1 732	1 569	4 015	. . .
1962	7 475	6 150	309	6 459	297	-20	6 142	846	488	1 830	1 647	4 086	. . .
1963	8 123	6 655	395	7 051	349	-24	6 678	924	522	1 947	1 752	4 172	. . .
1964	8 808	7 316	330	7 647	376	-29	7 242	1 019	547	2 069	1 875	4 258	. . .
1965	9 713	8 051	374	8 425	407	-35	7 983	1 129	601	2 242	2 027	4 332	. . .
1966	10 695	9 023	385	9 408	545	-43	8 820	1 219	656	2 442	2 193	4 379	. . .
1967	11 625	9 829	383	10 212	624	-52	9 535	1 309	781	2 637	2 378	4 408	. . .
1968	12 873	11 011	341	11 352	682	-62	10 608	1 334	930	2 872	2 558	4 482	. . .
1969	14 317	12 274	416	12 690	786	-76	11 828	1 427	1 063	3 146	2 743	4 551	2 119
1970	15 556	13 140	394	13 535	836	-69	12 629	1 628	1 299	3 378	2 989	4 605	2 121
1971	17 197	14 398	453	14 851	951	-65	13 835	1 817	1 545	3 651	3 266	4 710	2 167
1972	19 340	16 305	467	16 772	1 127	-57	15 588	2 012	1 740	4 023	3 549	4 807	2 253
1973	21 988	18 369	783	19 153	1 444	-55	17 653	2 325	2 009	4 481	3 984	4 907	2 356
1974	24 235	20 004	666	20 670	1 626	-55	18 989	2 736	2 510	4 852	4 312	4 995	2 374
1975	26 088	20 923	633	21 555	1 679	-45	19 832	2 931	3 326	5 157	4 673	5 059	2 313
1976	29 155	23 887	625	24 513	1 945	-77	22 492	3 117	3 547	5 688	5 107	5 126	2 400
1977	32 319	27 068	360	27 428	2 188	-97	25 143	3 496	3 680	6 201	5 535	5 212	2 503
1978	36 742	30 792	562	31 354	2 550	-79	28 724	4 015	4 002	6 951	6 163	5 286	2 622
1979	41 292	34 539	592	35 130	2 972	-97	32 062	4 670	4 560	7 659	6 711	5 391	2 705
1980	46 192	38 226	34	38 260	3 309	-114	34 837	5 901	5 454	8 420	7 409	5 486	2 747
1981	52 395	42 185	517	42 702	3 929	-28	38 745	7 431	6 218	9 409	8 246	5 568	2 785
1982	56 834	45 089	679	45 767	4 283	-69	41 416	8 627	6 792	10 059	8 872	5 650	2 802
1983	62 289	49 717	471	50 188	4 794	-112	45 282	9 631	7 376	10 874	9 574	5 728	2 886
1984	71 237	56 949	950	57 899	5 610	-176	52 113	11 242	7 882	12 209	10 814	5 835	3 081
1985	78 332	63 162	781	63 943	6 359	-193	57 390	12 490	8 451	13 137	11 561	5 963	3 224
1986	85 000	69 039	822	69 860	7 115	-238	62 507	13 491	9 001	13 970	12 305	6 085	3 354
1987	91 395	74 555	891	75 446	7 642	-238	67 566	14 383	9 446	14 721	12 894	6 208	3 455
1988	99 402	80 830	1 151	81 981	8 534	-232	73 215	15 990	10 198	15 738	13 860	6 316	3 568
1989	107 069	85 130	1 349	86 479	9 075	-192	77 211	18 537	11 321	16 701	14 648	6 411	3 633
1990	114 643	90 735	1 257	91 991	9 719	-113	82 159	19 906	12 577	17 603	15 464	6 513	3 689
1991	120 222	93 943	1 552	95 495	10 196	-129	85 170	20 604	14 449	18 070	15 985	6 653	3 645
1992	130 041	102 108	1 638	103 746	10 930	-179	92 637	21 206	16 198	19 075	16 909	6 817	3 722
1993	137 607	108 791	1 480	110 271	11 683	-166	98 422	21 819	17 366	19 719	17 402	6 978	3 891
1994	148 234	116 226	1 947	118 173	12 644	-214	105 315	24 283	18 637	20 711	18 252	7 157	4 046
1995	158 858	125 131	1 784	126 914	13 582	-297	113 036	25 942	19 880	21 677	19 043	7 328	4 215
1996	172 113	134 974	1 881	136 855	14 509	-350	121 996	28 738	21 378	22 945	20 029	7 501	4 362
1997	182 868	144 033	1 861	145 894	15 538	-434	129 922	31 166	21 779	23 795	20 630	7 685	4 477
1998	198 782	157 534	1 823	159 357	16 845	-552	141 960	34 433	22 389	25 279	21 792	7 864	4 640
1999	212 081	171 018	1 994	173 012	18 195	-582	154 235	34 086	23 761	26 359	22 695	8 046	4 778
2000	230 356	185 385	1 650	187 035	19 367	-728	166 940	37 570	25 845	27 990	24 054	8 230	4 892
2001	240 616	192 105	1 985	194 091	20 178	-766	173 148	38 767	28 702	28 582	24 686	8 419	4 908
2002	244 957	195 576	1 470	197 046	20 587	-801	175 659	36 731	32 568	28 538	25 220	8 584	4 893
2003	250 806	201 111	2 010	203 121	21 078	-799	181 244	36 658	32 903	28 720	25 632	8 733	4 950
2004	264 854	213 766	1 843	215 608	22 863	-863	191 883	37 738	35 233	29 723	26 589	8 911	5 074
2005	284 277	227 018	2 009	229 026	24 072	-881	204 074	42 120	38 084	31 260	27 770	9 094	5 246
2006	300 982	239 149	1 177	240 327	25 376	-880	214 071	46 392	40 519	32 299	28 473	9 319	5 420
2007	319 018	250 387	1 595	251 982	26 540	-930	224 512	50 911	43 595	33 499	29 361	9 523	5 560
2008	329 071	254 341	1 308	255 649	27 017	-907	227 725	52 889	48 457	33 975	30 082	9 686	. . .

. . . = Not available.

Table 21-2. Personal Income and Employment by Region and State—*Continued*

(Millions of dollars, except as noted.)

| Region or state and year | Personal income, total | Derivation of personal income | | | | | | | | | Per capita (dollars) | | Population (thousands) | Total employment (thousands) |
| | | Earnings by place of work | | | Less: Contributions for government social insurance | Plus: Adjustment for residence | Equals: Net earnings by place of residence | Plus: Dividends, interest, and rent | Plus: Personal current transfer receipts | Personal income | Disposable personal income | | |
		Nonfarm	Farm	Total									
HAWAII													
1958	1 168	963	64	1 027	40	0	986	140	42	1 931	. . .	605	. . .
1959	1 306	1 077	73	1 151	45	0	1 106	155	46	2 100	. . .	622	. . .
1960	1 496	1 216	81	1 297	52	0	1 245	203	48	2 330	2 005	642	. . .
1961	1 619	1 316	75	1 391	57	0	1 334	227	59	2 457	2 112	659	. . .
1962	1 736	1 403	78	1 481	61	0	1 421	248	67	2 538	2 222	684	. . .
1963	1 850	1 505	87	1 592	76	0	1 516	264	70	2 712	2 377	682	. . .
1964	2 013	1 647	88	1 735	82	0	1 653	289	70	2 876	2 556	700	. . .
1965	2 205	1 795	91	1 885	85	0	1 800	323	81	3 132	2 796	704	. . .
1966	2 410	1 983	95	2 077	113	0	1 964	351	95	3 394	2 982	710	. . .
1967	2 620	2 145	98	2 243	130	0	2 112	387	121	3 623	3 176	723	. . .
1968	2 949	2 442	117	2 559	152	0	2 407	402	140	4 018	3 495	734	. . .
1969	3 375	2 826	119	2 946	183	0	2 763	452	160	4 543	3 893	743	416
1970	3 886	3 238	133	3 371	212	0	3 160	520	206	5 094	4 389	763	434
1971	4 225	3 476	131	3 607	236	0	3 371	585	270	5 338	4 677	792	437
1972	4 653	3 840	132	3 971	274	0	3 697	633	322	5 687	4 918	818	453
1973	5 172	4 297	139	4 436	349	0	4 087	715	370	6 143	5 328	842	473
1974	5 945	4 740	343	5 084	401	0	4 683	818	444	6 928	6 040	858	485
1975	6 483	5 252	203	5 454	443	0	5 011	895	577	7 409	6 613	875	499
1976	7 041	5 736	173	5 909	485	0	5 425	943	674	7 891	6 991	892	505
1977	7 650	6 244	185	6 428	523	0	5 905	1 038	707	8 353	7 368	916	509
1978	8 465	6 935	168	7 103	597	0	6 506	1 200	759	9 114	7 976	929	527
1979	9 602	7 838	194	8 032	701	0	7 331	1 432	839	10 107	8 818	950	556
1980	11 073	8 781	377	9 158	781	0	8 377	1 733	962	11 443	10 007	968	575
1981	12 015	9 482	200	9 682	901	0	8 781	2 102	1 132	12 283	10 748	978	569
1982	12 715	10 103	235	10 338	952	0	9 386	2 102	1 227	12 794	11 408	994	568
1983	14 087	10 863	339	11 202	1 040	0	10 162	2 576	1 349	13 910	12 412	1 013	579
1984	15 352	11 896	240	12 136	1 140	0	10 996	2 933	1 423	14 935	13 374	1 028	585
1985	16 311	12 744	222	12 966	1 242	0	11 724	3 078	1 509	15 688	13 990	1 040	602
1986	17 225	13 543	257	13 799	1 348	0	12 452	3 202	1 572	16 377	14 568	1 052	616
1987	18 386	14 669	241	14 910	1 474	0	13 436	3 324	1 627	17 217	15 106	1 068	647
1988	20 161	16 240	264	16 504	1 697	0	14 807	3 616	1 739	18 671	16 358	1 080	674
1989	22 462	17 930	246	18 176	1 892	0	16 283	4 251	1 927	20 521	17 789	1 095	702
1990	24 704	19 964	261	20 225	2 113	0	18 112	4 505	2 087	22 186	19 269	1 113	730
1991	26 026	21 069	230	21 299	2 278	0	19 021	4 702	2 304	22 895	19 769	1 137	751
1992	27 910	22 533	217	22 750	2 429	0	20 321	4 526	3 063	24 089	21 223	1 159	753
1993	28 799	23 125	213	23 339	2 471	0	20 868	5 002	2 929	24 555	21 655	1 173	749
1994	29 424	23 199	210	23 409	2 503	0	20 906	5 347	3 172	24 777	21 869	1 188	744
1995	29 926	23 202	200	23 402	2 484	0	20 918	5 444	3 564	25 004	22 190	1 197	740
1996	30 122	23 261	197	23 459	2 460	0	20 998	5 461	3 663	25 024	22 086	1 204	739
1997	31 002	23 747	208	23 956	2 462	0	21 493	5 834	3 675	25 587	22 565	1 212	740
1998	31 757	24 192	221	24 413	2 492	0	21 921	6 100	3 736	26 132	22 967	1 215	742
1999	32 646	24 881	252	25 133	2 561	0	22 572	6 191	3 882	26 973	23 651	1 210	742
2000	34 451	26 266	212	26 478	2 668	0	23 810	6 567	4 074	28 437	24 855	1 211	763
2001	35 126	26 745	215	26 960	2 786	0	24 174	6 596	4 357	28 840	25 207	1 218	767
2002	36 370	28 382	223	28 605	2 991	0	25 614	6 045	4 711	29 632	26 322	1 227	770
2003	37 837	30 187	217	30 404	3 227	0	27 177	5 782	4 877	30 555	27 328	1 238	787
2004	41 027	32 822	221	33 043	3 419	0	29 623	6 204	5 200	32 782	29 334	1 252	813
2005	44 111	35 300	213	35 513	3 641	0	31 872	6 581	5 659	34 885	30 846	1 264	838
2006	47 334	37 611	210	37 820	3 892	0	33 928	7 446	5 960	37 117	32 737	1 275	858
2007	50 125	39 311	213	39 524	4 032	0	35 492	8 096	6 537	39 242	34 524	1 277	873
2008	52 159	40 582	181	40 763	4 156	0	36 607	8 341	7 212	40 490	35 939	1 288	. . .

. . . = Not available.

Table 21-2. Personal Income and Employment by Region and State—*Continued*

(Millions of dollars, except as noted.)

Region or state and year	Personal income, total	Earnings by place of work Nonfarm	Farm	Total	Less: Contributions for government social insurance	Plus: Adjustment for residence	Equals: Net earnings by place of residence	Plus: Dividends, interest, and rent	Plus: Personal current transfer receipts	Per capita (dollars) Personal income	Disposable personal income	Population (thousands)	Total employment (thousands)
IDAHO													
1958	1 165	824	164	988	37	-3	948	139	78	1 804	1 627	646	. . .
1959	1 236	884	164	1 048	43	-3	1 002	149	85	1 881	1 693	657	. . .
1960	1 263	913	156	1 069	50	-3	1 016	156	90	1 882	1 683	671	. . .
1961	1 336	971	156	1 127	56	-3	1 068	166	102	1 954	1 760	684	. . .
1962	1 430	1 046	165	1 210	62	-3	1 145	179	106	2 067	1 866	692	. . .
1963	1 459	1 062	171	1 233	69	-2	1 162	188	109	2 137	1 920	683	. . .
1964	1 507	1 141	132	1 273	70	-2	1 201	194	112	2 215	2 017	680	. . .
1965	1 728	1 247	229	1 477	76	-2	1 399	209	120	2 519	2 296	686	. . .
1966	1 753	1 322	177	1 499	93	-1	1 405	219	129	2 544	2 308	689	. . .
1967	1 865	1 387	204	1 591	107	-1	1 484	226	155	2 711	2 450	688	. . .
1968	1 989	1 515	184	1 698	121	-1	1 576	239	174	2 862	2 573	695	. . .
1969	2 290	1 675	250	1 925	127	12	1 810	286	194	3 239	2 887	707	315
1970	2 525	1 828	264	2 092	137	14	1 969	328	229	3 520	3 165	717	324
1971	2 755	2 001	247	2 248	154	15	2 108	378	269	3 730	3 354	739	332
1972	3 144	2 279	317	2 596	183	16	2 429	409	306	4 119	3 727	763	347
1973	3 658	2 588	450	3 038	240	18	2 816	491	351	4 677	4 200	782	365
1974	4 316	2 963	625	3 588	282	22	3 328	567	421	5 341	4 758	808	381
1975	4 626	3 367	383	3 750	316	28	3 462	640	524	5 560	4 999	832	393
1976	5 218	3 917	339	4 256	370	35	3 922	705	591	6 088	5 466	857	419
1977	5 715	4 417	236	4 653	418	35	4 271	818	627	6 469	5 793	883	435
1978	6 595	5 124	304	5 427	487	42	4 982	944	669	7 240	6 465	911	460
1979	7 264	5 665	227	5 892	567	48	5 372	1 110	781	7 789	6 942	933	470
1980	8 198	6 040	402	6 442	605	61	5 899	1 365	934	8 648	7 719	948	466
1981	9 032	6 497	423	6 920	702	53	6 271	1 690	1 071	9 387	8 297	962	463
1982	9 368	6 479	391	6 869	718	62	6 214	1 925	1 229	9 621	8 590	974	453
1983	10 143	7 008	581	7 589	782	64	6 871	1 972	1 300	10 330	9 293	982	464
1984	10 973	7 715	496	8 211	874	77	7 414	2 212	1 346	11 074	10 002	991	474
1985	11 572	8 162	454	8 617	933	84	7 767	2 362	1 442	11 641	10 490	994	476
1986	11 833	8 305	475	8 780	961	100	7 919	2 392	1 521	11 949	10 827	990	476
1987	12 366	8 689	592	9 282	995	109	8 396	2 404	1 566	12 554	11 348	985	490
1988	13 300	9 437	670	10 106	1 127	124	9 104	2 515	1 682	13 493	12 172	986	512
1989	14 647	10 188	876	11 065	1 235	139	9 969	2 855	1 824	14 729	13 143	994	529
1990	15 918	11 099	990	12 089	1 358	152	10 884	3 067	1 968	15 724	13 988	1 012	552
1991	16 692	11 780	816	12 596	1 482	174	11 289	3 210	2 194	16 030	14 280	1 041	570
1992	18 318	13 082	858	13 940	1 613	191	12 518	3 340	2 460	17 093	15 135	1 072	590
1993	20 073	14 337	1 080	15 416	1 767	210	13 860	3 568	2 644	18 103	16 066	1 109	616
1994	21 422	15 629	761	16 390	1 951	238	14 676	3 957	2 789	18 707	16 593	1 145	651
1995	22 871	16 455	836	17 291	2 074	281	15 498	4 350	3 023	19 426	17 206	1 177	672
1996	24 360	17 184	947	18 131	2 134	326	16 323	4 718	3 319	20 248	17 898	1 203	694
1997	25 367	17 966	779	18 745	2 223	369	16 891	5 068	3 408	20 648	18 173	1 229	713
1998	27 287	19 127	959	20 086	2 337	437	18 185	5 544	3 557	21 789	19 192	1 252	740
1999	29 068	20 676	1 046	21 722	2 480	504	19 746	5 546	3 776	22 786	19 988	1 276	759
2000	31 290	22 587	867	23 453	2 676	524	21 302	5 909	4 079	24 079	20 962	1 299	788
2001	33 054	23 441	1 043	24 484	2 723	530	22 291	6 195	4 568	25 027	21 916	1 321	796
2002	33 849	24 131	953	25 085	2 801	544	22 827	6 051	4 971	25 234	22 747	1 341	802
2003	34 816	24 927	748	25 675	2 909	570	23 336	6 227	5 253	25 543	23 186	1 363	813
2004	38 079	26 895	1 013	27 908	3 100	614	25 421	7 057	5 601	27 389	24 931	1 390	841
2005	40 845	28 946	887	29 833	3 364	625	27 094	7 691	6 060	28 681	25 683	1 424	879
2006	44 383	31 795	689	32 484	3 757	657	29 385	8 450	6 548	30 374	26 944	1 461	918
2007	47 583	33 115	1 142	34 257	3 901	714	31 069	9 433	7 081	31 804	28 040	1 496	947
2008	48 965	33 416	958	34 374	3 936	756	31 195	9 911	7 859	32 133	28 638	1 524	. . .

. . . = Not available.

Table 21-2. Personal Income and Employment by Region and State—Continued

(Millions of dollars, except as noted.)

Region or state and year	Personal income, total	Earnings by place of work			Less: Contributions for government social insurance	Plus: Adjustment for residence	Equals: Net earnings by place of residence	Plus: Dividends, interest, and rent	Plus: Personal current transfer receipts	Per capita (dollars)		Population (thousands)	Total employment (thousands)
		Nonfarm	Farm	Total						Personal income	Disposable personal income		
ILLINOIS													
1958	24 601	20 156	856	21 012	704	-111	20 198	3 052	1 350	2 488	2 208	9 886	. . .
1959	26 130	21 778	657	22 435	852	-127	21 456	3 267	1 407	2 617	2 321	9 986	. . .
1960	26 950	22 507	636	23 143	1 073	-133	21 937	3 540	1 472	2 672	2 352	10 086	. . .
1961	27 971	22 922	800	23 723	1 088	-138	22 496	3 775	1 699	2 761	2 439	10 130	. . .
1962	29 527	24 220	785	25 004	1 195	-154	23 655	4 108	1 763	2 872	2 528	10 280	. . .
1963	30 678	25 126	805	25 931	1 329	-159	24 443	4 419	1 815	2 949	2 602	10 402	. . .
1964	32 775	26 982	651	27 633	1 337	-175	26 122	4 806	1 847	3 098	2 772	10 580	. . .
1965	35 524	28 969	888	29 857	1 356	-194	28 307	5 237	1 981	3 322	2 965	10 693	. . .
1966	38 473	31 888	960	32 848	1 820	-222	30 806	5 523	2 145	3 551	3 142	10 836	. . .
1967	40 917	33 884	922	34 806	1 986	-239	32 581	5 781	2 555	3 738	3 295	10 947	. . .
1968	43 848	36 625	680	37 306	2 192	-265	34 849	6 006	2 993	3 988	3 476	10 995	. . .
1969	47 931	39 958	897	40 854	2 717	93	38 230	6 465	3 236	4 342	3 715	11 039	5 179
1970	50 835	42 176	706	42 882	2 811	18	40 089	6 909	3 837	4 570	3 930	11 125	5 144
1971	54 555	44 885	870	45 755	3 075	-23	42 657	7 307	4 592	4 868	4 253	11 206	5 105
1972	59 248	48 794	980	49 774	3 518	-42	46 214	7 865	5 169	5 263	4 538	11 258	5 156
1973	66 374	54 070	1 822	55 892	4 491	-59	51 342	8 884	6 149	5 895	5 119	11 260	5 351
1974	72 753	59 101	1 649	60 750	5 079	-71	55 600	10 143	7 010	6 453	5 580	11 274	5 442
1975	79 270	62 185	2 439	64 625	5 196	-96	59 332	10 952	8 986	7 011	6 150	11 306	5 342
1976	86 597	69 306	1 693	70 999	5 882	-76	65 040	11 641	9 916	7 623	6 623	11 360	5 458
1977	95 420	76 897	1 695	78 592	6 516	-10	72 066	12 982	10 372	8 366	7 250	11 406	5 587
1978	105 497	85 870	1 482	87 352	7 467	78	79 963	14 494	11 039	9 226	7 972	11 434	5 748
1979	115 966	93 950	1 809	95 759	8 483	163	87 439	16 503	12 024	10 152	8 709	11 423	5 811
1980	125 838	99 447	350	99 797	8 955	262	91 104	20 148	14 585	11 005	9 464	11 435	5 688
1981	139 569	106 465	1 497	107 962	10 275	198	97 885	24 927	16 758	12 196	10 471	11 443	5 684
1982	147 604	109 368	899	110 267	10 717	126	99 676	29 528	18 401	12 921	11 284	11 423	5 583
1983	153 546	114 125	-498	113 627	11 259	90	102 458	31 385	19 703	13 459	11 829	11 409	5 542
1984	169 736	126 062	1 202	127 264	12 809	-15	114 440	35 223	20 073	14 873	13 150	11 412	5 746
1985	178 529	133 155	1 697	134 852	13 762	-83	121 007	36 571	20 951	15 661	13 801	11 400	5 814
1986	187 025	141 045	1 404	142 449	14 767	-142	127 540	37 776	21 710	16 424	14 487	11 387	5 927
1987	197 603	151 176	1 415	152 591	15 637	-230	136 723	38 717	22 163	17 347	15 145	11 391	6 072
1988	212 011	164 930	838	165 768	17 418	-361	147 989	41 099	22 923	18 613	16 346	11 390	6 232
1989	225 574	173 261	2 143	175 404	18 470	-376	156 558	44 657	24 358	19 770	17 247	11 410	6 342
1990	238 499	183 093	1 722	184 815	19 637	-281	164 897	47 026	26 576	20 824	18 168	11 453	6 440
1991	245 434	188 369	928	189 298	20 599	-294	168 405	48 337	28 693	21 215	18 634	11 569	6 416
1992	263 702	201 612	1 882	203 494	21 736	-337	181 421	49 557	32 724	22 550	19 905	11 694	6 397
1993	271 174	209 580	1 641	211 222	22 937	-497	187 788	49 132	34 254	22 962	20 164	11 810	6 487
1994	285 537	219 921	2 095	222 015	24 452	-515	197 048	53 003	35 486	23 969	20 964	11 913	6 658
1995	301 688	232 445	556	233 001	25 762	-778	206 461	57 378	37 849	25 123	21 920	12 008	6 822
1996	320 081	243 715	2 345	246 061	26 827	-831	218 403	61 828	39 850	26 449	22 924	12 102	6 925
1997	337 897	258 356	2 167	260 523	28 338	-874	231 312	65 874	40 712	27 729	23 849	12 186	7 029
1998	360 095	276 720	1 487	278 207	30 089	-853	247 265	71 525	41 305	29 343	25 103	12 272	7 185
1999	373 385	293 094	935	294 029	31 536	-1 049	261 445	69 859	42 081	30 212	25 763	12 359	7 282
2000	400 373	311 686	1 338	313 024	33 038	-1 343	278 642	76 913	44 818	32 190	27 416	12 438	7 416
2001	407 254	317 043	1 129	318 172	33 984	-1 505	282 683	76 281	48 290	32 553	27 883	12 511	7 371
2002	413 711	324 017	408	324 425	34 496	-1 457	288 472	73 143	52 096	32 925	28 871	12 565	7 284
2003	426 877	337 466	1 364	338 830	35 231	-1 516	302 083	70 081	54 713	33 849	30 118	12 611	7 260
2004	445 151	352 778	2 801	355 579	37 435	-1 607	316 538	72 279	56 334	35 146	31 377	12 666	7 336
2005	463 089	365 340	1 309	366 649	39 679	-1 597	325 373	76 214	61 502	36 452	32 201	12 704	7 440
2006	490 683	383 909	1 403	385 313	41 640	-1 713	341 960	86 564	62 160	38 456	33 694	12 760	7 536
2007	526 006	401 451	2 472	403 923	43 132	-1 963	358 828	95 860	71 318	41 012	35 778	12 826	7 609
2008	546 985	412 726	3 593	416 320	44 352	-1 956	370 012	99 039	77 934	42 397	37 298	12 902	. . .

. . . = Not available.

Table 21-2. Personal Income and Employment by Region and State—*Continued*

(Millions of dollars, except as noted.)

Region or state and year	Personal income, total	Earnings by place of work			Less: Contributions for government social insurance	Plus: Adjustment for residence	Equals: Net earnings by place of residence	Plus: Dividends, interest, and rent	Plus: Personal current transfer receipts	Per capita (dollars)		Population (thousands)	Total employment (thousands)
		Nonfarm	Farm	Total						Personal income	Disposable personal income		
INDIANA													
1958	9 197	7 480	420	7 900	295	35	7 640	986	570	2 007	1 816	4 583	. . .
1959	9 790	8 186	294	8 479	356	41	8 164	1 055	571	2 122	1 908	4 613	. . .
1960	10 286	8 534	359	8 893	415	40	8 518	1 164	604	2 201	1 964	4 674	. . .
1961	10 590	8 584	455	9 039	411	43	8 671	1 227	692	2 239	2 010	4 730	. . .
1962	11 343	9 289	444	9 733	461	48	9 320	1 326	697	2 395	2 137	4 736	. . .
1963	11 909	9 775	460	10 236	526	48	9 757	1 428	724	2 482	2 201	4 799	. . .
1964	12 684	10 603	293	10 896	545	46	10 397	1 538	749	2 612	2 341	4 856	. . .
1965	14 029	11 559	544	12 103	581	49	11 571	1 653	806	2 850	2 551	4 922	. . .
1966	15 137	12 807	470	13 277	818	55	12 515	1 756	866	3 028	2 684	4 999	. . .
1967	15 860	13 426	423	13 849	916	59	12 992	1 856	1 011	3 139	2 775	5 053	. . .
1968	17 245	14 664	373	15 037	992	69	14 113	1 951	1 180	3 386	2 968	5 093	. . .
1969	18 956	16 014	541	16 555	1 097	25	15 483	2 194	1 279	3 686	3 186	5 143	2 327
1970	19 678	16 472	371	16 843	1 116	58	15 785	2 393	1 500	3 782	3 309	5 204	2 291
1971	21 408	17 530	588	18 118	1 229	118	17 008	2 609	1 790	4 078	3 607	5 250	2 290
1972	23 453	19 484	496	19 980	1 442	151	18 689	2 794	1 970	4 428	3 876	5 296	2 367
1973	27 049	21 954	1 218	23 172	1 865	195	21 502	3 211	2 335	5 076	4 487	5 329	2 483
1974	28 975	23 614	721	24 335	2 091	256	22 500	3 718	2 757	5 416	4 713	5 350	2 493
1975	31 211	24 291	1 085	25 376	2 122	301	23 555	4 144	3 512	5 833	5 170	5 351	2 405
1976	34 912	27 780	1 065	28 846	2 440	351	26 756	4 491	3 665	6 500	5 704	5 372	2 489
1977	38 717	31 429	712	32 141	2 757	413	29 798	5 070	3 849	7 163	6 263	5 405	2 578
1978	43 272	35 403	716	36 119	3 196	467	33 390	5 646	4 236	7 945	6 916	5 446	2 671
1979	47 781	38 926	655	39 581	3 636	544	36 489	6 425	4 867	8 727	7 565	5 475	2 713
1980	51 469	40 144	361	40 505	3 725	667	37 447	7 937	6 085	9 374	8 188	5 491	2 632
1981	56 488	43 131	291	43 422	4 306	716	39 832	9 856	6 800	10 307	8 961	5 480	2 611
1982	58 448	43 147	297	43 445	4 399	781	39 827	11 044	7 577	10 689	9 376	5 468	2 530
1983	61 123	45 482	-265	45 218	4 660	830	41 388	11 576	8 159	11 214	9 902	5 450	2 550
1984	68 027	50 091	738	50 829	5 257	993	46 565	12 904	8 558	12 463	11 055	5 458	2 653
1985	71 838	53 092	668	53 760	5 685	1 080	49 155	13 675	9 008	13 159	11 631	5 459	2 709
1986	75 378	55 967	564	56 532	6 093	1 177	51 615	14 251	9 512	13 820	12 243	5 454	2 769
1987	79 846	60 020	753	60 773	6 466	1 249	55 556	14 592	9 698	14 589	12 872	5 473	2 865
1988	84 969	64 859	274	65 132	7 244	1 375	59 263	15 428	10 277	15 472	13 654	5 492	2 953
1989	92 341	68 990	946	69 937	7 759	1 442	63 619	17 555	11 167	16 717	14 678	5 524	3 030
1990	97 213	72 440	838	73 278	8 221	1 513	66 570	18 516	12 127	17 491	15 368	5 558	3 090
1991	100 361	75 515	212	75 728	8 700	1 536	68 563	18 421	13 377	17 869	15 752	5 616	3 091
1992	108 029	80 908	771	81 679	9 257	1 752	74 173	18 631	15 224	19 037	16 844	5 675	3 139
1993	113 428	85 485	849	86 334	9 860	1 940	78 415	18 951	16 062	19 764	17 431	5 739	3 216
1994	120 278	90 848	766	91 614	10 664	2 091	83 042	20 481	16 756	20 761	18 225	5 794	3 306
1995	125 269	94 943	330	95 273	11 170	2 342	86 445	21 817	17 006	21 408	18 757	5 851	3 400
1996	132 103	98 763	1 144	99 907	11 546	2 486	90 847	23 246	18 010	22 368	19 528	5 906	3 439
1997	138 794	103 913	1 185	105 098	12 122	2 648	95 625	24 734	18 435	23 306	20 247	5 955	3 496
1998	149 336	112 167	763	112 931	12 830	2 679	102 779	27 448	19 109	24 894	21 572	5 999	3 567
1999	154 842	118 361	300	118 660	13 446	3 032	108 246	26 616	19 980	25 615	22 206	6 045	3 626
2000	165 285	124 719	553	125 272	13 888	3 374	114 757	28 997	21 531	27 134	23 650	6 091	3 673
2001	167 881	125 841	469	126 310	14 113	3 472	115 669	28 530	23 682	27 414	23 935	6 124	3 611
2002	172 474	130 509	116	130 624	14 505	3 426	119 546	27 685	25 243	28 058	24 959	6 147	3 585
2003	178 675	136 566	742	137 309	15 019	3 475	125 764	26 626	26 285	28 917	26 004	6 179	3 579
2004	186 210	142 155	1 432	143 587	15 855	3 670	131 402	27 206	27 602	29 982	27 072	6 211	3 633
2005	191 163	146 190	990	147 180	16 546	3 866	134 500	26 823	29 839	30 593	27 387	6 249	3 685
2006	201 452	152 057	790	152 847	17 214	4 146	139 780	29 545	32 127	32 006	28 512	6 294	3 706
2007	210 448	157 210	1 298	158 509	17 732	4 547	145 323	32 191	32 933	33 215	29 452	6 336	3 728
2008	217 467	159 894	1 808	161 702	18 144	4 697	148 256	33 191	36 021	34 103	30 437	6 377	. . .

. . . = Not available.

Table 21-2. Personal Income and Employment by Region and State—*Continued*

(Millions of dollars, except as noted.)

Region or state and year	Personal income, total	Earnings by place of work			Less: Contributions for government social insurance	Plus: Adjustment for residence	Equals: Net earnings by place of residence	Plus: Dividends, interest, and rent	Plus: Personal current transfer receipts	Per capita (dollars)		Population (thousands)	Total employment (thousands)
		Nonfarm	Farm	Total						Personal income	Disposable personal income		
IOWA													
1958	5 394	3 437	1 005	4 442	135	27	4 335	729	331	1 992	1 803	2 708	. . .
1959	5 540	3 775	741	4 516	166	29	4 379	799	362	2 030	1 841	2 729	. . .
1960	5 674	3 889	720	4 609	186	33	4 457	833	385	2 059	1 850	2 756	. . .
1961	6 007	4 000	838	4 838	189	36	4 685	898	424	2 180	1 969	2 756	. . .
1962	6 271	4 184	870	5 054	203	39	4 890	938	444	2 281	2 060	2 750	. . .
1963	6 667	4 407	983	5 390	233	41	5 198	1 005	464	2 427	2 194	2 747	. . .
1964	6 984	4 727	905	5 633	247	44	5 430	1 075	479	2 543	2 318	2 746	. . .
1965	7 744	5 060	1 232	6 292	261	48	6 080	1 143	522	2 824	2 569	2 742	. . .
1966	8 428	5 626	1 328	6 955	352	52	6 655	1 207	566	3 051	2 746	2 762	. . .
1967	8 589	6 020	1 066	7 086	418	56	6 725	1 189	675	3 075	2 760	2 793	. . .
1968	9 226	6 491	1 009	7 500	457	60	7 103	1 340	782	3 292	2 931	2 803	. . .
1969	10 256	7 109	1 222	8 331	544	82	7 869	1 532	856	3 656	3 225	2 805	1 289
1970	10 931	7 541	1 197	8 738	568	89	8 259	1 680	992	3 865	3 436	2 829	1 295
1971	11 450	8 046	997	9 043	627	88	8 504	1 819	1 127	4 015	3 609	2 852	1 297
1972	12 835	8 774	1 464	10 237	720	94	9 611	2 008	1 216	4 487	3 968	2 861	1 316
1973	15 472	9 873	2 712	12 586	931	88	11 742	2 326	1 404	5 402	4 817	2 864	1 374
1974	16 035	11 078	1 694	12 772	1 094	84	11 762	2 647	1 626	5 591	4 853	2 868	1 407
1975	17 919	12 052	1 945	13 997	1 169	100	12 928	2 974	2 017	6 219	5 488	2 881	1 407
1976	19 111	13 718	1 204	14 922	1 324	92	13 689	3 207	2 215	6 582	5 758	2 904	1 455
1977	21 145	15 318	1 204	16 522	1 461	65	15 126	3 677	2 341	7 255	6 352	2 914	1 488
1978	24 433	16 950	2 412	19 362	1 675	61	17 748	4 104	2 581	8 370	7 352	2 919	1 514
1979	26 220	18 993	1 540	20 533	1 960	71	18 644	4 683	2 892	8 989	7 816	2 917	1 557
1980	27 930	20 155	683	20 838	2 067	92	18 863	5 661	3 405	9 585	8 320	2 914	1 541
1981	31 569	21 304	1 611	22 915	2 325	118	20 708	6 986	3 876	10 856	9 429	2 908	1 513
1982	32 477	21 296	797	22 093	2 354	192	19 931	8 126	4 419	11 245	9 870	2 888	1 476
1983	33 153	22 192	-7	22 185	2 430	206	19 961	8 456	4 737	11 550	10 226	2 871	1 479
1984	36 836	23 961	1 434	25 395	2 688	239	22 945	9 038	4 853	12 886	11 579	2 859	1 506
1985	38 171	24 690	1 729	26 419	2 815	278	23 882	9 139	5 151	13 490	12 122	2 830	1 503
1986	39 389	25 379	2 106	27 485	2 947	270	24 808	9 237	5 344	14 108	12 706	2 792	1 501
1987	41 242	27 165	2 442	29 606	3 158	266	26 714	9 068	5 460	14 905	13 297	2 767	1 523
1988	42 415	29 167	1 627	30 794	3 529	307	27 572	9 142	5 700	15 321	13 634	2 768	1 567
1989	45 981	30 999	2 366	33 365	3 774	315	29 906	9 985	6 091	16 596	14 707	2 771	1 611
1990	48 358	32 713	2 250	34 963	4 010	323	31 276	10 473	6 609	17 389	15 369	2 781	1 646
1991	49 808	34 164	1 730	35 894	4 221	373	32 047	10 663	7 098	17 804	15 785	2 798	1 665
1992	53 082	36 360	2 558	38 918	4 467	399	34 850	10 565	7 667	18 834	16 768	2 818	1 680
1993	53 098	38 164	846	39 010	4 718	380	34 672	10 408	8 018	18 716	16 590	2 837	1 702
1994	57 873	40 512	2 762	43 273	5 082	386	38 577	10 982	8 314	20 301	18 042	2 851	1 735
1995	60 012	42 462	1 817	44 279	5 345	446	39 380	11 848	8 785	20 929	18 559	2 867	1 796
1996	64 862	44 253	3 653	47 907	5 541	498	42 863	12 750	9 248	22 521	19 962	2 880	1 826
1997	68 297	46 672	3 610	50 283	5 838	578	45 023	13 731	9 543	23 623	20 794	2 891	1 852
1998	71 704	50 255	2 391	52 646	6 175	663	47 134	14 800	9 770	24 701	21 725	2 903	1 894
1999	73 285	53 167	1 402	54 569	6 422	737	48 885	14 310	10 090	25 118	22 076	2 918	1 914
2000	77 763	55 681	1 656	57 336	6 609	832	51 560	15 416	10 787	26 558	23 393	2 928	1 934
2001	79 456	57 013	1 290	58 302	6 820	783	52 265	15 556	11 635	27 125	23 944	2 929	1 916
2002	82 398	58 768	1 399	60 167	6 953	817	54 032	15 478	12 888	28 128	25 316	2 929	1 906
2003	83 920	61 262	1 437	62 698	7 256	850	56 292	14 679	12 949	28 608	25 942	2 933	1 898
2004	90 436	65 326	3 367	68 693	7 688	896	61 901	15 178	13 357	30 732	27 981	2 943	1 941
2005	93 203	68 420	3 119	71 538	8 083	844	64 300	14 761	14 142	31 575	28 484	2 952	1 963
2006	97 152	71 944	2 157	74 101	8 559	838	66 380	15 263	15 509	32 741	29 285	2 967	1 997
2007	104 168	75 420	3 799	79 219	9 004	991	71 206	16 711	16 251	34 916	31 134	2 983	2 035
2008	110 135	78 580	5 168	83 747	9 451	1 028	75 324	17 279	17 532	36 680	32 919	3 003	. . .

. . . = Not available.

Table 21-2. Personal Income and Employment by Region and State—*Continued*

(Millions of dollars, except as noted.)

Region or state and year	Personal income, total	Earnings by place of work			Less: Contributions for government social insurance	Plus: Adjustment for residence	Equals: Net earnings by place of residence	Plus: Dividends, interest, and rent	Plus: Personal current transfer receipts	Per capita (dollars)		Population (thousands)	Total employment (thousands)
		Nonfarm	Farm	Total						Personal income	Disposable personal income		
KANSAS													
1958	4 469	3 025	524	3 548	121	147	3 575	636	258	2 086	1 889	2 142	. . .
1959	4 514	3 180	365	3 545	142	163	3 567	667	280	2 090	1 892	2 160	. . .
1960	4 693	3 241	435	3 676	161	173	3 688	703	302	2 150	1 930	2 183	. . .
1961	4 895	3 394	442	3 836	177	176	3 835	725	335	2 210	1 986	2 215	. . .
1962	5 101	3 579	414	3 993	183	192	4 002	754	345	2 286	2 046	2 231	. . .
1963	5 226	3 683	394	4 077	206	212	4 083	777	366	2 357	2 100	2 217	. . .
1964	5 494	3 928	360	4 288	213	234	4 309	806	379	2 487	2 260	2 209	. . .
1965	5 855	4 100	454	4 554	222	257	4 589	853	413	2 654	2 410	2 206	. . .
1966	6 277	4 496	469	4 966	293	292	4 965	869	444	2 853	2 554	2 200	. . .
1967	6 573	4 791	400	5 191	339	322	5 174	868	532	2 992	2 672	2 197	. . .
1968	7 143	5 257	395	5 651	376	353	5 628	899	616	3 223	2 850	2 216	. . .
1969	7 937	5 721	457	6 178	423	441	6 196	1 052	689	3 550	3 111	2 236	1 029
1970	8 583	6 035	599	6 633	444	439	6 629	1 151	803	3 818	3 372	2 248	1 017
1971	9 320	6 510	700	7 210	494	430	7 146	1 258	916	4 149	3 718	2 246	1 022
1972	10 411	7 208	956	8 163	575	453	8 041	1 386	984	4 616	4 096	2 256	1 048
1973	11 936	8 099	1 378	9 477	737	468	9 208	1 577	1 151	5 271	4 669	2 264	1 090
1974	12 943	9 079	1 049	10 127	856	483	9 754	1 865	1 323	5 707	4 997	2 268	1 122
1975	14 136	10 059	797	10 856	938	497	10 415	2 108	1 613	6 204	5 501	2 279	1 133
1976	15 432	11 388	575	11 963	1 070	514	11 407	2 245	1 780	6 713	5 947	2 299	1 169
1977	16 876	12 551	489	13 040	1 176	559	12 423	2 527	1 926	7 281	6 407	2 318	1 208
1978	18 712	14 255	273	14 528	1 375	604	13 757	2 854	2 102	8 021	7 033	2 333	1 252
1979	21 422	16 102	695	16 796	1 617	652	15 832	3 272	2 318	9 126	7 924	2 347	1 298
1980	23 578	17 658	97	17 755	1 760	729	16 724	4 098	2 756	9 953	8 629	2 369	1 312
1981	26 764	19 350	333	19 683	2 059	755	18 378	5 210	3 176	11 223	9 638	2 385	1 326
1982	28 988	20 045	570	20 615	2 184	778	19 209	6 215	3 564	12 072	10 413	2 401	1 310
1983	30 221	21 125	373	21 498	2 289	754	19 963	6 457	3 800	12 511	11 018	2 416	1 327
1984	33 274	23 302	740	24 042	2 569	799	22 272	7 085	3 918	13 726	12 216	2 424	1 370
1985	35 078	24 466	802	25 268	2 735	844	23 376	7 570	4 131	14 451	12 810	2 427	1 375
1986	36 501	25 581	930	26 510	2 901	826	24 436	7 731	4 334	15 005	13 399	2 433	1 375
1987	38 146	26 820	1 168	27 988	3 017	901	25 872	7 818	4 456	15 599	13 818	2 445	1 428
1988	40 070	28 412	1 136	29 549	3 319	911	27 140	8 254	4 675	16 275	14 422	2 462	1 440
1989	42 157	30 030	818	30 847	3 504	960	28 303	8 725	5 128	17 048	14 988	2 473	1 463
1990	44 876	31 495	1 372	32 867	3 708	975	30 134	9 174	5 568	18 085	15 971	2 481	1 483
1991	46 541	32 815	1 017	33 832	3 928	953	30 857	9 652	6 032	18 626	16 517	2 499	1 498
1992	49 867	35 362	1 395	36 757	4 178	967	33 546	9 637	6 685	19 692	17 554	2 532	1 511
1993	51 729	36 977	1 338	38 315	4 384	1 062	34 992	9 670	7 067	20 234	17 973	2 557	1 534
1994	54 164	38 811	1 397	40 208	4 671	932	36 469	10 383	7 312	20 990	18 609	2 581	1 561
1995	56 073	40 611	786	41 396	4 843	1 099	37 653	10 758	7 662	21 558	18 995	2 601	1 609
1996	59 729	42 595	1 484	44 079	5 057	1 159	40 180	11 579	7 970	22 845	20 036	2 615	1 642
1997	63 356	45 464	1 405	46 869	5 387	1 066	42 548	12 456	8 352	24 041	20 923	2 635	1 686
1998	67 800	49 032	1 290	50 322	5 757	1 096	45 661	13 654	8 485	25 483	22 171	2 661	1 734
1999	70 158	51 703	1 364	53 066	6 013	996	48 050	13 305	8 804	26 195	22 775	2 678	1 752
2000	74 570	55 091	705	55 796	6 259	1 103	50 640	14 437	9 492	27 693	24 047	2 693	1 771
2001	77 564	57 480	778	58 258	6 496	993	52 755	14 350	10 459	28 713	25 056	2 701	1 782
2002	78 606	58 959	250	59 209	6 626	991	53 575	13 818	11 214	28 979	25 824	2 713	1 773
2003	81 116	60 957	1 193	62 150	6 785	871	56 236	13 120	11 760	29 799	26 852	2 722	1 758
2004	84 642	64 726	955	65 681	7 173	772	59 279	13 408	11 955	30 992	28 009	2 731	1 782
2005	88 106	67 416	991	68 407	7 530	849	61 726	13 768	12 612	32 130	28 701	2 742	1 799
2006	95 160	72 209	505	72 714	8 054	798	65 457	16 120	13 582	34 525	30 558	2 756	1 821
2007	101 444	76 462	903	77 365	8 399	910	69 877	17 237	14 330	36 525	32 111	2 777	1 856
2008	106 421	80 011	949	80 960	8 788	860	73 031	17 912	15 478	37 978	33 642	2 802	. . .

. . . = Not available.

Table 21-2. Personal Income and Employment by Region and State—*Continued*

(Millions of dollars, except as noted.)

Region or state and year	Personal income, total	Earnings by place of work			Less: Contributions for government social insurance	Plus: Adjustment for residence	Equals: Net earnings by place of residence	Plus: Dividends, interest, and rent	Plus: Personal current transfer receipts	Per capita (dollars)		Population (thousands)	Total employment (thousands)
		Nonfarm	Farm	Total						Personal income	Disposable personal income		
KENTUCKY													
1958	4 532	3 344	361	3 705	142	83	3 646	507	379	1 531	1 385	2 961	. . .
1959	4 769	3 575	336	3 911	169	97	3 839	537	393	1 590	1 438	2 999	. . .
1960	4 921	3 675	319	3 994	184	97	3 907	585	429	1 618	1 461	3 041	. . .
1961	5 238	3 770	392	4 162	184	89	4 066	618	555	1 715	1 558	3 054	. . .
1962	5 563	4 108	391	4 500	209	92	4 383	676	504	1 807	1 628	3 079	. . .
1963	5 848	4 374	400	4 774	240	92	4 625	719	504	1 889	1 706	3 096	. . .
1964	6 112	4 670	293	4 963	245	99	4 817	765	530	1 953	1 775	3 129	. . .
1965	6 631	5 044	361	5 405	258	107	5 255	798	579	2 112	1 915	3 140	. . .
1966	7 243	5 621	377	5 997	339	116	5 775	842	627	2 302	2 064	3 147	. . .
1967	7 840	6 117	378	6 495	399	95	6 191	903	746	2 472	2 227	3 172	. . .
1968	8 577	6 777	369	7 146	445	104	6 805	929	843	2 684	2 395	3 195	. . .
1969	9 444	7 416	423	7 839	511	174	7 502	998	944	2 953	2 585	3 198	1 332
1970	10 229	7 993	388	8 381	549	164	7 996	1 129	1 104	3 166	2 801	3 231	1 336
1971	11 132	8 708	403	9 110	616	107	8 601	1 233	1 298	3 375	3 014	3 298	1 360
1972	12 329	9 651	501	10 152	716	101	9 538	1 351	1 441	3 696	3 256	3 336	1 392
1973	13 901	10 965	573	11 538	922	59	10 675	1 508	1 719	4 123	3 676	3 372	1 461
1974	15 670	12 264	657	12 921	1 063	26	11 883	1 736	2 051	4 586	4 010	3 417	1 496
1975	17 119	13 218	475	13 693	1 124	11	12 580	1 956	2 583	4 935	4 413	3 469	1 465
1976	19 247	15 045	550	15 595	1 293	-23	14 279	2 146	2 822	5 452	4 857	3 530	1 523
1977	21 702	17 051	675	17 727	1 454	1	16 273	2 471	2 959	6 071	5 363	3 575	1 579
1978	24 378	19 341	595	19 936	1 690	12	18 259	2 949	3 171	6 750	5 945	3 611	1 645
1979	27 686	21 634	667	22 301	1 950	4	20 355	3 634	3 697	7 598	6 696	3 644	1 668
1980	29 965	22 940	549	23 488	2 064	28	21 453	4 059	4 453	8 178	7 238	3 664	1 646
1981	33 296	24 726	928	25 654	2 396	-8	23 250	5 022	5 025	9 072	7 981	3 670	1 639
1982	35 477	25 629	895	26 524	2 528	-18	23 979	6 013	5 485	9 631	8 498	3 683	1 621
1983	36 630	26 730	224	26 954	2 655	12	24 311	6 379	5 941	9 915	8 796	3 694	1 629
1984	41 139	29 648	1 109	30 757	3 001	-65	27 691	7 230	6 218	11 132	9 978	3 695	1 683
1985	42 974	31 166	865	32 031	3 219	-76	28 736	7 731	6 506	11 631	10 379	3 695	1 706
1986	44 492	32 459	636	33 095	3 420	-48	29 626	8 055	6 811	12 065	10 775	3 688	1 742
1987	47 171	34 929	722	35 651	3 652	-78	31 920	8 207	7 044	12 807	11 388	3 683	1 775
1988	49 914	37 047	770	37 817	4 064	-91	33 663	8 782	7 469	13 564	12 072	3 680	1 827
1989	53 733	39 213	1 125	40 338	4 355	-138	35 845	9 698	8 190	14 612	12 920	3 677	1 877
1990	57 026	41 431	1 045	42 475	4 677	-101	37 697	10 361	8 968	15 437	13 621	3 694	1 918
1991	60 160	43 101	1 068	44 168	4 961	-142	39 065	10 831	10 264	16 162	14 347	3 722	1 915
1992	64 671	47 009	1 306	48 315	5 389	-413	42 513	10 982	11 176	17 175	15 251	3 765	1 962
1993	66 791	49 229	1 104	50 333	5 737	-424	44 172	11 012	11 606	17 520	15 527	3 812	2 006
1994	70 148	51 763	1 139	52 901	6 169	-538	46 194	11 785	12 169	18 225	16 110	3 849	2 047
1995	73 389	54 066	714	54 780	6 482	-573	47 725	12 581	13 084	18 879	16 625	3 887	2 123
1996	77 819	56 573	1 131	57 704	6 740	-641	50 323	13 607	13 889	19 854	17 443	3 920	2 155
1997	82 436	59 950	1 163	61 112	7 129	-657	53 326	14 482	14 627	20 855	18 218	3 953	2 203
1998	87 851	64 022	1 042	65 064	7 498	-595	56 970	15 845	15 035	22 043	19 218	3 985	2 244
1999	91 462	68 223	796	69 019	7 993	-686	60 340	15 528	15 593	22 763	19 834	4 018	2 291
2000	98 845	72 430	1 442	73 872	8 182	-719	64 972	17 137	16 736	24 413	21 345	4 049	2 332
2001	101 346	74 503	953	75 456	8 478	-976	66 002	17 191	18 153	24 923	21 773	4 066	2 305
2002	103 866	77 377	391	77 768	8 777	-1 073	67 918	16 449	19 498	25 415	22 585	4 087	2 292
2003	106 319	80 444	564	81 009	9 042	-1 315	70 652	15 513	20 154	25 863	23 158	4 111	2 301
2004	111 847	84 610	992	85 602	9 522	-1 502	74 578	15 665	21 604	27 045	24 328	4 136	2 340
2005	116 941	88 683	1 500	90 183	9 992	-1 889	78 303	16 070	22 568	28 071	25 073	4 166	2 387
2006	124 058	93 320	1 036	94 356	10 526	-2 211	81 619	18 190	24 249	29 542	26 380	4 199	2 412
2007	130 581	97 624	813	98 437	11 024	-2 355	85 058	19 615	25 908	30 824	27 390	4 236	2 438
2008	135 873	100 356	932	101 288	11 406	-2 559	87 323	20 270	28 281	31 826	28 424	4 269	. . .

. . . = Not available.

Table 21-2. Personal Income and Employment by Region and State—*Continued*

(Millions of dollars, except as noted.)

Region or state and year	Personal income, total	Earnings by place of work			Less: Contributions for government social insurance	Plus: Adjustment for residence	Equals: Net earnings by place of residence	Plus: Dividends, interest, and rent	Plus: Personal current transfer receipts	Per capita (dollars)		Population (thousands)	Total employment (thousands)
		Nonfarm	Farm	Total						Personal income	Disposable personal income		
LOUISIANA													
1958	5 162	4 114	187	4 301	140	-3	4 159	625	378	1 636	1 496	3 155	...
1959	5 412	4 279	203	4 482	159	-2	4 321	679	411	1 687	1 524	3 208	...
1960	5 510	4 356	183	4 539	185	-2	4 353	721	436	1 690	1 541	3 260	...
1961	5 723	4 464	215	4 679	187	-1	4 491	747	486	1 741	1 587	3 287	...
1962	6 038	4 747	202	4 949	208	0	4 740	794	504	1 805	1 641	3 345	...
1963	6 441	5 042	257	5 300	246	-1	5 054	852	535	1 907	1 726	3 377	...
1964	6 894	5 494	223	5 717	262	-1	5 455	885	554	2 001	1 830	3 446	...
1965	7 456	6 007	195	6 202	285	-1	5 915	943	598	2 133	1 952	3 496	...
1966	8 242	6 763	236	6 999	389	2	6 613	987	642	2 322	2 093	3 550	...
1967	9 024	7 405	265	7 670	432	4	7 242	1 030	752	2 520	2 278	3 581	...
1968	9 880	8 159	297	8 455	489	4	7 970	1 059	850	2 742	2 458	3 603	...
1969	10 453	8 655	239	8 894	568	3	8 328	1 164	961	2 888	2 569	3 619	1 440
1970	11 281	9 160	280	9 441	591	3	8 852	1 275	1 154	3 090	2 788	3 650	1 429
1971	12 299	9 931	318	10 249	657	-9	9 583	1 398	1 318	3 314	2 994	3 711	1 445
1972	13 462	10 934	345	11 280	756	-22	10 502	1 511	1 450	3 578	3 210	3 762	1 488
1973	15 076	12 125	576	12 701	960	-38	11 703	1 688	1 685	3 979	3 582	3 789	1 550
1974	17 188	13 722	609	14 331	1 117	-55	13 159	2 055	1 974	4 499	4 013	3 821	1 598
1975	19 297	15 506	416	15 921	1 242	-84	14 595	2 262	2 439	4 964	4 478	3 887	1 641
1976	21 951	17 920	452	18 372	1 453	-114	16 805	2 456	2 689	5 555	4 962	3 952	1 702
1977	24 561	20 222	452	20 674	1 625	-141	18 907	2 760	2 893	6 116	5 448	4 016	1 756
1978	28 160	23 540	369	23 909	1 929	-188	21 791	3 219	3 150	6 913	6 113	4 073	1 848
1979	32 076	26 737	498	27 235	2 273	-234	24 727	3 764	3 585	7 749	6 801	4 139	1 899
1980	37 067	30 700	169	30 869	2 595	-339	27 934	4 857	4 276	8 777	7 680	4 223	1 968
1981	42 887	35 149	261	35 411	3 182	-365	31 864	6 247	4 775	10 013	8 692	4 283	2 036
1982	45 962	36 735	260	36 995	3 383	-343	33 268	7 185	5 509	10 560	9 307	4 353	2 029
1983	47 894	37 172	228	37 400	3 376	-324	33 701	7 922	6 271	10 897	9 716	4 395	1 990
1984	51 348	39 558	318	39 875	3 661	-317	35 897	8 921	6 530	11 669	10 466	4 400	2 032
1985	53 398	40 512	226	40 738	3 773	-286	36 679	9 685	7 034	12 113	10 853	4 408	2 020
1986	52 905	39 217	230	39 447	3 665	-231	35 551	9 633	7 720	12 005	10 887	4 407	1 939
1987	53 052	39 221	393	39 614	3 621	-196	35 797	9 438	7 818	12 212	11 052	4 344	1 915
1988	55 908	41 436	627	42 062	3 989	-176	37 898	9 817	8 193	13 036	11 845	4 289	1 947
1989	59 437	43 499	461	43 961	4 215	-142	39 604	10 879	8 955	13 976	12 620	4 253	1 966
1990	64 052	47 034	381	47 414	4 569	-119	42 726	11 456	9 870	15 173	13 689	4 222	2 019
1991	67 628	49 404	448	49 852	4 912	-137	44 803	11 583	11 242	15 900	14 381	4 253	2 044
1992	72 000	52 211	554	52 765	5 126	-137	47 503	11 497	13 000	16 771	15 233	4 293	2 052
1993	75 161	54 150	566	54 717	5 360	-139	49 218	11 725	14 218	17 413	15 788	4 316	2 100
1994	80 043	57 071	659	57 729	5 785	-165	51 779	12 536	15 727	18 411	16 667	4 347	2 140
1995	83 535	59 857	675	60 532	6 073	-193	54 265	13 530	15 741	19 077	17 228	4 379	2 209
1996	87 036	62 305	870	63 175	6 355	-217	56 603	14 435	15 999	19 786	17 690	4 399	2 254
1997	91 432	65 945	715	66 660	6 742	-233	59 685	15 415	16 331	20 681	18 373	4 421	2 305
1998	96 677	70 309	453	70 762	7 137	-255	63 370	16 684	16 622	21 772	19 385	4 440	2 355
1999	98 200	71 733	616	72 349	7 217	-249	64 884	16 193	17 123	22 014	19 650	4 461	2 374
2000	103 151	74 913	502	75 415	7 380	-260	67 775	17 700	17 676	23 082	20 577	4 469	2 404
2001	110 256	79 924	467	80 392	7 845	-139	72 408	17 429	20 420	24 719	22 062	4 460	2 409
2002	112 744	82 480	232	82 712	8 114	-125	74 473	16 539	21 732	25 249	22 875	4 465	2 412
2003	115 695	85 721	663	86 384	8 379	-166	77 839	15 895	21 962	25 862	23 686	4 474	2 436
2004	122 346	90 627	518	91 145	8 707	-166	82 272	16 133	23 941	27 262	25 014	4 488	2 462
2005	110 823	88 964	520	89 484	9 049	-140	80 295	-5 256	35 785	24 651	21 964	4 496	2 446
2006	139 329	100 700	448	101 148	10 118	-156	90 875	22 432	26 022	32 832	29 504	4 244	2 435
2007	153 504	107 902	642	108 544	10 921	-155	97 469	29 646	26 388	35 100	31 471	4 373	2 517
2008	159 983	114 811	699	115 510	11 656	-184	103 671	27 746	28 566	36 271	32 651	4 411	...

. . . = Not available.

Table 21-2. Personal Income and Employment by Region and State—*Continued*

(Millions of dollars, except as noted.)

Region or state and year	Personal income, total	Earnings by place of work			Less: Contributions for government social insurance	Plus: Adjustment for residence	Equals: Net earnings by place of residence	Plus: Dividends, interest, and rent	Plus: Personal current transfer receipts	Per capita (dollars)		Population (thousands)	Total employment (thousands)
		Nonfarm	Farm	Total						Personal income	Disposable personal income		
MAINE													
1958	1 678	1 294	100	1 395	52	-20	1 322	215	141	1 778	1 626	944	. . .
1959	1 749	1 409	59	1 468	60	-24	1 383	219	148	1 828	1 674	957	. . .
1960	1 854	1 473	102	1 575	70	-28	1 477	224	152	1 901	1 724	975	. . .
1961	1 872	1 513	66	1 579	73	-29	1 477	228	167	1 882	1 707	995	. . .
1962	1 950	1 576	65	1 641	78	-30	1 533	245	172	1 962	1 773	994	. . .
1963	2 014	1 626	58	1 684	87	-30	1 566	267	181	2 028	1 843	993	. . .
1964	2 179	1 734	88	1 823	92	-31	1 700	295	184	2 195	2 011	993	. . .
1965	2 357	1 832	125	1 957	92	-30	1 834	331	192	2 364	2 168	997	. . .
1966	2 510	1 998	106	2 104	118	-33	1 953	347	210	2 513	2 300	999	. . .
1967	2 641	2 145	54	2 199	137	-35	2 027	365	248	2 630	2 396	1 004	. . .
1968	2 824	2 326	54	2 381	157	-38	2 185	360	279	2 841	2 557	994	. . .
1969	3 106	2 505	74	2 578	181	-23	2 375	419	312	3 131	2 782	992	443
1970	3 400	2 705	77	2 782	193	-18	2 571	459	370	3 411	3 068	997	446
1971	3 647	2 872	66	2 937	211	-17	2 709	500	438	3 591	3 278	1 016	443
1972	3 993	3 159	64	3 223	241	-20	2 962	541	490	3 859	3 502	1 035	453
1973	4 509	3 497	147	3 644	301	-11	3 332	593	583	4 309	3 875	1 046	470
1974	5 034	3 799	195	3 993	337	-6	3 650	681	703	4 749	4 278	1 060	478
1975	5 397	4 063	81	4 143	357	-19	3 767	732	899	5 029	4 578	1 073	475
1976	6 215	4 722	163	4 885	422	-23	4 440	800	975	5 702	5 170	1 090	498
1977	6 766	5 177	128	5 305	461	-25	4 819	908	1 038	6 121	5 556	1 105	513
1978	7 483	5 820	89	5 909	531	-23	5 355	1 013	1 115	6 708	6 053	1 115	532
1979	8 349	6 478	74	6 552	607	-17	5 929	1 160	1 260	7 422	6 658	1 125	546
1980	9 406	7 140	48	7 189	670	-14	6 504	1 431	1 471	8 347	7 464	1 127	555
1981	10 415	7 663	117	7 780	773	-50	6 956	1 782	1 677	9 193	8 153	1 133	554
1982	11 282	8 134	103	8 238	835	-49	7 354	2 089	1 839	9 925	8 739	1 137	556
1983	12 108	8 841	71	8 913	912	-40	7 961	2 157	1 989	10 577	9 432	1 145	568
1984	13 506	9 831	117	9 948	1 045	-30	8 873	2 534	2 099	11 687	10 481	1 156	591
1985	14 602	10 729	102	10 831	1 133	-9	9 689	2 693	2 221	12 556	11 209	1 163	610
1986	15 789	11 659	92	11 751	1 246	29	10 535	2 951	2 304	13 494	11 976	1 170	635
1987	17 231	12 834	135	12 969	1 362	48	11 655	3 219	2 357	14 546	12 789	1 185	658
1988	18 912	14 270	117	14 387	1 549	61	12 900	3 513	2 500	15 710	13 851	1 204	692
1989	20 499	15 283	124	15 406	1 657	60	13 810	3 997	2 693	16 803	14 827	1 220	708
1990	21 402	15 741	166	15 907	1 704	58	14 261	4 135	3 006	17 376	15 387	1 232	707
1991	21 681	15 603	121	15 724	1 721	75	14 078	4 144	3 459	17 526	15 627	1 237	683
1992	22 606	16 216	176	16 392	1 818	119	14 692	4 099	3 815	18 253	16 343	1 239	686
1993	23 156	16 678	157	16 835	1 925	179	15 088	4 049	4 018	18 639	16 688	1 242	697
1994	24 092	17 239	148	17 387	2 033	240	15 593	4 298	4 201	19 387	17 292	1 243	708
1995	25 044	17 679	123	17 802	2 110	310	16 002	4 613	4 429	20 140	17 965	1 243	710
1996	26 484	18 406	151	18 558	2 171	364	16 750	4 991	4 743	21 203	18 801	1 249	720
1997	27 830	19 332	106	19 438	2 290	436	17 584	5 279	4 967	22 179	19 509	1 255	733
1998	29 710	20 612	138	20 750	2 417	511	18 844	5 744	5 122	23 596	20 576	1 259	753
1999	31 016	21 939	154	22 092	2 555	580	20 118	5 619	5 279	24 484	21 343	1 267	770
2000	33 173	23 226	146	23 371	2 666	701	21 406	6 179	5 588	25 974	22 493	1 277	792
2001	35 107	24 719	117	24 837	2 812	726	22 751	6 338	6 018	27 328	23 748	1 285	797
2002	35 998	25 492	76	25 569	2 847	710	23 432	6 089	6 478	27 827	24 723	1 294	799
2003	37 533	26 596	97	26 692	2 937	698	24 454	6 048	7 031	28 811	25 878	1 303	802
2004	39 488	28 110	116	28 226	3 083	740	25 882	6 145	7 461	30 191	27 190	1 308	821
2005	40 378	28 771	92	28 864	3 167	771	26 468	5 778	8 132	30 798	27 495	1 311	827
2006	42 404	29 878	103	29 981	3 314	820	27 486	6 632	8 285	32 287	28 709	1 313	828
2007	44 711	31 055	129	31 184	3 464	853	28 573	7 366	8 772	33 991	30 120	1 315	830
2008	46 578	31 995	162	32 157	3 611	875	29 421	7 684	9 473	35 381	31 593	1 316	. . .

. . . = Not available.

Table 21-2. Personal Income and Employment by Region and State—*Continued*

(Millions of dollars, except as noted.)

Region or state and year	Personal income, total	Derivation of personal income								Per capita (dollars)		Population (thousands)	Total employment (thousands)
		Earnings by place of work			Less: Contributions for government social insurance	Plus: Adjustment for residence	Equals: Net earnings by place of residence	Plus: Dividends, interest, and rent	Plus: Personal current transfer receipts	Personal income	Disposable personal income		
		Nonfarm	Farm	Total									
MARYLAND													
1958	6 580	5 040	103	5 143	188	466	5 422	848	311	2 207	1 940	2 982	. . .
1959	6 954	5 365	85	5 450	239	516	5 727	901	327	2 268	1 976	3 066	. . .
1960	7 312	5 622	93	5 715	289	582	6 008	964	340	2 349	2 041	3 113	. . .
1961	7 771	5 941	88	6 029	312	641	6 359	1 021	391	2 447	2 141	3 176	. . .
1962	8 403	6 417	84	6 500	350	720	6 870	1 117	416	2 575	2 226	3 263	. . .
1963	8 997	6 848	66	6 913	380	804	7 337	1 225	436	2 657	2 288	3 386	. . .
1964	9 822	7 435	85	7 520	396	886	8 010	1 352	460	2 813	2 460	3 492	. . .
1965	10 727	8 035	96	8 131	398	1 003	8 735	1 488	504	2 980	2 598	3 600	. . .
1966	11 841	9 015	77	9 093	526	1 117	9 684	1 600	557	3 205	2 754	3 695	. . .
1967	12 913	9 601	94	9 694	585	1 366	10 476	1 746	691	3 437	2 948	3 757	. . .
1968	14 305	10 668	86	10 755	641	1 528	11 641	1 837	826	3 750	3 128	3 815	. . .
1969	16 230	11 866	131	11 997	750	2 154	13 401	1 885	944	4 196	3 482	3 868	1 679
1970	17 951	12 944	120	13 064	815	2 512	14 761	2 064	1 126	4 558	3 857	3 938	1 702
1971	19 640	14 079	93	14 172	916	2 764	16 020	2 248	1 373	4 883	4 190	4 023	1 729
1972	21 555	15 481	127	15 608	1 059	3 000	17 549	2 433	1 574	5 282	4 457	4 081	1 781
1973	23 861	17 260	208	17 468	1 353	3 203	19 318	2 727	1 816	5 807	4 929	4 109	1 846
1974	26 329	18 949	163	19 112	1 531	3 478	21 058	3 166	2 105	6 370	5 369	4 133	1 868
1975	28 656	20 109	202	20 311	1 622	3 864	22 553	3 456	2 647	6 893	5 918	4 157	1 846
1976	31 444	22 281	173	22 454	1 806	4 179	24 827	3 767	2 850	7 537	6 473	4 172	1 866
1977	34 306	24 337	128	24 465	1 972	4 586	27 079	4 190	3 037	8 179	6 965	4 195	1 919
1978	38 027	27 080	182	27 262	2 258	4 953	29 957	4 720	3 350	9 029	7 673	4 212	2 003
1979	42 135	29 946	158	30 104	2 607	5 388	32 885	5 449	3 801	9 977	8 430	4 223	2 061
1980	47 296	32 846	56	32 902	2 861	5 961	36 002	6 767	4 526	11 187	9 511	4 228	2 075
1981	52 794	36 134	127	36 261	3 377	6 434	39 318	8 289	5 187	12 388	10 415	4 262	2 102
1982	57 330	38 006	142	38 149	3 613	7 008	41 544	10 013	5 774	13 386	11 336	4 283	2 090
1983	61 841	41 516	88	41 604	4 071	7 382	44 916	10 630	6 296	14 337	12 313	4 313	2 158
1984	68 984	46 396	263	46 659	4 672	8 079	50 065	12 282	6 636	15 803	13 558	4 365	2 253
1985	75 325	50 925	275	51 201	5 285	8 729	54 645	13 665	7 015	17 069	14 721	4 413	2 356
1986	81 069	55 292	285	55 577	5 863	9 361	59 075	14 510	7 484	18 068	15 593	4 487	2 443
1987	87 696	60 547	298	60 845	6 352	10 136	64 629	15 295	7 771	19 208	16 379	4 566	2 572
1988	95 867	66 462	364	66 826	7 276	11 230	70 780	16 800	8 288	20 582	17 765	4 658	2 668
1989	103 528	70 968	362	71 330	7 861	12 077	75 546	18 953	9 029	21 900	18 724	4 727	2 726
1990	109 686	75 228	351	75 579	8 417	12 546	79 708	20 088	9 890	22 852	19 591	4 800	2 760
1991	113 436	76 595	305	76 901	8 725	13 216	81 392	20 961	11 083	23 304	20 135	4 868	2 683
1992	118 847	79 974	353	80 327	9 032	14 068	85 363	21 012	12 472	24 139	20 951	4 923	2 656
1993	122 906	83 059	329	83 388	9 386	14 474	88 476	21 446	12 984	24 720	21 406	4 972	2 679
1994	128 523	86 718	311	87 029	9 944	14 942	92 026	22 861	13 636	25 587	22 085	5 023	2 726
1995	133 814	90 440	219	90 659	10 331	14 992	95 320	24 048	14 446	26 393	22 676	5 070	2 788
1996	140 035	93 880	398	94 279	10 678	15 347	98 947	25 566	15 522	27 393	23 396	5 112	2 827
1997	147 843	100 100	274	100 374	11 326	15 310	104 358	27 583	15 901	28 666	24 091	5 157	2 891
1998	157 784	106 978	331	107 309	12 034	16 649	111 924	29 550	16 310	30 317	25 610	5 204	2 947
1999	167 075	114 411	349	114 760	12 769	17 611	119 603	30 200	17 272	31 796	26 813	5 255	3 018
2000	181 957	124 081	354	124 435	13 613	19 892	130 715	32 998	18 245	34 264	28 806	5 310	3 092
2001	191 657	131 865	293	132 158	14 628	20 321	137 851	33 910	19 896	35 653	30 084	5 376	3 129
2002	198 824	138 561	179	138 740	15 339	20 996	144 396	32 939	21 488	36 553	31 543	5 439	3 162
2003	205 737	144 438	313	144 751	15 999	21 639	150 391	32 266	23 079	37 441	32 539	5 495	3 207
2004	220 127	155 135	413	155 547	17 263	23 614	161 898	34 271	23 958	39 741	34 569	5 539	3 271
2005	232 950	164 629	361	164 990	18 203	24 881	171 667	35 461	25 822	41 781	36 052	5 576	3 344
2006	245 879	173 059	269	173 328	19 183	25 412	179 557	39 336	26 986	43 889	37 679	5 602	3 399
2007	261 115	181 363	340	181 703	20 069	26 414	188 049	44 122	28 944	46 471	39 576	5 619	3 438
2008	270 924	186 909	293	187 202	20 825	27 617	193 994	45 437	31 492	48 091	41 325	5 634	. . .

. . . = Not available.

Table 21-2. Personal Income and Employment by Region and State—*Continued*

(Millions of dollars, except as noted.)

| Region or state and year | Personal income, total | Derivation of personal income | | | | | | | | Per capita (dollars) | | Population (thousands) | Total employment (thousands) |
| | | Earnings by place of work | | | Less: Contributions for government social insurance | Plus: Adjustment for residence | Equals: Net earnings by place of residence | Plus: Dividends, interest, and rent | Plus: Personal current transfer receipts | Personal income | Disposable personal income | | |
		Nonfarm	Farm	Total									
MASSACHUSETTS													
1958	11 553	9 446	67	9 513	353	-56	9 104	1 574	874	2 306	2 041	5 010	. . .
1959	12 350	10 226	59	10 285	427	-69	9 788	1 687	874	2 413	2 124	5 117	. . .
1960	12 869	10 657	68	10 725	499	-75	10 150	1 798	921	2 494	2 175	5 160	. . .
1961	13 510	11 151	60	11 211	528	-83	10 600	1 883	1 027	2 589	2 276	5 219	. . .
1962	14 303	11 829	60	11 889	617	-93	11 180	2 072	1 051	2 718	2 379	5 263	. . .
1963	14 866	12 229	60	12 289	679	-99	11 511	2 245	1 110	2 782	2 434	5 344	. . .
1964	15 890	12 952	62	13 014	697	-109	12 208	2 531	1 151	2 917	2 595	5 448	. . .
1965	16 966	13 749	68	13 818	714	-122	12 982	2 772	1 212	3 084	2 740	5 502	. . .
1966	18 318	15 028	71	15 099	942	-141	14 015	3 002	1 300	3 309	2 914	5 535	. . .
1967	19 937	16 197	56	16 252	1 032	-158	15 062	3 270	1 605	3 564	3 132	5 594	. . .
1968	21 805	17 670	64	17 735	1 138	-176	16 421	3 449	1 936	3 881	3 359	5 618	. . .
1969	23 734	19 262	66	19 328	1 259	-126	17 943	3 635	2 156	4 201	3 572	5 650	2 679
1970	25 568	20 590	69	20 659	1 323	-108	19 228	3 791	2 550	4 483	3 872	5 704	2 679
1971	27 271	21 783	63	21 846	1 443	-111	20 292	3 960	3 019	4 752	4 161	5 739	2 644
1972	29 436	23 667	62	23 729	1 647	-110	21 972	4 151	3 313	5 109	4 398	5 762	2 697
1973	32 081	26 017	70	26 088	2 069	-134	23 885	4 481	3 716	5 547	4 811	5 784	2 787
1974	34 754	27 700	69	27 769	2 269	-150	25 350	5 001	4 404	6 016	5 205	5 777	2 811
1975	37 217	28 668	68	28 737	2 290	-155	26 292	5 195	5 731	6 459	5 678	5 762	2 728
1976	40 233	31 440	76	31 516	2 550	-182	28 784	5 513	5 936	6 998	6 107	5 749	2 756
1977	43 770	34 557	79	34 636	2 811	-224	31 600	6 073	6 098	7 620	6 619	5 744	2 833
1978	48 413	38 736	103	38 839	3 242	-287	35 310	6 635	6 468	8 430	7 297	5 743	2 959
1979	53 926	43 372	90	43 461	3 788	-361	39 312	7 453	7 161	9 385	8 050	5 746	3 079
1980	60 920	48 178	105	48 283	4 217	-483	43 583	9 165	8 172	10 602	9 053	5 746	3 142
1981	68 062	52 825	116	52 940	4 985	-599	47 357	11 417	9 289	11 798	9 987	5 769	3 155
1982	74 684	56 835	131	56 966	5 488	-729	50 749	13 894	10 041	12 941	11 082	5 771	3 157
1983	81 246	62 745	164	62 909	6 135	-906	55 867	14 737	10 642	14 009	12 057	5 799	3 230
1984	91 835	71 536	182	71 719	7 218	-1 180	63 321	17 321	11 194	15 723	13 603	5 841	3 422
1985	99 445	78 467	160	78 627	7 995	-1 366	69 266	18 465	11 714	16 910	14 544	5 881	3 533
1986	107 119	85 208	175	85 383	8 777	-1 502	75 104	19 692	12 323	18 148	15 551	5 903	3 629
1987	116 181	93 682	153	93 835	9 558	-1 683	82 595	20 913	12 673	19 575	16 660	5 935	3 661
1988	127 622	103 283	173	103 456	10 690	-1 917	90 848	23 126	13 647	21 341	18 412	5 980	3 770
1989	134 399	107 024	152	107 175	11 056	-2 040	94 080	24 930	15 390	22 342	19 178	6 015	3 743
1990	138 782	108 597	151	108 748	11 227	-2 089	95 432	26 109	17 241	23 043	19 795	6 023	3 647
1991	141 024	108 226	171	108 396	11 401	-2 295	94 700	26 555	19 770	23 432	20 272	6 018	3 480
1992	147 930	114 834	171	115 005	11 992	-2 401	100 613	26 696	20 622	24 538	21 281	6 029	3 510
1993	152 578	119 513	166	119 679	12 610	-2 613	104 456	26 951	21 171	25 176	21 745	6 061	3 576
1994	160 322	125 587	151	125 738	13 431	-2 824	109 483	28 393	22 445	26 303	22 639	6 095	3 645
1995	168 623	132 142	148	132 289	14 231	-2 891	115 167	29 801	23 655	27 457	23 458	6 141	3 680
1996	178 797	140 371	169	140 540	15 029	-3 153	122 358	32 042	24 397	28 933	24 439	6 180	3 744
1997	189 885	149 449	169	149 619	16 164	-3 428	130 027	34 439	25 419	30 498	25 500	6 226	3 833
1998	203 987	161 510	107	161 617	17 279	-3 656	140 683	37 686	25 618	32 524	26 916	6 272	3 917
1999	216 221	175 021	106	175 127	18 592	-4 247	152 288	37 540	26 393	34 227	28 126	6 317	3 989
2000	240 209	195 723	116	195 839	20 551	-5 116	170 173	42 108	27 928	37 753	30 308	6 363	4 097
2001	249 095	200 623	97	200 721	21 152	-5 074	174 495	43 988	30 613	38 877	31 744	6 407	4 125
2002	249 954	200 721	115	200 836	21 040	-4 871	174 924	41 670	33 360	38 855	33 310	6 433	4 065
2003	253 993	203 619	109	203 728	21 323	-4 776	177 630	40 778	35 586	39 431	34 102	6 441	4 032
2004	266 635	216 733	127	216 859	23 055	-4 964	188 840	41 009	36 786	41 420	35 854	6 437	4 074
2005	278 704	225 150	100	225 250	23 971	-4 956	196 323	42 889	39 492	43 315	37 094	6 434	4 124
2006	298 363	236 800	95	236 895	25 201	-5 112	206 582	50 736	41 045	46 305	39 417	6 443	4 154
2007	316 896	249 549	104	249 653	26 463	-5 719	217 471	55 286	44 139	48 995	41 366	6 468	4 199
2008	329 673	258 486	78	258 564	27 485	-6 049	225 030	56 854	47 789	50 735	43 134	6 498	. . .

. . . = Not available.
* = Less than $50,000, but the estimates for this item are included in the total.

Table 21-2. Personal Income and Employment by Region and State—*Continued*

(Millions of dollars, except as noted.)

Region or state and year	Personal income, total	Derivation of personal income								Per capita (dollars)		Population (thousands)	Total employment (thousands)
		Earnings by place of work			Less: Contributions for government social insurance	Plus: Adjustment for residence	Equals: Net earnings by place of residence	Plus: Dividends, interest, and rent	Plus: Personal current transfer receipts	Personal income	Disposable personal income		
		Nonfarm	Farm	Total									
MICHIGAN													
1958	17 188	13 954	295	14 249	560	30	13 719	2 286	1 183	2 242	2 025	7 667	. . .
1959	18 278	15 158	220	15 378	695	34	14 717	2 488	1 073	2 353	2 115	7 767	. . .
1960	19 088	15 800	234	16 034	824	37	15 246	2 730	1 112	2 437	2 174	7 834	. . .
1961	19 156	15 411	293	15 704	786	38	14 956	2 868	1 332	2 427	2 183	7 893	. . .
1962	20 582	16 724	269	16 993	888	41	16 146	3 131	1 304	2 595	2 314	7 933	. . .
1963	22 021	18 018	292	18 310	1 038	44	17 317	3 377	1 327	2 733	2 429	8 058	. . .
1964	24 210	19 813	289	20 101	1 077	49	19 074	3 771	1 366	2 957	2 662	8 187	. . .
1965	26 937	22 103	268	22 371	1 122	54	21 303	4 158	1 476	3 223	2 890	8 357	. . .
1966	29 419	24 418	342	24 760	1 571	63	23 252	4 550	1 617	3 456	3 083	8 512	. . .
1967	30 765	25 205	271	25 476	1 652	68	23 892	4 871	2 002	3 565	3 175	8 630	. . .
1968	34 072	28 062	300	28 362	1 853	76	26 585	5 175	2 312	3 918	3 429	8 696	. . .
1969	36 523	30 769	345	31 115	2 203	107	29 019	4 945	2 559	4 159	3 571	8 781	3 640
1970	37 346	31 039	334	31 374	2 193	112	29 293	4 837	3 216	4 198	3 654	8 897	3 558
1971	40 372	33 744	305	34 049	2 446	104	31 706	4 827	3 839	4 500	3 951	8 972	3 571
1972	44 824	37 704	420	38 124	2 901	112	35 336	5 170	4 318	4 967	4 285	9 025	3 687
1973	50 345	42 829	555	43 384	3 794	138	39 728	5 691	4 925	5 550	4 824	9 072	3 858
1974	53 956	44 629	640	45 270	4 077	140	41 333	6 471	6 153	5 923	5 174	9 109	3 854
1975	57 435	45 633	570	46 204	4 087	154	42 271	7 088	8 076	6 306	5 595	9 108	3 695
1976	64 660	52 806	471	53 277	4 789	197	48 685	7 665	8 311	7 092	6 200	9 117	3 844
1977	72 818	60 448	552	61 000	5 485	223	55 737	8 547	8 534	7 952	6 888	9 157	4 016
1978	80 986	68 222	500	68 722	6 394	270	62 598	9 312	9 076	8 801	7 551	9 202	4 188
1979	89 110	74 493	534	75 027	7 197	310	68 140	10 504	10 467	9 635	8 269	9 249	4 234
1980	95 460	75 328	525	75 853	7 181	355	69 026	12 625	13 809	10 314	8 983	9 256	4 039
1981	102 206	79 421	505	79 927	8 188	384	72 123	15 456	14 627	11 098	9 634	9 209	3 992
1982	105 189	78 622	402	79 025	8 242	393	71 176	17 682	16 331	11 540	10 147	9 115	3 837
1983	111 468	83 679	214	83 893	8 948	427	75 372	18 812	17 284	12 320	10 797	9 048	3 881
1984	123 531	93 384	540	93 924	10 351	491	84 064	21 990	17 477	13 651	11 999	9 049	4 059
1985	134 083	102 618	653	103 271	11 659	512	92 124	23 920	18 039	14 773	12 895	9 076	4 257
1986	142 459	109 552	482	110 035	12 629	495	97 900	25 643	18 915	15 607	13 642	9 128	4 373
1987	147 486	113 544	660	114 204	12 973	512	101 743	26 291	19 452	16 053	13 984	9 187	4 511
1988	156 961	122 341	580	122 921	14 386	523	109 058	27 631	20 272	17 028	14 901	9 218	4 612
1989	168 637	129 411	967	130 378	15 261	517	115 634	31 067	21 937	18 225	15 878	9 253	4 742
1990	176 189	134 549	757	135 305	15 869	457	119 893	32 537	23 758	18 922	16 571	9 311	4 825
1991	181 655	137 697	645	138 343	16 406	472	122 409	32 558	26 688	19 324	17 028	9 400	4 754
1992	192 788	148 021	740	148 760	17 435	599	131 924	32 883	27 981	20 338	18 040	9 479	4 783
1993	201 574	155 626	742	156 368	18 536	663	138 494	33 204	29 876	21 129	18 567	9 540	4 843
1994	217 812	169 356	566	169 922	20 325	763	150 360	37 309	30 143	22 694	19 888	9 598	5 016
1995	227 466	177 753	711	178 464	21 386	734	157 812	38 018	31 635	23 508	20 487	9 676	5 175
1996	237 193	183 594	629	184 222	21 903	758	163 077	40 784	33 333	24 306	21 040	9 759	5 282
1997	248 821	191 430	655	192 086	22 969	849	169 966	43 479	35 376	25 367	21 857	9 809	5 363
1998	265 098	205 821	633	206 454	24 035	892	183 312	46 690	35 096	26 919	23 077	9 848	5 416
1999	278 062	218 175	838	219 013	25 441	995	194 567	45 859	37 635	28 095	24 099	9 897	5 519
2000	294 227	230 621	560	231 181	26 411	1 005	205 775	49 515	38 938	29 555	25 438	9 955	5 629
2001	299 542	233 516	359	233 875	26 358	1 063	208 580	47 635	43 327	29 941	25 996	10 004	5 540
2002	303 465	238 109	413	238 522	26 764	1 086	212 844	45 766	44 855	30 234	26 820	10 037	5 483
2003	313 503	246 581	556	247 136	27 557	1 136	220 716	45 494	47 293	31 145	27 943	10 066	5 461
2004	318 736	249 227	960	250 188	28 176	1 239	223 251	46 511	48 974	31 588	28 471	10 090	5 502
2005	325 293	253 656	847	254 504	28 973	1 301	226 832	46 400	52 061	32 229	28 879	10 093	5 545
2006	332 617	256 029	792	256 821	29 475	1 409	228 755	48 181	55 681	32 985	29 472	10 084	5 493
2007	345 940	261 242	1 024	262 266	29 977	1 469	233 758	52 340	59 842	34 423	30 684	10 050	5 455
2008	353 113	261 458	1 196	262 655	30 100	1 539	234 094	53 889	65 130	35 299	31 719	10 003	. . .

. . . = Not available.
* = Less than $50,000, but the estimates for this item are included in the total.

Table 21-2. Personal Income and Employment by Region and State—*Continued*

(Millions of dollars, except as noted.)

Region or state and year	Personal income, total	Earnings by place of work			Less: Contribu- tions for govern- ment social insurance	Plus: Adjust- ment for residence	Equals: Net earnings by place of residence	Plus: Dividends, interest, and rent	Plus: Personal current transfer receipts	Per capita (dollars)		Population (thou- sands)	Total employ- ment (thou- sands)
		Nonfarm	Farm	Total						Personal income	Disposable personal income		
MINNESOTA													
1958	6 645	4 886	594	5 480	179	1	5 302	879	464	2 006	1 800	3 313	...
1959	6 905	5 287	409	5 695	220	0	5 475	942	488	2 052	1 836	3 366	...
1960	7 332	5 575	505	6 080	260	-1	5 819	1 006	507	2 141	1 907	3 425	...
1961	7 706	5 818	529	6 347	269	-3	6 075	1 061	571	2 221	1 980	3 470	...
1962	8 129	6 263	456	6 719	303	-3	6 414	1 125	590	2 314	2 054	3 513	...
1963	8 620	6 521	608	7 128	339	-4	6 785	1 210	625	2 441	2 175	3 531	...
1964	8 968	6 979	390	7 370	348	-4	7 018	1 299	651	2 520	2 271	3 558	...
1965	9 914	7 531	641	8 172	372	-7	7 793	1 413	708	2 760	2 478	3 592	...
1966	10 749	8 308	721	9 028	522	-13	8 493	1 495	761	2 972	2 650	3 617	...
1967	11 562	9 035	633	9 668	601	-17	9 050	1 587	925	3 160	2 808	3 659	...
1968	12 731	10 001	672	10 673	683	-24	9 966	1 707	1 058	3 438	3 038	3 703	...
1969	14 157	11 177	709	11 886	782	-33	11 071	1 925	1 161	3 767	3 270	3 758	1 691
1970	15 411	11 948	863	12 811	826	-29	11 956	2 081	1 373	4 039	3 554	3 815	1 699
1971	16 417	12 736	786	13 522	911	-28	12 582	2 242	1 593	4 262	3 789	3 852	1 706
1972	17 845	13 821	946	14 767	1 038	-30	13 699	2 384	1 762	4 615	4 040	3 867	1 780
1973	21 033	15 462	2 165	17 628	1 336	-38	16 254	2 713	2 065	5 414	4 804	3 885	1 878
1974	22 671	17 045	1 626	18 671	1 528	-34	17 110	3 139	2 423	5 815	5 059	3 898	1 921
1975	24 432	18 413	1 247	19 660	1 615	-34	18 011	3 497	2 924	6 223	5 454	3 926	1 920
1976	26 580	20 697	767	21 464	1 847	-43	19 574	3 797	3 210	6 718	5 854	3 957	1 977
1977	29 978	22 914	1 485	24 398	2 045	-55	22 298	4 305	3 375	7 533	6 552	3 980	2 034
1978	33 703	26 160	1 605	27 765	2 412	-70	25 283	4 795	3 624	8 416	7 284	4 005	2 123
1979	37 603	29 778	1 221	30 998	2 858	-88	28 052	5 498	4 052	9 312	7 983	4 038	2 222
1980	41 898	32 485	934	33 418	3 111	-92	30 215	6 826	4 857	10 256	8 838	4 085	2 254
1981	46 460	35 134	1 018	36 152	3 609	-131	32 411	8 474	5 575	11 299	9 705	4 112	2 241
1982	49 807	36 680	804	37 484	3 842	-154	33 488	10 050	6 268	12 056	10 420	4 131	2 201
1983	52 586	39 255	107	39 362	4 165	-183	35 014	10 814	6 758	12 698	11 023	4 141	2 228
1984	59 664	44 180	1 421	45 601	4 800	-238	40 563	12 009	7 092	14 350	12 587	4 158	2 335
1985	63 458	47 404	1 322	48 726	5 238	-286	43 202	12 721	7 535	15 166	13 306	4 184	2 399
1986	67 102	50 169	1 622	51 791	5 657	-327	45 807	13 423	7 873	15 957	14 047	4 205	2 432
1987	71 516	53 912	2 125	56 036	6 067	-378	49 591	13 802	8 123	16 886	14 738	4 235	2 526
1988	75 230	58 303	1 237	59 540	6 819	-458	52 263	14 392	8 575	17 511	15 311	4 296	2 598
1989	82 088	62 152	2 022	64 174	7 304	-442	56 428	16 338	9 322	18 923	16 520	4 338	2 653
1990	87 318	66 158	1 916	68 073	7 823	-469	59 781	17 517	10 020	19 891	17 304	4 390	2 712
1991	90 050	68 981	1 159	70 140	8 310	-477	61 354	17 909	10 787	20 278	17 739	4 441	2 736
1992	96 401	74 824	1 396	76 220	8 954	-513	66 753	17 938	11 710	21 443	18 707	4 496	2 781
1993	98 571	77 927	177	78 104	9 436	-519	68 149	18 065	12 357	21 636	18 790	4 556	2 835
1994	105 971	82 409	1 287	83 696	10 146	-568	72 983	19 968	13 021	22 985	19 964	4 610	2 923
1995	112 209	87 062	503	87 565	10 708	-614	76 244	22 161	13 804	24 078	20 814	4 660	3 015
1996	121 195	92 732	1 886	94 618	11 367	-684	82 567	24 182	14 447	25 716	21 986	4 713	3 077
1997	128 388	98 786	1 152	99 938	12 044	-777	87 117	26 524	14 747	26 953	22 994	4 763	3 129
1998	139 553	107 639	1 556	109 195	12 946	-837	95 412	28 941	15 200	28 993	24 649	4 813	3 202
1999	146 722	115 346	1 071	116 418	13 821	-946	101 650	29 205	15 867	30 106	25 784	4 873	3 275
2000	157 964	124 400	1 016	125 416	14 734	-1 040	109 642	31 339	16 983	32 017	27 186	4 934	3 344
2001	162 578	128 707	448	129 156	15 342	-1 136	112 677	30 918	18 982	32 631	27 844	4 982	3 363
2002	166 968	132 755	569	133 323	15 723	-1 164	116 437	29 926	20 605	33 283	28 952	5 017	3 362
2003	173 498	137 466	1 206	138 672	16 355	-1 209	121 108	30 707	21 683	34 378	30 242	5 047	3 381
2004	183 821	146 048	1 569	147 617	17 337	-1 278	129 002	32 184	22 635	36 199	32 005	5 078	3 437
2005	190 286	150 715	2 465	153 180	17 940	-1 298	133 942	32 865	23 479	37 275	32 590	5 105	3 503
2006	200 296	156 887	1 604	158 491	18 791	-1 278	138 422	36 073	25 801	38 944	33 859	5 143	3 537
2007	213 022	165 112	2 256	167 368	19 676	-1 401	146 291	39 075	27 655	41 105	35 574	5 182	3 562
2008	223 288	171 199	3 491	174 690	20 486	-1 393	152 811	40 501	29 976	42 772	37 300	5 220	...

. . . = Not available.
* = Less than $50,000, but the estimates for this item are included in the total.

Table 21-2. Personal Income and Employment by Region and State—*Continued*

(Millions of dollars, except as noted.)

Region or state and year	Personal income, total	Earnings by place of work			Less: Contributions for government social insurance	Plus: Adjustment for residence	Equals: Net earnings by place of residence	Plus: Dividends, interest, and rent	Plus: Personal current transfer receipts	Per capita (dollars)		Population (thousands)	Total employment (thousands)
		Nonfarm	Farm	Total						Personal income	Disposable personal income		
MISSISSIPPI													
1958	2 396	1 758	271	2 029	72	9	1 966	226	204	1 149	1 076	2 086	. . .
1959	2 651	1 922	333	2 255	87	10	2 178	254	219	1 240	1 155	2 138	. . .
1960	2 680	1 990	278	2 268	101	12	2 179	268	233	1 228	1 136	2 182	. . .
1961	2 895	2 074	350	2 423	104	13	2 332	301	262	1 312	1 223	2 206	. . .
1962	3 023	2 228	294	2 522	115	15	2 422	328	273	1 348	1 245	2 243	. . .
1963	3 331	2 374	428	2 801	136	17	2 682	359	290	1 484	1 370	2 244	. . .
1964	3 454	2 543	366	2 909	143	20	2 785	366	303	1 541	1 434	2 241	. . .
1965	3 749	2 823	348	3 171	152	22	3 041	380	328	1 669	1 547	2 246	. . .
1966	4 078	3 158	343	3 501	197	23	3 327	391	360	1 816	1 670	2 245	. . .
1967	4 417	3 384	383	3 767	226	25	3 565	421	431	1 983	1 825	2 228	. . .
1968	4 834	3 768	361	4 129	252	32	3 908	437	489	2 179	1 994	2 219	. . .
1969	5 303	4 160	346	4 506	291	35	4 249	503	552	2 389	2 172	2 220	909
1970	5 813	4 432	391	4 823	311	36	4 549	575	689	2 617	2 369	2 221	917
1971	6 450	4 860	433	5 293	351	58	4 999	637	814	2 847	2 619	2 266	939
1972	7 352	5 594	490	6 084	422	73	5 735	699	918	3 187	2 889	2 307	979
1973	8 439	6 321	688	7 010	539	93	6 564	810	1 065	3 591	3 276	2 350	1 019
1974	9 308	7 013	510	7 523	616	123	7 029	966	1 313	3 913	3 534	2 379	1 031
1975	10 086	7 510	372	7 882	654	150	7 378	1 077	1 631	4 203	3 859	2 400	1 001
1976	11 529	8 587	572	9 159	757	182	8 584	1 167	1 779	4 744	4 321	2 430	1 039
1977	12 870	9 678	606	10 284	851	223	9 655	1 312	1 903	5 232	4 779	2 460	1 071
1978	14 345	10 993	449	11 442	984	279	10 737	1 513	2 095	5 766	5 206	2 488	1 102
1979	16 263	12 205	699	12 904	1 131	337	12 110	1 762	2 392	6 485	5 835	2 508	1 117
1980	17 695	13 168	178	13 346	1 216	425	12 555	2 275	2 865	7 007	6 305	2 525	1 114
1981	19 928	14 416	327	14 743	1 429	455	13 770	2 909	3 250	7 849	7 011	2 539	1 110
1982	21 064	14 802	421	15 223	1 505	473	14 191	3 298	3 575	8 238	7 494	2 557	1 083
1983	22 021	15 557	99	15 656	1 597	530	14 589	3 494	3 939	8 576	7 768	2 568	1 091
1984	24 278	16 979	473	17 452	1 777	594	16 270	3 935	4 074	9 417	8 581	2 578	1 121
1985	25 602	17 983	433	18 416	1 917	624	17 123	4 211	4 268	9 892	9 010	2 588	1 129
1986	26 440	18 749	198	18 946	2 045	609	17 511	4 409	4 520	10 194	9 323	2 594	1 136
1987	27 962	19 641	584	20 224	2 135	647	18 736	4 516	4 710	10 802	9 845	2 589	1 147
1988	29 832	20 962	731	21 693	2 387	688	19 994	4 819	5 019	11 561	10 576	2 580	1 176
1989	32 164	22 257	562	22 819	2 564	731	20 986	5 682	5 496	12 495	11 374	2 574	1 196
1990	33 754	23 567	433	24 001	2 712	754	22 042	5 754	5 958	13 089	11 910	2 579	1 210
1991	35 607	24 634	538	25 172	2 885	813	23 100	5 871	6 635	13 702	12 525	2 599	1 218
1992	38 199	26 425	641	27 066	3 073	832	24 824	5 926	7 449	14 559	13 319	2 624	1 241
1993	40 596	28 534	547	29 081	3 335	852	26 598	6 057	7 940	15 290	13 941	2 655	1 294
1994	43 805	30 802	818	31 620	3 668	854	28 805	6 598	8 402	16 291	14 801	2 689	1 343
1995	45 973	32 211	681	32 892	3 850	943	29 985	6 900	9 088	16 885	15 314	2 723	1 374
1996	48 646	33 488	1 067	34 555	3 977	986	31 565	7 416	9 665	17 702	16 004	2 748	1 398
1997	51 514	35 315	1 174	36 490	4 175	1 124	33 439	8 016	10 058	18 550	16 733	2 777	1 424
1998	54 820	37 875	958	38 833	4 421	1 204	35 616	8 889	10 315	19 545	17 593	2 805	1 462
1999	56 719	39 635	955	40 590	4 614	1 310	37 286	8 748	10 685	20 053	18 038	2 828	1 488
2000	59 837	41 267	724	41 991	4 707	1 506	38 790	9 547	11 500	21 008	18 938	2 848	1 493
2001	62 739	42 332	905	43 237	4 819	1 658	40 077	9 782	12 880	21 990	19 870	2 853	1 470
2002	63 979	43 834	334	44 168	5 009	1 724	40 883	9 207	13 889	22 386	20 484	2 858	1 473
2003	66 305	45 713	950	46 663	5 193	1 786	43 256	8 596	14 452	23 129	21 336	2 867	1 470
2004	69 700	48 115	1 193	49 309	5 459	1 938	45 788	8 469	15 443	24 163	22 367	2 885	1 492
2005	73 292	49 713	1 342	51 055	5 681	2 077	47 451	6 516	19 324	25 289	23 380	2 898	1 495
2006	78 419	53 064	416	53 480	6 078	2 275	49 677	11 198	17 544	27 072	24 776	2 897	1 530
2007	83 368	55 166	801	55 967	6 300	2 530	52 197	12 869	18 302	28 541	26 024	2 921	1 568
2008	86 891	57 477	932	58 409	6 580	2 603	54 433	12 364	20 095	29 569	27 077	2 939	. . .

. . . = Not available.

* = Less than $50,000, but the estimates for this item are included in the total.

Table 21-2. Personal Income and Employment by Region and State—*Continued*

(Millions of dollars, except as noted.)

Region or state and year	Personal income, total	Earnings by place of work			Less: Contribu-tions for govern-ment social insurance	Plus: Adjust-ment for residence	Equals: Net earnings by place of residence	Plus: Dividends, interest, and rent	Plus: Personal current transfer receipts	Per capita (dollars)		Population (thou-sands)	Total employ-ment (thou-sands)
		Nonfarm	Farm	Total						Personal income	Disposable personal income		
MISSOURI													
1958	8 692	8 692	6 822	7 381	260	-149	6 971	1 122	598	2 076	1 864	4 186	. . .
1959	9 211	9 211	7 372	7 840	311	-165	7 363	1 215	633	2 163	1 938	4 258	. . .
1960	9 483	9 483	7 623	8 060	358	-176	7 526	1 286	671	2 192	1 950	4 326	. . .
1961	9 796	9 796	7 793	8 269	375	-182	7 713	1 338	745	2 252	2 004	4 349	. . .
1962	10 325	10 325	8 265	8 743	408	-198	8 137	1 417	771	2 370	2 100	4 357	. . .
1963	10 840	10 840	8 771	9 202	469	-222	8 511	1 521	808	2 468	2 182	4 392	. . .
1964	11 452	11 452	9 403	9 730	491	-246	8 993	1 628	830	2 578	2 316	4 442	. . .
1965	12 449	12 449	10 084	10 609	517	-271	9 820	1 741	888	2 787	2 486	4 467	. . .
1966	13 314	13 314	11 094	11 502	695	-310	10 497	1 857	960	2 944	2 617	4 523	. . .
1967	14 170	14 170	11 852	12 249	796	-346	11 107	1 943	1 120	3 122	2 773	4 539	. . .
1968	15 683	15 683	13 052	13 524	898	-382	12 244	2 127	1 313	3 433	3 028	4 568	. . .
1969	16 551	16 551	14 162	14 604	954	-758	12 892	2 232	1 427	3 567	3 085	4 640	2 216
1970	18 037	18 037	15 085	15 600	1 004	-702	13 895	2 451	1 691	3 850	3 376	4 685	2 203
1971	19 431	19 431	16 087	16 649	1 108	-683	14 858	2 623	1 950	4 114	3 643	4 723	2 200
1972	21 140	21 140	17 456	18 161	1 261	-703	16 197	2 833	2 111	4 448	3 889	4 753	2 242
1973	23 542	23 542	19 089	20 295	1 584	-737	17 975	3 119	2 449	4 931	4 358	4 775	2 325
1974	25 235	25 235	20 650	21 277	1 766	-763	18 748	3 596	2 890	5 273	4 624	4 785	2 341
1975	27 602	27 602	21 920	22 607	1 841	-773	19 993	3 955	3 654	5 756	5 120	4 795	2 291
1976	30 433	30 433	24 747	25 208	2 095	-850	22 263	4 277	3 893	6 309	5 570	4 824	2 365
1977	33 839	33 839	27 557	28 263	2 330	-990	24 943	4 832	4 064	6 984	6 167	4 845	2 424
1978	37 743	37 743	30 825	31 730	2 695	-1 143	27 892	5 431	4 420	7 748	6 792	4 871	2 513
1979	42 199	42 199	34 195	35 359	3 087	-1 307	30 965	6 234	5 000	8 631	7 529	4 889	2 580
1980	45 893	45 893	36 617	36 843	3 284	-1 524	32 034	7 778	6 082	9 324	8 143	4 922	2 554
1981	51 359	51 359	39 478	40 237	3 795	-1 663	34 779	9 743	6 836	10 413	9 054	4 932	2 549
1982	54 839	54 839	41 306	41 644	4 051	-1 730	35 863	11 522	7 454	11 125	9 625	4 929	2 525
1983	58 534	58 534	44 455	44 345	4 387	-1 758	38 199	12 327	8 008	11 840	10 468	4 944	2 571
1984	65 162	65 162	49 343	49 754	4 995	-1 886	42 873	13 930	8 359	13 097	11 642	4 975	2 679
1985	69 812	69 812	52 925	53 710	5 477	-2 003	46 230	14 765	8 817	13 962	12 364	5 000	2 753
1986	73 310	73 310	55 978	56 549	5 908	-2 052	48 589	15 438	9 282	14 595	12 937	5 023	2 816
1987	77 057	77 057	59 356	60 084	6 219	-2 177	51 687	15 811	9 559	15 239	13 466	5 057	2 854
1988	81 340	81 340	63 171	63 819	6 842	-2 265	54 712	16 541	10 087	16 006	14 179	5 082	2 905
1989	86 570	86 570	66 431	67 324	7 283	-2 395	57 646	17 997	10 927	16 988	14 975	5 096	2 960
1990	90 407	69 167	682	69 849	7 670	-2 626	59 553	19 014	11 839	17 627	15 536	5 129	2 993
1991	94 900	71 308	561	71 869	8 001	-2 639	61 229	19 883	13 789	18 353	16 312	5 171	2 962
1992	100 945	76 098	804	76 903	8 440	-2 814	65 648	20 548	14 749	19 349	17 240	5 217	2 977
1993	104 699	79 308	493	79 801	8 857	-2 922	68 022	20 881	15 796	19 862	17 654	5 271	3 061
1994	111 005	84 013	680	84 693	9 506	-2 917	72 270	22 179	16 556	20 848	18 466	5 324	3 134
1995	115 948	88 669	232	88 901	10 081	-3 143	75 678	22 666	17 604	21 559	19 013	5 378	3 218
1996	122 469	92 921	1 040	93 961	10 514	-3 277	80 170	23 802	18 497	22 548	19 777	5 432	3 277
1997	129 992	98 557	1 096	99 654	11 141	-3 484	85 029	25 766	19 197	23 716	20 701	5 481	3 349
1998	137 619	105 196	614	105 810	11 671	-3 691	90 448	27 453	19 718	24 923	21 683	5 522	3 405
1999	142 925	111 165	247	111 411	12 281	-3 767	95 363	26 837	20 725	25 697	22 345	5 562	3 450
2000	152 722	117 772	657	118 429	12 842	-4 056	101 530	29 030	22 162	27 243	23 678	5 606	3 497
2001	156 937	120 401	555	120 956	13 288	-3 938	103 729	28 768	24 439	27 816	24 183	5 642	3 481
2002	161 104	124 405	243	124 647	13 642	-4 036	106 969	27 904	26 231	28 385	25 247	5 676	3 471
2003	166 129	127 955	583	128 538	14 022	-3 873	110 643	27 961	27 526	29 122	26 194	5 705	3 478
2004	173 906	133 713	1 447	135 161	14 627	-3 855	116 679	28 284	28 943	30 283	27 360	5 743	3 527
2005	180 509	139 929	940	140 868	15 469	-4 132	121 268	28 216	31 024	31 202	27 913	5 785	3 593
2006	189 653	146 188	696	146 884	16 297	-4 305	126 281	30 541	32 831	32 514	28 892	5 833	3 632
2007	199 655	152 343	941	153 284	17 064	-4 608	131 611	33 145	34 899	33 964	30 022	5 878	3 663
2008	208 255	157 435	1 231	158 666	17 761	-4 703	136 202	34 182	37 871	35 228	31 339	5 912	. . .

. . . = Not available.
* = Less than $50,000, but the estimates for this item are included in the total.

Table 21-2. Personal Income and Employment by Region and State—*Continued*

(Millions of dollars, except as noted.)

| Region or state and year | Personal income, total | Derivation of personal income | | | | | | | | | Per capita (dollars) | | Population (thousands) | Total employment (thousands) |
| | | Earnings by place of work | | | Less: Contributions for government social insurance | Plus: Adjustment for residence | Equals: Net earnings by place of residence | Plus: Dividends, interest, and rent | Plus: Personal current transfer receipts | | Personal income | Disposable personal income | | |
		Nonfarm	Farm	Total										
MONTANA														
1958	1 380	906	235	1 142	44	0	1 098	182	100		2 072	1 891	666	...
1959	1 352	956	146	1 102	51	0	1 052	193	107		2 021	1 806	669	...
1960	1 405	996	160	1 156	62	0	1 094	203	108		2 069	1 864	679	...
1961	1 402	1 041	107	1 149	62	*	1 086	198	117		2 014	1 801	696	...
1962	1 646	1 104	274	1 378	64	0	1 314	213	119		2 358	2 144	698	...
1963	1 631	1 153	209	1 362	72	0	1 290	220	121		2 319	2 094	703	...
1964	1 662	1 206	166	1 373	74	0	1 298	238	126		2 355	2 153	706	...
1965	1 787	1 282	187	1 470	76	0	1 394	259	134		2 531	2 300	706	...
1966	1 915	1 367	223	1 590	99	0	1 491	282	143		2 709	2 451	707	...
1967	1 952	1 408	188	1 596	108	0	1 487	296	169		2 785	2 510	701	...
1968	2 052	1 487	194	1 680	115	-1	1 565	296	191		2 932	2 642	700	...
1969	2 276	1 613	239	1 853	127	-1	1 724	342	209		3 279	2 872	694	298
1970	2 518	1 736	289	2 025	137	-1	1 886	390	241		3 611	3 215	697	301
1971	2 684	1 897	249	2 145	152	-1	1 992	411	280		3 774	3 404	711	307
1972	3 116	2 133	398	2 531	179	0	2 352	454	310		4 332	3 863	719	319
1973	3 628	2 389	573	2 961	229	0	2 733	535	360		4 987	4 432	727	333
1974	3 947	2 700	462	3 162	264	1	2 899	626	423		5 354	4 743	737	344
1975	4 347	3 012	396	3 409	285	3	3 126	707	514		5 802	5 190	749	344
1976	4 696	3 447	222	3 669	326	3	3 346	781	569		6 191	5 495	759	359
1977	5 104	3 886	68	3 954	371	4	3 588	903	613		6 617	5 835	771	372
1978	5 998	4 430	299	4 729	435	3	4 297	1 027	674		7 650	6 791	784	390
1979	6 466	4 887	115	5 003	500	6	4 509	1 197	759		8 193	7 171	789	397
1980	7 144	5 204	118	5 322	537	14	4 799	1 453	892		9 058	7 955	789	394
1981	8 124	5 659	223	5 881	626	25	5 281	1 811	1 032		10 214	9 007	795	396
1982	8 566	5 811	168	5 979	656	18	5 341	2 069	1 155		10 654	9 502	804	392
1983	9 009	6 143	123	6 265	701	9	5 573	2 170	1 266		11 067	9 912	814	400
1984	9 609	6 570	42	6 611	760	6	5 857	2 401	1 351		11 706	10 528	821	410
1985	9 793	6 745	-86	6 659	792	3	5 871	2 494	1 429		11 909	10 718	822	409
1986	10 148	6 704	233	6 938	810	-2	6 126	2 496	1 525		12 470	11 331	814	404
1987	10 448	6 895	314	7 209	833	-3	6 373	2 477	1 598		12 978	11 700	805	408
1988	10 640	7 260	106	7 366	931	0	6 435	2 519	1 686		13 296	11 917	800	419
1989	11 707	7 646	413	8 059	997	-2	7 059	2 801	1 847		14 641	13 043	800	427
1990	12 361	8 097	386	8 483	1 077	-4	7 402	2 935	2 024		15 448	13 795	800	436
1991	13 213	8 693	544	9 237	1 182	-11	8 043	3 045	2 125		16 318	14 656	810	447
1992	13 928	9 376	467	9 843	1 291	-2	8 550	3 087	2 291		16 867	15 115	826	459
1993	15 012	10 094	769	10 863	1 432	1	9 432	3 112	2 467		17 770	15 939	845	473
1994	15 384	10 634	366	11 001	1 518	6	9 489	3 343	2 552		17 861	15 939	861	497
1995	16 084	10 964	322	11 286	1 534	9	9 761	3 604	2 719		18 349	16 402	877	507
1996	16 880	11 402	295	11 697	1 538	12	10 171	3 835	2 874		19 047	16 983	886	523
1997	17 688	11 814	329	12 143	1 555	14	10 602	4 174	2 912		19 877	17 660	890	529
1998	18 857	12 596	337	12 932	1 598	18	11 353	4 489	3 015		21 130	18 738	892	540
1999	19 373	13 176	391	13 567	1 651	22	11 938	4 443	2 991		21 585	19 087	898	548
2000	20 716	14 077	244	14 321	1 733	26	12 614	4 763	3 339		22 934	20 238	903	559
2001	22 359	15 295	286	15 581	1 853	32	13 760	4 995	3 605		24 683	21 896	906	566
2002	22 819	15 794	180	15 973	1 948	31	14 056	4 974	3 789		25 080	22 610	910	572
2003	24 177	16 601	357	16 958	2 072	29	14 915	5 316	3 946		26 373	23 977	917	579
2004	25 813	17 922	440	18 361	2 173	33	16 222	5 419	4 172		27 877	25 364	926	598
2005	27 520	19 254	488	19 742	2 373	33	17 401	5 664	4 454		29 436	26 487	935	616
2006	29 366	20 700	99	20 799	2 589	31	18 241	6 299	4 825		31 061	27 718	945	631
2007	31 783	21 954	339	22 293	2 765	34	19 562	7 073	5 149		33 225	29 507	957	647
2008	33 140	22 753	192	22 945	2 886	36	20 095	7 437	5 609		34 256	30 627	967	...

. . . = Not available.
* = Less than $50,000, but the estimates for this item are included in the total.

Table 21-2. Personal Income and Employment by Region and State—*Continued*

(Millions of dollars, except as noted.)

Region or state and year	Personal income, total	Earnings by place of work			Less: Contributions for government social insurance	Plus: Adjustment for residence	Equals: Net earnings by place of residence	Plus: Dividends, interest, and rent	Plus: Personal current transfer receipts	Per capita (dollars)		Population (thousands)	Total employment (thousands)
		Nonfarm	Farm	Total						Personal income	Disposable personal income		
NEBRASKA													
1958	2 863	1 824	521	2 345	75	-9	2 261	442	160	2 070	1 891	1 383	. . .
1959	2 892	1 992	357	2 349	93	-9	2 247	471	174	2 070	1 885	1 397	. . .
1960	3 072	2 129	385	2 514	116	-11	2 387	500	185	2 168	1 957	1 417	. . .
1961	3 138	2 235	312	2 547	119	-11	2 417	516	205	2 170	1 943	1 446	. . .
1962	3 411	2 359	430	2 789	128	-10	2 652	544	216	2 330	2 109	1 464	. . .
1963	3 502	2 441	384	2 825	140	-9	2 676	597	229	2 373	2 140	1 476	. . .
1964	3 592	2 586	304	2 891	146	-8	2 736	619	236	2 423	2 214	1 482	. . .
1965	3 951	2 701	490	3 191	148	-8	3 035	659	258	2 686	2 462	1 471	. . .
1966	4 252	2 908	583	3 490	196	-8	3 287	685	280	2 920	2 655	1 456	. . .
1967	4 403	3 141	481	3 622	228	-8	3 386	676	341	3 022	2 734	1 457	. . .
1968	4 692	3 433	438	3 871	245	-8	3 618	679	394	3 198	2 868	1 467	. . .
1969	5 261	3 800	596	4 397	269	-100	4 028	804	430	3 570	3 140	1 474	704
1970	5 642	4 121	534	4 655	289	-107	4 259	885	498	3 792	3 363	1 488	715
1971	6 197	4 438	681	5 120	320	-110	4 689	946	562	4 120	3 719	1 504	728
1972	6 874	4 879	800	5 679	364	-119	5 196	1 059	619	4 527	4 014	1 518	748
1973	8 042	5 466	1 219	6 685	467	-123	6 095	1 207	741	5 261	4 678	1 529	775
1974	8 379	6 078	759	6 837	541	-133	6 164	1 369	847	5 449	4 785	1 538	793
1975	9 523	6 579	1 099	7 677	579	-140	6 959	1 528	1 036	6 178	5 535	1 541	790
1976	9 970	7 478	579	8 056	661	-147	7 248	1 620	1 103	6 437	5 743	1 549	811
1977	10 817	8 151	522	8 673	723	-146	7 805	1 838	1 174	6 959	6 128	1 554	831
1978	12 534	9 128	1 074	10 202	832	-169	9 201	2 030	1 303	8 030	7 111	1 561	855
1979	13 527	10 202	740	10 943	970	-198	9 775	2 300	1 451	8 647	7 555	1 564	877
1980	14 403	11 053	98	11 151	1 051	-215	9 885	2 824	1 693	9 160	8 015	1 572	879
1981	16 722	11 887	822	12 708	1 209	-255	11 244	3 526	1 952	10 593	9 351	1 579	874
1982	17 984	12 352	760	13 111	1 287	-262	11 562	4 272	2 151	11 370	9 889	1 582	864
1983	18 630	12 989	540	13 528	1 355	-276	11 897	4 405	2 327	11 759	10 498	1 584	870
1984	20 826	14 329	1 150	15 479	1 525	-328	13 627	4 758	2 441	13 109	11 846	1 589	889
1985	21 978	15 089	1 442	16 531	1 651	-353	14 527	4 859	2 593	13 869	12 527	1 585	902
1986	22 565	15 614	1 406	17 020	1 756	-351	14 913	4 942	2 710	14 333	12 942	1 574	902
1987	23 549	16 436	1 630	18 066	1 859	-347	15 860	4 916	2 772	15 032	13 521	1 567	930
1988	25 095	17 477	2 026	19 503	2 069	-380	17 054	5 148	2 893	15 969	14 355	1 571	953
1989	26 497	18 526	1 834	20 360	2 209	-389	17 761	5 633	3 102	16 825	15 022	1 575	971
1990	28 444	19 736	2 182	21 918	2 372	-382	19 164	5 915	3 365	17 983	16 031	1 582	994
1991	29 563	20 678	1 979	22 658	2 508	-420	19 730	6 226	3 608	18 524	16 566	1 596	998
1992	31 184	21 948	2 087	24 034	2 630	-458	20 947	6 313	3 924	19 349	17 329	1 612	1 005
1993	32 105	23 084	1 735	24 818	2 769	-472	21 577	6 341	4 187	19 750	17 656	1 626	1 027
1994	34 012	24 518	1 787	26 306	2 961	-479	22 865	6 779	4 367	20 751	18 515	1 639	1 068
1995	36 006	26 296	1 311	27 607	3 101	-524	23 982	7 377	4 647	21 730	19 290	1 657	1 077
1996	39 382	27 887	2 555	30 442	3 264	-579	26 599	7 822	4 961	23 530	20 879	1 674	1 103
1997	40 576	29 465	1 823	31 288	3 462	-653	27 173	8 272	5 131	24 061	21 132	1 686	1 118
1998	43 314	31 387	1 723	33 110	3 686	-684	28 741	9 096	5 477	25 542	22 392	1 696	1 144
1999	45 116	33 311	1 472	34 783	3 874	-762	30 146	9 148	5 822	26 465	23 175	1 705	1 166
2000	47 329	35 157	963	36 120	4 031	-825	31 263	9 991	6 075	27 626	24 090	1 713	1 183
2001	49 303	36 471	1 201	37 672	4 200	-833	32 639	9 998	6 666	28 703	25 140	1 718	1 182
2002	50 390	37 857	660	38 517	4 350	-869	33 299	10 023	7 069	29 225	26 170	1 724	1 180
2003	53 391	39 443	1 951	41 394	4 520	-911	35 963	10 002	7 426	30 811	27 932	1 733	1 181
2004	55 424	41 659	1 878	43 537	4 724	-933	37 880	9 835	7 710	31 827	28 851	1 741	1 199
2005	57 517	43 531	1 723	45 254	4 970	-951	39 333	10 062	8 122	32 847	29 520	1 751	1 212
2006	59 927	45 770	1 052	46 822	5 304	-915	40 602	10 618	8 706	34 053	30 266	1 760	1 226
2007	64 360	48 197	1 791	49 988	5 512	-1 013	43 464	11 697	9 200	36 372	32 237	1 769	1 245
2008	67 288	50 154	1 956	52 110	5 744	-1 077	45 289	12 110	9 889	37 730	33 678	1 783	. . .

. . . = Not available.
* = Less than $50,000, but the estimates for this item are included in the total.

Table 21-2. Personal Income and Employment by Region and State—*Continued*

(Millions of dollars, except as noted.)

Region or state and year	Personal income, total	Earnings by place of work			Less: Contributions for government social insurance	Plus: Adjustment for residence	Equals: Net earnings by place of residence	Plus: Dividends, interest, and rent	Plus: Personal current transfer receipts	Per capita (dollars)		Population (thousands)	Total employment (thousands)
		Nonfarm	Farm	Total						Personal income	Disposable personal income		
NEVADA													
1958	705	595	22	617	26	-2	589	79	37	2 622	2 309	269	...
1959	776	663	19	682	30	-2	650	88	38	2 780	2 470	279	...
1960	851	730	14	744	36	-2	706	104	41	2 923	2 573	291	...
1961	941	805	13	817	40	-3	775	117	49	2 988	2 606	315	...
1962	1 134	985	18	1 004	50	-4	950	133	51	3 222	2 829	352	...
1963	1 276	1 127	20	1 147	66	-6	1 075	143	58	3 213	2 804	397	...
1964	1 387	1 222	11	1 234	67	-5	1 161	161	65	3 257	2 909	426	...
1965	1 487	1 285	13	1 299	66	-5	1 228	187	72	3 348	2 999	444	...
1966	1 570	1 359	18	1 377	80	-4	1 294	199	78	3 521	3 144	446	...
1967	1 668	1 429	17	1 446	86	-3	1 356	217	95	3 715	3 309	449	...
1968	1 935	1 642	19	1 661	100	-4	1 557	265	113	4 170	3 632	464	...
1969	2 164	1 888	32	1 921	132	-34	1 754	285	125	4 509	3 830	480	244
1970	2 435	2 096	34	2 130	144	-39	1 947	340	148	4 936	4 360	493	256
1971	2 719	2 322	35	2 357	165	-42	2 151	384	184	5 229	4 674	520	267
1972	3 043	2 589	42	2 631	194	-45	2 393	433	218	5 566	4 944	547	280
1973	3 474	2 976	56	3 032	256	-55	2 721	499	254	6 107	5 429	569	304
1974	3 873	3 277	34	3 311	287	-57	2 967	591	315	6 491	5 752	597	317
1975	4 365	3 622	33	3 655	312	-58	3 284	644	438	7 043	6 404	620	326
1976	5 009	4 191	35	4 226	367	-68	3 791	730	489	7 745	6 938	647	349
1977	5 786	4 919	27	4 946	438	-84	4 424	829	534	8 533	7 593	678	384
1978	6 996	6 029	23	6 052	552	-117	5 383	1 010	603	9 725	8 566	719	432
1979	8 157	7 005	9	7 014	678	-132	6 204	1 242	711	10 661	9 314	765	468
1980	9 480	7 965	57	8 022	775	-160	7 087	1 529	863	11 700	10 300	810	490
1981	10 809	8 927	27	8 954	928	-170	7 857	1 900	1 053	12 752	11 192	848	502
1982	11 594	9 228	32	9 261	951	-171	8 139	2 283	1 172	13 152	11 651	882	497
1983	12 317	9 778	26	9 804	1 048	-179	8 576	2 458	1 283	13 656	12 193	902	502
1984	13 521	10 716	35	10 751	1 190	-191	9 369	2 777	1 374	14 618	13 080	925	528
1985	14 723	11 601	28	11 630	1 313	-199	10 118	3 095	1 510	15 481	13 776	951	551
1986	15 856	12 531	27	12 559	1 458	-217	10 884	3 289	1 683	16 170	14 346	981	577
1987	17 260	13 799	48	13 847	1 621	-241	11 985	3 479	1 796	16 865	14 880	1 023	623
1988	19 531	15 800	64	15 864	1 878	-280	13 706	3 850	1 975	18 168	15 966	1 075	670
1989	22 019	17 627	78	17 705	2 125	-325	15 254	4 485	2 281	19 360	17 012	1 137	719
1990	24 837	19 831	81	19 912	2 387	-381	17 144	5 085	2 607	20 346	17 866	1 221	766
1991	26 910	20 891	73	20 964	2 551	-351	18 062	5 645	3 203	20 761	18 383	1 296	779
1992	29 844	23 028	70	23 098	2 779	-313	20 006	6 209	3 629	22 084	19 526	1 351	786
1993	32 143	25 017	117	25 134	3 041	-354	21 739	6 567	3 837	22 777	20 053	1 411	829
1994	35 641	27 653	81	27 734	3 398	-367	23 969	7 649	4 023	23 772	21 015	1 499	909
1995	39 250	30 519	69	30 588	3 736	-365	26 487	8 397	4 366	24 817	21 941	1 582	964
1996	43 466	33 715	72	33 787	4 041	-386	29 360	9 395	4 711	26 085	22 803	1 666	1 035
1997	47 388	36 638	72	36 710	4 310	-340	32 059	10 321	5 008	26 862	23 531	1 764	1 102
1998	52 371	40 341	95	40 436	4 582	-349	35 504	11 529	5 338	28 260	24 576	1 853	1 145
1999	56 462	44 151	89	44 240	4 831	-379	39 030	11 855	5 577	29 184	25 349	1 935	1 215
2000	61 428	47 304	97	47 401	4 701	-339	42 361	13 067	5 999	30 436	26 322	2 018	1 268
2001	64 367	49 386	102	49 487	4 988	-302	44 198	13 351	6 819	30 739	26 799	2 094	1 289
2002	66 632	50 914	81	50 995	5 256	-311	45 428	13 545	7 659	30 784	27 348	2 165	1 304
2003	71 183	54 600	86	54 686	5 641	-370	48 675	14 471	8 037	31 866	28 566	2 234	1 363
2004	80 250	60 928	102	61 030	6 234	-447	54 348	17 304	8 597	34 533	30 853	2 324	1 450
2005	90 018	67 652	99	67 752	6 909	-543	60 299	20 409	9 310	37 481	33 110	2 402	1 543
2006	96 512	72 637	79	72 716	7 512	-571	64 633	21 774	10 105	38 850	34 336	2 484	1 626
2007	101 799	76 311	91	76 402	7 867	-639	67 895	22 900	11 003	39 853	34 936	2 554	1 667
2008	104 924	77 157	105	77 261	7 941	-619	68 701	23 860	12 364	40 353	35 768	2 600	...

. . . = Not available.
* = Less than $50,000, but the estimates for this item are included in the total.

Table 21-2. Personal Income and Employment by Region and State—*Continued*

(Millions of dollars, except as noted.)

Region or state and year	Personal income, total	Earnings by place of work Nonfarm	Farm	Total	Less: Contributions for government social insurance	Plus: Adjustment for residence	Equals: Net earnings by place of residence	Plus: Dividends, interest, and rent	Plus: Personal current transfer receipts	Per capita (dollars) Personal income	Disposable personal income	Population (thousands)	Total employment (thousands)
NEW HAMPSHIRE													
1958	1 163	887	21	908	39	57	926	155	83	2 002	1 807	581	. . .
1959	1 265	976	16	992	46	70	1 016	163	86	2 122	1 912	596	. . .
1960	1 336	1 025	19	1 044	55	79	1 068	178	90	2 194	1 959	609	. . .
1961	1 407	1 068	20	1 089	56	85	1 118	188	102	2 277	2 040	618	. . .
1962	1 509	1 142	19	1 160	62	94	1 193	211	105	2 387	2 134	632	. . .
1963	1 569	1 185	17	1 202	68	100	1 234	223	113	2 418	2 150	649	. . .
1964	1 686	1 271	18	1 289	71	108	1 326	244	116	2 543	2 309	663	. . .
1965	1 822	1 365	21	1 386	75	119	1 430	268	123	2 695	2 435	676	. . .
1966	2 005	1 519	24	1 543	103	139	1 579	294	132	2 945	2 630	681	. . .
1967	2 191	1 668	17	1 685	116	154	1 723	313	155	3 143	2 805	697	. . .
1968	2 424	1 838	20	1 858	128	173	1 902	342	180	3 418	3 029	709	. . .
1969	2 705	1 992	21	2 012	129	232	2 116	386	203	3 736	3 295	724	334
1970	2 883	2 113	16	2 130	135	220	2 215	427	241	3 886	3 409	742	334
1971	3 123	2 270	14	2 284	150	230	2 364	467	292	4 098	3 662	762	336
1972	3 454	2 525	16	2 541	176	252	2 617	515	322	4 419	3 888	782	350
1973	3 905	2 882	21	2 902	229	284	2 957	568	380	4 870	4 340	802	374
1974	4 304	3 119	13	3 132	257	329	3 204	644	455	5 267	4 673	817	381
1975	4 655	3 266	17	3 283	266	359	3 375	694	586	5 608	5 049	830	370
1976	5 298	3 787	19	3 806	310	411	3 906	768	624	6 255	5 588	847	394
1977	5 992	4 304	18	4 322	353	480	4 449	883	660	6 873	6 109	872	418
1978	6 918	5 032	19	5 051	420	572	5 203	993	723	7 739	6 817	894	446
1979	7 933	5 762	21	5 784	503	681	5 962	1 144	827	8 700	7 653	912	469
1980	9 104	6 397	14	6 410	560	849	6 699	1 435	969	9 850	8 698	924	483
1981	10 323	7 062	23	7 084	669	959	7 375	1 812	1 135	11 021	9 703	937	494
1982	11 382	7 629	19	7 648	741	1 050	7 957	2 180	1 246	12 010	10 698	948	500
1983	12 517	8 563	17	8 580	841	1 174	8 913	2 274	1 331	13 064	11 631	958	520
1984	14 211	9 694	21	9 715	977	1 390	10 129	2 674	1 408	14 547	12 997	977	556
1985	15 763	10 930	24	10 954	1 125	1 513	11 342	2 947	1 474	15 815	14 018	997	589
1986	17 407	12 256	24	12 280	1 285	1 598	12 594	3 267	1 546	16 981	14 957	1 025	622
1987	19 252	13 814	43	13 856	1 430	1 723	14 150	3 524	1 579	18 261	16 067	1 054	639
1988	21 178	15 254	45	15 299	1 621	1 876	15 554	3 910	1 714	19 563	17 335	1 083	665
1989	22 615	15 864	34	15 898	1 700	1 968	16 166	4 531	1 918	20 475	18 157	1 105	665
1990	22 817	15 773	43	15 817	1 720	2 004	16 101	4 568	2 149	20 512	18 292	1 112	648
1991	23 518	15 619	44	15 663	1 740	2 190	16 113	4 543	2 863	21 189	19 031	1 110	621
1992	24 594	16 706	51	16 758	1 845	2 247	17 159	4 384	3 051	22 002	19 777	1 118	633
1993	25 273	17 449	43	17 492	1 924	2 370	17 938	4 383	2 953	22 376	20 016	1 129	647
1994	26 972	18 492	41	18 532	2 082	2 468	18 919	4 696	3 358	23 607	21 141	1 143	670
1995	28 647	19 637	36	19 673	2 228	2 456	19 901	5 131	3 615	24 748	22 094	1 158	685
1996	31 045	20 859	42	20 901	2 352	2 624	21 173	6 302	3 570	26 427	23 434	1 175	701
1997	32 420	22 536	39	22 575	2 536	2 829	22 869	5 830	3 721	27 257	23 770	1 189	722
1998	35 149	24 694	42	24 736	2 753	2 946	24 928	6 363	3 858	29 147	25 403	1 206	745
1999	37 125	26 424	45	26 469	2 929	3 410	26 949	6 244	3 932	30 380	26 278	1 222	763
2000	41 429	29 364	42	29 405	3 210	4 043	30 239	6 986	4 204	33 401	28 571	1 240	785
2001	42 624	30 315	38	30 353	3 354	4 015	31 014	7 044	4 566	33 919	29 264	1 257	795
2002	43 393	31 138	38	31 176	3 437	3 865	31 604	6 794	4 995	34 149	30 462	1 271	795
2003	44 327	32 470	41	32 511	3 572	3 796	32 734	6 517	5 076	34 596	31 203	1 281	804
2004	47 190	34 772	50	34 822	3 851	3 960	34 930	6 715	5 545	36 523	33 098	1 292	825
2005	48 682	36 519	39	36 558	4 040	3 946	36 465	6 443	5 775	37 432	33 585	1 301	843
2006	51 964	38 478	31	38 509	4 237	4 027	38 298	7 518	6 148	39 703	35 423	1 309	846
2007	54 640	39 668	41	39 709	4 393	4 560	39 875	8 319	6 446	41 639	36 957	1 312	848
2008	56 356	40 624	38	40 661	4 552	4 756	40 865	8 552	6 939	42 830	38 304	1 316	. . .

. . . = Not available.
* = Less than $50,000, but the estimates for this item are included in the total.

Table 21-2. Personal Income and Employment by Region and State—*Continued*

(Millions of dollars, except as noted.)

Region or state and year	Personal income, total	Derivation of personal income								Per capita (dollars)		Population (thousands)	Total employment (thousands)
		Earnings by place of work			Less: Contributions for government social insurance	Plus: Adjustment for residence	Equals: Net earnings by place of residence	Plus: Dividends, interest, and rent	Plus: Personal current transfer receipts	Personal income	Disposable personal income		
		Nonfarm	Farm	Total									
NEW JERSEY													
1958	14 369	11 477	133	11 610	469	684	11 825	1 698	847	2 440	2 160	5 890	. . .
1959	15 456	12 474	105	12 580	557	769	12 792	1 809	855	2 570	2 279	6 015	. . .
1960	16 288	13 087	120	13 207	660	855	13 403	1 989	896	2 669	2 357	6 103	. . .
1961	17 112	13 633	119	13 752	694	912	13 970	2 118	1 024	2 731	2 411	6 265	. . .
1962	18 410	14 592	108	14 700	771	1 013	14 943	2 389	1 079	2 887	2 545	6 376	. . .
1963	19 320	15 227	106	15 333	869	1 088	15 552	2 608	1 159	2 958	2 605	6 531	. . .
1964	20 731	16 175	102	16 277	881	1 205	16 601	2 925	1 205	3 113	2 793	6 660	. . .
1965	22 283	17 303	118	17 421	934	1 317	17 804	3 194	1 285	3 293	2 932	6 767	. . .
1966	24 138	18 890	118	19 008	1 212	1 514	19 310	3 442	1 385	3 523	3 135	6 851	. . .
1967	26 025	20 250	104	20 354	1 345	1 680	20 689	3 694	1 642	3 757	3 319	6 928	. . .
1968	28 601	22 151	102	22 253	1 533	1 888	22 608	4 030	1 964	4 083	3 575	7 005	. . .
1969	32 013	24 081	104	24 186	1 827	3 117	25 476	4 325	2 212	4 512	3 913	7 095	3 061
1970	34 663	26 049	99	26 149	1 957	3 071	27 263	4 712	2 689	4 821	4 225	7 190	3 125
1971	37 285	27 829	93	27 922	2 168	3 155	28 908	5 100	3 276	5 120	4 549	7 282	3 119
1972	40 492	30 383	88	30 472	2 482	3 354	31 343	5 485	3 664	5 519	4 835	7 337	3 184
1973	44 253	33 599	126	33 725	3 128	3 511	34 109	6 012	4 132	6 033	5 331	7 335	3 288
1974	48 161	36 184	137	36 320	3 458	3 701	36 564	6 748	4 848	6 566	5 779	7 335	3 301
1975	51 810	37 723	96	37 819	3 541	3 983	38 261	7 211	6 338	7 057	6 299	7 341	3 191
1976	56 579	41 568	101	41 669	3 930	4 326	42 065	7 673	6 842	7 704	6 809	7 344	3 248
1977	62 009	45 747	111	45 858	4 313	4 720	46 265	8 526	7 218	8 446	7 383	7 342	3 325
1978	68 857	51 302	126	51 428	4 985	5 301	51 744	9 431	7 681	9 360	8 160	7 356	3 464
1979	76 525	56 860	126	56 985	5 744	6 057	57 298	10 684	8 544	10 379	8 956	7 373	3 555
1980	86 355	62 436	114	62 549	6 325	7 159	63 384	13 209	9 763	11 707	10 084	7 376	3 608
1981	96 485	68 287	148	68 436	7 378	7 797	68 854	16 668	10 963	13 025	11 188	7 407	3 643
1982	104 313	73 032	165	73 198	8 007	8 339	73 529	18 766	12 018	14 038	12 070	7 431	3 651
1983	112 659	79 741	191	79 932	8 979	8 573	79 526	20 155	12 978	15 086	13 118	7 468	3 753
1984	124 744	88 809	199	89 008	10 422	8 976	87 562	23 648	13 533	16 598	14 501	7 515	3 933
1985	133 915	96 368	226	96 594	11 391	9 355	94 558	25 171	14 186	17 701	15 321	7 566	4 049
1986	143 017	104 150	228	104 378	12 485	9 953	101 846	26 320	14 852	18 763	16 212	7 622	4 146
1987	154 440	114 160	260	114 420	13 605	10 505	111 321	27 770	15 350	20 134	17 237	7 671	4 248
1988	169 577	126 764	260	127 024	15 329	10 836	122 531	30 701	16 345	21 988	19 041	7 712	4 349
1989	181 461	133 204	254	133 458	15 980	10 339	127 816	36 138	17 506	23 487	20 354	7 726	4 386
1990	190 753	139 588	234	139 821	16 641	10 556	133 736	37 702	19 315	24 572	21 381	7 763	4 344
1991	194 174	140 848	220	141 068	17 191	10 647	134 524	37 633	22 016	24 847	21 700	7 815	4 204
1992	207 904	150 184	237	150 421	18 256	12 656	144 821	37 478	25 604	26 382	23 084	7 881	4 201
1993	213 222	156 037	268	156 305	18 953	13 077	150 429	36 017	26 776	26 824	23 357	7 949	4 228
1994	220 859	162 295	286	162 581	20 037	13 144	155 688	38 032	27 139	27 558	23 897	8 014	4 264
1995	233 937	170 507	284	170 790	20 840	14 226	164 176	40 712	29 049	28 941	25 158	8 083	4 330
1996	248 320	179 807	303	180 110	21 722	15 672	174 060	43 856	30 404	30 470	26 299	8 150	4 386
1997	263 420	189 111	248	189 359	22 502	18 451	185 309	47 048	31 063	32 051	27 411	8 219	4 446
1998	282 721	203 154	261	203 415	23 902	20 798	200 311	50 775	31 636	34 115	28 914	8 287	4 524
1999	294 385	213 763	234	213 997	25 071	22 436	211 362	50 143	32 881	35 215	29 600	8 360	4 595
2000	323 554	233 138	304	233 441	26 854	25 657	232 244	56 234	35 076	38 377	32 020	8 431	4 755
2001	332 951	238 171	269	238 440	27 970	27 219	237 689	56 587	38 676	39 213	32 876	8 491	4 789
2002	337 009	245 182	261	245 444	28 752	24 087	240 779	54 151	42 080	39 428	34 085	8 547	4 804
2003	342 858	252 280	253	252 533	29 274	24 133	247 391	51 940	43 527	39 916	34 888	8 590	4 846
2004	361 822	266 375	270	266 645	30 458	27 104	263 291	53 976	44 555	41 971	36 813	8 621	4 936
2005	376 912	277 754	241	277 995	31 837	29 839	275 996	54 171	46 745	43 651	37 762	8 635	5 034
2006	404 474	292 000	242	292 242	33 258	33 787	292 771	61 296	50 407	46 813	40 331	8 640	5 089
2007	428 425	303 410	239	303 648	34 929	39 059	307 779	68 262	52 384	49 511	42 327	8 653	5 128
2008	442 116	311 545	225	311 770	36 189	40 438	316 019	69 366	56 730	50 919	43 921	8 683	. . .

. . . = Not available.
* = Less than $50,000, but the estimates for this item are included in the total.

Table 21-2. Personal Income and Employment by Region and State—*Continued*

(Millions of dollars, except as noted.)

Region or state and year	Personal income, total	Earnings by place of work			Less: Contributions for government social insurance	Plus: Adjustment for residence	Equals: Net earnings by place of residence	Plus: Dividends, interest, and rent	Plus: Personal current transfer receipts	Per capita (dollars)		Population (thousands)	Total employment (thousands)
		Nonfarm	Farm	Total						Personal income	Disposable personal income		
NEW MEXICO													
1958	1 630	1 322	113	1 435	45	-13	1 377	168	84	1 840	1 672	886	...
1959	1 754	1 448	99	1 546	54	-14	1 478	184	93	1 909	1 728	919	...
1960	1 807	1 494	86	1 580	61	-14	1 505	200	102	1 894	1 719	954	...
1961	1 891	1 533	101	1 634	61	-14	1 558	214	118	1 959	1 778	965	...
1962	1 965	1 622	82	1 703	66	-15	1 623	223	120	2 008	1 816	979	...
1963	2 029	1 672	85	1 757	74	-16	1 667	233	129	2 052	1 857	989	...
1964	2 144	1 785	65	1 850	78	-17	1 755	254	135	2 131	1 955	1 006	...
1965	2 272	1 877	77	1 954	81	-19	1 854	272	145	2 245	2 041	1 012	...
1966	2 393	1 967	99	2 066	104	-19	1 943	294	156	2 376	2 161	1 007	...
1967	2 481	2 040	89	2 129	121	-20	1 989	297	195	2 481	2 257	1 000	...
1968	2 683	2 182	101	2 284	124	-21	2 138	316	228	2 699	2 443	994	...
1969	2 942	2 399	107	2 506	152	-22	2 332	350	261	2 910	2 588	1 011	395
1970	3 262	2 592	131	2 723	163	-22	2 538	399	325	3 188	2 849	1 023	399
1971	3 601	2 856	129	2 986	188	-22	2 775	448	378	3 419	3 106	1 053	416
1972	4 043	3 225	136	3 362	221	-20	3 121	500	422	3 752	3 380	1 078	440
1973	4 551	3 610	179	3 789	283	-17	3 489	562	500	4 122	3 716	1 104	461
1974	5 143	4 078	147	4 225	328	-15	3 881	662	601	4 553	4 086	1 130	478
1975	5 876	4 596	176	4 772	367	-13	4 393	745	738	5 054	4 618	1 163	491
1976	6 601	5 263	123	5 386	421	-12	4 953	823	825	5 523	5 003	1 195	512
1977	7 429	5 981	134	6 116	481	-11	5 623	937	869	6 064	5 486	1 225	539
1978	8 515	6 872	167	7 039	565	-11	6 463	1 098	954	6 802	6 091	1 252	568
1979	9 666	7 746	206	7 952	667	-9	7 275	1 290	1 101	7 549	6 751	1 281	593
1980	10 929	8 561	179	8 740	740	-3	7 996	1 623	1 310	8 346	7 483	1 309	598
1981	12 415	9 637	128	9 765	893	-15	8 857	2 062	1 497	9 316	8 255	1 333	613
1982	13 559	10 281	115	10 396	972	-17	9 407	2 506	1 647	9 942	8 789	1 364	621
1983	14 594	10 921	126	11 046	1 035	-13	9 998	2 797	1 800	10 467	9 476	1 394	633
1984	16 030	12 030	145	12 176	1 165	-6	11 005	3 102	1 923	11 315	10 286	1 417	658
1985	17 376	12 929	207	13 136	1 272	1	11 865	3 450	2 060	12 080	10 958	1 438	678
1986	17 993	13 270	193	13 463	1 333	9	12 139	3 637	2 217	12 301	11 212	1 463	684
1987	18 769	13 784	240	14 024	1 376	24	12 671	3 753	2 345	12 695	11 443	1 479	703
1988	19 816	14 537	320	14 857	1 514	35	13 378	3 926	2 512	13 296	11 995	1 490	739
1989	21 173	15 319	381	15 700	1 614	43	14 129	4 246	2 797	14 078	12 637	1 504	754
1990	22 708	16 407	416	16 822	1 737	51	15 136	4 525	3 046	14 924	13 413	1 522	767
1991	24 302	17 549	402	17 951	1 887	64	16 128	4 783	3 391	15 625	14 088	1 555	790
1992	25 963	18 776	484	19 260	2 006	81	17 335	4 848	3 781	16 273	14 687	1 595	803
1993	27 753	20 215	533	20 748	2 167	99	18 680	4 977	4 096	16 959	15 254	1 636	831
1994	29 662	21 511	463	21 974	2 357	117	19 734	5 506	4 421	17 631	15 831	1 682	863
1995	31 701	22 924	397	23 321	2 524	130	20 926	5 925	4 849	18 426	16 566	1 720	905
1996	33 345	23 626	413	24 039	2 597	150	21 592	6 472	5 282	19 029	17 034	1 752	915
1997	34 961	24 728	559	25 287	2 722	173	22 739	6 804	5 418	19 698	17 529	1 775	929
1998	37 046	26 134	614	26 748	2 852	196	24 091	7 261	5 694	20 656	18 382	1 793	945
1999	38 046	26 974	726	27 700	2 967	224	24 957	7 061	6 028	21 042	18 681	1 808	951
2000	40 318	28 692	504	29 196	3 115	250	26 332	7 545	6 441	22 144	19 586	1 821	973
2001	44 138	31 234	712	31 946	3 337	251	28 860	8 080	7 198	24 141	21 543	1 828	978
2002	44 987	32 637	498	33 134	3 497	252	29 890	7 190	7 906	24 330	21 975	1 849	988
2003	46 650	34 211	528	34 739	3 660	259	31 338	6 882	8 430	24 975	22 749	1 868	1 013
2004	49 813	36 482	681	37 162	3 885	266	33 542	7 313	8 957	26 366	24 113	1 889	1 039
2005	53 383	38 930	646	39 576	4 155	281	35 702	8 076	9 605	27 907	25 303	1 913	1 052
2006	56 870	41 795	386	42 181	4 524	297	37 954	8 554	10 361	29 346	26 369	1 938	1 092
2007	60 318	43 519	609	44 128	4 754	331	39 704	9 406	11 209	30 706	27 481	1 964	1 116
2008	63 680	45 583	504	46 086	4 997	347	41 437	9 914	12 330	32 091	28 922	1 984	...

. . . = Not available.
* = Less than $50,000, but the estimates for this item are included in the total.

Table 21-2. Personal Income and Employment by Region and State—*Continued*

(Millions of dollars, except as noted.)

Region or state and year	Personal income, total	Derivation of personal income										Per capita (dollars)		Population (thousands)	Total employment (thousands)
		Earnings by place of work			Less: Contributions for government social insurance	Plus: Adjustment for residence	Equals: Net earnings by place of residence	Plus: Dividends, interest, and rent	Plus: Personal current transfer receipts			Personal income	Disposable personal income		
		Nonfarm	Farm	Total											
NEW YORK															
1958	42 844	35 970	374	36 344	1 434	-589	34 321	5 925	2 597			2 581	2 263	16 601	. . .
1959	45 478	38 431	314	38 745	1 711	-663	36 371	6 385	2 721			2 726	2 373	16 685	. . .
1960	47 504	40 258	348	40 607	2 040	-738	37 828	6 882	2 794			2 821	2 452	16 838	. . .
1961	49 537	41 747	359	42 106	2 191	-792	39 123	7 207	3 207			2 904	2 511	17 061	. . .
1962	52 265	44 181	282	44 463	2 489	-879	41 095	7 875	3 295			3 021	2 615	17 301	. . .
1963	54 369	45 662	330	45 992	2 712	-945	42 335	8 485	3 549			3 114	2 696	17 461	. . .
1964	58 119	48 468	313	48 781	2 681	-1 042	45 058	9 338	3 723			3 304	2 902	17 589	. . .
1965	61 648	51 125	361	51 486	2 803	-1 129	47 554	10 079	4 016			3 476	3 042	17 734	. . .
1966	66 196	55 520	421	55 941	3 719	-1 284	50 938	10 623	4 636			3 710	3 226	17 843	. . .
1967	71 480	59 466	376	59 842	4 031	-1 429	54 382	11 198	5 900			3 985	3 437	17 935	. . .
1968	78 777	65 221	385	65 606	4 444	-1 611	59 551	12 012	7 213			4 364	3 736	18 051	. . .
1969	83 071	70 374	435	70 810	5 283	-3 370	62 156	13 177	7 738			4 588	3 866	18 105	8 496
1970	89 047	74 870	415	75 285	5 525	-3 320	66 440	13 696	8 912			4 874	4 182	18 272	8 468
1971	94 929	79 090	405	79 495	6 021	-3 426	70 047	14 132	10 750			5 169	4 499	18 365	8 348
1972	101 465	84 851	347	85 199	6 786	-3 682	74 731	14 735	11 999			5 529	4 758	18 352	8 350
1973	108 510	91 179	465	91 644	8 402	-3 900	79 342	15 873	13 295			5 964	5 159	18 195	8 468
1974	117 015	96 764	435	97 199	9 177	-4 124	83 898	17 692	15 425			6 475	5 582	18 073	8 395
1975	125 715	101 226	372	101 598	9 443	-4 471	87 683	18 518	19 514			6 972	6 100	18 032	8 175
1976	134 312	108 634	395	109 029	10 240	-4 915	93 875	19 655	20 782			7 472	6 514	17 975	8 128
1977	145 284	117 785	325	118 110	11 004	-5 468	101 638	21 900	21 746			8 138	7 069	17 852	8 202
1978	158 202	129 462	425	129 887	12 359	-6 121	111 407	24 010	22 785			8 928	7 721	17 720	8 381
1979	173 257	142 323	530	142 853	14 064	-6 979	121 810	27 111	24 336			9 825	8 437	17 634	8 591
1980	193 492	156 467	521	156 988	15 326	-8 203	133 459	32 079	27 955			11 015	9 424	17 567	8 622
1981	216 592	172 221	535	172 756	17 978	-8 989	145 788	39 247	31 556			12 329	10 454	17 568	8 700
1982	235 868	185 233	512	185 745	19 580	-9 865	156 300	45 045	34 523			13 409	11 352	17 590	8 710
1983	252 521	197 967	363	198 331	21 209	-10 334	166 787	48 380	37 353			14 277	12 282	17 687	8 771
1984	281 237	219 483	484	219 967	23 922	-11 005	185 040	56 657	39 540			15 848	13 687	17 746	9 058
1985	300 275	236 364	552	236 916	26 256	-11 661	198 999	59 537	41 739			16 877	14 473	17 792	9 293
1986	320 223	254 715	645	255 360	28 610	-12 570	214 180	61 820	44 223			17 956	15 381	17 833	9 494
1987	341 560	275 384	727	276 111	30 469	-13 388	232 255	63 931	45 375			19 115	16 212	17 869	9 552
1988	372 771	301 956	642	302 598	34 131	-14 183	254 284	70 236	48 252			20 777	17 818	17 941	9 768
1989	400 769	316 180	764	316 944	35 868	-13 782	267 294	80 513	52 962			22 286	18 986	17 983	9 841
1990	423 897	332 467	745	333 212	37 849	-14 083	281 280	84 547	58 069			23 523	20 183	18 021	9 817
1991	434 304	334 699	617	335 316	38 691	-14 151	282 475	86 538	65 291			23 965	20 750	18 123	9 567
1992	453 737	354 874	728	355 602	40 470	-17 429	297 702	83 690	72 344			24 867	21 525	18 247	9 494
1993	462 008	362 389	792	363 181	41 543	-17 363	304 275	80 922	76 811			25 143	21 650	18 375	9 516
1994	475 979	370 458	665	371 123	43 347	-17 370	310 406	85 003	80 570			25 785	22 197	18 459	9 551
1995	501 667	389 360	545	389 905	44 952	-19 760	325 193	90 770	85 704			27 082	23 268	18 524	9 601
1996	528 363	411 259	777	412 036	46 314	-22 529	343 193	95 589	89 580			28 424	24 212	18 588	9 686
1997	557 024	436 661	474	437 135	48 332	-25 017	363 785	103 491	89 748			29 857	25 245	18 657	9 819
1998	591 847	469 379	716	470 096	51 014	-28 639	390 443	108 539	92 864			31 555	26 461	18 756	10 015
1999	619 659	498 632	827	499 459	53 642	-30 402	415 415	108 354	95 889			32 816	27 296	18 883	10 220
2000	663 005	537 852	770	538 623	57 239	-34 495	446 888	115 784	100 334			34 898	28 881	18 998	10 455
2001	679 886	550 300	851	551 151	59 470	-35 416	456 264	113 585	110 036			35 618	29 166	19 088	10 491
2002	677 604	548 912	596	549 508	60 353	-31 537	457 618	103 078	116 908			35 363	30 088	19 162	10 415
2003	693 533	560 473	772	561 246	61 947	-31 238	468 060	102 458	123 015			36 064	31 065	19 231	10 460
2004	739 969	598 660	925	599 586	65 286	-35 099	499 201	108 460	132 308			38 338	32 941	19 301	10 611
2005	788 561	632 699	879	633 577	67 916	-38 171	527 490	129 938	131 133			40 781	34 646	19 336	10 773
2006	846 795	678 966	683	679 649	72 176	-42 828	564 645	143 248	138 902			43 724	36 763	19 367	10 882
2007	900 819	725 871	1 127	726 998	76 008	-48 546	602 444	153 142	145 232			46 364	38 553	19 429	11 040
2008	937 010	752 457	1 015	753 472	78 547	-50 275	624 650	156 508	155 851			48 076	40 254	19 490	. . .

. . . = Not available.
* = Less than $50,000, but the estimates for this item are included in the total.

Table 21-2. Personal Income and Employment by Region and State—*Continued*

(Millions of dollars, except as noted.)

Region or state and year	Personal income, total	Earnings by place of work			Less: Contributions for government social insurance	Plus: Adjustment for residence	Equals: Net earnings by place of residence	Plus: Dividends, interest, and rent	Plus: Personal current transfer receipts	Per capita (dollars)		Population (thousands)	Total employment (thousands)
		Nonfarm	Farm	Total						Personal income	Disposable personal income		
NORTH CAROLINA													
1958	6 552	5 065	625	5 690	214	9	5 485	666	400	1 497	1 383	4 376	. . .
1959	7 014	5 609	518	6 127	257	9	5 879	705	430	1 573	1 435	4 458	. . .
1960	7 414	5 879	600	6 478	306	9	6 181	776	457	1 621	1 473	4 573	. . .
1961	7 834	6 140	639	6 779	314	10	6 474	836	524	1 680	1 526	4 663	. . .
1962	8 416	6 653	621	7 275	346	10	6 939	924	552	1 788	1 615	4 707	. . .
1963	8 849	7 072	599	7 670	412	11	7 270	985	595	1 866	1 682	4 742	. . .
1964	9 596	7 687	628	8 316	435	11	7 892	1 081	623	1 998	1 823	4 802	. . .
1965	10 349	8 440	526	8 966	467	11	8 510	1 160	679	2 128	1 922	4 863	. . .
1966	11 484	9 499	611	10 110	617	10	9 504	1 243	738	2 346	2 107	4 896	. . .
1967	12 429	10 362	602	10 964	714	10	10 259	1 311	859	2 510	2 257	4 952	. . .
1968	13 702	11 642	514	12 156	825	12	11 343	1 377	981	2 738	2 429	5 004	. . .
1969	15 272	12 885	667	13 553	899	16	12 670	1 495	1 107	3 036	2 655	5 031	2 458
1970	16 661	13 881	666	14 546	971	13	13 589	1 734	1 337	3 267	2 879	5 099	2 469
1971	18 181	15 184	622	15 805	1 101	10	14 714	1 898	1 568	3 496	3 108	5 201	2 490
1972	20 569	17 280	743	18 023	1 308	4	16 720	2 094	1 756	3 884	3 409	5 296	2 602
1973	23 407	19 492	1 155	20 647	1 677	2	18 972	2 398	2 038	4 349	3 844	5 382	2 720
1974	25 830	21 304	1 101	22 405	1 900	8	20 513	2 784	2 532	4 730	4 155	5 461	2 743
1975	27 932	22 239	1 058	23 297	1 977	14	21 334	3 077	3 521	5 046	4 541	5 535	2 647
1976	31 206	25 131	1 141	26 272	2 271	15	24 016	3 409	3 781	5 579	4 966	5 593	2 754
1977	34 239	28 005	849	28 854	2 512	22	26 364	3 884	3 992	6 040	5 352	5 668	2 851
1978	38 715	31 757	1 133	32 890	2 922	21	29 989	4 424	4 303	6 744	5 950	5 740	2 948
1979	42 946	35 519	746	36 264	3 390	18	32 892	5 133	4 921	7 403	6 474	5 802	3 051
1980	48 344	38 941	639	39 580	3 727	23	35 875	6 599	5 870	8 195	7 172	5 899	3 060
1981	54 553	42 821	1 040	43 860	4 393	-20	39 448	8 334	6 772	9 158	8 000	5 957	3 082
1982	58 508	44 892	1 058	45 950	4 648	-30	41 272	9 694	7 542	9 720	8 615	6 019	3 051
1983	63 973	49 669	628	50 296	5 177	-49	45 070	10 770	8 132	10 527	9 304	6 077	3 138
1984	72 997	56 515	1 283	57 798	5 974	-83	51 741	12 659	8 596	11 842	10 517	6 164	3 306
1985	79 417	61 714	1 152	62 866	6 593	-147	56 126	14 075	9 217	12 699	11 245	6 254	3 410
1986	85 223	66 483	1 136	67 619	7 231	-210	60 179	15 243	9 802	13 481	11 928	6 322	3 512
1987	91 611	72 355	1 137	73 492	7 803	-292	65 397	16 016	10 198	14 306	12 552	6 404	3 631
1988	99 786	78 675	1 477	80 152	8 776	-351	71 025	17 733	11 028	15 398	13 589	6 481	3 774
1989	108 309	83 928	1 712	85 640	9 430	-403	75 807	20 186	12 316	16 497	14 460	6 565	3 864
1990	114 926	88 090	2 122	90 212	10 017	-447	79 748	21 605	13 573	17 246	15 196	6 664	3 928
1991	119 927	90 607	2 382	92 989	10 504	-430	82 055	22 291	15 581	17 677	15 648	6 784	3 889
1992	129 957	99 375	2 308	101 682	11 395	-451	89 836	22 782	17 339	18 842	16 720	6 897	3 989
1993	137 865	105 214	2 587	107 800	12 178	-467	95 155	23 608	19 101	19 575	17 325	7 043	4 113
1994	146 620	111 617	2 804	114 421	13 105	-520	100 797	25 958	19 865	20 400	17 982	7 187	4 227
1995	156 407	118 415	2 701	121 115	13 922	-592	106 601	27 715	22 091	21 295	18 716	7 345	4 380
1996	167 416	124 934	3 001	127 935	14 596	-648	112 691	30 754	23 972	22 320	19 548	7 501	4 487
1997	180 163	134 089	3 024	137 114	15 663	-716	120 735	34 165	25 263	23 530	20 508	7 657	4 631
1998	193 223	144 640	2 365	147 005	16 692	-704	129 609	37 408	26 206	24 743	21 400	7 809	4 746
1999	203 187	155 058	2 158	157 216	17 797	-771	138 648	36 606	27 933	25 560	22 136	7 949	4 850
2000	218 668	166 192	2 579	168 771	18 748	-885	149 137	39 633	29 898	27 067	23 395	8 079	4 925
2001	225 395	170 532	2 766	173 298	19 564	-781	152 953	39 156	33 286	27 487	23 832	8 200	4 885
2002	228 684	174 832	1 363	176 195	19 900	-779	155 515	37 195	35 975	27 515	24 334	8 311	4 878
2003	234 983	180 432	1 584	182 017	20 864	-720	160 432	37 038	37 514	27 942	24 953	8 410	4 891
2004	250 921	191 274	1 901	193 175	22 015	-752	170 408	40 405	40 108	29 440	26 381	8 523	5 015
2005	268 512	202 877	2 540	205 417	23 519	-875	181 023	44 024	43 465	31 002	27 509	8 661	5 146
2006	285 445	216 875	2 019	218 893	25 223	-1 057	192 613	45 863	46 968	32 271	28 387	8 845	5 307
2007	305 022	228 801	2 055	230 856	26 704	-1 222	202 930	50 848	51 244	33 735	29 486	9 042	5 461
2008	317 613	235 243	1 853	237 095	27 617	-1 258	208 220	52 882	56 512	34 439	30 311	9 222	. . .

. . . = Not available.
* = Less than $50,000, but the estimates for this item are included in the total.

Table 21-2. Personal Income and Employment by Region and State—*Continued*

(Millions of dollars, except as noted.)

Region or state and year	Personal income, total	Derivation of personal income								Per capita (dollars)		Population (thousands)	Total employment (thousands)
		Earnings by place of work			Less: Contributions for government social insurance	Plus: Adjustment for residence	Equals: Net earnings by place of residence	Plus: Dividends, interest, and rent	Plus: Personal current transfer receipts	Personal income	Disposable personal income		
		Nonfarm	Farm	Total									
NORTH DAKOTA													
1958	1 156	624	321	945	31	-10	904	179	73	1 908	1 766	606	. . .
1959	1 069	680	185	865	34	-11	820	170	78	1 729	1 594	618	. . .
1960	1 185	706	269	974	41	-11	922	180	83	1 869	1 724	634	. . .
1961	1 077	735	140	875	43	-11	820	166	90	1 680	1 543	641	. . .
1962	1 516	796	472	1 268	47	-14	1 207	215	94	2 379	2 206	637	. . .
1963	1 401	847	321	1 168	56	-14	1 097	206	98	2 176	2 000	644	. . .
1964	1 392	913	235	1 148	59	-17	1 072	215	104	2 145	1 976	649	. . .
1965	1 621	971	376	1 347	62	-17	1 268	238	114	2 497	2 315	649	. . .
1966	1 638	1 023	343	1 366	74	-16	1 276	239	123	2 531	2 330	647	. . .
1967	1 640	1 052	305	1 357	89	-16	1 252	241	147	2 620	2 395	626	. . .
1968	1 708	1 121	280	1 402	95	-16	1 291	252	164	2 750	2 510	621	. . .
1969	1 910	1 227	379	1 605	103	-52	1 450	277	183	3 076	2 759	621	274
1970	1 999	1 367	300	1 667	115	-55	1 497	291	212	3 230	2 920	619	281
1971	2 314	1 500	428	1 928	130	-58	1 741	325	248	3 693	3 397	627	284
1972	2 769	1 681	661	2 342	148	-62	2 132	361	276	4 388	4 027	631	288
1973	3 914	1 901	1 521	3 422	190	-65	3 167	437	310	6 189	5 686	632	300
1974	3 878	2 155	1 153	3 308	225	-78	3 005	517	356	6 114	5 444	634	308
1975	4 063	2 443	934	3 377	257	-84	3 037	606	420	6 363	5 695	638	314
1976	3 990	2 796	470	3 266	295	-99	2 872	654	464	6 183	5 531	645	326
1977	4 160	3 038	266	3 304	304	-106	2 894	760	506	6 409	5 764	649	331
1978	5 258	3 471	855	4 326	355	-118	3 852	853	553	8 082	7 246	651	345
1979	5 392	3 890	491	4 382	414	-136	3 831	948	613	8 269	7 390	652	354
1980	5 174	4 232	-396	3 837	448	-153	3 235	1 216	723	7 907	6 932	654	356
1981	6 819	4 733	361	5 094	530	-176	4 388	1 601	830	10 340	9 098	660	360
1982	7 383	5 006	298	5 304	574	-179	4 551	1 902	930	11 036	9 929	669	361
1983	7 734	5 256	358	5 614	615	-182	4 817	1 882	1 035	11 430	10 361	677	366
1984	8 410	5 555	599	6 154	654	-188	5 312	1 988	1 110	12 358	11 252	680	368
1985	8 710	5 682	688	6 370	680	-188	5 502	2 029	1 179	12 866	11 731	677	365
1986	8 796	5 704	682	6 386	702	-184	5 500	2 011	1 285	13 137	12 032	670	359
1987	9 057	5 927	780	6 707	732	-186	5 789	1 924	1 344	13 699	12 489	661	365
1988	8 343	6 144	-70	6 074	798	-192	5 083	1 912	1 348	12 731	11 485	655	369
1989	9 338	6 373	426	6 798	846	-198	5 754	2 116	1 468	14 447	13 075	646	373
1990	10 166	6 714	751	7 465	908	-194	6 363	2 231	1 573	15 943	14 457	638	376
1991	10 351	7 091	594	7 685	978	-203	6 504	2 245	1 602	16 282	14 746	636	385
1992	11 277	7 550	1 021	8 570	1 044	-222	7 304	2 214	1 759	17 669	16 085	638	390
1993	11 351	8 033	602	8 635	1 131	-242	7 262	2 236	1 853	17 703	16 006	641	400
1994	12 255	8 481	994	9 475	1 207	-258	8 011	2 368	1 876	19 006	17 244	645	414
1995	12 221	8 888	404	9 292	1 255	-283	7 754	2 490	1 977	18 865	17 008	648	421
1996	13 702	9 354	1 272	10 627	1 312	-319	8 995	2 631	2 075	21 068	19 084	650	429
1997	13 440	9 791	336	10 127	1 357	-344	8 425	2 861	2 154	20 686	18 560	650	433
1998	14 810	10 390	950	11 340	1 414	-371	9 555	3 065	2 190	22 872	20 620	648	440
1999	14 934	10 837	658	11 495	1 446	-402	9 647	2 994	2 293	23 180	20 863	644	443
2000	16 097	11 360	962	12 322	1 503	-428	10 391	3 244	2 462	25 105	22 594	641	447
2001	16 465	12 059	542	12 601	1 559	-461	10 581	3 352	2 531	25 880	23 204	636	449
2002	16 743	12 584	314	12 898	1 600	-486	10 812	3 256	2 675	26 429	24 097	634	451
2003	18 179	13 261	1 215	14 476	1 687	-515	12 274	3 139	2 766	28 733	26 466	633	451
2004	18 645	14 289	608	14 897	1 792	-569	12 536	3 177	2 932	29 307	26 988	636	464
2005	20 055	15 104	1 108	16 212	1 870	-620	13 722	3 239	3 094	31 571	28 910	635	474
2006	20 515	15 985	473	16 458	1 976	-677	13 806	3 440	3 270	32 233	29 134	636	481
2007	23 017	17 006	1 723	18 729	2 100	-712	15 917	3 628	3 472	36 082	32 604	638	487
2008	25 224	18 435	2 413	20 848	2 302	-815	17 731	3 772	3 720	39 321	35 824	641	. . .

. . . = Not available.
* = Less than $50,000, but the estimates for this item are included in the total.

Table 21-2. Personal Income and Employment by Region and State—*Continued*

(Millions of dollars, except as noted.)

Region or state and year	Personal income, total	Earnings by place of work			Less: Contributions for government social insurance	Plus: Adjustment for residence	Equals: Net earnings by place of residence	Plus: Dividends, interest, and rent	Plus: Personal current transfer receipts	Per capita (dollars)		Population (thousands)	Total employment (thousands)
		Nonfarm	Farm	Total						Personal income	Disposable personal income		
OHIO													
1958	20 843	17 271	378	17 649	700	-119	16 830	2 567	1 446	2 171	1 945	9 599	. . .
1959	22 308	18 960	261	19 221	860	-133	18 228	2 712	1 368	2 307	2 059	9 671	. . .
1960	23 209	19 579	327	19 906	1 002	-131	18 772	2 925	1 512	2 384	2 114	9 734	. . .
1961	23 635	19 548	365	19 914	984	-121	18 809	3 066	1 760	2 398	2 139	9 854	. . .
1962	24 920	20 810	328	21 138	1 125	-126	19 888	3 302	1 731	2 510	2 229	9 929	. . .
1963	25 946	21 726	325	22 051	1 236	-129	20 686	3 477	1 782	2 598	2 304	9 986	. . .
1964	27 708	23 369	297	23 666	1 354	-134	22 178	3 742	1 789	2 749	2 474	10 080	. . .
1965	30 005	25 317	350	25 667	1 408	-147	24 112	4 000	1 893	2 941	2 630	10 201	. . .
1966	32 757	27 971	487	28 458	1 864	-166	26 428	4 290	2 038	3 171	2 821	10 330	. . .
1967	34 362	29 268	322	29 590	1 957	-161	27 472	4 512	2 379	3 300	2 933	10 414	. . .
1968	37 916	32 238	407	32 645	2 133	-184	30 328	4 899	2 690	3 606	3 167	10 516	. . .
1969	41 407	35 347	409	35 757	2 360	-187	33 210	5 298	2 899	3 920	3 394	10 563	4 695
1970	43 597	36 742	426	37 167	2 409	-178	34 580	5 623	3 394	4 086	3 589	10 669	4 683
1971	46 381	38 669	407	39 076	2 605	-128	36 343	6 026	4 012	4 321	3 856	10 735	4 627
1972	50 350	42 095	497	42 592	2 987	-125	39 479	6 435	4 436	4 685	4 116	10 747	4 710
1973	56 071	47 155	658	47 813	3 865	-153	43 795	7 113	5 163	5 208	4 581	10 767	4 902
1974	61 593	50 967	784	51 752	4 312	-129	47 311	8 081	6 200	5 721	5 020	10 766	4 964
1975	65 710	52 665	802	53 468	4 338	-75	49 055	8 726	7 929	6 101	5 402	10 770	4 809
1976	72 585	58 965	777	59 742	4 944	-85	54 713	9 389	8 483	6 750	5 946	10 753	4 889
1977	80 707	66 238	664	66 902	5 557	-98	61 246	10 549	8 912	7 493	6 561	10 771	5 034
1978	89 417	73 903	613	74 515	6 407	-116	67 993	11 843	9 581	8 283	7 233	10 795	5 207
1979	99 084	81 302	745	82 047	7 332	-138	74 578	13 566	10 940	9 176	7 960	10 799	5 298
1980	108 500	85 191	559	85 750	7 615	-153	77 983	16 735	13 783	10 046	8 770	10 801	5 215
1981	118 192	91 268	155	91 423	8 706	-463	82 254	20 621	15 316	10 956	9 510	10 788	5 151
1982	123 709	92 078	260	92 338	8 892	-585	82 861	23 070	17 778	11 500	10 105	10 757	4 983
1983	131 008	97 188	-77	97 111	9 600	-706	86 805	25 186	19 017	12 201	10 737	10 738	4 978
1984	144 833	107 686	857	108 543	10 920	-841	96 782	28 427	19 624	13 488	11 941	10 738	5 183
1985	153 758	114 774	855	115 630	11 858	-930	102 842	29 995	20 921	14 323	12 641	10 735	5 316
1986	160 469	120 111	669	120 780	12 681	-964	107 135	31 178	22 157	14 955	13 220	10 730	5 430
1987	167 984	126 814	722	127 536	13 449	-1 001	113 086	31 871	23 026	15 612	13 688	10 760	5 582
1988	179 628	137 023	772	137 795	14 928	-1 053	121 815	33 627	24 186	16 634	14 648	10 799	5 720
1989	192 358	144 303	1 149	145 453	15 919	-1 092	128 441	38 088	25 828	17 763	15 559	10 829	5 843
1990	203 630	151 641	1 166	152 807	16 872	-1 079	134 856	40 065	28 709	18 743	16 446	10 864	5 905
1991	209 066	155 532	663	156 195	17 692	-1 082	137 421	40 360	31 285	19 100	16 824	10 946	5 882
1992	221 277	165 885	1 121	167 006	18 756	-1 284	146 967	40 372	33 938	20 062	17 709	11 029	5 893
1993	229 065	173 029	912	173 941	19 815	-1 346	152 780	41 056	35 230	20 634	18 149	11 101	5 998
1994	242 146	183 511	1 127	184 638	21 316	-1 485	161 837	43 717	36 592	21 712	19 067	11 152	6 175
1995	252 003	190 711	892	191 603	22 425	-1 408	167 769	45 671	38 563	22 495	19 675	11 203	6 341
1996	262 201	196 924	1 231	198 156	23 039	-1 367	173 749	48 328	40 124	23 322	20 217	11 243	6 437
1997	278 049	207 342	1 734	209 076	23 706	-1 451	183 918	52 712	41 419	24 656	21 308	11 277	6 541
1998	294 292	220 595	1 258	221 853	24 264	-1 567	196 022	56 190	42 079	26 017	22 405	11 312	6 660
1999	304 464	232 218	752	232 970	25 366	-1 597	206 007	55 044	43 413	26 859	23 164	11 335	6 747
2000	320 538	243 185	936	244 121	25 426	-1 526	217 168	57 209	46 161	28 207	24 264	11 364	6 836
2001	325 623	246 588	689	247 277	26 189	-1 405	219 684	55 602	50 337	28 585	24 667	11 391	6 759
2002	333 158	253 786	199	253 985	26 334	-1 438	226 212	53 187	53 758	29 197	25 639	11 411	6 691
2003	341 146	261 589	662	262 251	27 553	-1 429	233 270	51 287	56 589	29 846	26 494	11 430	6 664
2004	352 103	272 128	923	273 051	29 258	-1 434	242 359	50 938	58 806	30 765	27 329	11 445	6 741
2005	362 676	279 445	849	280 294	30 082	-1 513	248 699	52 432	61 545	31 672	27 963	11 451	6 805
2006	378 124	288 960	714	289 674	31 503	-1 613	256 558	56 654	64 912	33 000	29 000	11 458	6 820
2007	395 614	298 598	1 171	299 769	32 464	-1 778	265 526	60 643	69 445	34 468	30 223	11 478	6 830
2008	407 874	304 125	1 429	305 553	33 153	-1 728	270 673	61 999	75 203	35 511	31 370	11 486	. . .

. . . = Not available.
* = Less than $50,000, but the estimates for this item are included in the total.

Table 21-2. Personal Income and Employment by Region and State—*Continued*

(Millions of dollars, except as noted.)

Region or state and year	Personal income, total	Earnings by place of work Nonfarm	Farm	Total	Less: Contributions for government social insurance	Plus: Adjustment for residence	Equals: Net earnings by place of residence	Plus: Dividends, interest, and rent	Plus: Personal current transfer receipts	Per capita (dollars) Personal income	Disposable personal income	Population (thousands)	Total employment (thousands)
OKLAHOMA													
1958	4 085	3 022	326	3 348	113	4	3 239	514	331	1 802	1 636	2 267	. . .
1959	4 265	3 207	262	3 469	130	5	3 344	562	359	1 863	1 685	2 289	. . .
1960	4 488	3 303	331	3 634	150	7	3 491	619	378	1 921	1 736	2 336	. . .
1961	4 638	3 432	297	3 728	159	8	3 578	644	416	1 949	1 754	2 380	. . .
1962	4 836	3 659	236	3 895	178	11	3 728	668	441	1 993	1 791	2 427	. . .
1963	4 997	3 825	209	4 035	208	12	3 839	688	471	2 049	1 844	2 439	. . .
1964	5 355	4 116	204	4 320	207	14	4 127	737	491	2 189	1 989	2 446	. . .
1965	5 736	4 347	273	4 620	216	17	4 422	788	526	2 351	2 136	2 440	. . .
1966	6 142	4 734	263	4 996	286	21	4 731	827	584	2 503	2 261	2 454	. . .
1967	6 695	5 188	273	5 461	336	25	5 150	845	700	2 690	2 425	2 489	. . .
1968	7 341	5 777	216	5 993	384	31	5 640	912	789	2 933	2 626	2 503	. . .
1969	8 111	6 305	272	6 576	402	63	6 237	1 018	855	3 200	2 818	2 535	1 107
1970	8 919	6 802	355	7 157	431	65	6 791	1 147	981	3 475	3 098	2 566	1 120
1971	9 729	7 391	332	7 723	484	64	7 303	1 295	1 130	3 716	3 356	2 618	1 132
1972	10 675	8 155	413	8 568	558	73	8 084	1 351	1 240	4 017	3 574	2 657	1 183
1973	12 172	9 095	729	9 825	720	83	9 188	1 578	1 406	4 518	4 058	2 694	1 221
1974	13 600	10 387	446	10 832	846	107	10 094	1 842	1 663	4 977	4 400	2 732	1 256
1975	15 237	11 530	399	11 928	928	142	11 142	2 043	2 052	5 497	4 936	2 772	1 269
1976	16 879	12 960	333	13 293	1 054	177	12 416	2 217	2 245	5 978	5 339	2 823	1 305
1977	18 853	14 807	178	14 985	1 198	153	13 940	2 525	2 388	6 578	5 841	2 866	1 359
1978	21 405	17 011	167	17 178	1 417	149	15 911	2 923	2 571	7 348	6 456	2 913	1 428
1979	24 956	19 487	628	20 115	1 687	164	18 592	3 413	2 952	8 403	7 364	2 970	1 483
1980	28 906	22 648	257	22 905	1 964	171	21 113	4 383	3 410	9 506	8 279	3 041	1 551
1981	33 952	26 334	324	26 657	2 443	196	24 411	5 667	3 874	10 966	9 414	3 096	1 630
1982	37 938	28 875	483	29 358	2 741	201	26 817	6 753	4 368	11 833	10 086	3 206	1 678
1983	38 747	28 987	208	29 196	2 738	239	26 697	7 257	4 794	11 776	10 372	3 290	1 642
1984	41 833	31 099	368	31 467	2 968	288	28 787	8 072	4 974	12 732	11 328	3 286	1 672
1985	43 614	32 036	375	32 411	3 108	330	29 632	8 668	5 314	13 332	11 874	3 271	1 656
1986	43 291	31 358	638	31 996	3 118	378	29 256	8 388	5 647	13 309	12 100	3 253	1 595
1987	43 171	31 321	558	31 880	3 135	425	29 169	8 126	5 875	13 448	12 062	3 210	1 607
1988	45 023	32 621	760	33 381	3 457	473	30 397	8 414	6 212	14 216	12 753	3 167	1 617
1989	48 111	34 557	792	35 349	3 696	497	32 151	9 342	6 618	15 272	13 632	3 150	1 632
1990	50 971	36 644	847	37 490	3 966	560	34 084	9 765	7 121	16 187	14 280	3 149	1 664
1991	52 565	38 020	610	38 630	4 241	590	34 978	9 845	7 742	16 554	14 749	3 175	1 678
1992	55 958	40 450	815	41 266	4 469	610	37 406	9 876	8 676	17 376	15 553	3 221	1 690
1993	57 937	42 261	865	43 125	4 721	645	39 049	9 774	9 115	17 814	15 947	3 252	1 726
1994	60 283	43 590	821	44 412	4 979	701	40 133	10 474	9 676	18 374	16 410	3 281	1 759
1995	62 395	45 122	275	45 397	5 194	739	40 942	11 142	10 311	18 861	16 826	3 308	1 810
1996	65 944	47 523	373	47 896	5 379	767	43 284	11 886	10 773	19 743	17 523	3 340	1 861
1997	69 720	50 339	680	51 018	5 605	840	46 253	12 369	11 098	20 671	18 213	3 373	1 908
1998	74 118	53 674	572	54 246	5 882	874	49 238	13 431	11 448	21 766	19 161	3 405	1 957
1999	77 565	56 264	872	57 136	6 050	925	52 011	13 537	12 017	22 567	19 887	3 437	1 975
2000	84 310	60 883	715	61 598	6 355	1 008	56 251	15 290	12 770	24 410	21 520	3 454	2 015
2001	90 161	65 716	625	66 341	6 798	1 010	60 553	15 478	14 130	26 033	23 021	3 463	2 025
2002	90 178	65 338	774	66 112	7 012	1 043	60 143	14 914	15 121	25 891	23 281	3 483	2 007
2003	92 599	67 734	724	68 458	7 310	1 065	62 213	14 475	15 911	26 486	24 006	3 496	1 986
2004	100 024	73 656	852	74 508	7 824	1 113	67 798	15 419	16 807	28 481	25 911	3 512	2 024
2005	106 740	78 157	836	78 993	8 307	1 153	71 838	16 787	18 115	30 237	27 183	3 530	2 075
2006	116 876	85 648	318	85 966	9 032	1 207	78 141	19 018	19 716	32 755	29 214	3 568	2 123
2007	126 273	91 749	504	92 252	9 608	1 203	83 847	21 208	21 218	34 997	31 195	3 608	2 160
2008	134 400	98 304	-158	98 147	10 362	1 231	89 015	22 222	23 162	36 899	33 143	3 642	. . .

. . . = Not available.
* = Less than $50,000, but the estimates for this item are included in the total.

Table 21-2. Personal Income and Employment by Region and State—*Continued*

(Millions of dollars, except as noted.)

Region or state and year	Personal income, total	Earnings by place of work Nonfarm	Farm	Total	Less: Contributions for government social insurance	Plus: Adjustment for residence	Equals: Net earnings by place of residence	Plus: Dividends, interest, and rent	Plus: Personal current transfer receipts	Per capita (dollars) Personal income	Disposable personal income	Population (thousands)	Total employment (thousands)
OREGON													
1958	3 596	2 826	175	3 001	145	-11	2 846	467	283	2 093	1 834	1 718	. . .
1959	3 896	3 120	178	3 297	180	-14	3 103	507	286	2 232	1 957	1 746	. . .
1960	4 021	3 238	172	3 410	207	-17	3 185	532	304	2 269	1 987	1 772	. . .
1961	4 170	3 321	159	3 480	211	-19	3 250	568	352	2 333	2 061	1 787	. . .
1962	4 441	3 554	170	3 724	232	-22	3 470	612	359	2 443	2 150	1 818	. . .
1963	4 678	3 792	161	3 953	266	-27	3 660	647	371	2 524	2 202	1 853	. . .
1964	5 041	4 123	148	4 270	271	-32	3 967	690	384	2 670	2 348	1 888	. . .
1965	5 492	4 484	166	4 650	276	-38	4 337	741	414	2 835	2 512	1 937	. . .
1966	5 929	4 883	193	5 076	352	-42	4 681	800	447	3 011	2 650	1 969	. . .
1967	6 296	5 141	183	5 324	392	-46	4 886	877	533	3 181	2 802	1 979	. . .
1968	6 864	5 632	182	5 814	444	-54	5 315	948	600	3 425	2 986	2 004	. . .
1969	7 554	6 145	224	6 369	483	-91	5 795	1 097	662	3 664	3 138	2 062	920
1970	8 242	6 542	214	6 756	506	-67	6 183	1 254	805	3 924	3 424	2 100	926
1971	9 027	7 143	203	7 345	569	-56	6 720	1 376	932	4 199	3 696	2 150	951
1972	10 110	8 062	257	8 320	680	-50	7 589	1 498	1 022	4 605	4 014	2 195	1 001
1973	11 442	9 112	369	9 481	881	-56	8 545	1 685	1 213	5 110	4 473	2 239	1 058
1974	13 010	10 141	475	10 615	1 004	-63	9 549	1 965	1 496	5 704	4 959	2 281	1 089
1975	14 389	10 975	391	11 367	1 057	-31	10 278	2 210	1 901	6 190	5 470	2 325	1 105
1976	16 374	12 735	368	13 103	1 235	-16	11 852	2 454	2 067	6 903	6 046	2 372	1 156
1977	18 371	14 488	318	14 805	1 421	-74	13 311	2 826	2 235	7 531	6 504	2 439	1 223
1978	21 122	16 878	315	17 192	1 694	-132	15 366	3 315	2 441	8 416	7 244	2 510	1 297
1979	24 001	19 107	387	19 494	1 989	-205	17 300	3 964	2 737	9 309	7 984	2 578	1 352
1980	26 710	20 445	474	20 919	2 125	-253	18 541	4 920	3 248	10 113	8 731	2 641	1 353
1981	28 882	21 280	403	21 683	2 367	-263	19 052	6 070	3 760	10 825	9 388	2 668	1 324
1982	29 672	21 153	290	21 443	2 400	-250	18 793	6 640	4 239	11 134	9 687	2 665	1 274
1983	31 490	22 284	296	22 580	2 559	-234	19 787	7 145	4 557	11 869	10 431	2 653	1 300
1984	34 350	24 480	397	24 877	2 892	-280	21 704	7 939	4 706	12 882	11 381	2 667	1 348
1985	36 197	25 930	423	26 353	3 073	-317	22 963	8 308	4 925	13 543	11 923	2 673	1 379
1986	37 965	27 265	545	27 809	3 264	-362	24 184	8 769	5 013	14 148	12 386	2 684	1 414
1987	39 999	29 155	512	29 667	3 451	-422	25 795	9 014	5 191	14 809	12 966	2 701	1 464
1988	43 446	32 087	702	32 789	3 936	-493	28 359	9 566	5 522	15 849	14 044	2 741	1 532
1989	47 580	34 664	666	35 330	4 270	-546	30 514	11 007	6 060	17 050	14 833	2 791	1 586
1990	51 515	37 807	694	38 501	4 615	-608	33 278	11 646	6 591	18 010	15 823	2 860	1 638
1991	54 256	39 622	706	40 328	4 936	-664	34 729	12 212	7 316	18 527	16 214	2 929	1 647
1992	57 547	42 441	716	43 158	5 291	-748	37 118	12 310	8 119	19 235	16 813	2 992	1 665
1993	61 349	45 294	860	46 154	5 661	-838	39 655	13 005	8 689	20 046	17 471	3 060	1 709
1994	65 735	48 530	759	49 289	6 127	-888	42 275	14 426	9 034	21 060	18 284	3 121	1 792
1995	70 990	51 716	678	52 394	6 591	-1 061	44 742	16 228	10 020	22 293	19 393	3 184	1 858
1996	75 975	55 840	819	56 659	7 245	-1 284	48 129	17 149	10 697	23 398	20 232	3 247	1 933
1997	80 854	59 858	945	60 802	7 703	-1 467	51 632	18 176	11 046	24 469	20 986	3 304	1 999
1998	85 629	63 656	877	64 533	8 097	-1 589	54 848	19 314	11 467	25 542	21 951	3 352	2 037
1999	89 873	67 936	829	68 765	8 477	-1 737	58 551	18 929	12 393	26 480	22 657	3 394	2 065
2000	96 402	73 256	849	74 105	9 090	-1 904	63 111	20 303	12 988	28 099	23 906	3 431	2 111
2001	99 020	74 810	763	75 572	9 158	-1 891	64 523	19 999	14 498	28 530	24 530	3 471	2 104
2002	101 882	77 128	783	77 912	9 301	-1 952	66 659	19 502	15 721	28 960	25 526	3 518	2 092
2003	105 161	79 882	968	80 850	9 610	-1 992	69 248	19 800	16 113	29 607	26 286	3 552	2 108
2004	109 718	83 316	1 092	84 408	10 256	-2 003	72 149	21 024	16 545	30 679	27 220	3 576	2 168
2005	114 379	87 379	1 068	88 447	10 842	-2 087	75 518	21 189	17 671	31 580	27 616	3 622	2 234
2006	123 857	93 095	976	94 070	11 570	-2 218	80 283	24 718	18 857	33 648	29 289	3 681	2 284
2007	131 278	97 542	1 192	98 734	12 059	-2 486	84 188	26 970	20 120	35 143	30 487	3 736	2 320
2008	136 277	99 879	1 014	100 893	12 392	-2 558	85 943	28 311	22 022	35 956	31 643	3 790	. . .

. . . = Not available.
* = Less than $50,000, but the estimates for this item are included in the total.

Table 21-2. Personal Income and Employment by Region and State—*Continued*

(Millions of dollars, except as noted.)

| Region or state and year | Personal income, total | Earnings by place of work | | | Less: Contributions for government social insurance | Plus: Adjustment for residence | Equals: Net earnings by place of residence | Plus: Dividends, interest, and rent | Plus: Personal current transfer receipts | Per capita (dollars) | | Population (thousands) | Total employment (thousands) |
		Nonfarm	Farm	Total						Personal income	Disposable personal income		
PENNSYLVANIA													
1958	23 858	19 746	339	20 086	846	-45	19 195	2 861	1 803	2 158	1 925	11 058	...
1959	25 072	21 023	252	21 275	1 042	-57	20 177	3 024	1 871	2 232	1 986	11 234	...
1960	25 978	21 843	294	22 137	1 211	-75	20 851	3 205	1 922	2 293	2 036	11 329	...
1961	26 517	22 021	297	22 318	1 225	-81	21 012	3 322	2 183	2 328	2 080	11 392	...
1962	27 632	23 123	214	23 337	1 334	-97	21 905	3 560	2 167	2 433	2 161	11 355	...
1963	28 637	23 897	255	24 153	1 473	-106	22 573	3 818	2 245	2 507	2 222	11 424	...
1964	30 646	25 658	264	25 922	1 530	-129	24 264	4 124	2 259	2 660	2 388	11 519	...
1965	32 850	27 511	273	27 785	1 593	-149	26 043	4 438	2 370	2 827	2 530	11 620	...
1966	35 384	30 213	260	30 473	2 147	-193	28 133	4 676	2 575	3 034	2 694	11 664	...
1967	37 885	32 020	355	32 375	2 316	-222	29 837	4 980	3 068	3 243	2 883	11 681	...
1968	41 142	34 675	310	34 985	2 420	-258	32 307	5 323	3 512	3 504	3 089	11 741	...
1969	44 729	37 860	367	38 227	2 810	-413	35 003	5 726	4 000	3 810	3 311	11 741	5 250
1970	48 088	39 971	382	40 353	2 930	-379	37 044	6 121	4 923	4 071	3 566	11 812	5 226
1971	51 007	41 943	331	42 274	3 190	-362	38 722	6 501	5 783	4 292	3 802	11 884	5 159
1972	55 719	45 934	341	46 275	3 658	-372	42 246	6 935	6 537	4 680	4 060	11 905	5 247
1973	61 303	50 803	479	51 282	4 632	-336	46 314	7 675	7 315	5 158	4 504	11 885	5 402
1974	67 547	55 417	455	55 872	5 228	-341	50 302	8 695	8 550	5 693	4 947	11 864	5 419
1975	73 581	58 711	417	59 128	5 407	-374	53 347	9 395	10 840	6 184	5 460	11 898	5 302
1976	80 825	64 453	510	64 963	6 010	-362	58 591	10 207	12 027	6 799	5 984	11 887	5 353
1977	88 847	71 112	462	71 574	6 607	-361	64 606	11 463	12 778	7 478	6 545	11 882	5 429
1978	98 035	79 020	497	79 518	7 526	-372	71 620	12 692	13 723	8 263	7 205	11 865	5 564
1979	108 608	87 084	631	87 715	8 596	-395	78 724	14 431	15 452	9 147	7 935	11 874	5 672
1980	119 692	93 188	412	93 600	9 194	-431	83 975	18 022	17 695	10 085	8 769	11 868	5 638
1981	132 196	100 071	625	100 697	10 573	-413	89 710	22 563	19 923	11 148	9 628	11 859	5 605
1982	141 241	102 416	557	102 972	10 986	-246	91 740	26 684	22 817	11 924	10 389	11 845	5 495
1983	147 915	106 470	352	106 822	11 570	-86	95 166	28 072	24 677	12 495	11 020	11 838	5 455
1984	160 164	115 749	837	116 585	13 094	104	103 596	31 729	24 839	13 556	11 964	11 815	5 606
1985	170 050	122 548	836	123 384	14 059	251	109 576	34 479	25 995	14 447	12 738	11 771	5 714
1986	178 939	129 176	875	130 051	14 998	356	115 408	36 121	27 409	15 187	13 418	11 783	5 808
1987	189 585	139 281	876	140 157	15 991	453	124 619	36 926	28 040	16 052	14 096	11 811	5 998
1988	203 661	151 121	737	151 857	17 810	685	134 733	39 391	29 537	17 193	15 134	11 846	6 165
1989	220 748	161 204	980	162 184	18 766	878	144 296	44 984	31 467	18 603	16 334	11 866	6 265
1990	234 334	170 686	973	171 659	19 763	959	152 855	47 166	34 314	19 687	17 344	11 903	6 342
1991	242 822	174 787	794	175 581	20 611	908	155 877	48 130	38 814	20 265	17 949	11 982	6 259
1992	255 874	185 645	1 169	186 813	21 879	1 229	166 163	47 330	42 381	21 235	18 796	12 049	6 262
1993	263 462	192 717	1 039	193 756	23 147	1 243	171 853	47 321	44 289	21 738	19 236	12 120	6 302
1994	272 695	199 647	919	200 566	24 499	1 607	177 675	49 517	45 504	22 414	19 776	12 166	6 369
1995	283 764	207 402	648	208 051	25 368	1 868	184 551	51 675	47 539	23 262	20 443	12 198	6 471
1996	297 494	214 929	1 128	216 057	25 875	2 242	192 423	54 532	50 538	24 344	21 258	12 220	6 525
1997	311 509	225 787	786	226 573	27 021	2 549	202 101	57 746	51 662	25 475	22 096	12 228	6 631
1998	330 161	240 915	921	241 836	28 206	2 465	216 095	61 899	52 167	26 961	23 301	12 246	6 724
1999	342 611	253 111	881	253 992	29 424	2 889	227 456	60 613	54 542	27 937	24 101	12 264	6 836
2000	364 838	267 020	1 148	268 169	30 697	3 355	240 827	66 085	57 926	29 698	25 576	12 285	6 973
2001	372 339	272 455	943	273 398	31 880	3 389	244 907	65 227	62 205	30 310	26 160	12 285	6 979
2002	382 251	281 086	675	281 761	32 768	3 470	252 463	63 611	66 177	31 080	27 456	12 299	6 956
2003	393 908	291 030	1 103	292 132	33 835	3 640	261 937	62 117	69 854	31 979	28 511	12 318	6 936
2004	413 855	308 680	1 413	310 093	35 582	3 908	278 418	62 658	72 779	33 550	29 990	12 336	7 038
2005	429 522	322 034	1 166	323 200	37 544	4 327	289 983	61 767	77 772	34 774	30 747	12 352	7 167
2006	455 884	337 701	941	338 642	39 616	4 770	303 796	70 657	81 431	36 800	32 340	12 388	7 235
2007	481 806	353 978	1 297	355 275	41 455	4 648	318 469	76 475	86 863	38 793	33 919	12 420	7 305
2008	501 225	365 642	1 416	367 058	43 041	4 635	328 652	78 546	94 026	40 265	35 413	12 448	...

. . . = Not available.
* = Less than $50,000, but the estimates for this item are included in the total.

Table 21-2. Personal Income and Employment by Region and State—*Continued*

(Millions of dollars, except as noted.)

Region or state and year	Personal income, total	Earnings by place of work			Less: Contributions for government social insurance	Plus: Adjustment for residence	Equals: Net earnings by place of residence	Plus: Dividends, interest, and rent	Plus: Personal current transfer receipts	Per capita (dollars)		Population (thousands)	Total employment (thousands)
		Nonfarm	Farm	Total						Personal income	Disposable personal income		
RHODE ISLAND													
1958	1 793	1 443	8	1 450	75	44	1 418	225	149	2 090	1 865	858	. . .
1959	1 893	1 543	6	1 550	86	51	1 514	232	146	2 209	1 978	857	. . .
1960	1 934	1 581	7	1 589	96	54	1 547	237	150	2 262	2 012	855	. . .
1961	2 023	1 634	7	1 641	98	57	1 601	256	166	2 358	2 090	858	. . .
1962	2 169	1 751	7	1 758	108	63	1 713	287	169	2 490	2 215	871	. . .
1963	2 265	1 807	7	1 814	117	67	1 764	323	179	2 586	2 299	876	. . .
1964	2 416	1 933	8	1 940	122	73	1 892	340	184	2 729	2 459	885	. . .
1965	2 600	2 078	8	2 086	133	82	2 035	367	198	2 912	2 617	893	. . .
1966	2 840	2 296	9	2 305	162	96	2 239	383	218	3 159	2 818	899	. . .
1967	3 082	2 468	7	2 474	174	105	2 405	411	265	3 390	3 038	909	. . .
1968	3 367	2 700	8	2 708	200	116	2 625	434	308	3 652	3 235	922	. . .
1969	3 591	2 901	8	2 909	230	65	2 744	500	347	3 853	3 392	932	440
1970	3 902	3 117	9	3 126	245	66	2 948	531	423	4 104	3 653	951	440
1971	4 137	3 278	8	3 286	267	61	3 081	560	497	4 292	3 824	964	436
1972	4 510	3 614	8	3 621	306	56	3 371	593	546	4 619	4 066	976	447
1973	4 853	3 873	6	3 880	381	71	3 569	659	625	4 962	4 372	978	452
1974	5 142	3 973	9	3 982	410	88	3 660	749	734	5 393	4 744	954	439
1975	5 543	4 113	9	4 121	415	82	3 788	783	972	5 857	5 257	946	424
1976	6 090	4 631	9	4 641	472	89	4 257	840	993	6 408	5 699	950	442
1977	6 670	5 096	8	5 104	520	103	4 687	943	1 040	6 983	6 224	955	459
1978	7 317	5 661	9	5 670	597	102	5 176	1 031	1 111	7 644	6 714	957	475
1979	8 141	6 305	7	6 312	684	110	5 738	1 168	1 235	8 510	7 401	957	484
1980	9 181	6 882	8	6 890	746	124	6 268	1 484	1 428	9 677	8 476	949	486
1981	10 263	7 431	9	7 440	851	155	6 744	1 885	1 634	10 769	9 441	953	486
1982	11 036	7 803	27	7 831	902	209	7 137	2 105	1 794	11 566	10 196	954	477
1983	11 890	8 425	37	8 462	988	265	7 739	2 238	1 913	12 432	10 998	956	482
1984	13 183	9 384	32	9 416	1 135	334	8 615	2 603	1 965	13 705	12 183	962	507
1985	14 161	10 162	42	10 204	1 220	394	9 378	2 696	2 087	14 615	12 968	969	522
1986	15 174	10 991	43	11 034	1 336	419	10 118	2 886	2 171	15 526	13 697	977	541
1987	16 310	11 910	41	11 951	1 435	488	11 004	3 071	2 236	16 482	14 393	990	550
1988	17 980	13 160	42	13 202	1 603	563	12 162	3 427	2 391	18 045	15 865	996	564
1989	19 559	13 860	32	13 892	1 669	625	12 848	4 098	2 612	19 546	17 184	1 001	565
1990	20 126	14 136	31	14 167	1 716	665	13 117	4 123	2 887	20 006	17 639	1 006	555
1991	20 262	13 810	32	13 842	1 722	693	12 814	3 940	3 509	20 049	17 741	1 011	528
1992	21 129	14 666	30	14 696	1 835	712	13 573	3 902	3 654	20 867	18 541	1 013	534
1993	21 913	15 207	30	15 237	1 924	754	14 067	3 880	3 966	21 586	19 141	1 015	538
1994	22 450	15 657	26	15 683	2 011	828	14 500	4 007	3 943	22 097	19 553	1 016	538
1995	23 620	16 395	25	16 420	2 080	860	15 200	4 253	4 167	23 225	20 544	1 017	541
1996	24 609	16 919	24	16 943	2 113	929	15 759	4 623	4 227	24 106	21 213	1 021	544
1997	25 983	17 758	16	17 774	2 218	990	16 547	4 940	4 497	25 341	22 080	1 025	550
1998	27 501	18 856	16	18 872	2 348	1 074	17 598	5 315	4 587	26 670	23 111	1 031	558
1999	28 568	19 810	16	19 826	2 459	1 177	18 544	5 232	4 792	27 459	23 757	1 040	570
2000	30 697	21 255	16	21 271	2 619	1 344	19 996	5 713	4 988	29 215	25 059	1 051	584
2001	32 478	22 360	15	22 376	2 748	1 341	20 969	5 951	5 559	30 696	26 415	1 058	587
2002	33 635	23 231	18	23 249	2 875	1 305	21 679	6 057	5 899	31 555	27 810	1 066	589
2003	35 072	24 632	18	24 650	3 020	1 273	22 903	6 036	6 133	32 737	29 116	1 071	595
2004	36 818	25 932	19	25 951	3 138	1 377	24 190	6 108	6 520	34 375	30 622	1 071	605
2005	37 868	26 984	16	27 000	3 283	1 381	25 097	5 975	6 796	35 575	31 495	1 064	611
2006	39 891	28 153	16	28 168	3 440	1 438	26 167	6 703	7 021	37 669	33 179	1 059	614
2007	41 946	29 042	17	29 059	3 525	1 544	27 079	7 257	7 610	39 829	34 990	1 053	615
2008	43 091	29 388	15	29 404	3 575	1 659	27 488	7 402	8 202	41 008	36 336	1 051	. . .

. . . = Not available.

* = Less than $50,000, but the estimates for this item are included in the total.

Table 21-2. Personal Income and Employment by Region and State—*Continued*

(Millions of dollars, except as noted.)

Region or state and year	Personal income, total	Derivation of personal income								Per capita (dollars)		Population (thousands)	Total employment (thousands)
		Earnings by place of work			Less: Contributions for government social insurance	Plus: Adjustment for residence	Equals: Net earnings by place of residence	Plus: Dividends, interest, and rent	Plus: Personal current transfer receipts	Personal income	Disposable personal income		
		Nonfarm	Farm	Total									
SOUTH CAROLINA													
1958	3 014	2 438	182	2 620	95	13	2 538	287	189	1 308	1 211	2 304	. . .
1959	3 249	2 678	164	2 842	113	15	2 745	305	199	1 384	1 267	2 348	. . .
1960	3 416	2 824	168	2 991	135	17	2 874	333	210	1 428	1 306	2 392	. . .
1961	3 585	2 913	194	3 107	138	19	2 988	359	238	1 488	1 360	2 409	. . .
1962	3 853	3 153	183	3 336	153	22	3 205	395	253	1 590	1 444	2 423	. . .
1963	4 074	3 355	186	3 541	189	25	3 377	425	272	1 656	1 505	2 460	. . .
1964	4 389	3 645	178	3 823	202	30	3 650	455	284	1 773	1 625	2 475	. . .
1965	4 839	4 030	180	4 210	221	35	4 024	506	310	1 940	1 770	2 494	. . .
1966	5 433	4 611	194	4 804	290	43	4 557	533	342	2 156	1 947	2 520	. . .
1967	5 876	4 994	196	5 190	341	49	4 898	577	401	2 320	2 096	2 533	. . .
1968	6 519	5 618	154	5 772	386	57	5 443	605	471	2 547	2 283	2 559	. . .
1969	7 229	6 159	186	6 345	416	115	6 044	648	536	2 813	2 495	2 570	1 170
1970	7 928	6 657	187	6 844	448	116	6 511	748	669	3 051	2 738	2 598	1 196
1971	8 690	7 253	202	7 456	509	128	7 075	837	778	3 265	2 935	2 662	1 215
1972	9 766	8 206	212	8 417	599	145	7 963	927	876	3 592	3 168	2 718	1 262
1973	11 148	9 348	300	9 648	773	159	9 035	1 070	1 043	4 017	3 562	2 775	1 328
1974	12 652	10 492	339	10 830	897	174	10 107	1 228	1 318	4 450	3 939	2 843	1 365
1975	13 721	10 992	274	11 266	927	185	10 524	1 384	1 814	4 731	4 297	2 900	1 326
1976	15 460	12 649	232	12 880	1 088	220	12 013	1 528	1 919	5 256	4 713	2 941	1 376
1977	16 945	13 977	185	14 162	1 198	243	13 207	1 733	2 005	5 669	5 066	2 989	1 411
1978	19 167	15 871	243	16 114	1 389	261	14 985	1 978	2 204	6 303	5 616	3 041	1 467
1979	21 577	17 805	256	18 062	1 607	285	16 740	2 294	2 544	6 990	6 160	3 087	1 510
1980	24 270	19 666	33	19 699	1 777	320	18 242	2 939	3 088	7 743	6 846	3 135	1 527
1981	27 402	21 686	168	21 854	2 095	350	20 110	3 721	3 571	8 619	7 584	3 179	1 541
1982	29 155	22 456	192	22 649	2 199	383	20 832	4 401	3 922	9 089	8 081	3 208	1 518
1983	31 715	24 588	49	24 637	2 470	396	22 564	4 967	4 184	9 806	8 717	3 234	1 552
1984	35 810	27 767	266	28 033	2 850	443	25 627	5 769	4 414	10 945	9 789	3 272	1 631
1985	38 534	29 706	194	29 899	3 096	500	27 303	6 447	4 783	11 666	10 407	3 303	1 664
1986	40 900	31 674	88	31 762	3 393	564	28 934	6 922	5 045	12 235	10 915	3 343	1 706
1987	43 838	34 116	248	34 364	3 631	608	31 341	7 310	5 188	12 968	11 518	3 381	1 748
1988	47 510	37 151	347	37 498	4 110	628	34 016	7 959	5 535	13 924	12 439	3 412	1 820
1989	51 381	39 690	363	40 053	4 463	581	36 171	8 569	6 640	14 864	13 172	3 457	1 871
1990	55 647	42 754	295	43 049	4 817	505	38 737	9 845	7 064	15 894	14 095	3 501	1 926
1991	57 987	43 771	394	44 164	5 035	492	39 621	10 219	8 148	16 241	14 522	3 570	1 898
1992	61 377	46 294	376	46 671	5 305	502	41 867	10 391	9 119	16 953	15 186	3 620	1 910
1993	64 220	48 564	338	48 902	5 641	506	43 767	10 666	9 788	17 531	15 681	3 663	1 944
1994	68 050	50 654	484	51 138	5 982	611	45 767	11 730	10 553	18 365	16 384	3 705	1 992
1995	71 688	53 328	381	53 709	6 326	731	48 115	12 272	11 301	19 124	16 980	3 749	2 051
1996	76 144	55 854	463	56 318	6 540	851	50 628	13 319	12 197	20 058	17 724	3 796	2 094
1997	81 004	59 171	474	59 645	6 942	1 000	53 702	14 486	12 816	20 987	18 473	3 860	2 154
1998	86 854	63 512	341	63 853	7 403	1 074	57 524	15 912	13 418	22 161	19 440	3 919	2 209
1999	91 716	67 945	418	68 363	7 786	1 169	61 747	15 705	14 264	23 075	20 238	3 975	2 257
2000	98 270	71 951	489	72 441	8 132	1 398	65 707	17 289	15 274	24 425	21 501	4 023	2 291
2001	101 468	73 736	587	74 323	8 425	1 371	67 270	17 216	16 982	24 981	22 059	4 062	2 266
2002	104 046	76 089	190	76 279	8 721	1 390	68 948	16 654	18 445	25 364	22 796	4 102	2 259
2003	107 203	79 106	563	79 669	9 040	1 408	72 036	15 765	19 402	25 873	23 443	4 143	2 277
2004	113 603	83 401	589	83 990	9 500	1 516	76 006	16 684	20 912	27 069	24 603	4 197	2 326
2005	120 224	87 984	540	88 524	9 984	1 680	80 220	17 926	22 078	28 292	25 375	4 249	2 381
2006	129 920	93 365	381	93 746	10 693	1 893	84 946	21 218	23 756	30 041	26 801	4 325	2 444
2007	137 006	97 470	331	97 801	11 177	2 097	88 721	22 849	25 436	31 103	27 633	4 405	2 508
2008	142 836	99 961	226	100 187	11 509	2 148	90 826	23 950	28 060	31 884	28 556	4 480	. . .

. . . = Not available.

* = Less than $50,000, but the estimates for this item are included in the total.

Table 21-2. Personal Income and Employment by Region and State—*Continued*

(Millions of dollars, except as noted.)

| Region or state and year | Personal income, total | Derivation of personal income | | | | | | | | | Per capita (dollars) | | Population (thousands) | Total employment (thousands) |
| | | Earnings by place of work | | | Less: Contributions for government social insurance | Plus: Adjustment for residence | Equals: Net earnings by place of residence | Plus: Dividends, interest, and rent | Plus: Personal current transfer receipts | | Personal income | Disposable personal income | | |
		Nonfarm	Farm	Total										
SOUTH DAKOTA														
1958	1 156	648	308	956	26	0	930	153	73		1 762	1 620	656	. . .
1959	1 048	707	140	847	34	0	814	153	82		1 571	1 454	667	. . .
1960	1 290	740	320	1 060	35	0	1 026	179	86		1 889	1 752	683	. . .
1961	1 297	811	246	1 057	39	0	1 019	184	94		1 872	1 723	693	. . .
1962	1 482	865	364	1 229	45	1	1 184	198	100		2 102	1 941	705	. . .
1963	1 429	875	293	1 168	51	1	1 118	205	106		2 018	1 853	708	. . .
1964	1 397	918	211	1 129	50	1	1 080	208	109		1 993	1 853	701	. . .
1965	1 574	950	330	1 279	51	2	1 230	226	119		2 275	2 124	692	. . .
1966	1 701	1 016	388	1 404	64	2	1 342	230	129		2 491	2 311	683	. . .
1967	1 726	1 070	340	1 411	77	3	1 336	236	154		2 573	2 383	671	. . .
1968	1 853	1 162	359	1 521	83	3	1 440	236	177		2 770	2 542	669	. . .
1969	2 010	1 272	353	1 625	90	6	1 541	275	194		3 009	2 739	668	303
1970	2 177	1 371	369	1 740	96	6	1 650	305	222		3 265	3 005	667	305
1971	2 381	1 498	400	1 897	107	6	1 797	329	255		3 546	3 304	671	306
1972	2 757	1 662	560	2 221	121	7	2 107	368	282		4 070	3 795	677	309
1973	3 502	1 879	1 022	2 901	159	7	2 749	426	327		5 158	4 776	679	323
1974	3 515	2 107	681	2 789	184	8	2 613	520	382		5 169	4 717	680	326
1975	3 877	2 303	701	3 004	201	10	2 814	607	456		5 689	5 271	681	326
1976	3 837	2 622	273	2 895	225	12	2 682	654	501		5 586	5 108	687	336
1977	4 368	2 871	439	3 310	238	13	3 085	755	528		6 339	5 875	689	342
1978	5 023	3 267	609	3 877	275	15	3 617	832	574		7 287	6 708	689	355
1979	5 545	3 603	644	4 247	323	16	3 941	956	648		8 048	7 387	689	360
1980	5 577	3 839	128	3 966	344	18	3 640	1 180	758		8 073	7 317	691	354
1981	6 507	4 070	437	4 507	391	14	4 130	1 508	869		9 437	8 582	690	349
1982	6 887	4 196	368	4 564	411	12	4 165	1 756	966		9 972	9 022	691	345
1983	7 142	4 492	249	4 741	442	5	4 304	1 798	1 040		10 306	9 486	693	354
1984	8 159	4 956	680	5 636	493	-2	5 141	1 918	1 099		11 701	10 887	697	364
1985	8 401	5 186	604	5 791	532	-5	5 254	1 978	1 169		12 029	11 172	698	367
1986	8 755	5 406	656	6 062	572	-11	5 478	2 060	1 217		12 578	11 691	696	368
1987	9 223	5 725	837	6 563	617	-19	5 926	2 040	1 257		13 251	12 251	696	383
1988	9 577	6 156	708	6 865	691	-26	6 148	2 116	1 313		13 717	12 669	698	390
1989	10 267	6 550	713	7 263	750	-36	6 476	2 360	1 431		14 737	13 548	697	398
1990	11 273	7 115	1 005	8 120	821	-56	7 243	2 505	1 525		16 172	14 822	697	412
1991	11 803	7 647	879	8 526	891	-69	7 567	2 599	1 638		16 774	15 396	704	423
1992	12 687	8 253	1 045	9 298	958	-85	8 255	2 645	1 787		17 799	16 328	713	434
1993	13 207	8 827	935	9 761	1 025	-99	8 638	2 693	1 877		18 289	16 682	722	445
1994	14 172	9 401	1 173	10 574	1 113	-128	9 333	2 849	1 989		19 392	17 775	731	467
1995	14 390	9 854	629	10 482	1 167	-152	9 163	3 106	2 121		19 501	17 777	738	475
1996	15 948	10 262	1 446	11 708	1 216	-192	10 300	3 396	2 252		21 488	19 661	742	482
1997	16 335	10 781	1 102	11 883	1 278	-191	10 413	3 609	2 313		21 949	19 849	744	488
1998	17 523	11 534	1 255	12 789	1 366	-243	11 180	3 967	2 376		23 488	21 251	746	497
1999	18 367	12 309	1 185	13 494	1 459	-258	11 777	4 116	2 474		24 475	22 019	750	509
2000	19 438	13 099	1 116	14 215	1 535	-280	12 400	4 393	2 645		25 723	23 165	756	519
2001	20 429	13 832	863	14 696	1 593	-235	12 867	4 703	2 859		26 927	24 309	759	517
2002	20 596	14 462	266	14 728	1 641	-216	12 871	4 655	3 070		27 039	24 786	762	519
2003	22 386	15 122	1 244	16 366	1 704	-208	14 454	4 760	3 172		29 207	27 163	766	518
2004	23 853	16 117	1 434	17 551	1 807	-228	15 516	5 007	3 330		30 837	28 669	774	530
2005	25 088	16 889	1 436	18 326	1 900	-204	16 221	5 275	3 593		32 193	29 694	779	540
2006	25 427	17 756	401	18 157	2 021	-195	15 941	5 608	3 879		32 293	29 390	787	551
2007	28 454	18 813	1 558	20 371	2 160	-209	18 002	6 316	4 135		35 760	32 545	796	564
2008	30 057	19 832	1 692	21 524	2 305	-229	18 990	6 600	4 467		37 375	34 216	804	. . .

. . . = Not available.
* = Less than $50,000, but the estimates for this item are included in the total.

Table 21-2. Personal Income and Employment by Region and State—*Continued*

(Millions of dollars, except as noted.)

Region or state and year	Personal income, total	Derivation of personal income								Per capita (dollars)		Population (thousands)	Total employment (thousands)
		Earnings by place of work			Less: Contributions for government social insurance	Plus: Adjustment for residence	Equals: Net earnings by place of residence	Plus: Dividends, interest, and rent	Plus: Personal current transfer receipts	Personal income	Disposable personal income		
		Nonfarm	Farm	Total									
TENNESSEE													
1958	5 272	4 206	313	4 520	175	27	4 372	531	370	1 519	1 393	3 471	...
1959	5 657	4 589	305	4 893	207	23	4 709	562	386	1 606	1 471	3 522	...
1960	5 808	4 771	243	5 014	242	23	4 794	610	404	1 625	1 478	3 575	...
1961	6 144	4 966	290	5 256	247	22	5 031	654	459	1 696	1 547	3 622	...
1962	6 525	5 336	250	5 586	273	22	5 335	713	477	1 777	1 595	3 673	...
1963	6 912	5 687	273	5 959	323	22	5 658	751	502	1 859	1 687	3 718	...
1964	7 436	6 188	234	6 422	339	21	6 104	807	525	1 972	1 808	3 771	...
1965	8 109	6 756	250	7 006	363	21	6 664	867	578	2 135	1 949	3 798	...
1966	8 935	7 605	253	7 858	502	21	7 377	922	636	2 338	2 115	3 822	...
1967	9 577	8 150	215	8 366	564	35	7 836	978	763	2 482	2 252	3 859	...
1968	10 675	9 077	222	9 299	634	33	8 697	1 103	875	2 753	2 467	3 878	...
1969	11 487	9 905	252	10 157	659	-155	9 342	1 168	977	2 948	2 607	3 897	1 789
1970	12 480	10 539	265	10 804	695	-155	9 954	1 330	1 197	3 170	2 827	3 937	1 785
1971	13 776	11 592	262	11 854	789	-165	10 900	1 481	1 396	3 435	3 087	4 010	1 817
1972	15 518	13 153	321	13 475	937	-192	12 346	1 634	1 538	3 796	3 407	4 088	1 924
1973	17 714	14 916	488	15 403	1 211	-181	14 011	1 886	1 816	4 280	3 842	4 138	2 025
1974	19 663	16 476	312	16 788	1 383	-191	15 214	2 230	2 220	4 680	4 202	4 202	2 055
1975	21 405	17 344	244	17 588	1 430	-190	15 968	2 503	2 933	5 024	4 557	4 261	1 983
1976	24 104	19 654	366	20 021	1 639	-184	18 197	2 714	3 193	5 568	5 030	4 329	2 052
1977	26 795	22 168	294	22 463	1 846	-241	20 376	3 066	3 354	6 087	5 503	4 402	2 135
1978	30 593	25 576	312	25 888	2 151	-308	23 429	3 500	3 664	6 857	6 164	4 462	2 228
1979	34 236	28 396	333	28 730	2 480	-358	25 891	4 079	4 266	7 552	6 777	4 533	2 282
1980	37 994	30 627	188	30 815	2 675	-425	27 714	5 143	5 136	8 259	7 406	4 600	2 264
1981	42 404	33 394	352	33 746	3 142	-460	30 144	6 435	5 825	9 163	8 216	4 628	2 263
1982	45 249	34 683	297	34 979	3 338	-417	31 224	7 632	6 393	9 739	8 780	4 646	2 224
1983	48 130	37 357	-38	37 318	3 650	-430	33 238	8 022	6 869	10 329	9 331	4 660	2 247
1984	53 966	41 775	402	42 178	4 188	-430	37 559	9 213	7 194	11 515	10 468	4 687	2 354
1985	57 984	45 092	326	45 419	4 588	-447	40 384	9 952	7 648	12 297	11 140	4 715	2 411
1986	61 771	48 341	232	48 574	5 017	-487	43 069	10 493	8 209	13 035	11 819	4 739	2 490
1987	66 412	52 507	297	52 804	5 430	-520	46 855	10 907	8 650	13 885	12 531	4 783	2 593
1988	71 640	56 628	382	57 011	6 057	-534	50 420	11 925	9 294	14 856	13 464	4 822	2 680
1989	76 859	59 936	430	60 366	6 500	-560	53 306	13 327	10 225	15 833	14 298	4 854	2 753
1990	81 700	63 314	423	63 737	6 916	-595	56 226	14 157	11 317	16 692	15 122	4 894	2 796
1991	85 914	66 124	490	66 613	7 353	-592	58 668	14 403	12 842	17 298	15 728	4 967	2 795
1992	93 807	72 514	653	73 167	7 953	-432	64 782	14 590	14 435	18 577	16 893	5 050	2 855
1993	99 074	77 377	577	77 954	8 566	-562	68 825	14 785	15 463	19 284	17 504	5 138	2 960
1994	105 846	83 132	626	83 758	9 339	-666	73 752	15 881	16 212	20 233	18 318	5 231	3 079
1995	112 793	88 380	437	88 818	9 959	-757	78 102	17 027	17 665	21 174	19 132	5 327	3 164
1996	118 374	92 275	374	92 649	10 314	-732	81 602	18 221	18 551	21 854	19 628	5 417	3 214
1997	124 699	97 431	485	97 916	10 941	-935	86 039	19 343	19 317	22 676	20 290	5 499	3 288
1998	133 620	104 721	235	104 955	11 589	-1 088	92 278	21 026	20 316	23 989	21 452	5 570	3 373
1999	140 395	111 391	103	111 494	12 204	-1 285	98 006	21 138	21 252	24 898	22 293	5 639	3 435
2000	148 833	116 833	383	117 216	12 650	-1 456	103 110	22 659	23 065	26 097	23 409	5 703	3 496
2001	154 416	120 939	298	121 237	13 069	-1 517	106 651	22 614	25 150	26 839	24 127	5 753	3 459
2002	159 173	126 489	-15	126 474	13 656	-1 525	111 293	20 939	26 942	27 448	25 098	5 799	3 452
2003	165 402	131 766	198	131 964	14 279	-1 454	116 231	20 569	28 602	28 276	26 065	5 850	3 475
2004	174 636	140 406	264	140 671	15 135	-1 571	123 965	20 401	30 270	29 565	27 337	5 907	3 567
2005	183 714	146 721	502	147 223	15 793	-1 288	130 142	21 207	32 365	30 705	28 211	5 983	3 638
2006	195 197	155 356	195	155 551	16 723	-1 215	137 612	23 897	33 687	32 167	29 305	6 068	3 699
2007	205 350	161 253	-180	161 073	17 406	-1 379	142 288	26 148	36 914	33 395	30 267	6 149	3 746
2008	213 359	165 423	-150	165 274	17 998	-1 303	145 972	27 101	40 286	34 330	31 327	6 215	...

. . . = Not available.
* = Less than $50,000, but the estimates for this item are included in the total.

Table 21-2. Personal Income and Employment by Region and State—*Continued*

(Millions of dollars, except as noted.)

Region or state and year	Personal income, total	Earnings by place of work			Less: Contributions for government social insurance	Plus: Adjustment for residence	Equals: Net earnings by place of residence	Plus: Dividends, interest, and rent	Plus: Personal current transfer receipts	Per capita (dollars)		Population (thousands)	Total employment (thousands)
		Nonfarm	Farm	Total						Personal income	Disposable personal income		
TEXAS													
1958	17 399	13 629	1 058	14 687	472	14	14 229	2 282	888	1 881	1 697	9 252	...
1959	18 411	14 502	992	15 495	567	14	14 942	2 517	951	1 958	1 765	9 405	...
1960	18 913	14 976	914	15 890	677	15	15 228	2 687	998	1 965	1 764	9 624	...
1961	19 964	15 638	1 078	16 716	695	15	16 036	2 806	1 122	2 033	1 824	9 820	...
1962	20 965	16 567	938	17 505	748	15	16 772	2 971	1 222	2 085	1 866	10 053	...
1963	21 932	17 491	769	18 260	831	16	17 444	3 166	1 321	2 159	1 930	10 159	...
1964	23 502	18 914	716	19 630	877	16	18 770	3 361	1 371	2 288	2 079	10 270	...
1965	25 263	20 260	853	21 113	929	18	20 201	3 564	1 498	2 434	2 206	10 378	...
1966	27 561	22 499	907	23 406	1 259	15	22 162	3 769	1 630	2 627	2 358	10 492	...
1967	30 103	24 846	768	25 614	1 458	13	24 169	3 966	1 969	2 840	2 543	10 599	...
1968	33 593	27 825	901	28 726	1 630	12	27 108	4 124	2 360	3 105	2 747	10 819	...
1969	37 122	31 086	917	32 003	2 013	-86	29 905	4 575	2 642	3 361	2 941	11 045	5 005
1970	40 820	33 530	1 159	34 689	2 150	-97	32 443	5 240	3 137	3 633	3 221	11 237	5 045
1971	44 282	36 357	1 008	37 365	2 400	-102	34 864	5 754	3 664	3 847	3 451	11 510	5 123
1972	49 166	40 363	1 248	41 611	2 784	-128	38 699	6 354	4 114	4 181	3 709	11 759	5 334
1973	56 072	45 501	2 136	47 636	3 610	-155	43 871	7 254	4 947	4 665	4 150	12 019	5 608
1974	63 498	52 244	1 143	53 387	4 251	-132	49 004	8 593	5 901	5 176	4 562	12 268	5 822
1975	72 230	58 934	1 302	60 236	4 722	-130	55 384	9 469	7 377	5 747	5 131	12 568	5 938
1976	81 994	68 068	1 282	69 351	5 514	-94	63 743	10 205	8 047	6 355	5 638	12 903	6 207
1977	91 735	77 063	1 269	78 332	6 290	-308	71 734	11 442	8 560	6 954	6 118	13 192	6 521
1978	106 096	89 904	1 015	90 918	7 495	-428	82 995	13 562	9 539	7 860	6 925	13 498	6 898
1979	122 776	103 506	1 727	105 234	9 039	-434	95 760	16 133	10 883	8 841	7 696	13 887	7 222
1980	141 659	118 911	598	119 509	10 479	-544	108 486	20 452	12 721	9 880	8 563	14 338	7 511
1981	167 287	138 253	1 954	140 207	13 099	-356	126 753	26 073	14 460	11 344	9 736	14 746	7 925
1982	183 782	149 693	1 344	151 037	14 494	-427	136 116	31 201	16 466	11 987	10 406	15 331	8 098
1983	194 872	156 409	1 728	158 137	15 029	-410	142 699	33 576	18 598	12 372	10 940	15 752	8 088
1984	215 633	172 540	1 609	174 149	16 884	-471	156 795	39 062	19 777	13 471	11 989	16 007	8 469
1985	232 242	184 943	1 482	186 424	18 291	-499	167 635	43 472	21 135	14 272	12 708	16 273	8 721
1986	235 416	185 811	1 256	187 067	18 535	-459	168 072	44 177	23 167	14 215	12 784	16 561	8 560
1987	240 661	189 243	2 070	191 313	18 606	-457	172 250	44 052	24 360	14 479	12 975	16 622	8 773
1988	255 422	201 850	2 306	204 156	20 405	-461	183 290	46 527	25 605	15 325	13 812	16 667	8 934
1989	274 145	214 722	2 215	216 937	21 751	-471	194 715	51 286	28 144	16 312	14 626	16 807	9 064
1990	297 146	232 867	3 006	235 873	23 633	-504	211 737	53 929	31 480	17 421	15 623	17 057	9 304
1991	311 926	245 094	2 731	247 824	25 471	-585	221 768	55 152	35 005	17 929	16 165	17 398	9 465
1992	335 941	263 896	3 314	267 209	27 111	-609	239 489	55 185	41 267	18 916	17 128	17 760	9 545
1993	354 213	280 534	3 984	284 518	28 782	-633	255 104	54 972	44 137	19 503	17 633	18 162	9 844
1994	374 791	296 382	3 387	299 769	30 815	-698	268 256	59 105	47 430	20 189	18 236	18 564	10 163
1995	398 192	314 855	2 758	317 613	32 834	-790	283 990	63 236	50 966	21 003	18 928	18 959	10 507
1996	427 810	339 131	2 385	341 516	34 898	-865	305 753	67 676	54 380	22 120	19 802	19 340	10 808
1997	466 182	372 947	3 099	376 046	38 041	-1 006	337 000	72 351	56 831	23 616	20 991	19 740	11 236
1998	507 681	409 793	2 867	412 660	41 453	-1 102	370 104	78 933	58 644	25 186	22 282	20 158	11 646
1999	539 661	440 935	4 499	445 434	44 041	-1 151	400 241	78 918	60 502	26 250	23 251	20 558	11 895
2000	593 139	486 842	2 765	489 607	47 231	-1 254	441 122	87 612	64 405	28 317	24 968	20 946	12 245
2001	619 642	509 298	3 058	512 355	49 836	-1 442	461 077	87 505	71 060	29 045	25 720	21 334	12 356
2002	626 604	514 504	3 039	517 543	50 507	-1 452	465 585	83 046	77 973	28 858	26 157	21 713	12 370
2003	649 419	531 879	3 793	535 672	53 069	-1 449	481 154	85 079	83 186	29 436	26 953	22 062	12 490
2004	694 925	574 137	3 783	577 920	55 911	-1 507	520 502	87 828	86 595	30 989	28 518	22 425	12 656
2005	758 443	617 778	3 361	621 140	59 987	-1 622	559 531	102 707	96 205	33 249	30 243	22 811	13 069
2006	821 642	673 529	1 686	675 214	65 345	-1 783	608 087	111 216	102 339	35 162	31 724	23 368	13 615
2007	884 191	723 519	2 822	726 340	70 236	-2 069	654 036	118 402	111 753	37 083	33 248	23 843	14 157
2008	938 406	766 129	2 074	768 203	74 506	-2 242	691 456	121 227	125 723	38 575	34 850	24 327	...

. . . = Not available.
* = Less than $50,000, but the estimates for this item are included in the total.

Table 21-2. Personal Income and Employment by Region and State—*Continued*

(Millions of dollars, except as noted.)

| Region or state and year | Personal income, total | Earnings by place of work | | | Less: Contributions for government social insurance | Plus: Adjustment for residence | Equals: Net earnings by place of residence | Plus: Dividends, interest, and rent | Plus: Personal current transfer receipts | Per capita (dollars) | | Population (thousands) | Total employment (thousands) |
		Nonfarm	Farm	Total						Personal income	Disposable personal income		
UTAH													
1958	1 591	1 308	53	1 360	54	0	1 307	189	95	1 883	1 708	845	...
1959	1 710	1 415	49	1 464	62	1	1 402	207	101	1 965	1 770	870	...
1960	1 827	1 514	43	1 557	75	1	1 483	239	105	2 030	1 826	900	...
1961	1 951	1 628	34	1 662	79	1	1 583	250	117	2 084	1 869	936	...
1962	2 131	1 770	53	1 822	87	1	1 736	273	122	2 225	2 002	958	...
1963	2 214	1 867	40	1 907	105	1	1 803	279	132	2 273	2 041	974	...
1964	2 326	1 952	29	1 982	106	1	1 876	309	141	2 378	2 167	978	...
1965	2 462	2 043	46	2 089	109	1	1 982	329	152	2 485	2 266	991	...
1966	2 615	2 199	48	2 247	144	1	2 105	349	162	2 592	2 353	1 009	...
1967	2 763	2 311	62	2 373	159	1	2 216	356	191	2 711	2 454	1 019	...
1968	2 974	2 497	66	2 563	175	1	2 390	364	220	2 890	2 587	1 029	...
1969	3 238	2 694	73	2 766	176	2	2 593	397	248	3 093	2 734	1 047	444
1970	3 611	2 960	77	3 036	191	2	2 847	465	298	3 389	3 032	1 066	455
1971	4 023	3 280	76	3 356	218	3	3 141	530	353	3 655	3 296	1 101	467
1972	4 516	3 682	87	3 769	260	5	3 515	599	402	3 980	3 569	1 135	494
1973	5 052	4 137	129	4 266	339	8	3 936	645	472	4 323	3 873	1 169	523
1974	5 688	4 687	95	4 782	396	11	4 398	752	538	4 745	4 244	1 199	545
1975	6 392	5 211	66	5 277	433	14	4 859	860	673	5 180	4 693	1 234	553
1976	7 328	6 013	73	6 086	502	17	5 601	997	730	5 760	5 157	1 272	580
1977	8 356	6 910	63	6 972	575	22	6 419	1 151	786	6 348	5 671	1 316	613
1978	9 623	7 971	70	8 041	678	27	7 390	1 357	876	7 054	6 291	1 364	651
1979	11 035	9 048	81	9 129	810	36	8 354	1 683	998	7 792	6 923	1 416	679
1980	12 519	10 013	58	10 071	897	52	9 226	2 118	1 175	8 501	7 584	1 473	689
1981	14 206	11 235	41	11 276	1 082	54	10 247	2 582	1 377	9 374	8 325	1 515	699
1982	15 541	11 929	45	11 974	1 170	54	10 857	3 100	1 583	9 973	8 852	1 558	709
1983	16 803	12 704	36	12 739	1 268	43	11 514	3 564	1 726	10 535	9 469	1 595	721
1984	18 546	14 162	55	14 216	1 449	38	12 805	3 961	1 779	11 431	10 325	1 622	764
1985	19 794	15 128	55	15 183	1 579	40	13 644	4 217	1 932	12 048	10 849	1 643	793
1986	20 663	15 740	85	15 825	1 666	35	14 193	4 380	2 090	12 426	11 176	1 663	805
1987	21 361	16 368	129	16 497	1 729	25	14 792	4 328	2 241	12 729	11 392	1 678	835
1988	22 287	17 390	208	17 598	1 931	24	15 691	4 263	2 333	13 192	11 803	1 689	870
1989	23 891	18 574	202	18 777	2 095	22	16 703	4 613	2 575	14 005	12 546	1 706	903
1990	25 817	20 227	246	20 473	2 293	17	18 197	4 795	2 825	14 913	13 197	1 731	944
1991	27 573	21 772	228	22 000	2 518	11	19 493	4 973	3 106	15 492	13 786	1 780	967
1992	29 601	23 606	278	23 883	2 726	6	21 164	5 013	3 424	16 115	14 331	1 837	985
1993	31 810	25 462	303	25 765	2 956	7	22 817	5 244	3 750	16 756	14 857	1 898	1 032
1994	34 437	27 633	222	27 855	3 253	7	24 609	5 966	3 862	17 566	15 481	1 960	1 109
1995	37 218	30 017	170	30 187	3 545	1	26 643	6 434	4 141	18 478	16 210	2 014	1 158
1996	40 386	32 475	182	32 657	3 777	1	28 881	7 115	4 390	19 529	17 085	2 068	1 225
1997	43 667	35 231	206	35 436	4 050	1	31 387	7 681	4 599	20 600	17 977	2 120	1 277
1998	47 019	38 008	240	38 248	4 301	-5	33 943	8 258	4 818	21 708	18 937	2 166	1 317
1999	49 343	40 340	256	40 596	4 519	-1	36 076	8 188	5 078	22 393	19 488	2 203	1 349
2000	53 561	43 559	201	43 760	4 797	4	38 967	9 148	5 447	23 866	20 792	2 244	1 388
2001	56 594	45 996	277	46 273	5 030	18	41 261	9 372	5 961	24 702	21 661	2 291	1 393
2002	58 172	47 353	181	47 534	5 172	13	42 374	9 302	6 495	24 919	22 328	2 334	1 394
2003	59 412	48 467	209	48 676	5 394	19	43 301	9 251	6 860	24 958	22 506	2 380	1 409
2004	63 565	52 156	279	52 435	5 807	26	46 653	9 749	7 163	26 053	23 547	2 440	1 457
2005	69 747	56 402	246	56 649	6 290	40	50 398	11 554	7 795	27 885	24 832	2 501	1 524
2006	75 598	61 715	110	61 825	6 927	52	54 950	12 184	8 464	29 243	25 766	2 585	1 603
2007	79 618	66 186	186	66 372	7 402	42	59 012	11 656	8 949	29 831	25 979	2 669	1 674
2008	82 890	68 579	82	68 660	7 672	38	61 026	11 984	9 880	30 291	26 641	2 736	...

. . . = Not available.
* = Less than $50,000, but the estimates for this item are included in the total.

Table 21-2. Personal Income and Employment by Region and State—*Continued*

(Millions of dollars, except as noted.)

Region or state and year	Personal income, total	Earnings by place of work			Less: Contributions for government social insurance	Plus: Adjustment for residence	Equals: Net earnings by place of residence	Plus: Dividends, interest, and rent	Plus: Personal current transfer receipts	Per capita (dollars)		Population (thousands)	Total employment (thousands)
		Nonfarm	Farm	Total						Personal income	Disposable personal income		
VERMONT													
1958	653	493	54	547	19	-5	523	77	52	1 718	1 553	380	...
1959	703	542	50	592	22	-5	564	83	55	1 816	1 634	387	...
1960	744	571	56	626	27	-5	594	90	59	1 912	1 718	389	...
1961	774	584	55	639	28	-5	606	101	67	1 985	1 787	390	...
1962	813	624	46	670	31	-5	634	109	70	2 068	1 863	393	...
1963	843	653	43	696	36	-5	655	114	74	2 124	1 893	397	...
1964	903	693	49	742	38	-5	698	128	77	2 264	2 034	399	...
1965	990	770	45	814	41	-7	765	144	81	2 451	2 218	404	...
1966	1 124	883	58	941	58	-10	873	164	87	2 722	2 426	413	...
1967	1 217	962	46	1 008	71	-10	927	183	107	2 878	2 562	423	...
1968	1 342	1 050	50	1 100	74	-11	1 015	201	126	3 121	2 750	430	...
1969	1 473	1 167	57	1 224	83	-27	1 113	215	144	3 370	2 921	437	203
1970	1 614	1 256	61	1 318	89	-27	1 202	241	172	3 617	3 154	446	205
1971	1 745	1 337	60	1 397	98	-24	1 276	265	205	3 841	3 444	454	206
1972	1 924	1 467	67	1 534	111	-21	1 402	291	230	4 153	3 657	463	211
1973	2 118	1 626	71	1 697	141	-20	1 536	320	262	4 521	4 028	469	220
1974	2 293	1 736	58	1 794	155	-17	1 622	356	315	4 847	4 319	473	222
1975	2 494	1 826	60	1 886	162	-11	1 712	380	401	5 197	4 654	480	220
1976	2 786	2 056	77	2 133	184	-6	1 943	411	431	5 742	5 172	485	228
1977	3 028	2 259	65	2 325	203	-2	2 119	467	441	6 152	5 494	492	236
1978	3 478	2 637	94	2 731	244	-2	2 485	526	467	6 980	6 227	498	252
1979	3 924	2 960	104	3 064	284	5	2 785	609	530	7 760	6 878	506	261
1980	4 414	3 220	107	3 327	310	14	3 031	756	627	8 613	7 607	513	266
1981	4 983	3 535	122	3 657	366	18	3 309	950	724	9 664	8 505	516	271
1982	5 359	3 708	122	3 831	393	24	3 461	1 093	805	10 324	9 175	519	272
1983	5 735	4 067	82	4 150	431	22	3 740	1 131	864	10 959	9 764	523	279
1984	6 341	4 510	82	4 592	490	28	4 130	1 321	889	12 040	10 759	527	290
1985	6 873	4 972	100	5 071	549	30	4 552	1 394	928	12 968	11 528	530	302
1986	7 388	5 414	98	5 512	607	33	4 939	1 494	956	13 834	12 238	534	313
1987	8 037	5 987	123	6 110	661	41	5 490	1 576	971	14 875	13 053	540	323
1988	8 792	6 599	120	6 720	752	47	6 014	1 753	1 025	15 992	14 109	550	337
1989	9 685	7 105	121	7 226	814	50	6 461	2 097	1 126	17 365	15 268	558	344
1990	10 096	7 362	111	7 473	845	49	6 677	2 163	1 256	17 876	15 759	565	344
1991	10 227	7 396	100	7 497	869	56	6 684	2 173	1 369	17 985	15 951	569	337
1992	10 919	7 881	175	8 056	918	64	7 202	2 165	1 552	19 065	17 310	573	344
1993	11 257	8 265	127	8 392	967	72	7 498	2 140	1 619	19 485	17 310	578	352
1994	11 809	8 586	128	8 714	1 022	86	7 778	2 311	1 719	20 226	17 998	584	361
1995	12 370	8 901	100	9 001	1 079	100	8 022	2 490	1 858	21 002	18 697	589	365
1996	13 040	9 321	146	9 467	1 123	115	8 460	2 655	1 925	21 964	19 418	594	370
1997	13 738	9 779	111	9 890	1 175	138	8 853	2 850	2 035	23 002	20 160	597	375
1998	14 788	10 457	137	10 594	1 238	164	9 521	3 153	2 115	24 629	21 515	600	386
1999	15 650	11 180	153	11 333	1 313	187	10 207	3 188	2 255	25 881	22 577	605	394
2000	16 883	12 070	163	12 234	1 392	219	11 060	3 407	2 416	27 683	24 012	610	404
2001	17 742	12 692	144	12 836	1 486	232	11 582	3 513	2 647	28 983	25 252	612	408
2002	18 051	13 067	102	13 169	1 531	237	11 875	3 329	2 847	29 352	26 075	615	410
2003	18 711	13 595	121	13 716	1 584	266	12 398	3 325	2 988	30 340	27 335	617	409
2004	19 776	14 440	169	14 609	1 664	289	13 234	3 426	3 116	31 977	28 878	618	419
2005	20 273	15 040	167	15 207	1 746	322	13 784	3 119	3 370	32 736	29 212	619	426
2006	21 810	15 720	81	15 801	1 839	355	14 317	3 780	3 712	35 166	31 234	620	427
2007	23 267	16 242	198	16 441	1 913	383	14 911	4 363	3 994	37 483	33 188	621	427
2008	24 155	16 727	167	16 894	1 993	388	15 289	4 528	4 338	38 880	34 634	621	...

. . . = Not available.
* = Less than $50,000, but the estimates for this item are included in the total.

Table 21-2. Personal Income and Employment by Region and State—*Continued*

(Millions of dollars, except as noted.)

| Region or state and year | Personal income, total | Derivation of personal income | | | | | | | | Per capita (dollars) | | Population (thousands) | Total employment (thousands) |
| | | Earnings by place of work | | | Less: Contributions for government social insurance | Plus: Adjustment for residence | Equals: Net earnings by place of residence | Plus: Dividends, interest, and rent | Plus: Personal current transfer receipts | Personal income | Disposable personal income | | |
		Nonfarm	Farm	Total									
VIRGINIA													
1958	6 872	5 383	258	5 641	184	361	5 818	723	331	1 756	1 579	3 914	. . .
1959	7 327	5 840	192	6 033	234	386	6 185	781	361	1 854	1 662	3 951	. . .
1960	7 598	5 992	212	6 203	268	432	6 367	859	373	1 906	1 693	3 986	. . .
1961	8 089	6 317	222	6 538	284	463	6 717	944	428	1 975	1 760	4 095	. . .
1962	8 741	6 829	219	7 047	317	512	7 242	1 046	452	2 091	1 853	4 180	. . .
1963	9 353	7 409	133	7 542	369	565	7 738	1 130	485	2 187	1 921	4 276	. . .
1964	10 338	8 118	219	8 337	383	615	8 569	1 258	512	2 373	2 126	4 357	. . .
1965	11 158	8 710	205	8 915	402	704	9 217	1 381	560	2 529	2 254	4 411	. . .
1966	12 078	9 592	153	9 745	544	779	9 981	1 486	610	2 710	2 395	4 456	. . .
1967	13 230	10 380	199	10 579	630	933	10 882	1 614	734	2 935	2 589	4 508	. . .
1968	14 683	11 639	176	11 816	696	1 008	12 128	1 701	855	3 221	2 819	4 558	. . .
1969	16 396	13 209	210	13 419	800	956	13 575	1 842	978	3 554	3 046	4 614	2 148
1970	17 658	14 220	210	14 430	871	851	14 411	2 068	1 179	3 789	3 265	4 660	2 158
1971	19 443	15 651	191	15 842	1 000	877	15 719	2 312	1 413	4 091	3 561	4 753	2 196
1972	21 655	17 464	251	17 715	1 167	933	17 480	2 553	1 621	4 485	3 849	4 828	2 263
1973	24 393	19 683	351	20 034	1 484	1 005	19 555	2 902	1 937	4 971	4 300	4 907	2 384
1974	27 300	21 863	312	22 175	1 701	1 134	21 608	3 391	2 301	5 484	4 710	4 978	2 451
1975	30 141	23 555	262	23 816	1 821	1 394	23 389	3 804	2 947	5 961	5 245	5 056	2 425
1976	33 619	26 394	233	26 627	2 071	1 617	26 173	4 227	3 219	6 550	5 730	5 133	2 501
1977	37 455	29 520	165	29 685	2 302	1 857	29 240	4 763	3 452	7 195	6 259	5 206	2 585
1978	42 386	33 282	286	33 568	2 621	2 191	33 137	5 432	3 816	8 021	6 936	5 284	2 697
1979	47 656	37 211	151	37 362	3 050	2 588	36 900	6 376	4 380	8 950	7 730	5 325	2 769
1980	54 457	41 357	64	41 421	3 388	3 164	41 198	8 052	5 208	10 144	8 770	5 368	2 802
1981	61 447	45 860	265	46 125	4 022	3 394	45 497	9 937	6 013	11 287	9 696	5 444	2 820
1982	66 758	49 328	119	49 447	4 381	3 464	48 530	11 657	6 572	12 154	10 521	5 493	2 832
1983	72 551	53 913	42	53 955	4 947	3 450	52 459	12 984	7 108	13 038	11 411	5 565	2 905
1984	81 186	60 988	321	61 309	5 702	3 561	59 168	14 498	7 520	14 385	12 677	5 644	3 054
1985	87 821	66 828	223	67 051	6 436	3 680	64 295	15 489	8 037	15 366	13 459	5 715	3 198
1986	94 892	72 660	270	72 930	7 211	3 835	69 555	16 820	8 517	16 328	14 311	5 812	3 335
1987	102 769	79 524	366	79 890	7 910	4 048	76 029	17 893	8 847	17 324	15 066	5 932	3 501
1988	111 768	86 420	520	86 939	8 962	4 431	82 408	19 911	9 449	18 514	16 190	6 037	3 582
1989	120 816	92 214	634	92 848	9 725	4 664	87 787	22 688	10 342	19 740	17 185	6 120	3 681
1990	127 129	96 150	670	96 819	10 329	5 419	91 909	23 997	11 223	20 449	17 872	6 217	3 726
1991	131 913	98 849	604	99 453	10 804	5 950	94 600	24 995	12 318	20 934	18 384	6 301	3 666
1992	139 901	104 961	658	105 619	11 403	6 420	100 636	25 388	13 876	21 811	19 200	6 414	3 684
1993	146 273	109 985	524	110 509	11 991	6 862	105 381	26 218	14 674	22 470	19 726	6 510	3 758
1994	153 654	115 007	629	115 636	12 705	6 853	109 783	28 374	15 497	23 305	20 389	6 593	3 842
1995	160 470	120 085	553	120 637	13 240	7 072	114 469	29 315	16 686	24 056	21 007	6 671	3 931
1996	169 001	126 723	570	127 292	13 902	6 519	119 910	31 117	17 974	25 034	21 761	6 751	4 012
1997	179 654	135 507	428	135 935	14 876	7 060	128 119	33 037	18 498	26 307	22 746	6 829	4 111
1998	191 711	145 903	436	146 339	15 969	6 758	137 128	35 425	19 158	27 780	23 662	6 901	4 185
1999	204 586	157 576	360	157 936	17 243	8 158	148 851	35 604	20 132	29 226	24 664	7 000	4 282
2000	220 845	171 986	521	172 507	18 568	6 275	160 214	39 100	21 531	31 086	26 214	7 104	4 407
2001	233 770	182 604	449	183 052	19 642	6 037	169 448	40 332	23 991	32 521	27 564	7 188	4 439
2002	240 534	187 668	408	188 076	20 303	7 555	175 328	39 648	25 557	33 055	28 749	7 277	4 440
2003	250 605	196 177	418	196 594	21 274	7 862	183 183	40 222	27 200	34 034	29 838	7 363	4 498
2004	267 521	213 075	582	213 656	23 225	7 929	198 360	40 587	28 573	35 886	31 557	7 455	4 634
2005	286 685	228 542	628	229 171	24 825	7 937	212 284	43 450	30 951	37 988	33 061	7 547	4 719
2006	306 918	240 821	381	241 203	26 253	8 555	223 504	49 785	33 629	40 234	34 860	7 628	4 831
2007	321 245	251 893	382	252 275	27 401	9 106	233 980	51 304	35 961	41 727	35 877	7 699	4 936
2008	333 110	259 796	328	260 124	28 380	9 641	241 386	52 432	39 292	42 876	37 194	7 769	. . .

. . . = Not available.
* = Less than $50,000, but the estimates for this item are included in the total.

Table 21-2. Personal Income and Employment by Region and State—*Continued*

(Millions of dollars, except as noted.)

Region or state and year	Personal income, total	Earnings by place of work			Less: Contributions for government social insurance	Plus: Adjustment for residence	Equals: Net earnings by place of residence	Plus: Dividends, interest, and rent	Plus: Personal current transfer receipts	Per capita (dollars)		Population (thousands)	Total employment (thousands)
		Nonfarm	Farm	Total						Personal income	Disposable personal income		
WASHINGTON													
1958	6 270	5 026	221	5 246	239	16	5 023	778	469	2 261	2 019	2 773	. . .
1959	6 668	5 380	232	5 612	281	21	5 351	833	484	2 364	2 122	2 821	. . .
1960	6 901	5 523	253	5 777	313	25	5 489	898	514	2 417	2 163	2 855	. . .
1961	7 248	5 802	244	6 046	327	29	5 747	938	563	2 515	2 248	2 882	. . .
1962	7 832	6 304	268	6 572	357	34	6 248	1 017	567	2 662	2 375	2 942	. . .
1963	8 024	6 445	271	6 716	395	42	6 363	1 063	598	2 715	2 419	2 955	. . .
1964	8 406	6 742	248	6 990	394	51	6 647	1 128	631	2 839	2 582	2 961	. . .
1965	9 066	7 247	268	7 515	417	62	7 159	1 244	663	3 056	2 770	2 967	. . .
1966	10 272	8 376	362	8 738	593	71	8 216	1 367	689	3 360	3 011	3 057	. . .
1967	11 255	9 215	325	9 540	687	82	8 935	1 491	829	3 546	3 163	3 174	. . .
1968	12 515	10 273	339	10 612	769	99	9 942	1 622	951	3 827	3 390	3 270	. . .
1969	13 645	11 160	396	11 556	910	83	10 729	1 840	1 077	4 082	3 578	3 343	1 539
1970	14 323	11 365	344	11 709	913	65	10 861	2 028	1 435	4 191	3 748	3 417	1 491
1971	15 058	11 724	390	12 114	981	63	11 196	2 191	1 671	4 368	3 945	3 447	1 457
1972	16 275	12 685	505	13 190	1 117	73	12 146	2 344	1 784	4 722	4 218	3 477	1 558
1973	18 408	14 340	754	15 094	1 438	90	13 746	2 651	2 011	5 294	4 715	3 548	1 622
1974	20 939	16 177	889	17 065	1 659	133	15 540	3 048	2 351	5 902	5 262	3 548	1 622
1975	23 684	18 134	905	19 039	1 840	200	17 399	3 378	2 907	6 545	5 859	3 619	1 659
1976	26 475	20 773	752	21 526	2 140	247	19 633	3 686	3 156	7 174	6 407	3 691	1 739
1977	29 449	23 591	603	24 194	2 459	227	21 962	4 184	3 304	7 807	6 953	3 772	1 815
1978	34 308	27 803	752	28 555	2 977	270	25 848	4 876	3 583	8 828	7 781	3 886	1 939
1979	39 572	32 275	737	33 013	3 567	323	29 769	5 792	4 011	9 861	8 616	4 013	2 061
1980	45 004	35 527	859	36 386	3 862	389	32 913	7 185	4 907	10 832	9 486	4 155	2 110
1981	50 295	38 858	861	39 719	4 540	433	35 612	8 980	5 703	11 874	10 373	4 236	2 126
1982	53 328	40 311	764	41 075	4 762	465	36 778	10 134	6 416	12 470	11 106	4 277	2 101
1983	56 666	42 325	1 063	43 388	5 119	485	38 754	10 902	7 010	13 177	11 860	4 300	2 147
1984	61 086	45 497	1 020	46 518	5 653	543	41 408	12 308	7 370	14 063	12 720	4 344	2 224
1985	64 924	48 599	748	49 347	6 094	587	43 840	13 157	7 927	14 755	13 316	4 400	2 290
1986	69 203	51 969	1 055	53 024	6 627	608	47 006	13 791	8 406	15 542	14 052	4 453	2 365
1987	73 461	55 615	1 083	56 698	7 068	659	50 289	14 317	8 855	16 210	14 545	4 532	2 486
1988	79 648	60 944	1 023	61 967	7 976	749	54 740	15 274	9 634	17 166	15 461	4 640	2 617
1989	88 084	66 431	1 148	67 579	8 722	833	59 690	17 816	10 578	18 558	16 542	4 746	2 737
1990	97 399	74 023	1 195	75 218	9 615	926	66 528	19 251	11 620	19 865	17 676	4 903	2 863
1991	103 974	79 073	1 262	80 335	10 483	989	70 841	20 085	13 049	20 689	18 502	5 026	2 897
1992	112 035	86 214	1 513	87 727	11 457	1 085	77 354	20 165	14 516	21 709	19 441	5 161	2 928
1993	117 266	90 128	1 765	91 893	11 972	1 177	81 098	20 650	15 517	22 214	19 945	5 279	2 972
1994	123 294	94 099	1 402	95 501	12 642	1 217	84 076	22 888	16 329	22 938	20 528	5 375	3 082
1995	129 845	98 300	1 457	99 757	13 232	1 367	87 892	24 488	17 464	23 690	21 163	5 481	3 123
1996	139 650	104 792	1 919	106 711	13 831	1 570	94 451	26 841	18 359	25 073	22 202	5 570	3 215
1997	150 119	113 444	1 619	115 063	14 590	1 720	102 193	28 875	19 050	26 454	23 223	5 675	3 320
1998	163 762	124 979	1 731	126 710	16 062	1 827	112 474	31 528	19 760	28 384	24 615	5 770	3 402
1999	175 491	136 680	1 496	138 175	16 951	1 939	123 163	31 363	20 966	30 037	25 627	5 843	3 471
2000	187 853	145 419	1 607	147 026	18 189	2 182	131 019	34 521	22 314	31 780	27 309	5 911	3 551
2001	193 498	148 619	1 404	150 023	17 821	2 312	134 515	33 906	25 078	32 319	28 208	5 987	3 557
2002	197 452	151 522	1 490	153 012	18 165	2 385	137 232	33 595	26 625	32 606	29 254	6 056	3 527
2003	202 942	155 458	1 849	157 307	18 952	2 403	140 757	34 254	27 931	33 214	30 091	6 180	3 631
2004	218 432	164 535	1 701	166 236	20 289	2 436	148 383	41 866	28 183	35 347	32 208	6 180	3 631
2005	226 585	173 606	1 539	175 144	21 503	2 542	156 184	40 787	29 614	36 227	32 703	6 255	3 744
2006	245 765	187 244	1 401	188 646	23 085	2 701	168 262	45 784	31 719	38 639	34 610	6 361	3 847
2007	265 738	200 120	1 811	201 931	24 359	2 983	180 554	51 450	33 734	41 203	36 685	6 450	3 949
2008	277 397	207 674	1 656	209 330	25 330	3 068	187 069	53 750	36 579	42 356	38 009	6 549	. . .

. . . = Not available.
* = Less than $50,000, but the estimates for this item are included in the total.

Table 21-2. Personal Income and Employment by Region and State—*Continued*

(Millions of dollars, except as noted.)

Region or state and year	Personal income, total	Earnings by place of work			Less: Contributions for government social insurance	Plus: Adjustment for residence	Equals: Net earnings by place of residence	Plus: Dividends, interest, and rent	Plus: Personal current transfer receipts	Per capita (dollars)		Population (thousands)	Total employment (thousands)
		Nonfarm	Farm	Total						Personal income	Disposable personal income		
WEST VIRGINIA													
1958	2 921	2 421	58	2 479	114	-21	2 344	275	301	1 583	1 444	1 845	. . .
1959	3 014	2 526	45	2 571	135	-20	2 415	296	303	1 625	1 470	1 855	. . .
1960	3 062	2 566	49	2 615	155	-20	2 440	318	304	1 653	1 484	1 853	. . .
1961	3 101	2 557	42	2 599	153	-20	2 426	331	344	1 696	1 524	1 828	. . .
1962	3 238	2 673	31	2 703	168	-19	2 517	354	367	1 790	1 609	1 809	. . .
1963	3 378	2 798	24	2 821	186	-18	2 618	381	379	1 881	1 684	1 796	. . .
1964	3 601	2 977	23	2 999	173	-17	2 809	407	385	2 004	1 816	1 797	. . .
1965	3 850	3 180	24	3 205	184	-13	3 008	431	411	2 155	1 957	1 786	. . .
1966	4 080	3 450	14	3 463	244	-10	3 209	437	434	2 298	2 072	1 775	. . .
1967	4 329	3 634	28	3 662	268	-8	3 386	451	492	2 447	2 210	1 769	. . .
1968	4 590	3 854	22	3 876	298	2	3 579	467	544	2 603	2 325	1 763	. . .
1969	4 868	4 138	30	4 169	324	-79	3 766	503	599	2 788	2 443	1 746	652
1970	5 428	4 548	25	4 573	350	-82	4 141	566	722	3 108	2 752	1 747	660
1971	5 965	4 945	25	4 970	395	-100	4 474	620	870	3 369	2 999	1 770	670
1972	6 601	5 465	30	5 495	455	-114	4 926	678	997	3 673	3 256	1 797	684
1973	7 240	5 929	44	5 973	567	-117	5 288	765	1 186	4 010	3 579	1 805	700
1974	8 051	6 562	28	6 590	647	-131	5 812	897	1 343	4 438	3 916	1 814	711
1975	9 157	7 399	14	7 412	709	-158	6 545	1 012	1 600	4 975	4 407	1 841	717
1976	10 268	8 408	3	8 412	817	-195	7 400	1 115	1 753	5 469	4 821	1 877	739
1977	11 488	9 497	-2	9 495	915	-226	8 354	1 263	1 871	6 028	5 324	1 906	758
1978	12 796	10 617	12	10 629	1 056	-263	9 309	1 407	2 080	6 663	5 903	1 920	781
1979	14 293	11 710	17	11 727	1 211	-273	10 242	1 616	2 435	7 371	6 488	1 939	791
1980	15 841	12 567	8	12 575	1 297	-301	10 978	2 034	2 829	8 118	7 129	1 951	784
1981	17 249	13 280	-23	13 257	1 467	-280	11 511	2 542	3 196	8 827	7 765	1 954	764
1982	18 325	13 687	-29	13 659	1 552	-234	11 872	2 948	3 505	9 399	8 318	1 950	743
1983	18 700	13 448	-16	13 432	1 569	-191	11 672	3 143	3 885	9 614	8 555	1 945	724
1984	20 063	14 404	22	14 426	1 735	-139	12 551	3 544	3 968	10 408	9 303	1 928	735
1985	20 777	14 860	20	14 880	1 826	-118	12 936	3 698	4 143	10 896	9 729	1 907	735
1986	21 444	15 139	46	15 185	1 905	-91	13 189	3 856	4 400	11 392	10 221	1 882	735
1987	22 010	15 602	6	15 608	1 977	-26	13 605	3 883	4 523	11 849	10 624	1 858	742
1988	22 922	16 238	4	16 242	2 166	8	14 084	4 066	4 772	12 524	11 283	1 830	755
1989	24 305	16 886	31	16 917	2 268	87	14 736	4 535	5 034	13 454	12 034	1 807	762
1990	25 980	18 133	44	18 177	2 420	70	15 827	4 759	5 394	14 493	12 965	1 793	783
1991	27 152	18 794	34	18 828	2 580	41	16 289	4 793	6 071	15 095	13 554	1 799	784
1992	29 105	19 919	62	19 981	2 756	103	17 328	4 819	6 959	16 112	14 543	1 806	794
1993	30 077	20 721	64	20 785	2 971	106	17 919	4 758	7 400	16 548	14 936	1 818	806
1994	31 301	21 758	60	21 819	3 113	149	18 854	4 971	7 477	17 194	15 464	1 820	827
1995	32 328	22 444	23	22 467	3 255	194	19 406	5 202	7 721	17 727	15 924	1 824	844
1996	33 622	23 016	11	23 026	3 350	208	19 885	5 599	8 139	18 445	16 540	1 823	853
1997	35 005	23 825	3	23 827	3 435	360	20 753	5 890	8 363	19 243	17 200	1 819	864
1998	36 722	24 847	7	24 853	3 566	401	21 689	6 367	8 666	20 226	18 068	1 816	878
1999	37 557	25 707	-4	25 704	3 654	455	22 504	6 204	8 849	20 729	18 509	1 812	879
2000	39 582	26 926	26	26 951	3 905	568	23 615	6 676	9 292	21 905	19 540	1 807	887
2001	41 902	28 201	-10	28 192	3 952	663	24 902	6 689	10 312	23 298	20 809	1 799	883
2002	43 312	28 886	-31	28 855	3 974	722	25 603	6 413	11 296	24 070	21 807	1 799	884
2003	43 841	29 711	-24	29 687	4 116	787	26 358	5 917	11 566	24 325	22 195	1 802	878
2004	45 686	31 680	14	31 694	4 238	819	28 275	5 885	11 525	25 334	23 222	1 803	894
2005	47 565	33 182	-12	33 170	4 436	926	29 660	5 882	12 022	26 366	23 935	1 804	908
2006	50 472	34 804	-72	34 731	4 527	1 007	31 212	6 399	12 862	27 935	25 287	1 807	917
2007	53 181	36 353	-75	36 278	4 714	1 144	32 708	6 890	13 583	29 385	26 496	1 810	922
2008	55 941	38 432	-134	38 297	5 035	1 103	34 365	7 162	14 414	30 831	27 926	1 814	. . .

. . . = Not available.
* = Less than $50,000, but the estimates for this item are included in the total.

Table 21-2. Personal Income and Employment by Region and State—*Continued*

(Millions of dollars, except as noted.)

Region or state and year	Personal income, total	Earnings by place of work — Nonfarm	Earnings by place of work — Farm	Earnings by place of work — Total	Less: Contributions for government social insurance	Plus: Adjustment for residence	Equals: Net earnings by place of residence	Plus: Dividends, interest, and rent	Plus: Personal current transfer receipts	Per capita (dollars) — Personal income	Per capita (dollars) — Disposable personal income	Population (thousands)	Total employment (thousands)
WISCONSIN													
1958	7 940	6 126	451	6 578	233	52	6 397	1 033	510	2 066	1 843	3 843	. . .
1959	8 620	6 733	472	7 205	282	59	6 982	1 113	524	2 215	1 969	3 891	. . .
1960	8 911	7 012	421	7 432	341	63	7 155	1 199	557	2 249	1 982	3 962	. . .
1961	9 199	7 087	487	7 575	348	67	7 294	1 260	646	2 295	2 040	4 009	. . .
1962	9 735	7 559	484	8 043	374	74	7 743	1 334	658	2 404	2 127	4 049	. . .
1963	10 074	7 884	430	8 314	433	81	7 962	1 417	695	2 450	2 159	4 112	. . .
1964	10 869	8 506	470	8 976	449	91	8 618	1 527	724	2 610	2 327	4 165	. . .
1965	11 765	9 146	537	9 683	479	104	9 307	1 678	779	2 780	2 469	4 232	. . .
1966	12 877	10 084	661	10 745	668	123	10 200	1 815	862	3 013	2 652	4 274	. . .
1967	13 645	10 709	557	11 266	759	137	10 644	1 938	1 063	3 171	2 769	4 303	. . .
1968	14 904	11 574	640	12 214	815	158	11 557	2 109	1 237	3 430	2 992	4 345	. . .
1969	16 398	12 676	630	13 307	934	249	12 622	2 418	1 359	3 746	3 212	4 378	1 944
1970	17 609	13 399	631	14 030	974	253	13 308	2 702	1 599	3 979	3 460	4 426	1 954
1971	18 906	14 252	686	14 938	1 070	264	14 132	2 904	1 870	4 239	3 737	4 460	1 957
1972	20 679	15 717	721	16 437	1 248	287	15 477	3 123	2 080	4 597	4 007	4 498	2 014
1973	23 149	17 717	907	18 624	1 615	313	17 322	3 462	2 365	5 123	4 476	4 518	2 116
1974	25 472	19 421	793	20 215	1 841	339	18 713	3 948	2 811	5 613	4 878	4 538	2 159
1975	27 810	20 632	855	21 488	1 928	345	19 905	4 378	3 527	6 086	5 345	4 570	2 148
1976	30 606	23 199	752	23 951	2 188	390	22 154	4 634	3 818	6 676	5 829	4 585	2 211
1977	34 137	25 939	1 133	27 072	2 444	432	25 061	5 027	4 049	7 400	6 437	4 613	2 293
1978	38 190	29 355	1 114	30 468	2 847	487	28 108	5 609	4 472	8 245	7 113	4 632	2 382
1979	42 922	32 724	1 391	34 115	3 307	526	31 334	6 457	5 131	9 199	7 958	4 666	2 465
1980	47 623	34 859	1 429	36 288	3 507	550	33 330	8 044	6 249	10 107	8 786	4 712	2 469
1981	51 994	37 195	1 157	38 352	4 011	604	34 945	9 943	7 107	11 001	9 506	4 726	2 424
1982	54 851	38 243	1 011	39 254	4 170	623	35 707	11 216	7 928	11 599	10 118	4 729	2 382
1983	57 004	40 307	457	40 764	4 363	677	37 079	11 405	8 520	12 073	10 632	4 721	2 385
1984	62 462	44 316	982	45 298	4 908	794	41 185	12 553	8 724	13 190	11 645	4 736	2 478
1985	65 709	46 704	1 012	47 716	5 212	883	43 387	13 053	9 269	13 840	12 219	4 748	2 509
1986	69 089	49 203	1 289	50 491	5 536	966	45 920	13 608	9 560	14 528	12 822	4 756	2 551
1987	73 006	52 599	1 405	54 004	5 840	1 071	49 235	13 994	9 777	15 280	13 406	4 778	2 621
1988	77 433	57 064	840	57 904	6 557	1 240	52 587	14 715	10 132	16 057	14 102	4 822	2 702
1989	83 936	60 344	1 712	62 056	6 980	1 272	56 348	16 660	10 927	17 283	15 140	4 857	2 759
1990	88 635	64 219	1 342	65 561	7 464	1 356	59 453	17 470	11 711	18 072	15 801	4 905	2 834
1991	92 124	67 086	963	68 049	7 912	1 381	61 518	17 875	12 731	18 557	16 260	4 964	2 860
1992	98 917	72 633	1 204	73 837	8 530	1 515	66 822	18 353	13 742	19 683	17 253	5 025	2 913
1993	103 379	76 993	914	77 907	9 073	1 575	70 409	18 663	14 306	20 331	17 768	5 085	2 969
1994	109 927	81 854	1 141	82 995	9 780	1 695	74 910	20 265	14 752	21 413	18 666	5 134	3 060
1995	115 180	85 733	764	86 497	10 258	1 793	78 032	21 513	15 636	22 215	19 310	5 185	3 140
1996	121 718	89 456	1 363	90 819	10 682	1 947	82 085	23 420	16 214	23 273	20 091	5 230	3 191
1997	129 099	95 081	1 024	96 106	11 316	2 167	86 957	25 394	16 748	24 514	21 034	5 266	3 245
1998	138 667	101 690	1 421	103 111	11 930	2 314	93 495	28 024	17 148	26 175	22 382	5 298	3 303
1999	144 702	108 102	1 333	109 435	12 631	2 502	99 306	27 509	17 887	27 135	23 236	5 333	3 374
2000	153 548	114 023	877	114 900	13 138	2 736	104 498	29 870	19 179	28 572	24 499	5 374	3 431
2001	158 888	117 907	923	118 830	13 522	2 868	108 176	29 303	21 409	29 380	25 307	5 408	3 419
2002	163 309	122 036	864	122 900	13 917	2 952	111 936	28 332	23 042	29 994	26 407	5 445	3 411
2003	168 120	126 895	1 323	128 217	14 393	3 016	116 841	27 530	23 750	30 710	27 280	5 474	3 435
2004	174 655	132 806	1 407	134 213	15 201	3 173	122 185	28 238	24 232	31 705	28 249	5 509	3 502
2005	181 153	137 591	1 232	138 822	15 774	3 320	126 368	28 773	26 013	32 706	28 911	5 539	3 558
2006	191 895	143 827	929	144 756	16 523	3 476	131 709	32 681	27 504	34 461	30 264	5 569	3 579
2007	203 084	148 691	1 768	150 459	17 078	3 779	137 161	36 234	29 688	36 272	31 748	5 599	3 595
2008	209 999	152 550	1 589	154 139	17 631	3 910	140 417	37 552	32 031	37 314	32 835	5 628	. . .

. . . = Not available.
* = Less than $50,000, but the estimates for this item are included in the total.

Table 21-2. Personal Income and Employment by Region and State—*Continued*

(Millions of dollars, except as noted.)

Region or state and year	Personal income, total	Derivation of personal income								Per capita (dollars)		Population (thousands)	Total employment (thousands)
		Earnings by place of work			Less: Contributions for government social insurance	Plus: Adjustment for residence	Equals: Net earnings by place of residence	Plus: Dividends, interest, and rent	Plus: Personal current transfer receipts	Personal income	Disposable personal income		
		Nonfarm	Farm	Total									
WYOMING													
1958	687	498	75	573	23	-1	549	100	38	2 182	1 973	315	. . .
1959	730	546	64	610	27	-1	582	107	42	2 282	2 053	320	. . .
1960	765	597	50	647	34	-1	611	109	45	2 312	2 068	331	. . .
1961	803	611	56	667	34	-1	632	119	53	2 384	2 146	337	. . .
1962	832	619	66	685	35	-1	649	128	54	2 498	2 238	333	. . .
1963	848	638	66	703	40	-1	662	130	56	2 524	2 235	336	. . .
1964	874	681	46	727	43	-1	684	135	55	2 577	2 348	339	. . .
1965	904	688	52	741	41	-1	700	147	58	2 724	2 479	332	. . .
1966	931	705	57	762	48	0	714	155	61	2 882	2 606	323	. . .
1967	999	748	70	818	53	0	764	163	71	3 101	2 787	322	. . .
1968	1 066	822	62	884	59	0	825	161	81	3 291	2 946	324	. . .
1969	1 173	902	69	971	66	*	905	180	89	3 567	3 148	329	158
1970	1 303	983	78	1 060	72	0	989	212	103	3 904	3 466	334	159
1971	1 449	1 084	87	1 172	81	-1	1 090	240	119	4 261	3 811	340	165
1972	1 626	1 215	125	1 340	96	-3	1 242	255	129	4 689	4 240	347	172
1973	1 905	1 436	152	1 588	128	-7	1 453	299	152	5 390	4 806	353	182
1974	2 242	1 774	109	1 883	159	-14	1 711	360	172	6 151	5 388	365	194
1975	2 557	2 071	66	2 137	182	-16	1 939	411	208	6 722	5 986	380	203
1976	2 857	2 356	47	2 403	213	-23	2 167	458	232	7 224	6 383	395	214
1977	3 357	2 809	44	2 853	249	-30	2 574	529	254	8 157	7 210	412	231
1978	4 033	3 402	63	3 465	309	-39	3 118	630	286	9 361	8 254	431	250
1979	4 752	4 012	95	4 107	381	-56	3 670	752	331	10 517	9 137	452	267
1980	5 556	4 677	84	4 761	442	-77	4 243	922	392	11 718	10 216	474	280
1981	6 335	5 304	51	5 354	542	-88	4 724	1 140	471	12 883	11 159	492	290
1982	6 794	5 400	29	5 429	566	-85	4 779	1 474	541	13 417	11 831	506	288
1983	6 528	5 129	37	5 166	523	-62	4 581	1 306	640	12 791	11 409	510	275
1984	6 854	5 385	14	5 399	561	-56	4 782	1 440	633	13 576	12 208	505	277
1985	7 154	5 619	17	5 636	600	-55	4 982	1 501	672	14 317	12 871	500	278
1986	6 971	5 355	39	5 394	584	-43	4 767	1 464	740	14 064	12 754	496	265
1987	6 762	5 076	58	5 134	553	-28	4 553	1 458	751	14 177	12 801	477	260
1988	6 938	5 218	59	5 276	601	-23	4 652	1 504	782	14 918	13 463	465	265
1989	7 536	5 530	88	5 618	622	-16	4 979	1 714	842	16 440	14 729	458	267
1990	8 167	5 916	148	6 064	671	-12	5 381	1 881	906	18 002	16 149	454	272
1991	8 579	6 096	209	6 305	717	-2	5 586	1 988	1 005	18 680	16 816	459	279
1992	9 020	6 412	218	6 630	748	-7	5 874	2 034	1 112	19 346	17 430	466	282
1993	9 450	6 771	247	7 018	785	-10	6 224	2 012	1 215	19 976	17 925	473	286
1994	9 845	7 077	119	7 197	832	-9	6 356	2 211	1 278	20 498	18 364	480	299
1995	10 207	7 248	102	7 350	854	-7	6 489	2 366	1 352	21 039	18 848	485	302
1996	10 678	7 472	87	7 558	872	-2	6 685	2 559	1 434	21 875	19 159	488	306
1997	11 459	7 884	193	8 076	905	3	7 175	2 806	1 478	23 412	20 413	489	309
1998	12 189	8 323	88	8 411	952	6	7 465	3 209	1 515	24 836	21 613	491	315
1999	13 050	8 849	170	9 020	998	5	8 027	3 439	1 584	26 536	23 044	492	319
2000	14 063	9 576	115	9 692	1 051	13	8 653	3 706	1 704	28 470	24 505	494	328
2001	14 972	10 371	149	10 520	1 132	6	9 394	3 733	1 846	30 374	26 412	493	333
2002	15 463	10 813	81	10 894	1 182	4	9 716	3 754	1 994	31 115	27 870	497	337
2003	16 420	11 310	139	11 449	1 236	3	10 216	4 069	2 135	32 902	29 836	499	339
2004	17 756	12 269	140	12 409	1 327	2	11 084	4 428	2 244	35 314	32 124	503	348
2005	19 610	13 313	175	13 488	1 452	1	12 037	5 200	2 373	38 755	34 685	506	360
2006	22 236	15 139	38	15 177	1 683	-5	13 489	6 235	2 512	43 381	38 018	513	375
2007	24 618	16 570	-2	16 568	1 840	-7	14 721	7 242	2 655	47 047	40 935	523	390
2008	26 484	18 024	-10	18 014	2 005	-18	15 992	7 620	2 872	49 719	43 607	533	. . .

. . . = Not available.
* = Less than $50,000, but the estimates for this item are included in the total.

NOTES AND DEFINITIONS

TABLE 21-1
GROSS DOMESTIC PRODUCT BY REGION AND STATE

SOURCE: U.S. DEPARTMENT OF COMMERCE, BUREAU OF ECONOMIC ANALYSIS (BEA)

A state's gross domestic product (GDP) is the sum of the value added or GDP originating in all the industries in a state. For explanation of GDP, see the notes and definitions to Tables 1-1 through 1-15. In concept, the sum of state GDPs is identical with national GDP except for Federal military and civilian activity located overseas, which cannot be attributed to a particular state. GDP by state is only calculated on an annual basis.

Definitions and notes on the data

The value of an industry's GDP is equal to the market value of its gross output (which consists of sales or receipts and other operating income, taxes on production and imports, and inventory change) minus the value of its intermediate inputs (which consist of energy, raw materials, semifinished goods, and services that are purchased from domestic industries or foreign sources). In concept, this definition is equal to the sum of labor and property-type income earned in that industry in the production of GDP, plus commodity taxes. Property-type income is the sum of corporate profits, proprietors' income, rental income of persons, net interest, capital consumption allowances, business transfer payments, and the current surplus of government enterprises less subsidies.

In practice, GDP by state, like GDP by industry, is measured using the incomes data rather than data on gross output and intermediate inputs, which are not available on a sufficiently detailed and timely basis.

Therefore, the *value* of *GDP by state* is defined as the sum of labor and property-type incomes originating in each of 63 industries in that state, plus commodity taxes, and plus the allocated value of the statistical discrepancy between national GDP and national gross national income. Starting with the 2004 comprehensive revision of the data from 1997 forward, the annual industry accounts and the GDP-by-state accounts allocate the statistical discrepancy across all private-sector industries, making the GDP by state estimates more similar to GDP estimates than they had been in the past. In the SIC-based measures for 1977 through 1997, the statistical discrepancy has not been allocated to industries and states.

The *quantity indexes* of state GDP are aggregates of the real output of each industry in the state, net of intermediate inputs, based on chained constant-dollar estimates and expressed as index numbers, 2000 = 100. They are derived by applying national implicit deflators calculated for each industry group to the current-dollar GDP estimates for that industry group, and then applying the chain-type index formula used in the national accounts to aggregate the industry groups to the state total.

To the extent that a state's output is produced and sold in national markets at relatively uniform output and input prices, or sold locally at national prices, GDP by state captures the differences across states that reflect the relative differences in the mix of goods and services produced by the states. However, real GDP by state does not capture geographic differences in the output and input prices of goods and services produced and sold locally.

Estimates for the latest year (2007) are made using more limited source data and an abbreviated estimation methodology.

GDP by state is now calculated on a North American Industry Classification System (NAICS) basis back through 1997. Data for earlier years, beginning with 1977, were calculated on the Standard Industrial Classification (SIC) basis. According to BEA (in a "Cautionary note" on the Web site, dated June 7, 2007), "There is a discontinuity in the GDP by state time series at 1997, where the data change from SIC industry definitions to NAICS industry definitions. This discontinuity results from many sources, including differences in source data and different estimation methodologies. In addition, the NAICS-based GDP by state estimates are consistent with U.S. gross domestic product (GDP) while the SIC-based GDP by state estimates are consistent with U.S. gross domestic income (GDI). This data discontinuity may affect both the levels and the growth rates of the GDP by state estimates. Users of the GDP by state estimates are strongly cautioned against appending the two data series in an attempt to construct a single time series of GDP by state estimates for 1963 to 2006."

Business Statistics provides SIC-based data for 1977 to 1997 for those who require information about economic growth before 1997 by state. If a continuous series spanning the two time periods is needed despite the cautions just quoted, the earlier data can be linked to the later data using the values of the two series in the overlap year 1997.

Data availability and references

The latest estimates are presented and explained in "Gross Domestic Product by State: Advance Estimates for 2007 and Revised Estimates for 2004–2006" in the *Survey of Current Business*, July 2008. In addition to the data reproduced here, this article includes per capita real GDP by state and the contributions of the major industry sectors to economic growth in each state. This article and all historical data can be found on the Bureau of Economic Analysis (BEA) Web site <http://www.bea.gov>. The next release is scheduled for June 2, 2009.

TABLE 21-2
PERSONAL INCOME AND EMPLOYMENT BY REGION AND STATE

SOURCE: U.S. DEPARTMENT OF COMMERCE, BUREAU OF ECONOMIC ANALYSIS (BEA)

This table presents annual time-series data on personal income and employment for the United States as a whole, each individual state, the District of Columbia, and eight geographic regions for 1958 through 2008. In almost all respects, the data are consistent with the national personal income data as defined and presented in Chapters 1 and 4. BEA also publishes quarterly estimates of state personal income, which are not shown here.

The sum of state personal incomes for the United States shown in this table is somewhat smaller than U.S. personal income as shown in the national income and product accounts (NIPAs) in Chapters 1 and 4, due to slightly different definitions. The national total of the state estimates consists only of the income earned by persons who live in the United States and of foreign residents who work in the United States. The measure of personal income in the NIPAs is broader. It includes the earnings of federal civilian and military personnel stationed abroad (see below for a change in the definition of "stationed abroad") and of U.S. residents on foreign assignment for less than a year. It also includes the investment income received by federal retirement plans for federal workers stationed abroad. Earnings of foreign residents are included only if they live and work in the United States for a year or more. There are also statistical differences that reflect different timing of the availability of source data.

In an article entitled "State Personal Income: Second Quarter of 2005 and Revised Estimates for 2002–2005:I" in the October 2005 *Survey of Current Business*, BEA announced "New Treatment of State Estimates of Military Compensation." This announcement says, "BEA's state estimates of military compensation are based on troop data by base and national estimates of average pay from the Department of Defense (DOD). For 2001–2004, the DOD estimates of troops stationed at U.S. bases do not show a large decrease for troops sent to Afghanistan and Iraq. Those estimates reflect the DOD's new method of reporting active duty military personnel for the Army and the Air Force. The DOD now reports active duty regular military personnel according to the troops' home bases and reserve personnel according to the state of the reservists' bases. However, for the Marines, DOD continues to use an approach that reduces domestic base personnel figures when troops are sent overseas. Since BEA's state estimates of military earnings reflect the geographic distribution of military personnel as reported by the DOD, the surge in military earnings due to the activation of reservists and the special pay associated with the war is recorded in the states from which the forces were deployed. This practice is consistent with the pay being received by family members at home and with

news reports of strong retail sales at affected military bases.... Since the Persian Gulf war, the demographics of the armed forces have evolved, and BEA has changed its military residency definition accordingly. The current Army has a larger proportion of mature troops with families to support, in contrast to the typical young, single soldiers of the past."

Definitions

A state's *personal income* is the sum of earnings, dividends, interest, rental income, and current transfer receipts, net of government contributions for social insurance, of persons resident in that state, not persons working in that state. Its derivation from source data on earnings by place of work is shown in Table 21-2 and is explained below.

Earnings by place of work consists of payments to persons working in the state of wage and salary disbursements, all supplements to wages and salaries (including employer contributions for government social insurance and all other benefits), and farm and nonfarm proprietors' income.

Contributions for government social insurance, which is subtracted from total earnings, includes both the employer and the employee contributions for persons working in the state. Personal income is defined as net of all contributions for government social insurance, though not net of other taxes on wages or other income.

Adjustment for residence. BEA adjusts earnings by place of work to a place-of-residence basis, to account for interstate and international commuting. The difference between earnings by place of residence and earnings by place of work is shown in the "Adjustment for residence" column. This adjustment is a net figure, equaling income received by state (or area) residents from employment outside the state minus income paid to persons residing outside the state but working in the state. There is a negative adjustment to total personal income for the United States as a whole, reflecting net payments to foreign residents working in the United States.

The effect of interstate commuting can be seen in its most extreme form by comparing 2008 data for the District of Columbia, with its adjustment for residence of negative $41 billion—representing net payments to persons living outside D.C.—with Maryland, with its adjustment for residence of positive $28 billion net from the District of Columbia and other employment sources outside the state.

Dividends, interest, and rent are aggregates for state residents of these categories as defined in U.S. personal income. The rental income component of personal income, which includes the imputed rent on owner-occupied homes, is net of capital consumption with capital consumption adjustment. In the case of a catastrophe such as Hurricane Katrina in 2005, not only "normal" capital consumption but also the property destruction in excess of normal depreciation caused by the event are subtracted from gross rental income; the treatment is described more fully in the article at the beginning of this book. The effect of this can be seen in the personal income accounts for Louisiana in 2005, when the destruction of property was so great that the total "dividends, interest, and rent" component of income is negative.

Personal current transfer receipts are aggregates for state residents of such receipts as defined in U.S. personal income.

Population is the U.S. Census Bureau estimate for the *middle* of the year. Note that because Hurricane Katrina occurred in September of 2005, the population decline in Louisiana caused by that event does not appear until the entry for 2006.

Total employment is the total number of jobs, full-time plus part-time; each job that any person holds is counted at full weight. The employment estimates are on a place-of-work basis. Both wage and salary employment and self-employment are included. The main source for the wage and salary employment estimates is the Bureau of Labor Statistics estimates from unemployment insurance data (the ES-202 data), which also provides benchmarks for the payroll employment measures (see Table 10-7 and its notes and definitions). Self-employment is estimated mainly from individual and partnership federal income tax returns.

This concept of employment differs from the concept of employment in the Current Population Survey (CPS), which is derived from a monthly count of persons employed; any individual will appear only once in the CPS in a given month, no matter how many different jobs he or she might hold. (See the notes and definitions to Tables 10-1 through 10-5.) In addition, a self-employed individual who files more than one Schedule C income-tax filing will be counted more than once in the state figures. Finally, the state figures include members of the armed forces, who are not covered in the CPS. Due to these differences and other possible reporting inconsistencies, the BEA estimates are different from, and usually larger than, state employment estimates from the CPS.

The employment estimates correspond closely in coverage to the earnings estimates by place of work. However, the earnings estimates include the income of limited partnerships and of tax-exempt cooperatives, for which there are no corresponding employment estimates.

Per capita income is total income divided by the state's midyear population. (Because, as noted above, Hurricane Katrina was reflected in the 2005 income data but not in the population figure for that year, the 2005 decline in per capita income may be exaggerated.) It is therefore an average or "mean," subject to the qualifications discussed in the article at the beginning of this volume, under the "Whose Standard of Living?" heading. For recent data on median household income by state, which give a better idea of the income received by typical residents of the state, see Table 3-6 in Chapter 3.

The states and the District of Columbia are divided into regions by BEA as follows:

- **New England:** Connecticut, Maine, Massachusetts, New Hampshire, Rhode Island, and Vermont
- **Mideast:** Delaware, District of Columbia, Maryland, New Jersey, New York, and Pennsylvania
- **Great Lakes:** Illinois, Indiana, Michigan, Ohio, and Wisconsin
- **Plains:** Iowa, Kansas, Minnesota, Missouri, Nebraska, North Dakota, and South Dakota
- **Southeast:** Alabama, Arkansas, Florida, Georgia, Kentucky, Louisiana, Mississippi, North Carolina, South Carolina, Tennessee, Virginia, and West Virginia
- **Southwest:** Arizona, New Mexico, Oklahoma, and Texas
- **Rocky Mountain:** Colorado, Idaho, Montana, Utah, and Wyoming
- **Far West:** Alaska, California, Hawaii, Nevada, Oregon, and Washington

These BEA regional groupings differ from the region and division definitions used by the Census Bureau.

Data availability and references

The most recent updates to annual state personal income were issued in a BEA news release of March 24, 2009, available on the BEA Web site at <http://www.bea.gov/bea/rels.htm>. Quarterly state personal income data are issued approximately 2½ months after the end of each quarter and can be found at the same site.

The most recent comprehensive revision of state personal income, consistent with the 2003 comprehensive revision of the NIPAs, was presented in "Comprehensive Revision of State Personal Income: Preliminary Estimates for 2003, Revised Estimates for 1969–2002," *Survey of Current Business,* May 2004. Descriptions of subsequent updates can be found in articles in the *Survey of Current Business* on the BEA Web site at <http://www.bea.gov>. All current and historical data are on the BEA Web site at <http://www.bea.gov/bea/regional/spi>.

Also on the BEA Web site are some annual state data that go back even farther than shown here. Included are data on personal income, per capita personal income, and population back to 1929; disposable personal income and per capita disposable personal income back to 1948; and various levels of industry detail for income and wages and salaries within the state data back to 1929. For a complete listing, see the article "State Personal Income: Second Quarter of 2005 and Revised Estimates for 2002–2005:I" in the October 2005 issue of the *Survey of Current Business.*

INDEX